THE
MODERN ENGLISH VERSION

SpiritLed Woman
Bible

IS PRESENTED TO

....

BY

....

ON THIS DATE OF

....

SpiritLed Woman Bible

SpiritLed Woman

Bible

MEV

MODERN
ENGLISH
VERSION

SpiritLed Woman Bible
Published by Passio
Charisma Media/Charisma House Book Group
600 Rinehart Road
Lake Mary, Florida 32746
www.charismahouse.com

Published in cooperation with The Livingstone Corporation.

Like all translations of the Bible, this translation of the Scriptures is subject to human limitations and imperfections. Recognizing these limitations, the publisher sought God's guidance and wisdom throughout this project. Our prayer is that He will use this translation for the benefit of the church and His kingdom. Should a mistake be found, please feel free to contact the publisher.

14 15 16 17 18 — 987654321
Printed in the United States of America

Table of Contents

The Books of the Old Testament

The Books of the New Testament

Appendixes

TO HER MAJESTY ELIZABETH II, BY THE GRACE OF GOD, OF THE UNITED KINGDOM OF GREAT BRITAIN AND NORTHERN IRELAND, AND OF HER OTHER REALMS AND TERRITORIES, QUEEN, HEAD OF THE COMMONWEALTH, DEFENDER OF THE FAITH.

THE TRANSLATORS OF THE BIBLE WISH GRACE, MERCY, AND PEACE THROUGH JESUS CHRIST OUR LORD.

Preface to the Reader

In January 1604, King James I convened the Hampton Court Conference at the Hampton Court Palace. Meeting with King James I were two parties representing the Church of England. One party comprised the Archbishop of Canterbury, John Whitgift, and eight bishops who represented the episcopacy, supported by eight deans and one archdeacon. The second party comprised several Anglicans who were moderate Puritans led by John Rainolds, who was the president of Corpus Christi College, Oxford. The conference comprised three meetings over a period of three days.

The conference was called in response to a series of requests for reform set down in the Millenary Petition by the Puritans, a document that contained the signatures of one thousand Puritan ministers. The petition detailed complaints about the terms *absolution* and *confirmation*, water baptism administered by women rather than by ministers, excommunication for "trifles and twelvepenny matters" and ecclesiastical discipline administered by governmental authority, and various other issues.

King James I persuaded the bishops that only ministers should administer baptisms. He also abolished excommunication for "trifles and twelvepenny matters," though he maintained that bishops should not be the sole administers of ecclesiastical discipline and that the trial policies of the commissaries' court should be reviewed by the Lord Chancellor and Lord Chief Justice. The King alleviated many of the Puritans' concerns and brought much peace between the two parties.

Trouble mounted for the Puritans when Archbishop John Whitgift died soon after the conference. Richard Bancroft was appointed to the See of Canterbury, and due to the King's concerns, the Puritan ministers were expected to adhere to each of the Thirty-Nine Articles that upheld the hierarchical nature of the Church of England, which the Puritans sought to abolish.

But the major outcome of the conference was that King James I commissioned a new translation of the Holy Bible into the English vernacular, which became the predecessor to the Modern English Version. The translation was to be pleasing both to the episcopacy and to the moderate Puritans who emphasized that man should be able to study the Holy Bible, not only with the help of the ministers but also privately. The translation became known as the Authorized Version because only this translation would be authorized to be read in the Church of England once it replaced portions of the Great Bible inserted in the 1662 edition of the *Book of Common Prayer*. In some parts of the world it is known as the King James Version. The translation enabled King James I to broaden his support in the Church and among the populace. It demonstrated his moderate and inclusive approach to concerns in the Church.

King James I gave certain instructions to the translators: The new translation would contain no marginal notes, it would conform to the ecclesiology of the Church of England, the translation of certain words should reflect old ecclesiastical words such as "church" and were not to be translated as "congregation," and the new translation would reflect the episcopal structure of the Church of England and traditional beliefs about ordained clergy.

He also required the Church to use the Bishop's Bible as the primary guide for the translation and retain the familiar names of the biblical characters. However, for additional textual support, he permitted the Church to use the Tyndale Bible, the Coverdale Bible, Matthew's Bible, the Great Bible, and the Geneva Bible. This instruction is the basis for the statement in the flyleaf of the Authorized Version: "translated out of the original tongues, and with the former translations diligently compared and revised, by His Majesty's special command." William Tyndale's translation from the Greek text, now known as the Textus Receptus, comprises eighty percent of the King James Version New Testament. The King James Version Old Testament is based on the Jacob ben Hayyim edition of the Masoretic Text.

Forty-seven scholars represented the Church of England, both Puritans and High Churchmen, including the Anglican scholar Sir Henry Savile, who was not a clergyman. They formed six committees: two at the University of Oxford, two at the University of Cambridge, and two at the Collegiate Church of St. Peter at Westminster, popularly known as Westminster Abbey. The King's printer printed forty unbound copies of the 1602 Bishop's Bible for the committees. This meant that the scholars could record their agreed-upon changes in the margins for the printer to insert into the text. The committees were assigned various sections of Scriptures. They then compared their drafts and revised them until they achieved consistency in the translation.

The Anglican clergy working on the King James Version stated their purpose: not to make a new translation, but to make a good one better. They also wanted to make the Bible more known and accessible to the people. Thus they produced the King James Version in 1611.

Later, the University of Oxford produced a standard text of the King James Version, known as the 1769 Oxford Update and edited by Dr. Benjamin Blayney. Dr. Blayney standardized the punctuation and spelling to update the King James Version. The 1769 Oxford Update is the edition commonly used today.

The King James Version has been the standard version for Protestants throughout the English-speaking world for over four hundred years now. Its flowing language, prose rhythm, and powerful and majestic style made it a literary classic, with many of its phrases and expressions embedded in contemporary English.

Today, realizing the need to update the King James Version for the twenty-first century, forty-seven scholars serving as professors, or chaplains to the Armed Forces of Her Majesty Queen Elizabeth II and to the United States Armed Forces, comprising the Committee on Bible Translation under the leadership of the senior editorial advisor Dr. Stanley M. Horton and the chief editor Dr. James F. Linzey, have joined forces to produce a more updated edition of the King James Version called the Modern English Version, which is based on a modern English vernacular.

The Modern English Version is a translation of the Textus Receptus and the Jacob ben Hayyim edition of the Masoretic Text, using the King James Version as the base manuscript. The Committee on Bible Translation adhered to the principle of formal equivalence, the meaning of which is to be as literal as proper English syntax and grammar will allow. At times it is impossible to translate every word or thought from Greek into English with proper syntax or a modern English vernacular. In such instances, it is important to realize certain words may go untranslated. For example, the Semitism in Matthew 11:4 transliterated as, "*kai apokritheis Ho Iesous eipen autois*," is translated in the King James Version as "Jesus answered and said unto them." This is not an effective rendition in the modern English vernacular due to the redundant speech, nor is it translated literally in the King James Version. So, to translate the Greek into the modern English vernacular, the phrase is translated as "Jesus answered them." Additionally, the original translators of the King James Version did not translate the Greek "*Ho*," translated as "the," nor did they translate "*apokritheis*" literally as "'answering." Their goal was to use proper English syntax in the modern English vernacular of their day. Yet, by leaving certain terms untranslated in this update, it may appear that a Greek text other than the Textus Receptus may have been used. Such is not the case. A different English rendering is being used to re-translate the Textus Receptus while updating the King James Version manuscript.

When using the Textus Receptus as the base text for a contemporary English translation, the translators cannot use archaic, non-standard, purely literalistic English, nor fail to use what is known today about linguistics and ancient literary and cultural understandings in contemporary English translations. The original translators of the King James Version had this same approach for their own cultural and linguistic setting.

The original motive for creating this translation was to provide an update by military chaplains for the troops so they could understand the King James Version better. This project grew larger than anticipated in the search for academically qualified scholars when the chaplains "enlisted" the help of those who were not chaplains to get the job done, and when an unexpected publishing opportunity was offered. The target audience grew from the military to the entire English-speaking world. The translators began their work on June 2, 2005; they completed the New Testament on October 25, 2011, and the Old Testament on May 28, 2014.

The forty-seven American and English translators, being in great Christian unity and cooperation, who have a personal relationship with God through Jesus Christ and who have formed an interdenominational translation committee, represent churches such as the Baptist Union of Great Britain, Charismatic Episcopal Church, Central Church of the Nazarene, Church of Christ, Church of England, Church of God, Elim Church, Evangelical Lutheran Church of America, Free Methodist Church of North America, General Council of the Assemblies of God, International Church of the Foursquare Gospel, Methodist Church of Great Britain, Methodist Episcopal Church, Presbyterian Church of America, Reformed Presbyterian Church of North America, Southern Baptist Convention, United Church of Christ, United Methodist Church, and the United Reformed Church. The translators represent a cross section of the English-speaking Church. So it is their prayer that the Modern English Version will please the entire English-speaking world.

As professors or graduates of some of the world's leading colleges, seminaries, and universities, they represent institutions such as the Assemblies of God Theological Seminary, the College of William and Mary, Evangel University, Fuller Theological Seminary, Geneva College, Golden Gate Baptist Theological Seminary, Gordon-Conwell Theological Seminary, Harvard University, Hebrew Union College, Midwestern Baptist Theological Seminary, New Orleans Baptist Theological Seminary, Oklahoma Baptist University, Oral Roberts University, the Oxford Centre for Hebrew and Jewish Studies, Pentecostal Theological Seminary, Princeton Theological Seminary, Reformed Presbyterian Theological Seminary, Saint Leo University, the Southern Baptist Theological Seminary, Southwestern Baptist Theological Seminary, Stanford University, the University of Notre Dame, Vanguard University of Southern California, Westminster Seminary California, Westminster Theological Seminary, and Yale University. The translators are devoted to making a good translation better and ensuring that the Modern English Version is an accurate and responsible update of the King James Version.

The work of translating Scripture has always been an important part of Christian missions. Due to the work of missionary Bible translators, the complete Bible is available in over four hundred languages today. Missionaries normally have not used ancient Greek, Hebrew, or Aramaic texts in translation work. Instead, they usually have relied on the King James Version. In like manner, the Modern English Version is useful to continue translation work on the mission field. The Modern English Version is a translator's Bible for missions work to provide the Word of God to all English-speaking people and the entire world.

Compare the original Tyndale Translation with the updates of the following passage:

> For when the worlde thorow wysdome knew not God in ye wysdome of God: it pleased God thorow folisshnes of preachinge to save them yt beleve (1Co 1:21, Tyndale Translation, 1534).
>
> For after that, in the wisedom of God, the world by wisedome knew not God, it pleased God by the foolishnesse of preaching, to saue them that beleeue (1Co 1:21, KJV, 1611).
>
> For after that in the wisdom of God the world by wisdom knew not God, it pleased God by the foolishness of preaching to save them that believe (1Co 1:21, KJV, 1769).
>
> For since, in the wisdom of God, the world through wisdom did not know God, it pleased God through the foolishness of the message preached to save those who believe (1Co 1:21, NKJV, 1982).
>
> For since, in the wisdom of God, the world through its wisdom did not know God, it pleased God through the foolishness of preaching to save those who believe (1Co 1:21, MEV, 2014).

The clergymen and scholars comprising the Committee on Bible Translation offer up to God the Modern English Version, the inspired Word of God, in the spirit of praise and gratitude, for the purpose of making disciples and teaching all nations in the name of the Father and of the Son and of the Holy Spirit.

The Committee on
Bible Translation

Welcome to the SpiritLed Woman Bible!

In 1998 God gave me the vision and direction for a devotional magazine that would increase women's hunger for Him and help them get to know Him more intimately through teaching articles, firsthand testimonies of His power, and profiles of women past and present who have made a difference in His kingdom. That vision became *SpiritLed Woman* magazine, which our company, Charisma Media, published for ten years in print and continues to make available in digital form online today.

Over the course of those ten years I heard from countless women who shared the way our articles impacted them and encouraged them to fulfill God's plan for their lives. I also learned several things about encouraging women in the SpiritLed life:

1. **You can be whatever God calls you to be.** God uses women like you to impact His kingdom, even when the world defines you as ineligible. Don't allow the enemy to count you out.
2. **There is no more fulfilling way to live than pursuing God's purpose for your life.** You are called to make a difference for God within your sphere of influence, and because you may be the only expression of Jesus and His love many people will ever encounter, you must make an effort to represent Him well.
3. **There are no limitations in God.** When God's assignments seem overwhelming, you are often tempted to think of all the reasons you can't obey. But when you become "God-conscious" rather than "self-conscious," you can accomplish all God asks because of His great power that "works in" you (Eph 3:20). You can move beyond yourself into the realm in which He dwells, where all things are possible.
4. **God is in the storms.** When you obey God, you may encounter storms. But they can be used by God to build your character and take you to a new place in Him.
5. **Failure leads to victory.** While fulfilling God's assignments, you will make mistakes, and the enemy will use your failures to try to discourage you. But failure is simply a reminder that you cannot do anything worthwhile of yourself. By repenting and relying on God's grace and strength, you will live a life of victory.
6. **When God calls you to do something, you must trust Him.** When God gives you direction, you might encounter some uncertainty, but you must always step out in faith and obey.

A number of years have passed since we published the magazine, and now we see a new generation of women rising up with the same hunger and thirst for more of God in their lives, their families, and their communities. Whether you are young, old, or somewhere in between, my prayer is that this *SpiritLed Woman Bible* will fan that flame of passion in your heart until it becomes a brightly burning fire of zeal for God.

This desire has been the driving force behind the beautiful Bible you now hold in your hands. I thank everyone involved in its creation, including our editors who gathered content from today's leading authors and from past issues of *SpiritLed Woman* to make this Bible a unique and much-needed help in your spiritual walk.

The *SpiritLed Woman Bible* is for women like you, women who will take up the mantle of Deborah, Esther, Ruth, and other women of the Bible who have gone before us. Heroines of the faith, like Maria Woodworth-Etter and Phoebe Palmer, who have inspired me personally through their wholehearted pursuit of God. Pioneers. Trailblazers. Victorious women. Virtuous women of fasting and prayer. Godly women whose tears of intercession watered the way for those of us who are SpiritLed women today.

May you find within these pages everything you need as you seek to embrace and fulfill all that God has purposed for you to do.

Joy F. Strang

Contributors

The following Christian authors and leaders have contributed to the *SpiritLed Woman Bible*, with original articles, excerpts or adaptations from books that were published by Charisma Media, or from articles in the digital magazine *SpiritLed Woman*, published by Charisma Media. The list below shows the names of these contributors and the books or articles from which text has been excerpted or adapted.

We greatly appreciate these writers' contributions and would encourage readers to purchase the individual books they wrote. Books are available to order from the Charisma House website at www.strang.christianbook.com.

Charisma House Books

Nancy Alcorn, *Mission of Mercy* (Lake Mary, FL: Charisma House, 2013).
Nancy Alcorn is the founder and president of Mercy Ministries, an organization dedicated to helping young women find freedom from life-controlling issues. She is a sought-after international speaker and author, spreading the message of true hope and transformation.

Heidi Baker, *Compelled by Love* (Lake Mary, FL: Charisma House, 2008).
Rolland and Heidi Baker, founders of Iris Global (formerly Iris Ministries), served as missionaries in Indonesia and Hong Kong before following God's calling in 1995 to Mozambique. Having faced overwhelming need, the Bakers now watch God provide miraculously for well over ten thousand children at their centers. Iris Global has expanded to more than ten thousand churches throughout Mozambique and neighboring countries.

Kate Battistelli, *Growing Great Kids* (Lake Mary, FL: Charisma House, 2012).
Kate Battistelli is a wife, former stage actress, and mom to one of Christian music's most celebrated recording artists—Grammy-nominated Christian contemporary singer-songwriter Francesca Battistelli.

Lisa Bevere, *Out of Control and Loving It!* (Lake Mary, FL: Charisma House, 2006).
———. *The True Measure of a Woman* (Lake Mary, FL: Charisma House, 2007).
Lisa Bevere is the best-selling author of *Fight Like a Girl, Kissed the Girls and Made Them Cry, Out of Control and Loving It!,* and *Be Angry but Don't Blow It!* In addition to speaking at national and international conferences, she is a frequent guest on Christian television and radio shows. Lisa is the cofounder with her husband, John, of Messenger International.

Faith Bogdan, *Who Are All These Children, and Why Are They Calling Me Mom?* (Lake Mary, FL: Charisma House, 2013).
Faith Bogdan writes and speaks to moms and general audiences about living "well loved" by God. She also serves alongside her husband as co-pastor of Wellsburg Neighborhood Church in Wellsburg, New York.

Rachel Burchfield, *Miracle Moments* (Lake Mary, FL: Charisma House, 2013).
Rachel Burchfield has served as president of Texas Bible Institute since 1991 and draws thousands of women to her National Women's Retreats. She and her husband, Tommy, have been in ministry for more than twenty-five years, and during that time they have seen God move in miraculous ways and have learned much about how to facilitate His movement by relying on the power of the Holy Spirit.

Kimberly Daniels, *Clean House, Strong House* (Lake Mary, FL: Charisma House, 2003).
———. *Prayers That Bring Change* (Lake Mary, FL: Charisma House, 2009).
———. *Spiritual Boot Camp* (Lake Mary, FL: Charisma House, 2012).
———. *Spiritual Housekeeping* (Lake Mary, FL: Charisma House, 2011).

Apostle Kimberly Daniels, pastor of Spoken Word Ministries in Jacksonville and Fort Lauderdale, Florida, and a Jacksonville councilwoman, is a sought-after conference speaker, preacher, and powerful prayer warrior.

Brenda J. Davis, former editor of *SpiritLed Woman* magazine

Brenda J. Davis served as editor of *SpiritLed Woman* magazine from its inception. She spoke regularly at the Charisma Women's Conferences and was on the worship team. She also served as acquisitions editor for Creation House until early 2014.

Iris Delgado, *Satan, You Can't Have My Children* (Lake Mary, FL: Charisma House, 2011).

———. *Satan, You Can't Have My Marriage* (Lake Mary, FL: Charisma House, 2012).

———. *Satan, You Can't Have My Miracle* (Lake Mary, FL: Charisma House, 2012).

———. *Satan, You Can't Have My Promises* (Lake Mary, FL: Charisma House, 2013).

Dr. Iris Delgado is founder and president of Crowned With Purpose Ministries. She is a dynamic speaker and author who shares the vision of her ministry with her husband, Dr. John Delgado, as they travel and minister together.

Iris and John Delgado, *Destroy the Works of the Enemy* (Lake Mary, FL: Charisma House, 2013).

Drs. John and Iris Delgado travel the globe together, ministering a message of hope and restoration. John is founder and president of Vision International University of Florida and the author of *Prayer Training Manual*. Iris is the founder and president of Crowned With Purpose Ministries.

Barbara Dycus, former executive director of product development for Charisma House Book Group

Barbara Dycus is a freelance writer/editor with more than thirty years of experience in the publishing field. She worked for nearly twenty years at Charisma Media, retiring in November 2011 from her position as executive director of product development.

Misty Edwards, *What Is the Point?* (Lake Mary, FL: Passion, 2012).

Misty Edwards has been a worship leader at the International House of Prayer in Kansas City for more than ten years. She is one of four permanent board members at the Missions Base, the head section leader of the Global Prayer Room, and the executive producer of Forerunner Music.

Rebecca Greenwood, *Let Our Children Go* (Lake Mary, FL: Charisma House, 2011).

Rebecca Greenwood is cofounder and president of Christian Harvest International and Strategic Prayer Action Network. She is an internationally known speaker who conducts seminars and conferences on prayer, spiritual warfare, deliverance, prophecy, and the kingdom of God.

Diana Hagee, *What Every Woman Wants in a Man* (Lake Mary, FL: Charisma House, 2007).

Diana Hagee is author of *Not by Bread Alone*, a cookbook encouraging creative ministry through food, and *The King's Daughter*, which received a Retailers Choice Award.

Rita Hancock, *Radical Well-Being* (Lake Mary, FL: Siloam, 2013).

Rita Hancock, MD, is a board-certified physical medicine specialist with subspecialty board certification in pain management. She has been in full-time practice in Norman, Oklahoma, for more than fifteen years.

Marilyn Hickey, *The Bible Can Change You* (Lake Mary, FL: Creation House, 1989).

More than three decades ago Marilyn Hickey responded to God's call on her life to cover the earth with His Word, as referenced in Isaiah 11:9. The natural inclination to reach out and to celebrate people and culture was traceable in Marilyn's formative years, yet she had no idea how God would send her around the globe teaching the Bible and building bridges with people of all cultures and religious backgrounds, especially in the Muslim world.

Julie Hiramine, *Guardians of Purity* (Lake Mary, FL: Charisma House, 2012).
Julie Hiramine is founder and executive director of Generations of Virtue, a ministry that equips parents to empower their children for purity in our world today.

Shelley Hundley, *A Cry for Justice* (Lake Mary, FL: Charisma House, 2011).
Shelley Hundley was one of the original interns who helped launch the International House of Prayer under Mike Bickle's leadership and has been on the senior leadership of IHOPKC since its inception in 1999. She currently serves as vice president of training at the International House of Prayer University in Kansas City, Missouri.

Judy Jacobs, *Stand Strong* (Lake Mary, FL: Charisma House, 2007).
———. *You Are Anointed for This!* (Lake Mary, FL: Charisma House, 2013).
Judy Jacobs, founder of His Song Ministries, is a recording artist, sought-after conference speaker, and best-selling author. She and her husband, Jamie Tuttle, pastor Dwelling Place Church International in Cleveland, Tennessee.

Larry Keefauver, general editor, *Holy Spirit Encounter Bible* (Lake Mary, FL: Charisma House, 1997).
Larry Keefauver, DMin, writes extensively and is a contributing editor for various Christian magazines. He and his wife, Judi, travel internationally, leading seminars and conferences on family, marriage, parenting, church leadership, and church growth.

Mercy Lokulutu, *As You Wish* (Lake Mary, FL: Passio, 2013).
Mercy Lokulutu is a passionate and dynamic communicator of God's Word. As an ordained pastor and conference speaker, she carries with her a mandate to preach the gospel, reach the lost, and build the local church.

Babbie Mason, *FaithLift* (Lake Mary, FL: Charisma House, 2003).
Babbie Mason is a Dove Award–winning singer, songwriter, and recording artist. She is also the author of *Treasures of Heaven in the Stuff of Earth*. Babbie is in great demand at conferences (often with Women of Faith) and concerts worldwide.

Michelle McClain-Walters, *The Prophetic Advantage* (Lake Mary, FL: Charisma House, 2012).
Michelle McClain-Walters serves as director of prayer ministry on staff at Crusaders Church in Chicago under the leadership of John Eckhardt. She has traveled to more than forty nations, partnering with senior church leaders to release strategies that advance the kingdom of God.

Reina Olmeda, *Fit for Your Assignment* (Lake Mary, FL: Siloam, 2014).
Reina Olmeda is senior pastor of Third Day Worship Center in Allentown, Pennsylvania, alongside her husband, Rev. Charles Olmeda. With a passion to see women rise up to the Lord's standards for their lives, she has worked with abused women as well as young women in crisis.

Fuchsia Pickett, *For Such a Time as This* (Lake Mary, FL: Charisma House, 1997).
———. *How to Search the Scriptures* (Lake Mary, FL: Charisma House, 1999).
———. *Possess Your Promised Land* (Lake Mary, FL: Charisma House, 2003).
———. *Receiving Divine Revelation* (Lake Mary, FL: Charisma House, 1997).
———. *The Prophetic Romance* (Lake Mary, FL: Charisma House, 1996).
———. *Walking in the Anointing of the Holy Spirit* (Lake Mary, FL: Charisma House, 2004).
The late Dr. Fuchsia Pickett was a best-selling author and international conference speaker and teacher. Her books and speaking presentations were filled with fresh revelation and deep spiritual truths.

Chuck D. Pierce, *Redeeming the Time* (Lake Mary, FL: Charisma House, 2009).
Dr. Charles D. "Chuck" Pierce has been used by God to intercede and mobilize

prayer throughout the world. An ordained minister and best-selling author, he is president of Glory of Zion International Ministries in Denton, Texas, and of Global Sphere, Inc.

Kimberly Ray, *Spiritual Intervention* (Lake Mary, FL: Charisma House, 2013).
Kimberly Ray is an accomplished speaker and gifted singer and songwriter. She has been delivering messages that inspire, encourage, and bring effective change in people's lives for more than twenty-five years.

John Rea, *Charisma's Bible Handbook on the Holy Spirit* (Lake Mary, FL: Charisma House, 1998).
John Rea, ThD, professor emeritus of Old Testament at Regent University, has theological degrees from Wheaton College, Grace Theological Seminary, and Princeton University. He has been an author and/or contributing editor for many books, including the *Holy Spirit Encounter Bible*.

Joyce Rodgers, *Fatal Distractions* (Lake Mary, FL: Charisma House, 2003).
Joyce Rodgers is an evangelist and sought-after conference speaker who frequently writes for *Charisma* and *SpiritLed Woman* magazines. She is the founder and CEO of Primary Purpose Ministry and serves on an international, jurisdictional, and district level with the Church of God in Christ.

Katherine Ruonala, *Living in the Miraculous* (Lake Mary, FL: Charisma House, 2013).
Katherine Ruonala has a prophetic and healing ministry. She and her husband, Tom, are founders and senior ministers of Glory City Church in Brisbane, Australia, and oversee the international Glory Gathering church-planting network.

Peggy Joyce Ruth, *Psalm 91* (Lake Mary, FL: Charisma House, 2010).
———. *Psalm 91 for Mothers* (Lake Mary, FL: Charisma House, 2013).
Peggy Joyce Ruth and her husband, Jack, are former pastors from Brownwood, Texas. Peggy has taught an adult Bible study each week at her church for the past thirty years and continues her teaching on a weekly radio broadcast. She is the author of ten books.

Karen Jensen Salisbury, *Why, God, Why?* (Lake Mary, FL: Charisma House, 2013).
Karen Jensen Salisbury is an instructor at Rhema Bible Training College, an itinerant minister, and the editor and principal writer of the *Connections* alumni magazine.

John Loren and Paula Sandford and Lee Bowman, *Choosing Forgiveness* (Lake Mary, FL: 2007).
John Sandford pastored churches for many years and founded Elijah House Ministries. He is considered a pioneer in the prophetic and healing movements and is a best-selling author of many books. Paula Sandford joined her husband in the team ministry of Elijah House from its beginning and was ordained in 1995. Lee Bowman is a graduate of William Jewell College and holds a graduate degree in theology and a master's degree in art.

Rita Springer, *Finding Eve* (Lake Mary, FL: Passio, 2013).
Rita Springer is known for her unscripted, spontaneous worship and has written many popular worship songs, such as "Make Us a Prayer" and "This Blood." She is part of the worship ministry staff at Gateway Church in Southlake, Texas. Out of her music has grown a passion to mentor and empower women to rise up and take their place in the kingdom of God.

Jeannette Storms, *Connexion* (Lake Mary, FL: Charisma House, 2010).
Prior to joining the faculty at the King's College and Seminary to teach, Jeanette Storms served as a missionary in Mexico, Zambia, Japan, and London for sixteen years. In London she founded Agape Christian Fellowship and served as its pastor for several years. Now she serves as founder of Kingdom Connexion, a

nonprofit organization that equips and empowers leaders in prayer, leadership, and missions.

Jenny Swindall, *Freedom From Depression* (Lake Mary, FL: Charisma House, 2013).
Jenny Swindall has a bachelor of science degree in microbiology from Auburn University and started her career in clinical pharmaceutical and biotech sales. *Freedom From Depression* was birthed out of Jenny's personal struggle with and triumph over depression more than a decade ago.

Riva Tims, *When It All Falls Apart* (Lake Mary, FL: Charisma House, 2012).
Riva Tims is pastor of Majestic Life Ministries, a nondenominational congregation in Orlando, Florida. She has served in ministry for more than fifteen years as a pastor and speaker and is the cohost of her own TV and radio programs.

Jennifer Toledo, *Children and the Supernatural* (Lake Mary, FL: Charisma House, 2012).
Jennifer Toledo and her husband, Jonatan, are founders and directors of Global Children's Movement and pastors at Expression58 in Los Angeles. They speak at churches, conferences, and community and educational gatherings to raise awareness about the issues of children at risk and to get people involved.

Cindy Trimm, *The Art of War for Spiritual Battle* (Lake Mary, FL: Charisma House, 2010).
———. *Commanding Your Morning* (Lake Mary, FL: Charisma House, 2007).
———. *The Prayer Warrior's Way* (Lake Mary, FL: Charisma House, 2011).
———. *'Til Heaven Invades Earth* (Lake Mary, FL: Charisma House, 2013).
———. *When Kingdoms Clash* (Lake Mary, FL: Charisma House, 2012).
Cindy Trimm has dedicated her life to serving God and humanity. A best-selling author and former senator, Dr. Trimm is a sought-after empowerment specialist, revolutionary thinker, and transformational leader.

Tish Hagee Tucker, *Master of the Impossible* (Lake Mary, FL: Charisma House, 2013).
Tish Hagee Tucker teaches at Cornerstone Christian School in San Antonio, Texas, and has undergraduate degrees in both journalism and Spanish and a master's degree in education. She is the author of *Hear My Cry: How Grace Conquered Cancer.*

SpiritLed Woman Articles

Each of the following articles appeared in the digital magazine *SpiritLed Woman* or in one of the blogs published by Charisma Media and are accessible at www.spiritledwoman.com.

Wendy Alsup, "Honesty and Truth Will Always Overcome Darkness," December 30, 2013. (www.theologyforwomen.org)

Shirley Arnold, "Break Out of Mediocrity," January 3, 2014. (www.tlcfamilychurch.org)

Jill Austin, "The Bride Awaits Her King," August 14, 2013. (www.masterpotter.com)

Sue Birdseye, "When Being Right Is Wrong," April 30, 2013. (www.suebirdseye.com)

Cynthia Brazelton, "Can You See His Glory?" April 29, 2013.

Felicity Dale, "Heroine of the Faith: Amy Carmichael," May 15, 2013. (http://simplychurch.com)
———. "Heroine of the Faith: Corrie ten Boom," May 1, 2013.
———. "Heroine of the Faith: Jessie Penn-Lewis," June 4, 2013.
———. "Heroine of the Faith: Lottie Moon," April 24, 2013.
———. "Heroine of the Faith: Phoebe Palmer," June 12, 2013.

Jennifer Kennedy Dean, "Created by God's Hand," March 14, 2014. (www.prayinglife.org)

Stasi Eldredge, "Finding God's Purpose in Your Femininity," July 17, 2013. (www.ransomedheart.com)

June Evans, "Pursue His Presence," May 3, 2013. (http://makejesusfamous.net)

Elisabeth Farrell, "Modern-Day Martyrs: Women Endure Torture, Rape, and Losing Family to Follow Christ," July 25, 2013.

Pat Francis, "How to Open the Windows of Heaven," October 24, 2013. (www.patfrancis.org)

J. Lee Grady, "Delay Is Not Denial," Fire in My Bones (blog), August 1, 2010. (www.themordecaiproject.com)

Kathy Gray, "How to Keep the Flow of Prophetic Intercession," February 11, 2013. (www.worldrevivalchurch.com)

———. "Joy That Ignites Your Faith," September 4, 2013.

Greg Hinnant, "How to Show Your Kids the Way to God," March 6, 2013. (www.greghinnantministries.org)

Jo Kadlecek, "Four Ways to Feed Your Spirit," August 19, 2013.

Susie Larson, "Can God Trust You With His Glory?" May 24, 2013. (www.susielarson.com)

———. "Six Words That Will Reignite Your Prayer Life," October 1, 2013.

———. "When God Doesn't Answer," October 22, 2013.

Cathy Lechner, "Staying Steady in Your Faith During Change," March 12, 2014. (http://cathylechner.com)

Anne Graham Lotz, "How an Encounter With Jesus Changes Everything," February 6, 2014.

Winifred W. Morris, "Let Go of the Guilt," May 31, 2005. (http://www.mtairycogic.com/new1/mothermorris.html)

Fuchsia Pickett, "Possess Your Spiritual Inheritance," July 26, 2013. (www.fuchsiapickett.com)

Anna Rountree, "Three Keys to Moving in the Supernatural Love of God," February 4, 2014. (http://annarountree.com)

Teresa Seputis, "Did God Really Say That?" April 19, 2013. (www.godspeak.net)

———. "Two Keys to Surviving God's Refining Fire," April 10, 2014.

Ellen Stumbo, "The Effective, Fervent Prayer of a Woman Unlocks Tremendous Power," June 26, 2013. (www.ellenstumbo.com)

Thetus Tenney, "How Angels Minister Today," June 25, 2013. (www.focusedlight.net)

Barbara J. Yoder, "Take Authority in Your Day of Trouble," July 16, 2013. (wwww.shekinahchurch.org)

———. "Unleash the Power to Break Through to Victory," March 11, 2013.

How to Study the Bible

The Bible deserves our devoted systematic study.

Preliminary Considerations

Regular and systematic reading of the Bible is essential for Christian growth. Spiritual success for both an individual and a church can come only through Bible study and meditation. A greater use and deeper understanding of the Word of God by believers is essential to a living, dynamic church. D. L. Moody said, "I never saw a useful Christian who was not a student of the Bible. If a man neglects his Bible, he may pray and ask God to use him in His work, but God cannot make much use of him, for there is not much for the Holy Spirit to work upon. We must have the Word itself, which is sharper than any two-edged sword."

The Bible is God's Book, given to us to tell us about God. We know there is a God because we see His creation—the sun, the moon, the stars, the mountains, the plains, the rivers, the lakes, and the oceans. All these and a thousand more are indications of the presence of a powerful Creator.

But we know little about God until we study the Bible. There we learn who God is, what He is, what He has done, what He is doing, and what He shall yet do. Man comes to the end of his search for truth when he sees the manifestation of God in the Person of the Lord Jesus Christ as revealed in God's written Word. From the Bible we learn that God is holy and that He hates our sins. But the Bible shows us that God loves us so much that He gave His Son to save us from our sins.

The Bible tells us that we have sinned. It tells us that Jesus came into the world to save sinners, that He took our place at Calvary, that He arose from the dead, and that He is seated at the right hand of the Father, from whence He shall come to receive His own unto Himself.

These are the glorious truths related in fascinating detail in the Bible. Pray with the psalmist: "Open my eyes, that I may behold wondrous things from Your law" (Ps 119:18). Prayerful study of the Bible will help us gain a full-length picture of God's provision and plan for us.

Many Christians do not get much joy and satisfaction—that extra something—from their Bible study. They have failed to learn how to make studying the Word a feeding process that results in spiritual nourishment and growth. Most Christians read a portion of Scripture each day as a devotional exercise. This is good; it is necessary and profitable. But too many believers follow the practice of merely reading Bible portions; they never read the Bible in any other way.

The Bible should be studied systematically. A knowledge of the Bible—or of any one book of the Bible—comes by a definite plan of reading and studying. Reading Bible portions will feed the soul, but a Christian needs to grasp and understand the great truths and doctrines the Bible teaches.

Bible study must not be an end in itself. God has given us the Bible; it is to do something *in* us and *through* us.

A Plan of Action

Study daily.

Study prayerfully.

Study systematically.

Study with enjoyment.

Preparation for Study

> My son, if you will receive my words, and hide my commandments within you, so that you incline your ear to wisdom, and apply your heart to understanding; yes, if you cry out for knowledge, and lift up your voice for understanding, if you seek her as silver, and search for her as for hidden treasures, then you will understand the fear of the Lord, and find the knowledge of God.
>
> —Proverbs 2:1–5

Personal Bible study is a battle. One does not find too many people today who seek a quiet place with a book; the number is even fewer when it comes to Bible study. Distractions are manifold, and time runs short.

Christians need to evaluate how they spend their time. Unwise use of time is one of the greatest deterrents to Christian growth.

Bible study is the most effective tool of the Holy Spirit to bring the Christian into conformity to Christ. Understandably, Satan uses every device possible to keep us from the Word of God.

Rules to follow

1. The Bible is God's Word.

"My son, if you will receive my words." We must come to the Bible with the conviction that it is the Word of God through which God will surely speak to us. We do not need to prove the Bible first and then accept it; we accept it and then let it prove itself. If we doubt the authority of the Word, we cannot expect to receive anything from the Lord (Jas 1:6–7). We need to be like the Thessalonians and receive the Word of God as truth (1Th 2:13). Many receive no benefit because they do not receive the Word with faith (Heb 4:2).

2. Obedience is required.

"And hide my commandments within you…" The soul must be exercised by the Word. The Word must school us and change our lives. If we fail to translate the Word into daily practice, we will be spiritually anemic. Bible study brings renewed devotion to God. Even more, it produces discipline and determination, resulting in the transformation of human nature. There is no better way to blind ourselves to Bible truth than to refuse to heed and obey it. The prophet Hosea said, "My people are destroyed for lack of knowledge. Because you have rejected knowledge, I will reject you" (Hos 4:6). We do not truly study the Word—or really know it—until we put it into practice in our lives. "Be doers of the word" (Jas 1:22).

3. Listening is demanded.

"Incline your ear to wisdom." The word *incline* means "to listen, to take heed." Luke 8:18 says, "Take heed therefore how you hear." We need to incline our ears to the voice of the Holy Spirit. A first principle in Bible study is to learn to read intelligently. But more than that, we need the illumination of the Holy Spirit, for the Bible is a revelation of spiritual truth and its understanding is dependent upon spiritual sensitivity. Consider every phrase and every word of Scripture. Let the Holy Spirit make it real to the listening ear.

4. The heart must be yielded.

"Apply your heart to understanding." Heart-searching should precede Bible study. The Word has been likened in Scripture to seed. We must prepare the soil of our hearts to receive the Word so it will bear fruit. The psalmist prayed, "Search me, O God, and know my heart; try me, and know my concerns, and see if there is any rebellious way in me, and lead me in the ancient way" (Ps 139:23–24). Unless the heart is prepared, we will miss the truths of the Word. We must have a regenerated heart (Jn 3:3), a humble heart (Mt 11:25), a willing heart (Jn 7:17), and a devoted heart (Ps 119:67). We need to open our hearts to God and let Him prepare them to receive the truth of His Word.

5. Prayer is necessary.

"Yes, if you cry out for knowledge, and lift up your voice for understanding." We cannot, by our own wisdom, understand the Bible. In all our study we must carefully seek the help of the Holy Spirit. He alone can remove the veil from our minds. It is impossible to know the Bible without prayer. We need to join the psalmist in his prayer: "Open my eyes, that I may behold wondrous things from Your law" (Ps 119:18). When we breathe this prayer in faith, we can expect the Lord to open our understanding as He did for the two men on the Emmaus road after His resurrection: "Their eyes were opened, and they recognized Him.…They said…'Did not our hearts burn within us…while He opened the Scriptures to us?'" (Lk 24:31–32). It is the same understanding given to Lydia, the seller of purple: "A woman named Lydia…the Lord opened her heart" (Ac 16:14).

6. Seek as for silver.

"If you seek her as silver." Silver is a standard of money. Women will do almost anything for money because money gives them so many of the things they want. The Bible states, "Money resolves everything" (Ecc 10:19). We work for the paycheck. But there is something of far greater worth than the silver of this world. David said, "The words of the LORD are pure words; they are silver tried in an earthen furnace refined seven times" (Ps 12:6). As a woman disciplines herself to hard toil to get a share of this world's goods, the Christian must prepare for the discipline of businesslike Bible study, coupled with businesslike prayer. It takes earnestness of purpose, concentration of effort, and determination of mind and heart.

7. Search as for hidden treasure.

"And search for her as for hidden treasures." The word *search* is equivalent to dig. The Vulgate translation reads "to dig out." The treasures of God's Word will be found by the woman who gives herself to diligently dig for them. We need to use the same untiring energy with which women dig for hidden treasure in our search for the riches of the Word. The perseverance of the seeker after material wealth often puts to shame the seeker after spiritual wealth. This matter of searching is important. Jesus said, "Search the Scriptures" (Jn 5:39).

Results to expect

The serious seeker after spiritual wealth can expect the following results from study:

- Understanding: "Then you will understand the fear of the LORD…" (Pr 2:5). Our hearts will be filled with wonder and praise, and we will receive "the things of the Spirit of God" (1Co 2:14).
- Knowledge: "…and find the knowledge of God" (Pr 2:5). Purposeful study will do more than merely give us the facts of the Bible; we will learn to know God. The divine personality, infinite and unfathomable, will reveal Himself. We know the living Word as we understand His revelation given to us in the written Word.

Provision for Study

> But the Counselor, the Holy Spirit, whom the Father will send in My name, will teach you everything and remind you of all that I told you.
> —John 14:26

> But when the Spirit of truth comes, He will guide you into all truth. For He will not speak on His own authority. But He will speak whatever He hears, and He will tell you things that are to come. He will glorify Me, for He will receive from Me and will declare it to you. All that the Father has is Mine. Therefore I said that He will take what is Mine and will declare it to you.
> —John 16:13–15

The Bible is God's message to us.

Every word has value and importance in the total revelation. The general theme of the Bible is redemption through the Lord Jesus Christ. Every part of the Bible is perfect because it is the Word of God. But the Old Testament by itself is incomplete, for it is anticipatory. It looks forward to the coming of the promised Redeemer. From beginning to end, it is a book of promise, looking forward to something not yet fulfilled.

On the other hand, the New Testament speaks of the fulfillment of that expectation. The mighty sweep of God's purpose is given to us in Matthew 16:13–27. Here we have:

- The revelation of His person: "You are the Christ, the Son of the living God" (v. 16).
- The revelation of His purpose: "On this rock I will build My church" (v. 18).
- The revelation of His program: "He must go to Jerusalem and suffer many things from the elders and chief priests and scribes, and be killed, and be raised on the third day" (v. 21). In the Gospel of Luke God's purpose for this age is given in three steps: "It was necessary for the Christ to suffer and to rise from the dead the third day, and that repentance and remission of sins should be preached in His name to all nations, beginning at Jerusalem" (Lk 24:46–47).
- The revelation of the opposition to His program: "Far be it from You, Lord! This shall not happen to You" (Mt 16:22).
- The revelation of the cost to be His follower: "If anyone will come after Me, let him deny himself, and take up his cross, and follow Me" (v. 24).
- The revelation of the culmination of His purpose: "For the Son of Man shall come with His angels in the glory of His Father, and then He will repay every man according to his works" (v. 27).

The Bible is clear in its central message.

There are depths of meaning that challenge the greatest minds and elude the grasp of the greatest thinkers, but generally the truths of the Scriptures are plain and clear. Satan wants to make us think that it is very difficult for the ordinary person to understand the Bible. Anyone who stands upon the Word need not be troubled with the fear of not being able to understand it, for understanding and enlightenment do not rest with us.

The Bible deals with matters that are divine, infinite, and eternal.

The Bible transcends man's understanding. But divine enablement comes to us through the Holy Spirit (Jn 14:26; 16:13–15; 1Co 2:13–14). A yielded Christian, even though she may have a limited intellectual capacity and may lack formal education, can nevertheless make great progress in her understanding of the Bible, because she knows the Teacher and has daily fellowship with Him.

God has made provision for us to understand His Word by giving us the Holy Spirit. The Spirit who authored the Word is the divine Teacher who explains it. We must allow Him to guide us. Then it will be amazing how He will open our spiritual eyes.

The Word of God will not degenerate into a mere textbook of history or a manual on religion if we come to it always expecting an encounter with the Lord. Study, illumined by the Holy Spirit, will bring us to worship. Meditation will bring us to praise, and praise will bring us to adoration. No better illustration can be found than the warmth of worship expressed by the psalmist as he dwelt on the wonders of the Word in Psalms 1, 19, and 119.

Principles of Study

> All Scripture is inspired by God and is profitable for teaching, for reproof, for correction, and for instruction in righteousness.
>
> —2 Timothy 3:16

God wants us to study the Bible. He has provided the Book and the Teacher. Through His servants we have an abundance of help in the form of Bible study books and study methods. If we have a desire to know the Word, a willingness to give time for that purpose, and a resolve to keep on despite obstacles, we will find the joy of learning and living in the Word. Come hungry to the Word, for the hungry are never disappointed (Mt 5:6).

Bible study must be personal, practical, perpetual, and presented to others.

Personal Bible study

"Oh, how I love Your law! It is my meditation all the day" (Ps 119:97). Note the personal pronouns *I* and *my*. Bible study will be tedious until it becomes personal. Then it can be delightful, intensely interesting, thrilling, and profitable. In Bible study, we must be participants rather than spectators.

Practical Bible study

Bible study requires a systematic approach. Do not stay only with those portions that have brought blessing or seem more inviting. If a less interesting passage falls into the plan, resist the inclination to turn aside. *All* Scripture is inspired. *All* is God's Word. "Man shall not live by bread alone, but by every word that proceeds out of the mouth of God" (Mt 4:4). Aim to cover *all* the Bible. Approach the uninviting passage with a real spirit of study. Pray over it; meditate upon it; compare it with parallel passages; read what others have written about it. Watch it become real!

Actual study should involve reading the passage or the book over again and again. Read available translations. Make notes for later study. Keep a record of your observations just as they occur to you, whether they seem significant or not. Writing down your thoughts will serve to stimulate thinking and concentration. We discover how little we know when we try to write it down. Use a study Bible that can be marked. Marking your Bible will help to make your reading more concrete. Try underlining passages that are especially meaningful. Jot in the margins thoughts that the Spirit makes real.

Effective Bible study involves asking the following sequential questions:

- Observation—What does the passage say (content)?
- Interpretation—What does it mean?
- Application—How does it apply to me?

As you seek to apply God's Word to your life, continue by asking: What does it say to me (personal application)? What does it say to me today (relevant personal application)? What am I going to do about it today (immediate personal action on the Word)?

It is necessary to *observe* carefully what the passage actually says before *interpreting* it and then *applying* the truths personally.

A simple, practical approach to study is suggested in 2 Timothy 3:16. Just as John 3:16 gives us the central verse of the Bible on how to become a Christian, 2 Timothy 3:16 gives us an important verse on how to grow as a Christian:

> All Scripture is given by inspiration of God and is profitable for teaching, for reproof, for correction, for instruction in righteousness.

Any passage in the Bible—a verse, a chapter, a book—is God's Word and is profitable in four ways. Note them:

- Doctrine—The Bible presents a system of truth containing all the knowledge of God, man, and the universe essential to spiritual growth. Find the teaching of the passage.
- Reproof—Biblical reproof makes us feel keenly to what extent we have strayed from the divine standard.
- Correction—The Scripture is the plumb line by which we test the correctness of our thinking and the uprightness of our conduct. Some read the Bible to criticize and attempt to correct it. Blessing comes to those who read it for the purpose of allowing it to criticize and correct them.
- Instruction in righteousness—Biblical instruction applies the lessons learned in the passage to your personal life. As we compare our character and conduct with the precepts of the Scriptures, we are being practical about Bible study. Instruction is effective only to the extent that it is applied.

Perpetual Bible study

> These [the Bereans] were more noble than those in Thessalonica, for they received the word with all eagerness, daily examining the Scriptures, to find out if these things were so.
>
> —Acts 17:11

The Bereans were marked as noble people for two reasons: They welcomed the Word of God, and they searched the Scriptures daily.

Bible study has been compared to eating. If we expect to stay alive spiritually, we must keep feeding ourselves. We do not eat a week's supply of food for the natural body in a day; there must be a daily assimilation of food. Neither can we absorb enough Bible study in a day to last for a lengthy period of time. If spiritual strength is to be maintained, there must be constant feeding on the Word of God.

Presented to others

> Share the things that you have heard from me in the presence of many witnesses with faithful men who will be able to teach others also.
>
> —2 Timothy 2:2

What we learn in Bible study must be passed on to others. If not, our study can become dull and uninteresting. The constant outflow of water from a body of water keeps it fresh and free from the stagnant odors and scum of a dead body of water. We use what we have learned by sharing it with others. Sharing is an excellent way to make a truth real to us.

Illustrative and Practical

Other books we may read and criticize. To the Scriptures we must bow the entire soul, with all its faculties.

—E. N. Kirk

The Scriptures were written, not to make us astronomers, but to make us saints.

—Matthew Henry

The Bible is the most thought-suggesting book in the world. No other deals with such grand themes.

—Herrick Johnson

When you are reading a book in a dark room, and come to a difficult part, you take it to a window to get more light. So take your Bible to Christ.

—Robert McCheyne

I am convinced that the Bible becomes even more beautiful the more one understands it; that is, the more one gets insight to see that every word, which we take generally and make special applications of it to our own wants, has had, in connection with certain circumstances, with certain relations of time and place, a particular, directly individual reference of its own.

—Goethe

Make it the first morning business of your life to understand some part of the Bible clearly, and make it your daily business to obey it in all that you do understand.

—John Ruskin

Nobody ever outgrows Scripture; the Book widens and deepens with the years.

—Charles H. Spurgeon

There is no book that will so repay time spent on its pages as will the Word of God.

—F. B. Meyer

Benefits of committing the Scriptures to memory

The benefits of memorizing Scripture are many. Unquestionably the presence of the Word of God in the inner mind does tend, by God's grace, to sweeten and sanctify. And then in solitary moments, whether on the job, in private meditation, or lying awake at night, how beautiful it is to be able to listen to the voice of God talking out of one's memory by His Word unto the mind and heart. What a power to guide, to warn, and to cheer us. Many a moment that would be invaded by sin or darkened by sorrow is turned into purity and hope by a portion of Scripture—a verse, a passage, a psalm—said from memory. "Your word I have hidden in my heart, that I might not sin against You" (Ps 119:11).

Fuchsia Pickett

How to Use This Bible

The purpose of the *SpiritLed Woman Bible* is to provide the reader with opportunities to study the principles and teachings contained in either the Modern English Version text of this Bible or the various additional teaching elements added by the publishers to help the reader deepen her relationship with Christ and utilize the power and strength of the Holy Spirit to help her to mature as a SpiritLed woman, prepared to be an effective servant of Christ who is actively impacting her world for God.

The additional teaching elements are written in the present tense so that their impact will address the reader's life at the moment of studying the Word and teachings. The Scripture texts used in the additional teachings use the Modern English Version of the Bible.

While the inclusive pronoun *us* is often used to involve the reader, the pronoun *you* is used whenever possible so as to confront and engage the reader with the impact of the teaching.

SpiritLed Woman teachings may be found throughout the Bible to give further insight, inspiration, and depth from the perspectives of outstanding Christian pastors and authors.

Additional Study Elements

There are six different tools in the *SpiritLed Woman Bible* for your personal study and devotions. Here is a list of the tools and how to use them.

SpiritLed Woman's Daily Inspirational Thoughts

There are 366 SpiritLed Woman's Daily Inspirational Thoughts to be found within the text of this Bible. These are presented as one-sentence, Scripture-based inspirational thoughts affirming the SpiritLed woman's access to the power of the Holy Spirit's help. These inspirational thoughts include a Scripture reference, showing the Bible verse that is the basis for that thought. You may:

- Choose an inspirational thought as your daily focus.
- Read progressively from Genesis through Revelation, reading the inspirational thoughts as you read the Bible text in your daily time of study and devotions. As you read, pause to reflect on the truth of each declaration.
- Choose to commit one inspirational thought to memory each day.

SpiritLed Woman's Counsel From the Spirit Basics

There are nearly one hundred SpiritLed Woman's Counsel From the Spirit Basics, which are found in each book of the Bible. These are usually one-quarter to one-half column in length. They are short, succinct teachings from the Holy Spirit to you and cover many of the very basic things you will need to know as you prepare to mature into a SpiritLed woman of God.

Some ways to use these SpiritLed Woman's Counsel From the Spirit Basics include:

- Reading a SpiritLed Woman's Counsel From the Spirit Basic each day for your daily devotional time.
- Reading progressively from Genesis through Revelation, completing one SpiritLed Woman's Counsel From the Spirit Basic each day and applying the revelation to your daily life.

- Keeping a journal of your insights and responses to these SpiritLed Woman's Counsel From the Spirit Basics and the other study elements in this Bible. The journal can serve as your personal training manual.

Profile of a SpiritLed Woman

The study materials include twenty-one character profiles of Old and New Testament women or women who became heroines of the faith in history and were equipped and anointed by the Holy Spirit to become SpiritLed women. Each profile shows how the Spirit enabled that woman for a specific moment's need. The profiles could easily be adapted for a three-week small-group study about spiritual warfare or as part of a specific devotional plan for three weeks. Be sure to journal your responses as you read about each character, and include your specific prayer requests for God to equip and prepare you in a similar way for maturing in the SpiritLed woman's lifestyle. The profiles included are:

Spirit-to-Spirit Prayers

Scattered throughout the Bible are thirty-five prayers that focus on a specific prayer topic. You may choose to pray one prayer daily for an entire month, during which you will be focused on developing a more intimate relationship with our Father God.

These prayers may also be prayed when you are facing a similar spiritual challenge, or they may be used as material for a small-group discussion on prayer and intercession for maturing in the SpiritLed life. You may choose to use the specific words that are included, or you can make the prayers your own by expressing your own thoughts and desires around that particular spiritual challenge. The prayers included are:

Growing as a SpiritLed Woman study elements

Interspersed throughout the Bible are twenty-one opportunities for you to spend some time in deeper reflection and study and to use various study methods to internalize what the Word of God says specifically about growing spiritually in a SpiritLed lifestyle. Use these opportunities to make specific preparations for your spiritual growth. They would make excellent small-group study starters and could also be used as part of a deeper devotional focus at various times throughout your reading God's Word.

The subjects included in these Growing as a SpiritLed Woman study elements, with their focus Scripture reference, include:

Woman of the Spirit articles

There is a one- to two-page focus article included with each book of the Bible. These articles give a deeper, more complete teaching about a specific element of the SpiritLed lifestyle. They are excellent resources for deeper study as you become stronger in your faith and mature in the Spirit. The specific topical articles included are:

Appendixes at the back of the Bible

We have included some appendixes that we feel are important additional materials related to the preparation and equipping of the SpiritLed woman. We encourage you to read these appendixes and use them as tools as you step forward into the SpiritLed life. The appendixes included are:

- Appendix A—The Anointing Is for You
- Appendix B—Ten Tactics of Prayer
- Appendix C—Family Devotions—Eliminating the Yawn Factor
- Appendix D—One Hundred Advantages of the Word of the Lord

Small group or class study

The *SpiritLed Woman Bible* is an excellent resource for a small group or class Bible study focused on the subject of SpiritLed women. This Bible may be used for:

- Small group studies
- Home groups
- Cell groups
- Sunday school classes
- Midweek classes
- Group seminars or retreats

- Women's and men's groups
- Accountability groups
- Youth groups, campus groups, or college and career groups

It is our prayer that this *SpiritLed Woman Bible* will become an invaluable tool for you to use continually as you grow in your relationship with your heavenly Father. Remember that the Holy Spirit is the One who will guide you and empower you to be a woman of great spiritual power—one who will be used to show many other women how to be empowered by God's Holy Spirit to impact their world for God's glory.

Prayer of Salvation

Maybe you're reading this Bible because you have questions, but you've never met the God you're seeking answers from. Maybe you've never asked Him into your life. I want to invite you into a relationship with Him. He holds all the answers, He knows you inside and out, and He loves you! He knows what your heart desires.

There was a point in my life when I had to be introduced to Him, just like anyone who is a Christian. Now I can honestly say, if it wasn't for Him in my life, I wouldn't be where I am today. We are all born into sin (Ro 3:23). Sin separates you from God. Two thousand years ago God sent His only Son, Jesus, to the earth as a man, and He died on the cross to bear the consequences of our sin so that we could be restored to a perfect relationship (right standing) with God (1Pe 2:24). He became sin so that we could become righteousness (2Co 5:21). He traded places with us.

God loves you, not because you've done everything right or because you're good, but because *He* is good. He loved you so much that He sent Jesus to pay a price you could never pay (Jn 3:16). He wants to have a personal, one-on-one, day-to-day relationship with you. You are the apple of His eye (Ps 17:8).

It is God's will for you to be saved. If you've never received Jesus as your Savior, then you've never received the benefits of what He did for you on the cross, and you're still in a sinful state.

You can receive Him today. It is not hard. The Bible says:

> If you confess with your mouth Jesus is Lord, and believe in your heart that God has raised Him from the dead, you will be saved, for with the heart one believes unto righteousness, and with the mouth confession is made unto salvation. For the Scripture says, "Whoever believes in Him will not be ashamed." For there is no distinction between Jew and Greek, for the same Lord over all is generous toward all who call upon Him. For, "Everyone one who calls on the name of the Lord shall be saved."
>
> —Romans 10:9–13

All of God's blessings and the benefits of salvation can be yours if you receive Him into your heart. You can do this by praying this prayer:

> *Dear God, I come to You admitting that I am a sinner. I believe that Your Son, Jesus, died on the cross to take away my sins. I also believe He rose from the dead so I could be justified and made righteous through faith in Him. I call upon the name of Jesus Christ to be the Savior and Lord of my life. Jesus, thank You for washing away my sin. I choose to follow You, and I ask that You fill me with the power of the Holy Spirit. I declare right now that I am a born-again child of God. I am free from sin, and I am the righteousness of God in Christ. I am saved, in Jesus's name. Amen.*

Congratulations, and welcome to the family of God! I encourage you to get into a good Word-believing church so you can learn and grow.

Karen Jensen Salisbury

An Invitation to Become a SpiritLed Woman

You're born again. Jesus is your Savior, Lord, and Master. You have wonderful times with Him in prayer, and sometimes sense His presence during praise and worship. Your prayers are answered, the family is doing fine, life seems to have its normal share of highs and lows—but mostly things are stable. This is good…isn't it?

Yet perhaps there's a nagging thought that something is missing in your spiritual walk—an absence of power, a lack of testimonies about the miraculous, wonder-working God of the New Testament church. Or have you wondered whether miracles, signs, and wonders have simply passed away?

Is your spiritual life so safe and stable that it lacks the luster of excitement and adventures in Christ? Then perhaps it's time to step out of the boat and go for it: pray to be filled with the Holy Spirit so the power of God can flow out from you and touch the lives of others.

But if you do, be prepared for change, because it is this remarkable transforming power—the power of the Holy Spirit—that transformed Peter from frightened, wimpish denier of Christ to mighty rock of apostolic works…transformed Saul of Tarsus from Christian killer to church founder…transformed the hundred and twenty from timid Christ-followers to mountain-moving world-shapers. Be prepared to change, for to become Spirit filled is to become Spirit directed…SpiritLed. It is to become a Spirit-taught, Spirit-walking, Spirit-praying, Spirit-inspired woman of God. It is to become Spirit-yielded to His marvelous plan for your life. Will you?

If you desire to be baptized in the Holy Spirit, may I suggest that you read and study the wonderful promises contained in Luke 11:5–13; Acts 1:5, 8; 2:1–8; 11:16. Get to know and trust the operation of the Holy Spirit through these passages even before you pray. Rest in the knowledge that the Holy Spirit is no invader, and certainly no counterfeit Spirit. He requires your permission to baptize you in the Holy Spirit; He will not simply rush in, unless you hunger and thirst for more of Him. You are accustomed to asking Jesus for answers in prayer; now ask Him for the Holy Spirit. From these verses in Luke 11 you can easily see that if you ask Him for the Holy Spirit, He will personally vouch for your receiving the Holy Spirit—and only the Holy Spirit. He will send exactly what you ask for—not a counterfeit.

Ask in faith to be filled with the Holy Spirit, and believe you'll receive just what you ask for. He is a glorious God who delights to fill His children with the Holy Spirit. And He will take you on adventures in prayer and in practice that will one day fill His Book in heaven.

You may pray as the Lord directs you to pray, or you may wish to pray a prayer like this:

> *Lord Jesus, thank You for saving me and for washing me in Your blood. I renounce all sin. I renounce all rebellion and disobedience. I renounce the devil and all his works, and I ask that You forgive me for anything I was even involved with that displeased or dishonored You. Jesus, I know You promised to send the Comforter when You ascended to the Father. You promised that He—the Holy Spirit—would never leave us. Now fill me, Lord, with the Holy Spirit and give me the evidence of my heavenly language. Thank You that as You fill me with the Spirit, You also begin to teach and instruct me in the deeper application of Your Word in my daily*

walk. Lead me to the plan You always purposed for my life. Show me how You would use me in my world to reach out to others. Develop within me the fruit of the Spirit and send the gifts of the Spirit that You wish for me to have in daily activation. Thank You, Lord, for baptizing me in the Spirit. In Jesus' name, amen.

God bless you richly as you enter into the SpiritLed life and all of its seasons.

There are many seasons in the life of every SpiritLed woman. Unlikely as it may seem, the cycle of spiritual seasons does not begin with spring. No, winter is where it actually begins, when the Word of God is first sown in the heart. The spiritual walk begins at spiritual ground zero without any fruit to show for all the initial months of effort. That's when faith is the candle that takes you through the cold, gray days.

Just when the SpiritLed woman feels that she has adjusted to winter and trusting God regardless of whether or not there is fruit to show for it, a bud begins to appear, and then a few blades. Spring has begun to produce a simple crop of fruit from the prayers and the faithful lifestyle that was cloaked in winter's cover.

And when spring has had its cycle, summer presents a bumper crop of results from the seeds of the secret times when all the SpiritLed woman could do was pray and walk and go by faith and trust.

Finally, fall comes—the time to harvest and enjoy a lifetime of bounty from the endless supply of the storehouse of God!

As you read through this Bible each day, devote every day and every season to God. Your faithful obedience will produce a lifetime of blessing and a legacy of godliness—just as it did for all the faithful women who went before you.

How to Live as a SpiritLed Woman

Children of God are described in the Scriptures as those who are led by the Spirit (Ro 8:14). The Bible has much to say about the three developmental stages of walking with God: *babyhood*, *youth*, and *adulthood*. There is a vast difference between being a baby born into a family and being a daughter who has come to maturity. Being a daughter of God who has come into adulthood in the Scriptures indicates a mature relationship with the Father, involving both privilege and responsibility. God wants not just daughters, but daughters with knowledge. Daughters with knowledge are those who walk in revelation and who know what their Father is thinking. There are some grown children who can't "run the company." The spiritual daughter with knowledge is the one who has been trained in the ways of the Father so that she can reign with Him.

The first requirement for becoming a mature daughter of God—a SpiritLed woman—is that you must first be born of the Spirit. What does it mean to be born of the Spirit? Nicodemus asked Jesus, "How can a man be born when he is old? Can he enter a second time into his mother's womb and be born?" (Jn 3:4). Jesus told Nicodemus that unless he was born again, he could not see the kingdom of God. Do we really know what He meant? Evangelicals have taught people that they must be born again to get to heaven. One day they will die, and that in order to go to heaven they must be born again. That is true, but that is not all God intended in offering eternal life through the new birth.

In this world there are two kingdoms. One is the satanic kingdom of darkness and of lies. The other is the kingdom of light, love, and truth—the kingdom of God. Those who live in sin are being controlled by a satanic power that rules that kingdom. Though they might be considered moral, pay their bills, and choose a decent lifestyle, they are living in the kingdom of darkness that is opposed to the kingdom of God. When Jesus walked this earth, He said, "The kingdom of heaven is at hand" (Mt 4:17). His kingdom has come for those who are willing to receive it through repentance. Asking Jesus to forgive your sins and to be Lord of your life and acknowledging His sacrifice on Calvary bring the kingdom of God to you and usher you into that kingdom here on earth.

Entering the kingdom of God through the new birth means your inner man has entered into eternity now. When you are born of the Spirit, you are alive to the eternal realities of the kingdom of God. You am not simply going into eternity when you die. Your spirit is already living in the eternal kingdom of God as a born-again daughter of God. You can't see the kingdom of God unless you are born of the Spirit, taught by the Spirit, and led by the Spirit—because the kingdom is a spiritual kingdom. Jesus said, "That which is born of the flesh is flesh, and that which is born of the Spirit is spirit" (Jn 3:6). To be born of the Spirit means to be born from above, to receive a new spiritual life of divine origin.

Paul told the Corinthians, "'Eye has not seen, nor ear heard, nor has it entered into the heart of man the things which God has prepared for those who love Him.' But God has revealed them to us by His Spirit" (1Co 2:9–10). He understood that only by the Spirit of God can you know the mind and purpose of God for you. It is not possible for the natural man to be able to comprehend and see what is in the kingdom of God. Why? The kingdom is a spirit world ruled by King Jesus and administered by the Holy Spirit. He is the Executor, Divine Administrator, and the Teacher. He came to make the kingdom real and to put you into the kingdom. You are a citizen of another world. Without experiencing a supernatural new birth by the Spirit of God, a person cannot enjoy this wonderful kingdom—a kingdom of peace, joy, and righteousness in the Holy Spirit (Ro 14:17).

Even as a Christian, having experienced the new birth, you must be careful to focus your mind and heart on the eternal kingdom. Although you must live and work in this world, you dare not set your affections and pursuits on the values of this world system. The more you crave what is here, and the more the system of this world takes hold of you, the less you will know about the kingdom of God. If you expect to grow from babyhood to youth and into a daughter with knowledge, you will have to concentrate your energies on the pursuit of God and His holiness and righteousness in every area of your life.

Paul declared, "I have been crucified with Christ. It is no longer I who live, but Christ who lives in me. And the life I now live in the flesh, I live by faith in the Son of God, who loved me and gave Himself for me" (Gal 2:20). The death of your sin nature has been legally accomplished; it was nailed to the cross on which Jesus died. Your old Adamic, sinful, ungodly nature is reckoned dead, powerless to rule you any longer, as you bring it to the cross and refuse to yield to its ways. You are powerless to change yourself, but as you allow the Holy Spirit to birth the life of Christ within you, you can continually yield to Him and be changed into the image of Christ. And you can then fulfill the requirements for and receive the blessings of being a SpiritLed woman.

Requirements for Being a SpiritLed Woman

Let's look at the divine requirements for being a SpiritLed woman.

Dependence

You are completely dependent on the Holy Spirit for your future. Not only does He save you and give you spiritual gifts, but also He is responsible for your entire well-being: spirit, soul, and body. You are completely dependent on Him, whether or not you consciously feel His presence. All believers know what it is at times to enjoy the conscious presence of the Holy Spirit. When I was first filled with the Spirit, I thought I was always going to feel His presence and be aware of Him.

Then one day when I was distressed because I did not feel His nearness, He gave me a beautiful object lesson. He said to me, "You loved your daddy dearly." That is true. He continued, "When you went to bed and said good-night to your daddy, did he have to stay in the room all night to prove to you he was there? Did he have to wake you up every few minutes and say, 'Daughter, I am here'? Or did you go to sleep trusting him, knowing that he was there and, if the slightest disturbance came, you would be conscious of his presence?" I understood then that I did not always have to have a consciousness of the presence of the Holy Spirit with me. I needed only to trust Him with my life as I had trusted my earthly daddy unreservedly as a child.

Your total dependence on the Holy Spirit makes available to you the help you need from God. He doesn't expect you to be perfect; He came because you weren't perfect. He didn't come because you already knew, but because you don't know. He came to bring you what you don't have and can't receive any other way.

Obedience

If your disposition must be one of dependence in order to be a SpiritLed woman, your response must be that of obedience to His Word. The first step of obedience is to hearken to what He says. You must be sure you are listening to His Word and set yourself to hear Him. Then, after hearing Him, you must come to Him with a surrendered will so you can obey Him.

Failure to continually walk in obedience will result in discontent and despondency. The cause of every despondent cloud that falls over the soul can be traced to the neglect of some particular instruction from the "divine monitor." Of course, this does not apply to places of testing where God may allow you to experience darkness for a season. It does explain, however, the difficult places you may find yourself in because you didn't listen to or obey the voice of the Spirit but insisted that God let you go your own way.

Keeping in step

Not only must you learn obedience to be a SpiritLed woman, but you must also learn to keep in step with Him in your obedience. Sometimes you may fall way behind in your obedience, not finding a willingness in your heart to commit to Him completely or depend on Him fully. A halfhearted obedience will not allow you to keep in step with His purposes in your life.

A shepherd knows all the names of his sheep, but he can't talk to those that are not walking close to him. The ones he talks to the most are those that keep in step with him, rubbing his leg to get his attention. What a picture of Jesus, the Good Shepherd! He has given the Holy Spirit to be your gentle guide—kind, tender, merciful, understanding. He is patient and willing to walk with you all the way. When you acknowledge that you want to be near Him, then you will do what is necessary to keep in step with your Lord.

Availability

As you learn to walk in step with your Lord, you will make yourself available to Him to fulfill His purposes, not your own. Continual availability is one of the greatest prerequisites for being a SpiritLed woman. The secret of abiding in Him is to continually make yourself available as a servant who is waiting for His instructions.

Friendship

You also need to acknowledge that the Holy Spirit is your indwelling Friend. Jesus called His disciples *friends*, and He told them it was expedient for Him to go away so He could send them the Comforter who would dwell in them. The Holy Spirit is your Friend. How great a value you place on friendship will help determine how you value your relationship with the Holy Spirit.

A real friend is one who cuts covenant with you, promising not to leave you when you are facing trouble. When you are a SpiritLed woman, you are never without a friend. You can count on the Holy Spirit in all situations of life. He is all-sufficient in every crisis, and He is your constant companion. He wants to be included in the details of your life. You might be surprised at what this Friend would do for you if you asked for His help more often.

The Blessings of Being a SpiritLed Woman

As you choose to obey the Word of God and make yourself available to be a servant of God, walking closely to Him, you will find yourself cultivating a divine friendship with Him, which results in eternal blessings for you and for His church.

Deliverance from sin

One of the first blessings that come as a result of being a SpiritLed woman is a complete and delightful deliverance from sin. As you yield to the Holy Spirit, you will know a life freed from the destructive power of sin. Daily walking as a SpiritLed woman is the only guarantee of having power over sin.

Peace

The second blessing is experiencing a delightful serenity, tranquility, and steadfastness. God's wonderful intention for His daughters is that they walk in peace, free from the tyranny of fleshly drives and impulses. You will experience the peace of God and not be subject to ups and downs, becoming a victim of circumstances or of your own emotions. His rest gives us a stability in the face of every life situation.

God's providences

The third blessing that comes to the SpiritLed woman is the ability to meet the *providences* of God as they come. A providence is something that God chooses for you and promotes, although you may not always perceive it as something positive. As a SpiritLed woman you will be able to maintain perfect harmony between your inward disposition and God's outward leadings or providences. Living in such a way that the providences of God can come into your life always results in blessings.

Remember that what God requires of you is always for your ultimate good. Then you will surrender your life without reservation, becoming available to Him, dependent on Him, and learning to be obedient to His instructions. This will result in a deepening friendship with God. In learning to know the Holy Spirit, you will come into intimate relationship with God that will satisfy your heart and fulfill the eternal purpose of God in you.

Fuchsia Pickett

THE OLD TESTAMENT

Author: Traditionally Moses

Written: Between 1440 and 1400 BC

Themes: Creation, Humanity, Israel

GENESIS

Dear Spirit Led Woman,

From the very first pages of the Bible—from the beginning of Creation—we can see that God desires a loving relationship with the people He has created, longing to commune with them. Throughout Genesis we find evidence of His Spirit moving in people's lives to fulfill that divine desire and plan.

We must never forget that we have been created in His image, with His breath breathed into us, just as Adam and Eve were. We have been created to fulfill His purpose, and we will forever be protected by Him. God our Father loves us more than we can ever imagine, and our relationship with Him formed in the very beginning—in Genesis. May you follow the leading of His Spirit today and draw closer in your relationship with Him as you read His Word.

Joy F. Strang

SPIRITLED WOMAN

COUNSEL FROM THE SPIRIT BASICS

Anointed at Creation

There's only one place to start when it comes to talking about the anointing, and that is from the beginning. I believe that when God said "Let there be...," the entire host of heaven, including the angels, was involved in Creation. Genesis opens with the arrangement of the solar system, the separation of the waters, and the forming of land for habitation for what was coming—man! Then after completing His prized creations, God blessed Adam and Eve and told them:

> Be fruitful and multiply, and replenish the earth and subdue it. Rule over the fish of the sea and over the birds of the air and over every living thing that moves on the earth.
>
> —GENESIS 1:28

So from the beginning, God appointed us sons and daughters of the first Adam, and then by faith we became sons and daughters of God, brothers and sisters of the second Adam, Jesus Christ, as heirs to this earth domain. (See 1 Corinthians 15:22, 45–50.) *We were made to dominate, reproduce, multiply, and replenish the earth with godly seed.* That power and anointing was rightfully given to us by God in the beginning, as descendants of His first creations, and today we have that authority to do the same in every sphere of our lives.

Judy Jacobs

The Creation

1 In the beginning God created the heavens
and the earth. 2 The earth was formless and
void,[1] darkness was over the surface of the
deep, and the Spirit of God was moving[2] over
the surface of the water.

3 God said, "Let there be light," and there was
light. 4 God saw that the light was good, and
God separated the light from the darkness.
5 God called the light Day, and the darkness
He called Night. So the evening and the
morning were the first day.
6 Then God said, "Let there be an expanse
in the midst of the waters, and let it separate
the waters from the waters." 7 So God
made the expanse and separated the waters
which were under the expanse from the waters
which were above the expanse. And it
was so. 8 God called the expanse Heaven.
So the evening and the morning were the
second day.
9 Then God said, "Let the waters under the
heavens be gathered together into one
place, and let the dry land appear." And
it was so. 10 God called the dry land Earth,
and the gathering together of the waters He
called Seas. Then God saw that it was good.
11 Then God said, "Let the earth produce
vegetation:[3] plants yielding seed and fruit
trees on the earth yielding fruit after their
kind with seed in them." And it was so. 12 The
earth produced vegetation, plants yielding
seed after their kind and trees yielding fruit
with seed in them after their kind. And God
saw that it was good. 13 So the evening and
the morning were the third day.
14 And God said, "Let there be lights in the
expanse of the heavens to separate the
day from the night, and let them be signs
to indicate seasons, and days, and years.
15 Let them be lights in the expanse of the
heavens to give light on the earth." And it
was so. 16 God made two great lights: the
greater light to rule the day and the lesser
light to rule the night. He made the stars
also. 17 Then God set them in the expanse of
the heavens to give light on the earth, 18 to
rule over the day and over the night, and to
divide the light from the darkness. Then God
saw that it was good. 19 So the evening and
the morning were the fourth day.
20 Then God said, "Let the waters swarm with
swarms of living creatures and let the birds
fly above the earth in the open expanse of
the heavens." 21 So God created great sea
creatures and every living thing that moves,
with which the waters swarmed, according
to their kind, and every winged bird according
to its kind. And God saw that it was
good. 22 Then God blessed them, saying, "Be
fruitful and multiply and fill the waters in
the seas, and let the birds multiply on the
earth." 23 So the evening and the morning
were the fifth day.
24 Then God said, "Let the earth bring forth living
creatures according to their kinds: livestock,
and creeping things, and beasts of the
earth according to their kinds." And it was
so. 25 So God made the beasts of the earth

1:1 Heb 11:3
1:2 Ps 104:30
1:3 2Co 4:6
1:5 Ps 74:16

1:7 Ps 148:4
1:8 Ge 1:5
1:9 Jer 5:22
1:16 Job 38:7
1:18 Jer 31:35
1:22 Ge 8:17

[1] 2 Or *a waste and emptiness.* [2] 2 Or *hovering.*
[3] 11 Or *grass.*

according to their kind, and the livestock
according to their kind, and everything that
creeps on the earth according to its kind.
And God saw that it was good.
26 Then God said, "Let us make man in our
image, after our likeness, and let them have
dominion over the fish of the sea, and over
the birds of the air, and over the livestock,
and over all the earth, and over every creep-
ing thing that creeps on the earth."

27 So God created man in His own image;
in the image of God He created him;
male and female He created them.

28 God blessed them and said to them, "Be
fruitful and multiply, and replenish the earth
and subdue it. Rule over the fish of the sea
and over the birds of the air and over every
living thing that moves on the earth."
29 Then God said, "See, I have given you
every plant yielding seed which is on the
face of all the earth and every tree which
has fruit yielding seed. It shall be food for
you. 30 To every beast of the earth and to
every bird of the air and to everything that
creeps on the earth which has the breath of
life in it, I have given every green plant for
food." And it was so.
31 God saw everything that He had made,
and indeed it was very good. So the evening
and the morning were the sixth day.

2 So the heavens and the earth, and all their
hosts, were finished.
2 On the seventh day God completed His work
which He had done, and He rested on the
seventh day from all His work which He had
done. 3 Then God blessed the seventh day
and made it holy, because on it He had rest-
ed from all His work which He had created
and made.

Adam and Eve

4 This is the account[1] of the heavens and the
earth when they were created.

In the day that the LORD God made the earth
and the heavens, 5 no shrub of the field was yet
on the earth, and no plant of the field had yet
sprouted, for the LORD God had not caused it
to rain on the earth, and there was no man to
cultivate the ground. 6 But a mist[2] arose from
the earth and watered the whole surface of
the ground. 7 Then the LORD God formed man
from the dust of the ground and breathed into
his nostrils the breath of life, and man became
a living being.
8 The LORD God planted a garden in the east,
in Eden, and there He placed the man whom
He had formed. 9 Out of the ground the LORD
God made to grow every tree that is pleasant
to the sight and good for food. The tree of life
was also in the midst of the garden, along with
the tree of knowledge of good and evil.
10 A river flowed out of Eden to water the gar-
den, and from there it parted and became four
rivers. 11 The name of the first is Pishon; it en-
compasses the whole land of Havilah, where
there is gold. 12 The gold of that land is good;
bdellium and the onyx stone are there. 13 The
name of the second river is Gihon; it encom-
passes the whole land of Cush. 14 The name of
the third river is Tigris; it goes toward the east
of Assyria. The fourth river is the Euphrates.
15 The LORD God took the man and put him
in the garden of Eden to till it and to keep

1:26 Jas 3:9
1:27 Mt 19:4
1:28 Ge 9:1
1:29 Ge 9:3
1:30 Ps 147:9
1:31 1Ti 4:4
2:1 Dt 4:19
2:2 Ex 31:17
2:7 Ge 3:19
2:8 Ge 13:10
2:9 Ge 3:22

2:10 Ps 46:4
2:11 Ge 25:18
2:14 Da 10:4
2:15 Ge 2:8

SPIRITLED WOMAN

COUNSEL FROM THE SPIRIT BASICS

God's Purpose for Marriage

God's design and purpose for marriage was for a man and woman to have a lasting and satisfying union to nurture and rear healthy offspring. God established marriage as the only institution to nurture a family before sin came into existence. To take care of loneliness, God created woman to be a helper and companion to man (Ge 2:18), as well as to procreate and prevent fornication (Ge 1:28; 1Co 7:1–2).

Marriage is the most sacred of all vows or oaths a man and woman will ever make. It is not like a promise that can be forgotten or broken. When a couple makes this vow before God and witnesses, they are making a sacred commitment and covenant "till death do us part," not "till divorce separates us." *Vows remain intact even if the marriage is full of problems*—and too many are experiencing warfare because of all the excess baggage they refuse to release to Jesus. Satan is in hot pursuit of your marital vows. He can't break the vows, so instead he diligently works at sowing dissension and strife until he succeeds in breaking up the marriage.

Iris Delgado

[1]4 Lit. *These are the generations.* [2]6 Or *flow.*

The Role of the Helpmeet

I do not believe that men and women can do whatever or be whomever they feel like they can be in the household. I believe that God has established roles in the family. The roles in the family unit make up the organism of the family—which God created. The family is not an institution; it is an organism. It lives because it is filled with lives. The Word of the Lord declares that Jesus came that we might have abundant life (Jn 10:10). This means that having abundant life in our homes is conditional. Somehow society has gotten off course for what God's original plan was for the family. He meant for marriage to be between one man and one woman. Their union was blessed by God to be fruitful to have children. Because of new customs, new laws, and new ways of thinking, all that God meant for the family to be is at stake. The tolerance of alternative lifestyles in our churches has bred antichrist doctrines that relate to family and marriage.

The devil wants to pervert the role of the family and change the order in our homes. He wants the men to be followers and to be soft, and he wants the women to lead and to be hard. There is nothing wrong with women taking leadership in the house. It just becomes a problem when we allow the enemy to pervert the roles. Men can cook and women can bring home provisions, but the order of God must stay intact.

The woman was created *after* the man. God said that it was not good "that the man should be alone" (Ge 2:18). Something was going on in Adam's life before God created Eve that made God notice that something was missing in his life. God did not create another man for Adam; He created a woman. God made Eve to look similar to Adam, but there was something different about her. She was a weaker vessel, but there was an inner strength in her. God made her from Adam's rib so that she could be bone of his bone and flesh of his flesh. She was created to be his helpmeet. The word *helpmeet* is a combination of the Hebrew words *ezer* and *neged*, which mean "help" and "counterpart or mate." It means "to render aid, assist, or give help." It means "to succor, to surround and protect." The word *succor* means:

- To get beneath
- To give assistance in times of want, difficulty, or distress
- To run to help when in any kind of need

When the woman takes her place, it really makes it easier for men to get in place. It is like a Rubik's Cube. When everybody gets in place, all the colors line up. When everyone is in line, the greater picture and plan that God has for the family can be seen.

Even after the devil has attacked the order of the house and things are a mess, it is never too late. I have seen God save marriages that seemed hopeless and over. Only He can make a way where there is no way and work a miracle. I thank God for His mercy and grace flowing through our relationships and our homes!

Make it personal and receive it for yourself.

Kimberly Daniels

it. 16 And the LORD God commanded the man,
saying, "Of every tree of the garden you may
freely eat, 17 but of the tree of the knowledge
of good and evil you shall not eat, for in the
day that you eat from it you will surely die."
18 Then the LORD God said, "It is not good that
the man should be alone. I will make him a
helper suitable for him."

> The Lord is faithful to guard us from the evil one (Ge 2:16–17).

19 Out of the ground the LORD God formed
every beast of the field and every bird of the
sky, and brought them to the man to see what
he would call them. Whatever the man called
every living creature, that was its name. 20 The
man gave names to all the livestock, to the
birds of the sky, and to every beast of the field,
but for Adam[3] there was not found a helper
suitable for him.

> The devil was cast out of heaven, and You will establish me and guard me from the evil one (Ge 2:16–17).

21 So the LORD God caused a deep sleep to
fall on Adam, and he slept. Then He took one
of his ribs and closed up the place with flesh.
22 Then the rib which the LORD God had taken
from man, He made into a woman, and He
brought her to the man.
23 Then Adam said,

"This is now bone of my bones
 and flesh of my flesh;
she will be called Woman,
 for she was taken out of Man."

24 Therefore a man will leave his father and his
mother and be joined to his wife, and they will
become one flesh.
25 They were both naked, the man and his
wife, and were not ashamed.

The Fall

3 Now the serpent was more subtle than
any beast of the field which the LORD God
had made. And he said to the woman, "Has
God said, 'You shall not eat of any tree of the
garden'?"
2 And the woman said to the serpent, "We
may eat of the fruit from the trees of the gar-
den; 3 but from the fruit of the tree which is in
the midst of the garden, God has said, 'You
will not eat of it, nor will you touch it, or else
you will die.' "
4 Then the serpent said to the woman, "You
surely will not die! 5 For God knows that on the

2:17 Ro 6:23
2:18 Ge 3:12
2:19 Ge 1:28
2:21 Ge 15:12
2:23 Ge 29:14
2:24 Ps 45:10
2:25 Ge 3:7
3:1 2Co 11:3
3:4 Jn 8:44
3:5 Eze 28:2

....

3:6 1Ti 2:14
3:7 Ge 2:25
3:8 Job 31:33
3:9 Ge 4:9
3:10 Ge 2:25
3:12 Job 31:33
3:13 2Co 11:3
3:14 Isa 65:25
3:15 Ro 16:20
3:16 1Co 11:3

day you eat of it your eyes will be opened and
you will be like God, knowing good and evil."
6 When the woman saw that the tree was
good for food, that it was pleasing to the eyes
and a tree desirable to make one wise, she
took of its fruit and ate; and she gave to her
husband with her, and he ate. 7 Then the eyes
of both were opened, and they knew that they
were naked. So they sewed fig leaves together
and made coverings for themselves.
8 Then they heard the sound of the LORD God
walking in the garden in the cool of the day,
and the man and his wife hid themselves from
the presence of the LORD God among the trees
of the garden. 9 The LORD God called to the man
and said to him, "Where are you?"
10 He said, "I heard Your voice in the garden
and was afraid because I was naked, so I hid
myself."
11 And He said, "Who told you that you were
naked? Have you eaten from the tree of which
I commanded you not to eat?"

> The devil has no part or portion in our lives (Ge 3:15).

12 The man said, "The woman whom You
gave to be with me, she gave me *fruit* of the
tree, and I ate."
13 Then the LORD God said to the woman,
"What have you done?"
And the woman said, "The serpent deceived
me, and I ate."

> Thank You, Father, because Jesus defeated the devil on the cross of Calvary (Ge 3:15).

14 The LORD God said to the serpent: "Because
you have done this,

You are cursed above all livestock,
 and above every beast of the field;
you will go on your belly,
 and you will eat dust
 all the days of your life.
15 I will put enmity
 between you and the woman,
 and between your offspring and her
  offspring;
he will bruise your head,
 and you will bruise his heel."

16 To the woman He said,

"I will greatly multiply your pain in
  childbirth,

[3] *20* MT *the man*, or *the Adam*.

EVE

THE POWER OF CHOICE

If Adam and Eve were given a "do over" in the garden, I doubt anything in our world would change. Even if Eve had found the strength to resist the serpent that day, the enemy would have tried to deceive her on another. The problem was not in the fact that Eve was given the power to choose. Choice is not a bad thing. God gave us this gift because He wants us to choose to obey Him.

But why did He give us free will? Without choice we would be automatons, loving God out of obligation instead of delight. But this is not what the Father wanted.

For all the knowledge she lacked, Eve was educated in how to live out the reason for her being, which was relationship. Her purpose was to love God and reflect His goodness by loving Adam. Eve is usually remembered for her most famous mistake, but she is much more than one bad decision. And so are we.

I wonder why God even mentioned that tree in the first place. Why let Adam and Eve know it even existed? Why not just take it out of the garden or keep it under lock and key? But God chose not only to place that tree in the center of the garden but also to warn mankind against eating of it.

A profound thought occurred to me: choice must have existed before Creation. Scripture doesn't say much about the fall of Lucifer beyond what is recorded in Ezekiel 28 and Isaiah 14, so we really don't know what went down. What we can infer is that if Lucifer got puffed up enough to choose to rebel against God, free will had to have been in operation at that time.

If Lucifer could lead a third of the angels in rebelling against God, then in the realm of the angelic and the supernatural a choice existed to believe or not to believe. Somehow a standard was set, and God's desire to be obeyed was made known. We were not created without the ability to obey; we were given the opportunity to decide whether we would. Our actions would then determine the direction we would take and the one we would serve.

Choice is important in our understanding of God and His relationship with humanity. When we make choices, they are usually provoked by a desire or need, intent or determination. God has always longed to be our choice. When we choose Him, He can reach us even faster with His transforming love because we've stopped running from Him. Choice, yes, is key.

Rita Springer

and in pain you will bring forth children;
your desire will be for your husband,
and he will rule over you."

17 And to Adam He said, "Because you have
listened to the voice of your wife and have
eaten from the tree about which I commanded
you, saying, 'You shall not eat of it,'

Cursed is the ground on account of you;
in hard labor you will eat of it
all the days of your life.
18 Thorns and thistles it will bring forth for
you,
and you will eat the plants of the field.
19 By the sweat of your face
you will eat bread
until you return to the ground,
because out of it you were taken;
for you are dust,
and to dust you will return."

20 The man called his wife's name Eve be-
cause she was the mother of all the living.
21 The LORD God made garments of skins for
both Adam and his wife and clothed them.
22 The LORD God said, "The man has become
like one of us, knowing good and evil. And
now, he might reach out his hand, and take
also from the tree of life, and eat, and live for-
ever"— 23 therefore the LORD God sent him out
from the garden of Eden, to till the ground
from which he was taken. 24 He drove the man
out, and at the east of the garden of Eden He
placed the cherubim and a flaming sword
which turned in every direction, to guard the
way to the tree of life.

Cain and Abel

4 Adam had relations with his wife Eve,
and she conceived, gave birth to Cain
and said, "I have gotten a man with the help
of the LORD." 2 Then she gave birth again to his
brother Abel.

And Abel was a keeper of flocks, but Cain
was a tiller of the ground. 3 In the course of
time Cain brought an offering to the LORD of
the fruit of the ground. 4 Abel also brought the
firstborn of his flock and of their fat portions.
And the LORD had respect for Abel and for his
offering, 5 but for Cain and for his offering, He
did not have respect. And Cain was very angry
and his countenance fell.
6 The LORD said to Cain, "Why are you angry?
Why is your countenance fallen? 7 If you do
well, shall you not be accepted?[l] But if you
do not do well, sin is crouching at the door.
It desires to dominate you, but you must rule
over it."

3:17 Ge 5:29
3:19 Ps 104:29
3:22 Ge 1:26
3:24 Heb 1:7
4:1 Ge 3:15
4:2 Ge 47:3
4:3 Nu 18:12
4:4 Heb 11:4
4:8 Mt 23:35
4:9 Jn 8:44
4:10 Heb 12:24
4:14 Nu 35:19
4:15 Eze 9:4
4:17 Ps 49:11
4:19 Ge 2:24
4:25 Ge 4:8

8 Cain told Abel his brother. And it came
about, when they were in the field, that Cain
rose up against his brother Abel and killed him.
9 The LORD said to Cain, "Where is Abel your
brother?"

He said, "I do not know. Am I my brother's
keeper?"
10 And then He said, "What have you done?
The voice of your brother's blood is crying out
to Me from the ground. 11 Now you are cursed
from the ground which opened its mouth to
receive your brother's blood from your hand.
12 From now on when you till the ground, it will
not yield for you its best. You will be a fugitive
and a wanderer on the earth."
13 Then Cain said to the LORD, "My punish-
ment is more than I can bear. 14 You have driv-
en me out this day from the face of the earth,
and from your face will I be hidden; and I will
be a fugitive and a vagabond in the earth, and
it will happen that anyone who finds me will
kill me."
15 So the LORD said to him, "Therefore whoev-
er kills Cain, vengeance will be taken on him
sevenfold." Then the LORD put a mark upon
Cain, so that no one finding him would kill
him. 16 Then Cain went out from the presence
of the LORD and settled in the land of Nod,
east of Eden.
17 Cain had relations with his wife, and she
conceived and gave birth to Enoch. He built a
city and called the name of the city after the
name of his son, Enoch. 18 To Enoch was born
Irad, and Irad was the father of Mehujael, and
Mehujael was the father of Methushael, and
Methushael was the father of Lamech.
19 Lamech took two wives. The name of one
was Adah, and the name of the other Zillah.
20 Adah gave birth to Jabal. He was the father
of those who dwell in tents and have livestock.
21 His brother's name was Jubal. He was the
father of all those who play the harp and flute.
22 Zillah gave birth to Tubal-Cain, a forger of
every tool of bronze and iron. The sister of
Tubal-Cain was Naamah.
23 Lamech said to his wives:

"Adah and Zillah, hear my voice,
you wives of Lamech, and listen to my
speech.
For I have killed a man for wounding me,
a young man who hurt me.
24 If Cain will be avenged sevenfold,
then truly Lamech seventy-sevenfold."

25 Adam had relations with his wife again,
and she had another son and called his name
Seth, for she said, "God has granted me anoth-
er offspring instead of Abel because Cain killed

[l]7 Or *uplifted.*

him."[26] To Seth also was born a son, and he called his name Enosh.

At that time men began to call on the name of the LORD.

Adam's Descendants

5 This is the book of the generations of Adam.

In the day when God created man, He made him in the likeness of God. [2] He created them male and female. He blessed them and called them Mankind in the day when they were created.

[3] Adam lived a hundred and thirty years and became the father of a son in his own likeness, after his own image, and called his name Seth. [4] The days of Adam after he became the father of Seth were eight hundred years, and he had other sons and daughters. [5] So all the days that Adam lived were nine hundred and thirty years, and he died.

[6] Seth lived one hundred and five years and became the father of Enosh. [7] Seth lived after the birth of Enosh eight hundred and seven years and had other sons and daughters. [8] So all the days of Seth were nine hundred and twelve years, and he died.

[9] Enosh lived ninety years and became the father of Kenan. [10] Enosh lived after the birth of Kenan eight hundred and fifteen years and had other sons and daughters. [11] So all the days of Enosh were nine hundred and five years, and he died.

[12] Kenan lived seventy years and became the father of Mahalalel. [13] Kenan lived after the birth of Mahalalel eight hundred and forty years and had other sons and daughters. [14] So all the days of Kenan were nine hundred and ten years, and he died.

[15] Mahalalel lived sixty-five years and became the father of Jared. [16] Mahalalel lived after the birth of Jared eight hundred and thirty years and had other sons and daughters. [17] So all the days of Mahalalel were eight hundred and ninety-five years, and he died.

[18] Jared lived one hundred and sixty-two years and became the father of Enoch. [19] Jared lived after the birth of Enoch eight hundred years and had other sons and daughters. [20] So all the days of Jared were nine hundred and sixty-two years, and he died.

[21] Enoch lived sixty-five years and became the father of Methuselah. [22] Enoch walked with God after the birth of Methuselah for three hundred years and had other sons and daughters. [23] So all the days of Enoch were three hundred and sixty-five years. [24] Enoch walked with God, and then he was no more because God took him.

4:26 Ps 116:17
5:1 Ge 1:26–27
5:5 Ge 3:19
5:22 Ge 6:9
5:24 2Ki 2:11

....

6:3 Ps 78:39
6:4 Nu 13:33
6:5 Ge 8:21
6:6 Isa 63:10
6:8 Ge 19:19
6:9 Lk 1:6
6:11 Eze 8:17

[25] Methuselah lived one hundred and eighty-seven years and became the father of Lamech. [26] Methuselah lived after the birth of Lamech seven hundred and eighty-two years and had other sons and daughters. [27] So all the days of Methuselah were nine hundred and sixty-nine years, and he died.

[28] Lamech lived one hundred and eighty-two years and had a son. [29] He named his son Noah, saying, "This one will comfort us concerning our work and the toil of our hands because of the ground which the LORD has cursed." [30] Lamech lived after the birth of Noah five hundred and ninety-five years and had other sons and daughters. [31] So all the days of Lamech were seven hundred and seventy-seven years, and he died.

[32] Noah was five hundred years old and became the father of Shem, Ham, and Japheth.

Man's Wickedness

6 When men began to multiply on the face of the earth and daughters were born to them, [2] the sons of God saw that the daughters of men were fair and took as wives any they chose. [3] The LORD said, "My Spirit will not always strive with man, for he is flesh; yet his days will be a hundred and twenty years."

[4] The Nephilim were on the earth in those days, and also after that, when the sons of God came in to the daughters of men, and they bore children to them. These were the mighty men who were of old, men of renown.

[5] The LORD saw that the wickedness of man was great on the earth, and that every intent of the thoughts of his heart was continually only evil. [6] The LORD was sorry that He had made man on the earth, and it grieved Him in His heart. [7] So the LORD said, "I will destroy man, whom I have created, from the face of the earth—both man and beast, and the creeping things, and the birds of the sky, for I am sorry that I have made them." [8] But Noah found grace in the eyes of the LORD.

Noah and the Flood

[9] These are the generations of Noah.

Noah was a just man and blameless among his contemporaries. Noah walked with God. [10] Noah had three sons: Shem, Ham, and Japheth.

[11] The earth was corrupt before God and filled with violence. [12] God looked on the earth and saw it was corrupt, for all flesh had corrupted their way on the earth. [13] So God said to Noah, "The end of all flesh is come before Me, for the earth is filled with violence because of them. Now I will destroy them with the earth. [14] Make an ark of cypress wood for yourself. Make rooms in the ark, and cover it inside and out

with pitch. 15 And this is how you must make it:
The length of the ark will be three hundred cu-
bits, the width of it fifty cubits, and the height
of it thirty cubits.[1] 16 Make an opening[2] one
cubit[3] below the top of the ark all around; and
you must set the door of the ark on the side.
Make it with a lower, a second, and a third
story. 17 I will bring a flood of waters on the
earth to destroy all flesh, wherever there is the
breath of life under heaven, and everything
that is on the earth will die. 18 But I will estab-
lish My covenant with you; you must go into
the ark—you, and your sons, and your wife,
and your sons' wives with you. 19 Bring every
living thing of all flesh, two of every kind, into
the ark to keep them alive with you. They shall
be male and female. 20 Two of every kind of
bird, of every kind of animal, and of every
kind of creeping thing of the earth will come
to you to be kept alive. 21 Also, take with you
of every kind of food that is eaten and gather
it to yourself, and it will be for food for you
and for them."

22 Noah did this; he did all that God com-
manded him.

7 The LORD said to Noah, "You and your
entire household go into the ark, for you
alone I have seen to be righteous before Me
among this generation. 2 Take with you seven
each of every clean animal, the male and its
female, and two each of every unclean animal,
the male and its female, 3 and seven each of
birds of the air, the male and female, to keep
offspring alive on the face of all the earth. 4 In
seven days I will cause it to rain on the earth
for forty days and forty nights, and every living
thing that I have made I will destroy from the
face of the earth."

5 And Noah did according to all that the LORD
commanded him.

6 Noah was six hundred years old when the
floodwaters came upon the earth. 7 And Noah
went with his sons and his wife and his sons'
wives into the ark because of the floodwaters.
8 Everything that creeps on the land from clean
and unclean animals and birds 9 came in two
by two, male and female, to Noah into the ark,
as God had commanded Noah. 10 After seven
days, the waters of the flood were on the earth.

11 In the six hundredth year of Noah's life, in
the second month, on the seventeenth day of
the month, the same day, all the fountains of
the great deep burst open and the floodgates
of the heavens were opened. 12 The rain fell
upon the earth for forty days and forty nights.

13 On the very same day Noah and the sons
of Noah, Shem, Ham, and Japheth, and No-
ah's wife, and the three wives of his sons with
them, entered the ark. 14 They and every wild
animal according to its kind, and all the live-
stock according to their kind, and every creep-
ing thing that creeps on the earth according to
its kind, and every bird according to its kind,
every bird of every sort, 15 went with Noah into
the ark, two by two of all flesh in which was
the breath of life. 16 So they went in, male and
female of all flesh, just as God had command-
ed him; then the LORD shut him in.

17 The flood was on the earth forty days, and
the water increased and lifted up the ark, so
that it rose up above the earth. 18 The water
prevailed and increased greatly upon the
earth, and the ark floated on the surface of
the water. 19 The water prevailed exceedingly
on the earth, and all the high mountains that
were under the whole heaven were covered.
20 The waters prevailed upward and the moun-
tains were covered fifteen cubits deep.[4] 21 All
flesh that moved on the earth died: birds and
livestock and beasts, and every creeping thing
that crept on the earth, and every man. 22 All in
whose nostrils was the breath of life, all that
was on the dry land, died. 23 So He blotted out
every living thing which was on the face of
the ground, both man and animals and the
creeping things and the birds of the heavens.
They were blotted out from the earth, and only
Noah and those who were with him in the ark
remained alive.

24 The waters prevailed on the earth for one
hundred and fifty days.

The Flood Recedes

8 God remembered Noah and every living
thing and all the livestock that were with
him in the ark. So God made a wind to pass
over the earth, and the water receded. 2 Also
the fountains of the deep and the floodgates
of heaven were closed, and the rain from the
heavens was restrained. 3 The water receded
steadily from the earth, and after the end of
one hundred and fifty days the waters de-
creased. 4 The ark rested in the seventh month,
on the seventeenth day of the month, on the
mountains of Ararat. 5 The water continually
decreased until the tenth month. In the tenth
month, on the first day of the month, the tops
of the mountains became visible.

6 Then at the end of forty days, Noah opened
the window of the ark which he had made,
7 and he sent forth a raven, which went to and
fro until the waters were dried up on the earth.
8 Then he sent out a dove to see if the waters
had subsided from the face of the ground.
9 But the dove found no rest for the sole of

6:17 Ge 7:4
6:18 Ge 7:7
6:21 Ge 1:29–30
6:22 Ge 7:5
7:1 Ge 6:9
7:2 Ge 8:20
7:4 Ge 6:17
7:5 Ge 6:22
7:6 Ge 5:32
7:10 Ge 7:4
7:11 Ge 8:2
7:12 Ge 7:4

7:16 Ge 7:2–3
7:17 Ge 7:4
7:21 Ge 6:13
7:22 Ge 2:7
7:23 2Pe 2:5
8:1 Ge 19:29
8:2 Ge 7:11
8:3 Ge 7:24
8:6 Ge 6:16

[1] *15* About 450 feet long, 75 feet wide, and 45 feet high; or 135 meters long, 23 meters wide, and 14 meters high.
[2] *16* Or *roof.* [3] *16* About 18 inches, or 45 centimeters.
[4] *20* About 23 feet, or 6.8 meters.

her foot, so she returned to him into the ark,
for the waters were on the surface of all the
earth. Then he put forth his hand, and took
her, and brought her into the ark to himself.
10 He waited yet another seven days, and again
he sent out the dove from the ark. 11 The dove
came to him in the evening, and in her mouth
there was a freshly plucked olive leaf. So Noah
knew that the waters had receded from the
earth. 12 He waited another seven days and
sent out the dove again, but it did not return
to him again.

13 So in the six hundred and first year, in the
first month, the first day of the month, the wa-
ters were dried up from the earth; and Noah
removed the covering of the ark, and looked,
and saw the surface of the ground was dry.
14 In the second month, on the twenty-seventh
day of the month, the earth was dry.

15 Then God spoke to Noah, saying, 16 "Go out
of the ark, you and your wife, and your sons
and your sons' wives with you. 17 Bring out
with you every living thing of all flesh that is
with you, birds and animals, and every creep-
ing thing that creeps on the earth, so that they
may breed abundantly on the earth and be
fruitful and multiply on the earth."

18 So Noah and his sons and his wife and
his sons' wives went out. 19 Every beast, every
creeping thing, every bird, and everything that
moves on the earth, according to their families,
went out of the ark.

20 Then Noah built an altar to the LORD and
took of every clean animal and of every clean
bird and offered burnt offerings on the altar.
21 The LORD smelled a soothing aroma; and the
LORD said in His heart, "I will never again curse
the ground because of man, for the inclination
of man's heart is evil from his youth, nor will I
again destroy every living thing as I have done.

22 While the earth remains,
seedtime and harvest,
cold and heat,
summer and winter,
and day and night
will not cease."

The Noahic Covenant

9 Then God blessed Noah and his sons and
said to them, "Be fruitful and multiply and
fill the earth. 2 Every beast of the earth and
every bird of the sky and all that moves on the
earth and all the fish of the sea will fear you
and be terrified of you. They are given into
your hand. 3 Every moving thing that lives will
be food for you. I give you everything, just as I
gave you the green plant.

4 "Only you shall not eat flesh with its life, *that
is*, its blood. 5 But for your own lifeblood I will

8:16 Ge 7:13
8:17 Ge 1:22
8:20 Ge 12:7–8
8:21 Ge 3:17
8:22 Jer 5:24
9:1 Ge 1:28
9:2 Jas 3:7
9:4 Dt 12:16
9:5 Ex 21:28–29

9:6 Ge 1:26–27
9:7 Ge 9:1
9:9 Ge 6:18
9:11 Isa 54:9
9:12 Ge 17:11
9:13 Eze 1:28
9:15 Eze 16:60
9:16 Ge 17:13
9:18 Ge 10:1
9:21 Pr 20:1

surely require a reckoning; from every animal
will I require it; of man, too, will I require a
reckoning for human life, of every man for
that of his fellow man.

6 Whoever sheds the blood of man,
by man shall his blood be shed;
for God made man
in His own image.

7 And as for you, be fruitful and multiply; in-
crease abundantly in the earth and multiply
in it."

8 Again God spoke to Noah and to his sons
with him, saying, 9 "As for Me, I establish My
covenant with you, and with your descendants
after you; 10 and with every living creature that
is with you, the birds, the livestock, and every
beast of the earth with you; of all that comes
out of the ark, every beast of the earth. 11 I
establish My covenant with you. Never again
shall all flesh be cut off by the waters of a
flood. Never again shall there be a flood to
destroy the earth."

12 Then God said, "This is the sign of the cov-
enant which I am making between Me and you
and every living creature that is with you, for
all future generations. 13 I have set My rain-
bow in the cloud, and it shall be a sign of a
covenant between Me and the earth. 14 When
I bring a cloud over the earth, the rainbow will
be seen in the cloud; 15 then I will remember
My covenant, which is between Me and you
and every living creature of all flesh, and the
waters will never again become a flood to de-
stroy all flesh. 16 The rainbow will appear in
the cloud, and I will see it and remember the
everlasting covenant between God and every
living creature of all flesh that is on the earth."

17 So God said to Noah, "This is the sign of
the covenant that I have established between
Me and all flesh that is on the earth."

The Sons of Noah

18 The sons of Noah who went forth from the
ark were Shem, Ham, and Japheth. Ham was
the father of Canaan. 19 These were the three
sons of Noah, and from them the whole earth
was populated.

20 Noah began to be a man of the soil, and
he planted a vineyard. 21 Then he drank some
of the wine and became drunk, and lay un-
covered in his tent. 22 And Ham, the father of
Canaan, saw the nakedness of his father, and
told his two brothers outside. 23 So Shem and
Japheth took a garment, and laid it upon both
their shoulders, and went backward, and cov-
ered the nakedness of their father. Their faces
were turned away, and they did not see their
father's nakedness.

[24] When Noah awoke from his wine and knew what his younger son had done to him, [25] he said,

"Canaan be cursed!
He will be a servant of servants
to his brothers."

[26] He also said,

"Blessed be the LORD God of Shem,
and let Canaan be his servant.
[27] May God enlarge Japheth,
and may he dwell in the tents of Shem,
and may Canaan be his servant."

[28] Noah lived after the flood three hundred and fifty years. [29] All the days of Noah were nine hundred and fifty years, and then he died.

The Table of Nations

10 Now these are the generations of Shem, Ham, and Japheth, the sons of Noah. And sons were born to them after the flood.

The Japhethites

1Ch 1:5–7

[2] The sons of Japheth were
Gomer, Magog, Madai, Javan, Tubal,
Meshek, and Tiras.
[3] The sons of Gomer were
Ashkenaz, Riphath, and Togarmah.
[4] The sons of Javan were
Elishah, Tarshish, the Kittites, and the
Rodanites. [5] From these the coastlands
of the nations were divided[1] into their
lands, everyone according to his tongue,
according to their families, by their
nations.

The Hamites

1Ch 1:8–16

[6] The sons of Ham were
Cush, Egypt, Put, and Canaan.
[7] The sons of Cush were
Seba, Havilah, Sabtah, Raamah, and
Sabteka;
and the sons of Raamah were
Sheba and Dedan.

[8] Cush was the father of Nimrod. He became a mighty one on the earth. [9] He was a mighty hunter before the LORD. Therefore it is said, "Even like Nimrod the mighty hunter before the LORD." [10] The beginning of his kingdom was Babel,[2] Uruk, Akkad, and Kalneh in the land of Shinar. [11] From that land he went to Assyria and built Nineveh, the city Rehoboth Ir, and Calah, [12] and Resen between Nineveh and Calah (that is the principal city).

[13] Egypt was the father of
the Ludites, Anamites, Lehabites,
Naphtuhites, [14] Pathrusites, Kasluhites
(from whom came the Philistines), and
Caphtorites.
[15] Canaan was the father of
Sidon his firstborn and Heth, [16] and
the Jebusites, Amorites, Girgashites,
[17] Hivites, Arkites, Sinites, [18] Arvadites,
Zemarites, and the Hamathites.

Later the families of the Canaanites spread abroad. [19] The border of the Canaanites was from Sidon toward Gerar to Gaza, and then to Sodom, Gomorrah, Admah, Zeboyim, as far as Lasha.

[20] These are the sons of Ham, according to their families, according to their languages, in their lands and in their nations.

The Semites

Ge 11:10–27; 1Ch 1:17–27

[21] To Shem, who was the father of all the children of Eber, whose older brother was Japheth,[3] were sons born also.

[22] The sons of Shem were
Elam, Ashur, Arphaxad, Lud, and Aram.
[23] The sons of Aram were
Uz, Hul, Gether, and Meshek.
[24] Arphaxad was the father of Shelah,
and Shelah was the father of Eber.
[25] To Eber were born two sons.
The name of one was Peleg, for in his
days the earth was divided; his brother's
name was Joktan.
[26] Joktan was the father of
Almodad, Sheleph, Hazarmaveth, Jerah,
[27] Hadoram, Uzal, Diklah, [28] Obal, Abimael, Sheba, [29] Ophir, Havilah, and Jobab.
All these were the sons of Joktan.

[30] Their dwelling place was from Mesha all the way to Sephar, the hill country of the east.

[31] These are the sons of Shem, by their families and their language, in their lands and their nations.

[32] These are the families of the sons of Noah, according to their generations, in their nations. From these were the nations divided in the earth after the flood.

The Tower of Babel

11 Now the whole earth had one language and the same words. [2] As the people journeyed from the east, they found a plain in the land of Shinar and settled there.

[3] They said to each other, "Let us make bricks and bake them thoroughly." And they had brick for stone and tar for mortar. [4] Then they said, "Come, let us build us a city and a

9:25 Jos 9:23
10:1 Ge 2:4
10:2 Eze 38:2
10:7 Eze 27:22
10:10 Ge 11:2
10:11 Mic 5:6
10:14 Jer 47:4
10:19 Ge 14:2
10:21 Nu 24:24
10:22 Isa 66:19
10:23 Job 1:1
10:25 1Ch 1:19
10:29 1Ki 9:28
10:32 Ge 9:19
11:2 Ge 10:10
11:3 Ge 14:10
11:4 Dt 1:28

[1] 5 Or *separated themselves.* [2] 10 Or *Babylon.*
[3] 21 Or *the older brother of Japheth.*

tower, whose top will reach to heaven, and let
us make a name for ourselves; otherwise we
will be scattered abroad over the face of the
whole earth."
5 But the LORD came down to see the city and
the tower that the sons of men built. 6 The LORD
said, "The people are one and they have one
language, and this is only the beginning of
what they will do; now nothing that they pro-
pose to do will be impossible for them. 7 Come,
let us go down and there confuse their lan-
guage, so that they may not understand one
another's speech."
8 So the LORD scattered them abroad from
there over the face of all the earth, and they
stopped building the city. 9 Therefore the name
of it was called Babel, because there the LORD
confused the language of all the earth. From
there the LORD scattered them abroad over the
face of all the earth.

Shem's Descendants

Ge 10:21–31; 1Ch 1:17–27

10 These are the generations of Shem.

Shem was a hundred years old, and two
years after the flood he became the father of
Arphaxad. 11 Shem lived after the birth of Ar-
phaxad five hundred years, and had other sons
and daughters.
12 Arphaxad lived thirty-five years, and be-
came the father of Shelah. 13 Arphaxad lived
after the birth of Shelah four hundred and
three years, and had other sons and daughters.
14 Shelah lived thirty years, and became the
father of Eber. 15 Shelah lived after the birth of
Eber four hundred and three years, and had
other sons and daughters.
16 Eber lived thirty-four years, and became
the father of Peleg. 17 Eber lived after the birth
of Peleg four hundred and thirty years, and
had other sons and daughters.
18 Peleg lived thirty years, and became the
father of Reu. 19 Peleg lived after the birth of
Reu two hundred and nine years, and had oth-
er sons and daughters.
20 Reu lived thirty-two years, and became the
father of Serug. 21 Reu lived after the birth of
Serug two hundred and seven years, and had
other sons and daughters.
22 Serug lived thirty years, and became the
father of Nahor. 23 Serug lived after the birth
of Nahor two hundred years, and had other
sons and daughters.
24 Nahor lived twenty-nine years, and be-
came the father of Terah. 25 Nahor lived after
the birth of Terah one hundred and nineteen
years, and had other sons and daughters.

11:5 Ge 18:21
11:6 Ge 11:1
11:7 Ge 1:26
11:8 Lk 1:51
11:9 Ge 10:10
11:10 1Ch 1:17–27
11:20 Lk 3:35
11:24 Lk 3:34

....

11:26 Jos 24:2
11:27 Ge 11:31
11:28 Ge 15:7
11:29 Ge 17:15
11:31 Ne 9:7
12:1 Heb 11:8
12:2 Ge 18:18
12:3 Ge 22:18
12:5 Ge 14:14
12:6 Dt 11:30
12:7 Ge 13:15
12:8 Ge 4:26
12:9 Ge 13:3

26 Now Terah lived seventy years, and be-
came the father of Abram, Nahor, and Haran.

Terah's Descendants

27 These are the generations of Terah.

Terah became the father of Abram, Nahor,
and Haran, and Haran became the father of
Lot. 28 Haran died before his father Terah in
the land of his birth, in Ur of the Chaldeans.
29 Abram and Nahor took wives. The name of
Abram's wife was Sarai, and the name of Na-
hor's wife, Milkah, the daughter of Haran, the
father of Milkah and the father of Iskah. 30 But
Sarai was barren; she had no child.
31 Terah took his son Abram and his grand-
son Lot, son of Haran, and his daughter-in-law
Sarai, his son Abram's wife, and they went out
together from Ur of the Chaldeans to go into
the land of Canaan; but when they came to
Harran, they settled there.
32 The days of Terah were two hundred and
five years, and Terah died in Harran.

The Call of Abram

12 Now the LORD said to Abram, "Go from
your country, your family, and your
father's house to the land that I will show you.

2 I will make of you a great nation;
I will bless you
and make your name great,
so that you will be a blessing.
3 I will bless them who bless you
and curse him who curses you,[1]
and in you all families of the earth
will be blessed."

4 So Abram departed, as the LORD had spoken
to him, and Lot went with him. Abram was
seventy-five years old when he departed from
Harran. 5 Abram took Sarai his wife, Lot his
brother's son, and all their possessions that
they had accumulated, and the people that
they had acquired in Harran, and they set out
for the land of Canaan. They came to the land
of Canaan.
6 Then Abram passed through the land to the
place of Shechem, to the oak of Moreh. The
Canaanites were in the land at that time. 7 The
LORD appeared to Abram and said, "To your
descendants I will give this land." So he built
an altar to the LORD, who had appeared to him.
8 From there he continued on to a moun-
tain to the east of Bethel and pitched his tent,
having Bethel on the west and Ai on the east.
There he built an altar to the LORD and called
on the name of the LORD. 9 Then Abram contin-
ued his journey toward the Negev.

[1] 3 Or *treats you lightly.*

Abram in Egypt
Ge 20:1–18; 26:1–11

10 Now there was a famine in the land, so
Abram went down to Egypt to live there, for
the famine was severe in the land. 11 When
he was getting near to Egypt, he said to Sarai
his wife, "I know you are a beautiful woman.
12 Therefore, when the Egyptians see you, they
will say, 'This is his wife.' They will then kill me,
but they will let you live. 13 Say you are my sis-
ter so that I may be treated well for your sake.
Then my life will be spared because of you."

14 So when Abram entered Egypt, the Egyp-
tians saw that Sarai was very beautiful. 15 The
princes of Pharaoh saw her and commended
her to Pharaoh, and she was taken into Pha-
raoh's house. 16 He treated Abram well for her
sake and he had sheep and livestock, male and
female donkeys, male and female servants,
and camels.

17 But the LORD afflicted Pharaoh and his
house with great plagues because of Abram's
wife, Sarai. 18 So Pharaoh called Abram, and
said, "What have you done to me? Why did you
not tell me that she was your wife? 19 Why did
you say, 'She is my sister'? I might have taken
her as my wife. Now here is your wife; take her
and leave." 20 Pharaoh commanded his men
concerning him, and they sent him away with
his wife and all that he had.

Abram and Lot

13 So Abram went up from Egypt to the
Negev, he and his wife and all that
he had, and Lot with him. 2 Abram was very
wealthy in livestock, in silver and in gold.

3 He continued on his journey from the Ne-
gev and came to Bethel, to the place where his
tent had been at the beginning, between Beth-
el and Ai, 4 to the place where he first made
an altar. There Abram called on the name of
the LORD.

5 Now Lot, who went with Abram, also had
flocks and herds and tents. 6 But the land was
not able to support them both dwelling togeth-
er because their possessions were so great.
7 And there was strife between the herdsmen
of Abram's livestock and the herdsmen of Lot's
livestock. The Canaanites and the Perizzites
dwelled in the land at that time.

8 So Abram said to Lot, "Let there be no strife,
I ask you, between me and you, and between
my herdsmen and your herdsmen, for we are
close relatives. 9 Is not the whole land before
you? Please separate from me. If you will go
to the left, then I will go to the right, or if you
take the right, then I will go to the left."

10 Lot lifted up his eyes, and looked at all the
valley of the Jordan, that it was well watered
everywhere like the garden of the LORD, like the
land of Egypt as you go to Zoar. This was be-
fore the LORD destroyed Sodom and Gomorrah.
11 Then Lot chose for himself the entire valley
of the Jordan and journeyed east, and the two
of them separated from each other. 12 Abram
dwelled in the land of Canaan, and Lot dwelled
in the cities of the valley and pitched his tent
as far as Sodom. 13 Now the men of Sodom
were exceedingly wicked and sinners against
the LORD.

14 After Lot had departed from him, the LORD
said to Abram, "Lift up now your eyes, and
look from the place where you are, northward
and southward and eastward and westward.
15 All the land that you see I will give to you
and to your descendants forever. 16 I will make
your descendants like the dust of the earth,
so that if a man could number the dust of the
earth, then your descendants could also be
numbered. 17 Arise, and walk throughout the
land across its length and its width, for I will
give it to you."

18 So Abram moved his tent and came and
settled by the oaks of Mamre, which are in
Hebron, and built an altar to the LORD there.

Abram Rescues Lot

14 In the days that Amraphel was king
of Shinar, Arioch king of Ellasar, Ked-
orlaomer king of Elam, and Tidal king of
Goyim, 2 they made war with Bera king of So-
dom, Birsha king of Gomorrah, Shinab king
of Admah, Shemeber king of Zeboyim, and
the king of Bela (that is, Zoar). 3 All these were
joined together in the Valley of Siddim (that
is, the Dead Sea). 4 For twelve years they had
served Kedorlaomer, but in the thirteenth year
they rebelled.

5 In the fourteenth year, Kedorlaomer and
the kings who were with him came and de-
feated the Rephaites in Ashteroth Karnaim,
the Zuzites in Ham, and the Emites in Shaveh
Kiriathaim, 6 and the Horites in their hill coun-
try of Seir, as far as El Paran, which is by the
wilderness. 7 Then they turned back and came
to En Mishpat (that is, Kadesh) and conquered
all the country of the Amalekites and also the
Amorites who lived in Hazezon Tamar.

8 Then the king of Sodom, the king of Gomor-
rah, the king of Admah, the king of Zeboyim,
and the king of Bela (that is, Zoar) came out,
and they joined together in battle in the Valley
of Siddim 9 against Kedorlaomer, the king of
Elam, Tidal king of Goyim, Amraphel king of
Shinar, and Arioch king of Ellasar—four kings
against five. 10 Now the Valley of Siddim was
full of tar pits, and as the kings of Sodom and
Gomorrah fled, some fell in them, and the rest
fled to the hill country. 11 Then they took all

12:10 Ge 43:1
12:12 Ge 20:11
12:13 Ge 20:2
12:15 Ge 20:2
12:17 1Ch 16:21
12:18 Ge 20:9–10
13:2 Ge 24:35
13:4 Ge 12:7–8
13:6 Ge 36:6–7
13:7 Ge 12:6
13:10 Dt 34:3

....

13:12 Ge 19:29
13:13 Ge 18:20
13:14 Ge 28:14
13:15 Ge 12:7
13:16 Ge 28:14
13:18 Ge 14:13
14:1 Ge 10:10
14:2 Ge 13:10
14:3 Nu 34:12
14:5 Ge 15:20
14:6 Dt 2:22
14:7 2Ch 20:2
14:10 Ge 19:17

the possessions of Sodom and Gomorrah, and
all their provisions, and departed. 12 They also
took Lot, Abram's brother's son, who lived in
Sodom, and his possessions, and went their
way.
13 Then one who had escaped came and told
Abram the Hebrew, who was living near the
oaks of Mamre the Amorite, brother of Eshkol
and Aner, and these were allies with Abram.
14 When Abram heard that his relative was
taken captive, he armed his three hundred
and eighteen trained servants born in his
own house, and pursued them as far as Dan.
15 During the night he divided his men to attack
them and defeated them, and pursued them
as far as Hobah, which is north of Damascus.
16 He brought back all the possessions, along
with his relative Lot and his possessions, and
also the women and the people.

Melchizedek Blesses Abram

17 After his return from the defeat of Kedor-
laomer and the kings who had joined with
him, the king of Sodom went out to meet him
in the Valley of Shaveh (that is, the King's Val-
ley).
18 Then Melchizedek king of Salem brought
out bread and wine. He was the priest of God
Most High. 19 And he blessed him and said,

"Blessed be Abram by God Most High,
Creator[1] of heaven and earth;
20 and blessed be God Most High,
who has delivered your enemies into
your hand."

Then Abram gave him a tenth of everything.
21 The king of Sodom said to Abram, "Give
me the people and take the goods for yourself."
22 But Abram said to the king of Sodom, "I
have lifted up my hand to the LORD, God Most
High, the Possessor of heaven and earth, 23 that
I will take nothing that is yours, not a thread
or a sandal strap; lest you say, 'I have made
Abram rich.' 24 I will accept only that which my
men have eaten and the portion that belongs
to the men who went with me, Aner, Eshkol,
and Mamre. Let them take their portion."

The Abrahamic Covenant

15 After this the word of the LORD came to
Abram in a vision, saying,

"Do not fear, Abram.
I am your shield,
your exceedingly great reward.[2]"

2 But Abram said, "Lord GOD, what will You
give me, seeing I am childless and the heir of
my house is Eliezer of Damascus?" 3 Abram
said, "Since You have not given me any chil-
dren, my heir is a servant born in my house."
4 Then the word of the LORD came to him,
saying, "This man will not be your heir, but a
son that is from your own body will be your
heir." 5 He brought him outside and said, "Look
up toward heaven and count the stars, if you
are able to count them." And He said to him,
"So will your descendants be."
6 Abram believed the LORD, and He credited
it to him as righteousness.
7 He also said to him, "I am the LORD who
brought you out of Ur of the Chaldeans to give
you this land to possess[3] it."
8 But Abram said, "Lord GOD, how may I know
that I will possess it?"
9 So He said to him, "Bring Me a three-year-
old heifer, a three-year-old female goat, a
three-year-old ram, a turtledove, and a young
pigeon."
10 Then Abram brought all of these to Him
and cut them in two and laid each piece op-
posite the other, but he did not cut the birds in
half. 11 When the birds of prey came down on
the carcasses, Abram drove them away.
12 As the sun was going down, a deep sleep
fell on Abram, and terror and a great darkness
fell on him. 13 Then He said to Abram, "Know
for certain that your descendants will live as
strangers in a land that is not theirs, and they
will be enslaved and mistreated for four hun-
dred years. 14 But I will judge the nation that
they serve, and afterward they will come out
with great possessions. 15 As for you, you will
go to your fathers in peace and you will be bur-
ied at a good old age. 16 In the fourth genera-
tion, your descendants will return here, for the
iniquity of the Amorites is not yet complete."
17 When the sun went down and it was dark,
a smoking fire pot with a flaming torch passed
between these pieces. 18 On that same day the
LORD made a covenant with Abram, saying, "To
your descendants I have given this land, from
the river of Egypt to the great Euphrates Riv-
er— 19 the land of the Kenites, the Kenizzites,
the Kadmonites, 20 the Hittites, the Perizzites,
the Rephaites, 21 the Amorites, the Canaanites,
the Girgashites, and the Jebusites."

The Birth of Ishmael

16 Now Sarai, Abram's wife, had borne
him no children, and she had a maid-
servant, an Egyptian, whose name was Hagar.
2 So Sarai said to Abram, "The LORD has pre-
vented me from having children. Please go in
to my maid; it may be that I will obtain children
through her."
Abram listened to Sarai. 3 So after Abram
had been living for ten years in the land of

14:13 Ge 13:18
14:14 Ge 15:3
14:17 2Sa 18:18
14:18 Ps 110:4
14:19 Ge 14:22
14:20 Ge 28:22
14:22 Ex 6:8
14:23 2Ki 5:16
15:1 Ge 26:24
15:2 Ac 7:5
15:3 Ge 14:14
15:4 Ge 17:16
15:5 Dt 1:10
15:6 Jas 2:23
15:8 Lk 1:18
15:10 Lev 1:17
15:12 Ge 2:21
15:13 Gal 3:17
15:15 Job 5:26
15:16 1Ki 21:26
15:17 Jer 34:18–19
15:18 Ge 12:7
16:1 Gal 4:24
16:3 Ge 12:4–5

[1] 19 Or *Possessor* [2] 1 Or *your reward will be great.*
[3] 7 Or *inherit.*

Canaan, Sarai, his wife, took Hagar her maid, the Egyptian, and gave her to her husband Abram to be his wife. 4 He went in to Hagar, and she conceived.

When she saw that she had conceived, she began to despise her mistress. 5 Then Sarai said to Abram, "May the wrong done to me be on you! I gave my maid into your arms; and when she saw that she had conceived, I became despised in her eyes. May the LORD judge between you and me."

6 But Abram said to Sarai, "Indeed, your maid is in your power; do to her as you please." Then Sarai dealt harshly with her, and she fled from her presence.

7 The angel of the LORD found her by a spring of water in the wilderness. It was the spring on the way to Shur. 8 And he said, "Hagar, Sarai's maid, where have you come from and where are you going?"

And she said, "I am fleeing from the presence of my mistress Sarai."

9 Then the angel of the LORD said to her, "Return to your mistress, and submit yourself to her authority." 10 The angel of the LORD also said to her, "I will multiply your descendants exceedingly so that they will be too many to count."

11 Then the angel of the LORD said to her,

"You are pregnant
and will bear a son.
You shall call his name Ishmael,
because the LORD has heard your
affliction.
12 He will be a wild man;
his hand will be against every man,
and every man's hand will be against
him.
And he will dwell
in the presence of all his brothers."

13 Then she called the name of the LORD that spoke to her, "You are the God who sees," for she said, "Have I now looked on Him who sees me?" 14 Therefore the well was called Beer Lahai Roi. It is between Kadesh and Bered.

15 So Hagar bore Abram a son, and Abram called the son she bore Ishmael. 16 Abram was eighty-six years old when Hagar bore Ishmael to Abram.

The Covenant of Circumcision

17 When Abram was ninety-nine years old, the LORD appeared to him and said, "I am Almighty God. Walk before Me and be blameless. 2 And I will make My covenant between you and Me and will exceedingly multiply you."

3 Abram fell on his face and God said to him, 4 "As for Me, My covenant is with you, and you shall be the father of a multitude of nations. 5 No longer will your name be called Abram, but your name will be Abraham, for I have made you the father of a multitude of nations. 6 I will make you exceedingly fruitful; and I will make nations of you, and kings will come from you. 7 I will establish My covenant between Me and you and your descendants after you throughout their generations for an everlasting covenant, to be God to you and your descendants after you. 8 All the land of Canaan, where you now live as strangers, I will give to you and to your descendants for an everlasting possession, and I will be their God."

9 Then God said to Abraham, "As for you, you shall keep My covenant, you and your descendants after you throughout their generations. 10 This is My covenant, which you shall keep, between Me and you and your descendants after you; every male among you shall be circumcised. 11 You shall circumcise the flesh of your foreskins, and it shall be a sign of the covenant between Me and you. 12 Every male throughout every generation that is eight days old shall be circumcised, whether born in your household or bought with money from a foreigner who is not your descendant. 13 He who is born in your house and he who is bought with your money must be circumcised. My covenant shall be in your flesh as an everlasting covenant. 14 Any uncircumcised male whose flesh of his foreskin is not circumcised shall be cut off from his people. He has broken My covenant."

15 Then God said to Abraham, "As for Sarai your wife, you will not call her name Sarai, but her name will be Sarah. 16 I will bless her and also give you a son by her. I will bless her, and she will be the mother of nations. Kings of peoples will come from her."

God's covenant to me and to my children is everlasting (Ge 17:7).

17 Then Abraham fell on his face and laughed and said in his heart, "Shall a child be born to a man that is a hundred years old? Shall Sarah, who is ninety years old, bear a child?" 18 Abraham said to God, "Oh, that Ishmael might live before You!"

19 Then God said, "No, but your wife Sarah will bear you a son, and you will call his name Isaac. I will establish My covenant with him as an everlasting covenant and with his descendants after him. 20 And as for Ishmael, I have heard you. I have blessed him, and will make him fruitful and will multiply him exceedingly. He will be the father of twelve princes, and I

16:5 Ge 31:53
16:7 Ge 25:18
16:8 Ge 3:9
16:10 Ge 17:20
16:11 Ex 3:7
16:12 Ge 25:18
16:13 Ge 32:30
16:15 Ge 25:12
17:1 Ge 6:9
17:2 Ge 13:16
17:3 Ge 17:17
17:4 Ge 35:11
....
17:5 Ne 9:7
17:6 Ge 35:11
17:7 Ge 26:24
17:8 Ge 12:7
17:10 Ac 7:8
17:11 Ro 4:11
17:12 Lev 12:3
17:13 Ex 12:44
17:14 Ex 4:24–26
17:16 Ge 35:11
17:17 Ge 21:6
17:19 Ge 21:2–3
17:20 Ge 21:18

will make him a great nation. 21 But I will establish My covenant with Isaac, whom Sarah will bear to you at this set time next year." 22 Then He stopped talking with Abraham, and God went up from him.

23 Then Abraham took Ishmael, his son, and all that were born in his house, and all that were bought with his money, every male among the men of Abraham's household, and circumcised the flesh of their foreskins that very same day as God had said to him. 24 Abraham was ninety-nine years old when he was circumcised in the flesh of his foreskin. 25 His son, Ishmael, was thirteen years old when he was circumcised in the flesh of his foreskin. 26 Abraham and Ishmael were circumcised on the same day. 27 All the men born in Abraham's household or bought from foreigners were circumcised with him.

Isaac's Birth Foretold

18 The LORD appeared to Abraham near the great oak trees of Mamre while he sat in the tent door in the heat of the day. 2 Abraham lifted up his eyes and looked and saw three men standing across from him. When he saw them, he ran from the tent door to meet them and bowed himself toward the ground.

3 He said, "My Lord, if I have found favor in Your sight, do not pass by Your servant. 4 Please let a little water be brought and wash your feet and rest yourselves under the tree. 5 I will bring a piece of bread so that you may refresh yourselves. After that you may pass on, now that you have come to your servant."

And they said, "So do, as you have said."

6 So Abraham hurried into the tent to Sarah, and said, "Quickly prepare three measures[1] of fine flour, knead it, and make cakes."

7 Then Abraham ran to the herd and took a choice and tender calf and gave it to a servant, who hurried to prepare it. 8 He then brought butter and milk and the calf that he had prepared and set it before them; and he stood by them under the tree while they ate.

9 They said to him, "Where is Sarah your wife?"

And he said, "There, in the tent."

10 One of them said, "I will certainly return to you about this time next year, and Sarah your wife will have a son."

And Sarah heard it in the tent door, which was behind him. 11 Now Abraham and Sarah were old and very advanced in age, and Sarah was well past childbearing. 12 Therefore Sarah laughed to herself, saying, "After I am so old and my lord is old also, shall I have pleasure?"

13 Then the LORD said to Abraham, "Why did Sarah laugh and say, 'Shall I surely bear a child when I am old?' 14 Is anything too difficult for the LORD? At the appointed time I will return to you, at this time next year, and Sarah will have a son."

15 Then Sarah denied it, saying, "I did not laugh," because she was afraid.

But He said, "Yes, you did laugh."

Sodom and Gomorrah

16 Then the men rose up and looked toward Sodom, and Abraham went with them to see them on their way. 17 Then the LORD said, "Should I hide from Abraham what I am doing, 18 since Abraham will surely become a great and mighty nation, and all the nations of the earth will be blessed in him? 19 I chose him, and he will instruct his children and his household after him to keep the way of the LORD by doing righteousness and justice, so that the LORD may bring to Abraham what He promised him."

20 Then the LORD said, "Because the outcry against Sodom and Gomorrah is great, and because their sin is very grave, 21 I will go down and see if what they have done is as bad as the outcry that has come to Me. If not, I will know."

22 The men turned away from there and went toward Sodom, but Abraham remained standing before the LORD. 23 Then Abraham drew near and said, "Shall You also destroy the righteous with the wicked? 24 What if there are fifty righteous in the city? Shall You also destroy, and not spare the place, for the fifty righteous who are in it? 25 Far be it from You to do such a thing as this, to slay the righteous with the wicked, so that the righteous should be treated like the wicked; far be it from You. Should not the Judge of all the earth do right?"

26 So the LORD said, "If I find in Sodom fifty righteous within the city, then I will spare the entire place for their sakes."

27 Then Abraham answered and said, "I who am but dust and ashes have taken it upon myself to speak to the Lord. 28 Suppose there were five less than the fifty righteous. Will You destroy all the city for lack of five?"

And He said, "If I find forty-five there, I will not destroy it."

29 And he spoke to Him yet again and said, "Suppose there will be forty found there?"

So He said, "I will not do it for the sake of forty."

30 Then he said to Him, "Let not the Lord be angry, and I will speak. Suppose there will be thirty found there?"

17:22 Ge 18:33
17:24 Ro 4:11
18:1 Ge 13:18
18:2 Heb 13:2
18:4 Ge 19:2
18:5 Jdg 13:15
18:8 Ge 19:3
18:9 Ge 24:67
18:10 Ge 21:2
18:11 Ge 17:17
18:12 Ge 17:17

....

18:14 Jer 32:17
18:17 Am 3:7
18:18 Gal 3:8
18:20 Ge 19:13
18:21 Ge 11:5
18:22 Ge 19:1
18:23 Nu 16:22
18:24 Jer 5:1
18:25 Job 8:3
18:26 Jer 5:1
18:27 Ge 3:19

[1] 6 Likely about 36 pounds, or 16 kilograms.

Again He said, "I will not do it if I find thirty there."

31 He said, "Behold, I have undertaken to speak to the Lord. Suppose twenty are found there?"

He said, "I will not destroy it for the sake of twenty."

32 Then he said, "Let not the Lord be angry, and I will speak only once more. Suppose ten will be found there?"

Then He said, "I will not destroy it for the sake of ten."

33 So the LORD went His way as soon as He had stopped speaking to Abraham, and Abraham returned to his place.

Sodom and Gomorrah Destroyed

19 Now the two angels came to Sodom in the evening, and Lot was sitting at the gate of Sodom. When Lot saw them he rose up to meet them, and he bowed himself with his face toward the ground. 2 Then he said, "Here, my lords, please turn in to your servant's house and spend the night and wash your feet; and then you may rise early and go on your way."

They said, "No, we will stay in the open square all night."

3 But he strongly insisted, so they turned aside with him and entered his house. Then he made them a feast and baked unleavened bread, and they ate. 4 Before they lay down, the men of the city, the men of Sodom, both old and young, all the people from every quarter, surrounded the house. 5 They then called to Lot and said to him, "Where are the men who came to you tonight? Bring them out to us, so that we may have relations with them."

6 So Lot went out through the door to them and shut the door behind him. 7 Then he said, "Please, my brothers, do not act so wickedly. 8 Look, I have two daughters who have not been with a man. Please, let me bring them out to you, and you may do to them as you wish. Only do nothing to these men, for they have come under the shelter of my roof."

9 But they replied, "Stand back!" Also, they said, "This man came here as an alien, and he keeps acting like a judge. We will deal worse with you than with them." So they pressed hard against Lot, and came close to breaking down the door.

10 But the men reached out their hands and pulled Lot into the house with them and shut the door. 11 Then they struck the men that were at the door of the house, both small and great, with blindness so that they wore themselves out groping for the door.

12 Then the men said to Lot, "Have you anyone else here? Sons-in-law, sons, daughters, or anyone you have in the city, take them out of this place! 13 For we are about to destroy this place, because the outcry against its people has grown great before the presence of the LORD, and the LORD has sent us to destroy it."

14 So Lot went out and spoke to his sons-in-law, who had married his daughters, and said, "Get up, get out of this place, for the LORD will destroy this city!" But to his sons-in-law he seemed to be joking.

15 When the morning dawned, the angels urged Lot, saying, "Arise, take your wife and your two daughters who are here. Otherwise you will be consumed in the punishment of the city."

16 And while he lingered, the men took hold of his and his wife's hands, along with the hands of his two daughters, the LORD being merciful to him, and brought him out and set him outside the city. 17 When they had brought them out, one of them said to them, "Escape for your lives! Do not look behind you or stay anywhere in the plain. Escape to the mountain, lest you be destroyed."

> Your mercy is saving my life (Ge 19:19).

18 Then Lot said to them, "Please, no, my lords! 19 Your servant has found grace in your eyes, and you have shown your mercy, which you have shown to me by saving my life. However, I cannot escape to the mountain. Otherwise some evil will overtake me, and I will die. 20 Look, this city is close enough to flee to, and it is a little one. Please, let me escape there (is it not a little one?), and my life will be saved."

21 He said to him, "I have granted your request in this matter also. I will not overthrow this city of which you have spoken. 22 Hurry, escape there, for I cannot do anything until you arrive there." Therefore the name of the city was called Zoar.

23 The sun had risen over the land when Lot entered Zoar. 24 Then the LORD rained brimstone and fire on Sodom and Gomorrah. It was from the LORD out of heaven. 25 So He overthrew those cities, all the valley, all the inhabitants of the cities, and what grew on the ground. 26 But his wife, behind him, looked back, and she became a pillar of salt.

27 Now Abraham got up early in the morning and went to the place where he stood before the LORD. 28 Then he looked toward Sodom and Gomorrah, and toward all the land of the valley, and he saw the smoke of the land going up like the smoke of a furnace.

18:32 Jdg 6:39
19:1 Ge 18:22
19:2 Ge 18:4
19:3 Ge 18:6–8
19:5 Jdg 19:22
19:6 Jdg 19:23
19:8 Jdg 19:24
19:9 Ex 2:14
19:11 2Ki 6:18

19:13 Ge 18:20
19:14 Nu 16:21
19:15 Rev 18:4
19:17 Ge 19:26
19:22 Ge 14:2
19:24 Dt 29:23
19:25 Ps 107:34
19:26 Ge 19:17
19:28 Rev 18:9

29 So it was that when God destroyed the cit-
ies of the valley, God remembered Abraham,
and sent Lot out of the middle of the destruc-
tion, when He overthrew the cities in which
Lot lived.

Lot and His Daughters

30 Then Lot left Zoar, and lived in the moun-
tains, along with his two daughters who were
with him, for he was afraid to dwell in Zoar. He
and his two daughters lived in a cave. 31 And
the firstborn said to the younger, "Our father is
old, and there is no man on the earth to have
relations with us after the manner of all the
earth. 32 Let us make our father drink wine and
let us lie with him, so that we may preserve the
lineage of our father."

33 So they made their father drink wine that
night, and the firstborn went in and had rela-
tions with her father. He did not know when
she lay down or when she arose.

34 On the next day the firstborn said to the
younger, "Indeed, last night I had relations
with my father. Let us make him drink wine
tonight also, so that you may go in and have
relations with him, so that we may preserve
the lineage of our father." 35 So they made
their father drink wine that night also. Then
the younger arose and lay down with him, and
he did not know when she lay down or when
she arose.

36 Therefore both the daughters of Lot were
pregnant by their father. 37 The firstborn bore
a son and called his name Moab. He is the fa-
ther of the Moabites to this day. 38 The younger
also gave birth to a son and called his name
Ben-Ammi. He is the father of the Ammonites
to this day.

Abraham and Abimelek

Ge 12:10–20; 26:1–11

20 Abraham journeyed from there toward
the Negev, settled between Kadesh
and Shur, and then he sojourned in Gerar.
2 Then Abraham said about Sarah his wife,
"She is my sister." So Abimelek, king of Gerar,
sent for her and took Sarah.

3 But God came to Abimelek in a dream by
night and said to him, "You are a dead man
because of the woman whom you have taken,
for she is a man's wife."

4 Abimelek had not gone near her, and he
said, "Lord, will You slay a righteous nation?
5 Did he not say to me, 'She is my sister,' and
did not even she herself say, 'He is my broth-
er'? In the integrity of my heart and innocence
of my hands I have done this."

6 And God said to him in a dream, "Yes, I
know that you did this in the integrity of
your heart. For I also kept you from sinning
against Me. Therefore, I did not let you touch
her. 7 Therefore return the man's wife, for he is
a prophet and he will pray for you. Moreover,
you will live. However, if you do not return
her, know that you will surely die, you and all
who are yours."

8 So Abimelek rose early in the morning,
and called all his servants and told them all
these things, and the men were very afraid.
9 Then Abimelek called Abraham and said to
him, "What have you done to us? How have I
offended you that you would bring on me and
on my kingdom a great sin? You have done
things to me that should not have been done."
10 Then Abimelek said to Abraham, "What were
you thinking of, that you did this thing?"

11 Abraham said, "Because I thought, surely
there is no fear of God in this place, and they
will slay me because of my wife. 12 Still, in-
deed, she is my sister. She is the daughter of
my father, but not the daughter of my mother.
She became my wife. 13 When God caused me
to travel from my father's house, I said to her,
'This is your kindness which you must show
me: Every place where we go, say concerning
me, He is my brother.' "

14 Then Abimelek took sheep, oxen, and
male and female servants, and gave them to
Abraham, and returned his wife Sarah to him.
15 Abimelek said, "My land is before you; settle
wherever it pleases you."

16 To Sarah he said, "I have given your broth-
er a thousand shekels of silver.[1] It is a sign of
your innocence in the eyes of all who are with
you, and before everyone you are vindicated."

17 So Abraham prayed to God, and God
healed Abimelek, his wife, and his female ser-
vants. Then they bore children. 18 For the LORD
had closed up all the wombs of the house of
Abimelek because of Sarah, Abraham's wife.

The Birth of Isaac

21 The LORD visited Sarah as He had said,
and the LORD did for Sarah as He had
spoken. 2 For Sarah conceived and bore Abra-
ham a son in his old age, at the set time that
God had spoken to him. 3 Abraham called the
name of his son who was born to him, whom
Sarah bore to him, Isaac. 4 Then Abraham
circumcised his son Isaac when he was eight
days old, as God had commanded him. 5 Now
Abraham was one hundred years old when his
son Isaac was born to him.

6 And Sarah said, "God has made me laugh.
All who hear will laugh with me." 7 Also she
said, "Who would have said to Abraham that
Sarah would nurse children? Yet I have borne
him a son in his old age."

19:30 Ge 19:19
19:37 Dt 2:9
19:38 Dt 2:19
20:1 Ge 26:6
20:2 Ge 12:15
20:3 Job 33:15
20:6 1Sa 25:26
20:7 1Sa 7:5
20:9 Ge 12:18
20:11 Ge 12:12
20:12 Ge 11:29
20:13 Ge 12:1
20:14 Ge 12:16
20:15 Ge 13:9
20:16 Ge 20:5
20:17 Jas 5:16
20:18 Ge 12:17
21:1 Ge 18:10
21:2 Gal 4:22
21:3 Ge 17:19
21:4 Ac 7:8
21:5 Ge 17:17
21:6 Isa 54:1
21:7 Ge 18:11–12

[1] *16* About 25 pounds, or 12 kilograms.

Hagar and Ishmael Depart

8 So the child grew and was weaned. Then Abraham made a great feast the same day that Isaac was weaned. 9 Sarah saw the son of Hagar the Egyptian, whom she had borne to Abraham, mocking. 10 Therefore she said to Abraham, "Throw out this slave woman and her son, for the son of this slave woman shall not be heir with my son, Isaac."

11 This matter was very displeasing in Abraham's sight because of his son. 12 But God said to Abraham, "Do not be upset concerning the boy and your slave wife. Whatever Sarah has said to you, listen to what she says, for in Isaac your descendants will be called. 13 Yet I will also make a nation of the son of the slave woman, because he is your offspring."

14 So Abraham rose up early in the morning, and took bread and a skin of water and gave it to Hagar, putting it on her shoulder, and sent her away with the child. So she departed and wandered in the Wilderness of Beersheba.

15 When the water in the skin was gone, she placed the child under one of the shrubs. 16 Then she went and sat down across from him at a distance of about a bowshot, for she said to herself, "Let me not see the death of the child." She sat across from him, and lifted up her voice and wept.

17 And God heard the boy's voice. Then the angel of God called to Hagar out of heaven and said to her, "What is the matter with you, Hagar? Do not be afraid, for God has heard the voice of the boy where he is. 18 Arise, pick up the boy and hold him in your hands, for I will make him a great nation."

19 Then God opened her eyes, and she saw a well of water. And she went and filled the skin with water and gave the boy a drink.

20 God was with the boy; and he grew and lived in the wilderness and became an archer. 21 He lived in the Wilderness of Paran, and his mother found a wife for him out of the land of Egypt.

The Treaty With Abimelek

22 Now it came to pass at that time that Abimelek and Phicol, the commander of his army, spoke to Abraham, saying, "God is with you in all that you do. 23 Now therefore, swear to me by God that you will not deal deceitfully with me, or with my children, or with my descendants. Instead, according to the kindness that I have shown to you, you will show to me and to the land where you have lived."

24 Abraham said, "I will swear."

25 Then Abraham complained to Abimelek about a well of water that Abimelek's servants had violently seized. 26 And Abimelek said, "I do not know who has done this. You did not tell me, and I have not heard of it until today."

27 So Abraham took sheep and oxen and gave them to Abimelek, and the two of them made a covenant. 28 Then Abraham set seven ewe lambs of the flock by themselves. 29 And Abimelek said to Abraham, "What is the meaning of these seven ewe lambs that you have set by themselves?"

30 And he said, "You shall take these seven ewe lambs from my hand so that they may be a witness that I have dug this well."

31 Therefore he called that place Beersheba, because the two of them swore an oath there.

32 Thus they made a covenant at Beersheba. Then Abimelek rose with Phicol, the commander of his army, and they returned to the land of the Philistines. 33 Abraham planted a tamarisk tree in Beersheba, and there he called on the name of the LORD, the Everlasting God. 34 Abraham stayed in the land of the Philistines many days.

The Sacrifice of Isaac

22 After these things God tested Abraham and said to him, "Abraham!"

And he said, "Here I am."

2 Then He said, "Take your son, your only son Isaac, whom you love, and go to the land of Moriah, and offer him there as a burnt offering on one of the mountains of which I will tell you."

3 So Abraham rose up early in the morning and saddled his donkey, and took two of his young men with him and Isaac his son; and he split the wood for the burnt offering, and arose and went to the place that God had told him. 4 Then on the third day Abraham lifted up his eyes and saw the place from a distance. 5 Abraham said to his young men, "Stay here with the donkey. The boy and I will go over there and worship and then return to you."

6 So Abraham took the wood of the burnt offering and laid it on Isaac his son; and he took the fire in his hand and the knife. So the two of them walked on together. 7 But Isaac spoke to Abraham his father and said, "My father!"

And he said, "Here I am, my son."

Then he said, "Here is the fire and the wood, but where is the lamb for the burnt offering?"

8 Abraham said, "My son, God will provide for Himself the lamb for a burnt offering." So the two of them went together.

9 Then they came to the place that God had told him. So Abraham built an altar there and arranged the wood; and he bound Isaac his son and laid him on the altar, on the wood. 10 Then Abraham stretched out his hand and took the knife to slay his son. 11 But the angel

21:9 Ge 16:15
21:10 Jn 8:35
21:11 Ge 17:18
21:12 Heb 11:18
21:13 Ge 21:18
21:17 Ge 16:11
21:18 Ge 21:13
21:19 Nu 22:31
21:20 Ge 28:15
21:22 Ge 20:2
21:23 Jos 2:12
21:25 Ge 26:15–22
21:30 Ge 31:52
21:31 Ge 26:33
21:33 Ge 4:26
22:1 Heb 11:17
22:2 2Ch 3:1
22:6 Jn 19:17
22:8 Jn 1:36
22:9 Jas 2:21

SPIRITED WOMAN

COUNSEL FROM THE SPIRIT BASICS

The Anointed Knife

The Bible is full of godly men and women whose lives demonstrated the anointing God had entrusted to them. Let's look at Abraham, the father of many nations (Ge 17:1–8). God told him, "Take your son, your only son Isaac, whom you love, and go to the land of Moriah, and offer him there as a burnt offering on one of the mountains of which I will tell you" (Ge 22:2).

One thing that has always seemed so interesting to me is how the Bible says, "So Abraham *rose up early* in the morning" and got going (v. 3, emphasis added). I can't imagine how Abraham felt as he got up and prepared to do what God had told him. I don't know, I might have waited until at least around midday to see if God might change His mind. Not Abraham! He was determined to obey God and flow in the leading of His Spirit, power, and anointing.

The true picture of the anointing in this story is Abraham raising that knife upward and getting ready to slay his son as a sacrifice to God. He was so bent on obeying God that the angel of the Lord had to call out his name twice to stop him (vv. 10–11). Abraham was anointed to obey God, even to the point of killing his only son, because the Bible says he was convinced that God would absolutely raise Isaac from the dead. (See Hebrews 11:17–19.) Of course, this encounter is a type and shadow of what Father God did for us by giving us His one and only Son to die for our sins.

Judy Jacobs

of the LORD called to him out of heaven and
said, "Abraham, Abraham!"
And he said, "Here I am."
12 Then He said, "Do not lay your hands on
the boy or do anything to him, because now I
know that you fear God, seeing you have not
withheld your only son from Me."
13 Then Abraham lifted up his eyes and
looked, and behind him was a ram caught in
a thicket by his horns. So Abraham went and
took the ram and offered him up as a burnt
offering in the place of his son. 14 Abraham
called the name of that place The LORD Will
Provide, as it is said to this day, "In the mount
of the LORD it will be provided."

> You are Jehovah-Jireh, my provider (Ge 22:14).

15 Then the angel of the LORD called to Abra-
ham out of heaven a second time, 16 and said,
"By Myself I have sworn, says the LORD, be-
cause you have done this thing, and have
not withheld your son, your only son, 17 I will
indeed bless you and I will indeed multiply
your descendants as the stars of the heavens
and as the sand that is on the seashore. Your
descendants will possess the gate of their ene-
mies. 18 Through your offspring all the nations
of the earth will be blessed, because you have
obeyed My voice."

> If you are obedient to God, not only is He going to give you favor, but He is also going to give you *release* and *increase* (Ge 22:16–18).

19 So Abraham returned to his young men,
and they arose and went together to Beershe-
ba. Then Abraham lived at Beersheba.

> Through Jesus, let me possess the gate of the enemy (Ge 22:17).

Sons of Nahor

20 After these things Abraham was told,
"Milkah has also borne children to your broth-
er Nahor: 21 Uz his firstborn, Buz his brother,
Kemuel the father of Aram, 22 Kesed, Hazo,
Pildash, Jidlaph, and Bethuel." 23 Bethuel be-
came the father of Rebekah. Milkah gave birth
to these eight to Nahor, Abraham's brother.
24 His concubine, whose name was Reumah,
also bore Tebah, Gaham, Tahash, and Maakah.

The Death of Sarah

23 Sarah lived one hundred and twen-
ty-seven years. These were the years
of the life of Sarah. 2 Then Sarah died in Kiriath
Arba (that is, Hebron) in the land of Canaan,
and Abraham went in to mourn for Sarah and
to weep for her.
3 Then Abraham stood up from before his
dead and spoke to the Hittites,[1] saying, 4 "I am
a stranger and a foreigner among you. Give me

22:12 1Sa 15:22
22:14 Ge 22:8
22:16 Lk 1:73
22:17 Ge 15:5
22:18 Ge 12:3
22:19 Ge 21:31
22:20 Ge 11:29
22:21 Job 1:1
22:23 Ge 24:15
23:2 Ge 23:19
23:3 Ge 10:15
23:4 Ge 17:8

[1]3 Or *the sons of Heth*; also in vv. 5, 7, 10, 16, 18, and 20.

property for a burying place among you, that I
may bury my dead out of my sight."
5 So the Hittites answered Abraham, 6 "Hear
us, my lord. You are a mighty prince among
us. Bury your dead in the choicest of our burial
places. None of us will withhold from you his
burial place that you may bury your dead."
7 Then Abraham stood up and bowed him-
self to the people of the land, the Hittites. 8 He
spoke with them, saying, "If it be your wish
that I bury my dead out of my sight, hear me
and entreat Ephron the son of Zohar for me,
9 that he may give me the cave of Machpelah,
which he owns, at the end of his field. Let him
give it to me in your presence for the full price
for a burial site."
10 Now Ephron was sitting among the Hit-
tites; and Ephron the Hittite answered Abra-
ham in the presence of all the Hittites, all who
went in at the gate of his city, saying, 11 "No,
my lord. Hear me: I give you the field and the
cave that is in it. I give it to you in the presence
of the sons of my people. Bury your dead."
12 Then Abraham bowed before the people
of the land. 13 Then he spoke to Ephron in the
hearing of the people of the land, saying, "In-
deed, if you will give it, please hear me. I will
give you money for the field; take it from me
and I will bury my dead there."
14 Then Ephron answered Abraham, saying
to him, 15 "My lord, listen to me. The land is
worth four hundred shekels of silver.[1] What is
that between me and you? So bury your dead."
16 Abraham listened to Ephron; and Abraham
weighed out for Ephron four hundred shekels
of silver, the price that he had named in the
hearing of the Hittites, according to the stan-
dard commercial measure.
17 So the field of Ephron, which was in Mach-
pelah, which was before Mamre, the field and
the cave that was in it, and all the trees that
were in the field that were within all the sur-
rounding borders were deeded 18 to Abraham
as a possession in the presence of the Hittites,
before all who went in at the gate of his city.
19 After this, Abraham buried Sarah his wife
in the cave of the field of Machpelah before
Mamre (that is, Hebron) in the land of Canaan.
20 So the field and the cave that was in it were
deeded to Abraham by the Hittites as property
for a burial place.

Isaac and Rebekah

24 Now Abraham was old, well advanced
in age; and the LORD had blessed Abra-
ham in all things. 2 So Abraham said to his
servant, the oldest of his household, who was
in charge over all that he had, "Please, place
your hand under my thigh, 3 and I will make
you swear by the LORD, the God of heaven and
the God of the earth, that you will not take
a wife for my son from the daughters of the
Canaanites, among whom I live. 4 But you shall
go to my country and to my family, and take a
wife for my son Isaac."
5 Then the servant said to him, "Perhaps the
woman will not be willing to follow me to this
land. Must I take your son back to the land
from which you came?"
6 Abraham said to him, "See to it that you do
not take my son back there. 7 The LORD God of
heaven, who took me from my father's family
and from the land of my relatives, and who
spoke to me and swore to me, saying, 'To your
descendants I will give this land,' He shall send
His angel before you and you shall take a wife
for my son from there. 8 If the woman is not
willing to follow you, then you will be free from
my oath. Only do not take my son back there."
9 So the servant put his hand under the thigh
of Abraham his master and swore to him con-
cerning this matter.
10 Then the servant took ten of his master's
camels and departed, for all the goods of his
master were in his hand. And he arose and
went to the city of Nahor in Aram Naharaim.
11 He made his camels kneel down outside the
city by a well of water in the evening when the
women came out to draw water.
12 Then he said, "O LORD, the God of my mas-
ter Abraham, please let me have success this
day and show kindness to my master Abra-
ham. 13 See, here I stand by the well of water,
and the daughters of the men of the city are
coming out to draw water. 14 Let it be that the
young woman to whom I shall say, 'Please
lower your pitcher, that I may drink,' and she
shall say, 'Drink, and I will give your camels
water also'—let her be the one that You have
appointed for Your servant Isaac. Then I will
know that You have shown kindness to my
master."
15 Before he had finished speaking, Rebekah,
who was born to Bethuel, son of Milkah, the
wife of Nahor, Abraham's brother, came out
with a pitcher on her shoulder. 16 The young
woman was very beautiful to look at, a virgin,
and no man had ever been with her. She went
down to the well and filled her pitcher and
came up.
17 Then the servant ran to meet her and said,
"Please let me drink a little water from your
pitcher."
18 So she said, "Drink, my lord." Then she
quickly let down her pitcher to her hand and
gave him a drink.

23:6 Ge 24:35
23:10 Ge 34:20
23:15 Eze 45:12
23:16 Jer 32:9
23:17 Ge 25:9
23:20 Ru 4:7–10
24:1 Ge 13:2
24:2 Ge 47:29
24:3 Ge 26:34–35
24:4 Ge 28:2
24:7 Ge 13:15
24:8 Jos 2:17–20
24:9 Ge 24:2
24:11 1Sa 9:11
24:12 Ge 24:27
24:13 Ge 24:43
24:14 Jdg 6:17
24:15 Ge 11:29
24:16 Ge 26:7
24:17 Jn 4:7

[1] *15* About 10 pounds, or 4.6 kilograms.

19 When she had finished giving him a drink,
she said, "I will draw water for your camels
also, until they have finished drinking." 20 Then
she quickly emptied her pitcher into the trough
and ran to the well to draw water and drew
for all his camels. 21 The man, gazing at her,
remained silent, trying to discern whether the
LORD had made his journey a success or not.

22 When the camels had finished drinking,
the man took a gold nose ring of half a shekel
weight[1] and two bracelets for her wrists of ten
shekels weight[2] in gold, 23 and said, "Whose
daughter are you? Please tell me, is there room
in your father's house for us to lodge?"

24 She said to him, "I am the daughter of
Bethuel the son of Milkah, whom she bore
to Nahor." 25 Again she said to him, "We have
both straw and provision enough, and room
in which to lodge."

26 Then the man bowed down his head and
worshipped the LORD. 27 And he said, "Blessed
be the LORD God of my master Abraham, who
has not forsaken His mercy and His truth to-
ward my master. As for me, the LORD led me to
the house of my master's relatives."

28 So the young woman ran and told her
mother's household of these things. 29 Now
Rebekah had a brother whose name was La-
ban, and Laban ran out to the man at the well.
30 When he saw the nose ring and bracelets
on his sister's hands and when he heard the
words of Rebekah his sister, saying, "This is
what the man said to me," he went to the man
who stood by the camels at the well. 31 And he
said, "Come in, blessed of the LORD. Why do
you stand outside? I have prepared the house
and a place for the camels."

32 So the man came to the house. Then he
unloaded his camels and gave straw and pro-
vision to the camels and water to wash his
feet and the feet of the men who were with
him. 33 He then set food before him to eat, but
he said, "I will not eat until I have told about
my errand."

And he said, "Speak on."

34 So he said, "I am Abraham's servant. 35 The
LORD has greatly blessed my master, and he
has become wealthy. He has given him flocks
and herds, and silver and gold, and male and
female servants, and camels and donkeys.
36 Sarah my master's wife bore a son to my
master when she was old, and he has given
to him all that he has. 37 My master made me
swear, saying, 'You must not take a wife for
my son from the daughters of the Canaanites,
in whose land I live. 38 But you shall go to my
father's house, and to my relatives, and take a
wife for my son.'

39 "So I said to my master, 'Perhaps the wom-
an will not follow me.'

40 "Then he said to me, 'The LORD, before
whom I walk, will send His angel with you and
prosper your way, and you will take a wife for
my son from my relatives and from my father's
house. 41 You will be free from my oath, when
you come to my family, if they will not give her
to you; then you will be released from my oath.'

42 "So today I came to the well and said, 'O
LORD, the God of my master Abraham, if You
will now give me success in my task; 43 I am
standing by the well of water, and let it be that
when the virgin comes forth to draw water,
and I say to her, "Please give me a little water
from your pitcher to drink," 44 and she says to
me, "Drink, and I will also draw for your cam-
els," let her be the woman whom the LORD has
appointed for my master's son.'

45 "Before I had finished speaking in my
heart, there was Rebekah coming out with her
pitcher on her shoulder; and she went down
to the well and drew water. Then I said to her,
'Please let me drink.'

46 "She then quickly let down her pitcher from
her shoulder and said, 'Drink, and I will give
your camels a drink also.' So I drank, and she
gave the camels a drink also.

47 "Then I asked her, 'Whose daughter are
you?'

"And she said, 'The daughter of Bethuel, Na-
hor's son, whom Milkah bore for him.'

"So I put the nose ring on her nose and the
bracelets on her wrists. 48 And I bowed down
my head and worshipped the LORD, and bless-
ed the LORD God of my master Abraham, who
had led me in the right way to take the daugh-
ter of my master's brother for his son. 49 And
now if you will deal kindly and truly with my
master, tell me; and if not, tell me, so that I
may turn to the right hand or to the left."

50 Then Laban and Bethuel answered and
said, "This thing comes from the LORD; we
cannot speak to you bad or good. 51 Here is
Rebekah before you; take her and go, and let
her be the wife of your master's son, as the
LORD has spoken."

52 When Abraham's servant heard their
words, he worshipped the LORD, bowing him-
self to the earth. 53 Then the servant brought
out jewels of silver and gold, and clothing and
gave them to Rebekah. He also gave precious
things to her brother and to her mother. 54 Then
they ate and drank, he and the men who were
with him, and stayed all night.

The next morning they arose, and he said,
"Send me away to my master."

24:19 Ge 24:14
24:21 Ge 24:12
24:22 Ex 32:2–3
24:24 Ge 24:15
24:26 Ge 24:48
24:27 Ge 24:48
24:29 Ge 29:5
24:31 Ge 26:29
24:32 Ge 43:24
24:35 Ge 13:2
24:36 Ge 25:5
24:38 Ge 24:4

....

24:40 Ge 17:1
24:41 Ge 24:8
24:42 Ne 1:11
24:43 Ge 24:13–14
24:44 Ge 24:14
24:48 Ge 24:26–27
24:49 Ge 47:29
24:50 Ge 31:24
24:51 Ge 24:15
24:52 Ge 24:26
24:54 Ge 24:56

[1] *22* About ⅕ ounce, or 5.7 grams. [2] *22* About 4 ounces, or 115 grams.

55 But her brother and her mother said, "Let
the young woman remain with us a few days,
at least ten; after that she may go."
56 So he said to them, "Do not delay me, see-
ing the LORD has given me success. Let me go
that I may go to my master."
57 They said, "We will call the girl and ask
her." 58 Then they called Rebekah and said to
her, "Will you go with this man?"
And she said, "I will go."
59 So they sent away Rebekah their sister and
her nurse, and Abraham's servant and his men.
60 They blessed Rebekah and said to her,

"May you, our sister, become the mother
of thousands of ten thousands;
and may your descendants possess
the gate of those who hate them."

61 Then Rebekah and her maids arose and
they rode on the camels and followed the man.
So the servant took Rebekah and went his way.
62 Now Isaac came from the way of Beer La-
hai Roi, for he lived in the Negev. 63 Isaac went
out in the evening to meditate in the field; and
he lifted up his eyes and looked, and surely
the camels were coming. 64 And Rebekah lift-
ed up her eyes, and when she saw Isaac, she
dismounted from her camel 65 and said to the
servant, "Who is this man walking in the field
to meet us?"
The servant said, "It is my master." Therefore
she took a veil and covered herself.
66 Then the servant told Isaac all the things
he had done. 67 So Isaac brought her into the
tent of his mother Sarah; and he took Rebekah
and she became his wife and he loved her. So
Isaac was comforted after his mother's death.

The Death of Abraham
1Ch 1:32–33

25 Then Abraham took another wife,
whose name was Keturah. 2 And she
bore to him Zimran, Jokshan, Medan, Midian,
Ishbak, and Shuah. 3 Jokshan was the father of
Sheba and Dedan. The descendants of Dedan
were the Ashurites, the Letushites, and the
Leummites. 4 The sons of Midian were Ephah,
Epher, Hanok, Abida, and Eldaah. All these
were the children of Keturah.
5 Abraham gave all that he had to Isaac. 6 But
to the sons of his concubines Abraham gave
gifts, and while he was still living, he sent them
away from his son Isaac eastward to the east
country.
7 These are the years of Abraham's life that
he lived: one hundred and seventy-five years.
8 Then Abraham breathed his last and died at a
good old age, an old man and full of years; and
he was gathered to his people. 9 His sons Isaac
and Ishmael buried him in the cave of Mach-
pelah, in the field of Ephron the son of Zohar
the Hittite, east of Mamre, 10 the field that Abra-
ham purchased from the sons of Heth. There
Abraham was buried with his wife Sarah. 11 Af-
ter the death of Abraham, God blessed his son
Isaac. Isaac lived at Beer Lahai Roi.

Sons of Ishmael
1Ch 1:29–31

12 These are the generations of Ishmael,
Abraham's son, whom Hagar the Egyptian,
Sarah's maidservant, bore to Abraham.

13 These are the names of the sons of Ish-
mael, by their names, according to their gen-
erations: the firstborn of Ishmael, Nebaioth,
and then Kedar, Adbeel, Mibsam, 14 Mishma,
Dumah, Massa, 15 Hadad, Tema, Jetur, Na-
phish, and Kedemah. 16 These were the sons
of Ishmael, and these were their names, by
their towns and their settlements, twelve princ-
es according to their peoples. 17 These were
the years of the life of Ishmael: one hundred
and thirty-seven years. He breathed his last
and died; and he was gathered to his people.
18 They lived from Havilah as far as Shur, which
is east of Egypt, as you go toward Assyria. He
died in the presence of all his relatives.

The Births of Jacob and Esau

19 These are the generations of Isaac, Abra-
ham's son.

Abraham was the father of Isaac. 20 Isaac was
forty years old when he took Rebekah as his
wife, the daughter of Bethuel the Syrian of
Paddan Aram, the sister to Laban the Syrian.
21 Now Isaac pleaded with the LORD for his
wife, because she was barren; and the LORD
granted his plea, and Rebekah his wife con-
ceived. 22 But the children struggled together
within her, and she said, "If all is well, why am
I like this?" So she went to inquire of the LORD.
23 Then the LORD said to her,

"Two nations are in your womb,
and two peoples will be separated from
your body;
one people will be stronger than the other,
and the older will serve the younger."

24 Now when the time of her delivery came,
there were twins in her womb. 25 The first came
out red all over, like a hairy garment, and they
called his name Esau. 26 After that his brother
came out, and his hand took hold of Esau's
heel, so he was named Jacob. Isaac was sixty
years old when she bore them.
27 So the boys grew. Esau was a cunning
hunter, a man of the field, while Jacob was a
calm man, living in tents. 28 Isaac loved Esau,

24:59 Ge 35:8
24:60 Ge 17:16
24:62 Ge 16:14
24:63 Ps 1:2
25:2 1Ch 1:32–33
25:5 Ge 24:36
25:6 Ge 21:14
25:7 Ge 12:4
25:8 Ge 49:33
25:9 Ge 35:29
25:10 Ge 23:16
25:11 Ge 16:14
25:13 1Ch 1:29–31
25:15 1Ch 5:19
25:16 Ge 17:20
25:18 Ge 16:12
25:19 Mt 1:2
25:20 Ge 24:29
25:21 1Ch 5:20
25:22 1Sa 9:9
25:23 Ge 27:29
25:25 Ge 27:11
25:26 Ge 27:36
25:27 Heb 11:9
25:28 Ge 27:19

because he ate of his game, but Rebekah loved
Jacob.

Esau Sells His Birthright

29 Now Jacob cooked a stew; and Esau came
in from the field and he was famished. 30 So
Esau said to Jacob, "Please feed me some of
that red stew, for I am famished." Therefore
his name was called Edom.

31 Then Jacob said, "First sell me your birth-
right."

32 Esau said, "Look, I am about to die; of what
use is the birthright to me?"

33 Then Jacob said, "Swear to me this day."
So he swore to him, and he sold his birthright
to Jacob.

34 Then Jacob gave Esau bread and lentil
stew. Then he ate and drank, arose, and went
his way.

Thus Esau despised his birthright.

Isaac and Abimelek

Ge 12:10–20; 20:1–18

26 There was a famine in the land, in
addition to the first famine that was
during the days of Abraham. Isaac went to Abi-
melek king of the Philistines in Gerar. 2 The
LORD appeared to him and said, "Do not go
down to Egypt. Live in the land of which I will
tell you. 3 Sojourn in this land, and I will be with
you and will bless you; for I will give to you and
all your descendants all these lands, and I will
fulfill the oath which I swore to Abraham your
father. 4 I will make your descendants multiply
as the stars of the heavens and will give your
descendants all these lands. By your descen-
dants all the nations of the earth will be bless-
ed,[1] 5 because Abraham obeyed Me and kept
My charge, My commandments, My statutes,
and My laws." 6 So Isaac lived in Gerar.

7 The men of the place asked him about his
wife. And he said, "She is my sister," for he
was afraid to say, "She is my wife," *thinking*,
"The men of the place might kill me on ac-
count of Rebekah, because she is beautiful in
appearance."

8 When he had been there a long time, Abim-
elek the king of the Philistines looked out of a
window and saw Isaac caressing Rebekah his
wife. 9 Abimelek summoned Isaac and said,
"She is surely your wife, so how is it you said,
'She is my sister'?"

Then Isaac said to him, "Because I said, 'I
might die on account of her.' "

10 Abimelek said, "What is this you have done
to us? One of the people might have easily lain
with your wife, and you might have brought
guilt upon us!"

25:33 Heb 12:16
26:1 Ge 12:10
26:2 Ge 12:1
26:3 Ge 13:15
26:4 Ge 15:5
26:5 Ge 22:16
26:7 Ge 12:13

....

26:11 Ps 105:15
26:12 Ge 26:3
26:15 Ge 21:30
26:16 Ex 1:9
26:18 Ge 21:31
26:20 Ge 21:25
26:22 Ge 17:6
26:24 Ge 15:1
26:25 Ge 13:18
26:27 Ge 26:16
26:28 Ge 21:22–23
26:29 Ge 24:31

11 Abimelek charged all his people, saying,
"He who touches this man or his wife will sure-
ly be put to death."

12 Then Isaac sowed in that land and reaped
in the same year a hundredfold; the LORD bless-
ed him. 13 The man became rich and continued
to prosper until he became very wealthy. 14 For
he had possessions of flocks and herds and a
great number of servants so that the Philistines
envied him. 15 For the Philistines had stopped
up all the wells which his father's servants had
dug in the days of Abraham his father by filling
them with dirt.

16 Abimelek said to Isaac, "Go away from us,
for you are much more powerful than we are."

17 So Isaac departed from there and pitched
his tent in the Valley of Gerar and settled there.
18 Isaac dug again the wells of water, which
they had dug in the days of Abraham his fa-
ther, for the Philistines had stopped them up
after the death of Abraham. He called their
names after the names his father had called
them.

19 But when Isaac's servants dug in the valley
and found a well of running water there, 20 the
herdsmen of Gerar contended with Isaac's
herdsmen, saying, "The water is ours." So
he called the name of the well Esek, because
they contended with him. 21 They dug another
well and quarreled over that also. So he called
the name of it Sitnah. 22 Then he moved away
from there and dug another well, and they did
not quarrel over it. So he called the name of
it Rehoboth, for he said, "For now the LORD
has made room for us, and we will be fruitful
in the land."

23 He went up from there to Beersheba. 24 The
LORD appeared to him that same night and
said, "I am the God of Abraham your father.
Do not fear, for I am with you. I will bless you
and multiply your descendants for the sake of
My servant Abraham."

25 He built an altar there, called on the name
of the LORD, and pitched his tent there. And
there Isaac's servants dug a well.

26 Then Abimelek went to him from Gerar,
along with Ahuzzath, one of his friends, and
Phicol the commander of his army. 27 Isaac said
to them, "Why have you come to me, since you
hate me and have sent me away from you?"

28 And they said, "We saw plainly that the
LORD was with you. So we said, 'Let there now
be an oath between us, between you and us,
and let us make a covenant with you, 29 so that
you will do us no harm, just as we have not
touched you, and have done you nothing but
good and have sent you away in peace. You
are now the blessed of the LORD.' "

[1] 4 Or *will bless themselves.*

30 Then he made them a feast, and they ate
and drank. 31 They rose up early in the morn-
ing and swore an oath with one another. Isaac
sent them away, and they departed from him
in peace.

32 That same day Isaac's servants came and
told him about the well that they had dug and
said to him, "We have found water." 33 And he
called it Shibah. Therefore, the name of the city
is Beersheba to this day.

34 Esau was forty years old when he took as
wives Judith the daughter of Beeri the Hittite,
and Basemath the daughter of Elon the Hit-
tite, 35 and they brought grief to Isaac and to
Rebekah.

Isaac Blesses Jacob

27 When Isaac was old and his eyes
were so weak that he could not see,
he called Esau his oldest son and said to him,
"My son."

And he answered him, "Here I am."

2 He said, "I am old. I do not know the day of
my death. 3 Therefore, please take your weap-
ons, your quiver and your bow, and go out to
the field and hunt game for me. 4 And prepare
for me savory food, such as I love, and bring
it to me that I may eat, so that my soul may
bless you before I die."

5 Rebekah was listening when Isaac spoke
to Esau his son. So when Esau went to the
field to hunt for wild game and bring it back,
6 Rebekah said to her son Jacob, "I heard your
father speak to your brother Esau, saying,
7 'Bring me wild game, and prepare for me
savory food, that I may eat and bless you in the
presence of the LORD before my death.' 8 Now
therefore, my son, listen to me as I command
you. 9 Go now to the flock, and get me two
choice young goats, so that I may prepare from
them savory food for your father, such as he
loves. 10 Then you will take it to your father, so
that he may eat and so that he may bless you
before his death."

11 But Jacob said to his mother Rebekah,
"Look, my brother Esau is a hairy man, and
I am a man of smooth *skin*. 12 Perhaps my fa-
ther will feel me, and I will seem to him as a
deceiver, and I will bring a curse on myself
and not a blessing."

13 His mother said to him, "Let your curse be
upon me, my son. Only listen to me and go
get them for me."

14 He went and got them and brought them
to his mother. Then his mother prepared sa-
vory food such as his father loved. 15 Then Re-
bekah took the best clothes belonging to her
older son Esau, which were with her in the
house, and put them on Jacob her younger
son. 16 Then she put the skins of the young
goats on his hands and on the smooth part
of his neck. 17 She put the savory food and the
bread, which she had prepared, into the hands
of her son Jacob.

18 He came to his father and said, "My father."

And he said, "Here I am. Who are you, my
son?"

19 And Jacob said to his father, "I am Esau
your firstborn. I have done just as you asked
me. Please arise, sit and eat of my wild game,
so that your soul may bless me."

20 Isaac said to his son, "How is it that you
have found it so quickly, my son?"

And he said, "Because the LORD your God
brought it to me."

21 Isaac said to Jacob, "Please come near, so
that I may feel you, my son, whether you are
really my son Esau or not."

22 Jacob went near to his father Isaac, and
he felt him and said, "The voice is the voice of
Jacob, but the hands are the hands of Esau."
23 He did not recognize him because his hands
were hairy, just like his brother Esau's hands;
so he blessed him. 24 He asked, "Are you really
my son Esau?"

And he said, "I am."

25 He said, "Bring it near to me, and I will eat
of my son's wild game, so that my soul may
bless you."

And he brought it near to him, and he ate.
He also brought him wine, and he drank. 26 His
father Isaac said to him, "Come near now and
kiss me, my son."

27 He came near and kissed him; and he
smelled the smell of his clothing and blessed
him and said,

"See, the smell of my son
  is like the smell of the field
  which the LORD has blessed.
28 Therefore, may God give you of the dew of
    heaven
  and the fatness of the earth,
  and plenty of grain and new wine.
29 Let peoples serve you,
  and nations bow down to you.
Be master over your brothers,
  and let your mother's sons bow down
    to you.
Cursed be everyone who curses you,
  and blessed be those who bless you!"

30 As soon as Isaac had finished blessing Ja-
cob, and Jacob had barely gone out from the
presence of his father Isaac, Esau his brother
came in from his hunting. 31 He also had pre-
pared savory food and brought it to his father,
and said to his father, "Let my father arise and

26:30 Ge 19:3
26:33 Ge 21:31
26:34 Ge 36:2
27:1 Ge 48:10
27:3 Ge 25:27–28
27:4 Ge 27:25
27:8 Ge 27:13
27:11 Ge 25:25
27:12 Dt 27:18
27:13 Mt 27:25
27:15 Ge 27:27
27:21 Ge 27:12
27:27 Heb 11:20
27:28 Dt 33:28
27:29 Ge 12:3

SPIRIT-TO-SPIRIT PRAYER

A Mother's Prayer of Blessing for Her Children

My child, I love you! You are exceptional. You are a gift and treasure from God. I thank God for permitting me to be your mother. I bless you with the healing of all wounds of rejection, neglect, and abuse that you have endured. I bless you with bubbling-over peace—the peace that only the Prince of Peace can give, a peace beyond comprehension. I bless your life with fruitfulness—good fruit, much fruit, and fruit that remains. I bless you with the spirit of sonship. You are a son (or daughter) of the King of kings. You have a rich inheritance in the kingdom of God.

I bless you with success. You are the head and not the tail; you are above and not below. I bless you with health and strength of body, soul, and spirit. I bless you with overflowing success, enabling you to be a blessing to others. I bless you with spiritual influence, for you are the light of the world and the salt of the earth. You are like a tree planted by rivers of water. You will thrive in all your ways.

I bless you with a depth of spiritual understanding and an intimate walk with your Lord. You will not stumble or falter, for God's Word will be a lamp to your feet and a light to your path. I bless you with pure, edifying, encouraging, and empowering relationships in life. You have favor with God and man. I bless you with abounding love and life. I bless you with power, love, and a sound mind. I bless you with wisdom and spiritual gifts from on high. You will minister God's comforting grace and anointing to others. You are blessed, my child! You are blessed with all spiritual blessings in Christ Jesus. Amen!

Rebecca Greenwood

eat of his son's wild game, so that your soul
may bless me."
32 Isaac his father said to him, "Who are you?"
And he said, "I am your son, your firstborn,
Esau."
33 Then Isaac trembled violently, and said,
"Who? Where then is he who hunted game
and brought it to me? I ate all of it before you
came, and I have blessed him. Yes, and he
shall be blessed."
34 When Esau heard the words of his father,
he cried with a great and exceedingly bitter
cry, and said to his father, "Bless me, even me
also, O my father!"
35 He said, "Your brother came deceitfully and
has taken away your blessing."
36 Esau said, "Is he not rightly named Jacob?
For he has supplanted me these two times. He
took away my birthright, and now he has taken
away my blessing." And he said, "Have you not
reserved a blessing for me?"
37 Then Isaac answered and said to Esau, "I
have made him your lord, and I have given
to him all his brothers as servants; and I have
sustained him with grain and new wine. What
can I now do for you, my son?"
38 And Esau said to his father, "Do you have
only one blessing, my father? Bless me, even
me also, O my father!" Then Esau lifted up his
voice and wept.
39 Isaac his father answered and said to him,

"Your dwelling shall be
away from the fatness of the earth
and away from the dew of heaven from above.
40 You will live by your sword
and will serve your brother.
When you become restless,

27:33 Ge 28:3–4
27:34 Heb 12:17
27:36 Ge 25:26

27:38 Heb 12:17
27:39 Ge 27:28
27:40 Ge 25:23

you will break his yoke
from your neck."

Jacob Escapes From Esau

[41] So Esau hated Jacob because of the blessing with which his father blessed him. And Esau said in his heart, "The days of mourning for my father are at hand; then I will kill my brother Jacob."

[42] These words of Esau her older son were told to Rebekah; and she sent and called Jacob her younger son, and said to him, "Your brother Esau consoles himself regarding you by planning to kill you. [43] Now therefore, my son, listen to me and get up and flee to Laban, my brother in Harran. [44] Stay with him a few days until your brother's fury subsides, [45] until your brother's anger against you turns away, and he forgets what you have done to him. Then I will send and get you from there. Why should I lose both of you in one day?"

[46] Then Rebekah said to Isaac, "I am tired of my life because of the daughters of Heth. If Jacob takes a wife from the daughters of Heth, such as these who are of the daughters of the land, what good will my life be to me?"

28 Then Isaac called Jacob and blessed him. Then he charged him and said to him, "You must not take a wife of the daughters of Canaan. [2] Arise, go to Paddan Aram to the house of Bethuel your mother's father, and take for yourself a wife from there, from the daughters of Laban your mother's brother. [3] May God Almighty bless you and make you fruitful and multiply you, so that you may become a multitude of people. [4] May He give you the blessing of Abraham, to you and your descendants with you, that you may inherit the land where you are a stranger, which God gave to Abraham." [5] Then Isaac sent Jacob away, and he went to Paddan Aram to Laban, the son of Bethuel the Syrian, the brother of Rebekah, Jacob's and Esau's mother.

[6] Esau saw that Isaac had blessed Jacob and sent him away to Paddan Aram to take for himself a wife from there, and that as he blessed him he gave him a charge, saying, "You must not take a wife of the daughters of Canaan," [7] and that Jacob obeyed his father and his mother and had gone to Paddan Aram. [8] Esau saw that the daughters of Canaan did not please Isaac his father. [9] So Esau went to Ishmael and took as his wife Mahalath the daughter of Ishmael, Abraham's son, the sister of Nebaioth, in addition to the wives he had.

Jacob's Dream at Bethel

[10] Then Jacob went out from Beersheba and went toward Harran. [11] He came to a certain place and stayed there all night, because the sun had set. He took one of the stones of that place and put it under his head, and lay down in that place to sleep. [12] He dreamed and saw a ladder set up on the earth with the top of it reaching to heaven. The angels of God were ascending and descending on it. [13] The LORD stood above it and said, "I am the LORD God of Abraham your father and the God of Isaac. The land on which you lie, to you will I give it and to your descendants. [14] Your descendants will be like the dust of the earth, and you will spread abroad to the west and to the east and to the north and to the south, and in you and in your descendants all the families of the earth will be blessed. [15] Remember, I am with you, and I will protect you wherever you go, and I will bring you back to this land. For I will not leave you until I have done what I promised you."

[16] Jacob awoke out of his sleep, and he said, "Surely the LORD is in this place, and I did not know it." [17] He was afraid and said, "How awesome is this place! This is none other but the house of God, and this is the gate of heaven."

[18] So Jacob rose up early in the morning and took the stone that he had put under his head, set it up as a pillar, and poured oil on top of it. [19] He called the name of that place Bethel, but previously the name of the city was called Luz.

[20] Jacob vowed a vow, saying, "If God will be with me and will protect me in this way that I go, and will give me bread to eat and clothing to put on, [21] so that I return to my father's house in peace, then the LORD will be my God. [22] Then this stone, which I have set for a pillar, will be the house of God, and from all that You give me I will surely give a tenth to You."

Jacob Meets Rachel

29 Then Jacob went on his journey and came into the land of the people of the east. [2] As he looked, he saw a well in the field and three flocks of sheep lying by it, for out of that well the flocks were watered. A large stone was on the well's opening. [3] When all the flocks were gathered there, the shepherds rolled the stone from the well's opening, watered the sheep, then put the stone back on the well's opening in its place.

[4] Jacob said to them, "My brothers, where are you from?"

And they said, "We are from Harran."

[5] Then he said to them, "Do you know Laban the son of Nahor?"

And they said, "We know him."

[6] He said to them, "Is he well?"

And they said, "He is well, and here is Rachel his daughter coming with the sheep."

27:41 Ge 37:4
27:43 Ge 11:31
27:44 Ge 31:38
27:46 Ge 24:3
28:1 Ge 24:3
28:2 Ge 25:20
28:3 Ge 35:11
28:4 Ge 12:7
28:8 Ge 24:3
28:9 Ge 36:3
....
28:12 Jn 1:51
28:13 Ge 13:15
28:14 Ge 12:3
28:15 Ge 26:24
28:16 Ex 3:5
28:18 Ge 35:14
28:19 Ge 48:3
28:20 Ge 31:13
28:21 Dt 26:17
28:22 Ge 14:20
29:1 Jdg 6:3
29:4 Ge 28:10

7 He said, “Since it is yet midday, it is not the time that the livestock should be gathered together. Water the sheep, and go and feed them.”

8 They said, “We cannot until all the flocks are gathered together and the stone is rolled from the well’s opening. Then we may water the sheep.”

9 While he was still speaking with them, Rachel came with her father’s sheep, for she kept them. 10 When Jacob saw Rachel the daughter of Laban his mother’s brother and the sheep of Laban his mother’s brother, Jacob went near and rolled the stone from the well’s opening and watered the flock of Laban his mother’s brother. 11 Jacob kissed Rachel and wept aloud. 12 Jacob told Rachel that he was her father’s relative and that he was Rebekah’s son. Then she ran and told her father.

13 When Laban heard the news of Jacob his sister’s son, he ran to meet him and embraced him and kissed him and brought him to his house. Then Jacob told Laban all these things. 14 Laban said to him, “Surely you are my bone and my flesh.”

And he stayed with him for a month. 15 Laban said to Jacob, “Since you are my relative, should you therefore serve me for nothing? Tell me, what shall your wages be?”

Jacob Marries Leah and Rachel

16 Now Laban had two daughters. The name of the older was Leah, and the name of the younger was Rachel. 17 Leah’s eyes were tender, but Rachel was beautiful in form and appearance. 18 Jacob loved Rachel, so he said, “I will serve you seven years for Rachel your younger daughter.”

19 Laban said, “It is better that I give her to you than that I should give her to another man. Stay with me.” 20 So Jacob served seven years for Rachel, and they seemed to him but a few days because of the love he had for her.

21 Then Jacob said to Laban, “Give me my wife, for my days are fulfilled, so that I may have relations with her.”

22 Laban gathered together all the men of the place and prepared a feast. 23 But in the evening he took Leah his daughter and brought her to Jacob, and Jacob had relations with her. 24 Laban gave Zilpah his maid to his daughter Leah for a maidservant.

25 In the morning Jacob discovered it was Leah, and he said to Laban, “What is this you have done to me? Did I not serve you for Rachel? Why then have you tricked me?”

26 Then Laban said, “It is not the custom in our country to marry off the younger before the firstborn. 27 Fulfill the period of seven days for this one, and we will give you the other also in return for serving me another seven years.”

28 Jacob did so and completed her week. Then Laban gave him Rachel his daughter as his wife also. 29 Laban gave Bilhah his maidservant to Rachel his daughter to be her maid. 30 So Jacob also had relations with Rachel, and he loved Rachel more than Leah and served Laban another seven years.

Jacob’s Children

31 When the LORD saw that Leah was unloved, He opened her womb, but Rachel was barren. 32 Leah conceived and gave birth to a son, and she called his name Reuben, for she said, “Surely the LORD has looked upon my affliction. Now therefore my husband will love me.”

33 She conceived again and gave birth to a son and said, “Because the LORD has heard that I was unloved, He has therefore given me this son also.” Then she called his name Simeon.

34 She conceived again and gave birth to a son and said, “Now this time my husband will be joined to me, because I have borne him three sons.” Therefore his name was called Levi.

35 She conceived again and gave birth to a son, and she said, “Now I will praise the LORD!” Therefore she called his name Judah. Then she stopped giving birth.

30 When Rachel saw that she could not give Jacob children, she became jealous of her sister. She said to Jacob, “Give me children, or I will die.”

2 Jacob became angry with Rachel and said, “Am I in the place of God, who has withheld from you the fruit of the womb?”

3 Then she said, “Here is my maid Bilhah. Have relations with her so that she may bear *a child* on my knees,[1] so that I may also have children through her.”

4 So she gave him Bilhah her maidservant as a wife, and Jacob had relations with her. 5 Bilhah conceived and gave Jacob a son. 6 Rachel said, “God has vindicated me, and He has also heard my voice and has given me a son.” Therefore she called his name Dan.

7 Bilhah, Rachel’s maid, conceived again and gave Jacob a second son. 8 Then Rachel said, “With great wrestling have I wrestled with my sister, and I have prevailed.” So she called his name Naphtali.

9 When Leah saw that she had stopped having children, she took Zilpah her maid and gave her to Jacob as a wife. 10 Zilpah, Leah’s maid, gave Jacob a son. 11 Then Leah said, “How fortunate!” So she called his name Gad.

29:10 Ex 2:17
29:11 Ge 33:4
29:12 Ge 24:28
29:13 Ge 24:29
29:14 Ge 2:23
29:17 Ge 12:11
29:18 Hos 12:12
29:20 Hos 12:12
29:21 Jdg 15:1
29:24 Ge 30:9–12

....

29:27 Jdg 14:12
29:30 Ge 31:41
29:31 Dt 21:15
29:32 Ex 4:31
29:33 Ge 34:25
29:34 Ge 49:5–7
29:35 Mt 1:2
30:1 Ge 29:31
30:2 Ge 16:2
30:3 Ge 50:23
30:6 Ps 35:24
30:9 Ge 30:4
30:11 Ge 49:19

[1] 3 Meaning “on my behalf.”

12 Zilpah, Leah's maid, gave Jacob a second
son. 13 Then Leah said, "Happy am I, for wom-
en will call me happy." So she called his name
Asher.
14 At the time of the wheat harvest, Reuben
went and found mandrakes in the field and
brought them to his mother Leah. Then Rachel
said to Leah, "Please give me some of your
son's mandrakes."
15 Leah said to her, "Is it a small matter that
you have taken my husband? Would you take
away my son's mandrakes also?"
So Rachel said, "All right, he may lie with you
tonight in exchange for your son's mandrakes."
16 When Jacob came out of the field in the
evening, Leah went out to meet him and said,
"You must sleep with me, because I have paid
for you with my son's mandrakes." And he
slept with her that night.
17 God listened to Leah, and she conceived
and gave Jacob a fifth son. 18 Leah said, "God
has given me my reward because I have given
my maid to my husband." So she called his
name Issachar.
19 Leah conceived again and gave Jacob a
sixth son. 20 Leah said, "God has given me a
good gift. Now my husband will dwell with
me, because I have given him six sons." So
she called his name Zebulun.
21 Afterwards she gave birth to a daughter
and called her name Dinah.
22 Then God remembered Rachel, and God
listened to her and opened her womb. 23 She
conceived and gave birth to a son and said,
"God has taken away my reproach." 24 And she
called his name Joseph, saying, "The LORD will
add to me another son."

Jacob's Agreement With Laban

25 When Rachel had given birth to Joseph,
Jacob said to Laban, "Send me away, so that I
may go to my own place, to my country. 26 Give
me my wives and my children, for whom I
have served you, and let me go. For you know
the service that I have given you."
27 Laban said to him, "If I have found favor
in your eyes, please stay. For I have learned
by divination that the LORD has blessed me on
account of you." 28 He said, "Name me your
wages, and I will give it."
29 Jacob said to him, "You know how I have
served you, and how your livestock have fared
with me. 30 For you had little before I came, and
it is now increased to a multitude. The LORD has
blessed you since I came, and now when may
I also provide for my own house?"
31 Laban said, "What may I give you?"
And Jacob said, "You may not give me any-
thing, but if you will do this *one* thing for me,
I will continue to feed and keep your flock.
32 I will pass through all your flock today, re-
moving from it all the speckled and spotted
sheep, and every brown sheep from among the
lambs, and the spotted and speckled among
the goats. These shall be my wages. 33 So my
integrity will answer for me in time to come.
When you come to examine my wages, every
one that is not speckled and spotted among
the goats, and brown among the sheep that
are with me will be considered stolen."
34 Laban said, "Agreed. Let it be according to
your word." 35 He removed that day the male
goats that were striped and spotted and all the
female goats that were speckled and spotted,
every one that had some white in it, and all the
brown ones among the sheep, and gave them
into the care of his sons. 36 He put three days'
journey between himself and Jacob, and Jacob
fed the rest of Laban's flocks.
37 Then Jacob took rods of fresh-cut poplar,
almond, and plane trees, and peeled white
streaks in them, exposing the white which was
in the rods. 38 He set the rods which he had
peeled before the flocks in the troughs, that
is, the watering places, where the flocks came
to drink, so that they would mate when they
came to drink. 39 The flocks mated before the
rods and gave birth to *young* that were striped,
speckled, and spotted. 40 Jacob separated the
lambs and made the flocks face toward the
striped and all the brown in the flock of Laban.
He put his own flocks by themselves and did
not put them with Laban's sheep. 41 Whenever
the stronger sheep mated, Jacob laid the rods
before the eyes of the sheep in the troughs, so
that they might mate among the rods. 42 But
when the livestock were feeble, he did not put
them in. So the weaker were Laban's and the
stronger Jacob's. 43 The man became exceed-
ingly prosperous and had many sheep and fe-
male servants and male servants and camels
and donkeys.

Jacob Flees From Laban

31 Now *Jacob* heard the words of Laban's
sons, saying, "Jacob has taken away
all that was our father's, and he has gotten all
his wealth from what was our father's." 2 Jacob
saw the look of Laban and saw he was not
congenial toward him as before.
3 Then the LORD said to Jacob, "Return to the
land of your fathers, to your family, and I will
be with you."
4 So Jacob sent and called Rachel and Leah
to the field where his flock was, 5 and said
to them, "I see your father's demeanor, that
it is not congenial toward me as before; but
the God of my father has been with me. 6 You

30:13 Lk 1:48
30:14 SS 7:13
30:15 Nu 16:13
30:20 Mt 4:13
30:22 Ge 29:31
30:23 Isa 4:1
30:25 Ge 24:54
30:26 Ge 29:30
30:27 Ge 26:24
30:28 Ge 29:15
30:29 Ge 31:6
30:30 1Ti 5:8
....
30:32 Ge 31:8
30:43 Ge 24:35
31:1 Ecc 4:4
31:2 Ge 4:5
31:3 Ge 28:15
31:5 Ge 31:2–3
31:6 Ge 30:29

know that with all my strength I have served
your father. 7 Your father has deceived me and
changed my wages ten times, but God did not
allow him to hurt me. 8 If he said, 'The speckled
will be your wages,' then all the flock produced
speckled. If he said, 'The striped will be your
pay,' then all the flock produced striped. 9 In
this way God has taken away your father's
flock and given them to me.

10 "When the livestock conceived, I lifted up
my eyes and saw in a dream that the male
goats mating with the flock were striped,
speckled, and spotted. 11 The angel of God
spoke to me in a dream, saying, 'Jacob.' And I
said, 'Here I am.' 12 He said, 'Now lift up your
eyes and see all the male goats which mate
with the flock are striped, speckled, and spot-
ted, for I have seen all that Laban has done
to you. 13 I am the God of Bethel, where you
anointed the pillar, where you vowed a vow to
Me. Now arise, and get out of this land, and
return to the land of your family.' "

14 Rachel and Leah answered him, "Is there
any portion or inheritance left for us in our
father's house? 15 Are we not seen by him as
foreigners? For he has sold us and has com-
pletely spent our money also. 16 For all the rich-
es which God has taken from our father are
ours and our children's. Now then, whatever
God has said to you, do it."

17 Then Jacob rose up and set his sons and
his wives on camels. 18 Then he carried away
all his livestock and all his goods which he had
obtained, his acquired livestock which he had
gotten in Paddan Aram, in order to go to Isaac
his father in the land of Canaan.

19 When Laban went to shear his sheep, Ra-
chel stole the household idols that were her
father's. 20 Jacob also deceived Laban the Syr-
ian by not telling him that he was fleeing. 21 So
Jacob fled with all that he had, and he rose up
and passed over the river and headed toward
the mountains of Gilead.

Laban Pursues Jacob

22 Laban was told on the third day that Jacob
had fled. 23 He took his kinsmen with him and
pursued him for seven days until he caught up
with him in the mountains of Gilead. 24 But God
came to Laban the Syrian in a dream by night
and said to him, "Take care that you speak to
Jacob neither good nor bad."

25 Then Laban overtook Jacob. Now Jacob
had pitched his tent on the mountain, and La-
ban with his kinsmen pitched in the mountains
of Gilead. 26 Laban said to Jacob, "What have
you done that you have stolen away without
my knowing and carried away my daughters
like captives taken with the sword? 27 Why
did you flee away secretly and sneak away
from me and not tell me? I would have sent
you away with joy and with songs, with the
tambourine and harp. 28 And why did you not
permit me to kiss my sons and my daughters
farewell? You have acted foolishly in so do-
ing. 29 It is in my power to do you harm, but
the God of your father spoke to me last night,
saying, 'Take care that you not speak to Jacob
either good or bad.' 30 Now you surely have
gone away because you longed desperately
after your father's house, yet why have you
stolen my gods?"

31 Then Jacob answered and said to Laban,
"Because I was afraid, for I thought that you
would take your daughters from me by force.
32 But anyone with whom you find your gods,
let him not live. In the presence of our kins-
men, point out what I have that is yours and
take it." For Jacob did not know that Rachel
had stolen them.

33 So Laban went into Jacob's tent and into
Leah's tent and into the two female servants'
tents, but he did not find them. Then he went
out of Leah's tent and entered into Rachel's
tent. 34 Now Rachel had taken the household
idols and put them in the camel's saddle and
sat on them. Laban searched the entire tent,
but could not find them.

35 She said to her father, "Let not my lord be
displeased that I cannot rise before you, for the
manner of women is on me." So he searched,
but he did not find the household idols.

36 Then Jacob became angry and berated
Laban. And Jacob asked Laban, "What is my
offense? What is my sin that you have so hot-
ly pursued after me? 37 You have searched all
my things, and yet what have you found of all
your household things? Set it here before my
kinsmen and your kinsmen, so that they may
judge between us both.

38 "This twenty years I have been with you.
Your ewes and your female goats have not
miscarried their young, and the male goats of
your flock I have not eaten. 39 That which was
torn by beasts I did not bring to you. I bore
the loss of it. You required it from my hand
whether it was stolen by day or stolen by night.
40 It was like this with me: In the day the heat
consumed me and the frost by night, and my
sleep fled from my eyes. 41 I have been twen-
ty years in your house. I served you fourteen
years for your two daughters and six years for
your flock, and you have changed my wages
ten times. 42 If the God of my father, the God of
Abraham and the Fear of Isaac, had not been
with me, surely you would have sent me away
empty now. God has seen my affliction and the
labor of my hands and rebuked you last night."

31:8 Ge 30:32
31:9 Ge 31:1
31:11 Ge 31:13
31:12 Ex 3:7
31:13 Ge 32:9
31:19 Ge 31:30
31:21 2Ki 12:17
31:24 Ge 20:3
31:26 1Sa 30:2
31:27 Ex 15:20
31:28 Ge 31:55
31:29 Ge 31:53
31:30 Ge 31:19
31:35 Lev 19:32
31:41 Ge 31:7
31:42 Ge 29:32

Laban's Covenant With Jacob

43 Laban answered and said to Jacob, "These
daughters are my daughters, and these chil-
dren are my children, and the flocks are my
flocks, and all that you see is mine. But what
can I do this day to my daughters or to their
children whom they have borne? 44 Now there-
fore come, let us make a covenant, you and I,
and let it be as a witness between you and me."
45 So Jacob took a stone and set it up for a
pillar. 46 Jacob said to his kinsmen, "Gather
stones." So they took stones and made a pile,
and they ate there on the pile. 47 And Laban
called it Jegar Sahadutha, but Jacob called it
Galeed.
48 Laban said, "This pile is a witness between
me and you this day." Therefore its name was
called Galeed, 49 and Mizpah, for he said, "May
the LORD watch between you and me, when we
are apart from one another. 50 If you mistreat
my daughters, or if you take other wives beside
my daughters, although no one else is with us,
remember that God is witness between you
and me."
51 Then Laban said to Jacob, "See this pile
and see this pillar which I have thrown be-
tween you and me. 52 This heap is a witness,
and this pillar is a witness, so that I will not
cross over this pile to you and so that you will
not pass over this pile and this pillar to me
for harm. 53 The God of Abraham, the God of
Nahor, and the God of their father, judge be-
tween us."
Then Jacob vowed by the Fear of his father
Isaac. 54 Then Jacob offered a sacrifice on the
mountain and called his kinsmen to eat bread.
And they ate bread and stayed all night on the
mountain.
55 Early in the morning Laban rose up, kissed
his grandchildren and his daughters, and
blessed them. Then Laban departed and re-
turned to his place.

Jacob Prepares to Meet Esau

32 Jacob went on his way, and the an-
gels of God met him. 2 When Jacob
saw them, he said, "This is God's camp." So
he called the name of that place Mahanaim.
3 Jacob sent messengers before him to his
brother Esau in the land of Seir, the country
of Edom. 4 He commanded them, saying,
"This is what you must say to my lord Esau:
This is what your servant Jacob says, 'I have
sojourned with Laban and stayed there until
now. 5 I have oxen and donkeys, flocks, and
male servants and female servants, and I am
sending *this message* to tell my lord, so that I
may find favor in your sight.' "

6 The messengers returned to Jacob, saying,
"We went to your brother Esau. He is coming
to meet you, and what is more, four hundred
men are with him."
7 Then Jacob was very afraid and distressed,
and he divided the people that were with him,
along with the flocks and herds and the cam-
els, into two groups. 8 He said, "If Esau comes
to the one camp and attacks it, then the other
camp which is left may escape."
9 And Jacob said, "O God of my father Abra-
ham and God of my father Isaac, the LORD
who said to me, 'Return to your country and
to your relatives, and I will prosper you,' 10 I
am not worthy of all the lovingkindness and
of all the faithfulness which You have shown
to Your servant. For with my staff I crossed
over this Jordan, and now I have become two
encampments. 11 Deliver me, I pray, from the
hand of my brother, from the hand of Esau.
For I fear him, that he will come and attack
me and the mothers with the children. 12 You
said, 'I will surely prosper you and make your
descendants as the sand of the sea, which is
too many to be counted.' "
13 So he spent the night there. Then he se-
lected from what he had with him a gift for
his brother Esau: 14 two hundred female goats
and twenty male goats, two hundred ewes and
twenty rams, 15 thirty female camels with their
colts, forty cows and ten bulls, twenty female
donkeys and ten male donkeys. 16 He gave
them to his servants, every drove by itself, and
said to his servants, "Pass over before me, and
keep a distance between each drove."
17 He commanded the one leading, saying,
"When my brother Esau meets you and asks
you, saying, 'To whom do you belong, and
where are you going, and to whom do these
animals belong?' 18 then you are to say, 'They
belong to your servant Jacob. They are a gift
sent to my lord Esau, and he is also behind
us.' "
19 Likewise he commanded the second and
the third and all that followed the droves, say-
ing, "This is what you are to say to Esau when
you find him. 20 Moreover, say, 'Your servant Ja-
cob is behind us.' " For he said, "I will appease
him with the gift that goes before me, and then
I will see his face. Perhaps he will accept me."
21 So the gift went before him, but he lodged
that night in the encampment.

Jacob Wrestles With God

22 The same night he arose and took his
two wives, his two female servants, and his
eleven sons, and crossed over the ford of the
Jabbok. 23 He took them and sent them across
the stream along with all that he had. 24 Jacob

31:48 Jos 24:27
31:49 Jdg 11:29
31:50 Jer 42:5
31:53 Ge 31:42
31:54 Ex 18:12
31:55 Ge 31:28
32:1 Ps 91:11
32:2 2Sa 2:8
32:3 Ge 25:30
32:5 Ge 33:8

......

32:6 Ge 33:1
32:7 Ge 35:3
32:9 Ge 28:13
32:10 Ge 24:27
32:12 Ge 28:13–15
32:13 Ge 43:11
32:20 Job 42:8–9
32:22 Dt 3:16

was left alone, and a man wrestled with him
there until daybreak. 25 When the man saw that
He did not prevail against Jacob, He touched
the socket of his thigh, so the socket of Ja-
cob's thigh was dislocated, as he wrestled with
Him. 26 Then He said, "Let Me go, for the day
breaks."

But Jacob said, "I will not let You go, unless
You bless me."

27 So He said to him, "What is your name?"

And he said, "Jacob."

28 Then the man said, "Your name will no
more be called Jacob, but Israel. For you have
fought with God and with men, and have pre-
vailed."

29 Then Jacob asked Him, "Tell me, I pray
You, Your name."

But He said, "Why do you ask Me My name?"
Then He blessed him there.

30 Jacob called the name of the place Peniel,
saying, "I have seen God face to face, and my
life has been preserved."

31 As he crossed over Peniel, the sun rose
over him, and he was limping on his thigh.
32 Therefore to this day the children of Israel
do not eat the sinew which is attached to the
socket of the thigh, because He touched the
socket of Jacob's thigh in the sinew of the hip.

Jacob Meets Esau

33 Then Jacob looked up and saw Esau
coming and four hundred men with
him. So he divided the children among Leah,
Rachel, and the two female servants. 2 He put
the female servants and their children in front,
then Leah and her children next, and then Ra-
chel and Joseph last. 3 He went on before them,
bowing himself to the ground seven times, un-
til he came near to his brother.

4 But Esau ran to meet him and embraced
him and fell on his neck and kissed him, and
they wept. 5 When Esau looked up and saw
the women and the children, he said, "Who
are those with you?"

Jacob said, "The children whom God has
graciously given your servant."

6 Then the female servants came near, they
and their children, and they bowed down.
7 Leah also with her children came near and
bowed themselves. Afterward Joseph and Ra-
chel came near, and they bowed themselves.

8 Esau said, "What do you mean by all this
company that I met?"

Jacob answered, "These are to find favor in
the sight of my lord."

9 Esau said, "I have enough, my brother. Keep
what you have for yourself."

10 Jacob said, "No, I pray you, if I have now
found favor in your sight, then receive my gift

32:25 Ge 32:32
32:26 Hos 12:4
32:28 Ge 35:10
32:30 Ge 16:13
33:3 Ge 42:6
33:4 Ge 45:14–15
33:5 Ge 48:9
33:8 Ge 32:5
33:9 Ge 27:39

....

33:11 1Sa 25:27
33:14 Ge 32:3
33:15 Ru 2:13
33:17 Jos 13:27
33:18 Jos 24:1
33:19 Jos 24:32
34:1 Ge 30:21
34:4 Jdg 14:2
34:7 Jdg 20:6

from my hand. For I have seen your face, and
it is as though I have seen the face of God, with
you having received me favorably. 11 Please
take my blessing that has been brought to
you, because God has dealt graciously with
me and because I have plenty." So he urged
him, and he took it.

12 Then Esau said, "Let us journey on our
way, and I will go ahead of you."

13 But Jacob said to him, "My lord knows that
the children are weak, and the flocks and herds
with young are with me. If they are driven too
hard one day, all the flock will die. 14 Please
let my lord pass over before his servant, and
I will lead on slowly, according to the pace of
the livestock that goes before me and the pace
the children will be able to endure, until I come
to my lord at Seir."

15 So Esau said, "Let me leave some of the
people that are with me with you."

But Jacob said, "What need is there? Let me
find favor in the sight of my lord."

16 So Esau returned that day making his way
back to Seir. 17 But Jacob journeyed to Sukkoth
and built himself a house and made booths for
his livestock. Therefore the name of the place
is called Sukkoth.

18 Jacob came peacefully to the city of
Shechem, which is in the land of Canaan, on
his way from Paddan Aram, and camped be-
fore the city. 19 He bought a parcel of a field,
where he had pitched his tent, from the chil-
dren of Hamor, Shechem's father, for a hun-
dred pieces[1] of silver. 20 He erected an altar
there and called it El Elohe Israel.

Dinah Is Defiled

34 Now Dinah, the daughter of Leah,
whom she bore to Jacob, went out
to see the daughters of the land. 2 When
Shechem, the son of Hamor the Hivite, prince
of the land, saw her, he took her and lay with
her and defiled her. 3 He was very smitten by
Dinah the daughter of Jacob, and he loved the
girl and spoke kindly to her. 4 Shechem spoke
to his father Hamor, saying, "Get me this girl
for *my* wife."

5 Now Jacob heard that Shechem had vio-
lated his daughter Dinah, but his sons were
with his livestock in the field, so Jacob held
his peace until they came.

6 Hamor the father of Shechem went out to
Jacob to commune with him. 7 The sons of
Jacob came out of the field when they heard
it, and the men were grieved and were very
disturbed, because Shechem had disgraced
Israel by lying with Jacob's daughter, a thing
that should not be done.

8 Hamor spoke with them, saying, "The soul
of my son Shechem longs for your daughter.
I pray that you will give her to him to mar-
ry. 9 Make marriages with us, and give your
daughters to us, and take our daughters for
yourselves. 10 You may dwell with us, and the
land will be before you. Dwell and trade in it
and get possessions in it."
11 Shechem said to her father and to her
brothers, "Let me find favor in your eyes, and
whatever you say to me I will give. 12 You can
make the dowry and gift I must bring high,
and I will give according to what you say to
me. Just give me the girl to marry."
13 The sons of Jacob answered Shechem and
Hamor his father deceitfully, because he had
defiled Dinah their sister. 14 They said to them,
"We cannot do this. To give our sister to one
who is uncircumcised would be a disgrace to
us. 15 But we will consent to you in this: If you
will become as we are, that is, every one of
your males be circumcised, 16 then we will give
our daughters to you, and we will take your
daughters to us, and we will dwell with you,
and we will become one people. 17 But if you
will not listen to us and be circumcised, then
we will take our daughter, and we will leave."
18 Their words pleased Hamor and Shechem,
Hamor's son. 19 The young man did not delay
to do the thing, because he wanted Jacob's
daughter. Now he was more respected than
all the household of his father. 20 So Hamor
and Shechem his son came to the gate of their
city, and they spoke with the men of their city,
saying, 21 "These men are at peace with us.
Therefore let them dwell in the land and trade
in it. For the land is large enough for them.
Let us take their daughters as our wives, and
let us give them our daughters. 22 Only on this
condition will the men consent to dwell with
us and be one people: if every male among us
will be circumcised as they are circumcised.
23 Will not their livestock and their possessions
and every animal of theirs be ours? Only, let us
agree with them, and they will dwell with us."
24 All who went out of the gate of his city
listened to Hamor and Shechem his son, and
every male was circumcised, all who went out
of the gate of his city.
25 On the third day, when they were in pain,
two of Jacob's sons, Simeon and Levi, Dinah's
brothers, took their swords and went to the un-
suspecting city and killed all the males. 26 They
killed Hamor and Shechem his son with the
edge of the sword and took Dinah out of the
house of Shechem and departed. 27 The sons of
Jacob came upon the slain and looted the city,
because they had defiled their sister. 28 They
took their flocks and their herds, their donkeys
and whatever was in the city and in the fields.
29 They took captive and looted all their wealth,
all their little ones, and their wives, even all
that was in each house.
30 Then Jacob said to Simeon and Levi, "You
have brought trouble on me by making me
revolting among the inhabitants of the land,
among the Canaanites and the Perizzites. Our
being few in number, they will gather them-
selves together against me and slay me, and I
will be destroyed, both I and my household."
31 But they said, "Should he treat our sister
like a prostitute?"

Jacob Returns to Bethel

35 Then God said to Jacob, "Arise, go up
to Bethel, dwell there, and there make
an altar to God, who appeared to you when
you fled from the face of Esau your brother."
2 So Jacob said to his household and to all
who were with him, "Put away the foreign
gods that are among you. Purify yourselves
and change your clothes. 3 Let us arise and
go up to Bethel, and there I will make an al-
tar to God, who answered me in the day of
my distress and has been with me wherever I
have gone." 4 So they gave Jacob all the foreign
gods which were in their possession and all
their earrings which were in their ears, and
Jacob hid them under the oak which was near
Shechem. 5 As they traveled, the terror of God
was on the cities that were around them, and
they did not pursue the sons of Jacob.
6 So Jacob came to Luz (that is, Bethel), which
is in the land of Canaan, he and all the people
who were with him. 7 There he built an altar
and called the place El Bethel, because God
had appeared to him there when he fled from
his brother.
8 Now Deborah, Rebekah's nurse, died and
was buried beneath Bethel under the oak. So
it was called Allon Bakuth.
9 God appeared to Jacob again when he came
out of Paddan Aram and blessed him. 10 God
said to him, "Your name is Jacob. Your name
shall not be called Jacob any more, but Israel
shall be your name." So He called his name
Israel.
11 God said to him, "I am God Almighty. Be
fruitful and multiply. A nation and a compa-
ny of nations will come from you, and kings
shall come forth from you. 12 The land that I
gave Abraham and Isaac, I will give to you,
and to your descendants after you I will give
the land." 13 Then God went up from him in the
place where He had spoken with him.

34:10 Ge 13:9
34:11 Ge 33:15
34:12 Ex 22:16–17
34:20 Ru 4:1
34:24 Ge 23:10
34:25 Ge 49:5–7
34:30 Ex 5:21
35:2 Ge 18:19
35:3 Ge 31:3
35:5 Ex 23:27
35:6 Ge 28:19
35:8 Ge 24:59
35:10 Ge 17:5
35:11 Ge 17:1
35:12 Ge 12:7
35:13 Ge 17:22

[1] 19 Heb. *a hundred qesitahs*; a *qesitah* was a coin of unknown weight and value.

14 Jacob set up a pillar in the place where He had spoken with him, a pillar of stone, and he poured out a drink offering on it, and he poured oil on it *too*. 15 So Jacob called the name of the place where God had spoken with him Bethel.

The Deaths of Rachel and Isaac
1Ch 2:1–2

16 They journeyed from Bethel, and when they were still some distance from Ephrath, Rachel went into labor, and she had a difficult labor. 17 When she was in hard labor, the midwife said to her, "Do not fear. You will have this son also." 18 As her soul was departing (for she died), she called his name Ben-Oni, but his father called him Benjamin.

19 Rachel died and was buried on the way to Ephrath, which is Bethlehem. 20 Jacob set a pillar on her grave. It is the pillar of Rachel's grave to this day.

21 Israel journeyed and pitched his tent beyond the tower of Eder. 22 When Israel lived in that land, Reuben went and lay with Bilhah, his father's concubine, and Israel heard about it.

Now the sons of Jacob were twelve:
23 The sons of Leah were
Reuben, Jacob's firstborn,
and Simeon and Levi and Judah and
Issachar and Zebulun.
24 The sons of Rachel were
Joseph and Benjamin.
25 And the sons of Bilhah, Rachel's maidservant, were
Dan and Naphtali.
26 And the sons of Zilpah, Leah's maidservant, were
Gad and Asher.
These are the sons of Jacob, which were born to him in Paddan Aram.

27 Jacob came back to Isaac his father in Mamre of Kiriath Arba (which is Hebron), where Abraham and Isaac had sojourned. 28 Now the days of Isaac were one hundred and eighty years. 29 And Isaac breathed his last and died and was gathered to his people, being old and full of days, and his sons Esau and Jacob buried him.

Esau's Descendants
1Ch 1:35–42

36 Now these are the generations of Esau, who is Edom.

2 Esau took his wives from the daughters of Canaan: Adah the daughter of Elon the Hittite, and Oholibamah the daughter of Anah the daughter of Zibeon the Hivite, 3 and Basemath, Ishmael's daughter, sister of Nebaioth.

35:15 Ge 28:19
35:16 Mic 5:2
35:17 Ge 30:24
35:19 Mic 5:2
35:20 1Sa 10:2
35:22 1Ch 5:1
35:27 Ge 13:18
35:29 Ge 15:15
. . . .
36:4 1Ch 1:35
36:7 Ge 13:6
36:8 Ge 32:3

4 Adah bore to Esau Eliphaz, and Basemath bore Reuel, 5 and Oholibamah bore Jeush, Jalam, and Korah. These are the sons of Esau, who were born to him in the land of Canaan.

6 Then Esau took his wives, his sons, his daughters, and all the people of his house, his livestock, all his animals, and all his property that he had acquired in the land of Canaan, and he moved to a land some distance from his brother Jacob. 7 For their possessions were too great for them to dwell together, and the land where they were foreigners could not sustain them because of their livestock. 8 So Esau settled in the hill country of Seir. Esau is Edom.

9 These are the generations of Esau the father of the Edomites in the hill country of Seir.

10 These are the names of Esau's sons:
Eliphaz the son of Adah the wife of Esau, and Reuel the son of Basemath the wife of Esau.
11 The sons of Eliphaz were
Teman, Omar, Zepho, Gatam, and Kenaz.
12 Timna was a concubine to Eliphaz, Esau's son, and she bore to Eliphaz Amalek. These were the sons of Adah, Esau's wife.
13 These are the sons of Reuel:
Nahath, Zerah, Shammah, and Mizzah. These were the sons of Basemath, Esau's wife.
14 These were the sons of Oholibamah, the daughter of Anah the daughter of Zibeon, Esau's wife: she bore to Esau Jeush, Jalam, and Korah.

The Chiefs of Edom

15 These were chiefs of the sons of Esau.
The sons of Eliphaz the firstborn son of Esau were
Chief Teman, Chief Omar, Chief Zepho, Chief Kenaz, 16 Chief Korah, Chief Gatam, and Chief Amalek. These are the chiefs who came from Eliphaz in the land of Edom. These were the sons of Adah.
17 These were the sons of Reuel Esau's son:
Chief Nahath, Chief Zerah, Chief Shammah, and Chief Mizzah. These are the chiefs who came from Reuel in the land of Edom. These were the sons of Basemath, Esau's wife.
18 These were the sons of Oholibamah, Esau's wife:
Chief Jeush, Chief Jalam, and Chief Korah. These were the chiefs who came from Oholibamah, the daughter of Anah, Esau's wife.
19 These were the sons of Esau, who is Edom, and these were their chiefs.

The Sons of Seir

20 These were the sons of Seir the Horite, who inhabited the land:

Lotan, Shobal, Zibeon, Anah, 21 Dishon,
Ezer, and Dishan. These were the chiefs
of the Horites, the children of Seir in the
land of Edom.

22 The children of Lotan were
Hori and Homam, and Lotan's sister was
Timna.

23 The children of Shobal were these:
Alvan, Manahath, Ebal, Shepho, and
Onam.

24 These were the children of Zibeon:
Aiah and Anah. This was the Anah who
found the water in the wilderness as he
fed the donkeys of Zibeon, his father.

25 The children of Anah were these:
Dishon and Oholibamah, the daughter
of Anah.

26 These are the children of Dishon:
Hemdan, Eshban, Ithran, and Keran.

27 The children of Ezer were these:
Bilhan, Zaavan, and Akan.

28 The children of Dishan were these:
Uz and Aran.

29 These were the chiefs that came from the
Horites:
Chief Lotan, Chief Shobal, Chief Zibeon,
Chief Anah, 30 Chief Dishon, Chief Ezer,
and Chief Dishan. These are the chiefs
who came from Hori, among their chiefs
in the land of Seir.

The Kings of Edom

1Ch 1:43–54

31 These were the kings who reigned in the
land of Edom before there reigned any king
over the children of Israel.

32 Bela the son of Beor reigned in Edom,
and the name of his city was Dinhabah.

33 Bela died, and Jobab the son of Zerah of
Bozrah reigned in his stead.

34 Jobab died, and Husham of the land of
Temani reigned in his stead.

35 Husham died, and Hadad the son of Be-
dad, who defeated Midian in the field of
Moab, reigned in his stead, and the name
of his city was Avith.

36 Hadad died, and Samlah of Masrekah
reigned in his stead.

37 Samlah died, and Shaul of Rehoboth by
the river reigned in his stead.

38 Shaul died, and Baal-Hanan the son of
Akbor reigned in his stead.

39 Baal-Hanan the son of Akbor died, and
Hadad reigned in his stead, and the
name of his city was Pau. His wife's
name was Mehetabel, the daughter of
Matred, the daughter of Me-Zahab.

36:20 Ge 14:6
36:23 1Ch 1:40
36:29 Ge 36:20
36:31 Ge 17:6
. . . .
36:40 1Ch 1:51–54
37:1 Ge 17:8
37:2 Ge 35:25–26
37:3 Ge 37:23
37:4 Ge 27:41
37:5 Ge 28:12
37:7 Ge 42:6
37:10 Ge 27:29
37:11 Lk 2:19

40 These are the names of the chiefs who
came from Esau, according to their families,
according to their places, by their names:
Chief Timnah, Chief Alvah, Chief Jetheth,
41 Chief Oholibamah, Chief Elah, Chief
Pinon, 42 Chief Kenaz, Chief Teman,
Chief Mibzar, 43 Chief Magdiel, and Chief
Iram. These were the chiefs of Edom,
according to their settlements in the land
of their possession.

Esau *was* the father of the Edomites.

Joseph's Dreams

37 Now Jacob lived in the land where his
father was a foreigner, in the land of
Canaan.

2 These are the generations of Jacob.

Joseph, being seventeen years old, was feed-
ing the flock with his brothers, and the boy
was with the sons of Bilhah and with the sons
of Zilpah, his father's wives. Joseph brought
back a bad report about them to their father.
3 Now Israel loved Joseph more than all his
sons, because he was the son of his old age,
and he made him a coat of many colors.[1] 4 But
when his brothers saw that their father loved
him more than all his brothers, they hated him
and could not speak peaceably to him.
5 Now Joseph dreamed a dream, and when
he told it to his brothers, they hated him even
more. 6 He said to them, "Please listen to this
dream which I have dreamed. 7 We were bind-
ing sheaves in the field. All of a sudden my
sheaf rose up and stood upright, and your
sheaves stood around it and bowed down to
my sheaf."
8 His brothers said to him, "Will you really
reign over us, or will you really have domin-
ion over us?" So they hated him even more
because of his dreams and his words.
9 Then he dreamed another dream and told
it to his brothers and said, "I have dreamed
another dream. The sun and the moon and
eleven stars were bowing to me."
10 But when he told it to his father and his
brothers, his father rebuked him and said
to him, "What is this dream that you have
dreamed? Will I and your mother and your
brothers really come to bow down ourselves
to you to the ground?" 11 So his brothers were
jealous of him, but his father kept the matter
in mind.

Joseph Sold Into Slavery

12 Now his brothers went to feed their father's
flock in Shechem. 13 Israel said to Joseph,

[1] *3* From the Septuagint, a cloak with long sleeves, a full-length cloak, or an embroidered cloak, showing favoritism.

"Are not your brothers feeding the flock in Shechem? Come, and I will send you to them."

He answered, "Here I am."

14 Israel said to him, "Please go and see if it is well with your brothers and well with the flocks, and bring back word to me." So he sent him out of the Valley of Hebron, and he came to Shechem.

15 A certain man found him wandering in the field. The man asked him, "What are you looking for?"

16 And he said, "I am looking for my brothers. Please tell me where they are feeding their flocks."

17 The man said, "They have departed from here. I heard them say, 'Let us go to Dothan.' "

So Joseph went after his brothers and found them in Dothan.

18 When they saw him some distance away, before he came near to them, they conspired against him to kill him.

19 They said one to another, "The master of dreams comes! 20 Come now, let us kill him and throw him into some pit, and we will say, 'Some evil beast has devoured him.' Then we will see what will become of his dreams."

21 But when Reuben heard it, he rescued him out of their hands, saying, "Let us not kill him." 22 Reuben said to them, "Shed no blood, but throw him into this pit here in the wilderness, but lay no hand on him," so that he might rescue him out of their hands and deliver him to his father again.

23 When Joseph came to his brothers, they stripped Joseph of his coat—his coat of many colors that he had on. 24 And they took him and threw him into a pit. The pit was empty, and there was no water in it.

25 Then they sat down to eat. And looking up, they saw a caravan of Ishmaelites coming from Gilead, with their camels bearing spices, balm, and myrrh, carrying it down to Egypt.

26 Then Judah said to his brothers, "What profit is it if we kill our brother and cover up his blood? 27 Come, let us sell him to the Ishmaelites, and let us not lay our hand on him, for he is our brother and our own flesh." So his brothers agreed.

28 Then when the Midianite merchants passed by, they drew Joseph up and lifted him out of the pit and sold Joseph to the Ishmaelites for twenty shekels of silver.[1] They took Joseph to Egypt.

29 When Reuben returned to the pit and saw that Joseph was not in the pit, he tore his clothes. 30 He returned to his brothers, and said, "The boy is not *there*, and I, where can I go?"

31 They took Joseph's coat and killed a young goat and dipped the coat in the blood. 32 Then they took the coat of many colors and brought it to their father and said, "This we have found. Do you know whether it is your son's robe or not?"

33 He knew it and said, "It is my son's coat. A wild beast has devoured him. Joseph has without a doubt been torn into pieces."

34 Jacob tore his clothes and put sackcloth on his waist and mourned for his son many days. 35 All his sons and all his daughters rose up to comfort him, but he refused to be comforted. And he said, "For I will go down into the grave mourning for my son." So his father wept for him.

36 Meanwhile the Midianites sold him in Egypt to Potiphar, an officer of Pharaoh and captain of the guard.

Judah and Tamar

38 At that time Judah left his brothers and visited a certain Adullamite, whose name was Hirah. 2 There Judah saw the daughter of a certain Canaanite, whose name was Shua, and he took her and had relations with her. 3 She conceived and bore a son, and he called his name Er. 4 She conceived again and bore a son, and she called his name Onan. 5 She again conceived and bore a son and called his name Shelah. He was at Kezib when she bore him.

6 Judah took a wife for Er his firstborn, whose name was Tamar. 7 But Er, Judah's firstborn, was wicked in the sight of the LORD, so the LORD killed him.

8 Then Judah said to Onan, "Go have relations with your brother's wife, and marry her, and raise up descendants for your brother." 9 But Onan knew that the descendant would not be his, so when he had relations with his brother's wife, he let his semen go on the ground, so that he would not give a descendant to his brother. 10 What he did displeased the LORD; therefore He killed him also.

11 Then Judah said to Tamar, his daughter-in-law, "Remain a widow at your father's house until Shelah my son grows up." For he thought, "He may die also, just as his brothers did." So Tamar went and lived in her father's house.

12 As time went on, the daughter of Shua, Judah's wife, died. After Judah was consoled, he went up to his sheepshearers in Timnah, he and his friend Hirah the Adullamite.

13 It was told to Tamar, "Your father-in-law is going up to Timnah to shear his sheep." 14 She took off her widow's clothing, covered herself with a veil, wrapped herself up, and sat in an open place, which is by the road to Timnah.

37:14 Ge 35:27
37:17 2Ki 6:13
37:18 Ps 37:12
37:21 Ge 42:22
37:25 Ge 37:28
37:26 Ge 37:20
37:27 Ge 42:21
37:28 Ps 105:17
37:29 Ge 37:34
37:30 Ge 42:13
....
37:31 Ge 37:23
37:33 Ge 37:20
37:34 Ge 37:29
37:36 Ge 37:28
38:1 1Sa 22:1
38:2 1Ch 2:3
38:3 Ge 46:12
38:7 1Ch 2:3
38:10 Ge 46:12
38:12 Jos 15:10
38:14 Ge 38:26

[1] *28* About 8 ounces, or 230 grams.

For she saw that Shelah was grown, and she
was not given to him as *his* wife.
15 When Judah saw her, he thought she was
a prostitute, because she had covered her face.
16 He turned to her by the road and said, "Come
now, let me have relations with you" (for he did
not know that she was his daughter-in-law).
And she said, "What will you give me, so that
you may have relations with me?"
17 And he said, "I will send you a young goat
from the flock."
And she said, "Will you give me a pledge,
until you send it?"
18 And he said, "What pledge should I give
you?"
And she said, "Your signet, your bracelets,
and your staff that is in your hand." So he gave
them to her and had relations with her, and
she conceived by him. 19 She arose and went
away, and taking off her veil, she put on her
widow's clothing.
20 Judah sent the young goat by his friend
the Adullamite to receive his pledge from
the woman's hand, but he could not find her.
21 Then he asked the men of the place, "Where
is the cult prostitute who was at Enaim by the
road?"
And they said, "There was no prostitute in
this place."
22 So he returned to Judah and said, "I cannot
find her. Also, the men of the place said there
was no cult prostitute in this place."
23 Judah replied, "Let her keep them for her-
self, or we shall be laughed at. I sent this young
goat, and you did not find her."
24 After about three months, it was told Ju-
dah, "Tamar your daughter-in-law has turned
to prostitution, and what is more, as a result
of prostitution she is pregnant."
Then Judah said, "Bring her forth, and let
her be burned!"
25 When she was brought forth, she sent *word*
to her father-in-law, saying, "By the man to
whom these belong am I with child." And she
said, "Please identify whose these are—the
signet and bracelet and staff."
26 Judah recognized them and said, "She has
been more righteous than I, because I did not
give her to Shelah my son." He did not have
relations with her again.
27 When it was time for her to give birth,
there were twins in her womb. 28 While she
was giving birth, one put out his hand, and
the midwife took and tied on his hand a scarlet
thread, saying, "This one came out first." 29 But
as he drew back his hand, his brother came
out. Then she said, "How have you made a
breach for yourself?" Therefore his name was
called Perez. 30 Afterward his brother came out,
the one that had the scarlet thread on his hand,
and his name was called Zerah.

38:18 Ge 38:25–26
38:19 Ge 38:14
38:24 Lev 21:9
38:25 Ge 38:18
38:26 1Sa 24:17
38:29 Ge 46:12

39:1 Ge 37:25
39:2 Ge 21:22
39:3 Ps 1:3
39:4 Ge 19:19
39:5 Ge 30:27
39:6 1Sa 16:12
39:7 2Sa 13:11
39:9 2Sa 12:13
39:12 Ecc 7:26
39:17 Ex 23:1

Joseph and Potiphar's Wife

39 Now Joseph was brought down to
Egypt, and Potiphar, an officer of
Pharaoh, captain of the guard, an Egyptian,
bought him from the Ishmaelites who had
brought him down there.
2 The LORD was with Joseph, so that he be-
came a prosperous man. He was in the house
of his master, the Egyptian. 3 His master saw
that the LORD was with him and that the LORD
made all that he did to prosper. 4 Joseph found
favor in his sight and served him. So he made
him overseer over his house, and all that he
had he put under his charge. 5 From the time
that he had made him overseer in his house
and over all that he had, the LORD blessed the
Egyptian's house on account of Joseph. So the
blessing of the LORD was on all that he had
in the house and in the field. 6 So he left all
that he had in Joseph's charge, and he had no
concerns regarding anything except the food
he ate.
Now Joseph was handsome and well-built.
7 After a time, his master's wife took notice of
Joseph and said, "Lie with me."
8 But he refused and said to his master's wife,
"My master does not concern himself with *any-
thing* concerning me in the house, and he has
committed all that he has to my charge. 9 There
is none greater in this house than I. He has
kept nothing back from me but you, because
you are his wife. How then can I do this great
wickedness and sin against God?" 10 She spoke
to Joseph every day, but he did not listen to her
about lying with her or being with her.
11 But it happened one day that Joseph went
into the house to do his work, and none of
the men of the house was there. 12 She caught
him by his clothing, saying, "Lie with me." But
he left his clothing in her hand and fled and
got outside.
13 When she saw that he had left his clothing
in her hand and had fled outside, 14 she called
to the men of her house and spoke to them,
saying, "See, he has brought in a Hebrew
among us to humiliate us. He came in to me
to lie with me, and I cried out with a loud voice.
15 When he heard that I lifted up my voice and
cried out, he left his clothing with me, fled,
and got outside."
16 She laid up his clothing next to her until
his master came home. 17 She spoke to him
using these words, saying, "The Hebrew ser-
vant, whom you have brought to us, came in
to me to mock me. 18 When I lifted up my voice

and cried out, he left his clothing with me and
fled outside."
19 When his master heard the words of his
wife, which she spoke to him, saying, "This
is what your servant did to me," he became
enraged. 20 Joseph's master took him and put
him into the prison, a place where the king's
prisoners were confined.

So he was there in the prison. 21 But the LORD
was with Joseph and showed him mercy and
gave him favor in the sight of the keeper of the
prison. 22 The keeper of the prison committed
all the prisoners that were in the prison to the
charge of Joseph. So whatever they did there,
he was the one responsible for it. 23 The keeper
of the prison did not concern himself with any-
thing that was under Joseph's charge because
the LORD was with him. And whatever he did,
the LORD made it to prosper.

Joseph Interprets Dreams

40 Sometime after this, the cupbearer of
the king of Egypt and his baker of-
fended their lord, the king of Egypt. 2 Pharaoh
was angry with his two officials, with the chief
of the cupbearers and with the chief of the
bakers. 3 So he put them in confinement in
the house of the captain of the guard, in the
prison, the place where Joseph was confined.
4 The captain of the guard charged Joseph with
them, and he attended to them.

They continued to be in confinement for
some time. 5 Then the cupbearer and the baker
for the king of Egypt, who were confined in the
prison, both had a dream the same night, each
man with his own dream and each dream with
its *own* interpretation.
6 Joseph came in to them in the morning and
looked at them and realized they were sad. 7 So
he asked Pharaoh's officials who were with
him in the care of his lord's house, saying,
"Why do you look so sad today?"
8 And they said to him, "We have dreamed a
dream, and there is no interpreter for it."

Then Joseph said to them, "Do not interpre-
tations belong to God? Please tell them to me."
9 The chief cupbearer told his dream to Jo-
seph and said to him, "In my dream, a vine
was in front of me. 10 And in the vine there
were three branches. As it budded, its blos-
soms shot forth and its clusters brought forth
ripe grapes. 11 Pharaoh's cup was in my hand,
and I took the grapes, and pressed them into
Pharaoh's cup, and I put the cup into Pharaoh's
hand."
12 Joseph said to him, "This is the interpreta-
tion of it. The three branches are three days.
13 Within three days Pharaoh will lift up your
head and restore you to your place, and you

39:20 Ge 40:15
39:21 Ex 3:21
39:22 Ge 39:4
39:23 Ge 39:2–3
40:2 Pr 16:14
40:3 Ge 39:20
40:7 Ne 2:2
40:8 Ge 41:15–16
40:12 Ge 41:12

. . . .

40:14 Jos 2:12
40:18 Ge 40:12
40:20 Ge 40:13
40:21 Ge 40:13
40:22 Ge 40:19
40:23 Job 19:14
41:8 Ex 7:11
41:10 Ge 39:20

will deliver Pharaoh's cup into his hand in the
same way you did before when you were his
cupbearer. 14 But remember me when it is well
with you, and show kindness, I pray you, to
me, and make mention of me to Pharaoh, and
get me out of this house. 15 For I was indeed
kidnapped out of the land of the Hebrews, and
I have done nothing that they should put me
in the dungeon."
16 When the chief baker saw that the interpre-
tation was good, he said to Joseph, "I also was
in my dream, and I had three white baskets
on my head. 17 In the uppermost basket there
was all manner of baked goods for Pharaoh,
and the birds ate them out of the basket on
my head."
18 Joseph answered and said, "This is the in-
terpretation: The three baskets are three days.
19 Within three days Pharaoh will lift your head
from off you and will hang you on a tree, and
the birds will eat your flesh from you."
20 It happened on the third day, which was
Pharaoh's birthday, that he made a feast for
all his servants. He lifted up the heads of the
chief cupbearer and the chief baker among his
servants. 21 He restored the chief cupbearer to
his position again, and he put the cup into Pha-
raoh's hand. 22 However, he hanged the chief
baker, just as Joseph had interpreted to them.
23 Yet, the chief cupbearer did not remember
Joseph, but forgot him.

Pharaoh's Dreams

41 After two whole years, Pharaoh had
a dream that he was standing by the
Nile. 2 Seven fine-looking and fattened cows
suddenly came up out of the river, and they
grazed in the meadow. 3 Then seven other
cows came up after them out of the river, ugly
and gaunt, and stood by the other cows on
the riverbank. 4 The ugly and gaunt cows ate
up the seven fine-looking and fattened cows.
Then Pharaoh awoke.
5 He slept and dreamed a second time. Sev-
en ears of grain suddenly came up on one
stalk, plump and good. 6 Then seven thin ears,
scorched by the east wind, sprang up after
them. 7 The seven thin ears devoured the sev-
en plump and full ears. Then Pharaoh awoke
and realized it was a dream.
8 In the morning his spirit was troubled,
and he sent and called for all the magicians
of Egypt and all its wise men. Pharaoh told
them his dreams, but there was no one who
could interpret them to Pharaoh.
9 Then the chief cupbearer spoke to Pha-
raoh, saying, "Today I remember my offenses.
10 Pharaoh was angry with his servants and
put me in confinement in the captain of the

guard's house, both me and the chief baker. 11 And we had a dream in the same night, he and I. We, each of us, dreamed according to the interpretation of his *own* dream. 12 A young Hebrew man was with us there, a servant to the captain of the guard. We told him and he interpreted our dreams for us. To each man he interpreted according to his *own* dream. 13 It happened just as he interpreted. He restored me to my position, and the baker was hanged."

14 So Pharaoh sent and called for Joseph, and they brought him hastily out of the dungeon. He shaved himself, changed his clothes, and came to Pharaoh.

15 Pharaoh said to Joseph, "I have dreamed a dream, and there is no one who can interpret it. I have heard it said of you that you can understand a dream to interpret it."

16 Joseph answered Pharaoh, saying, "It is not in me. God will give Pharaoh a favorable answer."

17 Then Pharaoh said to Joseph, "In my dream, I stood on the bank of the Nile. 18 And suddenly there came up out of the river seven cows, fattened and fine-looking, and they grazed in the reeds. 19 Then seven other cows came up after them, poor and very ugly and gaunt. I have never seen such ugliness in all the land of Egypt. 20 And the gaunt and ugly cows ate up the first seven fat cows. 21 And when they had eaten them up, no one would have known that they had eaten them, for they were still as ugly as before. Then I awoke.

22 "I also saw in my dreams seven ears *of grain*, full and good, suddenly come up on one stalk. 23 Then seven ears, thin and scorched by the east wind, sprang up after them. 24 And the thin ears swallowed the seven good ears. So I told this to the magicians, but there was no one who could explain it to me."

25 Then Joseph said to Pharaoh, "The dreams of Pharaoh are *one and the same*. God has shown Pharaoh what He is about to do. 26 The seven good cows are seven years, and the seven good ears are seven years. The dreams are one. 27 The seven gaunt and ugly cows that came up after them are seven years, and the seven empty ears scorched by the east wind will be seven years of famine.

28 "It is as I have spoken to Pharaoh. God has shown Pharaoh what He is about to do. 29 Seven years of great abundance will come throughout all the land of Egypt. 30 However, there will arise after them seven years of famine. All the abundance will be forgotten in the land of Egypt, and the famine will consume the land. 31 The abundance will be unknown in the land because of the famine following, for it will be very severe. 32 The reason the dream was repeated to Pharaoh twice is because the matter is established by God, and God will soon bring it to pass.

33 "Now, therefore, let Pharaoh seek out a man *who is* discerning and wise and set him over the land of Egypt. 34 Let Pharaoh do this, and let him appoint officials over the land and collect the fifth part of the produce of the land of Egypt in the seven abundant years. 35 Let them gather all the food from those good years that come and lay up grain under the authority of Pharaoh, and let them keep food in the cities. 36 This food will be for a reserve for the land for the seven years of famine which will be in the land of Egypt, so that the land does not perish during the famine."

Joseph Rises to Power

37 The counsel seemed good to Pharaoh and to all of his servants. 38 Pharaoh said to his servants, "Can we find anyone like this man, in whom is the Spirit of God?"

39 And Pharaoh said to Joseph, "Since God has shown you all this, there is no one as discerning and wise as you. 40 You will be over my house, and according to your word all my people will be ruled. Only in regard to the throne will I be greater than you."

41 Then Pharaoh said to Joseph, "See, I have set you over all the land of Egypt." 42 Pharaoh took off his ring from his hand and put it on Joseph's hand and arrayed him in clothes of fine linen and put a gold chain around his neck. 43 Then he had him ride in the second chariot which was his, and they cried out before him, "Bow the knee!" So he set him over all the land of Egypt.

44 Pharaoh said to Joseph, "I am Pharaoh, and without your consent no man will lift up his hand or foot in all the land of Egypt." 45 Pharaoh called Joseph's name Zaphenath-Paneah, and he gave him a wife, Asenath the daughter of Potiphera priest of On.[1] And Joseph went out over all the land of Egypt.

46 Joseph was thirty years old when he stood before Pharaoh, the king of Egypt. And Joseph went out from the presence of Pharaoh and went throughout all the land of Egypt. 47 In the seven abundant years the earth brought forth plentifully. 48 So he gathered up all the food of the seven years which was in the land of Egypt and laid up the food in the cities. He put in every city the food of the fields which surrounded the city. 49 Joseph gathered great quantities of grain as the sand of the sea until he stopped measuring it, for it was beyond measure.

41:14 Ps 113:7–8
41:15 Da 5:16
41:16 Ge 40:8
41:24 Ge 41:8
41:25 Da 2:45
41:27 2Ki 8:1
41:28 Ge 41:25
41:30 Ge 41:54
41:32 Nu 23:19
41:38 Da 4:18
41:41 Da 6:3
41:42 Da 5:7
41:43 Ge 45:8
41:46 Ge 37:2

[1] *45 On* is also called *Heliopolis*.

50 Before the years of famine came, two sons were born to Joseph, whom Asenath, the daughter of Potiphera priest of On, bore to him. 51 Joseph called the name of the firstborn Manasseh, "For God," he said, "has made me forget all my trouble and all my father's house." 52 The name of the second he called Ephraim, *saying,* "For God has caused me to be fruitful in the land of my affliction."

53 The seven years of abundance that were in the land of Egypt ended. 54 The seven years of famine began to come, just as Joseph had said. The famine was in all lands, but there was food in all the land of Egypt. 55 When all the land of Egypt was hungry, the people cried to Pharaoh for food, and Pharaoh said to all the Egyptians, "Go to Joseph. Do whatever he says to you."

56 The famine was over all the face of the earth, so Joseph opened all the storehouses and sold to the Egyptians, and the famine was severe throughout the land of Egypt. 57 Moreover, all countries came to Egypt to Joseph to buy grain, because the famine was so severe in all the lands.

Joseph's Brothers Go to Egypt

42 Now when Jacob saw that there was grain in Egypt, Jacob said to his sons, "Why do you look at one another?" 2 And he said, "I have heard that there is grain in Egypt. Go down there and buy *some* for us, so that we may live and not die."

3 Joseph's ten brothers went down to buy grain in Egypt. 4 But Jacob did not send Benjamin, Joseph's brother, with his brothers for he said, "Perhaps some harm might happen to him." 5 Thus the sons of Israel came to buy grain among those who came, for the famine was in the land of Canaan.

6 Now Joseph was the governor over the land, and it was he who sold to all the people of the land. So Joseph's brothers came and bowed themselves down before him with their faces to the ground. 7 Joseph saw his brothers, and he recognized them, but he pretended to be a stranger to them and spoke harshly to them. He said to them, "From where do you come?"

And they said, "From the land of Canaan to buy food."

8 Joseph knew his brothers, but they did not know him. 9 Joseph also remembered the dreams that he had dreamed of them. He said to them, "You are spies! You came to see the nakedness of the land!"

10 They said to him, "No, my lord, your servants have come only to buy food. 11 We are all one man's sons. We are honest men. Your servants are not spies."

12 But he said to them, "No, you have come to see the nakedness of the land!"

13 They said, "Your servants are twelve brothers, the sons of one man in the land of Canaan. The youngest is with our father today, and one is no longer living."

14 Joseph said to them, "It is as I said to you, 'You are spies!' 15 Here is how you will be tested. By the life of Pharaoh, you will not leave here unless your youngest brother comes here. 16 Send one of you, and let him get your brother, and you will be kept in prison, so that your words may be tested, whether there be any truth in you. Or else, by the life of Pharaoh, you are surely spies." 17 He put them all together in custody for three days.

18 Joseph said to them the third day, "Do this and live, for I fear God. 19 If you are honest men, let one of your brothers be confined in your prison house. The rest of you go and carry grain for the famine of your households. 20 Nevertheless, bring your youngest brother to me so that your words may be verified and you shall not die." And they did so.

21 Then they said one to another, "We are guilty concerning our brother, because we saw the anguish of his soul when he pleaded with us, but we would not listen. Therefore, this distress has come upon us."

22 Reuben answered them, saying, "Did I not speak to you, saying, 'Do not sin against the boy'; and you would not listen? Therefore, his blood is now required of us." 23 They did not know that Joseph understood them, for he spoke to them through an interpreter.

24 He turned himself away from them and wept, but then turned back to them again and spoke with them. Then he took Simeon from them and bound him before their eyes.

25 Joseph then gave the command to fill their sacks with grain and to restore every man's money to his sack and to give them provisions for the way. And it was done for them.

Joseph's Brothers Return Home

26 They loaded their donkeys with the grain and departed from there.

27 As one of them opened his sack to give his donkey feed in the lodging place, he saw his money. It was in the mouth of his sack. 28 And he said to his brothers, "My money has been returned. Here it is in my sack!"

Then their hearts sank, and they were afraid, saying to one another, "What is this that God has done to us?"

29 They came to Jacob their father in the land of Canaan and told him all that had happened

41:50 Ge 46:20
41:52 Ge 49:22
41:54 Ac 7:11
42:1 Ac 7:12
42:2 Ge 43:8
42:4 Ge 42:38
42:5 Ge 12:10

42:13 Ge 37:30
42:15 1Sa 17:55
42:17 Ge 40:4
42:18 Lev 25:43
42:20 Ge 42:34
42:21 Hos 5:15
42:22 1Ki 2:32
42:24 Ge 43:30

to them, saying, 30 “The man, the lord of the land, spoke harshly to us and took us for spies of the country. 31 And we said to him, ‘We are honest men. We are not spies. 32 We are twelve brothers, *all* sons of our father. One is no longer living, and the youngest is with our father today in the land of Canaan.’

33 “The man, the lord of the country, said to us, ‘Here is how I may know that you are honest men. Leave one of your brothers here with me, take food for the famine of your households, and be gone. 34 But bring your youngest brother back to me. Then I will know that you are not spies, but that you are honest men. Then I will deliver your brother to you, and you may trade in the land.’ ”

35 As they emptied their sacks, every man’s bundle of money was in his sack. When both they and their father saw the bundles of money, they were afraid. 36 Then Jacob their father said to them, “You have bereaved me of my children! Joseph is no more, Simeon is no more, and you will take Benjamin away. All these things are against me.”

37 Reuben spoke to his father, saying, “Kill my two sons if I fail to bring him to you. Put him in my hands, and I will bring him back to you.”

38 But Jacob said, “My son must not go down with you, for his brother is dead, and he alone is left. If harm should happen to him on the journey you are to make, then you will bring down my gray hairs with sorrow to the grave.”

Joseph’s Brothers Return With Benjamin

43 Now the famine was severe in the land. 2 When they had eaten up the grain which they had brought out of Egypt, their father said to them, “Go back and buy us a little food.”

3 Judah spoke to him, saying, “The man solemnly warned us, saying, ‘You will not see my face unless your brother is with you.’ 4 If you will send our brother with us, we will go down and buy food for you. 5 But if you will not send him, we will not go down. For the man said to us, ‘You will not see my face unless your brother is with you.’ ”

6 Israel said, “Why did you treat me so badly as to tell the man that you had *another* brother?”

7 And they said, “The man asked us directly about ourselves and our family, saying, ‘Is your father still alive? Do you have another brother?’ So we answered his questions. How could we even know that he would say, ‘Bring your brother down’?”

8 And Judah said to Israel his father, “Send the boy with me, and we will arise and go, so that we may live and not die, both we and you, and also our little ones. 9 I will be a surety for him. You may hold me personally responsible for him. If I fail to bring him back to you and set him before you, then let me bear the blame forever. 10 For if we had not delayed, we could have returned twice.”

11 Their father Israel said to them, “If it must be so, do this. Take some of the best fruits in the land in your bags, and carry down a present for the man: a little balm and a little honey, spices, and myrrh, pistachio nuts and almonds. 12 Take double the money with you, along with the money that was brought back in the mouths of your sacks. Carry it with you again. Perhaps it was a mistake. 13 Also, take your brother and arise, return to the man. 14 And may God Almighty give you mercy before the man, so that he may send away your other brother, along with Benjamin. As for me, if I am bereaved, I am bereaved.”

15 The men took the gift, and they took double the money with them, along with Benjamin. Then they went on their way down to Egypt and stood before Joseph. 16 When Joseph saw Benjamin with them, he said to the house steward, “Bring these men home, slaughter an animal and prepare it, for these men will dine with me at noon.”

17 The man did as Joseph ordered, so the man brought the men into Joseph’s house. 18 The men were afraid because they were brought into Joseph’s house. They said, “We have been brought in because of the money that was returned in our sacks the first time, so that he may seek occasion against us and fall upon us and take us for slaves with our donkeys.”

The Feast With Joseph

19 They approached the steward of Joseph’s house, and they spoke with him at the entrance of the house. 20 They said, “My lord, we indeed came down the first time to buy food. 21 When we came to the lodging place, we opened our sacks and realized every man’s money was in the mouth of his sack, our money in full weight. So we have brought it again with us. 22 We have also brought additional money with us to buy food. We cannot tell who put our money in our sacks.”

23 He said, “Be at peace; do not be afraid. Your God and the God of your father has given you treasure in your sacks. I had your money.” Then he brought Simeon out to them.

24 The man brought the men into Joseph’s house and gave them water to wash their feet and gave feed to their donkeys. 25 Then they made ready the gift for Joseph’s coming at

42:33 Ge 42:19–20
42:34 Ge 34:10
42:35 Ge 43:21
42:36 Ge 43:14
42:38 Ge 37:35
43:3 Ge 44:23
43:7 Ge 43:3
43:8 Ge 42:2

43:9 Ge 42:37
43:11 Ge 37:25
43:12 Ge 42:25
43:14 Ge 17:1
43:16 Ge 44:1
43:20 Ge 42:3
43:23 Ge 42:24
43:24 Ge 18:4
43:25 Ge 43:11

noon, for they heard that they would be eat-
ing a meal there.
26 When Joseph came home, they brought
into the house to him the present that they
had with them and bowed themselves to him
to the ground. 27 He asked them about their
well-being and said, "Is your father well, the
old man of whom you spoke? Is he still alive?"
28 And they answered, "Your servant our fa-
ther is in good health. He is still alive." And
they bowed down their heads and prostrated
themselves.
29 He lifted up his eyes and saw his brother
Benjamin, his mother's son, and said, "Is this
your younger brother of whom you spoke to
me?" And he said, "God be gracious to you, my
son." 30 Joseph hurried *out*, for he was deeply
moved over his brother and sought a place
to weep. So he entered into his chamber and
wept there.
31 Then he washed his face and came out.
Controlling himself, he said, "Serve the food."
32 They served him by himself and them by
themselves and the Egyptians who ate with
him by themselves, because the Egyptians
could not eat a meal with the Hebrews, for
that is an abomination to the Egyptians. 33 They
sat before him, the firstborn according to his
birthright and the youngest according to his
youth, and the men looked at one another in
astonishment. 34 He gave them portions from
his own table, but Benjamin's serving was five
times more than any of theirs. So they drank
and feasted with him.

Joseph Detains Benjamin

44 Then he commanded the steward of
his house, saying, "Fill the men's sacks
with food, as much as they can carry, and put
every man's money in the mouth of his sack.
2 Put my cup, the silver cup, in the mouth of
the sack of the youngest, along with his grain
money." And he did according to what Joseph
had spoken.
3 As soon as the morning was light, the
men were sent away, they and their donkeys.
4 When they were gone out of the city, but not
yet far off, Joseph said to his steward, "Get up,
follow after the men. When you overtake them,
say to them, 'Why have you rewarded evil for
good? 5 Is this not the one from which my lord
drinks and uses as he practices divination? You
have done evil in doing this.' "
6 So he overtook them, and he spoke to them
these same words. 7 They said to him, "Why
does my lord say these words? Far be it from
your servants that they should do such a thing.
8 Look, we brought back to you from the land
of Canaan the money that we found in the top

43:28 Ge 37:7
43:29 Ge 42:13
43:30 Ge 42:24
43:31 Ge 45:1
43:32 Ge 46:34
43:34 Ge 45:22
44:1 Ge 42:25
44:5 Ge 30:27

....

44:9 Ge 31:32
44:13 Nu 14:6
44:16 Ge 44:9
44:18 Ex 32:22
44:19 Ge 43:7
44:20 Ge 37:3
44:21 Ge 42:15
44:23 Ge 43:3
44:25 Ge 43:2
44:27 Ge 46:19
44:28 Ge 37:33

of our sacks. Why then would we steal silver
or gold from your lord's house? 9 Whichever
of your servants is found with it shall die, and
the rest of us will become my lord's slaves."
10 He said, "Now let it also be according to
your words. He with whom it is found shall be
my slave, and you will be blameless."
11 Then every man hurriedly took down his
sack to the ground, and every man opened
his sack. 12 He searched, beginning with the
oldest and ending with the youngest. The cup
was found in Benjamin's sack. 13 Then they tore
their clothes, and every man loaded his donkey
and returned to the city.
14 When Judah and his brothers came to Jo-
seph's house, he was still there; and they fell to
the ground before him. 15 Joseph said to them,
"What deed is this that you have done? Did you
not know that such a man as I can certainly
practice divination?"
16 And Judah said, "What shall we say to my
lord? What shall we speak? Or how shall we
clear ourselves? God has found out the iniq-
uity of your servants. Here we are, my lord's
servants, both we and he also in whose pos-
session the cup was found."
17 But he said, "Far be it from me that I should
do so. The man in whose possession the cup
was found shall be my slave; but as for you,
go up in peace to your father."

Judah's Plea for Benjamin

18 Then Judah approached him and said, "O
my lord, please let your servant speak a word
in my lord's ears, and do not be angry with
your servant, for you are equal to Pharaoh.
19 My lord asked his servants, saying, 'Have
you a father or a brother?' 20 And we said to
my lord, 'We have a father, an old man, and
a young brother, the child of his old age. His
brother is dead, and he alone is left of his
mother, and his father loves him.'
21 "You said to your servants, 'Bring him
down to me, so that I may set my eyes on
him.' 22 We said to my lord, 'The boy cannot
leave his father, for if he should leave his fa-
ther, his father would die.' 23 You said to your
servants, 'Unless your youngest brother comes
down with you, you will not see my face again.'
24 When we went back to your servant, my fa-
ther, we told him the words of my lord.
25 "Our father said, 'Go again and buy us a
little food.' 26 We said, 'We cannot go down. If
our youngest brother is with us, then we will
go down, for we may not see the man's face,
unless our youngest brother is with us.'
27 "Your servant, my father, said to us, 'You
know that my wife bore me two sons. 28 And
the one went out from me, and I said, "Surely

he was torn in pieces," and I have not seen him since. 29 And if you take this one also from me and he is harmed, you will bring down my gray hairs with sorrow to the grave.'

30 "Now therefore when I come to your servant, my father, and the boy is not with us, as his life is bound up in the boy's life, 31 when he sees that the boy is not with us, he will die, and your servants will bring down the gray hairs of your servant, our father, with sorrow to the grave. 32 For your servant became surety for the boy to my father, saying, 'If I fail to bring him to you, then I shall bear the blame to my father forever.'

33 "Now therefore, please let your servant stay as a slave to my lord instead of the boy, and let the boy go up with his brothers. 34 For how can I go up to my father if the boy is not with me, lest perhaps I see the evil that would find my father?"

Joseph Reveals His Identity

45 Then Joseph could not restrain himself before all who stood by him, and he cried out, "Make every man go out from me." So no man stood with him when Joseph made himself known to his brothers. 2 He wept so loudly that the Egyptians and the house of Pharaoh heard about it.

3 Joseph said to his brothers, "I am Joseph. Is my father still alive?" But his brothers could not answer him, for they were dismayed in his presence.

4 Joseph said to his brothers, "Please come near to me," and they came near. Then he said, "I am your brother, Joseph, whom you sold into Egypt. 5 Now do not be upset or angry with yourselves because you sold me here, for God sent me before you to preserve life. 6 For these two years the famine has been in the land, and there are still five years in which there will be neither plowing nor harvesting. 7 God sent me ahead of you to preserve you *as* a remnant on the earth and to save your lives by a great deliverance.

8 "So now it was not you who sent me here, but God. He has made me a father to Pharaoh and lord of his entire household and a ruler throughout all the land of Egypt. 9 Hurry and go up to my father and say to him, 'This is what your son Joseph says, "God has made me lord of all Egypt. Come down to me; do not delay. 10 And you will dwell in the land of Goshen, and you will be near me, you and your children and your children's children, along with your flocks, your herds, and all that you have. 11 I will provide for you there, for there are still five years of famine *to come, lest* you and your household, and all that you have, come to poverty." '

12 "Your eyes and the eyes of my brother Benjamin see that it is my mouth that is speaking to you. 13 You must tell my father of all my glory in Egypt and of all that you have seen, and you must hurry and bring my father down here."

14 Then he fell on his brother Benjamin's neck and wept, and Benjamin wept on his neck. 15 Moreover he kissed all his brothers and wept on them. After that his brothers talked with him.

16 When the news reached Pharaoh's palace that Joseph's brothers had come, it pleased Pharaoh and his servants. 17 Pharaoh said to Joseph, "Say to your brothers, 'Do this. Load your animals and go to the land of Canaan. 18 Get your father and your households and come to me, and I will give you the best of the land of Egypt, and you shall eat the fat of the land.'

19 "You are also commanded to say, 'Do this: Take your wagons out of the land of Egypt for your little ones and for your wives, and get your father and come. 20 Also do not concern yourself with your goods, for the best of all the land of Egypt is yours.' "

21 So the sons of Israel did so, and Joseph gave them wagons, according to the commandment of Pharaoh, and gave them provisions for the journey. 22 To each of them he gave a change of clothes, but he gave to Benjamin three hundred shekels of silver[1] and five changes of clothes. 23 To his father he sent the following: ten donkeys loaded with the best things of Egypt and ten female donkeys loaded with grain and bread and provisions for his father on the journey. 24 So he sent his brothers away, and they departed. He said to them, "Do not quarrel on the way."

25 They went up out of Egypt and came to the land of Canaan to Jacob their father. 26 They told him, "Joseph is still alive, and he is governor over all the land of Egypt." And Jacob's heart stood still because he could not believe them. 27 They told him all the words of Joseph, which he had said to them, and when he saw the wagons that Joseph had sent to carry him, the spirit of their father Jacob revived. 28 Then Israel said, "Enough! Joseph my son is still alive. I will go and see him before I die."

Jacob's Journey to Egypt

46 So Israel set out with all that he had and came to Beersheba and offered sacrifices to the God of his father Isaac.

2 God spoke to Israel in visions of the night and said, "Jacob, Jacob."

44:29 Ge 42:38
44:30 1Sa 18:1
44:31 Ge 44:29
45:3 Ac 7:13
45:4 Ge 37:28
45:5 Ge 50:20
45:8 Jdg 17:10
45:11 Ge 47:12

....

45:12 Ge 42:23
45:13 Ac 7:14
45:18 Ge 27:28
45:19 Ge 46:5
45:21 Ge 45:19
45:22 Ge 43:34
46:1 Ge 21:33
46:2 Ge 15:1

[1] *22* About 7½ pounds, or 3.5 kilograms.

And he said, "Here I am."
3 Then He said, "I am God, the God of your
father. Do not be afraid to go down to Egypt,
for I will make you into a great nation there.
4 I will go down with you to Egypt, and I will
also surely bring you back again. And Joseph's
own hand shall close your eyes."
5 Jacob arose from Beersheba, and the sons
of Israel carried Jacob their father and their
little ones and their wives in the wagons that
Pharaoh had sent to carry him. 6 They took
their livestock and their possessions that they
had acquired in the land of Canaan, and came
to Egypt, Jacob and all his descendants with
him. 7 He brought with him to Egypt his sons
and his sons' sons, his daughters and his sons'
daughters, and all his descendants.
8 These were the names of the sons of Israel,
Jacob and his sons, who came to Egypt:

Reuben, Jacob's firstborn.
9 The sons of Reuben were
Hanok, Pallu, Hezron, and Karmi.
10 The sons of Simeon were
Jemuel, Jamin, Ohad, Jakin, Zohar, and
Shaul the son of a Canaanite woman.
11 The sons of Levi were
Gershon, Kohath, and Merari.
12 The sons of Judah were
Er, Onan, Shelah, Perez, and Zerah (but
Er and Onan died in the land of Canaan).
The sons of Perez were
Hezron and Hamul.
13 The sons of Issachar were
Tola, Puah, Job, and Shimron.
14 The sons of Zebulun were
Sered, Elon, and Jahleel.
15 These were the sons of Leah, whom she
bore to Jacob in Paddan Aram, with his daugh-
ter Dinah. All his sons and his daughters *num-
bered* thirty-three.

16 And the sons of Gad were
Zephon, Haggi, Shuni, Ezbon, Eri, Arodi,
and Areli.
17 The sons of Asher were
Imnah, Ishvah, Ishvi, Beriah,
and Serah their sister.
The sons of Beriah:
Heber and Malkiel.
18 These were the sons of Zilpah, whom La-
ban gave to Leah his daughter; and these she
bore to Jacob, sixteen in all.
19 The sons of Rachel, Jacob's wife, were
Joseph and Benjamin. 20 To Joseph in the
land of Egypt were born Manasseh and
Ephraim, whom Asenath the daughter of
Potiphera, the priest of On, bore to him.
21 The sons of Benjamin were
Bela, Beker, Ashbel, Gera, Naaman, Ehi,
Rosh, Muppim, Huppim, and Ard.
22 These were the sons of Rachel who were
born to Jacob, fourteen in all.

23 The son of Dan was
Hushim.
24 The sons of Naphtali:
Jahziel,[1] Guni, Jezer, and Shillem.[2]
25 These were the sons of Bilhah, whom La-
ban gave to Rachel his daughter, and she bore
these to Jacob, seven in all.

26 All those who came with Jacob to Egypt,
who were direct descendants, besides the
wives of Jacob's sons, were sixty-six in all.
27 And the sons of Joseph, who were born to
him in Egypt, were two. All those of the house
of Jacob who came to Egypt were seventy.

Jacob Settles in Goshen

28 Now he sent Judah ahead of him to Joseph
to get directions to Goshen. And they came into
the land of Goshen. 29 Joseph readied his char-
iot and went up to Goshen to meet Israel his
father. As soon as he appeared to him, he fell
on his neck and wept on his neck a long time.
30 Israel said to Joseph, "Now let me die,
since I have seen your face, because you are
still alive."
31 Joseph said to his brothers and to his fa-
ther's household, "I will go up and tell Pharaoh
and say to him, 'My brothers and my father's
household, who were in the land of Canaan,
have come to me. 32 The men are shepherds;
their work has been to feed livestock, and they
have brought their flocks and their herds and
all that they have.' 33 When Pharaoh calls you
and asks, 'What is your occupation?' 34 you
shall say, 'Your servants have been keepers of
livestock from our youth even until now, both
we and our fathers,' so that you may dwell in
the land of Goshen, because every shepherd
is an abomination to the Egyptians."
47 Then Joseph went and told Pharaoh,
"My father and my brothers and their
flocks and their herds and all that they possess
have come from the land of Canaan and are
now in the land of Goshen." 2 He took five men
from among his brothers and presented them
before Pharaoh.
3 Pharaoh asked his brothers, "What is your
occupation?"
And they said to Pharaoh, "Your servants
are shepherds, both we and also our fathers."
4 They said to Pharaoh, "We have come to so-
journ in the land, for your servants have no
pasture for their flocks, because the famine is

46:3 Ge 12:2
46:4 Ge 28:15
46:5 Ge 45:19
46:6 Jos 24:4
46:10 Ex 6:15
46:16 Nu 26:15–17
46:18 Ge 29:24
46:20 Ge 41:50–52
....
46:21 1Ch 7:6–12
46:25 Ge 29:29
46:26 Ex 1:5
46:27 Ac 7:14
46:28 Ge 45:10
46:34 Ge 43:32
47:1 Ge 46:31
47:2 Ac 7:13
47:3 Ge 46:33–34
47:4 Ge 15:13

[1] *24 Jahzeel* in Nu 26:48. [2] *24 Shallum* in 1Ch 7:13.

severe in the land of Canaan. Now therefore,
please allow your servants to dwell in the land
of Goshen."
5 Pharaoh spoke to Joseph, saying, "Your fa-
ther and your brothers have come to you. 6 The
land of Egypt is before you. Have your father
and your brothers dwell in the best of the land.
Have them dwell in the land of Goshen, and if
you know any capable men among them, then
put them in charge over my livestock."
7 Then Joseph brought in Jacob his father
and presented him to Pharaoh, and Jacob
blessed Pharaoh. 8 Pharaoh said to Jacob,
"How old are you?"
9 And Jacob said to Pharaoh, "The days of
the years of my pilgrimage are one hundred
and thirty years. My days of the years of my
life have been few and evil, and they have not
attained to the days of the years of the lives
of my fathers in the days of their pilgrimage."
10 And Jacob blessed Pharaoh and went out
from his presence.
11 So Joseph settled his father and his broth-
ers and gave them a possession in the land
of Egypt, in the best *part* of the land, in the
land of Rameses, as Pharaoh had command-
ed. 12 Joseph provided food for his father, his
brothers, and his father's entire household,
according to the number *of their* children.

Joseph and the Famine

13 There was no food in all the land, for the
famine was very severe, so that the land of
Egypt and all the land of Canaan languished
because of the famine. 14 Joseph gathered
up all the money that was found in the land
of Egypt and in the land of Canaan for the
grain that they bought, and Joseph brought
the money into Pharaoh's house. 15 When
the money was all spent in the land of Egypt
and in the land of Canaan, all the Egyptians
came to Joseph and said, "Give us food, for
why should we die in your presence? For our
money is gone."
16 Joseph said, "Give your livestock, and I
will give you *food* for your livestock, if *your*
money is gone." 17 They brought their livestock
to Joseph, and Joseph gave them food in ex-
change for the horses, the flocks, the herds,
and the donkeys; and he fed them with food
in exchange for all their livestock for that year.
18 When that year was ended, they came to
him the second year and said to him, "We will
not hide it from our lord, that our money is all
spent. Our lord also has our herds of livestock.
There is nothing left in the sight of my lord but
our bodies and our lands. 19 Why should we die
before your eyes, both we and our land? Buy
us and our land for food, and we and our land

47:6 Ge 47:11
47:7 Ge 47:10
47:9 Ge 35:28
47:10 Ge 47:7
47:11 Ex 1:11
47:13 Ac 7:11
47:14 Ge 41:56

47:22 Ezr 7:24
47:24 Ge 41:34
47:26 Ge 47:22
47:27 Ge 46:3
47:29 Ge 24:2
47:30 Ge 49:29–32
47:31 1Ki 1:47
48:4 Ge 17:8

will be slaves to Pharaoh. Also give us seed, so
that we may live and not die, so that the land
will not be desolate."
20 So Joseph bought all the land of Egypt
for Pharaoh, for every Egyptian man sold his
field because the famine was severe on them.
So the land became Pharaoh's. 21 As for the
people, he removed them to cities from one
end of the borders of Egypt to the other end.
22 Only the land of the priests he did not buy;
for the priests had an allotment from Pharaoh,
and they lived off their allotment that Pharaoh
gave them. Therefore they did not sell their
lands.
23 Then Joseph said to the people, "I have
bought you and your land today for Pharaoh;
here is seed for you so you may sow the land.
24 At the harvest, you must give a fifth part to
Pharaoh and four parts will be your own, as
seed for the field and for your food and for
those of your households and for food for your
little ones."
25 They said, "You have saved our lives. Let
us find grace in the sight of my lord, and we
will be Pharaoh's slaves."
26 So Joseph made it a law over the land of
Egypt to this day, that Pharaoh should have the
fifth part, except from the land of the priests,
which did not become Pharaoh's.

Jacob's Request of Joseph

27 Israel lived in the land of Egypt, in the land
of Goshen, and they had possessions there and
grew and became very numerous.
28 And Jacob lived in the land of Egypt sev-
enteen years, so the years of Jacob's life were
one hundred and forty-seven years. 29 When
the time drew near when Israel would die, he
called his son Joseph and said to him, "If now
I have found grace in your sight, please put
your hand under my thigh and deal kindly and
truly with me. Please do not bury me in Egypt,
30 but let me lie with my fathers. Carry me out
of Egypt and bury me in their burial place."
And he said, "I will do as you have said."
31 And he said, "Swear to me," and he swore
to him. Then Israel bowed himself at the head
of his bed.

Jacob Blesses Joseph's Sons

48 After these things, Joseph was told,
"Your father is sick." So he took his
two sons Manasseh and Ephraim with him.
2 When Jacob was told, "Your son Joseph is
coming to you," Israel strengthened himself
and sat up in the bed.
3 Jacob said to Joseph, "God Almighty ap-
peared to me at Luz in the land of Canaan, and
blessed me. 4 And He said to me, 'I will make
you fruitful and multiply you, and I will make

you into a multitude of people and will give
this land to your descendants after you for an
everlasting possession.'
5 "Now your two sons, Ephraim and Ma-
nasseh, who were born to you in the land of
Egypt before I came to you in Egypt, are mine;
as Reuben and Simeon, they shall be mine.
6 Any children you have after them will be
yours and will be called by the names of their
brothers in their inheritance. 7 As for me, when
I came from Paddan, Rachel died beside me
in the land of Canaan on the way, when there
was still some distance to get to Ephrath, and
I buried her there on the way to Ephrath (that
is, Bethlehem)."
8 Then Israel saw Joseph's sons and said,
"Whose are these?"
9 And Joseph said to his father, "They are my
sons, whom God has given me in this place."
And he said, "Please bring them to me, and
I will bless them."
10 Now the eyes of Israel were dim with age,
so that he could not see. So Joseph brought
them near to him, and he kissed them and
embraced them.
11 Israel said to Joseph, "I never thought I
would see your face, but here God has also
shown me your children."
12 So Joseph took them from beside his
knees, and he bowed down with his face to
the ground. 13 Joseph took them both, Ephraim
in his right hand toward Israel's left hand, and
Manasseh in his left hand toward Israel's right
hand, and brought them near him. 14 Israel
stretched out his right hand and laid it on
Ephraim's head, who was the younger, and
his left hand on Manasseh's head, crossing his
hands, for Manasseh was the firstborn.
15 He blessed Joseph and said,

"God, before whom my fathers
Abraham and Isaac walked,
the God who fed me
all my life long to this day,
16 the angel who redeemed me from all evil,
bless the boys;
let them be called by my name,
and the name of my fathers, Abraham
and Isaac;
and let them grow into a multitude
in the midst of the earth."

17 When Joseph saw that his father laid his
right hand on the head of Ephraim, it dis-
pleased him, and he took hold of his father's
hand to remove it from Ephraim's head to
Manasseh's head. 18 Joseph said to his father,
"Not so, my father, for this one is the firstborn.
Put your right hand on his head."

48:5 Ge 41:50–52
48:9 Ge 27:4
48:10 Ge 27:1
48:14 Ge 41:51
48:15 Ge 17:1
....
48:21 Ge 46:4
48:22 Jos 24:32
49:1 Nu 24:14
49:2 Ps 34:11
49:3 Dt 21:17
49:4 Ge 35:22
49:6 Ps 26:9
49:8 1Ch 5:2
49:9 Nu 24:9

19 His father refused and said, "I know it, my
son, I know it. He will also become a people,
and he will also be great, but truly his younger
brother will be greater than he, and his de-
scendants will become a multitude of nations."
20 He blessed them that day, saying,

"By you Israel will bless, saying,
'May God make you like Ephraim and
Manasseh.'"

So he set Ephraim before Manasseh.
21 Israel said to Joseph, "I am about to die,
but God will be with you and return you again
to the land of your fathers. 22 Moreover, I have
given to you one portion more than your broth-
ers, which I took out of the hand of the Amor-
ites with my sword and my bow."

Jacob Blesses His Sons
Dt 33:1–29

49 Jacob called to his sons and said,
"Gather yourselves together, so that I
may tell you what will befall you in the last
days.

2 Gather yourselves together and hear, sons
of Jacob,
and listen to your father Israel.

3 Reuben, you are my firstborn,
my might and the beginning of my
strength,
the excellency of dignity, and the
excellency of power.
4 Unstable as water, you shall not excel,
because you went up to your father's
bed;
then you defiled it—he went up to my
couch.

5 Simeon and Levi are brothers;
weapons of violence are their swords.
6 Let my soul not enter into their council;
let my glory not be united with their
assembly;
for in their anger they killed men
and in their self-will they hamstrung
oxen.
7 Cursed be their anger, for it is fierce;
and their wrath, for it is cruel!
I will divide them in Jacob
and scatter them in Israel.

8 Judah, your brothers shall praise you;
your hand shall be on the neck of your
enemies;
your father's sons will bow down before
you.
9 Judah is a lion's cub;
from the prey, my son, you have
gone up.
He crouches and lies down like a lion;
and as a lion, who dares rouse him?

10 The scepter shall not depart from Judah,
nor a lawgiver from between his feet,
until Shiloh comes;
and to him will be the obedience of the
people.
11 He tethers his foal to the vine,
and his colt to the choicest vine;
he washes his garments in wine,
his clothes in the blood of grapes.
12 His eyes are darker than wine,
and his teeth whiter than milk.

13 Zebulun shall dwell at the haven of the sea;
and he shall be a haven of ships.
His border shall be at Sidon.

14 Issachar is a strong donkey,
lying down between two burdens;
15 he saw that a resting place was good,
and that the land was pleasant;
so he bowed his shoulder to bear the
burden
and became a slave to forced labor.

16 Dan shall judge his people
as one of the tribes of Israel.
17 Dan shall be a serpent by the road,
a viper on the path,
that bites the horse's heels
so that its rider will fall backward.
18 I wait for Your salvation, O LORD!

19 Gad shall be attacked by raiding bands,
but he shall raid at their heels.

20 Asher's food shall be rich,
and he shall yield royal delicacies.

21 Naphtali is a doe set loose;
he gives beautiful words.

22 Joseph is a fruitful bough,
a fruitful bough by a spring,
whose branches run over the wall.

I rebuke in the name of Jesus every lion that would stoop and crouch down to attack me (Ge 49:9).

23 The archers bitterly attacked him,
they shot at him and hated him.
24 But his bow remained firm.
His arms were agile
because of the hands of the Mighty One of
Jacob,
because of the Shepherd, the Rock of
Israel,
25 because of the God of your father who will
help you,
and by the Almighty who will bless you
with blessings from heaven above,

49:10 Nu 24:17
49:11 2Ki 18:32
49:12 Pr 23:29
49:13 Dt 33:18–19
49:16 Ge 30:6
49:18 Ps 119:166
49:19 Ge 30:11
49:20 Ge 30:13
49:21 Dt 33:23
49:22 Ge 41:52
49:23 Ge 37:24
49:24 Ps 132:2
49:25 Ge 28:13
....
49:26 Dt 33:15–16
49:29 Ge 47:30
49:31 Ge 25:9
49:33 Ge 49:29
50:1 Ge 46:4
50:2 Ge 50:26
50:3 Nu 20:29
50:5 2Ch 16:14

blessings from the deep that lies
beneath,
the blessings of the breasts and the
womb.
26 The blessings of your father have
surpassed
the blessings of my fathers,
up to the utmost bound of the
everlasting hills.
They will be on the head of Joseph,
and on the crown of the head of him
who was set apart from his brothers.
27 Benjamin is a ravenous wolf;
in the morning he devours the prey,
and at night he divides the spoil."

28 These are all the twelve tribes of Israel, and
this is what their father said to them when he
blessed them. He blessed them, each with the
blessing appropriate to him

The Death of Jacob

29 Then he charged them and said to them, "I
am about to be gathered to my people. Bury
me with my fathers in the cave that is in the
field of Ephron the Hittite, 30 in the cave that
is in the field of Machpelah, which is before
Mamre in the land of Canaan, which Abraham
bought along with the field from Ephron the
Hittite as a burial place. 31 They buried Abra-
ham and Sarah his wife there. They buried
Isaac and Rebekah his wife there, and I bur-
ied Leah there. 32 The field and the cave that
is there were purchased from the children of
Heth."
33 When Jacob finished instructing his sons,
he drew his feet into the bed, breathed his last,
and was gathered to his people.

The Burial of Jacob

50 Then Joseph fell on his father's face
and wept over him and kissed him.
2 Joseph commanded his servants the physi-
cians to embalm his father. So the physicians
embalmed Israel. 3 Forty days were required
for him, for such is the time required for those
who are embalmed. Then the Egyptians
mourned for him seventy days.
4 When the days of his mourning were past,
Joseph spoke to the household of Pharaoh,
saying, "If now I have found favor in your eyes,
speak to Pharaoh, saying, 5 'My father made
me swear, saying, "I am about to die. Bury me
in my tomb which I dug for myself in the land
of Canaan." Now therefore please let me go up
and bury my father, and then I will return.' "
6 Pharaoh said, "Go up and bury your father,
as he made you swear to do."
7 Joseph went up to bury his father, and all
the servants of Pharaoh went up with him too,

the elders of his household and all the elders
of the land of Egypt, 8 all the house of Joseph
and his brothers and his father's household.
They left only their little ones and their flocks
and their herds in the land of Goshen. 9 Both
the chariots and horsemen also went up with
him. It was a very great company.
10 When they came to the threshing floor of
Atad, which is beyond the Jordan, they mourn-
ed with a great and very sorrowful lamenta-
tion. He observed seven days of mourning
for his father. 11 When the inhabitants of the
land, the Canaanites, saw the mourning at the
threshing floor of Atad, they said, "This is a
grievous mourning for the Egyptians." There-
fore the place was called Abel Mizraim, which
is beyond the Jordan.
12 So his sons did with him just as he had
commanded them. 13 For his sons carried him
into the land of Canaan and buried him in the
cave of the field of Machpelah, near Mamre,
which Abraham bought with the field as a buri-
al site from Ephron the Hittite. 14 After he had
buried his father, Joseph returned to Egypt, he
and his brothers and all who went up with him
to bury his father.

Joseph Reassures His Brothers

15 When Joseph's brothers saw that their fa-
ther was dead, they said, "Perhaps Joseph will
hate us and will certainly pay us back for all
the wrong we did to him." 16 So they sent a
message to Joseph, saying, "Your father gave
this command before he died: 17 'Say to Jo-
seph, "I beg you, forgive the transgressions of
your brothers and their sin. For they did evil to
you."' Now, please forgive the transgressions
of the servants of the God of your father." And
Joseph wept when they spoke to him.
18 Then his brothers also went and fell down
before his face and said, "We are your ser-
vants."
19 Joseph said to them, "Do not be afraid, for
am I in the place of God? 20 But as for you,
you intended to harm me, but God intended it
for good, in order to bring it about as it is this
day, to save many lives. 21 So now, do not fear.
I will provide for you and your little ones." So
he comforted them and spoke kindly to them.

The Death of Joseph

22 Joseph stayed in Egypt, he and his father's
household, and Joseph lived one hundred and
ten years. 23 Joseph saw Ephraim's children to
the third generation. Also, the children of Ma-
kir, the son of Manasseh, were brought up on
Joseph's knees.
24 Joseph said to his brothers, "I am about to
die. God will surely come to you and bring you
out of this land to the land of which He swore
to Abraham, to Isaac, and to Jacob." 25 Then
Joseph made the sons of Israel swear, saying,
"God will surely visit you, and you shall carry
up my bones from here."
26 So Joseph died at the age of one hundred
and ten years old, and they embalmed him,
and he was put in a coffin in Egypt.

50:10 Ac 8:2
50:17 Ge 49:25
50:20 Ro 8:28
50:21 Ge 47:12
50:23 Ge 30:3
50:24 Ge 26:3
50:25 Ex 13:19

Author: Traditionally Moses

Written: Between 1440 and 1400 BC

Themes: Deliverance, Instruction

EXODUS

Dear Spirit Led Woman,

The Book of Exodus is a record of Israel's journey from bondage to the Promised Land. Even though they were visibly being led by the Spirit with a cloud by day and fire by night, many times the children of Israel lost sight of God's promises to them and even asked to return to their old life of slavery.

Becoming like Jesus requires a similar journey in all of our lives—and often involves difficult periods of transition. The changes brought about by times of transition can be momentary, like shifting a gear in a car. Other times transition can seem as if it will never end—a long dark night of the soul when all around you seems dim and you lose sight of God's promises to you.

Don't give up! Trust God. He will lead you by day and night, just as He led His people through the desert long ago. Each period of transition in your life will lead you to a glorious new place. Allow God to use each one to take you to a higher level spiritually, with the ultimate goal of becoming like Him.

Joy F. Strang

Israel Oppressed

1 Now these are the names of the sons of Israel, which came into Egypt (each man and his household came with Jacob): 2 Reuben, Simeon, Levi, and Judah; 3 Issachar, Zebulun, and Benjamin; 4 Dan, Naphtali, Gad, and Asher. 5 All the people who came from the seed of Jacob were seventy people, but Joseph was in Egypt *already*.

6 Joseph died, as did all his brothers, and all that generation. 7 Nevertheless, the sons of Israel were fruitful, and increased abundantly, and multiplied, and became exceedingly mighty,[1] so that the land was filled with them.

8 Now there rose up a new king over Egypt, who did not know Joseph. 9 He said to his people, "Surely, the people of the sons of Israel are more numerous and powerful than we. 10 Come, let us deal wisely with them, lest they multiply, and it come to pass that when any war breaks out, they also join our enemies, and fight against us, and escape from the land."

11 Therefore they set taskmasters over them to afflict them with their labor. They built for Pharaoh storage cities: Pithom and Rameses. 12 But the more they afflicted them, the more they multiplied and grew so that as a result they abhorred the sons of Israel. 13 The Egyptians made the children of Israel to serve with rigor, 14 and they made their lives bitter with hard service—in mortar and in brick, and in all manner of service in the field, all their service in which they made them serve was with rigor.

15 The king of Egypt spoke to the Hebrew midwives, of which the name of one was Shiphrah, and the name of the other Puah, 16 and he said, "When you perform the office of a midwife to the Hebrew women and see them on the stools, if it is a son, then you must kill him, but if it is a daughter, then she may live." 17 However, the midwives feared God, and did not do as the king of Egypt commanded them, but kept the male children alive. 18 The king of Egypt called for the midwives and said to them, "Why have you done this thing and preserved the male children's lives?"

19 The midwives said to Pharaoh, "Because the Hebrew women are not like the Egyptian women, for they are vigorous and give birth before the midwives come to them."

20 Therefore God dealt well with the midwives, and the people multiplied and grew very mighty. 21 So it happened that because the midwives feared God, He gave them families.

22 Pharaoh charged all his people, saying, "You must cast every son that is born into the river, and you must preserve every daughter's life."

The Birth of Moses

2 Now a man of the house of Levi went and married a daughter of Levi. 2 And the woman conceived and bore a son, and when she saw him, that he was a beautiful child, she hid him three months. 3 When she could no longer hide him, she took for him a container *made* of bulrushes and daubed it with tar and with pitch. She then put the child in it and set it in the reeds by the river's bank. 4 Then his sister stood afar off so that she might know what would happen to him.

5 The daughter of Pharaoh came down to wash herself at the river while her maidens walked along by the river's side, and when she saw the container among the reeds, she sent her maid, and she retrieved it. 6 When she opened it, she saw the child. He was crying. She had compassion on him and said, "This is one of the Hebrews' children."

7 Then his sister said to Pharaoh's daughter, "Shall I go and call for you a nursing woman of the Hebrew women so that she may nurse the child for you?"

8 And Pharaoh's daughter said to her, "Go." So the young girl went and called the child's mother. 9 Pharaoh's daughter said to her, "Take this child away, and nurse him for me, and I will give you your wages." So the woman took the child and nursed him. 10 Now the child grew, and she brought him to Pharaoh's daughter, and he became her son. And she called his name Moses and said, "Because I drew him out of the water."

11 In those days, when Moses was grown, he went out to his brothers and looked on their burdens; and he saw an Egyptian striking a Hebrew, one of his brothers. 12 He looked this way and that way, and when he saw no one, he killed the Egyptian and hid him in the sand. 13 When he went out the next day, two men of the Hebrews struggled with each other; and he said to him that did the wrong, "Why do you strike your companion?"

14 He said, "Who made you a prince and a judge over us? Do you intend to kill me as you killed the Egyptian?" Moses feared and said, "Surely this thing is known."

Moses Flees to Midian

15 Now when Pharaoh heard this thing, he sought to slay Moses. But Moses fled from the presence of Pharaoh and settled in the land of Midian, and he dwelled by a well. 16 Now the priest of Midian had seven daughters, and they came and drew water, and filled the troughs to water their father's flock. 17 Then shepherds

1:1 Ge 46:8–26
1:5 Ge 46:26–27
1:6 Ge 50:26
1:7 Ge 46:3
1:8 Ac 7:18
1:9 Ps 105:24–25
1:10 Ac 7:19
1:11 Ge 15:13
1:14 Ex 2:23
1:17 Ac 5:29
1:20 Ex 1:12
1:21 1Sa 2:35
1:22 Ac 7:19

2:1 Nu 26:59
2:2 Ac 7:20
2:3 Isa 18:2
2:4 Ex 15:20
2:10 Heb 11:24
2:11 Heb 11:24–26
2:15 Ac 7:29
2:16 Ge 24:11
2:17 Ge 29:10

[1] 7 Or *numerous*; also in v. 20.

came and drove them away, but Moses stood
up and helped them, and watered their flock.
18 When they came to Reuel their father, he
said, "Why is it you have come *back* so soon
today?"
19 And they said, "An Egyptian delivered us
out of the hand of the shepherds and also
drew water for us and watered the flock."
20 He said to his daughters, "So where is he?
Why is it that you have left the man? Call him
so that he may eat bread."
21 Moses was content to dwell with the man,
and he gave Zipporah, his daughter, to Moses.
22 Then she gave birth to a son, and he called
his name Gershom, for he said, "I have been a
sojourner in a foreign land."
23 In the passing of time the king of Egypt
died. And the children of Israel sighed because
of the bondage, and they cried out, and their
cry came up to God on account of the bondage.
24 God heard their groaning, and God remem-
bered His covenant with Abraham, Isaac, and
Jacob. 25 God looked on the children of Israel,
and God had concern for them.

Moses at the Burning Bush

3 Now Moses kept the flock of Jethro his
father-in-law, the priest of Midian, and
he led the flock to the far side of the desert
and came to the mountain of God, to Horeb.
2 The angel of the LORD appeared to him in a
flame of fire from the midst of a bush, and he
looked, and the bush burned with fire, but the
bush was not consumed. 3 So Moses said, "I
will now turn aside and see this great sight,
why the bush is not burnt."
4 When the LORD saw that he turned aside to
see, God called to him from out of the midst of
the bush and said, "Moses, Moses."
And he said, "Here am I."
5 He said, "Do not approach here. Remove
your sandals from off your feet, for the place
on which you are standing is holy ground."
6 Moreover He said, "I am the God of your fa-
ther, the God of Abraham, the God of Isaac,
and the God of Jacob." And Moses hid his face,
for he was afraid to look upon God.

Lead me into the land flowing with milk and honey (Ex 3:8).

7 The LORD said, "I have surely seen the afflic-
tion of My people who are in Egypt and have
heard their cry on account of their taskmasters,
for I know their sorrows. 8 Therefore, I have
come down to deliver them out of the hand
of the Egyptians, and to bring them up out
of that land to a good and spacious land, to a
land flowing with milk and honey, to the place
of the Canaanites, the Hittites, the Amorites,
the Perizzites, the Hivites, and the Jebusites.
9 Now therefore, the cry of the children of Isra-
el has come to Me. Moreover, I have also seen
the oppression with which the Egyptians are
oppressing them. 10 Come now therefore, and
I will send you to Pharaoh so that you may
bring forth My people, the children of Israel,
out of Egypt."
11 Moses said to God, "Who am I that I should
go to Pharaoh and that I should bring forth the
children of Israel out of Egypt?"
12 And He said, "Certainly I will be with you,
and this will be a sign to you, that I have sent
you: When you have brought forth the people
out of Egypt, all of you shall serve God on this
mountain."
13 Moses said to God, "I am going to the chil-
dren of Israel and will say to them, 'The God
of your fathers has sent me to you.' When they
say to me, 'What is His name?' what shall I
say to them?"
14 And God said to Moses, "I AM WHO I AM,"[1]
and He said, "You will say this to the children
of Israel, 'I AM has sent me to you.' "
15 God, moreover, said to Moses, "Thus you
will say to the children of Israel, 'The LORD, the
God of your fathers, the God of Abraham, the
God of Isaac, and the God of Jacob, has sent
me to you. This is My name forever, and this
is My memorial to all generations.'
16 "Go, and gather the elders of Israel togeth-
er, and say to them, 'The LORD, the God of your
fathers, the God of Abraham, of Isaac, and of
Jacob, appeared to me, saying, "I am indeed
concerned about you and what has been done
to you in Egypt. 17 Therefore, I said, I will bring
you up out of the affliction of Egypt to the land
of the Canaanites, the Hittites, the Amorites,
the Perizzites, the Hivites, and the Jebusites, to
a land flowing with milk and honey." '
18 "They shall listen to your voice, and you
shall come, you and the elders of Israel, to the
king of Egypt, and you must say to him, 'The
LORD, the God of the Hebrews has met with us.
Therefore, now, let us go, we ask you, three
days' journey into the wilderness so that we
may sacrifice to the LORD our God.' 19 However, I
know that the king of Egypt will not let you go,
no, not even under a forceful hand. 20 So I will
stretch out My hand and strike Egypt with all
My wonders which I will perform in its midst,
and after that he will let you go.
21 "I will give this people favor in the sight of
the Egyptians, and it will come to pass, that,
when you go, you will not go empty-handed.

2:18 Ex 3:1
2:20 Ge 31:54
2:22 Ac 7:29
2:23 Jas 5:4
2:24 Ex 6:5
2:25 Ex 4:31
3:1 1Ki 19:8
3:2 Dt 33:16
3:3 Ac 7:31
3:4 Dt 33:16
3:5 Jos 5:15
3:6 Ex 4:5
3:7 Ps 106:44
3:8 Ge 50:24
3:9 Ex 2:23
3:10 Mic 6:4
3:11 Ex 6:12
3:12 Jos 1:5
3:14 Ex 6:3
3:15 Ps 135:13
3:16 Ex 4:29
3:18 Ex 7:16
3:19 Ex 5:2
3:20 Ex 9:15
3:21 Ex 12:36

[1] *14* The Heb. *to be*, related to the covenantal name of God translated LORD.

22 But every woman will borrow of her neigh-
bor, and of her that sojourns in her house, arti-
cles of silver, and articles of gold, and clothing,
and you will put them on your sons, and on
your daughters—in this way you will plunder
the Egyptians."

Moses' Miraculous Signs

4 And Moses answered and said, "But they
will not believe me, nor listen to my voice.
For they will say, 'The LORD has not appeared
to you.' "
2 The LORD said to him, "What is that in your
hand?"
And he said, "A rod."
3 He said, "Throw it on the ground."
And he threw it on the ground, and it became
a serpent. Then Moses fled from it. 4 Then the
LORD said to Moses, "Put forth your hand and
take it by the tail." And he put forth his hand,
and caught it, and it became a rod in his hand.
5 "*This is so* that they may believe that the LORD,
the God of their fathers, the God of Abraham,
the God of Isaac, and the God of Jacob, has
appeared to you."
6 The LORD said furthermore to him, "Now put
your hand into your bosom." He put his hand
into his bosom, and when he took it out, his
hand was as leprous as snow.
7 He said, "Put your hand into your bosom
again." So he put his hand into his bosom
again and brought it out of his bosom, and it
was restored like his other flesh.
8 "If they will not believe you, nor listen to the
voice of the first sign, then they may believe
the voice of the latter sign. 9 But if they will not
believe also these two signs or listen to your
voice, then you shall take water from the river
and pour it on the dry land, and the water
which you take out of the river will become
blood on the dry land."
10 Then Moses said to the LORD, "O my Lord, I
am not eloquent, neither before nor since You
have spoken to Your servant. But I am slow of
speech, and of a slow tongue."
11 The LORD said to him, "Who has made
man's mouth? Or who made the dumb, or deaf,
or the seeing, or the blind? Have not I, the
LORD? 12 Now therefore go, and I will be with
your mouth and teach you what you must say."
13 He said, "O my Lord, send, I pray, by the
hand of whomever else You will send."
14 The anger of the LORD was inflamed against
Moses, and He said, "Is not Aaron the Levite
your brother? I know that he can speak well.
And also, he comes out to meet you, and when
he sees you, he will be glad in his heart. 15 You
shall speak to him and put the words in his
mouth, and I will be with your mouth, and with

3:22 Eze 39:10
4:1 Ex 3:18
4:2 Ex 4:17
4:5 Ex 19:9
4:6 Nu 12:10
4:7 2Ki 5:14
4:10 Ex 6:12
4:11 Ps 94:9
4:12 Isa 50:4
4:14 Ex 4:27
4:15 Isa 51:16
....
4:16 Ex 7:1–2
4:17 Ex 4:2
4:18 Ex 3:1
4:19 Ex 2:15
4:20 Ex 17:9
4:21 Ex 3:20
4:22 Jer 31:9
4:23 Ex 11:5
4:24 Ge 17:14
4:25 Jos 5:2–3
4:27 Ex 3:1
4:28 Ex 4:8–9
4:29 Ex 3:16
4:31 Ex 3:18
5:1 Ex 10:9
5:2 Ex 3:19

his mouth, and will teach you what you must
do. 16 What's more, he will be your spokesman
to the people, and he will be as a mouth for
you, and you will be as God to him. 17 You must
take this rod in your hand, with which you will
perform the signs."

Moses Returns to Egypt

18 Moses went and returned to Jethro his fa-
ther-in-law and said to him, "Please let me go
and return to my brothers who are in Egypt,
and see whether they be yet alive."
And Jethro said to Moses, "Go in peace."
19 The LORD said to Moses in Midian, "Go, re-
turn to Egypt, for all the men are dead who
sought your life." 20 Moses took his wife and
his sons and set them on a donkey, and he
returned to the land of Egypt. And Moses took
the rod of God in his hand.
21 The LORD said to Moses, "When you go to
return into Egypt, see that you do all those
wonders before Pharaoh, which I have put in
your hand, but I will harden his heart, so that
he shall not let the people go. 22 You shall say
to Pharaoh, 'Thus says the LORD: Israel is My
son, even My firstborn. 23 So I say to you, "Let
My son go, that he may serve Me. And if you
refuse to let him go, I will slay your son, even
your firstborn." ' "
24 At a lodging place on the way, the LORD met
him and sought to kill him. 25 Then Zipporah
took a sharp stone, and cut off the foreskin
of her son, and threw it at his feet, and said,
"Surely a bloody husband are you to me." 26 So
He let him go. Then she said, "A bloody hus-
band *you are*, because of the circumcision."
27 Now the LORD said to Aaron, "Go into the
wilderness to meet Moses." So he went, and
met him at the mount of God, and kissed him.
28 Moses told Aaron all the words of the LORD
who had sent him, and all the signs which He
had commanded him.
29 Moses and Aaron went and gathered to-
gether all the elders of the children of Israel.
30 And Aaron spoke all the words which the
LORD had spoken to Moses and did the signs in
the sight of the people. 31 And the people be-
lieved. And when they heard that the LORD had
visited the children of Israel and that He had
looked on their affliction, they bowed down
and worshipped.

Bricks Without Straw

5 And afterward Moses and Aaron went in
and said to Pharaoh, "Thus says the LORD,
the God of Israel, 'Let My people go, that they
may hold a feast to Me in the wilderness.' "
2 And Pharaoh said, "Who is the LORD that I
should obey His voice to let Israel go? I do not
know the LORD, nor will I let Israel go."

3 They said, "The God of the Hebrews has met with us. Let us go, we pray you, three days' journey into the wilderness, and sacrifice to the LORD our God, lest He fall upon us with pestilence or with the sword."

4 But the king of Egypt said to them, "Why do you, Moses and Aaron, take the people from their work? Get back to your labor." 5 Pharaoh said, "Look, the people of the land now are numerous, and you make them rest from their labor."

6 Pharaoh commanded the same day the taskmasters of the people and their officers, saying, 7 "You shall no more give the people straw to make brick, as before. Let them go and gather straw for themselves. 8 However, the quota of the bricks, which they were making previously, you shall lay upon them. You shall not diminish any of it. For they are idle. Therefore they cry out, saying, 'Let us go and sacrifice to our God.' 9 Let there be more work laid upon the men so that they may labor therein, and let them not regard deceptive words."

10 The taskmasters of the people and their officers went out, and they spoke to the people, saying, "Thus says Pharaoh, 'I will not give you straw. 11 Go, get straw where you can find it, yet nothing of your work shall be diminished.' " 12 So the people scattered abroad throughout all the land of Egypt to gather stubble for straw. 13 The taskmasters pushed them, saying, "Fulfill your works, your daily tasks, just as when there was straw." 14 The officers of the children of Israel, which Pharaoh's taskmasters had set over them, were beaten and were asked, and demanded, "Why have you not fulfilled your task in making brick both yesterday and today, as previously?"

15 Then the officers of the children of Israel came and cried to Pharaoh, saying, "Why do you deal this way with your servants? 16 There is no straw being given to your servants, and they say to us, 'Make brick.' And indeed, your servants are beaten, but the fault is in your *own* people."

17 But he said, "You are slackers! Slackers! Therefore you say, 'Let us go and do sacrifice to the LORD.' 18 Go therefore now and work, for there shall no straw be given you, yet shall you deliver the quota of bricks."

19 The officers of the children of Israel saw that they were in trouble, after it was said, "You shall not diminish anything from your bricks of your daily task." 20 Then they met Moses and Aaron, who stood in the way, as they came forth from Pharaoh. 21 And they said to them, "May the LORD look on you and judge, because you have made our scent stink in the estimation of Pharaoh and in the estimation of his servants, to put a sword in their hand to slay us."

God Promises Deliverance

22 Moses returned to the LORD, and said, "Lord, why have You caused trouble for this people? Why is it that You have sent me? 23 For since I came to Pharaoh to speak in Your name, he has done evil to this people; neither have You delivered Your people at all."

6 Then the LORD said to Moses, "Now you shall see what I will do to Pharaoh, for with a strong hand shall he let them go, and with a strong hand shall he drive them out of his land."

2 Then God spoke to Moses, and said to him, "I am the LORD, 3 and I appeared to Abraham, to Isaac, and to Jacob, by the name of God Almighty, but by My name, The LORD, I was not known to them. 4 I have also established My covenant with them, to give them the land of Canaan, the land of their pilgrimage, wherein they sojourned. 5 I have also heard the groaning of the children of Israel, whom the Egyptians keep in bondage, and I have remembered My covenant.

Stretch out Your arm and deliver me, and rid me of all bondage (Ex 6:6).

6 "Therefore say to the children of Israel: 'I am the LORD, and I will bring you out from under the burdens of the Egyptians, and I will rid you out of their bondage, and I will redeem you with a stretched-out arm and with great judgments. 7 And I will take you to Me for a people, and I will be to you a God. And you shall know that I am the LORD your God, who brings you out from under the burdens of the Egyptians. 8 I will bring you into the land, which I swore to give to Abraham, to Isaac, and to Jacob, and I will give it to you for a heritage. I am the LORD.' "

9 Moses spoke so to the children of Israel, but they did not listen to Moses on account of *their* anguish of spirit and for cruel bondage.

10 The LORD spoke to Moses, saying, 11 "Go in, tell Pharaoh king of Egypt to let the children of Israel go out of his land."

12 Moses spoke before the LORD, saying, "The children of Israel have not listened to me. How then shall Pharaoh listen to me, as I am of uncircumcised lips?"

13 And the LORD spoke to Moses and to Aaron, and gave them a command for the children of Israel, and for Pharaoh, king of Egypt, to bring the children of Israel out of the land of Egypt.

5:3 Ex 3:18
5:4 Ex 1:11
5:6 Ex 5:10
5:10 Ex 1:11
5:21 Ge 34:30

6:1 Ex 12:33
6:3 Ps 83:18
6:4 Ge 15:18
6:5 Ex 2:24
6:6 Dt 26:8
6:7 Dt 4:20
6:8 Ge 15:18
6:9 Ex 5:21
6:12 Ex 4:10

The Genealogy of Moses and Aaron

14 These are the heads of their fathers' houses:

The sons of Reuben the firstborn of Israel: Hanok, Pallu, Hezron, and Karmi. These are the families of Reuben.

15 The sons of Simeon: Jemuel, Jamin, Ohad, Jakin, Zohar, and Shaul the son of a Canaanite woman. These are the families of Simeon.

16 These are the names of the sons of Levi according to their generations: Gershon, Kohath, and Merari, and the years of the life of Levi were one hundred and thirty-seven years.

17 The sons of Gershon: Libni, and Shimei, according to their families.

18 The sons of Kohath: Amram, Izhar, Hebron, and Uzziel, and the years of the life of Kohath were one hundred and thirty-three years.

19 The sons of Merari: Mahli and Mushi.

These are the families of Levi according to their generations.

20 Now Amram married Jochebed his father's sister, and she bore him Aaron and Moses. And the years of the life of Amram were one hundred and thirty-seven years.

21 The sons of Izhar: Korah, Nepheg, and Zikri.

22 The sons of Uzziel: Mishael, Elzaphan, and Sithri.

23 Aaron took to himself Elisheba, daughter of Amminadab, sister of Nahshon, to wife; and she bore him Nadab, Abihu, Eleazar, and Ithamar.

24 The sons of Korah: Assir, Elkanah, and Abiasaph. These are the families of the Korahites.

25 Eleazar, Aaron's son, married one of the daughters of Putiel, and she bore him Phinehas.

These are the heads of the fathers of the Levites according to their families.

26 *It* was that Aaron and Moses to whom the LORD said, "Bring out the children of Israel from the land of Egypt according to their armies." 27 They are the ones who spoke to Pharaoh king of Egypt to bring out the children of Israel from Egypt. *It* was that Moses and Aaron.

Aaron to Speak for Moses

28 On the day when the LORD spoke to Moses in the land of Egypt, 29 the LORD spoke to Moses, saying, "I am the LORD. Speak to Pharaoh the king of Egypt all that I say to you."

30 However, Moses said before the LORD, "Listen! I am unskilled in speech, so how will Pharaoh listen to me?"

7 So the LORD said to Moses, "See, I have made you a god to Pharaoh, and Aaron your brother will be your prophet. 2 You shall speak all that I command you, and Aaron your brother shall tell Pharaoh to send the children of Israel out of his land. 3 But I will harden Pharaoh's heart and multiply My signs and My wonders in the land of Egypt. 4 Nevertheless, Pharaoh will not listen to you, so that I may lay My hand upon Egypt and bring forth My armies and My people, the children of Israel, out of the land of Egypt by great judgments. 5 And the Egyptians shall know that I am the LORD when I stretch forth My hand upon Egypt and bring out the children of Israel from among them."

6 So Moses and Aaron did *it*. Just as the LORD commanded them, so they did. 7 Moses was eighty years old, and Aaron was eighty-three years old when they spoke to Pharaoh.

Aaron's Rod Becomes a Snake

8 Now the LORD spoke to Moses and to Aaron, saying, 9 "When Pharaoh shall speak to you, saying, 'Show a miracle,' then you shall say to Aaron, 'Take your rod, and throw it before Pharaoh,' and it shall become a serpent."

10 So Moses and Aaron went to Pharaoh, and they did what the LORD had commanded. And Aaron threw down his rod before Pharaoh and before his servants, and it became a serpent. 11 Then Pharaoh also called the wise men and the sorcerers. Then the magicians of Egypt likewise performed with their secret arts. 12 For every man threw down his rod, and they became serpents. But Aaron's rod swallowed up their rods. 13 Nonetheless, Pharaoh's heart hardened so that he would not listen to them, just as the LORD had said.

The First Plague: Waters Turn to Blood

14 The LORD said to Moses, "Pharaoh's heart is hardened. He refuses to let the people go. 15 Go to Pharaoh in the morning as he goes out to the water, and you shall stand by the river's bank to meet him. You must take the rod which was turned to a serpent in your hand. 16 Then you are to say to him, 'The LORD, the God of the Hebrews, has sent me to you, saying, "Let My people go, so that they may serve Me in the wilderness." But up to this point you have not listened! 17 Thus says the LORD, "In this you shall know that I am the LORD: Indeed, I will strike the waters of the Nile with the rod that is in my hand, and they shall be turned to blood. 18 And the fish that are in the river shall die, and the river shall stink so that the Egyptians shall be weary of drinking the river's water." ' "

19 Then the LORD spoke to Moses, "Say to Aaron, 'Take your rod, and stretch out your hand over the waters of Egypt, over their rivers, over their canals, over their ponds, and over all their pools of water, so that they may become blood.

6:14 Ge 46:9
6:15 Ge 46:10
6:16 Ge 46:11
6:17 1Ch 6:17
6:18 1Ch 6:2
6:19 Nu 3:20
6:20 Ex 2:1–2
6:21 Nu 16:1
6:22 Lev 10:4
6:23 Ru 4:19–20
6:24 1Ch 6:22–23
6:25 Jos 24:33
6:26 Ex 7:4
6:29 Ex 6:11
6:30 Ex 6:12
7:2 Ex 4:15
7:3 Ex 4:21
7:4 Ex 6:6
7:5 Ex 7:17
7:6 Ex 7:2
7:7 Dt 31:2
7:9 Isa 7:11
7:10 Ex 4:3
7:11 Ex 7:22
7:13 Ex 4:21
7:15 Ex 8:20
7:16 Ex 3:18
7:17 Ex 4:9
7:18 Ex 7:24
7:19 Ex 8:5–6

And there will be blood throughout all the land of Egypt, both in *vessels* of wood, and in *vessels* of stone.' "

20 Moses and Aaron did so, just as the LORD commanded. And he lifted up the rod and struck the waters that were in the river, in the sight of Pharaoh, and in the sight of his servants, and all the waters that were in the river were turned to blood. 21 The fish that were in the river died, the river stank, and the Egyptians could not drink of the water of the river. Blood was everywhere throughout the land of Egypt.

22 Nevertheless, the magicians of Egypt did the same with their secret arts, and Pharaoh's heart was hardened, and he did not listen to them, as the LORD had said. 23 Then Pharaoh turned and went into his house, and he did not concern himself with this either. 24 So all the Egyptians dug around about the river for water to drink, because they could not drink of the water of the river.

25 Seven days passed after the LORD had struck the river.

The Second Plague: Frogs

8 Then the LORD said to Moses, "Go to Pharaoh and say to him, 'Thus says the LORD: Let My people go, so that they may serve Me. 2 But if you refuse to let them go, then I will plague all your borders with frogs. 3 And the river will swarm with frogs, which shall go up and come into your house, and into your bedchamber, and on your bed, and into the houses of your servants, and on your people, and into your ovens, and into your kneading troughs. 4 So the frogs shall come upon you, upon your people, and upon all your servants.' "

5 Then the LORD said to Moses, "Say to Aaron, 'Stretch forth your hand with your rod over the streams, over the rivers, and over the ponds, and cause frogs to come up on the land of Egypt.' "

6 Aaron stretched out his hand over the waters of Egypt, and the frogs came up, and covered the land of Egypt. 7 The magicians did the same with their secret arts and brought up frogs upon the land of Egypt.

8 Then Pharaoh called for Moses and Aaron, and said, "Entreat the LORD, that He may take away the frogs from me, and from my people, and I will let the people go, so that they may sacrifice to the LORD."

9 Moses said to Pharaoh, "Glory yourself over me: When shall I entreat for you, your servants, and your people, to destroy the frogs from you and your houses, that they may remain in the river only?"

10 And he said, "Tomorrow."

Then he said, "Be it according to your word, in order that you may know that there is no one like the LORD our God. 11 The frogs shall depart from you, and from your houses, from your servants, and from your people. They shall remain in the river only."

12 Moses and Aaron went out from Pharaoh, and Moses cried out to the LORD concerning the frogs which he had brought against Pharaoh. 13 Then the LORD did according to the word of Moses. And the frogs died out of the houses, the villages, and the fields. 14 So they gathered them together in heaps, and the land stank. 15 But when Pharaoh saw that there was relief, he hardened his heart and did not listen to them, as the LORD had said.

The Third Plague: Gnats

16 Then the LORD said to Moses, "Say to Aaron, 'Stretch out your rod, and strike the dust of the land, so that it may become gnats throughout all the land of Egypt.' " 17 They did so, for Aaron stretched out his hand with his rod and smote the dust of the earth, and it became gnats on man and on beast. All the dust of the land became gnats throughout all the land of Egypt. 18 Then the magicians tried with their secret arts to bring forth gnats, but they could not, so there were gnats upon man and beast.

19 Then the magicians said to Pharaoh, "This is the finger of God." Nevertheless, Pharaoh's heart was hardened, and he did not listen to them, just as the LORD had said.

The Fourth Plague: Flies

20 So the LORD said to Moses, "Rise up early in the morning and stand before Pharaoh as he comes forth to the water and say to him, 'Thus says the LORD: Let My people go, so that they may serve Me. 21 Otherwise, if you will not let My people go, indeed I will send swarms *of flies* on you, and on your servants, and on your people, and into your houses. And the houses of the Egyptians shall be full of swarms *of flies* and also the ground wherever they are.

22 " 'I will in that day set apart the land of Goshen, in which My people dwell, so that no swarms of flies shall be there, in order that you may know that I am the LORD in the midst of the earth. 23 I will put a division between My people and your people. Tomorrow this sign will happen.' "

24 The LORD did so, and great swarms *of flies* came into the house of Pharaoh, and into his servants' houses, and into all the land of Egypt. The land was corrupted because of the swarms *of flies*.

25 Pharaoh called for Moses and Aaron, and said, "Go, sacrifice to your God in the land."

7:20 Ps 78:44
7:21 Ex 7:18
7:22 Ex 7:11
8:1 Ex 3:18
8:5 Ex 7:19
8:6 Ps 78:45
8:7 Ex 7:11
8:8 Ex 9:28
8:10 Ex 9:14

8:17 Ps 105:31
8:18 Ex 7:11
8:19 Ps 8:3
8:20 Ex 7:15
8:22 Ex 9:4
8:24 Ps 78:45
8:25 Ex 8:8

26 Moses said, "It is not right to do so, for what we shall sacrifice to the LORD our God would be an abomination to the Egyptians. If we shall sacrifice what is an abomination of the Egyptians before their eyes, will they not stone us? 27 We will go three days' journey into the wilderness, and then we will sacrifice to the LORD our God, as He shall command us."

28 Pharaoh said, "I will let you go, that you may sacrifice to the LORD your God in the wilderness. Only you shall not go very far away. Make entreaty for me."

29 Moses said, "Indeed, I am leaving you, and I will plead with the LORD that the swarms *of flies* may depart from Pharaoh, from his servants, and from his people tomorrow. But let not Pharaoh deal deceitfully any more by not letting the people go to sacrifice to the LORD."

30 Moses went away from Pharaoh and entreated the LORD. 31 Then the LORD did according to the word of Moses, and He removed the swarms *of flies* from Pharaoh, from his servants, and from his people. Not one remained. 32 Nevertheless, Pharaoh hardened his heart at this time also, nor would he let the people go.

The Fifth Plague: Livestock Die

9 Then the LORD said to Moses, "Go to Pharaoh, and speak to him, 'Thus says the LORD, the God of the Hebrews: Let My people go, so that they may serve Me. 2 For if you refuse to let *them* go and continue holding them, 3 indeed, the hand of the LORD will be upon your livestock which are in the field, upon the horses, upon the donkeys, upon the camels, upon the oxen, and upon the sheep. There shall be a very grievous pestilence. 4 The LORD shall separate between the livestock of Israel and the livestock of Egypt, and nothing shall die of all that belongs to the children of Israel.' "

5 So the LORD appointed a set time, saying, "Tomorrow the LORD shall do this thing in the land." 6 Then the LORD did this thing the next day, so that all the livestock of Egypt died, but not one of the livestock of the children of Israel died. 7 Pharaoh sent, and there was not one of the livestock of the children of Israel dead. And the heart of Pharaoh was hardened, so that he did not let the people go.

The Sixth Plague: Boils

8 Then the LORD said to Moses and to Aaron, "Take for yourselves handfuls of ashes from a kiln, and let Moses toss it toward the heavens in the sight of Pharaoh. 9 It shall become fine dust over all the land of Egypt and shall be a boil breaking forth with blisters upon man and beast, throughout all the land of Egypt."

10 So they took the ashes from a kiln and stood before Pharaoh. Then Moses tossed it up toward the heavens, and it became a boil breaking forth with blisters upon man and beast. 11 The magicians could not stand before Moses because of the boils, for the boils were upon the magicians and upon all the Egyptians. 12 Moreover, the LORD hardened the heart of Pharaoh, so that he did not listen to them, just as the LORD had spoken to Moses.

The Seventh Plague: Hail

13 Then the LORD said to Moses, "Rise up early in the morning, and stand before Pharaoh, and say to him, 'Thus says the LORD, the God of the Hebrews: Let My people go, so that they may serve Me. 14 For I will at this time send all My plagues upon you and your servants and your people, so that you may know that there is none like Me in all the earth. 15 For by now I could have stretched out My hand, so that I might strike you and your people with pestilence, and you would be cut off from the earth. 16 But, indeed, for this cause I have raised you up, in order to show in you My power and so that My name may be declared throughout all the earth. 17 Still, you exalt yourself against My people by forbidding them to go. 18 Certainly, tomorrow about this time I will cause it to rain a very severe hail, such as has not happened in Egypt since it was founded until now. 19 Send therefore now and bring your livestock and all that you have in the field to safety. Every man and beast which shall be found in the field and not brought home when the hail comes down upon them will die.' "

20 He that feared the word of the LORD among the servants of Pharaoh made his servants and his livestock flee into the houses. 21 But he that failed to regard the word of the LORD left his servants and his livestock in the field.

22 So the LORD said to Moses, "Stretch forth your hand toward the heavens, so that there may be hail in all the land of Egypt, upon man and beast, and upon every herb of the field, throughout the land of Egypt." 23 Moses stretched forth his rod toward the heavens, and the LORD sent thunder and hail, and fire ran along upon the ground. So the LORD rained hail upon the land of Egypt. 24 So there was hail, and fire mingled with the hail. It was so severe that there had been none like it in all the land of Egypt since it became a nation. 25 The hail struck all the land of Egypt, all that was in the field, both man and beast, and the hail struck every herb of the field and broke every tree of the field. 26 Only in the land of Goshen, where the children of Israel *were*, was there no hail.

8:26 Ge 43:32
8:27 Ex 3:18
8:28 Ex 8:8
8:29 Ex 8:15
8:30 Ex 8:12
8:32 Ex 8:15
9:1 Ex 8:1
9:2 Ex 8:2
9:3 Ex 7:4
9:4 Ex 8:22
9:6 Ps 78:48
9:7 Ex 7:14
9:9 Dt 28:27

....

9:12 Ex 4:21
9:13 Ex 8:20
9:14 Ex 8:10
9:15 Ex 3:20
9:16 Ro 9:17
9:22 Rev 16:21
9:23 Jos 10:11
9:26 Ex 9:4

27 Then Pharaoh sent and called for Moses and Aaron, and said to them, "I have sinned this time. The LORD is righteous, and I and my people are wicked. 28 Entreat the LORD, for there has been enough of God's mighty thunder and hail, and I will let you go, and you shall stay no longer."

29 Moses said to him, "As soon as I am gone out of the city, I will spread out my hands to the LORD. The thunder shall cease, and there shall no longer be any more hail, so that you may know that the earth is the LORD's. 30 But as for you and your servants, I know that you will not yet fear the LORD God."

31 Now the flax and the barley were struck, for the barley was in the ear, and the flax was in bud. 32 But the wheat and the spelt were not struck, for they grow up later.

33 So Moses went out of the city from Pharaoh and spread out his hands to the LORD, and the thunders and hail ceased, and the rain was no longer poured upon the earth. 34 However, when Pharaoh saw that the rain and the hail and the thunders were ceased, he sinned yet more, and hardened his heart, he and his servants. 35 The heart of Pharaoh hardened, and he would not let the children of Israel go, just as the LORD had spoken by Moses.

The Eighth Plague: Locusts

10 Then the LORD said to Moses, "Go to Pharaoh, for I have hardened his heart and the heart of his servants, that I might show these signs of Mine before him, 2 in order that you may tell in the hearing of your son, and of your son's son, what things I have done in Egypt, and My signs which I have done among them, that you may know that I am the LORD."

3 Moses and Aaron came to Pharaoh and said to him, "Thus says the LORD, the God of the Hebrews, 'How long will you refuse to humble yourself before Me? Let My people go, that they may serve Me. 4 For if you refuse to let My people go, indeed, tomorrow I will bring locusts into your territory. 5 And they shall cover the face of the earth, such that no one will be able to see the earth. What's more, they shall eat the remainder of that which has escaped—that which remains to you from the hail—and shall eat every tree which grows for you out of the field. 6 And they shall fill your houses, and the houses of all your servants, and the houses of all the Egyptians—which neither your fathers, nor your fathers' fathers have seen since the day that they were on the earth until this day.' " And he turned and went out from Pharaoh.

7 Then Pharaoh's servants said to him, "How long shall this man be a snare to us? Let the men go, so that they may serve the LORD their God. Do you not yet know that Egypt is destroyed?"

8 So Moses and Aaron were brought back to Pharaoh, and he said to them, "Go, serve the LORD your God! But who are the ones that shall go?"

9 And Moses said, "We will go with our young and our old, with our sons and our daughters, with our flocks and our herds will we go, for *we must hold* a feast to the LORD."

10 Then he said to them, "The LORD indeed be with you when I let you and your little ones go. Beware, for evil is before you. 11 Not so! Go now, you that are men, and serve the LORD, for that is what you desire." Then they were driven out from Pharaoh's presence.

12 Then the LORD said to Moses, "Stretch out your hand over the land of Egypt for the locusts, so that they may come up upon the land of Egypt and eat every herb of the land, even all that the hail has left."

13 So Moses stretched forth his rod over the land of Egypt; then the LORD brought an east wind upon the land all that day and all that night. And when it was morning, the east wind brought the locusts. 14 The locusts went up over all the land of Egypt and settled down in all the territory of Egypt. They were very grievous. Never before had there been such locusts as they, nor would there be such ever again. 15 For they covered the face of the whole earth, so that the land was darkened, and they ate every herb of the land, and all the fruit of the trees which the hail had left. As a result, nothing green remained there in the trees or herbs of the field, through all the land of Egypt.

16 Then Pharaoh called for Moses and Aaron in haste and said, "I have sinned against the LORD, your God, and against you. 17 Now therefore please forgive my sin only this once, and entreat the LORD your God, so that He may take away from me this death only."

18 So he went out from Pharaoh and prayed to the LORD. 19 Then the LORD turned a mighty strong west wind, which took away the locusts and threw them into the Red Sea. Not one locust remained in all the territory of Egypt. 20 But the LORD hardened Pharaoh's heart, so that he would not let the children of Israel go.

The Ninth Plague: Darkness

21 Then the LORD said to Moses, "Stretch out your hand toward the heavens, so that there may be darkness over the land of Egypt, a darkness *which* may be felt." 22 So Moses stretched forth his hand toward the heavens, and there was a thick darkness in all the land of Egypt for three days. 23 They did not see one

9:27 Ex 10:16
9:28 Ex 8:8
9:29 1Ki 8:22
9:30 Isa 26:10
9:31 Ru 1:22
9:33 Ex 9:29
9:34 Ex 7:14
9:35 Ex 4:21
10:1 Ex 4:21
10:2 Ex 13:14
10:3 1Ki 21:29
10:4 Rev 9:3
10:5 Ex 9:32
10:6 Ex 8:3
10:7 Ex 23:33

....

10:8 Ex 10:24
10:11 Ex 10:28
10:12 Ex 7:19
10:14 Ps 78:46
10:15 Ex 10:5
10:16 Ex 9:27
10:17 Ex 8:8
10:19 Joel 2:20
10:20 Ex 4:21
10:22 Ps 105:28
10:23 Ex 8:22

another; nor did anyone rise from his place for three days. But all the children of Israel had light in their dwellings.

24 Then Pharaoh called to Moses and said, "Go, serve the LORD. Only let your flocks and your herds be detained. Even let your little ones also go with you."

25 But Moses said, "You must also give us sacrifices and burnt offerings, so that we may sacrifice to the LORD our God. 26 Our livestock will go with us also. Not a hoof will be left behind, for we must take of them to serve the LORD our God. And we do not know with what we must serve the LORD, until we get there."

27 But the LORD hardened Pharaoh's heart, and he would not let them go. 28 So Pharaoh said to him, "Get away from me! Watch yourself, do not see my face anymore; for in the day you see my face you shall die."

29 Then Moses said, "As you wish. I will never see your face again."

Warning of the Final Plague

11 Now the LORD said to Moses, "I will still bring one plague more upon Pharaoh, and upon Egypt. Afterwards he will let you go from here. When he lets you go, he shall surely thrust you out from here altogether. 2 Speak now in the hearing of the people, and let every man borrow of his neighbor and every woman of her neighbor, articles of silver and articles of gold." 3 Then the LORD gave the people favor in the sight of the Egyptians. Moreover, the man Moses was very great in the land of Egypt, in the sight of Pharaoh's servants, and in the sight of the people.

4 Moses said, "Thus says the LORD, 'About midnight I will go out into the midst of Egypt, 5 and all the firstborn in the land of Egypt shall die, from the firstborn of Pharaoh who sits on his throne, even to the firstborn of the maidservant that is behind the mill, as well as all the firstborn of beasts. 6 Then there shall be a great cry throughout all the land of Egypt, such as there has never been, nor shall ever be again. 7 But against any of the children of Israel a dog will not even move his tongue, against man or beast, in order that you may know how that the LORD distinguishes between Egypt and Israel.' 8 Then all these your servants shall come down to me and bow themselves to me, saying, 'Get out, and all the people who follow you!' After that I will go out." And he went out from Pharaoh in great anger.

9 Then the LORD said to Moses, "Pharaoh shall not listen to you so that My wonders may be multiplied in the land of Egypt." 10 So Moses and Aaron did all these wonders before Pharaoh, and the LORD hardened Pharaoh's heart, and he would not let the children of Israel go out of his land.

The Passover Instituted

Lev 23:4–8; Nu 28:16–25; Dt 16:1–8

12 Now the LORD spoke to Moses and Aaron in the land of Egypt, saying: 2 This month shall be the beginning of months to you. It shall be the first month of the year to you. 3 Speak to all the congregation of Israel, saying: On the tenth day of this month every man shall take a lamb, according to the house of their fathers, a lamb for a household. 4 And if the household be too little for the lamb, let him and his neighbor next to his house take it according to the number of the persons; according to what each man shall eat, divide the lamb. 5 Your lamb shall be without blemish, a male of the first year. You shall take it out from the sheep, or from the goats. 6 You shall keep it up until the fourteenth day of the same month, and then the whole assembly of the congregation of Israel shall kill it in the evening. 7 They shall take some of the blood and put it on the two side posts and on the upper doorpost of the houses in which they shall eat it. 8 They shall eat the flesh on that night, roasted with fire, and they shall eat it with unleavened bread and bitter herbs. 9 Do not eat it raw, nor boiled at all with water, but roasted with fire, its head with its legs and its entrails. 10 And you shall let nothing of it remain until the morning, but that of it which remains until the morning you shall burn with fire. 11 In this way shall you eat it: with your waist girded, your sandals on your feet, and your staff in your hand. So you shall eat it in haste. It is the LORD's Passover.

12 For I will pass through the land of Egypt this night and will smite all the firstborn in the land of Egypt, both man and beast, and against all the gods of Egypt I will execute judgment. I am the LORD. 13 The blood shall be to you for a sign on the houses where you are. And when I see the blood, I will pass over you, and the plague shall not be upon you to destroy *you* when I smite the land of Egypt.

14 This day shall be a memorial to you, and you shall keep it as a feast to the LORD. Throughout your generations you shall keep it a feast by an eternal ordinance. 15 Seven days you shall eat unleavened bread. On the first day you shall put away leaven out of your houses, for whoever eats leavened bread from the first day until the seventh day, that person shall be cut off from Israel. 16 On the first day there shall be a holy convocation, and on the seventh day there shall be a holy convocation for you. No manner of work shall be done on them; but that which every man must eat—that only may be prepared for you.

10:24 Ex 10:8–10
10:27 Ex 10:20
10:29 Heb 11:27
11:2 Ex 3:22
11:3 Ex 3:21
11:4 Ex 12:29
11:5 Ps 78:51
11:6 Ex 12:30
11:8 Ex 12:31–33
11:9 Ex 7:3–4
11:10 Ex 4:21

....

12:2 Dt 16:1
12:6 Lev 23:5
12:8 Ex 34:25
12:9 Ex 12:8
12:10 Ex 23:18
12:11 Ex 12:27
12:12 Ex 6:2
12:13 Heb 11:28
12:14 Ex 12:17
12:15 Dt 16:3
12:16 Lev 23:7–8

17 You shall observe the Feast of Unleavened
Bread. For on this very day I brought your
armies out of the land of Egypt. Therefore you
shall observe this day throughout your gener-
ations as an ordinance forever. 18 In the first
month, on the fourteenth day of the month at
evening, you shall eat unleavened bread until
the twenty-first day of the month at evening.
19 Seven days shall there be no leaven found
in your houses, for whoever eats that which
is leavened, that person shall be cut off from
the congregation of Israel, whether he be a
stranger or born in the land. 20 You shall eat
nothing leavened. In all your dwellings you
shall eat unleavened bread.

> The destroyer cannot come into my life or family, in the name of Jesus (Ex 12:23).

21 Then Moses called for all the elders of Is-
rael and said to them, "Draw out and take for
yourselves a lamb according to your families
and kill the Passover *lamb*. 22 You shall take a
bunch of hyssop, and dip it in the blood that is
in the basin, and apply the lintel and the two
side posts with the blood that is in the basin,
and none of you shall go out from the door of
his house until the morning. 23 For the Lord will
pass through to kill the Egyptians. And when
He sees the blood upon the lintel and on the
two side posts, the Lord will pass over the door
and will not permit the destroyer to come to
your houses to kill *you*.
24 "And you shall observe this thing as an
ordinance to you and to your sons forever.
25 When you enter the land which the Lord
will give you, according as He has promised,
that you shall observe this service. 26 And when
your children shall say to you, 'What does this
service mean to you?' 27 that you shall say, 'It
is the sacrifice of the Lord's Passover, who
passed over the houses of the children of Is-
rael in Egypt, when He smote the Egyptians,
and delivered our households.'" And the peo-
ple bowed down and worshipped. 28 Then the
children of Israel went and did *so*. Just as the
Lord had commanded Moses and Aaron, so
they did.

The Tenth Plague: Death of the Firstborn

29 At midnight the Lord smote all the firstborn
in the land of Egypt, from the firstborn of Pha-
raoh that sat on his throne to the firstborn of
the captive who was in the dungeon and all
the firstborn of livestock. 30 Pharaoh rose up
in the night, he and all his servants and all the
Egyptians, and there was a great cry in Egypt,
for there was not a house where there was not
someone dead.

The Exodus

31 Then he called for Moses and Aaron at
night and said, "Rise up, and get out from
among my people, both you and the children
of Israel, and go, serve the Lord, as you have
said. 32 Also take your flocks and your herds,
as you have said, and be gone, and bless me
also."

12:17 Ex 13:3
12:19 Ex 12:15
12:21 Ex 12:3
12:22 Heb 11:28
12:23 Heb 11:28
12:24 Ex 12:14
12:26 Ex 13:14–15
12:27 Ex 4:31
12:29 Ex 4:23
12:30 Ex 11:6
12:31 Ex 10:9
12:32 Ex 10:26

SPIRITLED WOMAN

COUNSEL FROM THE SPIRIT BASICS

Our Fear Protection

How do we keep from being afraid? Very simply! In Psalm 91 God gives us instructions to quiet the fear that rises in our hearts: "You shall not be afraid of the terror by night, nor of the arrow that flies by day" (v. 5). These words also address the anxiety that comes the night before battle.

Fear comes when we think we are responsible for bringing about this protection ourselves. Too often we think, "Oh, if I can just believe hard enough, maybe I'll be protected." That's wrong thinking! Protection has already been provided, whether we receive it or not. Faith is simply the *choice* to receive what Jesus has already done. The Bible gives classic examples of how to deal with terror.

The answer is in the blood of Jesus. Exodus 12:23 tells us that when Israel put blood on the door facings, the destroyer could not come in. The animal blood they used serves as a type and shadow, or a picture of the blood of Jesus that ratifies our better protection—under our better covenant (Heb 8:6).

When we confess aloud, "I am protected by the blood of Jesus"—and believe it, the devil literally cannot come in. Remember, Psalm 91:2 tells us, "I will say of the Lord, 'He is my refuge and my fortress.'" It is heart and mouth—believing with our hearts and confessing with our mouths.

Peggy Joyce Ruth

33 The Egyptians urged the people, so that
they might send them out of the land in haste,
for they said, “We all will be dead.” 34 So the
people took their dough before it was leav-
ened, *with* their kneading troughs being bound
up in their clothes on their shoulders. 35 Now
the children of Israel did according to the word
of Moses, and they requested of the Egyptians
articles of silver and articles of gold, and cloth-
ing. 36 And the LORD gave the people favor in
the sight of the Egyptians, so that they gave
them *what they requested*. Thus they plundered
the Egyptians.

37 Then the children of Israel journeyed from
Rameses to Sukkoth, about six hundred thou-
sand men on foot, besides children. 38 A mixed
multitude also went up with them along with
flocks and herds, a large amount of livestock.
39 They baked unleavened cakes of the dough
which they brought forth out of Egypt, for it
was not leavened because they were driven
out of Egypt and could not linger, nor had they
prepared for themselves any food.

40 Now the sojourning of the children of
Israel who lived in Egypt was four hundred
and thirty years. 41 And at the end of the four
hundred and thirty years, on the very day, all
the hosts of the LORD went out from the land of
Egypt. 42 It is a night to be observed to the LORD
for bringing them out from the land of Egypt.
This is that night for the LORD to be observed by
all the children of Israel in their generations.

The Ordinance of Passover

43 So the LORD said to Moses and Aaron: This
is the ordinance of the Passover:

No foreigner may eat of it. 44 But every man’s
servant bought with money, when you have
circumcised him, may eat it. 45 A foreigner or
a hired servant shall not eat it.

46 In one house shall it be eaten. You shall not
carry any of the flesh outside of the house, nor
shall you break a bone of it. 47 All the congre-
gation of Israel shall keep it.

48 Now when a stranger sojourns with you
and keeps the Passover to the LORD, let all his
males be circumcised, and then let him come
near and keep it. And he shall be as one that is
born in the land. However, no uncircumcised
person shall eat of it. 49 The same law shall
apply to him that is a native and to the stranger
who sojourns among you.

50 So all the children of Israel did it. They
did just as the LORD commanded Moses and
Aaron. 51 And that same day the LORD brought
the children of Israel out of the land of Egypt
by their hosts.

12:33 Ps 105:38
12:37 Ex 38:26
12:38 Nu 11:4
12:39 Ex 6:1
12:40 Ge 15:13
12:42 Dt 16:1–6
12:43 Ex 12:48
12:44 Ge 17:12–13
12:45 Lev 22:10
12:46 Nu 9:12
12:47 Ex 12:6
12:48 Nu 9:14
12:49 Nu 15:15–16
12:51 Ex 12:41

....

13:2 Nu 3:13
13:3 Ex 6:1
13:4 Ex 23:15
13:5 Ex 3:8
13:6 Ex 12:15–20
13:7 Ex 12:19
13:8 Ex 13:14
13:9 Dt 6:8
13:10 Ex 12:14
13:12 Nu 18:15
13:13 Ex 34:20
13:14 Jos 4:6
13:15 Ex 12:29
13:16 Ex 13:9

Consecration of the Firstborn

13 Then the LORD spoke to Moses, saying:
2 Sanctify unto Me all the firstborn, the
firstborn of every womb among the children
of Israel, both of man and of beast. It is Mine.

The Feast of Unleavened Bread

3 Moses said to the people, “Remember this
day, in which you came out from Egypt, out of
the house of bondage, for by strength of hand
the LORD brought you out from this place. Noth-
ing leavened shall be eaten. 4 On this day, you
are going out, in the month of Aviv. 5 It shall be
when the LORD brings you into the land of the
Canaanites and the Hittites and the Amorites
and the Hivites and the Jebusites, which He
swore to your fathers to give you, a land flow-
ing with milk and honey, that you shall keep
this ceremony in this month. 6 Seven days you
shall eat unleavened bread, and on the seventh
day shall be a feast to the LORD. 7 Unleavened
bread shall be eaten seven days. And there
shall be no leavened bread seen among you,
nor shall there be leaven seen among you in
all your borders. 8 You shall declare to your son
on that day, saying, ‘This is done because of
that which the LORD did for me when I came
forth out of Egypt.’ 9 It shall be as a sign to
you on your hand and as a memorial on your
forehead, in order that the LORD’s law may be
in your mouth. For with a strong hand the LORD
brought you out of Egypt. 10 You shall, there-
fore, keep this ordinance at its appointed time
from year to year.

The Law of the Firstborn

11 “It shall be when the LORD brings you into
the land of the Canaanites, just as He swore to
you and to your fathers, and shall give it you,
12 that you shall set apart to the LORD the first
offspring of every womb and the first offspring
of every beast which you have. The males shall
be the LORD’s. 13 But every first offspring of a
donkey you shall redeem with a lamb. And if
you do not redeem it, then you shall break its
neck, and all the firstborn of man among your
sons you shall redeem.

14 “It shall be when your son asks you in
time to come, saying, ‘What is this?’ that you
shall say to him, ‘With a strong hand the LORD
brought us out from Egypt, from the house
of bondage. 15 And when Pharaoh stubbornly
refused to let us go, that the LORD killed all
the firstborn in the land of Egypt, both the
firstborn of man, and the firstborn of beast.
Therefore, I sacrifice to the LORD the first male
offspring of every womb, but all the firstborn
of my sons I redeem.’ 16 It shall be as a sign on
your hand and as frontlets on your forehead,

for with a strong hand the LORD brought us out of Egypt."

The Route of the Exodus

17 Now when Pharaoh had let the people go, God did not lead them through the way of the land of the Philistines, although it was nearby. For God said, "Lest the people change their minds when they see war, and they return to Egypt." 18 Therefore, God led the people around, *through* the way of the wilderness to the Red Sea, and the children of Israel went up prepared for war out of the land of Egypt.

19 Moses took the bones of Joseph with him, for he had made the children of Israel solemnly swear, saying, "God will surely attend to you, and you shall carry my bones away from here with you."

20 They took their journey from Sukkoth and camped in Etham, on the edge of the wilderness. 21 The LORD went before them by day in a pillar of cloud to lead them *along* the way, and by night in a pillar of fire, to give them light, so that they might travel by day and by night. 22 He did not remove the pillar of cloud by day or the pillar of fire by night from before the people.

Crossing the Red Sea

14 Now the LORD spoke to Moses, saying: 2 Speak to the children of Israel, so that they turn and camp before Pi Hahiroth, between Migdol and the sea, before Baal Zephon. Opposite it you shall camp by the sea. 3 For Pharaoh will say of the children of Israel, "They are confused in the land. The wilderness has shut them in." 4 So I will harden Pharaoh's heart, so that he shall pursue them. And I will be honored because of Pharaoh and because of all his army, so that the Egyptians may know that I am the LORD. And they did so.

5 When it was told the king of Egypt that the people fled, the heart of Pharaoh and of his servants was turned against the people, and they said, "Why have we done this, that we have let Israel go from serving us?" 6 So he made ready his chariot and took his people with him. 7 And he took six hundred select chariots, and all the chariots of Egypt, and officers over every one of them. 8 The LORD hardened the heart of Pharaoh king of Egypt, and he pursued after the children of Israel. However, the children of Israel went out with confidence. 9 But the Egyptians pursued after them, all the horses and chariots of Pharaoh, and his horsemen, and his army, and overtook them camping by the sea, beside Pi Hahiroth, before Baal Zephon.

10 When Pharaoh drew near, the children of Israel lifted up their eyes, and indeed, the Egyptians were marching after them, and they were extremely terrified, so the children of Israel cried out to the LORD. 11 Then they said to Moses, "Is it because there were no graves in Egypt that you have taken us away to die in the wilderness? Why have you dealt with us in this way, bringing us out of Egypt? 12 Is not this the word that we spoke to you in Egypt, saying, 'Let us alone, that we may serve the Egyptians'? For it would have been better for us to serve the Egyptians than to die in the wilderness."

13 But Moses said to the people, "Fear not! Stand firm! And see the salvation of the LORD, which He will show you today. For the Egyptians whom you have seen today, you shall never see again. 14 The LORD shall fight for you, while you hold your peace."

15 The LORD said to Moses, "Why do you cry out to Me? Speak to the children of Israel, so that they go forward. 16 And as for you, lift up your rod, and stretch out your hand over the sea, and divide it; then the children of Israel shall go on dry ground through the midst of the sea. 17 As for Me, surely, I will harden the hearts of the Egyptians, so that they shall follow them, and I will be honored through Pharaoh, through all his army, his chariots, and his horsemen. 18 Then the Egyptians shall know that I am the LORD when I am honored through Pharaoh, his chariots, and his horsemen."

19 Then the angel of God, which went before the camp of Israel, moved and went behind them, and the pillar of the cloud moved before them and stood behind them. 20 So it came between the camp of the Egyptians and the camp of Israel, and there was a cloud and darkness to them, but it gave light by night. Therefore, the one did not come near the other the entire night.

21 Then Moses stretched out his hand over the sea, and the LORD caused the sea to go back by a strong east wind all that night, and made the sea dry land, so that the waters were divided. 22 The children of Israel went into the midst of the sea on the dry ground, and the waters were a wall unto them on their right hand, and on their left.

23 Then the Egyptians pursued and went in after them into the midst of the sea, even all Pharaoh's horses, his chariots, and his horsemen. 24 And in the morning watch the LORD looked down on the army of the Egyptians through the pillar of fire and of the cloud and threw the camp of the Egyptians into confusion. 25 He removed their chariot wheels, so that they drove them with difficulty, and the Egyptians said, "Let us flee from the face of

13:17 Nu 14:1–4
13:19 Jos 24:32
13:21 Dt 1:33
14:2 Jer 44:1
14:4 Ex 7:5
14:5 Ps 105:25
14:7 Ex 15:4
14:8 Nu 33:3
14:9 Ex 15:9
14:10 Jos 24:7

14:11 Ps 106:7–8
14:12 Ex 5:21
14:13 Ex 14:30
14:14 Ex 14:25
14:16 Ex 4:17
14:17 Ex 14:4
14:18 Ex 7:5
14:21 Ex 15:8
14:22 Ex 15:19
14:23 Ex 14:17
14:25 Ex 14:14

Israel, for the LORD is fighting for them against
Egypt."
26 Then the LORD said to Moses, "Stretch out
your hand over the sea, so that the waters
may come back upon the Egyptians, upon
their chariots, and their horsemen." 27 So Mo-
ses stretched forth his hand over the sea, and
the sea returned to its normal place when the
morning appeared, while the Egyptians fled
against it, so the LORD overthrew the Egyptians
in the midst of the sea. 28 The waters returned
and covered the chariots, and the horsemen,
and all the host of Pharaoh that came into the
sea after them. There remained not so much
as one of them.
29 But the children of Israel walked on dry
land in the midst of the sea. And the waters
were a wall to them on their right hand and
on their left. 30 Thus the LORD saved Israel that
day from the hand of the Egyptians, and Israel
saw the Egyptians dead upon the seashore.
31 When Israel saw the great power which the
LORD used upon the Egyptians, the people
feared the LORD, and they believed in the LORD
and in His servant Moses.

A Song of Moses

15 Then Moses and the children of Israel
sang this song to the LORD and spoke,
saying:

"I will sing to the LORD,
for He has triumphed gloriously!
He has thrown the horse and his rider
into the sea!
2 The LORD is my strength and song,
and He has become my salvation.
He is my God, and I will praise Him;
my father's God, and I will exalt Him.
3 The LORD is a man of war;
the LORD is His name.

> Let every pharaoh who would pursue my life be drowned in the sea (Ex 15:4).

4 Pharaoh's chariots and his army
He has thrown into the sea;
his chosen captains also
are drowned in the Red Sea.
5 The depths have covered them;
they sank to the bottom like a stone.

6 "Your right hand, O LORD,
is glorious in power.
Your right hand, O LORD,
shatters the enemy.
7 In the greatness of Your excellence,
You overthrow those who rise up against
You.
You send out Your wrath;
it consumes them like stubble.
8 With the blast of Your nostrils
the waters were gathered together.
The flowing waters stood upright as a
heap;
and the depths were congealed in the
heart of the sea.
9 "The enemy said,
'I will pursue. I will overtake.
I will divide the spoil;
my lust shall be satisfied upon them.
I will draw my sword,
my hand shall destroy them.'
10 You blew with Your wind,
and the sea covered them;
they sank like lead
in the mighty waters.
11 "Who is like You, O LORD, among the gods?
Who is like You,
glorious in holiness,
fearful in praises,
doing wonders?
12 You stretched out Your right hand,
and the earth swallowed them.

13 "In Your mercy You have led
the people whom You have redeemed;
You have guided them by Your strength
to Your holy dwelling.
14 The peoples have heard and are afraid;
sorrow has taken hold on the inhabitants
of Philistia.
15 Then the chiefs of Edom were amazed;
the mighty men of Moab, trembling
takes hold of them;
all the inhabitants of Canaan are melted
away.
16 Fear and dread fall upon them;
by the greatness of Your arm
they are as still as a stone,
until Your people pass over, O LORD,
until the people whom You have
purchased pass over.
17 You shall bring them in, and plant them
on the mountain of Your inheritance,
in the place, O LORD, which You have made
for Your dwelling,
in the sanctuary, O LORD, which Your
hands have established.
18 The LORD will reign
forever and ever."
19 For the horses of Pharaoh went in with
his chariots and with his horsemen into the
sea, and the LORD brought back the waters of
the sea upon them, but the children of Israel
walked on dry land in the midst of the sea.

14:26 Ex 14:16
14:27 Jos 4:18
14:29 Ex 14:22
14:30 Ps 106:8
14:31 Jn 2:11
15:1 Ps 106:12
15:2 Isa 12:2
15:3 Ps 24:8
15:5 Ne 9:11
15:6 Ps 118:15–16
15:7 Isa 5:24
....
15:8 Ps 78:13
15:9 Jdg 5:30
15:11 Dt 3:24
15:13 Ps 77:20
15:15 Jos 5:1
15:16 Ps 74:2
15:17 Ps 44:2
15:18 Ps 10:16
15:19 Ex 14:28–29

God Heals

If you diligently listen to the voice of the LORD your God, and do what is right in His sight, and give ear to His commandments, and keep all His statutes, I will not afflict you with any of the diseases with which I have afflicted the Egyptians. For I am the LORD who heals you.

—EXODUS 15:26

Exodus 15:26 declares God to be *Jehovah Rophe*, "The God Who Heals Us." God does not put disease on His children to teach them things. That is ludicrous! He is a loving Father. If there was a father who was a doctor and had access to petri dishes of the polio virus, what would you think of him if he used that virus on his son because the boy would never sit down and do his homework? You would think he was a monster, wouldn't you? Not a loving father! Well, if that is true, then the same goes for our heavenly Father. We live in enemy territory, where disease is a weapon the enemy uses to open fire upon humanity. Certainly God can teach and strengthen you through your sickness, but He is not the inflicter of illness any more than a physician would make you sick in order for you to seek treatment.

Certainly sickness and disease are in the world today because of sin, and sometimes disease comes as a direct result of our sin—smoking leads to lung cancer, promiscuity can lead to sexually transmitted infections, gluttony is directly connected to heart disease, and worry can contribute to high blood pressure—but other times illness takes hold regardless of our choices or whether or not we "deserve" it. Take, for example, the man born blind whom Jesus is asked about in John 9:2: "Rabbi, who sinned, this man or his parents, that he was born blind?" Jesus' answer?

Neither this man nor his parents sinned. But it happened so that the works of God might be displayed in him. I must do the works of Him who sent Me while it is day. Night is coming when no one can work. While I am in the world, I am the light of the world.

—JOHN 9:3–5

In other words, the man's blindness wasn't the direct result of sin—and I do not believe Jesus was saying the man was born blind just so that Jesus could come by one day and heal him to the glory of God. Jesus isn't concerned with cause and effect here—because there isn't any—but He is concerned with healing! God is not the one who puts diseases on people, but when we come to Him in faith, abiding in His Spirit and His Word abiding in us, then He is *Jehovah Rophe*, "The God Who Heals Us."

Cindy Trimm

The Song of Miriam

20 Miriam the prophetess, the sister of Aaron, took a timbrel in her hand, and all the women went out after her with timbrels and with dancing. 21 Miriam answered them,

"Sing to the LORD,
  for He triumphed gloriously!
The horse and his rider
  He has hurled into the sea."

The Waters of Marah and Elim

22 Then Moses led Israel from the Red Sea, and they went out into the Wilderness of Shur, and they went three days in the wilderness and found no water. 23 When they came to Marah, they could not drink of the waters of Marah, for they were bitter. Therefore, the name of it was called Marah. 24 So the people murmured against Moses, saying, "What shall we drink?"

The Lord is my healer (Ex 15:26).

25 And he cried to the LORD, and the LORD showed him a tree. When he had thrown *it* into the waters, the waters were made sweet.

There He made for them a statute and an ordinance, and there He tested them. 26 He said, "If you diligently listen to the voice of the LORD your God, and do what is right in His sight, and give ear to His commandments, and keep all His statutes, I will not afflict you with any of the diseases with which I have afflicted the Egyptians. For I am the LORD who heals you."

27 Then they came to Elim, where there were twelve wells of water and seventy palm trees, and they camped there by the waters.

Bread and Quail

16 Then they set out from Elim, and all the congregation of the children of Israel came to the Wilderness of Sin, which is between Elim and Sinai, on the fifteenth day of the second month after their departing out of the land of Egypt. 2 The whole congregation of the children of Israel murmured against Moses and Aaron in the wilderness. 3 Now the children of Israel said to them, "Would to God we had died by the hand of the LORD in the land of Egypt, when we sat by the pots of meat, when we ate bread to the full, for you have brought us forth into this wilderness to kill this whole assembly with hunger."

4 Then the LORD said to Moses, "Indeed, I will rain bread from heaven for you. And the people shall go out and gather a certain amount every day, that I may test them, whether they will walk in My law or not. 5 And it shall come to pass that on the sixth day they shall prepare that which they bring in, and it will be twice as much as they gather daily."

6 So Moses and Aaron said to all the children of Israel, "At evening, you shall know that the LORD has brought you out from the land of Egypt. 7 And in the morning you shall see the glory of the LORD, because He hears your murmurings against the LORD. And what are we that you murmur against us?" 8 Then Moses said, "This will happen when the LORD gives you meat to eat in the evening and bread in the morning to satisfy, for the LORD hears your murmurings which you murmur against Him. And what are we? Your murmurings are not against us, but against the LORD."

9 Then Moses said to Aaron, "Say to all the congregation of the children of Israel, 'Come near before the LORD, for He has heard your murmurings.' "

10 So as Aaron spoke to the whole congregation of the children of Israel, they looked toward the wilderness, and indeed, the glory of the LORD appeared in the cloud.

11 Then the LORD spoke to Moses, saying, 12 "I have heard the murmurings of the children of Israel. Speak to them, saying, '*In* the evening you shall eat meat, and in the morning you shall be filled with bread. And you shall know that I am the LORD your God.' "

13 So in the evening the quail came up and covered the camp, and in the morning a layer of dew was surrounding the camp. 14 When the layer of dew evaporated, on the surface of the wilderness there lay a small flaky thing, as fine as the frost on the ground. 15 When the children of Israel saw it, they said one to another, "What is it?" For they did not know what it was.

And Moses said to them, "This is the bread which the LORD has given you to eat. 16 This is what the LORD has commanded, 'Every man is to gather of it according to what he will eat, an omer[1] for every man, according to the number of your people. Every man should take for them for whoever lives in his tent.' "

17 The children of Israel did so, and gathered, some more, some less. 18 When they measured it with an omer, he that gathered much had nothing left over, and he that gathered little had no lack. They gathered every man according what he could eat.

19 Moses said to them, "Let no man leave any of it until the morning."

20 However, they did not listen to Moses, and some of them left part of it until the morning, and it bred worms, and stank, and Moses was angry with them.

15:20 Jdg 11:34
15:21 Ex 15:1
15:22 Ge 16:7
15:23 Nu 33:8
15:24 Ex 16:2
15:25 Ex 14:10
15:26 Dt 7:15
15:27 Nu 33:9
16:1 Nu 33:10–12
16:2 Ex 15:24
16:3 La 4:9
16:4 Ex 15:25
16:6 Ex 6:7
16:7 Nu 16:11
16:8 1Sa 8:7
16:9 Nu 16:16
16:10 Ex 16:7
16:13 Nu 11:9
16:14 Nu 11:7–9
16:15 Ex 16:4
16:16 Ex 16:36
16:19 Ex 12:10

[1] *16* Likely about 3 pounds, or 1.4 kilograms; and in vv. 18, 32, 33, and 36.

21 So they gathered it every morning, every man according to what he could eat. And when the sun got hot, it melted. 22 Now on the sixth day they gathered twice as much bread, two omers[1] per man, and then all the leaders of the congregation came and told Moses. 23 He said to them, "This is what the LORD has said, 'Tomorrow is the Sabbath, a holy Sabbath to the LORD. Bake that which you will bake today, and boil that you will boil, and all that which remains over lay up for yourselves to be kept until the morning.' "

24 So they laid it up until the morning, just as Moses commanded, and it did not stink, nor was there any worm in it. 25 Moses said, "Eat it today, for today is a Sabbath to the LORD. Today you will not find it in the field. 26 Six days you shall gather it, but on the seventh day, the Sabbath, there will be none."

27 It happened that some of the people went out on the seventh day to gather, but they found nothing. 28 Then the LORD said to Moses, "How long will you refuse to keep My commandments and My instructions? 29 See, the LORD has given you the Sabbath; therefore He gives you bread for two days on the sixth day. Every man remain in his place. Let no man go out of his place on the seventh day." 30 So the people rested on the seventh day.

31 The house of Israel named it manna, and it was like coriander seed and was white, and its taste was like wafers made with honey. 32 Then Moses said, "This is what the LORD has commanded, 'Fill an omer of it to be kept for your generations *to come*, so that they may see the bread that I fed you in the wilderness, when I brought you forth from the land of Egypt.' "

33 Moses said to Aaron, "Take a pot and put an omer full of manna in it, and place it before the LORD, to be kept for generations *to come*."

34 As the LORD commanded Moses, so Aaron placed it before the testimony, to be kept. 35 The children of Israel ate manna forty years, until they came to an inhabited land. They ate the manna until they came to the border of the land of Canaan.

36 Now an omer is one-tenth of an ephah.

Water From the Rock

17 All the congregation of the children of Israel journeyed from the Wilderness of Sin, from place to place, according to the commandment of the LORD, and pitched in Rephidim, but there was no water for the people to drink. 2 Therefore the people contended with Moses and said, "Give us water so that we may drink."

And Moses said to them, "Why do you contend with me? Why do you test the LORD?"

16:22 Ex 16:5
16:23 Lev 23:3
16:24 Ex 16:20
16:25 Ex 16:23
16:28 Ps 78:10
16:31 Ex 16:15
16:33 Heb 9:4
16:34 Ex 25:16
16:35 Jos 5:12
16:36 Ex 16:16
17:1 Ex 16:1
17:2 Dt 6:16

17:3 Ex 16:2–3
17:4 Nu 14:10
17:6 Ps 114:8

SPIRITED WOMAN

COUNSEL FROM THE SPIRIT BASICS

A Pit Stop at Rephidim

On their journey from Egypt to the Promised Land, God took Israel from Elim through the Wilderness of Sin to Rephidim, where "there was no water for the people to drink" (Ex 17:1). Can you imagine their reaction?

It probably went something like this: "We don't understand. Why leave Elim? The blessings were flowing, the teaching was good, the house was nice, and the palm trees swayed in the breeze. Then God shocked us by telling us to move on! And where does He take us? He leads us straight to Rephidim, where there is no water. That's not fair. Why would God take us from wells and palms to Rephidim?"

God wants to prove Himself to you right now. In the hard places where there is no water and everything seems unfair, God is shaping you to possess greater things than you have ever known. This is not the devil's hour; this is God's hour.

What is happening right now is not the devil's plan but God's plan, so that we can grow up and put a sharp edge to our spirit. God wants to bring forth a strong people. Rest assured, Rephidim is only a pit stop on the way to the Promised Land.

Cathy Lechner

3 But the people thirsted there for water, and the people murmured against Moses, and said, "Why is it that you have brought us up out of Egypt, to kill us and our children and our livestock with thirst?"

4 Then Moses cried out to the LORD, saying, "What shall I do to this people? They are almost ready to stone me."

5 The LORD said to Moses, "Pass over before the people, and take with you some of the elders of Israel. And take in your hand your rod with which you struck the Nile, and go. 6 Indeed, I will stand before you there on the rock in Horeb, and you shall strike the rock, and there water shall come out of it, so that the people may drink." Then Moses did so in

[1] *22* Likely about 6 pounds, or 2.8 kilograms.

the sight of the elders of Israel. 7 He called the name of the place Massah, and Meribah, because of the contending of the children of Israel, and because they tested the LORD, saying, "Is the LORD among us, or not?"

The Amalekites Defeated

8 Then Amalek came and fought with Israel in Rephidim. 9 So Moses said to Joshua, "Choose men for us and go out, fight against Amalek. Tomorrow I will stand on the top of the hill with the rod of God in my hand."

10 So Joshua did as Moses had said to him and fought against Amalek. And Moses, Aaron, and Hur went up to the top of the hill. 11 Now when Moses held up his hand, Israel prevailed, but when he let down his hand, Amalek prevailed. 12 But Moses' hands became heavy. So they took a stone, and put it under him, and he sat on it. And Aaron and Hur supported his hands, one on one side, and the other on the other side. And his hands were steady until the going down of the sun. 13 So Joshua laid low Amalek and his people with the edge of the sword.

14 Then the LORD said to Moses, "Write this as a memorial in a book and rehearse it to Joshua, for I will utterly wipe out the remembrance of Amalek from under heaven."

15 Then Moses built an altar and called the name of it, The LORD Is My Banner; 16 for he said, "For the LORD has sworn that the LORD will have war with Amalek from generation to generation."

Jethro Counsels Moses

18 Jethro, the priest of Midian, Moses' father-in-law, heard of all that God had done for Moses, and for Israel His people, and that the LORD had brought Israel out of Egypt.

2 Then Jethro, Moses' father-in-law, took Zipporah, Moses' wife, after he had sent her back, 3 and her two sons, one of whom was named Gershom; for he said, "I have been a sojourner in a foreign land." 4 And the name of the other was Eliezer, for *he said*, "The God of my father was my help, and He delivered me from the sword of Pharaoh."

5 Then Jethro, Moses' father-in-law, came with his sons and his wife to Moses in the wilderness, where he camped at the mountain of God. 6 And he said to Moses, "I, your father-in-law, Jethro, am coming to you, and your wife, and her two sons with her."

7 Then Moses went out to meet his father-in-law, and bowed down and kissed him; and they asked each other of the other's welfare, and then they went into the tent. 8 Moses told his father-in-law all that the LORD had done to Pharaoh and to the Egyptians for Israel's sake, and all the hardships that had come on them along the way, and how the LORD delivered them.

9 Jethro rejoiced because of all the goodness which the LORD had done for Israel, whom He had delivered out of the hand of the Egyptians. 10 Jethro said, "The LORD be blessed, who has delivered you out of the hand of the Egyptians, and out of the hand of Pharaoh, who has delivered the people from under the hand of the Egyptians. 11 Now I know that the LORD is greater than all gods, for in the matter in which they treated the *people* insolently, *He was* above them." 12 Then Jethro, Moses' father-in-law, took a burnt offering and sacrifices for God, and Aaron and all the elders of Israel came to eat bread with Moses' father-in-law before God.

13 On the next day, Moses sat to judge the people, and the people stood around Moses from the morning until the evening. 14 When Moses' father-in-law saw all that he was doing for the people, he said, "What is this thing that you are doing for the people? Why are you sitting by yourself while all the people stand around you from morning until evening?"

15 Then Moses said to his father-in-law, "Because the people come to me to inquire of God. 16 When they have a dispute, it comes to me, and I judge between a man and his neighbor, and I make known the statutes of God and His laws."

17 Moses' father-in-law said to him, "What you are doing is not good. 18 You will surely wear yourself out, both you, and these people who are with you, for this thing is too heavy for you. You are not able to do it by yourself. 19 Now listen to me, I will advise you, and may God be with you: You be a representative for the people to God so that you may bring *their* disputes to God. 20 And you shall teach them the statutes and laws and shall show them the way in which they must walk and the work that they must do. 21 Moreover, you shall choose out of all the people capable men who fear God, men of truth, hating dishonest gain, and place *these men* over them, to be rulers of thousands, rulers of hundreds, rulers of fifties, and rulers of tens. 22 Let them judge the people at all times, and let it be that every difficult matter they shall bring to you, but every small matter they shall judge, so that it will be easier for you, and they will bear *the burden* with you. 23 If you shall do this thing and God commands you *so*, then you will be able to endure, and all these people also will go to their place in peace."

24 So Moses listened to his father-in-law and did everything that he had said. 25 Moses chose

17:7 Nu 20:13
17:8 Ge 36:12
17:9 Ex 4:20
17:10 Ex 24:14
17:12 Isa 35:3
17:14 Ex 34:27
17:15 Ge 22:14
18:1 Ex 2:16
18:2 Ex 2:21
18:3 Ex 2:22
18:5 Ex 3:1
18:7 Ge 29:13
. . . .
18:10 Ge 14:20
18:11 2Ch 2:5
18:12 Ge 31:54
18:16 Ex 24:14
18:19 Nu 27:5
18:20 Dt 1:18
18:21 2Ch 19:5–10
18:22 Nu 11:17
18:23 Ex 18:18
18:25 Dt 1:15

capable men out of all Israel and made them
heads over the people, rulers of thousands,
rulers of hundreds, rulers of fifties, and rulers
of tens. 26 They judged the people at all times.
They brought the difficult cases to Moses, but
they judged every small matter themselves.
27 Moses sent out his father-in-law, and he
went his way to his own land.

Israel at Mount Sinai

19 In the third month after the children of
Israel had gone forth out of the land
of Egypt, on the same day they came into
the Wilderness of Sinai. 2 When they set out
from Rephidim, they came to the Wilderness
of Sinai and camped in the wilderness. Israel
camped there before the mountain.
3 Moses went up to God, and the LORD called
to him from the mountain, saying, "Thus you
shall say to the house of Jacob and tell the
children of Israel: 4 'You have seen what I did
to the Egyptians, and how I lifted you up on ea-
gles' wings, and brought you to Myself. 5 Now
therefore, if you will faithfully obey My voice
and keep My covenant, then you shall be My
special possession out of all the nations, for
all the earth is Mine. 6 And you will be to Me a
kingdom of priests and a holy nation.' These
are the words which you shall speak to the
children of Israel."
7 So Moses came and called for the elders
of the people and laid before them all these
words which the LORD commanded him. 8 Then
all the people answered together and said, "All
that the LORD has spoken we will do." And Mo-
ses brought back the words of the people to
the LORD.
9 The LORD said to Moses, "Indeed, I am going
to come to you in a thick cloud, so that the
people may hear when I speak with you and
always believe in you." Then Moses told the
words of the people to the LORD.
10 The LORD said to Moses, "Go to the people
and sanctify them today and tomorrow, and
have them wash their clothes, 11 and be ready
for the third day, for on the third day the LORD
will come down in the sight of all the people
on Mount Sinai. 12 You shall set boundaries
for the people all around, saying, 'Take heed
to yourselves so that you not go up onto the
mountain or touch its border. Whoever touches
the mountain will surely be put to death. 13 No
hand will touch him, but he shall surely be
stoned or shot through, whether it be beast
or man. He shall not live.' When the trumpet
sounds a long *blast*, they shall come up to the
mountain."
14 So Moses went down from the mountain to
the people and sanctified the people, and they
washed their clothes. 15 He said to the people,
"Be ready for the third day. Do not go near
your wives."
16 So on the third day, in the morning, there
was thunder and lightning, and a thick cloud
on the mountain, and the sound of an exceed-
ingly loud trumpet. All the people who were in
the camp trembled. 17 Then Moses brought the
people out of the camp to meet with God, and
they stood at the foot of the mountain. 18 Now
Mount Sinai was completely covered in smoke
because the LORD had descended upon it in
fire, and the smoke ascended like the smoke
of a furnace, and the whole mountain shook
violently. 19 When the sound of the trumpet
grew louder and louder, Moses spoke, and God
answered him with a voice.[1]
20 The LORD came down on Mount Sinai, on
the top of the mountain. And the LORD called
Moses up to the top of the mountain, and Mo-
ses went up. 21 Then the LORD said to Moses,
"Go down, warn the people, lest they force
their way to the LORD to look, and many of
them perish. 22 Let the priests also, which come
near to the LORD, sanctify themselves, lest the
LORD break through against them."
23 Moses said to the LORD, "The people cannot
come up to Mount Sinai, for You warned us,
saying, 'Set boundaries around the mountain,
and sanctify it.' "
24 Then the LORD said to him, "Go, get down,
and come up, you and Aaron with you, but do
not let the priests and the people force their
way through to come up to the LORD, lest He
break through against them."
25 So Moses went down to the people and
spoke to them.

The Ten Commandments
Dt 5:6–21

20 Now God spoke all these words, say-
ing:

2 I am the LORD your God, who brought you
out of the land of Egypt, out of the house
of bondage.

> I will put no other gods before You,
> Lord (Ex 20:3).

3 You shall have no other gods before Me.
4 You shall not make for yourself any graven
idol, or any likeness of anything that is
in heaven above, or that is in the earth
beneath, or that is in the water below the
earth. 5 You shall not bow down to them
or serve them; for I, the LORD your God,
am a jealous God, visiting the iniquity of

18:26 Ex 18:22
18:27 Nu 10:29–30
19:2 Ex 3:1
19:3 Ex 3:4
19:4 Isa 63:9
19:5 Ex 9:29
19:6 Dt 7:6
19:7 Ex 4:29–30
19:8 Ex 24:3
19:9 Dt 4:36
19:10 Ge 35:2
19:11 Ex 19:16
19:16 Heb 12:21
19:17 Dt 4:10
19:18 Ps 144:5
19:19 Ps 81:7
19:20 Ne 9:13
19:21 1Sa 6:19
19:22 Ex 24:5
19:23 Ex 19:12
20:1 Dt 5:22
20:2 Ex 13:3
20:3 Jer 35:15
20:4 Lev 26:1
20:5 Ex 34:14

[1] 19 *Or thunder.*

the fathers on the children to the third and fourth generation of them who hate Me, 6 and showing lovingkindness to thousands of them who love Me and keep My commandments.

7 You shall not take the name of the LORD your God in vain, for the LORD will not hold guiltless anyone who takes His name in vain.

8 Remember the Sabbath day and keep it holy. 9 Six days you shall labor and do all your work, 10 but the seventh day is a Sabbath to the LORD your God. On it you shall not do any work, you, or your son, or your daughter, or your male servant, or your female servant, or your livestock, or your sojourner who is within your gates. 11 For in six days the LORD made heaven and earth, the sea, and all that is in them, and rested on the seventh day. Therefore the LORD blessed the Sabbath day and made it holy.

12 Honor your father and your mother, that your days may be long in the land which the LORD your God is giving you.

13 You shall not murder.

14 You shall not commit adultery.

15 You shall not steal.

16 You shall not bear false witness against your neighbor.

17 You shall not covet your neighbor's house; you shall not covet your neighbor's wife, or his manservant, or his maidservant, or his ox, or his donkey, or anything that is your neighbor's.

18 All the people witnessed the thunder and the lightning and the sound of the trumpet and the mountain smoking; and when the people saw it, they trembled and stood at a distance. 19 They said to Moses, "You speak to us, and we will listen, but do not let God speak to us, lest we die."

20 Moses said to the people, "Do not fear, for God has come to test you, so that the fear of Him may be before you so that you do not sin."

21 The people stood a distance away as Moses drew near to the thick darkness where God was.

The Law About the Altar

22 Then the LORD said to Moses: Thus you shall say to the children of Israel, "You yourselves have seen that I have spoken to you from heaven. 23 You shall not make gods of silver alongside Me or make gods of gold for yourselves.

24 "You shall make an altar of earth for Me and on it you shall sacrifice your burnt offerings and your peace offerings, your sheep, and your oxen. In every place where I cause My name to be honored, I will come to you and bless you. 25 If you will make Me an altar of stone, you shall not build it of cut stones, for if you use your tool on it, you will have polluted it. 26 And you shall not go up by steps to My altar, so that your nakedness will not be exposed on it."

20:6 Dt 7:9
20:7 Lev 19:12
20:8 Lev 19:3
20:9 Lk 13:14
20:11 Ge 2:2–3
20:12 Lev 19:3
20:13 Ro 13:9
20:14 Lev 18:20
20:15 Lev 19:11
20:17 Ro 7:7
20:18 Ex 19:16–18
20:20 Dt 13:3
20:22 Ne 9:13
20:24 Dt 12:5

....

20:25 Dt 27:5–6
21:1 Dt 4:14
21:5 Dt 15:16–17
21:6 Ex 22:8–9
21:7 Ne 5:5
21:12 Ge 9:6
21:13 Jos 20:2–9
21:14 1Ki 2:28–34
21:16 Dt 24:7
21:17 Pr 20:20

The Law About Servants

Dt 15:12–18; Lev 25:39–55

21 Now these are the judgments which you will set before them.

2 If you buy a Hebrew servant, he will serve for six years, but in the seventh he shall go out free without paying anything. 3 If he came in by himself, he shall go out by himself. If he is married, then his wife will go out with him. 4 If his master gives him a wife, and she bears him sons or daughters, the wife and her children shall belong to her master, and he will go out by himself.

5 However, if the servant plainly says, "I love my master, my wife, and my children. I will not go out free," 6 then his master will bring him to the judges, then he shall also bring him to the door or to the doorpost, and his master shall bore his ear through with an awl, and he shall serve him forever.

7 If a man sells his daughter to be a female servant, she shall not go out as the male servants do. 8 If she does not please her master, who has betrothed her to himself, then he shall let her be redeemed. He has no authority to sell her to a foreign nation, because he has dealt deceitfully with her. 9 If he has designated her for his son, then he shall deal with her according to the customary rights of daughters. 10 If he marries another wife, then he must not diminish *the first one's* food, her clothing, or her marital rights. 11 If he does not provide these three for her, then she shall go out free, without paying money.

The Law About Violence

12 He that strikes a man so that he dies shall surely be put to death. 13 However, if it was not premeditated, but God let *him* fall into his hand, then I will appoint you a place where he may flee. 14 But if a man willfully comes upon his neighbor in order to kill him cunningly, then you must take him from My altar, that he may die.

15 He who strikes his father or his mother shall surely be put to death.

16 He who kidnaps a man and sells him, or if he is found in his possession, shall surely be put to death.

17 He who curses his father or his mother shall surely be put to death.

18 If men fight and one strikes the other with a stone or with his fist, and he does not die, but must remain in bed, 19 and then if he gets up and walks around on his staff, then he who struck him shall go unpunished. Only he must pay for his loss of time and shall see to it that he is thoroughly healed.

20 If a man strikes his male servant or his female servant with a rod so that he *or she* dies at his hand, then he shall surely be punished. 21 Nevertheless, if he survives for a day or two, then he shall not be punished, for it is his money.

22 If men fight and hurt a pregnant woman so that her child is born prematurely,[1] yet there is no serious injury, then he shall be surely punished in accordance with what the woman's husband demands of him, and he shall pay as the judges determine. 23 But if there is any serious injury, then you shall give life for life, 24 eye for eye, tooth for tooth, hand for hand, foot for foot, 25 burn for burn, wound for wound, bruise for bruise.

26 If a man strikes the eye of his male servant or the eye of his female servant so that it is destroyed, then he must let him go free on account of his eye. 27 If he knocks out his male servant's tooth or his female servant's tooth, then he shall let him *or her* go free on account of *the* tooth.

Laws About Property

28 If an ox gores a man or a woman to death, then the ox must surely be stoned and its flesh must not be eaten, but the owner of the ox will be acquitted. 29 But if the ox has had the habit of goring, and the owner has been made aware of it, and he has not kept it in, and it has killed a man or a woman, then the ox shall be stoned and its owner also shall be put to death. 30 If a ransom is set for him, then he shall give for the ransom of his life whatever is demanded of him. 31 Whether it gored a son or gored a daughter, it will be done to him according to this rule. 32 If the ox gores a male servant or a female servant, then its owner shall give thirty shekels[2] of silver to their master, and the ox must be stoned.

33 If a man opens a pit or if a man digs a pit and does not cover it, and an ox or a donkey falls into it, 34 the owner of the pit must make restitution. He must give money to their owner, and the dead animal will be his.

35 If one man's ox hurts another's so that it dies, then they shall sell the live ox and divide its proceeds and divide the dead ox also. 36 Or if it be known that the ox has had the habit of goring and its owner has not kept it in, then he shall surely pay ox for ox and the dead *animal* will become his own.

Laws About Restitution

22 If a man steals an ox or a sheep and kills it or sells it, then he shall repay five oxen for an ox, and four sheep for a sheep.

2 If a thief is caught breaking in and is struck so that he dies, then there will be no blood guilt for him. 3 If the sun has risen on him, then there is blood guilt for him.

He must make full restitution. If he has nothing, then he will be sold for his theft. 4 If the stolen item is in fact found alive in his possession, whether it be an ox, or donkey, or sheep, then he shall repay double.

5 If a man causes a field or vineyard to be eaten and puts out his beast so that it feeds in another man's field, he must make restitution of the best of his own field and of the best of his own vineyard.

6 If fire breaks out and catches in thorn bushes, so that stacked grain or the standing grain or the field are consumed, then he who started the fire must surely make restitution.

7 If a man gives his neighbor money or items to be kept *for him*, and it is stolen from the man's house, if the thief is caught, he must repay double. 8 If the thief is not caught, then the owner of the house will be brought before the judges to determine if he has laid his hand on his neighbor's goods. 9 For any kind of trespass, whether it be for an ox, for a donkey, for a sheep, for clothing, or for any type of lost thing, where another says it is his, the case of both parties shall come before the judges. And whoever the judges find guilty will pay double to his neighbor.

10 If a man gives his neighbor a donkey, or an ox, or a sheep, or any beast to keep *for him*, and it dies, or is injured, or is driven away while no one sees it, 11 then there will be an oath before the LORD between both of them that he has not laid his hand upon his neighbor's property. And its owner must accept this, and he will not have to make restitution. 12 However, if it was stolen from him, he shall make restitution to its owner. 13 If it is torn in pieces, then let him bring it as evidence, and he will not have to repay for that which was torn.

14 If a man borrows anything from his neighbor, and it is hurt or dies when the owner was not with it, then he shall surely make restitution. 15 But if the owner was with it, he shall not make restitution. If it was a hired thing, it came with his hire.

21:18 Ex 21:20
21:22 Dt 22:18–19
21:23 Dt 19:21
21:24 Dt 19:21
21:28 Ex 21:32
21:30 Ex 21:22
21:32 Mt 26:15

22:1 2Sa 12:6
22:2 Mt 24:43
22:3 Ex 21:2
22:6 Ex 22:9
22:9 Dt 25:1
22:11 Heb 6:16
22:12 Ge 31:39

[1]22 Or *she has a miscarriage.* [2]32 About 12 ounces, or 345 grams.

Moral and Ceremonial Laws

16 If a man seduces a virgin who is not engaged and has relations with her, he must surely endow her to be his wife. 17 If her father absolutely refuses to give her to him, he must pay money according to the dowry of virgins.

18 You must not allow a sorceress to live.

19 Whoever has relations with a beast must surely be put to death.

20 He who sacrifices to any god other than the LORD alone shall be utterly destroyed.

21 You must neither wrong a foreigner nor oppress him, for you were foreigners in the land of Egypt.

22 You shall not afflict any widow or orphan. 23 If you afflict them in any way and they cry at all to Me, I will surely hear their cry. 24 And My anger will burn, and I will kill you with the sword, and your wives will become widows, and your children fatherless.

25 If you lend money to any of My people who is poor among you, do not be a creditor to him, and do not charge him interest. 26 If you take your neighbor's garment as a pledge, you shall return it to him before the sun goes down, 27 for that is his only covering; it is his garment for his body. In what else will he sleep? And when he cries out to Me, I will hear, for I am gracious.

28 You shall not curse God or curse the ruler of your people.

29 You must not delay to offer the first of your harvest and of your vats.

You must give to Me the firstborn of your sons. 30 Likewise you must do the same with your oxen and with your sheep. Seven days it shall remain with its mother, but on the eighth day you must give it to Me.

31 You will be holy men to Me; therefore you must not eat any flesh that is torn by beasts in the field. You must throw it to the dogs.

Laws of Justice and Mercy

23 You must not give a false report. Do not join your hand with the wicked to be a malicious witness.

2 You must not follow the masses to do evil, and do not testify in a dispute that agrees with the crowd to pervert *justice*. 3 You must not show partiality to a poor man in his dispute.

4 If you meet your enemy's ox or his donkey going astray, you shall surely return it to him. 5 If you see the donkey of someone who hates you lying under its burden, you must not ignore it; you must surely help with him.

6 You shall not turn justice away from your poor in his dispute. 7 Keep far away from a false charge, and do not kill the innocent and the righteous, for I will not justify the wicked.

8 You shall not take a bribe, for a bribe blinds those who see and subverts the words of the righteous.

9 Also you shall not oppress a foreigner, for you know the life of a foreigner, seeing you were foreigners in the land of Egypt.

The Laws of Sabbaths

10 You shall sow your land for six years and shall gather in its produce, 11 but in the seventh year you shall let it rest and lie fallow, so that the poor of your people may eat, and what they leave the beasts of the field may eat. You shall do likewise with your vineyard and with your olive grove.

12 For six days you are to do your work, but on the seventh day you must cease, so that your ox and your donkey may rest, and the son of your female servant and the foreigner may refresh themselves.

13 In all things that I have said to you, watch yourselves, and do not mention the name of other gods, nor let *them* be heard from your mouth.

The Three Annual Feasts

14 Three times in the year you must celebrate a feast to Me.

15 You shall observe the Feast of Unleavened Bread. For seven days you shall eat unleavened bread, as I commanded you, in the appointed time of the month Aviv, for in it you came out from Egypt.

No one shall appear before Me empty-handed.

16 You shall observe the Feast of Harvest, the first fruits of your labors, which you have sown in the field.

You shall observe the Feast of Ingathering at the end of the year, when you have gathered in the fruit of your labors from the field.

17 Three times in the year all your males shall appear before the Lord GOD.

18 You shall not offer the blood of My sacrifice with leavened bread, nor shall the fat of My sacrifice remain until the morning.

19 The first of the first fruits of your land you shall bring into the house of the LORD your God.

You shall not boil a young goat in its mother's milk.

The Angel Prepares the Way

20 Indeed, I am going to send an angel before you to guard you along the way and to bring you into the place which I have prepared. 21 Be on guard before him and obey his voice. Do not provoke him, for he will not pardon your transgressions, for My name is in him. 22 But if you diligently obey his voice and do all that I say, then I will be an enemy to your enemies and an adversary to your adversaries. 23 For

22:16 Dt 22:28–29
22:17 Ge 34:12
22:18 Lev 20:27
22:19 Lev 18:23
22:20 Dt 17:2–5
22:21 Dt 10:19
22:22 Dt 24:17
22:23 Ps 18:6
22:24 Ps 109:9
22:25 Ps 15:5
22:26 Dt 24:6
22:27 Ex 34:6
22:28 Ecc 10:20
22:29 Ex 13:2
22:30 Lev 22:27
22:31 Eze 4:14
23:1 Ps 35:11
23:4 Dt 22:1–4
23:5 Dt 22:4
23:7 Ex 34:7
23:8 Dt 16:19
23:12 Ex 20:8–11
23:13 Dt 4:9
23:14 Dt 16:16
23:15 Ex 34:20
23:16 Ex 34:22
23:17 Dt 16:16
23:18 Ex 34:25
23:19 Ex 34:26
23:20 Ex 14:19
23:21 Ps 78:40
23:22 Ge 12:3
23:23 Ex 23:20

My angel will go before you and bring you to the Amorites, and the Hittites, and the Perizzites, and the Canaanites, the Hivites, and the Jebusites, and I will completely destroy them. 24 You must not bow down to their gods, or serve them, or do according to their practices, but you shall utterly overthrow them and break down their images in pieces. 25 You shall serve the LORD your God, and He shall bless your bread and your water, and I will remove sickness from your midst. 26 No one shall be miscarrying or be barren in your land. I will fulfill the number of your days.

27 I will send My fear before you, and I will throw into panic all the people to whom you shall come. I will make all your enemies turn their backs to you. 28 I will send hornets before you which shall drive out the Hivite, the Canaanite, and the Hittite from before you. 29 I will not drive them out before you in one year, lest the land become desolate and the beasts of the field multiply against you. 30 Little by little I will drive them out before you, until you become fruitful and inherit the land.

31 I will set your boundaries from the Red Sea to the sea of the Philistines, and from the desert to the River;[1] for I will deliver the inhabitants of the land into your hand, and you will drive them out before you. 32 You must not make a covenant with them or with their gods. 33 They shall not live in your land, lest they cause you to sin against Me, for if you serve their gods, it will surely be a snare to you.

The Covenant Confirmed

24 Then He said to Moses, "Come up to the LORD, you, and Aaron, Nadab, and Abihu, and seventy of the elders of Israel, and you shall worship from a distance. 2 Moses alone shall come near the LORD, but they shall not come near, nor may the people go up with him."

3 Moses came and told the people all the words of the LORD and all the ordinances. Then all the people answered with one voice and said, "All the words which the LORD has said we will do." 4 Moses wrote all the words of the LORD, and rose up early in the morning, and built an altar at the foot of the mountain with twelve pillars for the twelve tribes of Israel. 5 He sent young Israelite men who offered burnt offerings and sacrificed peace offerings of young bulls to the LORD. 6 Moses took half of the blood and put it in basins, and half of the blood he sprinkled on the altar. 7 He took the Book of the Covenant and read in the hearing of the people, and they said, "All that the LORD has said we will do, and we will be obedient."

23:24 Ex 20:5
23:25 Ex 15:26
23:26 Dt 7:14
23:27 Dt 2:25
23:28 Dt 7:20
23:29 Dt 7:22
23:31 Ge 15:18
23:32 Ex 34:12
23:33 Dt 7:16
24:1 Ex 6:23
24:3 Ex 19:8
24:4 Dt 31:9
24:5 Ex 18:12
24:6 Heb 9:18
24:7 Ex 24:3–4

24:8 Mt 26:28
24:9 Ex 24:1
24:10 Jn 1:18
24:12 Ex 31:18
24:13 Ex 33:11
24:14 Ex 17:10
24:15 Ex 19:9
24:16 Ex 16:10
24:17 Ex 3:2
24:18 Ex 34:28
25:2 Ezr 2:68
25:6 Ex 27:20
25:7 Ex 28:4
25:8 Ex 29:45
25:9 Ex 25:40

8 So Moses took the blood, and sprinkled it on the people, and said, "This is the blood of the covenant, which the LORD has made with you in accordance with all these words."

Moses on Mount Sinai

9 Then Moses went up with Aaron, Nadab, and Abihu, and seventy of the elders of Israel, 10 and they saw the God of Israel, and under His feet there was something like a paved work of sapphire stone as clear as the sky itself. 11 He did not lay His hand upon the nobles of the children of Israel. Also they saw God, and they ate and they drank.

12 The LORD said to Moses, "Come up to Me to the mountain and stay there, and I will give you the stone tablets with law and the commandments which I have written, so that you may teach them."

13 Moses rose up with Joshua his attendant, and Moses went up to the mountain of God. 14 He said to the elders, "Wait for us in this place until we return to you. Aaron and Hur are with you. Whoever has any matters of dispute let him come to them."

15 Moses went up to the mountain, and the cloud covered the mountain. 16 The glory of the LORD rested on Mount Sinai, and the cloud covered it for six days. And on the seventh day He called to Moses from the midst of the cloud. 17 Now the appearance of the glory of the LORD was like a consuming fire on the top of the mountain to the eyes of the children of Israel. 18 Moses went into the midst of the cloud and went up to the mountain. And Moses was on the mountain for forty days and forty nights.

Offerings for the Tabernacle

Ex 35:4–9

25 The LORD said to Moses: 2 Tell the children of Israel to bring Me an offering. From every man who gives willingly with his heart you shall receive My offering. 3 This is the offering which you shall take from them: gold, silver, and bronze, 4 blue, purple, scarlet, fine linen, goats' hair, 5 rams' skins dyed red, porpoise skins, acacia wood, 6 oil for the light, spices for anointing oil and for fragrant incense, 7 onyx stones, and stones to be set in the ephod and in the breastplate.

8 Let them make Me a sanctuary that I may dwell among them. 9 According to all that I show you—the pattern of the tabernacle and the pattern of all its furniture—you shall make it just so.

[1] 31 *Euphrates River.*

The Ark of the Covenant
Ex 37:1–9

10 They shall make an ark of acacia wood
two and a half cubits long, and one and a half
cubits wide, and one and a half cubits high.[1]
11 You shall overlay it with pure gold, inside
and out shall you overlay it, and you shall
make a gold border around it. 12 You shall cast
four gold rings for it and put them on the four
feet with two rings on the one side of it and
two rings on the other side of it. 13 You shall
make poles of acacia wood and overlay them
with gold. 14 You shall put the poles into the
rings on the sides of the ark in order to carry
the ark with them. 15 The poles must remain in
the rings of the ark. They must not be removed
from it. 16 You shall put into the ark the testimo-
ny which I shall give you.
17 You shall make a mercy seat of pure gold,
two and a half cubits long and one and a half
cubits wide. 18 You shall make two cherubim
of gold, make them of hammered work at the
two ends of the mercy seat. 19 Make one cherub
on the one end and the other cherub on the
other end. From the mercy seat you shall make
the cherubim on its two ends. 20 The cherubim
shall stretch forth their wings upward, covering
the mercy seat with their wings and facing one
another. The faces of the cherubim are to face
toward the mercy seat. 21 You shall put the mer-
cy seat above upon the ark, and in the ark you
shall put the testimony that I will give you. 22 I
will meet with you there, and I will meet with
you from above the mercy seat, from between
the two cherubim which are upon the ark of
the testimony. I will speak with you all that I
will command you for the children of Israel.

The Table for the Showbread
Ex 37:10–16

23 You shall also make a table of acacia wood,
two cubits long, one cubit wide, and a half cu-
bit high.[2] 24 You shall overlay it with pure gold
and make a gold border around it. 25 You shall
make a border around it of a handbreadth, and
you shall make a gold molding for the frame all
around. 26 You shall make four gold rings for it
and put the rings on the four corners that are
on its four feet. 27 The rings shall be close to the
frame to provide places for the poles to carry
the table. 28 You shall make the poles of acacia
wood and overlay them with gold, so that the
table may be carried with them. 29 You shall
make the dishes, its spoons, its pitchers, and its
bowls with which to pour drink offerings. You
shall make them of pure gold. 30 You shall set
the showbread on the table before Me always.

The Gold Lampstand
Ex 37:17–24

31 You shall make a lampstand of pure gold.
The lampstand and its base and its shaft are
to be made of hammered metal. Its cups, its
buds, and its flowers shall be of one piece.
32 Six branches shall go out from its sides,
three branches of the lampstand from its one
side and three branches of the lampstand
from its other side. 33 Three cups shall be
made shaped like almond *flowers* with buds
and blossoms on one branch, and three cups
made like almond *flowers* in the other branch,
with buds and blossoms, and the same for the
six branches that come out of the lampstand.
34 On the lampstand shall be four cups shaped
like almond *flowers*, with their buds and their
blossoms. 35 There shall be a bud under two
branches of the same, and a bud under two
branches of the same, and a bud under *the
next* two branches of the same, according to
the six branches that proceed out of the lamp-
stand. 36 Their buds and their branches shall be
of the same *piece*, all of it shall be one ham-
mered work of pure gold.
37 You shall make its seven lamps, and they
shall light its lamps so that they may give light
to the area in front of it. 38 Its snuffers and their
snuff dishes shall be of pure gold. 39 It shall be
made from a talent[3] of pure gold along with
all these utensils. 40 See that you make them
according to their pattern which was shown
to you on the mountain.

The Tabernacle
Ex 36:8–38

26 Moreover you shall make the taber-
nacle with ten curtains of fine twisted
linen, and blue, and purple, and scarlet. Make
them with cherubim, the work of a skilled
workman. 2 The length of each curtain shall
be twenty-eight cubits, and the width of each
curtain four cubits.[4] All of the curtains shall
have the same measurements. 3 Five curtains
shall be joined together, one to another. And
the other five curtains are to be joined, one to
another. 4 You shall make loops of blue on the
edge of the end curtain in one set, and likewise
you shall make *loops* in the outermost edge of
the end curtain in the second set. 5 You shall
make fifty loops in the one curtain, and you
shall make fifty loops in the edge of the curtain
that is in the second set. The loops are to be
opposite to one another. 6 You shall make fifty
clasps of gold and join the curtains together

25:10 Heb 9:4
25:15 1Ki 8:8
25:16 Dt 31:26
25:17 Ex 37:6
25:20 1Ki 8:7
25:21 Ex 26:34
25:22 Ex 29:42–43
25:23 Ex 37:10–16
25:24 Ex 25:11
25:29 Nu 4:7
25:30 Ex 39:36
25:31 1Ki 7:49
25:37 Nu 8:2
25:40 Ex 26:30
26:1 Ex 26:36

[1] *10* About 3¾ feet long and 2¼ feet wide and high, or 1.1 meters long and 68 centimeters wide and high; similarly in v. 17. [2] *23* About 3 feet long, 1½ feet wide, and 2¼ feet high, or 90 centimeters long, 45 centimeters wide, and 68 centimeters high. [3] *39* About 75 pounds, or 34 kilograms. [4] *2* About 42 feet long and 6 feet wide, or 13 meters long and 1.8 meters wide.

with the clasps so that the tabernacle shall be one unit.

7 You shall make curtains of goats' hair to be a covering upon the tabernacle. You shall make eleven curtains. 8 The length of each curtain shall be thirty cubits, and the width of each curtain four cubits,[1] and the eleven curtains shall all have the same measure. 9 You shall join five curtains by themselves, and six curtains by themselves. You shall double over the sixth curtain at the front of the tabernacle. 10 You shall make fifty loops on the edge of the end curtain in one set and fifty loops on the edge of the curtain that joins the second set. 11 You shall make fifty bronze clasps, and put the clasps into the loops, and join the tent together so that it may be one unit. 12 The part that remains of the curtains of the tent, the half curtain that remains, shall hang over the back of the tabernacle. 13 A cubit[2] on the one side and a cubit on the other side of that which remains in the length of the curtains of the tent shall hang over the sides of the tabernacle on this side and on that side to cover it. 14 You shall make a covering for the tent out of rams' skins dyed red and a covering above of porpoise skins.

15 You shall make boards for the tabernacle of acacia wood, standing upright. 16 Ten cubits[3] shall be the length of each board, and a cubit and a half shall be the width of each board. 17 There shall be two tenons for each board, fitted to one another. You shall make all the boards of the tabernacle in this way. 18 You shall make the boards for the tabernacle, twenty boards for the south side. 19 You shall make forty sockets of silver under the twenty boards, two sockets under one board for its two tenons and two sockets under another board for its two tenons. 20 For the second side of the tabernacle, on the north side, there shall be twenty boards, 21 and their forty sockets of silver, two sockets under one board, and two sockets under another board. 22 For the back of the tabernacle, to the west, you shall make six boards. 23 You shall make two boards for the corners of the tabernacle at the back. 24 They shall be doubled together beneath and finished together at the top of it into one ring. So it shall be for both of them. They shall form the two corners. 25 There shall be eight boards with their sockets of silver, sixteen sockets, two sockets under one board and two sockets under another board.

26 You shall make bars of acacia wood, five for the boards of the one side of the tabernacle, 27 and five bars for the boards of the other side of the tabernacle, and five bars for the boards of the side of the tabernacle for the back to the west. 28 The middle bar in the center of the boards shall reach from end to end. 29 You shall overlay the boards with gold and make their rings of gold to provide places for the bars, and you shall overlay the bars with gold.

30 You shall set up the tabernacle according to the plan which you have been shown on the mountain.

31 You shall make a veil of blue, and purple, and scarlet, and fine twined linen. It shall be made with cherubim, the skillful work of a workman. 32 You shall hang it on four pillars of acacia wood overlaid with gold. Their hooks *also* shall be of gold on four sockets of silver. 33 You shall hang up the veil under the clasps, so that you may bring in the ark of the testimony within the veil; and the veil shall serve for you as a partition between the holy place and the Most Holy. 34 You shall put the mercy seat on the ark of the testimony in the Most Holy. 35 You shall set the table outside the veil, and the lampstand opposite the table on the side of the tabernacle toward the south, and you shall put the table on the north side.

36 You shall make a screen for the doorway of the tent of blue, and purple, and scarlet, and fine twined linen, the work of an embroiderer. 37 You shall make five pillars of acacia wood for the screen and overlay them with gold, with their hooks also made of gold, and you shall cast five sockets of bronze for them.

26:14 Ex 36:19
26:15 Ex 36:20–33
26:19 Ex 38:27
26:30 Ex 25:40
26:31 Ex 36:35
26:33 Ex 40:21
26:34 Ex 25:21
26:35 Ex 40:22
26:36 Ex 36:37
26:37 Ex 36:38
27:1 Ex 38:1–7
27:2 Ps 118:27
27:3 1Ki 7:45
27:8 Ex 25:40

The Altar of Burnt Offering

Ex 38:1–7

27 You shall make an altar of acacia wood, five cubits long and five cubits wide.[4] The altar shall be square, and its height shall be three cubits.[5] 2 You shall make its horns on its four corners. Its horns shall be part of it, and you shall overlay it with bronze. 3 You shall make its pots for its ashes, and its shovels, and its basins, and its meat hooks, and its fire pans. You shall make all of its vessels out of bronze. 4 You shall make a grating for it, a network of bronze, and on the net you shall make four bronze rings at its four corners. 5 You shall put it under the ledge of the altar beneath, so that the net will reach halfway up the altar. 6 You shall make poles for the altar, poles of acacia wood, and overlay them with bronze. 7 The poles shall be put into the rings, so that the poles shall be on the two sides of the altar when carrying it. 8 You shall make it hollow with boards. Just as it was shown you on the mountain, so shall they make it.

[1] *8* About 45 feet long and 6 feet wide, or 13.5 meters long and 1.8 meters wide. [2] *13* About 18 inches, or 45 centimeters. [3] *16* About 15 feet long and 2¼ feet wide, or 4.5 meters long and 68 centimeters wide. [4] *1* About 7½ feet, or 2.3 meters long and wide. [5] *1* About 4½ feet, or 1.4 meters.

The Court of the Tabernacle
Ex 38:9–20

9 You shall make the court of the tabernacle. On the south side there shall be curtains for the court of fine twined linen one hundred cubits long[1] for one side; 10 and it *shall have* twenty pillars with twenty bronze sockets. The hooks of the pillars and their bands shall be of silver. 11 Likewise for the north side in length there shall be curtains one hundred cubits long, and its twenty pillars and their twenty sockets of bronze. The hooks of the pillars and their bands *shall be* of silver.

12 For the width of the court on the west side shall be curtains of fifty cubits[2] with their ten pillars and their ten sockets. 13 The width of the court on the east side shall be fifty cubits. 14 The curtains on one side of the gate shall be fifteen cubits[3] with their three pillars and their three sockets. 15 On the other side shall be curtains fifteen cubits with their three pillars and their three sockets.

16 For the gate of the court there shall be a curtain of twenty cubits,[4] of blue, and purple, and scarlet, and fine twined linen, the work of an embroiderer, with their four pillars and their four sockets. 17 All the pillars around about the court shall be furnished with silver bands. Their hooks shall be of silver, and their sockets of bronze. 18 The length of the court shall be one hundred cubits, and the width fifty[5] throughout, and the height five cubits[6] of fine twisted linen, and their sockets of bronze. 19 All the utensils of the tabernacle used in all its service, and all its tent pegs, and all the tent pegs of the court shall be of bronze.

The Oil for the Lamp
Lev 24:1–3

20 You shall command the children of Israel that they bring you pure oil of olive pressed for the light, to cause the lamp to burn continually. 21 In the tent of meeting, outside the veil which is before the testimony, Aaron and his sons shall arrange it from evening to morning before the LORD. It shall be a perpetual statute for the children of Israel for generations to come.

The Priestly Garments

28 And bring near to yourself Aaron, your brother, and his sons with him from among the children of Israel, so that they may minister to Me as priests—Aaron, Nadab and Abihu, Eleazar and Ithamar, Aaron's sons. 2 You shall make holy garments for your brother Aaron, for glory and for beauty. 3 You shall speak to all who are specially skilled, whom I have filled with the spirit of wisdom, that they may make Aaron's garments to consecrate him, that he may minister to Me as a priest. 4 These are the garments which they shall make: a breastplate, and an ephod, and a robe, and an embroidered coat, a turban, and a sash. They shall make holy garments for Aaron your brother and his sons, that he may minister to Me as priest. 5 They shall take the gold, the blue, the purple, and the scarlet, and fine linen.

> I have been filled with the spirit of wisdom (Ex 28:3).

The Ephod
Ex 39:2–7

6 They shall make the ephod of gold, of blue, and of purple, of scarlet, and fine twined linen, the work of a skilled workman. 7 It shall have the two shoulder pieces attached to its two corners, so it shall be joined together. 8 The skillfully woven waistband of the ephod, which is on it, shall be of the same workmanship, of the same material: of gold, of blue and purple, and scarlet, and fine twisted linen.

9 You shall take two onyx stones and engrave on them the names of the children of Israel, 10 six of their names on one stone, and the other six names of the rest on the other stone, according to their birth. 11 With the work of an engraver in stone, like the engravings of a signet, you shall engrave the two stones with the names of the children of Israel. You shall set them in filigree of gold. 12 You shall put the two stones on the shoulders of the ephod as stones of memorial for the children of Israel, and Aaron shall bear their names before the LORD on his two shoulders as a memorial. 13 You shall make filigree settings of gold, 14 and two chains of pure gold. You shall make them of twisted cord and fasten the braided chains to the filigree settings.

The Breastplate
Ex 39:8–21

15 You shall make the breastplate of judgment, the work of a skillful workman. You shall make it in the same manner as the ephod. Of gold, of blue, and of purple, and of scarlet, and of fine twisted linen you shall make it. 16 It is to be square when doubled: a span[7] in length and a span in width. 17 You shall set in it four rows of stones. The first row shall be a sardius, a topaz, and a carbuncle; 18 the second row an emerald, a sapphire, and a diamond; 19 the third row a jacinth, an agate, and an amethyst; 20 and the fourth row a beryl, an onyx, and a

27:9 Ex 38:9–20
27:16 Ex 26:36
27:21 Nu 18:23
28:1 Nu 18:7
28:2 Ex 31:10
28:4 Ex 28:39–40
28:12 Ex 28:29
28:17 Eze 28:13

[1] *9* About 150 feet, or 45 meters; and in v. 11. [2] *12* About 75 feet, or 23 meters; and in v. 13. [3] *14* About 23 feet, or 6.8 meters; and in v. 15. [4] *16* About 30 feet, or 9 meters. [5] *18* About 150 feet long and 75 feet wide, or 45 meters long and 23 meters wide. [6] *18* About 7½ feet, or 2.3 meters. [7] *16* About 9 inches, or 23 centimeters.

jasper. They shall be set in gold filigree. 21 The stones shall be according to the names of the children of Israel, twelve, according to their names, each like the engravings of a signet, every one according to his name for the twelve tribes.

22 You shall make for the breastplate braided chains of pure gold. 23 You shall make on the breastplate two rings of gold and shall put the two rings on the two ends of the breastplate. 24 You shall put the two braided chains of gold on the two rings which are on the ends of the breastplate. 25 You shall fasten the other two ends of the two braided chains in the two filigree settings and put them on the front of the shoulder pieces of the ephod. 26 You shall make two rings of gold and shall put them on the two ends of the breastplate, on the edge of it which is toward the inner side of the ephod. 27 You shall make two other rings of gold and shall put them on the two shoulder pieces of the ephod underneath toward the front, close to the place where it is joined above the skillfully woven waistband of the ephod. 28 They shall bind the breastplate by its rings to the rings of the ephod with a blue cord, so that it may be above the skillfully woven waistband of the ephod, and so that the breastplate will not come loose from the ephod.

29 Aaron shall bear the names of the children of Israel on the breastplate of judgment over his heart when he goes into the holy place, as a memorial before the LORD continually. 30 You shall put the Urim and the Thummim in the breastplate of judgment, and they shall be over Aaron's heart when he goes in before the LORD. And Aaron shall bear the judgment of the children of Israel over his heart before the LORD continually.

Other Priestly Garments

Ex 39:22–31

31 You shall make the robe of the ephod completely blue. 32 There shall be a hole at the top of it, in the middle of it. Around its opening it shall have a binding of woven work, like the opening of a coat of mail, so that it will not be torn. 33 You shall make on its hem pomegranates of blue, and of purple, and of scarlet, all around its hem, and bells of gold between them all around: 34 a golden bell and a pomegranate, a golden bell and a pomegranate, all around on the hem of the robe. 35 It shall be on Aaron when he ministers. And its sound shall be heard when he goes into the holy place before the LORD, and when he comes out, so that he does not die.

36 You shall make a plate of pure gold and engrave on it, like the engravings of a signet,

HOLINESS TO THE LORD.

37 You shall put it on a blue cord, so that it may be upon the turban. It is to be on the front of the turban. 38 It shall be on Aaron's forehead, so that Aaron may bear the iniquity of the holy things which the children of Israel shall consecrate in regard to all their holy gifts. And it shall always be on his forehead, so that they may be accepted before the LORD.

39 You shall embroider the tunic of fine linen, and you shall make the turban of fine linen, and you shall make the sash, the work of an embroiderer. 40 For Aaron's sons you shall make tunics. You shall make sashes for them, and you shall make caps for them, for glory and for beauty. 41 You shall put them on Aaron your brother, and on his sons with him, and shall anoint them, and consecrate them, and sanctify them, that they may minister to Me as priests.

42 You shall make linen undergarments for them to cover their naked skin. They shall reach from the waist to the thighs. 43 They shall be on Aaron and on his sons when they come into the tent of meeting or when they come near to the altar to minister in the holy place, so that they may not bear iniquity and die.

It shall be a perpetual statute to him and his descendants after him.

Consecration of the Priests

Lev 8:1–36

29 Now this is the thing that you shall do to them to consecrate them, to minister as priests to Me: Take one young bull and two rams without blemish, 2 and unleavened bread, and unleavened cakes mixed with oil, and unleavened wafers anointed with oil—you shall make them of wheat flour. 3 You shall put them into one basket and bring them in the basket with the bull and the two rams. 4 Then you shall bring Aaron and his sons to the door of the tent of meeting and wash them with water. 5 You shall take the garments and clothe Aaron *with* the tunic and the robe of the ephod and the ephod and the breastplate, and gird him with the skillfully woven band of the ephod. 6 And you shall put the turban on his head and put the holy crown on the turban. 7 Then shall you take the anointing oil and pour it on his head and anoint him. 8 You shall bring his sons and put tunics on them. 9 You shall gird them with sashes, Aaron and his sons, and put the headbands on them, and the priest's office shall be theirs for a perpetual statute.

Thus you shall consecrate Aaron and his sons.

10 Then you shall bring a bull before the tent of meeting, and Aaron and his sons shall put

28:28 Nu 15:38
28:29 Ex 28:12
28:30 Lev 8:8
28:36 Zec 14:20
28:38 Lev 10:17
28:40 Ex 39:41
28:41 Ex 29:7
28:42 Lev 6:10
28:43 Ex 27:21
29:2 Nu 6:15
29:4 Ex 40:12
29:6 Lev 8:9
29:7 Lev 21:10
29:8 Lev 8:13
29:9 Nu 18:7
29:10 Lev 1:4

their hands on the head of the bull. 11 You shall
kill the bull before the Lord by the door of the
tent of meeting. 12 You shall take of the blood
of the bull, and put it on the horns of the altar
with your finger, and pour all the blood beside
the bottom of the altar. 13 You shall take all the
fat that covers the entrails, and the lobe that
is above the liver, and the two kidneys, and
the fat that is on them, and burn them on the
altar. 14 But the flesh of the bull, its skin, and
its dung, you shall burn with fire outside the
camp. It is a sin offering.

15 You shall also take one ram, and Aaron
and his sons shall put their hands on the head
of the ram. 16 You shall slay the ram, and you
shall take its blood and sprinkle it around on
the altar. 17 Then you shall cut the ram in pieces,
and wash its entrails and its legs, and put
them with its pieces and its head. 18 You shall
burn the whole ram on the altar. It is a burnt
offering to the Lord. It is a soothing aroma, an
offering made by fire to the Lord.

19 Then you shall take the other ram, and
Aaron and his sons shall put their hands on
the head of the ram. 20 You shall kill the ram
and take some of its blood and put it on the
tip of the right ear of Aaron, and on the tip of
the right ear of his sons, and on the thumb of
their right hand, and on the great toe of their
right foot, and sprinkle the blood around on
the altar. 21 You shall take some of the blood
that is on the altar and some of the anointing
oil and sprinkle it on Aaron and on his garments,
and on his sons, and on the garments
of his sons with him. So he and his garments
shall be consecrated, along with his sons and
his sons' garments with him.

22 Also you shall take the fat and the rump of
the ram, and the fat that covers the entrails and
the lobe above the liver, and the two kidneys,
and the fat that is on them and the right shoulder
(for it is a ram of consecration), 23 and one
loaf of bread, and one cake of oiled bread, and
one wafer out of the basket of the unleavened
bread that is before the Lord. 24 And you shall
put all of these in the hands of Aaron and in
the hands of his sons, and shall wave them
for a wave offering before the Lord. 25 Then
you shall take them from their hands and burn
them on the altar for a burnt offering, for a
soothing aroma before the Lord. It is an offering
made by fire to the Lord. 26 You shall take
the breast of Aaron's ram of consecration, and
wave it as a wave offering before the Lord, and
it shall be your portion.

27 You shall consecrate the breast of the
wave offering that is waved and the thigh of
the priest's portion that is contributed from the
ram of the consecration, from that which was
for Aaron and from that which was for his sons.
28 It shall be for Aaron and his sons by a statute
forever, for it is a contribution. It shall be a contribution
from the children of Israel from their
peace offerings, their contributions to the Lord.

29 The holy garments belonging to Aaron are
to belong to his sons after him, so that they
may be anointed in them and be consecrated
in them. 30 The son that is priest in his stead
shall put them on seven days when he comes
into the tent of meeting to minister in the holy
place.

31 You shall take the ram of the consecration
and boil its flesh in a holy place. 32 Aaron and
his sons shall eat the flesh of the ram and the
bread that is in the basket by the door of the
tent of meeting. 33 They shall eat those things
by which the atonement was made in order to
consecrate and sanctify them, but no one else
shall eat *them*, because they are holy. 34 If any
of the flesh from the consecrations or from
the bread remain until the morning, then you
shall burn the remainder with fire. It shall not
be eaten, because it is holy.

35 Thus shall you do to Aaron and his sons according
to all that I have commanded you. You
shall consecrate them for seven days. 36 Every
day you must offer a bull as a sin offering for
atonement, and you must cleanse the altar
when you make atonement for it. You must
anoint it to consecrate it. 37 For seven days you
must make atonement for the altar and consecrate
it, and then the altar will be most holy,
and whatever touches the altar will be holy.

The Daily Offerings

38 Now this is what you are to offer on the
altar: two one-year-old lambs every day, continually.
39 The one lamb you must offer in the
morning, and the other lamb you must offer
at sundown. 40 And with the first lamb *will be*
a tenth *of an ephah*[1] of flour mingled with the
fourth part of a hin[2] of beaten oil, and the
fourth part of a hin of wine for a drink offering.
41 The other lamb you must offer at sundown
and must offer with it the same grain offering
and the same drink offering as in the morning,
for a soothing aroma, an offering made by fire
to the Lord.

42 This will be a continual burnt offering
throughout your generations at the door of
the tent of meeting before the Lord, where I
will meet with you, to speak to you there. 43 I
will meet there with the children of Israel, and
it will be consecrated by My glory.

44 I will sanctify the tent of meeting and the
altar. I will also sanctify both Aaron and his

29:12 Ex 27:2
29:13 Lev 3:3–4
29:14 Lev 4:11–12
29:15 Ex 29:19
29:18 Ge 8:21
29:19 Ex 29:3
29:22 Ex 29:13
29:23 Ex 29:2–3
29:24 Lev 7:30
29:25 Lev 8:28
29:26 Lev 8:29
29:27 Lev 10:15
29:29 Nu 18:8
29:30 Nu 20:28
29:31 Lev 8:31
29:32 Mt 12:4
29:33 Nu 18:4
29:34 Ex 12:10
29:36 Heb 10:11
29:37 Ex 40:10
29:38 Nu 28:3–8
29:39 Eze 46:13–15
29:40 Lev 23:13
29:42 Ex 25:22
29:43 1Ki 8:11
29:44 Lev 21:15

[1] *40* Likely about 3½ pounds, or 1.6 kilograms. [2] *40* Likely about 1 quart, or 1 liter.

sons to minister as priests to Me. 45 I will dwell among the children of Israel and will be their God. 46 Then they will know that I am the LORD their God who brought them out of the land of Egypt, so that I may dwell among them. I am the LORD their God.

The Altar of Incense
Ex 37:25–28

30 Also, you must make an altar for burning incense. You must make it of acacia wood. 2 It must be a cubit in length, and its width a cubit. It will be square. Its height will be two cubits;[1] the horns shall be of one piece with it. 3 You must overlay it with pure gold, its top, its sides all around, and its horns; and you must make a molding of gold all around it. 4 You must make two golden rings for it under its molding. You must make *them* on its two sides, on opposite sides of it, and they will be holders for the poles with which to carry it. 5 Then you must make the poles of acacia wood and overlay them with gold. 6 You must put it before the veil that is by the ark of the testimony, in front of the mercy seat that is over the testimony, where I will meet with you.

7 Aaron must burn sweet incense on it. Every morning, when he trims the lamps, he must burn incense. 8 When Aaron lights the lamps at sundown, he must burn incense on it. It is to be a perpetual incense before the LORD throughout your generations. 9 You must offer no strange incense on it, nor burnt sacrifice, nor grain offering, and you must not pour out a drink offering on it. 10 Aaron must make atonement on its horns once a year with the blood of the sin offering of atonement. Once a year he must make atonement on it throughout your generations. It is most holy to the LORD.

The Atonement Money

11 The LORD spoke to Moses, saying: 12 When you take the census of the children of Israel according to their number, then each man is to pay a ransom for his life to the LORD when you count them, so that there be no plague among them when you number them. 13 This is what everyone who is counted must give: half a shekel according to the shekel of the sanctuary[2] (a shekel is twenty gerahs). The half shekel will be the offering to the LORD. 14 Everyone who is counted, from twenty years old and above, must give an offering to the LORD. 15 The rich must not give more and the poor must not give less than half a shekel when they give the offering to the LORD, to make atonement for your lives. 16 You must take the atonement money of the children of Israel and give it for the service of the tent of meeting, so that it may be a memorial to the children of Israel before the LORD, to make atonement for your lives.

The Bronze Basin

17 The LORD spoke to Moses, saying: 18 You must also make a basin of bronze, with its base also of bronze, for washing, and you must put it between the tent of meeting and the altar, and you must put water in it. 19 For Aaron and his sons must wash their hands and their feet from it. 20 When they go into the tent of meeting, or when they come near the altar to minister by burning incense as an offering made by fire to the LORD, they must wash with water so that they will not die. 21 So they must wash their hands and their feet, so that they will not die. And it will be a perpetual statute for them, even to him and to his seed throughout their generations.

The Anointing Oil

22 Moreover the LORD spoke to Moses, saying: 23 Take for yourself choice spices: five hundred shekels[3] of pure myrrh, half as much sweet-smelling cinnamon (two hundred and fifty shekels[4]), two hundred and fifty shekels of sweet-smelling cane, 24 five hundred shekels of cassia, according to the shekel of the sanctuary, and a hin[5] of olive oil. 25 And you must make with it a holy anointing oil, a perfumed compound, the work of a perfumer. It will be a holy anointing oil. 26 And you must anoint the tent of meeting with it, along with the ark of the testimony, 27 and the table and all its utensils, and the lampstand and its utensils, and the altar of incense, 28 and the altar of burnt offering with all its utensils, and the basin and its stand. 29 You must consecrate them, so that they may be most holy. Whatever touches them must be holy.

30 You must anoint Aaron and his sons and consecrate them, so that they may minister as priests to Me. 31 You must speak to the children of Israel, saying, "This will be a holy anointing oil to Me throughout your generations. 32 It must not be poured out on anyone's body, nor shall you make any other like it in composition. It is holy, and it will be holy to you. 33 Whoever makes anything like it or whoever puts any of it on a layman will be cut off from his people."

The Incense

34 Then the LORD said to Moses: Take for yourself sweet spices, stacte and onycha and galbanum, sweet spices with pure frankincense of equal amounts. 35 You shall make of these

29:45 Ex 25:8
29:46 Ex 20:2
30:1 Ex 37:25–28
30:2 Ex 27:2
30:4 Ex 25:27
30:6 Ex 25:21–22
30:7 1Sa 2:28
30:9 Lev 10:1
30:10 Lev 16:18
30:12 Nu 31:50
30:13 Lev 27:25
....
30:18 Ex 38:8
30:19 Isa 52:11
30:21 Ex 28:43
30:23 SS 4:14
30:25 Ex 37:29
30:26 Nu 7:1
30:29 Ex 29:37
30:30 Lev 8:12
30:32 Ex 30:25
30:33 Ex 30:38

[1] *2* About 1½ feet long and wide and 3 feet high, or 45 centimeters long and wide and 90 centimeters high. [2] *13* About ⅕ ounce, or 5.8 grams; and in v. 15. [3] *23* About 12½ pounds, or 5.8 kilograms; and in v. 24. [4] *23* About 6¼ pounds, or 2.9 kilograms. [5] *24* Likely about 1 gallon, or 3.8 liters.

SPIRITLED WOMAN

COUNSEL FROM THE SPIRIT BASICS

Jehovah M'Kaddesh

For centuries and even today the Hebrew people have been set aside from the rest of the world by their observance of the Sabbath—the period starting at sundown on Friday evening and ending at sundown on Saturday. It was a time to rest, yes, but it also began with a ceremony of blessing, during which the parents, particularly the father, spoke a blessing over his children.

> Speak also to the children of Israel, saying, "You must surely keep My Sabbaths, for it is a sign between Me and you throughout your generations, that you may know that I am the LORD who sanctifies you."
>
> —EXODUS 31:13

The word *sanctification* signifies a "setting apart of something for a special purpose." It denotes separating something out as special. The Greek word for "church" is *ecclesia*, which means, "the called-out ones." We have been called out of the troubles and limitations of the world to be used for good—as catalysts of positive change and as a people looking to establish the city of God on the earth. "The God Who Sanctifies," *Jehovah M'Kaddesh*, is the God who has called us out of the chaos of the world system to manifest His grace and transformational power.

Cindy Trimm

an incense, a compound expertly blended,
mingled with salt, pure and holy. 36 You must
beat some of it very fine and put part of it
before the testimony in the tent of meeting
where I will meet with you. It will be most
holy to you. 37 As for the perfume which you
will make, you may not make *it* for yourselves
using the same recipe. It must be holy for the
LORD to you. 38 Whoever makes anything like
it in order to use it as perfume must be cut off
from his people.

30:36 Ex 25:22
30:38 Ex 30:33

....

31:2 Ex 36:1
31:3 1Ki 7:14
31:7 Ex 36:8–37:9
31:8 Ex 37:10–28
31:9 Ex 38:1–8
31:11 Ex 37:29
31:13 Eze 20:12
31:15 Ex 16:23
31:17 Ge 1:31
31:18 Ex 24:12
32:1 Ex 24:18

The Tabernacle Artisans
Ex 35:30–35

31 Now the LORD spoke to Moses, saying:
2 See, I have called by name Bezalel
the son of Uri, the son of Hur, of the tribe of
Judah. 3 I have filled him with the Spirit of God
in wisdom, in understanding, in knowledge,
and in all manner of craftsmanship 4 to devise
artistic works for work with gold, with silver,
and with bronze, 5 and in the cutting of stones
for settings, and in carving of wood, to work
in all manner of craftsmanship. 6 I, indeed, I
have given him Oholiab, the son of Ahisamak,
of the tribe of Dan, and I have given skill to all
who are specially skilled, that they may make
everything that I have commanded you: 7 the
tent of meeting, the ark of the testimony, and
the mercy seat that is on it, and all the furniture
of the tent, 8 the table and its utensils, and the
pure lampstand with all its utensils, and the
altar of incense, 9 the altar of burnt offering
with all its utensils, and the basin and its stand,
10 the woven garments, the holy garments for
Aaron the priest and the garments of his sons,
to minister as priests, 11 the anointing oil and
sweet incense for the holy place. They must
make *them* according to all that I have commanded you.

The Sabbath Law

12 The LORD spoke to Moses, saying: 13 Speak
also to the children of Israel, saying, "You
must surely keep My Sabbaths, for it is a sign
between Me and you throughout your generations, that you may know that I am the LORD
who sanctifies you.

14 "You shall keep the Sabbath, for it is holy
to you. Everyone who defiles it will surely be
put to death. For whoever does any work on
it, that person will be cut off from among his
people. 15 Six days may work be done, but on
the seventh is the Sabbath of complete rest,
holy to the LORD. Whoever does any work on
the Sabbath day will surely be put to death.
16 Therefore the children of Israel must keep
the Sabbath, to observe the Sabbath throughout their generations, for a perpetual covenant.
17 It is a sign between Me and the children of
Israel forever, for in six days the LORD made
heaven and earth, but on the seventh day He
rested and was refreshed."

18 When He had made an end of communing
with him on Mount Sinai, He gave Moses the
two tablets of testimony, tablets of stone, written with the finger of God.

The Golden Calf

32 Now when the people saw that Moses
delayed coming down from the mountain, the people gathered themselves together

REBEKAH

A GREAT LOVE ADVENTURE

The story of Isaac and Rebekah is a picture of the great love adventure between Christ and His bride. Abraham (Father God) commissions his servant (the Holy Spirit) to find a bride for his son, Isaac (Christ).

In Genesis 24:10 the servant leaves the father and goes through the wilderness with ten camels loaded down with a large dowry. When he arrives at the town, it is evening, the time when the women would go draw water at the well. The servant prays to God and puts forth a fleece: "Let it be that the young woman to whom I shall say, 'Please lower your pitcher, that I may drink,' and she shall say, 'Drink, and I will give your camels drink also'—let her be the one that You have appointed for Your servant Isaac" (v. 14).

Before the servant even finished his prayer, Rebekah came to the well, going about her daily chores. The servant asked her for a drink, and immediately something quickened her heart. She answered, "Yes, of course, and may I also water your camels?"

In the natural all Rebekah saw were thirsty camels. She didn't know about the son. But hidden beneath this simple request for a drink was a prophetic invitation for her. Often the Holy Spirit comes to us asking for what could be compared to only a drink of water, and we reject His invitation because we can't see what is concealed within it.

After Rebekah watered the camels, the servant presented her with jewelry. When she told her brother Laban about the visitor and the gifts, Laban ran to meet the servant and extended him a personal invitation to his home (v. 31).

When the servant entered Laban's home, he refused to eat anything before he first explained his mission. Then he shared the story of Isaac's miraculous birth and recounted the series of events from earlier that day.

After the servant related the story, they ate and fellowshipped all night. The next morning, as the servant prepared to leave, Rebekah's family asked if he would stay another ten days before taking Rebekah to his master. The servant refused the invitation because he had a mission. He had to get the bride to the son! When Rebekah's family asked her if she was willing to go with the servant, she replied, "I will go."

The Holy Spirit is looking for voluntary lovers who will say, "Yes, I will go with You! Yes, I want to know the Bridegroom King! Yes, I am willing to leave my family to follow You now."

Rebekah didn't know how to get to Isaac on her own. But she was willing to leave her comfort zone, totally dependent upon the servant.

The Holy Spirit is jealous to bring a pure, lovesick bride to Jesus. He knows the fears and weaknesses we have. He knows the times our hearts faint, and He will protect us. He takes away everything that hinders love and wants to do a radical work of healing, cleansing, and deliverance so that we will mature into the beautiful bride we were created to be.

Every time we say yes to the Holy Spirit's leading, our Bridegroom's heart must leap as He sees His bride moving closer to Him in love. Jesus wears many crowns, but the one crown the bride can give Him is her love.

Jill Austin

around Aaron and said to him, "Come, make
us gods which will go before us. As for this
Moses, the man who brought us up out of the
land of Egypt, we do not know what has be-
come of him."

2 Aaron said to them, "Break off the gold ear-
rings that are in the ears of your wives, your
sons, and your daughters, and bring *them* to
me." 3 So all the people broke off the gold ear-
rings that were in their ears and brought *them*
to Aaron. 4 He received *them* from their hand,
and fashioned it with an engraving tool, and
made it into a molded calf. Then they said,
"This is your god, O Israel, who brought you
up from the land of Egypt."

5 When Aaron saw *it*, he built an altar before
it. And Aaron made a proclamation and said,
"Tomorrow will be a feast to the LORD." 6 So
they rose up early on the next day, and offered
burnt offerings, and brought peace offerings.
And the people sat down to eat and to drink,
and rose up to play.

7 The LORD spoke to Moses, "Go, and get
down, for your people, whom you brought
out of the land of Egypt, have corrupted
themselves. 8 They have quickly turned aside
from the way which I commanded them. They
have made for themselves a molded calf, and
have worshipped it, and have sacrificed to it,
and said, 'This is your god, O Israel, which
has brought you up from the land of Egypt.' "

9 Then the LORD said to Moses, "I have seen
this people, and certainly, it is a stiff-necked
people. 10 Now therefore let Me alone, so that
My wrath may burn against them and I may
destroy them. And I will make of you a great
nation."

11 But Moses sought the favor of the LORD his
God, and said, "LORD, why does Your wrath
burn against Your people, whom You have
brought forth from the land of Egypt with great
power and with a mighty hand? 12 Why should
the Egyptians speak, saying, 'With evil *intent*
He brought them out, to kill them in the moun-
tains and to destroy them from the face of the
earth'? Turn from Your fierce wrath and relent
of this harm against Your people. 13 Remem-
ber Abraham, Isaac, and Israel, Your servants,
to whom You swore by Yourself, and said to
them, 'I will multiply your descendants as the
stars of the heavens, and all this land that I
have spoken of will I give to your descendants,
and they will inherit *it* forever.' " 14 Then the
LORD relented of the harm which He said He
would do to His people.

15 Moses turned and went down from the
mountain with the two tablets of testimony
in his hand. The tablets were written on both
their sides. They were written on one side and
on the other. 16 The tablets were God's work,
and the writing was God's writing, engraved
on the tablets.

17 When Joshua heard the noise of the people
as they shouted, he said to Moses, "There is a
sound of war in the camp."

18 But he said:

"It is not the sound of those who shout for
victory,
nor is it the sound of those who cry
because of being overcome,
but I hear the sound of singing."

19 As soon as he came near the camp, he
saw the calf and the dancing, and Moses' an-
ger burned, so he threw the tablets from his
hands and shattered them at the bottom of the
mountain. 20 Then he took the calf which they
had made and burned it in the fire, ground it
to powder, and scattered it on the water, and
made the children of Israel drink it.

21 Moses said to Aaron, "What did this people
do to you, that you have brought so great a sin
upon them?"

22 Aaron said, "Do not let the anger of my lord
burn. You know that the people are set on evil.
23 For they said to me, 'Make a god for us which
will go before us, for this Moses, the man that
brought us up from the land of Egypt, we do
not know what has become of him.' 24 I said to
them, 'Whoever has any gold, let them break it
off.' So they gave *it* to me, and then I threw it
into the fire, and this calf came out.' "

25 Now when Moses saw the people were in
a frenzy, for Aaron had let them get complete-
ly out of control, causing derision from their
enemies, 26 then Moses stood in the gate of
the camp and said, "Whoever is on the LORD's
side, come to me." And all the Levites gathered
themselves together around him.

27 He said to them, "Thus says the LORD, the
God of Israel, 'Every man fasten his sword on
his side, and go back and forth from gate to
gate throughout the camp, and let every man
kill his brother, and every man his friend, and
every man his neighbor.' " 28 The Levites did
according to the word of Moses, and about
three thousand men of the people died that
day. 29 For Moses had said, "Consecrate your-
selves today to the LORD, that He may bestow
a blessing on you this day, for every man op-
poses his son and his brother."

30 On the next day Moses said to the people,
"You have committed a great sin, and now I
will go up to the LORD. Perhaps I can make
atonement for your sin."

31 Then Moses returned to the LORD and said,
"Oh, this people has committed a great sin and
have made a god of gold for themselves. 32 Yet

32:4 Dt 9:16
32:5 2Ki 10:20
32:6 1Co 10:7
32:7 Dt 9:12
32:8 Ex 20:3–4
32:9 Ex 33:3
32:10 Dt 9:14
32:11 Dt 9:18–20
32:12 Nu 14:13–16
32:13 Ge 12:7
32:14 Ps 106:45
32:15 Dt 9:15
32:16 Ex 31:18
32:19 Dt 9:16–17
32:20 Dt 9:21
32:21 Ge 20:9
32:22 Dt 9:24
32:23 Ex 32:1–4
32:24 Ex 32:4
32:27 Nu 25:5
32:28 Dt 33:9
32:30 1Sa 12:20
32:31 Ex 20:23
32:32 Ps 69:28

now, if You will, forgive their sin, but if not,
I pray, blot me out of Your book which You
have written."
33 Then the LORD said to Moses, "Whoever
has sinned against Me, I will blot him out of
My book. 34 So go now, lead the people to the
place of which I have spoken to you. Indeed,
My angel will go before you. Nevertheless in
the day when I punish, I will indeed punish
them for their sin."
35 And the LORD plagued the people because
they had made the calf, the one that Aaron
made.

The Command to Leave Sinai

33 Then the LORD said to Moses, "Depart,
go up from here, you and the people
whom you have brought up from the land of
Egypt, to the land which I swore to Abraham,
Isaac, and Jacob, saying, 'To your descendants
I will give it.' 2 I will send an angel before you,
and I will drive out the Canaanite, the Amorite,
the Hittite, the Perizzite, the Hivite, and the
Jebusite. 3 *Go up* to a land flowing with milk
and honey. However, I will not go up in your
midst, for you are a stiff-necked people, and I
might destroy you on the way."
4 When the people heard this disturbing
word, they mourned. And no one put on his
ornaments. 5 For the LORD had said to Moses,
"Say to the children of Israel, 'You are a stiff-
necked people. If I went up among you for one
moment, I might destroy you. Now therefore,
take off your ornaments, so that I may know
what I will do to you.' " 6 The children of Isra-
el stripped themselves of their ornaments by
Mount Horeb.

The Tent of Meeting

7 Moses took the tent and pitched it outside
the camp, a good distance from the camp,
and called it the tent of meeting. And anyone
who sought the LORD would go out to the tent
of meeting which was outside the camp. 8 So
whenever Moses went out to the tent, all the
people would rise up and stand, every man
at the entrance of his tent, and gaze after Mo-
ses until he entered the tent. 9 And whenever
Moses entered the tent, the pillar of cloud de-
scended and stood at the entrance of the tent,
and the LORD spoke with Moses. 10 When all
the people saw the pillar of cloud standing at
the entrance of the tent, all the people rose up
and worshipped, every man at the entrance
of his tent. 11 The LORD spoke to Moses face to
face, just as a man speaks to his friend. When
he returned to the camp, his servant Joshua,
the son of Nun, a young man, did not depart
from the tent.

32:33 Eze 18:4
32:34 Ex 23:20
33:1 Ge 12:7
33:2 Ex 32:34
33:3 Ex 3:8
33:4 Nu 14:39
33:6 Ex 33:4
33:7 Ex 29:42–43
33:8 Nu 16:27
33:9 Ps 99:7
33:11 Nu 12:8

. . . .

33:12 Ex 33:17
33:13 Dt 9:29
33:14 Jos 21:44
33:15 Ex 33:3
33:16 Nu 14:14
33:17 Ge 19:21
33:18 Ex 33:20
33:20 Isa 6:5
33:22 Ps 91:4
33:23 Ex 33:20
34:1 Ex 32:19
34:2 Ex 19:20
34:3 Ex 19:12–13
34:5 Ex 33:19
34:6 Ro 2:4

The Glory of God

12 Moses said to the LORD, "See, You say to me,
'Bring up this people,' but You have not let me
know whom You will send with me. Yet You
have said, 'I know you by name, and you have
also found grace in My sight.' 13 Now therefore,
I pray You, if I have found favor in Your sight,
show me now Your way, that I may know You,
and that I may find favor in Your sight. Consid-
er too that this nation is Your people."
14 And He said, "My Presence will go with
you, and I will give you rest."
15 Then he said to Him, "If Your Presence
does not go with us, do not bring us up from
here. 16 For how will it be known that I have
found favor in Your sight, I and Your people?
Is it not by Your going with us, so that we will
be distinguished, I and Your people, from all
the people who are on the face of the earth?"
17 The LORD said to Moses, "I will do this thing
of which you have spoken, for you have found
favor in My sight, and I know you by name."
18 Then Moses said, "I pray, show me Your
glory."
19 Then He said, "I will make all My goodness
pass before you, and I will proclaim the name
of the LORD before you. I will be gracious to
whom I will be gracious and will show mercy
on whom I will show mercy." 20 He said, "You
cannot see My face, for no man can see Me
and live."
21 Then the LORD said, "Indeed, there is a
place by Me. You must stand on the rock.
22 While My glory passes by, I will put you in
a cleft of the rock and will cover you with My
hand while I pass by. 23 Then I will take away
My hand, and you will see My back, but My
face may not be seen."

The New Stone Tablets

34 Now the LORD said to Moses, "Cut out
for yourself two tablets of stone like
the first, and I will write on these tablets the
words that were on the first tablets, which you
broke. 2 Be ready in the morning, and come up
in the morning to Mount Sinai, and present
yourself there to Me on the top of the moun-
tain. 3 No one is to come up with you. Do not
let anyone be seen anywhere on the mountain,
and the flocks or herds may not graze in front
of the mountain."
4 So he cut out two tablets of stone like the
first, and Moses rose up early in the morning
and went up to Mount Sinai, just as the LORD
had commanded him, and took in his hand the
two tablets of stone. 5 Then the LORD descended
in the cloud, and stood with him there, and
proclaimed the name of the LORD. 6 The LORD
passed by before him, and proclaimed, "The

Looking Beyond the Veil

The Christian religion does not require that women veil themselves outwardly. We are often proud that we are free from the bondage of physical veiling. Yet often we are unknowingly draped in a multitude of veils.

Veils can be used deliberately to hide us from the view of others. After forty days on the mountain with God, Moses used a veil to cover the reflected radiance of his face, which still shone brightly with the glory of God:

> But whenever Moses went in before the LORD to speak with Him, he took the veil off until he came out. Then he came out and spoke to the children of Israel what he had been commanded. The children of Israel saw the face of Moses, that the skin of Moses' face shone, and then Moses put the veil over his face again until he went in to speak with Him.
>
> —EXODUS 34:34–35

Before the sacrifice of Jesus, each of us was separated from the presence of God by a veil. The holy of holies was hidden from the sight of all mankind except the high priest. A thick curtain separated the holy of holies from the holy place. It could only be entered by the high priest, and then only when he brought the blood for atonement.

With the death of Jesus, this heavy, multilayered, and colored veil was torn asunder:

> At that moment the curtain of the temple was torn in two, from the top to the bottom. And the ground shook, and the rocks split apart.
>
> —MATTHEW 27:51

A veiled heart is not hidden from God. It only obscures our vision. This causes us to believe we're unseen. Looking at our image does nothing to transform us; it simply discourages us. It limits us to ourselves. It is when we behold the glory of the Lord that we are being transformed into the same image.

To look deeper by the Spirit is to turn our focus from ourselves and toward Christ in us, the hope of glory. He speaks loving and comforting words to us as He patiently points us beyond the obvious toward the glorious unseen.

These study questions will help you take off the spiritual veil and really see yourself. However, because seeing your own image is often discouraging, remember that as a SpiritLed woman, you have been transformed into the image of God. Reflect carefully on each question below, and then write your responses on the lines.

1. Do you feel your relationship with the Lord is shrouded and cold?

____

____

____

2. Are you fighting confusion over whether God accepts you when you come into His presence?

3. When you go before God, is it easier for you to behold your flaws and image, or do you see His goodness and mercy?

4. Was your reaction to reading the Bible different when you were first saved? How did you see it then, and how do you see it now?

5. Try to identify the veils you use to shroud yourself from God's light:

- ❑ Fear
- ❑ Religion
- ❑ Unbelief
- ❑ Materialism
- ❑ Doubt
- ❑ Rebellion
- ❑ Pride
- ❑ Other: ____________

Pray, asking God to rent these veils in two. Then sit and "Son-bathe" in the warmth of God's presence, basking in His truth.

Lisa Bevere

Lord, the Lord God, merciful and gracious,
slow to anger, and abounding in goodness and
truth, 7 keeping mercy for thousands, forgiving
iniquity and transgression and sin, but who
will by no means clear *the guilty*, visiting the
iniquity of fathers on the children and on the
children's children, to the third and the fourth
generation."
8 Moses made haste and bowed to the ground
and worshipped. 9 He said, "If now I have
found favor in Your sight, O Lord, let my Lord,
I pray, go among us, for we are a stiff-necked
people. Pardon our iniquity and our sin, and
take us for your inheritance."

The Covenant Renewed

10 Then He said: Indeed, I am going to make a
covenant before all your people. I will do won-
ders such as have not been done in all the earth
nor in any nation. And all the people among
whom you live will see the work of the Lord,
for it is a fearful thing that I will do with you.
11 Obey what I command you this day. Indeed,
I am going to drive out before you the Amorite,
the Canaanite, the Hittite, the Perizzite, the Hi-
vite, and the Jebusite. 12 Watch yourself so that
you make no covenant with the inhabitants of
the land where you are going, lest it become
a snare in your midst. 13 But you shall destroy
their altars, break their *sacred* pillars, and cut
down their Asherah poles[1] 14 (for you shall not
worship any other god, for the Lord, whose
name is Jealous, is a jealous God), 15 lest you
make a covenant with the inhabitants of the
land, and they prostitute themselves with their
gods, and sacrifice to their gods, and someone
invites you to eat of his sacrifice. 16 And then
you take of their daughters for your sons, and
their daughters prostitute themselves after
their gods. They will make your sons prostitute
themselves after their gods.
17 You shall make no molded gods for your-
selves.
18 You shall keep the Feast of Unleavened
Bread. For seven days you are to eat un-
leavened bread, as I commanded you, in the
month of Aviv, for in the month of Aviv you
came out of Egypt.
19 Every firstborn of the womb belongs to
Me, and every firstborn male among your live-
stock, whether ox or sheep. 20 But you must
redeem with a lamb the firstborn of a donkey,
and if you fail to redeem him, then you must
break his neck. You must redeem all the first-
born of your sons.
No one may appear before Me empty-handed.

34:7 Ex 20:5–6
34:8 Ex 4:31
34:9 Ps 33:12
34:11 Ex 33:2
34:12 Ex 23:32–33
34:13 Ex 23:24
34:15 Nu 25:2
34:17 Ex 32:8
34:18 Ex 13:4
34:19 Ex 13:2
34:20 Ex 23:15

....

34:21 Ex 23:12
34:22 Ex 23:16
34:23 Ex 23:14
34:24 Ex 33:2
34:25 Ex 23:18
34:26 Ex 23:19
34:27 Ex 17:14
34:28 Ex 24:18
34:29 Ex 32:15
34:34 2Co 3:16
35:1 Ex 34:32
35:2 Ex 20:9–10

21 You shall work six days, but on the seventh
day you must rest. Even at the time of plowing
and harvest you must rest.
22 You must observe the Feast of Weeks, the
first fruits of the wheat harvest, and the Feast
of Ingathering at the end of the year. 23 Three
times in the year all your males must appear
before the Lord God, the God of Israel. 24 For I
will drive out the nations before you and en-
large your borders. No man will covet your
land when you go up to appear before the Lord
your God three times in the year.
25 You must not offer the blood of My sacrifice
with leaven, nor is the sacrifice of the Feast
of the Passover to be left until the following
morning.
26 The first of the first fruits of your land you
must bring to the house of the Lord your God.
You must not boil a young goat in its moth-
er's milk.
27 Then the Lord said to Moses: Write down
these words, for in accordance with these
words I have made a covenant with you and
with Israel. 28 So he was there with the Lord
forty days and forty nights. He did not eat
bread or drink water. And He wrote on the
tablets the words of the covenant, the Ten
Commandments.

Moses' Radiant Face

29 When Moses came down from Mount Si-
nai with the two tablets of testimony in the
hands of Moses, when he came down from
the mountain, Moses did not know that the
skin of his face shone while he talked with
Him. 30 So when Aaron and all the children of
Israel saw Moses, amazingly, the skin of his
face shone, and they were afraid to come near
him. 31 But Moses called to them, and Aaron
and all the rulers of the congregation returned
to him, and Moses spoke to them. 32 Afterward
all the children of Israel drew near, and he
commanded them all that the Lord had spoken
to him on Mount Sinai.
33 When Moses finished speaking with them,
he put a veil over his face. 34 But whenever
Moses went in before the Lord to speak with
Him, he took the veil off until he came out.
Then he came out and spoke to the children
of Israel what he had been commanded. 35 The
children of Israel saw the face of Moses, that
the skin of Moses' face shone, and then Moses
put the veil over his face again until he went
in to speak with Him.

Sabbath Regulations

35 Moses gathered all the congregation
of the children of Israel together, and
said to them: These are the things the Lord has
commanded you to do. 2 Six days shall work

[1]13 Carved images of a female deity.

be done, but on the seventh day you shall
have a holy day, a Sabbath of rest to the LORD.
Whoever does any work on it must be put to
death. 3 You must not kindle fire in any of your
dwellings on the Sabbath day.

Offerings for the Tabernacle

Ex 25:1–7; 39:32–41

4 Moses said to all the congregation of the
children of Israel: This is the thing which the
LORD commanded, saying: 5 Take from among
you an offering to the LORD. Whoever is of a
willing heart, let him bring it as an offering to
the LORD: gold, silver, and bronze, 6 and blue,
purple, and scarlet, fine linen, goats' hair,
7 rams' skins dyed red, and porpoise skins,
and acacia wood, 8 oil for the light, and spices
for anointing oil, and for the fragrant incense,
9 onyx stones, and gemstones to be set for the
ephod and for the breastplate.

10 Every skilled craftsman among you shall
come and make all that the LORD has com-
manded: 11 the tabernacle with its tent and its
covering, its hooks and its boards, its bars, its
pillars, and its sockets; 12 the ark with its poles,
the mercy seat, and the veil that conceals it;
13 the table with its poles, and all its utensils,
and the showbread; 14 the lampstand also for
the light and its utensils and its lamps, and
the oil for the light; 15 and the incense altar
with its poles, and the anointing oil and the
fragrant incense, and the hanging for the door
at the entrance of the tabernacle; 16 the altar
of burnt offering with its bronze grating, its
poles, and all its utensils, the basin and its
stand; 17 the hangings of the court, its pillars
and their sockets, and the curtain for the gate
of the court; 18 the pegs of the tabernacle and
the pegs of the court and their cords; 19 the
woven garments for serving in the holy place,
the holy garments for Aaron the priest and the
garments of his sons, to minister as priests.

20 Then all the congregation of the children
of Israel departed from the presence of Mo-
ses. 21 Everyone whose heart stirred him and
everyone whose spirit was willing came and
brought the LORD's offering for the work of the
tent of meeting and for all its service and for
the holy garments. 22 They came, both men and
women, as many as had willing hearts, and
brought brooches, earrings, rings and brace-
lets, all kinds of gold jewelry, and everyone
that offered an offering of gold to the LORD.
23 Everyone who had blue, purple, and scarlet,
and fine linen, and goats' hair, and red skins
of rams, and porpoise skins, brought them.
24 Everyone who was making a contribution
of silver and bronze brought the LORD's offer-
ing, and everyone who had acacia wood for
any work of the service brought it. 25 All the
women that were skilled spun with their hands
and brought what they had spun, both of blue,
purple, and scarlet, and of fine linen. 26 All the
women whose hearts stirred them to action
and were skilled spun goats' hair. 27 The lead-
ers brought onyx stones and gemstones to be
set for the ephod and for the breastplate, 28 and
spice and oil for the light, and for the anointing
oil, and for the fragrant incense. 29 The chil-
dren of Israel brought a willing offering to the
LORD, every man and woman whose heart was
willing to bring *material* for all the work which
the LORD had commanded through Moses to
be made.

Bezalel and Oholiab

Ex 31:2–6

30 Moses said to the children of Israel: See,
the LORD has called by name Bezalel the son
of Uri, the son of Hur, of the tribe of Judah.
31 And He has filled him with the Spirit of God,
in wisdom, in understanding, and in knowl-
edge, and in all manner of craftsmanship, 32 to
design artistic works, to work in gold, in silver,
and in bronze, 33 and in the cutting of stones
for settings and in the carving of wood in order
to make every manner of artistic work. 34 He
also has put in his heart to teach, both he and
Oholiab, the son of Ahisamak, of the tribe of
Dan. 35 He has filled them with skill to do all
manner of work as craftsmen; as designers; as
embroiderers in blue, in purple, in scarlet, and
in fine linen; and as weavers: as craftsmen of
every work and artistic designers.

36 So Bezalel and Oholiab, and every
skilled person, in whom the LORD has
put skill and understanding to know how to
do all manner of work for the service of the
sanctuary, are to do the work according to all
that the LORD has commanded.

2 Moses called Bezalel and Oholiab and ev-
ery skilled person in whom the LORD had put
wisdom, everyone whose heart stirred him to
come to the work to do it. 3 They received from
Moses all the offerings which the children of
Israel had brought to do the work of the ser-
vice of the sanctuary, and they *continued* to
bring to him freewill offerings every morning.
4 And all the skilled men who were doing all
the work of the sanctuary came from the work
they were doing, 5 and they said to Moses, "The
people are bringing much more than is need-
ed for the service of the work which the LORD
commanded *us* to do."

6 So Moses issued a command, and they cir-
culated a proclamation throughout the camp,
saying, "Let no man or woman do any more
work for the offering of the sanctuary." So the
people were restrained from bringing *any*

35:3 Ex 16:23
35:5 Ex 25:2–7
35:11 Ex 26:1–37
35:12 Ex 25:10–22
35:13 Ex 25:23–30
35:14 Ex 25:31–39
35:15 Ex 30:1–10
35:16 Ex 27:1–8
35:18 Ex 27:19
35:19 Ex 31:10
35:21 Ex 25:2
35:23 1Ch 29:8
35:25 Ex 28:3
35:26 Ex 35:21
35:27 1Ch 29:6
35:28 Ex 30:23–38
35:29 Ex 35:4
35:34 Ex 31:6
35:35 Ex 35:31
36:1 Ex 28:3
36:3 Ex 35:29
36:5 2Ch 24:14

more. 7 For the material they had was sufficient
for all the work and more than enough to do it.

Construction of the Tabernacle
Ex 26:1–37

8 Every skilled man among those who were
doing the work made the tabernacle with ten
curtains of fine twisted linen, and blue, and
purple, and scarlet, with cherubim that were
the work of skillful workmen. 9 The length of
each curtain was twenty-eight cubits, and the
width of each curtain four cubits.[1] All of the
curtains were the same size. 10 He joined
the five curtains to one another, and the other
five curtains he joined to one to another. 11 He
made loops of blue on the edge of the outer-
most curtain in the first set. He did likewise
along the edge of the outermost curtain in the
second set. 12 He made fifty loops in the one
curtain and made fifty loops on the edge of
the curtain which was in the second set. The
loops were opposite one another. 13 He made
fifty gold clasps and joined the curtains to one
another with the clasps, so that the tabernacle
was a unit.

14 He made curtains of goats' hair for a tent
over the tabernacle. He made eleven curtains
in all. 15 The length of each curtain was thirty
cubits, and the width of each curtain was four
cubits.[2] The eleven curtains were all the same
size. 16 He joined five curtains by themselves
and six curtains by themselves. 17 He made
fifty loops on the outermost edge of the cur-
tain in the *first* set, and he made fifty loops
on the edge of the curtain which joined the
second set. 18 He made fifty bronze clasps to
join the tent together, so that it would be one
unit. 19 He made a covering for the tent out of
rams' skins dyed red and a covering of por-
poise skins above.

20 Then he made boards for the tabernacle
out of acacia wood, standing upright. 21 The
length of each board was ten cubits, and the
width of each board was one and a half cu-
bits.[3] 22 Each board had two tenons, equally
distant from each other. He did this for all the
boards of the tabernacle. 23 He made boards
for the tabernacle: twenty boards for the
south side. 24 He made forty sockets of silver
under the twenty boards; two sockets under
one board for its two tenons and two sockets
under another board for its two tenons. 25 For
the other side of the tabernacle, which is to-
ward the north corner, he made twenty boards,
26 and their forty sockets of silver: two sockets
under one board, and two sockets under an-
other board. 27 For the back of the tabernacle
westward he made six boards. 28 He made two
boards for the corners of the tabernacle at the
back. 29 They were doubled beneath and joined
together at the top in one ring. He did this with
both of them in both the corners. 30 There were
eight boards with their sockets of silver, sixteen
sockets, two under every board.

31 He made bars of acacia wood, five for the
boards of one side of the tabernacle, 32 and
five bars for the boards of the other side of the
tabernacle, and five bars for the boards of the
tabernacle for the back to the west. 33 He made
the middle bar to pass through the boards from
the one end to the other. 34 He overlaid the
boards with gold, and made their rings of gold
to be places for the bars, and overlaid the bars
with gold.

35 He made a veil of blue, and purple, and
scarlet, and fine twined linen. He made cher-
ubim, the work of a skillful designer. 36 He
made four pillars of acacia wood and overlaid
them with gold with their hooks of gold, and
he cast four sockets of silver for them. 37 He
made a hanging for the tabernacle entrance
of blue, purple, scarlet, and fine twisted linen,
the work of an embroiderer. 38 And he made
its five pillars with their hooks, and he overlaid
their tops and their bands with gold, but their
five sockets were of bronze.

Making the Ark of the Covenant
Ex 25:10–20

37 Now Bezalel made the ark of acacia
wood. Its length was two and a half
cubits, and its width a cubit and a half, and its
height a cubit and a half.[4] 2 He overlaid it with
pure gold, inside and out, and made a gold
molding for it all around. 3 He cast four rings
of gold for it on its four feet, with two rings on
one side and two rings on the other side of it.
4 He made poles of acacia wood and overlaid
them with gold. 5 He put the poles into the
rings on the sides of the ark to carry the ark.

6 He made the mercy seat of pure gold, two
and a half cubits long and one and a half cu-
bits wide. 7 He made two cherubim of gold.
He made them of hammered metal on the two
ends of the mercy seat: 8 one cherub on one
end, and one cherub on the other end. Of one
piece with the mercy seat he made the cheru-
bim on its two ends. 9 The cherubim spread out
their wings upward, covering the mercy seat
with their wings, with their faces toward each
other. The faces of the cherubim were looking
toward the mercy seat.

36:12 Ex 26:5
36:14 Ex 26:7–13
36:20 Ex 25:5
....
36:31 Ex 26:26–29
36:35 Mt 27:51
37:6 Heb 9:5

1 *9* About 42 feet long and 6 feet wide, or 13 meters long and 1.8 meters wide. *2* *15* About 45 feet long and 6 feet wide, or 14 meters long and 1.8 meters wide. *3* *21* About 15 feet long and 2¼ feet wide, or 4.5 meters long and 68 centimeters wide. *4* *1* About 3¾ feet long and 2¼ feet wide and high, or 1.1 meters long and 68 centimeters wide and high; similarly in v. 6.

Making the Table for the Showbread
Ex 25:23–29

10 He made the table of acacia wood, two cubits long and a cubit wide and a cubit and a half high.[1] 11 And he overlaid it with pure gold and made a gold molding for it all around. 12 Also he made a rim for it of a handbreadth[2] all around, and he made a gold molding for the rim all around. 13 He cast four rings of gold for it and put the rings on the four corners that were on its four feet. 14 Close by the rim were the rings, the holders for the poles to carry the table. 15 He made the poles of acacia wood and overlaid them with gold, to carry the table. 16 He made the utensils which were on the table, its dishes and its pans and its bowls and its jars, to be used in pouring out offerings, of pure gold.

Making the Lampstand
Ex 25:31–39

17 Then he made the lampstand of pure gold. He made it of hammered work, its base and its shaft. Its cups, its buds, and its blossoms were of the same *piece*. 18 Six branches were extending from its sides, three branches of the lampstand from one side of it, and three branches of the lampstand from the other side of it. 19 Three cups shaped like almond flowers, a bulb and a flower were on the first branch, and three cups shaped like almond flowers, a bulb and a flower were on the next branch, and the same for the six branches going out of the lampstand. 20 In the lampstand there were four cups made like almond flowers, its bulbs and its flowers. 21 And a bulb was under the first two branches from it, and a bulb under the next two branches from it, and a bulb under the third two branches from it, according to the six branches coming out of it. 22 Their bulbs and their branches were of the same *piece*. All of it was one hammered work of pure gold.

23 He made its seven lamps with its snuffers and its trays of pure gold. 24 He made it and all of its utensils from a talent[3] of pure gold.

Making the Altar of Incense
Ex 30:1–5

25 He made the incense altar of acacia wood. Its length was a cubit, and the width a cubit, a square, and two cubits high.[4] Its horns were of the same *piece*. 26 He overlaid it with pure gold, its top, its sides all around, and its horns. He also made a gold molding for it all around. 27 He also made two rings of gold for it under its molding, on its two sides, on opposite sides, to be places for the poles to carry it. 28 He made the poles of acacia wood and overlaid them with gold.

37:17 Ex 25:31–39
37:25 Ex 30:1–5

38:1 Ex 27:1–8
38:8 Ex 40:7
38:9 Ex 27:9–19

29 He made the holy anointing oil and the pure incense of sweet spices, according to the work of a perfumer.

Making the Altar of Burnt Offering
Ex 27:1–8

38 He made the altar of burnt offering of acacia wood. It was five cubits[5] long and five cubits wide. It was square, and it was three cubits high.[6] 2 He made its horns on its four corners. The horns were part of the same *piece*, and he overlaid it with bronze. 3 He made all the utensils of the altar, the pots, and the shovels, and the basins, the flesh hooks, and the fire pans. He made all its utensils of bronze. 4 He made for the altar a bronze grating, a network beneath, under its ledge, reaching halfway up. 5 He cast four rings for the four ends of the bronze grating to provide places for the poles. 6 He made the poles of acacia wood and overlaid them with bronze. 7 He put the poles into the rings on the sides of the altar with which to carry it. He made *the altar* hollow, out of boards.

Making the Bronze Basin

8 He made the basin of bronze with its base of bronze from the mirrors of the women who served at the entrance of the tent of meeting.

Making the Court of the Tabernacle
Ex 27:9–19

9 He made the courtyard: On the south side southward the hangings of the courtyard were of fine twisted linen, one hundred cubits;[7] 10 their twenty pillars and their twenty bases were of bronze. The hooks of the pillars and their bands *were* of silver. 11 For the north side the hangings were one hundred cubits; their twenty pillars and their twenty sockets *were* of bronze. The hooks of the pillars and their bands *were* of silver.

12 For the west side the hangings were fifty cubits[8] *with* their ten pillars and their ten sockets. The hooks of the pillars and their bands *were* of silver. 13 For the east side eastward, fifty cubits. 14 The hangings of one side of the gate were fifteen cubits[9] *with* their three pillars and their three sockets, 15 and also for the other side of the court gate. On both sides of the gate of the courtyard the hangings *were* fifteen cubits *with* their three pillars and their three sockets. 16 All the hangings of the courtyard all around were of fine twisted linen. 17 The sockets for the pillars were of bronze, the hooks of the

[1] *10* About 3 feet long, 1½ feet wide, and 2¼ feet high, or 90 centimeters long, 45 centimeters wide, and 68 centimeters high. [2] *12* About 3 inches, or 7.5 centimeters. [3] *24* About 75 pounds, or 34 kilograms. [4] *25* About 1½ feet long and wide and 3 feet high, or 45 centimeters long and wide and 90 centimeters high. [5] *1* About 7½ feet, or 2.3 meters long and wide. [6] *1* About 4½ feet, or 1.4 meters. [7] *9* About 150 feet, or 45 meters. [8] *12* About 75 feet, or 23 meters. [9] *14* About 22 feet, or 6.8 meters.

pillars and their bands *were* of silver, and the overlaying of their tops of silver, and all the pillars of the courtyard were furnished with silver bands.

18 The screen for the gate of the courtyard was embroidered of blue, and purple, and scarlet, and fine twisted linen. Its length was twenty cubits,[1] and its height was five cubits,[2] corresponding to the hangings of the courtyard. 19 Their four pillars and their four sockets *were* of bronze. Their hooks and their bands *were* of silver, and the overlaying of their tops and their bands *were* of silver. 20 All the tent pegs of the tabernacle and of the courtyard all around were bronze.

The Inventory of the Tabernacle

21 This is the inventory of the tabernacle, the tabernacle of testimony, as it was counted according to the commandment of Moses for the service of the Levites by the hand of Ithamar, son of Aaron the priest. 22 Bezalel, the son of Uri the son of Hur of the tribe of Judah, made all that the LORD commanded Moses. 23 With him was Oholiab the son of Ahisamak, of the tribe of Dan, an engraver and designer, an embroiderer in blue and purple and scarlet yarns, and fine linen. 24 All the gold that was used for the work, in all the work of the sanctuary, even the gold of the wave offering, was twenty-nine talents, and seven hundred and thirty shekels,[3] according to the shekel of the sanctuary.

25 The silver of those who were numbered of the congregation was one hundred talents,[4] and a thousand, seven hundred and seventy-five shekels,[5] according to the shekel of the sanctuary; 26 a bekah for every man, that is, half a shekel,[6] according to the shekel of the sanctuary, for everyone who was numbered, from twenty years old and upward, for six hundred and three thousand, five hundred and fifty men. 27 The hundred talents of silver were for casting the sockets of the sanctuary and the sockets of the veil—a hundred sockets of the hundred talents, a talent for a socket. 28 Of the one thousand seven hundred seventy-five shekels, he made hooks for the pillars and overlaid their tops and made bands for them.

29 The bronze of the wave offering was seventy talents and two thousand four hundred shekels.[7] 30 With it he made the sockets for the door of the tent of meeting, and the bronze altar and its bronze grating, and all the utensils of the altar, 31 and the sockets of the courtyard all around, and the sockets of the courtyard gate, and all the tent pegs of the tabernacle, and all the tent pegs of the courtyard all around.

Making the Priestly Garments

39 Now from the blue, purple, and scarlet they made woven garments for serving in the holy place and made the holy garments for Aaron, just as the LORD commanded Moses.

Making the Ephod

Ex 28:6–14

2 He made the ephod of gold, blue, purple, and scarlet, and fine twisted linen. 3 Then they hammered the gold into thin sheets and cut it into threads to work them into the blue, the purple, the scarlet, and the fine linen, with skillful work. 4 They made shoulder pieces for it, in order to attach it together. It was joined by the two edges together. 5 The skillfully woven waistband of his ephod that was on it was like it, of the same material, of gold, blue, purple, and scarlet, and fine twisted linen, just as the LORD commanded Moses.

6 They set the onyx stones enclosed in gold filigree settings; they were engraved like the engravings of a signet, according to the names of the children of Israel. 7 And he put them on the shoulder pieces of the ephod, to be stones for a memorial to the children of Israel, just as the LORD commanded Moses.

Making the Breastplate

Ex 28:15–28

8 He made the breastplate, the work of a skillful workman, like the workmanship of the ephod: of gold, blue, purple, and scarlet, and fine twisted linen. 9 It was square. They made the breastplate folded double, a span[8] long and a span wide when doubled. 10 They set in it four rows of stones. A row of sardius, topaz, and carbuncle was the first row; 11 the second row, an emerald, a sapphire, and a diamond; 12 the third row, a jacinth, an agate, and an amethyst; 13 and the fourth row, a beryl, an onyx, and a jasper. They were enclosed in settings of gold filigree. 14 The stones were corresponding to the names of the children of Israel, twelve, corresponding to their names, *like* the engravings of a signet, each with its name, corresponding to the twelve tribes.

15 They made on the breastplate braided chains like cords of pure gold. 16 They made two gold filigree settings and two gold rings and put the two rings in the two ends of the breastplate. 17 They put the two braided chains of gold in the two rings on the ends of the breastplate. 18 The *other* two ends of the two braided chains they fastened in the two filigree *settings* and put them on the shoulder pieces of

38:21 Nu 1:50
38:23 Ex 35:34
38:24 Lev 27:25
38:26 Nu 1:46
38:27 Ex 26:19
38:30 Ex 26:37

39:1 Ex 31:10
39:2 Ex 28:6–12
39:6 Ex 28:9
39:14 Rev 21:12

1 18 About 30 feet, or 9 meters. *2 18* About 7½ feet, or 2.3 meters. *3 24* A little over a ton, or 1 metric ton. *4 25* About 3¾ tons, or 3.4 metric tons; and in v. 27. *5 25* About 44 pounds, or 20 kilograms; and in v. 28. *6 26* About ⅕ ounce, or 5.7 grams. *7 29* About 2½ tons, or 2.4 metric tons. *8 9* About 9 inches, or 23 centimeters.

the ephod at the front of it. 19 They made two
rings of gold and put them on the two ends
of the breastplate, on the edge of it which was
on the inner side of the ephod. 20 They made
two other golden rings and put them on the
two sides of the ephod underneath, toward the
front of it, over against where it joined, above
the waistband of the ephod. 21 They bound
the breastplate by its rings to the rings of the
ephod with a blue cord, so that it might be
above the waistband of the ephod, and that
the breastplate might not come loose from the
ephod, just as the LORD commanded Moses.

Making Other Priestly Garments
Ex 28:31–43

22 Then he made the robe of the ephod of
woven work, all of blue. 23 There was an open-
ing in the middle of the robe, like the opening
of a coat of mail, with a band all around the
opening so that it should not be torn. 24 They
made on the hems of the robe pomegranates
of blue, purple, and scarlet, and twisted linen.
25 They made bells of pure gold and put the
bells between the pomegranates all around on
the hem of the robe. 26 There was a bell and a
pomegranate, a bell and a pomegranate, all
around about the hem of the robe to be used
in service, just as the LORD commanded Moses.
27 They made tunics of finely woven linen for
Aaron and his sons, 28 and the turban of fine
linen, and the decorated caps of fine linen, and
linen breeches of fine twisted linen. 29 The sash
was of fine twisted linen and blue, purple, and
scarlet, the work of an embroiderer, just as the
LORD commanded Moses.
30 They made the plate of the holy crown of
pure gold and wrote on it an inscription, like
the engravings of a signet:

HOLINESS TO THE LORD.

31 They attached to it a blue cord, to fasten it to
the turban above, just as the LORD commanded
Moses.

The Work Completed
Ex 35:10–19

32 Thus all the work of the tabernacle of the
tent of meeting was finished, and the children
of Israel did according to all that the LORD com-
manded Moses—so they did. 33 They brought
the tabernacle to Moses, the tent and all its
furnishings: its clasps, its boards, its bars, and
its pillars, and its sockets; 34 and the covering of
rams' skins dyed red, and the covering of por-
poise skins, and the screening veil; 35 the ark
of the testimony and its poles and the mercy
seat; 36 the table, and all its utensils, and the
showbread; 37 the pure gold lampstand, with its
arrangement of lamps, and all its utensils, and
the oil for the light; 38 and the gold altar, and

39:27 Eze 44:18
39:28 Ex 28:4
39:32 Ex 39:42–43
39:38 Ex 30:7
....
39:42 Ex 35:10
39:43 Lev 9:22–23
40:3 Nu 4:5
40:6 Ex 40:29
40:9 Lev 8:10
40:10 Ex 29:36–37
40:12 Lev 8:1–13
40:13 Ex 28:41
40:15 Nu 25:13
40:17 Nu 7:1

the anointing oil, and the fragrant incense, and
the curtain for the entrance to the tent; 39 the
bronze altar, and its bronze grating, its poles
and all its utensils, the basin and its stand;
40 the hangings of the courtyard, its pillars, and
its sockets, and the curtain for the courtyard
gate, its cords, and its pegs, and all the utensils
for the service of the tabernacle, for the tent
of meeting; 41 the woven garments of service
to do service in the holy place, and the holy
garments for Aaron the priest and his sons'
garments, to minister as priests.
42 The children of Israel did all the work ac-
cording to all that the LORD commanded Moses.
43 Moses looked over all the work, and indeed
they had done it; as the LORD had commanded,
so they had done. Then Moses blessed them.

The Tabernacle Erected

40 Now the LORD spoke to Moses, saying:
2 On the first day of the first month you
shall set up the tabernacle of the tent of meet-
ing. 3 You shall put the ark of the testimony in
it and screen the ark with the veil. 4 You shall
bring in the table and arrange the things that
are to be arranged on it, and you shall bring
in the lampstand and set up its lamps. 5 You
shall set the gold altar of incense before the
ark of the testimony and put the curtain for the
entrance to the tabernacle.
6 You shall set the altar of the burnt offering
in front of the entrance of the tabernacle of
the tent of meeting. 7 You shall set the basin
between the tent of meeting and the altar and
put water in it. 8 You shall set up the court-
yard around it and hang up the curtain at the
courtyard gate.
9 You shall take the anointing oil and anoint
the tabernacle and all that is in it and shall
consecrate it and all its furnishings, and it shall
be holy. 10 Then you shall anoint the altar of the
burnt offering and all its utensils, and conse-
crate the altar, and the altar shall be most holy.
11 You shall anoint the basin and its stand, and
consecrate it.
12 Then you shall bring Aaron and his sons to
the entrance of the tent of meeting and wash
them with water. 13 You shall put the holy gar-
ments on Aaron and anoint him and conse-
crate him, so that he may minister to Me as
a priest. 14 You shall bring his sons and clothe
them with tunics. 15 Then you shall anoint them
just as you anointed their father, so that they
may minister to Me as priests, for their anoint-
ing will surely be an everlasting priesthood
throughout their generations. 16 Thus Moses
did. According to all that the LORD commanded
him, so he did.
17 In the first month of the second year, on
the first day of the month, the tabernacle was

erected. 18 Moses erected the tabernacle and
fastened its sockets, and set up its boards, and
inserted its bars, and erected its pillars. 19 Then
he spread the tent over the tabernacle and put
the covering of the tent on top of it, just as the
LORD commanded Moses.
20 He took the testimony and put it into the
ark, attached the poles to the ark, and put the
mercy seat on top of the ark. 21 And he brought
the ark into the tabernacle, and set up the veil
of the screening, and screened the ark of the
testimony, just as the LORD commanded Moses.
22 Then he put the table in the tent of meeting
on the north side of the tabernacle outside the
veil. 23 He set the bread in order on it before the
LORD, just as the LORD had commanded Moses.
24 And he put the lampstand in the tent of
meeting, opposite the table, on the south side
of the tabernacle. 25 He lighted the lamps be-
fore the LORD, just as the LORD commanded
Moses.
26 Then he put the gold altar in the tent of
meeting before the veil. 27 And he burned fra-
grant incense on it, just as the LORD command-
ed Moses. 28 Then he set up the curtain at the
entrance of the tabernacle.
29 He put the altar of burnt offering by the
entrance of the tabernacle of the tent of meet-
ing and offered on it the burnt offering and the
grain offering, just as the LORD commanded
Moses.
30 Then he set the basin between the tent of
meeting and the altar and put water in it for
washing. 31 It was there Moses and Aaron and
his sons washed their hands and their feet.
32 Whenever they went into the tent of meeting,
and whenever they came near the altar, they
washed, just as the LORD commanded Moses.
33 He erected the courtyard all around the tab-
ernacle and the altar, and set up the curtain of
the courtyard gate. So Moses finished the work.

The Glory of the LORD

34 Then the cloud covered the tent of meeting,
and the glory of the LORD filled the tabernacle.
35 Moses was not able to enter into the tent of
meeting because the cloud settled on it, and
the glory of the LORD filled the tabernacle.
36 When the cloud was lifted up from over the
tabernacle, the children of Israel would set out
in all their journeys. 37 But if the cloud was not
lifted up, then they did not set out until the day
that it was lifted. 38 For the cloud of the LORD
was on the tabernacle by day, and fire was on it
by night, in the sight of all the house of Israel,
throughout all their journeys.

40:20 Ex 16:34
40:21 Ex 26:33
40:22 Ex 26:35
40:25 Ex 25:37
40:26 Ex 40:5
40:27 Ex 30:7
40:28 Ex 40:5
40:29 Ex 40:6
40:30 Ex 40:7
40:33 Ex 40:8
40:34 Nu 9:15–23
40:35 1Ki 8:11
40:36 Ne 9:19
40:37 Nu 9:19–22
40:38 Ex 13:21

Author: Traditionally Moses

Written: Between 1440 and 1400 BC

Themes: Holiness, Sacrifice

LEVITICUS

Dear Spirit Led Woman,

One of the most often quoted verses from Leviticus is, "You shall be holy, for I am holy" (Lev 11:45). Because God is holy, He requires holiness from His people. All of the instructions for sacrifice, worship, purification, and consecration in Leviticus are symbolic of the sanctifying work that the Holy Spirit does in our lives today.

That's why in 1 Peter 1:16 the same command to be holy is repeated for the early church. God desires that you, as a follower of Christ, lay your life on the altar so that He may consume it with His fire. When you embrace the fire and allow it to work in you, old things are burned out and a new passion for God is released. You desire to stay in close communion with Him because you realize that without continual grace, it is impossible to be holy.

If the flame of passion for the things of God has grown dim in your life or halfhearted faith has set in, I encourage you to pray right where you are, "Lord, send Your fire!" When you do, I know He will both consume and empower you with new passion and purpose.

Joy F. Strang

The Burnt Offering

1 And the LORD called Moses and spoke to him from the tent of meeting, saying: 2 Speak to the children of Israel and say to them: When an individual among you brings an offering to the LORD, you shall bring your offering from the livestock, either from the herd or from the flock.

3 If his offering is a burnt sacrifice, and it is from the herd, he shall offer a male without blemish. At the door of the tent of meeting, he shall offer it of his own free will before the LORD. 4 Then he shall lay his hand on the head of the burnt offering, and it shall be accepted for him to make atonement[1] for him. 5 And he shall slaughter the bull before the LORD, and the sons of Aaron, the priests, shall bring the blood and sprinkle the blood on all the sides of the altar that is at the door of the tent of meeting. 6 Then he shall skin the burnt offering and cut it up into parts. 7 The sons of Aaron the priest shall put fire on the altar and arrange the wood on the fire. 8 Then the priests, the sons of Aaron, shall arrange the parts, with the head and the fat, on the wood that is on the fire that is on the altar. 9 But he shall wash its entrails and its legs in water, and the priest shall burn everything on the altar. It is a burnt sacrifice, a food offering made by fire, which is a pleasing aroma for the LORD.

10 If his gift for a burnt offering is from the flocks, whether from the sheep or from the goats, he shall bring a male without blemish. 11 He shall slaughter it at the north side of the altar before the LORD. And the sons of Aaron, the priests, shall sprinkle its blood on all the sides of the altar. 12 He shall cut it up into parts, with its head and its fat, and the priest shall arrange them on the wood that is on the fire that is on the altar. 13 But he shall wash the entrails and the legs with water. The priest shall bring it all and burn it on the altar. It is a burnt sacrifice, a food offering made by fire, which is a pleasing aroma for the LORD.

14 If his offering to the LORD is a burnt sacrifice of birds, then he shall bring his offering from turtledoves or from young pigeons. 15 The priest shall bring it to the altar, wring off its head, and burn it on the altar. Its blood shall be drained out on the side of the altar. 16 He shall remove its entrails with its feathers and throw it to the east side of the altar to the place of the ashes. 17 And he shall split it open by its wings, but not tear it in two. The priest shall burn it on the altar on the wood that is on the fire. It is a burnt sacrifice, a food offering made by fire, which is a pleasing aroma for the LORD.

[1]4 To appease wrath, remove sin, and reconcile with God.

1:1 Ex 19:3
1:2 Lev 22:18–19
1:3 Ex 12:5
1:4 Ex 29:10
1:5 Lev 1:11
1:6 Lev 7:8
1:9 Lev 1:13
1:11 Lev 1:5
1:14 Lev 5:7
1:17 Ge 15:10

2:1 Lev 6:14–18
2:2 Lev 5:12
2:3 Lev 10:12–13
2:4 Ex 29:2
2:9 Lev 2:2
2:10 Lev 2:3
2:12 Ex 23:19
2:13 Eze 43:24
2:14 Lev 23:10
3:1 Lev 1:3

The Grain Offering

2 When a person offers a grain offering to the LORD, his offering shall be of wheat flour. He shall pour olive oil on it and put frankincense on it. 2 And he shall bring it to the sons of Aaron, the priests, and he shall scoop out a handful of the flour and its oil, along with all its frankincense. And the priest shall burn this memorial portion on the altar, a food offering made by fire, which is a pleasing aroma for the LORD. 3 And the remainder of the grain offering shall belong to Aaron and to his sons, which is a most holy part of the food offerings to the LORD made by fire.

4 When you bring an oven-baked grain offering, it shall be unleavened cakes of fine flour mixed with oil or unleavened wafers spread with oil. 5 If your offering is grain on a griddle, it shall be of unleavened wheat flour mixed with olive oil. 6 Break it into pieces and pour oil on it. It is a grain offering. 7 If your offering is grain in a skillet, it shall be made of wheat flour in olive oil. 8 You shall bring the grain offering that is made of these things to the LORD, and when it is presented to the priest, he shall take it to the altar. 9 The priest shall remove a memorial portion from the grain offering and burn it on the altar, a food offering made by fire, which is a pleasing aroma for the LORD. 10 The remainder of the grain offering shall belong to Aaron and to his sons, which is a most holy part of the food offerings to the LORD made by fire.

11 No grain offering that you bring to the LORD shall be made with leaven, for you shall not burn leaven nor any honey as a food offering by fire to the LORD. 12 As an offering of first fruits, you may offer them to the LORD, but they shall not be offered on the altar for a pleasing aroma. 13 You shall season all your grain offerings with salt. You shall not fail to use the salt of the covenant of your God on your grain offering. With all your offerings you shall offer salt.

14 If you offer a grain offering of your first fruits to the LORD, you shall offer for the grain offering of your first fruits fresh ripe grain roasted by fire, coarsely ground new grain. 15 You shall put olive oil on it and frankincense on it. It is a grain offering. 16 The priest shall burn its memorial portion and some of its coarsely ground new grain and oil, along with all its frankincense as a food offering made by fire to the LORD.

The Peace Offering

3 If his offering is a peace sacrifice, and if he is offering from the herd, whether male or female, then he shall offer it without blemish before the LORD. 2 He shall lay his hand on the head of his offering and slaughter it at the door of the tent of meeting, and the sons of Aaron, the priests, shall sprinkle the blood on the sides of the altar. 3 He shall offer from the peace sacrifice, as a food offering made by fire to the LORD, the fat that covers the entrails and all the fat that is on the entrails, 4 and the two kidneys with the fat that is above them, which is on the loins, and the appendage on the liver which he shall remove with the kidneys. 5 Then the sons of Aaron shall burn it on the altar on the burnt sacrifice that is on the wood that is on the fire, as a food offering made by fire, which is a pleasing aroma for the LORD.

6 If his offering for a peace sacrifice to the LORD is from the flock, male or female, he shall offer it without blemish. 7 If he is offering a sheep for his offering, he shall offer it before the LORD. 8 He shall lay his hand upon the head of his offering and slaughter it before the tent of meeting, and the sons of Aaron shall sprinkle its blood on the sides of the altar. 9 He shall offer from the peace sacrifice, a food offering made by fire for the LORD, its fat, and the whole fatty tail which he shall remove close to the backbone, and the fat that covers the entrails, and all the fat that is on the entrails, 10 and the two kidneys with the fat that is above them, which is on the loins, and the appendage on the liver which he shall remove with the kidneys. 11 The priest shall burn it on the altar as a food offering made by fire for the LORD.

12 If his offering is a goat, he shall offer it before the LORD. 13 He shall lay his hand on its head and slaughter it before the tent of meeting, and the sons of Aaron shall sprinkle its blood on the sides of the altar. 14 He shall offer from it as his offering, an offering made by fire for the LORD, the fat that covers the entrails and all the fat that is on the entrails, 15 and the two kidneys with the fat that is above them, which is on the loins, and the appendage on the liver which he shall remove with the kidneys. 16 The priest shall burn them on the altar as a food offering made by fire for a pleasing aroma. All the fat belongs to the LORD.

17 As a continual statute for your generations in all your settlements, you shall not eat any fat or any blood.

The Sin Offering

4 And the LORD spoke to Moses, saying: 2 Speak to the children of Israel, saying: When a person sins unintentionally against any of the commandments of the LORD that should not be done, and he violates one of them, 3 if the anointed priest sins, so as to bring guilt on the people, he shall bring for his sin that he has committed a bull without blemish to the LORD for a sin offering. 4 He shall bring the bull to the opening of the tent of meeting before the LORD, and he shall lay his hand on the bull's head and slaughter the bull before the LORD. 5 The anointed priest shall take some of the bull's blood and bring it into the tent of meeting. 6 The priest shall dip his finger in the blood and sprinkle some of the blood seven times before the LORD in front of the veil of the sanctuary. 7 Then the priest shall put some of the blood on the horns of the altar of fragrant incense before the LORD which is in the tent of meeting, and shall pour *the rest of* the blood of the bull at the base of the altar of the burnt offering which is at the door of the tent of meeting. 8 Then he shall remove all the fat of the bull that is for the sin offering—the fat that covers the entrails—and all the fat that is on the entrails, 9 and the two kidneys with the fat that is above them, which is on the loins, and the appendage on the liver which he shall remove with the kidneys, 10 just as these are removed from the bull of the peace sacrifice, and the priest shall burn them on the altar of the burnt offering. 11 The skin of the bull, and all its flesh, with its head, its legs, its entrails, and its dung, 12 all *the rest of* the bull, he shall bring outside the camp to a *ritually* clean[1] place at the ash pile and burn it on wood with fire. It shall be burned on the ash heap.

13 If the whole congregation of Israel commits an unintentional sin, and the matter is hidden from the eyes of the assembly, and they do any one of the things that by the commandments of the LORD should not be done, and they are *found* guilty, 14 and the sin that they committed against *the commandment* becomes known, the congregation shall offer a bull for a sin offering, and they will bring it before the tent of meeting. 15 The elders of the congregation shall lay their hands on the head of the bull before the LORD, and the bull will be slaughtered before the LORD. 16 The anointed priest shall bring some of the bull's blood to the tent of meeting. 17 And the priest shall dip his finger in some of the blood and sprinkle it seven times before the LORD in front of the veil. 18 He shall put some of the blood on the horns of the altar that is before the LORD, which is in the tent of meeting, and he shall pour all *the rest* of the blood at the base of the altar of the burnt offering that is at the opening of the tent of meeting. 19 He shall remove all the fat from it and burn it on the altar. 20 He shall do to this bull just as he did to the bull of the

3:3 Ex 29:13
3:4 Lev 3:10
3:5 Lev 6:12
3:7 1Ki 8:62
3:8 Lev 1:5
3:11 Lev 21:6
3:13 Lev 3:8
3:16 Lev 7:23–25
3:17 Ge 9:4
4:2 Lev 4:27
4:3 Lev 4:14
4:4 Lev 1:3–4
4:5 Lev 16:14
4:7 Lev 8:15
4:8 Lev 3:3–5
4:9 Lev 3:4
4:11 Nu 19:5
4:12 Heb 13:11
4:13 Lev 5:17
4:15 Lev 1:4
4:16 Lev 4:5–12
4:20 Nu 15:25

[1] 12 "Clean" and "unclean" refer to ceremonial aspects of places, objects, or people.

sin offering; this is what he will do to it. And the priest shall make atonement for them, and they shall be forgiven. 21 He shall bring the bull outside the camp, and he shall burn it just as he burned the first bull. It is the sin offering of the congregation.

22 Whenever a leader sins, and he does unintentionally any one of the things that by the commandments of the LORD his God should not be done and is *found* guilty, 23 or his sin that he committed was made known to him, he shall bring as his offering a male goat without blemish, 24 and he shall lay his hand on the head of the goat, and he shall slaughter it in the place where they slaughter the burnt offering before the LORD. It is a sin offering. 25 The priest shall take some of the blood of the sin offering on his finger and put it on the horns of the altar of the burnt offering, and he shall pour out its blood at the base of the altar of the burnt offering. 26 And he shall burn all its fat on the altar, like the fat of the peace sacrifice, and the priest shall make atonement for him for his sin, and he shall be forgiven.

27 If any one of the common people should sin unintentionally by doing one of the things that by the commandments of the LORD should not be done, and is *found* guilty, 28 or his sin that he committed was made known to him, he shall bring as his offering a female goat without blemish, for his sin that he committed. 29 He shall lay his hand on the head of the sin offering, and he shall slaughter the sin offering in the place of the burnt offering. 30 The priest shall take some of its blood on his finger and put it on the horns of the altar of the burnt offering, and he shall pour out *the rest of* its blood at the base of the altar. 31 And he shall remove all its fat, just as the fat is removed from the peace sacrifice, and the priest shall burn it on the altar for a pleasing aroma to the LORD, and the priest shall make atonement for him, and he shall be forgiven.

32 And if he brings a sheep for a sin offering, he shall bring a female without blemish, 33 and lay his hand on the head of the sin offering, and he shall slaughter it for a sin offering in the place where they slaughter the burnt offering. 34 The priest shall take some of the blood of the sin offering on his finger and put it on the horns of the altar of the burnt offering, and all the *rest of* its blood he shall pour out at the base of the altar. 35 And he shall remove all the fat, just as the fat of the sheep is removed from the peace sacrifice, and the priest shall burn it on the altar as a food offering to the LORD made by fire. And the priest shall make atonement for his sin that he committed, and he shall be forgiven.

The Guilt Offering

5 When a person sins in hearing the spoken oath, and he is a witness, whether he saw or knew *about the incident*, if he does not report it, he bears guilt.

2 Or *when* a person touches any *ceremonially* unclean thing, whether it is a carcass of unclean wildlife, or a carcass of an unclean domesticated animal, or the carcass of an unclean crawling thing, and he did not realize it, then he has become unclean and guilty.

3 Or when he touches human uncleanness, any uncleanness by which he may become *ceremonially* unclean, and he did not realize it, when he realizes it, then he shall be guilty.

4 Or when a person swears by speaking rashly with his lips to do evil or to do good, anything that a man may speak rashly by oath, and he did not realize it, but when he realizes it, then he has become guilty of any of these things.

5 When he becomes guilty of one of these things, he shall confess that he has sinned in that thing. 6 And he shall bring his guilt offering to the LORD for his sin which he has committed, a female from the flock, a lamb or goat, for a sin offering. And the priest shall make atonement for him concerning his sin.

7 If he cannot afford an animal, then he shall bring for his guilt offering, on account of the sin that he committed, two turtledoves or two pigeons to the LORD, one for a sin offering and one for a burnt offering. 8 He shall bring them to the priest who shall offer the one for the sin offering first. He will wring off its head at its neck, but he shall not sever it. 9 Then he shall sprinkle some of the blood of the sin offering on the side of the altar, and the rest of the blood shall be poured out at the base of the altar. It is a sin offering. 10 But the second he shall treat as a burnt offering according to the regulation. The priest shall make atonement for him for his sin that he committed, and he shall be forgiven.

11 But if he cannot afford to bring two turtledoves or two pigeons, he shall bring for his offering *for the sin* that he committed one-tenth of an ephah[1] of wheat flour for a sin offering. He shall not place olive oil on it, nor shall he put frankincense on it, for it is a sin offering. 12 Then he shall bring it to the priest, and *the priest* shall scoop out a handful from it as a memorial portion and burn it on the altar as a food offering to the LORD made by fire. It is a sin offering. 13 The priest shall make atonement for

4:21 Lev 16:15
4:22 Lev 4:2
4:23 Lev 4:14
4:25 Lev 4:7
4:26 Lev 4:20
4:27 Lev 4:2
4:28 Lev 4:23
4:29 Lev 4:4
4:31 Lev 4:26
4:32 Lev 4:28
4:35 Lev 4:26

5:1 Lev 5:17
5:2 Lev 5:17
5:5 Nu 5:7
5:6 Lev 4:28
5:7 Lev 12:8
5:8 Lev 1:15
5:9 Lev 4:7
5:10 Lev 1:14–17
5:11 Nu 5:15
5:12 Lev 2:9
5:13 Lev 2:3

[1] 11 Likely about 3½ pounds, or 1.6 kilograms.

him concerning his sin that he committed from any of these *offenses*, and he shall be forgiven. The *remainder* will belong to the priest, like the grain offering.

Offerings With Restitution

14 The LORD spoke to Moses, saying: 15 When a person acts unfaithfully and sins unintentionally in regard to the holy things of the LORD, then for his restitution offering to the LORD he shall bring a ram without blemish from the flock—*or its equivalent*, in your estimation, *in* silver shekels (using the sanctuary shekel[1])—for a guilt offering. 16 And he shall repay *the sin* that he committed with regard to the holy thing and shall add a fifth to it and give it to the priest. The priest shall make atonement for him with the ram of the guilt offering, and he shall be forgiven.

17 If a person sins unintentionally and does any one of the things that by commandments of the LORD should not be done and he is *found* guilty, he shall bear his iniquity. 18 He shall bring to the priest a ram without blemish from the flock—or its equivalent value[2]—for a guilt offering. The priest shall make atonement for him concerning his error that he made unintentionally, and he shall be forgiven. 19 It is a guilt offering: He has indeed incurred guilt before the LORD.

6 And the LORD spoke to Moses, saying: 2 When a person sins and acts unfaithfully against the LORD by lying to another concerning *something left in* storage, or entrusted *to him*, or theft, or by extorting his neighbor, 3 or by finding a lost item and lying about it, and he swears falsely concerning one of all the things that a man may do to sin in these things, 4 when he sins and he is *found* guilty, he shall return whatever he stole, or whatever he extorted, or whatever was left in storage with him, or the lost item which he found, 5 or about which he swore falsely, then he shall repay it in full and shall add one-fifth to it. He shall give it to whom it belongs on the day that he is found guilty. 6 And he shall bring his guilt offering to the LORD, a ram without blemish from the flock—or its equivalent value[3]—for a guilt offering to the priest. 7 And the priest shall make atonement for him before the LORD, and he shall be forgiven for anything he may have done to incur guilt.

The Law of the Burnt Offering

8 The LORD spoke to Moses, saying: 9 Command Aaron and his sons, saying: This is the law for the burnt offering. The burnt offering shall be on the hearth upon the altar all night until the morning, and the fire of the altar shall be kept burning on it. 10 The priest shall put on his linen robe, and his linen undergarments on his body. Then he shall remove the ashes from the fire of the burnt offering on the altar, and he shall put them beside the altar. 11 Then he shall take off his garments and put on other garments, and he shall bring the ashes outside the camp to a clean place. 12 The fire on the altar shall be kept burning on it. It shall not go out. The priest shall feed it with wood every morning. He will arrange the burnt offering on it, and he shall burn the fat of the peace offerings on it. 13 A perpetual fire shall be kept burning on the altar. It shall never go out.

The Law of the Grain Offering

14 This is the law of the grain offering. The sons of Aaron shall offer it before the LORD on the altar. 15 He shall take from it a handful of the flour of the grain offering, and of the oil and all the frankincense which is on the grain offering, and shall burn it on the altar for a pleasing aroma as a memorial to the LORD. 16 Aaron and his sons shall eat the remainder of it; it shall be eaten without leaven in a holy place. They shall eat it in the court of the tent of meeting. 17 It shall not be baked with leaven. I have given it to them for their portion of My food offerings made by fire. It is most holy, as is the sin offering and as is the guilt offering. 18 All the males among the children of Aaron shall eat of it. It shall be a perpetual statute in your generations concerning the food offerings of the LORD made by fire. Everyone who touches them shall become holy.

19 The LORD spoke to Moses, saying: 20 This is the offering of Aaron and of his sons which they shall offer to the LORD in the day when he is anointed: a tenth part of an ephah[4] of wheat flour for a regular grain offering, half of it in the morning and half at night. 21 It shall be made on a griddle with olive oil. When it is well mixed, you shall bring it; and the baked pieces of the grain offering you shall offer as a pleasing aroma to the LORD. 22 The priest from among the sons of Aaron who is anointed to succeed him shall offer it. It is a perpetual statute to the LORD. It shall be completely burned up. 23 For every grain offering for the priest shall be completely burned up. It shall not be eaten.

The Law of the Sin Offering

24 The LORD spoke to Moses, saying: 25 Speak to Aaron and to his sons, saying: This is the law of the sin offering: In the place where the burnt offering is killed shall the sin offering

5:15 Ex 30:13
5:16 Lev 22:14
5:17 Lev 4:13
5:18 Lev 5:15–16
6:3 Ex 23:4
6:5 Lev 5:16
6:6 Lev 5:15
6:7 Lev 4:26
6:9 Nu 28:3
6:10 Ex 28:39–43

....

6:11 Lev 4:12
6:14 Nu 15:4
6:15 Lev 2:2
6:16 Lev 2:3
6:17 Lev 2:11
6:18 Lev 6:29
6:20 Ex 16:36
6:21 Lev 2:5
6:25 Lev 4:24

[1] *15* About ⅖ ounce, or 12 grams. [2] *18* This is a shorthand version of the full formula found in Lev 5:15. [3] *6* Shorthand version of the full formula found in Lev 5:15. [4] *20* Likely about 3½ pounds, or 1.6 kilograms.

also be killed before the LORD. It is most holy. 26 The priest who offers it for sin shall eat it. In a holy place it shall be eaten in the court of the tent of meeting. 27 Whatever touches its flesh shall be holy, and when blood is sprinkled on any garment, you shall wash it in a holy place. 28 And the clay vessel where it is boiled shall be broken, and if it is boiled in a bronze pot, it shall be both scoured and rinsed in water. 29 All the males among the priests shall eat *from this offering*. It is most holy. 30 Any sin offering where blood is brought into the tent of meeting to make atonement in the holy place shall not be eaten. It shall be burned up in the fire.

The Law of the Guilt Offering

7 Likewise this is the law of the guilt offering. It is most holy. 2 In the place where they kill the burnt offering they shall kill the guilt offering, and its blood shall he sprinkle on the sides of the altar. 3 He shall offer all the fat. The fatty tail and the fat that covers the entrails, 4 and the two kidneys and the fat that is on them, which is on the loins, and the appendage that is above the liver, along with the kidneys, he shall take away. 5 And the priest shall burn them on the altar for a food offering made by fire to the LORD. It is a guilt offering. 6 Every male among the priests shall eat from it. It shall be eaten in a holy place. It is most holy.

7 As the sin offering, so is the guilt offering; there is one law for them: the priest who makes atonement shall have it. 8 The priest who offers anyone's burnt offering shall have for himself the skin of the burnt offering that he has offered. 9 Every grain offering that is baked in the oven and all that is prepared in a pan or griddle shall be for the priest who offers it. 10 And every grain offering, *whether* mixed with oil or dry, shall be equally shared among all the sons of Aaron.

The Law of Peace Offerings

11 This is the law of the sacrifice of peace offerings that a person shall offer to the LORD.

12 If he gives it as a thanksgiving *offering*, then he shall offer with the thanksgiving sacrifice unleavened cakes mixed with oil, and unleavened wafers smeared with oil, and cakes of wheat flour mixed with olive oil. 13 Besides the cakes, he shall offer for his offering leavened bread with the sacrifice of his thanksgiving peace offerings. 14 From this he shall offer one loaf from each offering, as a gift to the LORD. It shall be for the priest who sprinkles the blood of the peace offerings. 15 The flesh of the sacrifice of his peace offerings for thanksgiving shall be eaten the same day that it is offered; he shall not leave any of it until the morning.

16 But if the sacrifice of his offering is a vow or a voluntary offering, it shall be eaten the same day that he offers his sacrifice, and on the next day also the remainder of it can be eaten. 17 But the remainder of the flesh of the sacrifice on the third day shall be burned up with fire. 18 If any of the flesh of the sacrifice of his peace offerings is eaten at all on the third day, the one eating shall not be accepted, nor shall it be imputed to him who offers it. It shall be contaminated, and the one who eats of it shall bear his iniquity.

19 The flesh that touches any unclean thing shall not be eaten. It shall be burned up with fire. And as for the *other* flesh, all who are *ritually* clean can eat of it. 20 But the person who eats of the flesh of the sacrifice of peace offerings that belong to the LORD, and who has any uncleanness on him, that individual shall be cut off from his people. 21 Moreover the person who shall touch any unclean thing, whether the uncleanness of man or any unclean beast or any detestable unclean creature, and then eats of the flesh of the sacrifice of the peace offering that belongs to the LORD, that individual shall be cut off from his people.

Eating Fat and Blood Forbidden

22 The LORD spoke to Moses, saying: 23 Speak to the children of Israel, saying: You shall not eat any fat of an ox, a sheep, or a goat. 24 The fat of an animal that dies of itself and the fat of that which is torn by beasts may be used in any other way, but you shall certainly not eat of it. 25 For whoever eats the fat of an animal that is a food offering made by fire to the LORD, that individual shall be cut off from his people. 26 Moreover you shall not eat any manner of blood, whether from a fowl or animal, in any of your dwellings. 27 Whoever eats any manner of blood, that individual shall be cut off from his people.

The Priests' Share

28 The LORD spoke to Moses, saying: 29 Speak to the children of Israel, saying: He who offers the sacrifice of his peace offerings to the LORD shall bring his sacrifice to the LORD from his peace offerings. 30 His own hands shall bring the food offerings of the LORD made by fire, the fat with the breast that the breast may be waved for a wave offering before the LORD. 31 The priest shall burn the fat on the altar, but the breast shall be for Aaron and his sons. 32 The right thigh you shall give to the priest for a contribution offering for the sacrifice of your peace offerings. 33 The one among the sons of Aaron who offers the blood of the peace

6:26 Lev 10:17–18
6:27 Ex 29:37
6:28 Lev 11:33
7:2 Lev 1:5
7:3 Ex 29:13
7:6 Lev 6:29
7:7 Lev 6:25–26
7:12 Lev 2:4
7:13 Am 4:5
7:14 Nu 18:19

7:16 Lev 19:5–8
7:17 Ex 12:10
7:18 Lev 19:7–8
7:23 Lev 3:16–17
7:24 Ex 22:31
7:26 Ge 9:4
7:30 Nu 6:20
7:32 Lev 7:34

offerings and the fat shall have the right thigh for his portion. [34] For the breast that is waved and the thigh that is contributed I have taken from the children of Israel, from the sacrifices of their peace offerings, and have given them to Aaron the priest and to his sons as a perpetual portion from the children of Israel.

[35] This is the consecrated portion for Aaron and his sons, from the food offerings of the LORD made by fire, in the day when *Moses* presented them to minister as priests before the LORD, [36] which the LORD commanded that they be given this, in the day that he anointed them, from the children of Israel as a perpetual portion throughout their generations.

[37] This is the law of the burnt offering, of the grain offering, and of the sin offering, and of the guilt offering, and of the ordinations, and of the sacrifice of the peace offerings, [38] which the LORD commanded Moses on Mount Sinai, in the day that He commanded the children of Israel to offer their offerings to the LORD in the Wilderness of Sinai.

The Consecration of Aaron and His Sons
Ex 29:1–37

8 And the LORD spoke to Moses, saying: [2] Take Aaron and his sons with him, and the garments, and the anointing oil, and a bull for the sin offering, and two rams, and a basket of unleavened bread, [3] and gather all the congregation together at the entrance of the tent of meeting. [4] And Moses did as the LORD commanded him, and the assembly was gathered together at the entrance of the tent of meeting.

Like Moses, I bring my family before the Lord and wash them with the water of the Word (Lev 8:6).

[5] Moses said to the congregation, "This is the thing which the LORD commanded to be done." [6] Moses brought Aaron and his sons and washed them with water. [7] Then he put the tunic on him, and tied the sash around him, and clothed him with the robe, and put the ephod upon him, and he girded him with the decorative band of the ephod and bound the ephod to him. [8] He put the breastplate on him. He also put the Urim and the Thummim in the breastplate. [9] Then he put the turban upon his head. Also on the turban at the front he put the golden plate, the holy crown, as the LORD commanded Moses.

[10] Moses took the anointing oil, and anointed the tabernacle and all that was in it, and sanctified them. [11] He sprinkled oil on the altar seven times and anointed the altar and all its

7:34 Nu 18:18–19
7:36 Lev 8:12
7:37 Ex 29:1
7:38 Lev 1:1–2
8:2 Ex 28:2–4
8:6 Ex 29:4
8:7 Ex 28:4
8:8 Ezr 2:63

....

8:12 Ex 30:30
8:13 Ex 29:8–9
8:14 Eze 43:19
8:15 Lev 4:7
8:16 Ex 29:13
8:17 Lev 4:11–12
8:18 Lev 8:2
8:21 Ex 29:18
8:22 Lev 8:2
8:26 Ex 29:23
8:28 Ex 29:25

vessels, both the laver and its stand, to sanctify them. [12] Then he poured some of the anointing oil on the head of Aaron and anointed him to sanctify him. [13] Moses brought the sons of Aaron and put tunics on them, and girded them with sashes, and put headbands on them, as the LORD commanded Moses.

[14] He brought the bull for the sin offering, and Aaron and his sons laid their hands on the head of the bull for the sin offering. [15] He slaughtered it, and Moses took the blood, and put it on the horns of the altar around it with his finger, and purified the altar, and poured the blood at the base of the altar, and sanctified it to make reconciliation on it. [16] He took all the fat that was on the entrails, and the appendage above the liver, and the two kidneys with their fat, and Moses burned them on the altar. [17] But the bull, and its hide, its flesh, and its refuse he burned with fire outside the camp, as the LORD commanded Moses.

[18] Then he brought the ram for the burnt offering, and Aaron and his sons laid their hands on the head of the ram. [19] He killed it, and Moses sprinkled the blood on the sides of the altar. [20] He cut the ram into pieces, and Moses burned the head, the pieces, and the fat. [21] He washed the entrails and the legs in water, and Moses burned the whole ram on the altar. It was a burnt offering for a pleasing aroma, and a food offering made by fire to the LORD, as the LORD commanded Moses.

[22] Next he brought the other ram, the ram of consecration, and Aaron and his sons laid their hands on the head of the ram. [23] He slaughtered it, and Moses took some of its blood and put it on the tip of the right ear of Aaron, and on the thumb of his right hand, and on the big toe of his right foot. [24] He brought the sons of Aaron, and Moses put some of the blood on the tips of their right ears, and on the thumbs of their right hands, and on the big toes of their right feet. Then Moses sprinkled the blood on the sides of the altar. [25] He took the fat, and the fatty tail, and all the fat that was on the entrails, and the appendage above the liver, and the two kidneys, and their fat, and the right thigh, [26] and out of the basket of unleavened bread that was before the LORD he took one unleavened cake, and a cake of oiled bread, and one wafer and put them on the fat and on the right thigh. [27] And he put all *these* on the hands of Aaron and on the hands of his sons and waved them for a wave offering before the LORD. [28] Then Moses took them from off their hands and burned them on the altar with the burnt offering. This was a consecration for a pleasing aroma, an offering made by fire to the LORD. [29] Moses took the breast and waved it for

a wave offering before the LORD. This part of
the ram of consecration was for Moses, as the
LORD commanded Moses.
30 Then Moses took some of the anointing
oil and some of the blood which was on the
altar and sprinkled it on Aaron, and on his gar-
ments, and on his sons, and on the garments
of his sons with him and sanctified Aaron, and
his garments, and his sons, and the garments
of his sons with him.
31 Moses said to Aaron and to his sons, "Boil
the flesh at the entrance of the tent of meeting
and eat it there with the bread that is in the
basket of consecrations just as I command-
ed, saying, 'Aaron and his sons shall eat it.'
32 That which remains of the flesh and of the
bread you shall burn up. 33 You shall not go out
of the door of the tent of meeting for seven
days, until the days of your consecration are
at an end, for your consecration will take seven
days. 34 As he has done this day, so the LORD
has commanded what is to be done to make
atonement for you. 35 Therefore you shall abide
at the entrance of the tent of meeting day and
night for seven days and keep the charge of
the LORD that you do not die, for so I have been
commanded."
36 So Aaron and his sons did all things which
the LORD commanded by the hand of Moses.

The Priestly Ministry Begins

9 And it came to pass on the eighth day that
Moses called Aaron and his sons and the
elders of Israel. 2 Then he said to Aaron, "Take
a young calf for a sin offering and a ram for
a burnt offering, without blemish, and offer
them before the LORD. 3 To the children of Israel
you shall speak, saying, 'Take a male goat for
a sin offering, and a calf and a lamb—both a
year old without blemish—for a burnt offering,
4 also an ox and a ram for peace offerings to
sacrifice before the LORD, and a grain offering
mixed with oil. For today the LORD will appear
to you.' "
5 They brought that which Moses command-
ed before the tent of meeting, and the entire
congregation drew near and stood before the
LORD. 6 Moses said, "This is the thing which
the LORD commanded that you should do; then
the glory of the LORD shall appear to you."
7 Then Moses said to Aaron, "Go to the altar,
and offer your sin offering and your burnt of-
fering, and make atonement for yourself and
for the people, and offer the sacrifice of the
people, and make atonement for them, as the
LORD commanded."
8 Aaron therefore went to the altar and
slaughtered the calf of the sin offering which
was for himself. 9 The sons of Aaron brought
the blood to him, and he dipped his finger in
the blood, and put it on the horns of the altar,
and poured out the blood at the base of the
altar. 10 But the fat, the kidneys, and the ap-
pendage above the liver of the sin offering he
burned on the altar, as the LORD commanded
Moses. 11 The flesh and the hide he burned
with fire outside the camp.
12 He slaughtered the burnt offering, and the
sons of Aaron presented the blood to him,
which he sprinkled on the sides of the altar.
13 They presented the burnt offering to him,
with its pieces, and the head, and he burned
them on the altar. 14 He then washed the en-
trails and the legs and burned them with the
burnt offering on the altar.
15 He brought the people's offering, and took
the goat which was the sin offering for the
people, and slaughtered it, and offered it for
sin as the first offering.
16 And he brought the burnt offering and of-
fered it according to its regulation. 17 Then he
brought the grain offering, took a handful of
it, and burned it on the altar, besides the burnt
sacrifice of the morning.
18 He slaughtered the ox and the ram as a
sacrifice of peace offerings for the people, and
the sons of Aaron presented the blood to him,
which he sprinkled on the sides of the altar,
19 and the fat of the ox and of the ram, the
fatty tail, and that which covers the entrails,
and the kidneys, and the appendage above the
liver. 20 They put the fat pieces on the breasts,
and he burned the fat on the altar. 21 But the
breasts and the right thigh Aaron waved for a
wave offering before the LORD just as Moses
commanded.
22 Aaron lifted up his hand toward the people,
and blessed them, and came down from of-
fering the sin offering, the burnt offering, and
peace offerings.
23 Moses and Aaron went into the tent of
meeting, and when they came out they blessed
the people, and the glory of the LORD appeared
to all the people. 24 A fire came out from before
the LORD, and it consumed the burnt offering
and the fat that were on the altar. When all
the people saw this, they shouted and fell on
their faces.

The Death of Nadab and Abihu

10 Now Nadab and Abihu, the sons of
Aaron, each took his censer and put
fire in it, and put incense on it, and offered
strange fire before the LORD, which He did not
command them *to do*. 2 Then a fire came out
from the LORD and devoured them, and they
died before the LORD. 3 Then Moses said to
Aaron, "This is what the LORD spoke, saying:

8:30 Nu 3:3
8:31 Ex 29:31–32
8:32 Ex 29:34
8:33 Ex 29:35
8:34 Heb 7:16
8:35 Nu 3:7
9:2 Lev 4:3
9:4 Ex 29:43
9:6 Ex 24:16
9:7 Heb 5:3

....

9:11 Lev 4:11–12
9:14 Lev 8:21
9:15 Lev 4:27–31
9:17 Lev 2:1–2
9:21 Lev 7:30–34
9:22 Dt 21:5
9:23 Lev 9:6
9:24 Jdg 6:21
10:1 Lev 16:12
10:2 Nu 26:61
10:3 Eze 28:22

'I will be sanctified
by those who come near Me;
and before all the people
I will be glorified.' "

And Aaron held his peace.

4 Moses called Mishael and Elzaphan, the sons of Uzziel the uncle of Aaron, and said to them, "Come near, and carry your brothers from before the sanctuary out of the camp." 5 So they went near, and carried them in their tunics out of the camp as Moses had said.

6 Moses said to Aaron, and to Eleazar and Ithamar his sons, "Do not let your hair be loosely disheveled, nor rend your clothes, lest you die, and lest wrath come upon all the people. Instead, let your brothers, the whole house of Israel, mourn the burning which the LORD has caused. 7 You shall not go out from the entrance of the tent of meeting, lest you die, for the anointing oil of the LORD is upon you." And they did according to the word of Moses.

8 The LORD spoke to Aaron, saying: 9 Do not drink wine nor strong drink, you or your sons with you, when you go into the tent of meeting, lest you die. It shall be a perpetual statute throughout your generations, 10 so that you may differentiate between what is holy and common and between what is unclean and clean. 11 And so you may teach the children of Israel all the statutes that the LORD has spoken to them by the hand of Moses.

12 Moses spoke to Aaron, and to Eleazar and Ithamar, his sons who were left: Take the grain offering that remains of the food offerings of the LORD made by fire and eat it without leaven beside the altar. For it is most holy. 13 And you shall eat it in a holy place, because it is your due and your sons' due from the food sacrifices of the LORD made by fire. For so I have been commanded. 14 The breast that is waved and the thigh that is contributed you shall eat in a clean place, you, and your sons, and your daughters with you, for they are your due and your sons' due which are given out of the sacrifices of peace offerings of the children of Israel. 15 The thigh that is contributed and the breast that is waved they shall bring with the fat pieces of the food offerings made by fire to wave them as a wave offering before the LORD, and it shall be yours and your sons' with you as a perpetual statute, as the LORD has commanded.

16 Moses diligently sought the goat of the sin offering and saw it was burned up. And he was angry with Eleazar and Ithamar, the sons of Aaron who were left alive, saying, 17 "Why have you not eaten the sin offering in the sacred area, knowing that it is most holy and God has given it to you to bear the iniquity of the congregation to make atonement for them before the LORD? 18 Its blood was not brought into the inner part of the sanctuary. Indeed you should have eaten it in the sanctuary as I commanded."

19 Aaron said to Moses, "Today they have offered their sin offering and their burnt offering before the LORD, and such things have happened to me! If I had eaten the sin offering today, should it have been accepted in the sight of the LORD?" 20 And when Moses heard that, he approved.

10:4 Ex 6:22
10:6 Nu 16:22
10:7 Lev 21:12
10:9 Lk 1:15
10:10 Lev 11:47
10:11 Dt 24:8
10:12 Lev 21:22
10:14 Nu 18:11
10:15 Lev 7:34
10:16 Lev 9:3
10:18 Lev 6:30
10:19 Lev 9:12
11:6 Dt 14:7
11:7 Isa 65:4
11:10 Lev 7:18

Clean and Unclean Foods
Dt 14:3–20

11 The LORD spoke to Moses and Aaron, saying to them: 2 Speak to the children of Israel, saying: These are the living things which you shall eat among all the animals that are on the earth. 3 Whatever animal has a parted hoof (that is, split-hoofed), and chews the cud among the animals, that one you shall eat.

4 Nevertheless these you shall not eat of those that chew the cud or of those that have a divided hoof: The camel, because it chews the cud but does not have a divided hoof, is unclean to you; 5 the rock badger, because it chews the cud but does not have a divided hoof, is unclean to you; 6 the hare, because it chews the cud but does not have a divided hoof, is unclean to you; 7 the pig, though it does have a divided hoof (that is, split-hoofed), yet it does not chew the cud, is unclean to you; 8 you shall not eat of their flesh, and their carcasses you must not touch; they are unclean to you.

9 These you shall eat of all that are in the waters: Whatever has fins and scales in the waters, in the seas and in the rivers, these you shall eat; 10 all that do not have fins and scales in the seas and in the rivers, from all that move in the waters and from any living thing that is in the waters, they are detestable to you; 11 they shall be detestable to you. You shall not eat of their flesh, and you shall detest their carcasses. 12 Whatever has no fins or scales in the waters is detestable to you.

13 These you shall detest among the birds; they shall not be eaten; they are detestable: the griffon vulture, the bearded vulture, and the black vulture, 14 the kite, and buzzard of any kind, 15 the raven of any kind, 16 and the eagle owl, the short-eared and long-eared owls, and the hawk of any kind, 17 and the little owl, the cormorant, and the screech owl, 18 and the white owl, the scops owl, and the osprey, 19 and the stork, the heron of any kind, the hoopoe, and the bat.

20 All flying insects that walk, moving on all fours, shall be detestable to you. 21 Yet these

you may eat of every flying insect that creeps on all fours: those that have jointed legs above their feet with which to hop on the ground. 22 Even of these you may eat: the locust of any kind, the bald locust of any kind, the cricket of any kind, and the grasshopper of any kind. 23 But all other flying insects that have four feet shall be detestable to you.

24 And by these you shall be unclean. Whoever touches the carcass of these shall be unclean until the evening.

Unclean Animals

25 Whoever carries any of the carcasses of these shall wash his clothes and be unclean until the evening. 26 The carcass of every animal that divides the hoof but is not completely split-hoofed nor chews the cud is unclean to you. Everyone who touches them shall be unclean. 27 Whatever animal that walks on its paws, among all manner of animals that go on all fours, those are unclean to you. Whoever touches their carcass shall be unclean until the evening. 28 He who carries the carcass of these shall wash his clothes and be unclean until the evening; they are unclean to you.

29 These also shall be unclean to you among the crawling things that move on the ground: the mole rat, the mouse, and the great lizard of any kind, 30 and the gecko, the lizard, the wall gecko, the sand lizard, and the chameleon. 31 These are unclean to you among all that crawl. Whoever touches them when they are dead shall be unclean until the evening. 32 And anything on which any of them falls when they are dead shall be unclean, whether it be an article of wood or clothing or a skin or a sack, any article that is used for any purpose. It must be put in water. And it shall be unclean until the evening; then it shall be clean. 33 Every clay vessel into which any of these falls, everything in it shall be unclean, and you shall break it. 34 Any food in it that may be eaten on which water is poured shall be unclean, and any drink that may be drunk in every such vessel shall be unclean. 35 Everything on which any part of their carcass falls shall be unclean; whether it is an oven or stove, it shall be broken to pieces. They are unclean and shall be unclean to you. 36 Nevertheless a fountain or cistern where there is plenty of water shall be clean, but whoever touches their carcass shall be unclean. 37 If any part of their carcass falls on any grain seed that is to be sown, it shall be clean. 38 But if any water is put on the seed, and any part of their carcass fall on it, it shall be unclean to you.

39 If any animal from which you may eat dies, whoever touches the carcass shall be unclean until the evening. 40 And the person who eats of the carcass shall wash his clothes and be unclean until the evening. The person who carries the carcass shall wash his clothes and be unclean until the evening.

41 Every crawling thing that moves on the ground shall be detestable. It shall not be eaten. 42 Whatever goes on its belly, and whatever goes on all fours, or whatever has many feet from any crawling things that move on the earth, you shall not eat them for they are detestable. 43 You shall not make yourselves detestable with any crawling thing that moves, nor shall you make yourselves unclean with them, that you should thereby be defiled by them. 44 For I am the LORD your God. You shall therefore sanctify yourselves, and you shall be holy, for I am holy. Neither shall you defile yourselves with any manner of crawling thing that moves on the ground. 45 For I am the LORD who brings you up out of the land of Egypt to be your God. Therefore you shall be holy, for I am holy.

46 This is the law for the animals, and the fowls, and every living creature that moves in the waters, and every creature that crawls on the ground, 47 to differentiate between the unclean and the clean, and between the animal that may be eaten and the animal that may not be eaten.

Purification After Childbirth

12 Then the LORD spoke to Moses, saying: 2 Speak to the children of Israel, saying: If a woman has conceived and bears a male child, then she shall be unclean seven days, as in the days of her *monthly* menstruation she shall be unclean. 3 On the eighth day the flesh of his foreskin shall be circumcised. 4 And she shall then continue in the blood of her purifying for thirty-three days. She shall not touch anything holy, nor come into the sanctuary until the days of her purifying are fulfilled. 5 But if she gives birth to a female child, then she shall be unclean for two weeks as in her monthly menstruation, and she shall continue in the blood of her purifying for sixty-six days.

6 When the days of her purifying are fulfilled, whether for a son or for a daughter, she shall bring a year-old lamb for a burnt offering, and a young pigeon or a turtledove for a sin offering, to the priest at the entrance of the tent of meeting, 7 who shall offer it before the LORD and make atonement for her. Then she shall be cleansed from the issue of her blood.

This is the law for the woman who has given birth to a male or a female child. 8 If she cannot afford a lamb, then she shall bring two turtledoves or two pigeons, one for the burnt

11:22 Mt 3:4
11:25 Lev 11:40
11:29 Lev 11:41–42
11:32 Lev 15:12
11:40 Lev 22:8
11:41 Lev 11:29
11:43 Lev 20:25
11:44 Lev 19:2
11:45 Ex 6:7
11:47 Lev 10:10
12:2 Lev 15:19
12:3 Lk 1:59
12:6 Lk 2:22
12:8 Lev 4:26

offering and the other for a sin offering, and
the priest shall make atonement for her, and
she shall be clean.

The Law Concerning Leprosy

13 And the LORD spoke to Moses and Aar-
on, saying: 2 When a man has on the
skin of his body a swelling, a scab, or spot, and
it turns on the skin of his body like a mark of a
leprous sore, then he shall be brought to Aar-
on the priest or to one of his sons the priests.
3 And the priest shall examine the mark on the
skin of the body, and when the hair on the
diseased area is white, and the mark appears
to be deeper than the skin of his body, then it
is a leprous sore. So the priest shall look on
him and pronounce him unclean. 4 If the spot
is white on the skin of his body, and it appears
to be no deeper than the skin, and the hair is
not white, then the priest shall isolate the per-
son who has the mark for seven days. 5 Then
the priest shall examine him on the seventh
day, and if the mark is still visible, and the
mark has not spread into the skin, then the
priest shall isolate him for seven days more.
6 And the priest shall examine him again on
the seventh day, and if the mark has faded and
not spread into the skin, then the priest shall
pronounce him clean; it is only a scab, and he
shall wash his clothes and be clean. 7 But if the
scab spreads in the skin after he has been seen
by the priest for his cleansing, he shall be seen
by the priest again. 8 And if the priest sees that
the scab has spread in the skin, then the priest
shall pronounce him unclean. It is leprosy.

9 When a person has leprosy, then it shall be
reported to the priest. 10 And the priest shall
examine him, and if there is a white swelling
in the skin, and it has turned the hair white,
and there is raw flesh in the swelling, 11 it is a
recurring leprosy in the skin of his body, and
the priest shall pronounce him unclean, but he
shall not isolate him, for he is unclean.

12 If the leprosy breaks out all over the skin,
and the disease covers all the skin of the per-
son who has the disease from his head to his
feet, wherever the priest looks, 13 then the
priest shall examine, and if the leprosy has
covered all his body, he shall pronounce him
clean from the disease. It has all turned white,
and he is clean. 14 But when raw flesh appears
on him, he shall be unclean. 15 The priest shall
see the raw flesh and pronounce him to be
unclean, for the raw flesh is unclean. It is
leprosy. 16 Or if the raw flesh turns again, and
it is changed to white, then he shall come to
the priest. 17 And the priest shall see him, and
if the disease is changed to white, then the
priest shall pronounce him clean who has the
disease. He is clean.

18 And when the skin has a boil, and it is
healed, 19 and in the place of the boil there
is a white swelling or a reddish-white spot,
then it will be shown to the priest. 20 And if the
priest sees it, and it is deeper than the skin,
and the hair has turned white, then the priest
shall pronounce him unclean. It is a leprous
sore that has broken out in the boil. 21 But if
the priest looks at it, and there are no white
hairs in it, and if it is not deeper than the skin
but has faded, then the priest shall isolate the
person for seven days. 22 If it spreads around
the skin, then the priest shall pronounce him
unclean. It is a leprous sore. 23 But if the spot
stays in its place and does not spread, then it
is the scar of a boil, and the priest shall pro-
nounce him clean.

24 Or if there is some of the skin on the
body where there is a burn, and the raw flesh
that has a burn becomes a reddish or white
spot, 25 then the priest shall examine it, and
if the hair in the spot has turned white, and
it is deeper than the skin, then it is a leprous
disease broken out from the burn. Therefore
the priest shall pronounce him unclean. It is
a leprous sore. 26 But if the priest looks at it,
and there is no white hair in the spot, and it
is no deeper than the other skin and is faded,
then the priest shall isolate him for seven days.
27 And the priest shall examine him on the sev-
enth day, and if it has spread around the skin,
then the priest shall pronounce him unclean.
It is a leprous sore. 28 If the spot stays in its
place and it does not spread in the skin, but is
faded, then it is a swelling from the burn, and
the priest shall pronounce him clean, for it is
a scar from the burn.

29 If a man or woman has a sore on the head
or in the beard, 30 then the priest shall examine
the sore, and if it is deeper than the skin and
there is in it a yellow thin hair, then the priest
shall pronounce him unclean. It is a scaly
leprosy of the head or beard. 31 If the priest
examines the scaly sore, and it is no deeper
than the skin, and there is no black hair in it,
then the priest shall isolate the person with
the scale for seven days. 32 And on the seventh
day the priest shall examine the sore, and if
the scale has not spread, and there is no yel-
low hair in it, and the scale is not deeper than
the skin, 33 then he shall shave, but the scale
he shall not shave, and the priest shall isolate
the person with the scale another seven days.
34 And on the seventh day the priest shall ex-
amine the scale. If the scale has not spread
in the skin and is no deeper than the skin,
the priest shall pronounce him clean. He shall

13:2 Dt 24:8
13:3 Ro 3:19–20
13:4 Nu 12:15
13:6 Lev 11:25
13:10 2Ki 5:27
13:18 Ex 9:9

wash his clothes and be clean. 35 But if the
scale spreads over the skin after his cleansing,
36 then the priest shall examine him. If the scale
has spread over the skin, the priest shall not
look for yellow hair. He is unclean. 37 But if the
scale appears not to have changed and there
is black hair growing in it, then the scale is
healed. He is clean and the priest shall pro-
nounce him clean.

38 If a man or a woman has spots on the skin
of the body, even white bright spots, 39 then the
priest shall examine, and if the bright spots on
the skin of the body are a faded white, then it
is just a rash that has broken out on the skin.
He is clean.

40 When a man has lost hair from his head,
then he is bald. He is still clean. 41 And when a
man has lost hair from his forehead, then he
is bald on the forehead. He is still clean. 42 But
if there is on the bald head or bald forehead
a reddish-white sore, it is a leprous disease
breaking out on his bald head or his bald fore-
head. 43 Then the priest shall examine it. If the
diseased swelling is reddish-white on his bald
head or on his bald forehead, resembling a lep-
rous disease in the skin of the body, 44 he is lep-
rous. He is unclean. The priest shall pronounce
him unclean. His disease is on his head.

45 The man who has the leprous disease shall
have torn clothes and disheveled hair; and he
shall cover his mustache and shall cry, "Un-
clean, unclean." 46 All the days that he has the
disease, he shall be defiled. He is unclean. He
shall dwell alone, and he shall live outside the
camp.

The Law About Leprous Garments

47 If a garment has a leprous disease, whether
it is a wool or a linen garment, 48 whether it is
in the warp or woof of the linen or wool fabric,
or in the leather or anything made of leather,
49 and if the disease is greenish or reddish in
the garment, or in the leather, or in the warp
or woof, or in anything made of leather, it is
a leprous disease and shall be shown to the
priest. 50 And the priest shall examine the dis-
ease, and isolate the infected article for seven
days. 51 And he shall examine the disease on
the seventh day. If the disease has spread in
the garment, either in the warp or in the woof,
or in the leather, or in any work that is made
of leather, this is a spreading leprous disease.
It is unclean. 52 He shall therefore burn that
garment, whether warp or woof, wool or linen,
or anything of leather that has the disease, for
it is a spreading leprous disease. It shall be
burned in the fire.

53 If the priest examines *it*, and the disease
has not spread in the garment, either in the
warp or the woof, or in anything of leather,
54 then the priest shall command that they
wash the article in which the disease appears,
and he shall isolate it for seven days more.
55 The priest shall examine the infected article
after it has been washed. If the infected spot
has not changed its color, even if the disease
has not spread, it is unclean. You shall burn
it in the fire, whether the leprous spot is on
the inside or on the outside of the article. 56 If
the priest examines and the disease has fad-
ed after washing it, he shall tear the spot out
of the garment, or out of the leather, or out
of the warp or the woof. 57 If it still appears
in the garment, either in the warp or in the
woof, or in anything of leather, it is spread-
ing. You shall burn in the fire that in which
the disease appears. 58 The garment that you
have washed, either in the warp or woof, or
anything of leather, if the disease is gone from
it, then it shall be washed a second time and
shall be clean.

59 This is the law of the leprous disease in a
garment of wool or linen, either in the warp
or woof, or anything of leather to determine
if it is clean or unclean.

The Law for Cleansing Lepers

14 The LORD spoke to Moses, saying: 2 This
shall be the law of the leper in the day
of his cleansing: It shall be reported to the
priest, 3 and the priest shall go out of the camp,
and the priest shall examine him and see if
the disease is healed in the leprous person.
4 Then the priest shall command that two live
clean birds and cedar wood and scarlet fabric
and hyssop be brought for him who is to be
cleansed. 5 The priest shall command that one
of the birds be slaughtered in a clay vessel over
running water. 6 As for the living bird, he shall
take it, the cedar wood, the scarlet, and the
hyssop, and shall dip them and the living bird
in the blood of the bird that was killed over the
running water. 7 Then he shall sprinkle *it* seven
times on him who is to be cleansed from lepro-
sy, and he shall pronounce him clean and shall
let the living bird loose into the open field.

8 He that is to be cleansed shall wash his
clothes, and shave off all his hair, and wash
himself in water, so that he may be clean. After
that he shall come into the camp and shall stay
outside of his tent seven days. 9 But it shall be
on the seventh day that he shall shave all his
hair off his head and his beard and his eye-
brows, all his hair he shall shave off, and he
shall wash his clothes. Also he shall wash his
body in water, and he shall be clean.

10 On the eighth day he shall take two male
lambs without blemish, and one ewe lamb a

13:45 Lev 10:6
13:46 2Ki 7:3
13:47 Jude 1:23
13:51 Lev 14:44

14:2 Lk 17:14
14:3 Lev 13:46
14:4 Nu 19:6
14:7 2Ki 5:10
14:8 Lev 11:25
14:9 Nu 6:9
14:10 Lev 2:1

year old without blemish, and three-tenths of an *ephah*[1] of wheat flour mixed with oil for a grain offering, and one log of oil.[2] 11 The priest who makes him clean shall present the man who is to be made clean and those things before the LORD at the entrance of the tent of meeting.

12 Then the priest shall take one male lamb and offer it for a guilt offering, along with the log of oil, and wave them for a wave offering before the LORD. 13 Then he shall slaughter the lamb in the place where they kill the sin offering and the burnt offering in the holy sanctuary. For as the sin offering is the priest's, so is the guilt offering. It is most holy. 14 And the priest shall take some of the blood of the guilt offering, and the priest shall put it on the tip of the right ear of him who is to be cleansed, and on the thumb of his right hand, and on the big toe of his right foot. 15 And the priest shall take some of the log of oil and pour it into the palm of his own left hand. 16 Then the priest shall dip his right finger in the oil that is in his left hand, and shall sprinkle from the oil with his finger seven times before the LORD. 17 And some of the rest of the oil that is in his hand the priest shall put on the tip of the right ear of him who is to be cleansed, and on the thumb of his right hand, and on the big toe of his right foot, and on the blood of the guilt offering. 18 And the rest of the oil that is in the priest's hand he shall pour upon the head of him who is to be cleansed, and the priest shall make atonement for him before the LORD.

19 The priest shall offer the sin offering, and make atonement for him who is to be cleansed from his *ceremonial* uncleanness, and afterward he shall kill the burnt offering. 20 Then the priest shall offer the burnt offering and the grain offering on the altar, and the priest shall make atonement for him, and he shall be clean.

21 But if he is poor and cannot afford so much, then he shall take one male lamb for a guilt offering to be waved to make atonement for him, and one-tenth of an *ephah*[3] of wheat flour mixed with oil for a grain offering, and a log of oil, 22 and two turtledoves or two pigeons, such as he is able to afford. The one shall be a sin offering and the other a burnt offering.

23 He shall bring them on the eighth day for his cleansing to the priest at the entrance of the tent of meeting before the LORD. 24 The priest shall take the lamb of the guilt offering, along with the log of oil, and the priest shall wave them for a wave offering before the LORD. 25 Then he shall kill the lamb of the guilt offering; and the priest shall take some of the blood of the guilt offering and put it on the tip of the right ear of him who is to be cleansed and on the thumb of his right hand and on the big toe of his right foot. 26 Next the priest shall pour some of the oil into the palm of his own left hand, 27 and the priest shall sprinkle with his right finger some of the oil that is in his left hand seven times before the LORD. 28 Then the priest shall put some of the oil that is in his hand on the tip of the right ear of him who is to be cleansed, and on the thumb of his right hand, and on the big toe of his right foot on the place of the blood of the guilt offering. 29 The rest of the oil that is in the priest's hand he shall pour on the head of him who is to be cleansed to make atonement for him before the LORD. 30 He shall offer one of the turtledoves or the pigeons, such as he can afford, 31 even such as he is able to get, one for a sin offering and the other for a burnt offering, along with the grain offering, and the priest shall make atonement for him who is to be cleansed before the LORD.

32 This is the law for a person who has a leprous sore who cannot afford the offerings for his cleansing.

The Law About Leprous Houses

33 The LORD spoke to Moses and to Aaron, saying: 34 When you have come into the land of Canaan, which I am giving to you for a possession, and I put a leprous disease in a house of the land of your possession, 35 then he who owns the house shall come and tell the priest, "It seems to me there is some disease in the house." 36 Then the priest shall command that they empty the house before the priest goes into it to examine the disease, so that all that is in the house is not made unclean. Afterwards, the priest shall go in to examine the house. 37 He shall examine the disease and see if the disease is in the walls of the house with greenish or reddish spots, which appear to go deeper than the wall. 38 Then the priest shall go out to the door of the house and close off the house seven days. 39 The priest shall return on the seventh day and shall examine and see if the disease has spread in the walls of the house. 40 Then the priest shall command that they take away the stones in which the disease appears and throw them into an unclean place outside the city. 41 And he shall cause the house to be scraped all around, and they shall pour out the plaster that they scrape off outside the city into an unclean place. 42 And they shall take other stones and put them in the place of

14:12 Ex 29:24
14:13 Ex 29:11
14:14 Ex 29:20
14:18 Lev 4:26
14:19 Lev 14:12
14:20 Lev 14:10
14:21 Lev 12:8
14:23 Lev 14:10–11
14:29 Lev 14:18
14:30 Lev 14:22
14:34 Ge 17:8
14:35 Ps 91:10

[1] *10* Likely about 11 pounds, or 5 kilograms. [2] *10* About ⅓ quart, or 0.3 liter; and in vv. 12, 15, 21, and 24. [3] *21* Likely about 3½ pounds, or 1.6 kilograms.

those stones, and he shall take other plaster
and shall plaster the house.

43 If the disease comes again and breaks out
in the house after he has taken away the stones
and after he has scraped the house and after it
is plastered, 44 then the priest shall come and
examine and see if the disease has spread in
the house. If the disease has spread in the
house, it is a persistent leprosy in the house; it
is unclean. 45 He shall break down the house,
the stones and the timber, and all the plaster
of the house, and he shall carry them out of
the city into an unclean place.

46 Moreover, he who goes into the house
while it is closed off shall be unclean until the
evening. 47 And he who sleeps in the house
shall wash his clothes, and he who eats in the
house shall wash his clothes.

48 If the priest comes in and examines it and
sees the disease has not spread in the house
after the house was plastered, then the priest
shall pronounce the house clean, because the
disease is healed. 49 He shall take two birds,
and cedar wood, and scarlet, and hyssop to
cleanse the house. 50 Then he shall kill one of
the birds in a clay vessel over running water.
51 He shall take the cedar wood, and the hys-
sop, and the scarlet, and the living bird, and
dip them in the blood of the slain bird, and
in the running water, and sprinkle the house
seven times. 52 Then he shall cleanse the house
with the blood of the bird, and with the run-
ning water, and with the living bird, and with
the cedar wood, and with the hyssop, and with
the scarlet. 53 But he shall let the living bird
loose outside the city into the open fields and
make atonement for the house, and it shall
be clean.

54 This is the law for all manner of leprous
sore and scale, 55 and for the disease of a gar-
ment, or of a house, 56 and for a swelling, or
for a scab, or for a spot, 57 to discern when it is
unclean and when it is clean.

This is the law of leprosy.

The Law About Bodily Discharges

15 Then the LORD spoke to Moses and to
Aaron, saying: 2 Speak to the children
of Israel, and say to them: When any man has
a discharge out of his body, his discharge is un-
clean. 3 This is the instruction for his unclean-
ness in his discharge, whether the discharge
from his body flows or his body is stopped up
by his discharge, it is his uncleanness.

4 Every bed on which the man with the dis-
charge lies shall be unclean, and everything
on which he sits shall be unclean. 5 Whoever
touches the bed shall wash his clothes, and
bathe himself in water, and be unclean until
the evening. 6 And whoever sits on anything
where the man sat who has the discharge shall
wash his clothes, and bathe himself in water,
and be unclean until the evening.

7 And whoever touches the body of him who
has the discharge shall wash his clothes, and
bathe himself in water, and be unclean until
the evening.

8 If the man with the discharge spits on
someone who is clean, then he shall wash his
clothes, and bathe himself in water, and be
unclean until the evening.

9 Any saddle on which the man with a dis-
charge rides shall be unclean. 10 Whoever
touches anything that was under him shall be
unclean until the evening, and he who carries
any of those things shall wash his clothes, and
bathe himself in water, and be unclean until
the evening.

11 Whomever he who has the discharge
touches, and has not rinsed his hands in water,
he shall wash his clothes and bathe in water,
and be unclean until evening.

12 The earthen vessel that he who has the
discharge touches shall be broken, and every
vessel of wood shall be rinsed in water.

13 When he who has a discharge is cleansed
of his issue, then he shall count to himself sev-
en days for his cleansing, and wash his clothes,
and bathe his body in running water, and shall
be clean. 14 On the eighth day he shall take two
turtledoves or two pigeons and come before
the LORD at the entrance of the tent of meeting
and give them to the priest. 15 And the priest
shall offer them, one for a sin offering and the
other for a burnt offering, and the priest shall
make atonement for him before the LORD for
his discharge.

16 If any man has a seminal emission, then
he shall wash all his body in water and be un-
clean until the evening. 17 Every garment and
all leather on which there is seminal emission
shall be washed with water and be unclean
until the evening. 18 If a man lies with a wom-
an, and there is an emission of semen, they
shall both bathe themselves in water and be
unclean until the evening.

19 If a woman has a discharge, and the dis-
charge from her body is blood, she shall be set
apart for seven days; and whoever touches her
shall be unclean until the evening.

20 Everything that she lies on in her menstru-
al impurity shall be unclean. Also, everything
that she sits on shall be unclean. 21 Whoever
touches her bed shall wash his clothes and
bathe himself in water, and be unclean un-
til the evening. 22 Whoever touches anything
on which she sits shall wash his clothes and
bathe himself in water, and be unclean until

14:44 Lev 13:51–52
14:46 Nu 19:21–22
14:49 Lev 14:4
14:56 Lev 13:2
14:57 Lev 10:10
15:2 Lev 22:4
15:5 Lev 11:25

15:12 Lev 6:28
15:13 Lev 8:33
15:14 Lev 12:8
15:16 Lev 22:4
15:19 Lev 12:2
15:20 Lev 15:4–9

the evening. 23 Whether it is the bed or any-
thing on which she sits, when he touches it he
shall be unclean until the evening.
24 If any man lies with her, and her menstrual
impurity is on him, he shall be unclean sev-
en days, and every bed where he lies shall be
unclean.
25 If a woman has a discharge of blood for
many days, not at the time of her menstru-
al impurity, or if she has a discharge beyond
the time of her impurity, all the days of the
discharge she shall be in uncleanness, as in
the days of her impurity. She shall be unclean.
26 Every bed that she lies on all the days of her
discharge shall be for impurity, and whatever
she sits on shall be unclean, as the unclean-
ness of her menstrual impurity. 27 Whoever
touches those things shall be unclean and shall
wash his clothes and bathe himself in water
and be unclean until the evening.
28 But if she is cleansed of her discharge, then
she shall count to herself seven days, and after
that she shall be clean. 29 On the eighth day she
shall take two turtledoves or two pigeons and
bring them to the priest at the entrance of the
tent of meeting. 30 The priest shall offer one for
a sin offering and the other for a burnt offering,
and the priest shall make atonement for her
before the LORD for her unclean discharge.
31 Thus you shall separate the children of
Israel from their uncleanness, so that they do
not die in their uncleanness by defiling My
tabernacle that is among them.
32 This is the law for him who has a discharge
and for him who has a seminal emission and
thus becomes unclean, 33 and for her who is
sick from her menstruation, and for him who
has a discharge, for anyone male or female,
and for the man who lies with a woman who
is unclean.

The Day of Atonement
Lev 23:26–32; Nu 29:7–11

16 The LORD spoke to Moses after the
death of the two sons of Aaron, when
they drew near to the LORD and died. 2 The LORD
said to Moses: Speak to Aaron your brother so
that he does not come at any time into the Holy
Place within the veil before the mercy seat,
which is on the ark, so that he will not die, for
I will appear in the cloud on the mercy seat.
3 Thus Aaron shall come into the Holy Place
with a young bull for a sin offering and a ram
for a burnt offering. 4 He shall put on the holy
linen tunic, and he shall have the linen under-
garment on his body, and shall be girded with
a linen sash, and shall be wearing the linen
turban. These are holy garments. Therefore
he shall wash his body in water and then put
them on. 5 He shall take from the congregation
of the children of Israel two male goats for a
sin offering and one ram for a burnt offering.
6 Aaron shall offer his bull for the sin offering,
which is for himself, and make atonement for
himself and for his house. 7 Then he shall take
the two goats and present them before the
LORD at the entrance of the tent of meeting.
8 Aaron shall cast lots for the two goats: one lot
for the LORD and the other lot for the scapegoat.
9 Aaron shall bring the goat on which the lot of
the LORD falls and offer him for a sin offering.
10 But the goat on which the lot falls to be the
scapegoat shall be presented alive before the
LORD to make atonement with it, that it may be
sent away as a scapegoat into the wilderness.
11 Aaron shall bring the bull of the sin of-
fering, which is for himself, and shall make
atonement for himself, and for his house, and
shall kill the bull of the sin offering for himself.
12 And he shall take a censer full of burning
coals of fire from the altar before the LORD, and
two handfuls of sweet incense beaten small,
and bring it within the veil. 13 And he shall put
the incense on the fire before the LORD, that the
cloud of the incense may cover the mercy seat
that is over the testimony, so that he does not
die. 14 And he shall take of the blood of the bull,
and sprinkle it with his finger on the mercy
seat on the eastern side, and before the mercy
seat he shall sprinkle from the blood with his
finger seven times.
15 Then he shall kill the goat of the sin offer-
ing, which is for the people, and bring its blood
within the veil, and do with that blood as he
did with the blood of the bull, and sprinkle
it over and in front of the mercy seat. 16 And
he shall make atonement for the Holy Place,
because of the uncleanness of the children of
Israel and because of their transgressions in
all their sins, and so he shall do for the tent
of meeting that remains among them in the
midst of their uncleanness. 17 There shall be
no man in the tent of meeting when he goes
in to make atonement in the Holy Place, until
he comes out and has made atonement for
himself, and for his household, and for all the
congregation of Israel.
18 Then he shall go out to the altar that is
before the LORD and make atonement for it,
and he shall take some of the blood of the bull
and some of the blood of the goat, and put it
on the horns of the altar all around. 19 He shall
sprinkle from the blood on it with his finger
seven times, and cleanse it, and consecrate it
from the uncleanness of the children of Israel.
20 When he has made an end of atonement
for the Holy Place, and the tent of meeting,
and the altar, then he shall bring the live goat.
21 And Aaron shall lay both his hands on the

15:24 Lev 20:18
15:25 Mt 9:20
15:28 Lev 15:13–15
15:31 Nu 5:3
16:1 Lev 10:1–2
16:2 Ex 30:10
16:3 Lev 4:3
16:4 Ex 30:20
16:5 2Ch 29:21
16:6 Lev 9:7
16:10 1Jn 2:2
16:11 Lev 16:6
16:12 Lev 10:1
16:13 Ex 25:21
16:14 Heb 9:25
16:15 Heb 9:7
16:17 Lk 1:10
16:18 Lev 4:7

head of the live goat, and confess over it all
the iniquities of the children of Israel, and all
their transgressions in all their sins, putting
them on the head of the goat, and shall send
it away by the hand of a designated man into
the wilderness. 22 And the goat shall bear on
it all their iniquities to a desolate land, and
he shall let the goat go free in the wilderness.
23 Then Aaron shall come into the tent of
meeting, and shall take off the linen garments
which he put on when he went into the Holy
Place, and shall leave them there. 24 And he
shall wash his body with water in a holy place,
and put on his garments, and come out, and
offer his burnt offering, and the burnt offering
of the people, and make atonement for himself
and for the people. 25 The fat of the sin offering
he shall burn on the altar.
26 He who releases the goat as the scapegoat
shall wash his clothes, and bathe his body in
water, and afterward come into the camp.
27 The bull for the sin offering and the goat for
the sin offering, whose blood was brought in
to make atonement in the Holy Place, shall be
carried outside the camp. They shall burn in
the fire their hides, their flesh, and their refuse.
28 He who burns them shall wash his clothes,
and bathe his body in water, and afterward he
shall come into the camp.

> The man of God who is consecrated to minister as priest will seek God in prayer on my behalf (Lev 16:32–33).

29 This shall be a perpetual statute for you so
that in the seventh month, on the tenth day
of the month, you shall humble yourselves,
and do no work of any kind, whether it is the
native citizen or the stranger who sojourns
among you. 30 For on that day the priest shall
make atonement for you to cleanse you, so that
you may be clean from all your sins before the
LORD. 31 It shall be a sabbath, a solemn rest for
you, and you shall humble yourselves. It is a
perpetual statute. 32 The priest, who is anoint-
ed and consecrated to minister as a priest in
the place of his father, shall make atonement,
and shall put on the linen garments, the holy
garments. 33 And he shall make atonement for
the Holy Sanctuary, for the tent of meeting,
and for the altar, and he shall make atonement
for the priests, and for all the people of the
congregation.
34 This shall be a perpetual statute for you to
make atonement for the children of Israel for
all their sins once a year.
And Moses did as the LORD commanded him.

16:23 Eze 42:14
16:24 Lev 16:3–5
16:26 Lev 16:10
16:27 Lev 4:21
16:29 Nu 29:7
16:30 Jer 33:8
16:31 Lev 23:32
16:33 Lev 16:16
16:34 Heb 9:7

....

17:4 Ge 17:14
17:6 Nu 18:17
17:7 Ex 34:15
17:8 Lev 1:2–3
17:9 Lev 17:4
17:10 Lev 3:17
17:11 Heb 9:22
17:13 Dt 12:16
17:14 Ge 9:4

The Law About Eating Blood

17 And the LORD spoke to Moses, saying:
2 Speak to Aaron, and to his sons, and
to all the children of Israel, and say to them:
This is the thing which the LORD has command-
ed, saying: 3 If anyone of the house of Israel
ritually slaughters an ox, a lamb, or goat in
the camp, or slaughters it outside of the camp,
4 and does not bring it to the entrance of the
tent of meeting to offer it as a gift to the LORD
before the tabernacle of the LORD, then blood
guilt shall be accounted to that man. He has
shed blood, and that man shall be cut off from
among his people. 5 This is so that the children
of Israel may bring their sacrifices which they
offer in the open field, even that they may
bring them to the LORD at the entrance of the
tent of meeting, to the priest, and offer them
for peace offerings to the LORD. 6 The priest
shall sprinkle the blood on the altar of the
LORD at the entrance of the tent of meeting,
and burn the fat for a pleasing aroma to the
LORD. 7 They shall no more offer their sacrifices
to goat demons, after whom they have acted
like whores. This shall be a perpetual statute
for them throughout their generations.

> I nullify in the name of Jesus the power of any sacrifice made to devils in my city, region, or nation (Lev 17:7).

8 You shall say to them: Any man from the
house of Israel, or from the foreigners who
sojourn among you, who offers a burnt offer-
ing or sacrifice, 9 and does not bring it to the
entrance of the tent of meeting to offer it to
the LORD, even that man shall be cut off from
among his people.
10 Whoever from the house of Israel, or from
the strangers who sojourn among you, who
eats any manner of blood, I will set My face
against that person who eats blood, and will
cut him off from among his people. 11 For the
life of the flesh is in the blood, and I have giv-
en it to you on the altar to make atonement
for your lives; for it is the blood that makes
atonement for the soul. 12 Therefore I said to
the children of Israel: No person among you
shall eat blood, nor shall any stranger who so-
journs among you eat blood.
13 Whoever from the children of Israel, or
from the foreigners who sojourn among you,
who hunts and catches any wild animal or fowl
that may be eaten, he shall even pour out the
blood and cover it with dirt. 14 For the life of
every creature is its blood; in its blood is its life.
Therefore I said to the children of Israel: You

shall not eat the blood of any creature, for the life of every creature is its blood. Whoever eats it shall be cut off.

15 Every person who eats that which died of itself, or that which was torn by animals, whether he is a native citizen or a foreigner, he shall both wash his clothes and bathe himself in water, and be unclean until the evening. Then he shall be clean. 16 But if he does not wash them or bathe his body, then he shall bear his iniquity.

Laws on Immoral Relations

18 The LORD spoke to Moses, saying: 2 Speak to the children of Israel, and say to them: I am the LORD your God. 3 After the practices of the land of Egypt, from where you lived, you shall not follow, and after the practices of the land of Canaan, to where I will bring you, you shall not follow; nor shall you walk in their ordinances. 4 You shall follow My decrees and keep My ordinances to walk in them: I am the LORD your God. 5 You shall therefore keep My statutes and My judgments, which if a man does them, then he shall live by them: I am the LORD.

6 None of you shall approach any of his near relatives to have relations: I am the LORD.

7 You shall not have relations with your father or have relations with your mother. She is your mother. You shall not have relations with her.

8 You shall not have relations with your father's wife, for this exposes your father's nakedness.

9 You shall not have relations with your sister, whether your father's or mother's daughter, whether raised in the family or another home.

10 You shall not have relations with your son's daughter or your daughter's daughter, for this exposes your own nakedness.

11 You shall not have relations with your father's wife's daughter who is raised in your father's family, for she is your sister.

12 You shall not have relations with your father's sister, for she is your father's relative.

13 You shall not have relations with your mother's sister, for she is your mother's relative.

14 You shall not expose the nakedness of your father's brother. You shall not approach his wife for relations; she is your aunt.

15 You shall not have relations with your daughter-in-law, for she is your son's wife—you shall not have relations with her.

16 You shall not have relations with your brother's wife, for this exposes your brother's nakedness.

17 You shall not have relations with a woman and her daughter, nor shall you have her son's daughter or her daughter's daughter, for this exposes the woman's nakedness. They are all near relatives. It is depravity.

18 And you shall not have a woman as a rival wife, who is the sister of your other wife, for this is to expose her nakedness while her sister, your other wife, is still alive.

19 Also you shall not approach a woman to have relations as long as she is in her menstrual uncleanness.

20 Moreover, you shall not have relations with your neighbor's wife to defile yourself with her.

21 You shall not let any of your children be offered through the fire to Molek, and so profane the name of your God: I am the LORD.

22 You shall not lie with a man as one does with a woman. It is an abomination.

23 You shall not lie with an animal to defile yourself, nor shall any woman lie with an animal. It is a perversion.

24 Do not defile yourselves in any of these ways, for in these practices the nations I am casting out before you have defiled themselves. 25 And the land has become defiled; therefore I have punished its iniquity, and the land has vomited out her inhabitants. 26 But you shall therefore keep My statutes and My decrees, and you shall not commit any of these abominations, either the native citizen or any foreigner who sojourns among you 27 (for the people of the land, who were before you, committed all of these abominations, and the land became defiled), 28 lest the land vomit you out also when you defile it, as it vomited out the nations that were before you.

29 For whoever shall commit any of these abominations, those persons who commit them shall be cut off from among their people. 30 Therefore you shall keep My ordinances, that you do not commit any one of these abominable customs which were committed before you, so that you do not defile yourselves by them: I am the LORD your God.

Moral and Ceremonial Laws

19 And the LORD spoke to Moses, saying: 2 Speak to all the congregation of the children of Israel, and say to them: You shall be holy, for I the LORD your God am holy.

3 Every one of you shall revere his mother and his father, and you will keep My Sabbaths: I am the LORD your God.

4 Do not turn to idols, nor make for yourselves cast metal gods: I am the LORD your God.

5 When you offer a sacrifice of peace offerings to the LORD, you shall offer it so that you might be accepted. 6 It shall be eaten the same day you offer it or on the next day, and if any remains until the third day, it shall be burned

17:15 Ex 22:31
17:16 Lev 5:1
18:2 Ex 6:7
18:3 Ex 23:24
18:5 Eze 20:11
18:6 Lev 18:7–19
18:7 Lev 20:11
18:8 Lev 20:11
18:9 Lev 20:17
18:12 Lev 20:19
18:14 Lev 20:20
18:15 Lev 20:12
18:16 Lev 20:21
18:17 Lev 20:14
18:19 Lev 15:24
18:20 Ex 20:14
18:21 Lev 19:12
18:22 Lev 20:13
18:23 Ex 22:19
18:24 Dt 18:12
18:25 Lev 18:28
18:26 Lev 18:5
18:30 Lev 20:23
19:3 Ex 20:12
19:4 Lev 26:1

in the fire. 7 If it is eaten at all on the third day, then it is contaminated. It shall not be accepted. 8 Therefore everyone who eats it shall bear his iniquity, because he has defiled what is holy of the Lord, and that person shall be cut off from among his people.

9 When you reap the harvest of your land, you shall not reap up to the edge of your field, nor shall you gather the gleanings of your harvest. 10 You shall not glean bare your vineyard, nor shall you gather every fallen grape of your vineyard. You shall leave them for the poor and stranger: I am the Lord your God.

11 You shall not steal, nor deal falsely, nor lie to one another.

12 You shall not swear falsely by My name, and so defile the name of your God: I am the Lord.

13 You shall not defraud your neighbor or rob him. The wages of him who is hired shall not stay with you all night until the morning.

14 You shall not curse the deaf, nor put a stumbling block before the blind, but you shall fear your God: I am the Lord.

15 You shall do no unrighteousness in a court. You shall not be partial to the poor, nor honor the person who is great, but in righteousness you shall judge your neighbor.

16 You shall not go around as a slanderer among your people, nor shall you stand by while the life of your neighbor is in danger: I am the Lord.

17 You shall not hate your brother in your heart. You shall surely reason honestly with your neighbor, and not suffer sin because of him.

18 You shall not take vengeance, nor bear any grudge against the children of your people, but you shall love your neighbor as yourself: I am the Lord.

19 You shall keep My statutes.

You shall not let your livestock breed with a different kind.

You shall not sow your field with mixed seed, nor shall your garment be mixed from two types of fabric.

20 Whoever lies with a slave woman who is betrothed to another man and not yet ransomed or given freedom, compensation will be made. They shall not be put to death, because she was not free. 21 He shall bring his guilt offering to the Lord at the entrance of the tent of meeting, a ram for a guilt offering. 22 The priest shall make atonement for him with the ram of the guilt offering before the Lord for his sin which he has done, and he will be forgiven for the sin that he has committed.

23 When you come into the land and plant any kind of tree for food, then you shall count the fruit as forbidden.[1] Three years it shall be forbidden to you. It shall not be eaten. 24 But in the fourth year all the fruit shall be holy and an offering of praise to the Lord. 25 And in the fifth year you shall eat of the fruit that it may yield an increase to you: I am the Lord your God.

26 You shall not eat anything with the blood in it, nor shall you practice divination or fortune-telling.

27 You shall not round the corners of the hair on your head, nor shall you mar the edges of your beard.

28 You shall not make any cuttings in your flesh for the dead nor make any tattoo marks on yourselves: I am the Lord.

29 Do not prostitute your daughter and cause her to be defiled, lest the land fall into whoredom and become full of wickedness.

30 You shall keep My Sabbaths and revere My sanctuary: I am the Lord.

31 Do not turn to spirits through mediums or necromancers. Do not seek after them to be defiled by them: I am the Lord your God.

32 You shall rise up before a gray head, and honor the face of an old man, and fear your God: I am the Lord.

33 When a foreigner sojourns with you in your land, you shall not do him wrong. 34 The foreigner who dwells with you shall be to you as one born among you, and you shall love him as yourself for you were foreigners in the land of Egypt: I am the Lord your God.

35 You shall do no unrighteousness in judgment regarding measures in length, weight, or quantity. 36 You shall have honest balances, honest weights, an honest ephah,[2] and an honest hin:[3] I am the Lord your God, who brought you out of the land of Egypt.

37 Therefore you shall observe all My statutes and all My judgments and do them: I am the Lord.

Penalties for Violating the Law

20 Then the Lord spoke to Moses, saying: 2 Again, you shall say to the children of Israel: Whoever from the children of Israel or from the foreigners who sojourn in Israel who gives any of his children to Molek, he shall surely be put to death. The people of the land shall stone him. 3 I will set My face against that man and will cut him off from among his people, because he has given some of his descendants to Molek to defile My sanctuary and to defile My holy name. 4 If the people of the land in any way hide their eyes from the man when he gives of his children to Molek and do not put him to death, 5 then I will set My

19:11 Ex 20:15
19:12 Ex 20:7
19:13 Jas 5:4
19:14 Dt 27:18
19:15 Dt 1:17
19:16 Ex 23:1
19:17 Lk 17:3
19:18 Ro 12:19
19:19 Dt 22:9–11
19:20 Dt 22:23–24
19:26 Dt 12:23
19:27 Lev 21:5
19:28 Dt 14:1
19:30 Lev 19:3
19:31 Isa 8:19
19:32 Lev 19:14
19:33 Ex 22:21
19:34 Lev 19:18
19:35 Dt 25:13
19:37 Lev 18:4–5
20:2 Lev 18:21
20:3 Lev 18:21
20:4 Dt 17:2–5

[1] 23 Or *uncircumcised*. [2] 36 A dry measure of about ⅗ of a bushel, or 22 liters. [3] 36 A liquid measure of about 1 gallon, or 3.8 liters.

face against that man and against his family;
and I will cut them off from their people, both
him and those who follow after him as whores
after Molek.
6 The person who turns to spirits through me-
diums and necromancers in order to whore
after them, I will even set My face against that
person and will cut him off from among his
people.
7 Consecrate yourselves therefore, and be
holy, for I am the LORD your God. 8 You shall
keep My statutes, and do them; I am the LORD
who sanctifies you.
9 For anyone who curses his father or his
mother shall be surely put to death. He has
cursed his father or his mother, and his blood
guilt shall be upon him.
10 If a man commits adultery with another
man's wife, even he who commits adultery
with his neighbor's wife, the adulterer and the
adulteress shall surely be put to death.
11 If a man lies with his father's wife, he has
exposed his father's nakedness. Both of them
shall surely be put to death. Their blood guilt
shall be upon them.
12 If a man lies with his daughter-in-law, both
of them shall surely be put to death. They have
committed a perversion. Their blood guilt shall
be upon them.
13 If a man lies with another man as with
a woman, both of them have committed an
abomination. They shall surely be put to death.
Their blood guilt shall be upon them.
14 If a man lies with a woman and also her
mother, it is wickedness. Both he and they
shall be burned with fire, so that there is no
wickedness among you.
15 If a man lies with an animal, he shall surely
be put to death, and you shall kill the animal.
16 If a woman approaches an animal and lies
with it, you shall kill the woman and the ani-
mal. They shall surely be put to death. Their
blood guilt shall be upon them.
17 If a man lies with his sister, whether the
daughter of his father or mother, they have
exposed each other's nakedness; it is a wicked
thing and they shall be cut off from the sight of
their people. He has exposed his sister's naked-
ness, and he shall bear his iniquity.
18 If a man lies with a woman during her
menstrual period and exposes her nakedness,
her fountain of blood is then exposed. Both of
them shall be cut off from among their people.
19 You shall not have relations with your
mother's sister or your father's sister, for this
is to expose the nakedness of one's relative.
They shall bear their iniquity.

20:6 Lev 19:31
20:7 Eph 1:4
20:8 Ex 31:13
20:9 Ex 21:17
20:12 Lev 18:15
20:13 Lev 18:22
20:14 Lev 18:17
20:15 Lev 18:23
20:17 Lev 18:9
20:18 Lev 15:24
20:19 Lev 18:6
....
20:20 Lev 18:14
20:21 Lev 18:16
20:22 Lev 18:25–28
20:23 Lev 18:3
20:24 Ex 33:16
20:25 Lev 11:1–47
20:27 Lev 19:31
21:1 Eze 44:25
21:5 Dt 14:1
21:6 Lev 3:11
21:7 Lev 21:13–14
21:8 Lev 21:6

20 If a man lies with his uncle's wife, he has
exposed his uncle's nakedness. They shall bear
their sin. They shall die childless.
21 If a man lies with his brother's wife, it is
impurity. He has exposed his brother's naked-
ness. They shall be childless.
22 You shall therefore keep all My statutes and
all My decrees and do them, so that the land
to where I am bringing you will not vomit you
out. 23 You shall not walk in the customs of the
nation that I am driving out before you, for
they committed all these things, and therefore
I abhorred them. 24 But I have said to you: You
shall inherit their land, and I will give it to you
to possess it, a land that flows with milk and
honey. I am the LORD your God, who has sep-
arated you from other peoples.
25 You shall therefore make distinction be-
tween the clean animal from the unclean, and
the unclean fowl from the clean, and you shall
not make yourselves detestable by animal, or
by fowl, or by any manner of living thing that
crawls on the ground, which I have separated
from you as unclean. 26 You shall be holy unto
Me; for I the LORD am holy and have separated
you from other peoples, that you should be
Mine.
27 A man or woman who speaks to spirits as
a medium or necromancer shall surely be put
to death. They shall stone them. Their blood
guilt shall be upon them.

Rules for Priestly Conduct

21 Then the LORD said to Moses: Speak to
the priests, the sons of Aaron, and say
to them: None shall make himself unclean for
the dead among his people, 2 but for his closest
relatives, that is, for his mother, his father, his
son, his daughter, his brother, 3 and his virgin
sister (who is near him because she has not
had a husband), for her he may be made un-
clean. 4 And he shall not make himself unclean
as a husband among his people *because of the
dead* and so defile himself.
5 They shall not make bald areas on their
heads, nor shall they shave off the edges of
their beards, nor make any cuts in their flesh.
6 They shall be holy unto their God, and not
profane the name of their God; for they offer
the offerings of the LORD made by fire, and the
food of their God. Therefore they shall be holy.
7 They shall not take a wife who is a whore or
has been defiled, nor shall they take a woman
divorced from her husband, for he is holy unto
his God. 8 You shall sanctify him, for he offers
the food of your God. He shall be holy to you,
for I the LORD, who sanctifies you, am holy.

9 The daughter of any priest, if she defiles
herself by being a whore, she also defiles her
father. She shall be burned with fire.

10 He who is the high priest among his broth-
ers, on whose head the anointing oil was
poured and who is consecrated to wear the
garments, shall not dishevel his hair, nor tear
his clothes; 11 nor shall he approach any dead
body, nor make himself unclean, even for his
father or his mother; 12 nor shall he go out of
the sanctuary, so as not to defile the sanctuary
of his God, for the consecration of the anoint-
ing oil of his God is upon him: I am the LORD.

13 He shall take a wife in her virginity. 14 A
widow, or a divorced woman, or a defiled
woman, or a prostitute, these he shall not
marry. But he shall take for a wife a virgin of
his own people, 15 so that he does not defile his
offspring among his people, for I am the LORD
who sanctifies him.

16 The LORD spoke to Moses, saying: 17 Speak
to Aaron, saying: None of your offspring in
their generations who has any blemish may
approach to offer the food of his God. 18 For
whoever has a blemish, he shall not approach,
whether a blind or lame man, or one who has
a physical flaw on his face or a limb that is
too long, 19 or a man who has a broken foot or
broken hand, 20 or a hunchback, or a dwarf,
or who has a defect in his eye, or eczema or
scabs, or is a eunuch. 21 No man who has a
blemish from the offspring of Aaron the priest
shall come near to offer the food offerings of
the LORD made by fire. He has a blemish; he
shall not come near to offer the bread of his
God. 22 He shall eat the food of his God, both of
the most holy and of the holy. 23 Only he shall
not go in through the veil or come to the altar,
because he has a blemish, so that he does not
defile My sanctuaries, for I am the LORD who
sanctifies them.

24 Moses spoke this to Aaron, and to his sons,
and to all the children of Israel.

Holy Offerings

22 And the LORD spoke to Moses, saying:
2 Speak to Aaron and to his sons that
they should be very respectful with the holy
things of the children of Israel, and that they
do not defile My holy name with those things
which the people have consecrated to Me: I
am the LORD.

3 Say to them: Whoever from your offspring
through your generations approaches the holy
things, which the children of Israel have ded-
icated to the LORD, while he has uncleanness,
that person shall be cut off from My presence:
I am the LORD.

21:9 Ge 38:24
21:10 Lev 10:6–7
21:11 Nu 19:14
21:12 Lev 10:7
21:14 Lev 21:7
21:18 Lev 22:19–25
21:20 Dt 23:1
21:21 Lev 21:6
21:23 Lev 21:12
22:2 Lev 18:21
22:3 Lev 7:20–21
22:5 Lev 15:7
22:7 Lev 21:22
22:8 Lev 17:15
22:9 Ex 28:43
22:11 Ge 17:13
22:15 Nu 18:32
22:16 Lev 22:9
22:18 Lev 1:2
22:19 Lev 1:3
22:20 Dt 17:1
22:21 Nu 15:3
22:22 Lev 22:20

4 If a man of the offspring of Aaron is a lep-
er or has a discharge, he shall not eat of the
holy offerings until he is clean. And whoever
touches anything that is unclean by contact
with the dead or a man who had an emission
of semen, 5 or whoever touches any crawling
thing whereby he may be made unclean, or
a man from whom he may receive unclean-
ness, whatever uncleanness he has, 6 the per-
son who has touched any such thing shall be
unclean until evening, and shall not eat of the
holy things unless he washes his body with
water. 7 When the sun goes down, he shall be
clean, and afterward he shall eat of the holy
things, because it is his food. 8 That which dies
of itself or is torn by animals he shall not eat,
becoming unclean by it: I am the LORD.

9 They shall therefore keep My ordinance, lest
they bear sin from it and therefore die if they
defile it: I am the LORD who sanctifies them.

10 There shall be no outsider[1] who eats of
a holy thing, whether a foreign guest of the
priest or a hired servant, he shall not eat of a
holy offering. 11 But if a priest buys a person
with his money, the person acquired shall eat
of it, and he that is born in his house shall eat
of his food. 12 If the priest's daughter marries
an outsider, she may not eat of an offering of
the holy things. 13 But if the priest's daughter
is a widow or divorced, and has no child and
has returned to her father's house as in her
youth, she may eat of her father's food; but no
outsider may eat of it.

14 If a man eats the holy thing unwittingly,
then he shall add a fifth of the value to it and
shall give the holy thing to the priest. 15 They
shall not defile the holy things of the children
of Israel, which they offer to the LORD, 16 and
cause them to suffer and to bear the iniquity
of guilt when they eat their holy things, for I
am the LORD who sanctifies them.

Acceptable Offerings

17 The LORD spoke to Moses, saying: 18 Speak
to Aaron, and to his sons, and to all the chil-
dren of Israel, and say to them: Whoever from
the house of Israel or from the foreigners in
Israel who offers his burnt offering for any
vows or freewill offerings that he offers to
the LORD, 19 then if it is to be accepted for you,
the offering shall be a male without blemish,
a bull, sheep, or goat. 20 But whatever has a
blemish you shall not offer, for it shall not be
acceptable for you. 21 Whoever offers a sacrifice
of peace offerings to the LORD to fulfill his vow
or a freewill offering, whether from the herd or
flock, to be accepted it shall be perfect, with no
blemish on it. 22 Blind, or disabled, or maimed,
or having an ulcer or eczema or scabs, you

[1] 10 Or *stranger*.

shall not offer these to the LORD, nor make a
food offering by fire on the altar to the LORD.
23 A herd animal or a flock animal that has a
limb that is too long or short you may offer
for a freewill offering, but for a vow it shall
not be accepted. 24 You shall not offer to the
LORD an animal that is bruised or crushed or
torn or cut; nor shall you make any offering
of them in your land. 25 Nor from a foreigner
shall you offer an animal as the food of your
God, because a blemish is in them from their
mutilation. They shall not be accepted for you.
26 The LORD spoke to Moses, saying: 27 When
an ox, or a sheep, or a goat is born, then it shall
be seven days with its mother, and from the
eighth day and thereafter it shall be accepted
for a food offering made by fire to the LORD.
28 But you shall not slaughter on the same day
an ox or a sheep and her young.
29 When you offer a sacrifice of thanksgiving
to the LORD, offer it so that it may be accepted.
30 On the same day it shall be eaten. You shall
leave none of it until the next day: I am the
LORD.
31 Therefore you shall keep My command-
ments and do them: I am the LORD. 32 You shall
not defile My holy name, but I will be sanc-
tified among the children of Israel: I am the
LORD who sanctifies you, 33 who brought you
out of the land of Egypt, to be your God: I am
the LORD.

The Appointed Feasts

23 And the LORD spoke to Moses, saying:
2 Speak to the children of Israel, and
say to them: Concerning the feasts of the LORD
that you shall proclaim to be holy convoca-
tions, these are My appointed feasts.

The Sabbath

3 For six days work shall be done, but the
seventh day is the Sabbath of complete rest,
a holy convocation. You shall do no work. It is
the Sabbath of the LORD in all your dwellings.

The Passover and the Feast of Unleavened Bread

Ex 12:14–20; Nu 28:16–25; Dt 16:1–8

4 These are the appointed feasts of the LORD,
holy convocations which you shall proclaim
in their appointed times. 5 On the fourteenth
day of the first month at evening is the LORD's
Passover. 6 On the fifteenth day of the same
month is the Feast of Unleavened Bread to the
LORD. For seven days you must eat unleavened
bread. 7 On the first day you shall have a holy
convocation. You shall do no regular work.
8 But you shall offer a food offering made by
fire to the LORD for seven days. On the sev-
enth day is a holy convocation. You shall do
no regular work.

22:23 Lev 21:18
22:24 Lev 22:20
22:27 Ex 22:30
22:28 Dt 22:6–7
22:29 Ps 107:22
22:31 Dt 4:40
22:32 Lev 18:21
22:33 Lev 11:45
23:2 Lev 23:4
23:3 Lev 19:3
23:4 Lev 23:2
23:5 Dt 16:1–8
23:7 Lev 23:8

....

23:10 Ex 23:19
23:11 Ex 29:24
23:12 Lev 1:10
23:13 Lev 2:14–16
23:14 Ex 34:26
23:16 Ac 2:1
23:17 Lev 23:10
23:19 Nu 28:30
23:20 Dt 18:4
23:21 Lev 23:2
23:22 Lev 19:9–10

Offering the First Fruits

9 The LORD spoke to Moses, saying: 10 Speak to
the children of Israel, and say to them: When
you have come into the land that I am giving to
you and reap its harvest, then you shall bring a
sheaf bundle of the first fruits of your harvest
to the priest. 11 And he shall wave the sheaf
before the LORD so that you may be accepted.
On the day after the Sabbath the priest shall
wave it. 12 You shall offer that day when you
wave the sheaf a year-old male lamb without
blemish for a burnt offering to the LORD. 13 The
grain offering shall be two-tenths of an ephah[1]
of wheat flour mixed with oil, a food offering
made by fire to the LORD for a pleasing aroma;
its drink offering shall be of wine, a fourth of
a hin.[2] 14 You shall eat neither bread nor grain,
parched or fresh, until the same day that you
have brought an offering to your God. It shall
be a perpetual statute throughout your gener-
ations in all your dwellings.

The Feast of Weeks

Nu 28:26–31; Dt 16:9–12

15 You shall count seven full weeks from the
next day after the Sabbath, from the day that
you brought the sheaf bundle of the wave of-
fering. 16 You shall count fifty days to the day
after the seventh Sabbath; then you shall offer
a new grain offering to the LORD. 17 You shall
bring out of your habitations two wave loaves
of two-tenths of an ephah. They shall be of
wheat flour, baked with leaven. They are the
first fruits to the LORD. 18 You shall offer with
the bread seven lambs without blemish of the
first year, one bull, and two rams. They shall
be for a burnt offering to the LORD, with their
grain offering and their drink offerings, that is,
a food offering made by fire, of a pleasing aro-
ma to the LORD. 19 Then you shall sacrifice one
male goat for a sin offering, and two lambs of
the first year for a sacrifice of peace offerings.
20 The priest shall wave them with the bread
of the first fruits for a wave offering before the
LORD with the two lambs. They shall be holy
to the LORD for the priest. 21 You shall make a
proclamation on the same day and shall hold
a holy convocation. You shall do no regular
work. It shall be a perpetual statute in all your
dwellings throughout your generations.
22 When you reap the harvest of your land,
you shall not reap your field up to the edge,
nor shall you gather any gleaning of your har-
vest. You shall leave them to the poor and to
the foreigner: I am the LORD your God.

[1] *13* Likely about 7 pounds, or 3.2 kilograms; and in v. 17.
[2] *13* About 1 quart, or 1 liter.

SPIRIT-TO-SPIRIT PRAYER

Prayer to Renounce the Power of Satan

Dear Lord Jesus, I desire to really know You and the depth of Your love for me. Today I open my heart and welcome You completely into my life, asking You to heal all my painful situations and memories, as well as all the brokenness and traumatic experiences of my past. You alone are the Light of the World, my Savior and Lord. Have mercy on me. I surrender my life and my will to You. Please cleanse and forgive me of all sins and iniquities. Heal and sanctify every area of my spirit, soul, and body that has been controlled and tormented by evil spirits. I declare that Jesus is my Lord and my Healer. I plead the blood of Jesus over my spirit, soul, and body.

I now renounce the power of Satan over my life and my destiny. I declare that Jesus Christ is my Lord! Today I declare that I am free! No weapon formed against me shall prosper [Isa 54:17]. Fear no longer has any place in me. I cast fear out of my heart! The love of God now rules my heart. I will submit myself to God. I will resist the devil, and he must flee from me. I release all guilt and condemnation accusing me. Thank You, my Lord, because I am in Christ, and I will walk according to the Spirit of the Lord. In the name of Jesus Christ, amen!

Iris Delgado

The Feast of Trumpets
Nu 29:1–6

23 The Lord spoke to Moses, saying: 24 Speak
to the children of Israel, saying: In the seventh
month, on the first day of the month, you shall
have a sabbath, a memorial with the blowing
of trumpets, a holy convocation. 25 You shall
do no regular work, and you shall offer a food
offering made by fire to the Lord.

The Day of Atonement
Lev 16:2–34; Nu 29:7–11

26 The Lord spoke to Moses, saying: 27 Also on
the tenth day of this seventh month there shall
be the Day of Atonement. It shall be a holy convocation to you, and you shall humble yourselves, and offer a food offering made by fire to
the Lord. 28 You shall do no work on that same
day, for it is the Day of Atonement to make
atonement for you before the Lord your God.
29 For whoever is not humbled on that same
day, he shall be cut off from among his people.
30 And whoever does any work in that same
day, that person I will destroy from among his
people. 31 You shall do no manner of work. It
shall be a perpetual statute throughout your
generations in all your dwellings. 32 It shall be
to you a sabbath of complete rest, and you
shall afflict your souls. On the ninth day of the month starting at the evening, from evening to evening, you shall celebrate your sabbath.

The Feast of Tabernacles
Nu 29:12–39; Dt 16:13–17

33 The Lord spoke to Moses, saying: 34 Speak
to the children of Israel, saying: The fifteenth
day of this seventh month shall be the Feast of
Tabernacles for seven days to the Lord. 35 On
the first day shall be a holy convocation. You
shall do no regular work. 36 For seven days
you shall offer food offerings made by fire to
the Lord. On the eighth day it shall be a holy
convocation to you, and you shall offer a food
offering made by fire to the Lord. It is a solemn
assembly, and you shall do no regular work.

37 These are the appointed feasts of the Lord,
which you shall proclaim to be holy convocations, to offer a food offering made by fire
to the Lord, burnt offerings and grain offerings, sacrifices and drink offerings, each on
its proper day, 38 besides the Sabbaths of the
Lord, besides your gifts, besides all your vows,
and besides all your freewill offerings which
you give to the Lord.

39 On the fifteenth day of the seventh month,
when you have gathered in the produce of the

23:24 Lev 25:9
23:25 Lev 23:21
23:28 Lev 16:34
23:29 Ge 17:14
23:30 Lev 20:3

23:34 Ezr 3:4
23:36 Ne 8:18
23:37 Lev 23:2
23:38 Nu 29:39
23:39 Ex 23:16

land, you shall keep a feast to the LORD for seven days. On the first day shall be a sabbath, and on the eighth day shall be a sabbath. [40] You shall take on the first day the branches of majestic trees—branches of palm trees, branches of leafy trees, and willows from a brook, and you shall rejoice before the LORD your God for seven days. [41] You shall keep it as a feast to the LORD for seven days in the year. It shall be a perpetual statute in your generations. You shall celebrate it in the seventh month. [42] You shall dwell in booths for seven days. All who are native children of Israel shall dwell in booths, [43] that your generations may know that I made the children of Israel dwell in booths when I brought them out of the land of Egypt: I am the LORD your God.

[44] Moses declared to the children of Israel the feasts of the LORD.

The Tabernacle Lamps

Ex 27:20–21

24 And the LORD spoke to Moses, saying: [2] Command the children of Israel that they bring to you pure olive oil beaten for the lamp, to cause the lamps to burn continually. [3] Outside the veil of the sanctuary, in the tent of meeting, Aaron shall arrange it continually, from the evening until the morning before the LORD. It shall be a perpetual statute in your generations. [4] He shall arrange the lamps continually on the pure *gold* lampstand before the LORD.

The Bread of the Tabernacle

[5] You shall take wheat flour and bake twelve cakes. Two-tenths of an ephah[1] shall be in each cake. [6] You shall set them in two rows, six in a row, on the pure *gold* table before the LORD. [7] You shall put pure frankincense on each row, so that it may be on the bread for a memorial, a food offering made by fire to the LORD. [8] Every Sabbath he shall set it in order continually before the LORD, with the portion taken from the children of Israel by a perpetual covenant. [9] It shall be for Aaron and his sons, and they shall eat it in a holy place, for it is most holy to him of the food offerings of the LORD made by fire by a perpetual statute.

The Punishment for Blasphemy

[10] The son of an Israelite woman, whose father was an Egyptian, went out among the children of Israel, and this son of the Israelite woman and a man of Israel fought together in the camp. [11] And the Israelite woman's son blasphemed the name of the LORD and cursed. And they brought him to Moses. (His mother's name was Shelomith, the daughter of Dibri, of the tribe of Dan.) [12] And they put him in custody, so that the words of the LORD might be shown to them.

[13] The LORD spoke to Moses, saying: [14] Bring outside the camp him who has cursed, and let all who heard him lay their hands on his head, and let the entire congregation stone him. [15] You shall speak to the children of Israel, saying: Whoever curses his God shall bear his sin. [16] Whoever blasphemes the name of the LORD, he shall surely be put to death, and the entire congregation shall certainly stone him. The foreigner as well as the native in the land, when he blasphemes the name, then he shall be put to death.

[17] Whoever kills any man shall surely be put to death. [18] Whoever kills an animal shall make restitution, animal for animal. [19] If anyone causes injury to his neighbor, as he has done, so shall it be done to him, [20] fracture for fracture, eye for eye, tooth for tooth; as he has caused an injury to another, so shall it be done to him. [21] Whoever kills an animal shall make restitution. And whoever kills a man shall be put to death. [22] You shall have one manner of law for the foreigner as for the native, for I am the LORD your God.

[23] So Moses spoke to the children of Israel, and they brought outside the camp him who had cursed, and stoned him. And the children of Israel did as the LORD commanded Moses.

The Sabbath Year

25 Then the LORD spoke to Moses on Mount Sinai, saying: [2] Speak to the children of Israel, and say to them: When you come into the land that I give you, the land shall keep a sabbath to the LORD. [3] For six years you shall sow your field, and six years you shall prune your vineyard and gather in its fruit, [4] but in the seventh year there shall be a sabbath of complete rest for the land, a sabbath for the LORD. You shall neither sow your field nor prune your vineyard. [5] That which grows by itself from your harvest you shall not reap, nor gather the grapes of your unpruned vines, for it is a year of complete rest for the land. [6] The sabbath produce of the land shall be food for you: for you, and for your male and female servants, and for your hired servant, and for your stranger who sojourns with you, [7] and for your livestock, and for the wild animals in your land, shall all its increase be food.

The Year of Jubilee

Dt 15:1–11; Ex 21:2–11; Dt 15:12–18

[8] You shall count seven *sabbath* weeks of years, seven times seven years, and the time of the seven sabbaths of years shall be to you forty-nine years. [9] Then you shall sound the

23:40 Dt 16:14–15
23:41 Nu 29:12
23:42 Ne 8:14–17
23:43 Dt 31:10–13
24:2 Ex 27:20–21
24:4 Ex 31:8
24:5 Ex 25:30
24:6 1Ki 7:48
24:7 Lev 2:2
24:8 Nu 4:7
24:9 Lev 8:31
24:12 Ex 18:15–16

24:14 Dt 17:7
24:16 Mt 12:31
24:18 Lev 24:21
24:20 Dt 19:21
24:21 Lev 24:17–18
24:22 Ex 12:49
25:8 Lev 23:15
25:9 Lev 23:24

[1] 5 Likely about 7 pounds, or 3.2 kilograms.

horn blasts on the tenth day of the seventh
month. On the Day of Atonement you shall
make the sound of the horn throughout all
your land. 10 You shall consecrate the fiftieth
year, and proclaim liberty throughout all the
land to all the inhabitants. It shall be a Jubi-
lee to you, and each of you shall return to his
possession, and every person shall return to
his family. 11 That fiftieth year will be a Jubilee
for you. You shall neither sow nor reap that
which grows by itself, nor gather the grapes of
your unpruned vines. 12 For it is the Jubilee. It
shall be holy to you. You shall eat the produce
of the field.

13 In the Year of Jubilee you shall return to
your property.

14 If you sell anything to your neighbor or
buy anything from your neighbor, you shall
not oppress one another. 15 According to the
number of years after the Jubilee you shall pay
your neighbor, and according to the number
of years of the crops he shall sell to you. 16 Ac-
cording to the increase of years you shall in-
crease the price, and according to the decrease
of years you shall diminish the price of it. For
he shall sell to you according to the number
of years of crops. 17 You shall not therefore op-
press one another, but you shall fear your God.
For I am the LORD your God.

18 Therefore you shall do My statutes, and
keep My decrees, and do them, and you shall
dwell securely in the land. 19 The land shall
yield its fruit, and you shall eat your fill and
live securely in it. 20 If you shall say, "What shall
we eat in the seventh year, if we shall not sow
nor gather in our crop?" 21 then I will command
My blessing upon you in the sixth year, and it
shall bring forth produce for three years. 22 You
shall sow in the eighth year, and eat yet of old
crops until the ninth year until its crops come
in for you.

Redemption of Property

23 The land shall not be permanently sold,
for the land is Mine. For you are foreigners
and sojourners with Me. 24 In all the land of
your possession you shall grant a redemption
for the land.

25 If your brother becomes poor and has sold
some of his possession, then his nearest re-
deemer will come to redeem it, and buy back
that which his brother sold. 26 If the man has
none to redeem it, but he himself is able to
redeem it, 27 then let him count the years since
the sale and pay back the balance to the man
to whom he sold it, so that he may return to his
property. 28 But if he is not able to restore it to
himself, then that which he sold shall remain
in the hand of him who has bought it until the
Year of Jubilee, and in the Jubilee it shall be
released, and he shall return to his possession.

29 If a man sells a house in a walled city, then
he may redeem it within a year after it is sold,
within a full year he may have the right to
buy it back. 30 If it is not redeemed within the
time of a full year, then the house that is in the
walled city shall be given permanently to him
who bought it throughout his generations. It
shall not be returned in the Jubilee. 31 But the
houses of the villages that have no wall around
them shall be counted as the fields of the land.
They may be redeemed, and they shall be re-
turned in the Jubilee.

32 For the cities of the Levites, they may re-
deem at any time the houses in the cities that
they possess. 33 If a Levite purchases back the
house that was sold in the city of his posses-
sion, then it shall be returned in the Jubilee.
For the houses of the cities of the Levites are
their possession among the children of Isra-
el. 34 But the fields of the land of their cities
may not be sold, for they are their perpetual
possession.

Helping the Poor

35 If your brother becomes poor and cannot
maintain himself with you, then you shall
support him as if he were a foreigner or a so-
journer, so that he may live with you. 36 Take no
usury or interest from him; but fear your God,
so that your brother may live with you. 37 You
shall not lend him your money at interest, nor
lend him your food for profit. 38 I am the LORD
your God, who brought you out of the land of
Egypt, to give you the land of Canaan and to
be your God.

The Law About Slavery

39 If your brother who dwells near you be-
comes poor and sells himself to you, you shall
not compel him to serve as a bondservant.
40 But as a hired servant and as a sojourner
he shall be with you. He shall serve you until
the Year of Jubilee. 41 And then he shall depart
from you, both he and his children with him,
and he shall return to his own family and to
the possession of his fathers. 42 For they are My
servants, whom I brought out of the land of
Egypt. They shall not be sold as slaves. 43 You
shall not rule over him with harshness, but you
shall fear your God.

44 Both your male and female slaves, whom
you may have, they shall be bought from the
nations that are around you. 45 Moreover of
the foreigners who sojourn among you and of
their families who are with you, who were born
in your land, you may also buy from them,
and they may be your possession. 46 You may
take them as an inheritance for your children

25:10 Jer 34:8
25:12 Lev 25:6–7
25:13 Lev 25:10
25:14 Lev 19:13
25:17 Lev 19:14
25:18 Dt 12:10
25:21 Dt 28:8
25:23 1Ch 29:15
25:25 Ru 2:20

25:35 Dt 15:7–8
25:36 Ex 22:25
25:38 Lev 11:45
25:39 Ex 21:2
25:41 Lev 25:28
25:43 Col 4:1

after you, for their possession. They shall be
your slaves forever. But over your brothers, the
children of Israel, you shall not rule over one
another with rigor.
47 If a sojourner or foreigner becomes rich by
you, and your brother who dwells beside him
becomes poor and sells himself to the foreign-
er or sojourner with you, or to a member of
the stranger's family, 48 then after he is sold he
may be redeemed again. One of his brothers
may redeem him, 49 or either his uncle or his
cousin may redeem him, or any who is near
of kin to him of his family may redeem him.
Or if he is able, he may redeem himself. 50 He
shall calculate with him who bought him from
the year that he was sold to the Year of Jubilee,
and the price of his sale shall be according to
the number of years, according to the time of
a hired servant. 51 If there are still many years
left *until the Jubilee*, he shall pay the price pro-
portionately for his redemption as some of the
price that he was bought for. 52 If there remain
but a few years until the Year of Jubilee, then
he shall calculate and pay the price proportion-
ately for his redemption according to his years
of service. 53 As a yearly hired servant he shall
be treated, and the other shall not rule harshly
over him in your sight.
54 If he is not redeemed in these years, then
he shall go out in the Year of Jubilee, both
he and his children with him. 55 For to Me the
children of Israel are servants. They are My
servants whom I brought out of the land of
Egypt: I am the LORD your God.

Rewards for Obedience

26 You shall not make for yourselves
idols; neither set up a carved image
nor a standing stone, nor shall you set up any
sculpted stone in your land to bow down to it,
for I am the LORD your God.
2 You shall keep My Sabbaths and reverence
My sanctuary: I am the LORD.

> Let me dwell in my land safely
> (Lev 26:5).

3 If you walk in My statutes and keep My
commandments and do them, 4 then I will
give you rain in due season, and the land shall
yield its increase, and the trees of the field shall
yield their fruit. 5 Your threshing shall last till
the grape harvest, and the grape harvest shall
last till the time for sowing, and you shall eat
your bread till you are full and dwell in your
land safely.
6 I will give peace in the land, and you shall
lie down *for sleep*, and none shall make you
afraid; I will remove harmful beasts from the
land, and the sword shall not go through your
land. 7 You shall chase your enemies, and they
shall fall before you by the sword. 8 Five of
you shall chase a hundred, and a hundred of
you shall put ten thousand to flight, and your
enemies shall fall before you by the sword.
9 I will turn toward you and make you fruitful
and multiply you, and I will confirm My cove-
nant with you. 10 You shall eat the old harvest
long stored, and clear out the old to make way
for the new. 11 I will set My tabernacle among
you, and I shall not abhor you. 12 I will walk
among you, and I will be your God, and you
shall be My people. 13 I am the LORD your God,
who brought you out of the land of Egypt,

25:48 Ne 5:5
25:49 Lev 25:26
25:50 Isa 16:14
25:54 Ex 21:2–3
25:55 Lev 25:42
26:1 Lev 19:4
26:2 Lev 19:30
26:3 Dt 28:1–14
26:4 Ps 67:6
26:5 Am 9:13
26:6 Isa 35:9
....
26:8 Dt 32:30
26:9 Ge 17:6–7
26:10 Lev 25:22
26:11 Ex 25:8
26:12 2Co 6:16
26:13 Eze 34:27

SPIRITLED WOMAN

COUNSEL FROM THE SPIRIT BASICS

Give What Belongs to Him

What could we possibly give to the Lord for all His benefits? Psalm 116:18–19 has the answer: "I will pay my vows unto the LORD now in the presence of all His people, in the courts of the house of the LORD."

When you give God what belongs to Him, it releases the anointing to prosper upon your life. And this kind of prosperity is much greater than what the world can give. When God prospers you, it impacts every area of your life. Leviticus 26:9–10 declares, "I will turn toward you and make you fruitful and multiply you, and I will confirm My covenant with you. You shall eat the old harvest long stored, and clear out the old to make way for the new."

We are anointed to prosper abundantly in this season so the end-time harvest will yield many souls for God! Remember, He honors our faith and humility. No matter what you may be working through, remember all of His benefits. Bless God, walk in His purpose, and never stop giving Him your very best. And while you're at it, keep your eyes wide open to everything God has for you. I pray you will be blessed to overflowing!

Judy Jacobs

Spiritual Allies

Five of you shall chase a hundred, and a hundred of you shall put ten thousand to flight, and your enemies shall fall before you by the sword.

—Leviticus 26:8

When hearts gather together and unite, the force of their prayers is multiplied exponentially in the Spirit. No matter how many are assembled, their prayers ascend as multiples of hundreds and thousands for each person present. When we gather together to pray, there is a corporate anointing that harnesses the prayer of agreement to bind, loose, tear down, pluck up, and sound the trumpet for spiritual advancement. (See Matthew 18:18–19.) The foundations of the earth are shaken by corporate prayer, shaking whatever can be shaken so only that which cannot be shaken will remain. All flesh and diabolical schemes are overridden. The threats and whispers of the adversary are silenced and annihilated as we pray.

In the days shortly after the resurrection of Jesus the entire church came together to pray. Look at the power that was released:

> When the day of Pentecost had come, they were all together in one place. Suddenly a sound like a mighty rushing wind came from heaven, and it filled the whole house where they were sitting. There appeared to them tongues as of fire, being distributed and resting on each of them, and they were all filled with the Holy Spirit and began to speak in other tongues, as the Spirit enabled them to speak.
>
> —Acts 2:1–4

The result? Three thousand were saved that day. Later, in response to the persecution they were experiencing at the hands of the religious leaders in Jerusalem, the church gathered to pray again.

And again, thousands more were saved as a result.

In order for there to be a synergy within our churches for spreading the kingdom of God, every part of the body of Christ within that church must be "joined together and connected by every joint and ligament, as every part effectively does its work and grows, building itself up in love" (Eph 4:16). The determination of what is to be supplied is in the hands of the Father. The Lord has inscribed in our DNA the code that determines the talents and abilities He has placed within us that are for the sake of our communities even more than they are for ourselves. He has placed His Spirit in our bellies in such a manner that when we receive His Son as Savior, we are quickened and made alive. Now, as the sons and daughters of God, we are called to constantly be in His presence and in His service.

God has a homing device in the Spirit calling us to Him. We are called to be in His Son, in Christ, and when each of us is in our proper place, abiding in Him, we are one. In Christ we live and move in the divine synchronization of a military under command. The synergistic nature of our movements is in response to His calls to action for those around us. There is a call to see and feel the pain that God feels as the works of the enemy devastate our lands, but there is also an incredible wave of deliverance that happens when the membership of our churches move in unified synergy.

Cindy Trimm

that you should not be their slaves, and I have broken the bars of your yoke and made you walk upright.

Punishment for Disobedience

14 But if you will not listen to Me, and will not do all these commandments, 15 if you despise My statutes, or if you abhor My judgments, so that you will not do all My commandments, but you break My covenant, 16 then I will do this to you: I will visit you with terror, with wasting disease, and with a fever that shall consume the eyes and cause sorrow of heart, and you shall sow your seed in vain, for your enemies shall eat it. 17 I will set My face against you, and you shall be slain before your enemies. They that hate you shall reign over you, and you shall flee when none pursues you.

18 If you will not yet listen to Me after all this, then I will punish you seven times more for your sins. 19 I will break the pride of your power, and I will make your heaven as iron and your land as bronze. 20 Your strength shall be spent in vain, for your land shall not yield her increase, nor shall the trees of the land yield their fruits.

21 If you continue to walk contrary to Me and will not listen to Me, I will bring seven times more plagues upon you according to your sins. 22 I will also send wild beasts among you, which shall rob you of your children, destroy your livestock, and make you few in number. And your roads shall be desolate.

23 And if by these things you are not turned to Me, but walk contrary to Me, 24 then I will also walk contrary to you and will punish you yet seven times for your sins. 25 I will bring a sword upon you that shall extract vengeance for My covenant. And when you are gathered together within your cities, I will send pestilence among you, and you shall be delivered into the hand of the enemy. 26 When I have broken the supply of your bread, ten women shall bake your bread in one oven, and they shall ration your bread again by weight, and you shall eat and not be satisfied.

Lord, destroy the idols in high places (Lev 26:30).

27 If you will not listen to Me for all this, but walk contrary to Me, 28 then I will walk contrary to you also in fury, and I Myself will chastise you seven times for your sins. 29 You shall eat the flesh of your sons and the flesh of your daughters. 30 I will destroy your high places, and cut down your images, and cast your funeral offerings on the lifeless forms of your idols, and I shall abhor you. 31 I will make your cities a waste and bring your sanctuaries to desolation, and I will not smell the savor of your fragrant offerings. 32 I will bring the land into desolation, and your enemies that dwell there shall be astonished at it. 33 I will scatter you among the nations and I will draw out a sword after you. And your land shall be desolate and your cities a waste. 34 Then the land shall enjoy its sabbaths as long as it lies desolate, while you are in your enemies' land; then the land shall rest and enjoy its sabbaths. 35 As long as it lies desolate it shall rest because it did not rest during your sabbaths when you lived upon it.

36 And on those who are left alive of you I will send faintness into their hearts in the lands of their enemies; and the sound of a shaken leaf shall make them flee, and they shall flee as from a sword, and they shall fall when no one pursues. 37 They shall fall one upon one another, as to escape before the sword, though no one pursues, and you shall have no power to stand before your enemies. 38 You shall perish among the nations, and the land of your enemies shall consume you. 39 And those who are left of you shall rot away in their iniquity in your enemies' lands, and also because of the iniquities of their fathers, they shall rot away with them.

40 But if they confess their iniquity, and the iniquity of their fathers, with their treachery that they committed against Me, and also that they have walked contrary to Me, 41 and that I also have walked contrary to them and have brought them into the land of their enemies; if then their uncircumcised hearts are humbled, and they then accept the punishment of their iniquity, 42 then will I remember My covenant with Jacob, and also My covenant with Isaac, and also My covenant with Abraham, and I will remember the land. 43 But the land shall be abandoned by them, and enjoy its sabbaths while it lies desolate without them. They shall make amends for their iniquity, because they despised My judgments and because they abhorred My statutes. 44 Yet for all that, when they are in the land of their enemies, I will not cast them away, nor will I abhor them to destroy them utterly and to break My covenant with them, for I am the LORD their God. 45 But for their sake I will remember the covenant with their fathers, whom I brought out of the land of Egypt in the sight of the nations, that I might be their God: I am the LORD.

46 These are the statutes and judgments and laws that the LORD made between Himself and the children of Israel on Mount Sinai by the hand of Moses.

26:14 Dt 28:15–68
26:15 2Ki 17:15
26:16 Job 31:8
26:17 Ps 53:5
26:18 Lev 26:21
26:19 Dt 28:23
26:20 Ps 127:1
26:22 Dt 32:24
26:23 Jer 5:3
26:25 Nu 14:12
26:26 Isa 3:1
26:28 Isa 59:18
26:30 2Ki 23:20
26:31 Ne 2:3
26:32 Jer 9:11
26:33 Dt 4:27
26:34 2Ch 36:21
26:36 Eze 21:7
26:39 Eze 4:17
26:41 Eze 44:7
26:43 Lev 26:15
26:44 Ro 11:2
26:46 Lev 27:34

Laws About Vows

27 And the LORD spoke to Moses, saying: 2 Speak to the children of Israel, and say to them: When a man makes a special vow to the LORD based on the equivalent value[1] of persons, 3 then the equivalent value of a male from twenty to sixty years old shall be fifty shekels[2] of silver, according to the sanctuary shekel.[3] 4 If the person is a female, then the equivalent value shall be thirty shekels.[4] 5 If the person is five to twenty years old, then the equivalent value shall be twenty shekels[5] for a male and ten shekels[6] for a female. 6 If the person is one month to five years old, then the equivalent value shall be five shekels[7] for a male and three shekels[8] of silver for a female. 7 If the person is sixty years old or older, then the equivalent value shall be fifteen shekels[9] for a male and ten shekels for a female. 8 But if he is too poor *to afford* the equivalent value, then he shall present himself before the priest and the priest shall set his value. According to what the person making the vow can afford, so the priest shall set his value.

9 And if it be an animal, of which men bring an offering to the LORD, all that any man gives of such to the LORD shall be holy. 10 He shall not exchange it nor substitute it, good for bad or bad for good. If he in fact substitutes an animal for another, then both it and its substitute shall be holy. 11 If it is any sort of unclean animal that is not permitted as an offering to the LORD, then he shall present the animal before the priest. 12 And the priest shall set its value, whether good or bad; according to the equivalent value set by the priest, so shall it be. 13 But if he plans on redeeming it, then he shall add one-fifth to the equivalent value.

14 When a man consecrates his house as holy to the LORD, then the priest shall set its value, whether good or bad, according to the equivalent value set by the priest, so shall it be established. 15 If he who consecrates the house should redeem it, then he shall add one-fifth to its equivalent value, and it shall be his.

16 If a man shall consecrate to the LORD some of his land, then the equivalent value shall be according to the seed *needed to sow it*: fifty shekels of silver per homer[10] of barley seed. 17 If he consecrates his field from the Year of Jubilee, the equivalent value shall stay fixed, 18 but if he consecrates his field after the Jubilee, then the priest shall calculate for him the price according to the years that remain until the *next* Year of Jubilee, and the equivalent value shall be reduced. 19 And if he who consecrated the field plans on redeeming it, then he shall add one-fifth to the equivalent value, and it will be established as his. 20 If he does not redeem the field, but rather sells the field to another man, it may not be redeemed again. 21 But when the field is released in the Jubilee, it shall be holy to the LORD as a devoted field; it shall become the possession of the priest.

22 If a man consecrates to the LORD a field that he purchased, which is not part of his land property, 23 then the priest shall calculate for him the amount of the valuation, up to the Year of Jubilee, and he shall give your valuation on that day as a holy thing to the LORD. 24 In the Year of Jubilee the field shall return to the one from whom it was bought, to him to whom the property of land belongs. 25 All your estimations shall be according to the shekel of the sanctuary: Twenty gerahs[11] shall be one shekel.

26 A firstborn of animals, which as firstborn belongs to the LORD, no man may consecrate; whether ox or sheep, it is the LORD's. 27 If it is among the unclean animals, then he shall ransom it at the equivalent value and shall add one-fifth to it, but if it is not redeemed, then it shall be sold at the equivalent value.

28 Anything that a man shall devote to the LORD from all that he has, whether human, animal, or land, shall not be sold or redeemed. Every devoted thing is most holy to the LORD.

29 No one devoted of men, who shall be doomed to death, shall be redeemed; he shall surely be put to death.

30 Any tithe of the land, whether seed of the land or fruit of the trees, belongs to the LORD. It is holy to the LORD. 31 If a man plans on redeeming some of his tithe, he shall add one-fifth to it. 32 Any tithe of herd or flock, all that passes under the *counting* staff, the tenth one shall be holy to the LORD. 33 A person shall not differentiate between good or bad, nor shall he make a substitute for it, but if he does, then both it and its substitute shall be holy. It shall not be redeemed.

34 These are the commandments that the LORD commanded Moses for the children of Israel on Mount Sinai.

27:2 Nu 6:2
27:3 Ex 30:13
27:8 Lev 14:21–22
27:13 Lev 27:15
27:15 Lev 27:13
27:18 Lev 25:15–16
27:21 Eze 44:29
27:23 Lev 27:18
27:24 Lev 25:28
27:25 Ex 30:13
27:26 Ex 13:2
27:28 Jos 6:17–19
27:30 Ge 28:22
27:32 Jer 33:13
27:33 Lev 27:10
27:34 Lev 26:46

[1] *2* Shorthand for the formula in Lev 5:15. [2] *3* About 1¼ pounds, or 575 grams; and in v. 16. [3] *3* About ⅖ ounce, or 12 grams; and in v. 25. [4] *4* About 12 ounces, or 345 grams. [5] *5* About 8 ounces, or 230 grams. [6] *5* About 4 ounces, or 115 grams; and in v. 7. [7] *6* About 2 ounces, or 58 grams. [8] *6* About 1¼ ounces, or 35 grams. [9] *7* About 6 ounces, or 175 grams. [10] *16* Likely about 300 pounds, or 135 kilograms. [11] *25* About 1⁄50 ounce or 0.6 gram.

Author: Traditionally Moses

Written: Between 1440 and 1400 BC

Theme: Wilderness Wanderings

NUMBERS

Dear SpiritLed Woman,

One year my family traveled to London, and during the flight there was unexpected turbulence. It was uncomfortable, and in some people it stirred feelings of fear that we might not make it to our destination. But I knew the plane and its crew had been through inclement weather many times and had arrived safely.

The key in an airplane, as in your journey with God, is to stay in your place and rest in the fact that those who know better than you are in control. If you get out of your seat and walk around, you may be hurt; if you try to bail out, you will die.

The children of Israel faced unexpected hardships during their journey through the wilderness. Many times they focused on the problems instead of on God, who was in control. They even tried to bail out, wanting to return to slavery in Egypt.

The lesson for you, as a SpiritLed Woman, is that no matter how securely anchored you are, you will still experience the turbulence of life. But remember that everything that happens to you on the journey is either part of God's plan or occurs with His permission. He is in control.

Joy F. Strang

Israel's First Census

1 And the LORD spoke to Moses in the Wil-
derness of Sinai in the tent of meeting on
the first day of the second month in the second
year after they went out from the land of Egypt,
saying: 2 Take the sum of all the congregation
of the children of Israel, after their families, by
the house of their fathers, with the number of
their names, every male by their polls, 3 from
twenty years old and upward, all who are able
to go out to war in Israel. You and Aaron will
number them by their armies. 4 With you there
will be a man of every tribe, each one the head
of his father's house. 5 These are the names of
the men who will stand with you:

of the tribe of Reuben, Elizur the son of
Shedeur;
6 of Simeon, Shelumiel the son of Zuri-
shaddai;
7 of Judah, Nahshon the son of Ammin-
adab;
8 of Issachar, Nethanel the son of Zuar;
9 of Zebulun, Eliab the son of Helon;
10 of the children of Joseph:
of Ephraim, Elishama the son of Ammi-
hud;
of Manasseh, Gamaliel the son of
Pedahzur;
11 of Benjamin, Abidan the son of Gideoni;
12 of Dan, Ahiezer the son of Ammishaddai;
13 of Asher, Pagiel the son of Okran;
14 of Gad, Eliasaph the son of Deuel;
15 of Naphtali, Ahira the son of Enan.

16 These were the renowned of the congre-
gation, leaders of the tribes of their fathers,
heads of thousands in Israel.
17 Moses and Aaron took these men who had
been mentioned by name, 18 and they assem-
bled all the congregation on the first day of the
second month, and they declared their pedi-
grees according to their families, by the house
of their fathers, according to the number of the
names, from twenty years old and upward, by
their polls. 19 As the LORD commanded Moses,
so he numbered them in the Wilderness of
Sinai.

20 The children of Reuben, the oldest son
of Israel,
by their generations, after their families,
by the house of their fathers, according
to the number of the names, by their
polls, every male from twenty years old
and upward, all who were able to go out
to war, 21 those who were numbered of
them, even of the tribe of Reuben, were
forty-six thousand five hundred.

1:1 Ex 19:1
1:2 Ex 30:12
1:3 Ex 30:14
1:4 Nu 1:16
1:5 Nu 7:30
1:6 Nu 7:36
1:7 Lk 3:32
1:8 Nu 7:18
1:9 Nu 7:24
1:11 Nu 7:60
1:12 Nu 7:66
1:13 Nu 7:72
1:14 Nu 2:14
1:15 Nu 7:78
1:16 Ex 18:21
1:18 Ezr 2:59
1:20 Nu 26:5–7
1:21 Nu 26:7
....
1:22 Nu 26:12–14
1:23 Nu 26:14
1:24 Nu 26:15–18
1:25 Nu 26:18
1:26 Ge 29:35
1:29 Nu 26:25
1:30 Nu 26:26–27
1:31 Nu 26:27
1:32 Nu 26:35–37
1:33 Nu 26:37

22 Of the children of Simeon,
by their generations, after their families,
by the house of their fathers, those who
were numbered of them, according to
the number of the names, by their polls,
every male from twenty years old and
upward, all who were able to go out to
war, 23 those who were numbered of
them, even of the tribe of Simeon, were
fifty-nine thousand three hundred.

24 Of the children of Gad,
by their generations, after their families,
by the house of their fathers, according
to the number of the names, from twenty
years old and upward, all who were able
to go out to war, 25 those who were num-
bered of them, even of the tribe of Gad,
were forty-five thousand six hundred
and fifty.

26 Of the children of Judah,
by their generations, after their families,
by the house of their fathers, according
to the number of the names, from twenty
years old and upward, all who were
able to go out to war, 27 those who were
numbered of them, even of the tribe of
Judah, were seventy-four thousand six
hundred.

28 Of the children of Issachar,
by their generations, after their families,
by the house of their fathers, according
to the number of the names, from twenty
years old and upward, all who were
able to go out to war, 29 those who were
numbered of them, even of the tribe of
Issachar, were fifty-four thousand four
hundred.

30 Of the children of Zebulun,
by their generations, after their families,
by the house of their fathers, according
to the number of the names, from twenty
years old and upward, all who were
able to go out to war, 31 those who were
numbered of them, even of the tribe of
Zebulun, were fifty-seven thousand four
hundred.

32 Of the children of Joseph,
namely, of the children of Ephraim,
by their generations, after their families,
by the house of their fathers, according
to the number of the names, from twenty
years old and upward, all who were
able to go out to war, 33 those who were
numbered of them, even of the tribe
of Ephraim, were forty thousand five
hundred.

34 Of the children of Manasseh,
by their generations, after their families,
by the house of their fathers, according
to the number of the names, from twenty
years old and upward, all who were
able to go out to war, 35 those who were
numbered of them, even of the tribe of
Manasseh, were thirty-two thousand two
hundred.

36 Of the children of Benjamin,
by their generations, after their families,
by the house of their fathers, according
to the number of the names, from twenty
years old and upward, all who were
able to go out to war, 37 those who were
numbered of them, even of the tribe of
Benjamin, were thirty-five thousand four
hundred.

38 Of the children of Dan,
by their generations, after their families,
by the house of their fathers, according
to the number of the names, from twenty
years old and upward, all who were able
to go out to war, 39 those who were num-
bered of them, even of the tribe of Dan,
were sixty-two thousand seven hundred.

40 Of the children of Asher,
by their generations, after their families,
by the house of their fathers, according
to the number of the names, from twenty
years old and upward, all who were able
to go out to war, 41 those who were num-
bered of them, even of the tribe of Asher,
were forty-one thousand five hundred.

42 Of the children of Naphtali,
by their generations, after their families,
by the house of their fathers, according
to the number of the names, from twenty
years old and upward, all who were
able to go out to war, 43 those who were
numbered of them, even of the tribe of
Naphtali, were fifty-three thousand four
hundred.

44 These are those who numbered,
which Moses and Aaron numbered, and the
leaders of Israel, being twelve men. Each one
was for the house of his fathers. 45 So were
all those who were numbered of the children
of Israel, by the house of their fathers, from
twenty years old and upward, all who were
able to go out to war in Israel. 46 Even all they
who were numbered were six hundred and
three thousand five hundred and fifty.

47 But the Levites after the tribe of their fa-
thers were not numbered among them. 48 For
the LORD had spoken to Moses, saying: 49 Only
you will not number the tribe of Levi, nor take
the census of them among the children of Is-
rael, 50 but you will appoint the Levites over the
tent of the testimony, and over all its vessels,
and over all things that belong to it. They will
carry the tabernacle, and all its vessels, and
they will minister to it, and will camp around
the tabernacle. 51 When the tabernacle sets out,
the Levites will take it down, and when the
tabernacle is to be set up, the Levites will set
it up, and the foreigner that approaches will
be put to death. 52 The children of Israel will
pitch their tents, every man by his own camp,
and every man by his own standard, through-
out their armies. 53 But the Levites will camp
around the tabernacle of the testimony, so
there will be no wrath on the congregation of
the children of Israel. And the Levites will keep
the charge of the tabernacle of the testimony.

54 Thus the children of Israel did according to
all that the LORD commanded Moses.

Tribes and Leaders by Armies

2 And the LORD spoke to Moses and to Aar-
on, saying: 2 Every man of the children of
Israel will camp by his own standard, with the
ensign of his father's house. Facing the tent of
meeting they will camp.

3 On the east side toward the rising of the
sun the standard of the camp of Judah will
camp throughout their armies, and Nahshon
the son of Amminadab will be captain of the
children of Judah. 4 His host, and those who
were numbered of them, were seventy-four
thousand six hundred.

5 Those who camp next to him will be the
tribe of Issachar, and Nethanel the son of Zuar
will be captain of the children of Issachar. 6 His
host, and those who were numbered of them,
were fifty-four thousand four hundred.

7 Then comes the tribe of Zebulun, and Eliab
the son of Helon will be captain of the children
of Zebulun. 8 His host, and those who were
numbered of them, were fifty-seven thousand
four hundred.

9 All who were numbered throughout the
armies in the camp of Judah were one hun-
dred and eighty-six thousand four hundred.
They will march out first.

10 On the south side will be the standard of
the camp of Reuben according to their armies,
and the captain of the children of Reuben will
be Elizur the son of Shedeur. 11 His host, and
those who were numbered of them, were for-
ty-six thousand five hundred.

12 Those who camp by him will be the tribe of
Simeon, and the captain of the children of Sim-
eon will be Shelumiel the son of Zurishaddai.
13 His host, and those who were numbered of
them, were fifty-nine thousand three hundred.

1:35 Nu 26:34
1:36 Ge 49:27
1:37 Nu 26:41
1:38 Ge 46:23
1:39 Nu 26:43
1:41 Nu 26:47
1:43 Nu 26:50
1:44 Nu 26:64
1:46 Ex 12:37
1:47 Nu 2:33
1:49 Nu 26:62

....

1:50 Ex 38:21
1:51 Nu 3:38
1:52 Nu 2:2
1:53 Nu 16:46
2:3 Ru 4:20
2:5 Nu 1:8
2:7 Nu 1:9
2:9 Nu 10:14
2:10 Nu 1:5
2:12 Nu 1:6

14 Then comes the tribe of Gad, and the captain of the sons of Gad will be Eliasaph the son of Reuel. 15 His host, and those who were numbered of them, were forty-five thousand six hundred and fifty.

16 All who were numbered in the camp of Reuben were one hundred and fifty-one thousand four hundred and fifty, throughout their armies. And they will set out in the second rank.

17 Then the tent of meeting will set out with the camp of the Levites in the middle of the camp. As they camp, so they will set out, every man in his place by their standards.

18 On the west side will be the standard of the camp of Ephraim according to their armies, and the captain of the sons of Ephraim will be Elishama the son of Ammihud. 19 His host, and those who were numbered of them, were forty thousand five hundred.

20 By him will be the tribe of Manasseh, and the captain of the children of Manasseh will be Gamaliel the son of Pedahzur. 21 His host, and those who were numbered of them, were thirty-two thousand two hundred.

22 Then comes the tribe of Benjamin, and the captain of the sons of Benjamin will be Abidan the son of Gideoni. 23 His host, and those who were numbered of them, were thirty-five thousand four hundred.

24 All who were numbered of the camp of Ephraim were one hundred and eight thousand one hundred, throughout their armies. And they will go out in the third rank.

25 The standard of the camp of Dan will be on the north side by their armies, and the captain of the children of Dan will be Ahiezer the son of Ammishaddai. 26 His host, and those who were numbered of them, were sixty-two thousand seven hundred.

27 Those who camp by him will be the tribe of Asher, and the captain of the children of Asher will be Pagiel the son of Okran. 28 His host, and those who were numbered of them, were forty-one thousand five hundred.

29 Then the tribe of Naphtali, and the captain of the children of Naphtali will be Ahira the son of Enan. 30 His host, and those who were numbered of them, were fifty-three thousand four hundred.

31 All they who were numbered in the camp of Dan were one hundred and fifty-seven thousand six hundred. They will set out in the back with their standards.

32 These are those who were numbered of the children of Israel by the house of their fathers. All those who were numbered of the camps throughout their hosts were six hundred and three thousand five hundred and fifty. 33 But the Levites were not numbered among the children of Israel, as the LORD commanded Moses.

34 The children of Israel did according to all that the LORD commanded Moses. So they camped by their standards, and so they set out, each one after his family, according to their fathers' houses.

2:14 Nu 1:14
2:16 Nu 10:18
2:17 Nu 10:21
2:18 Nu 1:10
2:20 Nu 1:10
2:22 Nu 1:11
2:24 Nu 10:22
2:25 Nu 1:12
2:27 Nu 1:13
2:29 Nu 1:15
2:31 Nu 10:25
2:32 Nu 1:46

....

3:1 Ex 6:20
3:2 Ex 6:23
3:3 Ex 28:41
3:4 Lev 10:1–2
3:7 Nu 1:50
3:9 Nu 8:19
3:10 Nu 1:51
3:12 Nu 3:41
3:13 Ex 13:2
3:15 Nu 26:62

The Sons of Aaron

3 These also are the generations of Aaron and Moses in the day that the LORD spoke with Moses in Mount Sinai.

2 These are the names of the sons of Aaron: Nadab the firstborn, and Abihu, Eleazar, and Ithamar. 3 These are the names of the sons of Aaron, the priests who were anointed, whom he consecrated to minister as priests. 4 Nadab and Abihu died before the LORD when they brought strange fire before the LORD in the Wilderness of Sinai, and they had no children, and Eleazar and Ithamar ministered as priests in the sight of Aaron their father.

Duties of the Levites

5 The LORD spoke to Moses, saying: 6 Bring the tribe of Levi near, and present them before Aaron the priest, and they will minister to him. 7 They will keep his directives, and serve the whole congregation before the tent of meeting, to do the service of the tabernacle. 8 They will keep all the instruments of the tent of meeting, and attend to the needs of the children of Israel, to do the service of the tabernacle. 9 You will give the Levites to Aaron and to his sons. They are wholly given to him from the children of Israel. 10 You will appoint Aaron and his sons, and they will attend to their priesthood, and the foreigner that approaches will be put to death.

11 The LORD spoke to Moses, saying: 12 I Myself have taken the Levites from among the children of Israel instead of all the firstborn that open the womb among the children of Israel. Therefore the Levites will be Mine 13 because all the firstborn are Mine, for on the day that I struck all the firstborn in the land of Egypt I set apart to Me all the firstborn in Israel, both man and beast. They will be Mine. I am the LORD.

A Census of the Levites

14 The LORD spoke to Moses in the Wilderness of Sinai, saying: 15 Number the children of Levi after the house of their fathers, by their families. You will number every male from a month old and older. 16 Moses numbered them according to the word of the LORD, as he was commanded.

17 These were the sons of Levi by their
names:
Gershon, and Kohath, and Merari.
18 These are the names of the sons of Ger-
shon by their families:
Libni and Shimei;
19 the sons of Kohath by their families:
Amram, and Izhar, Hebron, and Uzziel;
20 the sons of Merari by their families:
Mahli and Mushi.
These are the families of the Levites accord-
ing to the house of their fathers.

21 From Gershon was the family of the Lib-
nites and the family of the Shimeites. These
are the families of the Gershonites. 22 Those
who were numbered of them, according to the
number of all the males, from a month old and
older, those who were numbered of them were
seven thousand five hundred. 23 The families of
the Gershonites were to camp behind the west
side of the tabernacle. 24 The chief of the house
of the father of the Gershonites was Eliasaph
the son of Lael. 25 The charge of the sons of
Gershon in the tent of meeting *included* the
tabernacle, and the tent, its covering, and the
hanging for the door of the tent of meeting,
26 the hangings of the court, the curtain for
the opening of the court that is around the
tabernacle and the altar, and its cords—all the
service pertaining to these.

27 Of Kohath was the family of the Am-
ramites, and the family of the Izharites, and
the family of the Hebronites, and the family of
the Uzzielites. These are the families of the Ko-
hathites. 28 The number of all the males, from
a month old and older, were eight thousand
six hundred, keeping the guard of the sanctu-
ary. 29 The families of the sons of Kohath were
to camp on the south side of the tabernacle.
30 The chief of the house of the father of the
families of the Kohathites was Elizaphan the
son of Uzziel. 31 Their duty included the ark,
and the table, and the lampstand, and the al-
tars, and the vessels of the sanctuary they min-
ister with, and the hanging, and all its service.
32 Eleazar the son of Aaron the priest was to
be chief over the leaders of the Levites and to
have the oversight of those who kept the guard
of the sanctuary.

33 Of Merari was the family of the Mahlites
and the family of the Mushites. These are the
families of Merari. 34 Those who were num-
bered of them, according to the number of all
the males from a month old and older, were
six thousand two hundred. 35 The chief of the
house of the father of the families of Mera-
ri was Zuriel the son of Abihail. These were
to camp on the north side of the tabernacle.

36 Under the oversight and guard of the sons of
Merari were the frames of the tabernacle, the
bars, the pillars, the sockets, all their accesso-
ries, all the service pertaining to these, 37 and
the pillars of the court all around, with their
sockets, and pins, and cords.

38 But those who were to camp before the
tabernacle toward the east, even before the
tent of meeting on the east side, were Moses,
and Aaron and his sons, keeping the guard of
the sanctuary for the guard of the children of
Israel, and the foreigner who approached was
to be put to death.

39 All who were numbered of the Levites,
which Moses and Aaron numbered at the
commandment of the LORD, throughout their
families, all the males from a month old and
older, were twenty-two thousand.

The Redemption of the Firstborn

40 The LORD said to Moses: Number all the
firstborn of the males of the children of Isra-
el from a month old and older and take the
number of their names. 41 You will take the
Levites for Me (I am the LORD) instead of all
the firstborn among the children of Israel, and
the livestock of the Levites instead of all the
firstborn among the livestock of the children
of Israel.
42 Moses numbered, as the LORD commanded
him, all the firstborn among the children of Is-
rael. 43 All the firstborn males, by the number of
names, from a month old and upward, of those
who were numbered of them, were twenty-two
thousand two hundred and seventy-three.
44 The LORD spoke to Moses, saying: 45 Take
the Levites instead of all the firstborn among
the children of Israel, and the livestock of the
Levites instead of their livestock, and the Le-
vites will be Mine. I am the LORD. 46 For those
who are to be redeemed of the two hundred
and seventy-three of the firstborn of the chil-
dren of Israel, which are more than the Levites,
47 you will take five shekels[1] apiece by the poll;
according to the shekel of the sanctuary you
will take them (the shekel is twenty gerahs).
48 And you will give the money, by which the
number of them is to be redeemed, to Aaron
and to his sons.
49 Moses took the redemption money of those
who were over and above those who were re-
deemed by the Levites. 50 Of the firstborn of the
children of Israel he took the money, one thou-
sand three hundred and sixty-five shekels,[2] af-
ter the shekel of the sanctuary. 51 And Moses
gave the money of those who were redeemed

3:17 Ge 46:11
3:18 1Ch 6:17
3:19 Ex 6:18
3:20 Ex 6:19
3:23 Nu 1:53
3:25 Ex 25:9
3:26 Ex 35:18
3:27 1Ch 26:23
3:29 Nu 1:53
3:35 Nu 1:53

......

3:38 Nu 1:53
3:39 Nu 26:62
3:40 Nu 3:15
3:41 Nu 3:12
3:45 Nu 3:12
3:46 Ex 13:13
3:47 Ex 30:13
3:50 Nu 3:46–47
3:51 Nu 3:48

[1] *47* About 2 ounces, or 58 grams. [2] *50* About 35 pounds, or 16 kilograms.

to Aaron and to his sons, according to the word of the LORD, as the LORD commanded Moses.

Duties of the Kohathites

4 And the LORD spoke to Moses and to Aaron, saying: 2 Take the sum of the sons of Kohath from among the sons of Levi, after their families, by the house of their fathers, 3 from thirty years old and older, even to fifty years old, all that enter into the host, to do the work in the tent of meeting.

4 This will be the service of the sons of Kohath in the tent of meeting, concerning the holiest things. 5 And when the camp sets out, Aaron will come, and his sons, and they will take down the covering curtain, and cover the ark of the testimony with it, 6 and will put on it the covering of porpoise skins, and will spread over it a cloth completely of blue, and will put in its poles.

7 Upon the table of showbread they will spread a cloth of blue, and put the dishes on it, and the spoons, and the bowls, and covers to cover it, and the showbread will be on it. 8 And they will spread on them a cloth of scarlet, and cover the same with a covering of porpoise skins, and will put in its poles.

9 They will take a cloth of blue, and cover the lampstand of the light, and its lamps, and its tongs, and its snuff dishes, and all its oil vessels, with which they minister to it. 10 And they will put it and all its vessels within a covering of porpoise skins and will put it on a carrying pole.

11 Upon the golden altar they will spread a cloth of blue, and cover it with a covering of porpoise skins, and will put in its poles.

12 And they will take all the instruments of ministry, with which they minister in the sanctuary, and put them in a cloth of blue, and cover them with a covering of porpoise skins, and will put them on a carrying pole.

13 And they will take away the ashes from the altar and spread a purple cloth on it. 14 They shall put on it all the instruments with which they minister there, the censers, the flesh hooks, the shovels, the basins, all the utensils of the altar. And they will spread on it a covering of porpoise skins and insert its poles.

15 When Aaron and his sons have finished covering the sanctuary, and all the instruments of the sanctuary, as the camp is to set out, after that, the sons of Kohath will come to carry it. But they will not touch any holy thing, lest they die. These things are the burden of the sons of Kohath in the tent of meeting.

16 To the office of Eleazar, Aaron the priest's son, pertains the oil for the light, and the sweet incense, and the daily grain offering, and the anointing oil, and the oversight of all the tabernacle, and of all that is in it, in the sanctuary, and in the instruments thereof.

17 The LORD spoke to Moses and to Aaron, saying: 18 Do not cut the tribe of the families of the Kohathites from among the Levites. 19 But do this to them, that they may live and not die, when they approach the most holy things. Aaron and his sons will go in, and appoint each one to his service and to his burden. 20 But they will not go in to see when the holy things are covered, lest they die.

Duties of the Gershonites

21 The LORD spoke to Moses, saying: 22 Take also the sum of the sons of Gershon, throughout the houses of their fathers, by their families. 23 From thirty years old and older to fifty years old you will number them, all that enter in to perform the service, to do the work in the tent of meeting.

24 This is the service of the families of the Gershonites, to serve, and to work. 25 And they will carry the curtains of the tabernacle, and the tent of meeting, its covering, and the covering of the porpoise skins that is on it, and the hanging for the door of the tent of meeting, 26 and the hangings of the courtyard, and the hanging for the opening of the gate of the courtyard, which is by the tabernacle and by the altar all around, and their cords, and all the instruments of their service, and all that is made for them. So they will serve. 27 At the appointment of Aaron and his sons will be all the service of the sons of the Gershonites, in all their burdens, and in all their service. And you shall assign to them all their tasks as their duty. 28 This is the service of the families of the sons of Gershon in the tent of meeting. And their charge will be under the hand of Ithamar the son of Aaron the priest.

Duties of the Merarites

29 As for the sons of Merari, you will number them by their families, by the house of their fathers. 30 From thirty years old and older, even to fifty years old, you will number them, everyone who enters into the service, to do the work of the tent of meeting. 31 This is the charge of their burden, according to all their service in the tent of meeting. The boards of the tabernacle, and its bars thereof, and its pillars, and its sockets, 32 and the pillars of the court round about, and their sockets, and their pins, and their cords, with all their instruments, and with all their service, and by name you will list the instruments of the charge of their burden. 33 This is the service of the families of the sons of Merari, according to all their service, in the

4:3 Nu 4:23
4:4 Nu 4:19
4:6 Ex 25:13–15
4:7 Lev 24:5–8
4:9 Ex 25:31–39
4:12 1Ch 9:29
4:15 2Sa 6:6–7
4:16 Ex 25:6

4:20 Ex 19:21
4:23 Nu 4:3
4:25 Ex 26:14
4:28 Nu 4:33
4:31 Nu 3:36–37
4:32 Ex 38:21
4:33 Nu 4:28

tent of meeting, under the hand of Ithamar the son of Aaron the priest.

Census of the Levites

[34] Moses, Aaron, and the leaders of the congregation numbered the sons of the Kohathites by their families, and by the house of their fathers, [35] from thirty years old and older to fifty years old, everyone who entered into the service, for the work in the tent of meeting. [36] And those who were numbered by their families were two thousand seven hundred and fifty. [37] These were the ones listed of the families of the Kohathites, all who might do service in the tent of meeting, which Moses and Aaron numbered according to the commandment of the LORD by the hand of Moses.

[38] Those who were numbered of the sons of Gershon, throughout their families, and by the house of their fathers, [39] from thirty years old and older to fifty years old, everyone who entered into the service, for the work in the tent of meeting, [40] even those who were numbered of them, throughout their families, by the house of their fathers, were two thousand six hundred and thirty. [41] These were the ones listed by the families of the sons of Gershon, of all who might do service in the tent of meeting, whom Moses and Aaron numbered according to the commandment of the LORD.

[42] Those who were numbered of the families of the sons of Merari, throughout their families, by the house of their fathers, [43] from thirty years old and older to fifty years old, everyone who entered into the service, for the work in the tent of meeting, [44] even those who were numbered by their families, were three thousand two hundred. [45] These were the ones listed of the families of the sons of Merari, whom Moses and Aaron numbered according to the word of the LORD by the hand of Moses.

[46] All those who were numbered of the Levites, whom Moses, Aaron, and the leaders of Israel numbered, by their families, and by the house of their fathers, [47] from thirty years old and older to fifty years old, everyone who came to do the service of the ministry, and the service of the work in the tent of meeting, [48] even those who were numbered were eight thousand five hundred and eighty. [49] According to the commandment of the LORD they were numbered by the hand of Moses, each according to his service, and according to his burden.

Thus they were numbered by him, as the LORD commanded Moses.

The Unclean

5 And the LORD spoke to Moses, saying: [2] Command the children of Israel that they put out of the camp every leper, and everyone who has a discharge, and whoever is defiled by the dead. [3] Both male and female you will put out. You will put them outside the camp, so they do not defile their camps in the midst of which I dwell. [4] The children of Israel did so, and put them outside the camp. As the LORD spoke to Moses, so the children of Israel did.

Restitution for Wrongs

[5] The LORD spoke to Moses, saying: [6] Tell the children of Israel: When a man or woman commits any sin against another, acting unfaithfully against the LORD, that person is guilty, [7] and shall confess his sin which he has committed, and he will repay his offense with its principal, and add to it one-fifth, and give it to him who was wronged. [8] But if the man has no relative to repay the offense to, let the offense be repaid to the LORD, even to the priest, beside the ram of the atonement, whereby an atonement will be made for him. [9] Every offering of all the holy things of the children of Israel, which they bring to the priest, will be his. [10] Every man's holy things will be his. Whatever any man gives the priest, it will be his.

The Test for Adultery

[11] The LORD spoke to Moses, saying: [12] Speak to the children of Israel and say to them: If any man's wife goes astray, and acts treacherously against him, [13] and a man lies with her carnally, and it is hidden from the eyes of her husband, and it is concealed though she has defiled herself, and there is no witness against her, nor is she caught in the act, [14] and if the spirit of jealousy comes on him, and he is jealous of his wife who has defiled herself, or if the spirit of jealousy comes on him and he is jealous of his wife, though she has not defiled herself, [15] then the man shall bring his wife to the priest and he shall bring her offering for her, a tenth of an ephah[1] of barley flour. He shall pour no oil on it nor put frankincense on it, for it is a grain offering of jealousy, a grain offering of remembrance, bringing iniquity to remembrance.

[16] The priest will bring her near, and set her before the LORD. [17] And the priest will take holy water in an earthen vessel, and the priest will take some of the dust that is on the floor of the tabernacle and put it into the water. [18] And the priest will set the woman before the LORD, and uncover the woman's head, and put the memorial offering in her hands, which is the grain offering of jealousy, and the priest will have in his hand the bitter water that causes the curse. [19] And the priest will charge her by an oath, and say to the woman, "If no man has

4:47 Nu 4:3
4:48 Nu 3:39
5:2 Lev 13:46

5:7 Lev 5:5
5:8 Lev 6:6–7
5:12 Nu 5:19–20
5:13 Lev 18:20
5:14 Pr 6:34
5:15 Eze 29:16

[1] *15* Likely about 3½ pounds, or 1.6 kilograms.

lain with you, and if you have not gone astray to impurity with another instead of your husband, be free from this bitter water that causes the curse. 20 But if you have gone astray to another instead of your husband, and if you are defiled, and a man besides your husband has lain with you"— 21 then the priest will charge the woman with an oath of cursing, and the priest will say to the woman, "The LORD make you a curse and an oath among your people, when the LORD makes your thigh rot and your belly swell. 22 And this water that causes the curse will go into your bowels, to make your belly swell and your thigh rot."

And the woman will say, "Amen, amen."

23 The priest will write these curses in a book, and he will wash them out with the bitter water. 24 And he will cause the woman to drink the bitter water that causes the curse. And the water that causes the curse will enter into her and become bitter. 25 Then the priest will take the grain offering of jealousy out of the woman's hand and will wave the offering before the LORD and offer it on the altar. 26 And the priest will take a handful of the offering, the memorial portion, and burn it on the altar, and afterward will cause the woman to drink the water. 27 When he has made her to drink the water, then it will be that, if she is defiled and has acted treacherously against her husband, the water that causes the curse will enter into her, and become bitter, and her belly will swell, and her thigh will rot, and the woman will be a curse among her people. 28 If the woman is not defiled, but is clean, then she will be free and will conceive offspring.

29 This is the law of jealousies, when a wife goes astray to another instead of her husband, and is defiled, 30 or when the spirit of jealousy comes on him, and he is jealous over his wife, and will set the woman before the LORD, and the priest will perform on her all this law. 31 Then the man will be guiltless from iniquity, and this woman will bear her iniquity.

The Nazirite Vow

6 And the LORD spoke to Moses, saying: 2 Speak to the children of Israel and say to them: When either a man or woman will make a hard vow, the vow of a Nazirite, to separate themselves to the LORD, 3 he will separate himself from wine and strong drink and will drink no vinegar of wine, or vinegar of strong drink. Neither shall he drink any juice of grapes, nor eat fresh or dry grapes. 4 All the days of his separation he will eat nothing that is made of the grapevine, from the seed to the skin.

5 All the days of the vow of his separation no razor will come on his head until the days are fulfilled in which he separates himself to the LORD. He will be holy and will let the locks of the hair of his head grow. 6 All the days that he separates himself to the LORD he will not approach a dead body. 7 He will not defile himself for his father or for his mother, for his brother or for his sister if they die because the separation of his God is on his head. 8 All the days of his separation he is holy to the LORD.

9 If any man dies very suddenly beside him, and he has defiled his consecrated head, then he will shave his head in the day of his cleansing, on the seventh day will he shave it. 10 On the eighth day he will bring two turtledoves or two young pigeons to the priest, to the door of the tent of meeting. 11 And the priest will offer one as a sin offering and the other as a burnt offering and make an atonement for him, since he sinned because of the dead, and will sanctify his head that same day. 12 He will consecrate to the LORD the days of his separation and bring a male lamb in its first year as a guilt offering. But the previous days will be lost because his separation was defiled.

13 This is the law of the Nazirite. When the days of his separation are fulfilled, he will be brought to the door of the tent of meeting. 14 And he will offer his offering to the LORD, one male lamb a year old without blemish as a burnt offering, one ewe lamb a year old without blemish as a sin offering, one ram without blemish as a peace offering, 15 a basket of unleavened bread, loaves of fine flour mixed with oil, unleavened wafers anointed with oil, and their grain offering with their drink offerings.

16 The priest will bring them before the LORD and will offer his sin offering and his burnt offering. 17 And he will offer the ram as a sacrifice of a peace offering to the LORD with the basket of unleavened bread. The priest will offer also his grain offering and his drink offering.

18 The Nazirite will shave his consecrated head at the door of the tent of meeting, and will take the hair from his consecrated head and put it in the fire which is under the sacrifice of the peace offerings.

19 The priest will take the cooked shoulder of the ram, and one unleavened cake out of the basket, and one unleavened wafer and will put them on the hands of the Nazirite, after he has shaved his consecrated hair. 20 And the priest will wave them as a wave offering before the LORD. This is holy for the priest, with the breast waved and the shoulder offered. And after that the Nazirite may drink wine.

21 This is the law of the Nazirite who has vowed to the LORD, his offering for his separation, besides whatever else his hand is able to provide. According to the vow which he

5:21 Jos 6:26
5:22 Ps 109:18
5:25 Lev 8:27
5:26 Lev 2:2
5:27 Jer 29:18
5:29 Nu 5:19
6:2 Jdg 13:5
6:3 Lk 1:15
6:4 Nu 6:5
6:5 1Sa 1:11

6:6 Lev 19:28
6:7 Nu 9:6
6:9 Nu 6:18
6:12 Lev 5:6
6:13 Ac 21:26
6:15 Ex 29:2
6:18 Ac 21:24
6:20 Ecc 9:7

spoke, so he must do, according to the law of his separation.

The Priestly Blessing

22 The LORD spoke to Moses, saying: 23 Speak to Aaron and to his sons, saying, This is how you will bless the children of Israel, saying to them,

24 The LORD bless you
  and keep you;
25 the LORD make His face to shine upon you,
  and be gracious unto you;
26 the LORD lift His countenance upon you,
  and give you peace.

27 They will put My name upon the children of Israel, and I will bless them.

Offerings at the Tabernacle's Dedication

7 And it was on the day that Moses had fully set up the tabernacle and anointed it and sanctified it and all its instruments, both the altar and all its vessels, and anointed them, and sanctified them, 2 that the leaders of Israel, heads of their fathers' houses, who were the leaders of the tribes, and were over them who were counted, made an offering. 3 And they brought their offering before the LORD, six covered wagons, and twelve oxen, a wagon for two of the leaders, and for each one an ox. And they brought them before the tabernacle.

4 The LORD spoke to Moses, saying: 5 Accept these things from them, that they may be used in the service of the tent of meeting. Give them to the Levites, to each man according to his service.

6 Moses took the wagons and the oxen and gave them to the Levites. 7 Two wagons and four oxen he gave to the sons of Gershon, according to their service. 8 And four wagons and eight oxen he gave to the sons of Merari, according to their service, under the hand of Ithamar the son of Aaron the priest. 9 But to the sons of Kohath he gave none because the service of the sanctuary belonging to them was that they should carry on their shoulders.

10 The leaders brought their dedication offerings when the altar was anointed, and offered their offerings before the altar. 11 The LORD said to Moses: They will offer their offering, each leader on his day, for the dedicating of the altar.

12 He that offered his offering the first day was Nahshon the son of Amminadab, of the tribe of Judah.

13 And his offering was one silver charger, the weight of which was one hundred and thirty shekels,[1] one silver bowl of seventy shekels,[2] after the shekel of the sanctuary, both of them full of fine flour mixed with oil as a grain offering; 14 one spoon of ten shekels[3] of gold, full of incense; 15 one young bull, one ram, and one male lamb in its first year as a burnt offering; 16 one goat kid as a sin offering; 17 and as a sacrifice of peace offerings, two oxen, five rams, five male goats, and five male lambs in their first year. This was the offering of Nahshon the son of Amminadab.

6:23 1Ch 23:13
6:25 Ps 31:16
6:26 Ps 4:6
6:27 2Ch 7:14
7:1 Lev 8:10–11
7:10 2Ch 7:9
7:13 Ex 30:13

7:16 Lev 4:23
7:18 Nu 1:8
7:23 Lev 7:11–13
7:24 Nu 1:9
7:30 Nu 1:5

18 On the second day Nethanel the son of Zuar, leader of Issachar, presented an offering.

19 He offered as his offering one silver charger, the weight of which was one hundred and thirty shekels, one silver bowl of seventy shekels, after the shekel of the sanctuary, both of them full of fine flour mingled with oil as a grain offering; 20 one spoon of ten shekels of gold, full of incense; 21 one young bull, one ram, and one male lamb in its first year as a burnt offering; 22 one goat kid as a sin offering; 23 and as a sacrifice of peace offerings, two oxen, five rams, five male goats, and five male lambs in their first year. This was the offering of Nethanel the son of Zuar.

24 On the third day Eliab the son of Helon, leader of the children of Zebulun, presented an offering.

25 And his offering was one silver charger, the weight of which was one hundred and thirty shekels, one silver bowl of seventy shekels, after the shekel of the sanctuary, both of them full of fine flour mixed with oil as a grain offering; 26 one spoon of ten shekels of gold, full of incense; 27 one young bull, one ram, one male lamb in its first year as a burnt offering; 28 one goat kid as a sin offering; 29 and as a sacrifice of peace offerings, two oxen, five rams, five male goats, five male lambs in their first year. This was the offering of Eliab the son of Helon.

30 On the fourth day Elizur the son of Shedeur, leader of the children of Reuben, presented an offering.

31 And his offering was one silver charger, the weight of which was one hundred and thirty shekels, one silver bowl of seventy shekels, after the shekel of the sanctuary, both of them full of fine flour mixed with oil as a grain offering; 32 one spoon of ten shekels of gold, full of incense; 33 one young bull, one ram,

[1] 13 About 3¼ pounds, or 1.5 kilograms; and throughout this chapter.
[2] 13 About 1¾ pounds, or 800 grams; and throughout this chapter.
[3] 14 About 4 ounces, or 115 grams; and throughout this chapter.

LEAH

THE HERITAGE OF LEAH

Leah's story is one of the most powerful stories of the Bible. It contains all the drama of a modern soap opera, but unfortunately with the ring of authentic truth to which so many women can relate. It is a story of betrayal, frustration, sibling rivalry, and family dysfunction that rivals any modern courtroom drama. It is the compelling love story of Rachel and Jacob, but it is also the somewhat pathetic story of the hopeless love of Leah for Jacob. However, in the end it is also a story filled with hope and the faithfulness of God.

The description that the Bible gives of Rachel and Leah reflects the reality that so many women face even today. As beautiful and alluring as Rachel was, Leah was her opposite:

> Leah's eyes were tender, but Rachel was beautiful in form and appearance. Jacob loved Rachel.
>
> —Genesis 29:17–18

Leah's job was to take care of the house, and such activity kept her indoors, but Rachel tended the sheep. Rachel was outdoors with the men, outdoors in the sunshine, most likely tanned and beautiful, at ease with the shepherds. And she was the first to meet the new cousin, Jacob, at the well. An instant chemistry sparked between the two of them, and Jacob was smitten—he proposed shortly thereafter. Jacob's uncle, Laban, accepted Jacob's proposal, but a plot was underway. Laban's plan was to secretly marry off Leah, the older sister, first—to Jacob! Laban gave one condition to his acceptance of the proposal: Jacob must work seven years of free labor to "purchase" his wife (whom he presumed would be Rachel).

During the wedding ceremony, a party that lasted for several days and featured a great deal of wine, Leah was substituted for her sister in the bridal chamber. The resulting deception was not discovered by Jacob until the following morning—but it was too late. Even as Jacob raged at his new father-in-law about the trick, he knew it was too late.

But Jacob wasn't the one who was harmed the most in the exchange. Both husband and father beat down Leah's self-esteem as she heard Jacob declare he did not love her but loved her sister, Rachel, instead. Leah heard her father bargain away her life as he promised Jacob he could wed Rachel after another seven years of labor. So, after a brief "honeymoon" with an unwilling husband, Leah was to share him with the love of his life—her own sister, her oldest and deepest rival.

If ever there was a potentially fatal distraction in Leah's life, this situation should have been it! Under these circumstances Leah might have become emotionally unstable, depressed, or even suicidal. Women in our day have cracked under lesser pressures than Leah faced. For years she lingered in a relationship that threatened to destroy her both emotionally and spiritually and to detour her permanently from her God-ordained path.

In fact, the names Leah gave her children during this incredibly difficult time in her life show the mental turmoil and emotional heartbreak she was experiencing. Scripture records that because God "saw that Leah was unloved, He opened her womb, but Rachel was barren" (Ge 29:31). When her first son was born, Leah named him Reuben, which means "Behold, a son." Every time Jacob called his son's name, he would be made to remember that Leah had done what every man wanted: she had given him a firstborn son.

Nevertheless, the distraction in Leah's life continued. Nothing changed in her relationship with her husband. But the Bible says that God again took pity on Leah and opened her womb a second time. She named her second son Simeon, which means "God hears," a sign that Leah still had faith God could turn her situation around. Surely God had heard her sorrow and prayers for her marriage to be healed. Surely God had seen her tears of rejection and heartbreak. But there was still no change. Wasn't He listening?

A third son was born. This one Leah named Levi, a name that means "joined." Leah's desire for a loving husband had become desperate. At this point she was so starved for love and attention that she craved simple companionship—and she began to seek fulfillment of this craving in her children. Her distraction was on the brink of becoming a fatal distraction.

Leah was losing sight of her God-given purpose. She was allowing her bad marriage and her emotional needs to blind her to the *rhema*, the life-giving word that was meant to be her destiny.

Fortunately Leah was able to shift her focus. She took her eyes off her circumstances and put her eyes—weak as they were—on God. She stopped looking to find her life in another person and instead began to recognize that her life, joy, fulfillment, and purpose all came from walking the path of destiny God had ordained for her.

How do we know that this change took place? When Leah's fourth son was born, she demonstrated that her "love line" was now directed vertically toward God instead of horizontally to Jacob. She named this son Judah, which means "praise." Moreover, Scripture says that she "stopped giving birth" (Ge 29:35). While this literally means that she ceased to have any more children, in a metaphorical sense it could mean that she stopped living for Jacob and began living for God. In other words, Leah derailed the distraction before it had a chance to become fatal to her future. She changed her focus from an earthly one to a heavenly one, and God put her back on course to fulfill her rightful destiny.

Even the heartbreak of broken relationships, something that millions of women can relate to, does not have to become a fatal distraction in your life! Once Leah understood the power of praise in her life, her "tender eyes" saw more clearly than they had ever seen before.

There is a purpose. God has a plan. If Satan had been able to fatally distract Leah, God's ultimate plan would still have been fulfilled, but the whole blessing of Judah would have been lost. Instead, Judah's praises rang out through the centuries. Jehoshaphat's great victory was won by sending the praises of Judah, the descendants of Leah, first.

This word is to encourage you wherever you are in your life as you struggle with family issues. Don't let the distraction of family heartbreak become a fatal distraction. Remember the model of Leah. She stayed on track and reached the promised end that God had ordained for her.

Joyce Rodgers

one male lamb in its first year as a burnt
offering; 34 one goat kid as a sin offering;
35 and as a sacrifice of peace offerings,
two oxen, five rams, five male goats, five
male lambs in their first year. This was
the offering of Elizur the son of Shedeur.

36 On the fifth day Shelumiel the son of Zuri-
shaddai, leader of the children of Simeon,
presented an offering.
37 And his offering was one silver charger,
the weight of which was one hundred
and thirty shekels, one silver bowl of
seventy shekels, after the shekel of
the sanctuary, both of them full of fine
flour mixed with oil as a grain offering;
38 one spoon of ten shekels of gold, full
of incense; 39 one young bull, one ram,
one male lamb in its first year, as a burnt
offering: 40 one goat kid as a sin offering;
41 and as a sacrifice of peace offerings,
two oxen, five rams, five male goats,
five male lambs in their first year. This
was the offering of Shelumiel the son of
Zurishaddai.

42 On the sixth day Eliasaph the son of Deuel,
leader of the children of Gad, presented an
offering.
43 And his offering was one silver charger,
the weight of which was one hundred
and thirty shekels, one silver bowl of
seventy shekels, after the shekel of
the sanctuary, both of them full of fine
flour mixed with oil as a grain offering;
44 one spoon of ten shekels of gold, full
of incense; 45 one young bull, one ram,
one male lamb in its first year as a burnt
offering; 46 one goat kid as a sin offering;
47 and as a sacrifice of peace offerings,
two oxen, five rams, five male goats, five
male lambs in their first year. This was
the offering of Eliasaph the son of Deuel.

48 On the seventh day Elishama the son of
Ammihud, leader of the children of Ephraim,
presented an offering.
49 And his offering was one silver charger,
the weight of which was one hundred
and thirty shekels, one silver bowl of
seventy shekels, after the shekel of
the sanctuary, both of them full of fine
flour mixed with oil as a grain offering;
50 one spoon of ten shekels of gold, full
of incense; 51 one young bull, one ram,
one male lamb in its first year as a burnt
offering; 52 one goat kid as a sin offering;
53 and as a sacrifice of peace offerings,
two oxen, five rams, five male goats,
five male lambs in their first year. This
was the offering of Elishama the son of
Ammihud.

54 On the eighth day Gamaliel the son of
Pedahzur, leader of the children of Manasseh,
presented an offering.
55 And his offering was one silver charger,
the weight of which was one hundred
and thirty shekels, one silver bowl of
seventy shekels, after the shekel of the
sanctuary, both of them full of fine flour
mixed with oil as a grain offering; 56 one
spoon of ten shekels of gold, full of
incense; 57 one young bull, one ram, and
one male lamb in its first year as a burnt
offering; 58 one goat kid as a sin offering;
59 and as a sacrifice of peace offerings,
two oxen, five rams, five male goats,
five male lambs in their first year. This
was the offering of Gamaliel the son of
Pedahzur.

60 On the ninth day Abidan the son of Gideoni,
leader of the children of Benjamin, presented
an offering.
61 And his offering was one silver charger,
the weight of which was one hundred
and thirty shekels, one silver bowl of
seventy shekels, after the shekel of the
sanctuary, both of them full of fine flour
mixed with oil as a grain offering; 62 one
spoon of ten shekels of gold, full of
incense; 63 one young bull, one ram, and
one male lamb in its first year as a burnt
offering; 64 one goat kid as a sin offering;
65 and as a sacrifice of peace offerings,
two oxen, five rams, five male goats, and
five male lambs in their first year. This
was the offering of Abidan the son of
Gideoni.

66 On the tenth day Ahiezer the son of Ammis-
haddai, leader of the children of Dan, present-
ed an offering.
67 And his offering was one silver charger,
the weight of which was one hundred
and thirty shekels, one silver bowl of
seventy shekels, after the shekel of the
sanctuary, both of them full of fine flour
mixed with oil as a grain offering; 68 one
spoon of ten shekels of gold, full of
incense; 69 one young bull, one ram, and
one male lamb in its first year as a burnt
offering; 70 one goat kid as a sin offering;
71 and as a sacrifice of peace offerings,
two oxen, five rams, five male goats, and
five male lambs in their first year. This
was the offering of Ahiezer the son of
Ammishaddai.

7:36 Nu 1:6
7:42 Nu 1:14
7:48 Nu 1:10

7:54 Nu 1:10
7:60 Nu 1:11
7:66 Nu 1:12

72 On the eleventh day Pagiel the son of Okran, leader of the children of Asher, presented an offering.

73 And his offering was one silver charger,
the weight of which was one hundred
and thirty shekels, one silver bowl of
seventy shekels, after the shekel of the
sanctuary, both of them full of fine flour
mixed with oil as a grain offering; 74 one
spoon of ten shekels of gold, full of
incense; 75 one young bull, one ram, and
one male lamb in its first year as a burnt
offering; 76 one goat kid as a sin offering;
77 and as a sacrifice of peace offerings,
two oxen, five rams, five male goats,
and five male lambs in their first year.
This was the offering of Pagiel the son
of Okran.

78 On the twelfth day Ahira the son of Enan, leader of the children of Naphtali, presented an offering.

79 And his offering was one silver charger,
the weight of which was one hundred
and thirty shekels, one silver bowl of
seventy shekels, after the shekel of the
sanctuary, both of them full of fine flour
mixed with oil as a grain offering; 80 one
spoon of ten shekels of gold, full of
incense; 81 one young bull, one ram, and
one male lamb in its first year as a burnt
offering; 82 one goat kid as a sin offering;
83 and as a sacrifice of peace offerings,
two oxen, five rams, five male goats,
and five male lambs in their first year.
This was the offering of Ahira the son of
Enan.

84 This was the dedication of the altar, in the
day when it was anointed, by the leaders of
Israel: twelve silver plates, twelve silver bowls,
and twelve gold spoons, 85 each silver plate
weighing one hundred and thirty shekels, each
bowl seventy. All the silver vessels weighed
two thousand four hundred shekels,[1] according to the shekel of the sanctuary. 86 The gold
spoons were twelve, full of incense, weighing
ten shekels apiece, according to the shekel of
the sanctuary. All the gold of the spoons was
one hundred and twenty shekels.[2] 87 All the
oxen for the burnt offering were twelve bulls,
twelve rams, twelve male lambs in their first
year, with their grain offering, and twelve goat
kids for a sin offering. 88 And all the oxen for
the sacrifice of the peace offerings were twenty-four bulls, the rams sixty, the goats sixty, the
one-year-old lambs sixty. This was the dedication of the altar after it was anointed.

89 And then Moses went into the tent of meeting to speak with Him, and he heard the voice
of One speaking to him from the mercy seat
that was on the ark of the testimony, from between the two cherubim, and He spoke to him.

The Seven Lamps

8 And the LORD spoke to Moses, saying:
2 Speak to Aaron and say to him: When
you set up the lamps, the seven lamps will give
light before the lampstand.

3 Aaron did so. He lit the lamps before the
lampstand, as the LORD commanded Moses.
4 And this was the work of the lampstand:
hammered gold, to its shaft, to its flowers was
beaten work. According to the pattern which
the LORD had shown Moses, so he made the
lampstand.

Consecrating the Levites

5 The LORD spoke to Moses, saying: 6 Take the
Levites from among the children of Israel and
cleanse them. 7 Thus you will do to them to
cleanse them: Splash purifying water on them,
and let them shave their whole body, and let
them wash their clothes, and so make themselves clean. 8 Then let them take a young bull
with its grain offering, also fine flour mixed
with oil, and you will take another young bull
as a sin offering. 9 You will bring the Levites
before the tent of meeting. And you will gather
the whole assembly of the children of Israel
together. 10 And you will bring the Levites before the LORD. And the children of Israel will
put their hands on the Levites. 11 And Aaron
will offer the Levites before the LORD as a wave
offering of the children of Israel, that they may
do the service of the LORD.

12 The Levites will lay their hands on the
heads of the bulls, and you will offer one as
a sin offering and the other as a burnt offering to the LORD, to make an atonement for the
Levites. 13 You will set the Levites before Aaron
and before his sons, and offer them as a wave
offering to the LORD. 14 Thus will you separate
the Levites from among the children of Israel,
and the Levites will be Mine.

15 And afterwards the Levites will go in to
do the service of the tent of meeting, and you
will cleanse them and offer them as a wave
offering. 16 For they are completely set aside
for Me by the children of Israel. Instead of all
who open the womb, instead of the firstborn
of all the children of Israel, I have taken them
for Myself. 17 For all the firstborn of the children
of Israel are Mine, both man and animal. On
the day that I struck every firstborn in the land
of Egypt I sanctified them for Myself. 18 I have
taken the Levites instead of all the firstborn of
the children of Israel. 19 I have given the Levites

7:72 Nu 1:13
7:78 Nu 1:15
7:84 Nu 7:10
7:88 Nu 7:1
7:89 Ps 80:1

....

8:2 Ex 25:37
8:4 Ex 25:9
8:8 Lev 2:1
8:9 Ex 40:12
8:10 Lev 1:4
8:11 Lev 7:30
8:12 Ex 29:10
8:14 Nu 3:45
8:15 Nu 8:11
8:16 Nu 3:12
8:17 Ex 13:2
8:19 Nu 1:53

[1] *85* About 60 pounds, or 28 kilograms. [2] *86* About 3 pounds, or 1.4 kilograms.

as a gift to Aaron and to his sons from among the children of Israel, to serve the service of the children of Israel in the tent of meeting and to make an atonement for the children of Israel, so there will be no plague among the children of Israel when the children of Israel approach the sanctuary.

20 Moses and Aaron and all the congregation of the children of Israel did to the Levites; according to all that the LORD commanded Moses concerning the Levites, so the children of Israel did to them. 21 The Levites cleansed themselves from sin, and they washed their clothes, and Aaron offered them as a wave offering before the LORD, and Aaron made an atonement for them to cleanse them. 22 And after that the Levites went in to do their service in the tent of meeting before Aaron and before his sons. As the LORD had commanded Moses concerning the Levites, so they did to them.

23 The LORD spoke to Moses, saying: 24 This is what belongs to the Levites: From twenty-five years old and older they will go in to do their duty concerning the service of the tent of meeting. 25 And from the age of fifty years they will cease doing their duty concerning its service and will serve no more. 26 But *they* will minister with their brothers in the tent of meeting, to attend to their needs, but will not do the work. Thus you will do to the Levites concerning their duties.

The Passover at Sinai

9 And the LORD spoke to Moses in the Wilderness of Sinai, in the first month of the second year after they came out of the land of Egypt, saying: 2 Let the children of Israel also keep the Passover at its appointed time. 3 On the fourteenth day of this month, at evening, you will keep it at its appointed time. According to all its rites and according to all its ceremonies, you will keep it.

4 Moses spoke to the children of Israel, that they should keep the Passover. 5 They kept the Passover on the fourteenth day of the first month at evening in the Wilderness of Sinai. According to all that the LORD commanded Moses, so the children of Israel did.

6 There were men who were unclean by the dead body of a man, so they could not keep the Passover on that day, and they came before Moses and before Aaron on that day. 7 And those men said to him, "We are defiled by the dead body of a man. Why are we kept back, that we may not offer an offering of the LORD at its appointed time among the children of Israel?"

8:21 Nu 8:7
8:24 Nu 4:3
8:26 Nu 1:53
9:1 Nu 1:1
9:3 Ex 12:6–11
9:5 Jos 5:10
9:6 Ex 18:15

....

9:8 Nu 27:5
9:11 2Ch 30:2–15
9:12 Ex 12:10
9:13 Ge 17:14
9:14 Ex 12:48–49
9:15 Ex 13:21
9:16 Ne 9:12
9:17 Ex 40:36–38
9:18 1Co 10:1
9:22 Ex 40:36–37
9:23 Nu 9:19

8 And Moses said to them, "Stand still, and I will hear what the LORD will command concerning you."

9 The LORD spoke to Moses, saying: 10 Speak to the children of Israel, saying: If any man of you or of your posterity is unclean because of a dead body, or is far off on a journey, he will still keep the Passover to the LORD. 11 The fourteenth day of the second month at evening they will keep it, and eat it with unleavened bread and bitter herbs. 12 They will leave none of it until the morning, nor break any of its bones. According to all the ordinances of the Passover they will keep it. 13 But the man who is ceremonially clean, and is not on a journey, and fails to keep the Passover, even the same person will be cut off from his people. Because he did not bring the offering of the LORD at its appointed time, that man will bear his sin.

14 If a stranger will sojourn among you and will keep the Passover to the LORD, according to the ordinance of the Passover, and according to the manner of it, so he will do. You will have one ordinance both for the resident alien and for the natural born citizen of the land.

The Cloud and the Fire

15 And on the day that the tabernacle was erected, the cloud covered the tabernacle, the tent of the testimony, and at evening there was over the tabernacle the appearance of fire until the morning. 16 So it was always. The cloud covered it by day, and the appearance of fire by night. 17 When the cloud was lifted up from over the tabernacle, then after it the children of Israel journeyed, and in the place where the cloud settled, there the children of Israel camped. 18 At the commandment of the LORD the children of Israel journeyed, and at the commandment of the LORD they camped. As long as the cloud dwelt over the tabernacle they camped. 19 When the cloud remained many days over the tabernacle, then the children of Israel kept the charge of the LORD and did not journey. 20 When the cloud remained a few days over the tabernacle, according to the commandment of the LORD they dwelt in their tents, and according to the commandment of the LORD they journeyed. 21 When the cloud dwelt from evening until morning and the cloud was lifted up in the morning, then they journeyed. Whether it was by day or by night that the cloud was lifted up, they journeyed. 22 Whether it was two days, or a month, or a long time that the cloud dwelt over the tabernacle, the children of Israel dwelt in their tents and did not journey. But when it was lifted up they journeyed. 23 At the command of the LORD they camped, and at the command of the

LORD they journeyed. They kept the charge of the LORD at the command of the LORD by the hand of Moses.

The Silver Trumpets

10 And the LORD spoke to Moses, saying: 2 Make for yourself two silver trumpets. Of a hammered work you will make them, and you will use them for summoning of the assembly and directing the breaking up of the camps. 3 When they blow both of them, all the assembly will assemble themselves to you at the door of the tent of meeting. 4 If they blow only one, then the leaders, who are heads of the thousands of Israel, will gather themselves to you. 5 When you blow an alarm, then the camps that lie on the east will set out. 6 When you blow an alarm the second time, then the camps that lie on the south will set out. They will blow an alarm for their setting out. 7 But when the assembly is to be gathered together, you will blow, but you will not sound an alarm.

8 The sons of Aaron, the priests, will blow the trumpets, and they will be to you as an ordinance forever throughout your generations. 9 And if you go to war in your land against the enemy that oppresses you, then you will blow an alarm with the trumpets, and you will be remembered before the LORD your God, and you will be saved from your enemies. 10 Also in the day of your gladness, and at your appointed days, and in the beginnings of your months, you shall blow the trumpets over your burnt offerings, and over the sacrifices of your peace offerings that they may be a memorial for you before your God. I am the LORD your God.

The Departure From Sinai

11 And it was on the twentieth day of the second month, in the second year, that the cloud was lifted up from over the tabernacle of the testimony. 12 The children of Israel set out from the Wilderness of Sinai. And the cloud dwelt in the Wilderness of Paran. 13 And they set out for the first time at the command of the LORD by the hand of Moses.

14 And the standard of the camp of the sons of Judah set out first by their armies, and over his armies was Nahshon the son of Amminadab. 15 Over the armies of the tribe of the children of Issachar was Nethanel the son of Zuar. 16 Over the armies of the tribe of the children of Zebulun was Eliab the son of Helon. 17 The tabernacle was taken down, and the sons of Gershon and the sons of Merari set out, carrying the tabernacle.

18 The standard of the camp of Reuben set out by their armies, and over his armies was Elizur the son of Shedeur. 19 Over the armies of the tribe of the children of Simeon was Shelumiel the son of Zurishaddai. 20 Over the armies of the tribe of the children of Gad was Eliasaph the son of Deuel. 21 The Kohathites set out, carrying the sanctuary, and they set up the tabernacle before they came.

22 The standard of the camp of the children of Ephraim set out by their armies, and over his armies was Elishama the son of Ammihud. 23 Over the armies of the tribe of the children of Manasseh was Gamaliel the son of Pedahzur. 24 Over the armies of the tribe of the children of Benjamin was Abidan the son of Gideoni.

25 Then the standard of the camp of the children of Dan set out, which was the rear guard of all the camps by their armies, and over his armies was Ahiezer the son of Ammishaddai. 26 Over the armies of the tribe of the children of Asher was Pagiel the son of Okran. 27 Over the armies of the tribe of the children of Naphtali was Ahira the son of Enan. 28 This was the order of march of the children of Israel, company by company, when they set out.

29 Moses said to Hobab, the son of Reuel the Midianite, Moses' father-in-law, "We are setting out to the place of which the LORD said, 'I will give it to you.' Come with us, and we will do good to you because the LORD has spoken good concerning Israel."

30 Hobab said to him, "I will not go. But I will depart to my own land, and to my kindred."

31 So Moses said, "Please do not leave us, because you know where to camp in the wilderness, and you may be our eyes. 32 Moreover, if you go with us, then it will be that whatever good the LORD will do for us, we will likewise do for you."

33 They set out three days from the mountain of the LORD, and the ark of the covenant of the LORD went before them the three days' journey, to find a resting place for them. 34 And the cloud of the LORD was over them by day when they set out from of the camp.

35 And it was, when the ark set out, that Moses said,

"Rise up, O LORD,
and let Your enemies be scattered,
and let them that hate You flee before You."

36 And when it rested, he said,

"Return, O LORD,
to the multitude of thousands of Israel."

Complaints in the Desert

11 Now when the people complained openly before the LORD, the LORD heard, and His anger burned. Then the fire of the LORD burned among them and consumed the outskirts of the camp. 2 And the people cried out

10:2 Isa 1:13
10:3 Jer 4:5
10:4 Ex 18:21
10:7 Joel 2:1
10:8 Nu 31:6
10:9 Ge 8:1
10:10 Ps 81:3
10:12 Ge 21:21
10:14 Nu 2:3–9
10:18 Nu 2:10–16
10:19 Nu 1:6
....
10:21 Nu 10:17
10:22 Nu 2:18–24
10:24 Nu 1:11
10:25 Jos 6:9
10:26 Nu 1:13
10:27 Nu 1:15
10:28 Nu 2:34
10:29 Ge 12:7
10:31 Job 29:15
10:33 Dt 1:33
10:35 Ps 68:1–2
10:36 Dt 1:10
11:1 Lev 10:2
11:2 Nu 21:7

Harmful Roots of Criticism and Ridicule

Criticism is rated as one of the most pernicious spirits to invade the sanctity of marriage. To *criticize* means "to express disapproval, disparage, assess, censure, pass judgment, complain, condemn, blast, lash out, nitpick, and pick holes." To criticize your spouse or children is to condemn and belittle them. Millions of people walk around ashamed and feeling unworthy because of someone who has criticized and humiliated them, never looking back to say, "I'm sorry; please forgive me."

To *ridicule* is to mock or make fun of a person. You'll find people in all walks of life wandering around with a broken spirit. These are evil roots that, if allowed to remain in a relationship, will bring discontentment and eventually separation.

I like what Kay Arthur says about a broken spirit: "Never, never break another person's spirit. *You will lose him! You will lose her!* Don't ever make your mate—or anyone else—the brunt of your jokes. Never ridicule. Never mock. Be very, very careful with barbed humor. Your words, so lightly spoken, may remain in an individual's soul until his or her dying day. Ridicule and mockery is cruel and kills communication. As Solomon wrote, 'A brother offended is harder to be won than a strong city' (Proverbs 18:19). If you have offended your mate or another in this way, go and ask forgiveness."[1]

In Numbers 12 we find that God inflicted the prophetess Miriam with leprosy for criticizing Moses. Criticism and murmuring go hand in hand—they both cut down and accuse a person. Many relationships, especially in marriage, suffer in agony and silence because of a critical spirit. When criticism is allowed to persist and the offended person is never redeemed or restored, it can cause a spirit of bitterness and low self-esteem to take root. I've seen many young women devastated and affected by this form of mental abuse.

The person who constantly nitpicks, murmurs, and criticizes his or her spouse is leaving an open door for demonic attacks to inflict the entire family. God looks at a critical, murmuring person just as he looked at Miriam.

One of the reasons why we encounter so many defeated and anemic Christians is because they are suffering with the curse of leprosy. Leprosy is a skin-and-nerve disease. Spiritual leprosy may not physically kill you today, but it will make a person spiritually dead. Repentance and forgiveness will be the only way out of this one. "Wow," you may say, "I never saw it like this!" Millions of people walk around hurt and deprived of joy because of these offenses.

In a marital relationship some of the most common criticisms are these:

- "You're too fat now. Why don't you lose weight? You look awful."
- "Your breasts are too small; why don't you get a boob job?"
- "Your nose is too big."
- "You're a bad cook."

- "Can't you do anything right?"
- "Your legs look like drumsticks."
- "I can't believe you're so stupid!"
- "You're dumb."
- "You're ignorant."
- "I can't believe I married you."
- "When are you going to learn to do things right?"
- "Stay home; I don't want to be seen with you in public."
- "You can't even get it up. You're like a lump in bed."
- "Sex is no fun with you."

You may think of many more. This kind of personal criticism attacks the core of a person, and that person may never rise above or recover unless divine and professional intervention is applied. Only forgiveness and reconciliation will initiate the process of healing in a relationship that has been assaulted by this kind of behavior.

It is Satan's intention to keep people bound by conflict and ridicule, which cause agitation and disturb the well-being of relationships. Why do I think these are so important to overcome?

I learned years ago that coping is not good enough. *Coping is managing and surviving. My desire was to be set free.* I discovered that my freedom came by applying the Word of God to my life consistently.

When you apply the Word to very aspect of your life and remain consistently connected to the Holy Spirit for wisdom and understanding, you will mature and understand the spiritual warfare we are involved in.

Iris Delgado

1. Kay Arthur, *A Marriage Without Regrets* (Eugene, OR: Harvest House, 2000), 150.

to Moses, and Moses prayed to the LORD, and
the fire was quenched. 3 He called the name of
the place Taberah because the fire of the LORD
burned among them.
4 The mixed multitude that was among them
lusted, and the children of Israel wept again
and said, "Who will give us meat to eat? 5 We
remember the fish, which we ate in Egypt for
free, the cucumbers, and the melons, and the
leeks, and the onions, and the garlic. 6 But now
our life is dried up. There is nothing at all ex-
cept this manna before our eyes."
7 The manna was as coriander seed, and it
looked like bdellium. 8 The people went about
and gathered it, and ground it in mills or beat
it in a mortar, and boiled it in pots, and made
cakes of it, and the taste of it was like the taste
of cakes baked in oil. 9 When the dew fell on
the camp at night, the manna fell on it.
10 Then Moses heard the people weep
throughout their families, every man in the
opening of his tent, and the anger of the LORD
burned greatly. Moses was also displeased.
11 Moses said to the LORD, "Why have You hurt
Your servant? And why have I not found fa-
vor in Your eyes, that You lay the burden of
all this people on me? 12 Have I conceived all
this people? Have I given them birth, that You
should say to me, 'Carry them in your bosom,
as a nurse bears the nursing child,' to the land
which You swore to their fathers? 13 Where am
I to get meat to give to all these people? For
they weep to me, saying, 'Give us meat, that
we may eat.' 14 I am not able to bear all these
people alone, because the burden is too heavy
for me. 15 If You do this to me, please kill me at
once, if I have found favor in Your eyes, and
do not let me see my misery."

The Seventy Elders

16 Then the LORD said to Moses, "Gather to
Me seventy men of the elders of Israel, whom
you know to be the elders of the people, and
officers over them, and bring them to the tent
of meeting, that they may take a stand there
with you. 17 And I will come down, and I will
speak with you there, and I will take of the
Spirit which is on you and will put it on them,
and they will bear the burden of the people
with you, and you will not bear it by yourself.
18 "And say to the people: Consecrate your-
selves for tomorrow, and you shall eat meat,
for you have wept in the hearing of the LORD,
saying, 'Who will give us meat to eat? For
it was better for us in Egypt.' Therefore the
LORD will give you meat, and you shall eat.
19 You shall eat, not one day, or two days, or
five days, or ten days, or twenty days, 20 but a
whole month, until it comes out at your nos-
trils, and it will be nauseating to you because
you rejected the LORD who is among you and
have wept before Him, saying, 'Why did we
come out of Egypt?' "
21 And Moses said, "The people I am with
number six hundred thousand foot soldiers,
and You have said, 'I will give them meat that
they may eat a whole month.' 22 Will the flocks
and the herds be slaughtered for them, to sat-
isfy them? Or will all the fish of the sea be
gathered together for them, to satisfy them?"
23 And the LORD said to Moses, "Is the hand
of the LORD shortened? Now you will see if My
word will happen to you or not."
24 Moses went out, and he spoke to the people
the words of the LORD and gathered the seventy
men of the elders of the people and set them
around the tabernacle. 25 And the LORD came
down in a cloud, and spoke to him, and took
of the Spirit that was on him, and gave it to the
seventy elders, and when the Spirit rested on
them, they prophesied, but did not do it again.
26 But two men remained in the camp. The
name of one was Eldad, and the name of the
other, Medad. And the Spirit rested on them.
They were among those listed, but they had
not gone out to the tent, and so they proph-
esied in the camp. 27 And a young man ran
and told Moses and said, "Eldad and Medad
prophesy in the camp."
28 Then Joshua the son of Nun, the assistant
of Moses from his youth, answered and said,
"My lord Moses, forbid them."
29 Moses said to him, "Are you jealous for my
sake? Oh, that all the people of the LORD were
prophets, and that the LORD would put His Spir-
it upon them!" 30 And Moses returned to the
camp, he and the elders of Israel.

The LORD Sends Quail

31 Now a wind from the LORD started up, and
it swept quail from the sea and let them fall
beside the camp, about a day's journey on
this side and a day's journey on the other
side, around the camp, and about two cubits[1]
above the ground. 32 And the people stayed
up all that day, all night, and all the next day,
and gathered the quail. Those who gathered
least gathered ten homers.[2] And they spread
them out for themselves all around the camp.
33 While the meat was between their teeth,
before it was chewed, the anger of the LORD
burned against the people, and the LORD struck
the people with a very great slaughter. 34 And
he called the name of that place Kibroth Hat-
taavah because there they buried the people
who had the craving.

11:3 Dt 9:22
11:4 Ex 12:38
11:5 Ex 16:3
11:6 Nu 21:5
11:7 Ex 16:31
11:9 Ex 16:13–14
11:11 Dt 1:12
11:12 Ex 13:5
11:14 Ex 18:18
11:16 Ex 24:1
11:17 Nu 11:25
11:18 Ex 19:10
11:20 Ps 106:15
11:21 Ex 12:37
11:22 Mt 15:33
11:23 Isa 50:2
11:24 Nu 11:16
11:25 Nu 11:17
11:29 1Co 14:5
11:31 Ex 16:13
11:32 Eze 45:11
11:33 Ps 78:30–31
11:34 Dt 9:22

[1] *31* About 3 feet, or 90 centimeters. [2] *32* Likely about 1¾ tons, or 1.6 metric tons.

35 The people journeyed from Kibroth Hattaa-
vah to Hazeroth, and they camped at Hazeroth.

Miriam and Aaron Oppose Moses

12 And Miriam and Aaron spoke against
Moses because of the Cushite woman
whom he married, for he had married a Cush-
ite woman. 2 They said, "Has the LORD spoken
only by Moses? Has He not spoken also by us?"
And the LORD heard it.
3 (Now the man Moses was very humble,
more than all the men on the face of the earth.)
4 And the LORD spoke at once to Moses and
to Aaron and to Miriam, "Come out, you three,
to the tent of meeting." And those three came
out. 5 The LORD came down in a pillar of cloud,
and stood in the opening of the tabernacle,
and called Aaron and Miriam, and they both
came forward. 6 He said, "Hear now My word.

If there is a prophet among you,
I the LORD will make Myself known to
him in a vision,
and I will speak to him in a dream.
7 Not so with My servant Moses;
he is entrusted with all My house.
8 Face to face I speak with him clearly,
and not in riddles,
and the likeness of the LORD will he
behold.
Then why were you not afraid
to speak against My servant, against
Moses?"

9 And the anger of the LORD burned against
them, and He set out.
10 When the cloud went away from over the
tabernacle, Miriam became leprous as snow,
and Aaron turned toward Miriam and saw
that she was leprous. 11 Aaron said to Moses,
"Alas, my lord, do not lay the sin on us, which
we have done foolishly, and which we have
sinned. 12 Do not let her be as dead, who when
he goes out of his mother's womb half his flesh
is eaten."
13 And Moses cried out to the LORD, saying, "O
God, heal her, I pray!"
14 But the LORD said to Moses, "If her father
had but spit in her face, would she not be
ashamed seven days? Let her be shut out of
the camp seven days, and afterward she may
be received again." 15 Miriam was shut out from
the camp seven days, and the people did not
set out until Miriam was brought in again.
16 Afterward the people set out from Hazeroth
and camped in the Wilderness of Paran.

Spying in Canaan

13 And the LORD spoke to Moses, saying,
2 "Send men that they may explore
the land of Canaan, which I am giving to the

11:35 Nu 33:17
12:1 Ex 2:21
12:2 Nu 11:1
12:3 Mt 11:29
12:5 Nu 11:25
12:6 Ge 46:2
12:7 Ps 105:26
12:8 Dt 34:10
12:10 Dt 24:9
12:11 2Sa 19:19
12:14 Dt 25:9
12:16 Nu 11:35

SPIRITLED WOMAN

COUNSEL FROM THE SPIRIT BASICS

Fear: Battling for Power

Fear is an insidious force. It causes reason and wisdom to escape us. It drives and compels, pushing us to the brink of unbelief. To overcome fear we must know its nature. Fear is not a mental state of mind or a bad attitude. Fear is a spirit sent by the enemy to torment our souls and defile our human spirits. Because it is a spiritual force, fear must be confronted spiritually.

The destination of the children of Israel was the Promised Land, but they forsook God's promises to embrace their fears. They placed their faith in their fears. In doing this, they chose the devil's lies over God's truth. God had told them He would lead them into a land flowing with milk and honey; His angel would go ahead of them to guard them. (See Exodus 3:8; 23:20.) But here is what fear said to them: "We are not able to go up against the people because they are stronger than we....The land through which we have gone as spies is a land that devours its inhabitants, and all the people whom we saw in it are men of great stature. And there we saw the giants...and in our eyes we were like grasshoppers, and so we were in their eyes" (Nu 13:31–33).

God never planned for a generation of Israelites to die as they wandered the wilderness. His plan was to rescue them from the Egyptians and bring them, escorted by an angel, to a good land. But when they chose fear's lie over God's truth, they forfeited their power to possess the Promised Land God had given them.

Fear is after our faith. It wants us to place our faith in it and not in the promises of God. Our faith will always work—but will it work for us or against us?

Lisa Bevere

children of Israel. Of every tribe of their fa-
thers you will send a man, each one a chief
among them."
3 And Moses sent them from the Wilderness
of Paran according to the LORD. All those men
were heads of the children of Israel. 4 These
were their names:

of the tribe of Reuben, Shammua the son of Zakkur;
5 of the tribe of Simeon, Shaphat the son of Hori;
6 of the tribe of Judah, Caleb the son of Jephunneh;
7 of the tribe of Issachar, Igal the son of Joseph;
8 of the tribe of Ephraim, Hoshea the son of Nun;
9 of the tribe of Benjamin, Palti the son of Raphu;
10 of the tribe of Zebulun, Gaddiel the son of Sodi;
11 of the tribe of Joseph, namely, of the tribe of Manasseh, Gaddi the son of Susi;
12 of the tribe of Dan, Ammiel the son of Gemalli;
13 of the tribe of Asher, Sethur the son of Michael;
14 of the tribe of Naphtali, Nahbi the son of Vophsi;
15 of the tribe of Gad, Geuel the son of Maki.

16 These are the names of the men whom Mo-
ses sent to explore the land. And Moses called
Hoshea the son of Nun Joshua.
17 Moses sent them to explore the land of Ca-
naan and said to them, "Go up to this south-
land, and go up into the mountain. 18 And see
what the land is, and the people that dwell in
it, whether they are strong or weak, few or
many; 19 and what the land is that they dwell
in, whether it is good or bad, and what cities
are that they dwell in, whether in tents, or in
fortifications; 20 and what the land is, whether
it is fat or lean, whether there is wood in it or
not. And you be courageous and bring some
of the fruit of the land." Now the time was the
time of the first ripe grapes.
21 So they went up and explored the land
from the Wilderness of Zin to Rehob, near
Lebo Hamath. 22 They went up by the Negev
and came to Hebron where Ahiman, Sheshai,
and Talmai, the children of Anak, were (now
Hebron was built seven years before Zoan in
Egypt). 23 And they came to the Valley of Es-
hkol, and cut down from there a branch with
one cluster of grapes, and they carried it on a
pole between two of them, and they brought
some of the pomegranates and of the figs.
24 The place was called the Valley of Eshkol
because of the cluster of grapes which the chil-
dren of Israel cut down from there. 25 They re-
turned from exploring the land after forty days.

13:6 Nu 14:6
13:16 Nu 13:8
13:17 Ge 12:9
13:20 Dt 31:23
13:21 Nu 20:1
13:22 Ps 78:12
13:23 Nu 32:9
13:26 Nu 32:8
13:27 Ex 3:8
13:28 Dt 1:28
13:29 Nu 14:43
13:30 Nu 14:24
13:31 Dt 1:28
13:32 Nu 14:36–37
13:33 Ge 6:4
14:5 Nu 16:4
14:7 Nu 13:27

The Spies' Report

26 And they returned and came to Moses and
to Aaron and to all the assembly of the chil-
dren of Israel, to the Wilderness of Paran, to
Kadesh, and brought back word to them and
to the entire assembly and showed them the
fruit of the land. 27 They reported to him and
said, "We came to the land where you sent us,
and surely it flows with milk and honey, and
this is the fruit of it. 28 However, the people are
strong that dwell in the land, and the cities are
fortified and very great, and also we saw the
children of Anak there. 29 The Amalekites dwell
in the land of the Negev, and the Hittites, and
the Jebusites, and the Amorites dwell in the
mountains, and the Canaanites dwell by the
sea and by the edge of the Jordan."
30 Caleb silenced the people before Moses
and said, "Let us go up at once and possess it,
for we are able to overcome it."
31 But the men that went up with him said,
"We are not able to go up against the people
because they are stronger than we." 32 They
gave the children of Israel a bad report of the
land which they had spied out, saying, "The
land through which we have gone as spies is
a land that devours its inhabitants, and all the
people whom we saw in it are men of great
stature. 33 And there we saw the giants, the
sons of Anak, which come from the giants, and
in our eyes we were like grasshoppers, and so
we were in their eyes."

Israel Refuses to Enter Canaan

14 And the whole assembly lifted up their
voices and cried, and the people wept
that night. 2 All the children of Israel grum-
bled against Moses and against Aaron, and
the whole assembly said to them, "O that we
had died in the land of Egypt! Or that we had
died in this wilderness! 3 And why has the LORD
brought us to this land to fall by the sword,
that our wives and our children should become
prey? Is it not better for us to return to Egypt?"
4 And they said one to another, "Let us select a
leader, and let us return to Egypt."

All God moments involve choices
(Nu 14:7–9).

5 Then Moses and Aaron fell on their faces be-
fore all the congregation of the assembly of the
children of Israel. 6 Joshua the son of Nun, and
Caleb the son of Jephunneh, from the ones
who explored the land, tore their clothes. 7 And

they spoke to all the assembly of the children of Israel, saying, "The land which we passed through to explore it is a very, very good land. 8 If the LORD delights in us, then He will bring us into this land and give it to us, a land which flows with milk and honey. 9 Only do not rebel against the LORD, nor fear the people of the land because they are bread for us. Their defense is gone from them, and the LORD is with us. Do not fear them."

10 But all the assembly said, "Stone them with stones." And the glory of the LORD appeared at the tent of meeting before all the children of Israel. 11 The LORD said to Moses, "How long will this people disgrace Me? And how long will they not believe Me, in spite of all the signs which I have done among them? 12 I will strike them with the pestilence, and disinherit them, and will make from you a nation greater and mightier than they."

Moses Intercedes for the People

13 Moses said to the LORD, "Then the Egyptians will hear of it, for by Your power You brought this people up from among them, 14 and they will say to the inhabitants of this land that they heard that You, LORD, are among this people, that You, LORD, are seen face to face, and Your cloud stands over them, and in the pillar of cloud You go before them by day and by a pillar of fire at night. 15 Now if You kill all this people as one man, then the nations which have heard the fame of You will speak, saying, 16 'The LORD was not able to bring this people into the land which He swore to them, so He slaughtered them in the wilderness.'

17 "So now, I pray, let the power of my Lord be great, just as You have spoken, saying, 18 'The LORD is slow to anger and abounding in mercy, forgiving iniquity and transgression; but He will by no means clear the guilty, visiting the iniquity of the fathers upon the children to the third and fourth generation.' 19 Pardon the iniquity of this people, I pray, according to the greatness of Your grace, just as You have pardoned this people, from Egypt even until now."

Thank You, Lord, for being slow to anger and quick to forgive (Nu 14:18).

20 The LORD said, "I have forgiven according to your word. 21 But truly as I live, all the earth will be filled with the glory of the LORD. 22 Because all those men seeing My glory and My signs which I did in Egypt and in the wilderness, and have tempted Me now these ten times, and have not listened to My voice, 23 surely they will not see the land which I swore to their fathers, nor will any of them who disgraced Me see it. 24 But My servant Caleb, because he had a different spirit with him and followed Me fully, I will bring him into the land where he went, and his seed will possess it. 25 Now the Amalekites and the Canaanites lived in the valley. Tomorrow you will turn, and you will set out for the wilderness by the way of the Red Sea."

Death of Rebels Predicted

26 The LORD spoke to Moses and to Aaron, saying: 27 How long will this evil assembly be murmuring against Me? I have heard the murmurings of the children of Israel which they murmur against Me. 28 Say to them, "As I live," says the LORD, "just as you have spoken in My ears, so I will do to you. 29 In this wilderness your corpses will fall, and all who were numbered of you, according to your whole number, from twenty years old and upward, who have murmured against Me, 30 you will not go into the land which I swore by My hand to cause you to dwell in it, except Caleb the son of Jephunneh and Joshua the son of Nun. 31 But your children, whom you said would be a prey, I will bring them in and they will know the land, which you rejected. 32 But as for you, your corpses will fall in this wilderness. 33 Your children will be shepherds in the wilderness forty years, and they will suffer for your fornications, until your corpses are in the wilderness. 34 According to the number of the days in which you spied out the land, forty days, a year for each day you will bear your iniquity, forty years, and you will know My displeasure." 35 I the LORD have spoken. I will surely do this to all this evil assembly gathered against Me. In this wilderness they will be finished, and there they will die.

36 The men whom Moses sent to explore the land, who returned and made all the assembly murmur against him by bringing up an evil report about the land, 37 the men who brought an evil report about the land, died by the pestilence before the LORD. 38 But Joshua the son of Nun and Caleb the son of Jephunneh, from the men that went to explore the land, lived.

Defeat in Battle

39 Moses spoke these words to all the children of Israel, and the people mourned greatly. 40 They rose up early in the morning, and they went up to the top of the mountain, saying, "Here we are. We will go up to the place which the LORD has promised, for we have sinned."

41 Moses said, "Why do you now transgress the commandment of the LORD? This will not prosper. 42 Do not go up, for the LORD is not among you; do not let yourselves be defeated

14:8 Dt 10:15
14:9 Dt 7:18
14:10 Ex 17:4
14:11 Ps 106:24
14:12 Ex 32:10
14:13 Ps 106:23
14:14 Ex 15:14
14:18 Ex 20:5
14:19 Ex 34:9
14:21 Hab 2:14
14:23 Nu 32:11
14:24 Nu 14:6–9
14:25 Nu 13:29
14:27 Ex 16:12
14:28 Nu 14:21
14:29 Nu 1:45
14:31 Ps 106:24
14:32 1Co 10:5
14:34 Nu 13:25
14:35 Nu 23:19
14:37 1Co 10:10
14:38 Nu 26:65
14:39 Ex 33:4
14:40 Dt 1:41
14:41 2Ch 24:20
14:42 Dt 1:42

by your enemies. 43 For the Amalekites and the
Canaanites are there before you, and you will
fall by the sword because you are turned from
the LORD, and the LORD will not be with you."
44 But they presumed to go up to the top of
the mountain. But the ark of the covenant of
the LORD and Moses did not depart from the
midst of the camp. 45 Then the Amalekites and
the Canaanites who dwelt on that mountain
went down and defeated them, pursuing them
as far as Hormah.

Laws of Grain and Drink Offerings

15 And the LORD spoke to Moses, saying:
2 Speak to the children of Israel, and
say to them: When you come into the land
of your dwelling, which I am giving to you,
3 when you make an offering by fire to the
LORD, a burnt offering, or a sacrifice in perform-
ing a vow, or as a freewill offering, or in your
appointed feasts, to make a pleasing aroma to
the LORD, of the herd or of the flock, 4 then he
who brings his offering to the LORD will bring
a grain offering of a tenth of an ephah[1] of
flour mixed with the fourth part of a hin[2] of
oil. 5 One-fourth of a hin of wine as a drink of-
fering you will prepare with the burnt offering
or sacrifice, for each lamb.
6 Or for a ram, you will make a grain offering
of two-tenths of an ephah[3] of flour mixed with
one-third of a hin[4] of oil. 7 As a drink offering
you will offer one-third of a hin of wine, as a
pleasing aroma to the LORD.
8 When you prepare a bull as a burnt offer-
ing, or as a sacrifice in performing a vow, or
as a peace offering to the LORD, 9 then shall
be brought with the bull a grain offering of
three-tenths of an ephah[5] of flour mixed with
one-half a hin[6] of oil. 10 You will bring as a
drink offering one-half a hin of wine, as a
fire offering, as a pleasing aroma to the LORD.
11 Thus it will be done for one herd animal, or
for one ram, or for a flock animal, whether
from the sheep or from the goats. 12 According
to the number that you will make, so you will
do for every one according to their number.
13 Every native Israelite will do these things
in this manner, in offering a fire offering as
a pleasing aroma to the LORD. 14 A foreigner
who lives with you, or who resides among
you throughout your generations, and would
present a fire offering, a pleasing aroma to the
LORD, shall do as you do. 15 One ordinance will
be for you of the assembly and for the foreign-
er who lives with you, an ordinance forever
throughout your generations. As you are, so
will the foreigner be before the LORD. 16 One
law and one justice will be for you and for the
foreigner who lives with you.
17 The LORD spoke to Moses, saying: 18 Speak
to the children of Israel, and say to them:
When you come into the land where I bring
you, 19 then it will be, when you eat of the
bread of the land you will offer up an offering
to the LORD. 20 From the first of your dough you
will offer a cake as an offering. As you make
the offering of the threshing floor, so will you
offer it. 21 Of the first of your dough you will
give to the LORD an offering throughout your
generations.

Laws About Unintentional Sins

22 If you have erred and not observed all
these commandments which the LORD has
spoken to Moses, 23 even all that the LORD has
commanded you by the hand of Moses, from
the day that the LORD commanded Moses and
onward through your generations, 24 then it
will be, if it is committed by ignorance without
the knowledge of the assembly, that all the
assembly will offer one young bull as a burnt
offering, as a pleasing aroma to the LORD, with
its grain offering and its drink offering, accord-
ing to the rule, and one kid of the goats as a
sin offering. 25 The priest will make atonement
for all the assembly of the children of Israel,
and it will be forgiven them because it is ig-
norance, and they will bring their offering, a
sacrifice made by fire to the LORD, and their sin
offering before the LORD, for their ignorance.
26 And it will be forgiven all the assembly of the
children of Israel and the foreigner who lives
among them, because all the people were in
ignorance.
27 If a person sins unintentionally, then he
will bring a year-old female goat as a sin of-
fering. 28 The priest will make an atonement for
the person who sins unintentionally, when he
sins by ignorance before the LORD, to make an
atonement for him; and it will be forgiven him.
29 You shall have one law for the person who
acts through ignorance, for the natural-born
citizen among the children of Israel and for-
eigner who lives in your midst.

Laws About Intentional Sins

30 But the person who acts by a high hand,
the natural-born citizen or the foreigner, the
same reviles the LORD, and that person will be
cut off from among his people. 31 Because he
has despised the word of the LORD and has
broken His commandment, that person will
be totally cut off. His iniquity will be on him.

14:44 Dt 1:43
14:45 Nu 21:3
15:2 Lev 23:10
15:3 Ex 29:18
15:4 Ex 29:40
15:5 Nu 28:7
15:8 Lev 3:1
15:15 Nu 9:14
15:18 Nu 15:2
15:19 Jos 5:11–12
15:20 Lev 2:14
15:22 Lev 4:2
15:25 Lev 4:20
15:27 Lev 4:27–28
15:28 Lev 4:35
15:29 Nu 15:15
15:30 Dt 1:43
15:31 2Sa 12:9

[1] *4* Likely about 3½ pounds, or 1.6 kilograms. [2] *4* About 1 quart, or 1 liter; and in v. 5. [3] *6* Likely about 7 pounds, or 3.2 kilograms. [4] *6* About 1⅓ quarts, or 1.3 liters; and in v. 7. [5] *9* Likely about 11 pounds, or 5 kilograms. [6] *9* About 2 quarts, or 1.9 liters; and in v. 10.

The Sabbath-Breaker Executed

32 While the children of Israel were in the wilderness, they found a man who gathered sticks on the Sabbath day. 33 The ones who found him gathering sticks brought him to Moses and Aaron and to all the assembly. 34 They put him in confinement because it was not declared what should be done to him. 35 The LORD said to Moses, "The man will surely die. All the assembly will stone him with stones outside the camp." 36 All the assembly brought him outside the camp and stoned him with stones, and he died as the LORD commanded Moses.

Tassels on Garments

37 The LORD spoke to Moses, saying: 38 Speak to the children of Israel, and tell them to make for themselves tassels on the corners of their garments throughout the generations to come, and they will put a ribbon of blue on the corners of their garments. 39 And it will be for you a tassel, and you will see it, and you will remember all the commandments of the LORD, and you will do them, and you will not follow the lust of your own heart and your own eyes. 40 So shall you remember and do all My commandments, and be holy to your God. 41 I am the LORD your God who brought you out of the land of Egypt, to be your God: I am the LORD your God.

Opposition to Moses and Aaron

16 Now Korah the son of Izhar, the son of Kohath, the son of Levi, and Dathan and Abiram the sons of Eliab, and On the son of Peleth, sons of Reuben, took men, 2 and they rose up before Moses and men of the children of Israel, two hundred and fifty chiefs of the assembly, famous in the assembly, well-known men. 3 They assembled against Moses and against Aaron, and said to them, "You take too much upon yourselves, seeing all the congregation are holy, every one of them, and the LORD is among them. So why do you exalt yourselves above the assembly of the LORD?"

4 And when Moses heard it, he fell on his face, 5 and he spoke to Korah and to all his company, saying, "In the morning the LORD will show who is His and who is holy, and He will bring him to come near to Him. Whom He has chosen He will bring near to Him. 6 Do this: Take censers, Korah and all his company; 7 put fire in them, and put incense in them before the LORD tomorrow, and it will be that the man whom the LORD chooses, he will be holy. You take too much upon yourselves, sons of Levi."

8 Moses said to Korah, "Listen, please, sons of Levi. 9 Does it seem a small thing to you that the God of Israel has separated you from the assembly of Israel to bring you near to Himself to do the service of the tabernacle of the LORD, and to stand before the assembly to minister to them? 10 And He has brought you near to Him, and all your brothers, the sons of Levi, with you, and you also seek the priesthood? 11 Therefore both you and all your company are gathered together against the LORD, and who is Aaron that you murmur against him?"

12 And Moses sent for Dathan and Abiram the sons of Eliab, who said, "We will not come up. 13 Is it a small thing that you have brought us up out of a land that flows with milk and honey to kill us in the wilderness because you make yourself a prince over us? 14 Moreover you have not brought us into a land that flows with milk and honey nor given us inheritance of fields and vineyards. Will you put out the eyes of these men? We will not come up."

15 Moses was very angry and said to the LORD, "Do not respect their offering. I have not taken one donkey from them, nor have I hurt one of them."

16 Moses said to Korah, "You and all your company be before the LORD, you and them and Aaron, tomorrow. 17 Let each man take his censer and put incense in it, and each of you bring his censer before the LORD, two hundred and fifty censers. Also you and Aaron shall each bring his censer." 18 Every man took his censer and put fire in it, and laid incense on it, and stood at the door of the tent of meeting with Moses and Aaron. 19 Korah gathered all the assembly against them to the door of the tent of meeting, and the glory of the LORD appeared to all the assembly. 20 The LORD spoke to Moses and to Aaron, saying: 21 Separate yourselves from among this assembly, that I may consume them in a moment.

22 They fell on their faces and said, "O God, the God of the spirits of all flesh, will one man sin and You will be angry with all the assembly?"

23 And the LORD spoke to Moses, saying: 24 Speak to the assembly, saying: Get up from around the tents of Korah, Dathan, and Abiram.

25 Moses rose up and went to Dathan and Abiram, and the elders of Israel followed him. 26 He spoke to the assembly, saying, "Depart now from the tents of these wicked men, and touch nothing of theirs, lest you be swept away for all their sins." 27 So they got up from the tents of Korah, Dathan, and Abiram, on every side, and Dathan and Abiram came out and stood in the opening of their tents, and their wives, and their sons, and their children.

28 Moses said, "By this you will know that the LORD has sent me to do all these works, because I have not done them of my own mind.

15:32 Ex 35:2–3
15:34 Lev 24:12
15:35 Ex 31:14–15
15:38 Dt 22:12
15:39 Ps 73:27
15:41 Lev 22:33
16:1 Jude 1:11
16:2 Nu 26:9
16:3 Ps 106:16
16:4 Nu 14:5
16:5 Lev 10:3
16:6 Lev 10:1
16:7 Nu 16:3
16:9 Dt 10:8
16:13 Ac 7:35
16:14 Lev 20:24
16:15 Ge 4:4–5
16:19 Nu 14:10
16:21 Ex 32:10
16:22 Nu 27:16
16:26 Isa 52:11
16:28 Ex 3:12

29 If these men die the common death of all
men, or if they are visited after the visitation of
all men, then the LORD has not sent me. 30 But
if the LORD makes a new thing, and the earth
opens its mouth and swallows them with all
that belongs to them, and they go down alive
into the pit, then you will know that these men
have despised the LORD."
31 So it was, when he finished speaking all
these words, that the ground that was under
them split open. 32 And the earth opened its
mouth and swallowed them, and their hous-
es, and all the men that belonged to Korah,
and all their goods. 33 And they and all that
belonged to them went down alive into the
pit, and the earth closed on them, and they
perished from among the assembly. 34 All Israel
that was around them fled at their cry because
they said, "The earth will swallow us also."
35 A fire went out from the LORD and con-
sumed the two hundred and fifty men that
offered incense.
36 The LORD spoke to Moses, saying: 37 Tell
Eleazar the son of Aaron the priest to take up
the censers out of the blaze, for they are holy.
Then scatter the fire far and wide. 38 As for the
censers of these men who have sinned at the
cost of their own lives, make them into ham-
mered plates as a covering for the altar, for
they presented them before the LORD and they
are holy. They shall be a sign to the children
of Israel.
39 So Eleazar the priest took the bronze cen-
sers, which those who were burned had of-
fered, and they were hammered out as a cov-
ering on the altar, 40 to be a memorial to the
children of Israel, that no outsider, who is not
of the descendants of Aaron, shall approach
to offer incense before the LORD, that he might
not become like Korah and his company, as the
LORD has said to him through Moses.

> Every plague is stopped when it comes near me through the atonement of Jesus Christ (Nu 16:50).

The People Complain

41 But the next day all the assembly of the
children of Israel murmured against Moses
and against Aaron, saying, "You have killed
the people of the LORD."
42 When the assembly was gathered against
Moses and Aaron, they looked toward the tent
of meeting. The cloud covered it, and the glo-
ry of the LORD appeared. 43 Moses and Aaron
went before the tent of meeting. 44 And the
LORD spoke to Moses, saying, 45 "Get up from
among this assembly, that I may destroy them
in a moment." And they fell on their faces.
46 Moses said to Aaron, "Take a censer and
put fire in it from off the altar, and put in in-
cense, and go quickly to the assembly, and
make an atonement for them, because wrath
has gone out from the LORD. The plague has
begun." 47 Aaron took it as Moses commanded
and ran into the midst of the assembly, where
the plague had begun among the people. He
put in incense and made an atonement for the
people. 48 He stood between the dead and the
living, and the plague was stopped. 49 Now
those who died in the plague were fourteen
thousand seven hundred, besides those that
died concerning the thing of Korah. 50 Aaron
returned to Moses, to the door of the tent of
meeting, and the plague was stopped.

The Budding of Aaron's Rod

17 And the LORD spoke to Moses, saying:
2 Speak to the children of Israel, and
take from them a rod, a rod for the house of
their fathers, from all their leaders according
to the house of their fathers, twelve rods. Write
each man's name on his rod. 3 You will write
the name of Aaron on the rod of Levi, because
one rod will be for each father's house. 4 You
will lay them in the tent of meeting before the
testimony, where I will meet with you. 5 It will
be that the rod of the man whom I choose will
bud. Thus I will rid myself of the complaints
of the children of Israel, that they have been
making against you.
6 Moses spoke to the children of Israel, and
each one of their leaders gave him a rod, one
for each leader, according to their fathers'
houses, even twelve rods, and the rod of Aar-
on was among their rods. 7 Moses laid the rods
before the LORD in the tent of witness.
8 When Moses went into the tent of witness
the next day, the rod of Aaron, for the house of
Levi, had sprouted. It brought forth buds, pro-
duced blossoms, and yielded almonds. 9 Moses
brought out all the rods from before the LORD
to all the children of Israel, and they looked,
and each man took his rod.
10 The LORD said to Moses, "Return the rod
of Aaron before the testimony, to be kept for
a warning to rebels, that you may put an end
to their complaints before Me, or else they will
die." 11 Moses did so. As the LORD commanded
him, so he did.
12 The children of Israel spoke to Moses,
saying, "Behold, we expire, we perish, we all
perish. 13 Anyone approaching the tabernacle
of the LORD will die. Are we all to perish?"

16:29 1Ki 22:28
16:30 Ps 55:15
16:32 Nu 26:11
16:33 Jude 1:11
16:35 Lev 10:2
16:38 Nu 26:10
16:40 Nu 3:10
16:41 Nu 14:2
16:42 Nu 16:19
16:45 Nu 16:24

16:46 Lev 10:6
16:48 2Sa 24:25
16:49 Nu 25:9
17:5 Nu 16:5
17:7 Ex 38:21
17:8 Eze 17:24

Duties of Priests and Levites

18 And the Lord said to Aaron: You and
your sons and your father's house with
you will bear the iniquity of the sanctuary, and
you and your sons with you will bear the in-
iquity of your priesthood. 2 Your brothers also
of the tribe of Levi, the tribe of your father,
bring with you, and let them be joined with
you, and minister to you. But you and your
sons with you will minister before the tent of
witness. 3 They will perform duties for you and
for the whole tent; but they will not come near
the vessels of the sanctuary or the altar, so
that neither they nor you die. 4 They will be
joined to you and perform the duties of the
tent of meeting, for all the service of the tent;
no foreigner will come near you.
5 You yourselves will perform the duties of
the sanctuary and the duties of the altar, so
that wrath may never come upon the children
of Israel again. 6 I Myself have taken your
brothers, the Levites, from among the children
of Israel; they are given to you as a gift from
the Lord to perform the service of the tent of
meeting. 7 And you and your sons with you will
attend to your priesthood for everything at the
altar, and within the veil, and you will serve.
I have given your priesthood to you as a gift
service, and the foreigner that comes near will
be put to death.

Offerings for Priests and Levites

8 The Lord spoke to Aaron: I have certainly
given you the charge of the offerings made to
Me, all the hallowed gifts of the children of
Israel. To you and to your sons have I given
them as a portion, as an ordinance forever.
9 This will be yours of the most holy things,
reserved from the fire: All of their offerings,
all of their grain offerings and all of their sin
offerings, and all of their guilt offerings, which
they render to Me, will be most holy for you
and for your sons. 10 In a most holy place shall
you eat it; every male shall eat it. It shall be
holy to you.
11 This is yours: the offering of their gift, with
all the wave offerings of the children of Israel.
I have given them to you and to your sons
and to your daughters with you, as an eternal
statute. Everyone who is clean in your house
will eat of it.
12 All the best of the oil, and all the best of the
wine, and of the wheat, the first fruits of what
they will offer to the Lord, those have I given
to you. 13 The first ripe fruit of all which is in
their land, which they will bring to the Lord,
will be yours. Everyone who is clean in your
house will eat of it.

18:1 Ex 28:38
18:3 Nu 4:15
18:5 Ex 27:21
18:6 Nu 3:9
18:7 Nu 3:10
18:8 Lev 6:16
18:9 Lev 7:7
18:10 Lev 6:29
18:11 Dt 18:3
18:12 Ex 23:19
18:13 Ex 22:29

18:14 Lev 27:28
18:15 Ex 34:20
18:16 Ex 30:13
18:19 2Ch 13:5
18:20 Dt 10:9
18:22 Lev 22:9
18:23 Nu 3:7
18:24 Nu 18:26
18:26 Ne 10:38
18:27 Nu 18:30

14 Everything devoted in Israel will be yours.
15 Everything that opens the womb of all flesh,
which they bring to the Lord, whether it is
of men or animals, will be yours. However,
you will surely redeem the firstborn of man,
and the firstborn of unclean beasts you will
redeem. 16 Their redemption price, reckoned
from one month of age, is five shekels,[1] after
the shekel of the sanctuary, which is twenty
gerahs.
17 But the firstborn of a herd animal, or the
firstborn of a sheep, or the firstborn of a goat,
you will not redeem. They are holy. You will
splash their blood on the altar and will burn
their fat as a fire offering, as a pleasing aro-
ma to the Lord. 18 Their flesh will be yours, as
the wave breast and as the right shoulder are
yours. 19 All the offerings of the holy things
which the children of Israel offer to the Lord I
have given to you, and to your sons and your
daughters with you, as an eternal statute. It is
a covenant of salt forever before the Lord, to
you and to your seed with you.
20 The Lord said to Aaron: You will not have
an inheritance in their land, nor will you have
any territory among them. I am your territory
and your inheritance among the children of
Israel.

Tithes for Supporting the Levites

21 I have given the children of Levi all the
tithes in Israel for an inheritance, for their ser-
vice, which they serve, even the service of the
tent of meeting. 22 Hereafter, the children of
Israel shall not come near the tent of meeting,
lest they bear sin and die. 23 But the Levites will
do the service of the tent of meeting, and they
will bear their iniquity. It will be an eternal stat-
ute throughout your generations, that among
the children of Israel they have no inheritance.
24 But the tithes of the children of Israel, which
they offer as an offering to the Lord, I have
given to the Levites to inherit. Therefore I have
said to them, among the children of Israel they
will have no inheritance.

The Tithe of the Levites

25 The Lord spoke to Moses, saying: 26 You will
speak to the Levites, and say to them: When
you take from the children of Israel the tithes
that I have given you from them for your in-
heritance, then you will offer up an offering
of it to the Lord, even one-tenth of the tithe.
27 And this offering will be counted to you, as
though it was the grain of the threshing floor,
and as the fullness of the winepress. 28 Thus
you also will set apart an offering to the Lord
from all the tithes which you receive from the

[1] 16 About 2 ounces, or 58 grams.

children of Israel. Out of them you will give the
offering of the LORD to Aaron the priest. 29 Out
of all your gifts you shall present every offering
due to the LORD, from all the best of them, the
consecrated part of them.
30 You will say to them: When you have of-
fered the best from it, then it will be counted
to the Levites as the increase of the threshing
floor, and as the increase of the winepress.
31 You will eat it in every place, you and your
households, because it is your reward for your
service in the tent of meeting. 32 You will bear
no sin because of it, when you have offered
the best of it. The holy things of the children of
Israel you will not pollute, and you will not die.

Laws of Purification

19 And the LORD spoke to Moses and to
Aaron, saying: 2 This is the statute of
the law which the LORD has commanded, say-
ing: Tell the children of Israel that they will
bring you a healthy red heifer, which has no
blemish, and on which a yoke has never gone,
3 and you will give it to Eleazar the priest, and
he will bring it outside the camp, and it will
be slaughtered before him. 4 And Eleazar the
priest will take from its blood with his finger
and sprinkle some of its blood directly before
the tent of meeting seven times. 5 Then it will
be burned in his sight. Its hide and its flesh
and its blood, with her dung, will be burned.
6 And the priest will take cedar wood, and hys-
sop, and scarlet and throw it into the midst of
the burning of the heifer. 7 Then the priest will
wash his clothes, and he will bathe his body
in water, and afterward he will come into the
camp, and the priest will be unclean until eve-
ning. 8 He who burns it will wash his clothes in
water, and bathe his body in water, and will be
unclean until evening.
9 A man who is clean will gather the ashes of
the heifer and deposit them outside the camp
in a clean place, and it will be guarded for the
assembly of the children of Israel for water of
purification. It is for purifying from sin. 10 He
that gathers the ashes of the heifer will wash
his clothes and be unclean until evening, and
it will be for the children of Israel and for the
foreigner that lives among them, for an eternal
statute.
11 He that touches the dead body of any man
will be unclean seven days. 12 He will make
himself clean on the third day, and on the sev-
enth day he will be clean. But if he does not
make himself clean on the third day, then the
seventh day he will not be clean. 13 Whoever
touches the body of any man that is dead and
does not purify himself defiles the tabernacle
of the LORD, and that person will be cut off from

18:32 Lev 19:8
19:2 Dt 21:3
19:3 Lev 4:12
19:4 Lev 4:17
19:5 Ex 29:14
19:6 Lev 14:4
19:7 Lev 11:25
19:9 Nu 19:13
19:11 Nu 5:2
19:12 Nu 31:19
19:13 Lev 15:31

....

19:16 Nu 31:19
19:20 Nu 19:13
19:22 Hag 2:13
20:1 Nu 13:21
20:2 Nu 16:19
20:3 Ex 17:2
20:4 Ex 17:3
20:5 Nu 16:14

Israel. Because the water of purification was
not sprinkled on him, he will be unclean. His
uncleanness is still on him.
14 This is the law, when a man dies in a tent.
Each person who comes into the tent and all
that is in the tent will be unclean seven days.
15 Every open vessel which has no covering
fastened on it is unclean.
16 Whoever in the field touches one that is
slain with a sword, or a dead body, or a bone of
a man, or a grave will be unclean seven days.
17 For an unclean person they will take from
the ashes of the burnt sin offering, and run-
ning water will be on it in a vessel. 18 A clean
person will take hyssop, and dip it in the water,
and splash it on the tent, and on all the vessels,
and on the people who were there, and on him
that touched a bone, or one slain, or one dead,
or a grave. 19 The clean person will splash on
the unclean person on the third day and on the
seventh day. And on the seventh day he shall
purify himself, wash his clothes, and bathe in
water; and he will be clean at evening. 20 But
the man who is unclean and does not purify
himself, that person will be cut off from among
the assembly because he has defiled the sanc-
tuary of the LORD. The water of purification has
not been sprinkled on him. He is unclean. 21 It
will be an eternal statute to them.
He that sprinkles the water of purification
will wash his clothes, and he that touches the
water of purification will be unclean until eve-
ning. 22 Whatever the unclean person touches
will be unclean, and the person that touches
it will be unclean until evening.

Moses Strikes the Rock

20 Then the children of Israel, the whole
assembly, came to the Wilderness of
Zin in the first month, and the people dwelt
in Kadesh, and Miriam died there and was
buried there.

> I will speak to the rock of my salvation, and He shall bring forth His water so that I can drink (Nu 20:8).

2 And there was no water for the assembly,
and they gathered themselves together against
Moses and against Aaron. 3 The people argued
with Moses, and spoke, saying, "O that we had
died when our brothers died before the LORD!
4 And why have you brought up the assembly
of the LORD into this wilderness, that we and
our livestock should die here? 5 And why have
you brought us up from Egypt, to bring us into
this evil place? It is no place of seed, or of figs,

or of vines, or of pomegranates. Nor is there
any water to drink."
6 Moses and Aaron went from the presence of
the assembly to the door of the tent of meeting,
and they fell on their faces, and the glory of
the LORD appeared to them. 7 The LORD spoke to
Moses, saying: 8 Take the rod, and gather the
assembly together, you and Aaron your broth-
er, and speak to the rock before their eyes, and
it will give its water, and you will bring out to
them water from the rock; so you will give the
assembly and their livestock drink.
9 So Moses took the rod from before the LORD,
as He commanded him. 10 Moses and Aaron
gathered the assembly before the rock, and
he said to them, "Hear now, you rebels. Will
we bring out water from this rock for you?"
11 And Moses lifted up his hand, and he struck
the rock twice with his rod, and plenty of water
came out, and the assembly drank, and their
livestock.
12 The LORD spoke to Moses and Aaron, "Be-
cause you did not believe in Me, to sanctify Me
in the eyes of the children of Israel, therefore
you will not bring this assembly into the land
which I have given them."
13 This is the water of Meribah because the
children of Israel argued with the LORD, and
He was sanctified among them.

Edom Denies Israel Passage

14 Moses sent messengers from Kadesh to the
king of Edom,

"Thus says your brother Israel: You know
all the hardship that has found us, 15 how
our fathers went down into Egypt, and we
lived in Egypt a long time, and the Egyp-
tians distressed us and our fathers. 16 And
when we cried out to the LORD, He heard
our voice and sent an angel and brought
us out of Egypt.

Lord, hear my voice, and send Your angels to deliver me (Nu 20:16).

"And here we are in Kadesh, a city on the
edge of your territory. 17 Please let us pass
through your land. We will not pass through
the fields or the vineyards, or drink of the
water of the wells. We will travel the king's
highway. We will not turn to the right hand
nor the left, until we have passed through
your territory."
18 Edom said to him,

"You will not pass through me, lest with
the sword I come out against you."

20:6 Nu 14:5
20:8 Ex 4:17
20:9 Nu 17:10
20:10 Ps 106:32–33
20:11 1Co 10:4
20:12 Nu 27:14
20:13 Ex 17:7
20:14 Jdg 11:16–17
20:15 Ge 46:6
20:16 Ex 14:19
20:17 Dt 2:27

SPIRITLED WOMAN

COUNSEL FROM THE SPIRIT BASICS

Anger Is Danger

Moses and Aaron gathered the assembly before the rock, and he said to them, "Hear now, you rebels. Will we bring out water from this rock for you?" And Moses lifted up his hand, and he struck the rock twice with his rod, and plenty of water came out....The LORD spoke to Moses and Aaron, "Because you did not believe in Me...you will not bring this assembly into the land which I have given them."

—NUMBERS 20:10–12

"I can't help it. It's just the way I am!" I don't know how many times I've used that line, but I do now what prompted me. That statement was usually hurled in justification of my anger. My excuses covered a wide range of topics, from the way I was raised to being pregnant to being stuck at home with young children to being under spiritual attack. (The last one was especially useful since it absolved me of all responsibility.) But the truth was, I had a problem with anger. Deep down I knew this, but I didn't want to face it.

In fact, I felt certain I could control my anger as long as all my circumstances and everyone around me cooperated by being perfect! But my circumstances, mainly those involving my husband and children, were not cooperating. It is impossible for anyone to be perfect, and their human flaws served to magnify and point out mine. If the heat turned up and I was under pressure, I became consumed with anger and lashed out at the ones I loved. So did Moses in Numbers 20—and it kept him out of the Promised Land.

God forgave Moses, and He forgave me—even though there were consequences. But when we humble ourselves, renounce anger, and acknowledge it for what it is, God forgives us and gives us His strength to overcome it.

Lisa Bevere

19 The children of Israel said to him,

> "We will travel the highway, and if we and our livestock drink of your water, then we will pay for it. I will only go through on my feet without doing anything else."

20 He said,

> "You will not go through."

And Edom came out against them with many people and with a strong hand. 21 Edom refused to give Israel passage through his territory, so Israel turned away from him.

The Death of Aaron

22 They journeyed from Kadesh, and the children of Israel, even the whole assembly, came to Mount Hor. 23 The LORD spoke to Moses and Aaron in Mount Hor, by the border of the land of Edom, saying, 24 "Aaron will be gathered to his people because he will not enter into the land which I have given to the children of Israel because you rebelled against Me at the water of Meribah. 25 Take Aaron and Eleazar his son, and bring them up to Mount Hor, 26 and strip Aaron of his garments, and put them on Eleazar his son, and Aaron will be gathered to his people, and he will die there."

27 Moses did as the LORD commanded, and they went up onto Mount Hor in the sight of all the assembly. 28 Moses stripped Aaron of his garments and put them on Eleazar his son. And Aaron died there on the top of the mountain, and Moses and Eleazar came down from the mountain. 29 When all the assembly saw that Aaron was dead, they wept for Aaron thirty days, all the house of Israel.

Arad Destroyed

21 When King Arad the Canaanite, who lived in the Negev, heard that Israel came by the way of Atharim, he fought against Israel and took some of them captive. 2 Israel vowed a vow to the LORD and said, "If You will indeed deliver this people into my hand, then I will utterly destroy their cities." 3 The LORD listened to the voice of Israel and delivered up the Canaanites, and they utterly destroyed them and their cities, and he called the name of the place Hormah.

The Bronze Serpent

4 They journeyed from Mount Hor by the way of the Red Sea, to go around the land of Edom, and the soul of the people was very discouraged because of the way. 5 The people spoke against God and against Moses, "Why have you brought us up from Egypt to die in the wilderness? For there is no bread or water, and our soul loathes this worthless manna."

20:19 Dt 2:6
20:20 Jdg 11:17
20:21 Jdg 11:18
20:24 Ge 25:8
20:26 Nu 20:24
20:28 Dt 10:6
20:29 Dt 34:8
21:1 Nu 33:40
21:2 Ge 28:20
21:3 Nu 14:45
21:4 Ex 6:9
21:5 Ps 78:19
....
21:6 Dt 8:15
21:7 Ex 8:8
21:9 2Ki 18:4
21:12 Dt 2:13–14
21:13 Nu 22:36
21:15 Nu 21:28
21:17 Ps 105:2
21:20 Nu 23:28
21:22 Nu 20:17
21:23 Jdg 11:20

6 So the LORD sent poisonous serpents among the people, and they bit the people, and many children of Israel died. 7 So the people came to Moses and said, "We have sinned for we have spoken against the LORD and against you. Pray to the LORD, and He will take away the serpents from us." And Moses prayed for the people.

8 The LORD said to Moses, "Make a poisonous serpent, and put it on a pole, and it will be, that everyone who is bitten, when he looks at it, will live." 9 Moses made a bronze serpent and put it on a pole, and if a serpent had bitten any man, when he looked at the bronze serpent he lived.

The Journey to Moab

10 The children of Israel set out and camped in Oboth. 11 They journeyed from Oboth and camped at Iye Abarim in the wilderness, which is before Moab toward the sunrise. 12 From there they journeyed and camped in the Valley of Zered. 13 From there they journeyed and camped on the other side of Arnon, which is in the wilderness that comes out of the borders of the Amorites, for Arnon is the border of Moab, between Moab and the Amorites. 14 Therefore it is said in the Book of the Wars of the LORD:

> "Zahab in Suphah, and in the brooks
> of Arnon, 15 and at the stream of the
> brooks
> that goes down to the dwelling of Ar,
> and lies on the border of Moab."

16 From there they went to Beer. That is the well of which the LORD spoke to Moses, "Gather the people together, and I will give them water."

17 Then Israel sang this song:

> "Spring up, O well!
> sing to it—
> 18 the leaders dug the well;
> the nobles of the people dug,
> by the lawgiver, with their staffs."

And from the wilderness they went to Mattanah, 19 and from Mattanah to Nahaliel, and from Nahaliel to Bamoth, 20 and from Bamoth in the valley that is in the country of Moab to the top of Pisgah, which looks toward Jeshimon.

King Sihon Defeated

21 Israel sent messengers to Sihon king of the Amorites, saying,

> 22 "Let me pass through your land. We will not turn into the fields nor into the vineyards. We will not drink of the waters of the well. But we will go along by the king's highway until we are past your borders."

23 Sihon would not allow Israel to pass through his border. But Sihon gathered all his people together and went out against Israel

into the wilderness, and he came to Jahaz and
fought against Israel. 24 Israel defeated him
with the edge of the sword and possessed his
land from Arnon to Jabbok, all the way to the
children of Ammon, because the border of
the children of Ammon was strong. 25 Israel
took all these cities, and Israel lived in all the
cities of the Amorites, in Heshbon, and in all
its villages. 26 Because Heshbon was the city
of Sihon the king of the Amorites, who had
fought against the former king of Moab and
taken all his land out of his hand, to Arnon.

27 Therefore they that speak in proverbs say:

"Come into Heshbon; let it be built,
and let the city of Sihon be established,
28 because a fire went out of Heshbon,
a flame from the city of Sihon;
it has devoured Ar of Moab
and the masters of the high places of
Arnon.
29 Woe to you, Moab!
You have perished, O people of
Chemosh!
He has made his sons fugitives,
and his daughters captives,
to Sihon king of the Amorites.
30 "We have overthrown them;
Heshbon is perished to Dibon,
and we have desolated them to Nophah,
which reaches to Medeba."

31 Thus Israel lived in the land of the Am-
orites.

King Og Defeated

32 Moses sent to spy out Jazer, and they took
its villages and drove out the Amorites who
were there. 33 They turned and went up by the
way of Bashan, and Og the king of Bashan
went out against them, he and all his people,
to the battle at Edrei.

34 The LORD said to Moses, "Do not fear him
because into your hand I have given him, and
all his people, and his land, and you will do to
him as you did to Sihon king of the Amorites,
who dwelt at Heshbon."

35 So they killed him, and his sons, and all his
people, until there was not a survivor left to
him alive, and they possessed his land.

Balak Summons Balaam

22 Then the children of Israel set out and
camped in the plains of Moab on the
other side of the Jordan from Jericho.

2 Balak the son of Zippor saw all that Israel
had done to the Amorites. 3 Moab was very
afraid of the people because they were many,
and Moab was distressed because of the chil-
dren of Israel.

21:24 Am 2:9
21:28 Nu 21:15
21:29 Jdg 11:24
21:30 Isa 15:2
21:32 Nu 32:1
21:33 Jos 13:12
22:2 Jdg 11:25
22:3 Ex 15:15

....

22:5 Dt 23:4
22:9 Ge 20:3
22:12 Ge 12:2
22:17 Nu 24:11
22:18 Nu 24:13

4 Moab said to the elders of Midian, "Now this
company will lick up all that are around us, as
the ox licks up the grass of the field."

And Balak the son of Zippor was king of the
Moabites at that time. 5 He sent messengers
to Balaam the son of Beor at Pethor, which is
by the Euphrates in the land of the sons of his
people, to call him, saying,

"A people went out from Egypt. They cover
the face of the earth, and they dwell next
to me. 6 And now, please come curse this
people for me because they are too mighty
for me. Perhaps I will prevail, and we will
defeat them, and I will drive them out of
the land because I know that he whom you
bless is blessed, and he whom you curse
is cursed."

7 The elders of Moab and the elders of Midi-
an went with the divination payments in their
hand, and they came to Balaam and spoke to
him the words of Balak.

8 He said to them, "Lodge here tonight, and
I will bring you word again, as the LORD will
speak to me." And the leaders of Moab dwelt
with Balaam.

9 God came to Balaam and said, "Who are
these men with you?"

10 And Balaam said to God, "Balak the son
of Zippor, king of Moab, has sent word to me,
saying, 11 'A people went out of Egypt who
covers the face of the earth. Now come, curse
them for me. Perhaps I will be able to battle
them and drive them out.' "

12 God said to Balaam, "You will not go with
them. You will not curse the people because
they are blessed."

13 So Balaam rose up in the morning and
said to the princes of Balak, "Go to your land
because the LORD refuses to let me to go with
you."

14 The princes of Moab rose up, and they
went to Balak and said, "Balaam refuses to
come with us."

15 Again Balak sent officials, more numerous
and more honorable than they. 16 They came to
Balaam and said to him,

"Thus says Balak the son of Zippor,
'Please, let nothing hold you back from
coming to me, 17 because I will promote
you to very great honor, and anything you
say to me I will do. Come please, curse this
people for me.' "

18 Balaam answered the servants of Balak,
"If Balak gave me his house full of silver and
gold, I am not able to go beyond the command
of the LORD my God, to do less or more. 19 Now

please remain here tonight, that I may know
what more the LORD will say to me."
20 God came to Balaam at night and said to
him, "If the men come to call you, rise up and
go with them. But surely the word which I will
say to you, that will you do."

Balaam, the Donkey, and the Angel

21 Balaam rose up in the morning, and sad-
dled his donkey, and went with the princes
of Moab. 22 The anger of God was inflamed
because he went, and the angel[1] of the LORD
stood in the way as an adversary against him.
Now he was riding on his donkey, and his two
servants were with him. 23 The donkey saw the
angel of the LORD standing in the way, and His
sword was drawn in His hand, so the donkey
turned out of the way and went into the field.
Balaam struck the donkey to turn her onto the
road.
24 But the angel of the LORD stood in a narrow
path of the vineyards, a wall on this side and a
wall on that side. 25 When the donkey saw the
angel of the LORD, she threw herself into the
wall and crushed the foot of Balaam against
the wall, and he struck her again.
26 The angel of the LORD went further and
stood in a narrow place where there was no
way to turn either to the right hand or to the
left. 27 When the donkey saw the angel of
the LORD, she fell down under Balaam, and
the anger of Balaam was inflamed, and he
struck the donkey with a staff. 28 Then the LORD
opened the mouth of the donkey, and she said
to Balaam, "What have I done to you, that you
have struck me these three times?"
29 And Balaam said to the donkey, "You have
mocked me. O that there was a sword in my
hand, for now I would kill you."
30 The donkey said to Balaam, "Am I not
your donkey, whom you have ridden since I
became yours, to this day? Do I normally do
this to you?"
And he said, "No."
31 Then the LORD opened the eyes of Balaam,
and he saw the angel of the LORD standing
in the way, and His sword was drawn in His
hand, and he bowed his head and fell flat on
his face.
32 The angel of the LORD said to him, "Why
have you struck your donkey these three times?
I have come out to oppose you, because your
way is perverse before Me. 33 And the donkey
saw Me and turned from Me these three times.
If she had not turned from Me, surely by now
I would have slain you and saved her alive."

[1] *22* At times the Lord speaks directly through an angel (cf. the story of the burning bush in Ex 3:2–4).

22:20 Nu 22:35
22:28 2Pe 2:16
22:29 Pr 12:10
22:31 Ge 21:19
22:32 Nu 22:22
22:34 Job 34:31–32
22:37 Nu 24:11
22:38 Nu 22:18
22:40 Nu 23:14
22:41 Nu 23:13
23:1 Nu 23:29
23:2 Nu 23:14
23:3 Nu 23:15
23:4 Nu 23:16
23:5 Dt 18:18
23:7 Nu 22:5–6
23:9 Ex 33:16

34 Balaam said to the angel of the LORD, "I
have sinned because I did not know that You
stood in the way against me. Now therefore,
if it displeases You, I will return."
35 The angel of the LORD said to Balaam, "Go
with the men. But only speak the word that I
tell you to speak." So Balaam went with the
leaders of Balak.
36 When Balak heard that Balaam had come,
he went out to meet him in a city of Moab
which is on the border of Arnon, which is at
the furthest end of the border. 37 Balak said to
Balaam, "Did I not earnestly send to summon
you? Why did you not come to me? Indeed am
I not able to honor you?"
38 And Balaam said to Balak, "I have come to
you now. But am I able to speak just anything?
The word God puts in my mouth is what I will
speak."
39 Balaam went with Balak, and they came
to Kiriath Huzoth. 40 Balak offered oxen and
sheep and sent them to Balaam and to the
officials who were with him.

Balaam's First Prophecy

41 It came to pass on the next day that Balak
took Balaam and brought him up to Bamoth
Baal, and from there he saw the extent of the
people.
23 And Balaam said to Balak, "Build for
me seven altars, and prepare for me
seven oxen and seven rams." 2 Balak did as
Balaam had spoken, and Balak and Balaam
offered on every altar a bull and a ram.
3 Balaam said to Balak, "Stand by your burnt
offering, and I will go. Perhaps the LORD will
come to meet me, and whatever He shows me
I will tell you." And he went to a high place.
4 God met Balaam, and he said to Him, "I
have prepared seven altars, and I have offered
on every altar a bull and a ram."
5 The LORD put a word in the mouth of Ba-
laam and said, "Return to Balak, and thus you
will speak."
6 So he returned to Balak, who was standing
by his burnt offering with all the princes of
Moab. 7 Then Balaam uttered his oracle, say-
ing:

"Balak has brought me from Aram,
the king of Moab from the mountains of
the east,
saying, 'Come, curse Jacob for me,
and come, defy Israel!'
8 How will I curse
whom God has not cursed?
Or how will I defy
whom the LORD has not defied?
9 For from the top of the rocks I see him,
and from the hills I behold him;

there, the people will dwell alone
and will not be counted among the nations.
10 Who can count the dust of Jacob
and the number of the fourth part of Israel?
Let me die the death of the righteous,
and let my last end be like his!"

11 And Balak said to Balaam, "What have
you done to me? I brought you to curse my
enemies, but now you have certainly blessed
them."
12 He answered and said, "Must I not take
heed to speak what the LORD puts in my
mouth?"

Balaam's Second Prophecy

13 And Balak said to him, "Please come with
me to another place from where you may see
them. You will see part of them, but will not
see them all. Curse them for me from there."
14 He brought him into the field of Zophim, to
the top of Pisgah, and built seven altars and
offered a bull and a ram on each altar.
15 He said to Balak, "Stand here by your burnt
offerings while I meet the LORD over there."
16 The LORD met Balaam and put a word in
his mouth and said, "Go again to Balak, and
thus you will speak."
17 When he came to him, he was standing by
his burnt offerings with the princes of Moab.
And Balak said to him, "What has the LORD
spoken?"
18 And he took up his parable and said:

"Rise up, Balak, and hear!
Listen to me, you son of Zippor!
19 God is not a man, that He should lie,
nor a son of man, that He should repent.
Has He spoken, and will He not do it?
Or has He spoken, and will He not make it good?
20 See, I have received a commandment to bless,
and He has blessed, and I cannot reverse it.
21 "He has not beheld iniquity in Jacob,
nor has He seen perverseness in Israel.
The LORD his God is with him,
and the shout of a king is among them.
22 God, who brings them out of Egypt,
has strength like a wild ox.
23 Surely there is no enchantment against Jacob,
nor is there any divination against Israel.
For this time it will be said of Jacob and of Israel,
'See what God has done!'
24 A people rises up as a great lion,
and lifts itself up like a lion;
it shall not lie down until it eats the prey
and drinks the blood of the slain."

25 Balak said to Balaam, "Do not curse them
at all, nor bless them at all."
26 But Balaam answered and said to Balak,
"Did I not tell you, saying, 'All that the LORD
speaks, I must do'?"

Balaam's Third Prophecy

27 And Balak said to Balaam, "Please come.
I will bring you to another place. Perhaps it
will please God that you may curse them for
me from there." 28 Balak brought Balaam to
the top of Peor, which looks toward Jeshimon.
29 Balaam said to Balak, "Build for me sev-
en altars, and prepare for me seven bulls and
seven rams." 30 Balak did as Balaam said and
offered a bull and a ram on each altar.

24 And when Balaam saw that it pleased
the LORD to bless Israel, he did not go
as other times to seek for enchantments, but
he set his face toward the wilderness. 2 Balaam
lifted up his eyes, and he saw Israel dwelling
in their tents by their tribes, and the Spirit of
God came on him. 3 He took up his proverb
and said:

"Balaam the son of Beor has said,
and the man whose eyes are open has said,
4 he has said, who heard the words of God,
who saw the vision of the Almighty,
falling into a trance, but having his eyes open:

He will pour out His Spirit over me like gushing buckets of water, and my seed will be supplied with all they need (Nu 24:5–7).

5 "How lovely are your tents, O Jacob,
and your tabernacles, O Israel!
6 "Like palm trees are they spread out,
like gardens by the river's side,
like the aloe plant, which the LORD has planted,
and like cedar trees beside the waters.
7 He will pour the water out of his buckets,
and his seed will be in many waters.

"His king will be higher than Agag,
and his kingdom will be exalted.
8 "God brings him out of Egypt;
he has the horns of a wild ox;
he will eat up the nations, his enemies,
and will break their bones,

23:10 Ge 13:16
23:11 Nu 24:10
23:12 Nu 22:38
23:14 Nu 23:1–2
23:15 Nu 23:3
23:16 Nu 23:5
23:19 1Sa 15:29
23:20 Ge 22:17
23:21 Jer 50:20
23:22 Nu 24:8
23:23 Nu 24:1
23:24 Ge 49:9
23:26 Nu 22:18
23:28 Nu 21:20
24:1 Nu 23:23
24:2 1Sa 19:20
24:6 Ps 1:3
24:7 2Sa 5:12
24:8 Nu 23:22

and pierce them through with his
arrows.
9 He crouches, he lies down as a lion, and as
a lion,
who will stir him up?

"Blessed is he who blesses you,
and cursed is he who curses you."

10 The anger of Balak was inflamed against
Balaam, and he struck his hands together. And
Balak said to Balaam, "I called you to curse
my enemies, and indeed, you have certainly
blessed them these three times. 11 Now flee to
your own place. I thought to promote you to
great honor. But certainly, the LORD has kept
you back from honor."
12 Balaam said to Balak, "Did I not speak to
your messengers which you sent to me, saying,
13 'If Balak would give me his house full of sil-
ver and gold, I cannot go beyond the mouth of
the LORD, to do either good or bad of my own
mind. But what the LORD speaks, I will speak'?
14 And now, I am going to my people. Come, I
will advise you what this people will do to your
people in the latter days."

Balaam's Fourth Prophecy

15 He took up his parable and said:

"The oracle of Balaam the son of Beor,
and the oracle of the man whose eyes
are open;
16 the oracle of the one hearing the words of
God,
and knowing the knowledge of the Most
High,
who sees the vision of the Almighty,
falling into a trance, but having his eyes
open:
17 "I will see him, but not now;
I will behold him, but not near;
a star will come out of Jacob,
and a scepter will rise out of Israel,
and will crush the borderlands of Moab,
and destroy all the children of Sheth.
18 Edom will be a possession,
and Seir, a possession of its enemies,
while Israel does valiantly.
19 One out of Jacob shall have dominion,
and destroy the survivors of the city."

20 Then he looked on Amalek; he took up his
proverb and said:

"Amalek was the first of the nations,
but his end will be that he perishes
forever."

21 He looked on the Kenites and took up his
proverb and said:

"Strong is your dwelling place,
and you put your nest in a rock;

24:9 Ge 12:3
24:10 Nu 23:11
24:11 Nu 22:17
24:12 Nu 22:18
24:14 Ge 49:1
24:16 Nu 24:4
24:17 Ge 49:10
24:18 Am 9:12
24:20 Ex 17:14
24:21 Ge 15:19
24:24 Ge 10:4
24:25 Nu 31:8
25:1 Jos 2:1
25:2 1Co 10:20
25:3 Jos 22:17
25:4 Dt 13:17
25:5 Ex 18:21
25:6 Joel 2:17
25:7 Ex 6:25
25:8 Nu 16:46–48
25:9 1Co 10:8
25:11 Dt 32:16
25:12 Mal 2:4–5
25:15 Nu 31:8

22 nevertheless the Kenite will be wasted.
How long until Ashur carries you away
captive?"

23 He took up his proverb and said:

"Alas, who will live when God does this?
24 And ships will come from the coasts of
Cyprus
and will afflict Ashur and will afflict Eber,
and he also will perish forever."

25 Balaam rose up and went and returned to
his place, and Balak also went his way.

Moab Seduces Israel

25 While Israel dwelt in Shittim, the peo-
ple began to commit harlotry with the
women of Moab. 2 They called the people to
the sacrifices of their gods, and the people ate
and bowed down to their gods. 3 Israel joined
himself to the Baal of Peor, and the anger of
the LORD was inflamed against Israel.
4 The LORD said to Moses, "Take all the chiefs
of the people and hang them before the LORD
in the sun, that the fierce anger of the LORD
turn from Israel."
5 Moses said to the judges of Israel, "Kill each
of the men who have aligned themselves with
the Baal of Peor."
6 Behold, one of the children of Israel came
and brought to his brothers a Midianite wom-
an in the sight of Moses and in the sight of
all the assembly of the children of Israel, who
were weeping before the door of the tent of
meeting. 7 When Phinehas the son of Eleazar,
the son of Aaron the priest, saw it, he rose up
from among the assembly and took a spear in
his hand, 8 and he went after the man of Israel
into the tent, and thrust both of them through,
the man of Israel and the woman through her
belly. So the plague was stopped from the chil-
dren of Israel. 9 Those that died in the plague
were twenty-four thousand.
10 The LORD spoke to Moses, saying, 11 "Phine-
has the son of Eleazar, the son of Aaron the
priest, has turned My wrath away from the
children of Israel, because he was zealous for
My sake among them, so I did not extermi-
nate the children of Israel in My zeal. 12 There-
fore say, 'I hereby grant him My covenant of
peace. 13 And it will be for him and his seed
after him, even the covenant of an everlasting
priesthood, because he was zealous for his God
and made an atonement for the children of
Israel.' "
14 Now the name of the slain Israelite who
was slain with the Midianite woman was Zim-
ri the son of Salu, a leader of a chief house
among the Simeonites. 15 The name of the
Midianite woman that was slain was Kozbi the

daughter of Zur. He was chief over a people
and of a father's house in Midian.
16 The LORD spoke to Moses, saying, 17 "Be
hostile to the Midianites, and defeat them,
18 because they have been hostile to you with
their wiles, with which they have deceived
you in the matter of Peor and in the matter of
Kozbi the daughter of a leader of Midian, their
sister, who was slain on the day of the plague
because of Peor."

The Second Census

26 After the plague, the LORD spoke to Mo-
ses and to Eleazar the son of Aaron
the priest, saying, 2 "Take the count of all the
assembly of the children of Israel from twenty
years old and older, throughout their fathers'
houses, all that are able to go to war in Israel."
3 Moses and Eleazar the priest spoke with them
in the plains of Moab by Jordan near Jericho,
saying, 4 "Take the count of the people from
twenty years old and older," as the LORD com-
manded Moses.

The children of Israel, who went out of the
land of Egypt, were these:

5 Reuben, the oldest son of Israel. The chil-
dren of Reuben:
of Hanok, from whom comes the family
of the Hanokites;
of Pallu, the family of the Palluites;
6 of Hezron, the family of the Hezronites;
of Karmi, the family of the Karmites.
7 These are the families of the Reubenites:
those who were counted were forty-three thou-
sand seven hundred and thirty.
8 The son of Pallu was Eliab. 9 The sons of
Eliab were Nemuel, and Dathan, and Abiram.
This is that Dathan and Abiram, called out
from the assembly, who argued against Moses
and against Aaron in the company of Korah
when they argued against the LORD. 10 And the
earth opened its mouth and swallowed them
with Korah when that company died, when
the fire devoured two hundred and fifty men,
and they became a sign. 11 But the children of
Korah did not die.

12 The sons of Simeon by their families
were:
of Nemuel, the family of the Nemuelites;
of Jamin, the family of the Jaminites;
of Jakin, the family of the Jakinites;
13 of Zerah, the family of the Zerahites;
of Shaul, the family of the Shaulites.
14 These are the families of the Simeonites:
twenty-two thousand two hundred.
15 The children of Gad by their families
were:

25:18 Rev 2:14
26:1 Nu 25:9
26:2 Ex 38:25–26
26:3 Nu 22:1
26:4 Nu 1:1
26:5 1Ch 5:3
26:9 Nu 1:16
26:10 Nu 16:38
26:11 Ex 6:24
26:12 1Ch 4:24
26:13 Ge 46:10
26:15 Ge 46:16
26:19 Ge 46:12
26:20 Ge 46:12
26:23 Ge 46:13
26:24 Ge 46:13
26:26 Ge 46:14
26:28 Ge 46:20
26:29 Jos 17:1
26:30 Jdg 6:11

of Zephon, the family of the Zephonites;
of Haggi, the family of the Haggites;
of Shuni, the family of the Shunites;
16 of Ozni, the family of the Oznites;
of Eri, the family of the Erites;
17 of Arodi, the family of the Arodites;
of Areli, the family of the Arelites.
18 These are the families of the children of Gad
according to those by their count: forty thou-
sand five hundred.

19 The sons of Judah were Er and Onan, and Er
and Onan died in the land of Canaan.
20 The sons of Judah after their families
were:
of Shelah, the family of the Shelanites;
of Perez, the family of the Perezites;
of Zerah, the family of the Zerahites.
21 The sons of Perez were:
of Hezron, the family of the Hez-
ronites;
of Hamul, the family of the Hamulites.
22 These are the families of Judah by their
count: seventy-six thousand five hundred.

23 The sons of Issachar by their families
were:
of Tola, the family of the Tolaites;
of Puah, the family of the Puites;
24 of Jashub, the family of the Jashubites;
of Shimron, the family of the Shim-
ronites.
25 These are the families of Issachar by their
count: sixty-four thousand three hundred.

26 The sons of Zebulun by their families
were:
of Sered, the family of the Seredites;
of Elon, the family of the Elonites;
of Jahleel, the family of the Jahleelites.
27 These are the families of the Zebulunites by
their count: sixty thousand five hundred.
28 The sons of Joseph according to their fami-
lies, by Manasseh and Ephraim, were:
29 The sons of Manasseh:
of Makir, the family of the Makirites, and
Makir begot Gilead;
of Gilead, the family of the Gileadites.
30 These are the sons of Gilead:
of Iezer, the family of the Iezerites;
of Helek, the family of the Helekites;
31 and of Asriel, the family of the
Asrielites;
and of Shechem, the family of the
Shechemites;
32 and of Shemida, the family of the
Shemidaites;
and of Hepher, the family of the
Hepherites.

33 Zelophehad the son of Hepher had
no sons, but daughters, and the names
of the daughters of Zelophehad were
Mahlah, Noah, Hoglah, Milkah, and
Tirzah.
34 These are the families of Manasseh, and
those who were numbered of them were fif-
ty-two thousand seven hundred.

35 These are the sons of Ephraim according
to their families:
of Shuthelah, the family of the Shuthela-
hites;
of Beker, the family of the Bekerites;
of Tahan, the family of the Tahanites.
36 These are the sons of Shuthelah:
of Eran, the family of the Eranites.
37 These are the families of the sons of Ephraim
by their count: thirty-two thousand five hun-
dred.

These are the sons of Joseph by their families.

38 The sons of Benjamin by their families
were:
of Bela, the family of the Belaites;
of Ashbel, the family of the Ashbelites;
of Ahiram, the family of the Ahiramites;
39 of Shupham, the family of the
Shuphamites;
of Hupham, the family of the Hupham-
ites.
40 The sons of Bela were Ard and
Naaman:
of Ard, the family of the Ardites;
and of Naaman, the family of the
Naamites.
41 These are the sons of Benjamin by their fam-
ilies, and by their count: forty-five thousand
six hundred.

42 These are the sons of Dan according to
their families:
of Shuham, the family of the Shuham-
ites.
These are the families of Dan after their fam-
ilies. 43 All the families of the Shuhamites, by
their count, were sixty-four thousand four
hundred.

44 The sons of Asher by their families were:
of Imnah, the family of the Imnites;
of Ishvi, the family of the Ishvites;
of Beriah, the family of the Beriites.
45 of the sons of Beriah were:
of Heber, the family of the Heberites;
of Malkiel, the family of the Mal-
kielites.
46 The name of the daughter of Asher
was Serah.
47 These are the families of the sons of Asher by
their count: fifty-three thousand four hundred.

26:33 Nu 27:1
26:38 1Ch 8:1
26:40 1Ch 8:3
26:42 Ge 46:23
26:44 Ge 46:17
26:48 Ge 46:24
26:49 1Ch 7:13
26:51 Nu 1:46
26:53 Jos 11:23
26:54 Nu 33:54
26:55 Nu 33:54
26:57 Ge 46:11
26:59 Ex 6:20
26:60 Nu 3:2
26:61 Lev 10:1–2
26:62 Nu 1:49
26:64 Dt 2:14–15
26:65 Nu 14:28–30

48 Of the sons of Naphtali by their families
were:
of Jahzeel, the family of the Jahzeelites;
of Guni, the family of the Gunites;
49 of Jezer, the family of the Jezerites;
of Shillem, the family of the Shillemites.
50 These are the families of Naphtali according
to their families; those who were numbered of
them were forty-five thousand four hundred.

51 These were the counted of the children of
Israel: six hundred and one thousand, seven
hundred and thirty.

52 The LORD spoke to Moses, saying: 53 To
these the land will be divided for an inheri-
tance by the number of names. 54 To a large
tribe you shall give a large inheritance, and to
small tribe you shall give a small inheritance.
To each one his inheritance will be given ac-
cording to those who were numbered of him.
55 But the land will be divided by lot. By the
names of the tribes of their fathers they will
inherit. 56 According to the lot his possession
will be divided between large and small.

57 These are those counted of the Levites by
their families:
of Gershon, the family of the Ger-
shonites;
of Kohath, the family of the Kohathites;
of Merari, the family of the Merarites.
58 These are the families of the Levites:
the family of the Libnites,
the family of the Hebronites,
the family of the Mahlites,
the family of the Mushites,
the family of the Korahites.
And Kohath begot Amram. 59 And
the name of the wife of Amram was
Jochebed, the daughter of Levi, whom
her mother bore to Levi in Egypt, and
she bore to Amram Aaron and Moses
and Miriam their sister. 60 To Aaron was
born Nadab, and Abihu, Eleazar, and
Ithamar. 61 Nadab and Abihu died when
they offered foreign fire before the LORD.
62 Those who were numbered of them were
twenty-three thousand, each male from a
month old and older; for they were not count-
ed among the children of Israel, because there
was no inheritance given them among the chil-
dren of Israel.

63 These were counted by Moses and Eleazar
the priest, who counted the children of Israel
in the plains of Moab by Jordan near Jericho.
64 But among these there was not a man count-
ed by Moses and Aaron the priest when they
counted the children of Israel in the Wilder-
ness of Sinai 65 because the LORD had said of

them, "They will surely die in the wilderness."
And there was not a man left of them, except
Caleb the son of Jephunneh and Joshua the
son of Nun.

Laws of Inheritance
Nu 36:1–12

27 Then came near the daughters of Zelo-
phehad, the son of Hepher, the son of
Gilead, the son of Makir, the son of Manasseh,
of the families of Manasseh the son of Joseph,
and these are the names of his daughters:
Mahlah, Noah, Hoglah, Milkah, and Tirzah.
2 They stood before Moses, and before Eleazar
the priest, and before the leaders and all the
assembly by the door of the tent of meeting,
saying, 3 "Our father died in the wilderness,
and he was not in the company of them that
gathered against the LORD, in the company of
Korah, but died in his own sin and had no
sons. 4 Why should the name of our father di-
minish from among his family, because he has
no son? Give to us a possession among the
brothers of our father."

5 Moses brought their case before the LORD.
6 The LORD spoke to Moses, saying: 7 The
daughters of Zelophehad speak right. You
will certainly give them an inheritance among
their father's brothers, and you will cause the
inheritance of their father to pass on to them.

8 You will speak to the children of Israel,
saying, "If a man dies, and has no son, then
you will cause his inheritance to pass on to his
daughter. 9 If he has no daughter, then you will
give his inheritance to his brothers. 10 If he has
no brothers, then you will give his inheritance
to his father's brothers. 11 If his father has no
brothers, then you will give his inheritance to
his closest kinsman in his family, and he will
possess it. And it will be for the children of
Israel a statute of judgment, as the LORD com-
manded Moses."

Joshua to Succeed Moses

12 The LORD said to Moses, "Go up into this
mountain of Abarim, and see the land which
I have given to the children of Israel. 13 When
you have seen it, you also will be gathered
to your people as Aaron your brother was
gathered. 14 For you rebelled against My com-
mandment in the Wilderness of Zin when the
congregation argued against Me. You did not
show My holiness at the waters before their
eyes." (These are the waters of Meribah in
Kadesh in the Wilderness of Zin.)

15 Moses spoke to the LORD, saying, 16 "Let the
LORD, the God of the spirits of all flesh, appoint
a man over the assembly 17 who will go out
before them, and who will go in before them,
and who will lead them out, and who will bring
them in, so the assembly of the LORD will not
be like sheep who do not have a shepherd."

18 The LORD said to Moses, "Take Joshua
the son of Nun, a man in whom is the Spirit,
and lay your hand on him, 19 and cause him
to stand before Eleazar the priest and before
all the assembly, and command in their sight.
20 You will put some of your majesty on him,
in order that all the assembly of the children
of Israel will listen. 21 He will stand before Elea-
zar the priest, who will ask for him about the
judgment of the Urim before the LORD. At his
word will they go out, and at his word they will
come in, both he and all the children of Israel
with him, even all the assembly."

22 Moses did as the LORD commanded him,
and he took Joshua, and he caused him to
stand before Eleazar the priest and before all
the assembly. 23 And he laid his hands on him
and commanded him as the LORD spoke by the
hand of Moses.

Daily Offerings

28 And the LORD spoke to Moses, saying:
2 Command the children of Israel and
say to them: My offering, My bread for My sac-
rifices made by fire, as a pleasing aroma to Me,
you will guard to offer to Me at their time. 3 You
will say to them: This is the fire offering which
you will bring near to the LORD: two male lambs
in their first year, without blemish, day by day,
as a regular burnt offering. 4 The one lamb you
will offer in the morning, and the other lamb
you will offer at evening, 5 and one-tenth of an
ephah[1] of flour as a grain offering, mingled
with one-fourth of a hin[2] of beaten oil. 6 It is a
regular burnt offering, which was ordained at
Mount Sinai as a pleasing aroma, a sacrifice
made by fire to the LORD. 7 Its drink offering
will be one-fourth of a hin for the one lamb. In
a holy place you will pour the strong wine to
the LORD as a drink offering. 8 The other lamb
you will offer at evening. As the morning grain
offering and its drink offering, you will offer it
as an offering made by fire, a pleasing aroma
to the LORD.

Sabbath Offerings

9 On the Sabbath day two lambs in their first
year, without blemish, and two-tenths of an
ephah[3] of flour as a grain offering, mixed with
oil, and its drink offering— 10 this is the burnt
offering of every Sabbath, in addition to the
regular burnt offering and its drink offering.

Monthly Offerings

11 At the beginnings of your months you will
offer a burnt offering to the LORD: two young

27:1 Nu 26:33
27:3 Nu 26:64–65
27:4 Jos 17:4
27:11 Nu 35:29
27:12 Nu 33:47–48
27:13 Nu 31:2
27:14 Ex 17:7
27:16 Nu 16:22
27:17 Dt 31:2
27:18 Dt 34:9
27:19 Dt 3:28
27:20 Jos 1:16–18
27:21 Ex 28:30
27:23 Nu 27:19
28:2 Lev 3:11
28:3 Lev 6:9
28:5 Lev 2:1
28:6 Am 5:25
28:7 Ex 29:42
28:10 Eze 46:4–5
28:11 Nu 10:10

[1] *5* Likely about 3½ pounds, or 1.6 kilograms; and in vv. 13, 21, and 29.
[2] *5* About 1 quart, or 1 liter; and in vv. 7 and 14.
[3] *9* Likely about 7 pounds, or 3.2 kilograms; and in vv. 12, 20, and 28.

bulls, one ram, seven lambs in their first year, without blemish; 12 three-tenths of an ephah[1] of flour as a grain offering, mixed with oil, for one bull; and two-tenths of an ephah of flour as a grain offering, mixed with oil, for one ram; 13 and one-tenth of an ephah of flour mixed with oil as a grain offering for one lamb; as a burnt offering of a pleasing aroma, a sacrifice made by fire to the LORD. 14 Their drink offerings will be one-half a hin[2] of wine for a bull, and one-third of a hin[3] for a ram, and one-fourth of a hin for a lamb. This is the burnt offering of each month throughout the months of the year. 15 Also one male goat as a sin offering to the LORD shall be offered, besides the regular burnt offering and its drink offering.

Passover Offerings
Ex 12:14–20; Lev 23:4–8; Dt 16:1–8

16 On the fourteenth day of the first month is the Passover of the LORD. 17 On the fifteenth day of this month is the feast. Unleavened bread will be eaten for seven days. 18 On the first day there will be a holy convocation. You will not do any ordinary work, 19 but you will offer a sacrifice made by fire as a burnt offering to the LORD: two young bulls, and one ram, and seven lambs in their first year. Be sure they are without blemish. 20 And their grain offering will be of flour mixed with oil. Three-tenths of an ephah you will offer for a bull, and two-tenths of an ephah for a ram. 21 One-tenth of an ephah you will offer for each of the seven lambs, 22 and one goat as a sin offering, to make an atonement for you. 23 You will offer these in addition to the burnt offering in the morning, which is for a regular burnt offering. 24 The same way you will offer daily, throughout the seven days, the food of the sacrifice made by fire, as a pleasing aroma to the LORD. It will be offered in addition to the regular burnt offering and its drink offering. 25 And on the seventh day you will have a holy assembly. You will not do any ordinary work.

Offerings at the Feast of Weeks
Lev 23:15–22; Dt 16:9–12

26 And on the day of the first fruits, when you bring a new grain offering to the LORD at your Feast of Weeks, you will have a holy assembly. You will do no ordinary work. 27 But you will offer the burnt offering as a pleasing aroma to the LORD: two young bulls, one ram, and seven lambs in their first year; 28 and their grain offering of flour mixed with oil, three-tenths of an ephah for one bull, two-tenths of an ephah for one ram, 29 one-tenth of an ephah for each of the seven lambs; 30 and one goat, to make an atonement for you. 31 Make sure they are without blemish. You will offer them with their drink offerings, besides the regular burnt offering and its grain offering.

Offerings at the Feast of Trumpets
Lev 23:23–25

29 In the seventh month, on the first day of the month, you will have a holy assembly. You will do no ordinary work. It is a day of blowing the trumpets for you. 2 You will offer a burnt offering as a pleasing aroma to the LORD: one young bull, one ram, and seven lambs in their first year, without blemish; 3 their grain offering will be of flour mixed with oil, three-tenths of an ephah[4] for a bull, and two-tenths of an ephah[5] for a ram, 4 and one-tenth of an ephah[6] for one lamb, for the seven lambs; 5 also one goat as a sin offering, to make an atonement for you; 6 besides the burnt offering of the month and its grain offering, and the daily burnt offering and its grain offering, and their drink offerings, according to their rule, as a pleasing aroma, a sacrifice made by fire to the LORD.

Offerings on the Day of Atonement
Lev 16:2–34; 23:26–32

7 You will have a holy assembly on the tenth day of this seventh month, and you will afflict yourselves. You will not do any work on it. 8 But you will offer a burnt offering to the LORD as a pleasing aroma: one young bull, one ram, and seven lambs in their first year. Be sure they are without blemish. 9 Their grain offering will be of flour mixed with oil, three-tenths of an ephah for the bull, and two-tenths of an ephah for one ram, 10 and one-tenth of an ephah for each of the seven lambs; 11 also one goat as a sin offering in addition to the sin offering of atonement, and the regular burnt offering, and its grain offering, and their drink offerings.

Offerings at the Feast of Tabernacles
Lev 23:33–43; Dt 16:13–17

12 On the fifteenth day of the seventh month you will have a holy convocation. You will do no ordinary work, and you will keep a feast to the LORD seven days. 13 And you will offer a burnt offering, a sacrifice made by fire, as a pleasing aroma to the LORD: thirteen young bulls, two rams, and fourteen lambs in their first year, without blemish. 14 And their grain offering will be of flour mixed with oil, three-tenths of an ephah to a bull, and two-tenths of an ephah to each ram of the two rams, 15 and one-tenth to each lamb of the fourteen lambs; 16 and one goat as a sin offering in addition to

28:12 Nu 15:4–12
28:15 Nu 28:3
28:16 Ex 12:18
28:17 Lev 23:6
28:18 Ex 12:16
28:19 Dt 15:21
28:23 Nu 28:3
28:25 Lev 23:8
28:26 Ex 23:16
28:27 Lev 23:18–19
28:31 Nu 28:19
29:11 Lev 16:3
29:12 Dt 16:13–14

[1] *12* Likely about 11 pounds, or 5 kilograms; and in vv. 20 and 28.
[2] *14* About 2 quarts, or 1.9 liters.
[3] *14* About 1⅓ quarts, or 1.3 liters.
[4] *3* Likely about 11 pounds, or 5 kilograms; and in vv. 9 and 14.
[5] *3* Likely about 7 pounds, or 3.2 kilograms; and in vv. 9 and 14.
[6] *4* Likely about 3½ pounds, or 1.6 kilograms; and in vv. 10 and 15.

the regular burnt offering, its grain offering, and its drink offering.

17 On the second day present twelve young bulls, two rams, fourteen lambs in their first year without blemish, 18 and their grain offering and their drink offerings, for the bulls, for the rams, and for the lambs, by their number according to the ordinance; 19 also one goat as a sin offering, besides the regular burnt offering, and its grain offering, and their drink offerings.

20 On the third day present eleven bulls, two rams, fourteen lambs in their first year without blemish, 21 and their grain offering and their drink offerings, for the bulls, for the rams, and for the lambs, by their number according to the ordinance; 22 also one goat as a sin offering, besides the regular burnt offering, and its grain offering, and its drink offering.

23 On the fourth day present ten bulls, two rams, and fourteen lambs in their first year without blemish, 24 and their grain offering and their drink offerings, for the bulls, for the rams, and for the lambs, by their number according to the ordinance; 25 also one goat as a sin offering in addition to the regular burnt offering, its grain offering, and its drink offering.

26 On the fifth day present nine bulls, two rams, and fourteen lambs in their first year without blemish, 27 and their grain offering and their drink offerings, for the bulls, for the rams, and for the lambs, by their number according to the ordinance; 28 also one goat as a sin offering in addition to the regular burnt offering, and its grain offering, and its drink offering.

29 On the sixth day present eight bulls, two rams, and fourteen lambs in their first year without blemish, 30 and their grain offering and their drink offerings, for the bulls, for the rams, and for the lambs, by their number according to the ordinance; 31 also one goat as a sin offering in addition to the regular burnt offering, its grain offering, and its drink offering.

32 On the seventh day present seven bulls, two rams, and fourteen lambs in their first year without blemish, 33 and their grain offering and their drink offerings, for the bulls, for the rams, and for the lambs, by their number according to the ordinance; 34 also one goat as a sin offering in addition to the regular burnt offering, its grain offering, and its drink offering.

35 On the eighth day you will have a solemn assembly. You will do no ordinary work on it. 36 But you will offer a burnt offering, a sacrifice made by fire as a pleasing aroma to the LORD: one bull, one ram, seven lambs in their first year, without blemish. 37 Their grain offering and their drink offerings, for the bull, for the ram, and for the lambs, will be according to their number, according to the rule; 38 also one goat as a sin offering in addition to the regular burnt offering, and its grain offering, and its drink offering.

39 These things you will do to the LORD in your set feasts in addition to your vows and your freewill offerings, as your burnt offerings, and as your grain offerings, and as your drink offerings, and as your peace offerings.

40 Moses told the children of Israel everything, according to all that the LORD commanded Moses.

29:18 Nu 28:7
29:35 Lev 23:36
. . . .
29:39 Lev 23:2
30:1 Nu 7:2
30:2 Job 22:27
30:6 Ps 56:12
30:8 Ge 3:16
30:12 Nu 30:8

The Law About Vows

30 And Moses spoke to the heads of the tribes of the children of Israel, saying: This is the thing that the LORD has commanded. 2 If a man vows a vow to the LORD, or swears an oath to bind himself with a bond, he will not break his word. He will do according to all that proceeds out of his mouth.

3 If a woman makes a vow to the LORD, and binds herself by a bond, while in her father's house in her youth, 4 and her father hears her vow and her bond with which she has bound herself, and her father is silent to her, then all her vows will stand, and every bond with which she has bound herself will stand. 5 But if her father restrains her in the day he hears, none of her vows or her bonds with which she has bound herself will stand, and the LORD will forgive her, because her father restrained her.

6 If she had a husband when she vowed, or uttered anything out of her lips with which she bound herself, 7 and her husband heard it and was silent to her in the day that he heard it, then her vows will stand, and her bonds with which she bound herself will stand. 8 But if her husband restrains her on the day that he heard it, then he will make her vow which she vowed and that which she uttered with her lips, with which she bound herself, of no effect, and the LORD will forgive her.

9 But every vow of a widow and of her that is divorced, with which she has bound herself, will stand against her.

10 If she vowed in her husband's house, or bound herself by a bond with an oath, 11 and her husband heard it and was silent to her and did not restrain her, then all her vows will stand, and every bond with which she bound herself will stand. 12 But if her husband has clearly voided them on the day he heard them, then whatever proceeded out of her lips concerning her vows, or concerning the bond of herself, will not stand. Her husband has voided them, and the LORD will forgive her. 13 Every vow, and every binding oath to afflict her soul, her husband may establish, or her husband

may nullify. 14 But if her husband says nothing to her from day to day, then he confirms all her vows, or all her pledges, which bind her. He confirms them because he said nothing to her on the day that he heard them. 15 But if he clearly makes them void after he has heard them, then he will bear her iniquity.

16 These are the statutes which the LORD commanded Moses, between a man and his wife, and between the father and his daughter, while she is still young and in her father's house.

Vengeance on the Midianites

31 And the LORD spoke to Moses, saying, 2 "Avenge the children of Israel on the Midianites. Afterward you will be gathered to your people."

3 Moses spoke to the people, saying, "Arm some of your men for war, and let them go against the Midianites to give the vengeance of the LORD against Midian. 4 A thousand from each tribe, throughout all the tribes of Israel, you will send to the war." 5 So there were delivered from the thousands of Israel a thousand of each tribe, twelve thousand armed for war. 6 Moses sent them to the war, a thousand from each tribe, with Phinehas the son of Eleazar the priest, with the holy vessels and the trumpets to sound the alarm in his hand.

7 They waged war against the Midianites, as the LORD commanded Moses, and they killed every male. 8 They killed the kings of Midian, in addition to the rest of those who were killed: Evi, and Rekem, and Zur, and Hur, and Reba, five kings of Midian. Balaam the son of Beor they also killed with the sword. 9 The children of Israel returned with the women of Midian and their children and took their livestock, and all their flocks, and all their wealth for plunder. 10 They burned with fire all their cities in which they lived and all their camps. 11 They took all the plunder and all the prey of men and of beasts. 12 They brought the captives, the prey, and the plunder to Moses, to Eleazar the priest, to the assembly of the children of Israel, and to the camp on the plains of Moab, which are by Jordan across from Jericho.

13 Moses and Eleazar the priest and all the leaders of the assembly went to meet them outside the camp. 14 Moses was angry with the officers of the army, with the captains over thousands, and captains over hundreds, who came from the battle.

15 Moses said to them, "Have you saved all the women alive? 16 These caused the children of Israel, through the word of Balaam, to act unfaithfully against the LORD concerning the thing of Peor, and there was a plague among the assembly of the LORD. 17 So now kill every male among the little ones, and kill every woman who has known a man by lying with him. 18 But keep alive for yourselves all the young girls who have not known a man by lying with him.

19 "And you stay outside the camp seven days. Whoever has killed any person and whoever has touched any slain, purify both yourselves and your captives on the third day and on the seventh day. 20 Purify all your clothes, and all that is made of skins, and all work of goats' hair, and all things made of wood."

I will be purified with the water of separation (Nu 31:23).

21 Eleazar the priest said to the fighting men of Israel who went to the battle, "This is the ordinance of the law which the LORD commanded Moses: 22 Only the gold, and the silver, the bronze, the iron, the tin, and the lead, 23 everything that can go through the fire, you will make it go through the fire, and it will be clean, but some of it will be purified with the water of purification, and all that cannot pass through the fire you will make go through the water. 24 You will wash your clothes on the seventh day, and you will be clean, and afterward you will come into the camp."

Dividing the Plunder

25 The LORD spoke to Moses, saying, 26 "Take the count of the plunder that was taken, of man and of beast, you and Eleazar the priest, and the chief of the fathers of the assembly. 27 And divide the prey into two parts between those that took the war on themselves, who went out to battle, and between all the assembly. 28 And levy a tribute to the LORD from the fighting men of Israel who went out to battle: one person out of five hundred, of the people and of the oxen, and of the donkeys, and of the sheep; 29 take it from their half, and give it to Eleazar the priest as an offering to the LORD. 30 Of the half of the children of Israel, you will take one portion of fifty, of the people, of the oxen, of the donkeys, and of the flocks, of all manner of beasts, and give them to the Levites, who keep the guard of the tabernacle of the LORD." 31 Moses and Eleazar the priest did as the LORD commanded Moses.

32 The plunder, being the rest of the prey, which the fighting men of Israel had caught, was six hundred and seventy-five thousand sheep, 33 seventy-two thousand oxen, 34 and sixty-one thousand donkeys, 35 and thirty-two

30:15 Lev 5:1
31:2 Nu 27:13
31:3 Lev 26:25
31:6 Nu 14:44
31:7 Jdg 21:11
31:8 Nu 25:15
31:11 Dt 20:14
31:12 Nu 22:1
31:15 1Sa 15:3
31:16 2Pe 2:15
31:17 Jdg 21:11–12
31:18 Dt 21:10–14
31:23 Nu 19:9
31:24 Lev 11:25
31:27 Jos 22:8
31:28 Nu 18:26

thousand people in all, of women who had not
known a man by lying with him.
36 The half, which was the portion of those
that went out to war, was three hundred and
thirty-seven thousand five hundred sheep.
37 And the LORD's tribute of the sheep was
six hundred and seventy-five.
38 The oxen were thirty-six thousand, of
which the LORD's tribute was seventy-two.
39 The donkeys were thirty thousand five
hundred, of which the LORD's tribute was
sixty-one.
40 The people were sixteen thousand, of
which the LORD's tribute was thirty-two
people.
41 Moses gave the tribute which was the
LORD's offering to Eleazar the priest, as the LORD
commanded Moses.
42 Of the half of the children of Israel, which
Moses divided from the men who fought, 43 the
half belonging to the assembly was three hun-
dred and thirty-seven thousand five hundred
sheep, 44 thirty-six thousand oxen, 45 thirty
thousand five hundred donkeys, 46 and six-
teen thousand people. 47 From the half of the
children of Israel Moses took one out of fifty,
of man and of beast, and gave them to the
Levites, who kept the guard of the tabernacle
of the LORD, as the LORD commanded Moses.
48 The officers who were over thousands of
the army, the captains of thousands, and cap-
tains of hundreds, came near to Moses, 49 and
they said to Moses, "Your servants have taken
the count of the fighting men of Israel who are
in our hand, and not a man of us is missing.
50 We have brought an offering for the LORD,
what every man has gotten of jewels of gold,
chains, and bracelets, rings, earrings, and
pendants, to make an atonement for ourselves
before the LORD."
51 Moses and Eleazar the priest took the gold
from them, all in the form of fashioned articles.
52 All the gold of the offering that they offered
up to the LORD, of the captains of thousands
and of the captains of hundreds, was sixteen
thousand seven hundred and fifty shekels.[1]
53 The fighting men of Israel had taken plun-
der, each man for himself. 54 And Moses and
Eleazar the priest took the gold of the captains
of thousands and of hundreds and brought it
into the tent of meeting as a memorial for the
children of Israel before the LORD.

The Tribes Settling in Gilead

32 Now the children of Reuben and the
children of Gad had a very great num-
ber of livestock, and when they saw the land
of Jazer and the land of Gilead was a place for
livestock, 2 the children of Gad and the children
of Reuben came and spoke to Moses, and to
Eleazar the priest, and to the leaders of the
assembly, saying, 3 "Ataroth, and Dibon, and
Jazer, and Nimrah, and Heshbon, and Elealeh,
and Sebam, and Nebo, and Beon, 4 the land
which the LORD defeated before the assembly
of Israel is a land for livestock, and your ser-
vants have livestock." 5 And they said, "If we
have found mercy in your sight, let this land
be given to your servants for a possession, and
do not take us over the Jordan."
6 Moses said to the children of Gad and to the
children of Reuben, "Will your brothers go to
war, and you will dwell here? 7 And why would
you discourage the hearts of the children of
Israel from going over into the land which the
LORD has given to them? 8 Thus your fathers
did, when I sent them from Kadesh Barnea
to see the land. 9 When they went up to the
Valley of Eshkol and saw the land, they dis-
couraged the hearts of the children of Israel
so they would not go into the land which the
LORD had given them. 10 And the anger of the
LORD was inflamed on that day, and He swore,
saying, 11 'Surely none of the men who came
up out of Egypt, from twenty years old and
older, will see the ground which I swore to
Abraham, to Isaac, and to Jacob, because they
did not completely follow Me, 12 except Caleb
the son of Jephunneh the Kenizzite, and Josh-
ua the son of Nun, because they completely
followed the LORD.' 13 The anger of the LORD was
inflamed against Israel, and He made them
wander in the wilderness forty years, until all
the generation that did evil in the eyes of the
LORD was finished.
14 "Behold, you have risen up in your fathers'
place, an increase of sinful men, to increase
more the burning anger of the LORD toward
Israel. 15 If you turn away from following Him,
He will again abandon them in the wilderness,
and you will destroy all this people."
16 They approached him and said, "We will
build sheepfolds here for our livestock and cit-
ies for our children. 17 But we ourselves will be
armed, ready before the children of Israel, until
we have brought them to their place. Our little
ones will dwell in the fortified cities because
of the inhabitants of the land. 18 We will not
return to our houses until all the children of
Israel have inherited their inheritance. 19 We
will not inherit with them on the other side of
the Jordan or beyond, because our inheritance
fell to us on this side of the Jordan to the east."
20 Moses said to them, "If you will do this
thing, if you will be armed before the LORD
for war, 21 and all of you, each armed, will go

31:41 Nu 18:8
31:47 Nu 31:30
31:50 Ex 30:12
31:53 Dt 20:14
31:54 Ex 30:16
32:1 Nu 21:32
32:4 Nu 21:34
32:10 Nu 14:11
32:11 Nu 14:28–30
32:12 Dt 1:36
32:13 Nu 14:33–35
32:15 2Ch 15:2
32:17 Jos 4:12–13
32:19 Jos 13:8
32:20 Jos 4:12–13

[1] 52 About 420 pounds, or 190 kilograms.

over the Jordan before the LORD until He has driven out His enemies from before Him 22 and the land is subdued before the LORD, then after that you will return and be exempt before the LORD and before Israel, and this land will be your possession before the LORD.

23 "But if you will not do so, you have sinned against the LORD, and be sure your sin will find you out. 24 Build for yourselves cities for your children and folds for your sheep, and do that which has proceeded out of your mouth."

25 The children of Gad and the children of Reuben spoke to Moses, saying, "Your servants will do as my lord commands. 26 Our children, our wives, our flocks, and all our livestock will be there in the cities of Gilead, 27 but your servants will cross over, each man armed for war, before the LORD to battle, as my lord says."

28 So Moses commanded Eleazar the priest, and Joshua the son of Nun, and the chief fathers of the tribes of the children of Israel. 29 And Moses said to them, "If the children of Gad and the children of Reuben will cross over the Jordan with you, each man armed for battle before the LORD, and the land will be subdued before you, you are to give them the land of Gilead as a possession. 30 But if they do not cross over with you armed, they will have possessions among you in the land of Canaan."

31 The children of Gad and the children of Reuben answered, saying, "As the LORD has said to your servants, so we will do. 32 We will cross over, armed before the LORD into the land of Canaan, so the possession of our inheritance on this side of the Jordan may be ours."

33 Moses gave to the children of Gad, to the children of Reuben, and to half the tribe of Manasseh the son of Joseph, the kingdom of Sihon king of the Amorites and the kingdom of Og king of Bashan, the land with the cities within the borders, the cities of the surrounding land.

34 The children of Gad built Dibon and Ataroth and Aroer, 35 Atroth Shophan and Jazer and Jogbehah, 36 Beth Nimrah and Beth Haran, fortified cities, and folds for sheep. 37 And the children of Reuben built Heshbon and Elealeh and Kiriathaim, 38 Nebo and Baal Meon (their names being changed) and Sibmah; and they named the other cities which they built.

39 The children of Makir the son of Manasseh went to Gilead and captured it and drove out the Amorites who were in it. 40 Moses gave Gilead to Makir the son of Manasseh, and he lived in it. 41 Jair the son of Manasseh went and captured its small towns and called them Havvoth Jair. 42 Nobah went and captured Kenath and its villages and called it Nobah, after his own name.

32:22 Jos 22:9
32:23 Ge 44:16
32:24 Nu 32:16
32:26 Jos 1:14
32:27 Jos 4:12
32:28 Jos 1:13
32:33 Jos 12:6
32:34 Dt 2:36
32:36 Nu 32:3
32:38 Nu 32:3
32:39 Ge 50:23
32:40 Jos 17:1
32:41 Dt 3:14

33:1 Ps 77:20
33:2 Nu 9:17–23
33:3 Ex 14:8
33:4 Ex 12:12
33:5 Ex 12:37
33:6 Ex 13:20
33:7 Ex 14:2
33:9 Ex 15:27
33:11 Ex 16:1
33:15 Ex 19:1–2
33:16 Nu 11:34
33:17 Nu 11:35
33:18 Nu 12:16

Recounting Israel's Journey

33 These are the journeys of the children of Israel, who went out of the land of Egypt with their armies under the hand of Moses and Aaron. 2 Moses recorded the starting points of their journeys at the command of the LORD. These are their journeys according to their starting points.

3 They set out from Rameses in the first month, on the fifteenth day of the first month. On the day after the Passover the children of Israel went out with a high hand in the sight of all the Egyptians, 4 because the Egyptians buried all their firstborn, whom the LORD had killed among them. Upon their gods the LORD executed judgments.

5 The children of Israel set out from Rameses and camped in Sukkoth.

6 They set out from Sukkoth and camped in Etham, which is on the edge of the wilderness.

7 They set out from Etham and turned to Pi Hahiroth, which is before Baal Zephon, and they camped before Migdol.

8 They set out from before Pi Hahiroth, and passed through the midst of the sea into the wilderness, and went three days' journey in the Wilderness of Etham, and camped in Marah.

9 They set out from Marah, and came to Elim, and in Elim were twelve fountains of water and seventy palm trees, and they camped there.

10 They set out from Elim and camped by the Red Sea.

11 They set out from the Red Sea and camped in the Wilderness of Sin.

12 They set out from the Wilderness of Sin and camped in Dophkah.

13 They set out from Dophkah and camped in Alush.

14 They set out from Alush and camped at Rephidim, where there was no water for the people to drink.

15 They set out from Rephidim and camped in the Wilderness of Sinai.

16 They set out from the Wilderness of Sinai and camped at Kibroth Hattaavah.

17 They set out from Kibroth Hattaavah and camped at Hazeroth.

18 They set out from Hazeroth and camped in Rithmah.

19 They set out from Rithmah and camped at Rimmon Perez.

20 They set out from Rimmon Perez and camped in Libnah.

21 They set out from Libnah and camped at Rissah.

22 They set out from Rissah and camped in Kehelathah.

23 They set out from Kehelathah and camped at Mount Shepher.

24 They set out from Mount Shepher and
camped in Haradah.
25 They set out from Haradah and camped
in Makheloth.
26 They set out from Makheloth and camped
at Tahath.
27 They set out from Tahath and camped at
Terah.
28 They set out from Terah and camped in
Mithkah.
29 They went from Mithkah and camped in
Hashmonah.
30 They set out from Hashmonah and camped
at Moseroth.
31 They set out from Moseroth and camped
in Bene Jaakan.
32 They set out from Bene Jaakan and
camped at Hor Haggidgad.
33 They set out from Hor Haggidgad and
camped in Jotbathah.
34 They set out from Jotbathah and camped
at Abronah.
35 They set out from Abronah and camped
at Ezion Geber.
36 They set out from Ezion Geber and camped
in the Wilderness of Zin, which is Kadesh.
37 They set out from Kadesh and camped at
Mount Hor, at the edge of the land of Edom.
38 Aaron the priest went up onto Mount Hor at
the word of the LORD and died there in the for-
tieth year after the children of Israel came out
of the land of Egypt, in the first day of the fifth
month. 39 Aaron was one hundred and twen-
ty-three years old when he died on Mount Hor.
40 King Arad the Canaanite, who lived in the
south in the land of Canaan, heard of the com-
ing of the children of Israel.
41 They set out from Mount Hor and camped
in Zalmonah.
42 They set out from Zalmonah and camped
in Punon.
43 They set out from Punon and camped in
Oboth.
44 They set out from Oboth and camped in Iye
Abarim, on the border of Moab.
45 They set out from Iye Abarim and camped
in Dibon Gad.
46 They set out from Dibon Gad and camped
in Almon Diblathaim.
47 They set out from Almon Diblathaim and
camped in the mountains of Abarim, before
Nebo.
48 They set out from the mountains of Abarim
and camped in the plains of Moab near Jor-
dan of Jericho. 49 They camped by Jordan, from
Beth Jeshimoth to Abel Shittim in the plains
of Moab.

Instructions for Conquering Canaan

50 The LORD spoke to Moses in the plains of
Moab by Jordan near Jericho, saying: 51 Speak
to the children of Israel, and say to them:
When you are crossing over Jordan into the
land of Canaan, 52 then you will drive out all
the inhabitants of the land from before you,
and destroy all their carved images, and de-
stroy all their molded images, and destroy all
their high places, 53 and you will drive out the
inhabitants of the land and dwell in it, because
I have given you the land to inherit it. 54 You
will possess the land by lot for an inheritance
among your families, and to the larger you will
give the larger inheritance, and to the smaller
you will give the smaller inheritance. Every
man's inheritance will be in the place where
his lot falls. By the tribes of your fathers you
will inherit.

I pluck down the high places of the enemy (Nu 33:52).

55 But if you do not drive out the inhabitants
of the land from before you, then those whom
you let remain will be like thorns in your eyes
and thorns in your sides. They will show hos-
tility to you in the land in which you live. 56 And
what I had planned to do to them, I will do
to you.

The Borders of Canaan

34 And the LORD spoke to Moses, saying:
2 Command the children of Israel, and
say to them: When you are going into the land
of Canaan, this is the land that will fall to you
for an inheritance, the land of Canaan with
its borders.
3 Then your south side will be from the Wil-
derness of Zin along by the border of Edom,
and your south border will be the end of the
Dead Sea to the east. 4 And your border will
turn from the south to the Ascent of Akrabbim,
and continue to Zin, and the end of it will be
from the south to Kadesh Barnea. Then it will
continue to Hazar Addar, and pass on to Az-
mon. 5 And the border will circle around from
Azmon to the Brook of Egypt, and the end of
it will be at the *Mediterranean* Sea.
6 For the western border, you will have the
Mediterranean Sea and its coastline. This will
be your western border.
7 This will be your northern border: From
the *Mediterranean* Sea you will mark a line to
Mount Hor; 8 from Mount Hor you will mark a
line of your border to Lebo Hamath, and the
limits of the border will be to Zedad. 9 And the
border will go on to Ziphron, and the limits
of it will be at Hazar Enan. This will be your
northern border.

33:31 Dt 10:6
33:32 Dt 10:7
33:33 Dt 10:7
33:35 Dt 2:8
33:36 Nu 20:1
33:37 Nu 21:4
33:38 Dt 10:6
33:43 Nu 21:10
33:44 Nu 21:11
33:47 Dt 32:49
33:48 Nu 22:1
33:51 Jos 3:17

33:52 Ex 23:24
33:54 Nu 26:53–56
33:55 Jdg 2:3
33:56 Dt 28:63
34:2 Ge 17:8
34:3 Ge 14:3
34:4 Nu 32:8
34:5 Jos 15:4
34:7 Nu 33:37
34:8 Nu 13:21
34:9 Eze 47:17

10 You will mark a line for your eastern bor-
der from Hazar Enan to Shepham. 11 And the
border will go down from Shepham to Riblah,
on the east side of Ain, and the border will go
down and will reach the side of the Sea of
Kinnereth to the east. 12 And the border will
go down to the Jordan, and the limits of it will
be at the Dead Sea.

This will be your land with its borders all
around.

13 Moses commanded the children of Israel,
saying: This is the land which you will possess
by lot, which the LORD commanded to give to
the nine tribes, and to the half-tribe 14 because
the tribe of the children of Reuben by the
house of their fathers and the tribe of the chil-
dren of Gad by the house of their fathers have
received their inheritance, and half the tribe of
Manasseh has received their inheritance. 15 The
two tribes and the half-tribe have received their
inheritance on this side of the Jordan near Jer-
icho to the east, toward the sunrise.

The Leaders to Divide the Land

16 The LORD spoke to Moses, saying: 17 These
are the names of the men who will divide the
land for you: Eleazar the priest and Joshua the
son of Nun. 18 You will take one leader of each
tribe to divide the land by inheritance. 19 These
are the names of the men:

of the tribe of Judah,
Caleb the son of Jephunneh;
20 of the tribe of the children of Simeon,
Shemuel the son of Ammihud;
21 of the tribe of Benjamin,
Elidad the son of Kislon;
22 the leader of the tribe of the children of
Dan,
Bukki the son of Jogli;
23 the leader of the children of Joseph, for
the tribe of the children of Manasseh,
Hanniel the son of Ephod;
24 the leader of the tribe of the children of
Ephraim,
Kemuel the son of Shiphtan;
25 the leader of the tribe of the children of
Zebulun,
Elizaphan the son of Parnak;
26 the leader of the tribe of the children of
Issachar,
Paltiel the son of Azzan;
27 the leader of the tribe of the children of
Asher,
Ahihud the son of Shelomi;
28 the leader of the tribe of the children of
Naphtali,
Pedahel the son of Ammihud.

34:11 Dt 3:17
34:12 Nu 34:3
34:14 Nu 32:33
34:17 Jos 14:1
34:19 Nu 26:65

35:1 Nu 22:1
35:2 Jos 14:3–4
35:6 Jos 21:3
35:8 Nu 26:54
35:11 Ex 21:13
35:12 Dt 19:6
35:15 Nu 15:16
35:16 Lev 24:17

29 These are the ones whom the LORD com-
manded to divide the inheritance among the
children of Israel in the land of Canaan.

The Levites' Cities

Dt 4:41–43; 19:1–14; Jos 20:1–9

35 And the LORD spoke to Moses in the
plains of Moab by Jordan near Jericho,
saying: 2 Command the children of Israel, and
they will give to the Levites of the inheritance
of their possession cities to dwell in, and you
will give the Levites pasturelands around the
city. 3 The cities will be for them to dwell in, and
their pasturelands will be for their livestock,
and for their property, and for all their animals.

4 The pasturelands of the cities, which you
will give to the Levites, will reach from the wall
of the city and beyond one thousand cubits[1]
all around. 5 You will measure from without
the city on the east side two thousand cubits,[2]
and on the south side two thousand cubits, and
on the west side two thousand cubits, and on
the north side two thousand cubits, and the city
will be in the middle. This will be for them the
pasturelands of the cities.

Cities of Refuge

6 Among the cities which you will give to the
Levites there will be six cities of refuge, which
you will appoint for the manslayer, that he may
flee there, and to them you will add forty-two
cities. 7 So all the cities which you will give to
the Levites will be forty-eight cities. You will
give them with their pasturelands. 8 The cities
which you shall give shall be from the posses-
sion of the children of Israel. From the larger
tribes you shall give many, and from the smaller
tribes you shall give few. Each tribe, in propor-
tion to the inheritance that it receives, shall give
of its cities to the Levites.

9 The LORD spoke to Moses, saying: 10 Speak
to the children of Israel and say to them: When
you are crossing over the Jordan into the land
of Canaan, 11 then you shall designate cities
as your cities of refuge, so that a manslayer
who unintentionally kills a person may flee
there. 12 The cities will be for you a refuge from
the avenger, so that the manslayer does not
die until he stands trial before the assembly.
13 The cities which you designate shall be your
six cities of refuge. 14 You will give three cities
across the Jordan, and three cities you will give
in the land of Canaan, which will be cities of
refuge. 15 For the children of Israel, and for the
stranger, and for the foreign sojourner among
them will be six cities. These will be for a ref-
uge. Everyone that unintentionally kills any
person may flee there.

16 If he strikes him with an instrument of iron,
so that he dies, he is a murderer. The murderer

[1] *4* About 1,500 feet, or 450 meters. [2] *5* About 3,000 feet, or 900 meters.

shall surely be put to death. [17] If he strikes him with a stone in hand, by which he could die, and he dies, he is a murderer. The murderer shall surely be put to death. [18] Or if he strikes him with a weapon of wood in hand, by which he could die, and he dies, he is a murderer. The murderer shall surely be put to death. [19] The avenger of blood himself will slay the murderer. When he meets him, he will slay him. [20] But if he pushed him out of hatred, or threw something at him, lying in wait, so he dies, [21] or in hatred struck him with his hand, so he died, he that struck him shall surely be put to death, because he is a murderer. The avenger of blood will slay the murderer when he meets him.

[22] But if he pushed him suddenly without hatred, or threw anything at him without lying in wait, [23] or used a stone that may cause death, unintentionally throwing it at him, resulting in death, though they were not enemies, and was not trying to harm him, [24] then the assembly will judge between the manslayer and the avenger of blood according to these judgments. [25] And the assembly will deliver the manslayer out of the hand of the avenger of blood, and the assembly will restore him to the city of his refuge where he fled, and he will dwell in it until the death of the high priest, who was anointed with the holy oil.

[26] But if the manslayer will go out at any time beyond the border of the city of his refuge where he fled, [27] and the avenger of blood finds him outside the borders of the city of his refuge, and the avenger of blood kills the manslayer, he will not be guilty of blood, [28] because the manslayer should have remained in the city of his refuge until the death of the high priest. But after the death of the high priest the manslayer may return to the land of his possession.

[29] So these things will be for a statute of judgment to you throughout your generations in all your dwelling places.

[30] Whoever kills a person, the murderer will be put to death by the testimony of witnesses, but one witness will not testify against a person for death.

[31] And you will not take a ransom for the life of a murderer who is guilty of death, but he will surely be put to death.

[32] You will not take a ransom for him who fled to the city of his refuge, that he should come out again to dwell in the land, until the death of the priest.

[33] So you will not defile the land which you are in, because blood defiles the land, and the land cannot be cleansed of the blood that is shed in it, except by the blood of him that shed it. [34] So do not defile the land which you are dwelling in, where I am residing, because I the LORD am residing among the children of Israel.

35:20 Ex 21:14
35:22 Ex 21:13
35:24 Jos 20:6
35:25 Ex 29:7
35:29 Nu 27:11
35:30 Dt 19:15
35:33 Mic 4:11

....

35:34 Nu 5:3
36:1 Nu 27:1
36:2 Nu 33:54
36:5 Nu 27:7
36:6 Nu 36:12
36:7 1Ki 21:3
36:8 1Ch 23:22
36:11 Nu 27:1
36:13 Lev 27:34

Marriage of Female Heirs

Nu 27:1–11

36 And the chief fathers of the families of the children of Gilead the son of Makir, the son of Manasseh, of the families of the sons of Joseph, came near, and spoke before Moses and before the leaders, the chief fathers of the children of Israel. [2] And they said, "The LORD commanded my lord to give the land for an inheritance by lot to the children of Israel, and my lord was commanded by the LORD to give the inheritance of Zelophehad our brother to his daughters. [3] If they are married to any of the sons of the other tribes of the children of Israel, then their inheritance will be taken from the inheritance of our fathers and will be added to the inheritance of the tribe to which they are married, so will it be taken from the lot of our inheritance. [4] When the jubilee of the children of Israel happens, then their inheritance will be added to the inheritance of the tribe to which they are married, so their inheritance will be taken away from the inheritance of the tribe of our fathers."

[5] Moses commanded the children of Israel according to the word of the LORD, saying: "The tribe of the sons of Joseph has spoken right. [6] This is the thing which the LORD commands concerning the daughters of Zelophehad, saying, 'Let them marry whom they think best. But they may marry only within a clan of their father's tribe. [7] So the inheritance of the children of Israel will not turn from tribe to tribe, because every one of the children of Israel will keep the inheritance of the tribe of his fathers. [8] Every daughter that possesses an inheritance in any tribe of the children of Israel will be wife to one of the families of the tribe of her father, so every man of the children of Israel may enjoy the inheritance of his fathers. [9] Thus no inheritance will turn from one tribe to another tribe, but every tribe of the children of Israel will keep its own inheritance.' "

[10] Just as the LORD commanded Moses, thus the daughters of Zelophehad did, [11] for Mahlah, Tirzah, Hoglah, Milkah, and Noah, the daughters of Zelophehad, were married to their uncles' sons. [12] And they were married into the families of the sons of Manasseh the son of Joseph, and their inheritance remained in the tribe of the family of their father.

[13] These are the commandments and the judgments which the LORD commanded by the hand of Moses to the children of Israel in the plains of Moab by Jordan near Jericho.

Author: Traditionally Moses

Written: 1410 BC

Theme: Obedience to God's Instruction

DEUTERONOMY

Dear Spirit Led Woman,

We read in Deuteronomy that the children of Israel faced a choice on the edge of the Promised Land: "I have set before you life and death, blessing and curse. Therefore choose life, that both you and your descendants may live" (Dt 30:19). They could choose to love and obey God, inviting blessings and life on themselves and their descendants, or to turn their hearts away from God and invite curses and destruction upon themselves. In like manner you are faced with choices every day that carry with them the potential of being life givers or life drainers. If you choose to skip your daily Bible reading and prayer time, you think less and less about God and more about other things. The most minor distractions will begin to keep you from pursuing Him. These are signs that your spiritual life is fading fast.

God is our life giver, so choosing His ways is choosing life. Ask the Holy Spirit to show you what stands between you and a passionate life in Christ. Make choices that bring life to your life and the lives of generations to come.

Joy F. Strang

The Command to Leave Horeb

1 These are the words which Moses spoke to all Israel on the other side of the Jordan in the wilderness, in the plain opposite Suph, between Paran and Tophel and Laban and Hazeroth and Dizahab. 2 (It is an eleven-day *journey* from Horeb by the way of Mount Seir to Kadesh Barnea.)

3 In the fortieth year, in the eleventh month, on the first day of the month, Moses spoke to the children of Israel, according to all that the LORD had commanded him *to give* to them. 4 *It was* after he had slain Sihon the king of the Amorites, who lived in Heshbon, and Og the king of Bashan, who lived at Ashtaroth in Edrei.

5 Across the Jordan, in the land of Moab, Moses began to declare this law, saying: 6 The LORD our God spoke to us in Horeb, saying, "You have dwelt long enough at this mountain. 7 Turn, and take your journey, and go to the mountains of the Amorites, and to all their neighbors, in the plain, in the mountains and in the lowland, in the Negev and by the seacoast, to the land of the Canaanites and to Lebanon, as far as the great river, the River Euphrates. 8 See, I have set the land before you. Go in and possess the land which the LORD swore to your fathers, Abraham, Isaac, and Jacob, to give to them and to their descendants after them."

Leaders Appointed

9 I spoke to you at that time, saying, "I am not able to bear you by myself. 10 The LORD your God has multiplied you, and surely you are this day as numerous as the stars of heaven. 11 May the LORD, the God of your fathers, make you a thousand times more numerous and bless you, just as He has promised you! 12 How can I myself bear your load and your burden and your strife? 13 Choose wise, discerning, and knowing men, among your tribes, and I will appoint them as leaders over you."

14 You answered me, and said, "The thing which you have said is good for us to do."

15 So I took the leaders of your tribes, wise and well-known men, and appointed them as leaders over you, leaders over thousands, and leaders over hundreds, and leaders over fifties, and leaders over tens, and officers among your tribes. 16 I charged your judges at that time, saying, "Hear the issues between your countrymen, and judge righteously between every man and his fellow countryman, and the foreigner that is with him. 17 You shall not show partiality in judgment, but you shall hear the small as well as the great. You shall not be afraid in any man's presence, for the judgment is God's. The case that is too hard for you, you shall bring it to me, and I will hear it." 18 At that time, I commanded you all the things you should do.

Israel Sends Spies

19 When we departed from Horeb, we went through all that great and terrible wilderness, which you saw by the way of the mountain of the Amorites, as the LORD our God commanded us, and we came to Kadesh Barnea. 20 I said to you, "You have come to the mountains of the Amorites, which the LORD our God is giving to us. 21 See, the LORD your God has set the land before you. Go up and possess it, just as the LORD, the God of your fathers, spoke to you. Do not fear or be discouraged."

22 So all of you came near to me and said, "Let us send men before us, so that they shall scout out the land, and bring back to us word concerning what way we should go up and into what cities we shall come."

23 The thing pleased me, and I took twelve men from you, one out of each tribe. 24 They turned and went up into the hill country and came to the Valley of Eshkol and scouted it out. 25 They took the fruit of the land in their hands, and brought it down to us, and brought us word again, and said, "It is a good land which the LORD our God is giving us."

Israel Rebels

26 Yet you were not willing to go up, but rebelled against the commandment of the LORD your God. 27 You murmured in your tents, and said, "Because the LORD hates us, He has brought us out of the land of Egypt to deliver us into the hand of the Amorites to destroy us. 28 Where shall we go up? Our brothers have discouraged our hearts, saying, 'The people are greater and taller than we. The cities are great and walled up to heaven. And moreover, we have seen the sons of the Anakites there.' "

29 Then I said to you, "Do not be terrified, or afraid of them. 30 The LORD your God who goes before you, He shall fight for you, just as all that He did for you in Egypt before your eyes, 31 and in the wilderness, where you saw how the LORD your God carried you, as a man carries his son, in all the way that you went, until you came to this place."

32 Yet in this thing you did not believe the LORD your God, 33 who went in the way before you, to find you a place to pitch your tents, in fire by night and in a cloud by day, to show you by what way you should go.

34 The LORD heard the sound of your words, and was angry, and vowed, saying, 35 "Not one of these men of this evil generation will see the good land which I swore to give to your

1:1 1Sa 25:1
1:2 Nu 13:26
1:3 Nu 33:38
1:7 Dt 11:24
1:8 Ge 12:7
1:9 Ex 18:18
1:10 Ge 15:5
1:11 Ge 22:17
1:13 Ex 18:21
1:16 Jn 7:24
1:17 Ex 18:26
1:19 Dt 1:2
1:21 Jos 1:9
1:24 Nu 13:21–27
1:26 Nu 14:1–4
1:27 Dt 9:28
1:28 Dt 9:1–2
1:30 Ex 14:14
1:31 Isa 46:3–4
1:32 Ps 106:24
1:33 Nu 10:33

fathers. 36 The exception will be Caleb the son
of Jephunneh. He shall see it, and to him I will
give the land upon which he has walked, and
to his children, because he has wholly followed
the LORD."
37 Also the LORD was angry with me on your
account, saying, "You also shall not go in. 38 But
Joshua the son of Nun, who stands before
you, he shall go in. Encourage him, for he will
cause Israel to inherit it. 39 Moreover, your little
ones, who you said would be a prey, and your
children, who in that day had no knowledge
between good and evil, they shall go in, and
to them will I give it, and they shall possess it.
40 But as for you, turn around, and take your
journey into the wilderness by the way of the
Red Sea."
41 Then you answered and said to me, "We
have sinned against the LORD. We will go up
and fight, just as the LORD our God commanded
us." So each of you girded on his weapons of
war and you thought it easy to go up into the
hill country.
42 Then the LORD said to me, "Tell them, 'Do
not go up nor fight, for I am not among you;
lest you be defeated before your enemies.' "
43 So I spoke to you, but you would not listen.
Instead, you rebelled against the command-
ment of the LORD and went presumptuously
up into the hill country. 44 The Amorites, who
lived in the hill country, came out against you,
and chased you as bees do, and destroyed you
in Seir as far as Hormah. 45 Then you returned
and wept before the LORD, but the LORD would
neither listen to your voice nor give ear to you.
46 So you dwelt in Kadesh many days, accord-
ing to the days you dwelt there.

The Wilderness Years

2 Then we turned, and set out toward the
wilderness by the way of the Red Sea, as
the LORD spoke to me, and we circled Mount
Seir for many days.
2 Then the LORD spoke to me, saying, 3 "You
have circled this mountain long enough. Now
turn north. 4 Command the people, saying: You
are to pass through the territory of your broth-
ers the children of Esau, who dwell in Seir, and
they shall be afraid of you. So carefully watch
yourselves. 5 Do not provoke them, for I will not
give you any of their land, no, not so much as
a footprint, because I have given Mount Seir
to Esau for a possession. 6 You may buy food
from them with money so that you may eat,
and you may also buy water from them with
money so that you may drink.

1:36 Nu 14:24
1:37 Nu 20:12
1:38 Nu 14:30
1:39 Nu 14:3
1:40 Nu 14:25
1:43 Nu 14:44
1:44 Ps 118:12
1:46 Nu 20:1
2:1 Nu 21:4
2:3 Dt 1:6
2:4 Nu 20:14–21
2:5 Ge 36:8
2:7 Dt 8:2–4
2:8 1Ki 9:26
2:9 Ge 19:36–37
2:10 Ge 14:5
2:12 Dt 2:22
2:13 Nu 21:12
2:14 Dt 1:34–35
2:15 Ps 106:26
2:19 Dt 2:9
2:20 Ge 14:5
2:22 Ge 36:8
2:23 Ge 10:14

7 "For the LORD your God has blessed you in
all the works of your hands. He knows your
wanderings through this great wilderness.
These forty years the LORD your God has been
with you. You have lacked nothing."
8 So we passed by our brothers, the children
of Esau, who lived in Seir, through the way of
the plain from Elath and from Ezion Geber,
and we turned and passed by the way of the
Wilderness of Moab.
9 The LORD said to me, "Do not harass the
Moabites, nor contend with them in battle, for I
will not give you any of their land for a posses-
sion, because I have given Ar to the children
of Lot as a possession."
10 (The Emites lived there in times past, a
people as great and as many and as tall as
the Anakites. 11 These people, as well as the
Anakites, also were regarded as giants,[1] but
the Moabites call them Emites. 12 The Horites
also formerly lived in Seir, but the children of
Esau dispossessed and destroyed them, and
settled there in their place, just as Israel did
to the land of its possession, which the LORD
gave to them.)
13 "Cross over the Zered Valley." So we went
over the Zered Valley.
14 Now the length of time it took for us to
come to Kadesh Barnea until we crossed over
the brook Zered was thirty-eight years, until
all the generation of the men of war perished
from among the army, just as the LORD swore
to them. 15 For indeed the hand of the LORD
was against them, to destroy them from among
their midst, until they were gone.
16 So it came to pass, when all the men of war
were gone and dead from among the people,
17 then the LORD spoke to me, saying, 18 "Today,
you are to pass over through Ar, the border of
Moab. 19 When you come close to the Ammo-
nites, do not harass them or provoke them,
for I will not give you any of the land of the
Ammonites as a possession, because I have
given it to the children of Lot for a possession."
20 (That also is considered the land of giants.
Giants formerly lived there, but the Ammonites
call them Zamzummites. 21 They were a great
people, as numerous and tall as the Anakites.
But the LORD destroyed them before *the Am-
monites*. Then they dispossessed them and
lived in their place, 22 just as He had done *for*
the children of Esau, who lived in Seir, when
He destroyed the Horites from before them,
and they dispossessed them, and lived in their
place even to this day. 23 And the Avvites, who
lived in villages as far as Gaza, the Caphtorites,
who came out of Caphtor, destroyed them, and
lived in their place.)

[1] *11 Rephaites*, English trans.of Heb. *Rephaim*, also 2:20; 3:11; Jos 13:12; 17:15.

King Sihon Defeated

24 "Arise, set out, and cross the River Arnon.
See, I have given Sihon the Amorite, king of
Heshbon, and his land into your hand. Begin
to possess it and contend with him in battle.
25 This day I will begin to put the dread of you
and the fear of you on the nations that are
under the whole heaven, who shall hear the
report of you, and shall tremble, and be in an-
guish because of you."

26 I sent messengers out of the Wilderness
of Kedemoth to Sihon, king of Heshbon,
with words of peace, saying, 27 "Let me pass
through your land. I will only go on the main
road. I will not turn aside to the right or the
left. 28 You shall sell me food for money so that
I may eat, and give me water for money so that
I may drink, only allow me to pass through on
foot, 29 just as the children of Esau who dwell in
Seir and the Moabites who dwell in Ar did for
me, until I pass over the Jordan into the land
which the LORD our God is giving us." 30 But Si-
hon, king of Heshbon, would not let us pass by
him, for the LORD your God hardened his spirit
and made his heart obstinate, so that He might
deliver him into your hand as he is to this day.

31 The LORD said to me, "See, I have begun
to give Sihon and his land to you. Begin to
possess *it*, so that you may inherit his land."

32 Then Sihon came out against us, he and
all his people, to fight at Jahaz. 33 Then the
LORD our God delivered him over to us, and
we struck him down with his sons and all his
people. 34 We took all his cities at that time and
utterly destroyed the men, the women, and the
children of every city. We left no survivors.
35 We took only the livestock for plunder and
the spoils of the cities which we took. 36 From
Aroer, which is on the bank of the River Arnon,
and from the city that is in the valley, all the
way to Gilead, there was not one city too strong
for us. The LORD our God delivered all to us.
37 Only you did not come near the land of the
Ammonites, nor to any place on the River Jab-
bok, nor to the cities in the hill country, nor to
any place the LORD our God had forbidden us.

King Og Defeated

3 Then we turned and went up the way
to Bashan, and Og, the king of Bashan,
came out against us, he and all his people, to
battle at Edrei. 2 Then the LORD said to me, "Do
not fear him, for I will deliver him and all his
people and his land into your hand; and you
shall do to him as you did to Sihon, king of the
Amorites, who lived at Heshbon."

3 So the LORD, our God, delivered Og, the king
of Bashan, with all his people, into our hands
also, and we struck him down until there was

2:25 Ex 15:14–16
2:26 Jos 13:18
2:27 Jdg 11:19
2:28 Nu 20:19
2:30 Ex 4:21
2:31 Dt 1:8
2:32 Nu 21:23–30
2:33 Dt 7:2
2:34 Dt 7:2
2:36 Jos 13:9
2:37 Ge 32:22
3:2 Nu 21:23–25
3:3 Nu 21:35

....

3:4 1Ki 4:13
3:6 Dt 2:34
3:7 Dt 2:35
3:9 1Ch 5:23
3:11 Ge 14:5
3:12 Dt 2:36
3:13 Nu 32:39–42
3:14 Nu 32:41
3:15 Nu 32:39–40
3:16 Nu 21:24
3:17 Jos 12:3
3:18 Jos 4:12–13
3:20 Jos 22:4

no survivor remaining. 4 We took all his cities
at that time. There was not a city which we
did not take from them: sixty cities, all the re-
gion of Argob, the kingdom of Og in Bashan.
5 All these cities were fortified with high walls,
gates, and bars, besides a great many rural
towns. 6 We utterly destroyed them, as we did
to Sihon, king of Heshbon, utterly destroying
the men, women, and children of every city.
7 But we took all the livestock and the spoil of
the cities as plunder for ourselves.

8 So at that time we took from the hand of
the two kings of the Amorites the land that
was across the Jordan, from the River Arnon
to Mount Hermon 9 (the Sidonians call Hermon
Sirion, and the Amorites call it Senir), 10 all
the cities of the plain, and all Gilead, and all
Bashan, as far as Salekah and Edrei, cities of
the kingdom of Og in Bashan. 11 For only Og,
king of Bashan, remained of the remnant of
the giants. (Notably, his bedstead was a bed-
stead of iron. Is it not in Rabbah of the chil-
dren of Ammon? It is nine cubits long and four
cubits wide,[1] according to the cubit of a man.)

Division of the Land

12 This is the land which we possessed at
that time from Aroer, which is by the River
Arnon, and half the hill country of Gilead and
its cities I gave to the Reubenites and to the
Gadites. 13 The rest of Gilead, and all Bashan,
the kingdom of Og, I gave to the half-tribe of
Manasseh. (All the region of Argob, with all
Bashan, was called the land of giants. 14 Jair,
the son of Manasseh, took all the region of
Argob, that is, Bashan, as far as the border of
the Geshurites and the Maakathites, and called
the villages after his own name, Havvoth Jair,
as it is to this day.) 15 I gave Gilead to Makir. 16 To
the Reubenites and to the Gadites I gave *the
territory* from Gilead even as far as the stream
bed of the River Arnon, half the valley as the
border to the River Jabbok, which is the border
of the Ammonites; 17 the plain also, with the
Jordan as the border, from Kinnereth as far
as the east side of the Sea of the Arabah (that
is, the Dead Sea), below the slopes of Pisgah.

18 Then I commanded you at that time, say-
ing, "The LORD your God has given you this
land to possess it. All you men of valor shall
pass over armed before your brothers, the
children of Israel. 19 But your wives and your
little ones, and your livestock (for I know that
you have much livestock) shall remain in your
cities which I have given you 20 until the LORD
has given rest to your brothers, as well as to
you, and until they also possess the land which

[1] *11* About 14 feet long and 6 feet wide, or 4 meters long and 1.8 meters wide.

the LORD your God has given them beyond the Jordan. Then each of you shall return to his possession which I have given you."

Moses Forbidden to Cross the Jordan

21 I commanded Joshua at that time, saying, "Your eyes have seen all that the LORD your God has done to these two kings. So shall the LORD do to all the kingdoms where you pass. 22 Do not fear them, for the LORD your God, He shall fight for you."

23 I pleaded with the LORD at that time, saying, 24 "O LORD God, You have begun to show Your servant Your greatness, and Your mighty hand, for what god is there in heaven or in earth that can do according to Your works and according to Your might? 25 Let me, I pray, go over and see the good land that is beyond the Jordan, that good hill country, and Lebanon."

26 But the LORD was angry with me because of you and would not listen to me, and the LORD said to me, "Enough of that! Speak to Me no more of this matter. 27 Get up to the top of Pisgah and lift up your eyes to the west and north and south and east, and see it with your eyes, for you shall not cross over this Jordan. 28 But charge Joshua and encourage him and strengthen him, for he shall cross over before this people, and he shall cause them to inherit the land which you will see." 29 So we remained in the valley over against Beth Peor.

Moses Commands Obedience

4 Now therefore, listen, O Israel, to the statutes and to the judgments which I am teaching you to do, so that you may live; and go in and possess the land which the LORD, the God of your fathers, is giving you. 2 You shall not add to the word which I am commanding you, nor shall you take anything from it, so that you may keep the commandments of the LORD your God which I command you.

3 Your eyes have seen what the LORD did at Baal Peor; for the LORD your God has destroyed from among you all the men who followed Baal of Peor. 4 But you who held fast to the LORD your God are alive to this day, every one of you.

5 See, I have taught you statutes and judgments, just as the LORD my God commanded me, that you should do so in the land where you are entering to possess it. 6 Therefore, keep and do *them*, for this is your wisdom and your understanding in the sight of the nations which shall hear all these statutes, and say, "Surely this great nation is a wise and understanding people." 7 For what nation is there so great, who has a god so near to it as the LORD our God is in all things whenever we call on Him? 8 And what nation is there so great that

3:22 Ex 14:14
3:24 Ex 15:11
3:25 Ex 3:8
3:26 Dt 1:37
3:27 Nu 27:12
3:28 Dt 31:3
3:29 Dt 4:46
4:1 Dt 8:1
4:2 Dt 12:32
4:3 Nu 25:1–9
4:6 Job 28:28
4:7 2Sa 7:23

....

4:9 Ge 18:19
4:10 Ex 19:9
4:11 Dt 5:23
4:12 Ex 20:22
4:13 Ex 34:28
4:15 Jos 23:11
4:17 Ro 1:23
4:19 Dt 17:3
4:20 1Ki 8:51
4:21 Dt 1:37
4:22 Dt 3:25
4:23 Dt 4:9

has statutes and judgments so righteous as all this law, which I am setting before you today?

9 Only give heed to yourself and keep your soul diligently, lest you forget the things which your eyes have seen and lest they depart from your heart all the days of your life; but teach them to your sons, and your grandsons. 10 Especially concerning the day you stood before the LORD your God at Horeb, when the LORD said to me, "Gather the people together to Me, so that I will let them hear My words so that they may learn to fear Me all the days they shall live on the earth, and so that they may teach their children." 11 Then you came near and stood at the foot of the mountain, and the mountain burned with fire up to the midst of heaven, with darkness, a cloud, a thick cloud. 12 Then the LORD spoke to you out of the midst of the fire. You heard the sound of the words but saw no form—only a voice was heard. 13 He declared to you His covenant, which He commanded you to perform, even the Ten Commandments, and He wrote them on two tablets of stone. 14 The LORD commanded me at that time to teach you statutes and judgments, so that you might do them in the land which you are crossing over to possess.

Idolatry Forbidden

15 Give good care to yourselves, for you saw no form on the day that the LORD spoke to you in Horeb from the midst of the fire, 16 lest you corrupt yourselves and make a graven image for yourselves in the form of any figure, the likeness of male or female, 17 the likeness of any beast that is on the earth, the likeness of any winged fowl that flies in the air, 18 the likeness of anything that creeps on the ground, the likeness of any fish that is in the waters beneath the earth. 19 And *beware*, lest you lift up your eyes to heaven, and when you see the sun, and the moon, and the stars, even all the host of heaven, you are led astray and worship them, and serve them, that which the LORD your God has allotted to all nations under the whole heaven. 20 But the LORD has taken you and brought you out of the iron furnace, from Egypt, to be to Him a people of inheritance, as you are today.

21 Furthermore, the LORD was angry with me because of you and swore that I should not cross over the Jordan, and that I would not go into that good land which the LORD your God is giving you for an inheritance. 22 So I must die in this land. I shall not cross over the Jordan, but you shall go over and possess that good land. 23 Watch yourselves, so that you do not forget the covenant of the LORD your God, which He made with you, and make yourself

a graven image or the likeness of anything as the LORD your God has forbidden you. 24 For the LORD your God is a consuming fire. He is a jealous God.

25 When you produce children and grandchildren and you have remained a long time in the land, and you corrupt yourselves and make a graven image, or the likeness of anything, and do evil in the sight of the LORD your God, to provoke Him to anger, 26 I call heaven and earth to witness against you today, that you will surely and suddenly perish from off the land that you are going across the Jordan to possess. You will not prolong your days on it, but shall be completely destroyed. 27 The LORD shall scatter you among the peoples, and you shall be left few in number among the nations where the LORD shall lead you. 28 There you will serve gods, the work of men's hands, wood and stone, which neither see nor hear nor eat nor smell. 29 But if from there you will seek the LORD your God, you will find Him, if you seek Him with all your heart and with all your soul. 30 When you are in distress and all these things come upon you, even in the latter days, if you turn to the LORD your God and shall be obedient to His voice 31 (for the LORD your God is a merciful God), He will not abandon you or destroy you or forget the covenant of your fathers which He swore to them.

I seek You, my God, with all my heart and soul (Dt 4:29).

32 Indeed, ask about the days that are past, which were before you, since the day that God created man[1] on the earth, and ask from one end of heavens to the other, whether there has ever been any such thing as this great thing, or has *anything* like it ever been heard? 33 Has a people ever heard the voice of God speaking out of the midst of the fire, as you have heard, and lived? 34 Or has God ever tried to take for Himself a nation from the midst of another nation, by trials, by signs, and by wonders, and by war, and by a mighty hand, and by a stretched-out arm, and by great terrors, according to all that the LORD your God did for you in Egypt before your eyes?

35 To you it was shown so that you might know that the LORD, He is God. There is no one else besides Him. 36 Out of heaven He let you hear His voice so that He might instruct you, and on earth He showed you His great fire, and you heard His words out of the midst of the fire. 37 Because He loved your fathers, therefore He chose their descendants after them and personally brought you out of Egypt with His mighty power 38 to drive out nations from before you greater and mightier than you are, to bring you in, to give you their land for an inheritance, as it is today.

39 Know therefore today, and consider it in your heart, that the LORD, He is God in heaven above and on the earth below. There is no other. 40 Therefore, you shall keep His statutes and His commandments which I command you this day, so that it may go well with you and with your children after you, and so that you may prolong your days in the land, which the LORD your God gives you, forever.

Cities of Refuge
Nu 35:6–34; Dt 19:1–14; Jos 20:1–9

41 Then Moses set apart three cities across the Jordan, toward the east, 42 that the manslayer might flee there, that is, anyone who killed his neighbor unintentionally without hating him in time past could flee to one of these cities and live: 43 Bezer in the wilderness in the plateau of the Reubenites, and Ramoth in Gilead of the Gadites, and Golan in Bashan of the Manassites.

Introduction to the Law

44 This is the law which Moses set before the children of Israel. 45 These are the testimonies, and the statutes, and the ordinances which Moses spoke to the children of Israel, after they came out of Egypt, 46 on this side of the Jordan, in the valley over against Beth Peor, in the land of Sihon, king of the Amorites, who lived at Heshbon, whom Moses and the children of Israel struck down, after they had come out of Egypt. 47 They possessed his land, and the land of Og, king of Bashan, the two kings of the Amorites, who were across the Jordan toward the east, 48 from Aroer, which is by the edge of the River Arnon, even as far as Mount Sion (that is, Hermon), 49 with all the Arabah across the Jordan to the east, even to the sea of the Arabah, under the slopes of Pisgah.

The Ten Commandments
Ex 20:1–17

5 Then Moses called all Israel and said to them: Hear, O Israel, the statutes and ordinances which I am speaking in your hearing today, so that you may learn them, and keep, and do them. 2 The LORD our God made a covenant with us in Horeb. 3 The LORD did not make this covenant with our fathers, but with us, we who are living now and here today. 4 The LORD talked with you face to face on the mountain from the midst of the fire. 5 I stood between the LORD and you at that time to declare to you the word of the LORD; for you were afraid

4:24 Ex 24:17
4:25 Dt 4:16
4:26 Isa 1:2
4:27 Lev 26:33
4:28 Dt 28:36
4:29 2Ch 15:4
4:30 Dt 31:29
4:31 2Ch 30:9
4:32 Job 8:8
4:34 Dt 26:8
4:35 1Sa 2:2
4:36 Ex 19:9
4:37 Dt 10:15
4:38 Dt 7:1
4:39 Jos 2:11
4:40 Lev 22:31
4:41 Nu 35:6
4:43 Jos 20:8
4:46 Dt 3:29
4:48 Dt 3:9
4:49 Dt 3:17
5:2 Dt 4:23
5:4 Dt 4:33
5:5 Gal 3:19

[1] 32 Or *Adam*.

SPIRITLED WOMAN

COUNSEL FROM THE SPIRIT BASICS

The Color of Hope

Many people only recognize each other's faults rather than choosing to see the image of God. Hope colors the way we see each other. Grace is the lens through which we must see one another. When we see someone, we look beyond the evil of the past. We have to look through the blood of Jesus into the heart of every man—we have to peer through the eyes of the Master.

Jesus is altogether lovely, never withholding mercy, and always extending kindness: "But showing mercy to thousands of them that love Me and keep My commandments" (Dt 5:10). He commands us to forgive seventy times seven, telling us that love always "bears all things, believes all things, hopes all things, and endures all things" (1Co 13:7). His blood is more than enough.

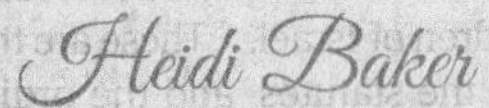

because of the fire and would not go up to the mountain. He said:

[6] I am the LORD, your God, who brought you out of the land of Egypt, from the house of bondage.
[7] You shall have no other gods before Me.
[8] You shall not make yourself any graven image, or any likeness of anything that is in heaven above, or that is in the earth beneath, or that is in the waters beneath the earth; [9] you shall not bow down to them, nor serve them. For I, the LORD your God, am a jealous God, visiting the iniquity of the fathers on the children, and on the third and fourth generations of those who hate Me, [10] but showing mercy to thousands of them that love Me and keep My commandments.
[11] You shall not take the name of the LORD your God in vain, for the LORD will not exonerate anyone who takes His name in vain.
[12] Keep the Sabbath day, to keep it holy, just as the LORD your God has commanded you. [13] Six days you shall labor and do all your work, [14] but the seventh day is the Sabbath of the LORD your God. *On it* you shall not do any work: you, nor your son, nor your daughter, nor your male servant, nor your female servant, nor your ox, nor your donkey, nor any of your livestock, nor the foreigner that is within your gates, so that your male servant and your female servant may rest as well as you. [15] Remember that you were a servant in the land of Egypt, and that the LORD your God brought you out from there with a mighty hand and by an outstretched arm; therefore your God commanded you to keep the Sabbath day.
[16] Honor your father and your mother, just as the LORD your God has commanded you, that your days may be prolonged, and that it may go well with you in the land which the LORD your God is giving you.
[17] You shall not murder.
[18] You shall not commit adultery.
[19] You shall not steal.
[20] You shall not bear false witness against your neighbor.
[21] You shall not covet your neighbor's wife, nor shall you covet your neighbor's house, his field, his male servant, his female servant, his ox, his donkey, or anything that belongs to your neighbor.

[22] These are the words the LORD spoke to all your assembly at the mountain out from the midst of the fire, the cloud, and the thick darkness with a great voice, and He added no more. He wrote them on two tablets of stone and gave them to me.

[23] When you heard the voice out of the midst of the darkness, while the mountain did burn with fire, you came near to me, all the heads of your tribes, and your elders. [24] You said, "See, the LORD our God has shown us His glory and His greatness, and we have heard His voice from the midst of the fire. We have seen this day that God speaks with man, yet he lives. [25] Now, therefore, why should we die? For this great fire will consume us. If we hear the voice of the LORD our God any more, then we will die. [26] For who is there of all flesh who has heard the voice of the living God speaking out of the midst of the fire, as we have, and lived? [27] Go near and hear all that the LORD our God will say. Then speak to us all that the LORD our God will speak to you, and we will hear and do it."

[28] The LORD heard the sound of your words when you spoke to me, and the LORD said to me, "I have heard the sound of the words of this people which they have spoken to you. They have done well in all that they have spoken. [29] O that there were such a heart in them that they would fear Me and always keep all My commandments, that it might be well with them and with their children forever!

5:6 Ex 20:2–17
5:7 Ex 20:3
5:8 Ex 20:4
5:9 Ex 34:7
5:10 Jer 32:18
5:11 Lev 19:12
5:12 Ex 20:8–11
5:14 Heb 4:4
5:16 Ex 20:12
5:17 Ex 20:13
5:18 Ex 20:14
5:19 Ex 20:15
5:21 Ro 13:9
5:22 Ex 24:12
5:24 Ex 19:19
5:25 Dt 18:16
5:26 Dt 4:33
5:27 Ex 20:19
5:28 Dt 18:17
5:29 Isa 48:18

30 "Go say to them, 'Return to your tents.'
31 But as for you, stand here by Me, so that
I may speak to you all the commandments,
and the statutes, and the ordinances which you
shall teach them, that they may keep them in
the land which I am giving them to possess."
32 Therefore, be careful to do as the LORD your
God has commanded you. You shall not turn
aside to the right hand or to the left. 33 You
shall walk in all the ways which the LORD your
God has commanded you, so that you may
live and that it may be well with you, and that
you may prolong *your* days in the land which
you shall possess.

The Greatest Commandment

6 Now these are the commandments, the
statutes, and the ordinances which the
LORD your God commanded to teach you, so
that you may observe them in the land which
you are crossing over to possess, 2 so that
you might fear the LORD your God in order to
keep all His statutes and His commandments
which I command you—you, and your son,
and your grandson—all the days of your life,
so that your days may be prolonged. 3 Hear
therefore, O Israel, and be careful to do it, so
that it may be well with you and so that you
may multiply greatly, as the LORD the God of
your fathers has promised you in the land that
flows with milk and honey.
4 Hear, O Israel: The LORD is our God. The
LORD is one! 5 And you shall love the LORD your
God with all your heart and with all your soul
and with all your might. 6 These words, which
I am commanding you today, shall be in your
heart. 7 You shall teach them diligently to your
children and shall talk of them when you sit
in your house, and when you walk by the way,
and when you lie down, and when you rise up.
8 You shall bind them as a sign on your hand,
and they shall be as frontlets between your
eyes. 9 You shall write them on the doorposts
of your house and on your gates.

As I fill my heart and obey the Word of God and His wisdom, my house will always be full of good things (Dt 6:6–11).

10 Then it shall be when the LORD your God
brings you into the land which He swore to
your fathers, to Abraham, Isaac, and Jacob,
to give you great and fine cities, which you
did not build, 11 and houses full of all good
things which you did not fill, and hewn cis-
terns which you did not dig, vineyards and
olive trees which you did not plant, and you
eat and are full, 12 then beware lest you forget
the LORD who brought you out of the land of
Egypt, out of the house of bondage.
13 You shall fear the LORD your God and serve
Him and shall swear by His name. 14 You shall
not go after other gods, the gods of the people
which surround you 15 (for the LORD your God
is a jealous God among you). Otherwise the
anger of the LORD your God will be inflamed
against you and destroy you from off the face
of the earth. 16 You shall not tempt the LORD
your God, as you tempted *Him* in Massah.
17 You shall diligently keep the commandments
of the LORD your God, and His testimonies and
His statutes which He has commanded you.
18 You shall do what is right and good in the
sight of the LORD that it may be well with you
and that you may go in and possess the good
land which the LORD swore to your fathers, 19 to
drive out all your enemies before you, just as
the LORD has spoken.
20 When your son asks you in time to come,
saying, "What do the testimonies and the
statutes and the judgments mean which the
LORD our God has commanded you?" 21 then
you shall say to your son, "We were slaves of
Pharaoh in Egypt, and the LORD brought us out
of Egypt with a mighty hand. 22 And the LORD
showed great and devastating signs and won-
ders upon Egypt, upon Pharaoh, and upon all
his household before our eyes. 23 He brought
us out from there, so that He might bring us
in, to give us the land which He swore to our
fathers. 24 The LORD commanded us to do all
these statutes, to fear the LORD our God, for our
good always, that He might preserve us, as He
has to this day. 25 It will be our righteousness
if we are careful to keep all these command-
ments before the LORD our God, just as He has
commanded us."

The Chosen People

7 When the LORD your God brings you into
the land which you are entering to possess
and has driven out many nations before you,
the Hittites and the Girgashites and the Amor-
ites and the Canaanites and the Perizzites and
the Hivites and the Jebusites, seven nations
greater and mightier than you, 2 and when the
LORD your God delivers them before you and
you strike them down, then you must utter-
ly destroy them. You shall make no covenant
with them nor show mercy to them. 3 What is
more, you shall not intermarry with them. You
shall not give your daughters to their sons or
take their daughters for your sons. 4 For they
will turn your sons away from following Me
to serve other gods. Then the anger of the
LORD will be inflamed against you, and He will

5:31 Gal 3:19
5:32 Dt 17:20
5:33 Jer 7:23
6:2 Ex 20:20
6:3 Ex 3:8
6:4 Jn 17:3
6:5 Mt 22:37
6:6 Dt 11:18
6:7 Dt 11:19
6:8 Ex 13:9
6:9 Dt 11:20
6:10 Jos 24:13
6:13 Dt 10:20
6:14 Jer 25:6
6:15 Dt 4:24
6:16 Ex 17:7
6:17 Dt 11:22
6:18 Dt 4:40
6:20 Ex 13:14
6:21 Ex 20:2
6:24 Ps 41:2
6:25 Dt 24:13
7:1 Dt 4:38
7:2 Dt 23:14
7:3 Ex 34:15–16
7:4 Dt 6:15

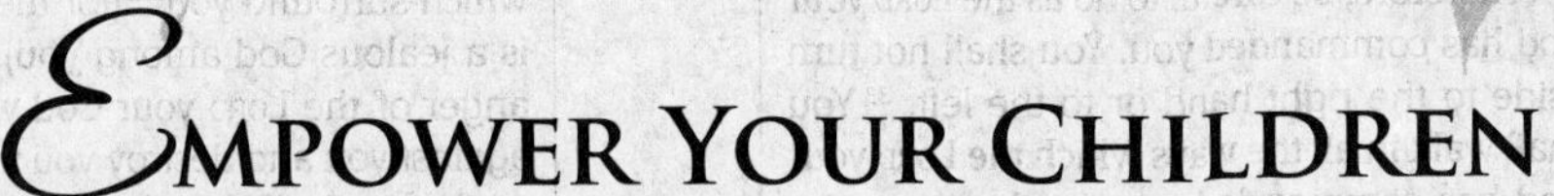

Empower Your Children

These words, which I am commanding you today, shall be in your heart. You shall teach them diligently to your children and shall talk of them when you sit in your house, and when you walk by the way, and when you lie down, and when you rise up. You shall bind them as a sign on your hand, and they shall be as frontlets between your eyes. You shall write them on the doorposts of your house and on your gates.

—Deuteronomy 6:6–9

Take a little time each day to pray and practice this advice. You will reap wonderful consequences. Train your children using God's precepts, and you will have a peaceful home.

On each line below, write how you will practice each statement of advice.

1. Teach them to bless and keep promises.

2. Lead them to welcome Jesus into their hearts.

3. Empower them to pray.

4. Teach them how to know Satan's tactics.

5. Teach them obedience.

6. Empower them to know the Holy Spirit.

7. Empower them by applying sound correction.

8. Teach them how to work.

9. Teach them how to be positive.

10. Teach them how to defend themselves.

Decide today that you will make your life count. Your children will thank you when they become older. Teach your children how to defend themselves and not be afraid of the enemy!

Iris Delgado

quickly destroy you. 5 But this is how you shall
deal with them: You shall destroy their altars
and break down their images and cut down
their Asherim[1] and burn their graven images
with fire. 6 For you are a holy people to the
LORD your God. The LORD your God has chosen
you to be His special people, treasured above
all peoples who are on the face of the earth.

> Let the idols and images of the land be broken by Your power, O Lord (Dt 7:5).

7 The LORD did not set His love on you nor
choose you because you were more in number
than any of the peoples, for you were the
fewest of all the peoples. 8 But it is because
the LORD loved you and because He kept the
oath which He swore to your fathers. The LORD
brought you out with a mighty hand and redeemed
you out of the house of slavery, from
the hand of Pharaoh, king of Egypt. 9 Know
therefore that the LORD your God, He is God, the
faithful God, who keeps covenant and mercy
with them who love Him and keep His commandments
to a thousand generations, 10 yet
He repays those who hate Him to their face,
to destroy them. He will not be slack with him
who hates Him. He will repay him to his face.
11 Therefore keep the commandments and the
statutes and the judgments which I command
you today, by doing them.

12 If you listen to these judgments, keep
them, and do them, then the LORD your God
shall keep with you the covenant and the mercy
which He swore to your fathers. 13 He will
love you and bless you and multiply you. He
will also bless the fruit of your womb and the
fruit of your land, your grain, and your wine,
and your oil, the increase of your herd and
the young of your flock, in the land which He
swore to your fathers to give you. 14 You shall
be blessed above all peoples. There will not be
male or female barren among you or among
your livestock. 15 The LORD will take away from
you all sickness, and will afflict you with none
of the evil diseases of Egypt, which you know,
but will lay them on all those who hate you.
16 You must consume all the peoples whom
the LORD your God will deliver to you. Your eye
shall have no pity on them, nor shall you serve
their gods, for that will be a snare to you.

17 If you say in your heart, "These nations are
greater than I—how can I dispossess them?"
18 you shall not be afraid of them. You must
surely remember what the LORD your God did
to Pharaoh and to all Egypt, 19 the great trials
which your eyes saw, and the signs, and
the wonders, and the mighty hand, and the
stretched-out arm, by which the LORD your God
brought you out. So the LORD your God will
do to all the peoples of whom you are afraid.
20 Moreover the LORD your God will send the
hornet among them, until they who are left
and hide themselves from you perish. 21 You
must not be frightened of them, for the LORD
your God is among you, a great and awesome
God. 22 The LORD your God will drive out those
nations before you, little by little. You will
not be able to destroy them all at once, lest
the beasts of the field become too numerous
for you. 23 But the LORD your God will deliver
them to you and will throw them into a great
confusion until they are destroyed. 24 He will
deliver their kings into your hand so that you
may erase their names from under heaven.
No man will be able to stand before you until
you have destroyed them. 25 You must burn
the graven images of their gods with fire. You
must not desire the silver or gold that is on
them nor take any of it, lest you be snared by
them, for it is an abomination to the LORD your
God. 26 You shall not bring an abomination into
your house, lest you become cursed like it, but
you must absolutely detest and abhor it, for it
is a cursed thing.

Remember the LORD Your God

8 You must carefully keep all the commandments
that I am commanding you today,
so that you may live, and multiply, and go in
and possess the land which the LORD swore to
your fathers. 2 You must remember that the
LORD your God led you all the way these forty
years in the wilderness, to humble you, and
to prove you, to know what was in your heart,
whether you would keep His commandments
or not. 3 He humbled you and let you suffer
hunger, and fed you with manna, which you
did not know, nor did your fathers know, that
He might make you know that man does not
live by bread alone; but man lives by every
word that proceeds out of the mouth of the
LORD. 4 Your clothing did not wear out on you,
nor did your feet swell these forty years. 5 You
must also consider in your heart that, as a man
disciplines his son, so the LORD your God disciplines
you.

6 Therefore you must keep the commandments
of the LORD your God, to walk in His
ways and to fear Him. 7 For the LORD your God
is bringing you into a good land, a land of
brooks of water, of fountains and springs that
flow out of valleys and hills, 8 a land of wheat,
barley, vines, fig trees, and pomegranates, a

7:5 Ex 23:24
7:6 Dt 14:2
7:7 Dt 10:22
7:8 Ex 32:13
7:9 Da 9:4
7:10 Isa 59:18
7:13 Jn 14:21
7:14 Ps 127:3
7:15 Ex 15:26
7:16 Ex 23:33
7:17 Nu 33:53
7:18 Ps 105:5

7:19 Dt 4:34
7:20 Jos 24:12
7:21 Dt 10:17
7:22 Ex 23:29–30
7:24 Jos 23:9
7:25 Ex 32:20
7:26 Dt 13:17
8:1 Dt 4:1
8:2 Am 2:10
8:3 Mt 4:4
8:4 Dt 29:5
8:5 2Sa 7:14
8:6 Dt 5:33

[1] 5 Or *groves*, referring to wooden symbols of a female deity.

SpiritLed Homeschooling

My husband and I made a decision when our daughter was young we weren't going to go along with the culture just because it was cool. And that's a big reason why we homeschooled Franny for most of her school years. It was just too important to us she not be influenced unduly by the culture and peer pressure.

I realize it's not practical or even possible for every family to homeschool, but if it is possible, I highly recommend looking into it. You remove an awful lot of influences from your children's lives and enable them to grow and learn in a safe, innocent, and parent-directed atmosphere when you homeschool. I love this scripture in Deuteronomy:

> These words, which I am commanding you today, shall be in your heart. You shall teach them diligently to your children and shall talk of them when you sit in your house, and when you walk by the way, and when you lie down, and when you rise up. You shall bind them as a sign on your hand, and they shall be as frontlets between your eyes. You shall write them on the doorposts of your house and on your gates.
>
> —Deuteronomy 6:6–9

This scripture assumes a parent is able to be with her children every day, day in and day out. It speaks of being able to continually have conversations about the things of God in the everyday of daily life.

Successful adults don't happen by accident. It takes intentional effort to raise a child into an adult who has a strong sense of their destiny in God, a passion to serve Him, and a deep knowledge of His gifts and callings. Parents, we know our children better than anyone else. By partnering with God, we can equip them to be all He called and created them to be. It's up to us to equip (not push or apply undue pressure) our children to go after their dreams.

Proverbs 22:6 says, "Train up a child in the way he should go, and when he is old he will not depart from it." These treasured words teach that we have a responsibility. We have to do the training. We will see the "way they should go." God will clearly show it to us. And we will lead them in that way.

Now that my daughter is a grown woman, she can look back at her childhood years and recognize the blessing of parents who sacrificed their own time and agenda to pour their lives into the training of their child. She writes: "I was blessed to have a dad who worked from home, a mom who homeschooled me, and a childhood full of some remarkable experiences. Whether it was getting to be involved in professional theater from the age of twelve on, taking hours and hours of ballet classes (my first love), going on trips to some incredible cities and countries around the world, going to ministry events with my mom, or learning how to cook from the world's greatest chef (also my mom), I have many memories from those years that I cherish. Life in those days felt like one giant adventure."

Raising a child to be a world-changer in any field takes discipline, time, diligence, and patience. As parents our actions greatly determine a child's ability to reach the full potential God designed for them.

Kate Battistelli

land of olive oil and honey, 9 a land where you may eat bread without scarcity, in which you will not lack anything, a land whose stones are iron, and out of whose hills you may dig copper.

> Bring me into a good land without scarcity or lack (Dt 8:9).

10 When you have eaten and are full, then you shall bless the LORD your God for the good land which He has given you. 11 Beware that you do not forget the LORD your God by not keeping His commandments, and His judgments, and His statutes, which I am commanding you today. 12 Otherwise, when you have eaten and are full and have built and occupied good houses, 13 and when your herds and your flocks multiply, and your silver and your gold multiply, and all that you have multiplies, 14 then your heart will become proud and you will forget the LORD your God who brought you out of the land of Egypt, from the house of slavery, 15 who led you through that great and terrible wilderness, where there were fiery serpents and scorpions and drought, where there was no water, who brought forth for you water out of the rock of flint, 16 who fed you in the wilderness with manna, which your fathers did not know, that He might humble you and that He might prove you, to do good for you in the end. 17 Otherwise, you may say in your heart, "My power and the might of my hand have gained me this wealth." 18 But you must remember the LORD your God, for it is He who gives you the ability to get wealth, so that He may establish His covenant which He swore to your fathers, as it is today.

19 If you ever forget the LORD your God and go after other gods and serve them and worship them, then I testify against you today that you will surely perish. 20 Just like the nations which the LORD will destroy before you, so shall you perish because you would not be obedient to the voice of the LORD your God.

Not Because of Righteousness

9 Hear, O Israel! You are to cross over the Jordan today, to go in to possess nations greater and mightier than you, great cities fortified up to heaven, 2 a great and tall people, the children of the Anakites, whom you know and of whom you have heard *it* said, "Who can stand before the children of Anak?" 3 Understand therefore today that the LORD your God is He who goes over before you as a consuming fire. He shall destroy them and shall bring them down before you, so that you drive them out and destroy them quickly, as the LORD has spoken to you.

4 Do not say in your heart, after the LORD your God has driven them out before you, "On account of my righteousness the LORD has brought me in to possess this land," but it is because of the wickedness of these nations the LORD is driving them out before you. 5 It is not because of your righteousness or the uprightness of your heart that you enter to possess their land, but because of the wickedness of these nations that the LORD your God drives them out before you, and that He may fulfill the word which the LORD swore to your fathers, Abraham, Isaac, and Jacob. 6 Understand, therefore, that the LORD your God is not giving you this good land to possess on account of your righteousness, for you are a stubborn people.

The Golden Calf

7 Remember, and do not forget how you provoked the LORD your God to wrath in the wilderness. From the day that you departed out of the land of Egypt until you came to this place, you have been rebellious against the LORD. 8 Also in Horeb you provoked the LORD to wrath, so that the LORD was angry enough with you to destroy you. 9 When I went up into the mountain to receive the tablets of stone, the tablets of the covenant which the LORD made with you, then I remained on the mountain forty days and forty nights. I did not eat bread or drink water. 10 The LORD delivered to me two tablets of stone, written with the finger of God, and on them was written all the words which the LORD spoke to you at the mountain out of the midst of the fire on the day of the assembly.

11 At the end of forty days and forty nights, the LORD gave me the two tablets of stone, the tablets of the covenant. 12 Then the LORD said to me, "Arise, go down from here quickly, for your people whom you brought out of Egypt have corrupted themselves. They are quickly turned aside from the way which I commanded them. They have made a molded image for themselves."

13 Furthermore the LORD spoke to me, saying, "I have seen this people, and indeed, they are a stubborn people. 14 Let Me alone, so that I may destroy them and blot out their name from under heaven, and I will make of you a nation mightier and greater than they."

15 So I returned and came down from the mount, and the mount burned with fire, and the two tablets of the covenant were in my two hands. 16 I looked, and indeed, you had sinned against the LORD your God and had made yourselves a molded calf. You had quickly turned

8:10 Ps 103:2
8:12 Pr 30:9
8:14 Ps 106:21
8:15 Nu 20:11
8:16 Ex 16:15
8:17 Dt 9:4
8:18 Pr 10:22
8:19 Dt 4:26
8:20 Da 9:11–12
9:1 Dt 4:38
9:2 Nu 13:22
9:3 Dt 4:24
9:4 Dt 8:17
9:5 Titus 3:5
9:6 Dt 9:13
9:9 Ex 34:28
9:10 Ex 31:18
9:11 Dt 9:9
9:12 Ex 32:7–8
9:13 Dt 9:6
9:14 Dt 29:20
9:15 Ex 19:18
9:16 Ex 32:19

aside out of the way which the LORD had com-
manded you. 17 I took the two tablets and threw
them out of my two hands and broke them
before your eyes.

18 I fell down before the LORD, as at the first,
forty days and forty nights. I did not eat bread
or drink water because of all your sins which
you committed, doing what was wicked in
the sight of the LORD to provoke Him to anger.
19 For I was afraid of the anger and hot displea-
sure with which the LORD was wrathful against
you to destroy you. But the LORD listened to me
at that time also. 20 The LORD was angry enough
with Aaron to destroy him, so I also prayed for
Aaron at the same time. 21 I took your sin, the
calf which you had made, and burned it with
fire, and crushed it, and ground it very small
until it was as small as dust. Then I threw the
dust into the brook that descended down from
the mountain.

22 Also at Taberah and at Massah and at
Kibroth Hattaavah you provoked the LORD to
wrath.

23 Likewise when the LORD sent you from
Kadesh Barnea, saying, "Go up and possess
the land which I have given you," then you
rebelled against the commandment of the LORD
your God, and you did not believe Him or lis-
ten to His voice. 24 You have been rebellious
against the LORD from the day I knew you.

25 So I fell down before the LORD forty days
and forty nights; I fell down because the LORD
had said He would destroy you. 26 I prayed
therefore to the LORD, and said, "O Lord GOD,
do not destroy Your people, Your inheritance,
which You have redeemed through Your great-
ness, which You have brought out of Egypt
with a mighty hand. 27 Remember Your ser-
vants, Abraham, Isaac, and Jacob. Do not look
at the stubbornness of this people or at their
wickedness or their sin. 28 Otherwise, the land
from which You brought us may say, 'Because
the LORD was not able to bring them into the
land which He promised them and because
He hated them, He has brought them out to
slay them in the wilderness.' 29 Yet they are
Your people, Your inheritance, whom You
brought out by Your mighty power and by Your
stretched-out arm."

The Second Pair of Tablets

10 At that time the LORD said to me, "Cut
out for yourself two tablets of stone like
the first and come up to Me onto the mountain
and make an ark of wood for yourself. 2 I will
write on the tablets the words that were on the
first tablets which you broke, and you shall put
them in the ark."

3 So I made an ark of acacia wood and cut
out two tablets of stone just like the first and
went up onto the mountain with the two tab-
lets in my hand. 4 He wrote on the tablets just
like the first writing, the Ten Commandments
which the LORD spoke to you at the mountain
out of the midst of the fire on the day of the
assembly, and the LORD gave them to me.
5 I turned around and came down from the
mountain and put the tablets in the ark which
I had made, and there they are, just as the LORD
commanded me.

6 (The children of Israel set out from Beeroth
of the sons of Jaakan to Moserah. There Aar-
on died and was buried, and his son Eleazar
ministered in the priest's office in his place.
7 From there they journeyed to Gudgodah, and
from Gudgodah to Jotbathah, a land of rivers
of waters. 8 At that time the LORD set apart the
tribe of Levi to carry the ark of the covenant of
the LORD, to stand before the LORD to minister
to Him, and to bless in His name, to this day.
9 Therefore, Levi has no portion or inheritance
with his brothers. The LORD is his inheritance,
just as the LORD your God promised him.)

10 As for me, I stayed on the mountain like
the first time, forty days and forty nights, and
the LORD listened to me at that time also. The
LORD was not willing to destroy you. 11 The LORD
said to me, "Arise, take your journey before the
people, so that they may go in and possess the
land which I swore to give to their fathers."

The Essence of the Law

12 Now, Israel, what does the LORD your God
require of you, but to fear the LORD your God,
to walk in all His ways, and to love Him, and
to serve the LORD your God with all your heart
and with all your soul, 13 to keep the command-
ments of the LORD and His statutes which I am
commanding you today for your good?

14 Indeed, heaven and the highest heavens
belong to the LORD your God, also the earth
with all that is in it. 15 The LORD delighted only
in your fathers, to love them; and He chose
their descendants after them, *even* you above
all people, as *it* is today. 16 Therefore, circum-
cise your heart, and do not be stubborn any-
more. 17 For the LORD your God is the God of
gods and Lord of lords, the great, the mighty,
and the fearsome God who is unbiased and
takes no bribe. 18 He executes the judgment of
the orphan and the widow and loves the for-
eigner, giving him food and clothing. 19 There-
fore, love the foreigner, for you were foreigners
in the land of Egypt. 20 You must fear the LORD
your God. You must serve Him and cling to
Him, and swear by His name. 21 He is your
praise, and He is your God, who has done for

9:18 Ex 34:28
9:19 Dt 10:10
9:21 Ex 32:20
9:22 Ex 17:7
9:23 Ps 106:24–25
9:24 Dt 31:27
9:25 Dt 9:18
9:26 Ex 32:11–13
9:28 Nu 14:16
9:29 Dt 4:20
10:1 Ex 34:1–2
10:3 Ex 34:4
10:4 Dt 9:10
10:5 Ex 34:29
10:6 Nu 33:38
10:8 Dt 18:5
10:9 Dt 18:1–2
10:10 Ex 34:28
10:12 Dt 6:5
10:13 Dt 6:24
10:14 1Ki 8:27
10:15 Dt 4:37
10:16 Dt 9:6
10:17 Jos 22:22
10:18 Ps 68:5
10:19 Ex 22:21
10:20 Dt 13:4
10:21 Jer 17:14

SPIRIT-TO-SPIRIT PRAYER

Breaking the Power of Generational Curses

Lord, we have come before You as a family. Where there has been generational curses of bondage, we repent on behalf of ourselves and our ancestors for allowing those patterns to be established. Where there has been family involvement in the occult, including freemasonry, Hinduism, Buddhism, shamanism, or witchcraft, we confess this as sin and repent. We break the power of all witchcraft, antichrist and lying spirits, and spirits of mammon. We renounce all generational curses attached to these occult practices and ask that all of these issues be now washed over by Your blood. We say that all generational curses are broken off of the lives of our family. We sever generational curses and unholy soul ties that have been in operation between our family and all past family members, in the name of Jesus.

Lord, Your Word says, "Listen diligently to Me, and eat what is good, and let your soul delight itself in abundance" (Isa 55:2). Today we choose to fill our souls with Your goodness and not the things of this world. We as a family choose to walk in Your ways and Your paths so we will find rest for our souls. Where there has been bondage, we speak and release freedom. We are not victims but victors in Christ. Where there has been witchcraft, divination, and antichrist spirits, we speak truth and the freedom of the Holy Spirit to move in our lives and to fill us up to overflowing.

Rebecca Greenwood

you these great and fearsome things which
your eyes have seen. [22] Your fathers went down
into Egypt with seventy people, and now the
LORD your God has made you as numerous as
the stars of heaven.

Love and Obey

11 You must love the LORD your God and
keep His charge, His statutes, His or-
dinances, and His commandments always.
[2] Know this day that I am not speaking with
your children who have not known and who
have not seen the discipline of the LORD your
God, His greatness, His mighty hand, and
His outstretched arm, [3] and His signs and His
works which He did in the midst of Egypt to
Pharaoh, the king of Egypt, and to all his land,
[4] and what He did to the army of Egypt, to their
horses, and to their chariots, when He made
the water of the Red Sea to flow over them as
they pursued after you, and how the LORD ut-
terly destroyed them, [5] and what He did to you
in the wilderness until you came to this place,
[6] and what He did to Dathan and Abiram, the
sons of Eliab, the son of Reuben, when the
earth opened its mouth and swallowed them
up, their households, their tents, and every-
thing that was in their possession, in the midst
of all Israel. [7] But your eyes have seen all the
great deeds of the LORD which He did.

[8] Therefore you must keep all the command-
ments which I am commanding you today, so
that you may be strong and go in and possess
the land which you are going to possess; [9] and
that you may prolong your days in the land
which the LORD swore to your fathers to give to
them and to their descendants, a land flowing
with milk and honey. [10] For the land which you
are entering to possess is not like the land of
Egypt from where you came, where you sowed
your seed and watered it with your foot like a
vegetable garden, [11] but the land, which you
are entering to possess, is a land of hills and
valleys and drinks water from the rain of heav-
en, [12] a land for which the LORD your God cares.
The eyes of the LORD your God are always on
it, from the beginning of the year even to the
end of the year.

10:22 Ge 15:5
11:1 Dt 6:5
11:2 Dt 5:24
11:3 Dt 7:19
11:6 Ps 106:17

……

11:8 Jos 1:6–7
11:9 Ex 3:8
11:12 1Ki 9:3

13 It will be, if you will diligently obey My
commandments which I am commanding you
today, to love the LORD your God, and to serve
Him with all your heart and with all your soul,
14 then I will give you the rain of your land in
its season, the early rain and the latter rain,
that you may gather in your grain and your
wine and your oil. 15 I will provide grass in your
fields for your livestock, that you may eat and
be full.

16 Take heed to yourselves that your heart be
not deceived, and you turn away and serve
other gods and worship them. 17 Then the
LORD's wrath will be inflamed against you, and
He will shut up the heavens so that there will
be no rain and the land will not yield its fruit,
and you will quickly perish from the good land
which the LORD is giving you. 18 Therefore you
must fix these words of mine in your heart
and in your soul, and bind them as a sign on
your hand, so that they may be as frontlets
between your eyes. 19 You shall teach them to
your children, speaking of them when you sit
in your house and when you walk by the way,
when you lie down, and when you rise up.
20 You shall write them on the doorposts of
your house and on your gates, 21 so that your
days and the days of your children may be
multiplied in the land which the LORD swore to
your fathers to give them, as long as the days
of heaven on the earth.

I choose blessing instead of cursing and life instead of death (Dt 11:26).

22 For if you diligently keep all these com-
mandments which I am commanding you to
do—to love the LORD your God, to walk in all
His ways, and to hold fast to Him— 23 then the
LORD will drive out all these nations from before
you, and you will dispossess nations greater
and mightier than you. 24 Every place where
the soles of your feet tread will be yours. Your
border will be from the wilderness to Lebanon,
from the river, the River Euphrates, as far as
the *Mediterranean* Sea. 25 No man will be able
to resist you, for the LORD your God shall lay
the fear of you and the dread of you on all
the land where you shall tread, just as He has
spoken to you.

I am blessed because I obey the commandments of the Lord (Dt 11:27).

26 See, I am setting before you today a bless-
ing and a curse: 27 the blessing if you obey the
commandments of the LORD your God, which
I am commanding you today, 28 and the curse,
if you will not obey the commandments of the
LORD your God, but turn from the way which I
am commanding you today, to go after other
gods which you have not known. 29 Now it shall
be, when the LORD your God has brought you
into the land which you are entering to pos-
sess, that you shall put the blessing on Mount
Gerizim and the curse on Mount Ebal. 30 Are
they not on the other side of the Jordan, west
where the sun goes down, in the land of the
Canaanites, who dwell in the plain opposite
Gilgal, beside the oaks of Moreh? 31 For you
will cross over the Jordan to go in to possess
the land which the LORD your God is giving you,
and you will possess it, and dwell in it. 32 You
must be careful to do all the statutes and judg-
ments which I am setting before you today.

The One Place of Worship

12 These are the statutes and judgments
which you shall be careful to observe
in the land, which the LORD, the God of your
fathers, has given you to possess, all the days
that you live on the earth. 2 You must utterly
destroy all the places where the nations which
you will possess served their gods, on the high
mountains, and on the hills, and under every
green tree. 3 And you shall overthrow their
altars, and break their pillars, and burn their
Asherah poles[1] with fire, and you shall cut
down the engraved images of their gods, and
eliminate their names out of that place.
4 You shall not act this way toward the LORD
your God. 5 But you must seek only the place
which the LORD your God shall choose out of
all your tribes to establish His name, and there
you must go. 6 There you shall bring your burnt
offerings, your sacrifices, your tithes, the of-
ferings of your hand, your vows, your freewill
offerings, and the firstborn of your herds and
of your flocks. 7 There you must eat before the
LORD your God, and you shall rejoice in all that
you put your hand to, you and your house-
holds, where the LORD your God has blessed
you.

8 You are not to do all the things that we are
doing here today, where every man does what-
ever is right in his own eyes. 9 For you have
not yet come to the rest and to the inheritance
which the LORD your God has given you. 10 But
when you cross the Jordan, and dwell in the
land which the LORD your God has given you
to inherit, and when He gives you rest from all
your enemies round about, so that you dwell
in safety, 11 then there will be a place which
the LORD your God will choose to cause His
name to dwell. There you must bring all that I

11:14 Lev 26:4
11:15 Dt 6:11
11:16 Job 31:27
11:17 Dt 4:26
11:19 Dt 4:9–10
11:20 Dt 6:9
11:21 Ps 72:5
11:22 Dt 6:17
11:23 Dt 4:38
11:24 Ex 23:31
11:25 Ex 23:27
11:26 Dt 30:1
11:27 Dt 28:1–14

....

11:28 Dt 28:15–68
11:30 Ge 12:6
11:31 Dt 9:1
11:32 Dt 12:32
12:1 1Ki 8:40
12:2 2Ki 16:4
12:3 Nu 33:52
12:5 2Ch 7:12
12:6 Dt 15:19–20
12:7 Dt 12:18
12:10 Dt 11:31
12:11 Dt 12:5

[1]3 Wooden symbols of a female deity.

command you: your burnt offerings, and your sacrifices, your tithes, the offering of your hand, and all your choice vows which you vow to the LORD. 12 You will rejoice before the LORD your God, you, your sons, your daughters, your male servants, your female servants, and the Levite who is within your gates, for he has no portion or inheritance with you. 13 Be careful that you do not offer your burnt offerings in every place that you see. 14 Rather, in the place which the LORD will choose in one of your tribes, there you must offer your burnt offerings, and there you must do all that I command you.

15 Notwithstanding, you may kill and eat meat within all your gates, whatever your heart desires, according to the blessing of the LORD your God which He has given you. The unclean and the clean may eat of it, of the gazelle and of the deer, 16 only you must not eat the blood. You shall pour it on the ground like water. 17 You may not eat within your gates the tithe of your grain, your wine, your oil, the firstborn of your herds or of your flock, any of your vows which you vow, your freewill offerings, or the offering of your hand. 18 Rather you must eat them before the LORD your God in the place which the LORD your God will choose—you, your son, your daughter, your male servant, your female servant, and the Levite that is within your gates—and you shall rejoice before the LORD your God in all that you undertake to do. 19 Take heed to yourself that you do not forsake the Levite as long as you live on the earth.

20 When the LORD your God shall enlarge your border as He has promised you, and you say, "I will eat meat," because you desire to eat meat, then you may eat as much meat as your heart desires. 21 If the place which the LORD your God has chosen to put His name is too far from you, then you shall kill of your herd and of your flock, which the LORD has given you, as I have commanded you, and you must eat in your gates whatever your heart desires. 22 Even as the gazelle and the deer are eaten, so you shall eat them. The unclean and the clean shall eat of them alike. 23 Only be sure that you do not eat the blood. For the blood is the life, and you may not eat the life with the meat. 24 You must not eat it. You must pour it on the ground like water. 25 You must not eat it, so that it may go well with you and with your children after you, when you do that which is right in the sight of the LORD.

26 You shall take only your holy things which you have, along with your vows, and go to the place which the LORD shall choose. 27 You must offer your burnt offerings, the meat and the blood, on the altar of the LORD your God, and the blood of your sacrifices will be poured out on the altar of the LORD your God, and you shall eat the meat. 28 Observe and hear all these words which I command you, so that it may go well with you and with your children after you forever, when you do that which is good and right in the sight of the LORD your God.

29 When the LORD your God shall cut off the nations from before you, where you go to possess them, and you dispossess them, and dwell in their land, 30 take heed to yourself so that you are not ensnared by following them, after they have been destroyed before you, and that you not inquire after their gods, saying, "How did these nations serve their gods? Even so I will do likewise." 31 You shall not do so to the LORD your God, for every abomination to the LORD, which He hates, they have done to their gods. They have even burned their sons and their daughters in the fire to their gods.

32 Whatever I command you, be careful to do it. You shall not add to it or take away from it.

Idolatry

13 If a prophet or a dreamer of dreams arises among you and gives you a sign or a wonder, 2 and the sign or the wonder comes to pass concerning that which he spoke to you, saying, "Let us go after other gods," which you have not known, "and let us serve them," 3 you must not listen to the words of that prophet or that dreamer of dreams, for the LORD your God is testing you, to know whether you love the LORD your God with all your heart and with all your soul. 4 You must follow after the LORD your God, fear Him, and keep His commandments, obey His voice, and you must serve Him, and cling to Him. 5 That prophet or that dreamer of dreams must be put to death because he has spoken in order to turn you away from the LORD your God, who brought you out of the land of Egypt and redeemed you out of the house of bondage, to entice you away from the way in which the LORD your God commanded you to walk. So you must put the evil away from your midst.

6 If your brother, the son of your mother, or your son, or your daughter, or your beloved wife, or your friend, who is as your own soul, entices you secretly, saying, "Let us go and serve other gods," which you have not known, neither you nor your fathers, 7 namely, of the gods of the people who are all around you, near you or far away from you, from one end of the earth to the other end of the earth, 8 you shall not consent to him or listen to him, neither should your eye pity him, nor shall you spare or conceal him, 9 but you must surely

12:12 Dt 12:7
12:15 Dt 14:5
12:16 Ge 9:4
12:18 Dt 12:7
12:20 Dt 19:8
12:21 Dt 12:5
12:23 Ge 9:4
12:25 Ex 15:26
12:26 Nu 5:9–10
12:27 Lev 1:9

....

12:29 Jos 23:4
12:30 Dt 7:16
12:31 Jer 32:35
12:32 Dt 4:2
13:3 Dt 8:2
13:4 Dt 10:20
13:5 1Co 5:13
13:8 Pr 1:10

kill him. Your hand must be first upon him to put him to death, and afterwards, the hand of all the people. 10 You shall stone him with stones so that he dies because he has sought to entice you away from the LORD your God who brought you out of the land of Egypt, from the house of bondage. 11 All Israel shall hear and fear and no more do any such wickedness as this among you.

12 If you hear it said in one of your cities, in which the LORD your God has given you to dwell, saying, 13 "Certain men, the sons of wickedness, are gone out from among you and have seduced the inhabitants of their city, saying, 'Let us go and serve other gods,'" which you have not known, 14 then you shall inquire, search out, and ask diligently. If it be true and certain that such an abomination has been among you, 15 you shall surely put the inhabitants of that city to the sword, utterly destroying it, all that is in it and its livestock—with the edge of the sword. 16 You must gather all the spoils of it into the middle of the street and burn the city with fire along with all the spoils within it for the LORD your God, and it will be a heap forever. It must not be rebuilt. 17 Nothing of the cursed thing there must cling to your hand, so that the LORD may turn from the fierceness of His anger and show you mercy, have compassion on you, and multiply you, just as He swore to your fathers, 18 if you listen to the voice of the LORD your God, to keep all His commandments which I command you today, and do that which is right in the eyes of the LORD your God.

Clean and Unclean Food

Lev 11:1–23

14 You are the sons of the LORD your God. You shall not cut yourselves or make any baldness between your eyes for the dead. 2 For you are a holy people to the LORD your God, and the LORD has chosen you to be a peculiar people to Himself, treasured above all the nations that are on the earth.

3 You must not eat any detestable thing. 4 These are the animals which you may eat: the ox, the sheep, and the goat, 5 the deer, the gazelle, the fallow deer, the wild goat, and the ibex, and the antelope, and the mountain sheep. 6 You may eat every animal with divided hooves, with the hoof divided into two parts, and that chews the cud. 7 Nevertheless, you may not eat of these that chew the cud, or of them that divide the hoof: the camel, the rabbit, and the coney. For they chew the cud, but their hoof is not divided, therefore they are unclean to you. 8 The pig is unclean to you because it divides the hoof, yet it does not chew the cud. You must not eat of their flesh or touch their dead carcass.

9 These you shall eat of all that are in the water: All that have fins and scales you may eat. 10 Whatever does not have fins and scales you may not eat. It is unclean to you.

11 You may eat of all clean birds. 12 However, these are the ones which you cannot eat: the eagle, the vulture, the buzzard, 13 the red kite, the falcon, and the kite after its kind, 14 every raven after its kind, 15 and the ostrich, the owl, the seagull, and the hawk after its kind, 16 the little owl, and the great owl, and the white owl, 17 the pelican, the carrion vulture, and the cormorant, 18 the stork, and the heron after its kind, and the hoopoe, and the bat.

19 Every creeping thing that flies is unclean to you. They must not be eaten. 20 You may eat all the clean birds.

21 You must not eat of anything that dies of itself, but you may give it to the foreigner that is in your gates, so that he may eat it, or you may sell it to a foreigner, for you are a holy people to the LORD your God.

You shall not boil a young goat in its mother's milk.

Tithes

22 You must be certain to tithe all the produce of your seed, so that the field produces year by year. 23 You must eat before the LORD your God, in the place in which He shall choose to place His name, the tithe of your grain, of your wine, of your oil, and of the firstborn of your herds and of your flocks so that you may learn to always fear the LORD your God. 24 If the distance is too long for you, so that you are not able to carry it, because the place is too far from you, where the LORD your God shall choose to set His name, when the LORD your God blesses you, 25 then you shall exchange it for money and bind up the money in your hand and go to the place which the LORD your God shall choose. 26 Then you may spend that money for whatever your heart desires, for oxen, or for sheep, or for wine, or for strong drink, or for whatever your heart desires, and you may eat there before the LORD your God, and you shall rejoice, you, and your household, 27 and the Levite that is within your gates. You must not forsake him, for he has no portion or inheritance with you.

28 At the end of three years you must bring forth all the tithe of your produce the same year and lay it up within your gates. 29 Then the Levite (because he has no portion or inheritance with you), the foreigner, the fatherless, and the widow, who are within your gates, shall come and shall eat and be satisfied, so

13:10 Jos 7:25
13:11 Dt 19:20
13:13 Dt 13:2
13:14 Dt 17:4
13:16 Jos 8:28
13:17 Ge 26:4
13:18 Dt 12:25
14:1 Ro 9:8
14:2 Dt 7:6
14:3 Eze 4:14
14:8 Lev 11:26–27
14:21 Ex 23:19
14:22 Dt 12:17
14:24 Dt 12:21
14:26 Dt 12:7
14:27 Nu 18:20
14:29 Dt 15:10

that the LORD your God may bless you in all the work of your hand which you do.

The Sabbatical Year

Lev 25:8–38

15 At the end of every seven years you shall grant a relinquishing *of debts.* 2 This is the manner of the relinquishing: Every creditor that has loaned anything to his neighbor shall relinquish it. He shall not exact it of his neighbor, or of his brother, because it is called the LORD's relinquishment. 3 You may collect it from a foreigner, but that which your brother has that is yours your hand shall release. 4 However, there will be no poor among you, for the LORD will greatly bless you in the land which the LORD your God has given you for an inheritance to possess, 5 if only you carefully obey the voice of the LORD your God, by carefully observing all these commandments which I command you today. 6 For the LORD your God will bless you, just as He promised you, and you will lend to many nations, but you shall not borrow. You will reign over many nations, but they will not reign over you.

7 If there be among you a poor man, one of your brothers within any of your gates in your land which the LORD your God has given you, you must not harden your heart or shut your hand from your poor brother. 8 But you shall open your hand wide to him and must surely lend him what is sufficient for his need, in that which he lacks. 9 Beware lest there be a wicked thought in your heart, saying, "The seventh year, the year of release, is at hand," and your eye be evil against your poor brother and you give him nothing, and he cry out to the LORD against you, and it become sin in you. 10 You must surely give to him, and your heart shall not be grieved when you give to him, because in this thing the LORD your God will bless you in all your works, and in all that you put your hand to do. 11 For the poor will never cease from being in the land. Therefore, I command you, saying, "You shall open your hand wide to your brother, to your poor and needy in your land."

Freeing Servants

Ex 21:2–6; Lev 25:38–55

12 If your brother, a Hebrew man, or a Hebrew woman, is sold to you and serves you six years, then in the seventh year you must let him go free from you. 13 When you send him out free from you, you must not let him go away empty-handed. 14 You shall supply him liberally out of your flock, out of your floor, and out of your winepress. From that with which the LORD your God has blessed you, you shall give to him. 15 You shall remember that you were a slave in the land of Egypt and the LORD your God redeemed you. Therefore, I command this to you today.

16 It shall be, if he says to you, "I will not go away from you," because he loves you and your house, because he is well off with you, 17 then you must take an awl and pierce it through his ear into the door, and he shall be your servant forever. And you shall also do likewise to your female servant.

18 It will not seem difficult for you when you send him away free from you, for he has been worth a double hired servant[1] in serving you six years. Then the LORD your God will bless you in all that you do.

The Firstborn Animals

19 You must sanctify all the firstborn males that come out of your herd and flock to the LORD your God. You must do no work with the firstborn of your bulls or shear the firstborn of your sheep. 20 You shall eat it before the LORD your God year by year in the place where the LORD shall choose, you and your household. 21 If there is any defect in it, if it is lame or blind or has a serious defect, you shall not sacrifice it to the LORD your God. 22 You shall eat it within your gates. The unclean and the clean person alike shall eat it, as if it were a gazelle or a deer. 23 Only you must not eat its blood. You shall pour it on the ground like water.

The Passover

Ex 12:14–20; Lev 23:4–8; Nu 28:16–25

16 Observe the month of Aviv[2] and keep the Passover to the LORD your God, for in the month of Aviv the LORD your God brought you out of Egypt by night. 2 Therefore, you must sacrifice the Passover to the LORD your God, from the flock or the herd, in the place where the LORD shall choose to place His name. 3 You must not eat leavened bread with it. For seven days you must eat unleavened bread, the bread of affliction, for you came out of the land of Egypt in a hurry, so that you may remember all the days of your life the day when you came out of the land of Egypt. 4 There must not be any leavened bread seen with you within all your borders for seven days, nor may any of the meat which you sacrificed in the evening on the first day remain overnight until morning.

5 You may not sacrifice the Passover within any of your gates that the LORD your God has given you. 6 But at the place where the LORD your God chooses to place His name, there you shall sacrifice the Passover in the evening at sunset, at the time that you came out of Egypt.

15:1 Dt 31:10
15:3 Dt 23:20
15:6 Dt 28:12–13
15:7 Dt 15:9
15:9 Dt 24:15
15:10 Dt 14:29
15:11 Mt 26:11
15:12 Jer 34:14
....
15:15 Dt 16:12
15:16 Ex 21:5–6
15:19 Ex 13:2
15:21 Dt 17:1
15:23 Dt 12:16
16:1 Ex 34:18
16:2 Dt 12:5
16:3 Ex 12:39
16:4 Ex 12:10

[1] *18* Or *double the amount.* [2] *1* March-April in the modern calendar.

7 You shall roast and eat it in the place where
the LORD your God will choose, and you must
return in the morning, and go to your tents.
8 For six days you must eat unleavened bread,
and on the seventh day there shall be a solemn
assembly to the LORD your God. You must do
no work *on that day*.

The Feast of Weeks
Lev 23:15–22; Nu 28:26–31

9 You must count seven weeks for your-
self. Begin counting the seven weeks from
the time you begin to put the sickle to the
standing grain. 10 You must keep the Feast of
Weeks to the LORD your God with a tribute of
a freewill offering from your hand, which you
must give to the LORD your God, in proportion
to how much the LORD your God has blessed
you. 11 You shall rejoice before the LORD your
God—you, your son, your daughter, your male
servant, your female servant, the Levite who
is within your gates, the foreigner, the orphan,
and the widow who are among you—in the
place where the LORD your God has chosen to
place His name. 12 You must remember that
you were a slave in Egypt, and you must be
careful to observe these statutes.

The Feast of Tabernacles
Lev 23:33–43; Nu 29:12–39

13 You shall observe the Feast of Tabernacles
seven days after you have gathered in your
threshing floor and your winepress, 14 and you
shall rejoice in your feast, you, your son, your
daughter, your male servant, your female ser-
vant, the Levite, the foreigner, the orphan, and
the widow who are within your gates. 15 You
are to celebrate the festival for seven days to
the LORD your God in the place where the LORD
will choose, because the LORD your God will
bless you in all your produce, and in all the
works of your hands. Therefore, you will in-
deed rejoice.
16 Three times a year all your males must
appear before the LORD your God in the place
where He will choose: at the Feast of Unleav-
ened Bread, at the Feast of Weeks, and at the
Feast of Tabernacles, and they must not ap-
pear before the LORD empty. 17 Every man must
give as he is able, in proportion to the blessing
of the LORD your God, which He has given you.

Judges

18 You must appoint judges and officers in
all your gates, which the LORD your God gives
you, throughout your tribes, and they shall
judge the people with righteous judgment.
19 You must not pervert judgment nor show
partiality. You must not accept a bribe, for a
bribe blinds the eyes of the wise and perverts
the words of the righteous. 20 You must follow
that which is altogether just, so that you may
live and inherit the land which the LORD your
God is giving you.

Idolatry Forbidden

21 You must not plant for yourself an Ashe-
rah[1] of any trees near the altar of the LORD your
God, which you make for yourself. 22 You shall
not set up for yourself any image, which the
LORD your God hates.

17 You must not sacrifice to the LORD your
God any bull or sheep that has a blem-
ish or any defect, for that is detestable to the
LORD your God.
2 If there be found among you, within any of
your gates which the LORD your God gives you,
man or woman, who has acted wickedly in the
sight of the LORD your God, by transgressing
His covenant, 3 and has gone and served other
gods and worshipped them, either the sun, or
moon, or any of the host of heaven, which I
have not commanded, 4 and if it is told to you,
and you have heard of it, and investigated dil-
igently, and it is true, and the matter is certain
that such a detestable thing has happened in
Israel, 5 then you must bring forth that man or
that woman who has committed that wicked
thing to your gates, that very man or wom-
an, and stone them with stones until they die.
6 On the testimony of two or three witnesses
he that is to die must be put to death, but on
the testimony of one witness he cannot be put
to death. 7 The hands of the witnesses shall
be first against him to put him to death, and
afterward the hands of all the people. So you
shall purge the evil from among you.

Courts of Law

8 If there arises a matter too difficult for you
in judgment, between one kind of bloodshed
and another, between one kind of lawsuit and
another, and between one kind of assault and
another, matters of controversy within your
gates, then you must arise and go up to the
place where the LORD your God shall choose.
9 You must go to the Levitical priests or to the
judge in *office* those days, and inquire, and
they will show you the verdict of judgment.
10 You shall do according to the verdict which
they declare to you from the place where the
LORD will choose to show you, and you must
be careful to do all that they instruct you to do.
11 You must do according to the terms of the
law which they instruct you and according to
the verdict which they tell you. You must not
deviate from the sentence which they show
you, to the right or to the left. 12 The man who
acts presumptuously and does not listen to

16:7 2Ch 35:13
16:8 Lev 23:36
16:9 Ex 23:16
16:10 1Co 16:2
16:11 Dt 12:7
16:12 Dt 15:15
16:13 Ex 23:16
16:16 Ex 23:14–17
16:19 Ex 23:2
16:20 Dt 4:1

16:21 2Ki 17:16
16:22 Lev 26:1
17:1 Dt 15:21
17:5 Lev 24:14
17:6 Nu 35:30
17:7 Dt 13:9
17:8 Dt 12:5
17:9 Eze 44:24
17:11 Jos 1:7
17:12 Nu 15:30

[1] *21* Wooden symbol of a female deity.

the priest who stands to minister before the LORD your God, or to the judge—that man must die, and you must purge the evil from Israel. 13 Then all the people will hear, and fear, and not act presumptuously again.

Appointing a King

14 When you have come into the land which the LORD your God gives you and possess it and dwell there and then say, "I will set a king over me just like all the nations that are around me," 15 you must set a king over you whom the LORD your God will choose. You must select a king over you who is from among your brothers. You may not select a foreigner over you who is not your countryman. 16 What is more, he shall not accumulate horses for himself or cause the people to return to Egypt in order that he accumulate horses, for as the LORD has said to you, "You must not go back that way ever again." 17 He shall not acquire many wives for himself, lest his heart turn away; nor shall he acquire for himself excess silver and gold.

18 It must be, when he sits on the throne of his kingdom, that he shall write a copy of this law for himself on a scroll before the priests, the Levites. 19 It must be with him, and he must read it all the days of his life so that he may learn to fear the LORD his God, and carefully observe all the words of this law and these statutes, and do them, 20 that his heart will not be lifted up above his brothers and so that he may not turn aside from the commandment, to the right or to the left, to the end, so that he may prolong his days in his kingdom, he and his children, in the midst of Israel.

Provision for Priests and Levites

18 The Levitical priests and all the tribe of Levi will not have any portion or inheritance with Israel. They must eat the offerings of the LORD made by fire and His portion. 2 They will have no inheritance among their brothers. The LORD is their inheritance, just as He has said to them.

3 This shall be the priest's due from the people, from them that offer a sacrifice, whether it be an ox or sheep: they shall give to the priest the shoulder, the two cheeks, and the stomach. 4 You must give him the first fruit of your grain, of your wine, and of your oil, and the first of the fleece of your sheep also. 5 For the LORD your God has chosen him out of all your tribes to stand to minister in the name of the LORD, him and his sons forever.

6 If a Levite comes from any of your gates out of all Israel, where he lives, and comes with all the desire of his mind to the place where the LORD shall choose, 7 then he shall minister in the name of the LORD his God, as all his brothers the Levites do, who stand there before the LORD. 8 They must have the same portions to eat, besides any profits he may receive from the sale of his father's inheritance.

17:13 Dt 13:11
17:14 1Sa 8:19–20
17:15 Jer 30:21
17:16 Ex 13:17
17:17 Ne 13:26
17:19 Jos 1:8
17:20 Dt 5:32
18:1 Dt 10:9
18:3 Lev 7:30–34
18:5 Dt 10:8
18:6 Nu 35:2–3
....
18:8 Ne 12:44
18:9 Dt 12:29–31
18:10 Lev 19:26
18:11 Lev 19:31
18:12 Lev 18:24
18:15 Ac 7:37
18:16 Ex 20:19
18:17 Dt 5:28
18:18 Jn 8:28
18:19 Ac 3:22–23
18:22 Dt 18:20
19:1 Dt 12:29
19:2 Ex 21:13

A Call to Holiness

9 When you enter into the land which the LORD your God gives you, you must not learn to practice the abominations of those nations. 10 There must not be found among you anyone who makes his son or his daughter pass through the fire, or who uses divination, or uses witchcraft, or an interpreter of omens, or a sorcerer, 11 or one who casts spells, or a spiritualist, or an occultist, or a necromancer. 12 For all that do these things are an abomination to the LORD, and because of these abominations the LORD your God will drive them out from before you. 13 You must be blameless before the LORD your God.

The Prophet

14 For these nations, which you shall possess, listened to soothsayers and to diviners, but as for you, the LORD your God has not permitted you to do so. 15 The LORD your God will raise up for you a prophet from the midst of you, of your brothers, like me. You must listen to him. 16 This is according to all that you desired of the LORD your God in Horeb on the day of the assembly, saying, "Let me not hear again the voice of the LORD my God, nor let me see this great fire anymore, so that I do not die."

17 The LORD said to me, "They have done well in what they have said. 18 I will raise up a prophet from among their brothers, like you, and will put My words in his mouth, and he will speak to them all that I command him. 19 It will be that whoever will not listen to My words which he will speak in My name, I will require it of him. 20 But the prophet, who presumes to speak a word in my name, which I have not commanded him to speak, or who shall speak in the name of other gods—that prophet shall die."

21 And you may say in your heart, "How can we know the word which the LORD has not spoken?" 22 When a prophet speaks in the name of the LORD, if the thing does not occur or come to pass, that is the thing which the LORD has not spoken; the prophet has spoken it presumptuously. You shall not be afraid of him.

Cities of Refuge

Nu 35:6–34; Dt 4:41–43; Jos 20:1–9

19 When the LORD your God has cut off the nations, whose land the LORD your God is giving you, and you dispossess them, and dwell in their cities, and in their houses, 2 you shall set apart three cities for yourselves in the midst of your land, which the LORD your God

is giving you to possess. 3 You shall prepare a roadway for yourself, and divide the territory of your land into three parts, which the LORD your God is giving you to inherit, so that every manslayer may flee there.

4 This is the word concerning the manslayer who will flee there, so that he may live: Whoever kills his neighbor unintentionally, whom he did not hate previously, 5 like when a man goes into the forest with his neighbor to cut wood, and his hand raises the axe to cut down the tree, and the axe head slips from the handle and lands on his neighbor causing him to die, then he may flee to one of those cities, and live. 6 Otherwise the avenger of blood might, while he is angry, pursue the manslayer and overtake him (because the way is long) and kill him, even though he was not worthy of death (since he did not hate him previously). 7 Therefore, I command you, saying, "You shall set apart three cities for yourselves."

8 If the LORD your God enlarges your borders as He promised your fathers, and gives you all the land which He promised to give to your fathers, 9 and if you will carefully keep all these commandments, which I command you today, to love the LORD your God, and to always walk in His ways, then you must add three cities more for yourself, besides these three. 10 Then innocent blood will not be shed in your land, which the LORD your God is giving you for an inheritance, and blood guiltiness be on you.

11 But if any man hates his neighbor, and lies in wait for him, and rises up against him, and mortally strikes him, causing him to die, and flees to one of these cities, 12 then the elders of his city must send and fetch him from there, and deliver him to the hand of the avenger of blood, so that he may die. 13 Your eye must not pity him, but you must remove the guilt of innocent blood from Israel, so that it may go well with you.

14 You shall not remove your neighbor's landmark, which they of old time have set in your inheritance, which you shall inherit in the land that the LORD your God is giving you to possess.

Witnesses

15 A single witness must not rise up against a man on account of any iniquity or any sin that he sins. At the testimony of two witnesses or at the testimony of three witnesses shall the matter be established.

16 If a false witness rises up against any man to testify against him to accuse him of doing wrong, 17 then both the men between whom the controversy is must stand before the LORD, before the priests and the judges, who are in *office* those days. 18 The judges will thoroughly investigate, and if the witness is a false witness and has testified falsely against his brother, 19 then you must do to him as he conspired to have done to his brother. In this way you must remove the evil from among you. 20 Those who remain will hear and fear, and will never again commit any such evil among you. 21 You must not show pity. But life will be for life, eye for eye, tooth for tooth, hand for hand, foot for foot.

19:6 Nu 35:12
19:9 Jos 20:7–8
19:13 1Ki 2:31
19:14 Dt 27:17
19:15 Nu 35:30
19:16 Ps 27:12
19:17 Dt 17:9
....
19:19 Pr 19:5
19:20 Dt 17:13
19:21 Dt 19:13
20:1 Dt 31:6
20:4 Dt 1:30
20:5 Ne 12:27
20:6 Lev 19:23–25
20:7 Dt 24:5
20:8 Jdg 7:3
20:14 Jos 8:2

Rules of Warfare

20 When you go out to battle against your enemies, and see horses, and chariots, and a people that outnumber you, do not be afraid of them, for the LORD your God is with you, who brought you up out of the land of Egypt. 2 It will be, when you approach the battle, that the priest will approach and speak to the people, 3 and he shall say to them, "Hear, O Israel, you approach today to do battle against your enemies. Do not be fainthearted. Do not fear, and do not tremble or be terrified because of them. 4 For the LORD your God is He that goes with you, to fight for you against your enemies, to save you."

5 The officers will speak to the people, saying, "What man is there who has built a new house and has not dedicated it? Let him go and return to his house, lest he die in the battle, and another man dedicate it. 6 What man is there who has planted a vineyard, and has not yet eaten of it? Let him also go and return to his house, lest he die in the battle, and another man eat of it. 7 What man is there who is engaged to a woman but has not married her? Let him go and return to his house, lest he die in the battle, and another man take her." 8 The officers are to speak further to the people, and they shall say, "What man is there that is fearful and fainthearted? Let him go and return to his house, lest his brother's heart faint as well as his heart." 9 It will be, when the officers have made an end of speaking to the people, that they must make captains of the armies to lead the people.

10 When you come near to a city to fight against it, then proclaim peace to it. 11 It shall be, if it gives you a reply of peace and opens to you, then it must be that all the people that are found within shall become slaves to you and they shall serve you. 12 If it will not make peace with you but makes war against you, then you are to besiege it. 13 And when the LORD your God has delivered it into your hands, you are to slay every male there with the edge of the sword. 14 But the women, and the little ones, and the livestock, and all that is in the city, all the spoil within, you are to take

to yourself, and you will eat the spoil of your enemies, which the LORD your God has given you. 15 Thus you are to do to all the cities which are far away, which are not the cities of these nearby nations.

16 But of the cities of these people, which the LORD your God is giving you for an inheritance, you must not leave alive anything that breathes. 17 But you shall completely destroy them: namely, the Hittites, and the Amorites, the Canaanites, and the Perizzites, the Hivites, and the Jebusites, just as the LORD your God has commanded you, 18 so that they do not teach you to participate in all their abominations, which they have done to their gods, causing you to sin against the LORD your God.

19 When you lay siege to a city for a long time, in making war against it in order to take it, you shall not destroy the trees there by chopping them down with an axe, for you may eat from them, and you shall not cut them down. For the tree of the field is not a man in which to lay siege. 20 However, you may destroy and cut down only the trees which you know are not fruit trees, so that you may build siege engines against the city that makes war with you until it falls.

Atonement for Unsolved Murders

21 If someone is found slain in the land which the LORD your God is giving you to possess, lying in the field, and it is not known who has slain him, 2 then your elders and your judges are to come forth, and they must measure *how far* it is to the cities which are around him who was slain. 3 And it must be, that the city which is closest to the slain man, that is, the elders of that city shall take a heifer which has not been worked, that has never pulled in yoke, 4 and the elders of that city must bring down the heifer to a valley with flowing water, which is neither plowed nor sown, and shall break the heifer's neck there in the valley. 5 Then the priests, the sons of Levi, must come near, for the LORD your God has chosen them to minister to Him, and to bless in the name of the LORD, and by their word every controversy and every assault will be settled. 6 And all the elders of that city, which is nearest to the slain man, shall wash their hands over the heifer whose neck was broken in the valley. 7 Then they must answer and say, "Our hands have not shed this blood, and our eyes have not seen it. 8 Be merciful, O LORD, to Your people Israel, whom You have redeemed, and lay not innocent blood in the midst of Your people Israel." And the blood guilt will be forgiven them. 9 In this way you are to remove the guilt of innocent blood from among you when you do that which is right in the eyes of the LORD.

20:16 Jos 11:14
20:18 Ex 23:33
21:3 Nu 19:2
21:5 1Ch 23:13
21:8 Jnh 1:14
....
21:14 Ge 34:2
21:15 Ge 29:33
21:16 1Ch 26:10
21:17 Ge 49:3
21:20 Pr 20:1
21:22 Dt 22:26
21:23 Gal 3:13

Marrying Female Captives

10 When you go forth to war against your enemies, and the LORD your God has delivered them into your hands, and you have taken them captive, 11 and you see among the captives a beautiful woman, and have a desire for her to have her as your wife, 12 then you are to bring her home to your house, and she is to shave her head and trim her nails. 13 She must also discard the clothing of her captivity and shall remain in your house, and mourn her father and her mother for a full month. After that you may have relations with her, and be her husband, and she will be your wife. 14 It will be, if you are not pleased with her, then you must let her go wherever she pleases, but you may not sell her at all for money, nor are you to make merchandise of her, because you have humbled her.

The Right of the Firstborn

15 If a man has two wives, one beloved and another unloved, and both have borne him children, both the loved one and the unloved one, and if the firstborn son is hers that is unloved, 16 then it must be, when he gives his sons the inheritance which he has, that he may not make the firstborn son of the loved come before the son of the unloved, who was indeed the firstborn. 17 On the contrary, he must acknowledge the son of the unloved for the firstborn, by giving him a double portion of all that he has, for he is the beginning of his strength. The right of the firstborn is his.

Dealing With a Rebellious Son

18 If a man has a stubborn and rebellious son, who will not obey the voice of his father or the voice of his mother, and who, when they have disciplined him, will not listen to them, 19 then his father and his mother are to lay hold of him and bring him out to the elders of his city, to the gate of his city. 20 They shall say to the elders of his city, "This son of ours is stubborn and rebellious. He will not listen to us. He is a glutton and a drunkard." 21 Then all the men of his city must stone him with stones, until he dies. In this way you are to remove the evil from among you, and all Israel shall hear and fear.

Various Laws

22 If a man has committed a sin worthy of death and is executed, and you hang him on a tree, 23 then his body must not remain all night on the tree, but you must bury him that day (for he that is hanged is accursed of God) so

that your land may not be defiled, which the
LORD your God is giving you for an inheritance.
22 You must not see your brother's ox or
his sheep go astray and hide yourself
from them. You must certainly bring them back
to your brother. 2 If your brother is not near
you or if you do not know him, then you are to
bring it to your own house, and it will be with
you until your brother seeks after it. Then you
must return it to him. 3 In the same way, you
must do so with his donkey, with his clothing,
and with anything lost by your brother which
he has lost and you have found. You must not
hide yourself *from him*.
4 You are not to see your brother's donkey or
his ox fall down by the way and hide yourself
from them. You certainly must help him to lift
them up.
5 A woman must not wear man's clothing,
nor is a man to put on a woman's clothing.
For all that do so are abominations to the LORD
your God.
6 If you happen to notice a bird's nest along
the way, in any tree or on the ground, whether
they be young ones or eggs, and the mother is
sitting on the young or on the eggs, you are not
to take the mother from the young. 7 You must
certainly let the mother go, but you may take
the young for yourself, so that it may be well
with you, and that you may prolong your days.
8 When you build a new house, you must
make a guard rail for your roof so that you
bring no blood guilt on your house, should
anyone fall from there.
9 You must not sow your vineyard with two
kinds of seeds, or the fruit of your seed which
you have sown and the fruit of your vineyard
will be defiled.
10 You must not plow with an ox and a donkey
together.
11 You must not wear clothing made of a ma-
terial of wool and linen together.
12 You must make tassels on the four quarters
of your clothing with which you cover yourself.

Laws About Marriage

13 If any man takes a wife and has sexual
relations with her and then rejects her, 14 and
accuses her of impropriety and publicly de-
fames her, saying, "I married this woman, but
when I had sexual relations with her, I found
her not to be a virgin," 15 then the father and
mother of the girl must produce *evidence* of
the girl's virginity to the elders of the city at the
gate. 16 The girl's father must say to the elders,
"I gave my daughter to this man to wife, and
he has rejected her. 17 What is more, he has ac-
cused her of impropriety, saying, 'I did not find
your daughter to be a virgin.' However, this is
the evidence of my daughter's virginity." And
they shall spread the cloth before the elders
of the city. 18 The elders of that city must take
that man and punish him, 19 and they must
fine him a hundred *shekels*[1] of silver and give
them to the father of the girl, because he has
publicly humiliated a virgin of Israel. Then she
is to remain his wife. He may not divorce her
all his days.
20 But if the accusation is true, and the evi-
dence of virginity does not exist for the girl,
21 then they shall bring the girl out to the door
of her father's house, and the men of her city
shall stone her with stones until she dies, be-
cause she has brought disgrace into Israel, to
act like a whore in her father's house. In this
way you may purge the evil from among you.
22 If a man is discovered lying with a married
woman, then both of them must die, both the
man that lay with the woman, and the woman.
In this way you may purge the evil from Israel.
23 If a girl who is a virgin is engaged to a
man, and *another* man finds her in the city
and has sexual relations with her, 24 then you
must bring them both out to the gate of that
city and you must stone them with stones until
they die, the girl because she did not cry out
even though in the city, and the man because
he has violated his neighbor's wife. In this way
you may purge the evil from among you.
25 But if a man finds an engaged girl in the
field, and the man forces her and rapes her,
then only the man that raped her shall die.
26 However, you are to do nothing to the girl.
There is no sin worthy of death in the girl, for
just as when a man rises against his neighbor
and murders him, so is this matter. 27 For he
found her in the field, the engaged girl cried
out, but there was no one to save her.
28 If a man finds a girl who is a virgin who
is not engaged and seizes her and lies with
her and they are discovered, 29 then the man
who lay with her must give fifty shekels[2] of
silver to the girl's father, and she shall be his
wife because he has violated her. He may not
divorce her all his days.
30 A man must not marry his father's wife and
in this way dishonor his father.

Exclusion From the Assembly

23 No one who is emasculated or has his
male organ cut off may enter the as-
sembly of the LORD.
2 No one of illegitimate birth may enter the
assembly of the LORD. Even to his tenth gen-
eration no one *related to him* may enter the
assembly of the LORD.

22:5 Dt 18:12
22:6 Lev 22:28
22:7 Dt 4:40
22:8 Ex 22:6
22:9 Lev 19:19
22:10 2Co 6:14–16
22:11 Lev 19:19
22:12 Mt 23:5
22:13 Ge 29:21
22:21 Ge 34:7
22:22 Lev 20:10
22:23 Mt 1:18–19
22:26 Dt 21:22
22:28 Ex 22:16–17
22:30 Lev 18:8
23:2 Zec 9:6

[1] *19* About 2½ pounds, or 1.2 kilograms. [2] *29* About 1¼ pounds, or 575 grams.

3 No Ammonite or Moabite may enter the assembly of the LORD. Even to their tenth generation they may not enter the assembly of the LORD forever, 4 because they refused you bread and water on the way, when you came from out of Egypt and because they hired Balaam, the son of Beor of Pethor of Mesopotamia, against you to curse you. 5 Nevertheless, the LORD your God would not listen to Balaam. Instead the LORD your God turned the curse into a blessing on you because the LORD your God loves you. 6 You are not ever to seek their peace nor their prosperity all your days.

7 You are not to abhor an Edomite, for he is your brother. You shall not abhor an Egyptian, because you were a foreigner in his land. 8 The children who are born of them may enter the assembly of the LORD in their third generation.

Uncleanness in the Camp

9 When the army goes out against your enemies, then keep yourself from every wicked thing. 10 If there be among you any man who is not clean because of a nocturnal emission, then he must leave the camp. He may not re-enter the camp. 11 And it must be that when evening comes, he must wash himself with water, and at sunset he may re-enter the camp.

12 You must also have a place outside the camp where one may go outside. 13 You must have a spade among your equipment, and it must be, when you relieve yourself outside, you must dig there and turn and cover up your excrement. 14 For the LORD your God walks in the midst of your camp, to deliver you, and to defeat your enemies before you. Therefore, your camp must be holy, so that He does not see any indecent thing among you, and turn away from you.

Various Laws

15 You must not deliver *back* to his master a slave who has escaped from his master to you. 16 He is to dwell with you, even among you, in a place which he shall choose in one of your towns, where he prefers. You must not oppress him.

17 There must never be a cult prostitute among the daughters of Israel nor a cult prostitute among the sons of Israel. 18 You must never bring the wage of a prostitute or the wage of a dog into the house of the LORD your God for any vow, for both of these are abominations to the LORD your God.

19 You must not charge interest on a loan to your brother: interest on money, interest on food, or on anything that may be lent with interest. 20 You may charge interest to a foreigner, but to your brother you may not lend with interest so that the LORD your God may bless you in all to which you set your hand in the land which you are entering to possess.

21 When you make a vow to the LORD your God, you must not be slow to pay it, for the LORD your God will surely require it of you, and it would be a sin to you. 22 But if you refrain from making a vow, it will not be a sin to you. 23 That which goes out of your lips you must keep and do, even a freewill offering, just as you have vowed to the LORD your God, what you have promised with your mouth.

24 When you go into your neighbor's vineyard, you may eat grapes to your fill at your own pleasure, but you may not put any in your basket. 25 When you enter into the standing grain of your neighbor, you may pluck the ears with your hand, but you may not use a sickle on your neighbor's standing grain.

Laws About Marriage and Divorce

24 When a man takes a wife and marries her, and it happens that she finds no favor in his eyes because he has found some indecency in her, then let him write her a bill of divorce and put it in her hand and send her out of his house. 2 When she departs out of his house, she may go and be another man's wife. 3 If the second husband rejects her and writes her a bill of divorce and puts it in her hand and sends her out of his house, or if the second husband who took her to be his wife dies, 4 her first husband, who sent her away, may not take her again to be his wife, since she is defiled, for that is abomination before the LORD, and you must not bring sin on the land, which the LORD your God is giving you for an inheritance.

5 When a man has taken a new wife, he shall not go out to war or be charged with any business; he is to be free at home one year, and must bring joy to his wife which he has taken.

Various Laws

6 No man shall take a lower or upper millstone as a pledge, for he would be taking a man's life as a pledge.

7 If a man is found kidnapping any of his brothers of the children of Israel, and makes property of him or sells him, then that kidnapper must die, and you must remove the evil from among you.

8 Be careful with an outbreak of leprosy, that you diligently observe and do according to all that the Levitical priests instruct you. As I have commanded them, so you must carefully do. 9 Remember what the LORD your God did to Miriam on the way, after you came out of Egypt.

10 When you do lend your brother anything, you may not go into his house to take his

23:3 Ne 13:1–2
23:6 Ezr 9:12
23:7 Ex 22:21
23:10 Lev 15:16
23:14 Lev 26:12
23:15 1Sa 30:15
23:16 Ex 22:21
23:17 Lev 19:29
23:18 Dt 23:21
23:19 Ex 22:25
23:20 Dt 15:10

....

23:21 Ecc 5:4–5
23:25 Mk 2:23
24:1 Mt 19:7–9
24:4 Jer 3:1
24:5 Dt 20:7
24:6 Dt 20:19
24:7 Ex 21:16
24:8 Lev 14:2
24:9 Nu 12:10–15
24:10 Dt 15:8

pledge. 11 You must stand outside, and the man to whom you lend must bring the pledge outside to you. 12 If the man is poor, you may not sleep with his pledge. 13 In any case, you must return the pledge to him when the sun goes down, so that he may sleep in his own cloak and bless you, and it will be righteousness to you before the LORD your God.

14 You may not oppress a hired servant that is poor and needy, whether he is one of your brothers or one of your foreigners who are in your land within your towns. 15 You must give him his wages on that very day before the sun sets, for he is poor, and sets his heart on it, lest he cry against you to the LORD, and it be a sin to you.

16 Fathers may not be put to death for the sons, nor shall sons be put to death for their fathers. Every man shall be put to death for his own sin.

17 You must not pervert the justice of the foreigner or of the fatherless, nor take a widow's cloak as a pledge. 18 On the contrary, you must remember that you were a slave in Egypt and the LORD your God redeemed you there. Therefore, I command you to do this.

19 Whenever you reap your harvest in your field and have forgotten a sheaf in the field, you may not go back to get it. It will be for the foreigner, for the fatherless, and for the widow, so that the LORD your God may bless you in all the work of your hands. 20 When you beat your olive tree, you may not go over the boughs again. It will be for the foreigner, for the fatherless, and for the widow. 21 When you gather the grapes of your vineyard, you shall not glean it again. It will be for the foreigner, for the fatherless, and for the widow. 22 You must remember that you were a slave in the land of Egypt. Therefore I command you to do this thing.

25 If there is a controversy between men, they are to go to court for judgment, so that the judges may judge them. Then they shall justify the righteous and condemn the wicked. 2 It must be, if the wicked man is worthy to be beaten, then the judge must make him lie down and be beaten in his presence, with the number of strikes his guilt deserves. 3 He may give him forty stripes, but no more, lest, if he should exceed and beat him more with numerous stripes, then your brother may appear contemptible to you.

4 You must not muzzle the ox when he treads out the grain.

Levirate Marriage

5 If brothers dwell together, and one of them dies without having had a child, the wife of the deceased may not marry outside *the family* to a stranger. Her husband's brother must go to her and take her to himself as a wife and perform the duty of a husband's brother to her. 6 It shall be, that the firstborn whom she bears shall continue in the name of his brother who is deceased, so that his name will not be blotted out of Israel.

7 If the man does not want to take his brother's wife, then let his brother's wife go up to the gate to the elders and say, "My husband's brother refuses to raise up his brother's name in Israel. He will not perform the duty of my husband's brother." 8 Then the elders of his city shall call him, and speak to him, and if he persists and says, "I do not want to take her," 9 then his brother's wife must come to him in the presence of the elders and remove his sandal from his foot, and spit in his face, and answer and say, "So shall it be done to that man who will not build up his brother's house." 10 His name will be called in Israel, "The house of him who has his sandal removed."

Various Laws

11 When a man and his brother fight one another, and the wife of the one draws near in order to deliver her husband out of the hand of him who fights him, and reaches out her hand and seizes him by the private parts, 12 then you must cut off her hand. You must not pity her.

13 You must not have in your bag different weights, a large and a small. 14 You must not have in your house differing measures, a large and a small. 15 But you must have a perfect and just weight—a perfect and just measure you must have, so that your days may be lengthened in the land which the LORD your God is giving you. 16 For all who do such things and all who act unjustly are an abomination to the LORD your God.

17 Remember what Amalek did to you by the road when you were coming out of Egypt, 18 how he met you by the way and attacked at your rear all that were stragglers behind you, when you were exhausted and weary. He did not fear God. 19 Therefore it shall be, when the LORD your God has given you rest from all your surrounding enemies, in the land which the LORD your God is giving you for an inheritance to possess, that you must blot out the remembrance of Amalek from under heaven. You must not forget it.

First Fruits and Tithes

26 And it must be, when you come into the land which the LORD your God is giving you for an inheritance, and you possess it, and dwell in it, 2 that you shall take from the first of all the produce of the ground which

24:12 Dt 24:17
24:13 Dt 6:25
24:15 Jas 5:4
24:16 Eze 18:20
24:17 Dt 16:19
24:18 Dt 5:15
24:19 Lev 23:22
24:22 Dt 24:18
25:2 Lk 12:47–48
25:3 Job 18:3
25:4 Pr 12:10
25:5 Mt 22:24

....

25:8 Ru 4:6
25:9 Nu 12:14
25:12 Dt 19:13
25:13 Pr 11:1
25:15 Ex 20:12
25:16 Pr 11:1
25:17 Ex 17:8–16
25:18 Ps 36:1
25:19 Ex 17:14
26:2 Ex 23:19

you shall bring from your land that the LORD your God is giving you, and put it in a basket and go to the place where the LORD your God chooses to make His name abide. 3 You shall go to the priest in office at that time and say to him, "I profess this day to the LORD your God that I have come into the land which the LORD promised to our fathers to give us." 4 The priest will take the basket out of your hand and set it down before the altar of the LORD your God. 5 Then you must answer and say before the LORD your God, "A wandering Aramean[1] was my father, and he went down into Egypt, and sojourned there *with only* a few in number, but there he became a great, mighty, and populous nation. 6 However, the Egyptians mistreated and afflicted us, and laid upon us harsh labor. 7 And when we cried to the LORD God of our fathers, the LORD heard our voice, and looked on our affliction, our labor, and our oppression. 8 And the LORD brought us forth out of Egypt with a mighty hand and with an outstretched arm and with great terror, and with signs and wonders. 9 Then He brought us into this place, and has given us this land, a land that flows with milk and honey. 10 Now, indeed, I have brought the first fruits of the land, which you, O LORD, have given me." Then you must set it before the LORD your God and worship before the LORD your God. 11 You must rejoice in every good thing which the LORD your God has given to you and your house, you, and the Levite, as well as the foreigner who is among you.

12 When you have finished tithing all the tithes of your income the third year, which is the year of tithing, and have given it to the Levite, the foreigner, the orphan, and the widow, that they may eat within your towns and be satisfied, 13 then you shall say before the LORD your God, "I have removed the sacred things out of my house and also have given them to the Levite, and to the foreigner, to the orphan, and to the widow, according to all Your commandments which You have commanded me. I have not transgressed Your commandments or forgotten them. 14 I have not eaten anything when in mourning, nor have I removed anything while unclean, nor offered anything to the dead. I have listened to the voice of the LORD my God and have done according to all that You have commanded me. 15 Look down from Your holy habitation, from heaven, and bless Your people Israel and the land which You have given us, as You swore to our fathers, a land flowing with milk and honey."

[1] *5* Rebekah, Jacob's mother, was an Aramean.

26:5 Ge 43:1–2
26:6 Ex 1:11
26:7 Ex 3:9
26:8 Dt 4:34
26:9 Ex 3:8
26:11 Dt 12:7
26:12 Lev 27:30
26:13 Ps 119:141
26:14 Lev 7:20
26:15 Isa 63:15

26:17 Ex 24:7
26:18 Dt 7:6
26:19 Dt 7:6
27:2 Jos 4:1
27:3 Dt 26:9
27:5 Ex 20:25
27:7 Dt 12:7
27:8 Hab 2:2
27:12 Jdg 9:7

An Exhortation to Obey

16 Today the LORD your God has commanded you to do these statutes and judgments. You must therefore keep and do them with all your heart and with all your soul. 17 You have affirmed today that the LORD is your God and vowed to walk in His ways, and to keep His statutes, and His commandments, and His judgments, and to listen to His voice. 18 And the LORD has affirmed today that you are His special people, just as He has promised you, and that you should keep all His commandments. 19 He will exalt you above all nations which He has made, in praise, and in name, and in honor; and that you may be a holy people to the LORD your God, just as He has spoken.

The Altar on Mount Ebal

27 Then Moses and the elders of Israel commanded the people, saying: Keep all the commandments which I am commanding you today. 2 On the day when you cross over the Jordan into the land which the LORD your God is giving you, you must set up for yourself great stones, and cover them with plaster. 3 Then you must write all the words of this law on them, when you cross over, so that you may enter into the land which the LORD your God is giving you, a land flowing with milk and honey, just as the LORD God of your fathers promised you. 4 Therefore, when you cross over the Jordan, you shall set up these stones, which I am commanding you today, on Mount Ebal, and you shall cover them with plaster. 5 There you must build an altar to the LORD your God, an altar of stones. You must not use any iron tool on them. 6 You must build the altar of the LORD your God with whole stones, and you must offer burnt offerings on it to the LORD your God. 7 You must offer peace offerings and eat there, and rejoice before the LORD your God. 8 You must write all the words of this law very clearly on the stones.

9 Moses and the Levitical priests spoke to all Israel, saying: Be silent and listen, O Israel. Today you have become the people of the LORD your God. 10 Therefore, you must obey the voice of the LORD your God and do His commandments and His statutes, which I am commanding you today.

11 Moses commanded the people the same day, saying:

12 These shall stand on Mount Gerizim to bless the people when you cross over the Jordan: Simeon, Levi, Judah, Issachar, Joseph, and Benjamin. 13 And these must stand on Mount Ebal for the curse: Reuben, Gad, Asher, Zebulun, Dan, and Naphtali.

14 The Levites will answer and say to all the men of Israel with a loud voice:

15 "Cursed is the man who makes any graven or molded image, an abomination to the LORD, the work of the hands of the craftsman, and puts it in a secret place." And all the people shall answer and say, "Amen."

16 "Cursed is he who disrespects his father or his mother." And all the people shall say, "Amen."

17 "Cursed is he who removes his neighbor's landmark." And all the people shall say, "Amen."

18 "Cursed is he who misleads the blind man on the road." And all the people shall say, "Amen."

19 "Cursed is he who perverts justice for the foreigner, orphan, and widow." And all the people shall say, "Amen."

20 "Cursed is he who lies with his father's wife, for he dishonors his father." And all the people shall say, "Amen."

21 "Cursed is he who lies with any kind of beast." And all the people shall say, "Amen."

22 "Cursed is he who lies with his sister, the daughter of his father, or the daughter of his mother." And all the people shall say, "Amen."

23 "Cursed is he who lies with his mother-in-law." And all the people shall say, "Amen."

24 "Cursed is he who strikes down his neighbor secretly." And all the people shall say, "Amen."

25 "Cursed is he who receives pay to slay an innocent person." And all the people shall say, "Amen."

26 "Cursed is he who does not confirm all the words of this law by doing them." And all the people shall say, "Amen."

Blessings for Obedience

28 Now it will be, if you will diligently obey the voice of the LORD your God, being careful to do all His commandments which I am commanding you today, then the LORD your God will set you high above all the nations of the earth. 2 And all these blessings will come on you and overtake you if you listen to the voice of the LORD your God.

3 You will be blessed in the city and blessed in the field.

4 Your offspring will be blessed, and the produce of your ground, and the offspring of your livestock, the increase of your herd and the flocks of your sheep.

5 Your basket and your kneading bowl will be blessed.

6 You will be blessed when you come in and blessed when you go out.

27:14 Da 9:11
27:15 Ex 20:4
27:16 Ex 20:12
27:17 Dt 19:14
27:18 Lev 19:14
27:19 Dt 10:18
27:20 Dt 22:30
27:21 Lev 18:23
27:22 Lev 18:9
27:23 Lev 20:14
27:24 Lev 24:17
27:25 Ex 23:7–8
27:26 Gal 3:10
28:1 Ex 15:26
28:2 Zec 1:6
28:3 Ge 39:5
28:4 Ge 49:25
28:6 Ps 121:8
....
28:9 Ex 19:5–6
28:10 2Ch 7:14
28:11 Dt 28:4
28:12 Lev 26:4
28:14 Dt 5:32
28:15 Mal 2:2
28:17 Dt 28:5
28:18 Dt 28:4

7 The LORD will cause your enemies who rise up against you to be defeated before you; they will come out against you one way and flee before you seven ways.

> I declare the Word of the Lord over my marriage, my children, and my household (Dt 28:7).

8 The LORD will command the blessing on you in your barns and in all that you set your hand to do, and He will bless you in the land which the LORD your God is giving you.

9 The LORD will establish you as a holy people to Himself, just as He swore to you, if you will keep the commandments of the LORD your God and walk in His ways. 10 All people of the earth shall see that you are called by the name of the LORD, and they shall be afraid of you. 11 The LORD will make you overflow in prosperity, in the offspring of your body, in the offspring of your livestock, and in the produce of your ground, in the land which the LORD swore to your fathers to give you.

> I am the head and not the tail (Dt 28:13).

12 The LORD will open up to you His good treasure, the heavens, to give the rain to your land in its season and to bless all the work of your hand. You will lend to many nations, but you will not borrow. 13 The LORD will make you the head and not the tail; you will only be above and you will not be beneath, if you listen to the commandments of the LORD your God, which I am commanding you today, to observe and to do them. 14 Also, you shall not turn aside from any of the words which I am commanding you today, to the right hand or to the left, to go after other gods to serve them.

Warnings Against Disobedience

15 But it will happen, if you will not listen to the voice of the LORD your God, by being careful to do all His commandments and His statutes which I am commanding you today, that all these curses will come upon you and overtake you.

16 You will be cursed in the city and cursed in the field.

17 Your basket and your kneading bowl will be cursed.

18 Your offspring will be cursed along with the fruit of your land, the produce of your herd, and the flocks of your sheep.

19 You will be cursed when you come in and
cursed when you go out.

20 The LORD will send cursing, vexation, and
rebuke on you in all that you set your hand to
do, until you are destroyed and until you per-
ish quickly because of the wickedness of your
doings, by which you have forsaken Me. 21 The
LORD will make pestilence cling to you until it
has consumed you from the land, which you
are going to possess. 22 The LORD will strike you
with a wasting disease, with a fever, with an
inflammation, with an extreme heat, with the
sword, with blight, and with mildew, and they
shall pursue you until you perish. 23 The heav-
ens which are over your head will be bronze,
and the earth that is under you will be iron.
24 The LORD will make the rain of your land
powder and dust. It will come from heaven
down on you until you are destroyed.

25 The LORD will cause you to be defeated be-
fore your enemies, and you will go out one
way against them and flee seven ways before
them, and will be become *an object* of terror to
all the kingdoms of the earth. 26 Your carcass
will be meat for all the fowls of the air and
beasts of the earth, and no man will frighten
them away. 27 The LORD will strike you with the
boils of Egypt and with tumors, eczema, and
with the itch, from which you cannot be healed.
28 The LORD will strike you with madness, and
blindness, and bewilderment of heart. 29 You
will grope at noon, as the blind man gropes
in darkness, and you will not prosper in your
ways. You will only be oppressed and continu-
ally robbed, and no man will save you.

30 You will be engaged to a woman and
another man shall rape her. You will build a
house, but you will not dwell in it. You will
plant a vineyard, but you will not gather its
grapes. 31 Your ox will be killed before your
eyes, and you will not eat of it. Your donkey
will be violently taken away from before you
and will not be returned to you. Your sheep will
be given to your enemies, and you will have
no one to rescue them. 32 Your sons and your
daughters will be given to another people.
Your eyes will look and fail with longing for
them all day long, but there will be nothing you
can do. 33 A nation that you do not know will
consume the produce of your land and all your
labors, and you will be nothing but oppressed
and crushed all the time. 34 You will go insane
because of what your eyes will see. 35 The LORD
will strike you in the knees and legs with sore
boils that cannot be healed, from the sole of
your foot to the top of your head.

36 The LORD will bring you and your king,
which you will set over you, to a nation which
neither you nor your fathers have known, and
there you will serve other gods, wood and
stone. 37 You will become a horror, a proverb,
and an object of ridicule among all nations
where the LORD shall lead you.

38 You will carry a lot of seed out into the
field but will gather but little in, for the locust
will consume it. 39 You will plant vineyards and
dress them, but will neither drink of the wine
nor gather the grapes, for worms will eat them.
40 You will have olive trees throughout all your
coasts, but you will not anoint yourself with
the oil, for your olive will drop off. 41 You will
give birth to sons and daughters, but you will
not enjoy them, for they will go into captivity.
42 The locust will consume all of your trees and
fruit of your land.

43 The foreigner who resides with you will get
up higher and higher, and you will go down
lower and lower. 44 He will lend to you, but you
will not lend to him. He will be the head, but
you will be the tail.

45 Moreover, all of these curses will come on
you and will pursue you and overtake you, un-
til you are destroyed, because you did not obey
the voice of the LORD your God, by keeping
His commandments and His statutes which He
commanded you. 46 They will be a perpetual
sign and wonder in regard to you and your
descendants, 47 because you did not serve the
LORD your God with joy and with gladness of
heart, for the abundance of all things. 48 There-
fore, you will serve your enemies whom the
LORD will send against you, in hunger, thirst,
nakedness, and need of all things, and He will
put a yoke of iron on your neck until He has
destroyed you.

49 The LORD will bring a nation against you
from far away, from the end of the earth, as
swift as the eagle flies, a nation whose lan-
guage you will not understand, 50 a nation with
a fierce countenance, which will not respect
the old or show favor to the young. 51 They
will eat the offspring of your livestock and the
produce of your land, until you are destroyed.
They will leave you no grain, wine, or oil, or
the offspring of your herd or the offspring of
your sheep, until they have destroyed you.
52 He will lay siege on you in all your towns
until your high and fortified walls in which you
trusted come down throughout all your land,
and he will lay siege on you in all your towns
throughout all your land which the LORD your
God has given you.

53 You will eat the offspring of your own body,
the flesh of your sons and of your daughters,
which the LORD your God has given you, during
the siege and distress in which your enemies
will persecute you. 54 The man who is tender

28:19 Dt 28:6
28:20 Isa 51:20
28:21 Lev 26:25
28:22 Lev 26:16
28:23 Lev 26:19
28:24 Dt 28:12
28:25 Isa 30:17
28:26 Jer 7:33
28:27 1Sa 5:6
28:29 Job 5:14
28:30 Am 5:11
28:32 Dt 28:41
28:33 Jer 5:17
28:35 Dt 28:27
28:36 Dt 4:28

28:37 Jer 24:9
28:38 Joel 1:4
28:40 Mic 6:15
28:41 Dt 28:32
28:43 Dt 28:13
28:44 Dt 28:12–13
28:45 Dt 28:15
28:46 Isa 8:18
28:48 Jer 28:13–14
28:49 La 4:19
28:50 Isa 47:6
28:51 Dt 28:33
28:53 La 2:20

among you, and very delicate, his eye shall be hostile toward his brother and toward his beloved wife and toward the rest of his children who remain, 55 so that he will not give to any of them any of the flesh of his children which he will eat, because he has nothing left to him because of the siege and the distress by which your enemies will persecute you in all your towns. 56 The tender and delicate woman among you, who would not venture to set the sole of her foot on the ground *because of her* delicateness and tenderness, will be hostile toward her beloved husband, and toward her son and her daughter, 57 and toward her afterbirth that comes out from between her legs, and toward her children whom she will bear. For she will secretly eat them because of lack during the siege and distress in which your enemy will persecute you in your towns.

58 If you are not careful to observe all the words of this law that are written in this book so that you may fear this glorious and fearful name, the LORD your God, 59 then the LORD will bring extraordinary plagues on you and your descendants, even great long-lasting plagues, and severe and long-lasting sicknesses. 60 Moreover, He will bring all the diseases of Egypt upon you, which you were afraid of, and they will cling to you. 61 Also every sickness and every plague which is not written in the Book of the Law will the LORD bring upon you until you are destroyed. 62 You will be left few in number, whereas you were as numerous as the stars of heaven, because you would not obey the voice of the LORD your God. 63 It will be that as the LORD rejoiced over you to do you good and to multiply you, so the LORD will take pleasure over you to destroy you and to bring you to nothing. You will be plucked from off the land which you go to possess.

64 The LORD will scatter you among all the peoples, from the one end of the earth to the other, and there you will serve other gods, wood and stone, which neither you nor your fathers have known. 65 Among these nations you will find no ease, nor will the sole of your foot have rest. But there the LORD will give you a trembling heart, failing of eyes, and despair of soul. 66 Your life shall hang in doubt before you. You will be in dread day and night and will have no assurance of your life. 67 In the morning you will say, "Would to God it were evening!" And at evening you will say, "Would to God it were morning!" because of the fear of your heart and because of the sights your eyes will see. 68 The LORD will bring you into Egypt again with ships, by the way by which I spoke to you, "You will not see it ever again." And there you will be sold to your enemies as male and female slaves, but no one will buy you.

Renewal of the Covenant

29 These are the words of the covenant which the LORD commanded Moses to make with the children of Israel in the land of Moab, besides the covenant which He made with them in Horeb.

2 Moses proclaimed to all Israel, and said to them:

You have seen all that the LORD did before your eyes in the land of Egypt, to Pharaoh and all his servants and to all his land— 3 the great temptations which your eyes have seen, those signs and great wonders. 4 Yet to this day the LORD has not given you a heart to know, eyes to see, and ears to hear. 5 I have led you forty years in the wilderness. Your clothes have not worn out on you, and your sandal has not worn out on your foot. 6 You have not eaten bread, nor have you drunk wine or strong drink, so that you might know that I am the LORD your God.

7 When you came to this place, Sihon, the king of Heshbon, and Og, the king of Bashan, came out against us to battle, and we defeated them. 8 We took their land and gave it as an inheritance to the Reubenites, the Gadites, and to half of the tribe of Manasseh.

9 Therefore, keep the words of this covenant and do them, so that you may prosper in all you do. 10 Today all of you stand before the LORD your God, the heads of your tribes, your elders, and your officers, with all the men of Israel, 11 your little ones, your wives, and your foreigners who are in your camp, from the one who chops your wood to the one who draws your water— 12 so that you should enter into a covenant with the LORD your God, and into His oath, which the LORD your God is making with you today. 13 Today He will establish that you are His people and that He is your God, just as He has said to you and He has sworn to your fathers, to Abraham, to Isaac, and to Jacob. 14 It is not with you alone that I am making this covenant and this oath, 15 but with him who stands here with us today before the LORD our God, and with him who is not here with us today 16 (for you know that we lived in the land of Egypt and how we came through the nations which you passed by, 17 and you have seen their abominations and their idols of wood and stone, of silver and gold, which were among them); 18 lest there be among you a man or woman or family or tribe whose heart turns away today from the LORD our God to go and serve the gods of these nations, and lest there be among you a root bearing

28:58 Isa 42:8
28:60 Dt 7:15
28:62 Dt 4:27
28:63 Pr 1:26
28:64 Lev 26:33
28:65 Lev 26:36
28:67 Dt 28:34

29:1 Dt 5:2–3
29:2 Ex 19:4
29:4 Ac 28:26–27
29:5 Dt 8:4
29:6 Dt 8:3
29:8 Nu 32:33
29:9 Dt 4:6
29:11 Ex 12:38
29:12 2Ch 15:12–15
29:13 Ge 17:7
29:15 Ac 2:39
29:18 Heb 12:15

SPIRITLED WOMAN

COUNSEL FROM THE SPIRIT BASICS

Divine Love and Fear

What are the love of God and the fear of the Lord? These became very real to me as I began to understand what Jesus was looking for in my own heart and in His church. The first commandment speaks of a radical love for God that requires spiritual violence as God's love takes primacy in our hearts. The fear of the Lord refers to a lovesick trembling that purifies the heart of Jesus' bride, leads us to a deeper knowledge of who God is, and shakes us from our complacency and compromise. The Lord was telling me that despite all of our religious activities, we have lost sight of the things Jesus wants the most.

I continue to be struck by the simplicity of what the Lord requires from us. We make it so complicated, and He has made it so clear: Love the Lord your God and fear Him only. One love and one fear—He made it absolutely clear. Deuteronomy 30:11–16 says it plainly.

Shelley Hundley

poisonous and bitter fruit; 19 and it happens that, when he hears the words of this covenant, he blesses himself in his heart, saying, "I shall have peace, even though I walk in the stubbornness of my heart," thus destroying the watered ground with the dry. 20 The LORD will not spare him; rather the anger of the LORD and His jealousy will smolder against that man. All the curses that are written in this book will rest on him, and the LORD will blot out his name from under heaven. 21 The LORD will single him out for disaster out of all the tribes of Israel, according to all the curses of the covenant that are written in this Book of the Law.

22 The generation to come, your children who will rise up after you and the foreigner who will come from a far land, when they see the plagues of that land, and the sicknesses which the LORD has laid on it, will say, 23 "The whole land is brimstone and salt, a burning waste, unsown and unproductive, and no grass grows there, like the overthrow of Sodom and Gomorrah, Admah and Zeboyim, which the LORD overthrew in His anger and wrath." 24 All nations will say, "Why has the LORD done such to this land? What does the heatedness of this great anger mean?"

25 Then men will say, "Because they have forsaken the covenant of the LORD God of their fathers, which He made with them when He brought them out of the land of Egypt. 26 For they went and served other gods, and worshipped them, gods which they did not know and which He had not given to them. 27 The anger of the LORD burned against this land, bringing on it all the curses that are written in this book. 28 The LORD rooted them out of their land in anger and in wrath and in great indignation, and threw them into another land, as it is today."

29 The secret things belong to the LORD our God, but those things which are revealed belong to us and to our children forever, so that we may keep all the words of this law.

29:19 Nu 15:30
29:20 Ps 74:1
29:23 Jer 17:6
....
29:24 Jer 22:8–9
29:28 2Ch 7:20
30:1 Dt 30:15
30:2 Ne 1:9
30:3 Ps 147:2
30:4 Ne 1:9
30:6 Dt 10:16
30:9 Jer 32:41

The Promise of Restoration

30 When all these things happen to you, the blessing and the curse, which I have set before you, and you remember them among all the nations, where the LORD your God has driven you, 2 then you must return to the LORD your God and obey His voice according to all that I am commanding you today, you and your children, with all your heart, and with all your soul. 3 Then the LORD your God will overturn your captivity and have compassion on you and will return and gather you from all the nations, where the LORD your God has scattered you. 4 If any of you are driven out to the outmost parts of heaven, from there will the LORD your God gather you, and from there He will get you. 5 The LORD your God will bring you to the land which your fathers possessed, and you shall possess it. He will prosper you and multiply you more than your fathers. 6 The LORD your God will circumcise your heart and the heart of your descendants to love the LORD your God with all your heart and with all your soul, so that you may live. 7 The LORD your God will put all these curses on your enemies, on them who hate you, who persecuted you. 8 You will return and obey the voice of the LORD, and obey all His commandments which I am commanding you today. 9 The LORD your God will make you prosper in every work of your hand, in the offspring of your body, and in the offspring of your livestock, and in the produce of your land, for good. For the LORD will once again rejoice over you for good, just as He rejoiced over your fathers, 10 if you obey the voice of the LORD your God, by keeping His commandments and His statutes which

are written in this Book of the Law, and if you
return to the LORD your God with all your heart
and with all your soul.

The Choice of Life or Death

11 This commandment which I am command-
ing you today is not hidden from you, nor is
it far off. 12 It is not in heaven, that you should
say, "Who will go up for us to heaven and bring
it to us, so that we may hear it and do it?" 13 It
is not beyond the sea, so that you should say,
"Who shall go over the sea for us and bring it
to us, so that we may hear it and do it?" 14 But
the word is very near to you, in your mouth,
and in your heart, so that you may do it.
15 See, today I have set before you life and
prosperity, and death and disaster. 16 What I
am commanding you today is to love the LORD
your God, to walk in His ways, and to keep
His commandments and His statutes and His
judgments, so that you may live and multiply.
Then the LORD your God will bless you in the
land which you go to possess.
17 But if your heart turns away, so that you
do not obey, but are drawn away, and worship
other gods and serve them, 18 then I declare
to you today that you will surely perish and
that you will not prolong your days in the land
which you are crossing the Jordan to go in
and possess.
19 I call heaven and earth to witnesses against
you this day, that I have set before you life and
death, blessing and curse. Therefore choose
life, that both you and your descendants may
live; 20 that you may love the LORD your God,
that you may obey His voice, and that you may
cling to Him, for He is your life and the length
of your days; and that you may dwell in the
land that the LORD swore to your fathers, to
Abraham, Isaac, and Jacob, to give them.

Joshua to Succeed Moses

31 Then Moses went and spoke these
words to all Israel. 2 He said to them,
"I am a hundred and twenty years old today.
I can no longer come and go. Also, the LORD
has said to me, 'You may not cross over the
Jordan.' 3 The LORD your God will cross over be-
fore you. He will destroy these nations before
you, you will possess them, and Joshua will
cross over before you, just as the LORD has said.
4 The LORD will do to them as He did to Sihon
and to Og, the kings of the Amorites, and to
their land, which He destroyed. 5 The LORD will
give them up before you, so that you may do
to them according to all the commandments
which I have commanded you. 6 Be strong and
of a good courage. Fear not, nor be afraid of
them, for the LORD your God, it is He who goes
with you. He will not fail you, nor forsake you."

30:11 Isa 45:19
30:15 Dt 11:26
30:16 Dt 30:6
30:19 Dt 4:26
30:20 Dt 10:20
31:2 Dt 34:7
31:3 Dt 9:3
31:4 Dt 2:33
31:5 Dt 7:2
31:6 Jos 10:25

....

31:7 Dt 3:28
31:8 Ex 33:14
31:9 Nu 4:15
31:10 Dt 15:1–2
31:11 2Ki 23:2
31:12 Dt 4:10
31:13 Dt 11:2
31:14 Nu 27:13
31:16 Jdg 2:12
31:17 Nu 14:42

7 Moses called to Joshua, and said to him in
the sight of all Israel, "Be strong and of good
courage, for you must go with this people to
the land which the LORD has sworn to their
fathers to give them, and you will enable them
to inherit it. 8 The LORD, He goes before you.
He will be with you. He will not fail you nor
forsake you. Do not fear, nor be dismayed."

I will not be afraid of evil, for my God goes before me (Dt 31:6).

9 Moses wrote this law and delivered it to the
priests, the sons of Levi who bore the ark of the
covenant of the LORD, and to all the elders of
Israel. 10 Moses commanded them, saying, "At
the end of every seven years, at the time of the
year of the cancellation of debts, at the Feast
of Tabernacles, 11 when all Israel has come to
appear before the LORD your God in the place
which He will choose, you must read this law
before all Israel in their hearing. 12 Gather the
people together, men, women, children, and
your foreigner who is within your towns, so
that they may hear and learn and fear the LORD
your God, and observe to do all the words of
this law. 13 Their children, who have not known
it, may hear and learn to fear the LORD your
God, as long as you live in the land which you
cross the Jordan to possess."

Prediction of Israel's Rebellion

14 The LORD said to Moses, "Indeed, your days
draw near when you must die. Call Joshua,
and present yourselves in the tent of meeting,
so that I may commission him." So Moses and
Joshua went, and presented themselves in the
tent of meeting.
15 The LORD appeared in the tent in a pillar of
cloud, and the pillar of cloud stood over the
door of the tent. 16 The LORD said to Moses, "You
are about to lie down with your fathers, and
this people will rise up and begin to prostitute
themselves after the gods of the foreigners of
the land, where they are going to be among
them, and will forsake Me and break My cov-
enant which I have made with them. 17 Then
My anger will burn against them on that day,
and I will forsake them, and I will hide My face
from them, and they will be devoured, and
many disasters and troubles will befall them,
so that they will say in that day, 'Have not these
disasters come upon us because our God is not
among us?' 18 And I will surely hide My face in
that day for all the evil things which they shall
have done, in that they turned to other gods.
19 "Now therefore write yourself this song
and teach it to the children of Israel. Put it

on their mouths, so that this song may be a
witness for Me against the children of Israel.
20 For when I have brought them into the land
which I swore to their fathers, flowing with
milk and honey, and they have eaten, and
filled themselves, and become fat, then they
will turn to other gods, and serve them, and
provoke Me, and break My covenant. 21 Then
when many disasters and troubles have fallen
on them, this song will testify against them as
a witness, for it must not be forgotten from
the mouths of their descendants. For I know
their intention which they are developing even
now, before I have brought them into the land
which I promised." 22 Therefore, Moses wrote
this song the same day, and taught it to the
children of Israel.
23 He gave Joshua, the son of Nun, an ex-
hortation, and said, "Be strong and of a good
courage, for you will bring the children of Is-
rael into the land which I swore to them, and
I will be with you."
24 When Moses had finished writing the
words of this law in a book, until they were
completed, 25 then Moses commanded the
Levites, who bore the ark of the covenant of
the LORD, saying, 26 "Take this Book of the Law,
and put it inside the ark of the covenant of the
LORD your God, so that it may be there for a wit-
ness against you. 27 For I know your rebellion
and your stiff neck. Even now, while I am yet
alive with you today, you have been rebellious
against the LORD. How much more after my
death? 28 Gather to me all the elders of your
tribes, and your officers, so that I may speak
these words in their hearing and call heav-
en and earth to witness against them. 29 For I
know that after my death you will utterly cor-
rupt yourselves and turn aside from the way
which I have commanded you, and disaster
will befall you in the latter days, because you
will do evil in the sight of the LORD, to provoke
Him to anger through the work of your hands."

The Song of Moses

30 Moses spoke the words of this song until
they were finished, in the hearing of all the
assembly of Israel:

32 Give ear, O heavens, and I will speak;
hear, O earth, the words of my mouth.
2 My teaching will drop like the rain,
my sayings will distill as the dew,
as the droplets on the grass,
and as the showers on the herb.

3 For I will proclaim the name of the LORD:
Ascribe greatness to our God!
4 He is the Rock; His work is perfect;
for all His ways are just.
He is a God of faithfulness and without
injustice;
righteous and upright is He.

5 They have acted corruptly to Him;
they are not His children, but blemished;
they are a perverse and crooked
generation.
6 Is this how you repay the LORD,
you foolish and unwise people?
Is He not your father, who has bought you?
Has He not made you, and established
you?

7 Remember the days of old,
consider the years of previous
generations.
Ask your father, and he will show you;
your elders, and they will tell you:
8 When the Most High gave the nations their
inheritance,
when He separated the sons of man,[1]
He set the boundaries of the peoples
according to the number of the children
of Israel.
9 For the LORD's portion is His people;
Jacob is the allotment of His inheritance.

> I imagine myself curled up and being rocked in God's lap, held close to His chest, clinging to folds of a linen robe as He caresses my hair (Dt 32:10).

10 He found him in a desert land
and in the howling waste of a
wilderness;
He led him about, He instructed him,
He protected him like the pupil of His
eye.
11 Like an eagle stirs up her nest,
that flutters over her young,
He spread out his wings and took him;
He lifted him on His pinions;
12 the LORD alone guided him,
and there was no foreign god with him.
13 He made him ride on the high places of the
earth,
and he ate of the produce of the fields;
He made him suck honey out of the rock
and oil out of the flinty rock,
14 butter from the herd,
and milk from the flock,
along with the fat of lambs,
and rams of the breed from Bashan,
and goats,
with the best of the kernels of wheat;
you drank the pure blood of the grape.

31:20 Ne 9:25–26
31:21 Hos 5:3
31:22 Dt 31:19
31:24 Dt 31:9
31:26 Dt 31:19
31:27 Dt 9:24
31:28 Dt 4:26
31:29 Jdg 2:19
32:1 Dt 4:26
32:2 Ps 72:6
32:3 Jer 10:6
32:4 Dt 32:18

32:5 Dt 31:29
32:6 Isa 63:16
32:7 Ps 44:1
32:8 Ac 17:26
32:9 Jer 10:16
32:10 Ps 17:8
32:11 Ex 19:4
32:12 Ps 78:52–53
32:13 Job 29:6
32:14 Ge 49:11

[1]8 Or *Adam.*

15 But Jeshurun grew fat and kicked;
you grew fat, you grew thick;
you are covered with fat.
Then he forsook God who made him,
and devalued the Rock of his salvation.
16 They made Him jealous with strange gods;
with abominations they provoked Him to anger.
17 They sacrificed to demons, not to God,
to gods whom they knew not,
to new gods that recently came along,
whom your fathers did not fear.
18 You have forgotten the Rock who begot you;
you are unmindful, and have forgotten the God who gave you birth.
19 When the LORD saw it, He despised them,
because of the provocation of His sons and daughters.
20 He said: I will hide My face from them;
I will see what their end will be,
for they are a very perverse generation,
children in whom there is no loyalty.
21 They have made Me jealous with that which is not God;
they have provoked Me to anger with their empty things.
And I will make them jealous of those who are not a people;
I will provoke them to anger with a foolish nation.
22 For a fire has been inflamed by My anger,
and it will burn to the lowest part of Sheol,[1]
and shall consume the earth and its produce,
and ignite the foundations of the mountains.

23 I will heap misfortunes on them;
I will use My arrows on them.
24 They will be starved by famine,
and consumed by plague and bitter destruction;
I will also send the teeth of beasts upon them,
with the poison of crawling creatures in the dust.
25 The sword outside and terror within will destroy both the young man and the virgin,
the infant along with the man of gray hair.
26 I said, "I want to cut them into pieces,
I will cause the memory of them to disappear from among men,"
27 however, I feared the wrath of the enemy,
that their adversaries would misunderstand
and say, "Our hand is victorious,
and the LORD has not done all this."

32:15 Dt 31:20
32:17 Jdg 5:8
32:18 Isa 17:10
32:19 Ps 106:40
32:20 Dt 32:5
32:21 1Ki 16:13
32:22 La 4:11
32:23 Eze 5:16
32:24 Lev 26:22
32:25 Eze 7:15
32:26 Dt 28:64
32:27 Ps 140:8
....
32:29 Dt 5:29
32:30 Lev 26:8
32:32 Dt 29:18
32:33 Ps 58:4
32:34 Job 14:17
32:35 Ro 12:19
32:36 Ps 135:14
32:37 Jdg 10:14
32:39 1Sa 2:6
32:40 Ge 14:22
32:41 Isa 66:16
32:42 Dt 32:23

28 For they are a nation devoid of counsel;
there is no understanding in them.
29 Would that they were wise,
so that they understood this,
so that they would comprehend their future!
30 How should one chase a thousand,
and two put ten thousand to flight,
unless their Rock had sold them,
and the LORD had given them up?
31 For their rock is not as our Rock;
even our enemies themselves concede this.
32 For their vine is from the vine of Sodom
and from the fields of Gomorrah;
their grapes are grapes of poison;
their clusters are bitter.
33 Their wine is the poison of dragons
and the deadly venom of cobras.
34 Is not this laid up in store with Me
and sealed up among My treasures?
35 Vengeance is Mine, and recompense;
their foot will slip in due time;
for the day of their calamity is at hand,
and the things to come hasten upon them.
36 For the LORD will judge His people,
and relent in regard to His servants,
when He sees that their power is gone
and there is no one left, whether restrained or free.
37 He will say: Where are their gods,
their rock in whom they trusted,
38 which ate the fat of their sacrifices
and drank the wine of their drink offerings?
Let them rise up and help you
and be your protection.

39 See now that I, even I, am He,
and there is no god besides Me;
I kill, and I make alive;
I wound, and I heal;
there is no one who can deliver out of My hand.
40 For I lift up My hand to heaven,
and say: As I live forever,
41 if I sharpen My flashing sword
and My hand takes hold on judgment,
I will render vengeance on My enemies
and will repay those who hate Me.
42 I will make My arrows drunk with blood,
and My sword shall devour flesh,
with the blood of the slain and of the captives,

[1] 22 Or *the lowest depths of the earth* or *underworld*.

from the heads of the leaders of the
enemies.

43 Rejoice, O you nations, with His people;
for He will avenge the blood of His
servants
and will render vengeance on His
adversaries
and will be merciful to His land and
people.

44 Moses came and spoke all the words of
this song in the hearing of the people, he,
with Joshua, the son of Nun. 45 When Moses
finished speaking all these words to all Israel,
46 he said to them, "Set your hearts on all the
words which I testify among you today, which
you shall command your children to be careful
to observe, all the words of this law. 47 For it
is no idle word for you, because it is your life,
and by this word you will prolong your days
in the land which you cross over the Jordan
to possess."

Moses to Die on Mount Nebo

48 The LORD spoke to Moses that same day, say-
ing, 49 "Go up to this mountain of the Abarim,
to Mount Nebo, which is in the land of Moab
opposite Jericho, and look at the land of Ca-
naan, which I am giving to the children of Israel
for a possession. 50 Die on the mount where
you go up, and be gathered to your people,
just as Aaron, your brother, died on Mount Hor
and was gathered to his people, 51 because you
trespassed against Me among the children of
Israel at the waters of Meribah Kadesh, in the
Wilderness of Zin, because you did not treat
Me as holy in the midst of the children of Is-
rael. 52 Nevertheless, you will see the land be-
fore you, but you may not go there, to the land
which I am giving to the children of Israel."

Moses Blesses Israel
Ge 49:1–28

33 Now this is the blessing with which
Moses, the man of God, blessed the
children of Israel before his death. 2 He said:

The LORD came from Sinai and rose up from
Seir to them;
He shone forth from Mount Paran,
and He came with ten thousands of holy
ones;
from His right hand went a fiery law[1] for
them.
3 Surely, He loved the people;
all His holy ones are in Your hand,
and they sit down at Your feet;
everyone receives Your words.
4 Moses decreed to us a law,
the inheritance of the assembly of Jacob.

32:43 Rev 19:2
32:44 Nu 13:8
32:46 Eze 40:4
32:47 Lev 18:5
32:49 Nu 27:12
32:50 Ge 25:8
32:51 Nu 27:14
32:52 Dt 34:1–4
33:1 Jos 14:6
33:2 Hab 3:3
33:3 Lk 10:39
33:4 Ps 119:111

33:5 Dt 32:15
33:6 Ge 49:3–4
33:7 Ge 49:8–12
33:8 Ex 17:7
33:10 Lev 10:11
33:13 Ge 49:22–26
33:15 Hab 3:6

5 He was king over Jeshurun,
when the heads of the people and
the tribes of Israel were gathered
together.
6 Let Reuben live, and not die,
and let not his men be few.

7 This is the blessing to Judah. He said:

Listen, O LORD, to the voice of Judah,
and bring him to his people;
may his hands contend for them,
and may You help him against his
enemies.

8 Of Levi he said:

Let Your Thummim and Your Urim be with
Your godly one,
whom You tested at Massah,
and with whom You contended at the
waters of Meribah,
9 who said to his father and to his mother,
"I have not seen him,"
and he did not acknowledge his brothers
or know his own children,
for they have kept Your word
and guarded Your covenant.
10 They will teach Jacob Your judgments
and Israel Your law.
They will put incense before You
and the whole burnt offerings on your
altar.
11 Bless, O LORD, his substance,
and accept the work of his hands;
run through the loins of them that rise
against him
and of them that hate him,
so that they rise never again.

12 Of Benjamin he said:

The beloved of the LORD
will dwell in safety by Him,
and the LORD will protect him all day long;
he will dwell between His shoulders.

13 Of Joseph he said:

May his land be blessed of the LORD,
from the harvest of the heavens,
by the dew,
and by the deep crouching beneath,
14 by the precious fruits brought forth by the
sun,
and by the choice things put forth by the
moon,
15 by the finest things of the ancient
mountains,
and by the choice things of the
everlasting hills,
16 by the best things of the earth and its
fullness,

[1] 2 Or *flashing lightning.*

and by the goodwill of Him who dwelt
in the bush.
May the blessing rest on the head of
Joseph,
on top of the head of him who was
separated from his brothers.
17 His glory is like the firstborn of his bull,
and his horns are like the horns of a
wild ox;
with them he will push the peoples
together to the ends of the
earth;
they are the ten thousands of Ephraim,
and they are the thousands of
Manasseh.

18 Of Zebulun he said:

Rejoice, Zebulun, in your going outside,
and Issachar in your tents.
19 They will call the peoples to the mountain;
there they will offer sacrifices of
righteousness,
for they will draw out the abundance of
the seas
and the treasures hid in the sand.

20 Of Gad he said:

Blessed be he who enlarges Gad;
he dwells as a lion
and tears an arm and the crown of a
head.
21 He provided the first part for himself,
because there, in a portion of the ruler,
he was seated.
He came with the heads of the people.
He executed the justice of the LORD,
and His ordinances with Israel.

22 Of Dan he said:

Dan is a lion's whelp;
he will leap forth from Bashan.

Let me be satisfied with favor and filled with Your blessing (Dt 33:23).

23 Of Naphtali he said:

O Naphtali, satisfied with favor
and full with the blessing of the LORD,
possess the west and the south.

24 Of Asher he said:

May Asher be blessed with children;
may he be acceptable to his brothers,
and may he dip his foot in oil.[1]
25 Your sandals will be iron and brass;
according to your days, so shall be your
strength.

33:17 Nu 23:22
33:18 Ge 49:13–15
33:19 Ps 4:5
33:20 Ge 49:19
33:21 Jos 1:14
33:23 Ge 49:21
33:24 Ge 49:20
....
33:26 Ex 15:11
33:28 Nu 23:9
33:29 2Sa 7:23
34:1 Dt 32:49
34:2 Dt 11:24
34:3 Jdg 1:16
34:4 Ge 12:7
34:5 Dt 32:50
34:6 Jude 1:9
34:7 Ge 27:1
34:8 Ge 50:3
34:9 Isa 11:2
34:10 Ex 33:11
34:11 Dt 4:34

26 There is none like the God of Jeshurun,
who rides through the heavens to help
you,
and in His majesty through the skies.
27 The eternal God is your refuge,
and underneath you are the everlasting
arms;
He will drive out the enemy before you,
and will say, "Destroy them."
28 Israel dwells in safety;
the fountain of Jacob will be secluded
in a land of grain and new wine;
its heavens will rain down dew.
29 Blessed are you, O Israel!
Who is like you,
a people saved by the LORD,
the shield of your help,
who is the sword of your majesty!
Your enemies will cringe before you,
and you will tread upon their high
places.

The Death of Moses

34 Moses went up from the plains of
Moab to Mount Nebo, to the top of Pis-
gah, which is opposite Jericho. Then the LORD
showed him all the land—from Gilead to Dan,
2 and all Naphtali and the land of Ephraim and
Manasseh, and all the land of Judah, to the
Mediterranean Sea, 3 and the Negev and the
plain of the valley of Jericho, the city of palm
trees, as far as Zoar. 4 The LORD said to him,
"This is the land which I swore to Abraham, to
Isaac, and to Jacob, saying, 'I will give it to your
descendants.' I have caused you to see it with
your eyes, but you will not cross over there."
5 So Moses, the servant of the LORD, died there
in the land of Moab, according to the word
of the LORD. 6 He buried him in a valley in the
land of Moab, opposite Beth Peor, but no man
knows of his burial place to this day. 7 Moses
was a hundred and twenty years old when he
died. His eye was not dim, nor was his vitality
diminished. 8 The children of Israel wept for
Moses in the plains of Moab thirty days. Then
the days of weeping and mourning for Moses
were ended.
9 Now Joshua, the son of Nun, was full of the
spirit of wisdom, for Moses had laid his hands
on him. And the children of Israel listened to
him and did as the LORD commanded Moses.
10 Since then there has not arisen a prophet
in Israel like Moses, whom the LORD knew face
to face, 11 in all the signs and wonders which
the LORD sent him to do in the land of Egypt,
to Pharaoh, to all his servants, and to all his
land, 12 and by all that mighty power and by
all the great terror which Moses displayed in
the sight of all Israel.

[1] 24 A metaphor depicting prosperity.

Author: Traditionally Joshua

Written: Between 1400 and 1370 BC

Theme: Conquering the Promised Land

JOSHUA

Dear Spirit Led Woman,

The Promised Land described in the Book of Joshua is a picture of what God has available for you. He has a promised land for your life—a destiny that only you can fulfill. Your promised land is the will of God for your life, and it is the only place you will find total fulfillment. But to take your land, you must heed the admonition given to Joshua: "Be strong and very courageous, in order to act carefully in accordance with all the law that My servant Moses commanded you" (Jos 1:7).

Be strong, not in your own strength, but in the power of God's Spirit, just as the prophet Zechariah wrote: "Not by might nor by power, but by My Spirit, says the Lord of Hosts" (Zec 4:6). It is by the power of God that you can go forth and take your promised land, just as the children of Israel conquered the Promised Land.

Joy F. Strang

The LORD Commissions Joshua

1 Now after the death of Moses the servant
of the LORD, the LORD spoke to Joshua son
of Nun, the assistant of Moses: 2 "Moses My
servant is dead, so now get up and cross over
the Jordan—you and all this people—to the
land that I am giving to the children of Israel.
3 I have given you every place that the sole of
your foot shall tread, as I said to Moses. 4 From
the wilderness and this Lebanon, as far as the
great river, the River Euphrates, all the land
of the Hittites, and to the *Mediterranean* Sea
toward the setting of the sun will be your terri-
tory. 5 No man will be able to stand against you
all the days of your life. As I was with Moses, I
will be with you. I will not abandon you. I will
not leave you.

> As I keep Your Word, You make me prosperous (Jos 1:8).

6 "Be strong and courageous, for you shall
provide the land that I swore to their fathers
to give them as an inheritance for this people.
7 Be strong and very courageous, in order to
act carefully in accordance with all the law that
My servant Moses commanded you. Do not
turn aside from it to the right or the left, so
that you may succeed wherever you go. 8 This
Book of the Law must not depart from your
mouth. Meditate on it day and night so that
you may act carefully according to all that is
written in it. For then you will make your way
successful, and you will be wise. 9 Have not I
commanded you? Be strong and courageous.
Do not be afraid or dismayed, for the LORD your
God is with you wherever you go."

Joshua Takes Command

10 Then Joshua commanded the officers of
the people, 11 "Pass through the midst of the
camp and command the people, 'Prepare food,
for in three days you will cross the Jordan to
go to take possession of the land that the LORD
your God is giving you to possess.' "
12 To the Reubenites, the Gadites, and to the
half-tribe of Manasseh, Joshua said, 13 "Re-
member the word that Moses the servant of
the LORD commanded you: 'The LORD your God
has given you a place for rest and will give
this land.' 14 Your wives, your children, and
your livestock may live in the land that Moses
gave you on the east side of the Jordan. But
you must cross over with your brothers fully
armed, your mighty men of valor, and help
them, 15 until the LORD has given your brothers
rest, as He has given you, and they also have
possessed the land that the LORD your God is
giving to them. Then you may return to your
own land and possess what Moses the servant
of the LORD gave you *on the east* side of the
Jordan where the sun rises."
16 They answered Joshua, "All that you com-
mand us we will do, and wherever you send
us we will go. 17 Just as we obeyed Moses in
all things, we will obey you. May the LORD
your God be with you, as He was with Moses!
18 Whoever rebels against your command and
disobeys your words, in all that you command
him, shall be put to death. Only be strong and
courageous."

Rahab and the Spies

2 Then Joshua son of Nun sent two men
out from Shittim to spy, saying, "Go see
the land, especially Jericho." So they went, and
they came to the house of a prostitute named
Rahab. They spent the night there.
2 The king of Jericho was told, "Israelite men
came here tonight to spy out the land." 3 So the
king of Jericho sent orders to Rahab, "Bring
out the men who came to you, who have en-
tered your house, for they came to spy out the
whole land."
4 Now the woman had taken the two men
and had hidden them. She said, "Yes, the men
came to me, but I did not know where they
were from. 5 The men went out when it was
time to shut the gate at dark. I do not know
where the men went. Chase after them quick-
ly, for you can overtake them." 6 Yet she had
brought them up to the roof. She hid them
in the stalks of flax that she had spread out
on the roof. 7 So the men chased after them
on the road to the Jordan as far as the fords.
They shut the gate as soon as the pursuers
went out after them.
8 Before the spies went to sleep, Rahab went
up to them on the roof. 9 She said to the men,
"I know that the LORD has given you the land,
for dread from you has fallen upon us, and all
the inhabitants of the land melt *in terror* before
you. 10 For we heard how the LORD dried up the
waters of the Red Sea before you when you
came out of Egypt, and what you did to Sihon
and Og, the two kings of the Amorites who
were on the other side of the Jordan, whom
you completely destroyed. 11 Our hearts melt-
ed when we heard *these things*, and no man
had any breath in him because of you, for the
LORD your God is God in heaven above and on
earth below.
12 "So now, since I have acted faithfully to-
ward you, please swear to me by the LORD that
you will also act faithfully toward my father's
house. Please give me a firm pledge 13 that you
will spare my father, my mother, my brothers,

1:1 Ex 24:13
1:3 Dt 11:24
1:4 Ex 23:31
1:5 Dt 7:24
1:7 Dt 5:32
1:11 Jos 3:2
1:13 Nu 32:20–28
....
1:17 Jos 1:5
2:1 Heb 11:31
2:4 2Sa 17:19–20
2:6 2Sa 17:19
2:7 Jdg 3:28
2:9 Ex 23:27
2:10 Nu 21:21–35
2:11 Dt 4:39
2:12 Jos 2:18

my sisters, and all whom they own, and that you will deliver our lives from death."

14 The men said to her, "Our lives for yours; if you do not report us, then when the LORD gives us the land, we will act faithfully and kindly with you."

15 Then Rahab lowered them by a rope through the window, for her home was set into the wall where she lived. 16 She said to them, "Go to the hill country so that the pursuers do not find you. Hide there three days until the pursuers return. After that, you can go on your way."

17 The men said to her, "We will be free from this oath that you have made us swear, 18 unless, when we come into the land, you tie this red cord to the window through which you let us down. You must bring your father, your mother, your brothers, and all who belong to your father's household into your home. 19 Anyone who comes out of the doors of your house into the street is responsible for his own blood, and we will be innocent. Yet for anyone who stays with you inside the house, we are responsible for his blood if someone should lay a hand on him. 20 But if you tell about this business of ours, then we will be released from the oath that you have made us swear."

21 She said, "Let it be so, according to your words."

Then she sent them off, and they departed. Then she tied the red cord in the window.

22 They went and came to the hill country. They stayed there three days, until the pursuers returned. The pursuers had sought them all along the way but had not found them. 23 So the two men returned. They descended from the hill country. They crossed the river, came to Joshua son of Nun, and told him all that they had discovered. 24 They said to Joshua, "The LORD has surely given the whole land into our hands! Indeed, all the inhabitants of the land melt *in terror* before us."

Israel Crossing the Jordan

3 In the morning Joshua got up early; then he and all the children of Israel set out from Shittim and came to the Jordan. They stayed there before crossing over. 2 After three days the officers went through the camp. 3 They commanded the people, "When you see the ark of the covenant of the LORD your God and the Levite priests carrying it, then you shall set out from where you are and go behind it. 4 There must be a distance of two thousand cubits[1] between you and it. Do not draw closer to it, in order that you may know the way you should go. For you have not passed this way before."

5 Joshua said to the people, "Consecrate yourselves, for tomorrow the LORD will perform wondrous deeds among you."

6 Joshua said to the priests, "Pick up the ark of the covenant, and proceed ahead of the people." So they picked up the ark of the covenant and went in front of the people.

7 The LORD said to Joshua, "Today I will begin to honor you in the sight of all Israel, so that they may know that just as I was with Moses, so I will be with you. 8 You shall command the priests who carry the ark of the covenant, 'When you come to the bank of the Jordan, stand still in the river.' "

9 So Joshua said to the children of Israel, "Draw near and hear the words of the LORD your God." 10 And Joshua said, "By this you will know that the living God is among you, and that He will thoroughly drive out the Canaanites, the Hittites, the Hivites, the Perizzites, the Girgashites, the Amorites, and the Jebusites from before you. 11 See, the ark of the covenant of the LORD of all the earth is passing before you into the Jordan. 12 Now select twelve men from the tribes of Israel, one man per tribe. 13 When the soles of the feet of the priests who bear the ark of the LORD, the Lord of all the earth, touch the water of the Jordan, the water of the Jordan that flows from upstream will be cut off and pile up."

14 When the people set out from their tents to cross over the Jordan, the priests were carrying the ark of the covenant before the people. 15 When the carriers of the ark came to the Jordan, the feet of the priests carrying the ark dipped into the edge of the water. (Now the Jordan overflows its banks all the days of the harvest.) 16 Then the water that flows down from upstream stood still and rose up in a heap very far away at Adam, the city beside Zarethan. The water that flows down toward the Sea of Arabah (the Dead Sea) stopped and was cut off. The people crossed over opposite Jericho. 17 The priests carrying the ark of the covenant of the LORD stood firmly on dry ground in the middle of the Jordan, and all Israel crossed over on dry ground until the entire people completed crossing over the Jordan.

Twelve Memorial Stones

4 When the entire people had completed crossing over the Jordan, the LORD said to Joshua, 2 "Take twelve men from among the people, one man per tribe. 3 Command them: 'Pick up twelve stones from the middle of the Jordan, from the place where the feet of the priests are standing; bring them over with

2:15 Ac 9:25
2:18 Jos 6:23
2:24 Ex 23:31
3:1 Jos 2:1
3:2 Jos 1:10–11
3:3 Dt 31:9
3:4 Ex 19:12
3:5 Jos 7:13
3:7 Jos 4:14
3:8 Jos 3:3
3:10 Ex 33:2
3:11 Zec 6:5
3:12 Jos 4:2
3:13 Ex 15:8
3:14 Ac 7:44–45
3:15 1Ch 12:15
3:16 Ge 14:3
3:17 Ex 14:29
4:1 Dt 27:2
4:2 Jos 3:12
4:3 Jos 4:19–20

[1] 4 About 3,000 feet, or 900 meters.

you, and set them in the place you will camp
tonight.' "
4 So Joshua summoned the twelve men he
had appointed from among the children of
Israel, one man per tribe. 5 Then Joshua said
to them, "Cross over before the ark of the LORD
your God into the middle of the Jordan. Each
of you lift up a stone upon your shoulder, one
for each of the tribes of the children of Israel,
6 so that this will be a sign among you. When
your children ask, 'What do these stones mean
to you?' 7 you will answer them that the waters
of the Jordan were cut off before the ark of
the covenant of the LORD. When it crossed the
Jordan, the waters of the Jordan were cut off.
These stones will be a memorial for the chil-
dren of Israel continually."
8 Then the children of Israel did as Joshua
commanded and picked up twelve stones
from the middle of the Jordan, one for each
of the tribes of the children of Israel, as the
LORD had spoken to Joshua. They crossed over
with them to the settlement and set them there.
9 Joshua also set twelve stones in the middle of
the Jordan at the place where the feet of the
priests who carried the ark of the covenant
were standing. The stones are there to this day.
10 The priests who were carrying the ark stood
in the middle of the Jordan until everything
was completed that the LORD had commanded
Joshua to say to the people, according to all
that Moses had commanded Joshua. The peo-
ple quickly crossed over. 11 When all the people
had finished crossing over, the ark of the LORD
and the priests crossed over in the presence
of the people. 12 The Reubenites, the Gadites,
and the half-tribe of Manasseh crossed over
in battle formation in front of the children of
Israel, according to what Moses had said to
them. 13 About forty thousand battle-ready men
crossed over before the LORD for battle on the
plains of Jericho.
14 On that day, the LORD honored Joshua in the
sight of all Israel. They feared him as they had
feared Moses, all the days of his life.
15 The LORD spoke to Joshua, 16 "Command
the priests carrying the ark of the testimony:
'Come up out of the Jordan!' "
17 So Joshua commanded the priests, "Come
up out of the Jordan!"
18 Then when the priests who were carrying
the ark of the covenant of the LORD came up
from the middle of the Jordan and the soles
of the priests' feet touched the dry ground, the
waters of the Jordan returned to their place
and overflowed all its banks as before.
19 Now the people came up from the Jordan
on the tenth day of the first month, and they
camped at Gilgal, on the eastern border of
Jericho. 20 Joshua set up in Gilgal those twelve
stones that they took from the Jordan. 21 He
said to the children of Israel, "When your
children someday ask their parents, 'What do
these stones mean?' 22 then you shall explain to
your children, 'Israel crossed over the Jordan
here on dry ground!' 23 For the LORD your God
dried up the waters of the Jordan before you
until you crossed over, as the LORD your God
did to the Red Sea when He dried it up before
us until we crossed over, 24 so that all the peo-
ples of the earth might know the hand of the
LORD, that it is mighty, and you would fear the
LORD your God always."

5 When all the kings of the Amorites west
of the Jordan and of the Canaanites by the
sea *to the east* heard that the LORD had dried
up the waters of the Jordan before the children
of Israel while they crossed over, their hearts
melted, and there was no longer any breath in
them because of the children of Israel.

Circumcision and Passover at Gilgal

2 At that time the LORD said to Joshua, "Make
flint knives and circumcise the children of Isra-
el a second time." 3 So Joshua made flint knives
and circumcised the children of Israel at the
Hill of the Foreskins called Gibeath Haaraloth.
4 Now this is the reason why Joshua circum-
cised them: All the males who came out of
Egypt who were men of fighting age had died
in the wilderness along the way after leaving
Egypt. 5 All of the people who had come out
were circumcised, but all the people born in
the wilderness along the way after leaving
Egypt were not circumcised. 6 The children of
Israel had traveled forty years in the wilderness
until all the people, the men of fighting age
who came out of Egypt, died, because they
did not obey the LORD. The LORD had sworn
not to let them see the land that He had sworn
to their fathers to give to us, a land flowing
with milk and honey. 7 Yet He raised up their
descendants in their place. These men Josh-
ua circumcised, for they were uncircumcised.
They had not been circumcised along the way.
8 So when the entire people was completely
circumcised, they stayed where they were in
the camp until they healed.
9 The LORD said to Joshua, "Today I have
rolled away the disgrace of Egypt from upon
you." So the name of that place is called Gilgal
even to this day.
10 The children of Israel camped in Gilgal and
kept the Passover on the fourteenth day of the
month in the evening on the plains of Jericho.
11 The day after the Passover, they ate of the
produce of the land, unleavened bread, and
roasted grain. 12 The manna stopped the day

4:6 Ex 13:14
4:7 Ex 12:14
4:14 Jos 3:7
4:18 Jos 3:15
4:19 Jos 5:9
4:20 Jos 4:3
4:21 Jos 4:6
4:22 Jos 3:17
4:23 Ex 14:21
4:24 Ex 14:31
5:1 Nu 13:29
5:2 Ex 4:25
5:6 Dt 2:7
5:8 Ge 34:25
5:11 Lev 23:14
5:12 Ex 16:35

after they ate from the produce of the land, and the children of Israel no longer had manna. That year they ate what the land of Canaan yielded.

The Fall of Jericho

13 Now when Joshua was by Jericho, he looked up and saw a man standing in front of him. In His hand was His drawn sword. Joshua went to Him and said, "Are You for us or for our enemies?"

14 He said, "Neither, for I am the commander of the army of the LORD. Now I have come." Then Joshua fell with his face to the ground and worshipped. Then he said, "What does my Lord wish to say to His servant?"

15 The commander of the army of the LORD said to Joshua, "Remove your sandals from your feet, for the place where you are standing is holy." So Joshua did this.

6 Now Jericho was tightly secured before the children of Israel. There was no one leaving or entering.

2 The LORD said to Joshua, "See, I have given Jericho, its king, and mighty men of valor into your hand. 3 All the men of fighting age shall march around the city. Circle the city once. Do this for six days. 4 Seven priests shall carry seven ram's horn trumpets before the ark. On the seventh day, march around the city seven times, with the priests blowing the trumpets. 5 When they blow a long blast on the ram's horn and when you hear the trumpet sound, all the people shall shout a loud battle cry. The walls of the city will fall down, and the people will go up, every man straight ahead."

I break down every wall of Jericho (Jos 6:5).

6 So Joshua son of Nun summoned the priests and said to them, "Take up the ark of the covenant. Seven priests bearing seven ram's horn trumpets shall be in front of the ark of the LORD." 7 He said to the people, "Advance and march around the city. Let the armed men pass on before the ark of the LORD."

8 So when Joshua had spoken to the people, the seven priests bearing seven ram's horn trumpets before the LORD advanced and blew their trumpets. The ark of the covenant of the LORD went after them. 9 The armed men went before the priests blowing the trumpets, and the rear guard went after the ark while the trumpets were blowing. 10 Now Joshua had commanded the people, "Do not shout a battle cry, and do not let your voices be heard. Do not let a word come out of your mouths until the time I say to you, 'Shout the battle cry!' Then shout." 11 So he had the ark of the LORD circle the city once. Then they came into the camp and spent the night there.

12 Then Joshua got up early in the morning, and the priests picked up the ark of the LORD. 13 Seven priests bearing seven ram's horn trumpets before the ark of the LORD moved on, blowing their trumpets continually. The armed men went before them, and the rear guard went after the ark of the LORD while the trumpets were blowing. 14 The second day they circled the city once, and they returned to the camp. They did this for six days.

15 Then on the seventh day they got up early as dawn was breaking and circled the city in this way seven times. Only on that day did they circle the city seven times. 16 On the seventh time, the priests blew the trumpets and Joshua said to the people, "Shout the battle cry, for the LORD has given you the city! 17 The city and all that is in it are dedicated to the LORD for destruction. Only Rahab the prostitute may live, she, and all who are with her in her house, for she hid the messengers we sent. 18 As for you, keep yourselves from that which is dedicated for destruction, lest you be destroyed. If you take from that which is dedicated for destruction, you will set the Israelite camp for destruction and bring trouble upon it. 19 All the silver, gold, and bronze and iron articles are set apart for the LORD. They will go into the treasury of the LORD."

20 So the people shouted, and they blew the trumpets. When the people heard the trumpet sound, they shouted a loud battle cry, and the wall fell down. So the people went up into the city, one man after the other, and they captured it. 21 They destroyed all that was in the city: man and woman, young and old, and oxen, sheep, and donkey with the edge of the sword.

22 Yet to the two men who had spied out the land, Joshua said, "Enter the prostitute's house, and bring out the woman and everyone who belongs to her, as you swore to her." 23 So the young men who had been spies entered and brought out Rahab, her father, her mother, her brothers, everyone who belonged to her, and her whole extended family. They brought them out and placed them outside of the camp of Israel.

24 They burned the city and everything in it with fire. Only the silver, the gold, the bronze and iron articles they gave to the treasury of the house of the LORD. 25 Yet Rahab the prostitute, her father's family, and everyone who belonged to her, Joshua let live. They live among Israel to this day because she hid the messengers Joshua sent to spy on Jericho.

5:13 Ge 18:2
5:14 Ge 17:3
5:15 Ex 3:5
6:2 Dt 7:24
6:7 Jos 4:13
6:9 Jos 6:13

6:17 Dt 20:17
6:18 Jos 7:1
6:19 1Ch 26:20
6:20 Heb 11:30
6:22 Heb 11:31
6:25 Heb 11:31

26 At that time Joshua made them swear, “Cursed before the LORD will be the man who arises and rebuilds this city of Jericho.

He will establish it
  at the cost of his firstborn
and erect its gates
  at the cost of his youngest child.”

27 So the LORD was with Joshua, and he became famous throughout the land.

Achan’s Sin

7 Yet the children of Israel violated their obligations with regard to the things dedicated for destruction. Achan, son of Karmi, son of Zimri, son of Zerah, from the tribe of Judah took from the things dedicated for destruction, and the anger of the LORD burned against the children of Israel.

2 Joshua sent men from Jericho to Ai (which is near Beth Aven, east of Bethel) and said to them, “Go up and spy on the land.” So the men went up and spied on Ai.

3 Then they returned to Joshua and said to him, “All the people need not go up. Let about two or three thousand men go up and strike Ai. Since they are so few, all the people need not weary themselves.” 4 So about three thousand men went up from among the people there, but they fled from before the men of Ai. 5 The men of Ai struck down thirty-six men and pursued them from the gate to Shebarim. They struck them down on the mountainside, and the hearts of the people melted like water.

6 Then Joshua ripped his clothes. He and the Israelite elders fell on their faces to the ground in front of the ark of the LORD until evening and threw dirt upon their heads. 7 Joshua said, “O Lord GOD, why did You bring this people across the Jordan to give us into the hands of the Amorites to destroy us? If only we had been content to dwell on the other side of the Jordan! 8 O my Lord, what should I say now that Israel has fled before its enemies? 9 The Canaanites and all the inhabitants of the land may hear, turn on us, and cut off our name from the earth. What will You do for Your great name?”

10 Then the LORD said to Joshua, “Stand up! Why have you fallen on your face? 11 Israel has sinned, and they have broken My covenant that I commanded them. They took from the things dedicated for destruction. They have stolen, acted deceitfully, and put them among their own possessions. 12 Therefore the children of Israel cannot stand before their enemies. They turn their backs to their enemies because they have become dedicated for destruction. I will not be with you anymore if you do not destroy the things dedicated for destruction in your midst.

13 “Get up! Consecrate the people and say, ‘Consecrate yourselves for tomorrow, for thus says the LORD, the God of Israel: “Things dedicated for destruction are in your midst, O Israel. You are not able to stand before your enemies until you remove the things dedicated for destruction from your midst.”

14 “ ‘In the morning you will be brought forward by tribes, and the tribe that the LORD selects by lot shall come forward by clans. The clan that the LORD selects by lot shall come forward by households, and the household that the LORD selects by lot shall come forward man by man. 15 And he who is taken with the things dedicated for destruction shall be burned with fire, he and all who belong to him, for he broke the covenant of the LORD and has done a disgraceful action in Israel.’ ”

16 So Joshua got up early in the morning and brought forward Israel by their tribes. The tribe of Judah was selected. 17 He brought forward the clans of Judah, and the clan of the Zerahites was selected. He brought forward the clan of the Zerahites man by man, and Zimri was selected. 18 He brought forward the household of Zimri man by man, and Achan son of Karmi, son of Zimri, son of Zerah, from the tribe of Judah, was selected.

19 Then Joshua said to Achan, “O my son, give glory to the LORD, the God of Israel, and give Him praise! Tell me what you have done! Do not hold back anything from me.”

20 Achan answered Joshua and said, “Indeed, I sinned against the LORD, the God of Israel. This is what I did: 21 When I saw among the plundered goods a beautiful robe from Babylon, two hundred shekels of silver,[1] and a gold bar weighing fifty shekels,[2] I coveted them, so I took them. They are hidden in the ground in my tent. The silver is underneath them.”

22 So Joshua sent messengers, and they ran to the tent. There it all was hidden in the ground with the silver underneath. 23 They took it from the tent and brought it to Joshua and all the children of Israel. They spread it out before the LORD.

24 Then Joshua, and all Israel with him, took Achan son of Zerah, the silver, the robe, the gold bar, his sons, his daughters, his oxen, his donkeys, his sheep, his tent, and all he had, and brought them up to the Valley of Achor. 25 Then Joshua said, “Why have you brought trouble on us? The LORD will trouble you today!”

6:26 1Ki 16:34
6:27 Jos 1:5
7:1 Jos 22:20
7:2 Jos 18:12
7:4 Lev 26:17
7:5 Jos 2:11
7:6 Ge 37:29
7:7 2Ki 3:10
7:9 Ex 32:12
7:11 Jos 6:17–19
7:12 Nu 14:45
7:13 Jos 3:5
7:14 Pr 16:33
7:15 Ge 34:7
7:17 Nu 26:20
7:19 1Sa 6:5
7:21 Dt 7:25
7:24 Jos 15:7
7:25 Jos 6:18

[1] *21* About 5 pounds, or 2.3 kilograms. [2] *21* About 1¼ pounds, or 575 grams.

So all Israel stoned him. They burned them
with fire and stoned them with stones. 26 Then
they erected over him a large pile of stones,
which is still there today. So the LORD turned
from His burning anger. Therefore the name
of the place is called the Valley of Achor to
this day.

Ai Destroyed

8 Then the LORD said to Joshua, "Do not be
afraid or dismayed. Take all the fighting
men with you. Arise, and go up to Ai. See,
I have given the king of Ai, his people, his
city, and his land into your hand. 2 Do to Ai
and its king what you did to Jericho and its
king, except you may plunder its spoils and
its livestock. Now set an ambush for the city
behind it."

3 So Joshua and all the fighting men arose
to go up to Ai. Joshua chose thirty thousand
men, mighty men of valor, and sent them out
at night. 4 He commanded them, "You shall
ambush the city from behind. Do not go very
far from the city. All of you be ready. 5 I and
all the people who are with me will approach
the city. When they come out to engage us as
before, we will flee from them. 6 They will come
after us until we have lured them away from
the city, for they will think, 'They are fleeing
from us as before!' So we will flee from them.
7 Then you shall rise up for the ambush and
take possession of the city. The LORD your God
will give it into your hands. 8 When you have
seized the city, set it on fire. Act according to
the word of the LORD. See, I have commanded
you."

9 So Joshua sent them out. They went to
the place of ambush and took up a position
between Bethel and Ai, westward of Ai, and
Joshua spent the night among the people.

10 Joshua got up early in the morning and
mustered the people. He and the elders of Is-
rael went up before the people to Ai. 11 All the
fighting men who were with him went up and
drew near to the city. They camped north of
Ai, and there was a valley between them and
Ai. 12 He took about five thousand men and
set them in ambush between Bethel and Ai,
westward of the city. 13 So they stationed the
people, all the army that was on the north of
the city, and its rear guard on the west of the
city, and Joshua spent that night in the midst
of the valley.

14 When the king of Ai saw this, the men of
the city hurriedly got up early and went out to
engage Israel in battle at the assembly point
near the Arabah. Yet he did not know that there
was an ambush for him behind the city. 15 So
Joshua and all Israel allowed themselves to be
beaten before them, and they fled in the direc-
tion of the wilderness. 16 All the people who
were in Ai were assembled to pursue them,
so they pursued Joshua and were drawn away
from the city. 17 Not a man was left in Ai or
Bethel who did not go out after Israel. They left
the city wide open, and they pursued Israel.

18 The LORD said to Joshua, "Point toward
Ai with the sword that is in your hand, for I
will give it into your hand." So Joshua pointed
toward the city with the sword in his hand.
19 When his hand pointed, the *men in* ambush
got up quickly from their place and ran. They
came into the city, captured it, and quickly set
the city on fire.

20 The men of Ai turned around and looked,
and there from the city came smoke rising to
the sky! They could not flee in any direction,
and the people who had fled into the wilder-
ness had turned back toward their pursuers.
21 When Joshua and all Israel saw that the
ambush had captured the city and that smoke
rose from it, they turned and struck down the
men of Ai. 22 Then the men in the city came
out to engage them in battle, so they were now
in the middle, with Israel on each side. Israel
struck them down until neither survivors nor
escapees were left. 23 They took the king of Ai
alive and brought him to Joshua.

24 When Israel completed killing all the in-
habitants of Ai in the open wilderness where
they had pursued them, and when all of them
had finally fallen by the edge of the sword, all
Israel returned to Ai and struck it with the edge
of the sword. 25 All who had fallen that day,
men and women, numbered twelve thousand,
all the people of Ai. 26 Joshua did not draw
back his hand with the stretched-out sword
until he destroyed all the inhabitants of Ai.
27 Israel plundered only the livestock and the
spoil of that city for themselves, according to
the word of the LORD that He had commanded
Joshua.

28 Joshua burned Ai and made it a heap for-
ever, a desolation to this day. 29 The king of
Ai hanged on a tree until evening. At sunset,
Joshua commanded that the people take down
the body from the tree and throw it down at the
city gate. They erected a large heap of stones
over it that remains to this day.

The Covenant Renewal at Mount Ebal

30 Then Joshua built an altar to the LORD God
of Israel on Mount Ebal, 31 as Moses the servant
of the LORD had commanded the children of
Israel. As is written in the Book of the Law of
Moses, it was "an altar of uncut stones not
shaped by iron tools." They sacrificed burnt
offerings to the LORD on it, as well as peace

7:26 Dt 13:17
8:1 Jos 1:9
8:2 Dt 20:14
8:4 Jdg 20:29
8:5 Jos 7:5
8:8 2Sa 13:28
8:15 Jos 18:12

8:16 Jdg 20:31
8:18 Jos 8:26
8:22 Dt 7:2
8:23 1Sa 15:8
8:27 Jos 8:2
8:28 Dt 13:16

offerings. 32 There in the presence of the children of Israel he wrote a copy of the Law of Moses on the stones. 33 All Israel, resident alien and native alike, with its elders, officials, and judges, were standing on either side of the ark in front of the Levite priests carrying the ark of the covenant of the LORD, half in front of Mount Gerizim and half in front of Mount Ebal, as Moses the servant of the LORD had commanded from the beginning, in order to bless the people of Israel.

34 After this, Joshua read out all the words of the law, both blessing and curse, according to all that is written in the Book of the Law. 35 There was not a word from all that Moses had commanded that Joshua did not read out before the whole assembly of Israel, with the women, the children, and the resident aliens who were among them.

The Gibeonite Deception

9 When all the kings west of the Jordan in the hill country, in the low country, and along all the coast of the *Mediterranean* Sea toward Lebanon—the Hittite, the Amorite, the Canaanite, the Perizzite, the Hivite, and the Jebusite kings—heard this, 2 they gathered together as one to wage war against Joshua and Israel.

3 But when the inhabitants of Gibeon heard what Joshua had done to Jericho and Ai, 4 they acted craftily, and took old sacks on their donkeys, and old wineskins, torn and mended, 5 old and patched sandals on their feet, and old garments on themselves. All the bread of their provision was dry and crumbly. 6 They went to Joshua at the Gilgal settlement and said to him and the children of Israel, "We have come from a distant land. Now make a pact with us."

7 Then the children of Israel said to these Hivites, "Perhaps you live among us, so how could we make a pact with you?"

8 Yet they said to Joshua, "We are your slaves."

Joshua said to them, "Who are you, and where do you come from?"

9 They said to him, "We, your slaves, have come from a very distant land because of the name of the LORD your God, for we heard news of Him and all He did in Egypt 10 and all that He did to the two Amorite kings on the other side of the Jordan, King Sihon of Heshbon and King Og of Bashan in Ashtaroth. 11 So our elders and all the inhabitants of our country said to us, 'Take food provisions for the journey and go to meet them. Say to them, "We are your slaves. So now, make a pact with us." ' 12 This bread of ours was hot as we took it from our homes on the day we left to come to you, but now, see, it is dry and crumbly. 13 These wineskins that we filled were new, but see, they are ripped open. These clothes and sandals wore out due to the very long journey."

14 So the men *examined* some of the food provisions, but they did not ask the LORD about it. 15 Joshua made peace with them and made a covenant with them to let them live, and the leaders of the congregation swore an oath to them.

16 Three days after they had made a covenant with them, they heard that they were neighbors to them and lived among them. 17 So the children of Israel set out and came to their cities on the third day. Their cities were Gibeon, Kephirah, Beeroth, and Kiriath Jearim. 18 Now the children of Israel did not attack them, for the leaders of the congregation had sworn an oath to them by the LORD, the God of Israel, so the congregation murmured against the leaders.

19 Yet all the leaders said to the whole congregation, "We swore to them by the LORD God of Israel, so now we may not harm them. 20 This is what we will do to them. We will let them live so that wrath will not come upon us due to the oath that we swore to them." 21 The leaders of the congregation also said to them, "Let them live!" So they became woodcutters and water carriers for the whole congregation, as the leaders told them.

22 Joshua met them and said, "Why did you trick us, saying, 'We are very distant from you,' but you are living in our midst? 23 Therefore now you are cursed, and you will always be slaves, cutting wood and carrying water for the house of my God."

24 They answered Joshua, "It was told to your slaves that the LORD your God commanded Moses His servant to give you all the land and to destroy all the inhabitants of the land before you. So we were very afraid for our lives, and we did this thing. 25 Now here we are, in your hands. Do to us whatever is good and right in your eyes."

26 Thus he did to them, and delivered them from the hand of the children of Israel; and they did not kill them. 27 That day he made them woodcutters and water carriers for the congregation and the altar of the LORD, even to this day, at the place He would choose.

The Sun Stands Still

10 Now when King Adoni-Zedek of Jerusalem heard that Joshua captured Ai and destroyed it, doing to Ai and its king as he had done to Jericho and its king, and how the inhabitants of Gibeon had made peace with Israel and were among them, 2 he *and*

8:32 Dt 27:2–3
8:33 Dt 11:29
8:35 Dt 31:12
9:1 Nu 34:6
9:3 Jos 10:2
9:6 Jos 5:10
9:7 Jos 11:19
9:8 Dt 20:11
9:9 Dt 20:15
9:11 Est 8:17

....

9:14 Nu 27:21
9:15 2Sa 21:2
9:18 Ps 15:4
9:21 Dt 29:11
9:22 Jos 9:6
9:24 Dt 7:1–2
9:25 Ge 16:6
9:27 Dt 12:5
10:1 Jos 6:21

his people were very afraid. Gibeon was a large city, like one of the royal cities. It was larger than Ai, and all its men were warriors. 3 So King Adoni-Zedek of Jerusalem sent this message to King Hoham of Hebron, King Piram of Jarmuth, King Japhia of Lachish, and King Debir of Eglon: 4 "Come and help me! Let us attack Gibeon, for it has made peace with Joshua and all the children of Israel."

5 So the five kings of the Amorites—the kings of Jerusalem, Hebron, Jarmuth, Lachish, and Eglon—and all their armies gathered, advanced, and camped against Gibeon. Then they waged war against it.

6 The men of Gibeon sent this message to Joshua at the Gilgal settlement: "Do not abandon your slaves. Come up to us quickly. Save us! Help us! For all the Amorite kings living in the hill country have gathered against us."

7 So Joshua went up from Gilgal, he and all the people of war with him, and all the mighty men of valor. 8 The LORD said to Joshua, "Do not be afraid of them, for I have given them into your hand. Not a single man can stand before you."

9 Then Joshua came upon them suddenly, having marched all night from Gilgal. 10 The LORD panicked them before Israel. They struck them with overwhelming force at Gibeon, then Israel pursued them on the road that rises to Beth Horon and struck them down as far as Azekah and Makkedah. 11 As they fled from Israel on the downslope from Beth Horon, the LORD hurled large hailstones down upon them from the sky as far as Azekah. They died, and *in fact* more died from the hailstones than the children of Israel killed with the sword.

12 On the day the LORD gave over the Amorites to the children of Israel, Joshua spoke to the LORD and said in full view of Israel:

"Sun, stand still over Gibeon;
and moon, in the Valley of Aijalon."
13 So the sun stood still,
and the moon stood in place
until the people brought vengeance on
their enemies.

Is this not written in the book of Jashar?

The sun stood still in the middle of the sky and did not set for about a full day. 14 There has not been a day like this either before or after it, when the LORD obeyed a man, for the LORD waged war for Israel.

15 Then Joshua, and all Israel with him, returned to the settlement at Gilgal.

The Execution of Five Amorite Kings

16 Yet these five kings fled and hid themselves in the cave at Makkedah. 17 Joshua was told, "The five kings have been found hiding themselves in the cave at Makkedah." 18 So Joshua said, "Roll large stones over the mouth of the cave, and station men to stand guard over it. 19 As for you, do not stop pursuing your enemies, but attack them from behind. Do not let them go back to their cities, for the LORD your God has given them into your hand."

Let every spirit hiding from me be exposed in the name of Jesus (Jos 10:16–20).

20 When Joshua and the children of Israel had finished striking them with overwhelming force until they were completely defeated, the survivors escaped from them and went back to their fortified cities. 21 Then all the people returned safely to Joshua at the Makkedah settlement, and no one spoke against any of the children of Israel.

22 Joshua said, "Open the mouth of the cave, and bring out to me those five kings from the cave." 23 They did this, and they brought out those five kings from the cave: the kings of Jerusalem, Hebron, Jarmuth, Lachish, and Eglon. 24 When they brought out those five kings to Joshua, he called out to all the men of Israel and the army commanders, "Come here and place your feet on the necks of these kings." So they came near and placed their feet on their necks.

25 Then Joshua said to them, "Do not be afraid or dismayed. Be strong and courageous! For this is what the LORD will do to all your enemies against whom you fight." 26 After that, Joshua struck them down, killed them, and hung them on five trees. They were hanging on the trees until evening.

27 At sundown Joshua commanded men to take them down from the trees and throw them into the cave in which they had hidden themselves. Over the mouth of the cave he placed large stones, which remain to this day.

Southern Cities Conquered

28 Joshua took Makkedah that day and struck it and its king with the edge of the sword. He destroyed it and all life within it. He did not leave any survivors. He did to the king of Makkedah just as he did to the king of Jericho. 29 Then Joshua passed from Makkedah to Libnah with all of Israel, and they fought against Libnah. 30 The LORD gave Libnah and its king into the hand of Israel, and they struck all who lived in it with the edge of the sword. There were no survivors left. They did to its king what they had done to the king of Jericho.

10:4 Jos 9:15
10:7 Jos 8:1
10:10 Jos 16:3
10:11 Isa 28:2
10:12 Hab 3:11
10:13 2Sa 1:18
10:14 Jos 10:42
10:15 Jos 10:43

10:20 Jos 8:24
10:21 Ex 11:7
10:24 Mal 4:3
10:26 Jos 8:29
10:27 Jos 8:29
10:28 Jos 6:21
10:29 Jos 21:13

Obedience or Disobedience?

If we don't know the cause of the battles in our lives, we will spend time fighting against people instead of our true enemy. Our real fight is against demonic strongholds (2Co 10:3–4). Our war is not with our rebellious child, our mean sister-in-law, our ex-husband, or our grumpy neighbor. The Bible tells us that all our struggles, both within ourselves and with others, are from the hand of the wicked one. It is the devil that tempts people with evil thoughts and is at the root of the attacks on the children of God.

Since we are in a spiritual fight, we must choose to fight with spiritual weapons. Let's look specifically into how we can resist the devil so that he will flee.

Disobedience opens the door to the demonic in our life. This is a *huge* concept to apply to our lives. God fights for His kids when His kids are obedient. Time and time again Israel fought against terrifying armies as Moses led the people toward the Promised Land. When the Israelites were obedient to the Lord, God did amazing works to defeat the idol-worshipping kingdoms. God even made the sun stand still for an entire day during the battle of Gilgal, when Joshua had to fight against five Amorite kings and their armies (Jos 10:1–15). When Israel was disobedient, however, they often met defeat. I don't know about you, but I would sure welcome some sun-stand-still miracles in my life. God comes out to fight our battles when we serve Him through obedience.

Believers, though saved through Jesus, can still piddle around in darkness by walking in sin and depending on what the world has to offer. But listen to what James had to say about that: "You adulterers and adulteresses, do you not know that the friendship with the world is enmity with God?" (Jas 4:4).

Let's look at James 4:7: "Therefore submit yourselves to God. Resist the devil, and he will flee from you." As we go forward, remember that it is pointless for us to do a bunch of resisting if we remain unsubmitted to the Lord. *Submitting to the Lord gives us the power to resist the devil.* We need to be careful that we are not resisting in our own power. Doing so will cause us to become really weary and give up. If you have recently given up in resisting the devil, if you have come to believe that it is pointless to fight him, then check your life to be sure that you have been faithful to the Lord in obedience and submission. Fix any problems you discover, and your spiritual battles will become easier for you to fight.

Jenny Swindall

31 Then Joshua passed from Libnah to Lachish with all of Israel, camped against it, and waged war against it. 32 The LORD gave Lachish into the hand of Israel. They captured it on the second day and struck all who lived in it with the edge of the sword, just as they had done to Libnah. 33 King Horam of Gezer came up to help Lachish, but Joshua attacked him and his people until he did not have a single survivor left.

34 From Lachish, Joshua and all of Israel passed to Eglon. They camped against it and waged war against it. 35 They captured it that day and struck it with the edge of the sword. All who lived in it were destroyed that day, just as Israel had done to Lachish.

36 Then Joshua and all of Israel went up from Eglon to Hebron and waged war against it. 37 They captured it and struck its king, and all who lived in it, and its *surrounding* towns with the edge of the sword. No survivor was left. Just as they had done to Eglon, they destroyed it and all who lived in it.

38 Then Joshua and all of Israel turned to Debir and waged war against it. 39 They captured it, its king, and all its *surrounding* towns and struck them with the edge of the sword. They destroyed all who lived in them, and no survivor was left. As he had done to Hebron, so he did to Debir and its king as they had done to Libnah and its king.

40 So Joshua attacked the whole land: the hill country, the Negev, the lowlands, the mountain slopes, and all their kings. No survivor was left. He destroyed all who breathed, as the LORD God of Israel had commanded. 41 Joshua attacked the land from Kadesh Barnea to Gaza and the land of Goshen as far as Gibeon. 42 Joshua captured all these kings and their land in one campaign because the LORD God of Israel waged war for Israel.

43 Then Joshua and all of Israel returned to the settlement at Gilgal.

Northern Kings Defeated

11 When King Jabin of Hazor heard these things, he sent word to King Jobab of Madon, the king of Shimron, the king of Akshaph, 2 and the kings of the northern hill country, the Arabah south of Kinnereth, the low country, and the heights of Dor in the west, 3 to the Canaanites in the east and in the west, the Amorites, the Hittites, the Perizzites, the Jebusites in the hill country, and the Hivites at Mount Hermon in the land of Mizpah. 4 So these kings went out with all their armies, people as numerous as *grains of* sand on the seashore, with a large number of horses and chariots. 5 These kings all met and camped together at the waters of Merom in order to wage war against Israel.

6 The LORD said to Joshua, "Do not be afraid of them, for about this time tomorrow I will make them dead before Israel. Hamstring their horses and burn their chariots with fire."

7 So Joshua and all his fighting forces came upon them by surprise at the waters of Merom and fell upon them. 8 The LORD gave them into the hand of Israel. They struck them down and pursued them all the way to Greater Sidon, Misrephoth Maim, and Mizpah Valley to the east. They struck them down until no survivor remained. 9 Joshua did to them as the LORD had said. He hamstrung their horses and burned their chariots with fire.

10 At that time Joshua turned, captured Hazor, and struck down its king with the sword. Hazor was formerly the head of all these kingdoms. 11 They struck all who lived in them with the edge of the sword, destroying them. No one who breathed was left, and he burned Hazor with fire.

12 Joshua captured all these kings and their towns. He struck with the edge of the sword, destroying them, as Moses the servant of the LORD had commanded. 13 However, Israel did not burn any of the cities that stood on mounds except Hazor. Joshua burned it. 14 The children of Israel plundered all the goods and the livestock of these cities, but they struck all the people with the edge of the sword until they destroyed them. They did not spare anyone who breathed. 15 As the LORD commanded Moses His servant, so Moses commanded Joshua, and Joshua did it. He did not ignore a word of all that the LORD commanded Moses.

16 So Joshua took all that land: the hill country, the Negev, all the land of Goshen, the lowland, the Arabah, the hill country of Israel and its lowland. 17 From Mount Halak to Seir, and as far as Baal Gad in the Lebanon Valley under Mount Hermon: All their kings he captured, struck down, and killed. 18 Joshua engaged all those kings in battle for a long time. 19 There was no city that made peace with the children of Israel except the Hivites living in Gibeon. They conquered all of them 20 because the LORD hardened their hearts to engage Israel in battle. They destroyed them without mercy, to put them to death, as the LORD had commanded Moses.

21 At that time Joshua came and wiped out the Anakites from the hill country: from Hebron, from Debir, from Anab, from all the hill country of Judah, and from all the hill country of Israel. Joshua utterly destroyed them and their cities. 22 No Anakites were left in the land of the children of Israel, but they did remain in

10:31 Jos 10:3
10:33 Jos 16:10
10:34 Jos 10:3
10:36 Jdg 1:10
10:38 Jos 15:15
10:41 Jos 11:16
10:42 Jos 10:14
10:43 Jos 10:15
11:1 Jos 11:10
11:2 Jos 12:3
11:3 Jdg 3:3
11:4 Jdg 7:12
....
11:6 Jos 10:8
11:7 Jos 10:9
11:8 Jos 13:6
11:9 Jos 11:6
11:11 Jos 10:40
11:12 Dt 7:2
11:15 Jos 1:7
11:16 Jos 10:41
11:17 Dt 7:24
11:21 Dt 9:2
11:22 1Sa 17:4

Gaza, Gath, and Ashdod. 23 So Joshua took the whole land according to all that the LORD had said to Moses. Joshua gave it to Israel as an inheritance according to their allotted portions by their tribes. Then the land rested from war.

The List of Defeated Kings

12 These are the kings on the east side of the Jordan, from the River Arnon to Mount Hermon and all the eastern Arabah, whom the children of Israel struck down to take over their land: 2 Sihon king of the Amorites, who lived at Heshbon and ruled from Aroer, which is on the bank of River Arnon, and from the middle of the valley as far as the River Jabbok, which is the border of the Ammonites, that is, half of Gilead, 3 and the Arabah to the Sea of Galilee eastward, and toward Beth Jeshimoth, to the Sea of Arabah, the Dead Sea, southward below the slopes of Pisgah; 4 and Og king of Bashan, one of the remnant of the giants, who lived at Ashtaroth and at Edrei 5 and ruled over Mount Hermon, Salekah, and all of Bashan to the border of the Geshurites and the Maakathites, and over half of Gilead to the border of Sihon king of Heshbon.

6 Moses the servant of the LORD and the children of Israel struck them down, and the servant of the LORD Moses gave their land to Reuben, Gad, and the half-tribe of Manasseh.

7 These are the kings of the land whom Joshua and the children of Israel defeated on the west side of the Jordan, from Baal Gad in the Valley of Lebanon to Mount Halak, that rises toward Seir. Joshua gave their land to the tribes of Israel according to their allotted portions as an inheritance, 8 in the hill country, in the lowland, in the Arabah, in the slopes, in the wilderness, and in the Negev—the land of the Hittites, the Amorites, the Canaanites, the Perizzites, the Hivites, and the Jebusites:

9 The king of Jericho, one;
the king of Ai, which is beside Bethel, one;
10 the king of Jerusalem, one;
the king of Hebron, one;
11 the king of Jarmuth, one;
the king of Lachish, one;
12 the king of Eglon, one;
the king of Gezer, one;
13 the king of Debir, one;
the king of Geder, one;
14 the king of Hormah, one;
the king of Arad, one;
15 the king of Libnah, one;
the king of Adullam, one;
16 the king of Makkedah, one;
the king of Bethel, one;
17 the king of Tappuah, one;
the king of Hepher, one;
18 the king of Aphek, one;
the king of Lasharon, one;
19 the king of Madon, one;
the king of Hazor, one;
20 the king of Shimron Meron, one;
the king of Akshaph, one;
21 the king of Taanach, one;
the king of Megiddo, one;
22 the king of Kedesh, one;
the king of Jokneam in Carmel, one;
23 the king of Dor in Naphoth Dor, one;
the king of the people in Gilgal, one;
24 the king of Tirzah, one—thirty-one kings in all.

Land Still to be Taken

13 Now Joshua was old and well advanced in years. The LORD said to him, "You are old and advanced in years, but very much of the land still remains to be possessed.

2 "This is the land that remains: all the districts of the Philistines and those of the Geshurites 3 (from the Shihor east of Egypt northward to the boundary of Ekron, which is counted as Canaanite; the cities of the five Philistine governors: Gaza, Ashdod, Ashkelon, Gath, and Ekron), and also the Avvites' lands. 4 Also remaining in the south is all the land of the Canaanites, Arah owned by the Sidonians, as far as Aphek at the Amorite boundary, 5 the land of the Gebalites and all Lebanon to the east, and from Baal Gad at the foot of Mount Hermon to Lebo Hamath.

6 "I will drive out from before the children of Israel all the inhabitants of the hill country from Lebanon to Misrephoth Maim and all the Sidonians. Be sure to divide these lands by lot as an inheritance for Israel as I have commanded you. 7 So now, divide this land as an inheritance for the nine tribes and the half-tribe of Manasseh."

Division of the Land East of the Jordan River

8 *With the other half-tribe of Manasseh,* Reuben and Gad took their inheritance that Moses gave to them on the east side of the Jordan, as Moses the servant of the LORD had given them: 9 from Aroer on the bank of the River Arnon, the city in the middle of the valley, all the plain from Medeba to Dibon, 10 all the cities of King Sihon of the Amorites who reigned in Heshbon, and the land up to the Ammonite border. 11 *Moses had also given them* Gilead, the territory of the Geshurites and Maakathites, all of Mount Hermon, and all of Bashan as far as Salekah, 12 and in Bashan all the kingdom of Og, one of the last remnant of the giants, who reigned in Ashtaroth and Edrei. Moses struck

12:1 Dt 3:8–9
12:2 Ge 32:22
12:3 Dt 3:17
12:4 Dt 1:4
12:5 Dt 3:14
12:6 Nu 32:33
12:7 Jos 11:17
12:8 Jos 11:16
12:10 Jos 10:23
12:12 Jos 10:33
12:13 Jos 10:38
12:14 Nu 21:1
12:17 1Ki 4:10
....
12:19 Jos 11:1
12:20 Jos 11:1
12:21 Jos 17:11
12:22 Jos 19:37
12:23 Jos 11:2
13:1 Jos 14:10
13:3 Dt 2:23
13:4 Jos 19:30
13:5 Jos 12:7
13:6 Jos 11:8
13:8 Jos 12:6
13:9 Nu 21:30
13:12 Jos 12:4

SPIRITLED WOMAN

COUNSEL FROM THE SPIRIT BASICS

Caleb's Inheritance

According to the Scriptures, only two of the Israelites who left Egypt went into the Promised Land. Among the twelve men Moses chose to spy out the land, ten came back and gave a negative report about the giants who lived there, causing the people's hearts to melt in fear. But Joshua and Caleb declared the beauty of the land and that God would make the giants defenseless before them (Nu 14:9).

Because of the Israelites' unbelief, God let them wander in the desert until they died. Their children inherited the Promised Land they were meant to enter.

However, Caleb followed the Lord fully and, along with Joshua, inherited the Promised Land. His was a winning battle strategy—complete abandonment to God (Jos 14:9–14).

Caleb's physical strength had not abated during those forty years in the wilderness. God was with him and drove out the enemy, giving him his inheritance in Hebron, which had been the stronghold of the strongest giants in the land, the Anakim.

Inheriting your promised land also will require a winning strategy. It will mean following the Lord wholly and yielding to the Holy Spirit at every point at which your will, your thoughts, and your desires differ from His divine purpose for your life.

The Holy Spirit comes to dwell in your spirit, filling you with the life of God and expressing that divine life through your soul—your mind, emotions, and will. When God's will becomes your will, His thoughts your thoughts, and His desires your desires, you can say with the apostle Paul, "I have been crucified with Christ. It is no longer I who live, but Christ who lives in me. And the life I now live in the flesh, I live by faith in the Son of God, who loved me and gave Himself for me" (Gal 2:20).

Fuchsia Pickett

13:13 Jos 13:11
13:16 Jos 13:9
13:18 Nu 21:23
13:19 Nu 32:37–38
13:21 Nu 31:8
13:22 Nu 31:8
13:26 2Sa 17:27
13:27 Ge 33:17
13:30 Jos 13:26
13:31 Jos 12:4
13:33 Jos 18:7

them down and took their lands. 13 Yet the children of Israel did not drive out the Geshurites or the Maakathites, and Geshur and Maakah live among Israel until this day.

14 However Moses did not give an inheritance to the tribe of Levi. The burnt offerings of the Lord God of Israel are their inheritance, as He said to them.

15 Moses assigned land to the tribe of the Reubenites according to their clans. 16 Their territory was from Aroer on the edge of the Arnon Valley, the city in the middle of the valley, all the plain of Medeba, 17 Heshbon and all its towns in the plain: Dibon, Bamoth Baal, Beth Baal Meon, 18 Jahaz, Kedemoth, Mephaath, 19 Kiriathaim, Sibmah, Zereth Shahar on the hill of the valley, 20 Beth Peor, the slopes of Pisgah, Beth Jeshimoth, 21 all the cities of the plain, and the whole kingdom of King Sihon of the Amorites, who reigned in Heshbon. Moses struck him down along with the leaders of Midian, Evi, Rekem, Zur, Hur, and Reba, who were princes of Sihon who lived in the land. 22 The children of Israel killed Balaam son of Beor, who practiced divination, with the sword along with the rest of the slain. 23 The border of the Reubenites was the banks of the Jordan. This was the inheritance of the Reubenites according to their clans: those towns and their settlements.

24 Moses assigned land to the tribe of Gad for the Gadites according to their clans. 25 Their territory was Jazer, all the cities of Gilead, and half of the Ammonite land as far as Aroer, which is east of Rabbah, 26 from Heshbon to Ramath Mizpah, Betonim, and from Mahanaim to the territory of Debir. 27 In the valley were Beth Haram, Beth Nimrah, Sukkoth, and Zaphon, the rest of the kingdom of King Sihon of Heshbon, the Jordan as its boundary to the lower Sea of Galilee to the east of the Jordan. 28 This was the inheritance of the Gadites according to their clans: those towns and their settlements.

29 Moses assigned land to the half-tribe of Manasseh for the descendants of Manasseh according to their clans. 30 Their territory was from Mahanaim, through all of Bashan, all the kingdom of King Og of Bashan, all the sixty villages of Jair that are in Bashan, 31 half of Gilead, Ashtaroth, and Edrei: cities of the kingdom of Og in Bashan. This was for the descendants of Makir son of Manasseh, half of the descendants of Makir by their clans.

32 This is the territory Moses assigned in the desert plains of Moab, on the eastern side of Jericho and the Jordan. 33 Yet Moses did not

assign land to the tribe of Levi as an inheritance. The LORD God of Israel was their inheritance, as He said to them.

Division of the Land West of the Jordan

14 These are the territories that the children of Israel inherited in the land of Canaan, which Eleazar the priest, Joshua son of Nun, and the family leaders of the Israelite tribes assigned to them. 2 Their inheritance fell to them by lot, as the LORD commanded through Moses, for the nine and a half tribes. 3 For Moses had assigned the inheritance of two and a half tribes on the other side of the Jordan, but he had not assigned an inheritance among them to the Levites. 4 The descendants of Joseph were two tribes: Manasseh and Ephraim. They did not give territory to the Levites in the land, but only towns in which to live, along with the pastures, livestock, and property. 5 Just as the LORD had commanded Moses, so the children of Israel did when they divided the land.

Hebron Given to Caleb

6 The descendants of Judah approached Joshua at Gilgal, and Caleb son of Jephunneh the Kenizzite said to him, "You know what the LORD said to Moses the man of God about you and me at Kadesh Barnea. 7 I was forty years old when Moses the servant of the LORD sent me from Kadesh Barnea to spy on the land, and I brought word back to him as it was in my heart. 8 My companions who went up with me made the hearts of the people melt, but I wholeheartedly followed after the LORD my God. 9 On that day Moses swore an oath, 'The land on which your foot treads shall be your inheritance, for your descendants perpetually, because you completely followed after the LORD my God.'

10 "Now, the LORD has kept me alive, just as He said, for forty-five years, since the LORD spoke this word to Moses while Israel wandered in the wilderness. Now, here I am this day, eighty-five years old. 11 I am still just as strong today as I was on the day that Moses sent me. My strength now is just like my strength then, both for battle and for going out and returning. 12 So now, give me this hill country that the LORD spoke about on that day. That day you heard that the Anakites live there in large, fortified cities. Perhaps the LORD will be with me, and I will drive them out, as the LORD said."

13 Then Joshua blessed him and gave Hebron to Caleb son of Jephunneh as an inheritance. 14 Therefore Hebron became an inheritance of Caleb son of Jephunneh the Kenizzite until this day because he completely followed after the LORD, the God of Israel. 15 The former name of Hebron was Kiriath Arba. Arba was the greatest man among the Anakites.

Then the land had rest from war.

14:1 Nu 34:17–29
14:2 Nu 33:54
14:3 Jos 13:14
14:4 Ge 48:5
14:5 Jos 21:2
14:6 Nu 14:30
14:7 Nu 13:6
14:8 Nu 14:24
14:11 Dt 34:7
14:12 Nu 13:33
14:13 Jos 22:6
14:14 Jos 14:8–9
14:15 Jos 11:23

....

15:3 Nu 34:4
15:4 Nu 34:5
15:5 Nu 34:12
15:6 Jos 18:17
15:7 2Sa 17:17
15:8 Jos 18:16
15:9 1Ch 13:6
15:10 Jdg 14:1
15:14 Jdg 1:10
15:15 Jos 10:38

Allotment for Judah

Jdg 1:11–15

15 The allotment for the tribe of Judah, by their clans, stretches southward to the border of Edom, to the Zin wilderness in the south.

2 Their southern border runs from the southern tip of the Salt Sea, 3 to south of the Ascent of Akrabbim, crosses to Zin, rises south of Kadesh Barnea, crosses to Hezron, then rises to Addar, turns toward Karka, 4 then crosses to Azmon, goes out to the Brook of Egypt, and then to the sea. This is your southern border.

5 The eastern border is the Salt Sea up to the mouth of the Jordan.

> Let all the giants of the valley be destroyed (Jos 15:8).

The northern border runs from the northern extremity of the Dead Sea at the mouth of the Jordan River, 6 then rises to Beth Hoglah, crosses north of Beth Arabah, rises to the Stone of Bohan son of Reuben, 7 and rises to Debir from the Achor Valley, turns northward to Gilgal opposite the Ascent of Adummim south of the valley, and crosses to the waters of En Shemesh and onward to En Rogel. 8 The border rises to Valley of Ben Hinnom, to the southern slope of the Jebusites (that is, Jerusalem), then rises to the top of the hill west of the Valley of Ben Hinnom, at the northern end of the Valley of Rephaim. 9 The border turns from the top of the hill to the waters of Nephtoah and goes out to the cities of Mount Ephron, then turns to Baalah (that is, Kiriath Jearim). 10 The border turns west of Baalah to Mount Seir, crosses to the northern slope of Mount Jearim (that is, Kesalon), descends to Beth Shemesh, and crosses to Timnah. 11 The border goes out to the northern slope of Ekron, turns to Shikkeron, crosses to Mount Baalah, goes out to Jabneel, and ends at the sea.

12 The western border was the coastline of the *Mediterranean* Sea.

These were the borders surrounding the tribe of Judah according to their clans.

13 According to the word of the LORD to Joshua, Caleb son of Jephunneh was given an allotment among the tribe of Judah: Kiriath Arba (that is, Hebron). Arba was the father of Anak. 14 Caleb drove out from there three Anakites: Sheshai, Ahiman, and Talmai, descendants of Anak. 15 He went up from there against the

inhabitants of Debir. Before the name of Debir was Kiriath Sepher. 16 Caleb said, "I will give my daughter Aksah in marriage to whoever attacks Kiriath Sepher and captures it." 17 Othniel son of Kenaz, the brother of Caleb, captured it, so Caleb gave him Aksah his daughter in marriage.

18 When she came to Othniel, she urged him to ask her father for a field. She dismounted from her donkey, and Caleb said to her, "What can I do for you?"

19 She answered, "Please give me a blessing. Since you have given me land in the Negev, now give me springs of water." So he gave her the upper and lower springs.

20 This is the inheritance of the tribe of Judah according to their clans.

21 The cities at the southern extremity of the tribe of Judah toward the border with Edom were Kabzeel, Eder, Jagur, 22 Kinah, Dimonah, Adadah, 23 Kedesh, Hazor, Ithnan, 24 Ziph, Telem, Bealoth, 25 Hazor Hadattah, Kerioth Hezron (that is, Hazor), 26 Amam, Shema, Moladah, 27 Hazar Gaddah, Heshmon, Beth Pelet, 28 Hazar Shual, Beersheba, Biziothiah, 29 Baalah, Iyim, Ezem, 30 Eltolad, Kesil, Hormah, 31 Ziklag, Madmannah, Sansannah, 32 Lebaoth, Shilhim, Ain, and Rimmon. The cities numbered twenty-nine with their villages.

33 In the lowland were Eshtaol, Zorah, Ashnah, 34 Zanoah, En Gannim, Tappuah, Enam, 35 Jarmuth, Adullam, Sokoh, Azekah, 36 Shaaraim, Adithaim, Gederah (Gederothaim): fourteen cities with their villages.

37 *Also there were* Zenan, Hadashah, Migdal Gad, 38 Dilean, Mizpah, Joktheel, 39 Lachish, Bozkath, Eglon, 40 Kabbon, Lahmas, Kitlish, 41 Gederoth, Beth Dagon, Naamah, and Makkedah: sixteen cities with their villages.

42 *Also there were* Libnah, Ether, Ashan, 43 Iphtah, Ashnah, Nezib, 44 Keilah, Akzib, and Mareshah: nine cities with their villages.

45 *Also there were* Ekron, its towns and villages; 46 from Ekron to the sea, all the land near Ashdod and their villages, 47 Ashdod, its towns and villages, Gaza, its towns and villages, as far as the Brook of Egypt and the *Mediterranean* Sea with its coast.

48 In the hill country were Shamir, Jattir, Sokoh, 49 Dannah, Kiriath Sannah (that is, Debir), 50 Anab, Eshtemoh, Anim, 51 Goshen, Holon, and Giloh: eleven cities with their villages.

52 *Also there were* Arab, Dumah, Eshan, 53 Janim, Beth Tappuah, Aphekah, 54 Humtah, Kiriath Arba (that is, Hebron), and Zior: nine cities with their villages.

55 *Also there were* Maon, Carmel, Ziph, Juttah, 56 Jezreel, Jokdeam, Zanoah, 57 Kain, Gibeah, and Timnah: ten cities with their villages.

58 *Also there were* Halhul, Beth Zur, Gedor, 59 Maarath, Beth Anoth, and Eltekon: six cities with their villages.

60 *Also there were* Kiriath Baal (that is, Kiriath Jearim) and Rabbah: two cities with their villages.

61 In the wilderness were Beth Arabah, Middin, Sekakah, 62 Nibshan, City of Salt, and En Gedi: six cities with their villages.

63 The people of Judah were not able to drive out the Jebusites living in Jerusalem, so the Jebusites live with the people of Judah in Jerusalem to this day.

Allotment for Ephraim and Manasseh

16 The allotment of land for the descendants of Joseph was from the Jordan by Jericho then east into the wilderness, rising from Jericho to the hill country of Bethel. 2 It goes out from Bethel to Luz and passes to the border of Arkite territory at Ataroth. 3 It goes down westward to the territory of the Japhletites, to the border of lower Beth Horon and Gezer, and then goes out to the sea.

4 So the descendants of Joseph, Manasseh and Ephraim, took their inheritance.

5 The territory of the Ephraimites, according to their clans, was as follows. The border of their inheritance on the east was Ataroth Addar as far as upper Beth Horon. 6 The border goes out toward the sea with Mikmethath on the north. It turns eastward toward Taanath Shiloh and passes it on the east toward Janoah. 7 It descends from Janoah to Ataroth and to Naarah, touches Jericho, and extends to the Jordan. 8 From Tappuah the border goes west to the Kanah Ravine and out to the sea. This is the inheritance of the tribe of the Ephraimites according to their clans. 9 The other cities for the Ephraimites were in the middle of the inheritance of the descendants of Manasseh, all the cities and their villages.

10 They did not drive out the Canaanites who lived in Gezer, so the Canaanites live in the midst of Ephraim until this day performing heavy labor as slaves.

17 Then allotment was made to the tribe of Manasseh, for he was the firstborn of Joseph. To Makir the firstborn of Manasseh, the father of Gilead, were allotted Gilead and Bashan, because he was a warrior. 2 And allotments were made to the rest of the tribe of Manasseh, according to their families: Abiezer, Helek, Asriel, Shechem, Hepher, and Shemida; these were the male descendants of Manasseh son of Joseph, according to their families.

15:17 Jdg 1:13
15:21 Ge 35:21
15:24 1Sa 23:14
15:26 1Ch 4:28
15:28 Ge 26:33
15:30 Jos 19:4
15:31 1Sa 27:6
15:33 Jdg 13:25
15:35 1Sa 17:1
15:38 2Ki 14:7
15:39 Jos 10:3
15:41 Jos 10:21
15:42 Jos 10:29
15:45 Jos 13:3
15:47 Jos 15:4
15:49 Jos 15:15
15:51 Jos 10:41
15:54 Jos 15:13

....

15:57 Jos 15:10
15:60 Jos 18:14
15:61 Jos 15:6
15:62 1Sa 23:29
15:63 Jdg 1:21
16:1 Jos 8:15
16:2 Jos 18:13
16:4 Jos 17:14
16:5 Jos 18:13
16:6 Jos 17:7
16:7 1Ch 7:28
16:8 Jos 17:8–9
16:10 Jdg 1:29
17:1 Ge 41:51

3 Yet Zelophehad, son of Hepher, son of Gilead, son of Makir, son of Manasseh had no sons, only daughters. These were his daughters' names: Mahlah, Noah, Hoglah, Milkah, and Tirzah. 4 They approached Eleazar the priest, Joshua son of Nun, and the leaders, saying, "The LORD commanded Moses to give us an inheritance among our relatives." So Joshua gave them an inheritance among their fathers' relatives according to the word of the LORD. 5 Therefore Manasseh received ten regions, apart from the lands of Gilead and Bashan on the east side of the Jordan, 6 because the daughters of Manasseh received an inheritance among his sons, and the rest of the people of Manasseh received the land of Gilead.

7 The boundary of Manasseh was from Asher to Mikmethath east of Shechem, and it runs south toward the inhabitants of En Tappuah. 8 Now Manasseh owned the land of Tappuah, but Tappuah on the border of Manasseh belonged to the Ephraimites. 9 Then the border descended to the Kanah Ravine, southward to the brook. These cities of Ephraim are among the cities of Manasseh. The border of Manasseh was on the north side of the brook, and it ended at the sea. 10 The land belonging to Ephraim was to the south, and the land belonging to Manasseh to the north. The *Mediterranean* Sea was the boundary of this territory, which bordered Asher in the north and Issachar in the east.

11 In Issachar and Asher, Manasseh was assigned districts: Beth Shan, Ibleam, Dor, Endor, Taanach, Megiddo, Naphoth, and their respective villages.

12 Yet the sons of Manasseh could not take possession of those cities, because the Canaanites were determined to live in that land. 13 But when the children of Israel became strong, they put the Canaanites to hard labor as slaves, but they did not actually drive them out.

14 The descendants of Joseph said to Joshua, "Why have you assigned us a single allotment, a single portion? We are a numerous people, as the LORD has blessed us."

15 Joshua said to them, "If you are a numerous people, go up to the forests and clear out a place there for yourselves in the land of the Perizzites and the giants, since the hill country of Ephraim is too small for you."

16 The descendants of Joseph said, "The hill country is not enough for us, and all the Canaanites living in the plains have iron chariots, both those in Beth Shan and the Jezreel Valley."

17 Joshua said to Ephraim and Manasseh, the descendants of Joseph, "You are a numerous people who have great strength. There will not be only one allotment for you. 18 The hill country shall be yours. Although it is a forest you shall clear it and own it to its borders. You shall drive out the Canaanites, even though they have iron chariots and are strong."

17:3 Nu 26:33
17:4 Jos 14:1
17:7 Jos 21:21
17:8 Jos 16:8
17:11 1Ch 7:29
17:12 Jdg 1:27–28
17:13 Jos 16:10
17:15 Ge 14:5
17:16 Jdg 1:19

....

18:1 Jos 19:51
18:3 Jdg 18:9
18:6 Jos 14:2
18:7 Jos 13:33
18:10 Jos 18:6
18:12 Jos 16:1
18:13 Ge 28:19
18:14 Jos 15:9

Dividing the Rest of the Land

18 The whole congregation of the children of Israel assembled at Shiloh and set up the tent of meeting there. The land was subdued before them. 2 Yet seven tribes among the children of Israel remained who had not yet received their inheritance.

3 So Joshua said to the children of Israel, "How long will you delay going in to possess the land that the LORD, the God of your fathers, has given you? 4 Select three men from each tribe, and I will send them out; and they will rise and go throughout the land, and describe it according to their inheritance, and they will come back to me. 5 They shall divide it into seven portions. Judah will stay in their territory in the south, and the house of Joseph will stay in their territory in the north. 6 So describe the land in seven portions and return to me. Then I will cast lots for you here before the LORD our God. 7 Yet there is no portion for the Levites among you, for the priesthood of the LORD is their inheritance. Gad, Reuben, and the half-tribe of Manasseh have acquired their inheritance on the east side of the Jordan, which Moses the servant of the LORD gave them."

8 So the men got up and left. Joshua commanded those who were leaving to survey the land, saying, "Go and walk back and forth throughout the land. Write a description of it, then return to me. Here in Shiloh I will cast lots for you before the LORD." 9 The men went and passed through the land. In a book they wrote a description of it by cities in seven portions, and they came back to Joshua at the Shiloh settlement. 10 Joshua cast lots for them in Shiloh before the LORD. There Joshua apportioned the land for the children of Israel according to their divisions.

The Allotment for Benjamin

11 The lot of the tribe of Benjamin, according to their clans, came up. The territory allotted to it fell between Judah and Joseph.

12 Their northern border goes from the Jordan up the northern slope of Jericho. It runs westward into the hill country and extends to the wilderness of Beth Aven. 13 The border passes from there southward toward Luz, to the slope of Luz (that is, Bethel), and descends to Ataroth Addar on the hill south of lower Beth Horon.

14 On the western side, the border turns south from the hill that lies to the south near Beth

Horon, and it extends to Kiriath Baal (that is, Kiriath Jearim), a city belonging to Judah. This is the western border.

15 The southern border starts from Kiriath Jearim and goes out westward to the spring of the waters of Nephtoah. 16 The border then descends to the foot of the mountain that lies by the Valley of Ben Hinnom, which is at the north end of the Valley of Rephaim. It descends from the Hinnom Valley to the slope of the Jebusites, then down to En Rogel. 17 The border runs north and goes out to En Shemesh and Geliloth, which is opposite the Ascent of Adummim, and descends to the Stone of Bohan the son of Reuben. 18 It passes toward the slope north of the Beth Arabah and descends to the Arabah. 19 The border passes north of the slope of Beth Hoglah, and it runs out to the northern tip of the Dead Sea at the southern end of the Jordan. This is the southern border.

20 The Jordan forms the eastern boundary.

This is the inheritance of the tribe of Benjamin, according to their clans, by its boundaries all around.

21 The cities belonging to the tribe of Benjamin, according to their clans, were Jericho, Beth Hoglah, Emek Keziz, 22 Beth Arabah, Zemaraim, Bethel, 23 Avvim, Parah, Ophrah, 24 Kephar Ammoni, Ophni, and Geba: twelve cities with their villages.

25 *Also there were* Gibeon, Ramah, Beeroth, 26 Mizpah, Kephirah, Mozah, 27 Rekem, Irpeel, Taralah, 28 Zelah, Haeleph, the Jebusite city (that is, Jerusalem), Gibeah, and Kiriath: fourteen cities with their villages.

This is the inheritance of the tribe of Benjamin according to their clans.

Allotment for Simeon

1Ch 4:28–33

19 The second lot came out for Simeon, for the tribe of Simeon according to their clans. Their inheritance was within the inheritance of the tribe of Judah. 2 Their inheritance was Beersheba, Sheba, Moladah, 3 Hazar Shual, Balah, Ezem, 4 Eltolad, Bethul, Hormah, 5 Ziklag, Beth Markaboth, Hazar Susah, 6 Beth Lebaoth, and Sharuhen: thirteen cities and their villages;

7 Ain, Rimmon, Ether, and Ashan: four cities and their villages; 8 and all the villages that were around these cities as far as Baalath Beer, Ramah of the Negev.

This was the inheritance of the tribe of Simeon according to their clans. 9 Simeon received a portion of the inheritance of Judah, for the inheritance of Judah was too large for them, so Simeon inherited land in the midst of the inheritance of Judah.

Allotment for Zebulun

10 The third lot came up for Zebulun according to their clans. Their territory extended to Sarid, 11 and their border ascended westward to Maralah, reaching Dabbesheth and the valley east of Jokneam. 12 From Sarid the border turned east to the border of Kisloth Tabor, out to Daberath, and up to Japhia. 13 From there it passes east to Gath Hepher and Eth Kazin. It turns out to Rimmon and turns toward Neah. 14 The boundary turns north to Hannathon and extends to the Valley of Iphtah El; 15 and Kattath, Nahalal, Shimron, Idalah, and Bethlehem: twelve cities and their villages.

16 This was the inheritance of the tribe of Zebulun according to their clans: these cities and their villages.

Allotment for Issachar

17 The fourth lot came out for Issachar, for the tribe of Issachar according to their clans. 18 Their territory included Jezreel, Kesulloth, Shunem, 19 Hapharaim, Shion, Anaharath, 20 Rabbith, Kishion, Ebez, 21 Remeth, En Gannim, En Haddah, and Beth Pazzez. 22 The border touches Tabor, Shahazumah, and Beth Shemesh, then extends to the Jordan: sixteen cities and their villages.

23 This is the inheritance of the tribe of Issachar according to their clans: the cities and their villages.

Allotment for Asher

24 The fifth lot came out for the tribe of Asher according to their clans. 25 Their territory included Helkath, Hali, Beten, Akshaph, 26 Allammelek, Amad, and Mishal. On the west their border touches Carmel and Shihor Libnath. 27 Then it turns eastward, goes to Beth Dagon, and touches Zebulun and the Valley of Iphtah El northward to Beth Emek and Neiel; then it continues in the north to Kabul, 28 Abdon, Rehob, Hammon, Kanah, as far as Greater Sidon. 29 Then the border turned to Ramah, reaching the fortified city of Tyre. Then the border turned to Hosah, and ended at the *Mediterranean* Sea by the region of Akzib, 30 Ummah, Aphek, and Rehob: twenty-two cities and their villages.

31 This is the inheritance of the tribe of Asher according to their clans: these cities and their villages.

Allotment for Naphtali

32 The sixth lot came out for the tribe of Naphtali according to their clans.

33 Their border runs from Heleph, from the oak of Zaanannim, to Adami Nekeb and Jabneel, as far as Lakkum, and extends to the Jordan. 34 The border turns west to Aznoth Tabor, goes out from there to Hukkok, and touches

18:15 Jos 15:9
18:16 2Ki 23:10
18:17 Jos 15:6
18:18 Jos 15:6
18:21 Jos 18:12
18:24 Ezr 2:26
18:25 Jos 9:17
18:28 Jos 15:8
19:1 Jos 19:9
19:2 1Ch 4:28–30
19:7 Jos 15:42

. . . .

19:11 Jos 12:22
19:15 Jos 11:1
19:18 1Sa 28:4
19:22 Jdg 4:6
19:27 1Ki 9:13
19:28 Jdg 1:31
19:29 Jdg 1:31
19:33 Jdg 4:11
19:34 Dt 33:23

Zebulun on the south, Asher on the west, and
Judah at the Jordan on the east. 35 Their forti-
fied cities were Ziddim, Zer, Hammath, Rak-
kath, Kinnereth, 36 Adamah, Ramah, Hazor,
37 Kedesh, Edrei, En Hazor, 38 Iron, Migdal El,
Horem, Beth Anath, and Beth Shemesh: nine-
teen cities and their villages.
39 This is the inheritance of the tribe of Naph-
tali according to their clans: the cities and their
villages.

Allotment for Dan

40 The seventh lot came out for the tribe of
Dan according to their clans. 41 The territory
of their inheritance included Zorah, Eshtaol,
Ir Shemesh, 42 Shaalabbin, Aijalon, Ithlah,
43 Elon, Timnah, Ekron, 44 Eltekeh, Gibbethon,
Baalath, 45 Jehud, Bene Berak, Gath Rimmon,
46 Me Jarkon, and Rakkon, along with the ter-
ritory near Joppa.
47 Yet the tribe of Dan lost their territory, so
they went up to wage war against Leshem and
captured it. They attacked it with the edge of
the sword, took possession of it, and settled
there. They called Leshem Dan after the name
of Dan their father.
48 This is the inheritance of the tribe of Dan
according to their clans: these cities and their
villages.

The Allotment for Joshua

49 When they had finished allotting the land
according to its boundaries, the children of
Israel gave an inheritance among them to
Joshua son of Nun. 50 According to the word
of the LORD, they gave him the city for which
he asked: Timnath Serah in the hill country of
Ephraim. He built up the city and lived in it.
51 These are the inheritances that Eleazar
the priest, Joshua son of Nun, and the family
leaders of the Israelite tribes assigned by lot
in Shiloh before the LORD at the entrance of the
tent of meeting. So they completed dividing
the land.

Cities of Refuge

Nu 35:9–34; Dt 4:41–43; 19:1–14

20 Then the LORD said to Joshua, 2 "Say to
the children of Israel, 'Choose refuge
cities, as I told you through Moses, 3 so that
anyone who kills a person without intent and
unknowingly may flee there. They shall be
your refuge from the avenger of blood.
4 "'The refugee can flee to one of these cities
then stand at the entrance of the city gate and
tell his case to the city elders. They will take
him into the city and give him a place to stay,
and he will live with them. 5 When the avenger
of blood comes after him, they shall not hand
over the manslayer to him, for he struck down
his neighbor unintentionally with no premedi-
tated malice. 6 He shall live in that city until he
stands before the congregation for judgment,
until the death of the high priest serving at that
time. Then the manslayer may return to his
home and to his city from which he had fled.'"
7 They selected Kedesh in Galilee in the hill
country of Naphtali, Shechem in the hill coun-
try of Ephraim, and Kiriath Arba (that is, He-
bron) in the hill country of Judah. 8 Across the
Jordan east of Jericho, they selected Bezer in
the wilderness plain from the tribe of Reuben,
Ramoth in Gilead from the tribe of Gad, and
Golan in Bashan from the tribe of Manasseh.
9 These were the cities designated for all the
children of Israel and resident foreigners liv-
ing among them, to which anyone who killed
someone inadvertently could flee and not die
at the hand of the avenger of blood until he
stood before the congregation.

Cities for the Levites

1Ch 6:54–80

21 The family leaders of the Levites ap-
proached Eleazar the priest, Joshua
son of Nun, and the family leaders of the Is-
raelite tribes. 2 At Shiloh in the land of Canaan
they said to them, "Through Moses the LORD
commanded that we be given cities in which
to live and grazing lands for our livestock."
3 So according to the word of the LORD, out of
their inheritance the children of Israel gave
the Levites these cities and their grazing lands.
4 The lot came out for the clans of the Kohath-
ites, so the Levites who were descendants of
Aaron received an allotment of thirteen cities
from the tribes of Judah, Simeon, and Benja-
min. 5 The remaining descendants of Kohath
received an allotment of ten cities from the
clans of the tribes of Ephraim, Dan, and the
half-tribe of Manasseh.
6 The descendants of Gershon received an
allotment of thirteen cities from the clans of
the tribes of Issachar, Asher, Naphtali, and the
half-tribe of Manasseh in Bashan.
7 Descendants of Merari by their clans re-
ceived an allotment of twelve cities from the
tribes of Reuben, Gad, and Zebulun.
8 The children of Israel allotted the Levites
these cities and their grazing lands, as the LORD
commanded through Moses.

9 From the tribes of Judah and Simeon they
assigned the following cities with these names.
10 They were assigned to the descendants of
Aaron, to the clans of the Kohathites of the
tribe of Levi, for theirs was the first lot.
11 They assigned them Kiriath Arba (Arba was
the father of Anak), which is Hebron, in the
hill country of Judah, and the grazing lands
around it. 12 (Now they had assigned the city's

19:35 Jos 11:2
19:30 Jos 11:1
19:42 Jdg 1:35
19:43 Ge 38:12
19:45 Jos 21:24
19:46 Jnh 1:3
19:47 Jdg 1:34–35
19:50 Jos 24:30
19:51 Jos 14:1
20:2 Nu 35:6
20:4 Jer 38:7
20:5 Nu 35:12

....

20:6 Nu 35:12
20:7 Jos 21:11
20:8 Jos 21:36
20:9 Nu 35:15
21:1 Jos 14:1
21:2 Jos 18:1
21:5 Jos 21:20–26
21:6 Jos 21:27–33
21:7 Jos 21:34–40
21:8 Jos 21:3
21:10 Jos 21:4
21:11 1Ch 6:55

fields and its surrounding villages to Caleb son
of Jephunneh as his property.)
13 So to the descendants of Aaron the priest
they assigned Hebron (a refuge city for people
who committed manslaughter), Libnah with its
pastures, 14 Jattir, Eshtemoa, 15 Holon, Debir,
16 Ain, Juttah, and Beth Shemesh, together
with the grazing lands of each: nine cities from
these two tribes.
17 From the tribe of Benjamin *they assigned*
Gibeon, Geba, 18 Anathoth, and Almon, togeth-
er with the grazing lands of each: four cities.
19 Altogether the descendants of Aaron re-
ceived thirteen cities and their grazing lands.

20 The rest of the Levites from the clans of the
descendants of Kohath received cities allotted
from the tribe of Ephraim.
21 They assigned them Shechem (a refuge city
for people who committed manslaughter) in
the hill country of Ephraim, Gezer, 22 Kibzaim,
and Beth Horon, together with the grazing
lands of each: four cities.
23 From the tribe of Dan *they assigned* Elte-
keh, Gibbethon, 24 Aijalon, and Gath Rimmon,
together with the grazing lands of each: four
cities.
25 From the half-tribe of Manasseh they as-
signed Taanach and Gath Rimmon, together
with the grazing lands of each: two cities.
26 Altogether the rest of the clans of the de-
scendants of Kohath received ten cities and
their grazing lands.

27 From the half-tribe of Manasseh *they as-
signed* to the descendants of Gershon (one of
the Levite clans): Golan in Bashan (a refuge city
for people who committed manslaughter) and
Be Eshterah, together with the grazing lands
of each: two cities.
28 From the tribe of Issachar *they assigned*
Kishion, Daberath, 29 Jarmuth, and En Gannim,
together with the grazing lands of each: four
cities.
30 From the tribe of Asher *they assigned*
Mishal, Abdon, 31 Helkath, and Rehob, togeth-
er with the grazing lands of each: four cities.
32 From the tribe of Naphtali *they assigned*
Kedesh in Galilee (a refuge city for people who
committed manslaughter), Hammoth Dor, and
Kartan, together with the grazing lands of
each: three cities.
33 Altogether the Gershonites according to
their clans received thirteen cities and their
grazing lands.

34 From the tribe of Zebulun *they assigned*
to the descendants of Merari (the remaining
Levites): Jokneam, Kartah, 35 Dimnah, and Na-
halal, together with the grazing lands of each:
four cities.

21:13 Jos 15:42
21:14 Jos 15:48
21:16 Jos 15:10
21:20 1Ch 6:66
21:21 Jos 20:7
21:27 1Ch 6:71
21:32 Jos 20:7
21:34 1Ch 6:77

....

21:36 Jos 20:8
21:38 Ge 32:2
21:44 Jos 11:23
22:2 Jos 1:12–18
22:4 Jos 13:8
22:5 Dt 6:17
22:6 Jos 14:13
22:7 Jos 17:1–12
22:8 Nu 31:27

36 From the tribe of Reuben *they assigned*
Bezer, Jahaz, 37 Kedemoth, and Mephaath,
together with the grazing lands of each: four
cities.
38 From the tribe of Gad *they assigned* Ramoth
in Gilead (a refuge city for people who com-
mitted manslaughter), Mahanaim, 39 Heshbon,
and Jazer, together with the grazing lands of
each: four cities in all.
40 So twelve cities were allotted for the de-
scendants of Merari according to their clans
(the remaining Levite clans).
41 Altogether the Levites received forty-eight
cities and their grazing lands within the pos-
sessions of the children of Israel. 42 Each of
these cities had grazing lands surrounding
them. It was this way with all these cities.
43 The LORD gave Israel all the land that He
swore to give to their fathers. They took pos-
session of it and lived in it. 44 The LORD gave
them rest all around, according to all that He
swore to their fathers. Not a man among their
enemies stood before them, and the LORD de-
livered all their enemies into their hands. 45 Not
a single word of all the good things that the
LORD had spoken to the children of Israel failed.
They all came to pass.

The Eastern Tribes Return Home

22 Then Joshua summoned the Reu-
benites, the Gadites, and the half-
tribe of Manasseh. 2 He said to them, "You
have done everything that Moses the servant
of the LORD commanded you and have obeyed
me in everything that I have commanded you.
3 You have not left your brothers these many
days down to this day, and you have observed
the obligations of the commandment of the
LORD your God. 4 Now the LORD your God has
given rest to your brothers, as He had said to
them. So now, turn and go to your homes, to
the land of your possession, which Moses the
servant of the LORD gave you on the other side
of the Jordan. 5 Only carefully obey the com-
mandment and the law that Moses the servant
of the LORD commanded you: to love the LORD
your God, to walk in all His ways, to obey His
commandments, to cling to Him, and to serve
Him with all your heart and soul."
6 Joshua blessed them and sent them off, and
they went to their tents. 7 Moses had assigned
land in Bashan to half the tribe of Manasseh,
and to the other half Joshua assigned land
among their brothers on the west side of the
Jordan. When Joshua sent them also to their
homes and blessed them, 8 he said, "Return
home with great wealth, much livestock, sil-
ver, gold, copper, iron, and great quantities

of clothing. Divide the spoil of your enemies
among your brothers."
9 So the Reubenites, Gadites, and the half-
tribe of Manasseh left the children of Israel at
Shiloh in the land of Canaan to go to the land
of Gilead, the land of their possession, accord-
ing to the word of the LORD through Moses.
10 The tribes of Reuben, Gad, and the half-
tribe of Manasseh came near the Jordan in
the land of Canaan and built a very large altar
by the Jordan. 11 The children of Israel heard
someone say, "The tribes of Reuben, Gad, and
the half-tribe of Manasseh have built an altar
by the land of Canaan by the Jordan on the
Israelite side." 12 When the children of Israel
heard this, they assembled the whole congre-
gation of the children of Israel at Shiloh to go
up against them in war.
13 Then the children of Israel sent Phinehas,
son of Eleazar the priest, to the sons of Reu-
ben, to the sons of Gad, and to the half-tribe
of Manasseh, into the land of Gilead, 14 and
with him ten chiefs, one chief each for each
father's household of every tribe of Israel; and
each one of them was the head of his father's
house among the thousands of Israel.
15 They came to the tribes of Reuben, Gad,
and the half-tribe of Manasseh in the land of
Gilead and said to them, 16 "The whole congre-
gation of the LORD says, 'What is this trespass
you have committed against the God of Israel?
Today you have turned from following the LORD
by building yourselves an altar to rebel against
Him! 17 Is the sin of Peor, from which we have
still not purified ourselves even today, not
enough for us, which brought a plague upon
the congregation of the LORD 18 that today you
have turned away from following the LORD?
" 'If today you are rebelling against the LORD,
then tomorrow He will be angry with the whole
congregation of Israel! 19 If indeed your own
land is unclean, then cross over to the land
of the LORD where the tabernacle of the LORD
stands and take land among us. Yet do not
rebel against the LORD or rebel against us by
building an altar other than the altar of the
LORD our God. 20 Did not Achan son of Zer-
ah commit a trespass in the things under the
ban, and wrath fall on all the congregation of
Israel? And that man did not perish alone in
his iniquity.' "
21 Then the tribes of Reuben, Gad, and the
half-tribe of Manasseh answered and said to
the heads of the Israelite clans, 22 "The LORD
God of gods, the LORD God of gods, He knows,
and may Israel know—if we *have acted* in re-
bellion or disloyalty against the LORD, do not
spare us today. 23 If we have built an altar to
turn away from following the LORD, to offer
burnt offerings and grain offerings or make
peace offerings upon it, may the LORD Himself
demand *an account*.
24 "We did this deed because we were worried
that in the future your descendants might say,
'What have you to do with the LORD God of Is-
rael? 25 The LORD made the Jordan a boundary
between us and you, the descendants of Reu-
ben and Gad. You have no share in the LORD!'
In this way your descendants might make our
descendants to stop worshipping the LORD.
26 "So we said to each other, 'Let us build
this altar, not for burnt offering or sacrifice,
27 but as a witness for us, for you, and for the
generations after us, that we may perform the
service of the LORD before Him with our burnt
offerings, sacrifices, and peace offerings, and
in the future your descendants will not be able
to say to our descendants, "You have no share
in the LORD!" '
28 "Therefore we said, 'In the future, if they
say this to us or to our descendants, we will
say, "Look at the replica of the altar of the LORD
that our fathers made, not for burnt offerings
or sacrifices, but as a witness between you
and us." '
29 "God forbid that we should rebel against
the LORD by turning from following the LORD
today by building an altar for burnt offerings,
grain offerings, and sacrifices other than the
altar of the LORD God that stands before His
tabernacle!"
30 When Phinehas the priest, the leaders of
the congregation, and the heads of the Isra-
elite clans who were with him heard what the
descendants of Reuben, Gad, and Manasseh
said, it pleased them. 31 Phinehas son of Elea-
zar the priest said to the descendants of Reu-
ben, Gad, and Manasseh, "Today we know that
the LORD is in our midst because you did not
violate your obligations to the LORD in this *mat-
ter*. Indeed, you have delivered the children of
Israel from the judgment of the LORD."
32 Then Phinehas son of Eleazar the priest
and the leaders returned from *meeting* the de-
scendants of Reuben and Gad in the land of
Gilead to the children of Israel in the land of
Canaan. They brought back a report. 33 This
report was good in the eyes of the children of
Israel, and the children of Israel blessed God.
They decided not to make war against the de-
scendants of Reuben and Gad to ruin the land
in which they lived.
34 The descendants of Reuben and Gad
named the altar Witness, "For it is a witness
between us that the LORD is God."

22:9 Nu 32:26
22:11 Dt 13:12–14
22:13 Nu 25:7
22:14 Nu 1:4
22:18 Nu 16:22
22:19 Jos 18:1
22:20 Jos 7:1
22:22 Dt 10:17
22:23 Dt 18:19

22:24 Jos 4:6
22:27 Jos 24:27
22:30 Jos 22:33
22:31 Lev 26:11–12
22:33 1Ch 29:20
22:34 Jos 22:27

Joshua's Charge to the Leaders

23 A long time later, after the LORD had given Israel rest from all their enemies around them, Joshua was old and advanced in years. 2 Joshua called for all Israel, their elders, clan heads, judges, and officials, and said to them, "I am old and advanced in years. 3 You have seen all that the LORD your God did to all these peoples before you, for it is the LORD your God who has waged war for you. 4 See, I have allotted to you as an inheritance *the land of* these peoples who remain, along with *the land of* the peoples whom I defeated, from the Jordan to the *Mediterranean* Sea in the west. 5 The LORD your God will drive them out and dispossess them from before you, and you will inherit their land, as the LORD your God told you.

6 "Now be very strong to observe and enact all that is written in the Book of the Law of Moses, so that you do not deviate from it to the right or the left. 7 Do not assimilate with these peoples remaining among you. Do not invoke the names of their gods, nor swear by, serve, or worship them. 8 Instead, cling to the LORD your God, as you have done until today.

9 "For the LORD has dispossessed before you great and mighty peoples, and as for you, not a single man has been able to stand against you until today. 10 One man from among you can make a thousand flee, for it is the LORD your God who wages war for you, as He told you. 11 Now be careful, therefore, to love the LORD your God!

12 "For if you should turn and cling to the remainder of these peoples who are left with you, and you intermarry and assimilate with them, and they with you, 13 know for certain that the LORD your God will no longer drive out these nations from before you. But they shall be snares and traps to you, a whip on your sides and thorns in your eyes, until you perish from off this good ground that the LORD your God has given you.

14 "Now, I am going the way of all the earth. You know in all your hearts and souls that not a single word has failed out of all the good things that the LORD your God has said concerning you. All came true for you. Not a single word among them failed. 15 So just as every good thing that the LORD your God said to you came to be, even so the LORD can bring every bad thing upon you until He has destroyed you from this good land that the LORD your God gave you. 16 If you break the covenant of the LORD your God that He commanded you, and go and serve other gods and worship them, the anger of the LORD will burn against you, and you will quickly perish from the good land that He gave you."

Covenant Renewed at Shechem

24 Joshua called for all the Israelite tribes at Shechem and summoned the elders, clan heads, judges, and officials of Israel. They presented themselves before God.

2 Joshua said to all the people, "Thus says the LORD God of Israel: Long ago your fathers—Terah father of Abraham and Nahor—lived beyond the Euphrates[1] and served other gods. 3 I took your father Abraham from beyond the Euphrates,[2] brought him through all the land of Canaan, and gave him many descendants. To him I gave Isaac. 4 To Isaac I gave Jacob and Esau, and to Esau I gave Mount Seir for his inheritance, but Jacob and his descendants went down into Egypt.

5 "I sent Moses and Aaron, I struck Egypt down with all I did in their midst, and afterward I brought you out. 6 I brought your fathers out of Egypt, then you came to the sea. The Egyptians pursued your fathers with chariots and horsemen to the Red Sea. 7 *Your fathers* cried out to the LORD, and He placed darkness between you and the Egyptians. He made the sea come upon them and cover them. Your own eyes saw what I did to Egypt, and you lived in the wilderness a long time.

8 "I brought you to the land of the Amorites who lived on the other side of the Jordan. They waged war against you, but I gave them into your hand so that you might inherit their land, and I destroyed them before you. 9 Then Balak son of Zippor, king of Moab, arose and waged war against Israel. He called for Balaam son of Beor to curse you, 10 but I refused to listen to Balaam. Therefore he blessed you still, and I delivered you out of his hand.

11 "You crossed the Jordan and came to Jericho. The leaders of Jericho, along with the Amorites, Perizzites, Canaanites, Hittites, Girgashites, Hivites, and Jebusites, waged war against you, but I gave them into your hand. 12 I sent the hornet and drove out the two Amorite kings from before you, but not with your sword or your bow. 13 I gave you a land for which you did not work, and cities that you did not build. You live in them, and you are eating from the produce of vineyards and olive groves you did not plant.

14 "Now fear the LORD, and serve Him with sincerity and faithfulness. Put away the gods your fathers served beyond the River[3] and in Egypt. Serve the LORD. 15 If it is displeasing to you to serve the LORD, then choose today whom you will serve, if it should be the gods

23:1 Jos 13:1
23:2 Jos 24:1
23:3 Ex 14:14
23:6 Dt 5:32
23:7 Ex 23:13
23:8 Dt 10:20
23:9 Dt 11:23
23:10 Lev 26:8
23:11 Jos 22:5
23:12 Dt 7:3
23:13 Dt 7:16
23:14 1Ki 2:2
23:15 Dt 28:15–68

24:1 Jos 23:2
24:2 Ge 31:53
24:4 Dt 2:5
24:5 Ex 3:10
24:7 Ex 14:20
24:8 Nu 21:21–35
24:9 Jdg 11:25
24:12 Ex 23:28
24:13 Jos 11:13
24:14 Jos 24:23
24:15 Jdg 6:10

[1] 2 Euphrates River. [2] 3 Euphrates River. [3] 14 Euphrates River.

your fathers served beyond the River[1] or the
gods of the Amorites' land where you are now
living. Yet as for me and my house, we will
serve the LORD."

> My children are sealed and marked
> (Jos 24:15).

16 The people answered and said, "God forbid
that we forsake the LORD and serve other gods!
17 For it is the LORD our God who brought us
and our fathers out from slavery in the land of
Egypt and performed these great signs in our
sight and guarded us all the way that we went
and among all the peoples through whom we
passed. 18 The LORD drove out before us all the
people, even the Amorites, who lived in the
land. So we will indeed serve the LORD, for He
is our God."

> I will serve the Lord my God, and His
> voice I will obey (Jos 24:24).

19 Then Joshua said to the people, "You are
not able to serve the LORD, for He is a holy God.
He is a jealous God, and He will not forgive
your transgressions nor your sins. 20 If you for-
sake the LORD and serve foreign gods, then He
will turn, bring disaster upon you, and finish
you off, after having been good to you."
21 The people said to Joshua, "No, we will
serve the LORD!"
22 Joshua said to the people, "You are wit-
nesses against yourselves, that you have cho-
sen the LORD, to serve Him."
Then they said, "We are witnesses."
23 "Now then," he said, "put away the foreign
gods in your midst, and stretch out your hearts
to the LORD God of Israel!"

24:19 Ex 20:5
24:20 1Ch 28:9
24:22 Ps 119:173
24:23 Jos 24:14

24:25 Ex 15:25
24:26 Jdg 9:6
24:27 Jos 22:34
24:28 Jdg 2:6
24:29 Jdg 2:8
24:30 Jos 19:50
24:31 Jdg 2:7
24:32 Ge 33:19

24 The people said to Joshua, "It is the LORD
our God we will serve, and His voice that we
will obey."
25 So that day Joshua made a covenant for the
people and established regulations and laws
for them at Shechem. 26 Joshua wrote these
words in the Book of the Law of God. He took
a large stone and set it up under the oak by
the sanctuary of the LORD.
27 Joshua said to all the people, "See, this
stone will be a witness for us, for it has heard
all the words of the LORD that He spoke to us.
It will be a witness for us, lest you deny your
God."
28 Then Joshua sent the people away, each
man to his inheritance.

Joshua's Death and Burial

29 After these events took place, Joshua son of
Nun, the servant of the LORD, died at the age of
one hundred and ten. 30 They buried him in the
territory of his inheritance in Timnath Serah,
which is in the hill country of Ephraim north
of Mount Gaash.
31 Israel served the LORD all the days of Josh-
ua and of the elders who outlived Joshua and
had known all the deeds that the LORD had
done for Israel.
32 They buried the bones of Joseph, which the
children of Israel had brought out of Egypt,
in Shechem in the part of the field that Jacob
bought from the descendants of Hamor the
father of Shechem for one hundred pieces of
silver.[2] It became an inheritance of the descen-
dants of Joseph.
33 Eleazar son of Aaron died, and they buried
him at Gibeah, the town of Phinehas his son,
which was in the hill country of Ephraim.

[1] *15* Euphrates River. [2] *32* Heb. *a hundred kesitahs*; a kesitah was a coin of unknown weight and value.

Author: Traditionally the prophet Samuel

Written: Between 1405 and 1000 BC

Theme: Defeat and Deliverance

JUDGES

Dear Spirit Led Woman,

Deborah's testimony is a portrait of what a dynamic woman of faith looked like in the days when judges ruled Israel. She was willing to go to the front lines of battle—to give her life if necessary—in response to God's call. As a result of her devotion and leadership, God brought deliverance to an entire nation.

Many times we believe that the people of the Bible were very different from us. But I doubt Deborah arose one day with the idea that she was going out to live the fourth and fifth chapters of Judges. It's more likely that she simply gave herself to God—*the same God we serve*—each day and took one obedient step after another. Her faithful actions, aligned with the mighty plan of God, took on eternal significance. Like Deborah, you have the awesome opportunity to hear the voice of God, act upon what He says, and see Him bring freedom and reconciliation through you.

We need Deborahs in this generation—courageous women who will abandon all for the glory of the almighty God, our God, the same God who called and empowered Deborah! Will you declare to be a Deborah in our day?

Brenda J. Davis

Israel Fights Remaining Canaanites

1 After the death of Joshua, the children of
Israel inquired of the LORD, "Who should
go up against the Canaanites first, in order to
wage war against them?"
2 The LORD said, "Judah shall go up. Indeed, I
have given the land into their hands."
3 Then the men of Judah said to Simeon, their
brothers, "Come up with us into our allotted
territory. We will wage war against the Canaan-
ites. Likewise we will go with you into your
allotted territory." So Simeon went with them.
4 Then Judah went up, and the LORD gave
the Canaanites and Perizzites into their hands.
They struck down ten thousand men in Bezek.
5 They found Adoni-Bezek in Bezek and fought
against him. They struck down the Canaanites
and Perizzites. 6 Yet Adoni-Bezek fled, and they
chased after him, seized him, and cut off his
thumbs and big toes.
7 Adoni-Bezek said, "Seventy kings whose
thumbs and big toes were cut off once collect-
ed scraps of food under my table. Just as I have
done, so God has repaid me." They brought
him to Jerusalem, and he died there.
8 Then Judah waged war against Jerusalem.
They captured it, struck it with the edge of the
sword, and sent the city up in flames.
9 Afterwards, Judah went down to wage war
against the Canaanites living in the hill coun-
try, the Negev, and the lowlands. 10 Judah went
against the Canaanites living in Hebron (pre-
viously the name of Hebron was Kiriath Arba)
and they struck down Sheshai, Ahiman, and
Talmai. 11 From there they went against the
inhabitants of Debir (previously the name of
Debir was Kiriath Sepher).
12 Caleb said, "He who attacks Kiriath Sepher
and takes it, I will give him my daughter Aksah
as wife." 13 Othniel son of Kenaz, the younger
brother of Caleb, captured it. So Caleb gave
him Aksah his daughter in marriage.
14 When she came to Othniel, she urged him
to ask her father for a field. As she dismounted
from her donkey, Caleb said to her, "What can
I do for you?"
15 She answered, "Please give me a special
gift. Since you have given me land in the
Negev, now give me springs of water." So
Caleb gave her the upper and lower springs.
16 The descendants of Moses' father-in-law,
the Kenite, went up with the descendants of
Judah from the City of Palms to the Negev
near Arad. Then they went and lived with the
people.
17 But Judah went with his brother Simeon
and struck down the Canaanites living in Zeph-
ath and utterly destroyed it. So now they call
the city Hormah. 18 Then Judah captured Gaza,
Ashkelon, Ekron, and the territory belonging
to each of these cities.

> I break the chariots of the enemies of the valley, in the name of Jesus (Jdg 1:19).

19 The LORD was with Judah, and they took
the hill country but could not drive out the in-
habitants of the coastal plain, for they had iron
chariots. 20 They gave Hebron to Caleb, as Mo-
ses had said, and he drove out the three sons
of Anak. 21 However, the tribe of Benjamin did
not drive out the Jebusites living in Jerusalem,
so the Jebusites live with the tribe of Benjamin
in Jerusalem to this day.
22 The descendants of Joseph went up
against Bethel, and the LORD was with them.
23 The descendants of Joseph sent spies into
Bethel (the former name of the city was Luz).
24 The spies saw a man coming out of the city
and said to him, "Please show us the entrance
to the city, and we will deal kindly with you."
25 So he showed them an entrance to the city.
They struck the city with the edge of the sword,
but they let the man and his extended family
go. 26 The man went to the land of the Hittites.
He built a city and named it Luz, and that is its
name to this day.
27 Manasseh did not drive out the inhabitants
of Beth Shan, Taanach, Dor, Ibleam, Megiddo,
or their daughter villages, for the Canaanites
were determined to live in that land. 28 When
the children of Israel became strong, they put
the Canaanites to hard labor as slaves, but they
did not actually drive them out. 29 Ephraim did
not drive out the inhabitants of Gezer, so the
Canaanites lived among them in Gezer. 30 Zeb-
ulun did not drive out the inhabitants of Kitron
and Nahalol, so the Canaanites lived among
them and became slave laborers. 31 Asher did
not drive out the inhabitants of Akko, Sidon,
Ahlab, Akzib, Helbah, Aphek, or Rehob. 32 Ash-
er lived among the Canaanites, the inhabitants
of the land, for they did not drive them out.
33 Naphtali did not drive out the inhabitants
of Beth Shemesh or Beth Anath, so they live
among the Canaanites, the inhabitants of the
land. The *Canaanites* of Beth Shemesh and
Beth Anath became slave laborers for them.
34 The Amorites pushed the tribe of Dan into
the hill country, for they would not let them
come down to the coastal plain. 35 The Amor-
ites were determined to live in Mount Heres,
Aijalon, and Shaalbim, but the hand of the de-
scendants of Joseph was heavy *on them*, and
they became slave laborers. 36 The border of

1:1 Nu 27:21
1:3 Jdg 1:17
1:4 1Sa 11:8
1:7 1Sa 15:33
1:8 Jos 15:63
1:11 Jos 15:15
1:13 Jdg 3:9
1:16 Nu 10:29–32
1:17 Nu 21:3
1:18 Jos 11:22

1:19 Jdg 1:2
1:20 Jdg 1:10
1:21 Jos 15:63
1:22 Jdg 1:19
1:23 Ge 28:19
1:27 Jos 17:11–13
1:29 Jos 16:10
1:30 Jos 19:15
1:31 Jos 19:24–30
1:33 Jos 19:32–38
1:34 Jos 19:47
1:35 Jos 19:42
1:36 Nu 34:4

the Amorites was from the Ascent of Akrabbim to Sela and beyond.

The Angel of the LORD at Bokim

2 The angel[1] of the LORD went up from Gilgal to Bokim and said, "I brought you up from Egypt and brought you into the land that I promised your fathers. I said, 'I will never break My covenant with you, 2 but you must not make a pact with the inhabitants of this land, and you must tear down their altars.' Yet you have not obeyed Me. What is this you have done? 3 So now I say, 'I will not drive them out before you. They will be thorns in your sides, and their gods will be a snare to you.' "

4 When the angel of the LORD spoke these words to all the children of Israel, the people raised their voices and wept aloud. 5 They named that place Bokim and sacrificed to the LORD there.

The Death of Joshua

6 When Joshua dismissed the people, each Israelite went to his inheritance to possess the land. 7 So the people served the LORD all the days of Joshua, and all the days of the elders who outlived Joshua, who had seen all the great works that the LORD had done for Israel.

8 Joshua, the son of Nun, the servant of the LORD, died at the age of one hundred and ten. 9 They buried him in the territory of his inheritance in Timnath Heres, in the hill country of Ephraim, north of Mount Gaash.

10 That entire generation passed away, and after them grew up a generation who did not know the LORD or the deeds that He had done for Israel.

Israel's Unfaithfulness

11 The children of Israel did evil in the sight of the LORD and served the Baals. 12 They abandoned the LORD God of their fathers, who brought them out of the land of Egypt. They followed after other gods, the gods of the peoples around them. They worshipped them and provoked the LORD to anger. 13 They abandoned the LORD and served Baal and the Ashtoreths. 14 The anger of the LORD burned against Israel, and He gave them into the hands of those who plundered them; and He sold them into the hands of their enemies around them, so that they were no longer able to stand against their enemies. 15 Whenever they marched out, the hand of the LORD was against them to bring disaster, as the LORD had said and as He had sworn to them. They were in great distress.

16 Then the LORD raised up judges who delivered them from the hand of those who plundered them. 17 Yet they would not listen to their judges, for they prostituted themselves to other gods and worshipped them. They quickly turned aside from the path their fathers had walked, who had obeyed the commandments of the LORD. They did not do *as their fathers had done.* 18 When the LORD raised up judges for them, the LORD was with the judge and delivered them from the hand of their enemies all the days of the judge; for their groaning before their oppressors and tormentors grieved the LORD. 19 When the judge died, the people turned back and acted more wickedly than their fathers, pursuing other gods to serve and worship them. They would not give up their practices and obstinate ways.

20 The anger of the LORD burned against Israel, and He said, "Because this nation has violated My covenant that I commanded their fathers and has not heeded My voice, 21 I will no longer drive out from before them any of the nations that Joshua left when he died, 22 so that through them I may test Israel and see whether or not they will keep the ways of the LORD, to walk in them as their fathers did." 23 So the LORD left those nations, not hurrying to drive them out; and He did not deliver them into the hand of Joshua.

3 Now these are the nations that the LORD left to test those in Israel who had not experienced war in Canaan 2 (so that *later* generations of the children of Israel who did not know *war* before might know it, to teach them how to fight): 3 the five Philistine lords, all the Canaanites, the Sidonians, and the Hivites living on Mount Lebanon, from Mount Baal Hermon to Lebo Hamath. 4 They were to test Israel, in order to know if they would obey the commandments of the LORD, which He commanded their fathers by the hand of Moses.

5 The children of Israel lived among the Canaanites, Hittites, Amorites, Perizzites, Hivites, and Jebusites. 6 They took their daughters for themselves as wives, and gave their own daughters to their sons, and served their gods.

Othniel

7 The children of Israel did what was evil in the sight of the LORD. They forgot the LORD their God and served the Baals and the Asherahs. 8 The anger of the LORD burned against Israel, and He sold them into the hands of Cushan-Rishathaim, king of Mesopotamia. The children of Israel served Cushan-Rishathaim for eight years. 9 Then the children of Israel cried out to the LORD, and the LORD raised up a deliverer in order to save the children of Israel—Othniel son of Kenaz, the younger brother of Caleb. 10 The Spirit of the LORD came

2:1 Ge 17:7–8
2:2 Dt 7:2–4
2:3 Nu 33:55
2:6 Jos 24:28–31
2:7 Jos 24:31
2:9 Jos 19:50
2:10 Ex 5:2
2:11 Jdg 3:7
2:12 Ex 20:5
2:13 Jdg 10:6
2:14 Dt 32:30
2:15 Dt 28:15–68
2:16 Ac 13:20
2:17 Jdg 2:7
2:18 Dt 32:36
2:19 Jdg 4:1
2:20 Jdg 2:14
2:21 Jos 23:13
2:22 Dt 8:2
3:1 Jdg 2:21–22
3:3 Jos 13:3
3:5 Ex 3:8
3:6 Ex 34:16
3:7 Ex 34:13
3:8 Jdg 2:14
3:9 Jdg 1:13
3:10 Jdg 6:34

[1] *1* At times the Lord speaks directly through an angel (cf. the story of the burning bush in Ex 3:2–4).

on him, and he judged Israel. He went out to battle, and the LORD gave Cushan-Rishathaim, king of Mesopotamia, into his hands, so that *Othniel* overpowered Cushan-Rishathaim. 11 The land rested forty years, then Othniel son of Kenaz died.

Ehud

12 Then the children of Israel once more did what was evil in the sight of the LORD, so the LORD strengthened King Eglon of Moab against Israel because they had done what was evil in the sight of the LORD. 13 Eglon joined forces with the Ammonites and Amalekites; then he went and attacked Israel and took possession of the City of Palms. 14 The children of Israel served King Eglon of Moab for eighteen years.

15 Then the children of Israel cried out to the LORD, and the LORD raised up a deliverer—Ehud son of Gera the Benjamite, a left-handed man. The children of Israel sent a tribute payment by him to King Eglon of Moab. 16 Ehud made a cubit-long[1] two-edged sword for himself and strapped it onto his right thigh under his cloak. 17 He brought the tribute payment to King Eglon of Moab. Now Eglon was a very fat man. 18 When Ehud finished offering the tribute payment, he sent away the people who carried it. 19 But he himself turned back from the stone idols that were at Gilgal, and said, "I have a secret message for you, O king."

And he said, "Keep silence!" And all who attended him departed from him.

20 Ehud approached him as he was sitting alone in his cool upper chamber. Ehud said, "I have a message from God for you." And *Eglon* rose from his seat. 21 Then Ehud reached with his left hand, drew the sword from his right thigh, and plunged it into the belly of *Eglon*. 22 The hilt went in after the blade and the fat closed over the blade and his entrails came out, for he did not pull the sword out of the belly of Eglon. 23 Then Ehud went out to the entrance hall and closed the doors of the upper chamber on him and locked them.

24 When he went out, the servants of *Eglon* came. They looked and noticed the doors of the upper chamber were locked. They thought, "Surely he is attending to his needs in the cool chamber." 25 They waited until they were embarrassed, but he still did not open the doors of the upper chamber. So they took a key and opened it. There, fallen dead on the floor, was their lord.

26 Yet Ehud escaped while they were waiting. He passed the sacred stones and escaped to Seirah. 27 Upon his arrival, he blew a ram's horn trumpet in the hill country of Ephraim. Then the children of Israel went down with him from the hill country, and he led them.

28 He said to them, "Follow me, for the LORD has given your enemies the Moabites into your hands." They followed him, and they captured the Jordan fords leading to Moab. They did not let anyone cross. 29 They struck down about ten thousand Moabites, all strong and valorous men, and not a single man escaped. 30 So Moab was humbled under the hand of Israel that day, and the land had peace for eighty years.

Shamgar

31 After *Ehud* was Shamgar son of Anath. He struck down six hundred Philistine men with an ox goad. He also saved Israel.

Deborah

4 When Ehud was dead, the children of Israel once more did what was evil in the sight of the LORD. 2 The LORD sold them into the hands of King Jabin of Canaan, who ruled in Hazor. The commander of his army was Sisera. He lived in Harosheth Haggoyim. 3 The children of Israel cried out to the LORD, for *Sisera* had nine hundred iron chariots and had forcefully oppressed the children of Israel for twenty years.

4 Now Deborah, the wife of Lappidoth, was a prophetess. She judged Israel at that time. 5 She would sit under the palm tree of Deborah between Ramah and Bethel in the hill country of Ephraim. The children of Israel would go up to her for *her to render* judgment. 6 She sent for Barak son of Abinoam from Kedesh in Naphtali and said to him, "The LORD God of Israel commands you, 'Go and deploy troops at Mount Tabor, and take ten thousand men from the tribes of Naphtali and Zebulun with you. 7 I will draw Sisera, the commander of the army of Jabin, with his chariots and large army to you at the River Kishon and give him into your hands.' "

8 Barak said to her, "If you will go with me, then I will go, but if you will not go with me, then I will not go."

9 She said, "I will indeed go with you. However, the way you are going will gain you no glory, for the LORD will deliver Sisera into the hand of a woman." Then Deborah got up and went with Barak to Kedesh. 10 Barak called Zebulun and Naphtali to Kedesh. Ten thousand men went up on foot with him, and Deborah went up with him *also*.

11 Now Heber the Kenite had moved away from the Kenites, who were descendants of Hobab, Moses' father-in-law. He pitched his tent at the oak in Zaanannim, near Kedesh.

3:12 1Sa 12:9
3:13 Jdg 1:16
3:15 Jdg 3:9
3:19 Jos 4:20
3:20 Am 3:15
3:24 1Sa 24:3
3:27 Jdg 6:34

3:28 Jdg 12:5
3:30 Jdg 3:11
3:31 Jdg 5:6
4:2 Jos 11:1
4:3 Jdg 1:19
4:5 Ge 35:8
4:6 Heb 11:32
4:9 Jdg 2:14
4:10 Jdg 5:18
4:11 Nu 10:29

[1] *16* About 18 inches, or 45 centimeters.

PROFILE OF A SPIRITLED WOMAN

DEBORAH

TAKE AUTHORITY IN YOUR DAY OF TROUBLE

What a gift—to live in our time! Today is a day of great opportunity for women. We can now break through to new positions and levels of authority in all spheres. Women currently lead in every sector of society. We direct schools, universities, corporations, churches, governments, and nations.

In the midst of this unparalleled opportunity there's also great trouble: war, earthquakes, tsunamis, famines, and devastating weather patterns. We live in a country divided by every kind of controversy. Unrighteousness is now being legislated so that people can "legally" sin. Call it a day of immense turmoil and pain.

The world has never needed answers as it does today. It needs bearers of good news, healers, and deliverers. It needs women who are captured by the very heart of God—women who don't see problems but see solutions.

Great Expectations

Consider Deborah, a woman who led a nation through times of great strife (Jdg 4–5). When she became Israel's leader, the nation was suffering under the consequences of its own sin.

The people had chosen new gods, and as a result there was war at the gates. An enemy army surrounded them. Life was so dangerous that highways were deserted and people traveled by hidden paths or simply stayed at home. Judges 5:7 says that life in the village had stopped.

But Deborah possessed a different spirit than others around her. Judges 5:6–7 recounts the situation: "In the days of Jael, main roads were abandoned and travelers used roundabout paths. Village life ceased. It ceased *until I, Deborah, arose; I arose like a mother in Israel*" (emphasis added).

What a statement for Deborah to make! She positively and confidently knew that she would turn her nation around.

Deborah perceived mothers to be more than just bearers of children. She saw motherhood as a leadership and problem-solving role extending beyond the family. Women with a true mother's heart are created to find solutions and lead people to victory. Deborah said, "I know I was made for this. I know I can solve this nation's problems." What faith! It was a faith that apprehended the promises of God.

The apostle Paul said, in Acts 14:22, that it's through "many afflictions" we enter the kingdom of God. According to *Strong's Concordance*, the word *affliction* comes from a Greek word denoting pressure. It means "to be crowded around by problems or caught in a narrow place where escape is impossible."

This isn't a pretty picture. But Deborah wasn't deterred. She said, "I'm getting in line. This is my day. I was made for this!" Paul's message isn't just for Deborah. It's for us too. Tribulation is our entry fee or ticket into the kingdom of God.

In the Book of Hosea we find that Israel was once again punished and restored. God said, "From there, I will give her vineyards to her, and the Valley of Achor as a door of hope"

(Hos 2:15). *Achor* means "trouble." And the "door of hope" isn't just wishful thinking. It is positive expectation.

The Hebrew translation also calls it a "rope." This means that hope wraps itself around the faithful in the valley of trouble and pulls them, through their attitude, to a place of triumph. So, when trouble comes, look ahead for the victory.

This is what Deborah believed. She was energized and confidently expectant. She expected to change her world. I remember my spiritual mentor preaching what Paul said in Acts 14:22. Back then I didn't get it. It bothered me so much that I took it up with God in prayer.

Suddenly, while praying, God painted a vivid picture for me that helped me understand. That day I learned this truth: trouble is the door to a new place in God's kingdom.

Standing up through a season of trouble does something to us that nothing else can do. Strength begins to line our backbone. We begin to understand we're part of a kingdom that will stand firm, no matter how much the world shakes. And the next time we experience trouble, there's within us a greater strength and grace to overcome.

Most believers have no idea what kind of power and authority is at their disposal. Many women don't comprehend that they're more than just a cultural subset in this nation. Their goal is to live a nice life with great kids, a wonderful husband and good friends. But God intended far more than that.

We are kingdom rulers because God, through Jesus Christ, has delegated to us the authority to administrate His kingdom on Earth (Luke 9:1; 10:19). Ephesians 2:6 says that we're both raised up and seated with Christ in heavenly places. We rule and reign through Him (Rev. 5:10).

Often women struggle with this concept because it doesn't seem feminine. We were taught to submit and be nice. It seems foreign to us because we're used to being Daddy's girl—a dancing princess, pirouetting through life.

However, we're to be fully women and fully feminine, displaying a wonderful heart filled with love. Being kingdom releasers and enforcers should never cancel out our femininity.

We as SpiritLed women have power and authority in Christ. Let's use it to further His kingdom!

Barbara J. Yoder

12 Then they told Sisera that Barak son of Abi-
noam had gone up to Mount Tabor. 13 So Sisera
summoned all his nine hundred iron chariots
and all the people with him, from Harosheth
Haggoyim to the River Kishon.
14 Then Deborah said to Barak, "Get up, for
this is the day that the LORD has given Sis-
era into your hands. Has not the LORD gone
out before you?" So Barak went down from
Mount Tabor with ten thousand men behind
him. 15 The LORD routed Sisera and all of his
chariots and all of his army with the edge of
the sword in front of Barak. Sisera dismounted
his chariot and fled on foot.
16 Barak chased after the chariots and the
army as far as Harosheth Haggoyim. The
whole army of Sisera fell by the edge of
the sword. Not a single man survived. 17 Sisera
fled on foot to the tent of Jael, the wife of
Heber the Kenite, for there was peace between
King Jabin of Hazor and the family of Heber
the Kenite.
18 Jael went out to meet Sisera and said to
him, "Turn aside, my lord. Turn aside to me.
Do not be afraid." So he turned aside to her
into the tent, and she covered him with a rug.
19 He said to her, "Please give me a little wa-
ter to drink, for I am thirsty." So she opened a
leather milk container, gave it to him to drink,
and covered him.
20 He said to her, "Stand in the entrance to
the tent, and if anyone comes and asks you, 'Is
there a man here?' then you say, 'No.' "
21 Then Jael the wife of Heber took a tent peg
and a hammer in her hand and went quietly
to him, for he was fast asleep and tired. She
drove the tent peg into his temple, and it went
down into the ground, so he died.
22 Now as Barak had been chasing Sisera,
Jael came out to meet him and said, "Come,
and I will show you the man whom you seek."
When he came in, there was Sisera fallen dead
with a tent peg in his temple.
23 So God humbled King Jabin of Canaan
before the children of Israel that day. 24 The
children of Israel grew more and more pow-
erful over King Jabin of Canaan until he was
no more.

The Song of Deborah

5 On that day, Deborah and Barak son of
Abinoam sang:

2 "When the leaders in Israel lead,
when the people freely volunteer,
bless the LORD!

3 "Hear, O kings! Listen, O rulers!
I will sing to the LORD;
I will sing praise to the LORD God of
Israel.

4:13 Jdg 4:2–3
4:14 Dt 9:3
4:15 Jos 10:10
4:19 Jdg 5:25–26
4:23 Ne 9:24
5:1 Ex 15:1
5:2 Jdg 5:9
. . . .
5:4 Dt 33:2
5:5 Ex 19:18
5:6 Jdg 3:31
5:9 Jdg 5:2
5:10 Jdg 10:4
5:11 1Sa 12:7
5:12 Ps 57:8
5:15 Jdg 4:14

4 "LORD, when You went out from Seir,
when You marched from the land of
Edom,
the ground shook and the skies poured,
indeed, the dense clouds poured water.

Let the mountains melt at Your presence, O God (Jdg 5:5).

5 The mountains quaked before the LORD,
this very Sinai, before the LORD God of
Israel.
6 "In the days of Shamgar son of Anath,
in the days of Jael, *main* roads were
abandoned
and travelers used roundabout paths.
7 Village life ceased. It ceased
until I, Deborah, arose;
I arose *like* a mother in Israel.
8 They were choosing new gods,
and warfare was at the city gates,
but not a shield or spear was to be seen
among forty thousand in Israel.
9 My heart is with the rulers of Israel
who offered themselves willingly among
the people.
Bless the LORD!
10 "You who ride on white donkeys,
you who sit in judges' attire,
you who walk on the road,
11 consider the voice of those who distribute
water among the watering places.
There they tell of the righteous deeds of
the LORD,
the righteous deeds of villagers in Israel.
"Then the people of the LORD
go down to the gates.
12 Awake, awake, Deborah!
Awake, awake, sing a song!
Stand up, Barak,
and capture your prisoners, son of
Abinoam!

13 "The survivors
came down to the nobles;
the people of the LORD
came down for me against the mighty.
14 Some came from Ephraim, whose roots
were in Amalek,
following you, Benjamin, with your
people.
From Makir rulers came down,
and from Zebulun those who carry the
staff of a scribe.
15 The princes of Issachar were with Deborah,
and Issachar was with Barak;
they were sent into the valley on foot.

Among the clans of Reuben
there was great resolve of heart.
16 Why do you sit among the sheepfolds
to hear playing of pipes for the flocks?
In the clans of Reuben
there was much searching of heart.
17 Gilead stayed beyond the Jordan.
As for Dan, why did he stay with the ships?
Asher stayed by the seacoast
and settled by its bays.
18 Zebulun is a people who risked their lives
to the *point of* death,
Naphtali also, on the heights of the battlefield.

19 "Kings came to wage war.
The kings of Canaan waged war
in Taanach, by the waters of Megiddo;
they took no money as profit.
20 From the heavens the stars fought,
from their courses they fought against Sisera.
21 The torrent of Kishon swept them away,
that ancient torrent, the torrent of Kishon.
My soul, march on in strength!
22 Then horses' hooves pounded,
the galloping, galloping of his steeds.
23 Curse Meroz, said the angel of the LORD,
curse its inhabitants,
for they did not come to the aid of the LORD,
to the aid of the LORD against the mighty warriors.

24 "Most blessed of women is Jael,
the wife of Heber the Kenite,
most blessed of tent-dwelling women.
25 He asked for water, she gave him milk.
In a magnificent bowl she brought cream.
26 Her hand on a tent peg,
her right hand on a workman's hammer;
she struck Sisera, she crushed his skull,
she shattered and pierced his temple.
27 Between her feet he sank, he fell, he lay;
between her feet he sank, he fell;
where he sank, there he fell,
overpowered.

28 "The mother of Sisera looked through the window,
and cried out through the lattice,
'Why is his chariot so late?
Why is the sound of his war chariots so delayed?'
29 Her wise attendants answered her,
indeed, she replied to herself,
30 'Are they not finding and dividing the spoils:
a girl or two for each man;
dyed garments as plunder for Sisera,
dyed and embroidered garments,
two pieces of dyed embroidery for the neck of the looter?'
31 "May all Your enemies perish like this,
O LORD!
But may those who love Him rise like the sun
when it rises in full strength."

Then the land was at peace for forty years.

5:16 Nu 32:24
5:17 Jos 13:25
5:18 Jdg 4:10
5:19 Jdg 1:27
5:20 Jos 10:11
5:21 Jdg 4:7
5:23 Jdg 21:9–10
5:24 Jdg 4:17
5:30 Ex 15:9

……

5:31 Jdg 3:11
6:2 1Sa 13:6
6:3 Jdg 3:13
6:4 Lev 26:16
6:5 Jdg 7:12
6:6 Jdg 3:9
6:9 Ps 44:2–3
6:10 Jer 10:2
6:11 Jos 17:2
6:12 Lk 1:28
6:13 Ps 44:1

Gideon

6 The children of Israel did evil in the sight
of the LORD, so the LORD gave them into the
hands of Midian for seven years. 2 The hands
of Midian dominated Israel, and because of
Midian the children of Israel made hiding plac-
es for themselves in the mountains, caves, and
strongholds. 3 Whenever Israel would plant
crops, the Midianites, Amalekites, and the
people from the east would come up against
them. 4 Then they would make camp by them
and ruin crops of the land all the way to Gaza.
They did not leave any provisions behind in
Israel—neither sheep, nor cattle, nor donkeys.
5 For they came with their livestock and tents
like a swarm of locusts. They and their camels
were too numerous to count, and they came
into the land to destroy it. 6 Israel was made
weak before Midian and cried out to the LORD.
7 When the children of Israel cried out to the
LORD because of Midian, 8 the LORD sent them
a prophet who said, "Thus says the LORD God
of Israel: I brought you up from Egypt and out
of that place of slavery. 9 I delivered you from
the hands of Egypt and all your oppressors. I
drove them out from before you and gave you
their land. 10 I said to you, 'I am the LORD your
God. Do not worship the gods of the Amorites
in whose land you are living.' But you have
disobeyed Me."
11 Now the angel[1] of the LORD came and
sat under the oak tree in Ophrah belonging
to Joash the Abiezrite. Gideon his son was
threshing wheat in a winepress to hide it from
the Midianites. 12 The angel of the LORD ap-
peared and said to him, "The LORD is with you,
O mighty man of valor."
13 Then Gideon said to him, "O my lord, if
the LORD is with us, then why has all this hap-
pened to us? Where are all His miracles that
our fathers told us about? They said, 'Did not
the LORD bring us out of Egypt?' Yet now the
LORD has forsaken us and delivered us into the
hands of the Midianites."

[1] *11* At times the Lord speaks directly through an angel (cf. the story of the burning bush in Ex 3:2–4).

SPIRITLED WOMAN

COUNSEL FROM THE SPIRIT BASICS

Jehovah Shalom

Then Gideon built an altar for the LORD there and called it The LORD Is Peace.

—JUDGES 6:24

Jehovah Shalom, "The Lord Is Peace," is our surety in times of trouble or conflict. Many think of peace treaties when they think of the word peace—an agreement to cease fire and end hostilities between different groups.

It is not just a *peace* where there is an absence of open conflict, but *shalom* is also a relationship of genuine good will and brotherly love toward the other party. It is an attitude of being sneaky in trying to bless the other, no matter what. It is another word that is indispensable in discussing the attitudes of one toward another in covenant relationships. Would only that more of our marriages were based on this kind of peace rather than simply nonconfrontational coexistence!

Cindy Trimm

14 Then the LORD turned to him and said, "Go
in this strength of yours. Save Israel from the
control of Midian. Have I not sent you?"
15 And he said to Him, "O my Lord, how can
I save Israel? Indeed my clan is the weakest
in Manasseh, and I am the youngest in my
father's house."
16 Then the LORD said to him, "But I will be
with you, and you will strike the Midianites
as one man."
17 And he said to Him, "If I have found favor
in Your sight, give me a sign that it is You who
are speaking with me.
18 Please do not depart
from here until I come to You and bring out
my gift and set it before You."
And He said, "I will stay until you return."
19 So Gideon went and prepared a young
goat and unleavened bread from an ephah of
flour. He put the meat in a basket, and he put
the broth in a pot, and brought them out and
offered them to Him under the oak.
20 And the angel of God said to him, "Take
the meat and the unleavened bread, lay them
on this rock, and pour out the broth." And so
he did.
21 The angel of the LORD reached out
the tip of the staff that was in His hand and
touched the meat and unleavened flatbread.
Fire rose out of the rock and consumed the
meat and unleavened bread. Then the angel
of the LORD departed from his sight.
22 Then
Gideon perceived that it was indeed the angel
of the LORD. So Gideon said, "Alas, O Lord GOD!
I have seen the angel of the LORD face to face."
23 Then the LORD said to him, "Peace be with
you. Do not be afraid. You will not die."
24 Then Gideon built an altar for the LORD
there and called it The LORD Is Peace. Even to
this day it stands in Ophrah of the Abiezrites.
25 That night the LORD said to him, "Take a
bull from your father's herd and a second bull
seven years old. Tear down your father's Baal
altar and cut down the Asherah pole beside it.
26 Then build an altar to the LORD your God on
top of this stronghold in an orderly way. Take
the second bull and offer it as a burnt offering
with the wood of the Asherah pole that you
will cut down."
27 So Gideon took ten men from among his
slaves and did as the LORD had told him, but
because he was too afraid of *the rest of* his
father's household and the men of the city to
do it by day, he did it at night.
28 When the men of the city got up early in
the morning, the altar of Baal was torn down,
the Asherah pole beside it was cut down, and
the second bull had been offered on the *new*
altar that had been built.
29 They said to each other, "Who has done
this?"
When they had inquired and asked, they responded, "Gideon son of Joash has done this."
30 Then the men of the city said to Joash,
"Bring out your son so that he may die, for he
tore down the altar of Baal and cut down the
Asherah pole beside it."
31 Joash then said to all who stood against
him, "Would you plead for Baal? Would you
save him? Whoever fights for him will be killed
by morning. If *Baal* is a god, let him fight for
himself, for someone has torn down his altar."
32 Therefore on that day he called him
Jerub-Baal, saying, "Let Baal fight him, for he
tore down the altar *of Baal.*"
33 All the Midianites, Amalekites, and the
people from the east gathered together, and
they crossed over, and camped in the Valley
of Jezreel.
34 The Spirit of the LORD enveloped
Gideon. He blew a ram's horn trumpet, and
the Abiezrites assembled behind him.
35 He
sent messengers throughout all of Manasseh
and they assembled behind him as well. He

6:14 Heb 11:34
6:15 Ex 3:11
6:16 Ex 3:12
6:19 Ge 18:6–8
6:20 Jdg 13:19

6:21 Lev 9:24
6:22 Ge 32:30
6:23 Da 10:19
6:24 Ge 22:14
6:25 Ex 34:13
6:32 1Sa 12:11
6:33 Jos 17:16
6:34 Jdg 3:10

Fleecing God?

Have you ever thought God was saying something to you, but you weren't sure it was really His voice you were hearing? Have you found yourself thinking, "How do I know it was really God I heard and not my own imagination—or worse, the enemy?"

God's solution is simple: "If any of you lacks wisdom, let him ask of God, who gives to all men liberally and without criticism, and it will be given to him" (Jas 1:5). When we need to know if we are hearing God's voice, all we have to do is ask Him—and not rely on a fleece as Gideon did.

We must not give God an ultimatum about how He is to confirm His word to us. Sometimes that's called "putting a fleece before the Lord," referring to the experience of Gideon found in Judges 6:36–40.

God wanted Gideon to lead Israel in battle against the Midianites, but Gideon was not feeling very confident in his calling—or in his hearing from God. So he laid a fleece (a sheepskin) on the floor and asked God to make the morning dew come only on the fleece and not on the ground around the fleece. God did this for him, but poor Gideon was still unconvinced. The next night he asked God to reconfirm His word by covering the ground with dew but leaving the fleece dry. Once again, God did as Gideon requested.

Based on this passage, some people assume they can tell God precisely how to confirm or correct what they believe they have heard Him say to them. In essence, they believe they can dictate the supernatural hoops through which God must jump to prove He really said what they believe they heard.

God allowed Gideon to fleece Him, but there is no indication He was setting a precedent for the rest of us to follow. In fact, there is a strong scriptural precedent against telling God specifically what to do.

Jesus Himself refused Satan's suggestion to put a fleece before God by casting Himself off the highest point of the temple. Instead, Jesus said, "You shall not tempt the Lord your God" (Mt 4:7).

When we go back to God for confirmation, we need to allow Him to choose how He will correct or confirm what we heard. It is not our place to dictate how He does this. Instead, we must trust that He will do it in a way that we can clearly recognize as being from Him.

Teresa Seputis

SPIRITLED WOMAN

COUNSEL FROM THE SPIRIT BASICS

"More Than" People

Our God loves to use impossible situations to prove His power and strength. He is constantly looking for people He can entrust with the impossible.

The story of Gideon is a perfect example. Though we tend to think there is strength in numbers, God's view is completely opposite.

When a large army of Midianites threatened Israel, the Lord said to Gideon, "You have too many people with you for Me to give the Midianites into their hands, lest Israel glorify themselves over Me, saying, 'Our own power saved us'" (Jdg. 7:2).

Through a series of qualifying tests God reduced Gideon's army from thirty-two thousand to three hundred—then sent him off to fight. Gideon's army was severely outnumbered, yet God led them to victory.

Like Gideon, "more than" people have learned their strength does not lie in their own ability but in the supernatural ability of God. Their attitude is, "I can do all things because of Christ who strengthens me" (Php 4:13).

Shirley Arnold

also sent messengers to Asher, Zebulun, and
Naphtali, so *these tribes* came up to meet them.
36 Gideon said to God, "If You will use my
hands to save Israel, as You have said— 37 I
am placing a fleece of wool on the threshing
floor. If there is dew on the fleece only and all
of the ground remains dry, then I will know
that You will save Israel with my hands, as You
have said." 38 So it happened. He got up early the next morning and squeezed the fleece.
Enough dew poured out of the fleece to fill a
bowlful of water.
39 Then Gideon said to God, "Do not let Your
anger burn against me as I speak only one
more time. Please let me perform a test with
the fleece one *more* time. Please, let the fleece
be the only *thing* dry, and let there be dew on
all of the ground." 40 So God did this during
that night. Only the fleece was dry, and the
dew was on all the ground.

6:36 Jdg 6:14
6:39 Ge 18:32

7:1 Ge 12:6
7:2 Dt 8:17
7:3 Dt 20:8
7:7 1Sa 14:6
7:11 Jdg 7:13–15
7:12 Jdg 6:5
7:14 Jos 2:9

Gideon Defeats the Midianites

7 Then Jerub-Baal (that is, Gideon) and all
the people who were with him got up early and set up camp at Harod Spring. There was
a camp of Midianites to the north of them in
the valley near the hill of Moreh. 2 The LORD
said to Gideon, "You have too many people
with you for Me to give the Midianites into
their hands, lest Israel glorify themselves over
Me, saying, 'Our own power saved us.' 3 So
now, call out so the people can hear, 'Whoever is afraid or anxious may turn back and
leave Mount Gilead.' " So twenty-two thousand
from among the people turned back, and ten
thousand were left.
4 But the LORD said to Gideon, "There are still
too many people. Bring them down to the water, and I will test them for you there. When I
say to you, 'This one will go with you,' he will
go with you. Everyone about whom I will say,
'This one will not go with you,' will not go."
5 So he brought the people down to the water, and the LORD said to Gideon, "You shall set
apart by himself everyone who laps the water
with his tongue like dogs; likewise, everyone
who kneels down to drink." 6 The number of
those who lapped, putting their hands to their
mouths, was three hundred. The rest of the
people had knelt to drink water.
7 The LORD said to Gideon, "With three hundred men who lapped *to drink*, I will save you
and give the Midianites into your hands. *All
the rest of* the people should go home." 8 So the
three hundred men took provisions and ram's
horn trumpets in their hands. Gideon sent all
the *other* Israelite men to their tents, but he
kept the three hundred men.
Now the Midianite camp was below him in
the valley. 9 That night the LORD said to him,
"Get up and go down into the camp, for I have
given it into your hands. 10 Yet if you are afraid
to go down, then go down to the camp with
Purah your servant. 11 Listen to what they
say, and afterward you will be emboldened
to go down to the camp." So he and Purah
his servant went down near the edge of the
camp. 12 Now the Midianites, Amalekites, and
the Kedemites covered the valley like locusts;
and their camels could not be counted, *for
they were* as numerous as *grains of* sand on
the seashore.
13 Gideon came and overheard one man who
was telling his dream to another. The man
said, "Listen to a dream I had. I saw a dry cake
of barley bread rolling into the Midianite camp.
It rolled up to a tent and struck it. It fell, turned
upside down, and collapsed."
14 The other man responded, "This is none
other than the sword of Gideon son of Joash

the Israelite. God has given Midian and the whole camp into his hands."

15 When Gideon heard the telling of the dream and its interpretation, he worshipped, returned to the camp of Israel, and said, "Get up, for the LORD has given the Midianite camp into your hands." 16 He divided the three hundred men into three combat units. He gave all of them ram's horn trumpets, empty jars, and torches within the jars.

> I release the sword of the Lord against the powers of hell, in the name of Jesus (Jdg 7:18).

17 He said to them, "Look at me and do likewise. Watch, and when I come to the perimeter of the camp, do as I do. 18 When I and all who are with me blow the horn, then you will blow the horns all around the camp and shout, 'For the LORD and for Gideon!' "

19 So Gideon and a hundred men with him went to the edge of the camp at the start of the middle night watch, just as they were setting the watch. Then they blew the horns and smashed the jars in their hands. 20 The three combat units blew the horns and broke the jars. They held the torches in their left hands and the horns for blowing in their right hands. They called out, "A sword for the LORD and for Gideon!" 21 Every man stood in his place all around the camp, but the men in the camp ran, shouted, and fled.

22 When they blew the three hundred horns, the LORD turned every man's sword against his fellow man throughout the camp. The *Midianite* camp fled to Beth Shittah in the direction of Zererah, up to the border of Abel Meholah, near Tabbath. 23 The men of Israel from Naphtali, Asher, and all of Manasseh were summoned, and they chased after the Midianites. 24 Now Gideon sent messengers throughout the hill country of Ephraim, saying, "Come down to engage Midian in battle. Take control of the water *ways* as far as Beth Barah and the Jordan."

All the men of Ephraim were summoned, and they took control of the water *ways* as far as Beth Barah and the Jordan. 25 They captured Oreb and Zeeb, the two Midianite commanders. They killed Oreb at the rock of Oreb and killed Zeeb at the winepress of Zeeb. They chased after the Midianites and brought the heads of Oreb and Zeeb to Gideon on the other side of the Jordan.

7:22 1Ki 4:12
7:23 Jdg 6:35
7:25 Isa 10:26

8:1 2Sa 19:41
8:3 Pr 15:1
8:5 Ge 33:17
8:6 1Ki 20:11
8:8 Ge 32:30–31
8:10 Jdg 7:12
8:11 Nu 32:35
8:12 Ps 83:11
8:16 Jdg 8:7
8:17 Jdg 8:9

Zebah and Zalmunna

8 Then the men of Ephraim said to him, "What have you done to us by not calling us to go and wage war against Midian?" They argued heatedly with him.

2 He said to them, "What have I done now compared to you? Are not the gleanings of the grapes of Ephraim better than the harvest of Abiezer? 3 It was into your hands that God gave the Midianite commanders, Oreb and Zeeb. What was I able to do compared to you?" When *Gideon* said this, their anger against him cooled down.

4 Then Gideon came to the Jordan and crossed over, he and the three hundred men who were with him, exhausted but still pursuing. 5 He said to the men of Sukkoth, "Please give some loaves of bread to the people who are following me, for they are exhausted, and I am pursuing Zebah and Zalmunna, kings of Midian."

6 The officials of Sukkoth said, "Are the hands of Zebah and Zalmunna already in your hands that we should give bread to your army?"

7 So Gideon said, "Because of this, when the LORD gives Zebah and Zalmunna into my hands, I will tear your bodies with desert thorns and briers."

8 He went up from there to Peniel and spoke to them in the same way. The men of Peniel answered him just as the men of Sukkoth had. 9 So he also said to the men of Peniel, "When I return safely, I will tear down this tower."

10 Now Zebah and Zalmunna were in Karkor with their armies, about fifteen thousand survivors; they were all who were left of all the army of the Kedemites, for one hundred twenty thousand arms-bearing men had fallen. 11 Gideon went up on the route of the tent dwellers east of Nobah and Jogbehah and attacked the camp while the army was off guard. 12 Zebah and Zalmunna fled, and Gideon chased after them. He captured Zebah and Zalmunna, the two kings of Midian, and the entire army was terrified.

13 Gideon son of Joash returned from battle by the Pass of Heres. 14 He captured a young man from among the men of Sukkoth and asked him to write the *names of* the leaders and elders of Sukkoth, seventy-seven men. 15 Then he came to the men of Sukkoth and said, "Here are Zebah and Zalmunna, about whom you taunted me. You said, 'Have you subjugated Zebah and Zalmunna that we should give bread to your weary army?' " 16 He took the city elders and disciplined the men of Sukkoth with thorns and briers of the wilderness. 17 He tore down the tower of Peniel and killed the men of the city.

18 Then he said to Zebah and Zalmunna, "What kind of men did you kill at Tabor?"

They said, "They were like you. Each one looked like the son of a king."

19 He said, "They were my brothers, the sons of my mother. As the LORD lives, if you had allowed them to live, I would not kill you." 20 Gideon said to his firstborn Jether, "Rise and kill them!" Yet the young man did not draw his sword because he was afraid, for he was still a young man.

21 Then Zebah and Zalmunna said, "You get up and attack us, for a man is judged by his strength." So Gideon got up and killed Zebah and Zalmunna and took the crescent-shaped ornaments that were on the necks of their camels.

Gideon's Ephod

22 Then the men of Israel said to Gideon, "Rule over us, you, and your son, and your grandson, for you have saved us from the hands of Midian."

23 Gideon said to them, "I will not rule over you, and my son will not rule over you. The LORD will rule over you." 24 Gideon continued, "I have a request to make of you, that each man would give me an earring from his spoils." (*Their enemy* had golden earrings because they were Ishmaelites.)

25 They said, "We will certainly give them." So they spread out a cloak, and each man threw a ring of his spoils there. 26 The weight of the golden earrings that he requested was seventeen hundred gold shekels.[1] This was in addition to the crescent-shaped ornaments, jewelry, and purple clothing worn by the kings of Midian, as well as the chains hanging on the necks of their camels. 27 Gideon used these things to make an ephod. He put it in his city, in Ophrah, and all Israel prostituted themselves to it there. It became a snare to Gideon and his family.

28 The Midianites were humbled before the children of Israel and did not lift their heads high again. The land had peace for forty years in the days of Gideon.

The Death of Gideon

29 Jerub-Baal son of Joash went to his house and lived there. 30 Gideon had seventy sons, for he had many wives. 31 His concubine who lived in Shechem also bore him a son, and he named him Abimelek. 32 Gideon son of Joash died at a good old age, and he was buried in the tomb of his father Joash in Ophrah of the Abiezrites.

33 After Gideon died, the children of Israel turned again to prostitute themselves with the Baals. They made Baal-Berith their god. 34 The children of Israel did not remember the LORD their God, who had delivered them from the hands of their enemies around them, 35 and they did not keep faith with the family of Jerub-Baal (that is, Gideon), for all the good he had done for Israel.

Abimelek

9 Abimelek son of Jerub-Baal went to Shechem, to his mother's brothers. He spoke to them and to the house of his mother's father saying, 2 "Please say in the hearing of all of the leaders of Shechem, 'Which is better for you, to have all seventy sons of Jerub-Baal rule over you, or for one man to rule over you? Remember that I am your own flesh and bone.' "

3 So his mother's brothers spoke all these things about him in the hearing of all the leaders of Shechem, and their hearts inclined toward Abimelek, for they said, "He is our brother." 4 They gave him seventy silver coins[2] from the temple of Baal-Berith. Abimelek hired unprincipled and undisciplined men, and they followed him. 5 He went to his father's house at Ophrah and killed his brothers, the seventy sons of Jerub-Baal, on a single stone. Yet Jotham, the youngest son of Jerub-Baal, survived because he hid himself. 6 All the leaders of Shechem and everyone from Beth Millo gathered together by the oak near the pillar in Shechem to make Abimelek king.

7 When Jotham heard this, he went and stood on the top of Mount Gerizim. He raised his voice and called out, saying to them, "Listen to me, leaders of Shechem, so that God may listen to you! 8 The trees once went out to anoint a king over them. They said to the olive tree, 'Rule over us!'

9 "Yet the olive tree said to them, 'Should I stop making oil, by which God and men are honored, to go and sway over the trees?'

10 "So the trees said to the fig tree, 'You come and rule over us.'

11 "Yet the fig tree said to them, 'Should I stop making my sweet aroma and my fruit, to go and sway over the trees?'

12 "So the trees said to the grapevine, 'You come and rule over us.'

13 "Yet the grapevine said to them, 'Should I stop making my fresh wine, which cheers God and men, to go and sway over the trees?'

14 "So the trees said to the thorn bush, 'You come and rule over us.'

15 "The thorn bush said to the trees, 'If you really want to anoint me king over you, then come and take refuge in my shade. If not, let

8:18 Jdg 4:6
8:23 1Sa 10:19
8:24 Ge 25:13
8:27 Jdg 17:5
8:28 Jdg 5:31
8:30 Jdg 9:2
8:32 Ge 25:8

....

8:33 Jdg 9:4
8:34 Ps 78:11
9:1 Jdg 8:31
9:2 Ge 29:14
9:3 Ge 29:15
9:4 Jdg 8:33
9:5 2Ki 11:1–2
9:6 2Sa 5:9
9:7 Dt 11:29
9:13 Ps 104:15
9:15 Jdg 9:20

[1] *26* About 43 pounds, or 20 kilograms. [2] *4* About 1¾ pounds, or 800 grams.

fire come out from the thorn bush and consume the cedars of Lebanon!’

16 “Now then, did you show good faith and integrity when you made Abimelek king? Did you deal well with Jerub-Baal and his family? Did you do to him as his actions deserved, 17 considering that my father waged war for you, risked his life for you, and delivered you from the hands of Midian? 18 Yet you have taken a stand against my father’s family today. You killed his seventy sons, each on a single stone. You made Abimelek, son of his slave woman, king over the leaders of Shechem because he is your brother. 19 So if you did show good faith and integrity in what you did with Jerub-Baal and his family today, then rejoice in Abimelek, and may he also rejoice in you. 20 If not, let fire come out from Abimelek and consume the leaders of Shechem and Beth Millo, and let fire come out from the leaders of Shechem and from Beth Millo and consume Abimelek!”

21 Then Jotham ran away and fled. He went to Beer and lived there because of Abimelek his brother.

The Downfall of Abimelek

22 After Abimelek ruled over Israel for three years, 23 God sent an evil spirit between Abimelek and the leaders of Shechem, and the leaders of Shechem dealt treacherously with Abimelek, 24 so that the violence done to the seventy sons of Jerub-Baal and their blood might come back upon Abimelek their brother, who killed them, and upon the leaders of Shechem, who empowered him to kill his brothers. 25 The leaders of Shechem set ambushes against him on the hilltops and robbed all who passed by them on the road. This was told to Abimelek.

26 Gaal, the son of Ebed, and his brothers came *to Shechem*, and the leaders of Shechem trusted him. 27 They went out to the field, gathered and trod their grapes, and had a celebration. They went to the temple of their god and ate, drank, and cursed Abimelek. 28 Gaal son of Ebed said, “Who is Abimelek, and who is Shechem, that we should serve him? Is he not the son of Jerub-Baal, and *is not* Zebul his officer? Serve the sons of Hamor, the father of Shechem. Why should we serve *Abimelek*? 29 If only this people were under my command, I would get rid of Abimelek.” So he said to Abimelek, “Muster your army and come out!”

30 Then Zebul the city ruler heard the words of Gaal son of Ebed and he burned with anger. 31 He secretly sent messengers to Abimelek, saying, “Gaal, the son of Ebed, and his brothers have come to Shechem and are fortifying the

9:16 Jdg 8:35
9:18 Jdg 9:5–6
9:19 Isa 8:6
9:20 Jdg 9:15
9:21 Nu 21:16
9:23 Isa 33:1
9:24 1Ki 2:32
9:27 Jdg 9:4
9:28 Ge 34:2
9:29 2Sa 15:4
9:33 1Sa 10:7
9:38 Jdg 9:28–29
9:45 2Ki 3:25
9:46 Jdg 8:33
9:48 Ps 68:14

city against you. 32 So now, get up at night, you and the people with you, and lie in wait in the field. 33 In the morning at sunrise, get up early and attack the city. He and the people with him will come out to you, then you can do to them as you find opportunity.”

34 So Abimelek and all the people who were with him got up at night and lay in wait by Shechem in four companies. 35 When Gaal son of Ebed went out and stood at the entrance of the city gate, then Abimelek and the people who were with him got up from their hiding places.

36 Gaal saw these people and said to Zebul, “Look, people are coming down from the hilltops.”

Zebul said to him, “The shadows of the hills look like men to you.”

37 Gaal spoke again and said, “Look, people are coming down the middle of the land, and a company is coming by way of the Diviner’s Oak.”

38 Then Zebul said to him, “Where is your mouth now, which said, ‘Who is Abimelek, that we should serve him?’ Are not these the people you dismissed out of hand? Go now, I pray, and fight against them.”

39 So Gaal went out before the leaders of Shechem and fought Abimelek. 40 Abimelek chased him, and Gaal fled from him. Many fell wounded at the entrance of the gate. 41 Abimelek stayed in Arumah, and Zebul drove out Gaal and his brothers from living in Shechem.

42 The next day the people went out into the field, and this was told to Abimelek. 43 So he took the people and divided them into three companies, and they laid in wait in the field. When the people came out from the city, he rose up against them and struck them down. 44 Abimelek and the company that was with him rushed forward and stood at the entrance of the city gate. The two other combat units attacked everyone in the field and struck them down. 45 Abimelek fought against the city all that day. He captured the city and killed the people inside it; he tore down the city and spread salt over it.

46 When the leaders of the Tower of Shechem heard this, they entered the fortified temple of El-Berith. 47 Abimelek was told that all the leaders of the Tower of Shechem had gathered together. 48 So Abimelek and all the people who were with him went up Mount Zalmon. He took an axe in his hand and cut off a tree branch, lifted it, and carried it on his shoulder. Then he said to the men who were with him, “What you have seen me do, hurry and do the same.” 49 So everyone likewise cut off a branch and followed Abimelek. They placed them on

the fortification and set the fortification on fire over them. So all the people of the Tower of Shechem died, about a thousand men and women.

50 Then Abimelek went to Thebez and encamped against Thebez and captured it. 51 But there was a fortified tower within the city, so all of the men and women and the leaders of the city fled there. They shut themselves in and went up to the top of the tower. 52 Abimelek came to the tower and fought against it. But as he drew near to the tower entrance to burn it with fire, 53 a certain woman dropped an upper millstone on the head of Abimelek, and it crushed his skull.

54 Urgently he called to the young man who carried his gear and said to him, "Draw your sword and kill me, so that people may not say about me, 'A woman killed him.' " So the young man pierced him through, and he died. 55 Then the men of Israel saw that Abimelek was dead, so everyone went home.

56 Thus God repaid the wickedness of Abimelek, which he committed against his father by killing his seventy brothers. 57 God also repaid the evil deeds of the men of Shechem, and the curse of Jotham son of Jerub-Baal came upon them.

Tola

10 After the death of Abimelek, Tola the son of Puah, the son of Dodo, a man of Issachar, arose to save Israel. He lived in Shamir, in the hill country of Ephraim. 2 He judged Israel for twenty-three years. Then he died and was buried in Shamir.

Jair

3 After him Jair the Gileadite arose and judged Israel for twenty-two years. 4 He had thirty sons who rode thirty donkeys and owned thirty cities that are in the land of Gilead. They are called Havvoth Jair to this day. 5 Jair died and was buried in Kamon.

Jephthah

6 Again the children of Israel did evil in the sight of the LORD. They worshipped the Baals, the Ashtoreths, and the gods of Syria, Sidon, Moab, the Ammonites, and the Philistines. They abandoned the LORD and did not serve Him. 7 The anger of the LORD burned against Israel, and He sold them into the hands of the Philistines and the Ammonites. 8 They brutally oppressed the children of Israel that year. For eighteen years *they oppressed* all the children of Israel beyond the Jordan in the land of the Amorites in Gilead. 9 The Ammonites also crossed over the Jordan to wage war against Judah, Benjamin, and Ephraim, so that Israel was greatly distressed. 10 Then the children of

9:53 2Sa 11:21
9:56 Ps 94:23
9:57 Jdg 9:20
10:1 Jdg 2:16
10:4 Nu 32:41
10:7 Jdg 2:14
10:10 1Sa 12:10
....
10:11 Ex 14:30
10:12 Jdg 6:3
10:13 Jer 2:13
10:14 Dt 32:37–38
10:15 1Sa 3:18
10:16 Isa 63:9
10:17 Jdg 11:29
10:18 Jdg 11:11
11:1 Heb 11:32
11:3 Jdg 9:4
11:7 Ge 26:27
11:8 Jdg 10:18
11:10 Jer 42:5
11:11 Jdg 10:17

Israel cried out to the LORD, "We have sinned against You, for we have abandoned our God and worshipped the Baals."

11 The LORD said to the children of Israel, "Did I not deliver you from Egypt, the Amorites, the Ammonites, the Philistines, 12 the Sidonians, the Amalekites, and the Maonites when they oppressed you? You cried out to Me, and I saved you from their hands. 13 Yet you have abandoned Me and worshipped other gods. Therefore I will not save you again. 14 Go and cry out to the gods that you have chosen. Let them save you in your time of distress."

15 Then the children of Israel said to the LORD, "We have sinned. Do to us whatever seems good in Your sight. Please, just deliver us today." 16 They removed the foreign gods from among them and worshipped the LORD, and He could no longer endure the suffering of Israel.

17 The Ammonites had been called out and set up camp in Gilead. The children of Israel assembled and set up camp in Mizpah. 18 The commanders of Gilead said to each other, "Who is the man who will begin to fight against the Ammonites? He will be the ruler of all the inhabitants of Gilead."

11 Now Jephthah the Gileadite was a mighty man of valor, but he was the son of a prostitute. Gilead was the father of Jephthah. 2 Gilead's wife also bore him sons. His wife's sons grew up and drove Jephthah away. They said to him, "You will not inherit anything from our father's house because you are the son of another woman." 3 So Jephthah fled from his brothers and lived in the land of Tob. Men of ill repute gathered around Jephthah and went out with him.

4 Some time passed, then the Ammonites waged war with Israel. 5 When the Ammonites waged war with Israel, the elders of Gilead went to bring Jephthah back from the land of Tob. 6 They said to Jephthah, "Come and be our leader so that we may fight the Ammonites."

7 Jephthah said to the elders of Gilead, "Did you not hate me and drive me out of my father's house? Why have you come to me now that you are in trouble?"

8 The elders of Gilead said to Jephthah, "Even so, we have turned to you. Come with us and fight the Ammonites. You will be ruler over all the inhabitants of Gilead."

9 Jephthah said to the elders of Gilead, "If you bring me back to wage war against the Ammonites, and the LORD gives them to me, then I will be your ruler."

10 The elders of Gilead said to Jephthah, "May the LORD be a witness between us if we do not act according to your word." 11 So Jephthah went with the elders of Gilead. The people

set him over them as ruler and leader. And Jephthah spoke all his words before the LORD in Mizpah.

12 Jephthah sent messengers to the Ammonite king to say, "What *problem* is there between you and me, that you have come to me to wage war in my land?"

13 The Ammonite king said to the messengers of Jephthah, "Because when Israel came up from Egypt, they took my land, from the Arnon to the Jabbok and as far as the Jordan. Now return it peacefully."

14 Again Jephthah sent messengers to the Ammonite king, 15 and said to him,

"Jephthah says this: Israel did not take the land of Moab, nor the Ammonite land; 16 for when Israel came up from Egypt, they went into the desert as far as the Red Sea and came to Kadesh. 17 Then Israel sent messengers to the king of Edom, saying, 'Please let us pass through your land.' Yet the king of Edom would not listen. They also sent messengers to the king of Moab, but he was unwilling. So Israel stayed at Kadesh.

18 "They went into the wilderness, around the lands of Edom and Moab. They went east of the land of Moab and set up camp on the other side of the River Arnon. They did not cross the boundary of Moab, for the River Arnon was the boundary of Moab.

19 "Then Israel sent messengers to Sihon king of the Amorites, who ruled in Heshbon. Israel said to him, "Please let us pass through your land to our home." 20 Yet Sihon did not trust Israel to pass through his territory, so Sihon gathered all his people and set up camp in Jahaz to fight with Israel.

21 "The LORD God of Israel gave Sihon and all his people into the hands of Israel, and they struck them down. So Israel took possession of all the land of the Amorites who lived in that land. 22 They took possession of all of the territory of the Amorites, from the Arnon to the Jabbok and from the desert to the Jordan.

23 "Now that the LORD God of Israel has driven out the Amorites from before His people Israel, should you take it? 24 Will you not take possession of whatever Chemosh your god gives you? So everything that the LORD our God possesses before us, we will take possession of it. 25 Now are you really better than Balak son of Zippor, the king of Moab? Did he ever contend with Israel or wage war with them? 26 Israel has lived in Heshbon and its nearby towns, in Aroer and its nearby towns, and in all the cities along the banks of the River Arnon for three hundred years. Why did you not take them back during that time? 27 So I have not sinned against you, but it is you who are doing evil to me by waging war against me. May the LORD, the Judge, judge today between the children of Israel and the Ammonites."

11:13 Ge 32:22
11:15 Dt 2:9
11:16 Nu 14:25
11:22 Dt 2:36
11:24 Nu 21:29
11:25 Mic 6:5
11:26 Dt 2:36
11:27 Ge 16:5
11:29 Jdg 3:10
11:30 Ge 28:20
11:31 1Sa 1:28
11:33 Eze 27:17
11:34 Ex 15:20
11:36 2Sa 18:19
11:37 Lk 1:25
11:39 Jdg 11:31
12:1 Jdg 8:1

28 Yet the Ammonite king would not listen to the message that Jephthah had sent him.

29 Then the Spirit of the LORD came on Jephthah and he passed through Gilead and Manasseh, and passed through Mizpah of Gilead, and went on to the Ammonites. 30 Jephthah made a vow to the LORD, "If You will indeed give the Ammonites into my hands, 31 then whatever comes out from the door of my house to meet me, when I return safely from the Ammonites, will surely be the LORD's, and I will offer it up as a burnt offering."

32 So Jephthah crossed over to the Ammonites to wage war against them, and the LORD gave them into his hands. 33 He struck them down from Aroer to Minnith, twenty cities, and as far as Abel Keramim. The defeat was very severe, and the Ammonites were humbled before the children of Israel.

34 When Jephthah went to his house at Mizpah, there was his daughter coming out to meet him, dancing with a tambourine. She was his only child. Other than her, he had neither son nor daughter. 35 When he saw her, he ripped up his clothes and said, "Alas, my daughter! You have brought utter disaster to me. You are my undoing, for I have given my word to the LORD, and I cannot take it back."

36 She said to him, "My father, you have opened your mouth to the LORD. Do to me what has come out of your mouth, because the LORD worked vengeance upon your enemies, the Ammonites." 37 Then she said to her father, "Let this be done for me: Give me two months, and I and my friends will wander the hill country and mourn over my virginity."

38 He said, "Go," and he sent her away for two months. She and her friends went and mourned over her virginity in the hill country. 39 At the end of two months she returned to her father, and he did to her according to the vow that he had made. She had not ever slept with a man.

So it became a custom in Israel 40 that the women of Israel would commemorate the daughter of Jephthah the Gileadite for four days each year.

Jephthah and Ephraim

12 The men of Ephraim gathered together and crossed over to Zaphon. They said to Jephthah, "Why did you go to wage war with the Ammonites and not call us to go with

you? We will burn down your house right on top of you."

2 Jephthah said to them, "My people and I were in a very great conflict with the Ammonites. I called you, but you did not save me from their hands. 3 When I saw that you were not going to save me, I took my life in my own hands and crossed over to the Ammonites. Then the LORD gave them into my hands. Now why have you come up to me today to wage war against me?"

4 Then Jephthah assembled all the men of Gilead and fought with Ephraim. The men of Gilead struck Ephraim down, for they had said, "You Gileadites are fugitives in Ephraim, living in Ephraim and Manasseh." 5 Gilead captured the fords of the Jordan River leading to Ephraim. Whenever an Ephraimite fugitive would say, "Let me cross," the Gileadite men would say to him, "Are you an Ephraimite?" If he said, "No," 6 then they would say to him, "Say, 'Shibboleth'!" Yet he would say, "Sibboleth," for he could not pronounce it *correctly*. Then they would grab him and kill him at the Jordan fords. During that time forty-two thousand from Ephraim fell.

7 Jephthah judged Israel for six years. When Jephthah the Gileadite died, he was buried among the cities of Gilead.

Ibzan, Elon, and Abdon

8 After him, Ibzan of Bethlehem judged Israel. 9 He had thirty sons, and he gave thirty daughters in marriage outside his clan; and he brought thirty daughters from outside for his sons. He judged Israel for seven years. 10 Then Ibzan died and was buried in Bethlehem.

11 After him, Elon the Zebulunite judged Israel. He judged Israel for ten years. 12 Elon the Zebulunite died and was buried in Aijalon in the land of Zebulun.

13 After him, Abdon son of Hillel the Pirathonite judged Israel. 14 He had forty sons and thirty grandsons who rode seventy donkeys. He judged Israel for eight years. 15 Abdon son of Hillel the Pirathonite died and was buried in Pirathon in the land of Ephraim, in the Amalekite hill country.

The Birth of Samson

13 Again the children of Israel did evil in the sight of the LORD, so the LORD gave them into the hands of the Philistines for forty years.

2 There was a certain man from Zorah, from the tribe of Dan. His name was Manoah. His wife was infertile and had borne no children. 3 The angel of the LORD appeared to the woman and said to her, "Indeed, you are infertile and have borne no children, yet you will conceive and bear a son. 4 Now be careful, I pray, that you drink no wine or strong drink and that you do not eat anything ritually unclean. 5 For you will conceive and bear a son. No razor may touch his head, for the boy will be a Nazirite to God from the womb. He will begin to save Israel from the hand of the Philistines."

6 Then the woman went to her husband and said, "A man of God came to me. He looked like a very fearsome angel of God. I did not ask him where he was from, and he did not tell me his name. 7 He said to me, 'You will conceive and bear a son. So now, do not drink wine or strong drink, and do not eat anything ritually unclean, for the boy will be a Nazirite to God from the womb until the day he dies.' "

8 Then Manoah prayed to the LORD, "O my Lord, let the man of God whom You sent come again to us, so that he can teach us what we should do for the boy who will be born."

9 God listened to the voice of Manoah, and the angel of God came again to the woman. She was sitting in the field; but her husband Manoah was not with her. 10 The woman hurried and ran to tell her husband, "The man who came to me the other day has appeared to me."

11 So Manoah got up and went after his wife. He came to the man and said to him, "Are you the man who spoke to my wife?"

He said, "I am."

12 Then Manoah said, "Now may your words come true! What will be the boy's way of life and his work?"

13 The angel of the LORD said to Manoah, "Your wife must observe everything that I said to her. 14 She must not consume anything that grows on the vine. She must not drink wine or strong drink, and she must not eat anything ritually unclean. She must observe everything that I commanded her."

15 Manoah said to the angel of the LORD, "Please let us detain you, and let us prepare a young goat for you."

16 The angel of the LORD said to Manoah, "If I stay, I will not eat your food, but if you want to make an offering to the LORD, you should offer it." (For Manoah did not know that he was an angel of the LORD.)

17 Manoah said to the angel of the LORD, "What is your name, so that we can honor you when your words come true?"

18 The angel of the LORD said to him, "Why do you ask my name? It is too wonderful." 19 Manoah took the young goat and the grain offering and offered them to the LORD upon a rock. Then he did a wondrous thing while Manoah and his wife watched. 20 When the flame went up from the altar toward the heavens, the

12:3 1Sa 19:5
12:4 1Sa 25:10
12:5 Jdg 3:28
12:14 Jdg 5:10
12:15 Jdg 5:14
13:1 Jdg 2:11
13:2 Jos 19:41
13:3 Lk 1:13

13:4 Nu 6:2–3
13:5 Nu 6:5
13:6 Jdg 13:17–18
13:14 Jdg 13:4
13:19 Jdg 6:19–21
13:20 Lev 9:24

angel of the LORD went up in the flames from the altar. Seeing this, Manoah and his wife fell face down on the ground. 21 The angel of the LORD did not appear again to Manoah and his wife. Then Manoah knew that he was an angel of the LORD.

22 Manoah said to his wife, "We are certainly going to die, for we have seen God."

23 Yet his wife said to him, "If the LORD wanted to kill us, He would not have taken the burnt offering and grain offering from us. He would not have shown us these things, nor let us hear things such as these at this time."

24 So the woman bore a son, and she called him Samson. The boy grew, and the LORD blessed him. 25 The Spirit of the LORD began to move upon him at Mahaneh Dan, between Zorah and Eshtaol.

Samson's Wedding

14 Samson went down to Timnah and saw a woman from the daughters of the Philistines. 2 He came back up and told his father and mother, "I have seen a woman in Timnah from the daughters of the Philistines; now get her for me as a wife."

3 His father and mother said to him, "Are there no women among your relatives, or all of our people, that you are intending to take a wife from among the uncircumcised Philistines?"

Yet Samson said to his father, "Get her for me, for she pleases me well." 4 His father and mother did not know that this was from the LORD, for He was seeking an opportunity *to act* against the Philistines. At that time the Philistines were ruling over Israel.

5 Samson went down with his father and mother to Timnah. As they came to the vineyards of Timnah, suddenly a young lion came roaring toward him. 6 Then the Spirit of the LORD came mightily upon him, and though unarmed, he tore the lion in two as one might tear a young goat in two. However, he did not tell his father and his mother what he had done. 7 So Samson went down and spoke with the woman, and she pleased Samson.

8 After a while, when he returned to take her, he turned aside to see the carcass of the lion. And a swarm of bees and honey were in the carcass of the lion. 9 He scooped it out into his hands and ate it as he went along. He came to his father and mother and gave some to them, and they also ate. Yet he did not tell them he had scooped the honey out of a lion's carcass.

10 Then his father went down to the woman. Samson put on a feast there, for this is what young men would do. 11 When *the Philistines* saw him, they brought thirty companions to be with him.

12 Samson said to them, "Let me tell you a riddle. If you can explain it to me within the seven days of the feast, then I will find thirty linen robes and thirty sets of clothes to give you. 13 However, if you are not able to explain it to me, then you will give me thirty linen robes and thirty sets of clothes."

They said to him, "Tell us your riddle, so we can hear it."

14 He said to them,

"Out of the eater came something to eat,
and out of the strong came something
sweet."

They could not explain the riddle after three days.

15 On the fourth day they said to Samson's wife, "Trick your groom into telling us the riddle, or we will burn you and your father's house with fire. Have you invited us to steal what we have? Is that not so?"

16 So Samson's wife wept all over him and said, "You must hate me. You do not love me. You have told a riddle to the young men and did not tell it to me."

Then he said to her, "I have not told it to my father and mother. Why should I tell it to you?" 17 She wept on him for the seven days of the feast, then on the seventh day he told it to her because she had nagged him. Then she explained the riddle to her people.

18 So on the seventh day before sunset, the men of the city said to Samson,

"What is sweeter than honey,
and what is stronger than a lion?"

Then he said to them,

"If you had not plowed with my heifer,
you would not have solved my riddle."

19 Then the Spirit of the LORD mightily came upon him, and he went down to Ashkelon and struck down thirty of their men. He took their clothes and gave them to the ones who had explained the riddle. His anger burned and he went up to his father's house. 20 So Samson's wife was given to his companion, who had been his best man.

Samson's Revenge

15 After a while, during the wheat harvest, Samson went to visit his wife, *taking* a young goat. He said, "I'm going in to my wife in her bedroom," but her father would not let him go in.

2 Her father said, "I thought that you thoroughly hated her, so I gave her to your best

13:21 Jdg 6:22
13:22 Ge 32:30
13:23 Ps 25:14
13:24 1Sa 3:19
13:25 Jdg 3:10
14:2 Ge 34:4
14:4 Jos 11:20
14:6 Jdg 3:10
....
14:12 Ge 45:22
14:15 Jdg 15:6
14:16 Jdg 16:15
14:17 Jdg 16:16
14:19 Jdg 3:10
14:20 Jdg 15:2
15:1 Ge 38:17
15:2 Jdg 14:20

man. Is not her younger sister better than she?
Please, let her be your wife instead."
3 Samson said to them, "This time I cannot
be blamed by the Philistines when I do them
harm." 4 Samson went and caught three hun-
dred foxes. He took torches and turned the
foxes tail to tail and put a torch between each
pair of tails. 5 He set fire to the torches and sent
the foxes into standing grain of the Philistines.
He burned the harvested grain, standing grain,
vineyards, and olive trees.
6 The Philistines asked, "Who did this?" They
said, "Samson, the son-in-law of the Timnite,
because the *Timnite* took the bride of *Samson*
and gave her to his best man."

So the Philistines went up and burned her
and her father with fire. 7 Samson said to them,
"Because you have done this, I will take re-
venge on you, and afterwards I will stop." 8 He
struck them down with a mighty blow, then
went to live in a cave in Etam Rock.
9 Then the Philistines went up and set up
camp in Judah. They deployed against Lehi.
10 The men of Judah said, "Why have you come
up against us?"

They said, "It is to take Samson prisoner that
we have come up, to do to him what he did
to us."
11 So three thousand men from Judah went to
the cave in Etam Rock and said to Samson, "Do
you not know that the Philistines are ruling us?
Why have you done this to us?"

He said to them, "As they did to me, so I have
done to them."
12 They said to him, "We have come to take
you prisoner, to give you into the hands of the
Philistines."

Samson said to them, "Swear to me that you
will not attack me."
13 They said to him, "No, we will bind you
securely and give you into their hands, but we
will not kill you." They bound him with two
new ropes and took him away from the rock.
14 He came to Lehi, and the Philistines shouted
as they approached him. Then the Spirit of
the LORD came mightily upon him. The ropes
on his arms became like burned flax and the
ties on his hands dissolved. 15 Then he found
a fresh jawbone of a donkey, reached out his
hand and took it, and with it struck down a
thousand men.
16 Samson said,

"With a jawbone of a donkey,
heaps upon heaps.
With a jawbone of a donkey
I have slain a thousand men."

15:6 Jdg 14:15
15:9 Jdg 15:17
15:11 Jdg 13:1
15:14 Jdg 14:19
15:15 Lev 26:8

....

15:19 Ge 45:27
15:20 Jdg 13:1
16:1 Jos 15:47
16:2 1Sa 23:26
16:5 Jos 13:3
16:10 Jdg 16:13

17 When he finished speaking, he threw the
jawbone away and called that place Ramath
Lehi.
18 He was very thirsty, and he called out to the
LORD, "You gave this great deliverance through
Your servant, but now may I die of thirst and
fall into the hands of the uncircumcised?" 19 So
God split open the basin at Lehi, and water
flowed out of it. He drank, was refreshed, and
revived. Because of this he called the place En
Hakkore, which is in Lehi to this day.
20 Samson judged Israel for twenty years in
the days of the Philistines.

Samson and Delilah

16 Samson went to Gaza. There he saw a
prostitute and spent the night with her.
2 The people of Gaza *were told*, "Samson has
come here!" So they surrounded him and laid
in wait for him all night at the city gate. They
kept quiet all night, thinking, "In the morning
light we will kill him."
3 Samson lay until midnight, then at midnight
he got up. He grabbed the doors of the city
gate and the two gateposts and pulled them
out along with the bar. He put them on his
shoulder and brought them to the top of the
mountain near Hebron.

I loose myself from every Delilah spirit operating in the valley (Jdg 16:4).

4 After this Samson loved a woman in the
Valley of Sorek, whose name was Delilah.
5 The Philistine rulers came up to her and said,
"Trick him! Find out about how his strength is
so great and how we can overcome him, bind
him, and humiliate him. Each one of us will
give you eleven hundred silver coins.[1]"
6 So Delilah said to Samson, "Please tell me
how your strength is so great and how you
could be bound in order to be subdued."
7 Samson said to her, "If they bind me with
seven fresh bowstrings that have not been
dried, then I will become weak and be like an
ordinary man."
8 So the Philistine rulers brought her seven
fresh bowstrings that had not been dried, and
she bound him with them. 9 They lay in wait
in her inner room. She said to him, "The Phi-
listines are upon you, Samson." Then he split
apart the bowstrings like a single thread is split
apart at the touch of fire. So the source of his
strength did not become known.
10 Delilah said to Samson, "You have deceived
me. You have told me lies. Now, please tell me
how you can be bound."

[1] 5 About 28 pounds, or 13 kilograms.

11 He said to her, "If they bind me with new ropes that have never been used, then I will become weak and be like an ordinary man."

12 So Delilah took new ropes and bound him with them. Then she said to him, "The Philistines are upon you, Samson." For men were lying in wait, remaining in the room. But he split apart the ropes on his arms like a thread.

13 Delilah said to Samson, "Up to now you have deceived me. You have told me lies. Tell how you can be bound."

He said to her, "If you weave seven locks of my hair into the fabric on the loom *and fasten it with the pin, then I will become weak and be like an ordinary man.*" 14 So Delilah lulled him to sleep and wove seven locks of his hair into the fabric on the loom. She fastened it with the pin and said to him, "The Philistines are upon you, Samson." He awakened from his sleep and tore away from the loom pin and the fabric.

15 She said to him, "How can you say, 'I love you,' when your heart is not with me? You have deceived me these three times and have not told me how your strength is so great." 16 Every day she nagged him with her words and pleaded with him until he was tired to death.

17 So he told her all his secrets and said to her, "No razor has touched my head, for I have been a Nazirite to God from my mother's womb. If I were shaven, my strength would leave me, and I would become weak and be like all other men."

18 Delilah saw that he had told her all his secrets, so she sent for the Philistine rulers, saying, "Come up this time, for he has told me all his secrets." So the Philistine rulers came up to her and brought the money in their hands. 19 Delilah lulled Samson to sleep on her knees and called for a man to shave off the seven locks of his hair. Then she began to humiliate him, and his strength left him.

20 She said, "The Philistines are upon you, Samson."

Then he awakened from his sleep and thought, "I will go out as before and shake myself free *of them*." He did not know that the LORD had left him.

21 The Philistines seized him and gouged out his eyes. They took him down to Gaza, bound him with bronze chains, and he ground grain in prison. 22 Yet after it had been shaven, the hair on his head began to grow back.

The Death of Samson

23 The Philistine rulers gathered to offer a great sacrifice to Dagon their god and to celebrate. They said, "Our god has given Samson our enemy into our hands."

24 The people saw him and praised their god, for they said,

"Our god has given into our hands
our enemy,
the one who ruined our land
and killed many of us."

25 When their hearts were merry, they said, "Call for Samson, so he can entertain us." So they called for Samson from the prison, and he entertained them.

They placed him between the pillars. 26 Samson said to the young man who held his hand, "Let me rest and touch the pillars on which the temple is set, then I can lean against them." 27 The temple was full of men and women, and all the Philistine rulers were there. There were about three thousand men and women on the roof watching Samson entertain. 28 Samson called out to the LORD, "Lord GOD, remember me, I pray! Please strengthen me just this once, God, so that I may get full revenge on the Philistines for my two eyes!" 29 Then Samson grasped the two middle pillars on which the temple was set and leaned against them, one with his right hand and one with his left. 30 Samson said, "Let me die with the Philistines!" He pushed with all his strength, and the temple fell upon the rulers and all the people who were in it. At his death he killed more than he had killed in his life.

31 Then his brothers and all his family came down, carried him, brought him up, and buried him between Zorah and Eshtaol in the grave of his father Manoah. He had judged Israel for twenty years.

Micah's Idols

17 There was a man from the hill country of Ephraim whose name was Micah. 2 He said to his mother, "The eleven hundred *shekels* of silver[1] that were taken from you, on which you put a curse, even speaking the curse in my ears—here is the silver with me. I took it."

Then his mother said, "May the LORD bless my son!"

3 Then he returned the eleven hundred silver coins to his mother. His mother said, "I certainly consecrated the silver to the LORD, for my son to make a carved idol and a metal idol, so now I return it to you."

4 When he returned the silver to his mother, she took two hundred *shekels* of silver[2] and gave them to a silversmith to make a carved idol and a metal idol. And they were put in the house of Micah.

16:15 Jdg 14:16
16:17 Jdg 13:5
16:18 Jdg 16:5
16:19 Pr 7:26–27
16:20 Jos 7:12
16:23 1Sa 5:2–5

16:24 Da 5:4
16:27 Dt 22:8
16:28 Jer 15:15
16:31 Jdg 15:20
17:2 Ne 13:25
17:3 Ex 20:4

[1] 2 About 28 pounds, or 13 kilograms. [2] 4 About 5 pounds, or 2.3 kilograms.

5 This man Micah owned a shrine. He made an ephod and household idols, and he hired one of his sons to be a priest for him. 6 In those days there was no king in Israel. Everyone did what was right in his eyes.

7 There was a young man from Bethlehem in Judah. He was a Levite from Judah, and he stayed as a resident foreigner there. 8 The man went from the city of Bethlehem in Judah to stay wherever he could find *a place*. He came to the hill country of Ephraim, to the house of Micah, to do his work.

9 Micah said to him, "Where do you come from?"

He said to him, "I am a Levite from Bethlehem in Judah, and I am going to stay wherever I can find *a place*."

10 Micah said to him, "Live with me, and be a father and a priest for me. I will give you ten silver coins[1] a year, a set of clothes, and food." So the Levite went in. 11 The Levite decided to live with the man, and the young man became like one of his sons. 12 Micah ordained the Levite, and the young man became his priest and lived in the house of Micah. 13 Then Micah said, "Now I know that the LORD will do good for me, for I have a Levite to be my priest."

The Danites Settle in Laish

18 In those days there was no king in Israel.

And in those days the tribe of the Danites was looking for an inheritance in which to live, for no territory had come into their possession among the tribes of Israel up to that time. 2 So the children of Dan sent out from their families five valorous men from Zorah and Eshtaol in order to spy out and explore the land. They said to them, "Go, explore the land."

They came to the hill country of Ephraim, to the house of Micah, and they spent the night there. 3 When they were at the house of Micah, they noticed the speech of the young Levite. They turned aside and said to him, "Who brought you here? What are you doing in this place? What is your business here?"

4 He told them what Micah had done for him, saying, "He hired me, and I became his priest."

5 They said to him, "Please ask God if we may know whether our mission will be a success as we go to do it."

6 The priest said to them, "Go in peace. The LORD is watching the way you are going."

7 The five men went away and came to Laish. They saw the people who were there, living securely according to the culture of the Sidonians. There were no rulers in the land who might put them to shame for anything. They were far from the Sidonians and had no ties with anyone.

8 When they came back to their brothers in Zorah and Eshtaol, their brothers asked them, "What do you have to say?"

9 They said, "Get up! Let us go up against them, for we have seen the land. It is very good. You are silent, but do not hesitate to go to take the land. 10 When you go, you will come to a secure people and to an expansive land. For God has given it into your hands: a place where there is no lack of anything on the earth."

11 So six hundred fully armed men set out from the family of the Danites, from Zorah and Eshtaol. 12 They went up and set up camp in Kiriath Jearim in Judah. Therefore they call that place Mahaneh Dan to this day. It is west of Kiriath Jearim. 13 From there they passed the hill country of Ephraim and came to the house of Micah.

14 The five men who went to spy out the land of Laish said to their brothers, "Did you know that in these houses are an ephod, household idols, a carved image, and a metal idol? Now think about what to do." 15 So they turned aside there and came to the house of the young Levite, to the house of Micah, and greeted him. 16 The six hundred men armed with their weapons of war, who were the children of Dan, stood at the entrance to the gate. 17 The five men who went to spy out the land went in and took the carved idol, ephod, household idols, and the metal idol. The priest was standing at the entrance to the gate with the six hundred fully armed men.

18 When these men went into the house of Micah and took the carved idol, ephod, household idols, and the metal idol, the priest said to them, "What are you doing?"

19 They said to him, "Quiet! Put your hand over your mouth and go with us. Be a father and priest for us. Is it better to be a priest for one man's house or for a tribe and a family in Israel?" 20 So the priest's heart was glad. He took the ephod, the household idols, and the carved image and went among the people. 21 So they turned and left, putting the children, livestock, and valuables in front of them.

22 They had gone far from the house of Micah, but the neighbors of Micah assembled and caught up to the children of Dan. 23 They called out to the children of Dan. So they turned and said to Micah, "What is wrong that have you assembled together?"

24 He said, "You took the gods that I made, and the priest, and then you left. What do I have left? So what is this that you say to me, 'What is wrong?' "

17:5 Ge 31:19
17:6 Dt 12:8
17:7 Ru 1:1–2
17:12 Jdg 18:30
18:1 Jdg 17:6
18:2 Jdg 13:25
18:4 Jdg 17:10
18:5 1Ki 22:5
18:6 1Ki 22:6
18:7 Jos 19:47

18:10 Jdg 18:7
18:12 Jdg 13:25
18:14 Jdg 17:5
18:15 Ge 43:27
18:17 Jdg 18:14
18:19 Jdg 17:10

[1] *10* About 4 ounces, or 115 grams.

25 The children of Dan said to him, "Do not let
us hear your voice again. Otherwise bitter men
might meet you and you will forfeit your life
and the lives of your family." 26 So the children
of Dan went their way. And when Micah saw
that they were too strong for him, he turned
and went back to his house.

27 They took what Micah had made and his
priest, and came to Laish to a quiet and se-
cure people. They struck them down with the
edge of the sword and burned the city with
fire. 28 There was no one to save them because
the city was far from Sidon and had no con-
tact with anyone. It was in the valley by Beth
Rehob.

They rebuilt the city and lived there. 29 They
called the city Dan, after their father Dan, who
was born to Israel (Laish was the former name
of the city). 30 The children of Dan set up the
carved idol for themselves. Jonathan the son
of Gershom, the son of Manasseh, and his sons
were priests to the tribe of Dan until the time of
exile from the land. 31 So they displayed Micah's
graven image that he had made, for the whole
time that the house of God was in Shiloh.

A Levite and His Concubine

19 In those days, when there was no king
in Israel, there was a certain Levite liv-
ing as resident foreigner in a remote part of the
hill country of Ephraim. He took a concubine
for himself from Bethlehem in Judah. 2 Yet his
concubine became angry with him and went
away from him to her father's house at Bethle-
hem in Judah. She was there for four months.
3 Her husband got up and went after her in
order to speak tenderly to her and bring her
back. His servant and two donkeys were with
him. When he came to her father's house, the
girl's father saw him and was happy to meet
with him. 4 His father-in-law, the girl's father,
prevailed upon him to stay with him for three
days. So they ate and drank and spent the
night there.

5 On the fourth day they woke up early in
the morning. He got ready to go, but the girl's
father said to his son-in-law, "Strengthen your-
self with a little food, and then you can go."
6 So the two of them sat down to eat and drink
together. Then the girl's father said to the man,
"Please spend the night and let your heart be
merry." 7 The man got up to go, but his father-
in-law urged him until he turned back and
spent the night there. 8 He got up early in the
morning on the fifth day to go. The girl's father
said, "Please, strengthen yourself and wait un-
til later in the day." So the two of them ate.

9 Then the man got up to go: he, his con-
cubine, and his servant. His father-in-law, the

18:27 Jos 19:47
18:28 2Sa 10:6
18:29 Ge 14:14
18:31 Jos 18:1
19:1 Jdg 18:1
19:5 Ge 18:5
19:6 Jdg 16:25

....

19:10 Jos 15:8
19:15 Jdg 19:18
19:18 Jdg 18:31
19:20 Jdg 6:23
19:22 Ge 19:4–5
19:23 Ge 34:7
19:24 Ge 19:8

girl's father, said to him, "Look! It is getting
dark. Spend the night! Settle in and spend the
night here, let your heart be merry. You can
get up early tomorrow and go home." 10 Yet
the man did not want to spend the night, so
he got up and left and approached Jebus (that
is, Jerusalem). Two saddled donkeys and his
concubine were with him.

11 When they were near Jebus, it was get-
ting very late. The servant said to his master,
"Come, let us turn aside to this Jebusite city
and spend the night in it."

12 His master said to him, "We must not turn
aside to a city of foreigners, who are not chil-
dren of Israel. We will continue on to Gibeah."
13 He said to his servant, "Come, let us go to
one of these places. We will spend the night in
Gibeah or Ramah." 14 They continued and went
on. The sun went down when they were near
Gibeah in Benjamin. 15 So they turned aside
there to go and spend the night in Gibeah.
They went in and sat in the city square, but
no one took them in to spend the night.

16 Just then, an old man came in at evening
time from his work in the field. The man was
from the hill country of Ephraim and lived as
a resident foreigner in Gibeah, but the towns-
people were Benjamites. 17 He looked up and
saw the traveler in the city square. The old
man said, "Where are you going, and where
do you come from?"

18 He said to him, "We are traveling from
Bethlehem in Judah to a remote part of the
hill country of Ephraim. I am from there. I
went to Bethlehem in Judah, and now I am
going to the house of the LORD. No one has
taken me into his home. 19 Yet there is enough
straw and fodder for our donkeys, with bread
and wine for me, your maidservant, and the
young man who is with your servant. We do
not lack anything."

20 The old man said, "Do not worry. I will take
care of whatever you need. Just do not spend
the night in the city square." 21 So he brought
him into his house and gave food to his don-
keys. They washed their feet, ate, and drank.

22 While they were enjoying themselves, the
men of the city, who were wicked men, sur-
rounded the house and pounded on the door.
They said to the old man, the master of the
house, "Bring out the man who came to your
house, so we can have relations with him."

23 The master of the house went out to them
and said, "No, my brothers, do not commit this
evil act, not after this man has come into my
house. Do not commit this disgrace. 24 Here are
my virgin daughter and the man's concubine.
Let me bring them out to you. Ravish them

and do to them what you please. But do not commit this vile act against this man."

25 The men were unwilling to listen to him, so the man seized his concubine and brought her out to them in the street. They knew her and abused her all night until morning. As the dawn began to break, they let her go. 26 The woman came back at daybreak and fell down at the door of the man's house where her master was, *lying there* until it was light.

27 Her master got up in the morning and opened the doors of the house. He went out to go on his way, but there was the woman, his concubine, fallen at the door of the house with her hands on the threshold. 28 He said to her, "Get up, let us be going," but there was no answer. So the man put her on a donkey and went home.

29 When he got home, he took a knife and seized his concubine, then cut her body into twelve pieces. Then he sent her throughout all the territory of Israel. 30 Everyone who saw this said, "Nothing like this has been done or seen since the day the children of Israel came out of the land of Egypt until today. Consider it, take counsel, and speak up!"

The Children of Israel Punish the Benjamites

20 All the children of Israel from Dan to Beersheba, and *also from* the land of Gilead, went out and gathered together in an assembly as one man before the LORD at Mizpah. 2 The leaders of all the people from all the tribes of Israel presented themselves in an assembly of the people of God, who numbered four hundred thousand infantrymen bearing swords. 3 (The Benjamites heard that the children of Israel had gone up to Mizpah.) The children of Israel said, "Tell how this evil happened!"

4 So the Levite, the husband of the murdered woman, answered, "My concubine and I came to Gibeah, in Benjamin, to spend the night. 5 Then the leaders of Gibeah rose up against me. At night they surrounded the house where I was staying. They wanted to kill me; instead they ravished my concubine so that she died. 6 I seized my concubine, cut her into pieces, and sent her throughout all the territory of Israel, because they committed an infamous and disgraceful act in Israel. 7 Now, all of you are children of Israel. Give your advice and counsel here."

8 All the people arose as one man and said, "Not a man among us will go to his tent, and no one will turn aside to his house. 9 Now this is what we will do to Gibeah. We will go against it by lot. 10 We will take ten men out of every hundred, from every tribe of Israel, a hundred from every thousand, and a thousand from every ten thousand, to bring provisions for the troops. Then when they come to Gibeah in Benjamin, they may repay them for all the evil that they committed in Israel." 11 So all the men of Israel gathered at the city, united like one man.

12 The tribes of Israel sent men throughout the whole tribe of Benjamin, saying, "What is this evil that has been committed among you? 13 Now hand over the wicked men in Gibeah, so that we can kill them and purge the evil from Israel."

Yet the Benjamites were not willing to listen to their fellow children of Israel. 14 The Benjamites gathered from their cities at Gibeah in order to go out and wage war against the children of Israel. 15 That day, the Benjamites mustered twenty-six thousand armed men from the cities and seven hundred specially chosen men from Gibeah. 16 Out of all these people there were seven hundred specially chosen men who were left-handed, all of whom could sling a stone at a hair and not miss.

17 The men of Israel, apart from Benjamin, gathered four hundred thousand armed men who drew the sword; all of them were men of war.

18 The children of Israel arose, went up to Bethel, and asked God, "Who should go up first to wage war against the Benjamites?"

The LORD said, "Judah first."

19 The children of Israel got up in the morning and camped against Gibeah. 20 The men of Israel went out for battle with Benjamin, and the men of Israel lined up for battle at Gibeah. 21 Then the Benjamites came out from Gibeah and struck twenty-two thousand Israelite men down to the ground. 22 The people, the men of Israel, rallied and lined up for battle again in the place where they had lined up on the first day. 23 Then the children of Israel went up and wept before the LORD until evening. They asked the LORD, "Should we advance and fight our brother-tribesmen the Benjamites again?"

The LORD said, "Advance against them."

24 So the children of Israel advanced against the Benjamites for the second day. 25 And on the second day, the Benjamites went out from Gibeah to meet them and again struck eighteen thousand men down to the ground, every one of them armed.

26 Then all the children of Israel, all the people, went up to Bethel where they wept and sat before the LORD. They fasted that day until evening and offered burnt offerings and peace offerings before the LORD. 27 The children of Israel asked the LORD (because the ark of the

19:28 Jdg 20:5
19:29 1Sa 11:7
19:30 Jdg 20:7
20:1 Jdg 11:11
20:2 Jdg 8:10
20:5 Jdg 19:22
20:6 Jdg 19:29
20:7 Jdg 19:30

....

20:12 Dt 13:14
20:13 Dt 13:13
20:15 Nu 26:41
20:16 Jdg 3:15
20:18 Nu 27:21
20:21 Jdg 20:25
20:23 Jdg 20:26–27
20:25 Jdg 20:21
20:26 Jdg 20:23
20:27 Jos 18:1

covenant of God was there in those days, 28 and Phinehas the son of Eleazar, the son of Aaron, stood before it then), "Should we go out again to wage war with our brother-tribesmen the Benjamites, or should we not?"

The LORD said, "Go up, for tomorrow I will give them into your hands."

29 So Israel set an ambushing force around Gibeah. 30 The children of Israel went up against the Benjamites on the third day and lined up at Gibeah as before. 31 The Benjamites went out to engage the people and were drawn away from the city. They began to strike the people down as before. On the main roads that go up to Bethel and Gibeah and in the field, they struck down about thirty children of Israel. 32 The Benjamites said, "They are struck down before us like at the beginning." But the children of Israel said, "Let us retreat and draw them away from the city toward the main roads."

33 So all the men of Israel rose up out of their place and assumed their battle positions at Baal Tamar. Then the men of Israel in ambush charged out of their places, out of the meadows of Gibeah. 34 Ten thousand specially chosen men from all of Israel came against Gibeah. The battle was fierce, and the Benjamites did not know that disaster was upon them. 35 The LORD defeated Benjamin before Israel, and that day the children of Israel struck down twenty-five thousand one hundred Benjamites, every one of them armed. 36 The Benjamites saw that they were defeated.

Now the men of Israel had withdrawn from Benjamin, because they relied on the men in ambush whom they had set against Gibeah. 37 So the ambushing force rushed on and attacked Gibeah. They struck down the whole city with the edge of the sword. 38 The men of Israel had made an agreement with the ambushing force that when they sent up a large amount of smoke from the city, 39 the children of Israel would turn around in battle.

When the Benjamites had begun to strike the children of Israel down, about thirty men, they said, "Surely they are struck down before us like at the beginning." 40 Yet when the smoke began to rise up from the city in a column, the Benjamites looked behind them and suddenly noticed the whole city going up in smoke to the sky. 41 Then the men of Israel turned around, and the men of Benjamin were horrified because they saw that disaster had come on them. 42 So they fled from the men of Israel toward the direction of the wilderness, but the battle overtook them. Whoever came out of the cities destroyed them in their midst. 43 They surrounded the Benjamites, chased them without rest, and trampled them down near Gibeah toward the east. 44 Eighteen thousand men from Benjamin fell; all these were men of valor. 45 The rest turned and fled toward the wilderness to Rimmon Rock, and they cut down five thousand men on the main roads. They pursued them relentlessly until they reached Gidom and killed two thousand of them.

46 So the Benjamites who fell that day numbered twenty-five thousand, every one of them armed, valorous men. 47 However, six hundred men turned and fled toward the wilderness, to Rimmon Rock. They dwelled at Rimmon Rock for four months. 48 Yet the men of Israel turned back against the Benjamites and struck them with the edge of the sword—city inhabitants, animals, and everything that could be found. Indeed, they set on fire every city that could be found.

Wives for the Benjamites

21 In Mizpah the men of Israel had taken an oath: "No one among us will give his daughter to a Benjamite as his wife."

2 So the people came to Bethel and sat there before God until evening. They raised their voices and wept, sobbing loudly. 3 They said, "Why, LORD God of Israel, has this happened in Israel, that today a tribe is missing from Israel?"

4 In the morning the people got up early and built an altar there. They offered burnt offerings and peace offerings.

5 The children of Israel said, "Who from all the tribes of Israel did not go up with the assembly to the LORD?" For they vowed a solemn oath regarding whoever did not go up to the LORD at Mizpah stating, "He must be killed."

6 The children of Israel lamented for Benjamin their brother, and said, "One tribe is cut off from Israel today. 7 What can we do to find wives for those who are left? For we swore by the LORD not to give them our daughters as wives." 8 So they said, "Is there anyone from among the tribes of Israel who did not go up to the LORD at Mizpah?" Then they learned that no one from the camp of Jabesh Gilead had come to the assembly. 9 When the people were counted, indeed, there was not a man there from among the inhabitants of Jabesh Gilead.

10 So the assembly sent twelve thousand valorous men there and commanded them, "Go and strike down the inhabitants of Jabesh Gilead with the edge of the sword, including women and children. 11 This is what you will do: You will kill every man and every woman who has slept with a man." 12 So among the inhabitants of Jabesh Gilead they found four hundred young virgins who had never slept

20:28 Dt 18:5
20:29 Jos 8:4
20:34 Jos 8:14
20:37 Jos 8:19
20:39 Jdg 20:32
20:40 Jos 8:20
20:45 Jos 15:32
21:1 Jdg 20:1
21:2 Jdg 20:26
21:4 2Sa 24:25
21:5 Jdg 5:23
21:6 Jdg 21:15
21:7 Jdg 21:1
21:8 1Sa 31:11–13
21:11 Nu 31:17–18
21:12 Jos 18:1

with a man, and they brought them to the
camp at Shiloh in the land of Canaan.
13 Then the whole assembly sent *someone* to
speak to the Benjamites who were at Rimmon
Rock, and they declared peace. 14 So the Ben-
jamites returned at that time, and they gave
to them the women who were still alive from
among the women of Jabesh Gilead. Yet they
did not find enough for them.
15 The people felt sorry for Benjamin, for the
Lord had made a gap among the tribes of Is-
rael. 16 The elders of the assembly said, "What
can we do to find wives for those who are
left? The Benjamite women were destroyed."
17 They said, "*There must be* an inheritance for
the remnant of Benjamin, so that a tribe will
not be wiped out from Israel. 18 Yet we cannot
give them our daughters for wives, for the chil-
dren of Israel swore, 'Cursed be anyone who
gives a wife to Benjamin.' " 19 They said, "Wait!
There is an annual festival of the Lord in Shi-
loh, which is north of Bethel, east of the main
road that goes up from Bethel to Shechem, and
south of Lebonah."

21:13 Dt 20:10
21:15 Jdg 21:6
21:18 Jdg 21:1
21:21 Ex 15:20
21:22 Jdg 21:1
21:23 Jdg 20:48
21:25 Jdg 17:6

20 So they commanded the Benjamites, "Go
and hide in the vineyards. 21 Watch, and then
when the daughters of Shiloh come out to
dance in the dances, come out from the vine-
yards and have every man grab a wife for
himself from among the daughters of Shiloh.
Then go to the land of Benjamin. 22 When their
fathers or their brothers come to us to com-
plain, we will say to them, 'Be favorable to
them for our sakes, because we did not take
for each man a wife in the battle; for you have
not given women to them at the time, thereby
making yourselves guilty.' "
23 So the Benjamites did this. They carried
away wives for each man from among the
dancers that they caught. Then they returned
to their inheritance, rebuilt the cities, and lived
in them.
24 At that time, the children of Israel departed
from there each man to his tribe and to his
family. They went out from there to their own
inheritance.
25 In those days there was no king in Israel;
everyone did what was right in his own eyes.

Author: Traditionally the prophet Samuel

Written: Between 1011 and 931 BC

Themes: Redemption, Love, Loyalty

RUTH

Dear Spirit Led Woman,

When a woman is planning to be married, she generally spends months preparing for the wedding ceremony. She shops for a wedding dress, chooses outfits for all her attendants, orders flowers, addresses and mails out invitations, and does scores of other tasks to ensure that her wedding will be a memorable occasion and a proper beginning for her new life. What some of us don't realize is that whether we have ever planned, or will ever plan, a wedding in the natural, we are preparing for a marriage in eternity with the Lamb of God—our Bridegroom.

The most important aspect of preparing for this role is getting to know your Bridegroom. You must become familiar with every facet of His nature and learn what pleases Him. To do this, you must make spending time with Him a priority. With even greater care than that with which you would plan your own earthly wedding, plan for a greater spiritual event—becoming the bride of Christ.

As you read the Book of Ruth, see Boaz, Ruth's redeemer and her husband, as a foreshadowing of Christ, our Redeemer and Husband.

Joy F. Strang

SPIRITLED WOMAN

COUNSEL FROM THE SPIRIT BASICS

Reckless Abandonment

Ruth abandoned her home country of Moab and returned with Naomi to Israel. During this process she grew, changed, and became a member of the lineage of Jesus.

We never really feel ready for life's challenges, tasks, or opportunities when they drop into our laps. And we shouldn't be shocked when we rise to the occasion and are better than we dreamed we ever could be, because the truth is, with God we are better than we believe we are.

That was the conflict churning inside me as I rolled out of my Nashville driveway and headed for Monroe, Louisiana, to open the first Mercy Ministries home for troubled girls. I didn't feel ready. I didn't feel capable. But, after all God had shown me during the past ten years, I knew without a doubt what *didn't* work, and I knew God had tutored me in what *would* work.

What was there to lose? I'd seen firsthand how the wisdom of man left girls empty. The experts had failed every single woman I'd worked with as an employee of the state of Tennessee. Frustration and compassion were my motivators, and witnessing girl after girl return to her same affliction upon release from bars and razor wire was what kept my car pointed toward Louisiana.

Years later thousands of young women have experienced new beginnings in Christ as we share the message of God's power to transform lives.

Nancy Alcorn

Naomi Loses

1 In the days when the judges ruled, there was a famine in the land. And a man from Bethlehem in Judah went to live in the land of Moab, he and his wife and his two sons. 2 The name of the man was Elimelek, the name of his wife was Naomi, and the names of his two sons were Mahlon and Kilion. They were Ephrathites from Bethlehem in Judah. And they went to Moab and lived there.

1:1 Ge 12:10
1:2 Ge 35:19

1:4 Mt 1:5
1:6 Ex 4:31
1:8 Ru 1:5
1:9 Ru 3:1
1:11 Ge 38:11
1:13 Jdg 2:15
1:15 Jdg 11:24
1:16 Ru 2:11–12
1:17 1Sa 3:17
1:18 Ac 21:14
1:19 Mt 21:10
1:20 Job 6:4
1:21 Job 1:21

3 Now Elimelek, the husband of Naomi, died, so she was left alone with her two sons. 4 They took Moabite wives for themselves; the name of one was Orpah and the name of the other Ruth. They lived there about ten years. 5 Then Mahlon and Kilion also died, and Naomi was left without her two sons and her husband.

6 So she got up with her daughters-in-law to return from the land of Moab, for in the land of Moab, she had heard that the LORD had visited His people by giving them food. 7 She set out from the place where she had been, with her two daughters-in-law, and they went on their way to return to the land of Judah.

8 Then Naomi said to her two daughters-in-law, "Go, return each to her mother's house. May the LORD deal kindly with you, as you have dealt with your deceased husbands and with me. 9 May the LORD grant that you each find rest in the house of *another* husband."

Then she kissed them, and they raised their voices and wept aloud. 10 They said to her, "We will return with you to your people."

11 But Naomi said, "Turn back, my daughters. Why would you go with me? Are there sons in my womb, who could become your husbands? 12 Turn back, my daughters! Go, for I am too old to have a husband. Even if I thought that there was still hope for me, that I could have a husband tonight and give birth to sons, 13 would you wait until they were grown? Would you refrain from getting married? No, my daughters. It is much more bitter for me than for you, for the hand of the LORD has turned against me."

14 Then they raised their voices and wept aloud once more. Orpah kissed her mother-in-law, but Ruth clung to her.

15 Naomi said, "Look, your sister-in-law has returned to her people and her gods. Return with her!"

16 But Ruth said, "Do not urge me to leave you or to turn back from following you. For wherever you go, I will go, and wherever you stay, I will stay. Your people shall be my people and your God my God. 17 Where you die, I will die, and there I will be buried. May the LORD do thus to me, and worse, if anything but death separates you and me!" 18 When Naomi saw that she was determined to go with her, she said no more to her.

19 So they both went on until they came to Bethlehem. When they came to Bethlehem, the whole town was stirred because of them, and the women asked, "Is this Naomi?"

20 But she said to them, "Do not call me Naomi. Call me Mara, because the Almighty has brought great bitterness to me. 21 I was full when I left, but the LORD has caused me to return empty. Why should you call me Naomi

when the LORD has opposed me? The Almighty has brought misfortune upon me!"

22 So Naomi returned from the land of Moab with Ruth the Moabite, her daughter-in-law. They came to Bethlehem at the start of the *spring* barley harvest.

Ruth Meets Boaz

2 Now Naomi had a relative of her husband, a man of prominence and means from the clan of Elimelek. His name was Boaz.

2 Ruth the Moabitess said to Naomi, "Please let me go into the field and glean among the heads of grain behind anyone in whose eyes I may find favor."

Naomi said to her, "Go, my daughter." 3 So she went to glean in the field behind the harvesters. She happened to come to a part of the field belonging to Boaz, who was from the clan of Elimelek.

4 Just then Boaz came from Bethlehem and said to the harvesters, "May the LORD be with you!"

And they said to him, "May the LORD bless you."

5 Then Boaz said to his servant who was in charge of his harvesters, "Whose young woman is this?"

6 So the servant who was in charge of his harvesters answered, "She is the young Moabitess woman who came back with Naomi from the land of Moab. 7 She said, 'Please let me glean and gather *grain* among the bundles behind the harvesters.' So she came and has remained from morning until now, though she rested a little while in the house."

8 Then Boaz said to Ruth, "Listen, my daughter. Do not go to glean in another field and leave this one. Stay close to my young women. 9 Keep your eyes on the field in which they reap and follow after them. I have commanded the men not to touch you. When you are thirsty, go to the vessels and drink from what the young men have drawn."

10 So she fell on her face, bowed down to the ground, and said to him, "Why have I found favor in your eyes, that you should acknowledge me, a foreigner?"

11 Boaz answered and said to her, "I have been told all that you have done for your mother-in-law after the death of your husband, and how you left your father and mother and your homeland and came to a people you did not know before. 12 May the LORD reward your deeds. May you have a full reward from the LORD, the God of Israel, under whose wings you have come to take refuge."

13 Then she said, "May I find favor in your eyes, my lord, for you have comforted me and have spoken kindly to your servant, though I am not like one of your servant girls."

1:22 Ru 2:23
2:1 Ru 3:2
2:2 Lev 19:9
2:4 Ps 129:7–8
2:6 Ru 1:22
2:10 1Sa 25:23
2:12 1Sa 24:19

2:14 Ru 2:18
2:18 Ru 2:14
2:19 Ru 2:10
2:20 2Sa 2:5
3:1 Ru 1:9
3:2 Ru 2:8
3:3 2Sa 14:2

Lord, let me find favor in Your sight today, and may You reward my actions as I take refuge in You (Ru 2:12–13).

14 At mealtime Boaz said to her, "Come over here, and eat some bread, and dip your piece in the vinegar."

So she sat down beside the harvesters, and he passed her some roasted grain. She ate and was full and had some left over. 15 When she got up to glean, Boaz commanded his young men, "Let her glean even among the bundles, and do not harm her. 16 Also pull out some *grain* for her from the bundles and leave it so that she may glean it, and do not rebuke her."

17 So she gleaned in the field until evening. Then she beat out what she had gleaned, and it was about an ephah[1] of barley. 18 She took it up and went into the city, and her mother-in-law saw what she had gleaned. She drew *it* out and gave her what she had left, after she had been satisfied.

19 Her mother-in-law said to her, "Where did you glean today, and where did you work? May he who took notice of you be blessed."

So she told her mother-in-law with whom she had worked, and said, "The name of the man with whom I worked today is Boaz."

20 Then Naomi said to her daughter-in-law, "May he be blessed of the LORD who has not withdrawn His kindness to the living and to the dead." Naomi said to her, "This man is a close relative of ours, one of our redeeming relatives."

21 Then Ruth the Moabitess said, "He even told me, 'You should stay close to my servants until they have finished all my harvest.' "

22 Naomi said to Ruth her daughter-in-law, "It is better, my daughter, that you go with his young women, for in someone else's field you might be harmed."

23 So she stayed close to the young women of Boaz to glean until the end of barley harvest and wheat harvest. And she lived with her mother-in-law.

Ruth's Redemption

3 One day Naomi her mother-in-law said to her, "My daughter, why should I not find a home that will be good for you? 2 Now is not Boaz our relative, with whose young women you have been working? Tonight he winnows barley on the threshing floor. 3 Now wash and anoint yourself, and put on your best clothes.

[1] *17* Likely about 30 pounds, or 13 kilograms.

PROFILE OF A SPIRITED WOMAN

RUTH

LEARN THAT SUBMISSION IS THE KEY TO REDEMPTION

A major revelation in the Book of Ruth is the power of redemption. The verb *redeem* means "to buy back and to protect." God can redeem your lost time. Just as in the case of the ten years that Naomi spent in Moab while her land and fortune were lost in Bethlehem, God, our Kinsman-Redeemer, can redeem our lost time, reposition us for victory, and give us a plan of security for the future.

Ruth chose to go with her mother-in-law, Naomi, back to Naomi's homeland rather than stay in her own land. But she had to learn the power of submission to gain redemption for herself and Naomi. Naomi perceived that Ruth had to make a shift if their inheritance was to be secured. On the night after Ruth had received the favor of Boaz by gleaning in his field, Naomi told Ruth, "Tonight is our *now*, Ruth! Get cleaned up, look good, get rid of that widow's garment that you have worn for a year, get anointed, and go to where the celebration is. When you get there, wait until midnight, and then, when Boaz is asleep, lie down and submit yourself to him. If you will do this, our future will be secured. Tonight is our future!" (See Ruth 3:1–4.) Can you imagine what must have been going through Ruth's mind? Naomi was telling her to lie down at the feet of a man. This was a true test of submission.

Ruth submitted to Naomi's request and lay down at Boaz's feet when he fell asleep. This startled Boaz, and he awoke and said, "Who are you?" Knowing the Jewish tradition of a close relative serving as the kinsman-redeemer for a widow, she responded, "I am Ruth, your maidservant. Spread your cloak over me, for you are a redeeming kinsman" (v. 9).

In asking for Boaz to cover her, Ruth was declaring, "I need a redeemer. I am a widow, disgraced, with no inheritance. You can take my shame, my poverty, and the bleakness of my future and give me a new beginning." Ruth was willing to be submissive to Naomi's request and to make big changes to secure her future and that of her mother-in-law. As you already know, Boaz married her, and everyone received the best of the redeemed time. That is what happens when we are willing to embrace change and find our new place.

Visualize what this act of submission meant to Naomi. Her bitterness has been let go. She has a smile on her face and laughter in her heart. Her life has been "bought back." Lost time has been redeemed. Her neighbors said, "A son has been born to Naomi!" They named him Obed, the father of Jesse, the father of King David (Ru 4:17), of the lineage of the Messiah, Jesus Christ (Mt 1:5). God had redeemed her.

God has a path for *your* redemption. Believe Him for the power to buy back lost years and move you into your future. You can conceive and birth your future if you will learn to be submissive to what He tells you to do!

Chuck D. Pierce

Then go down to the threshing floor, but do not let the man know you are there until he has finished eating and drinking. 4 When he lies down, notice the place where he is lying. Go in and uncover his feet and lie down. He will tell you what you will do."

5 She said to her, "All that you say to me I will do." 6 So she went down to the threshing floor and did all that her mother-in-law had instructed.

7 When Boaz had eaten and drunk and his heart was merry, he went to lie down at the end of the heap of grain. Then Ruth came softly, uncovered his feet, and lay down. 8 At midnight, the man was startled and rolled over; and there, a woman was lying at his feet. 9 He said, "Who are you?"

And she answered, "I am Ruth, your maidservant. Spread your cloak over me, for you are a redeeming kinsman."

10 He said, "May you be blessed of the LORD, my daughter. You have shown your last act of kindness to be greater than the first, because you have not pursued young men, whether poor or rich. 11 So now, my daughter, do not worry. All that you ask me, I will do for you. All of my fellow townsmen know that you are a woman of noble character. 12 Now it is true that I am a redeeming kinsman. Yet there is another redeemer closer than I am. 13 Stay here tonight, and in the morning if he wants to redeem you, very well. Let him do so. Yet if he does not want to redeem you, then I will redeem you. I will, as the LORD lives! Sleep here until morning."

14 So she lay at his feet until morning, but she arose before one could recognize another. Then he said, "It must not be known that a woman came to the threshing floor."

15 He said, "Bring me the shawl you have on you, and hold it." So she held it, and he poured six measures of barley into it and placed it on her. Then she went into the city.

16 When Ruth came to her mother-in-law, Naomi said, "How did it go, my daughter?"

Then she told her all that Boaz had done for her. 17 She said, "He gave me these six ephahs of barley, for he said to me, 'Do not return to your mother-in-law empty-handed.' "

18 Then Naomi said, "Wait here, my daughter, until you learn what happens. For the man will not rest until the matter is settled today."

Boaz Marries Ruth

4 So Boaz went up to the gate and sat down there. And now the redeemer of whom he had spoken passed by, and Boaz said, "Come over, friend, and sit here." So he went over and sat down.

2 Then Boaz took ten men from among the elders of the town and said, "Sit here." So they sat down. 3 He said to the redeemer, "Naomi, who has come back from the land of Moab, must sell the plot of land belonging to our brother Elimelek. 4 I thought I should inform you and say, 'Buy it in the presence of those sitting here and in the presence of the elders of my people. If you want to redeem it, redeem it. But if you will not redeem it, tell me so that I know, for there is no one prior to you to redeem it, and I am next after you.' "

So he said, "I will redeem it."

5 Then Boaz said, "On the day you buy the field from the hand of Naomi, you also acquire Ruth the Moabitess, the wife of the deceased, to perpetuate the name of the deceased through his inheritance."

6 The redeemer replied, "I am not able to redeem it for myself lest I ruin my own inheritance. Take my redemption rights for yourself, for I cannot do it."

7 (Now this was the custom in ancient times in Israel for redeeming and exchanging: to confirm a transaction, a man would remove his sandal and give it to his neighbor. This was a binding act in Israel.)

8 Therefore the redeemer said to Boaz, "Buy it yourself," and he removed his sandal.

9 Then Boaz said to the elders and all the people, "You are witnesses today that I have bought everything that belonged to Elimelek, Kilion, and Mahlon from Naomi. 10 Moreover I have also acquired Ruth the Moabitess, the wife of Mahlon, to be my wife, in order to preserve the name of the deceased man for his inheritance, so that his name will not be cut off from among his brothers or from his town. You are witnesses this day."

11 Then all the people who were at the gate, along with the elders, said, "We are witnesses. May the LORD make the woman who is coming to your house like Rachel and Leah, who together built up the house of Israel. May you do well in Ephrathah and be famous in Bethlehem! 12 May your house be like the house of Perez, whom Tamar bore to Judah, through the offspring that the LORD will give you by this young woman."

The Genealogy of David

13 So Boaz took Ruth, and she became his wife. When they came together, the LORD enabled her to conceive, and she bore a son. 14 Then the women said to Naomi, "Blessed be the LORD, who has not left you without a redeemer. May he become famous in Israel! 15 He will be a comfort for your soul and support you in your old age. For your daughter-in-law, who loves you and who is better to you than seven sons, has given birth to him."

3:7 Jdg 19:6
3:9 Ru 2:20
3:10 Ru 2:20
3:11 Pr 12:4
3:12 Ru 4:1
3:13 Jdg 8:19
3:14 Ro 14:16
3:18 Ps 37:3–5
4:1 Ru 3:12
4:2 1Ki 21:8
4:5 Ge 38:8
4:7 Dt 25:7–10
4:10 Dt 25:6
4:11 Dt 25:9
4:12 Ge 38:29
4:13 Ge 29:31
4:14 Lk 1:58
4:15 1Sa 1:8

WOMAN OF THE SPIRIT

Ruth's Sevenfold Declaration

We cannot fully appreciate Ruth's idyllic love story until we analyze the treaty that eventually brought to her such good fortune. By treaty, I do not mean a legal document, but rather the choices Ruth made before God. Those choices influenced her future as much as any legal treaty would have. Throughout the Book of Ruth we are made aware of the power of our choices for blessing or for ill. How could our own futures be altered if, through our choices, we pursued the godly principles revealed in this courageous lady's treaty?

Ruth's declaration to follow her mother-in-law rang out clearly of true commitment. It revealed a determination to face whatever the future held for her. I have an idea Ruth sat down somewhere and counted the cost. Was it going to be worth it to leave her land and her kindred to go to a place she'd never been? Ruth not only tried on the dress of consecration, but she was also willing to pay the cost of the garment, demonstrated by her decision to follow Naomi.

Ruth's treaty was a sevenfold declaration that revealed her heart's determination. The key words in Ruth's treaty were "I will." These two words expressed the intent of her heart and formed the basis of her decision. As we observe Orpah's tearful decision not to follow Naomi, we understand Ruth's choice was not based on emotion or sentiment but a decision of her will.

Decision itself is exhilarating and refreshing. Some people never know the joys and delights of walking with God because they do not choose to make decisions in favor of God, His Word, and His ways. Decisive people are seldom the subject of continued despair; they are steadfastly minded. As we decide to follow God's will, our decision will have wonderful results in our lives, as Ruth's did.

The treaty of "I wills" made by Ruth consists of these seven elements:

1. "Wherever you go, I will go" (Ru 1:16).
2. "Wherever you stay, I will stay" (Ru 1:16).
3. "Your people shall be my people" (Ru 1:16).
4. "And your God my God" (Ru 1:16).
5. "Where you die, I will die" (Ru 1:17).
6. "And there I will be buried" (Ru 1:17).
7. "May the LORD do thus to me, and worse, if anything but death separates you and me" (Ru 1:17).

Like Ruth, we should resolve to pursue God to the end, casting our lot with the separated, sanctified people of God, cleaving to the eternal God of the Bible. Like Ruth, we should enter God's field and be willing to serve. Like Ruth, we should abandon ourselves to our glorious, heavenly "Boaz" and stay at His feet until morning.

Fuchsia Pickett

I declare, O Lord, that You are the restorer of my life and the nourisher of my old age (Ru 4:15).

[16] Then Naomi took the child, laid him on
her lap, and became his nurse. [17] The neighbor
women gave him a name, saying, "A son has
been born to Naomi!" And they named him
Obed. He was the father of Jesse, the father
of David.

4:20 Nu 1:7
4:21 Mt 1:5

[18] Now these are the descendants of Perez:

Perez was the father of Hezron,
[19] Hezron the father of Ram,
Ram the father of Amminadab,
[20] Amminadab the father of Nahshon,
Nahshon the father of Salmon,
[21] Salmon the father of Boaz,
Boaz the father of Obed,
[22] Obed the father of Jesse,
and Jesse the father of David.

Author: The prophet Samuel
Written: After 960 BC
Theme: Israel's History (1100 to 1000 BC); Lives of Samuel, Saul, and David

1 SAMUEL

Dear SpiritLed Woman,

The Book of 1 Samuel opens with Hannah, the mother of Samuel, pleading with God for a son. Perhaps you can relate to Hannah's desperation. You're waiting on a miracle. Whether you're waiting on the blessing of a child, a husband, a financial miracle, or a career or ministry opportunity, there are times in life where you find yourself in a holding pattern. Some of you have dreams for your future that seem unattainable, some of you are claiming the promise of a miracle that has not yet come to pass, and others of you have a vision for the calling God has placed on your life. Whatever it is that you are waiting to "give birth to," right now it seems impossible from your current life situation.

Ask the Spirit to show you God's purpose and plan. Read the Word, press in to God, and pour your heart out to Him as Hannah did. Don't grow weary in praying and seeking God for the desires of your heart. Continue to worship God with a pure heart while you are in this season of waiting. Keep believing that your miracle is on the way!

Joy F. Strang

The Birth of Samuel

1 Now there was a certain man from Ramathaim Zuphim, in the hill country of Ephraim, and his name was Elkanah, the son of Jeroham, the son of Elihu, the son of Tohu, the son of Zuph, an Ephraimite. [2] And he had two wives; the name of one was Hannah and the name of the second was Peninnah. Now Peninnah had children, but Hannah had no children.

[3] This man went up out of his city annually to worship and to sacrifice to the LORD of Hosts in Shiloh. And there the two sons of Eli, Hophni and Phinehas, were priests to the LORD. [4] When the day came that Elkanah sacrificed, he gave portions to Peninnah his wife and to all her sons and her daughters. [5] But to Hannah he gave a double portion because he loved Hannah, but the LORD had closed her womb. [6] Now her rival provoked her greatly, making her miserable because the LORD had closed her womb. [7] Thus it was yearly, when she went up to the house of the LORD, that she provoked her. So Hannah wept and did not eat. [8] Then said Elkanah her husband to her, "Hannah, why are you weeping? And why do you not eat? Why is your heart grieved? Am I not better to you than ten sons?"

[9] So Hannah arose after they had eaten in Shiloh and after they had drunk. Now Eli the priest was sitting on a seat by the door of the tabernacle of the LORD. [10] And she was bitter, and prayed to the LORD, and wept severely. [11] So she made a vow and said, "O LORD of Hosts, if You will indeed look on the affliction of Your maidservant, and remember me and not forget Your maidservant, but will give to Your maidservant a baby boy, then I will give him to the LORD all the days of his life, and no razor shall touch his head."[1]

> I know God has heard my prayers and will grant me the desires of my heart (1Sa 1:11–18).

[12] And as she was praying before the LORD, Eli watched her mouth. [13] Now Hannah was speaking in her heart. Her lips were moving, but her voice was not heard. Therefore Eli thought she was drunk. [14] So Eli said to her, "How long will you be drunk? Put away your wine from you."

[15] And Hannah answered and said, "No, my lord, I am a woman of sorrow. I have drunk neither wine nor strong drink, but have poured out my soul before the LORD. [16] Do not consider your handmaid to be a sinful woman, for out of the abundance of my concern and provocation I have spoken until now."

[17] Then Eli answered and said, "Go in peace, and the God of Israel grant you your request that you have asked of Him."

[18] And she said, "Let your handmaid find grace in your sight." So the woman went her way and ate, and her face was not sad as before.

[19] They rose up in the morning early and worshipped before the LORD. And they returned and came to their house to Ramah. And Elkanah knew Hannah his wife, and the LORD remembered her. [20] And it came to pass that Hannah conceived and bore a son. And she called his name Samuel saying, "Because I have asked him of the LORD."

The Dedication of Samuel

[21] Then the man Elkanah and all his house went up to offer to the LORD the yearly sacrifice and his vow. [22] But Hannah did not go, for she said to her husband, "I will not go up until the child is weaned, and then I will bring him, that he may appear before the LORD and live there forever."

[23] So Elkanah her husband said to her, "Do what seems good to you. Wait until you have weaned him; only may the LORD establish His word." So the woman remained, and nursed her son until she weaned him.

[24] When she had weaned him, she took him up with her with three bulls, one ephah[2] of flour, and a bottle of wine. And she brought him to the house of the LORD in Shiloh, though the boy was young. [25] Then they slaughtered a bull, and they brought the boy to Eli. [26] And she said, "Oh, my lord! As you live, my lord, I am the woman that stood by you here praying to the LORD. [27] For this boy I prayed, and the LORD has given me my petition which I asked of Him. [28] Therefore also I have let the LORD have him. As long as he lives he will be dedicated to the LORD." And he worshipped the LORD there.

The Prayer of Hannah

2 Hannah prayed, saying:

"My heart rejoices in the LORD;
  my horn is exalted in the LORD.
My mouth is bold against my enemies,
  because I rejoice in Your salvation.

2 "There is none holy as the LORD,
  for there is none besides You,
  and there is no rock like our God.

1:1 1Sa 1:19
1:3 Ex 23:14
1:5 Ge 30:2
1:8 Ru 4:15
1:9 1Sa 3:3
1:10 Job 7:11
1:11 Jdg 13:5
1:13 Ge 24:42–45
1:15 Ps 42:4
1:16 1Sa 2:12
....
1:17 Jdg 18:6
1:18 Ru 2:13
1:19 Ge 30:22
1:20 Ge 41:51–52
1:21 1Sa 1:3
1:22 1Sa 1:11
1:23 2Sa 7:25
1:24 Jos 18:1
1:25 Lk 2:22
1:26 2Ki 2:2
1:27 1Sa 1:11–13
1:28 Ge 24:26
2:1 Ps 9:14
2:2 Ex 15:11

[1] *11* Hannah dedicates Samuel as a lifetime Nazirite (see Nu 6:2–21).
[2] *24* Likely about 36 pounds, or 16 kilograms.

SPIRIT-TO-SPIRIT PRAYER

BLESSING PRAYER FOR YOUR FAMILY

Heavenly Father,

I present to You this day my precious child, _______. Thank You for this gift that You have given our family. Father, I know You love _______ so much. I love you, my child.

Thank You for the unique gifts and talents You have bestowed upon this child. It is a blessing to see _______ walk in the fruit of Your Spirit and in the light of Your love.

Thank You for the calling and destiny that You have in store for my child. You have an amazing plan and future for his/her life. I commit _______ to You, Father, and ask that You would lead and guide this child in Your ways.

Lord, I invite You to mold, shape, and disciple _______ to be the instrument that You have designed him/her to be. I thank You for this time of preparation and how I see my child growing in mind, heart, and body. I am honored to be _______'s parent. I know that You will never leave or forsake _______.

You are my child, a joy and a blessing. May you fulfill all that God has in store for you. May you be a mighty child of the living God who serves, loves, and obeys the Lord always.

In Jesus' name, amen.

Julie Hiramine

3 "Do not multiply proud speech,
nor let arrogance come out of your mouth,
for the LORD is the God of knowledge,
and by Him actions are examined.

4 "The bows of the mighty are broken,
but those who stumbled are girded with strength.
5 Those that were full have hired out themselves for bread,
and those that were hungry ceased *to hunger*.
Even the barren has borne seven,
and she that has many children wastes away.

6 "The LORD kills and makes alive;
He brings down to the grave and brings up.
7 The LORD makes poor and makes rich;
He brings low and lifts up.
8 He raises up the poor out of the dust
and lifts up the oppressed from the dunghill
to make them sit with princes
and inherit a throne of glory.

"For the pillars of the earth belong to the LORD,
and He has set the world upon them.
9 He will guard the feet of His saints,
but the wicked will be silent in darkness.

The Lord will exalt the horn of His anointed; He will give strength to the man of God (1Sa 2:10).

"For by strength shall no man prevail.
10 The adversaries of the LORD will be broken to pieces;
He will thunder against them out of heaven.
The LORD will judge the ends of the earth.

"He will give strength to His king
and exalt the horn of His anointed."

2:3 1Ki 8:39
2:4 Ps 37:15
2:5 Ps 113:9
2:6 Dt 32:39
2:7 Job 5:11
2:8 Ps 113:7–8

2:9 Ps 33:16–17
2:10 Ps 2:9

11 Then Elkanah went to Ramah to his house. And the boy ministered to the LORD before Eli the priest.

Wicked Sons of Eli

12 Now the sons of Eli were corrupt. They did not know the LORD. 13 The priest's custom with the people was that when any man offered a sacrifice, the priest's servant came while the flesh was cooking with a three-pronged fork in his hand. 14 And he struck it into the pan, or kettle, or cauldron, or pot, *and* all that the fork brought up the priest took for himself. This they did in Shiloh to all the children of Israel who came there. 15 Even before they burned the fat, the priest's servant would come and say to the man sacrificing, "Give meat for the priest to roast. For he will not take boiled meat from you, but only raw."

16 If any man said to him, "Let them first burn the fat and then take as much as you wish," then he would answer him, "No, but you will give it *to me now*, and if not, I will take *it* by force."

17 Therefore the sin of the young men was very great before the LORD. For the men treated the offering of the LORD with contempt.

God Blesses Hannah

18 But Samuel ministered before the LORD, as a boy, wearing a linen ephod. 19 Now his mother would make him a little coat and brought it to him every year when she came up with her husband to offer the yearly sacrifice. 20 And Eli would bless Elkanah and his wife and say, "The LORD give you offspring from this woman for the sake of the request which was made to the LORD." Then they would return to their home. 21 The LORD visited Hannah, so that she conceived and bore three sons and two daughters. And the boy Samuel grew before the LORD.

Eli Confronts Hophni and Phinehas

22 Now Eli was very old, and he heard all that his sons were doing to all Israel, even that they lay with the women who served at the doorway of the tent of meeting. 23 He said to them, "Why are you doing these things? For I am hearing of your evil dealings from all these people. 24 No, my sons! Truly, it is not a good report that I hear the people of the LORD spreading. 25 If one man sins against another, God will judge him, but if a man sins against the LORD, who will intercede for him?" But they did not listen to the voice of their father, because the LORD desired to kill them.

26 Now the boy Samuel was growing both in stature and favor with the LORD and also with men.

God's Case Against the House of Eli

27 A man of God came to Eli and said to him, "Thus says the LORD, 'Did I *not* plainly reveal Myself to the house of your father, when they were in Egypt in Pharaoh's house? 28 And choose him out of all the tribes of Israel to be My priest, to offer upon My altar, to burn incense, to wear an ephod before Me? And I gave to the house of your father all the offerings made by fire by the children of Israel? 29 Why do you kick at My sacrifice and at My offering, which I have commanded in My dwelling, and honor your sons above Me, to make yourselves fat with the best of all the offerings of Israel My people?'

30 "Therefore the LORD God of Israel says, 'I surely said that your house, and the house of your father, should walk before Me forever,' but now the LORD says, 'Far be it from Me *to do so*, for those who honor Me, I will honor, and those that despise Me will be humbled. 31 The days are coming when I will cut off your authority and the strength of your father's house, so there shall not be an old man in your house. 32 You shall see the distress of *My* dwelling, despite all the good which will be done for Israel. And there shall not be an elderly man in your house perpetually. 33 Yet the one I do not cut off from My altar will be spared so your eyes will not stop *weeping* or your soul grieving. All the increase of your house will die in their prime.

34 " 'This will be the sign to you which will come upon your two sons, Hophni and Phinehas: In one day, they will both die. 35 And I will raise up for Myself a faithful priest; what is in My heart and in My soul he will do *it*. And I will build him a sure house, and it will walk before My anointed forever. 36 But it will be that everyone who is left in your house will come and bow down to him for a piece of silver and a morsel of bread, and will say, Please attach me to one of the priestly offices, that I may eat a piece of bread.' "

God Calls Samuel

3 Now the boy Samuel was ministering to the LORD before Eli. And the word of the LORD was rare in those days. There was no vision coming forth.

2 At that time, Eli was lying down in his place (now his eyes had begun to grow weak that he could not see), 3 and the lamp of God had not yet gone out, and Samuel was lying down in the house of the LORD where the ark of God was.

4 Then the LORD called to Samuel, and he answered, "Here I am." 5 He ran to Eli and said, "Here I am, for you called to me."

2:11 1Sa 2:18
2:12 Jer 2:8
2:15 Lev 3:16
2:17 Ge 6:11
2:18 1Sa 2:11
2:19 1Sa 1:3
2:20 1Sa 1:27–28
2:21 Ge 21:1
2:22 Ex 38:8
2:25 Jos 11:20
2:26 Lk 2:52

2:27 1Ki 13:1
2:28 Ex 28:1
2:29 1Sa 2:13–17
2:30 Ex 29:9
2:31 1Sa 22:17–20
2:32 Zec 8:4
2:34 1Sa 4:11
2:35 2Sa 7:11
2:36 1Ki 2:27
3:1 1Sa 2:11
3:2 1Sa 4:15

And he said, "I did not call. Return, lie down again." And he went and lay down.

> Let Your Word be revealed unto me (1Sa 3:7).

6 The LORD called Samuel again. So Samuel arose and went to Eli, and said, "Here I am, for you called me."

And he answered, "I did not call, my son. Return, lie down again."

7 Now Samuel did not yet know the LORD, nor had the word of the LORD been revealed to him.

8 The LORD again called Samuel a third time. So he arose and went to Eli and said, "Here I am, for you called me."

Then Eli understood that the LORD was calling to the boy. 9 Therefore Eli said to Samuel, "Go, lie down. And it will be, if He calls you, that you will say, 'Speak, LORD, for Your servant listens.' " So Samuel went and lay down in his place.

10 The LORD came and stood, and He called as at other times, "Samuel, Samuel."

Then Samuel said, "Speak, for Your servant listens."

11 The LORD said to Samuel, "See, I am doing something in Israel which will make both ears ring of every one that hears it. 12 In that day I will bring about against Eli everything which I have spoken with regard to his house, from beginning to end. 13 For I told him that I will judge his house forever, for the guilt which he knew, because his sons are cursed, and he did not rebuke them. 14 Therefore I have sworn to the house of Eli that the iniquity of Eli's house shall not be atoned for with sacrifice nor offering forever."

15 Samuel lay until the morning; then he opened the doors of the house of the LORD. Now Samuel feared to report the vision to Eli. 16 Then Eli called Samuel, and said, "Samuel, my son."

And he answered, "Here I am."

17 He said, "What is the thing that the LORD has spoken to you? Do not hide it from me. Thus may God do so to you, and more also, if you hide from me a word out of all the things that He spoke to you." 18 Samuel told him everything, and did not hide from him a thing. And he said, "It is the LORD; let Him do what is good in His eyes."

19 And Samuel grew, and the LORD was with him and did not let any of his words fall to the ground. 20 All Israel from Dan even to Beersheba knew that Samuel was proven to be a prophet of the LORD. 21 And the LORD appeared again in Shiloh. For the LORD revealed Himself to Samuel in Shiloh by the word of the LORD.

3:7 Ac 19:2
3:11 2Ki 21:12
3:12 1Sa 2:27–36
3:13 1Sa 2:12
3:14 Isa 22:14
3:17 Ru 1:17
3:18 Job 2:10
3:19 1Sa 2:21
3:20 Jdg 20:1
3:21 Ge 12:7

....

4:1 1Sa 7:12
4:4 2Sa 6:2
4:5 Jos 6:5
4:9 Jdg 13:1
4:10 Dt 28:25
4:11 1Sa 2:34
4:12 Jos 7:6
4:13 1Sa 1:9
4:15 1Sa 3:2
4:16 2Sa 1:4

4 And the word of Samuel came to all Israel.

The Ark of God Captured

And Israel went out to battle against the Philistines and they made camp beside Ebenezer, and the Philistines encamped in Aphek. 2 The Philistines arrayed themselves in a battle line against Israel, and when the battle was over, Israel was beaten before the Philistines, who struck down on the field of battle about four thousand men. 3 When the people came into the camp, the elders of Israel said, "Why has the LORD struck us today before the Philistines? Let us bring the ark of the covenant of the LORD out of Shiloh to us, that it might come among us and rescue us out of the hand of our enemies."

4 So the people sent to Shiloh, that they might bring from there the ark of the covenant of the LORD of Hosts, who dwells above the cherubim. And the two sons of Eli, Hophni and Phinehas, were there with the ark of the covenant of God.

5 When the ark of the covenant of the LORD came into the camp, all Israel shouted with a great shout, so that the ground was in an uproar. 6 When the Philistines heard the sound of the shout, they said, "What does this great shout in the camp of the Hebrews mean?" Then they understood that the ark of the LORD had come into the camp.

7 The Philistines were afraid, when they said, "God is come into the camp." And they said, "Woe to us! For this has never happened *to us* before. 8 Woe to us! Who will deliver us out of the hand of these mighty gods? These are the gods that struck the Egyptians with every plague in the wilderness. 9 Be strong and be men, O Philistines, lest you be servants to the Hebrews, as they have been to you. Now be men and fight."

10 So the Philistines fought and Israel was beaten. And they fled every man into his tent. It was a very great defeat, for there fell of Israel thirty thousand foot soldiers. 11 Now the ark of God was taken, and the two sons of Eli, Hophni and Phinehas, died.

12 There ran a man of Benjamin from the battle line, and he came to Shiloh the same day with his clothes torn and with dust upon his head. 13 When he came, Eli was sitting on a seat by the wayside watching. For his heart feared for the ark of God. Now the man came to tell *it* in the city, and all the city cried out.

14 When Eli heard the noise of the crying, he said, "What does the noise of this tumult mean?"

And the man hurriedly came and told Eli. 15 Now Eli was ninety-eight years old, and his eyes were dim, so that he could not see. 16 The

man said to Eli, "I am he that came out of the
army, and I fled today out of the battle line."
And he said, "What is the word, my son?"
17 The messenger answered and said, "Israel
has fled before the Philistines, and there also
has been a great slaughter among the people.
Your two sons also, Hophni and Phinehas, are
dead. And the ark of God is taken."
18 When he mentioned the ark of God, Eli fell
from off the seat backward by the side of the
gate. And his neck broke and he died, for he
was an old and heavy man. And he had judged
Israel forty years.
19 His daughter-in-law, Phinehas' wife, was
pregnant, about to give birth. And when she
heard the news that the ark of God was taken,
and that her father-in-law and her husband
were dead, she kneeled down and gave birth,
for her pains came upon her. 20 About the time
of her death the women that stood by her said
to her, "Do not fear, for you have borne a son."
But she did not answer or regard it.
21 She named the child Ichabod, saying, "The
glory is departed from Israel," because the ark
of God was taken, and because of her father-
in-law and her husband. 22 She said, "The glory
is departed from Israel, for the ark of God is
taken."

The Philistines and the Ark

5 Now the Philistines took the ark of God,
and brought it from Ebenezer to Ashdod.
2 When the Philistines took the ark of God, they
brought it into the house of Dagon and set it by
Dagon. 3 When the Ashdodites arose early in
the morning, Dagon had fallen upon his face
to the ground before the ark of the LORD. And
they took Dagon and set him in his place again.
4 When they arose early on the next morning,
again Dagon was fallen upon his face to the
ground before the ark of the LORD, and the
head of Dagon and both the palms of his
hands were cut off upon the threshold. Only
the *torso* of Dagon was left to him. 5 Therefore
neither the priests of Dagon, nor any coming
into Dagon's house, tread on the threshold of
Dagon in Ashdod to this day.
6 But the hand of the LORD was heavy upon
the Ashdodites. He desolated them and struck
them with tumors, even Ashdod and its terri-
tories. 7 When the men of Ashdod saw that it
was so, they said, "The ark of the God of Israel
cannot remain with us. For His hand is heavy
upon us and upon Dagon our god." 8 So they
sent and gathered all the lords of the Philis-
tines unto them, and said, "What shall we do
with the ark of the God of Israel?"

4:18 1Sa 4:13
4:20 Ge 35:17–18
4:21 Ps 26:8
5:1 1Sa 4:1
5:2 Jdg 16:23
5:3 Isa 19:1
5:4 Mic 1:7
5:5 Zep 1:9
5:6 1Sa 5:11
5:9 1Sa 5:6
5:11 1Sa 5:6
5:12 Ex 12:30
6:2 Ge 41:8
6:3 Ex 23:15
6:4 Jos 13:3
6:5 Jos 7:19
6:6 Ex 7:13
6:7 Nu 19:2
6:9 Jos 15:10

And they answered, "Let the ark of the God
of Israel be carried around to Gath." And they
carried the ark of the God of Israel *there*.
9 It happened that after they had carried it
about, the hand of the LORD was against the city
with a very great destruction. And He struck
the men of the city, both small and great. And
tumors broke out on them. 10 Therefore they
sent the ark of God to Ekron.
And it came about that as the ark of God
came to Ekron, that the Ekronites cried out,
saying, "They have brought about the ark of
the God of Israel to slay us and our people."
11 So they sent and gathered together all the
lords of the Philistines, and said, "Send away
the ark of the God of Israel, and let it go again
to His own place that He might not kill me and
my people," for there was a deadly destruction
throughout all the city. The hand of God was
very heavy there. 12 The men that did not die
were plagued with the tumors. And the cry of
the city went up to heaven.

The Ark Returned to Israel

6 Now the ark of the LORD had been in the
country of the Philistines seven months.
2 The Philistines called for the priests and the
diviners, saying, "What shall we do with the
ark of the LORD? Tell us how we should send
it to its place."
3 They said, "If you send away the ark of the
God of Israel, do not send it empty. But re-
turn to Him a guilt offering. Then you will be
healed, and it will be known to you why His
hand is not removed from you."
4 Then said they, "What will be the guilt offer-
ing which we will return to Him?"
They answered, "Five golden tumors and five
golden mice according to the number of the
lords of the Philistines. For one plague was on
you all, and on your lords. 5 Therefore you will
make images of your tumors and images of
your mice that ravage the land. And you will
give glory to the God of Israel. Perhaps He will
lighten His hand from off you, even from off
your gods and from off your land. 6 Why then
do you harden your hearts, as the Egyptians
and Pharaoh hardened their hearts? When He
dealt severely with them, did they not let the
people go, and they departed?
7 "Now therefore make a new cart, and take
two milk cows on which there has never been
a yoke. Then tie the cows to the cart and bring
their calves home, away from them. 8 Then take
the ark of the LORD and set it on the cart. And
put the images of gold, which you return to
Him for a guilt offering, in a box by the side.
And send it away, that it may go. 9 See, if it
goes up by the way of His own territory to Beth

Shemesh, then He has done us this great evil. But if not, then we will know that it is not His hand that struck us; it was by chance that it happened to us."

10 The men did so. And they took two milk cows, tied them to the cart, and shut up their calves at home. 11 And they set the ark of the LORD on the cart, as well as the box with the mice of gold and the images of their tumors. 12 Then the cows took the straight way to the way of Beth Shemesh, and went along the highway, lowing as they went. They did not turn aside to the right hand or to the left with the lords of the Philistines walking after them to the border of Beth Shemesh.

13 Now Beth Shemesh was reaping their wheat harvest in the valley. And they lifted up their eyes and saw the ark, and they rejoiced to see it. 14 The cart came into the field of Joshua, the Beth Shemite, and stood there where there was a great stone. And they split the wood of the cart, and offered the cows as a burnt offering to the LORD. 15 The Levites took down the ark of the LORD and the box that was with it, where the articles of gold were, and put them on the great stone. And the men of Beth Shemesh offered burnt offerings and made sacrifices the same day to the LORD. 16 When the five lords of the Philistines had seen it, they returned to Ekron the same day.

17 These are the golden tumors which the Philistines returned for a guilt offering to the LORD: for Ashdod one, for Gaza one, for Ashkelon one, for Gath one, for Ekron one. 18 And the golden mice, according to the number of all the cities of the Philistines belonging to the five lords, both of fortified cities, and of country villages. And the great stone, where they set the ark of the LORD, *is a witness* to this day in the field of Joshua, the Beth Shemite.

19 Then He struck the men of Beth Shemesh, because they had looked into the ark of the LORD. He struck fifty thousand and seventy men. And the people lamented, because the LORD had struck the people with a great slaughter. 20 The men of Beth Shemesh said, "Who is able to stand before the LORD, this holy God? And to whom will He go up from us?"

21 And they sent messengers to the inhabitants of Kiriath Jearim, saying, "The Philistines have brought back the ark of the LORD. Come down, and take it up to you."

7 So the men of Kiriath Jearim came and took up the ark of the LORD. And they brought it into the house of Abinadab on the hill, and sanctified Eleazar his son to keep the ark of the LORD. 2 And from the day the ark resided in Kiriath Jearim, the days increased to twenty years.

Samuel Judges Israel

And all the house of Israel lamented after the LORD. 3 Samuel spoke to all the house of Israel, saying, "If you are returning to the LORD with all your heart, then put away the foreign gods and Ashtoreths from your midst. And make firm your hearts unto the LORD, and serve Him only. Then He will deliver you out of the hand of the Philistines." 4 So the children of Israel put away the Baals and Ashtoreths and served the LORD only.

5 Then Samuel said, "Gather all Israel to Mizpah, and I will pray to the LORD for you." 6 They gathered together to Mizpah. And they drew water and poured it out before the LORD. And they fasted on that day, and said there, "We have sinned against the LORD." So Samuel judged the children of Israel in Mizpah.

7 When the Philistines heard that the children of Israel were gathered together to Mizpah, the lords of the Philistines went up against Israel. And when the children of Israel heard it, they were afraid of the Philistines. 8 The children of Israel said to Samuel, "Do not stop crying unto the LORD our God for us, that He might save us out of the hand of the Philistines." 9 Samuel took a suckling lamb, and offered it for a burnt offering unto the LORD. And Samuel cried to the LORD for Israel and the LORD heard him.

10 As Samuel was offering up the burnt offering, the Philistines drew near to battle against Israel, but the LORD thundered with a great thunder on that day against the Philistines, and confused them. So they were beaten before Israel. 11 Israel's fighting men went out of Mizpah, and pursued the Philistines, and struck them, as far as below Beth Kar.

12 Then Samuel took a stone and set it between Mizpah and Shen. And he called its name Ebenezer[1] saying, "Thus far the LORD has helped us."

13 So the Philistines were subdued, and they did not again come into the territory of Israel. And the hand of the LORD was against the Philistines all the days of Samuel. 14 The cities which the Philistines had taken from Israel were restored to Israel, from Ekron even to Gath. And Israel rescued their territory out of the hands of the Philistines. And there was peace between Israel and the Amorites.

15 So Samuel judged Israel all the days of his life. 16 He went annually in a circuit to Bethel, and Gilgal, and Mizpah. And he judged Israel in all those places. 17 But his return was to Ramah, for his house was there and there he

6:14 2Sa 24:22
6:19 Ex 19:21
6:20 2Sa 6:9
6:21 1Ch 13:5–6
7:3 Jos 24:14
7:5 Jdg 20:1
7:6 Jdg 10:10
7:7 1Sa 17:11
7:8 Isa 37:4
7:9 Ps 99:6
7:10 1Sa 2:10
7:12 Ge 35:14
7:13 Jdg 13:1
7:15 1Sa 7:6
7:17 1Sa 1:19

[1]12 Lit. *Stone of help.*

judged Israel. And there he built an altar to the LORD.

Israel Demands a King

8 And it came about when Samuel was old, that he installed his sons as judges for Israel. 2 Now the name of his firstborn son was Joel, and the name of his second son was Abijah. They were judging in Beersheba. 3 But his sons did not walk in his way, for they followed after unlawful gain, and they took bribes, and they perverted justice.

4 And all the elders of Israel gathered together and they came to Samuel at Ramah. 5 They said to him, "You are old and your sons do not walk in your ways. Now, install for us a king to govern us like all the nations."

6 But the thing was evil in the eyes of Samuel, because they said, "Give us a king to govern us." And Samuel prayed to the LORD. 7 The LORD said to Samuel, "Obey the voice of the people in relation to all that they say to you. For it is not you they have rejected, but Me they have rejected from reigning over them. 8 Just as all the deeds which they have done *to Me*, from the day I brought them up from Egypt even to this day, in that they have forsaken Me and have served other gods, so they are doing also to you *now*. 9 Now then, obey their voice. Only you will testify against them and proclaim to them the judgment concerning the king who will reign over them."

10 So Samuel said all the words of the LORD to the people who were asking from him a king. 11 And he said, "This will be the judgment concerning the king who will reign over you: Your sons he will take in order to place *them* for himself in his chariots and as his horsemen, and they will run before his chariot, 12 and in order to assign for himself captains of thousands and captains of fifties, and to plow his ground, and to gather in his harvest, and to make his weapons of war and the equipment of his chariots. 13 And your daughters he will take for perfumers, and cooks, and bakers. 14 And your choicest fields, and vineyards, and olive groves he will take and give them to his servants. 15 And of your seed fields and your vineyards he will take a tenth *of their harvest* and will give it to his high officials and to his servants. 16 And your menservants and your maidservants, and the best of your young men and asses he will take and make do his work. 17 Your flocks he will take a tenth of, but you will be his for slaves. 18 And you will cry out in that day because of your king, whom you have chosen for yourselves, but the LORD will not answer you in that day."

8:1 Dt 16:18–19
8:3 Dt 16:19
8:4 1Sa 7:17
8:5 Dt 17:14–15
8:6 1Sa 15:11
8:7 Ex 16:8
8:9 1Sa 8:11–18
8:11 1Sa 10:25
8:14 1Ki 21:7
8:18 Isa 1:15

....

8:19 Jer 44:16
8:20 1Sa 8:5
8:21 Jdg 11:11
8:22 1Sa 8:7
9:1 1Sa 14:51
9:4 2Ki 4:42
9:5 1Sa 10:2
9:6 Dt 33:1
9:7 1Ki 14:3
9:9 2Sa 24:11

19 But the people refused to obey the voice of Samuel. And they said, "No! But surely a king will be over us! 20 So that we also will be like all the nations! And so that our king will govern us, and will go out before us, and will fight our battles."

21 And after Samuel heard all the words of the people, he spoke them in the hearing of the LORD. 22 And the LORD said to Samuel, "Obey their voice, and make for them a king."

So Samuel said to Israel's fighting men, "Go every man to his city."

Samuel Anoints Saul

9 Now there was a man of Benjamin, whose name was Kish, the son of Abiel, the son of Zeror, the son of Bekorath, the son of Aphiah, a Benjamite, a mighty man of power. 2 He had a son, whose name was Saul, a choice and handsome man, and there was not a better looking man among the children of Israel. From his shoulders and up he was taller than any of the people.

3 Now the donkeys of Kish, the father of Saul, were lost. And Kish said to his son Saul, "Take now one of the servants with you, and arise, go find the donkeys." 4 He passed through the mountains of Ephraim, and passed through the land of Shalisha, but they did not find them. And they passed through the land of Shaalim, but *they were* not *there*. Then he passed through the land of the Benjamites, but they did not find them.

5 When they came to the land of Zuph, Saul said to his servant that was with him, "Come, and let us return lest my father stop *caring* about the donkeys and worry about us."

6 He said to him, "Look, there is in this city a man of God, and he is highly respected. All that he speaks surely comes about. Now let us go there. Perhaps he can show us the way that we should go."

7 Then Saul said to his servant, "But listen, if we go, what will we bring the man? For the bread is gone from our satchels, and there is no present to bring to the man of God. What do we have?"

8 And the servant answered Saul again, and said, "Look, I have here in my hand a quarter of a shekel[1] of silver. I will give *it* to the man of God, to tell us our way." 9 (Formerly in Israel, when a man went to inquire of God, thus he said, "Come, and let us go to the seer." For he that is now called a prophet was formerly called a seer.)

10 Then Saul said to his servant, "Well said. Come, let us go." So they went to the city where the man of God was.

[1] 8 About 1/10 ounce, or 3 grams.

11 As they went up the hill to the city, they
found young women going out to draw water
and said to them, "Is the seer here?"
12 And they answered them and said, "He is.
See, he is ahead of you. Hurry now, for today
he came to the city, because there is a sacrifice
for the people in the high place today. 13 As
soon as you come into the city, you will find
him before he goes up to the high place to
eat. For the people will not eat until he comes,
because he must bless the sacrifice. Afterwards
those invited will eat. Now therefore, go up,
for about this time of the day you will find
him *there*."
14 So they went up into the city. And when
they entered, Samuel was coming toward them
to go up to the high place.
15 Now the LORD had revealed in the ear of
Samuel one day before Saul came, saying,
16 "Tomorrow about this time I will send you a
man out of the land of Benjamin. And you will
anoint him to be leader over My people Israel,
that he may save My people out of the hand
of the Philistines. For I have looked upon My
people, because their cry has come unto Me."
17 When Samuel saw Saul, the LORD said to
him, "Here is the man of whom I spoke to you!
This one will rule over My people."
18 Then Saul drew near to Samuel in the gate,
and said, "Tell me, please, where is the seer's
house?"
19 Samuel answered Saul, and said, "I am the
seer. Go up before me to the high place, for
you will eat with me today. And tomorrow I
will let you go, and will tell you *then* all that is
in your heart. 20 As for your donkeys that were
lost three days ago, do not your worry about
them for they have been found. And on whom
is all the desire of Israel? Is it not on you and
on all your father's house?"
21 And Saul answered and said, "Am not I a
Benjamite, of the smallest of the tribes of Isra-
el? And my family the least of all the families
of the tribe of Benjamin? Why do you speak
to me this way?"
22 And Samuel took Saul and his servant, and
brought them into the hall, and gave them a
place at the head of those invited, which were
about thirty men. 23 Samuel said to the cook,
"Bring the portion which I gave you, of which
I said to you, 'Set it aside.' "
24 Then the cook took up the thigh and what
was on it and set it before Saul. And Samuel
said, "Here is what was set aside. Set it before
you and eat, because it has been kept for you
until this time, since I said I have invited the
people." So Saul ate with Samuel that day.
25 When they had come down from the high
place into the city, *Samuel* spoke with Saul up
on the roof. 26 They arose early, and it was at
the rising of the dawn that Samuel called to
Saul on the roof, saying, "Get up, that I may
send you away." So Saul arose, and both he
and Samuel went to the street. 27 As they were
going down to the outskirts of the city, Samuel
said to Saul, "Tell the servant to pass on before
us." So he passed on. "But you stand still and I
will proclaim to you the word of God."

10 Then Samuel took a vial of oil and
poured it upon his head. And he kissed
him and said, "Has not the LORD anointed you
over His inheritance as ruler? 2 When you
have departed from me today, you will find
two men by Rachel's tomb in the territory of
Benjamin at Zelzah. And they will say to you,
'The donkeys which you went to look for have
been found. And now, your father has stopped
caring about the donkeys, and worries for you,
saying, "What will I do for my son?" '

God is generous with His anointing oil (1Sa 10).

3 "Then you will go forward from there, and
you will come to the plain of Tabor. And there
you will meet three men going up to God to
Bethel: one carrying three kids, another carry-
ing three loaves of bread, and another carrying
a bottle of wine. 4 And they will greet you and
give you two loaves of bread, which you will
receive from their hands.
5 "After that you will come to the hill of God,
where the garrison of the Philistines is. And
when you come there to the city, you will meet
a group of prophets coming down from the
high place with a harp, a tambourine, a flute,
and a lyre before them. And they will prophesy.
6 And the Spirit of the LORD will come upon you,
and you will prophesy with them. And you will
be turned into another man. 7 And it will be
when these signs come to you, do for yourself
what the occasion requires; for God is with you.

The impartation of an anointing can happen in a moment, and so can the change that goes with it (1Sa 10:9–11).

8 "Then you will go down before me to Gil-
gal. And listen, I will be coming down to you,
in order to offer burnt offerings, *and* to offer
sacrifices of peace offerings. Seven days you
will wait, until I come to you. Then I will make
known to you what you will do."
9 And it happened, that when he turned his
back to go from Samuel, that God gave him

9:11 Ge 24:11
9:12 Ge 31:54
9:13 Jn 6:11
9:15 1Sa 15:1
9:16 1Sa 10:1
9:20 1Sa 8:5
9:21 1Sa 15:17
9:24 Lev 7:32–33
9:25 Dt 22:8

....

10:1 1Sa 16:13
10:2 1Sa 9:3–5
10:3 Ge 28:22
10:5 1Sa 13:3
10:6 1Sa 10:10
10:7 Jdg 6:12
10:8 1Sa 11:14–15

another heart. And all those signs came to pass that day. 10 When they came to the hill, a group of prophets met him. And the Spirit of God came upon him, and he prophesied among them. 11 So when all who previously knew him saw that he prophesied among the prophets, the people said one to another, "What is this that has come upon the son of Kish? Is Saul also among the prophets?"

12 And a man from there answered and said, "But who is their father?" Therefore it became a proverb, "Is Saul also among the prophets?" 13 When he had finished prophesying, he came to the high place.

14 And Saul's uncle said to him and to his servant, "Where did you go?"

And he said, "To seek the donkeys. And when we saw that *they were* nowhere *around*, we went to Samuel."

15 Saul's uncle said, "Please tell me what Samuel said to you."

16 Saul said to his uncle, "He told us plainly that the donkeys were found." But the matter of the kingdom, of which Samuel had spoken, he did not mention.

Saul Proclaimed King

17 Therefore Samuel called the people together unto the LORD at Mizpah. 18 And he said to the children of Israel, "Thus says the LORD, the God of Israel, 'I brought up Israel out of Egypt, and delivered you out of the hand of the Egyptians, and out of the hand of all kingdoms, and of them that oppressed you.' 19 But you have today rejected your God, who saves you from all your troubles and your distresses. And you have said to Him, 'No, but set a king over us.' Now therefore present yourselves before the LORD by your tribes, and by your clans."

20 So Samuel brought near all the tribes of Israel and the tribe of Benjamin was taken. 21 Then he brought near the tribe of Benjamin by its families. And the family of Matri was chosen. Then Saul the son of Kish was taken. But when they sought him, he could not be found. 22 Therefore they inquired again of the LORD, "Has the man come here yet?"

And the LORD answered, "He has hidden himself among the equipment."

23 So they ran and took him from there. When he stood among the people, he was taller than any of the people from his shoulders and upward. 24 Then Samuel said to all the people, "Do you see him whom the LORD has chosen? Truly there is none like him among all the people."

And all the people shouted and said, "*Long* live the king."

10:10 1Sa 10:5–6
10:11 1Sa 19:24
10:14 1Sa 14:50
10:16 1Sa 9:20
10:17 Jdg 20:1
10:18 Jdg 6:8–9
10:19 1Sa 12:12
10:23 1Sa 9:2
10:24 2Sa 21:6
....
10:25 Dt 17:14–20
10:26 1Sa 11:4
10:27 Dt 13:13
11:1 Jdg 21:8
11:2 1Sa 17:26
11:4 Jdg 2:4
11:5 1Ki 19:19
11:6 1Sa 10:10
11:7 Jdg 19:29
11:11 Jdg 7:16

25 Samuel told the people the ordinances of the kingdom, and wrote them in a book, and laid them up before the LORD. And Samuel sent all the people away, every man to his house.

26 Saul also went home to Gibeah. And there went with him *a band of* valiant *men* whose hearts God had touched. 27 But some worthless men said, "How will this man save us?" And they despised him, and did not bring him a present. But he remained silent.

Saul Rescues Jabesh Gilead

11 Then Nahash the Ammonite came up, and encamped against Jabesh Gilead. And all the men of Jabesh said to Nahash, "Make a covenant with us, and we will serve you."

2 Nahash the Ammonite answered them, "On this *condition* will I make a covenant with you, that I may pluck out all your right eyes. So I will inflict it as a reproach upon all Israel."

3 The elders of Jabesh said to him, "Give us seven days, that we may send messengers to all the territory of Israel. And *then* if there is no one to rescue us, we will come out to you."

4 So the messengers came to Gibeah of Saul, and spoke the words in the ears of the people. And all the people lifted up their voices, and wept. 5 Now Saul *was* coming out of the field after the cattle, and Saul said, "Why are the people weeping?" And they reported to him the words of the men of Jabesh.

6 The Spirit of God came strongly upon Saul when he heard these words, and he became very angry. 7 He took a yoke of oxen, and hewed them in pieces. And he sent them throughout all the territory of Israel by the hands of messengers, saying, "Whoever does not come out after Saul and after Samuel, so will it be done to his oxen." And the fear of the LORD fell on the people, and they came out as one man. 8 When he numbered them in Bezek, the children of Israel were three hundred thousand, and the men of Judah thirty thousand.

9 They said to the messengers that came, "Thus will you say to the men of Jabesh Gilead, 'Tomorrow, by the time the sun is hot, you will have help.'" And the messengers came and reported it to the men of Jabesh and they were glad. 10 Therefore the men of Jabesh said, "Tomorrow we will come out to you, and you may do to us all that seems good to you."

11 On the next day Saul put the people in three companies. And they came into the midst of the camp in the morning and struck down the Ammonites until the heat of the day. Those surviving were scattered, so that *even* two of them were not left together.

Saul Confirmed as King

12 The people said to Samuel, "Who said, 'Shall Saul reign over us?' Bring the men, that we may put them to death."

13 Saul said, "There will not be a man put to death this day. For today the LORD has worked deliverance in Israel."

14 Then Samuel said to the people, "Come, and let us go to Gilgal and renew the kingdom there." 15 All the people went to Gilgal and there they made Saul king before the LORD in Gilgal. And there they made sacrifices of peace offerings before the LORD. And there Saul and all Israel's fighting men rejoiced greatly.

Samuel's Farewell Address

12 Then Samuel said to all Israel: "I have listened to your voice in all that you said to me, and have made a king over you. 2 And now, see, the king walks before you, but I am old and gray-headed. As for my sons, they are with you. But I have walked before you from my childhood to this day. 3 Behold, here I am. Witness against me before the LORD and before His anointed. Whose ox have I taken? Or whose donkey have I taken? Or whom have I defrauded? Whom have I oppressed? Or from whose hand have I received any bribe to blind my eyes with? Indeed I will restore it you."

4 They said, "You have not defrauded us, nor oppressed us. Neither have you taken anything from any man's hand."

5 He said to them, "The LORD is witness against you, and His anointed is witness this day, that you have not found anything in my hand."

And they answered, "*He is* witness."

6 Samuel said to the people: "It is the LORD that prepared Moses and Aaron, and that brought your fathers up out of the land of Egypt. 7 Now therefore stand still that I may reason with you before the LORD, concerning all the righteous acts of the LORD, which He did for you and your fathers.

8 "When Jacob went into Egypt and your fathers cried out to the LORD, the LORD sent Moses and Aaron who brought forth your fathers out of Egypt and made them dwell in this place.

9 "When they forgot the LORD their God, He sold them into the hand of Sisera, captain of the host of Hazor, and into the hand of the Philistines, and into the hand of the king of Moab. And they fought against them. 10 They cried to the LORD, and said, 'We have sinned, because we have forsaken the LORD and have served the Baals and the Ashtoreths. But now deliver us out of the hand of our enemies, and we will serve You.' 11 The LORD sent Jerub-Baal, Bedan,[1] Jephthah, and Samuel. And He delivered you out of the hand of your enemies on every side, and you dwelled in safety.

12 "When you saw that Nahash, king of the Ammonites, came against you, you said to me, 'No, but a king will reign over us,' when the LORD your God was your king. 13 Now therefore, look at the king whom you have chosen and for whom you have asked! And see that the LORD has set a king over you. 14 If you will fear the LORD, and serve Him, and obey His voice, and not rebel against the commandment of the LORD, then both you and the king that reigns over you will continue following the LORD your God. 15 But if you will not obey the voice of the LORD, but rebel against the commandment of the LORD, then will the hand of the LORD be against you, *as it was* against your fathers.

16 "Even now, take your stand and see this great thing which the LORD is doing before your eyes. 17 Is it not the wheat harvest today? I will call to the LORD. And He will send thunder and rain, that you may know and see that your wickedness is great, which you have done in the sight of the LORD, by asking for yourselves a king."

18 So Samuel called to the LORD. And the LORD sent thunder and rain that day, and all the people greatly feared the LORD and Samuel.

19 All the people said to Samuel, "Pray for your servants to the LORD your God, that we will not die, for we have added to all our sins this evil, to ask for ourselves a king."

20 Samuel said to the people, "Do not fear. You have done all this wickedness, only do not turn aside from following the LORD, and serve the LORD with all your heart. 21 But do not turn aside, for *then you would be going* after empty things which cannot profit or deliver, for they are nothing. 22 As befits His great name, the LORD will not abandon His people. For it has pleased the LORD to make you His people. 23 Moreover as for me, God forbid that I should sin against the LORD in ceasing to pray for you. But I will teach you the good and the right way. 24 Fear the LORD; serve Him in truth with all your heart, and consider what great things He has done for you. 25 But if you still do wickedly, both you and your king will be swept away."

Saul Fails His Commission

13 Saul was *thirty* years old when he began to reign, and he reigned *forty*-two years over Israel.[2]

2 Saul chose for himself three thousand men of Israel. Two thousand were with Saul

11:12 1Sa 10:27
11:13 Ex 14:13
11:14 1Sa 10:8
11:15 1Sa 10:8
12:1 1Sa 10:24
12:2 1Sa 8:5
12:3 Nu 16:15
12:5 Ex 22:4
12:6 Mic 6:4
12:7 Isa 1:18
12:8 Ex 4:14–16
12:9 Jdg 3:12
12:10 Jdg 2:13
12:11 Jdg 6:32
12:12 Jdg 8:23
12:13 1Sa 10:24
12:14 Jos 24:14
12:15 Jos 24:20
12:16 Ex 14:13
12:17 1Sa 7:9–10
12:18 Ex 14:31
12:19 Ex 9:28
12:20 Dt 11:16
12:21 Hab 2:18
12:22 Jos 7:9
12:23 1Ki 8:36
12:24 Dt 10:21
12:25 Jos 24:20
13:2 1Sa 10:26

[1] *11* Perhaps *Barak* here (see LXX). [2] *1* Lit. "The son of a year was Saul in his ruling and two years he ruled over Israel." Most translations read in Saul's age and length of reign from external evidence (Josephus) or from the New Testament (Paul, who mentions a forty-year reign for Saul in Ac 13:21).

in Mikmash and in mountains of Bethel, and a thousand were with Jonathan in Gibeah of Benjamin. The rest of the people he sent each to his tent.

3 Jonathan struck the garrison of the Philistines that was in Geba, and the Philistines heard of it. And Saul blew the trumpet throughout all the land, saying, "Let the Hebrews hear." 4 All Israel heard that Saul had struck the garrison of the Philistines, and that Israel had become odious to the Philistines. And the people were called together after Saul to Gilgal.

5 The Philistines gathered together to fight with Israel, thirty thousand chariots and six thousand horsemen, with people like the sand which is on the seashore in multitude. And they came up and camped in Mikmash, east of Beth Aven. 6 When Israel's fighting men saw that they were in a strait (for the people were distressed), then the people hid themselves in caves, in hollows, *among* rocks, and in cellars and cisterns. 7 *Some* of the Hebrews went over Jordan to the land of Gad and Gilead.

But *as for* Saul, he was still in Gilgal, and all the people followed him, trembling. 8 He waited seven days, according to the set time that Samuel *had appointed*. But Samuel did not come to Gilgal, and the people were scattered from him. 9 Saul said, "Bring here to me the burnt offering and the peace offerings." Then he offered the burnt offering. 10 When he finished offering the burnt offering, Samuel came. And Saul went out to meet him to greet him.

11 Samuel said, "What have you done?"

And Saul said, "Because I saw that the people were scattered from me, and that you did not come to the appointed assembly days, and the Philistines are gathering themselves together at Mikmash, 12 therefore I said, 'The Philistines will come down now upon me to Gilgal, and I have not *yet* appeased the face of the LORD.' So I forced myself, and offered the burnt offering."

13 Samuel said to Saul, "You have done foolishly. You have not kept the commandment of the LORD your God, which He commanded you. Truly now, the LORD would have established your kingdom over Israel forever. 14 But now your kingdom will not continue. The LORD has sought for Himself a man after His own heart and the LORD has commanded him to be prince over His people, because you have not kept that which the LORD commanded you."

15 Samuel arose, and went up from Gilgal to Gibeah of Benjamin. And Saul numbered the people that were present with him, about six hundred men.

13:3 1Sa 10:5
13:4 Ge 34:30
13:5 Jos 11:4
13:6 Jdg 6:2
13:8 1Sa 10:8
13:9 1Ki 3:4
13:10 1Sa 15:13
13:11 1Sa 13:2
13:13 2Ch 16:9
13:14 1Sa 15:28
13:15 1Sa 13:2
....
13:17 Jos 18:23
13:18 Ne 11:34
13:19 2Ki 24:14
13:22 Jdg 5:8
13:23 Isa 10:28
14:2 1Sa 13:15–16
14:3 1Sa 2:28
14:4 1Sa 13:23
14:6 1Sa 17:26

Israel Unarmed

16 Now Saul, and Jonathan his son, and the people that were with them, were staying in Gibeah of Benjamin, but the Philistines encamped in Mikmash. 17 Then raiders came out of the camp of the Philistines in three companies. One company turned to the way that leads to Ophrah, to the land of Shual. 18 And another company turned the way to Beth Horon. And another company turned to the way of the border that looks to the Valley of Zeboyim toward the wilderness.

19 Now there was no blacksmith found throughout all the land of Israel. For the Philistines said, "Lest the Hebrews make for themselves swords or spears." 20 So all the children of Israel went down to the Philistines, to sharpen every man his plow-point, his axe, his adze and his hoe. 21 The sharpening *charge* was two-thirds of a shekel[1] for plow-points, axes, pitchforks, and adzes, and to fix an ox-goad.

22 So it came to pass on the day of battle, that neither sword nor spear were found in the hand of any of the people who were with Saul and Jonathan. But they were found *in the hand of* Saul and Jonathan his son.

23 And the garrison of the Philistines had marched out to the ravine of Mikmash.

Jonathan Defeats the Philistines

14 A day came that Jonathan, the son of Saul, said to the young man that bore his armor, "Come, and let us cross over to the Philistine garrison which is on the other side." But he did not tell his father.

2 Now Saul was staying on the outskirts of Gibeah under the pomegranate tree which is in Migron. And the people that were with him *were* about six hundred men. 3 And Ahijah, the son of Ahitub, Ichabod's brother, the son of Phinehas, the son of Eli, the priest of the LORD in Shiloh, was wearing the ephod. But the people did not know that Jonathan had gone.

4 Between the passages, by which Jonathan sought to go over to the Philistines' garrison, there was a sharp rock on the one side, and a sharp rock on the other side. And the name of the one was Bozez, and the name of the other Seneh. 5 The crag of the one rose north opposite Mikmash, and the other faced southward opposite Geba.

6 Jonathan said to the young man bearing his armor, "Come, and let us cross over to the garrison of these uncircumcised. Perhaps the LORD will work for us. For the LORD is not limited to save by many or by few."

[1] *21* About ¼ ounce, or 8 grams.

7 His armor bearer said to him, "Do all that is
in your heart. Turn yourself, *and* I *will be* with
you according to your heart."
8 Then Jonathan said, "Now we will cross
over to *these* men, and we will reveal ourselves
to them. 9 If they say to us, 'Wait until we come
to you,' then we will stand still in our place,
and we will not go up to them. 10 But if they
say, 'Come up to us,' then we will go up, for
the LORD has delivered them into our hand, and
this will be a sign to us."
11 So the two of them revealed themselves
to the garrison of the Philistines. And the
Philistines said, "Look, the Hebrews are com-
ing out of the caves where they have hidden
themselves." 12 The men of the garrison an-
swered Jonathan and his armor bearer, and
said, "Come up to us, and we will teach you
something."
So Jonathan said to his armor bearer, "Come
up after me. For the LORD has delivered them
into the hand of Israel."
13 Jonathan climbed up upon his hands and
upon his feet with his armor bearer behind
him. And they fell before Jonathan. And his
armor bearer was dealing death blows after
him. 14 That first slaughter, which Jonathan and
his armor bearer made, was about twenty men
within about a half-acre field.
15 There was trembling in the camp, in the
field, and among all the people. The garrison
and the raiders also trembled, and the ground
quaked. It was the fear of God.
16 The watchmen of Saul in Gibeah of Ben-
jamin looked, and behold, the multitude melt-
ed away, and they went even here *and there.*
17 Then Saul said to the people that were with
him, "Number now, and see who has gone
from us." And when they had numbered, Jon-
athan nor his armor bearer *were there.*
18 Saul said to Ahijah, "Bring here the ark of
God." For the ark of God was at that time with
the children of Israel. 19 It came to pass, while
Saul talked to the priest, that the noise which
was in the camp of the Philistines went on and
increased. So Saul said to the priest, "Withdraw
your hand."
20 Saul and all the people who were with him
assembled, and they went to the battle. And
every man's sword was against his fellow, so
that there was very great confusion. 21 Even
the Hebrews who were with the Philistines the
days before, who went up with them into the
camp from the country round about, even they
also turned to be with the children of Israel
that were with Saul and Jonathan. 22 Also all of
Israel's fighting men, who had hidden them-
selves in mountains of Ephraim, heard that the
Philistines fled, and even they followed hard
after them in the battle. 23 So the LORD saved
Israel that day, and the battle passed beyond
Beth Aven.

Saul's Rash Oath

24 Now Israel's fighting men were distressed
that day. For Saul had placed the people under
a curse, saying, "Cursed is the man that eats
any food before it is evening, and I have been
avenged on my enemies." So none of the peo-
ple tasted any food.
25 All *the people* of the land came to the
forest, and there was honey on the ground.
26 When the people came into the forest *there
was* flowing honey. But no man put his hand
to his mouth, because the people feared the
oath. 27 But Jonathan had not heard when his
father made the people swear. Therefore he
put forward the end of the rod that was in his
hand, and dipped it in the honeycomb. Then
he put his hand to his mouth, and his eyes
were brightened. 28 Then one of the people
answered, and said, "Your father surely made
the people swear, saying, 'Cursed is the man
that eats any food this day.' " And the people
were weary.
29 Then said Jonathan, "My father has trou-
bled the land. See how my eyes have bright-
ened, because I tasted a little of this honey.
30 How much more, if the people had surely
eaten freely today of the spoil of their enemies
which they found? But now the defeat of the
Philistines has not been great."
31 And they struck the Philistines that day
from Mikmash to Aijalon, and the people
were very weary. 32 The people rushed upon
the spoil; they took sheep, oxen, and calves
and slew them on the ground. And the people
ate *them* with the blood. 33 Then they reported
to Saul, saying, "Look, the people are sinning
against the LORD by eating the blood."
And he said, "You have dealt faithlessly.
Roll a great stone to me this day." 34 Saul said,
"Disperse yourselves among the people, and
say to them, 'Bring to me here every man his
ox or sheep. And slaughter them here, and eat.
But you shall not sin against the LORD by eating
with the blood.' "
And all the people brought every man his
ox with him that night, and slew *them* there.
35 And Saul built an altar to the LORD. It was the
first altar that he built to the LORD.
36 Saul said, "Let us go down after the Phi-
listines by night and plunder them until the
morning light. And let us not leave a man of
them."
And they said, "Do whatever seems good to
you."

14:8 Jdg 7:9–14
14:10 Ge 24:14
14:11 1Sa 13:6
14:12 1Sa 17:43–44
14:15 1Sa 13:17
14:19 Nu 27:21
14:20 Jdg 7:22
14:21 1Sa 29:4
14:22 1Sa 13:6

....

14:23 Ex 14:30
14:24 Jos 6:26
14:27 1Sa 30:12
14:29 1Ki 18:18
14:31 Jos 10:12
14:32 Lev 3:17
14:35 1Sa 7:17

Then the priest said, "Let us draw near here to God."

37 Saul asked of God, "Shall I go down after the Philistines? Will You deliver them into the hand of Israel?" But He did not answer him that day.

38 Saul said, "Come here, all you leaders of the people, and observe and see how this sin has come about this day. 39 For, as the LORD lives, who saves Israel, even if it is in Jonathan my son, he will surely die." But there was not one who answered him from among all the people.

40 Then he said to all Israel, "You will be on one side, and I and Jonathan my son will be on the other side."

And the people said to Saul, "Do what seems good to you."

41 Therefore Saul said to the LORD, the God of Israel, "Give a perfect lot." And Saul and Jonathan were taken, but the people escaped. 42 Saul said, "Cast lots between me and Jonathan my son." And Jonathan was taken.

43 Then Saul said to Jonathan, "Tell me what you have done."

And Jonathan told him, and said, "I indeed tasted a little honey with the end of the staff that was in my hand. Here I am. I must die."

44 Saul said, "May God do so *to me* and more also, for you will surely die, Jonathan."

45 The people said to Saul, "Will Jonathan die, who has worked this great salvation in Israel? God forbid. As the LORD lives, there will not one hair of his head fall to the ground. For he has worked with God this day." So the people rescued Jonathan, and he did not die.

46 Then Saul went up from following the Philistines, and the Philistines went to their own place.

47 So Saul took the kingdom over Israel and fought against all his enemies on every side, against Moab, and against the Ammonites, against Edom and against the kings of Zobah, and against the Philistines. Whatever place he turned himself, he defeated *them.* 48 He gathered an army, and struck the Amalekites, and delivered Israel out of the hand of its plunderers.

Saul's Family

49 Now the sons of Saul were Jonathan, Ishvi, and Malki-Shua. And the names of his two daughters were Merab, the firstborn, and Michal, the youngest. 50 And the name of the wife of Saul was Ahinoam, the daughter of Ahimaaz. And the name of the captain of his army was Abner, the son of Ner, the uncle of Saul. 51 Kish was the father of Saul, and Ner the father of Abner was the son of Abiel.

14:37 1Sa 28:6
14:38 1Sa 10:19–20
14:39 1Sa 14:44
14:41 Ac 1:24
14:43 Jos 7:19
14:44 Ru 1:17
14:45 2Sa 14:11
14:47 2Sa 10:6
14:49 1Sa 31:2
14:50 2Sa 2:8
14:51 1Sa 9:1

14:52 1Sa 8:11
15:1 1Sa 9:16
15:2 Dt 25:17–19
15:3 Nu 24:20
15:4 Jos 15:24
15:6 Jdg 1:16
15:7 Ge 16:7
15:8 1Sa 30:1
15:9 1Sa 15:15
15:11 Ge 6:6
15:12 Jos 15:55

52 There was strong war against the Philistines all the days of Saul, and when Saul saw any strong man, or any valiant man, he took him into his service.

The LORD Rejects Saul

15 Samuel said to Saul, "The LORD sent me to anoint you to be king over His people, over Israel. Now therefore listen to the voice of the words of the LORD. 2 Thus says the LORD of Hosts, 'I remember what Amalek did to Israel, how he laid wait for him in the way, when he came up from Egypt. 3 Now go and strike Amalek, and utterly destroy all that they have, and do not have compassion on them but put to death both man and woman, child and infant, ox and sheep, camel and donkey.' "

I need to be patient and at the same time ready to jump (1Sa 15:1–3).

4 So Saul summoned the people together, and numbered them in Telaim, two hundred thousand foot soldiers and ten thousand men of Judah. 5 Then Saul came to the city of Amalek and laid an ambush in the valley. 6 Saul said to the Kenites, "Go, depart, go down from among the Amalekites, lest I destroy you with them. For you showed kindness to all the children of Israel when they came up out of Egypt." So the Kenites departed from among the Amalekites.

7 Then Saul struck the Amalekites from Havilah until you come to Shur, which is near Egypt. 8 He took Agag the king of the Amalekites alive and utterly destroyed all the people with the edge of the sword. 9 But Saul and the people spared Agag, and the best of the sheep, oxen, fatlings, and lambs. And of all that was good, they were not willing to utterly destroy them. But everything that was despised and weak, that they completely destroyed.

10 Then came the word of the LORD to Samuel, saying, 11 "I regret that I have set up Saul to be king because he has turned back from following Me, and he has not carried out My words." And it grieved Samuel, and he cried to the LORD all night.

12 When Samuel rose early to meet Saul in the morning, it was told Samuel, saying, "Saul came to Carmel and set himself up a monument. Then he turned and has passed on down to Gilgal."

13 Samuel came to Saul. And Saul said to him, "Blessed are you of the LORD. I have carried out the word of the LORD."

14 Samuel said, "Then what is the sound of this flock of sheep in my ears? And the sound of the cattle which I am hearing?"

GROWING AS A SPIRITED WOMAN

You Are Not What They See

For the LORD sees not as man sees. For man looks on the outward appearance, but the LORD looks on the heart.

—1 SAMUEL 16:7

Young women make the mistake of putting their trust in their face or form while neglecting their incorruptible assets. We all know the verse in 1 Peter:

Do not let your adorning be the outward adorning of braiding the hair, wearing gold, or putting on fine clothing. But let it be the hidden nature of the heart, that which is not corruptible, even the ornament of a gentle and quiet spirit, which is very precious in the sight of God.

—1 PETER 3:3–4

God admonishes us to not allow our adornment to be merely outward or superficial. He is not telling us to not adorn ourselves, but that the emphasis of our adornment should be on the inside, not the outside. God is not advocating the neglect of our hair, the wearing of rags, or the absence of jewelry.

Remember, God's focus is not on the outward appearance; ours is. He doesn't judge the way we do. He judges not what is seen but the unseen condition of the heart. He warns us not to spend ourselves adorning what will not count for eternity. He wants us to adorn our hearts with His unfading, quiet, and gentle beauty. It doesn't age, it can't be stolen, and it doesn't turn gray.

Because God's perspective is eternity, He is letting us in on His secret beauty prescription. It is an intimate beauty, one reserved for the eyes of God. It is a kind of beauty others may not notice. But God does.

When you have that inner peace and rest, the world will notice it more than your newest designer outfit, hair color, or jewelry. Those in the world have those things, but what they don't have is peace, "which is very precious in the sight of God" (1Pe 3:4).

Those in the world have a confused standard for value and worth. They drape themselves to hide their emptiness while we purify ourselves to gain transparency. They hide while we shine. Unfortunately we have allowed the marketing of the world's illusions to influence our outward projections and veil our inward reflection.

1. How often are you intimidated by what you see outwardly in others?

2. What intimidates you the most about other women (weight, beauty, career, marital status, etc.)?

3. Do you draw your confidence from the outward or the inward aspect of who you are?

4. Which do you spend more time and thought on?

Action Step

Take a step today and make a commitment to God that you will stop judging others. Pray this prayer:

Father, I *repent of allowing outward appearances to affect my perceptions and relationships with others. Forgive me for comparisons and competition. You never compare us with others. Remove the cultural influences that distort my vision. In the days ahead, give me eyes to see others the way that You see them. Amen.*

Lisa Bevere

15 And Saul said, "They have brought them from the Amalekites. For the people spared the best of the sheep and oxen, to sacrifice to the LORD your God, and the rest we have utterly destroyed."

16 Then Samuel said to Saul, "Stop, and I will tell you what the LORD spoke to me this night."

And he said to him, "Speak."

17 Samuel said, "When you were little in your own sight, were you not made the head of the tribes of Israel, and the LORD anointed you king over Israel? 18 And the LORD sent you on a journey, and said, 'Go and utterly destroy the sinners, the Amalekites, and fight against them until they are destroyed.' 19 Why then did you not obey the voice of the LORD? And why did you rush upon the spoil and do evil in the sight of the LORD?"

20 And Saul said to Samuel, "I have obeyed the voice of the LORD. And I have followed in the way which the LORD sent me, and have brought Agag the king of Amalek, and have utterly destroyed the Amalekites. 21 But the people took from the plunder sheep and oxen, the first fruits of the banned things to sacrifice to the LORD your God in Gilgal."

22 Samuel said,

"Does the LORD delight in burnt offerings
and sacrifices
as much as in obeying the voice of the
LORD?
Obedience is better than sacrifice,
a listening ear than the fat of rams.
23 For rebellion is as the sin of witchcraft,
and stubbornness is as iniquity and
idolatry.
Because you have rejected the word of the
LORD,
He has also rejected you from being
king."

24 Saul said to Samuel, "I have sinned. For I have transgressed the commandment of the LORD, and your words, because I feared the people, and obeyed their voice. 25 Now therefore, please pardon my sin and return with me, that I may worship the LORD."

26 Samuel said to Saul, "I will not return with you. For you have rejected the word of the LORD, and the LORD has rejected you from being king over Israel."

27 As Samuel turned about to go, he seized the edge of his robe and it tore. 28 Samuel said to him, "The LORD has torn the kingdom of Israel from you this day, and has given it to a neighbor of yours who is better than you. 29 Also the Strength of Israel will not lie nor repent. For He is not a man, that He should repent."

30 Then he said, "I have sinned, yet please honor me before the elders of my people, and before Israel, and turn back with me, that I may worship the LORD your God." 31 So Samuel turned back after Saul, and Saul worshipped the LORD.

32 Then Samuel said, "Bring me Agag the king of the Amalekites."

And Agag came to him reluctantly. But Agag said, "Surely the bitterness of death is past."

33 Samuel said,

"As your sword has made women childless,
so will your mother be childless among
women."

And Samuel hacked Agag in pieces before the LORD in Gilgal.

34 Then Samuel went to Ramah, and Saul went up to his house to Gibeah of Saul. 35 Now Samuel did not see Saul up to the day of his death. But Samuel mourned for Saul and the LORD regretted that he had made Saul king over Israel.

Samuel Anoints David as King

16 The LORD said to Samuel, "How long will you mourn for Saul, since I have rejected him from ruling over Israel? Fill your horn with oil and go. I will send you to Jesse the Bethlehemite, for I have chosen a king for Myself *from* among his sons."

2 Samuel said, "How can I go? If Saul hears it, he will kill me."

And the LORD said, "Take a heifer with you and say, 'I have come to sacrifice to the LORD.' 3 Call Jesse to the sacrifice, and I will show you what you will do. And you will anoint for Me *him* whom I tell to you."

4 Samuel did that which the LORD spoke, and came to Bethlehem. The elders of the town trembled at his coming, and said, "Do you come in peace?"

5 And he said, "I have come in peace to sacrifice to the LORD. Consecrate yourselves, and come with me to the sacrifice." And he consecrated Jesse and his sons and called them to the sacrifice.

6 When they came, he looked on Eliab, and said, "Surely the anointed of the LORD is before Him."

7 But the LORD said to Samuel, "Do not look on his appearance or on the height of his stature, because I have rejected him. For the LORD sees not as man sees. For man looks on the outward appearance, but the LORD looks on the heart."

8 Then Jesse called Abinadab, and made him pass before Samuel. And he said, "Neither has the LORD chosen this *one*." 9 Then Jesse made Shammah to pass by. And he said, "Neither has the LORD chosen this *one*." 10 So Jesse

15:15 1Sa 15:9
15:17 1Sa 9:21
15:19 1Sa 14:32
15:20 1Sa 15:13
15:21 1Sa 15:15
15:22 Hos 6:6
15:23 1Sa 13:14
15:24 2Sa 12:13
15:25 Ex 10:17
15:26 1Sa 13:14
15:28 1Sa 28:17–18
15:29 Nu 23:19
15:30 Jn 5:44
15:33 Jdg 1:7
15:34 1Sa 11:4
15:35 1Sa 15:11
16:1 1Sa 15:23
16:2 1Sa 9:12
16:3 1Sa 9:16
16:4 1Ki 2:13
16:5 Ex 19:10
16:6 1Sa 17:13
16:7 1Ki 8:39
16:8 1Sa 17:13
16:9 1Sa 17:13

made seven of his sons pass before Samuel.
And Samuel said to Jesse, “The LORD has not
chosen these.” 11 Samuel said to Jesse, “Are
these all your young men?”
And he said, “There remains yet the youn-
gest, and *there* he is shepherding the flock.”
Then Samuel said to Jesse, “Send and bring
him, for we will not sit down until he comes
here.”
12 So he sent and brought him in. Now he
was ruddy with beautiful eyes and a good ap-
pearance.
And the LORD said, “Arise, anoint him, for
this is he.”
13 Then Samuel took the horn of oil, and
anointed him in the midst of his brothers.
And the Spirit of the LORD came on David from
that day forward. So Samuel arose and went
to Ramah.

David Serves Saul

14 Now the Spirit of the LORD departed from
Saul and an evil spirit from the LORD terrified
him.
15 So the servants of Saul said to him, “See, an
evil spirit from God troubles you. 16 Let our lord
now tell your servants, who are before you,
that they might seek out a man experienced
in playing the lyre. And it will come to pass,
when the evil spirit from God is on you, that he
will play with his hand, and you will be well.”
17 Saul said to his servants, “Find me now a
man that can play well, and bring him to me.”
18 Then one from the servants answered, and
said, “I have seen a son of Jesse the Bethle-
hemite, who is experienced in playing music,
a mighty man of valor, a man of battle, and
skillful in words, even a man of fine appear-
ance. And the LORD is with him.”
19 Therefore Saul sent messengers to Jesse,
and said, “Send me David your son, who is
with the sheep.” 20 Jesse took a donkey laden
with bread, a bottle of wine, and a young goat
and he sent them with his son David to Saul.
21 David came to Saul, and stood before him.
And Saul loved him greatly and he became
his armor bearer. 22 Saul sent to Jesse, saying,
“Let David stand before me, for he has found
favor in my sight.”

> I bind and rebuke every Goliath that would challenge me in the valley (1Sa 17:1–4).

23 It happened that when the evil spirit from
God came on Saul, David would take the lyre in
his hand and play. So Saul was refreshed and
was well, and the evil spirit departed from him.

16:12 1Sa 9:17
16:13 1Sa 10:1
16:14 Jdg 9:23
16:16 2Ki 3:15
16:18 1Sa 3:19
16:20 1Sa 10:27
16:21 Ge 41:46

17:1 Jos 15:35
17:2 1Sa 21:9
17:4 Jos 11:22

SPIRITLED WOMAN

COUNSEL FROM THE SPIRIT BASICS

Opportunities for Miracles

King David was no stranger to opposition. First Samuel 17 recounts the story of a young David being sent by his father to take supplies to his brothers. When he arrived, he witnessed Goliath’s taunts. The giant would come out and challenge the Israelites to send a man out to fight him, saying the Philistines would become Israel’s slaves if he lost but that Israel would have to become the Philistines’ slaves if he won. Full of faith in the Lord who had always proven Himself faithful and carrying God’s promise spoken through Samuel in his heart, David had a fresh and hope-filled view of the situation the army was facing. God is looking for this response—a new breed that sees challenges as opportunities for miracles (1Sa 17:20–27).

David saw the challenge that was causing Israel to tremble in fear as a glorious blessing from God. He had a righteous confidence based on God’s covenant with Israel that this was designed to work out for the nation’s good. God is for us, so who can be against us?

Katherine Ruonala

David and Goliath

17 Now the Philistines gathered their
armies for battle, and were gathered
at Sokoh, which belongs to Judah. And they
camped between Sokoh and Azekah in Ephes
Dammim. 2 Saul and Israel’s fighting men
were gathered, and they camped in the Valley
of Elah. And they drew up in battle order to
meet the Philistines. 3 Now the Philistines were
standing at *the base of* the mountain on the one
side, and Israel was standing at *the base of* the
mountain on the other side, and the valley was
between them.
4 There went out a champion from the camp
of the Philistines, Goliath was his name,
from Gath, whose height was six cubits and
a span.[1] 5 He had a helmet of bronze on his
head, and he was armed with a coat of mail.

[1] 4 About 9 feet 9 inches, or 3 meters.

SPIRITLED WOMAN

COUNSEL FROM THE SPIRIT BASICS

An Attack on David's Identity

Eliab, David's older brother, seemed to take offense at David's faith. He began to ridicule his little brother and accuse him of less-than-pure motives (1Sa 17:28).

It can be so hard when accusations are unfairly made against your heart. For prophetic people, who are generally super-sensitive anyway, this can be deeply painful. But the pain is significantly amplified when the attacks come from those you would expect to support you, such as family and those who are older in the faith. David's accuser was his own older brother, and the venom in his brother's words was obviously meant to intimidate, humiliate, and shut David down.

Eliab's attack was on David's identity. The attack was trying to link David's qualifications to his circumstances. It was as if Eliab were saying, "You are a nobody; you aren't part of the formal army, and you don't even have a uniform. All you do is look after a few sheep! How dare you come here and make us seem cowardly with your faith talk."

In this day of acceleration and awakening, a new breed is coming forth with radical faith based on the knowledge that God really is with them and for them. Perfect love that casts out fear is birthing a faith-filled, fearless generation that will do great exploits, miracles, signs, and wonders.

Katherine Ruonala

Now the weight of the bronze coat was five thousand shekels.[1] 6 He had greaves of bronze on his legs and a bronze javelin between his shoulders. 7 The staff of his spear was like a weaver's beam. His iron spearhead weighed six hundred shekels.[2] And a shield-bearer was walking before him.

8 He stood and called out to the ranks of Israel, "Why have you come out to line up for battle? Am not I the Philistine, and you the servants of Saul? Choose for yourselves a man and let him come down to me. 9 If he is able to fight with me and to strike me down, then we will be your servants. But if I prevail against him and strike him down, then you will be our servants and will serve us." 10 The Philistine said, "I defy the battle lines of Israel this day. Give me a man, and let us fight together." 11 When Saul and all Israel heard these words of the Philistine, they were filled with terror and were greatly afraid.

12 Now David was the son of that Ephrathite of Bethlehem in Judah whose name was Jesse, who had eight sons. And the man was old in the days of Saul *and* advanced in years. 13 The three eldest sons of Jesse went and followed Saul to the battle. And the names of his three sons that went to the battle were Eliab the firstborn, and next to him Abinadab, and the third was Shammah. 14 As for David, he was the youngest. The three eldest followed Saul, 15 but David would go back and forth from Saul to shepherd his father's flock in Bethlehem.

16 The Philistine stepped forward morning and evening and took his stand *daily* for forty days.

17 Then Jesse said to David his son, "Take now for your brothers an ephah[3] of this parched grain and these ten loaves and run to the camp to your brothers. 18 Carry these ten cheeses to the captain of their thousand, and look into your brothers' health, and bring back news of them." 19 Now Saul, and they, and all Israel's fighting men were in the Valley of Elah fighting with the Philistines.

20 So David rose up early in the morning and left the flock with a keeper. And he carried away *the food* and went as Jesse had commanded him. And when he came to the encampment, the army was going out to the battle line, and they shouted a war cry. 21 And Israel and the Philistines ordered themselves in battle lines, army against army. 22 David left his things with the keeper of the equipment, and he ran to the battle line. And he went and greeted his brothers. 23 As he was speaking with them, the champion, Goliath, the Philistine from Gath, was going up from the battle line of the Philistines. And he spoke these same words and David heard them. 24 When all Israel's fighting men saw the man, they fled from him, and were very afraid.

25 The men of Israel said, "Have you seen this man who has come up? Surely he has come up to defy Israel, and it will be that the man who kills him, the king will enrich him with great riches, will give him his daughter, and

17:6 1Sa 17:45
17:7 2Sa 21:19
17:8 1Sa 8:17
17:9 1Sa 11:1
17:10 1Sa 17:45
17:12 Ge 35:19
17:13 1Ch 2:13
17:14 1Sa 16:11
17:15 1Sa 16:11
17:17 1Sa 25:18
17:18 Ge 37:14
17:20 1Sa 26:5
17:25 Jos 15:16

[1] *5* About 125 pounds, or 58 kilograms. [2] *7* About 15 pounds, or 6.9 kilograms. [3] *17* Likely about 36 pounds, or 16 kilograms.

will make his father's house exempt *from taxes*
in Israel."
26 David spoke to the men that stood by him,
saying, "What will be done for the man that
kills this Philistine and takes away *this* re-
proach from Israel? For who is this uncircum-
cised Philistine that he should defy the armies
of the living God?"
27 And the people answered him in the same
way, saying, "So will it be done to the man
who kills him."
28 Eliab his eldest brother heard when he
spoke to the men. And Eliab's anger was kin-
dled against David, and he said, "Why have
you come down here? And with whom have
you left those few sheep in the wilderness? I
know your pride and the evil of your heart.
For you have come down that you might see
the battle."
29 David said, "What have I done now? Was
it not *only* a word?" 30 And he turned from him
toward another and spoke in the same way.
And the people answered him again as at the
first. 31 When the words which David spoke
were heard, they reported them to Saul and
he sent for him.
32 David said to Saul, "Let no man's heart fail
because of him. Your servant will go and fight
with this Philistine."
33 Saul said to David, "You are not able to go
against this Philistine to fight with him. For
you are but a youth, and he has been a man
of war from his youth."
34 David said to Saul, "Your servant was a
shepherd for my father's flock, and the lion
came and the bear, and took a lamb out of the
flock. 35 And I went out after him, and struck
him, and delivered it out of his mouth. And
when he arose against me, I took hold of
his beard, struck him, and killed him. 36 Your
servant slew both the lion and the bear. And
this uncircumcised Philistine will be as one of
them, because he has reviled the armies of
the living God." 37 David said, "The LORD who
delivered me out of the paw of the lion and
out of the paw of the bear, He will deliver me
out of the hand of this Philistine."
And Saul said to David, "Go, and the LORD
be with you."
38 Saul clothed David with his armor. And
he put a helmet of bronze on his head. He
also clothed him with a coat of mail. 39 David
secured his sword to his armor and tried to
walk, but he was not used to it, for he had not
tested *them*.
And David said to Saul, "I cannot walk with
these, for I have not tested *them*." So David
took them off. 40 He took his staff in his hand
and chose for himself five smooth stones out

17:26 Dt 5:26
17:28 Ge 37:4
17:30 1Sa 17:26–27
17:32 1Sa 16:18
17:33 Nu 13:31
17:35 Am 3:12
17:37 1Sa 20:13
17:40 Jdg 20:16
....
17:42 1Sa 16:12
17:43 1Sa 24:14
17:44 1Ki 20:10–11
17:45 2Ch 32:8

SPIRITLED WOMAN

COUNSEL FROM THE SPIRIT BASICS

Attacking David's Heart

One of the attacks Eliab, David's brother, made against him was an attack against his heart and motives (1Sa 17:28). This can be a hard thing to handle. Interestingly, David's brother Eliab was passed over by Samuel because the Lord said He looked on the heart. Wounded people who don't receive healing wound others. God loved David's heart, and now David had the opportunity to choose whom he would believe—God or his brother.

I love David's response to this attack:

> David said, "What have I done now? Was it not only a word?" And he turned from him toward another and spoke in the same way. And the people answered him again as at the first.
>
> —1 SAMUEL 17:29–30

Instead of being drawn into a fistfight with his brother or into a retaliatory war of words with him, David responded by focusing on what was important: "Is there not a cause?" Too often we can be caught up in the wrong fight. We need to remember what the call and the cause are and refuse to be distracted by the enemy's taunts.

Katherine Ruonala

of the brook. And he put them in his shep-
herd's bag, even in a pouch. And his sling
was in his hand. Then he drew near to the
Philistine.
41 The Philistine came walking and drew
near to David, and the man bearing the shield
went before him. 42 When the Philistine looked
and saw David, he despised him. For he was
a youth and ruddy with a handsome appear-
ance. 43 The Philistine said to David, "Am I a
dog, that you come to me with sticks?" Then
the Philistine cursed David by his gods. 44 The
Philistine said to David, "Come to me, and I
will give your flesh to the birds of the heavens
and to the beasts of the field."
45 Then David said to the Philistine, "You
come to me with a sword, a spear, and a shield,
but I come to you in the name of the LORD of

Hosts, the God of the armies of Israel, whom
you have reviled. 46 This day will the LORD de-
liver you into my hand. And I will strike you
down and cut off your head. Then I will give
the corpses of the Philistine camp this day to
the birds of the air and to the beasts of the
earth so that all the earth may know that there
is a God in Israel. 47 And then all this assembly
will know that it is not by sword and spear that
the LORD saves. For the battle belongs to the
LORD, and He will give you into our hands."

48 When the Philistine arose and came near
to meet David, David hurried and ran toward
the battle line to meet the Philistine. 49 David
put his hand in his bag and took from there a
stone. And he slung it and struck the Philistine
in his forehead. Therefore the stone sunk into
his forehead and he fell upon his face to the
ground.

50 So David prevailed over the Philistine with
a sling and with a stone. And he struck down
the Philistine and slew him, but there was no
sword in the hand of David.

51 Therefore David ran and stood over the
Philistine. Then he took his sword and drew it
from out of its sheath, and he finished him off
and he cut off his head with it.

> I spoil the tents of the enemy in the name of Jesus (1Sa 17:53).

When the Philistines saw their champion
was dead, they fled. 52 And the fighting men of
Israel and Judah arose and shouted. And they
pursued the Philistines from the entrance of
the Valley of Elah as far as the gates of Ekron.
So the Philistine dead lay slain on the road to
Shaaraim as far as Gath and Ekron. 53 Then the
children of Israel returned from chasing after
the Philistines and they plundered their tents.

54 David took the head of the Philistine and
brought it to Jerusalem, but he put his armor
in his tent.

55 When Saul saw David going out against the
Philistine, he said to Abner, the commander of
the army, "Whose son is this youth, Abner?"

And Abner said, "As your soul lives, O king,
I do not know."

56 The king said, "Inquire whose son the
young man is."

57 So when David returned from slaying the
Philistine, Abner took him and brought him
before Saul with the Philistine's head in his
hand.

58 Saul said to him, "Whose son are you,
young man?"

And David answered, "I am the son of your
servant, Jesse the Bethlehemite."

17:46 Dt 28:26
17:47 Hos 1:7
17:51 1Sa 21:9
17:52 Jos 15:11
17:55 1Sa 16:21–22
17:58 1Sa 17:12

18:1 2Sa 1:26
18:2 1Sa 17:15
18:4 Ge 41:42
18:6 Ex 15:20
18:7 1Sa 21:11
18:8 1Sa 15:28
18:10 1Sa 19:9
18:11 1Sa 20:33
18:12 1Sa 18:15
18:13 2Sa 5:2
18:14 Ge 39:2–3
18:16 1Sa 18:5
18:17 1Sa 17:25
18:18 1Sa 18:23

Saul Fears David

18 When he had finished speaking to Saul,
the soul of Jonathan was bound to the
soul of David, so that Jonathan loved him as
his own soul. 2 And Saul took him that day and
would not permit him to return home to his fa-
ther's house. 3 Then Jonathan and David made
a covenant because he loved him as his own
soul. 4 So Jonathan stripped himself of the robe
that was on him and gave it to David, even
his garments, his sword, his bow, and his belt.

5 David went out wherever Saul sent him, and
he was successful. So Saul set him over the
men of war, and it was pleasing in the sight
of all the people and also in the sight of the
servants of Saul.

6 When they came home, as David was re-
turning from slaying the Philistine, the women
came out from all cities of Israel to meet King
Saul, singing and dancing, with tambourines,
with joy, and with musical instruments. 7 The
dancing women sang and said,

"Saul has slain his thousands,
and David his ten thousands."

8 Saul became very angry, and this saying
was displeasing to him. Therefore he said,
"They have ascribed to David ten thousands,
but to me they have ascribed thousands. Now
what remains for him to have but the king-
dom?" 9 So Saul was suspicious of David from
that day and forward.

10 It came to pass the following day, that an
evil spirit from God came upon Saul, so that
he raved in the midst of the house. And David
was playing *the lyre*, as at other times. Now
there was a spear in Saul's hand. 11 And Saul
threw the spear. For he said, "I will pin David
to the wall." But David avoided him two times.

12 Saul was afraid of David because the
LORD was with him but had departed from
Saul. 13 Therefore Saul removed him from his
presence and placed him as his captain over
a thousand. And he went out and came in be-
fore the people. 14 David was successful in all
his ways and the LORD was with him. 15 When
Saul saw that he was very successful, he was
afraid of him. 16 Now all Israel and Judah loved
David, because he went out and came in be-
fore them.

David Marries Michal

17 Saul said to David, "Behold my elder
daughter Merab, I will give her to you as *your*
wife. Only be valiant for me, and fight the bat-
tles of the LORD." For Saul said, "Let not my
hand be against him, but let the hand of the
Philistines be against him."

18 But David said to Saul, "Who am I? And
what is my life, or my father's family in Israel,

Only in God's Presence

In my husband's presence I am able to find understanding and companionship. In the presence of my pastor I am able to receive encouragement and prayer. Many people are able to go to a psychiatrist, and they learn to cope with their problems. When they go to their physician, he will diagnose and prescribe medication to help them. If they go to their employer, they will receive training, new skills, and compensation. They also may go to their therapist, and he will give them help for one more day. In a mother's presence you will usually find nurturing and attention. In a friend's presence you'll find support and a listening ear.

But only when you enter into the presence of God will you be able to find and receive healing and restoration for your spirit, soul, and body. Not only that, but you will also find direction, communion, the guidance of the Holy Spirit, understanding and wisdom, provision, forgiveness, and power over all the works of the enemy. We can fill up several pages of the many wonderful things we can receive in God's presence.

I also find it very interesting when I find correction in His presence. The Lord will uncover the idols hidden in our lives as we proceed to enter and tarry in His presence. He also reveals unconfessed sins.

As we learn to walk in obedience, all of the old junk and excess baggage that we carry in our souls begins to come out, and it is replaced with God's love and the fruit of the Spirit.

How awesome to be able to trust the Lord completely and to surrender our lives and our family totally to His care. Only in God's presence are the battles won!

What you put into your heart will come out of your mouth. If you put guilt and negative thoughts into your mind, then they will come out of your mouth as a curse upon your family. If you put love, mercy, and grace into your heart, then love, mercy, and grace will come out of your mouth to bless your family. The choice is yours. David said to the Philistine Goliath:

> And then all this assembly will know that it is not by sword and spear that the LORD saves.
>
> —1 SAMUEL 17:47

Can you imagine a boy brave enough to fight a Philistine giant who was greatly feared by the Israelite army? What was it that gave a young shepherd the courage to wage war against a Philistine giant? It was his faith in God and his faith that God would deliver the enemy into his hand. The reason David had this type of faith is because he spent time in God's presence.

In His presence you will find peace, and in His Word you will find instruction for every need in your life. You don't have to spend the rest of your life coping and trying to make things work by yourself. Healing and deliverance are for you and all your family. God is able to do the impossible!

Iris Delgado

that I should be son-in-law to the king?" 19 So when it was time that Merab, daughter of Saul, should have been given to David, she was given to Adriel the Meholathite for a wife.

20 Now Michal, daughter of Saul, loved David and they told Saul, and the thing pleased him. 21 Saul said, "I will give her to him that she may be a snare to him, and so that the hand of the Philistines may be against him." Therefore Saul said to David, "For a second time, you may be my son-in-law today."

22 Saul commanded his servants, saying, "Speak to David in secret saying, 'Listen, the king delights in you and all his servants love you. Now therefore become the king's son-in-law.' "

23 So the servants of Saul spoke these words in the ears of David. And David said, "Does it seem to you a light thing to be a king's son-in-law, seeing that I am a poor man, and lightly esteemed?"

24 And the servants of Saul reported to him saying, "According to these words, David spoke." 25 Saul said, "Thus will you say to David, 'The king does not desire any dowry but a hundred foreskins of the Philistines, to be avenged of the king's enemies.' " But Saul thought to make David fall by the hand of the Philistines.

26 When his servants told David these words, it pleased David well to be the king's son-in-law. Now the days had not expired; 27 therefore David arose and went, he and his men, and killed two hundred men of the Philistines. Then David brought their foreskins and they gave them in full to the king, that he might be the king's son-in-law. And Saul gave him Michal his daughter for a wife.

28 When Saul saw and knew that the LORD was with David, and that Michal, his daughter, loved him, 29 Saul was yet the more afraid of David, and Saul became the enemy of David continually.

30 Then the commanders of the Philistines went out *to make war*. And when they went out David was more successful than all the servants of Saul, so that his name was highly honored.

Saul Tries to Kill David

19 And Saul spoke to Jonathan, his son, and to all his servants, that they should kill David. But Jonathan, Saul's son, delighted very much in David. 2 Jonathan told David, saying, "My father Saul seeks to kill you. Therefore, be on guard in the morning; stay in a secret place and hide yourself. 3 And I will go out and stand beside my father in the field where you are. Then I will speak about you to my father, and what I observe I will report to you."

4 Jonathan spoke positively of David to Saul his father and said to him, "Do not let the king sin against his servant, against David, because he has not sinned against you, and because his deeds have been very good toward you. 5 For he took his life in his hand and struck down the Philistine, and the LORD made a great salvation for all Israel. You saw it and rejoiced. Now why then would you sin against innocent blood, to kill David without cause?"

6 So Saul listened to the voice of Jonathan and Saul vowed, "As the LORD lives, he will not be killed."

7 Jonathan called David, and Jonathan reported to him all these words. Then Jonathan brought David to Saul, and he was in his presence as previously.

8 Then there was war again, and David went out and fought with the Philistines. He slew them with a great slaughter and they fled from him.

9 Now an evil spirit from the LORD was upon Saul as he was sitting in his house with his spear in his hand. And David was playing *the lyre*. 10 Then Saul sought to pin David to the wall with the spear, but he escaped from Saul's presence. He struck the spear into the wall. But David fled and escaped that night.

11 Saul also sent messengers to the house of David, to watch him and to slay him in the morning. But Michal, wife of David, told him, saying, "If you do not save your life tonight, tomorrow you will be dead." 12 So Michal let David down through a window, and he went and fled to safety. 13 Michal took an idol and laid it in the bed, and put a braided goat hair pillow for its head and covered it with clothes.

14 When Saul sent messengers to take David, she said, "He is sick."

15 Saul sent the messengers *again* to see David, saying, "Bring him up to me in the bed, that I may kill him." 16 When the messengers came in, there was the idol in the bed with a goat hair pillow for its head.

17 Saul said to Michal, "Why have you betrayed me and sent away my enemy, so that he escaped?"

And Michal said to Saul, "He said to me, 'Let me go. Why should I kill you?' "

18 Now David fled, and he escaped and came to Samuel at Ramah. And he reported to him all that Saul had done to him. And he and Samuel went and stayed in Naioth. 19 It was told Saul, saying, "David is at Naioth in Ramah." 20 Then Saul sent messengers to take David, but when they saw the company of the prophets prophesying and Samuel taking his

18:19 Jdg 7:22
18:20 1Sa 18:28
18:21 1Sa 18:17
18:25 Ge 34:12
18:27 2Sa 3:14
18:30 1Sa 18:5
19:1 1Sa 18:1
....
19:4 Jer 18:20
19:5 1Sa 11:13
19:7 1Sa 16:21
19:9 1Sa 16:14
19:10 1Sa 20:33
19:12 Jos 2:15
19:13 Ge 31:19
19:14 Jos 2:5
19:17 2Sa 2:22
19:18 1Sa 7:17
19:20 Jn 7:32

stand over them, the Spirit of God came upon
the messengers of Saul and they also proph-
esied. 21 When it was reported to Saul, he sent
other messengers. And they also prophesied.
So Saul sent messengers again a third time,
and they too prophesied. 22 Then he also went
to Ramah and came to the great well that is
in Seku. And he asked and said, "Where are
Samuel and David?"

And one said, "*They are* at Naioth in Ramah.
23 He went there to Naioth in Ramah, and
the Spirit of God came upon him also. And he
went on and he prophesied until he came to
Naioth in Ramah. 24 He stripped off his clothes
and he also prophesied before Samuel. And
he lay down naked all that day and all that
night. Therefore they say, "Is Saul also among
the prophets?"

David and Jonathan

20 David fled from Naioth in Ramah, and
came and said before Jonathan, "What
have I done? What is my offense? And what
is my sin before your father, that he seeks my
life?"

2 And he said to him, "Far from it! You shall
not die. Look, my father does nothing either
great or small that he does not reveal to me.
Why would my father hide this thing from me?
It is not so."

3 David vowed again and said, "Your father
certainly knows that I have found favor in your
sight. And he says, 'Do not let Jonathan know
this, lest he be distressed.' However, as the
LORD lives and as your soul lives, *there is* but a
step between me and death."

4 Jonathan said to David, "Whatever you say,
I will do it for you."

5 David said to Jonathan, "Tomorrow is the
New Moon, and I should not fail to sit with
the king to eat. But let me go that I may hide
myself in the field until the evening of the third
day. 6 If your father misses me at all, then say,
'David asked for leave from me that he might
run to Bethlehem his city, for there is a yearly
sacrifice there for all the family.' 7 If he says,
'Good,' it will be well for your servant. But if
he gets angry, know that evil is determined by
him. 8 Therefore deal kindly with your servant,
for you have brought your servant into a cov-
enant of the LORD with you. But if there is *any*
guilt in me, kill me yourself. For why should
you bring me to your father?"

9 Then Jonathan said, "Far be it from you.
For if I indeed knew that my father had deter-
mined evil against you, would I not tell it you?"

10 David said to Jonathan, "Who will tell me?
Or what if your father answers you roughly?"

11 So Jonathan said to David, "Come, let us go
out into the field." And the two of them went
out to the field.

12 Then Jonathan said to David, "The LORD
God of Israel *is witness*. When I have sounded
out my father about this time tomorrow, *or by*
the third day, and if he is favorable toward
David, then will I not send and reveal it to you?
13 May the LORD do so to Jonathan and much
more. If it pleases my father to do you evil,
then I will reveal it you and send you away
that you may go in peace. And may the LORD
be with you as He has been with my father.
14 And if I live, not only will you show me the
kindness of the LORD, that I shall not die, 15 but
you will not cut off your faithfulness from my
house forever, even when the LORD has cut off
each one of the enemies of David from the
face of the earth."

16 So Jonathan made a covenant with the
house of David *saying*, "May the LORD require
it at the hand of the enemies of David." 17 Jon-
athan made David swear again, because he
loved him. For he loved him as he loved his
own soul.

18 Then Jonathan said to David, "Tomorrow
is the New Moon, and you will be missed, be-
cause your seat will be empty. 19 When you
have stayed three days, you will surely go
down and come to the place where you hid
yourself on the day *this* happened, and wait
there beside the stone Ezel. 20 And I will shoot
three arrows to its side, as though I shot at a
target. 21 Then I will send a boy, saying, 'Go,
find the arrows.' If I expressly say to the boy,
'See, the arrows are on this side of you, take
them,' then come, for it will be safe for you.
And as the LORD lives, it is nothing *of concern*.
22 But if I say to the young man, 'See, the ar-
rows are beyond you,' go, for the LORD has sent
you away. 23 As for the matter *upon* which you
and I have spoken, the LORD is between you
and me forever."

24 So David hid himself in the field. And when
the New Moon appeared, the king sat down
over food to eat. 25 Now the king sat on his seat,
as at other times, even on a seat by the wall.
Then Jonathan arose and Abner sat by Saul's
side, but David's place was empty. 26 Neverthe-
less Saul did not say anything that day. For he
thought, "Something has happened. He is not
clean; surely he is not clean." 27 It happened
on the following day, which was the second
day of the month, that David's place remained
empty. So Saul said to Jonathan his son, "Why
has the son of Jesse not come to eat food either
yesterday or today?"

28 And Jonathan answered Saul, "David ear-
nestly asked leave from me to go to Bethlehem.

19:23 1Sa 10:10
19:24 2Sa 6:20
20:3 Dt 6:13
20:5 Nu 10:10
20:6 1Sa 9:12
20:7 1Sa 25:17
20:8 1Sa 18:3
20:13 Jos 1:5
20:15 2Sa 21:7
20:16 1Sa 25:22
20:17 1Sa 18:1
20:19 1Sa 19:2
20:22 1Sa 20:37
20:23 1Sa 20:14–15
20:25 1Sa 20:18
20:26 Lev 15:5
20:28 1Sa 20:6

29 And he said, 'Please let me go, for our family
has a sacrifice in the city and my brother has
commanded me *to come*. Now, if I have found
favor in your sight, please let me leave and see
my brothers.' This is why he has not come to
the king's table."

30 Then Saul was angry with Jonathan and he
said to him, "You son of a perverse rebellious
woman, do I not know that you are choosing
the son of Jesse to your own shame, and to
the shame of your mother's nakedness? 31 For
as long as the son of Jesse lives on the earth,
neither you nor your kingdom will be estab-
lished. Now, send and bring him to me, for he
is a dead man."

32 Jonathan answered Saul his father and said
to him, "Why should he be killed? What has he
done?" 33 So Saul cast a spear at him to strike
him. Therefore Jonathan knew that his father
was determined to kill David.

34 And Jonathan arose from the table in fierce
anger and did not eat food on the second day
of the month. For he was grieved for David,
because his father had dishonored him.

35 In the morning Jonathan went out to the
field at the time appointed with David, and a
little boy was with him. 36 And he said to his
boy, "Run, find the arrows which I shoot." He
ran, and he shot the arrow over him. 37 When
the boy came to the place of the arrow which
Jonathan had shot, Jonathan called after the
boy and said, "Is not the arrow beyond you?"
38 Then Jonathan cried after the boy, "Hurry
quickly! Do not stay!" And Jonathan's boy
gathered up the arrow and came to his master.
39 But the boy did not know anything. Only Jon-
athan and David knew the matter. 40 Jonathan
gave his weapons to his boy and said to him,
"Go, carry *them* to the city."

41 When the boy had gone, David arose from
the south side *of the stone*, and fell on his face
to the ground, and bowed himself three times.
They kissed one another and wept together,
but David *wept* more.

42 Jonathan said to David, "Go in peace, since
the two of us swore in the name of the LORD,
saying, 'The LORD will be between me and you,
and between my descendants and your de-
scendants forever.' " So he arose and departed,
but Jonathan went into the city.

David at Nob

21 Then David came to Nob to Ahimelek
the priest. And Ahimelek trembled
coming to meet David and said to him, "Why
are you alone and no man is with you?"

2 And David said to Ahimelek the priest, "The
king commanded me a matter and said to me,
'Let no man know anything of the business
which I am sending you and what I have com-
manded you.' But *to* the young men I made
known a certain place *to meet*. 3 Now therefore
what is in your hand? Give me five loaves of
bread in my hand, or whatever can be found."

4 The priest answered David and said, "There
is no common bread at hand. But there is holy
bread, if the young men have indeed been
kept from women."

5 David answered the priest and said to him,
"Indeed women have been kept from us. As
previously, when I went out the vessels of the
young men were holy even *if* it was an or-
dinary journey. How much more then today
will their vessels be holy?" 6 So the priest gave
him holy *bread*. For there was no bread there
but the showbread that was removed from be-
fore the LORD, in order to place hot bread *there*
on the day when it was taken away.

7 Now a certain man of the servants of Saul
was there that day, detained before the LORD.
And his name was Doeg, the Edomite, chief of
the shepherds of Saul.

8 David said to Ahimelek, "Is there not a spear
or a sword here at hand? For neither my sword
nor my weapons did I bring with me, because
the king's business was urgent."

9 The priest said, "The sword of Goliath the
Philistine, whom you struck down in the Valley
of Elah, is here, wrapped in a cloth behind the
ephod. If you will take that, take it. For there is
none other but that here."

And David said, "There is none like it. Give
it me."

David Flees to Gath

10 David arose and fled that day from Saul.
And he went to Achish the king of Gath. 11 The
servants of Achish said to him, "Is this not Da-
vid the king of the land? Did they not sing with
dances for him, saying,

'Saul has slain his thousands,
and David his ten thousands'? "

12 And David took these words to heart and
greatly feared Achish the king of Gath. 13 There-
fore he changed his behavior before them and
pretended to be insane in their hands. And he
scratched on the doors of the gate and let his
spittle run down his beard.

14 Then said Achish to his servants, "You see
the man is acting like a madman. Why then
have you brought him to me? 15 Am I one who
lacks lunatics, that you brought this one to be-
have as a madman in my presence? Will this
man come into my house?"

David Protects His Parents

22 David departed from there and es-
caped to the cave of Adullam. And
when his brothers and all his father's house
heard it, they went down to him there. 2 There

20:30 Pr 21:24
20:32 1Sa 19:5
20:37 1Sa 20:22
20:41 1Sa 18:3
20:42 1Sa 1:17
21:1 1Sa 16:4

21:4 Ex 19:15
21:6 Mt 12:3–4
21:7 1Sa 22:9
21:9 1Sa 17:2
21:11 1Sa 29:5
21:12 Lk 2:19

gathered to him every one that was in distress, and every one in debt, and every one that was discontented. So he became captain over them. Now there were with him about four hundred men.

3 Then David went from there to Mizpah of Moab. And he said to the king of Moab, "Please let my father and my mother come forth and be with you until I know what God will do for me." 4 He brought them before the king of Moab, and they lived with him all the while that David was in the stronghold.

5 The prophet Gad said to David, "Do not remain in the stronghold. Go to the land of Judah." So David went and came to the forest of Hereth.

Saul Kills the Priests of Nob

6 When Saul heard that David and the men who were with him were discovered, Saul was sitting in Gibeah under the tamarisk tree on the hill with his spear in his hand. And all his servants were standing about him. 7 Saul said to his servants that stood about him, "Hear now, Benjamites! Will the son of Jesse give every one of you fields and vineyards? Will he appoint you all as captains of thousands and captains of hundreds? 8 You have all conspired against me, and no one revealed to me that my son made a covenant with the son of Jesse. And not one of you is grieved for me and revealed it to me that my son raised up my servant against me to ambush me as at this day."

9 Then Doeg the Edomite, who was chief over the servants of Saul, answered and said, "I saw the son of Jesse coming to Nob, to Ahimelek the son of Ahitub. 10 And he inquired of the LORD for him and gave him provisions. And he gave him the sword of Goliath the Philistine."

11 So the king sent to summon Ahimelek the priest, the son of Ahitub, and all his father's house, the priests that were in Nob. And they all came to the king. 12 Saul said, "Hear now, son of Ahitub!"

And he answered, "Here I am, my lord."

13 Saul said to him, "Why have you conspired against me, you and the son of Jesse, in that you gave him bread and a sword, and have inquired of God for him, that he should rise against me to ambush *me*, as at this day?"

14 Then Ahimelek answered the king and said, "And who is as faithful among all your servants as David, who is the king's son-in-law, chief of your bodyguard, and is honored in your house? 15 Did I *just* today begin to inquire of God for him? Far be it from me! Let not the king assign any blame to his servant, or to all the house of my father. For your servant has known nothing of all this matter, whether small or great."

16 The king said, "You will surely die, Ahimelek, you and all your father's house."

17 The king said to the guards standing near him, "Turn and kill the priests of the LORD, because their hand is with David. And because they knew that he was fleeing and did not reveal it to me."

But the servants of the king would not put forth their hand to attack the priests of the LORD.

18 The king said to Doeg, "You turn and fall upon the priests." And Doeg the Edomite turned and struck the priests and killed on that day eighty-five men who wore a linen ephod. 19 And Nob, the city of the priests, he struck with the edge of the sword. Both men and women, children and babies, oxen, donkeys, and sheep, *he struck* with the edge of the sword.

David, Protector of the Priestly Line

20 But one of the sons of Ahimelek the son of Ahitub, named Abiathar, escaped and fled after David. 21 Abiathar reported to David that Saul had killed the priests of the LORD. 22 David said to Abiathar, "I knew it that day when Doeg the Edomite was there, that he would surely tell Saul. I have caused the death of all the persons of your father's house. 23 Remain with me. Do not fear. For the one who seeks my life seeks your life, but you are safe with me."

David Saves Keilah

23 Then they told David, "Listen, the Philistines are fighting against Keilah, and they are looting the threshing floors." 2 Therefore David inquired of the LORD, saying, "Shall I go and attack these Philistines?"

And the LORD said to David, "Go and attack the Philistines, and rescue Keilah."

3 The men of David said to him, "We are afraid here in Judah. How much more then, if we go down to Keilah against the armies of the Philistines?"

4 Then David again inquired of the LORD. And the LORD answered him and said, "Arise, go down to Keilah because I am giving the Philistines into your hand." 5 Then David and his men went to Keilah. He fought with the Philistines and carried off their livestock, and he struck them with a great slaughter. So David rescued the inhabitants of Keilah. 6 When Abiathar the son of Ahimelek fled to David at Keilah, he came down with the ephod in his hand.

Saul Pursues David

7 It was reported to Saul that David had come to Keilah. And Saul said, "God has delivered

22:8 1Sa 18:3
22:9 Ps 52:1–9
22:10 Nu 27:21
22:13 1Sa 22:8
22:15 1Sa 25:36
22:17 Ex 1:17
22:19 1Sa 15:3
22:20 1Sa 23:6
22:23 1Ki 2:26
23:1 Jos 15:44
23:2 1Sa 23:4
23:4 Jdg 7:7
23:6 1Sa 22:20

him into my hand. For he is shut in, by en-
tering into a town that has gates and bars."
8 Then Saul summoned all the people together
for war, to go down to Keilah to besiege David
and his men.
9 David found out that Saul was planning evil
against him. So he said to Abiathar the priest,
"Bring the ephod near." 10 And David said, "O
LORD, God of Israel, Your servant has certainly
heard that Saul seeks to come to Keilah, to
destroy the city on account of me. 11 Will the
leaders of Keilah deliver me into his hand? Will
Saul come down, as Your servant has heard? O
LORD, God of Israel, please tell Your servant."
And the LORD said, "He will come down."
12 Then said David, "Will the men of Keilah
deliver me and my men into the hand of Saul?"
And the LORD said, "They will deliver you."
13 So David and his men, which were about
six hundred, arose and left Keilah. And they
went wherever they could go. Now it was told
Saul that David had escaped from Keilah. So
he halted the expedition.
14 And David remained in the wilderness in
strongholds, and dwelled in mountains in the
Wilderness of Ziph. Saul sought him every day,
but God did not give him into his hand.
15 Now David saw that Saul had come out
to seek his life. And David was in the Wilder-
ness of Ziph in Horesh. 16 Jonathan, the son
of Saul, arose and went to David at Horesh.
And he strengthened his hand in God. 17 He
said to him, "Do not fear, for the hand of Saul
my father will not find you. You will be king
over Israel, and I will be next to you. Saul my
father knows this." 18 The two of them made
a covenant before the LORD. And David stayed
in Horesh, but Jonathan went to his house.
19 Then the Ziphites went up to Saul to Gibeah
saying, "Is David not hiding himself with us in
strongholds in Horesh, on the hill of Hakilah,
which is south of Jeshimon? 20 Now, O king,
come down according to all the desire of your
soul to come down. And our part will be to
deliver him into the king's hand."
21 Saul said, "Blessed are you of the LORD.
For you have had compassion on me. 22 Please
go, make sure again. Investigate and see the
place where his foot *rests*, and who has seen
him there. For it has been said to me that he
is very cunning. 23 So look and learn about all
the hiding places where he hides himself. And
come to me with certainty, and I will go with
you. And it will be that if he is in the land,
then I will track him throughout all the clans
of Judah."
24 So they arose and went to Ziph before Saul.
But David and his men were in the Wilder-
ness of Maon, in the desert south of Jeshimon.

23:9 1Sa 30:7
23:12 1Sa 23:20
23:13 1Sa 22:2
23:14 Ps 54:3–4
23:16 Ne 2:18
23:17 1Sa 20:31
23:18 1Sa 18:3
23:19 1Sa 26:1
23:20 1Sa 23:12
23:21 1Sa 22:8
23:24 Jos 15:55
....
23:26 Ps 17:9
23:27 2Ki 19:9
23:29 2Ch 20:2
24:1 1Sa 23:28–29
24:2 1Sa 26:2
24:3 Jdg 3:24
24:5 2Sa 24:10
24:7 Ps 7:4
24:8 1Sa 25:23–24
24:10 1Sa 24:4
24:11 1Sa 26:20

25 Saul and his men went to seek *him*, but they
told David. Therefore he came down to the
Rock, and lived in the Wilderness of Maon.
And when Saul heard *that*, he pursued after
David in the Wilderness of Maon.
26 Saul went on this side of the mountain
and David and his men on that side of the
mountain. And David hurried to get away from
Saul. Now Saul and his men were closing in
on David and his men to capture them. 27 But
a messenger came to Saul saying, "Hurry and
go! For the Philistines have invaded the land."
28 So Saul returned from pursuing after David,
and he went against the Philistines. Therefore
they called that place the Rock of Escape.
29 David then went up from there and lived in
the strongholds of En Gedi.

David Spares Saul's Life

24 When Saul had returned from follow-
ing the Philistines, it was reported to
him, saying, "David is in the Wilderness of En
Gedi." 2 Then Saul took three thousand chosen
men out of all Israel and went to seek David
and his men in front of the rocks of the wild
goats.
3 He came to the sheep pens by the way and
a cave was there. And Saul went in to relieve
himself. Now David and his men were sitting
in the rear of the cave. 4 The men of David
said to him, "This is the day of which the LORD
said to you, 'I am giving your enemy into your
hand. You may do with him as seems good in
your eyes.' " Then David arose and secretly cut
off the corner of Saul's robe.
5 Afterward David's heart troubled him be-
cause he had cut off a corner of Saul's robe.
6 He said to his men, "The LORD forbid that I
should do this thing to my lord, the LORD's
anointed, to stretch out my hand against him.
For he is anointed of the LORD." 7 So David dis-
persed his men by *these* words and did not let
them rise against Saul. And Saul arose from
the cave and went on his way.
8 David arose afterward and went out from
the cave. And he called after Saul saying, "My
lord the king!" And when Saul looked behind
him, David had bowed down with his face to
the ground and paid homage. 9 David said to
Saul, "Why do you listen to the words of men
saying, 'David seeks your harm'? 10 This day
you have seen with your own eyes that the
LORD delivered you today into my hand in the
cave. So that some said to kill you, but *my eye*
had compassion on you. And I said, 'I will not
put forth my hand against my lord, for he is
anointed of the LORD.' 11 See, my father! Look
at the corner of your robe in my hand. Indeed,
I cut off the corner of your robe, but I did not

kill you. Observe and see that there is no evil or
rebellion in my hand. I have not sinned against
you, but you are lying in wait for my life to take
it. 12 The LORD will judge between me and you,
and the LORD will avenge me on you, but my
hand will not be against you. 13 As the proverb
of the ancients says, 'From the wicked comes
forth wickedness,' but my hand will not be
against you.
14 "After whom has the king of Israel come
out? After whom are you pursuing? After a
dead dog? A single flea? 15 May the LORD be
judge, and decide between me and you. And
may He see and plead my case, and deliver me
out of your hand."
16 When David finished speaking these words
to Saul, Saul said, "Is this your voice, my son
David?" And Saul lifted up his voice and wept.
17 And he said to David, "You are more righ-
teous than I. For you have rewarded me with
good, while I have rewarded you with evil.
18 And you have shown today that you have
dealt well with me, when the LORD delivered
me into your hand and you did not kill me.
19 For if a man finds his enemy, will he let him
safely go away? Therefore may the LORD re-
ward you well for what you have done for me
this day. 20 Now, listen, I know that you will
surely be king and that the kingdom of Israel
will be established in your hand. 21 Therefore
swear to me now by the LORD that you will not
cut off my descendants after me and that you
will not destroy my name out of my father's
household."
22 So David swore to Saul and Saul went
home. But David and his men went up to the
stronghold.

Death of Samuel

25 Now Samuel died. And all the chil-
dren of Israel gathered together and
mourned him, and they buried him at his
home in Ramah. Then David arose and went
down to the Wilderness of Paran.

David, Nabal, and Abigail

2 Now there was a man in Maon whose work
was in Carmel. He was a rich man with three
thousand sheep and a thousand goats, and he
was shearing his sheep in Carmel. 3 The man's
name was Nabal and the name of his wife Abi-
gail. She was a woman of good understanding
and beautiful, but the man was harsh and evil
in his actions and he was a Calebite.
4 David heard in the wilderness that Nabal
was shearing his sheep. 5 So David sent out
ten young men, and David said to the young
men, "Go up to Carmel, and go to Nabal and
greet him in my name. 6 And thus you will you
say to him who lives *in prosperity*, 'Peace be to
you and peace to your house, and to all that
you have, peace.
7 " 'I have heard that you have shearers. Now
your shepherds were with us. We did not harm
them nor did they miss anything all the days
they were in Carmel. 8 Ask your young men and
they will tell you. Therefore let *my* young men
find favor in your eyes, for we have come on
a good day. Please give whatever you find at
hand to your servants, and to your son David.' "
9 When David's young men came, they spoke
to Nabal according to all these words in the
name of David, then they waited.
10 And Nabal answered David's servants, and
said, "Who is David? And who is the son of Jes-
se? Today many servants are breaking away
each one from his master. 11 Should I then take
my bread, and my water, and my meat, that
which I have killed for my shearers, and give it
to men whose origins are unknown?"
12 So David's young men turned themselves
around and went back. And they came and
reported to him all these words. 13 David said
to his men, "Each man strap on his sword."
And each man strapped on his sword. David
also put on his sword, and four hundred men
went up after David. But two hundred stayed
with the baggage.
14 Now one of the young men told Abigail,
Nabal's wife, "Listen, David sent messengers
out of the wilderness to bless our master; and
he railed against them. 15 But the men were
very good to us, and we were not harmed, nor
did we miss anything, all the days we went
about with them in the field. 16 They were a
wall to us both by night and day, all the days
we were with them keeping the flocks. 17 Now
therefore know and consider what you will do,
for evil is determined against our master and
against all his household. He is such a worth-
less man that *one* cannot speak to him."
18 Then Abigail hurried and took two hun-
dred loaves, two bottles of wine, five pre-
pared sheep, five measures[1] of roasted grain,
a hundred clusters of raisins, and two hundred
cakes of figs, and she loaded them on donkeys.
19 And she said to her servants, "Go on before
me. See, I will be coming after you." But she
did not tell her husband Nabal.
20 And as she was riding on the donkey and
going down into the cover of the mountain,
David and his men were coming down to meet
her and she met them. 21 Now David had said,
"Surely in vain have I guarded all that this *man*
has in the wilderness, so that nothing was
missed of all that belonged to him. And he
has returned me evil for good. 22 So may God

24:12 Ge 16:5
24:13 Mt 7:16–18
24:14 1Sa 26:20
24:15 1Sa 24:12
24:16 1Sa 26:17
24:17 1Sa 26:21
24:18 1Sa 26:23
24:20 1Sa 23:17
24:21 Ge 21:23
24:22 1Sa 23:29
25:1 Nu 20:29
25:2 Jos 15:55
25:6 1Ch 12:18
25:7 1Sa 25:21
25:8 Est 9:19
25:10 Jdg 9:28
25:11 Jdg 8:6
25:13 1Sa 23:13
25:15 1Sa 25:7
25:16 Job 1:10
25:17 1Sa 20:7
25:18 2Sa 16:1
25:19 Ge 32:20
25:21 Pr 17:13
25:22 1Sa 3:17

[1] *18* Likely about 60 pounds, or 27 kilograms.

do unto the enemies of David and more also,
if by morning I leave *even* one male of all who
belong to him."
23 When Abigail saw David, she hurriedly
got down from the donkey and fell before Da-
vid upon her face. And she bowed herself to
the ground. 24 So she fell at his feet and said,
"Against me alone, my lord, is the guilt. Please
let your handmaid speak in your ears, and hear
the words of your handmaid. 25 Please do not
let my lord set his heart against this worthless
man, against Nabal. For as his name is, so is
he. Nabal is his name and folly is with him.
But I, your handmaid, did not see the young
men of my lord, whom you sent. 26 Now my
lord, as the LORD lives, and as your soul lives,
because the LORD has restrained you from com-
ing in bloodshed and from avenging yourself
with your own hand, now let your enemies,
and those seeking to do evil to my lord, be
as Nabal. 27 Now let this blessing which your
maidservant has brought to my lord be given
to the young men who follow my lord.
28 "Please forgive the transgression of your
handmaid, for the LORD will certainly make my
lord a sure house, because my lord fights the
battles of the LORD, and evil will not be found
in you all your days. 29 Even *if* a man rises to
pursue you and to seek your life, the life of my
lord will be bound in the bundle of the living
with the LORD your God. But the lives of your
enemies He will sling out, as from the hollow
of a sling. 30 It will be, when the LORD does for
my lord according to all the good that He has
spoken concerning you and has appointed you
ruler over Israel, 31 that this will be no grief to
you, nor an offense of heart to my lord, either
that you have shed blood without cause, or
that my lord has avenged himself. But when
the LORD has dealt well with my lord, then re-
member your handmaid."
32 David said to Abigail, "Blessed be the LORD,
God of Israel, who sent you this day to meet
me. 33 And blessed is your discretion, and
blessed are you who have kept me this day
from coming to shed blood and from avenging
myself with my own hand. 34 For as the LORD,
the God of Israel lives, who has restrained me
from injuring you, if you had not hurried to
come and meet me, surely there would not
have been left *even* one male to Nabal by the
morning light."
35 So David received from her hand what she
had brought him and said to her, "Go up in
peace to your house. See, I have obeyed your
voice, and have granted your request."
36 Abigail came to Nabal, and he was feasting
in his house, like the feast of a king. And Na-
bal's heart was merry within him, for he was

25:23 1Sa 20:41
25:24 2Sa 14:9
25:25 1Sa 25:17
25:26 2Sa 18:32
25:27 Ge 33:11
25:28 1Sa 18:17
25:29 Jer 10:18
25:30 1Sa 13:14
25:31 Ge 40:14
25:32 Lk 1:68
25:33 1Sa 25:26
25:35 Ge 19:21
25:36 1Sa 25:19
....
25:38 1Sa 26:10
25:39 1Sa 25:26
25:41 Ru 2:10
25:42 Ge 24:61–67
25:43 Jos 15:56
26:1 1Sa 23:19
26:2 1Sa 24:2
26:5 1Sa 17:55
26:6 Jdg 7:10–11

very drunk. Therefore she told him nothing
until the morning light. 37 But in the morning
when the wine was gone out of Nabal, his
wife told him these things. And his heart died
within him, and he became as a stone. 38 And
about ten days after that, the LORD struck Nabal
and he died.
39 When David heard that Nabal was dead, he
said, "Blessed is the LORD, who has defended
the cause of my reproach from the hand of
Nabal, and has kept His servant from evil. For
the LORD has returned the wickedness of Nabal
upon his own head."
And David sent and spoke with Abigail, to
take her as his wife. 40 When the servants of
David came to Abigail at Carmel, they spoke to
her, saying, "David has sent us to you to take
you as his wife."
41 She arose, and bowed herself on her face
to the ground, and said, "Here is your hand-
maid, a servant to wash the feet of the servants
of my lord." 42 Abigail hurriedly arose and rode
on a donkey with her five young women who
attended her. And she went after the messen-
gers of David and became his wife. 43 David
also took Ahinoam of Jezreel. So both of them
were his wives. 44 But Saul had given Michal
his daughter, David's wife, to Paltiel the son of
Laish who was from Gallim.

David Again Spares Saul's Life

26 Then the Ziphites came to Saul at
Gibeah, saying, "Is David not hiding
himself on the hill of Hakilah, which is before
Jeshimon?"
2 Then Saul arose and went down to the Wil-
derness of Ziph, having three thousand chosen
men of Israel with him, to seek David in the
Wilderness of Ziph. 3 Saul camped on the hill
of Hakilah, which is before Jeshimon, by the
road. But David stayed in the wilderness, when
he saw that Saul came after him into the wil-
derness. 4 And David sent out spies and knew
that Saul had certainly come.
5 So David arose and came to the place where
Saul had camped. And David saw the place
where Saul was lying down and Abner son
of Ner, the commander of his army. Saul was
lying down in the encampment, while the peo-
ple encamped around him.
6 Then David answered and said to Ahimelek
the Hittite, and to Abishai the son of Zeruiah,
brother of Joab, saying, "Who will go down
with me to Saul to the camp?"
And Abishai said, "I will go down with you."
7 So David and Abishai came to the people by
night while Saul lay sleeping within the circle
of the camp. And his spear was stuck in the

ground at his head, and Abner and the people
were lying all around him.
8 Then Abishai said to David, "God has to-
day delivered your enemy into your hand. Now
please let me strike him with the spear through
to the ground with one stroke, and I will not
strike him a second time."
9 David said to Abishai, "Do not destroy him.
For who can stretch out his hand against the
LORD's anointed and remain unpunished?"
10 David said, "As the LORD lives, the LORD will
strike him, or his day will come to die, or he
will go down into battle and perish. 11 The
LORD forbid that I should stretch out my hand
against the LORD's anointed, but now please
take the spear that is at his head and the jug
of water, and let us go."
12 So David took the spear and the jug of
water from Saul's head and they went away.
No one saw, no one knew, and no one awoke,
for they were all asleep, because a deep sleep
from the LORD had fallen upon them.
13 Then David went over to the other side and
stood on the top of a hill at a distance. A great
space was between them. 14 And David called
to the people and to Abner the son of Ner,
saying, "Will you not answer, Abner?"
Then Abner answered and said, "Who are
you that calls to the king?"
15 And David said to Abner, "Are you not a
man? And who is like to you in Israel? Why
then have you not guarded your lord the king?
For one of the people came in to destroy the
king your lord. 16 This thing is not good which
you have done. As the LORD lives, you are wor-
thy of death because you have not guarded
your master, the LORD's anointed. And now, see
where is the king's spear? And the jug of water
that was at his head?"
17 Saul knew David's voice, and said, "Is this
your voice, my son David?"
And David said, "It is my voice, my lord king."
18 He said, "Why is my lord pursuing after his
servant? For what have I done? Or what evil
is in my hand? 19 Now please let my lord king
hear the words of his servant. If the LORD has
stirred you up against me, let Him accept an
offering. But if it was the sons of men, cursed
are they before the LORD. For they have driven
me today from having a share in the inher-
itance of the LORD, saying, 'Go, serve other
gods.' 20 Now do not let my blood fall to the
ground away from the presence of the LORD.
Truly the king of Israel has come out to seek
a single flea, as when one pursues a partridge
in the mountains."
21 Then said Saul, "I have sinned. Return, my
son David, for I will not harm you again, be-
cause my soul was precious in your eyes this

26:8 1Sa 24:4
26:9 2Sa 1:14
26:10 Ge 47:29
26:11 1Sa 24:6
26:12 Ge 2:21
26:17 1Sa 24:16
26:18 1Sa 24:9
26:19 2Sa 14:16
26:20 1Sa 24:14
26:21 1Sa 15:24

....

27:2 1Sa 21:10
27:3 1Sa 25:42–43
27:6 Ne 11:28
27:7 1Sa 29:3
27:8 Jos 13:2
27:9 1Sa 15:3
27:10 Jdg 1:16

day. I have acted foolishly and have seriously
gone astray."
22 David answered and said, "See, the king's
spear! Let one of the young men come over
and get it. 23 The LORD requites to every man
his right conduct and loyalty. So the LORD gave
you into my hand today, but I am not willing to
stretch my hand against the LORD's anointed.
24 As your life was highly valued in my eyes
this day, so may my life be highly valued in
the eyes of the LORD, and may He rescue me
out of all distress."
25 Then Saul said to David, "Blessed are you,
my son David. You will do great things, and
will surely prevail."
So David went on his way, and Saul returned
to his place.

David With the Philistines

27 Then David said in his heart, "Now
I will perish one day by the hand of
Saul. There is nothing better for me than that
I should escape to the land of the Philistines.
Then Saul will despair of continually seeking
me within all the territory of Israel. So will I
escape out of his hand."
2 David arose and passed over with the six
hundred men that were with him to Achish,
the son of Maok, king of Gath. 3 And David
lived with Achish at Gath, he and his men, each
man with his household, even David with his
two wives, Ahinoam the Jezreelitess, and Ab-
igail the Carmelitess, Nabal's widow. 4 It was
reported to Saul that David had fled to Gath,
so he no longer sought him.
5 David said to Achish, "If I have now found
favor in your eyes, let them give me a place in
one of the cities in the countryside, that I may
dwell there. For why should your servant dwell
in the royal city with you?"
6 Then Achish gave him Ziklag that day.
Therefore Ziklag has belonged to the kings of
Judah to this day. 7 The number of days that
David lived in the country of the Philistines
was a year and four months.
8 David and his men went up and invaded the
Geshurites, the Girzites, and the Amalekites.
For they were inhabitants of the land from of
old, as you come to Shur, even to the land of
Egypt. 9 So David would strike the land and
would not leave either man or woman alive.
And he would take the sheep, the cattle, the
donkeys, the camels, and the garments. And
then he came back to Achish.
10 Then Achish would say, "Where have you
made a raid today?" And David would say,
"Against the Negev of Judah," or "Against the
Negev of the Jerahmeelites," or "Against the
Negev of the Kenites." 11 Now David would

leave neither a man nor a woman alive, to bring tidings to Gath, saying, "Lest they should tell on us, saying, 'Thus David has done.'" This was his practice all the days which he lived in the country of the Philistines. 12 And Achish believed David, saying, "He has surely become a stench to his people Israel. Therefore he will be my servant forever."

28 And it came about in those days, that the Philistines gathered their armies together for war to fight with Israel. And Achish said to David, "Know assuredly that you will go out with me to battle, you and your men."

2 David said to Achish, "Surely you will know what your servant can do."

And Achish said to David, "Therefore I will appoint you my bodyguard for life."

The Medium of Endor

3 Now Samuel died and all Israel mourned him, and they buried him in Ramah, his own city. And Saul had removed the mediums and the necromancers from the land.

4 Then the Philistines gathered themselves together. And they came and camped in Shunem. So Saul gathered all Israel together, and they camped in Gilboa. 5 When Saul saw the camp of the Philistines, he was afraid and his heart trembled greatly. 6 Saul inquired of the LORD, but the LORD did not answer him by dreams, or by lots, or by prophets. 7 Then said Saul to his servants, "Seek for me a woman who is a medium, that I may go to her and inquire of her."

And his servants said to him, "There is woman medium in Endor."

8 So Saul disguised himself, put on other clothes, and he went with two of his men. And they came to the woman by night and he said, "Please divine for me by a spirit, and bring up for me whom I will name to you."

9 The woman said to him, "Listen, you know what Saul has done, how he has eliminated the mediums and necromancers from the land. Now why are you laying a trap for my life to cause my death?"

10 Saul swore to her by the LORD, saying, "As the LORD lives, no punishment will happen to you for this thing."

11 Then said the woman, "Whom shall I bring up for you?"

And he said, "Bring up Samuel for me."

12 When the woman saw Samuel, she cried out with a loud voice. And the woman said to Saul, "Why have you deceived me? For you are Saul."

13 The king said to her, "Do not be afraid. What did you see?"

28:3 Lev 19:31
28:4 Jos 19:18
28:6 Nu 12:6
28:7 Jos 17:11
28:8 1Ch 10:13
28:9 1Sa 28:3

28:14 1Sa 15:27
28:15 1Sa 18:12
28:18 1Ki 20:42
28:21 Jdg 12:3
28:23 1Ki 21:4
28:24 Lk 15:23
29:1 1Sa 4:1
29:2 1Sa 28:1–2

And the woman said to Saul, "I saw a divine being ascending out of the earth."

14 He said to her, "What is his appearance?"

And she said, "An old man is coming up, and he is covered with a robe."

And Saul perceived that it was Samuel. And he kneeled with his face to the ground and bowed himself.

15 Samuel said to Saul, "Why have you roused me to bring me up?"

And Saul answered, "I am greatly distressed, for the Philistines make war against me, and God has departed from me and does not answer me any longer by prophets or by dreams. Therefore I have called you that you might make known to me what I should do."

16 Then said Samuel, "Why then do you ask me, since the LORD has departed from you and has become your enemy? 17 The LORD has done for Himself as He spoke by me. The LORD has torn the kingdom from your hand and has given it to your neighbor, David. 18 As you did not obey the voice of the LORD and did not carry out His fierce wrath against Amalek, therefore the LORD has done this thing to you this day. 19 And moreover, the LORD will deliver Israel with you into the hand of the Philistines, and tomorrow you and your sons will be with me. The LORD will also deliver the army of Israel into the hand of the Philistines."

20 Saul immediately fell full length upon the ground because he greatly feared the words of Samuel. Also there was no strength in him, for he had eaten no bread all day and all night.

21 The woman came to Saul and saw that he was terrified. And she said to him, "Listen, your handmaid has obeyed your voice. I have taken my life in my hand and have listened to your words which you spoke to me. 22 Now therefore you also, please obey the voice of your maidservant and let me set before you a piece of bread, and eat so that you may have strength when you go on your way."

23 But he refused and said, "I will not eat."

But his servants, and also the woman, urged him and he listened to them. So he arose from the ground and sat on the bed.

24 Now the woman had a fattened calf in the house, and she hurried and killed it, and took flour, and kneaded it, and baked unleavened bread from it. 25 She brought it before Saul and his servants, and they ate. Then they arose and went away that night.

Philistines Reject David

29 Now the Philistines gathered together all their armies to Aphek, and the children of Israel were camping by the spring which is in Jezreel. 2 The lords of the Philistines

were advancing by hundreds and by thousands, and David and his men were advancing in the rear with Achish. 3 Then the princes of the Philistines said, "What are these Hebrews *doing here*?"

And Achish said to the princes of the Philistines, "Is this not David, the servant of Saul, king of Israel, who has been with me these days, or *rather* these years? And I have found no fault in him since the day of his desertion to this day."

4 But the princes of the Philistines became angry with him. And the princes of the Philistines said to him, "Make this man return and let him go again to his place which you have appointed him. He will not go down with us in battle, lest he might be an adversary to us in the battle. For with what could he make himself acceptable to his master, if not with the heads of these men? 5 Is this not David, whom they sing for in dances saying,

'Saul has slain his thousands,
and David his ten thousands'? "

6 Then Achish called David and said to him, "As the LORD lives, you have been upright, and your going out and your coming in with me in the camp has been pleasing in my sight. For I have not found evil in you since the day of your coming to me to this day. However, you are not acceptable in the eyes of the lords. 7 Therefore now, return and go in peace, that you do not displease the lords of the Philistines."

8 David said to Achish, "But what have I done? And what have you found in your servant, from the day which I came before you to this day, that I may not come and fight against the enemies of my lord the king?"

9 And Achish answered and said to David, "I know that you are pleasing in my sight like an angel of God. However the lords of the Philistines have said, 'He shall not go up with us in battle.' 10 Therefore rise up early in the morning with your master's servants who have come with you. And when you have risen early in the morning and it is light, then depart."

11 So David and his men rose early to depart in the morning *and* return to the land of the Philistines. But the Philistines went up to Jezreel.

David Defeats the Amalekites

30 Now when David and his men came to Ziklag on the third day, the Amalekites had raided the south as far as Ziklag. They had struck Ziklag and burned it with fire. 2 They had taken as captives all the women who were there. They did not kill anyone, but carried them off and went on their way.

29:3 1Sa 27:7
29:4 1Sa 14:21
29:5 1Sa 21:11
29:6 2Sa 3:25
29:9 2Sa 14:17
29:10 1Ch 12:19
30:1 1Sa 15:7
30:2 1Sa 27:11
30:4 Nu 14:1
30:5 1Sa 25:42–43
30:6 Ex 17:4
30:7 1Sa 22:20–21
30:8 1Sa 23:2
30:10 1Sa 30:21
30:12 Jdg 15:19
30:14 2Sa 8:18

3 David and his men came to the city, and they found it burned with fire, and their wives, their sons, and their daughters taken captive. 4 So David and the people that were with him lifted up their voice and wept until they had no strength in them to weep. 5 Now David's two wives were taken captive, Ahinoam the Jezreelitess and Abigail the wife of Nabal the Carmelite. 6 David was greatly distressed, for the people talked of stoning him, because all the people were bitter in spirit, each over his sons and daughters. But David encouraged himself in the LORD his God.

Father, during this time of discouragement and anguish in my life, help me not to lose heart, for my soul trusts in You (1Sa 30:6).

7 And David said to Abiathar the priest, the son of Ahimelek, "Please bring the ephod to me." So Abiathar brought the ephod to David. 8 David inquired at the LORD, saying, "Should I pursue after this raiding party? Will I overtake them?"

And He answered him, "Pursue *them*, for you will surely overtake them and will surely recover *all*."

9 So David went, he and the six hundred men who were with him. And they came to the brook Besor, where those that were left behind remained. 10 But David pursued, he and four hundred men, for two hundred who were too exhausted to cross over the brook Besor remained behind.

11 They found an Egyptian in the field and took him to David. He gave him bread and he ate, and they made him drink water. 12 And they gave him a part of a cake of figs and two cakes of raisins. When he had eaten, his spirit came back to him, for he had not eaten bread or drunk any water for three days and nights.

13 Then David said to him, "To whom do you belong? And where are you from?"

And he said, "I am a young man of Egypt, servant to an Amalekite. And my master left me, because three days ago I fell sick. 14 We raided the south of the Kerethites, the south of Judah, and the south of Caleb. And we burned Ziklag with fire."

15 David said to him, "Will you bring me down to this raiding party?"

And he said, "Swear to me by God that you will neither kill me, nor deliver me into the hand of my master, and I will bring you down to this raiding party."

16 When he brought him down, they were spread out over all the land, eating, drinking,

and dancing, because of all the great spoil which they had taken from the land of the Philistines and from the land of Judah. 17 David struck them from twilight until the evening of the next day, and no man escaped except four hundred young men who rode on camels and fled. 18 So David recovered all that the Amalekites had taken, and David rescued his two wives. 19 Now there was nothing missing, from the smallest *thing* to the greatest, neither sons, nor daughters, or plunder, or anything which they had taken. David brought back all *of it*. 20 And David took all the flocks and the herds, *which* they drove before the *other* livestock. And they said, "This is David's spoil."

21 Then David came to the two hundred men, who were too exhausted to follow David, whom they left at the brook Besor. And they went out to meet David and the people who were with him. And when David came near to the people, he greeted them. 22 Then all the wicked and worthless ones from the men who went with David answered and said, "Because they did not go with us, we will not give them anything from the spoil that we have rescued, except to every man his wife and his children, that they may lead them away and depart."

23 Then David said, "You will not do so, my brothers, with what the LORD has given us, for He has preserved us, and has delivered into our hand the raiding party that came against us. 24 And who will listen to you in this matter? Indeed as the share *is* of the one going down to battle, so *will be* the share of the one staying with the equipment. They will share equally." 25 So it was so from that day forward, that he set it *as* a statute and an ordinance for Israel to this day.

26 When David came to Ziklag, he sent part of the spoil to his friends, the elders of Judah, saying, "Here is a gift to you from the spoil of the enemies of the LORD": 27 to those who were in Bethel, in Ramoth of the Negev, and in Jattir; 28 to those who were in Aroer, Siphmoth, Eshtemoa, 29 and in Rakal; to those who were in the cities of the Jerahmeelites and the Kenites; 30 to those who were in Hormah, Bor Ashan, Athak 31 and in Hebron; and to those who were in all the other places where David and his men had roamed.

30:17 1Sa 11:11
30:19 1Sa 30:8
30:20 1Sa 30:26
30:21 1Sa 30:10
30:24 Nu 31:27
30:26 1Sa 25:27
30:27 Jos 15:48
30:28 Jos 13:16
30:29 Jdg 1:16
30:30 Jdg 1:17
30:31 2Sa 2:1

....

31:1 1Sa 28:4
31:2 1Ch 8:33
31:3 2Sa 1:6
31:4 Jdg 9:54
31:9 2Sa 1:20
31:10 Jos 17:11
31:12 2Ch 16:14
31:13 Ge 50:10

The House of Saul, Dead and Buried

2Sa 1:4–12; 1Ch 10:1–12

31 Now the Philistines were fighting against Israel, and Israel's fighting men fled before the Philistines and they fell slain on Mount Gilboa. 2 The Philistines overtook Saul and his sons. And the Philistines killed his sons, Jonathan, Abinadab, and Malki-Shua, Saul's sons. 3 The battle was heavy against Saul. The archers found him, and he was severely wounded by the archers.

4 Then Saul said to his armor bearer, "Draw your sword and thrust me through with it, lest these uncircumcised come and thrust me through and abuse me."

But his armor bearer would not, for he was very afraid. Therefore Saul took his sword and fell upon it. 5 When his armor bearer saw that Saul was dead, he also fell upon his sword and died with him. 6 So Saul died with his three sons and his armor bearer, together *with* all his men on that same day.

7 When Israel's fighting men who were on the other side of the valley, and those who were on the other side of the Jordan, saw that Israel's fighting men fled and that Saul and his sons were dead, they abandoned the cities and fled. So the Philistines came and lived in them.

8 The following day, when the Philistines came to strip the dead, they found Saul and his three sons fallen on Mount Gilboa. 9 They cut off his head, stripped off his armor, and sent *them* into the land of the Philistines round about, to make it known in the house of their idols and among their people. 10 They put his armor in the house of Ashtoreth, and they fastened his body to the wall of Beth Shan.

11 When the inhabitants of Jabesh Gilead heard what the Philistines had done to Saul, 12 all the valiant men arose and went all night, and they took the body of Saul and the bodies of his sons from the wall of Beth Shan, and they came to Jabesh and burned them there. 13 Then they took their bones and buried them under the tamarisk tree at Jabesh, and they *mourned,* fasting seven days.

Author: The prophet Samuel

Written: After 960 BC

Themes: Israel's History (1010 to 970 BC), David's Reign

2 Samuel

Dear Spirit Led Woman,

At one time during David's reign there was a drought in Israel (2Sa 21:1). God told David that the drought had been brought on by Israel's sin. When David dealt with the sin, the rains came.

While sin blocks the presence and rain of the Holy Spirit, and while it must be dealt with to restore the rain of God's presence, sin isn't the only reason you might find yourself in a dry season. God may be working in you to prepare you for a greater release of His Spirit. During these seasons He is teaching you to walk by faith rather than by sight or feeling. You are learning that whether you sense His presence or not, He is there. Don't despair! God has not abandoned you, and in His time He will bring you out of the dry season!

Joy F. Strang

The Death of Saul

1Sa 31:1–13; 1Ch 10:1–13

1 After the death of Saul, when David had returned from the slaughter of the Amalekites, David had remained two days in Ziklag. 2 On the third day, a man came from the camp of Saul with his clothes torn and dirt upon his head. As he approached David, he fell to the ground prostrate.

3 David asked him, "Where have you come from?"

He responded, "I fled from the camp of Israel."

4 David said to him, "Tell me, what is the report?"

So he reported, "The people fled from battle. Many of the people have fallen and died; even Saul and his son Jonathan are dead."

5 Then David asked the young man who was reporting to him, "How do you know that Saul and his son Jonathan are dead?"

6 The young man who was reporting to him answered, "I happened to be on Mount Gilboa when, in front of me, Saul was leaning on his spear with the chariots and horsemen drawing close. 7 When he turned around, he noticed me. He summoned me, and I responded, 'Here I am.'

8 "He asked me, 'Who are you?'

"I answered, 'I am an Amalekite.'

9 "Then he said to me, 'Stand over me and kill me, for I have been mortally wounded, yet I am still alive.'

10 "So I stood beside him and killed him because I knew that he could not live after he had fallen. Then I took the crown that was on his head and the armlet that was on his arm, and I have brought them here to my lord."

11 Then David took hold of his clothes and tore them, *as did* all of the men who were with him. 12 They mourned and wept and fasted until evening for Saul, Jonathan his son, the people of the LORD, and the house of Israel, because they had fallen by the sword.

13 Then David asked the young man who was reporting to him, "Where are you from?"

He responded, "I am the son of one who sought refuge, an Amalekite."

14 David said to him, "How is it that you did not fear raising your hand to destroy the anointed of the LORD?"

15 Then David called to one of the young men and said, "Step forward and execute him." So he struck him and killed him. 16 But David said to him, "Your blood is upon your own head, since your mouth has testified against you, saying, 'I put an end to the anointed of the LORD.' "

1:2 1Sa 4:12
1:4 1Sa 4:16
1:6 1Sa 28:4
1:8 1Sa 30:13
1:10 Jdg 9:54
1:11 Ge 37:29
1:14 1Sa 24:6
1:16 Mt 27:25

....

1:17 2Ch 35:25
1:18 Jos 10:13
1:19 2Sa 1:27
1:20 Mic 1:10
1:21 1Sa 31:1
1:22 1Sa 18:4
1:23 Jdg 14:18
1:25 2Sa 1:19
1:26 1Sa 18:1–4
1:27 2Sa 1:25
2:1 1Sa 23:2
2:2 1Sa 25:42–43

The Lament of David

17 Then David recited this lament over Saul and Jonathan his son, 18 and he told them to teach the sons of Judah the Song of the Bow. It is written in the book of Jashar:

19 Your splendor, O Israel, has been slain
upon your hills.
How the mighty ones have fallen.

20 Do not report it in Gath,
do not announce it in the streets of
Ashkelon,
lest the daughters of the Philistines rejoice,
or the daughters of the uncircumcised
exult.

21 O mountains of Gilboa,
may there be no rain or dew upon you
or your bountiful fields;
for there the shield of the mighty was
defiled!
The shield of Saul *is* no longer anointed
with oil.

22 From the blood of the slain,
from the fat of mighty,
the bow of Jonathan did not turn back,
nor did the sword of Saul return empty.
23 Saul and Jonathan,
beloved and delightful,
neither in life nor death will they be
separated.
They were swifter than eagles,
they were stronger than lions.

24 O daughters of Israel, weep over Saul,
who clothed you in scarlet and jewels,
who adorned your garments with gold
jewelry.

25 How the mighty ones have fallen in the
midst of battle!
Jonathan was slain on your high places.
26 I am distressed for you, my brother
Jonathan;
you were very dear to me;
your love was more remarkable than the
love of women.

27 How the mighty have fallen,
and the weapons of war have perished.

David Anointed King Over Judah

2 After this, David consulted the LORD, asking, "Shall I go to one of the cities of Judah?"

The LORD responded to him, "Go up."

David asked, "Where should I go?"

And He said, "Hebron."

2 So David went up there, along with his two wives, Ahinoam the Jezreelitess, and Abigail the widow of Nabal the Carmelite. 3 And David

brought the men who were with him, each man with his household, and they lived in the cities of Hebron. 4 Then the men of Judah came and there anointed David as king over the house of Judah, and they informed David that it was the men of Jabesh Gilead who had buried Saul.

5 So David sent messengers to the men of Jabesh Gilead saying, “May you be blessed by the LORD, you who have shown this loyalty to your lord Saul by burying him. 6 Now may the LORD show you loyalty and faithfulness, even as I deal kindly with you who have done this thing. 7 Now may your hands be strong and may you be courageous, since your lord Saul is dead and the house of Judah has anointed me as king over them.”

War Between the Houses of David and Saul
1Ch 3:1–4

8 However, Abner the son of Ner, commander of the army of Saul, had taken Ish-Bosheth the son of Saul and brought him over to Mahanaim. 9 He installed him as king over Gilead, the Ashurites, Jezreel, Ephraim, and Benjamin, over Israel in its entirety.

10 Ish-Bosheth the son of Saul was forty years old when he began to reign over Israel, and he ruled for two years. However, the house of Judah followed David. 11 The length of time during which David was king in Hebron over the house of Judah was seven years and six months.

12 Abner the son of Ner, with the servants of Ish-Bosheth the son of Saul, went out from Mahanaim toward Gibeon. 13 And Joab the son of Zeruiah, with the servants of David, went out in order to meet together at the pool of Gibeon. They sat down, one group on one side of the pool and the other group on the side of the pool opposite them.

14 Abner suggested to Joab, “Let the young men come forward and compete before us.”

And Joab replied, “Let them come.”

15 So they stepped forward and were counted, twelve from Benjamin and Ish-Bosheth and twelve from the servants of David. 16 Each one grabbed his opponent by the head and thrust his sword in his opponent’s side; so they fell down together. Therefore that place was called Helkath Hazzurim, which is at Gibeon.

17 The fighting was very fierce that day, but Abner and the men of Israel were defeated by the servants of David.

18 Now the three sons of Zeruiah were there: Joab, Abishai, and Asahel; and Asahel was as fast as a wild gazelle. 19 So Asahel pursued Abner, and as he went, he did not turn to the right hand or to the left from following Abner.

2:4 1Sa 31:11–13
2:5 1Sa 23:21
2:8 1Sa 14:50
2:11 1Ki 2:11
2:12 Jos 18:25
2:13 2Sa 8:16
2:14 2Sa 2:17
2:17 2Sa 3:1
2:18 1Ch 12:8
....
2:22 2Sa 3:27
2:23 2Sa 3:27
2:29 2Sa 2:8
3:1 1Ki 14:30
3:2 1Ch 3:1–4
3:3 1Sa 27:8

20 Abner looked behind him and said, “Is that you, Asahel?”

He answered, “It is I.”

21 Abner said to him, “Turn aside to your right or left, overtake one of the young men, and take his equipment for yourself,” but Asahel was not willing to desist.

22 Abner continued still to reason with Asahel, “Abandon your pursuit. Why should I strike you down? How then could I show my face to your brother Joab?”

23 But he refused to desist. So Abner struck him in the abdomen with the butt of his spear, so that the spear came out of his back. He fell there and died on the spot. When all of the others came to the place where Asahel fell and died, they halted.

24 But Joab and Abishai pursued Abner. As the sun was setting, they came to the hill of Ammah, which is next to Giah on the way to the Wilderness of Gibeon. 25 The sons of Benjamin gathered to the rear of Abner into a single formation, and they took their stand atop one of the hills.

26 Abner called to Joab, “Must the sword consume forever? Do you not understand that a bitter taste will result in the end? How long will you refuse to command the people to withdraw from chasing their brothers?”

27 Joab responded, “As God lives, I assure you that if you had not said this, the people would have each pursued his brother throughout the night.”

28 So Joab blew a trumpet, and all the people stood still. They pursued Israel no longer, nor did they continue to fight anymore.

29 So Abner and his men traveled through the Arabah all that night, crossed the Jordan, and marched all morning until they returned to Mahanaim.

30 Joab refrained from pursuing Abner, but instead mustered all of the people. There were nineteen men besides Asahel missing from among the servants of David. 31 But the servants of David routed Benjamin and the men of Abner; three hundred and sixty of their men died. 32 They carried Asahel back and interred him in his father’s tomb, which was at Bethlehem. Then Joab and his men traveled throughout the night and reached Hebron at dawn.

3 The struggle between the house of Saul and the house of David endured, but David grew stronger as Saul became weaker.

2 Sons were born to David in Hebron:
his firstborn was Amnon, by Ahinoam the Jezreelitess;
3 and his second, Kileab, by Abigail the widow of Nabal, the Carmelite;

and the third, Absalom the son of
Maakah the daughter of Talmai, the king
of Geshur;
4 and the fourth, Adonijah the son of
Haggith;
and the fifth, Shephatiah the son of
Abital;
5 and the sixth, Ithream, was born to
Eglah, the wife of David.
These were born to David in Hebron.

Abner Defects to David

6 While there was war between the house
of Saul and the house of David, Abner was
strengthening himself in the house of Saul.
7 Now Saul had a concubine whose name was
Rizpah, the daughter of Aiah, and Ish-Bosheth
said to Abner, "Why have you gone in to my
father's concubine?"
8 Abner became very angry over the words
of Ish-Bosheth. He said, "Am I a dog's head
that belongs to Judah? Each day I show loy-
alty to the house of Saul your father, to his
brothers, and to his friends by not allowing
you to fall into the hand of David. Yet today
you are charging me with guilt concerning this
woman. 9 May God do so to Abner, and more
also, for as the LORD has sworn to David, this
I will do for him, 10 to transfer the kingdom
from the house of Saul and to establish the
throne of David over Israel and Judah, from
Dan to Beersheba." 11 And he could not offer a
response to Abner, for fear of him.
12 So Abner sent messengers to David on his
behalf saying, "To whom does the land be-
long? Make your covenant with me, and my
hand will be with you to bring over all of Israel
to you."
13 He responded, "Very well, I will make a
covenant with you, but I require one thing
from you: you will not see my face unless you
bring Michal the daughter of Saul with you
when you come to see me." 14 Then David sent
messengers to Ish-Bosheth the son of Saul,
saying, "Give me my wife Michal, to whom
I was betrothed for one hundred Philistine
foreskins."
15 So Ish-Bosheth sent for her, and he took
her from her husband, Paltiel the son of Laish.
16 But her husband went with her, weeping as
he went, as far as Bahurim. Then Abner said to
him, "Go. Return." So he turned back.
17 Abner had a word with the elders of Israel,
"In days past, you were seeking David as king
over you. 18 So do it now, because the LORD said
to David: By the hand of David, I will save My
people Israel from the hand of the Philistines
and from the hand of every enemy."

3:6 2Sa 2:8–9
3:7 2Sa 21:8–11
3:8 2Sa 9:8
3:9 1Sa 15:28
3:10 Jdg 20:1
3:13 Ge 43:3
3:14 1Sa 18:27
3:15 1Sa 25:44
3:16 2Sa 16:5
3:18 1Sa 15:28

....

3:19 1Ch 12:29
3:21 2Sa 3:12
3:27 2Sa 20:9–10
3:29 2Sa 1:16
3:31 Ge 37:34
3:32 Pr 24:17

19 Abner also spoke privately with Benjamin.
Then Abner went to tell David privately at He-
bron all that was received favorably by Israel
and the entire house of Benjamin. 20 So Abner,
along with twenty men, went to David at He-
bron, and David held a festival for Abner and
the men who were with him. 21 Abner said to
David, "Let me arise, go, and gather all Israel
to my lord the king, so that they may make a
covenant with you, that you may rule over all
that your heart desires." So David sent Abner
away, and he went peaceably.

Joab Murders Abner

22 Now the servants of David and Joab came
from a raid and brought much plunder with
them, but Abner was no longer with David
at Hebron, because he had sent him away in
peace. 23 When Joab and the whole of the army
that was with him arrived, they reported to
Joab, "Abner the son of Ner came to the king
and he sent him away peaceably."
24 So Joab went to the king and said, "What
have you done? Abner came to you. Why is it
that you sent him away? Now he is long gone.
25 You know that Abner the son of Ner came
to deceive you, to learn of your coming and
going, to discern all that you are doing."
26 When Joab left David, he sent messengers
after Abner, and they brought him back from
the well of Sirah. However, David was not
aware of this. 27 So Abner returned to Hebron,
and Joab pulled him aside in the gateway so
as to speak with him undisturbed. There he
struck him in the midsection so that he died
on account of the blood of Asahel, his brother.
28 Afterward when David heard of this, he
said, "My kingdom and I are forever blame-
less before the LORD for the blood of Abner
the son of Ner. 29 May it fall upon the head of
Joab and upon all his father's house. May the
house of Joab never be without one who has
a discharge, or who is a leper, or who leans
on a staff, or who falls by the sword, or who
lacks food."
30 So Joab and his brother Abishai killed Ab-
ner, because he killed Asahel their brother at
Gibeon in the battle.

> God's timing is what I am looking for—not yesterday's time or next year's time, but today, now, this moment (2Sa 3:18).

31 David said to Joab and all of the people
with him, "Tear your clothes, put on sackcloth,
and mourn before Abner." As for King David,
he followed behind the bier. 32 When they

buried Abner at Hebron, the king raised his voice and wept at the grave of Abner, and all of the people wept.

33 Then, the king lamented for Abner, saying,

"Should Abner have died as a fool dies?
34 Your hands were not bound,
and your feet were not put in fetters;
as a man falls before the wicked, so you
have fallen."

And all of the people continued to weep over him.

35 Then all of the people came to persuade David to eat food while it was still day. But David took an oath, saying, "May God do to me, and more also, if I taste food or anything else before the sun sets."

36 All of the people recognized this, and it pleased them, as everything that the king did was pleasing to all of the people. 37 That very day, all of the people, all of Israel, understood that it was not *ordered* from the king to have Abner the son of Ner killed.

38 David said to his servant, "Do you not understand that a great leader has fallen this day in Israel? 39 Today, I am weak, even if an anointed king, and these men, the sons of Zeruiah, are too strong for me. May the LORD repay the evildoer according to his wickedness."

Ish-Bosheth Murdered

4 When the son of Saul heard that Abner had died in Hebron, his courage failed, and all of Israel was disheartened. 2 Now the son of Saul had two men who were leaders of raiding bands. The name of one was Baanah and the name of the other Rekab, both sons of Rimmon the Beerothite, from among the sons of Benjamin. Now Beeroth is also regarded as part of Benjamin, 3 because the Beerothites fled to Gittaim and have been sojourners there until this day.

4 Now Jonathan the son of Saul had a son with crippled feet. He was five years old when the report of Saul and Jonathan came from Jezreel. His nurse picked him up and fled, but in her haste to escape, he fell and became lame. His name was Mephibosheth.

5 The sons of Rimmon the Beerothite, Rekab and Baanah, went out and came to the house of Ish-Bosheth in the heat of the day, as he was resting in his bed at midday. 6 They entered the house as if to get wheat and stabbed him in the abdomen. Then Rekab and his brother Baanah fled to safety.

7 When they entered the house, he was lying on his bed in his bedroom; they struck him, killed him, and beheaded him. Then they took his head and traveled by way of the Arabah all night. 8 They brought the head of Ish-Bosheth to David in Hebron and said to the king, "Here is the head of Ish-Bosheth the son of Saul, your enemy who sought your life. This day, the LORD has given retribution against Saul and his descendent to my lord the king."

9 David answered Rekab and his brother Baanah, the sons of Rimmon the Beerothite, "As the LORD, who has delivered my life from every distress, lives, 10 when one reported to me that Saul was dead, although he was a bearer of good news in his own eyes, I seized him and killed him at Ziklag, which was my reward for his message. 11 How much more so, when guilty men have slain an innocent man in his own house on his own bed, should I not now require his blood from your hand and wipe you from the earth?"

12 David then gave orders to the young men. They killed them, cut off their hands and feet, and hung them at the pool in Hebron, but they took the head of Ish-Bosheth and buried it in the grave of Abner at Hebron.

David Anointed King Over Israel

1Ch 11:1–3

5 All of the tribes of Israel came to David at Hebron and said, "We are your bone and flesh. 2 Previously, when Saul was king over us, you were the one leading Israel out and in. Also, the LORD said to you: You will shepherd My people Israel, and you will be ruler over Israel."

3 So all of the elders of Israel came to the king at Hebron, and King David made a covenant with them before the LORD at Hebron. They anointed David king over Israel.

4 David was thirty years old when he began to reign, and he reigned forty years. 5 He reigned over Judah from Hebron for seven years and six months, and he reigned over all of Israel and Judah from Jerusalem for thirty-three years.

David Conquers Jerusalem

1Ch 3:5–9; 11:4–9; 14:1–7

6 The king and his men went to Jerusalem against the Jebusites, who were living in the land. They said to David, "You will not enter here; even the blind and the lame will turn you away"—thinking, "David cannot enter here." 7 Nevertheless, David overthrew the stronghold of Zion, which is now the City of David.

8 David said on that day, "Whoever defeats the Jebusites, let him go through the water shaft to reach the lame and the blind, who are despised by David." Therefore, it is said, "The blind and lame shall not come into the house."

9 So David occupied the stronghold, and he called it the City of David. He built on all sides

3:35 2Sa 1:12
3:39 1Ki 2:33–34
4:1 Ezr 4:4
4:2 Jos 18:25
4:3 Ne 11:33
4:4 2Sa 9:3
4:6 2Sa 2:23
4:8 1Sa 25:29
4:9 1Ki 1:29
4:10 2Sa 1:2–16
4:11 Ps 9:12
4:12 2Sa 1:15
5:1 1Ch 11:1–3
5:2 1Sa 18:13
5:3 2Sa 2:4
5:4 1Ch 26:31
5:5 2Sa 2:11
5:6 Jdg 1:8
5:7 1Ki 2:10
5:9 1Ki 9:15

from the terraces inward. 10 David went on and became great, because the LORD, the God of Hosts, was with him.

11 King Hiram of Tyre sent messengers to David with cedar wood, carpenters, and stonemasons, and they built a house for David. 12 Then David understood that the LORD had appointed him king over Israel, and that He had exalted his kingdom for the sake of His people Israel.

13 David took more concubines and wives in Jerusalem, after having come from Hebron, and they bore him more sons and daughters. 14 These are the names of the children born to him in Jerusalem: Shammua, Shobab, Nathan, Solomon, 15 Ibhar, Elishua, Nepheg, Japhia, 16 Elishama, Eliada, and Eliphelet.

David Defeats the Philistines

1Ch 14:8–17

17 When the Philistines heard that they had anointed David king over Israel, all of the Philistines went up to search for David, but David heard about this and went down to the stronghold. 18 Now the Philistines had come and were spread out in the Valley of Rephaim. 19 So David asked the LORD, "Shall I go up against the Philistines? Will You give them into my hand?"

The LORD said to David, "Go up, because I will certainly give them into your hand."

> You have broken forth against my enemies (2Sa 5:20).

20 So David came to Baal Perazim, and David defeated them there. He said, "The LORD has breached my enemies before me like bursting tides." Therefore, he named that place Baal Perazim. 21 The Philistines abandoned their idols there, and David and his men carried them away.

22 Once again, the Philistines went up and spread out in the Valley of Rephaim. 23 When David inquired of the LORD, He said, "You shall not go up. Circle around behind them and come against them opposite the trees. 24 When you hear the sound of marching in the tops of the trees, pay attention, because at that point the LORD is going before you to defeat the army of the Philistines." 25 So David did just as the LORD commanded, and he defeated the Philistines from Geba as far as Gezer.

The Ark Brought to Jerusalem

1Ch 13:1–14; 15:25–16:3

6 Again David gathered all of the chosen men in Israel, thirty thousand. 2 David and all of the people who were with him arose and went from Baalah of Judah to bring up the ark of God, so named for the name of the LORD of Hosts who sits enthroned among the cherubim that are upon it. 3 They loaded the ark of God on a new cart and brought it from the house of Abinadab, which was on the hill. Uzzah and Ahio the sons of Abinadab were driving the new cart. 4 They brought it with the ark of God from the house of Abinadab on the hill, and Ahio was walking in front of the ark. 5 Meanwhile, David and the entire house of Israel were celebrating before the LORD with all sorts of instruments made of fir wood, on harps, on stringed instruments, on tambourines, on sistrums, and on cymbals.

6 When they came to the threshing floor of Nakon, Uzzah reached out and took hold of the ark of God, because the oxen had stumbled. 7 The LORD became angry against Uzzah, and God struck him down on the spot for his irreverence. He died there beside the ark of God.

8 David became angry because of the outburst of the LORD against Uzzah; that place is called Perez Uzzah to this day.

9 David feared the LORD that day, and he thought, "How can the ark of the LORD come to me?" 10 So David did not allow the ark of the LORD to be brought to him in the City of David. Instead, David redirected it to the house of Obed-Edom the Gittite. 11 The ark of the LORD remained at the house of Obed-Edom the Gittite for three months, and the LORD blessed Obed-Edom and his entire household.

12 When it was reported to King David, "The LORD has blessed Obed-Edom and everything that belongs to him, for the sake of the ark of God," David went and brought up the ark of God from the house of Obed-Edom to the City of David with rejoicing. 13 When those who were carrying the ark of the LORD had taken six steps, David would sacrifice an ox and a fattened steer. 14 David danced before the LORD with all of his might, and he wore a linen ephod. 15 So David and the whole house of Israel escorted the ark of the LORD with shouting and the sound of the horn.

16 When the ark of the LORD entered the City of David, Michal the daughter of Saul looked down from the window, and upon seeing King David leaping and dancing before the LORD, she thought contemptuously of him in her mind.

17 They brought the ark of the LORD and set it in its place inside the tent that David had erected for it. Then David offered burnt offerings and peace offerings before the LORD. 18 When David had finished offering the burnt offerings and peace offerings, he blessed the people before the LORD of Hosts. 19 He distributed to all of the people, the entire multitude of Israel, both men and women, one bread cake, one

5:10 2Sa 3:1
5:11 1Ch 14:1
5:13 1Ch 3:9
5:17 2Sa 23:14
5:18 Jos 15:8
5:19 2Sa 2:1
5:20 Isa 28:21
5:21 Dt 7:5
5:24 Jdg 4:14
5:25 1Ch 14:16
6:2 1Sa 4:4

....

6:3 1Sa 6:7
6:4 1Ch 13:7
6:5 1Ch 13:8
6:6 Nu 4:15
6:7 1Sa 6:19
6:9 Ps 119:120
6:10 1Ch 26:4–8
6:11 Ge 30:27
6:12 1Ki 8:1
6:13 1Ki 8:5
6:14 Ex 15:20
6:16 1Ch 15:29
6:17 1Ch 15:1
6:18 1Ki 8:55
6:19 Ne 8:10

date cake, and one raisin cake to each one. Then all of the people left, each to his house.

20 David returned to bless his household, but Michal the daughter of Saul came out to meet him. She said, "How the king of Israel has dignified himself today, exposing himself this day in the sight of his servant's slave girls like one of the rabble might shamelessly expose himself."

21 Then David responded to Michal, "It was before the LORD, who chose me over your father and over everyone in his household, to appoint me ruler over the people of the LORD, over Israel. I was celebrating before the LORD. 22 I will humble myself even more than this and be abased in my own eyes. But by the maidservants, of whom you have spoken, I will be held in honor."

23 Michal the daughter of Saul had no children to the day of her death.

God's Covenant With David

1Ch 17:1–15

7 Now when the king settled into his house and the LORD had given him rest from all of his enemies on all sides, 2 the king said to Nathan the prophet, "I am dwelling in a cedar house, but the ark of God is sitting in a tent."

3 Nathan said to the king, "Go, do all that is in your heart because the LORD is with you."

4 That night the word of the LORD came to Nathan:

> 5 Go and say to My servant David: Thus says the LORD: Do you intend to build a house for Me in which I will dwell? 6 I have not dwelt in a house since the day I brought the sons of Israel from Egypt until this day. I have been moving about with a tent as My dwelling. 7 Wherever I have moved with all the sons of Israel, have I ever spoken a word to anyone from the tribes of Israel, whom I commanded to shepherd My people Israel, saying, "Why have you not built Me a house of cedar?"
>
> 8 Now therefore, you will say to My servant David: Thus says the LORD of Hosts: I took you from the pasture, from following after the sheep, to be ruler over My people Israel. 9 I have been with you wherever you have gone, and I have cut off all of your enemies before you. I will make your name great, like the great ones across the land. 10 Moreover, I will appoint a place for My people Israel. I will plant them, and they will dwell in that very place. They will be restless no longer, and the unjust will no longer oppress them, as in former times, 11 ever since the day in which I appointed judges over My people Israel. I will give you rest from all of your enemies.
>
> The LORD declares to you that He will instead bring about a house for you. 12 When your days are complete and you lie down with your fathers, I will raise up after you an offspring from your body, and I will establish his rule. 13 He will build a house for My name, and I will establish his royal throne forever. 14 I will be a father to him, and he will be a son to Me. When he goes astray, I will correct him with the rod of men and afflictions of the sons of men. 15 My commitment will not abandon him, as I removed it from Saul, whom I deposed before you. 16 Your house and dominion will endure before Me forever, and your throne will be established by the LORD forever.

17 So Nathan spoke to David in accordance with all of these words and the entirety of this vision.

The Prayer of David

1Ch 17:16–27

18 Then King David went in and sat before the LORD. He said,

> "Who am I, O Lord GOD, and what is my house that You have brought me this far? 19 Yet this was comparatively insignificant in Your sight, Lord GOD, for You have also spoken about Your servant's house into the distant future. Is this Your manner with man, Lord GOD?
>
> 20 "What more can David say to You? You know Your servant, Lord GOD. 21 Because of Your word, according to Your will, You have done all of this greatness to inform Your servant.
>
> 22 "Therefore You are great, LORD God. There is none like You, and there is no God except You, according to everything that we have heard with our ears. 23 And who is like Your people, like Israel—a single nation in the land, whom God went to redeem as a people for Himself, making a name for Himself by doing great and awesome things for Your land, before Your people whom You redeemed for Yourself from Egypt, a nation and its gods. 24 You established Your people Israel as Your own people forever, and You, LORD, became their God.
>
> 25 "Now, LORD God, confirm forever the word that You spoke regarding Your servant and his house and do as You have spoken. 26 May Your name be magnified forever by saying, 'The LORD of Hosts is God over Israel,' and may the house of Your servant David be established before You.

6:20 2Sa 6:16
6:21 1Sa 13:14
6:23 Mt 1:25
7:2 2Sa 5:11
7:3 1Ki 8:17–18
7:6 1Ki 8:16
7:7 Lev 26:11–12
7:8 2Sa 6:21
7:9 2Sa 5:10
7:10 Ps 89:22–23
7:11 1Sa 12:9–11
7:12 1Ki 8:20
7:13 1Ki 8:19
7:14 Heb 1:5
7:15 1Sa 15:23
7:16 2Sa 7:13
7:18 Ex 3:11
7:19 1Ch 17:17
7:20 1Sa 16:7
7:22 Ex 15:11
7:23 Dt 9:26
7:24 Dt 26:18
7:26 1Ch 17:23–24

SPIRIT-TO-SPIRIT PRAYER

Prayer When Facing Trouble

Heavenly Father, we come before You and thank You that when bad days come our way, Your Word says not to fear. We don't have to fear the circumstances because we know that You are the Alpha and the Omega, the beginning and the end. There is nothing that happens in our lives that takes You by surprise. You have already seen our terribly bad day even before we had the faintest idea things weren't going to go our way. Though we might not have a clue about what our future holds, we know who holds tomorrow. And if Your eye is on the sparrow, we know You're watching over us. We ask that in the middle of this storm You cover us with Your wings so that no harm might come near our dwelling. May You grant us Your peace that surpasses all understanding, and may this enormous challenge that we are facing somehow bring honor and glory to Your precious name. In Jesus' name, amen.

Tish Hagee Tucker

27 "For You, O Lord of Hosts, God of Isra-
el, have revealed a word to Your servant,
saying, 'I will build you a house.' Therefore,
Your servant has found the courage to pray
this prayer to You. 28 Now, Lord God, You
are God, and Your words are true. You have
spoken this good message to Your servant.
29 Now, be resolved and bless Your servant's
dynastic house, so that it may stand before
You forever. You, Lord God, have spoken,
and with Your blessing, the house of Your
servant will be blessed forever."

David's Victories
1Ch 18:1–13

8 Afterward, David defeated the Philistines
and subdued them, and David took Me-
theg Ammah from the hand of the Philistines.
2 He also defeated Moab. He measured them
with a length of rope, forcing them to lie down
on the ground. He measured two lengths of
rope to be put to death, but the entirety of one
length he allowed to live. So the Moabites be-
came subject to David, bearing tribute.
3 David also defeated Hadadezer the son of
Rehob, king of Zobah, when he went to restore
his authority over the River Euphrates. 4 David
seized from him one thousand seven hundred
horsemen and twenty thousand foot soldiers,
and David hamstrung all of the chariot horses,
save those for one hundred chariots.
5 The Arameans of Damascus came to help
Hadadezer king of Zobah, but David defeated
twenty-two thousand men of the Arameans.
6 David put garrisons in Aram of Damascus;
and the Arameans became servants who bore
tribute to David. The Lord helped David wher-
ever he went.
7 David took the shields of gold that were is-
sued to the servants of Hadadezer and brought
them to Jerusalem. 8 From Betah[1] and Beroth-
ai, cities of Hadadezer, King David took great
quantities of bronze.
9 When Toi king of Hamath heard that Da-
vid had defeated the entire army of Hadad-
ezer, 10 Toi sent his son Joram to King David
to greet him and bless him on account of his
fighting with Hadadezer and his defeat of him,
for Hadadezer was an opponent of Toi. Joram
brought with him implements of silver, gold,
and bronze, 11 which King David dedicated to
the Lord along with the silver and gold that
he dedicated from all of the nations that he
had subdued, 12 that is, from Aram,[2] Moab, the
Ammonites, the Philistines, Amalek, and the
plunder from Hadadezer the son of Rehob,
king of Zobah.
13 So David made a name for himself upon
his return from defeating eighteen thousand
Arameans[3] in the Valley of Salt.

7:28 Jn 17:17
7:29 Nu 6:24–26
8:1 1Ch 18:1–17
8:2 Nu 24:17
8:3 1Sa 14:47
8:4 Jos 11:6

8:5 1Ki 11:23–25
8:6 2Sa 8:14
8:8 1Ch 18:8
8:9 1Ki 8:65
8:11 1Ki 7:51
8:12 2Sa 10:14
8:13 2Ki 14:7

[1] 8 *Tibhath* in 1Ch 18:8. [2] 12 Possibly *Edom*. Cf. 2Sa 8:14, 1Ch 18:11–13, LXX and Syriac mss. See also note for v. 13. [3] 13 Possibly *Edomites*. Cf. 2Sa 8:14, 1Ch 18:11–13, LXX and Syriac mss.

14 He set up garrisons in Edom. Through-
out all of Edom, he set up garrisons, and all
of Edom became subject to David. The LORD
helped David wherever he went.

David's Officials
1Ch 18:14–17

15 David reigned over all of Israel, and he ad-
ministered fair judgments to all of his people.
16 Joab the son of Zeruiah was over the army.
Jehoshaphat the son of Ahilud was secretary.
17 Zadok the son of Ahitub and Ahimelek the
son of Abiathar were priests. Seraiah was
scribe. 18 Benaiah the son of Jehoiada was in
charge of the Kerethites and Pelethites. The
sons of David were chief ministers.

David's Kindness to Mephibosheth

9 David said, "Is there still anyone left from
the house of Saul to whom I may show
kindness on behalf of Jonathan?"

2 Now there was a servant from the house
of Saul whose name was Ziba. So they sum-
moned him to David. The king said to him,
"Are you Ziba?"

He replied, "I am your servant."

3 The king said, "Is there no one else from
the house of Saul to whom I may show the
kindness of God?"

Ziba responded to the king, "There is still a
son of Jonathan who is crippled in both feet."

4 The king said to him, "Where is he?"

Ziba told the king, "He is at the house of
Makir the son of Ammiel at Lo Debar."

5 So King David sent for and brought him
from the house of Makir the son of Ammiel,
from Lo Debar.

6 Mephibosheth the son of Jonathan the son
of Saul came to David and fell upon his face
and bowed down. Then David said, "Mephi-
bosheth," and he responded, "I am your ser-
vant."

7 David said to him, "Do not be afraid, for I
will certainly show you kindness on account
of Jonathan, your father. I will return to you
every field of Saul, your father, and you will
eat at my table perpetually."

8 He bowed low and said, "What is your ser-
vant that you should be concerned for a dead
dog like me?"

9 The king summoned Ziba the servant of
Saul, and he said to him, "All that belonged to
Saul and to all his house, I have given to the
son of your master. 10 You will work the ground
for him—you, your sons, and your servants.
You will bring in the produce so that the son
of your master will have food to eat; but Me-
phibosheth, the son of your master, will always
eat at my table." Now Ziba had fifteen sons and
twenty servants.

8:14 Ge 27:29
8:16 1Ki 4:3
8:18 1Sa 30:14
9:1 1Sa 20:42
9:2 2Sa 16:1–4
9:3 2Sa 4:4
9:4 2Sa 17:27–29
9:7 2Sa 9:1
9:8 2Sa 16:9
9:10 2Sa 9:7
....
9:13 2Sa 9:7
10:2 1Sa 11:1
10:4 Isa 20:4
10:6 2Sa 8:3
10:8 2Sa 10:6
10:12 Dt 31:6

11 Ziba said to the king, "Everything that my
lord the king has commanded his servant, your
servant will do." So Mephibosheth ate at the
table of David like one of the sons of the king.

12 Now Mephibosheth had a young son
whose name was Mika, and all who dwelled
in the house of Ziba were servants to Mephi-
bosheth. 13 So Mephibosheth lived in Jerusa-
lem, because he ate continually at the table of
the king. Now he was lame in both of his feet.

David Defeats the Ammonites and Arameans
1Ch 19:1–19

10 After this, the king of the Ammonites
died, and Hanun his son reigned in his
stead. 2 David said, "I will show kindness to Ha-
nun the son of Nahash, as his father showed
kindness to me." So David sent a message by
way of his servants to comfort him concerning
his father, and the servants of David went to
the land of the Ammonites.

3 But the Ammonite officials said to Hanun,
their lord, "Has David honored your father in
your eyes by sending comforters to you? Was
it not in an effort to search out the city, to scout
it in order to overthrow it, that he sent his ser-
vants to you?" 4 So Hanun seized the servants
of David, shaved half of the beard of each, cut
their robes in half so that they were exposed,
and sent them away.

5 When they reported what had happened
to David, he sent messengers to meet them,
because the men were severely ashamed. The
king instructed them, "Remain at Jericho until
your beards have regrown, then return."

6 When the Ammonites saw that they had
become odious to David, the Ammonites sent
and hired the Arameans of Beth Rehob and
the Arameans of Zobah, twenty thousand foot
soldiers, and from the king of Maakah, one
thousand men, and from Tob, twelve thousand
men.

7 When David heard of it, he sent Joab and
all the army with the warriors. 8 The Ammon-
ites came out and drew up in battle formation
at the entrance of the gate. But the Arameans
of Zobah, Rehob, Tob, and Maakah were by
themselves in the open field.

9 When Joab saw that the battlefronts were
both before and behind him, he selected some
from the best men in Israel and lined them
up opposite Aram. 10 The remainder of the
people he placed under the charge of Abishai
his brother, and lined them up opposite the
Ammonites. 11 Then he said, "If Aram starts to
prevail over me, you shall help me, but if the
Ammonites begin to prevail over you, then I
will come to help you. 12 Be strong and let us
fight with resolve for the sake of our people

SPIRITLED WOMAN

COUNSEL FROM THE SPIRIT BASICS

"Knowing"

The biblical word often used for intimacy is *knowing*. For example, some translations say that Adam "knew" his wife when she conceived. But contrast Adam's experience with David's one-night stand. The Bible says that David "lay" with Bathsheba.

David shared a moment of passion with Bathsheba, but he did not "know" her, for they had no ongoing relationship. They were not intimate in the biblical sense of the word.

God's desire for man from the very beginning has been for us to know Him and to walk in intimate fellowship with Him. He proved this by forming the body of the first man, Adam, with His own hands and breathing life into him face-to-face rather than simply speaking him into existence, as He had all other created things. He did not distance Himself from Adam until Adam sinned. At that moment God set into motion His redemptive plan.

The apostle Paul understood God's desire and considered everything in his life a loss other than the privilege of knowing Christ. He wrote, "But what things were gain to me, I have counted these things to be loss for the sake of Christ. Yes, certainly, I count everything as loss for the excellence of *the knowledge of Christ Jesus my Lord*, for whom I have forfeited the loss of all things and count them as rubbish that I may gain Christ, and be found in Him, not having my own righteousness which is from the law, but that which is through faith in Christ... *to know Him*" (Php 3:7–10, emphasis added).

Clearly Paul was seeking a level of relationship with God that cannot be attained through intellectual activity, religious works, or temporary emotional experiences. He was seeking intimacy. He wanted to know the width, length, depth, and height of God (Eph 3:18).

June Evans

10:13 1Ki 20:13–21
10:16 1Ch 19:16
10:18 1Ch 19:18
10:19 2Sa 8:6
11:1 1Ch 20:1
11:2 Dt 22:8
11:3 2Sa 23:39
11:4 Lev 18:19
11:5 Dt 22:22
11:8 Ge 18:4

and the cities of our God. May the LORD do what
seems good to Him."
13 Joab advanced the people that were with
him to fight against Aram, and they retreated
from before him. 14 When the Ammonites re-
alized that Aram had fled, they retreated from
before Abishai and entered the city. Then Joab
turned away from fighting against the Ammo-
nites, and he came to Jerusalem.
15 When Aram saw that they had been defeat-
ed by Israel, they assembled together. 16 Hada-
dezer sent for and summoned the Arameans
who were beyond the River,[1] and they came
to Helam. Shobak the commander of the army
of Hadadezer led them.
17 When David was informed of this, he as-
sembled all of Israel. They crossed over the
Jordan and came to Helam. Aram was drawn
up in formation opposite David, and they
fought against him. 18 Aram retreated before
Israel. David killed seven hundred charioteers,
forty thousand horsemen from Aram, and
wounded Shobak the commander of the army
so that he died there. 19 When all of the kings
who were subject to Hadadezer realized that
they were being defeated by Israel, they made
peace with Israel and became subject to them.
From then on, Aram was fearful of further
helping the Ammonites.

David and Bathsheba

11 In the spring of the year, the time when
the kings go out to battle, David sent
out Joab and his officers, all of Israel with
him. They brought to ruin the Ammonites
and besieged Rabbah, but David remained in
Jerusalem.
2 One evening when David arose from his
bed and was walking on the roof of the king's
house, from the roof he saw a woman bath-
ing; and the woman was very beautiful. 3 So,
David sent someone to inquire about the wom-
an. And it was asked, "Is this not Bathsheba
the daughter of Eliam, the wife of Uriah the
Hittite?" 4 So David sent messengers, and took
her; and she came to him, and he lay with
her. When she had purified herself from her
uncleanness, she returned to her house. 5 The
woman conceived. So she sent a message and
reported to David, "I am pregnant."
6 Then David sent an order to Joab, "Send
Uriah the Hittite to me." So, Joab sent Uriah to
David. 7 When Uriah came to him, David asked
about the welfare of Joab, the people, and the
fighting. 8 Then David said to Uriah, "Go down
to your house. Wash your feet." So Uriah left
the house of the king, and a gift from the king
followed him. 9 But Uriah slept at the entrance

[1] *16* Euphrates River.

of the house of the king with all of the servants of his lord; he did not go down to his house.

10 When they reported to David, saying, "Uriah did not go down to his house," David said to Uriah, "Have you not come from a journey? Why did you not go down to your house?"

11 Uriah responded to David, "The ark, Israel, and Judah dwell in makeshift shelters. My lord Joab and the officers of my lord are camping in the open field. But I may enter my house to eat, to drink, and to sleep with my wife? As you live and as your soul lives, I will not do this thing!"

12 So David said to Uriah, "Remain here another day, and I will send you back tomorrow." Uriah remained in Jerusalem that day and the following day. 13 Now David invited him to eat in his presence, and he drank until he got Uriah drunk. In the evening, he went to lie down in his lodging with the servants of his lord, but he did not go down to his house.

14 That morning, David wrote a message to Joab and sent it by way of Uriah. 15 He wrote in the message, "Send Uriah to the front of the line where the fighting is heaviest then withdraw from him, so that he may be struck down and die."

16 So as Joab was besieging the city, he stationed Uriah in a place where he knew fierce men were. 17 When the men of the city came out, they fought with Joab, and some people among those who served David fell; Uriah the Hittite died among them.

18 Joab sent word to inform David of all of the events of the battle. 19 He instructed the messenger, "When you finish telling the king all the details of the battle, 20 if his anger rises and he says to you, 'Why did you approach so near to the city? Did you not know that they might shoot from the city wall? 21 Who killed Abimelek the son of Jerub-Besheth? Did not a woman throw an upper millstone on him from the city wall so that he died at Thebez? Why did you approach so near to the city wall?' You shall then say, 'Additionally your servant Uriah the Hittite is dead.' "

22 So the messenger departed and came to report to David everything that Joab had sent with him. 23 The messenger reported to David, "The men prevailed over us when they came out against us in the open field, but we drove them back to the entrance of the gate. 24 Then the archers shot at your servants from upon the city wall, and some of those who serve the king are dead. Even your servant Uriah the Hittite died."

25 So David replied to the messenger, "Thus you shall report to Joab, 'Do not allow this thing to dismay you, for the sword devours one as well as another. Sustain your attack against the city and bring it to ruin.' Encourage him with this reply."

26 When the wife of Uriah heard that her husband was dead, she mourned for her husband. 27 When the time of mourning was concluded, David sent for her and brought her to his house. She became his wife and bore him a son. But the thing that David had done was displeasing to the LORD.

Nathan Rebukes David
1Ch 20:1–3

12 The LORD sent Nathan to David. He came to him and said, "There were two men in a certain city. One was wealthy, but the other was poor. 2 The wealthy man had a very large flock and herd, 3 but the poor man had nothing except a single small ewe lamb that he had acquired. He nourished it and raised it together with himself and his sons. From his crumbs, it would eat; from his cup, it would drink; and in his arms it would lie. It was like a daughter to him.

4 "There came a visitor to the wealthy man, but he was unwilling to take from his own flock or herd to prepare a meal for the wanderer who had come to him. Instead he took the poor man's ewe lamb and prepared food for the wanderer who had come to him."

5 David became very angry because of this man. He said to Nathan, "As the LORD lives, the man who did this deserves to die. 6 And he shall restore the lamb fourfold, because he did this thing, and because he had no pity."

> You have anointed me and delivered me from the hands of my enemies, just as You did for King David
> (2Sa 12:7).

7 Then Nathan told David, "You are this man! Thus says the LORD, the God of Israel: I anointed you as king over Israel and I rescued you from the hand of Saul. 8 I gave to you your master's house and your master's wives into your arms, and I gave to you the house of Israel and Judah. If this were too little, I would have continued to do for you much more. 9 Why have you despised the word of the LORD by doing evil in His sight? You struck down Uriah the Hittite with the sword, and you took his wife as a wife for yourself. You killed him with the sword of the Ammonites. 10 Now the sword will never depart from your house, because you have despised Me and have taken the wife of Uriah the Hittite to be your wife.

11 "Thus says the LORD: See, I will raise up trouble against you from within your own house. I will take your wives before your eyes

11:11 2Sa 7:2
11:14 1Ki 21:8–10
11:15 2Sa 12:9
....
11:27 2Sa 12:9
12:1 1Ki 20:35–41
12:3 2Sa 11:3
12:5 1Sa 26:16
12:6 Ex 22:1
12:7 1Sa 16:13
12:9 1Sa 15:19
12:10 2Sa 18:14–15
12:11 Dt 28:30

and will give them to your neighbor, and he will lie with your wives in broad daylight. 12 Although you did it secretly, I will do this thing before all of Israel, and under the sun."

13 Then David said to Nathan, "I have sinned against the LORD."

Nathan said to David, "Now the LORD has put away your sin; you shall not die. 14 Nevertheless, because by this deed you have utterly scorned the LORD, the child who is born to you shall die."

15 Then Nathan went to his house. The LORD struck the child that the wife of Uriah had born for David, and he became sick. 16 David entreated God on behalf of the child. He fasted for a period, and he would go in and lie throughout the night on the ground. 17 The elders of his house stood beside him to rouse him from the ground, but he was not willing, nor would he consume food with them.

18 The child died on the seventh day, and the servants of David were afraid to tell him that the child had died. They said, "When the child was alive, we would speak to him, but he would not acknowledge our voices. Now how can we say to him, 'The child is dead'? He may do harm."

19 When David noticed that his servants were whispering to one another, he perceived that the child was dead. So he asked his servants, "Is the child dead?"

They said, "He is dead."

20 So David arose from the ground, washed, anointed himself, and changed his garments. Then he entered the house of the LORD and worshipped. He then went in to his own house. When he asked, they set down food for him and ate.

21 His servants said to him, "What is this thing you have done? You fasted and wept for the sake of the living child, but when the child died, you arose and ate food."

22 He explained, "As long as the child was alive, I fasted and wept because I thought, 'Who knows? The LORD may be gracious to me, so that the child may live.' 23 But now he is dead. Why should I fast? Am I able to bring him back again? I will go to him, but he will not return to me."

The Birth of Solomon

24 Then David comforted Bathsheba, his wife. He went to her and lay with her, so that she conceived a son. They named him Solomon, and the LORD loved him. 25 So He sent a word by way of the prophet Nathan that he should be named Jedidiah for the sake of the LORD.

26 Now Joab fought against Rabbah of the Ammonites and assumed control of the royal city. 27 So Joab sent messengers to David and reported, "I have fought against Rabbah, and I have occupied the water supply of the city. 28 Now gather the remainder of the people, lay siege to the city, and take it. Otherwise, I myself will capture the city, and it will be called by my name."

29 So David gathered all of the people and they went to Rabbah, fought against it, and took it. 30 David took the crown of their king from his head, and its weight was a talent[1] of gold and precious stone. It was placed upon the head of David. He brought out large quantities of plunder from the city. 31 He brought out the people who were in it, and he put them to work with saws, and iron picks, and iron axes, and sent them to work in the brick kiln. Thus he did to all of the cities of the Ammonites. Then David and all of the people returned to Jerusalem.

Amnon and Tamar

13 After this, Absalom the son of David had a beautiful sister whose name was Tamar, and Amnon the son of David fell in love with her.

2 It depressed Amnon to the point of falling ill that Tamar his sister was a virgin, but it was impossible for Amnon to pursue her.

3 Now Amnon had a friend whose name was Jonadab the son of Shimeah, the brother of David, and Jonadab was a very crafty individual. 4 He asked him, "Why are you, the son of the king, so sullen morning after morning? Will you not tell me?"

Amnon told him, "I am in love with Tamar, the sister of Absalom my brother."

5 Jonadab instructed him, "Lie down on your bed and pretend to be ill. When your father comes to see you, say to him, 'Please allow Tamar, my sister, to come and prepare some food for me. She should make the food here, so that when I see it, I may eat it from her hand.' "

6 So Amnon lay down and pretended to be ill. When the king came to see him, Amnon said to the king, "Please let my sister Tamar come here to make a couple of cakes, so that I may be nourished from her hand."

7 Then David sent word to Tamar at the house, "Please go to the house of Amnon your brother, and prepare food for him." 8 So Tamar went to the house of Amnon her brother, where he was lying. She took the dough, kneaded it, and made the cakes before him. Then she baked them. 9 Then she took the baking tray and served the cakes to him, but he refused to eat.

12:12 2Sa 16:22
12:13 2Sa 24:10
12:14 Isa 52:5
12:15 1Sa 25:38
12:16 2Sa 13:31
12:17 2Sa 3:35
12:20 Job 1:20
12:22 Isa 38:1–3
12:23 Ge 37:35
12:24 Mt 1:6
12:25 Ne 13:26
12:30 1Ch 20:2
12:31 1Ch 20:3
13:1 2Sa 3:2–3
13:3 1Sa 16:9
13:6 Ge 18:6
13:9 Ge 45:1

[1] *30* About 75 pounds, or 34 kilograms.

Amnon said, "Send everyone away." So they all left him. 10 Then Amnon said to Tamar, "Bring the food into the bedroom that I may eat from your hand." So Tamar took the cakes that she had made and brought them in the bedroom to Amnon her brother. 11 When she brought them close for him to eat, he took hold of her and said, "Come, lie with me, my sister."

12 She pled with him, "No, my brother, do not violate me, for such a thing is not to be done in Israel. Do not carry out this awful thing. 13 As for me, where could I escape my disgrace? And you would be like one of the fools in Israel. Now, please speak to the king, for he will not withhold me from you." 14 But he refused to listen to her. So, being stronger than her, he overpowered her and lay with her.

15 Then Amnon hated her greatly, so that the hatred with which he hated her was greater than the love with which he had loved her. And Amnon said to her, "Get up, go away."

16 She said to him, "No, because this great offense of dismissing me is worse than the other which you did to me."

But he refused to listen to her. 17 He called his personal servant and said, "Send this woman out from me, and secure the door behind her." 18 Now she was wearing a long robe, because the virgin daughters of the king were clothed in such garments. So his servant put her out and secured the door behind her. 19 So Tamar put ashes on her head and tore the long robe that she was wearing. She put her hand on her head and left, wailing as she went.

20 Absalom her brother said to her, "Has Amnon your brother been with you? Keep silent for now, my sister. He is your brother. Do not take this thing to heart." So Tamar stayed in the house of Absalom, her brother, a desolate woman.

21 When King David heard about these things, he was very angry. 22 And Absalom would not speak with Amnon, either pleasantly or angrily; but Absalom hated Amnon because he had raped his sister Tamar.

Absalom Kills Amnon

23 Two full years later, the sheepshearers of Absalom were in Baal Hazor, near Ephraim, and Absalom invited all of the sons of the king. 24 Then Absalom came to the king and requested, "Your servant has sheepshearers; will the king and his servants kindly go with your servant?"

25 The king said to Absalom, "No, my son, we must not all go or we will be a burden to you." When he urged him, he refused to go, but gave him his blessing.

13:12 Lev 20:17
13:14 2Sa 12:11
13:18 Ge 37:3
13:19 Jos 7:6
13:21 Ge 34:7
13:22 Ge 31:24

....

13:28 Jdg 19:6
13:31 2Sa 1:11
13:33 2Sa 19:19
13:37 2Sa 3:3
14:1 2Sa 13:39
14:2 2Ch 11:6

26 Absalom said, "If not, allow my brother Amnon to go with us."

But the king replied to him, "Why should he go with you?" 27 But Absalom urged him until he sent Amnon and all of the king's sons along with him.

28 Now, Absalom had commanded his servant, "Look for Amnon to become carefree on account of the wine. Then I will say to you, 'Strike Amnon, and kill him.' Do not be afraid, for am not I myself commanding you? Be strong and brave." 29 So, the servants of Absalom did to Amnon that which Absalom had commanded. Then the sons of the king arose, each mounting his mule, and fled.

30 While they were on the way, the report reached David: "Absalom struck down all of the sons of the king, and there is not one of them remaining." 31 Then the king arose, tore his garments, and lay on the ground, while all of his servants who were standing nearby tore their garments.

32 But Jonadab, the son of David's brother Shimeah, said, "My lord should not think that they have killed all of the servants who are the king's sons. Amnon alone is dead, for this has been determined from the day he raped Tamar, his sister, by the very declaration of Absalom. 33 Now, my lord the king should not take this matter to heart, thinking that all of the king's sons are dead. Instead Amnon alone is dead."

34 Absalom fled.

Now when the servant who was keeping watch looked up, he saw many people coming on the road beyond him, around the hill.

35 So Jonadab said to the king, "See, the king's sons are coming. As your servant spoke, so it is."

36 As soon as he had finished speaking, the sons of the king arrived, lifted their voices, and wept. The king and all of his servants also wept loudly.

37 Now Absalom fled and went to Talmai the son of Ammihud, king of Geshur, but David mourned over his son every day.

38 When Absalom fled and went to Geshur, he was there for three years. 39 Then King David longed to go out to Absalom, for he was consoled over the death of Amnon.

Absalom Returns to Jerusalem

14 Now Joab the son of Zeruiah recognized that the king's mind was on Absalom. 2 So Joab sent a request to Tekoa and brought from there a wise woman. He instructed her, "Act as if you are observing mourning rites. Put on mourning garments, and do not anoint yourself with oil, but act like a woman

who has been mourning over the dead like this for many days. 3 Then come to the king and speak to him in this manner." Thus Joab put the words in her mouth.

4 As the Tekoan woman spoke to the king, she fell on her face toward the ground and bowed low. Then she said, "Help me, O king."

5 The king said to her, "What troubles you?"

She responded, "Alas, I am a widow, and my husband is dead. 6 Furthermore, your servant had two sons. The two of them were fighting in the field, but there was no one to separate them. One struck the other and killed him. 7 Now the entire family has risen up against your maidservant, and they said, 'Deliver him who struck his brother, so that we may kill him for the life of his brother whom he killed, and we will destroy the heir also.' So they will extinguish my remaining ember, and leave my husband neither name nor remnant on the face of the earth."

8 Then the king said to the woman, "Go to your house, and I will give orders concerning you."

9 The Tekoan woman responded to the king, "May guilt rest upon me and the house of my father, my lord the king, and may the king and his throne be blameless."

10 The king said, "Whoever speaks to you, bring him to me, and he will not cause you harm again."

11 Then she said, "May the king remember the LORD your God so that the avenger of blood will not continue to destroy, lest they exterminate my son."

He said, "As the LORD lives, not one hair of your son will fall to the ground."

12 Then the woman said, "Allow your servant to speak a word to my lord the king."

So he said, "Speak."

13 The woman said, "Why have you planned like this against the people of God? The king's speaking this word is like a self-conviction, for the king has not brought back his own banished one. 14 We will surely die and are like water spilled on the ground, which cannot be gathered up again. Yet God does not take away a life; He devises plans so that His banished ones will not be cast out from Him.

15 "So now I have come to speak to my lord the king about this matter because the people have made me afraid. So, I thought, 'I will speak to the king. Perhaps the king will perform the request of his servant. 16 For the king may accept my request to deliver his servant from the hand of the man who would destroy me and my son from the inheritance of God.'

17 "So, your servant thought, 'May the word of my lord the king provide rest. For like the angel of God, my lord the king discerns good from evil. May the LORD your God be with you.' "

18 Then the king answered and said to the woman, "Please do not conceal from me anything that I ask you."

The woman said, "May my lord the king please speak."

19 The king said, "Is the hand of Joab with you in all of this?"

The woman answered and said, "As your soul lives, my lord the king, there is no turning right or left from anything that you spoke, my lord the king, for your servant Joab is the very one who commanded me and placed all of these words in my mouth. 20 In order to change this situation, your servant Joab did this thing; but my lord is wise, as with the wisdom of the angel of God, so as to discern everything happening in the land."

21 Then the king said to Joab, "This is what I will do. Go and bring back the young man Absalom."

22 Then Joab fell with his face to ground and bowed low and blessed the king. Joab said, "Today your servant knows that I have found favor in your eyes, my lord the king, since the king has granted the request of his servant."

23 Then Joab arose and went to Geshur, and he brought Absalom to Jerusalem. 24 The king said, "Let him turn to his own house. He shall not come into my presence." So Absalom turned to his house and did not come into the king's presence.

David Forgives Absalom

25 In all of Israel, there was no man as handsome as Absalom. From the sole of his foot to the top of his head, there was not a blemish on him. 26 When he cut the hair of his head (and at the end of every year he cut it, for it was heavy on him), he weighed the hair from his head at two hundred shekels,[1] according to the king's standard.

27 There were born to Absalom three sons and one daughter whose name was Tamar. She was a beautiful woman.

> The enemy will not be able to burn up my harvest (2Sa 14:30).

28 Absalom lived in Jerusalem for two full years without coming into the king's presence. 29 Then Absalom sent a message to Joab, requesting that he send him to the king, but he was not willing to come to him. So he sent a second message, but still he was not willing

14:3 2Sa 14:19
14:7 Nu 35:19
14:9 1Sa 25:24
14:11 1Sa 14:45
14:13 2Sa 12:7
14:14 Nu 35:15
14:16 1Sa 26:19
14:17 1Sa 29:9
14:19 2Sa 14:3
14:20 2Sa 14:17
14:21 2Sa 14:11
14:25 Dt 28:35
14:27 2Sa 18:18

[1] *26* About 5 pounds, or 2.3 kilograms.

to come. 30 Then he said to his servants, "See, Joab's field is next to mine, and he has barley there. Go, set it on fire." So the servants of Absalom set the field on fire.

31 Then Joab arose, came to Absalom at his house, and said to him, "Why have your servants set my plot of land on fire?"

32 Absalom said to Joab, "I sent a message to you, saying: Come, so that I may send you to the king, asking, 'Why have I come from Geshur? It would be better for me to be there still.' Now, let me go before the king, and if there is still guilt with me, may he put me to death."

33 So Joab came and reported this to him. Then he summoned Absalom. So he came to the king, bowed low to him, his face on the ground before the king; then the king kissed Absalom.

Absalom's Conspiracy

15 After this Absalom acquired for himself a chariot, horses, and fifty men to run before him. 2 Absalom would go early and stand beside the way into the gate. When any man who had a dispute concerning which he had come to the king for a judgment approached, Absalom would call to him and say, "Which city are you from?" And he would say, "Your servant is from one of the tribes of Israel." 3 Then Absalom would say to him, "Look, your claim is good and right, but there is no one to hear you on behalf of the king." 4 Absalom would continue, "If I were appointed a judge in the land, then every man who had a claim could come and I would give him justice."

5 When a man would approach to bow before him, he would reach out, embrace him, and kiss him. 6 Absalom acted this way toward every Israelite who came to the king for a judgment. So Absalom stole the hearts of the men of Israel.

7 After forty years, Absalom said to the king, "Please allow me to go fulfill my vow that I made to the Lord in Hebron. 8 For your servant made a vow when I was dwelling in Geshur in Aram, saying: If indeed the Lord will bring me back to Jerusalem, then I will serve the Lord."

9 The king said to him, "Go in peace." So he arose and went to Hebron.

10 But Absalom sent scouts throughout all of the tribes of Israel, saying, "When you hear the sound of the horn, say: Absalom has become king in Hebron." 11 Now two hundred men went with Absalom from Jerusalem, invited and unsuspecting; they did not know anything. 12 Absalom sent for Ahithophel the Gilonite, the advisor of David, from his city Giloh, while he was offering the sacrifices. Now the conspiracy was strong, for the number of people with Absalom was continually growing.

David Flees Jerusalem

13 A messenger came to David and said, "The hearts of the men of Israel are following Absalom."

14 David said to all of his servants who were with him in Jerusalem, "Get up. We must flee or there will be no escape from Absalom for us. Hurry up and leave, or he will soon reach us and bring disaster upon us, striking the city with the edge of the sword."

15 The king's servants said to the king, "Whatever our lord the king decides, we are your servants."

16 So the king left with his entire house after him, but he left behind ten women, concubines, to watch over the house. 17 So the king left with all of the people after him, and they came to a stop at the furthest house. 18 Now all his servants passed on beside him, all the Kerethites, all the Pelethites, and all the Gittites, six hundred men who had followed him from Gath, passed on before the king.

19 The king said to Ittai the Gittite, "Why are you also going with us? Go back and dwell with the king, for you are a foreigner and, moreover, exiled from your own place. 20 You came only yesterday. Shall I cause you to go roaming around with us today? I am going where I go. Go back, and take back your brothers with you. Mercy and truth be with you."

21 Ittai answered the king and said, "As the Lord lives and as lives my lord the king, only in the place where my lord the king is, whether for death or for life, there alone will your servant be."

22 So David said to Ittai, "Go on, pass by." So Ittai the Gittite passed by, along with all of his men and all of the children and elderly who were with him.

23 The whole land wept with a loud voice as all the people passed by. Now the king was crossing over the brook Kidron, and all of the people were crossing over on the road to the wilderness.

24 And also Zadok and all of the Levites with him were carrying the ark of the covenant of God. They set down the ark of God, and Abiathar came up until all of the people had finished passing from the city.

25 The king said to Zadok, "Take the ark of God back to the city. If I have found favor in the eyes of the Lord, He will bring me back and allow me to see both it and its resting place. 26 But if He should say now, 'I take no delight in you,' here I am. May He do to me what seems good to Him."

14:30 Jdg 15:4–5
14:33 Ge 33:4
15:1 1Ki 1:5
15:4 Jdg 9:29
15:5 2Sa 14:33
15:6 Ro 16:18
15:8 Ge 28:20–21
15:11 1Sa 9:13
15:12 Jos 15:51

....

15:13 Jdg 9:3
15:14 2Sa 19:9
15:16 2Sa 16:21–22
15:18 2Sa 8:18
15:19 2Sa 18:2
15:20 1Sa 23:13
15:21 Ru 1:16–17
15:23 2Sa 16:2
15:24 Nu 4:15
15:26 1Sa 3:18

27 The king also said to Zadok the priest, "Are
you not a seer? Return to the city in peace with
your two sons, your son Ahimaaz and Jona-
than the son of Abiathar. 28 I will wait at the
fords of the wilderness until word from you
comes to inform me." 29 So Zadok and Abiathar
returned the ark of God to Jerusalem, and they
remained there.
30 David went up the ascent of the Mount
of Olives, weeping as he went. His head was
covered and he went barefoot. Then all of
the people who were with him each covered
his head and went up, weeping as they went.
31 Now it was reported to David that Ahithophel
was conspiring with Absalom, and David said,
"O LORD, make the advice of Ahithophel folly."
32 When David came to the summit where
he would worship God, Hushai the Arkite ap-
proached him with his coat torn and dirt on
his head. 33 David said to him, "If you pass on
with me, you will be a burden to me. 34 But
if you return to the city, you may say to Ab-
salom, 'I am your servant, O king, as I was a
servant of your father. As I was then, so now I
am your servant,' so as to counter the advice
of Ahithophel. 35 Will not Zadok and Abiathar
the priests be with you there? You shall report
everything that you hear from the king's house
to Zadok and Abiathar the priests. 36 Their two
sons Ahimaaz the son of Zadok and Jonathan
the son of Abiathar will be there with them.
You shall send word of everything that you
hear to me by their hand."
37 So Hushai, the friend of David, came to the
city as Absalom entered Jerusalem.

David and Ziba

16 When David had passed a little beyond
the summit, Ziba the servant of Mephi-
bosheth met him, with a couple of saddled
donkeys carrying two hundred loaves of bread,
one hundred clusters of raisins, one hundred
summer fruits, and one skin of wine.
2 The king said to Ziba, "Why do you have
these things?"
Ziba replied, "The donkeys are for the
household of the king to ride. The bread and
the summer fruit are for the servants to eat.
The wine is for those who become weary in
the wilderness to drink."
3 The king said, "And where is your master's
son?"
Ziba said to the king, "He is staying in Jerusa-
lem, for he said, 'Today they will return to me
the house of Israel and my father's kingdom.'"
4 Then David said to Ziba, "Everything that
belonged to Mephibosheth is now yours."
Ziba replied, "I bow before you. May I find
favor in your sight, my lord the king."

15:27 1Sa 9:9
15:28 2Sa 17:16
15:30 Est 6:12
15:31 2Sa 16:23
15:32 Jos 16:2
15:33 2Sa 19:35
15:35 2Sa 17:15–16
15:36 2Sa 17:17
15:37 2Sa 16:15–16
16:1 1Sa 25:18
16:2 2Sa 17:29
16:3 2Sa 9:9–10
16:5 2Sa 3:16
16:7 2Sa 12:9
16:8 2Sa 1:16
16:9 Ex 22:28
16:10 2Sa 19:22
16:12 Dt 23:5
16:15 2Sa 15:37
16:16 1Sa 10:24
16:17 2Sa 19:25
16:19 2Sa 15:34
16:21 2Sa 15:16

Shimei Curses David

5 When King David came to Bahurim, a
man of the family of the house of Saul came
out. His name was Shimei son of Gera, and
he came out continuously cursing. 6 He threw
stones at David and all of the servants of King
David, as well as all of the people and all of the
warriors who were at his right and left. 7 Shimei
said when he cursed: "Come out! Come out!
You bloodthirsty man, you scoundrel! 8 The
LORD has returned upon you all the blood of
the house of Saul, in whose place you have
reigned. And the LORD has given the kingdom
into the hand of your son Absalom. You are
taken in your own evil, because you are a man
of blood."
9 Then Abishai the son of Zeruiah said to the
king, "How can this dead dog curse my lord the
king! Let me go over and remove his head."
10 The king responded, "What do you have
against me, sons of Zeruiah? Suppose that he
curses because the LORD has said to him, 'Curse
David.' Who shall then say, 'Why do you do
so?'"
11 David then said to Abishai and to all of
his servants, "My son who came from my own
body seeks my life, and now also this Ben-
jamite. Leave him alone and let him curse if
the LORD has so instructed him. 12 Perhaps to-
day the LORD will look upon my guilt and return
kindness instead of his cursing."
13 So David and his men continued on the
road, and Shimei went along on the hillside
beside them, cursing, throwing stones, and
flinging dust at them as he went. 14 The king
and all of the people who were with him ar-
rived at their destination exhausted, but he
refreshed himself there.

The Advice of Ahithophel and Hushai

15 Now Absalom and all of the Israelite peo-
ple entered Jerusalem, and Ahithophel was
with him. 16 When Hushai the Arkite, the friend
of David, came to Absalom, Hushai said to Ab-
salom, "Long live the king! Long live the king!"
17 Then Absalom said to Hushai, "Is this the
extent of your commitment to your friend?
Why have you not gone with your friend?"
18 Hushai said to Absalom, "No! For whom
the LORD, this people, and all men of Israel
have chosen, his I will be and with him I will
remain. 19 Furthermore, whom shall I serve?
Should it not be his son? As I served your fa-
ther, so shall I be with you."
20 Absalom said to Ahithophel, "Give your
advice. What shall we do?"
21 Ahithophel said to Absalom, "Lie with your
father's concubines, whom he left to watch
over the palace. When all Israel hears that you

have made yourself abhorred by your father,
then the hands of all who are with you will be
strong." 22 So they set up a tent for Absalom on
the roof, and Absalom went in to his father's
concubines in the sight of all of Israel.
23 In those days, the advice that Ahithophel
gave was as when one inquired a word from
God. Such was all of the advice of Ahithophel,
whether that which he gave to David or to Ab-
salom.

17 Ahithophel also said to Absalom, "Let
me choose twelve thousand men so
that I may arise and pursue David tonight. 2 I
will overtake him while he is weary and weak
and strike him with terror; all of the people
who are with him will flee. Then I will strike
only the king, 3 and I will return all of the peo-
ple to you. When all return except the man
whom you are seeking, all of the people will
be at peace." 4 The advice pleased Absalom
and all of the elders of Israel.
5 So Absalom said, "Summon Hushai the
Arkite so that we may hear what he has to
say as well." 6 When Hushai came to Absalom,
Absalom said to him, "This is what Ahithophel
had advised. Should we do this thing? If not,
you should tell us."
7 Hushai said to Absalom, "At this time, the
advice that Ahithophel has given is not good."
8 Moreover, Hushai said, "You know that your
father and his men are warriors, and they have
been provoked like a bear robbed of her cubs.
Your father is a veteran of warfare. He will not
spend the night with the people. 9 Even now, he
has hidden himself in a ravine or some other
place, and when one of them falls in the first
attack, whoever hears will say, 'It was a defeat
for the people who follow Absalom.' 10 Then
even the valiant one, whose heart is like that of
a lion, will completely despair, for all of Israel
knows that your father is a warrior, and those
who are with him are brave.
11 "Therefore my advice is for all of Israel,
from Dan to Beersheba, to be completely gath-
ered to you like the multitude of the sand along
the shoreline and for you to go to battle in
person. 12 We will come upon him in one of the
places where he may be found, and we will fall
upon him like the dew upon the ground. Nei-
ther he nor any of the men who are with him
will remain, not a single one. 13 If he withdraws
into a city, then all of Israel will bring ropes to
that city. We will raze it until it is a valley, until
there cannot be found there even a pebble."
14 Then Absalom and all of the men of Israel
said, "The advice of Hushai the Arkite is better
than the advice of Ahithophel." For the LORD
had decided to undermine the prudent advice
of Ahithophel, so that the LORD might bring
calamity to Absalom.

Hushai Warns David to Escape

15 Then Hushai said to Zadok and Abiathar
the priests, "Ahithophel advised Absalom and
the elders of Israel to do one thing, but I ad-
vised them to do another thing. 16 Now quick-
ly send someone to report to David, 'Do not
spend the night at the fords of the wilderness,
but instead cross over. Otherwise, the king
and all of the people who are with him will be
swallowed up.' "
17 Now Jonathan and Ahimaaz were waiting
at En Rogel. A servant girl would go report to
them, and they would go report to King Da-
vid, because they could not be seen entering
the city. 18 But a young man saw them and
reported this to Absalom. So the two of them
went quickly and came to the house of a man
in Bahurim. He had a well in his courtyard,
and they went down into it. 19 The wife took a
covering and spread it over the opening of the
well. Then she scattered grain over it so that
nothing could be discerned.
20 The servants of Absalom came to the wom-
an at the house and said, "Where are Ahimaaz
and Jonathan?"
She said, "They crossed over the brook of
water." When they searched, they could not
find them. So they returned to Jerusalem.
21 After they left, they came up from the well,
went, and reported to King David. They said to
David, "Arise and quickly cross over the water
because thus has Ahithophel advised against
you." 22 So David and all of the people who
were with him arose and crossed over the Jor-
dan. By daybreak, there was not one left who
had not crossed over the Jordan.
23 When Ahithophel realized that his advice
was not followed, he saddled his donkey and
returned to his house in his own city. He gave
instruction to his household, then he hanged
himself and died; he was interred in the tomb
of his father.

Absalom's Death

24 David came to Mahanaim as Absalom
crossed the Jordan, he and every Israelite
with him. 25 Now Absalom had placed Amasa
over the army in the place of Joab. Now Amasa
was the son of a man named Jether the Ish-
maelite, who went in to Abigail the daughter
of Nahash and sister of Zeruiah, the mother
of Joab. 26 Israel and Absalom camped in the
land of Gilead.
27 When David came to Mahanaim, Shobi the
son of Nahash from Rabbah of the Ammo-
nites, Makir the son of Ammiel from Lo De-
bar, and Barzillai the Gileadite from Rogelim

16:22 2Sa 12:11–12
16:23 2Sa 15:12
17:2 2Sa 16:14
17:8 Hos 13:8
17:10 Jos 2:9–11
17:11 Ge 22:17
17:14 2Sa 15:34

....

17:16 2Sa 15:28
17:17 Jos 15:7
17:18 2Sa 3:16
17:20 Ex 1:19
17:21 2Sa 17:15–16
17:23 2Sa 15:12
17:24 Ge 32:2
17:25 2Sa 19:13
17:27 2Sa 9:4

28 brought bedding, metal bowls, ceramic ves-
sels, wheat, barley, flour, roasted grain, beans,
lentils, 29 honey, curds, sheep, and cheese from
the livestock for David and the people who
were with him to eat and use. For they said,
"The people are hungry, exhausted, and thirst-
ing in the wilderness."

18 David mustered the people who were
with him, and he set over them com-
manders of thousands and commanders of
hundreds. 2 Then David dispatched the people,
one-third under the command of Joab, one-
third under the command of Abishai the son
of Zeruiah and brother of Joab, and one-third
under the command of Ittai the Gittite. Then
David said to the people, "I myself will go out
with you."

3 But the people said, "You should not go, for
if we retreat, they will not be concerned about
us. Even if half of us die, they will not be con-
cerned about us. But now you are worth ten
thousand of us. Therefore, it would be better
to assist us from the city."

4 The king said to them, "I will do what seems
best to you."

So the king stood beside the gate while all
of the people went out by hundreds and thou-
sands. 5 The king commanded Joab, Abishai,
and Ittai, "Deal gently with the young man
Absalom." All of the people heard the king
instruct the commanders concerning Absalom.

6 So the people went out toward Israel in the
field, but the fighting occurred in the forest of
Ephraim. 7 The people of Israel were defeated
there by the servants of David. That day the
defeat was extensive, twenty thousand men.
8 The fighting spread across the land, and the
people consumed by the forest were more nu-
merous than those consumed by the sword
that day.

9 Absalom was encountered by some of the
servants of David. Now Absalom was riding
on his mule. When the mule went under the
branches of a very large tree, his head was
caught in the tree. He was left in midair while
the mule that was under him kept going.

10 One man saw him and reported it to Joab,
saying, "I saw Absalom hanging in a tree."

11 Joab said to the man who was reporting
to him, "What? You saw him? Why did you
not strike him on the spot, sending him to the
ground? I would have given you ten shekels[1]
of silver and a belt."

12 The man said to Joab, "Not even if I had felt
the weight of a thousand shekels[2] of silver in
my hand would I have laid a hand on the king's
son. In our hearing the king commanded you,
Abishai, and Ittai saying: Beware lest anyone
touch the young man Absalom! 13 Otherwise, I
would have worked falsehood against my own
life. For nothing is hidden from the king, and
you yourself would have set yourself against
me."

14 Then Joab said, "I will not waste any more
time with you." He took three spears in his
hand and thrust them into the heart of Absa-
lom while he was still alive in the midst of the
tree. 15 Then ten young men, armor bearers
for Joab, gathered around and struck down
Absalom, killing him.

16 When Joab blew the horn, the people
returned from pursuing Israel, for Joab held
back the people. 17 Then they took Absalom,
disposed of him in a large pit in the forest,
and piled over him a very large heap of stones.
Then all Israel fled, everyone to his home.

18 Now Absalom in his lifetime had taken
and set up for himself a memorial stone in
the Valley of the King, for he said, "I have no
son by whom my name may be remembered."
So he named the memorial stone after himself;
and to this day, it is called the monument of
Absalom.

David Mourns

19 Then Ahimaaz the son of Zadok said, "Al-
low me to run and bring the news to the king
that the LORD has delivered him from the hand
of his enemies."

20 But Joab said to him, "You will not be a
man who bears news today; you may bear
news another day. Today you will not bear
news because the king's son is dead."

21 Then Joab said to the Cushite, "Go, report
to the king what you have seen." The Cushite
bowed to Joab, then ran off.

22 Ahimaaz again said to Joab, "Whatever
may happen, let me run also, after the Cush-
ite."

Then Joab said, "Why is it that you want to
run, my son? There is no messenger's reward
for you to obtain."

23 "Whatever happens, I want to run."

So he said to him, "Run." So Ahimaaz ran
by way of the plain and passed the Cushite.

24 Now David was sitting between the two
gates when the watchman went up to the roof
of the gate, to the city wall. He lifted his eyes
and saw a man running by himself. 25 The
watchman called and told the king.

The king said, "If he is alone, there is news in
his mouth." And he came ever closer.

26 Then the watchman saw another man run-
ning. The watchman called to the gatekeeper
and said, "Look there is another man running
alone."

17:29 2Sa 16:2
18:2 Jdg 7:16
18:3 2Sa 21:17
18:4 2Sa 18:24
18:6 Jos 17:18
18:9 2Sa 14:26
18:13 2Sa 14:19–20
18:16 2Sa 2:28
18:17 Jos 7:26
18:18 1Sa 15:12
18:19 2Sa 15:36
18:24 2Sa 19:8

[1] 11 About 4 ounces, or 115 grams. [2] 12 About 25 pounds, or 12 kilograms.

The king said, "He also is bringing news."
27 The watchman said, "I think that the run-
ning of the first one is like the running of Ahi-
maaz."

The king said, "He is a good man and comes
with good news."
28 Then Ahimaaz called to the king and said,
"All is well." He bowed down to the ground
before the king and said, "Blessed be the LORD
your God who has handed over the men who
raised their hand against my lord the king."
29 The king said, "Is it well for the young man
Absalom?"

Ahimaaz said, "I saw a great commotion
when Joab sent the servant of the king, your
servant, but I do not know what it was."
30 The king said, "Step aside and stand here."
So he stepped aside and stood in position.
31 Then the Cushite came and said, "Good
news for my lord the king, for today the LORD
has delivered you from those who rose up
against you."
32 The king said to the Cushite, "Is it well for
the young man Absalom?"

The Cushite said, "May the enemies of my
lord the king and all who would rise up against
you to do harm become as the young man is."
33 The king was deeply moved and went up
to the upper chamber of the gate and wept.
As he went he said, "O my son Absalom, my
son, my son Absalom! If only I could have
given my death in your stead, Absalom, my
son, my son!"

19 It was reported to Joab that the king
was weeping and mourning over Ab-
salom. 2 The victory that day was turned into
mourning for all of the people, for the people
heard that day, "The king is grieving for his
son." 3 So the people entered the city by stealth
that day, as a people who have been disgraced
steal away when they flee from battle. 4 The
king covered his face and called with a loud
voice, "My son Absalom, my son, my son!"
5 Then Joab came to the king in his house
and said, "Today you have shamed the faces of
all of your servants who saved your life today,
as well as the lives of your sons and daugh-
ters, the lives of your wives, and the lives of
your concubines, 6 by loving those who hated
you and hating those who love you. You have
shown today that commanders and servants
are nothing to you. I know that if Absalom
were alive instead today and all of us were
dead, then this would be right in your eyes.
7 Now go out and speak reassuringly to your
servants, for I swear by the LORD that if you
do not go out, no man will stay with you this
night, and this will be worse for you than any

18:27 2Ki 9:20
18:29 2Sa 18:22
18:31 2Sa 18:19
18:33 2Sa 19:4
19:4 2Sa 15:30
19:7 Pr 14:28

. . . .

19:8 2Sa 18:24
19:9 2Sa 15:14
19:11 2Sa 15:29
19:12 2Sa 5:1
19:13 2Sa 17:25
19:14 Jdg 20:1
19:15 Jos 5:9
19:16 1Ki 2:8
19:17 2Sa 9:2
19:19 1Sa 22:15
19:20 2Sa 16:5
19:21 Ex 22:28
19:22 1Sa 11:13

calamity that has come against you from your
youth until now."
8 So the king arose and took his seat in the
gate, and the people were all told, "The king
is sitting in the gate." So all the people came
before the king, but the children of Israel had
fled, each to his tent.

David Returns to Jerusalem

9 Now all of the people began to quarrel
throughout all of the tribes of Israel, saying,
"The king delivered us from the hand of our
enemies, and he saved us from the hand of
the Philistines, but now he has fled from the
land on account of Absalom. 10 But Absalom,
whom we anointed over us, has died in battle.
Now why are you idle to bring back the king?"
11 Then David sent word to Zadok and Abi-
athar the priests, saying, "Speak to the elders
of Israel, saying, 'Why are you last to bring the
king back to his house when the word of all
Israel has come to the king, to his house? 12 You
are my brother. You are my bone and my flesh.
Why are you last to bring back the king?' 13 Say
to Amasa, 'Are you not my bone and my flesh?
May God do to me, and more so, if you are not
commander of the army before me from now
on in the place of Joab.' "
14 He swayed the heart of every man of Judah
as though they were one man, and they sent
a message to the king: "Return, you and all of
your servants."
15 So the king returned and came as far as
the Jordan, and Judah came to Gilgal to meet
the king and bring the king across the Jordan.
16 Shimei the son of Gera, the Benjamite who
was from Bahurim, hastened to go down with
the men of Judah to meet King David. 17 With
him were a thousand men from Benjamin. And
Ziba, the servant of the house of Saul, with his
fifteen sons and twenty servants, rushed down
to the Jordan before the king. 18 They crossed
the ford to bring the household of the king
across and to do what was pleasing in his eyes.

Shimei the son of Gera fell before the king as
he was crossing the Jordan, 19 and he said to
the king, "Do not regard me as guilty, my lord,
or remember how your servant went astray
the day when my lord the king went out from
Jerusalem. May the king not take it to heart.
20 For your servant knows that I have sinned.
Therefore, I have come this day, first from all
of the house of Joseph, to go down to meet
my lord the king."
21 Abishai the son of Zeruiah answered,
"Shall not Shimei be put to death for this, be-
cause he cursed the anointed of the LORD?"
22 David said, "What do you sons of Zeruiah
have against me that you should become an

adversary to me today? Should any man in Israel be put to death today? For do I not know that today I am king over Israel?" 23 The king said to Shimei, "You will not die." The king gave him his oath.

24 Then Mephibosheth the son of Saul went down to meet the king. He had neither dressed his feet, nor trimmed his mustache, nor washed his clothes from the day the king left until the day he came back in peace. 25 When he came from Jerusalem to meet the king, the king said to him, "Why did you not go with me, Mephibosheth?"

26 He said, "My lord, O king, my servant deceived me. For your servant said, 'I will saddle the mule for myself in order to ride on it and go with the king,' because your servant is lame. 27 But he has slandered your servant to my lord the king. Still my lord the king is as the angel of God, so do what seems best to you. 28 For all my father's house were but dead men before my lord the king. Yet you set your servant among those who eat at your table. What right do I have to cry out any more to the king?"

29 The king said to him, "Why do you still speak of your affairs? I say that you and Ziba shall divide the field."

30 Mephibosheth said to the king, "Let him even take everything, since my lord the king has come safely to his house."

31 Now Barzillai the Gileadite had come down from Rogelim in order to see the king across the Jordan. 32 Barzillai was very old, eighty years old. But he sustained the king during his stay in Mahanaim, for he was a very rich man. 33 The king said to Barzillai, "Cross over with me and I will sustain you with me in Jerusalem."

34 Barzillai said to the king, "How many days are left in my life that I should go up with the king to Jerusalem? 35 I am now eighty years old. Can I discern what is pleasant from what is harmful? Can your servant taste what I eat and what I drink? Can I still hear the voices of men and women who sing? Why, then, should your servant be a burden to my lord the king? 36 Your servant is merely crossing over the Jordan with the king. Why should the king repay me with this reward? 37 Now allow your servant to return, that I may die in my own city with the grave of my father and my mother. But here is your servant Kimham. He will cross over with my lord the king. Do for him what seems best to you."

38 The king said, "Kimham will cross over with me, and I will do for him what seems best to you. Whatever you require of me, I will do for you."

39 All of the people crossed over the Jordan. And when the king had crossed over, the king kissed Barzillai and blessed him and he returned to his own place.

40 The king passed on to Gilgal, and Kimham went on with him; all of the people of Judah and half of the people of Israel passed on with the king.

41 Now all of the men of Israel were coming to the king and said to the king, "Why have our brothers, the men of Judah, stolen you away and brought the king and his household across the Jordan, and all of the men of David with him?"

42 All of the men of Judah answered the men of Israel, "Because the king is our close relative. Why are you angry over this matter? Have we eaten at all at the king's expense? Has he given any gift to us?"

43 And the men of Israel answered the men of Judah and said, "We have ten shares in the king. Therefore we also have more claim on David than you. Why then did you treat us with contempt? Were we not the first to advise bringing back our king?"

But the words of the men of Judah were harsher than the words of the men of Israel.

Sheba Rebels Against David

20 There happened to be a worthless man there whose name was Sheba the son of Bikri, a Benjamite. He sounded the trumpet and said,

"We have no share in David,
nor do we have an inheritance in the son of Jesse;
every man to his tents, O Israel."

2 So every man of Israel withdrew from following David and followed after Sheba the son of Bikri, but the men of Judah stayed with their king, from the Jordan as far as Jerusalem.

3 When the king came to his house in Jerusalem, he took the ten women, the concubines whom he had left to keep watch over the house, and he placed them in custody. He provided for them but did not go in to them. They were shut up until the day of their deaths, living as in widowhood.

4 Then the king said to Amasa, "Summon for me the men of Judah in three days, then present yourself here." 5 So Amasa went to summon Judah, but he delayed beyond the deadline determined for him.

6 So David said to Abishai, "Now Sheba the son of Bikri will cause more harm for us than Absalom. You take your lord's servants and pursue after him. Otherwise, he will find fortified cities and escape from our sight." 7 The men of Joab went out after him, along with

19:25 2Sa 16:17
19:27 2Sa 14:17
19:28 2Sa 9:13
19:31 1Ki 2:7
19:32 1Sa 25:2
19:35 2Sa 15:33
19:37 1Ki 2:7
....
19:39 Ge 31:55
19:41 Jdg 8:1
19:42 2Sa 19:12
19:43 2Sa 5:1
20:1 1Ki 12:16
20:3 2Sa 15:16
20:4 2Sa 17:25
20:5 1Sa 13:8
20:6 2Sa 11:11
20:7 2Sa 8:18

the Kerethites, the Pelethites, and all of the warriors; and they went out from Jerusalem to pursue after Sheba the son of Bikri.

8 When they were at the large stone which is in Gibeon, Amasa came to meet them. Now Joab was dressed in his battle armor, and fastened on it was a belt with a sword in its sheath at the waist. As he went forward, it fell out.

9 Joab said to Amasa, "Is it well with you, my brother?" and he took Amasa by the beard with his right hand to kiss him. 10 Amasa was not on guard against the sword in the hand of Joab, and he struck him in the midsection spilling his entrails on the ground. He died without being struck a second time. Then Joab and Abishai his brother pursued after Sheba the son of Bikri.

11 Now one of the young men of Joab stood by him and said, "Whoever favors Joab and whoever is for David, *let him* follow Joab." 12 Now Amasa was wallowing in his own blood in the middle of the path. When the man saw that all of the people stood still, he moved Amasa from the path to the field and threw a covering over him, when he observed that everyone who passed by would stop. 13 Once he removed him from the path, all of the men passed by, following Joab in pursuit of Sheba the son of Bikri.

14 He passed through all of the tribes of Israel toward Abel Beth Maakah, also passing by all of the Bikrites. Once assembled, they also came after him. 15 They came and besieged him in Abel Beth Maakah. They constructed a siege ramp against the city, standing it against the rampart. As all of the people who were with Joab were battering the city wall in order to bring it down, 16 a wise woman called from the city, "Listen! Listen! Say to Joab, 'Come closer so that I may speak with you.' " 17 When he came near, the woman said, "Are you Joab?"

He said, "I am."

She said to him, "Listen to the words of your servant," and he said, "I'm listening."

18 She said, "In former times, they would say, 'Let them inquire carefully in Abel,' and thus they would resolve an issue. 19 I am a trustworthy and faithful one of Israel. You are attempting to destroy a city, even a mother, in Israel. Why do you swallow up the inheritance of the LORD?"

20 Joab responded, "Far be it, far be it from me to swallow up or destroy. 21 That is not true. But a man from the hill country of Ephraim, Sheba the son of Bikri by name, has lifted his hand against King David. Only deliver him, and I will depart from the city."

And the woman said to Joab, "His head will be thrown to you over the wall."

22 The woman, with her wisdom, came to all of the people in the city, and they cut off the head of Sheba the son of Bikri. When they threw it to Joab, he blew the horn, and they dispersed from the city, each going to his own tent. Joab returned to Jerusalem to the king.

David's Officials

23 Now Joab was over the entire army of Israel. Benaiah the son of Jehoiada was over the Kerethites and Pelethites. 24 Adoniram was over conscripted labor. Jehoshaphat the son of Ahilud was secretary. 25 Sheva was scribe. Zadok and Abiathar were priests, 26 and also Ira the Jairite was priest to David.

David Avenges the Gibeonites

21 Now there was a famine in the days of David for three years, year after year; and David called upon the LORD. The LORD said, "There is blood guilt upon Saul and upon his house because he put the Gibeonites to death."

2 So the king summoned the Gibeonites and spoke to them. Now the Gibeonites were not from the children of Israel. Instead they were a remnant of the Amorites. Although the children of Israel had made a pact with them, Saul attempted to destroy them in his zeal for the people of Israel and Judah. 3 David said to the Gibeonites, "What must I do for you, and with what may I appease you that you may bless the inheritance of the LORD?"

4 The Gibeonites said to him, "We have no concern for silver or gold from Saul or his household, nor is it for us to put any man in Israel to death."

He said to them, "What are you saying I should do for you?"

5 They said to the king, "Regarding the man who put an end to us and planned to exterminate us from the entire territory of Israel, 6 let seven of his male descendants be handed over to us, and we will hang them before the LORD at Gibeah of Saul, the chosen one of the LORD."

The king said, "I will hand them over."

7 But the king spared Mephibosheth the son of Jonathan, the son of Saul on account of the oath of the LORD that was between them, between David and Jonathan the son of Saul. 8 So the king took the two sons of Rizpah the daughter of Aiah, Armoni and Mephibosheth, whom she had born to Saul, and the five sons of Michal the daughter of Saul, whom she had born to Adriel the son of Barzillai the Meholathite. 9 He delivered them into the hands of the Gibeonites, and they hanged them on the mountain before the LORD; the seven of them fell together. They were put to death in the

20:10 2Sa 2:23
20:11 2Sa 20:13
20:14 2Ki 15:29
20:15 2Ki 19:32
20:16 2Sa 14:2
20:19 1Sa 26:19

20:22 2Sa 20:1
20:23 2Sa 8:16–18
20:24 1Ki 4:3
20:26 2Sa 23:38
21:1 Ge 12:10
21:3 2Sa 20:19
21:5 2Sa 21:1
21:6 1Sa 10:24
21:7 1Sa 18:3
21:8 1Sa 18:19
21:9 Ru 1:22

first days of harvest, in the beginning of the
barley harvest.
10 Rizpah the daughter of Aiah took sackcloth
and spread it for herself on the rock, from the
beginning of the harvest until the rains poured
on them from heaven. She did not allow the
birds of the air to rest on them by day nor
the animals of the field by night. 11 When it
was reported to David that which Rizpah the
daughter of Aiah, the concubine of Saul, had
done, 12 David went and took the bones of Saul
and the bones of Jonathan his son from the
men of Jabesh Gilead who had secretly taken
them from the plaza in Beth Shan, where the
Philistines had hung them the day the Philis-
tines struck down Saul on Gilboa. 13 He brought
up the bones of Saul and the bones of Jona-
than his son from there, and they gathered the
bones of those who had been hanged.
14 They interred the bones of Saul and Jona-
than his son in the land of Benjamin at Zela,
in the tomb of Kish, his father. They did every-
thing that the king commanded. After that God
was entreated regarding the land.

Wars With the Philistines
1Ch 20:4–8

15 Now once again there was a battle between
the Philistines and Israel. So David went down
and his servants with him to fight the Philis-
tines, and David grew weary. 16 Now Ishbi-Ben-
ob, who was among the descendants of the
giant and was girded with new weaponry, had
a spear weighing three hundred bronze shek-
els and had said that he would strike David
down. 17 But Abishai the son of Zeruiah came
to his aid. He struck down the Philistine and
killed him. Then the men of David made an
oath with him, saying, "You shall no longer
come out with us to battle, so that you do not
extinguish the lamp of Israel."
18 Now afterwards there was again a battle
with the Philistines at Gob. Then Sibbekai
the Hushathite struck down Saph, who was
among the descendants of the giant.
19 Once again, there was a battle with the Phi-
listines at Gob. On this occasion, Elhanan the
son of Jaare-Oregim the Bethlehemite struck
down Goliath the Gittite, whose spear shaft was
like a weaver's beam.
20 Once again, there was war at Gath. There
was a man of stature who had six fingers on
each hand and six toes on each foot, twen-
ty-four in number. Now he also was born to the
giant. 21 When he taunted Israel, Jonathan the
son of Shimeah, the brother of David, struck
him down.
22 Now these four were born to the giant in
Gath, and they fell by the hand of David and
by the hand of his servants.

21:10 Dt 21:23
21:12 Jos 17:11
21:14 Jos 18:28
21:16 2Sa 21:18
21:17 2Sa 18:3
21:18 1Ch 11:29
21:19 1Ch 20:5
21:20 2Sa 21:16
21:22 1Ch 20:8

....

22:1 Ex 15:1
22:2 Ps 31:3
22:3 Ge 15:1
22:5 Ps 69:14–15
22:6 Ps 116:3
22:7 Ps 116:4
22:8 Jdg 5:4
22:9 Heb 12:29
22:10 1Ki 8:12
22:11 Ps 104:3
22:12 2Sa 22:10
22:13 2Sa 22:9
22:15 Dt 32:23
22:16 Na 1:4

David's Song of Deliverance
Ps 18:1–50

22 Now on the day the LORD delivered him
from the hand of all of his enemies
and from the hand of Saul, David spoke to the
LORD the words of this song. 2 He said:

The LORD is my rock and my fortress and
my deliverer;
3 the God of my strength, in whom I will
trust;
my shield and the horn of my salvation,
my fortress and my sanctuary;
my Savior, You save me from violence.
4 I call upon the LORD, who is praiseworthy,
and I am saved from my enemies.
5 When the waves of death
encompassed me,
the currents of destruction made me
afraid.
6 The ropes of Sheol were wrapped
around me;
the snares of death were opposite me.
7 In my distress I called on the LORD,
and cried out to my God;
from His temple He heard my voice.
My cry *reached* His ears.
8 Then the earth quaked and trembled;
the foundations of the heavens rumbled
and shook,
because He was angry.
9 Smoke rose from His nostrils,
devouring fire from His mouth;
coals blazed forth from Him.
10 He bowed the heaven as He came down,
with thick darkness under His feet.
11 He rode upon a cherub as He flew,
and appeared upon the wings of the
wind.
12 He made darkness canopies around Him,
dark waters and thick clouds of the
skies.
13 From the brightness before Him
embers of fire are kindled.
14 The LORD thundered from heaven,
and the Most High uttered His voice.

Let the blast of your nostrils rebuke
the enemy (2Sa 22:16).

15 He sent out arrows and dispersed them;
with lightning He sent them into
confusion.
16 The channels of the sea appeared,
the foundations of the world were
exposed
with the rebuke of the LORD,
from the blast of breath from His
nostrils.

17 He reached from on high and took me;
He drew me out of mighty waters.
18 He rescued me from my strong enemy,
from those who hate me;
for they were stronger than I.
19 They confronted me in the day of my disaster,
but the LORD was my support.
20 He brought me to the open expanse;
He rescued me, for He delighted in me.

21 The LORD did for me according to my righteousness;
according to the cleanness of my hands
He recompensed me.
22 For I have kept the ways of the LORD,
and I have not become guilty against my God.
23 For all His judgments are before me,
and I have not abandoned His statutes.
24 I am blameless toward Him,
and I have kept myself from guilt.
25 The LORD has recompensed me according to my righteousness,
according to my cleanness in His sight.
26 With the faithful You prove Yourself faithful;
with the blameless You prove Yourself blameless;
27 with the pure You show Yourself pure;
but with the perverse You show Yourself shrewd.
28 You deliver a humble people;
but Your eyes are upon the exalted to bring them down.
29 For You are my lamp, O LORD;
the LORD illuminates my darkness.
30 For by You I can run *over* a channel;
by my God I can leap over a wall.

31 As for God, His way is perfect;
the word of the LORD is proven;
He is a shield
for all who take refuge in Him.
32 For who is God except the LORD?
And who is a rock except our God?
33 God is my strong fortress,
and He sets the blameless on His way.
34 He makes my feet like hinds' *feet*;
He sets me on my high places.
35 He trains my hand for battle,
so that my arm may bend a bow of bronze.
36 You have given me a shield of Your salvation,
and Your humility has made me great.
37 You widen my stride under me,
and my feet do stagger.

38 I pursued my enemies and destroyed them;
I did not turn back until they were consumed.

22:17 Ps 144:7
22:20 2Sa 15:26
22:21 1Sa 26:23
22:22 Ge 18:19
22:23 Ps 119:30
22:24 Ge 6:9
22:25 2Sa 22:21
22:26 Mt 5:7
22:27 Mt 5:8
22:28 Ps 72:12–13
22:29 Ps 27:1
22:31 Dt 32:4
22:32 1Sa 2:2
22:34 Dt 32:13
22:35 Ps 144:1
22:36 Eph 6:16
22:37 Pr 4:12
....
22:39 Mal 4:3
22:40 Ps 44:5
22:41 Ex 23:27
22:42 Isa 1:15
22:43 Mic 7:10
22:44 2Sa 8:1–14
22:45 Ps 66:3
22:46 Mic 7:17
22:47 Ps 89:26
22:48 Ps 144:2
22:49 Ps 140:1
22:50 Ro 15:9
22:51 Ps 144:10
23:1 2Sa 7:8–9
23:2 2Pe 1:21
23:3 2Sa 22:32

39 I consumed them and shattered them so that they did not rise;
they fell under my feet.
40 You girded me with strength for the battle;
You subjugated under me those who rose up against me.
41 You caused my enemies to retreat from me;
I destroyed those who hated me.
42 They looked, but there was no one to save them,
to the LORD, but He did not respond.
43 I crushed them like the dust of the land,
like the mud of the streets, I ground them and stamped them down.

44 You have also delivered me from the strivings of my people;
You have kept me as the head of the nations.
A people whom I have not known will serve me.
45 Foreigners submit to me, cringing;
as soon as they hear, they obey me.
46 Foreigners lose heart;
they gird themselves as they leave their fortresses.

47 The LORD lives; blessed be my rock.
May the God of the rock of my salvation be exalted,
48 the God who gave me retribution
and brought down peoples under me,
49 who brought me out from my enemies.
You exalted me above those who rose up against me;
You delivered me from violent ones.
50 Therefore, I praise You, O LORD, among the nations;
I sing praises to Your name.
51 He is a tower of salvation for His king,
and He acts faithfully toward His anointed,
toward David and his descendants forever.

David's Last Words

23 Now these are the last words of David:

The oracle of David the son of Jesse,
the oracle of the man who was raised on high,
the anointed of the God of Jacob,
and the favorite psalmist of Israel:

2 The Spirit of the LORD spoke by me,
and His word was on my tongue.
3 The God of Israel said,
the Rock of Israel spoke to me:
He who rules over man justly,
who rules in the fear of God,

How Angels Minister Today

Hanging in my grandmother's house was a picture that has left a lasting impact on me. It was titled *The Guardian*, and it featured a very large angel with a comforting expression and outreached hands hovering near a small boy and girl as they walked over a precariously dangerous bridge.

The simple framed print brought great comfort and security to my heart when I was a little girl and propelled my imaginative mind into the awesome arena of angels. In recent years the study of angels has continued to bring me much comfort and encouragement.

Angels have often been relegated to the shimmer and shine of Christmas, but actually they have been involved with God and His purposes since the dawn of creation. Wherever God is—and He fills every crack and crevice of the universe—you will find angels.

In my opinion, the evangelical world has underemphasized the ministry of angels. They are never to be our primary focus, but what overwhelming encouragement to be keenly aware of the myriad of angels who can be sent to minister to the children of God!

Angels, the Scriptures tell us, are innumerable (Heb 12:22). There are "ten thousand times ten thousand, and thousands of thousands" of them (Rev 5:11). I have been told by people more proficient in math than I am that there are possibly 100 trillion angels!

What Are Angels?

Angels are inhabitants of the heavenlies—a part of the eternal yet connected to time. They are celestial beings created by God whose principal purpose is to serve Him and help carry out His purposes in the heavens and the earth.

Angels are described in the Bible as mighty, strong, glorious, fearsome, wise, and flaming. They move swiftly from place to place. They fight. They shout. They speak. They go before. They go behind. They can bless. They can destroy. They move through lightning, thunder, storms, earthquakes, hailstones, and fire.

Angels are fierce enough to make a king plead for help (2Sa 24:16–17) and tender enough to bring comfort (Ge 21:17). They have tremendous power because they are propelled by God's Word, but their supernatural abilities are enlisted only at God's command, as we see in Psalm 103:20: "Bless the LORD, you His angels, who are mighty, and do His commands, and obey the voice of His word."

It is almost mind-boggling to realize these powerful beings are sent to minister to us—mere mortals yet the heirs of salvation (Heb 1:14). But it's true! This knowledge should bring us wonderful comfort and assurance.

To *minister* means "to serve, care for, attend to, help, aid, assist, relieve, comfort, console, accommodate, befriend." What more could we need on this, the earthly track of our heavenly journey?

Angels know the address for our prayers.

Prayer is our line of communication into the unseen world of God and angels, far beyond the bubble of our earthly existence. It is the believer's daily privilege to go boldly into the throne room of God where angels dwell and, through our prayers, to seek help and make our petitions and requests known.

When we enter into the throne room of heaven on the wings of prayer and speak the words "Our Father," heaven pays attention because we are God's children. When we find ourselves in weakness or in need, a heartfelt cry of "Father!" will give us instant access to God and can send the angels scurrying, for they have been given orders to keep us in all our ways (Ps 91:11). In the garden, with great distress of soul and perhaps a wail, Jesus uttered, "Father," and an angel from heaven appeared to Him and strengthened Him (Lk 22:42–43).

Incidents of angelic leading, guidance, deliverance, provision, and protection are numerous in the Scriptures. It would be surprising, I am sure, if all the events in the Bible were unfolded for us to see openly the corresponding activities of the spirit world. Could it be that whatever God does in the spirit world, He does with the assistance of angels, just as whatever He does in our world, He does with the assistance of men?

Two worlds—dramatically different, inexplicably intertwined. God rules in both. The connecting link is prayer, an expression from our limitations to the unlimited resources in God, which includes the ministry of an innumerable host of angels—ministers to the heirs of salvation.

Thetus Tenney

4 is like the light of the morning *when* the
sun rises,
a morning with no clouds,
gleaming after the rain
like grass from the land.

5 Is not my house like this with God?
For He made an everlasting covenant
with me,
ordered in all things and secure.
For *this is* all my salvation and all *my*
desire;
will He not make *it* flourish?
6 But the worthless individual is like a thorn
tossed away, all of them,
for they cannot be taken with the hand.
7 But the man who touches them
must have an iron *implement* and the
shaft of a spear,
and they must be burned with fire on
the spot.

David's Mighty Warriors

1Ch 11:10–41

8 These are the names of the warriors whom
David had:
Josheb-Basshebeth, a Tahkemonite, was
head of the three.[1] He was also known as Adi-
no the Eznite, on account of eight hundred
slain on one occasion.
9 After him was Eleazar the son of Dodai the
son of Ahohi. He was among the three war-
riors with David when they defied the Philis-
tines who were gathered together there to fight
when the men of Israel withdrew. 10 He arose
and attacked the Philistines until his hand
grew weary and stuck to the sword. The LORD
brought about a great victory that day, and the
people returned only to plunder.
11 After him was Shammah the son of Agee
the Hararite. The Philistines had gathered into
a troop, where the plot of the field was full of
lentils, and the people fled before the Philis-
tines. 12 He took his stand in the midst of the
plot of land, defended it, and defeated the Phi-
listines. The LORD brought about a great victory.
13 Then three[2] of the thirty chief men went
down and came to David at the cave of Adul-
lam during the harvest. Now the Philistine
army was in the Valley of Rephaim. 14 At that
time, David was in the stronghold while the
Philistine garrison was at Bethlehem. 15 David
said longingly, "O that someone would give me
a drink of water from the well in Bethlehem
by the gate!" 16 The three warriors breached
the Philistine camp and drew up water from
the well in Bethlehem by the gate, and they
brought it to David. However, he was not will-
ing to drink it, so he poured it out as a drink
offering to the LORD. 17 He said, "Far be it from
me, O LORD, to drink this, the blood of the men
who risked their lives." So he was not willing
to drink it.
These things the three warriors did.
18 Now Abishai, the brother of Joab and son
of Zeruiah, was chief of the thirty.[3] He wielded
his spear against three hundred men and killed
them, and won a name beside the three. 19 Was
he more honored than the three? He became
their commander, but he did not attain to the
three.
20 And Benaiah the son of Jehoiada was a
valiant man of Kabzeel, who had done great
acts. He struck down two sons of Ariel of
Moab. He also went down and killed a lion
in the middle of a pit on a snowy day. 21 He
struck down an Egyptian, an impressive man.
Now the Egyptian had a spear in his hand, but
Benaiah went down to him with a staff, seized
the spear from the Egyptian, and killed him
with his own spear. 22 These things Benaiah
the son of Jehoiada did and won for himself a
name alongside the three. 23 He was more hon-
ored than the thirty, but he did not attain to the
three. So David set him over his bodyguard.

24 Among the thirty were
Asahel the brother of Joab,
Elhanan the son of Dodo of Bethlehem,
25 Shammah the Harodite,
Elika the Harodite,
26 Helez the Paltite,
Ira the son of Ikkesh the Tekoite,
27 Abiezer the Anathothite,
Mebunnai the Hushathite,
28 Zalmon the Ahohite,
Maharai the Netophathite,
29 Heled the son of Baanah the Netopha-
thite,
Ithai the son of Ribai from Gibeah of
Benjamin,
30 Benaiah the Pirathonite,
Hiddai from the brooks of Gaash,
31 Abi-Albon the Arbathite,
Azmaveth the Barhumite,
32 Eliahba the Shaalbonite,
of the sons of Jashen,
Jonathan,
33 Shammah the Hararite,
Ahiam the son of Sharar the Hararite,
34 Eliphelet the son of Ahasbai, the son of
the Maakathite,
Eliam the son of Ahithophel the Gilonite,
35 Hezro the Carmelite,
Paarai the Arbite,
36 Igal the son of Nathan from Zobah,
the son of Hagri,
37 Zelek the Ammonite,

23:4 Jdg 5:31
23:5 Isa 55:3
23:7 Heb 6:8
23:8 1Ch 27:2
23:9 1Ch 27:4
23:12 2Sa 23:10
23:13 1Sa 22:1
23:14 1Sa 22:4–5
23:15 Jn 4:14
23:17 Lev 17:10
23:18 2Sa 10:10
23:20 Jos 15:21
23:24 2Sa 2:18
23:26 2Sa 14:2
23:27 Jos 21:18
23:30 Jdg 12:15
23:31 2Sa 3:16
23:34 2Sa 11:3
23:35 1Ch 11:37

[1] *8* Or *captains*, or *thirty*. Cf. 1Ch 11:11. [2] *13* Text reads *thirty*, but *three* has been translated here on the basis of other textual witnesses and Masoretic marginal notation. Cf. 22:16. [3] *18* Or *another three*, Cf. 11:20.

Naharai the Beerothite, the armor bearer
of Joab the son of Zeruiah,
38 Ira the Ithrite,
Gareb the Ithrite,
39 and Uriah the Hittite.
There were thirty-seven in all.

David's Census of Israel and Judah
1Ch 21:1–17

24 Again the LORD became angry against Israel, and He incited David against them, saying, "Go and count the people of Israel and Judah."

2 The king said to Joab the commander of the army who was with him, "Go throughout all of the tribes of Israel, from Dan to Beersheba, and muster the people so that I may know the number of the people."

3 Joab said to the king, "May the LORD your God add to the people however many they are one hundred times over in the sight of my lord the king. But why does my lord the king so desire this thing?"

4 However, the king's word prevailed against Joab and the commanders of the army. So Joab and the commanders of the army went out from before the king to register the people of Israel.

5 They crossed the Jordan and camped at Aroer, south of the city, in the middle of the ravine of Gad toward Jazer. 6 They went toward Gilead to the land of Tahtim Hodshi. Then they went toward Dan Jaan and around to Sidon. 7 They went to the fortress of Tyre and all of the towns of the Hivites and Canaanites. They went to the Negev and Beersheba.

8 They went throughout the entire land, and after nine months and twenty days, they came to Jerusalem.

9 Joab gave the count of the census of the people to the king. There were eight hundred thousand capable men who could draw a sword in Israel, and the men of Judah were five hundred thousand.

Judgment for David's Sin

10 Now the heart of David struck him after he had counted the people. David said to the LORD, "I have sinned greatly by what I have done. Now may the LORD take away the iniquity of your servant, for I have behaved very foolishly."

11 When David arose in the morning, the word of the LORD came to the prophet Gad, the seer for David, saying, 12 "Go and speak to David: Thus says the LORD: Three options I am laying before you. Choose for yourself one of them, and I will do this to you."

13 So Gad came to David and told him. He said to him, "Shall seven years of famine come to you in your land? Or shall you flee three months before your enemies while they pursue you? Or shall there be three days of plague in your land? Now consider and advise what answer I shall return to Him who sent me."

14 David said to Gad, "I am very distressed. Let us fall by the hand of the LORD, for His mercy is great. May I not fall by the hand of man."

15 So the LORD sent a plague upon Israel from the morning until the appointed time. Seventy thousand men from the people died, from Dan to Beersheba. 16 When the angel stretched out his hand toward Jerusalem to destroy it, the LORD relented from the calamity. He said to the angel who was annihilating the people, "Enough! Now stay your hand." The angel of the LORD was at the threshing floor of Araunah the Jebusite.

17 On seeing the angel who was striking down the people, David said to the LORD, "I am the one who has sinned and I am the one who has done wrong. These sheep, what have they done? Please, let your hand be against me and against the house of my father."

David Builds an Altar
1Ch 21:18–26

18 Gad came to David that day and said to him, "Go up and erect an altar to the LORD on the threshing floor of Araunah the Jebusite." 19 So David went up according to the word of Gad, as the LORD commanded. 20 When Araunah looked and saw the king and his servants coming toward him, he went out and bowed low to the king with his face on the ground.

21 Araunah said, "Why has my lord the king come to his servant?"

David replied, "To purchase the threshing floor from you in order to build an altar to the LORD, so that the plague may be averted from the people."

22 Araunah said to David, "Let my lord the king take and offer up what seems good to him. Here are the oxen for the burnt offering and the threshing sledges and yokes of the oxen for wood. 23 Everything, O king, Araunah gives to the king." Araunah also said to the king, "May the LORD your God be favorable toward you."

24 However, the king said to Araunah, "No, for I will certainly purchase from you for a fair price. I will not offer up to the LORD burnt offerings that cost me nothing."

So David purchased the threshing floor and the oxen for fifty shekels[1] of silver. 25 David built an altar to the LORD there and offered burnt offerings and peace offerings. Then the land pleaded with the LORD, and the plague was averted from Israel.

23:38 1Ch 2:53
23:39 2Sa 11:3
24:1 1Ch 27:23–24
24:2 2Sa 3:10
24:3 Dt 1:11
24:5 Dt 2:36
24:6 Jos 19:28
24:7 Jos 19:29
24:10 2Sa 12:13
24:11 1Sa 9:9
24:13 1Ch 21:12

24:14 Ps 51:1
24:16 Ge 6:6
24:17 Ps 74:1
24:22 1Ki 19:21
24:23 Eze 20:40–41
24:24 1Ch 21:24–25
24:25 2Sa 21:14

[1] *24* About 1.25 pounds, or 575 grams.

Author: Traditionally the prophet Jeremiah

Written: Between 560 and 540 BC

Themes: Ancient Israel United and Divided, Elijah's Ministry

1 Kings

Dear Spirit Led Woman,

Have you ever stopped to think about how many decisions you make in a day? If you're like most women, my guess is the answer might surprise you! We make countless decisions on a daily basis—many may seem trivial while others have a more long-term impact. The question is, whose wisdom are you relying on in your daily decision-making process?

In 1 Kings 3 God appeared to King Solomon in a dream and told him He would give him anything. All Solomon had to do was ask. Of all the things Solomon could have chosen—earthly fame, fortune, success—he asked for understanding to discern justice. He knew he would need supernatural discernment—godly wisdom, spiritual insight—to make good decisions as he ruled God's people.

Before you go about your day, making decisions based on your own limited wisdom, stop and pray. Ask the Holy Spirit for spiritual eyes to discern what's really going on in the situations you encounter with family, friends, or coworkers. The Holy Spirit will give you wisdom and discernment if you ask, just as He did for King Solomon.

Joy F. Strang

Adonijah Seeks Kingship

1 Now King David was old and advanced in years, and they covered him with clothes, but he could not get warm. 2 Therefore his servants said to him, "Let a young virgin be found for my lord the king, and let her stand before the king and care for him, and let her lie by your side so that my lord the king may keep warm."

3 So they searched for a beautiful young woman throughout the land of Israel and found Abishag, a Shunammite, and brought her to the king. 4 She was very beautiful and cared for the king and ministered to him, but the king did not know her intimately.

5 Then Adonijah the son of Haggith exalted himself, saying, "I will be king," and he assembled chariots and horsemen and fifty men to run before him. 6 His father had not confronted him at any time by asking, "Why have you done this?" He also was a very attractive man, and he was born next after Absalom.

7 He conferred with Joab the son of Zeruiah and with Abiathar the priest, and they agreed to help him. 8 But Zadok the priest and Benaiah the son of Jehoiada and Nathan the prophet and Shimei and Rei and David's mighty men did not join Adonijah.

9 Adonijah slaughtered sheep and oxen and fat cattle by the Stone of Zoheleth, which is by En Rogel, and invited all his brothers, the king's sons, and all the men of Judah, the king's servants. 10 But he did not invite Nathan the prophet, Benaiah, the mighty men, or his brother Solomon.

11 Therefore Nathan spoke to Bathsheba the mother of Solomon, saying, "Have you not heard that Adonijah the son of Haggith reigns and David our lord does not know *it*? 12 Now please come and let me give you some advice, so that you may save your own life as well as that of your son Solomon. 13 Go to King David and say to him, 'Did not you, my lord, O king, swear to your handmaid, saying: Assuredly Solomon your son shall reign after me, and he shall sit upon my throne? Why then does Adonijah reign?' 14 Then while you are still there talking with the king, I will come in and confirm your words."

15 So Bathsheba went to the king's chamber. Now the king was very old, and Abishag the Shunammite ministered to him. 16 Bathsheba bowed and prostrated herself before the king.

And the king said, "What do you want?"

17 And she said to him, "My lord, you swore by the LORD your God to your handmaid, saying: Assuredly Solomon your son shall reign after me, and he shall sit upon my throne. 18 But Adonijah reigns, and now, my lord, O king, you are unaware. 19 He has slain oxen and fat cattle and sheep in abundance and has invited all the sons of the king and Abiathar the priest and Joab the commander of the army, but he has not invited your servant Solomon. 20 And you, my lord, O king, all the eyes of Israel are upon you that you should tell them who shall sit on the throne of my lord the king after him. 21 Otherwise it shall be that when my lord the king sleeps with his fathers, I and my son Solomon shall be considered offenders."

22 While she was still talking with the king, Nathan the prophet also came in. 23 The king was told, "Nathan the prophet is here," and when he entered the king's presence, he bowed himself before the king with his face to the ground.

24 Nathan said, "My lord, O king, have you said, 'Adonijah shall reign after me, and he shall sit upon my throne'? 25 For he has gone down this day and has slain oxen, fat cattle, and sheep in abundance and has invited all the king's sons, the commanders of the guard, and Abiathar the priest, and they eat and drink with him, saying, 'God save King Adonijah!' 26 But he has not invited me, your servant, or Zadok the priest or Benaiah the son of Jehoiada or your servant Solomon. 27 Is this thing done by my lord the king, and you have not let your servants know who should sit on the throne of my lord the king after him?"

Solomon Becomes King

1Ch 29:21–25

28 Then King David answered and said, "Call Bathsheba to me." And she came into the king's presence and stood before the king.

29 The king vowed, "As the LORD lives, who has redeemed my soul out of all distress, 30 even as I swore to you by the LORD God of Israel, saying, 'Assuredly Solomon your son shall reign after me, and he shall sit upon my throne in my stead,' even so will I certainly do this day."

31 Then Bathsheba bowed with her face to the ground in reverence to the king and said, "Let my lord King David live forever."

32 King David said, "Call Zadok the priest, Nathan the prophet, and Benaiah the son of Jehoiada for me." So they came before the king. 33 And the king said to them, "Take with you the servants of your lord, and cause Solomon my son to ride upon my own mule, and bring him down to Gihon. 34 And let Zadok the priest and Nathan the prophet there anoint him king over Israel, and blow the trumpet and say, 'God save King Solomon!' 35 Then you shall come up after him. And he shall come and sit on my throne, for he will be king in my place as

1:3 Jos 19:18
1:5 2Sa 3:4
1:6 2Sa 3:3–4
1:7 2Sa 20:25
1:8 1Ki 4:18
1:9 2Sa 17:17
1:10 2Sa 12:24
1:11 2Sa 3:4
1:13 1Ki 1:30
1:17 1Ki 1:13
1:18 1Ki 1:24
1:21 Dt 31:16
1:25 1Sa 10:24
1:26 1Ki 1:8
1:29 2Sa 4:9
1:30 1Ki 1:13
1:31 Da 2:4
1:32 1Ki 1:8
1:33 2Ch 32:30
1:34 1Sa 10:1

I have appointed him to be ruler over Israel
and over Judah."
36 Benaiah the son of Jehoiada answered the
king and said, "Amen! May the LORD, the God
of my lord the king, also say so! 37 As the LORD
has been with my lord the king, may He also
be with Solomon and make his throne greater
than the throne of my lord King David."
38 So Zadok the priest, Nathan the prophet,
Benaiah the son of Jehoiada, and the Ker-
ethites and the Pelethites went down and
had Solomon ride on King David's mule and
brought him to Gihon. 39 Zadok the priest took
a horn of oil out of the tabernacle and anoint-
ed Solomon. Then they blew the trumpet, and
all the people said, "God save King Solomon!"
40 All the people came up to see him and played
flutes and greatly rejoiced, so that the earth
shook at the sound.
41 Adonijah and all the guests that were with
him heard the commotion as they were finish-
ing their meal, and when Joab heard the sound
of the trumpet, he said, "Why is the city so loud
and in an uproar?"
42 While he was speaking, Jonathan the son
of Abiathar the priest came. Adonijah said to
him, "Come in, for you are a valiant man and
bring good tidings."
43 Jonathan answered Adonijah, saying,
"Surely our lord King David has made Solo-
mon king. 44 The king has sent with him Za-
dok the priest, Nathan the prophet, Benaiah
the son of Jehoiada, and the Kerethites, and
the Pelethites. And they had him ride on the
king's mule. 45 And Zadok the priest and Na-
than the prophet have anointed him king in
Gihon, and they have come up from their re-
joicing, so that the city is in an uproar. This is
the noise that you heard. 46 Also Solomon sits
on the throne of the kingdom. 47 Moreover, the
king's servants came to bless our lord King
David, saying, 'May God make the name of
Solomon better than your name and make his
throne greater than your throne.' And the king
bowed himself upon the bed. 48 The king also
said, 'Blessed be the LORD God of Israel, who
has given one to sit on my throne this day so
that I could see with my own eyes.' "
49 All the guests that were with Adonijah
were afraid and rose up and went on their
way. 50 Adonijah feared Solomon. So he got
up and went to the altar and held on to its
horns. 51 Then Solomon was told, "Adonijah
fears King Solomon, for he has caught hold
of the horns on the altar, saying 'Let King Sol-
omon swear to me today that he will not slay
his servant with the sword.' "
52 And Solomon said, "If he will show himself
a worthy man, not one of his hairs will fall to
the ground, but if wickedness is found in him,
he shall die." 53 So King Solomon sent for him,
and they brought him down from the altar, and
he came and bowed himself to King Solomon.
And Solomon said to him, "Go to your house."

1:37 1Sa 20:13
1:38 2Sa 8:18
1:39 Ps 89:20
1:42 2Sa 15:36
1:45 1Ki 1:40
1:46 1Ch 29:23
1:47 Ge 47:31
1:48 1Ki 3:6
1:50 1Ki 2:28
1:52 1Sa 14:45

2:1 Ge 47:29
2:2 Jos 23:14
2:3 Dt 29:9
2:4 2Sa 7:25
2:5 2Sa 3:27
2:6 1Ki 2:9
2:7 2Sa 9:7
2:8 2Sa 16:5–8
2:9 1Ki 2:6
2:10 Ac 2:29
2:11 2Sa 5:4–5
2:12 2Ch 1:1

David's Charge to Solomon
1Ch 29:26–28

2 Now it was coming close to the day of Da-
vid's death, and he gave his son Solomon
a charge, saying:
2 "I am going the way of all the earth. Be
strong, and show yourself to be a man. 3 And
keep the charge of the LORD your God, walking
in His ways, keeping His statutes, His com-
mandments, His judgments, and His testimo-
nies, as it is written in the Law of Moses, that
you may prosper in all that you do and wher-
ever you turn, 4 that the LORD may carry out His
word that He spoke concerning me, saying, 'If
your children take heed to their way, to walk
before Me in faithfulness with all their hearts
and with all their souls, you shall not fail to
have a man on the throne of Israel.'
5 "Moreover, you know also what Joab the
son of Zeruiah did to me, what he did to the
two commanders of the army of Israel, to Ab-
ner the son of Ner and to Amasa the son of
Jether, whom he killed, shedding the blood of
war in a time of peace. He spilled their blood
on the belt that was around his waist and on
the shoes of his feet. 6 Do the right thing ac-
cording to your wisdom, and do not let his gray
head go down to the grave in peace.
7 "But show kindness to the sons of Barzillai
the Gileadite, and let them eat at your table,
for with such loyalty they supported me when
I fled from your brother Absalom.
8 "There is also with you Shimei the son of
Gera, a Benjamite from Bahurim, who cursed
me with a grievous curse in the day when I
went to Mahanaim. But when he came down
to meet me at the Jordan, I swore to him by
the LORD, saying, 'I will not put you to death
with the sword.' 9 Now therefore do not hold
him guiltless, for you are a wise man and know
what you ought to do to him. Bring his gray
head down to the grave with blood."
10 So David slept with his fathers and was
buried in the City of David.
11 David reigned over Israel forty years. He
reigned seven years in Hebron and thirty-three
years in Jerusalem. 12 So Solomon sat upon the
throne of his father David, and his kingdom
was firmly established.

The Throne of Solomon Established

13 Then Adonijah the son of Haggith came to
Bathsheba the mother of Solomon. And she
said, "Do you come in peace?"

And he said, "*I come* peaceably." [14] Then he said, "I have something to say to you."

And she said, "Speak."

[15] He said, "You know that the kingdom was mine and that all Israel viewed me as the king. However, the kingdom has become my brother's, for it was given to him by the LORD. [16] And now I ask one petition of you; do not deny me."

She said to him, "Keep speaking."

[17] And he said, "Please speak to Solomon the king, for he will not refuse you, that he may give me Abishag the Shunammite as a wife."

[18] Bathsheba said, "Very well, I will speak to the king on your behalf."

[19] So Bathsheba went to King Solomon to speak to him on behalf of Adonijah. The king rose up to meet her and bowed to her. Then he sat down on his throne and had a seat placed at his right hand for her to sit upon.

[20] Then she said, "I desire one small petition of you. Please do not deny me."

And the king said to her, "Ask, my mother, for I will not refuse you."

[21] She said, "Let Abishag the Shunammite be given as a wife to Adonijah your brother."

[22] King Solomon answered his mother, "Now why do you ask Abishag the Shunammite for Adonijah? Ask for him the kingdom also, for he is my elder brother. Ask not only for him, but also for Abiathar the priest, and for Joab the son of Zeruiah."

[23] Then King Solomon swore by the LORD, saying, "May God do so to me and more also if this word does not cost Adonijah his life. [24] Now therefore as the LORD lives, who has established me and set me on the throne of David my father and who has made me a house as He promised, Adonijah shall be put to death this day." [25] So King Solomon dispatched Benaiah the son of Jehoiada, and he executed him.

[26] The king said to Abiathar the priest, "Go to Anathoth, to your own fields, for you are worthy of death. But I will not at this time put you to death, because you bore the ark of the Lord GOD before David my father and because you shared in all the hardships my father endured." [27] So Solomon expelled Abiathar from being priest to the LORD, thus fulfilling the word of the LORD that He had spoken concerning the house of Eli in Shiloh.

[28] Then word came to Joab, for Joab had followed Adonijah, though he did not support Absalom. And Joab fled to the tabernacle of the LORD and caught hold of the horns of the altar. [29] King Solomon was told that Joab had fled to the tabernacle of the LORD and was by the altar. Then Solomon sent Benaiah the son of Jehoiada, saying, "Go and execute him."

2:15 1Ki 1:5
2:19 Ps 45:9
2:22 1Ch 3:2
2:23 Ru 1:17
2:24 1Ch 22:10
2:25 2Sa 8:18
2:26 Jos 21:18
2:27 1Sa 2:27–36
2:28 1Ki 1:7
2:29 1Ki 2:25

....

2:31 Nu 35:33
2:32 Jdg 9:24
2:33 1Ki 2:32
2:35 1Ki 2:27
2:37 2Sa 1:16
2:44 2Sa 16:5–13
2:45 Pr 25:5

[30] So Benaiah came to the tabernacle of the LORD and said to him, "Thus says the king, 'Come forth.' "

And he said, "No, I will die here."

And Benaiah told the king all Joab said.

[31] The king said to him, "Do as he has said, strike him down and bury him, and thus take away from me and my father's house the guilt for the blood Joab shed without cause. [32] The LORD shall return his blood upon his own head, for he attacked two men more righteous and better than he—Abner the son of Ner, commander of the army of Israel, and Amasa the son of Jether, commander of the army of Judah—and killed them with the sword when my father David was unaware. [33] Therefore their blood shall return upon the head of Joab and upon the head of his seed forever, but upon David and upon his seed and upon his house and upon his throne shall the peace of the LORD rest forever."

[34] So Benaiah the son of Jehoiada went up and attacked and killed him, and he was buried in his own house in the wilderness. [35] The king put Benaiah the son of Jehoiada over the army in place of Joab and put Zadok the priest in the place of Abiathar.

[36] The king sent and called for Shimei and said to him, "Build a house for yourself in Jerusalem, and dwell there, and never leave the city. [37] For on the day you go out and pass over the Kidron Valley, know for certain that you will surely die. Your blood shall be on your own head."

[38] Shimei said to the king, "What you say is good. As my lord the king has said, so will your servant do." And Shimei lived in Jerusalem many days.

[39] It came about that at the end of three years, two servants of Shimei ran away to Achish son of Maakah king of Gath. And they told Shimei, saying, "Your servants are in Gath." [40] Shimei arose, saddled his donkey, and went to Gath to Achish to look for his servants. And Shimei went and brought his servants from Gath.

[41] Solomon was told that Shimei had gone from Jerusalem to Gath and had returned. [42] The king sent and called for Shimei and said to him, "Did I not make you swear by the LORD and warned you, saying, 'Know for certain that on the day you go out and walk abroad anywhere, you shall surely die'? And you said to me, 'What you say is good; I will obey.' [43] Why then have you not kept the oath of the LORD and the commandment that I gave you?"

[44] The king also said to Shimei, "You know all the wickedness in your heart and what you did to David my father. Therefore the LORD shall return your wickedness on your own head. [45] But

King Solomon shall be blessed, and the throne of David shall be established before the LORD forever."

46 So the king commanded Benaiah the son of Jehoiada, who went out and attacked him so that he died.

And the kingdom was established in the hand of Solomon.

Solomon Asks for Wisdom

2Ch 1:2–13

3 Solomon made a treaty with Pharaoh king of Egypt. He married Pharaoh's daughter and brought her to the City of David until he finished building his palace, the house of the LORD, and the wall around Jerusalem. 2 The people were sacrificing at the high places, because no house had yet been built for the name of the LORD. 3 Solomon loved the LORD, walking in the statutes of his father David, though he sacrificed and burned incense at the high places.

4 The king went to Gibeon to sacrifice there, for that was the great high place, and he offered a thousand burnt offerings on that altar. 5 While he was in Gibeon, the LORD appeared to Solomon in a dream at night, and He said, "Ask what you want from Me."

6 Solomon answered, "You have shown great mercy to your servant David my father, because he walked before You in faithfulness, righteousness, and uprightness of heart toward You. And You have shown him great kindness in giving him a son to sit on his throne this day.

7 "Now, O LORD, my God, You have made Your servant king in place of my father David, and I am still a little child and do not know how to go out or come in. 8 And Your servant is in the midst of Your people whom You have chosen, a great people, so numerous that they cannot be numbered or counted. 9 Give Your servant therefore an understanding heart to judge Your people, that I may discern between good and bad, for who is able to judge among so great a people?"

10 It pleased the Lord that Solomon had asked this. 11 God said to him, "Because you have asked this and have not asked for yourself long life or riches or the lives of your enemies, but have asked for yourself wisdom so that you may have discernment in judging, 12 I now do according to your words. I have given you a wise and an understanding heart, so that there has never been anyone like you in the past, and there shall never arise another like you. 13 I have also given you what you have not asked, both riches and honor, so that no kings will compare to you all of your days. 14 If you will walk in My ways, keeping My statutes and My commandments as your father David did, then I will lengthen your days." 15 Solomon awoke and found it was a dream.

Then he came to Jerusalem and stood before the ark of the covenant of the LORD and offered up burnt offerings and peace offerings and made a feast for all of his servants.

The Wisdom of Solomon

16 At that time, two women who were prostitutes came and stood before the king. 17 The first woman said, "O my lord, this woman and I live in the same house, and I bore a child with her in the house. 18 Three days after I gave birth, she also had a child, and we were together. There was no one else with us in the house, only the two of us were in the house.

19 "Then this woman's child died during the night because she rolled over on it. 20 She got up at midnight and took my son from beside me while your servant slept and laid him at her bosom and laid her dead child at my bosom. 21 When I rose in the morning to feed my child, it was dead. But when I looked closely in the morning *light*, I recognized that it was not my son whom I bore."

22 The other woman said, "No, the living is my son, and the dead is your son."

And she said, "No, the dead is your son, and the living is my son." Thus they spoke before the king.

23 Then the king said, "One says, 'This is my son who lives, and your son is the dead,' and the other says, 'No, but your son is dead, and my son is the living.' "

24 So the king said, "Bring me a sword." And they brought a sword before the king. 25 The king said, "Divide the living child in two, and give half to the one and half to the other."

26 Then the woman whose child was the living one spoke to the king, for she yearned with compassion for her son, and she said, "O my lord, give her the living child, and do not kill it."

But the other said, "Let it be neither mine nor yours and divide it."

27 Then the king answered and said, "Give her the living child, and do not slay it. She is its mother."

28 All Israel heard of the king's judgment, and they feared the king, for they saw that the wisdom of God was in him, to execute sound judgment.

The Court of Solomon

4 So King Solomon was king over all Israel. 2 These were the officials in his court:

Azariah the son of Zadok was the priest.
3 Elihoreph and Ahijah, the sons of Shisha, were secretaries.

2:46 1Ki 2:12
3:1 1Ki 9:24
3:2 1Ki 22:43
3:3 Dt 6:5
3:4 1Ch 16:39
3:5 1Ki 9:2
3:6 1Ki 1:48
3:7 Nu 27:17
3:8 Ge 15:5
3:9 2Sa 14:17
3:12 1Ki 5:12
3:13 1Ki 4:21–24
3:14 Ps 91:16
3:15 Ge 41:7
3:16 Nu 27:2
3:26 Ge 43:30
3:28 Col 2:3
4:3 2Sa 8:16

Jehoshaphat the son of Ahilud was the
recorder;
4 Benaiah the son of Jehoiada was over the
army.
Zadok and Abiathar were priests.
5 Azariah the son of Nathan was over the
officers,
and Zabud the son of Nathan was principal
officer and the king's friend.
6 Ahishar was over the household,
and Adoniram the son of Abda was over
the forced labor.

7 Solomon had twelve officers over all Isra-
el who made provision for the king and his
household. Each man was assigned a month
to make provision. 8 These are their names:

the son of Hur in Mount Ephraim;
9 the son of Deker in Makaz and in
Shaalbim and Beth Shemesh and Elon
Bethhanan;
10 the son of Hesed in Arubboth (to him
belonged Sokoh and all the land of
Hepher);
11 the son of Abinadab in all the region of
Dor (he had Taphath the daughter of
Solomon as his wife);
12 Baana the son of Ahilud in Taanach,
Megiddo, and all Beth Shan that is by
Zarethan beneath Jezreel, and from Beth
Shan to Abel Meholah as far as the other
side of Jokmeam;
13 the son of Geber in Ramoth Gilead (to
him pertained the towns of Jair the son
of Manasseh which are in Gilead, and
also the region of Argob which is in
Bashan, sixty great cities with walls and
iron bars);
14 Ahinadab the son of Iddo in Mahanaim;
15 Ahimaaz in Naphtali (he had taken
Basemath the daughter of Solomon as
his wife);
16 Baana the son of Hushai in Asher and in
Aloth;
17 Jehoshaphat the son of Paruah in
Issachar;
18 Shimei the son of Ela in Benjamin;
19 Geber the son of Uri in the country of
Gilead, the country of Sihon king of the
Amorites and of Og king of Bashan.
He was the only officer who was in that
region.

The Wealth of Solomon

20 Judah and Israel had a large populace, as
numerous as the sand by the sea. They ate
and drank and were happy. 21 Solomon reigned
over all kingdoms from the River[1] to the land
of the Philistines and to the border of Egypt.
The people brought presents and served Sol-
omon all the days of his life.
22 Solomon's provision for one day was thir-
ty kors[2] of fine flour and sixty kors[3] of meal,
23 ten fat oxen and twenty pasture-fed cattle, a
hundred sheep in addition to deer, roebucks,
gazelle, and fatted poultry. 24 For he had do-
minion over all the region on this side of the
River[4] from Tiphsah to Gaza, over all the kings
on this side of the River,[5] and he had peace on
all borders of his land. 25 Judah and Israel lived
safely, every man under his vine and under his
fig tree, from Dan to Beersheba all the days
of Solomon.
26 Solomon had forty thousand stalls of
horses for his chariots and twelve thousand
horsemen.
27 Those officers made provision for King Sol-
omon and for all who came to King Solomon's
table, every man in his month, and they lacked
nothing. 28 Barley also and straw for the horses
and dromedaries were brought to the place
where the officers were, every man according
to his charge.
29 God gave Solomon wisdom and great
depth of understanding as well as compassion,
as vast as the sand on the seashore. 30 Solo-
mon's wisdom excelled the wisdom of all the
people of the East country and all the wisdom
of Egypt. 31 For he was wiser than all other
men, wiser than Ethan the Ezrahite, Heman,
Kalkol, and Darda, the sons of Mahol; his fame
spread throughout all the surrounding nations.
32 He spoke three thousand proverbs, and his
songs numbered a thousand and five. 33 He
spoke of trees, from the cedar tree that is in
Lebanon to the hyssop that springs out of the
wall. He also spoke of beasts and of fowl and
of insects and fish. 34 People from all over came
to hear the wisdom of Solomon, from all kings
of the earth, who had heard of his wisdom.

Plans to Build the Temple

2Ch 2:1–18

5 Now Hiram king of Tyre sent his servants
to Solomon, for he had heard that they had
anointed him king in place of his father, and
Hiram had always loved David. 2 And Solomon
sent *word* to Hiram, saying,

3 "You know how David my father was
unable to build a house for the name of the
LORD his God because of the wars all around
him, until the LORD put his enemies under
his feet. 4 But now the LORD my God has giv-
en me peace on every side, so that there is
neither adversary nor misfortune. 5 So know

4:4 1Ki 2:35
4:8 Jos 24:33
4:10 Jos 12:17
4:11 Jos 11:2
4:12 Jos 17:11
4:13 Nu 32:41
4:18 1Ki 1:8
4:20 Ge 22:17
4:21 Ge 15:18
4:24 1Ch 22:9
4:25 Mic 4:4
4:26 2Ch 1:14
4:28 Est 8:10
4:29 1Ki 3:12
4:30 Ac 7:22
4:31 1Ki 3:12
4:32 Ecc 12:9
4:34 1Ki 10:1
5:1 2Sa 5:11
5:2 2Ch 2:3
5:3 1Ch 28:3
5:4 1Ki 4:24
5:5 1Ch 17:12

[1] *21* Euphrates River. [2] *22* Likely about 5½ tons, or 5 metric tons.
[3] *22* Likely about 11 tons, or 10 metric tons. [4] *24* Euphrates River.
[5] *24* Euphrates River.

that I plan to build a house to honor the name of the LORD my God, just as the LORD spoke to my father David, saying, ‘Your son, whom I will set on your throne after you, shall build a house to honor My name.’

6 “Now therefore command that cedar trees from Lebanon be cut down for me, and my servants shall be with your servants, and I will pay your servants whatever you command, for you know that there are none among my people who can cut timber like the Sidonians.”

7 When Hiram heard the words of Solomon, he rejoiced greatly and said, “Blessed be the LORD this day, who has given David a wise son over this great people.”

8 Hiram sent to Solomon, saying,

“I have considered the things which you contacted me about, and I will do all you asked concerning timber of cedar and fir. 9 My servants shall bring them down from Lebanon to the sea, and I will send them by sea in floats to the place that you shall name and will cause them to be discharged into your care there, and in return you will meet my wishes by giving food for my household.”

10 So Hiram gave Solomon cedar trees and fir trees as he desired. 11 Solomon gave Hiram twenty thousand kors[1] of wheat for his household and twenty baths[2] of pure oil. This is what Solomon gave to Hiram each year. 12 The LORD gave Solomon wisdom, as He promised, and there was peace between Hiram and Solomon as they made a treaty together.

13 King Solomon drafted men from all Israel, totaling thirty thousand men. 14 He sent them to Lebanon in turns, ten thousand a month, with each spending a month in Lebanon and two months at home. Adoniram administered the labor force. 15 Solomon had seventy thousand porters and eighty thousand stonecutters in the mountains, 16 not counting the chief of Solomon’s officers who were over the work, three thousand three hundred, who ruled over the people who did the work. 17 At the king’s command, they quarried out great, costly stones in order to lay the foundation of the house with dressed stones. 18 Solomon’s builders and Hiram’s builders, along with the stonemasons, cut them and prepared timber and stones to build the house.

[1] *11* Likely about 3,600 tons, or 3,250 metric tons. [2] *11* About 120,000 gallons, or 440,000 liters. [3] *2* About 90 feet long, 30 feet wide, and 45 feet high, or 27 meters long, 9 meters wide, and 14 meters high. [4] *3* About 30 feet, or 9 meters; and in vv. 16 and 20. [5] *3* About 15 feet, or 4.5 meters; and in vv. 23–26. [6] *6* About 7½ feet, or 2.3 meters; and in vv. 10 and 24. [7] *6* About 9 feet, or 2.7 meters. [8] *6* About 11 feet, or 3.2 meters. [9] *17* About 60 feet, or 18 meters.

5:6 2Ch 2:8
5:9 Ezr 3:7
5:11 2Ch 2:10
5:12 1Ki 3:12
5:13 1Ki 9:15
5:15 1Ki 9:20–22
5:16 1Ki 9:23
5:17 1Ki 6:7
5:18 Jos 13:5

6:1 2Ch 3:1–2
6:4 Eze 40:16
6:5 1Ki 6:16
6:7 Dt 27:5–6
6:9 1Ki 6:14
6:12 1Ch 22:10
6:13 Ex 25:8
6:14 1Ki 6:9
6:15 1Ki 7:7
6:16 1Ki 8:6
6:18 1Ki 7:24

Solomon Builds the Temple

2Ch 3:1–14

6 In the four hundred and eightieth year after the children of Israel came out of the land of Egypt, in the fourth year of Solomon’s reign over Israel, in the month Ziv (which is the second month), he began to build the house of the LORD.

2 The house which King Solomon built for the LORD had a length of sixty cubits, a width of twenty cubits, and a height of thirty cubits.[3] 3 The porch in front of the temple was twenty cubits[4] in length, the same as the width of the house, and ten cubits[5] deep in front of the house. 4 He made beveled windows for the house. 5 He also built a structure against the wall of the house, running around the walls of the house, both of the temple and of the inner sanctuary, and he made side chambers all around. 6 The lowest story was five cubits[6] broad, the middle one was six cubits[7] broad, and the third was seven cubits[8] broad. For around the outside of the house, he made offsets on the wall so that the supporting beams should not be inserted into the walls of the house.

7 The house was built of stone prepared at the quarry, so that neither hammer nor axe nor any tool of iron was heard in the house while it was being built.

8 The door for the middle chamber was in the right side of the house, and it had winding stairs into the middle chamber and out of the middle into the third. 9 So he built the house and finished it and covered it with beams and boards of cedar. 10 Then he built chambers against the whole house, five cubits high, and they rested on the house with timber of cedar.

11 Now the word of the LORD came to Solomon, saying, 12 “Concerning this house which you are building, if you will walk in My statutes and execute My judgments and keep all My commandments and walk in them, then I will carry out My word with you, which I spoke to David your father, 13 and I will dwell among the people of Israel and will not forsake My people Israel.”

14 So Solomon built the house and finished it. 15 He built the interior walls of the house with boards of cedar. From the floor of the house to the ceiling, he covered them on the inside with wood; and he covered the floor of the house with planks of fir. 16 He lined twenty cubits on the sides of the house, both the floor and the walls, with boards of cedar, and he even lined them within, even the inner sanctuary and the Most Holy Place. 17 The house, that is, the nave in front of the inner sanctuary, was forty cubits[9] long. 18 The cedar of the house within

had carvings of gourds and open flowers. All was cedar. There was no stone seen.

19 He prepared the inner sanctuary in the inner part of the house in order to set there the ark of the covenant of the LORD. 20 The inner sanctuary was twenty cubits long, twenty cubits wide, and twenty cubits high. He overlaid it with pure gold. He also overlaid the altar of cedar. 21 So Solomon overlaid the interior of the house with pure gold, and he made a partition with gold chains in front of the inner sanctuary, and he overlaid it with gold. 22 He overlaid the whole house with gold as well as the whole altar that was by the inner sanctuary.

23 Within the inner sanctuary, he made two cherubim from olive wood, each ten cubits high. 24 One wing of the cherub was five cubits, and the other wing was also five cubits. From the furthest part of the one wing to the furthest part of the other was ten cubits. 25 The other cherub was ten cubits. Both the cherubim were the same shape and size. 26 The height of the one cherub was ten cubits, and so was that of the other cherub. 27 He set the cherubim within the inner sanctuary, and they stretched forth the wings of the cherubim, so that the wing of the one touched the one wall and the wing of the other cherub touched the other wall, and their wings touched one another in the middle of the house. 28 He overlaid the cherubim with gold.

29 He carved all the walls of the house with carved figures of cherubim and palm trees and open flowers both inside and out. 30 He overlaid the floor of the house with gold, both inside and out.

31 For the entrance to the inner sanctuary, he made doors of olive wood; the lintel and doorposts were five-sided. 32 The two doors were also made of olive wood. He carved on them cherubim, palm trees, and open flowers, overlaid them with gold, and spread gold upon the cherubim and upon the palm trees. 33 So also he made for the entrance to the nave four-sided posts of olive wood. 34 The two doors were made from fir tree, with two leaves of each door folding. 35 He carved on them cherubim and palm trees and open flowers and covered them with gold fitted upon the carved work.

36 He built the inner court with three rows of hewed stone and a row of cedar beams.

37 In the fourth year, in the month Ziv, the foundation of the house of the LORD was laid, 38 and in the eleventh year, in the month Bul (which is the eighth month), the house was completely finished. All the details and plans were met. So he took seven years to build it.

6:22 Ex 30:1
6:23 Ex 37:7–9
6:27 Ex 25:20
6:29 1Ki 6:32
6:34 Eze 41:23–25
6:36 1Ki 7:12
6:37 1Ki 6:1

....

7:1 1Ki 9:10
7:2 1Ki 10:17
7:7 Ps 122:5
7:8 1Ki 3:1
7:12 1Ki 6:36
7:13 2Ch 4:11
7:14 2Ch 2:14
7:15 Jer 52:21

Solomon's Palace Built

7 Solomon was building his own house for thirteen years, and he finished all his house. 2 He built the House of the Forest of Lebanon. Its length was a hundred cubits, and its width was fifty cubits, and its height was thirty cubits,[1] built on four rows of cedar pillars with cedar beams upon the pillars. 3 It was covered with cedar over the top of the beams, which sat upon forty-five pillars, fifteen in a row. 4 There were window frames in three rows and window opposite window in three tiers. 5 All the doors and posts were rectangular with the openings facing each other in three tiers.

6 He made a porch of pillars with a length of fifty cubits and a breadth of thirty cubits.[2] There was a porch in front with pillars, and a canopy in front of them.

7 Then he made a porch for the throne, from which he would judge, and called it the Hall of Judgment. It was covered with cedar from one side of the floor to the other. 8 His own house where he lived, in the other court back of the hall, was similar in style. Solomon also made a house like this for Pharaoh's daughter, whom he had taken as a wife.

9 All these were built with costly stones, cut to size and sawed with saws on the inside and outside, from the foundation up to the coping, throughout the outside toward the great court. 10 The foundation was of large, costly stones, stones of ten[3] and eight[4] cubits in size. 11 Above were costly stones cut to size, along with cedars. 12 The great court was enclosed with three rows of hewed stones and a row of cedar beams. So were the inner court of the house of the LORD and the porch of the house.

The Furnishings of the Temple

2Ch 4:2–5:1

13 Now King Solomon sent and called Huram out of Tyre. 14 He was the son of a widow from the tribe of Naphtali, and his father was a man of Tyre who worked in bronze, and he was filled with wisdom and understanding and skill to make all sorts of items in bronze. So he came to King Solomon and performed all his work.

15 He cast two pillars of bronze eighteen cubits high each and twelve cubits[5] in circumference. 16 He made two capitals of cast bronze to set on the tops of the pillars. The height of the one capital was five cubits,[6] and the height of the other capital was five cubits. 17 He

[1] *2* About 150 feet long, 75 feet wide and 45 feet high, or 45 meters long, 23 meters wide and 14 meters high. [2] *6* About 75 feet long and 45 feet wide, or 23 meters long and 14 meters wide. [3] *10* About 15 feet, or 4.5 meters; and in v. 23. [4] *10* About 12 feet, or 3.6 meters. [5] *15* About 27 feet high and 18 feet in circumference, or 8.1 meters high and 5.4 meters in circumference. [6] *16* About 7½ feet, or 2.3 meters; and in v. 23.

made lattices of checker work with wreaths of chainwork for the capitals on top of the pillars: seven for one capital and seven for the other. 18 Likewise he made pomegranates in two rows around the one latticework to cover the capital that was on the top of the pillar, and he did the same for the other capital. 19 The capitals that were on top of the pillars in the porch were four cubits[1] high and in the shape of lilies. 20 The capitals on top of the two pillars also had pomegranates above, by the convex surface which was next to the latticework. There were two hundred pomegranates in rows encircling each capital. 21 He set up the pillars in the porch of the temple. He set up the right pillar and called it Jakin, and he set up the left pillar and called it Boaz. 22 The tops of the pillars were in the shape of lilies. This completed the work on the pillars.

23 He made a cast metal sea, ten cubits from one side to the other. It was round and had a height of five cubits, and a line of thirty cubits[2] encircled it. 24 Under the brim all the way around there were gourds, ten in a cubit. When it was cast, the gourds were placed in two rows going all the way around it.

25 It stood on top of twelve oxen with three facing north, three facing toward the west, three facing toward the south, and three facing toward the east. The sea was set on them, and their hindquarters were turned inward. 26 It was a hand-breadth[3] thick, and the brim was made similar to the brim of a cup, like a lily blossom. It could hold two thousand baths.[4]

27 He made ten stands out of bronze, each measuring four cubits long, four cubits wide, and three cubits high.[5] 28 The work of the stands looked like this: They had panels, and the panels were set in the frames. 29 And on the panels that were set in the frames were lions, oxen, and cherubim. On the frames both above and below the lions and oxen, there were wreaths of beveled work. 30 Every stand had four bronze wheels and axles of bronze, and at the four corners were supports for a basin. The supports were cast with wreaths at the side of each. 31 Its opening was within a crown that projected upward one cubit. Its opening was round, like the work of a pedestal, a cubit and a half deep.[6] At its opening there were engravings, and its panels were four-sided, not round. 32 Underneath the panels were four wheels, and the axles of the wheels were joined to the stand, and the height of a wheel was a cubit and a half. 33 The wheels worked like chariot wheels in that their axles and rims and spokes and hubs were all cast metal.

34 There were four supports for the four corners of each stand, and the supports were part of one piece with the stand itself. 35 On the top of the stand, there was a round band half a cubit[7] high, and on the top of the stand its stays and its panels were of one piece with it. 36 On the surface of its stays and on its panels, he engraved cherubim, lions, and palm trees, according to the space of each, with wreaths all around. 37 In this way he made the ten stands, with them all having the same shape, measure, and size.

38 Then he made ten basins of bronze, with each basin able to hold forty baths,[8] each being four cubits. Upon every one of the ten stands sat one basin. 39 He put five stands on the right side of the house, and five on the left side of the house. He set the sea on the right side of the house toward the southeast. 40 Huram also made the pots, the shovels, and the basins.

So Huram finished all the work in making items for King Solomon for use in the house of the LORD: 41 the two pillars, the two bowls of the capitals that were on the top of the two pillars, the two latticeworks to cover the two bowls of the capitals that were upon the top of the pillars; 42 and the four hundred pomegranates for the two latticeworks, two rows of pomegranates for each latticework, to cover the two bowls of the capitals that were on the pillars; 43 the ten stands and ten basins on the stands; 44 one sea and twelve oxen under the sea; 45 the pots, the shovels, and the basins.

All these vessels that Huram made for King Solomon for the house of the LORD were of burnished bronze. 46 In the plain of the Jordan the king cast them, in the clay ground between Sukkoth and Zarethan. 47 Solomon left all the vessels unweighed because there were so many. The weight of the bronze was also never measured.

48 Solomon made all the vessels that were needed for the house of the LORD: the altar of gold, the table of gold on which was showbread, 49 the candlesticks of pure gold, five on the right side and five on the left before the inner sanctuary; the flowers, the lamps, and the tongs, of gold; 50 the cups, snuffers, basins, dishes for incense, fire pans, of pure gold; the sockets for the doors of the innermost part of the house, the Most Holy Place, and for the doors of the nave of the temple, of gold.

51 All the work that King Solomon made for the house of the LORD was completed. And Solomon brought in the things which David his father had dedicated—the silver, the gold,

7:20 2Ch 3:16
7:21 2Ch 3:17
7:23 2Ki 25:13
7:24 1Ki 6:18
7:25 Jer 52:20
7:26 2Ch 4:5
7:27 2Ch 4:14
7:40 2Ch 4:11–16
7:42 1Ki 7:20
7:45 Ex 27:3
7:46 Jos 3:16
7:47 1Ch 22:14
7:48 Ex 37:10–16
7:49 2Ch 4:7
7:51 2Ch 5:1

[1] *19* About 6 feet, or 1.8 meters; and in v. 38. [2] *23* About 45 feet, or 14 meters. [3] *26* About 3 inches, or 7.5 centimeters. [4] *26* About 12,000 gallons, or 44,000 liters. [5] *27* About 6 feet long and wide and 4½ feet high, or 1.8 meters long and wide and 1.4 meters high. [6] *31* About 2¼ feet, or 68 centimeters; and in v. 32. [7] *35* About 9 inches, or 23 centimeters. [8] *38* About 240 gallons, or 880 liters.

and the cups—and he put them among the treasures of the house of the LORD.

The Ark Brought to the Temple

2Ch 5:2–6:11

8 Then Solomon assembled the elders of Israel and all the heads of the tribes, the chief of the fathers of the children of Israel, before King Solomon in Jerusalem, so that they could ensure that the ark of the covenant of the LORD would be brought out of the City of David in Zion. 2 All the men of Israel assembled themselves before King Solomon at the feast in the month Ethanim, which is the seventh month.

3 All the elders of Israel came, and the priests carried the ark. 4 The priests and Levites brought up the ark of the LORD, the tabernacle of the congregation, and all the holy implements that were in the tabernacle. 5 King Solomon and all the congregation of Israel who were assembled before him stood together in front of the ark, sacrificing so many sheep and oxen that they could not be told or numbered.

6 The priests brought in the ark of the covenant of the LORD to its place in the inner sanctuary of the house, to the Most Holy Place under the wings of the cherubim. 7 For the cherubim spread forth their two wings over the place of the ark and covered the ark and the poles from above. 8 The poles were so long that the ends of the poles could be seen out in the holy place in front of the inner sanctuary, but they could not be seen from outside, and they are there to this day. 9 There was nothing in the ark except for the two tablets of stone that Moses put there at Horeb when the LORD made a covenant with the children of Israel after they had come out of the land of Egypt.

10 And when the priests came out of the holy place, the cloud filled the house of the LORD, 11 so that the priests could not continue to minister because of the cloud, for the glory of the LORD filled the house of the LORD.

12 Then Solomon spoke, saying, "The LORD said that He would dwell in the thick darkness. 13 I have surely built You a house to dwell in, a settled place for You to abide in forever."

14 Then the king turned around and blessed all the congregation of Israel (and all the congregation of Israel stood), 15 and he said,

> "Blessed be the LORD God of Israel, who spoke with His mouth to my father David and has with His hand fulfilled His word, saying, 16 'Since the day that I brought forth My people Israel out of Egypt, I chose no city from any tribe of Israel to build a house where My name might be praised, but I chose David to be over My people Israel.'

8:1 2Ch 5:2–10
8:2 Lev 23:34
8:3 Dt 31:9
8:4 1Ki 3:4
8:5 2Sa 6:13
8:6 2Sa 6:17
8:9 Ex 25:21
8:12 Ps 97:2
8:13 2Sa 7:13
8:14 2Sa 6:18
8:15 Lk 1:68
8:16 1Sa 16:1
8:17 2Sa 7:2–3
8:19 2Sa 7:5
8:20 1Ch 28:5–6
8:21 Dt 31:26
8:22 Ezr 9:5
8:23 Dt 7:9
8:24 1Ki 8:15
8:25 1Ki 2:4
8:27 Jer 23:24
8:29 Dt 12:11

17 "My father David had it in mind to build a house for the name of the LORD God of Israel. 18 The LORD said to my father David, 'Whereas it was in your heart to build a house for My name, you had good intentions. 19 Nevertheless, you shall not build the house, but your son who will come out of your loins, he shall build the house for My name.'

20 "The LORD has fulfilled His word that He spoke, and I have been elevated to the position of my father David, to sit on the throne of Israel as the LORD promised, and have built a house for the name of the LORD God of Israel. 21 I have set a place there for the ark, which houses the covenant of the LORD which He made with our fathers when He brought them out of the land of Egypt."

Solomon's Prayer of Dedication

2Ch 6:12–40

22 Then Solomon stood in front of the altar of the LORD in the presence of all the congregation of Israel and spread his hands toward heaven. 23 and he said,

> "LORD God of Israel, there is no God like You in heaven above or on earth below who keeps covenant and mercy with Your servants who walk before You with all their hearts, 24 who have kept what You promised Your servant David my father. You spoke also with Your mouth and have fulfilled it with Your hand, as it is this day.

25 "Therefore, LORD God of Israel, now keep what You promised Your servant David my father, saying, 'You will not fail to have a man sit before Me on the throne of Israel, so long as your sons take heed to their way, that they walk before Me as you have walked before Me.' 26 Now, O God of Israel, let Your word, I pray, be fulfilled, which You spoke to Your servant David my father.

God, I thank You that when You hear our prayers, You also forgive us (1Ki 8:30).

27 "But will God indeed dwell on the earth? See, heaven and the heaven of heavens cannot contain You. How much less can this house that I have built? 28 Yet give consideration to the prayer of Your servant and to his supplication, O LORD my God; listen to the cry and to the prayer which Your servant prays before You today, 29 that Your eyes may be upon this house night and day, even toward the place of which You have said, 'My name shall be there,' that You may

listen to the prayer which Your servant shall make toward this place. 30 Please listen to the supplication of Your servant and of Your people Israel when they pray toward this place. May You hear in heaven, Your dwelling place, and when You hear, forgive.

31 "If any man sins against his neighbor, and an oath be laid upon him to cause him to swear, and the oath comes before Your altar in this house, 32 then may You hear in heaven and act and judge Your servants, condemning the wicked, bringing his way on his own head, and justifying the righteous, giving him according to his righteousness.

33 "When Your people Israel are defeated by their enemies, because they have sinned against You, and they turn back to You and call upon Your name and pray and make supplication to You in this house, 34 then may You hear in heaven and forgive the sin of Your people Israel and bring them again to the land which You gave to their fathers.

35 "When heaven is shut up, and there is no rain, because they have sinned against You, if they pray toward this place and call upon Your name and turn from their sin when You afflict them, 36 then may You hear in heaven and forgive the sin of Your servants and Your people Israel, that You may teach them the good way in which they should walk and give rain upon Your land which You have given to Your people as an inheritance.

37 "When there is famine in the land, if there is plague, blight, mildew, locust, or grasshopper; if their enemy besieges them in the land of their cities; whatever plague, whatever sickness there is; 38 whatever prayer, whatever supplication is made by anyone, or by all Your people Israel, each knowing the affliction of his own heart, and spreading his hands toward this house; 39 then hear in heaven Your dwelling place, and forgive, and act, and render to everyone according to all his ways, whose hearts You know—for only You know the hearts of the sons of men— 40 so that they may fear You all the days that they live in the land that You gave to our fathers.

41 "Also concerning the foreigner who is not of Your people Israel and comes from a far country for Your name's sake 42 (for they will hear of Your great name and of Your strong hand and of Your outstretched arm), when he comes and prays toward this house, 43 may You hear in heaven, Your dwelling place, and do all that the foreigner asks of You, so all people of the earth will know Your name, to fear You as Your people Israel do, and that they may know that this house, which I have built, is called by Your name.

44 "If Your people go out to battle against their enemy wherever You send them, and they pray to the LORD toward the city which You have chosen and toward the house that I have built for Your name, 45 then may You hear their prayer and supplication in heaven and maintain their cause.

46 "If they sin against You (for there is no man who does not sin), and You get angry with them and hand them over to the enemy so that they are carried away as captives to the land of the enemy, far or near, 47 yet when they come to their senses while in the land where they were carried captives and repent and make supplication to You, saying, 'We have sinned and have acted perversely and have committed wickedness,' 48 and so return to You with all their hearts and with all their souls in the land of their enemies, who carried them away as captives, and pray to You toward their land, which You gave to their fathers, the city which You have chosen and the house which I have built for Your name, 49 then may You hear their prayers and supplications in heaven, Your dwelling place, and maintain their cause, 50 and forgive Your people who have sinned against You and all their transgressions which they committed against You and grant them compassion before those who carried them away as captives, so they will have compassion on them. 51 For they are Your people and Your inheritance whom You brought forth out of Egypt from the midst of the furnace of iron.

52 "Let Your eyes be open to the supplication of Your servant and to the supplication of Your people Israel, to listen to them regarding all for which they call upon You. 53 For You did call them out from among all the people of the earth to be Your inheritance, as You spoke by the hand of Moses Your servant when You brought our fathers out of Egypt, O Lord GOD."

54 Now when Solomon finished praying this prayer and making supplication to the LORD, he arose from before the altar of the LORD, from kneeling on his knees with his hands spread up to heaven. 55 He stood up and blessed all the congregation of Israel with a loud voice, saying,

56 "Blessed be the LORD who has given rest to His people Israel according to all that He promised. Not one word of His promises which He gave by the hand of Moses His

8:30 1Ki 8:34
8:31 Ex 22:8–11
8:32 Dt 25:1
8:33 Lev 26:17
8:35 Lev 26:19
8:36 1Sa 12:23
8:37 Lev 26:16
8:39 1Sa 16:7
8:40 Ps 130:4
8:41 1Ki 10:1–2
8:42 Dt 3:24
8:43 1Sa 17:46
8:46 Ecc 7:20
8:47 Ps 106:6
8:48 Da 6:10
8:50 Ps 106:46
8:51 Dt 4:20
8:52 1Ki 8:29
8:53 Ex 19:5–6
8:54 Lk 22:45
8:55 1Ki 8:14
8:56 Dt 12:10

servant has failed. 57 The LORD our God be with us, as He was with our fathers. Let Him neither leave us nor forsake us, 58 that He may incline our hearts to Him, to walk in all His ways and to keep His commandments, statutes, and judgments, which He commanded our fathers. 59 And let these my words, with which I have made supplication before the LORD, be close to the LORD our God day and night, that He will maintain the cause of His servant and the cause of His people Israel at all times as the situation demands, 60 so that all the people of the earth may know that the LORD is God and that there is none else. 61 Let your hearts, therefore, be perfect with the LORD our God, to walk in His statutes and keep His commandments, as at this day."

The Dedication of the Temple
2Ch 7:1–10

62 The king and all Israel with him offered sacrifices before the LORD. 63 Solomon offered a sacrifice of peace offerings, which he offered to the LORD, twenty-two thousand oxen and a hundred and twenty thousand sheep. So the king and all the children of Israel dedicated the house of the LORD.

64 The same day the king consecrated the middle of the court that was in front of the house of the LORD, for there he offered burnt offerings and meat offerings and the fat of the peace offerings, because the bronze altar that was before the LORD was too little to receive the burnt offerings and meat offerings and the fat of the peace offerings.

65 At that time, Solomon held a feast for all Israel, a great congregation, from the entry of Lebo Hamath to the Brook of Egypt, before the LORD our God, seven days and *another* seven days, a total of fourteen days. 66 On the eighth day he sent the people away, and they blessed the king and went to their tents rejoicing in their hearts for all the goodness that the LORD had done for David His servant and for Israel His people.

The LORD Appears to Solomon
2Ch 7:11–22

9 When Solomon had finished building the house of the LORD and the king's house and all else he desired, 2 the LORD appeared to Solomon a second time, as He had appeared to him at Gibeon. 3 The LORD said to him,

"I have heard your prayer and supplication, which you made before Me. I have consecrated this house which you built by putting My name there forever. And My eyes and My heart shall be there perpetually.

8:57 Dt 31:6
8:58 Ps 119:36
8:60 Dt 4:35
8:61 1Ki 11:4
8:62 2Sa 6:17–19
8:63 Ezr 6:16–17
8:64 2Ch 4:1
8:65 Nu 34:5
9:1 1Ki 9:19
9:2 1Ki 3:5
9:3 Dt 11:12
9:4 Ge 17:1
9:5 1Ki 2:4
9:7 Dt 28:37
9:8 Jer 22:8–9
9:10 1Ki 6:37–7:1
9:11 2Ch 8:2
9:13 Jos 19:27
9:14 1Ki 9:11
9:15 Jos 17:11
9:16 1Ki 3:1
9:17 Jos 16:3
9:18 Jos 19:44
9:19 1Ki 9:1

4 "If you will walk before Me, as your father David walked, in integrity of heart and uprightness, so that you are obedient to do all that I have commanded you, and will keep My statutes and My judgments, 5 then I will establish the throne of your kingdom upon Israel forever, just as I promised to your father David, saying, 'You shall not fail to have a man upon the throne of Israel.'

6 "But if you and your sons turn in any way from following Me and do not keep My commandments and My statutes which I have set before you, but go and serve other gods and worship them, 7 then I will cut Israel out of the land which I have given them, and I will cast this house, which I have consecrated for My name, out of My sight, and Israel shall be a proverb and a byword among all people. 8 And everyone who passes by this high house will be astonished and will hiss, and they shall say, 'Why has the LORD done this to this land, and to this house?' 9 And they will answer, 'Because they forsook the LORD their God, who brought their fathers out of the land of Egypt, and took hold of other gods and have worshipped and served them. That is why the LORD has brought all this disaster upon them.' "

Solomon's Other Activities
2Ch 8:1–18

10 When twenty years had passed since Solomon had built the two houses, the house of the LORD and the king's house 11 (now Hiram the king of Tyre had furnished Solomon with cedar and fir trees, along with gold, as he had requested), King Solomon gave Hiram twenty cities in the land of Galilee. 12 Hiram came out from Tyre to see the cities Solomon had given him, and he was not pleased with them. 13 He said, "What cities are these which you have given me, my brother?" And he called them the land of Kabul to this day. 14 Hiram sent to the king one hundred and twenty talents[1] of gold.

15 This is the account of the forced labor which King Solomon conscripted to build the house of the LORD and his own house, Millo, the wall of Jerusalem, Hazor, Megiddo, and Gezer. 16 For Pharaoh, king of Egypt, had gone up against and conquered Gezer and burned it with fire and slain the Canaanites that lived in the city and given it as a present to his daughter, Solomon's wife. 17 Solomon built Gezer and Lower Beth Horon 18 and Baalath and Tadmor in the wilderness, in the land, 19 and all the storage cities that Solomon had, cities for his chariots and cities for his horsemen and all that which Solomon desired to build

[1] *14* About 4½ tons, or 4 metric tons.

in Jerusalem and in Lebanon and in all the land of his dominion.

20 All the people who were left of the Amorites, Hittites, Perizzites, Hivites, and Jebusites, who were not children of Israel, 21 the descendants of those who were left in the land and whom the people of Israel were not able to utterly destroy, were conscripted by Solomon for slave labor to this day. 22 But Solomon did not make any children of Israel into slaves, but instead used them as men of war, as his servants, his leaders, his captains, rulers of his chariots, and his horsemen. 23 These were the chief officers over Solomon's work, five hundred and fifty, who ruled over the people who did the labor.

24 But Pharaoh's daughter moved out of the City of David to her house which Solomon had built for her, and he then built Millo.

25 Three times a year Solomon offered burnt offerings and peace offerings on the altar that he built to the LORD, and he burned incense on the altar that was before the LORD. So he finished the house.

26 King Solomon built a fleet of ships in Ezion Geber, which is beside Elath on the shore of the Red Sea in the land of Edom. 27 Hiram sent shipmen who had knowledge of the sea to serve alongside Solomon's men. 28 They went to Ophir and acquired four hundred and twenty talents[1] of gold there and brought it to King Solomon.

The Queen of Sheba

2Ch 9:1–12

10 Now when the queen of Sheba heard of Solomon's fame connected to the name of the LORD, she came to test him with hard questions. 2 She came to Jerusalem with a very great retinue, with camels bearing spices, and very much gold, and precious stones; and when she came to Solomon, she told him all that was on her mind. 3 Solomon answered all her questions; there was not anything too difficult for the king which he could not answer. 4 When the queen of Sheba observed Solomon's wisdom and the house he had built 5 and the meat of his table and the sitting of his servants and the attendance of his ministers and their clothing and his cupbearers and his entryway by which he went up to the house of the LORD, it took her breath away.

6 She said to the king, "What I heard in my own land about your acts and your wisdom was true! 7 I did not believe it until I came and saw it with my own eyes! In fact, I was not even told half. Your wisdom and prosperity are greater than the stories I heard! 8 Happy are your men, and happy are these your servants who stand continually before you and hear your wisdom! 9 Blessed be the LORD your God, who delighted in you and set you on the throne of Israel, because the LORD loved Israel forever; therefore He made you king in order to execute judgment and justice."

10 She gave the king a hundred and twenty talents[2] of gold and a great amount of spices and precious stones. No one gave as many spices as the queen of Sheba gave to King Solomon.

11 The ships of Hiram, which brought gold from Ophir, also brought from Ophir a large quantity of almug wood and precious stones. 12 The king made pillars for the house of the LORD out of the almug trees and harps also and psalteries for singers for the king's house. Never before had such almug wood *been brought*, nor has any such been seen to this day.

13 King Solomon gave to the queen of Sheba all she desired, no matter what she asked for, in addition to what Solomon gave her from his royal bounty. So she turned and went to her own country, she and her servants.

Solomon's Wealth

2Ch 1:14–17; 9:13–28

14 Now the weight of gold that came to Solomon in one year was six hundred and sixty-six talents[3] of gold. 15 In addition, he collected from the merchantmen and the traffic of the spice merchants and from all the kings of Arabia and the governors of the country.

16 King Solomon made two hundred large shields of beaten gold made of six hundred shekels[4] of gold each. 17 He made three hundred shields of beaten gold with three pounds[5] of gold in each shield. And the king put them in the House of the Forest of Lebanon.

18 The king also made a great throne of ivory and overlaid it with the best gold. 19 The throne had six steps, and the back of the throne was round, and there were armrests on either side of the seat with two lions standing beside the armrests. 20 Twelve lions stood on the sides of the six steps, and there was no other like it in any kingdom. 21 All of King Solomon's drinking cups were made of gold, and all the cups of the House of the Forest of Lebanon were made of pure gold. None were made of silver, for it was not considered valuable in the days of Solomon. 22 For the king had ships at sea at Tarshish with the ships of Hiram. Every three years the ships of Tarshish came bringing gold, silver, ivory, apes, and peacocks.

23 So King Solomon exceeded all the kings of the earth in terms of riches and wisdom. 24 All

9:21 Jos 15:63
9:22 Lev 25:39
9:23 1Ki 5:16
9:24 2Sa 5:9
9:26 1Ki 22:48
9:28 1Ch 29:4
10:1 Mt 12:42
10:5 1Ch 26:16
....
10:8 Pr 8:34
10:9 2Sa 8:15
10:10 1Ki 10:2
10:11 1Ki 9:27–28
10:14 1Ki 9:28
10:16 1Ki 14:26–28
10:17 1Ki 7:2
10:21 1Ki 10:17
10:22 1Ki 22:48
10:23 1Ki 3:12–13
10:24 1Ki 3:9

[1] *28* About 16 tons, or 14 metric tons. [2] *10* About 4½ tons, or 4 metric tons. [3] *14* About 25 tons, or 23 metric tons. [4] *16* About 15 pounds, or 6.9 kilograms; and in v. 29. [5] *17* About 3¾ pounds, or 1.7 kilograms, or if double minas, about 7½ pounds, or 3.5 kilograms.

the earth came to Solomon to hear his wisdom, which God had put in his heart. 25 Everyone brought an annual tribute in the form of presents, silver and gold cups, garments, armor, spices, horses, and mules.

26 Solomon gathered together chariots and horsemen. He had one thousand four hundred chariots and twelve thousand horsemen whom he stationed in the cities for chariots and with the king at Jerusalem. 27 The king made silver to be in Jerusalem as plentiful as stones, and he made cedars to be as plentiful as sycamore trees in the valley. 28 Solomon had horses brought out of Egypt along with linen yarn. The king's merchants received the linen yarn at a price. 29 He brought chariots from Egypt at a price of six hundred shekels of silver and a horse for a hundred and fifty.[1] And he exported them to all the kings of the Hittites and the kings of Aram, by their means.

Solomon's Apostasy

11 But King Solomon loved many foreign women in addition to the daughter of Pharaoh, women of the Moabites, Ammonites, Edomites, Sidonians, and Hittites, 2 from the nations which the LORD warned the children of Israel about, saying, "You shall not go in to them, nor shall they come in to you, for they will surely turn your heart away toward their gods." Solomon clung to these in love. 3 He had seven hundred wives who were princesses and three hundred concubines, and his wives turned his heart away. 4 For when Solomon was old, his wives turned his heart away after other gods, and his heart was not perfect with the LORD his God as the heart of David his father had been. 5 For Solomon went after Ashtoreth, the goddess of the Sidonians, and after Molek, the abomination of the Ammonites. 6 Solomon did what was evil in the sight of the LORD and did not fully follow the LORD as his father David had done.

7 Then Solomon built a high place for Chemosh, the abomination of Moab, in the hill that is close to Jerusalem, and for Molek, the abomination of the children of Ammon. 8 He did the same for all his foreign wives, who burned incense and sacrificed to their gods.

9 The LORD was angry with Solomon because he turned his heart away from the LORD God of Israel, who had appeared to him twice, 10 and had warned him about this, that he should not follow other gods, but he was disobedient to the LORD's command. 11 Therefore the LORD said to Solomon, "Since you have done this and have not kept My covenant and statutes, which I commanded you, I will surely take the kingdom from you and give it to your servant. 12 I will not do this in your lifetime for your father David's sake, but I will tear it out of the hand of your son. 13 However, I will not take the whole kingdom away, but will preserve one tribe for your son for David My servant's sake and for the sake of Jerusalem which I chose."

10:26 2Ch 9:25
10:28 Dt 17:16
11:1 Dt 17:17
11:2 Ex 34:16
11:3 2Sa 5:13–16
11:4 1Ki 9:4
11:5 Jdg 2:13
11:7 Nu 21:29
11:9 1Ki 3:5
11:11 1Ki 11:31
11:13 1Ki 12:20
11:15 2Sa 8:14
11:18 Nu 10:12
11:21 1Ki 2:10
11:23 2Sa 8:3
11:26 1Ki 12:2

Solomon's Adversaries

14 The LORD stirred up an adversary against Solomon, Hadad the Edomite. He was a prince of Edom. 15 For when David was in Edom, and Joab the commander of the army had gone to bury the slain, he had killed every male in Edom 16 (for six months Joab stayed there with his men until he had killed every male in Edom). 17 But Hadad fled to Egypt, he and some Edomites who served his father, Hadad still being a small child. 18 They set out from Midian and went to Paran, and they gathered men from Paran and then arrived in Egypt and presented him before Pharaoh king of Egypt, who gave him a house and provisions and land.

19 Pharaoh had great affection for Hadad, so much so that he gave him his sister-in-law, the sister of Tahpenes the queen, as a wife. 20 Tahpenes' sister gave birth to his son, Genubath, whom Tahpenes weaned in Pharaoh's house. Genubath lived in Pharaoh's house among the sons of Pharaoh.

21 When Hadad heard in Egypt that David slept with his fathers and that Joab, the commander of the army, was dead, he said to Pharaoh, "Allow me to depart and go to my own country."

22 Then Pharaoh said to him, "But what have you lacked with me that you want to go to your own country?"

And he answered, "Nothing, however let me go anyway."

23 God stirred up another adversary against him, Rezon the son of Eliada, who fled from his lord Hadadezer, king of Zobah. 24 He gathered a group of men and became leader over a band when David killed the men of Zobah, and they fled to Damascus and lived and reigned there. 25 He was an enemy of Israel all the days of Solomon in addition to the troubles caused by Hadad, and he hated Israel and reigned over Aram.

Jeroboam's Rebellion

26 Jeroboam the son of Nebat, an Ephraimite of Zeredah, who was Solomon's servant and whose mother's name was Zeruah, a widow woman, even he lifted up his hand against the king.

[1] *29* About 3¾ pounds, or 1.7 kilograms.

27 This is what led to his rebellion against the
king. Solomon built Millo and repaired the wall
of the City of David his father. 28 Jeroboam was
a mighty man of valor, and when Solomon
saw that the young man was industrious, he
made him ruler over all the labor force of the
house of Joseph.

29 At that time, when Jeroboam went out of
Jerusalem, the prophet Ahijah the Shilonite
found him along the way, and he had dressed
himself in a new garment, and the two *of*
them were alone in the field. 30 Ahijah took off
the new garment that he wore and tore it into
twelve pieces, 31 and he said to Jeroboam: Take
ten pieces, for thus says the LORD, the God of
Israel, "See, I will tear the kingdom out of the
hand of Solomon and will give ten tribes to you
32 (but he shall have one tribe for My servant
David's sake and for the sake of Jerusalem, the
city which I have chosen out of all the tribes of
Israel), 33 because they have forsaken Me and
have worshipped Ashtoreth the goddess of the
Sidonians, Chemosh the god of the Moabites,
and Molek the god of the children of Ammon
and have not walked in My ways and have
not done that which is right in My eyes, to
keep My statutes and judgments, as his father
David had done.

34 "However, I will not take the whole king-
dom out of his hand, but I will make him
prince all the days of his life for David My ser-
vant's sake, whom I chose, because he kept My
commandments and My statutes. 35 But I will
take the kingdom out of his son's hand and will
give ten tribes to you. 36 To his son will I give
one tribe, so that My servant David will always
have a light before Me in Jerusalem, the city in
which I have chosen to put My name. 37 I will
take you, and you shall reign according to all
that your soul desires and shall be king over
Israel. 38 It shall be, if you will listen to all that
I command you and will walk in My ways and
do what is right in My sight to keep My statutes
and My commandments, as David My servant
did, I will be with you and build you a sure
house, as I built for David, and will give Israel
to you. 39 I will thus afflict the seed of David,
but not forever."

40 Solomon therefore sought to kill Jero-
boam. And Jeroboam arose and fled to Egypt
to Shishak, king of Egypt, and he stayed in
Egypt until the death of Solomon.

The Death of Solomon
2Ch 9:29–31

41 The rest of the acts of Solomon and all that
he did and his wisdom, are they not written in
the book of the acts of Solomon? 42 And the
time that Solomon reigned in Jerusalem over
all Israel was forty years. 43 Solomon slept with
his fathers and was buried in the City of Da-
vid his father, and his son Rehoboam reigned
after him.

Israel Rebels Against Rehoboam
2Ch 10:1–11:4

12 And Rehoboam went to Shechem, for
all Israel had gone to Shechem to make
him king. 2 When Jeroboam the son of Nebat,
who was still in Egypt, heard of it (for he had
fled from King Solomon and stayed in Egypt),
3 they called and sent *for* him. And Jeroboam
and all the congregation of Israel came and
spoke to Rehoboam, saying, 4 "Your father
made our yoke unbearable. Now, therefore,
make the grievous service to your father and
the heavy yoke he put upon us lighter, and we
will serve you."

5 He said to them, "Depart for three days,
and then come back to me." And the people
departed.

6 King Rehoboam consulted with the old men
who advised his father Solomon while he was
still alive and asked, "How do you advise me
to answer the people?"

7 And they spoke to him, saying, "If you will
be a servant to this people this day and will
serve them and answer them and speak kind
words to them, they will be your servants for-
ever."

8 But he rejected the advice that the old men
gave him and consulted with the young men
who grew up with him and who stood before
him, 9 and he said to them, "What advice do
you give on how we should answer this peo-
ple, who have spoken to me saying, 'Make the
yoke your father put on us lighter'?"

10 And the young men who grew up with him
said, "Thus shall you answer this people who
said to you, 'Your father made our yoke heavy,
but make it lighter for us'; thus shall you say to
them, 'My little finger will be thicker than my
father's loins! 11 Whereas my father loaded you
with a heavy yoke, I will add to your burden.
My father chastised you with whips, but I will
chastise you with scorpions!' "

12 So Jeroboam and all the people came to
Rehoboam on the third day, just as the king
had appointed, saying, "Come to me again the
third day." 13 The king answered the people
roughly and forsook the counsel the old men
gave him, 14 and instead spoke to them follow-
ing the advice of the young men. He said, "My
father made your yoke heavy, and I will add
to your burden. My father chastised you with
whips, but I will chastise you with scorpions."
15 Thus the king did not listen to the people, for
the cause was from the LORD, that He might ful-
fill His saying, which the LORD spoke by Ahijah
the Shilonite to Jeroboam the son of Nebat.

11:27 1Ki 9:24
11:28 Pr 22:29
11:29 1Ki 12:15
11:30 1Sa 15:27–28
11:31 1Ki 11:11–12
11:32 1Ki 11:13
11:36 1Ki 11:13
11:37 2Sa 3:21
11:38 Jos 1:5
11:40 2Ch 12:2–9
11:41 2Ch 9:29–31
11:43 1Ki 2:10

....

12:1 2Ch 10:1–19
12:2 1Ki 11:40
12:4 1Sa 8:11–18
12:7 Pr 15:1
12:12 1Ki 12:5
12:15 1Ki 12:24

16 So when all Israel saw that the king did not listen to them, the people responded to the king, saying,

"What portion do we have in David?
  We also do not have an inheritance in
    the son of Jesse.
To your tents, O Israel,
  and see to your own house, David!"

So the people of Israel departed to their tents. 17 But the people of Israel living in the cities of Judah were ruled over by Rehoboam.

18 Then King Rehoboam sent Adoniram, who was in charge of the forced labor, and all Israel stoned him to death. As a result, King Rehoboam quickly mounted his chariot and fled to Jerusalem. 19 So Israel rebelled against the house of David, *and it remains so* even to this day.

20 When all Israel heard that Jeroboam had returned, they sent and called him before the congregation and made him king over all Israel. Only the tribe of Judah followed the house of David.

21 When Rehoboam arrived at Jerusalem, he assembled all the house of Judah along with the tribe of Benjamin, a hundred and eighty thousand chosen men who were warriors, to fight against the house of Israel and to bring the kingdom back to Rehoboam the son of Solomon.

22 But the word of God came to Shemaiah the man of God, saying: 23 Speak to Rehoboam the son of Solomon, king of Judah, and to all the house of Judah and Benjamin and to the remnant of the people, saying, 24 "Thus says the LORD: You shall not go up, nor fight against your brothers the children of Israel. Every man is to return to his house, for this thing is from Me." They listened therefore to the word of the LORD and turned to depart, according to the word of the LORD.

Jeroboam's Golden Calves

25 Then Jeroboam built Shechem in Mount Ephraim and lived there and went out from there and built Peniel.

26 Jeroboam said in his heart, "The kingdom will return to the house of David. 27 If this people go up to do sacrifice in the house of the LORD at Jerusalem, then shall the heart of this people turn again to their lord, even to Rehoboam king of Judah, and they shall kill me and go again to Rehoboam king of Judah."

28 At that point, the king got some advice and made two golden calves and said to the people, "It is too difficult for you to go up to Jerusalem. Here are your gods, O Israel, which brought you up out of the land of Egypt." 29 He set one in Bethel, and he put the other in Dan. 30 This was a sin, for the people went to worship before the one, even all the way in Dan.

Remove every false ministry in high places (1Ki 12:31).

31 He also made houses on high places and appointed priests from among all the people who were not Levites. 32 Jeroboam ordained a feast in the eighth month, on the fifteenth day of the month, like the feast in Judah, and he offered *sacrifice* on the altar. He did this in Bethel, sacrificing to the calves that he had made, and he stationed in Bethel the priests of the high places he had made. 33 So he made offerings on the altar that he had made in Bethel on the fifteenth day of the eighth month, a holiday he imagined in his own heart, and ordained a feast for the children of Israel, and he sacrificed on the altar and burned incense.

The Man of God From Judah

13 A man of God came out of Judah to Bethel by the word of the LORD while Jeroboam stood by the altar to burn incense. 2 He cried against the altar by the word of the LORD and said, "O altar, altar, thus says the LORD: 'A child named Josiah will be born in the house of David, and he will sacrifice upon you the priests of the high places who burn incense on you, and these men's bones shall be burned upon you.' " 3 He gave a sign the same day, saying, "This is the sign that the LORD has spoken: 'The altar will be torn apart, and the ashes that are upon it will be poured out.' "

4 When King Jeroboam heard the saying of the man of God who had cried against the altar in Bethel, he reached out his hand from the altar, saying, "Arrest him!" And the hand that he put forth against him dried up so that he could not pull it back in again. 5 The altar also was torn, and the ashes poured out from the altar, just as the man of God had said it would as a sign of the LORD.

6 The king answered and said to the man of God, "Seek the face of the LORD your God, and pray for me, that my hand will be healed." And the man of God interceded with the LORD, and the king's hand was healed and became as it was before.

7 The king said to the man of God, "Come home with me and refresh yourself, and I will give you a reward."

8 The man of God said to the king, "If you were to give me half your house, I would not go with you, nor will I eat bread nor drink water in this place, 9 for so I was commanded by the word of the LORD, saying: You shall eat no

12:16 2Sa 20:1
12:17 1Ki 11:13
12:18 1Ki 4:6
12:19 2Ki 17:21
12:20 1Ki 11:13
12:21 2Ch 11:1–3
12:22 2Ch 11:2
12:24 1Ki 12:15
12:25 Jdg 8:17
12:28 Ex 32:4
12:29 Ge 28:19
....
12:30 1Ki 13:34
12:31 1Ki 13:32–33
12:33 1Ki 13:1
13:1 2Ki 23:17
13:3 1Co 1:22
13:6 Ex 8:8
13:7 2Ki 5:15
13:8 Nu 22:18

Stuck in the Rut of Religion

Many believers are stuck in ruts whereby they are not experiencing new growth in Christ Jesus. When there is true new birth, it must be confirmed with new growth. The genuine new birth experience causes old things to be cut off and passed away. Once the old is pruned, the new can grow. If a believer continues to return to the old yoke of bondage, he or she will be bound by spiritually arrested development. They will not experience the level-to-level, glory-to-glory promised to them in the Word of God.

They will be condemned to a form of godliness, which makes a person appear to be victorious in Jesus on the outside. But in actuality, they will shut down the power on the inside of them that is greater than what is coming against them in life. There is no victory in the life of the believer who succumbs to the regiments, rudiments, and habits of religious forms.

Religion steals the youthful joy of young people in serving Jesus; it makes the elders become demonically *old*. In Matthew 19:14 Jesus forbid His disciples from stopping the little children from coming to Him. I do not believe in an age of spiritual accountability. Everything that has breath must praise and serve the Lord (Ps 150:6). Children must be raised up in the things of God so that they will not depart.

The Bible only has one account whereby a prophet is called old. In the Book of 1 Kings a man from Judah prophesied against the altar at Bethel. The king ordered that the man from Judah be seized. The king's arm froze as he pointed to the prophet from Judah, and the king could not pull his arm back to himself. The king asked the man from Judah to pray that his arm would be healed. He prayed, and the king was healed. Rumors of the authority of the prophet from Judah spread, and he was summoned by an "old prophet." This prophet was not necessarily old in age but actually washed up. He was spiritually or demonically old! (See 1 Kings 13.)

Religious people have no joy and, ultimately, no power! Nehemiah 8:10 declared that the joy of the Lord is our strength. It denotes that the person who lies in the dwelling place of the Lord (the place of joy—in the presence of the Lord there is fullness of joy) is reinforced with power.

To sum it all up, judgment will start at the house of God. Remember, it was religious spirits that nailed Jesus to the cross. Let us not religiously or repetitively serve God. We must worship Him in spirit and in truth.

Kimberly Daniels

bread, nor drink water nor return by the same
way that you came." 10 So he went another way
and did not return by the same way he came
to Bethel.
11 Now there lived an old prophet in Bethel,
and his sons came and told him all that the
man of God had done that day in Bethel. They
also told their father the words that he had
spoken to the king. 12 Their father said to them,
"What way did he go?" For his sons had seen
the way the man of God who came from Judah
had gone. 13 He said to his sons, "Saddle my
donkey." So they saddled the donkey for him,
and he rode on it. 14 He went after the man of
God and found him sitting under an oak, and
he said to him, "Are you the man of God who
came from Judah?"
And he said, "I am."
15 Then he said to him, "Come home with me
and eat bread."
16 He said, "I may not return with you or go in
with you, nor will I eat bread nor drink water
with you in this place, 17 for I was commanded
by the word of the LORD: You shall eat no bread
and drink no water there nor return by the way
you came."
18 He said to him, "I am a prophet like you,
and an angel spoke to me by the word of the
LORD, saying, 'Bring him back with you into
your house so that he may eat bread and drink
water.' " But he had lied to him. 19 So he went
back with him to his house and ate bread and
drank water.
20 Then as they sat at the table, the word of
the LORD came to the prophet who brought him
back, 21 and he cried out to the man of God
who came from Judah, saying, "Thus says the
LORD: Since you have disobeyed the mouth of
the LORD and have not kept the commandment
that the LORD your God commanded you, 22 but
instead came back and have eaten bread and
drunk water in the place of which the LORD
told you to eat no bread and drink no water,
your carcass will not be buried in the tomb of
your fathers!"
23 After he had eaten bread and had drunk,
he saddled the donkey for the prophet whom
he had brought back. 24 As he was going, a
lion met him on the way and killed him, and
his body was thrown in the road, and both
the donkey and lion stood by it. 25 Some men
passed by and saw the body thrown in the road
with the lion standing by the body, and they
came and told the story in the city where the
old prophet lived.
26 When the prophet who brought him back
from the way heard about it, he said, "It is the
man of God who was disobedient to the word
of the LORD, and thus the LORD has delivered
him to the lion, which has torn and slain him,
according to the word of the LORD that He
spoke to him."
27 He said to his sons, "Saddle my donkey,"
and they saddled it. 28 He then went and found
his body thrown in the road, and the donkey
and the lion were still standing by the body.
The lion had not eaten the body nor attacked
the donkey. 29 The prophet picked up the body
of the man of God and laid it on his donkey
and brought it back. The old prophet came to
the city to mourn and to bury him. 30 He laid
his body in his own tomb, and they mourned
over him, saying, "Alas, my brother!"
31 And after he had buried him, he said to his
sons, "When I am dead, bury me in the grave
in which the man of God is buried; lay my
bones beside his bones. 32 For the saying that
he cried out by the word of the LORD against
the altar in Bethel and against all the houses of
the high places that are in the cities of Samaria
shall surely come to pass."
33 After this event Jeroboam did not turn from
his evil ways, but made priests for the high
places again from among all the people. Any
who would, he consecrated to be priests of the
high places. 34 This matter became sin to the
house of Jeroboam, so as to cut it off and to
destroy it from the face of the earth.

Ahijah Prophesies Against Jeroboam

14 At that time, Jeroboam's son Abijah be-
came sick. 2 Jeroboam said to his wife,
"Please get up and disguise yourself, so that
you will not be recognized as the wife of Je-
roboam, and go to Shiloh. There you will find
Ahijah the prophet, who told me that I would
be king over this people. 3 Take ten loaves,
cakes, and a jar of honey, and go to him. He
will tell you what will happen to our child."
4 Jeroboam's wife did so and arose and went
to Shiloh, to the house of Ahijah.
But Ahijah could not see, for in his old age
he had gone blind. 5 The LORD said to Ahijah,
"The wife of Jeroboam has come to ask you
about her son, for he is sick. You shall say thus
and thus to her, for when she comes, she will
be disguised as another woman."
6 And so when Ahijah heard the sound of her
feet as she came in the door, he said, "Come
in, wife of Jeroboam. Why do you disguise
yourself as another? I have been sent to you
with bad news. 7 Go tell Jeroboam, 'Thus says
the LORD God of Israel: I raised you up from
among the people and made you prince over
My people Israel, 8 and took the kingdom away
from the house of David and gave it you. Yet
you have not been as My servant David, who
kept My commandments and who followed

13:11 2Ki 23:18
13:16 1Ki 13:8–9
13:17 1Ki 20:35
13:24 1Ki 20:36
13:30 Jer 22:18
13:32 1Ki 13:2
13:34 1Ki 12:30
14:2 1Sa 28:8
14:3 1Sa 9:7–8
14:4 1Ki 11:29
14:7 1Ki 16:2
14:8 1Ki 15:5

Me with all his heart to do only that which was right in My eyes, 9 but you have sinned more than all who were before you, for you have gone and made other gods and molded images and provoked Me to anger and have cast Me behind your back.

10 " 'Therefore I will bring disaster upon the house of Jeroboam and will cut off from Jeroboam all males, both slave and free in Israel, and will take away the remnant of the house of Jeroboam, as a man takes away refuse until it is all gone. 11 Descendants of Jeroboam who die in the city will be eaten by dogs, and those who die in the field will be eaten by the birds of the air, for the LORD has spoken it.'

12 "Arise therefore and go to your own house. When your feet enter the city, the child will die. 13 All Israel will mourn for him and bury him, for he alone from the house of Jeroboam will come to the grave, because in him there is found some good thing toward the LORD God of Israel.

14 "Moreover the LORD will raise up a king over Israel who will destroy the house of Jeroboam this day and from now on. 15 For the LORD will smite Israel, as a reed is shaken in the water, and He will uproot Israel from this good land, which he gave to their fathers, and will scatter them beyond the river, because they have made their Asherah poles, provoking the LORD to anger. 16 He shall give Israel up because of the sins of Jeroboam who sinned and who led Israel to sin."

17 Jeroboam's wife arose and departed and came to Tirzah. As she arrived at the threshold of the door, the child died, 18 and they buried him, and all Israel mourned for him, according to the word of the LORD, which He spoke by the hand of His servant Ahijah the prophet.

19 The rest of the acts of Jeroboam, how he waged war and how he reigned, are written in the book of the chronicles of the kings of Israel. 20 Jeroboam reigned twenty-two years, and then he slept with his fathers, and Nadab, his son, reigned in his stead.

Rehoboam, King of Judah
2Ch 12:9–16

21 Rehoboam the son of Solomon reigned in Judah. Rehoboam was forty-one years old when he began to reign, and he reigned seventeen years in Jerusalem, the city which the LORD had chosen out of all the tribes of Israel to put His name there. And his mother's name was Naamah, an Ammonitess.

22 Judah did evil in the sight of the LORD, and the people provoked Him to jealousy with the sins they committed, even worse than their fathers had done. 23 For they also built high places and images and Asherah poles on every high hill and under every green tree. 24 There were also male cult prostitutes in the land, and they did according to all the abominations of the nations that the LORD cast out before the children of Israel.

25 In the fifth year of King Rehoboam, Shishak king of Egypt came up against Jerusalem. 26 He took away all the treasures of the house of the LORD and the treasures of the king's house, even all the shields of gold which Solomon had made. 27 King Rehoboam replaced them with bronze shields and committed them to the hands of the chief of the guard who guarded the king's house. 28 And whenever the king entered the house of the LORD, the guards carried them and brought them back into the guard chamber.

29 Now the rest of the acts of Rehoboam and all that he did, are they not written in the book of the chronicles of the kings of Judah? 30 There was war between Rehoboam and Jeroboam all their days. 31 Rehoboam slept with his fathers and was buried with his fathers in the City of David. And his mother's name was Naamah, an Ammonitess. And Abijah his son reigned in his stead.

Abijah, King of Judah
2Ch 13:1–2; 13:22–14:1

15 Now in the eighteenth year of King Jeroboam the son of Nebat, Abijah became king over Judah. 2 He reigned three years in Jerusalem. His mother's name was Maakah, the daughter of Abishalom.

3 He walked in all the sins of his father that he had done before him, and his heart was not wholly devoted to the LORD his God as the heart of his father David had been. 4 Nevertheless, for David's sake, the LORD his God gave him a lamp in Jerusalem, to set up his son after him and to establish Jerusalem, 5 because David did that which was right in the eyes of the LORD and did not turn aside from anything that He commanded him all the days of his life, except in the matter involving Uriah the Hittite.

6 The war begun between Rehoboam and Jeroboam continued all the days of his life. 7 Now the rest of the acts of Abijah and all that he did, are they not written in the book of the chronicles of the kings of Judah? And there was war between Abijah and Jeroboam. 8 Abijah slept with his fathers, and they buried him in the City of David, and Asa his son reigned in his place.

Asa, King of Judah
2Ch 14:2–3; 15:16–17:1

9 In the twentieth year of Jeroboam king of Israel, Asa became king over Judah. 10 He reigned forty-one years in Jerusalem, and his

14:9 1Ki 12:28
14:10 Dt 32:36
14:11 1Ki 16:4
14:13 2Ch 19:3
14:14 1Ki 15:27–29
14:15 Jos 23:15–16
14:16 1Ki 12:30
14:17 1Ki 15:33
14:19 2Ch 13:2–20
14:21 2Ch 12:13
14:22 2Ch 12:1
14:23 Dt 12:2
....
14:24 Dt 23:17
14:25 1Ki 11:40
14:26 1Ki 15:18
14:31 2Ch 12:16
15:2 2Ch 13:2
15:3 1Ki 11:4
15:4 1Ki 11:36
15:5 1Ki 14:8
15:6 1Ki 14:30
15:7 2Ch 13:2–22
15:8 2Ch 14:1
15:10 1Ki 15:2

grandmother's name was Maakah, the daugh-
ter of Abishalom.
11 Asa did what was right in the eyes of the
LORD, just as his father David had done. 12 He
expelled the male cult prostitutes from the
land and removed all the idols that his fathers
had made. 13 In addition he even deposed his
grandmother Maakah as queen, because she
had made an idol in a grove. Asa destroyed her
idol and burned it by the Kidron brook. 14 But
the high places were not all removed, even
though Asa's heart was wholly devoted to the
LORD all his days. 15 He brought into the house
of the LORD the things that both his father and
he himself had dedicated, the silver and gold
and cups.

> Let any idol in my life or nation be destroyed and burned with Your fire (1Ki 15:13).

16 There was war between Asa and Baasha
king of Israel all their days. 17 Baasha king of
Israel went up against Judah and fortified Ra-
mah so he could prevent anyone from going
out or coming in to Asa king of Judah.
18 Then Asa took all the silver and the gold
that were left in the treasures of the house of
the LORD, as well as the treasures of the king's
house, and delivered them into the hand of his
servants, and he sent them to Ben-Hadad, the
son of Tabrimmon, the son of Hezion, king of
Aram, who lived at Damascus, saying, 19 "There
is a treaty between me and you and between
my father and your father. I have sent to you
a present of silver and gold. Come and break
your treaty with Baasha king of Israel, so he
will depart from me."
20 So Ben-Hadad listened to King Asa and
sent the commanders of his armies against the
cities of Israel and conquered Ijon, Dan, Abel
Beth Maakah, and all Kinnereth, along with
all the land of Naphtali. 21 When Baasha heard
about it, he halted the fortification of Ramah
and moved to Tirzah. 22 Then King Asa made a
proclamation throughout all Judah—none was
exempted—and they took away the stones of
Ramah and the timber with which Baasha had
built, and King Asa used them to build Geba of
Benjamin as well as Mizpah.
23 The rest of all the acts of Asa and all his
might and all that he did and the cities that
he built, are they not written in the book of
the chronicles of the kings of Judah? When
he was old, he got a disease in his feet. 24 Asa
then slept with his fathers and was buried with
them in the city of his father David, and Je-
hoshaphat his son reigned in his place.

15:11 2Ch 14:2
15:12 1Ki 22:46
15:13 Ex 32:20
15:14 1Ki 15:3
15:15 1Ki 7:51
15:16 1Ki 15:32
15:17 1Ki 12:27
15:18 1Ki 14:26
15:20 2Ki 15:29
15:21 1Ki 14:17
15:22 Jos 21:17
15:24 Mt 1:8

....

15:25 1Ki 14:20
15:26 1Ki 14:16
15:27 Jos 19:44
15:29 1Ki 14:9–16
15:30 1Ki 15:26
15:31 1Ki 14:19
15:32 1Ki 15:16
15:34 1Ki 15:26
16:1 2Ch 19:2
16:2 1Ki 14:7
16:3 1Ki 14:10
16:4 1Ki 14:11
16:5 1Ki 14:19
16:6 1Ki 14:17

Nadab, King of Israel

25 Nadab the son of Jeroboam began to reign
over Israel in the second year of Asa king of
Judah and reigned over Israel two years. 26 He
did evil in the sight of the LORD and walked in
the way of his father and in his sin with which
he made Israel to sin.
27 Baasha the son of Ahijah of the house of
Issachar conspired against him, and Baasha
killed him at Gibbethon, which belonged to
the Philistines, for Nadab and all Israel laid
siege to Gibbethon. 28 It was in the third year
of Asa king of Judah that Baasha killed him
and took his throne.
29 When he became king, Baasha killed all the
house of Jeroboam. No one from Jeroboam's
family was left breathing. He completely de-
stroyed them, according to the word of the
LORD which He spoke by His servant Ahijah the
Shilonite, 30 because of the sins of Jeroboam
which he sinned and which he made Israel sin,
by his provocation with which he provoked the
LORD God of Israel to anger.
31 Now the rest of the acts of Nadab and all
that he did, are they not written in the book
of the chronicles of the kings of Israel? 32 And
there was war between Asa and Baasha king
of Israel all their days.

Baasha, King of Israel

33 In the third year of Asa king of Judah,
Baasha the son of Ahijah began to reign over
all Israel in Tirzah, *and he did so* twenty-four
years. 34 He did evil in the sight of the LORD and
walked in the way of Jeroboam and in his sin
with which he made Israel to sin.

16 Then the word of the LORD came to Jehu
the son of Hanani against Baasha, say-
ing, 2 "I exalted you out of the dust and made
you prince over My people Israel, and you have
walked in the way of Jeroboam and have made
My people Israel to sin, to provoke Me to anger
with their sins. 3 See, I will take away the pos-
terity of Baasha and the posterity of his house
and will make your house like the house of
Jeroboam the son of Nebat. 4 Those from the
house of Baasha who die in the city will be
eaten by dogs, and those who die in the fields
will be eaten by the birds of the air."
5 Now the rest of the acts of Baasha and what
he did and his might, are they not written in
the book of the chronicles of the kings of Isra-
el? 6 So Baasha slept with his fathers and was
buried in Tirzah, and Elah his son reigned in
his place.
7 And so it was by the hand of the prophet
Jehu the son of Hanani that the word of the
LORD came against Baasha and his house, for
all the evil that he did in the sight of the LORD

in provoking Him to anger with the work of
his hands because he acted like the house of
Jeroboam and also because he killed it.

Elah, King of Israel

8 In the twenty-sixth year of Asa king of Ju-
dah, Elah the son of Baasha began to reign
over Israel in Tirzah, *and he did so* two years.
9 His servant Zimri, commander of half his
chariots, conspired against him, and when he
was in Tirzah, drinking himself drunk in the
house of Arza, manager of his house in Tirzah,
10 Zimri went in and smote him and killed him.
This took place in the twenty-seventh year of
Asa king of Judah, and Zimri reigned in his
place.
11 When he began to reign, as soon as he
was seated on his throne, he executed all the
household of Baasha. He left no males, neither
of his relatives nor of his friends. 12 Thus Zimri
destroyed all the house of Baasha, according
to the word of the LORD which He spoke against
Baasha by Jehu the prophet, 13 because of all
the sins of Baasha and the sins of Elah his son,
by which they sinned and by which they made
Israel to sin in provoking the LORD God of Israel
to anger with their vanities.
14 Now the rest of the acts of Elah and all that
he did, are they not written in the book of the
chronicles of the kings of Israel?

Zimri, King of Israel

15 In the twenty-seventh year of Asa king of
Judah, Zimri reigned seven days in Tirzah.
Now the troops were encamped against Gibbe-
thon, which belonged to the Philistines. 16 The
troops who were encamped heard how Zimri
had conspired and had slain the king. As a
result, all Israel made Omri, the commander of
the army, king over Israel that day in the camp.
17 Omri went up from Gibbethon and all Israel
with him, and they besieged Tirzah. 18 When
Zimri saw that the city had fallen, he went into
the citadel of the king's house and burned the
king's house over him with fire, and he died,
19 because of his sins which he sinned in doing
evil in the sight of the LORD, in walking in the
way of Jeroboam and in his sin which he did
to make Israel to sin.
20 Now the rest of the acts of Zimri and his
treason, are they not written in the book of the
chronicles of the kings of Israel?

Omri, King of Israel

21 Then the people of Israel were divided into
two parts. Half of the people followed Tibni
the son of Ginath to make him king, and half
followed Omri. 22 But the people who followed
Omri defeated the people who followed Tib-
ni, the son of Ginath. So Tibni died, and Omri
reigned.
23 In the thirty-first year of Asa king of Judah,
Omri began to reign over Israel, *and he did so*
twelve years. He reigned six years in Tirzah.
24 He bought the hill of Samaria from Shemer
for two talents[1] of silver. He fortified the hill
and named the city he built after the name of
Shemer, owner of the hill, calling it "Samaria."
25 But Omri did evil in the eyes of the LORD
and did worse than all who preceded him,
26 for he walked in all the ways of Jeroboam
the son of Nebat and in his sin with which he
made Israel to sin to provoke the LORD God of
Israel to anger with their vanities.
27 Now the rest of the acts Omri performed
and his might that he showed, are they not
written in the book of the chronicles of the
kings of Israel? 28 So Omri slept with his fathers
and was buried in Samaria, and Ahab his son
reigned in his place.

Ahab Reigns in Israel

29 In the thirty-eighth year of Asa king of Ju-
dah, Ahab the son of Omri began to reign over
Israel, and Ahab the son of Omri reigned over
Israel in Samaria twenty-two years. 30 Ahab the
son of Omri did more evil in the sight of the
LORD than all who were before him. 31 The sins
of Jeroboam the son of Nebat were seen as
minor for him to walk in, for he took Jezebel
the daughter of Ethbaal, king of the Sidonians,
as his wife and went and served Baal and wor-
shipped him. 32 He raised an altar for Baal in
the house of Baal, which he had built in Sa-
maria. 33 Ahab made an Asherah and did more
to provoke the LORD God of Israel to anger than
all the kings of Israel who preceded him.
34 In his days, Hiel the Bethelite built Jeri-
cho. He laid the foundation at the expense of
his firstborn Abiram and set up the gates at
the cost of the life of his youngest son Segub,
according to the word of the LORD, which He
spoke by Joshua the son of Nun.

Elijah's Prediction of Drought

17 Now Elijah the Tishbite, who was one
of the inhabitants of Gilead, said to
Ahab, "As the LORD God of Israel lives before
whom I stand, there will not be dew or rain
these years except by my word."
2 The word of the LORD came to him, saying,
3 "Go from here and turn eastward and hide by
the Kerith brook, which is east of the Jordan.
4 You shall drink from the brook, and I have
commanded the ravens to feed you there."
5 So he went and did according to the word
of the LORD, for he went and lived by the Kerith
brook, which is east of the Jordan. 6 The ravens
brought him bread and meat in the morning

16:12 1Ki 16:1
16:13 Dt 32:21
16:15 1Ki 15:27
16:18 2Sa 17:23
16:19 1Ki 15:26

16:24 1Ki 13:32
16:25 Mic 6:16
16:26 1Ki 16:19
16:30 1Ki 16:25
16:31 Jdg 18:7
16:32 2Ki 10:21
16:33 2Ki 13:6
16:34 Jos 6:26
17:1 2Ki 3:14
17:4 1Ki 17:9

[1] *24* About 150 pounds, or 68 kilograms.

and bread and meat in the evening, and he drank from the brook.

The Widow of Zarephath

7 After some time, the brook dried up because there had been no rain in the land. 8 The word of the LORD came to him, saying, 9 "Arise, go to Zarephath, which belongs to Sidon, and live there. I have commanded a widow there to provide for you." 10 So he got up and went to Zarephath, and when he came to the gate of the city, a widow was there gathering sticks. He called to her and said, "Please get a small cup of water for me to drink." 11 As she was going to get it, he called to her and said, "Please bring me a morsel of bread in your hand."

12 She said, "As the LORD your God lives, I do not have bread, but only a handful of meal in a barrel and a little oil in a jar. I am gathering two sticks, that I can go in and make it for me and my son, so we may eat it and die."

13 Elijah said to her, "Do not fear; go and do as you have said, but make a little cake for me first, and bring it to me, and afterward, make some for your son and you, 14 for thus says the LORD God of Israel: The barrel of meal will not run out, nor will the jar of oil empty, until the day that the LORD sends rain upon the earth."

15 She went and did what Elijah told her to do, and she, he, and her household ate many days. 16 The barrel of meal did not run out, nor did the jar of oil empty, according to the word of the LORD, which He spoke by Elijah.

17 Later on, the son of the woman, the mistress of the house, became terribly sick, so much so that he had no breath left in him. 18 She said to Elijah, "What do I have to do with you, O you man of God? Have you come to remind me of my sin and to kill my son?"

19 And he said to her, "Give me your son," and he took him out of her arms and carried him up to a loft where he slept and laid him on his own bed. 20 He cried to the LORD and said, "O LORD, my God, have You brought tragedy upon the widow with whom I live by killing her son?" 21 And he stretched himself upon the child three times and cried to the LORD and said, "O LORD, my God, I pray that You let this child's soul come into him again."

22 The LORD heard the voice of Elijah, and the soul of the child came into him again, and he was revived. 23 Elijah took the child and brought him down out of the chamber into the house and returned him to his mother, and Elijah said, "See, your son lives!"

24 The woman said to Elijah, "Now, because of this, I know that you are a man of God, and that the word of the LORD in your mouth is truth!"

17:9 Ob 1:20
17:10 Ge 24:17
17:12 1Ki 17:1
17:18 2Ki 3:13
17:21 Ac 20:10
17:24 Jn 3:2

18:1 Lk 4:25
18:3 Ne 7:2
18:4 1Ki 18:13
18:7 2Ki 1:6–8

SPIRITLED WOMAN

COUNSEL FROM THE SPIRIT BASICS

Raising Up a Deliverer

"Now Elijah the Tishbite, who was one of the inhabitants of Gilead, said to Ahab, 'As the LORD God of Israel lives before whom I stand, there will not be dew or rain these years except by my word'" (1Ki 17:1). God's prophets were very active in economic situations in biblical times, as they should be today. The economy was often affected by judgment that was a result of God's displeasure with man. In Judges 3:12–15 God gave His people over to the evil King Eglon for eighteen years. This king taxed the people harshly, and they began to cry out to God. As God always does, *He raised up a deliverer!*

The economic situations of the world can never affect the born-again believer who operates under the covering of the economy of God. As markets flip and flop and the deception of temporary riches grips the loins of many, stability and faithfulness in the principles of God will keep the righteous.

Kimberly Daniels

Elijah Confronts Ahab

18 After many days, in the third year, the word of the LORD came to Elijah, saying, "Go and present yourself to Ahab, and I will send rain upon the earth." 2 Elijah went to show himself to Ahab.

And there was a great famine in Samaria. 3 Ahab called Obadiah, who was the governor of his house. (Now Obadiah feared the LORD greatly. 4 When Jezebel killed the prophets of the LORD, Obadiah took a hundred prophets and hid them in groups of fifty in a cave and fed them with bread and water.) 5 And Ahab said to Obadiah, "Go into the land, to all the springs of water and to all the brooks. Perhaps we will find grass to save the horses and mules, so that we do not lose all the beasts." 6 So they divided the land between them to search throughout it. Ahab went one way by himself, and Obadiah went another way by himself.

7 As Obadiah was going along, he met Elijah, and he recognized him and fell on his face and said, "Is that you, my lord Elijah?"

8 And he answered him, "I am. Go, tell your
lord, 'Elijah is here.' "
9 He said, "What evil have I done that you
would hand your servant into the hand of
Ahab to put me to death? 10 As the LORD your
God lives, there is no nation or kingdom where
my lord has not looked for you, and when they
said, 'He is not here,' he made the kingdom
and nation swear that they could not find you,
11 and now you say, 'Go, tell your lord, "Elijah
is here!" ' 12 As soon as I am gone from you,
the Spirit of the LORD will carry you to a place
I do not know, and so when I come and tell
Ahab and he cannot find you, he will execute
me. But I, your servant, have feared the LORD
since my youth. 13 Were you not told what I
did when Jezebel killed the prophets of the
LORD, how I hid a hundred men of the LORD's
prophets in groups of fifty in a cave and fed
them with bread and water? 14 And now you
say, 'Go, tell your lord, "Elijah is here," ' and he
will execute me."
15 Elijah said, "As the LORD of Hosts lives, be-
fore whom I stand, I will surely show myself
to him today."

Elijah and the Prophets of Baal

16 So Obadiah went to meet Ahab and told
him. And Ahab went to meet Elijah. 17 When
Ahab saw Elijah, Ahab said to him, "Are you
he that troubles Israel?"
18 And he answered, "I have not troubled Isra-
el, but you and your father's house, in that you
have forsaken the commandments of the LORD
and you have followed the Baals. 19 Now send
word out and gather for me all Israel on Mount
Carmel, along with the four hundred and fifty
prophets of Baal and the four hundred proph-
ets of Asherah who eat at Jezebel's table."
20 So Ahab called out all the children of Israel
and gathered the prophets together on Mount
Carmel. 21 Elijah came to all the people and
said, "How long will you stay between two
opinions? If the LORD is God, follow Him, but
if Baal, then follow him."
And the people did not say a word.
22 Then Elijah said to the people, "I alone re-
main a prophet of the LORD, but Baal's prophets
number four hundred and fifty men. 23 There-
fore, let them give us two bulls, and let them
choose one bull for themselves and cut it in
pieces and lay it on some wood, but do not
light a fire under it, and I will prepare the other
bull, lay it on some wood, and not light a fire
underneath it. 24 And you call on the name of
your gods, and I will call on the name of the
LORD, and the God that answers by fire, let Him
be God."
And all the people answered and said, "It is
well spoken."
25 Elijah said to the prophets of Baal, "Choose
one bull for yourselves and prepare it first, for
there are many of you, and call on the name of
your god, but do not light a fire underneath."

> You are the God that answers by fire (1Ki 18:24).

26 They took the bull which was given to
them, and they prepared it and called on the
name of Baal from morning until noon, saying,
"O Baal, hear us." But there was no voice, and
no one answered. And they leaped upon the
altar which was made.
27 By noon, Elijah mocked them, saying, "Cry
out loud, for he is a god. Either he is talking or
is gone away or is on a journey, or perhaps he
is asleep and needs to be awakened." 28 They
cried out loud and cut themselves with knives
and spears according to their custom until the
blood gushed out on them. 29 And as midday
passed, they prophesied until the time of the
offering of the evening sacrifice. But there
was no voice. No one answered; no one paid
attention.
30 Elijah said to all the people, "Come near
to me." And all the people came near to him.
And he repaired the altar of the LORD that was
broken down. 31 Elijah took twelve stones, ac-
cording to the number of the tribes of the sons
of Jacob, to whom the word of the LORD came
saying, "Israel shall be your name," 32 and he
built an altar in the name of the LORD with
stones, and he made a trench around the al-
tar, so deep that it could contain two seahs[1] of
seed. 33 He arranged the wood and cut the bull
in pieces and laid him on the wood and said,
"Fill four barrels with water, and pour it on the
burnt sacrifice and on the wood."
34 He said, "Do it a second time," and they did
it a second time.
And he said, "Do it a third time," and they
did it the third time. 35 The water ran all around
the altar and also filled the trench with water.
36 At the time of the offering of the evening
sacrifice, Elijah the prophet came near and
said, "The LORD, God of Abraham, Isaac, and
of Israel, let it be known this day that You are
God in Israel and that I am Your servant and
that I have done all these things at Your word.
37 Hear me, O LORD, hear me, so that this people
may know that You are the LORD God and that
You have turned their hearts back again."
38 Then the fire of the LORD fell and con-
sumed the burnt sacrifice and the wood and

18:10 1Ki 17:1
18:12 2Ki 2:16
18:13 1Ki 18:4
18:15 1Ki 17:1
18:17 Jos 7:25
18:18 2Ch 15:2
18:19 Jos 19:26
18:21 Jos 24:15
18:22 1Ki 19:10
18:24 1Ki 18:38

18:26 Jer 10:5
18:28 Lev 19:28
18:30 1Ki 19:10
18:31 Ge 32:28
18:32 Col 3:17
18:33 Ge 22:9
18:36 Ex 3:6
18:38 Lev 9:24

[1] *32* Likely about 24 pounds, or 11 kilograms.

the stones and the dust and licked up the water
that was in the trench.
39 When all the people saw it, they fell on
their faces and said, "The LORD, He is God! The
LORD, He is God!"
40 Elijah said to them, "Arrest the prophets
of Baal, and do not let one of them escape."
And they arrested them, and Elijah brought
them down to the Kishon brook and executed
them there.

End of the Drought

41 Elijah said to Ahab, "Get up, eat and drink,
for there is a sound of a heavy rainfall." 42 So
Ahab got up to eat and drink. And Elijah went
up to the top of Carmel, and he threw himself
down on the ground and put his face between
his knees.
43 And he said to his servant, "Go up now, and
look toward the sea."
And he went up and looked and said, "There
is nothing."
And he said, "Go again," seven times.
44 On the seventh time, he said, "A small
cloud as small as a man's hand is rising out
of the sea."
And he said, "Go up and say to Ahab, 'Mount
your chariot and get down, so that the rain
does not stop you.' "
45 In the meantime, the sky turned black with
clouds and wind, and there was a great rain.
And Ahab rode and went to Jezreel. 46 The
hand of the LORD was on Elijah, and he girded
up his loins and ran ahead of Ahab to the en-
trance of Jezreel.

Elijah Flees From Jezebel

19 And Ahab told Jezebel all that Elijah
had done and how he had executed
all the prophets with the sword. 2 Then Jezebel
sent a messenger to Elijah, saying, "So let the
gods do to me and more also, if I do not make
your life as the life of one of them by tomorrow
about this time."
3 When he saw that she was serious, he
arose and ran for his life to Beersheba, which
belongs to Judah, and left his servant there.
4 But he went a day's journey into the wilder-
ness and came and sat down under a juniper
tree and asked that he might die, saying, "It is
enough! Now, O LORD, take my life, for I am not
better than my fathers."
5 As he lay and slept under the juniper tree,
an angel touched him and said to him, "Arise
and eat." 6 He looked, and there was a cake
baked on coals and a jar of water at his head.
And he ate and drank and then lay down
again.
7 The angel of the LORD came again a second
time and touched him and said, "Arise and

18:39 1Ki 18:24
18:40 Dt 13:5
18:44 Lk 12:54
18:46 2Ki 3:15
19:1 1Ki 18:40
19:2 Ru 1:17
19:3 Ge 21:31
19:4 Nu 11:15
19:6 Mt 4:11
....
19:8 Ex 34:28
19:10 1Ki 18:4
19:11 Ex 24:12
19:12 Job 4:16
19:13 1Ki 19:9
19:15 2Ki 8:7–15
19:16 1Ki 19:19–21
19:17 2Ki 8:12
19:18 Hos 13:2
19:19 2Ki 2:8
19:20 Mt 8:21–22

eat, because the journey is too great for you."
8 He arose and ate and drank and went in the
strength of that food forty days and forty nights
to Horeb, the mountain of God.

Elijah Hears the LORD

9 He came to a cave and camped there, and
the word of the LORD came to him, and He said
to him, "Why are you here, Elijah?"
10 And he said, "I have been very zealous for
the LORD, Lord of Hosts, for the children of Isra-
el have forsaken Your covenant, thrown down
Your altars, and killed Your prophets with the
sword, and I alone am left, and they seek to
take my life."
11 He said, "Go and stand on the mountain
before the LORD."
And, behold, the LORD passed by, and a great
and strong wind split the mountains and broke
in pieces the rocks before the LORD, but the
LORD was not in the wind. And after the wind,
an earthquake came, but the LORD was not in
the earthquake. 12 And after the earthquake, a
fire came, but the LORD was not in the fire, and
after the fire, a still, small voice. 13 When Elijah
heard it, he wrapped his face in his cloak and
went out and stood in the entrance to the cave.
And a voice came to him and said, "Why are
you here, Elijah?"
14 And he said, "I have been very zealous for
the LORD, Lord of Hosts, because the children
of Israel have forsaken Your covenant, thrown
down Your altars, and killed your prophets
with the sword, and I alone am left, and they
seek to take my life."
15 The LORD said to him, "Go, return on the
road through the Wilderness of Damascus, and
when you arrive, anoint Hazael to be king over
Aram. 16 And you shall anoint Jehu, the son of
Nimshi, to be king over Israel, and you shall
anoint Elisha, the son of Shaphat of Abel Me-
holah, to be prophet in your place. 17 He who
escapes the sword of Hazael will be killed by
Jehu, and he who escapes the sword of Jehu
will be killed by Elisha. 18 Still, I have preserved
seven thousand men in Israel for Myself, all
of whose knees have not bowed to Baal and
whose mouths have not kissed him."

The Call of Elisha

19 So he departed from there and found Eli-
sha the son of Shaphat, who was plowing
with twelve yoke of oxen before him and he
with the twelfth, and Elijah passed by him and
threw his cloak on him. 20 He left the oxen and
ran after Elijah and said, "Please let me kiss my
father and mother, and then I will follow you."
And he said to him, "Go back, for what have
I done to you?"

21 So he returned from following him and took a yoke of oxen and sacrificed them and boiled their flesh with the yokes from the oxen and gave it to the people, and they ate. Then he got up and went after Elijah and ministered to him.

Ben-Hadad Attacks Samaria

20 Now Ben-Hadad the king of Aram gathered his army together. Thirty-two kings were with him, with horses and chariots, and he went up and besieged Samaria and fought against it. 2 He sent messengers into the city to Ahab king of Israel and said to him, "Thus says Ben-Hadad: 3 Your silver and gold is mine, as are your most attractive wives and children."

4 The king of Israel answered, "My lord, O king, just as you have said, I and all that I own are yours."

5 The messengers came again and said, "Thus says Ben-Hadad: Although I have said that you must give me your silver and gold, your wives and your children, 6 instead I will send my servants tomorrow about this time, and they will search your house and the houses of your servants, and whatever is precious to you, they will put it in their hands and take it away."

7 Then the king of Israel called all the elders of the land and said, "Please notice how this man is looking for trouble, for he has demanded I give him my wives and children and my silver and gold, and I have not denied his request."

8 All the elders and all the people said to him, "Do not listen to him or consent to his demands."

9 Therefore he said to the messengers of Ben-Hadad, "Tell my lord the king: I will comply with the first request of your servant, but this thing I will not do." And the messengers departed and brought him word again.

10 Then Ben-Hadad sent *messengers* to him and said, "The gods do to me and then some if the dust of Samaria shall suffice for handfuls for all the people who follow me."

11 The king of Israel answered, "Tell him: Let not he who puts on *his armor* boast himself as he who takes *it* off."

12 When Ben-Hadad heard this message as he was drinking with the kings in the pavilions, he said to his servants, "Station yourselves!" And they stationed themselves against the city.

Ahab Defeats Ben-Hadad

13 Then a prophet came to Ahab king of Israel, saying, "Thus says the LORD: Have you seen this great multitude? See, I will deliver it into your hand this day, and you shall know that I am the LORD."

14 Ahab asked, "By whom?"

And he said, "Thus says the LORD: By the young leaders of the provinces."

Then he said, "Who shall order the battle?"

And he answered, "You."

15 Then he counted the young leaders of the provinces, and they were two hundred and thirty-two, and after them he counted all the people, all the children of Israel, and had seven thousand. 16 They went out at noon. But Ben-Hadad and the thirty-two kings who helped him were getting drunk in the pavilions. 17 The young leaders of the provinces went out first.

Ben-Hadad sent out scouts, and they told him, "Men from Samaria have come out."

18 He said, "If they have come out peacefully, take them alive, and if they have come out for battle, take them alive."

19 So these young leaders of the provinces came out of the city, followed by the army. 20 Each one killed his man, and the Arameans fled with Israel pursuing them, but Ben-Hadad, the king of Aram, escaped on a horse with the horsemen. 21 The king of Israel went out and attacked the horses and chariots and killed a great number of Arameans.

22 The prophet came to the king of Israel and said, "Go, strengthen yourself and prepare, and see what you do, for next year the king of Aram will come up against you."

23 The servants of the king of Aram said to him, "Their gods are gods of the hills. That is why they were stronger than us, but if we fight against them in the plain, we will surely be stronger than they. 24 Do this: Dismiss the kings, each from his position, and put commanders in their places, 25 and assemble an army like the army that you lost, horse for horse and chariot for chariot, and we will fight them in the plain and will surely be stronger than they." And he listened to their advice and followed it.

26 The next year Ben-Hadad assembled the Arameans and went up to Aphek to fight against Israel. 27 The children of Israel were assembled and were all present, and they went against them, and the children of Israel camped in front of them like two little flocks of kids, while the Arameans filled the country.

28 A man of God came and spoke to the king of Israel and said, "Thus says the LORD: Because the Arameans have said, 'The LORD is God of the hills, but He is not God of the valleys,' I will deliver all this great multitude into your hand, and you will know that I am the LORD."

19:21 2Sa 24:22
20:1 1Ki 15:18
20:7 2Ki 5:7
20:10 1Ki 19:2
20:11 Pr 27:1
20:12 1Ki 16:9
20:13 1Ki 20:28
. . . .
20:18 2Ki 14:8–12
20:22 2Sa 11:1
20:23 1Ki 14:23
20:26 2Ki 13:17
20:28 1Ki 20:13

29 They camped opposite each other for seven days, and on the seventh day, the battle was joined. The children of Israel killed a hundred thousand Aramean footmen in one day. 30 But the rest fled into the city of Aphek, where a wall fell on twenty-seven thousand of the men who were left. And Ben-Hadad fled and came into the city into an inner chamber.

31 His servants said to him, "We have heard that the kings of the house of Israel are merciful kings. Please let us put sackcloth on our loins and ropes on our heads and go out to the king of Israel. Perhaps he will spare your life."

32 So they girded sackcloth on their loins and put ropes on their heads and came to the king of Israel and said, "Your servant Ben-Hadad says, 'Please let me live.' "

And he said, "Is he still alive? He is my brother!"

33 Now the men were diligently looking for a positive sign and quickly took hold of it, and they said, "Your brother Ben-Hadad!"

Then he said, "Go. You bring him." Then Ben-Hadad came to him and got into the chariot.

34 Ben-Hadad said to him, "I will restore the cities which my father took from your father, and you shall make streets for yourself in Damascus, as my father made in Samaria."

Then Ahab said, "I will send you away with this covenant." So he made a covenant with him and sent him away.

A Prophet Condemns Ahab

35 Speaking in the word of the LORD, a certain man of the sons of the prophets said to his neighbor, "Strike me, please." But the man refused to strike him.

36 Then he said to him, "Because you have not obeyed the voice of the LORD, as soon as you leave me, a lion will kill you." And as soon as he left him, a lion found and killed him.

37 Then he found another man and said, "Strike me, please." And the man struck him so that he was wounded. 38 So the prophet departed and waited by the road for the king and disguised himself with ashes on his face. 39 As the king passed by, he cried to the king and said, "Your servant went out into the midst of the battle, and a man turned aside and brought a man to me and said, 'Keep this man, and if by any means he goes missing, then your life shall be given for his life, or else you shall pay a talent[1] of silver.' 40 As your servant was busy here and there, he disappeared."

And the king of Israel said to him, "So shall your judgment be; you have decided it yourself."

20:30 1Ki 22:25
20:31 Ge 37:34
20:32 1Ki 20:3–6
20:34 1Ki 15:20
20:35 1Ki 13:17–18
20:38 1Ki 14:2
20:39 2Ki 10:24

....

20:42 1Ki 22:31–37
20:43 1Ki 21:4
21:2 1Sa 8:14
21:3 Lev 25:23
21:4 1Ki 20:43
21:10 Ex 22:28
21:12 Isa 58:4
21:13 2Ki 9:26

41 He quickly took the ashes away from his face, and the king of Israel recognized him as one of the prophets. 42 He said to him, "Thus says the LORD, 'Because you have let go out of your hand a man whom I had appointed to utter destruction, you shall pay for his life with your life and his people with your people.' " 43 The king of Israel went to his house in Samaria angry and depressed.

Naboth's Vineyard

21 Now Naboth the Jezreelite had a vineyard in Jezreel right by the palace of Ahab king of Samaria. 2 And after this Ahab spoke to Naboth, saying, "Give me your vineyard, so that I can have it for a garden of herbs, because it is near to my house, and I will give you a better vineyard for it, or if you prefer, I will give you its worth in money."

3 Naboth said to Ahab, "The LORD forbid that I should give you the inheritance of my fathers."

4 Ahab returned home angry and depressed because of the answer Naboth the Jezreelite had given him, for he had said, "I will not give you the inheritance of my fathers." He lay down on his bed and sulked and would not eat any bread.

5 But Jezebel his wife came to him and said, "Why is your spirit so sad that you refuse to eat bread?"

6 And he said to her, "Because I spoke to Naboth the Jezreelite and said to him, 'Give me your vineyard for money; or else, if you prefer, I will give you another vineyard for it.' And he answered, 'I will not give you my vineyard.' "

7 Jezebel his wife said to him, "Are you not the governor of the kingdom of Israel? Get up and eat bread, and let your heart be happy, for I will get the vineyard of Naboth the Jezreelite for you."

8 So she wrote letters in Ahab's name and sealed them with his seal and sent the letters to the elders and to the nobles that were in the city where Naboth lived. 9 In the letters she wrote,

> "Proclaim a fast, and set Naboth on high among the people, 10 and set two men, sons of Belial,[2] before him, to bear witness against him, saying, 'You blasphemed God and the king.' And then carry him out and stone him, so that he will die."

11 The men of his city, the elders and the nobles who lived in his city, did as Jezebel had sent word to them, as it was written in the letters that she had sent to them. 12 They proclaimed a fast and set Naboth on high among the people. 13 Two men, children of

[1] 39 About 75 pounds, or 34 kilograms. [2] 10 *Or, evil men.*

Belial, came in and sat in front of him, and the men of Belial witnessed against Naboth in the presence of the people, saying, "Naboth blasphemed God and the king." Then they carried him out of the city and stoned him to death. 14 Then they sent word to Jezebel, saying, "Naboth has been stoned and is dead."

15 When Jezebel heard that Naboth had been stoned and was dead, she said to Ahab, "Arise, take possession of the vineyard of Naboth the Jezreelite, which he refused to sell to you for money, for Naboth is not alive, but dead." 16 When Ahab heard that Naboth was dead, he got up to go down to the vineyard of Naboth the Jezreelite, to take possession of it.

The LORD Condemns Ahab

17 The word of the LORD came to Elijah the Tishbite, saying: 18 Arise, go down to meet Ahab, king of Israel, who is in Samaria. He is now in the vineyard of Naboth, where he has gone down to possess it. 19 You shall speak to him, saying, "Thus says the LORD: Have you killed and also taken possession?" And you shall speak to him, saying, "Thus says the LORD: In the place where dogs licked the blood of Naboth, dogs will lick your own blood!"

20 Ahab said to Elijah, "Have you found me, my enemy?"

And he answered, "I have found you, because you have sold yourself to work evil in the sight of the LORD. 21 'See, I will bring disaster upon you and will take away your posterity and will cut off all your males, both free and slave, who are left in Israel, 22 and will make your house like the house of Jeroboam the son of Nebat and like the house of Baasha the son of Ahijah, for the provocation with which you have provoked Me to anger and made Israel to sin.'

23 "The LORD also spoke of Jezebel, saying, 'The dogs will eat Jezebel by the wall of Jezreel.'

24 "Those from Ahab's family who die in the city will be eaten by dogs, and those who die in the field will be eaten by birds of the air."

25 But there were none compared to Ahab, who sold himself to evil deeds in the sight of the LORD, which Jezebel his wife stirred up. 26 He performed the most abominable act in following idols like the Amorites, whom the LORD cast out before the children of Israel.

27 When Ahab heard those words, he tore his clothes and put on sackcloth on his flesh and fasted and lay in sackcloth and walked meekly.

28 The word of the LORD came to Elijah the Tishbite, saying, 29 "See how Ahab humbles himself before Me? Because he humbles himself before Me, I will not bring the disaster during his lifetime, but during his son's lifetime I will bring the disaster on his household."

21:17 Ps 9:12
21:19 1Ki 22:38
21:20 1Ki 18:17
21:21 1Ki 14:10
21:22 1Ki 16:3
21:23 2Ki 9:10
21:24 1Ki 14:11
21:25 1Ki 21:20
21:26 Ge 15:16
21:27 2Ki 6:30
21:29 2Ki 9:25–26

....

22:2 1Ki 15:24
22:3 Dt 4:43
22:4 2Ki 3:7
22:5 2Ki 3:11
22:6 1Ki 18:19
22:8 Am 5:10
22:11 Zec 1:18–21
22:14 Nu 24:13

Micaiah Prophesies Against Ahab

2Ch 18:1–27

22 And there were three years without war between Aram and Israel. 2 In the third year, Jehoshaphat king of Judah went to visit the king of Israel. 3 The king of Israel said to his servants, "You know that Ramoth in Gilead is ours, but we have done nothing to take it out of the hand of the king of Aram!"

4 And he said to Jehoshaphat, "Will you go with me to battle Ramoth Gilead?"

And Jehoshaphat said to the king of Israel, "I am as you are, my people as your people, my horses as your horses." 5 Jehoshaphat said to the king of Israel, "Please ask for a word from the LORD today."

6 Then the king of Israel gathered the prophets together, approximately four hundred men, and said to them, "Shall I go against Ramoth Gilead to battle, or shall I wait?"

And they said, "Go up, for the Lord shall deliver it into the hand of the king."

7 Jehoshaphat said, "Is there not a prophet of the LORD here whom we can ask?"

8 And the king of Israel said to Jehoshaphat, "There is still one man, Micaiah the son of Imlah, by whom we can inquire of the LORD. But I hate him because he never prophesies good for me, but always evil."

And Jehoshaphat said, "Let not the king say so."

9 Then the king of Israel called an officer and said, "Quickly, bring Micaiah the son of Imlah."

10 The king of Israel and Jehoshaphat the king of Judah *each* put on his robes and sat on his throne at the entrance of the gate of Samaria, and all the prophets prophesied before them. 11 Zedekiah the son of Kenaanah made horns of iron and said, "Thus says the LORD: With these you shall push the Arameans until you have consumed them."

12 All the prophets prophesied similarly, saying, "Go up to Ramoth Gilead and prosper, for the LORD will deliver it into the king's hand."

13 The servant who had gone to get Micaiah spoke to him, saying, "See here, the words of the prophets unanimously declare success for the king. Please let your word be like the word of one of them, and speak that which is good."

14 Micaiah said, "As the LORD lives, I will speak whatever the LORD says to me."

15 So he came to the king. And the king said to him, "Micaiah, shall we go against Ramoth Gilead to battle, or shall we wait?"

And he answered him, "Go and prosper, for the LORD will deliver it into the hand of the king."

16 The king said to him, "How many times must I admonish you to tell me only the truth in the name of the LORD?"

17 And he said, "I saw all Israel scattered upon the hills, as sheep without a shepherd, and the LORD said, 'These have no master. Let every man return to his own house in peace.' "

> Lord, protect my mind from believing the lies of the enemy (1Ki 22:19–23).

18 The king of Israel said to Jehoshaphat, "Did I not tell you that he would not prophesy good concerning me, but evil?"

19 And he said, "Hear, therefore, the word of the LORD: I saw the LORD sitting on His throne, and all the host of heaven standing beside Him on His right hand and on His left. 20 The LORD said, 'Who will persuade Ahab so that he will go up and die at Ramoth Gilead?'

"And one said this, and another said that. 21 Then a spirit came forth and stood before the LORD and said, 'I will persuade him.'

22 "The LORD said to him, 'How?'

"And he said, 'I will go and be a lying spirit in the mouth of all his prophets.'

"And He said, 'You will be successful and persuade him. Go forth, and do so.'

23 "Now therefore, the LORD has put a lying spirit in the mouths of all your prophets here, and He has spoken evil concerning you!"

24 Then Zedekiah the son of Kenaanah walked up and struck Micaiah on the cheek and said, "Which way did the spirit of the LORD go from me in order to speak to you?"

25 And Micaiah said, "You will see in that day, when you go into an inner chamber to hide."

26 The king of Israel said, "Take Micaiah back to Amon the governor of the city and to Joash the king's son, 27 and say, 'Thus says the king: Put this man in the prison, and feed him with reduced rations of bread and water until I return safely.' "

28 Micaiah said, "If you return safely, the LORD has not spoken through me." And he said, "Listen, all you people!"

Ahab Dies in Battle

2Ch 18:28–34

29 So the king of Israel and Jehoshaphat the king of Judah went up to Ramoth Gilead. 30 The king of Israel said to Jehoshaphat, "I will disguise myself and enter into the battle, but you wear your robes." And the king of Israel disguised himself and went into the battle.

31 But the king of Aram ordered his thirty-two commanders who had control over his chariots, saying, "Fight neither against small nor great, but only against the king of Israel." 32 So when the commanders of the chariots saw Jehoshaphat, they said, "Surely it is the king of Israel." And they turned aside to fight against him, and Jehoshaphat cried out. 33 When the commanders of the chariots realized that it was not the king of Israel, they turned away from pursuing him.

34 A certain man drew a bow at random and struck the king of Israel between the joints of the armor, and because of this, he said to the driver of his chariot, "Turn around and carry me out of the battle, for I am wounded." 35 The battle intensified that day, and the king was propped up in his chariot against the Arameans and died that evening, and the blood ran out of the wound into the floor of the chariot. 36 A proclamation went throughout the army as the sun was setting, saying, "Every man is to return to his city, and every man is to return to his own country."

37 So the king died and was brought to Samaria, and they buried him there. 38 The chariot was washed in the pool of Samaria, and the dogs licked up the king's blood, and they washed his armor according to the word which the LORD spoke.

39 Now the rest of the acts of Ahab and all that he did and the ivory house that he built and all the cities that he built, are they not written in the book of the chronicles of the kings of Israel? 40 So Ahab slept with his fathers. And Ahaziah his son reigned in his place.

Jehoshaphat, King of Judah

2Ch 20:31–21:1

41 Jehoshaphat the son of Asa began to reign over Judah in the fourth year of Ahab king of Israel. 42 Jehoshaphat was thirty-five years old when he began to reign, and he reigned twenty-five years in Jerusalem. His mother's name was Azubah, the daughter of Shilhi. 43 He walked in all the ways of Asa his father. He did not turn aside, doing that which was right in the eyes of the LORD. Nevertheless, the high places were not taken down, and the people continued to offer *sacrifices* and burn incense there. 44 So Jehoshaphat made peace with the king of Israel.

45 Now the rest of the acts of Jehoshaphat and the strength he showed and how he warred, are they not written in the book of the chronicles of the kings of Judah? 46 And he exterminated from the land the remnant

22:17 Nu 27:17
22:18 1Ki 22:8
22:19 Job 1:6
22:22 Jdg 9:23
22:23 Eze 14:9
22:24 Ac 23:2
22:25 1Ki 20:30
22:27 2Ch 16:10
22:28 Mic 1:2
22:30 2Ch 35:22
....
22:31 1Ki 20:24
22:34 2Ch 35:23
22:36 2Ki 14:12
22:38 1Ki 21:19
22:39 Am 3:15
22:41 2Ch 20:31
22:43 1Ki 15:14
22:46 1Ki 14:24

PROFILE OF A SPIRITED WOMAN

LOTTIE MOON

A LEGACY OF LOVE

Lottie Moon, at a height of four feet three inches, was a powerhouse for the gospel.

Born to affluent parents who owned a tobacco plantation in 1840, she was indifferent to her Baptist upbringing until the age of eighteen, when she underwent a spiritual awakening at a revival meeting on her college campus. At the age of thirty-three, with one of the first master of arts degrees accorded to a woman by a Southern university and with a few years of teaching experience, she followed her younger sister to the mission field in China. She spoke five languages, could read Hebrew, and would learn Chinese. She had turned down a marriage proposal and left everything behind, with no expectation of ever returning home, in order to follow God's call on her life.

Moon started teaching at a boys' school but soon discovered her real passion: evangelism. Most mission work at the time was done by men, but they could do nothing to reach the Chinese women. Frustrated at being tied to teaching in school, Moon soon viewed herself as part of an oppressed class—that of single female missionaries. She became relentless in her battle to see female missionaries given the freedom to minister and to have an equal voice in missions' proceedings. She wrote frequently to the head of the Southern Baptist Missions Board requesting more workers, male or female.

At the age of forty-five Moon moved from teaching into full-time evangelism. Her converts numbered in the hundreds.

Moon wrote numerous letters to people in the States, describing the life of a missionary and encouraging Southern Baptist women to create support groups for missionaries—and to consider becoming missionaries themselves. She also argued for regular furloughs for those on the mission field, convinced this would extend their lives on the field.

When she returned to China from her second furlough in 1904, Moon was deeply disturbed by the poverty and starvation she saw all around her and started sharing her meager supplies with those she encountered—to her own physical and mental detriment. She pleaded for more money, but the mission board had none to send her. By 1912 Moon weighed only fifty pounds. Fellow missionaries were so alarmed by her appearance that they arranged for her to be sent home with a companion. She died onboard the boat home.

But Moon's legacy lives on. In 1887 one of her letters home suggested that the week before Christmas be specially set aside for giving to missions. The idea caught on. The first offering raised more than $3,000, enough to send three more missionaries to China. In the years since, the Lottie Moon Christmas Offering for Missions has raised a total of $1.5 billion and finances half the Southern Baptist missions budget every year.

In a letter dated February 9, 1889, Moon wrote:

> Recently, on a Sunday which I was spending in a village near Pingtu city, two men came to me with the request that I would conduct the general services. They wished me to read and explain, to a mixed audience of men and women, the parable of the prodigal son. I replied that no one should undertake to speak without preparation, and that I had made none. (I had been busy all the morning teaching the women and girls.) After awhile they came again to know my decision. I said, "It is not the custom of the Ancient church that women preach to men." I could

not, however, hinder their calling upon me to lead in prayer. Need I say that, as I tried to lead their devotions, it was hard to keep back the tears of pity for those sheep not having a shepherd. Men asking to be taught and no one to teach them. We read of one who came forth and saw a great multitude, and he had compassion on them because they were as sheep not having a shepherd. "And how did he show his compassion?" He began to teach them many things. "Brethren, ministers and students for the ministry, who may read these lines, does there dwell in your hearts none of that divine compassion which stirred the heart of Jesus Christ, and which led him to 'teach' the multitude many things"?[1]

And from another letter:

> Women, too, may find [a place]. In city and in village, thousands of women will never hear the gospel until women bear it to them. They will admit women, but men cannot gain access to their homes, nor will they come to church. The only way for them to hear the good news of salvation is from the lips of foreign women. Are there not some, yea many, who find it in their hearts to say, "Here am I; send me"?[2]

Amazing what one outspoken little lady can do![3]

Felicity Dale

1. Lottie Moon, *Send the Light: Lottie Moon's Letters and Other Writings*, Keith Harper, ed. (N.p.: Mercer University Press, 2002), 239.
2. Ibid., 176.
3. Research for this article came from "Lottie Moon" on Wikipedia.com and information from the International Mission Board about Lottie Moon.

of the male cult prostitutes who remained in
the days of his father Asa. 47 At that time there
was no king in Edom, and a regent sat in the
king's place.
48 Jehoshaphat made ships of Tarshish to
go to Ophir for gold, but they never made it
there, for the ships were broken at Ezion Ge-
ber. 49 Then Ahaziah the son of Ahab said to
Jehoshaphat, "Let my servants go with your
servants in the ships." But Jehoshaphat did
not agree.
50 Jehoshaphat slept with his fathers and was
buried with his fathers in the City of David
his father, and Jehoram his son reigned in his
place.

22:47 2Sa 8:14
22:48 1Ki 9:26
22:50 2Ch 21:1

22:52 1Ki 15:26
22:53 1Ki 16:30–32

Ahaziah, King of Israel

51 Ahaziah the son of Ahab began to reign
over Israel in Samaria the seventeenth year of
Jehoshaphat king of Judah, and he reigned
two years over Israel. 52 He did evil in the sight
of the LORD and walked in the way of his father
and in the way of his mother and in the way of
Jeroboam the son of Nebat who made Israel
sin, 53 for he served Baal and worshipped him
and provoked the LORD God of Israel to anger,
according to all that his father had done.

Author: Traditionally the prophet Jeremiah

Written: Between 560 and 540 BC

Themes: History of Judah and Israel, Ministries of Elijah and Elisha

2 Kings

Dear Spirit Led Woman,

I once heard a story about a little boy who came upon a man shoveling pennies. When the boy asked the man what he was doing, the man told the boy to take what he wanted. The boy began stuffing pennies into his pockets until he saw the man shoveling quarters. Again the boy asked the man what he was doing, and the man responded that the boy could help himself. The boy immediately began to shove quarters into his pockets. Suddenly he noticed that the man was shoveling gold coins. When the boy asked him what he was doing, the man told him a third time to help himself.

The boy looked down at his bulging pockets filled with less valuable coins; he had no room for the gold. Without hesitation he emptied his pockets of what he already had so he could fill them with something of greater worth.

This story—and the account of the widow's empty vessels in 2 Kings 4—illustrates an important spiritual truth: if you want to be filled with God, you must be emptied of everything else. It is the first step in preparing for a move of the Holy Spirit in your life.

Joy F. Strang

God Judges Ahaziah

1 Then Moab rebelled against Israel after the
death of Ahab. 2 Ahaziah fell down through
a lattice in his upper chamber that was in Sa-
maria and became ill. So he sent messengers
and said to them, "Go, inquire of Baal-Zebub
the god of Ekron whether I will recover from
this illness."
3 But the angel of the LORD said to Elijah the
Tishbite, "Arise, go up to meet the messen-
gers of the king of Samaria, and say to them,
'Is it because there is not a God in Israel, that
you go to inquire of Baal-Zebub the god of
Ekron?' 4 Therefore thus says the LORD, 'You
will not come down from the bed on which
you have gone up but will surely die.' " Then
Elijah departed.
5 When the messengers returned to the king,
he said to them, "Why have you returned?"
6 And they said to him, "A man came up to
meet us and said to us, 'Go, return to the king
that sent you and say to him: Thus says the
LORD: Is it because there is no God in Israel
that you are sending to inquire of Baal-Zebub
the god of Ekron? Therefore you will not come
down from the bed on which you have gone
up, but you will surely die.' "
7 He said to them, "What sort of man was
he who came up to meet you and told you
these things?"
8 They answered him, "He was a hairy man
with a leather belt around his waist."
He said, "It was Elijah the Tishbite."
9 Then the king sent to him a captain of fifty
with his fifty men. He went up to Elijah, and
there he was, sitting on the top of a hill, and
he said to him, "Man of God, the king says,
'Come down.' "
10 But Elijah answered the captain of fifty: "If
I am a man of God, then let fire come down
from heaven and consume you and your fifty
men." Then fire came down from heaven and
consumed him and his fifty men.
11 Again the king sent to him another captain
of fifty with his fifty men. He said, "Man of
God, thus says the king: Come down quickly."
12 Elijah answered them, "If I am a man of
God, let fire come down from heaven and con-
sume you and your fifty men." Then the fire of
God came down from heaven and consumed
him and his fifty men.
13 Then again the king sent a third captain
of fifty with his fifty men. The third captain of
fifty went up, came and fell on his knees before
Elijah, and pleaded with him, "Man of God,
may my life and the life of these fifty servants
of yours be precious in your sight. 14 See, fire
came down from heaven and consumed the
two captains of the former fifties with their fif-
ty men. May my life now be precious in your
sight."
15 Then the angel of the LORD said to Elijah,
"Go down with him. Do not be afraid of him."
So he arose and went down with him to the
king.
16 Then he said to him, "Thus says the LORD:
Have you sent messengers to inquire of
Baal-Zebub the god of Ekron, because there is
no God in Israel to inquire of His word? There-
fore you will not come down from the bed on
which you have gone up, but you will surely
die." 17 So he died according to the word of the
LORD which Elijah had spoken.
Then Jehoram[1] reigned in his place in the
second year of Jehoram son of Jehoshaphat,
king of Judah, because he had no son. 18 Now
the rest of the acts of Ahaziah which he did,
are they not written in the book of the chron-
icles of the kings of Israel?

Elijah Ascends to Heaven

2 Then when the LORD was about to take
Elijah up to heaven by a whirlwind, Elijah
went with Elisha from Gilgal. 2 Elijah said to
Elisha, "Tarry here, I ask you, for the LORD has
sent me to Bethel."
But Elisha said to him, "As the LORD lives, and
as you live, I will not leave you." So they went
down to Bethel.
3 The sons of the prophets who were at Beth-
el came out to Elisha and said to him, "Do you
know that today the LORD is taking away your
master from you?"
And he said, "Yes, I know. Keep silent."
4 Elijah said to him, "Elisha, stay here, for the
LORD has sent me to Jericho."
And he said, "As the LORD lives, and as you
live, I will not leave you." So they entered Jer-
icho.
5 The sons of the prophets who were at Jer-
icho approached Elisha and said to him, "Do
you know that today the LORD is taking away
your master from you?"
And he said, "Yes, I know. Keep silent."
6 Then Elijah said to him, "Stay here, for the
LORD has sent me to the Jordan."
And he said, "As the LORD lives, and as you
live, I will not leave you." And the two of them
went on.

> Let a mantle of power rest upon my life (2Ki 2:8).

7 Fifty men of the sons of the prophets went
and stood at a distance, and the two of them

1:1 2Sa 8:2
1:2 Mt 10:25
1:3 1Ki 17:1
1:8 Zec 13:4
1:9 2Ki 6:13–14
1:10 Lk 9:54
1:13 Isa 1:5
....
1:15 Isa 51:12
1:17 2Ki 3:1
2:1 Ge 5:24
2:2 1Sa 1:26
2:3 2Ki 4:1
2:4 2Ki 2:2
2:5 2Ki 2:3
2:6 2Ki 2:2

[1] 17 *Joram* in 1Ch 3:11; 26:24.

stood by the Jordan. 8 Then Elijah took his robe
and rolled it up and struck the water, and it was
divided from one side to the other. Then the
two of them crossed on dry ground.
9 And as they were crossing, Elijah said to
Elisha, "Ask for something, and I will do it for
you before I am taken away from you."
And Elisha said, "Let a double portion of your
spirit be upon me."
10 He said, "You have asked for a difficult
thing, but if you see me when I am taken from
you, it will happen to you. If not, it will not."
11 As they continued walking and talking, a
chariot of fire and horses of fire separated the
two of them, and Elijah went up by a whirl-
wind into heaven. 12 Elisha was watching and
crying, "My father, my father, the chariot of
Israel and its horsemen!" And he did not see
him again. Then he grabbed his own clothes
and tore them in two pieces.
13 He picked up the robe of Elijah that fell
from him, and he returned and stood on the
bank of the Jordan. 14 And he took the robe of
Elijah that fell from him, and struck the water,
and said, "Where is the LORD, God of Elijah?"
When he had struck the water, it parted from
one side to the other, and Elisha crossed over.
15 When the sons of the prophets who were
at Jericho saw him from far off, they said, "The
spirit of Elijah rests on Elisha." And they came
to meet him and bowed down to the ground
before him. 16 They said to him, "Look now,
there are fifty strong men with your servants.
Let them go and look for your master. Perhaps
the Spirit of the LORD has lifted him up and
thrown him on some mountain or into some
valley."
He said, "Do not send them."
17 When they urged him until he was
ashamed, he said, "Send them." So they sent
fifty men, and they searched for three days but
did not find him. 18 When they returned to him
(for he had stayed at Jericho), he said to them,
"Did I not say to you, do not go?"

Elisha Performs Miracles

19 Now the men of the city said to Elisha, "The
location of this city is good, as my lord sees,
but the water is bad, and the land is unfruitful."
20 He said, "Bring me a new bowl and put salt
in it." So they brought it to him.
21 He went out to the spring of water and
threw the salt into it and said, "Thus says the
LORD: I have healed this water. No more death
or unfruitfulness will come from it." 22 So the
waters have been healthy until this day, ac-
cording to the word that Elisha spoke.
23 He went up from there to Bethel, and going
up on the way, little boys came out of the city
and made fun of him and said to him, "Go up,
you bald head! Go up, you bald head!" 24 He
turned around, saw them, and cursed them
in the name of the LORD. Then two she-bears
came out of the woods and ripped open for-
ty-two of the boys. 25 He went from there to
Mount Carmel, and from there he returned to
Samaria.

Jehoram Reigns Over Israel

3 Now Jehoram son of Ahab reigned over
Israel in Samaria in the eighteenth year of
Jehoshaphat king of Judah and reigned twelve
years. 2 He did evil in the sight of the LORD, but
not like his father and mother, for he removed
the pillar of Baal that his father had made.
3 Nevertheless he clung to the sins of Jeroboam
the son of Nebat, who had caused Israel to sin.
He did not depart from them.
4 Now Mesha king of Moab was a sheep-
breeder and gave back to the king of Israel
a hundred thousand lambs and the wool of
a hundred thousand rams. 5 But when Ahab
died, the king of Moab rebelled against the
king of Israel. 6 King Jehoram went out of
Samaria at that time and mustered all Israel.
7 He went and sent to Jehoshaphat the king of
Judah, saying, "The king of Moab has rebelled
against me. Will you go with me to Moab to
battle?"
He said, "I will go up. I am as you are, my
people as your people, and my horses as your
horses."
8 Then he said, "Which way should we go
up?"
And he said, "The way through the Wilder-
ness of Edom."
9 So the king of Israel, the king of Judah,
and the king of Edom went, and they marched
around seven days. But there was no water
for the camp or for the livestock that followed
them.
10 The king of Israel said, "Alas! The LORD has
called these three kings to give them into the
hand of Moab!"
11 But Jehoshaphat said, "Is there a prophet
of the LORD here, through whom we may in-
quire of the LORD?"
Then one of the king of Israel's servants
answered, "Elisha the son of Shaphat, who
poured water on the hands of Elijah, is here."
12 Jehoshaphat said, "The word of the LORD
is with him." So the king of Israel and Je-
hoshaphat and the king of Edom went down
to him.
13 Elisha said to the king of Israel, "What have
I to do with you? Go to your father's prophets,
or to your mother's prophets."

2:8 1Ki 19:19
2:9 Nu 11:17
2:11 2Ki 6:17
2:12 2Ki 13:14
2:16 1Ki 18:12
2:17 2Ki 8:11
2:21 2Ki 4:41
2:23 2Ch 36:16

2:25 2Ki 4:25
3:1 2Ki 1:17
3:2 1Ki 21:25
3:3 1Ki 14:16
3:4 2Sa 8:2
3:5 2Ki 1:1
3:7 1Ki 22:4
3:9 1Ki 22:47
3:11 1Ki 22:7
3:13 1Ki 18:19

Then the king of Israel said to him, "No. The LORD has called these three kings to deliver them into the hand of Moab."

14 Elisha said, "As the LORD of Hosts lives, before whom I stand, surely, were it not for my regard for Jehoshaphat the king of Judah, I would not look at you nor see you. 15 Now bring me a musician."

And when the musician played, the hand of the LORD came upon him. 16 He said, "Thus says the LORD, 'Make this valley full of pools.' 17 For thus says the LORD, 'You will not see wind, nor will you see rain, yet that valley will be filled with water, that you may drink, both you and your livestock, and your cattle.' 18 This is an easy thing in the sight of the LORD, and He will give the Moabites into your hand. 19 You will strike every fortified city and every choice city, and will cut down every good tree, and stop every spring of water, and you will ruin every good piece of land with stones."

20 So in the morning as the offering was offered up, suddenly water flowed from the way of Edom, and the land was filled with water.

21 When all the Moabites heard that the kings had come up to fight against them, all who were able to bear arms and older were summoned and stood at the border. 22 They got up early in the morning, and the sun shone on the water, and the Moabites saw the water opposite them was as red as blood. 23 Then they said, "This is blood. The kings have surely fought together; and they have killed one another. Now therefore, Moab, to the spoil!"

24 When they came to the camp of Israel, the children of Israel arose and struck the Moabites, so that they ran from them. And they went forward into their land, killing the Moabites. 25 They demolished the cities, and on every good piece of land every man threw a stone and filled it with stones, and they stopped every spring of water and cut down every good tree. Only in Kir Hareseth did the stones in the wall remain, until the slingers surrounded it and struck it.

26 When the king of Moab saw that the battle was overwhelming him, he took with him seven hundred swordsmen to break through to the king of Edom, but they were unable. 27 Then he took his firstborn son, who would have reigned in his place, and offered him for a burnt offering on the wall. And great wrath came upon Israel, and they departed from him and returned to their own land.

The Widow's Olive Oil

4 Now one of the wives of the sons of the prophets cried to Elisha, "Your servant my husband is dead, and you know that your servant feared the LORD, but a creditor has come to take my two sons as slaves."

2 Elisha said to her, "What shall I do for you? Tell me, what do you have in the house?"

She said, "Your servant has nothing in the house except a jar of oil."

3 Then he said, "Go, ask for vessels from all your neighbors, empty vessels and not just a few. 4 Then go in, shut the door behind you and your sons, and pour the oil into all these vessels. When each is full, set it aside."

5 So she left him and shut the door behind her and her sons, and they kept bringing vessels to her, and she kept pouring. 6 When the vessels were full, she said to her son, "Bring me another vessel."

But he said to her, "There is not another vessel." And the oil ceased.

7 Then she went and told the man of God. And he said, "Go, sell the oil, and pay your debt, and you and your children can live on the rest."

Elisha Raises the Shunammite's Son

8 One day Elisha passed through Shunem, and a noble woman was there who urged him to eat a meal. So whenever he passed through, he stopped there to eat a meal. 9 And she said to her husband, "I know that he is a holy man of God regularly passing through near us. 10 Let us make a little walled upper room and put for him there a bed, a table, a chair, and a lamp, so when he comes to us he can stay there."

11 One day he came by there, and he turned aside to the upper room and lay down. 12 He said to Gehazi his servant, "Call this Shunammite woman." So he called her and she stood before him. 13 He said to him, "Say to her, Look, you have gone to all this trouble for us. What may be done for you? Would you have a word spoken on your behalf to the king, or to the captain of the army?"

And she answered, "I am living among my people."

14 He said, "What may be done for her?"

And Gehazi said, "Actually, she has no son, and her husband is old."

15 He said, "Call her." When he had called her, she stood in the entrance. 16 He said, "At this season, when it is time, you will embrace a son."

And she said, "No, my lord, man of God, do not lie to your servant."

17 But the woman conceived and bore a son at that season, at the time that Elisha had told her.

18 When the child was older, he went out one day to his father with the reapers. 19 He said to his father, "My head, my head!"

3:14 1Ki 17:1
3:15 Eze 1:3
3:17 Ps 107:35
3:18 Jer 32:17
3:20 Ex 29:39–40
3:25 2Ki 3:19
3:27 Mic 6:7
4:1 2Ki 2:3

4:2 1Ki 17:12
4:6 Mt 14:20
4:8 Jos 19:18
4:10 Ro 12:13
4:12 2Ki 8:4–5
4:13 2Sa 19:13
4:16 2Ki 4:28

And he said to a servant, "Carry him to his mother." 20 When he had taken him and brought him to his mother, the boy sat on her knees until noon, and died. 21 She went up, and laid him down on the bed of the man of God, shut the door on him, and went out.

22 Then she called to her husband, "Send me one of the servants and one of the donkeys, so that I may run to the man of God and return."

23 He said, "Why are you going to him today? It is neither New Moon nor Sabbath."

She said, "It will be all right."

24 Then she saddled the donkey and said to her servant, "Lead on, and do not hold back for me unless I tell you." 25 So she went and came to the man of God at Mount Carmel.

And when the man of God saw her far off, he said to Gehazi his servant, "Look, over there is the Shunammite woman. 26 Now run to meet her, and say to her, Are you all right? Is your husband all right? Is the child all right?"

And she said, "It is all right."

27 When she came to the man of God at the mountain, she grabbed his feet. Gehazi approached to push her away. But the man of God said, "Let her alone, for she is in bitter distress, and the LORD has hidden it from me and has not told me."

28 Then she said, "Did I ask for a son from my lord? Did I not say, Do not give me false hope?"

29 Then he said to Gehazi, "Prepare yourself, take my staff in your hand, and go. If you find anyone, do not greet him, and if anyone greets you, do not answer him, and lay my staff on the face of the boy."

30 Then the boy's mother said, "As the LORD lives, and as you live, I will not leave without you." And he got up and followed her.

31 Gehazi passed through ahead of them and laid the staff on the face of the boy, but there was no sound or response. So he returned to meet him and told him, "The boy is not awake."

32 When Elisha came into the house, he saw that the boy was dead, lying on his bed. 33 So he went in, and shut the door on the two of them, and prayed to the LORD. 34 He went up and lay on the child, put his face on his face, and his eyes on his eyes, and his hands on his hands. Then he bent over the child, and the child's flesh warmed. 35 Then he got down, walked once back and forth in the house, and went up, and bent over him; the boy sneezed seven times, and the boy opened his eyes.

36 Then Elisha called Gehazi and said, "Call the Shunammite woman." So he called her, and she came to him. Then he said, "Pick up your son." 37 Then she came in, fell at his feet, and bowed down to the ground. Then she picked up her son and went out.

4:21 2Ki 4:32
4:23 Nu 10:10
4:25 2Ki 2:25
4:29 2Ki 2:14
4:31 Jn 11:11
4:33 Mt 6:6
4:34 1Ki 17:21
4:35 2Ki 8:5
4:36 Heb 11:35

4:38 2Ki 2:1
4:40 Ex 10:17
4:41 Ex 15:25
4:42 1Sa 9:7
4:43 Lk 9:13
5:1 Lk 4:27
5:2 2Ki 6:23
5:5 Jdg 14:12
5:7 1Sa 2:6

Elisha Purifies the Deadly Stew

38 When Elisha returned to Gilgal, there was a famine in the land. The sons of the prophets were sitting before him, and he said to his servant, "Put on the big cooking pot, and boil some stew for the sons of the prophets."

39 One went out into the field to gather herbs. He found a wild vine and gathered from it wild gourds, filling his clothes, and came and split them into the pot of stew, but they did not recognize them. 40 So they poured it out for the men to eat. But as they were eating the stew, they cried out, "Man of God, there is death in the pot." They could not eat it.

41 But he said, "Then bring flour." He threw it into the pot and said, "Pour it for the people and let them eat." And there was nothing bad in the pot.

Elisha Feeds One Hundred Men

42 A man came from Baal Shalishah, and he brought the man of God food from the first fruits—twenty loaves of barley and fresh ears of grain—in his sack. And Elisha said, "Give it to the people and let them eat."

43 But his servant said, "How can I set this before a hundred men?"

He said, "Give it to the people and let them eat, for thus says the LORD, 'They will eat and have some left.' " 44 So he set it before them, they ate, and some was left over, according to the word of the LORD.

Naaman Healed of Leprosy

5 Now Naaman, captain of the army of the king of Aram, was a great man before his master and held favor because by him the LORD had given deliverance to Aram. He was also a mighty warrior, but he had leprosy.

2 The Arameans had gone out raiding and had taken captive a little girl from the land of Israel, and she waited on the wife of Naaman. 3 She said to her mistress, "If only my lord were before the prophet who is in Samaria! Then he would take away his leprosy from him."

4 So Naaman went in and told his lord, "Thus and so spoke the girl from the land of Israel." 5 The king of Aram said, "Go, and I will send a letter to the king of Israel." So he went and took with him ten talents[1] of silver, six thousand shekels[1] of gold, and ten sets of clothes. 6 He brought the letter to the king of Israel, which read, "Now when this letter comes to you, know that I have sent Naaman my servant to you, that you may take away from him his leprosy."

7 When the king of Israel had read the letter, he tore his clothes and said, "Am I God, to kill

[1] 5 About 750 pounds, or 340 kilograms. [1] 5 About 150 pounds, or 69 kilograms.

and to give life, that this man sends a man
to me to take away his leprosy? But consider,
and see how he is seeking a quarrel with me."
8 But when Elisha the man of God heard that
the king of Israel had torn his clothes, he sent
word to the king, saying, "Why have you torn
your clothes? Let him come to me, and he will
know that there is a prophet in Israel." 9 So
Naaman came with his horses and chariot and
stood at the entrance to the house of Elisha.
10 Elisha sent a messenger to him, saying, "Go
and wash seven times in the Jordan, and your
flesh will be returned and cleansed."
11 But Naaman became angry and went away
and said to himself, "Surely he could have
come out, and stood and called on the name
of the LORD his God, and waved his hand over
the infected area, and taken away the leprosy.
12 Are not Abana and Pharpar, rivers of Damas-
cus, better than all the waters of Israel? Could I
not wash in them and be clean?" So he turned
and went away in a rage.

Father, open my spiritual eyes to discern the enemy's devices against my life (2Ki 5:13).

13 But his servants approached and spoke to
him, "My father, if the prophet had told you
to do some great thing, would you not have
done it? How much more when he said to you,
'Wash and be clean'?" 14 So he went down and
dipped himself in the Jordan seven times, ac-
cording to the word of the man of God, and
his flesh returned like the flesh of a little boy,
and he was clean.
15 Then he returned to the man of God, he
and all his company. He came and stood before
him, and he said, "Now I know that there is no
God in all the land, except in Israel. Now take
a gift from your servant."
16 But he said, "As the LORD lives, before
whom I stand, I will take no gift." He urged
him to take it, but he refused.
17 Then Naaman said, "If not, let two mule
loads of dirt be given to your servant, for your
servant will no longer offer a burnt offering or
sacrifice to any god, except the LORD. 18 But may
the LORD pardon your servant on one account:
When my master enters the house of Rimmon
to worship, and he leans on my hand, and I
bow down in the house of Rimmon, when I do
bow down in the house of Rimmon, may the
LORD pardon your servant on this one account."
19 He said to him, "Go in peace." So he de-
parted from him a short distance.

5:10 Jn 9:7
5:13 2Ki 6:21
5:14 Job 33:25
5:15 1Sa 25:27
5:16 2Ki 3:14
5:18 2Ki 7:2
5:19 1Sa 1:17

....

5:20 Ex 20:7
5:22 2Ki 5:5
5:25 2Ki 5:22
5:26 2Ki 5:16
5:27 Ex 4:6
6:1 2Ki 2:3
6:6 2Ki 2:21

Gehazi's Greed

20 Then Gehazi the servant of Elisha the man
of God said, "My master has spared Naaman
the Aramean by not taking from his hands
what he brought. As the LORD lives, I will run
after him and take something from him."
21 So Gehazi pursued Naaman. Then Naaman
saw him running after him, jumped down from
the chariot to meet him, and said, "Is every-
thing all right?"
22 And he said, "Everything is all right. My
master has sent me and says, 'Even now two
servants from Ephraim, from the sons of the
prophets, have come to me. Give them a talent[1]
of silver and two changes of clothes.'"
23 Naaman said, "Please, take two talents." He
urged him and tied up two talents of silver in
two bags with two changes of clothes and gave
them to two of his servants, who carried them
before Gehazi. 24 When he came to Ophel, he
took them from their hand and put them away
in the house. Then he sent the men away, and
they departed.
25 Then he entered and stood before his mas-
ter. And Elisha said to him, "Where have you
come from, Gehazi?"
And he said, "Your servant went here and
there."
26 He said to him, "Did my heart not go with
you when the man turned from his chariot to
meet you? Is it a time to take money, and to
take garments, olives and vineyards, sheep
and oxen, male and female servants? 27 The
leprosy of Naaman will cling to you and to
your descendants forever." So he went out
from his presence, leprous like snow.

The Floating Axe Head

6 Now the sons of the prophets said to Eli-
sha, "Look, the place where we are living
with you is too small for us. 2 Let us go to the
Jordan and take from there one beam per man,
and let us make for ourselves a place to live
there."
And Elisha said, "Go."
3 Then one of them said, "Please come with
your servants."
And he said, "I will come." 4 So he went with
them.
And they came to the Jordan and cut down
trees. 5 But as one was cutting down a tree,
the axe head fell into the water. He cried, "Ah,
master! It was borrowed."
6 Then the man of God said, "Where did it
fall?" When he showed him the place, he cut
off a stick, and threw it in there, and he made
the iron float. 7 So Elisha said, "Pick it up." And
he reached out his hand and took it.

1 22 About 75 pounds, or 34 kilograms.

The Blinded Arameans Captured

[8]Then the king of Aram was fighting against
Israel, and he took counsel with his servants,
saying, "At such and such a place will be my
camp."
[9]But the man of God sent word to the king of
Israel, saying, "Take care not to pass through
this place, for the Arameans are marching
down there." [10]The king of Israel sent word
to the place of which the man of God spoke.
He warned him and was on his guard there
more than once.
[11]The mind of the king of Aram was trou-
bled by this, so he called his servants and said
to them, "Will you not tell me who among us
sides with the king of Israel?"
[12]Then one of his servants said, "No one,
my lord, O king. Elisha, the prophet who is in
Israel, tells the king of Israel the words that
you speak in your bedroom."
[13]He said, "Go and see where he is, so that
I may send for him and take him." And it was
told to him, "He is in Dothan." [14]So he sent
horses, chariots, and a great army there. They
came by night and surrounded the city.
[15]When a servant of the man of God rose
early in the morning and went out, a force sur-
rounded the city both with horses and chariots.
And his servant said to him, "Alas, my master!
What will we do?"
[16]And he said, "Do not be afraid, for there are
more with us than with them."

I am going to spend more time looking into spiritual things than natural things by reading and meditating on His Word (2Ki 6:1–17).

[17]Then Elisha prayed, "LORD, open his eyes
and let him see." So the LORD opened the eyes
of the young man, and he saw that the moun-
tain was full of horses and chariots of fire sur-
rounding Elisha.
[18]When they came down to him, Elisha
prayed to the LORD, "Strike this people with
blindness." And He struck them with blindness
according to the word of Elisha.
[19]Elisha said to them, "This is not the way,
and this is not the city. Follow me, and let me
bring you to the man whom you seek." But he
led them to Samaria.
[20]When they entered Samaria, Elisha said,
"LORD, open the eyes of these men and let them
see." And the LORD opened their eyes, and they
saw that they were in the middle of Samaria.
[21]The king of Israel said to Elisha when he
saw them, "My father, shall I kill them? Shall
I kill them?"

6:13 Ge 37:17
6:16 Ro 8:31
6:17 2Ki 2:11
6:20 2Ki 6:17
6:21 2Ki 5:13

6:23 2Ki 5:2
6:24 1Ki 20:1

SPIRITLED WOMAN

COUNSEL FROM THE SPIRIT BASICS

Harvest Time

In 2 Kings 6 Elisha prays that his servant Gehazi's eyes would be opened to see that they were not left alone to face the Syrian army that was surrounding them. The Scripture says that "the LORD opened the eyes of the young man, and he saw that the mountain was full of horses and chariots of fire surrounding Elisha" (v. 17).

Today God is raising up a people who will believe Him and see His glory manifested in the earth. Why? Because it is harvest time. We must "lift up [our] eyes and look at the fields, for they are already white for harvest" (Jn 4:35).

As the people of God, what must we do in order to reflect Him? How do we become a living manifestation of His glory?

God wants His Word to be evidenced in us. We were predestined to be conformed into the image of His Son (Ro 8:29), who is the Word of God. Our heavenly Father made us to house and display His glorious Word to the world. God wants you and me to be living epistles of His Word. We should hear the Word, do the Word, and manifest the glory of His Word!

Cynthia Brazelton

[22]And he said, "You shall not kill them. Did
you capture with your sword and with your
bow those whom you want to kill? Set bread
and water before them, and let them eat and
drink and then go to their master." [23]So he
prepared for them a great banquet. When
they had eaten and had drunk, he sent them
away, and they went to their master. So the
Aramean raiders did not enter into the land
of Israel again.

Ben-Hadad Besieges Samaria

[24]After this, Ben-Hadad king of Aram gath-
ered all his army, went up, and besieged
Samaria. [25]There was a great famine in Sa-
maria, and they besieged it until a donkey's
head was sold for eighty shekels[1] of silver, and

[1]*25* About 2 pounds, or 920 grams.

one-fourth of a kab[1] of dove droppings for five
shekels[2] of silver.
26 As the king of Israel was walking across
the city wall, a woman cried out to him, "Help,
my lord king."
27 He said, "If the LORD will not help you, how
can I help you? From the threshing floor or
from the winepress?" 28 And the king said to
her, "What is wrong with you?"
And she said, "This woman said to me, 'Give
your son and let us eat him today, and we will
eat my son tomorrow.' 29 So we boiled my son
and ate him. The next day I said to her, 'Give
your son, that we may eat him.' But she has
hidden her son."
30 When the king heard the words of the
woman, he tore his clothes. And since he was
walking across the city wall, the people saw
that he had sackcloth on his body underneath.
31 Then he said, "So may God do to me, and
even more, if the head of Elisha the son of
Shaphat stands on his shoulders after today."
32 Now Elisha was sitting in his house, and
the elders were sitting with him. The king
sent a messenger, but before the messenger
came to him, Elisha said to the elders, "Are you
aware that this son of a murderer has sent a
man to take off my head? When the messenger
enters, shut the door and hold it against him. Is
not the sound of his master's feet behind him?"
33 And while he was speaking with them, the
messenger came down to him, and then the
king said, "This calamity is of the LORD! Why
should I hope in the LORD any longer?"
7 Then Elisha said, "Hear the word of the
LORD: Thus says the LORD: Tomorrow about
this time a measure[3] of fine flour will be sold
for a shekel,[4] and two measures[5] of barley for
a shekel, at the gate of Samaria."
2 Then an officer on whose hand the king
leaned answered the man of God, "If the LORD
were to make windows in heaven, could this
thing happen?"
And he said, "You will see it with your eyes,
but you will not eat from it."

The Arameans Flee

3 There were four leprous men at the entry of
the gate, and they said to one another, "Why
are we sitting here until we die? 4 If we say, 'Let
us enter the city,' the famine is in the city, and
we shall die there. But if we sit here, we die
also. Now come, let us fall into the camp of the
Arameans. If they spare our lives, we will live,
and if they kill us, we will die."
5 So they rose at twilight to enter the camp of
the Arameans. When they came to the edge of
the camp of the Arameans, there was no one
there. 6 For the Lord had caused the Aramean
camp to hear the sound of chariots, horses,
even the sound of a large army, so that they
said to one another, "Listen, the king of Isra-
el has hired the kings of the Hittites and the
kings of the Egyptians to come against us." 7 So
they got up and ran away in the twilight and
abandoned their tents, their horses, and their
donkeys. The camp remained just as it was,
and they ran for their lives.
8 When these leprous men came to the edge
of the camp, they went into one tent. They ate
and drank, carried off silver, gold, and clothes,
and went and hid them. Then they went back,
entered another tent, and carried off things
from there and went and hid them.
9 Then they said to one another, "We are not
doing right today. This is a day of good news.
If we are silent and wait until the morning
light, we will be found guilty. Let us go now
and enter the city and tell the king's house-
hold."
10 So they went and called to the gatekeepers
of the city, and they told them, "We came to the
camp of the Arameans, and there was no one
there. There was no sound of a man's voice,
only horses tied, donkeys tied, and the tents as
they were." 11 Then the gatekeepers called out
and told the king's household inside.
12 The king got up in the night and said to his
servants, "I will show you what the Arameans
have done to us. They know that we are starv-
ing, so they left the camp to hide themselves
in the field, saying, 'When they come out of
the city, we will capture them alive and get
into the city.' "
13 One of his servants answered, "Let some
men take five of the remaining horses, since
those remaining will suffer the fate of the
whole multitude of Israel that have perished
already; so let us send them and see."
14 So they took two chariots with horses, and
the king sent them after the army of the Ar-
ameans, saying, "Go and see." 15 So they went
after them to the Jordan, and the whole way
was full of clothes and vessels, which the Ar-
ameans had thrown away in their haste. Then
the messengers returned and told the king.
16 Then the people went out and looted the
camp of the Arameans. So a measure of fine
flour was sold for a shekel, and two measures
of barley for a shekel, according to the word
of the LORD.
17 The king had appointed the officer on
whose hand he leaned to have charge over
the gate, and the people trampled him in the

6:28 Jdg 18:23
6:30 1Ki 21:27
6:31 Ru 1:17
6:32 1Ki 18:4
6:33 Job 2:9
7:2 Ge 7:11
7:3 Nu 5:2–4

7:6 2Sa 5:24
7:7 Ps 48:4–6
7:8 Jos 7:21
7:16 2Ki 7:1

[1] 25 Likely about ¼ pound, or 100 grams. [2] 25 About 2 ounces, or 58 grams. [3] 1 Likely about 12 pounds, or 5.5 kilograms of flour, and in vv. 16 and 18. [4] 1 About ⅖ ounce, or 12 grams, and in vv. 16 and 18. [5] 1 Likely about 20 pounds, or 9 kilograms of barley, and in vv. 16 and 18.

gate, and he died, just as the man of God had
said when the king came down to him. 18 Then
the man of God had spoken to the king, saying,
"Two seahs of barley shall be sold for a shekel,
and a seah of fine flour for a shekel, about this
time tomorrow at the gate of Samaria."
19 The officer had answered the man of God,
"If the LORD should make windows in heaven,
could such a thing happen?" And he had said,
"You shall see it with your own eyes, but you
shall not eat of it." 20 So it happened to him,
for the people trampled him in the gate, and
he died.

The Shunammite's Land Restored

8 Then Elisha spoke to the woman whose
son he had restored to life, "Get up and go,
you and your household, and sojourn wherev-
er you can, for the LORD has called for a famine,
and it will come on the land for seven years."
2 So the woman got up and did according to
the word of the man of God. She went with
her household and sojourned in the land of
the Philistines for seven years.
3 At the end of seven years, the woman re-
turned from the land of the Philistines, and she
went forth to appeal to the king for her house
and her field. 4 Now the king was talking with
Gehazi the servant of the man of God, saying,
"Tell me all the great things that Elisha has
done." 5 As he was telling the king how he had
restored a dead body to life, the woman whose
son he had restored to life started appealing to
the king for her house and her land.
Gehazi said, "My lord king, this is the woman,
and this is her son whom Elisha restored to
life." 6 When the king questioned the woman,
she told him.
So the king appointed to her an official,
saying, "Restore all that was hers and all the
proceeds of the field from the day that she
abandoned the land until now."

Ben-Hadad Is Murdered

7 Then Elisha came to Damascus while
Ben-Hadad the king of Aram was ill, and he
was told, "The man of God has come here."
8 The king said to Hazael, "Take a present with
you and go to meet the man of God. Inquire of
the LORD through him, saying, 'Will I recover
from this illness?' "
9 So Hazael went to meet him and took a
present with him, all sorts of good things from
Damascus, forty camel loads. He came and
stood before him and said, "Your son Ben-Ha-
dad king of Aram has sent me to you, asking,
'Will I recover from this illness?' "
10 And Elisha said to him, "Go, say to him,
'You will certainly recover,' but the LORD has
shown me that he will certainly die." 11 Hazael

7:19 2Ki 7:2
8:1 Ps 105:16
8:4 2Ki 5:20–27
8:5 2Ki 4:35
8:7 1Ki 11:24
8:8 1Ki 19:15
8:11 Lk 19:41
....
8:12 2Ki 12:17
8:13 1Sa 17:43
8:14 2Ki 8:10
8:15 2Ki 8:13
8:16 2Ki 1:17
8:18 2Ki 8:26
8:19 1Ki 11:36
8:20 1Ki 22:47
8:22 Jos 21:13
8:25 2Ki 9:29
8:26 2Ch 22:2

stared at him until he was ashamed. Then the
man of God wept.
12 Hazael said, "Why are you weeping, my
lord?"
He said, "Because I know the evil that you
will do to the children of Israel. You will set
their fortresses on fire. You will kill their young
men with the sword. You will smash their chil-
dren and rip open their pregnant women."
13 Hazael said, "What? Is your servant a dog
that he should do this great thing?"
And Elisha said, "The LORD has shown me
that you will be king over Aram."
14 Then he left Elisha and went to his master,
who said to him, "What did Elisha say to you?"
And he said, "He told me that you would surely
recover." 15 But the next day he took a blanket,
dipped it in water, and spread it on his face, so
that he died. And Hazael reigned in his place.

Jehoram, King of Judah
2Ch 21:5–20

16 In the fifth year of Joram the son of
Ahab, king of Israel, Jehoram the son of Je-
hoshaphat, king of Judah, became king. 17 He
was thirty-two years old when he became king,
and he reigned eight years in Jerusalem. 18 He
walked in the way of the kings of Israel, just as
the house of Ahab had done, for the daughter
of Ahab was his wife. He did evil in the sight
of the LORD. 19 Yet the LORD was not willing to
destroy Judah, for the sake of His servant Da-
vid, since He promised to give a lamp to him
and his sons perpetually.
20 In his days Edom rebelled against the rule
of Judah, and they put a king over themselves.
21 So Jehoram crossed over to Zair, all his char-
iots with him, and he rose at night and struck
Edom and the captains of their chariots who
had surrounded him. But the people fled to
their tents. 22 So Edom has been in rebellion
against the rule of Judah until this day. Libnah
rebelled at the same time.
23 The rest of the deeds of Jehoram and all
that he did, are they not written in the book
of the annals of the kings of Judah? 24 So Je-
horam slept with his fathers and was buried
with his fathers in the City of David. Ahaziah
his son reigned in his place.

Ahaziah, King of Judah
2Ch 22:1–6

25 In the twelfth year of Joram the son of
Ahab, king of Israel, Ahaziah the son of Je-
horam, king of Judah, became king. 26 Ahazi-
ah was twenty-two years old when he became
king. He reigned one year in Jerusalem. His
mother's name was Athaliah, the daughter of
Omri, king of Israel. 27 He walked in the way of
the house of Ahab and did evil in the sight of

Right Time, Right Place

Second Kings 8 tells the story of the Shunammite woman. If you recall, she and her husband were having a hard time having a baby. They built a house for Elisha, and he blessed them and they had a baby. The son died. Elisha raised the baby up. Then there was a season of famine. When the famine came, Elisha told the family to leave the land. Then after the season of famine was up, he told them to go back (2Ki 8:1).

She followed the prophetic instructions; the prophet told her to leave and to come back in seven years. Then she walked in to the king's court at the same time Elisha's servant was telling her story to the king. God gave her favor, and the king gave her favor and all the money that she needed and her land (vv. 2–6)—all this because she was obedient to the prophetic timing of the Lord. She was fully restored.

Every time we disobey the voice of the Lord, we miss a divine setup. God is always after our growth. He is always promoting us to get to our destiny. He always wants us to move to a place of fulfillment. He always wants us to have exceedingly abundantly above all we can ask or think. He's always about the abundance. But if every time we are not where He tells us to be, we miss a divine setup.

God is a divine chess player. He is the master chess player. He likes to move us around and put us in certain places so we can be the winner of the game. He is the wise master builder. Your times are in His hands.

God is teaching us how to move with Him. He is pouring out His glory so we understand Him and love Him, so we can't be bought and there are no more strings tying us to the things of this world. There will be a remnant of people who will know the timing of God. The sons of Issachar were one of the smallest tribes of Israel and "those having understanding of times" (1Ch 12:32).

This is a season that the glory and grace of God will rest upon you. You will begin to have face-to-face encounters with the Lord, and from that place of encounter the Lord is going to ignite your passion. He is going to bring you to a place of assignment and alignment. From that place of alignment, nothing will be able to stop you. Even as the spirit of the fear of the Lord rests upon you, you will not fear man. You will be impregnated with destiny, so be mindful of your diet. Eat the meat of His Word, and drink from His cup that never runs dry.

The Lord says, "I shall give My people eyes to see, and they will began to understand their purpose and their destiny as never before because their confidence is in Me. Their confidence is in My love."

Michelle McClain-Walters

the LORD, as the house of Ahab did, for he was
the son-in-law of the house of Ahab.
28 He went with Joram the son of Ahab to the
war against Hazael king of Aram at Ramoth
Gilead, and the Arameans struck Joram. 29 King
Joram returned to be healed in Jezreel of the
wounds which the Arameans had inflicted on
him at Ramah when he fought against Hazael
king of Aram.
And Ahaziah the son of Jehoram, king of
Judah, went down to see Joram the son of
Ahab in Jezreel because he was ill.

Jehu Anointed King of Israel

9 Then Elisha the prophet called one of the
sons of the prophets, "Prepare yourself.
Take this flask of oil in your hand, and go to
Ramoth Gilead. 2 When you get there, look for
Jehu the son of Jehoshaphat, the son of Nim-
shi. Go in and make him rise from among his
brothers, and bring him into an inner chamber.
3 Then take the flask of oil, pour it on his head,
and say, 'Thus says the LORD: I have anointed
you king over Israel.' Then open the door and
flee. Do not wait."
4 So the young man, the prophet, went to
Ramoth Gilead. 5 When he arrived, the com-
manders of the army were sitting, and he said,
"I have a word for you, Commander."
Jehu said, "Which one of us?"
And he said, "For you, Commander."
6 So he arose, went into the house, poured
the oil on his head, and said to him, "Thus
says the LORD, God of Israel: I am anointing you
king over the people of the LORD, over Israel.
7 You will strike the house of Ahab your master,
and I will avenge the blood of my servants
the prophets and the blood of all the servants
of the LORD from the hand of Jezebel. 8 The
whole house of Ahab will perish, and I will
cut off from Ahab all the males in Israel, both
imprisoned and free. 9 I will make the house
of Ahab like the house of Jeroboam son of
Nebat and like the house of Baasha the son of
Ahijah. 10 Dogs will eat Jezebel in the territory
of Jezreel, and no one will bury her." Then he
opened the door and fled.
11 When Jehu had returned to his master's
servants, one said to him, "Is all well? Why did
this madman come to you?"
And he said to them, "You know this man
and his babble."
12 They said, "A lie! Tell us."
Then he said, "Thus and thus he spoke to me,
saying, 'Thus says the LORD: I am anointing you
king over Israel.' "
13 Then they hurried. Each took his clothes,
put them under him on the bare stairs, and
blew a horn, saying, "Jehu is king."

8:29 2Ki 9:15–16
9:1 1Sa 10:1
9:2 2Ki 9:5
9:3 1Ki 19:16
9:6 1Ki 19:16
9:7 1Ki 18:4
9:8 Dt 32:36
9:9 1Ki 15:29
9:10 1Ki 21:23
9:11 Jer 29:26
9:13 1Ki 1:34

9:14 2Ki 8:28
9:15 2Ki 8:29
9:17 1Sa 16:4
9:20 2Sa 18:27
9:21 1Ki 21:1–7
9:22 1Ki 16:30–33
9:23 2Ki 11:14
9:24 1Ki 22:34
9:25 1Ki 21:19

Joram of Israel Killed

2Ch 22:7–9

14 So Jehu the son of Jehoshaphat, the son of
Nimshi, conspired against Joram. Joram had
been guarding Ramoth Gilead, he and all Isra-
el, because of Hazael king of Aram. 15 But King
Joram had returned to be healed in Jezreel
from the wounds with which the Arameans
had stricken him when he fought with Hazael
king of Aram. So Jehu said, "If this be your
minds, let no fugitive exit the city to go tell
Jezreel." 16 Then Jehu rode in a chariot and
went to Jezreel, for Joram lay there. Ahaziah
king of Judah had come down to see Joram.
17 A watchman was standing on the tower in
Jezreel, and he saw the company of Jehu as
he was coming and said, "I see a company."
And Joram said, "Take a horseman and
send him to meet them, and let him say, 'Is
it peace?' "
18 So the horseman went to meet him and
said, "Thus says the king, 'Is it peace?' "
But Jehu said, "What have you to do with
peace? Circle in behind me."
So the watchman reported, "The messenger
came to them, but he is not returning."
19 Then he sent out a second horseman, who
came to them and said, "Thus says the king,
'Is it peace?' "
Again, Jehu said, "What have you to do with
peace? Circle in behind me."
20 The watchman reported, "He came to
them, but he is not returning. The driving is
like the driving of Jehu the son of Nimshi, for
he drives furiously."

I rebuke and cut off Jezebel and her witchcraft in the name of Jesus (2Ki 9:22).

21 Then Joram said, "Hitch my chariot." So his
chariot was hitched, and Joram king of Israel
and Ahaziah king of Judah went out, each in
his chariot. They went out to meet Jehu and
found him on the property of Naboth the Jez-
reelite. 22 When Joram saw Jehu he said, "Is it
peace, Jehu?"
And he said, "What peace, so long as the
harlotries of your mother Jezebel and her sor-
ceries are so many?"
23 Then Joram turned the reins, fled, and said
to Ahaziah, "There is treachery, Ahaziah."
24 Jehu drew a bow with his full strength and
shot Joram between his shoulder blades. The
arrow went out at his heart, and he kneeled
down in his chariot. 25 Then Jehu said to Bidkar
his officer, "Lift him up and throw him on the
property of the field of Naboth the Jezreelite.

Remember when you and I were riding to-
gether after Ahab his father and the LORD
pronounced this oracle about him: 26 'Surely I
have seen yesterday the blood of Naboth and
his sons, declares the LORD, and I will pay you
back on this property, declares the LORD.' Now
lift him up and throw him onto the property,
according to the word of the LORD."

Ahaziah of Judah Killed

27 But when Ahaziah the king of Judah saw
this, he fled on the path to the garden house.
Jehu chased after him and said, "Shoot him
too." So they shot him on the ascent to Gur,
which is by Ibleam. And he fled to Megiddo
and died there. 28 His servants carried him in
a chariot to Jerusalem and buried him in his
tomb with his fathers in the City of David. 29 In
the eleventh year of Joram the son of Ahab,
Ahaziah became king over Judah.

Jezebel Executed

30 When Jehu came to Jezreel, Jezebel heard
about it. She put black paint on her eyes,
adorned her head, and looked down through
the window. 31 As Jehu entered in at the gate,
she said, "Is everything all right, Zimri, mur-
derer of his master?"
32 And he lifted up his face toward the win-
dow and said, "Who is on my side? Who?" And
two or three eunuchs looked down to him.
33 He said, "Drop her down." So they dropped
her down and some of her blood splattered
on the wall and on the horses. Then he tram-
pled her.
34 Then he entered, ate and drank, and said,
"Attend to that cursed woman and bury her,
for she is a king's daughter." 35 So they went to
bury her, but they found nothing of her except
a skull, the feet, and the palms of her hands.
36 They returned and told Jehu, and he said,
"This is the word of the LORD, which He spoke
by His servant Elijah the Tishbite, saying, 'On
the property of Jezreel dogs will eat the flesh
of Jezebel. 37 The corpse of Jezebel will be like
dung in the field on the property of Jezreel, so
that they cannot say, This is Jezebel.' "

Ahab's Seventy Sons Killed

10 Now Ahab had seventy sons in Sa-
maria. So Jehu wrote letters and sent
them to Samaria to the captains of Jezreel, to
the elders, and to the guardians of the sons
of Ahab, saying, 2 "Now as soon as this letter
comes to you—since you are with your mas-
ter's sons, chariots, horses, a fortified city, and
weapons— 3 select the best and most fitting
of your master's sons, put him on his father's
throne, and fight for your master's house."

9:27 Jdg 1:27
9:29 2Ch 21:18–19
9:30 Jer 4:30
9:31 1Ki 16:9–20
9:34 1Ki 16:31
9:36 1Ki 21:23
9:37 Jer 8:2
10:2 2Ki 5:6
10:5 Jos 9:11
10:7 1Ki 21:21
10:9 2Ki 9:14–24
10:10 1Ki 21:29
10:11 Job 18:19
10:13 2Ki 8:29
10:15 1Ch 2:55
10:16 1Ki 19:10
10:17 2Ki 9:8

4 But they were extremely afraid and said,
"Two kings could not stand before him. How
can we stand?"
5 So he who was over the house, and he who
was over the city, the elders, and the guard-
ians sent word to Jehu, saying, "We are your
servants, and everything you say to us we will
do. We will not appoint a man king. Do what
is good in your eyes."
6 Then he wrote a second letter to them, say-
ing, "If you belong to me and will obey me,
take the heads of your master's sons and come
to me at Jezreel at this time tomorrow."
Now the king's sons, seventy men, were with
the great men of the city who brought them
up. 7 When the letter came to them, they took
the king's sons, slaughtered all seventy, put
their heads in baskets, and sent them to him
in Jezreel. 8 So the messenger came and told
him, saying, "They have brought the heads of
the king's sons."
Then he said, "Put them in two heaps at the
entry of the gate until morning."
9 When morning came, he went out and stood
and said to all the people, "You are innocent.
I conspired against my master and killed him,
but who struck all these? 10 Know then that
the words of the LORD which He spoke about
the house of Ahab will not fall to the ground.
The LORD has done that which He spoke by His
servant Elijah." 11 So Jehu struck all that re-
mained of the house of Ahab in Jezreel and all
his great men, his confidants, and his priests,
until he left him no survivor.

Ahaziah's Forty-Two Brothers Killed

12 Then he got up and went to Samaria. When
he was at Beth Eked of the Shepherds on the
way, 13 Jehu found the brothers of Ahaziah king
of Judah and said, "Who are you?"
And they said, "We are brothers of Ahaziah,
and we have come down to visit the sons of
the king and the sons of the queen mother."
14 He said, "Capture them alive." So they took
them alive and slaughtered them at the pit of
Beth Eked, forty-two men. Not a man of them
remained.
15 Then he left there and found Jehonadab
son of Rekab coming to meet him. He greeted
him and said to him, "Is your heart right with
me, as my heart is with yours?"
And Jehonadab said, "It is."
"If it is, give me your hand." So he gave him
his hand, and he pulled him up to him into
the chariot. 16 He said, "Come with me, and
see my zeal for the LORD." So he made him
ride in his chariot.
17 Then he came to Samaria and struck all
that remained to Ahab in Samaria until he ex-

terminated them, according to the word of the LORD which He spoke to Elijah.

Worshippers of Baal Killed

18 Then Jehu gathered all the people and said to them, "Ahab served Baal a little, but Jehu will serve him much. 19 Now call to me all the prophets of Baal, all his worshippers, and all his priests. Let none go unaccounted for, because I have a great sacrifice for Baal. All who are not accounted for will not live." But Jehu did it with cunning in order to destroy the servants of Baal.

20 Jehu said, "Sanctify a festive assembly for Baal." So they proclaimed it. 21 Jehu sent word through all Israel, and all the worshippers of Baal came. Not a man remained who did not come. They came into the house of Baal, and the house of Baal was full from one end to the other. 22 He said to the one in charge of the wardrobe, "Bring out garments for all the worshippers of Baal." So he brought them garments.

23 Then Jehu and Jehonadab the son of Rekab went into the house of Baal and said to the worshippers of Baal, "Search and see that there are no worshippers of the LORD here with you and only worshippers of Baal." 24 Then they went to offer sacrifices and burnt offerings, but Jehu put eighty men outside and said, "If any of the men whom I have brought into your hands escapes, the one who lets him go will die in his place."

25 As soon as he had finished making the burnt offering, Jehu said to the guards and the officers, "Go in. Kill them. No one comes out." So they struck them with the edge of the sword. The guards and the officers threw them out and went to the city of the house of Baal. 26 They brought out the sacred pillar from the house of Baal and burned it. 27 They broke down the sacred pillar of Baal, and tore down the house of Baal and made it a latrine to this day.

28 So Jehu exterminated Baal from Israel. 29 But from the sins of Jeroboam son of Nebat, who caused Israel to sin, Jehu did not turn aside (that is, the golden calves that were in Bethel and Dan).

30 And the LORD said to Jehu, "Because you have done well by doing what is right in My sight, and have done to the house of Ahab all that was in My heart, four generations of your sons will sit on the throne of Israel." 31 But Jehu was not careful to walk in the law of the LORD God of Israel with all his heart. He did not turn aside from the sins of Jeroboam, who caused Israel to sin.

The Death of Jehu

32 In those days the LORD began to trim off parts of Israel, and Hazael struck them in all the territory of Israel: 33 from the Jordan eastward, all the land of Gilead, the Gadites, the Reubenites, the Manassites from Aroer, which is by the River Arnon, even Gilead and Bashan.

34 Now the rest of the deeds of Jehu, all he did and all his power, are they not written in the book of the annals of the kings of Israel?

35 So Jehu slept with his fathers, and they buried him in Samaria. Jehoahaz his son became king in his place. 36 The days that Jehu reigned over Israel in Samaria were twenty-eight years.

Athaliah Reigns in Judah

2Ch 22:10–23:21

11 Now when Athaliah the mother of Ahaziah saw that her son was dead, she rose up and destroyed all the royal descendants. 2 But Jehosheba, the daughter of King Joram, sister of Ahaziah, took Joash[1] the son of Ahaziah, and stole him away from among the king's sons who were being murdered; and they hid him and his nurse in the bedroom, from Athaliah, so that he was not killed. 3 He was with her, hidden in the house of the LORD for six years, while Athaliah reigned over the land.

Joash Anointed King of Judah

4 But in the seventh year Jehoiada sent word and took the captains of hundreds from the Carites and the guards and brought them to him in the house of the LORD. He made a covenant with them, put them under oath in the house of the LORD, and then showed them the king's son. 5 He commanded them, saying, "This is the thing that you shall do: One-third of your unit, those who come on duty on the Sabbath, will guard the king's house. 6 One-third will be at the gate of Sur, and one-third will be at the gate behind the guards. You will take turns guarding the house. 7 Two of your companies from all who go out on the Sabbath will keep watch over the house of the LORD for the king. 8 You will encircle the king, each man with his weapons in his hand, and the one that comes within the ranks must be killed. They must be with the king when he goes out and comes in."

9 The captains of hundreds did according to everything that Jehoiada the priest commanded. Each took his men, those who came on duty on the Sabbath, with those that went off duty on the Sabbath, and came to Jehoiada the priest. 10 And the priest gave to the captains of hundreds spears and shields which belonged to King David that were in the house

10:18 1Ki 16:31–32
10:19 1Ki 22:6
10:20 Joel 1:14
10:21 1Ki 16:32
10:24 1Ki 20:30–42
10:25 1Ki 18:40
10:26 1Ki 14:23
10:27 Ezr 6:11
10:29 1Ki 12:28–30
10:30 2Ki 10:35
10:31 2Ki 10:29

....

10:32 1Ki 19:17
10:33 Am 1:3–4
11:1 2Ki 8:26
11:4 2Ki 11:9
11:5 1Ch 9:25
11:9 2Ch 23:8
11:10 2Sa 8:7

[1]2 An alternate spelling of *Jehoash*.

of the LORD. 11 The guards stood, each with his weapons in his hand, from the south side of the house to the north side of the house, along the altar and the house, surrounding the king.

12 Then he brought out the king's son and put the crown on him and gave him the testimony. They made him king and anointed him. Then they clapped their hands and said, "Live, O king!"

The Death of Athaliah

13 Then Athaliah heard the sound of the guards and the people, so she came to the people in the house of the LORD. 14 Then she looked, and the king was standing by a pillar according to custom, the captains and the trumpeters by the king, and all the people of the land were rejoicing and blowing trumpets. So Athaliah tore her clothes and cried, "Conspiracy, conspiracy!"

15 But Jehoiada the priest commanded the captains of hundreds, those appointed over the forces, "Bring her out of the house to the ranks, and kill with the sword whoever follows her." For the priest had said, "Let her not be killed in the house of the LORD." 16 So they laid hands on her, and she came through the horses' entrance into the king's house. Then she was put to death there.

17 Jehoiada made a covenant between the LORD and the king and the people, that they should be the people of the LORD, and also between the king and the people. 18 Then all the people of the land entered the house of Baal and broke down its altars. His images they thoroughly broke in pieces, and they killed Mattan the priest of Baal before the altars.

The priest put appointees over the house of the LORD. 19 He took the captains of hundreds, the Carites, the guards, and all the people of the land. Then they brought down the king from the house of the LORD and marched through the gate of the guards to the king's house. Then he sat on the throne of the kings. 20 All the people of the land rejoiced, and the city was quiet. They had killed Athaliah with the sword at the king's house.

21 Jehoash[1] was seven years old when he became king.

Jehoash Repairs the Temple

2Ch 24:1–27

12 In the seventh year of Jehu, Jehoash became king. He reigned forty years in Jerusalem. His mother's name was Zibiah of Beersheba. 2 Jehoash did what was right in the sight of the LORD all his days because Jehoiada the priest instructed him. 3 However, the high places were not taken away. The people still sacrificed and made offerings in the high places.

4 Now Jehoash said to the priests, "All the consecrated money that is brought into the house of the LORD, the money for which each man is currently assessed, and all the money that is brought voluntarily to the house of the LORD, 5 let the priests receive it, each from his donor, and repair the damages to the house wherever damages are found."

6 But in the twenty-third year of King Jehoash the priests had not repaired the damages to the house. 7 Then King Jehoash called for Jehoiada the priest and the other priests and said to them, "Why have you not repaired the damages to the house? So now money will no longer be taken from your donors. You will give it over for the damages to the house." 8 The priests agreed that they should take no more money from the people, nor repair the damages of the house.

9 So Jehoiada the priest took a chest, made a hole in its lid, and set it beside the altar on the right side as one enters the house of the LORD. The priests guarding the threshold put there all the money that was brought into the house of the LORD. 10 Whenever they saw that there was much money in the chest, the king's scribe and the high priest went up, emptied it, and counted the money that was found in the house of the LORD. 11 They gave the money that was weighed out into the hands of the workers who were appointed to the house of the LORD. Then they paid it out to the carpenters and builders working on the house of the LORD, 12 to the masons and stonecutters, and to buy timber and cut stone to repair the damages to the house of the LORD, that is, whatever went out for repairs to the house.

13 But for the house of the LORD silver bowls, snuffers, sprinkling basins, trumpets, and all the gold and silver vessels were not made with any of the money that was brought into the house of the LORD, 14 for they gave it to the workmen, and they repaired the house of the LORD with it. 15 They did not settle accounts with the men in whose hand they gave the money to give to the workmen, for they dealt faithfully. 16 The money from the guilt offerings and the money from the sin offerings were not brought into the house of the LORD. It belonged to the priests.

Hazael Threatens Jerusalem

17 Then Hazael king of Aram went up, fought against Gath, and seized it. Then Hazael set his face to go up to Jerusalem. 18 So Jehoash king of Judah took all the consecrated things that Jehoshaphat, Jehoram, and Ahaziah, his

11:12 Ex 25:16
11:14 2Ki 23:3
11:16 Ge 9:6
11:17 2Sa 5:3
11:18 Dt 12:3
11:20 Pr 11:10
11:21 2Ch 24:1–14
12:3 2Ki 14:4

12:4 2Ki 22:4
12:9 Mk 12:41
12:10 2Sa 8:17
12:12 2Ki 22:5–6
12:13 2Ch 24:14
12:15 2Ki 22:7
12:16 Lev 7:7
12:17 2Ch 24:23–24
12:18 1Ki 15:18

[1] 21 An alternate spelling of *Joash*.

fathers, kings of Judah, had dedicated and his own consecrated things, all the gold that was found in the treasures of the house of the LORD and in the king's house, and sent it to Hazael king of Aram. Then Hazael went away from Jerusalem.

The Death of Joash

19 Now the rest of the deeds of Joash, and all that he did, are they not written in the book of the annals of the kings of Judah? 20 His servants rose up, made a conspiracy, and struck Joash in the house of Millo, which goes down to Silla. 21 Jozabad the son of Shimeath and Jehozabad the son of Shomer, his servants, struck him, and he died. They buried him with his fathers in the City of David. Then Amaziah his son reigned in his place.

Jehoahaz, King of Israel

13 In the twenty-third year of Joash the son of Ahaziah, king of Judah, Jehoahaz the son of Jehu reigned over Israel in Samaria for seventeen years. 2 He did evil in the sight of the LORD and followed the sins of Jeroboam the son of Nebat, who caused Israel to sin. He did not turn aside from them. 3 The anger of the LORD was kindled against Israel, so He gave them into the hand of Hazael king of Aram and into the hand of Ben-Hadad the son of Hazael all their days.

4 But Jehoahaz appeased the LORD, and the LORD listened to him. For He saw the oppression of Israel, because the king of Aram oppressed them. 5 So the LORD gave Israel a savior, so that they got out from under the hand of Aram. Then the children of Israel dwelt in their tents as before. 6 Nevertheless, they did not turn aside from the sins of the house of Jeroboam, who caused Israel to sin, but walked in them. The Asherah pole also stood in Samaria.

7 So Jehoahaz had only fifty horsemen, ten chariots, and ten thousand footmen left, for the king of Aram had destroyed them and made them like the dust at threshing.

8 Now the rest of the deeds of Jehoahaz, all that he did and his power, are they not written in the book of the annals of the kings of Israel? 9 And Jehoahaz slept with his fathers, and they buried him in Samaria. Joash his son reigned in his place.

Jehoash, King of Israel

10 In the thirty-seventh year of Joash king of Judah, Jehoash the son of Jehoahaz reigned over Israel in Samaria for sixteen years. 11 He did evil in the sight of the LORD. He did not turn aside from all the sins of Jeroboam the son of Nebat, who caused Israel to sin, but he walked in them.

12:20 2Ki 14:5
13:2 1Ki 12:26–33
13:3 Jdg 2:14
13:4 2Ki 14:26
13:5 2Ki 13:25
13:6 1Ki 16:33
13:7 Am 1:3
13:11 2Ki 13:2
13:14 2Ki 2:12
13:17 1Ki 20:26
13:19 2Ki 13:25
13:20 2Ki 24:2
13:22 2Ki 8:12
13:23 2Ki 14:27
13:25 2Ki 13:18–19

12 The rest of the deeds of Joash, all that he did and his power with which he fought against Amaziah king of Judah, are they not written in the book of the annals of the kings of Israel? 13 So Joash slept with his fathers, and Jeroboam sat on his throne. Joash was buried in Samaria with the kings of Israel.

The Death of Elisha

14 Now Elisha had become sick with the illness of which he would die. So Joash the king of Israel went down to him and wept before him, and said, "My father, my father, the chariot of Israel and its horsemen."

15 Elisha said to him, "Take a bow and arrows." So he took a bow and arrows. 16 Then he said to the king of Israel, "Draw the bow." So he drew it. Elisha put his hands on the king's hands.

> I release the arrow of the Lord's deliverance in my life (2Ki 13:17).

17 Then he said, "Open the east window." So he opened it. Then Elisha said, "Shoot." So he shot. Then he said, "The arrow of the deliverance of the LORD, and the arrow of deliverance from Aram; for you must strike Aram in Aphek until you have destroyed them."

18 Then he said, "Take the arrows." So he took them. Then he said to the king of Israel, "Strike the ground." So he struck it three times and stood there. 19 Then the man of God was angry with him and said, "You should have struck it five or six times. Then you would have stricken Aram until you had finished them. Now you will strike Aram just three times."

20 So Elisha died, and they buried him.

Now Moabite raiders would enter the land in the spring. 21 As they were burying a man, they saw raiders. So they threw the man into the tomb of Elisha. When the man touched the bones of Elisha, he came to life and stood on his feet.

Israel Recaptures Cities from Aram

22 Now Hazael king of Aram oppressed Israel all the days of Jehoahaz. 23 But the LORD was gracious to them and had compassion on them. He turned toward them because of His covenant with Abraham, Isaac, and Jacob, and would not yet destroy them or cast them from His presence.

24 Then Hazael king of Aram died and Ben-Hadad his son reigned in his place. 25 And Jehoash the son of Jehoahaz took back the cities from Ben-Hadad the son of Hazael that had been taken from Jehoahaz his father in war.

Three times Joash struck him and recovered
the cities of Israel.

Amaziah, King of Judah
2Ch 25:1–26:2

14 In the second year of Joash son of
Jehoahaz, king of Israel, Amaziah the
son of Joash, king of Judah, became king.
2 He was twenty-five years old when he be-
came king and reigned twenty-nine years in
Jerusalem. His mother's name was Jehoaddan
from Jerusalem. 3 He did what was right in
the sight of the LORD, only not like David his
father. He did everything that Joash his father
did. 4 But he did not remove the high places.
Still the people sacrificed and made offerings
on the high places.
5 As soon as he seized the kingdom, he killed
his servants who had killed his father, the king.
6 But he did not kill the children of the murder-
ers, according to what is written in the Book
of the Law of Moses, in which the LORD com-
manded, "Fathers must not be put to death for
the children, nor the children be put to death
for the fathers. Rather, a man should be put to
death for his own sin."
7 He struck ten thousand Edomites in the
Valley of Salt and captured Sela in battle. He
called it Joktheel, as it is to this day.
8 Then Amaziah sent messengers to Jehoash
son of Jehoahaz, son of Jehu, king of Israel,
saying, "Come, let us look one another in the
face."
9 Then Jehoash the king of Israel sent word
to Amaziah king of Judah, saying, "The thorn
bush in Lebanon sent to the cedar in Lebanon,
saying, 'Give your daughter to my son for a
wife.' But a wild animal passed through in Leb-
anon and trampled the thorn bush. 10 You have
indeed struck Edom, and your heart has lifted
you up. Enjoy respect and sit at home. Why stir
up trouble and fall, you and Judah with you?"
11 But Amaziah would not listen. So Jehoash
king of Israel went up, and he and Amaziah
king of Judah looked one another in the face
at Beth Shemesh, which belongs to Judah.
12 Judah was beaten before Israel, and every
man fled to his tent. 13 Jehoash king of Israel
captured Amaziah king of Judah, the son of
Jehoash, the son of Ahaziah, at Beth Shemesh.
Then he came to Jerusalem and breached the
wall of Jerusalem from the Gate of Ephraim
to the Corner Gate, four hundred cubits.[1] 14 He
took all the gold and silver, all the vessels
found in the house of the LORD and in the trea-
suries of the king's house, and hostages, and
then returned to Samaria.

14:1 2Ki 13:10
14:4 2Ki 12:3
14:6 Eze 18:4
14:7 2Sa 8:13
14:8 2Ch 25:17–24
14:9 Jdg 9:8–15
14:10 Dt 8:14
14:11 Jos 19:38
14:12 2Sa 18:17
14:13 Ne 8:16
....
14:17 2Ch 25:25–28
14:19 Jos 10:31
14:20 2Ki 9:28
14:22 2Ki 16:6
14:25 Dt 3:17
14:26 Dt 32:36
14:27 2Ki 13:23
14:28 1Ki 11:24

15 Now the rest of the deeds Jehoash did, his
power and how he fought with Amaziah king
of Judah, are they not written in the book of
the annals of the kings of Israel? 16 So Jehoash
slept with his fathers and was buried in Sa-
maria with the kings of Israel. Jeroboam his
son reigned in his place.
17 Amaziah the son of Joash king of Judah
lived fifteen years after the death of Jehoash
son of Jehoahaz, king of Israel. 18 And the rest
of the deeds of Amaziah, are they not writ-
ten in the book of the annals of the kings of
Judah?
19 They made a conspiracy against him in
Jerusalem, and he fled to Lachish. But they
sent after him to Lachish, and killed him there.
20 They carried him on horses, and he was bur-
ied in Jerusalem with his fathers in the City
of David.
21 All the people of Judah took Azariah, who
was sixteen years old, and made him king in-
stead of his father Amaziah. 22 He built Elath
and restored it to Judah after the king slept
with his fathers.

Jeroboam II, King of Israel

23 In the fifteenth year of Amaziah the son
of Joash, king of Judah, Jeroboam the son of
Joash, king of Israel, became king in Samaria
for forty-one years. 24 He did evil in the sight of
the LORD. He did not turn aside from all the sins
of Jeroboam the son of Nebat, who caused
Israel to sin. 25 He restored the border of Isra-
el from the entrance of Lebo Hamath to the
Sea of the Arabah, according to the word of
the LORD God of Israel, which He spoke by His
servant Jonah the son of Amittai, the prophet,
who was from Gath Hepher.
26 For the LORD saw the very bitter affliction
of Israel. There was no one left, imprisoned or
free, and no helper for Israel. 27 The LORD had
not said that He would wipe out the name of
Israel from under heaven, so He saved them
by the hand of Jeroboam son of Joash.
28 Now the rest of the deeds of Jeroboam,
all that he did and his power, how he fought,
and how he recovered for Israel Damascus and
Hamath, which had belonged to Judah, are
they not written in the book of the annals of
the kings of Israel? 29 Jeroboam slept with his
fathers, with the kings of Israel. Zechariah his
son reigned in his place.

Azariah, King of Judah
2Ch 26:3–23

15 In the twenty-seventh year of Jero-
boam king of Israel, Azariah son of
Amaziah, king of Judah, became king. 2 He
was sixteen years old when he became king,
and he reigned fifty-two years in Jerusalem.

[1] *13* About 600 feet, or 180 meters.

His mother's name was Jekoliah from Jerusalem. 3 He did what was right in the sight of the LORD, according to all that his father Amaziah had done. 4 But the high places were not removed. The people continued sacrificing and making offerings on the high places.

5 The LORD afflicted the king, and he was leprous until the day of his death. He lived in a separate house. Jotham the king's son was in charge of the house, judging the people of the land.

6 Now the rest of the deeds of Azariah, and all that he did, are they not written in the book of the annals of the kings of Judah? 7 So Azariah slept with his fathers, and they buried him with his fathers in the City of David. Jotham his son reigned in his place.

Zechariah, King of Israel

8 In the thirty-eighth year of Azariah king of Judah, Zechariah the son of Jeroboam became king of Israel in Samaria for six months. 9 He did evil in the sight of the LORD, as his fathers had done. He did not turn aside from the sins of Jeroboam the son of Nebat, who caused Israel to sin.

10 Shallum the son of Jabesh conspired against him, struck him at Ibleam, and killed him. Then Shallum reigned in his place. 11 Now the rest of the deeds of Zechariah are written in the book of the annals of the kings of Israel. 12 This was the word of the LORD which He spoke to Jehu, "Your sons will sit on the throne of Israel to the fourth generation." And it was so.

Shallum, King of Israel

13 Shallum son of Jabesh became king in the thirty-ninth year of Uzziah king of Judah. He reigned for a month in Samaria. 14 Then Menahem son of Gadi went up from Tirzah, entered Samaria, and struck Shallum son of Jabesh in Samaria and killed him. Then Menahem reigned in his place.

15 Now the rest of the deeds of Shallum and the conspiracy he made are written in the book of the annals of the kings of Israel.

16 Then Menahem struck Tiphsah and all who were in it, and the territories around Tirzah. Because they did not open up the city to him, he attacked it. Then he split open all its pregnant woman.

Menahem, King of Israel

17 In the thirty-ninth year of Azariah king of Judah, Menahem son of Gadi became king over Israel for ten years in Samaria. 18 He did evil in the sight of the LORD. He did not turn aside all his days from the sins of Jeroboam the son of Nebat, who caused Israel to sin.

19 Pul the king of Assyria came against the land, and Menahem gave Pul a thousand talents[1] of silver, that he might help him strengthen his control of the kingdom. 20 Menahem exacted the money from Israel, from all the very wealthy men, fifty shekels[2] of silver each, to give to the king of Assyria. So the king of Assyria left and did not stay there in the land.

21 The rest of the deeds of Menahem, and all that he did, are they not written in the book of the annals of the kings of Israel? 22 And Menahem slept with his fathers, and Pekahiah his son reigned in his place.

Pekahiah, King of Israel

23 In the fiftieth year of Azariah king of Judah, Pekahiah the son of Menahem became king over Israel in Samaria for two years. 24 He did evil in the sight of the LORD. He did not turn aside from the sins of Jeroboam the son of Nebat, who caused Israel to sin. 25 But Pekah son of Remaliah, his officer, conspired against him and struck him in Samaria, in the palace of the king's house, with Argob, Arieh, and fifty men of the Gileadites with him. He killed him and reigned in his place.

26 Now the rest of the deeds of Pekahiah and all that he did are written in the book of the annals of the kings of Israel.

Pekah, King of Israel

27 In the fifty-second year of Azariah king of Judah, Pekah son of Remaliah became king over Israel in Samaria for twenty years. 28 He did evil in the sight of the LORD. He did not turn aside from the sins of Jeroboam son of Nebat, who caused Israel to sin.

29 In the days of Pekah king of Israel, Tiglath-Pileser king of Assyria came and took Ijon, Abel Beth Maakah, Janoah, Kedesh, Hazor, Gilead, Galilee, and all the land of Naphtali, and then exiled them to Assyria. 30 Then Hoshea son of Elah made a conspiracy against Pekah son of Remaliah and struck and killed him. Then he reigned in his place in the twentieth year of Jotham son of Uzziah.

31 The rest of the deeds of Pekah and all that he did are written in the book of the annals of the kings of Israel.

Jotham, King of Judah

2Ch 27:1–9

32 In the second year of Pekah son of Remaliah, king of Israel, Jotham son of Uzziah, king of Judah, became king. 33 He was twenty-five years old when he became king, and he reigned sixteen years in Jerusalem. His mother's name was Jerusha daughter of Zadok.

15:5 Lev 13:46
15:7 2Ch 26:23
15:12 2Ki 10:30
15:13 2Ki 15:1
15:14 1Ki 14:17
15:16 2Ki 8:12
15:19 2Ki 14:5
15:24 2Ki 15:9
15:25 2Ch 28:6
15:27 Isa 7:1
15:29 Jos 20:7
15:30 2Ki 17:1
15:32 2Ki 15:7
15:33 2Ch 27:1

[1] *19* About 38 tons, or 34 metric tons. [2] *20* About 1¼ pounds, or 575 grams.

[34] He did what was right in the sight of the
LORD. He did according to all that his father
Uzziah had done. [35] Only he did not remove the
high places. The people continued sacrificing
and making offerings on the high places. He
built the upper gate of the house of the LORD.
[36] Now the rest of the deeds of Jotham, and
all that he did, are they not written in the book
of the annals of the kings of Judah? [37] In those
days the LORD began to send Rezin king of
Aram and Pekah son of Remaliah against Ju-
dah. [38] Jotham slept with his fathers and was
buried with his fathers in the City of David his
father. Then Ahaz his son reigned in his place.

Ahaz, King of Judah
2Ch 28:1–27

16 In the seventeenth year of Pekah son of
Remaliah, Ahaz son of Jotham, king of
Judah, became king. [2] Ahaz was twenty years
old when he became king, and he reigned for
sixteen years in Jerusalem. He did not do what
was right in the sight of the LORD his God like
David his father. [3] He walked in the way of the
kings of Israel and even made his son pass
through the fire according to the abominations
of the nations whom the LORD dispossessed
before the children of Israel. [4] He sacrificed
and made offerings on the high places, on the
hills, and under every green tree.
[5] Then Rezin king of Aram and Pekah son of
Remaliah, king of Israel, came up to Jerusalem
to battle, and they besieged Ahaz but could
not subdue him. [6] At that time Rezin king of
Aram recovered Elath for Aram and expelled
the Judeans from Elath. The Edomites came
to Elath and live there to this day.
[7] So Ahaz sent messengers to Tiglath-Pileser
king of Assyria, saying, "I am your servant and
your son. Come up and save me from the hand
of the king of Aram and from the hand of the
king of Israel, who are rising up against me."
[8] Then Ahaz took the silver and gold that was
found in the house of the LORD and in the trea-
sures of the king's house, and sent a present
to the king of Assyria. [9] So the king of Assyria
listened to him. The king of Assyria went up
to Damascus, captured it, exiled the people to
Kir, and killed Rezin.
[10] Then King Ahaz went to Damascus to
meet Tiglath-Pileser king of Assyria and saw
an altar that was in Damascus. King Ahaz sent
to Uriah the priest a pattern of the altar and
model of it, according to the manner of its
construction. [11] Uriah the priest built an altar
according to all that King Ahaz had sent from
Damascus. Thus Uriah the priest worked until
King Ahaz came from Damascus. [12] When the
king came back from Damascus and saw the
altar, the king approached the altar and made

15:34 2Ch 26:4–5
15:37 2Ki 16:5
16:1 Isa 1:1
16:3 Dt 12:31
16:4 Dt 12:2
16:5 2Ki 15:37
16:6 2Ki 14:22
16:7 2Ki 15:29
16:8 2Ki 12:17–18
16:9 Isa 22:6
16:10 Isa 8:2
16:12 2Ch 26:16–19
16:14 2Ch 4:1
16:15 Ex 29:39–41
17:1 2Ki 15:30
17:3 Hos 10:14
17:6 Dt 28:64
17:7 Jos 23:16

offerings on it. [13] He offered his burnt offering
and his grain offering, poured out his libations,
and sprinkled the blood of his peace offerings
upon the altar. [14] And the bronze altar that was
before the LORD he moved from the front of the
house, from between the altar and the house
of the LORD. He put it on the north side of the
new altar.
[15] Then King Ahaz commanded Uriah the
priest, "Upon the great altar offer the morning
burnt offering, the evening grain offering, the
king's burnt offering, and his grain offering
with the burnt offering of all the people of the
land, their grain offering, and their libations.
Sprinkle on it all the blood of the burnt offer-
ing and all the blood of the sacrifice, and the
bronze altar will be for me to inquire by." [16] So
Uriah the priest did everything that King Ahaz
commanded.
[17] King Ahaz cut off the bases of the stands
and removed the basin from them. He took
down the sea from off the bronze oxen that
were under it and put it on stone pavement.
[18] The structure for the Sabbath that they had
built in the house and the king's outer entrance
he removed from the house of the LORD for the
king of Assyria.
[19] Now the rest of the deeds of Ahaz that he
did, are they not written in the book of the
annals of the kings of Judah? [20] Ahaz slept
with his fathers and was buried with his fa-
thers in the City of David. Then Hezekiah his
son reigned in his place.

Hoshea, King of Israel
2Kgs 18:9–12

17 In the twelfth year of Ahaz king of Ju-
dah, Hoshea son of Elah became king
in Samaria over Israel for nine years. [2] He did
evil in the sight of the LORD, only not as the
kings of Israel who were before him.
[3] Shalmaneser king of Assyria came up
against him. Hoshea became his servant and
gave him gifts. [4] But the king of Assyria found
conspiracy in Hoshea, for he had sent messen-
gers to So king of Egypt and offered up no gift
to the king of Assyria as he had done year by
year. So the king of Assyria detained him, and
then put him in prison.

Israel Exiled to Assyria

[5] Then the king of Assyria went throughout
all the land, went up to Samaria, and besieged
it for three years. [6] In the ninth year of Hoshea,
the king of Assyria seized Samaria and exiled
Israel to Assyria. He put them in Halah, in Ha-
bor by the River of Gozan, and in the cities of
the Medes.
[7] This happened because the children of Is-
rael had sinned against the LORD their God,

who had brought them up from the land of
Egypt from under the hand of Pharaoh king
of Egypt. They had feared other gods 8 and
walked in the statutes of the nations, whom
the LORD dispossessed before the children of
Israel, and walked in the statutes which the
kings of Israel had made. 9 The children of
Israel ascribed things to the LORD their God that
were not so, and they built for themselves high
places in all their cities from the watchtower to
the fortified city. 10 They set up standing stones
and Asherah poles on every high hill and un-
der every green tree. 11 There they burned in-
cense on all the high places, as the nations
did whom the LORD had carried away before
them. And they did wicked things to provoke
the LORD to anger, 12 for they served idols, of
which the LORD had said to them, "You shall
not do this thing." 13 But the LORD warned Is-
rael and Judah by all the prophets and by all
the seers, saying, "Turn from your evil ways,
and keep My commandments and My statutes,
according to all the law which I commanded
your fathers and which I sent to you by My
servants the prophets."

14 But they would not listen. They stiffened
their necks, like the neck of their fathers, who
did not believe in the LORD their God. 15 They
rejected His statutes and His covenant that He
had made with their fathers and the decrees
He had given them. They followed idols, and
became idolaters, and followed the surround-
ing nations, concerning whom the LORD com-
manded them, that they should not do like
them.

16 They forsook all the commandments of
the LORD their God, made themselves cast
images (two calves), made an Asherah pole,
worshipped all the host of heaven, and served
Baal. 17 They caused their sons and daughters
to pass through the fire, used divination and
omens, and sold themselves to do evil in the
sight of the LORD to anger Him.

18 Therefore the LORD was very angry with
Israel and removed them from His presence.
None remained except the tribe of Judah. 19 Ju-
dah also did not keep the commandments of
the LORD their God, but walked in the statutes
of Israel which they made. 20 The LORD rejected
all the seed of Israel, afflicted them, and gave
them into the hand of plunderers until He had
cast them out of His presence.

21 For He had torn Israel from the house of
David, and they made Jeroboam the son of
Nebat king. Jeroboam diverted Israel from fol-
lowing the LORD and caused them to sin great-
ly. 22 For the children of Israel walked in all the
sins which Jeroboam committed. They did not
turn aside from them 23 until the LORD removed
Israel from His presence as He had said by all
His servants the prophets. So Israel was exiled
from their land to Assyria until this day.

Assyria Resettles Samaria

24 Then the king of Assyria brought peo-
ple from Babylon, Kuthah, Avva, Hamath,
and Sepharvaim and put them in the cities
of Samaria instead of the children of Israel.
They possessed Samaria and lived in its cit-
ies. 25 Right at the beginning of their settling
there, they did not fear the LORD, so the LORD
sent lions among them, and they killed some
of them. 26 So they said to the king of Assyria,
"The nations which you have exiled and set-
tled in the cities of Samaria do not know the
law of the god of the land. Therefore He has
sent lions among them; they are killing them,
because they do not know the requirements of
the god of the land."

27 Then the king of Assyria commanded, "Es-
cort back one of the priests whom you exiled
from there and let him go and dwell there. Let
him teach them the law of the god of the land."
28 Then one of the priests whom they had ex-
iled from Samaria came and lived in Bethel.
He taught them how they should fear the LORD.

29 But each nation was making its own gods,
and they put them in the houses of the high
places that the people of Samaria had made,
each nation in the cities where they were liv-
ing. 30 The men of Babylon made Sukkoth
Benoth, the men of Kuthah made Nergal, the
men of Hamath made Ashima, 31 the Avvites
made Nibhaz and Tartak. The Sepharvites
were burning their children in fire to Adram-
melek and Anammelek, the gods of Sephar-
vaim. 32 They feared the LORD and made from
amongst themselves priests of the high places,
who were working for them in the houses of
the high places. 33 They feared the LORD, and
they were serving their own gods, after the
manner of the nations whom they exiled from
there.

34 To this day they continue to practice their
former customs. They do not fear the LORD, nor
are they doing according to the statutes, re-
quirements, the law or commandment that the
LORD commanded the children of Jacob, whom
He named Israel. 35 The LORD had made a cov-
enant and commanded them, saying, "You
shall not fear other gods, nor bow yourselves
to them. You shall not serve them or sacrifice
to them. 36 Rather, the LORD, who brought you
up out of the land of Egypt with great power
and an outstretched arm, Him you shall fear, to
Him you shall bow down, and to Him you shall
sacrifice. 37 The statutes, the ordinances, the
law, and the commandment, which He wrote

17:8 Lev 18:3
17:9 2Ki 18:8
17:10 1Ki 14:23
17:13 1Sa 9:9
17:14 Dt 31:27
17:15 Dt 12:30–31
17:16 1Ki 12:28
17:17 2Ki 21:6
17:18 1Ki 11:13
17:19 1Ki 14:22–23
17:20 2Ki 15:29
17:21 1Ki 11:11
17:23 2Ki 17:6
17:24 2Ki 18:34
17:31 2Ki 17:24
17:32 1Ki 12:31
17:34 Ge 32:28
17:35 Jdg 6:10
17:36 Ex 6:6

for you, you shall observe to do forever. And
you shall not fear other gods. 38 The covenant
that I have made with you, you shall not forget.
You shall not fear other gods. 39 Rather the LORD
your God you shall fear, and He will deliver you
from the hand of all your enemies."
40 But they did not listen; rather they were
practicing their former customs. 41 So these na-
tions feared the LORD and were serving their
carved images, both their children and their
grandchildren, as their fathers did, and so they
are doing to this day.

Hezekiah, King of Judah

2Ch 29:1–2; 31:1, 20–21; 2Ki 17:3–7

18 In the third year of Hoshea son of
Elah, king of Israel, Hezekiah the son
of Ahaz, king of Judah, became king. 2 He was
twenty-five years old when he became king,
and he reigned twenty-nine years in Jerusa-
lem. His mother's name was Abi daughter
of Zechariah. 3 He did what was right in the
sight of the LORD, according to everything that
David his father had done. 4 He removed the
high places, broke down the sacred pillars,
cut down the Asherah poles, and crushed the
bronze serpent that Moses had made, for until
those days the children of Israel had made of-
ferings to it. They called it Nehushtan.

> I break down the high places in the name of Jesus (2Ki 18:4).

5 He trusted in the LORD God of Israel. Af-
terwards, there was no one like him among
all the kings of Judah or among those who
were before him. 6 He clung to the LORD. He
did not depart from following him, but kept His
commandments, which the LORD commanded
Moses. 7 The LORD was with him. Wherever he
went, he prospered. He rebelled against the
king of Assyria and did not serve him. 8 He
struck the Philistines as far as Gaza and its
territory, from watchtower to fortified city.
9 In the fourth year of King Hezekiah, which
was the seventh year of Hoshea son of Elah,
king of Israel, Shalmaneser king of Assyria
came up against Samaria and besieged it.
10 He seized it at the end of three years. In the
sixth year of Hezekiah, that is, the ninth year
of Hoshea king of Israel, Samaria was taken.
11 Then the king of Assyria exiled Israel to As-
syria and put them in Halah and in Habor by
the River of Gozan and in the cities of the Me-
des, 12 because they did not obey the voice of
the LORD their God, but transgressed His cove-
nant and all that Moses the servant of the LORD
commanded, and would not obey or do them.

Sennacherib Invades Judah

Isa 36:1–22; 2Ch 32:9–19

13 In the fourteenth year of King Hezekiah,
Sennacherib king of Assyria came up against
all the fortified cities of Judah and captured
them. 14 Hezekiah king of Judah sent word to
the king of Assyria at Lachish, saying, "I have
done wrong; turn away from me. I will bear
whatever you put on me." So the king of As-
syria required of Hezekiah king of Judah three
hundred talents[1] of silver and thirty talents[2] of
gold. 15 So Hezekiah gave him all the silver that
was found in the house of the LORD and in the
treasuries of the king's house.
16 At that time Hezekiah cut off the gold from
the doors of the temple of the LORD and from
the doorposts that Hezekiah king of Judah had
overlaid and gave it to the king of Assyria.
17 Then the king of Assyria sent the Tartan,[3]
the Rabsaris,[4] and the Rabshakeh[5] from Lach-
ish to King Hezekiah with a great army against
Jerusalem. So they went up and came to Je-
rusalem. When they went up, they came and
stood by the conduit of the upper pool, which
is on the highway of the Fuller's Field. 18 Then
they called to the king, and Eliakim the son of
Hilkiah, who was over the household, Shebna
the scribe, and Joah the son of Asaph, the re-
corder, came out to them.
19 Then the Rabshakeh said to them, "Speak
to Hezekiah:

"Thus says the great king, the king of As-
syria: What is the basis of your confidence?
20 You speak empty words concerning coun-
sel and strength for the war. Now on whom
do you trust, that you have rebelled against
me? 21 Now, look! You trust in the staff of this
bruised reed, on Egypt, on which if a man
leans, it will enter his hand and pierce it. So
is Pharaoh king of Egypt to all who trust
in him. 22 But if you say to me, 'We trust in
the LORD our God,' is it not He, whose high
places and altars Hezekiah has removed,
saying to Judah and to Jerusalem, 'You shall
worship before this altar in Jerusalem'?
23 "Now, make a wager with my lord king
of Assyria. I will give you two thousand
horses if you are able to set riders on them.
24 How can you turn away one official of the
least of my master's servants and put your
trust on Egypt for chariots and horsemen?
25 Have I come up apart from the will of the
LORD against this place to destroy it? The
LORD said to me, Go up against this land and
destroy it."

17:38 Dt 4:23
17:41 Zep 1:5
18:3 2Ki 20:3
18:4 2Ch 31:1
18:5 2Ki 19:10
18:6 Dt 10:20
18:7 1Sa 18:14
18:8 2Ki 17:9
18:11 1Ch 5:26

18:13 Isa 36:1–22
18:15 2Ki 16:8
18:17 2Ki 20:20
18:18 2Ki 19:2
18:19 Isa 36:4
18:21 Isa 30:7
18:22 2Ch 31:1

[1] *14* About 11 tons, or 10 metric tons. [2] *14* About 1 ton, or 1 metric ton. [3] *17* Possibly *Commander in Chief.* [4] *17* Possibly *Chief of Staff.* [5] *17* Possibly *Commanding General.*

26 Then Eliakim the son of Hilkiah, Shebna,
and Joah said to the Rabshakeh, "Speak to
your servants in Aramaic, for we understand it.
Do not speak with us in the language of Judah
in earshot of the people who are on the wall."
27 But the Rabshakeh said to them, "Has my
master sent me to speak these words to your
master and to you, and not to the men sitting
on the wall, who are about to eat their own
dung and drink their own urine with you?"
28 Then the Rabshakeh stood and called with
a loud voice in the language of Judah, "Hear
the word of the great king, the king of Assyr-
ia. 29 Thus says the king: 'Do not let Hezekiah
deceive you, for he is not able to deliver you
from my hand. 30 Do not let Hezekiah make you
trust in the LORD, saying, The LORD will surely
deliver us, and this city will not be given into
the hand of the king of Assyria.'
31 "Do not listen to Hezekiah, for thus says
the king of Assyria: 'Submit to me; come out
to me, so that every man may eat from his own
vine and his own fig tree and drink water from
his own cistern, 32 until I come and take you
to a land like your own land, a land of grain
and wine, a land of bread and vineyards, a
land of olive oil and honey, that you may live
and not die.'
"Do not listen to Hezekiah when he leads you
astray saying, The LORD will deliver us. 33 Has
any of the gods of the nations at all delivered
its land from the hand of the king of Assyria?
34 Where are the gods of Hamath and Arpad?
Where are the gods of Sepharvaim, Hena, and
Ivvah? Have they delivered Samaria from my
hand? 35 Who among all the gods of the lands
have delivered their land out of my hand, that
the LORD should deliver Jerusalem from my
hand?"
36 But the people were silent and answered
him not a word, for the king's command was,
"Do not answer him."
37 Then Eliakim son of Hilkiah, who was over
the household, Shebna the scribe, and Joah the
son of Asaph, the recorder, came to Hezekiah
with their clothes torn and told him the words
of the Rabshakeh.

Hezekiah Consults Isaiah
Isa 37:1–13

19 When King Hezekiah heard it, he tore
his clothes, covered himself with sack-
cloth, and entered the house of the LORD. 2 He
sent Eliakim, who was over the household,
Shebna the scribe, and the elders of the priests,
covered with sackcloth, to Isaiah the prophet,
the son of Amoz. 3 They said to him, "Thus
says Hezekiah: This day is a day of distress,
chastisement, and disgrace, for children have
come to the mouth of the womb, but there is
no strength to birth them. 4 Perhaps the LORD
your God will hear all the words of the Rab-
shakeh, whom the king of Assyria, his master,
has sent to taunt the living God and will rebuke
the words that the LORD your God has heard,
and you might lift up a prayer for the remnant
that are left."
5 When the servants of King Hezekiah came
to Isaiah, 6 Isaiah said to them, "Thus shall you
say to your master, 'Thus says the LORD: Do not
be afraid of the words that you have heard,
with which the servants of the king of Assyria
have blasphemed Me. 7 I am putting a spirit in
him, and he will hear a report and return to his
own land. Then I will cause him to fall by the
sword in his own land.' "

Sennacherib Defies the LORD

8 Then the Rabshakeh returned and found
the king of Assyria warring against Libnah,
for he had heard that he had departed from
Lachish.
9 When the king heard concerning Tirhakah
king of Cush, "He has come out to fight against
you," he sent messengers to Hezekiah, saying,
10 "Thus you shall speak to Hezekiah king of
Judah, saying: Do not let your God in whom
you trust deceive you, saying: Jerusalem will
not be given into the hand of the king of Assyr-
ia. 11 You have heard what the kings of Assyria
have done to all lands by annihilating them.
Will you be delivered? 12 Have the gods of the
nations delivered them, the nations that my
fathers destroyed, Gozan, Harran, Rezeph,
and the sons of Eden who were in Tel Assar?
13 Where is the king of Hamath, the king of
Arpad, the king of the city of Sepharvaim, of
Hena, and Ivvah?"

Hezekiah's Prayer
Isa 37:14–20

14 Hezekiah received the letter from the hand
of the messengers and read it. Then Hezekiah
went up to the house of the LORD and spread it
before the LORD. 15 Then Hezekiah prayed be-
fore the LORD and said, "O LORD, God of Israel,
who sits on the cherubim, You alone are God
over all the kingdoms of the earth. You have
made the sky and the earth. 16 Incline, O LORD,
Your ear and hear. Open, O LORD, Your eyes
and see. Hear the words of Sennacherib, which
he sent to taunt the living God.
17 "Surely, O LORD, the kings of Assyria have
annihilated the nations and their lands 18 and
have put their gods in the fire, for they were
no gods but the work of men's hands, wood
and stone; thus they have been destroyed. 19 So
now, O LORD our God, save us from his hand,
that all the kingdoms of the earth may know
that You, O LORD, are God alone."

18:26 Ezr 4:7
18:31 1Ki 4:25
18:32 Dt 8:7–9
19:1 1Ki 21:27
19:2 Isa 1:1

19:4 2Sa 16:12
19:6 2Ki 18:17
19:8 2Ki 18:14
19:10 2Ki 18:5
19:12 Ge 11:31
19:13 2Ki 18:34
19:15 Ex 25:22
19:16 2Ki 19:4
19:18 Ac 17:29
19:19 1Ki 8:43

Isaiah Prophesies Sennacherib's Fall
Isa 37:21–38; 2Ch 32:20–21

20 Then Isaiah son of Amoz sent word to
Hezekiah, saying, "Thus says the LORD God
of Israel: That which you have prayed to Me
concerning Sennacherib king of Assyria I have
heard. 21 This is the word that the LORD has
spoken concerning him:

She despises you, she ridicules you—
virgin daughter of Zion.
Behind you, she shakes her head—
daughter of Jerusalem.
22 Whom have you taunted and blasphemed?
And against whom have you raised a voice
and lifted your eyes upward?
Against the Holy One of Israel.
23 By your messengers
you have taunted the Lord,
and have said,
'With my many chariots
I have gone up the height of the mountains,
to farthest reaches of Lebanon,
and I will cut down its tallest cedars,
its choicest junipers.
I will enter its most remote canopies of night,
its dense forest.
24 I have dug *wells*
and drunk foreign waters,
and I dried up with the sole of my foot
all the streams of Egypt.'

25 "Have you not heard?
Long ago I arranged it,
in ancient times I formed it;
now I bring it to pass,
that you will turn impregnable cities
into desolate heaps of stones.
26 Their inhabitants are powerless;
they are terrified and ashamed.
They are like grass of the field
and new vegetation,
grass on the roof tops,
scorched before it stands.

27 "But I know your dwelling place,
your going out and your coming in,
and your raging against Me.
28 Because you have raged against Me,
and your self-assuredness has come up to My ears,
I will put My hook in your nose
and My bridle on your lips,
and I will turn you back
on the way by which you came.

29 "This will be the sign to you:

This year you will eat what grows itself,
and in the second year the same.
Then in the third year sow, reap,
and plant vineyards, and eat their fruits.
30 The spared of the house of Judah who remain
will again take root below, and bear fruit above.
31 For from Jerusalem a remnant will go forth,
and escapees from Mount Zion.

"The zeal of the LORD of Hosts will do this.

32 "Therefore thus says the LORD concerning
the king of Assyria:

He will not enter this city,
shoot an arrow there,
approach it with shield,
or heap up a siege ramp against it.
33 By the way that he came, he will return;
he will not enter this city,
declares the LORD.
34 For I will protect this city to save it,
for My own sake and for the sake of
David My servant."

The Death of Sennacherib

35 On that night the angel of the LORD went
out and struck one hundred and eighty-five
thousand in the camp of the Assyrians. When
others woke up early in the morning, these
were all dead bodies. 36 So Sennacherib king
of Assyria departed and stayed in Nineveh.
37 As he was worshipping in the house of
Nisrok his god, Adrammelek and Sharezer his
sons struck him with the sword, and they es-
caped into the land of Ararat. Esarhaddon his
son reigned in his place.

Hezekiah's Life Extended
2Ch 32:24–26; Isa 38:1–8

20 In those days Hezekiah became ill and
was near death. The prophet Isaiah
son of Amoz came to him, and said to him,
"Thus says the LORD: Set your house in order,
for you shall die and not live."
2 Then he turned his face toward the wall
and prayed to the LORD, saying, 3 "Please, O
LORD, remember how I have walked before
You faithfully and with an undivided heart
and have done what is good in Your sight."
And Hezekiah wept bitterly.
4 Now before Isaiah had come out of the mid-
dle courtyard, the word of the LORD came to
him, saying, 5 "Turn back and say to Hezekiah
the leader of My people: Thus says the LORD,
the God of David your father: I have heard your
prayer; I have seen your tears. I will heal you.
On the third day you shall go up to the house
of the LORD. 6 I will add to your days fifteen
years, and I will deliver you and this city from
the hand of the king of Assyria. I will defend

19:20 2Ki 20:5
19:21 La 2:13
19:22 Isa 5:24
19:23 2Ki 18:17
19:25 Isa 45:7
19:28 2Ki 19:33
19:29 2Ki 20:8–9
....
19:30 2Ch 32:22–23
19:31 Isa 9:7
19:33 2Ki 19:28
19:34 2Ki 20:6
19:35 Ex 12:29–30
19:36 Jnh 1:2
19:37 Ge 8:4
20:1 2Sa 17:23
20:3 Ne 13:22
20:5 1Sa 9:16
20:6 2Ki 19:34

this city for My own sake and for the sake of David My servant."

7 Then Isaiah said, "Take a cake of figs." So they took it and laid it on the boil, and he recovered.

8 Hezekiah said to Isaiah, "What will be the sign that the LORD will heal me, and that I should go up to the house of the LORD on the third day?"

9 Isaiah said, "This is the sign to you from the LORD, that the LORD will do the thing that He has spoken: Should the shadow walk forward ten steps or go back ten steps?"

10 And Hezekiah answered, "It is an easy thing for the shadow to stretch ten steps, so let it go back ten steps."

11 Isaiah the prophet called to the LORD, and He made the shadow go back ten steps on the stairs of Ahaz.

Envoys From Babylon

Isa 39:1–8; 2Ch 32:32–33

12 At that time Marduk-Baladan son of Baladan, king of Babylon, sent letters and a gift to Hezekiah, for he had heard that Hezekiah had been ill. 13 Hezekiah welcomed them and showed them all the treasure house, the silver, the gold, the spices, the fine oil, all the armory, and all that was found in his storehouses. There was nothing in his house nor in all his dominion that Hezekiah did not show them.

14 Then Isaiah the prophet came to King Hezekiah and said to him, "What did these men say? From where did they come to you?"

Hezekiah said, "They came from a distant land, from Babylon."

15 He said, "What have they seen in your house?"

Hezekiah said, "They have seen everything in my house. There is nothing in my storehouses that I did not show them."

16 Isaiah said to Hezekiah, "Hear the word of the LORD: 17 The days are coming when everything that is in your house and that your fathers have stored up until this day will be carried off to Babylon. Nothing will be left, says the LORD. 18 Some of your sons who go out from you, who will be born to you, will be taken away. They will be eunuchs in the palace of the king of Babylon."

19 Then Hezekiah said to Isaiah, "The word of the LORD that you have spoken is good." And he said, "Why not, if there is peace and security in my days?"

The Death of Hezekiah

20 The rest of the deeds of Hezekiah, all his power, how he made a pool and a conduit and brought water into the city, are they not written in the book of the annals of the kings of Judah? 21 Hezekiah slept with his fathers, and Manasseh his son reigned in his place.

20:12 2Ch 32:31
20:17 2Ki 24:13
20:18 2Ch 33:11
20:19 1Sa 3:18
20:20 Ne 3:16

....

20:21 2Ch 32:33
21:3 2Ki 17:16
21:4 2Sa 7:13
21:5 1Ki 7:12
21:6 Lev 18:21
21:7 1Ki 8:29
21:8 2Sa 7:10
21:9 Pr 29:12
21:11 1Ki 21:26
21:12 1Sa 3:11
21:13 Isa 34:11
21:14 Jer 23:33

Manasseh, King of Judah

2Ch 33:1–20

21 Manasseh was twelve years old when he became king, and he reigned fifty-five years in Jerusalem. His mother's name was Hephzibah. 2 He did evil in the sight of the LORD, according to the abominations of the nations whom the LORD dispossessed before the children of Israel. 3 He went back and rebuilt the high places that Hezekiah his father had destroyed. He erected altars for Baal, made an Asherah pole as Ahab king of Israel had done, and worshipped all the host of heaven and served them. 4 He built altars in the house of the LORD, of which the LORD had said, "In Jerusalem I will put My name." 5 He built altars for all the host of heaven in the two courts of the house of the LORD. 6 He made his son pass through the fire, was conjuring and seeking omens, and dealt with mediums and soothsayers. He did much evil in the sight of the LORD, provoking Him to anger.

7 He put a carved image of Asherah that he had made in the house of which the LORD said to David and to Solomon his son, "In this house and in Jerusalem, which I have chosen out of all tribes of Israel, I will put My name forever. 8 I will not make the feet of Israel to wander homeless from the land that I gave to their fathers, if only they will be careful to do according to all that I have commanded them and according to all the law that My servant Moses commanded them." 9 But they did not listen. Manasseh led them to do more evil than the nations whom the LORD had destroyed before the children of Israel.

10 The LORD spoke by His servants the prophets, saying, 11 "Because Manasseh king of Judah has done these abominations, things more evil than all that the Amorites did, and has also caused Judah to sin with his idols, 12 therefore thus says the LORD God of Israel: I am bringing evil on Jerusalem and Judah, such evil that the ears of whoever hears about it will tingle. 13 I will stretch over Jerusalem the measuring line of Samaria and the level of the house of Ahab, and I will wipe out Jerusalem as one wipes out a bowl, wiping it and turning it upside down. 14 I will disregard the remnant of My inheritance and give them into the hand of their enemies. They shall become plunder and spoil for all their enemies, 15 because they have done evil in My sight and have provoked Me to anger, since the day their fathers came out of Egypt, even to this day."

16 Moreover, Manasseh shed innocent blood
very much, until he had filled Jerusalem from
one end to the other; besides his sin he caused
Judah to sin by doing evil in the sight of the
LORD.

17 Now the rest of the deeds of Manasseh, all
that he did, and his sin that he committed, are
they not written in the book of the annals of
the kings of Judah? 18 Manasseh slept with his
fathers, and was buried in the garden of his
house, in the garden of Uzza. Amon his son
reigned in his place.

Amon, King of Judah
2Ch 33:21–25

19 Amon was twenty-two years old when he
became king. He reigned two years in Jerusa-
lem. His mother's name was Meshullemeth,
daughter of Haruz of Jotbah. 20 He did evil in
the sight of the LORD, as his father Manasseh
had done. 21 He walked in all the ways that his
father walked, served the idols that his father
served, and worshipped them. 22 He aban-
doned the LORD God of his fathers, and he did
not walk in the way of the LORD.

23 The servants of Amon conspired against
him and killed the king in his house. 24 But the
people of the land struck all those who con-
spired against King Amon, and the people of
the land made Josiah his son king in his place.

25 Now the rest of the deeds of Amon that
he did, are they not written in the book of the
annals of the kings of Judah? 26 And he was
buried in his tomb in the garden of Uzza, and
Josiah his son reigned in his place.

Josiah, King of Judah
2Ch 34:1–28

22 Josiah was eight years old when he be-
came king, and he reigned thirty-one
years in Jerusalem. His mother's name was
Jedidah daughter of Adaiah from Bozkath. 2 He
did what was right in the sight of the LORD
and walked in all the ways of David his father.
He did not turn aside to the right hand or to
the left.

The Book of the Law Found

3 In the eighteenth year of King Josiah the
king sent Shaphan son of Azaliah, son of Me-
shullam, the scribe, to the house of the LORD,
saying, 4 "Go up to Hilkiah the high priest, and
have him prepare the money that has been
brought to the house of the LORD, which the
keepers of the threshold have gathered from
the people. 5 Let them deliver it to the hand
of the appointed workers of the house of the
LORD, and let them give it to the workers who
are in the house of the LORD to repair the dam-
ages to the house, 6 that is, to the carpenters,
the builders, and the masons to buy timber and
cut stone to repair the house. 7 But there need
be no settling of accounts with them concern-
ing the money that was given to their hand,
because they are behaving honestly."

8 Hilkiah the high priest said to Shaphan the
scribe, "I have found the Book of the Law in
the house of the LORD." Hilkiah gave the book
to Shaphan, and he read it. 9 Then Shaphan the
scribe came to the king and brought the king
a report. He said, "Your servants have emptied
the money that was found in the house and
have given it into the hand of the appointed
workers of the house of the LORD." 10 Shaphan
the scribe informed the king, saying, "Hilkiah
the priest has given me a book." So Shaphan
read it before the king.

11 When the king had heard the words of the
Book of the Law, he tore his clothes. 12 Then
the king commanded Hilkiah the priest,
Ahikam son of Shaphan, Akbor son of Mic-
aiah, Shaphan the scribe, and Asaiah, a servant
of the king, saying, 13 "Go, inquire of the LORD
for me, for the people, and for all Judah con-
cerning the words of this book that has been
found, for great is the wrath of the LORD that is
kindled against us, because our fathers have
not obeyed the words of this book by doing
according to all that is written concerning us."

14 So Hilkiah the priest, Ahikam, Akbor,
Shaphan, and Asaiah went to Huldah the
prophetess, wife of Shallum, son of Tikvah,
son of Harhas, keeper of the wardrobe (she
lived in Jerusalem in the second quarter), and
they spoke with her.

15 She said to them, "Thus says the LORD God
of Israel: Tell the man that sent you to Me,
16 Thus says the LORD: See, I will bring evil on
this place and on its inhabitants—all the words
of the book that the king of Judah has read.
17 Because they have forsaken Me and have
made offerings to other gods, so that they have
provoked Me to anger with all the works of
their hands, therefore My wrath will be kindled
against this place, and it will not be quenched.
18 But to the king of Judah who sent you to
inquire of the LORD, thus shall you say to him,
"Thus says the LORD God of Israel with regard
to the words you have heard: 19 Because your
heart was timid, and you humbled yourself
before the LORD when you heard what I spoke
against this place and against its inhabitants,
that they should become a desolation and a
curse, and you have torn your clothes and wept
before Me, I also have heard you, declares the
LORD. 20 Therefore, I will gather you to your fa-
thers, and you will be gathered to your grave in
peace. Your eyes will not see all the evil which
I am about to bring upon this place."

Then they brought the king a report.

21:16 2Ki 21:11
21:18 2Ch 33:20
21:22 1Ki 11:33
21:23 2Ki 12:20
21:24 2Ki 14:5
22:1 Jos 15:39
22:2 Dt 5:32
22:4 2Ki 12:4
22:5 2Ki 12:11–14
22:7 2Ki 12:15
22:8 Dt 31:24–26
22:12 Jer 26:24
22:14 2Ch 34:22
22:19 1Ki 21:29

Josiah Renews the Covenant

2Ch 34:3–33; 35:1–36:1

23 Then the king sent them away and
they gathered all the elders of Ju-
dah and Jerusalem to him. [2] The king went
up to the house of the LORD, and all the men
of Judah and all the inhabitants of Jerusalem
with him, the priests, the prophets, and all
the people, both small and great. He read in
their hearing all the words of the Book of the
Covenant that was found in the house of the
LORD. [3] The king stood by a pillar and made a
covenant before the LORD to follow the LORD,
to keep His commandments, His testimonies,
and His statutes with all his heart and all his
soul, to perform the words of this covenant
that were written in this book. All the people
agreed with the covenant.

[4] The king commanded Hilkiah the high
priest, the priests of the second order, and
the keepers of the threshold to bring out of
the temple of the LORD all the implements that
were made for Baal, for Asherah, and for all
the host of heaven. Then he burned them out-
side Jerusalem in the fields of Kidron and car-
ried their ashes to Bethel. [5] Then he removed
the idolatrous priests whom the kings of Judah
had ordained to burn incense on the high plac-
es at the cities of Judah and around Jerusalem;
those also who burned incense to Baal, to the
sun, to the moon, to the constellations, and
to all the host of heaven. [6] He brought out the
Asherah from the house of the LORD to the out-
side of Jerusalem, to the Kidron Valley. Then
he burned it at the Kidron Valley, crushed it
to dust, and threw its dust upon the graves of
the people. [7] He tore down the houses of the
male cult prostitutes that were in the house
of the LORD, where the women were weaving
hangings for the Asherah.

[8] He brought all the priests out of the cities
of Judah and defiled the high places where
the priests had made offerings, from Geba to
Beersheba. He broke down the high places of
the gates at the entry of the gates of Joshua
the governor of the city, which were on the left
at the gate of the city. [9] However the priests of
the high places did not go up to the altar of
the LORD in Jerusalem. Instead they ate unleav-
ened bread among their fellow priests.

[10] He defiled Topheth, which is in the Valley
of Ben Hinnom, so that no man would make
his son or his daughter pass through the fire
to Molek. [11] He removed the horses that the
kings of Judah had given to the sun, at the
entry of the house of the LORD, by the hall of
Nathan-Melek the eunuch, which was in the
vestibule. The chariots of the sun he burned
with fire.

23:2 2Ki 22:8
23:3 2Ki 11:14
23:4 2Ki 21:3
23:6 2Ch 34:4
23:7 1Ki 14:24
23:8 1Ki 15:22
23:9 Eze 44:10–14
23:10 Isa 30:33

23:12 2Ki 21:5
23:13 1Ki 11:5
23:14 Ex 23:24
23:17 1Ki 13:1
23:18 1Ki 13:31
23:19 2Ch 34:6–7
23:20 2Ki 11:18

[12] The altars that were on the roof of the up-
per chamber of Ahaz, which the kings of Ju-
dah had made, and the altars which Manasseh
had made in the two courts of the house of the
LORD the king tore down and banished from
there and threw their dust into the Kidron Val-
ley. [13] The high places east of Jerusalem, south
of the Mount of Corruption, which Solomon
the king of Israel had built for Ashtoreth the
abomination of the Sidonians, for Chemosh
the abomination of the Moabites, and for
Molek the abomination of the Ammonites, the
king defiled. [14] He broke the standing stones,
cut down the Asherah poles, and filled their
sites with human bones.

[15] Moreover, the altar that was at Bethel and
the high place which Jeroboam the son of Ne-
bat, who made Israel sin, had made, both that
altar and the high place he tore down. Then he
burned the high place and crushed it to pow-
der, and he burned the Asherah. [16] As Josiah
turned, he saw the tombs that were there on
the mount. He took the bones out of the tombs
and burned them on the altar and defiled it,
according to the word of the LORD that the man
of God proclaimed, the one who announced
these things.

[17] Then he said, "What is this monument that
I see?"

The men of the city said to him, "It is the
tomb of the man of God who came from Ju-
dah and proclaimed these things that you have
done against the altar of Bethel."

[18] He said, "Let him rest. No one shall dis-
turb his bones." So they let his bones alone,
with the bones of the prophet who came out
of Samaria.

Let all high places established by any ungodly ruler be removed in the name of Jesus (2Ki 23:19).

[19] Moreover, all the houses of the high places
that were in the cities of Samaria, which the
kings of Israel had made to provoke the LORD
to anger, Josiah removed. He did to them just
as he had done in Bethel. [20] He slaughtered on
the altars all the priests of the high places who
were there, and burned human bones on them.
Then he returned to Jerusalem.

[21] The king commanded all the people, "Keep
the Passover to the LORD your God as it is writ-
ten in this Book of the Covenant." [22] For such
a Passover had not been kept from the days
of the judges who judged Israel, nor in all the
days of the kings of Israel and the kings of
Judah. [23] But in the eighteenth year of King

Josiah, this Passover was kept to the LORD in
Jerusalem.
24 Moreover, Josiah disposed of the mediums,
the soothsayers, the teraphim, the idols, and all
the abominations that were seen in the land of
Judah and in Jerusalem, so that he established
the words of the law that were written in the
book that Hilkiah the priest found in the house
of the LORD. 25 Now there had been no king like
him before or after, who turned to the LORD
with all his heart, with all his soul, and with all
his might, according to all the Law of Moses.
26 However, the LORD did not turn from the
fierceness of His great wrath, by which His
anger was kindled against Judah, because of
all the provocations with which Manasseh had
provoked Him. 27 The LORD said, "I will also
remove Judah from before Me, as I have re-
moved Israel. I will reject this city that I have
chosen, Jerusalem, and the house of which I
said, My name shall be there."

Josiah Dies in Battle

28 Now the rest of the deeds of Josiah, and all
that he did, are they not written in the book of
the annals of the kings of Judah?
29 In his days Pharaoh Necho, king of Egypt,
went up against the king of Assyria to the River
Euphrates. King Josiah went to meet him, but
he killed him at Megiddo when he had seen
him. 30 His servants carried him dead in a char-
iot from Megiddo, brought him to Jerusalem,
and buried him in his own tomb. The people
of the land took Jehoahaz the son of Josiah,
anointed him, and made him king in place of
his father.

Jehoahaz, King of Judah

2Ch 36:2–4

31 Jehoahaz was twenty-three years old when
he became king, and he reigned three months
in Jerusalem. His mother's name was Hamu-
tal daughter of Jeremiah of Libnah. 32 He did
evil in the sight of the LORD, according to all
that his fathers had done. 33 Pharaoh Necho
imprisoned him at Riblah in the land of Ha-
math, so that he might not reign in Jerusalem,
and imposed tribute on the land of a hundred
talents[1] of silver and a talent[2] of gold. 34 Pha-
raoh Necho made Eliakim son of Josiah king
in place of Josiah his father and changed his
name to Jehoiakim. He took Jehoahaz away
and went to Egypt, and he died there. 35 Je-
hoiakim gave the silver and gold to Pharaoh,
but he taxed the land to give the money ac-
cording to Pharaoh's demand. According to
an assessed amount, he exacted the silver and
gold from the people of the land to give to
Pharaoh Necho.

Jehoiakim, King of Judah

2Ch 36:5–8

36 Jehoiakim was twenty-five years old when
he became king. He reigned eleven years in
Jerusalem. His mother's name was Zebidah
daughter of Pedaiah of Rumah. 37 He did evil
in the sight of the LORD, according to all that
his fathers had done.

Judah Overrun by Enemies

24 In his days Nebuchadnezzar king
of Babylon came up, and Jehoiakim
became his servant for three years. Then he
turned and rebelled against him. 2 The LORD
sent against him bands of Chaldeans, bands
of Arameans, bands of Moabites, and bands
of Ammonites. He sent them against Judah to
destroy it, according to the word of the LORD
that He spoke by His servants the prophets.
3 Surely at the decree of the LORD this came
upon Judah, to remove them from before Him,
for the sins of Manasseh, according to all that
he had done, 4 and also for the innocent blood
that he had shed, for he filled Jerusalem with
innocent blood, and the LORD was not willing
to pardon.
5 Now the rest of the deeds of Jehoiakim and
all that he did, are they not written in the book
of the annals of the kings of Judah? 6 So Je-
hoiakim slept with his fathers, and Jehoiachin
his son reigned in his place.
7 The king of Egypt did not come again from
his land, for the king of Babylon had taken
over from the Brook of Egypt to the River Eu-
phrates all that belonged to the king of Egypt.

Jehoiachin, King of Judah

2Ch 36:9–10

8 Jehoiachin was eighteen years old when he
became king. He reigned in Jerusalem three
months. His mother's name was Nehushta
daughter of Elnathan of Jerusalem. 9 He did
evil in the sight of the LORD, according to all
that his father had done.
10 At that time the servants of Nebuchadnez-
zar king of Babylon came up against Jerusa-
lem, and the city was under siege. 11 Nebu-
chadnezzar king of Babylon came up to the
city while his servants were besieging it, 12 and
Jehoiachin king of Judah went out to the king
of Babylon, he, his mother, his servants, his
princes, and his eunuchs. The king of Babylon
took him in the eighth year of his reign.

The Captivity of Jerusalem

13 He brought out from there all the treasures
of the house of the LORD and the treasures of
the king's house, and cut in pieces all the

23:24 Lev 19:31
23:25 2Ki 18:5
23:27 2Ki 18:11
23:29 Jer 46:2
23:30 2Ki 9:28
23:31 2Ki 24:18
23:33 1Ki 8:65
23:34 Eze 19:3–4

23:36 2Ch 36:5
24:1 Jer 25:1
24:2 Jer 35:11
24:3 2Ki 18:25
24:4 2Ki 21:16
24:6 Jer 22:18–19
24:7 Jer 37:5–7
24:8 1Ch 3:16
24:12 Jer 24:1
24:13 2Ki 20:17

[1] *33* About 3¾ tons, or 3.4 metric tons. [2] *33* About 75 pounds, or 34 kilograms.

implements of gold in the temple of the LORD,
which Solomon king of Israel had made, just
as the LORD had spoken. 14 He exiled all Je-
rusalem, all the princes, and all the mighty
men of valor, ten thousand captives, and all
the craftsmen and smiths. No one remained,
except the poorest people of the land.

15 He exiled Jehoiachin in Babylon. The king's
mother, the king's wives, his eunuchs, and the
elite of the land he took into exile from Jerusa-
lem to Babylon. 16 All the fighting men, seven
thousand, the craftsmen and smiths, one thou-
sand, all those strong and fit for war the king
of Babylon brought them into exile in Baby-
lon. 17 The king of Babylon made Mattaniah,
the uncle of Jehoiachin, king in his place and
changed his name to Zedekiah.

Zedekiah, King of Judah

2Ch 36:11–16; Jer 52:1–3

18 Zedekiah was twenty-one years old when
he became king. He reigned eleven years in
Jerusalem. His mother's name was Hamutal
daughter of Jeremiah of Libnah. 19 He did evil
in the sight of the LORD, according to all that
Jehoiakim had done. 20 Because of the anger
of the LORD this happened in Jerusalem and
Judah until He threw them out from His pres-
ence. But Zedekiah rebelled against the king
of Babylon.

The Fall and Exile of Judah

Jer 39:1–10; 40:7–9; 41:1–18; 52:4–27; 2Ch 36:17–20

25 In the ninth year of his reign, in the
tenth month, on the tenth day of the
month, Nebuchadnezzar king of Babylon
came, he and all his army, against Jerusa-
lem, and set up camp near it. They built siege
mounds against it all around. 2 The city came
under siege until the eleventh year of King Ze-
dekiah. 3 On the ninth day of the fourth month
the famine was severe in the city, and there
was no food for the people of the land. 4 The
city was breached, and all the fighting men
fled by night by the way of the gate between
the two walls, which is by the king's garden,
though the Chaldeans were all around the city.
They went along the way of the Arabah. 5 Then
the army of the Chaldeans pursued the king
and overtook him in the plains of Jericho. All
his army deserted him. 6 So they captured the
king and brought him up to the king of Baby-
lon at Riblah, and they passed sentence upon
him. 7 They slaughtered the sons of Zedekiah
before his eyes, and put out the eyes of Zedeki-
ah. They bound him with bronze fetters and
brought him to Babylon.

8 In the fifth month, on the seventh day of the
month (that was the nineteenth year of King
Nebuchadnezzar, king of Babylon), Nebuzara-
dan, the captain of the bodyguard, a servant
of the king of Babylon, came to Jerusalem.
9 He burned the house of the LORD, the king's
house, and all the houses of Jerusalem. Every
great house he burned with fire. 10 All the army
of the Chaldeans who were with the captain
of the guard tore down the walls of Jerusa-
lem all around. 11 The rest of the people who
remained in the city, the deserters who had
defected to the king of Babylon, and the rest
of the crowd Nebuzaradan the captain of the
bodyguard took into exile. 12 But the captain
of the bodyguard left some of the poor of the
land to be vinedressers and farmers.

13 The bronze pillars that were in the house
of the LORD, the stands, and the bronze sea that
were in the house of the LORD the Chaldeans
broke in pieces, and carried their bronze to
Babylon. 14 The pots, the shovels, the snuffers,
the incense bowls, and all the bronze imple-
ments which were used in service they took
away. 15 The fire pans and sprinkling basins
that were fine gold and fine silver the captain
of the bodyguard took.

16 The two pillars, the one sea, and the stands,
which Solomon had made for the house of the
LORD—the bronze of all these implements was
beyond weight. 17 The height of the one pil-
lar was eighteen cubits,[1] and a bronze capital
was on it. The height of the capital was three
cubits.[2] Latticework and pomegranates, all of
bronze, were on the capital all around. The
second pillar with its latticework was like it.

18 The captain of the bodyguard took Seraiah
the chief priest, Zephaniah the second priest,
and the three keepers of the threshold. 19 From
the city he took a eunuch who was an officer
over the fighting men, five men of the king's
council who were found in the city, the chief
scribe of the army who mustered the people
of the land, and sixty men from the people of
the land who were found in the city. 20 Nebu-
zaradan captain of the bodyguard took them,
and brought them to the king of Babylon at
Riblah. 21 Then the king of Babylon struck
them down and killed them at Riblah in the
land of Hamath.

Thus he exiled Judah from their land.

Gedaliah, Governor of Judah

22 Over the people who remained in the land
of Judah, whom Nebuchadnezzar king of Bab-
ylon had left, he appointed Gedaliah the son of
Ahikam, the son of Shaphan. 23 When all the
captains of the armies, they and their men,
heard that the king of Babylon had appointed
Gedaliah, they came to Gedaliah at Mizpah,
that is, Ishmael son of Nethaniah, Johanan

24:14 2Ki 25:12
24:15 2Ch 36:10
24:17 Jer 37:1
24:18 2Ki 23:31
24:19 2Ki 23:37
25:4 Eze 33:21
25:6 2Ki 23:33
25:9 Am 2:5
25:10 Ne 1:3
25:12 2Ki 24:14
25:13 1Ki 7:15
25:14 Ex 27:3
25:16 1Ki 7:47
25:18 1Ch 6:14
25:19 Est 1:14
25:21 Dt 28:64
25:22 Jer 39:14
25:23 Jer 40:7–9

[1] *17* About 27 feet, or 8.1 *meters.* [2] *17* About 4½ feet, or 1.4 meters.

son of Kareah, Seraiah son of Tanhumeth
the Netophathite, and Jaazaniah son of the
Maakathite, they and their men. 24 Gedaliah
swore to them and to their men, and said to
them, "Do not be afraid of being the servants
of the Chaldeans. Live in the land and serve the
king of Babylon, and it will go well for you."
25 But in the seventh month, Ishmael the son
of Nethaniah, the son of Elishama, of the roy-
al line, came with ten men and struck down
Gedaliah. He died along with the Judeans
and Chaldeans who were with him at Mizpah.
26 Then all the people, both small and great,
and the captains of the armies arose and went
to Egypt, for they were afraid of the Chaldeans.

25:26 Jer 43:4–7

25:27 Jer 52:31–34
25:29 2Sa 9:7

Jehoiachin Released from Prison
Jer 52:31–34

27 In the thirty-seventh year of the exile of Je-
hoiachin king of Judah, in the twelfth month,
on the twenty-seventh day of the month, Aw-
el-Marduk king of Babylon, in the year that
he became king, released Jehoiachin king of
Judah from prison. 28 He spoke kindly to him,
and gave him a throne above the thrones of
the kings that were with him in Babylon. 29 He
changed his prison garments, and he ate food
continually before him all the days of his life.
30 His allowance was a regular allowance giv-
en him by the king every day, all the days of
his life.

Author: Traditionally Ezra

Written: Between 450 and 425 BC

Themes: Genealogy, History of Israel

1 Chronicles

Dear SpiritLed Woman,

Patience is a virtue—one that we all struggle to achieve. We receive promises from the Lord, and we desire to see the outcomes instantly—especially now when technology has made so many things achievable within seconds. However, we must remember that God's promises are honored on His timing, not ours.

God promised Eve that the Savior for mankind would descend from her lineage. But Eve did not see that promise come to pass; hundreds of years passed before Christ was born. Follow the lineage of Christ through the centuries. Ruth was his ancestor. Had it not been for her promise to remain by her mother-in-law's side, she would never have met Boaz. If Rahab had not followed the instructions of the men whom she hid from the king of Jericho, she would have been destroyed. As a SpiritLed woman, you must remain confident in your promises from God and immersed in His Word.

Joy F. Strang

The Generations From Adam to Abraham

1 Adam, Seth, Enosh; 2 Kenan, Mahalalel,
Jared; 3 Enoch, Methuselah, Lamech;

4 Noah,
Shem, Ham, and Japheth.

Japhethites
Ge 10:2–5

5 The sons of Japheth *were*
Gomer, Magog, Madai, Javan, Tubal,
Meshek, and Tiras.
6 The sons of Gomer *were*
Ashkenaz, Riphath, and Togarmah.
7 The sons of Javan *were*
Elishah, Tarshish, the Kittites, and the
Rodanites.

Hamites
Ge 10:6–20

8 The sons of Ham *were*
Cush, Egypt, Put, and Canaan.
9 The sons of Cush *were*
Seba, Havilah, Sabta, Raamah, and
Sabteka.
The sons of Raamah *were*
Sheba and Dedan.
10 Cush became the father of
Nimrod, who began to be mighty on the
earth.
11 Egypt became the father of
the Ludites, Anamites, Lehabites, and
Naphtuhites, 12 Pathrusites, Kasluhites
(from whom came the Philistines), and
the Caphtorites.
13 Canaan became the father of
Sidon, his firstborn, and Heth 14 and the
Jebusites, the Amorites, the Girgashites,
15 the Hivites, the Arkites, the Sinites,
16 the Arvadites, the Zemarites, and the
Hamathites.

Semites
Ge 10:21–31; 11:10–27

17 The sons of Shem *were*
Elam, Ashur, Arphaxad, Lud, Aram,
Uz, Hul, Gether, and Meshek.
18 Arphaxad became the father of Shelah,
and Shelah became the father of Eber.
19 Two sons were born to Eber:
The name of one *was* Peleg, for in his
days the earth was divided, and the
name of his brother *was* Joktan.
20 Joktan became the father of
Almodad, Sheleph, Hazarmaveth, and
Jerah, 21 Hadoram, Uzal, and Diklah,
22 Ebal, Abimael, Sheba, 23 Ophir, Havilah,
and Jobab. All these *were* the sons of
Joktan.

24 Shem, Arphaxad, Shelah,
25 Eber, Peleg, Reu,
26 Serug, Nahor, Terah,
27 and Abram, who is Abraham.

The Generations of Abraham

28 The sons of Abraham *were*
Isaac and Ishmael.

Descendants of Hagar
Ge 25:12–16

29 These *are* their generations:
The firstborn of Ishmael *was* Nebaioth,
then Kedar, Adbeel, Mibsam, 30 Mishma,
Dumah, Massa, Hadad, Tema, 31 Jetur,
Naphish, and Kedemah. These *were* the
sons of Ishmael.

Descendants of Keturah
Ge 25:1–4

32 The sons of Keturah, Abraham's concubine:
She bore Zimran, Jokshan, Medan, Midian, Ishbak, and Shuah.
The sons of Jokshan *were*
Sheba and Dedan.
33 The sons of Midian *were*
Ephah, Epher, Hanok, Abida, and
Eldaah.
All these *were* the sons of Keturah.

Descendants of Sarah
Ge 36:10–14

34 Abraham *also* became the father of Isaac.
The sons of Isaac *were*
Esau and Israel.
35 The sons of Esau *were*
Eliphaz, Reuel, Jeush, Jalam, and Korah.
36 The sons of Eliphaz *were*
Teman, Omar, Zephi, Gatam, Kenaz,
Timna, and Amalek.
37 The sons of Reuel *were*
Nahath, Zerah, Shammah, and Mizzah.

Descendants of Esau in Edom
Ge 36:20–43

38 The sons of Seir *were*
Lotan, Shobal, Zibeon, Anah, Dishon,
Ezer, and Dishan.
39 The sons of Lotan *were*
Hori and Homam; the sister of Lotan *was*
Timna.
40 The sons of Shobal *were*
Alian, Manahath, Ebal, Shepho, and
Onam.
The sons of Zibeon *were*
Aiah and Anah.
41 The son of Anah *was*
Dishon.
The sons of Dishon *were*
Hamran, Eshban, Ithran, and Keran.
42 The sons of Ezer *were*
Bilhan, Zaavan, and Jaakan.

1:1 Lk 3:38
1:2 Lk 3:37
1:4 Ge 5:32
1:14 Ge 15:21
1:24 Ge 11:10–26
1:25 Lk 3:35
1:32 Ge 25:1–4
1:34 Ge 32:28
1:35 Ge 36:4–5

The sons of Dishan *were*
Uz and Aran.
43 These *are* the kings who reigned in the
land of Edom before *any* king reigned
over the children of Israel:
Bela the son of Beor (the name of his city
was Dinhabah).
44 When Bela died, Jobab the son of Zerah
from Bozrah reigned in his place.
45 When Jobab died, Husham from the land
of the Temanites reigned in his place.
46 When Husham died, Hadad the son of
Bedad, the one who struck Midian in the
open field of Moab, reigned in his place
(the name of his city *was* Avith).
47 When Hadad died, Samlah from Mas-
rekah reigned in his place.
48 When Samlah died, Shaul from Rehoboth
on the River reigned in his place.
49 When Shaul died, Baal-Hanan the son of
Akbor reigned in his place.
50 When Baal-Hanan died, Hadad reigned
in his place (the name of his city *was* Pai,
and the name of his wife *was* Mehetabel,
the daughter of Matred, the daughter of
Me-Zahab). 51 Then Hadad died.

The tribal chiefs of Edom *were*
Chief Timnah, Chief Alvah, Chief Jetheth,
52 Chief Oholibamah, Chief Elah, Chief
Pinon, 53 Chief Kenaz, Chief Teman,
Chief Mibzar, 54 Chief Magdiel, and Chief
Iram. These *were* the chiefs of Edom.

Sons of Israel
Ge 35:23–26; Ru 4:18–22; Mt 1:3–6

2 These *are* the sons of Israel:
Reuben, Simeon, Levi, Judah, Issachar,
Zebulun, 2 Dan, Joseph, Benjamin, Naph-
tali, Gad, and Asher.

From Judah to David
3 The sons of Judah *were*
Er, Onan, and Shelah: *These* three were
born to him by the daughter of Shua the
Canaanitess. Now Er, the firstborn of
Judah, was evil in the sight of the LORD,
and He put him to death. 4 Then Tamar
his daughter-in-law bore Perez and Zer-
ah for him. In all, Judah had five sons.
5 The sons of Perez *were*
Hezron and Hamul.
6 The sons of Zerah *were*
Zimri, Ethan, Heman, Kalkol, and Dara,
five of them in all.
7 The sons of Karmi *were*
Achar, the troubler of Israel, who acted
unfaithfully in regard to the ban.
8 The son of Ethan *was*
Azariah.

1:44 Isa 34:6
1:50 Ge 36:39
2:3 Ge 38:2–10
2:4 Mt 1:3
2:5 Ge 46:12
2:7 Jos 6:18

2:10 Mt 1:4
2:11 Ru 4:21
2:13 1Sa 17:13
2:17 2Sa 17:25
2:19 1Ch 2:50
2:20 Ex 31:2
2:21 Nu 27:1
2:24 1Ch 4:5

9 Now the sons of Hezron, who were born
to him, *were*
Jerahmeel, Ram, and Kelubai.

Sons of Ram
10 Ram became the father of
Amminadab, and Amminadab became
the father of Nahshon, a leader of the
sons of Judah. 11 Nahshon became the
father of Salma, and Salma became the
father of Boaz. 12 Boaz became the father
of Obed, and Obed became the father of
Jesse.
13 Now Jesse became the father of
his firstborn Eliab, and Abinadab the
second, and Shimea the third, 14 Nethanel
the fourth, Raddai the fifth, 15 Ozem the
sixth, David the seventh; 16 their sisters
were Zeruiah and Abigail. The sons of
Zeruiah *were* Abishai, Joab, and Asahel,
three *in all*. 17 Abigail bore Amasa: the fa-
ther of Amasa was Jether the Ishmaelite.

Sons of Caleb
18 Caleb the son of Hezron had *children* with
his wife Azubah and with Jerioth. These
are her sons: Jesher, Shobab, and Ardon.
19 Now Azubah died, and Caleb took
Ephrath *as a wife*. She bore Hur for him.
20 Hur became the father of Uri, and Uri
became the father of Bezalel.
21 Afterward Hezron had relations with the
daughter of Makir, the father of Gilead,
whom he took *as a wife* when he was
sixty years old, and she bore Segub
for him. 22 Segub became the father of
Jair, who had twenty-three cities in the
land of Gilead. 23 He took Geshur and
Aram, the towns of Jair, from them, with
Kenath and its villages, sixty towns. All
these were descendants of Makir, the
father of Gilead.
24 After the death of Hezron in Caleb Ephra-
thah, Hezron's wife Abijah bore him
Ashhur the father of Tekoa.

Sons of Jerahmeel
25 Now the sons of Jerahmeel the firstborn
of Hezron were
Ram the firstborn, Bunah, Oren, Ozem,
and Ahijah. 26 Jerahmeel also had anoth-
er wife. Her name was Atarah, and she
was the mother of Onam.
27 The sons of Ram the firstborn of Je-
rahmeel were
Maaz, Jamin, and Eker.
28 The sons of Onam were
Shammai and Jada.
And the sons of Shammai *were*
Nadab and Abishur.

29 The name of the wife of Abishur *was* Abi-
hail. She bore him Ahban and Molid.
30 The sons of Nadab *were*
Seled and Appaim, but Seled died with-
out children.
31 The son of Appaim *was*
Ishi. The son of Ishi *was* Sheshan,
and the son of Sheshan *was* Ahlai.
32 The sons of Jada the brother of Shammai
were
Jether and Jonathan, but Jether died
without children.
33 The sons of Jonathan *were*
Peleth and Zaza.
These were the sons of Jerahmeel.
34 Now Sheshan had no children except
daughters,
but he did have a servant, an Egyptian,
whose name *was* Jarha. 35 Sheshan gave
one of his daughters to Jarha his servant
as a wife, and she bore him Attai.
36 Attai became the father of Nathan,
and Nathan became the father of Zabad.
37 Zabad became the father of Ephlal,
and Ephlal became the father of Obed.
38 Obed became the father of Jehu,
and Jehu became the father of Azariah.
39 Azariah became the father of Helez,
and Helez became the father of Eleasah.
40 Eleasah became the father of Sismai,
and Sismai became the father of Shal-
lum.
41 Shallum became the father of Jeka-
miah,
and Jekamiah became the father of
Elishama.

Caleb's Clans

42 Now the sons of Caleb the brother of
Jerahmeel *were*
Mesha his firstborn, who was the father
of Ziph, and the sons of Mareshah the
father of Hebron.
43 The sons of Hebron *were*
Korah, Tappuah, Rekem, and Shema.
44 Shema became the father of Raham,
the father of Jorkeam, and Rekem be-
came the father of Shammai. 45 The son
of Shammai was Maon, and Maon was
the father of Beth Zur.
46 Ephah, Caleb's concubine, bore Haran,
Moza, and Gazez, and Haran became the
father of Gazez.
47 The sons of Jahdai *were*
Regem, Jotham, Geshan, Pelet, Ephah,
and Shaaph.
48 Maakah, Caleb's concubine, bore Sheber
and Tirhanah. 49 She also bore Shaaph
the father of Madmannah, Sheva the
father of Makbenah, and the father of
Gibea. The daughter of Caleb was Aksah.
50 These were the sons of Caleb the son of
Hur, the firstborn of Ephrathah:
Shobal the father of Kiriath Jearim, 51 Sal-
ma the father of Bethlehem, and Hareph
the father of Beth Gader.
52 Now sons were *born* to Shobal the father
of Kiriath Jearim:
Haroeh *and* half of the Manahathites.
53 The families of Kiriath Jearim *were* the
Ithrites, the Puthites, the Shumathites,
and the Mishraites. From these the
Zorathites and the Eshtaolites went forth.
54 The sons of Salma *were*
Bethlehem, the Netophathites, Atroth
Beth Joab, and half of the Manahathites,
the Zorites. 55 The families of the scribes
who lived at Jabez *were* the Tirathites,
the Shimeathites, *and* the Sucathites.
They are the Kenites who came from
Hammath, the father of the house of
Rekab.

2:36 1Ch 11:41
2:55 Jdg 1:16
3:1 2Sa 3:2–5
3:4 2Sa 2:11
3:5 2Sa 11:3
3:8 1Ch 14:7
3:10 1Ki 11:43
3:11 2Ki 8:24

The Generations of David

2Sa 3:2–5; 5:14–16; 1Ch 14:4–7

3 Now these were the sons of David, who
were born to him in Hebron:
The firstborn *was* Amnon by Ahinoam
the Jezreelitess;
the second, Daniel by Abigail the Car-
melitess;
2 the third *was* Absalom the son of
Maakah, the daughter of Talmai king of
Geshur;
the fourth, Adonijah the son of Haggith;
3 the fifth, Shephatiah by Abital;
the sixth, Ithream by Eglah his wife.
4 Six *sons* were born to him in Hebron,
and he reigned there seven years and six
months.
He also reigned thirty-three years in Jerusalem.
5 Now these were born to him in Jerusalem:
Shimea, Shobab, Nathan, and Solomon,
four sons by Bathsheba the daughter of
Ammiel; 6 then Ibhar, Elishama, Eliphelet,
7 Nogah, Nepheg, Japhia, 8 Elishama,
Eliada, and Eliphelet, nine. 9 These *were*
all the sons of David, besides the sons of
the concubines, and Tamar their sister.

The Kings of Judah

10 Solomon's son *was* Rehoboam;
Abijah *was* his son,
Asa his son,
Jehoshaphat his son,
11 Joram[1] his son,
Ahaziah his son,
Joash his son,

[1] 11 *Jehoram* in 2Ki 1:17; 8:16.

12 Amaziah his son,
Azariah his son,
Jotham his son,
13 Ahaz his son,
Hezekiah his son,
Manasseh his son,
14 Amon his son,
and Josiah his son.
15 The sons of Josiah *were*
the firstborn Johanan,
the second Jehoiakim,
the third Zedekiah,
and the fourth Shallum.
16 The sons of Jehoiakim *were*
Jeconiah his son
and Zedekiah his son.

The Post-Exilic Royal Line

17 The sons of Jeconiah *were* Assir,
Shealtiel his son, 18 Malkiram, Pedaiah,
Shenazzar, Jekamiah, Hoshama, and
Nedabiah.
19 The sons of Pedaiah *were*
Zerubbabel and Shimei,
and the sons of Zerubbabel *were*
Meshullam and Hananiah,
and Shelomith *was* their sister;
20 and Hashubah, Ohel, Berekiah, Hasadiah, *and* Jushab-Hesed, five.
21 The sons of Hananiah *were*
Pelatiah and Jeshaiah, the sons of
Rephaiah, the sons of Arnan, the sons of
Obadiah, and the sons of Shekaniah.
22 The sons of Shekaniah *were*
Shemaiah and the sons of Shemaiah:
Hattush, Igal, Bariah, Neariah, and
Shaphat, six *in all.*
23 The sons of Neariah *were*
Elioenai, Hizkiah, and Azrikam, three *in all.*
24 The sons of Elioenai *were*
Hodaviah, Eliashib, Pelaiah, Akkub, Johanan, Delaiah, and Anani, seven *in all.*

Other Sons of Judah

4 The sons of Judah *were*
Perez, Hezron, Karmi, Hur, and Shobal.
2 Reaiah the son of Shobal became the
father of Jahath, and Jahath became the
father of Ahumai and Lahad. These *are*
the families of the Zorathites.
3 These *were the sons of* the father of Etam:
Jezreel, Ishma, and Idbash. The name
of their sister *was* Hazzelelponi. 4 Penuel
was the father of Gedor, and Ezer *was* the
father of Hushah.
These *were* the sons of Hur, the firstborn of
Ephrathah, the father of Bethlehem.
5 Ashhur the father of Tekoa *had* two wives:
Helah and Naarah.

3:14 2Ki 23:30
3:16 2Ki 24:6
3:17 Ezr 3:2
3:19 Ezr 2:2
3:22 Ezr 8:2
4:1 Ge 46:12
4:4 1Ch 2:50
4:5 1Ch 2:24
4:13 Jos 15:17

6 Naarah bore him Ahuzzam, Hepher,
Temeni, and Haahashtari. These *were* the
sons of Naarah.
7 The sons of Helah *were*
Zereth, Zohar, and Ethnan. 8 Koz became
the father of Anub and Hazzobebah
and the families of Aharhel the son of
Harum.

I am blessed indeed, and my coasts have been enlarged (1Ch 4:10).

9 Now Jabez was more honorable than his
brothers, and his mother called his name
Jabez, saying, “Because I bore *him* in hard-
ship.” 10 Then Jabez called on the God of Israel,
saying, “Oh, that You would indeed bless me
and enlarge my territory, that Your hand might
be with me, and that You would keep *me* from
evil, that *it* may not bring me hardship!” So
God granted what he asked.

I pray that You would keep me from evil (1Ch 4:10).

11 Kelub the brother of Shuhah became the
father of Mehir, who *was* the father of
Eshton. 12 Eshton became the father of
Beth Rapha, Paseah, and Tehinnah the
father of Ir Nahash. These *were* the men
of Rekah.
13 The sons of Kenaz *were*
Othniel and Seraiah,
and the sons of Othniel *were*
Hathath *and Meonothai.* 14 Meonothai
became the father of Ophrah,
and Seraiah became the father of Joab,
the father of Ge Harashim, for they were
craftsmen.
15 The sons of Caleb the son of Jephunneh
were
Iru, Elah, and Naam,
and the son of Elah *was*
Kenaz.
16 The sons of Jehallelel *were*
Ziph, Ziphah, Tiria, and Asarel.
17 The sons of Ezrah *were*
Jether, Mered, Epher, and Jalon, and
Mered's wife bore Miriam, Shammai, and
Ishbah the father of Eshtemoa. 18 His Judean wife bore Jered the father of Gedor,
Heber the father of Soko, and Jekuthiel
the father of Zanoah. So these were the
sons of Bithiah the daughter of Pharaoh,
whom Mered took.

19 The sons of his wife Hodiah, the sister of
Naham, *were*
the father of Keilah the Garmite and
Eshtemoa the Maakathite.
20 The sons of Shimon *were*
Amnon, Rinnah, Ben-Hanan, and Tilon.
And the sons of Ishi *were*
Zoheth and Ben-Zoheth.
21 The sons of Shelah the son of Judah *were*
Er the father of Lekah, Laadah the
father of Mareshah, the families of the
house of workers of fine linen at Beth
Ashbea; 22 Jokim, the men of Kozeba,
Joash, Saraph, who was lord in Moab,
and Jashubi Lehem (these records are
ancient). 23 They *were* the potters, those
dwelling at Netaim and Gederah (they
dwelt there with the king for his work).

Sons of Simeon
Jos 19:2–10

24 The sons of Simeon *were*
Nemuel, Jamin, Jarib, Zerah, Shaul,
25 Shallum his son, Mibsam his son, *and*
Mishma his son.
26 The sons of Mishma *were*
Hammuel his son, Zakkur his son, *and*
Shimei his son.
27 Shimei had sixteen sons and six daugh-
ters, but his brothers did not have many sons,
nor did all their family multiply as much as
the sons of Judah. 28 Now they dwelt in Beer-
sheba, Moladah, and Hazar Shual 29 *as well as*
in Bilhah, Ezem, Tolad, 30 Bethuel, Hormah,
Ziklag, 31 Beth Markaboth, Hazar Susim, Beth
Biri, and Shaaraim. These *were* their cities until
the reign of David. 32 Their villages *were* Etam,
Ain, Rimmon, Token, and Ashan, five cities
in all, 33 and all the villages that *were* around
these cities as far as Baal. Such *are* their inhab-
ited cities, and those registered to them *were*
34 Meshobab, Jamlech, and Joshah the son of
Amaziah; 35 Joel, and Jehu the son of Joshib-
iah, the son of Seraiah, the son of Asiel; 36 El-
ioenai, Jaakobah, Jeshohaiah, Asaiah, Adiel,
Jesimiel, Benaiah; 37 Ziza the son of Shiphi,
the son of Allon, the son of Jedaiah, the son
of Shimri, the son of Shemaiah.
38 These mentioned by name *were* leaders
in their families, and their fathers' houses in-
creased greatly. 39 They went to the entrance
of Gedor, as far as the east side of the valley,
to seek pasture for their flocks. 40 There they
found rich, good pasture, and the land was
wide, quiet, and peaceful; for former inhabi-
tants there belonged to Ham.
41 In the days of Hezekiah king of Judah,
those written by name came and attacked
their tents, *along with* the Meunites who were
found there, and utterly destroyed them until
this day. Then they dwelt there in their place
because *there was* pasture for their flocks there.
42 Now *some* of them, *namely* five hundred men
from the sons of Simeon, went to Mount Seir
with Pelatiah, Neariah, Rephaiah, and Uzziel,
the sons of Ishi, as their captains. 43 *Then* they
struck down the rest of the Amalekites who
had escaped. So they have dwelt there until
this day.

Sons of Reuben

5 Now the sons of Reuben the firstborn of
Israel (for he was the firstborn, but since
he defiled his father's bed, his birthright was
given to the sons of Joseph the son of Israel,
so that the genealogy is not listed according to
the birthright; 2 though Judah prevailed over
his brothers and a ruler came from him, yet
the birthright belonged to Joseph), 3 the sons
of Reuben the firstborn of Israel *were*
Hanok, Pallu, Hezron, and Karmi.
4 The sons of Joel *were*
Shemaiah his son, Gog his son,
Shimei his son, 5 Micah his son,
Reaiah his son, Baal his son,
6 and Beerah his son, whom Tiglath-
Pileser the king of Assyria led into exile.
He was a leader of the Reubenites.
7 His brothers according to their families by
the registration of their generations *were*
Jeiel, the first, and Zechariah; 8 Bela the
son of Azaz, the son of Shema, the son
of Joel, who dwelt in Aroer, even as far
as Nebo and Baal Meon. 9 And he dwelt
toward the east as far as the entrance to
the wilderness from the Euphrates, for
their cattle were abundant in the land of
Gilead.
10 Now in the days of Saul, they made
war with the Hagrites, who fell by
their hand, and they dwelt in their
tents over all the eastern plains of
Gilead.

Sons of Gad

11 The sons of Gad dwelt opposite them in
the land of Bashan as far as Salekah.
12 Joel *was* the first, Shapham the second,
with Janai and Shaphat in Bashan.
13 Their brothers of their father's house *were*
Michael, Meshullam, Sheba, Jorai, Jakan,
Zia, and Eber, seven *in all*.
14 These *are* the sons of Abihail, the son
of Huri, the son of Jaroah, the son of
Gilead, the son of Michael, the son of
Jeshishai, the son of Jahdo, the son of
Buz;
15 Ahi the son of Abdiel, the son of Guni,
was the head of their father's house.

4:21 Ge 38:5
4:24 Ge 46:10
4:40 Jdg 18:7–10
4:43 1Sa 30:17
5:1 Ge 29:32
5:2 Mic 5:2
5:3 Ge 46:9
5:8 Nu 32:34
5:11 Jos 13:11

16 They dwelt in Gilead in Bashan, and in its
towns, and in all the outlands of Sharon
to *the edge of* their borders.
17 All of them were registered *by genealogy* in
the days of Jotham king of Judah and in the
days of Jeroboam king of Israel.
18 The sons of Reuben, and the Gadites, and
the half-tribe of Manasseh *numbered* forty-four
thousand seven hundred and sixty valiant
men, men able to bear shield and sword, to
shoot with a bow, and *who were* skillful in
battle, who went to war. 19 They made war
with the Hagrites, *namely* Jetur, Naphish, and
Nodab. 20 They were helped against them,
and the Hagrites and all who *were* with them
were delivered into their hand, for they cried
to God in the battle, and He heard their prayer
because they trusted in Him. 21 They captured
their livestock: fifty thousand of their camels,
two hundred and fifty thousand sheep, two
thousand donkeys, and one hundred thou-
sand men. 22 So many fell slain, because the
war was of God. And they dwelt in their place
until the exile.

The Half-Tribe of Manasseh

23 The children of the half-tribe of Manasseh
also dwelt in the land. They increased from
Bashan as far as Baal Hermon and Senir, even
to Mount Hermon.
24 These were the heads of their fathers'
houses: Epher, Ishi, Eliel, Azriel, Jeremiah,
Hodaviah, and Jahdiel, mighty men of valor,
men of reputation, *and* heads of their fathers'
houses. 25 They were unfaithful to the God of
their fathers and played the harlot after the
gods of the peoples of the land, whom God
had wiped out before them. 26 So the God of
Israel stirred up the spirit of Pul the king of
Assyria, *even* the spirit of Tiglath-Pileser king
of Assyria, and he led the Reubenites, the Ga-
dites, and the half-tribe of Manasseh into exile
and brought them to Halah, Habor, Hara, and
to the river of Gozan to this day.

Sons of Levi

6 The sons of Levi *were*
Gershon, Kohath, and Merari.
2 The sons of Kohath *were*
Amram, Izhar, Hebron, and Uzziel.
3 The children of Amram *were*
Aaron, Moses, and Miriam.
The sons of Aaron *were*
Nadab, Abihu, Eleazar, and Ithamar.
4 Eleazar became the father of Phinehas,
Phinehas the father of Abishua,
5 Abishua the father of Bukki, and Bukki
the father of Uzzi.
6 Uzzi became the father of Zerahiah, and
Zerahiah the father of Meraioth.

5:16 1Ch 27:29
5:17 2Ki 14:16
5:19 Ge 25:15
5:20 2Ch 18:31
5:22 2Ki 15:29
5:26 2Ki 15:19
6:1 Ge 46:11
6:3 Lev 10:1
6:8 2Sa 8:17
6:11 Ezr 7:3
6:14 2Ki 25:18
6:15 2Ki 25:18
6:16 Ex 6:16
6:19 1Ch 23:21
6:26 1Sa 1:1
6:27 1Sa 1:1
6:28 1Sa 8:2

7 Meraioth became the father of Amariah,
and Amariah father of Ahitub.
8 Ahitub became the father of Zadok, and
Zadok father of Ahimaaz.
9 Ahimaaz became the father of Azariah,
and Azariah father of Johanan.
10 Johanan became the father of Azariah
(he was the one who ministered as a
priest in the temple that Solomon built in
Jerusalem).
11 Azariah became the father of Amariah,
and Amariah the father of Ahitub.
12 Ahitub became the father of Zadok,
and Zadok the father of Shallum.
13 Shallum became the father of Hilkiah,
and Hilkiah the father of Azariah.
14 Azariah became the father of Seraiah,
and Seraiah of Jehozadak.
15 Jehozadak went *into exile* when the LORD
led Judah and Jerusalem into exile by
the hand of Nebuchadnezzar.
16 The sons of Levi *were*
Gershom, Kohath, and Merari.
17 These *are* the names of the sons of
Gershom:
Libni and Shimei.
18 The sons of Kohath *were*
Amram, Izhar, Hebron, and Uzziel.
19 The sons of Merari *were*
Mahli and Mushi.
Now these *are* the families of the Levites
according to their fathers.
20 Of Gershom *were*
Libni his son, Jahath his son,
Zimmah his son, 21 Joah his son,
Iddo his son, Zerah his son,
and Jeatherai his son.
22 The sons of Kohath *were*
Amminadab his son, Korah his son,
Assir his son, 23 Elkanah his son,
Ebiasaph his son, Assir his son,
24 Tahath his son, Uriel his son,
Uzziah his son, and Shaul his son.
25 The sons of Elkanah *were*
Amasai and Ahimoth.
26 As for Elkanah, the sons of Elkanah
were Zophai his son,
Nahath his son, 27 Eliab his son,
Jeroham his son, and Elkanah his son.
28 The sons of Samuel *were*
the firstborn Joel and Abijah.
29 The sons of Merari *were*
Mahli, Libni his son,
Shimei his son, Uzzah his son,
30 Shimea his son, Haggiah his son,
and Asaiah his son.

The Temple Musicians
Jos 21:4–39

31 These *are* the ones whom David appointed over the service of song in the house of the LORD, after the ark rested *there.* 32 Now they were ministering before the dwelling place of the tabernacle of meeting with singing until Solomon had built the house of the LORD in Jerusalem, and they were arranged by their order according to their service.

33 These *are* the ones standing in order with their sons.

Of the sons of the Kohathites *were*
Heman the singer,
the son of Joel, the son of Samuel,
34 the son of Elkanah, the son of Jeroham,
the son of Eliel, the son of Toah,
35 the son of Zuph, the son of Elkanah,
the son of Mahath, the son of Amasai,
36 the son of Elkanah, the son of Joel,
the son of Azariah, the son of Zephaniah,
37 the son of Tahath, the son of Assir,
the son of Ebiasaph, the son of Korah,
38 the son of Izhar, the son of Kohath,
the son of Levi, the son of Israel.
39 His brother Asaph, the one standing at his right hand, was
Asaph the son of Berekiah, the son of Shimea,
40 the son of Michael, the son of Baaseiah,
the son of Malkijah, 41 the son of Ethni,
the son of Zerah, the son of Adaiah,
42 the son of Ethan, the son of Zimmah,
the son of Shimei, 43 the son of Jahath,
the son of Gershom, the son of Levi.
44 Of the sons of Merari, their brothers, *standing* on the left hand *was*
Ethan the son of Kishi, the son of Abdi,
the son of Malluk, 45 the son of Hashabiah,
the son of Amaziah, the son of Hilkiah,
46 the son of Amzi, the son of Bani,
the son of Shemer, 47 the son of Mahli,
the son of Mushi, the son of Merari,
the son of Levi.

48 Their brothers the Levites also *were* appointed for all kinds of service to the tabernacle of the house of God. 49 But Aaron and his sons were making sacrifices on the altar of the burnt offering and on the altar of incense for all the work of the Most Holy Place and to make atonement for Israel, according to all that Moses the servant of God had commanded.

50 Now these *are* the sons of Aaron:
Eleazar his son, Phinehas his son,
Abishua his son, 51 Bukki his son,
Uzzi his son, Zerahiah his son,
52 Meraioth his son, Amariah his son,
Ahitub his son, 53 Zadok his son,
and Ahimaaz his son.

54 And these *are* their dwelling places according to their walled settlements in their territory, for they were given to them, *namely* to the sons of Aaron and to the families of the Kohathites, by lot.

55 They gave them Hebron in the land of Judah, and its surrounding outlands. 56 But the open fields of the city, and its villages, they gave to Caleb the son of Jephunneh.

57 To the sons of Aaron they gave the cities of Judah with the cities of refuge: Hebron and Libnah with its outlands, Jattir and Eshtemoa with their outlands, 58 Hilen with its outlands, Debir with its outlands, 59 Ashan with its outlands, and Beth Shemesh with its outlands. 60 From the tribe of Benjamin, *they gave* Geba with its outlands, Alemeth with its outlands, and Anathoth with its outlands.

All their cities throughout their families *were* thirteen.

61 To the sons of Kohath, those remaining from the family of *that* tribe, *they gave* ten cities by lot from half the tribe of Manasseh.

62 To the sons of Gershon, throughout their families, *they gave* from the tribe of Issachar, from the tribe of Asher, from the tribe of Naphtali, and from the tribe of Manasseh in Bashan, thirteen cities *in all.*

63 To the sons of Merari, throughout their families, *they gave* by lot from the tribe of Reuben, from the tribe of Gad, and from the tribe of Zebulun, twelve cities *in all.*

64 Thus, the sons of Israel gave cities with their outlands to the Levites. 65 They gave by lot from the tribe of the sons of Judah, and from the tribe of the sons of Simeon, and from the tribe of the sons of Benjamin, these cities, which are called by *their* names.

66 Then some from the families of the sons of Kohath *received* cities for their territory from the tribe of Ephraim.

67 They gave to them with the cities of refuge: Shechem in the mountains of Ephraim with its outlands, Gezer with its outlands, 68 Jokmeam with its outlands, Beth Horon with its outlands, 69 Aijalon with its outlands, and Gath Rimmon with its outlands.

70 Also the half-tribe of Manasseh *gave* Aner with its outlands and Bileam with its outlands for the remaining family of the sons of Kohath.

71 To the sons of Gershom, the family of the half-tribe of Manasseh *gave* Golan in Bashan

6:31 2Sa 6:17
6:33 1Ch 6:28
6:49 Ex 27:1–8

6:59 Jos 21:16
6:63 Jos 21:7
6:64 Jos 21:41–42
6:67 Jos 21:21
6:71 Jos 21:27

with its outlands and Ashtaroth with its out-
lands.
[72] From the tribe of Issachar, *they received*
Kedesh with its outlands, Daberath with its
outlands, [73] Ramoth with its outlands, and
Anem with its outlands.
[74] From the tribe of Asher, *they received*
Mashal with its outlands, Abdon with its out-
lands, [75] Hukok with its outlands, and Rehob
with its outlands.
[76] From the tribe of Naphtali, *they received*
Kedesh in Galilee with its outlands, Hammon
with its outlands, and Kiriathaim with its out-
lands.

[77] To the remaining sons of Merari, the tribe
of Zebulun *gave* Rimmono with its outlands
and Tabor with its outlands.
[78] Then on the other side of the Jordan *op-
posite* Jericho, to the east of the Jordan, from
the tribe of Reuben *they were given* Bezer in
the wilderness with its outlands, Jahzah with
its outlands, [79] Kedemoth with its outlands, and
Mephaath with its outlands.
[80] And from the tribe of Gad, *they received*
Ramoth in Gilead with its outlands, Mahanaim
with its outlands, [81] Heshbon with its outlands,
and Jazer with its outlands.

Sons of Issachar

7 Now the sons of Issachar *were*
Tola, Puah, Jashub, and Shimron, four
in all.
[2] The sons of Tola *were*
Uzzi, Rephaiah, Jeriel, Jahmai, Ibsam,
and Samuel. *They were* heads of their
father's house. The sons of Tola were
mighty men of valor in their generations.
Their number in the days of David *was*
twenty-two thousand six hundred.
[3] The son of Uzzi was
Izrahiah,
and the sons of Izrahiah were
Michael, Obadiah, Joel, and Ishiah, five
chiefs in all. [4] With them, by their gener-
ations, after the house of their fathers,
were thirty-six thousand troops of war,
battle-ready, for they had many wives
and sons.
[5] Now their brothers from all the families
of Issachar *were* mighty men of valor, in
all eighty-seven thousand registered by
genealogy.

Sons of Benjamin

[6] Benjamin *had*
Bela, Beker, and Jediael, three *sons in all.*
[7] The sons of Bela *were* five:
Ezbon, Uzzi, Uzziel, Jerimoth, and Iri.
They were heads of their fathers' houses,
mighty men of valor, and registered by
their genealogies, twenty-two thousand
and thirty four *in number*.
[8] The sons of Beker *were*
Zemirah, Joash, Eliezer, Elioenai,
Omri, Jeremoth, Abijah, Anathoth, and
Alemeth. All these *are* the sons of Beker.
[9] Now their registration according to
their generations, heads of their fathers'
houses, mighty men of valor, *was* twenty
thousand two hundred.
[10] The son of Jediael was
Bilhan,
along with the sons of Bilhan:
Jeush, Benjamin, Ehud, Kenaanah,
Zethan, Tarshish, and Ahishahar. [11] All
these sons of Jediael *were* heads of their
fathers' houses, mighty men of valor,
numbering seventeen thousand two
hundred soldiers, ready to go out to war
for battle.
[12] And the Shuppites and Huppites *were* the
sons of Ir; the Hushites the sons of Aher.

Sons of Naphtali

[13] The sons of Naphtali *were*
Jahziel, Guni, Jezer, and Shallum, de-
scendants of Bilhah.

Sons of Manasseh

[14] The sons of Manasseh *were*
Asriel, whom his Aramean concubine
bore. She *also* bore Makir the father of
Gilead. [15] Now Makir took a wife for Hup-
pim and Shuppim, whose sister's name
was Maakah.
The name of the second was Zelophe-
had, and Zelophehad had daughters.
[16] Maakah the wife of Makir bore a
son, and she called his name Peresh.
His brother's name *was* Sheresh, and
his sons *were* Ulam and Rakem.
[17] The son of Ulam was
Bedan.
These *were* the sons of Gilead, the son of
Makir, the son of Manasseh. [18] His sister
Hammoleketh bore Ishhod, Abiezer, and
Mahlah.
[19] The sons of Shemida were
Ahian, Shechem, Likhi, and Aniam.

Sons of Ephraim

[20] The sons of Ephraim *were*
Shuthelah, Bered his son,
Tahath his son, Eleadah his son,
Tahath his son, [21] Zabad his son,
Shuthelah his son, and Ezer and Elead,
whom the men of Gath born in that land
killed because they came down to take
their livestock. [22] Ephraim their father
mourned many days, and his brothers
came to comfort him. [23] Then he went in

6:76 Jos 21:32
6:80 Ge 32:2
6:81 Jos 21:39
7:1 Ge 46:13
7:6 Ge 46:21

7:13 Nu 26:48–49
7:17 1Sa 12:11

to his wife, and she conceived and bore
a son, so he called his name Beriah,
because evil had been in his house 24 (his
daughter was Sheerah, who built *both*
Lower and Upper Beth Horon as well as
Uzzen Sheerah).
25 Rephah *was* also his son, *as were*
Resheph,
Telah his son, Tahan his son,
26 Ladan his son, Ammihud his son,
Elishama his son, 27 Nun his son,
and Joshua his son.
28 Their possessions and settlements were
Bethel and its towns, and to the east Naaran,
and to the west Gezer with its towns, Shechem
and its towns, and Ayyah and its towns; 29 also
along the borders of the Manassites, Beth Shan
and its towns, Taanach and its towns, Megiddo
and its towns, and Dor and its towns. In these
lived the sons of Joseph the son of Israel.

Sons of Asher

30 Now the children of Asher *were*
Imnah, Ishvah, Ishvi, Beriah, and their
sister Serah.
31 The sons of Beriah *were*
Heber and Malkiel, who was the father
of Birzaith.
32 Heber became the father of Japhlet, Sho-
mer, Hotham, and their sister Shua.
33 The sons of Japhlet *were*
Pasak, Bimhal, and Ashvath.
These *were* the children of Japhlet.
34 The sons of Shomer *were*
Ahi, Rohgah, Hubbah, and Aram.
35 The sons of his brother Helem *were*
Zophah, Imna, Shelesh, and Amal.
36 The sons of Zophah *were*
Suah, Harnepher, Shual, Beri, Imrah,
37 Bezer, Hod, Shamma, Shilshah, Ithran,
and Beera.
38 The sons of Jether *were*
Jephunneh, Pispah, and Ara.
39 The sons of Ulla *were*
Arah, Hanniel, and Rizia.
40 All these *were* the children of Asher, heads
of their fathers' houses, choice men, mighty
men of valor, and heads of the leaders. They
were registered by their genealogy among the
army fit for war. Their number *was* twenty-six
thousand men.

The Generations of Benjamin
1Ch 9:34–44

8 Now Benjamin became the father of Bela
his firstborn,
Ashbel the second, Aharah the third,
2 Nohah the fourth, and Rapha the fifth.
3 The sons of Bela were

7:24 Jos 16:3
7:30 Ge 46:17
8:1 Ge 46:21

8:12 Ezr 2:33
8:33 1Sa 9:1
8:34 2Sa 9:12

Addar, Gera, Abihud, 4 Abishua, Naaman,
Ahoah, 5 Gera, Shephuphan, and Huram.
6 These *are* the sons of Ehud, who *were*
the heads of the fathers' *houses* to those
dwelling in Geba, and who exiled them
to Manahath.
7 So he exiled Naaman, Ahijah, and Gera
and *then* became the father of Uzza and
Ahihud.
8 Shaharaim had *sons* in the country of
Moab after he had sent away his wives
Hushim and Baara. 9 He had *sons* with
his wife Hodesh, *namely* Jobab, Zibia,
Mesha, Malkam, 10 Jeuz, Sakia, and
Mirmah. These *were* his sons, heads of
the fathers' *houses*. 11 He also had sons by
Hushim: Abitub and Elpaal.
12 The sons of Elpaal *were*
Eber, Misham, Shemed (he built Ono
and Lod with its towns), 13 Beriah, and
Shema, who were heads of the fathers'
houses to those dwelling in Aijalon *and*
who drove out the inhabitants of Gath,
14 *as well as* Ahio, Shashak, Jeremoth, 15 Ze-
badiah, Arad, Eder, 16 Michael, Ishpah,
and Joha, the sons of Beriah.
17 Zebadiah, Meshullam, Hizki, Heber,
18 Ishmerai, Izliah, and Jobab *were* the
sons of Elpaal.
19 Jakim, Zikri, Zabdi, 20 Elienai, Zillethai,
Eliel, 21 Adaiah, Beraiah, and Shimrath
were the sons of Shimei.
22 Ishpan, Eber, Eliel, 23 Abdon, Zikri, Hanan,
24 Hananiah, Elam, Anthothijah, 25 Iphdei-
ah, and Penuel *were* the sons of Shashak.
26 Shamsherai, Shehariah, Athaliah,
27 Jaareshiah, Elijah, and Zikri *were* the
sons of Jeroham.
28 These *were* heads of the fathers' houses
according to their generations, chief men who
dwelt in Jerusalem.

29 The father of Gibeon dwelt in Gibeon,
and Maakah *was* his wife's name. 30 His
firstborn son *was* Abdon, *along with* Zur,
Kish, Baal, Nadab, 31 Gedor, Ahio, and
Zeker. 32 Mikloth also became the father
of Shimeah. Now these also dwelt in
Jerusalem with their own families near
their brothers.
33 Ner became the father of Kish; Kish
the father of Saul; Saul the father of
Jonathan, Malki-Shua, Abinadab, and
Esh-Baal.
34 Jonathan's son *was*
Merib-Baal, and Merib-Baal became the
father of Micah.
35 The sons of Micah *were*
Pithon, Melek, Tarea, and Ahaz.

36 Ahaz became the father of Jehoad-
dah, and Jehoaddah became the father
of Alemeth, Azmaveth, and Zimri. Zimri
became the father of Moza, 37 and Moza
became the father of Binea. Now Ra-
phah *was* his son, Eleasah his son, *and*
Azel his son.
38 Azel had six sons, and their names *were*
Azrikam, Bokeru, Ishmael, Sheariah,
Obadiah, and Hanan. All these *were* the
sons of Azel.
39 The sons of his brother Eshek *were*
Ulam his firstborn, Jeush the second, and
Eliphelet the third. 40 The sons of Ulam
were mighty men of valor, *even* archers,
and had many sons and grandsons, one
hundred and fifty *in all*.
These *were* all the sons of Benjamin.

9 So all Israel was registered by genealo-
gies, and these were written in the book
of the kings of Israel. And Judah was led into
exile to Babylon for their unfaithfulness.
2 Now the first ones to dwell in their pos-
sessions in their cities *were* children of Israel,
priests, Levites, and temple servants.

A Post-Exilic Genealogy
Ne 11:3–19

3 Some of the sons of Judah dwelt in Jerusa-
lem *alongside* some of the sons of Benjamin,
Ephraim, and Manasseh:
4 Uthai the son of Ammihud, the son of
Omri, the son of Imri, the son of Bani, of
the sons of Perez the son of Judah;
5 of the Shilonites:
Asaiah the firstborn and his sons;
6 of the sons of Zerah:
Jeuel and their brothers, six hundred and
ninety.
7 *Those* of the sons of Benjamin *were*
Sallu the son of Meshullam, the son of
Hodaviah, the son of Hassenuah;
8 Ibneiah the son of Jeroham; Elah the
son of Uzzi, the son of Mikri; Meshullam
the son of Shephatiah, the son of Reuel,
the son of Ibnijah;
9 and their brothers according to their
generations, nine hundred and fifty-six.
All these men were heads of families
according to their fathers' houses.
10 *Those* of the priests *were*
Jedaiah, Jehoiarib, Jakin;
11 Azariah the son of Hilkiah, the son of
Meshullam, the son of Zadok, the son
of Meraioth, the son of Ahitub, the head
official of the house of God;
12 Adaiah the son of Jeroham, the son of
Pashhur, the son of Malkijah; Maasai the
son of Adiel, the son of Jahzerah, the son

9:2 Ne 7:73
9:4 Ge 46:12
9:11 Ne 11:11

9:18 Eze 46:1–2
9:21 1Ch 26:14
9:22 1Sa 9:9
9:25 2Ki 11:5
9:31 1Ch 9:19

of Meshullam, the son of Meshillemith,
the son of Immer;
13 and their brothers, heads of the houses
of their fathers, one thousand seven
hundred and sixty very able men for the
work of the service of the house of God.
14 *Those* of the Levites *were*
Shemaiah the son of Hasshub, the son
of Azrikam, the son of Hashabiah, of the
sons of Merari; 15 Bakbakkar, Heresh,
Galal, and Mattaniah the son of Mika, the
son of Zikri, the son of Asaph; 16 Obadiah
the son of Shemaiah, the son of Galal,
the son of Jeduthun; Berekiah the son of
Asa, the son of Elkanah, who lived in the
villages of the Netophathites.
17 Now the gatekeepers *were*
Shallum, Akkub, Talmon, Ahiman, and
their brothers (Shallum was the head
officer 18 who until then *had served* at
the king's eastern gate). They *were* the
gatekeepers for the camps of the Levites.
19 Shallum the son of Kore, the son of
Ebiasaph, the son of Korah, and his
brothers from his father's house, the
Korahites, *were* over the work of the ser-
vice, gatekeepers of the tabernacle. Their
fathers had been over the camp of the
LORD, guards at the entrance. 20 Phinehas
the son of Eleazar was the official over
them in previous *times*, *and* the LORD *was*
with him. 21 Zechariah the son of Meshel-
emiah was gatekeeper at the entrance to
the tent of meeting.
22 All those chosen as gatekeepers *were* two
hundred and twelve. They were registered by
their genealogy in their villages. *Now* David
and Samuel the seer established them in their
trusted offices. 23 So they and their sons *were*
in charge of the gates of the house of the LORD,
that is, the house of the tabernacle, as guards.
24 The gatekeepers were on four sides: east,
west, north, and south. 25 Their brothers in their
villages *were* to come for seven days from time
to time *to serve* with them. 26 For in their trusted
offices the four main gatekeepers who were
Levites *had charge* over the chambers and trea-
suries of the house of God. 27 They spent the
night around the house of God, for the watch
was entrusted to them, and they were respon-
sible for opening *it* every morning.
28 Some of them were in charge of the vessels
of service, that they should bring them in and
out by number. 29 Some *others were* appointed
over the furnishings and all the implements
of the sanctuary as well as the fine flour, the
wine, the oil, the frankincense, and the spices.
30 And some of the sons of the priests mixed
the ointment of the spices. 31 Mattithiah, one of

the Levites (he *was* the firstborn of Shallum the
Korahite), was entrusted with making the flat
cakes. 32 *Others* of the sons of the Kohathites
and from their brothers *were given charge* over
the showbread to prepare *it* every Sabbath.
33 Now these *are* the singers, heads of the
fathers' houses of the Levites, who stayed in
the *temple* chambers, free *from other service*,
because they *were occupied* with the work day
and night.
34 These *were* the heads of the fathers' houses
of the Levites according to their generations,
leaders, who dwelt in Jerusalem.

The Genealogy of Saul
1Ch 8:28–38

35 Now Jeiel the father of Gibeon,
whose wife's name was Maakah, dwelt in
Gibeon. 36 His firstborn son *was* Abdon,
then Zur, Kish, Baal, Ner, Nadab, 37 Ge-
dor, Ahio, Zechariah, and Mikloth. 38 Mik-
loth became the father of Shimeam.
These also dwelt in Jerusalem with their
own families near their brothers.
39 Ner became the father of Kish; Kish
the father of Saul; Saul the father of
Jonathan, Malki-Shua, Abinadab, and
Esh-Baal.
40 The son of Jonathan *was*
Merib-Baal, and Merib-Baal became the
father of Micah.
41 The sons of Micah *were*
Pithon, Melek, Tahrea, and Ahaz.
42 Ahaz became the father of Jarah, and
Jarah the father of Alemeth, Azmaveth,
and Zimri. Zimri became the father of
Moza, 43 and Moza became the father
of Binea, Rephaiah his son, Eleasah his
son, *and* Azel his son.
44 Azel had six sons, and these *were* their
names:
Azrikam, Bokeru, Ishmael, Sheariah,
Obadiah, and Hanan. These *were* the
sons of Azel.

The Death of Saul
1Sa 31:1–13; 2Sa 1:4–12

10 Now *when* the Philistines fought
against Israel, every Israelite *fighter*
fled before the Philistines, and the slain fell
on Mount Gilboa. 2 But the Philistines pursued
Saul and his sons and struck down Saul's sons
Jonathan, Abinadab, and Malki-Shua. 3 As the
battle with Saul became heavy, the archers'
bows found *their target* and mortally wounded
him.
4 So Saul said to his armor bearer, "Draw
your sword and pierce me through lest these
uncircumcised *Philistines* come and make a
fool of me."

9:32 Lev 24:5–8
9:41 1Ch 8:35
10:1 1Sa 31:1–13

....

10:13 Lev 19:31
10:14 1Sa 15:28
11:3 1Sa 16:1
11:4 Jdg 1:21
11:6 2Sa 8:16

But his armor bearer was unwilling to do
it because he was overwhelmed with fear,
so Saul took the sword and fell on it *himself*.
5 When the armor bearer saw that Saul was
dead, he too fell on his sword and died. 6 Thus,
Saul and his three sons, *namely* all his house,
died together.
7 Now *when* all the children of Israel in the
valley saw that they had fled *the battlefield*, and
Saul and his sons were dead, they abandoned
their cities and escaped, *leaving* the Philistines
to come and dwell in them.
8 The next day, *when* the Philistines came to
pillage the slain, they found Saul and his sons
fallen on Mount Gilboa. 9 So they stripped *Saul*,
removed his head and his armor, and circu-
lated the news of his demise throughout the
land of the Philistines to their idols *as well as*
the people. 10 Then they placed his armor in
the temple of their gods, while his head they
impaled in the house of Dagon.
11 Now all Jabesh Gilead heard about ev-
erything the Philistines did to Saul, 12 so their
valiant men rose up and carried the body of
Saul and the bodies of his sons to Jabesh. They
buried their bones under the oak in Jabesh and
fasted, *mourning* seven days.
13 So Saul died because of his unfaithful
deeds against the LORD, because of his failure
to keep the word of the LORD, and because he
sought to consult a spirit *of divination* 14 but did
not seek the LORD. So He killed him and turned
the kingdom over to David the son of Jesse.

David, King of Israel
2Sa 5:1–10

11 Then all Israel assembled before David
at Hebron, saying, "We are your *own*
people, *even* your flesh and blood. 2 Also from
times past until now, even when Saul was king,
you were the one who led Israel going out and
coming in, and the LORD your God said to you,
Indeed, you will shepherd My people Israel as
the ruler of Israel."
3 Then all the elders of Israel came to King
David at Hebron, and he made a covenant with
them there before the LORD. So they anointed
David king over Israel according to the word
of the LORD *delivered* by Samuel.

David Conquers Jerusalem

4 Now David and all Israel *with him* went to
Jerusalem (that is, Jebus, since the Jebusites
still dwelt there in the land). 5 And the Jebusites
said to David, "You will not come here," but
he captured the stronghold of Zion (it is the
City of David).
6 Now David had said, "Whoever strikes Jeb-
us first will be the commander and leader *of*

the army," so Joab, the son of Zeruiah, went up first and became the commander.

7 Then David dwelt in the stronghold, which is why they called it the City of David, 8 and he fortified the city all around from the Millo encircling *the stronghold*, while Joab preserved the rest of the city. 9 So David kept on going, becoming greater *and greater*, and the LORD of Hosts was with him.

David's Mighty Men
2Sa 23:8–39

10 Now these *are* the heads of the mighty men whom David had, who strengthened him in his kingdom, along with all Israel, to establish him as king according to the word of the LORD to Israel. 11 These *make up* the number of the mighty men who *fought* for David:

Jashobeam, the son of Hakmoni, the head of the thirty, who lifted his spear *in triumph* over three hundred slain at one time.

12 After him was Eleazar, the son of Dodai the Ahohite, who was among the three mighty men. 13 He was with David at Pas Dammim when the Philistines were gathered there for battle. There was a piece of ground full of barley. Now the men fled from the Philistines. 14 But they stood their ground in the middle of the field, defended it, and killed the Philistines; and the LORD saved them by a great victory.

15 Now three of the thirty captains climbed down the rock to David at the cave of Adullam while the camp of the Philistines was set up in the Valley of Rephaim. 16 (At that time, David was in the stronghold, but a garrison of the Philistines was in Bethlehem.) 17 Now David was overcome with longing and said, "Who will get me a drink of water from the well of Bethlehem by the gate?" 18 These three broke through the Philistine camp, drew water from the well of Bethlehem by the gate, and carried *it* back to David. However, he was not willing to drink it but poured out *the water* to the LORD. 19 For he said, "Far be it from me before my God to do this. Should I drink the life blood of these men who put their lives in jeopardy? For at the risk of their lives they brought it." Therefore he would not drink it.

The three mighty men did these things.

20 Also Abishai himself, the brother of Joab, was a captain of the three who lifted his spear *in triumph* over three hundred slain and was given a name among the three. 21 He was honored as a leader by the second *company* of the three, but he did not attain to the *first* three.

22 Benaiah son of Jehoiada was the son of a valiant man from Kabzeel, who had done many deeds. He killed two Moabite warriors. Indeed, once he went down into a well and struck a lion on a snowy day. 23 And he killed an Egyptian, a man of great stature, five cubits[1] tall. The Egyptian had in his hand a spear like a weaver's beam, and he went down to him with a staff, wrested the spear from the Egyptian's hand, and killed him with his own spear. 24 Benaiah, the son of Jehoiada, did these things, and won a name among the three mighty men. 25 Out of the thirty *captains*, he himself was honored, and although he did not attain to the three, David set him over his guard.

26 Now the *other* mighty men of valor of the army *were*
Asahel the brother of Joab,
Elhanan the son of Dodo of Bethlehem,
27 Shammoth the Harorite,
Helez the Pelonite,
28 Ira the son of Ikkesh the Tekoite,
Abiezer the Anathothite,
29 Sibbekai the Hushathite,
Ilai the Ahohite,
30 Maharai the Netophathite,
Heled the son of Baanah, the Netophathite,
31 Ithai the son of Ribai of Gibeah in Benjamin,
Benaiah the Pirathonite,
32 Hurai from the rivers of Gaash,
Abiel the Arbathite,
33 Azmaveth the Baharumite,
Eliahba the Shaalbonite,
34 the sons of Hashem the Gizonite,
Jonathan the son of Shagee, the Hararite,
35 Ahiam the son of Sakar, the Hararite,
Eliphal the son of Ur,
36 Hepher the Mekerathite,
Ahijah the Pelonite,
37 Hezro the Carmelite,
Naarai the son of Ezbai,
38 Joel the brother of Nathan,
Mibhar the son of Hagri,
39 Zelek the Ammonite,
Naharai the Berothite, the armor bearer of Joab, the son of Zeruiah,
40 Ira the Ithrite,
Gareb the Ithrite,
41 Uriah the Hittite,
Zabad the son of Ahlai,
42 Adina the son of Shiza, the Reubenite, a captain of the Reubenites, and thirty with him,
43 Hanan the son of Maakah,
Joshaphat the Mithnite,
44 Uzzia the Ashterathite,
Shama and Jeiel the sons of Hotham, the Aroerite,
45 Jediael the son of Shimri and
Joha his brother, the Tizite,

11:9 2Sa 3:1
11:11 2Sa 23:8
11:12 1Ch 27:4
11:15 1Ch 14:9
11:16 1Sa 10:5

[1] *23* About 7 feet 6 inches, or 2.3 meters.

46 Eliel the Mahavite,
and Jeribai and Joshaviah the sons of Elnaam,
Ithmah the Moabite,
47 Eliel, Obed, and Jaasiel the Mezobaite.

The Mighty Men Join David

12 Now these are the men who came
to David at Ziklag, while he yet kept
himself away from Saul the son of Kish. They
were among the brave men, helpers in the
war. 2 They were armed with bows, and could
use both the right hand and the left in hurling
stones and shooting arrows out of a bow. They
were Saul's brothers of Benjamin.
3 The chief was Ahiezer, then Joash, the sons
of Shemaah the Gibeathite; Jeziel and Pelet
the sons of Azmaveth; Berakah, and Jehu the
Anathothite; 4 and Ishmaiah the Gibeonite, a
brave warrior among the thirty, and over the
thirty; Jeremiah, Jahaziel, Johanan, and Joz-
abad the Gederathite; 5 and Eluzai, Jerimoth,
Bealiah, Shemariah, and Shephatiah the Ha-
ruphite; 6 and Elkanah, Ishiah, Azarel, Joezer,
and Jashobeam the Korahites; 7 and Joelah and
Zebadiah, the sons of Jeroham of Gedor.
8 From the Gadites mighty men of valor, men
of the war battalion, who could handle shield
and sword, whose faces were like the faces of
lions, and who were as swift as the gazelles on
the mountains, separated themselves for David
in the stronghold in the wilderness:

9 Ezer the captain,
Obadiah the second, Eliab the third,
10 Mishmannah the fourth, Jeremiah the fifth,
11 Attai the sixth, Eliel the seventh,
12 Johanan the eighth, Elzabad the ninth,
13 Jeremiah the tenth, Makbannai the eleventh.

14 These *were* from Gad, captains of the bat-
talions. One of the least *of them* was as a hun-
dred and the greatest as a thousand. 15 These
were the ones who crossed over the Jordan
during the first month when it had overflowed
its banks and caused the valley dwellers to flee
to the east and to the west.
16 Some of the sons of Benjamin and Judah
came to the stronghold of David. 17 So David
went out before them and said to them, "If you
have come in peace to help me, then I will *have*
a heart united with *yours*, but if to betray me
to my adversaries, when *there is* no violence
in my hand, may the God of our fathers see,
and may He decide *between us*."
18 Then the Spirit came upon Amasai the cap-
tain of the officers, *and he said,*

"*We are* for you, David,
and with you, son of Jesse.
Peace, peace to you,
and peace to the one helping you,
for your God helps you."

So David welcomed them and appointed
them as captains of the troops.
19 Now some from Manasseh joined forces
with David when he came with the Philistines
for battle against Saul, but they did not help
them. For after taking counsel, the lords of the
Philistines sent him away, saying, "*It will be*
our heads if he falls *back* to his lord Saul."
20 As he went to Ziklag, these men of Manasseh
deserted to join him: Adnah, Jozabad, Jediael,
Michael, Jozabad, Elihu, and Zillethai, chiefs
of thousands in Manasseh. 21 So they helped
David against the bands *of raiders* because all
of them were mighty men of valor and com-
manders in the army. 22 For at *that* time, day by
day, they came to help David until *they became*
a great camp like the camp of God.

David's Army at Hebron

23 Now these *make up* the number of the lead-
ers equipped for the battalion who came to
David at Hebron in order to turn the kingdom
of Saul over to him, as the mouth of the LORD
had spoken.

24 The sons of Judah who carried shields and spears: six thousand eight hundred equipped for war.
25 From the sons of Simeon, mighty men of valor, fit for war: seven thousand one hundred.
26 From the sons of the Levites: four thou-
sand six hundred. 27 Jehoiada *was* the
principal leader of the Aaronites, and *he*
brought with him three thousand seven
hundred, 28 while Zadok, a brave young
warrior, *brought* twenty-two leaders from
the house of his father.
29 From the sons of Benjamin, the brothers of Saul: three thousand (up to that time the greater number of them were keeping *their loyalty* with the house of Saul).
30 From the sons of Ephraim: twenty thousand eight hundred mighty men of valor, men of reputation in the house of their fathers.
31 From the half-tribe of Manasseh: eighteen thousand who were marked by name to come and crown David king.
32 From the sons of Issachar, those having understanding of times and what Israel should do: two hundred of their captains with all their brothers at their command.
33 Of Zebulun, fifty thousand seasoned troops, equipped for battle with all the weapons of war, to help David with singleness of purpose. From Zebulun,

12:2 Jdg 3:15
12:8 2Sa 2:18
12:14 Lev 26:8
12:15 Jos 3:15
12:18 Jdg 6:34
12:23 2Sa 2:3–4
12:28 2Sa 8:17
12:29 2Sa 2:8–9
12:32 Est 1:13
12:33 Ps 12:2

those going out to war, equipped for battle with all the weapons of war, to help David with an undivided heart: fifty thousand.

34 From Naphtali: one thousand leaders and thirty-seven thousand with shields and spears.

35 From the Danites, competent for battle: twenty-eight thousand six hundred.

36 From Asher, those going out to war, arranged for battle: forty thousand.

37 Also from the other side of the Jordan, from the Reubenites, the Gadites, and half of the tribe of Manasseh with all their battle array: one hundred and twenty thousand.

38 All these *made up* the men of war, arranged in ranks, *who* came to Hebron with a sincere heart to make David king over all Israel, along with the all the rest of Israel *who* with one heart *came* to make David king. 39 Now *all these* were there with David three days, eating and drinking, for their brothers had made provisions for them, 40 and also the ones who were as near to them as Issachar, Zebulun, and Naphtali were bringing bread on donkeys, on camels, on mules, and on oxen, food of fine flour, fig cakes, raisins, wine, oil, herds, and flocks in abundance, for there was joy in Israel.

The Ark
2Sa 6:1–11

13 So David conferred with the captains of the thousands and of the hundreds *and* with every leader. 2 Then he said to all the assembly of Israel, "If it seems good to you and to the LORD our God, let us send word to the rest of our brothers throughout all the land of Israel along with the priests and the Levites in their cities, that they might join us here. 3 Then let us bring the ark of the LORD our God back to us, for we did not seek it during the days of Saul." 4 Then all the assembly agreed to do it because the thing *seemed* right in the eyes of all the people.

5 So David assembled all Israel, from Shihor in Egypt as far as the entrance to Hamath, in order to bring the ark of God from Kiriath Jearim. 6 And he went up with all Israel to Baalah, *that is,* to Kiriath Jearim, which belongs to Judah, to bring up the ark of God, the LORD who dwells between the cherubim, where *His* name is called.

7 They transported the ark of God on a new cart from the house of Abinadab with Uzzah and Ahio driving the cart 8 while David and all Israel played *music* before God with all their might, *performing* songs on lyres, harps, tambourines, cymbals, and trumpets.

12:40 1Sa 25:18
13:3 1Sa 7:1–2
13:5 1Sa 6:21–7:1
13:6 Jos 15:9

13:9 2Sa 6:6
13:10 1Ch 15:13
14:9 1Ch 11:15
14:13 1Ch 14:9

9 When they had come as far as the threshing floor of Kidon, Uzzah stretched out his hand to take hold of the ark because the oxen had stumbled *on the path.* 10 Then the anger of the LORD burned against Uzzah, and He struck him because he reached his hand out to touch the ark. Thus, *Uzzah* died there before God.

11 Now David was angry because the LORD struck out against Uzzah, so he called that place Perez Uzzah, *as it is* to this day.

12 David was afraid of God that day, saying, "How can I *ever* bring the ark of God to myself?" 13 So David *stopped moving* the ark of God to himself in the City of David and diverted it to the house of Obed-Edom the Gittite, 14 and *while* the ark of God stayed in his house three months, the LORD blessed the house of Obed-Edom and all he had.

David Established at Jerusalem
2Sa 5:11–25; 1Ch 3:5–8

14 Then Hiram the king of Tyre sent messengers to David with cedar wood, stonemasons, and carpenters to build a palace for him. 2 So David knew that the LORD had established him as king over Israel because his kingdom was highly exalted for the sake of His people Israel.

3 Now David took more wives in Jerusalem, and David became the father of more sons and daughters. 4 These are the names of the children who were born to him in Jerusalem: Shammua, Shobab, Nathan, Solomon, 5 Ibhar, Elishua, Elpelet, 6 Nogah, Nepheg, Japhia, 7 Elishama, Beeliada, and Eliphelet.

David Defeats the Philistines

8 Now *when* the Philistines heard that David had been anointed king over all Israel, all the Philistines went up to seek out David, but David heard and went out to them. 9 So the Philistines came and raided the Valley of Rephaim. 10 Then David inquired of the LORD, saying, "Should I go up against the Philistines? Will You give them into my hand?"

The LORD answered, "Go up *against them,* and I will give them into your hand."

11 And they went up to Baal Perazim, and David struck them down there. Then David said, "God broke through my enemies by my hand as the breaking through of waters." Therefore they named that place Baal Perazim. 12 They abandoned their gods there, and David said *that* they should be burned with fire.

13 Now the Philistines raided the valley once more. 14 And David again inquired of God, and God *answered* him: "Do not go up after them, but turn around behind them and come to them in front of the balsam trees. 15 Whenever you hear the sound of marching in the tops

of the balsam trees, you will advance the bat-
tle, for God has gone out before you to strike
the camp of the Philistines.” 16 David did just
as God commanded him, and they struck the
camp of the Philistines from Gibeon as far as
Gezer.
17 So the fame of David went out in all the
lands, and the LORD put the dread of him on
all the nations.

The Ark Brought to Jerusalem
2Sa 6:12–19

15 So David built houses for himself in
the City of David, and he prepared a
place for the ark of God and pitched a tent for
it. 2 Then David said, “No one may carry the
ark of God except the Levites since the LORD
chose them to carry the ark of the LORD and to
minister before Him always.”
3 David assembled all Israel to Jerusalem in
order to bring up the ark of the LORD to the
place he had prepared for it. 4 And David gath-
ered *representatives* of the sons of Aaron and
the Levites, *as follows*:
5 from the sons of Kohath,
Uriel the leader and one hundred and
twenty of his brothers;
6 from the sons of Merari,
Asaiah the leader and two hundred and
twenty of his brothers;
7 from the sons of Gershom,
Joel the leader and one hundred and
thirty of his brothers;
8 from the sons of Elizaphan,
Shemaiah the leader and two hundred of
his brothers;
9 from the sons of Hebron,
Eliel the leader and eighty of his broth-
ers;
10 from the sons of Uzziel,
Amminadab the leader and one hundred
and twelve of his brothers.
11 Then David called for Zadok and Abiathar
the priests and for the Levites: Uriel, Asaiah,
Joel, Shemaiah, Eliel, and Amminadab. 12 He
said to them, “You are the captains of the
fathers’ houses for the Levites. Consecrate
yourselves, you and your brothers, so you
may bring up the ark of the LORD, the God of
Israel, to *the place* I have prepared for it 13 be-
cause *on* the first *attempt* without you the LORD
struck out against us since we did not seek
Him properly.” 14 So the priests and the Levites
consecrated themselves to bring up the ark of
the LORD, the God of Israel. 15 The sons of the
Levites lifted up the ark of God just as Moses
commanded, with the poles on their shoulders,
according to the word of the LORD.
16 Then David told the leaders of the Levites
to position their brothers the singers with mu-
sical instruments, harps, lyres, and cymbals to
resound with joyful songs.
17 So the Levites placed Heman the son of
Joel, and from his brothers, Asaph the son of
Berekiah, and from their brothers the sons
of Merari, Ethan the son of Kushaiah, 18 and
with them their brothers of the second rank:
Zechariah, Ben, Jaaziel, Shemiramoth, Jehiel,
Unni, Eliab, Benaiah, Maaseiah, Mattithiah,
Eliphelehu, Mikneiah, Obed-Edom, and Jeiel,
the gatekeepers.
19 So the singers, Heman, Asaph, and Ethan,
were directed to sound cymbals of brass.
20 Zechariah, Aziel, Shemiramoth, Jehiel, Unni,
Eliab, Maaseiah, and Benaiah *were to accom-
pany* with harps on Alamoth. 21 Mattithiah,
Eliphelehu, Mikneiah, Obed-Edom, Jeiel, and
Azaziah *were to lead* with lyres on the Shem-
inith. 22 Kenaniah, leader of the Levites, *was
to conduct* the music because he *was* skillful.
23 Berekiah and Elkanah were gatekeepers
for the ark. 24 Shebaniah, Joshaphat, Nethanel,
Amasai, Zechariah, Benaiah, and Eliezer, the
priests, *were assigned* to sound trumpets before
the ark of God. Obed-Edom and Jehiah were
gatekeepers for the ark.
25 So David, the elders of Israel, and the lead-
ers of the thousands went to bring up the ark
of the covenant of the LORD from the house of
Obed-Edom with rejoicing. 26 Since God helped
the Levites who carried the ark of the covenant
of the LORD, they sacrificed seven bulls and
seven rams. 27 Now David was clothed in a fine
linen robe, *as were* the Levites who carried the
ark, the singers, and Kenaniah, the conductor
of singing and singers. David *himself* wore a
linen ephod. 28 So all Israel brought up the ark
of the covenant of the LORD with a shout and
with the sound of the ram’s horn and with
trumpets and cymbals, making music on harps
and lyres.
29 Now as the ark of the covenant of the
LORD was entering the City of David, Michal
the daughter of Saul was looking down from
the window, and when she saw King David
dancing and spinning, she despised him in
her heart.

The Ark Set in the Tent

16 So they brought in the ark of God,
placed it in the midst of the tent that
David had erected for it, and drew near to
God with burnt offerings and peace offerings.
2 *When* David had finished offering the burnt
offerings and the peace offerings, he blessed
the people in the name of the LORD. 3 Then he
distributed to all the children of Israel, both
men and women, a loaf of bread, a piece of
meat, and a raisin cake for each.

14:17 Dt 2:25
15:1 1Ch 16:1
15:2 Dt 10:8
15:3 1Ki 8:1
15:11 1Ch 12:28
15:12 2Ch 35:6
15:13 2Sa 6:3
15:15 Nu 4:15
15:16 1Ch 13:8
15:17 1Ch 6:33
15:24 1Ch 16:6
15:26 Nu 23:29
16:1 1Ch 15:1

[4] And he appointed some of the Levites to
minister before the ark of the LORD, to com-
memorate, to thank, and to praise the LORD
God of Israel: [5] Asaph the chief, and next to him
Zechariah, then Jeiel, Shemiramoth, Jehiel,
Mattithiah, Eliab, Benaiah, and Obed-Edom:
Jeiel with stringed instruments and harps, but
Asaph made music with the cymbals. [6] More-
over, Benaiah and Jahaziel the priests sound-
ed trumpets continually before the ark of the
covenant of God.

David's Psalm of Thanksgiving
Ps 96:1–13; 105:1–15; 106:1, 47–48

[7] On that day then, David delivered for the
first time this psalm of thanksgiving to the
LORD into the hand of Asaph and his brothers:

[8] Give thanks to the LORD, call on His name;
make known His deeds among the
peoples.
[9] Sing to Him, sing praise to Him,
recount all His wonders.
[10] Glory in His holy name;
let the heart of those who seek the LORD
rejoice.
[11] Seek the LORD and His strength;
seek His face continually.
[12] Remember His wonders which He has
done,
His wonders and the judgments of His
mouth,
[13] O seed of Israel, His servant,
O sons of Jacob, His chosen.
[14] He is the LORD our God;
His judgments are in all the earth.
[15] Remember His covenant forever,
the word He commanded for a thousand
generations,
[16] that He made with Abraham,
even His oath to Isaac.
[17] He confirmed it to Jacob as a statute,
to Israel *for* an everlasting covenant,
[18] saying, "To you I will give the land of
Canaan
as the portion of your inheritance."

> I will not touch the Lord's anointed,
> and I will do His prophets no harm
> (1Ch 16:22).

[19] When you were few in number,
few indeed, and strangers *there*,
[20] when they wandered from nation to nation,
from one kingdom to another,
[21] He allowed no man to oppress them;
He rebuked kings on their account,
[22] saying, "Do not touch My anointed,
and do My prophets no harm."

16:7 2Sa 22:1
16:8 2Ki 19:19
16:16 Ge 17:2
16:18 Ge 13:15
16:19 Ge 34:30
16:21 Ge 12:17
16:22 Ge 20:7
16:23 Ps 96:1–13
16:25 Ps 89:7
16:26 Lev 19:4
16:29 Ps 29:2

SPIRITLED WOMAN

COUNSEL FROM THE SPIRIT BASICS

The Heart of Worship

One thing I know about worship is that it will always require something we have. It takes effort. It takes our undivided attention. It takes holy sacrifice. It has a value placed upon it from heaven. True worship always takes our focus off ourselves and our own needs and looks exclusively to God the Father and to His Son, Jesus. The heart of worship is not seeing what we can get from God but offering up what we can give to Him.

Worship comes from the overflow of a thankful heart: "Give thanks to the LORD, for He is good; for His mercy endures forever" (1Ch 16:34). No matter what has happened in our lives, blessings surround us. We need to take time to acknowledge and thank the Lord for our many gifts.

I do almost all the cooking and cleaning at our home, and every once in a while after dinner, my husband will go out of his way to thank me. I love the feeling I get when he shows me appreciation for the things I do for him and for our home every day. Our heavenly Father feels the same way when we express gratefulness to Him. What have you thanked Him for lately?

Jenny Swindall

[23] Sing to the LORD, all the earth.
Proclaim good tidings of His salvation
from day to day.
[24] Declare His glory among the nations,
His wonders among all the peoples.
[25] For great is the LORD and greatly to be
praised.
He is to be feared above all gods.
[26] For all the gods of the peoples are idols,
but the LORD made the heavens.
[27] Honor and majesty are before Him;
strength and joy are in His place.
[28] Give to the LORD, O families of the peoples,
give to the LORD glory and strength.
[29] Give to the LORD the glory due His name;
bring an offering and come before Him,
bow down to the LORD in holy array.

30 Tremble before Him, all the earth.
The world also is firmly established; it
shall not be moved.

31 Let the heavens rejoice, and let the earth be
glad.
Let them say among the nations, "The
LORD is King."
32 Let the sea roar, and all its fullness.
Let the field rejoice, and all that is in it.
33 Then the trees of the forest will ring out
before the LORD,
for He is coming to judge the earth.
34 Oh, give thanks to the LORD, for *He is* good;
for His mercy endures forever.
35 Now say, "Save us, O God of our salvation,
and gather us and deliver us from the
nations,
that we may give thanks to Your holy
name,
to glory in Your praise.
36 Blessed is the LORD, the God of Israel,
from everlasting to everlasting."

Then all the people said, "Amen," and "Praise
the LORD."

Worship Before the Ark

37 So he left Asaph and his brothers before
the ark of the covenant of the LORD to min-
ister before the ark regularly, as each day
required, 38 and also Obed-Edom and his six-
ty-eight brothers, while Obed-Edom, the son of
Jeduthun, and Hosah were to be gatekeepers.
39 And he left Zadok the priest and his priestly
brothers before the tabernacle of the LORD at
the high place that was at Gibeon 40 to offer
burnt offerings to the LORD on the altar of burnt
offering continually, morning and evening, ac-
cording to all that was written in the Law of the
LORD, which He commanded Israel.
41 With them were Heman and Jeduthun
and the rest who were chosen, who were
marked by name to give thanks to the LORD,
for His mercy endures forever. 42 Heman and
Jeduthun had with them trumpets and cym-
bals to sound aloud and instruments for sacred
song. The sons of Jeduthun were appointed
to the gate.
43 Then all the people departed, each man
to his house, and David returned to bless his
house.

The Davidic Covenant
2Sa 7:1–17

17 Now it happened as David dwelt in
his house that he said to Nathan the
prophet, "Here I am dwelling in a house of ce-
dar while the ark of the LORD is under curtains."

16:34 2Ch 5:13
16:35 Ps 106:47–48
16:36 1Ki 8:15
16:37 2Ch 8:14
16:39 1Ki 3:4
16:40 Nu 28:3–8
16:41 2Ch 5:13

....

17:5 2Sa 7:6
17:13 Heb 1:5

2 So Nathan said to David, "Do all that is in
your heart, for God is with you."
3 But it happened on that same night that
the word of the LORD came to Nathan, saying,
4 Go and tell David My servant: Thus says
the LORD: You will not build a house for Me
to dwell in, 5 for I have not dwelt in a house
since the day when I brought Israel up *even*
until this day, but I have gone from tent
to tent and from tabernacle *to tabernacle*.
6 Wherever I have gone in all Israel, have I
ever spoken a word to the any of the judges
of Israel that I commanded to shepherd My
people, saying, Why have you not built Me
a house of cedar?
7 And now say this to My servant David:
Thus says the LORD of Hosts: I took you from
the pasture, from following after the flock, to
be ruler over My people Israel, 8 and I have
been with you wherever you went, and I
have cut off all your enemies from before
you. Also I will make your name like the
names of the greatest on earth. 9 And I will
appoint a place for My people Israel, and I
will plant them there where they will dwell
securely and tremble no more, *so that* the
sons of wickedness will not oppress them
just as before 10 from the time when I com-
manded the judges of My people Israel. I
will subdue all your enemies.
And I declare to you the LORD will build a
house for you. 11 Then it will be when your
days are full and you go to your fathers, I
will raise up your seed after you from your
own sons. His kingdom I will establish. 12 He
is the one who will build Me a house, and I
will establish his throne forever. 13 I will be
a father to him, and he will be a son to Me.
I will not take away My favor from him as
I did from the one who was before you. 14 I
will assign him a place in My house and in
My kingdom forever, and his throne will be
established for all time.

15 Thus, Nathan spoke to David all these
words and according to all this vision.

The Prayer of David
2Sa 7:18–29

16 Then King David came and sat before the
LORD, and he said,
"Who am I, O LORD God, and what is my
house that You have brought me this far?
17 This was something small in Your eyes,
God, but You have spoken concerning the
house of Your servant for a great while to
come and have regarded me with the status
of a great man, O LORD God.

SPIRIT-TO-SPIRIT PRAYER

PRAYER FOR RELEASE FROM DEPRESSION

Dear God, I know that once again You have given me this challenge for a reason. I don't know why, and I can't say I'm particularly fond of this one. But if You could please make my path straight, if only for a little while...if You could reveal the unknown to me...if You could please let me know how I can get out from under this horrible fog, I will be forever grateful. I'm of no use to my children this way. I'm of no use to my husband. I'm of no use to anyone. Please bring me back to the joy of my salvation.

Thank You for the answer that is already on the way.

And Satan, I speak to you in Jesus' name. You can take this depression and stick it where the Son doesn't shine. I will no longer accept this as a way of life. I was created to live life more abundantly, and you cannot take that away from me. You will not steal my joy. You will not steal my peace. I'm telling you to back off right now, because I will praise the God of Abraham, Isaac, and Jacob until the day I no longer have air in my lungs. And then I will start praising Him for real.

O God, I praise You, and I worship You. I give You praise for both the good and the bad that come my way, for in You I find my strength. In You I find my peace. I can do all things through You, and I can't do anything without You. I ask that You give me strength for this journey and make me an overcomer in all areas of my life. Please take this depression from me. Amen.

Tish Hagee Tucker

[18] "What more can David *speak* to You for
the honor of Your servant? For You know
Your servant. [19] O LORD, for the sake of Your
servant and according to Your own heart
You have done all these great things and
made known all these great things.
[20] "O LORD, there is none like You, and there
is no god besides You as we have heard with
our ears. [21] Who is like Your people Israel, a
nation on earth whom God has redeemed
for Himself as a people to make for Yourself
a great name by great and awesome deeds
in driving out nations from before Your peo-
ple whom You redeemed from Egypt? [22] For
You made Your people Israel for Yourself
for a people forever, and You, O LORD, have
become their God.
[23] "And now, LORD, the word which You
have spoken concerning Your servant and
concerning his house, *let it* endure forever
and do just as You have spoken. [24] Let Your
name endure and be magnified forever, say-
ing, 'The LORD of Hosts, the God of Israel, is
God to Israel.' And let the house of David
Your servant be established before You.
[25] "For You, my God, have revealed to Your
servant that You will build a house for him.
Therefore Your servant has found courage
to pray before You. [26] And now, O LORD, You
are God, and You have promised this good
word to Your servant. [27] Now, You have been
pleased to bless the house of Your servant
that it may be forever before You. For You, O
LORD, have blessed it, and it shall be blessed
forever."

17:19 Isa 37:35
17:22 Ex 19:5–6

18:1 2Sa 8:1–18

David's Conquests
2Sa 8:1–18

18 Now it happened after this that David
attacked the Philistines and subdued
them, so he took Gath and its neighboring
towns from Philistine control.
[2] He also defeated Moab so that the Moabites
became servants to David and brought tribute.
[3] Next David struck down Hadadezer the king
of Zobah toward Hamath as he marched out

to establish his authority along the Euphrates. 4 David captured from him one thousand chariots, seven thousand horsemen, and twenty thousand infantry men. Then David hamstrung all the chariot *horses* except for the one hundred he spared.

5 When the Arameans of Damascus came to help Hadadezer king of Zobah, David struck down twenty-two thousand Arameans. 6 Then David set *garrisons* in Aram of Damascus; and Arameans became subject to David, and brought tribute. The LORD gave victory to David wherever he went.

7 So David took the shields of gold that were on the servants of Hadadezer, and brought them to Jerusalem. 8 Also from Tibhath[1] and Kun, cities of Hadadezer, David took a large amount of bronze; with it Solomon made the bronze Sea, the pillars, and the vessels of bronze.

9 When Tou king of Hamath heard that David had defeated all the army of Hadadezer king of Zobah, 10 he sent his son Hadoram to King David to ask about his welfare and to bless him because he fought and defeated Hadadezer (for Hadadezer had been at war with Tou). He sent all kinds of articles of gold, silver, and bronze.

11 King David also dedicated these to the LORD, together with the silver and gold which he had carried away from all the surrounding nations, from Edom, Moab, the Ammonites, the Philistines, and Amalek.

12 Also Abishai the son of Zeruiah struck down eighteen thousand men of Edom in the Valley of Salt. 13 He set up garrisons in Edom, and all the Edomites became servants to David. Wherever he went, the LORD gave David victory.

David's Officials

14 So David was king over all Israel, and he executed justice and righteousness for all his people. 15 Joab the son of Zeruiah *was* over the army, and Jehoshaphat the son of Ahilud was the historian. 16 Zadok the son of Ahitub and Abimelek the son of Abiathar *served as* priests, while Shavsha *was* scribe. 17 Benaiah the son of Jehoiada *was* over the Kerethites and the Pelethites, and the sons of David were the king's principal officials.

David Defeats the Ammonites

2Sa 10:1–19

19 Now it happened after this that Nahash the king of the Ammonites died, and his son reigned in his place. 2 Then David said, "I will show kindness to Hanun the son of Nahash, because his father showed kindness to me." So David sent messengers to comfort him concerning his father. And David's servants came to Hanun in the land of the Ammonites to comfort him.

3 But the leaders of the Ammonites said to Hanun, "Do you think that David is honoring your father because he sent consolers? Have not his servants come to you to search and to overthrow and to spy out the land?" 4 So Hanun took the servants of David, shaved them, cut their garments in half as far as the hip, and sent them away.

5 Then *some* came and told David about the men, so he sent to meet them, for the men were greatly humiliated. The king said, "Remain in Jericho until your beards grow full, and then return."

6 When the Ammonites saw that they had become a stench to David, Hanun and the Ammonites sent one thousand talents[2] of silver to hire chariots and horsemen from Aram Naharaim, Aram Maakah, and Zobah. 7 So they hired for themselves thirty-two thousand chariots, with the king of Maakah and his people. They camped before Medeba as the Ammonites gathered from their cities to go out to war. 8 When David heard of it, he sent Joab and all the army of the mighty men. 9 So the Ammonites went out and formed ranks for battle at the entrance to the city while the kings who had come were by themselves in the open country.

10 When Joab saw the battle line was drawn in front of him and behind him, he chose some of the best men in Israel and arrayed them against the Arameans. 11 The rest of the people he placed in the charge of his brother Abishai, and they took up positions to engage the Ammonites. 12 Then he said, "If the Arameans are too strong for me, then you will come help me, but if the Ammonites are too strong for you, I will come help you. 13 Take courage, and let us prove worthy of our people and the cities of our God. May the LORD do what seems right to Him."

14 So Joab and the people who *were* with him drew near to the Arameans for battle, and they fled before him. 15 When the Ammonites saw the Arameans fleeing, they also fled before Abishai his brother and entered the city. So Joab returned to Jerusalem.

16 When the Arameans saw that they had been defeated by Israel, they sent messengers and summoned the Arameans who were beyond the River,[3] and Shophak, the commander of Hadadezer's army *went* before them.

17 When David was told about it, he gathered all Israel, crossed over the Jordan, and came

18:4 2Sa 8:4
18:8 2Sa 8:8
18:13 1Ch 18:6
18:15 1Ch 11:6
18:16 2Sa 8:17
18:17 2Sa 8:18

19:7 Nu 21:30
19:16 2Sa 10:16

[1] *8 Betah* in 2Sa 8:8. [2] *6* About 38 tons, or 34 metric tons.
[3] *16* Euphrates River.

against them. He divided his ranks and pre-
pared to engage the Arameans in battle, so
they fought against him. 18 But the Arameans
fled before Israel, and David killed seven thou-
sand chariot drivers and forty thousand infan-
try men of the Arameans, and killed Shophak,
the commander of the army.
19 And when the servants of Hadadezer saw
that they were defeated before Israel, they
negotiated peace with David and served him.
So the Arameans were not willing to aid the
Ammonites in battle again.

Rabbah Captured
2Sa 11:1; 12:29–31

20 Now at the beginning of the year
when kings would go out *to war*,
Joab led the army and devastated the land of
the Ammonites. He came and besieged Rab-
bah. But David remained in Jerusalem. So
Joab struck Rabbah and overthrew it. 2 Then
David took the crown of their king from his
head and found it weighed about a talent[1] of
gold with a precious stone *set* in it. And it was
placed on David's head. He also brought out a
great abundance of plunder from the city. 3 He
brought out the people who were in it, and put
them to work with saws, sharp iron tools, and
axes. Thus David did to all the cities of the
Ammonites, and then he and all the people
returned to Jerusalem.

Philistine Giants Killed
2Sa 21:15–22

4 Now after *this*, *when* war broke out in Gezer
with the Philistines, Sibbekai of Hushah killed
Sippai, who was one of the descendants of the
giants, and they were humbled.
5 Again there was war with the Philistines,
and Elhanan the son of Jair killed Lahmi, the
brother of Goliath the Gittite, the shaft of whose
wooden spear was like a weaver's beam.
6 Yet again there was war at Gath, where
there was a man of great stature, who had
six fingers on each hand and six toes on each
foot, twenty-four in number; and he also was
descended from the giants. 7 When he taunted
Israel, Jonathan the son of Shimea, David's
brother, killed him.
8 These were descended from the giants in
Gath, and they fell by the hand of David and
his servants.

The Census of Israel and Judah
2Sa 24:1–25

21 Now Satan stood against Israel and
incited David to number Israel. 2 Then
David said to Joab and the leaders of the peo-
ple, "Go count Israel from Beersheba to Dan
and bring me a report, that I may know their
number."

3 But Joab said, "May the LORD increase the
number of His people one hundred times
more. My lord the king, are not all of them my
lord's servants? Why then should my lord re-
quire this? Why should it bring guilt on Israel?"
4 Nevertheless, the king's word prevailed
against Joab, so Joab departed and went
throughout all Israel. Then he returned to Je-
rusalem. 5 Joab gave the results of the census
of the people to David: All Israel had one mil-
lion one hundred thousand men who drew the
sword, and in Judah four hundred and seventy
thousand men drew the sword.
6 However, he did not include the Levites and
Benjamin because the word of the king was
abhorrent to Joab. 7 Now this thing was evil in
the sight of God, and He struck Israel.
8 So David said to God, "I have sinned greatly
in doing this thing. Now, please, take away
the iniquity of your servant, for I have acted
very foolishly."
9 And the LORD spoke to Gad, David's seer,
saying, 10 "Go and speak to David, 'Thus says
the LORD: Three things I offer you; choose one
of these for yourself that I may do to you.' "
11 So Gad came to David and said to him,
"Thus says the LORD, 'Select for yourself, 12 ei-
ther three years of famine, or three months of
being swept away before your foes while the
sword of your enemy overtakes you, or three
days of the sword of the LORD, even pestilence
in the land, with the angel of the LORD destroy-
ing throughout all the territory of Israel.' Now
then consider what answer I shall return to
Him who sent me."
13 David replied to Gad, "I am in great dis-
tress. Let me fall into the hands of the LORD,
for His mercies *are* very great, but do not let
me fall into the hand of man."
14 So the LORD sent a plague throughout Is-
rael, and seventy thousand men of Israel fell.
15 And God sent an angel to Jerusalem to de-
stroy it, but as he prepared to destroy it, the
LORD looked and relented from the calamity.
And He said to the angel bringing the destruc-
tion, "It is enough. Remove your hand." The
angel of the LORD was then standing by the
threshing floor of Ornan the Jebusite.
16 David lifted up his eyes and saw the angel
of the LORD standing between earth and heav-
en with his sword drawn in his hand stretched
out over Jerusalem. So David and the elders,
covered in sackcloth, fell on their faces.
17 David said to God, "Was it not I who gave
the command to number the people? I am the
one who has sinned and surely done evil. But
these sheep, what have they done? O LORD my

19:18 2Sa 10:18
20:1 2Sa 11:1
20:4 2Sa 21:18–22
20:5 2Sa 21:19
21:2 1Ch 27:23–24

21:5 2Sa 24:9
21:8 2Sa 12:13
21:9 1Sa 9:9
21:13 Ps 130:7
21:15 Ge 6:6

[1] 2 About 75 pounds, or 34 kilograms.

Trusting God's Timing

You can liken learning to trust in God's timing to working a jigsaw puzzle. There you sit, trying to make sense of the hundreds (even thousands) of tiny pieces scattered around the table. Life sometimes feels that way, with all the "happys" and "sads" scrambled around in one box. Where do you start? As a puzzle master, I'll tell you: with the four corner pieces. To make your life puzzle a pretty picture, I suggest these four cornerstones will help you trust God's timing.

Cornerstone #1: God is all-loving.

While dealing with what seems to be utter silence, remember the first cornerstone of your life puzzle is God's love. He takes no delight in watching you go through your day lonely or fearful, looking over your shoulder, and waiting for a heavenly hammer to fall. No. A thousand times no! God is a Father. Do you know any father who takes pleasure in his son's sorrow or sickness? He is your Father and won't withhold anything good from you. He loves you as much as Jesus: "He who did not spare His own Son, but delivered Him up for us all, how shall He not with Him also freely give us all things?" (Ro 8:32). Stop reading this instant and say this out loud: "Heavenly Father, help me to receive Your love right now."

Cornerstone #2: God is all-knowing.

God's omniscience confuses our finite minds. Psalm 139:2–3 reveals the touching truth that God knows all of us: "You know when I sit and when I get up; You understand my thought from far off. You search my path and my lying down and are aware of all my ways." The lyrics to the familiar children's song say, "Jesus loves me, this I know," but it could also be sung, "Jesus knows me, this I love." God knows you and still chose you. He knows the good and bad choices of your past and everything that people will do to you in the future. He knows all the parts of your life—the fair and the unfair, the just and the unjust, the positive and the negative. In His infinite foreknowledge this magnificent God sees every second of your life.

Cornerstone #3: God is all-powerful.

While waiting for God's perfect timing, many believers fall into the trap of blaming the devil for the delay. They conclude that it's the devil's fault that their dreams have not come true.

Ever hear the old joke about the Christian walking home from church when he notices the devil sitting on the curb? His face buried in his hands, Satan is sobbing uncontrollably. Distraught by the devil's anguish, the kindhearted believer sits down on the curb and compassionately says, "Tell me what is so terribly wrong that you are sobbing this uncontrollably." Barely lifting his head, the devil mutters, "It's those Christians! They blame me for everything."

Friends, God is all-powerful and exceedingly greater than the devil. According to 2 Chronicles 16:9, God will "strengthen the heart that is completely toward Him." Nothing is too difficult for God. He can bring you a fiancé from an underground church in China, translate him to Los Angeles, and put him on a Greyhound bus destined for your front door.

Cornerstone #4: God is faithful.

The fourth corner that will keep you sane while waiting on God's perfect timing is remembering His faithfulness. He is dependable and reliable. Remembering this will help you maintain the proper perspective on life. You can choose one of two outlooks: (1) God in *your* story or (2) you in God's story. The first is idolatry, and the other is truth. Here is a truth author Joy Dawson has shared and one that will help you avoid making demands on the Lord: It's not about you. It's not about making your life perfect but making His name known. The reason you absolutely must know this is because God is only faithful to His Word, not your every whim.

There is a bigger picture, and you have been invited to share in its fulfillment. Once you get this, your priorities will shift. You will stop fretting about unfulfilled personal needs. When you want what God wants more than what you want, life is wonderful. This is where the famous phrase from the Lord's Prayer, "Your will be done" (Mt 6:10), applies, revealing itself as a life of daily surrender to His plan. It is also where the phrase that "the desire of the righteous will be granted" (Pr 10:24) applies.

If you are battling disappointment, put God first in your life. You can trust Him with those buried hopes and dreams. He will be faithful to fulfill His Word in you. Remember, you have a beautiful promise waiting for you. As Ecclesiastes 3:11 promises, "He has made everything beautiful in its appropriate time." As you continually focus on a Father God who is all-loving, all-knowing, all-powerful, and faithful, you can expect a perfect peace to replace your impatience and anxieties. God's ways are perfect, and so is His timing.

Rachel Burchfield

God, I pray, let Your hand be against me and my father's house, but do not let Your people be plagued."

David Builds an Altar

18 Then the angel of the LORD commanded Gad to tell David that David should go up and raise an altar to the LORD on the threshing floor of Ornan the Jebusite. 19 So David went up at the word of Gad which he delivered in the name of the LORD.

20 Now Ornan turned and saw the angel, but his four sons *who were* with him hid themselves as Ornan threshed the wheat. 21 As David came to Ornan, Ornan looked and saw David and went out from the threshing floor and bowed down before David with *his* face to the ground.

22 Then David said to Ornan, "Give me the site of the threshing floor so that I may build an altar on it to the LORD. Sell it to me at full price so the plague on the people may be restrained."

23 So Ornan replied to David, "Take it for yourself, and let my lord the king do whatever seems good in his eyes. Look, I will give the oxen for the burnt offerings, the threshing wagons for wood, and the wheat for the grain offering. I will give it all."

24 Then King David said to Ornan, "No, for I will surely acquire it for the full price, for I will not take what is yours for the LORD nor offer burnt offerings that cost me nothing."

25 So David gave Ornan six hundred shekels[1] of gold by weight for the site, 26 and David built there an altar to the LORD and offered up burnt offerings and peace offerings. He called on the LORD, and the LORD answered him by fire from heaven on the altar of burnt offering.

27 So the LORD spoke to the angel, and he put away his sword in its sheath. 28 At that time, when David saw that the LORD had answered him at the threshing floor of Ornan the Jebusite, he sacrificed there. 29 For the tabernacle of the LORD and the altar of burnt offering that Moses had made in the wilderness *were* in the high place in Gibeon at that time. 30 But David was unable to go before it to inquire of God, because he was terrified by the sword of the angel of the LORD.

22 Then David said, "Here shall be the house of the LORD God and here the altar of the burnt offering for Israel."

Plans to Build the Temple

2 So David gave instructions to gather together those sojourning in the land of Israel, and he appointed stonemasons to cut hewn stones for building the house of God. 3 David also provided large quantities of iron for nails for the doors of the gates and for the clamps as well as an abundance of bronze beyond measure, 4 and cedar logs without number, for the Sidonians and the Tyrians brought much cedar wood to David.

5 Now David said, "Solomon my son *is* young and inexperienced, and the house that is to be built for the LORD *must* be exceedingly magnificent, of fame and glory throughout all the lands. Therefore I will make preparation for it now." So David made extensive preparations before his death.

6 Then David called Solomon his son and commanded him to build a house for the LORD, the God of Israel. 7 David said to Solomon, "My son, I had it in my heart to build a house for the name of the LORD my God, 8 but the word of the LORD came to me, saying, 'You have shed much blood and waged great wars. You shall not build a house for My name because you have shed much blood on the earth before Me. 9 A son shall be born to you who shall be a man of rest. I will give him rest from all his enemies all around. Solomon will be his name, and I will give peace and tranquility to Israel in his days. 10 He will be the one to build a house for My name. He shall be a son to Me, and I will be a father to him, and I will establish the throne of his kingdom over Israel forever.'

11 "Now, my son, may the LORD be with you, and may you have success in building the house of the LORD your God just as He has spoken concerning you. 12 Only may the LORD give you insight and understanding and give you charge over Israel so you may keep the law of the LORD your God. 13 Then you will prosper if you carefully observe the statutes and the judgments which the LORD commanded Moses for Israel. Be strong and of good courage. Do not be afraid or dismayed.

14 "With great difficulty I have prepared for the house of the LORD one hundred thousand talents[2] of gold and one million[3] talents of silver as well as innumerable quantities of bronze and iron, beyond measure. I have also prepared timber and stone to which you may add even more. 15 Moreover you have an abundance of workers: stonecutters, masons, carpenters, and men skilled in all *kinds of* work, 16 craftsmen in gold, silver, bronze, and iron without number. Rise up and work, and may the LORD be with you."

17 Then David commanded all the leaders of Israel to assist Solomon his son, *saying*, 18 "Is not the LORD your God with you? Has He not given you rest all around? For He has given the inhabitants of the land into my hand, and the land is subdued before the LORD and His

21:18 2Ch 3:1
21:26 Lev 9:24
21:29 1Ch 16:39
22:1 2Ch 3:1
22:2 1Ki 5:17–18
22:3 1Ch 22:14
22:5 1Ki 3:7
22:8 1Ch 28:3
22:9 1Ki 4:20
22:11 1Ch 22:16
22:12 1Ki 3:9–12
22:13 Jos 1:6–9
22:14 1Ch 22:3
22:16 1Ch 22:11
22:18 1Ch 22:9

[1] *25* About 15 pounds, or 6.9 kilograms. [2] *14* About 3,750 tons, or 3,400 metric tons. [3] *14* About 37,500 tons, or 34,000 metric tons.

people. 19 Now dedicate your heart and your soul to seek the LORD your God. Rise up and build the sanctuary of the LORD God, so that you may bring the ark of the covenant of the LORD along with the holy vessels of God into the house which is to be built for the name of the LORD."

The Levites

23 Now David was old and full of days when he made Solomon his son king over Israel. 2 So he gathered together all the leaders of Israel with the priests and the Levites.

3 The Levites from thirty years old and up were counted, and their head count of men was thirty-eight thousand. 4 Twenty-four thousand of these, David said, "shall have charge of the work in the house of the LORD; six thousand shall be officers and judges, 5 four thousand shall be gatekeepers, and four thousand shall offer praises to the LORD with the instruments that I have made for praise."

6 David assigned them to divisions according to the sons of Levi: Gershon, Kohath, and Merari.

Gershonites

7 From the Gershonites:
Ladan and Shimei.
8 The sons of Ladan *were*
first Jehiel, then Zetham and Joel, three *in all.*
9 The sons of Shimei *were*
Shelomith, Haziel, and Haran, three.
These *were* the heads of the fathers' houses of Ladan.
10 The sons of Shimei *were*
Jahath, Zina, Jeush, and Beriah.
These four *were* the sons of Shimei.
11 Now Jahath was the first and Ziza the second, but Jeush and Beriah did not have many sons, so they were counted as one unit for their father's house.

Kohathites

12 The sons of Kohath *were*
Amram, Izhar, Hebron, and Uzziel, four *in all.*
13 The sons of Amram *were*
Aaron and Moses,
but Aaron was set apart to consecrate the most holy things, he and his sons forever, to offer sacrifices before the LORD, to minister to Him, and to bless in His name forever. 14 As for Moses, the man of God, his sons were named among the tribe of Levi.
15 The sons of Moses *were*
Gershom and Eliezer.
16 The son of Gershom *was*
Shubael the chief.

22:19 1Ki 8:6
23:1 1Ch 29:28
23:4 2Ch 19:8
23:6 1Ch 6:1
23:12 Ex 6:18
23:13 Ex 6:20
23:14 Dt 33:1
23:16 1Ch 26:24
23:19 1Ch 24:23
23:24 Nu 10:17
23:25 1Ch 22:18
23:26 Nu 4:5
23:29 Lev 19:35–36
23:31 Isa 1:13–14
23:32 Nu 1:53
24:1 Ex 6:23
24:2 Lev 10:2

17 The son of Eliezer *was*
Rehabiah the chief.
Eliezer had no other sons, but the sons of Rehabiah were very many.
18 The son of Izhar *was*
Shelomith the chief.
19 The sons of Hebron *were*
Jeriah the first, Amariah the second, Jahaziel the third, *and* Jekameam the fourth.
20 The sons of Uzziel *were*
Micah the first and Ishiah the second.

Merarites

21 The sons of Merari *were*
Mahli and Mushi.
The sons of Mahli *were*
Eleazar and Kish.
22 Eleazar died having no sons, but only daughters, so the sons of Kish, their brothers, took them *as wives.*
23 The sons of Mushi were
Mahli, Eder, and Jerimoth, three.

24 These *were* the sons of Levi according to their fathers' houses, the heads of the fathers' houses as they were registered by the number of their names according to their head count, those doing the work for the service of the house of the LORD, from twenty years old and up.

25 For David said, "The LORD, the God of Israel, has given rest to His people, and He dwells in Jerusalem forever. 26 And so the Levites no longer need to carry the tabernacle and all its implements for its service." 27 For by the last words of David, the sons of Levi were numbered from twenty years old and up; 28 because their duty was to help the sons of Aaron in the service of the house of the LORD, in the courts and in the chambers, with the purifying of all holy things, even the work of service of the house of God, 29 and with the showbread, the fine flour for a grain offering, the wafers of unleavened bread, the baked offering, the offering mixed with oil, and all measures of quantity and size, 30 to stand morning by morning to thank and praise the LORD, and likewise in the evening, 31 and to offer up all burnt offerings to the LORD, for Sabbaths, New Moons, and appointed feasts, by number as the judgment concerning them, continually before the LORD, 32 and that they should keep charge of the tent of meeting and the sanctuary and attend to the sons of Aaron, their brothers, for the service of the house of the LORD.

Priestly Divisions Assigned

24 Now the divisions of the sons of Aaron *were* these.

The sons of Aaron: Nadab, Abihu, Eleazar, and Ithamar. 2 But Nadab and Abihu died

before their father, and they had no sons. So
Eleazar and Ithamar served as priests. 3 Then
David, along with Zadok of the sons of Eleazar
and Ahimelek of the sons of Ithamar, divided
them to their offices by their service. 4 Since the
sons of Eleazar were found *to have* more chief
men than the sons of Ithamar, they divided
them into sixteen heads of the fathers' houses
for the sons of Eleazar, and eight for the sons
of Ithamar, according to their fathers' houses.
5 So they divided them by lots, the one as the
other, for there were officers of the sanctuary
and officers of God among both the sons of
Eleazar and Ithamar.

6 Shemaiah the son of Nethanel, the Levite
scribe, wrote them down in the presence of the
king, the leaders, Zadok the priest, Ahimelek
the son of Abiathar, and the heads of the fa-
thers' houses of the priests and the Levites,
one father's house taken for Eleazar and one
for Ithamar.

7 The first lot fell to Jehoiarib,
the second to Jedaiah,
8 the third to Harim,
the fourth to Seorim,
9 the fifth to Malkijah,
the sixth to Mijamin,
10 the seventh to Hakkoz,
the eighth to Abijah,
11 the ninth to Jeshua,
the tenth to Shekaniah,
12 the eleventh to Eliashib,
the twelfth to Jakim,
13 the thirteenth to Huppah,
the fourteenth to Jeshebeab,
14 the fifteenth to Bilgah,
the sixteenth to Immer,
15 the seventeenth to Hezir,
the eighteenth to Happizzez,
16 the nineteenth to Pethahiah,
the twentieth to Jehezkel,
17 the twenty-first to Jakin,
the twenty-second to Gamul,
18 the twenty-third to Delaiah,
the twenty-fourth to Maaziah.

19 These were their appointments for their
service to come into the house of the LORD
according to the schedule prescribed for them
by Aaron their father, as the LORD God of Israel
had commanded him.

Remaining Levite Assignments

20 Now for the remaining sons of Levi:
from the sons of Amram, Shubael;
from the sons of Shubael, Jehdeiah.
21 For Rehabiah: from the sons of Reha-
biah,
the first *was* Ishiah.
22 From the Izharites, Shelomoth;

24:3 2Sa 8:17
24:10 Lk 1:5
24:19 1Ch 9:25
24:21 1Ch 23:17
24:22 1Ch 23:18

24:23 1Ch 23:19
24:31 1Ch 24:5–6
25:1 2Ki 3:15
25:2 1Ch 25:6
25:3 1Ch 16:41–42

from the sons of Shelomoth, Jahath.
23 The sons of Hebron: Jeriah *the first*, Am-
ariah the second, Jahaziel the third, *and*
Jekameam the fourth.
24 The sons of Uzziel, Micah;
from the sons of Micah, Shamir.
25 The brother of Micah, Ishiah;
from the sons of Ishiah, Zechariah.
26 The sons of Merari, Mahli and Mushi;
the son of Jaaziah, Beno.
27 The sons of Merari:
by Jaaziah *were* Beno, Shoham, Zakkur,
and Ibri.
28 For Mahli: Eleazar, who had no sons.
29 For Kish: the son of Kish,
Jerahmeel.
30 The sons of Mushi: Mahli, Eder, and
Jerimoth.

These *were* the sons of the Levites according
to their fathers' houses. 31 These also cast lots
just as their brothers, the sons of Aaron, in the
presence of David the king, Zadok, Ahimelek,
and the heads of the fathers' houses of the
priests and of the Levites, the head of the fa-
thers' houses as well as his younger brother.

The Musicians

25 Then David and the officers of the
army also set apart for the service
some of the sons of Asaph, and of Heman, and
of Jeduthun, those who prophesied with lyres,
harps, and cymbals. The number of those who
did the work according to their service was:

2 From the sons of Asaph:
Zakkur, Joseph, Nethaniah, and
Asarelah, the sons of Asaph under the
guidance of Asaph, who prophesied
according to the decree of the king.
3 For Jeduthun, the sons of Jeduthun:
Gedaliah, Zeri, Jeshaiah, Hashabiah, and
Mattithiah, six, under the guidance of
their father Jeduthun, who prophesied
with the lyre in giving thanks and praise
to the LORD.
4 For Heman, the sons of Heman:
Bukkiah, Mattaniah, Uzziel, Shubael and
Jerimoth, Hananiah, Hanani, Eliathah,
Giddalti, and Romamti-Ezer, Josh-
bekashah, Mallothi, Hothir, Mahazioth.
5 All these were the sons of Heman, the
king's seer, according to the words of
God, to exalt him, for God gave fourteen
sons and three daughters to Heman.

6 All these *were* under the direction of their
father for the music in the house of the LORD
with cymbals, harps, and lyres, for the service
of the house of God by decree of the king:
Asaph, Jeduthun, and Heman. 7 So the number

of them, with their brothers, who were trained
in singing to the LORD, all of whom were skill-
ful, *was* two hundred and eighty-eight. 8 They
cast lots for their duties, small and great, teach-
er and student alike.

9 The first lot fell for Asaph to Joseph;
the second to Gedaliah,
to him and his brothers and his sons,
twelve;
10 the third to Zakkur,
his sons and his brothers, twelve;
11 the fourth to Izri,
his sons and his brothers, twelve;
12 the fifth to Nethaniah,
his sons and his brothers, twelve;
13 the sixth to Bukkiah,
his sons and his brothers, twelve;
14 the seventh to Jesarelah,
his sons and his brothers, twelve;
15 the eighth to Jeshaiah,
his sons and his brothers, twelve;
16 the ninth to Mattaniah,
his sons and his brothers, twelve;
17 the tenth to Shimei,
his sons and his brothers, twelve;
18 the eleventh to Azarel,
his sons and his brothers, twelve;
19 the twelfth to Hashabiah,
his sons and his brothers, twelve;
20 for the thirteenth to Shubael,
his sons and his brothers, twelve;
21 for the fourteenth to Mattithiah,
his sons and his brothers, twelve;
22 for the fifteenth to Jerimoth,
his sons and his brothers, twelve;
23 for the sixteenth to Hananiah,
his sons and his brothers, twelve;
24 for the seventeenth to Joshbekashah,
his sons and his brothers, twelve;
25 for the eighteenth to Hanani,
his sons and his brothers, twelve;
26 for the nineteenth to Mallothi,
his sons and his brothers, twelve;
27 for the twentieth to Eliathah,
his sons and his brothers, twelve;
28 for the twenty-first to Hothir,
his sons and his brothers, twelve;
29 for the twenty-second to Giddalti,
his sons and his brothers, twelve;
30 for the twenty-third to Mahazioth,
his sons and his brothers, twelve;
31 for the twenty-fourth to Romamti-Ezer,
his sons and his brothers, twelve.

The Gatekeepers

26 *These were* the divisions of the gate-
keepers:
from the Korahites, Meshelemiah the son of
Kore, *one* of the sons of Asaph.

2 Meshelemiah had sons:
Zechariah the firstborn,
Jediael the second,
Zebadiah the third,
Jathniel the fourth,
3 Elam the fifth,
Jehohanan the sixth,
and Eliehoenai the seventh.
4 Obed-Edom had sons:
Shemaiah the firstborn,
Jehozabad the second,
Joah the third,
Sakar the fourth,
Nethanel the fifth,
5 Ammiel the sixth,
Issachar the seventh,
and Peullethai the eighth
(for God blessed him).

6 Also to his son Shemaiah sons were born
who ruled their fathers' houses, for they
were men of great ability. 7 The sons of
Shemaiah *were* Othni, Rephael, Obed,
and Elzabad, whose brothers were able
men: *namely* Elihu and Semakiah. 8 All
these were of the sons of Obed-Edom
with their sons and their brothers, able
men qualified for service, sixty-two of
Obed-Edom.
9 Meshelemiah had sons and brothers, able
men, eighteen *in all*.

10 Also Hosah, of the sons of Merari, had
sons: Shimri the first (although he was
not the firstborn, his father made him the
first), 11 Hilkiah the second, Tabaliah the
third, Zechariah the fourth: all the sons
and brothers of Hosah, thirteen.

12 These divisions of the gatekeepers, for
their chief men, had assignments to minister
in the house of the LORD just as their brothers.
13 They cast lots, small and great alike, accord-
ing to their fathers' houses, gate by gate.
14 The lot for the East Gate fell to Shelemiah.
Then they cast lots for Zechariah his son, a
wise counselor, and his lot came out for the
North Gate; 15 to Obed-Edom the South Gate,
and to his sons was allotted the storehouse.
16 For Shuppim and Hosah *the lot* came out for
the West Gate, at the Shalleketh Gate on the as-
cending road, guard corresponding to guard.
17 On the east there were six Levites *each
day*, on the north four each day, on the south
four each day, as well as two and two at the
storehouse. 18 For the colonnade on the west,
there were four at the highway, and two at the
colonnade.
19 These were the divisions of the gatekeep-
ers of the sons of Korah and of the sons of
Merari.

25:8 1Ch 26:13

26:10 1Ch 16:38
26:13 1Ch 25:8
26:15 2Ch 25:24
26:18 2Ki 23:11

The Treasurers and Other Officials

20 And of the Levites, Ahijah *was* over the
treasures of the house of God, and over the
treasures of the dedicated offerings.
21 The sons of Ladan, the sons of the Ger-
shonites, belonging to Ladan, the heads of the
fathers' houses belonging to Ladan the Ger-
shonite: Jehieli. 22 The sons of Jehieli, Zetham,
and Joel his brother, *were in charge of* the trea-
sures of the house of the LORD.
23 From the Amramites, the Izharites, the He-
bronites, and the Uzzielites:

24 Shubael the son of Gershom, the son of
Moses, *was* ruler of the treasures. 25 His
brothers by Eliezer *were* Rehabiah his
son, Jeshaiah his son, Joram his son,
Zikri his son, and Shelomith his son.
26 This Shelomith and his brothers *were*
in charge of all the treasures of the ded-
icated offerings, which David the king,
the heads of the fathers, the officers of
the thousands and the hundreds, and the
commanders of the army had dedicated.
27 Some of the spoils won in battles they
dedicated for the maintenance of the
house of the LORD. 28 Also all that Samuel
the seer and Saul the son of Kish and
Abner the son of Ner and Joab the son
of Zeruiah had dedicated—all dedicated
gifts were in the care of Shelomith and
his brothers.
29 From the Izharites, Kenaniah and his
sons were *assigned* the outside duties for
Israel, as officers and judges.
30 From the Hebronites: Hashabiah and his
brothers, one thousand seven hundred
able men, *were* administrators of Israel
on the west side of the Jordan for all
the work of the LORD and for the service
of the king. 31 Jeriah was chief of the
Hebronites according to the genealogical
records of his fathers. In the fortieth year
of the reign of David, mighty men of
valor were found in the records among
the Hebronites at Jazer of Gilead, 32 and
his brothers, able men, two thousand
seven hundred heads of the fathers, to
them King David entrusted all matters of
God and of the king concerning the Reu-
benites, the Gadites, and the half-tribe of
Manasseh.

The Military Divisions

27 Now *these are* the sons of Israel ac-
cording to their number, the heads of
fathers' houses, the commanders of thousands
and hundreds, and their officers who minis-
tered to the king in all matters concerning the
divisions, which came and went, month by
month throughout all the months of the year,
to each division of twenty-four thousand:

2 Jashobeam the son of Zabdiel led the first
division for the first month; in his division,
twenty-four thousand. 3 *He was* from the
sons of Perez *and was* the leader of all the
officers of the army for the first month.
4 Dodai the Ahohite and his division led the
division of the second month with Mikloth
as the ruler: in his division, twenty-four
thousand.
5 The third commander of the army for the
third month was Benaiah the son of Jehoia-
da, a chief priest: in his division, twenty-four
thousand. 6 Benaiah himself *was* the mighty
man of the thirty who led the thirty: Ammiz-
abad his son *led* his division.
7 The fourth for the fourth month, Asahel the
brother of Joab, and Zebadiah his son after
him: in his division, twenty-four thousand.
8 The fifth for the fifth month, the leader Sham-
huth the Izrahite: in his division, twenty-four
thousand.
9 The sixth for the sixth month, Ira the son of Ik-
kesh the Tekoite: in his division, twenty-four
thousand.
10 The seventh for the seventh month, Helez
the Pelonite, from the sons of Ephraim: in
his division, twenty-four thousand.
11 The eighth for the eighth month, Sibbekai
the Hushathite, of the Zerahites: in his divi-
sion, twenty-four thousand.
12 The ninth for the ninth month, Abiezer the
Anathothite, of the Benjamites: in his divi-
sion, twenty-four thousand.
13 The tenth for the tenth month, Maharai the
Netophathite, of the Zerahites: in his divi-
sion, twenty-four thousand.
14 The eleventh for the eleventh month, Be-
naiah the Pirathonite, from the sons of
Ephraim: in his division, twenty-four thou-
sand.
15 The twelfth for the twelfth month, Heldai
the Netophathite, of Othniel: in his division,
twenty-four thousand.

Leaders of the Tribes

16 Over the tribes of Israel:

The chief officer over the Reubenites was
Eliezer the son of Zikri;
over the Simeonites, Shephatiah the son of
Maakah;
17 over the Levites, Hashabiah the son of
Kemuel;
over the Aaronites, Zadok;
18 over Judah, Elihu, one of the brothers of
David;
over Issachar, Omri the son of Michael;

26:20 1Ch 26:22
26:28 1Sa 9:9
26:29 1Ch 23:4
26:31 1Ch 23:19
26:32 2Ch 19:11

27:2 2Sa 23:8
27:4 2Sa 23:9
27:7 1Ch 11:26
27:8 1Ch 11:27
27:9 1Ch 11:28
27:10 1Ch 11:27
27:11 2Sa 21:18
27:12 1Ch 11:28
27:13 1Ch 11:30
27:14 1Ch 11:31
27:15 2Sa 23:29
27:17 1Ch 26:30

19 over Zebulun, Ishmaiah the son of
Obadiah;
over Naphtali, Jerimoth the son of Azriel;
20 over the sons of Ephraim, Hoshea the son
of Azaziah;
over the half-tribe of Manasseh, Joel the
son of Pedaiah;
21 over the half-tribe of Manasseh in Gilead,
Iddo the son of Zechariah;
over Benjamin, Jaasiel the son of Abner;
22 over Dan, Azarel the son of Jeroham.
These *were* the leaders of the tribes of Israel.

23 But David did not take the number from
twenty years old and under because the LORD
had said He would multiply Israel as the stars
of the heavens. 24 Joab the son of Zeruiah be-
gan to count *them*, but he did not finish. And
because of this wrath came on Israel, and the
number was not recorded in the account of the
chronicles of King David.

Civic Officials

25 Azmaveth the son of Adiel was over the
king's treasures, and Jonathan the son of Uz-
ziah was over the storehouses in the fields, in
the cities, and in the villages, and in the towers.
26 Ezri the son of Kelub was over those who
did the work of the field to till the ground.
27 Shimei the Ramathite was over the vine-
yards, and Zabdi the Shiphmite was over what
was in the vineyards for the stores of wine.
28 Baal-Hanan the Gederite was over the ol-
ive trees and the sycamore trees that were in
the Shephelah, and Joash was over the stores
of oil.
29 Shitrai the Sharonite was over the herds
that fed in Sharon, and Shaphat the son of Ad-
lai was over the herds that were in the valleys.
30 Obil the Ishmaelite was over the camels,
and Jehdeiah the Meronothite was over the
donkeys.
31 Jaziz the Hagrite was over the flocks.
All these were the overseers of King David's
property.

32 Also Jonathan, David's uncle, *was* a coun-
selor, a man of understanding, and a scribe;
and Jehiel the son of Hakmoni was with the
king's sons.
33 Now Ahithophel was the king's counselor,
and Hushai the Arkite was the king's friend.
34 Jehoiada the son of Benaiah and Abiathar
came after Ahithophel, and Joab was the leader
of the king's army.

David's Plans for the Temple

28 Now David assembled all the leaders
of Israel in Jerusalem: the leaders
of the tribes, the officers of the divisions of
those ministering to the king, the captains of
thousands and the captains of hundreds, the
stewards over all the property and livestock of
the king and his sons with the eunuchs and
the fighting men and all the brave warriors.
2 So King David rose to his feet and said,
"Hear me, my brothers and my people. I *had*
it in my heart to build a house of rest for the
ark of the covenant of the LORD, a footstool
for the feet of our God, so I prepared to build
it. 3 But God said to me, 'You shall not build a
house for My name because you *are* a man of
war and have spilled much blood.'
4 "Still, the LORD God of Israel chose me from
all my father's house to be king over Israel for-
ever; for He chose Judah as leader, and in the
house of Judah, the house of my father, and
among the sons of my father, He took plea-
sure in me to make me king over all Israel. 5 Of
all my sons (for the LORD has given me many
sons), He has chosen my son Solomon to sit
on the throne of the kingdom of the LORD over
Israel. 6 For He said to me, 'Solomon your son
is the one who shall build My house and My
courts, for I have chosen him *to be* My son,
and I will be his Father. 7 I will establish his
kingdom forever if he is fully committed to
keep My commandments and My judgments
as it is this day.'
8 "Now therefore in the sight of all Israel, the
assembly of the LORD, and in the hearing of
our God, observe and seek out all the com-
mandments of the LORD your God, that you
may possess this good land and leave it for an
inheritance for your children after you forever.
9 As for you, Solomon my son, know the God
of your fathers and serve Him with a whole
heart and with a willing spirit, for the LORD
searches every heart and understands the
intent of every thought. If you seek Him, He
will be found by you, but if you forsake Him,
He will abandon you forever. 10 See now that
the LORD chose you to build the house for His
sanctuary. Be strong and do it."
11 Then David gave to Solomon his son the
building plans for the vestibule *of the temple*,
its house, its treasury, its roof chambers, its
inner rooms, and the place of the mercy seat;
12 and the plans, all of which were *given* to
him by the Spirit, for the courts of the house
of the LORD and for the surrounding rooms,
the storehouses of the house of God, and the
storehouses of the dedicated offerings; 13 for
the divisions of the priests and the Levites
for all the work of the service of the house
of the LORD and for all the implements of the
service of the house of the LORD; 14 the weight
of gold for all the golden implements of ser-
vice, the implements of silver by weight for
all implements of service, 15 and the weight

27:23 Ge 15:5
27:29 1Ch 5:16
27:33 2Sa 15:12
27:34 1Ki 1:7
28:1 1Ch 11:10–47

28:2 Ps 99:5
28:3 1Ch 22:8
28:4 1Sa 16:1
28:5 1Ch 3:1–9
28:6 2Sa 7:13–14
28:7 1Ch 22:13
28:9 1Sa 16:7
28:11 Ex 25:40
28:12 1Ch 26:20

of the golden lampstands and their lamps, the weight of gold for each lampstand and its lamps, the weight of silver for a lampstand and its lamps according to the use of each lampstand; 16 the weight of gold for the tables of the showbread, table by table, and silver for the tables of silver; 17 and the pure gold forks, the basins, and the pitchers; for the golden bowls with the weight for each bowl; the weight of silver for each silver dish; 18 and for the altar of incense, refined gold by weight; also his plan for the golden chariot of the cherubim that spread *their wings* and covered the ark of the covenant of the LORD.

19 "All *this*," *said David*, "the LORD made me understand in writing by His hand upon me, all the works of this pattern."

20 Then David said to Solomon his son, "Be strong and courageous, and take action. Do not be afraid nor be dismayed for the LORD God, my God, is with you. He will not leave you nor forsake you, until you have finished all the work of the service of the house of the LORD. 21 Now, here are the divisions of the priests and the Levites for all the service of the house of God, and all those who are willing and skillful for all the work will be with you for all the service; also the leaders and the people will be wholly at your command."

Temple Offerings

29 King David said to all the assembly, "Solomon my son, the one whom God has chosen, is young and inexperienced, and the work is great since the palace is not for a man but for the LORD God. 2 So with all my might I have prepared for the house of my God: gold for the *things of* gold, silver for the *things of* silver, bronze for the *things of* bronze, iron for the *things of* iron, and wood for the *things of* wood, *along with* onyx stones and stones for setting, stones of antimony, multicolored stones, and every precious stone, even alabaster in abundance. 3 Moreover, in my devotion to the house of my God I have offered from my own property, gold and silver, which I give for the house of my God, over and above that which I prepared for the holy dwelling place: 4 three thousand talents[1] of gold of the gold of Ophir and seven thousand talents[2] of refined silver for overlaying the walls of the house; 5 of gold for the *things of* gold and of silver for the *things of* silver, even for all the handiwork of the craftsmen. Now, who is willing to consecrate himself today to the LORD?"

6 Then the leaders of the fathers' houses, the leaders of the tribes of Israel, the captains of thousands and hundreds, and the officials of the king's workers offered willingly. 7 Also they donated to the service of the house of God five thousand talents[3] of gold and ten thousand darics[4] of gold, ten thousand talents[5] of silver, eighteen thousand talents[6] of bronze, and one hundred thousand talents[7] of iron. 8 Whoever had *precious* stones gave them to the treasury of the house of the LORD in the custody of Jehiel the Gershonite. 9 Then the people rejoiced because they had offered willingly, for with a whole heart they had offered freely to the LORD; and King David also rejoiced greatly.

A Prayer of David

10 So David blessed the LORD in the presence of all the assembly, and David said,

"Blessed are You, O LORD,
the God of Israel,
our Father forever and ever.
11 Yours, O LORD, is the greatness, and the power,
and the glory, and the victory, and the majesty,
for everything in the heavens and the earth *is Yours*.
Yours is the kingdom, O LORD,
and You exalt Yourself as head above all.
12 Riches and honor flow from You,
and You rule over all.
In Your hand are power and might,
and in Your hand *it is* to make great and to strengthen all.
13 So now, our God, we give thanks to You,
and praise Your glorious name.

Let power and might be released from Your hand (1Ch 29:12).

14 "But who am I, and who are my people, that we should be able to offer so freely as this? For everything comes from You, *even* from Your own hand we have given to You. 15 For we are strangers and sojourners before You, just as all our fathers were. Our days on earth are like a shadow, and there is no hope. 16 O LORD our God, all this abundance that we have prepared to build You a house for Your holy name has come from Your hand, and all belongs to You. 17 I know, my God, that You test the heart, and with uprightness You are pleased, so in the uprightness of my heart I have offered freely all these things, and now I have seen Your people, those present here, offer freely and joyously to You. 18 O LORD, the God of Abraham, Isaac, and Israel, our fathers, keep this forever in the thoughts and

28:18 Ex 25:18–22
28:19 1Ch 28:11–12
28:20 1Ch 22:13
29:1 1Ch 22:5
29:2 1Ch 22:3–5
29:4 1Ki 9:28
29:9 1Ki 8:61
29:11 Da 4:34–35
29:15 Job 14:2
29:17 1Ch 28:9

[1] *4* About 110 tons, or 100 metric tons. [2] *4* About 260 tons, or 235 metric tons. [3] *7* About 190 tons, or 170 metric tons. [4] *7* About 185 pounds, or 84 kilograms. [5] *7* About 380 tons, or 340 metric tons. [6] *7* About 675 tons, or 610 metric tons. [7] *7* About 3,800 tons, or 3,400 metric tons.

intentions of the heart of Your people and direct their heart to You. 19 Grant to Solomon my son a whole heart to keep Your commandments, Your testimonies, and Your statutes, to do all *these things* and to build the palace for which I have made preparation."

I will speak blessings and keep my heart from sinning (1Ch 29:19).

20 Then David said to all the assembly, "Bless now the LORD your God." So all the assembly blessed the LORD, the God of their fathers. They bowed down and paid homage to the LORD and the king.

Solomon, King of Israel

1Ki 1:28–53

21 On the following day, they made sacrifices to the LORD and offered burnt offerings to the LORD: one thousand bulls, one thousand rams, *and* one thousand lambs, with their drink offerings and sacrifices in abundance for all Israel. 22 So they ate and drank before the LORD on that day with great joy.

And they made Solomon the son of David king a second time, for they anointed *him* to the LORD as a ruler and Zadok as a priest. 23 Then Solomon sat on the throne of the LORD as king instead of David his father, and he prospered, and all Israel obeyed him. 24 All the leaders and the mighty men, and also the sons of King David, pledged their allegiance to King Solomon.

25 The LORD highly exalted Solomon in the sight of all Israel and bestowed on him such royal majesty as had never been on any king in Israel before him.

The Death of David

1Ki 2:10–12

26 Now David son of Jesse reigned over all Israel. 27 His tenure as king over Israel was forty years: In Hebron, he reigned seven years, and in Jerusalem he was king thirty-three years. 28 So he died at a good old age, full of days, riches, and honor. And Solomon his son reigned in his place.

29 Now the acts of David the king, first to last, are written in the book of Samuel the seer, and in the book of Nathan the prophet, and in the book of Gad the seer 30 with all his reign and his might and the times that overtook him, and Israel, and all the kingdoms of the lands.

29:19 Ps 72:1
29:20 Ex 4:31
29:22 1Ch 23:1

....

29:25 1Ki 3:13
29:26 1Ch 18:14
29:27 2Sa 5:4–5
29:28 Ge 15:15
29:29 1Sa 9:9

Author: Traditionally Ezra

Written: Between 450 and 425 BC

Theme: Religious History of Israel

2 Chronicles

Dear Spirit Led Woman,

Many Christian leaders believe we need another great awakening like the one that occurred in the mid-1700s to bring sweeping change to our culture. For America, just as it was for Israel in the events recorded in 2 Chronicles, our nation's return to God will only occur when individuals in great numbers are changed by the power of a personal relationship with God.

As a woman of God who is able to discern the times you are living in, you can help usher in the next great move of God that is needed in our land. Start by following the admonition to pray in 2 Chronicles 7:14. Pray that our nation will turn from its wicked ways and seek God. Pray for wisdom and direction for our national leadership. Look beyond your own situations to a world that needs Christ's love and determine to share it. Be led by the Holy Spirit, and look for opportunities to share the reason for your confidence concerning the future.

Joy F. Strang

Solomon Seeks Wisdom

1Ki 3:4–15; 10:26–29; 2Ch 9:25–28

1 Now Solomon the son of David strengthened himself over his kingdom, and the LORD his God was with him and made *Solomon* exceedingly great.

2 And Solomon spoke to all Israel, to the commanders of thousands and of hundreds, to the judges, and to all the leaders in all Israel, the heads of fathers' houses. 3 Then they all went, Solomon and all the assembly that was with him, to the high place that was at Gibeon, because the tent of meeting with God, which Moses the servant of the LORD had made in the wilderness, was there. 4 However, David had brought up the ark of God from Kiriath Jearim to the place he had prepared, for he had pitched a tent for it in Jerusalem. 5 And the bronze altar that Bezalel the son of Uri, the son of Hur, had made was set before the tabernacle of the LORD. And Solomon and the assembly sought it out *to seek the* LORD. 6 And Solomon went up to the bronze altar before the LORD, which was before the tent of meeting, and he offered up a thousand burnt offerings on it.

7 That night God appeared to Solomon and said to him, "Ask what I might give to you."

8 Then Solomon said to God, "You have given a great mercy to David my father and have made me king in his place. 9 Now, LORD God, may Your word to David my father be confirmed, for You have made me king over a people numerous as the dust of the earth. 10 Now give wisdom and knowledge to me so that I might know how to go before this people, for who can judge this great people of Yours?"

11 Then God responded to Solomon, "Because this was in your heart and you did not ask for possessions, wealth, and honor, or even the life of those who hate you, nor have you asked for many days of life, but you have asked Me for wisdom and knowledge that you might govern My people over whom I have made you king, 12 wisdom and knowledge are now given to you. Possessions, wealth, and honor I will also give to you; such has not been given to kings before you nor those who will follow after you."

13 So Solomon came from the high place at Gibeon, before the tent of meeting, to Jerusalem, and he reigned over Israel.

14 Solomon gathered together chariots and horses. He had one thousand four hundred chariots and twelve thousand horses, and he put them in designated cities and with the king in Jerusalem. 15 The king made silver and gold in Jerusalem as *abundant* as stones and cedar as plentiful as sycamore trees in the lowlands of the Shephelah. 16 The horses of Solomon were imported from Egypt and Kue, and the traders of the king would take them from Kue for a price. 17 They imported chariots from Egypt for six hundred shekels[1] of silver and a horse for one hundred and fifty pieces.[2] And they imported from these places to all the kings of the Hittites and Arameans.

1:1 1Ch 29:25
1:2 1Ch 28:1
1:4 2Sa 6:2
1:5 Ex 31:2
1:6 1Ki 3:4
1:8 1Ch 28:5
1:9 Ge 13:16
1:10 Nu 27:17
1:12 1Ch 29:25
1:14 1Ki 4:26
1:15 2Ch 9:27

2:1 1Ki 5:5
2:2 2Ch 2:18
2:3 1Ch 14:1

COUNSEL FROM THE SPIRIT BASICS

SPIRITLED WOMAN

The Power of Your Thoughts

Whatever your predominant focus is, that is what you permit to exist in your life. Many times people focus on the negative, and they live in a cycle of negativity. You have to choose to focus on the positive. You have to train your mind to think on whatever is honest, virtuous, and praiseworthy (Php 4:8). Whatever is going wrong in your life is a result of your focus. If you don't like it, change your focus!

If you plan to change your future, do not focus on things or people or circumstances that are smaller than what you are hoping for. Your focus will either feed your faith or confirm your fears. Learn to think like Abraham. Think intentionally, generationally, and even globally. You can never think too big, too grand, or too great!

Learn to think strategically, as Solomon did in establishing his kingdom after David's reign. Purposefully seek God's wisdom so that He can download specific timetables, goals, objectives, and resources into your mind. Read Solomon's prayer and God's response in 2 Chronicles 1:8, 10–12.

Cindy Trimm

Plans for Building the Temple

1Ki 5:1–16

2 Now Solomon wanted to build a temple for the name of the LORD and a royal house for his kingship. 2 And Solomon designated seventy thousand men to carry materials, eighty thousand men to cut stone in the hills, and three thousand six hundred supervisors to oversee these men.

3 And Solomon sent word to Hiram[3] king of Tyre saying,

[1] *17* About 15 pounds, or 6.9 kilograms. [2] *17* About 3¾ pounds, or 1.7 kilograms. [3] *3* Huram in the Heb. text.

"As you did for David my father and sent
him cedar trees in order to build for himself
a house in which to dwell, *so deal with me.*
4 I am going to build a temple for the name
of the LORD my God, sanctified for Him, for
making sacrifices before Him, and for in-
cense of fragrant spices, and for the contin-
ual showbread, for burnt offerings on both
morning and evening, and for Sabbaths,
New Moons, and appointed feasts of the
LORD our God, as an ordinance forever for
Israel.
5 "And the house that I am building will
be great because our God is greater than
all other gods. 6 But who is able to build a
house for Him, since the heavens and the
highest heavens cannot contain Him? Who
am I that I build a house for Him, except to
make offerings before Him?
7 "Now may you send to me a wise man
who works with gold, silver, bronze, iron,
and in purple, crimson, and violet threads
and knows how to engrave, who will be
with the skilled workers and me in Judah
and Jerusalem, which David my father es-
tablished.
8 "And may you send me trees of cedar,
cypress, and algum from Lebanon because
I realize that your slaves know how to cut
timber in Lebanon; and my servants will
be alongside your servants, 9 to prepare an
abundance of timber for me, because the
temple that I will build will be great and
marvelous. 10 I will provide for the woods-
men, your servants who cut timber, twenty
thousand dry kors[1] of crushed wheat, twen-
ty thousand kors[2] of barley, twenty thousand
liquid baths[3] of wine, and twenty thousand
liquid baths of oil."

11 Then Hiram king of Tyre responded in a
letter that he sent to Solomon,

"Because the LORD loves His people, He
has made you king over them."

12 And Hiram said,

"Blessed be the LORD God of Israel who
made heaven and earth and has given King
David a wise son, having insight and un-
derstanding, who is building a temple for
the LORD and a royal house for his kingship.
13 "And now I have sent a skilled man,
endowed with understanding, Huram-Abi,
14 the son of a woman from the daughters
of Dan and the son of a man of Tyre, who
knows gold, silver, bronze, iron, stone,
wood, and purple, violet, blue, and crim-
son threads, and who knows how to make
all types of engravings and to devise every
type of design that is given to him, with your
skilled men and the skilled men of my lord
David your father.
15 "Now the wheat, the barley, the oil, and
the wine that my lord has declared, may he
send *these items* to his slaves. 16 And let us
cut the timber from Lebanon, whatever you
need, and we will bring it to you on rafts on
the sea to Joppa, and you will bring it up
to Jerusalem."

17 Then Solomon numbered all the male for-
eigners who were in the land of Israel, after
the census that David his father had taken. And
there were found one hundred and fifty-three
thousand six hundred. 18 And he made seventy
thousand of them to carry materials, eighty
thousand to cut stone in the hills, and three
thousand six hundred supervisors to make the
people work.

Solomon Builds the Temple

1Ki 6:1–29

3 So Solomon began to build the house of
the LORD in Jerusalem on Mount Moriah,
where *He* appeared to David his father, at the
place that David established on the threshing
floor of Ornan the Jebusite. 2 He began to
build in the second month[4] on the second day
during the fourth year of his reign.[5]
3 These are the foundation *measurements*
that Solomon used for building the house of
God. The cubit[6] length in the former standard
measure was sixty cubits and the width twenty
cubits.[7] 4 The porch vestibule that was in front
of *the nave hall* had its length, like the width
of the house, as twenty cubits,[8] and its height
was one hundred and twenty cubits;[9] and he
overlaid the inside with pure gold.
5 And he paneled the great house with cy-
press trees and then covered it with fine gold.
Then he decorated it with palm trees and chain
work. 6 And he overlaid the house with pre-
cious stones for decoration, and the gold was
from Parvaim. 7 And he covered the house—
its beams, thresholds, walls, and doors—with
gold, and he engraved cherubim on the walls.
8 Then he made the dwelling of the Most Holy
Place. Its length was as the width of twenty
cubits, and its width also twenty cubits; and he
covered it with fine gold, six hundred talents[10]
worth. 9 And the weight in gold for the nails

2:4 Ex 30:7
2:5 1Ch 16:25
2:6 1Ki 8:27
2:10 1Ki 5:11
2:11 1Ki 10:9
2:12 Ps 33:6

2:15 2Ch 2:10
2:16 Jos 19:46
2:17 1Ch 22:2
3:1 1Ch 21:18
3:8 Ex 26:33

[1] *10* Likely about 3,600 tons, or 3,200 metric tons of wheat.
[2] *10* Likely about 3,000 tons, or 2,700 metric tons of barley.
[3] *10* About 120,000 gallons, or 440,000 liters. [4] *2* Ziv or Iyyar in the Hebrew calendar. [5] *2* April or May in 966 BC. [6] *3* The Egyptian cubit had a royal measure of 20.6 inches (52.3cm) and a commercial measure of 17.6 inches (44.7 cm). The cubit standards in Egypt and Mesopotamia were slightly different. [7] *3* About 90 feet long and 30 feet wide, or 27 meters long and 9 meters wide. [8] *4* About 30 feet, or 9 meters; and in vv. 8, 11, and 13. [9] *4* About 180 feet, or 54 meters.
[10] *8* About 23 tons, or 21 metric tons.

was fifty shekels.[1] And he covered the upper chamber in gold.

10 Then in the dwelling of the Most Holy Place, he made two cherubim that were cast metal and overlaid them with gold. 11 And the wings of the cherubim were the length of twenty cubits. The wing of one cherub was five cubits, reaching the wall of the house, and the wing of the other was five cubits,[2] reaching to the wing of the other cherub. 12 And the wing of this cherub was five cubits, reaching to the other wall of the house, and the other wing was five cubits, touching the wing of the first cherub. 13 So the wings of these cherubim spread out were twenty cubits; they were upright on their feet facing inward toward the house.

14 Then he made the curtain of violet, purple, crimson, and blue thread, and he wove cherubim into it.

15 And he made two pillars in front of the house thirty-five cubits[3] high, with a five cubit capital on the top of the pillar. 16 Then he made ornamental chain work, like in the Most Holy Place, and set it on the top of the pillars. Then he designed a hundred pomegranates and set them on the chain work. 17 He then raised the pillars in front of the temple, with one on the right *to the south* and the other on the left *to the north*, and the pillar to the south he called Jakin, and the pillar to the north he called Boaz.

The Furnishings of the Temple

1Ki 7:23–51

4 Then he made a bronze altar that was twenty cubits long, twenty cubits wide, and ten cubits[4] high. 2 And he made a cast metal sea *as a water basin*. It was round and ten cubits from edge to edge, five cubits high,[5] and a line of thirty cubits[6] measured its circumference. 3 Figures like oxen were underneath it, going all the way around the sea basin, ten cubits[7] on each side.[8] There were two rows of oxen that were poured as cast metal.

4 It stood on twelve oxen, three facing north, three facing west, three facing south, and three facing east. The sea was set on them, and their back sides were facing inward. 5 The thickness *of the sea* was a palm,[9] and its brim was like the brim of a cup, as the flower of a lily. It held three thousand baths[10] securely.

6 Then he made ten water basins, and he set five on the southern right side and five on the northern left side to rinse off in them the instruments of the burnt offering. And the sea basin was for the priests to wash in.

7 And he made ten lampstands of gold according to the specifications, and he set them in the temple, five on the southern, right side and five on the northern, left side.

8 Then he made ten tables and put them in the temple, five on the southern, right side and five on the northern, left side; and he made a hundred basins of gold.

9 Then he made the court of the priests and the great enclosure and the doors for the enclosure, and he overlaid the doors with bronze. 10 And he set the sea basin at the southeast side, opposite the southern side *of the house*.

11 And Huram made the pots, shovels, and bowls.

So Huram completed the work that he did for King Solomon on the house of God: 12 the two pillars, the bowls, and the two capitals on the top of the pillars; and the two latticeworks to cover the two bowls of the capitals that were on the top of the pillars; 13 and the four hundred pomegranates for the two pieces of grating, with two rows of pomegranates for each screen grate that covered the two bowl-shaped capitals on top of the pillars. 14 And he made the supporting stands and the basins on top of the stands, 15 and the sea basin and the twelve oxen underneath it; 16 the pots, shovels, utensils, and all the vessels from polished bronze, Huram-Abi made for King Solomon for the house of the LORD.

17 The king cast these *vessels* in the district of the Jordan in earthen foundries between Sukkoth and Zeredatha.[11] 18 And Solomon made all of these items in a great abundance such that they did not consider the weight of the bronze.

19 So Solomon made all the vessels that were in the house of God: the gold altar and the tables displaying the showbread, 20 and the finely hammered lampstands with their lamps to burn before the Most Holy Place as prescribed; 21 the golden flower-shaped ornaments, lamps, and tongs, of purest gold; 22 the snuffers, basins, ladles, and fire pans, of pure gold. As for the entrance to the temple: the inner doors to the Most Holy Place and the doors of the nave of the temple were of gold.

5 Thus all the work that Solomon did for the house of the LORD was finished. And Solomon brought in the things that David his father had dedicated: the silver and the gold and all the furnishings in the treasury of the house of God.

3:10 1Ki 6:23–28
3:17 1Ki 7:21
4:1 1Ki 8:64
4:5 1Ki 7:26
4:6 1Ki 7:38
4:7 Ex 25:31–40
4:8 1Ki 7:48
4:9 1Ki 6:36
4:10 1Ki 7:39
4:13 1Ki 7:20
4:16 2Ch 2:13
4:18 1Ki 7:47
5:1 1Ki 7:51

[1] *9* About 1¼ pounds, or 575 grams. [2] *11* About 7½ feet, or 2.3 meters; and in v. 15. [3] *15* About 53 feet, or 16 meters. [4] *1* About 30 feet long and wide and 15 feet high, or 9 meters long and wide and 4.5 meters high. [5] *2* About 7½ feet, or 2.3 meters. [6] *2* About 45 feet, or 14 meters. [7] *3* About 18 inches, or 45 centimeters. [8] *3* Or *ten oxen for a cubit.* [9] *5* About 3 inches, or 7.5 centimeters. [10] *5* About 18,000 gallons, or 66,000 liters. [11] *17 Zarethan* in 1Ki 7:46.

PROFILE OF A SPIRITLED WOMAN

NAOMI

THE TURNING OF NAOMI

Decisions that require great changes in our lifestyles are never easy to make. Though Naomi may have longed many times to return to her homeland of Bethlehem-Judah, where she was raised, she had undoubtedly grown accustomed to life in Moab during the years she lived there. She had buried her loved ones in Moab and had become attached to her daughters-in-law as well. It would require a painful uprooting of her life once more in order to return to her homeland. Yet when she heard God was visiting His people, her heart was stirred. It was this good news of God's visitation to His people that persuaded Naomi to return to the House of Bread:

> So she got up with her daughters-in-law to return from the land of Moab, for in the land of Moab, she had heard that the LORD had visited His people by giving them food. She set out from the place where she had been, with her two daughters-in-law, and they went on their way to return to the land of Judah.
>
> —RUTH 1:6–7

Spiritual hunger is wonderfully redemptive as we seek to satisfy it with God's provision. Naomi's life had become empty according to her own admission. She said, "I was full when I left, but the LORD has caused me to return empty" (v. 21). She did not seem to understand that hunger or emptiness could be a blessing, but in deciding to return to the House of Bread, she had placed her life in the Lord's hands. Perhaps He would fill her once again.

Many times difficult situations serve to turn us to God in a way that brings unexpected blessing into our lives. Often we do not recognize the disciplining hand of God in our negative circumstances. In order to get Naomi out of the land of Moab, the place of carnal compromise, God had to lay His hand heavily upon her. She suffered the loss of her husband and sons, who represented allegorically the presence of God in her life. When Naomi arrived home in Bethlehem-Judah, she testified to those who met her that she had been under the disciplining hand of God: "I was full when I left, but the LORD has caused me to return empty. Why should you call me Naomi when the LORD has opposed me! The Almighty has brought misfortune upon me!" (v. 21).

In the word *discipline* we can readily see the word *disciple*. When God disciplines us, it is to make us true disciples of Christ. God disciplined Naomi in the land of Moab by allowing her song and joy and the presence of her King to be taken from her. He laid His hand heavily upon her until, in her desperate situation, she was willing to leave Moab and return empty to the House of Bread. Many times that is what happens to us before we enter into the true blessing of God. There has to be a brokenness in our hearts that says, "Forgive me for not wanting to be corrected." God has promised to dwell with those who have a broken and contrite spirit (Isa 57:15). Brokenness, which is often a result of discipline, is a prerequisite for truly finding God.

Naomi returned to Bethlehem-Judah at the beginning of the barley harvest. According to historians, barley was one of the most important grains raised in Palestine. Firstfruits were waved as an offering before the Lord during the barley harvest (Lev 23:10). According to the Law, sheaves of barley were brought to the priest to be waved before the Lord as an offering of thanksgiving.

Naomi could not effect her own restoration; a kinsman-redeemer would be required for that. But she had positioned herself for redemption by returning to the House of Bread. In that same way, though the church is powerless to restore the holiness, evangelistic zeal, and manifest presence of God that she lost during the years of famine, she must choose to respond to the news of God's fresh visitation. For the church to be truly restored, she must turn, determining to position herself in the land where God is bringing fresh revelation of His Word and a demonstration of His mercies.

Fuchsia Pickett

The Ark Brought to the Temple

1Ki 8:1–21

2 Then Solomon assembled the elders of Israel and all the heads of the tribes and the leaders of the houses of the fathers among the sons of Israel to bring up the ark of the covenant of the LORD from the City of David, which is Zion. 3 And all the men of Israel were assembled before the king at the feast, which is the seventh month.[1]

4 All the elders of Israel came, and the Levites carried the ark. 5 Then they brought up the ark, and the tent of meeting, and all the holy vessels that were in the tent. So the Levitical priests brought them up. 6 And King Solomon and all the congregation of Israel, who were assembled with him before the ark, were sacrificing so many sheep and oxen that they could not be counted or numbered.

7 The priests brought the ark of the covenant of the LORD to its place—to the inner sanctuary of the temple, into the Most Holy Place, under the wings of the cherubim. 8 Then the cherubim wings were spread out over the place of the ark so that the cherubim covered the ark and its poles. 9 The poles were extended so that the ends of the poles of the ark were seen in front of the Most Holy Place, but they were not seen outside; and they are still there to this day. 10 In the ark there was nothing except the two tablets that Moses had given at Mount Horeb where the LORD made a covenant with the sons of Israel when they went out from Egypt.

11 When the priests came out from the Most Holy Place—for all the priests who were present had consecrated themselves, without keeping separate divisions— 12 and all the Levitical singers, Asaph, Heman, and Jeduthun, with their sons and relatives, all clothed in fine linen, with cymbals, harps, and lyres, stood to the east of the altar, and with them one hundred and twenty priests who were sounding with trumpets, 13 it happened, when the trumpet players and singers made one sound to praise and give thanks to the LORD, and when they lifted up their voice with the trumpets and cymbals and all the instruments of music and praised the LORD saying,

"For He is good
and His mercy endures forever,"

that the house, the house of the LORD, was filled with a cloud. 14 And the priests were not able to stand in order to serve because of the cloud, for the glory of the LORD had filled the house of God.

6 Then Solomon said, "The LORD has said that He would dwell in the dark cloud. 2 But I have built for You an exalted house, even a habitation where You can continually dwell."

Solomon's Speech

3 Then the king turned his face around, and he blessed the entire assembly of Israel while all the assembly of Israel was standing before him. 4 And he said:

"Blessed be the LORD God of Israel who spoke with David my father and fulfilled *His promise* saying, 5 'Since the day that I brought out My people from the land of Egypt, I did not choose any city from among the tribes of Israel to build a house for My name to dwell there, nor did I select a man to be the leader over My people Israel; 6 but I have chosen Jerusalem for My name to dwell there, and I have selected David to be over My people Israel.'

7 "And it was in the heart of David my father to build a house for the name of the LORD God of Israel. 8 But the LORD said to David my father, 'Whereas it was in your heart to build a house for My name, you did well because of what was in your heart; 9 only you will not be the one to build the house. For your son, who will be born to you, he will build a house for My name.'

10 "The LORD has fulfilled the word that He spoke. For I have risen up in the place of David my father and sit on the throne of Israel, as the LORD spoke, and I will build the house for the name of the LORD God of Israel. 11 And there I have set the ark, in which is the covenant of the LORD that He made with the children of Israel."

Solomon's Prayer of Dedication

1Ki 8:22–53; Ps 132:8–10

12 Then Solomon stood before the altar of the LORD before all the assembly of Israel and spread out his hands. 13 For Solomon made a bronze platform and set it in the midst of the enclosure. It was five cubits in length, five cubits in width, and three cubits in height.[2] And he stood on it and knelt down before all the assembly of Israel and spread out his hands to heaven. 14 And he said:

"O LORD God of Israel, there is no God like You in the heavens or on the earth, who keeps covenants and mercy with Your servants who walk before You with all their heart. 15 You have kept what You promised Your servant David my father. You have both spoken with Your mouth and fulfilled *it* with Your hand, as *it is* this day.

5:2 2Sa 6:12
5:3 1Ki 8:2
5:10 Heb 9:4
5:12 1Ch 15:24
5:13 2Ch 7:3
5:14 Ex 40:35

6:3 1Ki 8:14
6:6 1Ch 28:4
6:11 2Ch 5:10
6:13 1Ki 8:54
6:14 Ex 15:11
6:15 1Ch 22:9–10

1 3 Tishri or Ethanim in the Hebrew calendar. *2 13* About 7½ feet long and wide, and 4½ feet high; or 2.3 meters long and wide, and 1.4 meters high.

16 "And now, O LORD God of Israel, keep
what You promised Your servant David my
father saying, 'You will not lack a man sit-
ting on the throne of Israel before Me, if
only your sons take heed to their way to
walk in My law as you have walked before
Me.' 17 And now, O LORD God of Israel, may
Your word be confirmed which You have
spoken to Your servant David.
18 "For will God indeed dwell with man on
the earth? The heavens, even the highest
heavens, are not able to contain You, much
less this house that I have built. 19 But re-
spond to the prayer of Your servant and to
his plea, O LORD my God, to listen to the
cry and prayer of Your servant who prays
before You, 20 that Your eyes might be open
toward this house both day and night, to
the place that You have said that You will
set Your name, in order to hear the prayer
of Your servant for this place. 21 And listen
to the pleas of Your servant and Your people
Israel when they pray toward this place. And
may You respond from heaven, the place of
Your dwelling, so that You hear and forgive.
22 "If a man sins against his companion,
and the *companion* swears and puts him un-
der a curse, and the *wronged man* comes
with an oath before Your altar at this temple,
23 then You will hear from heaven, and You
will act and judge Your servants, to repay
the guilty one by bringing his way on his
own head; and to vindicate the innocent
one by rendering to him according to his
righteous behavior.
24 "If Your people Israel are struck before
enemies because they have sinned against
You, and they return and confess Your name
and pray and seek Your favor in this house,
25 then You will hear from heaven and for-
give the sin of Your people Israel, and You
will bring them back to the land that You
gave them and their fathers.
26 "When the sky is shut up and there is no
rain because they have sinned against You,
and they pray toward this place and confess
Your name and turn from their sin when You
afflict them, 27 then You will hear from heav-
en and forgive the sin of Your servants and
Your people Israel because You will teach
them the good path in which they will walk,
and You will send rain on the land that You
have given to Your people as a possession.
28 "When there is famine in the land or
when there is pestilence, blight, mildew,
winged locust, or grasshopper, or when en-
emies besiege them in the land up to their
city gates, in whatever plague or sickness,
29 whatever prayer or plea that is made by
any man or by all your people Israel, when
each man knows his own affliction and his
own sorrow, and stretches out his hands to-
ward this house, 30 then You will hear from
heaven, the place of the habitation of Your
dwelling, and forgive, and You will render
to each according to his conduct, for You
know their hearts (for You alone know the
heart of people), 31 so that they may fear
You and walk in Your ways all the days that
they live on the land that You have given
to our fathers.
32 "When foreigners are not from Your
people Israel and come from a distant land,
because of Your great name, mighty hand,
and outstretched arm, and they come and
pray toward this house, 33 then hear from
heaven, from Your dwelling place, and act
on everything for which the foreigner calls
on You, that all the peoples of the earth may
know Your name and fear You, as do Your
people Israel; and that they may know that
this house which I have built is called by
Your name.
34 "When Your people go out to battle
against their enemies, in the way that You
send them, and when they pray to You to-
ward this city that You have chosen and the
house that I have built for Your name, 35 then
hear from heaven their prayer and plea and
act for their cause.
36 "When they sin against You (for there
is no one who does not sin) and You are
angry against them and give them to their
enemies, and they are taken captive to a
land, whether distant or near, 37 and they
turn their hearts in the land that they have
been taken captive, and they repent and
seek Your favor in the land of captivity
saying, 'We have sinned, done wrong, and
acted wickedly,' 38 and if they turn in repen-
tance to You with all their heart and all their
soul in the land of their captivity that they
were taken to, and pray toward the land that
You have given to their fathers, and toward
the city that You have chosen, and toward
the house that I have built for Your name,
39 then hear from heaven, from Your dwell-
ing place, their prayer and supplication, and
maintain their cause, and forgive the people
who have sinned against You.
40 "Now, O my God, may Your eyes be open
and Your ears attentive to the prayer *that I*
offer in this place.

41 "Now rise up, O LORD God, to Your resting
place,
both You and the ark of Your strength.

6:16 1Ki 2:4
6:18 2Ch 2:6
6:20 Ps 34:15
6:21 Isa 43:25

6:30 1Ch 28:9
6:36 Ecc 7:20
6:40 2Ch 7:15
6:41 1Ch 28:2

And let Your priests, O LORD God, be
clothed in salvation
and Your loyal ones rejoice in goodness.
42 O LORD God, do not turn Your face from
Your anointed.
Remember the mercies of Your servant
David."

Solomon Dedicates the Temple
1Ki 8:62–66

7 And when Solomon finished praying, fire
came down from the heavens and con-
sumed the burnt offering and sacrifices, and
the glory of the LORD filled the temple. 2 And the
priests were not able to enter into the house
of the LORD, for the glory of the LORD filled the
LORD's house. 3 And all the sons of Israel saw
when the fire came down and the glory of the
LORD came on the temple, and they bowed
their faces low to the ground on the pavement,
and they worshipped confessing,

"The LORD is good,
and His mercy endures forever."

4 Then the king and all the people were mak-
ing sacrifices before the LORD. 5 King Solomon
sacrificed twenty-two thousand oxen and one
hundred and twenty thousand sheep. So the
king and all the people dedicated the house of
God. 6 The priests stood at their positions, with
the Levites and all their instruments of mu-
sic for the LORD that King David had made to
praise the LORD—for His mercy endures forev-
er—when David gave praise by their ministry,
and the priests sounded trumpets opposite the
Levites, and all Israel stood.
7 And Solomon consecrated the middle of the
court that was in front of the house of the LORD
because there he made burnt offerings and
the fat of peace offerings (because the bronze
altar that Solomon made was surely not able
to contain the burnt offerings, grain offerings,
and fat offerings).
8 And at the appointed time, Solomon made
a feast for seven days, and all Israel—as a very
great assembly—was with him, from the en-
trance of Lebo Hamath *in the north* to the Brook
of Egypt *in the south*. 9 Then on the eighth day
they made a solemn assembly because they
had made a consecration of the altar for seven
days and then the feast for seven days more.
10 Then on the twenty-third day of the seventh
month *Solomon* sent the people away to their
homes. They were joyful and good of heart
because of what the LORD had done for David,
Solomon, and His people Israel.
11 Thus Solomon finished the house of the
LORD and the king's house. And Solomon suc-
cessfully accomplished everything that came
into his heart to do in the house of the LORD
and in his own house.

The LORD Appears to Solomon
1Ki 9:1–9

12 Then the LORD appeared to Solomon at
night, and He said to Solomon,

"I have heard your prayer, and I have
chosen for Myself in this place a house of
sacrifice.
13 "When I shut up the heaven and there is
no rain, or when I command the locusts to
devour the land, or send pestilence on My
people, 14 if My people, who are called by
My name, will humble themselves and pray,
and seek My face and turn from their wick-
ed ways, then I will hear from heaven, and
will forgive their sin and will heal their land.
15 Now My eyes will be open and My ears at-
tentive to the prayer of this place. 16 So now
I have chosen and consecrated this house
that My name be there continually. My eyes
and heart will be there for all days.
17 "And you, if you walk before Me as Da-
vid your father did to do everything that I
command you to do, and you keep My stat-
utes and judgments, 18 then I will set the
throne of your kingdom as I made a cov-
enant with David your father saying, 'You
will not lack a man to rule Israel.'
19 "But if the people turn aside and aban-
don My statutes and commandments that
I have given to you, and you walk after
and serve other gods and worship them,
20 then I will uproot them from My land that
I have given to them; and the house that I
have consecrated for My name, I will throw
it from before Me and set it as a proverb
and taunt among the peoples. 21 And even
though this house was majestic, it will lie
desolate before all who pass by it, and they
will say, 'Why did the LORD do such a thing
to this land and this house?' 22 Then they will
say, 'Because they abandoned the LORD, the
God of their fathers who brought them up
from the land of Egypt, and they took hold
of other gods and worshipped and served
them; therefore He has brought on them all
this disaster.'"

Solomon's Other Activities
1Ki 9:10–28

8 It came that after twenty years, Solomon
built the house of the LORD and his royal
house, 2 and Solomon even rebuilt the cities
that Hiram had given to him, and he settled the
sons of Israel in them. 3 Then Solomon went
to Hamath Zobah and seized it. 4 He also built
Tadmor in the wilderness and all the store cit-
ies that he built in Hamath. 5 He also built the

6:42 Isa 55:3
7:1 1Ki 18:38
7:2 2Ch 5:14
7:3 2Ch 5:13
7:6 2Ch 5:12
7:8 Ge 15:18
7:9 Lev 23:36
7:11 1Ki 9:1–9

7:13 2Ch 6:26–28
7:15 2Ch 6:40
7:18 2Ch 6:16
7:19 Lev 26:14
7:20 Dt 28:37
8:5 1Ch 7:24

Upper and Lower Beth Horon, fortified cities
with walls, gates, and bars, 6 and Baalath, and
all the store cities that Solomon had, and all
the cities for his chariots, the cities for his cav-
alry, and whatever Solomon desired to build
in Jerusalem, Lebanon, and in all the land of
his dominion.
7 And all the people who remained from the
Hittites, Amorites, Perizzites, Hivites, and Jeb-
usites who were not from Israel, 8 and from
their descendants who remained *from these
peoples* in the land and whom the sons of Isra-
el did not finish destroying, Solomon brought
them up to be forced labor, even to this day.
9 But from the sons of Israel Solomon did not
make servants for his work. These were his
soldiers, officers, commanders of his chariots,
and horsemen. 10 And these were the two hun-
dred and fifty chief officers for King Solomon
who governed the people.
11 And Solomon brought up the daughter of
Pharaoh from the City of David to the house
that he built for her, for he said, "My wife will
not live in the house of David king of Israel,
for the places where the ark of the LORD have
been are holy."
12 At that time Solomon offered up burnt of-
ferings on the altar of the LORD that he built be-
fore the vestibule, 13 according to the daily duty
to offer up as the commandment of Moses for
Sabbaths, New Moons, and the three annual
festivals: the Feast of Unleavened Bread, the
Feast of Weeks, and the Feast of Tabernacles.
14 According to the ruling of David his father,
he set the divisions of the priests for their
service, and the Levites for their function to
praise and serve before the priests according
to the daily duty, and even the gatekeepers
for their divisions at each gate, for this was
the commandment of David the man of God.
15 And they did not turn from the command-
ment of the king, whether the priests or Lev-
ites, concerning any matter and concerning
the treasury.
16 So all the work of Solomon was established
from the day of the foundation of the house
of the LORD and until its completion; and the
house of the LORD was complete.
17 Then Solomon went to Ezion Geber and
Elath at the shore of the sea in Edom. 18 And
Hiram sent him ships by the hand of his ser-
vants, who knew the sea. And they went with
the servants of Solomon to Ophir, and took
from there four hundred and fifty talents[1] of
gold, and brought them to King Solomon.

8:11 1Ki 3:1
8:12 2Ch 4:1
8:13 Dt 16:16
8:14 1Ch 9:17
8:17 2Ki 14:22
8:18 2Ch 9:10

9:1 Mt 12:42
9:8 2Ch 2:11
9:10 2Ch 8:18

The Queen of Sheba Visits
1Ki 10:1–13

9 The queen of Sheba heard a report of Sol-
omon, and she came to Jerusalem with a
very impressive retinue—with camels carrying
spices, an abundance of gold, and precious
stones—to test Solomon with riddles. When
she came to Solomon she shared with him
everything that was on her heart. 2 Solomon
declared to her everything that she asked, and
there was not any matter concealed from Sol-
omon that he did not declare to her. 3 When
the queen of Sheba had observed the wisdom
of Solomon, the house that he had built, 4 the
food on his table, the seating of his officials,
and the attendance of his servants, and their
clothing, his valets, and their clothing, and his
burnt offerings that he offered at the house of
the LORD, there was no more spirit left in her.
5 Then she said to the king, "True was the
report that I heard in my land concerning your
words and wisdom. 6 But I did not believe their
reports until I came and my eyes saw; and in-
deed, half the greatness of your wisdom was
not declared to me. You have exceeded the re-
port that I heard. 7 How happy your men must
be! How happy these servants, those who are
continually before you listening to your wis-
dom. 8 May the LORD your God be blessed, who
has delighted in you, to set you as king on the
throne of the LORD your God. Your God has
loved Israel to establish them continually and
has set you as king over them to perform jus-
tice and righteousness."
9 Then she gave the king one hundred and
twenty talents[2] of gold and a great abundance
of spices and precious stones. And there were
no spices like those that the queen of Sheba
gave to King Solomon.
10 Moreover, the servants of Hiram and
Solomon who brought gold from Ophir also
brought algum wood and precious stones.
11 And the king used the algum wood for steps
for the house of the LORD and the palace of the
king, even for lyres and harps for the singers.
And there had not been anything seen like
these in the land of Judah.
12 And King Solomon gave everything to the
queen of Sheba in which she had pleasure,
even what she asked for in addition to what
she brought to the king. Then she turned and
left for her own land with her servants.

The Splendor of Solomon
1Ki 10:14–29; 2Ch 1:14–17

13 The weight of gold that came to Solomon
every year was six hundred and sixty-six tal-
ents[3] of gold. 14 In addition to what the explor-
ers and merchants brought in, all the kings of

[1] *18* About 17 tons, or 15 metric tons. [2] *9* About 4½ tons or 4 metric tons. [3] *13* About 25 tons, or 23 metric tons.

Arabia and governors of the land brought in gold and silver to Solomon.

15 King Solomon made two hundred large shields of hammered gold, and six hundred gold pieces[1] were used for each large shield. 16 And he made three hundred shields of hammered gold; three hundred gold pieces[2] were used for each shield. And the king put them in the House of the Forest of Lebanon.

17 And the king made a great throne of ivory, and he covered it with fine gold. 18 And there were six steps and a gold footstool attached to the throne, and on each side at the place of the seat were armrests with two lions standing beside the armrests. 19 So twelve lions stood there on the six steps, one on each side, and there was nothing like this in any kingdom. 20 Even all the drinking vessels of King Solomon were gold, and all the vessels in the House of the Forest of Lebanon were fine gold. And silver was not thought to be valuable in the days of Solomon. 21 The ships of Solomon went to Tarshish with the servants of Hiram. Once every three years the ships of Tarshish returned carrying gold, silver, ivory, apes, and peacocks.

22 So King Solomon was greater than all the kings of the earth in wealth and wisdom. 23 All the kings of the earth sought out an audience before Solomon to hear his wisdom that God gave to his mind. 24 Every year each man brought his own tribute, vessels of silver and gold, garments, myrrh, spices, horses, and mules.

25 Solomon had four thousand stalls for horses and chariots and twelve thousand horses, and he put them in designated cities and with him in Jerusalem. 26 He ruled over all the kings from the River[3] to the land of the Philistines and to the border of Egypt. 27 So the king made silver in Jerusalem as *abundant* as stones and cedar as plentiful as sycamore trees in the lowlands of the Shephelah. 28 The horses of Solomon were imported from Egypt and from all other lands.

The Death of Solomon
1Ki 11:41–43

29 And the rest of the acts of Solomon, from beginning to end, are they not written in the annals of Nathan the prophet, and the prophecy of Ahijah the Shilonite, and in the visions of Iddo the seer concerning Jeroboam the son of Nebat? 30 So Solomon reigned in Jerusalem over all Israel for forty years. 31 And Solomon slept with his fathers, and they buried him in the City of David his father. And Rehoboam his son then ruled in his place.

9:22 2Ch 1:12
9:25 1Ki 4:26
9:26 Ge 15:18
9:28 2Ch 1:16
9:29 1Ch 29:29
9:31 1Ki 2:10

10:2 1Ki 11:40
10:6 Job 32:7
10:7 Pr 15:1
10:8 2Sa 17:14
10:15 1Ki 11:29–39
10:16 2Sa 20:1

Israel Rebels Against Rehoboam
1Ki 12:1–24

10 Rehoboam went to Shechem because all Israel journeyed to Shechem to make him king. 2 It happened that Jeroboam the son of Nebat heard this—he was in Egypt, where he fled from King Solomon—so he returned from Egypt. 3 So they sent for him and called him. And Jeroboam and all Israel came and spoke to Rehoboam saying, 4 "Your father made our yoke heavy. Now therefore, lighten your father's labor and heavy yoke that he put on us, and we will serve you."

5 He responded, "Return again to me in three days." So the people left.

6 Then King Rehoboam consulted with the elders who stood in the presence of Solomon his father when he was alive saying, "How do you counsel that I should give a response to this people?"

7 They said to him, "If you are good to this people and please them and speak well to them, then they will be servants to you all your days."

8 But he abandoned the counsel of the elders that they gave to him. And he consulted the young men who grew up and stood before him. 9 Rehoboam said to them, "What do you counsel that we give as a response to this people who have spoken to me, 'Lighten the yoke that your father placed on us'?"

10 The young men who had grown up with him said, "So you should speak to the people who have spoken to you saying, 'Your father made our yoke heavy, but you lighten it from us.' So you will say to them, 'My little *finger* is thicker than my father's waist! 11 Whereas my father placed a heavy yoke on you, I will add to your yoke. My father chastened you with whips, but I will scourge you with scorpions.' "

12 So Jeroboam and all the people came to Rehoboam on the third day, as the king had ordered saying, "Return to me on the third day." 13 Then the king answered them harshly. King Rehoboam rejected the advice of the elders. 14 He spoke to them with the advice of the young men, saying, "My father made your yoke heavy, but I will increase it. My father chastised you with whips, but I will chastise you with scorpions." 15 The king did not listen to the people, for the event occurred because of God, that the LORD might establish His word that He spoke through Ahijah the Shilonite to Jeroboam the son of Nebat.

16 When all Israel saw that the king would not listen to them, the people answered the king saying,

[1] *15* About 15 pounds, or 6.9 kilograms. [2] *16* About 7½ pounds, or 3.5 kilograms. [3] *26* Euphrates River.

"What portion do we have in David?
We have no inheritance in the son of Jesse.
O Israel, each man to your tent.
Now look after your own house, O David!"

Then all Israel departed to their tents. 17 The sons of Israel dwelled in the cities of Judah, and Rehoboam reigned over them.

18 Then King Rehoboam sent Hadoram, who was over the forced labor, and the sons of Israel stoned him to death. And King Rehoboam hurried to mount his chariot and to flee to Jerusalem. 19 So Israel has rebelled against the house of David until this day.

11 When Rehoboam came to Jerusalem, he called together from the house of Judah and Benjamin one hundred and eighty thousand[1] choice men to make war and to battle with Israel in order to restore the kingdom to Rehoboam.

Lord, I am Your end-times warrior. Use me as Your weapon against the enemy (2Ch 11:1).

2 But the word of the LORD came to Shemaiah the man of God saying: 3 Speak to Rehoboam, son of Solomon and king of Judah, and to all Israel in Judah and Benjamin, 4 "So says the LORD: You are not to go up and fight against your brothers. Each man must return to his house, for this event is from Me." So they obeyed the word of the LORD and turned back from attacking Jeroboam.

Rehoboam Secures the Kingdom

5 So Rehoboam dwelled in Jerusalem and built siege cities in Judah. 6 He built Bethlehem, Etam, Tekoa, 7 Beth Zur *in the east*, Soko, Adullam, 8 Gath, Mareshah *in the west*, Ziph, 9 Adoraim, Lachish *in the south*, Azekah, 10 Zorah, Aijalon *in the northwest*, and *central* Hebron, all of which were fortified cities in Judah and Benjamin. 11 He strengthened the fortresses and set leaders in them with stockpiles of food, oil, and wine. 12 And in all the cities he placed shields and spears, and he greatly strengthened these *places*. So he held Judah and Benjamin.

13 And the priests and Levites in all Israel came before him from all their territories. 14 For the Levites left their pasture lands and properties, and they traveled to Judah and Jerusalem because Jeroboam and his sons excluded them from serving as priests to the LORD. 15 And he set for himself priests for the high places and for the goat and calf idols that he made. 16 And those who set their hearts to seek the LORD God of Israel followed after them from all the tribes of Israel, and they came to Jerusalem to sacrifice to the LORD God of their fathers. 17 So they strengthened the kingdom of Judah and supported Rehoboam, the son of Solomon, for three years, for they walked in the way of David and Solomon for three years.

I set my heart to seek the God of Israel (2Ch 11:16).

Rehoboam's Family

18 And Rehoboam took Mahalath for a wife, the daughter of both Jerimoth the son of David and of Abihail the daughter of Eliab the son of Jesse, 19 and she bore sons to him: Jeush, Shemariah, and Zaham. 20 Then after her he took Maakah the daughter of Absalom. And she bore to him Abijah, Attai, Ziza, and Shelomith. 21 And Rehoboam loved Maakah the daughter of Absalom more than his other wives and concubines (for he took eighteen wives and sixty concubines), and he had twenty-eight sons and sixty daughters.

22 And Rehoboam set Abijah the son of Maakah as chief and head over his brothers for he *planned* to make him king. 23 And he was discerning and spread out all his sons to all the lands of Judah and Benjamin, even among the fortified cities, and he provided for them an abundance of provisions and wives.

Egypt Attacks Jerusalem

1Ki 14:21–31

12 Now when the reign of Rehoboam was established and strong, he, and all of Israel with him, abandoned the law of the LORD. 2 And in the fifth year of King Rehoboam, Shishak king of Egypt went up against Jerusalem for they had acted unfaithfully against the LORD, 3 with one thousand two hundred chariots and sixty thousand horses. The people were without number who came with him from Egypt—Libyans, Sukkiktes, and Ethiopians. 4 And he captured the fortified cities that were in Judah, and he came even to Jerusalem.

5 Then Shemaiah the prophet came to Rehoboam and the rulers of Judah who were assembled in Jerusalem before Shishak, and he said to them, "So the LORD says: You have abandoned Me, so I have abandoned you into the hand of Shishak."

6 Then the king and the rulers of Israel humbled themselves and said, "The LORD is righteous."

10:18 1Ki 5:14
11:2 2Ch 12:15
11:7 Jos 15:35
11:14 2Ch 13:9
11:15 1Ki 12:28
11:16 2Ch 15:9
11:17 2Ch 12:1
11:18 1Sa 16:6
11:20 2Ch 13:2
11:21 Dt 17:17
11:22 Dt 21:15–17
12:1 2Ch 11:17
12:2 1Ki 11:40
12:3 2Ch 16:8
12:4 2Ch 11:5–12
12:5 2Ch 11:2
12:6 Ex 9:27

[1] *1* From population numbers in the region at this time, the Heb. term is *division* rather than *thousand*.

7 So when the LORD observed that they had humbled themselves, the word of the LORD came to Shemaiah, "They have humbled themselves, so I will not destroy them. I will let some of them escape, and My anger will not pour out against Jerusalem by the hand of Shishak. 8 For they will be slaves to him so that they experience My labor and the labor of the kingdoms of other lands."

9 So Shishak king of Egypt went up against Jerusalem and took away the treasures of the house of the LORD and of the palace of the king. He took everything, even the gold shields that Solomon made. 10 And King Rehoboam made bronze shields in their place and entrusted them to the hands of the rulers of the guards, those who guarded the entrance to the king's palace. 11 And it happened that whenever the king came to the house of the LORD, the guards came and carried the *shields* and then returned them to the guardroom.

12 And when he humbled himself, the anger of the LORD turned away from him so that there was not a complete annihilation. Moreover, there were some good things in Judah *during this time.*

The Death of Rehoboam

13 So King Rehoboam was strong and reigned in Jerusalem. For Rehoboam was forty-one years old when he became king, and he reigned for seventeen years in Jerusalem, the city that the LORD had chosen out of all the tribes of Israel, to put His name there. His mother's name was Naamah the Ammonite. 14 And he acted evil because he did not set his heart to seek out the LORD.

15 Now, are not the acts of Rehoboam written from beginning to end in the annals of Shemaiah the prophet and Iddo the seer, according to genealogy? And there were battles between Rehoboam and Jeroboam all their days. 16 And Rehoboam slept with his fathers and was buried in the City of David, and Abijah ruled in his place.

Abijah, King of Judah

1Ki 15:1–8

13 In the eighteenth year of King Jeroboam, Abijah became king of Judah. 2 He reigned for three years in Judah, and his mother's name was Micaiah,[1] the granddaughter of Uriel of Gibeah.

And there was a war between Abijah and Jeroboam. 3 Abijah set the battle in order with an army of valiant men of war, four hundred thousand choice men. Jeroboam also drew up battle lines against him with an army of eight hundred thousand men, mighty men of valor.

12:7 2Ch 34:25
12:9 1Ki 10:16–17
12:12 2Ch 19:3
12:13 1Ki 14:21
12:14 2Ch 19:3
12:15 2Ch 9:29
13:2 2Ch 11:20

....

13:4 Jos 18:22
13:5 Lev 2:13
13:6 1Ki 11:26
13:7 Jdg 9:4
13:8 1Ki 12:28
13:9 2Ch 11:14–15
13:11 2Ch 2:4
13:12 Nu 10:8–9
13:14 2Ch 14:11
13:15 2Ch 14:12

4 Then Abijah went up to Mount Zemaraim that is in the hills of Ephraim, and he said, "Listen to me, Jeroboam and all Israel! 5 Do you all not know that the LORD God of Israel has perpetually given the kingdom of Israel to David, even to him and to his sons with a covenant of salt? 6 And Jeroboam the son of Nebat, the servant of Solomon son of David, stood up and rebelled against his lord *Rehoboam.* 7 Then vain, worthless men gathered together around him and defied Rehoboam son of Solomon. And Rehoboam was young and timid in heart and was not strong before them.

8 "And now you think that you can withstand before the kingdom of the LORD by the hand of the sons of David. And you all are a great multitude, and with you are the golden calves that Jeroboam has made for you to be gods. 9 Have you all not driven out the priests of the LORD, even the Levites and sons of Aaron, and made for yourselves priests from the peoples of other lands? Whoever comes to be dedicated and has in his hand a young bull or seven rams becomes a priest to what is not a god.

10 "But for us, the LORD is our God, and we have not abandoned Him. And our priests serve the LORD and are sons of Aaron, Levites with their service. 11 They sacrifice burnt offerings to the LORD every morning and evening and put out an incense of spices. They also set the showbread in place on the ritual table and set the golden lampstand with its lamps to burn every evening. For we keep the duty of the LORD our God, but you all have abandoned Him. 12 God is with us as a leader, and His priests with their battle trumpets to call for battle against you all. O sons of Israel, do not fight against the LORD the God of your fathers because you will not find success."

13 So Jeroboam went around them with an ambush to come from behind them. Those from Israel were in front of Judah, while the ambush was behind them. 14 Then Judah turned and saw that the battle was both in front of and behind them. Then they cried out to the LORD, and the priests sounded their trumpets. 15 Then the men from Judah shouted out; and it happened when Judah shouted out, God struck down Jeroboam and all Israel before Abijah and Judah. 16 The men of Israel fled before Judah, and God gave them into their hand. 17 Abijah and his people struck them down with a great slaughter, and the slain from Israel who fell that day were five hundred thousand choice men. 18 So the sons of Israel were subdued at that time, and the people of

[1] *2 Maakah* in 1Ki 15:2.

Judah were strong for they depended on the
LORD God of their fathers.
19 And Abijah chased after Jeroboam and
captured cities from him: Bethel, Jeshanah,
and Ephron with their surrounding villages.
20 And Jeroboam did not again recover his
strength in the days of Abijah, and the LORD
struck down Jeroboam, and he died.
21 So Abijah grew strong and took fourteen
wives and had twenty-two sons and sixteen
daughters.
22 And the remainder of the acts of Abijah,
both his ways and words, are written in the
story of the prophet Iddo.

14 And Abijah slept with his fathers, and
they buried him in the City of David.
Asa his son then reigned in his place. In his
days the land was quiet for ten years.

Asa, King of Judah
1Ki 15:11–12

2 Asa did what was good and right in the eyes
of the LORD his God. 3 He took down the foreign
altars and high places, and he shattered the
pillars and cut down the images of Asherah.
4 Then he urged Judah to seek the LORD the
God of their fathers and to keep the law and
commandments. 5 And he also removed all the
high places and incense altars in the cities in
Judah. And the kingdom was at rest under Asa.
6 He built fortified cities in Judah because the
land was quiet; and there was no war in these
years, for the LORD gave peace to him.
7 And he said to Judah, "Let us build up these
cities and let us surround them with walls,
towers, gates, and bars for the land before us
is still ours because we have sought after the
LORD our God. We have sought Him, and He
has given us peace all around." So they built
and had success.
8 And it happened that Asa had an army
from Judah carrying large shields and spears
numbering three hundred thousand. And from
Benjamin he had an army carrying shields and
bows numbering two hundred eighty thou-
sand. All of these were mighty men of valor.
9 But Zerah the Ethiopian Cushite came out
against them with an army of a million men
and three hundred chariots. And he came up
to Mareshah. 10 Then Asa went out to engage
him, and they arranged for battle in the Valley
of Zephathah near Mareshah.
11 And Asa cried out the LORD his God, and
said, "LORD, it is nothing with You to help,
whether with many or with those who have
no power. Help us, O LORD our God; for we trust
in You, and in Your name we come against this
multitude. O LORD, You are our God. Let no man
prevail against You."

13:20 1Sa 25:38
13:22 2Ch 9:29
14:3 Dt 7:5
14:5 2Ch 34:4
14:6 2Ch 15:15
14:8 2Ch 13:3
14:9 2Ch 16:8
14:11 2Ch 13:14
14:12 2Ch 13:15
14:13 Ge 10:19
14:14 2Ch 17:10
15:1 2Ch 20:14
15:2 1Ch 28:9
15:3 Lev 10:11
15:5 Jdg 5:6
15:7 Jos 1:7
15:8 2Ch 8:12
15:9 2Ch 11:16
15:11 2Ch 14:13–15
15:12 2Ch 23:16
15:13 Ex 22:20

12 So the LORD struck down the Ethiopian
Cushites before Asa and Judah, and the Cush-
ites fled. 13 Then Asa and those with him pur-
sued them until Gerar. And the Cushites fell
till there was not one left alive because they
were struck down before the LORD and His
army. And those *in Judah* carried off a very
great plunder. 14 And they struck down all the
cities surrounding Gerar because the terror of
the LORD was on them. And they plundered all
the cities because there was a great amount
of possessions in them. 15 And they also struck
the tents holding livestock, and they carried
off sheep and a great amount of camels. Then
they returned to Jerusalem.

The Reforms of Asa
1Ki 15:13–16

15 Then the Spirit of God came on Azariah
the son of Oded, 2 and he went out to
meet Asa and said to him, "Listen to me, Asa,
and all Judah and Benjamin: The LORD is with
you while you are with Him. If you all seek
Him, He will be found with you. But if you
forsake Him, He will forsake you. 3 For a long
time Israel has been without the true God, and
without a teaching priest and without law, 4 but
when in their trouble they turned to the LORD
God of Israel, and sought Him, He was found
by them. 5 And at that time there was no peace
to the one traveling in or out because there
was a great panic on all those who dwelt in
the land. 6 They were broken to pieces, nation
against nation and city against city, because
God confused them with every type of distress.
7 But you all must be strong and not lose heart,
for there is a reward for your deeds."
8 And when Asa heard these words of the
prophecy of *Azariah son of* Oded the prophet,
he was encouraged and removed the detest-
able idols from the entire land of Judah and
Benjamin and from the cities that he captured
in the hills of Ephraim. And he repaired the
altar of the LORD that was before the vestibule
of the LORD.
9 And he gathered together all of Judah and
Benjamin and those who had settled among
them from Ephraim, Manasseh, and Simeon,
for these had come down to him from Israel in
a great number when they saw that the LORD
his God was with him.
10 These were gathered in Jerusalem in the
third month in the fifteenth year in the reign of
Asa. 11 They sacrificed to the LORD that day from
the plunder that they brought in, seven hun-
dred oxen and seven thousand sheep. 12 And
they entered into a covenant to seek the LORD
God of their fathers with all their heart and
soul. 13 But whoever would not seek the LORD
God of Israel would be put to death, whether

How to Keep the Flow of Prophetic Intercession

And when Asa heard these words of the prophecy of Azariah son of Oded the prophet, he was encouraged and removed the detestable idols from the entire land of Judah and Benjamin and from the cities that he captured in the hills of Ephraim. And he repaired the altar of the LORD that was before the vestibule of the LORD.

—2 CHRONICLES 15:8

We must give ourselves to prophetic intercession to meet the urgency of the hour we are living in. Here are my helps to keep the prophetic flowing in your life:

- *Ready yourself.* Believe and be filled with the enabling of God's Holy Spirit, and develop the fruit of the Holy Spirit too!
- *Get the Word of God in you.* His Word is the expression of His will. Revelation 19:10 tells us the testimony of Jesus is the spirit of prophecy. Sing it and speak it, and you'll keep the prophetic flowing.
- *Treasure the people you are praying for, and have the right motives for the prophetic to move through your life.* When I sing prophetically, I want to sing something that will set someone free.
- *Aim.* Get specific with your prayers. Ask God for a spirit of wisdom and revelation so you can see what's coming or what needs spiritual attention now.
- *Learn to see things in the spiritual realm.* Elisha asked God to open the eyes of his servant so he could see the chariots of God. There are more with us than against us.
- *Fire.* Launch your prayers with faith and with God's Word. Those bullets will never return to you empty or void.

As you move in prophetic intercession, keep your heart clean for God to pour through. Let the Holy Spirit convict you, and respond to His conviction. Together, let us arise and cry out for the advancement of God's kingdom on the earth!

Kathy Gray

young or old, man or woman. 14 They swore an oath to the LORD in a loud voice, with shouting, trumpets, and horns. 15 And all Judah rejoiced over this oath because they swore with their whole heart and they sought Him with all their desire; and He was found by them, and the LORD gave them rest all around.

16 King Asa even removed his mother Maakah from being queen mother because she had made a detestable image for Asherah. Asa cut down her image, crushed it, and burned it in the Kidron Valley. 17 But they did not remove the high places from Israel. Nevertheless the heart of Asa was wholly committed all his days. 18 He brought into the house of God the sacred gifts of his father and his own sacred gifts—silver, gold, and utensils.

19 And there was no war until the thirty-fifth year of the reign of Asa.

Asa's Last Years

1Ki 15:17–24

16 But in the thirty-sixth year of the reign of Asa, Baasha king of Israel went up against Judah and built Ramah and did not allow anyone to come in or go out to Asa king of Judah.

2 Then Asa removed silver and gold from the storehouses of the house of the LORD and palace of the king, and he sent it to Ben-Hadad king of Aram in Syria, who lived in Damascus, saying, 3 "There is a covenant between me and you as between my father and your father. I am sending you silver and gold. Go and break your covenant with Baasha king of Israel so that he might leave me."

4 And Ben-Hadad listened to King Asa, and he sent the commanders of his armies against the cities of Israel. They struck down Ijon, Dan, Abel Maim, and all the depot cities of Naphtali. 5 And it happened when Baasha heard this, that he stopped building Ramah and he ceased his work. 6 Then King Asa took all of Judah, and they took the stones of Ramah and its timber that Baasha had used to build, and he built with them Geba and Mizpah.

7 And at that time Hanani the seer came to King Asa of Judah saying, "Because you depended on the king of Aram and did not depend on the LORD your God, therefore the army of the king of Aram escaped from your hand. 8 Were not the Cushites and Libyans a very large army with chariots and horses, but when you depended on the LORD, He gave them to your hand. 9 For the eyes of the LORD move about on all the earth to strengthen the heart that is completely toward Him. You have acted foolishly in this, and from this point forward you will have wars."

15:16 1Ki 15:13–24
16:7 1Ki 16:1
16:8 2Ch 12:3
16:9 Pr 15:3

16:12 Jer 17:5
16:14 Ge 50:2
17:2 2Ch 15:8
17:4 1Ki 12:28
17:5 2Ch 18:1
17:6 2Ch 15:17
17:7 2Ch 35:3
17:10 2Ch 14:14
17:11 2Ch 26:8

10 Then Asa was angry with the seer and placed him in prison stocks, for he was enraged by these words. Asa even oppressed some of the people during this time.

The Death of Asa

11 The events of Asa from beginning to end are written in the book of the kings of Judah and Israel. 12 In the thirty-ninth year of the reign of Asa, he had a sickness in his feet until his sickness became grave. Even in his disease he did not seek after the LORD, but the physicians. 13 So Asa slept with his fathers; he died in the forty-first year of his reign. 14 And they buried him in the tomb that he cut for himself in the City of David. And they placed him on a place filled with all types of spices mixed with ointments, and then they burned him up with a very great conflagration.

Jehoshaphat, King of Judah

17 Then Jehoshaphat his son reigned in his place, and he grew strong against Israel. 2 He put an army in all the fortified cities of Judah and set military garrisons in the land of Judah, even in the cities of Ephraim that Asa his father had captured.

3 Now the LORD was with Jehoshaphat, for he walked in the previous ways of David his father, and he did not seek out the Baal cult. 4 For he sought out the God of his fathers and walked in his commandments, rather than the deeds of Israel. 5 So the LORD made firm the kingdom in his hand, and all Judah gave a tribute to Jehoshaphat. So he had an abundance of riches and honor. 6 His heart was raised up for the ways of the LORD. He even removed the high places and Asherah poles from Judah.

7 In the third year of his reign he sent officials, Ben-Hail, Obadiah, Zechariah, Nethanel, and Micaiah, to teach in the cities of Jerusalem, 8 and with them were also the Levites: Shemaiah, Nethaniah, Zebadiah, Asahel, Shemiramoth, Jehonathan, Adonijah, Tobijah, and Tob-Adonijah, who were Levites. And with these were also Elishama and Jehoram, who were priests. 9 They taught *the people* in Judah, and they used the Book of the Law of the LORD and they traveled about all the cities of Judah and taught the people.

10 The terror of the LORD came on all the kingdoms of the land that surrounded Judah, and they did not bring war against Jehoshaphat. 11 Some from the Philistine peoples brought gifts to Jehoshaphat such as silver for tribute. The Arabians even brought seven thousand seven hundred rams and seven thousand seven hundred goats to him.

12 Jehoshaphat continued to increase in greatness, and he built citadels and storehous-

es in Judah. 13 And he had much property in
the cities of Judah, and the men of war, mighty
men of valor, were in Jerusalem. 14 This was
their divisions by the houses of their father:

From Judah, the commanders of
thousands:
Adnah the commander with three hun-
dred thousand mighty men of valor.
15 Beside him was Jehohanan the
commander with two hundred eighty
thousand mighty men of war.
16 Beside him was Amasiah the son of
Zikri, a volunteer for the LORD with two
hundred thousand mighty men of war.
17 From Benjamin:
Eliada a mighty man of war with two
hundred thousand men armed with bow
and shield.
18 Beside him was Jehozabad with one
hundred and eighty thousand equipped
for warfare.

19 These were serving the king in addition to
those the king placed in the fortified cities
throughout Judah.

Micaiah Prophesies Against Ahab
1Ki 22:1–28

18 Now Jehoshaphat had great riches and
honor, and he married into the family
of Ahab. 2 At the end of some years he went
down to Ahab in Samaria. And Ahab slaugh-
tered a great amount of sheep and oxen for Je-
hoshaphat and those who journeyed with him
and then lured him up to Ramoth Gilead. 3 And
King Ahab of Israel said to King Jehoshaphat
of Judah, "Will you go up with me to Ramoth
Gilead?"

And he responded, "I am as you are, and
as your people also my people are. We will
be with you in this war." 4 And Jehoshaphat
further said to the king of Israel, "Inquire today
the word of the LORD on this."

5 So the king of Israel gathered together four
hundred prophets, and he inquired from them,
"Should I go up to Ramoth Gilead for battle, or
should I cease from this?"

They said, "Go up, for God will give this to
the hand of the king."

6 But Jehoshaphat said, "Is there not still here
another prophet for the LORD from whom we
might inquire?"

7 Then the king of Israel responded to Je-
hoshaphat, "There is still one man from whom
we can seek the LORD, but I hate him because
he does not prophesy anything good for me
but always disaster. He is Micaiah the son of
Imlah."

And Jehoshaphat said, "May the king not
speak like this."

17:16 Jdg 5:9
17:19 2Ch 17:2
18:1 2Ch 17:5

18:13 Nu 22:35
18:16 Mt 9:36
18:18 Da 7:9
18:21 Jn 8:44
18:22 Isa 19:14

8 So the king of Israel called to a court eunuch
and said, "Hurry and bring Micaiah the son
of Imlah."

9 And the king of Israel and Jehoshaphat
the king of Judah were sitting on their own
thrones, clothed in their *royal* garments, at the
threshing floor at the entrance at the gate of
Samaria, and all the prophets were prophesy-
ing before them. 10 Then Zedekiah the son of
Kenaanah made for himself iron horns, and
he said, "Thus says the LORD: With these you
will thrust out the Arameans in Syria until they
are finished."

11 And all the prophets were prophesying
the same, "Go up to Ramoth Gilead and find
success, because the LORD has given the king
into your hands."

12 And the messenger who went to call Mica-
iah said to him, "The words of the prophets are
as one voice and *only* for good to the king, so
may your word be like one of them, and you
speak favorably."

13 And Micaiah said, "As the LORD lives, what-
ever my God says, that will I speak."

14 When he came to the king, the king said
to him, "Micaiah, should we go up to Ramoth
Gilead for battle, or should I cease?"

He said, "All of you go up and be successful,
and they will be given into your hands."

15 Then the king said to him, "How many
times must I cause you to swear that you speak
to me only truth in the name of the LORD?"

16 Then he said, "I saw all Israel scattered on
the mountains like sheep that have no shep-
herd. The LORD said, 'There are no masters
for them. Let each man return to his home
in peace.' "

17 Then the king of Israel said to Jehosha-
phat, "Did I not say to you that he would not
prophesy good concerning me, but evil?"

18 So the *prophet* said, "Now hear the word of
the LORD: I saw the LORD sitting on His throne
and the heavenly assembly was standing at
His right and His left. 19 And the LORD said,
'Who will deceive Ahab king of Israel so that
he might go up and fall at Ramoth Gilead?'

"One was saying one thing, and another was
saying something else. 20 Then a spirit came
out and stood before the LORD, and he said, 'I
will deceive him.'

"Then the LORD said to him, 'How?'

21 "Then he said, 'I will go out and be a spirit
of deception in the mouth of all the prophets.'

"Then the LORD said, 'You will deceive and
find success. Go out and do this.'

22 "Now see that the LORD has put a spirit of
deception in the mouth of your prophets. So
the LORD has declared disaster over you."

23 Then Zedekiah the son of Kenaanah came
near to Micaiah and struck him on the cheek.
And he said, "Which way then did the spir-
it from the LORD pass from me to speak with
you?"

24 Then Micaiah said, "You will see *it* on the
day when you enter an inner chamber to hide
yourself."

25 And the king of Israel said, "Seize Micaiah
and take him to Amon, the governor of the
city, and to Joash the son of the king, 26 and
you will say, 'So says the king: Put him in a
prison, and feed him a little food and water
until I return in peace.' "

27 Then Micaiah said, "If you certainly return
in peace, then the LORD has not spoken by me.
Listen, all you people!"

The Death of Ahab
1Ki 22:29–36

28 So the king of Israel and Jehoshaphat
the king of Judah went up to Ramoth Gilead.
29 Then the king of Israel said to Jehoshaphat,
"I will disguise myself and go into battle, but
you will put on your clothes." So the king of
Israel disguised himself, and they both entered
into battle.

30 And the king of Aram ordered the com-
manders of his chariots, "Do not wage war
with the small or great but with the king of Is-
rael alone." 31 And it happened when the com-
manders of the chariots saw Jehoshaphat they
said, "It is the king of Israel." So they turned
on him to wage war. But Jehoshaphat cried
out, and the LORD helped him, then God drew
them away from the *king*. 32 And it happened
when the commanders of the chariots saw that
he was not the king of Israel, then they turned
away from him.

33 But a man pulled his bow at random and
struck the king of Israel between his armor
scales and body armor. He said to the com-
mander of the chariot, "Turn and remove me
from the battle because I am wounded." 34 And
the battle continued on that day, and the king
of Israel was set up in his chariot before the
Arameans until evening. Then he died when
the sun set.

19 But Jehoshaphat king of Judah re-
turned to his palace in Jerusalem in
peace. 2 And Jehu the son of Hanani the seer
went out to meet him, and he said to King
Jehoshaphat, "How do you help those who are
wicked and love those who hate the LORD? Be-
cause of this, wrath has gone out against you
from the LORD. 3 However, some good things
are found in you for you swept away the Asher-
ah poles from the land, and you set your heart
to seek after God."

The Reforms of Jehoshaphat

4 Jehoshaphat lived in Jerusalem, but he
went out among the people from Beersheba
to the hill country of Ephraim, and he brought
them back to the LORD God of their fathers.
5 And he set judges in the land among all the
fortified cities of Judah, one by one. 6 And he
said to the judges, "Consider carefully what
you do because you do not judge according
to man but the LORD, and He is with you in the
matter of judgment. 7 So now may the fear
of the LORD be on you. Consider and act *well*
because there is no injustice, partiality, or bribe
taking with the LORD our God."

8 Moreover, Jehoshaphat appointed in Jeru-
salem some from the Levites and the priests
and some from the heads of the families of
Israel, in order to render judgment and decide
disputes before the LORD; and they lived in Je-
rusalem. 9 And he commanded them, "So you
will act in the fear of the LORD, in honesty, and
with a complete heart. 10 And any dispute that
comes before you all from your brothers who
live in their cities, concerning bloodshed or of-
fenses against law or commandment, against
statutes or judgments, you will warn them, lest
they trespass against the LORD and wrath come
upon you and your brothers. Do this, and you
will not trespass.

11 "Note that Amariah the chief priest is over
you in all matters of the LORD; and Zebadiah
the son of Ishmael, the ruler of the house of
Judah, for all the king's matters; also, the Le-
vites will be officials before you. Deal coura-
geously, and the LORD will be with the good."

Jehoshaphat Defeats Moab and Ammon

20 After that, the Moabites and the Am-
monites, together with some Meu-
nites,[1] came against Jehoshaphat for battle.

2 And some came and declared this to Je-
hoshaphat, "A large multitude is coming
against you from across the Dead Sea from
Edom; and observe, they are in Hazezon Tam-
ar" (that is, En Gedi). 3 Then Jehoshaphat was
fearful and set himself to seek the LORD, and
he called for a fast throughout all Judah. 4 And
Judah was assembled to seek the LORD; even
from all the cities of Judah, they came to obtain
aid from the LORD.

5 And Jehoshaphat stood in the midst of the
assembly of Judah and Jerusalem in the house
of the LORD before the new courtyard, 6 and
he said:

> "O LORD God of our fathers, are You not
> God in the heavens? And do You not rule
> over all the kingdoms of the nations? In
> Your hand are strength and might, and

18:23 Jer 20:2
18:26 2Ch 16:10
18:31 2Ch 13:14
19:2 1Ki 16:1
19:3 2Ch 12:12
....
19:6 Dt 1:17
19:7 Ge 18:25
20:2 Ge 14:7
20:3 2Ch 19:3
20:6 1Ch 29:11–12

[1] 1 Heb. *and others with those from the Ammonites.*

there is no one who can oppose You. 7 Did
You not, our God, drive out those who lived
in this land before Your people Israel, and
You gave it perpetually to the descendants
of Abraham, who was in *covenant* love
with You. 8 And they have dwelled in it and
have built in it for You a sanctuary for Your
name saying, 9 'If disaster comes upon us,
the sword, or judgment, or pestilence, or
famine, then we will stand before this tem-
ple and before You because Your name is
in this temple. And we will cry out to You in
our distress, and You will hear and deliver.'

10 "Now here are the sons of Ammon and
Moab and Mount Seir, whom You did not
let Israel invade when they came out of the
land of Egypt, when they turned away from
them and did not destroy them. 11 See how
they are rewarding us by coming to drive
us out of Your possession, which You have
given us to inherit. 12 O our God, will You not
render judgment on them? For we have not
strength enough to stand before this great
army that is coming against us. And we do
not know what we should do, but our eyes
are on You."

13 Now all of Judah was standing before the
LORD, even their infants, wives, and children.

14 And in the midst of the assembly the Spirit
of the LORD came on Jahaziel the son of Zech-
ariah, the son of Benaiah, the son of Jeiel,
the son of Mattaniah, a Levite from the line
of Asaph.

15 And he said, "Pay attention all Judah, and
those dwelling in Jerusalem, and King Je-
hoshaphat: Thus says the LORD to you, 'Do not
fear, nor be dismayed because of this great
army, for the battle is not yours, but God's.
16 Tomorrow, go down against them. They will
travel up by the Ascent of Ziz. You will find
them at the back of the valley, before the Wil-
derness of Jeruel. 17 It will not be *necessary* for
you to fight in this *conflict*. Take your positions,
stand, and observe the deliverance of the LORD
for you, O Judah and Jerusalem.' Do not fear or
be filled with terror. Tomorrow, go out before
them, and the LORD will be with you."

18 Then Jehoshaphat bowed his face to the
ground, and all Judah and those dwelling in
Jerusalem fell before the LORD to worship Him.
19 And the Levites from the descendants of the
Kohathites and Korahites rose up to praise the
LORD God of Israel with a very loud voice.

20 So they rose up early in the morning and
went out to the Wilderness of Tekoa. And when
they went out, Jehoshaphat stood and said,
"Listen to me, Judah and those dwelling in Je-
rusalem. Believe in the LORD your God, and you
will be supported. Believe His prophets, and
you will succeed." 21 And he consulted with the

20:7 Isa 41:8
20:9 2Ch 6:20
20:10 Nu 20:17–21
20:12 Ps 25:15
20:14 2Ch 15:1
20:15 1Sa 17:47
20:17 2Ch 15:2
20:18 Ex 4:31
20:20 Isa 7:9
20:21 1Ch 16:29

....

20:27 Ne 12:43
20:29 2Ch 17:10
20:30 2Ch 14:6–7

people and then appointed singers for the LORD
and those praising Him in holy attire as they
went before those equipped for battle saying,

"Praise the LORD,
for His mercy endures forever."

I will give thanks to the Lord, for His love endures forever (2Ch 20:21).

22 When they began singing and praising, the
LORD set ambushes against Ammon, Moab, and
Mount Seir, who had come against Judah; so
they were defeated. 23 Then the Ammonites
and Moabites stood up against those dwelling
from Mount Seir to destroy and finish them.
Then when they made an end of the inhabi-
tants of Seir, each man attacked his companion
to destroy each other.

Loose confusion, and let my enemies attack each other, in the name of Jesus (2Ch 20:23).

24 And Judah came to the watchtower of the
wilderness, and they turned to the vast army
and saw only corpses lying on the ground.
And no one was spared. 25 Then Jehoshaphat
and his people came to gather their plunder,
and they found among them an abundance of
riches with the corpses, and precious jewelry,
which they took for themselves, more than
they could carry. They were gathering the
plunder for three days because there was so
much to carry. 26 On the fourth day they gath-
ered at the Valley of Berakah, because there
they blessed the LORD. For this reason people
have called the name of this place the Valley
of Berakah until this day.

27 Then they all returned, every man from
Judah and Jerusalem, with Jehoshaphat as
their head, to Jerusalem with joy because the
LORD made them rejoice because of the *death*
of their enemies. 28 So they entered Jerusalem
with harps, lyres, and trumpets to the house
of the LORD.

29 And it happened that the terror of God was
on all the kingdoms of the lands who heard
that the LORD had fought against the enemies
of Israel. 30 So the kingdom of Jehoshaphat
was quiet, because his God gave him rest on
all sides.

The End of Jehoshaphat's Reign
1Ki 22:41–50

31 And Jehoshaphat reigned over Judah.
He was thirty-five years old when he began
his reign, and he was king in Jerusalem for
twenty-five years. The name of his mother was

Azubah the daughter of Shilhi. 32 He walked in the way of his father Asa, and he did not turn aside from doing what was right in the eyes of the LORD. 33 Only the high places were not taken down. The people had yet to set their hearts to the God of their fathers.

34 And the remainder of the acts of Jehoshaphat, from beginning to end, are written in the annals of Jehu son of Hanani, which are taken up in the book of the kings of Israel.

35 Also, Jehoshaphat king of Judah was united with Ahaziah king of Israel, who acted wickedly. 36 Jehoshaphat joined with him to make ships to travel to Tarshish, and they made ships in Ezion Geber. 37 And Eliezer son of Dodavahu from Mareshah prophesied against Jehoshaphat saying, "Because you have joined with Ahaziah, the LORD will tear down your works." So the ships were wrecked, so that they were not able to journey to Tarshish.

21 So Jehoshaphat slept with his fathers and was buried with them in the City of David, and Jehoram his son ruled in his place. 2 And he had brothers, sons of Jehoshaphat king of Israel, Azariah, Jehiel, Zechariah, Azariahu, Michael, and Shephatiah. 3 And their father gave them great gifts of silver, gold, and excellent items, along with fortified cities in Judah, but he gave the kingdom to Jehoram because he was the firstborn.

Jehoram, King of Judah

2Ki 8:16–24

4 Then Jehoram rose up over the kingdom of his father and he became strong. And he killed all his brothers with the sword and even some of the officials in Israel. 5 Now Jehoram was thirty-two years old when he began as king, and he reigned eight years in Jerusalem. 6 And he walked in the ways of the kings of Israel as those from the house of Ahab did, for the daughter of Ahab was the wife of Jehoram. And he did evil in the eyes of the LORD. 7 But the LORD was not willing to destroy the house of David because of the covenant that He made with David, and because He said that He would give a lamp to David and his sons for all days.

8 In the days of Jehoram, Edom revolted from being under the hand of Judah, and they set a king for themselves. 9 So Jehoram passed over to the Edomite territory with his commanders and all his chariots, and it happened that he rose up at night and struck the Edomites, who had surrounded him and his chariot commanders. 10 So Edom revolted from being under the hand of Judah until this day.

20:33 2Ch 17:6
20:34 1Ki 16:1
20:35 1Ki 22:48–49
20:37 Pr 13:20
21:1 1Ki 22:50
21:4 Jdg 9:5
21:6 2Ch 18:1
21:7 1Ki 11:36
....
21:11 Lev 20:5
21:12 2Ch 14:2–5
21:13 2Ch 21:4
21:15 2Ch 21:18–19
21:16 2Ch 17:11
21:17 2Ch 22:1
21:18 2Ch 21:15
21:19 2Ch 16:14
21:20 Jer 22:18
22:1 2Ch 21:16–17

At that time Libnah also revolted from being under their rule, because Jehoram had abandoned the LORD God of his fathers. 11 He even made high places in the hill country of Judah and caused those in Jerusalem to be like prostitutes, and he led Judah astray.

12 And a letter came to him from Elijah the prophet, saying,

> "Thus says the LORD God of David your father: Because you have not walked in the ways of Jehoshaphat your father, or in the ways of Asa king of Judah, 13 but have walked in the way of the kings of Israel, and have led Judah and the inhabitants of Jerusalem into whoredom, as the house of Ahab led Israel into whoredom, and also have killed your brothers, those of your father's house, who were better than you, 14 the LORD will bring a great plague on your people, your children, your wives, and all your possessions; 15 and you will have great sickness with a disease of your intestines, until your intestines come out because of the disease, day by day."

16 Then the LORD stirred up the spirit of the Philistines against Jehoram and also the Arabians who were near the Cushites. 17 And they went up against Judah and broke through, and they took every possession found in the palace of the king, even his sons and wives, so that no son was left with him except his youngest *Ahaziah*.

The Death of Jehoram

18 And after all this, the LORD struck him in his entrails with an incurable disease. 19 And it happened after many days, at the end of two years, his entrails came out due to his disease, so he died by a despicable disease. And his people did not make for him a *memorial* fire like the fire for his fathers.

20 He was thirty-two when he began to reign, and he reigned eight years in Jerusalem. And he departed with no one's regret. They buried him in the City of David, but not in the tombs of the kings.

Ahaziah, King of Judah

2Ki 8:25–29; 9:21–29

22 Then those in Jerusalem made Ahaziah, the youngest son of Jehoram, king in his place because the raiding party, those coming with the Arabians to the camp, killed all the older sons. So Ahaziah the son of Jehoram reigned in Jerusalem.

2 Now Ahaziah was forty-two years[1] old when he began to reign, but he only reigned one year in Jerusalem. The name of his mother was Athaliah, a granddaughter of Omri.

[1] 2 2Ki 8:26 reads twenty-two years.

3 And he also walked in the ways of the house of Ahab because his mother was the one counseling him to do evil. 4 And he also did what was evil in the eyes of the LORD, like the house of Ahab, for they served as his counselors after his father *Jehoram* died, which *led* to his destruction. 5 Even Ahaziah walked in their counsel and went with Jehoram the son of Ahab king of Israel to war against Hazael king of Aram at Ramoth Gilead. And the Arameans wounded Joram, 6 and the king returned to Jezreel to heal from the wounds that he sustained in Ramah where he fought against Hazael king of Aram.

Then Ahaziah the son of Jehoram king of Judah went down to see Joram the son of Ahab in Jezreel because he was wounded.

7 And it was from God that a downfall would happen to Ahaziah in regard to his visit with Joram. And when he arrived he went out with Joram to see Jehu the son of Nimshi, whom the LORD anointed to cut off the house of Ahab. 8 And it happened that when Jehu was acting in judgment with the house of Ahab that he found the rulers of Judah and the sons of the brothers of Ahaziah, who were serving Ahaziah, and Jehu killed them. 9 He sought out Ahaziah, and they captured him while he hid in Samaria, and they brought him to Jehu, and they put him to death. And they buried him because they said, "He is the grandson of Jehoshaphat who sought the LORD with all his heart." And there was no one from the house of Ahaziah strong enough to retain the kingdom.

Athaliah Seizes the Throne
2Ki 11:1–21

10 So when Athaliah the mother of Ahaziah saw that her son was dead, she rose up and mounted a campaign to destroy all the royal offspring of the house of Judah. 11 But Jehoshabeath,[1] the daughter of the king, took Joash the son of Ahaziah and stole him away from the king's sons who were going to be put to death, and she placed him and his nurse in a bed chamber. So Jehoshabeath, the daughter of King Jehoram and wife of Jehoiada the priest (since she was a sister of Ahaziah), hid Joash from Athaliah. And she did not put the *royal child* to death. 12 And he was hidden away with them in the house of God for six years. And Athaliah ruled over the land.

Joash, King of Judah

23 Then in the seventh year Jehoiada strengthened himself and made a covenant with the commanders over hundreds: Azariah the son of Jeroham, Ishmael the son of Jehohanan, Azariah the son of Obed, Maaseiah the son of Adaiah, and Elishaphat the son of Zikri. 2 And they went throughout Judah and gathered the Levites from all the cities of Judah and even the heads of the fathers' houses in Israel. Then they all came to Jerusalem.

3 So the whole assembly made a covenant with the king in the house of God, and *Jehoiada* said to them, "The king's son will reign, as the LORD has said of the sons of David. 4 And this is the thing that you all will do: A third of you all from the priests and Levites who come on the Sabbath will be gatekeepers, 5 one-third will be at the palace of the king and another third at the Foundation Gate. And all the people will be in the courts of the house of the LORD. 6 And may no one enter the house of the LORD except the priests and those Levites who are serving. Those can enter because they are holy, but all the people will keep their assigned duty of the LORD. 7 Then the Levites will surround the king, each man with his weapon in his hand, and whoever enters the house will be put to death. They will be with the king when he enters and leaves."

8 The Levites and all Judah did everything that Jehoiada the priest commanded. Each brought his men, who were to come on duty on the Sabbath, with those who were to go off duty on the Sabbath, because Jehoiada the priest did not dismiss the divisions. 9 Then Jehoiada the priest gave to the commanders of hundreds the spears and the large and small shields which had been King David's, which were in the house of God. 10 Then he set all the people around the king, each man with his weapon in hand, from the south side to the north side of the temple, from the altar to the temple.

11 Then they brought out the son of the king and set on him the crown and the testimony and they proclaimed him as king. So Jehoiada and his sons anointed him and said, "Long live the king!"

The Death of Athaliah

12 And when Athaliah heard the sound of the people running and praising the king, she went toward the people in the temple of the LORD. 13 And she saw the king standing by the pillar at the entrance with the officials and trumpeters next to the king, and all of the people of the land were rejoicing and blowing trumpets, and singers with their instruments with songs were offering up praise. Then Athaliah tore her garments and yelled, "Treachery! Treachery!"

14 Then Jehoiada the priest brought out the commanders over hundreds, those entrusted over the army, and said to them, "Bring her out between the ranks, and let whoever follows

22:7 2Ki 9:21

23:3 2Sa 7:12
23:11 1Sa 10:24

[1] *11* Jehosheba in 2Ki 11:2.

her be killed with the sword." For the priest said, "Do not put her to death in the house of the LORD." 15 So they seized her, and she went to the entrance of the Horse Gate of the king's palace, and they put her to death there.

16 And Jehoiada made a covenant between himself, the people, and the king that they would be a people *dedicated* to the LORD. 17 Then all the people went to the temple of Baal, and they tore it down along with its altars, and they shattered its images. And Mattan the priest of Baal, they killed before the altars.

18 Then Jehoiada placed guards at the house of the LORD, under the supervision of the priests, the Levites whom David allotted for the house of the LORD to make burnt offerings to the LORD as is written in the Law of Moses, with rejoicing and music, according to the direction of David. 19 And he set the gatekeepers at the gates of the house of the LORD so that no one might enter who was in any manner unclean.

20 Then he took the commanders over hundreds, the nobles, those in authority over the people, and all the people of the land, and they brought down the king from the house of the LORD. And they went through the Upper Gate of the palace of the king, and they brought the king to sit on the royal throne. 21 And all the people of the land rejoiced. And the city had peace when they put Athaliah to death with the sword.

Joash Repairs the Temple
2Ki 12:1–21

24 Now Joash[1] was seven years old when he started his reign, and he was king in Jerusalem for forty years. The name of his mother was Zibiah of Beersheba. 2 Joash did what was correct in the eyes of the LORD all the days of Jehoiada the priest. 3 And Jehoiada gave *Joash* two wives, and he had sons and daughters.

4 And it happened after this that it was in the heart of Joash to restore the house of the LORD. 5 So he assembled the priests and Levites to speak with them, "Go out to the cities of Judah and collect money from all Israel to fortify the house of your God, what is necessary each year. Now hurry with this matter." But the Levites delayed.

6 So the king called Jehoiada, who was head over this, and said to him, "Why have you not required from the Levites that they bring in from Judah and Jerusalem the tax levied by Moses, the servant of the LORD, for the congregation of Israel for the tent of the testimony?"

7 For the sons of Athaliah, the wicked woman, had broken into the house of God and even used all the holy items of the house of the LORD for Baal *worship*.

8 Then the king spoke, and they made a chest, and put it outside the gate of the house of the LORD. 9 And they gave a report in Judah and Jerusalem to bring in to the LORD a tax levied by Moses the servant of God on Israel in the wilderness. 10 So all the officials and people rejoiced, and they brought in *the money* and cast it into the chest until it was full. 11 And it happened that at the time the Levites brought the chest to the guards of the king that there was a large amount of money. So the king's scribe and head priest's commissioner would bring it and empty the chest and then take it and return it to its place. They continued to do this every day and collected a great amount of money. 12 So the king and Jehoiada gave it to those doing a work of labor on the house of the LORD. And they hired masons and craftsmen to repair the house of the LORD, and even metal workers in iron and bronze to fortify the house of the LORD.

13 So the workmen worked, and the work was completed by them. They restored the house of God to its specifications and strengthened it. 14 When they had finished, they brought the rest of the money before the king and Jehoiada, who made vessels for the house of the LORD, vessels for serving and for making burnt offerings, spoons and vessels of gold and silver. They continually offered burnt offerings in the house of the LORD all the days of Jehoiada.

15 Then Jehoiada became old and full of days and died. He was one hundred and thirty years old when he died. 16 So they buried him in the City of David with the kings, because he had done good in Israel, both toward God and His house.

The Wickedness of Joash

17 After the death of Jehoiada the officials of Judah came and paid homage to the king. At that time the king listened to them. 18 Then they abandoned the house of the LORD and God of their fathers, and they served the Asherah poles and idols. And *divine* wrath was on Judah and Jerusalem because of this guilt. 19 And *God* sent prophets to return them to the LORD. These warned the *people*, but they would not listen.

20 Then the Spirit of God clothed Zechariah the son of Jehoiada the priest, and he stood above the people saying, "Thus says God: Why are you transgressing the commandments of the LORD so that you all will not be successful? Because you all have abandoned the LORD, He has abandoned you."

23:15 Ne 3:28
23:20 2Ki 11:19
24:6 Ex 30:12–16
24:7 2Ch 21:17

24:9 2Ch 24:6
24:18 Jos 22:20
24:20 Nu 14:41

[1] 1 Jehoash in 2Ki 12:1.

21 But they plotted against him, and at the command of the king they all stoned him in the court of the house of the LORD. 22 And Joash the king did not remember the kindness that Jehoiada the father of Zechariah had shown him, but killed his son. As he was dying, he said, "May the LORD see and avenge!"

The Death of Joash

23 And it happened that at the turn of the year the army of Aram came up against Joash. They came to Judah and Jerusalem and destroyed all the officials of the people, and they sent all their plunder to the king of Damascus. 24 Though the Aramean army came with a few men, the LORD delivered into their hand a very great Judean army because they abandoned the LORD God of their fathers. So they enacted judgment on Joash. 25 When they left him (for they abandoned him with severe wounds) his own servants plotted against him because of the blood of the son of Jehoiada the priest. So they killed him on his bed. So he died, and they buried him in the City of David, but they did not bury him in the tombs of the kings.

26 And those who conspired against him were Zabad the son of Shimeath the Ammonite and Jehozabad the son of Shimrith the Moabite. 27 Accounts of his sons and of the many oracles against him and of the rebuilding of the house of God are written in the annals of the kings. And Amaziah his son ruled in his place.

Amaziah, King of Judah
2Ki 14:1–20

25 Amaziah was twenty-five years old when he was king, and he reigned twenty-nine years in Jerusalem. The name of his mother was Jehoaddan from Jerusalem. 2 He did what was correct in the eyes of the LORD, only not with a complete heart. 3 And it happened that when the kingdom was firmly his that he killed his servants, those who struck down his father King Joash. 4 But he did not put to death their children because, as it is written in the Law in the Book of Moses, as the LORD commanded, "You will not put to death the fathers for their children's *actions* nor the children will you put to death for their fathers' *actions*, for every man will be put to death for his own sin."

Slaughter of the Edomites

5 Then Amaziah assembled Judah and set over them according to the house of the fathers commanders of thousands and hundreds in all Judah and Benjamin, and he appointed men who were twenty years old and above. And they found three hundred thousand choice men fit for war and able to use a long spear and large shield. 6 And he hired out from Israel one hundred thousand mighty men of war for one hundred talents[1] of silver.

7 Then a man of God came to him saying, "O king, do not let the army of Israel come with you because the LORD is not with Israel or with any of the sons of Ephraim. 8 But if you go, do it. Be strong for the battle. Yet God shall make you fall before the enemy, for God has power to help and to bring down."

9 Then Amaziah said to the man of God, "So what should I do about the one hundred talents of silver that I gave to the military party from Israel?"

And the man of God responded, "The LORD has more to give to you than this."

10 So Amaziah dismissed the military party that came to him from Ephraim to return to their place. And they were very angry with Judah and returned to their place in a great rage.

11 But Amaziah strengthened himself and led his people, and he journeyed to the Valley of Salt and struck down ten thousand of the people of Seir. 12 And the people of Judah took captive another ten thousand alive and brought them to the top of a cliff and threw them from the top of the rock so that they were all dashed to pieces.

13 But the men of the military party that Amaziah turned back from going with him in battle raided the cities of Judah from Samaria to Beth Horon. They struck down three thousand *Judeans* and took a great amount of plunder.

14 And it happened after Amaziah came back from striking down the Edomites, he brought back the gods of the people from Seir and set them up as gods for himself. He worshipped them and gave them sacrifices. 15 So the LORD was greatly angry with Amaziah, and He sent a prophet to the *king*. And he said, "Why do you seek from the gods of the people who were not even able to deliver the people from your hand?"

16 But while the *prophet* was speaking, the *king* said, "Have we made you a counselor to the king? Stop! Why should you be struck down?"

The prophet refrained, but he said, "I know that God has determined to destroy you because you have done this and not heeded my advice."

Israel Defeats Judah

17 Then Amaziah king of Judah received advice and sent for Jehoash[2] the son of Jehoahaz, the son of Jehu king of Israel, saying, "Come, let us meet together."

24:22 Ge 9:5
24:23 2Ki 12:17–18
25:2 2Ch 25:14
25:4 Dt 24:16
25:5 Nu 1:3
25:8 2Ch 20:6
25:11 2Ki 14:7
25:14 2Ch 28:23
25:17 2Ki 14:8–14

[1] 6 About 3¾ tons, or 3.4 metric tons; also in v. 9. [2] 17 Heb. text has *Joash*, but *Jehoash* is also given to distinguish between the Judean and Israelite kings.

18 So Jehoash king of Israel sent a *message*
for Amaziah king of Judah saying, “A thistle in
Lebanon sent for a cedar in Lebanon stating,
‘Give your daughter to my son as a wife.’ Then
an animal of the field in Lebanon passed by
and trampled the thistle. 19 You say that you
have struck down Edom, and your heart lifts
you up in arrogance. Now remain in your pal-
ace. Why do you provoke disaster so that you
fall, you and Judah with you?”

20 But Amaziah would not listen because
this was from God so that He might give them
into the hand of *Jehoash* because *Amaziah* had
sought after the gods of Edom. 21 So Jehoash
king of Israel went up, and they faced each
other, he and Amaziah king of Judah, at Beth
Shemesh, which is in Judah. 22 And Judah was
struck down by Israel, and each man fled to his
home. 23 So at Beth Shemesh, Jehoash king of
Israel seized Amaziah king of Judah the son of
Joash, the son of Ahaziah. And they brought
him to Jerusalem and broke through the walls
of the city from the Ephraim Gate to the Corner
Gate, a section of four hundred cubits.[1] 24 And
Jehoash took all the gold and silver and all
the vessels that were found in the house of
God with Obed-Edom, even the treasures of
the palace of the king and hostages. Then he
returned to Samaria.

The Death of Amaziah

25 And Amaziah, the son of Joash king of Ju-
dah, lived fifteen years more after the death of
Jehoash, the son of Jehoahaz king of Israel.
26 Now the rest of the acts of Amaziah, from
first to last, are they not written in the book
of the kings of Judah and Israel? 27 From the
time when Amaziah turned aside from the
Lord, they plotted a conspiracy against him in
Jerusalem, and he fled to Lachish. Then they
sent for him and put him to death in Lachish.
28 They brought him on horses and buried him
with his fathers in the City of David in Judah.

Uzziah, King of Judah

2Ki 14:21–22; 15:1–7

26 And all the people of Judah took Uzzi-
ah[2] and made him king in the place of
his father Amaziah when he was sixteen years
old. 2 He built Eloth and restored it to Judah
after *Amaziah* the king slept with his fathers.

3 Uzziah was sixteen years old when he be-
gan to reign, and he was king in Jerusalem for
fifty-two years. The name of his mother was
Jekoliah from Jerusalem. 4 And he did what
was correct in the eyes of the Lord as every-
thing his father Amaziah had done. 5 And he
sought after God in the days of Zechariah, the
one who instructed him in the fear of the Lord.
And in the days that he sought after the Lord,
God caused him to succeed.

6 He went out to make war with the Philis-
tines, and he broke through the walls at Gath
and Jabneh and Ashdod. Then he built cities
in Ashdod and among the Philistines. 7 And
God brought him aid against the Philistines
and Arabians, those living in Gur Baal, and
the Meunites. 8 And the Ammonites gave a
gift to Uzziah, and his name spread even to
the border of Egypt because he became quite
powerful.

9 Uzziah built towers in Jerusalem at the Cor-
ner Gate, at the Valley Gate, and at the corner
buttress; and he fortified them. 10 And he built
towers in the wilderness, and he dug out many
cisterns because he had a large amount of live-
stock, both in the lowland Shephelah and in
the plain. He also had workers in the fields and
vineyards in the hills and fertile orchards, for
he loved agriculture.

11 And Uzziah had an army prepared for
battle, those who went out for war as com-
panies in the number of their divisions by the
appointment of Jeiel the scribe, and Maaseiah
the officer, and Hananiah a commander of the
king. 12 The total number of chief officers of
the mighty men of valor was two thousand six
hundred. 13 And under their hand was a mighty
army of three hundred and seven thousand
five hundred who were able to go to battle
as a strong army and to help the king against
his enemies. 14 And Uzziah prepared for the
entire army shields, long spears, helmets, scale
armor, bows, and slings for stones. 15 In Jeru-
salem he made war machines by skilled men
to be placed on towers and corners to shoot
arrows and large stones. And his name went
out for a great distance. He received great help
until he was even more powerful.

Uzziah's Punishment for Pride

16 And as he grew strong, his heart grew more
proud, leading to his destruction. Then he act-
ed unfaithfully against the Lord his God, for
he entered the temple main hall of the Lord
to burn incense on the altar. 17 But Azariah the
priest entered in after him, and with him were
eighty priests of the Lord—men of valor. 18 And
they stood against King Uzziah and said to
him, “It is not for you, Uzziah, to burn incense
to the Lord for it is for the priests, the sons of
Aaron, who are consecrated to burn incense.
Leave from the sanctuary because you have
been unfaithful, and there will be no honor
for you from the Lord God.”

19 Then Uzziah was enraged, and in his hand
was a censer for incense. And when he became

25:18 Jdg 9:8–15
25:19 2Ch 26:16
25:23 2Ch 21:17
25:25 2Ki 14:17–22
26:3 2Ki 15:2–3
26:5 2Ch 24:2

26:6 Isa 14:29
26:7 2Ch 21:16
26:9 Ne 3:13
26:16 2Ch 25:19
26:17 1Ch 6:10
26:18 Ex 30:7–8
26:19 Nu 12:10

1 23 About 600 feet, or 180 meters. *2 1* Also known as Azariah in 2Ki 15.

angry with the priests, leprosy appeared on his forehead in front of the priests in the house of the LORD, near the altar of incense. 20 Then Azariah the head priest and all the priests turned to him, and he had leprosy on his forehead; and they hastened to remove him from there, and he also hurried to leave because the LORD had struck him.

21 So King Uzziah had leprosy until the day of his death. He dwelt in a separate house with his *unclean* disease because he was cut off from the house of the LORD. Then Jotham his son was over the house of the king, and he governed the people of the land.

22 Now the remainder of the acts of Uzziah, from beginning to end, Isaiah the prophet, son of Amoz, has written *them*. 23 So Uzziah slept with his fathers, and they buried him with his fathers in the burial field belonging to the kings because they said, "He is a leper." And Jotham his son ruled in his place.

Jotham, King of Judah

2Ki 15:33–38

27 Jotham was twenty-five years old when he began as king, and he reigned sixteen years in Jerusalem. The name of his mother was Jerushah the daughter of Zadok. 2 And he did what was correct in the eyes of the LORD just as his father Uzziah had done. However, he did not enter the temple of the LORD. But the people continued acting corruptly. 3 And he built the Upper Gate of the house of the LORD, and he built much on the wall of Ophel. 4 And he built cities in the hill country of Judah, and on the wooded heights he built citadels and towers.

5 He made war with the king of the Ammonites and prevailed against them. That year the Ammonites gave to him one hundred talents[1] of silver, ten thousand kors[2] of wheat, and ten thousand kors[3] of barley. The Ammonites paid him the same amount in the second and third years as well.

6 So Jotham was strengthened because he established his ways before the LORD his God.

7 And the remainder of the acts of Jotham, all his wars and ways, are written in the book of the kings of Israel and Judah. 8 He was twenty-five years old when he began to reign, and he was king for sixteen years in Jerusalem. 9 And Jotham slept with his fathers, and they buried him in the City of David. And Ahaz his son reigned in his place.

Ahaz, King of Judah

2Ki 16:1–20

28 Ahaz was twenty years old when he began to reign, and he was king in Jerusalem for sixteen years. And he did not do what was correct in the eyes of the LORD as David his father. 2 And he walked in the ways of the kings of Israel, and he cast images for Baal worship. 3 And he made sacrifices in the Valley of Ben Hinnom, and he burned his sons in the fire according to the detestable acts of the nations that the LORD had displaced before the sons of Israel. 4 He even made sacrifices and offered incense on the high places of the hills and under every green tree.

Judah Defeated

5 So the LORD his God gave him into the hand of the king of Aram. They struck *Ahaz* and took captive many prisoners and brought them to Damascus.

He was even given into the hand of the king of Israel, and he attacked *Ahaz* with a great slaughter. 6 And Pekah the son of Remaliah killed one hundred and twenty thousand in Judah in one day, and they were all strong men, but they abandoned the LORD God of their fathers. 7 And Zikri, a mighty warrior from Ephraim, killed Maaseiah the son of the king, and Azrikam the official of the palace, and Elkanah second to the king. 8 And the sons of Israel took captive two hundred thousand of their kin, women, sons, and daughters. They also took much plunder and brought the plunder to Samaria.

9 And there was a prophet there whose name was Oded, and he went out to the army as it approached Samaria and said to them, "See that the anger of the LORD God of your fathers is against Judah, and He gave them into your hand, and you all have killed them in a rage that has reached even to heaven. 10 And now you are planning to subdue for yourselves the people of Judah and Jerusalem as male and female slaves. Do you all not surely have among you guilt before the LORD your God? 11 And now listen to me. Return the captives whom you have taken captive from your relatives because the burning wrath of the LORD is on you all."

12 And some men who were heads of the people of Ephraim rose up before those coming from the war: Azariah the son of Jehohanan, Berekiah the son of Meshillemoth, Jehizkiah the son of Shallum, and Amasa the son of Hadlai. 13 And they said, "You will not bring the captives here, for guilt from the LORD will be on us, and you plan to add to our sin and guilt. Our guilt is great, and there is *already* a burning anger against Israel."

14 So the soldiers left the captives and spoil before the officials and all the assembly. 15 Then

26:21 Lev 13:46
26:22 Isa 1:1
27:3 2Ch 33:14
27:6 2Ch 26:5

28:2 Ex 34:17
28:3 Lev 18:21
28:5 Isa 7:1
28:6 2Ki 15:27
28:8 2Ch 11:4
28:9 Ezr 9:6
28:11 Jas 2:13
28:15 Dt 34:3

[1] *5* About 3¾ tons, or 3.4 metric tons. [2] *5* Likely about 1,800 tons, or 1,600 metric tons of wheat. [3] *5* Likely about 1,500 tons, or 1,350 metric tons of barley.

the men who were designated by name took the captives *and* clothed those who were naked from the plunder. So they clothed them, gave them sandals, offered them food and drink, anointed them with oil, and led them on donkeys, even all those who stumbled. They brought them to Jericho, the city of palm trees, which was near their kinsmen. Then the *officials* returned to Samaria.

16 At that time King Ahaz sent to the king of Assyria for help. 17 The Edomites continually came and struck Judah and carried off captives. 18 Even the Philistines made raids on the cities of the lowlands of the Shephelah and the Negev of Judah. And they captured Beth Shemesh, Aijalon, Gederoth, Soko and its villages, Timnah and its villages, and Gimzo and its villages; and they settled there. 19 For the LORD humbled Judah because of Ahaz king of Judah, for he allowed depravity to spread in Judah and continually transgressed against the LORD. 20 So Tiglath-Pileser king of Assyria came against him, but he brought him distress and not strength. 21 For Ahaz took a portion from the house of the LORD and palace of the king and the officials, and he gave it to the king of Assyria, but the king did not help Ahaz.

The Death of Ahaz

22 And at the time that he was oppressed he increased in unfaithfulness against the LORD. 23 So he sacrificed to the gods of Damascus that had devastated him, for he said, "Because the gods of the kings of Aram have helped them, I will sacrifice to them so that they might help me." But they were his downfall *in Judah* and the downfall for all of Israel.

24 And Ahaz gathered the vessels from the house of God, and he cut up the vessels. Then he shut the doors of the house of the LORD, and he made altars in every corner of Jerusalem. 25 Then in every city in Judah he made high places to make offerings to other gods. So he provoked the LORD God of his fathers.

26 Now the remainder of the acts and all his ways, from first to last, are written in the book of the kings of Judah and Israel. 27 So Ahaz slept with his fathers, and they buried him in the city of Jerusalem because they did not bring him to the tombs of the kings of Israel. Then Hezekiah his son was king in his place.

Hezekiah, King of Judah

2Ki 18:2–3

29 Hezekiah was twenty-five years old when he began to reign, and he was king in Jerusalem for twenty-nine years. The name of his mother was Abijah[1] the daughter of Zechariah. 2 And he did what was correct in the eyes of the LORD just as his father David had done.

Hezekiah Cleanses the Temple

3 And in the first year and first month of his reign he opened the doors of the house of the LORD and restored them. 4 He then brought in the priests and Levites and gathered them in the square on the eastern side 5 and said to them, "Listen to me, Levites. Consecrate yourselves and consecrate the house of the LORD God of your fathers. And bring out the detestable things from the holy sanctuary. 6 For our fathers have acted unfaithfully and have done what is evil in the eyes of the LORD our God, and they have abandoned Him. They have turned their face from the sanctuary of the LORD and have turned their back. 7 They also shut the doors of the vestibule and have extinguished the lamps, nor have they burned incense or burnt offerings in the Holy Place to the God of Israel. 8 Therefore the wrath of the LORD has come on Judah and Jerusalem for a terror, horror, and scorn as you all can see with your own eyes. 9 Observe, our fathers have fallen by the sword, and now our sons, daughters, and wives are in captivity for all this. 10 Now it is in my heart to make a covenant with the LORD God of Israel so that His burning anger might turn away from us. 11 My people, do not now be negligent for the LORD has chosen you all to stand in His presence, to serve Him, and to be ministers and make sacrifices for Him."

12 Then the Levites arose:
from the Kohathites,
Mahath son of Amasai and Joel son of Azariah;
from the Merarites,
Kish son of Abdi and Azariah son of Jehallelel;
from the Gershonites,
Joah son of Zimmah and Eden son of Joah;
13 from the descendants of Elizaphan,
Shimri and Jeiel;
from the descendants of Asaph,
Zechariah and Mattaniah;
14 from the descendants of Heman,
Jehiel and Shimei;
from the descendants of Jeduthun,
Shemaiah and Uzziel.

15 So they gathered their brothers together and consecrated themselves and entered in as the king commanded by the words of the LORD in order to cleanse the house of the LORD. 16 Then the priests came into the inner part of the house of the LORD to cleanse it, and they removed everything that they found that was unclean in the main hall of the temple of the LORD

28:18 Eze 16:57
28:19 2Ch 21:2
28:20 2Ki 15:29
28:23 2Ch 25:14
28:24 2Ch 29:7
28:26 2Ki 16:19–20
28:27 2Ch 21:20
29:1 2Ki 18:1–3

29:3 2Ch 28:24
29:5 2Ch 35:6
29:6 Eze 8:16
29:7 2Ch 28:24
29:8 Jer 25:9
29:9 2Ch 28:17
29:10 2Ch 23:16
29:13 1Ch 6:39
29:15 2Ch 30:12

[1] *1* Or Abi in 2Ki 18:2.

to the court. And the Levites took those things and brought them out to the Kidron Valley. 17 They began to consecrate themselves on the first day of the first month, and on the eighth day of the month they entered the vestibule of the LORD. They consecrated the house of the LORD for eight days. Then on the sixteenth day of the first month they completed *the task.*

18 Then they came toward Hezekiah the king and said, "We have cleaned the entire house of the LORD, the altar of burnt offerings and all its utensils, and the table for showbread and all its utensils. 19 All the vessels that King Ahaz discarded from use during his reign in his treachery we have prepared and consecrated. They are before the altar of the LORD."

Hezekiah Restores Temple Worship

20 So King Hezekiah got up early and gathered the officials of the city and went up to the house of the LORD. 21 And he brought seven bulls, seven rams, seven lambs, and seven male goats for a sin offering for the kingdom, sanctuary, and Judah. Then he commanded the priests, the sons of Aaron, to offer them up on the altar of the LORD. 22 So they slaughtered the bulls, and the priests took their blood and sprinkled it on the altar and then slaughtered the rams and sprinkled their blood on the altar. They did the same for the lambs. 23 And they brought the male goats for a sin offering before the king and the assembly, and they placed their hands on *the goats.* 24 And the priests slaughtered them and purified the altar with their blood to provide atoning reconciliation for all Israel because the king said that the burnt offering and sin offering would be for all Israel.

25 And he set the Levites at the house of the LORD with cymbals, harps, and lyres according to the commandment of David, and Gad the seer of the king, and Nathan the prophet. For the commandment came from the LORD through His prophets. 26 So the Levites stood with the instruments of David and the priests with the trumpets.

27 Then Hezekiah gave the command to offer the burnt offering on the altar. When they started the burnt offering, the song of the LORD began also, with the trumpets and the instruments of David, king of Israel. 28 The entire assembly worshipped, the singers sang, and the trumpeters sounded. All of this took place until the burnt offering was finished.

29 When the burnt offering was finished, the king and all those with him bowed down and worshipped. 30 Then Hezekiah the king and the officials ordered the Levites to praise the LORD with the words of David and Asaph the seer. So they praised with gladness and bowed down to worship.

31 Then Hezekiah responded, "Now you have dedicated yourselves to the LORD. Come near and bring sacrifices and thank offerings to the house of the LORD." So the assembly brought sacrifices and thank offerings, and all who had a willing heart brought burnt offerings.

32 The number of the burnt offerings that the assembly brought was seventy bulls, one hundred rams, and two hundred lambs; all these were for a burnt offering to the LORD. 33 The consecrated animals were six hundred bulls and three thousand sheep. 34 However there were too few priests, and they were not able to skin the burnt offerings. But their brothers the Levites helped them until the work was finished and more priests consecrated themselves, for the Levites were more upright in heart to consecrate themselves than the priests. 35 Also burnt offerings were in abundance with the fat of the peace offerings and the drink offerings for the burnt offerings.

So the service of the house of the LORD was set in order. 36 Then Hezekiah and all the people rejoiced that God had prepared the people, since the events happened suddenly.

Hezekiah Celebrates the Passover

30 And Hezekiah sent word to all Israel and Judah. He even wrote letters to Ephraim and Manasseh, that they come to the house of the LORD in Jerusalem to keep the Passover to the LORD God of Israel. 2 The king counseled with his officials and all the assembly in Jerusalem to have the Passover in the second month. 3 For they were not able to have it at the appropriate time *of the first month* because a sufficient amount of priests had not consecrated themselves, nor had the people assembled yet in Jerusalem. 4 And this matter was pleasing in the eyes of the king and all the assembly. 5 So they decreed to make a proclamation throughout all Israel, from Beersheba to Dan, that they come to keep the Passover to the LORD God of Israel in Jerusalem, for the *multitude of people* did not do as it was written.

6 So couriers ran throughout all Israel and Judah with a letter from the hand of the king and his officials as a command from the king:

> "Sons of Israel, return to the LORD of Abraham, Isaac, and Israel that He might turn to the remnant who has escaped from the king of Assyria. 7 Do not act like your fathers and brothers who were faithless before the LORD God of their fathers, and He appointed them for horror, as you observe. 8 So now do not harden your necks as your fathers, but give yourselves to the LORD and come to the

29:19 2Ch 28:24
29:22 Lev 4:18
29:23 Lev 4:15
29:25 2Ch 8:14
29:26 1Ch 23:5
29:27 2Ch 23:18
29:29 2Ch 20:18
29:31 2Ch 13:9
29:34 2Ch 30:3
29:35 Nu 15:5–10
30:2 Nu 9:10–11
30:3 2Ch 29:34
30:5 Jdg 20:1
30:6 Est 8:14
30:7 2Ch 29:8
30:8 Ex 32:9

sanctuary that He has consecrated permanently. Serve the LORD your God so that His burning anger might turn away from you all. 9 Because if you return to the LORD, your brothers and children will find compassion before those who have taken them captive, in order to return you to this land. For the LORD your God is gracious and compassionate. He will not turn His face from you if you all return to Him."

10 So the couriers ran from city to city in the land of Ephraim and Manasseh and up to Zebulun, but *the people* laughed at them and mocked them. 11 However some men from Asher, Manasseh, and Zebulun humbled themselves and journeyed to Jerusalem. 12 And even in Judah the hand of God was on them to give them one heart to do the commandment of the king and officials by the word of the LORD.

13 And many people assembled in Jerusalem to have the Feast of Unleavened Bread in the second month. There was a very large assembly. 14 They went out and removed the altars that were in Jerusalem, and they took away all the incense altars and threw *them* into the Kidron Valley.

15 They slaughtered the Passover lamb on the fourteenth day of the second month. The priests and Levites were ashamed, and they consecrated themselves and brought in burnt offerings to the house of the LORD. 16 They stood at their places according to the Law of Moses, the man of God; the priests sprinkled the blood they received from the hands of the Levites. 17 For there were many in the assembly who had consecrated themselves, so the Levites slaughtered the Passover lamb for those who were not clean in order to consecrate *the people* to the LORD. 18 For a multitude of the people—many from Ephraim, Manasseh, Issachar, and Zebulun—had not purified themselves. For they ate of the Passover contrary to what was written. But Hezekiah prayed over them saying, "The LORD is good, and may He pardon 19 everyone who sets his heart to seek God, the LORD God of his fathers, but is not pure according the *rules of the* holy sanctuary." 20 So the LORD heard Hezekiah and healed the people.

21 Then the sons of Israel present in Jerusalem kept the Feast of Unleavened Bread for seven days with great joy, and the Levites and priests praised the LORD every day, *singing* with loud instruments to the LORD.

22 Then Hezekiah spoke encouragingly to all the Levites who taught the good knowledge of the LORD. So they ate for the appointed seven days, sacrificing peace offerings and giving thanks to the LORD God of their fathers.

30:9 Ex 34:6–7
30:10 2Ch 36:16
30:11 2Ch 30:18
30:12 Php 2:13
30:14 2Ch 28:24
30:15 2Ch 29:34
30:17 2Ch 29:34
30:19 2Ch 19:3
30:21 Ex 12:15
30:22 2Ch 32:6

....

30:23 1Ki 8:65
30:24 2Ch 29:34
30:25 2Ch 30:11
30:27 Dt 26:15
31:1 2Ki 18:4
31:4 Mal 2:7
31:5 Ne 13:12
31:6 Lev 27:30

23 Then the whole assembly counseled to have the *feast* for another seven days, so they had seven more days of gladness. 24 For Hezekiah king of Judah lifted up for the assembly one thousand bulls and seven thousand sheep. And the officials offered up for the assembly one thousand bulls and ten thousand sheep. And a multitude of priests consecrated themselves. 25 So all the assembly of Judah and the priests and Levites and all the assembly who came from Israel rejoiced, even the sojourners who came from the land of Israel and those who resided in Judah. 26 And there was a great rejoicing in Jerusalem, for since the days of Solomon son of David king of Israel there had not been anything like this. 27 Then the priests and Levites went out and blessed the people, and their voices were heard. And their prayers came up to His holy habitation in the heavens.

31 And when this *celebration* was finished, all of Israel that was present went out to the cities of Judah and smashed the sacred pillars and cut down the Asherah poles and tore down the high places and the altars throughout all Judah and Benjamin, and in Ephraim and Manasseh, until everything was destroyed. Then all Israel returned to their cities, each man to his own possession.

Temple Contributions
2Ki 18:5–7

2 And Hezekiah set up the divisions of the priests and Levites according to their divisions, each man as he worked among the priests and Levites for burnt and fellowship offerings, to serve, give thanks, and offer praise at the gates of the camp of the LORD. 3 And the portion of the king that came from his own possessions was for burnt offerings, those given in the morning and evening, and those given for Sabbaths, New Moons, and appointed feasts, as written in the Law of the LORD. 4 And he ordered those people living in Jerusalem to give a portion for the priests and Levites, in order for them to devote themselves to the Law of the LORD. 5 And when the command spread, the sons of Israel gave generously the first fruits of grain, wine, oil, honey, and all the produce of the field. And they brought in abundance a tenth portion of everything. 6 And the sons of Israel and Judah and all who dwelled in the cities of Judah also brought in a tenth portion of cattle and sheep, and a tenth portion of the consecrated items that were to the LORD their God, and brought them in and set them in great piles. 7 In the third month they began to assign the piles of contribution, and they finished in the seventh month. 8 When Hezekiah and the officials saw the contribution piles, they blessed the LORD and His people Israel.

9 Then Hezekiah questioned the priests and Levites regarding the contribution piles. 10 Azariah the head priest from the house of Zadok said, "Since they began to bring the contributions into the house of the LORD, there has been plenty of food and a large amount left over. For the LORD has blessed His people, and this great abundance is left over."

11 Then Hezekiah ordered them to prepare chambers in the house of the LORD, and they did this. 12 They reliably brought in the contributions, tenth portions, and consecrated items. The leader over them was Konaniah the Levite, and Shimei his brother was second to him. 13 And Jehiel, Azaziah, Nahath, Asahel, Jerimoth, Jozabad, Eliel, Ismakiah, Mahath, and Benaiah were supervisors under Konaniah and Shimei his brother by the appointment of Hezekiah the king and Azariah the leader of the house of God.

14 And Kore the son of Imnah the Levite was gatekeeper for the East Gate and over the voluntary offerings to God, to designate the contributions of the LORD and most holy offerings. 15 Eden, Miniamin, Jeshua, Shemaiah, Amariah, and Shekaniah reliably assisted him in the cities of the priests to distribute the portions to their brothers by division, both great and small.

16 Besides those males registered from three years old and above, they distributed to all who entered into the house of the LORD his daily portion, for their services according to their duties and their divisions. 17 The registration of the priests was according to the house of their fathers and the Levites from twenty years and above, according to their duties and their divisions. 18 They were registered with all their little children, wives, sons, and daughters for the entire assembly for they consecrated themselves in faithfulness.

19 Also for the sons of Aaron, the priests, who were in the fields of common land of their cities, there were men in each city who were designated by name to allocate portions to every male among the priests and to everyone who was registered by genealogy among the Levites.

20 Hezekiah did this throughout all Judah, and he did what was good and just and faithful before the LORD his God. 21 And in every deed that he undertook in the service of the house of God and with the law and commandment to seek out his God, he did this with all his heart, and he found success.

Sennacherib Threatens Jerusalem

2Ki 18:17–35; 19:35–37; Isa 36:2–20; 37:36–38

32 After these things and these acts of faithfulness, Sennacherib king of Assyria came to Judah and encamped against the fortified cities thinking that he would break through them for himself. 2 When Hezekiah observed that Sennacherib had come and that he turned to war against Jerusalem, 3 he consulted with his officials and military men to stop up the waters of the springs that were outside the city, and they helped in this. 4 So, many people assembled and worked to stop up all the springs and the stream flowing through the area. They reasoned, "Why should the king of Assyria come and find a great amount of water?" 5 He then worked hard to build up all the walls that were broken down and to raise up towers. Then he built another wall outside that one and strengthened the Millo in the City of David. And he made weapons and shields in abundance.

6 And he designated commanders for fighting over the people, and he gathered them to himself at the open square of the gate of the city and spoke encouragingly to them saying, 7 "Be strong and brave. Do not fear or have terror before the king of Assyria or before all this army that is with him because there are more who are with us than with him. 8 With this king is a strong arm of flesh, but with us is the LORD our God who will help us and fight our battles." So the people leaned on the words of Hezekiah king of Judah.

9 After all this Sennacherib king of Assyria sent his servants to Jerusalem—while he was at Lachish with all his military force that was with him—to Hezekiah king of Judah and to all Judah that was in Jerusalem stating,

> 10 "Thus says Sennacherib king of Assyria: By what do you all trust that you remain in a besieged Jerusalem? 11 Is not Hezekiah leading you all astray to give you over to death by famine and thirst when he tells you, 'The LORD our God will deliver us from the hand of the king of Assyria'? 12 Has not Hezekiah himself taken down this god's high places and altars by ordering Judah and Jerusalem, 'You all will bow down at one altar and on it burn sacrifices'?
>
> 13 "Do you not know what I and my fathers have done to all the peoples of other lands? Were the gods of the nations of these lands surely able to rescue their lands from my hand? 14 Who from among all the gods of these nations that my fathers utterly destroyed was able to rescue his people from my hand? For will your god be able to rescue you all from my hand? 15 Now do not let Hezekiah trick or lead you all astray in this. And do not believe him, for no god from any nation or kingdom has been able to deliver his people from my hand or the hand of

31:10 Mal 3:10
31:15 Jos 21:9–19
31:17 1Ch 23:24
31:19 2Ch 31:12–15
31:20 2Ki 20:3

32:4 2Ch 32:30
32:5 2Ch 25:23
32:6 2Ch 30:22
32:7 2Ki 6:16
32:8 Jer 17:5
32:12 2Ch 31:1
32:15 Ex 5:2

my fathers. How much less will your God deliver you from my hand?"

16 And his servants continued to speak against the LORD God and Hezekiah his servant. 17 He also wrote letters to insult the LORD God of Israel, speaking against Him, "As the gods of the nations of other lands did not rescue their people from my hand, so the god of Hezekiah will not rescue his people from my hand." 18 And they proclaimed it also in a loud voice in the Judean language against the people of Jerusalem who were on the wall to frighten and terrify them in order to capture the city. 19 They spoke about the God of Jerusalem like the gods of the other peoples of the earth, which are only objects made by men's hands.

The Death of Sennacherib

20 So Hezekiah the king and Isaiah the prophet son of Amoz prayed concerning this. And they called out to heaven. 21 So the LORD sent an angel and destroyed the mighty army, leaders, and officials in the camp of the king of Assyria. So the king returned in shame to his own land. When he entered the temple of his god, some of his sons fell on him there with the sword.

22 So the LORD saved Hezekiah and the inhabitants of Jerusalem from the hand of Sennacherib king of Assyria, and from the hand of all others, and gave them rest on every side. 23 Many brought tribute to the LORD in Jerusalem and choice gifts to Hezekiah king of Judah so that he was lifted up before the eyes of all the nations from then on.

Hezekiah's Pride

24 In those days Hezekiah became ill even to the point of death, so he prayed to the LORD. He spoke to the *king* and gave him a sign. 25 But Hezekiah did not make recompense for what was given to him because his heart was proud. So *divine* anger was on him, Judah, and Jerusalem. 26 Then Hezekiah humbled himself from his arrogant heart, both he and those who lived in Jerusalem, and the anger of the LORD did not come over them in the days of Hezekiah.

27 And Hezekiah had a vast amount of riches and honor, and he made treasures for himself from silver, gold, costly stones, spices, shields, and all types of precious items. 28 He made storehouses for the produce of grain, wine, and oil; and stalls for all types of livestock and flocks. 29 He also built cities for himself and acquired numbers of flocks and herds, for God had given to him a vast amount of possessions.

30 And Hezekiah shut up the upper outlet of the waters of the Gihon and directed them downward to the western side of the City of David. And Hezekiah found success in all his works. 31 But the envoys came from the officials of Babylon who were sent to him to inquire about the sign that had been given in the land. God left him *alone* in order to test *Hezekiah*, to know what was in his heart.

32:23 2Ch 17:5
32:24 2Ki 20:1–11
32:25 2Ch 24:18
32:26 Jer 26:18–19
32:29 1Ch 29:12
32:30 1Ki 1:33

....

32:31 Dt 8:2
33:2 2Ch 28:3
33:3 Dt 16:21
33:4 2Ch 7:16
33:5 2Ch 4:9
33:6 2Ch 28:3
33:7 2Ch 33:4
33:8 2Sa 7:10
33:11 Dt 28:36

The Death of Hezekiah

2Ki 20:1–21; Isa 37:21–38; 38:1–8

32 And the remainder of the acts of Hezekiah and his kind acts, they are written in the vision of Isaiah the prophet, son of Amoz, in the book of the kings of Judah and Israel. 33 So Hezekiah slept with his fathers, and they buried him in the upper tombs of the sons of David. And all those from Judah and those living in Jerusalem paid him honor at his death. Then Manasseh his son reigned in his place.

Manasseh, King of Judah

2Ki 21:1–18

33 Manasseh was twelve years old when he became king, and he was king in Jerusalem for fifty-five years. 2 But he did evil in the sight of the LORD, according to the abominations of the nations whom the LORD *previously* cast out before the sons of Israel. 3 And he turned again to build the high places that his father Hezekiah had torn down, and he set up altars to the Baals, and made Asherah poles, and worshipped the starry assembly of heaven and served them. 4 And he built altars in the house of the LORD where the LORD said, "In Jerusalem My name will be perpetual." 5 And he built altars for the starry assembly of heaven in the two courtyards of the house of the LORD. 6 He even made his sons pass through the fire in the Valley of Ben Hinnom; and he had conjurers, and practitioners of divination and sorcery, and necromancers, and mediums. So he did a great amount of evil in the eyes of the LORD, so that God was provoked.

7 And he set the carved image of a statue that he made and put in the house of God where God said to David and to Solomon his son, "In this house and in Jerusalem where I have chosen from among all the tribes of Israel, there I have set My name perpetually. 8 And I will not again remove the foot of Israel from the ground that I have designated to your fathers, if only they will keep on doing everything that I have commanded them, the whole law, statutes, and judgments from the hand of Moses." 9 So Manasseh made Judah and those living in Jerusalem to wander and to perform more evil than the nations that the LORD destroyed from before Israel.

Manasseh's Repentance

10 The LORD spoke to Manasseh and his people, but they did not pay attention. 11 So the LORD brought on them the officials of the

army of the king of Assyria. They captured
Manasseh with hooks, and they bound him in
bronze chains and led him to Babylon. 12 And
when he was distressed, he entreated the face
of the LORD his God, and he greatly humbled
himself before the God of his fathers. 13 And
he prayed to *God*, and He was moved and re-
sponded to his plea and returned him to Jeru-
salem to his kingdom. Then Manasseh knew
that the LORD was God.
14 After this he built an outer wall for the
City of David, west of Gihon, in the valley and
toward the entrance of the Fish Gate, where
it went around Ophel, and raised it to a very
great height. Then he positioned military com-
manders in all the fortified cities in Judah.
15 And he removed the foreign gods and
statues from the house of the LORD, and all
the altars that he built on the hill of the house
of the LORD and Jerusalem, and he cast them
outside the city. 16 He also restored the altar
of the LORD, and he sacrificed fellowship and
thanksgiving offerings, and he ordered Judah
to serve the LORD God of Israel. 17 However, the
people continued to sacrifice at the high plac-
es, but only to the LORD their God.

The Death of Manasseh

18 And the remainder of the acts of Manasseh
and his prayer to God and the words of the
seers who spoke to him in the name of the
LORD God of Israel are written in the annals of
the kings of Israel. 19 And his prayer and how
God received his entreaty, and all his sin and
unfaithfulness, and the sites where he built
high places and where he set up the Asherah
poles and images before he humbled himself,
indeed they are written in the sayings of Hozai.
20 So Manasseh slept with his fathers, and they
buried him in his palace, and Amon his son
reigned in his place.

Amon, King of Judah

2Ki 21:19–24

21 And Amon was twenty-two years old when
he began to reign, and he was king for two
years in Jerusalem. 22 And he did what was evil
in the eyes of the LORD as his father Manasseh
had done. And Amon sacrificed to and served
all the idols that Manasseh his father had
made. 23 He did not humble himself before
the LORD as his father humbled himself. But
he increased his guilt all the more.
24 And his servants plotted against him, and
they killed him in his palace. 25 Then the people
of the land struck down all those who con-
spired against King Amon. The people of the
land made Josiah his son king in his place.

33:12 2Ch 32:26
33:13 1Ch 5:20
33:14 1Ki 1:33
33:15 2Ch 33:3–7
33:17 2Ch 32:12
33:23 2Ch 33:12

. . . . . .

34:2 2Ch 29:2
34:3 2Ch 15:2
34:4 Ex 32:20
34:5 1Ki 13:2
34:7 2Ch 31:1
34:11 2Ch 33:4–7
34:12 2Ki 12:15

Josiah, King of Judah

2Ki 22:1–7; 23:4–20

34 And Josiah was eight years old when
he began to reign, and he was king
for thirty-one years in Jerusalem. 2 And he did
what was correct in the eyes of the LORD, and
he walked in the ways of David his father and
did not turn either to the right or left.

> Let the high places be purged
> through Your anointing (2Ch 34:3).

3 And in the eighth year of his reign, while
he was still a young boy, he began to seek
out the God of David his father; and in the
twelfth year he began to cleanse Judah and
Jerusalem from high places, Asherah poles,
idols, and carved and cast images. 4 So they
tore down the altars for the Baals, and he cut
down the incense altars that were above them
and smashed the Asherah poles and carved
and cast images. And he crushed them to
dust and scattered them before the graves of
those who sacrificed to them. 5 Then he burned
the bones of the priests on their altars and so
cleansed Judah and Jerusalem. 6 In the cities
of Manasseh, Ephraim, and Simeon, and as
far as Naphtali, in their ruins all around, 7 he
broke down the altars, beat Asherah poles and
the images into powder, and cut down all the
incense altars throughout all the land of Israel.
Then he returned to Jerusalem.
8 In the eighteenth year of his reign, when
he had purged the land and the house, he
sent Shaphan the son of Azaliah, Maaseiah
the governor of the city, and Joah the son of
Joahaz, the recorder, to repair the house of
the LORD his God.
9 When they came to Hilkiah the high priest,
they delivered the money that was brought
into the house of God, which the Levites, the
keepers of the door, had collected from the
hand of Manasseh and Ephraim, and from all
the remnant of Israel, and from all Judah and
Benjamin, and from the inhabitants of Jeru-
salem. 10 And they gave it to those appointed
to do the work in the house of the LORD. And
those who were doing the work on the house
gave it to repair and restore the house. 11 And
they gave it to the craftsmen and builders to
acquire quarried stones and timber for joists
and beams for the buildings that the kings of
Judah had ruined.
12 So the men did the work faithfully. Their
overseers were Jahath and Obadiah the Le-
vites, of the sons of Merari, and Zechariah and
Meshullam, of the sons of the Kohathites, as
supervisors. And other Levites, all skillful with

musical instruments, 13 were over those laborers and supervised all those doing the work in every type of service, and other Levites were scribes, officials, and gatekeepers.

The Book of the Law Found

2Ki 22:8–20; 23:1–3

14 When they brought out the money that had been given to the house of the LORD, Hilkiah the priest found the Book of the Law of the LORD from Moses. 15 Then Hilkiah said to Shaphan the scribe, "I have found the Book of the Law in the house of the LORD." And Hilkiah gave the book to Shaphan.

16 Shaphan brought the book to the king and reported, "Everything that has been designated to your servants, they are doing. 17 They have given out the money that was in the house of the LORD and have allocated to those who are supervisors and those who are doing the work." 18 Then Shaphan the scribe also declared to the king, "Hilkiah the priest has given me a book." And Shaphan read from it to the king.

19 And it happened that when the king heard the words of the Law, he tore his garments. 20 Then the king ordered Hilkiah, Ahikam the son of Shaphan, Abdon the son of Micah, Shaphan the scribe, and Asaiah the attendant of the king: 21 "Go and seek the LORD on my behalf and on the behalf of the remnant in Israel and Judah concerning what is written in the book that was found, for the wrath of the LORD that is poured out on us is great because our fathers have not kept the word of the LORD, to do everything that is written in this book."

22 So Hilkiah and those with the king went to Huldah the prophetess, the wife of Shallum the son of Tokhath, son of Hasrah, who kept the wardrobe. She lived in Jerusalem in the Second Quarter, and they spoke to her about this.

I break all written curses that would affect my life, in the name of Jesus (2Ch 34:24).

23 And she said to them, "So says the LORD God of Israel: Speak to the man who sent you all to Me, 24 Thus says the LORD: I am bringing disaster on this place and all who dwell in it, even all the curses that are written in the book that they read before the king of Judah. 25 Because they have abandoned Me and offered sacrifices to other gods in order to provoke Me with everything they have made with their hands, so My rage will be poured out on this place, and it will not be quenched. 26 And the king of Judah who sent you all to seek out the LORD, so you will speak to him: So says the LORD God of Israel: The words that you have heard, 27 because your heart was tender and you humbled yourself before God when you heard His words against this place and those who dwell here, and you have brought yourself low before Me and torn your clothes and wept before Me, I have heard *you*, declares the LORD. 28 I am bringing you to be with your fathers, and you will be brought to your grave in peace, and your eyes will not see all the disaster that I am bringing on this place and on those who dwell here."

So they returned this word to the king.

Josiah Restores True Worship

29 Then the king sent for all the elders of Judah and Jerusalem. 30 Then the king went up to the house of the LORD with men from Judah and those living in Jerusalem, even the priests and Levites and all the people from the greatest to the least, and he read within their hearing all the words of the Book of the Covenant that was found in the house of the LORD. 31 Then the king stood in his place and made a covenant before the LORD, to walk after the LORD, and to keep His commandments and His testimonies and His statutes with all his soul, to perform the words of the covenant written in this book.

32 Then he appointed all who were in Jerusalem and Benjamin to carry this out, and those living in Jerusalem did according to the covenant of God, the God of their fathers.

33 So Josiah took away all the detestable things from the lands that belonged to the people of Israel and caused all who were found in Israel to serve their LORD God. And all his days they did not turn away from the LORD God of their fathers.

Josiah Celebrates the Passover

2Ki 23:21–23

35 Josiah kept a Passover for the LORD in Jerusalem; they slaughtered the Passover lamb on the fourteenth day of the first month. 2 He appointed priests for their duties and encouraged them in their service to the house of the LORD. 3 And he said to the Levites who gave insight to all Israel and were consecrated to the LORD, "Set the holy ark in the house that Solomon, the son of David and king of Israel, built. You should not carry it on your shoulders. Now serve the LORD your God and His people Israel. 4 Prepare yourselves according to your fathers' houses by your divisions, as instructed in the writing of David, king of Israel, and the document of Solomon his son.

5 "And stand in the Holy Place according to the divisions of the fathers' households of your brothers, the laypeople, and according to the

34:13 Ne 4:10
34:20 2Ki 22:12
34:24 2Ch 36:14–20
34:25 Jer 7:20
....
34:27 2Ch 32:26
34:29 2Ki 23:1–3
34:31 2Ch 23:16
34:33 2Ch 34:3–7
35:1 Ex 12:6
35:2 2Ch 31:2
35:3 Dt 33:10
35:4 2Ch 8:14

Levites, by division of a father's household. 6 Then slaughter the Passover lamb and consecrate yourselves and prepare for your brothers to do according to the word of the LORD by the hand of Moses."

7 Josiah contributed to the laypeople, as Passover *offerings* for all who were present, lambs and young goats from the flock to the number of thirty thousand, and three thousand bulls; these were from the king's possession.

8 His officials contributed willingly to the people, to the priests, and to the Levites. Hilkiah, Zechariah, and Jehiel, the chief officers of the house of God, gave to the priests for the Passover *offerings* two thousand six hundred lambs and three hundred bulls. 9 Konaniah, his brothers Shemaiah and Nethanel, and Hashabiah, Jeiel, and Jozabad, officers of the Levites, gave to the Levites for the Passover *offerings* five thousand lambs and five hundred bulls.

10 When the service was prepared, the priests stood in their places and the Levites in their divisions, according to the king's command. 11 And they slaughtered the Passover *offerings*, and the priests sprinkled the *blood* given to them while the Levites skinned *animals*. 12 And they set aside the burnt offering to distribute according to each house of the fathers for the people to bring near to the LORD, as written in the Book of Moses. And they did the same with the bulls. 13 And they cooked the Passover lamb with fire according to the rule, and they cooked the holy offerings in pots, jars, bowls, and quickly brought them to all the people. 14 Afterward they prepared the *offerings* for them and the priests because the priests, the sons of Aaron, offered the burnt offering and fat portions until night. So the Levites prepared for themselves and for the priests, the sons of Aaron.

15 The singers, the sons of Asaph, were in their places according to the command of David, Asaph, Heman, and Jeduthun the king's seer. The gatekeepers were at each of the gates; they did not need to leave their service, for their brothers the Levites made preparations for them.

16 So all the service of the LORD was carried out that day to have the Passover, and to offer the burnt offerings on the altar of the LORD according to the command of King Josiah. 17 And the sons of Israel who were present had the Passover at that time and the Feast of Unleavened Bread for seven days. 18 And no Passover had been made like this in Israel since the days of Samuel the prophet. And none of the kings of Israel had performed a Passover like Josiah had done. And the priests and Levites and all Judah and Israel were present along with those living in Jerusalem. 19 In the eighteenth year of the reign of Josiah this Passover was performed.

35:6 2Ch 29:5
35:7 1Ki 8:63
35:10 2Ch 30:16
35:11 2Ch 29:34
35:13 Ex 12:8–9
35:20 2Ki 23:29–30
35:22 Jdg 5:19
35:23 1Ki 22:34
35:24 Zec 12:11
35:25 Jer 22:10
36:4 Jer 22:10–12

The Death of Josiah
2Ki 23:28–30

20 After all this when Josiah had prepared the temple, Necho king of Egypt went up to war in Carchemish on the Euphrates, and Josiah went out to meet him. 21 And Necho sent messengers to him saying, "What is there between you and me, king of Judah? I am not against you this day, but *against* the house with which I am at war. And God has commanded that I hurry. Refrain from being against God who is with me so that He does not destroy you."

22 But Josiah did not turn away from him for he went to battle against him disguised. He did not listen to the words of Necho that came from the mouth of God, but he came to battle in the plain of Megiddo.

23 So the archers shot King Josiah, and the king said to his servants, "Take me away for I am severely wounded." 24 Then his servants took him from the chariot, and they set him in a second chariot, and they brought him to Jerusalem. He died and was buried in the tombs of his fathers. And all Judah and Jerusalem mourned for Josiah.

25 And Jeremiah composed a dirge for Josiah, and all the male and female singers speak of Josiah in their laments to this day. They set them as a statute over Israel. They are written in the Laments.

26 And the remainder of the acts of Josiah, his deeds and covenant faithfulness, according to what is written in the Law of the LORD, 27 and his acts from beginning to end are written in the book of the kings of Israel and Judah.

Jehoahaz, King of Judah
2Ki 23:31–34

36 Then the people of the land took Jehoahaz the son of Josiah and made him king in the place of his father in Jerusalem.

2 And Jehoahaz was twenty-three years old when he began to reign, and he reigned three months in Jerusalem. 3 Then the king of Egypt deposed him in Jerusalem and imposed on the land a tribute of a hundred talents[1] of silver and a talent[2] of gold. 4 The king of Egypt made his brother Eliakim king over Judah and Jerusalem, and changed his name to Jehoiakim. But Necho took his brother Jehoahaz and carried him to Egypt.

1 3 About 3¾ tons, or 3.4 metric tons. *2 3* About 75 pounds, or 34 kilograms.

Jehoiakim, King of Judah

2Ki 23:36–24:6

5 Jehoiakim was twenty-five years old when he began to reign, and he was king in Jerusalem for eleven years. He did what was evil in the eyes of the LORD his God. 6 And Nebuchadnezzar king of Babylon came up against him and bound him in bronze chains to lead him to Babylon. 7 Nebuchadnezzar also brought out some of the vessels of the house of the LORD to Babylon and put them in his temple in Babylon.

8 And the remainder of the acts of Jehoiakim, the detestable things that he did and were found against him, are written in the book of the kings of Israel and Judah. Then Jehoiachin his son reigned in his place.

Jehoiachin, King of Judah

2Ki 24:8–17

9 Jehoiachin was eighteen years old when he began to reign, and he was king in Jerusalem for three months and ten days. He did what was evil in the eyes of the LORD. 10 In the spring of that year King Nebuchadnezzar sent for him and brought him to Babylon with the precious items from the house of the LORD. Then Zedekiah his brother was king over Judah and Jerusalem.

Zedekiah, King of Judah

2Ki 24:18–20; Jer 52:1–3

11 Zedekiah was twenty-one years old when he began to reign, and he was king in Jerusalem for eleven years. 12 He did what was evil in the eyes of the LORD his God and did not humble himself before Jeremiah the prophet, who spoke from the LORD. 13 He also rebelled against King Nebuchadnezzar, who had made him swear by an oath by God. He stiffened his neck and hardened his heart against turning to the LORD God of Israel. 14 Even the officials over the priests and the people increased in their unfaithfulness in all the detestable practices of the nations, and they defiled the house of the LORD which He had consecrated in Jerusalem.

36:5 2Ki 23:36–37
36:7 2Ki 24:13
36:10 Jer 37:1
36:11 2Ki 24:18–20
36:12 2Ch 33:23

36:15 Jer 25:3–4
36:16 2Ch 30:10
36:17 Ps 74:20
36:18 2Ch 36:7
36:20 Jer 27:7
36:21 Jer 29:10
36:22 Jer 25:12

The Fall of Jerusalem

2Ki 25:1–21; Jer 52:4–27; Ezr 1:1–3

15 The LORD God of their fathers sent *warnings* to them over and over again by His messengers because He had compassion on His people and His dwelling place. 16 But they continued to jest regarding the messengers of God, despising His word and making fun of His prophets until the wrath of the LORD came up against His people, until there was no remedy. 17 So He brought up against them the king of the Chaldeans from Babylon, who killed their young men with the sword at the house of their sanctuary. He did not spare a young man or virgin, old or aged. *God* gave all of them into his hand. 18 Even all the vessels of the house of God, both large and small, and the treasures of the house of the LORD, the king, and his officials, all of this was taken to Babylon. 19 So they burned down the house of God, tore down the wall of Jerusalem, burned down all the palaces with fire, and destroyed all the precious items.

20 Then he carried into exile to Babylon the remnant, who survived the sword, and they were slaves to him and his sons until the kingdom of Persia ruled, 21 to fulfill the word of the LORD by the mouth of Jeremiah, until the land had enjoyed her Sabbaths. As long as she lay desolate, she kept Sabbath, to fulfill seventy years.

The Proclamation of Cyrus

22 In the first year of King Cyrus of Persia, that the word of the LORD spoken by the mouth of Jeremiah might be fulfilled, the LORD stirred up the spirit of King Cyrus of Persia, so that he sent a proclamation throughout all his kingdom and also declared in a written edict:

> 23 "Thus says King Cyrus of Persia:
>
> "The LORD God of heaven has given me all the kingdoms of the earth, and He has commanded me to build for Him a house at Jerusalem, which is in Judah. Whoever is among you of all His people, may the LORD his God be with him. Let him go up."

Author: Ezra

Written: Between 460 and 440 BC

Themes: Israel's History, Return from Exile

EZRA

Dear SpiritLed Woman,

As SpiritLed women, we are called to encourage those around us. At times it may seem as if others do not need the words of encouragement, but a kind word or a moment of prayer is always a good thing. We must confess our weaknesses, our fears, even our own sins so that others are led in the ways of Christ. As difficult as it may be, we should strive to be the living Bible because our lives may be the only example of Christ someone sees. When we are filled with God, we can't help but bring His presence to others. We could be the catalyst in the coming revival!

It is difficult to ignore those who seek to discourage us from our walk with Christ, but through constant prayer and intercession we could even lead the naysayers to the truth. Just as God's Spirit inspired Ezra to lead people to confess for the sins of Israel, we should seek God's inspiration to lead.

Joy F. Strang

SPIRITLED WOMAN

COUNSEL FROM THE SPIRIT BASICS

Victory in the Spirit

In Ezra 1 King Cyrus of Persia was stirred by the Spirit of God to prepare the documents that would give the Israelites the instructions they needed to build a temple to the Lord at Jerusalem. He wrote:

> The LORD God of heaven has given me all the kingdoms of the earth, and He has charged me to build Him a house at Jerusalem, which is in Judah. Whoever there is among you of all His people, may his God be with him, and may he go to Jerusalem, which is in Judah, and build the house of the LORD God of Israel. He is the God who is in Jerusalem. Whoever remains in any place where he sojourns, let the men of his place help him with silver, gold, goods, and animals, along with voluntary gifts for the house of God in Jerusalem.
>
> —EZRA 1:2–4

No decision can be rightly made and no battle ever won without the Spirit. King Cyrus could release the Israelites from captivity and allow them to return to Jerusalem, and he could give instructions to them to rebuild their temple to God only after the Spirit of the Lord gave him the instructions to follow. Yet how often we seek to discern wisely and to fight battles before the Spirit comes upon us with His specific instructions!

Larry Keefauver

The Proclamation of Cyrus
2Ch 36:22–23

1 Now in the first year of Cyrus king of Per-
sia, that the word of the LORD by the mouth
of Jeremiah might be fulfilled, the LORD stirred
up the spirit of Cyrus king of Persia, so that
he issued a proclamation throughout all his
kingdom, and also put it in writing, saying,

2 "Thus says Cyrus king of Persia:
"The LORD God of heaven has given me
all the kingdoms of the earth, and He has
charged me to build Him a house at Jeru-
salem, which is in Judah. 3 Whoever there is
among you of all His people, may his God
be with him, and may he go to Jerusalem,
which is in Judah, and build the house of
the LORD God of Israel. He is the God who
is in Jerusalem. 4 Whoever remains in any
place where he sojourns, let the men of his
place help him with silver, gold, goods, and
animals, along with voluntary gifts for the
house of God in Jerusalem."

5 Then the heads of the households of Judah
and Benjamin, and the Levitical priests, with
all those whose spirits God had stirred, rose up
to go up to build the house of the LORD in Jeru-
salem. 6 So everyone all around them strength-
ened their hands with vessels of silver, gold,
goods, animals, and precious things, besides
all that was given voluntarily. 7 Also Cyrus the
king brought forth the vessels of the house of
the LORD, which Nebuchadnezzar had brought
from Jerusalem and had put in the house of his
gods. 8 Cyrus king of Persia even brought forth
more for them, by the hand of Mithredath the
treasurer and had them numbered for Shesh-
bazzar, who was the prince of Judah.
9 This is the number of them: thirty containers
of gold, one thousand containers of silver, and
twenty-nine knives. 10 There were also thirty
smaller bowls of gold, four hundred and ten
smaller bowls of silver (of lesser value), and
one thousand other various containers.
11 All the articles of gold and silver were five
thousand four hundred. All these did Shesh-
bazzar bring up, when the exiles were brought
from Babylon to Jerusalem.

The List of Returning Exiles
Ne 7:6–73

2 Now these are the people of the prov-
ince who went up from the captivity of
the exiles, whom Nebuchadnezzar the king
of Babylon had carried away to Babylon, and
came again to Jerusalem and Judah. Each re-
turned to his own city. 2 Those who came with
Zerubbabel were Joshua, Nehemiah, Seraiah,
Reelaiah, Mordecai, Bilshan, Mispar, Bigvai,
Rehum, and Baanah.

The number of men of the people of Israel were:

3 The sons of Parosh—two thousand one hundred and seventy-two;
4 the sons of Shephatiah—three hundred and seventy-two;
5 the sons of Arah—seven hundred and seventy-five;
6 the sons of Pahath-Moab of the sons of Jeshua and Joab—two thousand eight hundred and twelve;

1:1 Jer 29:10
1:3 Da 6:26
1:5 Ezr 1:1
1:7 2Ki 24:13
1:8 Ezr 5:14
2:1 2Ki 24:14–16
2:2 Ne 7:7
2:3 Ezr 8:3
2:6 Ne 7:11

[7] the sons of Elam—one thousand two hundred and fifty-four;
[8] the sons of Zattu—nine hundred and forty-five;
[9] the sons of Zakkai—seven hundred and sixty;
[10] the sons of Bani—six hundred and forty-two;
[11] the sons of Bebai—six hundred and twenty-three;
[12] the sons of Azgad—one thousand two hundred and twenty-two;
[13] the sons of Adonikam—six hundred and sixty-six;
[14] the sons of Bigvai—two thousand and fifty-six;
[15] the sons of Adin—four hundred and fifty-four;
[16] the sons of Ater of Hezekiah—ninety-eight;
[17] the sons of Bezai—three hundred and twenty-three;
[18] the sons of Jorah—one hundred and twelve;
[19] the sons of Hashum—two hundred and twenty-three;
[20] the sons of Gibbar—ninety-five.

[21] The sons of Bethlehem—one hundred and twenty-three;
[22] the men of Netophah—fifty-six;
[23] the men of Anathoth—one hundred and twenty-eight;
[24] the sons of Azmaveth—forty-two;
[25] the sons of Kiriath Arim, Kephirah, and Beeroth—seven hundred and forty-three;
[26] the sons of Ramah and Geba—six hundred and twenty-one;
[27] the men of Mikmash—one hundred and twenty-two;
[28] the men of Bethel and Ai—two hundred and twenty-three;
[29] the sons of Nebo—fifty-two;
[30] the sons of Magbish—one hundred and fifty-six;
[31] the sons of the other Elam—one thousand two hundred and fifty-four;
[32] the sons of Harim—three hundred and twenty;
[33] the sons of Lod, Hadid, and Ono—seven hundred and twenty-five;
[34] the sons of Jericho—three hundred and forty-five;
[35] the sons of Senaah—three thousand six hundred and thirty.

[36] *Those who came with* the priests *were:*

the sons of Jedaiah, of the house of Jeshua—nine hundred and seventy-three;
[37] the sons of Immer—one thousand and fifty-two;
[38] the sons of Pashhur—one thousand two hundred and forty-seven;
[39] the sons of Harim—one thousand and seventeen.

[40] *Those who came with* the Levites were:

the sons of Jeshua and Kadmiel, of the sons of Hodaviah—seventy-four.

[41] *Those who came with* the singers were:

the sons of Asaph—one hundred and twenty-eight.

[42] The sons of the gatekeepers *were*:

the sons of Shallum, the sons of Ater, the sons of Talmon, the sons of Akkub, the sons of Hatita, the sons of Shobai—in all one hundred and thirty-nine.

[43] Those devoted to the temple as servants were:

the sons of Ziha, the sons of Hasupha, the sons of Tabbaoth,
[44] the sons of Keros, the sons of Siaha, the sons of Padon,
[45] the sons of Lebanah, the sons of Hagabah, the sons of Akkub,
[46] the sons of Hagab, the sons of Shalmai, the sons of Hanan,
[47] the sons of Giddel, the sons of Gahar, the sons of Reaiah,
[48] the sons of Rezin, the sons of Nekoda, the sons of Gazzam,
[49] the sons of Uzza, the sons of Paseah, the sons of Besai,
[50] the sons of Asnah, the sons of Meunim, the sons of Nephusim,
[51] the sons of Bakbuk, the sons of Hakupha, the sons of Harhur,
[52] the sons of Bazluth, the sons of Mehida, the sons of Harsha,
[53] the sons of Barkos, the sons of Sisera, the sons of Temah,
[54] the sons of Neziah, the sons of Hatipha.

[55] The sons of Solomon's servants were:

the sons of Sotai, the sons of Hassophereth, the sons of Peruda,
[56] the sons of Jaala, the sons of Darkon, the sons of Giddel,
[57] the sons of Shephatiah, the sons of Hattil, the sons of Pokereth-Hazzebaim, the sons of Ami.

[58] All those devoted to the temple as servants and the children of Solomon's

2:13 Ezr 8:13
2:34 1Ki 16:34

2:37 1Ch 24:14
2:38 1Ch 9:12
2:39 1Ch 24:8
2:43 1Ch 9:2
2:55 1Ki 9:21
2:57 Ne 7:59
2:58 1Ki 9:21

servants were three hundred and ninety-two.

[59] These were the ones who came up from Tel Melah, Tel Harsha, Kerub, Addon, and Immer; but they could not prove their father's house or their descent, whether they were of Israel:

[60] the sons of Delaiah, the sons of Tobiah, and the sons of Nekoda—six hundred and fifty-two;

[61] and of the sons of the priests:

the sons of Hobaiah, the sons of Hakkoz, and the sons of Barzillai (whose ancestor married one of the daughters of Barzillai the Gileadite and was thereafter called by their name).

[62] These sought their records in the
genealogy register, but they were not
found. Therefore, they were disqualified
(as polluted) from the priesthood. [63] The
governor advised them not to eat of the
most holy things until a priest consulted
with the Urim and Thummim.

[64] The whole congregation together
was forty-two thousand three hundred
and sixty, [65] besides their male and
female servants (these numbered seven
thousand three hundred and thirty-seven);
they also had two hundred singing
men and women. [66] Their horses
numbered seven hundred and thirty-six;
their mules, two hundred and forty-five;
[67] their camels, four hundred and thirty-five;
and their donkeys, six thousand
seven hundred and twenty.

[68] As some of the heads of households came
to the house of the Lord in Jerusalem, they
volunteered to erect the foundations for the
house of God. [69] They gave after their ability
to the treasure of the work sixty-one thousand
drachmas[1] of gold, five thousand pounds[2] of
silver, and one hundred priestly garments.
[70] So the priests and the Levites, along with
some of the people, the singers, the porters,
and those donated as temple servants, lived in
their cities, with the result that all Israel resettled
in their cities.

Rebuilding the Altar

3 When the seventh month had come, the
children of Israel *had resettled* in their
cities, and the people gathered themselves
together, as one man, to Jerusalem. [2] Then
Joshua the son of Jozadak and his brothers
the priests stood up, along with Zerubbabel the
son of Shealtiel and his brothers, and they built
the altar of the God of Israel in order to offer
burnt offerings on it, as it had been written in
the Law of Moses, the man of God. [3] They set
the altar upon its foundations and, because
they were living in fear of some of the peoples
of the region, they offered burnt offerings on
it to the Lord—morning and evening. [4] They
also kept the Feast of Tabernacles, as it had
been written, and offered the daily burnt offerings
in accordance with the daily schedule,
according to each day's custom. [5] Thereafter,
observance of the burnt offering became a perpetual
sacrifice with regard to the New Moon
sacrifices and all of the appointed feasts of the
Lord that had been consecrated, and all of the
voluntary freewill offerings to the Lord. [6] From
the first day of the seventh month they had
begun to offer burnt offerings unto the Lord,
but the foundation of the temple of the Lord
was not yet laid.

Rebuilding the Temple

[7] They gave money to the masons and carpenters,
and food, drink, and oil to the people
of Sidon and to the people of Tyre so that they
would bring cedar trees from Lebanon to the
sea, at Joppa, according to the grant they had
from Cyrus king of Persia.
[8] Now in the second month of the second
year of their coming to the house of God in
Jerusalem, Zerubbabel the son of Shealtiel,
Joshua the son of Jozadak, along with the
remnant of their brothers the Levitical priests
and all who had come out of captivity back to
Jerusalem, began work and appointed the Levites
twenty years old and older to supervise the
work on the house of the Lord. [9] Then Joshua
with his sons and brothers, and Kadmiel with
his sons, who are the sons of Judah, along
with the sons of Henadad with their sons and
their brothers—all Levites—stood together to
supervise the workers on the house of God.
[10] When the builders laid the foundation
of the temple of the Lord, the priests in their
apparel stood with trumpets and, from the
Levites, the sons of Asaph *stood* with cymbals
to praise the Lord, following the example of
David king of Israel. [11] They sang responsively,
praising and giving thanks unto the Lord,

"For He is good,
for His mercy endures forever toward
Israel."

And all the people responded with a great
shout when they praised the Lord, because the
foundation of the house of the Lord was laid.
[12] Now many of the older Levitical priests and
chiefs of the fathers' *households* who had seen

2:61 2Sa 17:27
2:62 Nu 3:10
2:63 Ex 28:30
3:2 1Ch 3:17
3:4 Ex 23:16
3:9 Ezr 2:40
3:11 1Ch 16:34
3:12 Hag 2:3

[1] *69* About 1,100 pounds, or 500 kilograms. [2] *69* About 3 tons, or 2.8 metric tons.

the first temple wept with a loud voice as the foundation of this temple was laid before their eyes, though many others shouted exuberantly for joy. 13 As a result, the people could not distinguish the noise of the shout of joy from the noise of the weeping of the people since the people had raised such a loud noise that could be heard from afar off.

Resistance to Rebuilding

4 Now when the adversaries of Judah and Benjamin heard that the descendants of the captivity built the temple unto the LORD God of Israel, 2 they came to Zerubbabel, and to the chiefs of the fathers' households, and said to them, "Let us build with you, for, like you, we seek your God and have been sacrificing to Him since the days of Esarhaddon king of Assyria, who brought us here."

3 But Zerubbabel, and Joshua, and the rest of the chiefs of the fathers' households of Israel said to them, "*This is* not for you! It is for us to build the temple of our God, so we ourselves together will build unto the LORD God of Israel, as Cyrus the king of Persia has commanded us."

4 Then the people of the land demoralized the people of Judah and terrified them while building, 5 and hired counselors against them to frustrate their purpose, all the days of Cyrus king of Persia, even until the reign of Darius king of Persia.

6 In the reign of Ahasuerus, in the beginning of his reign, they wrote an accusation against the inhabitants of Judah and Jerusalem.

The Letter to Artaxerxes

7 In the days of Artaxerxes, Bishlam, Mithredath, Tabeel, and the rest of their companions wrote to Artaxerxes king of Persia, and the writing of the letter was written in Aramaic, and interpreted in Aramaic.

8 Rehum the commander and Shimshai the scribe wrote a letter against Jerusalem to Artaxerxes the king in this manner:

9 (Rehum the commander, Shimshai the scribe, and the rest of their colleagues, the judges, the officials, the officers, the Persians, the men of Uruk, and of Babylon, and of Susa—that is, the Elamites— 10 and the rest of the nations whom the great and noble Ashurbanipal deported and settled in the city of Samaria and in the rest of the province Beyond the River—and now 11 this is the copy of the letter that they sent to him)—

"To Artaxerxes the king:

"Your servants the men of the province Beyond the River, and so forth.

12 "May it be known to the king, that the Jews who came from you have come near to us at Jerusalem and that they are building the rebellious and evil city, restoring its walls, and repairing the foundations.

13 "Be it known now to the king, that, if this city is rebuilt and the walls set up again, then they will not pay toll, tribute, and custom, and the revenue of the kings will be impacted. 14 Now because we are under obligation to the king's palace, and it was not appropriate for us to see the king's dishonor, therefore we have sent and notified the king, 15 so that a search may be made in the book of the records of your fathers. There you will find in the book of the records and realize that this city is a rebellious city, and hurtful to kings and provinces, and that they have incited revolt within it in former times—for which cause this city was destroyed. 16 We notify the king that if this city is rebuilt and the walls repaired by this means the portion Beyond the River will no longer be yours."

17 The king sent an answer:

"To Rehum the commander, to Shimshai the scribe, to the rest of their companions that dwell in Samaria, and to the remainder Beyond the River:

"Peace, and so forth.

18 "The letter which you sent to us has been translated and read before me. 19 I commanded, and a search has been made, and it is found that this city has in the past made insurrection against kings, and that rebellion and revolt have occurred there. 20 There have also been mighty kings over Jerusalem, who have ruled over the whole province Beyond the River, and toll, tribute, and custom was paid to them. 21 Command these men to cease now, so that this city is not built unless I give the command. 22 Take heed now that you do not fail to do this. Why should damage increase to the hurt of the king?"

23 Now when the copy of the letter by King Artaxerxes was read before Rehum, and Shimshai the scribe, and their companions, they went up in haste to Jerusalem to the Jews and made them cease by force and power.

24 Then the work of the house of God in Jerusalem ceased. So it ceased until the second year of the reign of Darius king of Persia.

Restoration of the Temple Resumed

5 Now the prophets, Haggai and Zechariah the son of Iddo, prophesied to the Jews that were in Judah and Jerusalem in the name

4:2 2Ki 19:37
4:3 Ne 2:20
4:4 Ezr 3:3
4:7 2Ki 18:26
4:9 Ezr 5:6
4:10 Ezr 4:17
4:13 Ezr 7:24
4:20 Ge 15:18

of the God of Israel who was over them. 2 Then Zerubbabel the son of Shealtiel and Joshua the son of Jozadak rose up and began to build the house of God which is at Jerusalem, and the prophets of God were with them, helping them.

3 At the same time Tattenai, governor of the province Beyond the River, and Shethar-Bozenai and their companions came to them and said to them, "Who issued a command for you to build this house and complete this structure?" 4 They also asked them, "What are the names of the men building this building?" 5 But the eye of their God was on the elders of the Jews, so that they could not cause them to cease building until a command came from Darius. Consequently, they sent a letter concerning this matter.

6 This is a copy of the letter that Tattenai, governor of the province Beyond the River, and Shethar-Bozenai and his colleagues, the officials who were in the province Beyond the River, sent to Darius the king.

7 This is the document that they sent to him, containing accordingly what follows:

"To Darius the king:

"All peace.

8 "May it be known to the king that we went into the province of Judah, to the temple of the great God, which is built with great stones, and timber is laid in the walls, and this work goes diligently, and prospers in their hands.

9 "Then we questioned those elders and said to them, 'Who issued a command for you to build this house and complete this structure?' 10 Also, we asked for their names in order to notify you and to document the names of the men that were their leaders.

11 "Thus they returned us an answer, saying,

" 'We are the servants of the God of heaven and earth and are rebuilding the temple that was built these many years ago, which a great king of Israel built and completed. 12 Afterwards, our fathers provoked the God of heaven to wrath, so He gave them into the hand of Nebuchadnezzar the king of Babylon, the Chaldean, who destroyed this temple and carried the people away into Babylon.

13 " 'However, in the first year of Cyrus the king of Babylon, King Cyrus made a decree to rebuild this house of God. 14 The vessels also of gold and silver of the house of God, which Nebuchadnezzar took from the temple in Jerusalem and placed them into the temple of Babylon, those Cyrus the king withdrew from the temple of Babylon and had them delivered to the one named Sheshbazzar, whom he had made governor. 15 King Cyrus said to him, "Take these vessels, go, carry them to the temple in Jerusalem and let the house of God be built its site."

16 " 'So that same Sheshbazzar came and laid the foundation of the house of God in Jerusalem. Since that time even until now it has been under construction, yet it is not finished.'

17 "Now therefore, if it seems good to the king, let there be search made in the king's treasure house there in Babylon to ascertain if it is so that a decree was made of Cyrus the king to build this house of God at Jerusalem. May the king send his pleasure to us concerning this matter."

The Decree of Darius

6 Then Darius the king issued a decree and a search was made in the house of records, where the treasures were stored in Babylon. 2 At Ecbatana, in the provincial palace of the Medes, a scroll was found, and in it the following record was written:

3 "In the first year of Cyrus the king, the same Cyrus the king issued a decree concerning the temple of God at Jerusalem:

"Let the house be rebuilt, the place where they offered sacrifices, and let the foundations of it be strongly laid, to a height of sixty cubits,[1] and a width of sixty cubits. 4 *Let it consist of* three rows of great stones and a row of new timber, and let the expenses be paid from the king's treasury. 5 Also, let the golden and silver vessels of the house of God, which Nebuchadnezzar took from the temple in Jerusalem and brought to Babylon, be returned and brought back to their places in the temple in Jerusalem. Put them in the house of God.

6 "Now therefore, Tattenai, governor of the province Beyond the River, and Shethar-Bozenai, along with your colleagues, the officials who are in the province Beyond the River, stay far away from there. 7 Let the work of this house of God alone. Let the governor of the Jews and the elders of the Jews build this house of God in its place.

8 "Moreover, I issue a decree concerning what you shall do for the elders of these Jews for the rebuilding of this house of God:

"The cost is to be paid to these men, in full and without delay, from the royal revenue,

5:2 Ezr 3:2
5:3 Ezr 6:6
5:5 Ezr 7:6
5:6 Ezr 4:9
5:12 2Ch 36:16–17
5:14 Ezr 6:5
5:16 Ezr 3:10
6:1 Ezr 5:17
6:4 1Ki 6:36
6:5 Ezr 5:14
6:6 Ezr 5:3
6:8 Ezr 6:4

1 3 About 90 feet, or 27 meters.

the tribute of the province Beyond the River. 9 Whatever they need—whether young bulls, rams, and lambs for the burnt offerings to the God of heaven, or wheat, salt, wine, and oil, according to the appointment of the priests in Jerusalem—let it be given them daily without fail, 10 so that they may offer acceptable sacrifices to the God of heaven, as well as pray for the life of the king and of his sons.

> I offer sacrifices of sweet savor unto God and pray for my life and the lives of my children (Ezr 6:10).

11 "Also, I have issued a decree that whoever shall violate this word, the timber will be pulled down from his house and arranged so that he may be hanged on it. Thus shall his house be made a dunghill for this. 12 May the God who has caused His name to dwell there overthrow all kings and people who stretch forth their hand to violate or destroy this house of God in Jerusalem.

"I, Darius, have issued the decree; so let it be done diligently."

Completion and Dedication of the Temple

13 In compliance, Tattenai, governor of the province Beyond the River, Shethar-Bozenai, and their companions speedily accomplished what Darius the king had decreed. 14 The rebuilding by the elders of the Jews prospered through the prophesying of Haggai the prophet and Zechariah the son of Iddo. And they built, and finished it, according to the decree of the God of Israel and according to the decrees of Cyrus, Darius, and Artaxerxes king of Persia. 15 This temple was finished on the third day of the month Adar during the sixth year of the reign of Darius the king.

16 The children of Israel, the priests and the Levites, and the rest of the descendants of the captivity kept the dedication of this house of God with joy. 17 At the dedication of this house of God, they offered a hundred bulls, two hundred rams, four hundred lambs; and as a sin offering for all Israel, they offered twelve goats (according to the number of the tribes of Israel). 18 They appointed the priests in their divisions and the Levites in their orders for the service of God in Jerusalem, as it had been written in the Book of Moses.

The Passover

19 The children of the captivity kept the Passover on the fourteenth day of the first month. 20 Because the priests and the Levites had purified themselves together, all of them were pure. So, they slaughtered the Passover *lambs* for all the descendants of the captivity, both for their brothers the priests and for themselves. 21 Then they ate together, both the children of Israel who had come out of captivity and all those who had separated themselves from the uncleanness of the nations of the land, in order to seek the LORD God of Israel. 22 With joy they observed the Feast of Unleavened Bread for seven days because the LORD had made them joyful. He had turned the heart of the king of Assyria toward them and strengthened their hands in the work on the house of God, who is the God of Israel.

The Arrival of Ezra

7 Now after these things, in the reign of Artaxerxes king of Persia, Ezra the son of Seraiah, the son of Azariah, the son of Hilkiah, 2 the son of Shallum, the son of Zadok, the son of Ahitub, 3 the son of Amariah, the son of Azariah, the son of Meraioth, 4 the son of Zerahiah, the son of Uzzi, the son of Bukki, 5 the son of Abishua, the son of Phinehas, the son of Eleazar, the son of Aaron the high priest—6 this Ezra went up from Babylon. He was a scribe skilled in the Law of Moses, given by the LORD God of Israel. Because the hand of the LORD his God was upon him, the king granted him all his requests. 7 Some of the children of Israel, along with some of the priests, and the Levites, the singers, the porters, and the temple servants, went up to Jerusalem in the seventh year of King Artaxerxes.

8 Ezra arrived at Jerusalem in the fifth month, during the king's seventh year. 9 From the first day of the first month when the journey from Babylon began, until the first day of the fifth month when he arrived at Jerusalem, the good hand of his God was upon him. 10 Because Ezra had prepared his heart to seek the Law of the LORD, he was doing *so* and teaching the statutes and judgments in Israel.

The Letter of Artaxerxes to Ezra

11 Now this is the copy of the letter that King Artaxerxes gave to Ezra the priest, who was likewise the scribe, the one responsible for the words of the commandments of the LORD and His statutes to Israel:

12 "Artaxerxes, king of kings,

"To Ezra the priest, scribe of the law of the God of heaven:

"Perfect peace, and so forth.

13 "I have issued a decree that all the people of Israel, and their priests, and the Levites in my realm, who are inclined to go up

6:10 Ezr 7:23
6:11 Da 2:5
6:12 1Ki 9:3
6:14 Ezr 7:1
6:15 Est 3:7
6:16 1Ki 8:63
6:17 Ezr 8:35
6:18 Nu 3:6
6:20 2Ch 35:11

6:21 Ezr 9:11
6:22 Ezr 1:1
7:1 Ne 2:1
7:6 Ezr 7:9
7:7 Ezr 8:1–20
7:9 Ezr 7:6
7:10 Dt 33:10
7:12 Eze 26:7

Learning to Prophesy

The rebuilding by the elders of the Jews prospered through the prophesying of Haggai the prophet and Zechariah the son of Iddo. And they built, and finished it, according to the decree of the God of Israel and according to the decrees of Cyrus, Darius, and Artaxerxes king of Persia.

—Ezra 6:14

Eli taught Samuel how to discern, respond, and become sensitive to the voice of God. The same is true today. Prophesying is cooperating with the activity of the Spirit as we discern, respond, and are sensitive to the voice of God.

1. Put on the priestly garments. We must spend quality time in the presence of God, understanding our responsibility to minister to God and then to His people. Worship is the doorway to receiving revelation from God. We must develop relationship and fellowship with the God who knows everything and about everything.

2. All of the Lord's words, no matter in what form we hear them, must be quickened and revealed by the Holy Spirit. The Greek word for "quicken" means to make alive. The words Jesus speaks have life and vitality. Other words are just dead language. The message can come in a variety of ways—flashes of pictures, Scripture verses, sentence fragments, or impressions.

3. Activate faith to operate in the gift of prophecy. We prophesy according to the portion of our faith. The word *proportion* refers to a ratio. We can have faith to prophesy to one person or faith to prophesy to one hundred people. It's all based on the proportion of our faith. The apostle Paul challenged Timothy to stir up (rekindle and arouse from dormancy) the gift that was given to him (2Ti 1:6).

4. Ask, seek, and knock (Mt 7:7–11). We can ask God for a prophetic word. Many are afraid to initiate conversation with the heavenly Father because of fear of deception or demonic interference. But Jesus states that if we ask the Father for gifts, He will not give us something contrary to what we ask. Jeremiah 33:3 says, "Call to Me, and I will answer you, and show you great and mighty things which you do not know."

5. God will immediately speak something to bless the body. God's first command was to bring light to chaos (Ge 1:3). God speaks as a means to bring life and order. Prophecy should speak light to dark situations.

6. Focus is the key. Ask, "What do I see, feel, or have a knowing about the situation?" God speaks through our spirits.

7. God will quicken one sentence, word, picture or thought to your spirit. Then you must exercise your faith to release the revelation given. The Holy Spirit will not move your mouth or override your will. You give voice to what He is speaking.

8. Manifestation of the Spirit is given to everyone, Paul wrote to the Corinthians: "But the manifestation of the Spirit is given to everyone for the common good" (1Co 12:7).

9. The end result of prophecy is to find a way to put honor and glory back on mankind and restore what we lost in the garden—relationship to the Father. People are made for validation, celebration, and appreciation. The psalmist wrote, "What is man that You are mindful of him, and the son of man that You attend to him? For You have made him a little lower than the angels, and crowned him with glory and honor" (Ps 8:4–5).

10. Prophecy releases the power of God. The focus is the heart of God being rightly communicated (1Sa 2:35)

11. God will give you a signal in your spirit to what He is about to do. You will know when to look, listen, and release.

12. God does not just manifest words; He manifests Himself, so do not quench your emotions. Recognize His thoughts in your mind. You must focus. You have the mind of Christ (1Co 2:16).

13. Recognize the voice of the Lord. God drops things into your spirit, and they manifest on the screen of the spirit called the imagination. Because the Lord speaks through your human spirit, the voice sounds like your voice. It's not normally an outside voice, but the Lord will quicken words to your human spirit, and the voice sounds like you. God speaks through your personality. God will add life to ordinary words, experiences, and things that you can relate to. Jesus said, "It is the Spirit who gives life. The flesh profits nothing. The words that I speak to you are spirit and are life" (Jn 6:63).

Remember, words that are given in prophecy by the Holy Spirit give life to what would otherwise be dead language.

Michelle McClain-Walters

to Jerusalem, may go with you. 14 For you
are sent by the king and his seven counsel-
ors to inquire concerning Judah and Jeru-
salem in accordance with the Law of your
God which is in your hand, 15 and to carry
the silver and gold, which the king and his
counselors have freely offered to the God
of Israel, whose habitation is in Jerusalem,
16 along with all the silver and gold that
you can find in all the province of Babylon,
plus the freewill offering of the people and
priests, who are voluntarily giving for the
house of their God in Jerusalem. 17 Diligently
use this money to buy bulls, rams, lambs,
with their grain offerings and their drink
offerings, and offer them on the altar of the
house of your God in Jerusalem.

18 "Whatever seems good to you and your
brothers to do with the rest of the silver and
the gold, do that according to the will of
your God. 19 The vessels also that are given
to you for the service of the house of your
God, deliver before the God of Jerusalem.
20 And whatever else is needed for the house
of your God and is your responsibility to pro-
vide, use the king's treasury to pay for it.

21 "I, even I Artaxerxes the king, issue a
decree to all the treasurers of the province
Beyond the River, that whatever Ezra the
priest, scribe of the law of the God of heav-
en, should request from you, you should
do it with all diligence— 22 as much as a
hundred talents[1] of silver, a hundred mea-
sures[2] of wheat, a hundred baths[3] of wine, a
hundred baths[4] of oil, and salt (without pre-
scribing how much). 23 Whatever is decreed
by the God of heaven, let it be zealously
done for the house of the God of heaven so
as to avoid there being wrath against the
realm of the king and his sons. 24 Also we
are informing you that with regard to all
the priests, Levites, singers, doorkeepers,
temple servants, or other servants of this
house of God, it is not permitted to impose
toll, tribute, or custom on them.

25 "You, Ezra, according to the wisdom
of your God who empowers you, appoint
magistrates and judges to judge all the peo-
ple of the province Beyond the River, all
those who know the laws of your God and
those who do not, whom you must teach.
26 Whoever will not observe the law of your
God or the law of the king, let judgment be
executed speedily on him, whether that be
death, banishment, confiscation of goods,
or imprisonment."

27 Blessed be the LORD God of our fathers,
who has put such a thing as this in the king's
heart, to beautify the house of the LORD in Je-
rusalem, 28 and has extended mercy to me be-
fore the king, his counselors, and all the king's
mighty princes. Thus I had been strengthened,
because the hand of the LORD my God was
upon me. As a result, I gathered together some
of the chief men of Israel to go up with me.

Family Leaders Returning With Ezra

8 Now these are the chiefs of the house-
holds of the fathers and the genealogical
register of those who went up with me from
Babylon, in the reign of King Artaxerxes:

2 of the sons of Phinehas, Gershom;
of the sons of Ithamar, Daniel;
of the sons of David, Hattush, 3 a descen-
dant of Shekaniah
and a descendant of Parosh, Zechariah,
plus another one hundred and fifty men
registered in the genealogical register;
4 of the sons of Pahath-Moab; Eliehoenai a
descendant of Zerahiah, plus two hun-
dred other males;
5 of the sons of Zattu, Shekaniah a descen-
dant of Jahaziel, plus three hundred
other males;
6 of the sons of Adin, Ebed a descendant of
Jonathan, plus fifty other males;
7 of the sons of Elam, Jeshaiah a descen-
dant of Athaliah, plus seventy other
males;
8 of the sons of Shephatiah, Zebadiah a
descendant of Michael, plus eighty other
males;
9 of the sons of Joab, Obadiah a descendant
of Jehiel, plus two hundred and eighteen
other males;
10 of the sons of Bani, Shelomith a descen-
dant of Josiphiah, plus one hundred and
sixty other males;
11 of the sons of Bebai, his son Zechariah,
plus twenty-eight other males;
12 of the sons of Azgad, Johanan a descen-
dant of Hakkatan, plus one hundred and
ten other males;
13 of the last sons of Adonikam, the ones
named Eliphelet, Jeuel, and Shemaiah,
plus sixty other males;
14 also of the sons of Bigvai, Uthai and
Zakkur, plus seventy other males.

Temple Servants

15 I gathered them together at the river that
runs to Ahava, and we camped in tents three
days. As I examined the people and the priests,
I discovered that none of the sons of Levi were
there. 16 So I sent for Eliezer, Ariel, Shemaiah,
Elnathan, Jarib, Elnathan, Nathan, Zechariah,

7:14 Est 1:14
7:15 2Ch 6:2
7:16 1Ch 29:6
7:17 Dt 12:5–11
7:20 Ezr 6:4
7:25 Dt 16:18
7:26 Ezr 6:11
7:27 Ezr 6:22
7:28 Ezr 9:9
8:2 1Ch 3:22
8:3 Ezr 2:3
8:6 Ezr 2:15
8:15 Ezr 7:7

[1] 22 About 3¾ tons, or 3.4 metric tons. [2] 22 Likely about 18 tons, or 16 metric tons. [3] 22 About 600 gallons, or 2,200 liters. [4] 22 About 600 gallons, or 2,200 liters.

and Meshullam, chief men; and also for Joiarib and Elnathan, discerning men. 17 I gave them orders for Iddo, chief at the place Kasiphia, and crafted exactly what they would say to Iddo, his brothers, and the temple servants at the place Kasiphia so that they would bring us ministering servants for the house of our God. 18 Because the good hand of our God was upon us, indeed they brought us a man of understanding descended from the sons of Mahli, who is a descendant of Levi, the son of Israel—Sherebiah along with his sons and his brothers, eighteen men; 19 and Hashabiah, and with him Jeshaiah of the sons of Merari, his brothers and their sons, twenty men; 20 and of the temple servants whom David and the leaders had appointed for the service of the Levites, two hundred and twenty temple servants, all of them designated by name.

21 Then I proclaimed a fast there, at the river of Ahava, that we might humble ourselves before our God, to seek from Him a good route for us, our little ones, and all our substance. 22 For I was ashamed to ask the king for an escort of foot and horse soldiers to help us against the enemy on the way, because we had spoken to the king, saying, "The hand of our God is upon all who seek Him for good, but His power and His wrath are against all who forsake Him." 23 So we fasted and sought our God for this, and He was moved by our prayers.

Temple Gifts

24 Then I separated twelve of the presiding priests—Sherebiah and Hashabiah, along with ten of their brothers— 25 and weighed out to them the silver, the gold, the vessels, as well as the contribution collected for the house of our God by the king, his counselors, his lords, in conjunction with what all Israel had offered. 26 I weighed out into their hand six hundred and fifty talents[1] of silver, silver articles *worth* one hundred talents,[2] one hundred talents[3] of gold, 27 twenty gold bowls *worth* a thousand darics,[4] and two vessels of fine shining bronze, precious as gold.

28 I said to them, "You are holy to the LORD. The vessels are holy also. The silver and the gold are a freewill offering to the LORD God of your fathers. 29 Watch and guard them until you weigh them before the presiding priests and Levites, and the presiding elders of Israel at Jerusalem, for the chambers of the house of the LORD." 30 So the priests and the Levites accepted the weighed-out silver and gold, along with the vessels, to bring them to Jerusalem to the house of our God.

8:17 Ezr 2:43
8:20 Ezr 2:43
8:21 2Ch 20:3
8:22 2Ch 15:2
8:23 Jer 29:12–13
8:24 Ezr 8:18–19
8:25 Ezr 8:33
8:28 Lev 22:2–3

....

8:31 Ezr 7:9
8:32 Ne 2:11
8:33 Ne 3:4
8:35 Ezr 6:17
8:36 Ezr 7:21–24
9:1 Ne 9:2
9:2 Ex 22:31
9:3 Ne 1:4
9:4 Ezr 10:3
9:6 2Ch 28:9

The Return to Jerusalem

31 Then we began the journey from the Ahava River on the twelfth day of the first month to go to Jerusalem. The hand of our God was upon us, and He delivered us from the hand of the attacker and the ambusher along the way. 32 When we arrived at Jerusalem, we stayed there three days.

33 Then on the fourth day the silver and the gold and the vessels were weighed out in the house of our God by the hand of Meremoth the son of Uriah the priest. With him was Eleazar the son of Phinehas as well as Jozabad the son of Jeshua, and Noadiah the son of Binnui—both Levites. 34 All of it was counted by number and by weight, and all the information was recorded at that time.

35 Then, the children of the exile who had come out of captivity offered burnt offerings to the God of Israel. On behalf of all Israel, they offered twelve bulls, ninety-six rams, seventy-seven lambs, and twelve male goats as a sin offering. All of it was offered as a burnt offering to the LORD. 36 Finally, they delivered the king's decrees to the satraps of the king as well as to the governors of the province Beyond the River. Accordingly, they supported the people and the house of God.

Ezra Prays About Intermarriage

9 Now when these things were done, the leaders contacted me, saying, "The people of Israel, the priests, and the Levites have not separated themselves from the people of the lands. They practice the abominations of the Canaanites, the Hittites, the Perizzites, the Jebusites, the Ammonites, the Moabites, the Egyptians, and the Amorites. 2 Specifically, they have taken some of their daughters *as wives* for themselves, as well as for their sons, so that the holy seed has been mingled with the people of the lands. In fact, the involvement of the leaders and rulers has been foremost in this vile behavior."

3 When I heard this, I tore my clothes and my robe, plucked out the hair of my head and from my beard, and sat down astonished. 4 Because of the vile behavior of those who had been in exile, every one that trembled at the words of the God of Israel gathered to me, but I sat astonished until the evening sacrifice.

5 At the evening sacrifice I rose up from my heaviness and, despite having my clothes and my robe torn, I knelt on my knees and stretched out my hands in prayer to the LORD my God 6 and said:

[1] *26* About 24 tons, or about 22 metric tons. [2] *26* About 3¾ tons, or about 3.4 metric tons. [3] *26* About 3¾ tons, or about 3.4 metric tons. [4] *27* About ¼ ounce or 8.5 grams.

The Benefits of Fasting

Then I proclaimed a fast there, at the river of Ahava, that we might humble ourselves before our God, to seek from Him a good route for us, our little ones, and all our substance.

—Ezra 8:21

Fasting positions us to acknowledge God's provision in our lives. It communicates that He alone is our source. We deny ourselves food and tell Him, "I only want You and what You provide."

When we lay aside the daily routine of food and drink or pleasures and leisure, we are able to reevaluate our priorities.

The Bible give us many benefits to fasting. Look up each of the verses below, and in the column beside the reference, write the benefits given.

Scripture	Benefit of Fasting
Luke 2:36–38	
Psalm 35:13	
Psalm 69:10	
Isaiah 58:6	
Isaiah 58:7	
Isaiah 58:8	
Isaiah 58:9	

If we are not hungry for God, it is because we have allowed our souls to be satisfied by other things. Fasting is not just about food; it is about separation. This separation represents a consecration to the Lord, a change in our relationship with Him.

God imparts His outlook on fasting by outlining the manner of fasting that truly pleases Him:

Is not this the fast that I have chosen: to loose the bonds of wickedness, to undo the heavy burdens, and to let the oppressed go free, and break every yoke? Is it not to divide your bread with the hungry and bring the poor who are outcasts into your house? When you see the naked, to cover him and not hide yourself from your own flesh?

—ISAIAH 58:6–7

God is challenging us to fast so that we might become women who are transformed. Whenever Israel truly fasted and turned to God for His assistance, He heard them. He responded with protection, provision, direction, and healing.

God told His people that if they would reach out beyond themselves, then everything they had tried to get for themselves would be provided by Him.

1. Read Isaiah 58:8–9, and write down what God promises to us in that verse:

2. In the past how have you viewed fasting?

3. What are some areas in your life where you could apply the principle of fasting (for example, TV, magazines, phone, etc.)?

When you make a commitment to God, it is important that you stick with it. It would be better to vow nothing than to pledge yourself casually. Take fasting seriously, and let your respect and awe of God guard you as you walk into this new season of spiritual growth and insight.

Lisa Bevere

"O my God, I am ashamed and embarrassed to lift up my face to You, my God, because our iniquities have expanded over our heads and our wrongdoing has grown up to the heavens. 7 Since the days of our fathers until this day, we have been in a great guilt. It is because of our iniquities that we, our kings, and our priests have been delivered—by the sword, by captivity, by spoil, and by being shamed—into the hand of the kings of the lands. This day is like that, too.

> Revive me, and repair every desolation in my life (Ezr 9:9).

8 "Yet now for a little while, there has been a favorable response from the LORD our God—leaving us a remnant to escape, giving us a tent peg from His holy place, having our eyes enlightened by our God, and giving us a little reviving in our bondage. 9 For though we were slaves, our God has not forsaken us in our bondage but has extended mercy to us in the sight of the kings of Persia, granting us a reviving for the rebuilding of the house of our God, for the repairing of its ruins, and for giving us a wall in Judah and in Jerusalem.

10 "Now, O our God, what shall we say after this? For we have forsaken Your commandments, 11 which You commanded by Your servants the prophets, saying, 'The land you are going to possess, it is an unclean land with the filthiness of the people of the lands. By their abominations, it is has been filled from one end to another with their uncleanness. 12 Now, therefore, cease giving your daughters as wives to their sons, do not take their daughters to your sons, and never seek their peace or prosperity, that you might grow strong and eat the good of the land and leave it as an eternal inheritance to your children.'

13 "After all that has come upon us because of our evil deeds and our great guilt, seeing that You our God have punished us less than our iniquities deserve and have given us such deliverance as this, 14 should we again break Your commandments and intermarry with the people of these abominations? Would You not become so completely angry with us that there would be no remnant nor any who escape? 15 O LORD God of Israel, You are righteous, for we who escaped exile yet remain to this very day. Here we stand before You in our guiltiness even though we should not stand before You because of this."

9:7 2Ch 29:6
9:8 Ps 13:3
9:11 Ezr 6:21
9:12 Dt 7:3
9:13 Ps 103:10
9:14 Dt 9:8
9:15 Ps 130:3

....

10:1 2Ch 20:9
10:2 Ne 13:27
10:3 Dt 7:2–3
10:4 1Ch 28:10
10:5 Ne 5:12
10:6 Dt 9:18
10:14 2Ch 29:10

The People's Confession of Sin

10 Now while Ezra prayed and confessed, weeping and prostrating himself before the house of God, a very large congregation of men, women, and children gathered around him from Israel, for the people too wept bitterly. 2 Shekaniah the son of Jehiel, one of the sons of Elam, answered and said to Ezra, "We have acted with vile unfaithfulness against our God and have wedded foreign women from the people of the land, yet there is now hope in Israel concerning this. 3 Now therefore let us make a covenant with our God to sever relations with all the women and their children according to the counsel of my lord and those who tremble at the commandment of our God. May this be done in accordance with the law. 4 Arise, for this matter is your responsibility. But we are standing with you. Be courageous and act!"

5 Then Ezra stood and made the presiding Levitical priests and all Israel to swear an oath to act according to this word. And they swore an oath. 6 Then Ezra stood in front of the house of God and went into the chamber of Jehohanan the son of Eliashib. When he arrived there, he ate no bread and drank no water because he was mourning over the vile unfaithfulness of the exiles.

7 They made a proclamation throughout Judah and Jerusalem for all the children of the exile to assemble in Jerusalem. 8 Whoever would not come within three days would forfeit all his possessions, according to the counsel of the leaders and the elders, and would himself be excluded from the congregation of the exiles.

9 Then all the men of Judah and Benjamin gathered themselves together to Jerusalem within the three days. It was the ninth month, on the twentieth day of the month. All the people sat on the grounds of the house of God, trembling about this matter and also because of the great rain. 10 Ezra the priest stood up and said to them, "You have acted unfaithfully by bringing home foreign women, adding to the guilt of Israel. 11 Now therefore make confession to the LORD God of your fathers and do what pleases Him: Sever your relationships with the people of the land, especially from the foreign women."

12 Then all the congregation answered loudly, "As you have said to us, that we will do. 13 But there are many people, and because it is the rainy season we will not be able to set up outside. Moreover, this is not a task for a day or two since we have so grievously transgressed in this matter. 14 Let now our rulers preside over

all the congregation so that, in each of our
cities, all who have married foreign women,
along with the elders and judges of that city,
will come at appointed times, until the fierce
wrath of our God for this matter is turned from
us." 15 Only Jonathan the son of Asahel and
Jahzeiah the son of Tikvah opposed this, with
Meshullam and Shabbethai the Levite support-
ing them.

16 Then the descendants of the captivity did
so. Ezra the priest selected men, heads of the
fathers' households, according to their fami-
lies, each of them by name. They sat down in
the first day of the tenth month to examine the
matter, 17 and finished *dealing with* every man
who had married foreign women by the first
day of the first month.

Those Guilty of Intermarriage

18 Some of the sons of the priests were dis-
covered to have wedded foreign women,
namely the sons of Joshua the son of
Jozadak, and his brothers: Maaseiah,
Eliezer, Jarib, and Gedaliah. 19 They com-
mitted to sever their relations with their
women, and, being guilty, they offered a
ram of the flock for their guilt.

20 Likewise, of the sons of Immer,
there were Hanani and Zebadiah.

21 Of the sons of Harim,
there were Maaseiah, Elijah, Shemaiah,
Jehiel, and Uzziah.

22 Of the sons of Pashhur,
there were Elioenai, Maaseiah, Ishmael,
Nethanel, Jozabad, and Elasah.

23 Also, from the Levites,
there were Jozabad, Shimei, Kelaiah, (the
same is Kelita), Pethahiah, Judah, and
Eliezer.

24 Among the singers,
there was Eliashib,
and from the porters,
there were Shallum, Telem, and Uri.

25 Further from Israel,
of the sons of Parosh,
there were Ramiah, Izziah, Malkijah, Mij-
amin, Eleazar, Malkijah, and Benaiah.

26 Of the sons of Elam,
there were Mattaniah, Zechariah, Jehiel,
Abdi, Jeremoth, and Elijah.

27 Of the sons of Zattu,
there were Elioenai, Eliashib, Mattaniah,
Jeremoth, Zabad, and Aziza.

28 Of the sons of Bebai,
there were Jehohanan, Hananiah, Zab-
bai, and Athlai.

29 Of the sons of Bani,
there were Meshullam, Malluk, Adaiah,
Jashub, Sheal, and Jeremoth.

30 Of the sons of Pahath-Moab,
there were Adna, Kelal, Benaiah, Maa-
seiah, Mattaniah, Bezalel, Binnui, and
Manasseh.

31 Of the sons of Harim,
there were Eliezer, Ishijah, Malkijah, She-
maiah, Shimeon, 32 Benjamin, Malluk,
and Shemariah.

33 Of the sons of Hashum,
there were Mattenai, Mattattah, Zabad,
Eliphelet, Jeremai, Manasseh, and
Shimei.

34 Of the sons of Bani,
there were Maadai, Amram, Uel, 35 Bena-
iah, Bedeiah, Keluhi, 36 Vaniah, Mere-
moth, Eliashib, 37 Mattaniah, Mattenai,
and Jaasu.

38 Of the sons of Binnui,
there were Shimei, 39 Shelemiah, Nathan,
Adaiah, 40 Maknadebai, Shashai, Sharai,
41 Azarel, Shelemiah, Shemariah, 42 Shal-
lum, Amariah, and Joseph.

43 Of the sons of Nebo,
there were Jeiel, Mattithiah, Zabad, Zebi-
na, Jaddai, Joel, and Benaiah.

44 All these married foreign women, and
some of them had wives that had children.

10:15 Ne 11:16
10:19 Lev 6:6

10:25 Ezr 2:3

Author: Traditionally Ezra

Written: Between 445 and 420 BC

Themes: Israel's History, Return from Exile, Rebuilding

NEHEMIAH

Dear Spirit Led Woman,

In Nehemiah God directs His leaders to rebuild what the enemy has destroyed so that God may be glorified, worshipped, and praised. What areas of your life are you trusting Him to rebuild today? Maybe your marriage has been falling apart and you need a miracle. Maybe your children's hearts are being tempted by the world and you feel they're losing their way. Perhaps you've lost a friend or family member, your job, or even your health. God is in the business of restoring and rebuilding. Like Nehemiah and the other Israelites, hold your sword (God's Word) in one hand while you work with the other. It reminds me of the saying "Pray as if everything depends on God, but work as if everything depends on you."

Sometimes we go through times where it seems that we face one battle after another. If this has been the season you've been in lately, you might look around and see nothing but ruins everywhere. Don't despair. God is in the middle of your situation. You can trust Him today to lead you in the way you should go as you seek to restore, repair, and rebuild what the enemy has destroyed.

Joy F. Strang

The Prayer of Nehemiah

1 The words of Nehemiah the son of Hakaliah.

In the month Kislev, in the twentieth year, while I was in Susa the palace, 2 Hanani, one of my relatives, and some men of Judah arrived. So I asked them concerning the returning Jews who had been in captivity, and concerning Jerusalem.

3 They said to me, "The remnant that returned from captivity is there in the province enduring great affliction and reproach. Also, the wall of Jerusalem remains broken down, and its gates have been burned with fire."

4 When I heard these words, I sat down and wept and mourned for days. Then I fasted, and prayed before the God of heaven, 5 and said:

> "I beseech You, O Lord God of heaven, the great and awesome God, who keeps covenant and mercy for those who love Him and keep His commandments. 6 Let Your ear now be attentive, and Your eyes open, that You may hear the prayer of Your servant, which I now pray before You, day and night, for the children of Israel Your servants, and confess the sins of the children of Israel, which we have sinned against You. Both my father's house and I have sinned. 7 We have acted very corruptly against You and have not obeyed the commandments, nor the statutes, nor the judgments, which You commanded Your servant Moses.
>
> 8 "Please remember the word that You commanded Your servant Moses, saying, 'If you behave unfaithfully, then I will scatter you among the nations, 9 but if you return to Me and keep My commandments and do them, though your outcasts are under the farthest part of the heavens, I will gather them from there and bring them back to the place where I have chosen to establish My name.'

I am Your servant, Lord; prosper me (Ne 1:11).

> 10 "Now these are Your servants and Your people, whom You have redeemed by Your great power and by Your strong hand. 11 O Lord, I implore You, let Your ear be attentive to the prayer of Your servant, and to the prayer of Your servants who delight to revere Your name. And let Your servant prosper this day, and grant him mercy in the sight of this man."

For I was the king's cupbearer.

1:1 Ne 10:1
1:2 Ne 7:2
1:3 Ne 2:17
1:4 Ne 2:4
1:5 Ex 20:6
1:6 Da 9:20
1:9 Dt 12:5
1:10 Dt 9:29
1:11 Ne 1:6

2:1 Ezr 7:1
2:2 Pr 15:13
2:3 Ne 1:3
2:4 Ne 1:4
2:6 Ne 13:6
2:8 Ezr 7:6
2:9 Ezr 8:22
2:10 Ne 2:19
2:11 Ezr 8:32
2:13 Ne 1:3
2:14 Ne 3:15

Nehemiah Sent to Jerusalem

2 In the month of Nisan, during the twentieth year of King Artaxerxes, when wine was before him, I took the wine and gave it to the king. Never had I been upset in his presence. 2 So the king said to me, "Why is your face troubled though you do not seem sick? This is nothing but a troubled heart."

Then I became very much afraid 3 and said to the king, "May the king live forever! Why should not my face be troubled when the city, the place of my fathers' tombs, lies waste, and its gates have been destroyed by fire?"

4 So the king said to me, "What are you requesting about this matter?"

Immediately, I prayed to the God of heaven 5 and then said to the king, "If this pleases the king and if this might be good for your servant who is before you, then would you send me to Judah, to the city of my fathers' tombs so that I may rebuild it?"

6 The king, with the queen sitting beside him, said to me, "How long would your journey be? And when will you return?" Because it pleased the king to send me, I established a timetable for him.

7 I further said to the king, "If this pleases the king, may letters be given to me for the governors of the province Beyond the River so that they would allow me to pass through until I come to Judah, 8 as well as a letter to Asaph the keeper of the king's forest, that he may give me timber to make beams for the gates of the temple mount, for the city wall, and for the house into which I will enter." The king granted me these things, because the good hand of my God was upon me. 9 When I came to the governors of the province Beyond the River, I gave them the king's letters. He also sent with me commanders of foot and horse soldiers.

10 When Sanballat the Horonite and Tobiah the Ammonite subordinate heard this, it deeply grieved them that there was a man coming to seek the welfare of the children of Israel.

Nehemiah Inspects Jerusalem's Walls

11 When I arrived in Jerusalem, I was there three days. 12 Then I arose in the night, I and a few men who were with me; I told no one what my God had put in my heart to do for Jerusalem. There was no animal with me, except the one on which I rode.

13 So I went out by night by the Valley Gate toward the Dragon's Well and then to the Dung Gate, because I was inspecting the broken-down walls of Jerusalem and its burned gates. 14 Next I passed by the Fountain Gate and then to the King's Pool, but there was no place for my mount to pass. 15 By going

up along the riverbed at night, I inspected the wall. Then I turned back so that I could enter by the Valley Gate, and then came back again. 16 The officials did not know where I went or what I did, since I had not yet told it to the Jews, the priests, the nobles, the officials, or to any of the others who would do the work.

17 Finally, I said to them, "You see the distress that we are in, how Jerusalem is devastated and its gates are burned with fire. Come, and let us rebuild the wall of Jerusalem so that we will no more be a reproach." 18 Then I told them that the hand of my God had been good to me and also about the king's words that he had spoken to me.

And they said, "Let us rise up and build!" So they strengthened their hands for the good work.

19 But when Sanballat the Horonite, Tobiah the Ammonite subordinate, and Geshem the Arabian heard it, they laughed us to scorn, and despised us, and said, "What is this thing that you are doing? Are you rebelling against the king?"

20 Then answered I them and said to them, "The God of heaven, He will enable us to prosper. Therefore we His servants will arise and build, but you will have no portion, or right, or memorial in Jerusalem."

Rebuilding the Wall

3 Then Eliashib the high priest rose up with his brothers the priests, and they built the Sheep Gate. They sanctified it and erected its doors. From the Tower of the Hundred to the Tower of Hananel, they sanctified the wall. 2 Next to him the men of Jericho built, and next to them Zakkur the son of Imri built.

3 The sons of Hassenaah built the Fish Gate, constructing its beams, erecting its doors, and *installing* locks and bars for it. 4 Next to them Meremoth the son of Uriah, the son of Hakkoz made repairs. Next to him, Meshullam the son of Berekiah, the son of Meshezabel made repairs. Next to him Zadok the son of Baana made repairs. 5 Next to them the Tekoites made repairs, but their noblemen would not put their shoulders to the work of their Lord.

6 Joiada the son of Paseah and Meshullam the son of Besodeiah repaired the Old Gate. They constructed its beams, erected its doors, and *installed* locks and bars for it. 7 Next to them repairs were made by Melatiah the Gibeonite and Jadon the Meronothite, the men of Gibeon and of Mizpah, places under the authority of the governor of the province Beyond the River. 8 Next to them Uzziel the son of Harhaiah, one of the goldsmiths, made repairs. Next to him Hananiah, the son of one of the apothecaries, made repairs, and they repaired Jerusalem as far as the Broad Wall. 9 Next to him Rephaiah the son of Hur, commander of half of the Jerusalem district, made repairs. 10 Next to him Jedaiah the son of Harumaph made repairs across from his house. Next to him Hattush the son of Hashabneiah made repairs. 11 Malkijah the son of Harim and Hasshub the son of Pahath-Moab repaired another section, as well as the Tower of the Furnaces. 12 Next to them Shallum the son of Hallohesh, commander of the other half of the Jerusalem district, made repairs along with his daughters.

13 Hanun and the inhabitants of Zanoah repaired the Valley Gate. They rebuilt it, erected its doors, and *installed* locks and bars for it, plus *repaired* one thousand cubits[1] along on the wall to the Dung Gate.

14 But the Dung Gate was repaired by Malkijah the son of Rekab, commander of the Beth Hakkerem district. He rebuilt it, and erected its doors, and *installed* the locks and bars for it.

15 Moreover, Shallun the son of Kol-Hozeh, commander of the Mizpah district, made repairs to the Fountain Gate. He rebuilt it, covered it, erected its doors, and *installed* the locks and bars for it. *He also repaired* the wall of the pool of Shelah by the king's garden as far as the steps going down from the City of David. 16 After him Nehemiah the son of Azbuk, commander of half of the Beth Zur district, made repairs as far as the area across from the Tomb of David plus to the constructed pool and to the house of the mighty.

17 After him the Levites, under Rehum the son of Bani, made repairs. Next to them Hashabiah, commander of half of the Keilah district, made repairs in his area. 18 After him their brothers, under Binnui the son of Henadad, commander of the other half of the Keilah district, made repairs. 19 Next to them Ezer the son of Jeshua, commander of Mizpah, made repairs to another section across from the ascent to the armory at the corner. 20 After him Baruch the son of Zabbai zealously repaired another section, from the corner to the door of the house of Eliashib the high priest. 21 After him Meremoth the son of Uriah the son of Hakkoz repaired another section from the door of the house of Eliashib to the end of it.

22 After him the priests, the men of the surrounding plain, made repairs. 23 After them Benjamin and Hasshub made repairs across from their house. After them Azariah the son of Maaseiah the son of Ananiah made repairs beside his house. 24 After him Binnui the son

2:17 Ne 1:3
2:18 2Sa 2:7
2:19 Ne 6:6
2:20 Ezr 4:3
3:1 Ne 12:39
3:2 Ne 7:36
3:3 Ne 12:39
3:5 2Sa 14:2
3:6 Ne 12:39
3:8 Ne 12:38

3:9 Ne 3:12
3:11 Ne 12:38
3:12 Ne 3:9
3:13 Ne 2:13
3:14 Jer 6:1
3:15 Ne 12:37
3:16 2Ki 20:20
3:19 2Ch 26:9
3:20 Ne 3:1
3:22 Ne 12:28

[1] *13* About 1,500 feet, or about 450 meters.

of Henadad repaired another section from the
house of Azariah as far as the corner plus the
corner tower. 25 Palal the son of Uzai *made re-
pairs* across from the corner and to the tower
protruding out of the king's upper house next
to the courtyard of the guards. After him Pe-
daiah the son of Parosh *made repairs*. 26 The
temple servants living in Ophel *made repairs*
from opposite the Water Gate eastward to the
protruding tower. 27 After them the Tekoites re-
paired another section across from the great
protruding tower as far as the wall of Ophel.

28 Up to the Horse Gate the priests made re-
pairs—each one across from his house. 29 After
them Zadok the son of Immer repaired across
from his house. After him Shemaiah the son
of Shekaniah, who was keeper of the East
Gate, made repairs. 30 After him Hananiah the
son of Shelemiah and Hanun the sixth son of
Zalaph repaired another section. After them
Meshullam the son of Berekiah made repairs
across from his chamber. 31 After him Malki-
jah the goldsmith's son made repairs as far
as the house of the temple servants and the
merchants. This was across from the Mustering
Gate *extending* as far as the upper room of
the corner tower. 32 Between the upper room
of the corner tower and the Sheep Gate, the
goldsmiths and the merchants made repairs.

Opposition to the Rebuilding

4 When Sanballat heard that we were re-
building the wall, he became angry and
was greatly irritated, and he mocked the Jews.
2 He spoke before his relatives and the army
of Samaria and said, "What are these feeble
Jews doing? Are they fortifying themselves?
Will they make sacrifices? Can they complete
this in a day? Can they revive the burned-up
stones out of the rubbish heaps?"

3 Now Tobiah the Ammonite was beside him,
and he said, "Even what they are rebuilding, if
even a fox climbed it, that would break down
their stone wall."

4 Hear, O our God, that we are despised. Turn
their reproach back upon their own head, and
give them as spoil in a land of captivity: 5 No
longer cover their iniquity nor blot out their
sin, which is before You since they have made
insults against the builders.

6 So we rebuilt the wall until all of it was so-
lidified up to half its height. The people had a
passion for the work.

7 When Sanballat, Tobiah, the Arabians, the
Ammonites, and the Ashdodites heard how the
restoration of Jerusalem's walls was progress-
ing and how the breaches had begun to be
sealed, it made them extremely furious. 8 So
they all conspired together to fight against
Jerusalem in order to cause it chaos. 9 Nev-
ertheless we prayed to our God, and, because
of them, we set up a watch for them day and
night.

10 Judah had said, "The strength of the bur-
den bearers is failing though there is much
rubble. And we ourselves are unable to rebuild
the wall."

11 Our adversaries said, "They will neither
know nor see until we have entered in among
them and slain them. Indeed, we will stop the
work!"

12 When the Jews living near them came, they
told us ten times, "From every place where you
turn, *they will be* against us."

13 Therefore I set *guards* at the lowest posi-
tions *along the wall* and just inside the wall at
the unrepaired areas. I also stationed the peo-
ple by families *providing them individually* their
own swords, spears, and bows. 14 After I looked
around, I stood up and said to the nobles, the
rulers, and the rest of the people, "Stop being
terrified because of them! Remember instead
that the Lord is great and awesome. So fight
for each other—and for your sons, your daugh-
ters, your wives, and your houses."

15 Now when our enemies heard that this had
become known to us and that God had brought
their counsel to nothing, then we all returned
to the wall, everyone to his work.

16 After that day, half of my servants did the
work while the other half handled the spears,
shields, bows, and body armor. Commanders
were *appointed* to support every house of Ju-
dah. 17 Those rebuilding the wall and those
hauling the loads were working with one
hand doing the task, but with the other hand
holding the weapon. 18 For the builders, ev-
eryone had his sword bound to his side, even
while rebuilding. The trumpet blower worked
beside me.

19 I said to the nobles, the rulers, and to the
rest of the people, "The work is vast and over a
large area. Since we are spread along the wall
far from each other, 20 assemble to us there at
the place where you hear the trumpet sound-
ed. Our God shall fight for us."

21 So we labored in the work with half of
them holding spears from sunrise to the rising
of the stars. 22 Likewise at the same time I said
to the people, "Every man and his servant must
lodge within Jerusalem. By night, they may be
a guard to us; by day, a *laborer for* the work."
23 So neither I nor my brothers nor my servants
nor the men of the guard who followed me
took off our clothes. Each carried his weapon,
even when washing.

3:25 Jer 32:2
3:26 Ne 8:1
3:28 2Ch 23:15
3:32 Ne 3:1
4:1 Ne 2:10
4:2 Ezr 4:9–10
4:4 Ps 79:12
4:5 Jer 18:23

4:14 Nu 14:9
4:15 2Sa 17:14
4:20 Ex 14:14

Nehemiah Stops Oppression

5 Now there was a great outcry of the people and their wives against their fellow Jews. 2 Some were saying, "We and our sons and our daughters are many. Therefore, let us acquire grain so that we may eat and live."

3 Others were saying, "We have mortgaged our fields, vineyards, and houses so that we might acquire grain because of hunger."

4 Still others were saying, "We have borrowed money for the king's tribute *against the value of* our fields and vineyards. 5 Now our flesh is the same as the flesh of our countrymen. Our children are like their children, but we are subjugating our sons and our daughters as servants. Indeed, some of our daughters are in bondage already, and we are powerless *to do anything* because our fields and vineyards belong to others."

6 I was very angry when I heard their outcry and these words. 7 So I contemplated about this for myself and, as a result, I rebuked the nobles and officials and said to them, "Based on the claim of each against his brother, you are exacting usury." Then I convened a great assembly against them, 8 and I said to them, "By whatever means we had, we purchased our Jewish countrymen who were being sold to the nations. So, will you once more sell your countrymen so that they might *again* be sold to us?" Then they kept silent, because they found nothing to answer.

9 Also I said, "What you are doing is not good! Should not you walk in the fear of our God because of the reproach of the nations, our enemies? 10 Moreover, I, my relatives, and my servants are loaning them money and grain. So, I urge you, cease from this practice of usury. 11 Please restore to them, even this day, their fields, their vineyards, their olive groves, and their houses, along with a hundredth part of the money, the grain, the wine, and the oil that you had exacted from them."

12 Then they said, "We will restore *it* and will require nothing of them. We will do what you have said."

Then I called the priests and made them swear an oath to keep this promise. 13 Also I shook out the front of my garment and said, "Like this, may God shake out every man from his house and from his labor who does not carry out this promise. Exactly like this, may he be shaken out and emptied."

And all the congregation said, "Amen," and praised the LORD. And the people did according to this promise.

5:4 Ezr 4:13
5:5 2Ki 4:1
5:7 Ex 22:25
5:12 Ezr 10:5
5:13 Ac 18:6

5:14 Ne 13:6
5:15 Ne 5:9
5:17 1Ki 18:19
5:18 1Ki 4:22–23
5:19 Ne 13:14
6:1 Ne 2:10
6:2 1Ch 8:12
6:6 Ne 2:19

Nehemiah's Generosity

14 Moreover from the time that I was appointed to be their governor in the land of Judah (from the twentieth year even until the thirty-second year of King Artaxerxes) twelve years *had passed*. And my companions and I had not eaten the governor's food *allotment*. 15 The former governors preceding me had extracted a heavy burden on the people, because they took from them food and wine, besides forty shekels[1] of silver. Moreover, even their servants domineered over the people. But I myself never did so, because of the fear of God. 16 Furthermore, I stayed determined in the work on this wall. We bought no field, and all my servants were gathered there for the sake of the work.

17 Moreover there were *regularly* at my table one hundred and fifty Jews and officials, besides those who came to us from the nations around us. 18 Daily there were one ox and six choice sheep prepared for me. Fowls were also prepared for me. Once in ten days all sorts of wine *were supplied* in abundance. Yet for all this, I never required the governor's food *allotment* because it was a heavy burden on this people.

19 Remember me, O my God, for good, according to all that I have done for this people.

Nehemiah's Enemies

6 When Sanballat, Tobiah, Geshem the Arabian, and the rest of our enemies heard that I had rebuilt the wall and that there was not a gap in it (though at that time I had not erected the doors on the gates), 2 Sanballat and Geshem sent to me, saying, "Come, that we might meet together in one of the villages in the plain of Ono."

But they planned to do evil to me. 3 So I sent messengers to them, saying, "I am doing a great work, so I am not able to come down. Why should the work cease while I leave it and come down to you?" 4 Four more times they sent for me like this, but I answered them the same way.

I bind and rebuke every spirit of Sanballat and Tobiah, in the name of Jesus (Ne 6:1–6).

5 Sanballat sent the same request a fifth time by his servant, but the letter was open in his hand. 6 In it was written,

> "It is reported among the nations, and Geshem confirms it, that you and the Jews are planning to rebel; consequently you are rebuilding the wall. According to these

[1] *15* About 1 pound, or 460 grams.

words, you are their king. 7 You have also
appointed prophets to preach on your be-
half in Jerusalem, saying, 'There is a king
in Judah!' According to these words, it will
now be reported to the king. So come now
and let us consult together."

8 I sent him *this response*, saying, "Nothing
like these reports that you are saying has oc-
curred. From your own mind, you are invent-
ing *them*."

9 Because they all wanted to frighten us, they
thought, "They will pull their hands back from
the work." But that would never be done.

So now, *O God*, strengthen my hands.

10 When I came to the house of Shemaiah the
crippled son of Delaiah the son of Mehetabel,
he said, "Let us meet together at the house of
God, inside the temple, and then we can shut
the temple doors. They are coming to kill you!
Even tonight, they could come to kill you!"

11 But I said, "Should a man like me flee?
Who is there like me who would go into the
temple to save his life? I would never go!"
12 Then I perceived and saw that God had not
sent him, but that he pronounced the prophecy
against me, because Tobiah and Sanballat had
hired him. 13 He was hired for this reason: that
I might become fearful, act accordingly, and
sin. Then they would have an evil report by
which they could reproach me.

14 Remember, O my God, concerning Tobiah
and Sanballat these deeds of theirs, as well
as the prophetess Noadiah and the rest of the
prophets who were trying to frighten me.

The Wall Completed

15 The wall was finished on the twenty-fifth
day of the month Elul, in fifty-two days.
16 When all our enemies heard *it* and all the
surrounding nations saw *it*, they were tremen-
dously humbled. They perceived that, because
of our God, this work had been accomplished.

17 Moreover in those days the nobles of Ju-
dah produced numerous letters in transit to
Tobiah. Likewise, the letters of Tobiah came
to them, 18 because so many in Judah were
bound by oath to him since he was the son-
in-law of Shekaniah the son of Arah, and his
son Jehohanan had married the daughter of
Meshullam the son of Berekiah. 19 Also they
reported his good deeds in front of me and
reported my words to him. Tobiah sent letters
to frighten me.

7 Once the wall was rebuilt and I had erect-
ed the doors, the gatekeepers, the singers,
and the Levites were appointed. 2 Over Jerusa-
lem, I put in charge both my brother Hanani
and Hananiah, the palace commander, be-
cause each was a faithful man and feared God
more than many. 3 I said to them, "The gates
of Jerusalem should not be opened until the
sun is hot. Until *guards* are posted, the doors
should be closed and bolted. Likewise, appoint
guards from Jerusalem's inhabitants—each at
his post, across from his own house."

4 Now the city was large and spacious, yet
the people in it were few since there had been
no houses built.

The List of Returned Exiles

Ezr 2:1–70

5 So my God put *an idea* in my mind, and I
gathered the nobles, the officials, and the peo-
ple together to conduct a genealogy registra-
tion. When I found the book of the genealog-
ical register, it *contained the list* of those who
first came back. I found written in it:

> 6 These are the people of the province who
> returned from the captivity of the exiles
> whom King Nebuchadnezzar of Babylon
> had carried away, but came back to Jeru-
> salem and to Judah, everyone to his city.
> 7 Those who came with Zerubbabel were
> Joshua, Nehemiah, Azariah, Raamiah,
> Nahamani, Mordecai, Bilshan, Mispereth,
> Bigvai, Nehum, and Baanah.
>
> The number of the men of the people of Israel was this:
>
> 8 The sons of Parosh, two thousand one hundred and seventy-two;
> 9 the sons of Shephatiah, three hundred and seventy-two;
> 10 the sons of Arah, six hundred and fifty-two;
> 11 the sons of Pahath-Moab, of the sons of Jeshua and Joab, two thousand eight hundred and eighteen;
> 12 the sons of Elam, one thousand two hundred and fifty-four;
> 13 the sons of Zattu, eight hundred and forty-five;
> 14 the sons of Zakkai, seven hundred and sixty;
> 15 the sons of Binnui, six hundred and forty-eight;
> 16 the sons of Bebai, six hundred and twenty-eight;
> 17 the sons of Azgad, two thousand three hundred and twenty-two;
> 18 the sons of Adonikam, six hundred and sixty-seven;
> 19 the sons of Bigvai, two thousand and sixty-seven;
> 20 the sons of Adin, six hundred and fifty-five;
> 21 the sons of Ater of Hezekiah, ninety-eight;

6:10 Jer 36:5
6:12 Eze 13:22
6:14 Ne 13:29
6:16 Ne 2:10
7:1 Ne 6:1
7:2 Ne 1:2

7:6 Ezr 2:1–70
7:7 Ezr 2:2

[22] the sons of Hashum, three hundred and twenty-eight;
[23] the sons of Bezai, three hundred and twenty-four;
[24] the sons of Hariph, one hundred and twelve;
[25] the sons of Gibeon, ninety-five.

[26] The men of Bethlehem and Netophah, one hundred and eighty-eight;
[27] the men of Anathoth, one hundred and twenty-eight;
[28] the men of Beth Azmaveth, forty-two;
[29] the men of Kiriath Jearim, Kephirah, and Beeroth, seven hundred and forty-three;
[30] the men of Ramah and Geba, six hundred and twenty-one;
[31] the men of Mikmash, one hundred and twenty-two;
[32] the men of Bethel and Ai, one hundred and twenty-three;
[33] the men of the other Nebo, fifty-two;
[34] the sons of the other Elam, one thousand two hundred and fifty-four;
[35] the sons of Harim, three hundred and twenty;
[36] the sons of Jericho, three hundred and forty-five;
[37] the sons of Lod, Hadid, and Ono, seven hundred and twenty-one;
[38] the sons of Senaah, three thousand nine hundred and thirty.

Priestly Leaders

[39] The priests:

the sons of Jedaiah, of the house of Jeshua, nine hundred and seventy-three;
[40] the sons of Immer, one thousand and fifty-two;
[41] the sons of Pashhur, one thousand two hundred and forty-seven;
[42] the sons of Harim, one thousand and seventeen.

[43] The Levites:

the sons of Jeshua, of Kadmiel, and of the sons of Hodaviah, seventy-four.

[44] The singers:

the sons of Asaph, one hundred and forty-eight.

[45] The gatekeepers:

the sons of Shallum, the sons of Ater, the sons of Talmon, the sons of Akkub, the sons of Hatita, the sons of Shobai, one hundred and thirty-eight.

[46] The temple servants:

the sons of Ziha, the sons of Hasupha, the sons of Tabbaoth,
[47] the sons of Keros, the sons of Sia, the sons of Padon,
[48] the sons of Lebana, the sons of Hagaba, the sons of Shalmai,
[49] the sons of Hanan, the sons of Giddel, the sons of Gahar,
[50] the sons of Reaiah, the sons of Rezin, the sons of Nekoda,
[51] the sons of Gazzam, the sons of Uzza, the sons of Paseah,
[52] the sons of Besai, the sons of Meunim, the sons of Nephusim,
[53] the sons of Bakbuk, the sons of Hakupha, the sons of Harhur,
[54] the sons of Bazluth, the sons of Mehida, the sons of Harsha,
[55] the sons of Barkos, the sons of Sisera, the sons of Temah,
[56] the sons of Neziah, the sons of Hatipha.

[57] The sons of Solomon's servants:

the sons of Sotai, the sons of Sophereth, the sons of Perida,
[58] the sons of Jaala, the sons of Darkon, the sons of Giddel,
[59] the sons of Shephatiah, the sons of Hattil,
the sons of Pokereth-Hazzebaim, the sons of Amon.

[60] All the temple servants and the sons of Solomon's servants were three hundred and ninety-two.

[61] These were they who came up from Tel
Melah, Tel Harsha, Kerub, Addon, and Immer,
but they could not show their fathers' houses
nor their lineage—whether they were of Israel:

[62] The sons of

Delaiah, the sons of Tobiah, the sons of Nekoda, six hundred and forty-two.

[63] Of the priests:

the sons of

Hobaiah, the sons of Hakkoz, the sons of Barzillai, who married one of the daughters of Barzillai the Gileadite, and was called by their name.

[64] These sought for their fathers' registra-
tion in the genealogical registry, but it was
not found. Therefore, they were considered
as unclean *and removed* from the priesthood.
[65] The magistrate said to them that they should
not eat of the most holy things until there was
an appointed priest with Urim and Thummim.

7:61 Ezr 2:59
7:65 Ne 8:9

66 The whole congregation together was for-
ty-two thousand three hundred and sixty, 67 be-
sides their male and female servants, which
numbered seven thousand three hundred and
thirty-seven; and they had two hundred and
forty-five male and female singers. 68 Their
horses were seven hundred and thirty-six; their
mules, two hundred and forty-five; 69 their cam-
els, four hundred and thirty-five; the donkeys,
six thousand seven hundred and twenty.

70 Some of the chiefs of the fathers' house-
holds gave to the work. The magistrate gave
to the treasury one thousand gold drachmas,[1]
fifty basins, and five hundred and thirty priests'
garments. 71 Others of the chiefs of the fathers'
households gave to the treasury for the work
twenty thousand gold drachmas[2] and two
thousand two hundred silver minas.[3] 72 What
the rest of the people gave was twenty thou-
sand gold drachmas, two thousand silver
minas,[4] and sixty-seven priests' garments.
73 So the priests, the Levites, the gatekeepers,
the singers, some of the people, the temple
servants, and all Israel lived in their cities.

Ezra Reads the Law

When the seventh month came, the children
of Israel were in their cities.

8 All the people gathered together as one
man in the area in front of the Water Gate,
and they asked Ezra the scribe to bring the
Book of the Law of Moses, which the LORD had
commanded to Israel.
2 On the first day of the seventh month, Ezra
the priest brought the Law before the congre-
gation of men, women, and all who could lis-
ten with understanding. 3 In the area in front
of the Water Gate, he read aloud from sunrise
until midday to the men, women, and those
who could understand. All the people listened
attentively to the Book of the Law.
4 Ezra the scribe stood on a raised wood plat-
form, which they had made for the purpose.
Beside him stood Mattithiah, Shema, Anaiah,
Uriah, Hilkiah, and Maaseiah on his right
hand; and on his left hand, Pedaiah, Mishael,
Malkijah, Hashum, Hashbaddanah, Zechariah,
and Meshullam.
5 Ezra opened the book in the sight of all
the people (because he was above all the peo-
ple), and, as he opened it, all the people stood
up. 6 When Ezra blessed the LORD as the great
God, all the people responded "Amen, Amen!"
By lifting up their hands as they bowed their
heads, they worshipped the LORD with their
faces to the ground.
7 Then Jeshua, Bani, Sherebiah, Jamin, Ak-
kub, Shabbethai, Hodiah, Maaseiah, Kelita,
Azariah, Jozabad, Hanan, Pelaiah, and the

8:1 Ezr 7:6
8:2 Lev 23:24
8:5 Jdg 3:20
8:6 Ex 4:31
8:7 Ne 9:4
....
8:9 Ne 7:65

SPIRITLED WOMAN

COUNSEL FROM THE SPIRIT BASICS

God's Joy Is Our Strength

God's joy is our strength. We must remember this, especially when the battle gets fierce. The last eighteen months have been, by far, the most difficult of my life. Friends and babies have died; there has been sickness, floods, emotional trauma, huge financial needs, great loss of prosperity, life threats, slander, and betrayal. The more difficult it gets, however, the more tenacious we become to fix our eyes on the beautiful, perfect prize: Christ Jesus. He is always worth it all.

In trials and tribulations our enemy will use every possible device to try to get us to focus on the problems. We will give him less attention and give more attention to Jesus, our Savior. We will not be led astray from the simplicity and purity of devotion to Him. We are advancing. Our weapons are a firm faith, gentleness, peace, patience, and a love that cannot be resisted. In Him we cannot lose.

Heidi Baker

Levites, explained the Law to the people while
the people stood in their place. 8 They read
from the book, from the Law of God, with in-
terpretation, and they gave the sense, so that
the people understood the reading.
9 Then Nehemiah the magistrate, Ezra the
priest and scribe, and the Levites who were
teaching the people said to all the people,
"This day is holy to the LORD your God. Stop
mourning and weeping." (This was because all
the people wept when they heard the words
of the Law.)

God will turn my sorrow to joy (Ne 8:10).

10 Then he said to them, "Go your way. Eat the
fat, drink the sweet *drink*, and send portions to
those for whom nothing is prepared; for this
day is holy to our Lord. Do not be grieved, for
the joy of the LORD is your strength."

[1] *70* About 19 pounds, or 8.4 kilograms. [2] *71* About 375 pounds, or 170 kilograms; and in v. 72. [3] *71* About 1⅓ tons, or 1.2 metric tons. [4] *72* About 1¼ tons, or 1.1 metric tons.

Four Ways to Feed Your Spirit

Even in the midst of difficult challenges, busy schedules, and awkward moments, God wants us to enjoy our time on the earth. He promised His joy would be our strength (Ne 8:10). He personally participates in our lives, eager to see us face each day with grace and confidence and holding us up when the hard places on our journey threaten our ability to stand. The good news of Christ is that God has not left us alone.

Neither has He left us to figure out life on our own. Scripture provides signposts for the journey, helping us live active and balanced lives in Christ, keeping us from falling along the way, and enabling us to partake of the feast of life as He intended.

Just as the four basic food groups help us live a healthy physical life, so the four spiritual food groups God has defined produce an energetic, balanced faith that help us live a vibrant spiritual life.

These four spiritual food groups are shown below. Read the brief illustration with each spiritual food group, and then on the lines below briefly relate a time when you discovered the importance of that particular food group.

1. Solitude

To be balanced Christians, we must seek solitude with God. Jesus often retreated to "lonely places," and we too must protect our alone time, when we can be still and know God. Too often we stay in overdrive and eventually burn out. But in solitude we learn the value of waiting on God while resting in His presence.

REFLECT: I learned the importance of solitude with God...

2. Service

When we care for the needs of others and share God's love with them, we stand firmly in the place we've been called to, our feet anchored in the hope we've discovered in Christ. When God takes up residence in our hearts, He longs to express His compassion outwardly through us. He will direct us by His Spirit to those activities that He has preordained for us to do (Eph 2:10).

REFLECT: I was prompted to care for the needs of __________ by doing...

3. Community

If service is the fruit of our fellowship with God, then community is its backdrop. Serving apart from the fellowship and encouragement of other Christians can cause us to burn out and do little good for God's kingdom. On the other hand, if we stay in a place of solitude, withdrawn from the presence and support of others, we can be overcome by the paralyzing ache of isolation and loneliness. We need people to spur us on in our faith and help us maintain our balance on the road to abundant living. Community is a coming together—but not coexistence without interaction.

REFLECT: I learned how important community is to me and others when...

---

4. Contemplation

Contemplation forces us to abandon the busyness of life so we may reflect on its purpose. Contemplative time is essential for our personal growth, and our growth affects our relationships with others. Notice how the psalmists continually call us to meditate on God's wonders, to remember His works, and to consider our ways.

REFLECT: In my busy life, I have learned how important it is to take time to meditate by...

Integrating these four ingredients into our lives produces an energetic, balanced faith in the midst of daily demands. We need solitude with God to restore, refresh, and direct us. Out of that time comes a natural outflow of service to others.

Balance brings to our souls much-needed rest (Mt 11:28; Heb 4:9–11), peace (Pr 14:30; Col 3:15), grace (Ro 5:17), mercy (La 3:22–23), and hope, which is "a sure and steadfast anchor of the soul" (Heb 6:19). These gifts keep us from turning to the left or the right, guarding our hearts along the way and infusing us with the necessary strength to "press toward the goal to the prize of the high calling of God in Christ Jesus" (Php 3:14).

Jo Kadlecek

11 So the Levites quieted all the people, say-
ing, "Hush! Because today is holy you should
stop being so sorrowful."
12 Then all the people went to eat, to drink,
to send portions, and to enjoy a great celebra-
tion because they had understood the words
declared to them.

The Feast of Tabernacles

13 On the second day, the chiefs of the fathers'
households of all the people, the priests, and
the Levites were gathered to Ezra the scribe
in order to understand the words of the Law.
14 They found written in the Law where the
LORD had commanded by Moses that the chil-
dren of Israel should dwell in booths in the
feast of the seventh month, 15 and that they
should publish and proclaim in all their cit-
ies and in Jerusalem, "Go out to the hills and
bring olive branches, along with wild olive
branches, myrtle branches, palm branches,
and other leafy branches to make booths, as
it was written."
16 So the people went out and brought back
branches and made themselves booths. Each
household did so on its roof, in their yard, on
the grounds of the house of God, in the area
in front of the Water Gate, or in the area at the
Gate of Ephraim. 17 All the congregation who
had returned from captivity made booths and
lived in them. Not since the days of Joshua
the son of Nun to that day had the children of
Israel done so, and there was a tremendously
great feast.
18 And day by day, from the first day to the last
day, he read from the Book of the Law of God.
They celebrated the feast seven days, and on
the eighth day there was a solemn assembly
as required.

The Israelites Confess Their Sins

9 Now on the twenty-fourth day of this
month the children of Israel were assem-
bled with fasting and sackcloth, and there was
dirt on them. 2 The offspring of Israel separated
themselves from all the foreigners and then
stood and confessed their sins and the iniqui-
ties of their fathers. 3 They stood in their place
and read from the Book of the Law of the LORD
their God for a fourth of the day. And for an-
other fourth, they confessed and worshipped
the LORD their God. 4 Jeshua, Bani, Kadmiel,
Shebaniah, Bunni, Sherebiah, Bani, and Ke-
nani stood up on the stairs of the Levites and
cried with a loud voice to the LORD their God.
5 Then the Levites, Jeshua, Kadmiel, Bani, Ha-
shabneiah, Sherebiah, Hodiah, Shebaniah, and
Pethahiah, said:

"Stand up and bless the LORD your God for-
ever and ever! Let them bless Your glorious
name, which is exalted above all blessing
and praise. 6 You alone are the LORD. You
have made heaven, the heaven of heavens,
with all their host, the earth and all that is on
it, the seas and all that is in them; and You
preserve them all. And the host of heaven
worships You.
7 "You are the LORD God who chose Abram
and brought him out of Ur of the Chaldeans.
You gave him the name Abraham 8 and
found his heart faithful before You. And You
made a covenant with him to give him the
land of the Canaanites, the Hittites, the Am-
orites, the Perizzites, the Jebusites, and the
Girgashites—to give it to his seed. Indeed,
You have fulfilled Your words because You
are righteous.
9 "When You saw the affliction of our fa-
thers in Egypt and heard their cry by the
Red Sea, 10 You enacted signs and wonders
against Pharaoh, against all his servants,
and against all the people of his land be-
cause You knew how arrogantly they had
acted against them. Thus, You made a name
for Yourself, as it is this day. 11 You divided
the sea before them, so they might pass
through the midst of the sea on dry ground,
and cast their pursuers into the deep like a
stone into stormy waters. 12 By day You led
them with a pillar of cloud, and by night
with a pillar of fire to light the way for them
to go.
13 "You came down on Mount Sinai and
spoke with them from heaven and gave
them just requirements, true laws, good
statutes and commandments. 14 You also
revealed to them Your Holy Sabbath and,
by the hand of Moses Your servant, set in
place for them the precepts, statutes, and
laws. 15 You gave them bread from heaven
for their hunger and brought water out of
the rock for them for their thirst. You told
them to enter in order to possess the land
which You had sworn to give them.
16 "But they and our fathers acted proudly
and hardened their necks and did not obey
Your commandments. 17 They refused to
obey and were not mindful of Your wonders
that You performed among them. But they
hardened their necks and in their rebellion
appointed a leader to return to their bond-
age. But You are a God ready to pardon,
gracious and merciful, slow to anger and
abounding in kindness, and did not forsake
them.
18 "Even when they had made themselves
a molded calf and said, 'This is your god
that brought you out of Egypt,' and com-
mitted terrible provocations, 19 yet You in

8:12 Ne 8:7–8
8:14 Lev 23:34
8:15 Lev 23:4
8:16 2Ki 14:13
8:17 2Ch 8:13
8:18 Lev 23:36
9:1 Jos 7:6
9:2 Ezr 10:11
9:4 Ne 8:7
....
9:6 Ge 1:1
9:7 Ge 11:31
9:8 Ge 15:6
9:10 Jer 32:20
9:11 Ps 78:13
9:12 Ex 13:21–22
9:13 Ex 20:1
9:14 Ge 2:3
9:15 Ex 17:6
9:17 Ps 78:11
9:19 Ne 9:12

Forgive Those Who Hurt You

You are a God ready to pardon, gracious and merciful, slow to anger, and abounding in kindness.

—Nehemiah 9:17

Whether we know it or not, unforgiveness is really a jail sentence. By harboring unforgiveness and withholding grace from those who have trespassed against us, we unknowingly lock a piece of our hearts away. It is a myth that we gain power by withholding forgiveness, although we may feel powerful when we decide to withhold forgiveness from someone. But that feeling of power fades fast, and we are left with nothing but bitterness and sorrow at the end of the day.

Forgiveness is just like that "get out of jail free" card we all covet when we play Monopoly. Unforgiveness keeps us behind bars, until one day we realize the key to the jail cell, unlike that Monopoly card, has been in our pocket all along. The key that unlocks the door to our cell is simply forgiveness. Some of us harbor things in our hearts for months, even years. Just the name of the person who hurt us brings a sting. If that's you, then I offer to you a heavenly key that will set you free.

We can never give to others what we have not experienced first ourselves. God has reached out and offered us forgiveness first—while we were still sinners—so that we would in turn have the power to forgive others. Sometimes our wounds run so deep that it must take God's power in us to truly forgive our enemies. In those cases, forgiving others is not only an act of the will but also a work of the Holy Spirit. It is amazing that the Lord always makes the first move in our lives. It is His Spirit that first draws us to Himself. God first loved us so that we may love Him back. He was also the first to forgive our trespasses so that we may have a will and way to forgive others.

Every gift the Father has given us He asks that we stand ready to give away as we see other people's need for it. This goes for spiritual gifts as well as material ones. There is always a chain reaction happening in the kingdom of God—God gives to us so that we may give to others. God's kingdom works so completely backward from our human systems that it requires us to develop a new mind-set that is free from religious customs and worldly principles.

We are challenged by Jesus to love those who are easy for us to love *and* those who seem impossible for us to love: "But I say to you who hear, love your enemies, do good to those who hate you, bless those who curse you, and pray for those who spitefully use you" (Lk 6:27–28). But we absolutely cannot love those whom we have not forgiven. We must first forgive and then make the great effort of loving those who have wronged us. Jesus told His disciples, "Freely you have received, freely give" (Mt 10:8), as He sent them out for the first time. He was reminding them of the spiritual gifts He had given them and asking them, in turn, to generously give these gifts to others. Forgiveness is a good gift to us from the Lord, and it is meant to be given away.

Jenny Swindall

Your great mercy did not forsake them in
the wilderness: The pillar of the cloud did
not depart from them by day, to lead them
in the way, nor the pillar of fire by night, to
light for them the way they should go. 20 You
gave Your good Spirit to instruct them, did
not withhold Your manna from their mouth,
and gave them water for their thirst. 21 Forty
years You sustained them in the wilderness,
so that they lacked nothing—their clothing
did not wear out nor did their feet swell.

22 "You gave them kingdoms and nations,
and You divided them as boundaries. They
possessed the land of Sihon, which was the
land of the king of Heshbon, and the land
of Og, the king of Bashan. 23 Their descen-
dants You increased like the stars of heaven,
and You brought them into the land, which
You had promised to their fathers that they
would enter and possess it. 24 So the descen-
dants went in and possessed the land, and
You subdued for them the inhabitants of the
land, the Canaanites, and gave them into
their hands—with their kings and the peo-
ples of the land—to do with them as they
would. 25 They captured unassailable cities
and a fertile land. They possessed houses
full of all goods, wells dug, vineyards, olive
groves, and fruit trees in abundance, so they
ate, were filled, and became fat, and they in-
dulged themselves in Your great goodness.

26 "Nevertheless they became disobedient,
and rebelled against You, and cast Your law
behind their backs, and killed Your prophets
who had warned them to turn back to You.
But they committed terrible provocations.
27 Therefore You delivered them into the
hand of their enemies, who afflicted them.
When they cried to You in the time of their
affliction, You heard from heaven, and, ac-
cording to Your abundant mercy, You gave
them deliverers who delivered them out of
the hand of their enemies.

28 "But after they had rest, they again did
evil before You. Therefore You abandoned
them to the hand of their enemies, so that
they had dominion over them. Yet when
they turned and cried to You, You heard
from heaven, and many times You delivered
them according to Your mercies.

29 "You warned them in order to restore
them again to Your law, but they acted
arrogantly and did not listen to Your com-
mandments. They sinned against Your ordi-
nances (which would enable a man to live,
if he would do them), stubbornly turning
away and becoming belligerent so that they
would not hear. 30 For many years You en-
dured them and warned them by Your Spirit

9:20 Nu 11:17
9:21 Dt 2:7
9:23 Ge 15:5
9:25 Dt 32:15
9:26 1Ki 14:9
9:29 Ne 9:16

....

9:31 Jer 4:27
9:32 2Ki 17:3
9:33 Ge 18:25
9:35 Dt 28:47
9:36 Dt 28:48
9:37 Dt 28:33
9:38 Ne 10:1
10:1 Ne 9:38

in Your prophets, yet they would not listen.
Therefore, You gave them into the hand of
the people of the lands. 31 Nevertheless,
for the sake of Your abundant mercy, You
did not completely destroy them or forsake
them. Indeed, You are a gracious and mer-
ciful God.

32 "Now therefore, our God, the great, the
mighty, and the awesome God, who keeps
covenant and mercy, let not all the hardship,
since the time of the kings of Assyria until
this day, that has come on us, our kings,
our princes, our priests, our prophets, our
fathers, and on all Your people seem in-
significant to You. 33 You are righteous for
everything that has come upon us! You
have acted faithfully while we have done
wickedly. 34 For our kings, princes, priests,
and fathers have failed to keep Your law and
did not obey Your commandments and Your
warnings even when You confronted them.
35 For whether in their kingdom or in Your
abundant goodness (that You gave them) or
in the spacious and fertile land (that You set
before them), they have neither served You
nor turned away from their wicked deeds.

36 "Here we are, slaves today. The land
that You gave to our fathers was for eating
its fruit and its goodness. Behold, we have
become slaves on account of it, 37 because
its abundant produce belongs to the kings
whom You have set over us due to our sins.
They have control over our bodies and over
our livestock, as they please. We are in great
distress."

Signatories to the Agreement

38 So on the basis of all this, we are executing
a written agreement that is being sealed by our
princes, Levites, and priests.

Signatories of the Covenant

10 Now *the names of* those on the sealed
agreement were:

Nehemiah, the magistrate, the son of
Hakaliah,
and Zedekiah. 2 Next were Seraiah, Azari-
ah, Jeremiah,
3 Pashhur, Amariah, Malkijah,
4 Hattush, Shebaniah, Malluk,
5 Harim, Meremoth, Obadiah,
6 Daniel, Ginnethon, Baruch,
7 Meshullam, Abijah, Mijamin,
8 Maaziah, Bilgai, and Shemaiah.
These were the priests.

9 The Levites were:

Jeshua the son of Azaniah, Binnui of the
sons of Henadad, and Kadmiel,
10 along with their relatives Shebaniah,

Hodiah, Kelita, Pelaiah, Hanan,
11 Mika, Rehob, Hashabiah,
12 Zakkur, Sherebiah, Shebaniah,
13 Hodiah, Bani, and Beninu.

14 The leaders of the people were:

Parosh, Pahath-Moab, Elam, Zattu, Bani,
15 Bunni, Azgad, Bebai,
16 Adonijah, Bigvai, Adin,
17 Ater, Hezekiah, Azzur,
18 Hodiah, Hashum, Bezai,
19 Hariph, Anathoth, Nebai,
20 Magpiash, Meshullam, Hezir,
21 Meshezabel, Zadok, Jaddua,
22 Pelatiah, Hanan, Anaiah,
23 Hoshea, Hananiah, Hasshub,
24 Hallohesh, Pilha, Shobek,
25 Rehum, Hashabnah, Maaseiah,
26 Ahiah, Hanan, Anan,
27 Malluk, Harim, and Baanah.

Summary of the Covenant

28 The remainder of the people, the priests,
the Levites, the gatekeepers, the singers, the
temple servants, and all those who on the
basis of the Law of God separated them-
selves from the people of the lands—their
wives, their sons, and their daughters, *that*
is, every one *capable of* knowledge *and* un-
derstanding— 29 have decisively joined in
with their countrymen and their nobles, and
obligated themselves—by both a curse and
an oath—to walk in the Law of God, which
was given by Moses the servant of God, and
to observe and do all the commandments
of the LORD who is our Lord, along with His
judgments and His statutes 30 so that we will
not give our daughters to the people of the
land nor take their daughters for our sons.

31 If the people of the land bring merchan-
dise or any grain on the Sabbath day to sell,
we will not buy from them on the Sabbath
or a holy day. We will also renounce the
seventh year *harvest* and the full payment
of every debt.

32 We also establish for ourselves the or-
dinance to collect from ourselves annually
one-third of a shekel for the service of the
house of our God: 33 for the showbread, the
continual grain offering, the continual burnt
offering, the Sabbaths, the New Moons, the
appointed feasts, the holy things, and the
sin offerings to make an atonement for Is-
rael, as well as for all the work of the house
of our God.

34 Also, we cast lots to determine *the duty*
of the supply of wood that the priests, the
Levites, and the people—according to the
houses of our fathers, *being* set by annually
appointed times—might bring to the house
of our God, in order to burn *it* on the altar of
the LORD our God, as it is written in the Law;
35 and, likewise, for the annual bringing of
the first fruits of our ground and the first
fruits of all fruit of all trees to the house of
the LORD; 36 and for bringing to the priests
who are ministering at the house of God, the
firstborn of our sons and livestock, as it is
written in the Law, plus the firstborn of our
herds and flocks.

37 Moreover, the first of our fresh dough,
our contributions, the fruit of every tree,
and the new wine and oil we will bring to
the priests at the chambers of the house of
our God, but the tithe of our crops *we will*
bring to the Levites, since they themselves
receive the tithes in all our agricultural cit-
ies. 38 There must be a priest, a descendant
of Aaron, with the Levites when they are
collecting tithes, and the Levites will offer
a tenth of the tithes to the house of our
God, for the chambers of the storehouse.
39 Both the children of Israel and the Levites
should bring the contribution of the grain,
new wine, and the fresh oil to the chambers
because the vessels of the sanctuary and the
ministering priests, the gatekeepers, and the
singers are there.

We resolve not to forsake the house of
our God.

The Residents of Jerusalem

1Ch 9:1–17

11 Now the rulers of the people lived at
Jerusalem, so the rest of the people
cast lots in order to bring one out of ten to
stay in Jerusalem, the holy city, while the oth-
er nine *remained* in *other* cities. 2 The people
blessed all the men who volunteered to dwell
in Jerusalem.

3 Now these are the leaders of the provinces
who lived in Jerusalem (though in the cities
of Judah every one lived on his own property
within their cities): Israel, the priests, the Lev-
ites, the temple servants, and the descendants
of Solomon's servants. 4 Some of the sons of
Judah and Benjamin lived in Jerusalem.

Those from Judah were:

Athaiah the son of Uzziah, the son of
Zechariah, the son of Amariah, the son
of Shephatiah, the son of Mahalalel—the
descendants of Perez, 5 and Maaseiah the
son of Baruch, the son of Kol-Hozeh, the
son of Hazaiah, the son of Adaiah, the
son of Joiarib, the son of Zechariah, the
son of Shelah. 6 All the descendants of
Perez who lived in Jerusalem were four
hundred and sixty-eight valiant men.

10:28 Ne 9:2
10:29 Ps 119:106
10:30 Ex 34:16
10:31 Ex 23:10–11
10:33 2Ch 2:4
10:34 Ne 13:31
10:35 Ex 23:19
10:36 Ex 13:2
10:37 Lev 23:17
11:1 Ne 11:18
11:2 Jdg 5:9
11:3 Ezr 2:43

7 These are the sons of Benjamin:

Sallu the son of Meshullam, the son of
Joed, the son of Pedaiah, the son of
Kolaiah, the son of Maaseiah, the son of
Ithiel, the son of Jeshaiah, 8 and after him
Gabbai and Sallai, *totaling* nine hundred
and twenty-eight. 9 Joel, the son of Zikri,
was their overseer, and Judah the son
of Hassenuah was second *to him* over
the city.

10 Of the priests there were:

Jedaiah the son of Joiarib and Jakin;
11 Seraiah the son of Hilkiah, the son of
Meshullam, the son of Zadok, the son of
Meraioth, the son of Ahitub, was a ruler
of the house of God. 12 Their relatives
performing the work of the house were
eight hundred and twenty-two. There
was also Adaiah the son of Jeroham,
the son of Pelaliah, the son of Amzi, the
son of Zechariah, the son of Pashhur,
the son of Malkijah, 13 plus his relatives
who were chiefs of the fathers' houses
were two hundred and forty-two; and
Amashsai the son of Azarel, the son of
Ahzai, the son of Meshillemoth, the son
of Immer, 14 and their brothers, mighty
men of valor, were one hundred and
twenty-eight. Their overseer was Zabdiel,
the son of Haggedolim.

15 From the Levites there were:

Shemaiah the son of Hasshub, the son
of Azrikam, the son of Hashabiah, the
son of Bunni; 16 plus Shabbethai and
Jozabad, who as leaders of the Levites
had oversight of the outside work of the
house of God. 17 Mattaniah the son of
Mika, the son of Zabdi, the son of Asaph,
was the first to begin the thanksgiving
at prayer, Bakbukiah was the second out
of his relatives, and then Abda the son
of Shammua, the son of Galal, the son
of Jeduthun. 18 All the Levites in the holy
city were two hundred and eighty-four.

19 Moreover, the gatekeepers,
Akkub, Talmon, and their relatives who
kept watch at the gates, were one hun-
dred and seventy-two.

20 The rest of Israel, the priests, and the Le-
vites were in all the cities of Judah, every one
tending to his own inheritance.
21 But the temple servants lived in Ophel, and
Ziha and Gishpa were over them.

22 The overseer of the Levites in Jerusalem
was Uzzi the son of Bani, the son of Hasha-
biah, the son of Mattaniah, the son of Mika.
Some of the sons of Asaph were the singers
attending to the work of the house of God,
23 for the king's regulation about them made
their unity a daily issue.
24 Pethahiah the son of Meshezabel, of the
sons of Zerah the son of Judah, was the king's
assistant[1] in all matters concerning the people.

The Residents Outside Jerusalem

25 For the villages *located* by their fields, some
of the people of Judah lived at Kiriath Arba
and its villages, *others* at Dibon and its villag-
es, or at Jekabzeel and its villages, 26 as well
as at Jeshua, at Moladah, and at Beth Pelet,
27 and at Hazar Shual, and at Beersheba and
its villages, 28 and at Ziklag, at Mekonah and
its villages, 29 and at En Rimmon, at Zorah, at
Jarmuth, 30 Zanoah, Adullam and their villages,
at Lachish and its fields, and at Azekah and its
villages. So they lived from Beersheba as far
as the Valley of Hinnom.
31 Some of the Benjamites settled from Geba
onward, at Mikmash, Aija, and Bethel and their
villages, 32 at Anathoth, Nob, Ananiah, 33 Hazor,
Ramah, Gittaim, 34 Hadid, Zeboim, Neballat,
35 Lod, and Ono, the valley of craftsmen.
36 From the Levites, some divisions in Judah
belonged to Benjamin.

The Priests and Levites

12 Now these are the priests and the Le-
vites who came up with Zerubbabel the
son of Shealtiel, and Joshua:
Seraiah, Jeremiah, Ezra,
2 Amariah, Malluk, Hattush,
3 Shekaniah, Rehum, Meremoth,
4 Iddo, Ginnethon, Abijah,
5 Mijamin, Moadiah, Bilgah,
6 Shemaiah, and Joiarib, Jedaiah,
7 Sallu, Amok, Hilkiah, Jedaiah.
These were the leaders of the priests and of
their relatives in the days of Joshua.
8 Moreover the Levites were Jeshua, Binnui,
Kadmiel, Sherebiah, Judah, and Mattaniah,
who was over the thanksgiving *songs*, in con-
junction with his relatives. 9 There were also
their relatives Bakbukiah and Unni, positioned
across from each other in the watches.
10 Joshua was the father of Joiakim, Joiakim
was the father of Eliashib, Eliashib was the fa-
ther of Joiada, 11 Joiada was the father of Jona-
than, and Jonathan was the father of Jaddua.
12 Now in the days of Joiakim, the priests,
these were the heads of the fathers' houses:
of Seraiah, Meraiah;
of Jeremiah, Hananiah;
13 of Ezra, Meshullam;

11:18 Ne 11:1
11:21 Ne 3:26
11:22 Ne 12:42
11:24 Ge 38:30
11:25 Jos 14:15
11:35 1Ch 8:12
12:1 Ezr 2:1–2
12:8 Ne 11:17

[1] 24 Lit. *at the king's hand.*

SPIRIT-TO-SPIRIT PRAYER

DECLARATION OF FAITH

I recognize that my real enemy is Satan, and he is already a defeated foe. Thank You, Father, for the blood of Jesus has redeemed me from every curse and stronghold of the enemy. I take my position in Christ Jesus, where no plan or strategy of Satan can enter to steal, kill, or destroy. I put on the whole armor of God, defeating every evil and foul spirit of hell. I have dominion over all the power of the enemy, and nothing shall hurt me. Thank You, Father, for this great promise. In the name of Jesus, amen.

Iris Delgado

of Amariah, Jehohanan;
14 of Malluk, Jonathan;
of Shebaniah, Joseph;
15 of Harim, Adna;
of Meraioth, Helkai;
16 of Iddo, Zechariah;
of Ginnethon, Meshullam;
17 of Abijah, Zikri;
of Miniamin and of Moadiah, Piltai;
18 of Bilgah, Shammua;
of Shemaiah, Jehonathan;
19 of Joiarib, Mattenai;
of Jedaiah, Uzzi;
20 of Sallu, Kallai;
of Amok, Eber;
21 of Hilkiah, Hashabiah;
and of Jedaiah, Nethanel.
22 The Levites, as well as the priests, were
recorded as the chiefs of the fathers' houses
in the days of Eliashib, Joiada, Johanan, and
Jaddua during the reign of Darius the Persian.
23 The descendants of Levi who *served* as the
chiefs of the fathers' house were recorded in
the book of the chronicles until the days of
Johanan the son of Eliashib. 24 The leaders of
the Levites were Hashabiah, Sherebiah, and
Jeshua the son of Kadmiel, with their brothers
across from them, to praise and to give thanks,
section opposite section, according to the commandment of David the man of God.
25 Mattaniah, Bakbukiah, Obadiah, Meshullam, Talmon, and Akkub were gatekeepers
maintaining the guard duty at the storehouse
of the gates. 26 These *leaders* served during
the days of Joiakim the son of Joshua, the
son of Jozadak, during the days of Nehemiah
the governor, and *during the days* of Ezra the
priest, the scribe.

12:26 Ne 8:9

12:27 1Ch 15:16
12:28 1Ch 9:16
12:31 Ne 2:13
12:36 Ne 12:24
12:37 Ne 2:14
12:38 Ne 3:8

Nehemiah Dedicates the City Wall

27 At the dedication of the wall of Jerusalem
they sought to bring the Levites from all their
places to Jerusalem to celebrate the dedication
appropriately with thanksgiving songs and
singing, accompanied by cymbals, harps, and
lyres. 28 The members of choirs had assembled
from the regions all around Jerusalem, from
the villages of the Netophathites, 29 from Beth
Gilgal, and from fields of Geba and Azmaveth,
because they had built villages for themselves
all around Jerusalem. 30 Then the priests and
the Levites purified themselves. They also purified the people, the gates, and the wall.
31 Then I led the commanders of Judah up
to the top of the wall and appointed two great
thanksgiving choirs. The first choir proceeded
to the right on the wall toward the Dung Gate.
32 Behind them followed Hoshaiah, and half of
the princes of Judah, 33 with Azariah, Ezra, and
Meshullam, 34 Judah, Benjamin, Shemaiah,
Jeremiah, 35 and some of the priests with trumpets—Zechariah, the son of Jonathan, the son
of Shemaiah, the son of Mattaniah, the son of
Micaiah, the son of Zakkur, the son of Asaph,
36 in conjunction with his relatives—Shemaiah, Azarel, Milalai, Gilalai, Maai, Nethanel,
Judah, and Hanani, being accompanied with
the musical instruments of David the man of
God. Ezra the scribe went before them. 37 At
the Fountain Gate, directly across from them,
they ascended the steps of the City of David,
following that sloped section of the wall up
to the house of David, then eastward to the
Water Gate.
38 The second thanksgiving choir proceeded
to the left where I followed them with the other
half of the people on top of the wall, from
the Tower of the Furnaces to the Broad Wall,

39 then from above the Ephraim Gate past the
Old Gate, the Fish Gate, the Tower of Hananel,
and the Tower of the Hundred, as far as the
Sheep Gate, but they stood *still* at the Gate of
the Guard.
40 So the two thanksgiving choirs stood in
the house of God, as did I and the half of the
officials with me, 41 and the priests, Eliakim,
Maaseiah, Miniamin, Micaiah, Elioenai, Zech-
ariah, and Hananiah, with trumpets, 42 and
Maaseiah, Shemaiah, Eleazar, Uzzi, Jehohan-
an, Malkijah, Elam, and Ezer. The singers sang
loudly. Jezrahiah was their director. 43 On that
day they offered great sacrifices and rejoiced
because God had given them great cause for
rejoicing. The wives and the children rejoiced,
too. From far away the joyful celebration of
Jerusalem was heard.

Temple Responsibilities

44 At that time men were appointed to gov-
ern over the chambers for the treasures, for
the contributions, for the first fruits, and for
the tithes, so that they might gather into them
out of the fields of the cities the legal portions
belonging to the priests and Levites. This was
because the celebration of Judah survived on
the basis of the priests and the Levites 45 who,
accompanied by the singers and the gate-
keepers, attentively preserved the practices
of their God and the practices of purification,
according to the commandment of David and
of his son Solomon. 46 For in the former days
of David and Asaph there were leaders for the
singers, the songs of praise, and thanksgivings
to God. 47 All Israel in the days of Zerubba-
bel and Nehemiah gave the singers and the
gatekeepers *their* portions, as specified daily.
Likewise, they consecrated what was due to
the Levites, who then consecrated what was
due to the descendants of Aaron.

The Reforms of Nehemiah

13 On that day they read aloud from the
Book of Moses in the hearing of the
people. In it there was found written that no
Ammonite or Moabite should ever enter the
congregation of God, 2 because they did not
meet the children of Israel with bread and
water, but hired Balaam to curse them. How-
ever, our God turned the curse into a blessing.
3 When they heard the Law, they separated
from Israel all the racially mixed.

I break every curse Balaam hired
against my life, in the name of Jesus
(Ne 13:2).

12:39 Ne 3:1
12:44 Ne 13:12–13
12:46 2Ch 29:30
13:1 Dt 23:3–5
13:2 Dt 23:5
13:3 Ne 9:2

....

13:4 Ne 12:44
13:6 Ne 5:14
13:7 Ne 13:5
13:9 2Ch 29:5
13:11 Ne 10:39
13:12 Ne 10:37–39
13:13 Ne 7:2
13:14 Ne 5:19
13:15 Ne 10:31

4 Before this, Eliashib the priest, who had
been appointed to govern the chambers of
the house of our God, was related to Tobiah.
5 So, he had prepared a great chamber hall for
him, where previously they had stored the con-
tributions, the frankincense, the vessels, and
the tithes of grain, new wine, and fresh oil, as
required, for the Levites, the singers, the gate-
keepers, and the contribution for the priests.
6 But during this time I was not in Jerusalem,
since in the thirty-second year of King Artax-
erxes of Babylon I had gone to the king. At the
conclusion of those days I requested a leave
of the king. 7 When I came to Jerusalem and
understood the evil that Eliashib did for Tobiah
by preparing him a chamber in the courts of
the house of God, 8 I was very grieved. So, from
the chamber I threw all of the household be-
longings of Tobiah outside. 9 Then I command-
ed, and they cleansed the chambers so that I
could return there the vessels of the house of
God, the contributions for the offerings, and
the frankincense.
10 When I perceived that the supplies for the
Levites had not been given and that the Le-
vites and the singers doing the work had fled,
everyone to his own field, 11 I confronted the
officials and asked, "Why is the house of God
forsaken?" So I gathered them and stationed
them at their posts.
12 Then all Judah brought the tithe of the
grain, the new wine, and the fresh oil to the
storehouses. 13 Overseeing the replenishing
of the storehouse, I appointed Shelemiah the
priest, Zadok the scribe, and Pedaiah from the
Levites, and to assist them Hanan the son of
Zakkur, the son of Mattaniah, for they were
considered reliable, and their task was to dis-
tribute to their relatives.
14 Remember me, O my God, concerning this.
Do not blot out my good deeds that I have
done for the house of my God and its work-
ings.

Lord, turn every curse spoken
against my life into a blessing
(Ne 13:2).

15 In those days I saw in Judah some treading
winepresses on the Sabbath or hauling loads
of grain or loading donkeys with wine, grapes,
figs, and all manner of burdens in order to
bring them to Jerusalem on the Sabbath day.
So, during the day while they were selling the
food goods, I warned them. 16 Men of Tyre
also stayed there, having hauled in fish and
all kinds of merchandise, and sold them on

the Sabbath to the people of Judah, and in
Jerusalem. 17 Then I confronted the nobles of
Judah and asked them, "What is this evil thing
that you are doing, profaning the Sabbath day?
18 Did not your fathers do likewise? Did not our
God bring all this evil against us and against
this city? Will you yet bring more wrath upon
Israel by profaning the Sabbath?"

19 As the gates of Jerusalem began to cast the
evening shadow before the Sabbath, I commanded that the gates should be shut, and
charged that they should not be opened until
after the Sabbath. Some of my servants I stationed at the gates so that there would be no
loads brought in on the Sabbath day. 20 Once
or twice the merchants and sellers of all kind
of merchandise lodged outside Jerusalem.
21 So I warned them and said to them, "Why
do you spend the night next to the wall? If you
do so again, I will send you away by force."
From that time on they stopped coming on
the Sabbath. 22 Then I commanded the Levites
to purify themselves so that they could come
and, as guardians of the gates, sanctify the
Sabbath day.

Remember me, O my God, concerning this
also, and spare me according to Your abundant mercy.

23 Moreover, in those days I also saw Jews
who had married the women of Ashdod, Ammon, and Moab. 24 Half of their children spoke
in the language of Ashdod, yet none of them
could recognize the language of the Jews.
This was true language by language. 25 So I
confronted them and cursed them. Some of
the men I beat. Others, I plucked out their
hair. Also, I made them swear an oath by God
and said to them, "You shall neither give your
daughters to their sons, nor marry their daughters to your sons or to yourselves. 26 Did not
Solomon king of Israel sin by these things?
Yet among many nations there was no king
like him. He was loved by his God, who made
him king over all Israel. Nevertheless, foreign
women caused even him to sin. 27 Should we
then listen to you, the ones doing all this great
evil, who are behaving unfaithfully against our
God by bedding foreign women?"

28 Also, one of the sons of Joiada, the son of
Eliashib the high priest, was a son-in-law to
Sanballat the Horonite, so I drove him away
from me.

29 Remember them, O my God, because they
have defiled the priesthood and the covenant
of the priesthood and the Levites.

30 Thus I purified them from everything foreign and appointed work crews for the priests
and the Levites, each to his task, 31 and I provided the wood offering, at the appointed
times, and the first fruits.

Remember me, O my God, for good.

13:17 Ne 13:11
13:18 Jer 17:21–23
13:22 Ne 12:30
13:23 Ne 10:30

13:25 Ezr 10:5
13:26 1Ki 3:13
13:27 Ezr 10:2
13:28 Ne 2:19
13:29 Ne 6:14
13:30 Ne 10:30
13:31 Ne 10:34

Author: Unknown

Written: Between 460 and 350 BC

Theme: Providential Care and Preservation of God's People

ESTHER

Dear Spirit Led Woman,

When you think of Esther, it's likely that being chosen by God "for such a time as this" comes to mind. But Esther was more than a pretty face! There were important things she had to do in order for God's plan to be accomplished through her.

First, Esther had to spend time—a whole year of her life—in preparation. Have you been wishing God would use you without being willing to go through a time of preparation? You can't cut corners in a season of preparation. The Holy Spirit is always at work, even when it looks like nothing is happening.

Esther also had to be willing to obey the advice of Mordecai. Do you seek the advice of those who hear from God? Even more important, do you obey it?

Next, Esther understood the importance of fasting and prayer. Do you fast and pray? Do you acknowledge the impact these spiritual steps can have on the world we live in?

Lastly, Esther had to have the courage to risk her life by standing for right. There are times when taking a stand for what is right may mean risking ridicule or even worse as our culture becomes less and less tolerant of those who speak the truth of God's Word. Don't back down. Instead, follow the example of Esther. Spend time in preparation. Listen to godly advice. Fast and pray for God's direction. And then be fearless in doing whatever He tells you to do!

Joy F. Strang

Queen Vashti Deposed

1 Now in the days of Ahasuerus, *also called*
Xerxes, who reigned from India to Ethiopia,
over one hundred and twenty-seven provinces,
2 in those days, the palace where King Aha-
suerus sat on the royal throne of his kingdom
was in Susa. 3 In the third year of his reign,
he prepared a feast for all his officials and his
servants. So the army commanders of Persia
and Media, the nobles, and the officials of the
provinces were before him.
4 He unveiled the riches of his glorious king-
dom and the costly luxury of his greatness
for many days, one hundred and eighty days.
5 When these days were completed, the king
prepared a seven-day feast for all the people
present, from the greatest to the least, in the
citadel of Susa. This feast was in the courtyard
garden of the king's palace 6 where white and
blue linen hangings were fastened with cords
of white and purple linen to silver rings and
columns of marble. The gold- and silver-*plat-*
ed couches were on a mosaic pavement of
porphyry, marble, mother-of-pearl, and *other*
costly stones. 7 They provided drinks in golden
vessels (the vessels being diverse one from an-
other) and royal wine in abundance, by the ex-
pense of the king. 8 In accordance with the law,
the drinking was not mandatory, because the
king had directed all the stewards of his house
to serve according to every man's pleasure.
9 Additionally, Vashti the queen prepared a
feast for the women in the royal house of King
Ahasuerus.
10 On the seventh day, when the heart of the
king was merry with wine, he commanded
Mehuman, Biztha, Harbona, Bigtha, Abagtha,
Zethar, and Karkas, the seven eunuchs attend-
ing to the needs of King Ahasuerus, 11 to bring
Queen Vashti before the king with the royal
crown, to unveil her beauty to the people and
the officials, for she was beautiful. 12 But Queen
Vashti refused to come at the king's command
delivered by his eunuchs. Therefore, the king
grew very angry, and his wrath burned within
him.
13 Then the king spoke to the wise men, who
understood the times (for in this way the king
would speak before all who understood law
and judgment). 14 Those nearest him were
Karshena, Shethar, Admatha, Tarshish, Meres,
Marsena, and Memukan. *They were* the seven
princes of Persia and Media and the king's
closest confidants who met with the king and
held the highest rank in the kingdom.
15 "According to law, what should be done
about Queen Vashti because she did not obey
the command of King Ahasuerus *when it was*
delivered by the eunuchs?"

1:1 Est 8:9
1:2 Ne 1:1
1:3 Est 2:18
1:6 Eze 23:41
1:10 Jdg 16:25
1:13 1Ch 12:32
1:14 2Ki 25:19

1:19 Est 8:8
1:20 Col 3:18
1:22 Est 3:12
2:6 2Ki 24:14–15
2:7 Est 2:15

16 And Memukan answered before the king
and the princes, "Queen Vashti has wronged
not only the king but also all the princes and
all the people who are in all the provinces of
King Ahasuerus. 17 For should this matter of
the queen spread to all wives, then they would
look with contempt on their husbands when it
is reported that, 'King Ahasuerus commanded
Queen Vashti to be brought before him, but
she never came.' 18 This very day the noble
ladies of Persia and Media, who hear of the
queen's act, will say the same thing to all the
king's princes. Then there will be more con-
tempt and wrath.
19 "If it pleases the king, let a royal decree
be sent by him, and let it be written in the
laws of the Persians and the Medes, that it
may not be altered, that Vashti can never enter
into the presence of King Ahasuerus, and that
the king will give her royal position to another
woman who is better than she. 20 When the
king's decree that he shall make is proclaimed
throughout all his empire (for it is vast), then all
the wives shall give honor to their husbands,
both the prominent and lowly."
21 The suggestion pleased the king and the
princes, so the king did according to the word
of Memukan. 22 He sent letters to all the king's
provinces, in the script of every province and
in the language of every people group, bearing
the message in the languages of his people
that each man should rule over his own house.

Esther Becomes Queen

2 After these things, as the rage of King
Ahasuerus abated, he became mindful of
Vashti, what she had done and what was de-
creed against her. 2 So the king's servants who
attended him said, "Let beautiful young virgins
be sought for the king! 3 Let the king appoint
officers in all the provinces of his kingdom so
that they may gather all the beautiful young
virgins to the citadel of Susa, to the harem un-
der the custody of Hegai the king's eunuch,
who is in charge of the harem, and let oint-
ments and cosmetics be given to them. 4 May
the young woman who pleases the king be
queen instead of Vashti." And the idea pleased
the king, so he acted accordingly.
5 Now in the citadel of Susa, there was a cer-
tain Jew named Mordecai, the son of Jair, the
son of Shimei, the son of Kish, a Benjamite.
6 He had been taken away from Jerusalem
among the exiles and carried into captivity
along with King Jeconiah of Judah by King
Nebuchadnezzar of Babylon. 7 He was the
guardian of Hadassah, that is Esther (who was
his uncle's daughter) because she had neither
father nor mother. The young woman was

SPIRITLED WOMAN

COUNSEL FROM THE SPIRIT BASICS

Human Nature Redeemed

In the story of Esther, Queen Vashti represents the *independent, rebellious* spirit that refuses to obey or to cooperate with the king. She must be put away so that Esther, the submissive, born-again spirit, can come to the palace. Mordecai typifies the *Holy Spirit,* whose rulership always brings peace and prosperity to the kingdom. Haman represents the *flesh,* or the natural nature. Haman has great influence with the king, or soul, and always rivals the Holy Spirit for honor, demanding preeminence. Haman does not tolerate Mordecai, whom he hates. Because of his hatred he decides to rid the earth of Mordecai and all Jews, including Queen Esther. The intensity of Haman's hatred and conflict allows no hope for coexistence.

This conflict accurately describes the reality of the struggle of every SpiritLed woman. Our natural life wars against the life of the Spirit of God within us. Paul wrote to the Galatians, "For the flesh lusts against the Spirit, and the Spirit against the flesh. These are in opposition to one another" (Gal 5:17). Paul explained to the Romans, "For those who live according to the flesh set their minds on the things of the flesh, but those who live according to the Spirit, the things of the Spirit. To be carnally minded is death, but to be spiritually minded is life and peace" (Ro 8:5–6). We can rejoice in the deliverance of Esther from Haman, expecting to see the same victory in our personal lives as we yield to the work of the Holy Spirit.

Fuchsia Pickett

lovely to look at and beautiful in form. When
her father and mother died, Mordecai took her
as his own daughter.
8 When the king's notice and his decree were
heard, many young women were then gathered to the citadel of Susa and *placed* under
the custody of Hegai. Esther was likewise
brought to the king's house and *placed* under
the custody of Hegai, who was in charge of
the harem. 9 Because the young lady appeared
pleasing to him and had gained favor in his sight, he quickly gave her the ointments and cosmetics, her allotted food, and seven young chosen women from the king's palace. He also transferred her and her young women to the best place of the harem.
10 Esther had not disclosed her people or
her lineage because Mordecai had charged
her not to disclose it. 11 Every day Mordecai
walked around the courtyard of the harem to find out how Esther fared and what might be done with her.
12 The turn came for each young woman to
go in to King Ahasuerus, after being twelve months under the regulations for the women, since this was the regular period of their beautifying, six months with oil of myrrh and six months with spices and ointments for
women. 13 When the young woman went in to
the king in this way, she was given whatever she desired to take with her from the harem
to take to the king's palace. 14 In the evening
she went in, and in the morning she returned to the second harem in custody of Shaashgaz, the king's eunuch, who was in charge of the concubines. She did not go in to the king again unless the king delighted in her and called for her by name.
15 When the turn came for Esther, the daughter of Abihail the uncle of Mordecai, who had taken her as his own daughter, to go in to the king, she asked for nothing except what the king's eunuch Hegai, who had charge of the women, advised. Now Esther obtained
favor in the sight of all who saw her. 16 So Es-
ther was taken to King Ahasuerus at his royal house in the month of Tebeth, which is the tenth month, in the seventh year of his reign.
17 The king loved Esther more than any other woman because she had gained grace and favor in his sight more than all the virgins. So he set the royal crown on her head and made
her queen instead of Vashti. 18 The king held
a great feast for all his officials and servants. It was a feast for Esther. He remitted his provinces from tax payments and gave gifts according to his royal generosity.

Mordecai Uncovers a Plot

19 At the second gathering of the virgins, Mor-
decai was sitting at the king's gate. 20 Esther
had not yet disclosed her lineage or her people, since Mordecai had so commanded her. Esther followed the command of Mordecai just as she had when under his protection.
21 During those days when Mordecai was
sitting at the king's gate, two of the king's

2:8 Est 2:3
2:9 Est 2:3
2:10 Est 2:20
2:19 Est 2:21
2:21 Est 6:2

eunuchs, Bigthan and Teresh, who served as
keepers of the door, became angry and sought
to attack King Ahasuerus. 22 But the matter be-
came known to Mordecai, and he reported it
to Queen Esther, and Esther reported it to the
king in the name of Mordecai. 23 When the
matter was investigated and confirmed, both
men were hanged on the gallows, and it was
written in the book of the chronicles in the
presence of the king.

Haman Plots to Destroy the Jews

3 After these things King Ahasuerus praised
Haman the son of Hammedatha the Agag-
ite, and promoted him, and set his seat above
all the officials who were with him. 2 All the
king's servants, when they were at the king's
gate, bowed or paid homage to Haman since
the king had commanded it. Mordecai, how-
ever, never bowed or paid homage.
3 So the king's servants tending the king's
gate said to Mordecai, "Why are you trans-
gressing the king's commandment?" 4 Though
they spoke to him daily, he never listened to
them, so they reported it to Haman to see if the
words of Mordecai would stand, for Mordecai
had told them that he was a Jew.
5 When Haman saw that Mordecai neither
bowed nor paid him homage, he was filled
with rage. 6 But he disdained to lay hands on
only Mordecai, since they had told him of the
people of Mordecai. So Haman sought to de-
stroy all the Jews throughout the whole king-
dom of Ahasuerus.
7 In the first month, which is the month Ni-
san, in the twelfth year of King Ahasuerus,
they cast Pur (that is, cast lots) before Haman
daily, and each month, until the twelfth month,
which is the month Adar, *to determine the time*.
8 Then Haman said to King Ahasuerus,
"There exists a scattered people dispersed
among the *other* peoples in all the provinc-
es of your kingdom. Their laws are different
from all others, and they are not complying
with the king's laws, so there may not be a
suitable reason for the king to allow them to
exist. 9 If it pleases the king, may it be written
that they are to be destroyed, and may there be
ten thousand talents[1] of silver deposited into
the king's treasuries so that I may distribute it
to the hands of those doing the work."
10 The king took his signet ring from his hand
and gave it to Haman, the son of Hammedatha
the Agagite, the enemy of the Jews. 11 The king
said to Haman, "The silver has been granted
to you, as have the people, so do with each as
it pleases you."
12 Then the king's scribes were summoned
on the thirteenth day of the first month, and
a decree was written just as Haman had com-
manded to the king's satraps and to the gov-
ernors over each province and to the officials
of all peoples and to every province according
to its own script, and to every people in their
language. It was written in the name of King
Ahasuerus and sealed with the king's signet
ring. 13 The letters were sent by mounted cou-
riers into all the king's provinces to cause the
destruction, slaughter, and annihilation of all
Jews, both young and old, little children and
women, in one day, the thirteenth day of the
twelfth month, which is the month Adar, and
even to plunder their possessions. 14 A copy of
the document, issued as law in every province,
was proclaimed, calling for all people to be
ready for the day.
15 The couriers went out, being hastened by
the king's command. At the citadel of Susa,
when the decree was issued, the king and
Haman sat down to drink, but the city of Susa
was in uproar.

Esther Helps the Jews

4 When Mordecai learned all that had been
done, he tore his clothes and put on sack-
cloth with ashes, and went out into the midst
of the city, and cried with a loud and bitter cry.
2 He went as far as the king's gate because no
one was allowed to enter into the king's gate
clothed with sackcloth. 3 In each and every
province where the king's command and his
decree came there was great mourning among
the Jews, and fasting, and weeping, and wail-
ing. Many lay in sackcloth and ashes.
4 So the young women of Esther and her eu-
nuchs came and told her of it. The queen was
then seized by anguish. She sent garments to
clothe Mordecai so that he could remove his
sackcloth, but he would not accept them. 5 So
Esther summoned Hathak, one of the king's
eunuchs appointed to attend her, and com-
manded him concerning Mordecai to learn
what this was about and why.
6 So Hathak went out to where Mordecai was
in the area of the city in front of the king's
gate. 7 Mordecai told him about all that had
happened to him and about the sum of sil-
ver that Haman had promised to pay to the
king's treasuries for the destruction of the
Jews. 8 Mordecai also gave him a copy of the
written decree issued in Susa concerning their
destruction so he could show Esther, tell her
about it, and then charge her to go to the king
in order to gain him favor with the king and
to make requests in the presence of the king
for her people.

3:1 Est 5:11
3:3 Est 3:2
3:5 Est 5:9
3:6 Ps 83:4
3:7 Ezr 6:15
3:8 Ac 16:20–21
3:10 Ge 41:42
3:12 1Ki 21:8
3:13 2Ch 30:6
3:14 Est 8:13–14
3:15 Est 8:15

[1] *9* About 375 tons, or 340 metric tons.

God Has Extended His Scepter to You

When Esther finally made her entry before King Ahasuerus, her preparation was not in vain. The king extended his scepter to her and honored her request for him to come and dine with her. Esther set a lavish table before her king and was glad to converse with him, showing no hint that she needed to rush through things so she could get to something else or that she was concerned with doing anything other than being in his presence. When he asked her for her petition at the end of their time together, she invited him to another evening with her. It was spending time with him that she wanted to show was important, not just getting an answer to whatever her petition was.

When Esther did finally present her petition, the king not only granted it once, but twice, extending the right to the Jewish people to arm themselves, defend themselves, and then make a spoil of their enemies, making sure it would be a long time before they were challenged again.

The life of prayer is a life of standing for and with others, just as Jesus is doing at this very minute. We focus on empowering others and seeing God's kingdom established in their lives. We reach out with the power and wisdom of God to lift people out of the traps evil has set for them and to find satisfaction and fulfillment in the presence of God. This is the life of seeing God's justice roll down, changing the hearts of the abusers and healing the abused.

Do not let it be said of our generation that when God looked for someone to stand in the gap for an issue, He could find no one willing do it. All those who say they belong to Christ should be willing to stand in that place—and need to do so regularly. God Himself issued the invitation in Jeremiah 33:3: "Call to Me, and I will answer you, and show you great and mighty things which you did not know."

Oh, there is so much to accomplish, but there are also so many resources available to us if we would trust God to reveal them to us! Pursue Him in prayer, and lift up the nations to Him that His will might be done in them just as they are in heaven. Justice always begins with a people who will stand for justice and not be denied. Enter before our King and demand His justice be realized.

The world, after all, is waiting for the sons and daughters of God to manifest. May we be that people for a world that still so needs our Savior.

Cindy Trimm

9 Hathak returned and told Esther the words
of Mordecai. 10 Again Esther spoke to Hathak
and ordered him *to reply* to Mordecai: 11 "All
the king's servants and the people of the king's
provinces know that whoever, whether man or
woman, wishes to come to the king at the in-
ner court but has not been summoned, there is
one law—to put him to death—unless for some
reason the king should hold out the golden
scepter so that he might live. I, however, have
not been summoned to come to the king for
these thirty days."

12 So all the words of Esther were told to Mor-
decai. 13 Then Mordecai told them to reply to
Esther, "Do not think that in the king's palace
you will be more likely to escape than all the
other Jews. 14 For if you remain silent at this
time, protection and deliverance for the Jews
will be ordained from some other place, but
you and your father's house shall be destroyed.
And who knows if you may have attained royal
position for such a time as this?"

15 Then Esther replied, sending back to Mor-
decai: 16 "Go, gather all the Jews who can be
found in Susa, then fast for me. Stop eating
and drinking for three days, night or day. I
and my young women will fast likewise. Only
then would I dare go to the king since it is not
allowed by law, and if I perish, I perish."

17 So Mordecai went away and did exactly as
Esther had commanded him.

Queen Esther's Banquet

5 On the third day, Esther put on her roy-
al apparel and positioned herself in the
king's palace courtyard so that she would be
directly in line with the *part of* the king's throne
room where the king sat facing the entrance
of the room on his royal throne in the royal
hall. 2 When the king saw Queen Esther stand-
ing quietly out in the courtyard, she gained
favor in his sight, so the king held out the
golden scepter in his hand to Esther. Esther
approached and touched the top of the scepter.

3 And the king said to her, "Queen Esther,
what do you want? What is your request? Even
if it is up to half of the kingdom, it will be
given to you."

4 Esther answered, "If it pleases the king, let
the king and Haman come today to a feast that
I have prepared for him."

5 Then the king said, "Quickly bring Haman
so that we may accept the invitation of Esther."

So the king and Haman came to the ban-
quet that Esther had prepared. 6 While drinking
wine the king said to Esther, "For whatever you
ask, it shall be granted you. So, what is your
request? Even if it is for as much as half of the
kingdom, it shall be done."

4:11 Est 5:1–2
4:16 Ge 43:14
5:1 Est 4:16
5:2 Est 4:11
5:3 Est 7:2
5:4 Est 5:8
5:6 Est 7:2

5:9 Est 3:5
5:10 Est 6:13
5:11 Est 9:7–10
5:14 Est 6:4
6:1 Est 2:23
6:4 Est 4:11

7 Then Esther replied and said, "This is my
petition and request. 8 If I have won the king's
favor, and if it pleases the king to grant my
petition and fulfill my request, then let the king
and Haman come to the banquet that I will
prepare for them, and tomorrow I will do what
the king says."

Haman's Plan to Destroy Mordecai

9 Haman left that day joyfully and with a glad
heart, but when Haman saw Mordecai at the
king's gate, that he neither stood up nor trem-
bled because of him, then Haman was full of
indignation against Mordecai. 10 Nevertheless,
Haman restrained himself, and when he came
to his home, he sent for his friends and for his
wife Zeresh.

11 Haman recounted to them the glory of
his riches, his many children, and everything
about him the king had praised, and how he
had promoted him over the princes and ser-
vants of the king. 12 Then Haman continued,
"Indeed, Queen Esther brought to the banquet
she had prepared no one but the king and me,
and tomorrow I am again invited by her with
the king. 13 Yet for all this, I am not satisfied
whenever I see Mordecai the Jew sitting at the
king's gate."

14 Then his wife Zeresh and all his friends
suggested to him, "Let a gallows fifty cubits[1]
tall be constructed, and in the morning ask the
king if Mordecai can be hanged on it. Then
go merrily with the king to the banquet." And
the suggestion pleased Haman, so he had the
gallows constructed.

The King Honors Mordecai

6 During that night the king could not sleep,
so he ordered that the book of memorable
acts (the chronicles) be brought, and they were
read before the king. 2 It was found written
that Mordecai had informed on Bigthana and
Teresh, the two eunuchs of the king *serving
as* the keepers of the door, who had sought to
assault King Ahasuerus.

3 So the king said, "What honor or dignity has
been done for Mordecai as a result of this?"

Then the king's servants attending him said,
"Nothing has been done for him."

4 So the king said, "Who is out in the court-
yard?" Now Haman had just then entered from
across the palace courtyard in order to speak
to the king about hanging Mordecai on the
gallows that he had prepared for him.

5 The king's attendants said to him, "Haman
is waiting in the court."

So the king said, "Let him enter."

[1] *14* About 75 feet, or 23 meters.

ESTHER

PREPARED FOR SUCH A TIME AS THIS

Mordecai asked Esther, "Who knows if you may have attained royal position for such a time as this?" (Est 4:14). But Esther did not get there overnight. She went through a period of preparation to reach her destiny.

When King Ahasuerus searched among the virgins of his kingdom to replace the rebellious Vashti, Esther was among the maidens chosen and placed in the custody of Hegai, the king's eunuch who was the keeper of the women. Esther had been orphaned as a child, and her cousin, Mordecai, raised her as his own daughter. Because of this, Esther's preparation to enter the presence of the king began many years before she was taken to Hegai. She had learned to love and trust Mordecai and follow his instructions explicitly. This obedience determined her destiny.

Though it was an honor for Esther to be chosen to be presented to the king, it was not easy for her to undergo the season of preparation required for that honor. For twelve months she was separated from family, friends, and everything that was familiar to her. But her willingness to submit to a lengthy time of preparation revealed the strength of her relationship with Mordecai. She had learned to listen to him and regard his instructions as she grew up in their home. That training helped her to be obedient in all the preparation that Hegai required of her. Her life of obedience brought her to the place or preparation.

So it is with us as SpiritLed women. The time element of separation and aloneness is part of God's preparation process in our lives. It takes time alone in prayer to cultivate a relationship with God. To search the Scriptures and meditate on them requires much time, during which we gain a truer perspective of God and become acquainted with His heart. We must allow God time to prepare our hearts before He brings us into His presence.

Having yielded to the time element required, Esther encountered other conditions that would bring change to her life. During the first six months of her preparation period myrrh, an oily extract taken from a bush, was used in her purification. As a chief cosmetic used in the house of preparation, myrrh represents grace for the dealings of God in our lives. Just as Esther was made beautiful by the myrrh, so we are made beautiful by myrrh as it works in the seasons of testings, brokenness, and aloneness in our lives. Treatment with the oil of myrrh required obedience, aloneness, and submission to the time element. All were part of the preparation needed to enter the presence of the king.

During the second six months Esther's purification process involved the application of sweet spices. These sweet spices represented her consecration to the will of God. There is a supernatural beauty in a consecrated life—a life that is submitted to the processes of purification without murmuring or complaining—that inspires the admiration of others. That beauty can only be received through obedience to the Holy Spirit.

Until we wear the fragrance of myrrh and have the sweet spices of consecration applied to our lives, we cannot be a dwelling place for God. Esther and the other girls were required to be in preparation for one year before appearing before the king. I don't know how long a year is in the sight of God regarding our time of preparation. Perhaps the length of our preparation depends upon how well we hear His commands and obey His decrees. May we be ready to step into our kingdom position "for such a time as this."

Fuchsia Pickett

6 And Haman entered. Now the king said to him, "What should be done for the man whom the king desires to honor?"

Haman thought in his heart, "Who more than me would the king desire to honor?" 7 So Haman answered the king, "For the man whom the king delights to honor, 8 let royal apparel be brought that the king himself has worn, and a horse on which the king has ridden, which has a royal insignia on its head. 9 Let the apparel and horse for this man be handled by one of the king's noble officials in order to dress the man whom the king delights to honor, as well as to lead him on horseback throughout the city. Finally, let him proclaim before him, 'Like this it shall be done for the man whom the king delights to honor.' "

10 Then the king said to Haman, "Quickly take the apparel and the horse, as you have said, and do so for Mordecai, the Jew sitting at the king's gate. Of everything you have spoken, do not fall short of any of it."

11 So Haman took the apparel and the horse, arrayed Mordecai, led him on horseback throughout the city, and proclaimed before him, "Like this it shall be done for the man whom the king delights to honor."

12 As Mordecai returned again to the king's gate, Haman hurried to his house, mourning with *his* head covered. 13 Haman recounted to his wife Zeresh and all his friends everything that had happened to him.

Then his wise friends and his wife Zeresh said to him, "If Mordecai, before whom you have begun to fall, is of Jewish lineage, then you will not be victorious over him. Rather, you will surely fall before him." 14 While they were still talking with him, the king's eunuchs arrived and rushed Haman to the banquet that Esther had prepared.

Haman Executed

7 So the king and Haman entered to feast and drink with Queen Esther. 2 The king repeated to Esther what he had said on the previous day while drinking wine, "For what are you asking, Queen Esther? It shall be granted to you. Now, what is your request? Even if it is half of the kingdom, it will be done!"

> If it pleases You and I have found favor in Your sight, let my life be given to me (Est 7:3).

3 Queen Esther replied, "If I have found favor in your sight, O king, and if it pleases the king, at my petition, let my life be given me, and my people at my request. 4 For we have been sold, I and my people, to be destroyed, to be slain, and to be annihilated. If only we had been sold as male and female slaves, I could have kept quiet, for that distress would not be sufficient to trouble the king."

5 Then King Ahasuerus answered and demanded of Queen Esther, "Who is he, and where is he, who would dare presume in his heart to do so?"

6 Esther said, "This wicked Haman is the adversary and enemy!"

Then Haman was seized with terror before the king and the queen. 7 And the king arose from the banquet of wine in his wrath and went into the palace garden. But Haman remained to plead for his life from Queen Esther, for he saw that harm was determined against him by the king.

8 Now the king returned from the palace garden back to the hall of the banquet as Haman was falling on the couch where Esther was.

Then the king said, "Will he also violate the queen while I am in the room?"

As the shout erupted from the king's mouth, they covered the face of Haman. 9 Then Harbona, one of the eunuchs in the king's presence, said, "The gallows, fifty cubits[1] high, which Haman had constructed for Mordecai (who had spoken good on behalf of the king), stands at the house of Haman."

10 Then the king said, "Hang him on it!" So they hanged Haman on the gallows that he had prepared for Mordecai. Then the king's wrath was pacified.

Esther Saves the Jews

8 On that day King Ahasuerus gave Queen Esther the house of Haman, the enemy of the Jews. Mordecai came before the king because Esther disclosed who he was to her. 2 The king took off his signet ring, which he had taken away from Haman, and gave it to Mordecai. Esther appointed Mordecai over the house of Haman.

3 Then Esther spoke again to the king and fell down at his feet and begged him with tears to avert the evil of Haman the Agagite, and the scheme that he had devised against the Jews. 4 When the king held out the golden scepter to Esther, she rose and stood before the king, 5 and said, "If it pleases the king, and if I have found favor in his sight, and the idea seems right before the king, and I have his approval, then let it be written to reverse the letters, devised by Haman the son of Hammedatha the Agagite, which he wrote to destroy the Jews in all the king's provinces. 6 For how am I able to watch the evil that will unfold against my

6:8 1Ki 1:33
6:9 Ge 41:43
6:12 2Sa 15:30
6:14 Est 5:8
7:2 Est 5:6
7:4 Est 3:9

7:7 Est 1:12
7:8 Est 1:6
7:9 Est 5:14
8:1 Est 2:7
8:2 Est 3:10
8:4 Est 4:11
8:5 Est 7:3
8:6 Est 7:4

[1] 9 About 75 feet, or 23 meters.

people? How can I endure to see the destruc-
tion of my kindred?"
7 Then King Ahasuerus said to Queen Esther
and to Mordecai the Jew, "See, I have given
Esther the house of Haman, and they have
hanged him on the gallows because he threat-
ened violence against the Jews. 8 Now, as it
suits you, write in the king's name on behalf
of the Jews and seal it with the king's signet
ring, because a document written in the king's
name and sealed with the king's signet ring
cannot be repealed."
9 The king's scribes were summoned at that
time, in the third month, which is the month
of Sivan, on the twenty-third day; and every-
thing was written, according to all that Mor-
decai commanded, to the Jews, to the satraps,
the governors, and the princes of the provinc-
es from India to Ethiopia, one hundred and
twenty-seven provinces, to every province in
its own script, to every people in their own
language, and to the Jews in their script and
language. 10 He wrote in the name of King Aha-
suerus, sealed it with the king's signet ring,
sent letters by couriers on horseback, riding
steeds bred from mares from the royal stables.

> I gather together with other believers and stand for my life (Est 8:11).

11 What the king granted to the Jews in each
and every city was *the right* to assemble and
to defend their lives by annihilating, slaying,
and destroying any army of any people or any
province that would assault them, the little
children and women included, and to plunder
their possessions. 12 *This would happen* on one
day in all the provinces of King Ahasuerus,
namely, on the thirteenth day of the twelfth
month (which is the month Adar). 13 A copy of
the edict being issued as law in each and every
province was published to all people, so that
the Jews could be ready for this day to avenge
themselves on their enemies.
14 So the couriers riding on royal steeds went
out with haste and urgency by the king's edict.
The decree was given at the citadel of Susa.
15 Mordecai went out from the king's pres-
ence in royal apparel of blue and white, with
a large crown of gold, and with a garment of
fine linen and purple. The city of Susa erupt-
ed with shouts of rejoicing. 16 To the Jews
belonged light, gladness, joy, and honor. 17 In
each and every province as well as in each and
every city, wherever the king's edict and his de-
cree reached, the Jews had joy and gladness,
a feast, and a holiday. Furthermore, many of

8:8 Est 1:19
8:9 Est 1:22
8:11 Est 3:13
8:12 Est 9:1
8:15 Ge 41:42
8:16 Ps 97:11
8:17 Est 9:19

....

9:1 Est 8:12
9:2 Est 8:11
9:3 Ezr 8:36
9:4 2Sa 3:1
9:10 Est 5:11
9:12 Est 5:6
9:13 Est 8:11
9:16 Est 8:11

the people of the land professed to be Jews
because the dread of the Jews fell on them.

The Jews Destroy Their Enemies

9 Now in the twelfth month (that is, the
month Adar), on the thirteenth day, when
the king's edict and his decree were to be car-
ried out on the day that the enemies of the
Jews had hoped to have power over them,
things were turned around. The Jews gained
power over those who hated them. 2 The Jews
had assembled in their cities throughout all the
provinces of King Ahasuerus in order to forci-
bly assault those seeking their injury. No man
could stand before them because the dread
of them had fallen on all people. 3 All the rul-
ers of the provinces, and the satraps, and the
governors, and all those doing the work of the
king were helping the Jews, because the fear
of Mordecai had fallen on them. 4 For Mordecai
had become great in the king's house, and his
fame went out throughout all the provinces
because Mordecai grew more powerful.
5 So the Jews struck all their enemies by
sword, slaughtering and destroying them,
and doing to those who hated them as they
pleased. 6 In the citadel of Susa, the Jews killed
and destroyed five hundred men, 7 along with
Parshandatha, Dalphon, Aspatha, 8 Poratha,
Adalia, Aridatha, 9 Parmashta, Arisai, Aridai,
and Vaizatha. 10 These were the ten sons of
Haman the son of Hammedatha, the enemy
of the Jews, whom they killed, but on their
plunder none *of the Jews* attempted to take it.
11 On that day the number of those who were
killed in the citadel of Susa was reported be-
fore the king. 12 The king said to Queen Esther,
"The Jews have slain and destroyed five hun-
dred men in the citadel of Susa and the ten
sons of Haman. What have they done in the
rest of the king's provinces? Now what is your
petition? It shall be granted you! What is your
request further? It shall be done!"
13 Then Esther said, "If it pleases the king, let
it be granted to the Jews in Susa to do again to-
morrow according to this day's decree. Let the
ten sons of Haman be hanged on the gallows."
14 So the king commanded that it be so done,
and the decree was given at Susa, and they
hanged the ten sons of Haman.
15 The Jews in Susa assembled again on the
fourteenth day of the month Adar and killed
three hundred more there, but on the plunder
no one attempted to take it.
16 But the rest of the Jews in the king's prov-
inces assembled to defend their lives. Some
had rest from their enemies, while others
killed seventy-five thousand of those who hat-
ed them, but no one took from the plunder.

17 Because *this occurred* on the thirteenth day of the month Adar, they rested on the fourteenth day and made it a day of feasting and rejoicing.

The Feast of Purim Established

18 Because the Jews in Susa had assembled on the thirteenth day and the fourteenth day of Adar, then on the fifteenth day they rested and made it a day of feasting and rejoicing. 19 Therefore, the Jews of the rural areas, who were living in the villages, made the fourteenth day of the month Adar a day of rejoicing and feasting and a special day for sending portions *of food* to one another.

20 Mordecai recorded these events and sent letters to all the Jews throughout all the provinces of King Ahasuerus, both near and far, 21 in order to institute for them the celebration for the fourteenth day and the fifteenth day of the month of Adar, each and every year, 22 like the days when the Jews had rest from their enemies, and *like* the month when things turned around for them—*changing* from sorrow to joy and from mourning into a favorable day—so that they could celebrate a season of feasting and rejoicing and sending *food* portions to one another and gifts to the poor.

23 So the Jews accepted what had begun *as tradition* as Mordecai had written to them. 24 Haman, the son of Hammedatha, the Agagite, the enemy of all the Jews, had plotted against the Jews to destroy them, and had cast Pur (that is, cast lots), to crush and destroy them. 25 But when Esther came before the king, he ordered by letter that the wicked plot which Haman had devised against the Jews should come upon his own head, and that he and his sons should be hanged on the gallows. 26 Therefore, they call these days Purim on the basis of the name Pur. Furthermore, based on all the information of this letter, along with what they had seen in this regard and what had happened to them, 27 the Jews instituted and accepted *as tradition* for themselves, for their descendants, and for all joining with them not to fail in observing the celebration of these two days as prescribed and as specified in each and every year. 28 These days should be remembered and celebrated throughout every generation, every family, province, and city, so that these days of Purim will not lose their significance among the Jews, and the commemoration of these days will not cease among their descendants.

29 Then Queen Esther, the daughter of Abihail, and Mordecai the Jew wrote with all authority, to confirm this second letter about Purim. 30 He sent the letters to all the Jews, to the one hundred and twenty-seven provinces of the kingdom of Ahasuerus, with instructions for peace and truth 31 in order to confirm these days of Purim at their appointed times, as Mordecai the Jew and Queen Esther had instituted for themselves and for their offspring, with the instructions for their times of fasting and their lamenting. 32 The command of Esther confirmed these traditions of Purim, and it was written in the book.

Mordecai's Greatness

10 Then King Ahasuerus charged a tribute on the land and on the coastal lands of the sea. 2 All the deeds of his power and of his might, and the detailed record of the greatness of Mordecai, after the king promoted him, are they not written in the book of the chronicles of the kings of Media and Persia? 3 Indeed, Mordecai the Jew was second in power to King Ahasuerus. He was great among the Jews and popular with many of his countrymen, for he sought favor for his people, and spoke of peace and prosperity for all of his posterity.

9:17 Est 9:1
9:19 Est 9:22
9:22 Ps 30:11
9:25 Ps 7:16

9:29 Est 9:20
9:30 Est 1:1
9:31 Est 4:3
10:1 Isa 24:15
10:2 Est 2:23
10:3 Ne 2:10

Author: Unknown

Written: Unknown

Themes: God's Sovereign Rule, God's Goodness and Justice, Suffering

JOB

Dear Spirit Led Woman,

Job's wife is the perfect example of what not to do! Every time she speaks, she brings more negativity to an already devastating situation.

It is so important as women of God to be mindful of the power of our words. In Proverbs we're told that "death and life are in the power of the tongue" (Pr 18:21). This means that by what we choose to say, we can either bring life, hope, and healing into the atmosphere of our homes and circumstances, or we can bring hopelessness, bitterness, strife, even curses—all things that lead to death.

If you struggle in this area, ask for forgiveness. Challenge yourself to only speak positive things and try to make this a habit in your life.

You may also need to ask the Lord to heal the hurts you may be carrying from harsh words that have been spoken to you in the past. Ask Him to break that cycle of pain so that you don't pass those negative things on to your children or to others around you. Then ask the Holy Spirit to renew your mind and to replace those negative thoughts and feelings with the truth of God's Word. Keep your heart and mind focused on the blessings of God, cultivating an attitude of thankfulness. Be mindful of the words you speak into any situation. Make it your goal to speak peace, hope, joy, love, and life.

Joy F. Strang

The Prologue

1 There was a man in the land of Uz whose
name was Job. That man was blameless
and upright, fearing God and avoiding evil.
2 Seven sons and three daughters were born
to him. 3 His possessions were seven thousand
sheep, three thousand camels, five hundred
yoke of oxen, five hundred female donkeys,
and very many servants. This man was the
greatest of all the people of the East.
4 His sons used to go and make a feast in the
house of each on his day, and they would send
and call for their three sisters to eat and drink
with them. 5 Now when the days of feasting
had run their course, Job sent and sanctified
them. He would rise up early in the morning,
and he would offer burnt offerings according
to the number of them all, because Job said:
"It may be that my sons have sinned, and
cursed God in their hearts." Thus Job would
do always.
6 Now there was a day when the sons of God
came to present themselves before the LORD,
and the Adversary also came among them.
7 And the LORD said to the Adversary, "From
where have you come?"
Then the Adversary answered the LORD, say-
ing, "From roaming on the earth, and from
walking up and down on it."
8 And the LORD said to the Adversary, "Have
you considered My servant Job, that there is
none like him on the earth, a blameless and an
upright man, who fears God, and avoids evil?"
9 Then the Adversary answered the LORD, say-
ing, "Has Job feared God for nothing? 10 Have
You not made a hedge around him, around his
household, and around all that he has on every
side? You have blessed the work of his hands,
and his possessions have increased in the land.
11 But stretch out Your hand now, and touch all
that he has, and he will curse You to Your face."
12 The LORD said to the Adversary, "Look, all
that he has is in your power; only do not stretch
out your hand against his person."
So the Adversary departed from the presence
of the LORD.
13 So a day came when his sons and his
daughters were eating and drinking wine in
their eldest brother's house, 14 and a messenger
came to Job and said, "The oxen were plowing,
and the donkeys were feeding beside them,
15 and the Sabeans attacked them, and took
them away, and they killed the servants with
the edge of the sword, and only I alone have
escaped to tell you."
16 While he was still speaking, another came
and said, "The fire of God fell from heaven
and burned up the sheep and the servants and
consumed them, and I alone have escaped to
tell you."
17 While he was still speaking, another came
and said, "The Chaldeans formed three com-
panies and made a raid on the camels and
have taken them away. They killed the servants
with the edge of the sword, and I alone have
escaped to tell you."
18 While he was still speaking, another came
and said, "Your sons and your daughters
were eating and drinking wine in their eldest
brother's house, 19 and suddenly a great wind
came from the wilderness and struck the four
corners of the house, and it fell on the young
people, and they are dead; and I alone have
escaped to tell you."
20 Then Job stood up, tore his robe, and
shaved his head. He fell to the ground and
worshipped. 21 He said,

"Naked I came from my mother's womb,
and naked will I return there.
The LORD gave, and the LORD has taken
away;
blessed be the name of the LORD."

22 In all this Job did not sin, and he did not
accuse God of wrongdoing.

2 Again there was a day when the sons of
God came to present themselves before
the LORD, and the Adversary came also among
them to present himself before the LORD. 2 The
LORD said to the Adversary, "From where do
you come?"
And the Adversary answered the LORD, say-
ing, "From roaming on the earth, and from
walking up and down on it."
3 The LORD said to the Adversary, "Have you
considered My servant Job, that there is none
like him on the earth, a blameless and an up-
right man, who fears God and avoids evil?
He still holds fast his integrity, although you
moved Me against him, to destroy him without
cause."
4 The Adversary answered the LORD, saying,
"Skin for skin; yes, all that a man has he will
give for his life. 5 Put forth Your hand now and
touch his bone and his flesh, and he will curse
You to Your face."
6 The LORD said to the Adversary, "Very well,
he is in your hand, but spare his life."
7 Therefore, the Adversary went out from the
presence of the LORD, and he afflicted Job with
severe sores from the sole of his foot to the
top of his head. 8 So he took a piece of broken
pottery with which to scrape himself while he
was sitting among the ashes.
9 His wife said to him, "Are you still maintain-
ing your integrity? Curse God and die."

1:1 Ge 17:1
1:3 Job 29:25
1:5 Ge 8:20
1:6 Job 2:1
1:7 1Pe 5:8
1:8 Job 1:1
1:10 Ps 34:7
1:11 Job 2:5
1:15 Ge 10:7
1:16 Ge 19:24
1:17 Ge 11:28
1:20 Ge 37:29
1:21 Ecc 5:15
1:22 Job 2:10
2:1 Job 1:6
2:3 Job 1:1
2:5 Job 1:11
2:7 Dt 28:35
2:8 Job 42:6

What About Job?

And the LORD said to the Adversary, "Have you considered My servant Job, that there is none like him on the earth, a blameless and an upright man, who fears God, and avoids evil?"

—Job 1:8

The story of Job is a perfect example of God multiplying someone after trouble hits. Much has been said about the Book of Job, and still many people don't understand it. The theme of Job's story is suffering, which most people don't necessarily want to talk about. In fact, at a glance, Job can seem like a book about decrease instead of increase. But it is not!

There are lots of good things to say about Job. First, the Bible says, "[Job] was blameless and upright, fearing God and avoiding evil" (Job 1:1). He had seven sons and three daughters, and his estate was substantial. Job 1:3 says, "This man was the greatest of all the people of the East."

Job had much, but one day everything collapsed. All that Job feared came upon him (Job 3:25), and everything he had was taken away from him. Marauding enemies stole his livestock and killed his servants, fire raged through his flocks and fields, all of his children died, he became deathly ill, and his wife turned on him.

Most of the Book of Job is about one man's personal suffering. But the suffering didn't last forever, and there was more to the story. Near the end of the book, Job 42:12 says, "So the LORD blessed the latter days of Job more than his beginning." The passage goes on to list all the belongings and family that were restored to Job. His story ends well too: "Job died, being old and full of days" (v. 17).

God is a restorer! He multiplies. You may feel as if you have lost some things. Obviously Job felt that way. But he didn't quit on God. He didn't have nearly as good a covenant with God as you have in the blood of Jesus, but he refused to turn his back on God. Despite everything bad that happened to him, he said, "Though He slay me, yet will I trust in Him" (Job 13:15).

Karen Jensen Salisbury

10 He said to her, "You talk like one of the
foolish women talks. Will we indeed accept the
good from God but not accept the adversity?"
In all this Job did not sin with his lips.

11 Three friends of Job heard about all this evil
that had come upon him, and each one came
from his own place: Eliphaz the Temanite, Bil-
dad the Shuhite, and Zophar the Naamathite.
They had agreed together to come to mourn
with him and to comfort him. 12 They saw him
from a distance and did not recognize him, so
they wept aloud. Each one tore his robe, and
they tossed dust into the air above their heads.
13 Then they sat down with him on the ground
seven days and seven nights. Meanwhile, no
one was speaking to him at all because they
saw that his pain was severe.

Job Laments His Birth

3 After this Job opened his mouth, and
cursed the day of his *birth*. 2 Job said:

3 "Let the day perish in which I was born
and the night in which it was said, 'A
male child is conceived.'
4 As for that day, let it be darkness;
let God above not regard it;
and let not light shine upon it.
5 Let darkness and the shadow of death
claim it;
let a cloud settle on it;
let the blackness of the day terrify it.
6 As for that night, let darkness capture it;
let it not rejoice among the days of the
year;
let it not come into the number of the
months.
7 Yes, as for that night, let it be barren!
Let no joyful cry come into it!
8 Let them curse it who curse any day,
those who are prepared to rouse
Leviathan.
9 Let its morning stars be dark;
let it look for light, but have none;
let it not see the rays of dawn,
10 because it did not shut the doors of my
mother's womb,
nor hide trouble from my eyes.

11 "Why did I not die at birth?
Why did I not expire when I came out of
the womb?
12 Why did *her* knees receive me?
And why *her* breasts that I should nurse?
13 For now I would be lying down and would
be at peace;
I would have slept; then there would be
rest for me,
14 with kings and counselors of the earth,
who built ruins for themselves,

2:10 Ps 39:1
2:11 Ge 25:2
2:12 Ne 9:1
2:13 Ge 50:10
3:3 Job 10:18–19
3:5 Job 10:21–22
3:8 Job 41:1
3:9 Job 41:18
3:12 Ge 30:3
3:14 Job 15:28
....
3:16 Ps 58:8
3:20 Job 7:15–16
3:21 Pr 2:4
3:23 Job 19:8
4:3 Isa 35:3
4:5 Job 19:21
4:6 Job 1:1
4:7 Ps 37:25
4:8 Pr 22:8

15 or with princes who had gold,
who filled their houses with silver.
16 Or why was I not hidden like a stillborn
child,
like infants who never saw light?
17 There the wicked will have stopped
causing trouble,
and there the exhausted will rest.
18 Captives will relax together;
they do not hear the voice of the
oppressor.
19 The small and great, they are there,
and the servant is free from his master.

20 "Why is light given to the miserable,
and life unto the bitter in soul,
21 who look for death, but it is not there;
and they search for it more than for
hidden treasures;
22 who rejoice exceedingly,
and they are glad when they find the
grave?
23 And why is light given to a man
whose way is hidden,
whom God has hedged in?
24 For my sighing comes before I eat,
and my groaning pours forth like the
waters.
25 For the thing which I greatly feared has
happened to me,
and that which I dreaded has come to
me.
26 I am not at peace; I have no quiet,
I cannot rest, and turmoil has come."

Eliphaz Speaks: Job Has Sinned

4 Then Eliphaz the Temanite answered:

2 "If one attempts a word with you, will you
be impatient?
But who can keep from speaking?
3 Surely you have instructed many,
and you have strengthened the weak
hands.
4 Your words have raised up him who was
falling,
and you have fortified the feeble knees.
5 But now it comes upon you, and you are
weary;
it reaches even you, and you are
terrified.
6 Is not your reverence your confidence?
And the integrity of your ways your
hope?

7 "Remember now, who being innocent ever
perished?
Or where were the upright ever wiped
out?
8 Just like I have seen, those who plow
iniquity

and sow trouble, reap the same.
[9] By the breath of God they perish,
and by the blast of His anger they are destroyed.
[10] The roaring of the lion, and the voice of the fierce lion,
and the teeth of the young lions are broken.
[11] The old lion perishes for lack of prey,
and the cubs of the lioness are scattered.

[12] "Now a word was brought to me secretly,
and my ear received a whisper of it.
[13] Amid disquieting thoughts from night visions,
when deep sleep falls on mortals,
[14] terror and trembling came to me,
which made all my bones shake.
[15] A breath of wind was passing before my face,
and the hair on my body was standing up.
[16] It stood still,
but I could not recognize its appearance;
a form was in front of my eyes,
there was stillness, then I heard a voice saying:
[17] 'Can a mortal be more righteous than God?
Can a man be more pure than his Maker?
[18] He does not trust in His servants,
and He charges His angels with error;
[19] Even more, those who dwell in houses of clay,
whose foundation is in the dust,
who are crushed before the moth.
[20] They are broken in pieces from morning to evening;
they perish forever without anyone regarding it.
[21] Are not their tent ropes plucked up,
so they die, even without wisdom?'

Eliphaz: Job Is Chastised by God

5 "Call out now; is anyone answering you?
And to whom among the holy ones will you turn?
[2] For anger slays the foolish man,
and jealousy kills the gullible.
[3] Yes, I saw the foolish taking root,
and quickly I cursed his dwelling.
[4] May his children be far from safety,
and may they be crushed in the gate without a deliverer;
[5] whose harvest the hungry eats up,
and takes it even out of the thorns,
and the thirsty captures his wealth.
[6] For affliction does not come out of the dust,
nor does trouble sprout up out of the ground;
[7] but man is born to trouble,
as the sparks fly upward.

[8] "Indeed, I would appeal to God,
and before God I would set forth my case,
[9] who does the great and the inscrutable,
wonders without number.
[10] He gives rain on the surface of the earth
and sends water on the outdoor places.
[11] He sets on high those who are lowly,
and those who mourn are lifted to safety.
[12] He frustrates the schemes of the crafty,
so that their hands cannot perform their plans.
[13] He catches the wise in their own craftiness,
and the scheme of the shrewd is swiftly stopped.
[14] In the daytime they encounter darkness,
and at noontime they grope as in the night.
[15] But the needy He saves from the sword,
from their mouth, and from the hand of the mighty.
[16] So the helpless has hope,
and injustice shuts her mouth.

[17] "How happy is the man whom God corrects!
Therefore do not despise the discipline of the Almighty,
[18] for He wounds, but He applies the bandage;
He injures, but His hands also heal.
[19] In six crises He will deliver you;
even in seven, disaster will not touch you.
[20] In famine He will redeem you from death,
and in war from the power of the sword.
[21] You will be hidden from the lash of the tongue,
and you will not fear violence when it comes.
[22] You will laugh at devastation and famine,
and you will not fear wild animals.
[23] For you will have a covenant with the stones of the field,
and the wild animals will be at peace with you.
[24] You will know that your tent is peaceful,
and you will inspect your property and find nothing missing.
[25] You will know that your offspring will be many
and your descendants as the grass of the earth.
[26] You go to the grave in a full age,

4:9 Job 15:30
4:10 Ps 58:6
4:11 Ps 34:10
4:17 Job 9:2
4:19 Ge 2:7
4:20 Job 20:7
4:21 Job 36:12
5:1 Job 15:15
....
5:7 Job 14:1
5:8 Ps 50:15
5:9 Ps 40:5
5:12 Ne 4:15
5:14 Job 12:25
5:15 Ps 35:10
5:16 Ps 107:42
5:17 Ps 94:12
5:18 Isa 30:26
5:19 Ps 34:19
5:20 Ps 33:19
5:21 Ps 31:20
5:22 Eze 34:25
5:25 Ps 112:2
5:26 Ge 15:15

as stalks of grain are gathered up in
season.
27"Look! We have investigated all this, and it
is so;
hear it, and know for yourself."

Job Replies: My Complaint Is Just

6 But Job answered:

2 "Oh, that my grief were fully weighed,
and my calamity laid with it on the
scales!
3 For now it would be heavier than the sand
of the sea;
therefore my words are stuck in my
throat.
4 For the arrows of the Almighty are
within me;
my spirit drinks in their poison;
the terrors of God are arrayed
against me.
5 Does the wild donkey bray when he has
grass?
Or the ox bellow over his fodder?
6 Is tasteless food eaten without salt?
Or is there any taste in the white of an
egg?
7 My soul refuses to touch them;
they are like loathsome food to me.
8 "Oh, that I might have my request,
and that God would grant me the thing
that I long for!
9 That it would please God to crush me,
that He would let loose His hand and cut
me off!
10Then I would still have comfort;
I would revel in pain; it will not subside,
for I have not concealed the words of the
Holy One.
11"What strength do I have, that I should
hope?
And what is my end, that I should
prolong my life?
12Is my strength the strength of stones?
Or is my flesh made of brass?
13Is there no help within me?
And is success banished from me?
14"A despairing man should be shown
kindness from his friend,
or he forsakes the fear of the Almighty.
15My brothers have acted deceitfully like a
riverbed,
like the streams of the riverbeds that
run dry;
16which are dark because of the ice,
and into which the snow disappears.
17In time they are scorched; they vanish!
When it is hot, they disappear from their
place.
18The caravans of their way turn aside;
they go nowhere, and they perish.
19The caravans of Tema looked,
the travelers of Sheba hoped for them.
20They were disappointed because they were
confident;
they arrived there and were dismayed.
21For now you are nothing;
you see terror and are afraid.
22Did I say, 'Give to me'?
Or, 'Out of your wealth, bribe me'?
23Or, 'Deliver me from the power of the
enemy'?
Or, 'From the power of the oppressors,
liberate me'?
24"Teach me, and I will hold my tongue,
and make me understand how I have
erred.
25How forceful are right words!
But what does your arguing prove?
26Do you mean to correct my words,
and treat my desperate words as wind?
27Yes, you cast lots for the fatherless,
and you bargain over your friend.
28"And now, please give me your attention,
for surely I will not lie to you.
29Turn, I pray, let there be no injustice!
Yes, turn again, my righteousness still
stands!
30Is there injustice on my tongue?
Cannot my taste discern pernicious
things?

Job: My Suffering Is Endless

7 "Is there not a time of hard service for a
man upon earth?
Are not his days also like the days of a
hired worker?
2 Like a servant, he longs for the shade,
and like a hired worker, he looks for his
wages,
3 so I have been assigned months of futility,
and nights of trouble have been
appointed to me.
4 When I lie down, I say,
'When will I arise and the night be
ended?'
And I am full of restlessness until the
dawn.
5 My flesh is covered with worms and caked
with dirt;
my skin is broken, and has become
loathsome.
6 "My days fly more swiftly than a weaver's
shuttle,
and are spent without hope.

6:3 Pr 27:3
6:4 Ps 38:2
6:9 1Ki 19:4
6:10 Lev 19:2
6:15 Jer 15:18
6:19 Ge 25:15
6:21 Ps 38:11
6:26 Job 8:2
6:30 Job 12:11
7:2 Lev 19:13
7:4 Dt 28:67
7:5 Job 17:14
7:6 Job 9:25

7 Oh, remember that my life is a breath!
My eye will never again see good.
8 The eye of him who sees me will behold me no more;
your eyes will be on me, but I will be no more.
9 As the cloud disappears and vanishes away,
so he who goes down to Sheol will come up no more.
10 He will never return to his house,
and his place will not recognize him anymore.

11 "Therefore, I will not restrain my mouth;
I will speak in the anguish of my spirit;
I will complain in the bitterness of my soul.
12 Am I the sea, or a sea monster,
that You set a guard over me?
13 When I say, 'My bed will comfort me,
my couch will ease my complaint,'
14 then You scare me with dreams
and terrify me with visions,
15 so that my soul chooses strangling,
even death rather than my life.
16 I loathe my life; I would not live forever;
let me alone, for my days are emptiness.
17 "What is man, that You should exalt him,
and that You should set Your heart on him,
18 and that You should visit him every morning,
and test him every moment?
19 How long until You look away from me?
Will You not let me alone until I swallow my saliva?
20 Have I sinned? What am I doing to You,
O You watcher of men?
Why have You set me as Your target,
so that I am a burden to myself?
21 And why do You not pardon my transgression
and take away my iniquity?
For now I will lie down in the dust;
and You will seek me diligently, but I will not be."

Bildad Speaks: Job Should Repent

8 Then Bildad the Shuhite answered:

2 "How long will you speak these things,
and the words of your mouth be like a strong wind?
3 Does God pervert judgment?
Or does the Almighty pervert justice?
4 If your children sinned against Him,
He cast them away for their transgression.
5 If you yourself would seek God earnestly,
and seek favor from the Almighty,
6 if you were pure and upright,
surely now He would rouse Himself on your behalf,
and He would prosper your righteous dwelling.
7 Though your beginning was small,
your end will increase greatly.

8 "Please, ask the former generation,
and prepare yourself for what their fathers searched out;
9 for we were born but yesterday and know nothing,
because our days on earth are a shadow.
10 Will they not teach you, and tell you,
and bring forth words out of their heart?
11 Can the papyrus grow up without a marsh?
Can the reed grow without water?
12 While it is yet green and not cut down,
it withers before any other plant.
13 So are the paths of all who forget God;
and the hypocrite's hope will perish,
14 whose confidence will be cut off,
and whose trust will be a spider's web.
15 He will lean upon his house, but it will not stand;
he will hold it fast, but it will not endure.
16 He is green before the sun,
and his branch shoots forth in his garden.
17 His roots are wrapped around the rock heap,
and *he* sees the place of stones.
18 If he is uprooted from his place,
then it will deny him, saying, 'I have not seen you.'
19 See, this is the joy of his way,
and out of the ground others will grow.

20 "Surely, God will not cast away a perfect man,
nor will He strengthen the evildoers,
21 until He fills your mouth with laughing,
and your lips with rejoicing.
22 Those who hate you will be clothed with shame,
and the dwelling place of the wicked will come to nothing."

Job Replies: There Is No Mediator

9 Then Job answered:

2 "Truly, I know it is so,
but how can a man be righteous with God?
3 If one would dispute with Him,
he cannot answer Him once in a thousand times.
4 He is wise in heart and mighty in strength.

7:7 Ps 78:39
7:8 Job 20:9
7:9 2Sa 12:23
7:10 Job 8:18
7:11 Ps 40:9
7:16 Job 10:1
7:17 Ps 8:4
7:19 Job 9:18
7:21 Job 10:14
8:2 Job 6:26
8:3 Ge 18:25
8:4 Job 1:5

....

8:8 Job 15:18
8:9 1Ch 29:15
8:13 Job 13:16
8:14 Isa 59:5–6
8:15 Job 27:18
8:18 Job 7:10
8:19 Job 20:5
8:21 Ps 126:2
8:22 Ps 132:18
9:2 Job 4:17
9:3 Job 10:2
9:4 Job 36:5

Who has hardened himself against Him
and prospered?
5 He who removes mountains, and they
know not,
who overturns them in His anger.
6 He who shakes the earth out of its place,
and its pillars tremble.
7 He who commands the sun, and it does not
rise;
he seals off the stars.
8 He who alone spreads out the heavens,
and treads on the waves of the sea.
9 He who makes the Bear, Orion, and
Pleiades,
and the constellations of the south.
10 He who does great things, beyond
discovery,
yes, and wonders beyond number.
11 Yes, He would cross before me, and I
would not see Him;
He would pass on by, but I would not
perceive Him.
12 Yes, He takes away; who can hinder Him?
Who will say to Him, 'What are You
doing?'
13 God will not withdraw His anger.
The proud helpers bow down beneath
Him.

14 "How, then, can I myself answer Him,
and choose my words to reason with
Him?
15 Even if I were righteous I could not
answer;
I would plead to my Judge for favor.
16 If I called, and He answered me,
I would not believe that He had listened
to my voice.
17 For He crushes me with a storm
and multiplies my wounds without
cause.
18 He will not allow me to get my breath,
but fills me with bitterness.
19 If it is a matter of strength, indeed, He is
strong;
and if of justice, who will set me a time
to plead?
20 Though I were righteous, my own mouth
would condemn me;
though I were perfect, it would prove me
perverse.

21 "Though I were perfect,
I would not know myself;
I would despise my life.
22 It is all one thing; therefore I said,
'He destroys both the perfect and the
wicked.'
23 If the whip kills suddenly,
He will laugh at the trial of the innocent.
24 The earth is given into the hand of the
wicked.
He covers the faces of its judges.
If it is not He, then who is it?

25 "Now my days are swifter than a runner;
they flee away; they see no good.
26 They pass by like reed skiffs,
like an eagle rushing upon its prey.
27 If I say, 'I will forget my complaint;
I will leave off my sad face and brighten
up,'
28 I am afraid of all my sorrows;
I know that You will not hold me
innocent.
29 If I am guilty,
why then do I labor in vain?
30 If I wash myself with snow water
and cleanse my hands with soap,
31 yet You will plunge me into the pit,
and my own clothes will abhor me.

32 "For He is not a man as I am, that I should
answer Him,
and we should come together in
judgment.
33 Nor is there a mediator between us,
who may lay his hand upon us both.
34 Let Him take His rod away from me,
and let not dread of Him terrify me.
35 Then I would speak and not fear Him,
but it is not so with me.

Job: I Abhor My Life

10 "My soul loathes my life;
I will freely give my complaint,
I will speak in the bitterness of my soul.
2 I will say to God, Do not condemn me;
show me why You contend with me.
3 Is it good for You that You should oppress,
that You should despise the work of
Your hands
and smile on the counsel of the wicked?
4 Do You have eyes of flesh?
Or do You see as man sees?
5 Are Your days as the days of man?
Are Your years as the days of a mortal,
6 that You inquire after my iniquity
and search after my sin?
7 You know that I am not wicked,
and there is none who can deliver out of
Your hand.

8 "Your hands have shaped me and made
me completely,
yet You destroy me.
9 Remember, I pray,
that You have made me as the clay.
And would You return me to dust?
10 Have You not poured me out as milk
and curdled me like cheese?

9:6 Isa 2:21
9:7 Isa 13:10
9:9 Am 5:8
9:10 Job 5:9
9:11 Job 23:8–9
9:12 Job 11:10
9:13 Job 26:12
9:15 Job 8:5
9:17 Job 2:3
9:18 Job 7:19
9:19 Job 9:4
....
9:26 Hab 1:8
9:28 Ps 119:120
9:30 Jer 2:22
9:32 Ecc 6:10
9:33 1Sa 2:25
9:34 Ps 39:10
10:1 Job 7:11
10:3 Job 14:15
10:4 1Sa 16:7
10:5 2Pe 3:8
10:8 Ps 119:73
10:9 Ge 2:7

11 You have clothed me with skin and flesh,
and have knit me together with bones
and sinews.
12 You have granted me life and loyal love,
and Your care has preserved my spirit.
13 "These things You have hid in Your heart.
I know that this is with You.
14 If I have sinned, then You would watch me,
and You would not acquit me from my
iniquity.
15 If I am wicked, woe unto me;
and if I am righteous, yet will I not lift up
my head.
I am full of shame;
look at my affliction!
16 For if *my head* is lifted up, You would hunt
me like a lion,
and again You show Yourself marvelous
to me.
17 You renew Your witnesses against me
and increase Your indignation upon me.
Your troops come against me.

18 "Why then did You bring me forth out of
the womb?
Oh, that I had died, and no eye had
seen me!
19 I should have been as though I had not
been;
I should have been carried from the
womb to the grave.
20 Are not my days few? Stop then,
and leave me alone that I may cheer up
a little,
21 before I go and do not return,
even to the land of darkness and the
shadow of death,
22 a land of darkness, as darkness itself;
and of the shadow of death, without any
order,
and where the light is as thick darkness."

Zophar Speaks: Job Is Guilty

11 Then Zophar the Naamathite answered:

2 "Should not the multitude of words be
answered?
And should a man full of talk be
justified?
3 Should your empty talk make men hold
their peace?
And when you mock, will no one shame
you?
4 For you have said, 'My teaching is pure,
And I am clean in your eyes.'
5 But oh, that God would speak
and open His lips against you,
6 and that He would show you the secrets of
wisdom!
For they would double your prudence.

10:13 Job 23:13
10:14 Job 7:21
10:15 Isa 3:11
10:16 Isa 38:13
10:17 Ru 1:21
10:20 Job 14:1
10:21 2Sa 12:23
11:3 Job 17:2
11:4 Job 10:7
11:6 Ezr 9:13

....

11:7 Ro 11:33
11:8 Job 22:12
11:11 Heb 4:13
11:13 1Sa 7:3
11:14 Job 22:23
11:15 Job 22:26
11:16 Isa 65:16
11:17 Ps 37:6
11:20 Dt 28:65
12:4 Job 17:6

And know that God overlooks some of
your iniquity.

7 "Can you search out the deep things of
God?
Can you find out the totality of the
Almighty?
8 It is as high as heaven; what can you do?
Deeper than Sheol; what can you know?
9 Its measure is longer than the earth
and broader than the sea.

10 "If He passes through, and shuts up, and
gathers together *for judgment*,
then who can hinder Him?
11 For He knows worthless men;
He sees wickedness also; will He not
then consider it?
12 For an empty-headed man will become
wise,
when a wild donkey's colt is born a man.

13 "If you prepare your heart
and stretch out your hands toward Him;
14 if iniquity is in your hand, put it far away,
and do not let wickedness dwell in your
tents;
15 for then you will lift up your face without
blemish;
yes, you will be steadfast and will not
fear,
16 because you will forget misery,
and remember it as waters that pass
away,
17 and your life will be brighter than noonday,
even your darkness will be as the
morning.
18 You will trust because there is hope;
yes, you will search about you,
and you will look around and rest in
safety.
19 Also you will lie down, and none will make
you afraid;
yes, many will court your favor.
20 But the eyes of the wicked will fail,
and they will not escape,
and their hope will be as the giving up
of breath."

Job Replies

12 And Job answered:

2 "No doubt but you are the people,
and wisdom will die with you!
3 But I have understanding as well as you;
I am not inferior to you.
Yes, who does not know such things as
these?

4 "I am a laughingstock to my neighbor,
who calls upon God, and He answers
him;

the righteous, upright man is a
laughingstock.
5 He whose foot is unsteady
is despised in the thoughts of him who
is at ease.
6 The tents of robbers are at peace,
and those who provoke God are secure,
into whose hand they bring their own
god.
7 "But now ask the beasts, and let them
teach you;
and the birds of the air, and let them tell
you;
8 or speak to the earth, let it teach you;
and let the fish of the sea declare to you.
9 Who among all these does not know
that the hand of the LORD has done this,
10 in whose hand is the soul of every living
thing
and the breath of all mankind?
11 Does not the ear test words
and the mouth taste its food?
12 Wisdom is with the elderly,
and understanding comes with long life.

13 "With Him are wisdom and strength;
He has counsel and understanding.
14 Surely, He tears down, and it cannot be
built again;
He imprisons a man, and there can be
no release.
15 Surely, He withholds the waters, and they
dry up;
also He sends them out, and they
overthrow the earth.
16 With Him are strength and wisdom.
The deceived and the deceiver are His.
17 He leads counselors away stripped
and makes fools of judges.
18 He has loosened the bonds imposed by
kings
and bound their waist with a belt.
19 He leads away priests stripped
and overthrows the mighty.
20 He removes speech from the trusted ones
and takes away the understanding of
the aged.
21 He pours contempt upon princes
and loosens the belt of the mighty.
22 He uncovers deep things out of darkness
and brings the shadow of death to light.
23 He increases the nations and destroys
them;
He enlarges the nations and guides
them.
24 He takes away the understanding of the
chiefs of the people of the earth,
and causes them to wander in a
wilderness where there is no way.

12:6 Job 9:24
12:10 Ac 17:28
12:11 Job 34:3
12:12 Job 32:7
12:13 Job 9:4
12:15 1Ki 17:1
12:20 Job 32:9
12:21 Ps 107:40
12:22 Da 2:22
12:23 Isa 9:3
12:24 Ps 107:40
12:25 Job 5:14
13:2 Job 12:3
13:4 Ps 119:69
13:5 Pr 17:28
13:15 Job 27:5
13:18 Job 23:4

25 They grope in the dark without light,
and He makes them to stagger like a
drunk man.

13 "Notice, my eye has seen all this;
my ear has heard and understood it.
2 What you know, I also know the same;
I am not inferior to you.
3 Surely I would speak to the Almighty,
and I desire to reason with God.
4 But you are plasterers of falsehood;
you are all physicians of no value.
5 Oh, that you would altogether hold your
peace,
and it would be your wisdom!
6 Hear now my reasoning,
and listen to the pleadings of my lips.
7 Will you speak wickedly for God?
And talk deceitfully for Him?
8 Will you take His side?
Will you plead for God?
9 Is it good that He would search you out?
Or as one man mocks another, do you so
mock Him?
10 He will surely rebuke you,
if you secretly show partiality.
11 Will not His excellence make you afraid,
and the dread of Him fall upon you?
12 Your reminders are parables made of
ashes;
your answers are answers made of clay.

13 "Hold your peace; leave me alone, that I
may speak,
and let come on me what may!
14 Why do I take my flesh in my teeth
and put my life in my hand?
15 Though He slay me, yet will I trust in Him,[1]
but I will defend my own ways before
Him.
16 He also will be my salvation,
for a hypocrite could not come before
Him.
17 Listen carefully to my speech,
and to my declaration with your ears.
18 See now, I have prepared my case;
I know that I will be justified.
19 Who is he who will plead with me?
For now, if I hold my tongue, I will give
up my breath.

20 "Only grant me two things,
then I will not hide myself from You:
21 Withdraw Your hand far from me,
and let not the dread of You make me
afraid.
22 Then call, and I will answer;
or let me speak, and You answer me.

[1] 15 Original Heb. *I have no hope.*

23 How many are my iniquities and sins?
Make known to me my transgression
and my sin.
24 Why do You hide Your face
and regard me as Your enemy?
25 Will You frighten a leaf driven to and fro?
And will You pursue dry stubble?
26 For You write bitter things against me
and make me inherit the iniquities of my
youth.
27 You put my feet in the stocks
and watch closely all my paths;
You draw a line around the soles of my
feet.

28 "Man, as a rotten thing, decays,
as a garment that is moth eaten.

14 "Man who is born of a woman
is of few days and full of trouble.
2 He comes forth like a flower and withers;
he flees like a shadow and does not
continue.
3 Do You open Your eyes on such a one,
and bring me into judgment with You?
4 Who can bring a clean thing out of an
unclean?
There is no one.
5 Seeing his days are determined,
the number of his months are with You;
You have appointed his bounds that he
cannot pass;
6 turn from him, that he may rest,
until he, as a hired man, finishes his day.

7 "For there is hope for a tree,
if it is cut down, that it will sprout again,
and that its tender shoots will not cease.
8 Though its root may grow old in the earth,
and its stump may die in the ground,
9 yet at the scent of water it will bud
and bring forth boughs like a plant.
10 But man dies and wastes away;
yes, man gives up his breath, and where
is he?
11 As the waters disappear from the sea,
and the flood shrivels and dries up,
12 so man lies down and does not rise;
until the heavens are no more, he will
not awake,
nor be raised out of his sleep.

13 "Oh, that You would hide me in the grave,
that You would conceal me until Your
wrath is past,
that You would appoint me a set time
and remember me!
14 If a man dies, will he live again?
All the days of my service I will wait,
until my relief comes.

13:24 Job 19:11
13:26 Ps 25:7
13:27 Job 33:11
14:1 Job 5:7
14:2 Job 8:9
14:3 Ps 143:2
14:4 Jn 3:6
14:5 Job 21:21
14:6 Job 7:19
....
14:15 Job 10:3
14:16 Job 10:6
14:17 Dt 32:34
14:21 Ecc 9:5
15:2 Job 6:26
15:6 Lk 19:22
15:7 Ps 90:2
15:8 Ro 11:34
15:9 Job 13:2
15:10 Job 32:6–7

15 You will call, and I will answer You;
You will long for the work of Your hands.
16 For now You number my steps;
do You not observe my sin?
17 My transgression is sealed up in a bag,
and You plaster over my iniquity.

18 "Surely the mountain falling comes to
nothing,
and the rock is removed out of its place.
19 The waters wear away the stones;
its overflow washes away the dust of the
earth;
and You destroy the hope of man.
20 You prevail forever against him, and he
passes on;
changing his countenance, You send
him away.
21 His sons come to honor, and he does not
know it;
and they are brought low, but he does
not perceive it.
22 But his flesh on him will have pain,
and his soul within him will mourn."

Eliphaz Speaks: Job Does Not Fear God

15 Then Eliphaz the Temanite answered:
2 "Should a wise man reply with empty
knowledge
and fill his lungs with the east wind?
3 Should he reason with unprofitable talk
or with speeches with which he can do
no good?
4 Yes, you cast off reverence
and hinder prayer before God.
5 For your mouth utters your iniquity,
and you choose the tongue of the crafty.
6 Your own mouth condemns you, and not I;
yes, your own lips testify against you.

7 "Are you the first man who was born?
Or were you made before the hills?
8 Have you heard the counsel of God?
And do you restrict wisdom to yourself?
9 What do you know that we do not know?
What do you understand that is not in
us?
10 Both the gray-haired and very aged are
among us—
much older than your father.
11 Are the consolations of God too small for
you?
Or the word spoken gently to you?
12 Why does your heart carry you away?
And what do your eyes wink at,
13 that you turn your spirit against God,
and let such words go out of your
mouth?

[14]"What is man that he should be pure?
And he who is born of a woman, that he should be righteous?
[15]Behold, He puts no trust in His holy ones,
and the heavens are not pure in His sight.
[16]How much more abhorred and corrupt is man,
who drinks iniquity like water!

[17]"I will tell you; hear me,
and what I have seen I will declare,
[18]what wise men have told,
not hiding anything received from their fathers,
[19]to whom alone the land was given,
and no foreigner passed among them:
[20]The wicked man travails with pain all his days,
and numbered are the years stored up for the oppressor.
[21]A dreadful sound is in his ears;
in prosperity the destroyer will come upon him.
[22]He does not believe that he will return from darkness,
and a sword awaits him.
[23]He wanders about for bread, saying, 'Where is it?'
He knows that the day of darkness is ready at his hand.
[24]Trouble and anguish will make him afraid;
they will prevail against him as a king ready to the battle.
[25]For he stretches out his hand against God,
and strengthens himself against the Almighty.
[26]He rushes upon Him, even on His neck,
with his thick embossed shield.

[27]"He has covered his face with his fatness
and gathered fat upon his waist.
[28]He dwells in desolate cities
and in houses which no man inhabits,
which are ready to become heaps.
[29]He will not be rich, nor will his wealth continue,
nor will his possessions spread over the earth.
[30]He will not depart out of darkness;
the flame will dry out his branches,
and by the breath of His mouth he will go away.
[31]Let him who is deceived not trust in futility,
for futility will be his reward.
[32]It will be accomplished before his time,
and his branch will not be green.
[33]He will shake off his unripe grape like the vine,
and will cast off his blossom like the olive.
[34]For the company of hypocrites will be desolate,
and fire will consume the tents of bribery.
[35]They conceive mischief, and give birth to futility;
their womb prepares deceit."

Job Replies: You Are Miserable Comforters

16 Then Job answered:

[2] "I have heard many such things;
miserable comforters are you all!
[3] Will windy words have an end?
Or what provokes you that you answer?
[4] I also could speak as you do,
if your soul were in my place.
I could heap up words against you
and shake my head at you;
[5] but I would strengthen you with my mouth,
and the moving of my lips *would* relieve your grief.

[6] "Though I speak, my grief is not relieved;
and though I stop, how am I eased?
[7] But now He has made me weary;
You have made desolate all my company.
[8] You have filled me with wrinkles, which is a witness against me;
and my leanness has risen up and bears witness to my face.
[9] He has torn me in His wrath, and He has carried a grudge against me.
He has gnashed me with His teeth;
my enemy sharpens His gaze upon me.
[10]They have gaped upon me with their mouth;
they have struck me upon the cheek with reproach;
they have gathered themselves together against me.
[11]God has delivered me to the ungodly
and turned me over into the hands of the wicked.
[12]I was at ease, but He has shattered me.
He also has taken me by my neck, and shaken me to pieces,
and set me up for His target.
[13] His archers surround me;
He splits open my kidneys and does not pity;
He pours out my gall upon the ground.
[14]He pierces me with thrust after thrust;
He rushes upon me like a warrior.
[15]"I have sewn sackcloth over my skin
and thrust my horn into the dust.

15:14 Job 14:4 **15:15** Job 4:18 **15:16** Job 34:7 **15:18** Job 8:8 **15:21** Job 18:11 **15:23** Ps 59:15 **15:27** Ps 17:10 **15:28** Job 3:14 **15:29** Job 27:16–17 **15:30** Job 4:9 **15:31** Isa 59:4 **15:32** Job 22:16 **15:35** Ps 7:14 **16:3** Job 6:26 **16:4** Ps 22:7 **16:7** Job 7:3 **16:8** Job 10:17 **16:9** Ps 35:16 **16:10** Ps 22:13 **16:12** Job 7:20 **16:13** Job 20:25 **16:15** Ps 7:5

SPIRIT-TO-SPIRIT PRAYER

My Daily Prayer for My Children

Father God, I worship and reverence You. You are Lord!

I declare that this is a day that You have made, and I will rejoice and be glad in it. Nothing can steal my joy today, because Your joy is my strength. I am Your child, and You are my God. I dedicate my day to You. As I participate in my daily activities, I thank You ahead of time for providing all my needs and protecting me from all danger. I put on the whole armor of God and plead the blood of Jesus over my day. My mind is buckled down with the helmet of salvation and being renewed every day. I am in tune with Your Holy Spirit, and I will make godly decisions today. I will not be influenced by peer pressure, the pressure of my flesh, or the pressures of this world. I am a child of the King, an heir of God, and a joint heir with Christ.

Every plan and trap of the enemy against me is bound and blocked. I am under an open heaven, and I bind every accident and incident that would rise up to interrupt the flow of the destiny of God for my life.

The favor of God is strong on my life. Every vehicle, plane, or other mode of transportation that I take is covered by the blood of Jesus. No freak accidents, incidents, arrows by day, or terrors by night can affect me as I participate in my school, work, and sports activities. Lord, I thank You ahead of time for delivering me from robberies, carjackings, terrorist attacks, kidnappings, sexual predators, sabotages, setups, demonic pranks, school fights, gang initiations, natural disasters, and anything the devil may plan for my day. My day is established in You. I am Your child, and the path for my day has been made safe and prosperous.

My destiny angel has gone before me. Guardian angels will surround me throughout the day. They will escort me from the morning until I am safely in my bed tonight. As I close my eyes, I will have divine rest and sweet sleep with no interference from nightmares, witchcraft, or demonic activity. Thank You, Jesus. Amen.

Kimberly Daniels

16 My face is inflamed with weeping,
and on my eyelids is the shadow of death,
17 *though* not for any violence in my hands,
and my prayer is pure.

18 "O earth, do not cover my blood,
and let my cry have no resting place.
19 Also now, look, my witness is in heaven,
and my record is on high.
20 My friends scorn me;
my eyes pour out tears unto God.
21 Oh, that one might plead for a man with God,
as a man pleads for his neighbor!
22 "For when a few years have passed,
I will go the way from which I will not return.

Job Prays for Relief

17 "My spirit is broken,
my days are extinguished,
the grave is ready for me.
2 Are not mockers with me?
And does not my eye dwell on their provocation?
3 "Now put down a pledge for me with Yourself.
Who is he who will shake hands with me?

16:18 Isa 26:21
16:19 Ro 1:9

17:2 1Sa 1:6–7
17:3 Pr 11:15

4 For You have hidden their heart from
understanding.
Therefore will You not exalt them.
5 He who speaks flattery to his friends,
even the eyes of his children will fail.

6 "And He has made me a byword of the
people,
someone in whose face they spit.
7 My eye also is dim because of sorrow,
and all my members are like a shadow.
8 Upright men will be astonished at this,
and the innocent will stir up himself
against the hypocrite.
9 The righteous also will hold to his way,
and he who has clean hands will be
stronger and stronger.

10 "But as for you all, return and come now,
for I cannot find one wise man among
you.
11 My days are past, my purposes are broken
off,
even the thoughts of my heart.
12 They change the night into day;
the light is short because of darkness.
13 If I wait, the grave is my house;
I have made my bed in the darkness.
14 I have said to the pit, 'You are my father';
to the worm, 'You are my mother and
my sister.'
15 Where now is my hope?
As for my hope, who will see it?
16 Will they go down to the gates of Sheol?
Will we descend together in the dust?"

Bildad Speaks: God Punishes the Wicked

18 Then Bildad the Shuhite answered:
2 "How long will it be until you put an end to
words?
Gain understanding, and afterwards we
will speak.
3 Why are we counted as beasts
and regarded as stupid in your sight?
4 You who tear yourself in anger,
will the earth be forsaken for you?
And will the rock be removed from its
place?

5 "Yes, the light of the wicked will be put out,
and the spark of his fire will not shine.
6 The light will be dark in his tent,
and his candle beside him will be put
out.
7 The steps of his strength will be shortened,
and his own counsel will cast him down.
8 For he is cast into a net by his own feet,
and he walks upon a snare.

17:6 Job 30:9
17:9 Pr 4:18
17:11 Job 7:6
17:16 Job 3:17–19
18:3 Ps 73:22
18:5 Pr 13:9

18:8 Job 22:10
18:11 Job 15:21

SPIRITLED WOMAN

COUNSEL FROM THE SPIRIT BASICS

Hang On to Hope

Hope is one of those qualities that we may not pay a whole lot of attention to until it is gone. And once it has gone missing in a certain area of life, it can be a little difficult to find it again. A loss of hope is one of the main markers of depression. But when we reintroduce hope into our lives, our depression will decrease. Hopelessness is a weary land to slog through, and it takes faith to walk out of it.

"Where now is my hope? As for my hope, who will see it?" (Job 17:15). We need to ask the same question Job did: Where did all our hope go?

"The eye of the LORD is on those who fear Him, on those who hope in His lovingkindness" (Ps 33:18). Our hope is in Him, through Him, because of Him. If your hope has been wrapped up in a relationship, in your career, in your future, in finding a spouse, in finding success, or in anything the world offers, then your hope anchor has been dropped into the wrong ocean. It is settling to know this instead: "We have this hope as a sure and steadfast *anchor* of the soul, which enters the Inner Place behind the veil. This is where Jesus has entered for us as a forerunner" (Heb 6:19–20, emphasis added).

Jenny Swindall

9 The trap will take him by the heel,
and the snare will prevail against him.
10 The snare is laid for him in the ground,
and a trap for him in the path.
11 Terrors will make him afraid on every side
and will drive him to his feet.
12 His strength will be hungry,
and destruction will be ready at his side.
13 It will devour the parts of his skin;
the firstborn of death will devour his
limbs.
14 His confidence will be rooted out of his
tent,
and it will bring him to the king of
terrors.

15 They dwell in his tent who have no part
with him;
brimstone will be scattered upon his
habitation.
16 His roots will be dried up beneath,
and above his branch will dry up.
17 The memory of him will perish from the
earth,
and he will have no name in the street.
18 He will be driven from light into darkness,
and chased out of the world.
19 He has neither descendant nor posterity
among his people,
nor anyone remaining in his dwellings.
20 They who come after him will be
astonished at his day,
as they who went before were seized
with fright.
21 Surely such are the dwellings of the
wicked,
and this is the place of him who does
not know God."

Job Replies: My Redeemer Lives

19 Then Job answered:

2 "How long will you torment my soul
and break me in pieces with words?
3 These ten times you have reproached me;
you are not ashamed that you have
wronged me.
4 And if indeed I have erred,
my error remains with me.
5 If indeed you exalt yourselves against me
and plead against me with my disgrace,
6 know now that God has bent me
and has surrounded me with His net.

7 "Look, I cry out concerning wrong, but I
am not heard;
I cry aloud, but there is no justice.
8 He has fenced up my way that I cannot
pass,
and He has set darkness in my paths.
9 He has stripped me of my glory
and taken the crown from my head.
10 He has destroyed me on every side, and I
am gone;
my hope He has uprooted like a tree.
11 He has also kindled His wrath against me,
and He counts me as one of His
enemies.
12 His troops come together
and build up their road against me;
they set up camp all around my tent.

13 "He has removed my brothers far from me,
and my acquaintances are completely
estranged from me.
14 My relatives have failed,
and my close friends have forgotten me.

18:15 Ps 11:6
18:16 Hos 9:16
18:17 Ps 34:16
18:20 Ps 37:13
18:21 Jer 9:3
19:5 Ps 35:26
19:8 Job 3:23
19:9 Ps 89:44
19:10 Job 24:20
19:11 Job 13:24
19:12 Job 30:12
19:13 Ps 69:8

....

19:18 2Ki 2:23
19:20 Ps 102:5
19:21 Job 1:11
19:22 Ps 69:26
19:23 Isa 30:8
19:26 Ps 17:15
19:28 Job 19:22

15 Those who dwell in my house, and my
maidservants,
count me for a stranger;
I am a foreigner in their sight.
16 I called my servant, but he gave me no
answer;
I begged him with my mouth.
17 My breath is offensive to my wife;
I am loathsome to the children of my
own body.
18 Yes, young children despise me;
I arose, and they spoke against me.
19 All my close friends abhorred me,
and they whom I love are turned against
me.
20 My bones cling to my skin and to my flesh,
and I have escaped by the skin of my
teeth.

21 "Have pity upon me, have pity upon me, O
you my friends,
for the hand of God has struck me!
22 Why do you persecute me as God does,
and are not satisfied with my flesh?

23 "Oh, that my words were written!
Oh, that they were inscribed in a book!
24 That they were engraved with an iron pen
and lead in the rock forever!
25 For I know that my Redeemer lives,
and He will stand at last on the earth;
26 and after my skin is destroyed,
yet in my flesh I will see God,
27 whom I will see for myself,
and my eyes will behold, and not
another.
How my heart yearns within me.

28 "If you should say, 'How shall we persecute
him?'
since the root of the matter is found in
me,
29 be afraid of the sword for yourselves;
for wrath brings the punishments of the
sword,
that you may know there is a judgment."

Zophar Speaks: The Wicked Will Suffer

20 Then Zophar the Naamathite answered:

2 "Therefore my thoughts cause me to
answer,
and for this I make haste.
3 I have heard the rebuke that disgraces me,
and the spirit of my understanding
causes me to answer.

4 "Do you not know this of old,
since man was placed upon earth,

[5] that the triumphing of the wicked is short,
and the joy of the hypocrite is but for a moment?
[6] Though his loftiness extends to the heavens,
and his head reaches to the clouds,
[7] yet he will perish forever like his own excrement;
those who have seen him will say,
'Where is he?'
[8] He will fly away like a dream and will not be found;
yes, he will be chased away as a vision of the night.
[9] The eye that saw him will see him no more;
nor will his place behold him anymore.
[10] His children will seek favor from the poor,
and his hands will give back his wealth.
[11] His bones are full of his youthful vigor,
but it will lie down with him in the dust.
[12] "Though evil is sweet in his mouth,
and he hides it under his tongue,
[13] though he spares it and does not forsake it,
but keeps it in his mouth,
[14] yet his food in his stomach turns sour;
it becomes the venom of cobras within him.
[15] He has swallowed down riches,
and he will vomit them up again;
God will cast them out of his belly.
[16] He will suck the poison of cobras;
the viper's tongue will slay him.
[17] He will not see the streams, the rivers,
the brooks of honey and butter.
[18] He will give back the produce of labor and will not swallow it down.
According to his wealth the restitution will be, and he will not rejoice in it;
[19] because he has oppressed and has forsaken the poor.
He has violently taken away a house that he did not build.

In times of famine He preserves me (Job 5:20–21).

[20] "Because he knows no quietness in his belly,
he will not save anything he desired.
[21] Nothing is left for him to eat;
therefore his prosperity will not endure.
[22] In his self-sufficiency he will be in distress;
every hand of misery will come upon him.
[23] When he is about to fill his belly,
God will cast the fury of His wrath on him
and will rain it on him while he is eating.
[24] He will flee from the iron weapon;
a bronze bow will pierce him through.
[25] It is drawn and comes out of the body;
yes, the glittering point comes out of his gall.
Terrors are upon him.
[26] Total darkness is stored up for his treasures.
An unfanned fire will consume him;
what is left in his tent will be consumed.
[27] The heavens will reveal his iniquity,
and the earth will rise up against him.
[28] The increase of his house will depart,
and his goods will flow away in the day of His wrath.
[29] This is the wicked man's portion from God,
and the inheritance appointed to him by God."

20:5 Ps 37:35–36
20:6 Isa 14:13–14
20:8 Ps 73:20
20:9 Job 7:8
20:10 Job 20:18
20:11 Job 13:26
20:17 Dt 32:13–14
20:18 Job 20:10
20:19 Job 35:9
20:20 Ecc 5:13–14
20:23 Ps 78:30–31
....
20:24 Isa 24:18
20:25 Job 16:13
20:26 Ps 21:9
20:29 Job 27:13
21:3 Job 16:10
21:5 Jdg 18:19
21:7 Job 12:6
21:10 Ex 23:26
21:13 Job 36:11
21:14 Job 22:17
21:15 Job 34:9
21:16 Job 22:18

Job Replies: The Wicked Do Prosper

21 But Job answered:
[2] "Listen carefully to my speech,
and let this be your consolation.
[3] Bear with me that I may speak,
and after I have spoken, mock on.
[4] "As for me, is my complaint against man?
And if it were so, why should not my spirit be troubled?
[5] Look at me and be astonished,
and put your hand over your mouth.
[6] Even when I remember I am afraid,
and trembling takes hold of my body.
[7] Why do the wicked live and become old;
yes, become mighty in power?
[8] Their descendants are established with them in their sight,
and their offspring before their eyes.
[9] Their houses are safe from fear,
nor is the rod of God upon them.
[10] Their bull breeds without failure;
their cow gives calves without miscarriage.
[11] They send forth their little ones like a flock,
and their children dance.
[12] They take up the tambourine and harp
and rejoice at the sound of the flute.
[13] They spend their days in wealth,
and in a moment go down to Sheol.
[14] Therefore they say to God, 'Depart from us,
for we do not desire the knowledge of Your ways.
[15] Who is the Almighty, that we should serve Him?
And what profit do we have if we pray to Him?'
[16] Indeed, their prosperity is not in their hand.
The counsel of the wicked is far from me.

17 "How often is the lamp of the wicked put out?
How often does their destruction come upon them,
the sorrows God distributes in His anger?
18 They are like straw before the wind,
and like chaff that a storm carries away.
19 God stores up their iniquity for their children;
let Him reward the people themselves,
and they will know it.
20 Let their eyes see their own destruction,
and let them drink of the wrath of the Almighty.
21 For what do they care about their households after them,
when the number of their months is cut off?

22 "Can anyone teach God knowledge,
since He judges those who are on high?
23 One dies in his full strength,
being wholly at ease and secure.
24 His pails are full of milk,
and the marrow of his bones is moist.
25 Another dies in the bitterness of his soul,
never having eaten with pleasure.
26 They will lie down alike in the dust,
and worms will cover them.

27 "Behold, I know your thoughts,
and the schemes with which you would wrong me.
28 For you say, 'Where is the house of the prince?
And where are the dwelling places of the wicked?'
29 Have you not asked them who travel the road?
And do you not know their signs?
30 For the wicked are reserved for the day of destruction;
they will be brought forth on the day of wrath.
31 Who will declare his way to his face?
And who will repay him for what he has done?
32 Yet will he be brought to the grave
and will remain in the tomb.
33 The clods of the valley will be sweet unto him;
and everyone will follow him,
as countless have gone before.

34 "How then can you comfort me with emptiness,
since deceit remains in your answers?"

21:17 Job 18:5–6
21:18 Job 13:25
21:19 Ex 20:5
21:20 Isa 51:17
21:21 Job 14:5
21:22 Ro 11:34
21:24 Pr 3:8
21:26 Ecc 9:2
21:30 Pr 16:4
21:31 Dt 7:10
21:34 Job 16:2

....

22:2 Lk 17:10
22:4 Job 14:3
22:6 Ex 22:26
22:7 Job 31:17
22:9 Job 24:3
22:11 La 3:54
22:13 Ps 10:11
22:16 Job 15:32
22:17 Job 21:14–15
22:18 Job 21:16
22:19 Ps 52:6

Eliphaz Speaks: Job's Wickedness Is Great

22 Then Eliphaz the Temanite answered:
2 "Can a man be profitable to God,
as he who is wise may be profitable to himself?
3 Is it any pleasure to the Almighty that you are righteous?
Or is it gain to Him that you make your ways blameless?

4 "Is it because of your fear of Him that He corrects you,
and enters into judgment with you?
5 Is not your wickedness great,
and your iniquity infinite?
6 For you have taken a pledge from your brother for nothing,
and stripped the naked of their clothing.
7 You have not given water to the weary to drink,
and you have withheld bread from the hungry.
8 But as for the mighty man, he possessed the earth,
and the honorable man lived in it.
9 You have sent widows away empty,
and the strength of the fatherless was crushed.
10 Therefore snares are all around you,
and sudden fear troubles you,
11 or darkness, so that you cannot see;
and an abundance of waters covers you.

12 "Is not God in the height of heaven?
And see the height of the stars, how high they are!
13 And you say, 'What does God know?
Can He judge through the dark cloud?
14 Thick clouds are His covering, so He cannot see;
and He walks above the circle of heaven.'
15 Will you keep to the old way,
that wicked men have trod?
16 They were cut down before their time;
their foundations were swept away by a flood.
17 They said to God, 'Depart from us,'
and, 'What can the Almighty do to us?'
18 Yet He filled their houses with good things;
but the counsel of the wicked is far from me.
19 "The righteous see it and are glad,
and the innocent laugh them to scorn:
20 'Surely our adversaries are cut down,
and the fire consumes their remnant.'

[21]"Now acquaint yourself with Him and be at peace;
thereby good will come to you.
[22]Receive, I pray, the teaching from His mouth,
and lay up His words in your heart.
[23]If you return to the Almighty, you will be built up;
you will put away iniquity far from your tents.
[24]Then you will lay up gold as dust,
and the gold of Ophir as the stones of the brooks.
[25]Yes, the Almighty will be your gold
and your precious silver;
[26]for then you will delight yourself in the Almighty,
and will lift up your face unto God.
[27]You will make your prayer to Him, and He will hear you,
and you will pay your vows.

As I declare it, God will establish it (Job 22:28).

[28]You will also declare a matter, and it will be established unto you;
and the light will shine upon your ways.

I stand up in the authority of God Himself and make pronouncements of truth (Job 22:28).

[29]When men are cast down, and you say, 'There is a time of exaltation!'
then He will save the humble person.
[30]He will even deliver one who is not innocent;
he will be delivered by the purity of your hands."

Job Replies: My Complaint Is Grievous

23 Then Job answered:
[2] "Today also my complaint is bitter;
my hand is heavy because of my groaning.
[3] Oh, that I knew where I might find Him,
that I might come even to His seat!
[4] I would present my case before Him
and fill my mouth with arguments.
[5] I would know the words that He would answer me
and understand what He would say to me.
[6] Will He plead against me with His great power?

22:23 Job 11:13–14
22:26 Job 27:10
22:27 Isa 58:9
22:29 1Pe 5:5
23:4 Job 13:18
....
23:8 Job 9:11
23:10 Ps 66:10
23:11 Ps 44:18
23:12 Jn 4:32
23:13 Ps 115:3
23:14 1Th 3:3
23:16 Job 27:2
23:17 Job 19:8
24:1 Ac 1:7
24:2 Dt 19:14
24:4 Pr 28:28
24:7 Ex 22:26–27

No! But He would take note of me.
[7] There the righteous might dispute with Him;
so would I be delivered forever from my Judge.
[8] "Look, I go forward, but He is not there,
and backward, but I cannot perceive Him;
[9] when He works on the left hand, I cannot behold Him;
He turns to the right hand, I cannot see Him.
[10]But He knows the way that I take;
when He has tested me, I will come forth as gold.
[11]My foot has held fast to His steps;
I have kept His way and have not turned aside.
[12]I have not departed from the commandment of His lips;
I have esteemed the words of His mouth more than my necessary food.
[13]"But He is resolute, and who can turn Him?
And whatever His soul desires, that He does.
[14]For He performs what is appointed for me,
and many such things are with Him.
[15]Therefore I am troubled at His presence;
when I consider, I am afraid of Him.
[16]For God makes my heart soft,
and the Almighty troubles me;
[17]because I was not cut off from the presence of darkness,
nor has He covered the darkness from my face.

24 "Since times of judgment are not kept by the Almighty,
why do they who know Him not see His days?
[2] Some remove the landmarks;
they violently take away flocks and feed on them.
[3] They drive away the donkey of the orphan;
they take the widow's ox for a pledge.
[4] They turn away the needy;
the poor of the earth are forced to hide.
[5] Behold, as wild donkeys in the desert,
they go out to their work, rising early for a prey.
The wilderness yields food for them and for their children.
[6] They gather their fodder in the field,
and they glean in the vineyard of the wicked.
[7] They cause the naked to lodge without clothing,
and they have no covering in the cold.

8 They are wet with the showers of the mountains
and embrace the rock for want of a shelter.
9 They snatch the fatherless from the breast
and take a pledge from the poor.
10 They cause him to go naked without clothing,
and they take away the sheaf from the hungry.
11 They press out oil within their walls
and tread their winepresses, yet suffer thirst.
12 Men groan from outside the city,
and the soul of the wounded cries out;
yet God does not charge them with wrong.

13 "They are those who rebel against the light;
they do not know its ways
nor abide in its paths.
14 The murderer, rising with the light, kills the poor and needy,
and in the night he is like a thief.
15 Also the eye of the adulterer waits for the twilight,
saying, 'No eye will see me';
and he disguises his face.
16 In the dark they break into houses,
which they had marked for themselves in the daytime;
they do not know the light.
17 For the morning is the same to them as the shadow of death;
if someone recognizes them,
they are in the terrors of the shadow of death.

18 "He is swift as the waters.
Their portion is cursed in the earth.
They do not turn toward the way of the vineyards.
19 Drought and heat consume the snow waters;
so the grave consumes those who have sinned.
20 The womb will forget him;
the worm will feed sweetly on him;
he will be remembered no more,
and wickedness will be broken like a tree.
21 He preys on the barren who do not bear,
and does no good for the widow.
22 But God draws the mighty away with His power;
He rises up, and no man is sure of life.
23 He gives them security, and they rely on it;
yet His eyes are on their ways.
24 They are exalted for a little while but are gone and brought low;
they are taken out of the way like all others
and cut off as the tops of the grain.

25 "If it is not so, who will prove me a liar
and make my speech worth nothing?"

24:8 La 4:5
24:13 Jn 3:19–20
24:15 Ps 10:11
24:16 Jn 3:20
24:20 Pr 10:7
24:24 Ps 37:10

25:3 Jas 1:17
25:4 Job 9:2
25:6 Ps 22:6
26:6 Ps 139:8
26:7 Job 9:8
26:8 Pr 30:4
26:9 Ps 97:2
26:10 Job 38:8–11
26:12 Isa 51:15
26:13 Isa 27:1

Bildad Speaks: Man Cannot Be Righteous

25 Then Bildad the Shuhite answered:
2 "Dominion and fear are with Him;
He makes peace in His high places.
3 Is there any number to His armies?
And upon whom does His light not rise?
4 How then can man be righteous with God?
Or how can he who is born of a woman be clean?
5 Behold, even the moon does not shine,
and the stars are not pure in His sight;
6 how much less man, who is a maggot?
And the son of man, who is a worm?"

Job Replies: God's Majesty Is Unsearchable

26 But Job answered:
2 "How have you helped him who is without power?
How have you saved the arm that has no strength?
3 How have you counseled him who has no wisdom?
And how have you plentifully declared sound knowledge?
4 To whom have you uttered words?
And whose breath came from you?

5 "The departed spirits tremble under the waters,
and their inhabitants.
6 The underworld is naked before Him,
and destruction has no covering.
7 He stretches out the north over empty space,
He hangs the earth upon nothing.
8 He binds up the waters in His thick clouds,
and the cloud is not broken under them.
9 He covers the face of the full moon
and spreads His cloud over it.
10 He has circled the waters with boundaries,
until the day and night come to an end.
11 The pillars of heaven tremble
and are astonished at His reproof.
12 He divides the sea with His power,
and by His understanding He strikes through the proud.
13 By His breath He has made fair the heavens;
His hand has formed the fleeing serpent.
14 Indeed, these are but a part of His ways,

and how small a whisper we hear of
Him!
But the thunder of His power who can
understand?"

Job's Last Words to His Friends

27 Moreover Job continued his discourse:
2 "As God lives, who has taken away my
judgment,
and the Almighty, who has made my
soul bitter,
3 all the while my spirit is in me,
and the breath of God is in my nostrils,
4 my lips will not speak wickedness,
nor my tongue utter deceit.
5 God forbid that I should justify you.
Until I die I will not put away my
integrity from me.
6 My righteousness I hold fast and will not
let it go;
my heart will not reproach me as long
as I live.

7 "Let my enemy be like the wicked,
and he who rises up against me like the
unrighteous.
8 For what is the hope of the hypocrite,
though he may gain much, when God
takes away his soul?
9 Will God hear his cry
when trouble comes upon him?
10 Will he delight himself in the Almighty?
Will he always call upon God?

11 "I will teach you about the hand of God;
what is with the Almighty I will not
conceal.
12 Look, all of you have seen it;
why then have you become altogether
vain?

13 "This is the portion of a wicked man with
God,
and the inheritance that oppressors
receive from the Almighty:
14 If his children are multiplied, it is for the
sword,
and his offspring will not be satisfied
with bread.
15 Those who survive him will be buried in
death,
and their widows will not weep.
16 Though he heaps up silver like the dust
and piles up clothing like the clay—
17 he may pile it up, but the just will wear it,
and the innocent will divide the silver.
18 He builds his house like a moth,
and like a booth that the watchman
makes.

27:2 Job 34:5
27:5 Job 2:9
27:6 Job 2:3
27:8 Job 11:20
27:9 Pr 1:28
27:14 Dt 28:41
27:15 Ps 78:64
27:16 Zec 9:3
27:17 Ecc 2:26
27:18 Job 8:14–15

....

27:20 Job 15:21
27:23 La 2:15
28:3 Ecc 1:13
28:15 Pr 16:16
28:18 Pr 3:15

19 The rich man will lie down, but he will not
be gathered;
he opens his eyes, and he is not.
20 Terrors overtake him like floodwaters;
a tempest steals him away in the night.
21 The east wind carries him away, and he
departs;
it sweeps him out of his place.
22 For God will cast it upon him and not
spare;
he would flee from its power.
23 Men will clap their hands at him
and will hiss him out of his place.

Interlude: Where Wisdom Is Found

28 "Surely there is a mine for the silver,
and a place where they refine gold.
2 Iron is taken out of the earth,
and copper is smelted from the ore.
3 Man puts an end to darkness,
and searches every extremity
for ore in the darkness and the shadow
of death.
4 He breaks open a shaft away from the
inhabitants;
in places forgotten by feet
they hang far away from men; and they
totter.
5 As for the earth, from it comes bread,
and underneath it is turned up as by fire.
6 Its stones are the source of sapphires,
and it has dust of gold.
7 There is a path that no bird knows,
and that the vulture's eye has not seen;
8 the lion cubs have not trodden it,
nor has the fierce lion passed by it.
9 He puts forth his hand upon the rock;
he overturns the mountains by the roots.
10 He cuts out rivers among the rocks,
and his eye sees every precious thing.
11 He prevents the floods from overflowing,
and the thing that is hidden he brings
forth to light.

12 "But where will wisdom be found?
And where is the place of
understanding?
13 Man does not know its price,
nor is it found in the land of the living.
14 The depth says, 'It is not in me,'
and the sea says, 'It is not with me.'
15 It cannot be bought for gold,
nor can silver be weighed for its price.
16 It cannot be valued in the gold of Ophir,
with the precious onyx or the sapphire.
17 The gold and the crystal cannot equal it,
and it cannot be exchanged for jewels of
fine gold.
18 No mention will be made of coral or of
pearls,

for the price of wisdom is above rubies.
19 The topaz of Ethiopia will not equal it,
nor will it be valued with pure gold.

20 "From where then does wisdom come?
And where is the place of understanding?
21 It is hidden from the eyes of all living
and concealed from the birds of the air.
22 Destruction and Death say,
'We have heard of its fame with our ears.'
23 God understands its way,
and He knows its place.
24 For He looks to the ends of the earth,
and sees under the whole heaven,
25 to make the weight of the wind,
and He weighs the waters by measure.
26 When He made a decree for the rain,
and a path for the lightning of the thunder,
27 then He saw it and declared it;
He prepared it, yes, and searched it out.
28 To man He said:
'Look, the fear of the Lord, that is wisdom;
And to depart from evil is understanding.' "

Job's Final Defense

29 Moreover Job continued his discourse:
2 "Oh, that I were as in months past,
as in the days when God watched over me;
3 when His lamp shone upon my head,
and when by His light I walked through darkness;
4 as I was in the days of my autumn youth,
when the friendly counsel of God was over my tent;
5 when the Almighty was still with me,
when my children were around me;
6 when my steps were bathed in butter,
and the rock poured out rivers of oil for me!

7 "When I went out to the gate of the city,
when I took my seat in the square,
8 the young men saw me and hid themselves,
and the aged arose and stood up.
9 The princes refrained from talking,
and put their hand on their mouth.
10 The nobles held their peace,
and their tongue stuck to the roof of their mouth.
11 When the ear heard, then it blessed me;
and when the eye saw, then it approved me,
12 because I delivered the poor who cried,
and the fatherless, and him who had none to help him.
13 The blessing of the perishing man came upon me,
and I caused the widow's heart to sing for joy.
14 I put on righteousness, and it clothed me;
my judgment was like a robe and a diadem.
15 I was eyes for the blind,
and I was feet for the lame.
16 I was a father to the poor,
and I searched out the case that I did not know.
17 I broke the jaws of the wicked
and plucked the victim from his teeth.

18 "Then I said, 'I will die in my nest,
and I will multiply my days as the sand.
19 My root was spread out by the waters,
and the dew lay all night upon my branch.
20 My glory was fresh in me,
and my bow was renewed in my hand.'

21 "Men listened to me and waited,
and kept silence for my counsel.
22 After my words they did not speak again,
and my speech settled on them like dew.
23 They waited for me as for the rain,
and they opened their mouth wide as for the spring rain.
24 If I mocked at them, they did not believe it,
and the light of my countenance they did not cast down.
25 I chose the way for them and sat as chief,
and lived as a king in the army,
as one who comforts mourners.

30 "But now those who are younger than I mock me,
whose fathers I disdained to put with the dogs of my flock.
2 Yes, how does the strength of their hands profit me?
Their vigor has perished.
3 For want and famine
they gnawed the parched land;
fleeing into the wilderness in former time, desolate and waste.
4 Who pluck mallow by the bushes,
and juniper roots for their food.
5 They were driven out from among men;
they shout after them as after a thief.
6 They had to dwell in the rocky riverbeds,
in caves of the earth, and in the rocks.
7 Among the bushes they brayed;
under the nettles they were gathered together.

28:24 Pr 15:3
28:25 Ps 135:7
28:26 Job 38:25
28:28 Ps 111:10
29:1 Job 27:1
29:3 Job 18:6
29:4 Ps 25:14
29:6 Job 20:17
29:9 Job 21:5
29:10 Ps 137:6
29:12 Ps 72:12
29:14 Ps 132:9
29:15 Nu 10:31
29:16 Pr 29:7
29:17 Ps 3:7
29:19 Job 18:16
29:20 Ge 49:24
29:22 Dt 32:2

[8] They were children of fools, yes, children
of vile men;
they were scourged from the earth.

[9] "Now I am their taunting song;
yes, I am their byword.
[10] They abhor me, they flee far from me;
they do not hesitate to spit in my face.
[11] Because He has loosed my bowstring and
afflicted me,
they have cast off the bridle before me.
[12] At my right hand their brood arises;
they push away my feet,
and they raise against me their ways of
destruction.
[13] They tear apart my path,
they promote my calamity;
they have no helper.
[14] They came upon me as a wide breach, with
a crash they came;
in the desolation they rolled themselves
upon me.
[15] Terrors are turned on me;
they pursue my dignity like the wind,
and my help passes away as a cloud.

[16] "Now my soul is poured out within me;
the days of affliction have taken hold
of me.
[17] My bones are pierced in me at night,
and my sinews have no rest.
[18] By the great force of my disease my
garment is changed;
it binds me about as the collar of my
coat.
[19] He has cast me into the mire,
and I have become like dust and ashes.

[20] "I cry unto You, but You do not hear me;
I stand up, and You do not regard me.
[21] You have become cruel to me;
with Your strong hand You oppose me.
[22] You lift me up to the wind and cause me to
ride on it;
You dissolve my success.
[23] For I know that You will bring me to death,
and to the house appointed for all living.

[24] "Surely He will not stretch out His hand to
the grave,
though they cry when He destroys it.
[25] Did I not weep for him who was in trouble?
Was not my soul grieved for the poor?
[26] When I looked for good, then evil disaster
came upon me;
and when I waited for light, darkness
came.
[27] My insides boiled and did not rest;
the days of affliction have met me.
[28] I went mourning without the sun;
I stood up, and I cried in the
congregation.
[29] I am a brother of jackals
and a companion of owls.
[30] My skin is black upon me,
and my bones are burned with fever.
[31] My harp is turned to mourning,
and my flute to the voice of those who
weep.

31 "I made a covenant with my eyes;
why then should I look upon a young
woman?
[2] For what portion of God is there from
above?
And what inheritance of the Almighty
from on high?
[3] Does not destruction belong to the wicked,
and calamity to the workers of iniquity?
[4] Does He not see my ways,
and count all my steps?

[5] "If I have walked in vanity,
or if my foot has hurried after deceit,
[6] let me be weighed in an even balance
that God may know my integrity.
[7] If my step has turned out of the path,
and my heart has gone after my eyes,
and if any spot has clung to my hands,
[8] then let me sow, but let another eat;
yes, let my offspring be rooted out.
[9] "If my heart has been deceived by a
woman,
or if I have laid wait at my neighbor's
door,
[10] then let my wife grind for another,
and let others bow down over her.
[11] For this is a heinous crime;
yes, it is an iniquity to be punished by
the judges.
[12] For it is a fire that consumes to destruction
and would root out all my increase.
[13] "If I have despised the cause of my male or
female servant
when they complained against me,
[14] what then will I do when God rises up?
And when He visits, what will I answer
Him?
[15] Did not He who made me in the womb
make him?
And did not the same One fashion us in
the womb?
[16] "If I have kept the poor from their desire,
or have caused the eyes of the widow
to fail,
[17] or have eaten my morsel by myself,
so that the fatherless could not eat of it

30:9 Job 17:6
30:10 Nu 12:14
30:12 Job 19:12
30:15 Hos 13:3
30:16 Ps 22:14
30:20 Job 19:7
30:25 Ps 35:13–14
30:26 Jer 8:15
30:27 La 2:11
30:28 Ps 38:6
30:29 Mic 1:8
30:30 Ps 102:3
31:2 Job 20:29
31:3 Job 21:30
31:4 2Ch 16:9
31:8 Lev 26:16
31:10 Jer 8:10
31:11 Lev 20:10

18 (but from my youth he was brought up with
me, as with a father,
and I have guided the widow from my
mother's womb);
19 if I have seen anyone perish for lack of
clothing,
or any poor without covering;
20 if his body has not blessed me,
and if he was not warmed with the
fleece of my sheep;
21 if I have lifted up my hand against the
fatherless,
when I saw I had help in the gate;
22 then let my arm fall from my shoulder
blade,
and my arm be broken from the bone.
23 For destruction from God is a terror to me,
and because of His highness I cannot
endure.

24 "If I have made gold my hope,
or have said to the fine gold, 'You are my
confidence';
25 if I rejoiced because my wealth was great,
and because my hand had gained much;
26 if I saw the sun when it shined,
or the moon moving in brightness;
27 and my heart has been secretly enticed,
or my mouth has kissed my hand;
28 this also would be an iniquity to be
punished by the judge,
for I would have denied the God who is
above.

29 "If I rejoiced at the destruction of him who
hated me,
or lifted up myself when disaster found
him
30 (nor have I allowed my mouth to sin
by wishing for a curse on his soul);
31 if the men of my tent have not said,
'Who is there who has not been satisfied
with his meat?'
32 (the stranger has not lodged in the street,
but I opened my doors to the traveler);
33 if I covered my transgressions as any man,
by hiding my iniquity in my heart,
34 did I fear a great multitude,
or did the contempt of families
terrify me,
so that I kept silence, and did not go out
of the door?

35 "Oh, that one would hear me!
Behold, my desire is that the Almighty
would answer me,
and that the One who contends against
me had written a book!
36 Surely I would carry it on my shoulder
and bind it on me like a crown.
37 I would declare to Him the number of my
steps;
like a prince I would approach Him.

38 "If my land cries out against me,
and its furrows also weep together;
39 if I have eaten its fruit without money,
or have caused its owners to lose their
life;
40 let thistles grow instead of wheat,
and weeds instead of barley."

The words of Job are ended.

Elihu Speaks: Job's Three Friends Rebuked

32 So these three men ceased answering
Job, because he was righteous in his
own eyes. 2 Then the wrath of Elihu the son of
Barakel the Buzite, of the family of Ram, was
aroused; his wrath was aroused against Job
because he justified himself rather than God.
3 His wrath was aroused also against his three
friends because they had found no answer
and yet had condemned Job. 4 Now Elihu had
waited until Job had spoken because they were
older than he. 5 When Elihu saw that there was
no answer in the mouth of these three men,
then his wrath was aroused.
6 Elihu the son of Barakel the Buzite an-
swered:

"I am young,
and you are very old;
therefore I was afraid
and dared not show you my opinion.
7 I said, 'Age should speak,
and multitude of years should teach
wisdom.'

A mentor can make it possible for the breath of God to bring my spirit alive (Job 32:7–8).

8 But there is a spirit in man,
and the breath of the Almighty gives
him understanding.
9 Great men are not always wise,
nor do the aged always understand
judgment.

10 "Therefore I say,
'Listen to me; I will also declare my
opinion.'
11 Indeed, I waited for your words;
I listened to your reasons,
while you searched out what to say.
12 Yes, I paid attention to you;
and surely none of you convinced Job
or answered his words.
13 Lest you say, 'We have found wisdom';

31:19 Job 22:6
31:21 Job 22:9
31:23 Job 13:11
31:26 Eze 8:16
31:28 Dt 17:2–7
31:29 Pr 17:5
31:32 Ge 19:2–3
31:33 Pr 28:13
31:34 Ex 23:2
31:39 1Ki 21:19
32:1 Job 10:7
32:2 Ge 22:21
32:6 Job 15:10
32:8 Job 33:4
32:13 Jer 9:23

God *will* subdue him, not man.
14 Now he has not directed his words against me,
so I will not answer him with your speeches.

15 "They are amazed; they answer no more;
they cease speaking.
16 And I have waited,
(for they did not speak, but stood still and answered no more).
17 I said, 'I also will answer my part;
I too will show my opinion.'
18 For I am full of words;
the spirit within me compels me.
19 See, my belly is like wine that has no vent;
it is ready to burst like new wineskins.
20 I will speak, that I may be refreshed;
I will open my lips and answer.
21 Let me not, I pray, show partiality to anyone,
nor let me give flattering titles to man.
22 For I do not know how to give flattering titles;
in so doing my Maker would soon take me away.

Elihu Addresses Job

33 "Therefore, Job, I pray, hear my speeches,
and listen to all my words.
2 Behold, now I have opened my mouth;
my tongue has spoken in my mouth.
3 My words will be from the uprightness of my heart,
and my lips will utter knowledge clearly.
4 The Spirit of God has made me,
and the breath of the Almighty has given me life.
5 If you can answer me,
set your words in order before me; stand up.
6 Surely I am before God like you;
I also am formed out of the clay.
7 Indeed, no dread of me will make you afraid,
nor will my hand be heavy upon you.

8 "Surely you have spoken in my hearing,
and I have heard the sound of your words, saying,
9 'I am clean, without transgression;
I am innocent, nor is there iniquity in me.
10 Behold, He finds occasions against me,
He counts me for His enemy;
11 He puts my feet in the stocks,
He watches all my paths.'

12 "Look, in this you are not just.

32:21 Lev 19:15
33:1 Job 13:6
33:3 Job 27:4
33:4 Ge 2:7
33:6 Job 4:19
33:7 Job 13:21
33:9 Job 10:7
33:11 Job 13:27
....
33:13 Job 40:2
33:14 Ps 62:11
33:15 Job 4:13
33:16 Job 36:10
33:19 Job 30:17
33:21 Job 19:20
33:25 2Ki 5:14
33:26 Ps 50:15
33:27 Ro 6:21
33:29 Eph 1:11
33:30 Ps 56:13

I will answer you, that God is greater than man.
13 Why do you strive against Him?
For He does not give an accounting for any of His words.
14 For God speaks once, yes twice,
yet man does not perceive it.
15 In a dream, in a vision of the night,
when deep sleep falls upon men,
in slumber on their beds,
16 then He opens the ears of men,
and seals their instruction,
17 that He *might* turn aside man from his purpose,
and conceal pride from man.
18 He keeps back his soul from the pit,
and his life from perishing by the sword.

19 "He is also chastened with pain on his bed,
and with strong pain in many of his bones,
20 so that his life abhors bread,
and his soul dainty food.
21 His flesh is consumed away that it cannot be seen,
and his bones that were not seen stick out.
22 Yes, his soul draws near to the grave,
and his life to the executioners.
23 If there is a messenger for him,
an interpreter, one among a thousand,
to show to man what is right for him,
24 then He is gracious to him, and says,
'Deliver him from going down to the pit;
I have found a ransom.'
25 His flesh will be fresher than a child's;
he will return to the days of his youth;
26 he will pray to God, and He will be favorable unto him,
and he will see His face with joy,
for He will render unto man His righteousness.
27 Then he looks at men and says,
'I have sinned and perverted what was right,
and it did not profit me.'
28 He will deliver his soul from going down to the pit,
and his life will see the light.

29 "Behold, God works all these things,
twice, three times with man,
30 to bring back his soul from the pit,
to be enlightened with the light of the living.

31 "Pay attention, Job, listen to me;
hold your peace, and I will speak.
32 If you have anything to say, answer me;
speak, for I desire to justify you.

33 If not, listen to me; hold your peace,
and I will teach you wisdom."

Elihu Proclaims God's Justice

34 Furthermore Elihu answered and said:
2 "Hear my words, O you wise men;
and give ear unto me, you that have knowledge.
3 For the ear tests words,
as the mouth tastes food.
4 Let us choose justice for ourselves;
let us know among ourselves what is good.

5 "For Job has said, 'I am righteous,
but God has taken away my judgment.
6 Should I lie concerning my right?
My wound is incurable, though I am without transgression.'
7 What man is like Job,
who drinks scorn like water,
8 who goes in company with the workers of iniquity
and walks with wicked men?
9 For he has said, 'It profits a man nothing
that he should delight himself in God.'

10 "Therefore listen to me, you men of understanding:
Far be it from God that He should do wickedness,
and from the Almighty that He should commit iniquity.
11 He will repay a man for his work,
and cause every man to find what is according to his ways.
12 Yes, surely God will not do wickedly,
nor will the Almighty pervert judgment.
13 Who has given Him charge over the earth?
Or who has set in order the whole world?
14 If He sets His heart on man,
if He gathers unto Himself His Spirit and His breath,
15 all flesh will perish together,
and man will turn again to dust.

16 "If now you have understanding, hear this;
listen to the voice of my words:
17 Should he who hates justice govern?
And will you condemn Him who is most just?
18 Is it fitting to say to a king, 'You are wicked'?
And to princes, 'You are ungodly'?
19 Yet He is not partial to princes,
nor does He regard the rich more than the poor.
For they all are the work of His hands.
20 In a moment they will die,
and the people will be troubled at midnight and pass away,
and the mighty will be taken away without a hand.

21 "For His eyes are upon the ways of man,
and He sees all his goings.
22 There is no darkness nor shadow of death
where the workers of iniquity may hide themselves.
23 For He will not lay upon man more than right,
that he should enter into judgment with God.
24 He will break in pieces mighty men without number,
and set others in their place.
25 Therefore He knows their works,
and He overturns them in the night
so that they are destroyed.
26 He strikes them as wicked men
in the open sight of others,
27 because they turned back from Him
and would not consider any of His ways,
28 so that they cause the cry of the poor to come unto Him;
and He hears the cry of the afflicted.
29 When He gives quietness, who then can make trouble?
And when He hides His face, who then can behold Him,
whether it is done against a nation or against a man only?
30 That the hypocrite should not reign,
lest the people be ensnared.

31 "Should anyone say to God,
'I have borne chastisement, I will offend no more;
32 teach me what I do not see;
if I have done iniquity, I will do no more'?
33 Should it be according to your mind?
He will repay it, whether you refuse or whether you choose,
and not I; therefore speak what you know.

34 "Let men of understanding say to me,
wise men who listen to me:
35 'Job has spoken without knowledge,
and his words were without wisdom.'
36 My desire is that Job may be tried unto the end,
because he answers like wicked men.
37 For he adds rebellion unto his sin;
he claps his hands among us,
and multiplies his words against God."

33:33 Ps 34:11
34:3 Job 12:11
34:4 1Th 5:21
34:5 Job 27:2
34:6 Job 6:4
34:7 Job 15:16
34:9 Job 35:3
34:10 Ge 18:25
34:11 Ps 62:12
34:12 Job 8:3
34:14 Ps 104:29
34:15 Ge 3:19
34:17 2Sa 23:3
34:18 Ex 22:28
34:19 Dt 10:17
....
34:21 Job 31:4
34:22 Am 9:2–3
34:27 1Sa 15:11
34:28 Job 35:9
34:35 Job 35:16
34:37 Job 27:23

Elihu Condemns Self-Righteousness

35 Elihu spoke again and said:

2 "Do you think this is right,
that you say, 'My righteousness is before God'?
3 For you said, 'What advantage will it be to me?
What profit will I have if I am cleansed from my sin?'

4 "I will answer you,
and your companions with you.
5 Look unto the heavens and see,
and behold the clouds that are higher than you.
6 If you sin, what do you accomplish against Him?
Or if your transgressions are multiplied, what does it do to Him?
7 If you are righteous, what does it give Him?
Or what does He receive from your hand?
8 Your wickedness may hurt a man like you,
and your righteousness may profit a son of man.

9 "Because of the many oppressions they cry out;
they cry out because of the arm of the mighty.
10 But none says, 'Where is God my Maker,
who gives songs in the night,
11 who teaches us more than the beasts of the earth,
and makes us wiser than the birds of heaven?'
12 There they cry out, but He does not answer
because of the pride of evil men.
13 Surely God will not hear vanity,
nor will the Almighty regard it.
14 Although you say you do not see Him,
yet judgment is before Him,
and you *must* trust in Him.
15 But now, because He has not punished in His anger,
nor taken much notice of folly,
16 therefore Job opens his mouth in vain;
he multiplies words without knowledge."

Elihu Proclaims God's Majesty

36 Elihu continued and said:

2 "Bear with me a little, and I will show you
that I have yet to speak on God's behalf.
3 I will bring my knowledge from afar
and will ascribe righteousness to my Maker.
4 For truly my words will not be false;
He who is perfect in knowledge is with you.

5 "Behold, God is mighty and despises no one;
He is mighty in strength and wisdom.
6 He does not preserve the life of the wicked,
but gives justice to the poor.
7 He does not withdraw His eyes from the righteous;
but they are on the throne with kings,
for He establishes them forever, and they are exalted.
8 If they are bound in chains
and held in cords of affliction,
9 then He shows them their work,
and their transgressions that they have exceeded;
10 and He opens their ear to discipline,
and commands that they turn from iniquity.
11 If they obey and serve Him,
they will spend their days in prosperity
and their years in pleasures.
12 But if they do not obey,
they will perish by the sword,
and they will die without knowledge.

13 "But the hypocrites in heart heap up wrath;
they do not cry out when He binds them.
14 They die in youth,
and their life ends among the unclean.
15 He delivers the poor in their affliction,
and opens their ears in oppression.

The Lord delivers the poor from their afflictions; the needy shall not always be forgotten (Job 36:15).

16 "Even so He would have removed you out of distress
into a broad place where there is no restraint;
and that which was set on your table would be full of richness.
17 But you are filled with the judgment due the wicked;
judgment and justice take hold of you.
18 Because there is wrath, beware lest He take you away with a blow;
even a great ransom cannot deliver you.
19 Will He esteem your riches?
No, not gold, nor all the force of your strength.
20 Do not desire the night,
when people are cut off in their place.
21 Take heed! Do not turn to iniquity,
for you have chosen this rather than affliction.

35:3 Job 34:9
35:5 Job 22:12
35:6 Pr 8:36
35:7 Job 22:2–3
35:9 Ex 2:23
35:10 Ps 42:8
35:11 Ps 94:12
35:12 Pr 1:28
35:13 Pr 15:29
35:14 Job 9:11
35:16 Job 38:2
36:4 Job 37:16

36:5 Ps 22:24
36:7 Ps 33:18
36:8 Ps 107:10
36:12 Job 4:21
36:14 Dt 23:17
36:15 Job 36:10
36:16 Ps 23:5
36:18 Job 33:24
36:21 Ps 66:18

22 "Behold, God is exalted in His power;
who teaches like Him?
23 Who has prescribed His way for Him?
Or who can say, 'You have worked
iniquity'?
24 Remember to magnify His work,
which men behold.
25 Every man may see it;
man may behold it from afar.
26 Look, God is great, and we do not know
Him,
nor can the number of His years be
searched out.

27 "For He draws up the drops of water;
they distill rain according to its mist,
28 which the clouds drop down,
and drip upon man abundantly.
29 Indeed, can anyone understand the
spreading of clouds,
or the noise of His tent?
30 See, He spreads His light upon it
and covers the bottom of the sea.
31 For by these He judges the people;
He gives food in abundance.
32 With clouds He covers the light,
and commands it to strike the mark.
33 Its thunder declares it,
the cattle also, concerning the rising
storm.

37 "At this also my heart trembles
and moves out of its place.
2 Hear attentively the thunder of His voice,
and the sound that goes out of His
mouth.
3 He lets it loose under the whole heaven,
and His lightning unto the ends of the
earth.
4 After it a voice roars; He thunders with His
majestic voice,
and He does not restrain them when His
voice is heard.
5 God thunders marvelously with His voice;
He does great things that we cannot
comprehend.
6 For He says to the snow, 'Come on the
earth,'
likewise to the gentle rain and to the
heavy rain of His strength.
7 He seals up the hand of every man,
that all men may know His work.
8 Then the beasts go into dens
and remain in their places.
9 Out of the south comes the whirlwind,
and cold out of the north.
10 By the breath of God frost is given,
and the broad waters are frozen.
11 Also He loads the thick clouds with
moisture;
He scatters His bright clouds,
12 and they are turned about by His guidance,
that they may do whatever He
commands them
upon the face of the inhabited earth.
13 He causes it to come, whether for
correction,
or for His land or for mercy.

14 "Listen to this, Job; stand still
and consider the wondrous works of
God.
15 Do you know when God dispatches them
and causes the light of His cloud to
shine?
16 Do you know how the clouds are balanced,
the wondrous works of Him who is
perfect in knowledge?
17 How your garments are warm,
when He quiets the earth by the south
wind?
18 Have you, with Him, spread out the sky,
which is strong and is like a molded
mirror?

19 "Teach us what we will say to Him,
for we cannot prepare our speech
because of the darkness.
20 Will it be told Him that I speak?
If a man speaks, surely he will be
swallowed up.
21 Now men do not see the bright light
which is in the clouds,
but the wind passes and cleanses them.
22 Fair weather comes out of the north;
with God is terrible majesty.
23 Concerning the Almighty, we cannot find
Him out;
He is excellent in power, and in
judgment,
and in much righteousness He will not
oppress.
24 Men therefore fear Him;
He shows no partiality to those who are
wise in heart."

The LORD Speaks to Job

38 Then the LORD answered Job out of the
whirlwind and said:
2 "Who is this who darkens counsel
by words without knowledge?
3 Prepare yourself like a man;
for I will question you,
and you shall answer Me.

4 "Where were you when I laid the
foundations of the earth?
Declare, if you have understanding.
5 Who has determined its measurements, if
you know?
Or who has stretched the line upon it?

36:23 Job 8:3
36:26 Ps 90:2
36:29 Job 37:16
36:31 Job 37:13
37:3 Job 38:13
37:5 Job 5:9
37:6 Job 36:27
37:8 Ps 104:22
37:9 Job 9:9
37:10 Job 38:29–30
....
37:12 Ps 148:8
37:13 1Ki 18:45
37:16 Job 36:4
37:18 Isa 44:24
37:23 1Ti 6:16
37:24 Mt 10:28
38:2 Job 35:16
38:3 Job 40:7
38:4 Ps 104:5
38:5 Isa 40:12

6 To what are its foundations fastened?
Or who laid its cornerstone
7 when the morning stars sang together,
and all the sons of God shouted for joy?

8 "Or who shut up the sea with doors
when it broke forth and went out of the womb?
9 When I made the cloud its garment,
and thick darkness its swaddling band,
10 and broke up for it My decreed place,
and set bars and doors,
11 and said, 'This far you will come but no farther,
and here your proud waves will be stopped'?

12 "Have you commanded the morning in your days,
and caused the dawn to know its place,
13 that it might take hold of the ends of the earth,
that the wicked might be shaken out of it?
14 It is turned like clay by the seal,
and it stands out as a garment.
15 From the wicked their light is withheld,
and the high arm will be broken.

16 "Have you entered into the springs of the sea?
Or have you walked in search of the depths?
17 Have the gates of death been opened to you?
Or have you seen the doors of the shadow of death?
18 Have you perceived the breadth of the earth?
Declare, if you know it all.

19 "Where is the path where light dwells?
And as for darkness, where is its place,
20 that you should take it to its boundary,
and that you should know the paths to its house?
21 Do you know it because you were born then,
or because the number of your days is many?

22 "Have you entered the treasuries of the snow?
Or have you seen the treasuries of the hail,
23 which I have reserved against the time of trouble,
against the day of battle and war?
24 By what way is the light diffused,
or the east wind scattered upon the earth?

38:6 Job 26:7
38:7 Job 1:6
38:8 Ge 1:9
38:10 Ps 104:9
38:11 Ps 89:9
38:13 Job 37:3
38:15 Ps 10:15
38:16 Ps 77:19
38:17 Ps 9:13
38:21 Job 15:7
38:22 Job 37:6
38:23 Jos 10:11

....

38:25 Job 28:26
38:28 Jer 14:22
38:29 Ps 147:16–17
38:30 Job 37:10
38:31 Job 9:9
38:33 Jer 31:35–36
38:36 Job 32:8
38:39 Ps 104:21
38:41 Ps 147:9
39:1 1Sa 24:2

25 Who has divided a channel for the overflowing waters,
or a path for the thunderbolt,
26 to cause it to rain on the earth where no man is,
on the wilderness in which there are no people,
27 to satisfy the desolate waste,
and to cause the bud of the tender herb to spring forth?
28 Does the rain have a father?
Or who has produced the drops of dew?
29 From whose womb came the ice?
And the frost of heaven, who gives it birth?
30 The waters harden like stone,
and the surface of the deep is frozen.

31 "Can you tie the cords to the Pleiades
or loosen the belt of Orion?
32 Can you bring out the constellation in its season?
Or can you guide the Bear with its cubs?
33 Do you know the ordinances of heaven?
Can you set their dominion over the earth?

34 "Can you lift up your voice to the clouds,
that abundance of waters may cover you?
35 Can you send lightning that they may go forth
and say to you, 'Here we are'?
36 Who has put wisdom in the inward parts,
or who has given understanding to the heart?[1]
37 Who can number the clouds by wisdom?
Or who *can* empty out the bottles of heaven,
38 when the dust turns into hard clumps
and the clods stick together?

39 "Will you hunt the prey for the lion?
Or fill the appetite of the young lions,
40 when they crouch in their dens
and lie in the thicket to wait in ambush?
41 Who provides for the raven his food
when his young ones cry unto God,
and they wander about for lack of food?

39 "Do you know the time when the wild mountain goats produce offspring?
Or can you observe when the deer gives birth?
2 Can you number the months that they fulfill,
or do you know the time when they bring forth?

[1] *36* The Heb. may refer to celestial bodies.

3 They bow themselves, they bring forth
their young ones,
they get rid of their labor pains.
4 Their young ones are healthy, they grow
strong with grain;
they go forth and do not return to them.

5 "Who has sent out the wild donkey free?
Or who has loosed the bands of the wild
donkey,
6 whose home I have made the wilderness,
and the barren land his dwelling?
7 He scorns the multitude in the city
and does not regard the shouts of the
driver.
8 The range of the mountains is his pasture,
and he searches after every green thing.

9 "Will the wild ox be willing to serve you
or spend the night by your manger?
10 Can you bind the wild ox in the furrow with
ropes?
Or will he plow the valleys behind you?
11 Will you trust him because his strength is
great?
Or will you leave your labor to him?
12 Will you trust him to bring home your grain
and gather it into your barn?

13 "Did you give the beautiful wings to the
peacocks?
Or wings and feathers to the ostrich,
14 who leaves her eggs in the earth,
and warms them in dust,
15 and forgets that a foot may crush them,
or that the wild beast may break them?
16 She is hardened against her young ones,
as though they were not hers;
her labor is in vain, without concern,
17 because God has deprived her of wisdom,
nor has He imparted understanding to
her.
18 When she lifts up herself on high,
she scorns the horse and his rider.

19 "Have you given the horse strength?
Have you clothed his neck with thunder?
20 Can you make him afraid like a
grasshopper?
The glory of his nostrils is awesome.
21 He paws in the valley and rejoices in his
strength;
he goes on to meet the armed men.
22 He mocks at fear and is not frightened,
nor does he turn back from the sword.
23 The quiver rattles against him,
the glittering spear and the shield.
24 He devours the distance with fierceness
and rage,
and he does not stand still at the sound
of the trumpet.

39:5 Job 6:5
39:6 Ps 107:34
39:9 Nu 23:22
39:16 La 4:3
39:17 Job 35:11
39:20 Jer 8:16
39:21 Jer 8:6

....

39:27 Jer 49:16
39:29 Job 9:26
39:30 Mt 24:28
40:2 Job 33:13
40:4 Job 29:9
40:6 Job 38:1
40:7 Job 38:3
40:10 Ps 93:1
40:11 Da 4:37
40:13 Isa 2:10

25 At the sound of the trumpet he says, 'Aha';
he smells the battle afar off,
the thunder of the captains, and the
shouting.

26 "Does the hawk fly by your wisdom,
and stretch her wings toward the south?
27 Does the eagle mount up at your command
and make her nest on high?
28 She dwells and remains on the rock,
upon the crag of the rock, and the strong
place.
29 From there she seeks the prey,
and her eyes see it from afar.
30 Her young ones also suck up blood,
and where the slain are, there she is."

40 Moreover, the LORD answered Job and
said:

2 "Will he who argues with the Almighty
instruct Him?
He who rebukes God, let him answer it."

Job Replies to the LORD

3 Then Job answered the LORD and said:

4 "Behold, I am vile; what shall I answer
You?
I will lay my hand over my mouth.
5 Once have I spoken, but I will not answer;
yes, twice, but I will proceed no further."

The LORD Challenges Job

6 Then the LORD answered Job out of the
whirlwind and said:

7 "Prepare yourself now like a man;
I will question you,
and you will answer Me.
8 "Will you indeed annul My judgment?
Will you condemn Me, that you may be
righteous?
9 Have you an arm like God?
Or can you thunder with a voice like
Him?
10 Adorn yourself now with majesty and
excellence,
and array yourself with glory and
beauty.
11 Let loose the rage of your wrath,
and look on every one who is proud and
abase him;
12 look on every one who is proud and bring
him low,
and tread down the wicked in their
place.
13 Hide them in the dust together,
and imprison them in the hidden place
of the grave.
14 Then I will also confess to you
that your own right hand can save you.

[15]"Look now at the behemoth
which I made along with you;
he eats grass like an ox.
[16]See now his strength is in his hips,
and his power is in the muscles of his belly.
[17]He moves his tail like a cedar;
the sinews of his thighs are wrapped together.
[18]His bones are like strong pieces of brass;
his bones are like bars of iron.
[19]He is the first of the works of God;
He who made him can bring near His sword.
[20]Surely the mountains bring forth food for him,
where all the beasts of the field play.
[21]He lies under the shady trees,
in the thicket of the reed and marsh.
[22]The shady trees cover him with their shadow;
the willows of the brook surround him.
[23]Look, the river rages, but he is not alarmed;
he trusts that he can draw up the Jordan into his mouth.
[24]Can anyone catch it by its eyes,
or pierce its nose with a snare?

41 "Can you draw out Leviathan with a hook[1]
or snare his tongue with a line which you let down?
2 Can you put a cord into his nose,
or pierce his jaw with a hook?
3 Will he make many supplications to you?
Will he speak soft words to you?
4 Will he make a covenant with you?
Will you take him for a servant forever?
5 Will you play with him as with a bird?
Or will you put him on a leash for your maidens?
6 Will your companions make a banquet of him?
Will they divide him among the merchants?
7 Can you fill his skin with harpoons
or his head with fishing spears?
8 Lay your hand on him;
remember the battle—you will do it no more.
9 Notice, any hope of overcoming him is in vain;
shall not one be overwhelmed at the sight of him?
10 No one is so fierce that he dares to stir him up.
Who then is able to stand before Me?
11 Who has preceded Me that I should repay him?
Everything under heaven is Mine.

12 "I will not conceal his limbs,
nor his power, nor his graceful proportions.
13 Who can remove his outer garment?
Or who can approach him with a double bridle?
14 Who can open the jaws of his face?
His teeth are terrible all around.
15 His scales are his pride,
shut up tightly as with a seal.
16 One is so near to another
that no air can come between them.
17 They are joined to each other;
they stick together that they cannot be separated.
18 His sneezing flashes forth light,
and his eyes are like the eyelids of the morning.
19 Out of his mouth go burning lights,
and sparks of fire leap out.
20 Out of his nostrils goes smoke
as out of a seething pot or cauldron.
21 His breath kindles coals,
and a flame goes out of his mouth.
22 In his neck remains strength,
and sorrow is turned into joy before him.
23 The folds of his flesh are joined together;
they are firm on him; they cannot be moved.
24 His heart is as firm as a stone,
yes, as hard as a piece of the lower millstone.
25 When he raises up himself even the gods are afraid;
because of his crashings they are beside themselves.
26 The sword that reaches him cannot avail,
nor does the spear, the arrow, or the javelin.
27 He counts iron as straw,
and brass as rotten wood.
28 The arrow cannot make him flee;
slingstones are turned into stubble by him.
29 Arrows are counted as straw;
he laughs at the shaking of a spear.
30 Sharp stones are his underside;
he leaves a mark in the mire like a sharp threshing sledge.
31 He makes the deep to boil like a pot;
he makes the sea like a pot of ointment.
32 He leaves a shining wake behind him;
one would think the deep had white hair.
33 On earth there is nothing like him,
a creature made without fear.
34 He beholds all high things;
he is a king over all the children of pride."

40:20 Ps 104:14
41:1 Job 3:8
41:2 Isa 37:29
41:4 Ex 21:6
41:11 Ps 24:1

41:18 Job 3:9
41:21 Ps 18:8
41:33 Job 40:19

[1]1 Heb. text 40:25

Job's Repentance

42 Then Job answered the LORD and said:

2 "I know that You can do everything,
and that no thought can be withheld
from You.
3 'Who is he who hides counsel without
knowledge?'
Therefore I have uttered what I did not
understand,
things too wonderful for me which I did
not know.

4 " 'Hear, and I will speak;
I will question you,
and you declare to Me.'
5 I have heard of You by the hearing of the
ear,
but now my eye sees You.
6 Therefore I abhor myself,
and repent in dust and ashes."

Epilogue

7 And so it was, that after the LORD had spoken
these words to Job, the LORD said to Eliphaz the
Temanite, "My wrath is kindled against you
and against your two friends, for you have not
spoken of Me what is right as My servant Job
has. 8 And now, take for yourselves seven bulls
and seven rams, and go to My servant Job, and
offer up for yourselves a burnt offering; and
My servant Job will pray for you. For him I will
accept, lest I deal with you according to your
folly, in that you have not spoken of Me the
thing which is right like My servant Job." 9 So
Eliphaz the Temanite, and Bildad the Shuhite,
and Zophar the Naamathite went and did as
the LORD had commanded them; the LORD also
accepted Job.
10 And the LORD restored the fortunes of Job
when he prayed for his friends, and also the
LORD gave Job twice as much as he had before.
11 Then all of his brothers, and all his sisters,
and all of those who had been of acquaintance
before came to Job, and they ate bread with
him in his house, and they consoled him and
comforted him for all the adversity that the
LORD had brought upon him. Every man also
gave him a piece of money and an earring
of gold.
12 So the LORD blessed the latter days of Job
more than his beginning, for he had fourteen
thousand sheep, and six thousand camels, and
a thousand yoke of oxen, and a thousand fe-
male donkeys. 13 He had also seven sons and
three daughters. 14 He called the name of the
first Jemimah; and the name of the second
Keziah; and the name of the third Keren-Hap-
puch. 15 In all the land, there were no women
as beautiful as the daughters of Job, and their
father gave them an inheritance along with
their brothers.
16 After this, Job lived a hundred and forty
years, and saw his sons, and their sons to the
fourth generation. 17 So Job died, being old and
full of days.

42:2 Mt 19:26
42:3 Job 38:2
42:4 Job 38:3
42:5 Ro 10:17
42:8 Nu 23:1

42:10 Ps 14:7
42:11 Job 2:11
42:12 Job 1:3
42:13 Job 1:2
42:17 Ge 15:15

Author: King David, Asaph, King Solomon, Moses, Sons of Korah, and Others

Written: Written over centuries, compiled by Jewish scribes in about 537 BC

Themes: Praise to God, Comfort for Struggles, Fears, and Concerns

PSALMS

Dear Spirit Led Woman,

One of my favorite things about Psalms is David's transparency about his weakness and his need for God. His life is a beautiful example to us that even the spiritually mature are in danger of allowing their hearts to wander away from God.

If your heart has wandered, recognize your condition and cry out for God's help. Ask forgiveness and be willing to forgive others. Get your heart right with others and with God. These are the first steps back into His empowering grace. Next, learn to walk in the Spirit, keeping your mind on God and His kingdom by praying continually. In this manner the Holy Spirit will become a filter for your thoughts. Daily pray Psalm 139:23–24, "Search me, O God, and know my heart; try me, and know my concerns, and see if there is any rebellious way in me, and lead me in the ancient way." God will be faithful to answer this prayer and to keep your heart stayed on Him.

Joy F. Strang

BOOK ONE
Psalms 1–41

PSALM 1

1 Blessed is the man
who walks not in the counsel of the ungodly,
nor stands in the path of sinners,
nor sits in the seat of scoffers;
2 but his delight is in the law of the LORD,
and in His law he meditates day and night.
3 He will be like a tree planted by the rivers of water,
that brings forth its fruit in its season;
its leaf will not wither,
and whatever he does will prosper.

4 The ungodly are not so,
but are like the chaff
which the wind drives away.
5 Therefore the ungodly will not stand in the judgment,
nor sinners in the congregation of the righteous.

6 For the LORD knows the way of the righteous,
but the way of the ungodly will perish.

PSALM 2

1 Why do the nations rage,
and the peoples plot in vain?
2 The kings of the earth set themselves,
and the rulers take counsel together,
against the LORD
and against His anointed, saying,
3 "Let us tear off their bonds
and cast away their ropes from us."

4 He who sits in the heavens laughs;
the LORD ridicules them.
5 Then He will speak to them in His wrath
and terrify them in His burning anger:
6 "I have installed My king
on Zion, My holy hill."

7 I will declare the decree of the LORD:

He said to me, "You are My son;
this day have I begotten you.

> I am a joint heir with Jesus Christ (Ps 2:8).

8 Ask of Me,
and I will give you the nations for your inheritance,
and the ends of the earth for your possession.
9 You will break them with a scepter of iron;
you will dash them in pieces like a potter's vessel."

10 Now then, you kings, be wise;
be admonished, you judges of the earth.
11 Serve the LORD with fear;
tremble with trepidation!
12 Kiss the son, lest He become angry,
and you perish in the way,
for His wrath kindles in a flash.
Blessed are all who seek refuge in Him.

PSALM 3

A Psalm of David, when he fled from Absalom his son.

1 LORD, how my foes have multiplied!
Many rise up against me!
2 Many are saying about my life,
"There is no help for him in God."
Selah[1]
3 But You, O LORD, are a shield for me,
my glory and the One who raises up my head.
4 I cried to the LORD with my voice,
and He answered me from His holy hill. Selah

5 I lay down and slept;
I awoke, for the LORD sustained me.
6 I will not be afraid of multitudes of people
who have set themselves against me all around.

7 Arise, O LORD;
save me, O my God!
For You have struck all my enemies on the cheek;
You have broken the teeth of the wicked.

8 Salvation belongs to the LORD.
Your blessing is on Your people. Selah

PSALM 4

For the Music Director. With stringed instruments. A Psalm of David.

1 Hear me when I call,
O God of my righteousness!
You have given me relief when I was in distress;
have mercy on me, and hear my prayer.

2 O people, how long will you turn my glory into shame?
How long will you love vanity and seek after lies? Selah

1:1 Jer 15:17
1:2 Jos 1:8
1:3 Ge 39:3
1:4 Job 21:18
1:5 Ps 5:5
1:6 2Ti 2:19
2:1 Ps 46:6
2:2 Ps 45:7
2:3 Jer 5:5
2:4 Ps 37:13
2:6 Ps 45:6
2:7 Ac 13:33
2:8 Ps 22:27
....
2:9 Ps 89:23
2:12 Jn 5:23
3:2 Ps 71:11
3:3 Ps 27:6
3:4 Ps 2:6
3:5 Ps 4:8
3:7 Job 16:10
3:8 Isa 43:11

[1] 2 Musical term for a pause or change in the music.

[3] Know that the LORD set apart the faithful for Himself;
the LORD hears when I call to Him.

[4] Tremble *in awe*, and do not sin.
Commune with your own heart on your bed,
and be still. Selah
[5] Offer sacrifices of righteousness,
and trust in the LORD.

[6] Many are saying, "Who will show us any good?"
Lift up the light of Your face over us.
[7] You have placed gladness in my heart
that is better than when their corn and their new wine abound.

[8] I will both lie down in peace and sleep;
for You, LORD,
make me dwell safely and securely.

PSALM 5

For the Music Director. With the flutes. A Psalm of David.

[1] Give ear to my words, O LORD;
consider my meditation.
[2] Listen to the voice of my cry,
my King and my God,
for to You will I pray.

[3] O LORD, in the morning You will hear my voice;
in the morning I will direct my prayer to You,
and I will watch expectantly.
[4] For You are not a God who has pleasure in wickedness,
nor will evil dwell with You.
[5] Those who boast will not stand in Your sight;
You hate all workers of iniquity.
[6] You will destroy those who speak lies;
the LORD abhors
the bloodthirsty and deceitful man.
[7] But as for me, in the abundance of Your mercy
I will enter Your house;
in fear of You I will worship
at Your holy temple.

[8] Lead me, O LORD, in Your righteousness
because of my enemies;
make Your way straight before me.
[9] For there is no uprightness in their mouth;
destruction is in their midst;
their throat is an open tomb;
they flatter with their tongue.
[10] Declare them guilty, O God;
may they fall by their own counsels;
cast them out in the multitude of their transgressions,
for they have rebelled against You.
[11] But may all those who seek refuge in You rejoice;
may they ever shout for joy,
because You defend them;
may those who love Your name be joyful in You.

[12] For You, LORD, will bless the righteous;
You surround him with favor like a shield.

PSALM 6

For the Music Director. With stringed instruments. According to The Sheminith. A Psalm of David.

[1] O LORD, do not rebuke me in Your anger,
nor discipline me in the heat of Your anger.
[2] Be gracious to me, O LORD, for I am weak;
O LORD, heal me, for my bones are terrified.
[3] My soul is greatly troubled,
but You, O LORD, how long?

[4] Return, O LORD, rescue my soul.
Save me for the sake of Your lovingkindness.
[5] For in death there is no remembrance of You;
in Sheol who will give You thanks?

[6] I am weary with my groaning;
all night I flood my bed *with weeping*;
I drench my couch with my tears.
[7] My eye wastes away from grief;
it grows weak because of all those hostile to me.

[8] Depart from me, all you workers of iniquity;
for the LORD has heard the voice of my weeping.
[9] The LORD has heard my supplication;
the LORD accepts my prayer.
[10] May all my enemies be ashamed and greatly terrified;
may they turn back and be suddenly ashamed.

PSALM 7

A Shiggaion of David, which he sang to the LORD concerning the words of Cush, a Benjamite.

[1] O LORD my God, in You I put my trust;
save me from all those who persecute me, and deliver me,
[2] lest they tear my soul like a lion,

4:4 Ps 77:6
4:5 Dt 33:19
4:6 Nu 6:26
4:7 Isa 9:3
4:8 Ps 3:5
5:3 Ps 88:13
5:5 Ps 1:5
5:6 Ps 55:23
5:7 Ps 138:2
5:8 Ps 27:11
5:9 Ro 3:13
6:1 Ps 38:1
6:2 Hos 6:1
6:3 Ps 90:13
6:4 Ps 17:13
6:5 Ps 30:9
6:6 Ps 69:3
6:7 Job 17:7
6:8 Ps 119:115
7:1 Ps 31:15
7:2 Ps 50:22

rending it in pieces, while there is none
to deliver.
3 O LORD my God, if I have done this,
if there is iniquity in the palms of my
hands,
4 if I have repaid evil to him who was at
peace with me,
or have delivered my adversary without
cause,
5 then may the enemy pursue my life and
overtake me;
may my enemy trample my life to the
ground,
and lay my honor in the dust. Selah

6 Arise, O LORD, in Your anger;
rise up because of the rage of my
adversaries,
and awaken Yourself for me; You have
commanded justice.
7 The congregation of the peoples surround
You;
return above it to heaven's heights.
8 The LORD will judge the peoples;
grant me justice, O LORD, according to my
righteousness,
and according to my integrity within me.
9 May the evil of the wicked come to an end;
may You vindicate the righteous one;
You are a righteous God who examines the
minds and hearts.

10 My defense depends on God,
who saves the upright in heart.
11 God is a righteous judge,
and God has indignation every day.
12 If one does not repent,
God will sharpen His sword;
He has bent His bow and made it ready.
13 He has prepared for Himself deadly
weapons;
He makes His arrows flaming shafts.

14 The wicked man writhes in pain of iniquity;
he has conceived mischief and brought
forth falsehood.
15 He who digs a hole and hollows it
will then fall into his own pit.
16 His mischief will return on his own head;
his violence will descend on the crown
of his own head.

17 I will thank the LORD according to His
righteousness,
and will sing praise to the name of the
LORD Most High.

7:3 1Sa 24:11
7:4 1Sa 24:7
7:6 Ps 44:23
7:8 Ps 26:1
7:9 Jer 11:20
7:10 Ps 125:4
7:12 Dt 32:41
7:14 Job 15:35
7:15 Job 4:8
7:16 Est 9:25
7:17 Ps 9:2

8:1 Ps 148:13
8:2 Ps 44:16
8:3 Ps 111:2
8:4 Job 7:17
8:5 Heb 2:9
8:6 Ge 1:28
8:9 Ps 8:1
9:1 Ps 86:12
9:2 Ps 5:11
9:4 Ps 140:12
9:5 Pr 10:7

PSALM 8

For the Music Director. According to
The Gittith. A Psalm of David.

1 O LORD, our Lord,
how excellent is Your name in all the
earth!

You have set Your glory
above the heavens.
2 Out of the mouth of babes and nursing
infants
You have ordained strength
because of Your enemies,
to silence the enemy and the avenger.
3 When I consider Your heavens,
the work of Your fingers,
the moon and the stars,
which You have established,
4 what is man that You are mindful of him,
and the son of man that You attend to
him?

5 For You have made him a little lower than
the angels,
and crowned him with glory and honor.
6 You have given him dominion over the
works of Your hands;
You have put all things under his feet,
7 all sheep and oxen,
and also the beasts of the field,
8 the birds of the air,
and the fish of the sea,
and whatever travels the paths of the
seas.

9 O LORD, our Lord,
how excellent is Your name in all the
earth!

PSALM 9

For the Music Director. To the melody of
"The Death of the Son." A Psalm of David.

1 I will give thanks to You, O LORD, with my
whole heart;
I will declare all Your marvelous works.
2 I will be glad and rejoice in You;
I will sing praise to Your name, O Most
High.

3 When my enemies are turned back,
they will stumble and perish at Your
presence.
4 For You have maintained my right and my
cause;
You sat on the throne judging what is
right.
5 You have rebuked the nations,
You have destroyed the wicked,

You have wiped out their name forever
and ever.
6 O you enemy, destructions have come to
you for a perpetual end.
You have destroyed cities;
their memory perished with them.

7 But the LORD remains forever;
He has established His throne for
judgment.
8 He will judge the world in righteousness;
He will give judgment to the peoples in
uprightness.
9 The LORD also will be a refuge for the
oppressed,
a refuge in times of trouble.
10 Those who know Your name will put their
trust in You,
for You, LORD, have not forsaken those
who seek You.

11 Sing praises to the LORD who dwells in
Zion;
declare His deeds among the people.
12 He who avenges deaths remembers them;
He does not forget the cry of the
humble.
13 Be gracious to me, O LORD; consider my
trouble from those who hate me,
O You who lifts me up from the gates of
death,
14 that I may recount all Your praise
in the gates of the daughter of Zion,
that I may rejoice in Your salvation.

15 The nations have sunk down in the pit that
they made;
their own foot is caught in the net which
they hid.
16 The LORD is known by the judgment that
He executes;
the wicked one is snared in the work of
his own hands. Meditation. Selah
17 The wicked will be turned to Sheol,
and all the nations that forget God.
18 For the needy will not always be forgotten,
nor will the hope of the poor perish
forever.

19 Arise, O LORD, may mortals not prevail;
let the nations be judged in Your sight.
20 Put them in fear, O LORD,
that the nations themselves may know
they are mortals. Selah

PSALM 10

1 Why do You stand far off, O LORD?
Why do You hide Yourself in times of
trouble?

9:8 Ps 96:13
9:9 Ps 32:7
9:10 Ps 91:14
9:11 Ps 107:22
9:12 Ge 9:5
9:14 Ps 13:5
9:15 Ps 7:15–16
9:16 Ex 7:5
9:17 Job 8:13
9:18 Pr 23:18
10:1 Ps 22:1

....

10:2 Ps 7:16
10:3 Ps 94:4
10:6 Mt 24:48
10:7 Ps 7:14
10:9 Ps 17:12
10:12 Ps 9:12
10:14 Ps 68:5
10:15 Ps 37:17
10:16 Ps 29:10
10:17 1Ch 29:18
10:18 Ps 82:3

2 In arrogance the wicked persecutes the
poor;
let them be caught in the devices they
have planned.
3 For the wicked boasts of his soul's desire;
he blesses the greedy and despises the
LORD.
4 The wicked, through the pride of his
countenance, will not seek *God*;
God is not in all his thoughts.
5 His ways are always prosperous;
Your judgments are high and distant
from him;
as for all his enemies, they scoff at him.
6 He says in his heart, "I shall not be moved;
for generations I shall not meet
adversity."
7 His mouth is filled with cursing and deceit
and oppression;
under his tongue is mischief and
iniquity.
8 He sits in the lurking places of the villages;
in the secret places he murders the
innocent;
his eyes lurk against the unfortunate.
9 He lies in wait secretly as a lion in his den;
he lies in wait to catch the poor;
he catches the poor, drawing them into
his net.
10 He crouches; he lies low,
so that the unfortunate fall by his
strength.
11 He says in his heart, "God has forgotten;
He hides His face; He will never see it."

12 Arise, O LORD! O God, lift up Your hand!
Do not forget the humble.
13 Why do the wicked despise God?
He says in his heart,
"You will require an account."
14 You have seen it, for You observe trouble
and grief,
to repay it with Your hand.
The unfortunate one entrusts it to You;
You are the helper of the orphan.
15 Break the arm of the wicked and the evil
man;
seek out his wickedness
until You find none.

16 The LORD is King forever and ever;
the nations perished from His land.
17 The desire of the humble You have heard,
O LORD;
You make their heart attentive; You bend
Your ear
18 to judge the orphan and the oppressed;
man on earth no longer trembles.

PSALM 11

For the Music Director. A Psalm of David.

1 In the LORD I seek refuge;
how do you say to my soul,
"Flee as a bird to your mountain,
2 for the wicked bend their bow;
they make ready their arrow on the string,
that they may treacherously shoot
the upright in heart.
3 If the foundations are broken,
what can the righteous do?"

4 The LORD is in His holy temple,
His throne is in heaven;
His eyes see,
His eyes examine mankind.
5 The LORD tests the righteous,
but the wicked and one who loves violence
His soul hates.
6 Upon the wicked He will rain
coals of fire and brimstone and a burning wind;
this will be the portion of their cup.

7 For the righteous LORD
loves righteousness;
His countenance beholds the upright.

PSALM 12

For the Music Director. According to The Sheminith. A Psalm of David.

1 Help, LORD, for the godly man comes to an end,
for the faithful disappear from sons of men.
2 They speak empty words, each with his own neighbor;
they speak with flattering lips and a double heart.

3 The LORD will cut off all flattering lips,
and the tongue that speaks proud things,
4 who have said, "With our tongue will we prevail;
our lips are in our control, who is master over us?"

5 "Because the poor are plundered,
because the needy sigh,
now I will arise," says the LORD;
"I will place him in the safety for which he yearns."
6 The words of the LORD are pure words;
they are silver tried in an earthen furnace
refined seven times.

7 You will keep them, O LORD;
You will preserve them from this generation.
8 The wicked walk on every side,
when the worthless of mankind are exalted.

PSALM 13

For the Music Director. A Psalm of David.

1 How long, O LORD? Will You forget me for good?
How long will you hide Your face from me?
2 How long will I harbor cares in my soul
and sorrow in my heart by day?
How long will my enemy loom over me?

3 Take note and answer me, O LORD my God!
Brighten my eyes, lest I sleep the sleep of death,
4 lest my enemy say, "I have him,"
lest my foes exult when I stumble.

5 I for my part confide in Your kindness;
may my heart exult in Your salvation!
6 I will sing to the LORD,
because He has dealt bountifully with me.

PSALM 14

Ps 53:1–6

For the Music Director. A Psalm of David.

1 The fool has said in his heart,
"There is no God."
They are corrupt, they do abominable deeds,
there is none who does good.

2 The LORD looks down from heaven
on the children of men,
to see if there are any who understand,
who seek God.
3 They all turn aside,
together they become corrupt;
there is none who does good,
not even one.

4 Have all the workers of iniquity no knowledge,
who eat my people as they eat bread,
but do not call on the LORD?
5 There they were in great fear,
for God is with the generation of the righteous.
6 You shame the counsel of the poor,
but the LORD is his refuge.

7 Oh, that the salvation of Israel would come from Zion!

11:3 Ps 82:5
11:4 Ps 18:6
11:5 Ge 22:1
11:6 Eze 38:22
11:7 Ps 17:15
12:1 Isa 57:1
12:2 Ps 41:6
12:3 Da 7:8
12:5 Isa 33:10
12:6 Ps 18:30
12:7 Ps 37:28
13:1 Job 13:24
13:3 Ezr 9:8
13:4 Ps 25:2
13:5 Ps 9:14
13:6 Ps 116:7
14:1 Ps 10:4
14:4 Ps 79:6
14:5 Ps 73:15
14:6 Ps 9:9
14:7 Ps 53:6

When the LORD turns back the captivity
of His people,
Jacob will rejoice, and Israel will be glad.

PSALM 15

A Psalm of David.

1 LORD, who will abide in Your tabernacle?
Who will dwell in Your holy hill?
2 He who walks uprightly,
and does righteousness,
and speaks truth in his heart;
3 he who does not slander with the tongue
and does no evil to his neighbor,
nor bears a reproach against his friend;
4 in whose eyes a vile person is despised,
but who honors those who fear the LORD;
he who swears to avoid evil
and does not change;
5 he who does not put his money out to
usury,
nor take a bribe against the innocent.
He who does these things
will never be moved.

PSALM 16

A Miktam of David.

1 Preserve me, O God,
for in You I take refuge.
2 I have said to the LORD, "You are my Lord;
my welfare has no existence outside of
You."
3 For the holy ones who are in the land,
they are the majestic ones; in them is all
my delight.
4 Those who chase after other *gods*,
their sorrows will be multiplied;
their drink offerings of blood I will not
offer,
nor lift their names on my lips.
5 The LORD is the portion of my inheritance
and of my cup;
You support my lot.
6 The lines have fallen for me in pleasant
places;
yes, an inheritance is beautiful for me.
7 I will bless the LORD who has given me
counsel;
my affections also instruct me in the
night seasons.
8 I have set the LORD always before me;
because He is at my right hand,
I will not be moved.
9 Therefore my heart is glad, and my glory
rejoices;
my flesh also will rest in security.
10 For You will not leave my soul in Sheol,
nor will You suffer Your godly one to see
corruption.
11 You will make known to me the path of
life;
in Your presence is fullness of joy;
at Your right hand there are pleasures
for evermore.

PSALM 17

A Prayer of David.

1 Hear a just cause, O LORD,
attend to my cry;
give ear to my prayer
that is not spoken from deceitful lips.
2 May my sentence go out from Your
presence;
may Your eyes see rightly.
3 You have examined my heart; You have
visited me in the night;
You have tried me and found nothing;
I have purposed that my mouth will not
transgress.
4 Concerning the works of men,
by the word of Your lips
I have avoided
the paths of the violent,
5 placing my steps in Your paths,
that my footsteps do not slip.
6 I called on You, for You will answer me,
O God;
incline Your ear to me, and hear my
speech.
7 Show marvelously Your lovingkindness,
O Deliverer of those who seek refuge
by Your right hand from those who arise
in opposition.
8 Keep me as the apple of Your eye;
hide me under the shadow of Your
wings,
9 from the wicked who bring ruin to me,
from my deadly enemies who surround
me.
10 They close their hard hearts;
with their mouth they speak proudly.
11 They have now encircled us in our steps;
they have set their eyes to bend down to
the earth;
12 it is like a lion that is anxious to rip its prey,
and as a young lion lurking in secrecy.
13 Arise, O LORD! Confront him, cast him
down!
Deliver my soul from the wicked by Your
sword,
14 from men by Your hand, O LORD,

15:1 Ps 61:4
15:2 Eph 4:25
15:4 Jdg 11:35
15:5 Ex 22:25
16:1 Ps 17:8
16:4 Ex 23:13
16:5 Ps 23:5
16:6 Ps 78:55
16:7 Ps 73:24
16:8 Ps 73:23
16:9 Ps 30:12
16:11 Mt 7:14
17:1 Ps 61:1
17:3 Job 23:10
17:5 Ps 18:36
17:6 Ps 116:2
17:7 Ps 31:21
17:8 Dt 32:10
17:10 1Sa 2:3
17:12 Ps 7:2
17:14 Lk 16:8

from men of the world whose portion is
in this life.
You fill their belly with Your treasure;
they are satisfied with children,
and they leave their abundance to their
infants.

15 As for me, I will see Your face in
righteousness;
I will be satisfied when I awake with
Your likeness.

PSALM 18

2Sa 22:1–51

For the Music Director. A Psalm of David the servant of the Lord. He spoke to the Lord the words of this song on the day that the Lord delivered him from the hand of all his enemies, and from the hand of Saul. He said:

1 I love You, O Lord, my strength.
2 The Lord is my pillar, and my fortress, and
my deliverer;
my God, my rock, in whom I take refuge;
my shield, and the horn of my salvation,
my high tower.
3 I will call on the Lord, who is worthy to be
praised,
and I will be saved from my enemies.
4 The cords of death encircled me,
and the torrents of destruction terrified
me.
5 The cords of Sheol surrounded me;
the snares of death confronted me.

6 In my distress I called on the Lord,
and cried for help to my God;
He heard my voice from His temple,
and my cry for help came before Him to
His ears.
7 Then the earth shook and quaked;
the foundations of the hills also moved;
they reeled because His anger burned.
8 Smoke went up out of His nostrils,
and fire from His mouth devoured;
coals were kindled by it.
9 He bent the heavens and came down,
and darkness was under His feet.
10 He rode on a cherub, and flew;
He flew swiftly on the wings of the wind.
11 He made darkness His secret place;
His pavilion was surrounding Him,
dark waters and thick clouds of the
skies.
12 At the brightness before Him His thick
clouds passed by,
hailstones and coals of fire.
13 The Lord also thundered in the heavens,
and the Most High gave His voice,
hailstones and coals of fire.

17:15 Ps 16:11
18:4 Ps 116:3
18:10 Ps 104:3
18:11 Ps 97:2
18:13 Ps 104:7
18:14 Ps 144:6
18:15 Ps 106:9
18:16 Ps 144:7
18:17 Ps 35:10
18:19 Ps 31:8
18:20 Ps 24:4
18:21 Ps 119:102
18:26 Pr 3:34
18:27 Ps 101:5
18:28 Job 18:6
18:30 Dt 32:4
18:31 Ps 86:8
18:32 Isa 45:5

14 He sent out His arrows and scattered them,
and He shot out lightning and distressed
them.
15 Then the channels of waters appeared,
and the foundations of the world were
discovered
at Your rebuke, O Lord,
at the blast of the breath of Your nostrils.
16 He sent from above, He took me;
He drew me out of many waters.
17 He delivered me from my strong enemy,
and from those who hated me,
for they were too strong for me.
18 They confronted me in the day of my
calamity,
but the Lord was my support.
19 He also brought me forth into a large place;
He delivered me because He delighted
in me.

20 The Lord rewarded me according to my
righteousness;
according to the cleanness of my hands
He has repaid me.
21 For I have kept the ways of the Lord,
and have not wickedly departed from
my God.
22 For all His judgments were before me,
and I did not put away His statutes from
me.
23 I was also upright before Him,
and I kept myself from my iniquity.
24 Therefore the Lord has repaid me
according to my righteousness,
according to the cleanness of my hands
in His view.

25 With the merciful You will show Yourself
merciful;
with the blameless man You will show
Yourself blameless;
26 with the pure You will show Yourself pure;
and with the crooked You will show
Yourself crooked.
27 For You will save the afflicted people,
but will bring down prideful eyes.
28 For You will cause my lamp to shine;
the Lord my God will enlighten my
darkness.
29 For by You I can run through a troop,
and by my God I can leap a wall.

30 As for God, His way has integrity;
the word of the Lord is proven;
He is a shield
to all those who take refuge in Him.
31 For who is God except the Lord?
Or who is a rock besides our God?
32 It is God who clothes me with strength,
and gives my way integrity.

33 He makes my feet like the feet of a deer,
and causes me to stand on my high places.
34 He trains my hands for war,
so that my arms bend a bow of bronze.
35 You have given me the shield of Your salvation,
and Your right hand has held me up,
and Your gentleness has made me great.
36 You have lengthened my stride under me,
so that my feet did not slip.

37 I pursued my enemies and overtook them;
I did not return until they were destroyed.
38 I wounded them, and they were not able to rise;
they are fallen under my feet.
39 For You clothed me with strength for the battle;
You subdued under me those who rose up against me.
40 You gave me the necks of my enemies,
and I destroyed those who hate me.
41 They cried for help, but there was none to save them;
even to the LORD, but He did not answer them.
42 Then I beat them small as the dust before the wind;
I cast them out as the dirt in the streets.
43 You have delivered me from the hostilities of the people,
and You have made me the head of nations;
a people whom I have not known serve me.
44 At hearing a report, they obey me;
foreigners come cringing to me.
45 Foreigners fade away,
and come quaking out of their prisons.

46 The LORD lives! And blessed be my Rock!
May the God of my salvation be exalted.
47 It is God who avenges me
and subdues the people under me;
48 He delivers me from my enemies.
You lift me up above those who rise up against me;
You have delivered me from the violent man.
49 Therefore I will give thanks to You, O LORD, among the nations,
and sing praises to Your name.
50 He gives great deliverance to His king,
and shows lovingkindness to His anointed,
to David and to his descendants for evermore.

18:33 Dt 32:13
18:34 Ps 144:1
18:36 Pr 4:12
18:41 Pr 1:28
18:43 Isa 52:15
18:44 Ps 66:3
18:45 Mic 7:17
18:47 Ps 47:3
18:49 Ro 15:9
18:50 Ps 144:10

19:1 Ro 1:19–20
19:2 Ps 74:16
19:4 Ro 10:18
19:6 Ecc 1:5
19:7 Ps 111:7
19:8 Ps 12:6
19:9 Ps 119:142
19:10 Ps 119:72
19:11 Pr 29:18
19:12 Ps 90:8
19:13 Ps 119:133
19:14 Isa 47:4

PSALM 19

For the Music Director. A Psalm of David.

1 The heavens declare the glory of God,
and the firmament shows His handiwork.
2 Day unto day utters speech,
and night unto night declares knowledge.

> I receive Your knowledge in the night (Ps 19:2).

3 There is no speech and there are no words;
their voice is not heard.
4 Their line has gone out through all the earth,
and their words to the end of the world.

In them has He set a tent for the sun,
5 which is like a bridegroom coming out of his chamber;
it rejoices as a strong man to run a race.
6 Its going forth is from one end of the heavens,
and its circuit extends to the other end,
and there is nothing hidden from its heat.

7 The law of the LORD is perfect,
converting the soul;
the testimony of the LORD is sure,
making wise the simple;
8 the statutes of the LORD are right,
rejoicing the heart;
the commandment of the LORD is pure,
enlightening the eyes;
9 the fear of the LORD is clean,
enduring forever;
the judgments of the LORD are true
and righteous altogether.

10 More to be desired are they than gold,
yes, than much fine gold;
sweeter also than honey and the honeycomb.
11 Moreover by them is Your servant warned,
and by keeping them comes great reward.
12 Who can understand his errors?
Cleanse me from secret faults.
13 Keep back Your servant also from presumptuous sins;
may they not rule over me.
Then I will be upright
and innocent from great transgression.

14 Let the words of my mouth and the meditation of my heart
be acceptable in Your sight,
O LORD, my strength and my Redeemer.

PSALM 20

For the Music Director. A Psalm of David.

[1] May the LORD answer you in the day of
trouble;
may the name of the God of Jacob
defend you;
[2] may He send you help from the sanctuary,
and strengthen you from Zion;
[3] may He remember all your offerings,
and accept your burnt offering. Selah
[4] May He grant you according to your own
heart,
and fulfill all your counsel.
[5] We will rejoice in your salvation,
and in the name of our God we will set
up our banners;
may the LORD fulfill all your petitions.

[6] Now I know that the LORD saves His
anointed;
He will answer him from His holy
heaven
with the saving strength of His right
hand.
[7] Some trust in chariots, and some in horses,
but we will remember the name of the
LORD our God.
[8] They are brought down and fallen,
but we arise and stand upright.
[9] Save, LORD!
May the King answer us when we call.

PSALM 21

For the Music Director. A Psalm of David.

[1] The king will rejoice in Your strength,
O LORD,
and in Your salvation how greatly will
he rejoice!

[2] You have given him his heart's desire,
and have not withheld the request of his
lips. Selah
[3] For You meet him with the blessings of
goodness;
You set a crown of pure gold on his
head.
[4] He asked life of You, and You gave it him,
length of days forever and ever.
[5] His glory is great in Your salvation;
honor and majesty You set on him.
[6] For You place blessings on him forever;
You make him rejoice with gladness with
Your presence.
[7] For the king trusts in the LORD,
and by the lovingkindness of the Most
High
he will not be moved.

20:1 Ps 46:7
20:4 Ps 21:2
20:5 Ps 60:4
20:6 Ps 28:8
20:7 2Ch 32:8
21:3 2Sa 12:30
21:4 Ps 91:16

. . . .

21:9 Mal 4:1
21:10 Ps 37:28
21:11 Ps 2:1
22:1 Mt 27:46
22:2 Ps 42:3
22:3 Dt 10:21
22:5 Isa 49:23
22:6 Job 25:6
22:7 Mk 15:29
22:8 Ps 91:14
22:9 Ps 71:6
22:10 Isa 49:1

[8] Your hand will find out all Your enemies;
Your right hand will find out those who
hate You.
[9] You will make them as a fiery oven
in the time of Your appearance;
the LORD will swallow them up in His
wrath,
and fire will devour them.
[10] You will destroy their offspring from the
earth,
and their descendants from among the
children of men.
[11] For they intended evil against You;
they devised evil thoughts they will not
be able to accomplish.
[12] For You will make them turn their back,
when You aim with Your bowstrings
against their face.
[13] Be exalted, LORD, by Your strength;
may we sing and make music to Your
might.

PSALM 22

For the Music Director. To the melody of
"The Doe of the Dawn." A Psalm of David.

[1] My God, my God, why have You forsaken
me?
Why are You so far from delivering me,
and from my roaring words of distress?
[2] O my God, I cry in the daytime, but You do
not answer;
and at night, but I have no rest.

[3] But You are holy,
O You who inhabits the praises of Israel.
[4] Our fathers trusted in You;
they trusted, and You did deliver them.
[5] They cried to You and were delivered;
they trusted in You and were not put to
shame.

[6] But I am a worm, and not a man;
a reproach of men and despised by the
people.
[7] All who see me laugh me to scorn;
they sneer with the lip, they shake the
head, saying,
[8] "Trust in the LORD,
let Him deliver him;
let Him rescue him,
seeing He delights in him."
[9] But You are He who took me out of the
womb;
You caused me to trust
while I was on my mother's breasts.
[10] I was cast on You from birth;
You are my God from my mother's
womb.

[11]Be not far from me
for trouble is near,
for there is none to help.
[12]Many bulls encircle me;
strong bulls of Bashan surround me.
[13]They open their mouths against me,
as a preying and roaring lion.
[14]I am poured out like water,
and all my bones are out of joint;
my heart is like wax;
it is melted inside my body.
[15]My strength is dried up like a potsherd,
and my tongue cleaves to my jaws;
and You have set me toward the dust of death.
[16]For dogs have encompassed me;
the assembly of the wicked has enclosed me;
like a lion they pin my hands and my feet;
[17]I can count all my bones;
they look and stare on me.
[18]They part my garments among them
and cast lots for my clothes.
[19]But do not be far from me, O LORD;
O my Help, hasten to my aid.
[20]Rescue my soul from the sword,
my only life from the power of the dog.
[21]Save me from the lion's mouth,
and from the horns of the wild ox,
answer me!
[22]I will declare Your name to my community;
in the midst of the congregation I will praise You.
[23]You who fear the LORD, praise Him;
all you descendants of Jacob, glorify Him,
and stand in awe of Him, all you descendants of Israel.
[24]For He has not despised nor abhorred
the affliction of the afflicted;
nor has He hid His face from him;
but when he cried to Him, He heard.
[25]From You my praise will be in the great congregation;
I will pay my vows before those who fear Him.
[26]The meek will eat and be satisfied;
those who seek Him will praise the LORD.
May your hearts live forever.
[27]All the ends of the world
will remember and turn to the LORD,
and all the families of the nations
will worship before You.
[28]For kingship belongs to the LORD,
and He rules among the nations.

22:11 Ps 72:12
22:12 Ps 68:30
22:13 Ps 35:21
22:14 Jos 7:5
22:15 Jn 19:28
22:16 Zec 12:10
22:17 Lk 23:35
22:18 Lk 23:34
22:20 Ps 35:17
22:23 Ps 135:19–20
22:24 Heb 5:7
22:25 Ps 35:18
22:26 Ps 69:32
22:27 Ps 2:8
22:28 Ps 47:7–8
....
22:29 Ps 45:12
22:31 Ps 78:6

SPIRITLED WOMAN

COUNSEL FROM THE SPIRIT BASICS

A Table Is Prepared Before Us

God prepares a table before us in the presence of our enemies. Do you know why a table and what is on that table? Do you know why it's set in the presence of our enemies? I believe that God provides everything that is necessary for our time of need!

All of the weapons and tools that you need for spiritual warfare can be found upon His table that's placed in the presence of our enemies. The Word of God that is alive and active is on that table. The table is not placed and set in your private bedroom—*no!* It is placed and set in front of your enemies because that is when you need assistance and powerful weapons. It is also a table full of fatness and provision.

> You prepare a table before me in
> the presence of my enemies.
> —PSALM 23:5

The Holy Spirit brings to your remembrance the Word of God that is stored up in the tablet of your heart, the Word that you have studied, applied, tested, proven, believed, and confessed. You are dynamite. You are a threat to Satan. A believer who is equipped and who is no longer ignorant about spiritual warfare is a person who is armed, powerful, and fearless. Satan should not be a threat to you.

Iris Delgado

[29]All the prosperous ones of the earth will eat and worship;
all who go down to the dust will bow before Him,
even he who cannot keep his own soul alive.
[30]Posterity will serve Him;
it will be told to generations about the Lord;
[31]they will come and declare His righteousness
to a people yet to be born,
that He has acted.

PSALM 23

A Psalm of David.

1 The LORD is my shepherd; I shall not want.
2 He makes me lie down in green pastures;
He leads me beside still waters.
3 He restores my soul;
He leads me in paths of righteousness
for His name's sake.
4 Even though I walk
through the valley of the shadow of death,

I will keep walking through the valley of the shadow and not set up camp there (Ps. 23:4).

I will fear no evil;
for You are with me;
Your rod and Your staff,
they comfort me.
5 You prepare a table before me
in the presence of my enemies;
You anoint my head with oil;
my cup runs over.
6 Surely goodness and mercy shall follow me
all the days of my life,
and I will dwell in the house of the LORD
forever.

PSALM 24

A Psalm of David.

1 The earth belongs to the LORD, and its fullness,
the world, and those who dwell in it.
2 For He has founded it on the seas,
and established it on the floods.
3 Who may ascend the hill of the LORD?
Who may stand in His holy place?
4 He who has clean hands and a pure heart;
who has not lifted up his soul unto vanity,
nor sworn deceitfully.
5 He will receive the blessing from the LORD,
and righteousness from the God of his salvation.
6 This is Jacob, the generation of those who seek Him,
who seek Your face. Selah
7 Lift up your heads, O you gates;
and be lifted up, you everlasting doors,
that the King of glory may enter.
8 Who is this King of glory?
The LORD strong and mighty,
the LORD mighty in battle.
9 Lift up your heads, O you gates;
lift up, you everlasting doors,
that the King of glory may enter.
10 Who is He—this King of glory?
The LORD of Hosts,
He is the King of glory. Selah

PSALM 25

A Psalm of David.

1 To You, O LORD,
do I lift up my soul.
2 O my God, I trust in You;
may I not be ashamed;
may my enemies not triumph over me.
3 Yes, let none who wait on You
be ashamed;
let them be ashamed
who transgress without cause.
4 Make me to know Your ways, O LORD;
teach me Your paths.
5 Lead me in Your truth and teach me,
for You are the God of my salvation;
on You I wait all the day.
6 Remember Your mercies, O LORD, and Your lovingkindness,
for they are from old.
7 Do not remember the sins of my youth
or my transgressions;
according to Your lovingkindness
remember me,
on account of Your goodness, O LORD.
8 Good and upright is the LORD;
therefore He will teach sinners in the way.
9 The meek will He guide in judgment,
and the meek He will teach His way.
10 All the paths of the LORD are lovingkindness and truth,
for those who keep His covenant and His testimonies.
11 For Your name's sake, O LORD, pardon my iniquity,
for it is great.
12 Who is the man who fears the LORD?
He will teach him in the way He should choose.
13 He will dwell at ease,
and his descendants will inherit the land.
14 The counsel of the LORD is with those who fear him,
and He will make His covenant known to them.
15 My eyes are ever toward the LORD,
for He will lead my feet from the net.
16 Turn to me, and be gracious to me,
for I am isolated and afflicted.

23:1 Isa 40:11
23:2 Rev 7:17
23:3 Ps 5:8
23:4 Ps 3:6
23:5 Ps 16:5
24:1 Ps 89:11
24:2 Ps 136:6
24:3 Ps 15:1
24:4 Mt 5:8
24:6 Ps 27:8
24:7 Isa 26:2

25:1 Ps 86:4
25:2 Ps 31:1
25:4 Ex 33:13
25:5 Ps 88:1
25:6 Ps 103:17
25:7 Job 13:26
25:8 Ps 92:15
25:9 Ps 23:3
25:11 Ps 31:3
25:12 Ps 37:23
25:13 Ps 37:11
25:14 Pr 3:32
25:15 Ps 141:8

[17]The troubles of my heart are enlarged;
bring me out of my distresses.
[18]Look on my pain and misery,
and forgive all my sins.
[19]Consider my enemies, for they are many,
and they hate me with violent hatred.

[20]Watch over my life, and deliver me!
Let me not suffer shame,
for I seek refuge in You.
[21]Truth and integrity will preserve me
while I wait for You.

[22]Redeem Israel, O God,
out of all their troubles.

PSALM 26

A Psalm of David.

1 Judge me, O LORD,
for I have walked in my integrity.
I have trusted in the LORD;
I will not slip.
2 Examine me, O LORD, and test me;
try my affections and my heart.
3 For Your lovingkindness is before my eyes,
and I have walked in Your truth.
4 I have not sat with the worthless,
nor will I go with hypocrites.
5 I have hated the congregation of evildoers,
and will not sit with the wicked.
6 I will wash my hands in innocence;
thus I will go around Your altar, O LORD,
7 that I may proclaim with the voice of thanksgiving,
and tell of all Your wondrous works.
8 LORD, I have loved the refuge of Your house,
and the place where Your honor dwells.
9 Do not gather my soul with sinners,
nor my life with murderers,
10 in whose hands is wickedness,
and their right hand is full of bribes.
11 But as for me, I will walk in my integrity;
redeem me and be gracious to me.

12 My foot stands in an even place;
with the congregations I will bless the LORD.

PSALM 27

A Psalm of David.

1 The LORD is my light and my salvation;
whom will I fear?
The LORD is the strength of my life;
of whom will I be afraid?
2 When the wicked came against me
to eat my flesh—
my enemies and my foes—
they stumbled and fell.
3 Though an army should encamp against me,
my heart will not fear;
though war should rise against me,
in this will I be confident.

4 One thing I have asked from the LORD,
that will I seek after—
for me to dwell in the house of the LORD
all the days of my life,
to see the beauty of the LORD,
and to inquire in His temple.
5 For in the time of trouble
He will hide me in His pavilion;
in the shelter of His tabernacle He will hide me;
He will set me up on a rock.

6 Now my head will be lifted up
above my enemies encircling me;
therefore I will offer sacrifices of joy in His tabernacle;
I will sing, yes, I will sing praises to the LORD.

7 Hear, O LORD, when I cry with my voice!
Be gracious to me and answer me.
8 When You said, "Seek My face,"
my heart said to You, "Your face, LORD, I will seek."
9 Do not hide Your face far from me;
do not thrust Your servant away in anger;
You have been my help.
Do not leave me nor forsake me,
O God of my salvation.
10 If my father and my mother forsake me,
then the LORD will take me in.
11 Teach me Your way, O LORD,
and lead me in an upright path,
because of my enemies.
12 Do not deliver me to the will of my enemies;
for false witnesses have risen against me,
and they breathe out violence.

13 I believe
I will see the goodness of the LORD
in the land of the living.
14 Wait on the LORD;
be strong, and may your heart be stout;
wait on the LORD.

PSALM 28

A Psalm of David.

1 To You, O LORD, will I cry;
my Rock, do not be silent to me;

25:18 2Sa 16:12
25:21 Ps 41:12
25:22 Ps 130:8
26:1 Ps 7:8
26:2 Ps 7:9
26:3 2Ki 20:3
26:4 Ps 1:1
26:5 Ps 31:6
26:6 Ps 73:13
26:11 Ps 69:18
26:12 Ps 27:11
27:1 Ex 15:2
27:2 Ps 14:4
27:3 Ps 3:6
27:4 Ps 23:6
27:5 Ps 31:20
27:6 Ps 3:3
27:8 Ps 105:4
27:9 Ps 69:17
27:10 Isa 40:11
27:11 Ps 5:8
27:12 Ps 35:11
27:13 Ps 52:5
27:14 Ps 31:24
28:1 Ps 83:1

lest if You were silent to me,
then I would become like those who go down to the pit.
2 Hear the voice of my supplications
when I cry to You,
when I lift up my hands
toward Your most holy place.

3 Do not draw me away with the wicked
and with the workers of iniquity,
who speak peace to their neighbors,
but mischief is in their hearts.
4 Give them according to their deeds,
and according to the wickedness of their endeavors;
give them according to the work of their hands;
return to them what they deserve.

5 Because they do not regard the works of the LORD,
nor the work of His hands,
He will destroy them
and not build them up.

6 Blessed be the LORD,
because He has heard the voice of my supplications.
7 The LORD is my strength and my shield;
my heart trusted in Him, and I was helped;
therefore my heart rejoices,
and with my song I will thank Him.

8 The LORD is the strength of His people,
and He is the saving strength of His anointed.
9 Save Your people,
and bless Your inheritance;
feed them and lift them up forever.

PSALM 29

A Psalm of David.

1 Give to the LORD, you heavenly beings,
give to the LORD glory and strength.
2 Give to the LORD the glory of His name;
worship the LORD in holy splendor.

3 The voice of the LORD is over the waters;
the God of glory thunders;
the LORD is over many waters.
4 The voice of the LORD *sounds* with strength;
the voice of the LORD—with majesty.
5 The voice of the LORD breaks the cedars;
the LORD breaks the cedars of Lebanon.
6 He makes them skip like a calf,
Lebanon and Sirion like a wild ox.
7 The voice of the LORD flashes
like flames of fire.
8 The voice of the LORD shakes the wilderness;

28:2 Ps 5:7
28:3 Ps 12:2
28:4 2Ti 4:14
28:5 Isa 5:12
28:7 Ps 13:5
28:8 Ps 20:6
28:9 Dt 9:29
29:1 Ps 96:7–9
29:2 2Ch 20:21
29:6 Dt 3:9
29:8 Nu 13:26

....

29:10 Ge 6:17
29:11 Ps 68:35
30:1 Ps 25:2
30:2 Ps 6:2
30:3 Ps 28:1
30:4 Ps 97:12
30:5 Ps 103:9
30:7 Ps 104:29
30:9 Ps 6:5
30:11 Jer 31:4
30:12 Ps 16:9

the LORD shakes the Wilderness of Kadesh.
9 The voice of the LORD makes the deer to give birth,
and strips the forests bare;
and in His temple everyone says, "Glory!"

10 The LORD sits enthroned above the flood,
the LORD sits as King forever.
11 The LORD will give strength to His people;
the LORD will bless His people with peace.

PSALM 30

A Psalm of David. A Song at the dedication of the temple.

1 I will extol You, O LORD, for You have drawn me up,
and have not caused my foes to rejoice over me.
2 O LORD my God, I cried to You,
and You healed me.
3 O LORD, You have brought up my soul from the grave;
You have kept me alive, that I should not go down to the pit.

4 Sing to the LORD, O you saints of His,
and give thanks at the remembrance of His holiness.
5 For His anger endures but a moment,
in His favor is life;
weeping may endure for a night,
but joy comes in the morning.

6 In my prosperity I said,
"I will never be moved."
7 LORD, by Your favor
You had set me strong as a mountain;
You hid Your face,
and I was terrified.

8 I cried to You, O LORD,
and to the LORD I made supplication:
9 "What profit is there in my death,
if I go down to the pit?
Will the dust give You thanks?
Will it declare Your truth?
10 Hear, O LORD, and be gracious to me;
LORD, be my helper."

11 For You have turned my mourning into dancing;
You have put off my sackcloth and girded me with gladness,
12 so that my glory may sing praise to You
and not be silent.
O LORD my God, I will give thanks to You forever.

PSALM 31

Ps 71:1–3

For the Music Director. A Psalm of David.

1 In You, O LORD, do I seek refuge;
may I never be ashamed;
deliver me in Your righteousness.
2 Incline Your ear to me;
deliver me speedily;
be my strong rock,
a strong fortress to save me.
3 For You are my rock and my fortress;
for Your name's sake lead me and guide me.
4 Lead me out of the net that they have hidden for me,
for You are my strength.
5 Into Your hand I commit my spirit;
You have redeemed me, O LORD, God of truth.
6 I have hated those who regard worthless vanity,
but I trust in the LORD.
7 I will be glad and rejoice in Your lovingkindness,
for You have seen my trouble;
You have known my soul in adversities,
8 and have not delivered me up into the hand of the enemy;
You have set my feet in a broad place.
9 Be gracious to me, O LORD, for I am in trouble;
my eye wastes away with grief,
yes, my soul and my body.
10 For my life is spent with grief,
and my years with sighing;
my strength fails because of my iniquity,
and my bones waste away.
11 I became a reproach among all my enemies,
but especially among my neighbors,
and a dread to my acquaintances;
those who saw me outside fled from me.
12 I am forgotten as a dead man out of mind;
I am like a broken vessel.
13 For I have heard the slander of many;
fear was on every side;
while they took counsel together against me,
they planned to take away my life.
14 But I trusted in You, O LORD;
I said, "You are my God."
15 My times are in Your hand;
deliver me from the hand of my enemies
and my pursuers.
16 Make Your face to shine on Your servant;
save me by Your lovingkindness.
17 Do not let me be ashamed, O LORD,
for I have called on You;
let the wicked be ashamed,
and let them be silent in the grave.
18 Let the lying lips be put to silence,
who speak arrogantly
in pride and contempt against the righteous.
19 Oh, how great is Your goodness,
which You have laid up for those who fear You,
which You have done for those
seeking refuge in You before people!
20 You will hide them in the secret of Your presence
from conspirators;
You will keep them secretly in a shelter
from the strife of tongues.
21 Blessed be the LORD,
for He has shown me His marvelous lovingkindness
in a fortified city.
22 For I said in my haste,
"I am cut off from before Your eyes."
Nevertheless You heard the voice of my supplications
when I cried to You.
23 Oh, love the LORD, all you His saints,
for the LORD preserves the faithful,
but amply repays the one who acts in pride.
24 Be strong, and He will strengthen your heart,
all you who wait for the LORD.

31:4 Ps 25:15
31:5 Lk 23:46
31:8 Dt 32:30
31:9 Ps 6:7
31:11 Ps 38:11
31:13 Jer 20:10
31:15 Job 24:1
31:16 Ps 4:6
31:17 Ps 115:17
31:18 Ps 94:4
31:19 Isa 64:4
31:20 Ps 27:5
31:21 Ps 17:7
31:22 Ps 116:11
31:23 Ps 30:4
31:24 Ps 27:14
32:1 Ps 85:2
32:2 Jn 1:47
32:4 Job 33:7
32:5 2Sa 12:13

PSALM 32

A Psalm of David. A Contemplative Maskil.

1 Blessed is he
whose transgression is forgiven,
whose sin is covered.
2 Blessed is the man
against whom the LORD does not count iniquity,
and in whose spirit there is no deceit.
3 When I kept silent,
my bones wasted away
through my groaning all day long.
4 For day and night
Your hand was heavy on me;
my strength was changed
into the drought of summer. Selah
5 I acknowledged my sin to You,
and my iniquity I did not conceal.
I said, "I will confess
my transgressions to the LORD,"
and You forgave
the iniquity of my sin. Selah

6 For this cause everyone who is godly will
pray to You
in a time when You may be found;
surely in the floods of great waters
they will not reach him.
7 You are my hiding place;
You will preserve me from trouble;
You will surround me with shouts of
deliverance. Selah

Surround me with songs of deliverance (Ps 32:7).

8 I will instruct you and teach you in the way
you should go;
I will counsel you with my eye on you.
9 Do not be as the horse or as the mule
that are without understanding,
that must be restrained with bit and bridle,
or they will not come near you.
10 Many sorrows come to the wicked,
but lovingkindness will surround
the man who trusts in the LORD.
11 Be glad in the LORD, and rejoice, you
righteous one;
and shout for joy, all you who are
upright in heart!

PSALM 33

The Sovereignty of the LORD.

1 Rejoice in the LORD, O you righteous,
for praise is fitting for the upright.
2 Give thanks to the LORD with the harp;
make music to Him with an instrument
of ten strings.
3 Sing to Him a new song;
play an instrument skillfully with a joyful
shout.
4 For the word of the LORD is upright,
and all His work is done in truth.
5 He loves righteousness and justice;
the earth is full of the lovingkindness of
the LORD.
6 By the word of the LORD the heavens were
made,
and all their host by the breath of His
mouth.
7 He gathers the waters of the sea together
as a heap;
He puts the depths in storehouses.
8 Let all the earth fear the LORD;
let all the inhabitants of the world stand
in awe of Him.
9 For He spoke, and it was done;
He commanded, and it stood fast.

32:6 Isa 43:2
32:7 Ps 9:9
32:8 Ps 33:18
32:9 Pr 26:3
32:10 Pr 16:20
32:11 Ps 64:10
33:1 Ps 32:11
33:2 Ps 144:9
33:3 Ps 96:1
33:4 Ps 19:8
33:5 Ps 11:7
33:6 Heb 11:3
33:7 Ex 15:8
33:9 Ge 1:3

....

33:10 Isa 19:3
33:11 Pr 19:21
33:12 Ps 144:15
33:13 Job 28:24
33:15 Jer 32:19
33:17 Ps 20:7
33:18 Job 36:7
33:19 Ps 37:19
33:21 Zec 10:7
34:1 Eph 5:20
34:2 Jer 9:24
34:3 Lk 1:46
34:4 Mt 7:7
34:7 Da 6:22

10 The LORD frustrates the counsel of the
nations;
He restrains the purposes of the people.
11 The counsel of the LORD stands forever,
the purposes of His heart to all
generations.
12 Blessed is the nation whose God is the
LORD,
the people whom He has chosen as His
inheritance.
13 The LORD looks from heaven;
He sees all the sons of men.
14 From the place of His habitation He gazes
on all the inhabitants of the earth;
15 He fashions their hearts alike;
He considers all their works.
16 No king is saved by a great army;
a mighty man is not delivered by great
strength.
17 A horse is a vain hope for safety;
it will not deliver by its great strength.
18 The eye of the LORD is on those who fear
Him,
on those who hope in His
lovingkindness,
19 to deliver their soul from death,
and to keep them alive in famine.
20 Our soul waits for the LORD;
He is our help and our shield.
21 For our heart will rejoice in Him,
because we have trusted in His holy
name.
22 Let Your lovingkindness, O LORD, be on us,
just as we hope in You.

PSALM 34

A Psalm of David, when he feigned madness before Abimelek, who drove him away, and he departed.

1 I will bless the LORD at all times;
His praise will continually be in my
mouth.
2 My soul will make its boast in the LORD;
the humble will hear of it and be glad.
3 Oh, magnify the LORD with me,
and let us exalt His name together.
4 I sought the LORD, and He answered me,
and delivered me from all my fears.
5 They looked to Him and became radiant,
and their faces are not ashamed.
6 This poor man cried, and the LORD heard,
and saved him out of all his troubles.
7 The angel of the LORD camps around those
who fear Him,
and delivers them.

8 Oh, taste and see that the LORD is good;
blessed is the man who takes refuge in
Him.
9 Oh, fear the LORD, you His saints;
for the ones who fear Him will not be in
need.
10 The young lions are in want and suffer
hunger,
but the ones who seek the LORD will not
lack any good thing.
11 Come, you children, listen to me;
I will teach you the fear of the LORD.
12 Who is the man who desires life,
and loves a long life in order to see
good?
13 Keep your tongue from evil,
and your lips from speaking deceit.
14 Turn away from evil, and do good;
seek peace, and pursue it.
15 The eyes of the LORD are on the righteous,
and His ears are open to their cry.
16 The face of the LORD is against the ones
doing evil,
to cut off the memory of them from the
earth.
17 The *righteous* cry out, and the LORD hears,
and delivers them out of all their
troubles.
18 The LORD is near to the broken-hearted,
and saves the contrite of spirit.
19 Many are the afflictions of the righteous,
but the LORD delivers him out of them all.
20 A righteous one keeps all his bones;
not one of them is broken.
21 Evil will slay the wicked,
and those who hate the righteous will be
condemned.
22 The LORD redeems the life of His servants,
and all who take refuge in Him will not
be punished.

Father, I believe Your angels encamp around and about me to defend me (Ps 34:7).

PSALM 35

A Psalm of David.

1 Plead my cause, O LORD, with my
adversaries;
fight those who fight me.
2 Take hold of the large shield and small
shield,
and rise up for my help.
3 Draw the spear and javelin
against those who pursue me.
Say to my soul,
"I am Your salvation."
4 May those who seek my life
be ashamed and humiliated;
may those who plan my injury
be turned back and put to shame.
5 May they be as chaff before the wind,
and may the angel of the LORD cast them
down.
6 May their way be dark and slippery,
and may the angel of the LORD pursue
them.
7 For without cause they have hidden their
net for me in a pit,
which they have dug without cause for
my soul.
8 Let destruction come on him without
warning,
and let the net that he hid ensnare him;
let him fall into it, to his destruction.
9 My soul will be joyful in the LORD;
it will rejoice in His salvation.
10 All my bones will say,
"LORD, who is like You,
who delivers the poor from a stronger one,
the poor and the needy from the one
who robs them?"
11 Witnesses intent on violence rose up;
they accused me of things I knew
nothing about.
12 They rewarded me evil for good,
the bereavement of my soul.
13 But as for me, when they were sick, my
clothing was sackcloth;
I humbled my soul with fasting;
and my prayer returns to my own heart.
14 I paced as though he were my friend or
brother;
I bowed down lamenting,
as one who mourns for a mother.
15 But in my adversity they rejoiced and
gathered together;
assailants gathered together against me,
though I was unaware;
they tore me apart and did not stop;
16 with hypocritical mockers in feasts,
they gnashed on me with their teeth.
17 Lord, how long will You look on?
Rescue my soul from their destructions,
my life from the lions.
18 I will give You thanks in the great
congregation;
I will praise You among a mighty people.
19 May my deceitful enemies
not rejoice over me;
nor may those who hate me without cause
wink with their eye.

34:8 Ps 2:12
34:9 Ps 23:1
34:10 Ps 84:11
34:11 Ps 32:8
34:13 1Pe 2:22
34:14 Ps 37:27
34:15 Ps 33:18
34:16 Jer 44:11
34:18 Isa 57:15
34:19 Ps 34:6
34:20 Jn 19:36
34:21 Ps 94:23
34:22 1Ki 1:29

......

35:4 Ps 129:5
35:5 Job 21:18
35:6 Ps 73:18
35:8 1Th 5:3
35:9 Isa 61:10
35:10 Ex 15:11
35:11 Ps 27:12
35:12 Jn 10:32
35:13 Job 30:25
35:16 Job 16:9
35:17 Hab 1:13
35:19 Ps 69:4

[20] For they do not speak peace,
but they devise deceitful matters
against the restful ones in the land.
[21] They opened their mouth wide against me,
and said, "Aha, aha, our eye has seen it."

[22] This You have seen, O LORD; do not be silent;
O Lord, be not far from me.
[23] Rouse Yourself and awake for my judgment,
for my cause, my God and my Lord.
[24] Judge me, O LORD my God, according to Your righteousness,
and may they not rejoice over me.
[25] May they not say in their hearts, "Ah, *we have* our soul's desire."
May they not say, "We have swallowed him up."

[26] May those who rejoice at my harm be ashamed
and altogether put to shame;
may they be clothed with shame and dishonor
who magnify themselves against me.
[27] May those who favor my righteous cause
shout for joy and be glad;
may they say continually, "The LORD be magnified,
who delights in the peace of His servant."

[28] My tongue will speak of Your righteousness
and of Your praise all the day long.

PSALM 36

For the Music Director. A Psalm of David, the servant of the LORD.

[1] An oracle within my heart
about the transgression of the wicked:
There is no fear of God
before their eyes.

[2] For they flatter themselves in their own eyes,
that their iniquity cannot be found out and hated.
[3] The words of their mouth are wickedness and deceit;
they have ceased to be wise and to do good.
[4] They devise mischief on their bed;
they set themselves on a path that is not good;
they do not reject evil.

[5] Your mercy, O LORD, is in the heavens,
and Your faithfulness reaches to the clouds.

35:21 Ps 22:13
35:22 Ex 3:7
35:23 Ps 44:23
35:25 La 2:16
35:26 Job 19:5
35:27 Ps 40:16
35:28 Ps 71:24
36:1 Ro 3:18
36:2 Dt 29:19
36:4 Pr 4:16

36:6 Ro 11:33
36:7 Ru 2:12
36:8 Ps 16:11
36:9 Jer 2:13
36:10 Jer 22:16
37:1 Ps 73:3
37:4 Isa 58:14
37:5 Ps 55:22
37:6 Job 11:17
37:7 Ps 40:1
37:8 Eph 4:31
37:9 Isa 60:21

[6] Your righteousness is like the great mountains,
Your judgments like the great deep;
O LORD, You preserve man and beast.
[7] How excellent is Your lovingkindness, O God!
Therefore mankind
seeks refuge in the shadow of Your wings.
[8] They will drink their fill from the abundance of Your house,
and You will cause them to drink from the river of Your pleasures.
[9] For with You is the fountain of life;
in Your light we see light.

[10] Oh, continue Your lovingkindness to those who know You,
and Your righteousness to the upright in heart.
[11] Do not let the foot of the arrogant come against me,
and do not let the hand of the wicked cause me to wander.
[12] There the workers of iniquity have fallen;
they are cast down and not able to rise.

PSALM 37

A Psalm of David.

[1] Do not fret because of evildoers,
nor be jealous of those who do injustice.
[2] For they will quickly wither like the grass,
and fade like the green herbs.
[3] Trust in the LORD, and do good;
dwell in the land, and practice faithfulness.
[4] Delight yourself in the LORD,
and He will give you the desires of your heart.
[5] Commit your way to the LORD;
trust also in Him, and He will bring it to pass.
[6] He will bring forth your righteousness as the light,
and your judgment as the noonday.

[7] Rest in the LORD, and wait patiently for Him;
do not fret because of those who prosper in their way,
because of those who make wicked schemes.

[8] Let go of anger, and forsake wrath;
do not fret—it surely leads to evil deeds.
[9] For evildoers will be cut off,
but those who hope in the LORD will inherit the earth.

10 For yet a little while, and the wicked will
not be;
you will look diligently for their place,
and it will not be.
11 But the meek will inherit the earth,
and will delight themselves in the
abundance of peace.
12 The wicked plot against the righteous,
and grind their teeth against them.
13 The Lord will laugh at him,
for He sees that his day is coming.

14 The wicked have drawn out the sword
and have bent their bow,
to cast down the poor and needy,
and to slay those on the upright path.
15 Their sword will enter into their own heart,
and their bows will be broken.

16 Better is a little that the righteous has
than the abundance of many wicked.
17 For the arms of the wicked will be broken,
but the LORD supports the righteous.
18 The LORD knows the days of people of
integrity,
and their inheritance will be forever.
19 They will not be ashamed in the evil time,
and in the days of famine they will be
satisfied.

20 But the wicked will perish,
and the enemies of the LORD will be like
the glory of pastures;
they will waste away, in smoke they will
waste away.

21 The wicked borrows and does not repay,
but the righteous is gracious and gives.
22 For those who are blessed of Him will
inherit the earth,
but those who are cursed of Him will be
cut off.

23 The steps of a man are made firm by the
LORD;
He delights in his way.
24 Though he falls, he will not be hurled
down,
for the LORD supports him with His hand.

25 I have been young, and now am old;
yet I have not seen the righteous
forsaken,
nor their offspring begging bread.
26 The righteous are gracious and lend,
and their offspring are a source of
blessing.

27 Depart from evil and do good,
and abide forevermore.
28 For the LORD loves justice,
and does not forsake His saints;
they are preserved forever,
but the descendants of the wicked will
be cut off.
29 The righteous will inherit the land,
and dwell on it forever.

30 The mouth of the righteous utters wisdom,
and their tongue speaks justice.
31 The law of their God is in their heart;
none of their steps will slip.

32 The wicked watch the righteous,
and seek to kill them.
33 The LORD will not forsake them to their
hand,
nor condemn them when they are
judged.

34 Hope in the LORD,
and keep His way,
and He will exalt you to inherit the land;
when the wicked are cut off, you will
see it.

35 I have seen the wicked in great power,
and spreading himself like a luxuriant
tree.
36 Yet he passed away, and he was not;
I sought him, but he could not be found.

37 Mark the blameless man, and consider the
upright,
for the end of that man is peace.
38 But the transgressors will be destroyed
together;
the end of the wicked is to be cut off.

39 But the salvation of the righteous is from
the LORD;
He is their refuge in the time of distress.
40 The LORD will help them and deliver them;
He will deliver them from the wicked,
and save them, because they take refuge
in Him.

37:10 Job 7:10
37:11 Mt 5:5
37:12 Ps 35:16
37:13 Ps 2:4
37:16 Pr 16:8
37:17 Job 38:15
37:18 Ps 1:6
37:19 Ps 33:19
37:20 Ps 102:3
37:21 Ps 112:5
37:22 Pr 3:33
37:23 1Sa 2:9
37:24 Ps 145:14
37:25 Heb 13:5
37:27 Ps 34:14
37:28 Ps 21:10
37:29 Ps 37:9
37:31 Dt 6:6
37:33 Ps 109:31
37:34 Ps 27:14
37:35 Job 5:3
37:39 Ps 3:8
37:40 1Ch 5:20
38:1 Ps 6:1
38:2 Job 6:4
38:3 Ps 6:2
38:4 Ezr 9:6

PSALM 38

A Psalm of David. To bring remembrance.

1 O LORD, do not rebuke me in Your wrath,
nor chasten me in Your hot displeasure.
2 For Your arrows pierce me,
and Your hand presses down on me.
3 There is no soundness in my flesh because
of Your indignation,
nor is there health in my bones because
of my sin.
4 For my iniquities have passed over my
head;
as a heavy burden they are too heavy
for me.
5 My wounds grow foul and fester
because of my foolishness.

6 I am bent, I am bowed down greatly;
I go mourning all the day long.
7 For my sides are filled with burning,
and there is no soundness in my flesh.
8 I am numb and completely crushed;
I have roared because of the groaning of my heart.
9 Lord, all my desire is before You,
and my sighing is not hidden from You.
10 My heart throbs, my strength fails me;
as for the light of my eyes, it also is gone from me.
11 My friends and my companions stand back because of my affliction,
and those close to me stand at a distance.
12 The people who seek my life strike at me;
those who seek my harm speak destruction,
and plan treacheries all the day long.
13 But I, like a deaf man, did not hear;
and like a dumb man, did not open my mouth.
14 Thus I was as a man who does not hear,
and in whose mouth are no reproofs.
15 For in You, O LORD, do I hope;
You will answer, O Lord my God.
16 For I said, "Lest otherwise they should rejoice over me.
When my foot slips, they magnify themselves against me."
17 For I am ready to stumble,
and my pain is continually before me.
18 For I will declare my iniquity;
I am anxious because of my sin.
19 But my enemies are lively, and they are strong;
and those who wrongfully hate me are many.
20 Those also who repay evil for good are my adversaries,
because I pursue good.
21 Do not abandon me, O LORD;
O my God, do not be far from me.
22 Make haste to help me,
O Lord, my salvation.

PSALM 39

For the Music Director. To Jeduthun. A Psalm of David.

1 I said, "I will take heed of my ways
so that I do not sin with my tongue;
I will keep my mouth muzzled
while the wicked are before me."
2 I was speechless in silence;
I was silent to no avail,

38:6 Job 30:28
38:10 Ps 6:7
38:11 Ps 31:11
38:12 Ps 35:20
38:13 Ps 39:2
38:15 Ps 39:7
38:17 Ps 35:15
38:18 Ps 32:5
38:19 Ps 35:19
38:20 Ps 35:12
38:22 Ps 27:1
39:1 1Ki 2:4

....

39:3 Jer 20:9
39:4 Ps 90:12
39:5 Ps 62:9
39:6 Ecc 2:26
39:7 Ps 38:15
39:8 Ps 44:13
39:9 Job 2:10
39:10 Job 9:34
39:11 Job 13:28
39:12 Heb 11:13
40:1 Ps 37:7
40:2 Ps 27:5
40:3 Ps 33:3
40:4 Ps 34:8

but my anguish was stirred up.
3 My heart was hot within me;
while I was musing, the fire burned,
then I spoke with my tongue:
4 "LORD, make me to know my end,
and what is the measure of my days,
that I may know how transient I am.
5 Indeed, You have made my days as a handbreadth,
and my age is as nothing before You;
indeed every man at his best is as a breath." Selah
6 Surely every man walks in a mere shadow;
surely he goes as a breath;
he heaps up riches, and does not know who will gather them.
7 Now, Lord, what do I wait for?
My hope is in You.
8 Deliver me from all my transgressions;
do not make me the reproach of the foolish.
9 I was speechless, I did not open my mouth,
because You did it.
10 Remove Your blow from me;
I am consumed by the hostility of Your hand.
11 When with rebukes You correct a man for iniquity,
You consume like a moth what is dear to him;
surely every man is vapor. Selah
12 Hear my prayer, O LORD,
and give ear to my cry;
do not be silent at my tears,
for I am a stranger with You,
and a sojourner, as all my fathers were.
13 Turn Your gaze *of displeasure* from me,
that I may smile,
before I go away and am no more.

PSALM 40

Ps 70:1–5

For the Music Director. A Psalm of David.

1 I waited patiently for the LORD,
and He turned to me, and heard my cry.
2 He also brought me up out of a horrible pit,
out of the miry clay,
and set my feet on a rock,
and established my steps.
3 He has put a new song in my mouth,
even praise to our God;
many will see it, and fear,
and will trust in the LORD.
4 Blessed is the man
who places trust in the LORD,
but does not turn toward the proud,

nor those falling away to falsehood.
5 O LORD my God,
You have done many wonderful works,
and Your thoughts toward us
cannot be compared;
if I would declare and speak of them,
they are more than can be numbered.

6 Sacrifice and offering You did not desire;
You have opened up my ears to listen.
Burnt offering and sin offering
You have not required.
7 Then I said, "Behold, I have come;
in the scroll of the book it is written of
me,
8 I delight to do Your will, O my God;
Your law is within my inward parts."

9 I have proclaimed righteousness in the
great congregation;
I have not held back my lips,
O LORD, You know.
10 I have not hidden Your righteousness
within my heart;
I have declared Your faithfulness and
Your salvation;
I have not concealed Your lovingkindness
and Your truth
from the great congregation.

11 Do not withhold Your compassion from
me, O LORD;
may Your lovingkindness and Your truth
always guard me.
12 For innumerable evils have surrounded
me;
my iniquities have overtaken me, so that
I am not able to look up;
they are more than the hairs of my head
so that my heart fails me.
13 Be pleased, O LORD, to deliver me;
O LORD, make haste to help me.

14 May those seeking to snatch away my life
be ashamed and confounded together;
may those who desire my harm
be driven backward and dishonored.
15 May those who say to me "Aha, aha!"
be appalled on account of their shame.
16 May all those who seek You
rejoice and be glad in You;
may those who love Your salvation say
continually,
"The LORD is magnified."
17 But I am poor and needy;
yet the LORD thinks about me.
You are my help and my deliverer;
do not delay, O my God.

40:5 Ps 71:15
40:6 1Sa 15:22
40:8 Jn 4:34
40:9 Ps 22:25
40:11 Ps 43:3
40:12 Ps 38:4
40:14 Ps 35:4
40:15 Ps 35:21
40:16 Ps 35:27
40:17 Ps 70:5

....

41:1 Pr 14:21
41:2 Ps 27:12
41:4 Ps 103:3
41:6 Ps 12:2
41:9 2Sa 15:12
41:12 Job 36:7
41:13 Ps 89:52
42:2 Ps 63:1

PSALM 41

For the Music Director. A Psalm of David.

1 Blessed are those who consider the poor;
the LORD will deliver them in the day of
trouble.
2 The LORD will preserve them and keep
them alive,
and they will be blessed on the earth,
and You will not deliver them to the will
of their enemies.
3 The LORD will sustain them on the sickbed;
You will restore all his lying down in his
illness.

4 I said, "LORD, be gracious to me;
heal my soul, for I have sinned against
You."
5 My enemies speak evil of me:
"When will he die, and his name
perish?"
6 And if people come to see me, they speak
insincerely;
their heart gathers iniquity to itself,
when they go outside, they tell it.

7 All who hate me whisper together against
me;
they devise harm against me.
8 "An evil disease clings to him.
And now that he lies down, he will not
rise up again."
9 Yes, my own close friend,
in whom I trusted, who ate of my bread,
has lifted up the heel against me.
10 But You, O LORD, be gracious to me,
and raise me up, that I may repay them.
11 By this I know that You favor me,
because my enemy does not triumph
over me.
12 As for me, You uphold me in my integrity,
and set me before You forever.

13 Blessed be the LORD God of Israel
from everlasting and to everlasting.
Amen and Amen.

BOOK TWO

Psalms 42–72

PSALM 42

For the Music Director. A Contemplative
Maskil of the sons of Korah.

1 As the deer pants after the water brooks,
so my soul pants after You, O God.
2 My soul thirsts for God, for the living God.
When will I come and appear before
God?

[3] My tears have been my food
day and night,
while they always say to me,
"Where is your God?"
[4] When I remember these things,
I pour out my soul within me.
For I would travel with the throng of
people;
I proceeded with them to the house of
God,
with the voice of joy and thanks,
with a multitude making a pilgrimage.

The Lord is the health of my countenance and my beauty (Ps 42:5).

[5] Why are you cast down, O my soul?
And why are you disquieted in me?
Hope in God,
for I will yet thank Him
for the help of His presence.
[6] O my God, my soul is cast down within me;
therefore I will remember You
from the land of Jordan,
and of the Hermon, from the hill of
Mizar.
[7] Deep calls to deep
at the noise of Your waterfalls;
all Your waves and Your billows
passed over me.
[8] Yet the LORD will command His
lovingkindness in the daytime,
and in the night His song will be with
me,
a prayer to the God of my life.
[9] I will say to God, my rock,
"Why have You forgotten me?
Why do I go mourning
because of the oppression of the
enemy?"
[10] With shattering in my bones,
those harassing me reproach me,
when they say to me every day,
"Where is your God?"

[11] Why, my soul, are you cast down?
Why do you groan within me?
Wait for God;
I will yet thank Him,
For He is my deliverance and my God.

PSALM 43

[1] Vindicate me, O God,
and plead my cause against an ungodly
nation;
deliver me from the deceitful and unjust
man.
[2] For You are the God of my refuge;
why have You rejected me?
Why do I walk about mourning
because of the oppression of the enemy?
[3] Send out Your light and Your truth.
Let them lead me;
let them bring me to Your holy hill,
and to Your dwelling place.
[4] Then I will go to the altar of God,
to the God of my joyful gladness;
with the harp I will give thanks to You,
O God, my God.

[5] Why are you cast down, O my soul?
And why are you disquieted within me?
Hope in God;
for I will yet give Him thanks,
the salvation of my countenance and
my God.

PSALM 44

For the Music Director. A Contemplative
Maskil of the sons of Korah.

[1] We have heard with our ears, O God,
our fathers have told us
what work You did in their days,
in the days of old:
[2] how You drove out the nations with Your
hand,
and planted others instead;
how You afflicted peoples,
and sent them away.
[3] For they did not take possession of the
land by their own sword,
nor did their own arm save them;
but it was Your right hand, and Your arm,
and the light of Your countenance,
because You had favor on them.

[4] You are my King, O God;
command deliverances for Jacob.
[5] Through You we will push down our
opponents;
through Your name we will trample
those who rise up against us.
[6] For I will not trust in my bow,
nor will my sword save me.
[7] But You have saved us from our
opponents,
and have put to shame those who hate
us.
[8] In God we boast all the day long,
and give thanks to Your name forever.
Selah

[9] But You have rejected us and put us to
shame,
and do not go out with our armies.
[10] You make us to turn back from the
opponent,

42:3 Ps 79:10
42:4 Isa 30:29
42:5 Ps 42:11
42:6 2Sa 17:22
42:7 Ps 88:7
42:8 Job 35:10
42:9 Ps 38:6
42:10 Ps 42:3
42:11 Ps 42:5
43:1 1Sa 24:15
....
43:2 Ps 42:9
43:3 Ps 2:6
43:5 Ps 42:5
44:2 Ex 15:17
44:3 Dt 7:7–8
44:4 Ps 74:12
44:5 Dt 33:17
44:8 Ps 34:2
44:9 Ps 60:10
44:10 Lev 26:17

and those who hate us make us their
spoil.
11 You have placed us like sheep for prey,
and have scattered us among the
nations.
12 You sell Your people for nothing,
and do not increase Your wealth by their
sale.

13 You make us a reproach to our neighbors,
a scorn and a derision to those who
surround us.
14 You make us a byword among the nations,
a shaking of the head among the
people.
15 All day long my reproach is before me,
and the shame of my face covers me,
16 from the voice of him who reproaches and
reviles,
by reason of the enemy and avenger.

17 All this is come on us,
yet we have not forgotten You,
nor have we dealt falsely in Your
covenant.
18 Our heart is not turned back,
nor have our steps deviated from Your
way,
19 though You have crushed us in the place of
jackals,
and covered us with the shadow of
death.

20 If we have forgotten the name of our God,
or stretched out our hands to a strange
god,
21 would not God search this out?
For He knows the secrets of the heart.
22 Yes, for Your sake we are killed all the day
long;
we are considered like sheep for the
slaughter.

23 Awake; why do You sleep, O Lord?
Arise; do not reject us forever.
24 Why do You hide Your face,
and forget our affliction and our
oppression?

25 For our soul is bowed down to the dust;
our body cleaves to the earth.
26 Arise, be our help,
and redeem us for the sake of Your
lovingkindness.

PSALM 45

For the Music Director. To the melody of "Lilies." A Contemplative Maskil of the sons of Korah. A love song.

1 My heart is overflowing with a good
thought;
I am speaking my works for the king;
my tongue is the pen of a skilled scribe.

2 You are fairer than all the sons of men;
favor is poured on your lips;
therefore God has blessed you forever.
3 Gird your sword on your thigh, O mighty
one,
with your splendor and your majesty.
4 In your majesty ride prosperously
because of truth and meekness and
righteousness;
and your right hand will teach you
awesome things.
5 Your arrows are sharp in the heart of the
king's enemies;
peoples will fall under you.
6 Your throne, O God, is forever and ever;
the scepter of Your kingdom is an
upright scepter.
7 You love righteousness and hate
wickedness;
therefore God, your God, anointed you
with the oil of gladness above your
companions.
8 All your garments are fragrant with myrrh
and aloes and cassia;
from the ivory palaces stringed
instruments make you glad.
9 Kings' daughters are among your
honorable women;
at your right hand stands the queen in
gold of Ophir.

10 Listen, O daughter, consider and incline
your ear;
forget your own people, and your
father's house,
11 and the king will desire your beauty.
Since he is your lord, bow to him.
12 The daughter of Tyre will be there with a
gift;
even the rich among the people will
entreat your favor.
13 The royal daughter is all glorious within *her
chamber*;
her clothing is plaited gold.
14 She shall be brought to the king in
embroidered garments;
the virgins, her companions who follow
her,
shall be brought to you.
15 With gladness and rejoicing they shall be
brought;
they shall enter into the king's palace.

16 Your sons shall succeed your fathers;
you will make them princes in all the
land.

44:11 Dt 4:27
44:12 Jer 15:13
44:13 Ps 79:4
44:14 Jer 24:9
44:16 Ps 8:2
44:17 Da 9:13
44:18 Ps 119:51
44:19 Job 3:5
44:21 Jer 17:10
44:22 Ro 8:36
44:23 Ps 7:6
44:24 Job 13:24
44:25 Ps 119:25

....

45:2 Lk 4:22
45:3 Heb 4:12
45:6 Ps 93:2
45:7 Ps 21:6
45:8 Jn 19:39
45:9 1Ki 2:19
45:10 Dt 21:13
45:11 Ps 95:6
45:12 Ps 22:29
45:14 Jdg 5:30

17 I will cause your name to be remembered
in all generations;
therefore the people will praise you
forever and ever.

PSALM 46

For the Music Director. A Psalm of the sons
of Korah. According to Alamoth. A Song.

1 God is our refuge and strength,
a well-proven help in trouble.
2 Therefore we will not fear, though the earth
be removed,
and though the mountains be carried
into the midst of the sea;
3 though its waters roar and foam,
though the mountains shake with its
swelling. Selah

4 There is a river whose streams make glad
the city of God,
the holy dwelling place of the Most
High.
5 God is in the midst of her; she will not be
moved;
God will help her in the early dawn.
6 The nations roared; the kingdoms were
moved;
He uttered His voice; the earth melted.
7 The LORD of Hosts is with us;
the God of Jacob is our refuge. Selah

8 Come, see the works of the LORD,
who makes desolations in the earth.
9 He makes wars cease to the end of the
earth;
He breaks the bow and cuts off the
spear;
He burns the chariot in the fire.
10 Be still and know that I am God;
I will be exalted among the nations,
I will be exalted in the earth.

11 The LORD of Hosts is with us;
the God of Jacob is our refuge. Selah

PSALM 47

For the Music Director. A Psalm
of the sons of Korah.

1 Clap your hands, all you people!
Shout to God with a joyful voice.

2 For the LORD Most High is awesome;
He is a great King over all the earth.
3 He subdued peoples under us,
and nations under our feet.
4 He chose our inheritance for us,
the excellency of Jacob whom He loved.
Selah

45:17 Mal 1:11
46:1 Dt 4:7
46:2 Ps 23:4
46:3 Ps 93:3–4
46:4 Ps 48:1
46:5 Isa 12:6
46:6 Am 9:5
46:7 2Ch 13:12
46:8 Ps 66:5
46:9 Isa 2:4
46:10 Isa 2:11
47:1 Ps 98:4
47:2 Dt 7:21
47:3 Ps 18:47
47:4 1Pe 1:4

....

47:7 Zec 14:9
47:8 1Ch 16:31
47:9 Ps 89:18
48:1 Ps 46:4
48:2 Ps 50:2
48:7 Jer 18:17
48:8 Ps 87:5
48:9 Ps 26:3
48:10 Dt 28:58
48:11 Ps 97:8

5 God went up with a shout,
the LORD with the sound of a trumpet.
6 Sing praises to God, sing praises;
sing praises to our King, sing praises.

7 For God is the King of all the earth;
sing praises with understanding.
8 God reigns over the nations;
God sits on His holy throne.
9 The princes of peoples are gathered
together,
even the people of the God of Abraham.
For the shields of the earth belong to God;
He is greatly exalted.

PSALM 48

A Song. A Psalm of the sons of Korah.

1 Great is the LORD, and greatly to be praised
in the city of our God, in His holy
mountain.

2 Beautiful in elevation,
the joy of the whole earth,
is Mount Zion, on the sides of the north,
the city of the great King.
3 God is known in her citadels
as a refuge.

4 For the kings were assembled,
they passed by together.
5 They saw it, and so they were astounded;
they were alarmed, they hurried away.
6 Trembling seized them there,
and pain like a woman in labor;
7 You break the ships of Tarshish
with an east wind.

8 As we have heard,
so have we seen
in the city of the LORD of Hosts,
in the city of our God;
God will establish it forever. Selah

9 We have thought of Your lovingkindness, O
God,
in the midst of Your temple.
10 According to Your name, O God,
so is Your praise to the ends of the earth;
Your right hand is full of righteousness.
11 May Mount Zion rejoice,
may the daughters of Judah be glad,
because of Your judgments.

12 Walk about Zion, and go round about her;
count her towers;
13 mark well her bulwarks;
consider her citadels;
that you may tell it to the generation
following.

[14]For this God is our God forever and ever;
He will be our guide even to death.

PSALM 49

For the Music Director. A Psalm of the sons of Korah.

[1] Hear this, all you people;
give ear, all you inhabitants of the world,
[2] both low and high,
rich and poor together.
[3] My mouth will speak wisdom,
and the meditation of my heart will be understanding.
[4] I will incline my ear to a parable;
I will expound my riddle with a harp.
[5] Why should I fear in the days of evil,
when the iniquity of my stalkers surrounds me?
[6] Those who trust in their wealth,
and boast in the multitude of their riches,
[7] none of them can by any means redeem the other,
nor give to God a ransom for anyone,
[8] for the redemption of their souls is costly;
even so people cease to exist forever,
[9] making efforts to live eternally,
and not see the pit.
[10]For one sees that wise men die,
together the fool and the brute perish,
and leave their wealth to others.
[11]Their graves become their perpetual homes,
and their dwelling places to all generations,
though they call their lands after their own names.
[12]But a man does not abide in honor;
mankind is like the beasts that come to ruin.
[13]This is their way, it is their folly;
yet their posterity approve their sayings. Selah
[14]Like sheep they are appointed for Sheol;
Death shall be their shepherd;
the upright shall rule over them in the morning,
and their form shall waste away in Sheol,
far from their dwelling.
[15]But God shall redeem my soul from the power of Sheol,
for He shall receive me. Selah
[16]Do not fear when one is made rich,
when the glory of his house is increased,
[17]for he takes nothing away in death;
his glory does not descend after him.
[18]Though while he lives he blesses his soul—
and men will praise you when you do well for yourself—
[19]that soul will go to the generation of his fathers;
they will never see light.
[20]A man in honor, and yet without understanding,
is like the animals that perish.

PSALM 50

A Psalm of Asaph.

[1] The Mighty One, God, is the LORD;
He has spoken and summoned the earth
from the rising of the sun to its setting.
[2] Out of Zion, the perfection of beauty,
God has shined.
[3] Our God will come, and will not keep silent;
a fire consumes before Him,
and a strong tempest is around Him.
[4] He calls to the heavens above,
and to the earth, that He may judge His people:
[5] "Gather My faithful ones together to Me,
those who have made a covenant with Me by sacrifice."
[6] The heavens will declare His righteousness,
for God Himself is judge. Selah
[7] "Hear, O My people, and I will speak,
O Israel, and I will testify against you;
I am God, even your God.
[8] I will not reprove you for your sacrifices
or for your burnt offerings that are continually before Me.
[9] I will take no young bull out of your house,
nor male goats out of your folds.
[10]For every wild animal of the forest is Mine,
and the cattle on a thousand hills.
[11]I know every bird of the mountains,
and the creatures that move in the field are Mine.
[12]If I were hungry, I would not tell you;
for the world is Mine, and all its fullness.
[13]Will I eat the flesh of bulls,
or drink the blood of goats?
[14]Sacrifice a thank offering to God,
and pay your vows to the Most High,
[15]and call on Me in the day of trouble;
I will deliver you, and you will glorify Me."
[16] But to the wicked God says:

"What right have you to declare My statutes,
or take My covenant in your mouth?
[17]You hate instruction,

48:14 Ps 73:24
49:1 Ps 78:1
49:2 Ps 62:9
49:4 Ps 78:2
49:6 Ps 52:7
49:9 Ps 89:48
49:10 Ps 39:6
49:11 Ge 4:17
49:13 Lk 12:20
49:14 Mal 4:3
49:15 Ps 73:24
49:17 1Ti 6:7
49:18 Dt 29:19
49:19 Ge 15:15
50:1 Jos 22:22
50:2 Dt 33:2
50:3 Da 7:10
50:4 Isa 1:2
50:6 Ps 75:7
50:7 Ex 20:2
50:8 Hos 6:6
50:12 Ex 19:5
50:14 Dt 23:21
50:15 Ps 22:23
50:17 Ne 9:26

and cast My words behind you.
18 When you see a thief, you are pleased,
and have a share in those who commit adultery.
19 You let loose your mouth to evil,
and your tongue is bound to deceit.
20 You sit and speak against your brother;
you accuse your own mother's son.
21 These things have you done, and I kept silent;
you thought that I was indeed like you;
but I will reprove you
and make a case before your eyes.

22 "Now consider this, you who forget God,
lest I tear you in pieces, and there be none to deliver:
23 Whoever sacrifices a thank offering
glorifies Me and makes a way;
I will show him the salvation of God."

PSALM 51

For the Music Director. A Psalm of David, when Nathan the Prophet came to him, after he had gone in to Bathsheba.

1 Have mercy on me, O God,
according to Your lovingkindness;
according to the abundance of Your compassion,
blot out my transgressions.
2 Wash me thoroughly from my iniquity,
and cleanse me from my sin.

My heavenly Father has forgiven me and cleansed me of all my sins and iniquities (Ps 51:2).

3 For I acknowledge my transgressions,
and my sin is ever before me.
4 Against You, You only, have I sinned,
and done this evil in Your sight,
so that You are justified when You speak,
and You are blameless when You judge.
5 I was brought forth in iniquity,
and in sin my mother conceived me.
6 You desire truth in the inward parts,
and in the hidden part You make me to know wisdom.

God has washed me and set me free from all the iniquities and sins of my parents and ancestors (Ps 51:7).

7 Purify me with hyssop, and I will be clean;
wash me, and I will be whiter than snow.
8 Make me to hear joy and gladness,
that the bones that You have broken may rejoice.
9 Hide Your face from my sins,
and blot out all my iniquities.

10 Create in me a clean heart, O God,
and renew a right spirit within me.
11 Do not cast me away from Your presence,
and do not take Your Holy Spirit from me.
12 Restore to me the joy of Your salvation,
and uphold me with Your willing spirit.

13 Then I will teach transgressors Your ways,
and sinners will return to You.
14 Deliver me from blood guiltiness, O God,
God of my salvation,
and my tongue will sing aloud of Your righteousness.
15 O Lord, open my lips,
and my mouth will declare Your praise.
16 For You do not desire sacrifice, or I would give it;
You do not delight in burnt offering.
17 The sacrifices of God are a broken spirit;
a broken and a contrite heart,
O God, You will not despise.

18 Do good to Zion in Your good pleasure;
build the walls of Jerusalem.
19 Then You will be pleased with the sacrifices of righteousness,
with burnt offering and whole burnt offering;
then they will offer young bulls on Your altar.

PSALM 52

For the Music Director. A Contemplative Maskil. A Psalm of David, when Doeg the Edomite came and told Saul, "David has come to the house of Ahimelek."

1 Why do you boast in evil, O mighty man?
The goodness of God endures continually.
2 Your tongue devises calamities,
like a sharp razor, you worker of treachery.
3 You love evil more than good,
and lying rather than speaking righteousness. Selah
4 You love all devouring words,
O you deceitful tongue.

5 God will likewise break you down forever;
He will snatch you away and pluck you from your home,
and uproot you from the land of the living. Selah
6 The righteous also will see and fear,

50:18 Ro 1:32
50:19 Ps 10:7
50:20 Mt 10:21
50:21 Ps 90:8
50:22 Ps 7:2
50:23 Ps 91:16
51:1 Isa 43:25
51:2 Ps 51:7
51:3 Isa 59:12
51:4 Ge 20:6
51:5 Job 14:4
51:6 Job 38:36
51:7 Isa 1:18
....
51:9 Jer 16:17
51:10 Mt 5:8
51:11 2Ki 13:23
51:12 Ps 13:5
51:14 2Sa 12:9
51:16 Ps 40:6
51:17 Ps 34:18
51:18 Ps 102:16
51:19 Ps 4:5
52:1 1Sa 21:7
52:2 Ps 57:4
52:5 Ps 27:13
52:6 Ps 40:3

and will laugh in contempt,
7 "See, this is the man
who did not make God his refuge,
but trusted in the abundance of riches,
and grew strong in his own wickedness."
8 But I am like a green olive tree
in the house of God;
I trust in the mercy of God
forever and ever.
9 I will give thanks to You forever, because
You have acted;
and I will wait on Your name,
for it is good before Your saints.

PSALM 53
Ps 14:1–7

For the Music Director. According to Mahalath. A Contemplative Maskil of David.

1 The fool has said in his heart,
"There is no God."
They are corrupt, and have done abhorrent
injustice;
there is none who does good.
2 God looked down from heaven
on the children of men,
to see if there were any who have insight,
who seek God.
3 Every one of them has turned aside;
they are altogether corrupt;
there is no one who does good,
not even one.
4 Have the workers of iniquity no
knowledge,
who eat up my people as they eat bread,
and do not call on God?
5 There they were in fear,
where there was nothing to fear,
for God has scattered the bones of him who
camps against you;
you have put them to shame, because
God has rejected them.
6 Oh, that the salvation of Israel would come
out of Zion!
When God brings back the captivity of
His people,
Jacob will rejoice and Israel will be glad.

PSALM 54

For the Music Director. With stringed instruments. A Contemplative Maskil of David, when the Ziphites went and told Saul, "Is David not hiding among us?"

1 O God, save me by Your name,
and judge me by Your strength.
2 O God, hear my prayer;
give ear to the words of my mouth.

52:8 Jer 11:16
52:9 Ps 54:6
53:1 Ps 14:1–7
53:2 2Ch 15:2
53:3 Ro 3:12
53:5 Lev 26:17
54:1 Ps 20:1
....
54:3 Ps 86:14
54:5 Ps 89:49
54:6 Ps 52:9
54:7 Ps 59:10
55:2 Isa 38:14
55:3 2Sa 16:7–8
55:4 Ps 116:3
55:5 Ps 119:120
55:9 Jer 6:7

3 For strangers rise up against me,
and formidable adversaries seek my life;
they do not set God before them. Selah
4 God is my helper;
the Lord is with those who support my
life.
5 He will repay my enemies for their evil.
In Your faithfulness, destroy them.
6 I will sacrifice a freewill offering to You;
I will give thanks to Your name, O LORD,
for it is good.
7 For He has delivered me out of all trouble;
and my eye has looked down on my
enemies.

PSALM 55

For the Music Director. With stringed instruments. A Contemplative Maskil of David.

1 Give ear to my prayer, O God,
and do not hide Yourself from my
supplication.
2 Attend to me, and answer me;
I am restless in my complaint, and I
murmur,
3 because of the voice of the enemy,
because of the pressure of the wicked,
for they cause trouble to drop on me,
and in wrath they have animosity
against me.
4 My heart is in pain within me,
and the terrors of death have fallen on
me.
5 Fear and trembling come into me,
and horror has overwhelmed me.
6 I said, "Oh, that I had wings like a dove!
For then I would fly away and be at rest.
7 Indeed, then I would wander far off,
and remain in the wilderness. Selah
8 I would hasten my escape
from the windy storm and tempest."
9 Confuse, O Lord, divide their tongues,
for I have seen violence and strife in the
city.
10 Day and night they go around it on its
walls;
trouble and sorrow are in its midst.
11 Destruction is in its midst;
oppression and treachery do not depart
from its streets.
12 For it is not an enemy who reproaches me;
then I could bear it.
Nor is it one who hates me who has exalted
himself against me;
then I could hide from him.

[13]But it was you, my peer,
my guide, and my acquaintance.
[14]We took pleasant counsel together,
and walked to the house of God in company.
[15]May death surprise them,
and may their lives go down to Sheol,
for wickedness is in their dwellings and among them.
[16]As for me, I will call on God,
and the LORD will save me.
[17]Evening and morning and at noon,
I will make my complaint and murmur,
and He will hear my voice.
[18]He has ransomed my life in peace
from the battle against me,
for there were many against me.
[19]God will hear and afflict them,
even He who sits enthroned from of old.
Selah
Because they do not change,
therefore they do not fear God.
[20]My friend has set his hands against those at peace with him;
he has violated his covenant.
[21]The words of his mouth were smoother than butter,
but battle was in his heart;
his words were softer than oil,
yet they were drawn swords.

> I will cast my burden upon the Lord, and He will sustain me (Ps 55:22).

[22]Cast your burden on the LORD,
and He will sustain you;
He will never allow
the righteous to be moved.
[23]But You, O God, will cast the wicked down
into the pit of destruction;
men of blood and deceitful men
will not live out half their days.
But I will trust in You.

PSALM 56

For the Music Director. To the melody of "Silent Dove at a Distance." A Miktam of David, when the Philistines seized him in Gath.

1 Be gracious to me, O God, for man would crush me;
all day long he who battles
oppresses me.
2 All day long my enemies would crush me,
for there are many who arrogantly battle against me.
3 In the day when I am afraid,
I will trust in You.
4 In God whose word I praise,
in God I have trusted; I will not fear.
What can mere flesh do to me?
5 Every day they twist my words;
all their thoughts are against me for evil.
6 They stir up strife, they lurk,
they watch my steps,
when they wait for my life.
7 Should there be deliverance for them on account of wickedness?
In Your anger cast down the peoples, O God.
8 You take account of my wandering;
put my tears in Your bottle;
are they not in Your book?
9 In the day I cry to You,
then my enemies will turn back;
this I know, that God is for me.
10 In God whose word I praise,
in the LORD whose word I praise,
11 in God I trust, I will not fear;
what can a man do to me?
12 Your vows are on me, O God;
I will complete them with thank offerings to You;
13 for You have delivered my soul from death,
even my feet from stumbling,
to walk before God
in the light of the living.

PSALM 57
Ps 108:1–5

For the Music Director. To the melody of "Do Not Destroy." A Miktam of David when he fled from Saul in the cave.

1 Be gracious to me, O God, be gracious to me!
For my soul seeks refuge in You;
in the shadow of Your wings I will make my refuge,
until the ruinous storm passes by.
2 I will cry to God Most High,
to God who vindicates me.
3 He will send from heaven and save me
from the taunt of the one who crushes me. Selah
God will send forth His mercy and His truth.
4 My soul is among lions,
and I lie among the sons of men who blaze like fire,
whose teeth are spears and arrows,
and their tongue a sharp sword.

55:13 2Sa 15:12
55:14 Ps 42:4
55:17 Ac 3:1
55:19 Dt 33:27
55:20 Ps 7:4
55:21 Ps 28:3
55:22 Ps 37:5
55:23 Job 15:32

56:3 Ps 55:4–5
56:4 Ps 118:6
56:6 Ps 59:3
56:7 Ps 55:23
56:8 Mal 3:16
56:9 Ro 8:31
56:13 Job 33:30
57:1 Isa 26:20
57:2 Ps 138:8
57:3 Ps 40:11
57:4 Ps 58:6

5 Be exalted, O God, above the heavens;
may Your glory be above all the earth.

6 They have prepared a net for my steps;
my soul is bowed down;
they have dug a pit before me,
but they have fallen into it. Selah

7 My heart is fixed, O God,
my heart is fixed;
I will sing and give praise.
8 Awake, my glory!
Awake, psaltery and harp!
I will awake the dawn.
9 I will thank You, O Lord, among the
peoples;
I will sing to You among the nations.
10 For Your mercy is great up to the heavens,
and Your truth extends to the clouds.

11 Be exalted, O God, above the heavens;
may Your glory be above all the earth.

PSALM 58

For the Music Director. To the melody of "Do Not Destroy." A Miktam of David.

1 Do you truly speak righteousness, O
heavenly gods?
Do you judge uprightly, O earthly men?
2 Indeed, in the heart you work wickedness;
you weigh the violence of your hands in
the earth.

3 The wicked are estranged from the womb
onward;
those who speak lies go astray from
birth.
4 Their poison is like the poison of a serpent;
they are like the deaf adder that plugs
its ear,
5 and will not listen to the voice of charmers,
even the best and wisest enchanter.

6 Break their teeth in their mouth, O God;
break out the great teeth of the young
lions, O LORD.
7 May they melt away as waters which run
continually;
when he bends his bow to shoot his
arrows, let them be trodden under.
8 May they become as a snail that melts as it
goes,
like the untimely birth of a woman, may
they not see the sun.

9 Before your pots can feel the thorns' heat,
green or burning,
may He sweep them away.
10 The righteous will rejoice when he sees the
vengeance;
he will wash his feet in the blood of the
wicked;

57:7 Ps 112:7
57:8 Ps 16:9
57:10 Ps 36:5
57:11 Ps 57:5
58:2 Ps 94:20
58:3 Ps 51:5
58:4 Ps 140:3
58:6 Ps 3:7
58:7 Jos 7:5
58:8 Job 3:16
58:9 Ps 118:12
58:10 Ps 68:23

....

58:11 Ps 67:4
59:2 Ps 139:19
59:3 Ps 56:6
59:4 Ps 35:23
59:6 Ps 59:14
59:7 Ps 57:4
59:8 Ps 2:4
59:9 Ps 9:9
59:10 Ps 54:7
59:12 Pr 12:13
59:13 Ps 83:18
59:15 Job 15:23

11 and people will say,
"Surely there is a reward for the
righteous;
surely there is a God who judges on the
earth."

PSALM 59

For the Music Director. To the melody of "Do Not Destroy." A Miktam of David, when Saul sent men, and they watched the house to kill him.

1 Deliver me from my enemies, O my God;
give me refuge from those who rise up
against me.
2 Deliver me from the workers of iniquity,
and save me from bloodthirsty people.

3 For they lie in wait for my life;
the mighty are gathered against me,
not for my transgression, nor for my sin,
O LORD.
4 For no guilt of mine, they run and prepare
themselves.
Arise to help me, and take notice.
5 You, O LORD God of Hosts, the God of Israel,
awake to punish all the nations;
do not be gracious to any wicked
transgressors. Selah

6 They return at evening,
they growl like a dog,
and go around the city.
7 Indeed, they burst out with their mouth;
swords are in their lips;
for who listens?
8 But You, O LORD, will laugh at them;
You will have all the nations in derision.

9 O my strength, I will wait on You;
for God is my refuge.

10 The God of lovingkindness will go before
me;
God will cause me to look in triumph on
my enemies.
11 Do not slay them,
lest my people forget;
scatter them by Your power,
and bring them down, O Lord our shield.
12 For the sin of their mouth
and the words of their lips,
may they be snared by their pride,
and because of curses and lies that they
speak.
13 Consume them in wrath,
consume them so they no longer exist;
and let them know that God rules in Jacob
to the ends of the earth. Selah

14 At evening they return,
and growl like a dog,
and go around the city.
15 They roam about to eat,

and if they are not satisfied, they
complain.
16 But I will sing of Your power;
I will sing aloud of Your lovingkindness
in the morning,
for You have been my refuge
and escape in the day of my trouble.

17 To You, O my strength, I will sing,
for God is my refuge, and the God of my
lovingkindness.

PSALM 60

Ps 108:6–13

For the Music Director. A Miktam of David to teach. To the melody of "Lily of the Testimony," when he struggled with Aram Naharaim and with Aram Zobah and when Joab returned from striking down twelve thousand Edomites in the Valley of Salt.

1 O God, You have rejected us, You have
scattered us;
You have been displeased; take us back.
2 You have made the earth tremble; You have
split it open;
heal its breaches, for it shook.
3 You have shown Your people hard times;
You have made us drink wine, causing
us to stagger.
4 You have given a banner to those who fear
You,
that they may flee to it from the bow.[1]
Selah
5 That Your beloved ones may be delivered,
save with Your right hand and
answer us.
6 God has spoken in His holiness:
"I will rejoice, I will divide Shechem,
and measure out the Valley of Sukkoth.
7 Gilead is Mine, and Manasseh is Mine;
Ephraim also is My helmet;
Judah is My scepter;
8 Moab is My wash basin;
over Edom I will cast My shoe;
shout the alarm, O Philistia, because of
Me."
9 Who will bring me into the fortified city?
Who will lead me into Edom?
10 You, O God, have You not cast us off?
And You, O God, did not go out with our
armies.
11 Give us help from trouble,
for the help of man is worthless.
12 Through God we will do valiantly,
for He will tread down our enemies.

[1]4 Or for the truth.

59:16 Ps 21:13
60:1 Ps 44:9
60:2 2Ch 7:14
60:3 Ps 71:20
60:4 Ps 20:5
60:5 Ps 17:7
60:6 Ge 12:6
60:7 Ge 49:10
60:8 2Sa 8:1–2
60:10 Jos 7:12
60:11 Ps 146:3
60:12 Ps 44:5

61:2 Ps 77:3
61:3 Pr 18:10
61:4 Ps 17:8
61:5 Ps 56:12
61:6 Ps 21:4
61:7 Ps 40:11
61:8 Ps 65:1
62:1 Ps 33:20
62:4 Ps 28:3
62:6 Ps 62:2
62:7 Jer 3:23
62:8 Ps 42:4
62:9 Ps 39:5

PSALM 61

For the Music Director. With stringed instruments. A Psalm of David.

1 Hear my cry, O God,
attend to my prayer.
2 From the end of the earth I will cry to You;
when my heart faints,
lead me to the rock that is higher than I.
3 For You have been a refuge for me,
and a strong tower from the enemy.

4 I will abide in Your tent forever;
I will seek refuge in the covering of Your
wings. Selah
5 For You, O God, have heard my vows;
You have given me the heritage of those
who fear Your name.

6 May You prolong the king's life,
and may his years be as many
generations.
7 May he sit enthroned before God forever;
oh, prepare mercy and truth, which may
preserve him.

8 Thus will I sing praise to Your name
forever,
that I may fulfill my vows day by day.

PSALM 62

For the Music Director. According to Jeduthun. A Psalm of David.

1 My soul waits in silence on God alone;
from Him comes my salvation.
2 He only is my rock and my salvation;
He is my refuge; I will not be greatly
shaken.

3 How long will you attack a man,
to batter him, all of you,
as you would a leaning wall, a tottering
fence?
4 They only conspire to cast him down
from his high position;
they delight in lies,
they bless with their mouth,
but they curse inwardly. Selah

5 My soul, wait silently for God,
for my hope is from Him.
6 He only is my rock and my salvation;
He is my refuge; I will not be moved.
7 In God is my salvation and my glory;
the rock of my strength, and my shelter,
is in God.
8 Trust in Him at all times;
you people, pour out your heart before
Him;
God is a shelter for us. Selah

9 Surely people of low degree are a breath,
and men of high degree are a lie;

if they are placed in the balance,
they are altogether lighter than vapor.
10 Do not trust in oppression,
and do not become vain in robbery;
if riches increase,
do not set your heart on them.

11 God has spoken once,
twice have I heard this:
that power belongs to God.
12 Also to You, O Lord, belongs mercy;
for You render to each one
according to his work.

PSALM 63

A Psalm of David, when he was in the Wilderness of Judah.

1 O God, You are my God;
early will I seek You;
my soul thirsts for You,
my flesh faints for You,
in a dry and thirsty land
with no water.
2 I have seen You in the sanctuary,
to see Your power and Your glory.
3 Because Your lovingkindness is better than life,
my lips will praise You.
4 Thus will I bless You while I live;
I will lift up my hands in Your name.
5 My soul will be satisfied as with marrow and fatness,
and my mouth will praise You with joyful lips.
6 When I remember You on my bed,
and meditate on You in the night watches,
7 because You have been my help,
therefore in the shadow of Your wings I will rejoice.
8 My soul clings hard to You;
Your right hand upholds me.
9 But those who seek my soul to destroy it
will go into the lower parts of the earth.
10 They will fall by the sword;
they will be a portion for jackals.
11 But the king will rejoice in God;
everyone who swears by Him will glory,
because the mouth of liars will be stopped.

PSALM 64

For the Music Director. A Psalm of David.

1 Hear my voice, O God, in my complaint;
guard my life from dread of the enemy.

62:11 Job 33:14
62:12 Job 34:11
63:1 Ps 84:2
63:2 Ps 27:4
63:3 Ps 69:16
63:4 Ps 104:33
63:5 Ps 71:23
63:6 Ps 42:8
63:8 Ps 18:35
63:9 Ps 55:15
63:11 Dt 6:13

64:2 Ps 56:6
64:3 Ps 58:7
64:4 Ps 55:19
64:5 Ps 10:11
64:7 Ps 7:12–13
64:8 Pr 18:7
64:9 Jer 51:10
65:1 Ps 62:1
65:2 Ps 86:9
65:3 Ps 38:4
65:4 Ps 33:12
65:5 Ps 22:27
65:6 Ps 93:1
65:7 Isa 17:12–13

2 Hide me from the secret counsel of the wicked,
from the throng of the workers of iniquity;
3 they sharpen their tongue like a sword,
and bend their bows to shoot their arrows—bitter words,
4 that they may shoot in secret at the blameless;
suddenly they shoot at him and do not fear.
5 They harden themselves in an evil matter;
they talk privately of laying snares;
they say, "Who will see them?"
6 They devise injustice,
saying "We have perfected a secret plot."
Both the inward thought of man and the heart are deep.
7 But God will suddenly shoot them with an arrow;
they will be wounded.
8 They will bring ruin on themselves
by their own tongues;
all who see them will flee away.
9 All people will fear,
and declare the work of God;
they will wisely consider His deeds.
10 The righteous will be glad in the Lord,
and seek refuge in Him,
and all the upright in heart will glory.

PSALM 65

For the Music Director. A Psalm of David. A Song.

1 Praise awaits You, O God, in Zion;
and to You a vow will be fulfilled.
2 O You who hears prayer,
to You all flesh will come.
3 Iniquities are stronger than me;
as for our transgressions, You atone for them.
4 Blessed is the man You choose and allow to draw near;
he will dwell in Your courts.
We will be satisfied with the goodness of Your house,
even of Your holy temple.
5 In righteousness You will answer us gloriously,
O God of our salvation,
You, who are the confidence of all the ends of the earth,
and of those who are afar off on the sea;
6 who established the mountains by His strength,
being clothed with might;
7 who stills the noise of the seas,

the noise of their waves,
and the tumult of peoples.
8 Those who dwell in the uttermost parts
are in awe because of Your signs;
You make the going out of the morning
and evening rejoice.

9 You visit the earth, and water it;
You enrich it
with the river of God, which is full of water;
You prepare their grain,
for thus You have established it.
10 You water its furrows abundantly;
You settle its ridges;
You soften it with showers;
You bless its sprouting.
11 You crown the year with Your goodness,
and Your paths drip abundance.
12 They drip on the pastures of the
wilderness,
and the hills clothe themselves with
rejoicing.
13 The pastures are clothed with flocks;
the valleys also are covered with grain;
they shout for joy, they also sing.

PSALM 66

For the Music Director. A Song. A Psalm.

1 Shout joyfully to God, all you lands!
2 Sing out the glory of His name;
make His praise glorious.
3 Say to God, "How awesome are Your
works!
Through the greatness of Your power
Your enemies cringe before You.
4 All the earth will worship You
and will sing to You;
they will sing to Your name." Selah

5 Come and see the works of God;
He is awesome in His doings toward
mankind.
6 He turned the sea into dry land;
they crossed the river on foot;
there we rejoiced in Him.
7 He rules by His power forever;
His eyes keep watch on the nations;
do not let the rebellious exalt
themselves. Selah

8 Oh, bless our God, you people,
and make the voice of His praise to be
heard,
9 who keeps our soul among the living,
and does not allow our feet to slip.
10 For You, O God, have proved us;
You have refined us, as silver is refined.
11 You brought us into the net;
You placed distress on our backs.
12 You have allowed people to ride over our
heads;
we went through fire and through water;
but You brought us out into a well-
watered place.

13 I will go into Your house with burnt
offerings;
I will fulfill my vows to You,
14 which my lips have uttered,
and my mouth spoke when I was in
trouble.
15 I will offer You burnt sacrifices of fat
animals,
with the incense of rams;
I will offer bulls with goats. Selah

16 Come and hear, all you who fear God,
and I will declare what He has done for
my soul.
17 I cried to Him with my mouth,
and He was extolled with my tongue.
18 If I regard iniquity in my heart,
the Lord will not hear me;
19 but certainly God has heard me;
He has attended to the voice of my
prayer.
20 Blessed be God,
who has not turned away my prayer,
nor His mercy from me.

PSALM 67

For the Music Director. With stringed
instruments. A Psalm. A Song.

1 May God be gracious to us, and bless us,
and cause His face to shine on us;
Selah
2 that Your way may be known on earth,
Your salvation among all nations.
3 Let the peoples praise You, O God;
let all the peoples praise You.
4 Oh, let the nations be glad and sing for joy;
for You will judge the people uprightly,
and lead the nations on earth. Selah
5 Let the peoples praise You, O God;
let all the peoples praise You.

6 Then will the earth yield its produce,
and God, our God, will bless us.
7 God will bless us,
and all the ends of the earth will fear
Him.

PSALM 68

For the Music Director. A Psalm of David. A Song.

1 Let God arise, let His enemies be scattered;
let those who hate Him flee before Him.
2 As smoke is driven away,

65:8 Ps 2:8
65:9 Ps 46:4
65:10 Ps 147:8
65:12 Job 38:26–27
65:13 Isa 55:12
66:1 Ps 100:1
66:3 Ps 18:44
66:4 Ps 22:27
66:5 Ps 46:8
66:6 Jos 3:16
66:7 Ps 11:4
66:9 Ps 121:3
66:10 Ps 17:3
66:11 La 1:13
66:12 Isa 51:23
66:13 Ecc 5:4
66:16 Ps 34:11
66:17 Ps 30:1
66:18 Jas 4:3
66:19 Ps 116:1–2
67:1 Ps 4:6
67:2 Titus 2:11
67:5 Ps 67:3
67:6 Lev 26:4
67:7 Ps 22:27
68:1 Nu 10:35
68:2 Ps 37:20

You drive them away;
as wax melts before the fire,
so may the wicked perish before God.
3 But let the righteous be glad;
let them rejoice before God;
let them rejoice exceedingly.

4 Sing to God, sing praises to His name;
raise a song to Him who rides through the deserts—
His name is the LORD;
exult before Him.
5 A father of the fatherless, and a protector of the widows,
is God in His holy habitation.
6 God sets the deserted in families;
He brings out prisoners into prosperity,
but the rebellious dwell in a dry land.

7 O God, when You went forth before Your people,
when You marched through the wasteland, Selah
8 the earth shook;
the heavens also poured down *rain*
at the presence of God; even Sinai shook
at the presence of God, the God of Israel.
9 You, O God, sent plentiful rain;
You established Your inheritance when it was weary.
10 Your congregation has lived in it;
You, O God, by Your goodness have prepared for the poor.

11 The Lord gave the word;
great was the company of women who proclaimed it:
12 "Kings of armies flee; they flee!"
Even the women who were at home divided the spoil.
13 Though you sleep between the sheepfolds,
yet you will be like the wings of a dove overlaid with silver,
and its feathers with yellow gold.
14 When the Almighty scattered kings in it,
it was white as snow on Mount Zalmon.

15 The mountain of God is as the mountain of Bashan;
a mountain of many peaks like the mountain of Bashan.
16 Why are you envious, you mountains of many peaks?
This is the mountain which God desires to dwell in;
yes, the LORD will dwell in it forever.
17 The chariots of God are twice ten thousand,
even thousands of thousands;
the Lord is among them, as in Sinai, in the holy place.
18 You have ascended on high,
You have led captivity captive;
You have received gifts from people,
yes, even from the rebellious,
that the LORD God might dwell among them.

19 Blessed be the Lord, who daily loads us with benefits,
even the God who is our salvation. Selah
20 That God is for us, the God of saving acts;
and to GOD the Lord belongs escape from death.
21 But God will shatter the head of His enemies,
and the scalp of one who walks in his trespasses.
22 The Lord said, "I will cause them to return from Bashan,
I will bring my people again from the depths of the sea,
23 that your foot may stomp in the blood of your enemies,
and the tongue of your dogs may have a portion in it."

24 They have seen Your processions, O God,
the processions of my God, my King, in the sanctuary.
25 The singers went before,
the players on instruments followed after;
among them were the young women playing tambourines.
26 Bless God in the congregations,
the LORD, from the fountain of Israel.
27 There is little Benjamin leading them,
the princes of Judah and their throng of people,
the princes of Zebulun, and the princes of Naphtali.

28 Your God has commanded your strength;
strengthen, O God, what You have done for us.
29 From Your temple above Jerusalem,
kings will bring gifts to You.
30 Rebuke the animals that live among the reeds,
the herd of bulls, with the calves of the people,
until everyone submits himself with pieces of silver;
scatter peoples who delight in war.
31 Ambassadors will come out of Egypt;
Ethiopia will stretch out its hands to God.

32 Sing to God, you kingdoms of the earth;
oh, sing praises to the Lord; Selah
33 to Him who rides on the heavens, the ancient heavens;

68:4 Ex 6:3
68:5 Dt 10:18
68:6 Ps 107:10
68:7 Ex 13:21
68:8 Ex 19:18
68:9 Eze 34:26
68:10 Ps 74:19
68:11 Ex 15:20
68:12 Jos 10:16
68:13 Ge 49:14
68:16 Dt 12:5
68:17 Dt 33:2
68:18 Jdg 5:12
68:20 Dt 32:39
68:21 Hab 3:13
68:22 Nu 21:33
68:23 1Ki 21:19
68:25 Jdg 11:34
68:26 Isa 48:1
68:27 1Sa 9:21
68:29 1Ki 10:10
68:31 Isa 45:14
68:33 Ps 18:10

He who sends out His voice, a mighty
voice.
34 Ascribe strength to God;
His majesty is over Israel,
and His strength is in the clouds.
35 O God, You are awesome from Your
sanctuaries;
the God of Israel is He who gives
strength and power to people.

Blessed be God!

PSALM 69

For the Music Director. To the melody
of "Lilies." A Psalm of David.

1 Save me, O God!
For the waters have come up to my
throat.
2 I sink in deep mire;
there is no standing place;
I have come into the watery depths,
and a stream overflows me.
3 I am weary of my crying;
my throat is parched;
my eyes fail
while I wait for my God.
4 Those who hate me without cause
are more than the hairs of my head;
they are mighty
who would destroy me, being my
wrongful enemies,
so that I must pay back
what I did not steal.

5 O God, You know my folly,
and my sins are not hidden from You.

6 May those who wait on You,
O Lord God of Hosts,
not be ashamed because of me;
may those who seek You
not be humiliated because of me,
O God of Israel.
7 Because for Your sake I have endured
insult;
humiliation has covered my face.
8 I have become estranged to my relatives,
and a foreigner to my mother's children;
9 for the zeal of Your house has
consumed me,
and the insults of those who insulted
You fell on me.
10 When I wept with fasting for my soul,
it became an insult to me.
11 I also made sackcloth my garment,
and I became a byword to them.
12 Those who sit in the gate speak against
me,
and I am the song of the drunkards.

13 But as for me, my prayer is to You, O Lord;
in an acceptable time, O God,
in the abundance of Your mercy,
answer me in the truth of Your salvation.
14 Deliver me out of the mire
that I may not sink;
may I be delivered from those who
hate me,
and out of the watery depths.
15 May the stream not overflow me;
neither may the deep swallow me up,
nor the pit close its mouth on me.

16 Answer me, O Lord, for Your
lovingkindness is good;
turn Your face to me according to the
abundance of Your tender mercies.
17 Do not hide Your face from Your servant,
for I am in trouble; answer me quickly.
18 Draw near to my soul, and redeem it;
deliver me because of my enemies.

19 You have known how I am insulted, and
my shame and my dishonor;
my adversaries are all before You.
20 Insults have broken my heart,
and I am sick;
and I looked for some to take pity, but there
was none;
and for comforters, but I found none.
21 They also gave me poison for my food,
and in my thirst they gave me vinegar
to drink.

22 May their table become a snare before
them,
and may security become a trap.
23 May their eyes be darkened so they do not
see,
and make their sides shake continually.
24 Pour out Your indignation on them,
and may Your wrathful anger overtake
them.
25 May their habitation be desolate,
and may no one dwell in their tents.
26 For they persecute him whom You have
struck down,
and they recount the pain of those You
have wounded.
27 Add punishment to their iniquity,
and do not let them come into Your
righteousness.
28 Let them be blotted out of the book of the
living,
and not be written along with the
righteous.

29 But I am poor and in pain;
may Your salvation, O God, set me
secure on high.
30 I will praise the name of God with a song,
and will magnify Him with thanksgiving.

68:35 Ps 29:11
69:1 Ps 69:14–15
69:2 Ps 40:2
69:3 Ps 6:6
69:4 Ps 35:19
69:7 Jer 15:15
69:8 Ps 31:11
69:9 Ro 15:3
69:10 Ps 35:13
69:13 Isa 49:8
69:14 Ps 144:7
69:16 Ps 63:3
69:17 Ps 27:9
69:19 Heb 12:2
69:20 Job 16:2
69:21 Mt 27:34
69:23 Da 5:6
69:24 Ps 79:6
69:25 Mt 23:38
69:26 Isa 53:4
69:27 Isa 26:10
69:28 Eze 13:9
69:30 Ps 28:7

31 This also will please the LORD
more than an ox or bull with horns and hoofs.
32 The humble will see this and be glad;
and you who seek God, may your heart live.
33 For the LORD hears the poor,
and does not despise His prisoners.

34 Let heaven and earth praise Him,
the seas and everything that moves in them.
35 For God will save Zion,
and will build the cities of Judah;
that they may dwell there, and take possession of it.
36 The descendants of His servants will inherit it;
and those who love His name will dwell in it.

PSALM 70

Ps 40:13–17

For the Music Director. A Psalm of David. To bring remembrance.

1 Make haste, O God, to deliver me!
Make haste to help me, O LORD.

2 May those who seek my life
be ashamed and confused;
may those who desire my harm
be driven back and humiliated.
3 May they turn back as a consequence of their shame
who say "Aha! Aha!"
4 May all those who seek You
rejoice and be glad in You;
and may those who love Your salvation
continually say,
"God be magnified!"

5 But I am poor and needy;
make haste to me, O God!
You are my help and my deliverer;
O LORD, do not delay!

PSALM 71

Ps 31:1–4

1 In You, O LORD, I seek refuge;
may I never be put to shame.
2 Deliver me in Your righteousness and help me escape;
incline Your ear to me and save me.
3 Be my rock of refuge
to enter continually;
You have given commandment to save me;
for You are my rock and my stronghold.

69:31 Ps 50:13–14
69:32 Ps 22:26
69:33 Ps 68:6
69:34 Ps 96:11
69:35 Ps 51:18
69:36 Ps 102:28
70:1 Ps 40:13–17
70:2 Ps 35:4
70:3 Ps 40:15
70:5 Ps 141:1
71:1 Ps 25:2–3
71:2 Ps 17:6
71:3 Ps 18:2
....
71:5 Jer 17:7
71:6 Ps 22:9–10
71:7 Isa 8:18
71:8 Ps 35:28
71:9 Ps 71:18
71:10 Ps 56:6
71:11 Ps 7:2
71:12 Ps 35:22
71:13 Ps 35:4
71:15 Ps 40:5
71:16 Ps 51:14
71:18 Ps 71:9
71:19 Ps 35:10
71:20 Ps 60:3

4 Deliver me, O my God, out of the hand of the wicked,
out of the hand of the unjust and cruel man.

5 For You are my hope, O Lord GOD;
You are my confidence from my youth.
6 On You I have supported myself from the womb;
You took me out of my mother's womb.
My praise will continually be about You.
7 I am like a wondrous sign to many;
You are my strong refuge.
8 My mouth will be filled with Your praise
and with Your glory all the day.

9 Do not cast me off in the time of old age;
do not forsake me when my strength fails.
10 For my enemies speak against me;
and those who watch for my life take counsel together,
11 saying, "God has forsaken him;
pursue and catch him,
for there is none to deliver him."
12 O God, do not be far from me;
O my God, act quickly to help me.
13 May the adversaries of my life be ashamed and confused;
may those who seek my harm
be enveloped in scorn and dishonor.

14 But I will hope continually,
and will add to all Your praise.
15 My mouth will declare Your righteousness
and Your salvation all the day,
for I cannot know their numbers.
16 I will go in the strength of the Lord GOD;
I will make mention of Your righteousness, of Yours only.
17 O God, You have taught me from my youth;
and until now I have proclaimed Your wondrous works.
18 Now also when I am old and gray,
O God, do not forsake me,
until I have proclaimed Your strength to this generation,
and Your power to everyone who is to come.
19 Your righteousness, O God, reaches to the heights;
You have done great deeds;
O God, who is like You?
20 You who have shown me great distresses and troubles
will revive me again,
and will bring me up again
from the depths of the earth.
21 You will increase my greatness,
and You will encircle and comfort me.

22 I will give You thanks with the harp,
even Your truth, O my God;
to You I will sing with the lyre,
O Holy One of Israel.
23 My lips will rejoice
when I sing to You,
and my soul, which You have redeemed.
24 My tongue also will speak of Your
righteousness
all the day long;
for those who seek my harm are ashamed,
for they have been put to shame.

PSALM 72

A Psalm of Solomon.

1 Give the king Your judgments, O God,
and Your righteousness to the king's son.
2 May he judge Your people with
righteousness,
and Your poor with justice.
3 May the mountains bring well-being to the
people,
and the hills, in righteousness.
4 May he judge the poor of the people,
may he save the children of the needy,
and crush the oppressor.
5 May they fear You as long as the sun
endures,
and the moon, throughout all
generations.
6 May he descend like rain on the mown
grass,
as showers dripping on the earth.
7 In his days may the righteous flourish,
and abundance of peace until the moon
is no more.
8 May he have dominion from sea to sea,
and from the River to the ends of the
earth.
9 May those who dwell in the wilderness
bow before him,
and his enemies lick the dust.
10 May the kings of Tarshish and of the isles
bring presents;
the kings of Sheba and Seba offer a gift.
11 May all kings bow down before him;
may all nations serve him.
12 Indeed, may he deliver the needy when he
cries;
the poor also, and him who has no
helper.
13 May he have compassion on the poor and
needy,
and save the lives of the needy.
14 May he redeem their life from deceit and
violence;

71:22 2Ki 19:22
71:23 Ps 103:4
71:24 Ps 71:13
72:1 1Ch 22:12–13
72:2 Isa 32:1
72:3 Isa 52:7
72:4 Isa 11:4
72:5 Ps 89:36–37
72:6 Dt 32:2
72:7 Isa 2:4
72:8 Ex 23:31
72:9 Isa 49:23
72:10 1Ki 10:1
72:11 Ps 86:9
72:12 Job 29:12
72:14 Ps 116:15
72:17 Ge 12:3
72:18 Ps 41:13
72:19 Nu 14:21
72:20 2Sa 23:1
73:1 Mt 5:8
73:2 Ps 94:18
73:3 Job 21:7
73:5 Ps 73:12
73:6 Ps 109:18
73:7 Job 15:27
73:8 Jude 1:16
73:9 Rev 13:6

and may their blood be precious in his
sight.
15 May he live long,
and may one give him the gold of
Sheba;
and pray for him continually;
and all day long may he be blessed.
16 May there be abundance of grain in the
earth
on the top of the mountains;
may its fruit shake like Lebanon;
and may those from the city flourish like
grass of the earth.
17 May his name endure forever;
may his name increase as long as the
sun.
May men be blessed in him;
may all nations call him blessed!

18 Blessed be the LORD God, the God of Israel,
who alone does wondrous deeds.
19 Blessed be His glorious name forever;
and may the whole earth be filled with
His glory.
Amen, and Amen.

20 The prayers of David the son of Jesse are ended.

BOOK THREE

Psalms 73–89

PSALM 73

A Psalm of Asaph.

1 Truly God is good to Israel,
to the pure in heart.
2 But as for me, my feet almost stumbled;
my steps had almost slipped.
3 For I was envious at the boastful;
I saw the prosperity of the wicked.
4 For there are no pains in their death;
their bodies are fat.
5 They are not in trouble as other people;
nor are they plagued like others.
6 Therefore pride is their necklace;
violence covers them as a garment.
7 Their eyes bulge with fatness;
they have more than a heart could wish.
8 They mock and speak with evil oppression;
they speak loftily.
9 They set their mouth against the heavens,
and their tongue struts through the
earth.
10 Therefore people turn to them,
and abundant waters are drunk by them.
11 They say, "How does God know?

And is there knowledge with the Most
High?"
12 Observe, these are the wicked, always at
ease;
they increase in riches.
13 Surely I have kept my heart pure for
nothing,
and washed my hands in innocence.
14 For all the day long I am plagued,
and chastened every morning.
15 If I said, "I will speak thus,"
I would have betrayed the generation of
Your children.
16 When I thought to understand this,
it was troublesome in my eyes,
17 until I went into the sanctuary of God;
then I understood their end.
18 Surely You have set them in slippery
places;
You have brought them down to ruin.
19 How they come to desolation, as in a
moment!
They have come to an end, utterly
consumed with terrors.
20 As a dream when one awakes,
so, O Lord, when You awake,
You will despise their form.

21 Thus my heart was embittered,
and I was pierced in my feelings.
22 I was a brute and did not understand;
I was as a beast before You.
23 Nevertheless I am continually with You;
You have held me by my right hand.
24 You will guide me with Your counsel,
and afterward receive me to glory.
25 Whom have I in heaven but You?
And there is nothing on earth that I
desire besides You.
26 My flesh and my heart fails,
but God is the strength of my heart
and my portion forever.
27 For those who are far from You will perish;
You destroy everyone who is unfaithful
to You.
28 But it is good for me to draw near to God;
I have taken my refuge in the Lord GOD,
that I may declare all Your works.

PSALM 74

A Contemplative Maskil of Asaph.

1 O God, why have You cast us off forever?
Why does Your anger smoke against the
sheep of Your pasture?
2 Remember Your congregation, which You
have purchased of old,

73:12 Ps 52:7
73:13 Job 34:9
73:16 Ecc 8:17
73:17 Ps 77:13
73:18 Ps 35:6
73:20 Job 20:8
73:22 Ps 92:6
73:24 Ps 32:8
73:25 Php 3:8
73:26 Ps 84:2
73:27 Ps 119:155
73:28 Jas 4:8
74:1 Dt 29:20
74:2 Ex 15:16

....

74:3 Ps 79:1
74:4 La 2:7
74:6 1Ki 6:18
74:7 2Ki 25:9
74:8 Ps 83:4
74:9 1Sa 3:1
74:11 La 2:3
74:12 Ps 44:4
74:13 Ex 14:21
74:14 Isa 27:1
74:15 Nu 20:11
74:16 Ps 136:7–9
74:17 Ge 8:22
74:18 Ps 39:8
74:19 SS 2:14

the rod of Your inheritance, which You
have redeemed,
this Mount Zion, where You have lived.
3 Move Your footsteps to the perpetual
desolations,
to all the harm the enemy has done in
the sanctuary.
4 Your enemies roar in the midst of Your
meeting place;
they set up their miracles for signs.
5 They seem like men who lift up axes
on a thicket of trees.
6 But now they strike down its carved work
altogether
with axes and hammers.
7 They have cast fire into Your sanctuary;
they have defiled the dwelling place of
Your name to the ground.
8 They said in their hearts, "Let us destroy
them together."
They have burned up all the meeting
places of God in the land.
9 We do not see our signs;
there is no longer any prophet,
nor is there among us any who knows
how long.
10 O God, how long will the adversary scorn?
Will the enemy blaspheme Your name
forever?
11 Why do You withdraw Your hand, Your
right hand?
Draw it out of Your bosom and destroy
them!
12 For God is my King of old,
working salvation in the midst of the
earth.
13 You divided the sea by Your strength;
You broke the heads of the dragons on
the waters.
14 You crushed the heads of Leviathan in
pieces,
and gave him for food to the people
inhabiting the wilderness.
15 You split the fountain and the flood;
You dried up ever-flowing rivers.
16 The day is Yours, the night also is Yours;
You have prepared the light and the sun.
17 You have established all the borders of the
earth;
You have made summer and winter.
18 Remember this, that the enemy has
scorned, O LORD,
and that the foolish people have
blasphemed Your name.
19 Do not give the life of Your turtledove to a
wild animal;

do not forget the life of Your poor
forever.
20 Have regard for the covenant;
for the dark places of the earth are full
of the habitations of violence.
21 May the oppressed not return ashamed;
may the poor and needy praise Your
name.
22 Arise, O God, plead Your own cause;
remember how the fool insults You daily.
23 Do not forget the voice of Your enemies,
the tumult of those who rise up against
You continually.

PSALM 75

For the Music Director. To the melody of "Do Not Destroy." A Psalm of Asaph. A Song.

1 We give thanks to You, O God;
we give thanks, and Your name is near;
Your wondrous works declare it.
2 When I select an appointed time,
I will judge with equity.
3 Though the earth and all its inhabitants are
swaying,
I steady its pillars. Selah
4 I said to the boastful, "Do not boast,"
and to the wicked, "Do not lift up your
horn.
5 Do not lift up your horn on high,
or speak with an arrogant neck."
6 For neither from the east nor west,
nor from the wilderness comes victory.
7 But God is the judge;
He brings one low, and lifts up another.
8 For in the hand of the LORD there is a cup,
and it is full of mixed, foaming wine,
and He pours from it;
surely all the wicked of the earth will
find and drink its dregs.
9 But I will declare forever,
I will sing praises to the God of Jacob.
10 All the horns of the wicked I will cut off,
but the horns of the righteous will be
exalted.

PSALM 76

For the Music Director. With stringed instruments. A Psalm of Asaph. A Song.

1 In Judah God is known;
in Israel His name is great.
2 In Salem is His abode,
and His dwelling place in Zion.
3 There He broke the fiery arrows of the bow,
the shield, the sword, and the *weapons
of* war. Selah
4 You are more glorious and excellent
than the mountains of prey.
5 The strong of heart have been plundered;
they have been put to sleep;
and none of the mighty men
could use their hands.
6 At Your rebuke, O God of Jacob,
both the chariot and horse lay stunned.
7 You, even You, are to be feared;
and who may stand in Your sight from
the moment of Your anger?
8 From the heavens You gave their
judgment,
and the earth feared and was silent,
9 when God arose to judgment,
to save all the meek of the earth. Selah
10 Surely the wrath of people shall bring You
praise;
the remainder of wrath You shall put on.
11 Make your vows to the LORD your God, and
fulfill them;
let all who surround Him
bring tribute to Him who is to be feared.
12 He reduces the spirit of princes,
and is feared among the kings of the
earth.

PSALM 77

For the Music Director. To Jeduthun. A Psalm of Asaph.

1 I cried out to God with my voice,
even to God with my voice; and He
listened to me.
2 In the day of my trouble I sought the Lord;
in the night my hand is stretched out
and does not weary,
my soul refuses to be comforted.
3 I remember God, and I groan;
I complain, and my spirit is
overwhelmed. Selah
4 You hold my eyelids open;
I am so troubled that I cannot speak.
5 I have considered the days of old,
the years long ago.
6 May I remember my song in the night;
may I meditate in my heart;
my spirit made a diligent search:
7 "Will the Lord cast off forever,
and will He be favorable no more?
8 Has His mercy ceased forever,
and have His promises failed for all
time?
9 Has God forgotten to be gracious,
and has He in anger shut up His tender
mercies?" Selah

74:20 Ps 106:45
74:22 Ps 74:18
74:23 Ps 65:7
75:3 1Sa 2:8
75:4 Zec 1:21
75:7 Ps 50:6
75:8 Job 21:20
75:10 Ps 89:17
76:1 Ps 4:1
76:2 Ge 14:18
76:3 Ps 46:9

....

76:5 Ps 13:3
76:6 Ex 15:1
76:7 Na 1:6
76:8 2Ch 20:29–30
76:11 Ps 50:14
77:1 Ps 3:4
77:2 Ge 37:35
77:3 Ps 61:2
77:5 Dt 32:7
77:6 Ps 4:4
77:7 Ps 85:1
77:8 Ro 9:6

10 Then I said, "This is my grief;
yet I will remember the years of the right
hand of the Most High."
11 I will remember the works of the LORD;
surely I will remember Your wonders
of old.
12 I will meditate also on all Your work
and ponder on Your mighty deeds.

13 Your way, O God, is holiness;
what god is as great as our God?
14 You are the God who can do wonders;
You have declared Your strength among
the nations.
15 You have with Your arm redeemed Your
people,
the children of Jacob and Joseph. Selah
16 The waters saw You, O God.
The waters saw You; they were afraid;
the depths also trembled.
17 The clouds poured out water;
the skies thundered.
Your arrows flashed about.
18 The sound of Your thunder was in the
whirlwind,
and Your lightning lit up the world;
the earth trembled and shook.
19 Your way is through the sea,
and Your path in the great waters,
and your footsteps are not seen.

20 You led Your people like a flock
by the hand of Moses and Aaron.

PSALM 78

A Contemplative Maskil of Asaph.

1 Give ear, O my people, to my teaching;
incline your ears to the words of my
mouth.
2 I will open my mouth in a parable;
I will utter insightful sayings of old,
3 which we have heard and known,
what our fathers have told us.
4 We will not hide them from their children,
but will tell the coming generation
the praises of the LORD,
and His strength, and the wonderful
works that He has done.
5 For He established a rule in Jacob,
and appointed a law in Israel,
which He commanded our fathers
that they should make them known to
their children,
6 that the generation to come might know
them,
even the children who are not yet born,
who will arise and declare them to their
children:
7 that they might set their hope in God

77:10 Ps 31:22
77:13 Ex 15:11
77:14 Ps 72:18
77:15 Ex 6:6
77:16 Ex 14:21
77:17 Ps 18:14
77:18 Ps 97:4
77:19 Hab 3:15
77:20 Ex 13:21
78:1 Isa 51:4
78:2 Ps 49:4
78:3 Ps 44:1
78:4 Dt 11:19
78:5 Ps 81:5
78:6 Ps 102:18
78:7 Dt 5:29

....

78:8 Ps 78:37
78:11 Ps 106:13
78:12 Nu 13:22
78:14 Ps 105:39
78:15 Ex 17:6
78:17 Isa 63:10
78:18 Nu 11:4
78:19 Nu 21:5
78:20 Nu 20:11
78:22 Heb 3:18–19
78:23 Ge 7:11
78:24 Ex 16:4
78:25 Ps 103:20
78:26 Nu 11:31

and not forget the works of God,
but keep His commandments,
8 and they might not be as their fathers,
a stubborn and rebellious generation,
a generation that did not set their heart
steadfast,
and whose spirit was not faithful to God.

9 The people of Ephraim, being armed with
bows,
turned back in the day of battle.
10 They did not keep the covenant of God
and refused to walk in His law;
11 and they forgot His works
and the wonders that He had shown
them.
12 In the sight of their ancestors He did
marvelous wonders
in the land of Egypt, in the field of Zoan.
13 He divided the sea and caused them to
pass through,
and He made the waters to stand as a
heap.
14 In the daytime He led them with a cloud,
and all the night with a light of fire.
15 He split rocks in the wilderness
and gave them abundance to drink as
out of the great depths.
16 He brought streams out of the rock
and caused waters to run down like
rivers.

17 They sinned yet more against Him
by provoking the Most High in the
wilderness.
18 They tested God in their heart
by demanding the food that they craved.
19 They spoke against God by saying,
"Can God furnish a table in the
wilderness?
20 Behold, He struck the rock, so that the
waters gushed out
and the streams overflowed.
Can He give bread
or provide meat for His people?"
21 Therefore the LORD heard this and was full
of wrath;
a fire was kindled against Jacob,
and anger also came up against Israel,
22 because they did not believe in God
nor trust in His deliverance.
23 Yet He had commanded the skies above
and opened the doors of heaven,
24 and He rained down manna upon them to
eat
and gave them the grain of heaven.
25 Man ate the food of mighty angels;
He sent them bread in abundance.
26 He caused an east wind to blow in the
heavens,

and by His power He brought out a
south wind.
27 He rained meat on them as dust,
and winged birds as the sand of the sea;
28 and He let them fall in the midst of their
camp
all around their habitations.
29 So they ate and were satisfied,
for He gave them their own desire;
30 while they were not yet filled up,
and while the meat was still in their
mouths,
31 the wrath of God came upon them,
and He killed the strongest of them
and struck down the young men of
Israel.

32 For all this they sinned still,
and did not believe despite His
wondrous works.
33 Therefore He made their days vanish like a
breath,
and their years in trouble.
34 When He killed them, then they sought
Him;
they turned back and longed for God.
35 They remembered that God was their rock,
and the Most High God their redeemer.
36 Nevertheless they flattered Him with their
mouth,
and they lied to Him with their tongues;
37 for their heart was not devoted to Him,
neither were they committed to His
covenant.
38 But He being full of compassion
forgave their iniquity
and did not destroy them.
He constantly restrained His anger,
and did not stir up all His wrath;
39 for He remembered that they were but
flesh,
like a wind that passes away and does
not return.

40 How often they provoked Him in the
wilderness
and grieved Him in the desert!
41 Yes, they tested God over and over,
and provoked the Holy One of Israel.
42 They did not remember His power,
nor the day when He delivered them
from the enemy,
43 how He had performed His signs in Egypt
and His wonders in the fields of Zoan:
44 and He turned their rivers into blood,
so that they could not drink from their
streams.
45 He sent swarms of flies among them,
which devoured them,
and frogs, which destroyed them.

78:31 Isa 10:16
78:33 Nu 14:29
78:34 Hos 5:15
78:35 Dt 32:4
78:36 Eze 33:31
78:37 Ps 78:8
78:39 Ge 6:3
78:40 Eph 4:30
78:41 Nu 14:22
78:44 Ps 105:29
....
78:46 Ex 10:12–15
78:51 Ps 105:23
78:52 Ps 77:20
78:53 Ex 14:19–20
78:54 Ex 15:17
78:55 Ps 44:2
78:56 Jdg 2:11–12
78:57 Hos 7:16
78:58 Lev 26:30
78:59 Ps 106:40
78:60 Jos 18:1
78:61 Ps 132:8
78:63 Jer 7:34
78:64 1Sa 4:17
78:65 Ps 44:23
78:66 1Sa 5:6

46 He gave also their crops to the grasshopper
and the fruit of their labor to the locust.
47 He destroyed their vines with hail
and their sycamore trees with frost.
48 He gave up their cattle also to the hail
and their flocks to thunderbolts.
49 He cast upon them the fierceness of His
anger,
wrath, indignation, and trouble,
by sending angels bringing disaster.
50 He made a path for His anger;
He did not spare them from death,
but gave their lives over to the plague,
51 And struck down all the firstborn in Egypt,
the first fruits of their strength in the
tents of Ham.
52 Then He led out His own people like sheep
and guided them in the wilderness like
a flock;
53 He led them in safety, so that they were not
afraid,
but the sea overwhelmed their enemies.
54 He brought them to the border of His holy
land,
to the mountain that His right hand had
acquired.
55 He cast out the nations also before them,
and divided for them their tribal
allotments,
and made the tribes of Israel dwell in
their tents.

56 Yet they tested and provoked the Most High
God,
and did not keep His commands,
57 but turned back and acted unfaithfully like
their fathers;
they turned aside like a deceitful bow.
58 For they provoked Him to anger with their
high places
and moved Him to jealousy with their
graven images.
59 When God heard this, He was full of wrath
and greatly rejected Israel
60 so that He left the tabernacle at Shiloh,
the tent where He lived among people,
61 and delivered His strength to captivity
and His glory into the enemy's hand.
62 He gave His people over also to the sword;
He was enraged with His inheritance.
63 The fire consumed their young men,
and their maidens were not given to
marriage in song.
64 Their priests fell by the sword,
and their widows made no lamentation.

65 Then the Lord awoke as one out of sleep,
and like a mighty man who shouts
because of wine.
66 He routed His enemies back,

and He made them a perpetual
reproach.
67 Moreover, He rejected the tent of Joseph,
and He did not choose the tribe of
Ephraim,
68 but chose the tribe of Judah,
Mount Zion which He loves.
69 He built His sanctuary like the high
heavens,
like the earth that He has established
perpetually.
70 He chose David His servant
and took him from the sheepfolds;
71 from following the nursing ewes He
brought him
to shepherd Jacob His people,
and Israel His inheritance.
72 So he shepherded them according to the
integrity of his heart
and guided them by the skillfulness of
his hands.

PSALM 79

A Psalm of Asaph.

1 O God, the nations have come into Your
inheritance;
Your holy temple they have defiled;
they have laid Jerusalem in ruins.
2 The dead bodies of Your servants
they have given to the birds of the sky
for food
and the flesh of Your faithful to the
animals of the land.
3 Their blood they have poured out like
water
all around Jerusalem,
and there was no one to bury them.
4 We have become a reproach to our
neighbors,
a scorn and derision to those who are
around us.
5 How long, O Lord? Will You be angry
forever?
Will Your jealousy burn like fire?
6 Pour out Your wrath
upon the nations who do not know You,
and upon the kingdoms
who have not called upon Your name.
7 For they have devoured Jacob,
and laid waste his dwelling place.

8 Do not choose to remember our former
iniquities;
let Your tender mercies come swiftly to
us,
for we are brought very low.
9 Help us, O God of our salvation,
for the glory of Your name;

78:68 Ps 87:2
78:70 1Sa 16:11–12
78:71 2Sa 5:2
78:72 1Ki 9:4
79:1 2Ch 36:19
79:2 Jer 7:33
79:3 Jer 14:16
79:4 Ps 80:6
79:5 Ps 89:46
79:6 Ps 14:4
79:8 Ps 116:6
79:9 2Ch 14:11

. . . .

79:10 Ps 42:10
79:11 Ps 102:20
79:12 Ge 4:15
79:13 Ps 74:1
80:1 1Sa 4:4
80:2 Nu 2:18–24
80:3 Ps 85:4
80:4 Ps 85:5
80:5 Ps 42:3
80:6 Ps 79:4
80:8 Jer 2:21
80:9 Jos 24:12

deliver us, and purge away our sins,
for Your name's sake.
10 Why should the nations say,
"Where is their God?"

May the avenging of the shed blood of
Your servants
be known among the nations before our
eyes.
11 Let the groans of the prisoners come
before You;
according to the greatness of Your
power
preserve those who are appointed to die.
12 And render unto our neighbors sevenfold
into their lap
the reproach that they have reproached
You, O Lord.
13 But we are Your people, the sheep of Your
pasture,
and will give You thanks forever;
we will declare Your praise
to all generations.

PSALM 80

For the Music Director. To the melody of
"Lilies of the Testimony." A Psalm of Asaph.

1 Give ear, O Shepherd of Israel,
You who lead Joseph like a flock;
You who are enthroned between the
cherubim, shine forth.
2 In the sight of Ephraim and Benjamin
and Manasseh,
stir up Your strength,
and come and rescue us.
3 Restore us again, O God,
and cause Your face to shine,
and we shall be delivered.
4 O Lord God of Hosts,
how long will You be angry
against the prayers of Your people?
5 You have fed them with the bread of tears
and have given them tears to drink in
great measure.
6 You make us contention for our neighbors,
and our enemies laugh among
themselves.
7 Restore us again, O God of Hosts,
and cause Your face to shine,
and we shall be delivered.
8 You have brought a vine out of Egypt;
You have cast out the nations and
planted it.
9 You cleared the *ground* for it;
it took deep root and filled the land.

[10]The mountains were covered with its
shadow
and the mighty cedars with its branches.
[11]It sent out its branches to the sea
and its shoots to the River.

[12]Why have You then broken down its walls,
so that all those who pass by the way
pluck its *fruit*?
[13]The boar from the woods ravages it,
and the insects of the field devour it.
[14]Return again, O God of Hosts;
look down from heaven, and behold,
have regard for this vine
[15] and the root that Your right hand has
planted,
and the shoots that You made strong for
Yourself.

[16]It is burned with fire; it is cut down;
may they perish at the rebuke from Your
presence.
[17]Let Your hand be upon the man of Your
right hand,
the son of man whom You made strong
for Yourself.
[18]So we will not turn back from You;
give us life, and we will call upon Your
name.

[19]Restore us again, O LORD God of Hosts;
cause Your face to shine,
and we shall be delivered.

PSALM 81

For the Music Director. According to
The Gittith. A Psalm of Asaph.

[1] Sing aloud unto God our strength;
make a joyful noise unto the God of
Jacob.
[2] Lift up a melody, and sound the
tambourine,
the pleasant lyre with the harp.
[3] Blow the trumpet at the New Moon,
at the full moon on our feast day.
[4] For this is a statute for Israel,
a decree of the God of Jacob.
[5] This He ordained in Joseph as a decree
when He went out against the land of
Egypt.

I heard a voice that I had not known:

[6] "I removed his shoulder from the burden;
his hands were released from holding
the basket.
[7] You called in trouble, and I delivered you;
I answered you in the secret place of
thunder;
I tested you at the waters of Meribah.
Selah
[8] Hear, O My people, and I will testify against
you.
O Israel, if you would listen to me!
[9] There shall be no strange god among you;
neither shall you bow down to any
strange god.
[10]I am the LORD your God,
who brought you out of the land of
Egypt;
open your mouth wide, and I will fill it.

[11]"But My people would not listen to My
voice;
Israel would not submit to Me.
[12]So I gave them up to their stubborn hearts,
to walk in their own counsels.

[13]"Oh, that My people would listen to Me,
and Israel would follow in My ways!
[14]I would soon subdue their enemies,
and turn My hand against their
adversaries.
[15]Let those who hate the LORD cower before
Him
and their fate might last forever.
[16]But I would feed them with the finest of
wheat,
and with honey out of the rock I would
satisfy you."

PSALM 82

A Psalm of Asaph.

[1] God stands among the divine council;
He renders judgment among the gods.
[2] "How long will you all judge unjustly
and accept partiality of the wicked?
Selah
[3] Defend the poor and fatherless;
vindicate the afflicted and needy.
[4] Grant escape to the abused and the
destitute,
pluck them out of the hand of the false.

[5] "They have neither knowledge nor
understanding;
they walk in darkness:
all the foundations of the earth are
shaken."

[6] I have said, "You are gods,
sons of the Most High, all of you,
[7] but you all shall die like men,
and fall like a man, O princes."

[8] Arise, O God, judge the earth,
for You shall inherit all nations.

80:11 Ps 72:8
80:12 Isa 5:5
80:13 Jer 5:6
80:14 Isa 63:15
80:15 Ps 80:8
80:16 Ps 39:11
80:17 Ps 89:21
80:19 Ps 80:3
81:1 Ps 66:1
81:2 Ps 92:3
81:5 Ps 114:1
81:6 Isa 9:4
81:7 Ex 2:23
81:8 Ps 50:7
81:9 Dt 32:12
81:10 Ex 20:2
81:11 Ex 32:1
81:12 Ac 7:42
81:13 Dt 5:29
81:14 Am 1:8
81:15 Ro 1:30
81:16 Dt 32:13–14
82:1 2Ch 19:6–7
82:2 Dt 1:17
82:3 Ps 10:18
82:4 Job 29:12
82:5 Ps 11:3
82:6 Ps 82:1
82:7 Ps 49:12
82:8 Ps 2:8

PSALM 83

A Song. A Psalm of Asaph.

1 Do not keep Your silence, O God;
do not hold Your peace or be still, O God.
2 For, look, Your enemies make an uproar,
and those who hate You have lifted up their heads.
3 They have given crafty counsel against Your people,
and have consulted against Your treasured ones.
4 They have said, "Come, and let us cut them off from being a nation,
that the name of Israel may be no more remembered."

5 For they have conspired together;
they make a covenant against You—
6 the tents of Edom and the Ishmaelites,
even Moab and the Hagrites;
7 Gebal and Ammon and Amalek,
the Philistines with the inhabitants of Tyre;
8 Assyria also is joined with them,
they are the strength of the descendants of Lot. Selah

9 Do to them as You did to the Midianites,
as to Sisera and Jabin at the river of Kishon,
10 who perished at Endor;
they became as dung for the ground.
11 Make their nobles like Oreb and Zeeb;
yes, all their princes as Zebah and Zalmunna,
12 who said, "Let us take for ourselves
the pastures of God as a possession."

13 O my God, make them like a tumbleweed,
as stubble before the wind.
14 As fire burns a forest,
and as the flame sets the mountains ablaze,
15 so pursue them with Your storm,
and make them afraid with Your hurricane.
16 Fill their faces with shame,
that they may seek your name, O LORD.

17 Let them be confounded and troubled forever;
yes, let them be put to shame and perish,
18 that they may know that You, whose name alone is the LORD,
are the Most High over all the earth.

83:1 Ps 28:1
83:2 Ps 81:15
83:3 Ps 27:5
83:4 Jer 11:19
83:5 Ps 2:2
83:6 1Ch 5:10
83:7 Jos 13:5
83:8 Dt 2:9
83:10 Zep 1:17
83:11 Jdg 7:25
83:12 2Ch 20:11
83:13 Job 21:18
83:14 Dt 32:22
83:15 Job 9:17
83:17 Ps 35:4
83:18 Ps 59:13

....

84:1 Ps 27:4
84:2 Ps 42:1–2
84:3 Ps 5:2
84:4 Ps 65:4
84:6 Joel 2:23
84:7 Pr 4:18
84:9 Ps 2:2
84:10 Ps 27:4
84:11 Pr 2:7
84:12 Ps 2:12
85:1 Ps 14:7
85:2 Ps 32:1

PSALM 84

For the Music Director. According to The Gittith. A Psalm of the sons of Korah.

1 How lovely is Your dwelling place,
O LORD of Hosts!
2 My soul longs, yes, even faints
for the courts of the LORD;
my heart and my body cry out
for the living God.

3 Yes, the sparrow has found a home
and the swallow a nest for herself,
where she may lay her young,
even at Your altars,
O LORD of Hosts, my King and my God.
4 Blessed are those who dwell in Your house;
they continually praise You. Selah

5 Blessed is the man whose strength is in You,
in whose heart are the paths to *Zion*.
6 As they pass through the Valley of Baca,
they makes it a spring;
the early rain also covers it with pools.
7 They go from strength to strength;
every one of them appears in Zion before God.

8 O LORD God of Hosts, hear my prayer,
and give ear, O God of Jacob. Selah
9 Behold, O God our shield,
and look upon the face of Your anointed.

10 For a day in Your courts is better
than a thousand elsewhere.
I had rather be a doorkeeper in the house of my God
than to dwell in the tents of wickedness.

The Lord is my sun and shield (Ps 84:11).

11 For the LORD God is a sun and shield;
the LORD will give favor and glory,
for no good thing will He withhold
from the one who walks uprightly.
12 O LORD of Hosts,
blessed is the man who trusts in You.

PSALM 85

For the Music Director. A Psalm of the songs of Korah.

1 LORD, You have been favorable to Your land;
You have brought back the captivity of Jacob.
2 You have forgiven the iniquity of Your people;

You have covered all their sin. Selah
3 You have withdrawn all Your wrath;
You have turned from the fierceness of Your anger.

4 Restore us, O God of our salvation,
and put away Your indignation toward us.
5 Will You be angry with us forever?
Will You draw out Your anger to all generations?
6 Will You not revive us again,
that Your people may rejoice in You?
7 Show us Your mercy, O LORD,
and grant us Your deliverance.

8 I will hear what God the LORD will speak,
for He will speak peace to His people
and to His saints,
but let them not turn again to folly.
9 Surely His salvation is near to them who fear Him,
that glory may dwell in our land.

10 Mercy and truth have met together;
righteousness and peace have kissed.
11 Truth springs from the ground,
and righteousness looks down from the sky.
12 Yes, the LORD gives that which is good,
and our land shall yield its increase.
13 Righteousness shall go before Him
and prepare a way for His footsteps.

PSALM 86

A Prayer of David.

1 Incline Your ear, O LORD, and answer me,
for I am oppressed and needy.
2 Preserve my soul, for I am godly;
You are my God; save Your servant
who trusts in You.
3 Have mercy on me, O Lord,
for to You I cry all day long.
4 Gladden the soul of Your servant,
for to You, O Lord,
I lift my soul.

5 For You, Lord, are good, and forgiving,
abounding in kindness to all who call on You.
6 Give ear, O LORD, to my prayer,
and attend to my plea for mercy.
7 In the day of my trouble I will call upon You,
for You will answer me.

8 Among the gods there is none like You, O Lord;
neither are there any works like Your works.
9 All nations whom You have made
shall come and worship before You, O Lord,
and shall glorify Your name.
10 For You are great and do wondrous deeds;
You are God alone.

11 Teach me Your way, O LORD,
that I will walk in Your truth;
bind my heart
to fear Your name.
12 I will give You thanks, O Lord my God, with all my heart,
and I will glorify Your name forever.
13 For great is Your mercy toward me,
and You have delivered my soul from the depths of Sheol.

14 O God, insolent men have risen against me,
and bands of violent men have sought my life;
they have not set You before them.
15 But You, O Lord, are a God full of compassion and gracious,
slow to anger, and abundant in mercy and truth.
16 Turn to me and have mercy on me;
give Your strength to Your servant,
and save the *humble* son of Your female servant.
17 Show me a sign of Your favor,
that those who hate me may see it and be ashamed
because You, LORD, have helped and comforted me.

PSALM 87

A Psalm of the sons of Korah. A Song.

1 The city of His foundation is on the holy mountain.
2 The LORD loves the gates of Zion
more than all the dwelling places of Jacob.

3 Glorious things are spoken of you,
O city of God. Selah.

4 I will make mention of Rahab and Babylon
to those who know Me;
look, Philistia and Tyre with Ethiopia;
"This man was born there."
5 But of Zion it shall be said,
"This one and that one were born in her,"
for the Most High shall make her secure.
6 The LORD shall count when He registers the people,
"This one was born there." Selah

7 As well the singers and the players of instruments say,
"All my springs are in you."

85:3 Dt 13:17
85:4 Ps 80:3
85:5 Ps 79:5
85:6 Ps 80:18
85:8 Zec 9:10
85:9 Isa 46:13
85:10 Ps 72:3
85:11 Isa 45:8
85:12 Ps 67:6
85:13 Ps 89:14
86:1 Ps 31:2
86:2 Ps 4:3
86:3 Ps 57:1
86:4 Ps 25:1
86:5 Joel 2:13
86:7 Ps 50:15
86:8 Ex 15:11
86:9 Ps 66:4
86:10 Ps 72:18
86:11 Ps 26:3
86:13 Ps 88:6
86:14 Ps 54:3
86:15 Ne 9:17
86:16 Ps 116:16
87:1 Isa 28:16
87:3 Ps 46:4
87:4 Ps 45:12
87:6 Isa 4:3

PSALM 88

For the Music Director. A Song. A Psalm of the sons of Korah. To the melody of "Suffering of Affliction." A Contemplative Maskil of Heman the Ezrahite.

1 O LORD, God of my salvation,
I cry out day and night before You.
2 Let my prayer come before You;
incline Your ear to my cry.

3 For my soul is full of troubles,
and my life draws near to Sheol.
4 I am counted with those who go down to
the grave;
I am a man who has no strength,
5 like one who is set free among the dead,
like the slain who lie in the grave,
like those whom You remember no more,
for they are cut off from Your hand.

6 You have laid me in the depths of the pit,
in dark and deep regions.
7 Your wrath lies heavy upon me,
and You have afflicted me with all Your
waves. Selah
8 You have caused my companions to be far
from me;
You have made me an abomination to
them;
I am shut up, and I cannot escape;
9 my eye is dim from my affliction.

LORD, I call daily upon You,
and I have stretched out my hands to
You.
10 Will You show wonders to the dead?
Shall the dead rise up to praise You?
Selah
11 Shall Your lovingkindness be declared in
the grave,
or your faithfulness in Abaddon?
12 Shall Your wonders be known in the
darkness
or Your righteousness in the land of
forgetfulness?

13 But unto You have I cried, O LORD,
and in the morning my prayer comes
before You.
14 O LORD, why do You cast away my soul?
Why do You hide Your face from me?

15 I am afflicted and close to death since my
youth;
while I suffer Your terrors I am helpless.
16 Your fierce wrath sweeps over me;
Your terrors destroy me.
17 They come around me daily like a flood;
they encircle me together.
18 You have caused to be far from me my
lovers and friends,
and my companion is darkness.

88:1 Ps 22:2
88:3 Ps 107:18
88:4 Ps 28:1
88:5 Isa 53:8
88:6 Ps 69:15
88:7 Ps 42:7
88:8 Ps 31:11
88:9 Job 11:13
88:10 Ps 6:5
88:12 Ecc 9:5
88:13 Ps 5:3
88:14 Job 13:24
88:15 Job 6:4
88:17 Ps 22:16
88:18 Ps 38:11

89:1 Ps 89:33
89:2 Ps 36:5
89:3 Ps 132:11
89:5 Ps 19:1
89:6 Ps 29:1
89:7 Ps 47:2
89:8 Ps 35:10
89:9 Ps 65:7
89:10 Ps 144:6
89:11 Ge 1:1
89:12 Jos 12:1
89:14 Ps 97:2
89:15 Ps 4:6

PSALM 89

A Contemplative Maskil of Ethan the Ezrahite.

1 I will sing of the mercies of the LORD
forever;
with my mouth I will make known Your
faithfulness to all generations.
2 For I have said, "Mercy shall be built up
forever;
Your faithfulness shall be established in
the heavens."
3 You have said, "I have made a covenant
with my chosen one;
I have sworn to David my servant:
4 'Your offspring I will establish forever,
and build up your throne for all
generations.' " Selah

5 Let the heavens praise Your wonders,
O LORD;
Your faithfulness also in the assembly of
the holy ones.
6 For who in the skies can be compared to
the LORD?
Who among the *heavenly* sons is like the
LORD?
7 God is greatly to be feared in the assembly
of the holy ones
and awesome to all those who surround
Him.
8 O LORD God of Hosts, who is a mighty LORD
like You,
with Your faithfulness all around You?

9 You rule the raging of the sea;
when the waves arise, You still them.
10 You crushed Rahab like a corpse;
You scattered Your enemies with Your
strong arm.
11 The heavens are Yours; the earth also is
Yours;
the world and all that is in it, You have
founded them.
12 The north and the south, You have created
them;
Tabor and Hermon rejoice in Your name.
13 You have a mighty arm,
and strong is Your hand, and victorious
is Your right hand.

14 Righteousness and justice are the
foundation of Your throne;
mercy and truth shall go before Your
presence.
15 Blessed are the people who know the
joyful shout.
They walk, O LORD, in the light of Your
presence.
16 In Your name they rejoice all the day,
and in Your righteousness they shall be
exalted.

17 For You are the beauty of their strength;
by Your favor our horn is exalted.
18 For the LORD is our shield of defense,
and the Holy One of Israel is our king.

19 Long ago You spoke in a vision
to Your godly one and said:
"I have given help to one who is mighty;
I have exalted one chosen from the
people.
20 I have found David, My servant;
with My holy oil I have anointed him:
21 By whom My hand shall be established;
My arm also shall strengthen him.
22 The enemy shall not take tribute from him,
nor the wicked humiliate him.
23 I will beat down his foes before him
and strike down those who hate him.
24 My faithfulness and My mercy shall be with
him,
and in My name his horn shall be
exalted.
25 I will set his hand on the sea
and his right hand on the rivers.
26 He shall cry unto Me, 'You are my Father,
my God,
and the Rock of my salvation.'
27 Also I will make him my firstborn,
the highest of the kings of the earth.
28 In My mercy I will keep him forever,
and My covenant shall stand firm with
him.
29 His offspring also I will establish forever
and his throne as the days of heaven.

30 "If his children forsake My law
and do not walk in My judgments,
31 if they break My statutes
and do not keep My commandments,
32 then I will punish their transgression with
the rod
and their iniquity with lashes.
33 Nevertheless My lovingkindness I will not
remove from him
nor be false in My faithfulness.
34 My covenant I will not violate
nor alter the word that has gone out
from My lips.
35 Once and for all I have sworn by My
holiness
that I will not lie to David:
36 His offspring shall endure forever,
and his throne as the sun before Me;
37 it shall be established forever as the moon
and as a faithful witness in the heavens."
Selah
38 But now You have cast off and rejected
him,
You have been wrathful with Your
anointed king.

89:17 Ps 75:10
89:18 Ps 47:9
89:19 1Ki 11:34
89:20 1Sa 16:1
89:22 2Sa 7:10
89:23 2Sa 7:9
89:26 2Sa 7:14
89:27 Nu 24:7
89:28 Isa 55:3
89:29 Ps 89:4
89:30 2Sa 7:14
89:32 2Sa 7:14
89:33 2Sa 7:15
89:34 Nu 23:19
89:35 Am 4:2
89:36 Ps 72:5
89:38 Dt 32:19

. . . .

89:39 Ps 74:7
89:40 Ps 80:12
89:41 Ps 79:4
89:45 Ps 109:29
89:46 Ps 79:5
89:47 Job 7:7
89:49 2Sa 7:15
89:50 Ps 74:18
89:52 Ps 41:13
90:1 Dt 33:27

39 You have renounced the covenant with
Your servant;
You have defiled his crown by casting it
to the ground.
40 You have broken down all his walls;
You have brought his strongholds to
ruin.
41 All who pass by the way plunder him;
he is a reproach to his neighbors.
42 You have set high the right hand of his
adversaries;
You have made all his enemies rejoice.
43 You have also turned back the edge of his
sword
and have not made him stand in battle.
44 You have made his glory cease
and cast his throne down to the ground.
45 The days of his youth You have shortened;
You have covered him with shame.
Selah

46 How long, O LORD? Will You hide Yourself
forever?
How long shall Your wrath burn like
fire?
47 Remember how short my time is!
Why have You made all people in such
emptiness?
48 What man can live and not see death?
Who can deliver his soul from the power
of Sheol? Selah
49 Lord, where are Your former
lovingkindnesses,
which You swore to David in Your
faithfulness?
50 Remember, O Lord, the reproach of Your
servants
and how I bear in my heart *the insults* of
the many nations,
51 which Your enemies taunt, O LORD,
with which they mock the footsteps of
Your anointed king.

52 Blessed be the LORD forever!
Amen and Amen.

BOOK FOUR
Psalms 90–106

PSALM 90

A Prayer of Moses, the man of God.

1 Lord, You have been our dwelling place
in all generations.
2 Before the mountains were brought forth,
or You had formed the earth and the
world,
even from everlasting to everlasting You
are God.

[3] You return man to the dust
and say, "Return, you children of men."
[4] For a thousand years in Your sight
are but as yesterday when it is past,
or as a night watch in the night time.
[5] You carry them away as with a flood;
they are as a dream, like renewed grass
in the morning:
[6] In the morning it flourishes and grows up;
in the evening it fades and withers.

[7] For we are consumed by Your anger,
and by Your wrath we are terrified.
[8] You have set our iniquities before You,
even our secret sins in the light of Your
presence.
[9] For all our days pass away in your wrath;
we end our years with a groan.
[10] The years of our life are seventy,
and if by reason of strength eighty;
yet their length is toil and sorrow,
for they soon end, and we fly away.
[11] Who knows the power of Your anger?
Or Your wrath according to Your fear?
[12] So teach us to number our days,
that we may apply our hearts to wisdom.

[13] Return, O LORD, how long?
Have mercy on Your servants.
[14] Satisfy us in the early morning with Your
mercy,
that we may rejoice and be glad all our
days.
[15] Make us glad according to the days that
You have afflicted us,
and the years that we have seen evil.
[16] Let Your work be displayed to Your
servants
and Your glory to their children.

[17] Let the beauty of the LORD our God be upon
us,
and establish the work of our hands
among us;
yes, establish the work of our hands.

PSALM 91

[1] He who dwells in the shelter of the Most
High
shall abide under the shadow of the
Almighty.

We are secure from pestilence, destruction, terror, and plagues (Ps 91).

[2] I will say of the LORD, "He is my refuge and
my fortress,
my God in whom I trust."

90:3 Ge 3:19
90:4 2Pe 3:8
90:5 Isa 40:6
90:6 Job 14:2
90:7 Ps 39:11
90:8 Ps 19:12
90:9 Ps 78:33
90:12 Ps 39:4
90:13 Dt 32:36
90:14 Ps 85:6
90:15 Dt 2:14–16
90:16 Hab 3:2
90:17 Isa 26:12
91:1 Ps 17:8
91:2 Ps 18:2

....

91:3 Ps 124:7
91:4 Ps 17:8
91:6 2Ki 19:35
91:8 Ps 37:34
91:10 Pr 12:21
91:11 Ps 34:7

SPIRITLED WOMAN

COUNSEL FROM THE SPIRIT BASICS

Enemy Assaults

Do you sometimes feel you have opposition facing you from every side? Psalm 91:3 addresses the enemy's assaults from both the physical and the spiritual sides.

One of our family members went to a certain country as a missionary and made the comment, "This is a country where there are lots of ways to die." Both the poor health conditions and the hostility in the country provided many dangers.

You will encounter enemies that attack your mind (thoughts), that attack your body internally (germs), and that attack with weapons (people). This is your verse, ensuring your deliverance from all the varieties of harm.

Peggy Joyce Ruth

[3] Surely He shall deliver you from the snare
of the hunter
and from the deadly pestilence.
[4] He shall cover you with His feathers,
and under His wings you shall find
protection;
His faithfulness shall be your shield and
wall.
[5] You shall not be afraid of the terror by
night,
nor of the arrow that flies by day;
[6] nor of the pestilence that pursues in
darkness,
nor of the destruction that strikes at
noonday.
[7] A thousand may fall at your side
and ten thousand at your right hand,
but it shall not come near you.
[8] Only with your eyes shall you behold
and see the reward of the wicked.

[9] Because you have made the LORD, who is
my refuge,
even the Most High, your dwelling,
[10] there shall be no evil befall you,
neither shall any plague come near your
tent;
[11] for He shall give His angels charge over
you
to guard you in all your ways.
[12] They shall bear you up in their hands,

lest you strike your foot against a stone.
13 You shall tread upon the lion and adder;
the young lion and the serpent you shall trample underfoot.

God commands His angels concerning me to guard me in all my ways (Ps. 91:11).

14 Because he has set his love upon Me,
therefore I will deliver him;
I will set him on high, because he has known My name.
15 He shall call upon Me, and I will answer him;
I will be with him in trouble,
and I will deliver him and honor him.
16 With long life I will satisfy him
and show him My salvation.

PSALM 92

A Psalm. A Song for the Sabbath day.

1 It is good to give thanks to the LORD,
and to sing praises unto Your name, O Most High:
2 to declare forth Your lovingkindness in the morning
and Your faithfulness in the night,
3 on a ten-stringed lute and on the harp,
and on the lyre with a solemn sound.
4 For you, O LORD, have made me glad through Your work;
I will sing joyfully at the works of Your hands.
5 O LORD, how great are Your works!
Your thoughts are very deep!
6 A brutish man does not recognize,
neither does the fool understand this.
7 Though the wicked spring up as the grass
and all those who do iniquity flourish,
they shall be destroyed forever:
8 But You, O LORD, are on high forever.
9 For Your enemies, O LORD,
for Your enemies shall perish;
all those who do iniquity shall be scattered.
10 But my horn You have exalted like the horn of the wild ox;
You have anointed me with fresh oil.
11 My eyes also shall see the downfall of my enemies,
and my ears shall hear the doom of my wicked adversaries.
12 The righteous shall flourish like the palm tree
and grow like a cedar in Lebanon.
13 Those that are planted in the house of the LORD
shall flourish in the courts of our God.
14 They shall still bring forth fruit in old age;
they shall be filled with vitality and foliage,
15 to show that the LORD is upright;
He is my rock, and there is no unrighteousness in Him.

PSALM 93

1 The LORD reigns; He is robed in majesty;
the LORD is robed; He has put on strength as His belt.
Indeed, the world is established;
it cannot be moved.
2 Your throne is established of old;
You are from everlasting.
3 The floods have lifted up, O LORD,
the floods have lifted up their voice;
the floods lift up their roaring waves.
4 The LORD on high is mightier than the noise of many waters,
yes, than the mighty waves of the sea.
5 Your statutes are very sure;
holiness is becoming to Your house,
O LORD, forever.

PSALM 94

1 O LORD God, to whom vengeance belongs;
O God to whom vengeance belongs, shine forth.
2 Rise up, O Judge of the earth;
render to the proud what they deserve.
3 O LORD, how long shall the wicked,
how long shall the wicked triumph?
4 They spew forth their arrogant words;
all those who do iniquity boast.
5 They break in pieces Your people, O LORD,
and afflict Your inheritance.
6 They kill the widow and the sojourner,
and murder the fatherless.
7 Yet they say, "The LORD does not see,
neither does the God of Jacob regard it."
8 Understand, you brutish among the people;
fools, when will you be wise?
9 He who made the ear, shall He not hear?
He who formed the eye, shall He not see?
10 He who chastises the nations, shall He not correct?
He teaches people knowledge!
11 The LORD, He knows the thoughts of people,
that they are a breath.

91:13 Da 6:22
91:14 Ps 9:10
91:15 1Sa 2:30
91:16 Ps 21:4
92:1 Ps 147:1
92:3 Ps 33:2
92:4 Ps 8:6
92:5 Ps 40:5
92:6 Ps 73:22
92:7 Ps 37:38
92:8 Ps 83:18
92:9 Ps 89:10
92:10 Ps 23:5
92:11 Ps 54:7
92:12 Ps 52:8
....
92:13 Ps 100:4
92:15 Ps 18:2
93:1 Ps 96:10
93:2 Ps 45:6
93:3 Ps 96:11
93:4 Ps 65:7
93:5 Ps 29:2
94:1 Na 1:2
94:2 Ge 18:25
94:3 Job 20:5
94:4 Ps 31:18
94:5 Isa 3:15
94:6 Isa 10:2
94:8 Ps 92:6
94:9 Ex 4:11
94:10 Job 35:11
94:11 1Co 3:20

A Secret Place of Refuge

When I think of dwelling in the shelter of God (Ps 91:1), a childhood memory always comes to mind. My parents would often take my younger brother and sister and me to a lake. There was a wonderful place to fish for perch that very few people knew about, and we children loved to perch fish. It was such a thrill to see the cork begin to bobble and then suddenly go completely out of sight. There were very few things that I liked better than jerking back on that old cane pole and landing a huge perch. Dad had a good reason for having us catch those perch. They were what he used for bait on the trotline that he had stretched out across one of the secret coves at the lake.

One of those outings proved to be more exciting than most, turning out to be an action-packed experience that I will never forget. It had been a beautiful day when we started out, but by the time we finished our perch fishing and were headed toward the trotline, everything changed. A storm came up on the lake so suddenly, there was no time to get back to the boat dock. The sky turned black, lightning was flashing, and drops of rain were falling so hard that they stung our skin when they hit. Then, moments later, we were in the middle of a hailstorm with large, marble-sized hail.

I could see the fear in my mother's eyes, and I knew we were in danger. But before I had time to wonder what we were going to do, Dad had driven the boat to the rugged shoreline of the only island on the lake. There are many boat docks that surround the island now, but back then it looked like an abandoned island with absolutely no place to take refuge from the storm.

In just moments Dad had us all out of the boat and ordered the three of us to lie down beside our mother on the ground. Quickly pulling a canvas tarp out of the bottom of the boat, he knelt down on the ground beside us and pulled that tarp up over all five of us. That storm raged outside the homemade tent he had made—the rain beat down, the lightning flashed, and the thunder rolled. But all I could think about was how it felt to have his arms around us. There was a certain peace that is hard to explain as we lay there under the protection of the shield my father had provided. In fact, I had never felt as safe and secure in my entire life. I can remember thinking that I wished the storm would last forever. I didn't want anything to spoil the wonderful security I felt that day—there in our secret hiding place. Feeling my father's strong, protective arms around me, I wanted it to never end.

Although I have never forgotten that experience when we were fishing at the lake, today it has taken on new meaning. Just as Dad put a tarp over us to shield us from the storm, our heavenly Father has a secret place in His arms that protects us from the storms that are raging in the world around us.

Peggy Joyce Ruth

12 Blessed is the man whom You chasten,
O LORD,
and teach from Your law,
13 that You may give him rest from the days
of adversity,
until a pit is dug for the wicked.
14 For the LORD will not forsake His people;
neither will He abandon His inheritance.
15 But justice shall return to those who are
righteous,
and all the upright in heart shall
follow it.

16 Who will rise up for me against the
wicked?
Who will stand up for me against those
who do iniquity?
17 Unless the LORD had been my help,
my soul would have lived in the land of
silent death.
18 When I said, "My foot slips,"
Your mercy, O LORD, held me up.
19 When there is a multitude of worries within
me,
Your comforts delight my soul.

20 Shall wicked rulers, who make oppressive
laws,
align with You?
21 They conspire together against the life of
the righteous
and condemn innocent blood to death.
22 But the LORD is my defense,
and my God is the rock of my refuge.
23 He shall bring upon them their own
iniquity
and shall cut them off for their own
wickedness;
yes, the LORD our God shall destroy them.

PSALM 95

1 O come, let us sing unto the LORD;
let us make a joyful noise to the rock of
our salvation!
2 Let us come before His presence with
thanksgiving;
let us make a joyful noise unto Him with
psalms!
3 For the LORD is a great God,
and a great King above all gods.
4 In His hand are the deep places of the
earth;
the heights of the mountains are also
His.
5 The sea is His, for He made it,
and His hands formed the dry land.

6 O come, let us worship and bow down;
let us kneel before the LORD, our Maker.
7 For He is our God,
and we are the people of His pasture
and the sheep of His hand.

Today if you hear His voice,
8 do not harden your hearts, as at
Meribah,
and as in the day of Massah in the
wilderness,
9 when your fathers tested Me and tried Me,
though they had seen My deeds.
10 For forty years I loathed that generation
and said, "They are a people who go
astray in their heart,
and they have not known My ways."
11 Therefore I swore in My wrath,
"They shall not enter into My rest."

PSALM 96
1Ch 16:23–33

1 O sing unto the LORD a new song;
sing unto the LORD, all the earth!
2 Sing unto the LORD, bless His name;
declare His salvation from day to day.
3 Proclaim His glory among the nations,
His wonders among all peoples.
4 For the LORD is great, and greatly to be
praised;
He is to be feared above all gods.
5 For all the gods of the nations are
worthless,
but the LORD made the heavens.
6 Honor and majesty are before Him;
strength and beauty are in His sanctuary.
7 Give unto the LORD, O families of the
people,
give unto the LORD glory and strength.
8 Give unto the LORD the glory due His name;
bring an offering, and come into His
courts.
9 Worship the LORD in the beauty of holiness;
tremble before Him, all the earth.
10 Say among the nations, "The LORD reigns!
Indeed, the world is established; it shall
not be moved;
He shall judge the peoples righteously."
11 Let the heavens rejoice, and let the earth be
glad;
let the sea roar, and all that fills it;
12 let the field be joyful, and all that is in it;
then all the trees of the forests shall rejoice
13 before the LORD, for He comes,
for He comes to judge the earth.
He shall judge the world with
righteousness
and the peoples with His faithfulness.

PSALM 97

1 The LORD reigns; let the earth rejoice;
let the many coastlands be glad!

94:12 Job 5:17
94:13 Ps 55:23
94:14 1Sa 12:22
94:15 Mic 7:9
94:17 Ps 124:1–2
94:18 Ps 38:16
94:20 Ps 58:2
94:21 Pr 17:15
94:22 Ps 18:2
94:23 Ps 7:16
95:1 Ps 81:1
95:3 Ps 96:4
95:4 Ps 135:6
95:5 Ge 1:9–10
95:6 2Ch 6:13
95:7 Heb 3:15
....
95:8 Ex 17:7
95:9 Nu 14:22
95:10 Heb 3:17
95:11 Nu 14:23
96:1 1Ch 16:23–33
96:2 Ps 71:15
96:4 Ps 18:3
96:5 Ps 115:15
96:6 Ps 104:1
96:7 Ps 22:27
96:9 Ps 29:2
96:10 Ps 93:1
96:11 Ps 69:34
96:12 Isa 55:12–13
96:13 Rev 19:11
97:1 Ps 96:10–11

[2] Clouds and darkness are all around Him;
righteousness and justice are the foundation of His throne.
[3] A fire goes before Him
and burns up His enemies all around.
[4] His lightning bolts light up the world;
the earth sees and shakes.
[5] The mountains melt like wax at the presence of the LORD,
at the presence of the Lord of the earth.
[6] The heavens declare His righteousness,
and all the peoples see His glory.

[7] All who serve graven images are ashamed,
who boast in worthless idols;
worship Him, all you gods.

[8] Zion hears and is glad,
and the daughters of Judah rejoice
because of Your judgments, O LORD.
[9] For You, O LORD, are Most High above all the earth;
You are exalted far above all gods.
[10] You who love the LORD, hate evil!
He preserves the lives of His devoted ones;
He delivers them from the hand of the wicked.
[11] Light goes out for the righteous,
and gladness for the upright in heart.
[12] Rejoice in the LORD, you righteous,
and give thanks at the memory of His holy name.

PSALM 98

A Psalm.

[1] Oh, sing to the LORD a new song,
for He has done marvelous deeds!
His right hand and His holy arm
have accomplished deliverance.
[2] The LORD has made known His salvation;
His righteousness He has revealed in the sight of the nations.
[3] He has remembered His mercy
and His faithfulness toward the house of Israel;
all the ends of the earth have seen
the deliverance of our God.

[4] Make a joyful noise unto the LORD, all the earth;
break out in loud songs, and sing praises.
[5] Sing unto the LORD with the harp,
with the harp and the sound of melody,
[6] with trumpets and sound of the horn;
make a joyful noise before the LORD, the King.

[7] Let the sea roar, and all that fills it,
the world and those who live in it;
[8] let the rivers clap their hands;
let the hills be joyful together
[9] before the LORD,
for He is coming to judge the earth.
With righteousness He will judge the world,
and the peoples with justice.

97:2 Ps 89:14
97:3 Ps 18:8
97:4 Ps 77:18
97:5 Na 1:5
97:6 Ps 50:6
97:7 Heb 1:6
97:8 Ps 48:11
97:9 Ps 83:18
97:10 Ps 34:14
97:11 Job 22:28
97:12 Ps 30:4
98:1 Ex 15:6
98:2 Isa 52:10
98:3 Ps 22:27
98:4 Isa 44:23
98:5 Isa 51:3
98:7 Ps 24:1
98:8 Isa 55:12
98:9 Ps 96:10
99:1 Ex 25:22
99:2 Ps 97:9
99:3 Dt 28:58
99:5 Ps 132:7
99:6 Jer 15:1
99:7 Ex 33:9
99:8 Nu 20:12
99:9 Ps 2:6
100:1 Ps 98:4
100:2 Ps 95:2
100:3 Ps 95:6–7
100:4 Ps 96:2

PSALM 99

[1] The LORD reigns;
let the peoples tremble!
He sits enthroned between the cherubim;
let the earth shake.
[2] The LORD is great in Zion;
He is high above all the peoples.
[3] Let them praise Your great and awesome name—
He is holy!
[4] The King's strength loves justice;
You establish righteousness,
and You execute judgment
and fairness in Jacob.
[5] Exalt the LORD our God,
and worship at His footstool—
He is holy!

[6] Moses and Aaron were among His priests,
even Samuel was among them who called upon His name;
they called upon the LORD,
and He answered them.
[7] He spoke to them in the pillar of cloud;
they kept His statues and the ordinance that He gave them.

[8] You answered them,
O LORD our God;
You were a God who forgave them,
though You took vengeance on their wrongdoing.
[9] Exalt the LORD our God,
and worship at His holy mountain;
for the LORD our God is holy!

PSALM 100

A Psalm of thanksgiving.

[1] Make a joyful noise unto the LORD, all the earth!
[2] Serve the LORD with gladness;
come before His presence with singing.
[3] Know that the LORD, He is God;
it is He who has made us, and not we ourselves;
we are His people, and the sheep of His pasture.

[4] Enter into His gates with thanksgiving,
and into His courts with praise;
be thankful to Him, and bless His name.

5 For the Lord is good; His mercy endures
forever,
and His faithfulness to all generations.

PSALM 101

A Psalm of David.

1 I will sing of mercy and justice;
to You, O Lord, I will sing.
2 I will consider the path that is blameless.
When will You come to me?

I will walk within my house
with a perfect heart.
3 I will set no wicked thing
before my eyes.

I hate the work of those who turn aside;
it shall not have part of me.
4 A perverted heart shall be far from me;
I will not know anything wicked.
5 Whoever privately slanders his neighbor,
him I will destroy;
whoever has a haughty look and a proud
heart
I will not endure.

6 My eyes shall be favorable to the faithful in
the land,
that they may live with me;
he who walks in a blameless manner,
he shall serve me.

7 He who practices deceit
shall not dwell within my house;
he who tells lies
shall not remain in my sight.

8 Every morning I will destroy
all the wicked in the land,
that I may cut off all wicked doers
from the city of the Lord.

PSALM 102

A Prayer of one afflicted, when he
is overwhelmed and pours out his
complaint before the Lord.

1 Hear my prayer, O Lord,
and let my cry come unto You.
2 Do not hide Your face from me
in the day when I am in trouble;
incline Your ear to me;
in the day when I call answer me
quickly.

3 For my days are consumed like smoke,
and my bones are burned as a furnace.
4 My heart is struck down and withered like
grass,
so that I forget to eat my bread.
5 Because of the sound of my groaning
my bones cling to my skin.
6 I am like an owl of the wilderness,
like a screech owl of the desert.
7 I stay awake and am
as a sparrow alone upon the housetop.
8 My enemies reproach me all the day,
and those who taunt me curse my name.
9 For I have eaten ashes like bread
and mixed my drink with weeping,
10 because of Your indignation and Your
wrath,
for You have lifted me up, and cast me
down.
11 My days are like an evening shadow that
vanishes,
and I wither away like grass.

12 But You, O Lord, shall endure forever
enthroned
and Your reputation to all generations.
13 You shall arise, and have mercy upon Zion,
for the time to favor her,
indeed, the appointed time has come.
14 For Your servants take pleasure in her
stones,
and have pity on her dust.
15 So the nations shall fear the name of the
Lord,
and all the kings of the earth Your glory.
16 For the Lord shall build up Zion;
He shall appear in His glory.
17 He will regard the prayer of the destitute
and will not despise their prayer.

18 Let this be written for the generation to
come,
that a people who shall be created shall
praise the Lord.
19 For He has looked down from the height of
His sanctuary;
from heaven the Lord looked down on
the earth,
20 to hear the groaning of the prisoners
and to set free those who are appointed
to death,
21 that they may declare the name of the Lord
in Zion
and His praise in Jerusalem;
22 when the peoples are gathered together,
and the kingdoms, to serve the Lord.

23 He has weakened my strength in my
midlife;
He has shortened my days.
24 I said,
"O my God, do not take me away in the
midst of my days—
Your years endure throughout all
generations."
25 From before You have laid the foundation
of the earth,

100:5 Ps 106:1
101:1 Ps 89:1
101:2 1Ki 9:4
101:3 Ps 40:4
101:4 Pr 11:20
101:5 Ps 18:27
101:8 Ps 75:10
102:1 Ex 2:23
102:2 Ps 69:17
102:3 Jas 4:14
102:4 Ps 37:2
102:5 Job 19:20
102:6 Zep 2:14
102:7 Ps 77:4
102:8 Ac 26:11
102:9 Ps 42:3
102:10 Ps 38:3
102:11 Job 14:2
102:12 Ps 9:7
102:14 Ne 4:2
102:15 1Ki 8:43
102:16 Isa 60:1–2
102:17 Ne 1:6
102:18 Ro 15:4
102:19 Dt 26:15
102:20 Ps 79:11
102:21 Ps 22:22
102:24 Hab 1:12
102:25 Ge 1:1

and the heavens are the work of Your
hands.
26 They shall perish, but You shall endure;
indeed, all of them shall wear out like a
garment;
like a robe You shall change them,
and they shall pass away,
27 but You are the same,
and Your years shall have no end.
28 The children of Your servants shall be
secure,
and their offspring shall be established
before You.

PSALM 103

A Psalm of David.

1 Bless the LORD, O my soul,
and all that is within me, bless His holy
name.
2 Bless the LORD, O my soul,
and forget not all His benefits,
3 who forgives all your iniquities,
who heals all your diseases,
4 who redeems your life from the pit,
who crowns you with lovingkindness
and tender mercies,

Daily I will praise the Lord, thanking Him for His blessings (Ps 103:1–5).

5 who satisfies your mouth with good things,
so that your youth is renewed like the
eagle's.
6 The LORD does righteousness
and justice for all who are oppressed.
7 He made known His ways to Moses,
His acts to the people of Israel.
8 The LORD is merciful and gracious,
slow to anger, and abounding in mercy.
9 He will not always accuse,
neither will He keep his anger forever.
10 He does not treat us according to our sins,
nor repay us according to our iniquities.
11 For as the heavens are high above the
earth,
so great is His mercy toward those who
fear Him;
12 as far as the east is from the west,
so far has He removed our
transgressions from us.
13 Like a father shows compassion to his
children,
so the LORD gives compassion to those
who fear Him.

102:26 Isa 34:4
102:27 Mal 3:6
103:3 Ex 15:26
103:4 Ps 56:13
103:5 Isa 40:31
103:6 Ps 146:7
103:7 Ps 147:19
103:8 Ps 86:15
103:9 Ps 30:5
103:10 Ezr 9:13
103:11 Ps 36:5
103:12 Isa 43:25
103:14 Ge 3:19
103:15 1Pe 1:24
103:16 Isa 40:7
103:17 Ex 20:6
103:18 Dt 7:9
103:19 Ps 47:2
103:20 Ps 148:2
103:21 1Ki 22:19
103:22 Ps 145:10
104:1 Ps 103:22
104:2 Isa 40:22
104:3 Am 9:6
104:4 Heb 1:7
104:5 Ps 24:2
104:6 Ge 7:19
104:10 Isa 41:18

14 For He knows how we are formed;
He remembers that we are dust.
15 As for man, his days are as grass;
as a flower of the field he flourishes.
16 For the *hot* wind passes over it, and it is
gone;
the place where it was is not known.
17 But the mercy of the LORD
is from everlasting to everlasting
upon those who fear Him,
and His righteousness to children's
children,
18 to those who keep His covenant,
and to those who remember to do His
commandments.
19 The LORD has established His throne in the
heavens,
and His kingdom rules over all.
20 Bless the LORD, you His angels,
who are mighty, and do His commands,
and obey the voice of His word.
21 Bless the LORD, all you His hosts;
you servants who do His pleasure.
22 Bless the LORD, all His works,
in all places of His dominion.

Bless the LORD, O my soul!

PSALM 104

1 Bless the LORD, O my soul!
O LORD my God, You are very great!
You are clothed with honor and majesty,
2 covering Yourself with light as a garment,
who stretches out the heavens like a tent
curtain,
3 who lays the upper beams of His
chambers on the waters above,
who makes the clouds His chariot,
who rides upon the wings of the wind,
4 who makes His angels as winds,
His ministers a flaming fire.
5 You laid the earth on its foundations,
so that it should never be moved.
6 You covered it with the deep as a garment;
the waters stood above the mountains.
7 At Your rebuke they fled;
at the sound of Your thunder they
departed away.
8 The mountains rose up;
the valleys went down
to the place that You appointed them.
9 You set a boundary that they may not pass
over,
that they may not again cover the earth.
10 You send the springs to gush forth in the
valleys,
which flow between the hills.

11 They give drink to every animal of the
field;
the wild donkeys quench their thirst.
12 By them the birds of the heavens have
their habitation;
they sing among the branches.
13 You water the mountains from Your lofty
chamber;
the earth is satisfied with the fruit of
Your works.
14 You cause the grass to grow for the cattle
and plants for the cultivation of man,
that he may bring forth food from the
earth
15 and wine that makes glad the heart of
man,
and oil that makes shine his face,
and bread that strengthens his heart.
16 The trees of the LORD are well watered,
the cedars of Lebanon that He has
planted,
17 where the birds make their nests,
where the stork has its home in the fir
trees.
18 The high mountains are for the wild goats,
and the rocks a refuge for the badgers.

19 He set the moon to mark the appointed
seasons;
the sun knows its time for going down.
20 You make darkness, and it is night,
when all the animals of the forest go
forth.
21 The young lions roar after their prey
and seek their food from God.
22 When the sun arises, they gather
themselves together
and lay down in their dens.
23 Man goes forth to his work
and to his labor until the evening.
24 O LORD, how manifold are Your works!
With wisdom You have made them all;
the earth is full of Your creatures—
25 so is this great and wide sea,
which is full of innumerable creatures,
living animals both small and great.
26 There go the ships,
and there is Leviathan, which You have
made to play in it.

27 These all wait upon You,
that You may give them their food in due
season.
28 When You give it to them,
they gather it;
when You open Your hand,
they are filled with good food.
29 When You hide Your face,
they are troubled;
You take away their breath,
and they die and return to their dust.
30 When You send forth Your Spirit,
they are created,
and You renew the surface of the
ground.

31 May the glory of the LORD endure forever;
may the LORD rejoice in His works.
32 He looks on the earth, and it trembles;
He touches the mountains, and they
smoke.

33 I will sing unto the LORD as long as I live;
I will sing praise to my God while I have
my being.
34 May my meditation be sweet to Him,
for I will be glad in the LORD.
35 Let sinners be consumed from the earth,
and let the wicked be no more.
Bless the LORD, O my soul!

Praise the LORD!

104:13 Ps 147:8
104:14 Job 28:5
104:15 Jdg 9:13
104:16 Nu 24:6
104:17 Ps 104:12
104:18 Pr 30:26
104:20 Isa 45:7
104:21 Job 38:39
104:22 Job 37:8
104:23 Ge 3:19
104:24 Ps 40:5
104:25 Ps 69:34
104:26 Ps 74:14
104:27 Ps 136:25
104:28 Ps 145:16
104:29 Ge 3:19
104:30 Job 33:4
104:31 Ge 1:31
104:32 Ex 19:18
104:33 Ps 63:4
104:35 Ps 37:38
105:1 Isa 12:4
105:2 Ps 77:12
105:4 Ps 27:8
105:5 Ps 77:11
105:7 Isa 26:9
105:8 Dt 7:9
105:9 Ge 17:2
105:11 Ge 13:15
105:12 Ge 34:30

PSALM 105
1Ch 16:8–22

1 Oh, give thanks unto the LORD; call upon
His name;
make known His deeds among the
peoples.
2 Sing unto Him, sing praises unto Him;
proclaim all His wondrous works.
3 Glory in His holy name;
let the heart rejoice for those who seek
the LORD.
4 Seek the LORD and His strength;
seek His presence continuously.

5 Remember His marvelous works that He
has done;
His wonders and the judgments from
His mouth,
6 O offspring of Abraham, His servant,
O children of Jacob, His chosen ones.
7 He is the LORD our God;
His judgments are in all the earth.

8 He remembers His covenant forever,
the word that He commanded, to a
thousand generations,
9 that covenant He made with Abraham,
and His oath to Isaac,
10 and confirmed to Jacob as a decree,
and to Israel for an everlasting covenant,
11 saying, "To you I will give the land of
Canaan
as the portion of your inheritance."

12 When they were but a few people in
number,
indeed, very few, and strangers in it,

13 when they went from one nation to
another,
from one kingdom to another people,
14 He did not permit anyone to do them
wrong;
indeed, He reproved kings on their
behalf,
15 saying, "Do not touch my anointed ones,
and do no harm to my prophets."

16 Moreover He called for a famine upon the
land;
He broke the whole supply of bread.
17 He sent a man before them,
Joseph, who was sold as a slave.
18 They hurt his feet with fetters;
his neck was put in an iron collar.
19 Until the time that his word came to pass,
the word of the LORD tested him.
20 The king sent and released him;
the ruler of the people let him go free.
21 He made Joseph lord of his house
and ruler of all his possessions,
22 to imprison his princes at Joseph's pleasure
and to teach his elders wisdom.

23 Then Israel came into Egypt,
and Jacob sojourned in the land of Ham.
24 The LORD increased His people greatly
and made them stronger than their
enemies.
25 He turned their hearts to hate His people,
to deal cleverly with His servants.
26 He sent Moses, His servant,
and Aaron whom He had chosen.
27 They showed His signs among them
and wonders in the land of Ham.
28 He sent darkness and made the land dark,
and Moses and Aaron did not rebel
against His word.
29 He turned their waters into blood
and caused their fish to die.
30 Their land brought forth frogs in
abundance,
even in the chambers of their kings.
31 He spoke, and there came swarms of flies
and gnats in all their country.
32 He gave them hail for rain
and flaming lightning in their land.
33 He struck their vines and their fig trees
and shattered the trees of their country.
34 He spoke, and the locusts came,
and caterpillars without number,
35 that devoured all the vegetation in their
land,
and ate all the fruit of their ground.
36 He struck down all the firstborn in their
land,
the first fruits of all their strength.

105:14 Ge 35:5
105:15 Ge 26:11
105:16 Ge 41:54
105:17 Ac 7:9
105:18 Ge 39:20
105:19 Ge 40:20–21
105:20 Ge 41:14
105:21 Ge 41:40–44
105:24 Dt 26:5
105:25 Ac 7:19
105:26 Ex 3:10
105:27 Ps 78:43–51
105:28 Ps 99:7
105:34 Ex 10:12–15

....

105:37 Ex 12:35–36
105:38 Ex 12:33
105:39 Ne 9:12
105:40 Ps 78:18
105:41 Ex 17:6
105:42 Ex 2:24
105:44 Ps 78:55
105:45 Dt 4:40
106:1 1Ch 16:34
106:3 Ps 15:2
106:4 Ps 119:132
106:6 1Ki 8:47
106:7 Ex 14:11–12
106:8 Ex 9:16

37 Then He brought them out with silver and
gold,
and no one among their tribes faltered.
38 Egypt was glad when they left,
for the fear of Israel fell upon them.

39 He spread a cloud for a covering,
and fire to give light in the night.
40 The people asked, and He brought quail,
and satisfied them with abundant bread
of heaven.
41 He opened the rock, and the waters gushed
out;
they ran in the desert like a river.

42 For he recalled His holy promise
to Abraham His servant.
43 He brought forth His people with joy,
and His chosen ones with gladness,
44 and gave them the lands of the nations,
and they took possession of the fruitful
labor of the people,
45 that they might observe His statutes
and keep His laws.

Praise the LORD!

PSALM 106

1Ch 16:34–36

1 Praise the LORD!

Oh, give thanks unto the LORD, for He is
good,
for His mercy endures forever.
2 Who can recount the mighty acts of the
LORD
or declare all His praise?
3 Blessed are those who keep justice
and who do righteousness at all times.
4 Remember me, O LORD, when You give
favor to Your people;
visit me with Your deliverance,
5 that I may see the goodness over Your
chosen ones,
that I may rejoice in the gladness of
Your nation,
that I may glory with Your inheritance.

6 We have sinned with our fathers;
we have committed iniquity; we have
done wickedly.
7 Our fathers did not consider
Your wonders in Egypt;
they did not remember the greatness of
Your mercy,
but rebelled against Him at the sea, by
the Red Sea.
8 Nevertheless He saved them for His name's
sake,
that He might make His mighty power
known.

9 He rebuked the Red Sea, and it was
dried up,
so He led them through the depths as
through the wilderness.
10 He saved them from the hand of him who
hated them
and redeemed them from the hand of
the enemy.
11 The waters covered their enemies;
there was not one of them left.
12 Then they believed His words;
they sang His praise.

13 But they soon forgot His works;
they did not wait for His counsel,
14 but they lusted exceedingly in the
wilderness
and tested God in the desert.
15 He gave them their request,
but He sent a wasting disease on them.

16 They envied in the camp Moses
and Aaron, the holy priest of the LORD.
17 The earth opened and swallowed up
Dathan
and engulfed those led by Abiram.
18 A fire broke out among their company;
the flame burned up the wicked.
19 They made a calf at Horeb,
and worshipped the molded image.
20 Thus they changed the glory of God
for the image of an ox that eats grass.
21 They forgot God, their Deliverer,
who had done great things in Egypt,
22 wondrous works in the land of Ham,
and marvelous deeds by the Red Sea.
23 Therefore He said that He would destroy
them,
had not Moses, His chosen one,
stood before Him to intercede,
to turn away His wrath from destroying
them.

24 Then they despised the pleasant land;
they did not believe His promise,
25 but they grumbled in their tents,
and did not listen to the voice of the
LORD.
26 Therefore He lifted up His hand against
them
and swore to overthrow them in the
wilderness,
27 and to overthrow their offspring among the
nations,
and to scatter them in the lands.

28 They joined themselves to Baal of Peor
and ate the sacrifices given for the dead.
29 Thus they provoked Him to anger with
their acts,
and a plague broke out upon them.
30 Then Phinehas stood up and interceded,

106:9 Ps 18:15
106:10 Ex 14:30
106:11 Ex 15:5
106:12 Ex 14:31–15:21
106:13 Ex 15:24
106:14 1Co 10:9
106:15 Isa 10:16
106:17 Dt 11:6
106:20 Jer 2:11
106:21 Ps 106:13
106:24 Nu 14:31
106:26 Eze 20:15
106:27 Ps 44:11
106:28 Hos 9:10

. . . .

106:31 Nu 25:11–13
106:32 Ps 81:7
106:33 Nu 20:10–11
106:34 Dt 7:16
106:35 Jdg 3:5–6
106:36 Dt 7:16
106:37 2Ki 16:3
106:38 Nu 35:33
106:39 Eze 20:18
106:40 Jdg 2:14
106:41 Jdg 2:14
106:43 Jdg 2:16–18
106:44 Jdg 3:9
106:45 Ps 105:8
106:46 Ezr 9:9
106:48 Ps 41:13

and so the plague ceased.
31 That was counted unto him for
righteousness
unto all generations forever.
32 They angered Him also at the waters of
Meribah,
so that Moses suffered because of them,
33 because they provoked his temper,
so that he spoke impulsively with his
lips.

34 They did not destroy the nations
as the LORD commanded them,
35 but they mixed among the nations
and learned their deeds;
36 they served their idols,
which were a snare to them.
37 Yes, they sacrificed their sons
and their daughters to demons,
38 and poured out innocent blood,
even the blood of their sons and of their
daughters,
whom they sacrificed to the idols of
Canaan,
and the land was polluted with blood.
39 Thus were they defiled by their acts
and acted like whores with these actions.

40 Therefore the wrath of the LORD was
kindled against His people,
and He abhorred His own inheritance.
41 He gave them into the hand of the nations,
and those who hated them ruled over
them.
42 Their enemies also oppressed them,
and Israel was brought into subjection
under their powerful hand.
43 Many times He delivered them,
but they were rebellious against Him
with their counsel,
and were afflicted for their iniquity.
44 Nevertheless, He regarded their affliction,
when He heard their cry:
45 and He remembered on their behalf His
covenant
and relented according to the greatness
of His mercies.
46 He made them pitied
among all those who held them captive.

47 Save us, O LORD our God,
and gather us from among the nations,
to give thanks unto Your holy name
and to boast in Your praise.

48 Blessed be the LORD God of Israel,
from everlasting to everlasting,
and let all the people say, "Amen!"

Praise the LORD!

BOOK FIVE
Psalms 107–150

PSALM 107

1 Oh, give thanks unto the LORD, for He is good,
for His mercy endures forever!
2 Let the redeemed of the LORD speak out,
whom He has redeemed from the hand of the enemy,
3 and gathered them from the lands,
from the east and from the west, from the north and from the south.
4 They wandered in the wilderness on a deserted path;
they found no city to dwell in.
5 Hungry and thirsty,
their soul fainted in them.
6 Then they cried unto the LORD in their trouble,
and He delivered them out of their distresses.
7 He led them on a level road,
that they might go to a city to live in.
8 Let them praise the LORD for His goodness
and for His wonderful works to the people!
9 For He satisfies the longing soul
and fills the hungry soul with goodness.
10 Some sit in darkness and in the shadow of death,
being prisoners in affliction and irons,
11 because they rebelled against the words of God
and rejected the counsel of the Most High.
12 Therefore He brought down their hearts with *hard* labor;
they fell down, and there was none to help.
13 Then they cried unto the LORD in their trouble,
and He delivered them out of their distress.
14 He brought them out of darkness and the shadow of death
and broke apart their bonds.
15 Let them praise the LORD for His goodness
and for His wonderful works to the people!
16 For He has broken the gates of bronze
and cut the bars of iron in two.
17 Some were fools because of their transgressions,
and because of their iniquities they are afflicted.
18 They loathed all manner of food,

107:1 Ps 106:1
107:2 Ps 106:10
107:3 Ps 106:47
107:4 Nu 14:33
107:6 Ps 50:15
107:9 Lk 1:53
107:10 Lk 1:79
107:12 Ps 22:11
107:13 Ps 107:6
107:14 Ps 116:16
107:16 Isa 45:1–2
107:17 La 3:39
107:18 Ps 88:3

107:20 Mt 8:8
107:22 Ps 9:11
107:25 Jnh 1:4
107:26 Ps 22:14
107:27 Job 12:25
107:29 Ps 65:7
107:32 Ps 22:22
107:33 Isa 42:15
107:34 Ge 13:10
107:35 Ps 114:8
107:36 Ps 107:7
107:38 Ge 12:2

and they drew near to the gates of death.
19 Then they cried unto the LORD in their trouble,
and He saved them out of their distress.
20 He sent His word and healed them
and delivered them from their destruction.
21 Let them praise the LORD for His goodness
and for His wonderful works to the people!
22 And let them offer the sacrifices of thanksgiving
and declare His works with rejoicing.

23 Some went down to the sea in ships,
to do business in the vast waters;
24 they saw the works of the LORD
and His wonders in the deep water.
25 For He commands and raises the stormy wind,
which lifts up the sea waves.
26 The *sailors* went up to the sky, they came down to the depths;
their strength melted because of the great danger.
27 They reeled to and fro and staggered like drunken men,
and were completely confused.
28 Then they cried out to the LORD in their trouble,
and He saved them out of their distress.
29 He made the storm calm,
and the sea waves were still.
30 They were glad because the waters were quiet,
so He brought them to their desired harbor.
31 Let them praise the LORD for His goodness
and for His wonderful works to the people!
32 Let them exalt Him in the congregation of the people,
and praise him in the assembly of the elders.

33 He turns rivers into a desert,
water springs into dry ground,
34 a fruitful land into salty wasteland,
because of the wickedness of those living there.
35 He turns a wilderness into pools of water,
a parched ground into springs of water.
36 There He makes the hungry dwell,
and they prepare a city to live in;
37 they sow fields and plant vineyards,
and yield a fruitful harvest.
38 He blesses them, so that they are greatly multiplied,

and He does not let their livestock
decrease.
39 But when they are diminished and brought
down
through oppression, affliction, and
sorrow,
40 He pours contempt upon princes,
and causes them to wander in a
wilderness with no road;
41 yet He raises up the poor from affliction
and cares for their families like flocks of
sheep.
42 The righteous shall see it and rejoice,
and all evil people shall stop their
mouth.
43 Whoever is wise let him observe these
things;
let them consider the lovingkindness of
the LORD.

PSALM 108

Ps 57:7–11; 60:5–12

A Song. A Psalm of David.

1 O God, my heart is determined;
I will sing and give praise with my whole
heart.
2 Awake, O lyre and harp!
I will awake at dawn!
3 I will praise you, O LORD, among the
peoples,
and I will sing praises unto You among
the nations.
4 For Your mercy is great above the heavens;
Your faithfulness reaches to the clouds.
5 Be exalted, O God, above the heavens,
may Your glory be above all the earth.
6 That Your beloved ones may be delivered,
provide salvation with Your right hand
and answer me.
7 God has spoken in His sanctuary:
"I will triumph and will divide up
Shechem
and portion out the Valley of Sukkoth.
8 Gilead is Mine; Manasseh is Mine;
Ephraim is My helmet;
Judah is My royal scepter;
9 Moab is My washbasin;
on Edom I throw My shoe;
over Philistia I shout in triumph."
10 Who will bring me into the fortified city?
Who will lead me into Edom?
11 Have You not rejected us, O God?
You surely do not go out, O God, with
our armies.
12 Grant us help against the foe,
for the help of man is worthless.

107:39 2Ki 10:32
107:40 Job 12:24
107:41 1Sa 2:8
107:42 Job 22:19
107:43 Ps 64:9
108:1 Ps 57:7–11
108:5 Ps 57:5
108:6 Ps 60:5–12
108:8 Ge 49:10
108:11 Ps 44:9
....
108:13 Isa 63:3
109:1 Dt 10:21
109:2 Ps 52:4
109:3 Ps 69:4
109:4 Ps 38:20
109:6 Zec 3:1
109:7 Pr 28:9
109:8 Ps 55:23
109:9 Ex 22:24
109:10 Ps 37:25
109:11 Job 5:5
109:13 Pr 10:7
109:14 Ex 20:5
109:15 Ps 34:16
109:16 Ps 34:18
109:17 Pr 14:14

13 Through God we shall be valiant,
for He shall tread down our enemies.

PSALM 109

For the Music Director. A Psalm of David.

1 Do not remain silent,
O God of my praise!
2 For the mouth of the wicked and deceitful
are opened against me;
they have spoken against me with a
lying tongue.
3 They encircled me with words of hatred
and fought against me without cause.
4 In return for my love they are my
adversaries,
but I give myself to prayer.
5 They have rewarded me evil for good
and hatred for my love.
6 Set a wicked man against him,
and let an accuser stand at his right
hand.
7 When he shall be judged, let him be
condemned,
and let his prayer be reckoned as sin.
8 Let his days be few,
and let another take his office.
9 Let his children be fatherless
and his wife a widow.
10 Let his children be wandering beggars;
let them seek their bread far from their
desolate places.
11 Let the creditor seize all that he has;
let the strangers plunder the fruit of his
labor.
12 Let there be none to extend mercy unto
him,
neither let there be any to pity his
fatherless children.
13 Let his posterity be cut off,
and in the generation following let his
name be blotted out.
14 Let the iniquity of his fathers be
remembered with the LORD,
and let not the sin of his mother be
blotted out.
15 Let them be before the LORD continually,
that the LORD may cut off the memory of
them from the earth.
16 For he did not remember to show
kindness,
but pursued the poor and needy and
broken-hearted
to their death.
17 As he loved cursing,
so let it come over him;
as he did not delight in blessing,
so let it be far from him.

[18]As he clothed himself with cursing like a
garment,
so let it soak into him like water,
and like oil into his bones.
[19]Let it be unto him as the garment that
covers him,
and a belt that he continually wears.
[20]Let this be the reward of my adversaries
from the LORD,
and of those who speak evil against my
soul.
[21]But You, O GOD my Lord,
work on my behalf for your name's sake;
because your mercy is good, deliver me.
[22]For I am poor and needy,
and my heart is wounded within me.
[23]I am gone like a shadow in the evening;
I am tossed as the locust.
[24]My knees are weak through fasting,
and my body is thin with no fat.
[25]I am a reproach to my accusers;
when they look upon me, they shake
their heads.

[26]Help me, O LORD my God!
Save me according to Your mercy,
[27]that they may know that this is by Your
hand,
that You, O LORD, have done it.
[28]Let them curse, but You will bless;
when they arise, let them be ashamed,
but let Your servant rejoice.
[29]Let my adversaries be clothed with shame,
and let them cover themselves with their
own disgrace like a cloak.

[30]I will greatly praise the LORD with my
mouth;
indeed, I will praise Him among the
multitude.
[31]For He stands at the right hand of the poor,
to save him from those who condemn
his soul to death.

PSALM 110

A Psalm of David.

[1] The LORD said to my lord,
"Sit at My right hand,
until I make your enemies
your footstool."

[2] The LORD shall send your mighty scepter
out of Zion;
rule in the midst of your enemies.
[3] Your people will follow you
in the day of your battle;
on the holy mountains
at dawn of the morning,
the dew of your youth belongs to you.

109:18 Nu 5:22
109:19 Ps 109:29
109:23 Ex 10:19
109:24 Heb 12:12
109:25 Ps 22:6–7
109:26 Ps 119:86
109:27 Job 37:7
109:29 Ps 35:26
109:30 Ps 35:18
109:31 Ps 16:8
110:1 1Co 15:25
110:3 Jdg 5:2

....

110:4 Nu 23:19
110:5 Ps 16:8
110:6 Ps 68:21
110:7 Jdg 7:5–6
111:1 Ps 138:1
111:2 Ps 143:5
111:3 Ps 119:142
111:4 Ps 103:8
111:5 Ps 105:8
111:7 Ps 19:7
111:8 Mt 5:18
111:9 Ps 99:3
111:10 Pr 9:10
112:1 Ps 128:1
112:2 Ps 102:28
112:3 Pr 3:16

[4] The LORD has sworn
and will not change,
"You are a priest forever
after the order of Melchizedek."

[5] The Lord is at your right hand;
He shall strike down kings in the day of
His wrath.
[6] He shall judge among the nations; He shall
fill them with dead bodies;
He shall scatter heads all over the land.
[7] He shall drink of the brook in the path;
then He shall lift up the head.

PSALM 111

[1] Praise the LORD!

I will praise the LORD with my whole heart,
in the assembly of the upright, and in
the congregation.

[2] The works of the LORD are great,
sought out by all who have pleasure in
them.
[3] His work is honorable and glorious,
and His righteousness endures forever.
[4] He has made His wonderful works to be
remembered;
the LORD is gracious and full of
compassion.
[5] He has given food to those who fear Him;
He will ever be mindful of His covenant.

[6] He has shown His people the power of His
works,
that He may give them the inheritance
of the nations.
[7] The works of His hands are true and just;
all His commands are sure.
[8] They stand forever and ever,
and are done in truth and uprightness.
[9] He sent redemption to His people;
He has commanded His covenant
forever;
holy and fearful is His name.

[10]The fear of the LORD is the beginning of
wisdom;
all who live it have insight.
His praise endures forever!

PSALM 112

[1] Praise the LORD!

Blessed is the man who fears the LORD,
who delights greatly in His
commandments.

[2] His offspring shall be mighty in the land;
the generation of the upright shall be
blessed.
[3] Wealth and riches shall be in his house,
and his righteousness endures forever.

4 To the upright there arises light in the darkness;
he is gracious, and full of compassion, and righteous.
5 A good man shows generous favor, and lends;
he will guide his affairs with justice.

6 Surely the righteous man shall not be moved;
the righteous shall be in everlasting remembrance.
7 He shall not be afraid of evil tidings;
his heart is fixed, trusting in the LORD.
8 His heart is established; he shall not be afraid,
until he sees triumph upon his enemies.
9 He has given away freely; he has given to the poor;
his righteousness endures forever;
his horn shall be exalted with honor.

10 The wicked shall see it and be grieved;
he shall gnash his teeth and melt away;
the desire of the wicked shall perish.

PSALM 113

1 Praise the LORD!

Praise, O you servants of the LORD,
praise the name of the LORD.
2 Blessed be the name of the LORD
from this time forth and for evermore.
3 From the rising of the sun to its going down,
the LORD's name is to be praised.

4 The LORD is high above all nations,
and His glory above the heavens.
5 Who is like the LORD our God,
who dwells on high,
6 who looks down on the things
that are in heaven and on the earth?

7 He raises up the poor out of the dust
and lifts the needy out of the ash heap,
8 to make them sit with princes,
even with the princes of His people.
9 He gives the barren woman a dwelling,
making her the joyful mother of children.

Praise the LORD!

PSALM 114

1 When Israel went out of Egypt,
the house of Jacob from a people of strange language,
2 Judah was His sanctuary,
and Israel His dominion.

3 The sea saw it and fled;
the Jordan was driven back;
4 the mountains skipped like rams
and the hills like lambs.

5 What alarmed you, O sea, that you fled,
O Jordan, that you turned back,
6 O mountains, that you skipped like rams,
O hills, like lambs?

7 Tremble, O earth, at the presence of the Lord,
at the presence of the God of Jacob
8 who turned the rock into a pool of water,
the hard stone into a spring of waters.

PSALM 115
Ps 135:15–20

1 Not unto us, O LORD, not unto us,
but unto Your name give glory,
for the sake of Your mercy, and for the sake of Your truth.

2 Why should the nations say,
"Where now is their God?"
3 But our God is in the heavens;
He does whatever He pleases.
4 Their idols are silver and gold,
the work of men's hands.
5 They have mouths, but they cannot speak;
eyes, but they cannot see;
6 they have ears, but they cannot hear;
noses, but they cannot smell;
7 they have hands, but they cannot feel;
feet, but they cannot walk;
neither can they speak with their throat.
8 Those who make them are like them;
so is everyone who trusts in them.

9 O Israel, trust in the LORD;
He is their help and their shield.
10 O house of Aaron, trust in the LORD;
He is their help and their shield.
11 You who fear the LORD, trust in the LORD;
He is their help and their shield.

12 The LORD has been mindful of us; He will bless us;
He will bless the house of Israel;
He will bless the house of Aaron.
13 He will bless those who fear the LORD,
both the small and great ones.

14 The LORD shall increase you more and more,
you and your children.
15 You are blessed of the LORD,
who made heaven and earth.

16 The heavens belong to the LORD,
but the earth He has given to the children of men.
17 The dead do not praise the LORD,
nor do any who go down into silence.

112:4 Job 11:17
112:6 Pr 10:7
112:7 Ps 57:7
112:8 Ps 59:10
112:9 Ps 75:10
112:10 Ps 37:12
113:2 Da 2:20
113:3 Isa 59:19
113:4 Ps 8:1
113:5 Ps 89:6
113:6 Ps 11:4
113:7 Ps 107:41
113:8 Job 36:7
113:9 1Sa 2:5
114:1 Ex 13:3
114:3 Ps 77:16
....
114:4 Ex 19:18
114:5 Hab 3:8
114:7 Ps 96:9
114:8 Nu 20:11
115:1 Isa 48:11
115:2 Ps 42:3
115:3 Da 4:35
115:4 Dt 4:28
115:8 Ps 135:18
115:9 Ps 62:8
115:13 Ps 112:1
115:14 Dt 1:11
115:15 Ge 1:1
115:16 Ps 89:11
115:17 Ps 6:5

18 But we will bless the Lord
from this time and for evermore.

Praise the Lord!

PSALM 116

1 I love the Lord, because He has heard my voice
and my supplications.
2 Because He has inclined His ear to me,
therefore I will call upon Him as long as I live.

3 The cords of death encircled me,
and the pains of Sheol took hold of me;
I found trouble and sorrow.
4 Then called I upon the name of the Lord:
"O Lord, I plead with You, deliver my soul."

5 Gracious is the Lord, and righteous;
indeed, our God is merciful.
6 The Lord protects the simple;
I was brought low, and He helped me.

7 Return to your rest, O my soul;
for the Lord has vindicated you.

8 For You have delivered my soul from death,
my eyes from tears,
and my feet from falling.
9 I will walk before the Lord
in the land of the living.

10 I believed, indeed I have spoken:
"I am greatly afflicted."
11 I said in my haste,
"All men are liars."

12 What shall I render unto the Lord
for all His benefits toward me?

13 I will take the cup of salvation
and call upon the name of the Lord.
14 I will pay my vows unto the Lord
now in the presence of all His people.
15 Precious in the sight of the Lord
is the death of His godly ones.
16 O Lord, I am Your servant;
I am Your servant, the son of Your female servant;
You have loosed my bonds.

17 I will offer to You the sacrifice of thanksgiving
and will call upon the name of the Lord.
18 I will pay my vows unto the Lord
now in the presence of all His people,
19 in the courts of the house of the Lord,
in your midst, O Jerusalem.

Praise the Lord!

115:18 Ps 113:2
116:4 Ps 118:5
116:5 Ezr 9:15
116:6 Ps 19:7
116:7 Ps 13:6
116:8 Ps 56:13
116:9 Ps 27:13
116:10 2Co 4:13
116:11 Ps 31:22
116:12 Ps 103:2
116:13 Ps 105:1
116:14 Ps 22:25
116:15 Ps 72:14
116:16 Ps 86:16
116:17 Ps 50:14
116:18 Ps 116:14
116:19 Ps 96:8
....
117:1 Ro 15:11
118:1 1Ch 16:8
118:2 Ps 115:9–11
118:5 Ps 18:19
118:6 Ps 56:4
118:7 Ps 54:4
118:8 Ps 40:4
118:11 Ps 88:17
118:12 Dt 1:44
118:13 Ps 140:4
118:14 Isa 12:2
118:15 Ps 89:13

PSALM 117

1 Praise the Lord, all you nations!
Exalt Him, all you peoples!
2 For His merciful kindness is great toward us,
and the faithfulness of the Lord endures forever.

Praise the Lord!

PSALM 118

1 Oh, give thanks unto the Lord, for He is good,
because His mercy endures forever.

2 Let Israel say,
"His mercy endures forever."
3 Let the house of Aaron say,
"His mercy endures forever."
4 Let those who fear the Lord say,
"His mercy endures forever."

5 I called upon the Lord from my distress;
the Lord answered me and *set me* in an open place.

> Despite any bad thing that may have happened in my life, God hasn't loosened His hold on me (Ps 118:6)!

6 The Lord is on my side; I will not fear.
What can people do to me?
7 The Lord is on my side to help me;
I shall look in triumph upon those who hate me.

8 It is better to trust in the Lord
than to put confidence in man.
9 It is better to trust in the Lord
than to put confidence in princes.
10 All nations encircled me,
but in the name of the Lord I will destroy them.
11 They circled me; indeed, they surrounded me,
but in the name of the Lord I will destroy them.
12 They circled me like bees;
they went forth as a fire over thorns,
but in the name of the Lord I will destroy them.
13 You have pushed against me, that I was falling,
but the Lord helped me.
14 The Lord is my strength and song;
He has become my salvation.

15 The voice of rejoicing and salvation
is in the tents of the righteous:
"The right hand of the Lord is valiant.

16 The right hand of the LORD is exalted;
the right hand of the LORD is valiant."
17 I shall not die, but I shall live
and declare the works of the LORD.
18 The LORD has severely chastened me,
but He has not given me over unto
death.
19 Open to me the gates of righteousness;
I will go into them, and I will praise the
LORD.
20 This is the gate of the LORD;
the righteous shall enter through.
21 I will thank You that You have heard me
and have become my deliverance.

22 The stone that the builders rejected
has become the cornerstone.
23 This is what the LORD has done;
it is marvelous in our eyes.
24 This is the day that the LORD has made;
we will rejoice and be glad in it.

25 Save us, we ask You, O LORD;
O LORD, we ask You, send now success.

26 Blessed be he that comes in the name of
the LORD:
we have blessed you out of the house of
the LORD.
27 The LORD is God,
and He has shown us His light;
bind the sacrifice with cords,
even unto the horns of the altar.

28 You are my God, and I will praise You;
You are my God, I will exalt You.

29 Oh, give thanks unto the LORD, for He is
good,
for His mercy endures forever.

PSALM 119

א ALEPH

1 Blessed are those whose way is blameless,
who walk in the law of the LORD.
2 Blessed are those who keep His
testimonies,
and who seek Him with all their heart.
3 They also do no wrong;
they walk in His ways.
4 You have commanded us
to keep Your precepts diligently.
5 Oh, that my ways were established
to keep Your statutes!
6 Then I shall not be ashamed,
when I have my focus on all Your
commandments.
7 I will praise You with an upright heart,
when I have learned Your righteous
judgments.
8 I will keep Your statutes;
do not completely abandon me.

118:16 Ex 15:6
118:17 Ps 6:5
118:18 2Co 6:9
118:19 Isa 26:2
118:21 Ps 116:1
118:22 Mt 21:42
118:26 Mt 21:9
118:27 1Pe 2:9
118:28 Ex 15:2
118:29 Ps 118:1
119:1 Ps 128:1
119:3 1Jn 3:9
....
119:9 Ps 25:7
119:10 2Ch 15:15
119:11 Ps 37:31
119:15 Ps 1:2
119:17 Ps 13:6
119:19 1Ch 29:15
119:20 Ps 63:1
119:21 Ps 119:10
119:22 Ps 39:8
119:24 Ps 119:16
119:25 Ps 44:25
119:26 Ps 25:4
119:27 Ps 105:2
119:28 Ps 107:26

ב BETH

9 How shall a young man keep his way pure?
By keeping it according to Your word.
10 With my whole heart I seek You;
do not allow me to wander from Your
commandments.
11 Your word I have hidden in my heart,
that I might not sin against You.
12 Blessed are You, O LORD;
teach me Your statutes.
13 With my lips I declare
all the decrees of Your mouth.
14 I rejoice in the way of Your testimonies,
as much as in all riches.
15 I will meditate on Your precepts
and keep my eyes on Your ways.
16 I will delight in Your statutes;
I will not forget Your word.

ג GIMEL

17 Deal kindly with Your servant, that I may
live
and keep Your word.
18 Open my eyes, that I may behold
wondrous things from Your law.
19 I am a sojourner in the land;
do not hide Your commandments
from me.
20 My soul is consumed all the time
with a longing for Your decrees.
21 You have rebuked the proud, those cursed,
who depart from Your commandments.
22 Remove from me reproach and contempt,
for I have kept Your testimonies.
23 Even if princes sit and conspire against me,
Your servant will meditate on Your
statutes.
24 Your testimonies are my delight
and my counselors.

ד DALETH

25 My soul clings to the dust;
revive me according to Your word.
26 I have declared my ways, and You heard
me;
teach me Your statutes.
27 Make me to understand the way of Your
precepts;
then I shall contemplate on Your
wondrous works.
28 My soul collapses on account of grief;
strengthen me according to Your word.
29 Remove from me the way of falsehood,
and graciously grant me Your law.
30 I have chosen the way of faithfulness;
Your judgments I have laid before me.
31 I have stayed with Your testimonies,
O LORD;
may I not be put to shame.

[32]I will run in the way of Your
commandments,
when You set my heart free.

ה HE

[33]Teach me, O Lord, the way of Your statutes,
and I shall keep it to the end.
[34]Give me understanding, and I shall keep
Your law
and observe it with my whole heart.

Father, turn away my eyes from looking at worthless things, and revive me in Your way (Ps 119:37).

[35]Lead me in the path of Your
commandments,
for I delight in them.
[36]Incline my heart unto Your testimonies,
and not for unjust gain.
[37]Turn away my eyes from beholding
worthlessness,
and revive me in Your way.
[38]Establish Your word to Your servant,
so that You are feared.
[39]Turn away my reproach that I dread,
for Your judgments are good.
[40]Behold, I have a longing for Your precepts;
revive me in Your righteousness.

ו WAW

[41]Let Your mercies come to me, O Lord,
even Your deliverance according to Your
word.
[42]So I shall have an answer for him who
reproaches me,
for I trust in Your word.
[43]Do not take the word of truth out of my
mouth,
for I have hoped in Your judgments.
[44]So I shall keep Your law continually,
forever and ever.
[45]I will walk in an open space,
for I seek Your precepts.
[46]I will speak of Your testimonies also before
kings
and will not be ashamed.
[47]I will delight in Your commandments,
which I have loved.
[48]My hands I will lift up unto Your
commandments, which I have loved;
I will meditate on Your statutes.

ז ZAYIN

[49]Remember Your word to Your servant,
on which You have caused me to hope.
[50]This is my comfort in my affliction,
for Your word revives me.

119:33 Ps 119:12
119:35 Ps 119:16
119:36 1Ki 8:58
119:37 Isa 33:15
119:39 Ps 119:22
119:40 Ps 119:20
119:45 Ps 119:94
119:46 Ac 26:1–2
119:48 Ps 119:15
119:50 Ro 15:4
....
119:51 Job 23:11
119:53 Ezr 9:3
119:54 Ge 47:9
119:55 Ps 42:8
119:57 Ps 16:5
119:58 Ps 119:41
119:61 Ps 119:176
119:63 Ps 101:6
119:64 Ps 33:5
119:66 Php 1:9
119:67 Jer 31:18–19
119:68 Ps 106:1
119:69 Job 13:4
119:70 Ps 17:10
119:71 Ps 119:67
119:72 Ps 19:10

[51]The proud ones have derided me,
yet I have not forsaken Your law.
[52]I remembered Your judgments of old,
O Lord,
and I have comforted myself.
[53]Fury has taken hold of me because of the
wicked
who forsake Your law.
[54]Your statutes have been my songs
in the house of my temporary dwelling.
[55]I have remembered Your name, O Lord, in
the night,
and have kept Your law.
[56]This is my blessing,
because I have kept Your precepts.

ח HETH

[57]You are my portion, O Lord;
I have said that I would keep Your
words.
[58]I seek Your favor with my whole heart;
be merciful to me according to Your
word.
[59]I consider my ways,
and I turn my feet to Your testimonies.
[60]I made haste, and I did not delay
to keep Your commandments.
[61]The bands of the wicked have trapped me,
but I have not forgotten Your law.
[62]At midnight I will rise to give thanks to
You,
because of Your righteous judgments.
[63]I am a companion of all who fear You,
and of those who keep Your precepts.
[64]The earth, O Lord, is full of Your mercy;
teach me Your statutes.

ט TETH

[65]You have been good to Your servant,
O Lord, according to Your word.
[66]Teach me good discernment and
knowledge,
for I have believed Your
commandments.
[67]Before I was afflicted I wandered,
but now I keep Your word.
[68]You are good and do good;
teach me Your statutes.
[69]The proud have spoken lies against me,
but I keep Your precepts with my whole
heart.
[70]Their heart is as thick as fat,
but I delight in Your law.
[71]It is good for me that I have been afflicted,
that I might learn Your statutes.
[72]The law from Your mouth is better to me
than thousands of gold and silver coins.

י YODH

73 Your hands have made me and
fashioned me;
give me understanding, that I may learn
Your commandments.
74 Those who fear You will be glad when they
see me,
because I have hoped in Your word.
75 I know, O LORD, that Your judgments are
right,
and that You in faithfulness have
afflicted me.
76 Let Your merciful kindness comfort me,
according to Your word to Your servant.
77 Let Your compassion come to me, that I
may live,
for Your law is my delight.
78 Let the proud be ashamed, for they have
been wicked to me in falsehood,
but I will meditate on Your precepts.
79 Let those who fear You turn to me,
that they might know Your testimonies.
80 Let my heart be blameless in Your statutes,
that I may not be ashamed.

כ KAPH

81 My soul longs for Your deliverance,
but I hope in Your word.
82 My eyes are weary for Your word,
saying, "When will You comfort me?"
83 For I have become like a wineskin *dried* in
the smoke,
yet I have not forgotten Your statutes.
84 How many days are given to Your servant?
When will You provide judgment on
those who persecute me?
85 The proud have dug pits for me,
and they do not live in accordance to
Your law.
86 All Your commandments are faithful;
I am persecuted without cause; help me!
87 They have almost consumed me on the
earth,
but I have not abandoned Your precepts.
88 Revive me according to Your
lovingkindness,
that I may keep the testimony from Your
mouth.

ל LAMEDH

89 Forever, O LORD, Your word
is established in heaven.
90 Your faithfulness is for all generations;
You have established the earth, and it
is firm.
91 They continue this day according to Your
ordinance,
for all are Your servants.
92 Unless Your law had been my delight,
I would have perished in my affliction.
93 I will never forget Your precepts,
for with them You have revived me.
94 I am Yours; deliver me,
for I have sought Your precepts.
95 The wicked have waited to destroy me,
but I will consider Your testimonies.
96 I have seen that all perfection has an end,
but Your commandment is quite broad.

מ MEM

97 Oh, how I love Your law!
It is my meditation all the day.
98 Your commandments have made me wiser
than my enemies,
for they are continually with me.
99 I have more understanding than all my
teachers,
for Your testimonies are my meditation.
100 I understand more than the elders,
because I keep Your precepts.
101 I have restrained my feet from every evil
way,
that I might keep Your word.
102 I have not departed from Your judgments,
for You have taught me.
103 How sweet are Your words to the taste of
my mouth!
Sweeter than honey to my mouth!
104 Through Your precepts I receive
understanding;
therefore I hate every false way.

נ NUN

105 Your word is a lamp to my feet
and a light to my path.
106 I have sworn, and I will perform it,
that I will keep Your righteous
judgments.
107 I am greatly afflicted;
revive me, O LORD, according to Your
word.
108 Accept the freewill offerings of my praise,
O LORD,
and teach me Your judgments.
109 My soul is continually in my hand,
yet I do not forget Your law.
110 The wicked have laid a trap for me,
yet I do not depart from Your precepts.
111 Your testimonies are my inheritance
forever,
for they are the rejoicing of my heart.
112 I have inclined my heart to perform Your
statutes always,
even unto the end.

ס SAMEKH

113 I hate those who are double-minded,
but I love Your law.

119:73 Ps 100:3
119:75 Heb 12:10–11
119:77 Ps 119:41
119:81 Ps 84:2
119:82 Ps 69:3
119:83 Job 30:30
119:85 Ps 35:7
119:86 Ps 35:19
119:89 1Pe 1:25
119:91 Jer 33:25
....
119:93 Ps 119:16
119:97 Ps 1:2
119:98 Dt 4:6
119:101 Pr 1:15
119:103 Ps 19:10
119:104 Ps 119:128
119:105 Pr 6:23
119:106 Ne 10:29
119:107 Ps 119:25
119:108 Hos 14:2
119:109 Jdg 12:3
119:110 Ps 119:10
119:111 Dt 33:4
119:112 Ps 119:33

114 You are my hiding place and my shield,
I hope in Your word.
115 Depart from me, you who are wicked,
for I keep the commandments of my
God.
116 Uphold me according to Your word, that I
may live,
and let me not be ashamed with my
hope.
117 Hold me up, and I shall be safe,
and I will have respect for Your statutes
continually.
118 You have rejected all those who stray from
Your statutes,
for their deceit is falsehood.
119 You put away all the wicked of the earth
like dross;
therefore I love Your testimonies.
120 My body trembles for fear of You,
and I am afraid of Your judgments.

ע AYIN

121 I have done what is right and just;
do not abandon me to my oppressors.
122 Be true to Your servant for good;
let not the proud ones oppress me.
123 My eyes long for Your deliverance
and for the promise of Your
righteousness.
124 Deal with Your servant according to Your
mercy,
and teach me Your statutes.
125 I am Your servant; grant me
understanding,
that I may know Your testimonies.
126 It is time for You, O LORD, to act,
for they have broken Your law.
127 Therefore I love Your commandments
above gold, even fine gold.
128 For I follow all Your precepts to be right,
and I hate every false way.

פ PE

129 Your testimonies are wonderful;
therefore my soul keeps them.
130 The giving of Your words gives light;
it grants understanding to the simple.
131 I opened my mouth and panted,
for I long for Your commandments.
132 Look upon me, and be merciful to me,
as You are for those who love Your
name.
133 Order my steps according to Your word,
and let not any iniquity have dominion
over me.
134 Deliver me from the oppression of man,
so I will keep Your precepts.
135 Make Your face to shine upon Your
servant,
and teach me Your statutes.
136 Rivers of waters run down my eyes,
because people do not keep Your law.

צ TSADHE

137 You are righteous, O LORD,
and upright are Your judgments.
138 You have set Your testimonies in
righteousness
and faithfulness.
139 My zeal has consumed me,
because my enemies have forgotten
Your words.
140 Your word is pure and true;
therefore Your servant loves it.
141 I am small and despised,
yet I do not forget Your precepts.
142 Your righteousness is an everlasting
righteousness,
and Your law is true.
143 Trouble and anguish have discovered me,
but Your commandments are my delight.
144 The righteousness of Your testimonies is
everlasting;
grant me understanding, and I shall live.

ק QOPH

145 I cried with my whole heart; hear me, O
LORD,
I will keep Your statutes.
146 I cried unto You; deliver me,
and I shall keep Your testimonies.
147 I arose before the dawn of the morning
and cried for help;
I hope in Your words.
148 My eyes are awake before the night
watches,
that I might meditate on Your word.
149 Hear my voice according to Your
lovingkindness, O LORD;
revive me according to Your judgment.
150 They draw close, those who persecute me
with evil;
they are far from Your law.
151 But You are near, O LORD,
and all Your commandments are true.
152 I have known of old
that You have established Your
testimonies forever.

ר RESH

153 Consider my affliction, and deliver me,
for I do not forget Your law.
154 Plead my cause, and defend me;
revive me according to Your word.
155 Salvation is far from the wicked,
for they do not seek Your statutes.
156 Great are Your compassions, O LORD;
revive me according to Your judgments.

119:114 Ps 32:7
119:115 Ps 6:8
119:116 Ps 25:2
119:117 Ps 119:6
119:119 Mal 3:2–3
119:120 Hab 3:16
119:121 2Sa 8:15
119:124 Ps 119:12
119:125 Ps 116:16
119:127 Ps 19:10
119:128 Ps 119:104
119:129 Ps 119:18
119:130 Ps 19:7
119:131 Ps 42:1
119:132 Ps 106:4
119:133 Ps 17:5
119:135 Ps 4:6
....
119:136 Jer 9:1
119:137 Ezr 9:15
119:138 Ps 19:7–9
119:139 Ps 69:9
119:140 Ps 12:6
119:141 Ps 22:6
119:145 Ps 119:10
119:147 Ps 5:3
119:148 Ps 63:6
119:149 Ps 119:25
119:151 Ps 145:18
119:152 Lk 21:33
119:153 La 5:1
119:154 1Sa 24:15
119:155 Job 5:4

SPIRIT-TO-SPIRIT PRAYER

COVENANT CONFESSION OF THE WORD

Father God, I thank You that Your Word is right and all of Your work is done in truth.

I thank You for the logos*. I thank You for the expressed and spoken word by interpretation. I thank You for sound doctrine, and I thank You for the* rhema *word of God. I thank You that You have anointed me to command the* rhema *word of God. It will take feet and become the Word in action because of the greater One who is inside me. I am a child of the King, an heir of God, and a joint heir with Christ. Because I am in covenant with God and with my brothers and sisters, what I speak shall come to pass.*

Lord, I thank You for Your chronicles. I thank You for Your commandments. Thank You, Holy Spirit, for communicating with Your people. I thank You for the conference of the Lord. I thank You for the counsel of the Lord, which will bring me forth in power, promise, provision, and purpose. God, I hide Your Word in my heart. I delight myself in Your Word, and I will not forget Your Word. I will observe Your Word—hearing it, receiving it, loving it, and obeying it.

Lord, open my eyes that I may behold the great and wondrous things in Your love. Hide not Your commandments from me, for it is for the love of God that I keep Your commandments, and they are not grievous in my soul. My comfort and my consolation in my affliction is that Your Word revives me and gives me life. Affliction helps me to learn Your statutes. God, affliction is good for my soul.

Forever, Lord, Your Word is established in the heavens. My destiny is connected to that. Your Word is a lamp to my feet and a light to my path. Order my steps, O God, in Your Word, and let not iniquity have dominion over me. I make covenant with the Word of God, and I break covenant with death, hell, and the grave. This is not just for me, but it is also for my future generations. My covenant with the Word is going forth for a thousand generations. My children's children's children will have covenant with the Word.

Lord, I thank You that Your Word is pure. Your Word is tried and well refined. I am Your servant, and I love it. I love Your Word. I eat Your Word for breakfast. I eat Your Word for lunch. And I eat Your Word for dinner. In Jesus' name I pray, amen.

Kimberly Daniels

157 Many are my persecutors and my
enemies,
yet I do not turn from Your testimonies.
158 I behold the transgressors with disgust,
because they have not kept Your word.
159 Consider how I love Your precepts;
revive me, O LORD, according to Your
lovingkindness.
160 Your word is true from the beginning,
and every one of Your righteous
judgments endures forever.

ש SIN AND SHIN

161 Princes have persecuted me without a
cause,
but my heart stands in awe of Your
words.
162 I rejoice at Your word,
as one who finds great plunder.

119:157 Ps 119:51
119:158 Ps 139:21
119:161 1Sa 26:18
119:162 1Sa 30:16

163 I hate and abhor lying,
but I love Your law.
164 Seven times a day I praise You,
because of Your righteous judgments.
165 Those who love Your law have great peace,
and nothing shall cause them to stumble.
166 LORD, I have hoped for Your deliverance,
and I carry out Your commandments.
167 My soul has kept Your testimonies,
and I love them greatly.
168 I have kept Your precepts and Your testimonies,
for all my ways are before You.

ת TAW

169 Let my cry come near before You, O LORD;
give me understanding according to Your word.
170 Let my supplication come before You;
deliver me according to Your word.
171 My lips shall declare praise,
for You have taught me Your statutes.
172 My tongue shall speak of Your word,
for all Your commandments are right.
173 Let Your hand help me,
for I have chosen Your precepts.
174 I have longed for Your salvation, O LORD,
and Your law is my delight.
175 Let my soul live and praise You,
and let Your judgments come to my aid.
176 I have wandered like a lost sheep;
seek Your servant,
for I do not forget Your commandments.

PSALM 120

A Song of Ascents.

1 In my distress I cried unto the LORD,
and He heard me.
2 Deliver my soul, O LORD, from lying lips
and from a deceitful tongue.

3 What shall be given to you,
or what shall be done to you, you false tongue?
4 Sharp arrows of the warrior,
with coals of the broom tree!

5 Woe is me, that I have sojourned in Meshek,
or that I have dwelled among the tents of Kedar!
6 My soul has long lived
with those who hate peace.
7 I am for peace,
but when I speak, they are for war!

119:163 Ps 119:128
119:165 Isa 32:17
119:166 Ge 49:18
119:168 Pr 5:21
119:169 Ps 18:6
119:173 Jos 24:22
119:176 Isa 53:6
120:1 Jnh 2:2
120:4 Ps 45:5
120:5 Ge 25:13

....

121:1 Ps 87:1
121:2 Ps 124:8
121:3 1Sa 2:9
121:5 Ps 16:8
121:6 Isa 49:10
121:7 Ps 41:2
121:8 Dt 28:6
122:1 Isa 2:3
122:3 2Sa 5:9
122:4 Dt 16:16
122:5 Dt 17:8
122:6 Ps 51:18
122:7 Ps 48:3
122:9 Ne 2:10
123:1 Ps 121:1

PSALM 121

A Song of Ascents.

1 I will lift up my eyes to the hills,
from where does my help come?
2 My help comes from the LORD,
who made heaven and earth.

3 He will not let your foot slip;
He who keeps you will not slumber.
4 Behold, He who guards Israel
shall neither slumber nor sleep.

5 The LORD is your guardian;
the LORD is your shade at your right hand.
6 The sun shall not harm you during the day,
nor the moon during the night.
7 The LORD shall protect you from all evil;
He shall preserve your soul.
8 The LORD shall preserve your going out and your coming in
from now and for evermore.

PSALM 122

A Song of Ascents. Of David.

1 I was glad when they said to me,
"Let us go into the house of the LORD."
2 Our feet shall stand
within your gates, O Jerusalem.

3 Jerusalem is built as a city
that is designed for a multitude,
4 where the tribes go up,
the tribes of the LORD,
as a decree of Israel,
to give thanks unto the name of the LORD.
5 There are set thrones of judgment,
the thrones of the house of David.

6 Pray for the peace of Jerusalem:
"May they prosper who love you!
7 Peace be within your walls
and security within your towers!"
8 For my brothers and companions' sake,
I will now say, "Peace be within you."
9 Because of the house of the LORD our God,
I will seek your good.

PSALM 123

A Song of Ascents.

1 To You I lift up my eyes,
O You who dwell in the heavens.
2 Behold, as the eyes of servants look to the hand of their master,
and as the eyes of a maiden to the hand of her mistress,

God's Promises for Parents

Look, children are a gift of the Lord, and the fruit of the womb is a reward. As arrows in the hand of a mighty warrior, so are the children of one's youth.

—Psalm 127:3–4

Praying according to God's Word is one of the most powerful ways you will ever pray. Scripture praying is putting God's Word into action. Open your heart and your mouth, and begin invading the darkness and taking back what rightfully belongs to you. Many of these declarations you will make by faith, believing in those things that are not as though they already are.

Describe the promise for each Scripture reference below. Then write a sentence prayer using the promise. Personalize these scriptures by adding your and your child's names.

1. Proverbs 22:6

2. Psalm 127:3–5

3. Psalm 103:17

4. Psalm 103:20

5. Hebrews 4:15

6. Joel 2:28

7. Luke 10:18–19

8. Matthew 8:14

9. Acts 16:31

Iris Delgado

so our eyes look upon the LORD our God,
until He has mercy upon us.

3 Have mercy upon us, O LORD, have mercy
upon us,
for we have been completely filled with
contempt.
4 Our soul is exceedingly filled with the
ridicule of those who are at ease,
and with the contempt of the proud
ones.

PSALM 124

A Song of Ascents. Of David.

1 If it had not been the LORD who was on our
side,
now may Israel say,
2 if it had not been the LORD who was on our
side,
when men rose up against us,
3 then they would have swallowed us up,
when their wrath was kindled
against us;
4 then the flood would have
overwhelmed us,
the torrent would have passed over our
lives;
5 then the surging waters
would have gone over us.

6 Blessed be the LORD,
who has not given us for a prey to their
teeth.
7 We have escaped
as a bird out of the snare of the hunters;
the snare is broken,
and we have escaped.
8 Our help is in the name of the LORD,
who made heaven and earth.

PSALM 125

A Song of Ascents.

1 Those who trust in the LORD shall be as
Mount Zion,
which cannot be removed, but abides
forever.
2 As the mountains are around Jerusalem,
so the LORD surrounds His people,
from now and forever.

3 For the scepter of the wicked shall not rest
upon the land allotted to the righteous,
lest the righteous put forth
their hands to do iniquity.

4 Do good, O LORD, for those who are good,
and to those who are upright in their
hearts.

5 As for those who turn aside to their twisted
ways,
the LORD shall lead them away with the
other workers of iniquity.

Peace be upon Israel!

PSALM 126

A Song of Ascents.

1 When the LORD restored the captives of
Zion,
we were like those who dream.
2 Then our mouth was filled with laughter,
and our tongue with singing.
Then they said among the nations,
"The LORD has done great things for
them."
3 The LORD has done great things for us;
we are glad.

4 Restore our captives, O LORD,
as the streams in the Negev.
5 Those who sow in tears
shall reap in joy.
6 He who goes forth and weeps,
bearing precious seed to sow,
shall come home again with rejoicing,
bringing his grain sheaves with him.

PSALM 127

A Song of Ascents. Of Solomon.

1 Except the LORD build the house,
those who build labor in vain;
except the LORD guards the city,
the watchman stays awake in vain.
2 It is in vain for you to rise up early,
to stay up late,
and to eat the bread of hard toil,
for He gives sleep to His beloved.

3 Look, children are a gift of the LORD,
and the fruit of the womb is a reward.
4 As arrows in the hand of a mighty warrior,
so are the children of one's youth.
5 Happy is the man
who has his quiver full of them;
he shall not be ashamed
when he speaks with the enemies at the
gate.

PSALM 128

A Song of Ascents.

1 Blessed is everyone who fears the LORD,
who walks in His ways.
2 For you shall eat the fruit of the labor of
your hands;
you will be happy, and it shall be well
with you.

124:1 Ps 129:1
124:5 Job 38:11
124:7 Ps 91:3
124:8 Ps 121:2
125:2 Zec 2:5
125:3 Pr 22:8

125:5 Ps 128:6
126:1 Ps 85:1
126:2 Job 8:21
127:1 Ps 120:1
127:2 Ecc 5:12
127:3 Ge 33:5
127:5 Pr 27:11
128:1 Ps 112:1
128:2 Isa 3:10

³ Your wife shall be as a fruitful vine
in your house,
your children like olive shoots
around your table.
⁴ Behold, this man shall be blessed
who fears the LORD.
⁵ The LORD shall bless you from Zion,
and may you see the welfare of
Jerusalem
all the days of your life.
⁶ Indeed, may you see your children's
children.
Peace upon Israel!

PSALM 129

A Song of Ascents.

1 "Often they have afflicted me from my
youth,"
may Israel now say,
2 "often they have afflicted me from my
youth,
yet they have not prevailed against me.
3 The plowmen plowed upon my back;
they made their furrows long."
4 The LORD is righteous;
He has cut the cords of the wicked.
5 Let all those be shamed
and turned back who hate Zion.
6 Let them be as the grass on the housetops,
which withers before it even grows,
7 where the reaper is unable to fill his hand,
or he who binds sheaves, his arms.
8 Neither do they who pass by say,
"The blessing of the LORD be upon you;
we bless you in the name of the LORD!"

PSALM 130

A Song of Ascents.

1 From the depths I call on You, O LORD!
2 O Lord, hear my voice;
let Your ears be attentive
to the sound of my supplications.
3 If you, O LORD, should keep track of
iniquities,
O Lord, who shall stand?
4 For there is forgiveness with You,
that You may be feared.
5 I wait for the LORD, with bated breath I wait;
I long for His Word!
6 My soul waits for the Lord,
more than watchmen for the morning,
more than watchmen for the morning.
7 Let Israel wait for the LORD!
For mercy is found with the LORD;
with Him is great redemption.

128:3 Ps 52:8
128:5 Ps 20:2
128:6 Job 42:16
129:1 Ps 124:1
129:2 Mt 16:18
129:3 Isa 51:23
129:6 Ps 37:2
129:8 Ru 2:4
130:1 Ps 42:7
130:2 2Ch 6:40
130:3 Ps 143:2
130:4 Isa 55:7
130:5 Ps 33:20
130:6 Ps 63:6
130:7 Ps 131:3
. . . .
130:8 Titus 2:14
131:1 Ro 12:16
131:2 1Co 14:20
131:3 Ps 130:7
132:1 Ps 120:1
132:2 Ge 49:24
132:4 Pr 6:4
132:6 1Sa 17:12
132:7 Ps 5:7
132:8 Ps 68:1
132:9 Job 29:14
132:11 2Sa 7:12
132:13 Ps 68:16
132:14 Ps 132:8

8 He shall redeem Israel
from all their iniquities.

PSALM 131

A Song of Ascents. Of David.

1 LORD, my heart is not haughty,
my eyes are not raised too high.
I have not striven for enormities,
for things too wonderful for me.
2 I composed and quieted my desire,
like a child given suck by his mother;
like a child who sucks is my desire
within me.
3 Let Israel hope in the LORD
from now and forever.

PSALM 132

2Ch 6:41–42

A Song of Ascents.

1 O LORD, remember David
and all his afflictions,
2 how he swore unto the LORD,
and vowed unto the mighty God of
Jacob:
3 "I will not come into my house,
nor go up to my bed;
4 I will not give sleep to my eyes,
or slumber to my eyelids,
5 until I find a place for the LORD,
a dwelling for the mighty God of Jacob."
6 We heard of it in Ephrathah;
we found it in the fields of Jaar.
7 "We will go to His dwelling place,
we will worship at His footstool."
8 Arise, O LORD, go to Your resting place,
You and the ark of Your strength.
9 Let Your priests be clothed with
righteousness,
and let Your godly ones shout for joy.
10 For Your servant David's sake,
do not turn away Your anointed king.
11 The LORD has sworn with a sure oath to
David
that He will not turn from it:
"From the fruit of your body
I will set a son on your throne.
12 If your children will keep My covenant
and My testimonies that I shall teach
them,
then their children shall also sit
upon your throne forever."
13 For the LORD has chosen Zion;
He has desired it for His dwelling:
14 "This is My resting place forever;
here I will dwell, for I have chosen it.

15 I will abundantly bless her provisions;
I will satisfy her poor with bread.
16 I will also clothe her priests with salvation,
and her godly ones shall shout for joy.

17 "There I will make a horn sprout for David;
I have prepared a lamp for My anointed one.
18 His enemies I will clothe with shame,
but on him his crown will shine."

PSALM 133

A Song of Ascents. Of David.

1 Behold, how good and how pleasant it is
for brothers to dwell together in unity!

2 It is like precious oil upon the head,
that runs down on the beard—
even Aaron's beard—
and going down to the collar of his garments;
3 as the dew of Hermon,
that descends upon the mountains of Zion,
for there the LORD has commanded the blessing,
even life forever.

PSALM 134

A Song of Ascents.

1 Come, bless the LORD, all you servants of the LORD,
who by night stand in the house of the LORD.
2 Lift up your hands in the sanctuary,
and bless the LORD.
3 May the LORD who made heaven and earth
bless you from Zion.

PSALM 135

Ps 115:4–11

1 Praise the LORD!

Praise the name of the LORD
praise Him, O servants of the LORD,
2 you who stand in the house of the LORD,
in the courts of the house of our God!

3 Praise the LORD, for the LORD is good;
sing praises unto His name, for it is pleasant.
4 For the LORD has chosen Jacob for Himself,
and Israel for His special possession.

5 For I know that the LORD is great,
and that our Lord is above all gods.
6 Whatever the LORD pleases,
He does in heaven and on earth,
in the seas and all the depths.
7 He causes the clouds to ascend from the ends of the earth;
He makes lightning for the rain;
He brings the wind out from His storehouses.

8 He struck down the firstborn of Egypt,
both of man and animal.
9 He sent signs and wonders into your midst, O Egypt,
against Pharaoh and all his servants;
10 He struck down great nations
and slew mighty kings—
11 Sihon, king of the Amorites,
and Og king of Bashan,
and all the kingdoms of Canaan—
12 and gave their land for an inheritance,
a possession to Israel His people.

13 Your name, O LORD, endures forever;
and Your renown, O LORD, throughout all generations.
14 For the LORD will defend His people,
and He will have compassion on His servants.

15 The idols of the nations are silver and gold,
the work of men's hands.
16 They have mouths, but do not speak;
they have eyes, but do not see;
17 they have ears, but do not hear;
neither is there any breath in their mouths.
18 Those who make them are like them;
so is everyone who trusts in them.

19 Bless the LORD, O house of Israel;
bless the LORD, O house of Aaron.
20 Bless the LORD, O house of Levi;
you who fear the LORD, bless the LORD.
21 Blessed be the LORD from Zion,
who dwells at Jerusalem.

Praise you the LORD!

PSALM 136

1 Oh, give thanks unto the LORD, for He is good,
for His mercy endures forever.
2 Oh, give thanks unto the God of gods,
for His mercy endures forever.
3 Oh, give thanks to the Lord of lords,
for His mercy endures forever:

4 to Him who alone does great wonders,
for His mercy endures forever;
5 to Him who by wisdom made the heavens,
for His mercy endures forever;
6 to Him who stretched out the earth above the waters,
for His mercy endures forever;
7 to Him who made the great *heavenly* lights,
for His mercy endures forever;

132:15 Ps 147:14
132:16 2Ch 6:41
132:17 1Ki 11:36
132:18 Job 8:22
133:1 Ge 13:8
133:2 Lev 8:12
133:3 Lev 25:21
134:1 1Ch 9:33
134:2 Ps 28:2
134:3 Ps 128:5
135:1 Ps 134:1
135:2 Ps 92:13
135:3 Ps 147:1
135:4 Dt 10:15
135:5 Ps 48:1
135:6 Ps 115:3

....

135:7 Jer 10:13
135:8 Ps 78:51
135:9 Ps 136:15
135:10 Ps 136:17–22
135:11 Jos 12:7–24
135:12 Ps 78:55
135:13 Ex 3:15
135:14 Dt 32:36
135:15 Ps 115:4–8
135:21 Ps 134:3
136:1 Ps 106:1
136:2 Dt 10:17
136:4 Ps 72:18
136:5 Ge 1:1
136:6 Ps 24:2

8 the sun to rule over the day,
for His mercy endures forever;
9 the moon and stars to rule over the night,
for His mercy endures forever;
10 to Him who struck down in Egypt their firstborn,
for His mercy endures forever;
11 and brought out Israel from among them,
for His mercy endures forever;
12 with a strong hand and a stretched-out arm,
for His mercy endures forever;
13 to Him who divided the Red Sea into two,
for His mercy endures forever;
14 and made Israel to pass through the midst of it,
for His mercy endures forever;
15 but overthrew Pharaoh and his host in the Red Sea,
for His mercy endures forever;
16 to Him who led His people through the wilderness,
for His mercy endures forever;
17 to Him who struck down great kings,
for His mercy endures forever;
18 and slew mighty kings,
for His mercy endures forever;
19 Sihon king of the Amorites,
for His mercy endures forever;
20 and Og king of Bashan,
for His mercy endures forever;
21 and gave their land for a possession,
for His mercy endures forever;
22 even an inheritance to Israel His servant,
for His mercy endures forever.

23 Who remembered us in our low place,
for His mercy endures forever;
24 and has redeemed us from our enemies,
for His mercy endures forever;
25 who gives food to all people,
for His mercy endures forever.
26 Give thanks unto the God of heaven,
for His mercy endures forever.

PSALM 137

1 By the rivers of Babylon, there we sat down and wept
when we remembered Zion.
2 We hung our harps
upon the poplars.
3 For there our captors made us sing
and our tormentors made us entertain,
saying, "Sing us one of the songs of Zion."
4 How shall we sing the song of the LORD
in a foreign land?
5 If I forget you, O Jerusalem,
let my right hand forget its skill.
6 If I do not remember you,
let my tongue stick to the roof of my mouth,
if I do not have Jerusalem
as my highest joy.

7 Remember, O LORD, the people of Edom
in the day of Jerusalem,
who said, "Raze it, raze it,
down to its foundations."

8 O daughter of Babylon, who is to be destroyed,
blessed is the one who rewards you
as you have done to us.
9 Blessed is the one who takes
and dashes your little ones against the rocks.

136:10 Ex 12:29 **136:11** Ex 12:51 **136:13** Ps 78:13 **136:14** Ex 14:22 **136:15** Ps 78:53 **136:16** Ex 13:18 **136:17** Ps 135:10–12 **136:20** Nu 21:33 **136:24** Ps 107:2 **136:25** Ps 104:27 **137:1** Eze 1:1

137:6 Eze 3:26 **137:7** Jer 49:7–22 **137:8** Rev 18:6 **137:9** Isa 13:16 **138:1** Ps 111:1 **138:2** Ps 5:7 **138:4** Ps 102:15 **138:5** Ps 21:5 **138:6** Pr 3:34 **138:7** Ps 60:5 **138:8** Ps 57:2 **139:1** Ps 17:3

PSALM 138

A Psalm of David.

1 I will praise You, O LORD, with my whole heart;
before the gods I will sing Your praise.
2 I will worship toward Your holy temple,
and praise Your name
for Your lovingkindness and for Your truth;
for You have exalted Your word
above all Your name.
3 On the day I called, You answered me,
and strengthened me in my soul.

4 All the kings of the earth shall praise You, O LORD,
for they have heard the words of Your mouth.
5 Indeed, they shall sing of the ways of the LORD,
for great is the glory of the LORD.

6 Though the LORD is exalted, yet He has concern for the lowly,
but the proud one He knows from a distance.
7 Though I walk in the midst of trouble,
You will preserve me;
You stretch forth Your hand against the wrath of my enemies,
and Your right hand saves me.
8 The LORD will fulfill His purpose for me;
Your mercy, O LORD, endures forever;
do not forsake the works of Your hands.

PSALM 139

For the Music Director. A Psalm of David.

1 O LORD, You have searched me
and known me.

SPIRITLED WOMAN

COUNSEL FROM THE SPIRIT BASICS

His Inescapable Presence

God's presence—His Spirit—is inescapable! God is passionate about being near us. He wants us to encounter Him. That is why Jesus went to the cross—so mankind would never have to be separated from God's love or His presence. Heaven is motivated by a desire to love and connect with humanity. In Psalm 139:13–16 we see how present, how near, how involved God is with each person while he or she is still in the womb. He personally weaves together each intricate part of who we are in the secret place.

Not only that, but God also writes a story for each one of us before we're ever born. He dreams up a beautiful story for our life while shaping us in the quiet dark of the womb. That is amazing! I tell people all the time, "Boredom is a choice." If you're bored in your life, that is not God's fault. God—the ultimate Creator, the King of creativity—has dreamed up an amazing, adventurous love journey for you, and He wrote this amazing story for you while you were still in your mother's womb.

Jennifer Toledo

2 You know when I sit down and when I get
up;
You understand my thought from far off.
3 You search my path and my lying down
and are aware of all my ways.
4 For there is not a word on my tongue,
but behold, O LORD, You know it fully.

God knows absolutely every little detail about me (Ps 139).

5 You put Yourself behind and before me,
and keep Your hand on me.
6 Such knowledge is too wonderful for me;
it is lofty, and I cannot fathom it.
7 Where shall I go from Your spirit,
or where shall I flee from Your presence?
8 If I ascend to heaven, You are there;
if I make my bed in Sheol, You are there.
9 If I take the wings of the morning
and dwell at the end of the sea,
10 even there Your hand shall guide me,
and Your right hand shall take hold of
me.

God's presence—His Spirit—is inescapable (Ps 139:7, 10)

11 If I say, "Surely the darkness shall
cover me,
and the light shall be as night
about me,"
12 even the darkness is not dark to You,
but the night shines as the day,
for the darkness is like light to You.
13 You brought my inner parts into being;
You wove me in my mother's womb.
14 I will praise you, for You made me with
fear and wonder;
marvelous are Your works,
and You know me completely.
15 My frame was not hidden from You
when I was made in secret,
and intricately put together in the lowest
parts of the earth.
16 Your eyes saw me unformed,
yet in Your book
all my days were written,
before any of them came into being.
17 How precious also are Your thoughts to
me, O God!

He personally weaves together each intricate part of who I am in the secret place (Ps 139:13–16).

How great is the sum of them!
18 If I should count them,
they are more in number than the sand;
when I awake,
I am still with You.

I am the object of His love and affection (Ps 139:18).

19 If only You would slay the wicked, O God!
O violent men, depart from me.
20 For they speak against You with malice,
and Your enemies take your *name* in
vain.
21 Do I not hate those, O LORD, who hate You?
And do I not abhor those who rise up
against You?

139:2 2Ki 19:27
139:3 Job 31:4
139:6 Job 42:3
139:7 Jnh 1:3
139:8 Job 26:6
139:10 Ps 23:3
139:12 Job 34:22
139:14 Ge 1:26–27
139:15 Ps 63:9
139:16 Ps 56:8
139:17 Ps 40:5
139:18 Ps 3:5
139:19 Isa 11:4
139:20 Jude 1:15
139:21 Ps 119:158

Mining the Greatness

Precious metals and precious stones are embedded in rocks and have to be extracted. Metals especially don't generally appear in nature in their pure form. Shafts and tunnels are cut into the earth. The rock is quarried and then smelted with heat to remove the dross from the ore. It's a difficult, tedious process, and it takes time and effort. The results, however, are certainly worth the effort to tap those precious veins beneath the earth.

In the same way, our children's gifts are sometimes buried deep. It's up to us to mine the gift in them, extract it, and allow it to be shaped and polished to be useful in building the kingdom of God. The effort requires selfless dedication on our part and an investment of time and finances, but it's one that pays lifelong dividends in the life of your child.

What is God showing you about your child? What traits is your child expressing? What most interests or intrigues him? Is he outgoing or introspective? Is he intellectual or athletic? Is he artistic and creative or mechanically minded and good with his hands? And what are the dreams you have inside for him? Do you have a knowing deep inside about his life? Has God given you a glimpse into his future? What do you see when you pray for him?

I believe it's my job to find out who God made my child to be. What particular path has He set for him? What's unique about his personality, gifts, talents, and aspirations? How do I help him find the life God has already planned for him? What is God's purpose for his life, and how do I train him to accomplish his purpose?

Psalm 139:13–16 says it so beautifully:

> You brought my inner parts into being; You wove me in my mother's womb. I will praise You, for You made me with fear and wonder; marvelous are Your works, and You know me completely. My frame was not hidden from You when I was made in secret, and intricately put together in the lowest parts of the earth. Your eyes saw me unformed, yet in Your book all my days were written, before any of them came into being.

He knows our paths and has already written them in His book!

I don't claim to be an expert in child rearing, but I am an expert in raising my child, just as you are an expert in raising your child. The fact is, no one knows your child better than you, and as your child grows and develops, his gifts and talents will be more obvious to you than anyone else.

I firmly believe God shows parents from the time their kids are small what He has invested in them. He shows us their bent, and our job is to dig deep and find the depth of the gifts and callings buried inside. It is important we are not too busy or distracted with life to see what God is eager to reveal to us in each of our children.

Kate Battistelli

22 I hate them with perfect hatred;
I count them my enemies.

23 Search me, O God, and know my heart;
try me, and know my concerns,
24 and see if there is any rebellious way
in me,
and lead me in the ancient way.

PSALM 140

For the Music Director. A Psalm of David.

1 Deliver me, O LORD, from evil men;
protect me from violent men,
2 who plan evil deeds in their heart
and continually gather together for
conflicts.
3 They have tongues as sharp as a serpent;
adders' poison is with their lips. Selah

4 Keep me, O LORD, from the hands of the
wicked;
preserve me from the violent men
who have planned to overthrow me.
5 The proud have hid a snare for me,
and with cords they have spread a net;
they have set traps for me. Selah

6 I said to the LORD, "You are my God;
hear the voice of my supplications,
O LORD."
7 O GOD my Lord, the strength of my
salvation,
You have covered my head in the day of
battle.
8 Grant not, O LORD, the desires of the
wicked;
do not allow his evil plot,
lest he be raised up. Selah

9 As for the head of those who
encompass me,
let the mischief of their own lips
overwhelm them;
10 let burning coals fall upon them;
let them be cast into the fire,
into deep pits that they do not rise up
again.
11 Let not an evil speaker be established in
the land;
let evil hunt the violent man to
overthrow him!

12 I know that the LORD will maintain the
cause of the afflicted
and will give justice to the poor.
13 Surely the righteous shall give thanks unto
Your name;
the upright shall dwell in Your presence.

139:23 Ps 26:2
139:24 Ps 5:8
140:1 Ps 18:48
140:2 Ps 56:6
140:3 Ps 58:4
140:4 Ps 71:4
140:5 Ps 35:7
140:6 Ps 16:2
140:7 Ps 144:10
140:9 Ps 7:16
140:10 Ps 11:6
140:11 Ps 34:21
140:12 Ps 9:4

141:1 Ps 70:5
141:2 Rev 5:8
141:3 Mic 7:5
141:4 Ps 119:36
141:5 Pr 19:25
141:7 Ps 53:5
141:9 Ps 140:5
141:10 Ps 35:8
142:2 Isa 26:16
142:3 Ps 140:5
142:4 Ps 31:11

PSALM 141

A Psalm of David.

1 LORD, I cry unto You; make haste to me;
give ear to my voice, when I cry unto
You.
2 Let my prayer be set forth before You as
incense,
and the lifting up of my hands as the
evening sacrifice.

3 Set a guard, O LORD, over my mouth;
keep watch over the door of my lips.
4 Do not let my heart be drawn to any evil,
to practice wicked deeds
with men who do iniquity,
and do not let me eat of their delights.

5 Let the righteous man strike me;
it shall be a kindness.
Let him rebuke me;
it shall be oil for my head;
let my head not refuse it.
For my prayer is continually against
their evil deeds.

6 When their judges are thrown to stony
places,
then they shall hear my words, for they
are sweet.
7 As when one plows to break up the land,
so our bones are scattered at the mouth
of Sheol.

8 But my eyes are unto You, O GOD my Lord,
in You is my trust; do not leave my soul
defenseless.
9 Keep me from the snares that they have
laid for me,
and the traps of those who do iniquity.
10 Let the wicked fall into their own nets,
while I pass by and escape.

PSALM 142

A Contemplative Maskil of David, when
he was in the cave. A Prayer.

1 I cried unto the LORD with my voice;
with my voice I made my supplication
unto the LORD.
2 I poured out my complaint before Him;
I declared to Him my trouble.

3 When my spirit was overwhelmed within
me,
then You knew my path.
In the way where I walk,
they have laid a snare for me.
4 I looked on my right and noticed,
but there was no one who would care
for me;

there is no refuge for me;
no one cares for my soul.
5 I cried unto You, O LORD;
I said, "You are my refuge
and my portion in the land of the living."
6 Attend to my cry,
for I am brought very low;
deliver me from my persecutors,
for they are stronger than me.
7 Bring my soul out of prison,
that I may praise Your name;
the righteous shall surround me,
for You shall deal bountifully with me.

PSALM 143

A Psalm of David.

1 Hear my prayer, O LORD,
give ear to my supplications;
in Your faithfulness answer me,
and in Your righteousness.
2 Enter not into judgment with Your servant,
for in Your sight no one living is
righteous.
3 For the enemy has persecuted my soul;
he has crushed my life down to the
ground;
he has made me to dwell in darkness,
as those who have been long dead.
4 Therefore my spirit is overwhelmed within
me;
my heart within me is desolate.
5 I remember the days of old;
I meditate on all Your works;
I consider the work of Your hands.
6 I stretch forth my hands unto You;
my soul thirsts after You as a thirsty land.
Selah
7 Respond to me quickly, O LORD,
my spirit fails;
do not hide Your face from me,
lest I be like those who go down into
the pit.
8 Cause me to hear Your lovingkindness in
the morning;
for in You I have my trust;
cause me to know the way I should walk,
for I lift up my soul unto You.
9 Deliver me, O LORD, from my enemies;
I flee unto You for my protection.
10 Teach me to do Your will,
for You are my God;
may Your good spirit
lead me onto level ground.
11 Revive me, O LORD, for Your name's sake,
for Your righteousness' sake bring my
soul out of trouble.

142:5 Ps 16:5
142:6 Ps 79:8
142:7 Ps 13:6
143:1 Ps 71:2
143:2 Ecc 7:20
143:3 Ps 88:4–6
143:4 Ps 77:3
143:6 Ps 63:1
143:7 Ps 69:17
143:8 Ps 27:11
143:10 Ne 9:20
143:11 Ps 31:1

....

143:12 Ps 54:5
144:1 Ps 18:2
144:2 Ps 18:2
144:3 Ps 8:4
144:4 Ps 102:11
144:5 Ps 18:9
144:7 Ps 18:16
144:8 Ps 12:2
144:9 Ps 33:2–3
144:10 Ps 18:50
144:12 Ps 128:3

12 In Your mercy cut off my enemies,
and destroy all them who afflict my soul,
for I am Your servant.

PSALM 144

A Psalm of David.

1 Blessed be the LORD my strength,
who prepares my hands for war,
and my fingers to fight;
2 my goodness, and my fortress;
my high tower, and my deliverer,
my shield, and in whom I trust;
who subdues nations under me.
3 O LORD, who is man that You take notice of
him
or the son of a man that You make
account of him?
4 Man is like a breath;
his days are as a shadow that passes
away.
5 Bow your heavens, O LORD, and come
down;
touch the mountains, and they shall
smoke.
6 Cast forth lightning, and scatter them;
shoot out Your arrows, and destroy
them.
7 Send Your hand from above;
rescue me, and deliver me
out of the great waters,
from the hand of foreigners,
8 whose mouth speaks lies,
and their right hand is a right hand of
falsehood.
9 I will sing a new song unto You, O God,
on a harp and an instrument of ten
strings I will sing praises unto You;
10 it is He who gives victory to kings,
who delivers David His servant from the
cruel sword.
11 Rescue me and deliver me
from the hand of foreigners,
whose mouths speak lies
and whose right hand is a right hand of
falsehood.
12 May our sons in their youth
be like plants full grown,
and our daughters like cornerstones,
cut in the similitude of a palace,
13 that our granaries may be full,
providing all manner of produce,
that our sheep may bring forth
thousands and ten thousands in our
fields,
14 and may our cattle be strong in labor.
May there be no breaking in

or going out,
and no wailing in our streets.
15 Blessed are the people who have such things;
indeed, blessed are the people whose God is the LORD.

PSALM 145

A Psalm of Praise. Of David.

1 I will exalt you, my God and King,
and I will bless Your name forever and ever.
2 Every day I will bless You,
and I will praise Your name forever and ever.
3 Great is the LORD, and greatly to be praised,
and His greatness is unfathomable.
4 One generation shall praise Your works to another
and shall declare Your mighty acts.
5 I will speak of the glorious honor of Your majesty
and of Your wondrous works.
6 They shall speak of the might of Your awesome acts,
and I will declare Your greatness.
7 They shall abundantly declare the fame of Your great goodness
and shall sing of Your righteousness.

8 The LORD is gracious and full of compassion,
slow to anger, and great in mercy.

9 The LORD is good to all,
and His compassion is over all His works.
10 All Your works shall praise You, O LORD,
and Your godly ones shall bless You.
11 They shall speak of the glory of Your kingdom
and talk of Your power,
12 to make known to people His mighty acts,
and the glorious majesty of His kingdom.
13 Your kingdom is an everlasting kingdom,
and Your dominion endures throughout all generations.

14 The LORD upholds all who fall,
and raises up all who are bowed down.
15 The eyes of all wait upon You,
and You give them their food in due season.
16 You open Your hand
and satisfy the desire of every living thing.
17 The LORD is righteous in all His ways
and loving in all His works.

144:15 Ps 33:12
145:1 Ps 30:1
145:3 Job 5:9
145:4 Isa 38:19
145:7 Isa 63:7
145:8 Ps 86:15
145:10 Ps 19:1
145:12 Ps 105:1
145:13 1Ti 1:17
145:14 Ps 37:24
145:15 Ps 104:27
145:16 Ps 104:28
....
145:18 Dt 4:7
145:19 Ps 37:4
145:20 Ps 97:10
145:21 Ps 71:8
146:1 Ps 103:1
146:2 Ps 104:33
146:3 Isa 2:22
146:4 Ecc 12:7
146:5 Ps 144:15
146:6 Rev 14:7
146:7 Ps 68:6
146:8 Mt 9:30
146:9 Ps 68:5
146:10 Ps 10:16
147:1 Ps 33:1
147:2 Dt 30:3
147:3 Isa 61:1

18 The LORD is near to all those who call upon Him,
to all who call upon Him in truth.
19 He will fulfill the desire of those who fear Him;
He also will hear their cry and will save them.
20 The LORD preserves all those who love Him,
but all the wicked He will destroy.

21 My mouth shall speak the praise of the LORD,
and let all people bless His holy name forever and ever.

PSALM 146

1 Praise the LORD!

Praise the LORD, O my soul!

2 While I live I will praise the LORD;
I will sing praises unto my God while I have my life.
3 Do not put your trust in princes,
nor in a son of man, in whom there is no help.
4 His breath leaves him, and he returns to the earth;
on that very day his plans perish.

5 Blessed is he who has the God of Jacob for his help,
whose hope is in the LORD his God,
6 who made heaven, and earth,
the sea, and all that is in them,
who keeps faithfulness forever,
7 who executes justice for the oppressed,
who gives food to the hungry.
The LORD releases the prisoners.
8 The LORD opens the eyes of the blind;
the LORD raises those who are brought down;
the LORD loves the righteous.
9 The LORD preserves the sojourners;
He lifts up the fatherless and widow,
but on the way of the wicked He brings disaster.

10 The LORD shall reign forever,
your God, O Zion, unto all generations.

Praise you the LORD!

PSALM 147

1 Praise the LORD!

For it is good to sing praises unto our God;
for it is pleasant, and a song of praise is fitting.

2 The LORD builds up Jerusalem;
He gathers together the outcasts of Israel.
3 He heals the broken in heart,

and binds up their wounds.
4 He counts the number of the stars;
He calls them all by their names.
5 Great is our Lord and great in power;
His understanding is without measure.
6 The LORD lifts up the meek;
He casts the wicked down to the ground.

7 Sing unto the LORD with thanksgiving;
sing praise upon the harp unto our God:
8 who covers the heaven with clouds,
who provides rain for the earth,
who makes grass to grow upon the mountains.
9 He gives food to the animals
and to the young ravens that chirp.

10 He delights not in the strength of the horse,
nor does He take pleasure in the legs of a man,
11 but the LORD takes pleasure in those who fear Him,
in those who hope in His mercy.

12 Praise the LORD, O Jerusalem;
praise your God, O Zion.

13 For He has strengthened the bars of your gates;
He has blessed your children within you.
14 He makes peace in your borders,
and fills you with the finest of the wheat.

15 He sends forth His commandment on the earth;
His word goes out swiftly.
16 He gives snow like wool;
He scatters the frost like ashes;
17 He casts forth His ice like morsels;
who can stand before His cold?
18 He sends out His word and melts them;
He causes His wind to blow and the waters flow.

19 He shows His word to Jacob,
and His statutes and His judgments to Israel.
20 He has not dealt so with any other nation;
they have not known His judgments.

Praise the LORD!

PSALM 148

1 Praise the LORD!

Praise the LORD from the heavens;
praise Him in the heights.
2 Praise Him, all His angels;
praise Him, all His heavenly hosts.
3 Praise Him, sun and moon;
praise Him, all you stars of light.
4 Praise Him, you highest of heavens,
and you waters that are above the skies.

147:4 Isa 40:26
147:5 Isa 40:28
147:6 Ps 146:8–9
147:7 Ps 95:1–2
147:8 Job 5:10
147:9 Job 38:41
147:10 1Sa 16:7
147:11 Ps 33:18
147:14 Isa 60:17–18
147:15 Job 37:12
147:16 Job 37:6
147:19 Mal 4:4
147:20 Dt 4:32–34
148:2 Ps 103:20–21
148:4 Ge 1:7
148:5 Ge 1:6
148:6 Jer 33:25
148:7 Ge 1:21
148:8 Ps 147:15–18
148:9 Isa 44:23
148:11 Ps 102:15
148:13 Ps 8:1
148:14 1Sa 2:1
149:1 Ps 33:3
149:2 Zec 9:9
149:3 Ex 15:20
149:4 Ps 35:27
149:5 Job 35:10
149:6 Heb 4:12
149:9 Ps 148:14

5 Let them praise the name of the LORD,
for He commanded, and they were created.
6 He has also established them forever and ever;
He has made a decree that shall not pass away.

7 Praise the LORD from the earth,
you great sea creatures, and all you depths,
8 fire and hail, snow and mist,
storming wind fulfilling His word,
9 mountains and all hills,
fruitful trees and all cedars;
10 animals and all cattle,
creeping things and flying birds;
11 kings of the earth and all peoples,
princes and all rulers of the earth;
12 both young men and maidens,
old men and children.

13 Let them praise the name of the LORD,
for His name alone is excellent;
His glory is above the earth and heaven.
14 He has raised up a *victory* horn for His people,
praise for all His saints,
even for the people of Israel near Him.

Praise the LORD!

PSALM 149

1 Praise the LORD!

Sing unto the LORD a new song,
and His praise in the assembly of the godly ones.

2 Let Israel rejoice in its Maker;
let the children of Zion be joyful in their King.
3 Let them praise His name with dancing;
let them sing praises unto Him with the tambourine and harp.
4 For the LORD takes pleasure in His people;
He will beautify the meek with salvation.
5 Let the godly ones be joyful in glory;
let them sing for joy on their beds.

6 Let the high praises of God be in their mouths,
and two-edged swords in their hands,
7 to execute vengeance on the nations,
and punishments on the peoples;
8 to bind their kings with chains,
and their nobles with shackles of iron;
9 to execute upon them the written judgment;
this is honor for all His godly ones.

Praise the LORD!

PSALM 150

1 Praise the LORD!

Praise God in His sanctuary;
praise Him in the firmament of His power!
2 Praise Him for His mighty acts;
praise Him according to His excellent greatness!
3 Praise Him with the sound of the trumpet;
praise Him with the lyre and harp!
4 Praise Him with the tambourine and dancing;
praise Him with stringed instruments and flute!
5 Praise Him with loud cymbals;
praise Him with the clanging cymbals!

6 Let everything that has breath praise the LORD.

Praise the LORD!

150:1 Ps 134:2
150:2 Dt 3:24
150:3 Ps 33:2

150:4 Ps 149:3
150:5 1Ch 15:16

Author: King Solomon, King Lemuel, Agur, and Others

Written: 900 BC

Themes: Wisdom for Daily Living, Virtue

PROVERBS

Dear Spirit-Led Woman,

I love to read Proverbs because of its practical wisdom and timeless truth. One of its most well-known passages is, "Trust in the LORD with all your heart, and lean not on your own understanding; in all your ways acknowledge Him, and He will direct your paths" (Pr 3:5–6).

I remember when I learned the truth of these verses the hard way. One day while I was driving, I asked the Lord to show me anything that was a hindrance to knowing Him. The presence of God filled my car, and rather than revealing some forgotten sin or offense, the Holy Spirit said, "Your independence is a stench to Me." Even though I had always been quick to seek God's intervention in circumstances beyond my control, I am independent by nature, and without realizing it I had always tried to handle the bulk of my life situations on my own. I came to understand that God didn't want me to wait until I had run out of my own resources to put things in His hands; He wanted me to depend on Him for everything. If we desire to be truly led by the Spirit, we are to depend not on ourselves but on Him.

Joy F. Strang

The Purpose and Theme

1 The proverbs of Solomon, the son of David, king of Israel:

2 To know wisdom and instruction,
to perceive the words of understanding,

I will know wisdom and instruction
(Pr 1:2).

3 to receive the instruction of wisdom,
justice, judgment, and equity;
4 to give subtlety to the simple,
to the young man knowledge and
discretion—
5 a wise man will hear and will increase
learning,
and a man of understanding will attain
wise counsel,
6 to understand a proverb and the
interpretation,
the words of the wise and their riddles.
7 The fear of the LORD is the beginning of
knowledge,
but fools despise wisdom and
instruction.

The Prologue: Embrace Wisdom

8 My son, hear the instruction of your father,
and do not forsake the teaching of your
mother;
9 for they will be a garland of grace on your
head,
and chains about your neck.

10 My son, if sinners entice you,
do not consent.
11 If they say, "Come with us,
let us lie in wait for blood;
let us lurk secretly for the innocent
without cause;
12 let us swallow them up alive as the grave,
and whole, as those who go down into
the pit;
13 we will find all kinds of precious
possessions;
we will fill our houses with spoil;
14 cast in your lot among us,
let us all have one purse"—
15 my son, do not walk in the way with them,
keep your foot from their path;
16 for their feet run to evil
and make haste to shed blood.
17 Surely in vain the net is spread
in the sight of any bird.
18 They lie in wait for their own blood;
they lurk secretly for their own lives.
19 So are the ways of everyone who is greedy
of gain,
which takes away the life of its owners.

The Call of Wisdom

20 Wisdom cries out in the street;
she utters her voice in the markets.
21 She cries at the corner of the streets, in the
openings of the gates;
she speaks her words in the city, saying:

22 "How long, you simple ones, will you love
simplicity?
For the scorners delight in their
scorning,
and fools hate knowledge.
23 Turn at my reproof;
surely I will pour out my spirit on you;
I will make my words known to you.
24 Because I have called and you refused,
I have stretched out my hand and no
man regarded,
25 because you neglected all my counsel,
and would have none of my reproof,
26 I also will laugh at your calamity;
I will mock when your fear comes,
27 when your fear comes as desolation
and your destruction comes as a
whirlwind,
when distress and anguish come upon
you.
28 "Then they will call on me, but I will not
answer;
they will seek me early, but they will not
find me.
29 Because they hated knowledge
and did not choose the fear of the LORD,
30 they would have none of my counsel
and despised all my reproof.
31 Therefore they will eat of the fruit of their
own way,
and be filled with their own devices.
32 For the turning away of the simple will slay
them,
and the prosperity of fools will destroy
them.
33 But whoever listens to me will dwell safely,
and will be secure from fear of evil."

The Value of Wisdom

2 My son, if you will receive my words,
and hide my commandments within
you,
2 so that you incline your ear to wisdom,
and apply your heart to understanding;
3 yes, if you cry out for knowledge,
and lift up your voice for understanding,
4 if you seek her as silver,

1:1 Pr 10:1
1:4 Pr 8:5
1:5 Pr 9:9
1:6 Ps 78:2
1:7 Pr 9:10
1:8 Pr 6:20
1:9 Pr 4:9
1:10 Eph 5:11
1:11 Pr 1:18
1:12 Ps 28:1
1:15 Ps 1:1
1:16 Pr 6:18
....
1:19 Pr 15:27
1:20 Pr 9:3
1:22 Ps 1:1
1:23 Joel 2:28
1:24 Isa 65:12
1:25 Ps 107:11
1:26 Ps 2:4
1:28 Job 27:9
1:29 Pr 1:22
1:30 Pr 1:25
1:31 Job 4:8
1:32 Jer 2:19
1:33 Ps 25:12–13
2:4 Mt 13:44

and search for her as for hidden
treasures,
5 then you will understand the fear of the
LORD,
and find the knowledge of God.
6 For the LORD gives wisdom;
out of His mouth come knowledge and
understanding.
7 He lays up sound wisdom for the
righteous;
He is a shield to those who walk
uprightly.
8 He keeps the paths of justice,
and preserves the way of His saints.

9 Then you will understand righteousness
and judgment
and equity, and every good path.
10 When wisdom enters your heart,
and knowledge is pleasant to your soul,
11 discretion will preserve you;
understanding will keep you,
12 to deliver you from the way of the evil
man,
from the man who speaks perverse
things,
13 from those who leave the paths of
uprightness
to walk in the ways of darkness;
14 who rejoice to do evil,
and delight in the perversity of the
wicked;
15 whose ways are crooked,
and who are devious in their paths;
16 to deliver you from the immoral woman,
even from the seductress who flatters
with her words,
17 who forsakes the guide of her youth,
and forgets the covenant of her God.
18 For her house leads down to death,
and her paths to the departed spirits;
19 none who go to her return again,
nor do they take hold of the paths of life.

20 So you may walk in the way of good men
and keep the paths of the righteous.
21 For the upright will dwell in the land,
and the innocent will remain in it;
22 but the wicked will be cut off from the
earth,
and the transgressors will be rooted out
of it.

The Rewards of Wisdom

3 My son, do not forget my teaching,
but let your heart keep my
commandments;
2 for length of days and long life
and peace will they add to you.

2:6 1Ki 3:12
2:7 Ps 84:11
2:8 1Sa 2:9
2:11 Pr 4:6
2:13 Pr 4:19
2:14 Pr 10:23
2:15 Ps 125:5
2:16 Pr 6:24
2:17 Jer 3:4
2:19 Ecc 7:26
2:20 Heb 6:12
2:21 Ps 37:29
2:22 Ps 52:5
3:1 Pr 4:5
3:2 Pr 4:10

3:3 Pr 7:3
3:4 Ps 111:10
3:5 Ps 37:3
3:6 1Ch 28:9
3:7 Job 1:1
3:8 Job 21:24
3:9 Ex 23:19
3:10 Dt 28:8
3:11 Job 5:17
3:12 Dt 8:5
3:14 Pr 8:19
3:15 Pr 8:11
3:16 Pr 3:2
3:18 Ge 2:9
3:19 Ps 104:24
3:20 Ge 7:11

3 Do not let mercy and truth forsake you;
bind them around your neck,
write them on the tablet of your heart,
4 so you will find favor and good
understanding
in the sight of God and man.

Every day I learn more of what it means to trust Him with *all* my heart (Pr 3:5).

5 Trust in the LORD with all your heart,
and lean not on your own
understanding;
6 in all your ways acknowledge Him,
and He will direct your paths.
7 Do not be wise in your own eyes;
fear the LORD and depart from evil.
8 It will be health to your body,
and strength to your bones.
9 Honor the LORD with your substance,
and with the first fruits of all your
increase;
10 so your barns will be filled with plenty,
and your presses will burst out with new
wine.

11 My son, do not despise the chastening of
the LORD,
nor be weary of His correction;
12 for whom the LORD loves He corrects,
even as a father the son in whom he
delights.

13 Happy is the man who finds wisdom,
and the man who gets understanding;
14 for her benefit is more profitable than
silver,
and her gain than *fine* gold.
15 She is more precious than rubies,
and all the things you may desire are not
to be compared with her.
16 Length of days is in her right hand,
and in her left hand riches and honor.
17 Her ways are ways of pleasantness,
and all her paths are peace.
18 She is a tree of life to those who take hold
of her,
and happy is everyone who retains her.

19 The LORD by wisdom has founded the
earth;
by understanding He has established the
heavens;
20 by His knowledge the depths are broken
up,
and the clouds drop down the dew.

SPIRITLED WOMAN

COUNSEL FROM THE SPIRIT BASICS

Communicate Love and Commitment to Your Children

Build up your children. Leave an inheritance of peace, joy, kindness, love, words of blessing, sound counsel, and admonition. Compliment them when they do something well. Affirm them. Take time to say that you love them dearly.

Bless your children every day. Place your hand upon their heads and speak words of blessing. Enjoy the weekends, holidays, and vacations. Never go to bed angry with them.

Ask God to help you be a great and loving mom. Lighten up! Don't be so serious. Smile, laugh, sing, and goof off with your kids. Take them to the park and ball games. Act silly sometimes.

Speak God's Word over your children all the time. Begin by speaking God's Word into your own life. The Word is like medicine—it heals (Pr 4:20–22).

Every time you plan something with your family, think *inheritance* and make memories that will never be forgotten.

Iris Delgado

21 My son, let them not depart from your
eyes—
keep sound wisdom and discretion;
22 so they will be life to your soul
and grace to your neck.
23 Then you will walk safely in your way,
and your foot will not stumble.
24 When you lie down, you will not be afraid;
yes, you will lie down and your sleep
will be sweet.
25 Do not be afraid of sudden terror,
nor of trouble from the wicked when it
comes;
26 for the LORD will be your confidence,
and will keep your foot from being
caught.

27 Do not withhold good from those to whom
it is due,
when it is in the power of your hand to
do it.
28 Do not say to your neighbor,
"Go, and come again, and tomorrow I
will give it,"
when you have it with you.
29 Do not devise evil against your neighbor,
seeing he dwells securely by you.
30 Do not strive with a man without cause,
if he has done you no harm.

31 Do not envy the oppressor,
and choose none of his ways;
32 for the perverse is an abomination to the
LORD,
but His secret *counsel* is with the
righteous.
33 The curse of the LORD is on the house of the
wicked,
but He blesses the habitation of the just.
34 Surely He scorns the scornful,
but He gives favor to the humble.
35 The wise will inherit glory,
but shame will be the legacy of fools.

Wisdom Is Supreme

4 Hear, O children, the instruction of a
father,
and attend to know understanding.
2 For I give you good precepts;
do not forsake my teaching.
3 For I was my father's son,
tender and the only beloved in the sight
of my mother.
4 He also taught me and said to me,
"Let your heart retain my words;
keep my commandments, and live.
5 Get wisdom! Get understanding!
Do not forget it, nor turn away from the
words of my mouth.
6 Do not forsake her, and she will preserve
you;
love her, and she will keep you.
7 Wisdom is principal; therefore get wisdom.
And with all your getting, get
understanding.
8 Exalt her, and she will promote you;
she will bring you honor, when you
embrace her.
9 She will place on your head an ornament
of grace;
a crown of glory she will deliver to you."

10 Hear, my son, and receive my sayings,
and the years of your life will be many.
11 I have taught you in the way of wisdom;
I have led you in right paths.
12 When you walk, your steps will not be
hindered,
and when you run, you will not stumble.
13 Take firm hold of instruction, do not let her
go;
keep her, for she is your life.
14 Do not enter the path of the wicked,

3:21 Pr 4:21
3:22 Pr 1:9
3:23 Pr 4:12
3:24 Ps 3:5
3:25 Ps 91:5
3:26 1Sa 2:9
3:27 Gal 6:10
3:28 Lev 19:13
....
3:29 Pr 6:14
3:31 Ps 37:1
3:32 Ps 25:14
3:33 Mal 2:2
3:34 Jas 4:6
4:1 Pr 1:8
4:2 Dt 32:2
4:3 1Ch 22:5
4:4 Pr 7:2
4:6 2Th 2:10
4:7 Mt 13:44–46
4:8 1Sa 2:30
4:9 Pr 1:9
4:10 Pr 3:2
4:12 Pr 3:23
4:13 Pr 3:18
4:14 Ps 1:1

and do not go in the way of evil men.
15 Avoid it, do not travel on it;
turn from it and pass on.
16 For they do not sleep unless they have
done mischief;
and their sleep is taken away unless they
cause some to fall.
17 For they eat the bread of wickedness
and drink the wine of violence.

18 But the path of the just is as the shining
light,
that shines more and more unto the
perfect day.
19 The way of the wicked is as darkness;
they do not know at what they stumble.

20 My son, attend to my words;
incline your ear to my sayings.
21 Do not let them depart from your eyes;
keep them in the midst of your heart;

> The Word is medicine and health to all my body (Pr 4:20–22).

22 for they are life to those who find them,
and health to all their body.
23 Keep your heart with all diligence,
for out of it are the issues of life.
24 Put away from you a deceitful mouth,
and put perverse lips far from you.
25 Let your eyes look right on,
and let your eyelids look straight before
you.
26 Ponder the path of your feet,
and let all your ways be established.
27 Do not turn to the right or to the left;
remove your foot from evil.

Warning Against Adultery

5 My son, attend to my wisdom,
and bow your ear to my understanding,
2 that you may regard discretion,
and that your lips may keep knowledge.
3 For the lips of an immoral woman drip as a
honeycomb,
and her mouth is smoother than oil.
4 But her end is bitter as wormwood,
sharp as a two-edged sword.
5 Her feet go down to death,
her steps take hold of Sheol.
6 She does not ponder the path of life;
her ways are unstable, and she does not
know it.

7 Hear me now therefore, O children,
and do not depart from the words of my
mouth.
8 Remove your way far from her,
and do not go near the door of her
house,
9 lest you give your honor to others,
and your years to the cruel;
10 lest strangers be filled with your wealth,
and your labors go to the house of a
stranger;
11 and you mourn at the last,
when your flesh and your body are
consumed,
12 and say, "How I have hated instruction,
and my heart despised reproof!
13 And I have not obeyed the voice of my
teachers,
nor inclined my ear to those who
instructed me!
14 I was almost in utter ruin
in the midst of the congregation and
assembly."

15 Drink waters out of your own cistern,
and running waters out of your own
well.
16 Should your fountains be dispersed abroad,
streams of water in the streets?
17 Let them be only your own,
and not for strangers with you.
18 Let your fountain be blessed,
and rejoice with the wife of your youth.
19 Let her be as the loving deer and pleasant
doe;
let her breasts satisfy you at all times;
and always be enraptured with her love.
20 Why should you, my son, be intoxicated by
an immoral woman,
and embrace the bosom of a seductress?
21 For the ways of man are before the eyes of
the LORD,
and He ponders all his goings.
22 His own iniquities entrap the wicked
himself,
and he is snared in the cords of his sins.
23 He will die for lack of instruction,
and in the greatness of his folly he will
go astray.

Warning Against Pledges

6 My son, if you put up a security for your
friend,
if you have shaken hands with a
stranger,
2 you are snared with the words of your
mouth;
you are taken with the words of your
mouth.
3 Do this now, my son, and deliver yourself;
when you have come into the hand of
your friend,
go and humble yourself;
plead with your friend.

4:16 Ps 36:4
4:18 2Sa 23:4
4:19 Isa 59:9–10
4:20 Pr 5:1
4:21 Pr 3:21
4:22 Pr 3:8
4:23 Lk 6:45
4:27 Dt 5:32
5:1 Pr 4:20
5:3 Ps 55:21
5:4 Ecc 7:26
5:5 Pr 7:27
5:6 Pr 4:26
5:7 Pr 4:1

....

5:12 Pr 12:1
5:16 Ps 68:26
5:18 Ecc 9:9
5:19 SS 2:9
5:21 Hos 7:2
5:22 Ps 7:15–16
5:23 Job 4:21
6:1 Pr 11:15

4 Give no sleep to your eyes,
nor slumber to your eyelids.
5 Deliver yourself as a doe from the hand of
the hunter,
and as a bird from the hand of the
fowler.

The Folly of Idleness

6 Go to the ant, you sluggard!
Consider her ways and be wise.
7 Which, having no guide,
overseer, or ruler,
8 provides her bread in the summer,
and gathers her food in the harvest.

9 How long will you sleep, O sluggard?
When will you arise out of your sleep?
10 Yet a little sleep, a little slumber,
a little folding of the hands to sleep—
11 so will your poverty come upon you like a
stalker,
and your need as an armed man.

The Wicked Man

12 A wayward person, a wicked man,
walks with a perverse mouth.
13 He winks with his eyes,
he signals with his feet,
he motions with his fingers;
14 perversity is in his heart,
he devises mischief continually, he sows
discord.
15 Therefore his calamity will come suddenly;
in a moment he will be broken without
remedy.

16 These six things the LORD hates,
yes, seven are an abomination to him:
17 a proud look,
a lying tongue,
and hands that shed innocent blood,
18 a heart that devises wicked
imaginations,
feet that are swift in running to
mischief,
19 a false witness who speaks lies,
and he who sows discord among
brethren.

Warning Against Adultery

20 My son, keep your father's commandment,
and do not forsake the instruction of
your mother.
21 Bind them continually upon your heart,
and tie them around your neck.
22 When you go, they will lead you;
when you sleep, they will keep you;
and when you awake, they will speak
with you.
23 For the commandment is a lamp, and the
law is light;

6:4 Ps 132:4
6:6 Pr 10:26
6:8 Pr 10:5
6:9 Pr 24:33–34
6:11 Pr 24:34
6:12 Pr 4:24
6:13 Ps 35:19
6:14 Mic 2:1
6:15 2Ch 36:16
6:17 Pr 12:22
6:18 Ge 6:5
6:19 Ps 27:12
6:20 Eph 6:1
6:21 Pr 3:3
6:23 Ps 119:105

....

6:24 Pr 2:16
6:25 2Ki 9:30
6:26 Pr 29:3
6:32 Pr 7:7
6:33 Pr 5:9–11
6:34 Pr 27:4
7:1 Pr 1:8
7:2 Dt 32:10
7:3 Pr 3:3
7:5 Pr 2:16
7:7 Pr 6:32

and reproofs of instruction are the way
of life,
24 to keep you from the evil woman,
from the flattery of the tongue of a
seductress.

25 Do not lust after her beauty in your heart,
nor let her allure you with her eyelids.
26 For by means of a harlot a man is reduced
to a piece of bread,
and the adulteress will prey upon his
precious life.
27 Can a man take fire in his bosom,
and his clothes not be burned?
28 Can one walk upon hot coals,
and his feet not be burned?
29 So he who goes in to his neighbor's wife;
whoever touches her will not be
innocent.
30 Men do not despise a thief if he steals
to satisfy himself when he is hungry.
31 But if he is found, he will restore sevenfold;
he will give all the substance of his
house.
32 But whoever commits adultery with a
woman lacks understanding;
he who does it destroys his own soul.
33 A wound and dishonor will he get,
and his reproach will not be wiped away.
34 For jealousy is the rage of a man;
therefore he will not spare in the day of
vengeance.
35 He will not regard any ransom,
nor will he rest content, though you give
many gifts.

Beware of the Adulteress

7 My son, keep my words,
and lay up my commandments within
you.
2 Keep my commandments and live,
and my teaching as the apple of your
eye.
3 Bind them on your fingers;
write them on the tablet of your heart.
4 Say to wisdom, "You are my sister,"
and call understanding your
kinswoman,
5 that they may keep you from the immoral
woman,
from the seductress who flatters with her
words.

6 For at the window of my house
I looked through my casement,
7 and saw among the simple ones,
I discerned among the youths,
a young man void of understanding,
8 passing through the street near her corner;
and he went the way to her house

9 in the twilight, in the evening,
in the black and dark night.

10 And there a woman met him,
with the attire of a harlot, and subtle of heart.
11 She is loud and stubborn;
her feet do not abide in her house.
12 Now she is without, now in the streets,
and lies in wait at every corner.
13 So she caught him, and kissed him;
and with an impudent face said to him:

14 "I have peace offerings with me;
this day have I paid my vows.
15 Therefore I came out to meet you,
diligently to seek your face, and I have found you.
16 I have decked my bed with coverings of tapestry,
with carved works, with fine linen of Egypt.
17 I have perfumed my bed
with myrrh, aloes, and cinnamon.
18 Come, let us take our fill of love until the morning;
let us solace ourselves with love.
19 For my husband is not at home;
he has gone on a long journey;
20 he has taken a bag of money with him,
and will come home at the day appointed."

21 With her enticing speech she caused him to yield,
with the flattering of her lips she seduced him.
22 He went after her straightway,
as an ox goes to the slaughter,
or as a fool to the correction of the stocks,
23 until a dart struck through his liver.
As a bird hastens to the snare,
he did not know that it would cost him his life.

24 Listen to me now therefore, O children,
and attend to the words of my mouth:
25 do not let your heart turn aside to her ways,
do not go astray in her paths;
26 for she has cast down many wounded,
and many strong men have been slain by her.
27 Her house is the way to Sheol,
going down to the chambers of death.

The Virtue of Wisdom

8 Does not wisdom cry out,
and understanding lift up her voice?
2 She stands on the top of high places,
by the way in the places of the paths.
3 She cries out at the gates,
at the entry of the city, at the entrance of the doors:
4 "To you, O men, I call,
and my voice is to the sons of men.
5 O you simple, understand wisdom,
and you fools, be of an understanding heart.
6 Hear, for I will speak of excellent things,
and from the opening of my lips will be right things;
7 for my mouth will speak truth,
and wickedness is an abomination to my lips.
8 All the words of my mouth are in righteousness;
there is nothing crooked or perverse in them.
9 They are all plain to him who understands,
and right to those who find knowledge.
10 Receive my instruction, and not silver,
and knowledge rather than choice gold;
11 for wisdom is better than rubies,
and all the things that may be desired are not to be compared to it.

12 "I, wisdom, dwell with prudence,
and find out knowledge and discretion.
13 The fear of the LORD is to hate evil;
pride and arrogance
and the evil way and the perverse mouth I hate.
14 Counsel is mine, and sound wisdom;
I am understanding, I have strength.
15 By me kings reign,
and princes decree justice.
16 By me princes rule,
and nobles, even all the judges of the earth.
17 I love those who love me,
and those who seek me early will find me.
18 Riches and honor are with me,
yes, enduring riches and righteousness.
19 My fruit is better than gold,
yes, than fine gold, and my revenue than choice silver.

Thank You for opening the doors of blessing and closing the doors of lack (Pr 8:21).

20 I lead in the way of righteousness,
in the midst of the paths of justice,
21 that I may cause those who love me to inherit wealth,
and I will fill their treasuries.

7:11 Pr 9:13
7:12 Pr 23:28
7:13 Ge 39:12
7:14 Lev 7:11
7:16 Isa 19:9
7:17 Ps 45:8
7:19 Mt 20:11
7:21 Pr 5:3
7:23 Ecc 9:12
7:24 Pr 5:7
7:25 Pr 5:8
7:26 Ne 13:26
7:27 Pr 5:5
8:1 Pr 1:20–21
8:3 Job 29:7
8:5 Pr 1:22
8:7 Jn 8:14
8:9 Pr 14:6
8:12 Pr 1:4
8:13 Pr 16:6
8:14 Ecc 7:19
8:15 Da 2:21
8:17 1Sa 2:30
8:18 Pr 3:16
8:19 Pr 3:14

22 "The LORD possessed me in the beginning of His way,
before His works of old.
23 I was set up from everlasting,
from the beginning, before there was ever an earth.
24 When there were no depths, I was brought forth,
when there were no fountains abounding with water.
25 Before the mountains were settled,
before the hills I was brought forth;
26 while as yet He had not made the earth or the fields,
or the first dust of the world.
27 When He prepared the heavens, I was there,
when He drew a circle on the face of the deep,
28 when He established the clouds above,
when He strengthened the fountains of the deep,
29 when He gave to the sea His decree,
that the waters should not pass His commandment,
when He appointed the foundations of the earth,
30 then I was by Him, as one brought up with Him;
and I was daily His delight,
rejoicing always before Him,
31 rejoicing in the habitable part of His earth,
and my delights were with the sons of men.

32 "Now therefore listen to me, O you children,
for blessed are those who keep my ways.
33 Hear instruction, and be wise,
and do not refuse it.
34 Blessed is the man who hears me,
watching daily at my gates,
waiting at the posts of my doors.
35 For whoever finds me finds life,
and will obtain favor of the LORD;
36 but he who sins against me wrongs his own soul;
all those who hate me love death."

The Way of Wisdom

9 Wisdom has built her house,
she has hewn out her seven pillars;
2 she has killed her beasts, she has mixed her wine,
she has also furnished her table.
3 She has sent out her maidens,
she cries out from the highest places of the city,
4 "Whoever is simple, let him turn in here."
As for him who wants understanding,
she says to him,
5 "Come, eat of my bread,
and drink of the wine which I have mixed.
6 Forsake foolishness and live,
and go in the way of understanding."
7 He who reproves a scorner gets shame for himself,
and he who rebukes a wicked man gets hurt.
8 Do not reprove a scorner, lest he hate you;
rebuke a wise man, and he will love you.
9 Give instruction to a wise man, and he will be yet wiser;
teach a just man, and he will increase in learning.

10 The fear of the LORD is the beginning of wisdom,
and the knowledge of the Holy One is understanding.
11 For by me your days will be multiplied,
and the years of your life will be increased.
12 If you are wise, you will be wise for yourself,
but if you scorn, you alone will bear it.

The Way of Foolishness

13 A foolish woman is clamorous;
she is simple, and knows nothing.
14 For she sits at the door of her house,
on a seat in the high places of the city,
15 to call those who pass by
who go right on their way:
16 "Whoever is simple, let him turn in here."
And as for him who lacks understanding,
she says to him,
17 "Stolen waters are sweet,
and bread eaten in secret is pleasant."
18 But he does not know that the dead are there,
and that her guests are in the depths of the grave.

The Proverbs of Solomon

10 The proverbs of Solomon.

A wise son makes a glad father,
but a foolish son is the grief of his mother.

2 Treasures of wickedness profit nothing,
but righteousness delivers from death.

3 The LORD will not allow the soul of the righteous to famish,
but He casts away the desire of the wicked.

8:22 Pr 3:19
8:23 Ps 2:6
8:25 Ps 90:2
8:29 Ps 104:9
8:30 Jn 1:1–3
8:31 Ps 16:3
8:32 Ps 119:1–2
8:33 Pr 4:1
8:34 Pr 3:13
8:35 Pr 12:2
9:1 Eph 2:20–22
9:2 Pr 23:30
9:3 Pr 9:14
9:4 Pr 6:32
9:5 SS 5:1
9:8 Ps 141:5
9:9 Pr 1:5
9:10 Pr 1:7
9:11 Pr 10:27
9:12 Job 22:2–3
9:13 Pr 7:11
9:14 Pr 9:3
9:17 Pr 20:17
9:18 Pr 7:27
10:1 Pr 1:1
10:2 Pr 11:4
10:3 Ps 34:9–10

4 He becomes poor who deals with a slack
hand,
but the hand of the diligent makes rich.

5 He who gathers in summer is a wise son,
but he who sleeps in harvest is a son
who causes shame.

6 Blessings are on the head of the just,
but violence covers the mouth of the
wicked.

7 The memory of the just is blessed,
but the name of the wicked will rot.

8 The wise in heart will receive
commandments,
but a prating fool will fall.

9 He who walks uprightly walks surely,
but he who perverts his ways will be
known.

10 He who winks with the eye causes sorrow,
but a prating fool will fall.

11 The mouth of a righteous man is a well of
life,
but violence covers the mouth of the
wicked.

12 Hatred stirs up strife,
but love covers all sins.

13 In the lips of him who has understanding
wisdom is found,
but a rod is for the back of him who is
void of understanding.

14 Wise men store up knowledge,
but the mouth of the foolish is near
destruction.

15 The rich man's wealth is his strong city;
the destruction of the poor is their
poverty.

16 The labor of the righteous tends to life,
the fruit of the wicked to sin.

17 He who keeps instruction is in the way of
life,
but he who refuses reproof errs.

18 He who hides hatred has lying lips,
and he who spreads slander is a fool.

19 In the multitude of words sin is not lacking,
but he who restrains his lips is wise.

20 The tongue of the just is as choice silver;
the heart of the wicked is worth little.

21 The lips of the righteous feed many,
but fools die for lack of wisdom.

22 The blessing of the Lord makes rich,
and He adds no sorrow with it.

10:4 Pr 13:4
10:6 Pr 10:11
10:7 Ps 112:6
10:9 Ps 23:4
10:10 Ps 35:19
10:11 Pr 10:6
10:12 1Pe 4:8
10:13 Pr 26:3
10:14 Pr 18:7
10:15 Pr 18:11
10:17 Pr 6:23
10:19 Jas 3:2
10:21 Hos 4:6
10:22 Ge 24:35

. . . .

10:23 Pr 15:21
10:24 Ps 145:19
10:25 Ps 15:5
10:27 Job 15:32–33
10:28 Job 8:13
10:29 Pr 21:15
10:30 Ps 37:22
10:31 Ps 37:30
10:32 Ecc 12:10
11:1 Pr 16:11
11:2 Pr 29:23
11:3 Pr 13:6
11:4 Ge 7:1
11:5 Pr 5:22
11:6 Ecc 10:8

23 To do mischief is like sport to a fool,
but a man of understanding has
wisdom.

24 The fear of the wicked will come upon him,
but the desire of the righteous will be
granted.

25 As the whirlwind passes, so is the wicked
no more,
but the righteous has an everlasting
foundation.

26 As vinegar to the teeth and as smoke to the
eyes,
so is the sluggard to those who send
him.

27 The fear of the Lord prolongs days,
but the years of the wicked will be
shortened.

28 The hope of the righteous will be gladness,
but the expectation of the wicked will
perish.

29 The way of the Lord is strength to the
upright,
but destruction will come to the workers
of iniquity.

30 The righteous will never be removed,
but the wicked will not inhabit the earth.

31 The mouth of the just brings forth wisdom,
but the perverse tongue will be cut out.

32 The lips of the righteous know what is
acceptable,
but the mouth of the wicked speaks
what is perverse.

11 A false balance is abomination to the
Lord,
but a just weight is His delight.

2 When pride comes, then comes shame;
but with the humble is wisdom.

3 The integrity of the upright will guide
them,
but the perverseness of transgressors
will destroy them.

4 Riches do not profit in the day of wrath,
but righteousness delivers from death.

5 The righteousness of the upright will direct
his way,
but the wicked will fall by his own
wickedness.

6 The righteousness of the upright will
deliver them,
but transgressors will be taken by their
schemes.

7 When a wicked man dies, his expectation will perish,
and the hope of unjust men perishes.

8 The righteous is delivered out of trouble,
and the wicked comes in his place.

9 A hypocrite with his mouth destroys his neighbor,
but through knowledge the just will be delivered.

10 When it goes well with the righteous, the city rejoices;
and when the wicked perish, there is shouting.

11 By the blessing of the upright the city is exalted,
but it is overthrown by the mouth of the wicked.

12 He who is void of wisdom despises his neighbor,
but a man of understanding holds his peace.

13 A talebearer reveals secrets,
but he who is of a faithful spirit conceals the matter.

14 Where there is no counsel, the people fall;
but in the multitude of counselors there is safety.

15 He who puts up a pledge for a stranger will suffer for it,
and he who hates being a pledge is secure.

16 A gracious woman retains honor,
but ruthless men retain riches.

17 The merciful man does good to his own soul,
but he who is cruel troubles his own body.

18 The wicked works a deceitful work,
but to him who sows righteousness will be a sure reward.

19 As righteousness tends to life,
so he who pursues evil pursues it to his own death.

20 Those who are of a perverse heart are abomination to the LORD,
but such as are upright in their way are His delight.

21 Though be assured, the wicked will not be unpunished,
but the posterity of the righteous will be delivered.

22 As a jewel of gold in a swine's snout,
so is a fair woman who is without discretion.

11:7 Pr 10:28
11:8 Pr 21:18
11:10 Pr 28:12
11:11 Pr 29:8
11:13 Lev 19:16
11:14 Pr 15:22
11:15 Pr 17:18
11:16 Pr 31:30–31
11:17 Mt 5:7
11:18 Gal 6:8–9
11:19 Pr 10:16
11:21 Pr 16:5

11:23 Ro 2:8–9
11:25 Mt 5:7
11:26 Job 29:13
11:27 Est 7:10
11:28 Jer 17:8
11:29 Ecc 5:16
11:30 Jas 5:20
11:31 Jer 25:29
12:1 Pr 9:7–8
12:2 Pr 8:35
12:3 Pr 10:25
12:4 Pr 14:30
12:6 Pr 14:3

23 The desire of the righteous is only good,
but the expectation of the wicked is wrath.

24 There is *one* who scatters, yet increases;
and there is *one* who withholds more than is right, but it leads to poverty.

25 The generous soul will be made rich,
and he who waters will be watered also himself.

26 The people will curse him who withholds grain,
but blessing will be upon the head of him who sells it.

27 He who diligently seeks good procures favor,
but he who seeks mischief, it will come to him.

28 He who trusts in his riches will fall,
but the righteous will flourish as a branch.

29 He who troubles his own house will inherit the wind,
and the fool will be servant to the wise of heart.

30 The fruit of the righteous is a tree of life,
and he who wins souls is wise.

31 If the righteous will be recompensed in the earth,
how much more the wicked and the sinner.

12 Whoever loves instruction loves knowledge,
but he who hates reproof is brutish.

2 A good man obtains favor of the LORD,
but a man of wicked devices will He condemn.

3 A man will not be established by wickedness,
but the root of the righteous will not be moved.

4 A virtuous woman is a crown to her husband,
but she who brings shame is as rottenness in his bones.

5 The thoughts of the righteous are right,
but the counsels of the wicked are deceit.

6 The words of the wicked are, "Lie in wait for blood,"
but the mouth of the upright will deliver them.

7 The wicked are overthrown, and are not,
but the house of the righteous will stand.

[8] A man will be commended according to his wisdom,
but he who is of a perverse heart will be despised.

[9] He who is lightly esteemed and has a servant is better
than he who honors himself and lacks bread.

[10] A righteous man regards the life of his animal,
but the tender mercies of the wicked are cruel.

[11] He who tills his land will be satisfied with bread,
but he who follows vain persons is void of understanding.

[12] The wicked covet the plunder of evil men,
but the root of the righteous yields fruit.

[13] The wicked is snared by the transgression of his lips,
but the just will come out of trouble.

[14] A man will be satisfied with good by the fruit of his mouth,
and the recompense of a man's hands will be rendered to him.

[15] The way of a fool is right in his own eyes,
but he who listens to counsel is wise.

[16] A fool's wrath is presently known,
but a prudent man covers shame.

[17] He who speaks truth shows forth righteousness,
but a false witness deceit.

[18] There is one who speaks like the piercings of a sword,
but the tongue of the wise is health.

[19] The truthful lip will be established forever,
but a lying tongue is but for a moment.

[20] Deceit is in the heart of those who imagine evil,
but to the counselors of peace is joy.

[21] There will no evil happen to the just,
but the wicked will be filled with mischief.

[22] Lying lips are abomination to the LORD,
but those who deal truly are His delight.

[23] A prudent man conceals knowledge,
but the heart of fools proclaims foolishness.

[24] The hand of the diligent will rule,
but the slothful will be put to forced labor.

12:10 Dt 25:4
12:11 Pr 28:19
12:12 Ps 10:9
12:13 2Pe 2:9
12:14 Pr 13:2
12:15 Pr 16:2
12:16 Pr 29:11
12:17 Pr 14:5
12:18 Ps 57:4
12:19 Pr 19:9
12:21 Ps 91:10
12:22 Rev 22:15
12:23 Pr 13:16
12:24 Pr 10:4

. . . .

12:25 Pr 15:13
12:27 Pr 13:4
12:28 3Jn 1:11
13:1 Pr 10:1
13:2 Pr 12:14
13:3 Pr 21:23
13:6 Pr 11:3
13:9 Pr 4:18
13:11 Pr 20:21

[25] Heaviness in the heart of man makes it droop,
but a good word makes it glad.

[26] The righteous is a guide to his neighbors,
but the way of the wicked leads them astray.

[27] The slothful man does not roast that which he took in hunting,
but the substance of a diligent man is precious.

[28] In the way of righteousness is life,
and in its pathway there is no death.

13 A wise son heeds his father's instruction,
but a scoffer does not listen to rebuke.

[2] A man will eat well by the fruit of his mouth,
but the soul of the transgressor will eat violence.

[3] He who guards his mouth preserves his life,
but he who opens wide his lips will have destruction.

[4] The soul of the sluggard desires, and has nothing;
but the soul of the diligent will be made fat.

[5] A righteous man hates lying,
but a wicked man is loathsome and comes to shame.

[6] Righteousness keeps him who is upright in the way,
but wickedness overthrows the sinner.

[7] There is one who makes himself rich, yet has nothing;
there is one who makes himself poor, yet has great riches.

[8] The ransom of a man's life is his riches,
but the poor does not hear rebuke.

[9] The light of the righteous rejoices,
but the lamp of the wicked will be put out.

[10] Only by pride comes contention,
but with the well-advised is wisdom.

[11] Wealth gained by vanity will be diminished,
but he who gathers by labor will increase.

[12] Hope deferred makes the heart sick,
but when the desire comes, it is a tree of life.

[13]Whoever despises the word will be destroyed,
but he who fears the commandment will be rewarded.

[14]The teaching of the wise is a fountain of life,
to depart from the snares of death.

[15]Good understanding gives favor,
but the way of transgressors is hard.

[16]Every prudent man deals with knowledge,
but a fool lays open his folly.

[17]A wicked messenger falls into mischief,
but a faithful envoy is health.

[18]Poverty and shame will be to him who refuses instruction,
but he who regards reproof will be honored.

[19]The desire accomplished is sweet to the soul,
but it is abomination to fools to depart from evil.

[20]He who walks with wise men will be wise,
but a companion of fools will be destroyed.

[21]Evil pursues sinners,
but to the righteous good will be repaid.

[22]A good man leaves an inheritance to his children's children,
and the wealth of the sinner is laid up for the just.

[23]Much food is in the tillage of the poor,
but for lack of justice it is destroyed.

[24]He who spares his rod hates his son,
but he who loves him disciplines him early.

[25]The righteous eats to the satisfying of his soul,
but the stomach of the wicked will want.

14 Every wise woman builds her house,
but the foolish pulls it down with her hands.

[2] He who walks in his uprightness fears the LORD,
but he who is perverse in his ways despises Him.

[3] In the mouth of the foolish is a rod of pride,
but the lips of the wise will preserve them.

[4] Where no oxen are, the crib is clean;
but much increase is by the strength of the ox.

13:13 2Ch 36:16
13:14 Pr 10:11
13:15 Pr 3:4
13:17 Pr 25:13
13:18 Pr 15:5
13:19 Pr 13:12
13:20 1Ki 12:8
13:21 Ps 32:10
13:22 Job 27:16–17
13:23 Pr 12:11
13:24 Pr 19:18
13:25 Ps 34:10
14:1 Ru 4:11
14:2 Pr 28:6
14:3 Pr 12:6
....
14:5 Pr 6:19
14:9 Pr 10:23
14:10 1Sa 1:10
14:11 Job 8:15
14:12 Pr 16:25
14:13 Ecc 2:2
14:14 Pr 12:14
14:16 Pr 22:3
14:17 Pr 14:29
14:19 Ge 42:6
14:20 Pr 19:4
14:21 Pr 11:12
14:22 Pr 12:2

[5] A faithful witness will not lie,
but a false witness will utter lies.

[6] A scorner seeks wisdom and does not find it,
but knowledge is easy to him who understands.

[7] Go from the presence of a foolish man,
when you do not perceive in him the lips of knowledge.

[8] The wisdom of the prudent is to understand his way,
but the folly of fools is deceit.

[9] Fools make a mock at sin,
but among the righteous there is favor.

[10]The heart knows its own bitterness,
and a stranger does not share its joy.

[11]The house of the wicked will be overthrown,
but the tent of the upright will flourish.

[12]There is a way that seems right to a man,
but its end is the way of death.

[13]Even in laughter the heart is sorrowful,
and the end of that cheer is grief.

[14]The backslider in heart will be filled with his own ways,
but a good man will be satisfied with his.

[15]The simple believes every word,
but the prudent man considers his steps.

[16]A wise man fears and departs from evil,
but the fool rages and is self-confident.

[17]He who is quick-tempered deals foolishly,
and a man of wicked devices is hated.

[18]The simple inherit folly,
but the prudent are crowned with knowledge.

[19]The evil bow before the good,
and the wicked at the gates of the righteous.

[20]The poor is hated even by his own neighbor,
but the rich has many friends.

[21]He who despises his neighbor sins,
but he who has mercy on the poor, happy is he.

[22]Do they not err who devise evil?
But mercy and truth will be to those who devise good.

[23]In all labor there is profit,
but mere talk leads only to poverty.

[24]The crown of the wise is their riches,
but the foolishness of fools is folly.

25 A true witness delivers souls,
but a deceitful witness speaks lies.

26 In the fear of the LORD is strong confidence,
and His children will have a place of
refuge.

27 The fear of the LORD is a fountain of life,
to depart from the snares of death.

28 In the multitude of people is a king's honor,
but in the lack of people is the
destruction of a prince.

29 He who is slow to wrath is of great
understanding,
but he who is hasty of spirit exalts folly.

30 A sound heart is the life of the flesh,
but envy the rottenness of the bones.

31 He who oppresses the poor reproaches his
Maker,
but he who honors Him has mercy on
the poor.

32 The wicked is driven away in his
wickedness,
but the righteous has hope in his death.

33 Wisdom rests in the heart of him who has
understanding,
but that which is in the midst of fools is
made known.

34 Righteousness exalts a nation,
but sin is a reproach to any people.

35 The king's favor is toward a wise servant,
but his wrath is against him who causes
shame.

15 A soft answer turns away wrath,
but grievous words stir up anger.

2 The tongue of the wise uses knowledge
aright,
but the mouth of fools pours out
foolishness.

3 The eyes of the LORD are in every place,
keeping watch on the evil and the good.

4 A wholesome tongue is a tree of life,
but perverseness in it crushes the spirit.

5 A fool despises his father's instruction,
but he who regards reproof is prudent.

6 In the house of the righteous is much
treasure,
but in the revenue of the wicked is
trouble.

7 The lips of the wise disperse knowledge,
but the heart of the foolish does not do
so.

8 The sacrifice of the wicked is an
abomination to the LORD,
but the prayer of the upright is His
delight.

9 The way of the wicked is an abomination
unto the LORD,
but He loves him who follows after
righteousness.

10 Correction is grievous to him who forsakes
the way,
and he who hates reproof will die.

11 Death and destruction are before the LORD;
so how much more the hearts of the
children of men.

12 A scorner does not love one who reproves
him,
nor will he go to the wise.

13 A merry heart makes a cheerful
countenance,
but by sorrow of the heart the spirit is
broken.

14 The heart of him who has understanding
seeks knowledge,
but the mouth of fools feeds on
foolishness.

15 All the days of the afflicted are evil,
but he who is of a merry heart has a
continual feast.

16 Better is little with the fear of the LORD
than great treasure with trouble.

17 Better is a dinner of herbs where love is
than a fatted calf with hatred.

18 A wrathful man stirs up strife,
but he who is slow to anger appeases
strife.

19 The way of the slothful man is as a hedge
of thorns,
but the way of the righteous is made
plain.

20 A wise son makes a father glad,
but a foolish man despises his mother.

21 Folly is joy to him who is destitute of
wisdom,
but a man of understanding walks
uprightly.

22 Without counsel, purposes are
disappointed,
but in the multitude of counselors they
are established.

23 A man has joy by the answer of his mouth,
and a word spoken in due season, how
good it is!

14:25 Pr 14:5
14:26 Pr 18:10
14:27 Pr 13:14
14:29 Ecc 7:9
14:30 Pr 12:4
14:31 Pr 17:5
14:32 2Ti 4:18
15:1 Pr 25:15
15:2 Pr 12:23
15:3 Jer 16:17
15:6 Pr 8:21
15:7 Mt 12:34

....

15:8 Pr 15:29
15:9 1Ti 6:11
15:11 2Ch 6:30
15:12 Am 5:10
15:13 Pr 17:22
15:16 Ps 37:16
15:17 Pr 17:1
15:18 Pr 26:21
15:19 Pr 22:5
15:20 Pr 10:1
15:21 Pr 10:23
15:22 Pr 11:14
15:23 Pr 12:14

[24]The way of life leads above for the wise,
that he may depart from Sheol below.

[25]The LORD will destroy the house of the proud,
but He will establish the border of the widow.

[26]The thoughts of the wicked are an abomination to the LORD,
but the words of the pure are pleasant words.

[27]He who is greedy of gain troubles his own house,
but he who hates bribes will live.

[28]The heart of the righteous studies to answer,
but the mouth of the wicked pours out evil things.

[29]The LORD is far from the wicked,
but He hears the prayer of the righteous.

[30]The light of the eyes rejoices the heart,
and a good report makes the bones healthy.

[31]The ear that hears the reproof of life
abides among the wise.

[32]He who refuses instruction despises his own soul,
but he who hears reproof gains understanding.

[33]The fear of the LORD is the instruction of wisdom,
and before honor is humility.

16

The preparations of the heart belong to man,
but the answer of the tongue is from the LORD.

[2] All the ways of a man are clean in his own eyes,
but the LORD weighs the spirit.

[3] Commit your works to the LORD,
and your thoughts will be established.

[4] The LORD has made all things for Himself,
yes, even the wicked for the day of evil.

[5] Everyone who is proud in heart is an abomination to the LORD;
be assured, he will not be unpunished.

[6] By mercy and truth iniquity is purged;
and by the fear of the LORD men depart from evil.

[7] When a man's ways please the LORD,
He makes even his enemies to be at peace with him.

15:25 Ps 146:9
15:27 Ex 23:8
15:28 1Pe 3:15
15:29 Ps 145:18–19
15:30 Pr 25:25
15:31 Pr 15:5
15:33 Pr 1:7
16:1 Pr 19:21
16:2 1Sa 16:7
16:3 Ps 55:22
16:4 Ro 9:22
16:5 Pr 11:21
16:6 Pr 14:16
16:7 Ge 33:4

....

16:9 Jer 10:23
16:11 Pr 11:1
16:12 Pr 25:5
16:13 Pr 14:35
16:14 Pr 19:12
16:15 Job 29:23–24
16:16 Pr 8:19
16:17 Isa 35:8
16:18 Pr 11:2
16:19 Ex 15:9
16:20 Ps 2:12
16:23 Pr 15:28
16:24 Ps 19:10
16:25 Pr 14:12

[8] Better is a little with righteousness
than great revenues with injustice.

[9] A man's heart devises his way,
but the LORD directs his steps.

[10]A divine sentence is in the lips of the king;
his mouth does not transgress in judgment.

[11]A just weight and balance belong to the LORD;
all the weights of the bag are His work.

[12]It is an abomination to kings to commit wickedness,
for the throne is established by righteousness.

[13]Righteous lips are the delight of kings,
and they love him who speaks right.

[14]The wrath of a king is as messengers of death,
but a wise man will pacify it.

[15]In the light of the king's countenance is life,
and his favor is as a cloud of the latter rain.

[16]How much better to get wisdom than gold!
And to get understanding is to be chosen rather than silver!

[17]The highway of the upright is to depart from evil;
he who keeps his way preserves his soul.

[18]Pride goes before destruction,
and a haughty spirit before a fall.

[19]Better it is to be of a humble spirit with the lowly
than to divide the spoil with the proud.

[20]He who handles a matter wisely will find good,
and whoever trusts in the LORD, happy is he.

[21]The wise in heart will be called prudent,
and the sweetness of the lips increases learning.

[22]Understanding is a wellspring of life to him who has it,
but the instruction of fools is folly.

[23]The heart of the wise teaches his mouth,
and adds learning to his lips.

[24]Pleasant words are as a honeycomb,
sweet to the soul and health to the bones.

[25]There is a way that seems right to a man,
but its end is the way of death.

[26]He who labors, labors for himself,
for his mouth craves it of him.

[27]An ungodly man digs up evil,
and in his lips there is as a burning fire.

[28]A perverse man sows strife,
and a whisperer separates the best of friends.

[29]A violent man entices his neighbor,
and leads him into the way that is not good.

[30]He shuts his eyes to devise perverse things;
moving his lips he brings evil to pass.

[31]The gray-haired head is a crown of glory,
if it is found in the way of righteousness.

[32]He who is slow to anger is better than the mighty,
and he who rules his spirit than he who takes a city.

[33]The lot is cast into the lap,
but the whole outcome is of the LORD.

17 Better is a dry morsel with quietness
than a house full of sacrifices with strife.

[2] A wise servant will have rule over a son who causes shame,
and will have part of the inheritance among the brothers.

[3] The refining pot is for silver and the furnace for gold,
but the LORD tries the hearts.

[4] A wicked doer gives heed to false lips,
and a liar gives ear to a wayward tongue.

[5] Whoever mocks the poor reproaches his Maker,
and he who is glad at calamities will not be unpunished.

[6] Grandchildren are the crown of old men,
and the glory of children are their fathers.

[7] Excellent speech is not becoming to a fool,
much less lying lips to a prince.

[8] A gift is as a precious stone in the eyes of him who has it;
wherever he turns, it prospers.

[9] He who covers a transgression seeks love,
but he who repeats a matter separates friends.

[10]A reproof enters deeper into a wise man
than a hundred stripes into a fool.

16:26 Ecc 6:7
16:27 Jas 3:6
16:28 Pr 15:18
16:31 Pr 20:29
16:32 Pr 14:29
17:1 Pr 15:17
17:3 Ps 26:2
17:5 Job 31:29
17:9 Pr 10:12
17:12 2Sa 17:8
17:13 Ps 35:12
17:14 Pr 20:3
17:15 Ex 23:7
17:16 Pr 23:23
17:17 Pr 18:24
17:18 Pr 11:15
17:19 Pr 16:18
17:21 Pr 10:1
17:22 Pr 15:13
17:23 Ex 23:8
17:24 Ecc 2:14
17:25 Pr 10:1
17:26 Pr 17:15
17:27 Jas 1:19

[11]An evil man seeks only rebellion;
therefore a cruel messenger will be sent against him.

[12]Let a man meet a bear robbed of her cubs
rather than a fool in his folly.

[13]Whoever rewards evil for good,
evil will not depart from his house.

[14]The beginning of strife is as when one lets out water;
therefore abandon contention before a quarrel starts.

[15]He who justifies the wicked, and he who condemns the just,
both of them are abomination to the LORD.

[16]Why is there a price in the hand of a fool to get wisdom,
seeing he has no heart for it?

[17]A friend loves at all times,
and a brother is born for adversity.

[18]A man void of understanding shakes hands,
and becomes a pledge in the presence of his friend.

[19]He loves transgression who loves strife,
and he who exalts his gate seeks destruction.

[20]He who has a deceitful heart finds no good,
and he who has a perverse tongue falls into mischief.

[21]He who fathers a fool does it to his sorrow,
and the father of a fool has no joy.

[22]A merry heart does good like a medicine,
but a broken spirit dries the bones.

[23]A wicked man takes a bribe out of a hidden place
to pervert the ways of judgment.

[24]Wisdom is before him who has understanding,
but the eyes of a fool are in the ends of the earth.

[25]A foolish son is a grief to his father,
and bitterness to her who bore him.

[26]Also to punish the just is not good,
nor to strike princes for their uprightness.

[27]He who has knowledge spares his words,
and a man of understanding is of an excellent spirit.

SPIRITLED WOMAN

COUNSEL FROM THE SPIRIT BASICS

You Are Not Alone

Sometimes when you are hurting, you feel very much alone. Maybe you feel like that today. Maybe you feel as if you are facing the storms of life all by yourself

One of the enemy's best lies is that no one understands what you're going through. Satan will try to convince you that no one cares. Believe it or not, he tells the same lie to anyone who will listen. At one time or another, everyone has felt disheartened and abandoned.

But another truth that will bring hope in seemingly hopeless moments is this: You always have someone with you who sticks closer than a brother (Pr 18:24). God is with you! And when He is with you, you can be sure that everything will turn out better than OK.

Karen Jensen Salisbury

28 Even a fool, when he holds his peace, is
counted wise;
and he who shuts his lips is esteemed a
man of understanding.

18 He who separates himself seeks his
own desire;
he seeks and quarrels against all
wisdom.

2 A fool has no delight in understanding,
but in expressing his own heart.

3 When the wicked comes, then comes also
contempt,
and with dishonor reproach.

4 The words of a man's mouth are as deep
waters,
and the wellspring of wisdom as a
flowing brook.

5 It is not good to favor the wicked,
or to turn aside the righteous in
judgment.

6 A fool's lips enter into contention,
and his mouth calls for flogging.

17:28 Job 13:5
18:1 Jude 1:19
18:4 Pr 20:5
18:5 Lev 19:15

18:7 Pr 10:14
18:8 Pr 16:28
18:9 Pr 28:24
18:10 2Sa 22:3
18:11 Pr 10:15
18:12 Pr 11:2
18:13 Jn 7:51
18:14 Pr 17:22
18:15 Pr 15:14
18:16 Ge 32:20
18:18 Pr 16:33
18:22 Pr 19:14
18:23 Jas 2:3

7 A fool's mouth is his destruction,
and his lips are the snare of his soul.

8 The words of a talebearer are as wounds,
and they go down into the innermost
parts of the body.

9 He also who is slothful in his work
is brother to him who is a great waster.

10 The name of the LORD is a strong tower;
the righteous run into it and are safe.

11 The rich man's wealth is his strong city,
and as a high wall in his own conceit.

Lord, You will keep me safe when I call upon You (Pr 18:10).

12 Before destruction the heart of man is
haughty,
and before honor is humility.

13 He who answers a matter before he
hears it,
it is folly and shame to him.

14 The spirit of a man will sustain his
infirmity,
but a wounded spirit who can bear?

15 The heart of the prudent gets knowledge,
and the ear of the wise seeks
knowledge.

16 A man's gift makes room for him,
and brings him before great men.

17 He who is first in his own cause seems just,
but his neighbor comes and searches
him.

18 The lot causes contentions to cease,
and keeps the mighty ones apart.

19 A brother offended is harder to be won
than a strong city,
and their contentions are like the bars of
a castle.

20 A man's stomach will be satisfied with the
fruit of his mouth;
and with the increase of his lips will he
be filled.

21 Death and life are in the power of the
tongue,
and those who love it will eat its fruit.

22 Whoever finds a wife finds a good thing,
and obtains favor of the LORD.

23 The poor *man* uses entreaties,
but the rich *man* answers roughly.

24 A man who has friends must show himself
friendly,
and there is a friend who sticks closer
than a brother.

19 Better is the poor who walks in his
integrity
than he who is perverse in his lips and
is a fool.

2 Also, it is not good for the soul to be
without knowledge,
and he who hastens with his feet sins.

3 The foolishness of man perverts his way,
and his heart frets against the LORD.

4 Wealth makes many friends,
but the poor is separated from his
neighbor.

5 A false witness will not be unpunished,
and he who speaks lies will not escape.

6 Many will entreat the favor of the prince,
and every man is a friend to him who
gives gifts.

7 All the brothers of the poor hate him;
how much more do his friends go far
from him!
He pursues them with words,
yet they abandon him.

8 He who gets wisdom loves his own soul;
he who keeps understanding will find
good.

9 A false witness will not be unpunished,
and he who speaks lies will perish.

10 Delight is not seemly for a fool,
much less for a servant to have rule over
princes.

11 The discretion of a man defers his anger,
and it is his glory to pass over a
transgression.

12 The king's wrath is as the roaring of a lion,
but his favor is as dew upon the grass.

13 A foolish son is the calamity of his father,
and the contentions of a wife are a
continual dripping of water.

14 House and riches are the inheritance of
fathers,
and a prudent wife is from the LORD.

15 Slothfulness casts into a deep sleep,
and an idle soul will suffer hunger.

16 He who keeps the commandment keeps
his own soul,
but he who is careless in his ways will
die.

18:24 Pr 17:17
19:1 Pr 28:6
19:2 Pr 21:5
19:3 Ps 37:7
19:4 Pr 14:20
19:5 Pr 21:28
19:6 Pr 17:8
19:7 Ps 38:11
19:8 Pr 16:20
19:9 Pr 19:5
19:11 Pr 16:32
19:12 Pr 16:14–15
19:13 Pr 21:9
19:14 Pr 18:22
19:15 Pr 20:13
19:16 Lk 10:28

....

19:17 Pr 28:27
19:18 Pr 13:24
19:20 Ps 37:37
19:21 Ps 33:10–11
19:23 Pr 12:21
19:24 Pr 15:19
19:25 Pr 21:11
19:28 Job 15:16
19:29 Pr 26:3
20:1 Pr 31:4
20:2 Pr 8:36
20:3 Pr 17:14

17 He who has pity on the poor lends to the
LORD,
and He will repay what he has given.

18 Chasten your son while there is hope,
and let not your soul spare for his crying.

19 A man of great wrath will suffer
punishment;
for if you deliver him, yet you must do
it again.

20 Hear counsel and receive instruction,
that you may be wise in your latter days.

21 There are many plans in a man's heart,
nevertheless the counsel of the LORD will
stand.

22 The desire of a man is his kindness,
and a poor man is better than a liar.

23 The fear of the LORD tends to life,
and he who has it will abide satisfied; he
will not be visited with evil.

24 A slothful man hides his hand in his bowl,
and will not so much as bring it to his
mouth again.

25 Smite a scorner, and the simple will
beware;
and reprove one who has
understanding, and he will
understand knowledge.

26 He who mistreats his father and chases
away his mother
is a son who causes shame and brings
reproach.

27 Cease, my son, to hear the instruction
that causes to err from the words of
knowledge.

28 An ungodly witness scorns judgment,
and the mouth of the wicked devours
iniquity.

29 Judgments are prepared for scorners,
and beatings for the back of fools.

20 Wine is a mocker, strong drink is
raging,
and whoever is deceived by it is not
wise.

2 The terror of a king is as the roaring of a
lion;
whoever provokes him to anger sins
against his own soul.

3 It is an honor for a man to cease from
strife,
but every fool will be meddling.

4 The sluggard will not plow because of the cold;
therefore he will beg during harvest and have nothing.

5 Counsel in the heart of man is like deep water,
but a man of understanding will draw it out.

6 Most men will proclaim everyone his own goodness,
but who can find a faithful man?

7 The just man walks in his integrity;
his children are blessed after him.

8 A king who sits on the throne of judgment
scatters away all evil with his eyes.

9 Who can say, "I have made my heart clean,
I am pure from my sin"?

10 Diverse weights and diverse measures,
both of them alike are an abomination to the LORD.

11 Even a child is known by his doings,
whether his work is pure and whether it is right.

12 The hearing ear and the seeing eye,
the LORD has made both of them.

13 Do not love sleep, lest you come to poverty;
open your eyes, and you will be satisfied with bread.

14 "It is bad, it is bad," says the buyer;
but when he has gone his way, then he boasts.

15 There is gold and a multitude of rubies,
but the lips of knowledge are a precious jewel.

16 Take the garment of him who is a pledge for a stranger,
and hold it as a security when it is for a wayward woman.

17 Bread of deceit is sweet to a man,
but afterwards his mouth will be filled with gravel.

18 Every purpose is established by counsel,
and with good advice wage war.

19 He who goes about as a talebearer reveals secrets;
therefore do not meddle with him who flatters with his lips.

20 Whoever curses his father or his mother,
his lamp will be put out in obscure darkness.

20:4 Pr 19:15
20:5 Pr 18:4
20:6 Ps 12:1
20:7 Ps 37:26
20:8 Pr 20:26
20:9 1Ki 8:46
20:10 Pr 11:1
20:11 Mt 7:16
20:12 Ps 94:9
20:13 Pr 19:15
20:15 Pr 3:15
20:16 Pr 27:13
20:18 Pr 24:6
20:19 Pr 11:13
20:20 Ex 21:17

20:22 Pr 24:29
20:23 Pr 20:10
20:24 Pr 16:9
20:26 Pr 20:8
20:27 1Co 2:11
20:28 Pr 29:14
20:29 Pr 16:31
20:30 Pr 22:15
21:2 Pr 16:2
21:3 1Sa 15:22
21:4 Pr 6:17
21:5 Pr 10:4
21:6 Pr 8:36

21 An inheritance may be gained hastily at the beginning,
but the end of it will not be blessed.

22 Do not say, "I will recompense evil";
but wait on the LORD, and He will save you.

23 Diverse weights are an abomination to the LORD,
and a false balance is not good.

24 Man's goings are of the LORD;
how can a man then understand his own way?

25 It is a snare to the man who dedicates rashly that which is holy,
and after the vows to make inquiry.

26 A wise king sifts out the wicked,
and drives the threshing wheel over them.

27 The spirit of man is the candle of the LORD,
searching all the inward parts of the heart.

28 Mercy and truth preserve the king,
and his throne is upheld by mercy.

29 The glory of young men is their strength,
and the beauty of old men is the gray head.

30 The blows of a wound cleanse away evil,
so do stripes the inward parts of the heart.

21

The king's heart is in the hand of the LORD,
as the rivers of water; He turns it to any place He will.

2 Every way of a man is right in his own eyes,
but the LORD weighs the hearts.

3 To do justice and judgment
is more acceptable to the LORD than sacrifice.

4 A high look, a proud heart,
and the plowing of the wicked are sin.

5 The thoughts of the diligent tend only to plenty,
but of everyone who is hasty only to want.

6 The getting of treasures by a lying tongue
is a vanity tossed back and forth by those who seek death.

7 The violence of the wicked will destroy them,
because they refuse to do justice.

8 The way of a guilty man is perverse;
but as for the pure, his work is right.

9 It is better to dwell in a corner of the housetop
than with a brawling woman in a wide house.

10 The soul of the wicked desires evil;
his neighbor finds no favor in his eyes.

11 When the scorner is punished, the simple is made wise;
and when the wise is instructed, he receives knowledge.

12 The righteous man wisely considers the house of the wicked,
but God overthrows the wicked for their wickedness.

13 Whoever shuts his ears at the cry of the poor,
he also will cry himself, but will not be heard.

14 A gift in secret pacifies anger,
and a concealed bribe strong wrath.

15 It is joy to the just to do justice,
but destruction will come to the workers of iniquity.

16 The man who wanders out of the way of understanding
will remain in the congregation of the dead.

17 He who loves pleasure will be a poor man;
he who loves wine and oil will not be rich.

18 The wicked will be a ransom for the righteous,
and the transgressor for the upright.

19 It is better to dwell in the wilderness
than with a contentious and angry woman.

20 There is treasure to be desired and oil in the dwelling of the wise,
but a foolish man squanders it.

21 He who follows after righteousness and mercy
finds life, righteousness, and honor.

22 A wise man scales the city of the mighty,
and casts down the strength of its confidence.

23 Whoever guards his mouth and his tongue
keeps his soul from trouble.

24 Proud and haughty—scorner is his name,
who deals in proud wrath.

25 The desire of the slothful kills him,
for his hands refuse to labor.

26 He covets greedily all the day long,
but the righteous gives and does not spare.

27 The sacrifice of the wicked is an abomination;
how much more when he brings it with a wicked intent!

28 A false witness will perish,
but a man who listens will speak forever.

29 A wicked man hardens his face,
but as for the upright, he directs his way.

30 There is no wisdom nor understanding nor counsel
against the LORD.

31 The horse is prepared against the day of battle,
but victory is of the LORD.

22 A good name is rather to be chosen than great riches,
and loving favor rather than silver and gold.

2 The rich and poor have this in common,
the LORD is the maker of them all.

3 A prudent man foresees the evil and hides himself,
but the simple pass on and are punished.

4 By humility and the fear of the LORD
are riches, and honor, and life.

5 Thorns and snares are in the way of the perverse;
he who guards his soul will be far from them.

6 Train up a child in the way he should go,
and when he is old he will not depart from it.

7 The rich rules over the poor,
and the borrower is servant to the lender.

8 He who sows iniquity will reap vanity,
and the rod of his anger will fail.

9 He who has a bountiful eye will be blessed,
for he gives of his bread to the poor.

10 Cast out the scorner, and contention will go out;
yes, strife and reproach will cease.

11 He who loves pureness of heart, for the grace of his lips
the king will be his friend.

21:8 Pr 2:15
21:9 Pr 21:19
21:11 Pr 19:25
21:12 Ps 37:35–36
21:14 Pr 18:16
21:15 Pr 10:29
21:16 Ps 49:14
21:17 Pr 23:21
21:18 Pr 11:8
21:19 Pr 21:9
21:20 Ps 112:3
21:21 Mt 5:6
21:22 Ecc 7:19
21:23 Pr 12:13
21:25 Pr 13:4
21:26 Ps 37:26
21:27 Pr 15:8
21:28 Pr 19:5
21:29 Pr 11:5
21:30 Jer 9:23
21:31 Isa 31:1
22:1 Ecc 7:1
22:2 Job 31:15
22:3 Pr 14:16
22:4 Pr 21:21
22:5 Pr 15:19
22:6 Eph 6:4
22:7 Jas 2:6
22:8 Job 4:8
22:9 Pr 19:17
22:10 Ge 21:9–10
22:11 Pr 16:13

SPIRITLED WOMAN

COUNSEL FROM THE SPIRIT BASICS

How Do I Discipline?

One of the problems we face today is how to discipline our children. The law forbids using the rod as the Bible instructs us in several verses, including Proverbs 22:15: "Foolishness is bound in the heart of a child, but the rod of correction will drive it far from him."

What can we do? I have two daughters, and we only had to use the "rod" two times since they were very young. We used a ruler, as was used in schools years ago. But my daughters never forgot about that experience. They only had to see the "rod," and they rapidly behaved.

Today, parents go to the school to argue with the teacher about their child's behavior, blaming the school for the problem. How absurd and counterproductive.

Ask for the Holy Spirit's help today in order to deal with your child's disciplinary problems. Never administer discipline in anger; wait until you calm down. Hug your child afterward. Be firm, fair, and caring. Don't be angry or cruel. Teach your child that you are the parent and you are in control. Don't discipline until you are under control.

It is a parent's responsibility to make sure her children are consistently and fairly disciplined. Even though our children have a sin nature and are not naturally inclined to be good, if we rear them in a good environment and parent them correctly, giving them self-esteem and building them up, as they grow older they will make right choices. Don't wait until it is too late.

Iris Delgado

12 The eyes of the LORD preserve knowledge,
and He overthrows the words of the
transgressor.
13 The slothful man says, "There is a lion
without!
I will be slain in the streets!"
14 The mouth of an immoral woman is a deep
pit;

22:14 Pr 23:27
22:15 Pr 13:24
22:16 Jas 2:13
22:17 Pr 23:12
22:18 Pr 2:10
22:19 Pr 3:5
22:20 Pr 8:6
22:21 Lk 1:3–4
22:22 Ex 23:6
22:23 1Sa 25:39
22:24 Pr 29:22
22:25 1Co 15:33
22:27 Pr 20:16
22:28 Dt 19:14

he who is detested by the LORD will fall
therein.
15 Foolishness is bound in the heart of a
child,
but the rod of correction will drive it far
from him.
16 He who oppresses the poor to increase his
riches,
and he who gives to the rich, will surely
come to want.

Thirty Sayings of the Wise

Saying One

17 Incline your ear and hear the words of the
wise,
and apply your heart to my knowledge;
18 for it is a pleasant thing if you keep them
within you;
they will readily be fitted in your lips.
19 That your trust may be in the LORD,
I have made known to you this day, even
to you.
20 Have I not written to you excellent things
in counsels and knowledge,
21 that I might make you know the certainty
of the words of truth,
that you might answer the words of
truth
to those who send to you?

Saying Two

22 Do not rob the poor because he is poor,
neither oppress the afflicted in the gate;
23 for the LORD will plead their cause,
and spoil the soul of those who spoiled
them.

Saying Three

24 Make no friendship with an angry man,
and with a furious man you will not go,
25 lest you learn his ways
and get a snare to your soul.

Saying Four

26 Do not be one of those who shakes hands
in a pledge,
or of those who use securities for debts;
27 if you have nothing to pay,
why should he take away your bed from
under you?

Saying Five

28 Do not remove the ancient landmark
which your fathers have set.

Saying Six

29 Do you see a man diligent in his business?
He will stand before kings;
he will not stand before obscure men.

SPIRIT-TO-SPIRIT PRAYER

PRAYER OF THANKFULNESS FOR OUR CHILDREN

Lord, thank You for the blessing of our children. We know that You have greatly and uniquely gifted them. Teach us to know and discern their gifting and to give them the freedom to flow in Your anointing. We welcome Your guidance. We speak a release of the anointing and authority in their lives. We say that there is freedom of the Lord in our home and in our youth. Holy Spirit, give them dreams, visions, prophetic revelations, prayer burdens, a heart for the lost, an authority to stand, and an understanding of the truth of who they are in You. Give them a passion to seek after You and to stand on Your truths and Word. Give us wisdom on how to encourage, release, and bless Your plans and purposes in their lives. Help us not to be religious but free in You. Give us the ability to impart this freedom and authority to the next generation. Thank You, Lord. Amen.

Rebecca Greenwood

Saying Seven

23 When you sit to eat with a ruler,
consider diligently what is before you;
2 and put a knife to your throat,
if you are a man given to appetite.
3 Be not desirous of his delicacies,
for they are deceptive food.

Saying Eight

4 Do not labor to be rich;
cease from your own wisdom.
5 Will you set your eyes on that which is not?
For riches certainly make themselves wings;
they fly away as an eagle toward heaven.

Saying Nine

6 Do not eat the bread of him who has an evil eye,
neither desire his delicacies;
7 for as he thinks in his heart,
so is he.
"Eat and drink!" he says to you,
but his heart is not with you.
8 The morsel you have eaten, you will vomit up,
and lose your sweet words.

Saying Ten

9 Do not speak in the ears of a fool,
for he will despise the wisdom of your words.

23:3 Pr 23:6
23:4 Pr 28:20
23:5 Pr 27:24
23:6 Ps 141:4
23:7 Ps 12:2
23:9 Mt 7:6

23:10 Pr 22:28
23:11 Pr 22:23
23:13 Pr 13:24
23:14 1Co 5:5
23:15 Pr 29:3
23:16 Pr 8:6
23:17 Pr 28:14
23:18 Ps 9:18
23:20 Isa 5:22

Saying Eleven

10 Do not remove the old landmark,
nor enter the fields of the fatherless;
11 for their Redeemer is mighty;
He will plead their cause with you.

Saying Twelve

12 Apply your heart to instruction,
and your ears to the words of knowledge.

Saying Thirteen

13 Do not withhold correction from a child,
for if you beat him with the rod, he will not die.
14 You shall beat him with the rod,
and deliver his soul from death.

Saying Fourteen

15 My son, if your heart is wise,
my heart will rejoice—even mine.
16 Yes, my inmost being will rejoice
when your lips speak right things.

Saying Fifteen

17 Do not let your heart envy sinners,
but continue in the fear of the Lord all day long;
18 for surely there is an end,
and your expectation will not be cut off.

Saying Sixteen

19 Hear, my son, and be wise;
and guide your heart in the way.
20 Do not be among winebibbers,
among riotous eaters of meat;

21 for the drunkard and the glutton will come
to poverty,
and drowsiness will clothe a man with
rags.

Saying Seventeen

22 Listen to your father who gave you life,
and do not despise your mother when
she is old.
23 Buy the truth, and do not sell it,
also wisdom and instruction and
understanding.
24 The father of the righteous will greatly
rejoice,
and he who fathers a wise child will
have joy of him.
25 Your father and your mother will be glad,
and she who bore you will rejoice.

Saying Eighteen

26 My son, give me your heart,
and let your eyes observe my ways.
27 For a prostitute is a deep ditch,
and a seductress is a narrow pit.
28 She also lies in wait as for a prey,
and increases the transgressors among
men.

Saying Nineteen

29 Who has woe? Who has sorrow?
Who has contentions? Who has
babbling?
Who has wounds without cause? Who
has redness of eyes?
30 Those who tarry long at the wine,
those who go to seek mixed wine.
31 Do not look on the wine when it is red,
when it sparkles in the cup,
when it swirls around smoothly;
32 at the last it bites like a serpent,
and stings like a viper.
33 Your eyes will see strange things,
and your heart will utter perverse things.
34 Yes, you will be as he who lies down in the
midst of the sea,
or as he who lies upon the top of a mast.
35 "They have stricken me," you will say, "and
I was not sick;
they have beaten me, and I did not feel
it.
When will I awake?
I will seek it yet again."

Saying Twenty

24 Do not be envious against evil men,
nor desire to be with them;
2 for their heart studies destruction,
and their lips talk of mischief.

Saying Twenty-One

3 Through wisdom is a house built,
and by understanding it is established;

23:21 Pr 21:17
23:22 Pr 1:8
23:23 Mt 13:44
23:24 Pr 10:1
23:25 Pr 17:25
23:27 Pr 22:14
23:28 Pr 7:12
23:30 Ps 75:8
23:35 Isa 56:12
24:1 Ps 37:1
24:2 Ps 10:7
24:3 Pr 14:1

24:5 Pr 21:22
24:6 Pr 11:14
24:7 Pr 14:6
24:8 Ro 1:30
24:10 Job 4:5
24:11 Ps 82:4
24:12 Job 34:11
24:13 SS 5:1
24:14 Pr 23:18
24:16 Job 5:19

4 and by knowledge the rooms will be filled
with all precious and pleasant riches.

Saying Twenty-Two

5 A wise man is strong;
yes, a man of knowledge increases
strength.
6 For by wise counsel you will wage your
war,
and in multitude of counselors there is
safety.

Saying Twenty-Three

7 Wisdom is too high for a fool;
he does not open his mouth in the gate.

Saying Twenty-Four

8 He who devises to do evil
will be called a schemer of plots.
9 The thought of foolishness is sin,
and the scorner is an abomination to
men.

Saying Twenty-Five

10 If you faint in the day of adversity,
your strength is small.
11 If you refrain to deliver those who are
drawn unto death,
and those who are ready to be slain;
12 if you say, "Surely we did not know this,"
does not He who ponders the heart
consider it?
And He who keeps your soul, does He not
know it?
And will He not render to every man
according to his works?

Saying Twenty-Six

13 My son, eat honey because it is good,
and the honeycomb that is sweet to your
taste;
14 so shall the knowledge of wisdom be to
your soul;
when you have found it, then there will
be a reward,
and your expectation will not be cut off.

> I will shout God's praises until I have become obnoxious to the enemy (Pr 24:15–16).

Saying Twenty-Seven

15 Do not lie in wait, O wicked man, against
the dwelling of the righteous;
do not spoil his resting place;
16 for a just man falls seven times and rises
up again,
but the wicked will fall into mischief.

Saying Twenty-Eight

[17]Do not rejoice when your enemy falls,
and do not let your heart be glad when he stumbles;
[18]lest the LORD see it, and it displease Him,
and He turn away His wrath from him.

Saying Twenty-Nine

[19]Do not fret because of evil men,
nor be envious of the wicked;
[20]for there will be no reward to the evil man;
the candle of the wicked will be put out.

Saying Thirty

[21]My son, fear the LORD and the king;
and do not meddle with those who are given to change;
[22]for their calamity will rise suddenly,
and who knows the ruin of them both?

More Sayings of the Wise

[23]These *things* also *belong* to the wise:

It is not good to show partiality in judgment.
[24]He who says to the wicked, "You are righteous,"
him the people will curse; nations will abhor him.
[25]But to those who rebuke him will be delight,
and a good blessing will come upon them.

[26]Every man will kiss his lips
that gives a right answer.

[27]Prepare your work outside,
and make it fit for yourself in the field;
and afterwards build your house.

[28]Do not be a witness against your neighbor without cause,
and do not deceive with your lips.
[29]Do not say, "I will do so to him as he has done to me;
I will render to the man according to his work."

[30]I went by the field of the slothful,
and by the vineyard of the man void of understanding;
[31]and it was all grown over with thorns,
and nettles covered its surface,
and the stone wall was broken down.
[32]Then I saw, and considered it;
I looked on it and received instruction:
[33]Yet a little sleep, a little slumber,
a little folding of the hands to sleep,
[34]so your poverty will come like a stalker,
and your need as an armed man.

24:17 Job 31:29
24:19 Ps 37:1
24:20 Pr 13:9
24:21 Ro 13:1–7
24:23 Pr 18:5
24:24 Pr 17:15
24:25 Pr 28:23
24:28 Eph 4:25
24:29 Pr 20:22
24:34 Pr 10:4

25:1 Pr 1:1
25:2 Dt 29:29
25:4 2Ti 2:20–21
25:5 Pr 16:12
25:8 Mt 5:25
25:9 Pr 11:13
25:11 Pr 15:23
25:12 Ps 141:5
25:13 Pr 13:17
25:14 Pr 20:6
25:15 Pr 15:1
25:16 Pr 25:27

More Proverbs of Solomon

25 These are also proverbs of Solomon, which the men of Hezekiah king of Judah copied.

[2] It is the glory of God to conceal a thing,
but the honor of kings is to search out a matter.
[3] As the heaven for height, and the earth for depth,
so the heart of kings is unsearchable.

[4] Take away the dross from the silver,
and there will come forth a vessel for the refiner.
[5] Take away the wicked from before the king,
and his throne will be established in righteousness.

[6] Do not exalt yourself in the presence of the king,
and do not stand in the place of great men;
[7] for it is better that it be said to you, "Come up here,"
than that you should be put lower in the presence of the prince,
whom your eyes have seen.
[8] Do not go forth hastily to strive;
lest you do not know what to do in the end,
when your neighbor has put you to shame.

[9] Debate your cause with your neighbor himself,
and do not disclose a secret to another;
[10]lest he who hears it put you to shame,
and your reputation be ruined.

[11]A word fitly spoken
is like apples of gold in settings of silver.
[12]As an earring of gold and an ornament of fine gold,
so is a wise reprover to an obedient ear.

[13]As the cold of snow in the time of harvest,
so is a faithful messenger to those who send him,
for he refreshes the soul of his masters.
[14]Whoever boasts himself of a false gift
is like clouds and wind without rain.

[15]By long forbearing is a prince persuaded,
and a soft tongue breaks the bone.

[16]Have you found honey? Eat only as much as is sufficient for you,
lest you be filled with it and vomit it.
[17]Withdraw your foot from your neighbor's house,
lest he be weary of you and so hate you.

SPIRITLED WOMAN

COUNSEL FROM THE SPIRIT BASICS

Gossip: More Than Mere Words

Where there is no wood, the fire goes out; so where there is no talebearer, the strife ceases.

—PROVERBS 26:20

Gossip can be extremely painful. All of us at one time or another have suffered from the wounds of careless words. We have felt the isolation and rejection they bring. We have seen the averted eyes and sensed the distance in others' measured words, words that often carried additional unspoken messages. We have known the turned backs of those who have avoided us.

I wish I could say I have never gossiped as a Christian, but I can't. I would gossip and then be grieved in my spirit. I would vow never to do it again, but then I would be caught up in it again. It got to the place where I asked God to isolate me until I was able to rise above this stronghold in my life.

Gossip is rooted in unbelief and watered by fear. Since fear is a spirit and unbelief a condition of the heart, we can call gossip a heart condition. Though we may be tempted to make excuses for gossiping, it is crucial to see gossip as the painful and shameful thing that it is. Then we will turn to our loving Father and ask His forgiveness, renounce our involvement with gossip, and rejoice as God hurls it away!

Lisa Bevere

18 A man who bears false witness against his neighbor
is like a club, a sword, and a sharp arrow.
19 Confidence in an unfaithful man in time of trouble
is like a broken tooth and a foot out of joint.
20 As he who takes away a garment in cold weather,
and as vinegar on soda,
so is he who sings songs to a heavy heart.

25:18 Ps 57:4
25:19 Isa 36:6
25:20 Ro 12:15

25:21 Ex 23:4–5
25:22 2Sa 16:12
25:23 Ps 101:5
25:24 Pr 21:9
25:25 Pr 15:30
25:27 Pr 27:2
25:28 Pr 16:32
26:2 Nu 23:8
26:3 Ps 32:9
26:5 Pr 28:11
26:6 Pr 10:26
26:7 Pr 26:9
26:8 Pr 26:1
26:9 Pr 23:35
26:11 Ex 8:15
26:12 Pr 29:20

21 If your enemy is hungry, give him bread to eat;
and if he is thirsty, give him water to drink;
22 for you will heap coals of fire upon his head,
and the LORD will reward you.

23 The north wind brings rain,
and a backbiting tongue an angry countenance.
24 It is better to dwell in the corner of the housetop
than with a brawling woman in a wide house.

25 As cold waters to a thirsty soul,
so is good news from a far country.
26 A righteous man falling down before the wicked
is as a troubled fountain and a corrupt spring.

27 It is not good to eat much honey;
so for men to search their own glory is not glory.

28 He who has no rule over his own spirit
is like a city that is broken down and without walls.

26 As snow in summer, and as rain in harvest,
so honor is not seemly for a fool.
2 As the bird by flitting, as the swallow by flying,
so the curse without cause will not alight.
3 A whip for the horse, a bridle for the donkey,
and a rod for the fool's back.
4 Do not answer a fool according to his folly,
lest you also be like unto him.
5 Answer a fool according to his folly,
lest he be wise in his own conceit.
6 He who sends a message by the hand of a fool
cuts off the feet and drinks violence.
7 The legs of the lame are not equal;
so is a parable in the mouth of fools.
8 As he who binds a stone in a sling,
so is he who gives honor to a fool.
9 As a thorn goes into the hand of a drunkard,
so is a parable in the mouth of fools.
10 The great God who formed all things
rewards the fool and rewards the transgressor.
11 As a dog returns to its vomit,
so a fool returns to his folly.
12 Do you see a man wise in his own conceit?
There is more hope for a fool than for him.

13 The slothful man says, "There is a lion in
the way!
A lion is in the streets!"
14 As the door turns upon his hinges,
so does the slothful upon his bed.
15 The slothful buries his hand in his bowl;
it grieves him to bring it again to his
mouth.
16 The sluggard is wiser in his own conceit
than seven men who can answer
reasonably.
17 He who passes by and meddles with strife
not belonging to him
is like one who takes a dog by the ears.
18 As a madman who casts
firebrands, arrows, and death,
19 so is the man who deceives his neighbor,
and says, "I was only joking."
20 Where there is no wood, the fire goes out;
so where there is no talebearer, the strife
ceases.
21 As charcoal is to burning coals, and wood
to fire,
so is a contentious man to kindle strife.
22 The words of a talebearer are as wounds,
and go down into the innermost parts of
the body.
23 Burning lips and a wicked heart
are like earthenware covered with silver
dross.
24 He who hates dissembles with his lips,
and lays up deceit within him;
25 when he speaks kindly, do not believe him,
for there are seven abominations in his
heart;
26 though his hatred is covered by deceit,
his wickedness will be shown before the
whole congregation.
27 Whoever digs a pit will fall into it,
and he who rolls a stone, it will return
upon him.
28 A lying tongue hates those who are
afflicted by it,
and a flattering mouth works ruin.

27 Do not boast about tomorrow,
for you do not know what a day may
bring forth.
2 Let another man praise you, and not your
own mouth;
a stranger, and not your own lips.
3 A stone is heavy and the sand weighty,
but a fool's wrath is heavier than them
both.
4 Wrath is cruel, and anger is outrageous,
but who is able to stand before envy?

26:13 Pr 22:13
26:15 Pr 19:24
26:16 Pr 26:12
26:19 Eph 5:4
26:20 Pr 22:10
26:21 Pr 15:18
26:22 Pr 18:8
26:24 Pr 12:20
26:25 Ps 28:3
26:27 Pr 28:10
26:28 Pr 29:5
27:1 Lk 12:19–20
27:2 Pr 25:27
27:3 Pr 17:12
27:4 Pr 6:34
....
27:5 Pr 28:23
27:6 Ps 141:5
27:8 Isa 16:2
27:10 1Ki 12:6–8
27:11 Pr 10:1
27:12 Pr 22:3
27:13 Pr 20:16
27:15 Pr 19:13
27:18 1Co 9:7
27:20 Pr 30:15–16
27:21 Pr 17:3

5 Open rebuke is better
than secret love.
6 Faithful are the wounds of a friend,
but the kisses of an enemy are deceitful.
7 The full soul loathes a honeycomb,
but to the hungry soul every bitter thing
is sweet.
8 As a bird that wanders from her nest,
so is a man who wanders from his place.
9 Ointment and perfume rejoice the heart,
so does the sweetness of a man's friend
by hearty counsel.
10 Do not forsake your own friend or your
father's friend,
nor go into your brother's house in the
day of your calamity;
for better is a neighbor who is near than
a brother far off.
11 My son, be wise, and make my heart glad,
that I may answer him who
reproaches me.
12 A prudent man foresees the evil and hides
himself,
but the simple pass on and are
punished.
13 Take his garment that is security for a
stranger,
and take a pledge of him for an
adulterous woman.
14 He who blesses his friend with a loud
voice, rising early in the morning,
it will be counted a curse to him.
15 A continual dripping on a very rainy day
and a contentious woman are alike;
16 whoever restrains her restrains the wind,
and grasps oil in his right hand.
17 Iron sharpens iron,
so a man sharpens the countenance of
his friend.

I will seek Him, and then keep seeking Him some more (Pr 27:17).

18 Whoever keeps the fig tree will eat its fruit;
so he who waits on his master will be
honored.
19 As in water face answers to face,
so the heart of man to man.
20 Death and destruction are never full;
so the eyes of man are never satisfied.
21 As the refining pot for silver, and the
furnace for gold,
so is a man to his praise.

22 Though you should grind a fool in a mortar
among wheat with a pestle,
yet his foolishness will not depart from
him.

23 Be diligent to know the state of your flocks,
and look well to your herds;
24 for riches are not forever,
nor does the crown endure to every
generation.
25 The hay appears, and the tender grass
shows itself,
and herbs of the mountains are
gathered.
26 The lambs are for your clothing,
and the goats are the price of the field.
27 You will have goats' milk enough
for your food, for the food of your
household,
and for the maintenance of your
maidens.

28

1 The wicked flee when no man
pursues,
but the righteous are bold as a lion.

2 Because of the transgression of a land,
many are its princes;
but by a man of understanding and
knowledge, it shall be prolonged.

3 A poor man who oppresses the poor
is like a sweeping rain that leaves no
food.

4 Those who forsake instruction praise the
wicked,
but such as keep instruction contend
with them.

5 Evil men do not understand justice,
but those who seek the LORD understand
all things.

6 Better is the poor who walks in his
uprightness
than he who is perverse in his ways,
though he be rich.

7 Whoever keeps the law is a wise son,
but he who is a companion of riotous
men shames his father.

8 He who by usury and unjust gain increases
his substance
will gather it for him who will pity the
poor.

9 He who turns away his ear from hearing
instruction,
even his prayer will be an abomination.

10 Whoever causes the righteous to go astray
in an evil way,
he himself will fall into his own pit;
but the upright will have good things in
possession.

11 The rich man is wise in his own conceit,
but the poor who has understanding
searches him out.

12 When righteous men rejoice, there is great
glory;
but when the wicked rise, a man hides
himself.

13 He who covers his sins will not prosper,
but whoever confesses and forsakes
them will have mercy.

14 Happy is the man who always fears,
but he who hardens his heart will fall
into mischief.

15 As a roaring lion and a charging bear,
so is a wicked ruler over the poor
people.

16 The prince who lacks understanding is also
a great oppressor,
but he who hates covetousness will
prolong his days.

17 A man burdened with bloodshed of any
person
will flee until death;
let no man help him.

18 Whoever walks uprightly will be saved,
but he who is perverse in his ways will
fall at once.

19 He who tills his land will have plenty of
bread,
but he who follows after vain things will
have poverty enough.

20 A faithful man will abound with blessings,
but he who makes haste to be rich will
not be innocent.

21 To show partiality is not good,
because for a morsel of bread that man
will transgress.

22 He who hastens to be rich has an evil eye,
and does not consider that poverty will
come upon him.

23 He who rebukes a man will find more favor
afterward
than he who flatters with the tongue.

24 Whoever robs his father or his mother
and says, "It is no transgression,"
the same is the companion of a
destroyer.

25 He who is of a proud heart stirs up strife,
but he who puts his trust in the LORD will
prosper.

27:22 Pr 23:35
27:23 1Pe 5:2
27:24 Pr 23:5
28:1 Lev 26:17
28:4 1Ki 18:18
28:5 Ps 92:6
28:6 Pr 19:1
28:7 Pr 29:3
28:8 Lev 25:36
28:9 Ps 109:7
28:10 Pr 26:27
28:11 Pr 26:16
28:12 Pr 11:10
28:13 Job 31:33
28:14 Pr 23:17
28:15 Mt 2:16
28:16 Isa 3:12
28:17 Ge 9:6
28:18 Pr 10:9
28:19 Pr 12:11
28:20 Pr 28:22
28:21 Eze 13:19
28:22 Pr 23:6
28:23 Pr 27:5–6
28:24 Pr 18:9
28:25 Pr 11:25

[26]He who trusts in his own heart is a fool,
but whoever walks wisely will be delivered.

[27]He who gives to the poor will not lack,
but he who hides his eyes will have many a curse.

[28]When the wicked rise, men hide themselves;
but when they perish, the righteous increase.

29 He who is often reproved, yet hardens his neck,
will suddenly be destroyed, and that without remedy.

2 When the righteous are in authority, the people rejoice;
but when the wicked rule, the people mourn.

3 Whoever loves wisdom rejoices his father,
but he who keeps company with harlots spends his substance.

4 The king establishes the land by judgment,
but he who receives bribes overthrows it.

5 A man who flatters his neighbor
spreads a net for his feet.

6 In the transgression of an evil man there is a snare,
but the righteous sing and rejoice.

7 The righteous considers the cause of the poor,
but the wicked regards not to know it.

8 Scornful men bring a city into a snare,
but wise men turn away wrath.

9 If a wise man contends with a foolish man,
whether he rage or laugh, there is no rest.

10 The bloodthirsty hate the upright,
but the just seek his soul.

11 A fool utters all his mind,
but a wise man keeps it in until afterwards.

12 If a ruler listens to lies,
all his servants are wicked.

13 The poor and the deceitful man have this in common:
The LORD gives light to the eyes of both.

14 The king who faithfully judges the poor,
his throne will be established forever.

15 The rod and reproof give wisdom,
but a child left to himself brings his mother to shame.

28:26 Pr 3:5
28:27 Pr 10:17
28:28 Pr 28:12
29:1 Pr 6:15
29:2 Est 8:15
29:3 Pr 10:1
29:4 Pr 29:14
29:5 Ps 5:9
29:6 Ecc 9:12
29:7 Job 29:16
29:8 Pr 11:11
29:10 Ge 4:5–8
29:11 Pr 12:16
29:13 Pr 22:2
29:14 Pr 16:12
29:15 Pr 10:1
29:16 Ps 37:36
29:17 Pr 13:24
29:18 Jn 13:17
29:20 Pr 26:12
29:22 Pr 15:18
29:23 Pr 15:33
29:24 Lev 5:1
29:25 Ge 20:2
29:26 Pr 19:6
30:2 Ps 73:22
30:3 Pr 9:10

16 When the wicked are multiplied, transgression increases;
but the righteous will see their fall.

17 Correct your son, and he will give you rest;
yes, he will give delight to your soul.

Good discipline means I am emotionally on top of training my kids in excellent character and behavior (Pr 29:17).

18 Where there is no vision, the people perish;
but happy is he who keeps the teaching.

19 A servant will not be corrected by words,
for though he understands he will not answer.

20 Do you see a man who is hasty in his words?
There is more hope for a fool than for him.

21 He who delicately brings up his servant from a child
will have him as a son in the end.

22 An angry man stirs up strife,
and a furious man abounds in transgression.

23 A man's pride will bring him low,
but honor will uphold the humble in spirit.

24 Whoever is partner with a thief hates his own soul;
he hears the oath but tells nothing.

25 The fear of man brings a snare,
but whoever puts his trust in the LORD will be safe.

26 Many seek the ruler's favor,
but every man's judgment comes from the LORD.

27 An unjust man is an abomination to the just,
and he who is upright in the way is an abomination to the wicked.

The Sayings of Agur

30 The words of Agur the son of Jakeh, the oracle.

The man declares to Ithiel,
to Ithiel and Ukal:

2 Surely I am more brutish than any man,
and have not the understanding of a man.

3 I neither learned wisdom,
nor have the knowledge of the holy.

4 Who has ascended up into heaven, or
descended?
Who has gathered the wind in his fists?
Who has bound the waters in a garment?
Who has established all the ends of the
earth?
What is His name, and what is the name of
His son,
if you know?

God is a shield to my children
(Pr 30:5).

5 Every word of God is pure;
He is a shield to those who put their trust
in Him.
6 Do not add to His words,
lest He reprove you, and you be found
a liar.

7 Two things I have required of you;
do not deny me them before I die:
8 Remove vanity and lies far from me—
give me neither poverty nor riches;
feed me with food convenient for me;
9 lest I be full, and deny You,
and say, "Who is the LORD?"
or lest I be poor, and steal,
and take the name of my God in vain.

10 Do not accuse a servant to his master,
lest he curse you, and you be found
guilty.

11 There is a generation that curses their
father,
and does not bless its mother.
12 There is a generation that is pure in its own
eyes,
and yet is not washed from its filthiness.
13 There is a generation—oh, how lofty are
their eyes!
And their eyelids are lifted up.
14 There is a generation whose teeth are as
swords,
and their jaw teeth as knives,
to devour the poor from off the earth,
and the needy from among men.

15 The leech has two daughters,
crying, "Give, give."

There are three things that are never
satisfied,
indeed, four things never say, "It is
enough":
16 the grave, the barren womb,
the earth that is not filled with water,
and the fire that never says, "It is
enough."

30:4 Jn 3:13
30:5 Ps 12:6
30:6 Dt 4:2
30:8 Mt 6:11
30:9 Ex 20:7
30:11 Pr 20:20
30:12 Lk 18:11
30:13 Pr 6:17
30:14 Job 29:17
30:16 Pr 27:20
30:17 Pr 23:22
30:18 Job 42:3
30:22 Pr 19:10
30:25 Pr 6:6–8
30:26 Ps 104:18
30:27 Joel 2:25
30:30 Jdg 14:18
30:32 Job 21:5
30:33 Pr 29:22
31:2 Isa 49:15

17 The eye that mocks at his father,
and despises to obey his mother,
the ravens of the valley will pick it out,
and the young eagles will eat it.

18 There are three things which are too
wonderful for me,
indeed, four which I do not know:
19 the way of an eagle in the air,
the way of a serpent on a rock,
the way of a ship in the midst of the sea,
and the way of a man with a maid.

20 Such is the way of an adulterous woman;
she eats and wipes her mouth,
and says, "I have done no wickedness."

21 For three things the earth is disquieted,
and for four which it cannot bear:
22 for a servant when he reigns,
and a fool when he is filled with food,
23 for a hateful woman when she is married,
and a handmaid who is heir to her
mistress.

24 There are four things which are little upon
the earth,
but they are exceeding wise:
25 The ants are a people not strong,
yet they prepare their food in the
summer;
26 the badgers are but a feeble folk,
yet they make their houses in the rocks;
27 the locusts have no king,
yet they go forth all of them by bands;
28 the spider takes hold with her hands,
and is in kings' palaces.

29 There are three things which go well,
indeed, four are comely in going:
30 a lion which is strongest among beasts,
and does not turn away for any;
31 a strutting rooster, a male goat also,
and a king, against whom there is no
rising up.

32 If you have been foolish in lifting up
yourself,
or if you have thought evil,
put your hand on your mouth.
33 Surely the churning of milk brings forth
butter,
and the wringing of the nose brings
forth blood,
so the forcing of wrath brings forth
strife.

The Sayings of King Lemuel's Mother

31 The words of King Lemuel, an oracle
that his mother taught him:

2 What, my son? And what, the son of my
womb?
And what, the son of my vows?

Confession of the Proverbs 31 Woman

Use these confessions in your prayer time to decree and declare the virtues of the Proverbs 31 woman over your life. Read the points aloud, and then pray them prophetically as the Holy Spirit gives you utterance.

"I will open my mouth to speak on the behalf of those who are left desolate and defenseless. I will be a voice for the innocent unborn babies who are murdered continually in my city.

"I will open my mouth to judge righteously and administer justice to the poor and needy. I will open my hand to the poor and fill the hands of the needy, whether they are needs of mind, body, or spirit.

"The virtue that God has given me makes me capable and intellectually equipped to do whatever He has called me to do.

"My husband (or husband-to-be) confidently trusts in me in his heart and relies on me in strong security. Because of this, he has no lack in honest gain and no need of dishonest spoils.

"I am anointed to comfort, encourage, and do good to my husband as long as there is life within me.

"I am girded with spiritual, mental, and physical strength. I am healthy, my mind is clear, and I will walk with God in the cool of the day. My arms are strengthened to carry the load of my days. I can do many things at one time and excel in all of them.

"I have the ability to taste and see that the labor of my hands is good. I have good endurance, and my lamp will burn continually. I will not be overwhelmed or burned out.

"My husband is well known in the gate of my city. He sits among the elders of the land, and his counsel is sought after around the world. He does not walk in the counsel of the ungodly, stand in the way of sinners, or sit in the seat of the scornful. Other men seek his counsel because they desire what he has in his marriage. My husband is fulfilled spiritually, emotionally, and physically through my relationship with him. There are no doors open in his life to cause him to give ungodly counsel.

"I am clothed with strength and dignity, and my position is strong and secure. I am secure and confident in who I am, and my husband does not have any hangups about it.

"I rejoice over my future. Great things are ahead for my personal endeavors, my marriage, my children, and even my extended family. Every omen or demonic prognostication against my future is overturned by my rejoicing in the great things that God is about to do.

"My mouth is opened in skillful and godly wisdom. The law of kindness is on my tongue to give godly counsel and instruction.

"My children will rise up and call me blessed. My husband will boast and praise me, saying, 'Many daughters have done virtuous and noble things, but my wife excels them all. She is a woman of virtue and excellence!'

"Charm and grace are deceptive, and beauty is vain because it is temporary. This is why I will be a woman who reverently and worshipfully fears the Lord. Because of this I will be praised."

There may be things in this confession that you are far away from in your marriage. Despite this, confess each one with boldness! Speak things that are not as though they were—*and soon they will become a reality!* Whose report will you believe for your household?

Kimberly Daniels

3 Do not give your strength to women,
nor your ways to that which destroys kings.

4 It is not for kings, O Lemuel,
it is not for kings to drink wine,
nor for princes strong drink;
5 lest they drink and forget the law,
and pervert the justice of any of the afflicted.
6 Give strong drink to him who is ready to perish,
and wine to those who are of heavy hearts.
7 Let him drink, and forget his poverty,
and remember his misery no more.

8 Open your mouth for the speechless
in the cause of all such as are appointed to destruction.
9 Open your mouth, judge righteously,
and plead the cause of the poor and needy.

Epilogue: The Virtuous Wife

10 Who can find a virtuous woman?
For her worth is far above rubies.
11 The heart of her husband safely trusts in her,
so that he will have no lack of gain.
12 She will do him good and not evil
all the days of her life.
13 She seeks wool and flax,
and works willingly with her hands.
14 She is like the merchant ships,
she brings her food from afar.
15 She also rises while it is yet night,
and gives food to her household,
and a portion to her maidens.
16 She considers a field and buys it;
with the fruit of her hands she plants a vineyard.
17 She clothes herself with strength,
and strengthens her arms.
18 She perceives that her merchandise is good;
her candle does not go out by night.
19 She lays her hands to the spindle,
and her hands hold the distaff.
20 She stretches out her hand to the poor;
yes, she reaches forth her hands to the needy.
21 She is not afraid of the snow for her household,
for all her household are clothed with scarlet.
22 She makes herself coverings of tapestry;
her clothing is silk and purple.
23 Her husband is known in the gates,
when he sits among the elders of the land.
24 She makes fine linen and sells it,
and delivers sashes to the merchant.
25 Strength and honor are her clothing,
and she will rejoice in time to come.
26 She opens her mouth with wisdom,
and in her tongue is the teaching of kindness.
27 She looks well to the ways of her household,
and does not eat the bread of idleness.
28 Her children rise up and call her blessed;
her husband also, and he praises her:
29 "Many daughters have done virtuously,
but you excel them all."
30 Charm is deceitful, and beauty is vain,
but a woman who fears the LORD, she shall be praised.
31 Give her of the fruit of her hands,
and let her own works praise her in the gates.

31:3 Dt 17:17
31:4 Ecc 10:17
31:6 1Ti 5:23
31:8 Ps 82:3–4
31:9 Lev 19:15
31:10 Ru 3:11
31:15 Lk 12:42

31:20 Eph 4:28
31:22 Ge 41:42
31:23 Ru 4:1
31:25 1Ti 2:10

Author: Traditionally King Solomon

Written: 935 BC

Themes: Meaning of Life, Searching for Purpose

ECCLESIASTES

Dear Spirit Led Woman,

As you probably know from experience, God has different plans for different seasons of your life. Ecclesiastes reminds us of this: "To everything there is a season, a time for every purpose under heaven" (Ecc 3:1). When seasons change and the Holy Spirit leads you in a new direction, step out in faith to obey. Do not be afraid of what our Lord has designed. No one except God knows the end from the beginning, but if you take hold of His plan for your life, you will see Him do mighty works through you!

It might be difficult to relinquish our control, to step off of the path we have created for ourselves and follow the one God has created instead. At times we may not know how we can achieve the tasks God has laid out for us. However, when we follow God's orders, He will make the way. We don't have to rely on our own strength.

Joy F. Strang

All Is Vanity

1 These are the words of the Preacher, the
son of David and king in Jerusalem.

2 "Vanity[1] of vanities,"
says the Preacher;
"vanity of vanities,
all is vanity."

3 What benefit is there to a man in all his
labors
that he toils under the sun?
4 A generation comes, and a generation
goes,
but the earth continually remains.
5 The sun comes up, and the sun goes down,
and hurries to the place where it rises.
6 It moves to the south,
and then moves around to the north;
the wind continually travels around,
and it keeps turning on its circuit.
7 All the streams flow into the sea,
and the sea is never filled up.
And to the place where the streams flow,
there they continually return to flow.
8 All matters are wearisome;
a man is not able to speak to them.
The eye is not satisfied with what it sees,
and the ear is not content with what it
hears.
9 What has been is the same as what will be,
and what has been done is the same as
what will be done;
there is nothing new under the sun.
10 Is there a matter where it is said,
"See, this is truly new"?
Long ago in the past
every matter has already been in our
midst.
11 There is not a memory for the former
things,
and moreover, there will not be
a memory for the things coming after,
even those things that are yet to come.

The Burden of Wisdom

12 I, the Preacher, have been king over Israel
in Jerusalem. 13 I set my heart to seek and to in-
vestigate with wisdom everything that is done
under heaven. It is a burdensome task that God
has given to the sons of men, by which they
may be occupied. 14 I have seen everything that
is done under the sun, and indeed, all is vanity
and like chasing the wind.

15 What is bent cannot be straightened,
and what is missing cannot be counted.

16 I spoke in my heart, saying, "I have been
great and increased in wisdom more than any-

[1] 2 Heb. suggests something futile, temporal, or obscure.

1:1 Ecc 1:12
1:2 Ecc 12:8
1:3 Ecc 2:11
1:4 Ps 104:5
1:5 Ps 19:4–6
1:6 Jn 3:8
1:8 Pr 27:20
1:9 Ecc 3:15
1:11 Ecc 2:16
1:12 Ecc 1:1
1:13 Ecc 3:10
1:14 Ecc 2:11
1:16 1Ki 4:30
....
1:17 Ecc 2:3
2:1 Ecc 8:15
2:2 Pr 14:13
2:3 Pr 20:1
2:4 1Ki 7:1–12
2:6 Ne 2:14
2:8 2Sa 19:35
2:9 1Ch 29:25
2:10 Ecc 3:22
2:11 Ecc 1:14
2:12 Ecc 1:17

one else who has been before me in Jerusa-
lem, and my heart has had great experience of
wisdom and knowledge." 17 And I set my heart
to know wisdom and to know the folly of ideas
and to know foolish behavior, and I know that
this as well is like chasing the wind.

18 For in an abundance of wisdom is an
abundance of frustration,
and he who increases in knowledge also
increases in sorrow.

The Vanity of Pleasure

2 And I said in my heart, "Come, and I will
test you with selfish pleasures to experi-
ence desires." And notice that this too is vanity.
2 And I said of frivolous fun, "They are only
senseless ideas"; and regarding selfish plea-
sure, "What purpose is this?" 3 I investigated
how to cheer up my body with wine, while my
heart was still guiding me with wisdom, in or-
der to grasp folly until I might experience what
is good for sons of men to do under heaven
during the number of days that they might
have life.
4 I accomplished great works. I built hous-
es for myself, and planted myself vineyards.
5 I made for myself royal gardens and parks,
and I planted in them all sorts of fruit trees. 6 I
made for myself pools of water to irrigate the
forests of growing trees. 7 I even bought male
and female slaves; even some were born to me
in my house. I had also great possessions of
herds and flocks more than any who had been
in Jerusalem before me. 8 I also gathered for
myself silver and gold and treasures of kings
and provinces. I obtained singers, both men
and women, and the delights of the sons of
men, and many concubines. 9 So I became
great and surpassed anyone who had been in
Jerusalem before me. All the while my wisdom
remained with me.

10 And everything that my eyes wanted I did
not refuse them.
And I did not withhold my heart from
any selfish pleasure,
for my heart was glad from all my efforts;
and this was my reward for all my
efforts.
11 Then I turned to all the work that my hands
had designed
and all the labor that I had toiled to
make;
and notice, all of it was vanity and chasing
the wind.
And there was no benefit under the sun.

The Fate of the Wise and the Fool

12 So I turned to consider wisdom,
the folly of ideas, and foolish behavior;
for what else can a man do who comes
after the king?

Or what more than those have already
done?
13 Then I saw that there is more benefit in
wisdom than in foolishness,
more benefit in light than in darkness.
14 A wise man has eyes in his head so he sees
where he walks,
but the fool continues in darkness.
Yet I perceived
that the same fate overtakes them all.

15 Then I said in my heart,

"What happens to the fool will happen to
me also.
So to what advantage is my wisdom?"
Then I said to myself,
"This also is vanity."
16 For there is no lasting memory for the wise
or the fool,
by which in the coming days everyone
will be forgotten.
How the wise dies just like the fool!

17 And I began to hate life for the labor that
was done under the sun was contemptible to
me, for all of this was vanity and chasing the
wind. 18 And I despised all the toil in which I
labored under the sun, which I will give up
to the man who comes after me. 19 And who
knows if this man will be wise or a fool? Yet
he will gain power over every labor that I have
toiled and *my use of* wisdom under the sun.
Also this is vanity. 20 So I turned to give my
heart up to despair concerning all the toil of
my labors under the sun. 21 For there is a man
who labors with wisdom, knowledge, and skill;
yet to a man who did not labor for this, he
leaves it as his inheritance. This also is vanity
and a great distress. 22 For what becomes of
a man with all his labor and with the striving
in his heart that he toils under the sun? 23 For
all his days are sorrowful, and his work is a
vexation; even at night his heart finds no rest.
Also this is fleeting.
24 There is nothing better for a man than to
eat and drink, and find enjoyment in his labor.

> I am good in the sight of the Lord,
> for He gives me wisdom, knowledge,
> and joy (Ecc 2:26).

This also, I saw, is from the hand of God. 25 For
who can even eat or have enjoyment more
so than I?[1] 26 For to a man who is pleasing
before Him, God gives wisdom, knowledge,
and joy; but to the sinner He gives the work
of gathering and collecting to give him who
is pleasing before God. Also this is vanity and
chasing the wind.

2:13 Ecc 7:11–12
2:14 Ps 49:10
2:15 Ecc 6:8
2:16 Ecc 1:11
2:17 Ecc 2:11
2:18 Ps 39:6
2:22 Ecc 1:3
2:23 Job 5:7
2:24 Ecc 3:12–13
2:26 Pr 13:22

3:1 Ecc 3:17
3:2 Heb 9:27
3:4 Ex 15:20
3:7 Am 5:13
3:8 Lk 14:26

SPIRITLED WOMAN

COUNSEL FROM THE SPIRIT BASICS

The Seasons of Life

In life there can be times of multiplication, but there can also be times of drought and hardship. Have you ever noticed how these seasons of life mirror the passing of the natural seasons of winter, spring, summer, and fall?

Just as there are seasons in nature, our lives have seasons. Some are barren and cold. Some are filled with new hope and new life. In some seasons we plant and we water, and we don't see anything come up for a while. But then comes the harvest season.

If you're in a winter season right now, don't quit or get discouraged. Spring is coming in your life, just as surely as it comes in the natural realm every year. God hasn't stopped multiplying you. Your season of increase is coming if you'll simply keep believing.

Karen Jensen Salisbury

A Time for Everything

3 To everything there is a season,
a time for every purpose under heaven:

2 a time to be born, and a time to die;
a time to plant, and a time to uproot
what is planted;
3 a time to kill, and a time to heal;
a time to break down, and a time to
build up;
4 a time to weep, and a time to laugh;
a time to mourn, and a time to dance;
5 a time to cast away stones, and a time to
gather stones;
a time to embrace, and a time to refrain
from embracing;
6 a time to gain, and a time to lose;
a time to keep, and a time to cast away;
7 a time to tear, and a time to sew;
a time to keep silence, and a time to
speak;
8 a time to love, and a time to hate;
a time of war, and a time of peace.

[1] 25 Some Heb. and Gk. texts, *apart from Him.*

The God-Given Task

9 What benefit does the worker have in his
toil? 10 I have seen the task that God has given
to sons of men to be concerned with. 11 He has
made everything beautiful in its appropriate
time. He has also put obscurity in their hearts[1]
so that no one comes to know the work that
God has done from the beginning to the end.
12 I experienced that there is nothing better for
them than to be glad and do good in their life.
13 And also that everyone should eat and drink
and experience good in all their labor. This is a
gift of God. 14 I have perceived that everything
that God has done will be lasting. And to this
there is nothing to be added, and from it there
is nothing to be taken away. And God has done
this so that in His presence men fear Him.

15 That which is has already been,
and what is to come has also already
been;
and God seeks out what has been driven
away.

The Vanity of Injustice

16 Moreover I saw what was under the sun:

In the place of justice, there was
wickedness;
and in the place of righteousness, there
was wickedness.

17 I thought in my heart:

God will bring judgment
to the righteous and the wicked,
for there is an appropriate time
for every matter and deed.

18 Then I thought in my heart: Regarding the
account of sons of men, God is making clear to
them to show that they are but animals. 19 For
what befalls the sons of men befalls animals;
as one dies, so dies the other. There is one
breath for all of them; there is no advantage for
man any more than animals, for all is vanity.
20 All go to one place: All are from the dust and
all return to dust. 21 Who knows whether the
spirit of man goes upward and the spirit of
animals goes down to the earth?
22 So I saw that there is nothing better than
that a man should rejoice in his labor, for that
is his reward. For who will bring him to see
what will happen after his life?

Evil Under the Sun

4 Again I saw all types of oppression that
are done under the sun:

Look! The tears of the oppressed,
and no one was there to comfort them.
And there was force from the hand of the
oppressors,
and no one was there to comfort them.
2 And I thought that fortunate were the dead
who had already died,
even more than the living
who were still alive.
3 And still better than both
is he who has not been,
who has not seen the evil deeds
that are done under the sun.

4 Then I saw that all toil and every skillful
work come from one man's envy of another.
This also is vanity and like chasing the wind.

5 The fool folds his hands
and eats his own flesh.
6 Better is a full hand of quietness
than handfuls of toil and chasing the
wind.

7 Again, I saw vanity under the sun:

8 There is a man who is alone,
neither having son or brother,
and there is not an end to all his toil,
and his eyes are not satisfied with riches
to say,
"For whom do I labor
and cause my life to lack good things?"
Also this is vanity
and a burdensome task.
9 Two are better than one,
because there is a good reward for their
labor together.
10 For if they fall,
then one will help up his companion.
But woe to him who is alone when he falls
and has no one to help him up.
11 Also if two lie down together, then they will
keep warm;
but how can one keep warm by himself?
12 And if someone might overpower another
by himself,
two together can withstand him.
A threefold cord is not quickly broken.

The Vanity of Status

13 Better is a poor and wise youth than an
old and foolish king who will no longer be
admonished. 14 For out of prison he has come
to reign, even though he was born poor in the
kingdom. 15 Then I saw all those who live and
walk under the sun, along with the next youth
who will arise in the *king's* place. 16 There is no
end of all the people, to all who were before
them. Yet those who come later will not rejoice
in him. Surely this also is vanity and chasing
the wind.

3:9 Ecc 1:3
3:11 Ecc 8:17
3:13 Ecc 2:24
3:14 Jas 1:17
3:16 Ecc 4:1
3:17 Ecc 3:1
3:18 Ps 73:22
3:19 Ps 49:12
3:20 Ge 3:19
3:21 Ecc 12:7
3:22 Ecc 2:24
4:1 Ecc 3:16
....
4:2 Ecc 2:17
4:3 Lk 23:29
4:4 Ecc 1:14
4:5 Isa 9:20
4:6 Pr 15:16–17
4:7 Ecc 4:1
4:8 Pr 27:20
4:13 Ecc 9:15–16
4:14 Ge 41:14
4:16 Ecc 1:14

[1] 11 Or *timelessness*, or *perpetuity*.

Revere God

5 Guard your steps when you enter the
house of God, and draw near to listen
rather than to offer the sacrifice of fools, for
they do not know that they are doing evil.[1]

2 Do not be quick *to speak* with your mouth,
nor let your heart be hasty to utter a
word
before God.
For God is in heaven,
and you are on the earth;
therefore may your words be few.
3 For a dream comes when there is a great
burden,
and a foolish voice when there are many
words.

4 When you make a vow to God, do not delay
in fulfilling it because He has no pleasure in
fools. Fulfill what you have vowed. 5 Better it
is that you do not make a vow than you make
a vow and not fulfill it. 6 Do not let your mouth
cause you to sin, and do not say before the
messenger that it was an error. Why should
God be angry with your words and destroy
the work of your hands? 7 For when there is
an abundance of dreams and futilities, then
words increase too. Therefore it is God you
should fear.

The Vanity of Loving Money

8 If you see in a district the oppression of the
poor and the violent perversion of justice and
righteousness, do not be astounded at the mat-
ter; for the high official is watched over by an
even higher official, and there are even higher
officials over them. 9 But this is an advantage
to the land in every way, like a king committed
to a cultivated field.

10 He who loves money will not be satisfied
with money;
nor he who loves abundance with
increase.
This also is vanity.
11 When there is an increase of good things,
then there is an increase of those who
devour them.
And what profit have the owners
except to see them with their eyes?

12 Sweet is the sleep of a laboring man,
whether he eats a little or much;
but the abundance of the rich
will not let him sleep.

13 There is a grave misery that I have seen
under the sun:

when riches were kept by an owner to his
hurt,
14 and those riches were lost in a
misfortunate business deal;
and although he has a son,
there is nothing at all to put in his hand.
15 As he came from his mother's womb,
naked shall he return, to go as he came;
he shall take nothing from his labor
which he may carry away in his hands.

16 This also is a grievous evil:

Just as he came,
so shall he go.
And what profit is there to him who toils
for the wind?
17 Moreover, in all his days he eats in
darkness,
while he is greatly irritated in sickness
and anger.

18 This is what I have seen to be good: It is
fitting to eat and drink and find enjoyment in
all his labor in which he toils under the sun
all the days of his life, which God has given to
him; for this is his reward. 19 And also everyone
to whom God has given wealth and posses-
sions, and given him power to enjoy them,
and to receive his reward and to rejoice in his
labor—this is the gift of God. 20 For he will not
much remember the days of his life because
God keeps him occupied with joy in his heart.

6 There is an evil that I have seen under the
sun, and it lies heavy on mankind: 2 a man
to whom God gives wealth, possessions, and
honor so that there is no want in his life from
among anything that he desires; yet God does
not give him ability to eat from them because
another man eats and enjoys from *his posses-
sions*. This is vanity and a tormenting injustice.
3 If a man fathers a hundred children and
lives many years, so that the days of his years
are many, but his soul is not satisfied with life's
good things, and he has no burial, I say that
a stillborn child is better off than he— 4 for it
comes in vanity and departs in darkness, and
in darkness its name is covered up. 5 Moreover,
it has not seen the sun or known anything, yet
it finds rest rather than he. 6 Though the man
may live a thousand years, twice over, yet he
does not see the good things. Does not every-
one go to the same place?

7 All the labor of man is for his mouth,
yet his appetite is not satisfied.
8 For what benefit is there for the wise
over the fool?
And what more does the poor man know
who walks before others?
9 Better to be content with the sight of eyes
than to have a wandering appetite.

5:1 Ex 3:5
5:2 Pr 10:19
5:4 Nu 30:2
5:5 Pr 20:25
5:6 1Co 11:10
5:7 Ecc 12:13
5:8 Ps 12:5
5:10 Ecc 4:8
5:12 Pr 3:24
5:13 Ecc 6:1–2
....
5:15 Job 1:21
5:16 Pr 11:29
5:17 Ps 127:2
5:18 Ecc 2:10
5:19 Ecc 6:2
6:1 Ecc 5:13
6:2 Ps 17:14
6:3 Job 3:16
6:7 Pr 16:26
6:9 Ecc 1:14

1 1 4:17 in the Heb. text.

GROWING AS A SPIRITLED WOMAN

The Pursuit of Real Meaning in Life

As a young child, Solomon was tutored in the ways and wisdom of the Lord by his mother, Bathsheba. He was her closest and most treasured son. David had promised her that Solomon would sit upon the throne and succeed him (1Ki 1:30). The Lord had loved Solomon from the moment of his birth and sent confirmation of Solomon's destiny by the mouth of the prophet Nathan (2Sa 12:24–25).

In the light of this, Bathsheba raised Solomon from infancy to be set apart as a prince and ruler over God's people. She instructed him daily in the statutes and fear of the Lord. Solomon confirms this repeatedly in Proverbs.

Look up Proverbs 4:3–4; 6:20. What do these verses tell us that Solomon learned from his mother's instruction and God's revelation about her instructions?

Solomon's father gave him commandments, and his mother taught him. David would speak God's laws or principles, and then Bathsheba would explain to the young Solomon how they were to be applied to life. Her words bore insight into relationships, gave warning and instruction, and imparted an even deeper desire within Solomon for wisdom.

When Solomon became king, he was still a young man. He began his exploration of all that was under the sun.

Read Ecclesiastes 2:1, 3. What does this scripture tell us is one of the first things Solomon pursued as an adult?

Doesn't that sound like a lot of us? We were raised by parents who instructed us the best they knew how, teaching us right from wrong in the hope that we would learn from their mistakes. But most of us, as soon as we were on our own, pursued the same thing. How have you attempted to pursue this same thing in your own life?

It wasn't long before Solomon decided he wanted more out of life. Read Ecclesiastes 2:4–9. What is the next thing that Solomon began to pursue?

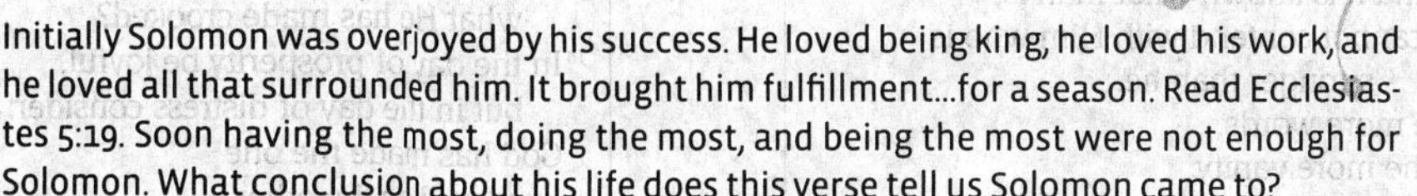

Initially Solomon was overjoyed by his success. He loved being king, he loved his work, and he loved all that surrounded him. It brought him fulfillment...for a season. Read Ecclesiastes 5:19. Soon having the most, doing the most, and being the most were not enough for Solomon. What conclusion about his life does this verse tell us Solomon came to?

It is important to note that there is nothing wrong with having goals and dreams. God made us with the creative capacity to dream. However, according to Ecclesiastes 5:19, what is important to understand in order to enjoy our successes?

God gives wealth, possessions, and contentment. Outside of His provision, we may have "things" but not peace. This means we cannot enjoy them. Often those with the greatest possessions are tormented with the most worry. They cannot rest and enjoy what they have because they are consumed with thinking of ways they might safeguard and even expand their riches. Then there is another torment that plagues them: Though they have much, they notice there are those who have even more. They strive, trying to gain as much as their neighbor, and so are never satisfied with what they have in their hands. They lose what they possess, either by holding it too tightly or by grasping for more.

This is a telltale sign of those who have measured themselves by what they have. Possessions are a deceptive measure of worth. There is no lasting stability because a person's worth is not dependent on the increase or decrease of possessions.

Read 1 Timothy 6:6. What two important ingredients are necessary in our lives?

Our lives are of a much greater worth than things, and therefore our lives cannot be measured by things. If our worth were equal to a whole world of things, then God would not have ransomed us with the life of His only Son. Instead He would have ransomed us with the boundless riches of heaven, where the riches are so immense that gold paves the streets. In God's eyes, our worth is far more precious than gold.

Lisa Bevere

This is vanity
and like chasing the wind.

10 Whatever happens, it has already been
given a name,
and it is known what man is;
he cannot contend with Him who is
stronger than he.
11 The more words,
the more vanity,
so what profit is there to mankind?

12 For who knows what is good for man while
he lives the few days of his vain life which pass
like a shadow? For who can tell men what will
be after them under the sun?

The Value of Wisdom

7 A good name is better than precious
ointment,
and the day of death than the day of
birth.
2 It is better to go to a house of mourning
than to go to a house of feasting,
for this is the end of all mankind;
and the living will lay it to heart.
3 Grief is better than laughter,
for with a downcast face the heart
considers the good.
4 The heart of those who are wise is in the
house of mourning,
but the heart of those who are foolish in
the house of feasting.
5 It is better to hear the rebuke from a wise
man
than a man listen to the song of
fools.
6 For like the crackling sound of thorns
under a pot,
so is the mocking laughter of fools.
And this is also vanity.

7 For oppression brings confusion to the
wise man,
and a bribe destroys a man's heart.

8 The end of a matter is better than the
beginning of it,
and the patient in spirit than the haughty
in spirit.
9 Do not be quick in your spirit to be angry,
for irritation settles in the bosom of fools.

10 Do not say, "Why were the earlier days
better than these days?"
For it is not from wisdom that you
inquire this.

11 Wisdom is good with an inheritance,
and an advantage to those who see the
sun.
12 For the protection of wisdom
is like the protection of money,
and the advantage of knowledge is
that wisdom preserves the life of him
who has it.

13 Consider the work of God:

Who is able to make straight
what He has made crooked?
14 In the day of prosperity be joyful,
but in the day of distress consider:
God has made the one
as well as the other.
For this reason man will not be able to
understand
anything that comes after him.

15 I have seen everything in my days of vanity:

There is the righteous man who dies in his
righteousness,
and there is the wicked man who
extends his life of evil.
16 Do not be excessively righteous,
and do not be extremely wise;
why should you destroy yourself?
17 Do not be overly wicked,
and do not be a fool;
why should you die before your time?
18 It is good that you should take hold of this,
and from the other not withhold your
hand;
for he who fears God will come out from
them all.

19 Wisdom strengthens the wise man
more than ten rulers who are in the city.

20 For there is not a righteous man on earth
who only does good and refrains from
sin.

21 Do not give heed to everything people say,
lest you hear your servant cursing you.
22 Your heart knows
that many times you have spoken a
curse against others.

23 All this I have tested by wisdom. I said,

"I will be wise,"
but it was far from me.
24 That which is, is far off,
and exceedingly deep.
Who can find it out?
25 And I turned my heart to know,
and seek and search out wisdom in how
things are
and to experience wicked folly,
even foolishness and madness.

6:10 Job 9:32
6:12 Job 14:2
7:1 Pr 22:1
7:2 Ps 90:12
7:5 Ps 141:5
7:6 Ps 58:9
7:7 Dt 16:19
7:8 Pr 14:29
7:9 Pr 14:17
7:11 Ecc 11:7
7:12 Pr 3:18

....

7:13 Ecc 1:15
7:14 Ecc 3:22
7:15 Ecc 8:12–14
7:16 Ro 12:3
7:17 Ps 55:23
7:20 1Ki 8:46
7:21 Pr 30:10
7:23 Ro 1:22
7:24 Ro 11:33
7:25 Ecc 10:13

The possession of God's wisdom is a defense to me (Ecc 7:12).

26 I find more bitter than death
the woman whose heart is snares
and nets,
and whose hands are fetters.
He who pleases God escapes her,
but the sinner is taken by her.

27 "See, this is what I found," says the Preacher,

"adding one thing to another to find the
sum,
28 which my soul still seeks
but I do not find:
One man among a thousand I have found,
but a woman among all these I have not
found.
29 See, this only have I found:
that God made man upright,
but they have sought out many
schemes."

8 Who is like a wise man?
And who knows the interpretation of a
matter?
A man's wisdom makes his face shine,
and the harshness of his face is
softened.

The Value of Obedience

2 I say, "Keep the king's command, because of your oath to God. 3 Do not be hasty to leave his presence. Do not take a stand in an unpleasant matter, for he does whatever pleases him." 4 For the word of the king is powerful, and who would say to him, "What are you doing?"

5 He who keeps his command will know no
evil thing;
and a wise heart will know the
appropriate time and just way.
6 For to every matter there is an appropriate
time and just way,
though a man's distress weighs heavily
on him.
7 For he does not know what will happen;
for who can declare to him what will
occur?
8 There is not a man with mastery over the
wind to restrain it,
nor with power over the day of death.
And no one can discharge a battle,
nor can wickedness rescue the one
possessing it.

9 All this I saw while applying my heart to every work that is done under the sun, when one man rules over another to the other's hurt.

God's Unknowable Ways

10 Then I saw the wicked buried. They used to go in and out of the holy place, and they were praised[1] in the city where they did works. This is also vanity.

11 Because the sentence against an evil deed is not executed swiftly, the heart of the sons of men is fully set to do evil. 12 Since one who sins may do evil a hundred times and extend his life, I also have experienced that it will be good for those who fear God when they have reverence before Him. 13 But it will not be well for the wicked, and he will not prolong his days, like a shadow, because he does not fear before God.

14 There is a vanity that takes place on the earth that there are righteous men who are treated according to the deeds of the wicked, and there are wicked men who are treated according to the deeds of the righteous. I said that this also is vanity. 15 And I commend joy, for man has nothing better under the sun than to eat and drink and be joyful; for this will go with him in his labor all the days of his life that God has given him under the sun.

16 When I set my heart to know wisdom and to experience the affairs that are done on earth, though day and night there is no sleep for one's eyes, 17 then I saw all the work of God, that a man cannot comprehend the work that is done under the sun. Inasmuch as a man labors to seek, he will not understand. Even if a wise man claims to know, he cannot grasp it.

A Common Fate

9 For I considered all this in my heart, so that I could declare it all: that the deeds of the righteous and the wise are in the hand of God. No man knows whether love or hate awaits them; both are before him. 2 The same fate comes to all: There is one fate for the righteous and the wicked, for the good and the evil,[2] for the clean and the unclean, for him who sacrifices and him who does not sacrifice.

As is the good,
so is the sinner;
he who takes an oath
as he who fears an oath.

3 And this is an evil in all that is done under the sun: that the same event happens to all. Truly the hearts of the sons of men are filled with evil, and folly is in their hearts while they have life, and after that they go to the dead. 4 But for him who is joined to all the living there is hope, for a living dog is better than a dead lion.

5 The living know that they will die,
but the dead know nothing;
they have no more reward,
for the memory of them is forgotten.

7:26 Pr 22:14
7:28 Job 33:23
7:29 Ge 3:6–7
8:1 Dt 28:50
8:2 1Ki 2:43
8:3 Ecc 10:4
8:6 Ecc 3:1
8:7 Ecc 6:12
8:9 Ecc 5:8
8:10 Ecc 9:5
8:12 Ps 37:11
8:13 Job 14:2
8:14 Ecc 7:15
8:15 Ecc 2:24
8:17 Ecc 3:11
9:1 Dt 33:3
9:3 Ecc 1:17
9:5 Job 14:21

[1] 10 Or the Heb. *forgotten*. [2] 2 *Evil* from Gk. is missing in some Heb. mss.

WOMAN OF THE SPIRIT

What Do You Model?

Whatever your hands find to do, do with your strength.

—Ecclesiastes 9:10

How hard do your children see you work at what you do? Are you setting an example of excellence in your household for them to emulate? What you do, they will follow, and the pace you set is the pace they will run. My husband likes to say, "The speed of the leader is the speed of the group." If you sit at home during the day, watching television or playing computer games for hours, you risk having your kids grow up to do exactly the same with their precious time.

Walking into one's destiny probably ought not to be called a walk. In reality, it can often be a strenuous climb. Success is not going to happen by accident, and successful adults don't just spontaneously coalesce. Most successful adults we know were raised to believe hard work and tenacious dedication are the pathways to success. The tangible rewards of financial, social, and spiritual success naturally follow the work needed to achieve them. To those who say success is a matter of luck, I offer the theory that the harder we work, the luckier we become. It's our job to set the example and to teach our children the value of diligence. What you model, they will follow.

We intentionally created an atmosphere in our house where our daughter's gifts were nurtured, celebrated, and honored, and we set high expectations. We set a standard of excellence in every area of our home life. She knew we wouldn't let her slack off in any area because we modeled a job well done in our own work. We endeavored to exemplify daily, in large things and small, that anything worth doing is worth doing well and that anything worth having is worth working for.

Franny knew growing up that I loved to cook and entertain, and I tend to go all out when we have people over. I make pretty much everything I cook from scratch, and I have a passion for good food and making people feel special and welcome when they come to my house. It is such a passion for me that I started my own blog about a year ago to share my favorite recipes and cooking how-tos. So she knew when we entertained that we weren't going to be cutting corners. We used the good china and the good silverware. We were going to be cooking, baking, cleaning, and all the other things it takes to entertain and offer hospitality. And she was going to help me! I knew I was setting an example for her not only in hospitality but also in taking the time to do things well and with excellence. As a wife and mom now, she is a gracious hostess who provides wonderful hospitality for her friends and family.

Kate Battistelli

6 What they loved, hated,
and envied has already perished;
and there is no reward for them from long ago
in everything that is done under the sun.

7 Go and eat your food with gladness, and
drink your wine with a pleasant heart; for
God is already pleased with your deeds. 8 At
all times may your clothing be white, and let
not oil ever lack on your head. 9 Enjoy life with
the wife whom you love all the days of your
vain life which He has given you under the
sun; because that is your reward in life and in
your toil because you have labored under the
sun. 10 Whatever your hands find to do, do with
your strength; for there is no work or planning
or knowledge or wisdom in Sheol, the place
where you are going.

11 Again I saw under the sun that—

the race is not to the swift,
nor the battle to the strong,
nor food to the wise,
nor riches to the intelligent,
nor favor to those with knowledge;
but time and chance happen to them all.

12 For man does not know his time:
Like fish caught in an unfortunate net,
like birds caught in a snare,
so the sons of men are ensnared at a tragic, yet appointed time,
when it suddenly falls on them.

The Excellence of Wisdom

13 I have also seen this wisdom under the
sun, and it seemed great to me: 14 There was a
small city with a few men in it; and a great king
came and surrounded it, and he built up great
siege works against it. 15 But a poor, wise man
was found there, and he himself in his wisdom
delivered the city, but no one remembered that
poor man. 16 Then I said, "Wisdom is better
than strength; yet the poor man's wisdom is
despised, and his words are not heard."

17 The words of the wise heard in quietness are better
than the shouting of a ruler among fools.
18 Wisdom is better than weapons of war,
but only one sinner can destroy much that is good.

10 1 A dead fly causes a stench in mixed anointing oil,
so a little folly is more weighty than wisdom and honor.
2 The heart of the wise inclines to the right,
but the heart of a fool to the left.
3 Even when a fool walks on the road,
he lacks sense,
and he shows everyone that he is a fool.

9:7 Ecc 8:15
9:8 Ps 23:5
9:9 Ecc 2:10
9:10 Ro 12:11
9:11 Jer 9:23
9:12 Pr 29:6
9:15 Ecc 4:13
9:16 Ecc 7:19
9:18 Jos 7:1
10:3 Pr 13:16
....
10:4 Pr 25:15
10:6 Est 3:1
10:7 Pr 19:10
10:8 Am 5:19
10:11 Jer 8:17
10:12 Lk 4:22
10:14 Pr 15:2
10:16 Isa 3:12
10:18 Pr 20:4

4 If the anger of a ruler rises against you,
do not leave your post;
for calmness pacifies great offenses.

5 There is an evil that I have seen under the sun
like an error that goes out from a ruler:
6 Folly is set in many high places,
but the rich sit in a low place.
7 I have seen slaves riding on horses,
and officials walking along the ground like slaves.

I pray for every broken hedge in my life to be restored in the name of Jesus (Ecc 10:8).

8 He who digs a pit will fall into it,
and whoever breaks through a wall will be bitten by a serpent.
9 He who quarries stones is injured by them,
and he who splits wood is in danger from them.

Wisdom is a benefit to help me succeed (Ecc 10:10).

10 If an iron piece is blunt
and there is no one to sharpen it,
then he must prevail with more strength;
but wisdom is a benefit to succeed.

11 If a serpent bites before it is charmed,
there is no advantage to the charmer.

12 The words of a wise man's mouth bring favor,
but the speech of a fool consumes him;
13 the beginning of the words of his mouth is foolishness,
and the end of his talk is evil madness.
14 A fool multiplies words,
though no man knows what is to be;
who can tell him what will be after him?

15 The labor of the foolish makes him weary,
such that he does not know the way to the city!

16 Woe to you, O land, when your king is a lad,
and your princes are feasting in the morning!
17 Happy are you, O land, when your king is from nobility,
and your princes are feasting at the appropriate time—
with self-control and not drunkenness!

18 The roof beams sink in with slothfulness,
and with the idleness of one's hands the house drips.

[19] They make feasts for laughter,
and wine gladdens life;
but money resolves everything.

[20] Even in your mind do not curse the king;
and in your bedchamber do not curse
the rich;
for a bird in the sky may carry your voice,
and a winged creature may declare the
matter.

The Value of Diligence

11 Cast your bread upon the waters,
for you will find it after many days.
2 Give a portion to seven, or even eight,
for you do not know what calamity may
happen on the earth.

3 If the clouds are full of rain,
they empty out on the land;
and if a tree falls to the north or south,
in the place that the tree falls, there it
will be.
4 He who observes the wind will not sow,
and he who regards the clouds will not
reap.
5 As you do not know the way of the wind,
or how the bones grow in the womb of
her who is with child;
likewise you do not know the work of God
who has made everything.
6 In the morning sow your seed,
and in the evening do not let your hand
rest;
because you do not know which activity
will find success,
this way or that way,
or if the both will be good.

Remember Your Creator in Your Youth

7 Light is sweet,
and good for the eyes to see the sun;
8 for if a man lives many years,
may he rejoice in all of them.
But let him also remember
that the days of darkness are many.
Everything that comes is vanity.

9 Rejoice, O young man, in your youth,
and in your early years may your heart
do you good;
walk in the path of your heart
and the desire of your eyes;
but know that in all these things
God will bring you into judgment.
10 Take away anger from your heart,
and remove distress from your body,
for youth and the dawn are vanity.

10:19 Ps 104:15
10:20 Ex 22:28
11:1 Pr 19:17
11:2 Ps 112:9
11:5 Jn 3:8
11:6 Ecc 9:10
11:7 Ecc 7:11
11:9 Ecc 12:14
11:10 2Co 7:1

....

12:1 Ecc 11:8
12:5 Job 17:13
12:7 Ge 3:19
12:8 Ecc 1:2
12:9 1Ki 4:32
12:12 Ecc 1:18
12:13 Dt 10:12
12:14 1Co 4:5

12 Remember your Creator
in the days of your youth,
before the difficult days come
and the years arrive when you say,
"I have no pleasure in them":
2 before the sun, light,
moon, and stars are darkened,
and the clouds leave after the rain;
3 in the day when those watching the house
tremble,
and the strong men are bent over;
when the grinders cease because they are
few,
and those looking through the windows
have dimmed *eyes*;
4 and the doors on the street are shut,
and the sound of grinding is low;
and one rises up at the sound of a bird,
and all the daughters of song are
brought low;
5 when they are afraid of heights,
even the terrors along the road;
the almond tree blossoms,
the grasshopper drags itself along
and desire fails,
because man goes to his eternal home,
and the mourners go about the streets.

6 *Remember your Creator* before the cord of
silver is snapped,
or the bowl of gold smashed,
or the jar by the spring broken
or the wheel at the cistern crushed.
7 The dust returns to the earth where it was,
and the spirit returns to God who gave it.

8 It is all vanity, says the Preacher;
all is vanity.

Epilogue

9 And in addition to being wise, the Preach-
er still taught the people knowledge, and he
considered, sought out, and arranged many
proverbs. 10 And the Preacher sought to discov-
er words of delight, and to write in uprightness
words of truth.
11 The words of the wise are like goads, and
the collected sayings are like firmly embed-
ded nails, given by one shepherd. 12 My son,
beware of anything beyond these.
Of making many books there is no end, and
much study is a weariness to the flesh.

13 Now all has been heard.
Let us hear the conclusion of the matter:
Fear God and keep His commandments,
for this is the whole *duty* of man.
14 For God will bring every deed into
judgment,
including every secret thing,
whether good or evil.

Author: Traditionally King Solomon

Written: 965 BC

Themes: Love, God's Gift of Intimacy Between a Man and a Woman

SOLOMON

Dear Spirit Led Woman,

Nowhere is the relationship God envisions more clearly described than in the Song of Solomon, beginning with the words of the beloved to her lover, who represents Jesus: "Let him kiss me with the kisses of his mouth! For your love is better than wine" (SS 1:2). Though we may shy away from it, the place of intimate spiritual fellowship these words allude to is available to us all.

Intimacy is not just for selfish satisfaction, though. As you become more like Jesus, He puts His desires into your heart. The intimacy leads somewhere. You begin to release your desires for Christ's desires. His thoughts replace the carnal ones of your past. Things that would separate you from God become easier to release. Old agendas go and new plans emerge. You find yourself dreaming dreams too big to carry out and doing things foreign to your old nature in order to remain in close fellowship with Him. That is because you have His vision and heart for His people.

Listen for His voice, and respond to His leading. He desires intimacy even more than you do.

Joy F. Strang

Introduction

1 The Song of Songs, which is Solomon's.

The Woman

2 Let him kiss me with the kisses of his
mouth!
For your love is better than wine.
3 Your anointing oils are fragrant,
your name is oil poured out;
therefore the virgins love you.
4 Draw me after you, let us run.
The king has brought me into his
chambers.

Friends of the Woman

We will exult and rejoice in you;
we will remember your love more than
wine;
rightly do they love you.

The Woman

5 I am dark, but still lovely, O daughters of
Jerusalem,
like the tents of Kedar,
like the curtains of Solomon.
6 Do not gaze at me, because I am dark,
because the sun has looked
upon me.
My mother's sons were angry with me;
they made me the keeper of the
vineyards,
but my own vineyard I have not kept.
7 Tell me, you whom my soul loves,
where you pasture your flock,
where you make it lie down at noon;
for why should I be like one who
veils herself by the flocks of your
companions?

Friends of the Woman

8 If you do not know, O fairest among
women,
follow in the tracks of the flock,
and pasture your young goats
beside the shepherds' tents.

The Man

9 I compare you, my love, to a mare among
Pharaoh's chariots.
10 Lovely are your cheeks with ornaments,
your neck with chains of gold.

Friends of the Woman

11 We will make you ornaments of gold,
with studs of silver.

The Woman

12 While the king was on his couch,
my nard gave forth its fragrance.
13 My beloved is to me a bundle of myrrh
that lies all night between my breasts.
14 My beloved is to me a cluster of henna
blossoms
in the vineyards of En Gedi.

The Man

15 How fair you are, my love.
How fair you are! Your eyes are doves.

The Woman

16 How fair you are, my beloved!
Yes, pleasant!
Our bed is verdant;
17 the beams of our house are cedar,
and our rafters of fir.

2 I am the rose of Sharon,
the lily of the valleys.

The Man

2 As a lily among thorns,
so is my love among the maidens.

The Woman

3 As an apple tree among the trees of the
forest,
so is my beloved among the young men.
In his shadow I sat with great delight,
and his fruit was sweet to my taste.
4 He brought me to the banquet house,
and his banner over me was love.
5 Sustain me with raisins,
refresh me with apples;
for I am faint with love.
6 His left hand is under my head,
and his right hand embraces me.
7 I charge you, O daughters of Jerusalem,
by the gazelles or the does of the field,
do not stir up or awaken love
until it pleases.

8 The voice of my beloved!
Look, he comes
leaping over the mountains,
bounding over the hills.
9 My beloved is like a gazelle or a young
stag.
Look, he stands behind our wall, gazing
through the windows,
looking through the lattice.
10 My beloved speaks and says to me:
"Rise up, my love,
my fair one, and come away.
11 For now the winter has past;
the rain is over and gone.
12 The flowers appear on the earth;
the time of singing has come,
and the voice of the turtledove is heard in
our land.
13 The fig tree puts forth its green figs,
and the vines their blossoms;
and they give forth fragrance.
Rise up, my love, my beautiful one, and
come away.

1:1 1Ki 4:32
1:2 SS 4:10
1:3 Ecc 7:1
1:4 Ps 45:14–15
1:5 Ps 120:5
1:6 Ps 69:8
1:7 SS 3:1–4
1:8 SS 5:9
1:12 Jn 12:3
1:13 Ps 45:8
....
1:15 SS 4:1
1:16 SS 2:3
2:4 SS 1:4
2:5 SS 5:8
2:7 SS 3:5
2:9 SS 8:14
2:10 SS 2:13
2:13 SS 2:10

Knowing Your Value

I often wonder how we as women have convinced ourselves that we do not have value in Christ, and I always find it interesting when I see women trying hard to prove they are equal to men. I think this happens because we allow being equal to overshadow the importance of just being. What do I mean by this?

I have spent the bulk of my years in ministry in what is loosely known as the worship music industry. I use the word *loosely* because worship is not really supposed to be a business, but the industry I refer to is one whose primary focus is on creating and producing music that is used in church settings. Despite its aims, positive though they may be, it still is an industry, and it often perpetuates stereotypes.

One of the stereotypes this industry promotes is that most worship leaders are men. This was hard for me to deal with for many reasons. In my traveling I have met more female worship leaders than male, yet the role popularly belongs to men. Because of the perception that worship leaders are or should be male, I have had to push my way through a lot of unnecessary debris in an effort to prove myself as a worship leader and be recognized for the gifts God has put within me.

I learned from experience that if I allowed the obstacles in my field to intimidate me, I would limit myself from reaching the potential I was meant to attain. There are plenty of things to be frustrated by, for sure, and there are plenty of obstacles to overcome in life, no matter what field you are in. But only we can prevent ourselves from walking in our calling.

It took me years to realize that I never really needed anyone to validate me as a worship leader because I had God's approval. Realizing that started me down the road of not being affected by what others thought. I have come to believe that my life and livelihood are in God's hands. He opens doors no man or woman can shut and shuts doors no one can open.

I know I am not alone. So often we as women feel as though we are hitting a wall as we try to get noticed. Our sense of value is attacked from many different fronts—home, church, our friendships, and relational circles. This is why I have prayed for peace about having my gifts validated, and I encourage other women to do the same. We need peace that passes everything we will never understand. God can leave us with a peace so complete that it will keep all of the stress we run up against from preventing us from reaching our purpose in Him.

God is ready and willing to teach us the way to follow. He has not made anything that He didn't fall in love with. It is time for us to believe His opinion of us. It is time to hear Him speaking, "How fair you are, my love. How fair you are! Your eyes are doves" (SS 1:15). Believing God's opinion is what sets us free from being bound to what others think. It shows us our true value.

Rita Springer

SPIRITLED WOMAN

COUNSEL FROM THE SPIRIT BASICS

Little Foxes

If you are married and happy, reinforce your personal life by paying attention to the little foxes that will come to steal your happiness. Stay anchored to Jesus Christ, your Savior, and build yourself up in your faith. Pay specific attention to your spiritual life, and pray powerful warfare prayers. We are in a war. Our struggle is not with humans but with demonic entities that are constantly looking for an open door to sneak in and begin their work of destruction. If your marriage is healthy and solid, invest some time in another young couple, and teach them what you practice and know.

Don't fall asleep. Declare boldly: "Satan, you can't have my marriage!" "Satan, you can't have my children!" "Satan, you can't have what belongs to me!" Don't just stroll through la-la land. We must tread upon evil spirits that come to steal our substance and our faith. To *tread upon* is warfare action terminology. It means "to trample, walk, crush, and march." To be effective, you have to put on your spiritual cleats!

You can't remain passive in your daily spiritual walk. To conquer something difficult, you must engage the enemy before he engages you. Trample and crush evil with the Word of God and with your prayers. God will do the rest. We must do what God expects from us to love, obey, and believe that He will fight our battles. Then He will enable us to do the impossible things. Only then can you have your cake and eat it too.

Iris Delgado

14 O my dove, in the clefts of the rock,
in the secret places of the cliffs,
let me see your face,
let me hear your voice;
for your voice is sweet,
and your face is lovely.
15 Catch the foxes for us,
the little foxes
that spoil the vineyards,
for our vineyards are in blossom."
16 My beloved is mine, and I am his;
he feeds *his flock* among the lilies.
17 Until the day breathes
and the shadows flee,
turn, my beloved,
be like a gazelle
or a young stag
on the cleft mountains.[1]

3 On my bed by night I sought him
whom my soul loves;
I sought him, but found him not.
2 I will rise now and go about the city,
in the streets and in the squares;
I will seek him whom my soul loves.
I sought him, but found him not.
3 The watchmen found me,
as they went about the city.
"Have you seen him whom my soul loves?"
4 Scarcely had I passed them,
when I found him whom my soul loves.
I held him, and would not let him go
until I brought him to my mother's house,
and into the chamber of her who conceived me.
5 I charge you, O daughters of Jerusalem,
by the gazelles or does of the field,
do not stir up or awaken love
until it pleases.

6 Who is that coming up from the wilderness,
like columns of smoke,
perfumed with myrrh and frankincense,
with all the fragrant powders of the merchant?
7 Look, it is the litter of Solomon!
Around it are sixty mighty men,
of the mighty men of Israel,
8 all of them holding swords
and expert in war,
each with his sword at his thigh,
because of terrors by night.
9 King Solomon made himself a palanquin
from the wood of Lebanon.
10 He made its posts of silver,
its back of gold,
its seat of purple;
its interior was inlaid with love
by the daughters of Jerusalem.
11 Go forth, O daughters of Zion,
and see King Solomon with the crown
with which his mother crowned him
on the day of his wedding,
on the day of the gladness of his heart.

2:14 SS 1:5
2:15 SS 2:13
2:16 SS 6:3
2:17 SS 4:6
3:1 SS 5:6
3:3 SS 5:7
3:5 SS 2:7
3:6 SS 8:5
3:8 Ps 45:3
3:11 Isa 62:5

[1] 17 Or *mountains of Bether*.

The Man

4 How fair you are, my love!
How very fair!
Your eyes are doves behind your veil.
Your hair is like a flock of goats,
streaming down the hills of Gilead.
2 Your teeth are like a flock of shorn ewes
that have come up from the washing,
all of which bear twins,
and not one among them has lost its
young.
3 Your lips are like a scarlet thread,
and your mouth is lovely.
Your cheeks are halves of a pomegranate
behind your veil.
4 Your neck is like the tower of David,
built in rows of stone;
on it hang a thousand shields,
all of them shields of mighty men.
5 Your two breasts are like two fawns,
twins of a gazelle,
that feed among the lilies.
6 Until the day breathes
and the shadows flee,
I will go away to the mountain of myrrh
and the hill of frankincense.
7 You are altogether fair, my love;
there is no flaw in you.

8 Come with me from Lebanon, my bride;
come with me from Lebanon.
Depart from the peak of Amana,
from the peak of Senir and Hermon,
from the dens of lions,
from the mountains of leopards.
9 You have ravished my heart, my sister, my
bride;
you have ravished my heart
with one *glance* of your eyes,
with one jewel of your necklace.
10 How fair is your love, my sister, my bride!
How much better than wine is your love,
and the fragrance of your oils than any
spice!
11 Your lips drip honey, my bride;
honey and milk are under your tongue;
and the fragrance of your garments is
like the scent of Lebanon.
12 A garden locked is my sister, my bride,
a fountain sealed.
13 Your plants are an orchard of
pomegranates
with all choicest fruits,
henna with nard,
14 nard and saffron,
calamus and cinnamon,
with all trees of frankincense,
myrrh and aloes,
with all the chief spices—

4:1 SS 1:15
4:2 SS 6:6
4:3 SS 6:7
4:4 SS 7:4
4:5 SS 2:16
4:6 SS 2:17
4:7 SS 1:15
4:8 Dt 3:9
4:9 SS 5:1–2
4:10 SS 1:2–4
4:11 Ge 27:27
4:12 Pr 5:15–18
4:13 SS 1:14
4:14 Ex 30:23
4:15 Jn 4:10
4:16 SS 5:1
5:1 SS 6:2
5:2 SS 6:9
5:3 Lk 11:7
5:5 SS 5:13
5:6 SS 5:2
5:7 SS 3:3
5:8 SS 2:7
5:9 SS 1:8

15 a garden fountain,
a well of living water,
and flowing streams from Lebanon.

> A fountain of gardens, a well of living waters, and streams from Lebanon dwell within me (SS 4:15).

The Woman

16 Awake, O north wind,
and come, O south wind!
Blow upon my garden,
that its spices may flow out.
Let my beloved come to his garden,
and eat its choicest fruits.

The Man

5 I come to my garden, my sister, my
bride;
I gather my myrrh with my spice;
I eat my honeycomb with my honey;
I drink my wine with my milk.

Friends of the Man

Eat, friends!
Drink, and be drunk with love!

The Woman

2 I slept, but my heart was awake.
A sound! My beloved is knocking. "Open to
me, my sister, and my love,
my dove, my perfect one;
for my head is wet with dew,
my locks with the drops of the night."
3 I had taken off my garment;
how could I put it on again?
I had bathed my feet;
how could I soil them?
4 My beloved put his hand by the latch,
and my heart yearned for him.
5 I rose up to open to my beloved,
and my hands dripped with myrrh,
my fingers with liquid myrrh
on the handles of the bolt.
6 I opened to my beloved,
but my beloved had turned and was
gone.
My soul failed me when he spoke.
I sought him, but found him not;
I called him, but he gave no answer.
7 The watchmen found me
as they went about the city;
they struck me, they wounded me;
they took away my mantle,
those watchmen of the walls.
8 I charge you, O daughters of Jerusalem,
if you find my beloved,
that you tell him I am faint with love.

Friends of the Woman

9 What is your beloved more than another
beloved,

SPIRITLED WOMAN

COUNSEL FROM THE SPIRIT BASICS

Love From a Suffering Heart

God's presence is always with us, but we can't always feel it. It is in the moment of greatest darkness, when we are barraged with every reason not to believe and trust, that Jesus gives a simple command that is the most difficult thing for a suffering heart to do. He simply says, "Open to me" (SS 5:2). Throughout her journey described in the Song of Solomon, the bride of Christ is given many commands—to arise, run over mountains, go out to the vineyard and labor, and so on. But when His bride is suffering, Christ has only one request: that she respond to His knocking and open the deepest places of her heart to Him.

As you read Song of Solomon, it is easy to pick up on the bride's passion for the Bridegroom as she recalls attributes of Jesus she can no longer see. After the bride's declaration of His beauty, Jesus proclaims in poetic language how touched and impacted God is when He is loved and adored in those times of darkness and suffering when we cannot see Him or feel His presence.

In Song of Solomon 6:4–5 we see a picture of just how deeply it moves Jesus to see someone who, in her moment of suffering, is able to remember the beauty of who He is and declare it to others. Armies cannot conquer Jesus, hell's demons cannot defeat Him, the wealth and might of all of the nations of the earth cannot overwhelm Him, but one reality can captivate Him: love from a suffering heart.

Shelley Hundley

O fairest among women?
What is your beloved more than another
beloved,
that you so charge us?

The Woman

10 My beloved is white and ruddy,
distinguished among ten thousand.
11 His head is the finest gold;
his locks are wavy,
black as a raven.
12 His eyes are like doves
beside rivers of water,
bathed in milk,
fitly set.
13 His cheeks are like beds of spices,
mounds of scented herbs.
His lips are lilies,
dripping liquid myrrh.
14 His arms are rods of gold,
set with jewels.
His body is bright ivory,
inlaid with sapphires.
15 His legs are alabaster columns,
set on bases of gold.
His appearance is like Lebanon,
choice as the cedars.
16 His mouth is most sweet,
and he is altogether desirable.
This is my beloved and this is my
friend,
O daughters of Jerusalem.

Friends of the Woman

6 Where has your beloved gone,
O fairest among women?
Where has your beloved turned aside,
that we may seek him with you?

The Woman

2 My beloved has gone down to his garden,
to the beds of spices,
to feed *his flock* in the gardens,
and to gather lilies.
3 I am my beloved's and my beloved is mine;
he feeds *his flock* among the lilies.

The Man

4 You are beautiful as Tirzah, my love,
comely as Jerusalem,
awesome as an army with banners!
5 Turn your eyes away from me,
for they overwhelm me!
Your hair is like a flock of goats
streaming down from Gilead.
6 your teeth are like a flock of ewes
that have come up from the washing;
all of them bear twins; not one among
them has lost its young;
7 your cheeks are like halves
of a pomegranate behind your veil.
8 There are sixty queens
and eighty concubines,
and virgins without number.
9 My dove, my perfect one, is the only one,
the only one of her mother,
choice to her who bore her.
The maidens saw her and called her
blessed;
the queens and concubines also, and
they praised her.

5:10 Ps 45:2
5:12 SS 1:15
5:13 SS 1:10
5:14 Ex 24:10
5:15 1Ki 4:33
6:1 SS 1:8
6:2 SS 5:13
6:3 SS 2:16
6:4 SS 6:10
6:6 SS 4:2
6:7 SS 4:3
6:8 Ps 45:14
6:9 SS 5:2

SPIRIT-TO-SPIRIT PRAYER

Prayer for Marriage Relationships

Father, in the name of Christ Jesus, we totally dedicate our marriage relationship to You. We consecrate ourselves unto holy matrimony. You beget marriage, and we wholly submit to its covering according to Your precepts and Your Holy Spirit. Our marriage is anointed, and every yoke must bow down and be cauterized in the name of Jesus. We repent of the sins of our forefathers, and the bloodline curses that came through are cauterized four generations back. We renounce every curse that crossed over through our union and send it back to the pit of hell. Our marriage bed is blessed, our finances are blessed, our children from this union are blessed, and those who are from any other union are now covered under this blessing because of the blood of Christ. Our home and business affairs are blessed.

The blessings of Abraham are running us down because we have dedicated our lives to obey the precepts of God. Curses have no rule over us. We renounce all outside ungodly influences over our marriage from family members, associates, or previous relationships. All soul ties and cords are broken, and sympathetic magic is under our feet. We bind memory recall whereby the enemy would present us with past challenges. All old things have passed away, and all things in our marriage have become new. Our marriage is growing toward God, level to level and glory to glory.

We come into agreement and bind all rebellion against the perfect will of God for our lives. We bind imagery, magnification, mental locutions, blocking spirits, curses through negative confession, and the working of the akashic records against where we are presently in God. We bind sexual perversion away from our household and take authority over the covenant-breaking spirit. We renounce all idols and permanently remove them from our hearts and home in the name of Jesus. We bind enchantment, bewitchment, assassination, faultfinding, vexation, confusion, division, distrust, dishonesty, disloyalty, suspicion, celibacy, impotency, the zombie spirit, the warring spirit, the spirit of the hypocrite, financial stress, and argument stirred up by financial disagreements, and we bind the spirit of ungodly counsel. Lilith, Lamia, Ahab, Jezebel, Ishmael, Arachne, Batman, and Poltergeist—get out of our home; it belongs to Jesus! And now that all of these forces have been bound, we release the perfect will of God for our family. We now declare that as for this house, we will serve the Lord!

Kimberly Daniels

10 Who is this who looks forth like the dawn,
fair as the moon, radiant as the sun,
awesome as an army with banners?

11 I went down to the nut orchard
to look at the blossoms of the valley,
to see whether the vines had budded,
whether the pomegranates were in
bloom.
12 Before I was aware, my soul set me in a
chariot beside my prince.

6:10 SS 6:4
6:11 SS 7:12
6:13 Ge 32:2

Friends of the Woman

13 Return, return, O Shulammite![1]
Return, return, that we may look upon
you.

The Man

Why should you look upon the
Shulammite,
as upon a dance before two armies?[2]

[1] *13* 7:1 in the Heb. text. [2] *13* Or *dance of Mahanaim.*

Six Ways to Romance Your Husband

Before we take a look at ways to romance your husband, please understand that romance is not sex. Romance is so much more. Romance lasts. Romance generates a love so deep that if sex were not possible for whatever reason, love would still grow. Romantic affection creates the necessary environment for a good marriage, and sex is one of the main events. Romance is precious.

Read carefully both the Scripture verse for each number and the comments about each verse. Then on the lines below each number, add the things that you have done—or will do in the future—to romance your husband in this way.

1. Tell him you love him.

Tell me, you whom my soul loves...

—Song of Solomon 1:7

One way to do this is with a phone call during the day with a simple "I love you." Ladies, don't overdo—remember, quality versus quantity; you don't want to smother the man!

2. Praise him.

You are altogether fair, my love; there is no flaw in you.

—Song of Solomon 4:7

Encouragement is so important. Telling your husband you are proud of him does more for him than you know. A wife's support of her husband contributes more to his success than any other factor.

3. Give him gifts.

The mandrakes give forth fragrance, and at our doors are all choice fruits, new as well as old, which I have laid up for you, my beloved.

—Song of Solomon 7:13

The gift doesn't have to be expensive. The fact that you thought of it with him in mind will be more than sufficient.

4. Surprise him.

Rise up, my love, my fair one, and come away.

—Song of Solomon 2:10

Date nights make for great surprises. Call your husband and ask him if he would like to have an exciting date for the evening. Make arrangements for dinner and a movie.

5. The power of your touch

Let him kiss me with the kisses of his mouth! For your love is better than wine.

—Song of Solomon 1:2

One of the most beautiful pictures of romance I have ever seen is one I witness every Sunday at our church. On the front row center sit a wonderful man and his precious wife. They are in their late eighties. Every Sunday they hold each other's hand. These two wrinkled and gnarled hands are clasped tightly, and the other two hands are raised to the Lord.

6. Loyalty

I am my beloved's and my beloved is mine.

—Song of Solomon 6:3

Proverbs 31 describes the perfect woman as being one in whom "the heart of her husband safely trusts" (v. 11). Trust is the fabric of every human connection. Without trust, there can be no confidence, emotional stability, or hope for the future. Trust is the cornerstone of your marriage relationship.

Diana Hagee

7 How beautiful are your feet in sandals,
O prince's daughter!
The curves of your thighs are like jewels,
the work of a master hand.
2 Your navel is a round bowl
that never lacks mixed wine.
Your belly is a heap of wheat,
encircled with lilies.
3 Your two breasts are like two fawns,
twins of a gazelle.
4 Your neck is like an ivory tower,
your eyes pools in Heshbon,
by the gate of Bath Rabbim.
Your nose is like a tower of Lebanon,
overlooking Damascus.
5 Your head crowns like Carmel,
and your flowing hair is like purple;
a king is held captive in the tresses.
6 How fair and pleasant you are,
O loved one, with all your delights!
7 Your stature is like a palm tree,
and your breasts are like its clusters.
8 I say I will climb the palm tree
and take hold of its branches.
Oh, may your breasts be like clusters of the
vine,
and the scent of your breath like apples,
9 and your mouth like the best wine.
It goes down smoothly for my beloved,
gliding over lips and teeth.

The Woman

10 I am my beloved's,
and his desire is for me.
11 Come, my beloved, let us go forth into the
fields,
and lodge in the villages;
12 let us go out early to the vineyards,
and see whether the vines have budded,
whether the grape blossoms have opened
and the pomegranates are in bloom.
There I will give you my love.
13 The mandrakes give forth fragrance,
and at our doors are all choice fruits,
new as well as old,
which I have laid up for you, my
beloved.

8 Oh, that you were like a brother to me,
who nursed at my mother's breasts!
If I found you outside,
I would kiss you,
and no one would despise me.
2 I would lead you and bring you
into the house of my mother,
she who used to instruct me.
I would give you spiced wine to drink,
the juice of my pomegranates.
3 His left hand is under my head,
and his right arm embraces me!

7:1 Ps 45:13
7:3 SS 4:5
7:4 SS 4:4
7:5 Isa 35:2
7:6 SS 1:15–16
7:7 SS 4:5
7:9 SS 5:16
7:10 Ps 45:11
7:11 SS 4:8
7:12 SS 6:11
7:13 Ge 30:14
8:2 SS 3:4
8:3 SS 2:6

....

8:4 SS 2:7
8:5 SS 3:6
8:6 Isa 49:16
8:7 Pr 6:35
8:11 Ecc 2:4
8:12 SS 1:6
8:13 SS 1:7
8:14 SS 2:17

4 I charge you, O daughters of Jerusalem,
do not stir up or awaken love
until it pleases.

Friends of the Woman

5 Who is that coming up from the
wilderness,
leaning upon her beloved?

The Woman

Under the apple tree I awakened you.
There your mother was in labor with
you;
there she who bore you was in labor.
6 Set me as a seal upon your heart,
as a seal upon your arm;
for love is strong as death,
passion fierce as the grave.
Its fires of desire are as ardent flames,
a most intense flame.
7 Many waters cannot quench love,
neither can floods drown it.
If a man offered for love
all the wealth of his house,
it would be utterly condemned.

Brothers of the Woman

8 We have a little sister,
and she has no breasts.
What will we do for our sister
on the day when she is spoken for?
9 If she is a wall,
we will build upon her a battlement of
silver;
but if she is a door,
we will enclose her with boards of cedar.

The Woman

10 I was a wall,
and my breasts were like towers;
then I was in his eyes
as one who finds peace.
11 Solomon had a vineyard at Baal Hamon;
he leased the vineyard to keepers;
each man was to bring for its fruit a
thousand pieces of silver.
12 My vineyard, my very own, is before me;
you, O Solomon, may have the
thousand,
and the keepers of the fruit two hundred.

The Man

13 O you who dwell in the gardens,
my companions listen for your voice;
let me hear it!

The Woman

14 Make haste, my beloved,
and be like a gazelle or a young stag
on the mountains of spices!

Author: Traditionally the prophet Isaiah

Written: Between 701 and 681 BC

Themes: Victory by the Holy One of Israel, Expectation of the Messiah and New Creation

ISAIAH

Dear Spirit Led Woman,

I once heard a story of a farmer who found an eagle with a broken wing. He rescued the eagle, but because of its injury, the eagle was forced to live like a chicken. But it wasn't a chicken; it was an eagle.

One day after the wing was healed, the farmer took the bird to a nearby mountaintop to set it free. The eagle flapped its wings but didn't try to take off. It still saw itself as a chicken. Day after day the same thing happened. But one day there was a strong wind, and when the eagle flapped its wings, the current began lifting it upward. Suddenly revelation hit: eagles are born to fly! The bird rose with the wind and began to soar.

Perhaps you see yourself in that eagle. When you go through difficult situations in life, you sometimes find yourself in a figurative chicken pen. You need a revelation of your true destiny—to soar with wings like eagles (Isa 40:31). If you've been recovering from a tough time, wait upon the Lord and renew your strength. There's a time and place for healing. But don't stay there. Rise up on the wind of the Spirit to fulfill your destiny. Like the eagle, you were born to soar!

Joy F. Strang

1 The vision of Isaiah the son of Amoz, which he saw concerning Judah and Jerusalem in the days of Uzziah, Jotham, Ahaz, and Hezekiah, kings of Judah.

The Wickedness of Judah

2 Hear, O heavens, and give ear, O earth.
For the LORD has spoken:
I have nourished and brought up children,
and they have rebelled against Me;
3 the ox knows his owner,
and the donkey his master's crib,
but Israel does not know;
My people do not consider.

4 Alas, sinful nation,
a people laden with iniquity,
a brood of evildoers,
children who deal corruptly!
They have forsaken the LORD,
they have provoked the Holy One of
Israel to anger,
they are estranged and backward.

5 Why should you be beaten again,
that you revolt more and more?
The whole head is sick,
and the whole heart faint.
6 From the sole of the foot even to the head
there is no soundness in it.
Wounds, bruises,
and open sores;
they have not been closed,
nor bandaged, nor soothed with oil.

7 Your country is desolate,
your cities are burned with fire;
strangers devour your land
in your presence;
and it is desolate, as overthrown by
strangers.
8 The daughter of Zion is left
like a shelter in a vineyard,
like a hut in a field of melons,
like a besieged city.
9 Unless the LORD of Hosts
had left to us a very small remnant,
we would have been as Sodom;
we would have been like Gomorrah.

10 Hear the word of the LORD,
you rulers of Sodom;
listen to the law of our God,
you people of Gomorrah:
11 For what purpose is the multitude
of your sacrifices to Me? says the LORD.
I am full of the burnt offerings of rams,
and the fat of fed animals.
I do not delight in the blood of bulls,
or of lambs, or of male goats.
12 When you come to appear before Me,
who has required this at your hand,
to trample My courts?

1:1 Isa 2:1
1:2 Mic 1:2
1:3 Jer 8:7
1:4 Isa 5:24
1:6 Jer 6:14
1:8 Isa 10:32
1:9 Ge 19:24
1:10 Rev 11:8
1:11 Jer 6:20
1:12 Ex 23:17

1:13 Isa 66:3
1:14 Isa 43:24
1:15 Isa 59:2–3
1:17 Jer 22:3
1:18 Ps 51:7
1:19 Dt 30:15–16
1:20 Isa 40:5
1:23 Ex 23:8

13 Bring no more vain offerings;
incense is an abomination to Me.
New Moons, Sabbaths, and convocations—
I cannot bear with evil assemblies.
14 My soul hates
your New Moons and your appointed
feasts;
they are a burden to Me;
I am weary of bearing them.
15 When you reach out your hands,
I will hide My eyes from you;
even when you make many prayers,
I will not hear.

Your hands are full of blood.

With Your help and the guidance of the Holy Spirit I will seek to help others and to be a light in the darkness (Isa 1:16–19).

16 Wash yourselves, make yourselves clean;
put away the evil from your deeds, from
before My eyes.
Cease to do evil,
17 learn to do good; seek justice,
relieve the oppressed;
judge the fatherless,
plead for the widow.

18 Come now, and let us reason together,
says the LORD.
Though your sins be as scarlet,
they shall be as white as snow;
though they be red like crimson,
they shall be as wool.
19 If you are willing and obedient,
you shall eat the good of the land;
20 but if you refuse and rebel,
you shall be devoured with the sword;
for the mouth of the LORD has spoken it.

The Degenerate City

21 How the faithful city
has become a prostitute!
She was full of justice;
righteousness lodged in her,
but now murderers.
22 Your silver has become dross,
your wine mixed with water.
23 Your princes are rebellious
and companions of thieves;
everyone loves a bribe
and follows after rewards.
They do not defend the fatherless,
nor does the cause of the widow come
before them.

24 Therefore the Lord, the LORD of Hosts,
the Mighty One of Israel, says:

Ah, I will get relief from My adversaries,
and avenge Myself on My enemies.
25 And I will turn My hand against you,
thoroughly purge away your dross,
and take away all your impurities.
26 I will restore your judges as at the first,
and your counselors as at the beginning.
Afterward you shall be called
the city of righteousness,
a faithful town.
27 Zion shall be redeemed with justice
and her converts with righteousness.
28 But the destruction of the transgressors
and sinners shall be together,
and those who forsake the LORD shall be
consumed.
29 For they shall be ashamed of the oaks
which you have desired,
and you shall be humiliated for the gardens
that you have chosen.
30 For you shall be as an oak whose leaf
fades,
and as a garden that has no water.
31 The strong shall be as tinder,
and his work like a spark;
they will both burn together,
and no one will quench them.

The Mountain of the LORD
Mic 4:1–3

2 The word that Isaiah the son of Amoz saw concerning Judah and Jerusalem.

2 In the last days,
the mountain of the LORD's house shall be
established
on the top of the mountains,
and shall be exalted above the hills,
and all nations shall flow to it.
3 Many people shall go and say,

"Come, and let us go up to the mountain of
the LORD,
to the house of the God of Jacob,
and He will teach us of His ways,
and we will walk in His paths."
For out of Zion shall go forth the law,
and the word of the LORD from
Jerusalem.
4 He shall judge among the nations,
and shall rebuke many peoples;
and they shall beat their swords into
plowshares,
and their spears into pruning hooks;
nation shall not lift up sword against
nation,
nor shall they learn war any more.
5 O house of Jacob, come,
and let us walk in the light of the LORD.

1:25 Mal 3:3
1:26 Jer 33:7
1:29 Isa 57:5
1:31 Isa 66:24
2:1 Isa 1:1
2:2 Isa 27:13
2:3 Lk 24:47
2:4 Hos 2:18

2:6 2Ki 1:2
2:7 Isa 30:16
2:9 Isa 5:15
2:10 Rev 6:15–16
2:11 Ps 18:27
2:12 Mal 4:1
2:13 Isa 14:8
2:14 Isa 30:25
2:16 1Ki 10:22
2:17 Isa 2:11
2:19 Isa 2:10
2:20 Isa 30:22
2:21 Isa 2:19

The Day of the LORD

6 For You have forsaken Your people,
the house of Jacob,
because they are replenished from the east,
and are soothsayers like the Philistines,
and they please themselves with the
children of strangers.
7 Their land also is full of silver and gold,
and there is no end to their treasures;
their land is also full of horses,
and there is no end to their chariots.
8 Their land also is full of idols;
they worship the work of their own
hands,
that which their own fingers have made.
9 And the *common* man bows down,
and the *great* man humbles himself;
therefore, do not forgive them.
10 Enter into the rock,
and hide in the dust
from the fear of the LORD
and from the glory of His majesty.
11 The lofty looks of man shall be humbled,
and the haughtiness of men shall be
bowed down,
and the LORD alone shall be exalted in that
day.
12 For the day of the LORD of Hosts shall be
upon everything that is proud and lofty,
and upon everything that is lifted up,
and it shall be brought low;
13 and *it will be* upon all the cedars of
Lebanon that are high and lifted up,
and upon all the oaks of Bashan,
14 and upon all the high mountains,
and upon all the hills that are lifted up,
15 and upon all the high towers,
and upon every fenced wall,
16 and upon all the ships of Tarshish,
and upon all pleasant sloops.
17 The loftiness of man shall be humbled,
and the haughtiness of men shall be
brought low;
the LORD alone will be exalted in that day;
18 the idols He shall utterly abolish.
19 They shall go into the holes of the rocks,
and into the caves of the earth,
from the fear of the LORD,
and from the glory of His majesty,
when He shall arise to shake the earth
mightily.
20 In that day a man shall cast away
his idols of silver and his idols of gold,
which they made for themselves to
worship,
to the moles and to the bats,
21 to enter the caverns of the rocks,
and into the clefts of the cliffs,

from the terror of the LORD,
and from the glory of His majesty,
when He arises to shake the earth
mightily.

22 Cease regarding man,
whose breath is in his nostrils;
for why should he be esteemed?

Judgment on Judah and Jerusalem

3 For now the Lord,
the LORD of Hosts,
takes away from Jerusalem and from Judah
the stock and the store,
the whole supply of bread, and the whole
supply of water;
2 the mighty man and the man of war,
the judge and the prophet,
and the prudent and the ancient,
3 the captain of fifty and the honorable man,
the counselor and the skillful artisan,
and the eloquent orator.

4 I will give youths to be their princes,
and unweaned children shall rule over
them.

5 The people shall be oppressed,
every one by another, and every one by
his neighbor;
the youth shall behave himself proudly
against the elder,
and the inferior against the honorable.

6 When a man shall take hold of his brother
in the house of his father saying,
"You have clothing; be our ruler,
and let this ruin be under your power,"
7 in that day he shall swear saying,
"I will not be a healer.
For in my house is neither bread nor
clothing;
do not make me a ruler of the people."

8 For Jerusalem is ruined,
and Judah is fallen,
because their tongue and their deeds are
against the LORD,
to provoke the eyes of His glory.
9 The expression of their countenance
witnesses against them,
and they declare their sin as Sodom;
they hide it not.
Woe to them!
For they have brought evil on
themselves.

10 Say to the righteous that it shall be well
with them,
for they shall eat the fruit of their deeds.
11 Woe to the wicked! It shall be ill with him,
for the reward of his hands shall be given
him.

2:22 Ps 146:3
3:1 Lev 26:26
3:2 Eze 17:13
3:4 Ecc 10:16
3:5 Jer 9:3–8
3:6 Isa 4:1
3:7 Hos 5:13
3:9 Ge 13:13
3:10 Ecc 8:12

....

3:12 Isa 3:4
3:13 Mic 6:2
3:14 Job 22:4
3:15 Ps 94:5
3:16 Isa 4:4
3:18 Jdg 8:21
3:20 Ex 39:28
3:21 Ge 24:47
3:24 Isa 22:12
3:26 Jer 14:2
4:1 Ge 30:23

12 As for My people, children are their
oppressors,
and women rule over them.
O My people, those who lead you cause
you to err,
and destroy the way of your paths.
13 The LORD stands up to plead
and stands to judge the people.
14 The LORD will enter into judgment
with the elders and the princes of His
people:
For you have eaten up the vineyard;
the spoil of the poor is in your houses.
15 What do you mean that you beat My
people to pieces
and grind the faces of the poor?
says the Lord GOD of Hosts.

16 Moreover the LORD says:
Because the daughters of Zion are
haughty
and walk with outstretched necks
and wanton eyes,
walking and mincing as they go,
and making a tinkling with their feet,
17 therefore, the Lord will strike with a
scab the crown of the head of the
daughters of Zion,
and the LORD will make their foreheads
bare.

18 In that day the Lord will take away the
finery of the ankle ornaments, and the head-
bands, and the crescent ornaments, 19 the
chains, and the bracelets, and the veils, 20 the
bonnets, the leg ornaments, the sashes, per-
fume boxes, amulets, 21 the finger rings, nose
rings, 22 festal robes, outer tunics, cloaks, purs-
es, 23 hand mirrors, and undergarments, hoods,
and veils.

24 Instead of sweet perfume there shall be a
stench;
and instead of a belt, a rope;
and instead of well-set hair, baldness;
and instead of fine clothes, a girding of
sackcloth;
and branding instead of beauty.
25 Your men shall fall by the sword,
and your mighty in the war.
26 Her gates shall lament and mourn,
and she, being desolate, shall sit on the
ground.

4 And in that day seven women
shall take hold of one man, saying,
"We will eat our own bread,
and wear our own apparel,
only let us be called by your name,
to take away our reproach."

The Branch of the LORD

[2] In that day the branch of the LORD shall be
beautiful and glorious, and the fruit of the
earth shall be excellent and comely for those
of Israel who have escaped. [3] He who is left in
Zion and he who remains in Jerusalem shall
be called holy, even everyone who is written
among the living in Jerusalem. [4] When the
Lord has washed away the filth of the daugh-
ters of Zion and has purged the blood of Je-
rusalem from the midst by the spirit of justice
and by the spirit of burning, [5] then the LORD
will create upon every dwelling place of Mount
Zion, and upon her assemblies, a cloud and
smoke by day and the shining of a flaming
fire by night. For over all the glory shall be a
covering. [6] There shall be a tabernacle for a
shadow in the daytime from the heat, and for
a place of refuge, and for a shelter from storm
and from rain.

The Song of the Vineyard

5 Now I will sing to my well-beloved a
song of my beloved
concerning His vineyard:
My well-beloved has a vineyard
in a very fruitful hill.
[2] And He fenced it, and removed its stones,
and planted it with the choicest vine.
And He built a tower in the midst of it,
and also made a winepress in it;
and He expected it to bring forth good
grapes,
but it brought forth wild grapes.
[3] Now, O inhabitants of Jerusalem and men
of Judah,
judge between My vineyard and Me.
[4] What more could have been done to My
vineyard
that I have not done in it?
Why, when I expected it to bring forth good
grapes,
did it bring forth wild grapes?
[5] So now I will tell you
what I will do to My vineyard:
I will take away its hedge,
and it shall be consumed;
I will break down its wall,
and it shall be trodden down.
[6] And I will lay it waste:
It shall not be pruned or dug,
but briers and thorns shall come up.
I will also command the clouds
that they rain no rain on it.
[7] For the vineyard of the LORD of Hosts
is the house of Israel,
and the men of Judah
His pleasant plant.

4:2 Jer 23:5
4:3 Lk 10:20
4:4 Mal 3:2–3
4:6 Isa 25:4
5:1 Ps 80:8
5:2 Jer 2:21
5:4 Mt 23:37
5:5 Isa 28:18
5:6 Isa 7:23–25
5:7 Ps 80:8–11
....
5:8 Mic 2:2

SPIRITLED WOMAN

COUNSEL FROM THE SPIRIT BASICS

A Day of Judgment and Justice

The Bible warns us that there will be days when right is called wrong and wrong is declared right. Isaiah released a warning to those who did this. Isaiah 5:20 says, "Woe to those who call evil good, and good evil." He goes further by saying that some people exchange "darkness for light, and light for darkness" and "put bitter for sweet, and sweet for bitter."

The Scripture says that people who do these things are "wise in their own eyes" (v. 21). They justify the wicked for reward and take "away the justice of the righteous from him" (v. 23).

How can a man take away the justice of another man? This can easily be done through natural and spiritual legal attacks. For example, a religious person with a legalistic spirit can take away the justice of a young lady who is a new believer because of what she wears. He takes away her justice in his own mind because of his ideas about what is righteous. In actuality, a righteous person's justice cannot be taken away. Our righteousness is in Jesus. It can only be taken away in the accuser's mind.

I praise God that the Book of Isaiah says that a day will come when Jesus will execute judgment and justice in the earth (Isa 16:3). In the meantime, we must stand in truth; if we do, we will be delivered from the attacks of darkness.

Kimberly Daniels

Thus He looked for justice, but saw
oppression;
for righteousness, but heard a cry.

Woes and Judgment

[8] Woe to those who join house to house,
who add field to field,
until there is no more space
where they may live alone in the midst
of the land!

9 In my ears the LORD of Hosts said:
Truly, many houses shall be desolate,
even great and beautiful, without
inhabitants.
10 For ten acres of vineyard shall yield one
bath,[1]
and the homer[2] of seed shall yield an
ephah.[3]

11 Woe to those who rise up early in the
morning
that they may pursue strong drink;
who continue late in the evening
until wine inflames them!
12 The lyre and the harp, the tambourine and
pipe,
and wine are in their feasts;
but they do not regard the deeds of the
LORD,
or consider the work of His hands.
13 Therefore My people go into captivity
because they have no knowledge;
and their honorable men are famished,
and their multitude dried up with thirst.
14 Therefore Sheol has enlarged itself
and opened its mouth without measure;
so their glory, and their multitude, and
their pomp,
and he who rejoices shall descend into it.
15 The *common* man shall be brought down,
and the *great* man shall be humbled,
and the eyes of the lofty shall be
humbled.
16 But the LORD of Hosts shall be exalted in
judgment,
and God who is holy shall be hallowed
in righteousness.
17 Then the lambs shall feed in their pasture,
and strangers shall eat *in* the waste
places of the wealthy.

18 Woe to those who draw iniquity with cords
of falsehood
and sin as if with a cart rope,
19 who say, "Let Him make speed
and hasten His work,
that we may see it;
and let the counsel of the Holy One of
Israel
draw near and come,
that we may know it!"

20 Woe to those who call evil good,
and good evil;
who exchange darkness for light,
and light for darkness;
who exchange bitter for sweet,
and sweet for bitter!

5:9 Mt 23:38
5:10 Lev 26:26
5:11 Pr 23:29–30
5:12 Job 34:27
5:13 Hos 4:6
5:14 Hab 2:5
5:15 Isa 2:9
5:16 Isa 29:23
5:17 Isa 7:25
5:18 Jer 23:14
5:19 Eze 12:22
5:21 Pr 3:7
5:22 Isa 5:11
5:23 Ps 94:21
5:24 Job 18:16
5:25 2Ki 9:37
5:26 Dt 28:49
5:27 Job 12:18
5:28 Ps 45:5
5:29 Isa 42:22
5:30 Isa 8:22
6:1 Jn 12:41
6:2 Rev 4:8

21 Woe to those who are wise in their own
eyes
and prudent in their own sight!

22 Woe to those who are mighty to drink
wine,
and men of strength to mingle strong
drink,
23 who justify the wicked for a reward,
and take away the justice of the
righteous from him!
24 Therefore, as the fire devours the stubble
and the flame consumes the chaff,
so their root shall be as rottenness,
and their blossom shall go up as dust;
because they have cast away the law of the
LORD of Hosts
and despised the word of the Holy One
of Israel.
25 Therefore the anger of the LORD burns
against His people,
and He has stretched out His hand
against them, and has stricken them,
and the hills trembled.
Their corpses were torn in the midst of
the streets.

For all this His anger is not turned away,
and His hand is still stretched out.

26 He will lift up a banner to the nations from
afar
and will hiss at them from the ends of
the earth;
certainly they shall come
with speed, swiftly.
27 No one shall be weary or stumble among
them;
no one shall slumber or sleep;
neither shall the girdle of their loins be
loosed,
nor the strap of their shoes be broken;
28 their arrows are sharp
and all their bows bent;
their horses' hooves will seem like flint,
and their wheels like a whirlwind.
29 Their roaring shall be like a lion,
they shall roar like young lions;
they shall roar and lay hold of the prey;
and shall carry it away, and no one shall
deliver it.
30 In that day they shall roar against them
like the roaring of the sea.
And if one looks to the land—
only darkness and sorrow,
and the light is darkened by the clouds.

The Commission of Isaiah

6 In the year that King Uzziah died I saw the
Lord sitting on a throne, high and lifted
up, and His train filled the temple. 2 Above it

[1] *10* About 6 gallons, or 22 liters. [2] *10* Likely about 360 pounds, or 160 kilograms. [3] *10* Likely about 36 pounds, or 16 kilograms.

Responding to a Fresh Revelation of Jesus

With a face that must have burned crimson from shame, Isaiah burst into a startled confession: "I am a man of unclean lips, and I dwell in the midst of a people of unclean lips. For my eyes have seen the King, the LORD of Hosts" (Isa 6:5). In other words, he was saying, "I'm no better than the people at whom I've been pointing my finger!" That wasn't just a humbling admission; it was a humiliating confession.

Just when Isaiah was spiraling into the dark night of despair, just when he surely thought he'd plummeted as far into the pit of abandonment as anyone could go, things got even worse: "Then one of the seraphim flew to me with a live coal which he had taken with the tongs from off the altar in his hand. And he laid it on my mouth" (vv. 6–7).

As the live coal was pressed to Isaiah's lips, the searing pain must have been agonizing. But painful blisters would lead to the joy of sins forgiven. For even as his lips were seared, the angel's words must have felt like a soothing balm to Isaiah's tortured soul: "This has touched your lips, and your iniquity is taken away, and your sin purged" (v. 7).

From that moment on, Isaiah's life was never the same. I expect that with his lips, now purified by holy fire, he never again talked, thought, or lived the same way. Praise God! There's hope for ruined sinners like Isaiah! For me! And for you! The hope is found not in a burning coal of fire, but in what it represents: the blood of Jesus, shed on the altar of the cross and applied to every area of our lives—mind, spirit, soul, and body.

My own searing conviction and confession of sin have left me feeling desperate for cleansing. I've longed to hear the same words of reassurance Isaiah heard. And I have. I've heard God whisper to my heart through His Word: "Anne, the blood of Jesus, My Son, purifies you from every sin—past, present, and even future sin. Because you have confessed your sin, I will be faithful and just to forgive you and purify you from all unrighteousness. Though your sins are like scarlet, they shall be as white as snow. As far as the east is from the west, so far have I removed your transgressions from you." Thank God for the blood of Jesus that hasn't lost its power to cleanse us of our sin—all of it!

As Isaiah bowed in the flickering light of the burning coals, having repented of his sin and returned to the cross, his heart must have started to beat in sync with that same divine rhythm. His entire being also must have been wholly captivated by the compelling desire to serve the One whose grace and mercy had been extended to him at the altar. And in that moment Isaiah knew his life would never be the same. A genuine experience of personal revival that results from a fresh encounter with Jesus is not a fleeting thing. It's not just educational or inspirational or motivational or emotional. It's life-changing.

It truly is like waking up in our personal relationship with God so that now our lives entirely revolve around our passionate love for Jesus. You'll know your heart's been set aflame by the fire of revival when nothing else matters to you as much as your love for Him.

Anne Graham Lotz

stood the seraphim. Each one had six wings.
With two he covered his face, and with two he
covered his feet, and with two he flew. 3 One
cried to another and said:

"Holy, holy, holy, is the LORD of Hosts;
the whole earth is full of His glory."

> God's holiness becomes an anointing on me as I pursue God's holy presence relentlessly (Isa 6:1–6).

4 The posts of the door moved at the voice of
him who cried, and the house was filled with
smoke.
5 And I said: "Woe is me! For I am undone be-
cause I am a man of unclean lips, and I dwell
in the midst of a people of unclean lips. For my
eyes have seen the King, the LORD of Hosts."
6 Then one of the seraphim flew to me with
a live coal which he had taken with the tongs
from off the altar in his hand. 7 And he laid
it on my mouth, and said, "This has touched
your lips, and your iniquity is taken away, and
your sin purged."
8 Also I heard the voice of the Lord saying,
"Whom shall I send, and who will go for us?"
Then I said, "Here am I. Send me."
9 He said, "Go, and tell this people:

'Keep on hearing, but do not understand;
keep on seeing, but do not perceive.'
10 Make the heart of this people dull,
and their ears heavy,
and shut their eyes;
lest they see with their eyes,
and hear with their ears,
and understand with their heart,
and turn and be healed."

11 Then I said, "Lord, how long?"
And He answered:

"Until the cities are laid waste
without inhabitants,
and the houses without man,
and the land is utterly desolate,
12 and the LORD has removed men far away,
and there is a great forsaking in the
midst of the land.
13 But yet in it shall be a tenth,
and it shall return, and shall be burned,
as a terebinth tree or as an oak,
whose stump remains when it is cut
down,
so the holy seed is its stump."

6:3 Ps 72:19
6:4 Rev 15:8
6:5 Ex 33:20
6:6 Rev 8:3–5
6:7 Jer 1:9
6:8 Ge 1:26
6:9 Lk 8:10
6:10 Jer 5:21
6:11 Isa 1:7
6:12 Jer 4:29
6:13 Ezr 9:2

7:1 2Ki 15:37
7:2 Isa 7:13
7:3 2Ki 18:17
7:4 Dt 20:3
7:7 Isa 8:10
7:8 Isa 17:1–3
7:9 2Ch 20:20
7:13 Isa 43:24
7:14 Isa 8:8
7:15 Isa 7:22
7:16 Isa 8:4

Isaiah Reassures King Ahaz

7 And it came to pass in the days of Ahaz the
son of Jotham, the son of Uzziah, king of
Judah, that Rezin the king of Aram, and Pekah
the son of Remaliah, king of Israel, went up
toward Jerusalem to war against it, but could
not prevail against it.
2 It was said to the house of David, "Aram is
allied with Ephraim." Then his heart trembled
and the heart of his people, as the trees of the
wood tremble with the wind.
3 Then the LORD said to Isaiah: Go out now to
meet Ahaz, you, and Shear-Jashub your son, at
the end of the conduit of the upper pool in the
highway of the fuller's field, 4 and say to him,
Take heed, and be quiet. Do not fear nor be
fainthearted because of the two tails of these
smoking firebrands, because of the fierce an-
ger of Rezin with Aram and of the son of Re-
maliah, 5 because Aram, Ephraim, and the son
of Remaliah have taken evil counsel against
you, saying, 6 Let us go up against Judah, and
trouble it, and let us make a breach there for
us, and set a king in the midst of it, even the
son of Tabeel. 7 Thus says the Lord GOD:

It shall not stand,
nor shall it come to pass.
8 For the head of Aram is Damascus,
and the head of Damascus is Rezin.
Now within sixty-five years
Ephraim shall be broken so that it is not
a people.
9 The head of Ephraim is Samaria,
and the head of Samaria is the son of
Remaliah.
If you will not believe,
surely you shall not be established.

The Sign of Immanuel

10 Moreover the LORD spoke again to Ahaz,
saying: 11 Ask for a sign from the LORD your
God. Make it either as deep as Sheol or as high
as heaven.
12 But Ahaz said, I will not ask, nor will I
tempt the LORD.
13 Then he said, "Hear now, O house of David.
Is it a small thing for you to weary men, but
will you weary my God also? 14 Therefore the
Lord Himself shall give you a sign: The virgin[1]
shall conceive, and bear a son, and shall call
his name Immanuel.[2] 15 Curds and honey he
shall eat at the time that he knows enough
to refuse the evil and choose the good. 16 For
before the child shall know to refuse the evil
and choose the good, the land that you dread
shall be forsaken of both her kings. 17 The LORD
shall bring upon you, and upon your people,
and upon your father's house, days that have

[1]14 Heb. *young woman.* [2]14 Or *God with us.*

not come from the day that Ephraim departed
from Judah, even the king of Assyria."
18 In that day the LORD shall whistle for the
fly that is in the uttermost part of the rivers
of Egypt, and for the bee that is in the land
of Assyria. 19 They shall come, and all of them
shall rest in the desolate valleys, and in the
holes of the rocks, and on all thorns, and on all
bushes. 20 In that same day the Lord shall shave
with a hired razor, from regions beyond the
River,[1] with the king of Assyria, the head, and
the hair of the legs, and it shall also remove
the beard. 21 In that day a man shall nourish
a young cow and two sheep, 22 and because
of the abundance of milk that they give, he
shall eat curds; for everyone who is left in
the land shall eat curds and honey. 23 In that
day every place where there were a thousand
vines, *worth* a thousand *shekels*[2] of silver, shall
become briers and thorns. 24 With arrows and
with bows shall men come there because all
the land shall become briers and thorns. 25 On
all hills that used to be cultivated with the hoe,
you will not go there for fear of briers and
thorns. But it shall be for pasturing oxen and
for sheep to tread.

The Coming Assyrian Invasion

8 Moreover the LORD said to me, Take for
yourself a large book and write in it with
a man's pen: "Swift is the booty, speedy is the
prey."[3] 2 I will take to Myself faithful witnesses
for testimony, Uriah the priest and Zechariah
the son of Jeberekiah. 3 So I went in to the
prophetess, and she conceived and bore a son.
Then the LORD said to me, Call his name Maher-
Shalal-Hash-Baz.[4] 4 For before the child knows
how to cry "My father" and "My mother," the
riches of Damascus and the spoil of Samaria
shall be taken away before the king of Assyria.
5 The LORD spoke to me again, saying:

6 Because this people refuses
the gently flowing waters of Shiloah
and rejoices in Rezin
and the son of Remaliah,
7 now therefore the Lord certainly is about to
bring upon them
the strong and plentiful waters of the
River,[5]
even the king of Assyria and all his
glory;
and he shall come up over all his channels
and go over all his banks.
8 And he shall pass through Judah, he shall
overflow and go over,
he shall reach even to the neck,
and the stretching out of his wings shall fill
the breadth of your land,
O Immanuel.

7:18 Isa 5:26
7:19 Isa 2:19
7:22 Isa 7:15
7:23 Isa 5:6
8:1 Isa 30:8
8:2 2Ki 16:10–11
8:6 Jn 9:7
8:7 Isa 17:12–13
8:8 Isa 7:14
....
8:10 Ro 8:31
8:11 Eze 3:14
8:12 1Pe 3:14–15
8:14 Eze 11:16
8:16 Da 12:4
8:17 Isa 54:8
8:18 Ps 9:11
8:19 Isa 19:3
8:20 Mic 3:6
8:21 Isa 9:20
8:22 Isa 5:30

9 Be broken, O you peoples, and be broken
in pieces.
And give ear, all you from far countries.
Gird yourselves, but be broken in pieces;
gird yourselves, but be broken in pieces.
10 Take counsel together, but it shall come to
nothing;
speak the word, but it shall not stand
for God is with us.

Fear God

11 For the LORD spoke thus to me with a strong
hand and instructed me that I should not walk
in the way of this people, saying:

12 You should not say, "It is a conspiracy,"
concerning all that this people calls a
conspiracy,
neither fear their threats
nor be afraid of them.
13 Sanctify the LORD of Hosts Himself,
and let Him be your fear,
and let Him be your dread.
14 He shall become a sanctuary,
but a stone of stumbling and a rock of
offense
to both the houses of Israel,
and a trap and a snare to the inhabitants
of Jerusalem.
15 Many among them shall stumble
and fall and be broken
and be snared and be taken.
16 Bind up the testimony;
seal the law among My disciples.
17 I will wait on the LORD,
who hides His face from the house of
Jacob,
and I will eagerly look for Him.

18 See, I and the children whom the LORD
has given me are for signs and for wonders
in Israel from the LORD of Hosts who dwells
in Mount Zion.
19 When they say to you, "Seek after the me-
diums and the wizards, who whisper and mut-
ter," should not a people seek after their God?
Should they consult the dead for the living?
20 To the law and to the testimony; if they do
not speak according to this word, it is because
there is no light in them. 21 They shall pass
through the land hard-pressed and hungry;
when they are hungry, they shall be furious
and curse their king and their God as they look
upward. 22 Then they shall look to the earth and
see trouble and darkness, gloom of anguish.
And they shall be driven away into darkness.

[1] *20* Euphrates River. [2] *23* About 25 pounds, or 12 kilograms.
[3] *1* See v. 3. [4] *3* See v. 1. [5] *7* Euphrates River.

The Coming King

9 Nevertheless there shall be no more gloom for her who was in anguish. In the former time He contemptuously treated the land of Zebulun and the land of Naphtali, but in the latter time He shall make it glorious, by the way of the sea, beyond the Jordan, in Galilee of the nations.

2 The people who walked in darkness
have seen a great light;
those who dwell in the land of the shadow of death,
upon them the light has shined.
3 You have multiplied the nation
and increased the joy;
they rejoice before You
according to the joy of harvest
and as men rejoice
when they divide the spoil.
4 For You have broken the yoke of his burden
and the bar of his shoulder,
the rod of his oppressor
as in the day of Midian's defeat.
5 For all the sandals of the tramping warriors
and all the garments rolled in blood
shall be burned as fuel for the fire.
6 For unto us a child is born,
unto us a son is given,
and the government shall be upon his shoulder.
And his name shall be called
Wonderful Counselor, Mighty God,
Eternal Father, Prince of Peace.
7 Of the increase of his government and peace
there shall be no end,
upon the throne of David
and over his kingdom,
to order it and to establish it
with justice and with righteousness,
from now until forever.
The zeal of the LORD of Hosts
will perform this.

The Message Against Israel

8 The Lord sent a word against Jacob,
and it falls upon Israel.
9 All the people shall know,
even Ephraim and the inhabitants of Samaria,
who say in the pride
and stoutness of heart,
10 "The bricks are fallen down,
but we will build with hewn stones;
the sycamores are cut down,
but we will replace them with cedars."
11 Therefore, the LORD shall set up the adversaries of Rezin against him,
and join his enemies together.
12 The Arameans shall be before and the Philistines behind;
and they shall devour Israel with open jaws.

For all this His anger is not turned away,
and His hand is stretched out still.
13 For the people do not turn to Him who struck them,
nor do they seek the LORD of Hosts.
14 Therefore the LORD will cut off from Israel head and tail,
branch and bulrush, in one day.
15 The elder and honorable man, he is the head;
and the prophet that teaches lies, he is the tail.
16 For the leaders of this people cause them to err,
and those who are led by them are destroyed.
17 Therefore the Lord shall have no joy in their young men,
nor shall He have mercy on their fatherless and widows;
for every one of them is a hypocrite and an evildoer,
and every mouth speaks folly.

For all this His anger is not turned away,
and His hand is stretched out still.
18 For wickedness burns as a fire;
it shall devour the briers and thorns,
and shall ignite in the thickets of the forest,
and they shall mount up like rising smoke.
19 Through the wrath of the LORD of Hosts
is the land burned up,
and the people shall be as fuel for the fire;
no man shall spare his brother.
20 They shall snatch on the right hand,
but still be hungry;
and they shall eat on the left hand,
and shall not be satisfied;
every man shall eat the flesh of his own arm.
21 Manasseh *consumes* Ephraim, and Ephraim, Manasseh,
and they together shall be against Judah.

For all this His anger is not turned away,
and His hand is stretched out still.

10 Woe to those who decree unrighteous decrees
and who write unjust judgments which they have prescribed
2 to turn aside the needy from justice

9:1 2Ki 15:29
9:2 Eph 5:8
9:3 1Sa 30:16
9:4 Isa 14:25
9:6 Isa 7:14
9:7 Isa 37:32
9:9 Isa 46:12
9:10 Mal 1:4
....
9:12 2Ch 28:18
9:13 Hos 7:10
9:14 Isa 19:15
9:16 Isa 3:12
9:17 Isa 10:6
9:18 Mal 4:1
9:19 Mic 7:2
9:20 Isa 49:26
9:21 Isa 5:25
10:1 Ps 58:2
10:2 Isa 3:14

and to take away the right from the poor
of My people,
that widows may be their prey,
and that they may rob the fatherless!
3 And what will you do in the day of
punishment
and in the desolation which shall come
from afar?
To whom will you flee for help,
and where will you leave your wealth?
4 Nothing remains but to bow down among
the prisoners,
and they shall fall among the slain.

For all this His anger is not turned away,
and His hand is stretched out still.

Judgment on Assyria

5 Woe to Assyria, the rod of My anger
and the staff in whose hand is My
indignation.
6 I will send him against an ungodly nation,
and against the people of My wrath I
will give him a command,
to seize the plunder, to take the prey,
and to tread them down like the mire of
the streets.
7 However he does not so intend,
nor does he plan so in his heart;
but his purpose is to destroy
and to cut off many nations.
8 For he says, "Are not my princes altogether
kings?
9 Is not Kalno as Carchemish?
Is not Hamath as Arpad?
Is not Samaria as Damascus?
10 As my hand has found the kingdoms of the
idols
whose graven images were greater than
those of Jerusalem and Samaria,
11 shall I not, as I have done to Samaria and
her idols,
so do to Jerusalem and her idols?"

12 When the Lord has performed all His work
on Mount Zion and on Jerusalem, *He will say*,
"I will punish the fruit of the stout heart of
the king of Assyria and the glory of his high
looks." 13 For he says:

"By the strength of my hand and by my
wisdom,
I have done it, for I am prudent;
and I have removed the bounds of the
people,
and have robbed their treasures,
and I have put down the inhabitants like
a valiant man.
14 And my hand has found as a nest
the riches of the people,
and as one gathers eggs that are left,

10:3 Hos 9:7
10:4 Isa 5:25
10:6 Isa 9:17
10:7 Ge 50:20
10:8 2Ki 18:24
10:9 2Ki 16:9
10:13 Da 4:30
10:14 Job 31:25
10:15 Isa 10:5
10:16 Ps 106:15
10:17 Nu 11:1–3
10:20 2Ki 16:7
10:21 Isa 9:6
10:22 Ro 9:27–28
10:24 Isa 37:6
10:25 Da 11:36

I have gathered all the earth
and there was no one who moved the wing
or opened the mouth or peeped."

15 Shall the axe boast itself against him who
hews with it?
Or shall the saw magnify itself against
him who wields it?
That is as if the rod wields itself against
those who lift it up,
or as if the staff should lift itself up as if
it were not wood.
16 Therefore the Lord, God of Hosts,
shall send leanness among his stout
ones,
and under his glory he shall kindle a
burning
like the burning of a fire.
17 The light of Israel shall be a fire,
and his Holy One a flame,
and it shall burn and devour
his thorns and his briers in one day,
18 and shall consume the glory of his forest,
and of his fruitful field, both soul and
body;
and it shall be as when a sick man faints.
19 The rest of the trees of his forest shall be so
few
that a child may write them down.

The Returning Remnant of Israel

20 In that day the remnant of Israel
and those who have escaped of the
house of Jacob
shall never again depend on him
who struck them,
but shall depend on the Lord,
the Holy One of Israel, in truth.
21 The remnant shall return, even the
remnant of Jacob,
to the mighty God.
22 For though your people, O Israel, are as the
sand of the sea,
yet a remnant of them shall return;
the destruction is decreed,
overflowing with righteousness.
23 For the Lord God of Hosts shall make a
complete destruction,
as decreed, in the midst of all the land.

24 Therefore, thus says the Lord God of Hosts:

O My people who dwell in Zion,
do not be afraid of the Assyrian.
He shall strike you with a rod
and shall lift up his staff against you,
after the manner of Egypt.
25 For yet a very little while, and the
indignation shall cease,
and My anger will be directed to their
destruction.

26 The LORD of Hosts shall stir up a scourge
for him
according to the slaughter of Midian at
the rock of Oreb;
and as His rod was over the sea, so shall
He lift it up
after the manner of Egypt.
27 In that day his burden shall be taken away
from off your shoulder,
and his yoke from off your neck;
and the yoke shall be destroyed
because of the anointing oil.

28 He has come against Aiath,
he has passed through Migron;
at Mikmash he has laid up his carriages.
29 They are gone over the pass,
they have taken up their lodging at
Geba.
Ramah is afraid,
Gibeah of Saul has fled.
30 Lift up your voice, O daughter of Gallim.
Listen, Laishah
and poor Anathoth.
31 Madmenah has fled,
the inhabitants of Gebim gather
themselves to flee.
32 Yet today he shall remain at Nob;
he shakes his fist
against the mount of the daughter of Zion,
the hill of Jerusalem.

33 See, the Lord, the LORD of Hosts,
shall lop the bough with terror;
and the tall ones of stature shall be hewn
down,
and the haughty shall be humbled.
34 He shall cut down the thickets of the forest
with iron,
and Lebanon shall fall by the Mighty
One.

The Righteous Branch of Jesse

11 And there shall come forth a shoot
from the stump of Jesse,
and a Branch shall grow out of his roots.
2 The Spirit of the LORD shall rest upon him,
the Spirit of wisdom and understanding,
the Spirit of counsel and might,
the Spirit of knowledge and of the fear
of the LORD.
3 He shall delight in the fear of the LORD,
and he shall not judge by what his eyes
see,
nor reprove by what his ears hear;
4 but with righteousness he shall judge the
poor,
and reprove with fairness for the meek
of the earth.

10:26 Isa 9:4
10:27 Isa 9:4
10:28 1Sa 14:2
10:29 1Sa 7:17
10:30 1Sa 25:44
10:32 1Sa 21:1
10:33 Am 2:9
10:34 Isa 37:24
11:1 Isa 11:10
11:2 Isa 61:1
11:3 Jn 7:24
11:4 Mal 4:6
11:5 Eph 6:14
11:6 Isa 65:25
11:9 Hab 2:14
11:10 Isa 11:1
11:11 Ge 10:22
11:12 Isa 11:10
11:13 Jer 3:18
11:14 Isa 25:10
11:15 Isa 19:16

He shall strike the earth with the rod of his
mouth,
and with the breath of his lips he shall
slay the wicked.
5 Righteousness shall be the belt of his loins,
and faithfulness the belt about his waist.

6 The wolf also shall dwell with the lamb,
and the leopard shall lie down with the
young goat,
and the calf and the young lion and the
fatling together;
and a little child shall lead them.
7 The cow and the bear shall graze;
their young ones shall lie down together;
and the lion shall eat straw like the ox.
8 The nursing child shall play by the hole of
the asp,
and the weaned child shall put his hand
in the viper's den.
9 They shall not hurt or destroy
in all My holy mountain,
for the earth shall be full of the knowledge
of the LORD,
as the waters cover the sea.

10 In that day there shall be a Root of Jesse,
who shall stand as a banner to the peoples.
For him shall the nations seek. And his rest
shall be glorious. 11 In that day the Lord shall
set His hand again the second time to recover
the remnant of His people, who shall be left,
from Assyria, from Egypt, from Pathros, from
Cush, from Elam, from Shinar, from Hamath,
and from the islands of the sea.

12 He shall set up a banner for the nations,
and shall assemble the outcasts of Israel,
and gather together the dispersed of Judah
from the four corners of the earth.
13 The envy also of Ephraim shall depart,
and the adversaries of Judah shall be
cut off;
Ephraim shall not envy Judah,
and Judah shall not harass Ephraim.
14 But they shall swoop down on the slopes
of the Philistines towards the west;
they shall plunder the sons of the east
together;
they shall lay their hand on Edom and
Moab,
and the children of Ammon shall obey
them.
15 The LORD shall utterly destroy
the tongue of the Egyptian sea,
and with His mighty wind He shall shake
His hand
over the River,[1]
and shall strike it into seven streams,
and make men walk over dry-shod.

[1] *15* Euphrates River.

[16]There shall be a highway for the remnant
of His people,
who will be left from Assyria,
as it was for Israel
when he came up from the land of
Egypt.

Hymns of Praise

12 And in that day you shall say:

O LORD, I will praise You;
though You were angry with me,
Your anger has turned away,
and You comforted me.
[2] Certainly God is my salvation;
I will trust and not be afraid;
for the LORD GOD is my strength and my
song;
He also has become my salvation.
[3] Therefore with joy you shall draw water
out of the wells of salvation.

[4] In that day you shall say:

Praise the LORD, call upon His name,
declare His deeds among the peoples,
make them remember that His name is
exalted.
[5] Sing to the LORD, for He has done excellent
things;
let this be known in all the earth.
[6] Cry out and shout for joy, O inhabitant of
Zion.
For great is the Holy One of Israel in
your midst.

A Prophecy Against Babylon

13 The burden of Babylon, which Isaiah
the son of Amoz saw.

[2] Lift up a banner on the high mountain,
exalt the voice to them,
shake the hand,
that they may go into the gates of the
nobles.
[3] I have commanded My sanctified ones,
I have also called My mighty ones for
My anger,
even those who rejoice in My exaltation.

[4] The noise of a multitude in the mountains,
like as of a great people!
A tumultuous noise of the kingdoms
of nations gathered together!
The LORD of Hosts musters
the army for battle.
[5] They come from a far country,
from the end of heaven,
the LORD and the weapons of His
indignation,
to destroy the whole land.

[6] Wail, for the day of the LORD is at hand!
It shall come as destruction from the
Almighty.
[7] Therefore all hands shall be faint,
and every man's heart shall melt,
[8] and they shall be afraid.
Pangs and sorrows shall take hold of
them;
they shall be in pain as a woman who
travails;
they shall be amazed one at another;
their faces shall be as flames.

[9] See, the day of the LORD comes,
cruel, both with wrath and fierce anger,
to lay the land desolate,
and He shall destroy its sinners out of it.
[10]For the stars of heaven and their
constellations
shall not give their light;
the sun shall be dark when it rises,
and the moon shall not cause her light
to shine.
[11]I will punish the world for its evil,
and the wicked for their iniquity;
and I will cause the arrogance of the proud
to cease,
and will lay low the haughtiness of the
ruthless.
[12]I will make a man more rare than fine gold,
and mankind than the golden wedge of
Ophir.
[13]Therefore, I will shake the heavens,
and the earth shall be shaken out of her
place
at the wrath of the LORD of Hosts
and in the day of His fierce anger.
[14]It shall be as the chased roe,
and as a sheep that no man takes up;
every man shall turn to his own people
and flee every one into his own land.
[15]Every one who is found shall be thrust
through,
and every one who is joined to them
shall fall by the sword.
[16]Their children also shall be dashed to
pieces before their eyes;
their houses shall be devastated and
their wives ravished.

[17]See, I will stir up the Medes against them,
who shall not regard silver;
and as for gold, they shall not delight
in it.
[18]Their bows also shall dash the young men
to pieces,
and they shall have no pity on the fruit
of the womb;
their eye shall not spare children.
[19]Babylon, the glory of kingdoms,
the beauty of the Chaldean's excellency,

11:16 Isa 10:23
12:1 Isa 25:1
12:2 Ex 15:2
12:3 Jer 2:13
12:4 Ps 105:1
12:5 Ex 15:1
12:6 Zep 3:14–17
13:1 Isa 1:1
13:2 Isa 5:26
13:3 Joel 3:11
13:4 Joel 3:14
13:6 Joel 1:15
13:7 Eze 21:7
13:8 Isa 26:17
13:9 Ps 104:35
13:10 Mt 24:29
13:12 Isa 4:1
13:13 La 1:12
13:14 1Ki 22:17
13:16 Na 3:10
13:17 Pr 6:34–35
13:18 2Ki 8:12
13:19 Ge 19:24

Recognizing Iniquity Patterns

Every one of our kids has the precious spirit part of them that has been cleansed by God and now functions in the power of the Holy Spirit. This is wonderful. They also arrived with areas that, even fairly early on, God wants them to overcome.

As our children grow day by day, we can see the specific areas of iniquity they struggle with. If we dive in and help them begin to overcome these stumbling blocks while they are still young, they will not be left to wrestle with them for the rest of their lives. This is the incredible opportunity we have as parents to be used by God to stand against the power of iniquity patterns that govern our kids' lives.

In the one passage of Scripture quoted below, we can see five patterns of iniquity that, as parents, we need to help our children guard against:

> For you have said in your heart, "I will ascend into heaven, I will exalt my throne above the stars of God; I will sit also on the mount of the congregation, in the recesses of the north; I will ascend above the heights of the clouds, I will be like the Most High."
>
> —ISAIAH 14:13–14

Let's consider a modern-day application of how these principles of iniquity patterns work in our world today. On the lines provided under each pattern, indicate if you have seen this pattern in your own child's life. Then describe how you can help your child to overcome this iniquity pattern.

1. The Chore Chart MVP ("I will ascend into heaven . . .")

This iniquity pattern causes a child to try to climb into heaven by his or her own works rather than by the grace of God. This child's desire to earn the esteemed Most Valuable Player (MVP) award stems from the wrong motive. It does not come from a loving motive ("I want to help others") but instead from a selfish motive ("I want everyone to see how good I am.") Self-righteous, religious, "goody-goody" children fall into this pattern. Wanting to appear to be the best kid on the planet, this is the one who can never be wrong or get in trouble. At the core of this iniquity pattern is the lie "What I do is more important than who I am."

Have I seen this pattern in my child's life? ❑ Yes ❑ No

I will help my child overcome this pattern by:

____

____

2. The Little Steam Engine ("I will exalt my throne above the stars of God . . .")

This is not "the little engine that could"—it's the little engine that you can't stop! These little people will stop at nothing to be the best. Competition is the arena they thrive in. The problem is that they are driven to flatten and level everyone in their path to get their way. They exalt themselves above others and will step on someone else to climb up their ladder of success. At the core of this iniquity pattern is the lie "I'm nothing if I'm not the best."

Have I seen this pattern in my child's life? ❑ Yes ❑ No

I will help my child overcome this pattern by:

3. The Aspiring Hollywood Star ("I will also sit on the mount of the congregation . . .")

This child is always at the center of everyone's attention. We have all seen it. Their drive causes them to stop at nothing to be the focal point in every situation. Drama, drama, drama surrounds their every move and decision. The desire to be looked at, listened to, and given extreme recognition over every other child produces a whirlwind in any family or set of friends. At the core of this iniquity pattern is the lie "I deserve all the attention."

Have I seen this pattern in my child's life? ❑ Yes ❑ No

I will help my child overcome this pattern by:

4. The Never-Never Land Native ("I will ascend above the heights of the clouds . . .")

This child's *modus operandi* is checking out of reality. When anything seems difficult or challenging, he is the first one to go find another "world" to live in where life is easier and more controllable. This child would rather be playing a video game, reading a book, or lost in a movie than be a functional part of the family. He dwells in an alternate reality where everything has the perfect fairy-tale ending. At the core of this iniquity pattern is the lie "This life is too hard, so I need to escape it."

Have I seen this pattern in my child's life? ❑ Yes ❑ No

I will help my child overcome this pattern by:

5. Unelected dictator ("I will be like the Most High...")

This is the "take control" child. The only problem is that these children are not just being responsible for themselves; they are also demanding to control everyone in their environment! Are mom and dad allowed to be Command Central? No. Dominance and supremacy in this household has been self-bestowed on this preeminent one (and not because God or any other authority has declared it to be there!). At the core of this iniquity pattern is the lie "I, not God, can and must control every situation and the people in my life."

Have I seen this pattern in my child's life? ❑ Yes ❑ No

I will help my child overcome this pattern by:

Julie Hiramine

shall be as when God overthrew
Sodom and Gomorrah.
20 It shall never be inhabited,
nor shall it be lived in from generation to generation,
nor shall the Arabian pitch a tent there,
nor shall the shepherds make their fold there.
21 But wild beasts of the desert shall lie down there,
and their houses shall be full of owls,
ostriches also shall dwell there,
and shaggy goats shall dance there.
22 The wild beasts of the islands shall cry in their desolate houses
and jackals in their pleasant palaces.
And her time is near to come,
and her days shall not be prolonged.

The Restoration of Judah

14 For the LORD will have mercy on Jacob,
and will yet choose Israel,
and set them in their own land.
Then the strangers shall be joined with them,
and they shall cleave to the house of Jacob.
2 The people shall take them
and bring them to their place,
and the house of Israel shall possess them
in the land of the LORD for servants and handmaids;
and they shall take them captive, whose captives they were,
and they shall rule over their oppressors.

He shall give me rest, and sorrow will be turned into joy (Isa 14:3).

The Fall of Babylon's King

3 In the day the LORD gives you rest from your
sorrow, and from your fear, and from the hard
bondage in which you were made to serve,
4 you shall take up this proverb against the king
of Babylon, and say:

How has the oppressor ceased!
The golden city ceased!
5 The LORD has broken the staff of the wicked,
and the scepter of the rulers;
6 he who struck the people in wrath with unceasing strokes,
he who ruled the nations in anger, is persecuted, and no one hinders.
7 The whole earth is at rest and is quiet;
they break forth into singing.
8 Indeed, the fir trees rejoice at you,
and the cedars of Lebanon, saying,
"Since you are laid down,
no tree cutter has come up against us."
9 Hell from beneath is moved for you
to meet you at your coming;
it stirs up the dead for you,
even all the chief ones of the earth;
it has raised up from their thrones
all the kings of the nations.
10 They all shall speak
and say to you:
"Have you also become as weak as we have?
Have you become like us?"
11 Your pomp is brought down to Hell,
and the noise of your harps;
maggots are spread under you,
and the worms cover you.

12 How are you fallen from heaven,
O Lucifer, son of the morning!
How you are cut down to the ground,
you who weaken the nations!
13 For you have said in your heart,
"I will ascend into heaven,
I will exalt my throne
above the stars of God;
I will sit also on the mount of the congregation,
in the recesses of the north;
14 I will ascend above the heights of the clouds,
I will be like the Most High."
15 Yet you shall be brought down to Hell,
to the sides of the pit.
16 Those who see you shall stare at you
and ponder over you:
"Is this the man who made the earth
to tremble and shook kingdoms,
17 who made the world as a wilderness
and destroyed its cities,
who did not open the house of his prisoners?"
18 All the kings of the nations, even all of them, lie in glory,
each one in his own tomb;
19 but you are cast out of your grave
like an abominable branch
and clothed with those who are slain,
thrust through with a sword,
who go down to the stones of the pit
as a corpse trodden underfoot.
20 You shall not be joined with them in burial
because you have destroyed your land
and slain your people.

The seed of evildoers
shall never be renowned.

13:20 Isa 14:23
13:21 Rev 18:2
14:1 Ps 102:13
14:2 Isa 61:5
14:7 Ps 126:1–3
14:8 Eze 31:16
....
14:12 Lk 10:18
14:13 Eze 28:2
14:14 Isa 47:8
14:15 Mt 11:23
14:16 Jer 50:23
14:17 Joel 2:3
14:19 Jer 41:7
14:20 Job 18:19

[21]Prepare a place of slaughter for his children
for the iniquity of their fathers;
they must not rise nor possess the land,
nor fill the face of the world with cities.
[22]For I will rise up against them,
says the LORD of Hosts,
and cut off from Babylon the name, and remnant,
and son, and nephew,
says the LORD.
[23]I will also make it a possession for the hedgehog
and pools of water,
and I will sweep it with the broom of destruction,
says the LORD of Hosts.

An Oracle Concerning Assyria

[24]The LORD of Hosts has sworn, saying:

Surely as I have thought, so shall it come to pass,
and as I have purposed, so shall it stand:
[25]that I will break the Assyrian in My land,
and on My mountains tread him under foot.
Then shall his yoke depart from off them
and his burden depart from off their shoulders.

[26]This is the purpose that is purposed on the whole earth,
and this is the hand that is stretched out on all the nations.
[27]For the LORD of Hosts has purposed, and who shall disannul it?
And His hand is stretched out, and who shall turn it back?

An Oracle Concerning Philistia

[28]In the year that King Ahaz died was this oracle:

[29]Rejoice not, O Philistia, all of you,
because the rod that struck you is broken;
for out of the serpent's root shall come forth a viper,
and his fruit shall be a fiery flying serpent.
[30]The firstborn of the poor shall feed,
and the needy shall lie down in safety:
and I will kill your root with famine,
and he shall slay your remnant.

[31]Wail, O gate. Cry, O city.
Melt away, O Philistia, all of you;
for smoke shall come from the north,
and there is no straggler in his ranks.
[32]What shall one then answer
the messengers of the nation?
That the LORD has founded Zion,
and the poor of His people shall trust in it.

A Prophecy Against Moab

Jer 48:29–36

15 The oracle of Moab.

Surely in the night Ar of Moab is laid waste
and brought to silence,
surely in the night Kir of Moab is laid waste
and brought to silence,
[2]he has gone up to the temple and to Dibon,
the high places, to weep.
Moab shall wail over Nebo and over Medeba;
on all their heads shall be baldness,
and every beard cut off.
[3]In their streets they shall clothe themselves with sackcloth;
on the tops of their houses and in their streets,
everyone shall wail,
weeping abundantly.
[4]Heshbon shall cry, and Elealeh;
their voice shall be heard even to Jahaz;
therefore the armed soldiers of Moab shall cry out;
his life shall be grievous to him.

[5]My heart shall cry out for Moab;
his fugitives shall flee to Zoar,
like a three-year-old heifer.
For by the Ascent of Luhith
they shall go up with weeping;
for in the way of Horonaim
they shall raise up a cry of destruction,
[6]for the waters of Nimrim shall be desolate;
surely the grass is withered away;
the grass fails,
there is no green thing.
[7]Therefore the abundance they have gained,
and that which they have laid up,
they shall carry away to the Brook of the Willows.
[8]For the cry has gone all around the borders of Moab;
its wailing to Eglaim,
and its wailing to Beer Elim.
[9]For the waters of Dimon shall be full of blood;
for I will bring more woes on Dimon,
lions on the fugitives of Moab,
and on the remnant of the land.

16 Send the lamb
to the ruler of the land
from Sela by way of the wilderness,
to the mount of the daughter of Zion.
[2]For it shall be that as a wandering bird

14:21 Ex 20:5
14:23 Zep 2:14
14:24 Ac 4:28
14:25 Isa 9:4
14:27 2Ch 20:6
14:28 2Ki 16:20
14:29 2Ch 26:6
14:30 Isa 7:21–22
14:31 Jer 1:14
14:32 Ps 87:5

15:1 Nu 21:28
15:2 Lev 21:5
15:3 Jnh 3:6–8
15:4 Jer 48:34
15:5 Jer 48:5
15:7 Jer 48:36
15:9 2Ki 17:25
16:1 2Ki 3:4
16:2 Pr 27:8

cast out of the nest,
so the daughters of Moab shall be
at the fords of Arnon.

3 "Take counsel,
execute justice,
make your shadow as the night
at the height of noon.
Hide the outcasts,
do not betray the fugitive.
4 Let my outcasts dwell with you, Moab;
be a hiding place to them from the face
of the destroyer."

For the extortioner has come to an end;
the destroyer ceases;
the oppressors are *consumed* out of the
land.
5 In mercy the throne shall be established;
and one who judges and seeks justice
and is diligent in righteousness
shall sit on it in truth
in the tabernacle of David, judging.

6 We have heard of the pride of Moab;
he is very proud,
even of his haughtiness and his pride and
his wrath;
but his lies shall not be so.
7 Therefore Moab shall wail for Moab;
everyone shall wail.
For the loss of raisin cakes of Kir Hareseth
you shall mourn;
surely they are destroyed.
8 For the fields of Heshbon languish,
and the vine of Sibmah;
the lords of the nations
have broken down its choice plants;
they have come as far as Jazer
and wandered through the wilderness.
Her branches are stretched out;
they are passed over the sea.
9 Therefore I will weep bitterly for Jazer,
the vine of Sibmah;
I will water you with my tears,
O Heshbon and Elealeh.
For the shouting for your summer fruits
and for your harvest has fallen away.
10 Gladness and joy are taken away out of the
plentiful field,
and in the vineyards there shall be no
singing,
nor shall there be shouting;
the treaders shall tread out no wine in their
presses.
I have made their vintage shouting to
cease.
11 Therefore my heart shall sound like a harp
for Moab,
and my inward parts for Kir Hareseth.

16:5 Da 7:14
16:6 Am 2:1
16:7 2Ki 3:25
16:9 Jer 40:12
16:10 Jer 48:33
16:11 Isa 15:5
....
16:12 Isa 15:2
16:14 Isa 21:16
17:1 Zec 9:1
17:2 Eze 25:5
17:3 Isa 7:16
17:4 Isa 10:16
17:5 2Sa 5:18
17:6 Isa 24:13
17:7 Mic 7:7
17:8 Isa 27:9
17:9 Isa 27:10
17:10 Dt 32:4

12 When it is seen that Moab
is weary on the high place,
he shall come to his sanctuary to pray;
but he shall not prevail.

13 This is the word that the LORD has spoken
earlier concerning Moab. 14 But now the LORD
has spoken, saying, Within three years, as the
years of a hireling, the glory of Moab shall be
brought into contempt with all his great pop-
ulation, and his remnant shall be very small
and feeble.

An Oracle Concerning Damascus

17 The oracle of Damascus.

See, Damascus will cease from being a city;
it shall be a ruinous heap.
2 The cities of Aroer are forsaken;
they shall be for flocks, which shall lie
down,
and no one shall make them afraid.
3 The fortress also shall cease from Ephraim,
and the kingdom from Damascus,
and the remnant of Aram;
they shall be as the glory of the sons of
Israel,
says the LORD of Hosts.

4 In that day the glory of Jacob shall
decrease,
and the fatness of his flesh shall grow
lean.
5 It shall be as when the harvestman gathers
the corn
and reaps the ears with his arm,
and it shall be as he who gathers ears
in the Valley of Rephaim.
6 Yet gleaning grapes shall be left in it,
as the shaking of an olive tree,
two or three berries in the top of the
uppermost bough,
four or five in its outmost fruitful
branches,
says the LORD God of Israel.

7 On that day a man shall look to his Maker,
and his eyes shall have respect for the
Holy One of Israel.
8 He shall not look to the altars,
the work of his hands,
nor shall he respect what his fingers have
made,
either the groves or the images.

9 In that day his strong cities shall be as a
forsaken bough and an uppermost branch,
which they left because of the sons of Israel;
and there shall be a desolation.

10 Because you have forgotten the God of
your salvation

and have not been mindful of the rock
of your strength,
therefore you plant pleasant plants
and set them with vine slips of a strange
god;
11 in the day that you plant it, you carefully
fence it in,
and in the morning you make your seed
to flourish;
but the harvest shall be a heap of ruins
in the day of grief and desperate pain.

12 Woe to the multitude of many people
who make a noise like the noise of the
seas,
and the rushing of many peoples
who make a rumble like the rumbling of
mighty waters!
13 The nations rumble like the rumbling of
many waters;
but God shall rebuke them, and they
shall flee far off,
and shall be chased as the chaff of the
mountains before the wind,
and like rolling dust before the
whirlwind.
14 At evening time, sudden terror!
And before the morning, they are no
more.
This is the portion of those who plunder us,
and the lot of those who rob us.

An Oracle Concerning Ethiopia

18 Woe to the land vibrating with wings,
which is beyond the rivers of Ethiopia,
2 which sends ambassadors by the sea,
even in vessels of reeds on the waters,
saying,
"Go, swift messengers,
to a nation tall and smooth,
to a people feared far and wide,
a nation strong and oppressive,
whose land the rivers have divided."

3 All you inhabitants of the world,
and dwellers on the earth:
When he lifts up a banner on the
mountains,
you will see it;
and when he blows a trumpet,
you will hear it.
4 For so the LORD said to me:
I will look from My dwelling place
quietly,
like dazzling heat in the sunshine,
like a cloud of dew in the heat of
harvest.
5 For before the harvest, when the bud is
perfect

17:11 Job 4:8
17:12 Ps 18:4
17:13 Ps 9:5
17:14 2Ki 19:35
18:1 2Ki 19:9
18:2 Ge 10:8–9
18:3 Isa 5:26
18:4 Isa 26:21
18:5 Eze 17:6–10
18:6 Jer 7:33
19:1 Ex 12:12
19:2 Jdg 7:22
19:3 Isa 8:19
19:4 Isa 20:4
19:5 Jer 51:36
19:6 Isa 37:25

and the sour grape is ripening in the
flower,
then He shall both cut off the sprigs with
pruning hooks
and take away and cut down the
branches.
6 They shall be left together for the fowl of
the mountains
and for the beasts of the earth;
and the fowl shall spend the summer
feeding on them,
and all the beasts of the earth shall
spend the winter on them.

7 In that time a present shall be brought to
the LORD of Hosts
from a people tall and smooth,
and from a people feared far and wide,
a nation strong and oppressive,
whose land the rivers have divided,
to the place of the name of the LORD of Hosts,
even Mount Zion.

An Oracle Concerning Egypt

19 The oracle of Egypt.
See, the LORD is riding on a swift cloud
and shall come into Egypt;
and the idols of Egypt shall tremble at His
presence,
and the heart of Egypt shall melt in its
midst.

2 I will set the Egyptians against the
Egyptians,
and they shall fight every one against
his brother,
and every one against his neighbor,
city against city,
and kingdom against kingdom.
3 The spirit of Egypt shall be discouraged in
their midst,
and I will destroy their counsel;
then they shall seek for the idols and for
the charmers
and for the mediums and the sorcerers.
4 The Egyptians I will give over
into the hand of a cruel lord,
and a fierce king shall rule over them,
says the Lord, the LORD of Hosts.

5 The waters from the sea shall dry up,
and the river shall be parched and dry.
6 The canals shall emit a stench;
the streams of Egypt shall diminish and
dry up;
the reeds and rushes shall wither.
7 The papyrus reeds by the brooks,
by the mouth of the brooks,
and everything sown by the brooks,

shall wither, be driven away, and be no
more.

8 The fishermen also shall mourn,
and all those who cast a line into the
brooks shall lament,
and those who spread nets on the waters
shall languish.

9 Moreover those who work with fine flax
and those who weave white cloth shall
be humiliated;

10 and the pillars *of Egypt* shall be crushed.
All the hired workers shall be grieved
in soul.

11 Surely the princes of Zoan are fools;
the counsel of the wise counselors of
Pharaoh has become stupid.
How can you say to Pharaoh,
"I am a son of the wise,
a son of ancient kings?"

12 Where are they? Where are your wise men?
Let them tell you now, and let them
understand
what the LORD of Hosts
has purposed against Egypt.

13 The princes of Zoan have become fools;
the princes of Memphis are deceived;
they have also seduced Egypt,
even those who are the cornerstone of
her tribes.

14 The LORD has mingled
a perverse spirit in her;
so they have caused Egypt to err in her
every work,
as a drunken man staggers in his vomit.

15 Nor shall there be any work for Egypt,
which its head or tail, its branch or
bulrush, may do.

16 In that day Egypt shall become like women.
And it shall be afraid and be in dread because
of the shaking of the hand of the LORD of Hosts
which He is about to shake over it. 17 The land
of Judah shall become a terror to Egypt. Ev-
eryone to whom it is mentioned shall be in
dread of it, because of the counsel of the LORD
of Hosts which He has determined against it.

18 In that day five cities in the land of Egypt
shall speak the language of Canaan and swear
to the LORD of Hosts. One shall be called the
City of Destruction.

19 In that day there shall be an altar to the
LORD in the midst of the land of Egypt, and a
pillar to the LORD at its border. 20 It shall be for
a sign and for a witness to the LORD of Hosts in
the land of Egypt. For they shall cry to the LORD
because of the oppressors, and He shall send
them a Savior and a Champion. And He shall

19:8 Eze 47:10
19:9 Eze 27:7
19:11 Nu 13:22
19:12 1Co 1:20
19:13 Jer 2:16
19:15 Isa 9:14–15
19:16 Isa 11:15
19:17 Isa 14:24
19:18 Zep 3:9
19:19 Ge 28:18
19:22 Dt 32:39
19:23 Isa 11:16
19:24 Isa 65:8
19:25 Isa 29:23
20:1 2Ki 18:17
20:2 1Sa 19:24
20:3 Isa 8:18
20:4 Isa 19:4
20:5 Isa 30:3
20:6 Mt 23:33
21:1 Isa 13:1
21:2 Isa 33:1
21:3 Isa 13:8

deliver them. 21 The LORD shall be known to
Egypt, and the Egyptians shall know the LORD
in that day, and shall worship with sacrifice
and offering, they shall make a vow to the LORD
and perform it. 22 The LORD shall strike Egypt.
He shall strike and heal it. Then they shall re-
turn to the LORD, and He shall be entreated by
them and shall heal them.

23 In that day there shall be a highway out of
Egypt to Assyria, and the Assyrian shall come
into Egypt, and the Egyptian into Assyria, and
the Egyptians shall worship with the Assyrians.
24 In that day Israel shall be the third group
with Egypt and Assyria, even a blessing in the
midst of the earth, 25 whom the LORD of Hosts
has blessed, saying, "Blessed is Egypt My peo-
ple, and Assyria the work of My hands, and
Israel My inheritance."

A Prophecy Against Egypt and Ethiopia

20 In the year that the Tartan[1] came to
Ashdod, when Sargon the king of As-
syria sent him, and he fought against Ashdod
and took it, 2 at the same time the LORD spoke
by Isaiah the son of Amoz saying, "Go and
loosen the sackcloth from your waist and take
off your shoes from your feet." And he did so,
walking naked and barefoot.

3 The LORD said, "Even as My servant Isaiah
has walked naked and barefoot three years for
a sign and wonder against Egypt and Ethio-
pia, 4 so the king of Assyria shall lead away
the Egyptians as prisoners and the Ethiopians
as captives, young and old, naked and bare-
foot, even with their buttocks uncovered, to
the shame of Egypt. 5 Then they shall be dis-
mayed and ashamed of Ethiopia their hope
and Egypt their boast. 6 So the inhabitants of
this coastland shall say in that day, 'Certainly
such is our hope, where we flee for help to be
delivered from the king of Assyria! And how
shall we escape?' "

A Prophecy Against Babylon

21 The oracle of the desert of the sea.

As whirlwinds in the Negev pass through,
so it comes from the desert,
from a terrible land.

2 A grievous vision is declared to me;
the treacherous one still deals
treacherously, and the destroyer still
destroys.
Go up, O Elam. Lay siege, O Media.
All her sighing I have made to cease.

3 Therefore, my loins are filled with pain;
pangs have taken hold of me as the
pangs of a woman who travails.

[1] 1 Possibly *Commander-in-Chief.*

I am so perplexed at the hearing of it;
I am so dismayed at the seeing of it.
4 My heart panted,
fearfulness overwhelmed me;
the night for which I longed
has turned into trembling for me.

5 Prepare the table,
watch in the watchtower,
eat and drink.
Arise, you princes,
and oil the shields.

6 For thus the Lord has said to me:

"Go, station a watchman;
let him declare what he sees.
7 When he sees chariots
with horsemen in pairs,
a chariot of donkeys,
and a chariot of camels,
then let him pay close attention,
very close attention."

8 Then the watchman called:

"O Lord, I stand continually on the
watchtower in the daytime,
and I am stationed at my guard post
every night.
9 Look, here comes a chariot of men,
horsemen in pairs."
And he answered and said,
"Fallen, fallen is Babylon.
And all the graven images of her gods
lie shattered on the ground."
10 O my threshed people and my afflicted of
the threshing floor!
What I have heard from the LORD of
Hosts,
the God of Israel,
I have declared to you.

A Prophecy Against Edom

11 The oracle of Dumah.

He calls to me out of Seir,
"Watchman, how far gone is the night?
Watchman, how far gone is the night?"
12 The watchman says,
"The morning comes and also the night.
If you would inquire, inquire;
return again."

A Prophecy Against Arabia

13 The oracle about Arabia.

In the forest of Arabia you shall lodge,
O traveling companies of Dedanites.
14 Bring water for the thirsty,
O inhabitants of the land of Tema;
meet the fugitive with bread.

21:6 2Ki 9:17–20
21:7 Isa 21:9
21:9 Jer 51:8
21:10 Jer 51:33
21:11 Ge 25:14
21:13 Jer 25:23–24
21:14 Ge 25:15
....
21:16 Ps 120:5
22:1 Jer 21:13
22:2 Isa 32:13
22:4 Jer 9:1
22:5 Isa 10:6
22:6 2Ki 16:9
22:8 1Ki 7:2
22:9 2Ki 20:20

15 For they fled from the swords,
from the drawn sword,
and from the bent bow,
and from the grievousness of war.

16 For thus the Lord has said to me: Within a
year, according to the years of a hireling, all the
glory of Kedar shall fail. 17 And the remainder
of the number of archers, the mighty men of
the children of Kedar, shall be diminished, for
the LORD God of Israel has spoken it.

An Oracle Concerning Jerusalem

22 The oracle of the Valley of Vision.

What ails you now,
that you all have gone up to the
housetops,
2 you who were full of noise,
a tumultuous city, a joyous city?
Your slain are not slain with the sword,
nor did they die in battle.
3 All your rulers have fled together;
they are captured by the archers.
All of you who were found were taken
captive together,
although they had fled from afar.
4 Therefore, I say, "Look away from me,
I will weep bitterly;
do not try to comfort me
because of the destruction of the
daughter of my people."

5 For it is a day of trouble and of treading
down and of perplexity
by the Lord GOD of Hosts
in the Valley of Vision,
a breaking down of the walls
and a crying to the mountains.
6 Elam took up the quiver
with chariots of men and horsemen,
and Kir uncovered the shield.
7 Your choicest valleys shall be full of
chariots,
and the horsemen shall set themselves
in array at the gate.

8 And He shall remove the protection of
Judah.
You shall depend in that day
on the weapons of the house of the
forest;
9 you have seen also that the breaches
of the City of David are many;
and you gathered together the waters
of the lower pool.
10 You have numbered the houses of
Jerusalem,
and the houses you have broken down
to fortify the wall.

11 You also made a reservoir between the two
walls
for the water of the old pool.
But you have not looked to its Maker,
nor did you respect Him who fashioned
it long ago.
12 In that day the Lord God of Hosts
called you to weeping and mourning,
and to tear your hair and wear sackcloth.
13 Yet, there is joy and gladness,
slaying of oxen and killing of sheep,
eating of meat and drinking wine:
"Let us eat and drink,
for tomorrow we may die."

14 It was revealed in my hearing by the Lord
of Hosts: Surely this iniquity shall not be for-
given you until you die, says the Lord God of
Hosts.

15 Thus says the Lord God of Hosts:

Come, go to this treasurer,
even to Shebna, who is over the royal
household, and say:
16 What right do you have here? And whom
do you have here
that you have dug out for yourself a
tomb here,
as he who hews out for himself a tomb on
high,
and who cuts a habitation for himself in
a rock?

17 Indeed, the Lord is about to hurl you
headlong, O man;
He is about to seize you firmly.
18 He will surely violently turn
and toss you like a ball into a large
country;
there you shall die,
and there the chariots of your glory shall
be
the shame of your lord's house.
19 I will drive you from your office
and pull you down from your station.

20 In that day I will call My servant Eliakim
the son of Hilkiah. 21 And I will clothe him with
your robe and tie him securely with your sash.
And I will entrust him with your authority, and
he shall be a father to the inhabitants of Jeru-
salem and to the house of Judah. 22 The key of
the house of David I will lay on his shoulder.
Then he shall open, and no one shall shut.
And he shall shut, and no one shall open. 23 I
will fasten him as a nail in a firm place, and he
shall become a glorious throne to his father's
house. 24 They shall hang on him all the glo-
ry of his father's house, the offspring and the

[1] 3 Nile River.

22:11 2Ki 25:4
22:12 Joel 2:17
22:13 Isa 56:12
22:14 1Sa 3:14
22:15 2Ki 18:18
22:16 Mt 27:60
22:18 Isa 17:13
22:20 2Ki 18:18
22:21 Ge 45:8
22:22 Job 12:14
22:23 1Sa 2:8
22:25 Isa 46:11
23:1 Joel 3:4–8
23:2 Isa 47:5
23:6 Isa 23:12
23:7 Isa 22:2
23:9 Isa 13:11
23:11 Zec 9:3–4
23:12 Rev 18:22

issue, all vessels of small quantity, from the
bowls to all the jars.

25 In that day, says the Lord of Hosts, the nail
that is fastened in the firm place shall be re-
moved, and be cut down and fall. And the load
that was on it shall be cut off, for the Lord has
spoken it.

An Oracle Concerning Tyre

23 The oracle of Tyre.

Wail, O ships of Tarshish,
for Tyre is laid waste
so that there is no house or harbor;
from the land of Cyprus
it is reported to them.

2 Be still, you inhabitants of the coastland,
you merchants of Sidon;
your messengers passed over the sea,
3 and were on many waters;
the grain of the Nile,
the harvest of the River[1] was her revenue;
and she was the market of nations.

4 Be ashamed, O Sidon; for the sea has
spoken,
even the stronghold of the sea, saying,
"I have not travailed nor brought forth
children;
neither have I brought up young men
nor raised virgins."
5 When the report *reaches* Egypt,
they shall be sorely pained at the report
of Tyre.

6 Pass over to Tarshish;
wail, O inhabitants of the coastland.
7 Is this your joyous city,
whose origin is from ancient days,
whose feet used to carry her
to sojourn in distant locations?
8 Who has planned this against Tyre,
the crowning city,
whose merchants are princes,
whose traffickers are the honorable of
the earth?
9 The Lord of Hosts has purposed it,
to stain the pride of all glory
and to bring into contempt all the
honorable of the earth.

10 Pass through your land as the Nile,
O daughter of Tarshish;
there is no more restraint.
11 He stretched out His hand over the sea,
He shook the kingdoms;
the Lord has given a command against the
merchant city,
to destroy its strongholds.
12 He said: You shall rejoice no more,
O oppressed virgin daughter of Sidon.

Arise, pass over to Cyprus;
there also you shall have no rest.
13 Look at the land of the Chaldeans;
this was a people who was not;
Assyria founded it
for those who dwell in the wilderness.
They set up their siege towers,
they stripped its palaces,
and brought it to ruin.

14 Wail, O ships of Tarshish,
for your stronghold is laid waste.

15 In that day Tyre shall be forgotten for seventy years, according to the days of one king. After the end of seventy years Tyre shall sing as a harlot:

16 Take your harp, go about the city,
O forgotten harlot;
make sweet melody, sing many songs,
that you may be remembered.

17 At the end of seventy years, the LORD will
punish Tyre. Then she shall turn to her harlot's
wages and shall commit fornication with all
the kingdoms on the face of the earth. 18 Her
merchandise and her harlot's wages shall be
set apart to the LORD. It shall not be treasured
nor stored up, for her merchandise shall be
for those who dwell before the LORD, to eat
sufficiently, and for choice clothing.

Judgment on the Earth

24 Now the LORD makes the earth
empty,
and makes it waste,
and turns it upside down,
and scatters its inhabitants abroad.
2 It shall be:
as with the people, so with the priest;
as with the servant, so with his master;
as with the maid, so with her mistress;
as with the buyer, so with the seller;
as with the lender, so with the borrower;
as with the creditor, so with the debtor.
3 The land shall be utterly emptied,
and utterly despoiled,
for the LORD has spoken this word.
4 The earth mourns and fades away,
the world languishes and fades away,
the haughty people of the earth
languish.
5 The earth also is defiled by its inhabitants
because they have transgressed the
laws,
violated the ordinances,
broken the everlasting covenant.
6 Therefore, the curse devours the earth,
and those who dwell in it are held guilty.

23:14 Isa 23:1
23:15 Jer 25:22
23:17 Na 3:4
23:18 Ps 72:10
24:2 Hos 4:9
24:6 Zec 5:3–4
....
24:7 Isa 16:10
24:8 Hos 2:11
24:14 Isa 54:1
24:15 Mal 1:11
24:16 Isa 21:2
24:17 Jer 48:43–44
24:18 Ge 7:11
24:20 Isa 19:14
24:21 Ps 76:12

Therefore, the inhabitants of the earth are
burned,
and few men are left.
7 The new wine fails, the vine languishes,
all the merry-hearted sigh.
8 The joy of tambourines ceases,
the noise of those who rejoice ends,
the joy of the harp ceases.
9 They shall not drink wine with song;
strong drink shall be bitter to those who
drink it.
10 The city of confusion is broken down;
every house is shut up so that no one
may come in.
11 There is an outcry for wine in the streets,
all joy is turned to gloom,
the joyfulness of the earth is gone.
12 Desolation is left in the city,
and the gate is battered to destruction.
13 For thus it shall be in the midst of the earth
among the peoples,
as the shaking of an olive tree,
and as the gleaning of grapes when the
vintage is done.

14 They lift up their voices; they sing for the
majesty of the LORD;
they cry aloud from the west.
15 Therefore glorify the LORD in the east,
even the name of the LORD God of Israel
in the coastlands of the sea.
16 From the uttermost part of the earth we
hear songs,
that is, "Glory to the Righteous One."

But I say, Woe to me! Woe to me!
Alas for me!
The treacherous deal treacherously;
indeed, the treacherous deal very
treacherously.
17 Terror and the pit and the snare are upon
you,
O inhabitant of the earth.
18 He who flees from the report of disaster
shall fall into the pit,
and he who comes up out of the midst of
the pit
shall be taken in the snare.
For the windows from on high are open,
and the foundations of the earth shake.
19 The earth is utterly broken down,
the earth is split through,
the earth is shaken violently.
20 The earth reels to and fro like a drunkard,
and it totters like a shack,
and its transgression is heavy upon it,
and it shall fall, never to rise again.

21 In that day the LORD shall punish
the host of heaven on high
and the kings of the earth on the earth.

22 They shall be gathered together,
as prisoners are gathered in the dungeon,
and shall be shut up in the prison,
and after many days they shall be punished.
23 Then the moon shall be humiliated and the sun ashamed,
when the LORD of Hosts reigns
in Mount Zion and in Jerusalem,
and His glory shall be before His elders.

Praise to the LORD

25 O LORD, You are my God.
I will exalt You, I will praise Your name,
for You have done wonderful things;
Your plans formed of old
are faithfulness and truth.
2 For You have made a city into a heap,
a fortified city into a ruin;
a palace of strangers is a city no longer;
it shall never be built.
3 Therefore a strong people shall glorify You;
cities of ruthless nations shall fear You.
4 For You have been a defense to the poor,
a defense to the needy in his distress,
a refuge from the storm,
a shadow from the heat;
for the breath of the ruthless ones
is as a storm against the wall.
5 You bring down the noise of strangers,
as heat in drought;
as the heat by the shadow of a cloud,
the song of the ruthless ones shall be brought low.
6 In this mountain the LORD of Hosts shall prepare
for all people a lavish feast,
a feast of aged wines,
choice pieces full of marrow, and refined, aged wines.
7 He will destroy in this mountain
the covering which is over all peoples,
even the veil that is spread over all nations.
8 He will swallow up death for all time,
and the Lord GOD will wipe away tears
from all faces;
and the reproach of His people He shall take away
from all the earth,
for the LORD has spoken it.

9 It shall be said in that day:

Look, this is our God
for whom we have waited that He might save us.
This is the LORD for whom we have waited;
we will be glad and rejoice in His salvation.
10 For in this mountain the hand of the LORD shall rest,
and Moab shall be trodden down in his place
as straw is trodden down in the water for the manure pile.
11 He shall spread out his hands in the midst of it,
as a swimmer spreads out *his hands* to swim,
yet *the LORD* shall bring down his pride
together with the trickery of his hands.
12 The unassailable fortresses of your walls
He shall bring down, lay low,
and bring to the ground,
even to the dust.

A Song of Victory

26 In that day this song shall be sung in the land of Judah:

We have a strong city;
He appoints walls
and bulwarks for security.
2 Open the gates,
that the righteous nation may enter,
the one who remains faithful.
3 You will keep him in perfect peace,
whose mind is stayed on You,
because he trusts in You.
4 Trust in the LORD forever,
for in GOD the LORD we have an everlasting rock.
5 For He brings down those who dwell on high,
the lofty city; He lays it low; He lays it low,
even to the ground;
He brings it even to the dust.
6 The foot shall tread it down,
even the feet of the poor
and the steps of the needy.
7 The way of the righteous is smooth;
O Upright One, make the path of the righteous level.
8 In the way of Your judgments, O LORD,
we have waited for You eagerly;
the desire of our souls is Your name,
even Your memory.
9 With my soul I have desired You in the night;
my spirit within me seeks You diligently;
for when Your judgments are in the earth,
the inhabitants of the world learn righteousness.
10 Though favor is shown to the wicked,
yet he will not learn righteousness;

24:22 Zec 9:11
24:23 Isa 13:10
25:1 Ex 15:2
25:2 Isa 17:1
25:6 Isa 2:2–3
25:7 Eph 4:18
25:8 Rev 21:4
25:9 Ps 20:5
25:11 Isa 5:25
25:12 Isa 26:5
26:1 Isa 60:18
26:4 Isa 12:2
26:5 Job 40:11–13
26:9 Ps 63:1
26:10 Hos 11:7

in the land of uprightness he deals unjustly
and does not perceive the majesty of the
LORD.
11 LORD, Your hand is lifted up,
but they do not see it.
They see Your zeal for the people and are
put to shame;
the fire of Your enemies shall devour
them.

12 LORD, You will ordain peace for us,
for You also have done all our works
for us.
13 O LORD our God, other lords besides You
have had dominion over us,
but through You alone we confess Your
name.
14 The dead shall not live;
the departed spirits shall not rise.
Therefore, You have punished and
destroyed them
and made all remembrance of them to
perish.
15 You have increased the nation, O LORD,
You have increased the nation;
You are glorified;
You have extended all the borders of the
land.

16 LORD, in trouble they have sought You;
they poured out a prayer
when Your chastening was on them.
17 Like a woman with child, who is in pain
and cries out in her pangs
when she draws near the time of her
delivery,
so have we been in Your sight, O LORD.
18 We have been with child, we have been in
pain,
we have, as it were, brought forth wind;
we have not accomplished any deliverance
in the earth,
nor were the inhabitants of the world
born.

19 Your dead shall live,
their corpses shall arise.
Awake and sing,
you who dwell in dust,
for your dew is as the dew of the dawn,
and the earth shall give birth to the
departed spirits.

20 Come, my people, enter your chambers,
and shut your doors behind you;
hide for a little while
until the indignation is over.
21 For the LORD comes out of His place
to punish the inhabitants of the earth for
their iniquity;
the earth also shall disclose her bloodshed
and shall cover her slain no more.

26:13 Isa 2:8
26:14 Isa 8:19
26:15 Isa 9:3
26:16 Hos 5:15
26:17 Isa 13:8
26:18 Ps 17:14
26:19 Isa 25:8
26:20 Ps 30:5
26:21 Job 16:18

....

27:1 Ps 104:26
27:2 Jer 2:21
27:3 Isa 58:11
27:4 Isa 10:17
27:5 Job 22:21
27:6 Isa 37:31
27:7 Isa 37:36–38
27:10 Isa 17:2
27:11 Isa 1:3

The Deliverance of Israel

27 In that day
the LORD with His fierce and great
and strong sword shall punish
Leviathan the fleeing serpent,
even Leviathan the twisted serpent;
and He shall slay the dragon that is in the
sea.
2 In that day:

Sing of it! A vineyard of red wine.
3 I, the LORD, am its keeper;
I water it every moment;
lest anyone damage it,
I protect it night and day.
4 I have no fury.
Should someone give Me briers and thorns
in battle,
then I would step on them,
I would burn them fully.
5 Or let him rely on My strength;
let him make peace with Me;
let him make peace with Me.
6 In the days to come Jacob shall take root;
Israel shall blossom and bud
and shall fill the whole world with fruit.

7 Has He struck them,
as He struck those who struck them?
Or like the slaughter of His slain,
have they been slain?
8 You fought with them by banishing them,
by driving them away.
He has expelled them
on the day of the east wind with His
fierce wind.
9 Through this, therefore, the iniquity of
Jacob shall be forgiven,
and this will be the full price of the
removal of his sin:
when he makes all the stones of the altar
as chalkstones that are pulverized,
when the groves and incense altars
shall not stand.
10 For the fortified city shall be desolate,
a homestead forlorn and forsaken like a
wilderness;
there the calf shall graze,
and there it shall lie down
and eat its branches.
11 When its boughs are withered, they are
broken off;
the women come and make a fire with
them,
for they are not a people of understanding;
therefore, their Maker will not have
mercy on them,

and their Creator will show them no
grace.

12 In that day the LORD shall thresh from the
channel of the River[1] to the stream of Egypt,
and you shall be gathered one by one, O sons
of Israel. 13 And in that day the great trumpet
shall be blown, and those who were ready to
perish in the land of Assyria and the outcasts
in the land of Egypt shall worship the LORD in
the holy mount at Jerusalem.

Woe to the Leaders of Ephraim and Judah

28 Woe to the proud crown of the drunkards of Ephraim,
whose glorious beauty is a fading flower
which is at the head of the fertile valley
of those who are overcome with wine!
2 See, the LORD has a mighty and strong one,
as a tempest of hail and a destroying storm,
as a flood of mighty overflowing waters,
He has cast it down to the earth with His hand.
3 The proud crown of the drunkards of Ephraim
is trodden under foot;
4 and the fading flower of its glorious beauty,
which is at the head of the fertile valley,
shall be like a first-ripe fig before the summer,
which when one sees, while it is yet in his hand,
he eats it up.

5 In that day the LORD of Hosts
shall become a crown of glory
and a diadem of beauty
to the remnant of His people,
6 a spirit of justice
for him who sits in judgment,
and strength
to those who turn away the battle at the gate.

7 But they also have erred through wine
and stagger from strong drink;
the priest and the prophet have erred through strong drink,
they are confused by wine,
they stagger from strong drink;
they err while having visions,
they stumble *when rendering* judgment.
8 For all the tables are full of vomit
and filthiness so that there is no *clean* place.
9 "To whom shall He teach knowledge,
and to whom shall He interpret the message?
Those just weaned from the milk
and drawn from the breasts?
10 For He says,
'Precept upon precept, precept upon precept,
line upon line, line upon line,
here a little, there a little.' "

11 For with stammering lips and foreign tongue
He will speak to this people,
12 He who said to them,
"This is the rest. Give rest to the weary,"
and, "This is repose,"
yet they would not listen.
13 So the word of the LORD will be to them,
"Precept upon precept, precept upon precept,
line upon line, line upon line,
here a little, there a little,"
that they might go and fall backward,
be broken, snared, and taken captive.

14 Therefore, hear the word of the LORD,
O scoffers,
who rule this people who are in Jerusalem,
15 because you have said, "We have made a covenant with death,
and with hell we are in agreement.
The overflowing scourge shall not come to us
when it passes through,
for we have made lies our refuge
and under falsehood we have hid ourselves."

A Cornerstone in Zion

16 Therefore, thus says the Lord GOD:

See, I lay in Zion a stone,
a tested stone,
a precious cornerstone, firmly placed;
he who believes shall not act hastily.
17 I shall make justice the measuring line
and righteousness the plummet;
then the hail shall sweep away the refuge of lies
and the waters shall overflow the hiding place.
18 Your covenant with death shall be annulled,
and your agreement with hell shall not stand;
when the overflowing scourge passes through,
then you shall be trodden down by it.
19 As often as it passes through, it shall seize you;

27:12 Ge 15:18
27:13 Lev 25:9
28:1 Hos 7:5
28:2 Isa 30:30
28:3 Isa 26:6
28:4 Mic 7:1
28:5 Isa 62:3
28:6 1Ki 3:28
28:8 Jer 48:26
28:9 Ps 131:2
....
28:11 1Co 14:21
28:12 Mt 11:28–29
28:13 Mt 21:44
28:14 Isa 1:10
28:15 Isa 8:7–8
28:16 Ps 118:22
28:17 2Ki 21:13
28:18 Isa 7:7

[1] *12* Euphrates River.

for morning by morning it shall pass
through,
anytime by day or night.

It shall be terror only
to understand the report.
20 The bed is too short to stretch out,
and the covering is too small to wrap
oneself in it.
21 For the LORD shall rise up as at Mount
Perazim,
He shall be wrathful as in the Valley of
Gibeon
to do His work, His unusual work,
and bring to pass His task, His
exceptional task.
22 Now therefore, do not continue as mockers,
lest your bonds be made stronger;
for I have heard from the Lord GOD of Hosts
of determined destruction upon the
whole earth.

23 Give ear and hear my voice;
listen and hear my speech.
24 Does the plowman plow all day to sow?
Does he continually turn and break the
clods of his ground?
25 Does he not level its surface
and sow dill and scatter the cumin
and plant wheat in rows,
barley in its place
and the rye within its area?
26 For his God instructs
and teaches him appropriately.

27 For the dill is not threshed with a threshing
instrument,
nor is a cartwheel driven over the cumin;
but the dill is beaten out with a staff,
and the cumin with a rod.
28 *Grain for* bread is crushed;
so he does not continue to thresh it
forever,
nor break it with the wheel of his cart,
nor crush it with his horsemen.
29 This also comes from the LORD of Hosts,
who is wonderful in counsel and
excellent in wisdom.

Woe to the City of David

29 Woe to Ariel, to Ariel,
the city where David lived!
Add year to year,
observe your feasts on schedule.
2 Yet I will distress Ariel,
and she shall be *a city of* lamenting and
sorrow,
and she shall be as an Ariel to me.
3 I will encamp against you all around,
and will lay siege against you with a
mound,
and I will raise forts against you.
4 You shall be brought down, and shall
speak from the ground,
and from the dust where you are
prostrate your speech shall come;
your voice shall also be as that of a ghost
from the ground;
and your speech shall whisper from the
dust.

5 Moreover the multitude of your enemies
shall become like fine dust,
and the multitude of the ruthless ones as
chaff which blows away;
and it shall happen in an instant, suddenly.
6 You shall be punished from the LORD of
Hosts
with thunder and earthquake and loud
noise,
with storm and tempest, and the flame
of a devouring fire.
7 The multitude of all the nations who fight
against Ariel,
even all who fight against her and her
stronghold, and who distress her,
shall be as a dream
of a night vision.
8 It shall even be as when a hungry man
dreams, and he eats;
but when he awakens, his hunger is not
satisfied;
or as when a thirsty man dreams, and he is
drinking;
but when he awakens, he is faint, and
his thirst is not quenched;
so shall the multitude of all the nations be
who fight against Mount Zion.

9 Be delayed and wait,
blind yourselves and be blind.
They are drunk, but not with wine.
They stagger, but not with strong drink.
10 For the LORD has poured out on you the
spirit of deep sleep
and has closed your eyes, the prophets;
and He has covered your heads, the
seers.

11 The whole vision will be to you as the
words of a book that is sealed, which when
they deliver it to one who is learned, saying,
"Read this, please," he shall say, "I cannot, for
it is sealed." 12 Then the book shall be delivered
to him who is not learned, saying, "Read this,
please." And he shall say, "I cannot read."

13 Therefore, the Lord said:
Because this people draw near with their
mouths
and honor Me with their lips,
but have removed their hearts far
from Me,

28:21 Jos 10:10
28:22 Isa 10:22–23
28:27 Am 1:3
28:29 Isa 9:6
29:1 2Sa 5:9
29:3 Lk 19:43–44

....

29:4 Isa 8:19
29:5 1Th 5:3
29:6 Mt 24:7
29:7 Job 20:8
29:9 Isa 51:21–22
29:10 Ro 11:8
29:11 Isa 8:16
29:13 Col 2:22

and their fear toward Me
is tradition by the precept of men,
14 therefore I will once again do a marvelous work among this people,
even a marvelous work and a wonder;
for the wisdom of their wise men shall perish,
and the understanding of their prudent men shall be hidden.

15 Woe to those who deeply
hide their counsel from the LORD
and whose works are done in the dark, and they say,
"Who sees us?" and "Who knows us?"
16 Surely you turn things upside down!
Shall the potter be esteemed as the potter's clay?
Shall what is made say to its maker,
"He did not make me"?
Or shall the thing formed say to him who formed it,
"He has no understanding"?

17 Is it not yet a very little while before
Lebanon shall be turned into a fruitful field,
and the fruitful field shall be counted as a forest?
18 And on that day the deaf shall hear the words of a book,
and the eyes of the blind shall see
out of obscurity and darkness.
19 The meek also shall increase their joy in the LORD,
and the poor among men shall rejoice in the Holy One of Israel.
20 For the ruthless shall come to nothing,
and the scorner will be consumed,
and all who are intent on doing iniquity shall be cut off—
21 those who cause a man to be indicted by a word,
and lay a snare for him who reproves in the gate,
and turn aside the righteous with meaningless arguments.

22 Therefore thus says the LORD, who re-
deemed Abraham, concerning the house of
Jacob:

Jacob shall not now be ashamed,
nor shall his face now turn pale;
23 but when he sees his children,
the work of My hands, in his midst,
they shall sanctify My name
and sanctify the Holy One of Jacob,
and fear the God of Israel.
24 Those also who err in spirit shall know the truth,
and those who murmured shall accept instruction.

29:14 Hab 1:5
29:15 Isa 30:1
29:17 Isa 32:15
29:18 Isa 35:5
29:19 Jas 2:5
29:20 Mic 2:1
29:21 Am 5:10–12
29:22 Isa 51:2
29:23 Isa 8:13
29:24 Isa 28:7

....

30:1 Isa 1:2
30:3 Isa 20:5
30:4 Isa 19:11
30:5 Jer 2:36
30:6 Dt 8:15
30:8 Isa 8:1
30:9 Isa 30:1
30:10 Am 7:13
30:12 Isa 5:24

The Warning of Judah

30 Woe to the rebellious children,
says the LORD,
who take counsel, but not from Me,
and make an alliance, but not of My Spirit,
in order to add sin to sin;
2 they walk down to Egypt
and have not asked from My mouth,
to strengthen themselves in the safety of Pharaoh
and to trust in the shadow of Egypt!
3 Therefore the safety of Pharaoh shall be your shame
and the trust in the shadow of Egypt your humiliation.
4 For their princes were at Zoan,
and their ambassadors came to Hanes.
5 They all will be ashamed
of a people who cannot profit them,
who are not a help or profit,
but a shame and also a reproach.

6 The burden of the beasts of the Negev.

Through a land of trouble and anguish,
from which comes the lioness and lion,
the viper and fiery flying serpent,
they will carry their riches on the shoulders of young donkeys,
and their treasures on the humps of camels,
to a people who shall not profit them.
7 For the Egyptians shall help in vain and to no purpose.
Therefore, I have called her,
"Rahab who has been exterminated."

8 Now go, write it before them on a tablet,
and note it in a book,
that it may serve in the time to come
as a witness forever;
9 for this is a rebellious people, lying children,
children who refuse to listen to the law of the LORD;
10 they say to the seers,
"You must not see *visions*,"
and to the prophets,
"You must not prophesy to us right things;
speak to us pleasant things,
prophesy illusions.
11 Get out of the way,
turn aside from the path,
let us hear no more
about the Holy One of Israel."

12 Therefore, thus says the Holy One of Israel:

Because you despise this word
and trust in oppression and perverseness,
and rely on them,

13 therefore this iniquity shall be to you
as a breach ready to fall, swelling up in a high wall,
whose collapse comes suddenly, in an instant.
14 He shall break it as the breaking of the potter's vessel
that is broken in pieces;
He shall not spare so that there shall not be found in the breaking of it a shard
to take fire from the hearth
or with which to take water out of a cistern.

> Laying hold of my destiny will happen when I am closeted with God, waiting, pondering, soaking up His presence (Isa 30:15).

15 For thus says the Lord God, the Holy One
of Israel:

In returning and rest you shall be saved;
in quietness and in confidence shall be your strength.
Yet you were not willing,
16 and you said, "No, for we will flee on horses";
therefore you shall flee.
"And we will ride on swift horses";
therefore those who pursue you shall be swift.
17 One thousand *shall flee*
at the threat of one man;
at the threat of five
you shall flee
until you are left
as a flag on the top of a mountain
and as a banner on a hill.

God's Promise to Zion

18 Therefore, the Lord longs to be gracious to you,
and therefore, He waits on high to have mercy on you;
for the Lord is a God of justice;
how blessed are all who long for Him.

19 O people in Zion, inhabitants in Jerusalem,
you shall weep no more. He will be very gra-
cious to you at the sound of your cry. When
He hears it, He will answer you. 20 Though the
Lord has given you the bread of adversity and
the water of affliction, yet He, your Teacher,
will no longer hide Himself, but your eyes shall
see your Teacher. 21 Your ears shall hear a word
behind you, saying, "This is the way, walk in
it," whenever you turn to the right hand and
when you turn to the left. 22 You shall defile also

30:13 1Ki 20:30
30:14 Ps 2:9
30:15 Isa 32:17
30:16 Isa 31:1
30:17 Lev 26:8
30:18 Isa 25:9
30:19 Ps 50:15
30:20 1Ki 22:27
30:22 Jdg 17:3–4
....
30:23 Isa 32:20
30:24 Ge 45:6
30:26 Isa 60:19–20
30:28 Isa 8:8
30:29 Ps 42:4
30:30 Ps 18:13–14
30:32 Isa 11:15
30:33 2Ki 23:10

your graven images overlaid with silver, and
your molded images ornamented with gold.
You shall scatter them as an impure thing, and
say to them, "Be gone!"

23 Then He shall give you rain for the seed
which you shall sow in the ground and bread
of the increase of the earth. And it shall be rich
and plentiful. On that day your cattle shall feed
in large pastures. 24 The oxen likewise and the
young donkeys that work the ground shall eat
cured fodder, which has been winnowed with
the shovel and fork. 25 There shall be on every
high mountain and on every high hill rivers
and streams of waters in the day of the great
slaughter, when the towers fall. 26 Moreover the
light of the moon shall be as the light of the
sun, and the light of the sun shall be sevenfold,
as the light of seven days, in the day that the
Lord binds up the breach of His people and
heals the wound from His blow.

Judgment on Assyria

27 See, the name of the Lord comes from afar,
burning with His anger, and its burden is heavy;
His lips are full of indignation,
and His tongue as a devouring fire.
28 And His breath is as an overflowing stream
which reaches to the middle of the neck,
to sift the nations with the sieve of vanity;
and there shall be a bridle in the jaws of the people,
causing them to err.
29 You shall have songs,
as in the night when a festival is kept,
and gladness of heart,
as when one goes with a flute
to come into the mountain of the Lord,
to the Mighty One of Israel.
30 The Lord shall cause His glorious voice to be heard,
and shall show the descending of His arm
with the indignation of His anger, and with the flame of a devouring fire,
with scattering, and cloudburst, and hailstones.
31 For through the voice of the Lord the Assyrian shall be beaten down
when He strikes with a rod.
32 And every blow of the rod of punishment
which the Lord shall lay on him
shall be with tambourines and harps;
and in battles, brandishing weapons, He will fight them.
33 For Topheth has been long prepared,
indeed, for the king it has been prepared.

He has made it deep and large,
a pile of fire with much wood;
the breath of the LORD,
like a stream of brimstone,
kindles it.

Woe to Those Who Trust Egypt

31 Woe to those who go down to Egypt for help,
and rely on horses,
and trust in chariots because they are many,
and in horsemen because they are very strong,
but they do not look to the Holy One of Israel
nor seek the LORD!
2 Yet He also is wise and will bring disaster
and will not call back His words,
but will arise against the house of the evildoers
and against the help of those who work iniquity.
3 Now the Egyptians are men and not God;
and their horses flesh and not spirit.
When the LORD shall stretch out His hand,
both he who helps shall fall
and he who is helped shall fall down,
and they all shall fail together.

4 For thus the LORD has spoken to me:

Like the lion, and the young lion,
roars over his prey,
against which a multitude of shepherds
is called out against him,
he will not be afraid of their voice,
nor disturbed at their noise,
so shall the LORD of Hosts come down
to fight for Mount Zion, and for its hill.
5 Like flying birds,
so the LORD of Hosts will defend Jerusalem.
He will defend and deliver it;
He will pass over and preserve it.

6 Turn to Him whom you have deeply be-
trayed, O sons of Israel. 7 For in that day every
man shall cast away his idols of silver and
his idols of gold which your own hands have
made for you as a sin.

8 "Then the Assyrian shall fall by the sword
that is not of man,
and the sword not of man shall devour him.
So he shall not escape the sword,
and his young men shall become forced laborers.

31:1 Ps 20:7
31:2 Nu 23:19
31:3 Isa 9:17
31:4 Am 3:8
31:5 Ps 91:4
31:7 Isa 2:20
31:8 Isa 14:25

....

32:2 Isa 25:4
32:3 Isa 29:18
32:4 Isa 29:24
32:5 Isa 5:20
32:7 Jer 5:26–28
32:9 Isa 28:23
32:10 Isa 7:23
32:13 Isa 22:2

9 He shall cross over to his stronghold for fear,
and his princes shall be afraid of the banner,"
says the LORD,
whose fire is in Zion,
and whose furnace is in Jerusalem.

The Kingdom of Righteousness

32 See, a king shall reign in righteousness,
and princes shall rule justly.
2 A man shall be as a hiding place from the wind,
and a shelter from the tempest,
as rivers of water in a dry place,
as the shadow of a great rock in a weary land.

3 The eyes of those who see shall not be blinded,
and the ears of those who hear shall listen.
4 The heart also of the hasty shall understand knowledge,
and the tongue of the stammerers shall be ready to speak plainly.
5 The vile person shall no more be called noble,
nor the rogue be spoken of as generous;
6 for the vile person will speak nonsense,
and his heart will work iniquity:
to practice hypocrisy
and to utter error against the LORD,
to keep the hungry unsatisfied
and to withhold drink from the thirsty.
7 The instruments also of the rogue are evil;
he devises wicked schemes
to destroy the poor with lying words,
even when the needy speaks right.
8 But the noble devises noble things,
and by noble things he stands.

The Women of Jerusalem

9 Rise up, you women who are at ease,
hear my voice;
you careless daughters,
give ear to my speech.
10 Within a year and a few days
you shall be troubled, you careless daughters;
for the vintage is ended
and the fruit gathering shall not come.
11 Tremble, you *women* who are at ease;
be troubled, you careless *daughters*;
strip, undress,
and put *sackcloth* on your waist.
12 Beat your breasts for the pleasant fields,
for the fruitful vine,
13 for the land of my people

in which thorns and briers shall come up,
yes, for all the joyful houses
and for the jubilant city;
14 because the palaces have been forsaken,
the populated city is forsaken.
The forts and towers shall be caves forever,
a joy of wild donkeys, a pasture of flocks,
15 until the Spirit is poured on us from on high,
and the wilderness is a fruitful field,
and the fruitful field is counted as a forest.

The Peace of God's Reign

16 Then justice shall dwell in the wilderness,
and righteousness will abide in the fruitful field.
17 The work of righteousness shall be peace,
and the effect of righteousness,
quietness and assurance forever.
18 My people shall dwell in a peaceable habitation
and in secure dwellings
and in quiet resting places;
19 and it shall hail when the forest comes down,
and the city shall be utterly laid low.
20 How blessed are you
who sow beside all waters,
who send out freely the ox and the donkey.

A Prophecy of Deliverance

33 Woe to you, O destroyer,
though you were not destroyed,
and he who is treacherous,
though others did not deal treacherously with you!
When you cease destroying,
you shall be destroyed;
and when you finish dealing treacherously,
others shall deal treacherously with you.
2 O LORD, be gracious to us;
we have waited for You.
Be our strength every morning,
our salvation also in the time of trouble.
3 At the noise of the tumult, the people flee;
at the lifting up of Yourself, the nations scatter;
4 your spoil is gathered like the caterpillar gathers;
as locusts rush about, men rush about on it.
5 The LORD is exalted, for He dwells on high;
He has filled Zion with justice and righteousness.
6 He shall be the stability of your times,

32:15 Isa 29:17
32:17 Ps 119:165
32:18 Hos 2:18–23
32:19 Isa 28:17
32:20 Ecc 11:1
33:1 Isa 21:2
33:2 Isa 25:9
33:5 Isa 2:17
33:6 Mt 6:33

33:8 Jdg 5:6
33:9 Isa 35:2
33:10 Ps 12:5
33:11 Ps 7:14
33:13 Ps 48:10
33:14 Heb 12:29
33:15 Ps 119:37
33:17 Isa 6:5
33:19 Isa 28:11

a wealth of salvation, wisdom, and knowledge;
the fear of the LORD is His treasure.
7 Listen! Their valiant ones cry in the streets;
the ambassadors of peace weep bitterly.
8 The highways lie waste,
the wayfaring man ceases.
He has broken the covenant,
he has despised the cities,
he has no regard for man.
9 The earth mourns and languishes;
Lebanon is ashamed and hewn down.
Sharon is like a wilderness,
and Bashan and Carmel shake off *their* fruits.

Impending Judgment on Israel

10 "Now I will rise," says the LORD,
"now I will be exalted,
now I will be lifted up.
11 You have conceived chaff,
you shall bring forth stubble;
My breath, as fire, shall devour you.
12 The people shall be burned to lime,
as thorns cut up are burned in the fire."
13 Hear what I have done, you who are far away;
and you who are near, acknowledge My might.
14 The sinners in Zion are afraid;
fearfulness has seized the hypocrites:
"Who among us can live with the continual fire?
Who among us can live with everlasting burning?"
15 He who walks righteously
and speaks uprightly,
he who rejects unjust gain
and shakes his hands from holding bribes,
who stops his ears from hearing of bloodshed,
and shuts his eyes from seeing evil:
16 He shall dwell on high;
his place of defense shall be the impregnable rock;
his bread shall be given him,
his waters shall be sure.

The Land of the Majestic King

17 Your eyes shall see the King in His beauty;
they shall see the land that is very far away.
18 Your heart shall meditate on terror:
"Where is he who counts?
Where is he who weighs?
Where is he who counts the towers?"
19 You shall not see a fierce people any more,
a people of unintelligible speech which no one comprehends,

of a stammering tongue which no one
understands.

[20]Look upon Zion, the city of our appointed
feasts;
your eyes shall see Jerusalem,
a quiet habitation, a tabernacle that shall
not be taken down;
not one of its stakes shall ever be removed,
nor shall any of its cords be broken.
[21]But there the glorious LORD will be to us
a place of broad rivers and streams
on which no boat with oars shall go
and on which no gallant ship shall pass,
[22]for the LORD is our judge,
the LORD is our lawgiver,
the LORD is our king;
He will save us.

[23]Your tackle hangs loose;
it cannot hold the base of its mast
securely,
nor spread out the sail.
Then the prey of an abundant spoil shall
be divided;
the lame shall take the prey.
[24]The inhabitant shall not say, "I am sick";
the people who dwell there shall be
forgiven their iniquity.

Judgment on the Nations

34 Come near, O nations, to hear;
and listen, O peoples!
Let the earth hear, and all that is in it,
the world, and all that comes from it.
[2] For the indignation of the LORD is upon all
nations
and His fury upon all their armies;
He has utterly destroyed them,
He has delivered them to the slaughter.
[3] Their slain also shall be cast out,
and their corpses shall emit their stench,
and the mountains shall be drenched
with their blood.
[4] All the host of heaven shall be dissolved,
and the heavens shall be rolled together
as a book;
and all their host shall fall down
as the leaf falls from the vine,
and as a falling fig from the fig tree.

[5] For My sword is filled in heaven;
see, it shall come down for judgment on
Edom,
and on the people whom I have devoted
to destruction.
[6] The sword of the LORD is filled with blood,
it is made full with fatness,
and with the blood of lambs and goats,
with the fat of the kidneys of rams.
For the LORD has a sacrifice in Bozrah,
and a great slaughter in the land of
Edom.
[7] The wild oxen shall also fall with them,
and the young bulls with the mighty
bulls;
so their land shall be soaked with blood,
and their dust become greasy with fat.

[8] For it is the day of the vengeance of the
LORD,
and the year of recompense for the
cause of Zion.
[9] Its streams shall be turned into pitch,
and its dust into brimstone,
and its land shall become burning pitch.
[10]It shall not be quenched night or day;
its smoke shall go up forever.
From generation to generation it shall lie
waste;
no one shall pass through it forever and
ever.
[11]But the cormorant and the hedgehog shall
possess it,
the owl also and the raven shall dwell
in it.
And He shall stretch out on it
the line of desolation,
and the plumb line of emptiness.
[12]They shall call its nobles to the kingdom,
but no one shall be there,
and all her princes shall be nothing.
[13]Thorns shall come up in her palaces,
nettles and brambles in the fortresses;
and it shall be a habitation of jackals
and a home for owls.
[14]The wild beasts of the desert shall also
meet with the wolves,
and the wild goat shall cry to its kind;
the screech owl also shall rest there
and find for herself a place of rest.
[15]There shall the tree snake make its nest
and lay eggs,
and it shall hatch and gather them under
its protection;
yes, there shall the vultures also be
gathered,
every one with its kind.
[16]Seek from the book of the LORD, and read.

Not one of these shall be missing,
not one shall lack its mate.
For His mouth has commanded,
and His Spirit has gathered them.
[17]He has cast the lot for them,
and His hand has divided it to them by
line.
They shall possess it forever,
from generation to generation they shall
dwell in it.

33:20 Ps 46:5
33:21 Ps 46:4–5
33:22 Jas 4:12
33:23 2Ki 7:8
33:24 Jer 50:20
34:1 Dt 32:1
34:3 Joel 2:20
34:4 Mt 24:29
34:5 Mal 1:4
34:6 Isa 63:1

34:7 Nu 23:22
34:8 Isa 63:4
34:9 Dt 29:23
34:10 Rev 19:3
34:11 2Ki 21:13
34:13 Jer 9:11
34:14 Isa 13:21–22
34:15 Dt 14:13
34:16 Isa 30:8
34:17 Isa 34:10

The Future Glory of Zion

35 The wilderness and the solitary place
shall be glad,
and the desert shall rejoice and blossom
as the rose;
2 it shall blossom abundantly
and rejoice even with joy and singing.
The glory of Lebanon shall be given to it,
the excellency of Carmel and Sharon.
They shall see the glory of the LORD
and the excellency of our God.

3 Strengthen the weak hands,
and support the feeble knees.
4 Say to those who are of a fearful heart,
"Be strong, fear not.
Your God will come
with vengeance,
even God with a recompense;
He will come and save you."

5 Then the eyes of the blind shall be opened,
and the ears of the deaf shall be
unstopped.
6 Then the lame man shall leap as a deer,
and the tongue of the mute sing for joy.
For in the wilderness waters shall break out
and streams in the desert.
7 The parched ground shall become a pool,
and the thirsty land springs of water;
in the habitation of jackals where each lay,
there shall be grass with reeds and
rushes.

8 A highway shall be there, a roadway,
and it shall be called the Highway of
Holiness.
The unclean shall not pass on it,
but it shall be for the wayfaring men,
and fools shall not wander on it.
9 No lion shall be there,
nor any ravenous beast shall go up on it;
these shall not be found there,
but the redeemed shall walk there,
10 and the ransomed of the LORD shall
return
and come to Zion with songs
and everlasting joy upon their heads.
They shall obtain joy and gladness,
and sorrow and sighing shall flee away.

Sennacherib Invades Judah

2Ki 18:13–37; 2Ch 32:9–19

36 Now it came to pass in the fourteenth
year of King Hezekiah that Sennach-
erib king of Assyria came up against all the
fortified cities of Judah and took them. 2 The
king of Assyria sent the Rabshakeh[1] from La-
chish to Jerusalem to King Hezekiah with a
great army. And he stood by the conduit of the
upper pool in the highway of the fuller's field.

35:1 Isa 51:3
35:2 Isa 60:13
35:3 Heb 12:12
35:4 Isa 34:8
35:5 Isa 29:18
35:6 Lk 11:14
35:8 Isa 52:1
35:9 Isa 62:12
35:10 Rev 21:4
36:1 2Ch 32:1
36:2 Isa 7:3
36:5 2Ki 18:7
36:6 Eze 29:6–7
36:7 2Ki 18:4–5
36:9 Isa 10:8
36:10 1Ki 13:18
36:11 Ezr 4:7
36:13 2Ch 32:18
36:16 1Ki 4:25

3 Then Eliakim came to him, the son of Hilki-
ah, who was over the household, and Shebna
the scribe, and Joah, the son of Asaph, the
recorder.
4 The Rabshakeh said to them:

"Say now to Hezekiah: Thus says the great
king, the king of Assyria: What confidence
is this that you have? 5 I say, Your counsel
and strength for war are only empty words.
Now on whom do you rely that you rebel
against me? 6 You rely on the staff of this
broken reed, on Egypt, on which if a man
leans, it will go into his hand and pierce it.
So is Pharaoh king of Egypt to all who rely
on him. 7 But if you say to me, 'We trust in
the LORD our God,' is it not He whose high
places and whose altars Hezekiah has taken
away, and said to Judah and to Jerusalem,
'You shall worship before this altar'?
8 "Now therefore, come make a bargain
with my master the king of Assyria, and I
will give you two thousand horses, if you
are able on your part to set riders on them.
9 How then will you turn away one captain
of the least of my master's servants and rely
on Egypt for chariots and for horsemen?
10 Have I now come up without the approv-
al of the LORD against this land to destroy
it? The LORD said to me, Go up against this
land, and destroy it."

11 Then Eliakim and Shebna and Joah said to
the Rabshakeh, "Speak now to your servants
in Aramaic, for we understand it. And do not
speak to us in Hebrew in the ears of the people
who are on the wall."
12 But the Rabshakeh said, "Has my mas-
ter sent me only to your master and to you
to speak these words? Has he not sent me to
the men who sit on the wall, that they may
eat their own dung and drink their own urine
with you?"
13 Then the Rabshakeh stood and cried out
with a loud voice in Hebrew, and said, "Hear
the words of the great king, the king of Assyr-
ia. 14 Thus says the king, 'Do not let Hezekiah
deceive you, for he shall not be able to deliver
you; 15 nor let Hezekiah make you trust in the
LORD, saying, The LORD will surely deliver us.
This city shall not be delivered into the hand
of the king of Assyria.'
16 "Do not listen to Hezekiah, for thus says
the king of Assyria: 'Make your peace with me
and come out to me, and eat every one of his
vine and every one of his fig tree, and drink
every one the waters of his own cistern, 17 until
I come and take you away to a land like your

[1] 2 Possibly *Commanding General.*

own land, a land of corn and new wine, a land
of bread and vineyards.
18 “ ‘*Beware* lest Hezekiah persuade you, say-
ing, The LORD will deliver us. Has any one of
the gods of the nations delivered his land out
of the hand of the king of Assyria? 19 Where
are the gods of Hamath and Arpad? Where
are the gods of Sepharvaim? And when have
they delivered Samaria out of my hand? 20 Who
are they among all the gods of these lands
that have delivered their land out of my hand,
that the LORD should deliver Jerusalem out of
my hand?’ ”
21 But they held their peace, and answered
him not a word, for the king’s commandment
was, “Do not answer him.”
22 Then Eliakim the son of Hilkiah, who was
over the household, and Shebna the scribe,
and Joah the son of Asaph, the recorder, came
to Hezekiah with their clothes torn and told
him the words of the Rabshakeh.

Isaiah Foretells Deliverance
2Ki 19:1–13

37 And it came to pass when King Heze-
kiah heard it that he tore his clothes,
and covered himself with sackcloth, and went
into the house of the LORD. 2 He sent Eliakim,
who was over the household, and Shebna the
scribe, and the elders of the priests, covered
with sackcloth, to Isaiah the prophet, the son of
Amoz. 3 They said to him, “Thus says Hezekiah:
This day is a day of trouble, and of rebuke,
and of blasphemy. For children have come to
birth, and there is no strength to bring them
forth. 4 Perhaps the LORD your God will hear
the words of the Rabshakeh, whom the king
of Assyria his master has sent to reproach the
living God, and will reprove the words which
the LORD your God has heard. Therefore, lift up
a prayer for the remnant that is left.”
5 So the servants of King Hezekiah came to
Isaiah. 6 Isaiah said to them, “Thus you shall
say to your master, ‘Thus says the LORD: Do not
be afraid of the words that you have heard,
with which the servants of the king of Assyria
have blasphemed Me. 7 Listen! I will put a spirit
in him so that he shall hear a rumor, and return
to his own land. And I will cause him to fall by
the sword in his own land.’ ”
8 So the Rabshakeh returned and found the
king of Assyria warring against Libnah. For
he had heard that the king had left Lachish.
9 He heard them say concerning Tirhakah
king of Ethiopia, “He has come out to make
war with you.” And when he heard it, he sent
messengers to Hezekiah, saying, 10 “Thus you
shall speak to Hezekiah king of Judah, saying:
Do not let your God in whom you trust deceive
you, saying, ‘Jerusalem shall not be given into

36:18 Isa 36:15
36:19 Jer 49:23
36:20 2Ch 32:19
36:21 Pr 26:4
36:22 Isa 36:3
37:2 Isa 1:1
37:3 Hos 13:13
37:4 Isa 1:9
37:6 Isa 7:4
37:7 Isa 37:9
37:8 Jos 10:29
37:10 Isa 36:15
37:11 Isa 36:18–20
37:12 Ge 11:31
37:16 Ex 25:22
37:17 2Ch 6:40
37:18 2Ki 15:29
37:20 Ps 46:10
37:22 Job 16:4
37:23 Eze 39:7
37:24 Isa 14:8

the hand of the king of Assyria.’ 11 Certainly
you have heard what the kings of Assyria have
done to all lands by utterly destroying them.
So shall you be delivered? 12 Have the gods of
the nations delivered them which my fathers
have destroyed, even Gozan and Harran and
Rezeph and the sons of Eden who were in Tel
Assar? 13 Where is the king of Hamath, and
the king of Arpad, and the kings of the city of
Sepharvaim, Hena, and Ivvah?”

The Prayer of Hezekiah
2Ki 19:14–19

14 And Hezekiah received the letter from the
hand of the messengers and read it. Then
Hezekiah went up to the house of the LORD,
and spread it before the LORD. 15 Hezekiah
prayed to the LORD, saying, 16 “O LORD of Hosts,
God of Israel, who dwells above the cherubim,
You are the God, even You alone, of all the
kingdoms of the earth. You have made heaven
and earth. 17 Incline Your ear, O LORD, and hear.
Open Your eyes, O LORD, and see, and hear all
the words of Sennacherib, which he has sent
to reproach the living God.
18 “Truly, O LORD, the kings of Assyria have
laid waste all the nations and their countries,
19 and have cast their gods into the fire. For
they were not gods, but the work of men’s
hands, wood and stone. Therefore, they have
destroyed them. 20 Now, O LORD our God, save
us from his hand that all the kingdoms of the
earth may know that You alone, LORD, are God.”

The Fall of Sennacherib
2Ki 19:20–37; 2Ch 32:20–21

21 Then Isaiah the son of Amoz sent to Heze-
kiah, saying, “Thus says the LORD God of Is-
rael: Because you have prayed to Me about
Sennacherib king of Assyria, 22 this is the word
which the LORD has spoken against him:

The virgin daughter of Zion
has despised you and mocked you;
the daughter of Jerusalem
has shaken her head at you.
23 Whom have you reproached and
blasphemed?
And against whom have you raised your
voice,
and lifted up your eyes haughtily?
Against the Holy One of Israel!
24 Through your servants
you have reproached the Lord
and have said,
‘With my many chariots
I have come up to the heights of the
mountains,
to the remotest parts of Lebanon;
and I cut down its tall cedars,
and its choice fir trees;

and I will go to its highest peak,
its thickest forest.
25 I have dug wells
and drunk water,
and with the sole of my feet
I have dried up all the rivers of Egypt.'

26 "Have you not heard?
Long ago I have done it,
from ancient times I have formed it.
Now I have brought it to pass,
that you should turn fortified cities
into ruinous heaps.
27 Therefore, their inhabitants were short of strength;
they were dismayed and humiliated;
they were as the grass of the field
and as the green herb,
as the grass on the housetops
is scorched before it is grown up.

28 "But I know your abode,
and your going out and your coming in,
and your rage against Me.
29 Because your rage against Me
and your tumult have come up into My ears,
therefore I will put My hook in your nose,
and My bridle in your lips,
and I will turn you back
on the way by which you came.

30 "This shall be a sign to you:

You shall eat this year what grows of itself,
and the second year what springs from the same,
and in the third year sow and reap
and plant vineyards, and eat their fruit.
31 The surviving remnant of the house of Judah
shall again take root downward and bear fruit upward.
32 For from Jerusalem shall go out a remnant,
and those who escape out of Mount Zion.
The zeal of the LORD of Hosts
shall do this.

33 "Therefore, thus says the LORD concerning
the king of Assyria:

He shall not come into this city,
nor shoot an arrow there,
nor come before it with shields,
nor build a siege ramp against it.
34 By the way that he came, by the same shall he return,
and shall not come into this city,
says the LORD.
35 For I will defend this city to save it
for My own sake and for the sake of My servant David."

36 Then the angel of the LORD went out and
struck one hundred eighty-five thousand in the
camp of the Assyrians. When others woke up
early in the morning, these were all dead bod-
ies. 37 So Sennacherib king of Assyria departed
and returned home and lived in Nineveh.
38 It came to pass as he was worshipping in
the house of Nisrok, his god, that Adrammelek
and Sharezer, his sons, struck him with the
sword, and they escaped into the land of Ar-
arat. And Esarhaddon his son reigned in his
stead.

Hezekiah's Illness

2Ki 20:1–11; 2Ch 32:24–26

38 In those days Hezekiah was mortally
ill. And Isaiah the prophet, the son of
Amoz, came to him and said to him, "Thus says
the LORD: Set your house in order, for you shall
die, and not live."
2 Then Hezekiah turned his face toward the
wall, and prayed to the LORD, 3 and said, "Re-
member now, O LORD, I beseech You, how I
have walked before You in truth and with a
perfect heart, and have done what is good in
Your sight." And Hezekiah wept bitterly.
4 Then the word of the LORD came to Isaiah,
saying: 5 "Go, and say to Hezekiah, Thus says
the LORD, the God of David your father: I have
heard your prayer, I have seen your tears. Sure-
ly I will add to your days fifteen years. 6 I will
deliver you and this city out of the hand of
the king of Assyria, and I will defend this city.
7 "This shall be a sign to you from the LORD,
that the LORD will do this thing that He has
spoken: 8 I will cause the shadow on the sun-
dial, which has gone down with the sun on the
sundial of Ahaz, to go back ten steps." So the
sun's *shadow* returned ten steps on the sundial
by which it had gone down.

9 This is the writing of Hezekiah king of Ju-
dah after his illness and recovery:
10 I said: In the middle of my days,
I shall go to the gates of Sheol;
I am to be deprived of the rest of my years.
11 I said, I shall not see the LORD,
even the LORD, in the land of the living;
I shall see man no more
with the inhabitants of the world.
12 My dwelling is pulled up
and removed from me as a shepherd's tent;
I rolled up my life like a weaver.
He cuts me off from the loom;

37:25 1Ki 20:10
37:26 Ac 2:23
37:27 Ps 129:6
37:29 Isa 30:28
37:31 Isa 27:6
37:32 Isa 9:7
37:34 Isa 37:29
37:35 Isa 31:5
37:36 Isa 10:12
37:37 Jnh 1:2
37:38 Ge 8:4
38:1 2Sa 17:23
38:3 1Ch 29:19
38:5 2Ki 18:2
38:6 Isa 37:35
38:8 Jos 10:12–14
38:10 2Co 1:9
38:11 Ps 27:13

from day even to night You make an end
of me.
13 I composed *my soul* until morning,
like a lion, so He breaks all my bones;
from day even to night You make an end
of me.
14 Like a crane or a swallow, so I twitter;
I mourn as a dove;
my eyes look wistfully upward.
O LORD, I am oppressed; undertake for
me.
15 What shall I say?
For He has spoken to me, and He
Himself has done it.
I shall wander about all my years
in the bitterness of my soul.
16 O Lord, by these things men live,
and in all these things is the life of my
spirit;
O restore me to health
and make me live!
17 Surely *it was* for *my own* peace
that I had great bitterness;
but You have kept my soul
from the pit of corruption,
for You have cast all my sins
behind Your back.
18 For Sheol cannot thank You,
death cannot praise You;
those who go down into the pit
cannot hope for Your faithfulness.
19 It is the living who give thanks to You,
as I do this day;
a father explains to his sons
about Your faithfulness.
20 The LORD shall surely save me;
therefore, we will sing my songs to the
stringed instruments
all the days of our lives
in the house of the LORD.

21 For Isaiah had said, "Let them take a cake
of figs and lay it on the boil, and he shall re-
cover."
22 Hezekiah also had said, "What is the sign
that I shall go up to the house of the LORD?"

Envoys From Babylon

2Ki 20:12–19

39 At that time Marduk-Baladan the son
of Baladan, king of Babylon, sent
letters and a present to Hezekiah, for he had
heard that he had been sick and had recov-
ered. 2 Hezekiah was glad and showed them
the house of his precious things: the silver,
and the gold, and the spices, and the precious
ointment, and his whole armory, and all that
was found in his treasuries. There was noth-
ing in his house, nor in all his dominion, that
Hezekiah did not show them.

38:13 Ps 51:8
38:14 Isa 59:11
38:15 1Ki 21:27
38:16 Dt 8:3
38:17 Ps 30:3
38:18 Ecc 9:10
38:19 Dt 6:7
39:1 2Ki 20:12–19
39:2 2Ch 32:25
39:3 Dt 28:49
39:6 2Ki 24:13
40:1 Isa 51:12
40:2 Isa 61:7
40:3 Mal 3:1
40:5 Isa 1:20
40:6 Job 14:2

3 Then Isaiah the prophet came to King Heze-
kiah and said to him, "What did these men say,
and from where did they come to you?"
And Hezekiah said, "They have come to me
from a far country, from Babylon."
4 Then he said, "What have they seen in your
house?"
And Hezekiah answered, "All that is in my
house they have seen. There is nothing among
my treasures that I have not shown them."
5 Then Isaiah said to Hezekiah, "Hear the
word of the LORD of Hosts. 6 The days are surely
coming when all that is in your house, and that
which your fathers have laid up in store until
this day, shall be carried to Babylon. Nothing
shall be left, says the LORD. 7 And some of your
sons who descend from you, whom you shall
father, shall be taken away. And they shall
become officials in the palace of the king of
Babylon."
8 Then Hezekiah said to Isaiah, "The word of
the LORD which you have spoken is good." For
he said, "For there shall be peace and truth
in my days."

Comfort for God's People

40 Comfort, O comfort, My people,
says your God.
2 Speak kindly to Jerusalem,
and cry to her
that her warfare has ended,
that her iniquity has been pardoned,
that she has received of the hand of the
LORD
double for all her sins.

3 The voice of him who cries out,
"Prepare the way of the LORD
in the wilderness,
make straight in the desert
a highway for our God.
4 Let every valley be lifted up,
and every mountain and hill be made
low,
and let the rough ground become a plain,
and the rough places a plain;
5 then the glory of the LORD shall be
revealed,
and all flesh shall see it together,
for the mouth of the LORD has spoken it."

6 The voice said, "Cry out."
And he said, "What shall I cry out?"
All flesh is grass,
and all its loveliness is as the flower of
the field.
7 The grass withers, the flower fades
because the Spirit of the LORD blows
upon it;
surely the people are grass.

[8] The grass withers, the flower fades,
but the word of our God shall stand forever.

[9] O Zion, bearer of good news,
get yourself up onto a high mountain;
O Jerusalem, bearer of good news,
lift up your voice with strength,
lift it up, do not be afraid;
say to the cities of Judah,
"Here is your God!"
[10] See, the Lord GOD will come with a strong hand,
and His arm shall rule for Him;
see, His reward is with Him,
and His recompense before Him.
[11] He shall feed His flock like a shepherd;
He shall gather the lambs with His arm,
and carry them in His bosom,
and shall gently lead those that are with young.

[12] Who has measured the waters in the hollow of His hand,
and meted out heaven with the span,
and calculated the dust of the earth by the measure,
and weighed the mountains in scales,
and the hills in a balance?
[13] Who has directed the Spirit of the LORD,
or as His counselor has taught Him?
[14] With whom did He take counsel, and who instructed Him,
and taught Him in the path of justice,
and taught Him knowledge,
and showed to Him the way of understanding?
[15] Certainly the nations are as a drop in a bucket,
and are counted as the small dust of the balance;
He takes up the coastlands as a very little thing.
[16] Lebanon is not sufficient to burn,
nor the beasts sufficient as a burnt offering.
[17] All nations before Him are as nothing,
and they are counted by Him as less than nothing
and meaningless.

[18] To whom then will you liken God?
Or what likeness will you compare to Him?
[19] The workman melts a graven image,
and the goldsmith spreads it over with gold,
and casts silver chains.
[20] He who is too impoverished for such an offering
chooses a tree that will not rot;
he seeks for himself a skillful workman
to prepare a graven image that shall not totter.

[21] Have you not known?
Have you not heard?
Has it not been told to you from the beginning?
Have you not understood from the foundations of the earth?
[22] It is He who sits upon the circle of the earth,
and the inhabitants are as grasshoppers,
who stretches out the heavens as a curtain,
and spreads them out as a tent to dwell in.
[23] He brings the princes to nothing;
He makes the judges of the earth meaningless.
[24] Scarcely shall they be planted;
scarcely shall they be sown;
scarcely shall their tree take root in the earth,
when He will also blow on them,
and they will wither,
and the whirlwind will take them away as stubble.

[25] To whom then will you liken Me,
that I should be equal to him? says the Holy One.
[26] Lift up your eyes on high,
and see who has created these things,
who brings out their host by number;
He calls them all by name,
by the greatness of His might and the strength of *His* power;
not one of them is missing.

[27] Why do you say, O Jacob,
and assert, O Israel,
"My way is hidden from the LORD,
and my justice escapes the notice of my God"?
[28] Have you not known?
Have you not heard,
that the everlasting God, the LORD,
the Creator of the ends of the earth,
does not faint, nor is He weary?
His understanding is inscrutable.
[29] He gives power to the faint,
and to those who have no might He increases strength.
[30] Even the youths shall faint and be weary,
and the young men shall utterly fall,
[31] but those who wait upon the LORD
shall renew their strength;
they shall mount up with wings as eagles,
they shall run and not be weary,
and they shall walk and not faint.

40:8 Mt 5:18
40:9 Isa 25:9
40:10 Isa 62:11
40:11 Eze 34:23
40:12 Pr 30:4
40:13 Ro 11:34
40:14 Col 2:3
40:15 Jer 10:10
40:16 Mic 6:6–7
40:17 Ps 62:9
40:18 Isa 46:5

....

40:21 Ac 14:17
40:22 Nu 13:33
40:23 Job 12:21
40:24 Isa 41:16
40:25 Isa 40:18
40:26 Ps 89:11–13
40:28 Ps 147:5
40:29 Isa 41:10
40:30 Isa 9:17
40:31 2Co 4:16

The Lord Helps Israel

41 Keep silent before Me, O islands,
and let the peoples renew their
strength.
Let them come near, then let them speak;
let us come near together to judgment.

2 Who raised up the righteous man from the
east,
called him to His foot,
gave the nations before him,
and made him rule over kings?
He makes them as the dust with his sword,
and as driven stubble with his bow.
3 He pursued them, and passed safely,
by paths his feet have not traveled.
4 Who has performed and done this,
calling the generations from the
beginning?
I, the Lord, am the first,
and with the last. I am He.

5 The coastlands saw it and feared,
the ends of the earth were afraid;
they drew near and came.
6 Every one helped his neighbor,
and every one said to his brother, "Be of
good courage."
7 So the carpenter encouraged the
goldsmith,
and he who smooths *metal* with the
hammer
encourages him who strikes the anvil,
saying, "It is ready for the soldering";
and he fastened it with nails so that it
should not totter.

8 But you, Israel, are My servant,
Jacob whom I have chosen,
the seed of Abraham, My friend.
9 You whom I have taken from the ends of
the earth,
and called from its remotest parts,
and said to you, "You are My servant;
I have chosen you and have not rejected
you."
10 Do not fear, for I am with you;
do not be dismayed, for I am your God.
I will strengthen you, I will help you,
yes, I will uphold you with My righteous
right hand.

11 Certainly all those who were incensed
against you
shall be ashamed and humiliated;
they shall be as nothing,
and those who strive with you shall
perish.
12 You shall seek them
and shall not find them, even those who
contended with you.
Those who war against you
shall be as nothing, as a thing of
nonexistence.
13 For I, the Lord your God,
will hold your right hand,
saying to you, "Do not fear;
I will help you."
14 Do not fear, you worm Jacob,
and you men of Israel.
I will help you, says the Lord
and your Redeemer, the Holy One of
Israel.
15 See, I will make you a new sharp threshing
instrument
with double edges;
you shall thresh the mountains, and beat
them small,
and shall make the hills as chaff.
16 You shall fan them, and the wind shall
carry them away,
and the whirlwind shall scatter them;
and you shall rejoice in the Lord,
and shall glory in the Holy One of Israel.

17 When the poor and needy seek water,
and there is none,
and their tongues fail for thirst,
I, the Lord, will hear them,
I, the God of Israel, will not forsake
them.
18 I will open rivers in high places,
and fountains in the midst of the valleys;
I will make the wilderness a pool of water,
and the dry land springs of water.
19 I will plant in the wilderness
the cedar, the acacia, the myrtle, and the
olive tree;
I will set in the desert
the fir tree, and the pine, and the box
tree together,
20 that they may see, and know,
and consider, and understand together,
that the hand of the Lord has done this,
and the Holy One of Israel has created it.

The Futility of Idols

21 Present your case, says the Lord.
Bring forth your arguments, says the
King of Jacob.
22 Let them bring them forth, and show us
what shall happen;
let them show the former things, what they
were,
that we may consider them
and know their outcome,
or declare to us things to come.
23 Show the things that are to come
hereafter,
that we may know that you are gods;
do good, or do evil,

41:1 Hab 2:20
41:2 Isa 40:24
41:4 Isa 41:26
41:7 Isa 40:19–20
41:8 2Ch 20:7
41:10 Jos 1:9
41:11 Isa 45:24
41:12 Ps 37:35–36
41:13 Isa 45:1
41:14 Ps 22:6
41:15 Mic 4:13
41:16 Jer 51:2
41:17 Isa 30:19
41:18 Ps 107:35
41:19 Isa 55:13
41:20 Job 12:9
41:22 Isa 45:21
41:23 Isa 42:9

that we may be dismayed and see it
together.
24 Indeed you are nothing,
and your work amounts to nothing;
he who chooses you is an abomination.

25 I have raised up one from the north, and he
shall come;
from the rising of the sun he shall call on
My name;
and he shall come on princes as on mortar,
and as the potter treads clay.
26 Who has declared from the beginning, that
we may know?
And from former times, that we may say,
"He is right!"?
There is no one who shows,
no one who declares,
no one who hears your words.
27 Formerly I said to Zion, "Look, here they
are,"
and to Jerusalem, "I will give one who
brings good news."
28 But when I look, there is no man,
even among them, and there is no
counselor
who, when I ask of them, could answer
a word.
29 See, they all are vanity;
their works are nothing;
their molded images are wind and
emptiness.

The Servant of the LORD

42 Here is My servant, whom I uphold,
My chosen one, in whom My soul
delights.
I have put My Spirit upon him;
he shall bring forth justice to the nations.
2 He shall not cry out, nor lift up his voice,
nor cause his voice to be heard in the
street.
3 A bruised reed he shall not break,
and the smoking flax he shall not
quench;
he shall bring forth justice faithfully.
4 He shall not be disheartened nor be
discouraged,
until he has set justice in the earth;
and the coastlands shall wait for his law.

5 Thus says God the LORD,
who created the heavens and stretched
them out,
who spread forth the earth and that
which comes out of it,
who gives breath to the people on it,
and spirit to those who walk in it:
6 I the LORD have called You in righteousness,
and will hold Your hand,
and will keep You and appoint You

41:24 Ps 115:8
41:25 Isa 41:2
41:26 Isa 41:22
41:27 Isa 40:9
41:28 Isa 63:5
41:29 Isa 41:24
42:1 Isa 43:10
42:2 Zec 9:9
42:4 Ge 49:10
42:5 Ac 17:25
42:6 Lk 2:32
42:7 Isa 35:5
42:8 Isa 48:11
42:9 Isa 43:19
42:10 Ps 33:3
42:11 Isa 32:16
42:15 Isa 50:2
42:16 Isa 29:18
42:17 Ps 97:7

for a covenant of the people,
for a light of the nations,
7 to open the blind eyes,
to bring out the prisoners from the
prison,
and those who sit in darkness out of the
prison house.
8 I am the LORD, that is My name;
and My glory I will not give to another,
nor My praise to graven images.
9 See, the former things have come to pass,
and new things I declare;
before they spring forth
I tell you of them.

A Song of Praise

10 Sing to the LORD a new song,
and His praise from the ends of the
earth,
you who go down to the sea, and all that
is in it,
the coastlands, and the inhabitants.
11 Let the wilderness and the cities lift up *their*
voices,
the villages that Kedar inhabits.
Let the inhabitants of Sela sing,
let them shout from the top of the
mountains.
12 Let them give glory to the LORD,
and declare His praise in the islands.
13 The LORD shall go forth like a mighty man;
He shall stir up zeal like a man of war.
He shall cry out, yes, raise a war cry;
He shall prevail against His enemies.

The LORD's Help Is Promised

14 I have for a long time held My peace;
I have been still and refrained Myself.
Now I will cry like a travailing woman;
I will destroy and devour at once.
15 I will lay waste mountains and hills
and dry up all their vegetation,
and I will make the rivers islands,
and I will dry up the pools.

The Lord will lead my children out of darkness and into His light (Isa 42:16).

16 I will bring the blind by a way that they did
not know;
I will lead them in paths that they have
not known.
I will make darkness light before them
and crooked things straight.
These things I will do for them
and not forsake them.
17 They shall be turned back, they shall be
greatly ashamed,

SPIRITLED WOMAN

COUNSEL FROM THE SPIRIT BASICS

Trust Him to Do It His Way

When you pass through waters, I will be with you. And through the rivers, they shall not overflow you. When you walk through the fire, you shall not be burned, nor shall the flame kindle on you.

—Isaiah 43:2

It is a well-known fact that human nature cries out to God when faced with trouble. Men in prison, soldiers in war, people in accidents—all seem to call out to God when they get in a crisis. Even atheists are known to call on the God they don't acknowledge when they are extremely afraid. A lot of criticism has been given to those kinds of "court of last resort" prayers. However, in defense of this kind of prayer, we must remember that when one is in pain, he usually runs to the one he loves the most and the one he trusts. The alternative is not calling out at all, so calling out to God when in trouble is a good place for a person to start!

God answers our prayers and rescues us in so many different ways. I am so thankful He is creative and not hindered by our seemingly impossible situations. But we have to ask in faith and not confine Him to our limited resources. God says, "If you love Me, I will be with you when you find yourself in trouble, and I will rescue you." But we have to trust Him to do it *His* way.

Peggy Joyce Ruth

who trust in graven images,
who say to the molded images, "You are our gods."

Israel's Disobedience

18 Hear, you deaf;
look, you blind, that you may see.
19 Who is blind, but My servant?
Or deaf, as My messenger whom I sent?
Who is blind as he who is at peace *with Me*,
and blind as the servant of the Lord?
20 You have seen many things, but you do not observe them;
your ears are open, but no one hears.
21 The Lord is well pleased
for His righteousness' sake
to magnify the law and make it honorable.
22 But this is a people robbed and despoiled;
they are all snared in holes,
and they are hidden in prison houses;
they are for a prey,
and no one delivers,
for a spoil,
and no one says, "Restore them."

23 Who among you will give ear to this?
Who will listen and hear for the time to come?
24 Who gave up Jacob as spoil,
and Israel to the robbers?
Did not the Lord,
against whom we have sinned?
For they would not walk in His ways,
nor were they obedient to His law.
25 Therefore, He has poured on him the fury of His anger
and the strength of battle;
and it has set him on fire all around, yet he did not recognize it;
and it burned him, yet he laid it not to heart.

The Redeemer of Israel

43 But now, thus says the Lord
who created you, O Jacob,
and He who formed you, O Israel:
Do not fear, for I have redeemed you;
I have called you by your name; you are Mine.
2 When you pass through waters,
I will be with you.
And through the rivers,
they shall not overflow you.
When you walk through the fire,
you shall not be burned,
nor shall the flame kindle on you.
3 For I am the Lord your God,
the Holy One of Israel, your Savior;
I gave Egypt for your ransom,
Ethiopia and Seba in your place.
4 Since you were precious in My sight, you have been honorable,
and I have loved you;
therefore, I will give men for you,
and people for your life.
5 Do not fear, for I am with you;
I will bring your descendants from the east,
and gather you from the west;

42:18 Isa 29:18
42:22 Isa 14:17
42:23 Isa 48:18
42:25 Hos 7:9
43:1 Isa 43:7
43:2 Ps 66:12
43:4 Ex 19:5–6
43:5 Isa 49:12

6 I will say to the north, "Give them up,"
and to the south, "Do not keep them back."
Bring My sons from afar,
and My daughters from the ends of the earth,
7 even everyone who is called by My name,
for I have created him for My glory;
I have formed him, and I have made him."

8 Bring forth the blind people who have eyes,
and the deaf who have ears.
9 Let all the nations be gathered together,
and let the people be assembled.
Who among them can declare this,
and show us former things?
Let them bring their witnesses, that they may be justified;
or let them hear and say, "It is true."
10 You are My witnesses, says the LORD,
and My servant whom I have chosen
that you may know and believe Me,
and understand that I am He.
Before Me there was no God formed,
nor shall there be after Me.
11 I, even I, am the LORD,
and besides Me there is no savior.
12 I have declared, and have saved, and I have shown,
when there was no strange god among you;
therefore, you are My witnesses, says the LORD, that I am God.
13 Indeed, from eternity I am He;
there is no one who can deliver out of My hand;
I act, and who can reverse it?

14 Thus says the LORD,
your Redeemer, the Holy One of Israel:
For your sake I have sent to Babylon,
and have brought down all their nobles,
and the Chaldeans,
into the ships in which they rejoice.
15 I am the LORD, your Holy One,
the Creator of Israel, your King.

16 Thus says the LORD,
who makes a way in the sea
and a path in the mighty waters,
17 who brings forth the chariot and horse,
the army and the mighty men
(they shall lie down together, they shall not rise;
they are extinguished, they are quenched like a wick):
18 Do not remember the former things
nor consider the things of old.

43:7 Ps 100:3
43:8 Isa 6:9
43:10 Isa 41:4
43:11 Hos 13:4
43:13 Ps 90:2
43:14 Isa 23:13
43:15 Isa 43:1
43:16 Ps 77:19
43:17 Isa 1:31
43:18 Isa 65:17

43:19 Ex 17:6
43:20 Isa 48:21
43:21 1Pe 2:9
43:22 Mic 6:3
43:23 Am 5:25
43:24 Isa 1:14
43:25 Isa 37:35
43:26 Isa 1:18
43:27 Jer 5:31
43:28 Jer 24:9
44:1 Isa 41:8
44:2 Dt 32:15
44:3 Joel 2:28

19 See, I will do a new thing,
now it shall spring forth; shall you not be aware of it?
I will even make a way in the wilderness,
and rivers in the desert.
20 The beast of the field shall honor Me,
the jackals and the owls,
because I give waters in the wilderness,
and rivers in the desert,
to give drink to My people, My chosen ones.
21 This people I have formed for Myself;
they shall declare My praise.

Pleading With Israel

22 But you have not called upon Me, O Jacob;
but you have been weary of Me, O Israel.
23 You have not brought Me the sheep for your burnt offerings,
nor have you honored Me with your sacrifices.
I have not burdened you with offerings,
nor wearied you with incense.
24 You have bought Me no sweet cane with money,
nor have you filled Me with the fat of your sacrifices;
but you have made Me burdened with your sins;
you have wearied Me with your iniquities.

25 I, even I, am He who blots out
your transgressions for My own sake,
and will not remember your sins.
26 Put Me in remembrance;
let us plead together;
state your *cause*, that you may be justified.
27 Your first father has sinned,
and your teachers have transgressed against Me.
28 Therefore, I have profaned the princes of the sanctuary,
and have given Jacob to the curse,
and Israel to reproaches.

God's Blessing on Jacob

44 Yet now listen, O Jacob, My servant,
and Israel, whom I have chosen.
2 Thus says the LORD
who made you, and formed you from the womb,
who will help you:
Do not fear, O Jacob, My servant, and you,
Jeshurun, whom I have chosen.
3 For I will pour water on him who is thirsty,
and floods on the dry ground;
I will pour out My Spirit on your descendants,
and My blessing on your offspring;

4 and they shall spring up as among the grass,
as willows by the water courses.
5 One will say, "I am the LORD's";
another will call himself by the name of Jacob;
and another will write on his hand,
"Belonging to the LORD,"
and name himself by the name of Israel.

Idolatry Condemned

6 Thus says the LORD the King of Israel,
and his Redeemer the LORD of Hosts:
I am the first, and I am the last;
besides Me there is no God.
7 Who is like Me? Let him proclaim
and declare it, and recount it in order for Me,
since I appointed the ancient people.
And let them declare to them the things that are coming,
and shall come.
8 Do not fear, nor be afraid;
have I not told you from of old, and declared it?
You are My witnesses!
Is there a God besides Me?
There is no Rock; I know not any.

9 Those who make a graven image are, all of them, vain,
and their delectable things shall not profit;
and they are their own witnesses;
they do not see nor know, that they may be ashamed.
10 Who has formed a god or molded a graven image
that is profitable for nothing?
11 All his companions shall be ashamed;
and the workmen, they are mere men.
Let them all be gathered together; let them stand up,
yet they shall fear; they shall be ashamed together.

12 The smith with the tongs
both works in the coals
and fashions it with hammers,
and works it with the strength of his arms.
He becomes hungry, and his strength fails;
He drinks no water and is faint.
13 The carpenter stretches out his measuring line;
he marks it out with a line;
he fits it with planes,
and he marks it out with the compass,
and makes it after the figure of a man,
according to the beauty of a man,
that it may remain in the house.

44:4 Ps 1:3
44:6 Rev 1:8
44:7 Isa 41:26
44:8 Isa 43:10
44:9 Isa 41:24
44:10 Jer 10:5
44:11 Isa 42:17
44:12 Isa 40:19
44:13 Jdg 17:4–5

....

44:14 Isa 40:20
44:15 2Ch 25:14
44:17 Isa 45:20
44:19 Dt 27:15
44:20 Job 15:31
44:21 Isa 44:1–2
44:22 Isa 43:25
44:23 Ps 69:34

14 He hews down cedars for himself,
and takes the cypress and the oak,
which he raises for himself among the trees of the forest.
He plants a fir, and the rain makes it grow.
15 Then it shall be for a man to burn,
for he will take some of it and warm himself;
he kindles it and bakes bread;
he also makes a god and worships it;
he makes it a graven image and bows down to it.
16 He burns half of it in the fire;
over this half he eats meat;
he roasts it and is satisfied.
Also he warms himself and says,
"Aha, I am warm, I have seen the fire."
17 And the rest he makes into a god, even his carved image.
He falls down to it, and worships it,
and prays to it, and says,
"Deliver me, for you are my god."
18 They have not known nor understood;
for He has shut their eyes so that they cannot see,
and their hearts so that they cannot understand.
19 No one considers in his heart,
nor is there knowledge nor understanding to say,
"I have burned part of it in the fire;
I also have baked bread on the coals;
I have roasted meat and eaten it;
and shall I make the rest into an abomination?
Shall I fall down to a block of wood?"
20 He feeds on ashes; a deceived heart has turned him aside
so that he cannot deliver his soul, nor say,
"Is there not a lie in my right hand?"

Israel Not Forgotten

21 Remember these things, O Jacob,
and Israel, for you are My servant;
I have formed you; you are My servant;
O Israel, you shall not be forgotten by Me.
22 I have blotted out, as a thick cloud,
your transgressions, and your sins, as a cloud.
Return to Me,
for I have redeemed you.
23 Sing, O heavens, for the LORD has done it.
Shout joyfully, you lower parts of the earth;
break forth into singing, you mountains,
O forest, and every tree in it.

For the LORD has redeemed Jacob,
and glorified Himself in Israel.

Jerusalem to Be Inhabited

24 Thus says the LORD,
your Redeemer, and He who formed you from the womb:

I am the LORD
who makes all things,
who stretches out the heavens alone,
who spreads abroad the earth by Myself,
25 who frustrates the omens of the boasters
and makes fools out of diviners,
who turns wise men backward
and makes their knowledge foolish,
26 who confirms the word of His servant
and performs the counsel of His messengers,
who says to Jerusalem, "You shall be inhabited,"
and to the cities of Judah, "You shall be built."
And I will raise up her ruins again;
27 it is I who says to the deep, "Be dried up!"
And I will dry up your rivers;
28 it is I who says of Cyrus, "He is My shepherd,
and shall perform all My desire";
and he declares to Jerusalem, "You shall be built,"
and to the temple, "Your foundation shall be laid."

Cyrus, God's Anointed

45 Thus says the LORD to Cyrus, His anointed,
whose right hand I have held—
to subdue nations before him
and to loosen the loins of kings,
to open doors before him
so that the gates will not be shut:
2 I will go before you
and make the crooked places straight;
I will break in pieces the gates of bronze
and shatter the bars of iron.
3 And I will give you the treasures of darkness
and hidden riches of secret places
so that you may know that I, the LORD,
who calls you by your name, am the God of Israel.
4 For Jacob My servant's sake
and Israel My chosen one,
I have even called you by your name;
I have named you,
though you have not known Me.
5 I am the LORD and there is no other;
there is no God besides Me.
I strengthen you,
though you have not known Me,

44:24 Isa 42:5 **44:25** 2Sa 15:31 **44:26** Zec 1:6 **44:28** 2Ch 36:22–1:3 **45:1** Isa 41:13 **45:2** Ps 107:16 **45:3** Isa 43:1 **45:4** Isa 41:8–9 **45:5** Isa 44:8

45:6 Mal 1:11 **45:7** Am 3:6 **45:8** Hos 10:12 **45:9** Isa 29:16 **45:11** Isa 29:23 **45:12** Isa 42:5 **45:13** Isa 41:2 **45:14** Isa 49:23

6 so that they may know from the rising of the sun
and from the west
that there is no one besides Me.
I am the LORD, and there is no other;
7 I form the light and create darkness;
I make peace and create calamity;
I, the LORD, do all these things.

8 Drip down, O heavens, from above,
and let the clouds pour down righteousness;
let the earth open up,
and let them bring forth salvation,
and let righteousness spring up together.
I, the LORD, have created it.

9 Woe to him who strives with his Maker,
the potsherd with the potsherds of the earth!
Shall the clay say to the potter,
"What are you making?"
Or the thing you are making say,
"He has no hands"?
10 Woe to him who says to his father,
"What are you begetting?"
Or to the woman,
"To what are you giving birth?"

11 Thus says the LORD,
the Holy One of Israel and his Maker:
Ask Me of things to come
concerning My sons,
and you shall commit to Me the work of My hands.
12 I have made the earth
and created man on it.
I, even My hands, have stretched out the heavens,
and I have ordained all their host.
13 I have raised him up in righteousness,
and I will direct all his ways;
he shall build My city,
and he shall let My captives go,
neither for price nor reward,
says the LORD of Hosts.

The Only Savior

14 Thus says the LORD:

The products of Egypt and merchandise of Ethiopia
and of the Sabeans—men of stature—
shall come over to you,
and they shall be yours;
they shall come after you;
in chains they shall come over,
and they shall fall down before you.
They shall make supplication to you, saying,
"Surely God is with you, and there is no other;
there is no other God."

[15]Truly You are a God who hides Yourself,
O God of Israel, the Savior.
[16]They shall be ashamed and also
humiliated, all of them;
the craftsmen of idols shall go away in
confusion together,
[17]but Israel shall be saved by the LORD
with an everlasting salvation;
you shall not be ashamed nor humiliated
to all eternity.

[18]For thus says the LORD,
who created the heavens,
who is God,
who formed the earth and made it,
who has established it,
who did not create it in vain,
who formed it to be inhabited:
I am the LORD,
and there is no other.
[19]I have not spoken in secret
in a dark place of the earth;
I did not say to the descendants of Jacob,
"Seek Me in a waste place";
I, the LORD, speak righteousness;
I declare things that are right.

[20]Assemble yourselves and come;
draw near together, you fugitives of the
nations.
They have no knowledge who set up the
wood of their carved image,
and pray to a god that cannot save.
[21]Declare and set forth your case;
let them take counsel together.
Who has declared this from ancient times?
Who has told it from that time?
Have not I, the LORD?
And there is no God besides Me,
a righteous God and Savior;
there is no other besides Me.

[22]Turn to Me and be saved,
all the ends of the earth.
For I am God, and there is no other.
[23]I have sworn by Myself,
the word has gone out of My mouth in
righteousness
and shall not return,
that to Me every knee shall bow,
every tongue shall take an oath.
[24]Surely, one shall say, "Only in the LORD
are righteousness and strength."
Men shall come to him,
and all who are incensed at Him shall be
ashamed.
[25]In the LORD shall all the seed of Israel
be justified and shall glory.

45:15 Ps 44:24
45:16 Isa 42:17
45:17 Isa 26:4
45:18 Isa 42:5
45:19 Isa 48:16
45:20 Isa 43:9
45:21 Isa 43:9
45:22 Nu 21:8–9
45:23 Php 2:10
45:24 Isa 41:11
45:25 Isa 41:16

46:1 Isa 21:9
46:2 Jdg 18:17–18
46:4 Ps 71:18
46:5 Isa 40:18
46:7 Isa 45:20
46:9 Dt 32:7
46:10 Pr 19:21
46:11 Nu 23:19
46:12 Ps 119:150
46:13 Isa 61:3

The Idols of Babylon

46 Bel bows down, Nebo stoops,
their idols are appointed to the beasts
and the cattle.
The things that you carry are burdensome;
they are a burden to the weary beast.
[2] They stoop, they bow down together;
they could not deliver the burden,
but themselves have gone into captivity.

[3] Listen to Me, O house of Jacob,
and all the remnant of the house of
Israel,
who are borne by Me from birth
and are carried from the womb:
[4] And even to your old age I am He,
and even to your graying years I will
carry you;
I have done it, and I will bear you;
even I will carry, and will deliver you.

[5] To whom will you liken Me, and make Me
equal,
and compare Me that we may be alike?
[6] They lavish gold out of the bag,
and weigh silver on the scales;
they hire a goldsmith, and he makes it a
god;
they fall down and worship it.
[7] They lift it on the shoulder, they carry it,
and they set it in its place, and it stands;
from its place it does not move.
If one shall cry to it, it cannot answer
nor save him out of his trouble.

[8] Remember this, and show yourselves men;
bring it to mind again, O transgressors.
[9] Remember the former things of old,
for I am God, and there is no other;
I am God, and there is no one like Me,
[10]declaring the end from the beginning,
and from ancient times the things that
are not yet done, saying,
"My counsel shall stand,
and I will do all My good pleasure,"
[11]calling a ravenous bird from the east,
the man who executes My counsel from
a far country.
Indeed, I have spoken it; I will also bring it
to pass.
I have purposed it; I will also do it.
[12]Listen to Me, you stubborn-hearted,
who are far from righteousness;
[13]I bring My righteousness near;
it shall not be far off,
and My salvation shall not tarry.
And I will grant salvation in Zion,
and My glory for Israel.

The Fall of Babylon

47 Come down, and sit in the dust,
O virgin daughter of Babylon;
sit on the ground; there is no throne,
O daughter of the Chaldeans.
For you shall no more be called
tender and delicate.
2 Take the millstones and grind meal.
Uncover your veil,
strip off the skirt, uncover the leg,
pass over the rivers.
3 Your nakedness shall be uncovered,
and your shame shall be seen;
I will take vengeance,
and I will not meet you as a man.
4 As for our Redeemer, the LORD of Hosts is
His name,
the Holy One of Israel.
5 Sit silently, and go into darkness,
O daughter of the Chaldeans;
for you shall no more be called
the queen of kingdoms.
6 I was angry with My people;
I have polluted My inheritance
and given them into your hand.
You did not show them mercy;
on the aged
you have laid your yoke very heavily.
7 You said, "I shall be a queen forever,"
but you did not take these things to
heart,
nor remember the outcome of them.
8 Therefore, now hear this, you who are
given to pleasures,
who dwell carelessly,
who say in your heart,
"I am, and there is no one besides me;
I shall not sit as a widow,
nor shall I know the loss of children";
9 but these two things shall come to you
in a moment, in one day,
the loss of children and widowhood.
They shall come upon you in their fullness
because of the multitude of your
sorceries
and for the great abundance of your
enchantments.
10 For you have trusted in your wickedness;
you have said, "No one sees me";
your wisdom and your knowledge have
perverted you;
and you have said in your heart,
"I am, and there is no one besides me."
11 Therefore, evil shall come upon you,
which you shall not know from where
it rises.
And disaster shall fall upon you,
for which you shall not be able to atone.
And desolation shall come upon you
suddenly,
which you shall not know.
12 Stand fast now with your enchantments,
and with the multitude of your sorceries
in which you have labored from your
youth.
Perhaps you shall be able to profit,
perhaps you may cause trembling.
13 You are wearied in the multitude of your
counsels;
let now the astrologers, the stargazers,
the monthly prognosticators stand up
and save you from these things that shall
come upon you.
14 Surely they shall be as stubble,
the fire shall burn them;
they shall not deliver themselves
from the power of the flame;
it shall not be coal to be warmed by
nor a fire to sit before.
15 Thus those shall be to you
with whom you have labored,
even your merchants, from your youth;
they shall wander, everyone to his quarter.
No one shall save you.

Israel Refined for God's Glory

48 Hear this, O house of Jacob,
who are called by the name of Israel,
and have come forth from the waters of
Judah;
who swear by the name of the LORD,
and invoke the God of Israel,
but not in truth or in righteousness;
2 for they call themselves after the holy city,
and lean on the God of Israel;
the LORD of Hosts is His name;
3 I have declared the former things from the
beginning;
and they went forth from My mouth, and
I announced them.
Suddenly I did them, and they came to
pass.
4 Because I knew that you are obstinate,
and your neck is an iron sinew,
and your brow bronze;
5 I have even from the beginning declared it
to you;
before it came to pass I announced it to
you,
lest you should say,
"My idol has done them,
and my carved image and my molded
image has commanded them."
6 You have heard; see all this.
And will you not declare it?
I have shown you new things from this
time,

47:1 Ps 137:8
47:2 Mt 24:41
47:3 Na 3:5
47:5 Isa 47:7
47:7 Dt 32:29
47:8 Zep 2:15
47:9 Na 3:4
47:10 Ps 52:7
47:11 1Th 5:3
47:13 Isa 44:25
47:14 Na 1:10
48:1 Ps 68:26
48:2 Mic 3:11
48:3 Isa 41:22
48:4 Ex 32:9
48:6 Isa 42:9

even hidden things, and you did not
know them.
7 They are created now and not from the
beginning;
even before the day when you did not
hear them,
lest you should say,
"Yes, I knew them."

You are the Lord my God who teaches me how to profit, and You lead me in the way I should go (Isa 48:17).

8 You have not heard, you have not known,
indeed, from long ago your ear has not
been open.
For I knew that you would deal very
treacherously,
and that from birth you have been called
a rebel.
9 For My name's sake I will defer My anger,
and for My praise I will restrain it for you
so that you are not cut off.
10 See, I have refined you, but not with silver;
I have chosen you in the furnace of
affliction.
11 For My own sake, even for My own sake, I
will do it;
for how can *My name* be polluted?
And I will not give My glory to another.

The Lord's Call to Israel

12 Listen to Me, O Jacob
and Israel, whom I called:
I am He;
I am the First, and I am the Last.
13 My hand also has laid the foundation of
the earth,
and My right hand has spanned the
heavens;
when I call to them,
they stand up together.

14 Assemble, all of you, and listen.
Who among them has declared these
things?
The Lord has loved him;
he will do His pleasure on Babylon,
and His arm *shall be against* the
Chaldeans.
15 I, even I, have spoken,
and I have called him;
I have brought him,
and his way will prosper.

16 Come near to Me, hear this:

I have not spoken in secret from the
beginning;
from the time that it was, there I am.
And now the Lord God has sent me
and His Spirit.

17 Thus says the Lord,
your Redeemer, the Holy One of Israel:
I am the Lord your God,
who teaches you to profit,
who leads you in the way you
should go.
18 Oh, that you had listened to My
commandments!
Then your peace would have been as a
river
and your righteousness as the waves of
the sea.
19 Your descendants also would have been as
the sand
and your offspring like grains of sand;
their name would not have been cut off
nor destroyed from before Me.

20 Go forth from Babylon!
Flee from the Chaldeans!
With a voice of singing declare,
proclaim this,
utter it even to the ends of the earth;
say, "The Lord has redeemed His servant
Jacob."
21 They did not thirst when He led them
through the deserts;
He caused the waters to flow out of the
rock for them;
He also split the rock,
and the waters gushed out.

22 "There is no peace," says the Lord, "for the
wicked."

The Servant of the Lord

49 Listen to me, O coastlands,
and pay attention, you peoples from
afar.
The Lord called me from the womb;
from the body of my mother He named
me.
2 He has made my mouth like a sharp sword;
in the shadow of His hand He has
hidden me
and made me a select arrow;
in His quiver He has hidden me.
3 He said to me, "You are My servant,
Israel, in whom I will be glorified."
4 Then I said, "I have labored in vain;
I have spent my strength for nothing and
vanity,
yet surely the justice due to me is with the
Lord,
and my reward with my God."
5 Now says the Lord,
who formed me from the womb to be
His servant,

48:8 Ps 58:3
48:9 Ps 78:38
48:10 Dt 4:20
48:11 Isa 42:8
48:12 Isa 41:4
48:13 Isa 40:26
48:14 Isa 43:9
48:16 Isa 45:19

48:17 Ps 32:8
48:18 Dt 32:29
48:19 Ge 22:17
48:20 Isa 52:9
48:21 Ex 17:6
48:22 Isa 57:21
49:1 Jer 1:5
49:2 Isa 11:4
49:3 Isa 44:23

to bring Jacob back to Him,
so that Israel might be gathered to Him
(yet I am honored in the eyes of the LORD,
and my God is my strength),
6 He says,
"It is a light thing that you should be My servant
to raise up the tribes of Jacob
and to restore the preserved ones of Israel;
I will also make you a light to the nations
so that My salvation may reach to the ends of the earth."
7 Thus says the LORD,
the Redeemer of Israel, and his Holy One,
to the despised one, to the one whom the nation abhors,
to the servant of rulers:
"Kings shall see and arise,
princes also shall worship,
because of the LORD who is faithful
and the Holy One of Israel who has chosen you."

The Restoration of Israel

8 Thus says the LORD:
In an acceptable time I have heard you,
and in a day of salvation I have helped you;
and I will preserve you, and give you
as a covenant of the people,
to restore the earth,
to make them inherit the desolate heritages,
9 saying to the prisoners, "Go forth,"
to those who are in darkness, "Show yourselves."
They shall feed along the paths,
and their pastures shall be in all desolate heights;
10 they shall not hunger nor thirst,
neither shall the heat nor sun strike them;
for He who has mercy on them shall lead them,
even by the springs of water He shall guide them.
11 I will make all My mountains a road,
and My highways shall be raised up.
12 See, these shall come from afar;
and these *will come* from the north and from the west,
and these from the land of Sinim.

13 Sing, O heavens!
And be joyful, O earth!
And break forth into singing,
O mountains!

49:6 Isa 42:6
49:7 Isa 52:15
49:8 Isa 42:6
49:9 Isa 42:7
49:10 Rev 7:16–17
49:11 Isa 11:16
49:12 Isa 43:5–6
49:13 Isa 44:23

49:14 Isa 40:27
49:15 Isa 44:21
49:16 SS 8:6
49:19 Zec 10:10
49:23 Isa 60:3

For the LORD has comforted His people
and will have mercy on His afflicted.

14 But Zion said, "The LORD has forsaken me,
and the Lord has forgotten me."

15 Can a woman forget her nursing child,
and have no compassion on the son of her womb?
Even these may forget,
yet I will not forget.
16 See, I have inscribed you on the palms of *My hands*;
your walls are continually before Me;
17 your builders hurry;
your destroyers and those who devastated you shall depart from you.
18 Lift up your eyes and look all around;
all these gather themselves together and come to you.
As I live, says the LORD,
you shall surely put on all of them as ornaments
and bind them on you as a bride does.

19 For your waste and your desolate places,
and the land of your destruction,
shall even now be too narrow by reason of the inhabitants,
and those who swallowed you up shall be far away.
20 The children whom you shall have,
after you have lost the others,
shall say again in your ears,
"The place is too cramped for me;
make room for me that I may dwell here."
21 Then you shall say in your heart,
"Who bore these for me,
since I have lost my children and am barren,
a captive and a wanderer?
And who has brought these up?
I was left alone;
from where did these come?"

22 Thus says the Lord GOD:
See, I will lift up My hand to the nations
and set up My standard to the peoples;
and they shall bring your sons in their arms,
and your daughters shall be carried on their shoulders;
23 kings shall be your foster fathers
and their queens your nursing mothers;
they shall bow down to you with their faces toward the ground
and lick up the dust of your feet.
And you shall know that I am the LORD,

PROFILE OF A SPIRITLED WOMAN

CORRIE TEN BOOM

HIDDEN IN HIS CARE

"There is no pit so deep that God's love is not deeper still."[1] These are among the final words Betsie ten Boom spoke to her sister, Corrie, as Betsie lay dying in a German death camp, a victim of starvation and torture.

Corrie ten Boom was a Dutch Christian who worked in her father's watch repair shop in Haarlem, Holland. When the Germans invaded Holland in 1940, the whole family became involved in the Dutch resistance movement. They constructed a secret hidden chamber, thirty inches deep, in Corrie's bedroom on the top floor of their home above the shop, where they hid Jews and others from the Nazi SS troops. Throughout 1943 and 1944 there were usually at least six people hiding in the ten Boom home. Additional refugees were given temporary accommodation until other places could be found for them to stay.

In February 1944 an informant betrayed the ten Boom family. The entire family was arrested, although the Nazis didn't find the Jews hidden in the secret room. Those Jews were rescued later by members of the resistance. The ten Booms' elderly father died ten days later in prison. Other members of the family were released, but Corrie and her sister, Betsie, were sent to the notorious Ravensbrück concentration camp. There they endured unspeakable horrors but held on to their faith. They were even able to conduct Bible studies using a contraband Bible.

Betsie died on December 16, 1944, and due to a clerical error, Corrie was released two weeks later, just one week before all women prisoners her age were executed.

After the war Corrie set up rehabilitation centers for concentration camp survivors and for Dutch people who had collaborated with the Germans and were unable to get jobs. She spoke everywhere about the need for forgiveness.

In 1947 this forgiveness was put to the test. Corrie had just finished speaking at a meeting in Germany when a man in an overcoat and brown hat came up to her. She recognized him instantly as one of the guards who had abused her and Betsie.

"I was a guard in Ravensbrück, but since then, I've become a Christian," he said to her. "I know Christ has forgiven me for the cruel things I did there. Will you forgive me?" Then he put out his hand.

It was the most difficult thing Corrie had ever been asked to do, but as she, by choice of will, gave him her hand, the love of Christ flooded her whole being, and she was able to say, "Yes, brother, I forgive you, with all of my heart!"[2]

Sometimes there are books that have such an impact on your life that you can remember them decades later. *The Hiding Place*, Corrie's autobiography, became a best-seller that was later made into a movie. I still remember its story and message.

Corrie traveled to more than sixty nations, preaching the message of Christ's forgiveness. Thousands became believers through her many books and her speaking. Israel honored her by giving her the title "Righteous Among the Nations." She was knighted by the queen of the Netherlands for her work during the war.

Corrie died in 1983 on her ninety-first birthday.[3]

Felicity Dale

1. CorrietenBoom.com, History, http://www.corrietenboom.com/history.htm (accessed April 29, 2014).
2. See Corrie ten Boom with Elizabeth and John Sherrill, *The Hiding Place* (Peabody, MA: Hendrickson Publishers, 2009), 261–262.
3. Research for this article was taken from the Corrie ten Boom Museum at www.corrietenboom.com and "Corrie ten Boom" on Wikipedia.com.

for those who wait for Me shall not be
ashamed.

24 Can the prey be taken from the mighty
or the captives of a tyrant be delivered?

25 For thus says the LORD:
Even the captives of the mighty shall be
taken away,
and the prey of the tyrant shall be
delivered;
for I will contend with him who contends
with you,
and I will save your sons.
26 I will feed those who oppress you with their
own flesh,
and they shall be drunk with their own
blood as with sweet wine.
And all flesh shall know
that I, the LORD, am your Savior
and your Redeemer, the Mighty One of
Jacob.

The Servant, Hope of Israel

50 Thus says the LORD:
Where is the certificate of divorce
by which I sent your mother away?
Or to which of My creditors
did I sell you?
For your iniquities you were sold,
and for your transgressions your mother
was sent away.
2 Why, when I came, was there no man?
When I called, was there no one to
answer?
Is My hand so short that it cannot redeem?
Or have I no power to deliver?
Indeed, at My rebuke I dry up the sea,
I make the rivers a wilderness;
Their fish stink because there is no water,
and die for thirst.
3 I clothe the heavens with blackness,
and I make sackcloth their covering.

4 The Lord GOD has given me the tongue of
the learned,
that I may know how to sustain him who
is weary with a word;
He awakens me morning by morning;
He awakens my ear to listen as the
learned.
5 The Lord GOD has opened my ear,
and I was not rebellious,
nor did I turn back.
6 I gave my back to those who struck me,
and my cheeks to those who plucked out
my beard;
I did not cover my face
from shame and spitting.
7 For the Lord GOD will help me;
therefore, I shall not be disgraced;
therefore, I have set my face like a flint,
and I know that I shall not be ashamed.
8 He who vindicates me is near;
who will contend with me?
Let us stand up to each other.
Who is my adversary?
Let him come near to me.
9 Certainly the Lord GOD will help me;
who is he who condemns me?
Indeed they all shall grow old as a
garment;
the moth shall eat them up.

10 Who among you fears the LORD,
who obeys the voice of His servant,
who walks in darkness
and has no light?
Let him trust in the name of the LORD,
and rely upon his God.
11 But now, all you who kindle a fire,
who encompass yourselves with sparks:
Walk in the light of your fire
and among the sparks that you have
ignited.
This you shall have from My hand:
You shall lie down in sorrow.

The Eternal Salvation of Zion

51 Listen to Me, you who pursue
righteousness,
you who seek the LORD:
Look to the rock from which you were
hewn
and to the quarry from which you were
dug.
2 Look to Abraham your father
and to Sarah who bore you;
for I called him alone,
and blessed him, and multiplied him.
3 For the LORD shall comfort Zion,
He will comfort all her waste places;
He will make her wilderness like Eden,
and her desert like the garden of the
LORD;
joy and gladness shall be found in it,
thanksgiving, and the voice of melody.

4 Listen to Me, O My people;
and give ear to Me, O My nation:
for a law shall proceed from Me,
and I will set My justice as a light of the
peoples.
5 My righteousness is near,
My salvation has gone forth,
and My arms shall judge the peoples;
the coastlands shall wait for Me,
and for My arm they shall expectantly
wait.
6 Lift up your eyes to the heavens,
and look on the earth beneath.

49:24 Mt 12:29
49:25 Jer 50:33–34
49:26 Isa 9:20
50:1 Jer 3:8
50:2 Nu 11:23
50:3 Rev 6:12
50:4 Mt 11:28
50:5 Jn 14:31
50:6 Mt 26:67
50:7 Eze 3:8–9
50:8 Isa 41:1
50:9 Job 13:28
50:10 Isa 9:2
51:1 Isa 51:7
51:2 Eze 33:24
51:3 Isa 52:9
51:4 Isa 2:3
51:5 Isa 46:13
51:6 Mt 24:35

For the heavens shall vanish away like smoke,
and the earth shall grow old like a garment,
and those who dwell in it shall die in like manner;
but My salvation shall be forever,
and My righteousness shall not be abolished.

7 Listen to Me, you who know righteousness,
the people in whose heart is My law;
do not fear the reproach of men
nor be afraid of their revilings.
8 For the moth shall eat them up like a garment,
and the worm shall eat them like wool;
but My righteousness shall be forever
and My salvation from generation to generation.

9 Awake, awake, put on strength,
O arm of the LORD.
Awake as in the ancient days,
in the generations of old.
Was it not You who cut Rahab to pieces
and wounded the dragon?
10 Was it not You who dried up the sea,
the waters of the great deep,
who made the depths of the sea a pathway
for the ransomed to pass over?
11 Therefore, the redeemed of the LORD shall return
and come with singing to Zion,
and everlasting joy shall be upon their head.
They shall obtain gladness and joy,
and sorrow and mourning shall flee away.

12 I, even I, am He who comforts you.
Who are you that you should be afraid of a man who shall die,
and of the son of man who shall be made as grass,
13 and forget the LORD your maker
who has stretched out the heavens
and laid the foundations of the earth?
And have feared continually every day
because of the fury of the oppressor
as he makes ready to destroy?
Yet where is the fury of the oppressor?
14 The exile shall soon be freed,
and shall not die in the dungeon,
nor will his bread be lacking.
15 But I am the LORD your God
who divided the sea whose waves roared;
the LORD of Hosts is His name.
16 I have put My words in your mouth,
and I have covered you in the shadow of My hand
that I may plant the heavens,
and lay the foundations of the earth,
and say to Zion, "You are My people."

The Wrath of God Ceases

17 Awake, awake,
stand up, O Jerusalem,
you who have drunk at the hand of the LORD
the cup of His fury;
the cup of reeling
you have drained to the dregs.
18 There is no one to guide her
among all the sons she has brought forth;
nor is there anyone to take hold of her hand
of all the sons that she has brought up.
19 These two things have befallen you;
who shall be mournful for you?
Desolation, and destruction, and famine, and sword—
how shall I comfort you?
20 Your sons have fainted;
they lie at the head of all the streets
as an antelope in a net;
they are full of the fury of the LORD,
the rebuke of your God.

21 Therefore please hear this,
you afflicted who are drunk but not with wine.
22 Thus says your Lord, the LORD,
and your God who pleads the cause of His people:
See, I have taken out of your hand
the cup of reeling,
even the dregs of the cup of My fury;
you will never drink it again.
23 But I will put it into the hand of those who afflict you,
who have said to you,
"Lie down that we may walk over you."
And you have laid your back as the ground
and as the street for those who walk on it.

52 Awake, awake!
Put on your strength, O Zion;
put on your beautiful garments,
O Jerusalem, the holy city.
For the uncircumcised and the unclean
will no longer enter you.
2 Shake yourself from the dust;
arise, O captive Jerusalem.
Loose yourself from the bonds of your neck,
O captive daughter of Zion.

3 For thus says the LORD:

You were sold for nothing,
and you shall be redeemed without money.

51:7 Ps 37:31
51:8 Isa 50:9
51:9 Isa 27:1
51:11 Isa 35:10
51:12 Ps 118:6
51:13 Ps 104:2
51:15 Jer 31:35
51:16 Isa 59:21
....
51:17 Job 21:20
51:18 Ps 88:18
51:19 Isa 47:9
51:20 La 2:11–12
51:22 Isa 51:17
51:23 Jos 10:24
52:1 Rev 21:27
52:3 Isa 45:13

4 For thus says the Lord God:

My people went down at the first into
Egypt to sojourn there;
then the Assyrian oppressed them
without cause.

5 Now therefore, what do I have here, says
the Lord,

seeing that My people have been taken
away for nothing?
Those who rule over them make them
wail,
says the Lord,
and My name is continually blasphemed
all day long.
6 Therefore, My people shall know My name;
therefore, they shall know in that day
that I am He who does speak:
Here I am.
7 How beautiful upon the mountains
are the feet of him who brings good
news,
who proclaims peace,
who brings good news of happiness,
who proclaims salvation,
who says to Zion,
"Your God reigns!"
8 Your watchmen lift up their voices;
they sing joyfully together;
for they shall see with their own eyes
when the Lord brings Zion back.
9 Break forth into joy, sing together,
you waste places of Jerusalem.
For the Lord has comforted His people;
He has redeemed Jerusalem.
10 The Lord has bared His holy arm
in the eyes of all the nations,
and all the ends of the earth shall see
the salvation of our God.

11 Depart, depart, go out from there,
touch no unclean thing;
go out of the midst of her; be clean,
you who bear the vessels of the Lord.
12 For you shall not go out with haste
nor go by flight.
For the Lord will go before you,
and the God of Israel will be your rear
guard.

The Suffering Servant

13 See, My servant shall deal prudently;
he shall be exalted and extolled, and be
very high.
14 Just as many were astonished at you,
his visage was so marred, more than
any man,
and his form more than the sons of men;
15 so he shall sprinkle many nations.

52:4 Ge 46:6
52:5 Ro 2:24
52:7 Isa 40:9
52:8 Isa 62:6
52:9 Isa 51:3
52:10 Isa 51:9
52:11 Isa 48:20
52:12 Ex 12:33
52:13 Isa 42:1
52:15 Isa 49:7
....
53:1 Jn 12:38
53:2 Isa 52:14
53:3 Isa 49:7
53:4 Mt 8:17
53:5 Ro 4:25
53:7 Mk 14:61
53:8 Da 9:26
53:9 1Pe 2:22
53:10 Ps 22:30

Kings shall shut their mouths at him;
for that which had not been told them they
shall see,
and that which they had not heard they
shall consider.

53 Who has believed our report?
And to whom has the arm of the Lord
been revealed?
2 For he grew up before Him as a tender
plant
and as a root out of a dry ground.
He has no form or majesty that we should
look upon him
nor appearance that we should desire
him.
3 He was despised and rejected of men,
a man of sorrows and acquainted with
grief.
And we hid, as it were, our faces from him;
he was despised, and we did not esteem
him.
4 Surely he has borne our grief
and carried our sorrows;
Yet we esteemed him stricken,
smitten of God, and afflicted.
5 But he was wounded for our
transgressions,
he was bruised for our iniquities;
the chastisement of our peace was upon
him,
and by his stripes we are healed.
6 All of us like sheep have gone astray;
each of us has turned to his own way,
but the Lord has laid on him
the iniquity of us all.
7 He was oppressed, and he was afflicted,
yet he opened not his mouth;
he was brought as a lamb to the slaughter,
and as a sheep before its shearers is
silent,
so he opened not his mouth.
8 By oppression and judgment he was taken
away,
and who shall declare his generation?
For he was cut off out of the land of the
living;
for the transgression of my people he
was struck.
9 His grave was assigned with the wicked,
yet with the rich in his death,
because he had done no violence,
nor was any deceit in his mouth.

10 Yet it pleased the Lord to bruise him; He
has put him to grief.
If he made himself as an offering for sin,
he shall see his offspring, he shall prolong
his days,

and the good pleasure of the LORD shall
prosper in his hand.
11 He shall see of the anguish of his soul
and be satisfied.
By his knowledge My righteous servant
shall justify the many,
for he shall bear their iniquities.
12 Therefore, I will divide him a portion with
the great,
and he shall divide the spoil with the
strong,
because he poured out his soul to death,
and he was numbered with the
transgressors,
thus he bore the sin of many
and made intercession for the
transgressors.

The Covenant of Peace

54 Sing, O barren,
you who did not bear a child.
Break forth into singing and cry aloud,
you who did not travail with child.
For more are the children of the desolate
than the children of the married wife,
says the LORD.
2 Enlarge the place of your tent,
and let them stretch out the curtains of
your habitations;
spare not,
lengthen your cords,
and strengthen your stakes.
3 For you shall spread out to the right hand
and to the left,
and your descendants shall inherit the
nations
and make the desolate cities to be
inhabited.
4 Do not fear, for you shall not be ashamed
nor be humiliated;
for you shall not be put to shame,
for you shall forget the shame of your
youth
and shall not remember the reproach of
your widowhood anymore.
5 For your Maker is your husband,
the LORD of Hosts is His name;
and your Redeemer is the Holy One of
Israel;
He shall be called the God of the whole
earth.
6 For the LORD has called you
as a woman forsaken and grieved in
spirit,
and a wife of youth
when you were refused, says your God.
7 For a small moment I have forsaken you,
but with great mercies I will gather you.
8 In a little wrath
I hid My face from you for a moment;
but with everlasting kindness
I will have mercy on you,
says the LORD your Redeemer.
9 For this is as the waters of Noah to Me;
for as I have sworn that the waters of
Noah should no longer cover the
earth,
so I have sworn that I would not be
wrathful with you
nor rebuke you.
10 For the mountains may be removed,
and the hills may shake,
but My kindness shall not depart from you,
nor shall My covenant of peace be
removed,
says the LORD who has mercy on you.

11 O afflicted one, tossed with tempest and
not comforted,
I will lay your stones with fair colors
and lay your foundations with sapphires.
12 I will make your windows of agates,
and your gates of crystal,
and all your borders of precious stones.
13 All your sons shall be taught of the LORD,
and great shall be the peace of your
sons.
14 In righteousness you shall be established;
you shall be far from oppression,
for you shall not fear,
and from terror,
for it shall not come near you.
15 Indeed they shall surely assail you fiercely,
but not from Me.
Whoever assails you shall fall for your
sake.
16 See, I have created the smith
that blows the coals in the fire
and who brings forth an instrument for
his work;
and I have created the destroyer in order to
cause ruin.

> No weapon formed against me shall prosper, and every tongue that rises up against me You shall condemn (Isa 54:17).

17 No weapon that is formed against you
shall prosper,
and every tongue that shall rise
against you in judgment, you shall
condemn.
This is the heritage of the servants of the
LORD,
and their vindication is from Me,
says the LORD.

53:11 Ro 5:18–19
53:12 Mk 15:27
54:1 1Sa 2:5
54:2 Isa 49:19–20
54:3 Isa 43:5–6
54:4 Jer 31:19
54:5 Jer 3:14
54:6 Isa 62:4
54:7 Isa 26:20
54:9 Ge 8:21
54:11 1Ch 29:2
54:13 Jn 6:45
54:14 Isa 1:26
54:17 Isa 50:8

The Invitation to the Waters

55 Ho! Everyone who thirsts,
come to the waters;
and you who have no money,
come, buy and eat.
Come, buy wine and milk
without money and without price.
2 Why do you spend money for that which is not bread,
and your labor for that which does not satisfy?
Listen diligently to Me, and eat what is good,
and let your soul delight itself in abundance.
3 Incline your ear, and come to Me.
Listen, so that your soul may live,
and I will make an everlasting covenant with you,
even the sure mercies of David.
4 See, I have given him as a witness to the people,
a leader and commander to the people.
5 Surely you shall call a nation that you do not know,
and nations that did not know you shall run to you
because of the LORD your God,
even the Holy One of Israel;
for He has glorified you.
6 Seek the LORD while He may be found,
call you upon Him while He is near.
7 Let the wicked forsake his way,
and the unrighteous man his thoughts;
and let him return to the LORD, and He will have mercy upon him,
and to our God, for He will abundantly pardon.
8 For My thoughts are not your thoughts,
nor are your ways My ways,
says the LORD.
9 For as the heavens are higher than the earth,
so are My ways higher than your ways,
and My thoughts than your thoughts.
10 For as the rain comes down,
and the snow from heaven,
and do not return there
but water the earth
and make it bring forth and bud
that it may give seed to the sower and bread to the eater,
11 so shall My word be that goes forth from My mouth;
it shall not return to Me void,
but it shall accomplish that which I please,
and it shall prosper in the thing for which I sent it.
12 For you shall go out with joy,
and be led out with peace;
the mountains and the hills
shall break forth into singing before you,
and all the trees of the field
shall clap their hands.
13 Instead of the thorn shall come up the fir tree,
and instead of the brier shall come up the myrtle tree;
and it shall be to the LORD for a memorial,
for an everlasting sign
that shall not be cut off.

Salvation for the Nations

56 Thus says the LORD:

Preserve justice
and do righteousness,
for My salvation is about to come
and My righteousness to be revealed.
2 Blessed is the man who does this,
and the son of man who takes hold of it,
who keeps from polluting the Sabbath
and keeps his hand from doing any evil.

I am constantly being transformed through my experiences and encounters with God (Isa 56).

3 Do not let the son of the foreigner
who has joined himself to the LORD
speak, saying,
"The LORD has utterly separated me from His people";
do not let the eunuch say,
"I am only a dry tree."
4 For thus says the LORD:
To the eunuchs who keep My Sabbaths,
and choose the things that please Me,
and take hold of My covenant,
5 to them I will give in My house and within My walls
a memorial, and a name
better than that of sons and of daughters;
I will give them an everlasting name
that shall not be cut off.
6 Also the sons of the foreigner who join themselves to the LORD
to serve Him,
and to love the name of the LORD,
and to be His servants,
to everyone who keeps from polluting the Sabbath
and takes hold of My covenant,
7 even them I will bring to My holy mountain
and make them joyful in My house of prayer.

55:1 SS 5:1
55:2 Ps 22:26
55:3 Isa 61:8
55:4 Jer 30:9
55:5 Isa 60:9
55:6 Ps 32:6
55:7 Isa 44:22
55:9 Ps 103:11
55:10 Isa 30:23
55:11 Isa 45:23
55:12 Isa 44:23
55:13 Isa 41:19
56:1 Ps 85:9
56:2 Isa 58:13
56:5 Isa 55:13
56:7 Mt 21:13

Their burnt offerings and their sacrifices
shall be accepted on My altar;
for My house shall be called
a house of prayer for all people.
8 The Lord God
who gathers the outcasts of Israel says,
Yet I will gather others to them
besides those who already are gathered
to him.

God Accuses the Wicked

9 All you beasts of the field,
all you beasts in the forest, come to
devour.
10 His watchmen are blind;
they all are ignorant;
they all are dumb dogs,
unable to bark;
sleepers lying down,
who love to slumber.
11 They are greedy dogs
which can never have enough,
and they are shepherds who cannot
understand;
they all turn to their own way,
every one for his gain, from his territory.
12 "Come," *they say*, "let us get wine,
and let us fill ourselves with strong
drink;
and tomorrow shall be as today,
only more so."

Israel's Futile Idolatry

57 The righteous man perishes,
and no man lays it to heart;
and merciful men are taken away
while no one understands,
for the righteous man is taken away
from the evil to come.
2 He shall enter into peace;
they shall rest in their beds,
each one walking in his uprightness.

3 But draw near to here, you sons of a
sorceress,
offspring of an adulterer and prostitute.
4 Whom do you mock?
Against whom do you open wide your
mouth
and stick out your tongue?
Are you not children of transgression,
offspring of falsehood,
5 inflaming yourselves with idols
under every green tree,
slaying the children in the valleys
under the clefts of the rocks?
6 Among the smooth stones of the stream is
your portion;
they are your lot.
Even to them you have poured out a drink
offering;
you have offered a grain offering.
Should I relent concerning these things?
7 On a lofty and high mountain you have set
your bed;
even there you went up to offer sacrifice.
8 Behind the doors and the doorposts
you have set up your memorial;
far removed from Me, you have uncovered
yourself;
you have enlarged your bed and made a
covenant with them;
you have loved their bed,
you have looked on their nakedness.
9 You went to the king with ointment,
and increased your perfumes,
and sent your messengers far off,
and made them go down to Sheol.
10 You were wearied by the length of your
road;
yet you did not say, "There is no hope."
You have found renewed strength;
therefore, you did not faint.

11 Of whom were you afraid or fearful
when you lied
and you did not remember Me,
nor give Me a thought?
Have I not held My peace for a long time
so that you do not fear Me?
12 I will declare your righteousness, and your
works,
yet they shall not profit you.
13 When you cry out,
let your collection of idols deliver you.
But the wind shall carry them all away,
a breath shall take them away.
But he who puts his trust in Me
shall possess the land
and shall inherit My holy mountain.

Healing for the Contrite

14 And it shall be said,

"Build up, build up, prepare the way,
take up every stumbling block out of the
way of My people."
15 For thus says the High and Lofty One
who inhabits eternity, whose name is
Holy:
I dwell in the high and holy place
and also with him who is of a contrite
and humble spirit,
to revive the spirit of the humble,
and to revive the heart of the contrite
ones.
16 For I will not contend forever,
nor will I always be angry;
for the spirit would grow faint before Me,
and the souls whom I have made.
17 For the iniquity of his unjust gain I was
angry and struck him;

56:8 Jn 10:16
56:9 Jer 12:9
56:11 Eze 13:19
56:12 Ps 10:6
57:1 2Ki 22:20
57:3 Mt 16:4
57:5 2Ki 16:3–4
57:6 Jer 3:9
....
57:7 Eze 16:16
57:9 Eze 23:16
57:10 Jer 2:25
57:11 Ps 50:21
57:12 Mic 3:2–4
57:13 Ps 37:9
57:14 Isa 62:10
57:15 Ps 34:18
57:16 Ps 85:5
57:17 Isa 56:11

I hid My face and was wrathful,
and he went on turning away in the way
of his heart.
18 I have seen his ways but will heal him;
I will lead him and restore comfort to
him and to his mourners,
19 by creating the fruit of the lips.
Peace, peace to him who is far off and to
him who is near,
says the LORD, and I will heal him.
20 But the wicked are like the troubled
sea when it cannot rest,
whose waters cast up mire and dirt.
21 There is no peace, says my God, for the
wicked.

The Chosen Fast

58 Cry aloud, do not hold back;
lift up your voice like a trumpet,
and show My people their transgression
and the house of Jacob their sins.
2 Yet they seek Me daily
and delight to know My ways,
as a nation that has done righteousness
and has not forsaken the ordinance of
their God.
They ask Me for the ordinances of justice;
they take delight in approaching God.
3 "Why have we fasted
and You do not see?
Why have we humbled ourselves
and You take no notice?"
Certainly, on the day of your fast you find
your desire
and are exacting on all your laborers.
4 Certainly, you fast for strife and debate
and to strike with the fist of wickedness.
You do not fast as you do this day,
to make your voice to be heard on high.
5 Is it such a fast that I have chosen,
a day for a man to humble himself?
Is it to bow down his head as a bulrush,
and to spread out sackcloth and ashes
under him?
Will you call this a fast
and an acceptable day to the LORD?
6 Is not this the fast that I have chosen:
to loose the bonds of wickedness,
to undo the heavy burdens,
and to let the oppressed go free,
and break every yoke?
7 Is it not to divide your bread with the
hungry
and bring the poor who are outcasts into
your house?
When you see the naked, to cover him
and not hide yourself from your own
flesh?
8 Then your light shall break forth as the
morning,
and your healing shall spring forth
quickly,
and your righteousness shall go before
you;
the glory of the LORD shall be your
reward.
9 Then you shall call, and the LORD shall
answer;
you shall cry, and He shall say, Here I
am.

If you take away the yoke from your midst,
the pointing of the finger, and speaking
wickedness,
10 and if you give yourself to the hungry
and satisfy the afflicted soul,
then your light shall rise in obscurity,
and your darkness shall become as the
noonday.
11 And the LORD shall guide you continually,
and satisfy your soul in drought,
and strengthen your bones;
and you shall be like a watered garden,
and like a spring of water, whose waters
do not fail.
12 Those from among you shall rebuild the
old waste places;
you shall raise up the foundations of
many generations;
and you shall be called, the Repairer of the
Breach,
the Restorer of Paths in which to Dwell.
13 If because of the Sabbath you turn away
your foot
from doing your pleasure on My holy
day,
and call the Sabbath a delight,
the holy day of the LORD honorable,
and honor it, not doing your own ways,
nor finding your own pleasure, nor
speaking your own words,
14 then you shall delight yourself in the LORD,
and I will cause you to ride upon the
high places of the earth,
and feed you with the heritage of Jacob
your father.
For the mouth of the LORD has spoken it.

The Consequence of Sin

59 Certainly, the hand of the LORD is not
so short that it cannot save,
nor is His ear so dull that it cannot hear.
2 But your iniquities have made a separation
between
you and your God,
and your sins have hidden His face from
you
so that He will not hear.

57:18 Jer 3:22
57:19 Ac 2:39
57:20 Job 18:5–14
57:21 Isa 48:22
58:2 Isa 29:13
58:3 Mal 3:14
58:5 Zec 7:5
58:6 Ne 5:10–12
58:7 Eze 18:7

....

58:8 Ex 14:19
58:9 Pr 6:13
58:10 Job 11:17
58:11 SS 4:15
58:12 Isa 61:4
58:13 Ps 84:2
58:14 Dt 32:13
59:1 Nu 11:23

3 For your hands are defiled with blood
and your fingers with iniquity;
your lips have spoken lies,
your tongue has muttered perverseness.
4 No one calls for justice,
nor does anyone plead for truth.
They trust in vanity and speak lies;
they conceive mischief and bring forth iniquity.
5 They hatch adders' eggs
and weave the spider's web;
he who eats of their eggs dies,
and that which is crushed breaks out into a viper.
6 Their webs shall not become garments,
nor shall they cover themselves with their works;
their works are works of iniquity,
and an act of violence is in their hands.
7 Their feet run to evil,
and they make haste to shed innocent blood;
their thoughts are thoughts of iniquity;
devastation and destruction are in their paths.
8 The way of peace they do not know,
and there is no justice in their ways;
they have made their paths crooked;
whoever walks in them does not know peace.

The Confession of Sin

9 Therefore, justice is far from us,
nor does righteousness overtake us;
we wait for light, but there is darkness,
for brightness, but we walk in gloom.
10 We grope along the wall like the blind,
and we grope as if we had no eyes;
we stumble at noonday as in the night;
among those who are vigorous, we are as dead men.
11 We all roar like bears
and mourn sadly like doves;
we look for justice, but there is none;
for salvation, but it is far from us.

12 For our transgressions are multiplied before You,
and our sins testify against us;
for our transgressions are with us.
And as for our iniquities, we know them:
13 transgressing, and lying against the LORD,
and departing away from our God,
speaking oppression and revolt,
conceiving and uttering from the heart words of falsehood.
14 Justice is turned backward,
and righteousness stands far off;
for truth is fallen in the street,
and equity cannot enter.

59:3 Isa 1:15
59:4 Job 15:35
59:7 Pr 1:16
59:8 Lk 1:79
59:9 Isa 5:30
59:10 Dt 28:29
59:11 Isa 38:14
59:12 Ezr 9:6
59:13 Mk 7:21–22
59:14 Hab 1:4
....
59:16 Ps 98:1
59:17 Isa 9:7
59:18 Isa 63:6
59:19 Ps 113:3
59:20 Ro 11:26–27
60:1 Eph 5:8
60:3 Isa 49:23

15 Truth is lacking,
and he who departs from evil makes himself a prey.

The Redeemer of Zion

Then the LORD saw it, and it displeased Him
that there was no justice.
16 He saw that there was no man
and was astonished that there was no intercessor;
therefore, His own arm brought salvation to Him,
and His righteousness sustained Him.
17 For He put on righteousness as a breastplate
and a helmet of salvation on His head;
He put on the garments of vengeance for clothing
and was clad with zeal as a cloak.
18 According to their deeds,
accordingly He will repay:
fury to His adversaries,
recompense to His enemies;
to the islands He will make recompense.

Lord, I believe that what the enemy has meant for defeat, You are able to turn into a victory (Isa 59:19).

19 So shall they fear the name of the LORD from the west
and His glory from the rising of the sun;
when the enemy shall come in like a flood,
the Spirit of the LORD shall lift up a standard against him.
20 The Redeemer shall come to Zion
and to those who turn from transgression in Jacob,
says the LORD.

21 As for Me, this is My covenant with them,
says the LORD: My Spirit who is upon you, and
My words which I have put in your mouth
shall not depart out of your mouth, nor out
of the mouth of your descendants, nor out of
the mouth of your descendants' descendants,
says the LORD, from this time forth and forever.

The Glory of Zion

60 Arise, shine, for your light has come,
and the glory of the LORD has risen upon you.
2 For the darkness shall cover the earth
and deep darkness the peoples;
but the LORD shall rise upon you,
and His glory shall be seen upon you.
3 The nations shall come to your light
and kings to the brightness of your rising.

4 Lift up your eyes all around, and see:
They all gather themselves together;
they come to you;
your sons shall come from afar,
and your daughters shall be carried at your side.
5 Then you shall see and be radiant,
and your heart shall thrill and rejoice
because the abundance of the sea shall be converted to you,
the wealth of the nations shall come to you.
6 The multitude of camels shall cover your *land*,
the young camels of Midian and Ephah;
all those from Sheba shall come;
they shall bring gold and incense
and shall bear good news of the praises of the LORD.
7 All the flocks of Kedar shall be gathered together to you,
the rams of Nebaioth shall minister to you;
they shall come up with acceptance on My altar,
and I will glorify My glorious house.
8 Who are these who fly as a cloud
and as the doves to their roosts?
9 Surely the coastlands shall wait for Me,
and the ships of Tarshish shall come first,
to bring your sons from afar,
their silver and their gold with them,
to the name of the LORD your God
and to the Holy One of Israel
because He has glorified you.
10 The sons of foreigners shall build up your walls,
and their kings shall minister to you;
for in My wrath I struck you,
but in My favor I have had mercy on you.
11 Therefore, your gates shall be open continually;
they shall not be shut day nor night,
so that men may bring to you the wealth of the nations,
and that their kings may be brought.

God wants to use me regardless of my age, my appearance, my education, my race, my gender, or my prior experience (Isa 60:1).

12 For the nation and kingdom that will not serve you shall perish,
and those nations shall be utterly destroyed.

60:4 Isa 49:18
60:5 Isa 61:6
60:6 Ps 72:10
60:7 Ge 25:13
60:9 Isa 2:16
60:10 Isa 49:23
60:11 Isa 60:5

....

60:13 Isa 35:2
60:14 Isa 49:23
60:16 Isa 49:23
60:18 Isa 26:1
60:19 Rev 21:23
60:20 Isa 35:10
60:21 Ps 37:11
60:22 Hab 2:3

13 The glory of Lebanon shall come to you,
the fir tree, the pine tree, and the box tree together,
to beautify the place of My sanctuary;
and I will make the place of My feet glorious.
14 The sons also of those who afflicted you
shall come bowing before you,
and all those who despised you shall
bow themselves down at the soles of your feet;
and they shall call you, The City of the LORD,
the Zion of the Holy One of Israel.

15 Whereas you have been forsaken
and hated so that no man went through you,
I will make you an eternal excellency,
a joy of many generations.
16 You shall also suck the milk of the nations
and suck the breast of kings;
then you shall know that I, the LORD, am your Savior
and your Redeemer, the Mighty One of Jacob.
17 Instead of bronze I will bring gold,
and instead of iron I will bring silver;
and instead of wood, bronze;
and instead of stones, iron.
I will also make your officers peace
and your exactors righteousness.
18 Violence shall no more be heard in your land,
nor devastation or destruction within your borders;
but you shall call your walls Salvation
and your gates Praise.
19 The sun shall no longer be your light by day,
nor for brightness shall the moon give light to you;
but the LORD shall be an everlasting light to you
and your God for your glory.
20 Your sun shall no more go down,
nor shall your moon wane;
for the LORD shall be your everlasting light,
and the days of your mourning shall end.
21 Then all your people shall be righteous;
they shall inherit the land forever,
the branch of My planting,
the work of My hands,
that I may be glorified.
22 A little one shall become a thousand,
and a small one a strong nation.
I, the LORD,
will hasten it in its time.

The LORD's Favor

61 The Spirit of the Lord GOD is upon me
because the LORD has anointed me
to preach good news to the poor;
He has sent me to heal the broken-hearted,
to proclaim liberty to the captives,
and the opening of the prison to those who are bound;
2 to proclaim the acceptable year of the LORD
and the day of vengeance of our God;
to comfort all who mourn,

God will take things of ruin and convert them into something of beauty—giving me "beauty for ashes" (Isa 61:3).

3 to preserve those who mourn in Zion,
to give to them beauty
for ashes,
the oil of joy
for mourning,
the garment of praise
for the spirit of heaviness,
that they might be called trees of righteousness,
the planting of the LORD,
that He might be glorified.
4 They shall build the old ruins;
they shall raise up the former desolations,
and they shall repair the waste cities,
the desolations of many generations.
5 Strangers shall stand and feed your flocks,
and the sons of the alien shall be your plowmen and your vinedressers.
6 But you shall be named the priests of the LORD;
men shall call you the ministers of our God.
You shall eat the riches of the nations,
and in their glory you shall boast.

7 Instead of your shame
you shall have double honor,
and instead of humiliation
they shall rejoice over their portion.
Therefore, in their land they shall possess a double portion;
everlasting joy shall be theirs.
8 For I, the LORD, love justice,
I hate robbery in the burnt offering;
and I will faithfully give them their recompense
and make an everlasting covenant with them.

61:1 Ps 45:7
61:2 Isa 34:8
61:3 Ps 45:7
61:4 Isa 58:12
61:5 Isa 14:1–2
61:6 Ex 19:6
61:7 Isa 40:2
61:8 Isa 55:3
61:9 Isa 44:3
61:10 Rev 21:2
61:11 Ps 85:11
62:2 Isa 62:4
62:3 Zec 9:16
62:4 Jer 32:41
62:5 Isa 65:19
62:6 Isa 52:8

9 Their descendants shall be known among the nations
and their offspring among the peoples.
All who see them shall acknowledge them
because they are the descendants whom the LORD has blessed.

10 I will greatly rejoice in the LORD,
my soul shall be joyful in my God;
for He has clothed me with the garments of salvation,
He has covered me with the robe of righteousness,
as a bridegroom decks himself with ornaments,
and as a bride adorns herself with her jewels.
11 For as the earth brings forth her buds,
and as the garden causes the things that are sown in it to spring forth,
so the Lord GOD will cause righteousness and praise
to spring forth before all the nations.

The Salvation of Zion

62 For the sake of Zion I will not keep silent,
and for the sake of Jerusalem I will not rest
until her righteousness goes forth as brightness
and her salvation as a lamp that burns.
2 The nations shall see your righteousness,
and all kings your glory.
And you shall be called by a new name,
which the mouth of the LORD shall name.
3 You shall also be a crown of glory in the hand of the LORD
and a royal diadem in the hand of your God.
4 You shall no more be termed Forsaken,
nor shall your land be termed Desolate;
but you shall be called My Delight Is In Her,
and your land Married;
for the LORD delights in you,
and your land shall be married.
5 For as a young man marries a virgin,
so your sons shall marry you;
and as the bridegroom rejoices over the bride,
so your God shall rejoice over you.

6 I have set watchmen on your walls, O Jerusalem,
who shall never hold their peace day nor night.
You who remind the LORD,
do not keep silent;
7 give Him no rest until He establishes
and makes Jerusalem a glory in the earth.

8 The LORD has sworn by His right hand
and by His strong arm:
Surely I will no longer give your grain
as food for your enemies;
and the sons of the foreigners shall not
drink your wine
for which you have labored.
9 But those who have gathered it shall eat it
and praise the LORD;
and those who have brought it shall drink it
in the courts of My sanctuary.

10 Go through, go through the gates.
Prepare the way of the people;
build up, build up the highway.
Remove the stones;
lift up a standard over the peoples.

11 The LORD has proclaimed
to the ends of the earth:
Say to the daughter of Zion,
"See, your salvation comes;
see, His reward is with Him,
and His recompense before Him."
12 They shall call them The Holy People,
the Redeemed of the LORD;
and you shall be called Sought Out,
a City Not Forsaken.

The Revenge of God

63 "Who is this who comes from Edom
with dyed garments from Bozrah?
This one who is glorious in His apparel,
traveling in the greatness of His
strength?"

"It is I who speak in righteousness,
mighty to save."

2 "Why is Your apparel red,
and Your garments like him who treads
in the wine vat?"

3 "I have trodden the winepress alone;
and from the peoples there was no one
with Me.
For I will tread them in My anger,
and trample them in My fury,
and their blood shall be sprinkled upon My
garments,
and I will stain all My raiment.
4 For the day of vengeance is in My heart,
and My year of redemption has come.
5 I looked and there was no one to help,
and I was astonished, and there was no
one to uphold;
therefore, My own arm brought salvation
to Me;
and My fury upheld Me.
6 I will tread down the peoples in My anger
and make them drunk in My fury,
and I will pour out their lifeblood on the
earth."

62:8 Dt 28:33
62:9 Dt 12:12
62:10 Isa 57:14
62:11 Zec 9:9
62:12 Isa 62:4
63:3 Mic 7:10
63:4 Isa 34:8
63:5 Ps 44:3
63:6 Isa 49:26

63:7 Ps 51:1
63:9 Dt 7:7–8
63:10 Ps 78:40
63:11 Nu 11:17
63:15 Dt 26:15
63:16 Isa 44:6

The Mercy of God Remembered

7 I will mention the steadfast love of the LORD
and the praises of the LORD,
according to all that the LORD has
bestowed on us,
and the great goodness toward the house
of Israel,
which He has bestowed on them
according to His mercy,
and according to the multitude of His
kindnesses.
8 For He said, "Surely they are My people,
sons who will not lie."
So He became their Savior.
9 In all their affliction He was afflicted,
and the angel of His presence saved
them;
in His love and in His mercy He redeemed
them;
and He lifted them and carried them
all the days of old.
10 But they rebelled
and grieved His Holy Spirit;
therefore, He turned Himself to be their
enemy,
and He fought against them.

11 Then His people remembered the days of
old,
of Moses, saying:
Where is He who brought them up out of
the sea
with the shepherds of His flock?
Where is He who put
His Holy Spirit in their midst,
12 who led them with His glorious arm
by the right hand of Moses,
dividing the water before them,
to make Himself an everlasting name,
13 who led them through the deep,
as a horse in the wilderness,
that they should not stumble?
14 As the cattle which go down into the valley,
the Spirit of the LORD caused them to
rest,
so You led Your people,
to make Yourself a glorious name.

A Prayer of Penitence

15 Look down from heaven and see,
from Your holy and glorious habitation.
Where are Your zeal and Your strength?
The stirrings of Your heart and Your
mercies toward me are restrained.
16 For You are our Father,
though Abraham is ignorant of us
and Israel does not recognize us.
You, O LORD, are our Father, our Redeemer;
Your name is from everlasting.

SPIRITLED WOMAN

COUNSEL FROM THE SPIRIT BASICS

The Might of His Church

The church of Jesus Christ has far more might than it realizes. We can penetrate heaven with our prayers and see the power of God released. Our access to God grants us enormous privileges. The church literally can tear the heavens open and summon the power of God. We can petition Him and cause heaven to react to what we pray. God's Word says that supernatural acts are available from a supernatural God to a certain kind of people. To people who will love Him, God is willing to give unlimited favor and miracles.

Paul the Apostle wrote, "Blessed be the God and Father of our Lord Jesus Christ, who has blessed us with every spiritual blessing in the heavenly places in Christ" (Eph 1:3). If the blessings of God are in the heavenly realms, how do we bring them down?

Isaiah prayed, "Oh, that You would rend the heavens and come down" (Isa 64:1). He was asking God to tear open the heavens and come down and manifest Himself in two very specific ways: (1) to make Himself known to the enemy in aggressive, destructive action; and (2) to come in mercy and love to His people (vv. 2, 8–9). To *rend* means "to tear, to rip to pieces, to part." We can stimulate the heart of God to open the windows of heaven for blessing in our lives.

Through a lifestyle of prayer and humble obedience, you can rend the heavens. Then the Holy Spirit can impart His anointing for your service unto God. Isaiah 64:4 states that no one has ever seen and no ear perceived what God will do for the one who waits on Him. This kind of waiting is not passive. It is serving with expectancy and patience, ministering to God in worship and prayer and knowing that He will act on your behalf.

Pat Francis

63:17 Nu 10:36
63:18 Ps 74:3–7
64:1 Mic 1:3–4
64:2 Ps 99:1
64:4 Ps 31:19
64:5 Ex 20:24
64:6 Ps 90:5–6
64:8 Isa 63:16

17 O LORD, why have You made us to err from
Your ways
and hardened our heart from fearing
You?
Return for Your servants' sake,
the tribes of Your inheritance.
18 Your holy people possessed Your sanctuary
for a little while;
our adversaries have trodden it down.
19 We have become
as those over whom You have never
ruled,
as those who were not called by Your
name.

64 Oh, that You would rend the heavens
and come down,
that the mountains might shake at Your
presence,
2 as when the melting fire burns,
as the fire causes the waters to boil,
to make Your name known to Your
adversaries,
that the nations may tremble at Your
presence!
3 When You did awesome things *for which*
we did not look,
You came down; the mountains quaked
at Your presence.
4 For since the beginning of the world men
have not heard,
nor perceived by ear,
neither has the eye seen a God besides
You,
who acts for the one who waits for Him.
5 You meet him who rejoices in doing
righteousness,
those who remember You in Your ways.
Indeed, You were angry, for we had sinned;
in *our sins* we remained a long time,
and shall we be saved?
6 But we all are as an unclean thing,
and all our righteousness is as filthy
rags;
and we all fade as a leaf,
and our iniquities, like the wind, have
taken us away.
7 There is no one who calls on Your name,
who stirs up himself to take hold of You;
for You have hidden Your face from us
and have consumed us because of our
iniquities.
8 But now, O LORD, You are our Father;
we are the clay, and You are our potter;
and we all are the work of Your hand.
9 Do not be wrathful beyond measure, O
LORD,
nor remember iniquity forever;
look upon us, we pray,

we all are Your people.
[10]Your holy cities are a wilderness;
Zion is a wilderness, Jerusalem a desolation.
[11]Our holy and beautiful house where our fathers praised You
is burned up with fire;
and all our precious things are laid waste.
[12]Will You refrain Yourself from these things, O LORD?
Will You hold Your peace and afflict us beyond measure?

Judgment and Salvation

65 I was sought by those who did not ask for Me;
I was found of those who did not seek Me.
I said, "Here I am, here I am,"
to a nation that did not call on My name.
[2] I have spread out My hands all day
to a rebellious people
who walk in a way that was not good,
after their own thoughts;
[3] a people who provoke Me continually
to My face,
presenting sacrifices in gardens
and burning incense on altars of brick;
[4] who sit among the graves
and lodge in the monuments;
who eat swine's flesh,
and the broth of abominable things is in their vessels;
[5] who say, "Stand by yourself; do not come near to me,
for I am holier than you!"
These are smoke in My nose,
a fire that burns all day.
[6] See, it is written before Me:
I will not keep silent, but I will recompense,
even recompense into their bosom,
[7] your iniquities and the iniquities of your fathers together,
says the LORD;
because they have burned incense on the mountains
and blasphemed Me on the hills,
therefore, I will measure their former work
into their bosom.

[8]Thus says the LORD:

As the new wine is found in the cluster,
and one says, "Do not destroy it
for a blessing is in it,"
so I will do for the sake of My servants
that I may not destroy them all.
[9] I will bring forth descendants from Jacob,

64:10 Isa 1:7
64:11 2Ki 25:9
64:12 Isa 42:14
65:1 Ro 10:20
65:2 Ro 10:21
65:3 Isa 1:29
65:4 Lev 11:7
65:5 Mt 9:11
65:6 Ps 50:3
65:7 Ex 20:5
65:9 Am 9:11–15

65:10 Isa 35:2
65:11 Isa 1:28
65:12 Jer 7:13
65:14 Mt 8:12
65:15 Zec 8:13
65:16 Ps 31:5
65:17 2Pe 3:13
65:18 Ps 98:1–9
65:19 Isa 35:10

and out of Judah an inheritor of My mountains;
and My chosen ones shall inherit it,
and My servants shall dwell there.
[10]Sharon shall be a fold of flocks,
and the Valley of Achor a place for the herds to lie down in,
for My people who seek Me.

[11]But you are those who forsake the LORD,
who forget My holy mountain,
who prepare a table for Fortune,
and who furnish the drink offering for Destiny.
[12]I will destine you for the sword,
and you all shall bow down to the slaughter;
because when I called, you did not answer;
when I spoke, you did not hear
but did evil before My eyes
and chose that in which I did not delight.

[13]Therefore, thus says the Lord GOD:

My servants shall eat,
but you shall be hungry;
My servants shall drink,
but you shall be thirsty;
My servants shall rejoice,
but you shall be ashamed;
[14]My servants shall sing for joy
with a glad heart,
but you shall cry
with a heavy heart
and shall wail with grief of spirit.
[15]You shall leave your name
for a curse to My chosen ones;
for the Lord GOD shall slay you,
but My servants shall be called by another name;
[16]because he who is blessed in the earth
shall bless himself in the God of truth;
and he who swears in the earth
shall swear by the God of truth;
because the former troubles are forgotten
and because they are hidden from My eyes.

The New Creation

[17]For I create
new heavens and a new earth;
the former things shall not be remembered
or come to mind.
[18]But be glad and rejoice forever
in that which I create;
for I create Jerusalem for rejoicing
and her people for joy.
[19]I will rejoice in Jerusalem
and be glad in My people;
and the voice of weeping shall no longer be heard in her,
nor the voice of crying.

[20]There shall no longer be
an infant *who lives only a few* days
nor an old man who has not filled out
his days.
For the child shall die
a hundred years old,
but the sinner being a hundred years old
shall be accursed.
[21]They shall build houses and inhabit them;
and they shall plant vineyards and eat
the fruit of them.
[22]They shall not build and another inhabit;
they shall not plant and another eat;
for as the days of a tree
are the days of My people,
and My chosen ones shall long enjoy
the work of their hands.
[23]They shall not labor in vain
nor bring forth children for trouble;
for they are the descendants of the blessed
of the LORD
and their offspring with them.
[24]Before they call, I will answer;
and while they are yet speaking, I will
hear.
[25]The wolf and the lamb shall feed together,
and the lion shall eat straw like the bull,
and dust shall be the serpent's food.
They shall not hurt nor destroy
in all My holy mountain,
says the LORD.

True Worship

66 Thus says the LORD:

Heaven is My throne,
and the earth is My footstool.
Where then is the house that you could
build for Me?
And where is the place of My rest?
[2] For My hand made all those things,
thus all those things have come to be,
says the LORD.

But to this man I will look,
even to him who is poor and of a
contrite spirit,
and trembles at My word.
[3] He who kills a bull
is as if he kills a man;
he who sacrifices a lamb,
as if he breaks a dog's neck;
he who offers a grain offering,
as if he offers swine's blood;
he who burns incense,
as if he blesses an idol.
They have chosen their own ways,
and their soul delights in their
abominations;
[4] I also will choose their punishments
and will bring their fears on them,
because when I called, no one answered;
when I spoke, they did not listen;
but they did evil before My eyes
and chose that in which I did not delight.

The Vindication of Zion

[5] Hear the word of the LORD,
you who tremble at His word:
Your brothers who hate you,
who cast you out for My name's sake,
said,
"Let the LORD be glorified
that we may see your joy."
Yet they shall be ashamed.
[6] A voice of noise from the city,
a voice from the temple,
the voice of the LORD
who renders recompense to His
enemies.

[7] Before she was in labor,
she gave birth;
before her pain came,
she delivered a son.
[8] Who has heard such a thing?
Who has seen such things?
Shall the earth be made to give birth in one
day?
Shall a nation be born at once?
For as soon as Zion was in labor,
she brought forth her sons.
[9] Shall I bring to the point of birth
and not cause delivery? says the LORD.
Shall I who cause delivery
shut *the womb*? says your God.
[10]Rejoice with Jerusalem and be glad for her,
all you who love her;
rejoice exceedingly with her,
all you who mourn for her,
[11]that you may feed and be satisfied
with her consoling breasts,
that you may feed
and be delighted with the abundance of
her bosom.
[12]For thus says the LORD:

I will extend peace to her like a river
and the glory of the nations like a
flowing stream.
Then you shall nurse, you shall be carried
on her sides,
and dandled on her knees.
[13]As one whom his mother comforts,
so I will comfort you;
and you shall be comforted in
Jerusalem.

God's Reign and Final Judgment

[14]Then you shall see this, and your heart
shall rejoice,

65:21 Am 9:14
65:22 Ps 92:12–14
65:23 Isa 61:9
65:24 Da 9:20–23
66:1 1Ki 8:27
66:2 Isa 57:15
66:3 Lev 2:2
66:4 Isa 65:12
....
66:5 Ps 38:20
66:6 Isa 59:18
66:7 Isa 54:1
66:8 Isa 64:4
66:9 Isa 37:3
66:10 Dt 32:43
66:11 Isa 60:16
66:12 Isa 48:18
66:13 Isa 51:3
66:14 Ezr 8:31

and your bones shall flourish like an
herb;
and the hand of the LORD shall be known
toward His servants,
and His indignation toward His enemies.
15 For the LORD shall come with fire
and with His chariots like a whirlwind,
to render His anger with fury
and His rebuke with flames of fire.
16 For by fire and by His sword on all flesh,
the LORD shall execute judgment;
and the slain of the LORD shall be many.

17 Those who sanctify themselves and purify
themselves in the gardens behind one tree in
the midst, eating swine's flesh, and abomina-
ble things, and mice shall be consumed togeth-
er, says the LORD.
18 For I know their works and their thoughts.
The time shall come to gather all nations and
tongues. And they shall come and see My
glory.
19 I will set a sign among them, and send
from them survivors to the nations: to Tarshish,

66:17 Isa 65:3–4
66:18 Isa 2:2
66:19 Eze 27:10

66:21 Ex 19:6
66:22 Isa 65:17
66:23 Eze 46:1
66:24 Isa 14:11

Pul, and Lud—who draw the bow—to Tubal,
and Javan, to the coastlands afar off who have
not heard My fame nor seen My glory. And
they shall declare My glory among the nations.
20 They shall bring all your brothers out of all
nations as an offering to the LORD on horses,
and in chariots, and in litters, and on mules,
and on swift beasts to My holy mountain Jeru-
salem, says the LORD, as the sons of Israel bring
an offering in a clean vessel into the house of
the LORD. 21 I will also take some of them for
priests and for Levites, says the LORD.

22 For as the new heavens and the new earth
which I will make shall remain before Me, says
the LORD, so shall your descendants and your
name remain. 23 From one New Moon to an-
other, and from one Sabbath to another, all
flesh shall come to worship before Me, says
the LORD. 24 And they shall go forth and look on
the corpses of the men who have transgressed
against Me. For their worm shall not die, nor
shall their fire be quenched. And they shall be
an abhorrence to all flesh.

Author: The prophet Jeremiah

Written: Between 630 and 580 BC

Themes: Warning, Judgment

JEREMIAH

Dear Spirit Led Woman,

In the middle of a difficult time you can feel abandoned by God and wonder where He is. You may feel that you are going through the "dark night of the soul." But you are not alone. God has not and will not abandon you. In the Book of Jeremiah He promised, "You shall seek Me and find Me, when you shall search for Me with all your heart" (Jer 29:13). And in Hebrews He tells us, "I will never leave you, nor forsake you" (Heb 13:5).

When you take your eyes off your circumstances and look for God in the situation, you'll find Him. Choose to look at your situation through spiritual eyes, based on what the Word of God says, rather than viewing it from a natural perspective and allowing your senses, your reason, or your feelings to dictate how you respond.

Joy F. Strang

The Commission of Jeremiah

1 The words of Jeremiah the son of Hilkiah,
of the priests who were in Anathoth in the
land of Benjamin, 2 to whom the word of the
LORD came in the days of Josiah the son of
Amon, king of Judah, in the thirteenth year
of his reign. 3 It came also in the days of Je-
hoiakim the son of Josiah, king of Judah, to
the end of the eleventh year of Zedekiah the
son of Josiah, king of Judah, until the captivity
of Jerusalem in the fifth month.

4 Now the word of the LORD came to me,
saying,

5 "Before I formed you in the womb I knew
you;
and before you were born I sanctified
you,
and I ordained you a prophet to the
nations."

6 Then I said, "Ah, Lord GOD! Truly, I cannot
speak, for I am a youth."

7 But the LORD said to me, "Do not say, 'I am a
youth.' For you shall go everywhere that I send
you, and whatever I command you, you shall
speak. 8 Do not be afraid of their faces. For I
am with you to deliver you," says the LORD.

9 Then the LORD put forth His hand and
touched my mouth. And the LORD said to me,
"Now, I have put My words in your mouth.
10 See, I have this day set you over the nations
and over the kingdoms, to root out and to pull
down, to destroy and to throw down, to build
and to plant."

Lord, perform Your Word in my life
(Jer 1:12).

The Almond Rod and Boiling Pot

11 Moreover the word of the LORD came to me,
saying, "Jeremiah, what do you see?"

And I said, "I see a branch of an almond
tree."

12 Then the LORD said to me, "You have seen
well. For I will hasten My word to perform it."

13 The word of the LORD came to me the sec-
ond time, saying, "What do you see?"

And I said, "I see a boiling pot, and it is facing
away from the north."

14 Then the LORD said to me: Out of the north
calamity will break forth on all the inhabitants
of the land. 15 For I will call all the families of
the kingdoms of the north, says the LORD.

And they will come and they will set each
one his throne
at the entrance of the gates of
Jerusalem,
and against all the walls all around,
and against all the cities of Judah.
16 I will utter My judgments against them
concerning all their wickedness,
whereby they have forsaken Me
and have burned incense to other gods,
and have worshipped the works of their
own hands.

17 You therefore gird up your loins and arise,
and speak to them all that I command you.
Do not be dismayed at their faces, lest I con-
found you before them. 18 For indeed, I have
made you this day a fortified city and an iron
pillar and bronze walls against the whole
land, against the kings of Judah, against the
officials, against the priests, and against the
people of the land. 19 They will fight against
you, but they will not prevail against you, for
I am with you, says the LORD, to deliver you.

God Pleads With Israel to Repent

2 Moreover the word of the LORD came to
me, saying, 2 Go and proclaim in the ears
of Jerusalem, saying,

Thus says the LORD:
I remember you, the kindness of your
youth,
the love of your espousals,
when you followed Me in the wilderness,
in a land that was not sown.
3 Israel is holy to the LORD,
and the first fruits of His harvest.
All who eat of it will become guilty;
disaster will come upon them,
says the LORD.

4 Hear the word of the LORD, O house of
Jacob
and all the families of the house of
Israel.
5 Thus says the LORD:

What iniquity have your fathers found
in Me,
that they have gone far from Me,
and have walked after vanity
and have become vain?
6 They did not say, "Where is the LORD
who brought us up out of the land of
Egypt,
who led us through the wilderness,
through a land of deserts and of pits,
through a land of drought and of the
shadow of death,
through a land that no man passed
through and where no man lived?"
7 And I brought you into a plentiful country
to eat its fruit and its goodness.
But when you entered, you defiled My land
and made My heritage an abomination.

1:1 1Ch 6:60
1:5 Isa 49:1
1:6 Ex 6:12
1:7 Nu 22:20
1:8 Ex 3:12
1:10 Jer 31:28
1:11 Am 7:8
1:15 Jer 4:16

1:16 Jer 7:9
1:17 1Ki 18:46
1:18 Isa 50:7
1:19 Jer 1:8
2:2 Dt 2:7
2:3 Jas 1:18
2:5 2Ki 17:15
2:6 Dt 32:10
2:7 Dt 8:7–9

[8] The priests did not say,
"Where is the LORD?"
And those who handle the law did not
know Me;
the shepherds also transgressed against
Me,
and the prophets prophesied by Baal
and walked after things that do not
profit.
[9] Therefore I will yet contend with you,
says the LORD,
and with your sons' sons I will contend.
[10] For pass over the coastlands of Cyprus and
see,
and send to Kedar and consider
diligently,
and see if there is such a thing.
[11] Has a nation changed their gods,
though they are not gods?
But My people have changed their glory
for that which does not profit.
[12] Be astonished at this, O heavens,
and be horribly afraid, be very desolate,
says the LORD.
[13] For My people have committed two evils.
They have forsaken Me,
the fountain of living waters,
and hewed out for themselves cisterns,
broken cisterns, that can hold no water.
[14] Is Israel a servant? Is he a homeborn slave?
Why has he been plundered?
[15] The young lions roared at him
and roared loudly,
and they made his land a waste;
his cities have been destroyed, without
inhabitant.
[16] Also the men of Memphis and Tahpanhes
have shaved the crown of your head.
[17] Have you not brought this on yourself,
in that you have forsaken the LORD your
God
when He led you in the way?
[18] And now what are you doing in the way of
Egypt,
to drink the waters of the Nile?
Or what are you doing in the way of
Assyria,
to drink the waters of the River?
[19] Your own wickedness will correct you,
and your backslidings will reprove you.
Know therefore and see
that it is an evil thing and bitter for you
to have forsaken the LORD your God,
and the fear of Me is not in you,
says the Lord GOD of Hosts.
[20] For long ago I have broken your yoke
and burst your bonds;
and you said, "I will not serve."

2:8 Hab 2:18
2:9 Eze 20:35–36
2:10 Ps 120:5
2:11 Ps 106:20
2:12 Isa 1:2
2:13 Ps 36:9
2:14 Ex 4:22
2:15 Jer 4:7
2:16 Jer 46:14
2:17 Jer 4:18
2:18 Jos 13:3
2:19 Isa 3:9
2:20 Dt 12:2

....

2:21 Ex 15:17
2:23 Jer 7:31
2:24 Jer 14:6
2:25 Dt 32:16
2:26 Jer 32:32
2:27 Isa 26:16
2:28 Dt 32:37
2:29 Jer 5:1
2:30 Ne 9:26
2:31 Dt 32:15

For upon every high hill
and under every green tree
you wander, playing the harlot.
[21] Yet I had planted you a noble vine,
a wholly faithful seed.
How then have you turned
into the degenerate plant of a strange
vine to Me?
[22] For though you wash yourself with lye,
and take much soap,
yet your iniquity is marked before Me,
says the Lord GOD.
[23] How can you say, "I am not polluted,
I have not gone after the Baals"?
See your way in the valley.
Know what you have done.
You are a swift young camel
entangling her ways,
[24] a wild donkey used to the wilderness
that sniffs the wind in her passion.
In the time of her heat, who can turn her
away?
All those who seek her will not weary
themselves;
in her month they shall find her.
[25] Withhold your foot from being unshod
and your throat from thirst.
But you said, "There is no hope. No!
For I have loved strangers,
and after them I will go."
[26] As the thief is ashamed when he is found,
so is the house of Israel ashamed.
They, their kings, their officials,
and their priests, and their prophets
[27] say to a tree, "You are my father."
And to a stone, "You gave birth to me."
For they have turned their back to Me,
and not their face.
But in the time of their trouble they will
say,
"Arise and save us."
[28] But where are your gods that you have
made for yourself?
Let them arise, if they can save you
in the time of your trouble;
for according to the number of your cities
are your gods, O Judah.
[29] Why will you plead with Me?
You all have transgressed against Me,
says the LORD.
[30] In vain I have smitten your children;
they received no correction.
Your own sword has devoured your
prophets
like a destroying lion.

[31] O generation, consider the word of the
LORD:

Have I been a wilderness to Israel?
A land of darkness?
Why do My people say, "We *are free* to
roam.
We will come no more to You"?
32 Can a virgin forget her ornaments,
or a bride her attire?
Yet My people have forgotten Me
for days without number.
33 You prepare your way very well to seek
love.
Therefore you have also taught the
wicked women your ways.
34 Also in your skirts is found
the blood of the souls of the innocent
poor.
I have not found it by breaking in,
but in spite of all these things.
35 Yet you say, "Because I am innocent,
surely His anger shall turn away
from me."
Now I will plead with you,
because you say, "I have not sinned."
36 Why do you go about so much
to change your way?
You also shall be ashamed of Egypt,
as you were ashamed of Assyria.
37 Indeed, you shall go forth from him
with your hands upon your head;
for the LORD has rejected those in whom
you trust,
and you shall not prosper in them.

Unfaithful Israel

3 If a man divorces his wife,
and she goes from him and becomes
another man's,
shall he return to her again?
Shall not that land be greatly polluted?
But you have played the harlot with many
lovers;
yet return again to Me,
says the LORD.
2 Lift up your eyes to the high places,
and see! Where have you not been
ravished?
In the roads you have sat for them
as the Arabian in the wilderness.
And you have polluted the land
with your harlotry and with your
wickedness.
3 Therefore the showers have been withheld,
and there has been no latter rain.
And you had a harlot's forehead;
you refused to be ashamed.
4 Shall you not from this time cry to Me,
"My Father, You are the guide of my
youth?
5 Shall He reserve His anger forever?
Shall He keep it to the end?"
Indeed, you have spoken
and done evil things as you could.

A Call to Repentance

6 The LORD said also to me in the days of Jo-
siah the king: Have you seen that which back-
sliding Israel has done? She has gone up on
every high mountain and under every green
tree, and there has played the harlot. 7 I said
after she had done all these things, "Turn to
Me." But she did not return. And her treach-
erous sister Judah saw it. 8 I saw that for all
the adulteries of backsliding Israel, I had put
her away and given her a bill of divorce. Yet
her treacherous sister Judah did not fear, but
went and played the harlot also. 9 Through the
lightness of her harlotry she defiled the land
and committed adultery with stones and with
trees. 10 Yet for all this, her treacherous sister
Judah has not turned to Me with her whole
heart, but feignedly, says the LORD.

God Invites Repentance

11 The LORD said to me: Backsliding Israel has
proved herself more righteous than treacher-
ous Judah. 12 Go and proclaim these words
toward the north, and say:

Return, backsliding Israel, says the LORD,
and I will not cause My anger to fall on
you.
For I am merciful, says the LORD,
and I will not keep anger forever.
13 Only acknowledge your iniquity,
that you have transgressed against the
LORD your God
and have scattered your ways to the
strangers
under every green tree,
and you have not obeyed My voice,
says the LORD.

14 Return, O backsliding sons, says the LORD.
For I am married to you. And I will take you,
one from a city and two from a family, and I
will bring you to Zion. 15 And I will give you
shepherds according to My heart, who shall
feed you with knowledge and understanding.
16 It shall come to pass when you are multiplied
and increased in the land in those days, says
the LORD, they will say no more, "The ark of the
covenant of the LORD." And it will not come to
mind, nor will they remember it, nor will they
call for it, nor will it be made any more. 17 At
that time they will call Jerusalem, the Throne
of the LORD, and all the nations will be gathered
to it, to Jerusalem, for the name of the LORD;
nor will they walk any more after the stub-
bornness of their evil hearts. 18 In those days
the house of Judah will walk with the house of
Israel, and they will come together out of the

2:32 Ps 106:21
2:34 2Ki 21:16
2:35 Pr 28:13
2:36 Jer 31:22
2:37 2Sa 13:19
3:1 Dt 24:1–4
3:2 Ge 38:14
3:3 Jer 6:15
3:4 Jer 2:2
3:5 Isa 57:16
....
3:7 Eze 16:46
3:8 Dt 24:1
3:9 Jer 2:27
3:10 Hos 7:14
3:11 Eze 16:51–52
3:12 Ps 86:15
3:13 Dt 12:2
3:15 Ac 20:28
3:16 Isa 65:17
3:17 Jer 11:8
3:18 Jer 31:8

land of the north to the land that I have given
to your fathers for an inheritance.

[19] But I said:

How can I put you among My sons
and give you a pleasant land,
the most beautiful heritage of the
nations?
And I said: You shall call Me, My Father,
and shall not turn away from Me.
[20] Surely as a wife treacherously departs from
her husband,
so you have dealt treacherously with Me,
O house of Israel,
says the LORD.

[21] A voice was heard upon the high places,
the weeping and the supplications of the
sons of Israel,
because they have perverted their way,
they have forgotten the LORD their God.

[22] Return, O backsliding sons,
and I will heal your backslidings.
"We come to You;
for You are the LORD our God.
[23] Truly in vain is salvation hoped for from
the hills,
and from the multitude of mountains.
Truly, in the LORD our God
is the salvation of Israel.
[24] For shame has devoured the labor
of our fathers from our youth,
their flocks and their herds,
their sons and their daughters.
[25] We lie down in our shame,
and our humiliation covers us.
For we have sinned against the LORD our
God,
we and our fathers,
from our youth even to this day,
and have not obeyed the voice of the
LORD our God."

Judah Threatened With Invasion

4 If you will return, O Israel,
says the LORD,
return to Me.
And if you will put away your
abominations out of My sight,
then you shall not be moved.
[2] You shall swear, "As the LORD lives,"
in truth, in justice, and in righteousness;
then the nations shall bless themselves in
Him,
and in Him they shall glory.

[3] For thus says the LORD to the men of Judah
and Jerusalem:

Break up your fallow ground,
and do not sow among thorns.

3:19 Jer 3:4
3:22 Hos 14:4
3:23 Ps 3:8
3:24 Hos 9:10
3:25 Jer 22:21
4:1 Joel 2:12
4:2 Isa 65:16
4:3 Hos 10:12

....

4:4 Dt 10:16
4:5 Jer 8:14
4:6 Jer 1:13–15
4:7 Jer 2:15
4:8 Isa 22:12
4:10 Jer 5:12
4:11 Eze 17:10
4:12 Jer 1:16
4:13 Isa 5:28
4:14 Jas 4:8

[4] Circumcise yourselves to the LORD,
and take away the foreskins of your
heart,
you men of Judah and inhabitants of
Jerusalem,
lest My fury come forth like fire,
and burn so that no one can quench it,
because of the evil of your deeds.

[5] Declare in Judah and publish in Jerusalem,
and say:
Blow the trumpet in the land.
Cry aloud and say,
"Assemble yourselves,
and let us go into the fortified cities."
[6] Set up the standard toward Zion.
Seek refuge, do not delay.
For I will bring disaster from the north,
and a great destruction.

[7] The lion has come up from his thicket,
and the destroyer of the nations is on
his way.
He has gone forth from his place
to make your land desolate.
And your cities shall be laid waste
without an inhabitant.
[8] For this gird yourself with sackcloth,
lament and howl.
For the fierce anger of the LORD
is not turned back from us.

[9] It shall come to pass in that day, says the
LORD,
that the heart of the king will fail and the
heart of the officials;
and the priests will be astonished
and the prophets will wonder.

[10] Then I said, "Ah, Lord GOD! Surely You have
greatly deceived this people and Jerusalem,
saying, 'You shall have peace,' whereas the
sword reaches the throat."
[11] At that time it will be said to this people and
to Jerusalem: A dry wind of the high places
in the wilderness toward the daughter of My
people, not to fan or to cleanse, [12] even a full
wind from those places, will come to Me. Now
also I will pronounce judgments against them.

[13] Look! He shall come up as clouds,
and his chariots shall be as a whirlwind.
His horses are swifter than eagles.
Woe to us, for we are ruined!

Heavenly Father, I repent of all
disobedience and acts of rebellion
against You (Jer 4:14).

[14] O Jerusalem, wash your heart from
wickedness, that you may be saved.

How long shall your evil thoughts lodge
within you?
15 For a voice declares from Dan,
and publishes wickedness from Mount
Ephraim:
16 "Report it to the nations, now!"
Indeed, proclaim against Jerusalem:
"Besiegers come from a far country,
and lift their voices against the cities of
Judah.
17 As watchmen of a field, they are against
her all around,
because she has been rebellious against
Me,
says the LORD.
18 Your way and your deeds
have procured these things to you.
This is your wickedness.
How bitter it is!
How it touches your heart!"

Sorrow for a Doomed Nation

19 My soul, my soul!
I am pained at my very heart.
My heart makes a noise in me.
I cannot hold my peace,
because you have heard, O my soul,
the sound of the trumpet, the alarm of
war.
20 Destruction upon destruction is
proclaimed,
for the whole land is devastated.
Suddenly are my tents devastated,
and my curtains in a moment.
21 How long shall I see the standard
and hear the sound of the trumpet?

22 "For My people are foolish,
they have not known Me.
They are foolish children,
and they have no understanding.
They are wise to do evil,
but to do good they have no
knowledge."

23 I looked on the earth,
and it was without form and void.
And to the heavens,
and they had no light.
24 I looked on the mountains,
and they trembled,
and all the hills moved to and fro.
25 I looked, and there was no man,
and all the birds of the heavens had fled.
26 I looked, and the fruitful place was a
wilderness,
and all the cities were broken down
at the presence of the LORD, and by His
fierce anger.

4:15 Jer 8:16
4:16 Jer 5:15
4:17 Jer 5:23
4:18 Jer 2:19
4:19 Isa 16:11
4:20 Ps 42:7
4:22 Ro 16:19
4:23 Ge 1:2
4:24 Isa 5:25
4:26 Ps 107:34

4:27 Jer 5:10
4:28 Nu 23:19
4:30 2Ki 9:30
4:31 Isa 1:15
5:1 2Ch 16:9
5:2 Titus 1:16
5:3 Jer 2:30
5:4 Jer 8:7

27 For thus says the LORD:

The whole land shall be desolate.
Yet I will not make a full end.
28 For this the earth shall mourn,
and the heavens above be black,
because I have spoken it, I have
purposed it,
and will not relent, nor will I turn back
from it.

29 The whole city shall flee
for the noise of the horsemen and
bowmen.
They shall go into thickets
and climb up upon the rocks.
Every city shall be forsaken,
and not a man dwell in it.

30 When you are devastated, what will
you do?
Though you clothe yourself with
crimson,
though you deck yourself with
ornaments of gold,
though you enlarge your eyes with paint,
in vain you will make yourself fair.
Your lovers will despise you;
they will seek your life.

31 For I have heard a voice as of a woman in
labor,
and the anguish as of her who brings
forth her first child,
the voice of the daughter of Zion,
that bewails herself, that spreads her
hands, saying,
"Ah, woe is me,
for my soul is wearied because of
murderers."

The Justice of God's Judgment

5 Run to and fro through the streets of
Jerusalem,
see now and know;
seek in the open places
if you can find a man,
if there is any who executes justice, who
seeks the truth,
that I may pardon her.
2 Though they say, "The LORD lives,"
surely they swear falsely.

3 O LORD, are not Your eyes upon the truth?
You have stricken them, but they have
not grieved.
You have consumed them, but they have
refused to receive correction.
They have made their faces harder than a
rock;
they have refused to return.
4 Therefore I said, "Surely these are the poor.
They are foolish;

for they know not the way of the LORD
or the judgment of their God.
5 I will go to the great men
and will speak to them,
for they have known the way of the LORD
and the judgment of their God."
But these have altogether broken the yoke
and burst the bonds.
6 Therefore a lion out of the forest will slay
them,
and a wolf from the deserts will destroy
them;
a leopard will watch over their cities.
Everyone who goes out from there will
be torn in pieces,
because their transgressions are many
and their backslidings have increased.

7 How shall I pardon you for this?
Your children have forsaken Me
and sworn by those who are not gods.
When I had fed them to the full,
then they committed adultery
and assembled themselves by troops in
the harlots' houses.
8 They were as fed horses in the morning;
everyone neighed after his neighbor's
wife.
9 Shall I not punish for these things? says the
LORD,
and shall not My soul be avenged on
such a nation as this?

10 Go up upon her walls and destroy,
but make not a full end.
Take away her battlements.
For they are not the LORD's.
11 For the house of Israel and the house of
Judah
have dealt very treacherously
against Me,
says the LORD.

12 They have lied about the LORD,
and said, "Not He.
Neither shall evil come upon us,
nor shall we see sword or famine."
13 And the prophets shall become wind,
and the word is not in them.
Thus it shall be done to them!

14 Therefore thus says the LORD God of Hosts:
Because you speak this word,
indeed I will make My words in your
mouth fire
and this people wood, and it shall
devour them.
15 Truly, I will bring a nation upon you from
far,
O house of Israel, says the LORD.
It is a mighty nation, it is an ancient nation,

5:5 Jer 2:20
5:6 Jer 4:7
5:7 Dt 32:21
5:8 Jer 13:27
5:9 Jer 9:9
5:10 Jer 4:27
5:11 Jer 3:20
5:12 2Ch 36:16
5:13 Jer 14:15
5:14 Jer 1:9
5:15 Dt 28:49

....

5:16 Ps 5:9
5:17 Lev 26:16
5:19 1Ki 9:8–9
5:21 Isa 6:9–10
5:22 Ps 119:120
5:23 Jer 6:28
5:24 Ge 8:22
5:25 Jer 3:3
5:26 Pr 1:11

a nation whose language you do not
know,
nor do you understand what they say.
16 Their quiver is as an open sepulcher,
they all are mighty men.
17 They will eat up your harvest and your
bread
which your sons and your daughters
should eat.
They will eat up your flocks and your
herds;
they will eat up your vines and your fig
trees;
they will impoverish your fenced cities,
in which you trusted, with the sword.

18 Nevertheless in those days, says the LORD, I
will not make a full end of you. 19 It shall come
to pass when they say, "Why does the LORD our
God do all these things to us?" then you shall
answer them, "As you have forsaken Me and
served strange gods in your land, so you will
serve strangers in a land that is not yours."

20 Declare this in the house of Jacob
and publish it in Judah, saying:
21 Hear this now, O foolish people and
without understanding,
who have eyes but do not see,
who have ears but do not hear.
22 Do you not fear Me? says the LORD.
Will you not tremble at My presence?
For I have placed the sand for the
boundary of the sea
by a perpetual decree so that it cannot
pass over it.
And though the waves toss themselves, yet
they cannot prevail;
though they roar, yet they cannot pass
over it.
23 But this people has a revolting and a
rebellious heart;
they have revolted and gone aside.
24 They do not say in their heart,
"Let us now fear the LORD our God,
who gives rain, both the former and the
latter, in its season.
He reserves for us the appointed weeks
of the harvest."
25 Your iniquities have turned away these
things,
and your sins have withheld good things
from you.

26 For among My people are found wicked
men.
They lie in wait, as he who sets snares;
they set a trap, they catch men.
27 As a cage is full of birds,
so are their houses full of deceit.

Therefore they have become great and
rich.
28 They are fat, they are sleek.
Indeed, they excel in deeds of wickedness.
They do not judge the cause of the
fatherless,
so that they may prosper;
and the right of the needy they do not
defend.
29 Shall I not punish them for these things?
says the LORD.
Shall not My soul be avenged
on such a nation as this?
30 An appalling and horrible thing
has been committed in the land.
31 The prophets prophesy falsely,
and the priests rule by their own
authority;
and My people love to have it so.
Yet what will you do in the end?

Siege of Jerusalem

6 O sons of Benjamin, gather yourselves
to flee from the midst of Jerusalem,
and blow the trumpet in Tekoa,
and set up a sign of fire in Beth
Hakkerem;
for disaster appears out of the north,
and great destruction.
2 I have likened the daughter of Zion
to a comely and delicate woman.
3 The shepherds with their flocks will come
to her.
They will pitch their tents against her all
around.
They will pasture each in his place.
4 "Prepare war against her;
arise, and let us go up at noon."
"Woe to us, for the day declines,
for the shadows of the evening are
stretched out."
5 "Arise, and let us go by night
and let us destroy her palaces."

6 For thus says the LORD of Hosts:

Hew down trees
and build a mound against Jerusalem.
This is the city to be punished.
She *is* full of oppression in her midst.
7 As a fountain casts out her waters,
so she casts out her wickedness.
Violence and devastation are heard in her;
before Me continually are grief and
wounds.
8 Be instructed, O Jerusalem,
lest My soul depart from you;
lest I make you desolate,
a land not inhabited.

9 Thus says the LORD of Hosts:

They will thoroughly glean
the remnant of Israel as a vine.
Turn back your hand
as a grape gatherer into the baskets.
10 To whom shall I speak and give warning
that they may hear?
See, their ears are closed,
and they cannot listen.
Indeed, the word of the LORD is a reproach
to them;
they have no delight in it.
11 Therefore I am full of the fury of the LORD;
I am weary with holding in.
I will pour it out upon the children in the
street
and upon the assembly of young men
together;
for even the husband with the wife shall
be taken,
the aged with him who is full of days.
12 Their houses shall be turned to others,
with their fields and wives together;
for I will stretch out My hand
upon the inhabitants of the land,
says the LORD.
13 For from the least of them even to the
greatest of them,
everyone is given to covetousness.
And from the prophet even to the priest,
everyone deals falsely.
14 They have healed also the brokenness
of the daughter of My people
superficially,
saying, "Peace, peace,"
when there is no peace.
15 Were they ashamed when they had
committed abomination?
They were not at all ashamed,
nor could they blush.
Therefore they shall fall among those who
fall;
at the time that I punish them they shall
be cast down,
says the LORD.

16 Thus says the LORD

Stand in the ways and see,
and ask for the old paths
where the good way is and walk in it,
and you shall find rest for your souls.
But they said, "We will not walk in it."
17 Also I set watchmen over you, saying,
"Listen to the sound of the trumpet."
But they said, "We will not listen."
18 Therefore hear, O nations,
and know, O congregation,
what is among them.

5:28 Dt 32:15
5:29 Jer 5:9
5:30 Jer 23:14
5:31 Eze 13:6
6:1 Ne 3:14
6:3 Lk 19:43
6:4 Jer 15:8
6:7 Eze 7:11
6:8 Eze 23:18
6:10 Ac 7:51
6:11 Jer 9:21
6:12 Jer 8:10
6:13 Jer 8:10
6:14 Eze 13:10
6:15 Jer 3:3
6:16 Jer 18:15
6:17 Isa 21:11

19 Hear, O earth.
I will bring calamity on this people,
even the fruit of their thoughts,
because they have not listened to My
words,
nor to My law, but rejected it.
20 To what purpose does incense from Sheba
come to Me,
and the sweet cane from a far country?
Your burnt offerings are not acceptable,
nor are your sacrifices sweet to Me.

21 Therefore thus says the LORD:

See, I will lay stumbling blocks before this
people,
and the fathers and the sons together
will fall upon them.
The neighbor and his friend will perish.

22 Thus says the LORD:

See, a people comes
from the north country,
and a great nation will be raised
from the remote parts of the earth.
23 They will lay hold on bow and spear;
they are cruel and have no mercy.
Their voice roars like the sea,
and they ride upon horses,
set in array as men for war
against you, O daughter of Zion.
24 "We have heard the report of it;
our hands grow feeble.
Anguish has taken hold of us,
and pain as of a woman in labor.
25 Do not go out into the field,
nor walk on the road.
For the sword of the enemy
and terror is on every side."
26 O daughter of my people, gird yourself
with sackcloth
and wallow in ashes.
Mourn as for an only son,
a most bitter lamentation;
for the destroyer
shall suddenly come upon us.

27 I have set you as an assayer
and fortress among My people
that you may know
and try their way.
28 They all are stubborn rebels
walking about practicing slander.
They are bronze and iron;
they all are corrupters.
29 The bellows blow fiercely,
the lead is consumed by the fire;
the founder melts in vain,
for the wicked are not plucked away.
30 Men will call them rejected silver,
because the LORD has rejected them.

6:19 Jer 8:9
6:20 Isa 1:11
6:21 Isa 8:14
6:22 Jer 10:22
6:23 Isa 13:18
6:24 Jer 4:31
6:25 Jer 49:29
6:26 Jer 4:8
6:27 Jer 1:18
6:28 Jer 9:4
6:30 Ps 119:119

7:2 Jer 26:2
7:3 Jer 18:11
7:4 Mic 3:11
7:6 Dt 8:19
7:7 Dt 4:40
7:8 Jer 7:4
7:9 Ex 20:3
7:10 Jer 32:34
7:11 Isa 56:7
7:12 1Sa 4:10–11
7:13 Isa 65:12
7:16 Ex 32:10
7:18 Jer 19:13
7:19 1Co 10:22
7:20 Jer 42:18

False Trust in the Temple

7 The word that came to Jeremiah from
the LORD, saying: 2 Stand in the gate of
the house of the LORD and proclaim there this
word:

Hear the word of the LORD, all you of Judah,
who enter at these gates to worship the LORD.
3 Thus says the LORD of Hosts, the God of Is-
rael: Amend your ways and your deeds, and I
will cause you to dwell in this place. 4 Do not
trust in lying words, saying, "The temple of
the LORD, the temple of the LORD, the temple
of the LORD." 5 For if you thoroughly amend
your ways and your deeds, if you thoroughly
execute justice between a man and his neigh-
bor, 6 if you do not oppress the stranger, the
fatherless, and the widow, and do not shed
innocent blood in this place, or walk after other
gods to your harm, 7 then I will cause you to
dwell in this place, in the land that I gave to
your fathers, forever and ever. 8 Indeed, you
trust in lying words that cannot profit.

9 Shall you steal, murder, and commit adul-
tery, and swear falsely, and burn incense to
Baal, and walk after other gods whom you do
not know, 10 and come and stand before Me in
this house, which is called by My name, and
say, "We are delivered," so that you may do all
these abominations? 11 Has this house, which is
called by My name, become a den of robbers
in your eyes? Certainly, even I have seen it,
says the LORD.

12 But go now to My place which was in Shi-
loh, where I set My name at the first, and see
what I did to it for the wickedness of My people
Israel. 13 And now, because you have done all
these works, says the LORD, and I spoke to you,
rising up early and speaking, but you did not
hear, and I called you, but you did not answer,
14 therefore I will do to this house, which is
called by My name, in which you trust, and
to the place which I gave to you and to your
fathers, as I have done to Shiloh. 15 I will cast
you out of My sight as I have cast out all your
brothers, even the whole seed of Ephraim.

16 As for you, do not pray for this people, nor
lift up a cry nor prayer for them, nor make
intercession to Me, for I will not hear you. 17 Do
you not see what they do in the cities of Judah
and in the streets of Jerusalem? 18 The children
gather wood, and the fathers kindle the fire,
and the women knead their dough, to make
cakes to the queen of heaven, and to pour out
drink offerings to other gods, that they may
provoke Me to anger. 19 Do they provoke Me
to anger? says the LORD. Do they not provoke
themselves to the shame of their own faces?

20 Therefore thus says the Lord GOD: My anger
and My fury will be poured out upon this place,

upon man and upon beast, and upon the trees
of the field, and upon the fruit of the ground;
and it shall burn, and shall not be quenched.
21 Thus says the LORD of Hosts, the God of
Israel: Add your burnt offerings to your sacri-
fices and eat flesh. 22 For I spoke not to your
fathers, nor commanded them in the day that
I brought them out of the land of Egypt, con-
cerning burnt offerings or sacrifices. 23 But this
thing I commanded them, saying, "Obey My
voice, and I will be your God, and you shall
be My people. And walk in all the ways that
I have commanded you, that it may be well
with you." 24 But they did not listen, nor incline
their ear, but walked in the counsels and in
the imagination of their evil heart, and went
backward and not forward. 25 Since the day that
your fathers came out of the land of Egypt to
this day, I have even sent to you all My ser-
vants the prophets, daily rising up early and
sending them. 26 Yet they did not listen to Me,
nor incline their ear, but hardened their neck.
They did worse than their fathers.
27 Therefore you will speak all these words to
them. But they will not listen to you. You will
also call to them, but they will not answer you.
28 You shall say to them: This is a nation that
does not obey the voice of the LORD their God,
nor receive correction. Truth has perished, and
has been cut off from their mouth.
29 Cut off your hair, O Jerusalem, and cast
it away, and take up a lamentation on high
places; for the LORD has rejected and forsaken
the generation of His wrath.
30 For the sons of Judah have done evil in
My sight, says the LORD. They have set their
abominations in the house which is called by
My name, to pollute it. 31 They have built the
high places of Topheth, which is in the Valley
of Ben Hinnom, to burn their sons and their
daughters in the fire, which I did not command
them, nor did it come into My heart. 32 There-
fore, truly the days are coming, says the LORD,
that it will no more be called Topheth, nor
the Valley of Ben Hinnom, but the Valley of
Slaughter; for they will bury in Topheth be-
cause there is no other place. 33 The corpses
of this people shall be food for the fowl of
the heaven and for the beasts of the earth;
and no one will frighten them away. 34 Then
I will cause to cease from the cities of Judah
and from the streets of Jerusalem the voice of
laughter and the voice of gladness, the voice
of the bridegroom and the voice of the bride;
for the land shall become desolate.

8 At that time, says the LORD, they will bring
out the bones of the kings of Judah, and
the bones of his officials, and the bones of the
priests, and the bones of the prophets, and
the bones of the inhabitants of Jerusalem out
of their graves. 2 And they will spread them
before the sun and the moon and all the host
of heaven, whom they have loved and whom
they have served, and after whom they have
walked and whom they have sought, and
whom they have worshipped. They will not
be gathered, nor be buried. They will be as
dung upon the face of the earth. 3 Death will be
chosen rather than life by all the rest of those
who remain of this evil family, which remains
in all the places wherever I have driven them,
says the LORD of Hosts.

Sin and Judgment

4 Moreover you shall say to them, Thus says
the LORD:

Do men fall and not arise?
Do they turn away and not repent?
5 Why then is this people of Jerusalem
turned away by a perpetual backsliding?
They hold fast to deceit;
they refuse to return.
6 I listened and heard,
but they did not speak what is right.
No man repented of his wickedness,
saying, "What have I done?"
Everyone turned to his course,
as the horse rushes into the battle.
7 Indeed, the stork in the sky
knows her appointed times.
And the turtledove and the crane and the
swallow
observe the time of their coming.
But My people do not know
the judgment of the LORD.

8 How do you say, "We are wise,
and the law of the LORD is with us"?
Certainly the lying pen of the scribes
has made it into a lie.
9 The wise men are ashamed;
they are dismayed and caught.
Indeed, they have rejected the word of the
LORD,
and what kind of wisdom do they have?
10 Therefore I will give their wives to others,
and their fields to those who shall inherit
them.
For everyone from the least even to the
greatest
is given to covetousness;
from the prophet even to the priest
everyone deals falsely.
11 For they have healed the brokenness
of the daughter of My people
superficially,
saying, "Peace, peace,"
when there is no peace.

7:21 Jer 6:20
7:22 Hos 6:6
7:23 Ex 15:26
7:24 Ps 81:11–12
7:25 2Ch 36:15
7:26 Jer 16:12
7:28 Isa 59:14–15
7:29 Job 1:20
7:30 Jer 32:34
7:31 Dt 17:3
7:32 Jer 19:6
7:33 Dt 28:26
7:34 Eze 26:13
8:1 Eze 6:5
8:2 2Ki 23:5
8:3 Rev 9:6
8:4 Pr 24:16
8:5 Jer 9:6
8:6 Ps 14:2
8:7 Isa 1:3
8:9 Jer 6:15
8:10 Jer 6:12–13
8:11 Jer 6:14

[12]Were they ashamed when they had
committed abomination?
They were not at all ashamed,
nor could they blush.
Therefore they will fall among those who
fall;
in the time of their punishment they will
be cast down,
says the LORD.

[13]I will surely consume them,
says the LORD.
There will be no grapes on the vine
nor figs on the fig tree,
and the leaf shall fade;
and the things that I have given them
will pass away from them.

[14]Why do we sit still?
Assemble yourselves,
and let us enter the fortified cities
and let us perish there.
For the LORD our God has doomed us
and given us water of gall to drink,
because we have sinned against the
LORD.
[15]We looked for peace,
but no good came;
and for a time of health,
but there was trouble!
[16]The snorting of his horses
was heard from Dan;
the whole land trembled
at the sound of the neighing of his
strong ones.
For they have come and have devoured
the land and all that is in it,
the city, and those who dwell in it.

[17]See, I will send serpents against you,
adders, which will not be charmed,
and they will bite you,
declares the LORD.

Jeremiah Mourns for His People

[18]My sorrow is beyond healing;
my heart is faint within me.
[19]Listen! The cry of the daughter of my
people
from a far country:
"Is not the LORD in Zion?
Is not her king in her?"

"Why have they provoked Me to anger with
their graven images,
with foreign vanities?"

[20]"The harvest is past,
the summer is ended,
and we are not saved."

[21]For the brokenness of the daughter of my
people am I broken;
I mourn; dismay has taken hold of me.

8:12 Jer 3:3
8:13 Joel 1:7
8:14 Jer 23:15
8:15 Jer 14:19
8:16 Jdg 5:22
8:17 Dt 32:24
8:19 Isa 39:3
8:21 Jer 14:17
....
8:22 Ge 37:25
9:1 Jer 13:17
9:2 Jer 5:7–8
9:3 Jdg 2:10
9:4 Jer 6:28
9:5 Mic 6:12
9:7 Isa 1:25
9:8 Ps 28:3
9:9 Jer 5:9
9:10 Jer 12:4

[22]Is there no balm in Gilead?
Is there no physician there?
Why then has not the health
of the daughter of my people recovered?

Failures of Judah

9 Oh, that my head were waters
and my eyes a fountain of tears,
that I might weep day and night
for the slain of the daughter of my
people!
[2] Oh, that I had in the wilderness
a lodging place of wayfaring men,
that I might leave my people
and go from them!
For they all are adulterers,
an assembly of treacherous men.
[3] They bend their tongues like their bow;
lies and not truth prevail upon the land;
for they proceed from evil to evil,
and they do not know Me,
says the LORD.
[4] Let everyone be on guard against his
neighbor,
and do not trust in any brother;
for every brother supplants,
and every neighbor walks about with
slanders.
[5] Everyone deceives his neighbor
and does not speak the truth.
They have taught their tongue to speak
lies;
they weary themselves in committing
iniquity.
[6] Your habitation is in the midst of deceit;
through deceit they refuse to know Me,
says the LORD.

[7]Therefore thus says the LORD of Hosts:

Now, I will refine them and assay them;
for what else shall I do
for the daughter of My people?
[8] Their tongue is a deadly arrow;
it speaks deceit.
One speaks peaceably to his neighbor with
his mouth,
but in his heart he lies in wait.
[9] Shall I not punish them for these things?
says the LORD.
Shall not My soul be avenged
on such a nation as this?
[10]For the mountains I will take up a weeping
and wailing,
and for the habitations of the wilderness
a lamentation,
because they are burned up so that no one
can pass through them;
nor can men hear the lowing of the
cattle.

Both the fowl of the heavens and the beast
have fled;
they are gone.

11 I will make Jerusalem a heap of ruins
and a den of jackals;
and I will make the cities of Judah
desolate,
without an inhabitant.

12 Who is the wise man who may understand
this? And who is he to whom the mouth of
the LORD has spoken, that he may declare it?
Why is the land ruined and burned up like a
wilderness, so that no one passes through?
13 And the LORD said: Because they have for-
saken My law which I set before them, and
have not obeyed My voice, nor walked in it,
14 but have walked after the imagination of
their own heart and after the Baals, which their
fathers taught them. 15 Therefore thus says the
LORD of Hosts, the God of Israel: I will feed
them, even this people, with wormwood and
give them water of gall to drink. 16 I will scatter
them also among the nations, whom neither
they nor their fathers have known. And I will
send a sword after them until I have consumed
them.

17 Thus says the LORD of Hosts:

Consider and call for the mourning
women, that they may come;
and send for wailing women, that they
may come.
18 And let them make haste
and take up a wailing for us,
that our eyes may run down with tears
and our eyelids gush out with waters.
19 For a voice of wailing is heard out of Zion,
"How devastated we are!
We are greatly humiliated,
because we have forsaken the land,
because our dwellings have cast us out."
20 Yet hear the word of the LORD, O you
women,
and let your ear receive the word of His
mouth;
and teach your daughters wailing,
and everyone her neighbor a
lamentation.
21 "For death has come up into our windows;
and has entered our palaces,
to cut off the children from the streets,
and the young men from the squares."

22 Speak, Thus says the LORD:

"The carcasses of men shall fall
as dung upon the open field,
and as the sheaf after the harvester,
and no one shall gather them."

9:11 Isa 25:2
9:12 Ps 107:43
9:13 2Ch 7:19
9:14 Jer 7:24
9:15 Jer 8:14
9:16 Lev 26:33
9:17 2Ch 35:25
9:18 Jer 14:17
9:19 Jer 4:13
9:20 Isa 32:9–13
9:21 2Ch 36:17
9:22 Jer 8:2

....

9:23 Ecc 9:11
9:24 Mic 7:18
9:25 Ro 2:8–9
9:26 Lev 26:41
10:2 Lev 20:23
10:4 Isa 40:19–20
10:5 Isa 46:7
10:6 Ex 15:11
10:7 Rev 15:4

23 Thus says the LORD:

Let not the wise man glory in his wisdom,
and let not the mighty man glory in his
might,
let not the rich man glory in his riches;
24 but let him who glories glory in this,
that he understands and knows Me,
that I am the LORD who exercises
lovingkindness,
justice, and righteousness in the earth.
For in these things I delight,
says the LORD.

25 The days are surely coming, says the LORD,
that I will punish all who are circumcised and
yet uncircumcised— 26 Egypt, Judah, Edom,
the children of Ammon, Moab, and all who
dwell in the wilderness who clip the hair on
their temples; for all these nations are uncir-
cumcised, and all the house of Israel are un-
circumcised of heart.

The True God and Idols
Jer 51:15–19

10 Hear the word which the LORD speaks
to you, O house of Israel. 2 Thus says
the LORD:

Do not learn the way of the nations;
do not be terrified at the signs of
heaven,
although the nations are terrified at
them.
3 For the customs of the people are vain;
for with the axe one cuts a tree out of
the forest,
the work of the hands of the workman.
4 They deck it with silver and with gold;
they fasten it with nails and with
hammers
so that it may not move.
5 They are as a scarecrow in a cucumber
field,
but do not speak;
they must be carried,
because they cannot walk.
Do not be afraid of them,
for they cannot do evil,
nor can they do good.

6 There is no one like You, O LORD.
You are great,
and Your name is great in might.
7 Who would not fear You,
O King of the nations?
Indeed, it is Your due.
For among all the wise men of the nations,
and in all their kingdoms,
there is no one like You.

8 But they are altogether unthinking and
foolish;
the tree is a doctrine of vanities.
9 Silver spread into plates is brought from
Tarshish,
and gold from Uphaz,
the work of the workman and of the hands
of the founder;
blue and purple are their clothing;
they all are the work of skilled men.
10 But the LORD is the true God;
He is the living God and an everlasting
King.
At His wrath the earth trembles,
and the nations cannot endure His
indignation.

11 Thus you shall say to them: The gods that
have not made the heavens and the earth,
even they shall perish from the earth and from
under these heavens.

12 He has made the earth by His power.
He has established the world by His
wisdom
and has stretched out the heavens by His
discretion.
13 When He utters His voice, there is a
multitude of waters in the heavens,
and He causes the vapors to ascend
from the remote parts of the earth;
He makes lightning with rain,
and brings out the wind from His
storehouses.

14 Every man is stupid, without knowledge;
every goldsmith is put to shame by an
idol;
for his molded image is false,
and there is no breath in them.
15 They are vain and a work of mockery;
in the time of their punishment they
shall perish.
16 The portion of Jacob is not like them,
for He is the Maker of all things,
and Israel is the rod of His inheritance.
The LORD of Hosts is His name.

The Exile Prophesied

17 Gather up your wares out of the land,
O inhabitant of the fortress.
18 For thus says the LORD:
I will sling out
the inhabitants of the land at this time,
and will distress them
that they may be found.

19 Woe is me because of my brokenness!
My wound is grievous.
But I said,
"Truly this is an illness, and I must bear
it."

10:9 Ps 115:4
10:10 Ps 76:7
10:11 Ps 96:5
10:12 Ge 1:1
10:13 Ps 135:7
10:14 Jer 10:8
10:15 Isa 41:24
10:16 Dt 32:9
10:17 Eze 12:3–12
10:18 1Sa 25:29
10:19 Mic 7:9
....
10:20 Jer 4:20
10:22 Jer 9:11
10:23 Pr 20:24
10:24 Ps 6:1
10:25 Ps 79:6–7
11:2 Jer 11:6
11:3 Dt 27:26
11:4 Lev 26:12
11:6 Ro 2:13
11:8 Jer 7:24

20 My tabernacle is devastated,
and all my cords are broken.
My sons have gone from me and are no
more.
There is no one to spread my tent
anymore,
and to set up my curtains.
21 For the shepherds have become unthinking
and have not sought the LORD.
Therefore they have not prospered,
and all their flocks are scattered.
22 Listen! The sound of the report has come,
and a great commotion out of the north
country,
to make the cities of Judah desolate
and a den of jackals.

The Prayer of Jeremiah

23 O LORD, I know that the way of man is not
in himself;
it is not in man who walks to direct his
steps.
24 O LORD, correct me, but with justice,
not in Your anger,
lest You bring me to nothing.
25 Pour out Your fury upon the nations
that do not know You
and upon the families that do not call on
Your name;
for they have eaten up Jacob
and devoured him, and consumed him,
and have made his habitation desolate.

The Broken Covenant

11 The word that came to Jeremiah from
the LORD, saying: 2 Hear the words of
this covenant, and speak to the men of Judah
and to the inhabitants of Jerusalem. 3 And say
you to them, Thus says the LORD God of Isra-
el: Cursed is the man who does not obey the
words of this covenant, 4 which I commanded
your fathers in the day that I brought them out
of the land of Egypt, from the iron furnace,
saying, Obey My voice, and do according to
all which I command you. So you shall be My
people, and I will be your God, 5 that I may
perform the oath which I have sworn to your
fathers, to give them a land flowing with milk
and honey, as it is this day.

Then I answered and said, "So be it, O LORD."
6 Then the LORD said to me: Proclaim all
these words in the cities of Judah and in the
streets of Jerusalem: saying, Hear the words
of this covenant, and do them. 7 For I earnestly
warned your fathers in the day that I brought
them up out of the land of Egypt, even to this
day, rising early and warning, saying, Obey My
voice. 8 Yet they did not obey or incline their
ear, but everyone walked in the imagination
of their evil heart. Therefore I will bring upon

them all the words of this covenant, which I
commanded them to do, but which they did
not do.
9 The LORD said to me: A conspiracy has been
found among the men of Judah and among
the inhabitants of Jerusalem. 10 They have
turned back to the iniquities of their forefa-
thers who refused to hear My words. And they
have gone after other gods to serve them. The
house of Israel and the house of Judah have
broken My covenant which I made with their
fathers. 11 Therefore thus says the LORD, Surely,
I will bring calamity upon them which they
will not be able to escape. And though they
cry to Me, I will not listen to them. 12 Then the
cities of Judah and inhabitants of Jerusalem
will go and cry to the gods to whom they offer
incense. But they will not save them at all in
the time of their trouble. 13 For according to the
number of your cities are your gods, O Judah.
And according to the number of the streets
of Jerusalem you have set up altars to that
shameful thing, even altars to burn incense
to Baal.
14 Therefore do not pray for this people, nor
lift up a cry or prayer for them. For I will not
hear them in the time that they cry to Me be-
cause of their trouble.

15 What right has My beloved in My house,
seeing that she has done many lewd
deeds?
Can the sacrificial meat take away from
you your disaster,
so that you can rejoice while doing evil?

16 The LORD called your name,
"A green olive tree, fair in fruit and
form."
With the noise of a great tumult
He has kindled fire upon it,
and its branches are broken.

17 For the LORD of Hosts, who planted you, has
pronounced disaster against you, because
of the evil of the house of Israel and of the
house of Judah, which they have done against
themselves to provoke Me to anger in offering
incense to Baal.

Jeremiah's Life Threatened

18 The LORD has made it known to me and
I knew it; then You showed me their deeds.
19 But I was like a gentle lamb that is brought
to the slaughter, and I did not know that they
had devised plots against me, saying,

"Let us destroy the tree with the fruit,
and let us cut him off from the land of
the living
so that his name may be remembered
no more."

11:9 Hos 6:9
11:11 Pr 1:28
11:12 Dt 32:37
11:14 Jer 11:11
11:15 Pr 2:14
11:16 Ps 52:8
11:17 Isa 5:2
11:19 Ps 83:4
....
11:20 Ps 7:9
11:22 Jer 18:21
11:23 Jer 23:12
12:1 Job 12:6
12:2 Isa 29:13
12:3 Jer 17:18
12:4 Jer 9:10
12:5 Jer 49:19
12:6 Pr 26:25

20 But, O LORD of Hosts, who judges
righteously,
who tries the feelings and the heart,
let me see Your vengeance on them,
for to You I have revealed my cause.

21 Therefore thus says the LORD of the men
of Anathoth who seek your life, saying, "Do
not prophesy in the name of the LORD so that
you not die by our hand." 22 Therefore thus
says the LORD of Hosts: I will punish them.
The young men shall die by the sword. Their
sons and their daughters shall die by famine.
23 And there shall be no remnant of them, for I
will bring calamity upon the men of Anathoth,
even the year of their punishment.

Jeremiah's Plea

12 Righteous are You, O LORD,
that I plead with You.
Indeed, let me talk with You about matters
of justice.
Why does the way of the wicked
prosper?
Why are all those happy who deal very
treacherously?
2 You have planted them; indeed, they have
taken root;
they grow; indeed, they bring forth fruit.
You are near in their mouth,
but far from their mind.
3 But You, O LORD, know me;
You have seen me and tested my heart
toward You.
Pull them out like sheep for the slaughter,
and prepare them for the day of
slaughter.
4 How long shall the land mourn
and the herbs of every field wither?
For the wickedness of those who dwell in
it,
the beasts and the birds have been
snatched away,
because they said,
"He will not see our latter end."

God Answers Jeremiah

5 If you have run with the footmen,
and they have wearied you,
then how can you contend with horses?
And if in the land of peace in which you
trusted, they wearied you,
then how will you do in the thicket of the
Jordan?
6 For even your brothers and the household
of your father,
even they have dealt treacherously with
you.
Indeed, they have cried aloud after you.
Do not believe them
though they speak fair words to you.

7 I have forsaken My house,
I have abandoned My heritage;
I have given the dearly beloved of My soul
into the hand of her enemies.
8 My heritage is to Me
as a lion in the forest.
She cries out against Me;
therefore I have hated her.
9 My heritage is to Me
as a speckled vulture;
the vultures all around are against her.
Come, assemble all the beasts of the field,
bring them to devour.
10 Many shepherds have destroyed My
vineyard;
they have trodden My portion under
foot;
they have made My pleasant portion
a desolate wilderness.
11 They have made it desolate,
and being desolate, it mourns to Me.
The whole land has been made desolate,
because no man lays it to heart.
12 The destroyers have come
upon all high places through the
wilderness,
for the sword of the LORD shall devour
from the one end of the land even to the
other end of the land.
No one shall have peace.
13 They have sown wheat, but reap thorns;
they have strained themselves, but shall
not profit.
And they shall be ashamed of your harvest
because of the fierce anger of the LORD.

14 Thus says the LORD: Against all My evil
neighbors who touch the inheritance which I
have caused My people Israel to inherit, I will
pluck them out of their land and pluck out the
house of Judah from among them. 15 It shall
come to pass that after I have plucked them
out, I will again have compassion on them,
and will bring them back, every man to his
heritage, and every man to his land. 16 It shall
come to pass if they will diligently learn the
ways of My people, to swear by My name, "As
the LORD lives," as they taught My people to
swear by Baal, then they will be built up in
the midst of My people. 17 But if they will not
obey, I will utterly pluck up and destroy that
nation, says the LORD.

A Linen Sash

13 Thus says the LORD to me, "Go and buy
yourself a linen waistband and put it
upon your loins, and do not put it in water."
2 So I bought a waistband according to the
word of the LORD and put it on my loins.

12:7 Jer 11:15
12:8 Hos 9:15
12:9 Isa 56:9
12:10 Isa 5:1–7
12:11 Isa 42:25
12:12 Jer 47:6
12:13 Dt 28:38
12:14 Zec 2:8
12:15 Jer 48:47
12:16 Jer 4:2
12:17 Isa 60:12
13:1 Jer 13:11

....

13:5 Ex 40:16
13:9 Lev 26:19
13:10 Jer 16:12
13:11 Jer 33:9
13:13 Ps 60:3
13:14 Dt 29:20
13:15 Isa 28:14–22
13:16 Isa 59:9
13:17 Jer 9:1

3 The word of the LORD came to me the sec-
ond time, saying, 4 "Take the waistband that
you have, which is upon your loins, and arise,
go to the Euphrates and hide it there in a hole
of the rock." 5 So I went and hid it by the Eu-
phrates, as the LORD had commanded me.
6 After many days the LORD said to me, "Arise,
go to the Euphrates and take the waistband
from there, which I commanded you to hide
there." 7 Then I went to the Euphrates, and
dug, and took the waistband from the place
where I had hidden it. But the waistband was
destroyed. It was profitable for nothing.
8 Then the word of the LORD came to me:
9 Thus says the LORD: After this manner I will
destroy the pride of Judah and the great pride
of Jerusalem. 10 This evil people, who refuse to
hear My words, who walk in the imagination
of their hearts, and walk after other gods, to
serve them, and to worship them, shall be even
as this waistband which is good for nothing.
11 For as the waistband cleaves to the loins of
a man, so I have caused the whole house of
Israel and the whole house of Judah to cleave
to Me, says the LORD, so that they might be to
Me a people for renown, and for a praise, and
for a glory; but they would not listen.

The Metaphor of Wine Bottles

12 Therefore you shall speak to them this
word: Thus says the LORD God of Israel: Every
bottle shall be filled with wine. And when they
say to you, "Do we not certainly know that
every bottle should be filled with wine?" 13 then
you shall say to them: Thus says the LORD: I
will fill all the inhabitants of this land—even
the kings that sit on the throne of David, and
the priests, and the prophets, and all the in-
habitants of Jerusalem—with drunkenness. 14 I
will dash them against one another, even the
fathers and the sons together, says the LORD. I
will not show pity nor spare nor have mercy,
but will destroy them.

Exile Threatened

15 Hear and give heed;
do not be proud,
for the LORD has spoken.
16 Give glory to the LORD your God,
before He causes darkness
and before your feet stumble
on the dark mountains,
and while you look for light,
He turns it into the shadow of death
and makes it gross darkness.
17 But if you will not listen to it,
my soul will weep in secret places
for your pride;
and my eyes will weep sorely
and run down with tears,

because the flock of the LORD is carried
away captive.

18 Say to the king and to the queen mother:
"Humble yourselves, sit down,
for your beautiful crown
shall come down from your head."
19 The cities of the Negev will be shut up,
and no one will open them;
all Judah will be carried away into
captivity;
it will be wholly carried away captive.

20 Lift up your eyes and see
those who come from the north.
Where is the flock that was given to you,
your beautiful flock?
21 What will you say when He appoints over
you
those you yourself had taught to be
companions to you?
Shall not sorrows take hold of you,
as a woman in labor?
22 And if you say in your heart,
"Why have these things come upon
me?"
for the greatness of your iniquity
your skirts have been removed
and your heels made bare.
23 Can the Ethiopian change his skin
or the leopard his spots?
Then you also can do good,
who are accustomed to doing evil.
24 Therefore I will scatter them as the stubble
that passes away by the wind of the
wilderness.
25 This is your lot,
the portion of your measures from Me,
says the LORD,
because you have forgotten Me
and trusted in falsehood.
26 Therefore I Myself have uncovered your
skirts over your face
so that your shame may appear.
27 I have seen your adulteries and your *lustful*
neighings,
the lewdness of your harlotry,
and your abominations
on the hills in the fields.
Woe to you, O Jerusalem!
How long will you remain unclean?

Drought, Famine, and Sword

14 The word of the LORD which came to Jeremiah concerning the drought:

2 Judah mourns,
and the gates languish;
they sit on the ground while mourning,
and the cry of Jerusalem has gone up.

13:18 2Ki 24:12
13:19 Jer 52:27
13:20 Jer 6:22
13:21 Isa 13:8
13:22 Na 3:5
13:24 Lev 26:33
13:25 Job 20:29
13:26 La 1:8
13:27 Eze 6:13
14:1 Jer 17:8
14:2 Isa 3:26

14:3 2Sa 15:30
14:5 Ps 29:9
14:6 Jer 2:24
14:7 Ps 25:11
14:8 Jer 17:13
14:9 Isa 59:1
14:10 Hos 8:13
14:11 Jer 7:16
14:12 Jer 6:20
14:13 Jer 6:14
14:14 Jer 27:9–10

3 Their nobles have sent their servants for
water;
they came to the cisterns and found no
water.
They returned with their vessels empty;
they were ashamed and humiliated,
and covered their heads.
4 Because the ground is chapped,
for there was no rain in the earth,
the plowmen were ashamed;
they have covered their heads.
5 Indeed, the hind also calved in the field
and abandoned *her young*
because there was no grass.
6 The wild donkeys stand in the high places;
they pant for air like jackals;
their eyes fail
because there is no grass.
7 O LORD, though our iniquities testify against
us,
do it for Your name's sake.
Indeed, our backslidings are many;
we have sinned against You.
8 O the Hope of Israel,
its Savior in time of trouble,
why should You be as a stranger in the
land,
and as a wayfaring man who turns aside
to pitch his tent for a night?
9 Why should You be as a man dismayed,
as a mighty man who cannot save?
Yet You, O LORD, are in our midst,
and we are called by Your name.
Do not forsake us!

10 Thus says the LORD to this people:
Even so they have loved to wander;
they have not restrained their feet.
Therefore, the LORD does not accept them;
He will now remember their iniquity
and punish their sins.

11 Then the LORD said to me: Do not pray for
the good of this people. 12 When they fast, I
will not hear their cry. And when they offer a
burnt offering and an oblation, I will not accept
them. But I will consume them by the sword,
and by the famine, and by the pestilence.

False Prophets

13 Yet I said, "Ah, Lord GOD! Here the proph-
ets say to them, 'You shall not see the sword
nor shall you have famine, but I will give you
assured peace in this place.' "

14 Then the LORD said to me: The prophets
prophesy lies in My name. I have not sent
them nor have I commanded them nor have I
spoken to them. They prophesy to you a false
vision and divination, and emptiness, and the
deceit of their heart. 15 Therefore thus says the

Learning to Walk Straight

The Bible says we need to separate "the precious from the worthless" (Jer 15:19), and that's what we need to do when dealing with our children and the power of iniquity in their lives. Parts of their lives have truly been crucified with Christ, and it is "no longer [they] who live, but Christ who lives in [them]" (Gal 2:20).

Every one of our kids has the precious spirit part of them that has been cleansed by God and now functions in the power of the Holy Spirit. This is wonderful. But when we are trying to deal with the part of their lives that iniquity governs, that is the vile part. This is the part that needs to be put to death on the cross of Jesus Christ. It needs to be crucified and buried so that the life of Christ can arise within them. This is true not only for our children but also for everyone on the planet. If we are willing for this cleansing work of sanctification to take place in us, then we truly will be governed by the Lord Jesus Christ, and the power of a holy God will flow through us. We will be what the Bible calls a "living sacrifice" (Ro 12:1), dead but with the power of God flowing through us.

Now, this is not something that happens at a special service at church in which the power of God strikes us, we are moved, and we leave perfected. No, this happens as the result of an everyday, moment-by-moment surrender of little areas of our lives, one by one, as the Spirit of God gently (or sometimes not-so-gently) points them out to us to give up. This is part of our role as parents with our children. God has given us authority to root out these crooked places of iniquity in their lives.

Face it: When each of our kids landed in our laps on the day they were born, they arrived with all the strengths and gifts God had given them. They also arrived with areas that, even fairly early on, God wanted them to overcome. As our children grow day by day, we can see the specific areas of iniquity they struggle with. If we dive in and help them begin to overcome these stumbling blocks while they are still young, they will not be left to wrestle with them for the rest of their lives. This is the incredible opportunity that we have as parents to be used by God to stand against the power of the iniquity patterns that govern our kids' lives.

Don't be discouraged when these iniquity patterns come up in your children. They are there, for sure. This is part of the journey God has placed us on with our families so that out of a repentant heart we will worship Him with all our hearts, all our souls, and all our strength (Dt 6:5).

If we are willing to dive into our kids' patterns of iniquity, we will truly be discipling them. This is what parenting is about—walking with our children, whether they are toddlers or teens, to bring these areas into submission to the Lord.

Julie Hiramine

Lord concerning the prophets who prophesy
in My name though I did not send them, yet
they say, "Sword and famine will not be in this
land." By sword and famine those prophets
will be consumed. 16 The people to whom they
prophesy will be cast out in the streets of Jeru-
salem because of the famine and the sword.
And they will have no one to bury them, not
them, nor their wives, nor their sons, nor their
daughters. For I will pour out their wickedness
upon them.

17 Therefore you will say this word to them:

Let my eyes run down with tears
night and day, and let them not cease;
for the virgin daughter of my people
has been broken with a great blow,
with a very infected wound.
18 If I go out into the field,
I see those slain with the sword!
And if I enter the city,
I see those who are sick with famine!
Indeed, both the prophet and the priest
go about into a land that they do not
know.

The People Ask for Mercy

19 Have You utterly rejected Judah?
Has Your soul loathed Zion?
Why have You stricken us
so that there is no healing for us?
We looked for peace,
but there was nothing good;
and for the time of healing,
but there is trouble!
20 We acknowledge, O Lord, our wickedness
and the iniquity of our fathers,
for we have sinned against You.
21 Do not abhor us. For Your name's sake,
do not disgrace Your glorious throne.
Remember and do not break
Your covenant with us.
22 Are there any among the idols of the
nations that can cause rain?
Or can the heavens give showers?
Is it not You, O Lord our God?
Therefore, we will wait upon You,
for You have done all these things.

The Lord Will Not Relent

15 Then the Lord said to me: Even though
Moses and Samuel were to stand be-
fore Me, yet My heart would not be with this
people. Cast them out of My sight and let them
go! 2 It shall come to pass if they say to you,
"Where should we go?" then you shall tell
them: Thus says the Lord:

Those destined for death, to death;
and those destined for the sword, to the
sword;
and those destined for the famine, to the
famine;
and those destined for the captivity, to the
captivity.

3 I will appoint over them four kinds of disas-
ter, says the Lord: the sword to slay, the dogs to
tear, the birds of the heaven, the beasts of the
earth to devour and destroy. 4 I will cause them
to be removed into all kingdoms of the earth,
because of Manasseh the son of Hezekiah king
of Judah, for that which he did in Jerusalem.

5 For who shall have pity on you,
O Jerusalem?
Or who shall bemoan you?
Or who shall go aside to ask how you
are doing?
6 You who have forsaken Me, says the Lord,
you keep going backward.
Therefore I will stretch out My hand against
you and destroy you.
I am weary of relenting!
7 I will winnow them with a winnowing fork
in the gates of the land;
I will bereave them of children. I will
destroy My people,
since they did not repent from their
ways.
8 Their widows will increase before Me
more than the sand of the seas;
I will bring against them, against the
mother of a young man,
a destroyer at noonday;
I will suddenly bring down on her
sorrow and terrors.
9 She who has borne seven sons languishes;
she has given up the spirit;
her sun has gone down while it was yet
day;
she has been ashamed and humiliated.
And the rest of them I will deliver to the
sword
before their enemies,
says the Lord.

Jeremiah's Sorrow

10 Woe is me, my mother, that you have borne
me
as a man of strife and a man of
contention to the whole earth!
I have not lent with usury, nor have men
lent to me on usury,
yet every one of them curses me!

11 The Lord said:

Truly I will set you free for good purposes.
Truly I will cause the enemy to entreat
you
in the time of evil and in the time of
affliction.

14:16 Pr 1:31
14:17 Jer 8:21
14:18 Eze 7:15
14:19 Jer 8:15
14:21 Ps 106:45
14:22 Dt 32:21
15:1 1Sa 7:9
15:2 Jer 14:12

15:3 Lev 26:16
15:4 Jer 24:9
15:5 Isa 51:19
15:6 Jer 7:24
15:7 Isa 9:13
15:8 Isa 3:25–4:1
15:9 1Sa 2:5
15:10 Ex 22:25

12 Can anyone break the northern iron
or the bronze?

13 Your wealth and your treasures
I will give to the destroyer without price,
and that for all your sins,
even within all your borders.
14 I will make you to pass with your enemies
into a land which you do not know;
for a fire is kindled in My anger,
which shall burn upon you.

15 O LORD, You who know, remember me,
and take notice of me,
and take vengeance on my persecutors.
Because of your longsuffering, do not take
me away.
Know that for Your sake I have suffered
rebuke.
16 Your words were found and I ate them.
And Your word became to me the joy
and rejoicing of my heart,
for I am called by Your name,
O LORD God of Hosts.
17 I did not sit in the assembly of mockers,
nor did I rejoice;
I sat alone because of Your hand,
for You have filled me with indignation.
18 Why is my pain perpetual
and my wound incurable, which refuses
to be healed?
Shall You be altogether to me as a
deceptive stream
and as waters that fail?

The LORD Reassures Jeremiah

19 Therefore thus says the LORD:
If you return, then I will bring you back,
and you shall stand before Me;
and if you take out the precious from the
worthless,
you will be My spokesman.
Let them return to you,
but do not return to them.
20 I will make you to this people
a fortified bronze wall;
and they shall fight against you,
but they shall not prevail against you;
for I am with you
to save you and to deliver you,
says the LORD.
21 I will deliver you out of the hand of the
wicked,
and I will redeem you out of the hand of
the violent.

The Day of Disaster

16 The word of the LORD came also to me,
saying: 2 You shall not take a wife, nor
shall you have sons or daughters in this place.
3 For thus says the LORD concerning the sons
and concerning the daughters who are born in
this place, and concerning their mothers who
bore them, and concerning their fathers who
fathered them in this land: 4 They will die of
deadly diseases. They will not be lamented,
nor shall they be buried. But they will be as
dung upon the face of the ground. And they
will be consumed by the sword and by famine.
And their carcasses will be food for the fowl of
heaven and for the beasts of the earth.
5 For thus says the LORD: Do not enter a house
of mourning, nor go to lament or bemoan
them; for I have taken away My peace from
this people, says the LORD, even lovingkindness
and mercy. 6 Both the great and the small will
die in this land. They will not be buried; neither
will men lament for them, cut themselves, nor
make themselves bald for them. 7 Neither will
men tear themselves for them in mourning, to
comfort them for the dead; nor will men give
them the cup of consolation to drink for their
father or for their mother.
8 Also you shall not go into the house of
feasting, to sit with them to eat and to drink.
9 For thus says the LORD of Hosts, the God of
Israel: I will cause to cease out of this place,
before your eyes and in your days, the voice of
laughter and the voice of gladness, the voice
of the bridegroom and the voice of the bride.
10 And when you tell this people all these
words, and they say to you, "Why has the LORD
pronounced all this great disaster against us?
Or what is our iniquity? Or what is our sin
that we have committed against the LORD our
God?" 11 then you shall say to them: Because
your fathers have forsaken Me, says the LORD,
and have walked after other gods and have
served them and have worshipped them, but
have forsaken Me and have not kept My law.
12 And you have done worse than your fathers,
for here you are, each one walking after the
imaginations of his evil heart so that they do
not listen to Me. 13 Therefore I will cast you out
of this land into a land that you do not know,
neither you nor your fathers; and there you will
serve other gods day and night because I will
not show you favor.

God Will Restore Israel

14 Therefore, surely the days are coming, says
the LORD, that it will no longer be said, "As the
LORD lives, who brought up the sons of Israel
out of the land of Egypt," 15 but, "As the LORD
lives, who brought up the sons of Israel from
the land of the north and from all the lands
wherever He had driven them." And I will
bring them again into their land that I gave
to their fathers.

15:13 Ps 44:12
15:14 Dt 32:22
15:15 Jer 12:3
15:16 Jer 14:9
15:17 Ps 1:1
15:18 Jer 30:15
15:19 Jer 15:1
15:20 Jer 1:18–19
15:21 Ge 48:16
16:2 1Co 7:26–27
....
16:4 Jer 25:33
16:5 Eze 24:16–23
16:6 Lev 19:28
16:7 Eze 24:17
16:8 Ecc 7:2–4
16:9 Jer 7:34
16:10 Jer 5:19
16:11 Ps 106:35–41
16:12 Jer 13:10
16:13 Dt 28:36
16:14 Dt 15:15
16:15 Jer 24:6

16 Now, I will send for many fishermen, says
the LORD, and they shall fish for them; and af-
terwards I will send for many hunters, and they
will hunt them from every mountain and from
every hill and out of the holes of the rocks.
17 For My eyes are upon all their ways; they are
not hidden from My face, nor is their iniquity
hidden from My eyes. 18 First I will doubly rec-
ompense their iniquity and their sin, because
they have defiled My land; they have filled My
inheritance with the carcasses of their detest-
able and abominable things.

19 O LORD, my strength and my fortress,
and my refuge in the day of affliction,
the nations will come to You
from the remote parts of the earth, and
will say:
Surely our fathers have inherited lies,
vanity,
and things in which there is no profit.
20 Shall a man make gods for himself,
which are not gods?

21 "Therefore, surely I will this once cause
them to know,
I will cause them to know
My hand and My might;
and they shall know
that My name is the LORD."

Judah's Sin and Punishment

17 The sin of Judah is written with an
iron pen
and with a diamond point;
it is engraved on the tablet of their heart
and on the horns of their altars;
2 as they remember their children,
so they remember their altars
and their groves by the green trees
on the high hills.
3 O My mountain in the field,
I will give your wealth
and all your treasures to the destroyer,
and your high places
for sin throughout all your borders.
4 You, even yourself, will discontinue
from your heritage that I gave you;
and I will cause you to serve your enemies
in the land which you do not know;
for you have kindled a fire in My anger
which will burn forever.

5 Thus says the LORD:

Cursed is the man who trusts in man
and makes flesh his strength,
and whose heart departs from the LORD.
6 For he will be like a bush in the desert
and will not see when good comes,
but will inhabit the parched places in the
wilderness,
in a salt land and not inhabited.

16:16 Am 4:2
16:17 Pr 15:3
16:18 Isa 40:2
16:19 Isa 25:4
16:20 Isa 37:19
16:21 Jer 33:2
17:1 Pr 3:3
17:2 2Ch 24:18
17:3 Jer 15:13
17:4 Jer 15:14
17:5 2Ch 32:8
17:6 Dt 29:23

17:7 Ps 34:8
17:8 Ps 1:3
17:9 Ecc 9:3
17:10 Jer 32:19
17:11 Lk 12:20
17:12 Jer 3:17
17:13 Isa 1:28
17:14 Dt 10:21
17:15 Isa 5:19
17:17 Jer 16:19
17:18 Ps 35:4

7 Blessed is the man who trusts in the LORD,
and whose hope is the LORD.
8 For he shall be as a tree planted by the
waters,
and that spreads out its roots by the
river,
and shall not fear when heat comes,
but its leaf shall be green,
and it shall not be anxious in the year of
drought,
neither shall cease from yielding fruit.

9 The heart is more deceitful than all things
and desperately wicked;
who can understand it?
10 I, the LORD, search the heart,
I test the mind,
even to give to every man according to his
ways,
and according to the fruit of his deeds.

11 As the partridge sits on eggs which it has
not laid,
so is he who gets riches, but not justly;
it will forsake him in the midst of his days,
and in the end he will be a fool.
12 A glorious high throne from the beginning
is the place of our sanctuary.
13 O LORD, the Hope of Israel,
all who forsake You will be ashamed.
"Those who depart from Me in the earth
will be written down,
because they have forsaken the LORD,
the fountain of living waters."

Jeremiah Prays for Deliverance

14 Heal me, O LORD, and I will be healed;
save me, and I will be saved,
for You are my praise.
15 See how they say to me,
"Where is the word of the LORD?
Let it come now!"
16 As for me, I have not hurried away from
being a shepherd after You,
nor have I desired the woeful day;
You Yourself know that which came out
of my lips was in Your presence.
17 Do not be a terror to me;
You are my hope in the day of disaster.
18 Let those who persecute me be humiliated,
but let me not be humiliated;
let them be dismayed,
but let me not be dismayed.
Bring upon them the day of evil,
and destroy them with double
destruction.

Keep the Sabbath Day Holy

19 Thus the LORD said to me: Go and stand in
the gate of the sons of the people whereby the

kings of Judah come in and by which they go out, and in all the gates of Jerusalem. 20 And say to them: Hear the word of the LORD, kings of Judah, and all Judah and all the inhabitants of Jerusalem who enter by these gates. 21 Thus says the LORD: Take heed to yourselves, and do not bear any load on the Sabbath day nor bring anything in by the gates of Jerusalem. 22 You shall not carry a load out of your houses on the Sabbath day, nor do any work, but keep the Sabbath day holy, as I commanded your fathers. 23 But they did not obey or incline their ears, but made their neck stiff, that they might not hear nor receive instruction. 24 It shall come to pass, if you diligently listen to Me, says the LORD, to bring in no load through the gates of this city on the Sabbath day, but sanctify the Sabbath day to do no work in it, 25 then there shall enter by the gates of this city kings and officials sitting on the throne of David, riding in chariots and on horses, they, and their officials, the men of Judah, and the inhabitants of Jerusalem. And this city will be inhabited forever. 26 They will come from the cities of Judah and from the places about Jerusalem, and from the land of Benjamin, and from the plain, and from the mountains, and from the Negev, bringing burnt offerings, and sacrifices, and grain offerings, and incense, and bringing sacrifices of praise to the house of the LORD. 27 But if you will not listen to Me to sanctify the Sabbath day and not to bear a load, even entering in at the gates of Jerusalem on the Sabbath day, then I will kindle a fire in the gates and it will devour the palaces of Jerusalem and it will not be quenched.

The Potter and the Clay

18 The word which came to Jeremiah from the LORD, saying: 2 "Arise and go down to the potter's house, and there I will cause you to hear My words." 3 Then I went down to the potter's house, and there he was making something on the wheel. 4 Yet the vessel that he made of clay was spoiled in the hand of the potter; so he made it again into another vessel, as seemed good to the potter to make it.

5 Then the word of the LORD came to me, saying: 6 O house of Israel, can I not do with you as this potter? says the LORD. As the clay is in the potter's hand, so are you in My hand, O house of Israel. 7 At one moment I may speak concerning a nation and concerning a kingdom to pluck up, and to pull down, and to destroy it. 8 If that nation against which I have spoken turns from its evil, I will relent of the disaster that I thought to do to it. 9 Or at another moment I may speak concerning a nation and concerning a kingdom to build and to plant it. 10 If it does evil in My sight by not obeying My voice, then I will relent of the good with which I said I would bless it.

17:20 Jer 19:3
17:21 Nu 15:32–36
17:22 Eze 20:12
17:23 Jer 11:10
17:24 Jer 17:21–22
17:25 Jer 22:4
17:26 Jer 32:44
17:27 2Ki 25:9
18:2 Jer 19:1–2
18:6 Isa 64:8
18:7 Jer 1:10
18:8 Jer 26:13
18:9 Jer 1:10

18:10 1Sa 2:30
18:11 2Ki 17:13
18:12 Jer 2:25
18:13 Jer 5:30
18:15 Isa 57:14
18:16 Ps 22:7
18:17 Jer 2:27
18:18 Jer 11:19
18:20 Ps 35:7

11 Now therefore speak to the men of Judah and to the inhabitants of Jerusalem, saying: Thus says the LORD: Look, I am shaping disaster against you and devising a plan against you. Repent now, everyone from his evil way, and make your ways and your deeds good. 12 But they say, "There is no hope! But we will walk after our own devices, and each of us will do according to the stubbornness of his evil heart."

13 Therefore thus says the LORD:

Ask now among the nations,
who has heard such things?
The virgin of Israel
has done a very horrible thing.
14 Shall a man leave the snow of Lebanon,
which comes from the rock of the field?
Shall the cold flowing water that comes
from another place
be forsaken?
15 Because My people have forgotten Me,
they have burned incense to vain gods
and they have stumbled in their ways
from the ancient paths,
to walk in bypaths,
not on a highway,
16 to make their land desolate,
and a perpetual hissing;
everyone who passes by shall be
astonished
and shake his head.
17 I will scatter them before the enemy
as with an east wind;
I will show them the back and not the face
in the day of their calamity.

Jeremiah Persecuted

18 Then they said, "Come and let us devise plans against Jeremiah. For the law will not be lost from the priest, nor counsel from the wise, nor the word from the prophet. Come and let us strike him with the tongue, and let us not give heed to any of his words."

19 Give heed to me, O LORD,
and listen to the voice of those who
contend with me.
20 Shall evil be recompensed for good?
For they have dug a pit for my soul.
Remember that I stood before You
to speak good for them,
and to turn away Your wrath from them.
21 Therefore, deliver up their children to the
famine

and pour out their blood by the power of
the sword;
and let their wives be bereaved of their
children and become widows
and let their men be put to death;
let their young men be slain by the
sword in battle.
22 Let a cry be heard from their houses,
when You bring a troop suddenly upon
them;
for they have dug a pit to take me
and hidden snares for my feet.
23 Yet, LORD, You know
all their counsel against me to slay me.
Do not forgive their iniquity
nor blot out their sin from Your sight;
but let them be overthrown before You;
deal thus with them in the time of Your
anger.

The Broken Jar

19 Thus says the LORD: Go and buy a potter's earthen bottle, and take some of the elders of the people and some of the elders of the priests. 2 Then go out to the Valley of Ben Hinnom, which is by the entry of the Potsherd Gate, and proclaim there the words that I will tell you, 3 and say: Hear the word of the LORD, O kings of Judah and inhabitants of Jerusalem. Thus says the LORD of Hosts, the God of Israel: I will bring such disaster upon this place, at which whoever hears of it, his ears shall tingle. 4 Because they have forsaken Me and have profaned this place by making offerings in it to other gods whom neither they, their fathers, nor the kings of Judah have known, and have filled this place with the blood of the innocent, 5 and have built the high places of Baal to burn their sons with fire for burnt offerings to Baal, which I did not command or decree, nor did it come into My mind— 6 therefore, surely the days are coming, says the LORD, when this place shall no more be called Topheth or the Valley of Ben Hinnom, but the Valley of Slaughter.

7 I will make void the counsel of Judah and Jerusalem in this place, and I will cause them to fall by the sword before their enemies, and by the hands of those who seek their lives. And their corpses I will give to be food for the fowl of the heaven and for the beasts of the earth. 8 I will make this city desolate and a hissing. Everyone who passes by will be astonished and hiss because of all the wounds. 9 I will cause them to eat the flesh of their sons and the flesh of their daughters, and everyone will eat the flesh of his friend in the siege and distress, with which their enemies and those who seek their lives will distress them.

10 Then you will break the bottle in the sight of the men that go with you, 11 and say to them: Thus says the LORD of Hosts: Even so I will break this people and this city, as one breaks a potter's vessel that cannot be made whole again; and they will bury them in Topheth until there is no other place to bury. 12 Thus I will do to this place and to the inhabitants, says the LORD, and even make this city as Topheth. 13 And the houses of Jerusalem and the houses of the kings of Judah will be defiled as the place of Topheth, because of all the houses upon whose roofs they have burned incense to all the host of heaven and have poured out drink offerings to other gods.

14 Then Jeremiah came from Topheth, where the LORD had sent him to prophesy. And he stood in the court of the house of the LORD and said to all the people: 15 Thus says the LORD of Hosts, the God of Israel. I am about to bring upon this city and upon all her towns all the disaster that I have pronounced against it, because they have stiffened their necks so that they might not heed My words.

Pashhur Strikes Jeremiah

20 Now Pashhur the son of Immer the priest, who was also chief officer in the house of the LORD, heard that Jeremiah prophesied these things. 2 Then Pashhur struck Jeremiah the prophet and put him in the stocks that were in the upper Gate of Benjamin, which was by the house of the LORD. 3 On the next day Pashhur brought Jeremiah out of the stocks. Then Jeremiah said to him, The LORD has not called your name Pashhur, but "Magor-missabib."[1] 4 For thus says the LORD: I will make you a terror to yourself and to all your friends. And they will fall by the sword of their enemies while your eyes will see it. Thus I will give all Judah into the hand of the king of Babylon, and he will carry them captive into Babylon and will slay them with the sword. 5 Moreover I will deliver all the wealth of this city, and all its produce, and all the precious things; and all the treasures of the kings of Judah I will give into the hand of their enemies who will destroy them, and take them, and carry them to Babylon. 6 You, Pashhur, and all who dwell in your house will go into captivity; and you will come to Babylon, and there you will die and will be buried there, you and all your friends to whom you have prophesied lies.

Jeremiah Dejected

7 O LORD, You have deceived me and I was
deceived;

18:22 Ps 140:5
18:23 Isa 2:9
19:1 Nu 11:16
19:2 Jos 15:8
19:3 1Sa 3:11
19:4 Jer 2:34
19:5 Jer 32:35
19:6 Jos 15:8
19:7 Lev 26:17
19:8 Jer 18:16
19:9 Lev 26:29
19:11 Ps 2:9
19:13 2Ki 23:12
19:14 2Ch 20:5
19:15 Jer 7:26
20:1 1Ch 24:14
20:2 Jer 37:13
20:3 Jer 20:10
20:4 Jer 29:21
20:6 Jer 14:14–15
20:7 La 3:14

[1] 3 Or *Terror on Every Side.*

You are stronger than I and have
prevailed.
I am held in derision daily;
everyone mocks me.
8 For each time I speak, I cry out;
I cry out, "Violence and devastation,"
because to me the word of the LORD has
resulted
in reproach and derision daily.
9 But if I say, "I will not make mention of
Him
nor speak any more in His name,"
then His word was in my heart
as a burning fire shut up in my bones;
and I was weary of forbearing it,
and I could not endure it.
10 For I heard the defaming of many,
"Terror on every side!
Denounce him. Yes, denounce him!"
All my familiar friends
who watch for my fall, say,
"Perhaps he will be enticed
so that we can prevail against him,
and we will take our revenge on him."

11 But the LORD is with me as a dread mighty
One.
Therefore my persecutors will stumble,
and will not prevail.
They will be greatly ashamed, for they will
not prosper.
Their everlasting shame will never be
forgotten.
12 But, O LORD of Hosts, who tests the
righteous
and sees the mind and the heart,
let me see Your vengeance on them,
for to You I have presented my cause.

13 Sing to the LORD,
praise the LORD.
For He has delivered the soul of the poor
from the hand of evildoers.

14 Cursed be the day in which I was born.
Let not the day be blessed in which my
mother bore me.
15 Cursed be the man who brought tidings to
my father,
saying, "A baby boy has been born to
you!"
and made him very glad.
16 Let that man be as the cities
which the LORD overthrew and did not
relent,
and let him hear the cry in the morning
and the shout of alarm at noon,
17 because he did not kill me from the womb,
so that my mother might have been my
grave,
and her womb be always pregnant.

20:8 Jer 6:10
20:9 Job 32:18–20
20:10 Ps 31:13
20:11 Jer 15:20
20:12 Jer 11:20
20:14 Jer 15:10
20:16 Jer 18:22
20:17 Job 3:10–11
....
20:18 Job 3:20
21:1 Jer 29:25
21:2 Jer 37:3
21:4 Jer 32:5
21:5 Ex 6:6
21:6 Jer 32:24
21:7 Jer 37:17
21:8 Dt 30:15
21:9 Jer 38:2
21:10 Jer 44:11
21:12 Isa 1:17
21:13 Ps 125:2

18 Why did I come forth from the womb
to see trouble and sorrow,
so that my days are spent in shame?

Zedekiah's Request Denied

21 The word which came to Jeremiah
from the LORD when King Zedekiah
sent to him Pashhur the son of Malkijah, and
Zephaniah the son of Maaseiah the priest, say-
ing, 2 "Please inquire of the LORD for us. For
Nebuchadnezzar king of Babylon is making
war against us. Perhaps the LORD will deal with
us according to all His wondrous works, so that
the enemy withdraws from us."
3 Then Jeremiah said to them: Thus you shall
say to Zedekiah: 4 Thus says the LORD God of
Israel: Behold, I will turn back the weapons
of war that are in your hands with which you
fight against the king of Babylon and against
the Chaldeans who besiege you outside the
walls; and I will assemble them into the midst
of this city. 5 I Myself will fight against you with
an outstretched hand and with a strong arm,
even in anger, and in fury, and in great wrath.
6 I will strike the inhabitants of this city, both
man and beast; they will die of a great pesti-
lence. 7 Afterwards, says the LORD, I will deliver
Zedekiah king of Judah and his servants and
the people and such as are left in this city from
the pestilence, from the sword, and from the
famine into the hand of Nebuchadnezzar king
of Babylon, and into the hand of their enemies
and into the hand of those who seek their life.
And he will strike them with the edge of the
sword. He will not spare them or have pity
or mercy.
8 To this people you shall say: Thus says the
LORD: See, I set before you the way of life, and
the way of death. 9 He who abides in this city
will die by the sword and by the famine and by
the pestilence. But he who goes out and falls
away to the Chaldeans who besiege you, he
will live, and he will have his own life as booty.
10 For I have set My face against this city for
disaster and not for good, says the LORD. It will
be given into the hand of the king of Babylon,
and he will burn it with fire.

Message to the House of David

11 Concerning the house of the king of Judah,
say, Hear the word of the LORD, 12 O house of
David; thus says the LORD:

Execute justice each morning,
and deliver him who has been robbed
from the hand of the oppressor,
lest My fury go out like fire
and burn so that no one can quench it,
because of the evil of your deeds.
13 See, I am against you,
O inhabitant of the valley,

O rocky plain,
says the LORD,
you men who say,
"Who shall come down against us?
Or who shall enter our dwellings?"
14 But I will punish you
according to the fruit of your deeds,
says the LORD,
and I will kindle a fire in the forest,
and it will devour all things around it.

Impending Judgment

22 Thus says the LORD: Go down to the
house of the king of Judah, and speak
this word there, 2 and say: Hear the word of the
LORD, O king of Judah who sits on the throne of
David, you and your servants and your people
who enter by these gates. 3 Thus says the LORD:
Execute justice and righteousness, and deliver
the robbed out of the hand of the oppressor.
And do no wrong or violence to the stranger,
the fatherless, or the widow, neither shed inno-
cent blood in this place. 4 For if you indeed do
these things, then kings sitting on the throne
of David will enter by the gates of this house,
riding in chariots and on horses, he and his
servants and his people. 5 But if you will not
obey these words, I swear by Myself, says the
LORD, that this house will become a desolation.
6 For thus says the LORD to the king's house
of Judah:

You are Gilead to Me,
and the peak of Lebanon;
yet surely I will make you a wilderness
and cities which are not inhabited.
7 I will prepare destroyers against you,
everyone with his weapons;
and they shall cut down your choice cedars
and cast them into the fire.

8 Many nations will pass by this city, and ev-
ery man will say to his neighbor, "Why has
the LORD done thus to this great city?" 9 Then
they will answer, "Because they have forsaken
the covenant of the LORD their God, and wor-
shipped other gods, and served them."

10 Do not weep for the dead nor bemoan him,
but weep constantly for him who goes
away;
for he will return no more
nor see his native country.

11 For thus says the LORD concerning Shallum
the son of Josiah king of Judah, who became
king instead of Josiah his father, who went
from this place: He will not return any more,
12 but will die in the place where they have led
him captive and will see this land no more.

21:14 2Ch 36:19
22:2 Lk 1:32
22:3 Jer 21:12
22:4 Jer 17:25
22:5 Heb 6:13
22:7 Isa 37:24
22:8 1Ki 9:8–9
22:9 2Ki 22:17
22:10 Ecc 4:2
22:12 2Ki 23:34
22:13 Lev 19:13
22:14 2Sa 7:2
22:15 2Ki 23:25
22:16 Ps 72:1–4
22:17 2Ki 24:4
22:18 1Ki 13:30
22:19 Jer 36:30
22:20 Nu 27:12
22:21 Jer 3:25
22:22 Jer 20:11
22:23 Jer 6:24

13 Woe to him who builds his house with
unrighteousness
and his chambers with injustice,
who uses his neighbor's services without
wages,
and gives him nothing for his work,
14 who says, "I will build myself a roomy
house
and large chambers,"
and cuts out its windows,
paneling it with cedar
and painting it with vermilion.

15 Do you reign
because you compete in cedar?
Did not your father eat and drink
and do justice and righteousness,
and then it was well with him?
16 He judged the cause of the poor and
needy;
then it was well with him.
Is not this what it means to know Me?
says the LORD.
17 But your eyes and your heart
are intent only on your covetousness
and on shedding innocent blood
and on oppression and violence.

18 Therefore thus says the LORD concerning
Jehoiakim the son of Josiah, king of Judah:

They will not lament for him, saying,
"Ah, my brother!" or, "Ah, sister!"
They will not lament for him, saying,
"Ah, lord!" or, "Ah, his glory!"
19 He will be buried with the burial of a
donkey,
drawn and cast out
beyond the gates of Jerusalem.

20 Go up to Lebanon and cry out,
and lift up your voice in Bashan,
and cry out from Abarim,
for all your lovers are destroyed.
21 I spoke to you in your prosperity,
but you said, "I will not listen!"
This has been your manner from your
youth,
that you have not obeyed My voice.
22 The wind will sweep away all your
shepherds,
and your lovers shall go into captivity;
surely then you will be ashamed and
humiliated
for all your wickedness.
23 O inhabitant of Lebanon,
who makes your nest in the cedars,
how you will groan when pangs come
upon you,
the pain as of a woman in labor!

[24] As I live, says the LORD, though Koniah the
son of Jehoiakim king of Judah were the sig-
net on My right hand, yet would I pluck you
from there. [25] And I will give you into the hand
of those who seek your life and into the hand
of those whose face you fear, even into the
hand of Nebuchadnezzar king of Babylon and
into the hand of the Chaldeans. [26] I will cast
you and your mother that bore you out into
another country where you were not born, and
there you shall die. [27] But to the land where
they desire to return, they will not return there.

[28] Is this man Koniah a despised broken jar?
 Is he a vessel in which is no desire?
Why are he and his seed cast out
 and thrown into a land which they had
  not known?
[29] O land, land, land,
 hear the word of the LORD!
[30] Thus says the LORD:
 Write down this man childless,
 a man who will not prosper in his days;
for no man of his seed shall prosper,
 sitting on the throne of David
 and ruling any more in Judah.

The Righteous Branch

23 Woe to the shepherds who destroy and
scatter the sheep of My pasture! says
the LORD. [2] Therefore thus says the LORD God
of Israel against the shepherds that feed My
people: You have scattered My flock and driven
them away and have not visited them. I am
about to punish you for the evil of your deeds,
says the LORD. [3] I will gather the remnant of My
flock out of all countries wherever I have driv-
en them and bring them again to their folds,
and they shall be fruitful and increase. [4] I will
also set up shepherds over them who will feed
them; and they will fear no more, nor be dis-
mayed, nor will they be missing, says the LORD.

[5] The days are coming, says the LORD,
 that I will raise up for David a righteous
  Branch,
and he shall reign as king and deal wisely,
 and shall execute justice and
  righteousness in the earth.
[6] In his days Judah will be saved,
 and Israel will dwell safely.
And this is the name by which he will be
  called:

THE LORD OUR RIGHTEOUSNESS.

[7] Therefore, surely the days are coming, says
the LORD, when they will no more say, "As the
LORD lives who brought up the sons of Israel
out of the land of Egypt," [8] but, "As the LORD
lives who brought up and led the descendants
of the house of Israel out of the north coun-
try and from all countries where I had driven
them." Then they will dwell in their own land.

22:24 SS 8:6
22:26 2Ki 24:15
22:28 Ps 31:12
22:29 Jer 6:19
22:30 Ps 94:20
23:1 Jer 10:21
23:2 Ex 32:34
23:3 Jer 32:37
23:4 1Pe 1:5
23:5 Isa 4:2
23:6 1Co 1:30
23:7 Jer 16:14–15
23:8 Isa 43:5–6

23:9 Hab 3:16
23:10 Ps 107:34
23:11 Jer 6:13
23:12 Ps 35:6
23:13 Jer 2:8
23:14 Isa 1:9–10
23:15 Jer 8:14
23:16 Jer 14:14
23:17 Mic 3:11

Lying Prophets

[9] My heart is broken within me,
 because of the prophets;
 all my bones shake;
I am like a drunken man,
 like a man overcome by wine,
because of the LORD,
 and because of His holy words.
[10] For the land is full of adulterers;
 for the land mourns because of the
  curse.
 The pleasant places of the wilderness
  have dried up.
And their course is evil
 and their might is not right.

[11] For both prophet and priest are profane;
 indeed, in My house I have found their
  wickedness,
 says the LORD.
[12] Therefore their way will be as slippery
  ways to them;
 they shall be driven into the darkness
 and fall in it;
for I will bring disaster upon them,
 even the year of their punishment,
 says the LORD.

[13] In addition, I have seen folly
 in the prophets of Samaria.
They prophesied by Baal
 and caused My people Israel to err.
[14] I have seen also among the prophets of
  Jerusalem
 a horrible thing.
 They commit adultery and walk in lies.
They also strengthen the hands of
  evildoers,
 so that no one repents from his
  wickedness.
All of them are as Sodom to Me
 and her inhabitants as Gomorrah.

[15] Therefore thus says the LORD of Hosts con-
cerning the prophets:

"I will feed them with wormwood
 and make them drink the water of gall,
for from the prophets of Jerusalem
 profaneness has gone out into all the
  land."

[16] Thus says the LORD of Hosts:

Do not listen to the words of the prophets
  who prophesy to you.
 They lead you into vanity;
they speak a vision of their own heart
 and not out of the mouth of the LORD.
[17] They still say to those who despise Me,
 "The LORD has said, 'You will have
  peace' ";

and they say to everyone who walks after
the imagination of his own heart,
"No evil will come upon you."
18 For who has stood in the counsel of the
LORD
and has perceived and heard His word?
Who has given heed to His word and
listened to it?
19 Look, a whirlwind of the LORD
has gone forth in fury,
a tempestuous whirlwind.
It will fall tempestuously upon the head
of the wicked.
20 The anger of the LORD will not turn back
until He has executed and performed
the thoughts of His heart.
In the latter days
you will understand it perfectly.
21 I have not sent these prophets,
yet they ran.
I have not spoken to them,
yet they prophesied.
22 But if they had stood in My counsel
and had caused My people to hear My
words,
then they would have turned them from
their evil way
and from the evil of their deeds.
23 Am I a God who is near,
says the LORD,
and not a God far off?
24 Can a man hide himself in secret places
so that I do not see him?
says the LORD.
Do I not fill heaven and earth?
says the LORD.

> Let Your Word out of my mouth be like a hammer that breaks the rocks in pieces (Jer 23:29).

25 I have heard what the prophets have said
who prophesy lies in My name, saying, "I had
a dream, I had a dream!" 26 How long shall this
be in the heart of the prophets who prophesy
lies? Indeed, they are prophets of the deceit of
their own heart, 27 who plan to cause My peo-
ple to forget My name by their dreams, which
they tell to their neighbor, as their fathers have
forgotten My name for Baal. 28 The prophet
who has a dream, let him tell his dream. And
he who has My word, let him speak My word
faithfully. What is the chaff to the wheat? says
the LORD. 29 Is not My word like fire, says the
LORD, and like a hammer that breaks the rock
in pieces?

23:18 Jer 23:22
23:19 Jer 25:32
23:20 Jer 30:24
23:21 Jer 14:14
23:22 Jer 23:18
23:23 Ps 139:1–10
23:24 1Ki 8:27
23:25 Jer 23:28
23:26 1Ti 4:1–2
23:27 Jdg 3:7
23:28 1Co 3:12–13
23:29 Jer 5:14
....
23:30 Dt 18:20
23:31 Jer 23:17
23:32 Jer 7:8
23:33 Mal 1:1
23:36 2Pe 3:16
23:39 Jer 23:33
23:40 Jer 20:11
24:1 Jer 29:2
24:2 Isa 5:4
24:3 Am 8:2

30 See, therefore I am against the prophets,
says the LORD, who steal My words, each from
his neighbor. 31 See, I am against the prophets,
says the LORD, who use their tongues and say,
"The LORD says." 32 See, I am against those who
prophesy false dreams, says the LORD, and re-
count them and cause My people to err by their
lies and reckless boasting. Yet I sent them not
nor commanded them. Therefore they shall
not profit this people at all, says the LORD.

False Prophecy

33 When this people or the prophet or a priest
asks you, saying, "What is the oracle of the
LORD?" you shall then say to them, "What ora-
cle? I will forsake you, says the LORD." 34 As for
the prophet and the priest and the people who
say, "The oracle of the LORD," I will punish that
man and his house. 35 Thus each of you will say
to his neighbor and to his brother, "What has
the LORD answered?" and, "What has the LORD
spoken?" 36 And the oracle of the LORD you shall
mention no more, for every man's word will be
his oracle. For you have perverted the words
of the living God, of the LORD of Hosts our God.
37 Thus you will say to that prophet, "What has
the LORD answered you?" and, "What has the
LORD spoken?" 38 But if you say, "The oracle of
the LORD"; therefore thus says the LORD: Be-
cause you say this word, "The oracle of the
LORD," I have also sent to you, saying, You shall
not say, "The oracle of the LORD." 39 Therefore,
surely, I, even I, will utterly forget you and cast
you and the city that I gave you and your fa-
thers out of My presence. 40 And I will bring an
everlasting reproach upon you and perpetual
shame which shall not be forgotten.

The Good and Bad Figs

24 The LORD showed me two baskets of
figs that were set before the temple of
the LORD after Nebuchadnezzar king of Baby-
lon had carried away captive Jeconiah the son
of Jehoiakim, king of Judah, and the officials
of Judah with the carpenters and smiths from
Jerusalem and brought them to Babylon. 2 One
basket had very good figs, even like the figs
that are first ripe, and the other basket had very
rotten figs, which were so rotten they could
not be eaten.

3 Then the LORD said to me, "What do you
see, Jeremiah?"

And I said, "Figs, the good figs, very good.
And the rotten, very rotten, that are so rotten
they cannot be eaten."

4 Again the word of the LORD came to me,
saying: 5 Thus says the LORD the God of Israel:
Like these good figs, so I will acknowledge
those who are carried away captive of Judah,
whom I have sent out of this place into the

land of the Chaldeans for their good. 6 For I will set My eyes upon them for good, and I will bring them again to this land. And I will build them up and not pull them down. And I will plant them and not pluck them up. 7 I will give them a heart to know Me, that I am the LORD; and they will be My people, and I will be their God, for they will return to Me with their whole heart.

8 But as the rotten figs, which cannot be eaten, they are so rotten, says the LORD, so I will forsake Zedekiah the king of Judah and his officials, and the rest of Jerusalem who remain in this land, and those who dwell in the land of Egypt. 9 And I will make them a horror and an evil to all the kingdoms of the earth, to be a reproach and a byword, a taunt and a curse, in all places wherever I shall drive them. 10 I will send the sword, the famine, and the pestilence among them until they are consumed from off the land that I gave to them and to their fathers.

Seventy Years of Captivity

25 The word that came to Jeremiah concerning all the people of Judah in the fourth year of Jehoiakim the son of Josiah, king of Judah, that was the first year of Nebuchadnezzar king of Babylon, 2 which Jeremiah the prophet spoke to all the people of Judah and to all the inhabitants of Jerusalem, saying: 3 From the thirteenth year of Josiah the son of Amon, king of Judah, even to this day, these twenty-three years the word of the LORD has come to me, and I have spoken to you, rising early and speaking, but you have not listened.

4 The LORD has sent to you all His servants the prophets, rising early and sending them, but you have not listened nor inclined your ear to hear. 5 They said, "Turn now again everyone from his evil way and from the evil of your deeds, and dwell in the land that the LORD has given to you and to your fathers forever and ever. 6 And do not go after other gods to serve them and to worship them, and provoke Me not to anger with the works of your hands; and I will do you no harm."

7 Yet you have not listened to Me, says the LORD, that you might provoke Me to anger with the works of your hands to your own harm.

8 Therefore thus says the LORD of Hosts: Because you have not obeyed My words, 9 I will send and take all the families of the north, says the LORD, and Nebuchadnezzar the king of Babylon, My servant, and will bring them against this land and its inhabitants, and against all these surrounding nations; I will utterly destroy them, and make them an astonishment, a hissing, and perpetual desolations. 10 Moreover I will take from them the voice of laughter and the voice of gladness, the voice of the bridegroom and the voice of the bride, the sound of the millstones and the light of the candle. 11 This whole land shall be a desolation and an astonishment, and these nations will serve the king of Babylon seventy years.

12 It shall come to pass when seventy years are finished that I will punish the king of Babylon and that nation, says the LORD, for their iniquity, and the land of the Chaldeans, and will make it perpetual desolations. 13 I will bring upon that land all My words which I have pronounced against it, even all that is written in this book, which Jeremiah has prophesied against all the nations. 14 For many nations and great kings will make slaves of them, even them. And I will recompense them according to their deeds and according to the works of their hands.

The Cup of God's Wrath

15 For thus says the LORD God of Israel to me: Take the wine cup of this fury at My hand and cause all the nations to whom I send you to drink it. 16 They will drink, and totter, and be mad, because of the sword that I will send among them.

17 Then I took the cup from the hand of the LORD and made all the nations, to whom the LORD had sent me, drink: 18 Jerusalem and the cities of Judah and the kings and the officials, to make them a desolation, an astonishment, a hissing, and a curse, as it is this day; 19 Pharaoh king of Egypt, and his servants, and his officials, and all his people; 20 and all the foreign people, and all the kings of the land of Uz, and all the kings of the land of the Philistines (even Ashkelon, and Gaza, and Ekron, and the remnant of Ashdod); 21 Edom, and Moab, and the children of Ammon; 22 and all the kings of Tyre, and all the kings of Sidon, and the kings of the coastlands which are beyond the sea; 23 Dedan, and Tema, and Buz, and all who cut the corners of their hair; 24 and all the kings of Arabia, and all the kings of the foreign people who dwell in the desert; 25 and all the kings of Zimri, and all the kings of Elam, and all the kings of the Medes; 26 and all the kings of the north, far and near, one with another; and all the kingdoms of the earth which are upon the face of the earth, and the king of Sheshak shall drink after them.

27 Therefore you shall say to them, Thus says the LORD of Hosts, the God of Israel: Drink and be drunk and spew and fall and rise no more because of the sword which I will send among you. 28 It will be, if they refuse to take the cup from your hand to drink, then you will say to

24:6 Jer 29:10
24:7 Jer 30:22
24:9 Jer 15:4
24:10 Isa 51:19
25:1 Jer 36:1
25:2 Jer 18:11
25:3 Jer 1:2
25:4 Jer 25:3
25:5 Jer 7:7
25:6 Dt 8:19
25:7 2Ki 21:15
25:9 Jer 1:15
25:10 Jer 7:34
25:11 Da 9:2
25:12 Isa 13:19
25:14 Jer 51:6
25:15 Ps 75:8
25:16 Na 3:11
25:17 Jer 1:10
25:20 Job 1:1
25:21 Jer 48:1–49:22
25:22 Jer 47:4
25:23 Jer 9:26
25:24 2Ch 9:14
25:25 Ge 10:22
25:26 Jer 51:41
25:27 Jer 25:16
25:28 Job 34:33

them: Thus says the LORD of Hosts: You shall
certainly drink! 29 For I am starting to bring ca-
lamity on the city which is called by My name,
and should you be utterly unpunished? You
shall not be unpunished. For I will call for a
sword upon all the inhabitants of the earth,
says the LORD of Hosts.
30 Therefore prophesy against them all these
words, and say to them:

The LORD will roar from on high,
and utter His voice from His holy
habitation;
He will mightily roar against His fold.
He will give a shout, as those who tread the
grapes,
against all the inhabitants of the earth.
31 A noise shall come even to the remote
parts of the earth,
for the LORD has a controversy with the
nations;
He shall enter into judgment with all flesh.
He shall give those who are wicked to
the sword,
says the LORD.

32 Thus says the LORD of Hosts:

See, disaster shall go forth
from nation to nation,
and a great whirlwind shall be raised up
from the remote parts of the earth.

33 The slain of the LORD on that day will be
from one end of the earth even to the other
end of the earth. They will not be lamented
or gathered or buried. They will be as dung
on the ground.

34 Howl, you shepherds, and cry;
and wallow in the ashes, you leaders of
the flock.
For the days of your slaughter and of your
dispersions are accomplished;
and you will fall like a choice vessel.
35 The shepherds will have no way to flee,
nor the leaders of the flock to escape.
36 A voice of the cry of the shepherds
and a howling of the leaders of the flock
shall be heard,
for the LORD has devastated their pasture.
37 The peaceable habitations are cut down
because of the fierce anger of the LORD.
38 He has left His lair as the lion;
for their land is desolate
because of the fierceness of the oppressor
and because of His fierce anger.

Jeremiah Threatened With Death

26 In the beginning of the reign of Je-
hoiakim the son of Josiah, king of
Judah, this word came from the LORD, saying:
2 Thus says the LORD: Stand in the court of the
house of the LORD, and speak to all the cities
of Judah who come to worship in the house of
the LORD all the words that I command you to
speak to them. Do not diminish a word. 3 Per-
haps they will listen and turn every man from
his evil way, that I may repent of the calamity
which I purpose to do to them because of the
evil of their deeds. 4 You will say to them: Thus
says the LORD: If you will not listen to Me, to
walk in My law which I have set before you, 5 to
listen to the words of My servants the prophets,
whom I sent to you, both rising up early and
sending them, but you have not listened, 6 then
I will make this house like Shiloh and will make
this city a curse to all the nations of the earth.
7 So the priests and the prophets and all the
people heard Jeremiah speaking these words
in the house of the LORD. 8 And when Jeremi-
ah had made an end of speaking all that the
LORD had commanded him to speak to all the
people, the priests and the prophets and all
the people took hold of him, saying, "You shall
surely die. 9 Why have you prophesied in the
name of the LORD, saying, 'This house shall
be like Shiloh, and this city shall be desolate
without an inhabitant'?" And all the people
were gathered against Jeremiah in the house
of the LORD.
10 When the officials of Judah heard these
things, then they came up from the king's
house to the house of the LORD and sat down
in the entry of the New Gate of the house of
the LORD. 11 Then the priests and the proph-
ets spoke to the officials and to all the people,
saying, "This man deserves to die! For he has
prophesied against this city, as you have heard
with your ears."
12 Then Jeremiah spoke to all the officials and
to all the people, saying, "The LORD sent me to
prophesy against this house and against this
city all the words that you have heard. 13 There-
fore now amend your ways and your deeds,
and obey the voice of the LORD your God; and
the LORD will repent of the disaster that He has
pronounced against you. 14 As for me, here I
am in your hand. Do with me as seems good
and right to you. 15 But know for certain that
if you put me to death, you will surely bring
innocent blood upon yourselves and upon
this city and upon the inhabitants. For truly
the LORD has sent me to you to speak all these
words in your ears."

Jeremiah Spared From Death

16 Then the officials and all the people said to
the priests and to the prophets, "This man is
not worthy of death. For he has spoken to us
in the name of the LORD our God."

25:29 Pr 11:31
25:30 Joel 3:10
25:31 Hos 4:1
25:32 Jer 23:19
25:33 Isa 66:16
25:34 Jer 6:26
25:35 Job 11:20
25:36 Jer 4:8
25:37 Isa 27:10–11
25:38 Jer 4:7

....

26:2 Dt 4:2
26:3 Jer 18:7–10
26:4 1Ki 9:6
26:5 Jer 25:3–4
26:6 2Ki 22:19
26:8 La 4:13–14
26:10 Jer 36:10
26:11 Jer 38:4
26:12 Jer 26:15
26:13 Jer 26:3
26:14 Jer 38:5
26:16 Ac 5:34–39

17 Then certain of the elders of the land rose
up and spoke to all the assembly of the people,
saying: 18 "Micah of Moresheth prophesied in
the days of Hezekiah king of Judah, and spoke
to all the people of Judah, saying, 'Thus says
the LORD of Hosts:

Zion shall be plowed like a field,
and Jerusalem shall become heaps,
and the mountain of the house as the
high places of a forest.'

19 Did Hezekiah king of Judah and all Judah
put him to death? Did he not fear the LORD
and entreat the LORD, and the LORD relented
of the disaster which He had pronounced
against them? Thus we might procure great
evil against ourselves."

20 There was also a man that prophesied in
the name of the LORD, Uriah the son of Shem-
aiah of Kiriath Jearim, who prophesied against
this city and against this land according to all
the words of Jeremiah. 21 And when Jehoiakim
the king, with all his mighty men and all the
officials, heard his words, the king sought to
put him to death. But when Uriah heard it,
he was afraid and fled and went into Egypt.
22 And Jehoiakim the king sent men into Egypt:
namely, Elnathan the son of Akbor and certain
men with him into Egypt. 23 They brought Uri-
ah out of Egypt and led him to Jehoiakim the
king, who slew him with the sword and cast
his dead body into the graves of the common
people.

24 Nevertheless the hand of Ahikam the son
of Shaphan was with Jeremiah, with the result
that he was not given into the hands of the
people to put him to death.

Judah to Serve Nebuchadnezzar

27 In the beginning of the reign of Ze-
dekiah the son of Josiah, king of Ju-
dah, this word came to Jeremiah from the LORD:
2 Thus says the LORD to me: Make bonds and
yokes and put them on your neck, 3 and send
them to the king of Edom, and to the king of
Moab, and to the king of the Ammonites, and
to the king of Tyre, and to the king of Sidon,
by the hand of the messengers who come to
Jerusalem to Zedekiah king of Judah. 4 And
command them to go to their masters, say-
ing: Thus says the LORD of Hosts, the God of
Israel: Thus you shall say to your masters: 5 I
have made the earth, the men, and the beasts
which are on the ground by My great power
and by My outstretched arm, and have given
it to whom it seemed good to Me. 6 Now I have
given all these lands into the hand of Nebu-
chadnezzar the king of Babylon, My servant.
And also I have given to him the beasts of the
field to serve him. 7 All nations shall serve him
and his son and his son's son until the time of
his own land comes; and then many nations
and great kings will make him their servant.

8 It shall come to pass that I will punish the
nation and kingdom which will not serve Ne-
buchadnezzar the king of Babylon, and that
will not put their neck under the yoke of the
king of Babylon, says the LORD. I will punish
that nation with the sword, and with famine,
and with pestilence, until I have consumed
them by his hand. 9 Therefore do not listen to
your prophets, or to your diviners, or to your
dreamers, or to your enchanters, or to your sor-
cerers who speak to you, saying, "You shall not
serve the king of Babylon." 10 For they prophe-
sy a lie to you in order to remove you far from
your land. And I will drive you out, and you
shall perish. 11 But the nations that bring their
neck under the yoke of the king of Babylon,
and serve him, those I will let remain still in
their own land, says the LORD, and they shall
till it and dwell in it.

12 I spoke also to Zedekiah king of Judah
according to all these words, saying: Bring
your necks under the yoke of the king of Bab-
ylon and serve him and his people, and live.
13 Why will you die, you and your people, by
the sword, by the famine, and by the pesti-
lence, as the LORD has spoken against the na-
tion that will not serve the king of Babylon?
14 Therefore do not listen to the words of the
prophets who speak to you, saying, "You will
not serve the king of Babylon," because they
prophesy a lie to you. 15 For I have not sent
them, says the LORD, yet they prophesy a lie
in My name, so that I might drive you out and
that you might perish, you and the prophets
that prophesy to you.

16 I also spoke to the priests and to all this
people: Thus says the LORD: Do not listen to
the words of your prophets that prophesy to
you, saying, "The vessels of the house of the
LORD will now soon be brought again from
Babylon." For they prophesy a lie to you. 17 Do
not listen to them; serve the king of Babylon,
and live. Why should this city be laid waste?
18 But if they are prophets, and if the word
of the LORD is with them, let them now make
intercession to the LORD of Hosts, that the ves-
sels which are left in the house of the LORD
and in the house of the king of Judah and in
Jerusalem not go to Babylon. 19 For thus says
the LORD of Hosts concerning the pillars, and
concerning the sea, and concerning the bas-
es, and concerning the rest of the vessels that
remain in this city, 20 which Nebuchadnezzar
king of Babylon did not take when he carried
away captive Jeconiah the son of Jehoiakim,
king of Judah from Jerusalem to Babylon, and

26:17 Ac 5:34
26:18 Ne 4:2
26:19 Ex 32:14
26:20 1Sa 7:2
26:21 Mt 10:23
26:23 Jer 2:30
27:5 Ps 115:15–16
27:6 Jer 28:14
27:10 Jer 32:31
27:11 Jer 21:9
27:12 Jer 28:1
27:13 Eze 18:31
27:14 Jer 14:14
27:15 Jer 27:10
27:16 2Ki 24:13
27:18 1Sa 7:8
27:19 2Ki 25:13
27:20 Jer 24:1

all the nobles of Judah and Jerusalem. 21 Indeed, thus says the LORD of Hosts, the God of Israel, concerning the vessels that remain in the house of the LORD and in the house of the king of Judah and in Jerusalem: 22 They will be carried to Babylon and they will be there until the day that I visit them, says the LORD. Then I will bring them up and restore them to this place.

The False Prophet Hananiah

28 In that same year, at the beginning of the reign of Zedekiah king of Judah, in the fourth year and in the fifth month, Hananiah the son of Azzur, the prophet, who was from Gibeon, spoke to me in the house of the LORD in the presence of the priests and of all the people, saying, 2 "Thus says the LORD of Hosts, the God of Israel: I have broken the yoke of the king of Babylon. 3 Within two full years I will bring back into this place all the vessels of the house of the LORD that Nebuchadnezzar king of Babylon took away from this place and carried to Babylon. 4 And I will bring back to this place Jeconiah the son of Jehoiakim, king of Judah, with all the captives of Judah who went into Babylon, says the LORD, for I will break the yoke of the king of Babylon."

5 Then the prophet Jeremiah said to the prophet Hananiah in the presence of the priests and in the presence of all the people that stood in the house of the LORD, 6 even the prophet Jeremiah said, "Amen. May the LORD do so; may the LORD perform your words which you have prophesied, to bring back the vessels of the house of the LORD and all that was carried away captive, from Babylon into this place. 7 Nevertheless hear now this word that I speak in your ears and in the ears of all the people. 8 The prophets of old who have been before me and before you prophesied both against many countries and against great kingdoms, of war and disaster and pestilence. 9 As for the prophet who prophesies of peace, when the word of the prophet comes to pass, then that prophet shall be known as one whom the LORD has truly sent."

10 Then Hananiah the prophet took the yoke from off the neck of the prophet Jeremiah and broke it. 11 Hananiah spoke in the presence of all the people, saying, "Thus says the LORD: Even so I will break the yoke of Nebuchadnezzar king of Babylon from the neck of all the nations within the space of two full years." Then the prophet Jeremiah went his way.

12 Then the word of the LORD came to Jeremiah the prophet, after Hananiah the prophet had broken the yoke from off the neck of the prophet Jeremiah, saying: 13 Go and tell Hananiah, saying, Thus says the LORD: You have broken the yokes of wood, but you have made instead of them yokes of iron. 14 For thus says the LORD of Hosts, the God of Israel: I have put a yoke of iron on the neck of all these nations, that they may serve Nebuchadnezzar king of Babylon; and they shall serve him. And I have given him the beasts of the field also.

15 Then the prophet Jeremiah said to Hananiah the prophet, "Listen now, Hananiah. The LORD has not sent you, and you make this people trust in a lie. 16 Therefore thus says the LORD: I am about to cast you from off the face of the earth. This year you shall die, because you have taught rebellion against the LORD."

17 So Hananiah the prophet died the same year in the seventh month.

Jeremiah's Letter to the Exiles

29 Now these are the words of the letter that Jeremiah the prophet sent from Jerusalem to the rest of the elders of the captivity, and the priests, and the prophets, and all the people whom Nebuchadnezzar had carried away captive from Jerusalem to Babylon. 2 (This was after Jeconiah the king, and the queen, and the eunuchs, and the officials of Judah and Jerusalem, and the carpenters, and the smiths had departed from Jerusalem.) 3 It was sent by the hand of Elasah the son of Shaphan and Gemariah the son of Hilkiah (whom Zedekiah, king of Judah, sent to Babylon to Nebuchadnezzar king of Babylon), saying:

4 Thus says the LORD of Hosts, the God of Israel, to all who have been carried away captive whom I have caused to be carried away from Jerusalem to Babylon: 5 Build houses and dwell in them; and plant gardens and eat their fruit. 6 Take wives and beget sons and daughters; and take wives for your sons and give your daughters to husbands, so that they may bear sons and daughters; so that you may increase there and not diminish. 7 Seek the peace of the city where I have caused you to be carried away captive, and pray to the LORD for it; for in its peace you will have peace. 8 For thus says the LORD of Hosts, the God of Israel: Do not let your prophets and your diviners who are in your midst deceive you, and do not listen to the dreams which they dream. 9 For they prophesy falsely to you in My name. I have not sent them, says the LORD.

10 For thus says the LORD: When seventy years have been completed for Babylon, I will visit you and perform My good word toward you, in causing you to return to this place. 11 For I know the plans that I have for

27:22 Jer 29:10
28:1 Jer 27:1
28:3 2Ki 24:13
28:4 Jer 22:24
28:5 Jer 28:1
28:6 1Ki 1:36
28:7 1Ki 22:28
28:9 Dt 18:22
28:10 Jer 27:2
28:12 Jer 1:2

....

28:14 Dt 28:48
28:15 La 2:14
28:16 Jer 29:32
29:1 Est 9:20
29:2 Jer 22:24–28
29:4 Jer 24:5
29:5 Jer 29:28
29:6 Jer 16:2–4
29:7 Ezr 6:10
29:9 Jer 27:15
29:10 Jer 25:12
29:11 Ps 40:5

SPIRITLED WOMAN

COUNSEL FROM THE SPIRIT BASICS

His Plan

Jeremiah 29:11 says, "For I know the plans that I have for you, says the Lord, plans for peace and not for evil, to give you a future and a hope."

There is a plan and purpose for your life. That is a promise from God to you. He knows the plan, and He wants to tell you all about it so that you can walk in it.

God's plan will produce good results in your life. I'm glad that the verse says He knows what He's doing! You can trust Him. He has your best interest at heart.

Karen Jensen Salisbury

you, says the LORD, plans for peace and not
for evil, to give you a future and a hope.
12 Then you shall call upon Me, and you shall
come and pray to Me, and I will listen to
you. 13 You shall seek Me and find Me, when
you shall search for Me with all your heart.
14 I will be found by you, says the LORD, and
I will turn away your captivity and gather
you from all the nations and from all the
places where I have driven you, says the
LORD, and I will bring you back into the place
from where I caused you to be carried away
captive.

Father, I know You haven't forgotten about me or changed Your mind about me for one moment (Jer 29:11).

15 Because you have said, "The LORD has
raised up prophets for us in Babylon,"
16 thus says the LORD concerning the king
who sits on the throne of David, and con-
cerning all the people who dwell in this city,
your brothers who did not go out with you
into exile, 17 thus says the LORD of Hosts: I
will send upon them the sword, the famine,
and the pestilence, and will make them like
vile figs that cannot be eaten, they are so
rotten. 18 I will pursue them with the sword,
with famine, and with pestilence; and will
make them a terror to all the kingdoms of
the earth, to be a curse and an astonish-
ment, a hissing and a reproach among all
the nations where I have driven them, 19 be-
cause they have not listened to My words,
says the LORD, which I sent to them by My
servants the prophets, rising up early and
sending them. But you would not listen,
says the LORD.
20 Therefore hear the word of the LORD, all
you in captivity whom I have sent from Je-
rusalem to Babylon. 21 Thus says the LORD of
Hosts, the God of Israel, concerning Ahab
the son of Kolaiah and concerning Zedeki-
ah the son of Maaseiah, who prophesy a
lie to you in My name: I will deliver them
into the hand of Nebuchadnezzar king of
Babylon, and he shall slay them before your
eyes. 22 And because of them a curse shall
be taken up by all the captives of Judah who
are in Babylon, saying, "May the LORD make
you like Zedekiah and Ahab, whom the king
of Babylon roasted in the fire," 23 because
they have committed folly in Israel, and
have committed adultery with their neigh-
bors' wives, and have spoken lying words
in My name, which I have not commanded
them. Indeed, I know and am a witness,
says the LORD.

A Message to Shemaiah

24 Thus you shall also speak to Shemaiah the
Nehelamite, saying: 25 Thus says the LORD of
Hosts, the God of Israel: Because you have
sent letters in your name to all the people who
are in Jerusalem, and to Zephaniah the son
of Maaseiah the priest, and to all the priests,
saying, 26 The LORD has made you priest instead
of Jehoiada the priest, that you should be of-
ficers in the house of the LORD, for every man
that is mad and makes himself a prophet, that
you should put him in the stocks and in prison.
27 Now therefore why have you not reproved
Jeremiah of Anathoth who prophesies to you?
28 For he has sent to us in Babylon, saying,
"*This captivity* will be long; build houses and
dwell in them, and plant gardens and eat their
fruit."
29 Zephaniah the priest read this letter in the
ears of Jeremiah the prophet. 30 Then the word
of the LORD came to Jeremiah, saying: 31 Send
to all the captives, saying, Thus says the LORD
concerning Shemaiah the Nehelamite: Be-
cause Shemaiah has prophesied to you though
I did not send, and he caused you to trust in a
lie, 32 therefore thus says the LORD: I will punish
Shemaiah the Nehelamite and his seed. He will
not have a man to dwell among this people,
nor will he see the good that I will do for My
people, says the LORD, because he has taught
rebellion against the LORD.

29:12 Jer 33:3
29:13 Jer 24:7
29:14 Jer 30:3
29:17 Jer 24:8–10
29:18 2Ch 29:8
29:19 Jer 6:19
29:20 Jer 24:5
29:22 Da 3:6
29:23 Jer 23:14
29:24 Jer 29:31–32
29:26 Jer 20:1–2
29:28 Jer 29:5
29:31 Jer 29:9
29:32 Jer 28:16

Israel and Judah Restored

30 The word that came to Jeremiah from
the LORD, saying: 2 Thus says the LORD
God of Israel: Write all the words that I have
spoken to you in a book. 3 For surely the days
are coming, says the LORD, when I will restore
the fortunes of My people Israel and Judah.
The LORD says, I also will cause them to return
to the land that I gave to their fathers, and they
shall possess it.
4 These are the words that the LORD spoke
concerning Israel and Judah. 5 For thus says
the LORD:

I have heard a sound of trembling,
of fear, and not of peace.
6 Ask now, and see,
can a male labor with child?
Why do I see every man
with his hands on his loins, as a woman in labor,
and all faces turned pale?
7 Alas! for that day is great,
so that no one is like it;
it is even the time of Jacob's trouble,
but he shall be saved out of it.

8 For it shall come to pass in that day, says the LORD of Hosts,
that I shall break his yoke from off their neck
and tear away their bonds,
and strangers shall no longer make them their slaves.
9 But they shall serve the LORD their God
and David their king,
whom I will raise up for them.

10 Therefore do not fear, O My servant Jacob,
says the LORD,
nor be dismayed, O Israel;
for I will save you from afar,
and your seed from the land of their captivity.
And Jacob shall return and shall be in rest and be quiet,
and no one shall make him afraid.
11 For I am with you, says the LORD,
to save you.
Although I make a full end of all nations
wherever I have scattered you,
yet I will not make a full end of you.
But I will correct you in measure
and will not leave you altogether unpunished.

12 For thus says the LORD:

Your bruise is incurable
and your wound is severe.
13 There is no one to plead your cause
that you may be bound up.
You have no healing medicines.
14 All your lovers have forgotten you;
they do not seek you;
for I have wounded you with the wound of an enemy,
with the chastisement of a cruel one,
because of the multitude of your iniquities,
because your sins are numerous.
15 Why do you cry because of your affliction?
Your sorrow is incurable.
Because of the multitude of your iniquities,
because your sins are numerous,
I have done these things to you.

16 Therefore all who devour you will be devoured;
and all your adversaries, every one of them, will go into captivity.
And those who plunder you will become plunder,
and all who prey upon you I will give for prey.
17 For I will restore health to you,
and I will heal you of your wounds,
says the LORD,
because they called you an outcast, saying,
"This is Zion whom no man cares for."

18 Thus says the LORD:

I will restore the fortunes of Jacob's tents
and have mercy on his dwelling places;
and the city will be built upon her own heap,
and the palace will remain on its rightful place.
19 Out of them will proceed thanksgiving
and the voice of those who make merry;
and I will multiply them,
and they will not be few.
I will also glorify them,
and they will not be small.
20 Their children also will be as before,
and their congregation will be established before Me;
and I will punish all who oppress them.
21 Their leader shall be one of them,
and their ruler shall proceed from their midst;
and I will cause him to draw near and he will approach Me;
for who is this that dares
to approach Me?
says the LORD.
22 You shall be My people,
and I will be your God.

23 Look, the whirlwind of the LORD
goes forth with fury,
a continuing whirlwind;
it will fall with pain upon the head of the wicked.
24 The fierce anger of the LORD shall not return

30:2 Isa 30:8
30:3 Jer 16:15
30:6 Jer 4:31
30:7 Joel 2:11
30:8 Eze 34:27
30:9 Hos 3:5
30:10 Isa 43:5
30:11 Jer 10:24
30:12 Jer 15:18
....
30:14 Job 30:21
30:16 Jer 10:25
30:17 Ex 15:26
30:18 Jer 30:3
30:19 Isa 35:10
30:21 Nu 16:5
30:24 Jer 23:20

until He has done it
and until He has performed the
intentions of His heart.
In the latter days
you will understand it.

The Exiles Return

31 At that time, says the LORD, I will be the
God of all the families of Israel, and
they shall be My people.
[2] Thus says the LORD:

The people who survived the sword
found grace in the wilderness,
when I went to give Israel rest.

[3] The LORD has appeared to him from afar,
saying:

Indeed, I have loved you with an
everlasting love;
therefore with lovingkindness I have
drawn you.
[4] Again I will build you
and you will be built, O virgin of Israel.
You will again be adorned with your
tambourines
and shall go forth in the dances of those
who make merry.
[5] You will yet plant vines
on the mountains of Samaria;
the planters will plant
and will enjoy them.
[6] For there will be a day when the watchmen
on the hills of Ephraim will proclaim,
"Arise, and let us go up to Zion,
to the LORD our God."

[7] For thus says the LORD:

Sing with gladness for Jacob,
and shout among the chief of the
nations;
publish, praise, and say,
"O LORD, save Your people,
the remnant of Israel."
[8] See, I will bring them from the north
country,
and gather them from the remote parts
of the earth,
and with them the blind and the lame,
the woman with child and her who is in
labor with child, together;
a great company will return here.
[9] They will come with weeping,
and with supplications I will lead them.
I will cause them to walk by the rivers of
waters,
in a straight way in which they shall not
stumble.
For I am a Father to Israel,
and Ephraim is My firstborn.

[10] Hear the word of the LORD, O nations,
and declare it in the coastlands far off,
and say,
"He who scattered Israel will gather him
and keep him, as a shepherd does his
flock."
[11] For the LORD has redeemed Jacob
and ransomed him from the hand of
him who was stronger than he.
[12] Therefore they will come and sing in the
height of Zion,
and will be joyful over the goodness of
the LORD,
for wheat and for wine and for oil
and for the young of the flock and of
the herd;
and their souls will be as a watered garden.
And they will not sorrow any more at all.
[13] Then the virgin shall rejoice in the dance,
both young men and old together;
for I will turn their mourning into joy,
and will comfort them, and make them
rejoice from their sorrow.
[14] I will satiate the soul of the priests with
abundance,
and My people shall be satisfied with My
goodness,
says the LORD.

[15] Thus says the LORD:

A voice is heard in Ramah,
lamentation and bitter weeping,
Rachel weeping for her children,
refusing to be comforted for her
children,
because they are no more.

[16] Thus says the LORD:

Keep your voice from weeping
and your eyes from tears;
for your work shall be rewarded,
says the LORD,
and they shall come back from the land
of the enemy.
[17] There is hope for your future,
says the LORD,
that your children will come back to
their own border.

[18] I have surely heard Ephraim pleading:
"You have chastised me,
and I was chastised, as an untrained calf;
turn me back and I will be turned,
for you are the LORD my God.
[19] Surely after I turned back,
I repented;
and after I was instructed,
I struck myself on my thigh;
I was ashamed and even humiliated

31:1 Jer 30:22
31:3 Hos 11:4
31:4 Jer 31:13
31:5 Am 9:14
31:6 Jer 50:4–5
31:7 Ps 14:7
31:8 Isa 42:16
31:9 Jer 3:4

31:10 Isa 40:11
31:11 Isa 44:23
31:12 Isa 35:10
31:13 Ps 30:11
31:14 Jer 31:25
31:15 Jos 18:25
31:16 Ru 2:12
31:18 Ps 80:3
31:19 Jer 3:25

because I bore the reproach of my
youth."
20 Is Ephraim My dear son?
Is he a pleasant child?
For since I spoke against him,
I *surely do* remember him *still*;
therefore My heart longs for him.
I will surely have mercy on him,
says the LORD.

21 Set up road marks,
place guideposts.
Set your heart toward the highway,
even the way by which you went.
Turn back, O virgin of Israel,
turn back to these your cities.
22 How long will you go about,
O faithless daughter?
For the LORD has created a new thing in the
earth:
A woman shall obtain a man.

23 Thus says the LORD of Hosts, the God of
Israel: Once again they shall use this speech
in the land of Judah and in the cities when I
restore their fortunes: "May the LORD bless you,
O habitation of righteousness and mountain
of holiness!" 24 And Judah and all its cities will
dwell there, the farmer and those who go out
with the flocks. 25 For I satiate the weary souls
and I replenish every languishing soul.
26 Upon this I awoke and looked, and my
sleep was sweet to me.
27 Surely, the days are coming, says the LORD,
when I will sow the house of Israel and the
house of Judah with the seed of man and with
the seed of beast. 28 It shall come to pass that
as I have watched over them to pluck up, and
to break down, and to throw down, and to de-
stroy, and to afflict, so I will watch over them,
to build, and to plant, says the LORD. 29 In those
days they will say no more:

"The fathers have eaten sour grapes,
and the children's teeth are set on edge."
30 But everyone will die for his own iniquity.
Every man that eats the sour grape, his teeth
will be set on edge.

A New Covenant

31 Surely, the days are coming, says the LORD,
when I will make a new covenant
with the house of Israel
and with the house of Judah.
32 It will not be according to the covenant
that I made with their fathers
in the day that I took them by the hand
to bring them out of the land of Egypt,
because they broke My covenant,
although I was a husband to them,
says the LORD.

31:20 Isa 55:7
31:21 Jer 50:5
31:22 Jer 2:23
31:23 Zec 8:3
31:24 Zec 8:4–8
31:25 Jer 31:14
31:27 Hos 2:23
31:28 Jer 1:10
31:29 La 5:7
31:30 Isa 3:11
31:31 Lk 22:20
31:32 Dt 1:31

....

31:33 2Co 3:3
31:34 Isa 54:13
31:35 Isa 51:15
31:36 Isa 54:9–10
31:37 Jer 33:22
31:38 2Ki 14:13
31:39 Zec 2:1–2
31:40 2Sa 15:23
32:1 2Ki 25:1–2
32:2 Ne 3:25

33 But this shall be the covenant that I will
make with the house of Israel
after those days, says the LORD:
I will put My law within them
and write it in their hearts;
and I will be their God,
and they shall be My people.
34 They shall teach no more every man his
neighbor
and every man his brother, saying,
"Know the LORD,"
for they all shall know Me,
from the least of them to the greatest of
them,
says the LORD,
for I will forgive their iniquity,
and I will remember their sin no more.

35 Thus says the LORD,
who gives the sun
for a light by day
and the ordinances of the moon and of the
stars
for a light by night,
who stirs up the sea
so that the waves roar,
the LORD of Hosts is His name:
36 If those ordinances depart from before Me,
says the LORD,
then the seed of Israel also will cease
from being a nation before Me forever.

37 Thus says the LORD:

If heaven above can be measured,
and the foundations of the earth
searched out beneath,
I will also cast off all the seed of Israel
for all that they have done,
says the LORD.

38 Surely, the days are coming, says the LORD,
when the city will be built to the LORD from the
Tower of Hananel to the Corner Gate. 39 The
measuring line shall stretch out straight to the
hill Gareb, and shall then turn to Goah. 40 The
whole valley of the dead bodies and of the
ashes, and all the fields to the Kidron Valley, to
the corner of the Horse Gate toward the east,
will be holy to the LORD. It will not be plucked
up nor thrown down any more forever.

Jeremiah Buys a Field

32 The word that came to Jeremiah from
the LORD in the tenth year of Zedeki-
ah king of Judah, which was the eighteenth
year of Nebuchadnezzar. 2 For then the king
of Babylon's army besieged Jerusalem, and
Jeremiah the prophet was shut up in the court

[1] *9* About 7 ounces, or 200 grams.

of the prison, which was in the house of the king of Judah.

3 For Zedekiah king of Judah had shut him up, saying, "Why do you prophesy? You say: Thus says the LORD: I am about to give this city into the hand of the king of Babylon, and he shall take it, 4 and Zedekiah king of Judah will not escape out of the hand of the Chaldeans, but will surely be delivered into the hand of the king of Babylon, and will speak with him face to face and see him eye to eye. 5 And he will lead Zedekiah to Babylon, and there he will be until I visit him, says the LORD. Though you fight against the Chaldeans, you will not succeed."

6 So Jeremiah said, The word of the LORD came to me, saying: 7 Hanamel the son of Shallum your uncle will come to you, saying, "Buy my field that is in Anathoth. For the right of redemption is yours to buy it."

8 So Hanamel my uncle's son came to me in the court of the prison according to the word of the LORD and said to me, "Please buy my field, that is in Anathoth, which is in the country of Benjamin; for the right of inheritance and the redemption is yours. Buy it for yourself."

Then I knew that this was the word of the LORD. 9 I bought the field of Hanamel my uncle's son, that was in Anathoth, and weighed him the money, even seventeen shekels[1] of silver. 10 I signed and sealed the deed, and summoned witnesses, and weighed the money from him in the balances. 11 So I took the deed of purchase, both that which was sealed according to the law and custom, and that which was open. 12 And I gave the deed of purchase to Baruch the son of Neriah, the son of Mahseiah, in the sight of Hanamel my uncle's son, and in the presence of the witnesses who signed the deed of purchase, before all the Jews who sat in the court of the prison.

13 I charged Baruch in their presence, saying, 14 Thus says the LORD of Hosts, the God of Israel: Take these deeds, this sealed deed of purchase and this deed which is open, and put them in an earthen vessel that they may last many days. 15 For thus says the LORD of Hosts, the God of Israel: Houses and fields and vineyards shall be possessed again in this land.

Jeremiah Prays for Understanding

16 Now when I had delivered the deed of purchase to Baruch the son of Neriah, I prayed to the LORD, saying:

> 17 Ah Lord GOD! Truly, You have made the heavens and the earth by Your great power and outstretched arm, and there is nothing too hard for You. 18 You show lovingkindness to thousands, and recompense the iniquity of the fathers into the bosom of their children after them, O great and mighty God. The LORD of Hosts is His name, 19 great in counsel and mighty in deed, whose eyes are open to all the ways of the sons of men, to give to everyone according to his ways and according to the fruit of his deeds. 20 You have set signs and wonders in the land of Egypt, even to this day, and in Israel, and among other men, and have made Yourself a name, as it is today. 21 And You have brought your people Israel out of the land of Egypt with signs, and with wonders, and with a strong hand, and with a stretched-out arm, and with great terror. 22 And You have given them this land, which You swore to their fathers to give them, a land flowing with milk and honey. 23 And they entered and possessed it. But they did not obey Your voice or walk in Your law. They have done nothing of all that You commanded them to do; therefore You have caused all this calamity to come upon them.
>
> 24 See, the siege ramps have come to the city to take it. And the city is given into the hand of the Chaldeans who fight against it, because of the sword, and of the famine, and of the pestilence, and what You have spoken has come to pass, as You can see. 25 O Lord GOD, You have said to me, "Buy the field for money and call in witnesses," although the city is given into the hand of the Chaldeans.

God Promises the People's Return

26 Then the word of the LORD came to Jeremiah, saying: 27 Behold, I am the LORD, the God of all flesh. Is anything too hard for Me? 28 Therefore thus says the LORD: I will give this city into the hand of the Chaldeans and into the hand of Nebuchadnezzar king of Babylon, and he shall take it. 29 And the Chaldeans who fight against this city will come and set this city on fire and burn it with the houses, upon whose roofs they have offered incense to Baal and poured out drink offerings to other gods, to provoke Me to anger.

30 Indeed the sons of Israel and the sons of Judah have only done evil before Me from their youth. For the sons of Israel have only provoked Me to anger with the work of their hands, says the LORD. 31 Indeed this city has been to Me a provocation of My anger and My fury from the day that they built it, even to this day, so that I should remove it from before My face, 32 because of all the evil of the sons of Israel and of the sons of Judah which they have done to provoke Me to anger, they, their kings, their officials, their priests, and

32:3 Jer 34:2–3
32:4 Jer 38:18
32:7 Jer 1:1
32:8 Jer 32:2
32:10 Jer 32:44
32:11 Lk 2:27
32:12 Jer 32:16
32:15 Jer 30:18
32:17 Ge 18:14
32:18 Jer 10:16

....

32:19 Isa 28:29
32:20 Ne 9:10
32:21 Ex 6:6
32:22 Ex 3:8
32:23 Ezr 9:7
32:24 Dt 4:26
32:25 Jer 32:24
32:27 Nu 16:22
32:28 Jer 32:3
32:29 Jer 19:13
32:31 2Ki 23:27
32:32 Isa 1:4–6

SPIRIT-TO-SPIRIT PRAYER

PRAYER FOR WISDOM AND REVELATION

Father, You say, "Call to Me, and I will answer you, and show you great and mighty things which you do not know" (Jer 33:3).

I thank You, Father, for granting me the spirit of wisdom and revelation in the knowledge of Christ, to understand the deeper things of the Word of God (Eph 1:17).

Iris Delgado

their prophets, and the men of Judah and the inhabitants of Jerusalem. 33 They have turned their back to Me and not their face. Though I taught them, rising up early and teaching them, yet they have not listened nor received instruction. 34 But they set their abominations in the house which is called by My name, to defile it. 35 They built the high places of Baal which are in the Valley of Ben Hinnom to cause their sons and their daughters to pass through *the fire* to Molek, which I had not commanded them, nor did it come into My mind that they should do this abomination, to cause Judah to sin.

36 Now therefore, thus says the LORD, the God of Israel, concerning this city of which you say, "It shall be delivered into the hand of the king of Babylon by the sword, and by famine, and by pestilence": 37 See, I will gather them out of all countries wherever I have driven them in My anger, and in My fury, and in great wrath; and I will bring them again to this place, and I will cause them to dwell safely. 38 And they shall be My people, and I will be their God. 39 And I will give them one heart and one way, that they may fear Me forever, for their good and for their children after them. 40 And I will make an everlasting covenant with them that I will not turn away from them, to do them good. But I will put My fear in their hearts so that they shall not depart from Me. 41 Indeed, I will rejoice over them to do them good, and I will plant them in this land assuredly with My whole heart and with My whole soul.

42 For thus says the LORD: Just as I have brought all this great calamity upon this people, so I will bring upon them all the good that I have promised them. 43 Fields will be bought in this land of which you say, It is desolate, without man or beast. It is given into the hand of the Chaldeans. 44 Men will buy fields for money, sign and seal deeds, and call in witnesses in the land of Benjamin, and in the places about Jerusalem, and in the cities of Judah, and in the cities of the mountains, and in the cities of the valley, and in the cities of the Negev; for I will restore their fortunes, says the LORD.

32:33 Jer 2:27
32:34 Jer 7:30
32:35 Jer 7:31
32:36 Jer 32:24
32:37 Jer 23:3
32:38 Jer 24:7
32:40 Isa 55:3
32:41 Jer 24:6
32:42 Jer 31:28

32:44 Jer 17:26
33:1 Jer 37:21
33:2 Ex 6:3
33:3 Jer 29:12
33:4 Jer 32:24
33:5 Isa 8:17
33:6 Isa 30:26
33:7 Isa 1:26

The Promise of Restoration

33 Moreover the word of the LORD came to Jeremiah the second time, while he was yet shut up in the court of the prison, saying: 2 Thus says the LORD, the Maker of the earth, the LORD who formed it to establish it; the LORD is His name: 3 Call to Me, and I will answer you, and show you great and mighty things which you do not know. 4 For thus says the LORD God of Israel concerning the houses of this city, and concerning the houses of the kings of Judah, which are thrown down *to make a defense* against the siege mounds and against the sword: 5 They come to fight with the Chaldeans, but it is to fill them with the dead bodies of men whom I have slain in My anger and in My fury, all for whose wickedness I have hidden My face from this city.

Father, You have said to call to You, and You will answer and show me great and mighty things that I do not know (Jer 33:3).

6 I will bring it health and healing, and I will heal them; and I will reveal to them the abundance of peace and truth. 7 I will restore the fortunes of Judah and the fortunes of Israel,

and will build them as at the first. 8 I will
cleanse them from all their iniquity whereby
they have sinned against Me. And I will pardon
all their iniquities whereby they have sinned
and whereby they have transgressed against
Me. 9 It will be to Me a name of joy, praise, and
honor before all the nations of the earth which
shall hear of all the good that I do to them; and
they will fear and tremble for all the goodness
and for all the prosperity that I procure for it.
10 Thus says the LORD: Again there shall be
heard in this place of which you say, "It is des-
olate, without man and without beast," even
in the cities of Judah, and in the streets of Je-
rusalem, that are desolate, without man and
without inhabitant, and without beast, 11 the
voice of joy, and the voice of gladness, the
voice of the bridegroom, and the voice of the
bride, the voice of those who shall say,

"Give thanks to the LORD of Hosts,
for the LORD is good;
for His mercy endures forever,"

and of those who bring the sacrifice of praise
into the house of the LORD. For I will restore
the fortunes of the land as at the first, says
the LORD.
12 Thus says the LORD of Hosts: Again in this
place which is desolate, without man and with-
out beast, and in all the cities, will be a habi-
tation of shepherds causing their flocks to lie
down. 13 In the cities of the mountains, in the
cities of the vale, and in the cities of the Negev,
and in the land of Benjamin, and in the places
about Jerusalem, and in the cities of Judah,
shall the flocks pass again under the hands of
him who numbers them, says the LORD.

The Davidic Covenant

14 Surely, the days are coming, says the LORD,
when I will perform that good word which I
have promised to the house of Israel and to
the house of Judah:

15 In those days and at that time,
I will cause a righteous Branch to spring
up for David;
and he shall execute justice and
righteousness in the earth.
16 In those days Judah will be saved,
and Jerusalem will dwell safely.
And this is *the name* by which she will be
called:
THE LORD OUR RIGHTEOUSNESS.

17 For thus says the LORD: David shall never
lack a man to sit on the throne of the house of
Israel; 18 nor shall the Levitical priests lack a
man before Me to offer burnt offerings, to kin-
dle grain offerings, and to sacrifice continually.

33:8 Ps 51:2
33:9 Jer 13:11
33:10 Jer 32:43
33:11 1Ch 16:34
33:12 Isa 65:10
33:13 Lev 27:32
33:14 Jer 29:10
33:15 Isa 4:2
33:16 Jer 23:6
33:17 1Ki 2:4
....
33:21 2Ch 7:18
33:22 Ge 15:5
33:25 Ps 74:16–17
33:26 Isa 14:1
34:1 Jer 1:15
34:2 Jer 21:10
34:3 Jer 32:4
34:5 2Ch 16:14
34:7 Jos 10:3

19 The word of the LORD came to Jeremiah,
saying: 20 Thus says the LORD: If you can break
My covenant of the day and My covenant of
the night so that there should not be day and
night in their season, 21 then also My covenant
may be broken with David My servant, that he
should not have a son to reign on his throne,
and with the Levitical priests, My ministers.
22 As the host of heaven cannot be numbered
nor the sand of the sea measured, so I will
multiply the seed of David My servant and the
Levites that minister to Me.
23 Moreover the word of the LORD came to
Jeremiah, saying: 24 Have you not considered
what this people have spoken, saying, "The
two families which the LORD has chosen, He
has cast them off"? Thus they have despised
My people, that they should be no more a na-
tion before them. 25 Thus says the LORD: If My
covenant for day and night does not stand,
and if I have not appointed the ordinances of
heaven and earth, 26 then I would cast away
the seed of Jacob and David My servant, so
that I would not take any of his seed to be
rulers over the seed of Abraham, Isaac, and
Jacob. Yet I will restore their fortunes and have
mercy on them.

Zedekiah to Die in Exile

34 The word which came to Jeremiah
from the LORD when Nebuchadnezzar
king of Babylon and all his army and all the
kingdoms of the earth of his dominion and
all the people fought against Jerusalem and
against all the cities, saying: 2 Thus says the
LORD, the God of Israel: Go and speak to Zed-
ekiah king of Judah and tell him: Thus says
the LORD: I will give this city into the hand of
the king of Babylon, and he will burn it with
fire. 3 And you will not escape out of his hand,
but will surely be taken and delivered into his
hand. And you will see the king of Babylon
eye to eye, and he will speak with you face to
face, and you will go to Babylon.
4 Yet hear the word of the LORD, O Zedekiah
king of Judah! Thus says the LORD concerning
you: You will not die by the sword. 5 But you
will die in peace; and as spices were burned
for your fathers, the former kings who were
before you, so they burn spices for you. And
they will lament for you, saying, "Alas, lord!"
For I have pronounced the word, says the LORD.
6 Then Jeremiah the prophet spoke all these
words to Zedekiah king of Judah in Jerusa-
lem, 7 when the king of Babylon's army fought
against Jerusalem, and against all the cities
of Judah that were left, against Lachish and
Azekah, for these fortified cities remained of
the cities of Judah.

Slaves to be Free

8 This is the word that came to Jeremiah from
the LORD after the king Zedekiah had made
a covenant with all the people who were in
Jerusalem to proclaim liberty to them: 9 that
every man should let his male slave and ev-
ery man his female slave, being a Hebrew
man or a Hebrew woman, go free so that no
one should keep them, a Jew his brother, in
bondage. 10 Now when all the officials and all
the people who had entered into the covenant
heard that everyone should let his male slave
and everyone his female slave go free, so that
no one should keep them any more in bond-
age, then they obeyed and let them go. 11 But
afterward they turned around and caused the
male slaves and the female slaves whom they
had set free to return, and brought them into
subjection for male slaves and female slaves.
12 Therefore the word of the LORD came to Jer-
emiah from the LORD, saying: 13 Thus says the
LORD, the God of Israel: I made a covenant with
your fathers in the day that I brought them
out of the land of Egypt, out of the house of
bondage, saying: 14 "At the end of seven years,
each of you shall set free his Hebrew brother
who has been sold to you; and when he has
served you six years, you shall let him go free
from you." But your fathers did not obey Me
nor incline their ear. 15 You recently turned and
did what was right in My sight by proclaiming
liberty, every man to his neighbor; and you
made a covenant before Me in the house that
is called by My name. 16 But then you turned
around and profaned My name when every
one of you took back his male and female
slaves, whom you had set free, at their plea-
sure, and you brought them into subjection to
be your slaves.
17 Therefore thus says the LORD: You have not
obeyed Me in proclaiming liberty, everyone to
his brother and every man to his neighbor. I
proclaim a liberty to you, says the LORD, to the
sword, to the pestilence, and to the famine;
and I will make you a terror to all the kingdoms
of the earth. 18 I will give the men who have
transgressed My covenant, who have not per-
formed the words of the covenant which they
had made before Me, when they cut the calf
in two and passed between the parts, 19 the of-
ficials of Judah and the officials of Jerusalem,
the court officers, and the priests, and all the
people of the land, who passed between the
parts of the calf, 20 I will even give them into
the hand of their enemies and into the hand of
those who seek their life; and their dead bodies
shall be food to the fowl of heaven and to the
beasts of the earth.
21 Zedekiah king of Judah and his officials I
will give into the hand of their enemies and
into the hand of those who seek their life and
into the hand of the king of Babylon's army,
which has gone away from you. 22 I will com-
mand, says the LORD, and cause them to return
to this city, and they will fight against it and
take it and burn it with fire; and I will make
the cities of Judah a desolation without an
inhabitant.

The Rekabites' Obedience

35 The word which came to Jeremiah
from the LORD in the days of Jehoiakim
the son of Josiah, king of Judah, saying: 2 Go
to the house of the Rekabites and speak to
them, and bring them into the house of the
LORD, into one of the chambers, and give them
wine to drink.
3 Then I took Jaazaniah the son of Jeremi-
ah, the son of Habazziniah, and his brothers
and all his sons and the whole house of the
Rekabites, 4 and I brought them into the house
of the LORD, into the chamber of the sons of
Hanan, the son of Igdaliah, a man of God,
which was by the chamber of the officials,
which was above the chamber of Maaseiah
the son of Shallum, the keeper of the door.
5 Then I set before the sons of the house of
the Rekabites pots full of wine and cups, and
I said to them, "Drink wine."
6 But they said, "We will drink no wine. For
Jonadab the son of Rekab our father com-
manded us, saying, 'You shall not drink wine,
neither you nor your sons forever. 7 You shall
not build a house, sow seed, plant a vineyard,
nor own one; but all your days you shall dwell
in tents so that you may live many days in
the land where you sojourn.' 8 Thus we have
obeyed the voice of Jonadab the son of Rekab,
our father, in all that he has charged us, to
drink no wine all our days, we, our wives, our
sons, nor our daughters, 9 nor to build houses
for us to dwell in; and we do not have vineyard,
or field, or seed. 10 But we have lived in tents
only and have obeyed and done according to
all that Jonadab our father commanded us.
11 But when Nebuchadnezzar king of Babylon
came up into the land, we said, 'Come, and let
us go to Jerusalem before the army of the Chal-
deans and before the army of the Arameans.'
So we have dwelt in Jerusalem."
12 Then the word of the LORD came to Jere-
miah, saying: 13 Thus says the LORD of Hosts,
the God of Israel: Go and tell the men of Judah
and the inhabitants of Jerusalem, Will you not
receive instruction by listening to My words?
says the LORD. 14 The words of Jonadab the son
of Rekab, that he commanded his sons not

34:8 Lev 25:10
34:13 Jos 24:17
34:14 Dt 15:12
34:15 Jer 34:8
34:16 Lev 19:12
34:17 Mt 7:2
34:18 Ge 15:10
34:19 Zep 3:3–4
34:20 Jer 7:33
34:21 Jer 39:6
34:22 Jer 9:11
35:2 1Ch 2:55
35:4 Dt 33:1
35:5 Am 2:12
35:6 2Ki 10:15
35:8 Col 3:20
35:9 1Ti 6:6
35:11 Jer 8:14
35:13 Jer 5:3
35:14 Isa 30:9

to drink wine, are performed. For to this day
they drink none, but they obey their father's
commandment. However, I have spoken to
you, rising early and speaking, but you did
not obey Me. 15 I also have sent to you all My
servants the prophets, rising up early and
sending them, saying, "Return now every man
from his evil way and amend your deeds, and
do not go after other gods to serve them, and
you will dwell in the land that I have given to
you and to your fathers." But you have not
inclined your ear nor obeyed Me. 16 Indeed,
the sons of Jonadab the son of Rekab have
performed the commandment of their father,
which he commanded them, but this people
has not obeyed Me.

17 Therefore thus says the LORD God of Hosts,
the God of Israel: I will bring upon Judah and
upon all the inhabitants of Jerusalem all the
disaster that I have pronounced against them;
because I have spoken to them but they have
not listened, and I have called them but they
have not answered.

18 Jeremiah said to the house of the Rek-
abites: Thus says the LORD of Hosts, the God
of Israel: Because you have obeyed the com-
mandment of Jonadab your father and kept
all his precepts and done according to all that
he has commanded you, 19 therefore thus says
the LORD of Hosts, the God of Israel, Jonadab
the son of Rekab shall not lack a man to stand
before Me always.

Jeremiah's Scroll Is Burned

36 In the fourth year of Jehoiakim the
son of Josiah, king of Judah, this word
came to Jeremiah from the LORD, saying: 2 Take
a scroll of a book, and write in it all the words
that I have spoken to you against Israel and
against Judah and against all the nations, from
the day I spoke to you, from the days of Josiah,
even to this day. 3 It may be that the house of
Judah will hear all the disaster which I intend
to do to them, so that every man may turn from
his evil way; then I will forgive their iniquity
and their sin.

4 Then Jeremiah called Baruch the son of
Neriah. And Baruch wrote on a scroll at the
dictation of Jeremiah all the words of the
LORD which He had spoken to him. 5 Jeremiah
commanded Baruch, saying, "I am shut in. I
cannot go into the house of the LORD. 6 There-
fore go and read from the scroll that you have
written at my dictation the words of the LORD
in the hearing of the people in the house of
the LORD on a fast day. And also you shall read
them in the ears of all Judah who come out
of their cities. 7 Perhaps their supplication will
come before the LORD, and everyone will turn

35:15 Jer 18:11
35:16 Mal 1:6
35:17 Isa 65:12
35:19 Jer 15:19
36:1 Jer 25:1
36:2 Jer 30:2
36:3 Jer 18:8
36:4 Jer 32:12
36:5 Jer 32:2
36:6 Jer 36:8–9
36:7 Jer 36:3

....

36:8 Jer 1:17
36:9 2Ch 20:3
36:10 Jer 36:11
36:12 Jer 26:22
36:13 2Ki 22:10
36:14 Jer 36:2
36:17 Jn 9:15
36:18 Jer 36:4
36:19 1Ki 17:3
36:20 Jer 36:12
36:21 2Ki 22:10
36:22 Am 3:15
36:23 1Ki 22:8

from his evil way, for great is the anger and
the fury that the LORD has pronounced against
this people."

8 Baruch the son of Neriah did according to
all that Jeremiah the prophet commanded him,
reading in the book the words of the LORD in
the house of the LORD. 9 In the fifth year of
Jehoiakim the son of Josiah, king of Judah, in
the ninth month, they proclaimed a fast before
the LORD to all the people in Jerusalem and
to all the people who came from the cities of
Judah to Jerusalem. 10 Then Baruch read from
the book the words of Jeremiah in the house of
the LORD, in the chamber of Gemariah the son
of Shaphan the scribe, in the higher court, at
the entry of the New Gate of the house of the
LORD, in the ears of all the people.

11 When Micaiah the son of Gemariah, the
son of Shaphan, had heard out of the book all
the words of the LORD, 12 then he went down
to the king's house, into the scribe's chamber.
And all the officials sat there, even Elishama
the scribe, and Delaiah the son of Shemaiah,
and Elnathan the son of Akbor, and Gemariah
the son of Shaphan, and Zedekiah the son of
Hananiah, and all the other officials. 13 Then
Micaiah declared to them all the words that
he had heard when Baruch read the book in
the ears of the people. 14 Then all the officials
sent Jehudi the son of Nethaniah, the son of
Shelemiah, the son of Cushi, to Baruch, saying,
"Take in your hand the scroll from which you
have read in the ears of the people and come."
So Baruch the son of Neriah took the scroll in
his hand and came to them. 15 They said to
him, "Sit down now, and read it in our ears."

So Baruch read it in their ears. 16 When they
heard all the words, they turned to one another
in fear and said to Baruch, "We will surely tell
the king of all these words." 17 They also asked
Baruch, saying, "Tell us now, how did you
write all these words? Was it at his mouth?"

18 Then Baruch answered them, "He pro-
nounced all these words to me with his mouth,
and I wrote them with ink in the book."

19 Then the officials said to Baruch, "Go hide,
you and Jeremiah, and let no man know where
you are."

20 Then they went to the king in the court, but
they laid up the scroll in the chamber of Elisha-
ma the scribe, and told all the words in the ears
of the king. 21 So the king sent Jehudi to fetch
the scroll, and he took it out of Elishama the
scribe's chamber. And Jehudi read it in the ears
of the king and in the ears of all the officials
who stood beside the king. 22 Now the king sat
in the winter house in the ninth month, and
there was a fire burning on the hearth before
him. 23 As Jehudi read three or four columns,

the king cut it with a scribe's knife and cast it
into the fire that was on the hearth, until all
the scroll was consumed in the fire that was
on the hearth. 24 Yet they were not afraid, nor
did they tear their garments, neither the king
nor any of his servants who heard all these
words. 25 Although Elnathan and Delaiah and
Gemariah entreated the king not to burn the
scroll, yet he would not listen to them. 26 But
the king commanded Jerahmeel the son of
Hammelech, and Seraiah the son of Azriel, and
Shelemiah the son of Abdeel to seize Baruch
the scribe and Jeremiah the prophet. But the
LORD hid them.

Jeremiah and Baruch Rewrite the Scroll

27 Then the word of the LORD came to Jere-
miah after the king had burned the book and
the words which Baruch had written at the
mouth of Jeremiah, saying: 28 Take again an-
other scroll and write in it all the former words
that were in the first book, which Jehoiakim
the king of Judah has burned. 29 You shall say
to Jehoiakim king of Judah: Thus says the
LORD: You have burned this book, saying, Why
have you written in it that the king of Babylon
will certainly come and destroy this land, and
will cause man and beast to cease from here?
30 Therefore thus says the LORD concerning Je-
hoiakim king of Judah: He shall have no one to
sit on the throne of David. And his dead body
shall be cast out to the heat of the day and the
frost of the night. 31 I will also punish him and
his seed and his servants for their iniquity. And
I will bring upon them and upon the men of Judah
tants of Jerusalem and upon the men of Judah
all the disaster that I have pronounced against
them; but they did not listen.
32 Then Jeremiah took another scroll and
gave it to Baruch the scribe, the son of Neriah
who wrote in it from the mouth of Jeremiah all
the words of the book which Jehoiakim king of
Judah had burned in the fire. And there were
added to them many like words.

Jeremiah Warns Zedekiah

37 And King Zedekiah the son of Josiah
reigned instead of Koniah the son
of Jehoiakim, whom Nebuchadnezzar king
of Babylon made king in the land of Judah.
2 But neither he nor his servants nor the people
of the land listened to the words of the LORD,
which He spoke through the prophet Jeremiah.
3 But Zedekiah the king sent Jehukal the son
of Shelemiah and Zephaniah the son of Maas-
eiah, the priest, to the prophet Jeremiah, say-
ing, "Please pray to the LORD our God for us."
4 Now Jeremiah was still coming in and go-
ing out among the people, for they had not yet
put him into prison. 5 At that time Pharaoh's

36:24 Ps 36:1
36:28 Zec 1:5–6
36:29 Isa 30:10
36:30 Jer 22:30
36:31 Pr 29:1
36:32 Jer 36:4
37:1 2Ki 24:17
37:3 Jer 21:1–2
37:4 Jer 37:15
37:5 Eze 17:15

37:7 La 4:17
37:12 Jer 1:1
37:13 Jer 38:7
37:15 Jer 38:26
37:16 Jer 38:6
37:17 Jer 21:7
37:18 Jn 10:32
37:20 Jer 36:7

army had come out of Egypt, and when the
Chaldeans who were besieging Jerusalem
heard the report of them, they departed from
Jerusalem.
6 Then the word of the LORD came to the
prophet Jeremiah, saying: 7 Thus says the LORD,
the God of Israel: Thus you shall say to the king
of Judah who sent you to Me to inquire of Me:
Pharaoh's army which has come out to help
you shall return to Egypt, to its own land. 8 The
Chaldeans will come again and fight against
this city, and take it, and burn it with fire.
9 Thus says the LORD: Do not deceive your-
selves, saying, "The Chaldeans will surely de-
part from us," for they will not depart. 10 For
though you had struck the whole army of the
Chaldeans who fight against you and there re-
mained but wounded men among them, yet
every man would rise up in his tent and burn
this city with fire.

Jeremiah Imprisoned

11 Now when the army of the Chaldeans had
withdrawn from Jerusalem at the approach
of Pharaoh's army, 12 Jeremiah set out from
Jerusalem to go into the land of Benjamin to
take possession of his property there among
the people. 13 When he was in the Gate of
Benjamin, a captain of the guard was there
whose name was Irijah the son of Shelemiah,
the son of Hananiah. And he seized Jeremiah
the prophet, saying, "You are falling away to
the Chaldeans!"
14 But Jeremiah said, "It is false! I am not
falling away to the Chaldeans," but he did not
listen to him. So Irijah seized Jeremiah and
brought him to the officials. 15 Therefore the of-
ficials were wrathful with Jeremiah, and struck
him, and put him in prison in the house of
Jonathan the scribe; for they had made that
the prison.
16 For Jeremiah had entered the dungeon,
that is, the vaulted cell, and Jeremiah had re-
mained there many days. 17 Then Zedekiah the
king sent and took him out; and the king asked
him secretly in his house, and said, "Is there
any word from the LORD?"
And Jeremiah said, "There is!" Then he said,
"You shall be delivered into the hand of the
king of Babylon."
18 Moreover Jeremiah said to King Zedekiah,
"How have I sinned against you or against
your servants or against this people that you
have put me in prison? 19 Where now are your
prophets who prophesied to you, saying, 'The
king of Babylon will not come against you,
nor against this land'? 20 Therefore now please
listen, O my lord the king. Please let my sup-
plication be accepted before you, that you not

cause me to return to the house of Jonathan
the scribe, lest I die there."
21 Then Zedekiah the king commanded that
they should commit Jeremiah into the court of
the prison and give him daily a piece of bread
out of the bakers' street, until all the bread in
the city was finished. Thus Jeremiah remained
in the court of the prison.

Jeremiah Thrown Into a Cistern

38 Now Shephatiah the son of Mattan,
and Gedaliah the son of Pashhur, and
Jukal the son of Shelemiah, and Pashhur the
son of Malkijah heard the words that Jeremiah
had spoken to all the people, saying: 2 Thus
says the LORD: He who remains in this city will
die by the sword, by famine, and by pestilence.
But he who goes out to the Chaldeans shall
live, for he shall have his life as plunder, and
shall live. 3 Thus says the LORD: This city shall
surely be given into the hand of the king of
Babylon's army, and he will capture it.
4 Therefore the officials said to the king, "We
beseech you, let this man be put to death, for
he thus weakens the hands of the men of war
who remain in this city and the hands of all
the people, in speaking such words to them;
for this man does not seek the welfare of this
people, but their harm."
5 Then Zedekiah the king said, "Here he is;
he is in your hand; for the king cannot do any-
thing against you."
6 Then they took Jeremiah and cast him into
the cistern of Malkijah the son of Hammelech
that was in the court of the prison, and they let
Jeremiah down with cords. And in the cistern
there was no water, only mud, so Jeremiah
sank in the mud.
7 Now Ebed-Melek the Ethiopian, one of the
eunuchs who was in the king's house, heard
that they had put Jeremiah in the cistern. Now
the king was sitting in the Gate of Benjamin.
8 Ebed-Melek went forth out of the king's house
and spoke to the king, saying, 9 "My lord the
king, these men have done evil in all that they
have done to Jeremiah the prophet whom they
have cast into the cistern. And he will die by
hunger in the place where he is, for there is no
more bread in the city."
10 Then the king commanded Ebed-Melek the
Ethiopian, saying, "Take thirty men with you
from here and take up Jeremiah the prophet
out of the cistern before he dies."
11 So Ebed-Melek took the men under his au-
thority and went into the house of the king un-
der the storeroom and took from there worn-
out clothes and worn-out rags and let them
down by cords into the cistern to Jeremiah.
12 Then Ebed-Melek the Ethiopian said to Jer-
emiah, "Now put these worn-out clothes and
worn-out rags under your armpits under the
cords," so Jeremiah did accordingly. 13 Then
they drew Jeremiah up with cords and took
him up out of the cistern, and Jeremiah re-
mained in the court of the prison.

Jeremiah Warns Zedekiah Again

14 Then Zedekiah the king sent and had Jer-
emiah the prophet brought to him at the third
entrance that is in the house of the LORD. And
the king said to Jeremiah, "I will ask you some-
thing; hide nothing from me."
15 Then Jeremiah said to Zedekiah, "If I de-
clare it to you, shall you not surely put me to
death? And if I give you counsel, you will not
listen to me."
16 So Zedekiah the king swore secretly to Jer-
emiah, saying, "As the LORD lives, who made
our souls, I surely will not put you to death,
nor will I give you into the hand of these men
who seek your life."
17 Then Jeremiah said to Zedekiah, "Thus
says the LORD, the God of Hosts, the God of Is-
rael: If you will surrender to the officers of the
king of Babylon, then your soul will live and
this city will not be burned with fire. Thus you
and your household will live. 18 But if you do
not surrender to the king of Babylon's officials,
then this city will be given into the hand of the
Chaldeans, and they will burn it with fire, and
you will not escape out of their hand."
19 Then Zedekiah the king said to Jeremiah,
"I am afraid of the Jews who have fallen over
to the Chaldeans, lest they deliver me into their
hand and mock me."
20 But Jeremiah said, "They will not deliver
you. Please obey the voice of the LORD which
I speak to you, so it will be well with you and
your soul will live. 21 But if you refuse to surren-
der, this is the word that the LORD has shown
me: 22 Then all the women who are left in the
house of the king of Judah will be brought
out to the officers of the king of Babylon; and
those women shall say:

'Your friends have misled
and prevailed against you;
while your feet were sunk in the mud,
they turned back.'

23 "So they will bring out all your wives and
your children to the Chaldeans. And you will
not escape out of their hand, but will be taken
by the hand of the king of Babylon; and you
will cause this city to be burned with fire."
24 Then Zedekiah said to Jeremiah, "Let no
man know of these words, and you will not
die. 25 But if the officials hear that I have talked
with you and they come to you and say to you,

37:21 Jer 38:13
38:2 Jer 34:17
38:3 Jer 21:10
38:4 Jer 26:11
38:5 2Sa 3:39
38:6 Jer 37:16
38:7 Jer 29:2
38:9 Jer 52:6

38:13 Jer 37:21
38:15 Lk 22:67–68
38:16 Isa 57:16
38:17 Jer 27:12
38:18 Jer 38:3
38:19 Jn 12:42
38:20 Isa 55:3
38:23 Jer 41:10

'Declare to us now what you said to the king and what the king said to you; do not hide it from us and we will not put you to death,' 26 then you will say to them, 'I presented my supplication before the king, that he would not cause me to return to the house of Jonathan, to die there.' "

27 Then all the officials came to Jeremiah and asked him. And he told them according to all these words that the king had commanded; so they stopped speaking with him, for the matter was not overheard.

28 So Jeremiah remained in the court of the prison until the day that Jerusalem was captured.

The Fall of Jerusalem

2Ki 25:1–12; Jer 52:4–16

39 In the ninth year of Zedekiah king of Judah, in the tenth month, Nebuchadnezzar king of Babylon and all his army came against Jerusalem and besieged it. 2 In the eleventh year of Zedekiah, in the fourth month, the ninth day of the month, the city wall was broken up. 3 All the officials of the king of Babylon entered and sat in the Middle Gate: Nergal-Sharezer, Samgar-Nebo, Sarsekim the Rabsaris,[1] Nergal-Sharezer the Rabmag,[2] and all the rest of the officials of the king of Babylon. 4 When Zedekiah the king of Judah saw them and all the men of war, then they fled and went out of the city by night, by way of the king's garden, by the gate between the two walls. And he went out the way of the Arabah.

5 But the Chaldeans' army pursued after them and overtook Zedekiah in the plains of Jericho. And when they had taken him, they brought him up to Nebuchadnezzar king of Babylon to Riblah in the land of Hamath, where he passed sentence on him. 6 Then the king of Babylon slew the sons of Zedekiah in Riblah before his eyes. Moreover, the king of Babylon slew all the nobles of Judah. 7 He also put out Zedekiah's eyes and bound him with chains to carry him to Babylon.

8 The Chaldeans burned the king's house and the houses of the people with fire and broke down the walls of Jerusalem. 9 Then Nebuzaradan the captain of the guard carried away captive into Babylon the remnant of the people who remained in the city, and those who fell away, who fell to him, with the rest of the people who remained. 10 But Nebuzaradan the captain of the guard left behind in the land of Judah the poor people who had nothing, and gave them vineyards and fields at that time.

38:26 Jer 37:20
38:28 Jer 37:21
39:3 Jer 21:4
39:5 2Ki 23:33
39:6 Jer 52:10
39:7 Eze 12:13
39:8 Ne 1:3
39:9 Jer 40:1
39:10 2Ki 25:12

39:12 Pr 16:7
39:13 Jer 39:3
39:14 Jer 38:28
39:16 Da 9:12
39:17 Ps 41:1–2
39:18 Jer 21:9
40:1 Jer 31:15
40:3 Ro 2:5
40:5 Jer 39:14

The Lord Delivers Jeremiah

11 Now Nebuchadnezzar king of Babylon gave charge concerning Jeremiah to Nebuzaradan the captain of the guard, saying, 12 "Take him and look after him, and do not harm him. But do to him just as he says to you." 13 So Nebuzaradan the captain of the guard, Nebushazban the Rabsaris, Nergal-Sharezer the Rabmag, and all the chief officers of the king of Babylon 14 sent and took Jeremiah out of the court of the prison and committed him to Gedaliah the son of Ahikam, the son of Shaphan, that he should take him home. So he lived among the people.

15 Now the word of the Lord came to Jeremiah while he was shut up in the court of the prison, saying: 16 Go and speak to Ebed-Melek the Ethiopian, saying: Thus says the Lord of Hosts, the God of Israel: I will bring My words upon this city for harm and not for good. And they shall be accomplished in that day before you. 17 But I will deliver you in that day, says the Lord, and you shall not be given into the hand of the men of whom you are afraid. 18 For I will surely deliver you, and you will not fall by the sword; but your life will be as plunder to you, because you have put your trust in Me, says the Lord.

Jeremiah With Gedaliah the Governor

40 The word that came to Jeremiah from the Lord after Nebuzaradan the captain of the guard had let him go from Ramah, when he had taken him bound in chains among all who were carried away captive of Jerusalem and Judah who were being carried away captive to Babylon. 2 The captain of the guard had taken Jeremiah, and said to him: "The Lord your God has pronounced this disaster upon this place. 3 And the Lord has brought it and done according as He has said. Because you have sinned against the Lord, and have not obeyed His voice, therefore this thing has come upon you. 4 Now look, I am loosening you this day from the chains which are on your hands. If it seems good to you to come with me to Babylon, come and I will look well after you. But if it seems bad to you to come with me into Babylon, never mind. See, all the land is before you. Go wherever it seems good and right for you to go." 5 Now while he was not yet going back, *he said*, "Go back also to Gedaliah the son of Ahikam, the son of Shaphan, whom the king of Babylon has made governor over the cities of Judah, and dwell with him among the people. Or go wherever it seems right for you to go."

[1] 3 Possibly *Chief of Staff.* [2] 3 Possibly *the high official.*

So the captain of the guard gave him rations and a gift and let him go. [6]Then Jeremiah went to Gedaliah the son of Ahikam to Mizpah and lived with him among the people who were left in the land.

Gedaliah Is Assassinated

2Ki 25:22–26

[7]Now all the captains of the forces which were in the fields, they and their men, heard that the king of Babylon had made Gedaliah the son of Ahikam governor in the land and had committed men to him, and women, and children, and some of the poorest of the land who were not carried away captive to Babylon. [8]Then they came to Gedaliah to Mizpah, even Ishmael the son of Nethaniah, and Johanan and Jonathan the sons of Kareah, and Seraiah the son of Tanhumeth, and the sons of Ephai the Netophathite, and Jezaniah the son of a Maakathite, they and their men. [9]Then Gedaliah the son of Ahikam, the son of Shaphan swore to them and to their men, saying, "Do not be afraid to serve the Chaldeans. Dwell in the land and serve the king of Babylon, and it will be well with you. [10]As for me, I will dwell at Mizpah to serve the Chaldeans who will come to us. But you, gather wine and summer fruits and oil, and put them in your vessels and dwell in your cities that you have taken."

[11]Likewise, also all the Jews who were in Moab, and among the Ammonites, and in Edom, and who were in all the countries, heard that the king of Babylon had left a remnant of Judah, and that he had set over them Gedaliah the son of Ahikam the son of Shaphan. [12]Then all the Jews returned out of all places wherever they were driven and came to the land of Judah, to Gedaliah at Mizpah, and gathered very much wine and summer fruits.

[13]Moreover Johanan the son of Kareah, and all the captains of the forces that were in the fields, came to Gedaliah at Mizpah, [14]and said to him, "Do you certainly know that Baalis, the king of the Ammonites, has sent Ishmael the son of Nethaniah to slay you?" But Gedaliah the son of Ahikam did not believe them.

[15]Then Johanan the son of Kareah spoke to Gedaliah in Mizpah secretly, saying, "Let me go, please, and I will slay Ishmael the son of Nethaniah and no man shall know it. Why should he slay you so that all the Jews who are gathered to you should be scattered and the remnant in Judah perish?"

[16]But Gedaliah the son of Ahikam said to Johanan the son of Kareah, "You shall not do this thing, for you speak falsely of Ishmael."

41 In the seventh month Ishmael the son of Nethaniah, the son of Elishama of the royal seed, and the officials of the king, even ten men with him, came to Gedaliah the son of Ahikam to Mizpah. While they were eating bread together in Mizpah, [2]Ishmael the son of Nethaniah and the ten men that were with him arose and struck Gedaliah the son of Ahikam, the son of Shaphan with the sword and slew him, whom the king of Babylon had made governor over the land. [3]Ishmael also slew all the Jews who were with him, even with Gedaliah at Mizpah, and the Chaldeans who were found there, and the men of war.

[4]On the day after he had slain Gedaliah, when no one knew it, [5]eighty men came from Shechem, from Shiloh, and from Samaria, having their beards shaven, and their clothes torn, and their bodies gashed, with offerings and incense in their hands to bring them to the house of the LORD. [6]Then Ishmael the son of Nethaniah went out from Mizpah to meet them, weeping all along as he went. As he met them, he said to them, "Come to Gedaliah the son of Ahikam!" [7]Yet it was so when they came into the midst of the city that Ishmael the son of Nethaniah, he and the men who were with him, slew them and cast them into the midst of the cistern. [8]But ten men were found among those who said to Ishmael, "Do not slay us, for we have stores in the field, of wheat and barley, and of oil and honey." So he refrained and did not slay them among their brothers. [9]Now the cistern in which Ishmael had cast all the dead bodies of the men, whom he had slain because of Gedaliah, was what Asa the king had made because of Baasha the king of Israel. And Ishmael the son of Nethaniah filled it with those who were slain.

[10]Then Ishmael carried away captive all the rest of the people who were in Mizpah, even the king's daughters, and all the people who remained in Mizpah whom Nebuzaradan the captain of the guard had committed to Gedaliah the son of Ahikam. And Ishmael the son of Nethaniah carried them away captive, and departed to go over to the Ammonites.

[11]But when Johanan the son of Kareah and all the captains of the forces that were with him heard of all the evil that Ishmael the son of Nethaniah had done, [12]then they took all the men and went to fight with Ishmael the son of Nethaniah, and found him by the great waters that are in Gibeon. [13]And when all the people who were with Ishmael saw Johanan the son of Kareah and all the captains of the forces that were with him, they were glad. [14]So all the people whom Ishmael had carried away captive from Mizpah turned about and returned, and went to Johanan the son of Kareah. [15]But Ishmael the son of Nethaniah escaped from

40:6 Jdg 20:1
40:7 Jer 39:10
40:8 Jer 42:1
40:9 Jer 27:11
40:10 Jer 40:12
40:11 Isa 16:4
40:12 Jer 43:5
40:14 Jer 41:10
41:1 Jer 40:8

41:2 2Ki 25:25
41:5 Dt 14:1
41:6 2Sa 3:16
41:9 Jdg 6:2
41:10 Jer 40:14
41:12 2Sa 2:13
41:15 Job 21:30

Johanan with eight men and went to the Ammonites.
16 Then Johanan the son of Kareah and all the
captains of the forces that were with him took
all the remnant of the people whom he had
recovered from Ishmael the son of Nethaniah,
from Mizpah, after he had slain Gedaliah the
son of Ahikam, even mighty men of war, and
the women, and the children, and the eunuchs,
whom he had brought back from Gibeon.
17 And they departed and lived in the habitation of Geruth Kimham, which is by Bethlehem, intending to go to Egypt,
18 because of
the Chaldeans. For they were afraid of them,
because Ishmael the son of Nethaniah had
slain Gedaliah the son of Ahikam, whom the
king of Babylon made governor in the land.

Jeremiah Warns Against Going to Egypt

42 Then all the captains of the forces, and
Johanan the son of Kareah, and Jezaniah the son of Hoshaiah, and all the people
from the least even to the greatest came near,
2 and said to Jeremiah the prophet, "Please let
our supplication be accepted before you, and
pray for us to the LORD your God, even for all
this remnant. For we are left but a few out
of many, as your eyes now see us.
3 Pray that
the LORD your God may show us the way in
which we should walk and the thing that we
should do."
4 Then Jeremiah the prophet said to them,
"I have heard you. I will pray to the LORD your
God according to your words. And it shall come
to pass, that whatever the LORD will answer
you, I will declare it to you. I will keep nothing
back from you."
5 Then they said to Jeremiah, "May the LORD
be a true and faithful witness against us, if we
do not act according to all things for which the
LORD your God shall send you to us.
6 Whether
it is good or whether it is bad, we will obey the
voice of the LORD our God, to whom we send
you so that it may be well with us when we
obey the voice of the LORD our God."
7 At the end of ten days the word of the LORD
came to Jeremiah.
8 Then he called Johanan
the son of Kareah and all the captains of the
forces that were with him and all the people
from the least even to the greatest,
9 and said
to them, "Thus says the LORD, the God of Israel,
to whom you sent me to present your supplication before Him:
10 If you will still abide in this
land, then I will build you up and not pull you
down, and I will plant you and not pluck you
up; for I will relent of the disaster that I have
brought on you.
11 Do not be afraid of the king
of Babylon of whom you are now afraid. Do
not be afraid of him, says the LORD. For I am
with you to save you and to deliver you from
his hand.
12 I will show mercies to you so that
he may have mercy on you and cause you to
return to your own land.
13 "But if you say, 'We will not dwell in this
land,' so as not to obey the voice of the LORD
your God,
14 saying, 'No, but we will go into
the land of Egypt where we shall see no war,
nor hear the sound of the trumpet, nor have
hunger for bread, and there we will dwell,'
15 now therefore hear the word of the LORD,
O remnant of Judah. Thus says the LORD of
Hosts, the God of Israel: If you wholly set your
faces to enter Egypt, and go to dwell there,
16 then it shall come to pass that the sword
which you feared shall overtake you there in
the land of Egypt and the famine of which you
were afraid shall follow close after you there
in Egypt. And there you shall die.
17 So it shall
be with all the men who set their faces to go
into Egypt to sojourn there. They shall die by
the sword, by famine, and by pestilence. And
none of them shall remain or escape from the
disaster that I will bring upon them.
18 For thus
says the LORD of Hosts, the God of Israel: As
My anger and My fury have been poured out
upon the inhabitants of Jerusalem, so will My
fury be poured out upon you when you go to
Egypt. And you will be an execration, and an
astonishment, and a curse, and a reproach.
And you shall see this place no more.
19 "The LORD has said concerning you, O remnant of Judah, Do not go into Egypt! Know
certainly that I have admonished you this day.
20 For you have only deceived yourselves when
you sent me to the LORD your God, saying, 'Pray
for us to the LORD our God. And according to
all that the LORD our God shall say, so declare
to us, and we will do it.'
21 Now I have this day
declared it to you. But you have not obeyed
the voice of the LORD your God, or anything for
which He has sent me to you.
22 Now therefore
certainly know that you will die by the sword,
by famine, and by pestilence, in the place
wherever you desire to go and to sojourn."

Jeremiah Taken to Egypt

43 When Jeremiah had finished speaking to all the people all these words of
the LORD their God, with which the LORD their
God had sent him to them,
2 Azariah the son
of Hoshaiah, and Johanan the son of Kareah,
and all the proud men said to Jeremiah, "You
speak falsely. The LORD our God has not sent
you to say, 'Do not go into Egypt to sojourn
there.'
3 But Baruch the son of Neriah sets you
against us to deliver us into the hand of the
Chaldeans, that they might put us to death and
carry us away captives into Babylon."

41:17 2Sa 19:37–38
41:18 Jer 40:5
42:1 Jer 6:13
42:2 Lev 26:22
42:3 Ps 86:11
42:4 Ex 8:29
42:5 Ge 31:50
42:6 Jer 7:23
42:7 Ps 27:14
42:8 Jer 42:1
42:10 Jer 24:6
42:11 Ro 8:31

....

42:12 Ne 1:11
42:13 Jer 44:16
42:14 Jer 4:19
42:15 Dt 17:16
42:16 Jer 44:27
42:17 Jer 42:22
42:18 Jer 7:20
42:19 Dt 17:16
42:21 Eze 2:7
42:22 Jer 42:17
43:1 Jer 26:8

4 So Johanan the son of Kareah and all the captains of the forces and all the people did not obey the voice of the LORD to dwell in the land of Judah. 5 But Johanan the son of Kareah and all the captains of the forces took all the remnant of Judah who had returned from all nations wherever they had been driven to dwell in the land of Judah, 6 even men, and women, and children, and the king's daughters, and every person that Nebuzaradan the captain of the guard had left with Gedaliah the son of Ahikam, the son of Shaphan, and Jeremiah the prophet, and Baruch the son of Neriah. 7 So they came into the land of Egypt because they did not obey the voice of the LORD. Thus they entered as far as Tahpanhes.

8 Then the word of the LORD came to Jeremiah in Tahpanhes, saying: 9 Take some large stones in your hand and hide them in the clay in the brick kiln which is at the entrance of Pharaoh's house in Tahpanhes, in the sight of the men of Judah, 10 and say to them, Thus says the LORD of Hosts, the God of Israel: I will send and take Nebuchadnezzar the king of Babylon, My servant, and will set his throne upon these stones that I have hid; and he shall spread his royal pavilion over them. 11 When he comes, he shall ravage the land of Egypt and deliver whoever is *meant* for death to death, and whoever is *meant* for captivity to captivity, and whoever is *meant* for the sword to the sword. 12 I will kindle a fire in the houses of the gods of Egypt and he shall burn them and carry them away captives. And he shall array himself with the land of Egypt, as a shepherd puts on his garment, and he shall depart from there in peace. 13 He shall also break the images of Heliopolis that is in the land of Egypt, and the houses of the gods of the Egyptians he shall burn with fire.

Idolatry Leads to Judgment

44 The word that came to Jeremiah concerning all the Jews which dwell in the land of Egypt, who dwell at Migdol, and Tahpanhes, and Memphis, and in the country of Pathros,[1] saying, 2 Thus says the LORD of Hosts, the God of Israel: You have seen all the calamity that I have brought upon Jerusalem and upon all the cities of Judah. Look at them; today they are a desolation, and no man dwells in them, 3 because of their wickedness, which they have committed to provoke Me to anger, in that they went to burn incense and to serve other gods, whom they did not know; they nor you nor your fathers. 4 However, I sent to you all My servants the prophets, rising early and sending them, saying, "Oh, do not do this abominable thing that I hate." 5 But they did not listen nor incline their ear to turn from their wickedness, not to burn incense to other gods. 6 Therefore My fury and My anger was poured out and was kindled in the cities of Judah and in the streets of Jerusalem; and they are ruined and desolate, as it is this day.

7 Now thus says the LORD God of Hosts, the God of Israel: Why are you committing this great evil against your souls, to cut off from you man and woman, child and infant, out of Judah, leaving you no one to remain, 8 provoking Me to wrath with the works of your hands, burning incense to other gods in the land of Egypt, where you have gone to dwell, so that you might cut yourselves off and become a curse and a reproach among all the nations of the earth? 9 Have you forgotten the wickedness of your fathers, and the wickedness of the kings of Judah, and the wickedness of their wives, and your own wickedness, and the wickedness of your wives, which they have committed in the land of Judah and in the streets of Jerusalem? 10 They are not humbled even to this day, nor have they feared, nor have they walked in My law and My statutes that I set before you and before your fathers.

11 Therefore thus says the LORD of Hosts, the God of Israel: I will set My face against you for disaster, and to cut off all Judah. 12 I will take the remnant of Judah who have set their faces to go into the land of Egypt to sojourn there, and they all will be consumed and fall in the land of Egypt. They will even be consumed by the sword and by the famine. They will die, from the least even to the greatest, by the sword and by the famine; and they will be an execration, and an astonishment, and a curse, and a reproach. 13 For I will punish those who dwell in the land of Egypt, as I have punished Jerusalem; by the sword, by famine, and by pestilence. 14 So none of the remnant of Judah who have gone into the land of Egypt to sojourn there will escape or remain, with the result that they return into the land of Judah to which they have a desire to return to dwell there. For no one shall return except those who escape.

15 Then all the men who knew that their wives had burned incense to other gods and all the women that stood by, a great multitude, even all the people who lived in the land of Egypt, in Pathros, answered Jeremiah, saying: 16 "As for the word that you have spoken to us in the name of the LORD, we will not listen to you. 17 But we will certainly do whatever we have vowed, to burn incense to the queen of heaven, and to pour out drink offerings to her, as we have done, we, and our fathers, our kings

43:4 Jer 42:5–6
43:5 Jer 40:11–12
43:6 Jer 39:10
43:7 Jer 2:16
43:11 Jer 15:2
43:12 Jer 46:25
44:1 Jer 46:14
44:2 Isa 6:11
44:3 Dt 13:6
44:4 Jer 7:13

44:7 Nu 16:38
44:8 Jer 42:18
44:9 Jer 7:17–18
44:11 Jer 21:10
44:12 Jer 42:15–18
44:14 Jer 22:26–27
44:17 Ne 9:34

[1] 1 Upper Egypt.

and our officials, in the cities of Judah and
in the streets of Jerusalem. For then we had
plenty of food, and were well off, and saw no
disaster. 18 But since we left off burning incense
to the queen of heaven and pouring out drink
offerings to her, we have been in want of all
things and have been consumed by the sword
and by the famine."

19 *The women also said*, "When we burned in-
cense to the queen of heaven, and poured out
drink offerings to her, did we make her cakes
to worship her and pour out drink offerings to
her without our husbands?"

Calamity for the Jews

20 Then Jeremiah said to all the people, to the
men and to the women, and to all the people
who had given him such an answer: 21 "The
incense offerings that you burned in the cities
of Judah and in the streets of Jerusalem, you,
and your fathers, your kings, and your officials,
and the people of the land, did not the LORD
remember them and did they not come into
His mind? 22 So the LORD could no longer bear it
because of the evil of your deeds and because
of the abominations which you have commit-
ted. Therefore your land is a desolation, and
an astonishment, and a curse, without an in-
habitant, as it is this day. 23 Because you have
burned incense and because you have sinned
against the LORD and have not obeyed the voice
of the LORD, nor walked in His law, nor in His
statutes, nor in His testimonies, therefore this
calamity has happened to you, as it is this day."

24 Moreover Jeremiah said to all the people
and to all the women, "Hear the word of the
LORD, all Judah who are in the land of Egypt.
25 Thus says the LORD of Hosts, the God of Isra-
el: You and your wives have both spoken with
your mouths and fulfilled with your hand, say-
ing, 'We will surely perform our vows that we
have vowed, to burn incense to the queen of
heaven and to pour out drink offerings to her.'

"Proceed to accomplish your vows and sure-
ly perform your vows! 26 Yet hear the word of
the LORD, all Judah who dwells in the land of
Egypt: I have sworn by My great name, says
the LORD, that My name shall no more be
named in the mouth of any man of Judah in
all the land of Egypt, saying, 'As the Lord GOD
lives.' 27 I will watch over them for disaster and
not for good. And all the men of Judah who
are in the land of Egypt shall be consumed by
the sword and by the famine until there is an
end of them. 28 Yet a small number who escape
the sword shall return out of the land of Egypt
into the land of Judah, and all the remnant of
Judah who have gone into the land of Egypt
to sojourn there will know whose words will
stand, Mine or theirs.

29 "This will be a sign to you, says the LORD,
that I will punish you in this place so that you
may know that My words shall surely stand
against you for disaster. 30 Thus says the LORD:
I will give Pharaoh Hophra the king of Egypt
into the hand of his enemies and into the
hand of those who seek his life, just as I gave
Zedekiah king of Judah into the hand of Ne-
buchadnezzar king of Babylon, who was his
enemy, and sought his life."

A Message to Baruch

45 The word that Jeremiah the prophet
spoke to Baruch the son of Neriah
when he had written these words in a book at
the mouth of Jeremiah, in the fourth year of
Jehoiakim the son of Josiah, king of Judah,
saying: 2 Thus says the LORD, the God of Israel,
to you, O Baruch: 3 You said, "Alas, woe is me!
For the LORD has added grief to my sorrow.
I fainted in my sighing, and I find no rest."
4 Thus you shall say to him, "Thus says the
LORD: That which I have built I will break down,
and that which I have planted I will pluck up,
even this whole land. 5 But are you seeking
great things for yourself? Do not seek them.
For I will bring disaster upon all flesh, says the
LORD, but I will give your life to you as booty in
all the places where you go."

Judgment on Egypt

46 The word of the LORD which came to
Jeremiah the prophet against the na-
tions:

2 Concerning Egypt, about the army of Pha-
raoh Necho king of Egypt, which was by the
River Euphrates in Carchemish, which Nebu-
chadnezzar king of Babylon defeated in the
fourth year of Jehoiakim the son of Josiah,
king of Judah:

3 Order the buckler and shield,
and draw near to battle!
4 Harness the horses;
mount the steeds!
Take your positions
with your helmets,
polish the spears,
put on the armor!
5 Why have I seen them
dismayed and drawing back?
Their mighty ones are beaten down
and have taken refuge in flight,
and not looking back.
Terror is on every side!
says the LORD.
6 Let not the swift flee away,
nor the mighty man escape;

44:18 Mal 3:13–15
44:19 Jer 7:18
44:21 Ps 79:8
44:22 Jer 25:18
44:23 1Ki 9:9
44:24 Jer 43:7
44:25 Mt 14:9
44:26 Ge 22:16
44:27 Jer 31:28
44:28 Jer 44:14
44:29 Pr 19:21
44:30 2Ki 25:4–7
45:1 Jer 36:1
45:4 Jer 18:7–10
45:5 Jer 21:9
46:1 Jer 1:10
46:2 2Ki 23:29
46:3 Isa 21:5
46:4 Eze 21:9–11
46:5 Jer 6:25
46:6 Da 11:19

they will stumble and fall
towards the north by the River
Euphrates.

7 Who is this that comes up as the Nile,
whose waters surge about as the rivers?
8 Egypt rises up like the Nile,
and his waters surge about like the
rivers.
And he has said, I will go up and will cover
the land.
I will surely destroy the city and its
inhabitants.
9 Come up, O horses,
and rage, O chariots!
And let the mighty men come forth:
the Ethiopians and the Libyans who
handle the shield,
and the Lydians who handle and bend
the bow.
10 For this is the day of the Lord God of Hosts,
a day of vengeance, so that He may
avenge Himself of His adversaries.
And the sword will devour;
and it will be satiated and made drunk
with their blood;
for the Lord God of Hosts has a slaughter
in the north country by the River
Euphrates.
11 Go up into Gilead and take balm,
O virgin daughter of Egypt;
in vain you shall use many medicines,
for you will not be cured.
12 The nations have heard of your shame,
and your cry has filled the land;
for the mighty man has stumbled over the
mighty,
and they both have fallen together.

Defeat of Egypt Foretold

13 The word that the LORD spoke to Jeremiah
the prophet, about Nebuchadnezzar king of
Babylon coming to strike the land of Egypt.

14 Declare in Egypt and publish in Migdol,
and publish in Memphis and in
Tahpanhes;
say, "Stand fast and prepare yourself,
for the sword will devour those about
you."
15 Why have your valiant men become
prostrate?
They do not stand because the LORD has
thrust them down.
16 He made many to fall.
Indeed, each one has fallen upon
another.
Then they said, "Arise and let us go back
to our own people and to the land of our
nativity,
away from the oppressing sword."

46:7 Jer 47:2
46:9 Isa 66:19
46:10 Joel 1:15
46:11 Jer 8:22
46:12 Na 3:8–10
46:14 Jer 44:1
46:15 Isa 66:15–16

....

46:17 Isa 19:11–16
46:18 Jer 48:15
46:19 Isa 20:4
46:20 Jer 47:2
46:21 2Ki 7:6
46:23 Jdg 7:12
46:24 Jer 1:15
46:26 Jer 44:30
46:27 Isa 43:5
46:28 Jer 4:27

17 They cried there,
"Pharaoh king of Egypt is a tumult.
He has let the time appointed pass by!"
18 As I live, says the King
whose name is the LORD of Hosts,
surely as Tabor is among the mountains,
and as Carmel by the sea, so he shall
come.
19 O daughter dwelling in Egypt,
prepare your baggage for captivity,
for Memphis will become desolate,
it will even be burned down without an
inhabitant.

20 Egypt is like a very fair heifer,
but destruction comes,
it comes out of the north.
21 Also her mercenaries are in her midst
like fat bulls,
for they also have turned back and have
fled away together.
They did not stand their ground
because the day of their calamity has come
upon them,
even the time of their punishment.
22 Its sound goes along like a serpent,
for they march on as an army,
and come against her with axes,
as choppers of wood.
23 They have cut down her forest,
says the LORD.
Surely it will not be found any more,
even though they are now more numerous
than the grasshoppers,
and are innumerable.
24 The daughter of Egypt has been
humiliated;
she has been delivered into the hand of
the people of the north.

25 The LORD of Hosts, the God of Israel, says:
See, I will punish Amon of Thebes, and Pha-
raoh, and Egypt, with their gods and their
kings, even Pharaoh and all those who trust in
him. 26 And I shall deliver them into the hand of
those who seek their lives and into the hand of
Nebuchadnezzar king of Babylon and into the
hand of his servants. But afterwards it will be
inhabited, as in the days of old, says the LORD.

God Will Save Israel

27 But do not fear, O My servant Jacob,
and do not be dismayed, O Israel.
For I will save you from afar off,
and your seed from the land of their
captivity;
and Jacob shall return and be in rest and
at ease,
and no one shall make him afraid.
28 Do not fear, O Jacob My servant,
says the LORD, for I am with you;

for I will make a full end of all the nations
where I have driven you.
However, I will not make a full end of
you,
but correct you in measure,
and I will not leave you wholly
unpunished.

Judgment on the Philistines

47 The word of the LORD which came to Jeremiah the prophet against the Philistines, before Pharaoh conquered Gaza.

2 Thus says the LORD:

See, waters rise up out of the north
and will be an overflowing flood,
and will overflow the land, and all that is
in it,
the city and those who dwell in it.
Then the men shall cry out
and all the inhabitants of the land will
howl
3 at the noise of the stamping of the hoofs of
his strong horses,
at the rushing of his chariots,
and at the rumbling of his wheels.
The fathers will not look back to their
children
because of the feebleness of their hands,
4 because of the day that comes
to destroy all the Philistines
and to cut off from Tyre and Sidon
every helper that remains.
For the LORD will destroy the Philistines,
the remnant of the country of Caphtor.
5 Baldness has come upon Gaza;
Ashkelon has been cut off.
O remnant of their valley,
how long shall you gash yourself?
6 O sword of the LORD,
how long shall you not be quiet?
Withdraw into your sheath,
rest, and be still.
7 How can it be quiet,
seeing the LORD has given it a charge
against Ashkelon and against the sea
shore?
There He has appointed it.

Judgment on Moab
Isa 16:6–12

48 Concerning Moab:

Thus says the LORD of Hosts, the God of Israel:

Woe to Nebo, for it is devastated.
Kiriathaim is humiliated and captured;
Misgab[1] is humiliated and dismayed.
2 There is no more praise for Moab;

47:1 Jer 25:20
47:4 Am 9:7
47:5 Jer 48:37
47:6 Jer 12:12
47:7 Eze 14:17
48:1 Nu 32:3
48:3 Isa 15:5

SPIRITLED WOMAN
COUNSEL FROM THE SPIRIT BASICS

The Judgment of God

One of the truths of Scripture that began to beautify and heal my heart at the very core was the knowledge that I was worth fighting for. As I studied Jesus the Judge in Isaiah 63 and several passages in Revelation, I was shocked to discover God actually asks us to give Him our greatest wounds of injustice because He will fight *for* us. In hindsight, this makes perfect sense. How can our worth and dignity be restored if we are not worth fighting for?

We should have long ago given up hope that a government or other system will bring justice to wrongdoers. No matter which political candidate is elected, the injustices continue. As a result, we consider ourselves and others worthless, and as a society, we degrade human life. We are in a hole that we dug and cannot get out of, and the last thought in our minds is that we need a judge.

God will not forget our case when we give it to Him. God is a just judge, and He is angry with the wicked (Ps 7:11). Throughout Scripture He promises to remember their iniquity and punish their sins (Jer 14:10; Hos 8:13; 9:9; Ps 90:7–9), and we know the Lord is faithful to keep His promises.

We can have complete assurance that the righteous Judge sees us and will fight for us, but that doesn't absolve us of the responsibility to forgive. Jesus displays an amazing power to forgive our sins, and He invites us to be like Him by forgiving others.

Shelley Hundley

in Heshbon they have devised evil
against her:
"Come and let us cut it off from being a
nation!"
Also you will be cut down, O Madmen.
The sword will pursue you.
3 A sound of crying will be from Horonaim:
"Devastation and great destruction!"

[1] 1 Or *the stronghold.*

4 "Moab is destroyed";
her little ones have caused a cry of
distress to be heard;
5 for by the Ascent of Luhith they will go up
with continual weeping;
for at the descent of Horonaim
they have heard a cry of destruction.
6 Flee, save your lives,
and be like the juniper in the wilderness.
7 For because you have trusted in your works
and in your treasures,
you will also be captured;
and Chemosh shall go forth into captivity
together with his priests and his officials.
8 The destroyer will come upon every city,
and no city will escape.
The valley also will perish,
and the plain will be destroyed,
as the LORD has spoken.
9 Give wings to Moab,
that she may flee and get away;
for the cities will become desolate,
without any to dwell in them.

10 Cursed be he who does the work of the
LORD negligently,
and cursed be he who keeps back his
sword from blood.

11 Moab has been at ease from his youth,
and he has also been undisturbed,
like wine on its dregs,
and he has not been emptied from vessel
to vessel,
nor has he gone into captivity.
Therefore his taste remained in him,
and his scent has not changed.
12 Therefore, surely the days are coming,
says the LORD,
when I will send to him those who tip
vessels,
and they will tip him over,
and will empty his vessels
and break his bottles.
13 Moab shall be ashamed of Chemosh,
as the house of Israel was ashamed
of Bethel, their confidence.

14 How do you say, "We are mighty
and strong men for the war"?
15 Moab has been devastated and gone up
out of her cities,
and her chosen young men have also
gone down to the slaughter,
says the King whose name is the LORD
of Hosts.
16 The calamity of Moab will come soon,
and his affliction hastens fast.
17 All you who are about him, mourn for him.
And all you who know his name,
say, "How the strong staff has been broken,
the beautiful rod!"

18 O daughter who inhabits Dibon,
come down from your glory
and sit on the parched ground,
for the destroyer of Moab
will come upon you,
and he will destroy your strongholds.
19 O inhabitant of Aroer,
stand by the road and keep watch.
Ask him who flees and her who escapes,
and say, "What has happened?"
20 Moab has been humiliated, for it has been
broken down.
Howl and cry out.
Tell it in Arnon,
that Moab has been devastated.
21 And judgment has come upon the plain
country:
upon Holon and Jahzah and Mephaath,
22 and Dibon and Nebo and Beth
Diblathaim,
23 and Kiriathaim and Beth Gamul and
Beth Meon,
24 and Kerioth and Bozrah,
and all the cities of the land of Moab, far
and near.
25 The horn of Moab has been cut off
and his arm has been broken,
says the LORD.
26 Make him drunk,
for he magnified himself against the
LORD.
Moab also will wallow in his vomit,
and he also will be held in derision.
27 For was not Israel a derision to you?
Or was he caught among thieves?
For each time you speak of him,
you shake your head in scorn.
28 O you who dwell in Moab,
leave the cities and dwell in the rock,
and be like the dove that makes her nest
in the sides of the hole's mouth.

29 We have heard of the pride of Moab
(he is very proud),
of his loftiness, and his arrogance, and his
pride,
and the haughtiness of his heart.
30 I know his wrath,
says the LORD,
but it is futile. His lies have
accomplished nothing.
31 Therefore I will howl for Moab,
and I will cry out for all Moab.
My heart shall mourn for the men of Kir
Hareseth.
32 O vine of Sibmah,
I will weep for you more than the
weeping of Jazer.
Your plants have stretched over the sea,

48:5 Isa 15:5
48:6 Jer 17:6
48:7 Nu 21:29
48:8 Jer 6:26
48:10 1Ki 20:42
48:11 Zep 1:12
48:14 Ps 33:16
48:15 Jer 46:18
48:16 Isa 13:22
48:17 Isa 9:4
48:18 Nu 21:30
48:19 Dt 2:36
48:20 Isa 16:2
48:21 Jos 13:18
48:23 Jos 13:17
48:24 Am 2:2
48:25 Ps 75:10
48:26 Isa 19:14
48:27 Jer 2:26
48:28 Jdg 6:2
48:29 Isa 16:6
48:30 Jer 50:36
48:31 2Ki 3:25
48:32 Isa 16:8–9

they reach even to the sea of Jazer.
The destroyer has fallen upon your
summer fruits
and upon your vintage.
33 Joy and gladness are taken away
from the plentiful field, even from the
land of Moab,
and I have caused wine to fail from the
winepresses;
no one will tread with shouting.
Their shouting will not be shouts of joy.

34 From the outcry of Heshbon even to
Elealeh, and even to Jahaz,
they have uttered their voice,
from Zoar even to Horonaim and to Eglath
Shelishiyah;
for also the waters of Nimrim shall
become desolate.
35 Moreover I will cause to cease in Moab,
says the LORD,
him who offers *sacrifice* in the high place
and him who burns incense to his gods.
36 Therefore My heart will wail for Moab like
pipes,
and My heart will wail like pipes for the
men of Kir Hareseth,
because the riches that they have gotten
have perished.
37 For every head will be bald
and every beard clipped;
upon all the hands will be gashes,
and upon the loins sackcloth.
38 There will be lamentation everywhere
upon all the housetops of Moab
and in the streets,
for I have broken Moab
like a vessel in which is no pleasure,
says the LORD.
39 How it is broken down! How they have
wailed!
How Moab has turned his back with
shame!
So Moab will be a derision
and a terror to all around him.

40 For thus says the LORD:

Look, one will fly as an eagle
and spread his wings against Moab.
41 Kerioth has been captured,
and the strongholds have been seized,
and the mighty men's hearts in Moab in
that day
will be as the heart of a woman in her
pangs.
42 Moab will be destroyed from being a
people
because he has magnified himself
against the LORD.

48:34 Isa 15:4–6
48:35 Isa 15:2
48:36 Isa 15:7
48:37 Ge 37:34
48:38 Jer 22:28
48:40 Dt 28:49
48:41 Isa 13:8
48:42 Jer 48:2

48:43 Isa 24:17–18
48:44 1Ki 19:17
48:45 Nu 24:17
48:46 Nu 21:29
48:47 Jer 49:39
49:2 Jer 4:19
49:3 Jer 48:7
49:4 Jer 9:23

43 Fear and the pit and the snare will be upon
you,
O inhabitant of Moab,
says the LORD.
44 He who flees from the terror
shall fall into the pit,
and he who gets up out of the pit
will be taken in the snare;
for I will bring upon it, even upon Moab,
the year of their punishment,
says the LORD.

45 The fugitives stand without strength
under the shadow of Heshbon;
for a fire will come out of Heshbon
and a flame from the midst of Sihon,
and will devour the forehead of Moab
and the crown of the head of the
tumultuous ones.
46 Woe to you, O Moab!
The people of Chemosh have perished;
for your sons have been taken away
captive
and your daughters into captivity.

47 Yet I will restore the fortunes of Moab
in the latter days,
says the LORD.

Thus far is the judgment of Moab.

Judgment on Ammon

49 Concerning the Ammonites:
Thus says the LORD:

Does Israel have no sons?
Or has he no heirs?
Why then does their king inherit Gad
and his people dwell in his cities?
2 Therefore, surely the days are coming,
says the LORD,
when I will cause an alarm of war
to be heard in Rabbah of the
Ammonites;
and it will be a desolate heap,
and her towns will be burned with fire.
Then Israel will be heir
to those who were his heirs,
says the LORD.
3 Howl, O Heshbon, for Ai has been
devastated!
Cry out, O daughters of Rabbah,
gird yourselves with sackcloth and lament,
and run to and fro inside the walls;
for their king shall go into captivity,
and his priests and his officials together.
4 Why do you glory in the valleys,
your flowing valley,
O backsliding daughter
who trusts in her treasures, saying,
"Who shall come against me?"

5 I will bring a fear upon you,
says the Lord GOD of Hosts,
from all those who are around you;
and each of you will be driven out
headlong,
and no one will gather together the
fugitives.

6 Yet afterward I will restore the fortunes of
the sons of Ammon,
says the LORD.

Judgment on Edom
Ob 1:1–6

7 Concerning Edom.

Thus says the LORD of Hosts:

Is there no more wisdom in Teman?
Has counsel perished from the prudent?
Has their wisdom vanished?
8 Flee, turn back, dwell in the depths,
O inhabitants of Dedan.
For I will bring the calamity of Esau upon
him,
the time that I punish him.
9 If grape gatherers came to you,
would they not leave some gleaning
grapes?
If thieves came by night,
they would destroy until they had
enough.
10 But I have made Esau bare,
I have uncovered his secret places
so that he will not be able to hide
himself.
His seed is devastated, and his brothers,
and his neighbors,
and he is no more.
11 Leave your fatherless children behind. I
will preserve them alive;
and let your widows trust in Me.

12 For thus says the LORD: They whose judg-
ment was not to drink of the cup have assur-
edly drunk. And are you the one who shall go
unpunished altogether? You will not go un-
punished, but you will surely drink of it. 13 For
I have sworn by Myself, says the LORD, that
Bozrah will become a desolation, a reproach,
a waste, and a curse. And all the cities will
become perpetual wastes.

14 I have heard a message from the LORD,
and an ambassador has been sent to the
nations:
"Gather together, and come against her,
and rise up to the battle!"
15 For I will make you small among the
nations,
and despised among men.
16 As for the terror of you,
the pride of your heart has deceived you,
O you who dwell in the clefts of the rock,
who hold the height of the hill.
Though you make your nest as high as the
eagle,
I will bring you down from there,
says the LORD.
17 Also Edom will become a desolation;
everyone who goes by it will be
astonished,
and will hiss at all its wounds.
18 As in the overthrow of Sodom and
Gomorrah
and the neighboring cities,
says the LORD,
no man will abide there,
nor will a son of man dwell in it.

19 He will come up like a lion from the
thickets of the Jordan
against the perpetually watered
meadow;
but I will suddenly make him run away
from her.
And I will appoint over her whomever I
choose.
For who is like Me? And who will summon
Me *into court*?
Who is the shepherd who can stand
against Me?

20 Therefore hear the counsel of the LORD that
He has planned against Edom,
and His purposes that He has purposed
against the inhabitants of Teman:
Surely the least of the flock will drag them
out;
surely He will make their habitations
desolate because of them.
21 The earth has shaken at the noise of their
fall;
there is an outcry. Its noise has been
heard at the Red Sea.
22 He will mount up and fly as the eagle
and spread his wings against Bozrah;
and in that day the hearts of the mighty
men of Edom
will be as the heart of a woman in her
pangs.

Judgment on Damascus

23 Concerning Damascus:

Hamath and Arpad have been humiliated,
for they have heard bad news.
They are faint-hearted;
there is sorrow on the sea; it cannot be
quieted.
24 Damascus has become helpless;
she has turned away to flee,
and panic has seized her.
Anguish and sorrows have seized her
as a woman in labor.

49:6 Jer 48:47
49:7 Ge 25:30
49:8 Jer 25:23
49:9 Ob 1:5–6
49:10 Isa 17:14
49:11 Ps 68:5
49:12 Jer 25:28–29
49:13 Ge 22:16
49:14 Isa 30:4
49:16 Job 39:27
49:17 Jer 50:13
49:18 Dt 29:23
49:19 Jer 12:5
49:20 Jer 50:45
49:21 Jer 50:46
49:22 Jer 48:40–41
49:23 2Ki 18:34

[25] How the city of praise has not been deserted,
the city of My joy!
[26] Therefore her young men will fall in her streets,
and all the men of war will be cut off in that day,
says the LORD of Hosts.
[27] I will kindle a fire to the wall of Damascus,
and it will consume the palaces of Ben-Hadad.

Judgment on Kedar and Hazor

[28] Concerning Kedar, and concerning the
kingdoms of Hazor, which Nebuchadnezzar
king of Babylon defeated:

Thus says the LORD:

Arise, go up to Kedar,
and destroy the men of the East.
[29] Their tents and their flocks they will take away.
They will carry away their curtains for themselves,
and all their vessels, and their camels;
and they will call out to one another,
"Terror is on every side!"
[30] Flee, go far away,
dwell in the depths, O inhabitants of Hazor,
says the LORD.
For Nebuchadnezzar king of Babylon has taken counsel against you,
and has conceived a purpose against you.

[31] Arise, go up to the nation at ease,
that dwells securely,
says the LORD.
It has neither gates nor bars;
they dwell alone.
[32] Their camels will become plunder,
and the multitude of their cattle booty.
And I will scatter into all winds those who cut the corners *of their hair*,
and I will bring their calamity from all sides,
says the LORD.
[33] Hazor will become a dwelling for jackals
and a desolation forever.
No man will abide there,
nor any son of man dwell in it.

Judgment on Elam

[34] The word of the LORD which came to Jere-
miah the prophet against Elam in the begin-
ning of the reign of Zedekiah king of Judah,
saying:

[35] Thus says the LORD of Hosts:

I will break the bow of Elam,
the chief of their might.
[36] Upon Elam I will bring the four winds
from the four quarters of heaven,
and will scatter them toward all those winds.
And there will be no nation
where the outcasts of Elam will not go.
[37] For I will cause Elam to be dismayed
before their enemies,
and before those who seek their life.
And I will bring disaster upon them,
even My fierce anger,
says the LORD;
and I will send the sword after them
until I have consumed them.
[38] And I will set My throne in Elam
and will destroy from there the king and the officials,
says the LORD.
[39] But it will come to pass in the latter days
that I will restore the fortunes of Elam,
says the LORD.

Judgment on Babylon

Jer 10:12–16

50 The word that the LORD spoke against
Babylon and against the land of the
Chaldeans by Jeremiah the prophet:

[2] Declare among the nations and publish,
and set up a standard;
do not conceal it, but say,
Babylon has been captured.
Bel has been humiliated.
Marduk has been broken in pieces;
her idols have been humiliated;
her images have been broken in pieces.
[3] For out of the north there comes up a nation against her,
which will make her land desolate,
and no one will dwell in it.
They will wander away;
they will depart,
both man and beast.

[4] In those days and at that time,
says the LORD,
the sons of Israel will come,
they and the children of Judah together.
They will go along weeping as they go,
and seek the LORD their God.
[5] They will ask for the way to Zion
with their faces in its direction.
They will come that they may join themselves to the LORD
in a perpetual covenant
that will not be forgotten.

[6] My people have been lost sheep.
Their shepherds have caused them to go astray;

49:25 Jer 33:9
49:26 Jer 50:30
49:28 Ge 25:13
49:29 Jer 6:25
49:31 Eze 38:11
49:32 Jer 9:26
49:33 Jer 9:11
49:34 Ge 10:22
49:35 Isa 22:6
49:36 Jer 49:32
49:37 Jer 9:16
49:39 Jer 48:47
50:2 Isa 46:1
50:3 Zep 1:3
50:4 Hos 3:5
50:5 Jer 32:40
50:6 Isa 53:6

they have turned them away on the
mountains.
They have gone from mountain to hill
and have forgotten their resting place.
7 All who found them have devoured them,
and their adversaries said, "We are not
guilty,
because they have sinned against the LORD,
the habitation of justice,
even the LORD, the hope of their fathers."

8 Wander away out of the midst of Babylon,
and go out of the land of the Chaldeans,
and be as the male goats before the
flocks.
9 For I will raise and cause to come up
against Babylon
an assembly of great nations from the
north country.
And they shall set themselves in array
against her;
from there she shall be taken captive.
Their arrows *will be* like *those* of a skilled
warrior;
no one shall return empty-handed.
10 Chaldea will become plunder;
all who destroy her will be satisfied,
says the LORD.

11 Because you were glad, because you
rejoiced,
O you destroyers of My heritage,
because you have grown fat as the heifer at
the grass,
and bellow as bulls,
12 your mother will be sorely humiliated;
she who bore you will be ashamed.
She will be the least of the nations,
a wilderness, a dry land, and a desert.
13 Because of the wrath of the LORD she will
not be inhabited,
but shall be wholly desolate.
Everyone who goes by Babylon will be
astonished
and hiss at all her wounds.

14 Put yourselves in battle array against
Babylon all around,
all you who bend the bow;
shoot at her, spare no arrows,
for she has sinned against the LORD.
15 Shout against her all around;
she has given herself up, her
foundations have fallen,
her walls have been thrown down.
For this is the vengeance of the LORD.
Take vengeance on her;
as she has done, do to her.
16 Cut off the sower from Babylon,
and him who handles the sickle in the
time of harvest.
For fear of the oppressing sword
everyone will turn to his people,
and everyone will flee to his own land.

17 Israel is a scattered flock.
The lions have driven him away.
First the king of Assyria
devoured him;
and this last one who has broken his bones
is Nebuchadnezzar king of Babylon.

18 Therefore thus says the LORD of Hosts, the
God of Israel:

I will punish the king of Babylon and his
land,
as I have punished the king of Assyria.
19 I will bring Israel again to his habitation,
and he will feed on Carmel and Bashan,
and his soul will be satisfied
upon Mount Ephraim and Gilead.
20 In those days and at that time,
says the LORD,
the iniquity of Israel will be sought for,
and there shall be none.
And the sins of Judah,
but they shall not be found;
for I will pardon those whom I leave as
a remnant.

21 Go up against the land of Merathaim, even
against it,
and against the inhabitants of Pekod.
Slay and utterly destroy them,
says the LORD,
and do according to all that I have
commanded you.
22 A noise of battle is in the land,
and great destruction.
23 How the hammer of the whole earth
has been cut asunder and broken!
How Babylon has become a desolation
among the nations!
24 I have laid a snare for you,
and you were also caught, O Babylon,
and you were not aware.
You have been found, and also caught,
because you have striven against the
LORD.
25 The LORD has opened His armory
and has brought out the weapons of His
indignation,
for this is the work of the Lord GOD of Hosts
in the land of the Chaldeans.
26 Come against her from the utmost border,
open her storehouses;
cast her up as heaps and destroy her
utterly;
let nothing of her be left.
27 Slay all her bulls,
let them go down to the slaughter.

50:7 Jer 14:8
50:8 Isa 48:20
50:10 Jer 25:12
50:11 Isa 47:6
50:12 Jer 51:43
50:13 Jer 18:16
50:14 Jer 50:29
50:15 Jer 51:58
50:16 Isa 13:14
50:17 Jer 2:15
50:18 Isa 10:12
50:20 Mic 7:19
50:21 Eze 23:23
50:22 Jer 4:19–21
50:23 Jer 51:20–24
50:24 Job 9:4
50:25 Jer 51:25
50:26 Isa 14:23
50:27 Isa 34:7

Woe to them! For their day has come,
the time of their punishment.
28 There is the sound of those who flee and escape out of the land of Babylon,
to declare in Zion
the vengeance of the LORD our God,
the vengeance of His temple.
29 Call together the archers against Babylon.
All you who bend the bow,
encamp against it all around;
let no one escape.
Recompense her according to her work;
according to all that she has done, do to her,
for she has been proud against the LORD,
against the Holy One of Israel.
30 Therefore her young men shall fall in the streets,
and all her men of war shall be cut off in that day,
says the LORD.
31 I am against you, O most proud,
says the Lord GOD of Hosts,
for your day has come,
the time when I will punish you.
32 The most proud will stumble and fall,
and no one will raise him up;
and I will kindle a fire in his cities,
and it will devour all all around him.

33 Thus says the LORD of Hosts:

The sons of Israel and the sons of Judah
were oppressed together;
and all who took them captives held them fast;
they refused to let them go.
34 Their Redeemer is strong;
the LORD of Hosts is His name.
He will thoroughly plead their case,
that He may give rest to the land,
but disquiet to the inhabitants of Babylon.

35 A sword is against the Chaldeans,
says the LORD,
and against the inhabitants of Babylon,
and against her officials, and against her wise men.
36 A sword is against the oracle priests,
and they will become fools.
A sword is against her mighty men,
and they shall be dismayed.
37 A sword is against their horses, and against their chariots,
and against all the foreigners who are in her midst;
and they will become as women.
A sword is against her treasures,
and they will be robbed.

50:28 Isa 48:20
50:29 Isa 47:10
50:30 Jer 49:26
50:31 Jer 21:13
50:32 Jer 21:14
50:33 Isa 14:17
50:34 Jer 51:36
50:35 Jer 47:6
50:36 Jer 49:22
50:37 Jer 51:30

....

50:38 Isa 44:27
50:39 Isa 13:20–22
50:40 Ge 19:24–25
50:41 Jer 51:27–28
50:42 Isa 5:30
50:44 Jer 49:19–21
50:45 Jer 49:20
50:46 Jer 49:21

38 A drought is against her waters,
and they will be dried up.
For it is the land of graven images,
and they are mad over their idols.
39 Therefore the wild beasts of the desert
with the wild beasts of the islands will dwell there,
and the ostriches will dwell in it.
It will be inhabited no more forever,
nor will it be lived in from generation to generation.
40 As God overthrew Sodom and Gomorrah
and the neighboring cities,
says the LORD,
so no man will abide there,
nor will any son of man dwell in it.
41 Look! A people shall come from the north
and a great nation, and many kings
will be raised up from the remote parts of the earth.
42 They will hold the bow and the lance;
they are cruel and will not show mercy.
Their voice shall roar like the sea;
and they shall ride on horses,
everyone put in array, like a man to the battle,
against you, O daughter of Babylon.
43 The king of Babylon has heard the report of them,
and his hands waxed feeble.
Anguish took hold of him,
and pangs as of a woman in labor.
44 He will come up like a lion from the thicket of the Jordan
to the perpetually watered meadow.
But I will make them suddenly run away from it,
and whoever is chosen I will appoint over it.
For who is like Me? And who will summon Me *into court*?
And who is the shepherd that can stand before Me?

45 Therefore hear the counsel of the LORD that He has planned against Babylon,
and His purposes that He has purposed against the land of the Chaldeans:
Surely the least of the flock will drag them out.
Surely He will make their habitation desolate because of them.
46 At the shout, "Babylon has been seized!"
the earth is shaken,
and the outcry is heard among the nations.

The Destruction of Babylon

51 Thus says the LORD:
I will raise up against Babylon,
and against those who dwell in Leb Kamai,
the spirit of a destroyer.
2 And I will send foreigners to Babylon
that they may winnow her and empty her land.
For in the day of trouble
they will be against her all around.
3 Let not him who bends his bow bend it,
and let him not rise up in his scale-armor,
and do not spare her young men;
utterly destroy all her host.
4 Thus the slain will fall in the land of the Chaldeans,
and those who are thrust through in her streets.
5 For Israel has not been forsaken, nor Judah,
by his God, the LORD of Hosts,
though their land was filled with sin
against the Holy One of Israel.

6 Flee out of the midst of Babylon,
and each of you deliver his soul!
Do not be cut off in her punishment,
for this is the time of the vengeance of the LORD;
He will render to her a recompense.
7 Babylon has been a golden cup in the hand of the LORD,
that made all the earth drunk.
The nations have drunk of her wine;
therefore the nations are mad.
8 Babylon is suddenly fallen and destroyed.
Howl for her.
Take balm for her pain;
perhaps she may be healed.

9 We applied healing to Babylon,
but she is not healed.
Forsake her, and let us each go into his own country;
for her judgment reaches to heaven
and is lifted up even to the skies.

10 The LORD has brought forth our righteousness.
Come, and let us declare in Zion
the work of the LORD our God.

11 Sharpen the arrows.
Gather the shields.
The LORD has raised up the spirit of the kings of the Medes.
For His device is against Babylon, to destroy it;
because it is the vengeance of the LORD,
the vengeance of His temple.
12 Set up the standard against the walls of Babylon,
make the watch strong,
set up the watchmen,
prepare the ambushes.
For the LORD has both devised and done
that which He spoke against the inhabitants of Babylon.
13 O you who dwell by many waters,
abundant in treasures,
your end has come,
and the measure of your end.
14 The LORD of Hosts has sworn by Himself,
saying: Surely I will fill you with men, as with locusts,
and they will lift up shouts of victory against you.
15 He has made the earth by His power;
He has established the world by His wisdom,
and has stretched out the heaven by His understanding.
16 When He utters His voice, there is a multitude of waters in the heavens,
and He causes the clouds to ascend from the remote parts of the earth;
He makes lightning with rain,
and brings out the wind from His storehouses.

17 Every man is ignorant by His knowledge;
every founder is humiliated by the graven image,
for his molded image is falsehood,
and there is no breath in them.
18 They are vanity, the work of errors;
in the time of their punishment they will perish.
19 The portion of Jacob is not like them,
for He is the former of all things,
and Israel is the rod of His inheritance.
The LORD of Hosts is His name.

20 *He says*: You are My battle-ax
and weapon of war:
for with you I will break in pieces the nations,
and with you I will destroy kingdoms;
21 and with you I will break in pieces the horse and his rider;
and with you I will break in pieces the chariot and his rider.
22 With you also I will break in pieces man and woman;
and with you I will break in pieces old and young;
and with you I will break in pieces the young man and the young woman.

51:2 Jer 15:7
51:3 Jer 46:4
51:4 Jer 49:26
51:5 Hos 4:1
51:6 Jer 50:8
51:7 Rev 14:8
51:8 Isa 21:9
51:9 Isa 13:14
51:10 Jer 50:28
51:11 Jer 46:4
51:12 Isa 13:2
51:13 Rev 17:1
51:15 Job 9:8
51:16 Ps 135:7
51:17 Jer 10:14
51:19 Jer 10:16
51:20 Isa 10:5
51:21 Ex 15:1
51:22 2Ch 36:17

23 I will also break in pieces with you the
shepherd and his flock;
and with you I will break in pieces the
farmer and his yoke of oxen;
and with you I will break in pieces
captains and rulers.

24 I will render to Babylon and to all the in-
habitants of Chaldea all their evil that they
have done in Zion in your sight, says the LORD.

25 I am against you, O destroying mountain,
says the LORD,
who destroys all the earth.
And I will stretch out My hand against you,
and roll you down from the rocks,
and will make you a burned mountain.
26 They will not take of you a stone for a
corner,
or a stone for foundations,
but you will be desolate forever,
says the LORD.
27 Set up a standard in the land,
blow the trumpet among the nations,
prepare the nations against her,
call together against her the kingdoms
of Ararat, Minni, and Ashkenaz;
appoint a captain against her.
Cause the horses to come up as the
rough locusts.
28 Prepare against her the nations,
the kings of the Medes,
the captains, and all the rulers,
and every land of their dominion.
29 So the land trembles and sorrows,
for the purposes of the LORD will be
performed against Babylon,
to make the land of Babylon a desolation
without an inhabitant.
30 The mighty men of Babylon have ceased
fighting;
they have remained in their strongholds.
Their might has failed;
they became as women.
They have burned her dwelling places;
the bars of her gates are broken.
31 One courier will run to meet another,
and one messenger to meet another,
to show the king of Babylon
that his city has been captured from end
to end,
32 and the passages have been seized,
and they have burned the reeds with
fire,
and the men of war are terrified.

33 For thus says the LORD of Hosts, the God
of Israel:

The daughter of Babylon is like a threshing
floor,
it is time to thresh her;
yet a little while and the time of her harvest
will come.

34 "Nebuchadnezzar the king of Babylon
has devoured me and crushed me;
he has made me an empty vessel.
He has swallowed me up like a dragon;
he has filled his belly with my delicacies,
he has cast me out.
35 May the violence done to me and to my
flesh be upon Babylon,"
the inhabitant of Zion will say;
and, "May my blood be upon the
inhabitants of Chaldea,"
Jerusalem will say.

36 Therefore thus says the LORD:

I will plead your cause,
and take vengeance for you.
And I will dry up her sea,
and make her springs dry.
37 Babylon will become heaps,
a dwelling place for jackals,
an astonishment, and a hissing,
without an inhabitant.
38 They will roar together like young lions;
they will growl as lions' whelps.
39 When they become heated up,
I will make their feasts,
and I will make them drunk,
that they may rejoice,
and sleep a perpetual sleep, and not
awake,
says the LORD.
40 I will bring them down
like lambs to the slaughter,
like rams with male goats.

41 How Sheshak has been captured!
And how the praise of the whole earth
has been seized!
How Babylon has become an astonishment
among the nations!
42 The sea has come up over Babylon;
she has been covered with the multitude
of the waves.
43 Her cities have become a desolation,
a dry land and a wilderness,
a land in which no man dwells,
through which no son of man passes.
44 I will punish Bel in Babylon,
and I will bring forth from his mouth
what he has swallowed up;
and the nations will not flow together any
more to him.
Indeed, the wall of Babylon will fall.

45 My people, go out of her midst,
and deliver every man his soul
from the fierce anger of the LORD,

51:24 Jer 50:15
51:25 Rev 8:8
51:26 Isa 13:19–22
51:27 Ge 8:4
51:28 Jer 51:11
51:29 Jer 8:16
51:30 Na 3:13
51:31 2Sa 18:19–31
51:33 Isa 21:10
51:34 Jer 50:17
51:36 Jer 50:38
51:37 Rev 18:2
51:38 Jer 2:15
51:39 Jer 51:57
51:40 Jer 50:27
51:41 Jer 25:26
51:42 Isa 8:7–8
51:43 Isa 13:20
51:44 Jer 51:34
51:45 Jer 51:6

[46]lest your heart grows faint, and you are
afraid
for the report that will be heard in the
land—
for the report will come one year, and
after that in another year will come
another report,
and violence will be in the land,
ruler against ruler—
[47]therefore the days are coming
when I will punish the graven images of
Babylon;
and her whole land will be humiliated,
and all her slain will fall in her midst.
[48]Then the heaven and the earth, and all that
is in it,
shall sing for joy over Babylon;
for the destroyers will come to her
from the north,
says the LORD.

[49]As Babylon has caused the slain of Israel to
fall,
so at Babylon the slain of all the earth
will fall.
[50]You who have escaped the sword,
go away, do not stand still.
Remember the LORD afar off,
and let Jerusalem come into your mind.

[51]We are humiliated
because we have heard reproach.
Shame has covered our faces,
for strangers have come into
the holy places of the house of the LORD.

[52]Therefore, surely the days are coming, says
the LORD,
when I will punish her graven images,
and the mortally wounded shall groan
through all her land.
[53]Though Babylon should mount up to
heaven,
and though she should fortify the height
of her strength,
yet from Me will destroyers come to her,
says the LORD.

[54]A sound of an outcry comes from Babylon,
and great destruction
from the land of the Chaldeans,
[55]because the LORD has devastated Babylon,
and destroyed the great voice out of her.
When her waves roar like great waters,
a noise of their voice is uttered.
[56]Because the destroyer is coming against
her, even upon Babylon,
and her mighty men will be captured,
every one of their bows are broken.
For the LORD is a God of recompense;
He will completely repay.

[57]I will make her officials drunk, and her
wise men,
her captains, and her rulers, and her
mighty men;
and they will sleep a perpetual sleep, and
not awake,
says the King whose name is the LORD
of Hosts.

[58]Thus says the LORD of Hosts:

The broad wall of Babylon will be utterly
broken,
and her high gates will be burned with
fire;
and the peoples will labor in vain,
and the nations become exhausted only
for fire.

Jeremiah's Command to Seraiah

[59]The word which Jeremiah the prophet
commanded Seraiah the son of Neriah, the
son of Mahseiah, when he went with Zedekiah
the king of Judah into Babylon in the fourth
year of his reign. Now Seraiah was a quarter-
master. [60]So Jeremiah wrote in a single scroll
all the evil that should come upon Babylon,
even all these words that are written against
Babylon. [61]Jeremiah said to Seraiah, "When
you come to Babylon, then see that you read
aloud all these words, [62]and say, 'O LORD, You
have spoken against this place to cut it off, that
no one will remain in it, neither man nor beast,
but that it shall be desolate forever.' [63]It will be
that when you have made an end of reading
this scroll that you will bind a stone to it, and
cast it into the midst of the Euphrates, [64]and
say, 'Thus Babylon will sink and not rise from
the disaster that I will bring upon her, and they
will become weary.' "

Thus far are the words of Jeremiah.

The Fall of Jerusalem Reviewed

2Ki 24:18–20; 25:1–21; 2Ch 36:11–20; Jer 39:1–10

52 Zedekiah was twenty-one years old
when he began to reign, and he
reigned eleven years in Jerusalem. And his
mother's name was Hamutal the daughter of
Jeremiah of Libnah. [2]He did what was evil in
the eyes of the LORD, according to all that Je-
hoiakim had done. [3]Through the anger of the
LORD this came to pass in Jerusalem and Judah
until He had cast them out from His presence.

Then Zedekiah rebelled against the king of
Babylon.

[4]In the ninth year of his reign, in the tenth
month, in the tenth day of the month, Neb-
uchadnezzar king of Babylon came, he and
all his army, against Jerusalem, and laid siege
to it; they built a siege wall all around it. [5]So
the city was besieged until the eleventh year
of King Zedekiah.

[6]In the fourth month, in the ninth day of
the month, the famine was so severe in the

51:46 2Ki 19:7
51:47 Jer 50:2
51:48 Isa 44:23
51:49 Jer 50:29
51:50 Jer 44:28
51:51 La 1:10
51:52 Jer 51:47
51:53 Jer 49:16
51:54 Jer 50:22
51:56 Ps 46:9
51:57 Jer 46:18
51:58 Jer 51:64
51:59 Jer 32:12
51:62 Jer 50:3
51:63 Jer 19:10–11
51:64 Jer 51:58
52:1 2Ki 24:18
52:2 1Ki 14:22
52:4 Jer 39:1
52:6 Isa 3:1

city that there was no bread for the people of the land. [7] Then the city was breached, and all the men of war fled and went out of the city by night by way of the gate between the two walls, which was by the king's garden, though the Chaldeans were all around the city, and they went by way of the Arabah. [8] But the army of the Chaldeans pursued after the king and overtook Zedekiah in the plains of Jericho, and all his army was scattered from him.

[9] Then they took the king and carried him up to the king of Babylon at Riblah in the land of Hamath where he passed sentence on him. [10] The king of Babylon slew the sons of Zedekiah before his eyes; he also slew all the officials of Judah in Riblah. [11] Then he put out the eyes of Zedekiah, and the king of Babylon bound him in chains and carried him to Babylon and put him in prison until the day of his death.

The Temple Burned

[12] Now in the fifth month, in the tenth day of the month, which was the nineteenth year of Nebuchadnezzar king of Babylon, Nebuzaradan the captain of the guard who served the king of Babylon came into Jerusalem, [13] and burned the house of the LORD, and the king's house, and all the houses of Jerusalem. Even all the large houses, he burned with fire. [14] And all the army of the Chaldeans who were with the captain of the guard broke down all the walls of Jerusalem all around. [15] Then Nebuzaradan the captain of the guard carried away captive some of the poorest of the people, and the rest of the people who remained in the city, and those who fell away, who fell to the king of Babylon, and the rest of the multitude. [16] But Nebuzaradan the captain of the guard left some of the poorest of the land to be vinedressers and farmers.

[17] Also the pillars of bronze that were in the house of the LORD, and the stands, and the bronze sea that was in the house of the LORD, the Chaldeans broke and carried all their bronze to Babylon. [18] The cauldrons also, and the shovels, and the snuffers, and the bowls, and the spoons, and all the vessels of bronze with which they ministered, they took away. [19] The captain of the guard also took away the basins, and the fire pans, and the bowls, and the cauldrons, and the lampstands, and the spoons, and the cups, what was of fine gold, and what was of fine silver.

[20] The two pillars, one sea, and twelve bronze bulls that were under the bases, which King Solomon had made in the house of the LORD, the bronze of all these vessels was beyond weight. [21] Concerning the pillars: the height of one pillar was eighteen cubits, and it was twelve cubits in circumference and in thickness it was four fingers,[1] and hollow. [22] A capital of bronze was upon it, and the height of one capital was five cubits,[2] with network and pomegranates upon the capital all around, all of bronze. The second pillar also and the pomegranates were like these. [23] There were ninety-six pomegranates on the sides; all the pomegranates were a hundred upon the network all around.

52:9 Nu 13:21
52:10 Jer 22:30
52:11 Eze 12:13
52:12 2Ki 25:8
52:13 2Ch 36:19
52:14 Ne 1:3
52:16 2Ki 25:12
52:17 Jer 27:19–22
52:18 Ex 27:3
52:19 1Ki 7:49–50
52:20 1Ki 7:47
52:21 2Ki 25:17
52:23 1Ki 7:20
52:24 2Ki 25:18
52:25 Est 1:14
52:29 Jer 52:12
52:33 2Sa 9:7
52:34 2Sa 9:10

The Babylonian Exile

[24] The captain of the guard took Seraiah the chief priest, and Zephaniah the second priest, and the three officers of the temple. [25] He also took out of the city one official who had charge of the men of war, and seven men of the advisers of the king who were found in the city, and the scribe of the commander of the army who mustered the people of the land, and sixty men of the people of the land who were found in the midst of the city. [26] So Nebuzaradan the captain of the guard took them and brought them to the king of Babylon to Riblah. [27] The king of Babylon struck them and put them to death in Riblah in the land of Hamath.

Thus Judah was carried away captive out of its own land. [28] These are the people whom Nebuchadnezzar carried away captive:

in the seventh year three thousand and
 twenty-three Jews.
[29] In the eighteenth year of Nebuchadnezzar
he carried away captive from Jerusalem
 eight hundred and thirty-two persons.
[30] In the twenty-third year of Nebuchadnezzar,
Nebuzaradan the captain of the guard
 carried away captive of the Jews seven hundred and forty-five.
All the persons were four thousand and
 six hundred.

Jehoiachin Released

2Ki 25:27–30

[31] In the thirty-seventh year of the captivity of Jehoiachin, king of Judah, in the twelfth month, on the twenty-fifth day of the month, Awel-Marduk, king of Babylon, in the first year of his reign lifted up the head of Jehoiachin king of Judah and brought him out of prison, [32] and spoke kindly to him, and set his throne above the throne of the kings who were with him in Babylon. [33] Therefore Jehoiachin changed his prison garments and continually ate meals before him all the days of his life. [34] For his allowance, there was a continual allowance given him by the king of Babylon, every day a portion all the days of his life until the day of his death.

[1] *21* About 27 feet high and 18 feet in circumference, or 8.1 meters high and 5.4 meters in circumference. [2] *22* About 7½ feet, or 2.3 meters.

Author: The prophet Jeremiah

Written: Between 586 and 575 BC

Themes: Mourning for Jerusalem

LAMENTATIONS

Dear Spirit Led Woman,

Years ago, when I was in worship one day following a particularly disappointing turn of events, the Lord reminded me of a verse from Lamentations: "'The LORD is my portion,' says my soul, 'therefore I will hope in Him'" (La 3:24). This verse has served me well during the years when the dreadful "if onlys" threatened me. Surely you're familiar with them: "If only I were married." "If only my dad were still here." "If only things were different."

Such musings are potentially very powerful in shaping a mood or mind-set. But praise God for the intervention of His reminder to me through Lamentations 3:24!

When your circumstances appear to have gone against you, God will intervene. If you trust Him, He will not allow Satan to thwart His plans for you. You are never at the mercy of your setbacks. Jesus Christ makes up the difference.

Brenda J. Davis

The Sorrows of Jerusalem

1 How lonely sits the city
that was full of people!
How she has become like a widow,
who was once great among the nations!
She who was a princess among the provinces
has become a slave!

2 She weeps sorely in the night,
her tears are on her cheeks;
among all her lovers
she has none to comfort her.
All her friends have dealt treacherously with her;
they have become her enemies.

3 Judah has gone into captivity,
under affliction and great servitude;
she dwells among the nations,
she finds no rest;
all her persecutors overtook her
in the midst of distress.

4 The roads to Zion mourn
because no one comes to the solemn feasts.
All her gates are desolate;
her priests sigh,
her virgins are afflicted,
and she herself suffers bitterly.

5 Her adversaries have become her masters,
her enemies prosper;
for the LORD has afflicted her
because of the multitude of her transgressions.
Her children have gone into captivity
before the enemy.

6 From the daughter of Zion
all her beauty has departed.
Her princes have become like deer
that find no pasture;
they fled without strength
before the pursuer.

7 In the days of her affliction and misery
Jerusalem remembers all her pleasant things
that she had in the days of old.
When her people fell into the hand of the enemy,
there was no one to help her.
The adversaries saw her
and mocked at her desolation.

8 Jerusalem has sinned grievously;
therefore she has become vile.
All who honored her despise her,
for they have seen her nakedness;
she herself sighs
and turns away.

9 Her uncleanness is in her skirts;
she took no thought of her future;
therefore her fall is astounding;
she has no comforter.
"O LORD, look upon my affliction,
for the enemy has triumphed!"

10 The adversary has spread his hand
over all her precious things;
for she has seen the nations
enter her sanctuary,
those whom You commanded
not to enter Your congregation.

11 All her people groan,
as they search for bread;
they trade their treasures for food
to restore their strength.
Look, O LORD, and consider,
for I am despised.

12 Is it nothing to you, all you who pass by?
Look and see
if there is any sorrow like my sorrow,
which was brought upon me,
which the LORD has inflicted
on the day of His fierce anger.

13 From on high He has sent fire into my bones,
and it prevailed against them;
He has spread a net for my feet;
He turned me back;
He has made me desolate
and faint all the day long.

14 The yoke of my transgressions
was bound; by His hand
they were fastened together; they were set upon my neck.
He made my strength fail;
the Lord delivered me into the hands
of those whom I am not able to withstand.

15 The Lord has trampled underfoot
all my mighty men in my midst;
He has called an assembly against me
to crush my young men;
The Lord has trodden the virgin daughter of Judah
as in a winepress.

16 For these things I weep;
my eyes flow with tears;
for the comforter, who should relieve my soul,
is far from me.
My children are desolate
for the enemy has prevailed.

17 Zion spreads out her hands,
but there is no one to comfort her;

1:1 1Ki 4:21
1:2 Ps 6:6
1:4 Jer 9:11
1:8 Isa 59:2–13

1:9 Dt 32:29
1:10 Dt 23:3
1:11 Jer 52:6
1:12 Da 9:12
1:13 Job 30:30
1:14 Dt 28:48
1:16 La 1:2
1:17 Jer 4:31

SPIRITLED WOMAN

COUNSEL FROM THE SPIRIT BASICS

The Watches of the Lord

Arise, cry out in the night,
at the beginning of the watches;
pour out your heart like water
before the face of the Lord.
Lift your hands to Him
for the lives of your young children,
who faint from hunger
at the head of every street.
—LAMENTATIONS 2:19

The watches of the Lord are mentioned in the Old and New Testaments. In the Old Testament there were three watches. These watches were designated shifts for the people of God to watch for enemy infiltration. Lamentations 2:19 teaches about the first watch.

Women are called to cry unto the Lord on behalf of their children and families. The scripture tells us to stay before God's face and to lift our hands toward Him. Staying before God's face represents persistence in prayer, and lifting our hands represents casting our cares on God and giving our problems to Him.

There is nothing like the prayers of a wife or mother for her family. God placed a special anointing on women to intercede for their families. He put fire in their mouths to decree the Word of the Lord in the home. When women close their mouths in disobedience to God's mandate on their lives, it is a sin. I believe this is why the devil is always telling the woman to be silent in the church.

Kimberly Daniels

the LORD has commanded against Jacob
that his neighbors should be his
adversaries;
Jerusalem has become a filthy thing
among them.

18 The LORD is in the right,
for I have rebelled against His
commandment.
Hear now, all peoples,
and see my sorrow;
my virgins and my young men
have gone into captivity.

19 I called for my lovers,
but they deceived me;
my priests and my elders
perished in the city,
while they sought food
to restore their strength.

20 Look, O LORD, for I am in distress;
my soul is greatly troubled;
my heart is overturned within me,
for I have grievously rebelled.
In the street the sword bereaves,
at home it is like death.

21 They have heard my groaning,
yet there is no one to comfort me.
All my enemies have heard of my trouble;
they are glad that You have done it.
Bring the day that You have announced,
that they become like me.

22 Let all their wickedness come before You,
and do to them
as You have done to me
for all my transgressions;
for my groans are many,
and my heart is faint.

1:18 1Sa 12:14–15

1:19 La 1:2
1:20 La 2:11
1:21 La 1:8
2:1 Ps 99:5
2:2 Ps 89:39–40
2:3 Ps 74:11
2:4 Isa 42:25

The Anger of God Over Jerusalem

2 How the Lord has covered the daughter
of Zion
with a cloud in His anger!
He has cast down from heaven to the earth
the beauty of Israel;
He has not remembered His footstool
in the day of His anger.

2 The Lord has swallowed up without mercy
all the habitations of Jacob;
In His wrath He has thrown down
the strongholds of the daughter of
Judah;
He has brought them down to the ground;
He has profaned the kingdom and its
princes.

3 He has cut off in fierce anger
all the might of Israel;
He has drawn back His right hand
from before the enemy.
He has burned against Jacob
like a flaming fire, devouring all around.

4 He has bent His bow like an enemy,
with his right hand set like an adversary;
He has killed all who were pleasant to
His eye;
in the tabernacle of the daughter of Zion,
He has poured out His fury like fire.

When God Doesn't Answer

Do you ever find yourself asking God questions that leave you feeling more despair than hope?

Though God has done some amazing things in our midst, we've also experienced our share of heartache and despair. Certain battles raged, the enemy flaunted our disappointments in our faces, and the sense of loss threatened to swallow me alive.

While I don't want to go into the details of my heartbreak, I will say I learned something very valuable that I never want to forget. Perhaps it'll help you too.

When in the midst of my disappointments, I'd stare at the barren field that was supposed to be flush and fruitful and wonder aloud, "Why didn't this field produce fruit? How did this happen? I planted seeds. I watered them with the Word. I lived by faith. Why am I not seeing the results I pictured in my head? What happened, Lord?"

I don't know about you, but I've realized those kinds of questions suck the life right out of me. Though God invites us to pray all kinds of prayers in every situation because He delights in every detail of our lives, for me, at least, certain kinds of prayers leave me feeling more burdened, not less so.

In fact, maybe they're not really prayers at all but instead misdirected questions.

On the flip side, when I step back from my barren field and look up, when I remind myself of whose I am and who He is, something in me changes. The Spirit-life within me flutters and awakens once again.

When I let go of my *how* and *why* questions and realize they're not for me to ask right now, I'm able to find my place of peace once again.

Years ago my son Luke said, "Mom, I've learned that the how question isn't ours to ask because it isn't ours to answer. The how is always God's to perform as He will. It's our job to show up and to do what He says. And the why question is for young children who don't know how to wait or trust. At some point, we have to grow up and trust Him with our whys."

The Lord makes strong and secure promises to us. He loves us with an everlasting love. And He loves to reveal Himself to those He loves.

He also promised we'd experience hardship during our time on this earth. He warned us that we'd have to live and walk by faith—which means we'll at times need to go forward without having all the answers. He knows we have a tendency to lean on our own understanding and logic, so He asked us to trust His heart more than we trust our sight.

Maybe these thoughts don't resonate with you, but I pray they do. Are you asking certain questions that God doesn't intend to answer right now? Are those questions holding you back when God beckons you forward?

Maybe it's time to let go and let God. Maybe it's time to ask some different questions. Jesus says things are proven right by their fruit. You'll know you're asking the right questions when peace and perspective return. You'll know you're on the right track when your disappointment takes a back seat to your divine appointment.

May the Lord lift your chin and give you a new perspective today.

Susie Larson

5 The Lord has become like an enemy;
He has swallowed up Israel,
He has swallowed up all her palaces;
He has destroyed her strongholds,
and has increased mourning and lamentation
in the daughter of Judah.

6 He has violently taken away His tabernacle
as if it were a garden;
He has destroyed His place of assembly;
the LORD has caused the solemn feasts and Sabbaths
to be forgotten in Zion.
In his fierce indignation He has despised
the king and the priest.

7 The Lord has scorned His altar,
He has disowned His sanctuary;
He has given up the walls of her palaces
into the hand of the enemy.
They have made a noise in the house of the LORD
as on the day of a solemn feast.

8 The LORD has purposed to destroy
the wall of the daughter of Zion.
He has stretched out a line;
He has not withdrawn His hand from destroying;
therefore He caused the rampart and the wall to lament;
they languished together.

9 Her gates have sunk into the ground;
He has destroyed and broken her bars.
Her king and her princes are among the nations;
the Law is no more,
and her prophets find
no vision from the LORD.

10 The elders of the daughter of Zion
sit on the ground in silence;
they throw dust on their heads
and gird themselves with sackcloth.
The virgins of Jerusalem
bow their heads to the ground.

11 My eyes fail with tears,
my spirit is greatly troubled;
my bile is poured on the ground
because of the destruction of the daughter of my people,
because the children and infants faint
in the streets of the city.

12 They say to their mothers,
"Where is grain and wine?"
when they faint like a wounded man
in the streets of the city,
as their life is poured out
on their mothers' bosom.

2:5 La 2:2
2:6 La 1:4
2:8 2Ki 21:13
2:9 Ne 1:3
2:10 Isa 3:26
2:11 Job 16:13

2:13 La 1:12
2:14 Isa 58:1
2:15 Ps 48:2
2:16 Ps 35:21
2:17 Ps 89:42
2:18 Ps 119:145
2:19 Ps 62:8
2:20 Jer 19:9

13 What can I say for you,
to what shall I liken you,
O daughter of Jerusalem?
What shall I compare with you,
that I may comfort you,
O virgin daughter of Zion?
For your devastation is great like the sea;
who can heal you?

14 Your prophets have seen for you
false and deceptive visions;
they have not revealed your iniquity,
to bring back your captives,
but have seen for you oracles
that are false and misleading.

15 All who pass by
clap their hands at you;
they hiss and shake their heads
at the daughter of Jerusalem, saying,
"Is this the city that men call
the perfection of beauty,
the joy of the whole earth?"

16 All your enemies
have opened their mouth against you;
they hiss and gnash their teeth.
They say, "We have swallowed her up!
Certainly this is the day that we longed for;
we have found it; we have seen it."

17 The LORD has done what He planned;
He has fulfilled His word
that He had commanded in the days of old.
He has thrown down and has not pitied,
and He has caused the enemy to rejoice over you;
He has exalted the power of your adversaries.

18 Their heart cried to the Lord:
O wall of the daughter of Zion,
let your tears run down
like a river day and night;
give yourself no rest,
your eyes no respite!

19 Arise, cry out in the night,
at the beginning of the watches;
pour out your heart like water
before the face of the Lord.
Lift your hands to Him
for the lives of your young children,
who faint for hunger
at the head of every street.

20 Look, O LORD, and consider!
To whom have You done this?
Should the women eat their offspring,
the children who were born healthy?
Should the priest and the prophet be killed
in the sanctuary of the Lord?

[21]The young and the old lie
on the ground in the streets;
my virgins and my young men
have fallen by the sword;
You have killed them in the day of Your anger,
You have slaughtered and not pitied.

[22]You have invited as to a feast day the terrors all around;
in the day of the LORD's anger
no one escaped or survived;
those whom I held and raised
my enemy destroyed.

The Prophet's Anguish

3 I am the man who has seen affliction
by the rod of His wrath.
[2] He has driven and brought me
into darkness without any light.
[3] Surely against me has He turned His hand
continually, the whole day long.

[4] My flesh and my skin He has made waste away;
He has broken my bones;
[5] He has besieged and enveloped me
with gall and travail.
[6] He has set me in dark places,
like the dead of long ago.

[7] He has hedged me in so that I cannot get out;
He has made my chain heavy.
[8] Even when I cry for help,
He shuts out my prayer.
[9] He has blocked my ways with hewn stone;
He has made my paths crooked.

[10]He is to me a bear lying in wait,
a lion in hiding.
[11]He has turned aside my ways and torn me in pieces;
He has made me desolate.
[12]He has bent His bow
and set me as a target for the arrow.

Father, Your compassions are new every morning (La 3:23).

[13]He has caused the arrows of His quiver
to pierce my inward parts.
[14]I have become the derision of all my people,
their mocking song all the day.
[15]He has filled me with bitterness,
He has sated me with wormwood.

[16]He has made my teeth grind on gravel,
and covered me with ashes.
[17]My soul is bereft of peace;
I have forgotten prosperity.
[18]So I say, "My strength and my hope
from the LORD have perished."
[19]Remember my affliction and my misery,
the wormwood and the gall.
[20]Surely my soul remembers
and is humbled within me.
[21]But this I call to mind,
and therefore I have hope:

[22]It is of the LORD's mercies that we are not consumed;
His compassions do not fail.
[23]They are new every morning;
great is Your faithfulness.
[24]"The LORD is my portion," says my soul,
"therefore I will hope in Him."

[25]The LORD is good to those who wait for Him,
to the soul who seeks Him.
[26]It is good that a man should wait quietly
for the salvation of the LORD.
[27]It is good for a man to bear the yoke
in his youth.

[28]Let him sit alone in silence
when it is laid on him;
[29]let him put his mouth in the dust—
there may yet be hope.
[30]Let him give his cheek to the one who strikes,
and let him be filled with insults.

[31]For the Lord
will not cast off forever.
[32]But though He causes grief, yet He will have compassion
according to the abundance of His mercies.
[33]For He does not afflict from His heart,
nor grieve the sons of men.

[34]To crush underfoot
all the prisoners of the earth,
[35]to turn aside the justice due a man
in the presence of the Most High,
[36]to subvert a man in his cause,
the Lord does not approve.

[37]Who is he who speaks and it comes to pass,
unless the Lord has commanded it?
[38]Is it not from the mouth of the Most High
that good and bad proceed?
[39]Why should a living man complain,
a man for the punishment of his sins?

[40]Let us search and try our ways,
and return to the LORD!
[41]Let us lift up our hearts and hands
to God in heaven:

2:21 2Ch 36:17
2:22 Jer 6:25
3:1 Ps 88:7
3:4 Ps 51:8
3:5 La 3:19
3:6 Ps 88:5–6
3:7 Job 3:23
3:8 Job 30:20
3:9 Isa 63:17
3:11 Hos 6:1
3:12 Job 7:20
3:13 Job 6:4
3:14 Jer 20:7
3:15 Jer 9:15
3:16 Pr 20:17
3:17 Isa 59:11
3:18 Job 17:15
3:19 La 3:5
3:20 Ps 42:5–6
3:21 Ps 130:7
3:22 Mal 3:6
3:23 Zep 3:5
3:24 Ps 16:5
3:25 Isa 25:9
3:26 Ps 37:7
3:27 Ecc 12:1
3:28 Jer 15:17
3:29 Job 40:4
3:30 Isa 50:6
3:31 Ps 94:14
3:32 Ps 78:38
3:33 Eze 33:11
3:36 Hab 1:13
3:37 Ps 33:9–11
3:38 Isa 45:7
3:39 Mic 7:9
3:40 Ps 119:59
3:41 Ps 25:1

42 We have transgressed and rebelled;
You have not pardoned.

43 You have covered Yourself with anger and pursued us;
You have killed and not pitied.
44 You have covered Yourself with a cloud,
so that no prayer should pass through.
45 You have made us filthy refuse
in the midst of the peoples.

46 All our enemies have opened their mouths against us.
47 Panic and snare have come upon us,
desolation and destruction.
48 My eyes flow with rivers of tears
for the destruction of the daughter of my people.

49 My eyes flow and do not cease,
without respite,
50 until the LORD from heaven
looks down and sees.
51 My eyes bring suffering to my soul
at the fate of all the daughters of my city.

52 My enemies chased me like a bird,
without cause.
53 They cut off my life in the pit
and cast stones on me.
54 Waters flowed over my head;
I said, "I am cut off!"

55 I called on Your name, O LORD,
from the lowest pit.
56 You have heard my plea:
"Do not close Your ear to my cry for help!"
57 You drew near on the day I called on You,
and You said, "Do not fear!"

You have redeemed my life (La 3:58).

58 O Lord, You have pleaded the case for my soul;
You have redeemed my life.
59 O LORD, You have seen the wrong done to me;
judge my case.
60 You have seen all their vengeance,
all their schemes against me.

61 You have heard their reproach, O LORD,
all their schemes against me,
62 the lips of my enemies and
their devices against me all the day.
63 Look at their sitting down and their rising up;
I am their mocking song.

3:43 La 2:21
3:44 La 3:8
3:45 1Co 4:13
3:46 La 2:16
3:47 Isa 24:17–18
3:48 La 2:11
3:49 Jer 14:17
3:50 Isa 63:15
3:52 Ps 35:7
3:53 Jer 38:6
3:54 Jnh 2:3–5
3:56 Ps 55:1
3:57 Isa 41:10
3:58 Jer 51:36
3:60 Jer 11:19–20
3:61 La 5:1
3:62 Eze 36:3
3:63 Ps 139:2

3:64 Ps 28:4
3:65 Isa 6:10
3:66 Ps 8:3
4:2 Jer 19:11
4:4 Ps 22:15
4:5 Am 6:3–7
4:6 Ge 19:25
4:7 Ps 51:7
4:8 Job 30:30
4:10 La 2:20
4:11 Jer 7:20

64 Render to them a recompense, O LORD,
according to the work of their hands.
65 Give them hardness of heart;
may Your curse be upon them!
66 In Your anger pursue and destroy them
from under Your heavens, O LORD!

The Punishment of Zion

4 How the gold has become dim!
How the most fine gold has changed!
The stones of the sanctuary lie scattered
at the head of every street.

2 The precious sons of Zion,
comparable to fine gold,
how they are esteemed as earthen pots,
the work of a potter's hands!

3 Even the jackals offer the breast;
they nurse their young,
yet the daughter of my people has become cruel,
like ostriches in the wilderness.

4 The tongue of the infant cleaves
to the roof of his mouth for thirst;
the children beg for bread,
but no one divides it for them.

5 Those who once ate delicacies
are desolate in the streets;
those who were brought up in scarlet
embrace ash heaps.

6 For the iniquity of the daughter of my people
is greater than the sin of Sodom,
which was overthrown in a moment,
and no hands were wrung for her.

7 Her princes were purer than snow,
whiter than milk;
their bodies were more ruddy than rubies,
their appearance like sapphire.

8 Their form is blacker than coal;
they are not recognized in the streets;
their skin cleaves to their bones,
it has become as dry as wood.

9 Those killed by the sword
are better off than those who die of hunger,
for they pine away,
stricken for want of the fruits of the field.

10 The hands of compassionate women
have boiled their own children;
they became their food in the destruction
of the daughter of my people.

11 The LORD has fulfilled His fury,
He has poured out His fierce anger.
He kindled a fire in Zion,
and it has devoured its foundations.

SPIRIT-TO-SPIRIT PRAYER

Prayer to Recover From Emotional Damage

Father God, in the name of Jesus, I thank You that Your peace surrounds my mind and spirit.

I do not have a spirit of fear but of power, love, and a sound mind. I am a carrier of the anointing. I renounce the load of extra burdens, undue stress, heaviness, unforgiveness, resentment, bitterness, envy, or strife in my heart. These things are displaced by Your yoke, for it is easy. I walk in divine release and relief, in unlimited forgiveness, in the sweetness of Your joy, and in the flow of the Holy Ghost in my life.

I take off the garment of heaviness, and I put on the garment of praise. I thank You that You have not appointed me to mourn or to be covered with spiritual ashes. I put on beauty for ashes and the oil of joy for mourning. I am a tree of righteousness, and my roots are deep in the soil of Your love. My body is the temple of the Holy Ghost. Because I am rooted and grounded in the love of Christ, my temple cannot be infiltrated by foreign spirits that bring gloom into my life. I declare that I have the mind of Christ—the same mind that is in Christ Jesus is in me. Lord, I am steadfast in the things of You and focused on the mark that You have for me in life.

Lord, I thank You for inner healing deep down in my soul. I am free from the things that my heart refuses to accept. Father, put counselors in my life who will minister chastisement, correction, and rebuke. I renounce stubborn spirits in my life and give You permission to deal with them. I renounce a stiff neck that will keep my mind in bondage.

Lord, create in me a clean heart and a right spirit. Let my inner man receive and be fed from Your light so that darkness will not fill my heart. I declare that the words of my mouth and the meditation of my heart will be acceptable in Your sight. Lord, You are my strength and redeemer.

I cast my cares on You, Jesus, because I know You love me. I thank You for filling every empty place in my life where You have removed things of darkness from my being. I am sanctified and satisfied with Your will in my life. I stand in the good will, the acceptable will, and the perfect will of God for my life. Confusion is far from me. Love, peace, long-suffering, gentleness, goodness, faith, meekness, and temperance flow fluently in my life because the Holy Spirit bears witness in my soul. The gifts of the Spirit accompany the fruit of the Spirit in my life. I am stable and steadfast in my calling and will not miss the high calling on my life because of attacks against my mind. It is settled in the heavens forever. In Jesus' name I pray, amen.

Kimberly Daniels

12 The kings of the earth, and all the
inhabitants of the world,
would not have believed
that the adversary and the enemy could
enter
the gates of Jerusalem.

13 This was for the sins of her prophets
and the iniquities of her priests,
who poured out in her midst the blood of
the righteous.

14 They wandered,
blind, in the streets;

4:13 Jer 5:31
4:14 Jer 2:34

they have defiled themselves with blood,
so that no one could touch their
garments.

15 They cried out to them, "Depart! Unclean!
Depart, depart, do not touch us!"
Therefore they fled and wandered;
men among the nations said,
"They shall live with us no longer."

16 The presence of the LORD scattered them;
He will regard them no more;
they do not respect the priests,
nor show favor to the elders.

17 Our eyes failed us,
watching vainly for help;
in our watchtowers we watched
for a nation that could not save us.

18 They tracked our steps
so that we could not walk in our streets.
Our end drew near; our days were
numbered,
for our end had come.

19 Our pursuers were swifter
than the eagles of the skies.
They pursued us on the mountains;
they lay in wait for us in the wilderness.

20 The breath of our life, the anointed king of
the LORD,
was captured in their traps,
of whom we said, "Under his shadow
we shall live among the nations."

21 Rejoice and be glad, O daughter of Edom,
you who dwell in the land of Uz!
The cup shall also pass to you;
you shall become drunk and strip
yourself bare.

22 The punishment of your iniquity, O
daughter of Zion, is accomplished;
He shall exile you no longer.
He shall punish your iniquity, O daughter
of Edom;
He will expose your sins!

A Prayer for Restoration

5 Remember, O LORD, what has come
upon us;
look, and see our reproach!

2 Our inheritance has been turned over to
strangers,
our homes to foreigners.
3 We have become orphans and fatherless;
our mothers are like widows.
4 We must pay for the water we drink;
our wood is sold to us.
5 Our pursuers are at our necks;
we labor and have no rest.
6 We have given our hand to Egypt and to
Assyria,
to be satisfied with bread.
7 Our fathers sinned and are no more,
but we bear their iniquities.
8 Slaves rule over us;
there is no one to deliver us from their
hand.
9 We get our bread at the peril of our lives,
because of the sword in the wilderness.
10 Our skin is hot as an oven,
because of the terrible famine.
11 They ravished the women in Zion,
the virgins in the cities of Judah.
12 Princes were hung up by their hands,
the faces of elders were not honored.
13 Young men ground at the millstones;
boys staggered under loads of wood.
14 The elders have left the city gate,
the young men stopped their music.
15 The joy of our hearts has ceased;
our dancing has turned into mourning.
16 The crown has fallen from our head;
woe to us, for we have sinned!
17 For this our heart is faint;
for these things our eyes grow dim;
18 because of Mount Zion, which is desolate,
with foxes walking upon it.

19 You, O LORD, remain forever;
Your throne endures from generation to
generation.
20 Why do You forget us forever,
and forsake us for so long a time?
21 Restore us to Yourself, O LORD, that we may
return!
Renew our days as of old,
22 unless You have utterly rejected us,
and are very angry with us.

4:16 Isa 9:14–16
4:17 Eze 29:16
4:18 Am 8:2
4:19 Isa 5:26–28
4:20 Ge 2:7
4:22 Isa 40:2
5:1 Ps 44:13–16

5:2 Zep 1:13
5:3 Jer 18:21
5:4 Isa 3:1
5:5 Ne 9:36–37
5:6 Hos 9:3
5:7 Jer 16:12
5:8 Ne 5:15
5:9 Jer 40:9–12
5:10 La 4:8
5:11 Zec 14:2
5:12 La 4:16
5:13 Jdg 16:21
5:14 Jer 7:34
5:15 Am 8:10
5:16 Ps 89:39
5:17 Isa 1:5
5:18 Mic 3:12
5:19 Ps 102:12
5:20 Ps 13:1
5:21 Ps 80:3
5:22 Ps 60:1–2

Author: The prophet Ezekiel

Written: Between 593 and 565 BC

Themes: Judgment of Judah, Glory of Restored Temple

EZEKIEL

Dear Spirit Led Woman,

God is looking for people who will stand in the gap—not only for their own situations, but also for the nations of the world. He tells us in Ezekiel, "I sought for a man among them who would build up the hedge and stand in the gap before Me for the land so that I would not destroy it" (Eze 22:30). Our nation desperately needs intercessors to stand in the gap for its future.

Prayer is powerless if you trust in yourself. But if you trust in God, who has all power, you will see results. You simply have to follow the direction of the Holy Spirit. God is calling for intercessors.

Will you respond to His call? Will you "build up the hedge and stand in the gap" for your family, your church, your nation...your world?

Joy F. Strang

The Vision of the LORD's Glory

1 In the thirtieth year, in the fourth month, on the fifth day of the month, as I was among the captives by the river of Kebar, the heavens were opened and I saw visions of God.

2 On the fifth day of the month, which was the fifth year of the captivity of King Jehoiachin, 3 the word of the LORD came expressly to Ezekiel the priest, the son of Buzi, in the land of the Chaldeans by the River Kebar. And the hand of the LORD was on him there.

4 As I looked, a whirlwind came out of the north, a great cloud with fire flashing forth continually, and a brightness was all around it, and in its midst something as glowing metal in the midst of the fire. 5 Also out of the midst came the likeness of four living creatures. And this was their appearance: They had the likeness of a man. 6 Every one had four faces, and every one had four wings. 7 Their legs were straight and the soles of their feet were like the sole of a calf's hoof. And they gleamed like the color of burnished bronze. 8 They had the hands of a man under their wings on their four sides. As for the faces and wings of the four of them, 9 their wings were joined to one another. Their *faces* did not turn when they went. Each went straight forward.

10 As for the likeness of their faces, each had the face of a man, and all four had the face of a lion on the right side, and the face of an ox on the left side, and the face of an eagle. 11 Thus were their faces. And their wings were stretched upward. Two wings of every one were joined to one another, and two covered their bodies. 12 Each went straight forward. Wherever the spirit was to go, they would go and not turn as they went. 13 As for the likeness of the living creatures, their appearance was like burning coals of fire and like the appearance of lamps. It went up and down among the living creatures. And the fire was bright, and out of the fire went forth lightning. 14 The living creatures ran to and fro as the appearance of a flash of lightning.

15 Now as I looked at the living creatures, one wheel was on the ground by the living creatures for each of the four faces. 16 The appearance of the wheels and their work was like the color of sparkling beryl. And all four of them had one likeness. And their appearance and their work was, as it were, a wheel in the middle of a wheel. 17 Whenever they went, they went in any of their four sides and did not turn as they went. 18 As for their rims, they were so high that they were dreadful. And the rims of all four of them were full of eyes all around.

19 Whenever the living creatures went, the wheels went with them. And whenever the living creatures were lifted up from the ground, the wheels also were lifted up. 20 Wherever the spirit was about to go, they would go in that direction. And the wheels rose close beside them. For the spirit of the living creatures was in the wheels. 21 Whenever those went, these went. And whenever those stood still, these stood still. And whenever those rose from the ground, the wheels rose close beside them. For the spirit of the living creatures was in the wheels.

22 The likeness of the expanse over the heads of the living creatures was as the awesome gleam of crystal, stretched out over their heads above. 23 Under the expanse their wings *were stretched out* straight, the one toward the other. Each one also had two wings which covered its body on the one side and the other. 24 When they went, I heard the noise of their wings, like the noise of abundant waters, as the voice of the Almighty, the noise of tumult as the noise of an army camp. Whenever they stood still, they let down their wings.

25 There was a voice from the expanse that was over their heads whenever they stood still and let down their wings. 26 Above the expanse that was over their heads was the likeness of a throne, as the appearance of a sapphire stone. And on the likeness of the throne was the likeness as the appearance of a man on it high up. 27 Then I saw as glowing metal, as the appearance of fire all around within it, from the appearance of His loins and upward; and from the appearance of His loins and downward I saw as it were the appearance of fire, and there was a brightness around Him. 28 As the appearance of the rainbow that is in the cloud on a day of rain, so was the appearance of the brightness all around.

This was the appearance of the likeness of the glory of the LORD. And when I saw it, I fell on my face and heard a voice of one speaking.

The Call of Ezekiel

2 Then He said to me: Son of man, stand on your feet, and I will speak to you! 2 When He spoke to me, the Spirit entered me and set me on my feet. Then I heard Him speaking to me.

3 And He said to me: Son of man, I send you to the sons of Israel, to a rebellious nation that has rebelled against Me. They and their fathers have transgressed against Me even to this very day. 4 And as for the impudent and obstinate children, I am sending you to them. And you shall say to them, "Thus says the Lord GOD." 5 As for them, whether they listen or not (for

1:1 Eze 11:24
1:2 Eze 8:1
1:3 2Ki 3:15
1:4 Eze 1:27
1:6 Eze 10:14
1:7 Rev 1:15
1:8 Eze 10:21
1:9 Eze 10:22
1:10 Eze 10:14
1:11 Isa 6:2
1:12 Eze 1:9
1:13 Ps 104:4
1:14 Zec 4:10
1:15 Eze 10:9
1:16 Da 10:6
1:17 Eze 1:9
1:18 Eze 10:12
1:19 Eze 10:16
1:20 Eze 1:12
1:21 Eze 10:17
1:22 Eze 10:1
1:24 Eze 43:2
1:26 Eze 10:1
1:27 Eze 1:4
1:28 Eze 3:23
2:1 Da 10:11
2:2 Eze 3:24
2:3 Jer 3:25
2:4 Eze 3:7
2:5 Eze 3:27

The Spirit of Knowledge

The spirit of knowledge is experience, living understanding, divine encounters, and personal relationship. It is the unveiling of the attributes of God by God Himself. It is more than informational facts. The spirit of knowledge paves the way for the spirit of the fear of the Lord.

> In the thirtieth year, in the fourth month, on the fifth day of the month, as I was among the captives by the river of Kebar, the heavens were opened and I saw visions of God. On the fifth day of the month, which was the fifth year of the captivity of King Jehoiachin, the word of the LORD came expressly to Ezekiel the priest, the son of Buzi, in the land of the Chaldeans by the River Kebar. And the hand of the LORD was on him there.
>
> —EZEKIEL 1:1–3

Ezekiel is an example of a prophet who walked in the spirit of knowledge. He said he saw heaven open. First, I would like to say that the Lord initiated the open heaven. *Open heaven* can be defined as a season when the supernatural invades the natural. It is when God gives an invitation to access the heavenly realm. It is an opening designed by God that starts in the third heaven, where the throne of God is located, travels through the second heaven, and lands as an opening on the earth. This portal releases light and revelation.

When the heavens are opened:

1. We see visions of God. The experiential knowledge of God is released. Then He begins to reveal His attributes.

2. The word of the Lord comes expressly, clearly, unhindered, and with certainty. This kind of prophetic encounter is a mouth-to-mouth, word-for-word conversation. It doesn't need any interpretation.

3. The hand of God is upon us, and we will receive supernatural empowerment from God. The Holy Spirit is in the earth to empower us to overcome. He is releasing keys that will allow the body of Christ to access our inheritance, which is in heavenly places.

Prophets will carry mantles of revelation and power. Revelation is being given to cause complete agreement between the heavens and the earth. (See Ephesians 1:10.) The spirit of truth is being released to prophets, allowing them to apprehend the heart of God and articulate with power and authority to this generation.

According to Webster's dictionary, revelation is "the act of disclosing or discovering to others what was before unknown to them." It is the communication of truth to men by God or by His authorized agents—the prophets and apostles. The key to saving this end-time generation is that revelation must come from God!

Michelle McClain-Walters

they are a rebellious house), they shall know that there has been a prophet among them. 6 And you, son of man, do not be afraid of them or be afraid of their words, though briers and thorns be with you, and you dwell among scorpions. Do not be afraid of their words or be dismayed at their looks, for they are a rebellious house. 7 You shall speak My words to them, whether they listen or not, for they are rebellious. 8 But you, son of man, hear what I say to you. Do not be rebellious like that rebellious house. Open your mouth and eat what I give you.

9 When I looked, a hand was sent to me. And a scroll was in it. 10 And He spread it before me. And there was writing on the inside and on the outside, and written on it were words of lamentation and mourning and woe.

3 Moreover He said to me, Son of man, eat what you find. Eat this scroll and go speak to the house of Israel. 2 So I opened my mouth, and He fed me this scroll.

3 He said to me, Son of man, feed your stomach and fill your inward parts with this scroll that I give you. Then I ate it, and it was as honey for sweetness in my mouth.

4 Then He said to me: Son of man, go to the house of Israel and speak with My words to them. 5 For you are not being sent to a people of foreign speech and hard language, but to the house of Israel, 6 nor to many peoples of foreign speech and hard language, whose words you cannot understand. But I have sent you to them who should listen to you. 7 But the house of Israel will not listen to you, because they will not listen to Me. For all the house of Israel is impudent and obstinate. 8 But I have made your face as hard as their faces and your forehead as hard as their foreheads. 9 As emery harder than flint, I have made your forehead. Do not be afraid of them or be dismayed at their looks, though they are a rebellious house.

10 Moreover He said to me: Son of man, all My words that I shall speak to you receive in your heart and hear with your ears. 11 Go to the captives, to the sons of your people, and speak to them and tell them, whether they listen or not, "Thus says the Lord God."

12 Then the Spirit took me up, and I heard behind me a great thundering voice: "Blessed be the glory of the Lord in His place." 13 I *heard* also the noise of the wings of the living creatures that touched one another and the noise of the wheels beside them, even a great rushing sound. 14 So the Spirit lifted me up and took me away, and I went in bitterness, in the heat of my spirit, and the hand of the Lord was strong upon me. 15 Then I came to the captives at Tel Aviv, who lived by the River Kebar, and I sat there where they sat seven days, causing consternation among them.

> I was in bitterness and in the heat of my spirit, but the hand of the Lord was strong upon me (Eze 3:14).

2:6 Jer 1:8
2:7 Jer 1:7
2:8 Rev 10:9
2:9 Eze 8:3
2:10 Rev 8:13
3:1 Eze 2:8–9
3:2 Jer 25:17
3:3 Ps 19:10
3:5 Jnh 1:2
3:7 Eze 2:4
3:8 Jer 1:18
3:9 Isa 50:7
3:11 Eze 2:7
3:12 Eze 8:3
3:13 Eze 1:24

3:14 Eze 37:1
3:15 Job 2:13
3:16 Jer 42:7
3:17 Isa 52:8
3:18 Eze 33:6
3:19 Eze 14:14
3:20 Eze 18:24
3:21 Ac 20:31
3:22 Ac 9:6
3:23 Eze 1:28
3:24 Eze 2:2
3:25 Eze 4:8
3:26 Eze 24:27
3:27 Eze 24:27
4:2 Eze 21:22

Ezekiel, a Watchman for Israel

16 At the end of seven days, the word of the Lord came to me, saying, 17 Son of man, I have made you a watchman to the house of Israel. Whenever you hear the word from My mouth, then warn them from Me. 18 When I say to the wicked, "You shall surely die," and you do not warn him, nor speak to warn the wicked from his wicked way that he may live, the same wicked man shall die in his iniquity, but his blood I will require at your hand. 19 Yet if you warn the wicked and he does not turn from his wickedness or from his wicked way, he shall die in his iniquity. But you have delivered your soul.

20 Again, when a righteous man turns from his righteousness and commits iniquity, and I lay a stumbling block before him, he shall die. Because you have not given him warning, he shall die in his sin, and his righteousness which he has done shall not be remembered. But his blood I will require at your hand. 21 Nevertheless if you warn the righteous man that the righteous should not sin and he does not sin, he shall surely live because he took warning. And you have delivered your soul.

22 The hand of the Lord was upon me there, and He said to me, Rise, go out into the plain, and I will talk with you there. 23 Then I arose, and went out into the plain. And the glory of the Lord stood there, as the glory which I saw by the river of Kebar, and I fell on my face.

24 Then the Spirit entered me, and set me on my feet, and spoke with me and said to me: Go, shut yourself up within your house. 25 As for you, son of man, they shall put bands on you and shall bind you with them, so that you cannot go out among them. 26 And I will make your tongue cleave to the roof of your mouth so that you shall be mute and cannot be one to rebuke them, for they are a rebellious house. 27 But when I speak with you, I will open your mouth, and you shall say to them, "Thus says the Lord God." He who hears, let him hear. And he who refuses, let him refuse. For they are a rebellious house.

The Siege of Jerusalem Portrayed

4 You also, son of man, take a brick and lay it before you and inscribe a city on it, even Jerusalem. 2 Then lay siege against it, and build a fort against it, and build a mound against it;

set camps and place battering rams against it
all around. 3 Moreover take for yourself an iron
plate and set it up for a wall of iron between
you and the city. And set your face against it so
that it is besieged, and lay siege against it. This
shall be a sign to the house of Israel.
4 As for you, lie down on your left side and
lay the iniquity of the house of Israel upon it.
According to the number of the days that you
lie on it, you shall bear their iniquity. 5 For I
have laid upon you the years of their iniquity
according to the number of the days, three
hundred and ninety days. So you shall bear
the iniquity of the house of Israel.
6 When you have accomplished them, lie
again on your right side, and you shall bear
the iniquity of the house of Judah forty days.
I have appointed you each day for a year.
7 Therefore you shall set your face toward the
siege of Jerusalem, and your arm shall be un-
covered, and you shall prophesy against it. 8 I
will lay bands upon you, and you shall not turn
yourself from one side to another until you
have ended the days of your siege.
9 Also take for yourself wheat, and barley, and
beans, and lentils, and millet, and spelt, and
put them in one vessel and make bread. Ac-
cording to the number of the days that you lie
on your side, three hundred and ninety days,
you shall eat it. 10 Your food which you shall
eat *shall be* by weight, twenty shekels[1] a day.
From time to time you shall eat it. 11 You also
shall drink water by measure, the sixth part
of a hin.[2] From time to time you shall drink it.
12 You shall eat it as barley cake, having baked
it in their sight with dung that comes out of
man. 13 Then the LORD said, "Even so the sons
of Israel shall eat their defiled bread among
the nations where I drive them."
14 Then I said, "Ah, Lord GOD! My soul has
not been defiled. For from my youth up even
until now I have not eaten of that which dies of
itself, or is torn in pieces, nor has abominable
meat come into my mouth."
15 Then He said to me, "I have given you cow
dung instead of man's dung over which you
shall prepare your bread."
16 Moreover He said to me, Son of man, I will
cut off the supply of bread in Jerusalem. They
shall eat bread by weight and with anxiety and
drink water by measure and with horror, 17 be-
cause bread and water will be scarce, and they
will be appalled with one another, and waste
away for their iniquity.

A Sword Against Jerusalem

5 As for you, son of man, take a sharp sword.
Take and cause it to pass upon your head
and upon your beard as a barber's razor. Then
take balances to weigh and divide the hair.
2 You shall burn with fire a third part in the
midst of the city when the days of the siege are
fulfilled. Then you shall take a third part and
strike it with the sword all around the city. And
a third part you shall scatter in the wind. And
I will draw out a sword after them. 3 You shall
also take a few in number from them and bind
them in the edges of your *robes*. 4 Then take
some of them again and cast them into the
midst of the fire and burn them in the fire. For
a fire shall come out into all the house of Israel.
5 Thus says the Lord GOD: This is Jerusalem.
I have set it in the midst of the nations, with
countries that are all around her. 6 But she has
rebelled against My judgments more wickedly
than the nations, and against My statutes more
than the countries that are all around her. For
they have refused My judgments and My stat-
utes, and have not walked in them.
7 Therefore thus says the Lord GOD: Because
you have more turmoil than the nations that
are round about you and have not walked in
My statutes, or have kept My judgments, and
have not even acted according to the judg-
ments of the nations that are all around you,
8 therefore thus says the Lord GOD: Pay atten-
tion. I, even I, am against you and will execute
judgments in your midst in the sight of the
nations. 9 I will do in you what I have not done,
and the like of which I will not do anymore,
because of all your abominations. 10 Therefore
the fathers shall eat their sons in your midst,
and the sons shall eat their fathers. For I will
execute judgments on you, and the whole rem-
nant of you I will scatter into all the winds.
11 Therefore, as I live, says the Lord GOD, surely,
because you have defiled My sanctuary with
all your detestable things and with all your
abominations, therefore I will also diminish
you, and My eye shall have no pity, nor will I
spare. 12 A third part of you shall die by pes-
tilence or by famine; they shall be consumed
in your midst. And a third part shall fall by the
sword all around you. And I will scatter a third
part into all the winds, and I will draw out a
sword after them.
13 Thus My anger shall be accomplished, and
I will cause My fury to rest upon them, and I
will be comforted. Then they shall know that I
the LORD have spoken it in My zeal when I have
accomplished My fury in them.
14 Moreover I will make you a desolation
and a reproach among the nations that are
all around you, in the sight of all who pass by.
15 So it shall be a reproach and a taunt, a warn-
ing and an astonishment to the nations that

4:3 Isa 8:18
4:4 Lev 16:22
4:6 Nu 14:34
4:7 Isa 52:10
4:8 Eze 3:25
4:13 Da 1:8
4:14 Eze 9:8
4:16 Lev 26:26
4:17 Lev 26:39
5:1 Lev 21:5

5:2 Eze 5:12
5:5 Eze 4:1
5:6 Jer 11:10
5:7 2Ch 33:9
5:8 Eze 15:7
5:9 Da 9:12
5:10 Dt 28:64
5:11 Eze 7:20
5:12 Eze 5:2
5:13 Isa 1:24
5:14 Ne 2:17
5:15 Eze 25:17

[1] *10* About 8 ounces, or 230 grams. [2] *11* About ⅔ quart, or 0.6 liter.

are all around you, when I execute judgments
in you in anger and in fury and in furious re-
bukes. I the LORD have spoken it. 16 When I send
upon them the deadly arrows of famine which
shall be for their destruction and which I will
send to destroy you, then I will also increase
the famine upon you and break your staff of
bread. 17 So I will send upon you famine and
wild beasts, and they shall bereave you of chil-
dren. And pestilence and bloodshed shall pass
through you. And I will bring the sword upon
you. I the LORD have spoken it.

Judgment on Idolatrous Israel

6 And the word of the LORD came to me,
saying: 2 Son of man, set your face toward
the mountains of Israel, and prophesy against
them, 3 and say, Mountains of Israel, hear the
word of the Lord GOD. Thus says the Lord GOD
to the mountains, and to the hills, to the rivers,
and to the valleys: Pay attention. I, even I, will
bring a sword upon you, and I will destroy
your high places. 4 Your altars shall be des-
olate, and your images shall be broken. And
I will cast down your slain men before your
idols. 5 I will lay the dead corpses of the sons of
Israel before their idols. And I will scatter your
bones all around your altars. 6 In all your dwell-
ing places, the cities shall be laid waste and
the high places shall be desolate so that your
altars may be laid waste and made desolate,
and your idols may be broken and cease, and
your images may be cut down, and your works
may be abolished. 7 The slain shall fall in your
midst, and you shall know that I am the LORD.
8 Yet I will leave a remnant, for you will have
some who escape the sword among the nations
when you are scattered among the countries.
9 Those of you who escape shall remember
Me among the nations wherever they shall be
carried captive, because I am broken by their
whorish heart which has departed from Me,
and with their eyes which play the harlot after
their idols. And they shall loathe themselves
for the evils which they have committed in all
their abominations. 10 They shall know that I
am the LORD, and that I have not said in vain
that I would bring this calamity upon them.
11 Thus says the Lord GOD: Clap your hand,
and stamp with your foot, and say, Alas for all
the evil abominations of the house of Israel!
For they shall fall by sword, by famine, and
by pestilence. 12 He who is far off shall die of
pestilence, and he who is near shall fall by the
sword, and he who remains and is besieged
shall die by famine. Thus I will accomplish My
fury upon them. 13 Then you shall know that
I am the LORD, when their slain men shall be
among their idols all around their altars, on

5:17 Eze 38:22
6:3 Lev 26:30
6:4 2Ch 14:5
6:6 Isa 6:11
6:8 Eze 14:22
6:9 Eze 20:43
6:11 Eze 5:12
6:12 Eze 5:13
6:13 Eze 20:28

6:14 Isa 5:25
7:2 Am 8:2
7:3 Eze 18:30
7:4 Eze 5:11
7:6 Zec 13:7
7:8 Eze 9:8
7:10 Isa 10:5

every high hill, in all the tops of the mountains,
and under every green tree, and under every
thick oak, the place where they offered sweet
savor to all their idols. 14 So, in all their habita-
tions I will stretch out My hand upon them and
make the land desolate, indeed, more desolate
than the wilderness toward Diblah. And they
shall know that I am the LORD.

The Day of the LORD's Wrath

7 Moreover the word of the LORD came to
me, saying: 2 And you, son of man, thus
says the Lord GOD to the land of Israel:

An end, the end is coming
upon the four corners of the land.
3 Now the end has come upon you,
and I will send My anger upon you,
and will judge you according to your ways,
and will recompense upon you all your
abominations.
4 My eye shall not spare you,
nor will I have pity;
but I will recompense your ways upon you,
and your abominations shall be in your
midst.

And you shall know that I am the LORD!

5 Thus says the Lord GOD:

A disaster, a singular disaster;
it is coming!
6 An end is coming,
the end has come;
it watches for you;
it has come!
7 Your doom has come to you,
O inhabitant in the land;
the time has come, the day of trouble is
near,
and not the joyful shouting on the
mountains.
8 Now I will shortly pour out My fury upon
you,
and accomplish My anger upon you;
and I will judge you according to your
ways,
and will recompense you for all your
abominations.
9 My eye shall not spare,
nor will I have pity;
I will recompense you according to your
ways,
and your abominations that are in your
midst.

And you shall know that I am the LORD who
strikes.

10 The day is coming!
Your doom has gone out;
the rod has blossomed,
pride has budded.

11 Violence has risen up
into a rod of wickedness;
none of them *shall remain,*
none of their people,
none of their wealth,
nor anything eminent among them.
12 The time has come,
the day has drawn near.
Do not let the buyer rejoice,
or the seller mourn,
for wrath is against all their multitude.
13 For the seller shall not return
to that which is sold,
although they both live;
for the vision concerning the whole
multitude
shall not return;
nor shall any strengthen his life
by his iniquity.

14 They have blown the trumpet
even to make all ready,
but none goes to the battle;
for My wrath is against all the multitude.
15 The sword is outside,
and the pestilence and the famine
within.
He who is in the field
shall die by the sword;
and he who is in the city,
famine and pestilence shall devour him.
16 Even when their survivors escape,
they shall be on the mountains
like doves of the valleys,
all of them mourning,
every one over his iniquity.
17 All hands shall be feeble,
and all knees shall be weak as water.
18 They shall also gird themselves with
sackcloth,
and horror shall cover them;
and shame shall be upon all faces,
and baldness upon all their heads.

19 They shall cast their silver in the streets,
and their gold shall become abhorrent;
their silver and their gold
shall not be able to deliver them
in the day of the wrath of the LORD;
they shall not satisfy their souls,
or fill their stomachs,
for their iniquity has become a
stumbling block.

20 They transformed the beauty of His
ornaments into pride,
and made the images of their
abominations
and of their detestable things with it;
therefore I will make it an abhorrent
thing to them.

7:11 Zep 1:18
7:12 Isa 5:13–14
7:13 Lev 25:24–28
7:14 Jer 4:5
7:15 Jer 14:18
7:16 Ezr 9:15
7:17 Eze 21:7
7:18 Isa 15:2–3
7:19 Pr 11:4
7:20 Eze 24:21

....

7:21 2Ki 24:13
7:22 Jer 18:17
7:23 Jer 27:2
7:24 Eze 28:7
7:26 Jer 4:20
8:1 Eze 20:1
8:2 Eze 1:4
8:3 Dt 32:16
8:4 Eze 3:22–23
8:5 Eze 8:3

21 I will give it into the hands of the strangers
as plunder and to the wicked of the
earth for destruction,
and they shall pollute it.
22 My face also I will turn from them,
and they shall pollute My secret place;
for the robbers shall enter
and defile it.

23 Make a chain,
for the land is full of bloody crimes,
and the city is full of violence.
24 Therefore I will bring the worst of the
nations,
and they shall possess their houses;
I will also make the pomp of the strong to
cease,
and their holy places shall be defiled.
25 When destruction comes,
then they shall seek peace, but there
shall be none.
26 Mischief shall come upon mischief,
and rumor shall be upon rumor.
Then they shall seek a vision of the
prophet;
but the law shall perish from the priest,
and counsel from the elders.
27 The king shall mourn,
and the prince shall be clothed with
desolation,
and the hands of the people of the land
shall tremble.
I will do to them according to their way,
and according to what they deserve I
will judge them.

And they shall know that I am the LORD!

Abominations in the Temple

8 In the sixth year, in the sixth month, on
the fifth day of the month, as I sat in my
house and the elders of Judah sat before me,
the hand of the Lord GOD fell upon me there.
2 Then I looked, and there was a likeness as
the appearance of a man. From His loins and
downward was the appearance of fire. And
from His loins and upward was the appearance
of brightness, as the appearance of glowing
metal. 3 He stretched out the form of a hand
and took me by a lock of my head. And the
Spirit lifted me up between the earth and the
heavens, and brought me in the visions of God
to Jerusalem, to the entrance of the north gate
of the inner court, where the seat of the image
of jealousy was, which provokes to jealousy.
4 The glory of the God of Israel was there, ac-
cording to the vision that I saw in the plain.
5 Then He said to me, "Son of man, lift up
your eyes now toward the north." So I lifted up
my eyes toward the north, and northward at

the gate of the altar was this image of jealousy in the entrance.

6 He said furthermore to me, "Son of man, do you see what they do, even the great abominations that the house of Israel commits here, so that I should go far off from My sanctuary? But yet you shall see still greater abominations."

7 Then He brought me to the door of the court. And when I looked, there was a hole in the wall. 8 So He said to me, "Son of man, now dig in the wall." And when I had dug in the wall, there was a door.

9 He said to me, "Enter and notice the wicked abominations that they do here." 10 So I went in and saw every form of creeping things, and abominable beasts, and all the idols of the house of Israel, portrayed upon the wall all around. 11 There stood before them seventy men of the elders of the house of Israel, and in their midst stood Jaazaniah the son of Shaphan, with every man his censer in his hand, and a thick cloud of incense went up.

12 Then He said to me, "Son of man, have you seen what the elders of the house of Israel do in the dark, every man in the chambers of his images? For they say, 'The LORD does not see us. The LORD has forsaken the land.'" 13 He also said to me, "Yet again you shall see greater abominations that they do."

14 Then He brought me to the door of the gate of the house of the LORD which was toward the north. And women sat there weeping for Tammuz. 15 Then He said to me, "Have you seen this, O son of man? Yet again you shall see greater abominations than these."

16 He brought me into the inner court of the house of the LORD, and at the door of the temple of the LORD, between the porch and the altar, were about twenty-five men with their backs toward the temple of the LORD and their faces toward the east. And they worshipped the sun toward the east.

17 Then He said to me, "Have you seen this, O son of man? Is it a light thing to the house of Judah that they commit the abominations which they commit here? For they have filled the land with violence and have continually provoked Me to anger. And they put the branch to their nose. 18 Therefore I will indeed deal in fury. My eye shall not spare, nor will I have pity. And though they cry in My ears with a loud voice, yet I will not listen to them."

The Slaughter of the Wicked

9 He cried out also in my ears with a loud voice, saying, "Cause those who have charge over the city to draw near, even every man with his destroying weapon in his hand." 2 Six men came from the way of the higher gate which lies toward the north, each with his battle weapon in his hand. And one man among them was clothed with linen with a writer's case by his side. And they went in and stood beside the bronze altar.

3 Then the glory of the God of Israel ascended from the cherub on which it had been, to the threshold of the temple. And He called to the man clothed with linen who had the writer's case by his side. 4 And the LORD said to him, "Go through the midst of the city, through the midst of Jerusalem, and set a mark upon the foreheads of the men who sigh and groan for all the abominations that are done in its midst."

5 To the others He said in my hearing, "Go after him through the city and strike. Do not let your eye spare or have pity. 6 Utterly slay old and young, both maidens and little children, and women. But do not touch any man on whom is the mark. And begin at My sanctuary." Then they began with the elders who were before the temple.

7 Then he said to them, "Defile the temple, and fill the courts with the slain. Go forth!" So they went out and killed in the city. 8 While they were killing, I was left alone; and I fell on my face and cried out, "Ah, Lord GOD! Will You destroy all the rest of Israel by Your pouring out of Your fury upon Jerusalem?"

9 Then He said to me, "The iniquity of the house of Israel and Judah is exceedingly great, and the land is full of blood, and the city is full of perverseness. For they say, 'The LORD has forsaken the land, and the LORD does not see.' 10 But as for Me, My eye shall not spare, nor will I have pity, but I will recompense their way upon their heads."

11 Then the man clothed with linen who had the case by his side reported the matter, saying, "I have done just as You have commanded me."

The Glory of God Leaves the Temple

10 Then I looked, and in the expanse that was above the heads of the cherubim there appeared over them, as it were, a sapphire stone, as the appearance of the likeness of a throne. 2 And He spoke to the man clothed with linen and said, "Go in between the wheels under the cherubim and fill your hands with coals of fire from among the cherubim and scatter them over the city." And he entered in my sight.

3 Now the cherubim stood on the right side of the temple when the man went in, and the cloud filled the inner court. 4 Then the glory of the LORD went up from the cherub and stood over the threshold of the temple. And the house was filled with the cloud, and the court was full of the brightness of the glory of the

8:6 Eze 5:11
8:8 Isa 29:15
8:10 Ex 20:4
8:11 Nu 11:16
8:12 Isa 29:15
8:13 Eze 8:6
8:16 Jer 2:27
8:17 Eze 7:23
8:18 Isa 1:15
9:1 Isa 6:8
9:2 Lev 16:4

....

9:3 Eze 10:4
9:4 Ex 12:7
9:5 Eze 5:11
9:6 2Ch 36:17
9:8 Eze 11:13
9:9 Eze 8:12
9:10 Eze 7:4
10:1 Ex 24:10
10:2 Rev 8:5
10:4 Eze 1:28

LORD. 5 The sound of the wings of the cheru-
bim was heard even in the outer court, like the
voice of the Almighty God when He speaks.
6 When He had commanded the man clothed
with linen, saying, "Take fire from between the
wheels, from among the cherubim," he went
in and stood beside the wheel. 7 One cherub
stretched out his hand from among the cher-
ubim to the fire that was between the cherubs,
and took some, and put it into the hands of
him who was clothed with linen, who took it
and went out. 8 There appeared among the
cherubim the form of a man's hand under
their wings.
9 Then I looked, and there were the four
wheels by the cherubim, one wheel by one
cherub, and another wheel by another cherub.
And the appearance of the wheels was as the
color of a beryl stone. 10 As for their appearanc-
es, all four had one likeness, as if one wheel
had been in the middle of a wheel. 11 When
they went, they went on their four sides. They
did not turn as they went, but they followed
to the place wherever the head looked. They
did not turn as they went. 12 Their whole body,
and their backs, and their hands, and their
wings, and the wheels that the four had were
full of eyes all round. 13 As for the wheels, they
were called in my hearing the whirling wheels.
14 Each one had four faces. The first face was
the face of a cherub, the second face was the
face of a man, the third the face of a lion, and
the fourth the face of an eagle.
15 Then the cherubim rose up. They are the
living creatures that I saw by the River Kebar.
16 When the cherubim went, the wheels went
by them. And when the cherubim lifted up
their wings to mount up from the earth, the
same wheels also would not turn from beside
them. 17 When the cherubim stood, the wheels
stood. And when they rose up, the wheels also
rose up with them. For the spirit of the living
creatures was in them.
18 Then the glory of the LORD departed from
off the threshold of the temple and stood over
the cherubim. 19 The cherubim lifted up their
wings and mounted up from the earth in my
sight. When they went out, the wheels were
beside them. They stood at the door of the east
gate of the house of the LORD; and the glory of
the God of Israel was above them.
20 These are the living creatures that I saw
under the God of Israel by the River Kebar.
So I knew that they were cherubim. 21 Every
one had four faces apiece, and every one four
wings. And the likeness of the hands of a man
was under their wings. 22 The likeness of their
faces was the same faces which I saw by the
River Kebar, their appearances and them-
selves. Each went straight forward.

10:5 Eze 1:24
10:6 Eze 10:2
10:8 Eze 1:8
10:9 Da 10:6
10:11 Eze 1:17
10:12 Eze 1:18
10:14 1Ki 7:36
10:15 Eze 1:5
10:17 Eze 1:20–21
10:18 Ps 18:10
10:20 Eze 1:1

....

11:1 Eze 3:12
11:5 Jer 17:10
11:6 Eze 7:23
11:7 Eze 24:3–13
11:8 Pr 10:24
11:9 Eze 5:8
11:10 2Ki 14:25
11:11 Eze 11:3
11:12 Eze 8:10
11:13 Eze 9:8
11:15 Eze 33:24
11:16 Isa 8:14
11:17 Eze 28:25

God's Judgment on Wicked Counselors

11 Moreover the Spirit lifted me up and
brought me to the east gate of the
house of the LORD which faces eastward. And
at the door of the gate *were* twenty-five men,
among whom I saw Jaazaniah the son of Az-
zur and Pelatiah the son of Benaiah, officials
of the people. 2 Then He said to me, "Son of
man, these are the men who devise mischief
and give wicked counsel in this city, 3 who say,
'*The time* is not near to build houses. This city
is the cauldron, and we are the flesh.' 4 There-
fore prophesy against them; prophesy, son of
man!"
5 Then the Spirit of the LORD fell upon me, and
He said to me, Say, Thus says the LORD: Thus
you have said, O house of Israel, for I know the
things that come into your mind, every one of
them. 6 You have multiplied your slain in this
city, and you have filled the streets with them.
7 Therefore thus says the Lord GOD: Your slain
whom you have laid in the midst of it, they
are the flesh and this city is the cauldron. But
I will bring you out of the midst of it. 8 You
have feared the sword, so I will bring a sword
upon you, says the Lord GOD. 9 I will bring you
out of the midst of the city and deliver you into
the hands of strangers and execute judgments
against you. 10 You shall fall by the sword. I
will judge you in the border of Israel. Then
you shall know that I am the LORD. 11 This city
shall not be your cauldron, nor shall you be
the flesh in the midst of it, but I will judge you
in the border of Israel. 12 Thus you shall know
that I am the LORD. For you have not walked
in My statutes, or executed My judgments, but
have done after the customs of the nations all
around you.
13 Now while I was prophesying, Pelatiah the
son of Benaiah died. Then fell I down upon my
face and cried out with a loud voice and said,
"Ah, Lord GOD! Will You make a full end of the
remnant of Israel?"

The Exiles' Return Promised

14 Again the word of the LORD came to me,
saying: 15 Son of man, your brothers, your kin-
dred, your fellow captives, and all the house
of Israel, all of them, are they to whom the
inhabitants of Jerusalem have said, "Go far
from the LORD. This land has been given to us
as a possession."
16 Therefore say, Thus says the Lord GOD: Al-
though I have cast them far off among the
nations, and although I have scattered them
among the countries, yet I will be a sanctuary
to them for a little while in the countries where
they have gone.
17 Therefore say, Thus says the Lord GOD: I
will gather you from the peoples and assemble

you out of the countries where you have been scattered, and I will give you the land of Israel.

18 When they come there, they shall take away all the detestable things and all the abominations from it. 19 I will give them one heart, and I will put a new spirit within them. And I will take the stony heart out of their flesh, and give them a heart of flesh, 20 that they may walk in My statutes, and keep My ordinances, and do them. And they shall be My people, and I will be their God. 21 But as for those whose hearts walk after the hearts of their detestable things and their abominations, I will recompense their way upon their own heads, says the Lord God.

22 Then the cherubim lifted up their wings with the wheels beside them. And the glory of the God of Israel was over them. 23 The glory of the Lord went up from the midst of the city and stood on the mountain which is on the east side of the city. 24 Afterwards the Spirit took me up and brought me in a vision by the Spirit of God into Chaldea to those of the captivity.

So the vision that I had seen went up from me. 25 Then I spoke to those of the captivity all the things that the Lord had shown me.

Judah's Captivity Symbolized

12 The word of the Lord also came to me, saying: 2 Son of man, you dwell in the midst of a rebellious house, which has eyes to see but does not see, and ears to hear but does not hear. For they are a rebellious house.

3 Therefore, son of man, prepare baggage for captivity and go into captivity by day in their sight. And you shall go into captivity from your place to another place in their sight. It may be that they understand, though they are a rebellious house. 4 You shall bring out your belongings by day in their sight, as baggage for exile; and you shall go out at evening in their sight, as those who go into exile. 5 Dig a hole through the wall in their sight, and go out thereby. 6 In their sight you shall bear it on your shoulders and carry it out in the twilight. You shall cover your face so that you cannot see the land. For I have set you as a sign to the house of Israel.

7 I did so as I was commanded. I brought out my baggage by day as baggage for captivity, and in the evening I dug through the wall with my own hands. I brought it out at twilight, carrying it on my shoulder in their sight.

8 In the morning the word of the Lord came to me, saying: 9 Son of man, has not the house of Israel, the rebellious house, said to you, "What are you doing?"

10 Say to them, "Thus says the Lord God: This oracle concerns the prince in Jerusalem and all the house of Israel who are in it." 11 Say, "I am your sign.

"As I have done, so it shall be done to them. They shall go into exile, into captivity."

12 The prince who is among them shall bear *his baggage* on his shoulder in the twilight and go out. They shall dig through the wall to carry it out thereby. He shall cover his face so that he cannot see the land with his eyes. 13 My net also I will spread upon him, and he shall be taken in My snare. And I will bring him to Babylon to the land of the Chaldeans. Yet he shall not see it, though he shall die there. 14 I will scatter toward every wind all who are about him, his helpers and all his troops. And I will draw out the sword after them.

15 Then they shall know that I am the Lord when I scatter them among the nations and disperse them among the countries. 16 But I will spare a few men of them from the sword, from famine, and from pestilence, so that they may declare all their abominations among the nations where they go and know that I am the Lord.

17 Moreover the word of the Lord came to me, saying: 18 Son of man, eat your bread with quaking, and drink your water with trembling and with anxiety. 19 And say to the people of the land, Thus says the Lord God concerning the inhabitants of Jerusalem in the land of Israel: They shall eat their bread with carefulness and drink their water with astonishment, because their land shall be desolate from all that is in it, because of the violence of all those who dwell in it. 20 The cities that are inhabited shall be laid waste, and the land shall be desolate. Then you shall know that I am the Lord.

21 The word of the Lord came to me, saying: 22 Son of man, what is this proverb that you people have in the land of Israel, saying, "The days are prolonged, and every vision fails"? 23 Tell them therefore, "Thus says the Lord God: I will make this proverb cease so that they shall no more use it as a proverb in Israel." But say to them, The days are at hand and the effect of every vision. 24 For there shall be no more any vain vision or flattering divination within the house of Israel. 25 For I the Lord will speak, and the word that I speak shall come to pass. It shall be no more prolonged. For in your days, O rebellious house, I will say the word, and will perform it, says the Lord God.

26 Again the word of the Lord came to me, saying: 27 Son of man, look, the house of Israel says, "The vision that he sees is for many days to come, and he prophesies of the times that are far off."

28 Therefore say to them, Thus says the Lord God: There shall none of My words be pro-

11:18 Eze 5:11
11:19 Eze 18:31
11:20 Ps 105:45
11:21 Eze 9:10
11:22 Eze 10:19
11:23 Zec 14:4
11:24 Eze 8:3
11:25 Eze 3:4
12:3 Jer 36:3
12:4 Jer 39:4
12:6 Eze 4:3
12:7 Eze 24:18
12:9 Eze 17:12

....

12:11 Jer 15:2
12:12 2Ki 25:4
12:13 Eze 17:20
12:14 Eze 5:2
12:15 Eze 6:7
12:16 Jer 22:8–9
12:19 Zec 7:14
12:20 Isa 7:23–24
12:22 Eze 11:3
12:23 Joel 2:1
12:24 Eze 13:23
12:25 Isa 14:24
12:27 Da 10:14

longed anymore, but the word which I have
spoken shall be done, says the Lord GOD.

False Prophets Condemned

13 And the word of the LORD came to me,
saying: 2 Son of man, prophesy against
the prophets of Israel who prophesy, and say
to those who prophesy out of their own hearts,
"Hear the word of the LORD!" 3 Thus says the
Lord GOD: Woe to the foolish prophets who fol-
low their own spirit and have seen nothing! 4 O
Israel, your prophets are like the foxes in the
ruins. 5 You have not gone up into the gaps,
nor did you build up the hedge for the house
of Israel to stand in the battle on the day of
the LORD. 6 They have seen vanity and lying
divination, saying, "The LORD says," when the
LORD has not sent them. And they have made
others to hope for the confirmation of their
word. 7 Have you not seen a vain vision, and
have you not spoken a lying divination when
you say, "The LORD says," yet it is not I who
have spoken?

8 Therefore thus says the Lord GOD: Because
you have spoken vanity and seen lies, there-
fore I am against you, says the Lord GOD. 9 Thus
My hand shall be against the prophets who
see vanity and who divine lies. They shall
not have a place in the council of My people,
nor shall they be written in the register of the
house of Israel, nor shall they enter into the
land of Israel so that you may know that I am
the Lord GOD.

10 It is surely because they have seduced My
people, saying, "Peace," when there was no
peace. And when anyone builds up a wall, they
daub it with whitewash. 11 Say to those who
daub it with whitewash that it shall fall. There
shall be an overflowing shower, and you, O
great hailstones, shall fall. And a stormy wind
shall break it. 12 When the wall has fallen, will
you not be asked, "Where is the whitewash
with which you have daubed it?"

13 Therefore thus says the Lord GOD: I will
make a violent wind break out in My fury. And
there shall be an overflowing shower in My
anger, and hailstones in My fury to consume it.
14 So I will break down the wall that you have
daubed with whitewash, and bring it down to
the ground so that its foundation is laid bare.
And when it falls, you shall be consumed in its
midst. And you shall know that I am the LORD.
15 Thus I will accomplish My wrath upon the
wall and upon those who have daubed it with
whitewash, and I will say to you, The wall is
no more, nor those who daubed it, 16 *along with*
the prophets of Israel who prophesy concern-
ing Jerusalem and who see visions of peace for
her when there is no peace, says the Lord GOD.

13:2 Jer 37:19
13:3 Jer 23:28–32
13:5 Isa 58:12
13:6 Eze 22:28
13:8 Eze 5:8
13:9 Ps 69:28
13:10 Jer 6:14
13:11 Eze 38:22
13:13 Isa 30:30
13:14 Jer 6:15
13:16 Jer 6:14

....

13:17 Eze 13:2
13:19 Pr 28:21
13:22 Jer 23:14
13:23 Eze 13:21
14:1 Eze 8:1
14:3 Eze 7:19
14:5 Isa 1:4
14:6 Isa 2:20
14:7 Ex 12:48
14:8 Eze 5:15

17 Now you, son of man, set your face against
the daughters of your people who prophesy
out of their own heart and prophesy against
them, 18 and say, Thus says the Lord GOD: Woe
to the women who sew magic bands on all
wrists and make veils on the heads of persons
of every stature to hunt souls! Will you hunt
the souls of My people but save the souls alive
of others for yourselves? 19 And you pollute Me
among My people for handfuls of barley and
pieces of bread to slay the souls of those who
should not die and to save the souls alive of
those who should not live by your lying to My
people who hear your lies.

20 Therefore thus says the Lord GOD: I am
against your magic bands with which you hunt
the souls there as birds, and I will tear them
from your arms, and will let the souls go, even
the souls that you hunt as birds. 21 Your veils
also I will tear off and deliver My people out of
your hands, and they shall be no more in your
hand to be hunted. And you shall know that
I am the LORD. 22 Because with lies you have
made the heart of the righteous sad, whom
I have not made sad, and strengthened the
hands of the wicked that he should not turn
from his wicked way and save his life, 23 there-
fore you women shall no more see vanity or
practice divinations, and I will deliver My peo-
ple out of your hand. Thus you shall know that
I am the LORD.

Idolatrous Elders Condemned

14 Then some of the elders of Israel came
to me and sat before me. 2 The word
of the LORD came to me, saying: 3 Son of man,
these men have set up their idols in their heart
and put the stumbling block of their iniquity
before their face. Should I be inquired of by
them at all? 4 Therefore speak to them and say
to them, Thus says the Lord GOD: Every man of
the house of Israel who sets up his idols in his
heart, and puts the stumbling block of his iniq-
uity before his face, and comes to the prophet,
I the LORD will answer him who comes accord-
ing to the multitude of his idols, 5 in order to
seize the heart of the house of Israel who are
estranged from Me through all their idols.

6 Therefore say to the house of Israel, Thus
says the Lord GOD: Repent and turn away from
your idols and turn away your faces from all
your abominations.

7 For every one of the house of Israel or of
the stranger who sojourns in Israel who sep-
arates himself from Me, and sets up his idols
in his heart, and puts the stumbling block of
his iniquity before his face, and comes to the
prophet to inquire of Me for himself, I the LORD
will answer him by Myself. 8 And I will set My

face against that man and will make him a sign and a proverb, and I will cut him off from the midst of My people. And you shall know that I am the LORD.

9 And if the prophet is deceived when he has spoken a word, I the LORD have deceived that prophet, and I will stretch out My hand against him and will destroy him from the midst of My people Israel. 10 They shall bear *the punishment of* their iniquity. The punishment of the prophet shall be even as the punishment of him who seeks him 11 in order that the house of Israel may no more go astray from Me or be polluted anymore with all their transgressions. Thus they shall be My people, and I shall be their God, says the Lord GOD.

Jerusalem's Imminent Judgment

12 The word of the LORD came to me again, saying: 13 Son of man, when the land sins against Me by trespassing grievously, then I will stretch out My hand against it, and break the staff of the bread, and send famine against it, and cut off man and beast from it. 14 Even though these three men, Noah, Daniel, and Job, were in it, they could deliver but their own souls by their righteousness, says the Lord GOD.

15 If I cause wild beasts to pass through the land, and they destroy it so that it becomes desolate, that no man may pass through because of the beasts, 16 though these three men were in it, as I live, says the Lord GOD, they could deliver neither their sons nor their daughters. They alone would be delivered, but the land would be desolate.

17 Or if I bring a sword on that land, and say, "Let the sword go through the land and cut off man and beast from it," 18 though these three men were in it, as I live, says the Lord GOD, they would deliver neither their sons nor their daughters, but they alone would deliver themselves.

19 Or *if* I send a pestilence into that land and pour out My fury on it in blood to cut off from it man and beast, 20 though Noah, Daniel, and Job were in it, as I live, says the Lord GOD, they would deliver neither their sons nor their daughters. They would deliver only their own souls by their righteousness.

21 For thus says the Lord GOD: How much more when I send My four sore judgments on Jerusalem, the sword, and the famine, and the wild beasts, and the pestilence, to cut off man and beast from it. 22 Yet a remnant shall be left in it who shall be brought out, both sons and daughters. They shall come out to you, and you shall see their way and their deeds. Then you shall be comforted concerning the disaster that I have brought against Jerusalem, even concerning all that I have brought upon it. 23 Then they shall comfort you when you see their ways and their deeds. And you shall know that I have not done without cause all that I have done in it, says the Lord GOD.

14:9 Jer 4:10
14:11 Eze 37:23
14:13 Lev 26:26
14:14 Jer 15:1
14:15 Eze 5:17
14:16 Ge 19:29
14:17 Lev 26:25
14:19 Eze 38:22
14:20 Eze 14:14
14:21 Eze 5:17
14:22 Eze 20:43
....
14:23 Jer 22:8–9
15:2 Isa 5:1–7
15:4 Jn 15:6
15:7 Eze 14:8
15:8 Eze 6:14
16:2 Eze 22:2
16:3 Eze 16:45
16:4 Hos 2:3
16:7 Ex 1:7
16:8 Ru 3:9

Jerusalem as a Useless Vine

15 And the word of the LORD came to me, saying: 2 Son of man, how is the wood of the vine tree better than any wood of a branch which is among the trees of the forest? 3 Can wood be taken from it to do any work, or can men take a peg of it to hang any vessel on it? 4 If it has been cast into the fire for fuel and the fire has devoured both ends of it and the middle of it is burned, is it useful for any work? 5 When it was whole, it was not made into anything. How much less is it useful for any work when the fire has devoured it and it is burned!

6 Therefore thus says the Lord GOD: As the wood of the vine tree among the trees of the forest, which I have given to the fire for fuel, so I will give the inhabitants of Jerusalem. 7 I will set My face against them. Though they go out from one fire, yet the fire shall devour them. Then you shall know that I am the LORD when I set My face against them. 8 I will make the land desolate, because they have committed a trespass, says the Lord GOD.

Jerusalem as an Adulterous Bride

16 Again the word of the LORD came to me, saying: 2 Son of man, cause Jerusalem to know her abominations, 3 and say, Thus says the Lord GOD to Jerusalem: Your birth and your nativity are from the land of Canaan. Your father was an Amorite, and your mother a Hittite. 4 As for your birth, on the day you were born your navel cord was not cut, nor were you washed in water to cleanse you. You were not rubbed with salt, nor wrapped in swaddling cloths. 5 No eye pitied you to do any of these to you, to have compassion on you. But you were cast out in the open field, to the loathing of your person, in the day that you were born.

6 When I passed by you and saw you polluted in your own blood, I said to you when you were in your blood, "Live!" Indeed, I said to you when you were in your blood, "Live!" 7 I have caused you to multiply as the bud of the field, and you have increased and become tall, and you have reached the age of fine ornaments. Your breasts were fashioned and your hair had grown, yet you were naked and bare.

8 Now when I passed by you and looked upon you, you were old enough for love. So I spread My garment over you and covered your nakedness. Indeed, I swore to you, and entered into

a covenant with you, says the Lord God, and
you became Mine.
9 Then I washed you with water. Indeed, I
thoroughly washed away your blood from you,
and I anointed you with oil. 10 I clothed you
also with embroidered work, and put sandals
of porpoise skin on your feet, and girded you
about with fine linen, and covered you with
silk. 11 I decked you also with ornaments, and
put bracelets on your hands, and a chain on
your neck. 12 I put a jewel on your forehead,
and earrings in your ears, and a beautiful
crown on your head. 13 Thus you were decked
with gold and silver. And your raiment was of
fine linen, and silk, and embroidered work.
You ate fine flour, and honey, and oil. And you
were exceedingly beautiful and advanced to
royalty. 14 Then your renown went out among
the nations for your beauty. For it was perfect
through My comeliness which I had put upon
you, says the Lord God.
15 But you trusted in your own beauty, and
played the harlot because of your renown, and
poured out your fornications on every willing
passerby. 16 Of your garments you took and
decked your high places with various colors
and played the harlot on them, which should
never come about or happen. 17 You have also
taken your fair jewels made of My gold and
My silver, which I had given you, and made for
yourself images of men that you might com-
mit harlotry with them. 18 Then you took your
embroidered garments and covered them. And
you have set My oil and My incense before
them. 19 My bread also which I gave you, fine
flour, and oil, and honey, with which I fed you,
you have even set before them for a sweet sa-
vor. And thus it was, says the Lord God.
20 Moreover you have taken your sons and
your daughters, whom you have borne to
Me, and these you have sacrificed to them to
be devoured. Were your harlotries so small
a matter? 21 You have slain My children and
delivered them up to idols by causing them
to pass through the fire. 22 Besides all your
abominations and your harlotries you have
not remembered the days of your youth when
you were naked and bare and were polluted
in your blood.
23 After all your wickedness (Woe, woe to you!
says the Lord God) 24 you also built for yourself
a shrine and have made yourself a high place
in every street. 25 You have built yourself a high
place at the head of every street, and have
made your beauty to be abhorred, and have
spread your legs to every passerby to multiply
your harlotries. 26 You have also committed for-
nication with the Egyptians, your lustful neigh-
bors, and increased your harlotries to provoke
Me to anger. 27 Therefore I have stretched out
My hand against you and have diminished
your ordinary food and delivered you to the
will of those who hate you, the daughters of
the Philistines who are ashamed of your lewd
conduct. 28 You have played the harlot also with
the Assyrians because you were insatiable. In-
deed, you have played the harlot with them,
and yet could not be satisfied. 29 You have
moreover multiplied your fornication with the
land of merchants, Chaldea. And yet you were
not satisfied even with this.
30 How weak is your heart, says the Lord God,
seeing you do all these things, the works of an
imperious harlot. 31 When you built your shrine
at the head of every street and made your high
place in every square, you have not been as a
harlot in that you scorned payment.
32 You have been as a wife who commits
adultery, who takes strangers instead of her
husband! 33 Men give gifts to all harlots. But
you give your gifts to all your lovers, and hire
them that they may come to you on every side
for your harlotry. 34 Thus you are different from
other women in your harlotries in that no one
follows you to commit harlotries, because you
give money, and no money is given to you.
Thus you are different.
35 Therefore, O harlot, hear the word of the
Lord. 36 Thus says the Lord God, Because your
filthiness was poured out and your nakedness
discovered through your harlotries with your
lovers, and with all the idols of your abomina-
tions, and by the blood of your children, which
you gave to idols, 37 therefore I will gather all
your lovers with whom you have taken plea-
sure and all those whom you have loved with
all those whom you have hated. I will even
gather them from all around against you and
will reveal your nakedness to them so that they
may see all your nakedness. 38 I will judge you
as women who commit adultery or shed blood
are judged. And I will bring on you the blood
of fury and jealousy. 39 I will also give you into
their hand, and they shall throw down your
shrines, and shall break down your high plac-
es. They shall strip you also of your clothes,
and shall take your fair jewels, and leave you
naked and bare. 40 They shall also bring up
a company against you, and they shall stone
you with stones, and thrust you through with
their swords. 41 They shall burn your houses
with fire and execute judgments on you in the
sight of many women. And I will cause you to
cease from playing the harlot, and you also
shall give no hire anymore. 42 So I will make
My fury toward you to rest, and My jealousy
shall depart from you, and I will be quiet, and
will be angry no more.

16:10 Eze 16:10
16:11 Ge 24:22
16:13 Dt 32:13–14
16:14 La 2:15
16:15 Isa 57:8
16:16 2Ki 23:7
16:19 Eze 16:13
16:20 Eze 23:37
16:21 2Ki 17:17
16:22 Jer 2:2
16:24 Ps 78:58
16:26 Eze 23:19–21

16:27 Isa 9:12
16:28 2Ki 16:7
16:30 Jer 3:3
16:33 Isa 57:9
16:36 Eze 23:10
16:37 Jer 13:22
16:38 Lev 20:10
16:39 Eze 23:26
16:40 Eze 23:47
16:41 Eze 23:48
16:42 Eze 5:13

43 Because you have not remembered the
days of your youth, but have enraged Me in
all these things, I also will recompense your
way upon your head, says the Lord God, so that
you shall not commit this lewdness above all
your other abominations.
44 Everyone who uses proverbs shall use this
proverb against you, saying, “Like mother, like
daughter.” 45 You are your mother’s daughter
who loathed her husband and her children.
And you are the sister of your sisters who
loathed their husbands and their children.
Your mother was a Hittite, and your father an
Amorite. 46 Now your elder sister is Samaria,
she and her daughters who dwell north of you.
And your younger sister who dwells south of
you is Sodom and her daughters. 47 Yet you
have not walked after their ways, or done ac-
cording to their abominations. But, as if that
were a very little thing, you were corrupted
more than they in all your ways. 48 As I live,
says the Lord God, Sodom your sister has not
done, she nor her daughters, as you and your
daughters have done.
49 This was the iniquity of your sister Sodom.
Pride, abundance of bread, and careless ease
was in her and in her daughters, but she did
strengthen the hand of the poor and needy.
50 They were haughty and committed abomi-
nations before Me. Therefore I took them away
when I saw it. 51 Moreover, Samaria did not
commit half of your sins. But you have multi-
plied your abominations more than they and
have made your sisters appear righteous in
all your abominations which you have done.
52 Also bear your own shame in that you have
made judgment favorable to your sisters. Be-
cause of your sins that you have committed
more abominable than they, they are more
righteous than you. Indeed, be humiliated also
and bear your shame in that you have made
your sisters appear righteous.
53 Yet I shall restore their captivity, the cap-
tivity of Sodom and her daughters, and the
captivity of Samaria and her daughters, and
along with them your own captivity, 54 in order
that you may bear your own shame and may
be humiliated in all that you have done in that
you are a comfort to them. 55 Your sisters, So-
dom and her daughters and Samaria and her
daughters, shall return to their former state,
and you and your daughters shall return to
your former state. 56 As the name of your sister
Sodom was not mentioned by your mouth in
the day of your pride, 57 before your wicked-
ness was uncovered, so now you have become
the reproach of the daughters of Edom and
all who are around her, the daughters of the
Philistines, those all around who despise you.

16:43 Eze 16:22
16:44 Eze 18:2–3
16:46 Eze 23:4
16:47 2Ki 21:9
16:48 Mt 10:15
16:49 Ge 13:10
16:50 Ge 13:13
16:51 Jer 3:8–11
16:54 Jer 2:26
16:57 2Ki 16:5–7

. . . .

16:58 Eze 23:49
16:62 Jer 24:7
16:63 Ro 3:19
17:2 Eze 20:49
17:3 Jer 48:40
17:5 Dt 8:7–9
17:6 Eze 17:14
17:10 Hos 13:15
17:12 Eze 24:19

58 You have borne *the punishment of* your lewd-
ness and your abominations, says the Lord.

An Everlasting Covenant

59 For thus, says the Lord God, I will even
deal with you as you have done, you who have
despised the oath by breaking the covenant.
60 Nevertheless I will remember My covenant
with you in the days of your youth, and I will
establish an everlasting covenant with you.
61 Then you shall remember your ways and be
ashamed when you receive your sisters, your
elder and your younger. And I will give them
to you as daughters, but not because of your
covenant. 62 Thus I will establish My covenant
with you, and you shall know that I am the
Lord, 63 in order that you may remember, and
be humiliated, and never open your mouth
anymore because of your shame, when I am
pacified toward you for all that you have done,
says the Lord God.

Two Eagles and a Vine

17 And the word of the Lord came to me,
saying: 2 Son of man, put forth a riddle,
and speak a parable to the house of Israel,
3 and say, Thus says the Lord God: A great eagle
with great wings, long-winged, full of feathers
which had various colors, came to Lebanon
and took away the highest branch of the cedar.
4 He cropped off the top of its young twigs and
carried it into a land of merchants. He set it in
a city of dealers.
5 He took also some of the seed of the land
and planted it in a fruitful field. He placed it by
great waters and set it as a willow tree. 6 It grew
and became a spreading vine of low stature,
whose branches turned toward him, and its
roots were under it. So it became a vine, and
brought forth branches, and shot forth sprigs.
7 There was also another great eagle with
great wings and many feathers. And this vine
bent its roots toward him and shot forth its
branches toward him, that he might water it by
the bed where it was planted. 8 It was planted
in a good soil by many waters, that it might
bring forth branches, and that it might bear
fruit, that it might be a splendid vine.
9 Say: Thus says the Lord God: Will it thrive?
Will he not pull up its roots and cut off its fruit,
so that it withers, so that all its spring leaves
wither? It will not take a great power or many
people to pull it from its roots. 10 Though it has
been planted, will it prosper? Shall it not utterly
wither when the east wind hits it? It shall with-
er in the furrows where it grew.
11 Moreover the word of the Lord came to me,
saying: 12 Say now to the rebellious house: Do
you not know what these things *mean*? Tell
them: The king of Babylon came to Jerusa-

lem, and took its king and its officials, and led
them to him in Babylon. 13 He took one of the
king's seed, and made a covenant with him,
and put him under oath. He has also taken
away the mighty of the land, 14 that the king-
dom might be debased, that it might not lift
itself up, but by the keeping of his covenant it
might stand. 15 But he rebelled against him in
sending his ambassadors into Egypt, that they
might give him horses and much people. Shall
he prosper? Shall he escape who does such
things? Can he indeed break the covenant and
be delivered?

16 As I live, says the Lord God, surely in the
country of the king who made him king,
whose oath he despised and whose covenant
he broke, in the midst of Babylon he shall die.
17 Nor shall Pharaoh with his mighty army and
great company help him in the war by cast-
ing up mounts and building forts to cut off
many persons. 18 Seeing he despised the oath
by breaking the covenant, when he had given
his allegiance and has done all these things,
he shall not escape.

19 Therefore thus says the Lord God: As I live,
surely My oath that he has despised and My
covenant that he has broken, I will inflict upon
his own head. 20 I will spread My net upon
him, and he shall be taken in My snare, and I
will bring him to Babylon and will enter into
judgment with him there for his trespass that
he has trespassed against Me. 21 All the choice
men in all his troops shall fall by the sword,
and those who remain shall be scattered to-
ward all winds. And you shall know that I the
Lord have spoken it.

22 Thus says the Lord God: I will also take
of the highest branch of the high cedar and
set it aside. I will crop off from the top of its
young twigs a tender one and will plant it on
a high and lofty mountain. 23 On the mountain
of the height of Israel I will plant it. And it shall
bring forth boughs, and bear fruit, and be a
splendid cedar. And under it all fowl of every
wing shall nest. In the shadow of its branches
they shall nest. 24 All the trees of the field shall
know that I the Lord have brought down the
high tree, have exalted the low tree, have dried
up the green tree, and have made the dry tree
to flourish.

I, the Lord, have spoken and will do it.

The Soul Who Sins Will Die

18 The word of the Lord came to me
again, saying: 2 What do you mean in
using this proverb concerning the land of Is-
rael, saying:

"The fathers have eaten sour grapes,
and the children's teeth are set on
edge"?

3 As I live, says the Lord God, you shall not
have occasion anymore to use this proverb in
Israel. 4 All souls are Mine. The soul of the fa-
ther, so also the soul of the son is Mine. The
soul who sins shall die.

5 But if a man is righteous
and does that which is lawful and right,
6 and has not eaten on the mountains;
nor has he lifted up his eyes to the idols
of the house of Israel,
nor has he defiled his neighbor's wife,
nor has he approached a woman during
her impurity;
7 and he has not oppressed anyone,
but has restored to the debtor his pledge;
has devastated no one by violence,
has given his bread to the hungry,
and has covered the naked with a
garment;
8 if he has not lent at interest,
nor has taken any increase,
but has withdrawn his hand from iniquity,
has executed true justice between man
and man;
9 has walked in My statutes,
and has kept My judgments to deal truly,
he is righteous
and shall surely live,
says the Lord God.

10 If he begets a son who is a robber, a shed-
der of blood, and who does any of these things
to a brother 11 (though he himself does not do
any of these things),

but even has eaten on the mountain
shrines
and defiled his neighbor's wife;
12 has oppressed the poor and needy,
has devastated by violence,
has not restored the pledge,
and has lifted up his eyes to the idols,
has committed abomination,
13 has lent at interest, and has taken increase,
shall he then live?

He shall not live. He has done all these abomi-
nations. He shall surely die. His blood shall be
upon his own head.

14 Now if he begets a son who sees all his fa-
ther's sins which he has done, and considering
does not do likewise:

15 He has not eaten on the mountain shrines,
nor has he lifted up his eyes to the idols
of the house of Israel,
has not defiled his neighbor's wife;
16 nor has he oppressed anyone,
has not withheld a pledge,
nor has he devastated by violence,
but has given his bread to the hungry,

17:13 2Ch 36:13
17:14 Eze 29:14
17:15 Dt 17:16
17:16 Eze 12:13
17:17 Jer 37:7
17:18 1Ch 29:24
17:20 Eze 12:13
17:21 2Ki 25:5
17:22 Eze 20:40
17:23 Eze 31:6
17:24 Eze 22:14
18:2 Isa 3:15

18:4 Eze 18:20
18:6 Eze 18:15
18:7 Eze 18:16
18:8 Ex 22:25
18:9 Am 5:4
18:10 Ex 21:12
18:12 Eze 8:6
18:14 2Ch 34:21
18:16 Eze 18:7

and has covered the naked with a
garment;
17 he keeps his hand from the poor,
has not received usury nor increase,
has executed My judgments, and has
walked in My statutes.

He shall not die for the iniquity of his father;
he shall surely live. 18 As for his father, because
he cruelly oppressed, devastated his brother
by violence, and did that which is not good
among his people, he shall die for his iniquity.

Repent and Live

19 Yet you say, "Why should the son not bear
the punishment of the iniquity of the father?"
When the son has done what is lawful and
right, and has kept all My statutes, and has
done them, he shall surely live. 20 The soul who
sins shall die. The son shall not bear the pun-
ishment of the iniquity of the father, nor shall
the father bear the punishment of the iniquity
of the son. The righteousness of the righteous
shall be upon himself, and the wickedness of
the wicked shall be upon himself.
21 But if the wicked turns from all his sins
that he has committed, and keeps all My stat-
utes, and does that which is lawful and right,
he shall surely live. He shall not die. 22 All his
transgressions that he has committed, they
shall not be remembered against him. Because
of his righteousness that he has done, he shall
live. 23 Do I have any pleasure in the death of
the wicked, says the Lord God, but rather that
he should turn from his ways and live?
24 But when a righteous man turns away
from his righteousness, and commits iniquity,
and does according to all the abominations
that the wicked man does, shall he live? All
his righteousness that he has done shall not
be remembered for his trespass that he has
committed and in his sin that he has done. In
them he shall die.
25 Yet you say, "The way of the Lord is not
right." Hear now, O house of Israel. Is not
My way right? Are not your ways not right?
26 When a righteous man turns away from his
righteousness and commits iniquity, he dies
in it. For his iniquity that he has done he shall
die. 27 Again, when the wicked man turns away
from his wickedness that he has committed
and does that which is lawful and right, he
shall save his soul. 28 Because he considered
and turned away from all his transgressions
that he has committed, he shall surely live. He
shall not die. 29 Yet the house of Israel says,
"The way of the Lord is not right." O house
of Israel, are not My ways right? Are not your
ways not right?

18:17 Eze 18:8–9
18:18 Eze 3:18
18:19 Ex 20:5
18:20 Dt 24:16
18:21 Eze 18:27–28
18:22 Ps 18:20–24
18:23 Eze 33:11
18:24 1Sa 15:11
18:25 Eze 33:17
18:27 Isa 1:18
18:30 Eze 18:21
18:31 Eze 11:19
18:32 Eze 18:23
19:1 2Ki 24:6
19:4 2Ki 23:33–34
19:7 Eze 30:12
19:9 2Ch 36:6
19:10 Ps 80:8–11
19:11 Eze 31:3

30 Therefore I will judge you, O house of
Israel, every one according to his ways, says
the Lord God. Repent, and turn away from all
your transgressions so that iniquity shall not be
your ruin. 31 Cast away from you all your trans-
gressions whereby you have transgressed, and
make yourselves a new heart and a new spirit.
For why will you die, O house of Israel? 32 For I
have no pleasure in the death of anyone who
dies, says the Lord God. Therefore, repent and
live.

A Lament for Israel's Princes

19 Moreover take up a lamentation for the
officials of Israel, 2 and say:

What was your mother?
A lioness among lions!
She lay down among young lions;
she nourished her whelps.
3 When she brought up one of her whelps,
he became a lion
and learned to catch his prey;
he devoured men.
4 The nations also heard of him;
he was taken in their pit,
and they brought him with chains
to the land of Egypt.
5 Now when she saw as she had waited
that her hope was lost,
then she took another of her whelps
and made him a young lion.
6 He went up and down among the lions;
he became a young lion,
and learned to catch the prey,
and devoured men.
7 He destroyed their fortified palaces,
and he laid waste their cities;
and the land and its fullness
were appalled by the noise of his
roaring.
8 Then the nations set against him
on every side from their provinces,
and spread their net over him;
he was taken in their pit.
9 They put him in a cage with hooks
and brought him to the king of Babylon;
they brought him in hunting nets,
so that his voice would be heard no
more
on the mountains of Israel.

10 Your mother was like a vine in your
vineyard,
planted by the waters;
it was fruitful and full of branches
by reason of many waters.
11 It had strong rods
for the scepters of those who rule.
And its stature

was exalted above the clouds,
so it appeared in its height
with the multitude of its branches.
12 But it was plucked up in fury,
it was cast down to the ground,
and the east wind dried up its fruit.
Its strong rod was broken and it
withered;
the fire consumed it.
13 Now it is planted in the wilderness,
in a dry and thirsty ground.
14 Fire has gone out from its branch;
it has devoured its shoots and fruit,
so that there is no strong rod in it,
a scepter to rule.

This is a lamentation, and has become a lamentation.

Israel's Continuing Rebellion

20 In the seventh year, in the fifth *month*,
on the tenth day of the month, certain
of the elders of Israel came to inquire of the
LORD and sat before me.
2 Then the word of the LORD came to me, say-
ing: 3 Son of man, speak to the elders of Israel,
and say to them: Thus says the Lord GOD: Do
you come to inquire of Me? As I live, says the
Lord GOD, I will not be inquired of by you.
4 Will you judge them, son of man, will you
judge them? Cause them to know the abomi-
nations of their fathers. 5 And say to them: Thus
says the Lord GOD: On the day when I chose
Israel, and lifted up My hand to the seed of
the house of Jacob, and made Myself known
to them in the land of Egypt, when I lifted up
My hand to them, saying, I am the LORD your
God, 6 on that day that I lifted up My hand to
them to bring them out of the land of Egypt
into a land that I had selected for them, flowing
with milk and honey, which is the glory of all
lands, 7 then I said to them: Cast away, each of
you, the abominations of his eyes, and do not
defile yourselves with the idols of Egypt. I am
the LORD your God.
8 But they rebelled against Me and would
not listen to Me. They did not cast away the
abominations of their eyes, nor did they for-
sake the idols of Egypt. Then I said I will pour
out My fury upon them, to accomplish My an-
ger against them in the midst of the land of
Egypt. 9 But I acted for My name's sake, that
it should not be polluted before the nations
among whom they were, in whose sight I
made Myself known to them in bringing them
out of the land of Egypt. 10 Therefore I caused
them to go forth out of the land of Egypt and
brought them into the wilderness. 11 I gave
them My statutes and showed them My judg-
ments, which if a man does them, he shall live.

19:12 Eze 17:10
19:13 Hos 2:3
20:1 Eze 8:1
20:3 Mic 3:7
20:4 Eze 22:2
20:6 Eze 20:15
20:7 Lev 18:3
20:8 Isa 63:10
20:9 Eze 20:14
20:11 Lev 18:5
....
20:13 Eze 20:21
20:14 Eze 20:9
20:15 Ps 95:11
20:16 Nu 15:39
20:17 Eze 11:13
20:20 Jer 17:22
20:21 Eze 20:13
20:22 Eze 20:9
20:23 Lev 26:33
20:24 Eze 6:9
20:25 Ps 81:12
20:26 Lev 18:21
20:27 Ro 2:24
20:28 Eze 6:13

12 Moreover I gave them My Sabbaths to be a
sign between them and Me, that they might
know that I am the LORD who sanctifies them.
13 But the house of Israel rebelled against
Me in the wilderness. They did not walk in
My statutes, and they despised My judgments,
which if a man does them, he shall live. And
My Sabbaths they greatly polluted. Then I said
I would pour out My fury upon them in the
wilderness to consume them. 14 But I acted for
My name's sake, that it should not be polluted
before the nations in whose sight I brought
them out. 15 Also I lifted up My hand to them
in the wilderness that I would not bring them
into the land which I had given them, flowing
with milk and honey, which is the glory of all
lands, 16 because they despised My judgments
and did not walk in My statutes, but polluted
My Sabbaths. For their hearts went after their
idols. 17 Nevertheless My eye spared them from
destroying them, nor did I make an end of
them in the wilderness. 18 But I said to their
children in the wilderness: Do not walk in
the statutes of your fathers, neither observe
their judgments, nor defile yourselves with
their idols. 19 I am the LORD your God: Walk in
My statutes, and keep My judgments, and do
them. 20 And hallow My Sabbaths. And they
shall be a sign between Me and you that you
may know that I am the LORD your God.
21 Yet the children rebelled against Me. They
did not walk in My statutes, nor did they
keep My judgments to do them, which if a
man does them, he shall live. They polluted
My Sabbaths. Then I said I would pour out
My fury upon them to accomplish My anger
against them in the wilderness. 22 Nevertheless
I withdrew My hand and acted for My name's
sake, that it should not be polluted in the sight
of the nations in whose sight I brought them
out. 23 I lifted up My hand to them also in the
wilderness, that I would scatter them among
the nations and disperse them through the
countries, 24 because they had not executed
My judgments, but had despised My statutes
and had polluted My Sabbaths, and their eyes
were after their fathers' idols. 25 Therefore I
gave them also statutes that were not good
and judgments by which they could not live.
26 And I pronounced them unclean because of
their gifts, in that they caused to pass through
the fire all who opened the womb, that I might
make them desolate in order that they might
know that I am the LORD.
27 Therefore, son of man, speak to the house
of Israel and say to them, Thus says the Lord
GOD: Yet in this your fathers have blasphemed
Me, in that they have committed a trespass
against Me. 28 When I had brought them into

the land for which I lifted up My hand to give it to them, then they saw every high hill and all the leafy trees, and there they offered their sacrifices, and there they presented the provocation of their offering. There also they made their sweet savor and there poured out their drink offerings. 29 Then I said to them: What is the high place to which you go? And the name is called Bamah to this day.

30 Therefore say to the house of Israel, Thus says the Lord GOD: Will you pollute yourselves after the manner of your fathers and commit harlotry after their abominations? 31 When you offer your gifts, when you make your sons to pass through the fire, you pollute yourselves with all your idols, even to this day. And shall I be inquired of by you, O house of Israel? As I live, says the Lord GOD, I will not be inquired of by you.

32 That which comes into your mind shall not come about when you say, "We will be as the nations, as the families of the countries, to serve wood and stone."

God Will Restore Israel

33 As I live, says the Lord GOD, surely with a mighty hand and with a stretched-out arm and with fury poured out, I will rule over you. 34 And I will bring you out from the peoples and will gather you out of the countries in which you are scattered with a mighty hand and with a stretched-out arm and with fury poured out. 35 I will bring you into the wilderness of the peoples, and there I will enter into judgment with you face to face. 36 As I entered into judgment with your fathers in the wilderness of the land of Egypt, so I will enter into judgment with you, says the Lord GOD. 37 I will cause you to pass under the rod, and I will bring you into the bond of the covenant. 38 And I will purge from among you the rebels and those who transgress against Me. I will bring them out of the country where they sojourn, and they shall not enter into the land of Israel. And you shall know that I am the LORD.

39 As for you, O house of Israel, thus says the Lord GOD: Go serve every one of you his idols, but later you shall surely listen to Me. But do not pollute My holy name anymore with your gifts and with your idols. 40 For on My holy mountain, on the mountain of the height of Israel, says the Lord GOD, there all the house of Israel, all of them, shall serve Me in the land. There I will accept them, and there I will seek your offerings and the first fruits of your gifts with all your holy things. 41 I will accept you with your sweet savor when I bring you out from the peoples and gather you out of the countries in which you have been scattered. And I will be sanctified among you before the nations. 42 You shall know that I am the LORD when I bring you into the land of Israel, into the country for which I lifted up My hand to give it to your fathers. 43 There you shall remember your ways and all your deeds in which you have been defiled. And you shall loathe yourselves in your own sight for all your evils that you have committed. 44 You shall know that I am the LORD when I have dealt with you for My name's sake, not according to your wicked ways, or according to your corrupt deeds, O house of Israel, says the Lord GOD.

A Prophecy Against the Negev

45 Moreover the word of the LORD came to me, saying: 46 Son of man, set your face toward the south, preach against the south, and prophesy against the forest land in the Negev. 47 And say to the forest of the Negev, Hear the word of the LORD. Thus says the Lord GOD: I will kindle a fire in you, and it shall devour every green tree in you and every dry tree. The flaming flame shall not be quenched, and all faces from the south to the north shall be burned in it. 48 All flesh shall see that I the LORD have kindled it. It shall not be quenched.

49 Then I said, "Ah, Lord GOD! They say of me, 'Does he not speak parables?' "

Babylon, the Sword of the LORD

21 And the word of the LORD came to me, saying: 2 Son of man, set your face toward Jerusalem, and speak against the holy places, and prophesy against the land of Israel, 3 and say to the land of Israel, Thus says the LORD: I am against you, and will draw My sword from its sheath, and will cut off from you the righteous and the wicked. 4 Seeing then that I will cut off from you the righteous and the wicked, therefore My sword shall be drawn from its sheath against all flesh from the south to the north, 5 that all flesh shall know that I the LORD have drawn forth My sword from its sheath. It shall not return anymore.

6 As for you, son of man, groan with breaking heart and bitter grief, groan before their eyes. 7 It shall be when they say to you, "Why do you groan?" that you shall answer, "Because of the news that is coming. And every heart shall melt, and all hands shall be feeble, and every spirit shall faint, and all knees shall be weak as water. It comes and shall be brought to pass," says the Lord GOD.

8 Again the word of the LORD came to me, saying: 9 Son of man, prophesy and say, Thus says the LORD! Say:

A sword, a sword is sharpened
and also furbished!
10 It is sharpened to make a slaughter;
it is furbished so that it may glitter like
lightning.

20:30 Jer 16:12
20:31 Ps 106:37–39
20:32 Jer 44:17
20:33 Jer 21:5
20:35 Hos 2:14
20:36 Nu 11:1–35
20:37 Lev 27:32
20:38 Eze 13:9
20:40 Isa 56:7
20:41 Eze 28:25
20:42 Eze 34:13
20:43 Eze 6:9
20:44 Eze 24:24
20:46 Eze 21:2
20:47 Jer 21:14
20:49 Jn 16:25
21:2 Eze 20:46
21:3 Job 9:22
21:4 Eze 20:47
21:5 Eze 21:30
21:7 Eze 7:17
21:9 Eze 21:3
21:10 Ps 110:5–6

Should we then make cheer, the rod of My
son despising every tree?

11 He has given it to be furbished,
that it may be handled;
the sword is sharpened,
and it is furbished to give it into the
hand of the slayer.
12 Cry out and howl, son of man;
for it shall be against My people,
it shall be against all the officials of
Israel.
Terrors by reason of the sword
shall be upon My people;
therefore strike your thigh.

13 Because it is a trial, and what if even the
rod which despises shall be no more? says the
Lord GOD.

14 You therefore, son of man, prophesy
and clap your hands together.
And let the sword be doubled
the third time,
the sword of the slain.
It is the sword of the great one slain,
which surrounds them.
15 That their hearts may faint,
and many fall at all their gates,
I have given the glittering sword.
Ah! It is made *for striking* like lightning;
it is wrapped up for the slaughter.
16 Show yourself sharp, go to the right hand.
Set yourself. Go to the left hand,
wherever your edge is set.
17 I will also clap My hands together,
and I will cause My fury to rest;
I the LORD have spoken.

I release battering rams against
the gates of hell (Eze 21:22).

18 The word of the LORD came to me again,
saying: 19 As for you, son of man, appoint two
ways for the sword of the king of Babylon to
come. Both of them shall come out of one
land. And make a signpost. Make it at the head
of the way to the city. 20 Appoint a way for the
sword to come to Rabbah of the sons of Am-
mon and to Judah in Jerusalem the fortified.
21 For the king of Babylon stands at the parting
of the way, at the head of the two ways, to use
divination: He shakes the arrows, he consults
the images, he looks in the liver. 22 At his right
hand was the divination for Jerusalem: to ap-
point battering rams, to open the mouth for
the slaughter, to lift up the voice with a battle
shout, to appoint battering rams against the
gates, to cast up a ramp, and to build a siege
tower. 23 It shall be to them as a false divination
in their sight, to those who have sworn oaths.
But he will call to remembrance the iniquity,
that they may be seized.

24 Therefore thus says the Lord GOD: Because
you have made your iniquity to be remem-
bered, in that your transgressions are uncov-
ered, so that in all your deeds your sins do
appear, because, I say, that you have come to
remembrance, you shall be seized with the
hand.

25 You, profane wicked prince of Israel,
whose day has come in the time of the pun-
ishment of the end, 26 thus says the Lord GOD:
Remove the diadem and take off the crown.
This shall not be the same anymore. Exalt what
is low, and abase what is high. 27 A ruin, a ruin,
a ruin I shall make it. And it shall be no more
until He comes whose right it is, and I shall
give it to Him.

A Sword Against the Ammonites

28 You, son of man, prophesy and say: Thus
says the Lord GOD concerning the sons of Am-
mon and concerning their reproach, and say,

The sword, the sword is drawn,
furbished for the slaughter,
to cause it to consume
that it may be like lightning,
29 while they see vanity for you,
while they divine a lie to you
to bring you upon the necks
of the wicked who are slain,
whose day has come
in the time of the punishment of the
end.

30 Return it to its sheath.
I will judge you
in the place where you were created,
in the land of your nativity.
31 I will pour out My indignation upon you;
I will blow against you in the fire of My
wrath,
and deliver you into the hand of cruel men,
skilled in destruction.
32 You shall be fuel to the fire;
your blood shall be in the midst of the
land.
You shall be no more remembered,
for I the LORD have spoken.

The Sins of Jerusalem

22 Moreover the word of the LORD came
to me, saying:

2 Now you, son of man, will you judge, will
you judge the bloody city? Indeed, you shall
show her all her abominations. 3 Then say,
Thus says the Lord GOD: The city sheds blood
in her midst, that her time may come, and

21:11 Eze 21:19
21:12 Eze 21:6
21:13 Eze 21:10
21:14 Nu 24:10
21:17 Eze 5:13
21:20 Jer 49:2
21:21 Ge 31:19
21:22 Eze 4:2
21:23 Nu 5:15
21:25 Eze 35:5
21:26 Eze 17:24
21:27 Ps 2:6
21:29 Eze 21:25
21:32 Eze 25:10
22:2 Eze 20:4
22:3 Eze 22:27

SPIRITLED WOMAN

COUNSEL FROM THE SPIRIT BASICS

The Cornerstone of Intercession

Ezekiel 22:29–30 is the cornerstone scripture on intercession...but it sounds a lot like the age we live in, doesn't it?

If you were to look back through history, corruption like this only changed in times of great societal awakening. Israel saw it under praying kings such as David, Hezekiah, and Josiah. The Great Awakening of the 1700s was birthed in the 24/7 prayer of the Moravians at Herrnhut and in the methodical devotion of John and Charles Wesley and George Whitefield. The Second Great Awakening was grounded in prayer as well, especially from intercessors such as Daniel Nash and Abel Clary, who were pivotal to the success of Charles Finney's ministry.

This kind of prayer is wonderful and indispensable in our lives. In it we do from time to time pray for others, especially our loved ones, friends, and coworkers—the people who touch our lives. We will lay our petitions at the foot of the cross on their behalf. This is intercession, and it is wonderful, but it is not the level of intercession I am talking about.

I am talking about a regular, systematic, strategic defense on behalf of individuals or entire people groups suffering from the forces of darkness. I am talking about a prepared, enduring, unswerving determination to see freedom won for people we may never meet. It is not about individual requests for individual people—though that will happen in the process. It is about laying down your life for a period of time (hours, days, weekends, perhaps) to call on heaven to invade earth. It is to lay siege to institutions of darkness—poverty, slavery, oppression, hunger, crime, drug abuse, domestic violence, war, divorce, you name it—and to plead for deliverance in the court of heaven.

Cindy Trimm

22:4 2Ki 21:16
22:6 Isa 1:23
22:7 Ex 22:21–22
22:8 Eze 20:13
22:9 Lev 19:16
22:10 Lev 18:19
22:11 Lev 18:15
22:12 Dt 27:25
22:13 Isa 33:15
22:14 Eze 17:24
22:15 Dt 4:27
22:16 Eze 6:7
22:18 Ps 119:119

makes idols against herself to defile herself.
4 You have become guilty in your blood that
you have shed and have defiled yourself with
your idols which you have made. And you have
caused your day to draw near and have come
to your years. Therefore I have made you a
reproach to the nations and a mocking to all
countries. 5 Those who are near and those who
are far from you shall mock you, you of infamy
and much turmoil.

6 The princes of Israel in you, every one
according to his power, have been bent on
shedding blood. 7 In you they have treated
father and mother lightly. In your midst they
have dealt with the stranger by oppression.
In you they have vexed the fatherless and the
widow. 8 You have despised My holy things
and have profaned My Sabbaths. 9 In you are
men who carry slanders to shed blood. And in
you they eat at the mountain *shrines*. In your
midst they commit lewdness. 10 In you they
have uncovered their fathers' nakedness. In
you they have humbled her who was unclean
in her menstrual impurity. 11 One has commit-
ted abomination with his neighbor's wife, and
another has lewdly defiled his daughter-in-law.
And another in you has humbled his sister,
his father's daughter. 12 In you they have taken
bribes to shed blood. You have taken usury and
increase, and you have injured your neighbors
for gain by extortion, and you have forgotten
Me, says the Lord God.

13 Therefore I have struck My hand toward
your dishonest gain which you have made,
and toward your blood which has been in your
midst. 14 Can your heart endure, or can your
hands be strong in the days that I shall deal
with you? I the Lord have spoken and will do
it. 15 I will scatter you among the nations and
disperse you in the countries and consume
your filthiness out of you. 16 You shall profane
yourself in the sight of the nations, and you
shall know that I am the Lord.

Jerusalem as God's Furnace

17 The word of the Lord came to me, saying:
18 Son of man, the house of Israel has become
dross to Me. All of them are bronze and tin
and iron and lead in the midst of the furnace.
They are the dross of silver. 19 Therefore thus
says the Lord God: Because you all have be-
come dross, therefore, I will gather you into
the midst of Jerusalem. 20 As they gather silver
and bronze and iron and lead and tin into the
midst of a furnace to blow fire on it to melt it,
so I will gather you in My anger and in My fury,
and I will lay you there and melt you. 21 Indeed,
I will gather you and blow upon you in the fire
of My wrath, and you shall be melted in the

midst of it. 22 As silver is melted in the midst of
a furnace, so you shall be melted in the midst
of it. And you shall know that I the LORD have
poured out My fury upon you.

Indictment of Sinful Leaders

23 The word of the LORD came to me, saying:
24 Son of man, say to her: You are the land
that is not cleansed nor rained upon in the day
of indignation. 25 There is a conspiracy of her
prophets in her midst like a roaring lion raven-
ing the prey. They have devoured souls. They
have taken the treasure and precious things.
They have made many widows in her midst.
26 Her priests have violated My law and have
profaned My holy things. They have made no
distinction between the holy and profane, nor
have they shown the difference between the
unclean and the clean, and they have hidden
their eyes from My Sabbaths, and I am pro-
faned among them. 27 Her officials in her midst
are like wolves ravening the prey by shedding
blood and destroying lives in order to obtain
dishonest gain. 28 Her prophets have daubed
them with whitewash, seeing vanity and divin-
ing lies for them, saying, "Thus says the Lord
GOD," when the LORD has not spoken. 29 The
people of the land have used oppression and
exercised robbery and have vexed the poor
and needy and have oppressed the sojourner
wrongfully.

I will not violate Your law or profane
Your holy things (Eze 22:26).

30 I sought for a man among them who would
build up the hedge and stand in the gap before
Me for the land so that I would not destroy it,
but I found no one. 31 Therefore I have poured
out My indignation on them. I have consumed
them with the fire of My wrath. Their own way
I have recompensed on their heads, says the
Lord GOD.

I will be faithful in prayer and
stand in the gap as I intercede
for my loved ones (Eze 22:30).

The Sins of Oholah and Oholibah

23 The word of the LORD came again to
me, saying: 2 Son of man, there were
two women, the daughters of one mother.
3 And they committed harlotries in Egypt. They
committed harlotries in their youth. There their
breasts were pressed, and there their virgin bo-
som was handled. 4 Their names were Oholah
the elder and Oholibah her sister. And they
were mine, and they bore sons and daughters.
As for their names, Samaria is Oholah, and
Jerusalem is Oholibah.

Samaria

5 Oholah played the harlot when she was
Mine. And she lusted after her lovers, on the
Assyrians her neighbors, 6 who were clothed in
purple, captains and rulers, all of them desir-
able young men, horsemen riding on horses.
7 Thus she committed her harlotries with them,
with all those who were the chosen men of
Assyria, and with all on whom she doted, with
all their idols she defiled herself. 8 She did not
forsake her harlotries from the time in Egypt.
For in her youth they lay with her, and they
handled her virgin bosom and poured their
harlotry upon her.

9 Therefore I have delivered her into the hand
of her lovers, into the hand of the Assyrians
after whom she doted. 10 They uncovered her
nakedness. They took her sons and her daugh-
ters and killed her with the sword. And she
became a byword among women, for they had
executed judgments on her.

Jerusalem

11 Now her sister Oholibah saw this, but she
was more corrupt in her inordinate love than
she, and in her harlotries more than her sister
in her harlotries. 12 She lusted after the Assyri-
ans her neighbors, captains and rulers clothed
most gorgeously, horsemen riding on horses,
all of them desirable young men. 13 Then I saw
that she was defiled, that they both took the
same way.

14 So she increased her harlotries. And she
saw men portrayed on the wall, the images
of the Chaldeans portrayed with vermilion,
15 girded with belts on their loins, exceeding
in dyed attire on their heads, all of them look-
ing like officials, after the manner of the Bab-
ylonians of Chaldea, the land of their nativity.
16 And as soon as she saw them with her eyes,
she lusted after them and sent messengers to
them into Chaldea. 17 The Babylonians came
to her into the bed of love, and they defiled
her with their harlotry, and she was polluted
with them, and her soul became disgusted
with them. 18 So she uncovered her harlotries
and uncovered her nakedness. Then My soul
became disgusted with her, as My soul became
disgusted with her sister. 19 Yet she multiplied
her harlotries while remembering the days of
her youth in which she had played the harlot
in the land of Egypt. 20 For she lusted after
their paramours, whose flesh is as the flesh of
donkeys and whose issue is like the issue of
horses. 21 Thus you longed for the lewdness of
your youth when the Egyptians handled your
bosom because of the breasts of your youth.

22:22 Eze 20:8
22:25 Hos 6:9
22:26 Lev 10:10
22:27 Eze 22:13
22:29 Eze 22:7
22:30 Jer 5:1
22:31 Eze 7:8–9
23:3 Lev 17:7
23:4 Eze 16:8

23:5 2Ki 15:19
23:7 Hos 5:3
23:8 Ex 32:4
23:11 Jer 3:8–11
23:12 2Ki 16:7–15
23:14 Eze 8:10
23:16 Eze 16:29
23:18 Ps 78:59
23:19 Eze 23:3

Judgment on Jerusalem

22 Therefore, O Oholibah, thus says the Lord God: I will raise up your lovers against you, from whom you were alienated, and I will bring them against you on every side: 23 the Babylonians and all the Chaldeans, Pekod and Shoa and Koa, and all the Assyrians with them. All of them are desirable young men, captains and rulers, officers and men of renown, all of them riding on horses. 24 They shall come against you with weapons, chariots and wagons, and with an assembly of peoples. They shall set themselves against you on every side with buckler and shield and helmet. And I will set the judgment before them, and they shall judge you according to their customs. 25 I will set My jealousy against you, so that they deal furiously with you. They shall take away your nose and your ears. And your remnant shall fall by the sword. They shall take your sons and your daughters. And your remnant shall be devoured by the fire. 26 They shall also strip you of your clothes and take away your fair jewels. 27 Thus I will make your lewdness and your harlotry *brought* from the land of Egypt to cease from you so that you shall not lift up your eyes to them or remember Egypt anymore.

28 For thus says the Lord God: I will deliver you into the hand of those whom you hate, into the hand of those from whom you were alienated. 29 And they shall deal with you hatefully, and shall take away all your labor, and shall leave you naked and bare. And the nakedness of your harlotries shall be uncovered, both your lewdness and your harlotries. 30 I will do these things to you because you have gone whoring after the nations, because you have polluted yourself with their idols. 31 You have walked in the way of your sister. Therefore I will give her cup into your hand.

32 Thus says the Lord God:

You shall drink of your sister's cup,
 which is deep and wide;
you shall be laughed to scorn and held in
 derision;
 it contains much.
33 You shall be filled with drunkenness and
 sorrow,
 the cup of horror and desolation,
 the cup of your sister Samaria.
34 You shall drink it and drain it,
 then you shall gnaw at its fragments
 and tear off your own breasts;

for I have spoken, says the Lord God.

35 Therefore thus says the Lord God: Because you have forgotten Me and cast Me behind your back, now bear *the punishment of* your lewdness and your harlotries.

23:22 Eze 16:37
23:23 Jer 50:21
23:25 Eze 23:47
23:26 Eze 16:39
23:27 Eze 16:41
23:28 Jer 34:20
23:30 Eze 6:9
23:31 2Ki 21:13
23:32 Ps 60:3
23:34 Ps 75:8
23:35 1Ki 14:9

....

23:36 Eze 22:2
23:37 Eze 16:36
23:38 Eze 20:13
23:39 2Ki 21:4
23:40 2Ki 9:30
23:41 Est 1:6
23:42 Eze 16:11–12
23:46 Eze 16:40
23:49 Eze 7:4
24:2 2Ki 25:1
24:3 Eze 11:3

Judgment on the Sisters

36 The Lord moreover said to me: Son of man, will you judge Oholah and Oholibah? Then declare to them their abominations. 37 For they have committed adultery, and blood is in their hands. Thus with their idols they have committed adultery and have also caused their sons whom they bore to Me to pass through *the fire* for them as food. 38 Moreover they have done this to Me: They have defiled My sanctuary in the same day and have profaned My Sabbaths. 39 For when they had slain their children to their idols, then they came the same day into My sanctuary to profane it. And thus they have done in the midst of My house.

40 Furthermore, they have even sent for men to come from afar, to whom a messenger was sent; and they came. For them you washed yourself, painted your eyes, and decked yourself with ornaments. 41 And you sat on a stately couch with a table prepared before it on which you had set My incense and My oil.

42 A sound of a multitude at ease was with her, and drunkards were brought from the wilderness with men of the common sort. And they put bracelets on the hands of the women and beautiful crowns on their heads. 43 Then I said to her who was worn out by adulteries, "Will they now commit harlotries with her when she is so?" 44 Yet they went in to her as they go in to a woman who plays the harlot. So they went in to Oholah and to Oholibah, the lewd women. 45 But righteous men shall judge them after the manner of adulteresses, and after the manner of women who shed blood, because they are adulteresses, and blood is on their hands.

46 For thus says the Lord God: Bring up a company against them and give them over to terror and devastation. 47 The company shall stone them with stones and cut them down with their swords. They shall slay their sons and their daughters, and burn up their houses with fire.

48 Thus I will cause lewdness to cease from the land, that all women may be warned and not commit lewdness as you have done. 49 Your lewdness shall be recompensed upon you, and you shall bear *the punishment of worshipping* your idols. Then you shall know that I am the Lord God.

The Siege of Jerusalem

24 And in the ninth year, in the tenth month, on the tenth day of the month, the word of the Lord came to me, saying: 2 Son of man, write the name of the day, this same day. The king of Babylon has laid siege to Jerusalem this same day. 3 Utter a parable to the rebellious house and say to them, Thus says the Lord God:

Put on the pot, put it on,
and also pour water into it.
4 Gather the pieces into it,
even every good piece, the thigh and the shoulder.
Fill it with the choice bones;
5 take the choicest of the flock,
and also pile the bones under it;
make it boil well,
also seethe its bones in it.

6 Therefore thus says the Lord GOD:

Woe to the bloody city,
to the pot whose rust is in it,
and whose rust has not gone out of it!
Take out of it piece by piece
without choosing.
7 For her blood is in her midst;
she set it on the bare rock;
she did not pour it on the ground
to cover it with dust.
8 That it may cause fury to come up to take vengeance,
I have set her blood on the bare rock,
that it may not be covered.

9 Therefore thus says the Lord GOD:

Woe to the bloody city!
I will also make the pile great.
10 Heap on wood,
kindle the fire;
boil the flesh,
and spice it well,
and let the bones be burned.
11 Then set it empty on its coals,
so that it may be hot and its bronze may glow,
and its filthiness may be melted in it,
and its rust may be consumed.
12 She has wearied Me with toil,
and her great rust has not gone from her.
Let her rust be in the fire.

13 In your filthiness is lewdness. Because
I *would* have purged you, yet you are not
purged, you shall not be purged from your
filthiness anymore until I have caused My fury
to rest on you.

14 I the LORD have spoken. It shall come to
pass and I will act. I will not go back, nor will
I spare, nor will I be sorry. According to your
ways and according to your deeds, I shall
judge you, says the Lord GOD.

The Death of Ezekiel's Wife

15 Also the word of the LORD came to me, say-
ing: 16 Son of man, I am about to take away
from you the desire of your eyes with a stroke.
Yet you shall not mourn or weep, nor shall

24:4 Mic 3:2–3
24:5 Jer 52:10
24:6 Eze 22:2
24:7 Lev 17:13
24:11 Jer 21:10
24:12 Jer 9:5
24:13 Jer 6:28–30
24:14 Eze 18:30
24:16 Jer 13:17
....
24:17 Hos 9:4
24:19 Eze 12:9
24:21 Eze 23:47
24:24 Eze 4:3
24:25 Eze 24:21
24:26 Job 1:15–19
24:27 Eze 33:22
25:2 Jer 49:1–6
25:3 Eze 36:2
25:4 Dt 28:33
25:5 Eze 21:20
25:6 Zep 2:8

your tears run down. 17 Groan silently. Make
no mourning for the dead. Bind on your tur-
ban and put your shoes on your feet and do
not cover your mustache and do not eat the
bread of men.

18 So I spoke to the people in the morning,
and in the evening my wife died. And in the
morning I did as I was commanded.

19 And the people said to me, "Will you not
tell us what these things mean for us, that you
are behaving this way?"

20 Then I answered them: The word of the
LORD came to me, saying: 21 Speak to the house
of Israel, Thus says the Lord GOD: I will profane
My sanctuary, the pride of your strength, the
desire of your eyes and the delight of your
soul. And your sons and your daughters whom
you have left behind shall fall by the sword.
22 You shall do as I have done. You shall not
cover your mustache, nor will you eat the
bread of men. 23 Your turbans shall be on your
heads, and your shoes on your feet. You shall
not mourn or weep. But you shall pine away
for your iniquities and groan toward one an-
other. 24 Thus Ezekiel is a sign to you. Accord-
ing to all that he has done you shall do. And
when it comes about, then you shall know that
I am the Lord GOD.

25 As for you, son of man, shall it not be on
the day when I take from them their strength,
the joy of their glory, the desire of their eyes,
and that on which they set their minds, their
sons and their daughters, 26 that on that day he
who escapes shall come to you to cause you
to hear it with your ears? 27 On that day your
mouth shall be opened to him who escaped,
and you shall speak and be mute no more.
Thus you shall be a sign to them. And they
shall know that I am the LORD.

A Prophecy Against Ammon

25 The word of the LORD came again to
me, saying: 2 Son of man, set your
face against the sons of Ammon and prophesy
against them, 3 and say to the sons of Ammon,
Hear the word of the Lord GOD. Thus says the
Lord GOD: Because you said, "Aha!" against My
sanctuary when it was profaned, and against
the land of Israel when it was made desolate,
and against the house of Judah when they
went into captivity, 4 therefore, I will deliver
you to the men of the East for a possession,
and they shall set their camps among you and
make their dwellings among you. They shall
eat your fruit and drink your milk. 5 I will make
Rabbah a meadow for camels, and the sons of
Ammon a couching place for flocks. Thus you
shall know that I am the LORD. 6 For thus says
the Lord GOD: Because you have clapped your

hands and stamped your feet and rejoiced in heart with all your spite against the land of Israel, 7 therefore, I will stretch out My hand against you and deliver you for destruction to the nations. And I will cut you off from the peoples and cause you to perish from the countries. I will destroy you. Then you shall know that I am the LORD.

A Prophecy Against Moab

8 Thus says the Lord GOD: Because Moab and Seir say, Look, the house of Judah is like all the nations, 9 therefore, I will deprive the side of Moab of its cities, of its cities which are on its frontiers, the glory of the country, Beth Jeshimoth, Baal Meon, and Kiriathaim, 10 and I will give it for a possession with the Ammonites to the men of the East, so that the sons of Ammon may not be remembered among the nations. 11 I will execute judgments on Moab. And they shall know that I am the LORD.

A Prophecy Against Edom

12 Thus says the Lord GOD: Because Edom has acted against the house of Judah by taking vengeance and has greatly offended and revenged themselves upon them, 13 therefore thus says the Lord GOD: I will also stretch out My hand against Edom and cut off man and beast from it. And I will make it desolate. From Teman even to Dedan they shall fall by the sword. 14 I will lay My vengeance upon Edom by the hand of My people Israel. And they shall do in Edom according to My anger and according to My fury. And they shall know My vengeance, says the Lord GOD.

A Prophecy Against Philistia

15 Thus says the Lord GOD: Because the Philistines have dealt by revenge and have taken vengeance with a spiteful heart to destroy with everlasting hatred, 16 therefore thus says the Lord GOD: I will stretch out My hand against the Philistines and will cut off the Kerethites and destroy the remnant of the seacoast. 17 I will execute great vengeance upon them with furious rebukes. And they shall know that I am the LORD when I lay My vengeance upon them.

A Prophecy Against Tyre

26 In the eleventh year, on the first day of the month, the word of the LORD came to me, saying: 2 Son of man, because Tyre has said against Jerusalem, "Aha, the gateway of the peoples is broken. It has opened to me. I shall be filled now that she is laid waste," 3 therefore thus says the Lord GOD: I am against you, O Tyre, and will cause many nations to come up against you, as the sea causes its waves to come up. 4 They shall destroy the walls of Tyre and break down her towers. I will also scrape her dust from her and make her a bare rock. 5 She shall be a place for the spreading of nets in the midst of the sea, for I have spoken, says the Lord GOD, and she shall become destruction to the nations. 6 Her daughters who are on the mainland shall be slain by the sword. And they shall know that I am the LORD.

7 For thus says the Lord GOD: From the north I will bring upon Tyre Nebuchadnezzar king of Babylon, a king of kings, with horses and with chariots and with cavalry and a great army. 8 He shall slay your daughters on the mainland with the sword. And he shall set up a siege wall against you and cast up a mound against you and lift up the roof of shields against you. 9 He shall set engines of war against your walls, and with his axes he shall break down your towers. 10 By reason of the abundance of his horses, their dust shall cover you. Your walls shall shake at the noise of the horsemen and of the wagons and of the chariots when he enters your gates as men enter a city that has been breached. 11 With the hoofs of his horses he shall tread down all your streets. He shall slay your people by the sword, and your strong garrisons shall go down to the ground. 12 They shall make a spoil of your riches, and a prey of your merchandise. And they shall break down your walls and destroy your pleasant houses. And they shall lay your stones and your timber and your dust in the midst of the water. 13 I will cause the noise of your songs to cease. And the sound of your harps shall be heard no more. 14 I will make you a bare rock. You shall be a place to spread nets upon. You shall be built no more, for I the LORD have spoken, says the Lord GOD.

15 Thus says the Lord GOD to Tyre: Shall not the coastlands shake at the sound of your fall when the wounded cry, when the slaughter is made in your midst? 16 Then all the officials of the sea shall come down from their thrones and lay away their robes and take off their embroidered garments. They shall clothe themselves with trembling. They shall sit on the ground and tremble every moment and be astonished at you. 17 They shall take up a lamentation over you and say to you:

How you are destroyed, O inhabited one of
 the seas,
 the renowned city,
which was strong in the sea,
 she and her inhabitants,
who caused her terror
 to be on all her inhabitants!
18 Now the coastlands shall tremble
 on the day of your fall; indeed,

25:7 Zep 1:4
25:9 Jos 13:17
25:10 Eze 21:32
25:12 Ps 137:7
25:13 Jer 25:23
25:14 Isa 11:14
25:15 Isa 14:29–31
25:16 1Sa 30:14
25:17 Eze 25:11
26:1 Eze 20:1
26:2 Isa 23:1–18
26:3 Isa 5:30
26:4 Isa 23:11
26:5 Eze 29:19
26:7 Ezr 7:12
26:8 Eze 21:22
26:11 Isa 5:28
26:12 Isa 23:8
26:13 Isa 23:16
26:14 Job 12:14
26:15 Eze 27:35
26:16 Eze 32:10
26:17 Eze 19:1

the coastlands that are by the sea
shall be troubled at your departure.

19 For thus says the Lord GOD: When I make
you a desolate city, like the cities that are not
inhabited, when I bring up the deep upon you
and great waters shall cover you, 20 then I shall
bring you down with those who descend into
the pit, to the people of old, and make you
dwell in the lower parts of the earth, in places
desolate of old, with those who go down to
the pit so that you will not be inhabited. But I
shall set glory in the land of the living. 21 I will
bring terrors on you and you shall be no more.
Though you will be sought, you shall never be
found again, says the Lord GOD.

A Lament for Tyre

27 The word of the LORD came again to
me, saying: 2 Now you, son of man,
take up a lamentation over Tyre. 3 And say to
Tyre who is situated at the entrance of the sea,
who is a merchant of the peoples for many
coastlands, Thus says the Lord GOD:

O Tyre, you have said,
"I am perfect in beauty."
4 Your borders are in the midst of the seas.
Your builders have perfected your
beauty.
5 They have made all your ship boards
of fir trees from Senir;
they have taken cedars from Lebanon
to make a mast for you.
6 Of the oaks of Bashan
they have made your oars;
with ivory they have inlaid your deck of
boxwood
out of the coastlands of Cyprus.
7 Fine linen with embroidered work from
Egypt was your sail,
so that it became your distinguishing
sign;
blue and purple from the coastlands of
Elishah
was your awning.
8 The inhabitants of Sidon and Arvad were
your mariners;
your wise men, O Tyre, were aboard;
they were your pilots.
9 The elders of Byblos and her wise men
were in you repairing your seams;
all the ships of the sea with their mariners
were in you to deal in your merchandise.

10 They of Persia and of Lydia and of Put
were in your army, your men of war;
they hung the shield and helmet in you;
they set forth your comeliness.
11 The sons of Arvad and your army
were upon your walls all around,
and the Gammad
were in your towers;
they hung their shields on your walls all
around;
they have made your beauty perfect.

12 Tarshish was your merchant by reason of
the multitude of all kinds of riches. With silver,
iron, tin, and lead, they traded in your wares.
13 Greece, Tubal, and Meshek, they were your
merchants. They traded in your market with
the lives of men and vessels of bronze.
14 Those of Beth Togarmah gave horses and
horsemen and mules for your wares.
15 The sons of Dedan were your merchants.
Many coastlands were your merchandise. They
brought you for a payment horns of ivory and
ebony.
16 Aram was your merchant by reason of the
multitude of your wares. They paid for your
wares with emeralds, purple, embroidered
work, fine linen, coral, and agate.
17 Judah and the land of Israel, they were
your merchants. They traded in your market
with the wheat of Minnith, cakes, honey, oil,
and balm.
18 Damascus was your merchant in the mul-
titude of your wares, because of the multitude
of all *kinds of* riches, because of the wine of
Helbon and white wool.
19 Dan and Javan paid for your wares from
Izal. Bright iron, cassia, and sweet cane were
in your market.
20 Dedan was your merchant in saddlecloths
for chariots.
21 Arabia and all the officials of Kedar, they
were your customers in lambs, rams, and
goats. For these they were your merchants.
22 The merchants of Sheba and Raamah, they
were your merchants. They paid for your wares
with the best of all kinds of spices and with all
kinds of precious stones and gold.
23 Harran, and Kanneh, and Eden, the mer-
chants of Sheba, Ashur, and Kilmad, were your
merchants. 24 They traded with you in choice
garments, in clothes of blue and embroidered
work, and in carpets of many colors and tightly
wound cords, *which were* among your mer-
chandise.

25 The ships of Tarshish were
the carriers for your market.
And you were filled and were very glorious
in the midst of the seas.
26 Your rowers have brought you
into great waters;
the east wind has broken you
in the midst of the seas.
27 Your riches and your wares, your
merchandise,

26:19 Isa 8:7–8
26:21 Eze 27:36
27:3 Eze 27:4
27:5 Dt 3:9
27:6 Ge 10:4
27:7 Ex 25:4
27:8 Ge 10:18
27:9 1Ki 5:18
27:10 Eze 30:5
. . . . . .
27:13 Ge 10:2
27:14 Ge 10:3
27:15 Ge 10:7
27:16 Jdg 10:6
27:17 Jdg 11:33
27:18 Isa 7:8
27:19 Ex 30:23–24
27:20 Ge 25:3
27:21 Isa 60:7
27:22 Ge 10:7
27:23 2Ki 19:12
27:25 Isa 2:16
27:26 Ps 48:7
27:27 Pr 11:4

your mariners and your pilots, your
caulkers,
and the dealers of your merchandise, and
all your men of war who are in you,
with all your company which is in your
midst,
shall fall into the midst of the seas
in the day of your ruin.
28 The meadowlands shall shake
at the sound of the cry of your pilots.
29 All who handle the oar,
the mariners and all the pilots of the sea,
shall come down from their ships;
they shall stand upon the land.
30 And they shall cause their voice to be heard
against you,
and shall cry bitterly,
and shall cast up dust upon their heads;
they shall wallow in ashes.
31 Also they shall make themselves utterly
bald for you,
and gird themselves with sackcloth;
and they shall weep for you with bitterness
of heart
and bitter wailing.
32 Also, in their wailing
they shall take up a lamentation for you
and lament over you, saying,
"Who is like Tyre, like her who is silent
in the midst of the sea?
33 When your wares went out by sea,
you filled many peoples;
you enriched the kings of the earth
with the multitude of your riches and of
your merchandise.
34 Now that you are broken by the seas
in the depths of the waters,
your merchandise and all your company
in your midst have fallen.
35 All the inhabitants of the coastlands
shall be astonished at you,
and their kings shall be sorely afraid;
they are troubled in countenance.
36 The merchants among the peoples hiss at
you;
you shall be a terror,
and you shall cease to be forever."

A Prophecy Against the King of Tyre

28 The word of the LORD came again to
me, saying: 2 Son of man, say to the
leader of Tyre, Thus says the Lord GOD:

Because your heart is lifted up,
and you have said, "I am a god;
I sit in the seat of gods
in the midst of the seas,"
yet you are a man, and not God,
though you set your heart as the heart
of God.

3 You are wiser than Daniel;
there is no secret that is a match for you.
4 With your wisdom and with your
understanding,
you have obtained riches for yourself,
and have obtained gold and silver
into your treasuries;
5 by your great wisdom, by your trade,
you have increased your riches,
and your heart is lifted up
because of your riches.

6 Therefore thus says the Lord GOD:

Because you have set your heart
as the heart of God,
7 therefore, I will bring strangers upon you,
the most cruel of the nations;
and they shall draw their swords against
the beauty of your wisdom,
and defile your brightness.
8 They shall bring you down to the pit,
and you shall die the death of those who
are slain
in the midst of the seas.
9 Will you yet say before him who slays you,
"I am a god,"
although you are a man and not God,
in the hands of those who wound you?
10 You shall die the death of the
uncircumcised
by the hand of strangers;
for I have spoken! says the Lord GOD.

A Lament for the King of Tyre

11 Moreover the word of the LORD came to me,
saying: 12 Son of man, take up a lamentation
over the king of Tyre and say to him, Thus
says the Lord GOD:

You had the seal of perfection,
full of wisdom and perfect in beauty.
13 You were in Eden,
the garden of God;
every precious stone was your covering:
the sardius, topaz, and the diamond,
the beryl, the onyx, and the jasper,
the sapphire, the emerald, and the
carbuncle, and gold.
The workmanship of your settings and
sockets was in you;
on the day that you were created, they
were prepared.
14 You were the anointed cherub that covers,
and I set you there;
you were upon the holy mountain of God;
you walked up and down in the midst of
the stones of fire.
15 You were perfect in your ways
from the day that you were created,
until iniquity was found in you.

27:28 Eze 26:10
27:30 Jer 6:26
27:31 Isa 16:9
27:32 Eze 26:17
27:33 Rev 18:19
27:36 Jer 18:16
28:2 Eze 28:9
28:3 Da 1:20
28:5 Ps 62:10
28:6 Eze 28:2
28:7 Eze 31:12
28:9 Eze 28:2
28:10 Eze 31:18
28:12 Eze 19:1
28:13 Eze 27:16
28:14 Ex 25:17–20

[16]By the multitude of your merchandise,
you were filled with violence in your midst,
and you sinned;
therefore I have cast you as profane out of the mountain of God;
and I have destroyed you, O covering cherub,
from the midst of the stones of fire.

Lord, keep my heart and my eyes from being lofty and arrogant (Eze 28:17).

[17]Your heart was lifted up
because of your beauty;
you have corrupted your wisdom
by reason of your brightness;
I cast you to the ground,
I lay you before kings, that they may see you.
[18]You have defiled your sanctuaries
by the multitude of your iniquities, by the iniquity of your trade;
therefore I have brought fire out from your midst;
it has devoured you,
and I have turned you to ashes upon the earth
in the sight of all those who see you.
[19]All those who know you among the people
are astonished at you;
you are a terror,
and you shall cease to be forever.

A Prophecy Against Sidon

[20] Again the word of the LORD came to me,
saying: [21] Son of man, set your face toward
Sidon and prophesy against her [22] and say,
Thus says the Lord GOD:

I am against you, O Sidon;
and I will be glorified in your midst;
and they shall know that I am the LORD,
when I execute judgments in her
and display My holiness in her.
[23]For I will send pestilence into her,
and blood into her streets;
and the wounded shall fall in her midst
by the sword upon her on every side;
and they shall know that I am the LORD.

[24] There shall be no more a pricking brier to the house of Israel, nor any painful thorn among all who are around them, who despised them. Then they shall know that I am the Lord GOD.

The Future Blessing for Israel

[25]Thus says the Lord GOD: When I gather the
house of Israel from the peoples among whom
they are scattered and display My holiness in
them in the sight of the nations, then they shall
dwell in their land that I have given to My servant Jacob. [26] They shall dwell safely in it and
shall build houses and plant vineyards and
dwell securely when I execute judgments on
all those around them who despise them. Then
they shall know that I am the LORD their God.

28:16 Hab 2:17
28:18 Mal 4:3
28:19 Eze 26:21
28:21 Eze 6:2
28:22 Eze 39:13
28:23 Eze 38:22
28:24 Nu 33:55
28:25 Ps 106:47
28:26 Eze 28:22
29:1 Eze 26:1
29:2 Eze 6:2
29:3 Isa 27:1
29:4 2Ki 19:28
29:5 Jer 7:33
29:6 2Ki 18:21
29:7 Eze 17:15–17
29:8 Eze 14:17
29:9 Eze 29:3
29:10 Eze 30:12
29:11 Eze 32:13
29:12 Jer 46:19

A Prophecy Against Egypt

29 In the tenth year, in the tenth month,
on the twelfth day of the month, the
word of the LORD came to me, saying: [2] Son of
man, set your face against Pharaoh king of
Egypt and prophesy against him and against
all Egypt. [3] Speak, and say, Thus says the Lord
GOD:

I am against you, Pharaoh king of Egypt,
the great dragon that lies in the midst of his rivers,
which has said, "My Nile is my own,
and I myself have made it."
[4] But I will put hooks in your jaws,
and will cause the fish of your rivers to stick to your scales,
and will bring you up out of the midst of your rivers,
and all the fish of your rivers shall stick to your scales.
[5] I will abandon you to the wilderness,
you and all the fish of your rivers;
you shall fall upon the open field;
you shall not be brought together or gathered.
I have given you for food
to the beasts of the field and to the fowl of the heavens.

[6] All the inhabitants of Egypt shall know that
I am the LORD, because they have been a staff
of reed to the house of Israel. [7] When they took
hold of you by your hand, you broke and tore
all their hands. And when they leaned upon
you, you broke and made all their legs shake.
[8] Therefore thus says the Lord GOD: I will
bring a sword upon you, and cut off man and
beast out of you. [9] The land of Egypt shall become a desolation and waste. Then they shall
know that I am the LORD.
Because you said, "The Nile is mine, and I
have made it," [10] therefore, I am against you
and against your rivers, and I will make the
land of Egypt an utter waste and desolation,
from Migdol to Syene, as far as the border of
Ethiopia. [11] No foot of man shall pass through
it, nor foot of beast pass through it, nor shall
it be inhabited for forty years. [12] Thus I will
make the land of Egypt desolate in the midst of
the countries that are desolate, and her cities
among the cities that are laid waste shall be

desolate for forty years. And I will scatter the
Egyptians among the nations and will disperse
them among the countries.
13 For thus says the Lord GOD: At the end of
forty years I will gather the Egyptians from the
peoples wherever they were scattered. 14 And I
will turn the fortunes of Egypt and will cause
them to return into the land of Pathros, into
the land of their origin, and there they shall be
a debased kingdom. 15 It shall be the basest of
the kingdoms, and it shall exalt itself no more
above the nations. For I will diminish them so
that they shall rule over the nations no more.
16 It shall be the confidence of the house of
Israel no more, bringing to mind the iniquity
of their having turned to Egypt. But they shall
know that I am the Lord GOD.

Babylonia to Plunder Egypt

17 In the twenty-seventh year, in the first
month, on the first day of the month, the
word of the LORD came to me, saying: 18 Son
of man, Nebuchadnezzar king of Babylon
caused his army to labor hard against Tyre.
Every head was made bald, and every shoul-
der was peeled. Yet he and his army had no
wages from Tyre for the labor that he had done
against it. 19 Therefore thus says the Lord GOD: I
will give the land of Egypt to Nebuchadnezzar
king of Babylon. And he shall carry off her
wealth and take her spoil and take her prey.
And it shall be wages for his army. 20 I have
given him the land of Egypt for his labor with
which he labored against it, because they acted
for Me, says the Lord GOD.
21 On that day I will cause the horn of the
house of Israel to spring forth, and I will open
your mouth in their midst. Then they shall
know that I am the LORD.

A Lament for Egypt

30 The word of the LORD came to me
again, saying: 2 Son of man, prophesy
and say, Thus says the Lord GOD:

Howl,
"Woe to the day!"
3 For the day is near,
even the day of the LORD is near,
a cloudy day,
it shall be the time *of doom* for the
nations.
4 The sword shall come upon Egypt,
and great pain shall be in Ethiopia,
when the slain fall in Egypt,
they take away her wealth,
and her foundations are broken down.
5 Ethiopia, and Libya, and Lydia, all Arabia,
Kub, and the men of the land that is in league
shall fall with them by the sword.

29:13 Isa 19:22
29:14 Eze 30:14
29:15 Eze 30:13
29:16 Hos 8:13
29:17 Eze 29:1
29:18 Jer 27:6
29:19 Jer 43:10–13
29:20 Isa 10:6–7
29:21 Ps 132:17
30:2 Isa 13:6
30:3 Eze 7:7
30:4 Eze 29:19
30:5 Jer 25:20
. . . . . .
30:6 Eze 29:10
30:7 Eze 29:12
30:8 Eze 29:6
30:9 Isa 18:1–2
30:10 Eze 29:19
30:11 Eze 28:7
30:12 Eze 29:3
30:13 Zec 10:11
30:14 Jer 46:25

6 Thus says the LORD:

Indeed, those who uphold Egypt shall fall,
and the pride of her power shall come
down.
From Migdol to Syene
they shall fall in her by the sword,
says the Lord GOD.
7 They shall be desolate
in the midst of the countries that are
desolate,
and her cities shall be
in the midst of the cities that are wasted.
8 They shall know that I am the LORD
when I have set a fire in Egypt
and when all her helpers are destroyed.

9 In that day messengers shall go forth from
Me in ships to make the careless Ethiopians
afraid, and great pain shall come upon them
as in the day of Egypt. For it is coming!
10 Thus says the Lord GOD:

I will also make the multitude of Egypt to
cease
by the hand of Nebuchadnezzar king of
Babylon.
11 He and his people with him, the terrible of
the nations,
shall be brought to destroy the land;
and they shall draw their swords against
Egypt,
and fill the land with the slain.
12 I will make the rivers dry,
and sell the land into the hand of the
wicked;
and I will make the land waste and all that
is in it,
by the hand of strangers.
I, the LORD, have spoken.

13 Thus says the Lord GOD:

I will also destroy the idols,
and I will cause their images to cease
from Memphis;
and no more shall there be a prince of the
land of Egypt.
And I will put a fear in the land of Egypt.
14 I will make Pathros desolate,
and will set fire in Zoan,
and will execute judgments in Thebes.
15 I will pour out My fury upon Pelusium,
the strength of Egypt;
and I will cut off the multitude of
Thebes.
16 I will set fire in Egypt;
Pelusium shall have great pain,
and Thebes shall be rent asunder,
and Memphis *shall have* distresses daily.

17 The young men of Heliopolis and of
Bubastis
shall fall by the sword,
and the women shall go into captivity.
18 In Tahpanhes also the day shall be
darkened,
when I break there the yokes of Egypt.
And the pomp of her strength shall
cease in her;
as for her, a cloud shall cover her,
and her daughters shall go into captivity.
19 Thus I will execute judgments in Egypt,
and they shall know that I am the LORD.

A Prophecy Against Pharaoh

20 In the eleventh year, in the first *month*, on
the seventh day of the month, the word of
the LORD came to me, saying: 21 Son of man, I
have broken the arm of Pharaoh king of Egypt.
And it has not been bound up to be healed
or wrapped with a bandage to make it strong
to hold the sword. 22 Therefore thus says the
Lord GOD: I am against Pharaoh king of Egypt
and will break his arms, both the strong and
the broken. And I will cause the sword to fall
out of his hand. 23 I will scatter the Egyptians
among the nations and disperse them among
the countries. 24 For I will strengthen the arms
of the king of Babylon and put My sword in
his hand. But I will break the arms of Pharaoh
so that he groans before him with the groan-
ings of a wounded man. 25 So I will strengthen
the arms of the king of Babylon, but the arms
of Pharaoh shall fall down. Then they shall
know that I am the LORD when I put My sword
into the hand of the king of Babylon and he
stretches it out upon the land of Egypt. 26 When
I scatter the Egyptians among the nations and
disperse them among the countries, then they
shall know that I am the LORD.

Pharaoh to Be Slain

31 In the eleventh year, in the third *month*,
on the first day of the month, the word
of the LORD came to me, saying: 2 Son of man,
speak to Pharaoh king of Egypt, and to his
multitude:

Whom are you like in your greatness?
3 Assyria was a cedar in Lebanon,
with fair branches and shade for a forest,
and high stature;
and its top was among the clouds.
4 The waters made it great;
the deep set it up on high.
With its rivers it continually ran
all around its plants,
and sent out its little rivers
to all the trees of the field.
5 Therefore its height was exalted
above all the trees of the field,

30:17 Ge 41:45
30:18 Eze 30:3
30:19 Eze 30:14
30:20 Eze 26:1
30:21 Jer 30:13
30:24 Eze 30:25
30:26 Eze 29:12
31:1 Eze 30:20
31:2 Eze 29:19
31:3 Isa 10:33–34
31:5 Da 4:11
....
31:6 Eze 17:23
31:8 Eze 28:13
31:10 Eze 28:17
31:12 Eze 28:7
31:13 Eze 32:4
31:16 Isa 14:15

and its boughs were multiplied,
and its branches became long
because of the abundance of water, as it
spread them out.
6 All the fowl of heaven
made their nests in its boughs;
and under its branches
all the beasts of the field gave birth;
and under its shadow
all great nations lived.
7 Thus it was fair in its greatness,
in the length of its branches,
for its roots were
by many waters.
8 The cedars in the garden of God
could not match it;
the fir trees
were not like its boughs,
and the chestnut trees
were not like its branches;
nor was any tree in the garden of God
like it in its beauty.
9 I made it beautiful with an abundance of
branches,
so that all the trees of Eden envied it,
that were in the garden of God.

10 Therefore, thus says the Lord GOD: Because
it is lifted up in height and has shot up its top
among the clouds, and its heart is arrogant in
its height, 11 I therefore will deliver it into the
hand of the mighty one of the nations. He shall
surely deal with it. I have driven it out for its
wickedness. 12 Aliens, the tyrants of the nations
have cut it off and left it. Upon the mountains
and in all the valleys its branches have fallen,
and its boughs have been broken by all the riv-
ers of the land. And all the peoples of the earth
have gone down from its shadow and have left
it. 13 Upon its ruin all the fowl of the heavens
shall remain, and all the beasts of the field
shall be upon its *fallen* branches 14 to the end
that none of all the trees by the waters exalt
themselves for their height, or shoot up their
tops among the clouds, or their well-watered
trees stand up in their height. For they all have
been delivered to death, to the nether parts of
the earth in the midst of the sons of men, with
those who go down to the pit.
15 Thus says the Lord GOD: On the day when it
went down to Sheol I caused mourning. I cov-
ered the deep over it and restrained its rivers,
and its many waters were stayed. And I caused
Lebanon to mourn for it, and all the trees of
the field fainted for it. 16 I made the nations to
shake at the sound of its fall when I cast him
down to Sheol with those who descend into the
pit. And all the well-watered trees of Eden, the
choice and best of Lebanon, were comforted

in the nether parts of the earth. 17 They also went down into Sheol with it to those who were slain with the sword. And those who were its power lived under its shadow in the midst of the nations.

18 To whom are you thus like in glory and in greatness among the trees of Eden? Yet you shall be brought down with the trees of Eden to the nether parts of the earth. You shall lie in the midst of the uncircumcised with those who were slain by the sword.

This is Pharaoh and all his multitude, says the Lord GOD.

A Lament for Pharaoh and Egypt

32 In the twelfth year, in the twelfth *month*, on the first day of the month, the word of the LORD came to me, saying: 2 Son of man, take up a lamentation for Pharaoh king of Egypt and say to him:

You likened yourself to a young lion of the
nations,
but you are as the monster in the seas;
and you burst forth in your rivers,
and muddied the waters with your feet,
and made foul their rivers.

3 Thus says the Lord GOD:

I will therefore spread out My net over you
with a company of many peoples,
and they shall bring you up in My net.
4 Then I will leave you upon the land;
I will cast you out on the open field,
and I will cause all the fowl of the heavens
to remain upon you.
And I will fill the beasts of the whole
earth with you.
5 I will lay your flesh upon the mountains,
and fill the valleys with your refuse.
6 I will also water the land with your blood,
as far as the mountains;
and the rivers shall be full of you.
7 When *I* put you out, I will cover the
heavens
and make their stars dark;
I will cover the sun with a cloud,
and the moon shall not give its light.
8 All the bright lights in the heavens
I will make dark over you,
and set darkness upon your land,
says the Lord GOD.

9 I will also vex the hearts of many peoples when I bring your destruction among the nations, into the countries which you have not known. 10 Indeed, I will make many peoples amazed at you, and their kings shall be horribly afraid for you when I brandish My sword before them. And they shall tremble at every moment, every man for his own life, on the day of your fall.

11 For thus says the Lord GOD:

The sword of the king of Babylon
shall come upon you.
12 By the swords of the mighty,
I will cause your multitude to fall.
All of them are tyrants of the nations;
they shall destroy the pride of Egypt,
and all its multitude shall be destroyed.
13 I also will destroy all the beasts
from beside many waters;
nor shall the foot of man muddy them
anymore,
nor the hoofs of beasts muddy them.
14 Then I will make their waters settle,
and cause their rivers to run like oil,
says the Lord GOD.
15 When I make the land of Egypt desolate,
and the country is destitute of that by
which it was full,
when I smite all those who dwell in it,
then shall they know that I am the LORD.

16 This is the lamentation, and they shall chant it. The daughters of the nations shall chant it. They shall chant it over Egypt and over all her multitude, says the Lord GOD.

A Dirge for Egypt

17 In the twelfth year, on the fifteenth day of the month, the word of the LORD came to me, saying: 18 Son of man, wail for the multitude of Egypt and cast it down, her and the daughters of the powerful nations, to the nether parts of the earth, with those who go down into the pit. 19 "Whom do you surpass in beauty? Descend and make your bed with the uncircumcised." 20 They shall fall in the midst of those who are slain by the sword. She is delivered to the sword. They have drawn her and all her multitudes away. 21 The strong among the mighty shall speak to him and those who help him out of the midst of Sheol: "They have gone down, they lie still, uncircumcised, slain by the sword."

22 Assyria is there and all her company. Her graves are around her. All of them are slain, fallen by the sword, 23 whose graves are set in the sides of the pit and her company is all around her grave. All of them are slain, fallen by the sword, who cause terror in the land of the living.

24 There is Elam and all her multitude all around her grave, all of them slain, fallen by the sword, who descended uncircumcised into the nether parts of the earth, who caused their terror in the land of the living and bore their shame with those who went down to the pit. 25 They have set a bed for her in the midst of

31:17 Ps 9:17
31:18 Eze 32:19
32:2 Eze 29:3
32:3 Eze 12:13
32:4 Isa 18:6
32:5 Eze 31:12
32:6 Isa 34:3
32:7 Isa 13:10
32:8 Ge 1:14
32:9 Rev 18:10–15
32:10 Eze 26:16
....
32:12 Eze 28:7
32:13 Eze 29:11
32:15 Ex 7:5
32:16 2Sa 1:17
32:17 Eze 32:1
32:18 Eze 31:14
32:19 Eze 31:18
32:20 Ps 28:3
32:21 Isa 14:9–10
32:22 Eze 32:26
32:23 Eze 26:20
32:24 Ge 10:22
32:25 Ps 139:8

the slain with all her multitude. Her graves are
all around it. All of them uncircumcised, slain
by the sword; though their terror was caused in
the land of the living, yet they have borne their
shame with those who go down to the pit. They
were put in the midst of those who are slain.
26 There is Meshek, Tubal, and all her mul-
titude. Their graves are all around them. All
of them uncircumcised, slain by the sword,
though they caused their terror in the land of
the living. 27 They shall not lie with the mighty
who are fallen of the uncircumcised, who have
gone down to Sheol with their weapons of war
and whose swords were laid under their heads.
But the punishment for their iniquity rested
upon their bones, though the terror of these
mighty ones was once in the land of the living.
28 Indeed, you shall be broken in the midst
of the uncircumcised and shall lie with those
who are slain with the sword.
29 There is Edom also, its kings and all its
officials, who for all their might are laid by
those who were slain by the sword. They shall
lie with the uncircumcised and with those who
go down to the pit.
30 There are also the officials of the north, all
of them, and all the Sidonians, who in spite of
the terror from their might have gone down
in shame with the slain. So they lie down un-
circumcised with those who are slain by the
sword, and bear their shame with those who
go down to the pit.
31 Pharaoh shall see them, and shall be com-
forted over all his multitude slain by the sword,
even Pharaoh and all his army, says the Lord
God. 32 Though I have caused a terror of him
in the land of the living, yet he shall be laid in
the midst of the uncircumcised with those who
are slain with the sword, even Pharaoh and all
his multitude, says the Lord God.

Renewal of Ezekiel's Call

33 Again the word of the Lord came to
me, saying: 2 Son of man, speak to
the children of your people and say to them:
If I bring a sword upon a land, and the peo-
ple of the land take a man from among them
and set him for their watchman, 3 and he sees
the sword come upon the land and blows the
trumpet and warns the people, 4 then whoever
hears the sound of the trumpet and does not
take warning, and a sword comes and takes
him away, his blood shall be upon his own
head. 5 He heard the sound of the trumpet yet
did not take warning. His blood shall be upon
himself. But he who takes warning delivers
his soul. 6 But if the watchman sees the sword
come and does not blow the trumpet and the
people are not warned and a sword comes and
takes a person from among them, he is taken
away in his iniquity. But his blood I will require
from the hand of the watchman.
7 Now as for you, son of man: I have set you
a watchman to the house of Israel. Therefore
you shall hear a word from My mouth and
warn them from Me. 8 When I say to the wick-
ed, "O wicked man, you shall surely die," and
you do not speak to warn the wicked from his
way, that wicked man shall die in his iniquity.
But his blood I will require from your hand.
9 Nevertheless, if you on your part warn the
wicked to turn from his way and he does not
turn from his way, he shall die in his iniquity.
But you have delivered your soul.

God's Justice and Mercy

10 Therefore as for you, son of man, say to
the house of Israel: Thus you have spoken,
saying, "Surely our transgressions and our
sins are upon us, and we pine away in them.
How should we then live?" 11 Say to them: As
I live, says the Lord God, I have no pleasure
in the death of the wicked, but rather that the
wicked turn from his way and live. Turn, turn
from your evil ways! For why will you die, O
house of Israel?
12 Therefore you, son of man, say to the sons
of your people: The righteousness of a righ-
teous man shall not deliver him in the day of
his transgression. As for the wickedness of the
wicked, he shall not fall by it in the day that he
turns from his wickedness. Nor shall the righ-
teous be able to live for his righteousness in the
day that he sins. 13 When I say to the righteous
that he shall surely live and he so trusts in his
righteousness that he commits iniquity, all his
righteousness shall not be remembered. But
for that iniquity of his that he has committed,
he shall die. 14 Again, when I say to the wicked,
"You shall surely die," and he turns from his
sin and does that which is lawful and right, 15 if
the wicked man restores a pledge, gives back
what he had robbed, walks in the statutes of
life without committing iniquity, he shall surely
live. He shall not die. 16 None of his sins that he
has committed shall be remembered against
him. He has done what is lawful and right. He
shall surely live.
17 Yet the sons of your people say, "The way
of the Lord is not right," when their way is
not right. 18 When the righteous turns from
his righteousness and commits iniquity, he
shall die by it. 19 But if the wicked turns from
his wickedness and does that which is lawful
and right, he shall live by them. 20 Yet you say,
"The way of the Lord is not right." O house of
Israel, I will judge you, every one according
to his ways.

32:26 Eze 27:13
32:27 Isa 14:18–19
32:29 Jer 49:7–22
32:30 Eze 38:6
32:31 Eze 31:16
32:32 Eze 32:27
33:2 Eze 3:11
33:3 Hos 8:1
33:4 Eze 18:13
33:7 Jer 26:2
33:8 Eze 18:4
33:9 Eze 3:19
33:10 Lev 26:39
33:11 Eze 18:23
33:12 2Ch 7:14
33:13 Eze 18:24
33:14 Eze 18:27
33:15 Eze 20:11
33:16 Eze 18:22
33:18 Eze 33:12–13
33:20 Eze 18:25

The Fall of Jerusalem

21 In the twelfth year of our captivity, in the tenth month, on the fifth day of the month, one who had escaped out of Jerusalem came to me, saying, "The city is taken." 22 Now the hand of the LORD was upon me in the evening, before those who escaped came. And He opened my mouth at the time they came to me in the morning. Therefore my mouth was opened and I was speechless no more.

23 Then the word of the LORD came to me, saying: 24 Son of man, those who inhabit these wastes in the land of Israel are saying, "Abraham was one, yet he inherited the land. But to us who are many, the land has been given for an inheritance." 25 Therefore say to them, Thus says the Lord GOD: You eat *meat* with the blood in it and lift up your eyes toward your idols as you shed blood. Should you then possess the land? 26 You rely upon your sword, you work abominations, and every one of you defiles his neighbor's wife. Should you then possess the land?

27 Thus you shall say to them, Thus says the Lord GOD: As I live, surely those who are in the ruins shall fall by the sword, and him who is in the open field I will give to the beasts to be devoured, and those who are in the forts and in the caves shall die of pestilence. 28 For I will make the land a desolation and a waste, and the pomp of her strength shall cease. And the mountains of Israel shall be desolate so that none shall pass through. 29 Then shall they know that I am the LORD, when I make the land a desolation and a waste because of all their abominations which they have committed.

30 As for you, son of man, the sons of your people are talking about you by the walls and in the doorways of the houses; and they speak to one another, each saying to his brother, "Come now, and hear what the word is that comes from the LORD." 31 They come to you as people come, and they sit before you as My people, and they hear your words; but they will not do them. For they do the lustful desires in their mouth, and their heart goes after their covetousness. 32 You are to them as a sensual song of one who has a pleasant voice and can play well on an instrument. For they hear your words, but they do not do them.

33 When this comes to pass, and it is coming to pass, then shall they know that a prophet has been among them.

A Prophecy Against Israel's Shepherds

34 And the word of the LORD came to me, saying: 2 Son of man, prophesy against the shepherds of Israel. Prophesy and say to those shepherds, Thus says the Lord GOD: Woe to the shepherds of Israel who feed themselves! Should not the shepherds feed the flock? 3 You eat the fat and clothe yourself with the wool; you kill those who are fed without feeding the flock. 4 The diseased you have not strengthened, nor have you healed that which was sick, nor have you bound up that which was broken, nor have you brought back that which was driven away, nor have you sought that which was lost. But with force and with cruelty you have subjugated them. 5 They were scattered because there was no shepherd. And they became meat to all the beasts of the field and were scattered. 6 My sheep wandered through all the mountains and upon every high hill. Indeed, My flock was scattered upon all the face of the earth, and no one searched or sought after them.

7 Therefore, you shepherds, hear the word of the LORD: 8 As I live, says the Lord GOD, surely because My flock became a prey, and My flock even became meat to every beast of the field, because there was no shepherd, nor did My shepherds search for My flock; but the shepherds fed themselves and did not feed My flock, 9 therefore, you shepherds, hear the word of the LORD. 10 Thus says the Lord GOD: I am against the shepherds. And I will require My flock from their hand and cause them to cease from feeding the flock. Nor shall the shepherds feed themselves anymore, for I will deliver My flock from their mouth so that they may not be meat for them.

The True Shepherd

11 For thus says the Lord GOD: I, even I, will search for My sheep and seek them out. 12 As a shepherd seeks out his flock in the day that he is among his sheep that are scattered, so I will seek out My sheep and will deliver them out of all the places where they have been scattered in a cloudy and dark day. 13 I will bring them out from the peoples, and gather them from the countries, and bring them to their own land, and feed them upon the mountains of Israel by the rivers and in all the inhabited places of the country. 14 I will feed them in a good pasture, and upon the high mountains of Israel their grazing ground shall be. There they shall lie on good grazing ground, and in a rich pasture they shall feed upon the mountains of Israel. 15 I will feed My flock, and I will cause them to lie down, says the Lord GOD. 16 I will seek that which was lost and bring back that which was driven away and bind up that which was broken and will strengthen that which was sick. But I will destroy the fat and the strong. I will feed them with judgment.

33:22 Eze 1:3
33:24 Isa 51:2
33:25 Ge 9:4
33:27 1Sa 13:6
33:28 Eze 7:24
33:29 Eze 6:7
33:31 Ps 78:36–37
33:32 Mk 6:20
33:33 Jer 28:9
34:2 Jer 23:1

34:3 Zec 11:16
34:5 Mt 9:36
34:6 Ps 142:4
34:10 Jer 21:13
34:11 Lk 19:10
34:12 Eze 30:3
34:13 Eze 11:17
34:14 Jn 10:9
34:16 Isa 10:16

17 As for you, O My flock, thus says the Lord God: I will judge between sheep and cattle, between the rams and the male goats. 18 Does it seem a small thing to you to have eaten up the good pasture, that you must tread down with your feet the rest of your pastures? Or that you should drink of the clear waters, that you must foul the rest with your feet? 19 And as for My flock, they eat that which you have trodden with your feet, and they drink that which you have fouled with your feet.

20 Therefore thus says the Lord God to them: I, even I, will judge between the fat sheep and between the lean sheep. 21 Because you have thrust with side and with shoulder, and pushed all the diseased with your horns until you have scattered them abroad, 22 therefore I will save My flock, and they shall no more be a prey. And I will judge between one sheep and another. 23 I will set up one shepherd over them, and he shall feed them, even My servant David. He shall feed them himself and be their shepherd. 24 I the Lord will be their God, and My servant David shall be prince among them. I the Lord have spoken.

I will dwell in safety; nothing shall make me afraid (Eze 34:28).

25 I will make with them a covenant of peace and will cause the wild beasts to cease from the land so that they dwell safely in the wilderness and sleep in the woods. 26 I will make them and the places all around My hill a blessing. And I will cause the showers to come down in their season. They shall be showers of blessing. 27 The tree of the field shall yield its fruit, and the ground shall yield its increase, and they shall be safe in their land. Then they shall know that I am the Lord, when I have broken the bands of their yoke and delivered them out of the hand of those who enslaved them. 28 They shall no more be a prey to the nations, nor shall the beast of the land devour them. But they shall dwell safely and no one shall make them afraid. 29 I will raise up for them a planting place of renown, and no more shall they be consumed with hunger in the land, nor shall they bear the shame of the nations anymore. 30 Thus shall they know that I, the Lord their God, am with them, and that they, the house of Israel, are My people, says the Lord God. 31 As for you, My flock, the flock of My pasture, you are men, and I am your God, says the Lord God.

A Prophecy Against Edom

35 Moreover the word of the Lord came to me, saying: 2 Son of man, set your face against Mount Seir and prophesy against it, 3 and say to it, Thus says the Lord God: I am against you, O Mount Seir, and I will stretch out My hand against you, and I will make you a desolation and a waste. 4 I will lay your cities waste, and you shall become a desolation. Then you shall know that I am the Lord.

5 Because you have had a perpetual hatred and have delivered the sons of Israel to the power of the sword in the time of their calamity, in the time of the punishment of the end, 6 therefore, as I live, says the Lord God, I will prepare you for bloodshed, and bloodshed shall pursue you. Since you have not hated bloodshed, therefore blood shall pursue you. 7 Thus I will make Mount Seir a desolation and a waste, and cut off from it the one who passes through and the one who returns. 8 I will fill its mountains with its slain men. On your hills and in your valleys and in all your rivers, they shall fall who are slain with the sword. 9 I will make you a perpetual desolation, and your cities shall not be inhabited. Then you shall know that I am the Lord.

10 Because you have said, "These two nations and these two countries shall be mine, and we will possess them," whereas the Lord was there, 11 therefore, as I live, says the Lord God, I will treat you according to your anger and according to your envy, which you have showed out of your hatred against them. And I will make Myself known among them when I have judged you. 12 Then you shall know that I, the Lord, have heard all your blasphemies which you have spoken against the mountains of Israel, saying, "They are laid desolate. They are given to us to consume." 13 Thus with your mouth you have boasted against Me and have multiplied your words against Me. I have heard them. 14 Thus says the Lord God: When the whole earth rejoices, I will make you a desolation. 15 As you rejoiced at the inheritance of the house of Israel because it was desolate, so I will do to you. You shall be a desolation, O Mount Seir, and all Edom, all of it. Then they shall know that I am the Lord.

A Prophecy to the Mountains of Israel

36 As for you, son of man, prophesy to the mountains of Israel and say: O mountains of Israel, hear the word of the Lord. 2 Thus says the Lord God: Because the enemy has said against you, "Aha! Even the ancient high places are our possession," 3 therefore, prophesy and say: Thus says the Lord God: For good reason they have made you desolate and swallowed you up on every side so that you might become a possession to the rest of the nations, and you have been taken up on the lips of talkers and are an infamy of the people. 4 Therefore, O mountains of Israel, hear the

34:17 Mt 25:32–33
34:22 Ps 72:12–14
34:23 Isa 40:11
34:25 Isa 11:6–9
34:26 Ge 12:2
34:27 Jer 30:8
34:28 Jer 30:10
34:29 Eze 36:29
34:31 Ps 100:3

....

35:3 Jer 6:12
35:4 Eze 35:9
35:5 Ps 137:7
35:6 Isa 63:2–6
35:8 Eze 31:12
35:10 Eze 36:5
35:11 Ps 9:16
35:12 Eze 36:2
35:13 Da 11:36
35:15 Isa 34:5–6
36:2 Dt 32:13
36:3 Ps 44:13–14
36:4 Dt 11:11

word of the Lord GOD: Thus says the Lord GOD
to the mountains and to the hills, to the rivers
and to the valleys, to the desolate wastes and
to the cities that are forsaken, which became
a prey and derision to the rest of the nations
that are all around; 5 therefore thus says the
Lord GOD: Surely in the fire of My jealousy I
have spoken against the rest of the nations and
against all Edom, who have arrogated My land
into their possession with the joy of all their
hearts and with a spiteful soul, to cast it out
for a prey. 6 Prophesy therefore concerning the
land of Israel and say to the mountains and to
the hills, to the rivers and to the valleys: Thus
says the Lord GOD: I have spoken in My jeal-
ousy and in My fury, because you have borne
the shame of the nations. 7 Therefore, thus
says the Lord GOD: I have lifted up My hand
that surely the nations who are about you shall
themselves bear their invectives.

8 But you, O mountains of Israel, you shall
shoot forth your branches and yield your fruit
for My people Israel. For they shall come soon.
9 For I am for you, and I will turn to you, and
you shall be tilled and sown. 10 And I will mul-
tiply men upon you, all the house of Israel,
all of it. And the cities shall be inhabited, and
the waste places shall be built. 11 And I will
multiply man and beast upon you. And they
shall increase and bring forth fruit. And I will
settle you as you were before and do better
to you than at the beginning. Thus you shall
know that I am the LORD. 12 Indeed, I will cause
men to walk upon you, My people Israel, and
they shall possess you, and you shall be their
inheritance, and you shall no longer bereave
them of children.

13 Thus says the Lord GOD: Because they say
to you, "You are a devourer of men and have
bereaved your nation of children," 14 therefore
you shall devour men no more or bereave your
nation of children anymore, says the Lord GOD.
15 Nor will I cause men to hear in you the in-
vectives of the nations anymore, nor shall you
bear the reproach of the peoples anymore, nor
shall you cause your nation to fall anymore,
says the Lord GOD.

The Restoration of Israel

16 Moreover the word of the LORD came to
me, saying: 17 Son of man, when the house
of Israel lived in their own land, they defiled
it by their ways and their deeds. Their way
was before Me as the uncleanness of a woman
in her impurity. 18 Therefore I poured My fury
upon them for the blood that they had shed
upon the land and for their idols with which
they had polluted it. 19 And I scattered them
among the nations, and they were dispersed
throughout the countries. According to their
ways and according to their deeds, I judged
them. 20 When they entered the nations, where
they went, they profaned My holy name, be-
cause they said of them, "These are the people
of the LORD and have gone out of His land."
21 But I had pity for My holy name, which the
house of Israel had profaned among the na-
tions where they went.

22 Therefore say to the house of Israel, Thus
says the Lord GOD: I do not do this for your
sake, O house of Israel, but for My holy name's
sake which you have profaned among the na-
tions where you went. 23 I will vindicate the
sanctity of My great name which was profaned
among the nations, which you have profaned
in their midst. Then the nations shall know that
I am the LORD, says the Lord GOD, when I shall
be sanctified among you before their eyes.

24 For I will take you from among the nations
and gather you out of all countries and will
bring you into your own land. 25 Then I will
sprinkle clean water upon you, and you shall
be clean. From all your filthiness and from
all your idols, I will cleanse you. 26 Also, I will
give you a new heart, and a new spirit I will
put within you. And I will take away the stony
heart out of your flesh, and I will give you a
heart of flesh. 27 I will put My Spirit within you
and cause you to walk in My statutes, and you
will keep My judgments and do them. 28 You
will dwell in the land that I gave to your fa-
thers. And you will be My people, and I will
be your God. 29 I will also save you from all
your uncleanness. And I will call for the grain
and increase it and lay no famine upon you.
30 I will multiply the fruit of the tree and the
increase of the field so that you shall receive
no more reproach of famine among the na-
tions. 31 Then you shall remember your evil
ways and your deeds that were not good, and
shall loathe yourselves in your own sight for
your iniquities and your abominations. 32 Not
for your sake am I doing this, says the Lord
GOD, let it be known to you. Be ashamed and
humiliated for your ways, O house of Israel!

33 Thus says the Lord GOD: On the day that I
cleanse you from all your iniquities, I will cause
you to dwell in the cities, and the waste plac-
es shall be built. 34 The desolate land shall be
tilled, whereas it lay desolate in the sight of all
who pass by. 35 They shall say, "This land that
was desolate has become like the garden of
Eden. And the waste and desolate and ruined
cities have become fenced and inhabited."
36 Then the nations that are left all around you
shall know that I the LORD have built the ruined
places and planted that which was desolate. I
the LORD have spoken it, and I will do it.

36:5 Eze 36:3
36:6 Ps 123:3–4
36:7 Eze 20:5
36:8 Isa 27:6
36:10 Eze 36:33
36:11 Mic 7:14
36:12 Jer 15:7
36:13 Nu 13:32
36:15 Ps 89:50
36:17 Jer 2:7
36:18 2Ch 34:21
36:19 Dt 28:64

....

36:20 Isa 52:5
36:21 Ps 74:18
36:22 Eze 36:32
36:23 Eze 20:41
36:24 Eze 37:21
36:25 Heb 10:22
36:26 Ps 51:10
36:27 Eze 37:14
36:28 Eze 37:27
36:30 Eze 34:27
36:31 Eze 6:9
36:32 Dt 9:5
36:33 Eze 36:10
36:35 Isa 51:3
36:36 Eze 17:24

37 Thus says the Lord GOD: This also I will let
the house of Israel ask Me to do for them: I will
increase their men like a flock. 38 As the flock
for sacrifices, as the flock of Jerusalem in her
solemn feasts, so shall the waste cities be filled
with flocks of men. Then they shall know that
I am the LORD.

The Valley of Dry Bones

37 The hand of the LORD was upon me,
and He carried me out in the Spirit of
the LORD and set me down in the midst of the
valley which was full of bones, 2 and He caused
me to pass among them all around. And *there*
were very many in the open valley. And *they*
were very dry. 3 He said to me, "Son of man,
can these bones live?"
And I answered, "O Lord GOD, You know."

Father, thank You that Your
breath brings life to dead dreams
(Eze 37:10).

4 Again He said to me, "Prophesy over these
bones and say to them, O dry bones, hear the
word of the LORD. 5 Thus says the Lord GOD to
these bones: I will cause breath to enter you so
that you live. 6 And I will lay sinews upon you
and will grow back flesh upon you and cover
you with skin and put breath in you so that you
live. Then you shall know that I am the LORD."
7 So I prophesied as I was commanded. And
as I prophesied, there was a noise and a shak-
ing. And the bones came together, bone to its
bone. 8 When I looked, the sinews and the flesh
grew upon them, and the skin covered them.
But there was no breath in them.
9 Then He said to me, "Prophesy to the wind;
prophesy, son of man, and say to the wind:
Thus says the Lord GOD: Come from the four
winds, O breath, and breathe upon these slain
so that they live." 10 So I prophesied as He com-
manded me, and the breath came into them,
and they lived and stood up upon their feet,
an exceeding great army.
11 Then He said to me, "Son of man, these
bones are the whole house of Israel. They say,
'Our bones are dried up, and our hope is lost.
We are cut off completely.' 12 Therefore proph-
esy and say to them, Thus says the Lord GOD:
Pay attention, O My people, I will open your
graves and cause you to come up out of your
graves and bring you into the land of Israel.
13 Then you shall know that I am the LORD,
when I have opened your graves, O My people,
and brought you up out of your graves. 14 And
I shall put My Spirit in you, and you shall live,
and I shall place you in your own land. Then
you shall know that I the LORD have spoken and
performed it, says the LORD."

36:37 Eze 14:3
36:38 Jn 10:16
37:1 Eze 1:3
37:3 1Sa 2:6
37:4 Jer 22:29
37:5 Ge 2:7
37:6 Eze 38:23
37:7 Jer 13:5–7
37:10 Rev 11:11
37:12 Isa 26:19
37:14 Eze 36:27

37:16 2Ch 15:9
37:17 Isa 11:13
37:18 Eze 12:9
37:20 Eze 12:3
37:21 Eze 36:24
37:22 Jer 3:18
37:23 Eze 36:28–29
37:24 Isa 40:11
37:25 Eze 28:25
37:26 Isa 55:3
37:27 Eze 37:23
37:28 Eze 20:12
38:2 Eze 39:1
38:3 Eze 13:8

Israel and Judah Unite

15 The word of the LORD came again to me,
saying: 16 Moreover, son of man, take one stick
and write on it: "For Judah and for the sons
of Israel his companions." Then take anoth-
er stick and write on it, "For Joseph the stick
of Ephraim and for all the house of Israel his
companions." 17 Then join them to one anoth-
er into one stick so that they become one in
your hand.
18 When the sons of your people speak to
you, saying, "Will you not show us what you
mean by these things?" 19 say to them, Thus
says the Lord GOD: I will take the stick of Jo-
seph, which is in the hand of Ephraim, and
the tribes of Israel his companions, and will
put them with it, with the stick of Judah, and
make them one stick; and they shall be one
in My hand. 20 The sticks on which you write
shall be in your hand before their eyes. 21 Say
to them, Thus says the Lord GOD: I will take the
sons of Israel from among the nations where
they have gone and will gather them on ev-
ery side and bring them into their own land.
22 And I will make them one nation in the land
upon the mountains of Israel. And one king
shall be king over them all. And they shall be
two nations no more, nor shall they be divided
into two kingdoms anymore. 23 Nor shall they
defile themselves anymore with their idols, nor
with their detestable things, nor with any of
their transgressions. But I will save them out
of all their dwelling places in which they have
sinned and will cleanse them. So they shall be
My people, and I will be their God.
24 David My servant shall be king over them.
And they all shall have one shepherd. They
shall also walk in My judgments, and ob-
serve My statutes and do them. 25 They shall
dwell in the land that I have given to Jacob
My servant, in which your fathers lived. And
they shall dwell in it, they and their sons and
their son's sons forever. And My servant David
shall be their prince forever. 26 Moreover I will
make a covenant of peace with them. It shall
be an everlasting covenant with them. And I
will place them and multiply them and will set
My sanctuary in their midst forevermore. 27 My
tabernacle also shall be with them. Indeed, I
will be their God and they shall be My people.
28 The nations shall know that I the LORD do
sanctify Israel when My sanctuary is in their
midst forevermore.

A Prophecy Against Gog

38 And the word of the LORD came to me,
saying: 2 Son of man, set your face
against Gog of the land of Magog, the prince
of Rosh, Meshek and Tubal, and prophesy
against him, 3 and say: Thus says the Lord GOD:
I am against you, O Gog, the prince of Rosh,

Meshek and Tubal. 4 And I will turn you back and put hooks into your jaws, and I will bring you out, and all your army, horses, and horsemen, all of them clothed with all sorts of armor, even a great company with buckler and shield, all of them handling swords. 5 Persia, Ethiopia, and Put with them, all of them with shield and helmet. 6 I will do so to Gomer and all its troops, Beth Togarmah of the north quarters and all its troops, and many peoples with you.

7 Be prepared and prepare yourself, you and all your companies that are assembled to you, and be a guard to them. 8 After many days you shall be called. In the latter years you shall come into the land that is restored from the sword, *whose inhabitants* have been gathered out of many peoples, against the mountains of Israel which had been always a waste. But its people were brought out of the nations, and they, all of them, are dwelling safely. 9 You shall ascend and come like a storm; you shall be like a cloud to cover the land, you and all your troops, and many peoples with you.

10 Thus says the Lord God: It shall come to pass on that day that things shall come into your mind and you shall think an evil thought, 11 and you shall say, "I will go up against the land of unwalled villages. I will go against those who are at rest, that dwell safely, all of them dwelling without walls and having neither bars nor gates," 12 to take spoil and to seize prey, to turn your hand against the desolate places that are now inhabited, and against the people who are gathered out of the nations, who have obtained livestock and goods, who dwell in the midst of the world. 13 Sheba and Dedan and the merchants of Tarshish with all its villages shall say to you, "Have you come to take spoil? Have you gathered your company to seize prey, to carry away silver and gold, to take away livestock and goods, to take great spoil?"

14 Therefore, son of man, prophesy and say to Gog: Thus says the Lord God: On that day when My people of Israel dwell safely, shall you not know it? 15 And you shall come from your place out of the north parts, you and many peoples with you, all of them riding on horses, a great company and a mighty army. 16 And you shall come up against My people of Israel as a cloud to cover the land. It shall come about in the latter days that I will bring you against My land so that the nations may know Me when I shall be sanctified in you, O Gog, before their eyes.

Judgment on Gog

17 Thus says the Lord God: Are you he of whom I have spoken in former days by My servants the prophets of Israel, who prophesied in those days for many years that I would bring you against them? 18 And it shall come to pass at the same time when Gog comes against the land of Israel, says the Lord God, that My fury shall come up in My anger. 19 For in My jealousy and in the fire of My wrath I have spoken: Surely in that day there shall be a great earthquake in the land of Israel. 20 The fish of the sea and the fowl of the heavens and the beasts of the field and all creeping things that creep upon the earth and all the men who are upon the face of the earth shall shake at My presence, and the mountains shall be thrown down, and the steep places shall fall, and every wall shall fall to the ground. 21 I will call for a sword against him on all My mountains, says the Lord God. Every man's sword shall be against his brother. 22 I will enter into judgment with him with pestilence and with blood. And I will rain upon him and upon his troops and upon the many peoples who are with him, an overflowing rain and hailstones, fire and brimstone. 23 Thus I will magnify Myself, and sanctify Myself, and I will be known in the eyes of many nations. Then they shall know that I am the Lord.

38:4 Eze 29:4
38:5 Eze 27:10
38:6 Ge 10:2–3
38:7 Isa 8:9–10
38:8 Isa 24:22
38:9 Isa 28:2
38:10 Ps 36:4
38:11 Zec 2:4–5
38:13 Eze 27:15
38:14 Eze 38:8
38:15 Eze 39:2
38:16 Eze 38:23

....

38:19 Hag 2:6–7
38:20 Hos 4:3
38:21 Jdg 7:22
38:22 Ps 11:6
38:23 Eze 36:23
39:1 Eze 38:2–3
39:2 Eze 38:15
39:3 Ps 76:3
39:4 Eze 33:27
39:6 Eze 30:8
39:7 Eze 38:16
39:8 Eze 38:17
39:9 Ps 46:9
39:10 Isa 33:1

The Destruction of Gog's Armies

39 Moreover you, son of man, prophesy against Gog and say: Thus says the Lord God: I am against you, O Gog, prince of Rosh, Meshek, and Tubal. 2 And I will turn you back, drive you on, and take you up the north parts and bring you against the mountains of Israel. 3 And I will strike your bow out of your left hand and will cause your arrows to fall out of your right hand. 4 You shall fall upon the mountains of Israel, you and all your troops and the peoples who are with you. I will give you to the ravenous birds of every sort, and to the beasts of the field to be devoured. 5 You shall fall upon the open field. For I have spoken, says the Lord God. 6 I will send a fire on Magog and among those who dwell safely in the coastlands. Then they shall know that I am the Lord.

7 So I will make My holy name known in the midst of My people Israel. And I will not let them pollute My holy name anymore. And the nations shall know that I am the Lord, the Holy One in Israel. 8 It is coming and it shall be done, says the Lord God. This is the day of which I have spoken.

9 Those who dwell in the cities of Israel shall go and make fires with the weapons and burn them, both the shields and the bucklers, the bows and the arrows, and the war clubs and the spears, and they shall burn them with fire for seven years. 10 They shall take no wood out of the field, or cut down any out of the forests, for they shall make fires with the weapons. And they shall despoil those who despoiled

them, and plunder those who plundered them, says the Lord God.

The Burial of Gog

11 It shall come to pass in that day that I will give to Gog a place of graves there in Israel, the valley of the passengers on the east of the sea, and it shall stop the passengers. And there they shall bury Gog and all his multitude, and they shall call it the Valley of Hamon Gog.

12 For seven months the house of Israel shall be burying them so that they may cleanse the land. 13 Indeed, all the people of the land shall bury them. And it shall be their renown on the day that I shall be glorified, says the Lord God. 14 They shall separate men who continually pass through the land to bury the passengers, even those who remain upon the face of the earth, to cleanse it.

After the end of seven months they shall search. 15 As the passengers pass through the land and anyone sees a man's bone, then he shall set up a sign by it until the buriers have buried it in the Valley of Hamon Gog. 16 Also the name of the city shall be Hamonah. Thus they shall cleanse the land.

17 As for you, son of man, thus says the Lord God: Speak to every kind of fowl and to every beast of the field: Assemble and come. Gather on every side to My sacrifice that I sacrifice for you, even a great sacrifice upon the mountains of Israel, that you may eat flesh and drink blood. 18 You shall eat the flesh of the mighty and drink the blood of the officials of the earth as *though of* rams, of lambs, and of goats, of bulls, all of them fatlings of Bashan. 19 You shall eat fat until you are full and drink blood until you are drunk from My sacrifice which I have sacrificed for you. 20 Thus you shall be filled at My table with horses and chariots, with mighty men, and with all the men of war, says the Lord God.

21 I will set My glory among the nations, and all the nations shall see My judgment that I have executed, and My hand that I have laid upon them. 22 So the house of Israel shall know that I am the Lord their God from that day and forward. 23 The nations shall know that the house of Israel went into captivity for their iniquity because they trespassed against Me, and I hid My face from them. And I gave them into the hand of their enemies, and all of them fell by the sword. 24 According to their uncleanness and according to their transgressions, I have done to them and hid My face from them.

The Restoration of Israel

25 Therefore thus says the Lord God: Now I will restore the fortunes of Jacob and have mercy on the whole house of Israel and will be jealous for My holy name. 26 They shall forget their shame and all their trespasses by which they have trespassed against Me when they lived safely in their land and no one made them afraid. 27 When I have brought them back from the peoples and gathered them out of the lands of their enemies, then I shall be sanctified in them in the sight of many nations. 28 Then they shall know that I am the Lord their God who caused them to be led into captivity among the nations, and then gathered them again to their own land and have left none of them there anymore. 29 Nor will I hide My face from them anymore. For I will have poured out My Spirit on the house of Israel, says the Lord God.

The Vision of the New Temple

40 In the twenty-fifth year of our captivity, in the beginning of the year, on the tenth day of the month, in the fourteenth year after the city was struck, on that very day the hand of the Lord was upon me and He brought me there. 2 In the visions of God He brought me into the land of Israel and set me upon a very high mountain, on which was as the frame of a city on the south. 3 He brought me there, and there was a man whose appearance was like the appearance of bronze, with a line of flax and a measuring reed in his hand. And he stood in the gate. 4 The man said to me, "Son of man, look with your eyes, and hear with your ears, and set your heart on all that I shall show you. For you have been brought here to show it to you. Declare all that you see to the house of Israel."

> I have the eyes to see what God is doing and the faith to partner with Him to accomplish it (Eze 40:4).

The East Gate

5 There was a wall all around the outside of the temple. In the man's hand was a measuring reed of six cubits[1] long, each being a cubit and a handbreadth.[2] So he measured the width of the building, one reed. And the height, one reed.

6 Then he went to the gateway facing east; and he went up its stairs and measured the threshold of the gate, which was one reed wide. And the other threshold of the gate was one reed wide. 7 Every little chamber was one reed long and one reed wide. And between the little chambers were five cubits.[3] And the threshold of the gate by the vestibule of the inside gate was one reed.

39:12 Dt 21:23
39:13 Eze 28:22
39:17 Zep 1:7
39:18 Ps 22:12
39:20 Rev 19:18
39:21 Ex 9:16
39:23 Isa 1:15
39:24 Jer 2:17
39:25 Isa 27:12–13
39:26 1Ki 4:25
39:27 Eze 36:23–24
39:28 Eze 39:22
39:29 Joel 2:28
40:1 Eze 33:21
40:2 Eze 1:1
40:3 Eze 47:3
40:4 Eze 44:5
40:5 Eze 42:20
40:6 Eze 8:16
40:7 Eze 40:36

[1]5 About 11 feet, or 3.2 meters. The long cubit of about 21 inches, or about 53 centimeters is used throughout ch. 40–48. [2]5 About 3 inches, or 7.5 centimeters. [3]7 About 8¾ feet, or 2.7 meters; and in v. 48.

8 He measured also the vestibule of the gate within, one reed. 9 Then he measured the vestibule of the gate, eight cubits.[1] And its posts, two cubits.[2] And the vestibule of the gate was the inner end.

10 The little chambers of the gate eastward were three on this side and three on that side. The three were of one measurement. And the posts had one measure on this side and on that side. 11 He measured the width of the entrance of the gate, ten cubits,[3] and the length of the gate, thirteen cubits.[4] 12 The space also before the little chambers was one cubit[5] on this side, and the space was one cubit on that side. And the little chambers were six cubits on this side, and six cubits on that side. 13 He measured then the gate from the roof of one little chamber to the roof of another; the width was twenty-five cubits,[6] door against door. 14 He measured the posts, sixty cubits,[7] even to the post of the court all around the gate. 15 From the face of the gate of the entrance to the face of the vestibule of the inner gate was fifty cubits.[8] 16 There were narrow windows in the little chambers and in their posts inside the gate all around, and likewise in the vestibules. And windows were all around inside. And on each post were palm tree ornaments.

The Outer Court

17 Then he brought me into the outer court, and there were chambers and a pavement made all around the court. Thirty chambers were on the pavement. 18 The pavement was by the side of the gates, corresponding to the length of the gates; this was the lower pavement. 19 Then he measured the width from the front of the lower gate to the outer front of the inner court, a hundred cubits[9] eastward and northward.

The North Gate

20 As for the gate of the outer court that faced north, he measured its length and its width. 21 Its little chambers, three on this side and three on that side, its posts, and its arches had the same measurements as the first gate; its length was fifty cubits, and its width twenty-five cubits. 22 Its windows, and those of its arches, and its palm trees had the same measurements as the gate facing east. Seven steps led up to it; and its arches were in front of it. 23 The gate of the inner court was opposite the gate on the north, as on the east. And he measured from gate to gate, a hundred cubits.

The South Gate

24 After that he brought me toward the south, and there was a gate facing south. And he measured its posts and its arches according to these same measurements. 25 There were windows in it and in its arches all around like those windows. The length was fifty cubits, and the width twenty-five cubits. 26 There were seven steps to go up to it, and its arches were before them. And it had palm tree ornaments, one on this side, and another on that side on its posts. 27 There was a gate in the inner court facing south. And he measured from gate to gate toward the south, a hundred cubits.

The Inner Court

28 He brought me to the inner court by the south gate. And he measured the south gate according to these same measurements. 29 And its little chambers and its posts and its arches were according to these same measurements. And there were windows in it and in its arches all around. It was fifty cubits long and twenty-five cubits wide. 30 The arches all around were twenty-five cubits long and five cubits wide. 31 Its arches faced the outer court. And palm tree ornaments were on its posts. And its staircase had eight steps.

32 He brought me into the inner court facing east. And he measured the gate according to these same measurements. 33 Its little chambers and its posts and its arches were according to these same measurements. And there were windows in it and in its arches all around. It was fifty cubits[10] long and twenty-five cubits wide. 34 Its arches faced the outer court. And palm tree ornaments were on its posts, on this side and on that side. And its staircase had eight steps.

35 He brought me to the north gate and measured it according to these same measurements; 36 its little chambers, its posts, and its arches, and it had windows all around: the length was fifty cubits, and the width twenty-five cubits. 37 Its posts faced the outer court. And palm tree ornaments were on its posts, on this side and on that side. And its staircase had eight steps.

Chambers for Washing the Sacrifice

38 The chambers and its entrance were by the posts of the gates where they washed the burnt offering. 39 In the vestibule of the gate were two tables on this side and two tables on that side, to slay on it the burnt offering and the sin offering and the trespass offering. 40 On the outside of the *vestibule*, as one goes up to the entrance of the north gate, were two tables.

40:14 Ex 27:9
40:16 1Ki 6:4
40:17 Eze 42:1
40:19 Eze 40:23
40:21 Eze 40:29–30
40:22 Eze 40:31
40:23 Eze 40:19

40:25 Eze 40:33
40:26 Eze 40:22
40:27 Eze 40:23
40:28 Eze 40:35
40:29 Eze 40:25
40:30 Eze 40:21
40:31 Eze 40:26
40:33 Eze 40:21
40:34 Eze 40:22
40:35 Eze 47:2
40:37 Eze 40:34
40:38 2Ch 4:6

[1] *9* About 14 feet, or 4.2 meters. [2] *9* About 3½ feet, or 1 meter. [3] *11* About 18 feet, or 5.3 meters. [4] *11* About 18 feet wide and 23 feet long, or 5.3 meters wide and 6.9 meters long. [5] *12* About 21 inches, or about 53 centimeters. [6] *13* About 44 feet, or 13 meters; and in vv. 21, 25, 29, 30, 33, and 36. [7] *14* About 105 feet, or 32 meters. [8] *15* About 88 feet, or 27 meters; and in vv. 21, 25, 29, 33, and 36. [9] *19* About 175 feet, or 53 meters; and in vv. 23, 27, and 47. [10] *33* About 88 feet, or 27 meters.

And on the other side of the vestibule of the gate were two tables. 41 Four tables were on this side and four tables on that side by the side of the gate, eight tables on which they slaughtered *their sacrifices*. 42 The four tables were of hewn stone for the burnt offering, of a cubit and a half long, and a cubit and a half wide, and one cubit high.[1] On which also they laid the instruments with which they slaughtered the burnt offering and the sacrifice. 43 Within were hooks, a handbreadth wide,[2] fastened all around. And on the tables was the flesh of the offering.

Chambers for the Singers and Priests

44 Outside the inner gate were the chambers for the singers in the inner court, one at the side of the north gate facing south, the other at the side of the east gate facing north. 45 He said to me, "This chamber that faces south is for the priests who have charge of the temple. 46 The chamber that faces north is for the priests who have charge of the altar. These are the sons of Zadok among the sons of Levi, who come near to the LORD to minister to Him."

47 So he measured the court, a hundred cubits long, and a hundred cubits wide, foursquare. And the altar was before the temple.

The Vestibule of the Temple

48 Then he brought me to the vestibule of the temple and measured each post of the vestibule, five cubits[3] on this side, and five cubits on that side. And the width of the gate was three cubits[4] on this side and three cubits on that side. 49 The length of the vestibule was twenty cubits[5] and the width eleven cubits.[6] And he brought me by the steps whereby they went up to it. And there were pillars by the posts, one on this side and another on that side.

The Inner Temple

41 Afterward he brought me to the temple and measured the posts, six cubits[7] wide on the one side and six cubits wide on the other side, which was the width of the tabernacle. 2 The width of the door was ten cubits.[8] And the sides of the door were five cubits[9] on the one side and five cubits on the other side. And he measured its length, forty cubits, and the width, twenty cubits.[10]

3 Then he went inward and measured the post of the door, two cubits,[11] and the door, six cubits, and the width of the door, seven cubits.[12] 4 So he measured its length, twenty cubits. And before the temple, the width was twenty cubits. And he said to me, "This is the Most Holy Place."

5 Afterward he measured the wall of the temple, six cubits, and the width of every side chamber, four cubits,[13] all around the temple on every side. 6 The side chambers were in three stories, one above the other, thirty in each story. There were offsets all around to serve as supports for the side chambers, so that they should not be supported by the wall of the temple. 7 The side chambers became wider with each successive story going up because the structures went up all around the temple. Therefore the width of the temple increased going upwards and thus one went up from the lowest to the highest level through the middle level.

8 I saw also the height all around the temple. The foundations of the side chambers were a full reed of six great cubits. 9 The thickness of the wall of the side chambers was five cubits. And that which was left was the place of the side chambers that were within. 10 Between the chambers was the wideness of twenty cubits all around the temple on every side. 11 The doors of the side chambers opened onto the open place, one door toward the north and another door toward the south. And the width of the open place was five cubits all around.

12 Now the building that was facing the separate yard on the west side was seventy cubits[14] wide. And the wall of the building was five cubits thick all around, and its length ninety cubits.[15]

13 So he measured the temple, a hundred cubits long; and the separate yard and the building with its walls, a hundred cubits long;[16] 14 also the width of the eastern face of the temple and the separate yard was a hundred cubits.

15 Then he measured the length of the building facing the yard at the west, together with its galleries on either side, one hundred cubits with the nave of the temple and the porches of the court, 16 the doorposts and the narrow windows. The galleries all around their three stories opposite the threshold were paneled with wood from the ground to the windows (the windows were covered), 17 from the space above the door, even to the inner room, as well as outside, and on every wall all around, inside and outside, by measure. 18 It was made with cherubim and palm trees, so that a palm tree was between cherub and cherub. And every cherub had two faces, 19 so that the face of a man was toward the palm tree on the one side,

40:42 Eze 40:39
40:44 1Ch 6:31–32
40:45 1Ch 9:23
40:46 Eze 44:15
41:2 1Ki 6:2
41:4 1Ki 6:20
41:6 1Ki 6:10
41:7 1Ki 6:8
41:8 Eze 40:5
41:9 Eze 41:11
41:11 Eze 41:9
41:12 Eze 41:13–15
41:13 Eze 40:47
41:15 Eze 42:3
41:16 1Ki 6:4
41:18 1Ki 7:36
41:19 Eze 10:14

[1] *42* About 2⅔ feet long and wide and 21 inches high, or 80 centimeters long and wide and 53 centimeters high. [2] *43* About 3½ inches, or 9 centimeters. [3] *48* About 8.75 feet, or 2.7 meters. [4] *48* About 5¼ feet, or 1.6 meters. [5] *49* About 35 feet, or 11 meters. [6] *49* About 19.25 feet, or 5.9 meters. [7] *1* About 11 feet, or 3.2 meters; and in vv. 3, 5, and 8. [8] *2* About 18 feet, or 5.3 meters. [9] *2* About 8¾ feet, or 2.7 meters; and in vv. 9, 11, and 12. [10] *2* About 70 feet long and 35 feet wide, or 21 meters long and 11 meters wide. [11] *3* About 3½ feet, or 1.1 meters; and in v. 22. [12] *3* About 12 feet, or 3.7 meters. [13] *5* About 7 feet, or 2.1 meters. [14] *12* About 123 feet, or 37 meters. [15] *12* About 158 feet, or 48 meters. [16] *13* About 175 feet, or 53 meters; and in vv. 14 and 15.

and the face of a young lion toward the palm
tree on the other side. It was made throughout
the temple all round. 20 From the ground to the
top of the door and on the wall of the nave,
cherubim and palm trees were carved.

21 The posts of the temple and the face of
the sanctuary were squared. The appearance
of the one was as the appearance of the other.
22 The altar of wood was three cubits[1] high,
and its length two cubits. And its corners and
its length and its walls were of wood. And he
said to me, "This is the table that is before the
LORD." 23 The temple and the sanctuary had
two doors. 24 The doors had two leaves apiece,
two turning leaves. Two leaves were for the
one door, and two leaves for the other door.
25 There were made on them, on the doors of
the temple, cherubim and palm trees like those
made on the walls. And there were thick planks
on the front of the vestibule outside. 26 There
were beveled windows and palm trees on
both sides, on the sides of the vestibule; thus
were the side chambers of the temple and the
thresholds.

The Chambers for the Priests

42 Then he brought me out into the out-
er court, toward the north; and he
brought me into the chamber that was oppo-
site the separate yard and which was opposite
the building on the north. 2 Before the length of
a hundred cubits was the north door, and the
width was fifty cubits.[2] 3 Opposite the twenty
cubits[3] that belonged to the inner court, and
opposite the pavement that belonged to the
outer court, was gallery against gallery in three
stories. 4 In front of the chambers was a pas-
sage on the inner side, ten cubits wide and one
hundred cubits[4] deep; and their doors faced
north. 5 Now the upper chambers were shorter.
For the galleries were higher than these, than
the lower and the middle ones of the build-
ing. 6 For they were in three stories, but had
no pillars as the pillars of the courts. There-
fore the building was set back more than the
lowest and the middle ones from the ground.
7 And a wall that was outside was parallel to
the chambers, toward the outer court, opposite
the chambers; its length was fifty cubits. 8 For
the length of the chambers that were in the
outer court was fifty cubits. And the length of
those before the temple was a hundred cubits.
9 From under these chambers was the entrance
on the east side as one goes into them from
the outer court.

10 The chambers were in the thickness of
the wall of the court toward the east, opposite
the separate yard and opposite the building,
11 with a passage in front of them; they were
like the appearance of the chambers which
were toward the north, of the same length and
width. And all their exits and arrangements
were according to plan. 12 Corresponding to
the doors of the chambers that were facing
south was a door at the head of the passage
way, the passage way directly in front of the
wall toward the east.

13 Then he said to me, "The north chambers
and the south chambers, which are before the
separate place, are the holy chambers where
the priests who approach the LORD shall eat the
most holy offerings. There they shall lay the
most holy offerings—the grain offering, the sin
offering, and the guilt offering—for the place
is holy. 14 When the priests enter it, then they
shall not go out of the holy place into the outer
court, but there they shall lay their garments
in which they minister, for they are holy. And
they shall put on other garments, and shall ap-
proach those things which are for the people."

15 Now when he had made an end of mea-
suring the inner temple, he brought me out
by the gate that faces east, and measured it
all around. 16 He measured the east side with
the measuring reed, five hundred cubits[5] with
the measuring reed all around. 17 He measured
the north side with the measuring reed round
about, five hundred reeds. 18 He measured
the south side with the measuring reed, five
hundred reeds. 19 He turned about to the west
side and measured five hundred reeds with the
measuring reed. 20 He measured it by the four
sides. It had a wall all around, five hundred
reeds long and five hundred wide,[6] to make
a separation between the sanctuary and the
profane place.

God's Glory Returns to the Temple

43 Afterward he brought me to the gate,
the gate facing east. 2 And the glory
of the God of Israel came from the way of the
east. And His voice was like a noise of many
waters. And the earth shone with His glory. 3 It
was according to the appearance of the vision
which I saw, even according to the vision that
I saw, when He came to destroy the city. And
the visions were like the vision that I saw by
the River Kebar. And I fell upon my face. 4 The
glory of the LORD came into the temple by the
way of the gate facing east. 5 So the Spirit took
me up and brought me into the inner court.
And the glory of the LORD filled the temple.

6 Then I heard one speaking to me out of the
temple. And a man stood by me. 7 He said to
me: Son of man, this is the place of My throne
and the place of the soles of My feet, where

41:21 Eze 41:1
41:22 Eze 23:41
41:23 1Ki 6:31–35
41:24 1Ki 6:34
41:25 Eze 41:18
41:26 Eze 41:16
42:1 Eze 40:17
42:3 Eze 41:15–16
42:4 Eze 46:19
42:6 Eze 41:6
42:9 Eze 46:19
42:10 Eze 42:1
42:13 Lev 7:6
42:14 Eze 44:19
42:15 Eze 43:1
42:16 Eze 40:3
42:20 Eze 45:2
43:1 Eze 42:15
43:2 Eze 11:23
43:3 Eze 9:1
43:4 Eze 44:2
43:5 Eze 8:3
43:6 Eze 40:3
43:7 Lev 26:30

[1] *22* About 5¼ feet, or 1.5 meters. [2] *2* About 175 feet long and 88 feet wide, or 53 meters long and 27 meters wide. [3] *3* About 35 feet, or 11 meters. [4] *4* About 18 feet wide and 175 feet long, or 5.3 meters wide and 53 meters long. [5] *16* Five hundred cubits equal about 875 feet, or 265 meters; and in vv. 17, 18, and 19. [6] *20* Five hundred cubits equal about 875 feet, or 265 meters.

I will dwell in the midst of the sons of Israel
forever. And My holy name shall the house of
Israel defile no more, nor they nor their kings
by their harlotry, nor by the corpses of their
kings when they die. 8 By setting their thresh-
old by My threshold and their post by My posts
and the wall between Me and them, they have
even defiled My holy name by their abomina-
tions that they have committed. Therefore I
have consumed them in My anger. 9 Now let
them put away their harlotry and the corpses
of their kings far from Me, and I will dwell in
their midst forever.

10 As for you, son of man, describe the tem-
ple to the house of Israel, that they may be
ashamed of their iniquities. And let them mea-
sure the pattern. 11 If they are ashamed of all
that they have done, show them the design of
the temple and its fashion and exits and its en-
trances and all its forms and all its ordinances
and all its laws. And write it in their sight so
that they may keep its whole form and all its
ordinances and do them.

12 This is the law of the temple: The whole
territory on the top of the mountain all around
shall be most holy. This is the law of the temple.

The Altar Restored

13 These are the measurements of the altar by
cubits[1] (the cubit is a cubit and a handbreadth):
The base shall be a cubit, and the width a cubit,
and its border by its edge all around shall be a
span.[2] And this shall be the height of the altar:
14 From the bottom on the ground even to the
lower ledge shall be two cubits, and the width
one cubit.[3] And from the lesser ledge even to
the greater ledge shall be four cubits, and the
width one cubit.[4] 15 So the altar shall be four
cubits. And from the altar and upward shall be
four horns. 16 The altar hearth shall be twelve
cubits long by twelve wide,[5] square in its four
corners. 17 The ledge shall be fourteen cubits[6]
long and fourteen wide in the four squares.
And the border about it shall be half a cubit.[7]
And its bottom shall be a cubit all around. And
its stairs shall face east.

18 He said to me: Son of man, thus says the
Lord God: These are the ordinances of the altar
in the day when they shall make it to offer
burnt offerings on it and to sprinkle blood on
it. 19 You shall give to the priests the Levites that
are of the seed of Zadok who approach Me to
minister to Me, says the Lord God, a young bull
as a sin offering. 20 You shall take of its blood
and put it on its four horns, and on the four
corners of the ledge and on the rim all around.
Thus you shall cleanse and purge it. 21 You shall
take the bull also of the sin offering, and it
shall be burned in the appointed place of the
temple, outside the sanctuary.

43:9 Eze 43:7
43:10 Eze 16:61
43:12 Eze 40:2
43:13 Ex 27:1–8
43:15 Ex 27:2
43:16 Ex 27:1
43:17 Ex 20:26
43:18 Ex 40:29
43:19 Eze 40:46
43:20 Lev 8:15
43:21 Ex 29:14
43:23 Ex 29:1
43:24 Lev 2:13
43:25 Lev 8:33
43:27 Lev 9:1
44:1 Eze 43:1
44:2 Eze 43:2–4
44:3 Eze 46:2
44:4 Eze 1:28
44:5 Eze 40:4
44:6 Eze 3:9
44:7 Lev 22:25
44:9 Eze 44:7

22 On the second day you shall offer a male
goat without blemish as a sin offering. And
they shall cleanse the altar as they cleansed it
with the bull. 23 When you have made an end
of cleansing it, you shall offer a young bull
without blemish and a ram out of the flock
without blemish. 24 You shall offer them be-
fore the Lord, and the priests shall cast salt on
them, and they shall offer them up as a burnt
offering to the Lord.

25 For seven days you shall prepare every day
a goat as a sin offering. They shall also prepare
a young bull and a ram out of the flock, with-
out blemish. 26 For seven days they shall purge
the altar and purify it. So they shall consecrate
it. 27 When they have completed the days, it
shall be that on the eighth day and forward,
the priests shall present your burnt offerings
and your peace offerings upon the altar. And I
will accept you, says the Lord God.

The East Gate for the Prince

44 Then he brought me back to the gate
of the outer sanctuary, which faces
east. And it was shut. 2 Then the Lord said
to me: This gate shall be shut; it shall not be
opened, and no man shall enter by it. Because
the Lord, the God of Israel, has entered by it,
therefore it shall be shut. 3 As for the prince, he
shall sit in it as prince to eat bread before the
Lord. He shall enter by the way of the vestibule
of the gate and shall go out by the same way.

4 Then he brought me by the way of the north
gate before the temple. And I looked, and the
glory of the Lord filled the house of the Lord,
and I fell upon my face.

5 The Lord said to me: Son of man, mark well,
and see with your eyes and hear with your
ears all that I say to you concerning all the
ordinances of the house of the Lord and all
its laws. And mark well those who may enter
the house, with all exits of the sanctuary. 6 You
shall say to the rebellious, even to the house
of Israel, Thus says the Lord God: O house of
Israel, let all your abominations suffice; 7 you
brought foreigners into My sanctuary, uncir-
cumcised in heart and uncircumcised in flesh,
to be in My sanctuary to pollute it, even My
house, when you offered My food, the fat and
the blood. For they have broken My covenant
because of all your abominations. 8 You have
not kept the charge of My holy things. But you
have set foreigners to keep charge of My sanc-
tuary. 9 Thus says the Lord God: No foreigner,
uncircumcised in heart nor uncircumcised in

[1] *13* About 21 inches, or 53 centimeters; and in vv. 14 and 17. [2] *13* About 11 inches, or 27 centimeters. [3] *14* About 3½ feet high and 1¾ feet wide, or 105 centimeters high and 53 centimeters wide. [4] *14* About 7 feet high and 1¾ feet wide, or 2.1 meters high and 53 centimeters wide. [5] *16* About 21 feet, or 6.4 meters. [6] *17* About 25 feet, or 7.4 meters. [7] *17* About 11 inches, or 27 centimeters.

flesh, shall enter into My sanctuary, of any for-
eigner who is among the sons of Israel.

Laws for the Priests

10 But the Levites who have gone far from Me
when Israel went astray, who went astray away
from Me after their idols, they shall bear the
punishment of their iniquity. 11 Yet they shall
be ministers in My sanctuary, having charge
at the gates of the house and ministering to
the house. They shall slay the burnt offering
and the sacrifice for the people, and they shall
stand before them to minister to them. 12 Be-
cause they ministered to them before their
idols and caused the house of Israel to fall
into iniquity, therefore I have lifted up My hand
against them, says the Lord God, that they shall
bear the punishment of their iniquity. 13 They
shall not come near to Me to do the office of
a priest to Me, nor to come near to any of My
holy things in the Most Holy Place. But they
shall bear their shame and their abominations
which they have committed. 14 But I will make
them keepers of the charge of the temple for
all its service and for all that shall be done in it.
15 But the Levitical priests, the sons of Zadok,
who kept the charge of My sanctuary when
the sons of Israel went astray from Me, they
shall come near to Me to minister to Me, and
they shall stand before Me to offer to Me the
fat and the blood, says the Lord God. 16 They
shall enter My sanctuary, and they shall come
near to My table to minister to Me, and they
shall keep My charge.
17 It shall come to pass that when they enter
at the gates of the inner court, they shall be
clothed with linen garments. And no wool shall
come upon them while they minister in the
gates of the inner court, and within. 18 They
shall have linen turbans on their heads and
shall have linen breeches on their loins. They
shall not gird themselves with *anything that
causes* sweat. 19 When they go out into the
outer court, even into the outer court to the
people, they shall put off their garments in
which they ministered and lay them in the
holy chambers, and they shall put on other
garments. And they shall not sanctify the peo-
ple with their garments.
20 Nor shall they shave their heads, nor suffer
their locks to grow long. They shall only trim
the hair of their heads. 21 Nor shall any priest
drink wine when they enter the inner court.
22 Nor shall they take for their wives a widow,
nor her who has been put away. But they shall
take maidens of the seed of the house of Israel,
or a widow who had a priest before. 23 They
shall teach My people the difference between
the holy and profane, and cause them to dis-
cern between the unclean and the clean.
24 In controversy they shall stand in judg-
ment. And they shall judge it according to My
judgments. And they shall keep My laws and
My statutes in all My assemblies. And they
shall hallow My Sabbaths.
25 They shall not go to a dead person to de-
file themselves. But for father, or for mother,
or for son, or for daughter, for brother, or for
sister that has had no husband, they may defile
themselves. 26 After he is cleansed, they shall
reckon to him seven days. 27 In the day that he
goes into the sanctuary, to the inner court, to
minister in the sanctuary, he shall offer his sin
offering, says the Lord God.
28 It shall be to them for an inheritance. I am
their inheritance. And you shall give them no
possession in Israel. I am their possession.
29 They shall eat the grain offering and the
sin offering and the guilt offering. And every
dedicated thing in Israel shall be theirs. 30 The
first of all the first fruits of all things and every
oblation of all of every sort of your oblations
shall be the priest's. You shall also give to the
priest the first of your dough to cause a bless-
ing to rest in your house. 31 The priests shall not
eat any bird or beast that has died naturally or
was torn to pieces.

The Holy District

45 Moreover, when you divide by lot the
land for inheritance, you shall offer an
allotment to the Lord, a holy portion of the
land. The length shall be the length of twen-
ty-five thousand cubits,[1] and the width shall be
twenty thousand.[2] It shall be holy throughout
its territory all around. 2 Of this there shall be
a square plot for the sanctuary, five hundred
by five hundred cubits,[3] with fifty cubits[4] for
an open space around it. 3 Of this measure
you shall measure the length of twenty-five
thousand cubits and the width of ten thou-
sand cubits.[5] And in it shall be the sanctuary
the Most Holy Place. 4 The holy portion of the
land shall be for the priests, the ministers of
the sanctuary, who shall come near to minister
to the Lord. And it shall be a place for their
houses and a holy place for the sanctuary. 5 An
area twenty-five thousand cubits in length and
ten thousand in width shall be for the Levites
the ministers of the temple, and for their pos
session cities in which to dwell.
6 You shall appoint the possession of the city
five thousand cubits[6] wide and twenty-five
thousand cubits long adjacent to the allotment
of the holy portion. It shall be for the whole
house of Israel.

44:10 Eze 48:11
44:11 Nu 16:9
44:12 2Ki 16:10–16
44:13 Nu 18:3
44:14 Nu 18:4
44:15 Eze 40:46
44:16 Eze 41:22
44:17 Rev 19:8
44:19 Lev 6:27
44:20 Nu 6:5
44:21 Lev 10:9
44:22 Lev 21:7
44:23 Eze 22:26
44:24 1Ch 23:4
44:27 Nu 6:9–11
44:28 Nu 18:20
44:29 Nu 18:14
44:30 Ne 10:35–37
44:31 Lev 22:8
45:1 Eze 48:29
45:2 Eze 42:16–20
45:3 Eze 48:10
45:5 Eze 48:13
45:6 Eze 48:15–18

[1] *1* About 8 miles, or 13 kilometers; and in vv. 3, 5, and 6. [2] *1* About 6½ miles, or 11 kilometers. [3] *2* About 875 feet, or 265 meters. [4] *2* About 88 feet, or 27 meters. [5] *3* About 3⅓ miles, or 5.3 kilometers. [6] *6* About 1⅔ miles, or 2.7 kilometers.

The Portion for the Prince

7 A portion shall be for the prince on the one
side and on the other side of the holy allotment
and property of the city, adjacent to the holy
allotment and the property of the city, from
the west side westward and from the east side
eastward. And the length shall correspond to
one of the *tribal* portions, from the west bor-
der to the east border. 8 In the land shall be
his possession in Israel. And My officials shall
no more oppress My people. And *the rest of*
the land they shall give to the house of Israel
according to their tribes.

Laws Governing the Prince

9 Thus says the Lord God: Let it suffice you of-
ficials of Israel. Remove violence and destruc-
tion, and execute justice and righteousness.
Take away your exactions from My people,
says the Lord God. 10 You shall have just bal-
ances and a just ephah[1] and a just bath.[2] 11 The
ephah and the bath shall be of one measure
so that the bath may contain the tenth part of
a homer,[3] and the ephah the tenth part of a
homer. Their measure shall be after the homer.
12 The shekel[4] shall be twenty gerahs.[5] Twenty
shekels, twenty-five shekels, and fifteen shek-
els shall be your mina.[6]
13 This is the offering that you shall offer: the
sixth part of an ephah[7] of a homer of wheat,
and you shall give the sixth part of an ephah[8]
of a homer of barley. 14 Concerning the ordi-
nance of oil that is the bath of oil, you shall
offer the tenth part of a bath[9] out of the kor,[10]
which is a homer or ten baths, for ten baths
are a homer. 15 And one lamb shall be out of
the flock, out of two hundred, out of the wa-
tering places of Israel, as a grain offering and
as a burnt offering and for peace offerings, to
make reconciliation for them, says the Lord
God. 16 All the people of the land shall give
this offering for the prince in Israel. 17 It shall
be the prince's part to give burnt offerings and
grain offerings and drink offerings in the feasts
and in the New Moons and in the Sabbaths, in
all solemnities of the house of Israel. He shall
prepare the sin offering and the grain offering
and the burnt offering and the peace offerings,
to make reconciliation for the house of Israel.

Observing the Feasts

18 Thus says the Lord God: In the first *month*,
on the first day of the month, you shall take
a young bull without blemish and cleanse the
sanctuary. 19 And the priest shall take some
of the blood of the sin offering and put it on
the doorposts of the temple and on the four
corners of the ledge of the altar and on the
gateposts of the inner court. 20 So you shall
do the seventh day of the month for everyone
who errs and for him who is naive. So you shall
make atonement for the temple.
21 In the first *month*, on the fourteenth day
of the month, you shall have the Passover, a
feast of seven days. Unleavened bread shall be
eaten. 22 On that day the prince shall prepare
for himself and for all the people of the land
a bull as a sin offering. 23 For seven days of
the feast he shall prepare a burnt offering to
the LORD, seven bulls and seven rams without
blemish daily for the seven days, and a male
of the goats daily as a sin offering. 24 He shall
prepare a grain offering of an ephah for a bull
and an ephah for a ram and a hin[15] of oil for
an ephah.
25 In the seventh *month*, on the fifteenth day
of the month, he shall do the like in the feast
of the seven days, according to the sin offering,
according to the burnt offering, and according
to the grain offering, and according to the oil.

45:7 Eze 48:21
45:8 Eze 46:18
45:9 Jer 22:3
45:10 Am 8:4–6
45:11 Isa 5:10
45:12 Ex 30:13
45:15 Lev 1:4
45:17 2Ch 31:3
45:18 Lev 16:16
45:19 Eze 43:20
....
45:21 Lev 23:5–8
45:22 Lev 4:14
45:23 Lev 23:8
45:24 Eze 46:5–7
45:25 Nu 29:12–38
46:1 Isa 66:23
46:2 Eze 44:3
46:3 Lk 1:10
46:4 Eze 45:17
46:5 Eze 45:24
46:7 Eze 46:5
46:8 Eze 46:2

The Prince and the Feasts

46 Thus says the Lord God: The gate of
the inner court that faces east shall be
shut the six working days. But on the Sabbath
it shall be opened, and in the day of the New
Moon it shall be opened. 2 The prince shall en-
ter by the way of the vestibule of that gate from
outside, and shall stand by the post of the gate,
and the priests shall prepare his burnt offering
and his peace offerings, and he shall worship
at the threshold of the gate. Then he shall go
out. But the gate shall not be shut until the
evening. 3 Likewise the people of the land shall
worship at the door of this gate before the LORD
in the Sabbaths and in the New Moons. 4 The
burnt offering that the prince shall offer to the
LORD in the Sabbath day shall be six lambs
without blemish and a ram without blemish.
5 The grain offering shall be an ephah[16] for a
ram and the grain offering for the lambs as
he shall be able to give and a hin[17] of oil to an
ephah. 6 In the day of the New Moon *it shall
be* a young bull without blemish and six lambs
and a ram. They shall be without blemish. 7 He
shall prepare a grain offering, an ephah[18] for a
bull and an ephah for a ram, and for the lambs
according as his hand shall attain to, and a hin
of oil to an ephah. 8 When the prince enters,
he shall go in by the way of the vestibule of
that gate, and he shall go out the same way.

[1] *10* An ephah was a dry measure of about ⅗ bushel, or 22 liters.
[2] *10* A bath was a liquid measure of about 6 gallons, or 22 liters.
[3] *11* In dry measure, six bushels or 220 liters; in liquid measure, 60 gallons or 220 liters.
[4] *12* A shekel weighed about ⅖ ounce, or 12 grams.
[5] *12* Weighs 1/20 of a shekel.
[6] *12* Sixty shekels equals about 1½ pounds, or 690 grams. The common mina was 50 shekels.
[7] *13* Likely about 6 pounds, or 2.7 kilograms.
[8] *13* Likely about 5 pounds, or 2.3 kilograms.
[9] *14* About 2½ quarts, or 2.2 liters.
[10] *14* Equals a homer in liquid measure, 60 gallons or 220 liters.
[15] *24* About 1 gallon, or 3.8 liters.
[16] *5* Likely about 35 pounds, or 16 kilograms.
[17] *5* About 1 gallon, or 3.8 liters.
[18] *7* Likely about 35 pounds, or 16 kilograms.

9 But when the people of the land shall come before the LORD in the solemn feasts, he who enters by the way of the north gate to worship shall go out by way of the south gate. And he who enters by the way of the south gate shall go out by way of the north gate. He shall not return by way of the gate by which he entered, but shall go out the opposite gate. 10 The prince shall be in their midst. When they enter, he shall enter; and when they go out, he shall go out. 11 At the feasts and the appointed festivals the grain offering shall be an ephah[1] for a bull, and an ephah for a ram, and with the lambs as much as he is able to give, together with a hin of oil for an ephah.

12 Now when the prince prepares a voluntary burnt offering or voluntary peace offering to the LORD, the gate facing east shall be opened for him; and he shall prepare his burnt offering and his peace offerings as he did on the Sabbath day. Then he shall go out. And after he goes out, the gate shall be shut.

13 You shall daily prepare a burnt offering to the LORD of a lamb of the first year without blemish. You shall prepare it every morning. 14 You shall prepare a grain offering for it every morning, the sixth part of an ephah,[2] and the third part of a hin[3] of oil to temper with the fine flour, a grain offering continually by a perpetual ordinance to the LORD. 15 Thus they shall prepare the lamb and the grain offering and the oil every morning as a continual burnt offering.

Inheritance Laws for the Prince

16 Thus says the Lord GOD: If the prince gives a gift out of his inheritance to any of his sons, it will belong to his sons. It is their possession by inheritance. 17 But if he gives a gift out of his inheritance to one of his servants, it will be his until the year of liberty. Then it will revert to the prince. His inheritance will be only his sons. It will belong to them. 18 Moreover the prince shall not take of the people's inheritance by oppression to thrust them out of their possession. But he shall give his sons inheritance out of his own possession so that My people not be scattered, every man from his possession.

Preparations for the Offerings

19 Then he brought me through the entrance, which was at the side of the gate, into the holy chambers of the priests which face toward the north. And there was a place at the extreme westward end of them. 20 Then he said to me, "This is the place where the priests shall boil the guilt offering and the sin offering, and where they shall bake the grain offering so that they not bear them out into the outer court, to sanctify the people."

21 Then he brought me out into the outer court and caused me to pass by the four corners of the court. And in every corner of the court *there was* a court. 22 In the four corners of the court there were courts joined of forty cubits long and thirty wide.[4] These four corners were of one measurement. 23 There was a row of *masonry* all around in them, all around the four of them; and it was made with hearths at the bottom of the rows all around. 24 Then he said to me, "These are the boiling places where the ministers of the temple shall boil the sacrifices of the people."

The River Flowing From the Temple

47 Then he brought me back to the door of the temple; and water was flowing out from under the threshold of the temple eastward, for the front of the temple faced east; the water was flowing down from under from the right side of the temple, south of the altar. 2 Then he brought me out by way of the north gate, and led me around on the outside to the outer gate that faces east; and the water was coming out on the south side.

3 When the man who had the line in his hand went eastward, he measured a thousand cubits, and he brought me through the water; the water reached the ankles. 4 Again he measured a thousand and brought me through the water. The water reached the knees. Again he measured a thousand and brought me through *the water*. The water *reached* the loins. 5 Afterward he measured a thousand. And it was a river that I could not pass over, for the water had risen, *enough* water to swim in, a river that could not be passed over. 6 He said to me, "Son of man, have you seen this?"

Then he brought me and caused me to return to the brink of the river. 7 When I had returned I saw on the bank of the river very many trees on the one side and on the other. 8 Then he said to me, "This water flows toward the eastern region and goes down into the valley, and enters the sea. When it flows into the sea, the water will become fresh. 9 Every living creature that swarms, wherever the rivers go, will live. And there shall be a very great multitude of fish, because these waters shall come there and the others become fresh. Thus everything shall live wherever the river comes. 10 It shall come to pass that the fishermen shall stand upon it. From En Gedi even to En Eglaim there shall be a place to spread out nets. Their fish shall be according to their kinds, as the fish of the *Mediterranean* Sea, exceedingly many. 11 But its miry places and its marshes shall not

46:10 Ps 42:4
46:11 Eze 46:5
46:12 Eze 45:17
46:13 Isa 50:4
46:14 Nu 28:5
46:16 2Ch 21:3
46:17 Lev 25:10
46:18 Eze 45:8
46:19 Eze 42:9
46:20 2Ch 35:13
....
46:24 Eze 46:20
47:1 Ps 46:4
47:3 Eze 40:3
47:5 Isa 11:9
47:7 Eze 47:12
47:8 Dt 3:17
47:10 Nu 34:6
47:11 Dt 29:23

[1] *11* Likely about 35 pounds, or 16 kilograms. [2] *14* Likely about 6 pounds, or 2.7 kilograms. [3] *14* About 1½ quarts, or 1.3 liters.
[4] *22* About 70 feet long and 53 feet wide, or 21 meters long and 16 meters wide.

be healed. They shall be given to salt. 12 By the river upon its bank, on this side and on that side, shall grow all *kinds of* trees for food, whose leaf shall not fade nor shall its fruit fail. They shall bring forth fruit according to their months, because their water issues out of the sanctuary. And their fruit shall be for food and their leaves for medicine."

The Borders of the Land

13 Thus says the Lord God: This shall be the border by which you shall divide the land for an inheritance according to the twelve tribes of Israel. Joseph *shall have two* portions. 14 You shall divide it for an inheritance, one as equally as another. For I lifted up My hand to give it to your fathers, and this land shall fall to you for inheritance.

15 This shall be the border of the land on the north: from the *Mediterranean* Sea by the way of Hethlon as men go to Zedad, 16 Hamath, Berothah, Sibraim (which lies between the border of Damascus and the border of Hamath), to Hazar Hattikon, which is on the border of Hauran. 17 The border from the sea shall be Hazar Enan at the border of Damascus, and on the north northward is the border of Hamath. And this is the north side.

18 The east side, from Hauran and from Damascus and from Gilead and the land of Israel, shall be the Jordan. You shall measure from the northern border to the eastern sea. And this is the east side.

19 The south side, toward the Negev, shall run from Tamar even to the waters of Meribah Kadesh, from there along the brook *of Egypt* to the *Mediterranean* Sea. This shall be the south side, toward the Negev.

20 The west side also shall be the *Mediterranean* Sea from the *southern* border to a point opposite Lebo Hamath. This is the west side.

21 So you shall divide this land among you according to the tribes of Israel. 22 It shall come to pass that you shall divide it by lot for an inheritance among yourselves and among the aliens who sojourn among you, who shall bear sons among you. And they shall be to you as born in the country among the sons of Israel. They shall have inheritance with you among the tribes of Israel. 23 It shall come to pass that in whatever tribe the alien sojourns, there you shall give him his inheritance, says the Lord God.

The Division of the Land

48 Now these are the names of the tribes: From the north end beside the way of Hethlon as one goes to Lebo Hamath, *as far as* Hazar Enan at the border of Damascus northward beside Hamath going from east to west, Dan, one portion;

2 by the border of Dan from the east side to the west side, a portion for Asher;

3 by the border of Asher from the east side even to the west side, a portion for Naphtali;

4 by the border of Naphtali from the east side to the west side, a portion for Manasseh;

5 by the border of Manasseh from the east side to the west side, a portion for Ephraim;

47:12 Rev 22:2
47:13 Ge 48:5
47:14 Ge 12:7
47:15 Nu 34:8
47:16 Nu 13:21
47:17 Eze 48:1
47:18 Ge 13:10
47:19 Dt 32:51
47:22 Eph 3:6
48:1 Eze 47:15–17
48:2 Jos 19:24–31
48:3 Jos 19:32–39
48:4 Jos 17:1–11
48:5 Jos 17:8–10

SPIRITLED WOMAN

COUNSEL FROM THE SPIRIT BASICS

Jehovah Shammah

The circumference shall be eighteen thousand cubits. And the name of the city from that day shall be, The Lord Is There.

—Ezekiel 48:35

The name *Jehovah Shammah* speaks not just of God's omnipresence but also His proximity to every question at hand. The above passage in Ezekiel speaks of a future city that would be named "The Lord Is There" to represent that the presence of God would always be in that city. However, centuries later Augustine took the term *City of God* to represent not a place but a people. He contrasted the City of God upon the earth with the City of Man to express the ways of God versus the ways of the world. Thus, it was the people who welcomed and embraced the presence of God versus those who rejected it and wanted to go their own way.

If we would but develop a sense of the presence of God with us at all times, wherever we go, we would in fact become radical agents of God's change. Certainly most of us know what it is like to be in church and feel the presence of God, but what about in our workplaces, in our homes, or when walking through our communities? God is no less there than He is at church. Perhaps it is not what God is doing that needs to change, but what we are doing. This is certainly one area where we have to take God at His name.

Cindy Trimm

6 by the border of Ephraim from the east side
even to the west side, a portion for Reuben;
7 by the border of Reuben from the east side
to the west side, a portion for Judah;
8 by the border of Judah from the east side to
the west side shall be the allotment which you
shall set apart, twenty-five thousand cubits[1] in
width and in length as one of the other parts,
from the east side to the west side. And the
sanctuary shall be in the middle of it.
9 The allotment that you shall set apart to
the LORD shall be twenty-five thousand cubits
in length, and ten thousand[2] in width. 10 For
them, even for the priests, shall be this holy
allotment, toward the north twenty-five thou-
sand cubits in length and toward the west
ten thousand in width and toward the east
ten thousand in width and toward the south
twenty-five thousand cubits in length. And the
sanctuary of the LORD shall be in its midst. 11 It
shall be for the priests who are sanctified of
the sons of Zadok, who have kept My charge,
who did not go astray when the sons of Isra-
el went astray as the Levites went astray. 12 It
shall be an allotment to them, a thing most
holy, the allotment of the land by the border
of the Levites.
13 Opposite the border of the priests, the
Levites shall have twenty-five thousand cubits
in length and ten thousand in width. All the
length shall be twenty-five thousand cubits,
and the width ten thousand. 14 They shall not
sell of it or exchange or alienate this choice
portion of the land, for it is holy to the LORD.
15 The five thousand cubits[3] in width that re-
main and the twenty-five thousand in length
shall be for common use for the city, for dwell-
ings and for suburbs. And the city shall be in
the midst. 16 These shall be its measurements:
the north side four thousand five hundred cu-
bits;[4] and the south side four thousand five
hundred cubits; and on the east side four thou-
sand five hundred cubits; and the west side
four thousand five hundred cubits. 17 The sub-
urbs of the city shall be: to the north, two hun-
dred and fifty cubits;[5] to the south, two hun-
dred and fifty cubits; to the east, two hundred
and fifty cubits; and to the west, two hundred
and fifty cubits. 18 The rest in length alongside
the holy portion shall be ten thousand cubits
eastward and ten thousand westward. And it
shall be alongside the holy portion. And its
increase shall be for food to those who serve
the city. 19 Those who serve the city, out of
all the tribes of Israel, shall cultivate it. 20 All
the allotment shall be twenty-five thousand
by twenty-five thousand cubits. You shall set
apart the holy allotment foursquare, with the
property of the city.
21 The rest shall belong to the prince, on both
sides of the holy allotment and the city prop-
erty, next to the twenty-five thousand cubits of
the allotment toward the eastern border, and
westward next to the twenty-five thousand to-
ward the western border, next to the portions
for the prince. And the holy allotment and the
sanctuary of the temple shall be in its midst.
22 Moreover excluding the property of the Lev-
ites and the property of the city, being in the
midst of that which is the prince's, everything
between the border of Judah and the border
of Benjamin shall be for the prince.
23 As for the rest of the tribes, from the east
side to the west side, Benjamin *shall have* one
portion.
24 By the border of Benjamin from the east
side to the west side, Simeon *shall have* one
portion.
25 By the border of Simeon from the east
side to the west side, Issachar *shall have* one
portion.
26 By the border of Issachar from the east
side to the west side, Zebulun *shall have* one
portion.
27 By the border of Zebulun from the east side
to the west side, Gad *shall have* one portion.
28 By the border of Gad at the south side
southward the border shall be even from Tam-
ar to the waters of Meribah Kadesh and to the
brook of *Egypt* toward the *Mediterranean* Sea.
29 This is the land which you shall divide by
lot to the tribes of Israel for inheritance, and
these are their portions, says the Lord GOD.

The Gates of the New City

30 These are the exits of the city on the north
side, four thousand five hundred cubits by
measurement. 31 The gates of the city shall be
named after the tribes of Israel, three gates
northward: one gate of Reuben, one gate of
Judah, one gate of Levi.
32 At the east side, four thousand five hundred
cubits, shall be three gates: one gate of Joseph,
one gate of Benjamin, one gate of Dan.
33 At the south side, four thousand five hun-
dred cubits[6] by measurement, shall be three
gates: one gate of Simeon, one gate of Is-
sachar, one gate of Zebulun.
34 At the west side, four thousand five hun-
dred cubits, shall be three gates: one gate of
Gad, one gate of Asher, one gate of Naphtali.
35 The circumference *shall be* eighteen thou-
sand cubits.[7]
And the name of the city from that day *shall
be*, The LORD Is There.

48:6 Jos 13:15–21
48:7 Jos 15:1–63
48:10 Eze 45:4
48:11 Eze 40:46
48:14 Lev 27:28
48:15 Eze 42:20
48:16 Rev 21:16
....
48:21 Eze 48:22
48:23 Jos 18:21–28
48:24 Jos 19:1–9
48:25 Jos 19:17–23
48:26 Jos 19:10–16
48:27 Jos 13:24–28
48:30 Eze 48:16
48:31 Rev 21:12–13
48:35 Jer 3:17

[1] *8* About 8 miles, or 13 kilometers; and in vv. 9, 10, 13, 15, 20, and 21. [2] *9* About 3⅓ miles, or 5.3 kilometers; and in vv. 10, 13, and 18. [3] *15* About 1⅔ miles, or 2.7 kilometers. [4] *16* About 1½ miles, or 2.4 kilometers; and in vv. 30, 32, 33, and 34. [5] *17* About 440 feet, or 135 meters. [6] *33* About 1½ miles, or 2.4 kilometers. [7] *35* About 6 miles, or 9.5 kilometers.

Author: Traditionally Daniel

Written: Between 540 and 530 BC

Themes: God's Sovereignty Over Human Affairs, Dreams

DANIEL

Dear SpiritLed Woman,

Daniel is one of many biblical examples of men and women who loved God but still had to walk through difficult times. When disaster strikes or you find yourself going through hard times, the Holy Spirit can show you what there is inside your heart that must be dealt with and how much you need God. Whether it's a personal situation or a broader disaster that affects you, the difficulty can be overwhelming.

In such circumstances you can believe that God's plan for you is good even when it doesn't appear to be so at first. God knows the best path for you to take. The more you get yourself out of the way and let Him take over, the more you become the SpiritLed woman He designed you to be. If you're in a tough situation right now, don't let your faith fail. God is calling those who know Him to do great exploits. Surrender to the process, and lay hold of your destiny!

Joy F. Strang

SPIRITLED WOMAN

COUNSEL FROM THE SPIRIT BASICS

God's Care in a Perilous Situation

Daniel 1 gives an excellent example of God's care for His people when they are in perilous situations. Daniel and three of his friends—Shadrach, Meshach, and Abednego—purposed in their hearts to obey God. The Bible says, "Daniel purposed in his heart that he would not defile himself with the portion of the king's food, nor with the wine which he drank. Therefore he requested of the master of the officials that he might not defile himself" (v. 8).

Daniel said to the chief of staff, "Please test your servants for ten days, and let them give us vegetables to eat and water to drink. Then let our countenances be looked upon before you, and the countenance of the youths who eat of the portion of the king's food. And as you see, deal with your servants" (vv. 12–13).

The Bible says these four young men looked *better* at the end of the ten days than the other candidates who ate the king's food! God supernaturally sustained them because they chose to believe Him. And as a result of their obedience under pressure, the Bible says God rewarded them with knowledge and wisdom above everyone in the kingdom (vv. 15–20).

Karen Jensen Salisbury

Daniel Taken to Babylon

1 In the third year of the reign of Jehoiakim king of Judah, Nebuchadnezzar king of Babylon came to Jerusalem and besieged it. 2 The Lord gave Jehoiakim king of Judah into his hand, with part of the vessels of the house of God, and he carried them into the land of Shinar to the house of his god. And he brought the vessels into the treasure house of his god.

3 The king spoke to Ashpenaz the master of his officials that he should bring some of the sons of Israel and some of the king's descendants and some of the nobles, 4 youths in whom was no blemish, who were handsome and skillful in every *branch of* wisdom and gifted with understanding and discerning knowledge, and such as had ability in them to serve in the king's palace, and whom they might teach the learning and the language of the Chaldeans. 5 The king appointed them a daily provision of the king's food and of the wine which he drank. They were to be educated for three years, that at the end of it they might serve before the king.

6 Now among them were of the sons of Judah: Daniel, Hananiah, Mishael, and Azariah, 7 to whom the commander of the officials gave names. And he gave to Daniel the name of Belteshazzar; to Hananiah, Shadrach; to Mishael, Meshach; and to Azariah, Abednego.

8 But Daniel purposed in his heart that he would not defile himself with the portion of the king's food, nor with the wine which he drank. Therefore he requested of the master of the officials that he might not defile himself. 9 Now God had brought Daniel into favor and compassion with the master of the officials. 10 The master of the officials said to Daniel, "I fear my lord the king who has appointed your food and your drink. For why should he see your faces worse-looking than the youths who are your age? Then you would endanger my head before the king."

11 Then Daniel said to the steward, whom the master of the officials had set over Daniel, Hananiah, Mishael, and Azariah, 12 "Please test your servants for ten days, and let them give us vegetables to eat and water to drink. 13 Then let our countenances be looked upon before you, and the countenance of the youths who eat of the portion of the king's food. And as you see, deal with your servants." 14 So he consented to them in this matter and tested them for ten days.

15 At the end of ten days their countenances appeared fairer and fatter than all the youths who ate the portion of the king's food. 16 Thus the guard continued to take away the portion of their food and the wine that they were to drink, and gave them vegetables.

17 As for these four youths, God gave them knowledge and skill in every *branch of* learning and wisdom. And Daniel had understanding in all *kinds of* visions and dreams.

18 Now at the end of the days that the king had set for them to be brought in, the master of the officials brought them in before Nebuchadnezzar. 19 The king spoke with them, and, among them all, none was found like Daniel, Hananiah, Mishael, and Azariah. Therefore they served before the king. 20 In all matters

1:1 2Ki 24:1–2
1:2 2Ch 36:7
1:3 Isa 39:7

1:4 2Sa 14:25
1:5 Da 1:19
1:6 Eze 14:14
1:7 Da 2:49
1:8 Eze 4:13–14
1:9 Ge 39:21
1:12 Da 1:16
1:15 Ex 23:25
1:16 Da 1:12
1:17 Da 2:23
1:19 Ge 41:46

of wisdom and understanding which the king
inquired of them, he found them ten times
better than all the magicians and astrologers
that were in all his realm.
21 Daniel continued even to the first year of
King Cyrus.

Nebuchadnezzar's Dream

2 And in the second year of the reign of
Nebuchadnezzar, Nebuchadnezzar had
dreams, and his spirit was troubled and his
sleep left him. 2 Then the king gave the com-
mand to call the magicians and the astrolo-
gers and the sorcerers and the Chaldeans to
tell the king his dreams. So they came and
stood before the king. 3 The king said to them,
"I have had a dream, and my spirit is anxious
to understand the dream."
4 Then the Chaldeans spoke to the king in Ar-
amaic,[1] "O king, live forever. Tell your servants
the dream, and we will tell the interpretation."
5 The king answered and said to the Chal-
deans, "The command from me is firm: If you
will not make known to me the dream with its
interpretation, you shall be cut in pieces and
your houses shall be made a dunghill. 6 But if
you tell the dream and its interpretation, you
shall receive from me gifts and rewards and
great honor. Therefore tell me the dream and
its interpretation."
7 They answered again and said, "Let the king
tell his servants the dream, and we will tell the
interpretation."
8 The king answered and said, "I know of
certainty that you are bargaining for time, be-
cause you see that the command from me is
firm: 9 If you will not make known to me the
dream, there is but one decree for you. For you
have agreed to speak lying and corrupt words
before me until the circumstance is changed.
Therefore tell me the dream so that I know that
you can tell me its interpretation."
10 The Chaldeans answered before the king
and said, "There is not a man on the earth
who can tell the king's matter, inasmuch as no
great king or ruler has ever asked such things
of any magician or astrologer or Chaldean.
11 Also, it is a rare thing that the king requires,
and there is no one else who can tell it before
the king, except the gods whose dwelling is
not with flesh."
12 For this cause the king was angry and very
furious, and commanded to destroy all the
wise men of Babylon. 13 Therefore the decree
went out that the wise men should be slain.
And they sought for Daniel and his compan-
ons to be slain.
14 Then Daniel answered with discretion and
wisdom to Arioch the captain of the king's

1:21 Da 6:28
2:1 Est 6:1
2:2 Da 1:20
2:4 Da 3:9
2:5 Ezr 6:11
2:6 Da 5:7
2:7 Da 2:4
2:9 Est 4:11
2:11 Da 5:11
2:12 Da 3:13
2:13 Da 1:19–20
2:14 Ge 37:36
....
2:18 Isa 37:4
2:19 Nu 12:6
2:20 Ps 113:2
2:21 Da 7:25
2:22 Job 12:22
2:23 Ex 3:15
2:24 Ac 27:24
2:25 Da 1:6

guard, who had gone out to kill the wise men
of Babylon. 15 He answered and said to Arioch
the king's captain, "Why is the decree from
the king so urgent?" Then Arioch made the
thing known to Daniel. 16 Then Daniel went
in and desired of the king that he would give
him time in order that he could tell the king
the interpretation.
17 Then Daniel went to his house and made
the thing known to Hananiah, Mishael, and
Azariah, his companions, 18 so that they might
ask for compassion from the God of heaven
concerning this secret, so that Daniel and his
companions might not perish with the rest of
the wise men of Babylon.

God is the only one who can change my times and seasons (Da 2:20–22).

God Reveals Nebuchadnezzar's Dream

19 Then the secret was revealed to Daniel in
a night vision. Then Daniel blessed the God of
heaven. 20 Daniel answered and said:

"Blessed be the name of God forever and
ever,
for wisdom and might are His.
21 It is He who changes the times and the
seasons;
He removes kings and sets up kings;
He gives wisdom to the wise
and knowledge to those who know
understanding.
22 He reveals the deep and secret things;
He knows what is in the darkness,
and the light dwells with Him.
23 I thank and praise You, O God of my
fathers;
for You have given me wisdom and
might,
and have made known to me now what we
asked of You,
for You have made known to us the
king's matter."

Daniel Interprets the Dream

24 Therefore Daniel went in to Arioch, whom
the king had ordained to destroy the wise men
of Babylon. He went and said to him: "Do not
destroy the wise men of Babylon. Bring me
in before the king, and I will tell the king the
interpretation."
25 Then in haste Arioch brought Daniel before
the king and said thus to him, "I have found a
man of the captives of Judah who can make
known to the king the interpretation."

[1] 4 2:4–7:28 is originally from the Aramaic language.

WOMAN OF THE SPIRIT

Putting Off Encumbrances

What is it that possesses your thoughts as you go through the day? What is it that takes you out of prayerfulness? Whatever it is, perhaps that is the thing you should be fasting from, even more than food!

Prayer is not just a place of laying our petitions before heaven and lifting up God's holy name in praise and worship. It is also a place of being refined and broken and remolded. It is where we come before the Lord to be pruned of the habits, desires, and ambitions that would hinder all God has for us. It is the furnace where the impurities are refined out of the gold of our lives.

Through fasting, we deny the natural world's domination over us and amplify our allegiance to God, who must be worshipped in spirit and in truth. After all, humanity first fell because we gave in to a physical hunger—because Adam and Eve couldn't resist eating a natural food that appealed to their physical eyes, even if it meant breaking a supernatural commandment. The first temptation of Jesus was that He should break His fast and turn stones into bread. Like Him, we are to deny the power of physical food to distract us from banqueting on God's Word. This is the starting place for resisting the other temptation Jesus would face—twisting the Word of God for His own glory or building His own kingdom rather than His Father's (Mt 4:1–11).

Fasting is also meant to lead to loving action. Jesus fasted to gain the strength to begin His ministry upon the earth. Paul fasted for the supernatural revelation that would deliver the Gentiles. It is a disciplining of self in preparation for doing the work and will of God.

> Do you not know that all those who run in a race run, but one receives the prize? So run, that you may obtain it. Everyone who strives for the prize exercises self-control in all things. Now they do it to obtain a corruptible crown, but we an incorruptible one. So, therefore, I run, not with uncertainty. So I fight, not as one who beats the air. But I bring and keep my body under subjection, lest when preaching to others I myself should be disqualified.
>
> —1 Corinthians 9:24–27

Fasting is thus a part of every life hungry for more of God. It is not to be an empty practice aimed only at increasing our own willpower, for what is willpower if it is not set to work in establishing God's kingdom? What is faith if it is not expressed in love? Great faith is only expressed in great works—and great works are defined only by the love they express. So just as with our prayers, there is to be an aim and a purpose to our fasting—namely love.

Fasting is the putting away of distractions and entangling habits so that we can be freer to work in love. Look at the example left to us by Daniel, Hananiah, Mishael, and Azariah (Da 1). Captured as children and taken to Babylon, they were selected for a special program by King Nebuchadnezzar. They were to be educated in the culture and religion of the Babylonians and become servants in the king's house. As part of their daily provision they would be given the same delicacies as the king received at his table, many of which violated Hebrew dietary laws. To keep themselves pure, these four Hebrew youths fasted, eating only vegetables and water. Upon a challenge that they would not be as healthy as the other servants because of their restricted diets, after a ten-day test period "their countenances appeared fairer and fatter than all the youths who ate the portion of the king's food" (Da 1:15).

Yet not only were these youths healthier, but also as they grew up living this fasted lifestyle, their spiritual power to interpret dreams and visions and to withstand persecution was like no other person in the Old Testament. When Nebuchadnezzar had a prophetic dream, not only could they tell him the meaning of the dream, but they also knew what the dream was without being told (Da 2). Some of the most profound prophecies of the Second Coming of Jesus Christ were given to Daniel for him to record.

Of all the stories of the Bible, Daniel and his friends were among those who showed the purest character and integrity. Nothing negative is recorded of Daniel, which is something that cannot be said for anyone else in the Bible except Jesus and John the Baptist. In Ezekiel 14, when the greatest intercessors of all time are mentioned, Daniel is prominent on the list alongside Noah and Job (vv. 14, 20). It is quite possible the three Hebrew children might have died in the fiery furnace of Nebuchadnezzar had they not had the spiritual power obtained through a lifetime of devotion marked by regular fasting (Da 3:19–25).

If your first thought in kneeling down to pray is that you need to go get something to eat before you start, that you need to check your e-mails or text messages, or that you need to look up something on the Internet, then you may have struck upon the very thing you should fast for a few days or a few weeks. Replace the time you would have spent on that activity with prayer. Then see what happens.

I believe that as you do this, your faith will be renewed. You will find your "first love" for God being rejuvenated, and you will step further into the life God has been trying to give you since you first gave Him your heart. It will begin stretching what you can trust God for and what you can accomplish in Him.

Cindy Trimm

26 The king answered and said to Daniel, whose name was Belteshazzar, "Are you able to make known to me the dream which I have seen, and its interpretation?"

27 Daniel answered in the presence of the king and said, "The secret which the king has demanded, the wise men, the astrologers, the magicians, and the soothsayers cannot tell the king. 28 But there is a God in heaven who reveals secrets and makes known to King Nebuchadnezzar what shall be in the latter days. Your dream and the visions of your head upon your bed are these:

29 "As for you, O king, your thoughts came into your mind upon your bed about what would come to pass hereafter, and He who reveals secrets makes known to you what shall come to pass. 30 But as for me, this secret is not revealed to me for any wisdom that I have more than any living man, but for the purpose of making known the interpretation to the king, and that you might understand the thoughts of your heart.

31 "You, O king, were watching, and there was a great image. This great image, whose brightness was excellent, stood before you. And its form was awesome. 32 This image's head was of fine gold, its breast and its arms of silver, its belly and its thighs of bronze, 33 its legs of iron, its feet partly of iron and partly of clay. 34 You watched until a stone was cut out without hands which struck the image upon its feet, which were of iron and clay, and broke them to pieces. 35 Then the iron, the clay, the bronze, the silver, and the gold were broken to pieces together, and became like the chaff of the summer threshing floors. And the wind carried them away so that not a trace of them was found. But the stone that struck the image became a great mountain and filled the whole earth.

36 "This was the dream. Now we will tell its interpretation before the king. 37 You, O king, are the king of kings. For the God of heaven has given you a kingdom, power, and strength, and glory. 38 Wherever the sons of men dwell, or the animals of the field, or the fowl of the heavens, He has given them into your hand and has made you ruler over them all. You are the head of gold.

39 "After you, another kingdom inferior to you shall arise, and a third kingdom of bronze, which shall rule over all the earth. 40 And the fourth kingdom shall be strong as iron, for iron breaks in pieces and shatters everything; and like iron that crushes, it shall crush and shatter all these. 41 As you saw the feet and toes, partly of potters' clay and partly of iron, the kingdom shall be divided. But there shall be in it some of the strength of the iron, inasmuch as you saw the iron mixed with miry clay. 42 As the toes of the feet were partly of iron and partly of clay, so the kingdom shall be partly strong and partly broken. 43 Whereas you saw iron mixed with miry clay, they shall mingle themselves with the seed of men, but they shall not cleave to one another, even as iron does not mix with clay.

44 "In the days of these kings the God of heaven shall set up a kingdom which shall never be destroyed. And the kingdom shall not be left to another people, but it shall break in pieces and consume all these kingdoms, and it shall stand forever. 45 Inasmuch as you saw that the stone was cut out of the mountain without hands and that it broke in pieces the iron, the bronze, the clay, the silver, and the gold, the great God has made known to the king what shall come to pass hereafter. And the dream is certain, and its interpretation sure."

The Promotion of Daniel

46 Then King Nebuchadnezzar fell upon his face and did homage to Daniel, and commanded that they should present an offering and sweet incense to him. 47 The king answered Daniel and said, "Truly your God is a God of gods, and a Lord of kings, and a revealer of secrets, since you could reveal this secret."

48 Then the king advanced Daniel and gave him many great gifts, and made him ruler over the whole province of Babylon and chief of the governors over all the wise men of Babylon. 49 Then Daniel requested of the king, and he set Shadrach, Meshach, and Abednego over the affairs of the province of Babylon. But Daniel sat at the court of the king.

The Image of Gold

3 Nebuchadnezzar the king made an image of gold, whose height was sixty cubits and its width six cubits.[1] He set it up in the plain of Dura in the province of Babylon. 2 Then Nebuchadnezzar the king sent to gather together the officials, the governors, and the captains, the judges, the treasurers, the counselors, the sheriffs, and all the rulers of the provinces to come to the dedication of the image which Nebuchadnezzar the king had set up. 3 Then the officials, the governors, and captains, the judges, the treasurers, the counselors, the sheriffs, and all the rulers of the provinces were gathered together to the dedication of the image that Nebuchadnezzar the king had set up, and they stood before the image that Nebuchadnezzar had set up.

2:26 Da 1:7
2:28 Da 10:14
2:29 Da 2:47
2:30 Ge 41:16
2:31 Hab 1:7
2:34 Da 8:25
2:35 Ps 37:10
2:37 Eze 26:7
2:38 Da 4:21–22
2:39 Da 2:32
2:40 Da 7:7
2:44 Isa 60:12
2:45 Isa 28:16
2:46 Ac 10:25
2:47 Dt 10:17
2:48 Da 2:6
2:49 Est 2:19
3:1 Isa 46:6
3:2 Da 3:27

1 1 About 90 feet high and 9 feet wide, or 27 meters high and 2.7 meters wide.

4 Then a herald cried aloud: "To you it is commanded, O peoples, nations, and languages, 5 that at the time you hear the sound of the cornet, flute, harp, sackbut, psaltery, dulcimer, and all kinds of music, you should fall down and worship the golden image that Nebuchadnezzar the king has set up. 6 And whoever does not fall down and worship shall the same hour be cast into the midst of a burning fiery furnace."

7 Therefore at that time, when all the people heard the sound of the cornet, flute, harp, sackbut, psaltery, and all kinds of music, all the peoples, the nations, and the languages fell down and worshipped the golden image that Nebuchadnezzar the king had set up.

The Fiery Furnace

8 Therefore at that time certain Chaldeans came near and accused the Jews. 9 They spoke and said to King Nebuchadnezzar, "O king, live forever. 10 You, O king, have made a decree, that every man who hears the sound of the cornet, flute, harp, sackbut, psaltery, and dulcimer, and all kinds of music should fall down and worship the golden image. 11 And whoever does not fall down and worship should be cast into the midst of a burning fiery furnace. 12 There are certain Jews whom you have set over the affairs of the province of Babylon: Shadrach, Meshach, and Abednego. These men, O king, have not regarded you. They do not serve your gods or worship the golden image which you have set up."

13 Then Nebuchadnezzar in his rage and fury commanded Shadrach, Meshach, and Abednego be brought. Then they brought these men before the king. 14 Nebuchadnezzar spoke and said to them, "Is it true, Shadrach, Meshach, and Abednego, that you do not serve my gods or worship the golden image which I have set up? 15 Now if you are ready at the time you hear the sound of the cornet, flute, harp, sackbut, psaltery, and dulcimer, and all kinds of music to fall down and worship the image which I have made, very well. But if you do not worship, you shall be cast the same hour into the midst of a burning fiery furnace. And who is that god who can deliver you out of my hands?"

16 Shadrach, Meshach, and Abednego answered and said to the king, "O Nebuchadnezzar, we do not need to give you an answer in this matter. 17 If it be so, our God whom we serve is able to deliver us from the burning fiery furnace, and He will deliver us out of your hand, O king. 18 But *even* if *He does* not, be it known to you, O king, that we will not serve your gods, nor worship the golden image which you have set up."

3:4 Da 4:1
3:5 Da 3:10
3:6 Jer 29:22
3:9 Da 5:10
3:10 Da 3:4–7
3:12 Da 2:49
3:13 Da 2:12
3:14 Isa 46:1
3:15 Ex 5:2
3:17 Job 5:19
3:18 Isa 51:12–13

....

3:19 Da 3:13
3:22 Ex 12:33
3:24 Da 6:7
3:25 Isa 43:2
3:27 Heb 11:34
3:28 Ac 5:19
3:29 Da 2:5

Protection in the Fiery Furnace

19 Then Nebuchadnezzar was full of fury, and the form of his visage was changed against Shadrach, Meshach, and Abednego. Therefore he spoke, and commanded that they should heat the furnace seven times more than it was usually heated. 20 He commanded the most mighty men in his army to bind Shadrach, Meshach, and Abednego and cast them into the burning fiery furnace. 21 Then these men were bound in their trousers, their coats, and their hats, and their other garments, and were cast into the midst of the burning fiery furnace. 22 Therefore, because the king's commandment was urgent and the furnace exceeding hot, the flame of the fire killed those men who took up Shadrach, Meshach, and Abednego. 23 These three men, Shadrach, Meshach, and Abednego, fell down bound into the midst of the burning fiery furnace.

24 Then Nebuchadnezzar the king was astonished, and rose up in haste, and spoke, and said to his counselors, "Did we not cast three men bound into the midst of the fire?"

They answered and said to the king, "True, O king."

25 He answered and said, "But I see four men loose and walking in the midst of the fire, and they are unharmed. And the form of the fourth is like the Son of God!"

Nebuchadnezzar Praises God

26 Then Nebuchadnezzar came near to the mouth of the burning fiery furnace, and spoke, and said, "Shadrach, Meshach, and Abednego, you servants of the Most High God, come out and come here!"

Then Shadrach, Meshach, and Abednego came out of the midst of the fire. 27 The officials, governors, and captains, and the king's counselors, being gathered together, saw these men upon whose bodies the fire had no power, nor was a hair of their head singed, neither were their coats changed, nor had the smell of fire even come upon them.

28 Then Nebuchadnezzar spoke and said, "Blessed be the God of Shadrach, Meshach, and Abednego, who has sent His angel and delivered His servants who trusted in Him. They have defied the king's word, and yielded their bodies, that they might not serve nor worship any god, except their own God. 29 Therefore I make a decree that every people, nation, and language which speaks anything amiss against the God of Shadrach, Meshach, and Abednego shall be cut in pieces, and their houses shall

be made a dunghill, because there is no other God who can deliver in this way."

30 Then the king promoted Shadrach, Meshach, and Abednego in the province of Babylon.

Nebuchadnezzar's Second Dream

4 Nebuchadnezzar the king,

to all peoples, nations, and languages, who dwell in all the earth:

Peace be multiplied to you.

2 I thought it good to declare the signs and wonders that the Most High God has done for me.

3 How great are His signs,
and how mighty are His wonders!
His kingdom is an everlasting kingdom,
and His dominion is from generation
to generation.

4 I, Nebuchadnezzar, was at rest in my house, and flourishing in my palace. 5 I saw a dream which made me afraid, and the thoughts upon my bed and the visions of my head troubled me. 6 Therefore I made a decree to bring in all the wise men of Babylon before me, that they might make known to me the interpretation of the dream. 7 Then came in the magicians, the astrologers, the Chaldeans, and the soothsayers, and I told the dream before them; but they did not make known to me its interpretation.

8 But at the last Daniel came in before me, whose name was Belteshazzar according to the name of my god and in whom is the Spirit of the Holy God, and before him I told the dream, saying, 9 "Belteshazzar, master of the magicians, because I know that the Spirit of the Holy God is in you and no secret troubles you, tell me the visions of my dream that I have seen, and its interpretation. 10 Now these were the visions of my mind *while* on my bed: I saw a tree in the midst of the earth, and its height was great. 11 The tree grew and became strong, and its height reached heaven, and it was visible to the end of all the earth. 12 Its leaves were fair, and its fruit much, and in it was food for all. The animals of the field had shadow under it, and the fowl of the heavens lived in its boughs, and all flesh was fed of it.

13 "I saw in the visions of my head upon my bed, and there was a holy watcher coming down from heaven. 14 He cried aloud and said thus: 'Hew down the tree and cut off its branches, shake off its leaves and scatter its fruit. Let the animals get away from under it, and the fowl from its branches. 15 Nevertheless leave the stump of its roots in the earth, even with a band of iron and bronze, in the tender grass of the field.

" 'And let it be wet with the dew of heaven, and let its portion be with the animals in the grass of the earth. 16 Let its heart be changed from that of a man, let him be given the heart of an animal. And let seven periods of time pass over it.

17 " 'This matter is by the decree of the watchers, and the demand by the word of the holy ones, in order that the living may know that the Most High rules over the kingdom of men and gives it to whomever He wills and sets up over it the basest of men.'

18 "This dream I, King Nebuchadnezzar, have seen. Now you, Belteshazzar, tell its interpretation to me, because all the wise men of my kingdom are not able to make known to me the interpretation. But you are able, for the Spirit of the Holy God is in you."

Daniel Interprets the Dream

19 Then Daniel, whose name was Belteshazzar, was astonished for a while, and his thoughts troubled him. The king spoke and said, "Belteshazzar, do not let the dream, or its interpretation, trouble you."

Belteshazzar answered and said, "My lord, *if only* the dream was for those who hate you, and its interpretation for your enemies! 20 The tree that you saw, which grew and became strong, whose height reached to the heavens, and was visible to all the earth, 21 and whose leaves were fair, and its fruit much, and in it was food for all, under which the animals of the field lived, and upon whose branches the fowl of the heavens had their habitation: 22 It is you, O king, who have grown and become strong. Your greatness has grown and reaches to heaven, and your dominion to the ends of the earth.

23 "Whereas the king saw a watcher and a holy one coming down from heaven and saying, 'Cut the tree down and destroy it, yet leave the stump of its roots in the ground, even with a band of iron and bronze, in the tender grass of the field. And let it be wet with the dew of heaven, and let its portion be with the animals of the field until seven periods of time pass over it'—

24 "This is the interpretation, O king, and this is the decree of the Most High, which has come upon my lord the king: 25 You shall be driven away from men, and your dwelling shall be with the wild animals. You shall be given grass to eat like oxen, and wet with the dew of heaven. And seven times shall pass over you, until you have learned that

3:30 Da 2:49
4:1 Da 6:25
4:2 Da 3:26
4:3 Da 2:44
4:4 Isa 47:7–8
4:5 Da 2:1
4:6 Da 2:2
4:7 Isa 44:25
4:8 Da 1:7
4:9 Da 2:48
4:10 Da 4:5
4:12 Eze 17:23
4:13 Dt 33:2
4:14 Mt 3:10
4:15 Job 14:7–9

4:16 Da 4:23
4:17 Da 4:25
4:18 Ge 41:8
4:19 Da 7:28
4:20 Da 4:10–12
4:22 2Sa 12:7
4:23 Da 5:21
4:24 Ps 107:40
4:25 Da 4:17

the Most High rules over the kingdom of
men and gives it to whomever He chooses.
26 Inasmuch as they commanded to leave
the stump of the tree roots, your kingdom
shall be assured to you after you acknowl-
edge that Heaven rules. 27 Therefore, O king,
let my counsel be acceptable to you, and
break off your sins by righteousness and
your iniquities by showing mercy to the
poor, in case there may be a lengthening
of your prosperity."

The Dream Is Fulfilled

28 All this came upon King Nebuchad-
nezzar. 29 At the end of twelve months he
walked on *the roof of* the palace of the king-
dom of Babylon. 30 The king spoke, saying,
"Is this not Babylon the Great that I myself
have built as a royal residence by my mighty
power and for the honor of my majesty?"
31 While the word was in the king's mouth,
there fell a voice from heaven: "O King
Nebuchadnezzar, to you it is spoken: The
kingdom has departed from you! 32 And
you shall be driven away from men, and
your dwelling shall be with the animals of
the field. You shall be given grass to eat as
oxen, and seven periods of time shall pass
over you until you know that the Most High
rules over the kingdom of men and gives it
to whomever He wills."
33 Immediately the thing was fulfilled con-
cerning Nebuchadnezzar. And he was driv-
en from men and ate grass as oxen, and his
body was wet with the dew of heaven until
his hairs were grown like eagles' *feathers*
and his nails like birds' *claws*.

Nebuchadnezzar Praises God

34 But at the end of the days, I, Nebuchad-
nezzar, lifted up my eyes to heaven, and my
understanding returned to me, and I blessed
the Most High, and I praised and honored
Him who lives forever:

For His dominion is an everlasting
dominion,
and whose kingdom endures from
generation to generation.
35 And all the inhabitants of the earth
are reputed as nothing;
and He does according to His will
in the army of heaven
and among the inhabitants of the
earth.
And no one can stay His hand or say to
Him,
"What have You done?"

36 At the same time my reason returned to
me. And for the glory of my kingdom, my
honor and splendor returned to me. And
my counselors and my lords sought me out.
Then I was established in my kingdom, and
excellent majesty was added to me. 37 Now
I, Nebuchadnezzar, praise and extol and
honor the King of heaven, for all His works
are true and His ways just, and those who
walk in pride He is able to abase.

Belshazzar's Feast

5 Belshazzar the king made a great feast
for a thousand of his lords and drank
wine before the thousand. 2 While he tasted
the wine, Belshazzar commanded that they
bring in the golden and silver vessels which
his father Nebuchadnezzar had taken from
the temple which was in Jerusalem, so that
the king, and his officials, his wives, and his
concubines might drink from them. 3 Then they
brought the golden vessels that were taken out
of the temple of the house of God which was
at Jerusalem. And the king and his officials, his
wives and his concubines drank from them.
4 They drank wine and praised the gods of gold
and of silver, of bronze, of iron, of wood, and
of stone.

The Writing on the Wall

5 Immediately fingers of a man's hand ap-
peared and wrote opposite the lampstand on
the plaster of the wall of the king's palace. And
the king saw the back of the hand that wrote.
6 Then the king's countenance was changed,
and his thoughts troubled him, so that the
joints of his loins were loosed, and his knees
struck against one another.
7 The king cried aloud to bring in the astrol-
ogers, the Chaldeans, and the soothsayers.
And the king spoke and said to the wise men
of Babylon, "Whoever shall read this writing
and show me its interpretation shall be clothed
with scarlet and have a chain of gold about
his neck and shall be the third ruler in the
kingdom."
8 Then all the king's wise men came in, but
they could not read the writing, nor make
known to the king its interpretation. 9 Then
King Belshazzar was greatly troubled, and his
countenance was changed in him, and his no-
bles were astonished.
10 Now the queen came into the banquet
house because of the words of the king and his
nobles. And the queen spoke and said, "O king,
live forever. Do not let your thoughts trouble

4:26 Da 4:15
4:27 1Ki 21:29
4:28 Nu 23:19
4:30 Isa 37:24–25
4:31 Lk 12:20
4:32 Da 5:21
4:34 Jer 10:10
4:35 Ps 115:3
4:36 Pr 22:4
....
4:37 Dt 32:4
5:1 Est 1:3
5:2 Da 1:2
5:4 Da 5:23
5:5 Da 4:31
5:6 Da 7:28
5:7 Da 5:16
5:8 Da 2:27
5:9 Da 5:6
5:10 Da 3:9

I was brought into the kingdom of
light and cleansed and healed and
turned into royalty (Da 5:11).

you, or let your countenance be changed. 11 There is a man in your kingdom in whom is the Spirit of the Holy God. And, in the days of your father, light and understanding and wisdom, like the wisdom of the gods, were found in him. And King Nebuchadnezzar, your father, your father the king, made him master of the magicians, astrologers, Chaldeans, and soothsayers. 12 Inasmuch as an excellent spirit and knowledge and understanding, interpreting dreams and explanation of enigmas and solving of problems, were found in the same Daniel, whom the king named Belteshazzar, now let Daniel be called, and he will give the interpretation."

Daniel Interprets the Writing

13 Then Daniel was brought in before the king. And the king spoke and said to Daniel, "Are you that Daniel who is one of the sons of the captivity of Judah, whom the king my father brought out of Judah? 14 Now I have heard of you, that the Spirit of God is in you; and that light, and understanding, and excellent wisdom have been found in you. 15 Now the wise men, the astrologers, have been brought in before me, that they should read this writing and make known to me its interpretation, but they could not give the interpretation of the matter. 16 And I have heard of you, that you can give interpretations and solve problems. Now if you can read the writing, and make known to me its interpretation, you shall be clothed with scarlet and have a chain of gold about your neck and shall be the third ruler in the kingdom."

17 Then Daniel answered and said before the king, "Let your gifts be for yourself, or give your rewards to another. Yet I will read the writing to the king and make known to him the interpretation.

18 "O king, the Most High God gave Nebuchadnezzar your father a kingdom and majesty and glory and honor. 19 And for the majesty that He gave him, all peoples, nations, and languages trembled and feared before him. Whom he would, he slaughtered, and whom he would, he kept alive; whom he would, he set up, and whom he would, he put down. 20 But when his heart was lifted up and his mind hardened in pride, he was deposed from his kingly throne and they took his glory from him. 21 And he was driven from the sons of men, and his heart was made like the animals, and his dwelling was with the wild donkeys. He was given grass to eat like oxen, and his body was wet with the dew of heaven until he knew that the Most High God rules in the kingdom of men, and that He appoints over it whomever He wills.

22 "Yet you, his son, O Belshazzar, have not humbled your heart, though you knew all this; 23 but have lifted up yourself against the Lord of heaven. And they have brought the vessels of His house before you, and you and your lords, your wives and your concubines, have drunk wine in them. And you have praised the gods of silver and gold, of bronze, iron, wood, and stone, which see not, nor hear, nor know. And the God in whose hand is your breath, and whose are all your ways, you have not glorified. 24 Then the hand was sent from Him, and this inscription was written.

25 "This is the inscription that was written:

MENE, MENE, TEKEL, UPHARSIN.

26 "This is the interpretation of the message: MENE:[1] God has numbered your kingdom and put an end to it.

27 TEKEL:[2] you have been weighed in the balances and are found wanting.

28 PERES:[3] your kingdom has been divided and given to the Medes and Persians."

29 Then Belshazzar gave the command, and they clothed Daniel with scarlet and put a chain of gold about his neck, and made a proclamation concerning him, that he should be the third ruler in the kingdom.

30 That same night Belshazzar the king of the Chaldeans was slain. 31 Then Darius the Mede received the kingdom, being about sixty-two years old.

Daniel and the Lions' Den

6 It pleased Darius to set over the kingdom one hundred and twenty officials, so that they would be over the whole kingdom, 2 and over them three presidents, of whom Daniel was first, so that the officials might give accounts to them and the king not suffer loss.

Let me have and walk in an excellent spirit (Da 6:3).

3 Then this Daniel was preferred above the presidents and officials because an excellent spirit was in him, and the king thought to set him over the whole realm. 4 Then the presidents and officials sought to find occasion against Daniel concerning the kingdom, but they could find no occasion or fault because he was faithful; nor was there any error or fault found in him. 5 Then these men said, "We shall not find any occasion against this Daniel, unless we find it against him concerning the law of his God."

5:11 Da 4:8–9
5:12 Da 1:7
5:13 Da 2:25
5:15 Da 5:7–8
5:16 Da 5:7
5:17 2Ki 5:16
5:18 Da 2:37–38
5:19 Da 2:12–13
5:20 Jer 13:18
5:21 Da 4:25
5:22 2Ch 33:23
5:23 Job 12:10
5:26 Jer 27:7
5:27 Ps 62:9
5:28 Isa 13:17
5:29 Da 5:7
5:30 Jer 51:31
5:31 Da 9:1
6:1 Est 1:1
6:2 Ezr 4:22
6:3 Da 5:12
6:5 Ac 24:13–16

[1] *26 Meaning to number.* [2] *27 Meaning to weigh.* [3] *28 Meaning to divide.*

6 Then these presidents and officials assem-
bled together to the king, and said to him:
"King Darius, live forever! 7 All the presidents
of the kingdom, the governors, and the offi-
cials, the counselors, and the captains have
consulted together to establish a royal statute
and to make a firm decree, that whoever shall
ask a petition of any god or man for thirty days,
save of you, O king, shall be cast into the den
of lions. 8 Now, O king, establish the decree
and sign the writing, that it not be changed, ac-
cording to the law of the Medes and Persians,
which may not be altered." 9 Therefore King
Darius signed the writing, even the decree.

Deliver me from the power of the lions (Da 6:7).

10 Now when Daniel knew that the writing
was signed, he went into his house. And his
windows being open in his chamber toward
Jerusalem, he kneeled on his knees three times
a day, and prayed, and gave thanks before his
God, as he had been doing previously. 11 Then
these men assembled and found Daniel pray-
ing and making supplication before his God.
12 Then they came near and spoke before the
king concerning the king's decree: "Have you
not signed a decree, that every man who asks
a petition of any god or man within thirty days,
save of you, O king, shall be cast into the den
of lions?"
The king answered and said, "The thing is
true, according to the law of the Medes and
Persians, which may not be altered."
13 Then they answered and said before the
king, "That Daniel, who is of the sons of the
captivity of Judah, does not regard you, O king,
or the decree that you have signed, but makes
his petition three times a day." 14 Then the king,
when he heard these words, was sorely dis-
pleased with himself and set his heart on Dan-
iel to deliver him. And he labored until sunset
to deliver him.
15 Then these men came by agreement to the
king and said to the king, "Know, O king, that
it is the law of the Medes and Persians that no
decree or statute which the king establishes
may be changed."
16 Then the king commanded, and they
brought Daniel and cast him into the den of
lions. Now the king spoke and said to Daniel,
"Your God whom you serve continually, He will
deliver you."

Daniel Saved From the Lions

17 A stone was brought and laid upon the
mouth of the den, and the king sealed it with
his own signet and with the signet of his lords
so that nothing might be changed concerning
Daniel. 18 Then the king went to his palace and
passed the night fasting, and no instruments of
music were brought before him. And his sleep
fled from him.
19 Then the king arose very early in the
morning and went in haste to the den of lions.
20 When he came to the den, he cried with a
voice full of sorrow to Daniel. And the king
spoke and said to Daniel, "Daniel, servant of
the living God, has your God whom you serve
continually been able to deliver you from the
lions?"
21 Then Daniel said to the king, "O king, live
forever! 22 My God has sent His angel and has
shut the lions' mouths so that they have not
hurt me, because innocence was found in me
before Him; and also before you, O king, I have
done no harm."
23 Then the king was exceeding glad for him
and commanded that they take Daniel up out
of the den. So Daniel was taken up out of the

6:6 Da 2:4
6:7 Ps 59:3
6:8 Est 1:19
6:10 Ps 55:17
6:12 Da 6:8
6:13 Da 2:25
6:14 Mk 6:26
6:15 Est 8:8
6:16 Job 5:19
6:17 La 3:53
....
6:18 Est 6:1
6:20 Da 3:17
6:21 Da 2:4
6:22 Da 3:28
6:23 1Ch 5:20

SPIRITLED WOMAN

COUNSEL FROM THE SPIRIT BASICS

Don't Doubt Him

Daniel and his friends knew God would take care of them—even when it looked as if honoring Him would get them into trouble. After all, how big a deal would it have been to just eat the king's food? Many people would have chosen the path of least resistance in that case.

But look what happened when they trusted God and chose His way. They received supernatural knowledge and wisdom. And it elevated them, even in the midst of their enemy's kingdom

You can trust God to take care of you. Don't doubt Him! He wants you to trust Him so He can perform miracles for you and promote you, just as He did for Daniel and his three friends. You can have the same assurance they did when you keep your eyes on God's Word and believe Him.

Karen Jensen Salisbury

den, and no manner of harm was found on
him, because he believed in his God.
24 Then the king commanded, and they
brought those men who had accused Daniel,
and they cast them into the den of lions—
them, their children, and their wives. And the
lions overpowered them and broke all their
bones in pieces before they came to the bottom
of the den.
25 Then King Darius wrote:

To all peoples, nations, and languages that
dwell in all the earth:

"Peace be multiplied unto you.

26 "I make a decree that in every dominion
of my kingdom men are to fear and tremble
before the God of Daniel.

"For He is the living God,
enduring forever;
His kingdom shall never be destroyed,
and His dominion shall be forever.
27 He delivers and rescues,
and He works signs and wonders
in heaven and on earth,
who has delivered Daniel
from the power of the lions."

28 So this Daniel prospered in the reign of
Darius and in the reign of Cyrus the Persian.

Daniel's Vision of the Four Beasts

7 In the first year of Belshazzar king of Bab-
ylon, Daniel had a dream and visions of
his mind *while* on his bed. Then he wrote the
dream and told the sum of the matters.
2 Daniel spoke and said: I saw in my vision
by night the four winds of the heaven striv-
ing upon the *Mediterranean* Sea. 3 Four great
beasts came up from the sea, diverse from one
another.
4 The first was like a lion and had eagle's
wings. I watched until its wings were plucked
and it was lifted up from the earth and made to
stand on the feet as a man, and a man's heart
was given to it.
5 Another beast appeared, a second, like a
bear, and it raised itself up on one side, and it
had three ribs in its mouth between its teeth.
And they said to it, "Arise, devour much flesh."
6 After this I looked and there was another,
like a leopard, which had on its back four
wings of a fowl. The beast also had four heads.
And dominion was given to it.
7 After this I saw in the visions at night a
fourth beast, dreadful and terrible, and ex-
ceedingly strong. And it had great iron teeth.
It devoured and broke in pieces, and stamped
the rest with its feet. And it was different from
all the beasts that were before it, and it had
ten horns.

6:24 Dt 24:16
6:25 Da 4:1
6:26 Da 4:34
6:27 Da 4:2–3
6:28 Da 1:21
7:1 Da 4:5
7:2 Rev 7:1
7:3 Rev 13:1
7:4 Jer 4:7
7:5 Da 2:39
7:6 Rev 13:2
7:7 Rev 12:3
....
7:8 Rev 13:5–6
7:9 Rev 1:14
7:10 Rev 5:11
7:11 Rev 19:20
7:13 Mt 26:64
7:14 Da 7:27
7:15 Da 7:28
7:18 Rev 20:4
7:19 Da 7:7

8 I considered the horns, when there came up
among them another little horn before whom
three of the first horns were plucked up by
the roots. And there, in this horn, were eyes
like the eyes of man, and a mouth speaking
great things.

Your throne, O Lord, is like
a fiery flame (Da 7:9).

The Ancient of Days Reigns

9 I watched until
the thrones were cast down
and the Ancient of Days was seated,
whose garment was white as snow,
and the hair of His head like the pure
wool.
His throne was like the fiery flame,
and its wheels as burning fire.
10 A fiery stream issued
and came out from before Him.
A thousand thousands ministered to Him;
and ten thousand times ten thousand
stood before Him.
The judgment was set,
and the books were opened.

11 Then I watched because of the sound of
the boastful words which the horn was speak-
ing. I watched even until the beast was slain,
and his body destroyed and given to the burn-
ing flame. 12 As for the rest of the beasts, they
had their dominion taken away; yet their lives
were prolonged for a season and time.
13 I saw in the night visions, and there was
one like a Son of Man coming with the clouds
of heaven. He came to the Ancient of Days and
was presented before Him. 14 There was given
to Him dominion, and glory, and a kingdom,
that all peoples, nations, and languages should
serve Him. His dominion is an everlasting do-
minion, which shall not pass away, and His
kingdom that which shall not be destroyed.

The Interpretation of the Dream

15 I, Daniel, was grieved in my spirit in the
midst of my body, and the visions of my head
troubled me. 16 I approached one of those who
were standing by and asked him the truth of
all this.

So he told me and made known to me the
interpretation of these things. 17 "These great
beasts, which are four, are four kings which
shall arise out of the earth. 18 But the saints
of the Most High shall take the kingdom and
possess the kingdom forever, even forever and
ever."
19 Then I desired to know the truth of the
fourth beast, which was different from all the

others, exceeding dreadful, whose teeth were
of iron and its nails of bronze, and which de-
voured, broke in pieces, and stamped the rest
with its feet; 20 and of the ten horns that were
in its head, and of the other which came up,
and before whom three fell, even of that horn
that had eyes and a mouth that spoke boast-
ful words, whose look was more stout than its
fellows. 21 I beheld, and the same horn was
warring with the saints and prevailing against
them 22 until the Ancient of Days came, and
judgment was passed in favor of the saints of
the Most High, and the time came when the
saints possessed the kingdom.

23 Thus he said: "The fourth beast shall be
the fourth kingdom upon earth, which shall be
different from all kingdoms, and shall devour
the whole earth and shall tread it down and
break it in pieces. 24 The ten horns out of this
kingdom are ten kings that shall arise; and
another shall rise after them, and he shall be
different from the first, and he shall subdue
three kings. 25 He shall speak words against
the Most High and shall wear out the saints of
the Most High and plan to change times and
law. And they shall be given into his hand until
a time and times and half a time.[1]

Let all dominions serve and obey You, O Lord (Da 7:27).

26 "But the court shall sit for judgment, and
they shall take away his dominion, to consume
and to destroy it forever. 27 Then the kingdom
and dominion, and the greatness of all the
kingdoms under the whole heaven, shall be
given to the people of the saints of the Most
High, whose kingdom is an everlasting king-
dom, and all dominions shall serve and obey
Him."

28 At this point the matter ended. As for me,
Daniel, my thoughts troubled me much, and
my countenance changed in me; but I kept the
matter in my heart.

Daniel's Vision of a Ram and a Goat

8 In the third year of the reign of King
Belshazzar a vision appeared to me, even
to me Daniel, after that which appeared to me
at the first. 2 I saw in the vision, and while I was
looking, I was at Susa in the palace which is in
the province of Elam. And I saw in the vision
that I was by the canal of Ulai. 3 Then I lifted
up my eyes and looked, and there stood before
the river a ram which had two horns, and the
two horns were high. But one was higher than
the other, and the higher one came up last. 4 I
saw the ram pushing westward and northward
and southward, so that no animal might stand
before him; nor was there any that could de-
liver out of his hand, but he did according to
his will and became great.

5 As I was considering this, suddenly a male
goat came from the west across the face of
the whole earth and did not touch the ground.
And the goat had a notable horn between his
eyes. 6 He came to the ram that had two horns,
which I had seen standing before the river,
and ran to him in the fury of his power. 7 I saw
him come close to the ram, and he was moved
with rage against him, and struck the ram and
broke his two horns. And there was no power
in the ram to stand before him, but he cast him
down to the ground and stamped on him. And
there was none who could deliver the ram out
of his hand. 8 Therefore the male goat grew
very great. And when he was strong, the great
horn was broken, and four conspicuous *horns*
came up in its place toward the four winds
of heaven.

The Little Horn

9 Out of one of them came a little horn, which
grew exceedingly great toward the south, to-
ward the east, and toward the Pleasant *Land*.
10 It grew great, even to the host of heaven.
And it cast down some of the host and of the
stars to the ground and stamped upon them.
11 Indeed, he magnified himself even to the
Prince of the host, and from Him the daily
sacrifice was taken away, and the place of
His sanctuary was cast down. 12 Because of
rebellion, an army was given *to the horn* to
oppose the daily sacrifice; and it cast truth to
the ground. It practiced this and prospered.

13 Then I heard one saint speaking, and an-
other saint said to that certain saint which
spoke, "How long shall be the vision concern-
ing the daily sacrifice and the transgression of
desolation, the giving of both the sanctuary
and the host to be trodden under foot?"

14 And he said to me, "For two thousand three
hundred evenings and mornings. Then the
sanctuary shall be cleansed properly."

Gabriel Interprets the Vision

15 When I, Daniel, had seen the vision, I
sought for the meaning. Then there before me
stood one who had the appearance of a man.
16 I heard a man's voice between *the banks of*
Ulai, which called, and said, "Gabriel, make
this man understand the vision."

17 So he came near where I stood. And when
he came, I was afraid and fell upon my face;
but he said to me, "Understand, son of man,
that the vision deals with the time of the end."

7:20 Da 7:8
7:23 Da 2:40
7:24 Da 7:20
7:25 Da 12:7
7:27 Da 2:44
7:28 Lk 2:19
8:1 Da 7:1
8:2 Ge 10:22
8:3 Da 8:20
8:4 Da 11:16
8:5 Da 8:21
8:8 Da 7:2
8:9 Da 11:16
8:10 Isa 14:13
8:11 Da 11:31
8:13 Da 4:13
8:14 Da 8:26
8:15 Da 10:16
8:16 Lk 1:19
8:17 Da 8:19

[1] *25 Or for a year, two years, and half a year.*

[18] Now as he was speaking with me, I was in
a deep sleep with my face toward the ground.
But he touched me and set me upright.

I take authority over the princes of darkness, in Jesus' name (Da 8:20).

[19] He said, "Listen, I will make you know
what shall be in the final period of the indig-
nation, for the end shall be at the appointed
time. [20] The ram which you saw having two
horns represents the kings of Media and Per-
sia. [21] The rough goat is the king of Greece,
and the great horn that is between his eyes is
the first king. [22] Now the broken horn and the
four horns that stood up in its place are four
kingdoms that shall stand up out of his nation,
but not with his power.

[23] "In the latter time of their kingdom, when
the transgressors have reached their limit, a
king will arise, having a fierce countenance,
skilled in intrigue. [24] His power shall be mighty,
but not by his own power. And he shall destroy
wonderfully and shall prosper and practice his
will and shall destroy the mighty men and the
holy people. [25] By his cunning, he shall cause
deceit to succeed under his hand, and he shall
magnify himself in his heart. He shall destroy
many in a time of peace. He shall also rise up
against the Prince of princes; but he shall be
broken, not by human hands.

[26] "And the vision of the evenings and the
mornings, which was told, is true. Therefore
shut up the vision, for it deals with many days
in the future."

[27] Then I, Daniel, fainted and was sick for
some days. Afterward I rose up again and did
the king's business. So I was astonished at the
vision, but there was none to explain it.

The Prayer of Daniel

9 In the first year of Darius the son of Aha-
suerus of the lineage of the Medes, who
was made king over the realm of the Chal-
deans, [2] in the first year of his reign, I, Daniel,
observed in the books the number of the years
which *were specified by* the word of the LORD
to Jeremiah the prophet for the accomplish-
ment of the desolations of Jerusalem, that is,
seventy years. [3] I set my face toward the Lord
God to seek by prayer and supplications with
fasting and sackcloth and ashes.

[4] And I prayed to the LORD my God, and made
my confession, and said,

"Alas, O Lord, the great and dreadful God,
keeping His covenant and mercy to those
who love Him, and to those who keep His
commandments. [5] We have sinned and have
committed iniquity and have done wickedly
and have rebelled, even by departing from
Your precepts and from Your judgments.
[6] We have not listened to Your servants the
prophets, who spoke in Your name to our
kings, our officials, and our fathers, and to
all the people of the land.

[7] "O Lord, righteousness belongs to You,
but to us shame of face, as it is this day, to
the men of Judah and to the inhabitants
of Jerusalem and to all Israel, who are
near and who are far off, through all the
countries wherever You have driven them,
because of their trespass that they have tres-
passed against You. [8] O Lord, to us belongs
shame of face, to our kings, to our officials,
and to our fathers, because we have sinned
against You. [9] To the Lord our God belong
mercies and forgiveness, though we have
rebelled against Him. [10] We have not obeyed
the voice of the LORD our God, to walk in His
laws, which He set before us by His servants
the prophets. [11] Indeed, all Israel has trans-
gressed Your law, even by departing that
they might not obey Your voice.

"Therefore the curse has been poured
upon us, and the oath that is written in the
Law of Moses the servant of God, because
we have sinned against Him. [12] He has
confirmed His words, which He had spo-
ken against us and against our judges who
judged us, by bringing on us great calamity.
For under the whole heaven there has not
been done such as has been done to Jeru-
salem. [13] As it is written in the Law of Moses,
great calamity has come on us. Yet we have
not sought the favor of the LORD our God so
that we might turn from our iniquities and
give attention to Your truth. [14] Therefore,
the LORD has kept the disaster in store and
brought it upon us. For the LORD our God is
righteous in all His works which He does,
but we have not obeyed His voice.

[15] "Now, O Lord our God, who brought
Your people out of the land of Egypt with a
mighty hand, and made Yourself a name,
even to this day, we have sinned, we have
done wickedly. [16] O Lord, according to all
Your righteousness, I beseech You, let Your
anger and Your fury be turned away from
Your city Jerusalem, Your holy mountain,
because for our sins and for the iniquities
of our fathers, Jerusalem and Your people
have become a reproach to all who are
around us.

[17] "Now therefore, O God, hear the prayer
of Your servant and his supplications, and
for Your sake, O Lord, cause Your face to
shine upon Your sanctuary, which is deso-

8:18 Da 10:18
8:20 Da 8:3
8:21 Da 10:20
8:24 Da 8:12
8:25 Da 8:11
8:26 Da 10:1
8:27 Da 7:28
9:1 Da 11:1
9:2 2Ch 36:21
9:4 Dt 7:9
9:5 Ps 106:6

....

9:7 Dt 4:27
9:9 Ps 130:4
9:10 2Ki 18:12
9:11 Isa 1:4–6
9:12 Eze 5:9
9:13 Isa 9:13
9:14 Ne 9:33
9:15 Ne 9:10
9:16 Zec 8:3
9:17 Ps 80:19

late. 18 O my God, incline Your ear and hear. Open Your eyes and look at our desolations and the city which is called by Your name, for we do not present our supplications before You for our righteousness, but for Your great mercies. 19 O Lord, hear! O Lord, forgive! O Lord, listen and act! Do not defer, for Your own sake, O my God. For Your city and Your people are called by Your name."

The Seventy Weeks

20 While I was speaking and praying and confessing my sin and the sin of my people Israel, and presenting my supplication before the LORD my God for the holy mountain of my God, 21 indeed, while I was speaking in prayer, the man Gabriel, whom I had seen in the vision at the beginning, being caused to fly swiftly, touched me about the time of the evening oblation. 22 He informed me and talked with me, and said, "Daniel, I have now come to give you insight and understanding. 23 At the beginning of your supplications the command went out, and I have come to tell you, for you are greatly beloved. Therefore understand the matter and consider the vision:

24 "Seventy weeks have been determined for your people and upon your holy city, to finish the transgression, and to make an end of sins, and to make atonement for iniquity, and to bring in everlasting righteousness, and to seal up the vision and prophecy, and to anoint the Most Holy *Place*.

25 "Know therefore and understand that from the going forth of the command to restore and to rebuild Jerusalem until the Prince Messiah shall be seven weeks, and sixty-two weeks. It shall be built again, with plaza and moat, even in times of trouble. 26 After the sixty-two weeks Messiah shall be cut off and shall have nothing. And the troops of the prince who shall come shall destroy the city and the sanctuary. The end of it shall come with a flood. And until the end of the war desolations are determined. 27 And he shall make a firm covenant with many for one week. But in the middle of the week he shall cause the sacrifice and the offering to cease. And on the wing of abominations shall come one who makes desolate, until the decreed destruction is poured out on the desolator."

Daniel's Vision of a Man

10 In the third year of Cyrus king of Persia a message was revealed to Daniel, whose name was called Belteshazzar, and the message was true and one of great conflict. And he understood the message and had understanding of the vision.

2 In those days I, Daniel, was mourning three full weeks. 3 I ate no tasty food, no meat or wine entered my mouth, nor did I anoint myself at all until three whole weeks were fulfilled.

4 On the twenty-fourth day of the first month, as I was by the side of the great river which is Tigris, 5 I lifted up my eyes and looked and saw a certain man clothed in linen, whose loins were girded with the fine gold of Uphaz. 6 His body also was like beryl, and his face had the appearance of lightning, and his eyes were like lamps of fire, and his arms and his feet were like the gleam of polished bronze, and the sound of his words like the sound of a tumult.

7 I, Daniel, alone saw the vision, while the men who were with me did not see the vision; but a great quaking fell upon them, so that they fled to hide themselves. 8 Therefore I was left alone and saw this great vision, and there remained no strength in me, and my countenance grew deathly pale, and I retained no strength. 9 Yet I heard the sound of his words; and while I heard the sound of his words, then I was in a deep sleep on my face with my face toward the ground.

Prophecies of Persia and Greece

10 But then a hand touched me, which set me on my knees and on the palms of my hands. 11 He said to me, "O Daniel, a man greatly beloved, understand the words that I speak to you, and stand upright, for I have been sent to you now." And when he had spoken this word to me, I stood trembling.

12 Then he said to me, "Do not be afraid, Daniel. For from the first day that you set your heart to understand this and to humble yourself before your God, your words were heard, and I have come because of your words. 13 But the prince of the kingdom of Persia withstood me for twenty-one days. So Michael, one of the chief princes, came to help me, for I had been left there with the kings of Persia. 14 Now I have come to make you understand what shall befall your people in the latter days. For the vision is yet for many days."

15 When he had spoken such words to me, I set my face toward the ground, and I became mute. 16 Then one in the likeness of the sons of men touched my lips. Then I opened my mouth and spoke and said to him who stood before me, "O my lord, because of the vision, sorrows have come upon me, and I have retained no strength. 17 How can the servant of my lord talk with you, my lord? And as for me, there remains no strength in me now, nor is there any breath left in me."

18 Then again, the one having the appearance of a man came and touched me, and he

9:18 Isa 37:17
9:20 Ps 145:18
9:21 Da 8:16
9:22 Da 8:16
9:23 Da 10:11–12
9:24 Eze 4:6
9:25 Ezr 4:24
9:26 Isa 53:8
9:27 Mt 24:15
10:1 Da 1:7

10:4 Ge 2:14
10:5 Jer 10:9
10:6 Rev 19:12
10:7 Ac 9:7
10:8 Da 7:28
10:9 Da 8:18
10:10 Jer 1:9
10:12 Ac 10:30–31
10:13 Da 12:1
10:14 Da 2:28
10:15 Eze 24:27
10:16 Isa 6:7
10:18 Da 10:16

> Lord, Your angels have touched me and strengthened me (Da 10:18).

strengthened me. 19 He said, "O man, greatly
beloved, do not fear. Peace be unto you. Be
strong and courageous!"

When he spoke to me, I was strengthened
and said, "Let my lord speak, for you have
strengthened me."

20 Then he said, "Do you understand why I
have come to you? But now I shall return to
fight against the prince of Persia, and when
I have gone forth, then truly the prince of
Greece will come. 21 But I will show you what
is inscribed in the Scripture of Truth. Yet there
is no one who stands firmly with me against
these forces, except Michael your prince.

The Kings of the South and the North

11 "Also, in the first year of Darius the
Mede, I, even I, stood to confirm and
to strengthen him.

2 "And now I will tell you the truth. Truly,
there shall stand up yet three kings in Persia,
and the fourth shall be far richer than all of
them; and by his strength, through his riches,
he shall stir up all against the realm of Greece.
3 A mighty king shall stand up who shall rule
with great dominion and do according to his
will. 4 When he shall stand up, his kingdom
shall be broken and shall be divided toward the
four winds of heaven, but not to his posterity,
nor according to his dominion which he ruled.
For his kingdom shall be plucked up, even for
others besides them.

5 "The king of the South shall be strong, as
well as one of his officials who shall be strong
above him and have dominion. His dominion
shall be a great dominion. 6 In the end of some
years they shall join themselves together. For
the king's daughter of the South shall come to
the king of the North to make an agreement.
But she shall not retain her position of power,
and neither he nor his power shall stand. But
she shall be given up with those who brought
her and with him who fathered her and with
him who strengthened her in those times.

7 "But out of a branch of her roots shall one
stand up in his place, who shall come with an
army and shall enter the fortress of the king of
the North and shall deal against them and shall
prevail. 8 And he shall also carry captive into
Egypt their gods, with their officials, and with
their precious vessels of silver and of gold. And
he shall continue more years than the king of
the North, 9 who will enter the kingdom of the
king of the South, but shall return to his own
land. 10 His sons shall wage war and assemble
a multitude of armed forces. One shall advance
like a flood and pass through, and again shall
wage the war as far as his fortress.

11 "The king of the South shall be moved with
rage, and shall go out and fight with him, with
the king of the North, who shall raise a great
multitude; but that multitude shall be given
into his *enemy's* hand. 12 When he has taken
away the multitude, his heart shall be lifted up;
and he shall cast down many ten thousands,
but he shall not be strengthened by it. 13 For the
king of the North shall return and shall raise
a multitude greater than the former, and shall
certainly come after certain years with a great
army and with much equipment.

14 "In those times many shall stand up against
the king of the South. Also the robbers of your
people shall exalt themselves to fulfill the vi-
sion, but they shall fall. 15 Then the king of the
North shall come and set up a siege mound
and capture a fortified city. And the forces of
the South shall not withstand him; neither shall
his chosen best troops have strength to resist.
16 But he who comes against him shall do ac-
cording to his own will, and none shall stand
before him. And he shall stand in the Pleasant
Land, which shall be consumed by his hand.
17 He shall also set his face to enter with the
strength of his whole kingdom, bringing with
him a proposal of peace which he shall put
into effect. And he shall give him the daugh-
ter of women to corrupt it. But she shall not
stand on his side or be for him. 18 After this
he shall turn his face to the coastlands and
shall capture many. But a commander shall
put a stop to his reproach against him, and he
shall repay him for his reproach. 19 Then he
shall turn his face toward the fortresses of his
own land, but shall stumble and fall and not
be found any more.

20 "Then one shall stand up in his place who
shall send an oppressor in the glory of his
kingdom. But within a few days he shall be
destroyed, but not in anger or in battle.

21 "In his place a vile person shall stand up,
to whom they shall not give the honor of the
kingdom. But he shall come in peaceably and
obtain the kingdom by flatteries. 22 A flood of
armies shall be swept away before him and
be broken, and the prince of the covenant as
well. 23 After the league *is* made with him, he
shall work deceitfully, and he shall come up
and shall become strong with a small force of
people. 24 He shall enter peaceably even upon
the richest places of the realm. And he shall
do that which his fathers have not done, nor
his fathers' fathers. He shall distribute among
them the plunder and spoil and riches. And he
shall plan his devices against the strongholds,
but only for a time.

10:19 Jos 1:9
10:20 Da 8:21
10:21 Da 10:13
11:1 Da 5:31
11:3 Da 8:21
11:4 Da 8:8
11:6 Da 11:13
11:8 Isa 37:19
11:11 Da 8:7
11:13 Da 4:16
11:16 Da 8:9
11:18 Hos 12:14
11:19 Ps 37:36
11:20 Isa 60:17
11:22 Da 11:10
11:23 Da 8:25

25 "He shall stir up his power and his courage against the king of the South with a great army. And the king of the South shall be stirred up to battle with a very great and mighty army. But he shall not stand, for schemes shall be devised against him. 26 Indeed, those who eat his choice food shall destroy him, and his army shall overflow, and many shall fall down slain. 27 As for both of these kings, their hearts shall plan on mischief, and they shall speak lies to one another at one table. But it shall not prosper, for the end shall yet be at the appointed time. 28 While turning back to his land with great wealth, his heart shall be against the holy covenant. He shall *wage war* and turn back to his own land.

Blasphemies of the Northern King

29 "At the appointed time he shall return and come into the south, but this latter time shall not be as the former. 30 For the ships of Kittim shall come against him. Therefore he shall be grieved and return and have indignation against the holy covenant and take action. He shall even return and show regard to those who forsake the holy covenant.

31 "His armies shall rise up and desecrate the sanctuary fortress. They shall abolish the daily sacrifice and set up the abomination that makes desolate. 32 By flatteries he will corrupt those who act wickedly toward the covenant. But the people who know their God will be strong and take action.

33 "The wise among the people shall instruct many. Yet for many days they shall fall by the sword and by flame, by captivity and by destruction. 34 Now when they fall, they shall be given a little help. But many shall cleave to them with flatteries. 35 Some of the wise will fall, so that they may be purged, purified, and made white, until the time of the end, for it is still for the appointed time.

36 "The king shall do according to his will. And he shall exalt himself, and magnify himself above every god, and shall speak blasphemous things against the God of gods, and shall prosper until the indignation is accomplished. For that which is determined shall be done. 37 He shall regard neither the gods of his fathers, nor the desire of women, nor regard any god; for he shall magnify himself above them all. 38 But instead he shall honor the god of forces, a god whom his fathers did not know. He shall honor him with gold and silver, and with precious stones, and pleasant things. 39 Thus he shall do in the strongest of fortresses with a foreign god. He shall give great honor to those who acknowledge him, and shall cause them to rule over the many and shall divide the land for gain.

Conquests of the Northern King

40 "At the time of the end the king of the South shall push at him. But the king of the North shall come against him like a whirlwind, with chariots and with horsemen and with many ships. And he shall enter the countries and shall overflow them and pass over. 41 He shall enter also the Pleasant Land, and many *countries* shall be overthrown. But these shall escape out of his hand, even Edom, and Moab, and the chief of the sons of Ammon. 42 Then he shall stretch out his hand against the countries, and the land of Egypt shall not escape. 43 But he shall have power over the hidden treasures of gold and of silver, and over all the precious things of Egypt. And the Libyans and the Ethiopians shall be at his steps. 44 But reports from the east and from the north shall trouble him. Therefore he shall go out with great fury to destroy and annihilate many. 45 He shall pitch the tabernacles of his palace between the seas in the beautiful holy mountain. Yet he shall come to his end, and no one shall help him.

The Prophecy of the End Times

12 "And at that time Michael shall stand up, the great prince who stands *guard* over the sons of your people. And there shall be a time of trouble such as never was since there was a nation even to that time. And at that time your people shall be delivered, everyone who shall be found written in the book. 2 Many of those who sleep in the dust of the earth shall awake, some to everlasting life, but others to shame and everlasting contempt. 3 Those who are wise shall shine as the brightness of the expanse of heaven, and those who turn the many to righteousness as the stars forever and ever. 4 But you, Daniel, shut up the words and seal the book until the time of the end. Many shall run to and fro, and knowledge shall increase."

5 Then I, Daniel, looked, and there before me stood two others, the one on this side of the bank of the river, and the other on that side of the bank of the river. 6 One said to the man clothed in linen, who was above the water of the river, "How long shall it be to the end of these wonders?"

7 And I heard the man clothed in linen, who was over the water of the river, when he held up his right hand and his left hand to heaven, and swore by Him who lives forever that it would be for a time, times, and half a time.[1] And when they finish shattering the power of the holy people, all these things shall be finished.

11:26 Da 11:10
11:27 Ps 12:2
11:30 Ge 10:4
11:31 Da 12:11
11:32 Mic 5:7–9
11:33 Mal 2:7
11:34 Mt 7:15
11:35 Zec 13:9
11:36 Dt 10:17

11:40 Isa 5:28
11:41 Jer 48:47
11:43 2Ch 12:3
12:1 Jer 30:7
12:2 Isa 26:19
12:3 Da 11:33
12:4 Da 12:9
12:6 Eze 9:2
12:7 Da 7:25

[1] 7 *Or a year, two years, and half a year.*

[8] As for me, I heard, but I could not under-
stand. So I said, "My lord, what shall be the
result of these things?"
[9] And he said, "Go your way, Daniel. For these
words are closed up and sealed until the time
of the end. [10] Many shall be purified and made
white and tried. But the wicked shall do wick-
edly, and none of the wicked shall understand,
but the wise shall understand.
[11] "From the time that the daily sacrifice
shall be taken away and the abomination that
makes desolate set up, there shall be one thou-
sand two hundred and ninety days. [12] Blessed
is he who waits and comes to the one thousand
three hundred and thirty-five days.
[13] "But as for you, go your way until the end.
Then you shall rest and rise *again* for your lot
at the end of the age."

12:9 Da 12:4
12:10 Da 11:35
12:11 Da 11:31
12:13 Rev 14:13

Author: The prophet Hosea

Written: Between 755 and 725 BC

Themes: Redeeming Love, Judgment, Restoration

HOSEA

Dear Spirit Led Woman,

If you want to be filled with God's Spirit, you must be emptied of everything else. How do you empty yourself? The prophet Hosea says to "break up your fallow ground; for it is time to seek the LORD, until He comes and rains righteousness upon you" (Hos 10:12). You break up the fallow ground of your heart by repenting of sins—first the ones you immediately recall and then others the Holy Spirit brings to mind as you make your confession to Him in prayer. Next, you spend time in the Word, letting it shine its light on your heart and revealing anything that is not pleasing to God. The psalmist wrote, "Your word is a lamp to my feet and a light to my path" (Ps 119:105). When the light of God's Word shines on you, the way is made clear.

I pray that the Holy Spirit uses these tools—repentance and the Word—to soften your heart to receive more of Him.

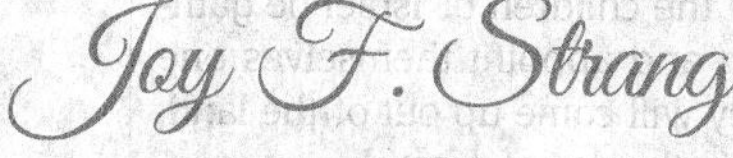

1 The word of the LORD that came to Ho-
sea son of Beeri, in the days of Uzziah,
Jotham, Ahaz, and Hezekiah, kings of Judah,
and in the days of Jeroboam the son of Joash,
king of Israel.

Hosea's Wife and Children

2 When the LORD first spoke by Hosea, the
LORD said to Hosea: "Go, take for yourself a
wife of harlotry and children of harlotry, for the
land has committed great harlotry, departing
from the LORD." 3 So he went and took Gomer
the daughter of Diblaim as a wife. She con-
ceived, and bore him a son.
4 The LORD said to him: "Call his name Jez-
reel,[1] for in a little while, I will punish the
house of Jehu for the blood of Jezreel, and
will bring to an end the kingdom of the house
of Israel. 5 On that day, I will break the bow of
Israel in the Valley of Jezreel."
6 Then Gomer conceived again, and bore a
daughter. And the LORD said to Hosea: "Call her
name Lo-Ruhamah,[2] for I will no longer have
mercy upon the house of Israel but will utterly
sweep them away. 7 But I will have mercy upon
the house of Judah, and will save them by the
LORD their God, and will not save them by bow,
or by sword, or by battle, or by horses, or by
horsemen."
8 When Gomer had weaned Lo-Ruhamah,
she conceived, and bore a son. 9 Then the LORD
said: "Call his name Lo-Ammi,[3] for you are not
My people, and I am not your God."
10 Yet the number of the children of Israel
will be as the sand of the sea, which cannot
be measured nor numbered. And in the place
where it was said to them, "You are not My
people," there it will be said to them, "You are
the children of the living God." 11 Then will the
Judahites and the children of Israel be gath-
ered together, and appoint themselves one
head, and they will come up out of the land,
for great will be the day of Jezreel.

2 Say to your brothers, Ammi,[4] and to your
sisters, Ruhamah.[5]

Israel's Unfaithfulness Punished

2 Plead with your mother, plead—
for she is not My wife,
and am I not her husband—
that she put away her harlotry from her face,
and her adultery from between her breasts,
3 lest I strip her naked
and leave her as in the day that she was born,
and turn her into a wilderness,
and turn her into a dry land,
and kill her with thirst.
4 I will not have mercy upon her children,
for they are children of harlotry.
5 For their mother has played the whore.
She that conceived them has acted shamefully.
For she said, "I will pursue my lovers,
who provide my bread and my water,
my wool and my flax, my oil and my drink."
6 Therefore, behold, I will hedge up your way with thorns,
and make a wall, so that she will not find her paths.
7 She will pursue her lovers, but she will not reach them;
and she will seek them but will not find them.
Then she will say,
"I will go and return to my first husband,
for it was better for me then than now."
8 But she did not know that it was I who provided her
the grain, the wine, and the oil,
and multiplied her silver and gold
that they used for Baal.
9 Therefore I will take back My grain in its time
and My wine in its season,
and I will recover My wool and My flax,
given to cover her nakedness.
10 Therefore I will uncover her shame
in the sight of her lovers,
and no one will deliver her from My hand.
11 I will also bring to an end all her joy,
her *annual* feasts, her New Moons,
and her Sabbaths, and all her solemn assemblies.
12 I will destroy her vines and her fig trees,
of which she has said, "These are my
rewards that my lovers have given me."
I will make them a forest,
and the beasts of the field will eat them.
13 I will punish her for the days of the Baals,
when she burned incense to them
and adorned herself with her earrings and her jewelry,
and pursued her lovers,
but forgot Me,
declares the LORD.

God's Mercy on Israel

14 Therefore, I will allure her,
and bring her into the wilderness,
and speak tenderly to her.

1:1 Isa 1:1
1:2 Hos 3:1
1:5 Jos 17:16
1:7 Zec 4:6
1:10 Hos 1:9
1:11 Isa 11:12–13
2:1 Hos 2:23
2:2 Isa 50:1
2:3 Isa 32:13–14
....
2:5 Isa 1:21
2:6 Job 19:8
2:7 Jer 2:2
2:8 Isa 1:3
2:9 Hos 2:3
2:10 Eze 23:29
2:11 Jer 7:34
2:12 Isa 5:5
2:13 Hos 11:2
2:14 Eze 20:35–36

[1] 4 That is, *May God make fertile.* [2] 6 That is, *Not pitied.* [3] 9 That is, *Not My people.* [4] 1 That is, *My people.* [5] 1 That is, *Pitied.*

[15]From there, I will give her vineyards to her,
and the Valley of Achor as a door of
hope.
She will respond there as in the days of her
youth,
and as in the day when she came up out
of the land of Egypt.

[16]On that day, declares the LORD,
you will call Me, "My husband,"
and will no longer call Me, "My Baal."[1]
[17]I will remove the names of the Baals from
her mouth,
and they will no longer be remembered
by their name.

Father, I will not reject Your knowledge and laws (Hos 4:6).

[18]On that day, I will make a covenant for
them
with the beasts of the field, with the
fowls of heaven,
and with the creeping things of the
ground.
I will break the bow and the sword and the
battle
from the earth,
and will make them to lie down safely.
[19]I will take you for My wife forever.
I will take you for My wife in
righteousness and in justice,
in mercy and in compassion.
[20]I will take you for My wife in faithfulness,
and you will know the LORD.

[21]On that day I will answer,
declares the LORD;
I will answer the heavens,
and they will answer the earth.
[22]The earth will answer the grain,
the wine, and the oil;
and they will answer Jezreel.
[23]Then I will sow her for Myself in the earth.
I will have mercy upon Lo-Ruhamah,
and I will say to Lo-Ammi, "You are My
people,"
and they will say, "You are my God."

Hosea Redeems His Wife

3 Then the LORD said to me, "Go, again, love
a woman who is loved by a lover and is
committing adultery, just as the LORD loves the
children of Israel, who look to other gods and
love raisin cakes."
[2] So I purchased her for myself for fifteen
shekels of silver, and for a homer of barley,
and a half homer of barley. [3]Then I said to her,
"You will remain with me many days. You will
not play the whore, and you will not belong
to *another* man. And also I *will be* with you."
[4] For the children of Israel will remain many
days without a king and without a prince,
without a sacrifice and without a standing
stone, and without an ephod and teraphim.
[5] Afterward the children of Israel will return
and seek the LORD their God and David their
king. They will come in fear to the LORD and to
His goodness in the latter days.

2:15 Jer 2:2
2:17 Ex 23:13
2:18 Eze 34:25
2:21 Zec 8:12
2:23 Hos 1:6
3:3 Dt 21:13

3:4 Jdg 17:5
3:5 Isa 2:2
4:1 Jer 4:22
4:2 Hos 6:9
4:3 Zep 1:3
4:4 Dt 17:12
4:5 Jer 15:8
4:6 Isa 5:13
4:7 Hos 13:6
4:8 Isa 56:11
4:9 Isa 24:2
4:10 Lev 26:26
4:11 Pr 20:1

God Accuses Israel

4 Hear the word of the LORD, O children of
Israel,
for the LORD has a dispute
with the inhabitants of the land:
There is no truth or mercy,
and no knowledge of God in the land.
[2] Swearing, lying, and killing,
and stealing and adultery
break out,
and bloodshed follows bloodshed.
[3] Therefore the land dries up,
and everyone who lives in it withers
with the beasts of the field
and the birds of the sky;
even the fish of the sea disappear.

[4] Yet let no one contend,
and let none reprove another,
for your people are like those
that contend with a priest.[2]
[5] You will stumble in the day,
and the prophet also will stumble with
you in the night,
and I will destroy your mother.
[6] My people are destroyed for lack of
knowledge.

Because you have rejected knowledge,
I will reject you from being My priest.
And because you have forgotten the law of
your God,
I will also forget your children.
[7] As they increased, so they sinned against
Me.
I will change[3] their glory[4] into shame.
[8] They feed upon the sin of My people,
and they are greedy for their iniquity.
[9] It will be like people, like priest.
I will punish them for their ways
and reward them for their deeds.

[10]They will eat, but not be satisfied;
they will play the whore, but not
multiply,
because they have forsaken the LORD
by devoting themselves to [11] harlotry;

[1]*16* Or *My master.* [2]*4* Meaning of Heb. uncertain. [3]*7* MT; Ancient Heb. tradition *They will change.* [4]*7* MT; Ancient Heb. tradition *My glory.*

Steps to National Downfall

From the time of Jonah on, the nation of Israel seemed committed to a lifestyle tha could only lead to destruction. The people of Israel no longer worshipped God o showed their thankfulness to Him for the times of prosperity and blessing He had grantec them. Each successive king seemed to be more evil than the last. The nation was filled witł anarchy and great insecurity.

However, God continued to raise up prophets to bring warning to the people of the con sequences of their actions. In His attempt to get the people to return to Him and leave thei sinning behind, God told the prophet Hosea to take a wife who was involved in the practice of prostitution—a prophetic picture of the whole nation of Israel, which had prostitutec itself to other gods, "departing from the LORD" (Hos 1:2).

In this study we will take a look at the successive steps in Israel's national downfal As you review each of the following steps, consider the similarities to the climate of evi in America. Work through each of the steps below, answering the questions and writin down how you believe God will respond to America's continued turning away from Him.

Step 1: Lack of knowledge (Hos 4:5–6)

It was because Israel had willfully ignored God that it was on the road to ruin. The knowl edge was available, but they rejected it.

1. What does Hosea 8:12 tell us about Israel's rejection of God's truth?

2. What parallels do you see in America today?

Step 2: Stubborn idolatry (Hos 4:12–19)

1. Even though Israel had rejected the knowledge of God and His Word, they still felt th need for guidance. To what did they turn to seek guidance?

2. How is America turning to idolatry today? How has the rise of fortune-telling, spiritism and astrology accelerated America's downfall?

Step 3: Proud apostates (Hos 5:1–15)

1. How do these verses describe the ways Israel's proud priests had used their position of leadership to trap the people into more sin?

____

____

2. What evidence can you list to show how America's spiritual leaders have become proud and have led the people into apostasy?

____

____

A plea for righteousness (Hos 6:1–11)

1. In Hosea 6:1–3 God offers Israel an opportunity to repent and be restored to God after a time of judgment. This promise of restoration is available for America today also. What do verses 1–2 say that God will do if we return to Him?

____

____

What must America do, according to verse 3?

____

____

2. Verse 6 is the key to understanding what God wants:

He wants _________, not _________. He wants _________ more than _________.

Hosea knew his people were as unfaithful to his loving God as Gomer, his adulterous wife, had been to him. Yet God taught Hosea that if he could love and forgive Gomer, God could love an unfaithful people and forgive those who repent. With great compassion, Hosea preached the love of God. Consider the following questions:

1. How can you witness to an unbelieving companion?

____

____

2. To rebellious children?

____

____

3. In what ways will you show God's love to the unbeliever?

____

____

Barbara Dycus

SPIRITLED WOMAN

COUNSEL FROM THE SPIRIT BASICS

The Cutting Away

We need to realize that God wants to purify our lives of the things that keep us from moving forward with His plan. Hosea 6:1–2 paints a picture of what God is doing:

> Come, let us return to the LORD,
> for He has torn,
> and He will heal us.
> He has struck,
> and He will bind us up.
> After two days He will revive us.
> On the third day He will raise us up,
> that we may live before Him.

When I first read that passage, I had a mental image of a lion mauling someone. I could not understand why a loving Father would maul His children in that manner, so I asked God about it.

He told me, "Teresa, you have the wrong picture. Let Me show you what it really means." Then I saw a picture in my mind's eye of a surgeon skillfully cutting around a cancerous growth so it could be removed.

The cutting away of the death within us can be painful. But God's goal for the surgery is to remove those things that work death in us and replace them with His life.

Even if you are already walking in holiness, you will go through a season of God's refinement because He desires to radiate His glory and His presence through your life. He wants pure vessels that He can pour His anointing into.

We can't control whether or not God will take us through His refiner's fire, but we can control how long we stay in the fire. The more we resist Him, the longer the process will take. The more we cooperate with Him, the faster it will go.

Teresa Seputis

wine and new wine
take away understanding.

The Idolatry of Israel

12 My people seek counsel from their wood,
and their staff informs them.
For the spirit of harlotry has led them
astray,
and they have played the whore in
defiance of their God.
13 They sacrifice upon the tops of the
mountains,
and burn incense upon the hills
under oak, poplar, and elm
because their shade is good.
Therefore your daughters play the whore,
and your daughters-in-law commit
adultery.

14 I will not punish your daughters
when they play the whore,
nor your daughters-in-law
when they commit adultery.
For the men separate themselves with
whores,
and they sacrifice with cult prostitutes.
A people without understanding will
come to ruin.

15 Though you play the whore, O Israel,
do not let Judah offend.

Do not come to Gilgal,
or go up to Beth Aven,
and do not swear, "As the LORD lives."
16 Like a stubborn heifer,
Israel is stubborn.
Now will the LORD feed them
like a lamb in a wide pasture?
17 Ephraim is joined to idols;
let him alone.
18 Their drink has soured,
they have played the whore continually.
Her rulers dearly love shame.
19 A wind has wrapped her in its wings,
and they will be ashamed because of
their sacrifices.

Judgment Against Israel and Judah

5 Hear this, O priests!
Pay attention, O house of Israel!
Listen, O house of the king!
For the judgment is for you,
because you have been a snare at Mizpah
and a net spread over Tabor,
2 and a pit dug deep in Shittim;
but I will discipline them all.
3 I know Ephraim,
and Israel is not hidden from Me;
for now, O Ephraim, you have played the
whore.
Israel is defiled.

4 Their deeds do not allow them
to return to their God;
for a spirit of harlotry is in their midst,
and they do not know the LORD.

4:12 Jer 2:27
4:13 Isa 1:29
4:14 Hos 4:1
4:15 Hos 9:15
4:18 Mic 3:11
4:19 Isa 1:29
5:1 Hos 9:8
5:2 Hos 9:15
5:3 Am 3:2
5:4 Hos 4:12

5 The pride of Israel testifies against him.
Israel and Ephraim stumble in their iniquity.
Judah also stumbles with them.
6 With their flocks and their herds they will go
to seek the LORD,
but they will not find Him.
He has withdrawn from them.
7 They have dealt faithlessly with the LORD,
for they have given birth to illegitimate children.
Now the New Moon will devour them
along with their portion.

War, Wrath, and Repentance

8 Blow the horn in Gibeah,
and the trumpet in Ramah.
Cry aloud at Beth Aven,
"*Look* behind you, O Benjamin!"[1]
9 Ephraim will become desolate
in the day of punishment.
Among the tribes of Israel
I make known that which is sure.
10 The princes of Judah have become
like those who remove a boundary marker.
Upon them I will pour out
My wrath like water.
11 Ephraim is oppressed
and broken in judgment,
because he eagerly followed after vanity.
12 Therefore I will be like pus to Ephraim
and like rottenness to the house of Judah.
13 When Ephraim saw his sickness
and Judah saw his wound,
then Ephraim went to Assyria,
and sent to King Jareb.[2]
Yet he cannot cure you
or heal your wound.
14 For I will be like a lion to Ephraim
and like a young lion to the house of Judah.
I, Myself, will tear and go away.
I will carry off, and no one will rescue.
15 I will again return to My place
until they acknowledge their offense
and seek My face.
In their affliction they will earnestly seek Me.

A Call to Repentance

6 Come, let us return to the LORD,
for He has torn,
and He will heal us.
He has struck,
and He will bind us up.
2 After two days He will revive us.
On the third day He will raise us up,
that we may live before Him.
3 Let us know, let us press on to know the LORD.
His appearance is as sure as the dawn.
He will come to us like the rain;
like the spring rains He will water the earth.

You will come as the rain—the latter and former rain—upon the earth (Hos 6:3).

Impenitence of Israel and Judah

4 What shall I do to you, O Ephraim?
What shall I do to you, O Judah?
Your faithfulness is like a morning cloud,
and like the early dew it goes away.
5 Therefore I have hewn them by the prophets.
I have killed them by the words of My mouth,
and My[3] judgments go forth like light.
6 For I desired mercy, and not sacrifice,
and the knowledge of God more than burnt offerings.
7 But like men[4] they have transgressed the covenant.
There they dealt faithlessly with Me.
8 Gilead is a city of evildoers,
polluted with blood.
9 As robbers lie in wait for someone,
so a company of priests
murder on the way to Shechem.
They commit a shameful deed.
10 I have seen a horrible thing
in the house of Israel.
The harlotry of Ephraim is there;
Israel is defiled.
11 Also, O Judah, a harvest is appointed for you,
when I restore the fortunes of My people.

7 When I would heal Israel,
the iniquity of Ephraim is revealed,
and the wickedness of Samaria.
For they deal deceitfully;
the thief breaks in;
the robbers raid outside,
2 but they did not consider in their hearts
that I remember all their wickedness.
Now their own deeds surround them;
they are before My face.

5:5 Hos 7:10
5:6 Pr 1:28
5:7 Hos 6:7
5:8 Hos 9:9
5:9 Isa 46:10
5:10 Dt 19:14
5:11 Dt 28:33
5:12 Isa 51:8
5:13 Hos 7:11
5:14 Ps 7:2
5:15 Jer 2:27
6:1 Dt 32:39
6:2 1Co 15:4
6:3 Ps 72:6
6:4 Hos 11:8
6:5 Jer 23:29
6:6 Mt 9:13
6:7 Hos 5:7
6:8 Hos 12:11
6:9 Hos 7:1
6:10 Hos 5:3
6:11 Joel 3:13
7:2 Jer 2:19

[1]8 Or *"After you, O Benjamin!"* [2]13 Or *the great king.* [3]5 Gk. Syr.: Heb. *Your.* [4]7 Or *like/at Adam.*

PROFILE OF A SPIRITLED WOMAN

AMY CARMICHAEL

"WHAT MORE CAN I GIVE?"

Amy Carmichael was born in Ireland in 1867 to a well-to-do family. She decided to follow Jesus at the age of thirteen. When she was eighteen, her father died, leaving the family in a difficult financial situation. They moved to Belfast, where Amy became involved with the "shawlies," mill girls who wore shawls rather than hats. She saw the appalling conditions in which they lived and worked. Her mission among the "shawlies" grew until she needed a hall seating five hundred. Later she moved to Manchester, England, where she did the same kind of work.

Amy had brown eyes but as a child always wished for blue ones. She was very disappointed when God didn't answer her prayers for her eyes to turn blue. But she was very grateful later on when God revealed His call on her life. Amy also suffered from neuralgia, a very painful neurological condition that often had her bedridden for weeks on end. She was an unlikely candidate for the mission field.

In 1887, at the Keswick Convention, Amy heard Hudson Taylor, founder of the China Inland Mission, speak about the missionary life. Soon she felt God's call to go overseas as a missionary. Initially she went to Japan, but she never really felt at home there. From there she went to Sri Lanka. Then, after a year at home, she set sail for India in 1895, where she did her life's work. She never returned home again, serving for fifty-five years without a furlough.

Amy did not fit into the missionary community in Bangalore—she hated the tea-drinking parties and gossip of the missionary wives. Soon she moved to join the Walker family on the very southern tip of India. Along with one of the Walker daughters and a few Indian Christian ladies, they began an itinerant ministry, speaking about Jesus throughout the surrounding villages. Their motto? "How much can I do without that I may have more to give?" Amy adopted Indian dress and lifestyle, sometimes dying her skin with dark coffee.

In 1901 a young five-year-old girl named Preena was brought to Amy. She had been sold by her mother into temple prostitution and was being taught all the degrading practices of the Hindu temple prostitutes. She had run away twice before, only to be found, taken back to the temple, and beaten. But this time the lady who found her, rather than taking her back to the temple, brought her to Amy. From that time onward Amy Carmichael set herself to rescue these young children from this terrible lifestyle. This work became known as the Dohnavur Fellowship. The organization has rescued literally thousands of children, mainly girls, from the horrific lifestyle of temple prostitute.

In 1931 Amy was crippled by a fall that left her bedridden for the nearly twenty remaining years of her life. She wrote many books during this time. Wheeled in a wheelchair onto the veranda outside her bedroom, children would come and sing songs to her in the evenings.

The impact of Amy Carmichael's life and writing continue to have an impact more than sixty years after her death.[1]

Felicity Dale

1. Research for this article came from "Amy Carmichael" on Wikipedia.com and the Gospel Fellowship Association at http://www.gfamissions.org/missionary-biographies/carmichael-amy-1867-1951.html (accessed April 29, 2014).

Corrupt and Disloyal Politics

[3] They make the king glad with their
wickedness,
and the princes with their lies.
[4] They are all adulterers,
like an oven heated by a baker,
who ceases stirring *the fire*
after kneading the dough until it is
leavened.
[5] On the day of our king the princes made
him sick
from the heat of wine.
He stretched out his hand with scorners.
[6] For they are kindled[1] like an oven.
Their heart burns within them;[2]
their anger smolders[3] all night;
in the morning it blazes like a flaming
fire.
[7] They are all hot as an oven,
and they devour their judges.
All their kings have fallen,
and none of them calls to Me.
[8] Ephraim mixes himself with the people.
Ephraim is a cake not turned.
[9] Foreigners devour his strength,
but he does not know it.
Gray hairs are here and there upon him,
but he does not know it.
[10] The pride of Israel testifies against him,
but they do not return to the LORD their
God,
nor seek Him for all this.
[11] Ephraim is like a dove,
silly and without sense;
they call to Egypt,
they go to Assyria.
[12] Wherever they go, I will spread My net over
them;
I will bring them down like the birds of
the sky;
I will discipline them according to
the report to their congregation.
[13] Woe to them,
for they have fled from Me!
Destruction to them,
for they have rebelled against Me!
Though I would redeem them,
yet they speak lies against Me.
[14] They do not cry to Me with their heart
when they howl on their beds.
They gather together for grain and wine,
they rebel against Me.
[15] Though I trained and strengthened their
arms,
yet they devise mischief against Me.
[16] They return, *but* not to the Most High.
They are like a loose bow.
Their princes will fall by the sword
for the rage of their tongue.
This will be their derision
in the land of Egypt.

7:3 Mic 7:3
7:4 Jer 9:2
7:5 Isa 28:1
7:8 Ps 106:35
7:9 Hos 8:7
7:10 Isa 9:13
7:11 Hos 5:13
7:12 Eze 12:13
7:13 Hos 9:12
7:14 Am 2:8
7:15 Na 1:9
7:16 Ps 78:57

8:1 Dt 28:49
8:4 Hos 2:8
8:5 Jer 13:27
8:7 Pr 22:8
8:8 Jer 22:28
8:9 Jer 2:24
8:10 Eze 16:37
8:11 Hos 12:11
8:12 Hos 4:6
8:13 Hos 9:6

The Apostasy of Israel

8 Set the trumpet to your mouth!
One like an eagle is on the house of the
LORD,
because they have transgressed My
covenant
and rebelled against My law.
[2] Israel cries to Me,
"My God, we know You."
[3] Israel has cast off the good;
the enemy will pursue him.
[4] They set up kings, but not through Me;
they made princes, but I did not know it.
With their silver and gold,
they made idols,
so that they will be cut off.
[5] Your calf, O Samaria, is rejected!
My anger is kindled against them.
How long will they be incapable of
innocence?
[6] For it is from Israel;
a craftsman made it,
and it is not God!
The calf of Samaria
will be broken to pieces.
[7] For they sow the wind,
and they will reap the whirlwind.
The standing grain has no head
and will yield no flour.
If it were to yield,
foreigners would swallow it up.
[8] Israel is swallowed up.
Now they are among the nations
as a vessel in which there is no pleasure.
[9] For they have gone up to Assyria
like a wild donkey alone by itself;
Ephraim has hired lovers.
[10] Though they hire among the nations,
I will now gather them.
They will begin to diminish due to the
burden
of the king of princes.
[11] Because Ephraim has multiplied altars for
sin,
they have become to him altars for
sinning.
[12] I have written for him the great things of
My law,
but they were regarded as a strange
thing.
[13] For the sacrifices of My offerings,
they sacrifice flesh and eat it;

[1]6 Gk. Syr.: Heb. *brought near.* [2]6 Or *while they lie in wait.*
[3]6 Or *Their baker sleeps.*

but the LORD does not accept them.
Now He will remember their iniquity
and punish their sins.
They will return to Egypt.
14 Israel has forgotten his Maker
and built temples,
and Judah has multiplied fortified cities;
so I will send a fire upon his cities,
and it will devour his palaces.

The Punishment of Israel

9 Do not rejoice, O Israel!
Do not exult[1] like the peoples,
for you have played the whore departing from your God.
You have loved a prostitute's wages
on every threshing floor.
2 The threshing floor and the winepress will not feed them,
and the new wine will fail in her.
3 They will not dwell in the land of the LORD;
but Ephraim will return to Egypt,
and they will eat unclean things in Assyria.
4 They will not offer wine offerings to the LORD,
and their sacrifices will not please Him.
Their sacrifices will be like the bread of mourners;
all who eat of it will be defiled.
For their bread will be only to satisfy their own hunger;
it will not come into the house of the LORD.

5 What will you do on the appointed day,
and on the day of the festival of the LORD?
6 For indeed they are gone because of destruction.
Egypt will gather them,
and Memphis will bury them.
Nettles will possess their pleasant things of silver,
and thorns will be in their tents.
7 The days of punishment have come;
the days of recompense have come.
Israel knows!
The prophet is a fool;
the man of the spirit is insane,
because of your great iniquity and great hatred.
8 The watchman of Ephraim is a prophet for my God;
yet a fowler's snare is on all his ways,
and hatred in the house of his God.
9 They have deeply corrupted themselves
as in the days of Gibeah.
He will remember their iniquity,
He will punish their sins.

10 Like grapes in the wilderness,
I found Israel.
Like the first fruit on the fig tree in its first season,
I saw your fathers.
But they went to Baal Peor
and consecrated themselves to *a thing of* shame,
and they became an abomination like *the thing* they loved.
11 As for Ephraim, their glory shall fly away like a bird:
no birth, no pregnancy, no conception!
12 Though they bring up their children,
I will bereave them until none are left.
Woe to them indeed,
when I depart from them!
13 Just as I saw Ephraim like Tyre,
planted in a pleasant place,
so now Ephraim will bring out
his children for slaughter.

14 Give them, O LORD—
what will You give?
Give them a miscarrying womb
and dry breasts.

15 All their wickedness is in Gilgal,
for there I hated them.
Because of the wickedness of their deeds,
I will drive them out of My house.
I will love them no more.
All their princes are rebels.
16 Ephraim is stricken,
their root is dried up,
they shall bear no fruit.
Even though they give birth,
I will slay the beloved offspring of their womb.

17 My God will reject them
because they did not listen to Him,
and they will be wanderers among the nations.

Israel's Sin and Captivity

10 Israel is a fertile vine
that brings forth its fruit.
As his fruit multiplied,
so his altars increased;
as his land prospered,
so he[2] improved *his* pillars.
2 Their heart is divided;
now they must bear their guilt.
He will break down their altars
and destroy their pillars.
3 For now they will say,
"We have no king,

8:14 Dt 32:18
9:1 Hos 10:5
9:2 Hos 2:9
9:3 Lev 25:23
9:4 Hos 8:13
9:5 Isa 10:3
9:6 Hos 10:8
9:7 Mic 7:4
9:8 Hos 5:1
9:9 Hos 10:9
9:10 Jer 11:13
9:12 Hos 7:13
9:13 Eze 26:1–21
9:14 Lk 23:29
9:15 Hos 4:15
9:17 Hos 7:13
10:1 Hos 8:11
10:2 1Ki 18:21

[1] 1 Gk.; Heb. *to exultation.* [2] 1 Heb. *they.*

because we do not fear the LORD;
and a king, what could he do for us?"
4 They speak mere words,
swearing falsely
in making a covenant.
Thus judgment springs up like a poisonous
plant
in the furrows of the field.
5 The inhabitants of Samaria fear
because of the calf of Beth Aven.
For its people mourn for it,
and its priests shriek for it,
because its glory has departed from it.
6 It will be carried to Assyria
as a tribute to King Jareb.[1]
Ephraim shall be put to shame,
and Israel shall be ashamed of his idol.[2]
7 As for Samaria, her king will perish
like a twig on the water.
8 The high places of Aven, the sin of Israel,
will be destroyed.
Thorn and thistle will grow
on their altars.
They will say to the mountains, Cover us,
and to the hills, Fall on us.

9 O Israel, you have sinned since the days of
Gibeah.
There they have continued.[3]
Will not the war in Gibeah against evildoers
overtake them?
10 When I desire, I will punish them.
The nations will be gathered against
them
when they are disciplined[4] for their two
transgressions.
11 Ephraim is a trained heifer
that loves to thresh grain,
but I harnessed her fair neck;
I will make Ephraim pull *a plow*.
Judah will plow;
Jacob shall furrow for himself.
12 Sow to yourselves righteousness,
reap mercy,
break up your fallow ground;
for it is time to seek the LORD,
until He comes
and rains righteousness upon you.
13 You have plowed wickedness.
You have reaped iniquity,
and you have eaten the fruit of lies.
Because you have trusted in your power
and in the numbers of your warriors,
14 therefore a tumult will arise among your
people,
and all your fortresses will be destroyed
as Shalman destroyed Beth Arbel in the
day of battle;
mothers were dashed to pieces upon
their children.

10:4 Am 5:7
10:5 Hos 9:11
10:6 Hos 5:13
10:7 Hos 10:3
10:8 Hos 9:6
10:9 Hos 9:9
10:10 Eze 5:13
10:12 Isa 45:8
10:13 Job 4:8
10:14 Hos 13:16

11:1 Ex 4:22
11:2 Hos 2:13
11:3 Dt 1:31
11:4 Lev 26:13
11:5 Hos 7:16
11:6 Hos 13:16
11:7 Jer 8:5
11:8 Ge 14:8
11:9 Nu 23:19
11:10 Isa 31:4
11:11 Isa 11:11

15 So will it be done to you, O Bethel,
because of your great wickedness.
At dawn
the king of Israel will be utterly cut off.

Let the fortresses of darkness
be destroyed, in the name of Jesus
(Hos 10:14).

God's Love for Israel

11 When Israel was a child, I loved him,
and out of Egypt I called My son.
2 As I[5] called them,
so they went from Me.[6]
They sacrificed to the Baals
and burned incense to idols.
3 I taught Ephraim to walk,
taking them up in My[7] arms,
but they did not know
that I healed them.
4 I drew them with cords of human
kindness,[8]
with bands of love.
I was to them as those who ease the yoke
on their neck,[9]
and I bent down and fed them.

5 He will return[10] to the land of Egypt,
and Assyria will be his king,
because they refused to return *to Me*.
6 The sword slashes in their cities,
consumes their oracle-priests,
and devours because of their own
counsels.
7 My people are bent on backsliding
from Me.
Though they called to the Most High,
none at all exalt Him.

8 How can I give you up, Ephraim?
How can I hand you over, Israel?
How can I make you like Admah?
How can I treat you like Zeboyim?
My heart churns within Me;
My compassion is stirred.
9 I will not execute the fierceness of My
anger;
I will not again destroy Ephraim.
For I am God, and not man,
the Holy One in your midst,
and I will not come in wrath.
10 They will walk after the LORD,
who roars like a lion.
When He roars,
His children will come trembling from
the west.
11 They will come trembling
like a bird out of Egypt

[1]6 Or *the great king*. [2]6 Or *counsel*. [3]9 Or *There they stood*.
[4]10 Gk.; Heb. *bound*. [5]2 Gk.; Heb. *they*. [6]2 Gk.; Heb. *them*.
[7]3 Gk. Syr. Vulg.; Heb. *his*. [8]4 Heb. *cords of a man*. [9]4 Or *jaws*.
[10]5 So LXX. Heb. *He not will return*.

and like a dove from the land of Assyria.
And I will let them dwell in their houses,
says the LORD.

God's Charge Against Ephraim

[12] Ephraim has surrounded Me with lies,
and the house of Israel with deceit.
But Judah still walks with God,
and is faithful to the Holy One.[1]

12

Ephraim feeds on the wind
and chases after the east wind all day long.
He multiplies lies and devastation.
They make a covenant with Assyria,
and oil is carried to Egypt.

A History of Rebellion

[2] The LORD has a dispute with Judah,
and will punish Jacob according to his ways,
and repay him according to his doings.
[3] In the womb, he took his brother by the heel,
and by his strength he strove with God.
[4] He struggled with the angel, and prevailed;
he wept, and sought favor from Him.
He found Him in Bethel,
and there He spoke with us.
[5] As for the LORD the God of Hosts,
the LORD is the name by which He is invoked!
[6] But as for you, return to your God,
hold fast to mercy and justice,
and wait on your God continually.

[7] A merchant, in whose hands are deceitful balances,
he loves to oppress.
[8] Ephraim said,
"Yet I am rich, I have found wealth for myself.
In all my labors, they shall find no offense in me
that would be sin."
[9] I am the LORD your God
from the land of Egypt.
I will again make you to dwell in tents,
as in the days of the appointed feast.
[10] I have spoken by the prophets,
and I have multiplied visions,
and through the prophets I will bring destruction.[2]

[11] In Gilead there is iniquity;
surely they will come to nothing.
In Gilgal they sacrifice bulls,
so their altars will be like stone heaps
in the furrows of the fields.
[12] Jacob fled to the land of Aram,
and Israel served for a wife,
and for a wife he kept *sheep.*
[13] By a prophet the LORD brought Israel up from Egypt,
and by a prophet he was preserved.
[14] Ephraim provoked Him to anger most bitterly,
so his Lord shall leave his bloodguilt on him
and repay him for his reproach.

God's Unrelenting Judgment on Israel

13

When Ephraim spoke, trembling,
he was exalted in Israel.
But he incurred guilt through Baal *worship* and he died.
[2] And now they continue sinning
and have made a cast image for themselves,
idols of their silver, according to their understanding;
all of them the work of craftsmen.
They say of them,
"Those who sacrifice[3]
are kissing calves!"
[3] Therefore they will be like the morning cloud,
or like the early dew that passes away,
like chaff blown off the threshing floor,
or like the smoke from a chimney.

[4] Yet I am the LORD your God
ever since the land of Egypt.
You know no God but Me,
and there is no savior besides Me.
[5] I knew[4] you in the wilderness,
in the land of great drought.
[6] When they had pasture, they were satisfied.
They were satisfied, and their heart was exalted;
therefore they forgot Me.
[7] So I will be like a lion to them,
like a leopard I will lurk by the path.
[8] I will attack them like a bear bereaved of her cubs,
and will tear open their rib cage.
There I will devour them like a lion,
as the wild beast would tear them to pieces.

[9] O Israel, you are destroyed,[5]
but in Me is your help.
[10] Where now is your king
that he may save you in all your cities?
And where are your judges of whom you said,
"Give me a king and princes"?
[11] I gave you a king in My anger,
and took him away in My wrath.

12:2 Hos 4:1
12:3 Ge 25:26
12:4 Ge 35:15
12:5 Ex 3:15
12:6 Mic 6:8
12:7 Pr 11:1
12:8 Rev 3:17
12:10 2Ki 17:13
12:11 Hos 8:11
12:14 Eze 18:13
13:1 Hos 11:2
13:2 Isa 44:17–20
13:3 Ps 68:2
13:4 Hos 12:9
13:5 Dt 2:7
13:6 Dt 32:13–15
13:7 Jer 5:6
13:8 2Sa 17:8
13:9 Dt 33:26
13:10 Hos 8:4
13:11 1Sa 10:19

[1] 12 Or *holy ones.* [2] 10 Or *speak in parables.* [3] 2 Or *those who offer human sacrifice.* [4] 5 Or *fed.* [5] 9 Heb. *he has destroyed you.*

WOMAN OF THE SPIRIT

In the Still of the Night

What is expected of you in the night season? Israel had been through a very tumultuous season when God spoke in Hosea 14:5 and said, "I will be like the dew to Israel." This little verse is packed with revelation. Dew is the tiny drops of moisture that appear on cool surfaces in the early morning. We often see it glistening on plants and blades of grass on clear days. But as my mom would say, "What does that have to do with the price of coffee?" I'm glad you asked.

Dew is usually produced late at night or early in the morning, before the sun rises. It brings relief to vegetation and livestock by providing water to sustain them when the sun is the hottest. Even when rain is scarce, it is possible for dew to form before the sun comes up.

In the same way, it is the dew formed in the night season that will nourish your soul and sustain you in the heat of your trial. This supernatural dew will give you everything you need.

The dew point is the temperature at which moisture in the air begins to condense. Objects receive heat from the sun during the day, but when night comes, the blade of grass is not able to retain the heat that has been stored. So it becomes cool, as does the air around it. When the air reaches the dew point, it can no longer hold all the moisture present, and the excess is deposited as dew on the grass and plants.

Natural dew can be produced only when everything is still; the process occurs in the quiet of the night. Likewise, God wants to produce something in our lives during the stillness of the night season. Before the day starts, God is waiting for us. He wants our attention on Him and Him alone. When we wait in His presence, He will begin to nourish us.

Dew doesn't collect when it's windy. It doesn't appear during rainstorms. It doesn't form when the air is hot. Dew forms when things are cool and still.

Before your joy comes in the morning, you must have a season of God-filled quietness when you can hear His voice. Isaiah 30:15 says we shall receive strength "in quietness and in confidence." You can't get clear direction when there is commotion; the noise in your environment frustrates communication. Rather, in stillness, the voice of God can be clearly heard.

In the darkest of night the enemy will torment your mind. He will make you restless and agitated. My heart was broken over and over during a significant transition process, and I was still wincing from spiritual wounds I suffered. On many nights I would drive for hours on end. My mind would not rest, and I had no peace. It was extremely difficult for me to get nourishment from the Lord. I was not still enough to hear His voice.

It wasn't until I got the mind of Christ and shut my mouth that God was able to intervene. He comforted me and held me in His arms. I felt the Holy Spirit envelop me. His presence sustained me when I stopped seeking vindication. I heard the Lord say, "Hold your peace, and I will fight your battle." As I rested in His bosom, I felt supernatural peace.

Riva Tims

12 The iniquity of Ephraim is bound up;
his sin is stored up.
13 The pains of childbirth come for him.
He is an unwise son,
for he does not present himself
at the opening of the womb.

14 I will ransom them from the power of
Sheol.
I will redeem them from Death.
O Death, where are your plagues?
O Sheol, where is your sting?
Compassion is hidden from My eyes.
15 Though he be fruitful among *his*
brothers,
the east wind will come, a wind of the
LORD,
rising from the wilderness.
And his spring shall become dry,
his fountain shall be dried up.
It shall plunder *his* treasury
of every desirable thing.
16 Samaria will be held guilty,
for she has rebelled against her God.
They will fall by the sword,
their infants will be dashed to pieces,
and their pregnant women will be
ripped open.

A Plea for Repentance

14 Return, O Israel, to the LORD your God,
for you have stumbled because of
your iniquity.
2 Take words with you
and return to the LORD.
Say to Him,
"Take away all iniquity,
and accept that which is good;
and we will offer the fruit[1] of our lips!
3 Assyria will not save us,
we will not ride on horses.
We will no longer say, 'Our God,'
to the work of our hands.
In You the orphan finds mercy."

4 I will heal their backsliding;
I will love them freely,
for My anger has turned away from him.
5 I will be like the dew to Israel;
he shall grow like the lily
and shall strike his roots
like Lebanon.
6 His branches will spread out,
and his beauty shall be like the olive tree,
and his fragrance like that of Lebanon.
7 Those that dwell under his shadow will
return,
they will flourish like the grain
and grow as a vine.
Their fragrance will be like the wine of
Lebanon.
8 O Ephraim, what have I to do with idols?
It is I who answer and look after him.
I am like a green fir tree;
your fruit is found in Me.

9 Whoever is wise, let him understand these
things;
whoever prudent, let him know them.
For the ways of the LORD are right,
and the just will walk in them;
but the transgressors stumble in them.

13:12 Job 14:17
13:13 Isa 13:8
13:14 Ps 49:15
13:15 Eze 19:12
13:16 2Ki 8:12
14:1 Hos 6:1
14:2 Heb 13:15
....
14:3 Ps 10:14
14:4 Zep 3:17
14:5 Isa 35:2
14:6 Ps 52:8
14:7 Ps 91:1
14:9 Ps 107:43

[1]2 Gk. Syr.; Heb. *bulls*.

Author: The prophet Joel

Written: Between 835 and 800 BC

Themes: The Day of the Lord, Deliverance, Restoration

JOEL

Dear Spirit Led Woman,

The prophet Joel told of a coming time when God would pour out His Spirit on all flesh (Joel 2:28–29). These words came true on the Day of Pentecost. They were also echoed by Peter in the first sermon he preached in the Book of Acts. During the days of the early church the new believers went straight to the marketplace after being baptized in the Spirit; there they declared what had happened. As far as we know from the biblical record, no one told them to do that; they just had such an intense awareness of who Jesus is—glorified and risen—that they were compelled to share it! Even in the midst of the persecution that attended their testimonies, they could not keep silent. The Bible tells us that miraculous signs followed those who believed.

I believe one key to experiencing the type of outpouring Joel foretold is to drive all areas of compromise out of your heart. This will give you a greater vision of who Jesus is. Then, as the early Christians did, you will dream dreams, see visions, and speak His Word to the whole earth.

Joy F. Strang

1 The word of the LORD, which came to Joel, son of Pethuel.

A Land Laid Waste

2 Hear this, elders,
and give ear, all inhabitants of the land!
Has anything like this happened in your days,
or in the days of your fathers?
3 Tell it to your children,
and let your children tell their children,
and let their children tell another generation.
4 What the fledging locust left,
the adult locust has eaten;
what the adult locust left,
the larval locust has eaten;
what the larval locust left,
the hopper locust has eaten.

5 Awaken, drunkards, and weep!
Wail, all wine-drinkers,
because the sweet wine
has been cut off from your lips.
6 For a nation powerful and innumerable
has invaded my land;
its teeth are like the teeth of a lion,
like the fangs of a lioness.
7 It has despoiled my vine,
and splintered my fig tree;
it has stripped off its bark
and cast it away,
leaving its branches white.

8 Lament like a virgin wearing sackcloth
for the husband of her youth.
9 The grain offering and the drink offering
are cut off from the house of the LORD;
the priests mourn, who are
ministers to the LORD.
10 The field is ravaged,
the ground mourns;
for the grain is ruined,
the new wine is dried up,
and the oil dwindles.

11 Despair, fieldworkers;
wail, vinedressers,
for the wheat and the barley,
because the harvest of the field has perished.
12 The vine is dried up,
and the fig tree is withered;
pomegranate, palm, and apple—
all the trees of the field are dry;
surely joy has withered away
from the sons of men.

A Call to Repentance

13 Put on sackcloth and lament, O priests;
wail, ministers of the altar.
Come, spend the night in sackcloth,
ministers of my God,
because the grain offering and the drink offering
are withheld from the house of your God.
14 Consecrate a fast,
call a sacred assembly,
assemble the elders
and all the inhabitants of the land
to the house of the LORD your God,
and cry out to the LORD.

15 Alas, for the day!
For the day of the LORD is near,
and like devastation from the Almighty it comes.

16 Has not the food been cut off
before our eyes,
joy and gladness
from the house of our God?
17 The seeds have shriveled
under their shovels,
the storehouses have been deserted;
the granaries have been torn down,
because the grain has dried up.
18 How the beasts groan!
The herds of cattle are confused,
because they have no pasture;
even the flocks of sheep suffer.

19 To You, O LORD, I call,
because fire has devoured the wild pastures,
and flame has burned all the trees of the field.
20 Even the beasts of the field long for You,
because the streams of water have dried up,
and fire has devoured the wild pastures.

The Day of the LORD

2 Blow the ram's horn in Zion,
sound the alarm on My holy mountain!

All the inhabitants of the earth will tremble,
because the day of the LORD has come,
because it is near—
2 a day of darkness and gloom,
a day of clouds and thick darkness.
Like blackness spreading over the mountain,
a great and mighty army comes,
such as was never before,
and will never be again,
even through the years of all generations.

3 Before them fire devours,
and behind them a flame blazes;
the land is like the garden of Eden before them,

1:1 Jer 1:2
1:2 Hos 5:1
1:4 Joel 2:25
1:6 Joel 2:25
1:7 Isa 5:6
1:8 Isa 22:12
1:9 Joel 2:14
1:11 Isa 17:11
1:12 Isa 24:11
1:13 Jer 4:8
1:14 Joel 2:15–16
1:15 Jer 30:7
1:18 Jer 12:4
1:19 Ps 50:15
1:20 Ps 104:21
2:1 Joel 1:15
2:2 Joel 1:6
2:3 Ge 2:8

but behind them a desolate wasteland,
and nothing escapes them.
4 They have the appearance of horses,
and like cavalry they run.
5 As with the sound of chariots,
they leap on the mountaintops,
as with the sound of a flame of fire
consuming stubble,
as a mighty army arrayed for war.

6 Before them, peoples are tormented;
every face turns pale.
7 Like mighty men they run,
like men of war they scale a wall;
each marches on his way,
they do not swerve from their paths.
8 They do not jostle one another;
each marches in his track.
Through the weapons they plunge;
they do not break rank.
9 They rush on the city,
they run on the wall;
they climb up into the houses,
they enter through the windows like
thieves.
10 Before them the earth quakes,
the heavens shake;
the sun and moon darken,
and the stars withdraw their radiance.
11 The LORD has sounded His voice
before His army,
for His camp is exceedingly great;
mighty is the one who accomplishes His
word.
For great is the day of the LORD,
and very awe-inspiring.
Who can endure it?

Return to the LORD

12 Yet even now, declares the LORD,
return to Me with all your heart,
and with fasting and with weeping and
with mourning.

13 Rend your heart,
and not your garments;
return to the LORD your God,
for He is gracious and merciful,
slow to anger, and abounding in steadfast
love;
and He relents from punishing.
14 Who knows? He might turn aside and
relent,
and He might leave behind a blessing—
a grain offering and a food offering
for the LORD your God.

15 Blow the ram's horn in Zion,
consecrate a fast,
call a sacred assembly.
16 Gather the people,
consecrate the congregation,
assemble the elders,
gather the children
and those nursing at the breast;
let the bridegroom leave his room
and the bride her chamber.
17 Between the temple porch and the altar,
let the priests, ministers of the LORD,
weep and say,
"Have pity upon Your people,
and do not make Your heritage a
disgrace,
a mockery among the nations.
Why should they say among the peoples,
'Where is their God?' "

Rescue and Restitution

18 Then the LORD became jealous for His land
and took pity upon His people.

19 So the LORD answered and said to His
people,

2:4 Rev 9:7
2:5 Isa 5:24
2:6 Na 2:10
2:7 Pr 30:27
2:9 Jer 9:21
2:10 Ps 18:7
2:11 Rev 18:8
2:12 Jer 4:1
2:13 Ps 34:18
2:14 Joel 1:13
2:15 Joel 1:14
....
2:17 Eze 8:16
2:18 Zec 1:14
2:19 Eze 34:29

SPIRITLED WOMAN

COUNSEL FROM THE SPIRIT BASICS

Candidate for Visions

And it will be that, afterwards, I will pour out My Spirit on all flesh; then your sons and daughters will prophesy, your old men will dream dreams, and your young men will see visions.

—JOEL 2:28

According to Joel, believers can expect to receive dreams and visions, a primary purpose for the Spirit's outpouring. Most dreams and visions reveal God's heart about a person or place and His plans to bring something to pass. Others are simply revelations of Himself.

Visions are real and occur more frequently than you might suspect. Have you ever had a dream or a vision? It may represent divine guidance or insight into a question you have posed. How should you respond? Paul's two questions on the Damascus Road provide the right response:

1. "Who are You, Lord?"
2. "Lord, what will You have me do?" (Ac 9:5–6).

They Will Come

Swing the sickle,
for the harvest is ripe.
Come and tread,
for the winepress is full.
The wine vats overflow,
because their evil is great.
—Joel 3:13

Many believers in the church are frustrated because they don't see a harvest. They're discouraged because they see so little fruit being produced, and they wonder why. But they keep going to the same people.

In the parable of the great banquet in Luke 14:15–24, the rich didn't want to come to the banquet. They were busy enjoying their money and possessions and made excuses. The poor can't do these things, and they are eager to come to the banquet when they are invited. God says there are no excuses, but believers keep going to the wealthy and well fed in the world, wondering why they don't respond. There are just as many lost in first-world nations, yet the church is often not equipped to reach them.

Jesus awakens us to love, but the church itself must wake up! We are not yet ready to go to the banquet at the wedding feast. The Father's house is still not full. We must reach the lost, but first we must learn how. The harvest is plentiful, but the laborers who carry His heart are few. Our lives must be living incarnations of the love of Christ Jesus if we will ever have an effective ministry.

What is our motivation for ministry? The Lord is looking for servant lovers—people who are passionate and filled with love for Him, people who desire and are longing for the Bridegroom's return, people who can already taste the feast and know it's about to begin. These people can no longer stand to stay in their comfort zones. They will literally run out and call in the poor, the crippled, the blind, and the lame. And if we will go out and call them—showing them the love of God—they will come.

Heidi Baker

Here! I am sending you grain, new wine,
and oil,
and you will be satisfied,
and I will never again make you
a disgrace among the nations.
20 I will remove the northerner far from you,
and I will banish him to a dry and
desolate land,
those in front to the eastern sea,
and those in back to the western sea,
and his stink will rise,
and his stench will rise,
for he has done great things.
21 Do not be afraid, land;
exult and rejoice,
for the LORD has done great things!
22 Do not be afraid, beasts of the field,
because the wild pastures flourish,
because the tree bears its fruit;
the fig tree and the vine yield their
abundance.
23 And children of Zion, exult
and rejoice in the LORD your God,
because He has given to you
the early rain for vindication.
He showers down rains for you,
the early rain and the latter rain, as
before.
24 Then the threshing floors will be filled with
grain,
and the vats will overflow with new
wine and oil.

My children will be restored (Joel 2:25).

25 And I will compensate you for the years the
locusts have eaten—
the larval locust, the hopper locust,
and the fledging locust—
My great army which I sent against you.

He satisfies me with bread and water,
and I lack no good thing (Joel 2:26).

26 You will eat abundantly and be satisfied,
and you will praise the name of the LORD
your God,
who has worked wonders for you;
and My people will never again be shamed.
27 Then you will know that I am in the midst
of Israel,
that I am the LORD your God,
and that there is no other.
And My people will never again be
shamed.

2:20 Zec 14:8
2:21 Isa 54:4
2:22 Ps 65:12
2:23 Zec 10:7
2:24 Lev 26:10
2:26 Lev 26:5
2:27 Joel 3:17

....

2:28 Eze 39:29
2:29 1Co 12:13
2:30 Lk 21:11
2:31 Mal 4:5
2:32 Isa 46:13
3:1 Jer 16:15
3:2 Isa 66:16
3:3 Am 2:6
3:4 Isa 34:8

The Outpouring of the Spirit

28 And it will be that, afterwards,
I will pour out My Spirit on all flesh;
then your sons and your daughters will
prophesy,
your old men will dream dreams,
and your young men will see visions.

I am anointed to prophesy (Joel 2:28).

29 Even on the menservants and
maidservants
in those days I will pour out My Spirit.
30 Then I will work wonders in the heavens
and the earth—
blood and fire and columns of smoke.
31 The sun will be turned to darkness,
and the moon to blood,
before the great and awe-inspiring day
of the LORD comes.

I call upon the Lord, and
He delivers me (Joel 2:32).

32 And it will be that everyone
who calls on the name of the LORD will
be saved.
For on Mount Zion and in Jerusalem
there will be deliverance,
as the LORD has said,
and among the survivors
whom the LORD calls.

Judging the Nations

3 In those days and at that time,
when I restore the fortunes of Judah and
Jerusalem,
2 I will gather all the nations,
and bring them down to the Valley of
Jehoshaphat.
I will enter into judgment with them there
regarding My people and My heritage
Israel,
whom they have scattered among the
nations;
they have also divided up My land.
3 They have cast lots for My people,
and have traded a boy for a prostitute;
they have sold a girl for wine,
that they might drink.

4 Also, what are you to Me, Tyre and Sidon
and all the regions of Philistia? Are you re-
paying Me for something? If you are repay-
ing Me, I will return your payment swiftly and
speedily on your head. 5 For you have taken
My silver and My gold, and you have carried
off My finest treasures to your temples. 6 You

have sold the people of Judah and Jerusalem
to the Greeks in order to remove them far from
their border.
[7] I am about to rouse them from the place to
which you have sold them, and I will return
your payment on your head. [8] I will sell your
sons and your daughters into the hand of the
people of Judah, and they will sell them to
the Sabeans—to a distant nation, for the LORD
has spoken.

[9] Proclaim this among the nations:
Consecrate a war!
Stir up the mighty men!
Let all the men of war draw near and rise.
[10] Beat your plowshares into swords
and your pruning hooks into spears;
let the weakling say,
"I am a warrior!"
[11] Hurry and come, all you surrounding nations,
and gather there.

Bring down Your warriors, O LORD.
[12] Let the nations be roused,
and go up to the Valley of Jehoshaphat;
for there I will sit
to judge all the surrounding nations.
[13] Swing the sickle,
for the harvest is ripe.
Come and tread,
for the winepress is full.
The wine vats overflow,
because their evil is great.

[14] Multitudes, multitudes,
in the valley of decision!
For the day of the LORD is near
in the valley of the decision.

3:7 Isa 43:5–6
3:8 Isa 60:14
3:10 Isa 2:4
3:11 Isa 13:3
3:12 Isa 2:4
3:13 Hos 6:11
3:14 Isa 34:2–8

3:15 Joel 2:10
3:16 Am 1:2
3:17 Joel 2:27
3:18 Isa 30:25
3:19 Isa 19:1–15
3:20 Eze 37:25
3:21 Isa 4:4

[15] The sun and moon darken,
and the stars withdraw their radiance.
[16] The LORD roars from Zion,
and sounds His voice from Jerusalem,
and heaven and earth quake.
But the LORD is a refuge for His people,
and a stronghold for the children of Israel.

The LORD Dwells in Zion

[17] Then you will know that I am the LORD your God,
who dwells in Zion, My holy mountain.
And Jerusalem will be holy,
and invaders will never again pass through her.

Let water flow into every valley place of my life (Joel 3:18).

[18] And it will be that in that day the
mountains will drip sweet wine,
and the hills will flow with milk,
and all the streambeds of Judah will flow with water;
a spring will proceed from the house of the LORD
and will water the Valley of Shittim.
[19] Egypt will become a desolation,
and Edom a desolate wasteland,
because of the violence done to the people of Judah—
they shed innocent blood in their land.
[20] But Judah will be inhabited forever,
and Jerusalem for generations and generations.
[21] I will avenge their blood,
which I have not yet avenged.

The LORD dwells in Zion!

Author: The prophet Amos

Written: Between 760 and 753 BC

Themes: Judgment, Social Injustice

AMOS

Dear Spirit Led Woman,

Amos was a shepherd and farmer during a time of idolatry and corruption in Israel, a time when the rich oppressed the poor. But God raised him up to condemn the social injustice of his day. Amos pleaded with the people of Israel to repent and return to God. "Seek good and not evil, so that you may live; then the LORD, the God of Hosts, will truly be with you" (Am 5:14). Verse 15 continues, "Hate evil and love good, and establish justice at the gate."

This shows us that our modern concept of justice has a biblical base. Amos 5:24 tells us that we should "let justice roll down like water, and righteousness like an ever-flowing stream."

The Bible often describes Jesus as being moved with compassion when He saw the needs of others. He then followed the Spirit's leading to accomplish the Father's will in each situation. When it comes to modern social justice issues, get involved! Be inspired by the words of Amos, be moved with compassion like Jesus, and follow the Spirit's leading to accomplish God's will.

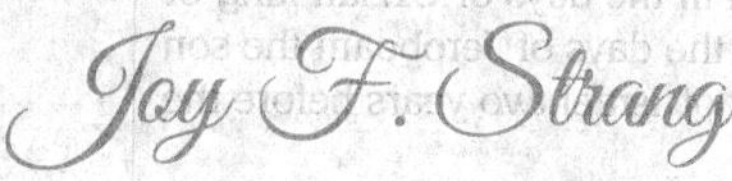

SPIRITLED WOMAN

COUNSEL FROM THE SPIRIT BASICS

SpiritLed Giving

Unconstrained, unstudied SpiritLed giving without pressure causes a new river of financial freedom. A person who gives under pressure may as well keep the money in her pocket. Pressure takes the joy out of giving, and God loves a cheerful giver. This does not mean we should have to pump ourselves up at every offering. It means we should live lifestyles of cheerfulness that create giving hearts. Giving hearts create giving atmospheres. This is the best offering we can give God. The attitudes and atmospheres from which we give mean everything to God.

In Amos 4:4–5 the people gave thanksgiving offerings in great distress and not out of thankful hearts. They were offering to try to gain God's favor, but God rejected them because they were not given with the right attitude of thanksgiving or an atmosphere of love. *Salem* is the Hebrew word for the thanksgiving offering. It is also called the *peace offering*. It gives true thanks and praise to God.

Kimberly Daniels

Judgment Against Israel's Neighbors

1 The words of Amos, who was among the
shepherds of Tekoa, which he saw concerning Israel in the days of Uzziah king of
Judah and in the days of Jeroboam the son
of Joash king of Israel two years before the
earthquake.

2 He said:

The LORD roars from Zion
and utters His voice from Jerusalem;
the pastures of the shepherds languish,
the top of Carmel withers.

3 Thus says the LORD:

For three transgressions of Damascus,
and for four, I will not revoke the punishment,
because they have threshed Gilead
with threshing sledges of iron.
4 So I will send fire against the house of Hazael,
and it will devour the fortresses of Ben-Hadad.
5 I will break the gate bar of Damascus;
from the Valley of Aven I will cut off the one enthroned,
and from Beth Eden the one who holds the scepter.
The people of Aram will go into captivity to Kir,
says the LORD.

6 Thus says the LORD:

For three transgressions of Gaza,
and for four, I will not revoke the punishment,
because they carried away into exile an entire deportation,
to deliver them up to Edom.
7 So I will send fire against the wall of Gaza,
and it will devour its fortresses.
8 From Ashdod I will cut off the one enthroned
and from Ashkelon the one who holds the scepter.
I will turn My hand against Ekron,
and the remnant of the Philistines will perish,
says the Lord GOD.

9 Thus says the LORD:

For three transgressions of Tyre,
and for four, I will not revoke the punishment,
because they delivered up an entire deportation to Edom,
and did not remember the covenant of kinship.
10 So I will send fire against the wall of Tyre,
and it will devour its fortresses.

11 Thus says the LORD:

For three transgressions of Edom,
and for four, I will not revoke the punishment,
because he pursued his brother with the sword,
and repressed all pity;
his anger tore with no ceasing,
and his wrath persisted with no end.
12 So I will send fire against Teman,
and it will devour the fortresses of Bozrah.

13 Thus says the LORD:

For three transgressions of the Ammonites,
and for four, I will not revoke the punishment,
because they ripped open the pregnant women of Gilead,
in order to enlarge their border.

1:1 2Sa 14:2
1:2 Joel 3:16
1:3 Isa 8:4
1:4 2Ki 6:24
1:5 2Ki 16:9
1:6 2Ch 28:18
1:8 Eze 25:16
1:9 1Ki 9:11–14
1:10 Zec 9:4
1:11 2Ch 28:17
1:13 Hos 13:16

SPIRIT-TO-SPIRIT PRAYER

PRAYER FOR DESPONDENT AND REBELLIOUS CHILDREN

Dear Father God,

My children are lost and without Your protection and guidance. Your Word declares, "Believe in the Lord Jesus Christ, and you and your household will be saved" (Ac 16:31).

Lord, Your promises never change. I rebuke the works of the enemy in my children's lives, and in the name of Jesus I come against all the strongholds of the enemy against my family. I come against all evil spirits that keep my children bound, confused, full of unbelief, and unwilling to give their lives to the will of God.

I bind their will to the will of God and to the truth in God's Word. Thank You, Lord, for Your promise in Matthew 16:19 that everything we bind on earth will be bound in heaven and everything we loose on earth will be loosed in heaven.

I declare that my children and my family will serve You. Father, I declare that I will stand fast in Your liberty and not be entangled again with the yoke of bondage, as Galatians 5:1 states. I thank You for setting us free and redeeming us with the blood of Jesus.

In the name of Jesus, amen.

Iris Delgado

14 So I will kindle a fire against the wall of
Rabbah,
and it will devour its fortresses,
with a war cry on the day of battle,
with a tempest on the day of the
whirlwind.
15 Their king shall go into captivity,
he and his princes together,
says the LORD.

2 Thus says the LORD:

For three transgressions of Moab,
and for four, I will not revoke the
punishment,
because he burned to lime
the bones of the king of Edom.
2 So I will send fire against Moab,
and it will devour the fortresses of
Kerioth;
Moab will die in uproar,
with a war cry and the alarm of the
trumpet.
3 I will cut off the ruler from its midst,
and will slay all its princes with him,
says the LORD.

1:14 Dt 3:11
1:15 Jer 49:3
2:1 Isa 15:1–9
2:2 Jer 48:24
2:3 Jer 48:7

2:4 Eze 20:24
2:5 Jer 17:27
2:6 Joel 3:3
2:7 Am 5:12

Judgment Against Judah

4 Thus says the LORD:

For three transgressions of Judah,
and for four, I will not revoke the
punishment,
because they have rejected the law of the
LORD,
and have not kept His commandments.
The lies which their fathers followed
have led them astray.
5 So I will send fire against Judah,
and it will devour the fortresses of
Jerusalem.

Judgment Against Israel

6 Thus says the LORD:

For three transgressions of Israel,
and for four, I will not revoke the
punishment,
because they sell the righteous for silver,
and the poor for a pair of sandals.
7 They trample the head of the poor
into the dust of the earth,
and push the oppressed out of the way.

The Lionlike Nature of God

Jesus went to the cross as a lamb, but He arose as the Lion of the tribe of Judah, prevailing over all the powers of darkness. The lionlike nature of the Lord is being expressed through His prophets and prophetic people. There is coming a reformation to the entire prophetic office and prophetic realm.

The word *reformation* comes from the Greek word *diorthosis*, and it means "making straight." In a physical sense it refers to restoring to its natural and normal condition something that in some way protrudes or has gotten out of line, such as a broken or misshapen limb. It is where we get our English word *orthopedic*, which is the study of the human skeletal structure. This word is associated with skeletal adjustments. It points to a change in the internal hidden skeleton that gives shape to the body.

The Lord is adjusting mentalities and heart positions to reflect the image and nature of Jesus Christ, the prophet.

> The lion has roared; who will not fear? The Lord God has spoken; who can but prophesy?
>
> —Amos 3:8

Amos declared the word of the Lord to Israel in a time of widespread rebellion and apostasy. He was the voice that represented the Lion's roar. His words were ones of dire warning. The people hearing them should have feared greatly.

Amos could not refrain from speaking. Prophetic people cannot refrain from declaring what the Lord is saying. When there is a stirring in the land, prophetic people cannot be silent.

The Lion of Judah lives inside of you. It is the nature of the lion to roar. The lion's roar is known to cause great fear in the animal kingdom. The lion's strength and power are manifested through his roar.

When God's people speak what God gives them with boldness, it is like a lion's roar. The roar of the lion will produce the fear of the Lord. This is one of the functions of true prophets: to release and help maintain the fear of the Lord in His church.

Prophetic voices are roaring against injustice. Prophetic voices are roaring against the powers of darkness. Prophetic voices are roaring against the enemies of the kingdom.

We are not zoo lions, caged by religion and tradition, losing our ability to speak truth, muzzled by laws and traditions of men. We are not circus lions, performing and entertaining prophetic words that tickle the ear and appease the flesh of men. The roar of the Lion of Judah is coming through His prophetic people even now.

Michelle McClain-Walters

A man and his father go in to the same
woman,
profaning My holy name.
8 They recline by every altar
on garments taken in pledge,
and in the house of their gods
they drink the wine from those who have
been fined.
9 Yet it was I who destroyed the Amorite
before them,
whose height was like the height of the
cedars.
He was strong as the oaks,
yet I destroyed his fruit above
and his roots below.
10 It was I who brought you up from the land
of Egypt,
and led you forty years through the
wilderness,
to possess the land of the Amorite.
11 I raised up some of your sons as prophets,
and some of your young men as
Nazirites.
Is it not so, O children of Israel?
says the LORD.
12 But you made the Nazirites drink wine,
and commanded the prophets, saying,
"Do not prophesy."
13 Indeed I will slow you down,
as a wagon is slowed that is full of
sheaves.
14 Flight will perish from the swift,
the strong will not retain his strength,
nor will the warrior save his life.
15 The bowman will not stand firm,
the swift-footed will not escape,
nor will the horseman save his life.
16 He that is courageous among the warriors
will flee away naked on that day,
says the LORD.

First Pronouncement of Punishment

3 Hear this word that the LORD has spoken
against you, O children of Israel, against
the whole family I brought up from the land
of Egypt, saying:

2 You alone have I known
of all the families of the earth;
therefore I will punish you
for all your iniquities.
3 Do two people walk together,
if they have not agreed?
4 Does a lion roar in the forest,
if it has no prey?
Does a young lion cry out from its den,
if it has not caught something?
5 Does a bird fall into a trap on the ground,
if there was no snare for it?
Does a trap spring up from the ground,
if it has not caught something?
6 If the trumpet blasts in the city,
are not the people frightened?
If there is disaster against a city,
is it not the LORD who has done it?
7 Surely the Lord GOD does nothing
without revealing His purpose
to His servants the prophets.
8 The lion has roared;
who will not fear?
The Lord GOD has spoken;
who can but prophesy?
9 Proclaim to the fortresses in Ashdod,
and the fortresses in the land of Egypt,
and say:
"Assemble yourselves on the mountains of
Samaria,
and see the great disorders within her,
and the oppression in her midst."
10 They do not know how to do right, says the
LORD,
storing up violence and destruction in
their fortresses.

Let the palaces and headquarters of darkness be plundered, in the name of Jesus (Am 3:11).

11 Therefore thus says the Lord GOD:
An enemy will surround your land;
he will tear down your defenses,
and your fortresses will be plundered.
12 Thus says the LORD:
As the shepherd rescues out of the mouth
of the lion
a pair of legs or a piece of an ear,
so will the children of Israel be rescued,
those who live in Samaria,
with the corner of a bed
or a piece of a couch.
13 Hear and testify against the house of Jacob,
says the Lord GOD, the God of Hosts:
14 Surely on the day I punish the
transgressions of Israel,
I will also punish the altars of Bethel;
the horns of the altar will be cut off
and fall to the ground.
15 I will destroy the winter house
as well as the summer house,
and the houses of ivory will perish;
the great houses will come to an end,
says the LORD.

2:8 Am 6:6
2:9 Mal 4:1
2:10 Ex 12:51
2:13 Isa 1:14
2:14 Jer 9:23
3:1 Am 2:10
3:2 Dt 7:6
3:4 Ps 104:21

3:6 Isa 45:7
3:7 Ge 18:17
3:8 Jer 20:9
3:9 Am 4:1
3:10 Jer 4:22
3:11 Am 2:5
3:14 2Ki 23:15
3:15 Jdg 3:20

Second Pronouncement of Punishment

4 Hear this word, you cows of Bashan,
who are on the mountain of Samaria,
who oppress the poor and crush the needy,
who say to their husbands, "Bring us something to drink!"
2 The Lord God has sworn by His holiness:
Indeed the days are coming upon you
when they will take you away with hooks,
the last one of you with fishhooks.
3 You will go out through breached walls,
every one straight ahead of her;
you will be exiled to Harmon,
says the Lord.
4 Come to Bethel and transgress,
to Gilgal and multiply transgression;
bring your sacrifices every morning
and your tithes every three days.
5 Burn leavened bread as a thank offering;
announce your voluntary offerings loudly,
for so you love to do, O children of Israel,
says the Lord God.

6 Though I gave you cleanness of teeth in all your cities
and lack of food in all your places,
yet you did not return to Me,
says the Lord.

7 I also withheld the rain from you,
when there were still three months to the harvest.
I would send rain on one town,
and send no rain on another town.
One field would receive rain,
but another field without rain would wither.
8 So two or three towns wandered to one town to drink water,
but they were not satisfied;
yet you did not return to Me,
says the Lord.

9 I struck you with blight and mildew.
Locusts devoured your many gardens and vineyards,
your fig trees and olive trees;
yet you did not return to Me,
says the Lord.

10 Pestilence like that of Egypt
I sent against you.
By the sword I killed your young men;
your horses were taken captive.
The stench of your camps I brought up into your nostrils;
yet you did not return to Me,
says the Lord.

4:1 Ps 22:12
4:2 Ps 89:35
4:3 Eze 12:5
4:4 Eze 20:39
4:5 Lev 22:18–21
4:6 Hag 2:17
4:7 Ex 9:26
4:9 Dt 28:22
4:10 Lev 26:25

4:11 Isa 13:19
4:13 Am 5:8
5:1 Eze 19:1
5:2 Jer 14:17
5:4 Isa 55:3
5:5 Am 4:4
5:6 Am 5:4
5:7 Am 6:12
5:8 Am 4:13

11 I destroyed some of you,
as God destroyed Sodom and Gomorrah.
You were like a firebrand plucked out of the fire;
yet you did not return to Me,
says the Lord.

12 Therefore thus will I do to you, O Israel,
and because I will do this to you,
prepare to meet your God, O Israel!

13 The One who forms the mountains
and creates the wind,
who reveals His thoughts to man,
who turns the darkness into dawn
and strides on the heights of the earth—
the Lord, the God of Hosts, is His name.

Third Pronouncement of Punishment

5 Hear this word which I take up as a dirge against you, O house of Israel:

2 Fallen, no more to rise
is maiden Israel;
forsaken on her land,
with no one to raise her up.

3 For thus says the Lord God:

The city that went out with a thousand
will be left with a hundred,
and the one that went out with a hundred
will be left with ten for the house of Israel.

4 Indeed, thus says the Lord to the house of Israel:

Seek Me and live!
5 But do not seek Bethel,
and do not enter into Gilgal
or cross over to Beersheba;
for Gilgal will surely go into captivity,
and Bethel shall be no more.
6 Seek the Lord and live,
or He will break out like fire in the house of Joseph,
and it will devour Bethel,
with no one to quench it.

7 You who turn justice into bitterness
and cast righteousness down to the ground!

8 The One who made the Pleiades and Orion,
who turns the deep darkness into dawn
and darkens the day into night,
who summons the waters of the sea
and pours them out on the surface of the earth—
the Lord is His name,
9 the One who flashes destruction against the strong,

so that destruction comes against the
fortress.
10 They hate the one who prosecutes at the
gate,
and abhor the one who speaks with
integrity.
11 Therefore, because you trample on the
poor
and take from him a levy of wheat,
though you have built houses of hewn
stone,
you will not dwell in them;
though you have planted pleasant
vineyards,
you will not drink their wine.
12 For I know your transgressions are many
and your sins are grievous,
you who oppress the just,
who take a bribe and subvert the needy
at the gate.
13 Therefore the prudent are silent at such a
time,
for it is an evil time.
14 Seek good and not evil,
so that you may live;
then the LORD, the God of Hosts, will truly
be with you,
as you claim.
15 Hate evil and love good,
and establish justice at the gate.
It may then be that the LORD God of Hosts
will be gracious
to the remnant of Joseph.

16 Therefore thus says the LORD, the God of
Hosts, the Lord:

Wailing will be in all the squares,
and in all the streets they will say, "Alas!
Alas!"
They shall call the farmer to mourning,
and to wailing those skilled in
lamentation.
17 In all vineyards there shall be wailing,
for I will pass through you,
says the LORD.

The Day of the LORD Is Darkness

18 Woe to you that desire
the day of the LORD!
Why do you want the day of the LORD?
It is darkness, and not light,
19 as if someone fled away from a lion,
but a bear attacked him,
or got into the house
and rested his hand on the wall,
but a snake bit him.
20 Will not the day of the LORD be darkness,
and not light?

5:10 1Ki 22:8
5:11 Mic 6:15
5:12 Am 2:6–7
5:13 Ecc 3:7
5:14 Mic 3:11
5:15 Ps 97:10
5:16 Joel 1:11
5:17 Ex 12:12
5:18 Joel 1:15
5:19 Isa 24:17–18
5:20 Isa 13:10

5:21 Lev 26:31
5:22 Isa 66:3
5:23 Am 6:5
5:24 Mic 6:8
5:25 Ac 7:42–43
6:1 Isa 32:9–11
6:2 Na 3:8
6:3 Am 9:10
6:5 Isa 5:12
6:7 Am 7:11

Will it not be deep darkness, with no
brightness in it?

21 I hate, I despise your festivals,
and I am not pleased by your solemn
assemblies.
22 Though you offer Me burnt offerings or
your grain offerings,
I will not accept them,
nor will I regard the offerings
of your fattened animals.
23 Take away from Me the noise of your
songs;
I will not listen to the melody of your
harps.
24 But let justice roll down like water,
and righteousness like an ever-flowing
stream.

25 Did you bring Me sacrifices and offerings
those forty years in the wilderness, O
house of Israel?
26 But you will carry away Sukuth your king
and Kaiwan your star-images,
your gods that you made for yourselves,
27 as I drive you away into exile beyond
Damascus,
says the LORD, whose name is the God
of Hosts.

Woe to the Complacent

6 Woe to those who are at ease in Zion,
and to those confident on the mount of
Samaria,
nobles of the first of the nations,
to whom the house of Israel comes!
2 Cross over to Kalneh and see,
and go from there to Hamath the great;
then go down to Gath of the
Philistines—
are you better than these kingdoms?
Or is their territory greater than your
territory?
3 You who brush off the day of disaster,
but bring on a session of lawlessness;
4 who lie upon beds of ivory, and lounge on
their couches,
eating lambs from the flock and calves
from the stall;
5 who sing to the sound of the harp
and invent musical instruments for
themselves like David;
6 who drink from bowls of wine
and anoint themselves with the finest
oils,
but are not grieved over the destruction
of Joseph.
7 Therefore now they will go at the head of
the captives into exile,
and the revelry of those who are
lounging will vanish.

8 The Lord God hath sworn by Himself, an
oracle of the Lord the God of Hosts:

I abhor the pride of Jacob
and hate his palaces,
so I will deliver up the city
with all that is in it.

9 If there remain ten people in one house,
they will die. 10 And when a relative or one who
prepares the bodies picks them up to carry
them out of the house, and says to someone in
the recesses of the house, "Is anyone else with
you?" and he says, "No," he will say, "Hush!"—
not to pronounce the name of the Lord.

11 But indeed the Lord gives a command,
and He will shatter the great house to
bits,
and the small house to pieces.

12 Can horses run on a rocky crag?
Can one plow the sea with oxen?
But you have turned justice into poison,
and the fruit of righteousness into
wormwood,
13 you who rejoice in Lo Debar, who say,
"Is it not by our own strength that we
captured Karnaim?"

14 Watch: I will raise up against you a nation,
O house of Israel,
says the Lord, the God of Hosts,
and they will oppress you
from Lebo Hamath to the Wadi Arabah.

Plague of Locusts

7 This is what the Lord God showed me: He
was forming a plague of locusts when the
latter growth was beginning to sprout up, the
latter growth after the king's reaping. 2 When
they had finished devouring the foliage of the
land, I said, "O Lord God, please forgive. How
can Jacob survive? For he is small."
3 The Lord relented concerning this:
"It shall not be," said the Lord.

Fire

4 This is what the Lord God showed me: The
Lord God was calling for a judgment by fire.
It was consuming the great deep and was devouring the fields. 5 I said, "O Lord God, please
stop. How can Jacob survive? For he is small."
6 The Lord relented concerning this:
"This also shall not be," said the Lord God.

Plumb Line

7 This is what He showed me: The Lord was
standing by a wall made using a plumb line,
with a plumb line in His hand. 8 The Lord said
to me, "Amos, what do you see?"
And I said, "A plumb line."

6:8 Ps 47:4
6:9 Am 5:3
6:10 1Sa 31:12
6:11 Am 3:15
6:12 Am 5:7
6:13 Isa 28:14–15
6:14 1Ki 8:65
7:1 Joel 1:4
7:2 Ex 10:15
7:3 Dt 32:36
7:5 Ps 85:4
7:7 2Ki 21:13
7:8 Am 8:2

....

7:9 2Ki 15:8–10
7:10 Jer 38:4
7:12 Mt 8:34
7:13 Am 2:12
7:14 2Ki 2:5
7:15 Eze 2:3–4
7:16 Eze 20:46
7:17 2Ki 17:6
8:1 Am 7:1
8:2 Am 7:8
8:3 Am 5:23

Then the Lord said, "See, I am putting a
plumb line in the midst of My people Israel. I
will forgive them no more.
9 The high places of Isaac will be destroyed,
the sanctuaries of Israel will be laid
waste,
and I will rise against the house of
Jeroboam with the sword."

The Priest Tries to Banish Amos

10 Then Amaziah the priest of Bethel sent a
message to Jeroboam king of Israel, saying,
"Amos has conspired against you at the very
center of the house of Israel. The country cannot endure all his words. 11 For this is what
Amos said:

'Jeroboam will die by the sword,
and Israel will surely be exiled
away from its land.' "

12 So Amaziah said to Amos, "O seer, go, flee
back to the land of Judah. Earn your sustenance there, and prophesy there. 13 But do not
prophesy any more at Bethel, for it is the king's
sanctuary and a royal temple."
14 But Amos answered Amaziah: "I am no
prophet, and I am no prophet's disciple. Rather, I am a herdsman and a dresser of sycamore
trees. 15 But the Lord took me away from the
flock, and the Lord said to me, 'Go, prophesy
to My people Israel.' 16 Now therefore hear the
word of the Lord: You say,

'Do not prophesy against Israel,
and do not preach against the house of
Isaac.'

17 "Therefore thus says the Lord:

'Your wife will be a prostitute in the city,
your sons and daughters will fall by the
sword,
and your land will be divided by measuring
line;
you yourself will die in an unclean land;
and Israel will surely go into exile
away from its land.' "

Basket of Fruit

8 This is what the Lord God showed me: a
basket of summer fruit. 2 He said, "Amos,
what do you see?"
And I said, "A basket of summer fruit."
Then the Lord said to me, "The end has come
upon My people Israel. I will forgive them no
more.
3 "The songs of the temple shall become
wailings on that day," says the Lord God. "The
corpses shall be many, cast down everywhere.
Hush!"

Against the Greedy

[4] Hear this, you who trample on the needy
to make the poor of the land fail,

[5] saying,

"When will the New Moon be over,
so that we may sell grain?
And the Sabbath,
that we may open the wheat sales,
making the ephah[1] too small,
and the shekel[2] too heavy,
cheating with dishonest scales,
[6] that we may buy the poor for silver,
the needy for a pair of sandals,
and sell the refuse as wheat?"

[7] The LORD has sworn by the pride of Jacob:
Surely I will never forget any of their deeds.

[8] Will not the land tremble because of this,
and everyone mourn who lives on it?
It will all rise up like the Nile,
and be tossed around, then sink
like the Nile of Egypt.

[9] On that day, says the Lord GOD,

I will make the sun go down at noon,
and darken the earth in mid-daylight;
[10] I will turn your feasts into mourning,
and all your songs into dirges;
I will put sackcloth upon all loins,
and baldness on every head;
I will make it like the mourning for an only child,
and its end like a bitter day.

[11] The time is coming, says the Lord GOD,
when I will send a famine on the land,
not a famine of bread, nor a thirst for water,
but of hearing the words of the LORD.
[12] They will wander from sea to sea,
and from north to east;
they will run back and forth to seek the word of the LORD,
but they will not find it.

[13] On that day

the beautiful maidens and the young men
will faint with thirst.
[14] Those who swear by Ashimah of Samaria,
and say,
"By the life of your god, O Dan,"
and, "By the life of the way of Beersheba"—
they shall fall
and never rise again.

Destruction of the Sanctuary

9 I saw the Lord standing upon the altar,
and He said:

Strike the capitals
so that the thresholds shake;
break them off onto the heads of all of them.
Those who remain I will slay with the sword.
Not one of them will get away;
not one fugitive will survive.
[2] Though they dig down to Sheol,
from there My hand will capture them;
though they climb up to the heavens,
from there I will bring them down;
[3] though they hide on the top of Carmel,
from there I will search and catch them;
though they hide from My sight on the bottom of the sea,
from there will I command the serpent to bite them;
[4] and though they go into captivity before their enemies,
from there will I command the sword to slay them.

I will set My eyes upon them
for evil and not for good.

[5] The Lord GOD of Hosts,
He who touches the earth and it melts,
and all who live on it mourn;
it all rises up like the Nile,
and subsides like the river of Egypt;
[6] who builds His chambers in the heavens,
and founds His vault over the earth;
who summons the waters of the sea,
and pours them out upon the surface of the earth—
the LORD is His name.

[7] Are you not like the Ethiopians to Me,
O children of Israel?
says the LORD.
Did I not bring Israel up from the land of Egypt,
but also the Philistines from Caphtor,
and the Arameans from Kir?

[8] The eyes of the Lord GOD
are upon the sinful kingdom,
and I will destroy it
from off the face of the earth,
though I will not completely destroy
the house of Jacob,
says the LORD.
[9] See, I am giving the command,
and I will sift the house of Israel
among all the nations,
as one sifts with a sieve,
and not a pebble falls to the ground.

8:4 Ps 14:4
8:5 Hos 12:7
8:6 Am 2:6
8:7 Hos 8:13
8:8 Am 9:5
8:9 Jer 15:9
8:10 Jer 6:26
8:11 1Sa 3:1
8:13 Hos 2:3
9:1 Ps 68:21

9:2 Jer 51:53
9:3 Jer 16:16
9:4 Lev 26:33
9:5 Am 8:8
9:6 Ps 104:3
9:7 Jer 47:4
9:8 Jer 30:11

[1] 5 A dry measure of about ⅗ bushel, or 22 liters. [2] 5 About ⅖ ounce, or 12 grams.

[10]All the sinners of My people
will die by the sword,
those who say,
"Never will disaster reach or
overtake us."

Restoration of the Davidic Kingdom

[11]On that day will I raise up
the hut of David that is fallen;
I will close up its breached walls,
raise up its ruins,
and rebuild it as in the days of old;
[12]that they may possess the remnant of
Edom,
and of all the nations called by My
name,
says the LORD who will do this.

[13]Indeed, the days are coming, says the LORD,

when the plowman will overtake the one
who is reaping,
and the treader of grapes the one who is
sowing the seed;
the mountains will drip sweet wine,
and all the hills will flow with it.
[14]I will restore the fortunes of My people
Israel;
they will rebuild the ruined cities and
inhabit them;
they will plant vineyards and drink their
wine;
they will make gardens and eat their
fruit.

Plant my roots deep in the land You have given me so that I will never be uprooted again (Am 9:15).

[15]I will plant them upon their land,
and no more will they be uprooted
out of their land which I have given
them.
The LORD your God has spoken.

9:10 Am 6:3
9:11 Ps 80:12
9:12 Isa 43:7
9:13 Lev 26:5

....

9:14 Jer 30:18
9:15 Isa 60:21

Author: The prophet Obadiah

Written: Sixth Century BC

Theme: Condemnation of Edom

OBADIAH

Dear Spirit Led Woman,

The message of Obadiah is one of judgment for the enemies of Israel. As we read this short book of the Bible, we see that God not only had a plan to deal with the enemies of His people, but He also had a plan to fully deliver and restore them.

Aren't you glad that you can trust God to take care of your enemies? Maybe you're dealing with false rumors, betrayal, or someone who honestly wants to see you fail, and they are doing everything in their power to make that happen. God will fight for you. You can rest assured that not only will He put your enemy in their place, but He will also vindicate your reputation and restore anything that's been lost. Wait upon Him, trust in Him, and follow the leading of His Spirit until He brings it to pass.

Joy F. Strang

SPIRITLED WOMAN

COUNSEL FROM THE SPIRIT BASICS

Human Pride Will Fail

The short book of Obadiah is the record of the prophet's vision, depicting the downfall of the proud nation of Edom in the face of God's divine judgment. The Edomites thought their strong defenses and mountainous homeland could never be penetrated by the enemy—even if it was God Himself who was coming to revoke Edom's fortunes, cause the nation to lose its influence, and cause it to become despised among its neighbors (Ob 1:2).

This nation's pride had gotten the best of it. But no matter how great a people may become, nothing places them beyond the reach of divine judgment. God declared that the military strength and wisdom of Edom would fall (vv. 8–9).

Obadiah's vision looked ahead to a time when Jerusalem would be restored (v. 17). The exiled Israelites would return to their homeland. The nation of Edom, however, would be no more (v. 18).

This prophecy's fulfillment is in progress. There are no known descendants of the Edomites today. Yet Jewish people around the world continue to return to the restored nation of Israel.

Though we live in a world where evil is active within every culture and followers of Christ may suffer at the hands of evil people, we must remember God is always at work. The promises of His Word never fail. God has already established His kingdom in the hearts of all who accept Jesus Christ as their Savior (v. 21). His authority is an unchanging reality that is already working miracles by changing countless lives.

Barbara Dycus

1:1 Eze 25:12–14
1:3 Isa 14:13–15
1:4 Hab 2:9
1:5 Dt 24:21
1:6 Jer 49:10
1:7 Ps 41:9
1:8 Isa 29:14
1:9 Ge 36:11
1:10 Am 1:11
1:11 Ps 137:7

Judgment on Edom
Jer 49:9–16

The vision of Obadiah.

Thus says the Lord God concerning Edom

(We have heard a report from the Lord
and a messenger has been sent among
the nations, saying:
"Rise up! Let us rise up against it for
battle!"):

2 See, I will make you small among the
nations;
you will be greatly despised.
3 The pride of your heart has deceived you,
you who live in the clefts of the rock,
whose dwelling is high;
you say in your heart,
"Who will bring me down to the
ground?"
4 Though you ascend high like the eagle,
and though you set your nest among the
stars,
I will bring you down from there,
says the Lord.
5 If thieves came to you,
if robbers by night—
how you have been destroyed!—
would they not steal only what they
want?
If grape gatherers come to you,
would they not leave gleanings?
6 How *the things of* Esau have been
ransacked!
How his hidden treasures hunted out!
7 All your confederates have driven you to
the border;
your allies have deceived and prevailed
against you.
Those who eat your bread have set a trap
for you.
You will not detect it.

8 On that day, says the Lord,
I will destroy the wise out of Edom,
and understanding out of Mount Esau.
9 Your mighty men shall be shattered,
O Teman,
so that everyone from Mount Esau will
be cut off.

Edom's Violence Against Jacob

10 For the slaughter and the violence done to
your brother Jacob,
shame shall cover you,
and you shall be cut off forever.
11 On the day that you stood aside,
on the day that strangers carried off his
wealth,
and foreigners entered his gates

The Little Books

The little books of the Bible should not seem insignificant because of their smallness. Their value is not diminished because of their size. For example, the brevity of Obadiah's challenging vision does not diminish the power of the divine truth it reveals.

The Book of Esther, another little book, beautifully foreshadows the personal relationship of the true worshipper with God. It portrays the miraculous deliverance of the bride of Christ from her enemies equally as well as the Book of Ruth, though set in a completely different historical and economical background. What profound drama and prophetic insight we would miss if the canon had not included the little book of Esther! I explore the richness of Esther in my book *For Such a Time as This*.

In the New Testament the Book of Philemon is a beautiful picture of redemption. Paul's poignant entreaty for a runaway slave to be restored not to his former state as a slave but as a beloved brother helps us understand God's compassion toward those bound to sin. Through redemption we are no longer slaves but members of the family of God—loved, accepted, and free from the debt of our sin. What priceless revelation of the love of God is found in these twenty-five verses of Scripture.

If the little Book of Jude had not been placed into the canon of Scripture, we would never have known that Enoch was a prophet (Jude 1:14). Nor would we have been given the understanding of the seven awful steps to apostasy (vv. 5–6, 8, 10–11) or have known that Satan wrestled for the body of Moses (v. 9). And we would not have been given the comforting promise, "Now to Him who is able to keep you from falling and to present you blameless before the presence of His glory with rejoicing, to the only wise God our Savior, be glory and majesty, dominion and power, both now and forever. Amen" (vv. 24–25).

We conclude, then, that the truths revealed by the smaller books of the canon are as powerful as the longest narratives. The Book of Ruth is one of those powerful little books that reveals to us allegorically what is involved in our own personal redemption as well as that of the body of Christ corporately. Not only Ruth's circumstances, but also her attitudes, desires, and decisions relating to those circumstances speak eternal truths on which the restoration of all the blessings of God for our lives depend. Other characters in the narrative teach us by example as well, mirroring the consequences of our own choices and attitudes and helping us evaluate our relationships with God.

Fuchsia Pickett

and cast lots on Jerusalem,
you also were like one of them.
12 But you should not have gloated
on the day of your brother,
on the day of his misfortune;
you should not have rejoiced over the
children of Judah
on the day of their destruction;
you should not have boasted
on the day of distress.

I will be a keeper of holiness in my house (Ob 1:17).

13 You should not have entered the gate of
My people
on the day of their calamity.
You should not have gloated over *the*
disaster *of Judah*[1]
on the day of his calamity;
you should not have seized his wealth
on the day of his calamity.
14 You should not have stood at the
crossroads
to cut off his fugitives;
you should not have handed over his
survivors,
on the day of distress.

The Day of the LORD Is Near

15 For the day of the LORD is near
upon all the nations;
as you have done, it shall be done to you;
your deeds shall return on your own
head.
16 For as you have drunk on My holy
mountain,
all the nations shall drink continually;
they shall drink and swallow
and shall be as though they had never
been.

1:12 Mic 4:11
1:15 Hab 2:8
1:16 Jer 49:12

1:17 Am 9:11–15
1:18 Zec 12:6
1:20 Jer 33:13
1:21 Ps 22:28

Let the nations receive deliverance on Mount Zion, and let them walk in holiness (Ob 1:17).

17 But on Mount Zion there shall be
deliverance,
and it shall be holy;
and the house of Jacob shall possess
those who dispossessed them.[2]
18 The house of Jacob shall be a fire,
the house of Joseph a flame,
but the house of Esau stubble;
they shall burn them and consume
them,
and there shall be no survivors
from the house of Esau,
for the LORD has spoken.

The Restoration of Israel

19 Those of the Negev shall possess
Mount Esau,
and those of the Shephelah the land
of the Philistines.
They shall possess the fields of Ephraim
and the fields of Samaria,
and Benjamin shall possess Gilead.
20 The exiles of this army of the sons of
Israel,
shall inherit the land of the Canaanites as
far as Zarephath,
and the exiles of Jerusalem who are in
Sepharad
shall inherit the cities of the Negev.
21 Saviors shall go up to Mount Zion
to rule Mount Esau,
and the kingdom shall be the LORD's.

[1] *13* Heb. *his.* [2] *17* Gk.; Heb. *their possessions.*

Author: Traditionally the prophet Jonah

Written: Between 793 and 758 BC

Themes: God's Mercy for Enemies and Foreigners

JONAH

Dear Spirit Led Woman,

Jonah was called to share God's message with foreigners, people who were different from him. His lack of compassion for people outside of his own culture is a sin that the Holy Spirit continues to confront in the church today: prejudice. For some people, this sin manifests itself as blatant discrimination against those we consider different. For others, it plays out merely as a subtle—perhaps even subconscious—avoidance of them. Either way, God's answer to prejudice is summed up in what Jesus called the second greatest commandment: "You shall love your neighbor as yourself" (Mt 22:39).

His command to love others goes beyond mere acceptance. Nor is it the same as tolerance. If you choose to live by the world's standard, you will learn to display "tolerance" for everything, including sin. But Scripture calls you to a different standard. You are called to love what God loves and hate what He hates. And God loves all His people—regardless of nation, tongue, or ethnicity.

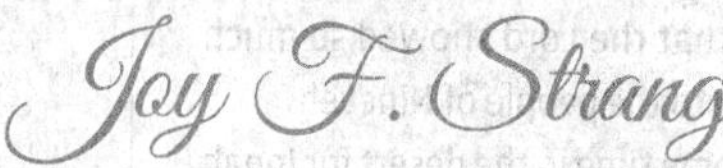

SPIRITLED WOMAN

COUNSEL FROM THE SPIRIT BASICS

Running Away

Jonah is the famous biblical character who was in the belly of a whale for three days before being spit out and delivered to safety. Although commonly depicted as a kids' cartoon, this real-life story is so much more than a sweet children's bedtime book.

Jonah was a prophet who was asked by the Lord to deliver a message to a very evil people in the city of Nineveh:

> Now the word of the LORD came to Jonah son of Amittai, saying, "Get up, go to Nineveh, the great city, and cry out against it, because their wickedness has come up before Me." But Jonah got up to flee to Tarshish from the presence of the LORD. He went down to Joppa and found there a ship going to Tarshish. He paid its fare and went down into it to go with them to Tarshish from the presence of the LORD.
>
> —JONAH 1:1–3

Since Jonah was a prophet, I imagine this was not the first time the Lord had spoken to him. Maybe Jonah had always done what the Lord had requested of him up until this point. But something about this particular assignment made Jonah decide he did not want to obey God's call. Read the entire Book of Jonah, and you will see that the prophet was upset that the Lord showed so much compassion to the people of Nineveh.

It took some time in the desert for Jonah to finally obey God's command. But the Lord had great mercy on Jonah, and He forgave him for running away from his call. An entire city could have experienced complete devastation if Jonah had not walked in obedience.

As He did with Jonah, sometimes the Lord will allow a storm to come into our lives so that we will repent for disobedience and surrender our will to Him.

Jenny Swindall

1:1 2Ki 14:25
1:2 Ge 10:11
1:3 Jos 19:46
1:4 Ps 135:7
1:5 Ac 27:18–19
1:6 Jnh 3:9
1:7 Pr 16:33
1:10 Jnh 1:3
1:12 2Sa 24:17
1:13 Pr 21:30
1:14 Ps 115:3
1:15 Ps 107:29

The Call of Jonah

1 Now the word of the LORD came to Jonah
son of Amittai, saying, 2 "Get up, go to
Nineveh, the great city, and cry out against it,
because their wickedness has come up before
Me."
3 But Jonah got up to flee to Tarshish from
the presence of the LORD. He went down to
Joppa and found there a ship going to Tarshish. He paid its fare and went down into it
to go with them to Tarshish from the presence
of the LORD.
4 But the LORD hurled a great wind upon the
sea, and a mighty storm came upon the sea,
so that the ship was in danger of breaking up.
5 Then the sailors were afraid, and each cried
to his god. They tossed the ship's cargo into
the sea in order to lighten the load.
But Jonah had gone down into the hold of
the ship, had lain down, and was fast asleep.
6 The captain came to him and said, "What are
you doing asleep? Get up, call to your god!
Perhaps *your* god will consider us, so that we
will not perish."
7 The sailors said to one another, "Come, let
us cast lots that we may know on whose account this disaster has come upon us." So they
cast lots, and the lot fell on Jonah.
8 Then the sailors said to Jonah, "Tell us why
this disaster has come upon us. What is your
occupation? Where do you come from? What is
your country? And from what people are you?"
9 Jonah replied, "I am a Hebrew, and I fear
the LORD, the God of heaven, who made the
sea and the dry land."
10 Then the men were very afraid and said
to him, "What is this you have done?" For the
men knew that he was fleeing from the presence of the LORD because he had told them.
11 Then they said to Jonah, "What shall we do
to you, so that the sea may quiet down for us?"
For the sea was growing stormier.
12 So Jonah said to them, "Pick me up and
toss me into the sea. Then the sea will quiet
down for you. For I know that it is on my account this great storm has come upon you."
13 Nevertheless, the men rowed hard to bring
the ship to land, but they could not do it, for
the sea grew more tempestuous against them.
14 Then they cried to the LORD and said, "Please,
LORD, do not let us perish for this man's life,
and do not make us guilty for innocent blood,
for You, LORD, have done as it pleased You."
15 So they picked up Jonah and tossed him into
the sea. Then the sea ceased from its raging.
16 Therefore the men were very afraid of the
LORD, and they offered a sacrifice to the LORD
and made vows.

SPIRIT-TO-SPIRIT PRAYER

PRAYER IN THE DAY OF TROUBLE

Heavenly Father, Your Word says that You have searched us and You know us. You are acquainted with all of our ways, not just some of them. There is nowhere we can go to escape Your love and mercy. If the darkness shall fall around us, Scripture records that with You there, the night will shine like the day. Darkness cannot hide us.

We thank You that no matter how crazy life gets, You are right beside us. We are never left alone to fend for ourselves. You can find us in the tightest spot and deliver us from the greatest enemy—seen or unseen. As we put on the full armor of God, You will surely deliver us in the day of trouble.

May Your mercy embrace us like the noonday sun, and may all who see us gain the victory know that the hand of God is upon us. In Jesus' name, amen.

Tish Hagee Tucker

The Prayer and Deliverance of Jonah

[17] Now the LORD appointed a great fish to
swallow Jonah. And Jonah was in the belly of
the fish three days and three nights.

2 Then Jonah prayed to the LORD his God
from the belly of the fish. [2] He said:

"I called to the LORD out of my distress,
and He answered me.
Out of the belly of Sheol I cried,
and You heard my voice.
[3] You cast me into the deep,
into the heart of the seas,
and the flood surrounded me.
All Your billows and Your waves
passed over me.
[4] Then I said, 'I am cast away
from Your sight;
yet I will look again
to Your holy temple.'

You have brought my life
up from the pit (Jnh 2:6).

[5] The waters encompassed me; *even* to my
soul
the deep surrounded me;
weeds were wrapped around my head.
[6] I went down to the foundations of the
mountains;
the earth with its bars *was* around me
forever;
yet You have brought up my life from the
pit,
O LORD my God.

[7] "When my life was ebbing away,
I remembered the LORD;
and my prayer came to You,
into Your holy temple.
[8] "Those who follow vain idols
forsake their true loyalty.
[9] But I will sacrifice to You
with the voice of thanksgiving;
I will pay what I have vowed.
Salvation is of the LORD!"

[10] Then the LORD spoke to the fish, and it vom-
ited Jonah out upon dry land.

Jonah Preaches at Nineveh

3 The word of the LORD came to Jonah a sec-
ond time, saying, [2] "Get up, go to Nineveh,
the great city, and proclaim to it the message
that I tell you."
[3] So Jonah got up and went to Nineveh, ac-
cording to the word of the LORD. Now Nineveh
was an exceedingly large city, a three-day
journey across. [4] Jonah began to enter the
city, going a day's walk. And he cried out, "In
forty days' time, Nineveh will be overthrown!"
[5] So the people of Nineveh believed God, and

1:17 Mt 12:40
2:2 Ps 120:1
2:3 Ps 42:7
2:4 Ps 31:22
2:5 Ps 69:1–2
2:7 2Ch 30:27
2:8 2Ki 17:15
2:9 Ps 3:8
2:10 Jnh 1:17
3:1 Jnh 1:1
3:5 Lk 11:32

Battle of Wills

On a warm Florida night three years after the ill-fated night I lost my mother, we had a women's gathering at church, and I tried to make excuses as to why I could not go. However, my then-boyfriend, now-husband, convinced me to attend. I am eternally grateful for his persistence, although it annoyed me a bit at the time.

Looking back, it was such a mundane, ordinary moment, but it proved to be a defining moment of the highest proportion. So many times you zero in on the big, major events in your life when, in fact, your life can be supernaturally and completely altered by an ordinary decision. By simply saying yes to the right thing or no to the wrong thing, you can change your life forever.

I reluctantly went to church that night, not caring enough to even take my Bible with me. As I sat listening to the minister, something began to happen in my heart. I didn't go to the altar or even raise my hand in response to the message. The best way I can describe it is that where there was once resistance to God in my heart, there no longer was. I had been thinking about my relationship with God and how off target I had drifted, and something gave way that night. It was as if there had been water shoring up behind a rock that had now broken through. It was a breakthrough. It was like an opening of my spiritual stance, a realization that I was desperate for the very person I had been ignoring. Even though my palms were sweaty and my mind was racing, I felt something I hadn't felt recently—peace.

After the event I hurried home and started reading my Bible for the first time in a long time. I underlined Ephesians 2:8–10 and wrote in green ink in the right margin of my Bible, "Call to destiny." It was at once a statement and a challenge. Those words remain there to this day.

Living my life God's way rather than my way drove the final nail into the coffin of my anger, bitterness, and selfishness. It was contagious. I couldn't help but fall in love with this new life. I was starting to understand that what I had just endured was both the act and the process of complete surrender to God. It did not look and feel like what I thought it would. I felt stronger, not weaker, full of faith rather than fear, and more alive than I had ever been. But to be completely honest, whenever I would hear the mention of the word *surrender* or *submit*, I would have a negative, emotional reaction.

It's not that I didn't like those words; it's that I didn't like the way they made me feel. Before now, they were simply "S" words in my Christian vocabulary, words I did not care for and certainly regarded with trepidation and suspicion. I still had flashbacks to the things I had seen as a young girl and preconceived notions I had about my identity as a woman. My defensive attitude and hostile posture toward the idea of surrender was rooted in fear. I was trying to compare a biblical principle with worldly experience, and it just doesn't work. If we decide to reject God's way of life because people have abused it, we will miss out on so many incredible blessings God has in store for us. Numbers 23:19 says, "God is not a man, that He should lie, nor a son of man, that He should repent. Has He spoken, and will He not do it? Or has He spoken, and will He not make it good?" God's ways are good and right, even when people are not good and right.

I had bought into the lie that strength and surrender can't coexist and that to be an independent woman means not allowing anyone dominate me. This protective mechanism may work when it comes to people, but those rules do not apply when it comes to God. He is a Father who loves His daughters relentlessly. God *is* love. He does not possess love, because if He did, that would mean there are times when He does not possess it or is unloving. Love is not something He has; it's who He is. God's love for us is not only the basis of our surrender to Him, but it also removes the fear of it.

True surrender to God will never diminish who you are; it actually does the opposite. It helps you discover who you really are. I am living proof of this. I lived as a sad shell of myself until I decided to think of myself less and think of God more. In order for me to be who God called me to be, I had to get over myself, get out of my daily routine, start thinking with a new mind, seeing with new eyes, and living with new purpose. My life had so much more meaning once I offered it to God.

Surrendered people are the ones God uses, and we see the lesson of surrender learned in the lives of several Bible characters. Sarah, the wife of Abraham, tried to help God and discovered in the end that surrender to God is the only way to go from a promise given to a promise fulfilled. Despite her doubting, Sarah eventually became the mother of all Jews. Your doubts do not prevent God from using you; a lack to surrender to Him will.

Jonah did not want to go to Nineveh. He didn't want to see those people—his enemies—saved from destruction. But he went. He surrendered to the call of God to go to Nineveh and preach, and the city was saved. True surrender always presents an opportunity to do something amazing for God. Your past won't disqualify you from being used by God, but an unsurrendered life will!

Mercy Lokulutu

proclaimed a fast. And everyone, great and small, put on sackcloth.

6 When the news reached the king of Nineveh, he arose from his throne, removed his robe, covered himself in sackcloth, and sat in ashes. 7 Then he made a proclamation in Nineveh:

"By decree of the king and his nobles:

No man or animal, no herd or flock, shall taste anything. They shall not eat or drink water. 8 Both man and animals shall cover themselves with sackcloth and cry mightily to God. All shall turn from their evil ways and from the violence that is in their hands. 9 Who knows? God may relent and change His mind. He may turn from His fierce anger, so that we will not perish."

10 When God saw their actions, that they turned from their evil ways, He changed His mind about the disaster that He had said He would bring upon them, and He did not do it.

Jonah's Anger and the LORD's Compassion

4 Now this greatly displeased Jonah, and he became angry. 2 He prayed to the LORD and said, "O LORD! Is this not what I said while I was still in my own land? This is the reason that I fled before to Tarshish, because I knew that You are a gracious God and merciful, slow to anger, abundant in faithfulness, and ready to relent from punishment. 3 Therefore, LORD, take my life from me, for it is better for me to die than to live."

4 Then the LORD said, "Is it right for you to be angry?"

5 So Jonah went out of the city and sat down east of the city and made for himself a booth there. He sat under it in the shade, waiting to see what would happen to the city. 6 Then the LORD God appointed a plant, and it grew up over Jonah to provide shade over his head, to provide comfort from his grief. And Jonah was very happy about the plant. 7 But at dawn the next day, God appointed a worm to attack the plant so that it withered. 8 When the sun rose, God appointed a scorching east wind, and the sun beat upon the head of Jonah so that he became faint and asked that he might die. He said, "It is better for me to die than to live."

9 Then God said to Jonah, "Is it right for you to be angry about the plant?"

And Jonah replied, "It is right for me to be angry, even to death."

10 The LORD said, "You are troubled about the plant for which you did not labor and did not grow. It came up in a night and perished in a night. 11 Should I not, therefore, be concerned about Nineveh, that great city, in which there are more than a hundred and twenty thousand people, who do not know their right hand from their left, and also many animals?"

3:6 Job 2:8
3:7 2Ch 20:3
3:8 Jnh 1:6
3:9 2Sa 12:22
3:10 Jer 18:8
4:1 Jnh 4:9
4:2 Ps 86:5
4:3 1Ki 19:4
4:7 Joel 1:12
4:8 Ps 121:6
4:11 Jnh 1:2

Author: The prophet Micah

Written: Between 735 and 700 BC

Themes: Warning and Hope

MICAH

Dear Spirit Led Woman,

What determines someone's goodness? Is it how she behaves in public? How she speaks? What she does in her spare time? The amount of time she dedicates to God's Word? None of the above determine goodness because we, as humans, are not good. Paul wrote, "There is no one who does good, no, not one" (Ro 3:12). Only God is good, and He has told us what He requires of us: "to do justice and to love kindness, and to walk humbly with your God" (Mic 6:8).

We must pray over our fallen world, warn our neighbors of God's judgment against sin. We must be the living Bible to those surrounding us, show our faith in the promise of our Redeemer. We most empty ourselves of the beliefs of the world and prepare our hearts for the movement of the Holy Spirit.

Joy F. Strang

1 The word of the LORD, which came to Micah the Morashite in the days of Jotham, Ahaz, and Hezekiah, kings of Judah, which he saw regarding Samaria and Jerusalem.

2 Hear, all you peoples!
Listen, earth and everything in it,
that the Sovereign LORD may be a witness against you,
the LORD from His holy temple.

Judgment Against Samaria and Jerusalem

3 Look! The LORD is coming out from His place,
so that He might come down and tread upon the high places of the earth.
4 The mountains will melt beneath Him,
and the valleys split apart
like wax before the fire,
like waters deluged down a slope.
5 All this because of the transgression of Jacob
and because of the sins of the house of Israel.
What is the transgression of Jacob?
Is it not Samaria?
And what is the high place of Judah?
Is it not Jerusalem?
6 Therefore I will make Samaria a heap in the field
for the planting of vineyards.
I will dump her stones into the valley
and expose her foundations.
7 All her idols will be shattered,
and her gifts burned with fire,
and I will annihilate her images,
because she gathered them as the wages of a prostitute,
and as the wages of a prostitute they will again be used.

The Lament of Micah

8 Because of this I will lament and wail,
I will go about barefoot and naked;
I will howl like the jackals
and moan like owlets.
9 For her wound is mortal,
for it has come to Judah;
it has extended to the gate of my people,
to Jerusalem.
10 Do not tell it in Gath,
do not weep at all;
in Beth Ophrah,
roll around in the dust.
11 Pass on your way,
inhabitants of Shaphir, naked and ashamed;
the inhabitants of Zaanan
have not come out.
The mourning of Beth Ezel
has taken from you its foothold.

1:1 Isa 1:1
1:2 Ps 11:4
1:3 Am 4:13
1:4 Na 1:5
1:5 Am 8:14
1:6 Eze 13:14
1:7 Dt 23:18
1:10 2Sa 1:20
1:11 Isa 20:4
1:12 Jer 14:19
1:14 Jos 15:44
1:15 Jos 15:44
1:16 Isa 22:12
2:1 Ps 36:4
2:2 Isa 5:8
2:3 Isa 2:11–12
2:4 Hab 2:6
2:5 Dt 32:8
2:6 Am 2:12
2:7 Ps 15:2

12 Indeed the inhabitants of Maroth
wait anxiously for good,
because calamity has come down from the LORD
to the gate of Jerusalem.
13 Harness the chariot to the steeds,
inhabitants of Lachish.
It was the beginning of sin
to the daughter of Zion,
because in you were found
the transgressions of Israel.
14 Therefore you will give parting gifts
to Moresheth Gath;
the houses of Akzib will be deception
to the kings of Israel.
15 I will again bring a conqueror to you,
inhabitants of Mareshah;
the glory of Israel
will come to Adullam.
16 Make yourself bald and shave your head
for the children of your delight;
make yourself as bald as the eagle,
for they will go from you into exile.

Woe to the Wicked

2 Woe to those who conceive wickedness,
to those who devise evil on their beds!
At morning's light they execute it,
because it is in the power of their hand.
2 They covet fields and seize them,
and houses and take them.
They defraud a man of his house,
and a fellow man of his inheritance.
3 Therefore, thus says the LORD:
I am devising disaster against this family,
from which you cannot remove your necks;
and you will not walk haughtily,
for it will be a time of calamity.
4 In that day they will take up a taunt against you,
and they will wail a wailing lament, and say:
"We are totally ruined!
He diminishes the portion of my people;
how He removes it from me!
To a traitor He reassigns our fields!"

5 Therefore you will not have anyone to apportion the land by lot
in the assembly of the LORD.

Prophets of Deceit

6 "Do not prophesy," they say.
"One should not prophesy about these things.
Disgrace will not overtake us."
7 Should it be said, O house of Jacob,
"Is the Spirit of the LORD impatient?
Are these His deeds?"

Do not My words benefit
him who walks uprightly?
8 But lately My people rise up
like an enemy.
You strip off the rich robe
from those who pass by trustingly,
like men returning from war.
9 The women of My people you drive out
from their delightful homes;
from their children
you take My adornment forever.
10 Get up and go,
for this is not the resting place,
because uncleanness ruins,
and ruin sickens.
11 If a man, going about vapidly and
deceitfully, lies,
"I will preach for you wine and beer,"
he would be just the preacher for this
people.

The Restoration of Israel

12 I will indeed assemble Jacob—all of you;
I will indeed gather the remnant of
Israel.
I will place them together like sheep in a
fold,
like a herd in its pasture—
thronging with people.

> The breaker is gone up before me and broken through every limitation and barrier of the enemy (Mic 2:13).

13 He who breaks through has gone up before
them;
they will break through and pass the
gate and go out by it.
Then their king will pass on before them,
the LORD at their head.

Leaders and Prophets Judged

3 Then I said:

Listen now, heads of Jacob,
and rulers of the house of Israel.
Should you not know justice?
2 You who hate good and love evil,
who tear the skin from My people
and the flesh from their bones;
3 you who have eaten the flesh of My
people,
and have flayed their skin from them,
and broken their bones in pieces;
who have chopped *them* up like meat in
the pot,
and like flesh in the cauldron.
4 Then they will cry out to the LORD,
but He will not answer them;

2:8 Ps 120:6–7
2:10 Dt 12:9
2:11 Jer 5:31
2:12 Mic 4:6–7
2:13 Isa 52:12
3:2 Ps 53:4
3:3 Ps 14:4
3:4 Isa 1:15

3:6 Isa 8:20–22
3:7 Isa 44:25
3:8 Isa 58:1
3:9 Ps 58:1–2
3:11 Isa 1:23
3:12 Jer 26:18
4:1 Ps 22:27
4:2 Ps 25:8–9

He will hide His face from them at that
time,
because they have wrought evil deeds.
5 Thus says the LORD:
Regarding the prophets
who mislead My people—
the ones who have something to eat
proclaim "Peace,"
but if one does not feed them,
then they prepare for war against him.
6 Therefore you will have night without
vision,
and you will have darkness without
divination;
the sun will set upon the prophets,
and black upon them will be the day.
7 The seers will be shamed
and the diviners disgraced,
and they will all cover their beards,
for there is no answer from God.
8 But as for me, I am filled with power,
with the Spirit of the LORD,
and with justice and might,
to declare to Jacob his transgression
and to Israel his sin.
9 Please hear this, heads of the house of
Jacob
and rulers of the house of Israel,
who detest justice
and warp all that is straight,
10 who build Zion with bloodguilt
and Jerusalem with wickedness.
11 Her leaders judge for a bribe,
her priests teach for a price,
and her prophets practice divination for
money.
Yet upon the LORD they lean, saying,
"Is not the LORD in our midst?
Evil will not come upon us."
12 Therefore, because of you,
Zion will be plowed like a field,
Jerusalem will be mounds of ruins,
and the mountain of the house will
become wooded heights.

The Mountain of the LORD

Isa 2:1–4

4 Then it will be that in the latter days,

the mountain of the house of the LORD will
be established
as head of the mountains,
and will be lifted up above the hills;
and people will stream to it.
2 And many nations will come and say,
"Come, that we might go up to the
mountain of the LORD,

and to the house of the God of Jacob,
that He might teach us His ways,
and that we might walk in His paths."
For from Zion will go forth the law,
and the word of the LORD from Jerusalem.

God's ways are not my ways,
but how glorious and how
beautiful His ways are (Mic 4:2).

3 Then He will judge between many peoples
and mediate for mighty nations far and wide;
they will beat their swords into plowshares,
and their spears into pruning hooks.
Nation will not take up sword against nation,
and they will no longer train for war.
4 Then each man will sit under his vine
and under his fig tree,
and no one will make them afraid;
for the mouth of the LORD of Hosts has spoken.
5 For all the peoples may walk,
each in the name of his God,
but we will walk in the name of the LORD
our God forever and ever.

The Promise of Restoration

6 In that day, declares the LORD,

I will assemble the lame
and gather the banished
and those whom I have afflicted;
7 and I will make the lame into a remnant,
and the banished into a mighty nation;
and the LORD will reign over them on Mount Zion
from this time forth and forevermore.
8 As for you, watchtower of the flock,
citadel of the daughter of Zion,
to you it will come, the former dominion will come,
kingship for the daughter of Jerusalem.

9 Now why do you cry loudly?
Have you no king?
Has your counselor perished,
that agony has seized you like the woman in labor?
10 Writhe and bring forth, daughter of Zion,
like the woman in labor,
because now you will go forth from the city
and reside in the field,
and you will come to Babylon.
There you will be rescued;
there the LORD will redeem you
from the hand of your enemies.

4:3 Isa 2:4
4:4 1Ki 4:25
4:5 Zec 10:12
4:6 Zep 3:19
4:7 Isa 24:23
4:8 Zec 9:10
4:9 Jer 8:19
4:10 2Ki 20:18

4:11 Ob 1:12
5:1 La 3:30
5:2 Zec 9:9
5:4 Mic 7:14
5:5 Lk 2:14
5:7 Mic 5:3

11 But now many nations
are gathered against you, saying,
"May she be defiled,
and may our eyes gaze upon Zion."
12 But they do not know
the thoughts of the LORD,
and they do not understand His plan,
that He has gathered them like sheaves
to the threshing floor.
13 Arise and thresh, daughter of Zion,
for I will make your horn iron;
your hoofs I will make bronze,
and you will shatter many peoples.
I will devote their pillage to the LORD,
their wealth to the Lord of all the earth.

The Ruler From Bethlehem

5 Now gather yourself in troops,
O daughter of troops;
he has laid siege against us.
With a rod they will strike
the judge of Israel on the cheek.

2 But you, Bethlehem Ephrathah,
although you are small among the tribes of Judah,
from you will come forth for Me
one who will be ruler over Israel.
His origins are from of old,
from ancient days.

3 Therefore He will give them up,
until the time when she who is in labor has given birth,
and the rest of his brothers will return
to the children of Israel.
4 He will stand and shepherd
in the strength of the LORD,
in the majesty of the name of the LORD his God;
then they will live securely, because now He will be great
until the ends of the earth;
5 and He will be their peace.

The Remnant of Jacob Delivered

When Assyria enters our land
and treads through our palaces,
then we will raise up against him seven shepherds
and eight commanders of men.
6 They will shepherd the land of Assyria with the sword,
and the land of Nimrod at her gates;
He will rescue us from Assyria,
when he enters our land
and when he treads within our border.
7 Then the remnant of Jacob will be
in the midst of many peoples,
like dew from the LORD,

like showers upon the grass,
which do not wait for a man
and do not linger for the sons of men.
8 The remnant of Jacob will be among the nations,
in the midst of many peoples,
like a lion among the beasts of the forest,
like a young lion among flocks of sheep,
which when it passes through, tramples and mauls,
without rescuer.
9 Your hand will be lifted up over your adversaries,
and all your enemies will be cut off.

10 And in that day, declares the LORD,

I will cut off your horses from among you,
and I will destroy your chariots.
11 Then I will cut off the cities of your land,
and I will overthrow your strongholds;
12 then I will cut off sorceries from your hand,
and you will no longer have fortune-tellers.
13 Then I will cut off your idols,
and your sacred stones from among you,
and you will no longer bow down
to the work of your hands;
14 then I will root out your Asherah idols from among you,
and I will annihilate your cities.
15 And in anger and wrath I will take vengeance
on the nations that have not listened.

The Indictment of the LORD

6 Listen to what the LORD says:

Arise, plead your case before the mountains,
that the hills may hear your voice.
2 Hear, mountains, the indictment of the LORD,
O enduring foundations of the earth—
that the LORD has an indictment against His people,
and against Israel He will dispute.

3 "My people, what have I done to you,
and how have I wearied you?
Answer Me!
4 For I have brought you up from the land of Egypt,
and from the house of slaves I have redeemed you;
and I sent before you Moses,
Aaron, and Miriam.
5 O My people, remember now
what Balak king of Moab counseled,
and what Balaam son of Beor answered him,
and *remember* what happened from Shittim to Gilgal,
so that you might know the righteous acts of the LORD."

The Requirement of the LORD

6 "With what should I come before the LORD,
and bow down before God on high?

5:8 Ps 50:22
5:9 Isa 26:11
5:10 Zec 9:10
5:11 Isa 2:12–17
5:13 Eze 6:9
5:14 Ex 34:13
6:2 Isa 1:18
6:3 Jer 2:5
6:4 Ex 12:51
6:5 Nu 25:1

SPIRITLED WOMAN

COUNSEL FROM THE SPIRIT BASICS

The Cross-Bearing Standard

Are there times when being right is wrong? When faced with this question, we must ask first, "Was it right that Jesus died on a cross for me?" No, but God's plan for it was good. My difficulties must be viewed through the lens of the cross.

When we are wronged by others, it is natural to wish to respond, usually in anger. When we suffer, it is natural to want to do anything to relieve our suffering. And those responses would be justified and understandable, but what does God call us to in the midst of suffering and persecution? Indeed, how does God call us to live?

I'm reminded of this verse from Micah: "He has told you, O man, what is good— and what does the LORD require of you, but to do justice and to love kindness, and to walk humbly with your God?" (Mic 6:8). In this verse God again shows Israel that He is not pleased by empty rituals or liturgy, but rather by justice, kindness (mercy), and humility.

I know when I pray that God is going to reveal how often His justice in my life has been tempered by His grace and mercy—that were I to feel the left hook of justice hitting my jaw...well, let's just say it would be deserved but not appreciated.

Thankfully He will give me the grace, the strength, and the ability to do all that He has called me to do with justice, mercy, and kindness. In the face of suffering I can humbly trust my God and His goodness. Praise God that He will always be right—and that His right is always best.

Sue Birdseye

Angels Execute the Judgment of God

God uses angels to carry out His vengeance against those who dare to defy Him. Angels work for God at His bidding, and when they are released, it is not always good news. Disobedience to the woes of God releases the judgment of God.

Judgment is a bad word in the world today. Few acknowledge the judgments of the Lord. They do not pay attention to the fact that God created heaven and hell. People—even preachers—make excuses about the judgments God releases to get our attention. God is a God of love but at the same time a God of vengeance. He literally takes it personally when He says that vengeance belongs to Him. Micah warns us:

> The voice of the Lord calls to the city—
> and wisdom will fear Your name:
> Heed the rod and Him who has appointed it.
>
> —Micah 6:9

There are two important understandings of the word *rod* in this passage. First, a rod (*matteh*) is an instrument of chastisement and looks like a branch taken from a tree to punish. This rod can be used for chastising and correction, and it is referred to as a supply of life.

We are warned by God that there will be repercussions if we fail to correct our children. The Bible goes as far to say that if we beat our children with the rod, they shall not die but live. The power of the rod delivers their soul from death (Pr 23:13–14).

The word *rod* also means "scepter of authority." So when we ignore or do not reverence the rod of God, we disrespect His authority. God commands His people not to ignore His rod, but to pay attention to His chastisement, correction, and the instruments that He chooses to give life.

God warns us that if He does not get our attention, we will die. He declares that He will not count us as pure or acquit us when we are as guilty as the wicked. This is why God commands us to be holy. Paul wrote, "Come out from among them" (2Co 6:17), and that is still the word of the Lord for the times in which we live.

Kimberly Daniels

Shall I come before Him with burnt
offerings,
with calves a year old?
7 Will the LORD be pleased with thousands of
rams,
with ten thousand rivers of oil?
Shall I give my firstborn for my
transgression,
the fruit of my body for the sin of my
soul?"
8 He has told you, O man, what is good—
and what does the LORD require of you,
but to do justice and to love kindness,
and to walk humbly with your God?

The Punishment of Israel's Guilt

9 The voice of the LORD calls to the city—
and wisdom will fear Your name:
Heed the rod and Him who has
appointed it.
10 Are there still in the house of the wicked
treasures of wickedness?
And the short ephah[1] which is accursed?
11 Should I acquit the scales of wickedness,
and the sack of dishonest weights?
12 Her wealthy men are full of violence,
and her inhabitants speak deception,
and their tongue in their mouth is
treachery.
13 Therefore, I have struck you a dreadful
blow,
devastating you because of your sins.
14 You will eat, but not be satisfied,
with hunger within you.
You will set aside, but not retain;
and what you retain I will give over to
the sword.
15 You will sow, but not reap;
you will tread olives, but not anoint
yourselves with oil;
you will crush grapes, but not drink
wine.
16 You observe the statutes of Omri,
and every practice of the house of Ahab,
and you walk in their counsels.
Therefore I will give you over to
destruction,
and the inhabitants to derision.
You will bear the contempt of My
people.

Wait on the LORD

7 Woe is me!
Because I am as the gathering of
summer fruit,
as the gleaning of grapes;
there is no cluster to eat,
no early fig that my soul desires.
2 The godly has perished from the earth,
and no one is upright among men.
All of them lie in wait for bloodshed;

6:7 2Ki 16:3
6:8 Isa 57:15
6:9 Isa 30:27
6:10 Am 3:10
6:11 Hos 12:7
6:12 Isa 1:23
6:14 Hos 4:10
6:15 Zep 1:13
6:16 Jer 7:24
7:1 Isa 24:13
7:2 Ps 12:1

7:3 Mic 3:11
7:4 Isa 22:5
7:5 Jer 9:4
7:6 Mt 10:35–36
7:7 Isa 25:9
7:8 Ps 112:4
7:9 Ps 37:6
7:10 Joel 2:17
7:12 Isa 19:23–25
7:13 Isa 3:10–11

each hunts his brother with a net.
3 Both hands are upon evil, to do it well.
The prince and the judge request the
bribe,
the powerful asserts the craving of his very
soul—
they intertwine together.
4 The best among them is like a brier,
the most upright among them a
bramble;
the day of your watchmen,
of your punishment, has come;
now their confusion is at hand.
5 Do not trust in a companion,
do not rely on a friend;
from her who lies in your embrace,
guard the doors of your mouth.
6 For the son dishonors the father,
the daughter rises up against her
mother,
the daughter-in-law against her mother-
in-law—
the enemies of a man are members of
his own household.

7 But as for me, I watch for the LORD;
I await the God of my salvation;
my God will hear me.

The Penitence of Israel

8 Do not rejoice over me, my enemy!
Although I have fallen, I will rise;
although I dwell in darkness,
the LORD is my light.
9 I will endure the rage of the LORD,
because I have sinned against Him,
until the time when He pleads my case
and executes judgment for me.
He will bring me out into the light;
I will look upon His vindication.
10 Then my enemy will see,
and shame will cover her
who said to me,
"Where is the LORD your God?"
My eyes will look upon her;
now she will be trampled
like muck in the streets.

11 A day for building your walls,
in that day the boundary will be
extended.
12 In that day they will come to you
from Assyria and the cities of Egypt,
and from Egypt to the River,
from sea to sea,
and from mountain to mountain.
13 The earth will become desolate because of
its inhabitants,
from the fruit of their deeds.

[1]10 A dry measure of about 3/5 bushel, or 22 liters.

The Restoration of Israel

14 Shepherd your people with your staff,
the flock of your inheritance,
which live alone in a forest,
in the midst of a fertile land;
let them graze in Bashan and Gilead,
as in the days of old.

15 As in the days when you came out of
Egypt,
I will display wonders.

16 Nations will see and be ashamed,
despite all their might;
they will put their hand on their mouth,
and their ears will be deaf.

17 They will lick dust like the serpent,
like crawling creatures of the earth;
they will come shuddering from their lairs.
They will turn in dread to the LORD our
God,
and they will be afraid of You.

18 Who is a God like You,
bearing iniquity and passing over
transgression
for the remnant of His inheritance?
He does not remain angry forever,
because He delights in benevolence.

19 He will again have compassion upon us.
He will tread down our iniquities,
and cast all of our sins into the depths
of the sea.

20 You will give faithfulness to Jacob
and benevolence to Abraham,
which You swore to our fathers
from the days of old.

7:14 Mic 5:4
7:15 Isa 11:16
7:16 Isa 26:11
7:17 Isa 49:23

7:18 Isa 43:25
7:19 Isa 38:17

Author: The prophet Nahum

Written: Between 663 and 612 BC

Themes: The Coming Destruction of Nineveh

NAHUM

Dear Spirit Led Woman,

How blessed we are to have a Father who is jealous for us—One who avenges and is furious for us! Our Father is, mercifully for you and me, slow to anger. He proclaims peace and brings good tidings (Na 1:15), and we are created in His image. We are created to be like our heavenly Father.

When He releases His wrath, no one can stand against Him. He is a whirlwind, drying seas and pouring His fury like a fire. Even mountains quake before Him (v. 5). And He *loves* us. He is our protector, our strength. Who shall stand against us when we have His incredible force in us? The enemy can have brandished spears, charging chariots, and mighty shields, and they will be defeated, for our Father is against our enemy. So do not be afraid, for we have a mighty God.

Joy F. Strang

SPIRITLED WOMAN

COUNSEL FROM THE SPIRIT BASICS

Choose the Right Stronghold

The LORD is good, a stronghold in the day of distress; and He knows those who take refuge in Him.
—NAHUM 1:7

The kingdom of God is at hand. Every believer has authority over every demonic stronghold. But just as a car without gasoline is going nowhere, so it is with a believer who has authority to resist the enemy and to intercede for God's deliverance but instead becomes fearful and anxious. She will never see or experience the victories and freedom available to her.

Humility, honesty, and a willingness to confess all known sin and to turn from all sin and contact with evil spirits are absolutely necessary to obtain complete freedom.

Iris & John Delgado

1 An oracle for Nineveh, a writing of the vision of Nahum, the Elkoshite.

God's Anger With Nineveh

2 The LORD is a jealous and avenging God;
the LORD avenges and is furious.
The LORD takes vengeance on His enemies,
and He reserves it for His adversaries;
3 the LORD is slow to anger and great in power,
and the LORD will in no way acquit the guilty.
In gale winds and a storm is His way,
and clouds are the dust of His feet.
4 He rebukes and dries up the sea,
and He makes waterless all the rivers.
Bashan and Carmel wither up,
and the sprout of Lebanon wastes away.
5 The mountains quake before Him,
and the hills melt;
the land rises up before Him,
the earth and everything that dwells on it.
6 Who can stand before His anger?
Who will rise up before His burning wrath?
His heat is poured out like fire,
and the rocks are broken up before Him.

1:1 Isa 13:1
1:2 Ex 20:5
1:3 Ex 34:6–7
1:4 Isa 33:9
1:5 Mic 1:4
1:6 Mal 3:2

....

1:7 Ps 1:6
1:9 Na 1:11
1:10 Mic 7:4
1:11 Na 1:9
1:12 Isa 37:36
1:13 Isa 9:4
1:14 Ps 109:13
1:15 Isa 52:7
2:1 Jer 51:20–23
2:2 Ps 80:12–13

7 The LORD is good,
a stronghold in the day of distress;
and He knows those who take refuge in Him.
8 As a flood running forth,
He will bring to an end the distress,
and He will pursue His adversaries into darkness.

9 Why do you all scheme against the LORD?
He will bring it to an end.
It will not rise up a second time.
10 Because they are like interwoven thorns
and as drunkards imbibing,
they are consumed like completely dry stubble.
11 Out of you, *O Nineveh*, comes one,
a worthless counselor,
who devises evil against the LORD.

12 So the LORD says:

"Even though they are full and many,
they will be cut down, and it will pass away.
Even though I have afflicted you,
I will no longer afflict you, *O Judah*;
13 now I will break apart his yoke from over you,
and I will tear apart your bonds."

14 The LORD has given a command concerning you:
"No longer will your name go forth.
I will cut off the carved image and metal image
from the house of your gods.
I will prepare your grave,
for you are despised."

15 Look, on the mountains
come the feet of him who brings good news,
who proclaims peace!
Make your feasts, O Judah,
and complete your vows.
For the wicked one will never again pass through your midst;
he is completely cut down.

The Fall of Nineveh

2 He who scatters has come to you.
Guard the fortifications!
Watch the road!
Prepare yourself,
and strengthen yourself!

2 For the LORD is restoring the prominence of Jacob,
even the prominence of Israel,
for others have certainly
laid waste their vines.

Knocked Down but Not Out

In their younger years our three children loved playing with a clown-faced, inflatable toy that stood about three feet tall and teetered back and forth. When you punched its smiling face, down to the ground it went before bouncing right back up, thanks to a weighted attachment on the bottom. Regardless of how hard or how often the kids punched it, the smiling clown would always bounce back up.

You can enjoy this same kind of resiliency due to the victories Jesus won for you at Calvary. Life might knock you down, but the Word will cause you to bounce right back up, because God's Word puts a fight inside your spirit.

Some people try to act as if they never have any problems because their faith is so strong. Right. That isn't reality Throughout Scripture we see people lamenting their woes; meditate on some of David's psalms and you will see "woe is me" to the max! Or look at the prophet Nahum, who acknowledged he experienced difficulties when he wrote, "The LORD is good, a stronghold in the day of distress; and He knows those who take refuge in Him" (Na 1:7).

Nahum's words give us answers to three of life's most difficult questions:

1. Did God do this? (No, He is a good God.)

2. Where is God in my pain? (He is holding on to you.)

3. What does He want from me? (He is inviting you to trust Him so that He can show Himself strong on your behalf.)

Notice that Nahum didn't write, "The Lord is your stronghold *from* the day of trouble," but rather "*in* the day of trouble." Everyone has such a day, but it won't destroy you unless you allow it.

Here are three settle-it-forever statements that will give the devil a black eye. They make divine knockout punches every time.

Knockout Punch #1: The Lord is good.

Blaming God is far too many people's initial reaction to bad news. They scream, "Why did God do this?" or "Why did He let this happen?" God didn't send tragedy into your life. God is a good God. He loves you. You will need to settle the goodness of God before you can move forward.

Knockout Punch #2: The Lord is your stronghold.

In biblical days a stronghold or strong tower served as a fortified place. It functioned as a refuge—a place of security, survival, and safety.

When calamity comes, you can run into God's stronghold. As the psalmist wrote, "For You have been a refuge for me, and a strong tower from the enemy" (Ps 61:3). You can literally hide in God's strength.

Knockout Punch #3: The Lord wants your trust.

When you are walking through your day of trouble, it is common to wonder why you are experiencing such despair. After all, if God is never the source of sickness, misery, or suffering, why did this hard thing happen? What does He want? What is He looking for? To summarize briefly my response: All He wants is your trust. He alone is faithful, dependable, and trustworthy.

Rachel Burchfield

[3] The shields of his mighty men are soaked
red,
even the mighty men are clad in red.
In the day he prepares the chariots,
they are like a fire of iron.
The cypress spears are ready.
[4] The chariots run wildly through the streets,
they rush to and fro in the open areas;
their appearance is like torches,
they dash to and fro like lightning.

[5] He remembers his officers
as they stumble about on the road;
they hurry on to the wall
as the siege tower is set up.
[6] The holding gates are opened wide,
and the palace washes away.
[7] It is decreed:
She is uncovered and led away captive;
her handmaidens shall lead her as with the
voice of doves,
beating their chests.
[8] Nineveh is like a pool
whose waters run away.
"Halt! Halt!" they cry,
but no one turns back.
[9] "Plunder the silver!
Plunder the gold!
There is no limit to the treasure,
or to the wealth of every precious thing."
[10] She is desolate, empty, and waste!
Hearts melt away, and knees shake;
pain is in all the loins, and all their faces
grow pale.
[11] Where is the den of the lions,
and the feeding place of the young lions,
where the lion and lioness prowl,
and the lion's cub goes, with no one to
disturb *them*?
[12] The lion tore enough food for his cubs,
and strangled prey for his lionesses;
he has filled his caves with prey,
and his dens with flesh.

[13] I am against you,
says the LORD of Hosts,
and I will burn your chariots in smoke,
and the sword will devour your lions.
I will cut off your prey from the earth,
and the voice of your messengers
will be heard no more.

Woe to Nineveh

3 Woe to the bloody city!
It is full of lies
and plunder.
The prey never departs.
[2] The noise of the whip
and the noise of the rattling of the
wheels,
galloping horses,
and rushing chariots!
[3] Horsemen charging
with flashing sword
and glittering spear.
Multitude of slain,
great number of corpses,
dead bodies without end—
they stumble on the corpses—
[4] because of the countless harlotries of the
seductive harlot,
the mistress of sorceries,
who sells nations through her harlotries
and families through her sorceries.

[5] I am against you, says the LORD of Hosts;
I will lift your skirts over your face,
and I will show the nations your
nakedness,
and the kingdoms your shame.
[6] I will throw filth on you,
and make you vile,
and make you a spectacle.
[7] All who look at you will flee from you, and
say,
"Nineveh is devastated! Who will lament
for her?"
Where shall I seek comforters for you?

[8] Are you better than Thebes
that sat by the Nile,
with water around her,
whose rampart was the sea,
and whose wall was the water?
[9] Ethiopia and Egypt were her strength, and
it was without limit;
Put and Libya were her helpers.
[10] Yet she went into exile,
she went into captivity;
her young children were dashed to pieces
at the head of every street;
they cast lots for her honorable men,
and all her great men were bound in
chains.
[11] You also will be drunk;
you will go into hiding;
you will seek refuge from the enemy.

[12] All your fortresses are like fig trees
with first-ripe figs:
If they are shaken,
they fall into the mouth of the eater.
[13] Your troops
are women in your midst!
The gates of your land
are wide open to your enemies;
fire has devoured your bars.

[14] Draw water for the siege!
Strengthen your forts!

2:3 Eze 23:14–15
2:4 Jer 4:13
2:5 Jer 46:12
2:7 Isa 38:14
2:10 Ps 22:14
2:11 Isa 5:29
2:12 Jer 51:34
2:13 2Ki 19:23

3:3 Hab 3:11
3:4 Isa 47:9
3:5 Na 2:13
3:6 Job 9:31
3:7 Isa 51:19
3:8 Am 6:2
3:9 Eze 27:10
3:10 Isa 20:4
3:11 Isa 2:10
3:12 Rev 6:13
3:13 Jer 51:30
3:14 Na 2:1

Go into the clay and
tread the mortar!
Take hold of the brick mold!
15 There the fire will devour you,
the sword will cut you off;
it will eat you up like the locust.
Multiply yourselves—like the locust!
Multiply—like the grasshopper!

Deliver me from the locust that plunders and then flies away (Na 3:16).

16 You have multiplied your merchants
more than the stars of heaven.
The locust plunders
and flies away.

17 Your leaders are like grasshoppers,
your commanders like swarms of
locusts,
which camp in the hedges on a cold day;
when the sun rises they fly away,
and the place where they are is not
known.

18 Your shepherds slumber, O king of Assyria;
Your nobles lie *in the dust*.
Your people are scattered on the
mountains,
and no one gathers them.
19 There is no healing of your injury,
your wound is grievous.
All who hear news about you
clap their hands over you,
for upon whom has not your wickedness
continually passed?

3:15 Joel 1:4

3:18 1Ki 22:17
3:19 La 2:15

Author: The prophet Habakkuk

Written: Between 610 and 605 BC

Theme: God's Involvement in the Lives of His People

HABAKKUK

Dear SpiritLed Woman,

As I look at the world surrounding me, I can't help but notice how many broken people I see. They have turned their hearts from God and try to live on their own with selfish pride. My heart breaks for these people, as should yours. They believe their wealth and their deeds will secure them a place in the kingdom of our Father, but they do not know what He has written. "The just shall live by his faith" (Hab 2:4) means that we have God's provision. We have trust in our Lord to honor His promises.

We do not need to fear for tomorrow or question if God has heard our pleas. God hears all of our prayers, and He answers us—even if it is not the answer we desire, no is an answer. How blessed are we that we do not need to worry about tomorrow! We only need to have faith that God is with us, always.

Joy F. Strang

1

1 The oracle that Habakkuk the prophet saw.

Habakkuk's Complaint

2 O LORD, how long shall I cry,
and You will not hear?
Or cry to You, "Violence!"
and You will not save?
3 Why do You make me see wickedness,
and cause me to see trouble?
Plundering and violence are before me;
strife and contention arise.
4 Therefore the law is powerless,
and justice never goes forth.
For the wicked surround the righteous;
therefore injustice proceeds.

The LORD's Answer

5 Look among the nations, and watch—
wonder and be amazed!
For I am doing a work in your days
that you would not believe,
though it were told you.
6 For I am raising up the Chaldeans,
that bitter and hasty nation
which marches through the breadth of the
earth,
to possess dwelling places that are not
theirs.
7 They are terrible and dreadful;
their justice and their dignity
proceed from themselves.
8 Their horses are swifter than leopards,
more fierce than evening wolves.
Their horsemen charge on;
their horsemen come from afar;
they fly like the eagle that hastens to eat.
9 They all come for violence;
their forces advance like the east wind.
They gather captives like sand.
10 They scoff at kings,
and they scorn rulers.
They deride every stronghold,
for they build up siege ramps to capture
it.
11 Then their mind changes,
and they transgress and commit offense;
their own power is their god.

Habakkuk's Second Complaint

12 Are You not from everlasting,
O LORD my God, my Holy One? We will
not die.
O LORD, You have appointed them for
judgment;
and You, O Rock, have established them
for correction.
13 Your eyes are too pure to look on evil,
and You cannot look on wickedness.
Why do You look on those who deal
treacherously,
and hold Your tongue when the wicked
devours the man who is more righteous
than he?
14 You make men like fish of the sea,
like crawling things that have no ruler.
15 They bring all of them up with a hook,
they catch them in their net;
they gather them in their dragnet.
Therefore they rejoice and are glad.
16 Therefore they sacrifice to their net
and burn incense to their dragnet;
for by them their portion is extravagant,
and their food plentiful.
17 Shall they continue to empty their net,
and continually kill the nations while not
sparing anyone?

2

1 I will stand at my watch
and station myself on the watchtower;
and I will keep watch to see what He will
say to me,
and what I will answer when I am
reproved.

1:1 Na 1:1
1:2 Ps 13:1–2
1:4 Ps 119:126
1:5 Isa 29:14
1:6 2Ki 24:2
1:7 Jer 39:5–9
1:8 Jer 4:13
1:10 2Ch 36:6
1:12 Dt 32:4

1:15 Jer 16:16
1:16 Hab 1:11
2:1 Ps 85:8

SPIRITLED WOMAN

COUNSEL FROM THE SPIRIT BASICS

Covet Not

The Old Testament prophets touched on the sin of coveting. Habakkuk said:

> Woe to him who gets evil gain for his house, to set his nest on high, to be delivered from the power of calamity!
>
> —HABAKKUK 2:9

Micah 2:2 also warns against coveting, speaking of a territorial and generational spirit of covetousness that rules over families and countries and even flows generationally through a man's heritage. Some people suffer from the manifestations of covetous spirits through these sources, and they must be dealt with through prayer and spiritual warfare. In dealing with territorial and generational spirits, they must be displaced.

This means that the negative influence must be removed and replaced with a positive one. To displace the spirit of coveting, it must be replaced with contentment. Let's define *contentment*. It is simple and not deep: "to be happy with what you have." It means "to be satisfied or full."

Kimberly Daniels

WOMAN OF THE SPIRIT

Waiting on the Lord

Most of the time when we enter into a battle, there is a period of waiting until we reach the battle's conclusion. You might be thinking, "How in the world will waiting help anything?" But throughout Scripture the Lord tells us again and again to wait upon Him. To us, waiting is simply passing the time until we get something that we want, but biblical waiting is altogether different.

Biblical waiting is full of activity; it is not wasted time. Even Jesus had to wait in obedience to His Father. I wonder how long Jesus knew He was the Messiah before He launched His ministry at age thirty-three. Perhaps He could have commanded miracles when He was six or cast out demons when He was two, but He didn't. Jesus' father, Joseph, passed away sometime between the time Jesus was twelve and when Jesus began His ministry at age thirty. As Jesus watched His earthly dad pass away, as much as He may have wanted to, He stood back and did not use His God-power to raise Joseph from the dead. It was not yet Jesus' time. Jesus had to wait to reveal His true identity until the Father's perfect time, even though it meant losing a member of His family.

But waiting is not without purpose. It is an important factor in God's kingdom, and God stresses that to us again and again.

Waiting on the Lord means choosing not to make something happen for ourselves outside God's will for us. Abraham wanted a child so badly that he slept with his maidservant, even though God had told him that his wife, Sarah, would bear him a child. Abraham just couldn't stand the wait.

We would avoid so many messes if we would be obedient in the waiting! A believer willing to wait on the Lord is not an easy target for the devil. The enemy may try to strike a few blows to such a Christian, but after a while he will realize that this believer will not be moved from faith, and he will eventually give up. Many Christians do not conquer simply because they tire out and therefore forfeit God's best.

Some of the most difficult times we will ever face as believers will be times of great waiting on the Lord. Satan can more easily disarm us when we are waiting without exercising faith. That's why when we are in a great battle and our faith is being challenged, it seems the blows from the devil increase. The wait in the battle has made us weary, so the enemy strikes again, creating a bigger battle.

Wait with a valiant heart. Do not lower your stance just because the wait seems longer than you first thought it would be. Fill your waiting with faith. Take a stand and decide that you will not grow impatient with God's plans. Do not let the devil convince you to take a bite of his carrot. Anything God has promised us is worth the wait.

Jenny Swindall

The Just Shall Live by Faith

2 And the LORD answered me:

Write the vision,
and make it plain on tablets,
that he who reads it may run.
3 For the vision is yet for an appointed time;
but it speaks of the end,
and does not lie.
If it delays, wait for it;
it will surely come, it will not delay.

4 Look, his soul is lifted up;
it is not upright in him;
but the just shall live by his faith.
5 Indeed, wine betrays the proud man,
who does not stay at home.
He enlarges his appetite as Sheol,
and like death he is never satisfied.
He gathers to himself all nations
and collects for himself all peoples.

Woe to the Wicked

6 Shall not all these take up a taunt against
him, with satire and riddles, and say,

"Woe to him who increases what is not
his—how long?
And to him who loads himself with
heavy debts!"
7 Shall not your debtors rise up suddenly,
and those awake who oppress you?
Then you will be their plunder.
8 Because you have plundered many
nations,
all the remnant of the people will
plunder you,
because of the bloodshed of men and
violence of the land,
of the cities and all who live in them.

9 "Woe to him who gets evil gain for his
house,
to set his nest on high,
to be delivered from the power of
calamity!"
10 You have given shameful counsel to your
house
by cutting off many peoples,
and forfeiting your life.
11 For the stone will cry out from the wall,
and the beam of the woodwork will
answer it.

12 "Woe to him who builds a town with
bloodshed
and establishes a city on iniquity!"
13 Is it not from the LORD of Hosts
that the people labor to feed fire,
and the nations weary themselves for
nothing?
14 For the earth will be filled with the
knowledge of the glory of the LORD,
as the waters cover the seas.

2:3 Da 10:14
2:4 Ro 1:17
2:5 Pr 27:20
2:7 Pr 29:1
2:8 Isa 33:1
2:9 Jer 49:16
2:11 Lk 19:40
2:12 Mic 3:10
2:13 Isa 50:11
2:14 Isa 11:9

....

2:16 Isa 47:3
2:17 Hab 2:8
2:18 Jer 10:8
2:19 Ps 135:17
2:20 Ps 11:4
3:2 Ps 85:6
3:3 Dt 33:2
3:4 Job 26:14
3:5 Ex 12:29–30

15 "Woe to him who makes his neighbor
drink,
pouring out your poison until they are
drunk,
that you may look on their nakedness!"
16 You will be filled with shame instead of
glory.
You yourself—drink and show your
uncircumcision!
The cup of the LORD's right hand will be
turned against you,
and utter shame will come on your
glory!
17 The violence done to Lebanon will cover
you,
as will the plunder of beasts that
terrified them,
because of the bloodshed of men and
violence of the land,
of the cities and all who live in them.

18 What profit is a carved image when its
maker has carved it,
a cast image, and a teacher of lies,
that its maker trusts in what he has shaped
when he makes mute idols?
19 Woe to him who says to the wood,
"Awake!"
To the silent stone, "Arise!" Can it teach?
It is overlaid with gold and silver,
and there is no breath at all in it.

20 But the LORD is in His holy temple.
Let all the earth keep silence before Him.

The Prayer of Habakkuk

3 A prayer of Habakkuk the prophet, on Shigionoth.

2 O LORD, I have heard the report of You,
and was afraid;
O LORD, revive Your work
in the midst of the years!
In the midst of these years
make them known;
in wrath remember mercy.

3 God came from Teman,
and the Holy One from Mount Paran.
Selah
His glory covered the heavens,
and the earth was full of His praise.

Let the power in Your hands be released in my life (Hab 3:4).

4 His brightness was like the light;
rays flashed from His hand,
and there His power was hidden.
5 Pestilence went out before Him,
and plague followed His feet.

SPIRIT-TO-SPIRIT PRAYER

REDEDICATION PRAYER

Heavenly Father, I am making a quality decision this day to rededicate my life to You. I pledge my heart and my entire being and everything that I am to You. I sincerely draw near to You and thank You for accepting me and helping me to recover what the enemy has stolen. Please forgive me of all my sins and iniquities. Father, I now choose to forgive everyone who has sinned against me. I receive Your love and Your mercy. Thank You for guiding my steps and granting me a new beginning. Help me to change the things I can change and to allow You to change the things I cannot. I surrender my life to You. I love You, my Lord and Savior. In Jesus' name, amen.

Iris Delgado

6 He stood and measured the earth;
He looked and shook the nations.
The eternal mountains were scattered,
the perpetual hills bowed.
His ways are everlasting.
7 I saw the tents of Cushan in affliction;
the curtains of the land of Midian
trembled.
8 Were you displeased with the rivers, O
LORD?
Was Your anger against the rivers,
and was Your wrath against the sea
when You rode on Your horses,
on Your chariots of salvation?
9 You made bare Your bow;
oaths were the arrows at Your
command. Selah
You divided the earth with the rivers.
10 The mountains saw You and trembled;
the overflowing water passed by.
The deep lifted its voice,
and lifted its hands on high.

Send out arrows of light into the kingdom of darkness (Hab 3:11).

11 The sun and moon stood still in their
places;
at the light of Your arrows they went,
at the flash of Your glittering spear.
12 You marched throughout the earth in
indignation;
You threshed the nations in anger.
13 You went forth to deliver Your people,
to deliver Your anointed one.
You wounded the head of the house of the
wicked,
laying him bare from head to
foot. Selah
14 You pierced with his own arrows
the leaders of his villages.
They came like a whirlwind to scatter me;
their rejoicing was like devouring the
poor in secret.
15 You trampled the sea with Your horses,
through the wakes of great waters.

16 I heard, and my body trembled;
my lips quivered at the sound;
rottenness entered my bones;
my legs tremble beneath me.
Yet I will wait quietly for the day
when calamity comes on the people
invading us.

A Hymn of Faith

17 Though the fig tree does not blossom,
nor fruit be on the vines;
though the yield of the olive fails,
and the fields produce no food;
though the flocks are cut off from the fold,
and there be no herd in the stalls—

I will walk upon the high places (Hab 3:19).

18 yet I will rejoice in the LORD;
I will exult in the God of my salvation.

19 The LORD God is my strength;
He will make my feet like hinds' feet,
and He will make me walk on my high
places.
To the Music Director: with my stringed
instruments.

3:7 Ex 15:14–16
3:8 Ps 68:17
3:9 Ps 7:12–13
3:10 Ps 93:3
3:13 Ps 110:6

3:15 Ps 77:19
3:16 Hab 3:2
3:18 Php 4:4
3:19 Dt 33:29

Author: The prophet Zephaniah

Written: Late Seventh Century BC

Theme: The Day of the Lord

ZEPHANIAH

Dear SpiritLed Woman,

When we stand before the Lord, how will He receive us? Will He know we accepted His love? Or will He not know us? Will we still be in need of repentance? I pray that "He will rejoice over you with gladness, He will renew you with His love, He will rejoice over you with singing" (Zep 3:17).

SpiritLed woman, our God is worthy of all praise. He is faithful to us, and we should rejoice with all of our hearts. He is full of praise for us too. He gathers us to Him, and He will make us distinct among those around us; people will ask why we are different, and we will be able to say it is because we walk with our Savior—a Savior who rejoices over us with gladness and singing.

Joy F. Strang

1 The word of the LORD which came to Zephaniah the son of Cushi, the son of Gedaliah, the son of Amariah, the son of Hezekiah, in the days of Josiah the son of Amon, king of Judah.

The Great Day of the LORD

2 I will utterly consume all things
on the face of the earth,
says the LORD;
3 I will consume man and beast;
I will consume the birds of the heavens
and the fish of the sea,
and the stumbling blocks with the wicked.
I will cut off man from the face of the land,
says the LORD.

4 I will stretch out my hand against Judah,
and against all the inhabitants of Jerusalem.
I will cut off from this place the remnant of Baal,
and the name of the idolatrous priests
along with the priests,
5 and those who bow down on the roofs
to the host of heaven;
those who worship and swear oaths by the LORD
and yet swear by Milcom;
6 those who have turned back from following the LORD,
who have not sought the LORD nor
inquired of Him.

7 Be silent before the Lord GOD!
For the day of the LORD is at hand;
the LORD has prepared the sacrifice;
He has consecrated His guests.

Punish the princes with Your power (Zep 1:8).

8 On the day of the LORD's sacrifice,
I will punish the officials
and the king's sons,
and all who clothe themselves
with foreign attire.
9 On that day I will punish
all who step over the threshold,
who fill their masters' houses
with violence and deceit.

10 On that day, says the LORD,
a cry will be heard from the Fish Gate,
a wail from the Second Quarter,
and a loud crash from the hills.
11 Wail, you inhabitants of the Mortar!
For all the merchants are cut down;
all those who weigh out silver are cut off.

1:1 2Ch 34:1–33
1:2 2Ki 22:16–17
1:3 Eze 7:19
1:4 Hos 10:5
1:5 1Ki 11:33
1:6 Isa 1:4
1:7 Isa 34:6
1:8 Isa 24:21
1:9 1Sa 5:5
1:10 2Ch 33:14
1:11 Jas 5:1
1:12 Jer 48:11
1:13 Am 5:11
1:14 Joel 2:11
1:15 Joel 2:2
1:16 Isa 2:12–15
1:17 Ps 83:10
1:18 Zep 3:8
2:1 2Ch 20:4
2:2 Isa 17:13
2:3 Am 5:14–15
2:4 Zec 9:5–7
2:5 Eze 25:16

12 At that time I will search Jerusalem with lamps,
and I will punish the men
who are settled on their lees,
who say in their heart,
"The LORD will not do good, nor will He do evil."
13 Their goods will be plundered,
and their houses laid waste.
Though they build houses,
they will not inhabit them;
though they plant vineyards,
they will not drink from their wine.

The Great Day of the LORD

14 The great day of the LORD is near,
near and hastening quickly.
The sound of the day of the LORD is bitter;
the mighty man shall cry out there.
15 That day is a day of wrath,
a day of trouble and distress,
a day of ruin and desolation,
a day of darkness and gloom,
a day of clouds and blackness,
16 a day of trumpet and alarms
against the fortified cities
and against the high towers.

17 I will bring distress on men,
so that they will walk like blind men.
Because they have sinned against the LORD,
their blood will be poured out like dust,
and their flesh like dung.
18 Neither their silver nor their gold
will be able to deliver them
on the day of the LORD's wrath.

But the whole earth will be consumed
by the fire of His jealousy,
for He will make a sudden end
of all those who dwell on the earth.

Judgment on the Nations

2 Gather together, yes, gather together,
O shameless nation,
2 before the decree takes effect,
before the day passes like chaff,
before the fierce anger of the LORD comes upon you,
before the day of the LORD's anger comes upon you.
3 Seek the LORD, all you humble of the land,
who carry out His judgment.
Seek righteousness, seek humility.
Perhaps you will be hidden
on the day of the LORD's anger.

4 For Gaza will be forsaken,
and Ashkelon a desolation;
Ashdod will be driven out at noon,
and Ekron will be uprooted.
5 Woe to the inhabitants of the seacoast,
the nation of Kerethites!

PHOEBE PALMER
SEEKER OF HOLINESS

Phoebe Palmer was the mother of the Holiness movement.

Born Phoebe Worrall in 1807, she was brought up in a devout Methodist home. She married a Methodist homeopathic physician, Walter Palmer. Their first two children died within months of their birth.

In early Methodism, conversion was an emotional experience, and the fact that Phoebe hadn't had such an encounter was a source of trial to her. Finally she came to understand that belief in God was enough—that if she laid her life on the altar, God Himself would make her holy.

Phoebe and Walter became very interested in John Wesley's writings, especially his doctrine of Christian perfection, which is the belief that a Christian can live free of voluntary sin and that this can happen instantly through a "second work of grace." Phoebe and her family experienced "entire sanctification" sometime during 1937 and felt they should teach others how to experience it for themselves. Phoebe developed a process that divided John Wesley's perfectionism into three parts:

1. Consecrate yourself totally to God.
2. Believe God will sanctify what is consecrated.
3. Tell others about it.

Phoebe and her sister began a series of women's prayer meetings in Phoebe's home, which became known as the "Tuesday Meeting for the Promotion of Holiness." Soon men were included too. They brought together people of many different backgrounds and inspired similar meetings around the country.

Phoebe soon became the most influential woman in the most rapidly growing group in America—the Holiness movement. She and her husband went on the road, teaching the concept of Christian holiness. She started missions and camp meetings, and around twenty-five thousand Americans became believers.

Phoebe inspired other women to follow her example, notably Catherine Booth of The Salvation Army and Frances Willard of the Women's Christian Temperance Union. Her theology gave rise to denominations, such as the Church of the Nazarene, the Salvation Army, the Church of God, and the Pentecostal-Holiness Church.[1]

Felicity Dale

1. Research for this article came from "Phoebe Palmer," ChristianHistory.net, http://www.christianitytoday.com/ch/131christians/moversandshakers/palmer.html (accessed April 29, 2014) and "Phoebe Palmer" on Wikipedia.com.

A Call for Joy

The LORD your God is in your midst,
a Mighty One, who will save.
He will rejoice over you with gladness,
He will renew you with His love,
He will rejoice over you with singing.

—ZEPHANIAH 3:17

Have you ever wondered if God really wants you to be happy? God wants us to live long lives of joy. It is a long-standing misconception that God is a harsh taskmaster only interested in burdening people with rules and catching them in their mistakes. Nothing could be further from the truth. God is the author of joy. And despite the introduction of sin into this world, God has worked to restore joy to His people. The story of salvation is the story of God rescuing people from the sorrow of sin and bringing His joy into their lives.

In Zephaniah 3:14 believers are commanded to be happy no less than four times.

"Sing," God commands.

"Shout," God commands.

"Be glad," God commands.

"Rejoice with all your heart," God commands.

Could this be any clearer? The command in verse 14 to be happy and rejoice is given in response to what God will do as people repent. May we never fail to rejoice in what God has done for us because we repented of our sins and turned to Him through faith in Christ.

Despite God's desire for us to be happy, there are many forces in life that come against our joy. Even during relatively good times our own attempts to find happiness are often flawed. And our ability to cope with painful circumstances is often incomplete. But as we draw close to God in faith, we discover that He brings joy into our lives that is not based on our limited abilities.

The promises in Zephaniah 3:15–20 point to the ultimate redemption God has planned for all who will trust in Him. The picture painted in these verses is one of idyllic existence. God's love will be fully expressed toward the righteous (v. 17). The sorrow of sin, the oppression of this world, and all sickness will be gone (vv. 18–19). In their place, the righteous will enjoy prestige and honor bestowed on them by God.

God has planned for all the righteous an eternal future of uninterrupted joy.

Barbara Dycus

The word of the LORD is against you,
O Canaan, land of the Philistines:
I will destroy you,
so that there will be no inhabitant.
6 The seacoast will be pastures,
with meadows for shepherds and folds
for flocks.
7 The coast will be for the remnant of the
house of Judah,
on which they will feed.
In the houses of Ashkelon
they will lie down at evening.
For the LORD their God will visit them
and restore their fortunes.

8 I have heard these taunts of Moab,
and the revilings of the Ammonites,
by which they have reproached My people,
and made boasts against their territory.
9 Therefore, as I live,
says the LORD of Hosts, the God of Israel,
surely Moab will be like Sodom,
and the Ammonites like Gomorrah—
a land of weeds and salt pits,
and a perpetual desolation.
The remnant of My people will plunder
them,
and the survivors of My nation will
possess them.

10 This will they have for their pride,
because they taunted and boasted
against
the people of the LORD of Hosts.
11 The LORD will be dreadful to them,
for He will weaken all the gods of the
earth;
men will worship Him, every one from his
place,
all the lands of the nations.

12 You also, O Ethiopians,
will be slain by My sword.

13 And He will stretch out His hand against
the north
and destroy Assyria;
and He will make Nineveh a desolation,
and dry like the desert.
14 Herds will lie down in her midst,
beasts of every kind;
the cormorant and the bittern
will lodge on her pillars.
Their voice will sing in the windows;
desolation will be on the threshold;
for He will lay bare the cedar work.
15 This is the rejoicing city
that dwelt securely,
that said in her heart,
"I am, and there is no one besides me."
How has she become a desolation,

2:7 Zep 3:20
2:9 Dt 29:23
2:10 Isa 16:6
2:13 Na 3:7
2:14 Jer 22:14
2:15 Eze 28:2

....

3:1 Jer 6:6
3:2 Jer 5:3
3:3 Hab 1:8
3:4 Eze 22:26
3:5 Dt 32:4

COUNSEL FROM THE SPIRIT BASICS

SPIRITLED WOMAN

God Promises to Restore

God sent the prophets to warn His people of the judgment He would send if they did not repent. But God wanted His people to understand that these judgments could be averted if they would repent. When people repent, God responds with love, cleansing their hearts so they can be restored to Him and serve Him.

God further spoke of how He would bring His people out of exile and return them to their land. Their return would be spiritual as well, for they would again offer worship to the Lord.

When God saves individuals, He not only removes the guilt of sin but also works in them to free them from the hold of sin. Old sinful habits are dealt with so that Christ-like character is formed in the believer. As believers trust in the Lord, they experience the peace of God.

Barbara Dycus

a place for beasts to lie down!
Everyone who passes by her will hiss
and shake his fist.

Woe to Jerusalem

3 Woe to her who is rebellious and defiled,
the oppressing city.
2 She obeys no voice,
she receives no correction;
she does not trust in the LORD,
she does not draw near to her God.
3 Her princes within her are roaring lions;
her judges are evening wolves
who leave nothing until the morning.
4 Her prophets are reckless,
treacherous men;
her priests have profaned the sanctuary
and done violence to the law.
5 The LORD is righteous in her midst;
He does no unrighteousness.
Every morning He brings His justice to
light;
He does not fail,
but the unjust knows no shame.

6 I have cut off nations,
their strongholds are devastated;
I have made their streets desolate,
with no one passing by.
Their cities are destroyed;
there is no man, no inhabitant.
7 I said,
"Surely you will fear Me;
and you will receive correction."
So her dwelling will not be cut off,
according to all that I have appointed
against her.
But they were more eager
to corrupt all their deeds.

The Conversion of the Nations

8 Therefore wait for Me, declares the LORD,
until the day when I rise up to seize the
plunder;
for My decision is to gather nations,
to assemble kingdoms,
to pour on them My indignation,
all My fierce anger;
for all the earth will be devoured
with the fire of My jealousy.

9 For then I will restore to the peoples a pure
speech
that all of them may call on the name of
the LORD,
to serve Him with one accord.
10 From beyond the rivers of Ethiopia
My worshippers, the daughter of My
dispersed ones,
will bring My offering.
11 On that day you will not be ashamed
for all your deeds by which you have
transgressed against Me;
for then I will remove from your midst
those who rejoice in your pride,
and you will no longer be haughty
in My holy mountain.
12 But I will leave in your midst
a meek and humble people,
and they will trust in the name of the
LORD.

3:7 Hos 9:9
3:8 Joel 3:2
3:9 Isa 19:18
3:10 Ps 68:31
3:11 Isa 54:4
3:12 Isa 14:32

....

3:13 Zep 2:7
3:14 Isa 12:6
3:15 Isa 51:22
3:16 Heb 12:12
3:17 Jer 32:41
3:19 Isa 60:14
3:20 Jer 29:14

13 The remnant of Israel will do no
unrighteousness,
nor speak lies;
nor will a deceitful tongue be found in
their mouth;
for they will feed and lie down,
and no one will make them afraid.

Israel's Song of Joy

14 Sing, O daughter of Zion!
Shout, O Israel!
Be glad and rejoice with all your heart,
O daughter of Jerusalem!
15 The LORD has taken away your judgments,
He has cast out your enemies.
The King of Israel, the LORD, is in your
midst;
you will see evil no more.
16 On that day it will be said to Jerusalem:
Fear not, O Zion;
let not your hands be slack.
17 The LORD your God is in your midst,
a Mighty One, who will save.
He will rejoice over you with gladness,
He will renew you with His love,
He will rejoice over you with singing.

18 I will gather those who grieve
for the appointed festival,
which is a reproach and burden on you.
19 At that time I will deal
with all who oppress you;
I will save the lame
and gather the outcast;
I will give them praise and fame
in every land where they have been put
to shame.
20 At that time I will bring you in,
at the time when I gather you;
for I will make you renowned and praised
among all peoples of the earth,
when I restore your fortunes
before your eyes,
says the LORD.

Author: The prophet Haggai

Written: 520 BC

Theme: Rebuilding the Temple

HAGGAI

Dear Spirit Led Woman,

There's a wonderful verse in Haggai that says, "According to the covenant that I made with you when you came out of Egypt, so My Spirit remains among you. Do not fear" (Hag 2:5). God was encouraging the remnant of His people that His Spirit was still with them. They had been through some devastating times, but He was letting them know they did not need to be afraid because His Spirit remained.

Where the Holy Spirit remains, all worry, anxiety, and fear must flee. You don't have to fear if your finances crumble. You don't have to fear if the doctor gives a bad report. You don't have to fear if your family faces attacks from every side. Fear is the enemy of faith, and without faith it is impossible to please God (Heb 11:6). When you listen to the Spirit and what He is calling you to do, fear disappears and faith rises up in your heart.

The Holy Spirit remains. His Spirit will lift you above every fear you face.

Joy F. Strang

SPIRITLED WOMAN

COUNSEL FROM THE SPIRIT BASICS

The Strongman of the Flesh

In Haggai 1:5 the prophet Haggai advises the Israelites who had returned to Jerusalem from their long captivity in Babylon by saying, "Consider your ways." The word *ways* in the Hebrew is *derek*, and it means "to consider the path of life that you have taken." It also means "to consider your methods, mannerisms, or how you conduct yourself." To put it in concise terms, it means to consider how your flesh acts out. You are a spirit, you possess a soul, and you live in a fleshly vessel. You cannot deny, overlook, or ignore your flesh. It must be sternly dealt with, or it will run the house.

The enemy is battling with you for control of your soul (mind) and your flesh, which stand in opposition to your spirit. This is the reason God wants you to renew your mind—because then your spirit man can be led by God's Spirit. Remember that the flesh has a mind of its own, and it is hostile against the things of God. Anything hostile against God or the things of God is evil.

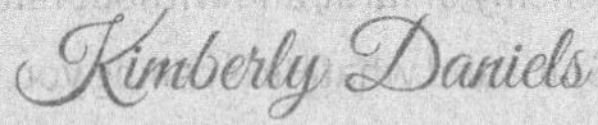

God's Command to Rebuild the Temple

1 In the second year of King Darius, in the sixth month, on the first day of the month, the word of the LORD came by Haggai the prophet to Zerubbabel the son of Shealtiel, governor of Judah, and to Joshua the son of Jehozadak, the high priest, saying,

2 Thus says the LORD of Hosts: These people say, The time has not yet come to rebuild the house of the LORD.

3 Then the word of the LORD came by Haggai the prophet, saying: 4 Is it time for you yourselves to live in paneled houses, while this house lies in ruins?

5 Now, therefore, thus says the LORD of Hosts: Consider your ways. 6 You have sown much, and harvested little. You eat, but you do not have enough; you drink, but you are not filled with drink; you clothe yourselves, but no one is warm; and he who earns wages earns wages to put them into a bag with holes.

1:1 Ezr 2:2
1:3 Ezr 5:1
1:4 2Sa 7:2
1:5 La 3:40
1:6 Hag 2:16

1:7 Hag 1:5
1:8 Ps 132:13–14
1:9 Hag 1:4
1:11 Hag 2:17
1:12 Isa 50:10
1:14 Hag 1:1
1:15 Hag 1:1
2:1 Hag 1:1
2:2 Hag 1:1
2:3 Ezr 3:12

Father, help me remain aware that it is You who provide all my needs and not my own strength or abilities (Hag 1:6).

7 Thus says the LORD of Hosts: Consider your ways. 8 Go up to the mountain and bring wood and rebuild the house, that I may take pleasure in it and be glorified, says the LORD. 9 You looked for much, and it came to little; and when you brought it home, I blew it away. Why? says the LORD of Hosts. Because of My house that lies in ruins while each of you runs to his own house. 10 Therefore the heavens above you have withheld the dew, and the earth has withheld its crops. 11 I called for a drought on the land and the mountains, on the grain, on the new wine, on the oil, on what the ground brings forth, on men, on livestock, and on all the labor of your hands.

The People Obey God's Command

12 Then Zerubbabel the son of Shealtiel, and Joshua the son of Jehozadak, the high priest, with all the remnant of the people, obeyed the voice of the LORD their God, and the words of Haggai the prophet, as the LORD their God had sent him. And the people feared the LORD.

Lord, stir up my spirit to do Your will (Hag 1:14).

13 Then Haggai, the messenger of the LORD, spoke the message of the LORD to the people, saying: I am with you, says the LORD. 14 And the LORD stirred up the spirit of Zerubbabel the son of Shealtiel, governor of Judah, and the spirit of Joshua the son of Jehozadak, the high priest, and the spirit of all the remnant of the people. And they came and worked on the house of the LORD of Hosts their God, 15 on the twenty-fourth day of the sixth month, in the second year of King Darius.

The Future Glory of the Temple

2 In the seventh month, on the twenty-first day of the month, the word of the LORD came by Haggai the prophet, saying: 2 Speak now to Zerubbabel the son of Shealtiel, governor of Judah, and to Joshua the son of Jehozadak, the high priest, and to all the remnant of the people, saying: 3 Who is left among you

Your Word declares that those who seek the Lord shall not lack any good thing (Hag 2:4–5).

"I've Heard From God" Checklist

In the Book of Haggai God spoke to His people, giving them specific instructions for correcting their ways. God will also speak directly to His people today, but it is sometimes difficult for us to determine if it was really God we were hearing or just our own thoughts about a specific thing.

This "I've Heard From God" checklist can help confirm whether you really heard something from God or simply ate too much pizza with anchovies before falling asleep.

1. Does it agree with Scripture?

God's voice never contradicts His Word. A ready example is marrying an unbeliever on the theory you can change him or simply because he is so attractive. God would never tell you to do this. His Word clearly says, "Do not be unequally yoked together with unbelievers" (2Co 6:14).

2. Do you have an inner witness?

Romans 8:16 says that all believers have an inward witness. I call it your "knower." In their deepest being, God's children recognize the things of God. You will know that you know that you know.

3. Are you accountable to your pastor? Teachable?

Pastors should not act as all-knowing masters, but if you face a major decision, it is wise to allow this person or someone with spiritual maturity to help guide you. God anoints pastors to guide and guard His people.

4. Do you have peace in your spirit?

You can have perfect peace in your spirit while your mind is screaming crazy thoughts. Remember the guidance of Proverbs: "Trust in the LORD with all your heart, and lean not on your own understanding" (Pr 3:5).

5. What would Jesus do?

When in doubt, consider Christ's example. It also helps to contemplate a spiritual mentor. Can you imagine that person doing what you feel led to do?

6. Would a loving father do this?

God is a loving Father, and His voice will reflect that. I would question any demanding voice that separates families (even emotionally) or is self-destructive.

7. Have you received a confirmation?

A confirmation is when God says the same exact thing more than once in a different way. If your decision is important or will affect many people, ask Him to confirm His voice, and He will—perhaps through a person, a scripture, or an unusual circumstance.

8. Are you willing to wait for God's timing?

You can do the right thing at the wrong time and really struggle. People tend to jump too soon, but God's timing is perfect.

Rachel Burchfield

SPIRIT-TO-SPIRIT PRAYER

Prayer for a Child's Deliverance From Oppression

In the name of Jesus, I take authority over all bad spiritual influences. Unbelief [or name of spirit you are addressing], *I rend you powerless in the life of_________. I bind your power right now. I break your influence, power, and lies off of_________'s mind, will, and emotions. I break all generational curses and influences of a spirit of unbelief passed down the family line to _________. We sever all ties to you on both sides of the family, all the way back to Adam and Eve. We command you to loose_________ from your grip. We cast you out and say go now! We speak cleansing of_________'s mind, will, emotions, imaginations, thought patterns, and thought life.*

Lord, we ask that You come and bring Your peace, the Father's love, and acceptance into _________'s life. Holy Spirit, fill them up to overflowing. Cause their path to be faith-filled and secure. We speak in agreement that all the plans and purposes You have for _________'s life will come to pass.

Now we seal the work that has been done here by the blood of the Lamb. In Jesus' name, amen!

Rebecca Greenwood

who saw this house in its former glory? How do you see it now? Is it not, in your eyes, as nothing in comparison? 4 Yet now be strong, O Zerubbabel, says the LORD, and be strong, O Joshua, son of Jehozadak, the high priest. Be strong all you people of the land, says the LORD. Work, for I am with you, says the LORD of Hosts. 5 According to the covenant that I made with you when you came out of Egypt, so My Spirit remains among you. Do not fear.

Shake the heavens and fill my house with Your glory (Hag 2:6–7).

6 For thus says the LORD of Hosts: Once more, in a little while, I will shake the heavens and earth, the sea and dry land. 7 And I will shake all the nations, and they will come with the wealth of all nations, and I will fill this house with glory, says the LORD of Hosts. 8 The silver is mine, and the gold is Mine, says the LORD of Hosts. 9 The glory of this latter house will be greater than the former, says the LORD of Hosts. And in this place I will give peace, says the LORD of Hosts.

Blessings on a Defiled People

10 On the twenty-fourth day of the ninth month, in the second year of Darius, the word of the LORD came by Haggai the prophet, saying: 11 Thus says the LORD of Hosts: Now ask the priests concerning the law, saying, 12 If a man carries holy meat in the fold of his garment, and touches with his fold bread or stew, or wine or oil, or any food, will it become holy?

The priests answered, "No."

13 Then Haggai said, "If one who is unclean by contact with a dead body touches any of these, will it become unclean?"

The priests answered, "It will become unclean."

14 Then Haggai said, So it is with this people, and so it is with this nation before Me, says the LORD, and so with every work of their hands; and what they offer there is unclean.

Help me to be satisfied and not tempted by the love of money (Hag 2:8).

15 Now consider from this day onward: from before stone was laid upon stone in the temple of the LORD, 16 from those days when one came to a heap of twenty measures, there were but ten. When one came to the wine vat to draw fifty measures, there were but twenty. 17 I struck you and all the labor of your hands with blight and mildew and hail; yet you did not turn to Me. 18 Consider from this day onward, from the

2:4 Zec 8:9
2:5 Ne 9:20
2:6 Isa 10:25
2:8 Isa 60:17
2:9 Isa 9:6–7
2:10 Hag 2:20
2:11 Lev 10:10–11
2:12 Lev 6:27
2:15 Hag 1:5
2:16 Hag 1:6
2:17 Dt 28:22
2:18 Zec 8:9

twenty-fourth day of the ninth month, from the
day when the foundation of the temple of the
LORD was laid, consider: [19] Is the seed yet in
the barn? As of yet, the vine, the fig tree, the
pomegranate, and the olive tree have yielded
nothing.

But from this day on I will bless you.

The Promise of God to Zerubbabel

[20] The word of the LORD came a second time
to Haggai on the twenty-fourth day of the
month: [21] Speak to Zerubbabel, governor of
Judah, saying, I will shake the heavens and
the earth. [22] I will overthrow the throne of the
kingdoms. I will destroy the strength of the
kingdoms of the nations. I will overthrow
the chariots and their riders. The horses and
their riders will come down, every one by the
sword of his brother.

[23] On that day, says the LORD of Hosts, I will
take you, O Zerubbabel My servant, the son of
Shealtiel, says the LORD, and I will make you
like a signet ring; for I have chosen you, says
the LORD of Hosts.

2:21 Ezr 5:2
2:22 Mic 5:10
2:23 Isa 43:10

Author: The prophet Zechariah

Written: Between 520 and 470 BC

Themes: Restoration of Jerusalem and the Temple, Judgment and Restoration of Gentile Nations

ZECHARIAH

Dear SpiritLed Woman,

Have you ever felt that other people are accomplishing things you will never have the ability to do? That feeling can come even after reading something meant to be uplifting—such as your *SpiritLed Woman Bible*. But how does God's Word say He will accomplish His purposes through us? By our strength? By our power? No. In Zechariah 4:6 He says, "Not by might nor by power, but by My Spirit, says the Lord of Hosts." It is by His Spirit. We are not limited in God. Our only needed ability is a willingness to press through the obstacles, listen to His voice, and follow His orders precisely.

You may not have a public role, but your role is significant. Imparting destiny to your children or mentoring other women can affect the world for years to come. Your prayers can change not only people and situations but also entire nations. God calls each of us to change the world, but we don't accomplish this through anything of ourselves. It is only by His Spirit.

Joy F. Strang

1
In the eighth month, during the second
year of King Darius, the word of the LORD
came to the prophet Zechariah, son of Bere-
kiah, son of Iddo, saying:

A Call to Repentance

2 The LORD was very angry with your fathers,
3 so you will say to them, Thus says the LORD of
Hosts: Return to Me, and I will return to you,
says the LORD of Hosts. 4 Do not be like your
fathers to whom the former prophets cried,
"Thus says the LORD of Hosts: Turn away from
your evil ways and deeds!" But they did not
listen or pay attention to Me, says the LORD. 5 So
where are your fathers, and do the prophets
live forever? 6 Surely My words and statutes
that I commanded to My servants, the proph-
ets, did they not persuade your fathers?

They turned back and said, "Whatever the
LORD of Hosts planned to do to us according
to our ways and deeds, so He has done to us."

Vision of the Horsemen

7 On the twenty-fourth day, in the eleventh
month, which is the month Shebat, during the
second year of Darius, the word of the LORD
came to the prophet Zechariah, son of Bere-
kiah, son of Iddo:

8 I saw during the night a man riding on a red
horse. But he was standing among the myrtle
trees that were in the ravine, and behind him
were red, sorrel, and white horses.

9 And I said, "What are these, my lord?"

Then the angel who was speaking with me
said, "I will show you what these are."

10 Then the man who was standing among
the myrtle trees responded and said, "These
are the ones whom the LORD has sent out to
walk to and fro on the earth."

11 They answered and said to the angel of
the LORD who was standing among the myrtle
trees, "We have gone to and fro on the earth,
and all the earth is resting and peaceful."

12 Then the angel of the LORD said, "How
much longer, O LORD of Hosts, will You with-
hold mercy from Jerusalem and the cities of
Judah with which You have been angry these
seventy years?" 13 And the LORD answered the
angel speaking to me with good and comfort-
ing words.

14 So the angel who spoke with me said, Cry
out, saying: Thus says the LORD of Hosts: I have
a great jealousy for Jerusalem and Zion. 15 And
I have a great anger for those nations who are
at ease, for while I was angry but a little, they
helped to increase evil.

16 Therefore thus says the LORD: I have re-
turned to Jerusalem with mercy, and My house
will be built in it, says the LORD of Hosts, and
a measuring line will be stretched over Jeru-
salem.

17 Cry out again, saying, Thus says the LORD
of Hosts: Yet again My cities will overflow with
goodness, and again the LORD will comfort
Zion and choose Jerusalem.

The Vision of the Horns and Craftsmen

18 And I then lifted up my eyes, and I saw
four horns. 19 And I said to the angel speaking
to me, "What are these?"

And he answered, "These are the horns that
have scattered Judah, Israel, and Jerusalem."

20 Then the LORD showed me four craftsmen.
21 And I said, "What are these coming to do?"

And he said, "These are the horns that scat-
tered Judah after which no one could raise his
head; and these four craftsmen have come to
terrify and throw down the horns of the na-
tions who lifted up their horn against the land
of Judah to scatter it."

The Vision of the Man With the Measuring Line

2
And I lifted up my eyes, and I saw a man
with a measuring cord in his hand. 2 And
I said, "Where are you going?"

And he responded, "To measure Jerusalem
and to note what is its width and length."

3 Then the angel who was speaking with me
went out, and then another angel came out to
meet him, 4 and said to him, "Run, say to this
young man: Jerusalem will be inhabited as vil-
lages without walls, because of the multitude
of men and animals in her. 5 And I will be like
a wall of fire all around her, says the LORD, and
I will be as glory in her midst."

Interlude: An Appeal to the Exiles

6 Up, up, flee from the northern land, says the
LORD, for I have spread you abroad like the four
winds of heaven, says the LORD.

7 Deliver yourself, O Zion, you who live with
the daughter of Babylon. 8 For thus says the
LORD of Hosts: He has sent Me after glory to the
nations which plunder you, for he who touches
you touches the apple of His eye. 9 For I will
swing My hand against them, and they will be-
come plunder for their servants. Then you will
know well that the LORD of Hosts has sent Me.

10 Sing and rejoice, O daughter of Zion, for I
am coming and will dwell in your midst, says
the LORD. 11 And many nations will join them-
selves with the LORD in that day, and they will
be My people. And I will reside in your midst,
and you will know that the LORD of Hosts has
sent Me to you. 12 And the LORD will possess
Judah as His portion in the holy land, and He
will again choose Jerusalem. 13 Be still, all flesh
before the LORD, for He is stirred from His holy
habitation.

1:1 Ne 12:4
1:2 Jer 44:6
1:3 Mal 3:7
1:4 Ps 78:8
1:6 La 2:17
1:7 Zec 1:1
1:8 Rev 6:4
1:9 Zec 4:4–5
1:10 Zec 1:11
1:11 Zec 1:10
1:12 Ps 102:13
1:14 Joel 2:18
1:16 Zec 4:9

1:17 Isa 51:3
1:19 Zec 1:21
2:1 Eze 40:3
2:3 Zec 1:19
2:5 Isa 4:5
2:6 Eze 17:21
2:7 Isa 48:20
2:8 Dt 32:10
2:9 Isa 14:2
2:10 Zec 8:3
2:12 Dt 32:9
2:13 Ps 68:5

The Joy of Significance

Through understanding the impact of prayer on the circumstances of our daily lives and the blessings it releases, a profound sense of significance envelops us. Every time a prayer is answered, it says we matter to the almighty Creator and King of the universe.

If I received a call from the White House to attend a private breakfast with the president and his top cabinet members, I would not hesitate to accept the invitation. Yet the welcome mat is out and the door is always open to the throne room in heaven, where our Father invites us to deliberate with Him about the humdrum events of our daily lives.

Remember, whatever happens to us is important to Him. So detailed and intimate is God's personal care that Jesus assures us the Father cares when worthless sparrows fall and that He knows every hair on our head (Mt 10:29–31). We matter to God. He created us in His image to enjoy and fellowship with Him forever. He rejoices to dwell in our midst (Zec 2:10–12).

As this reality penetrates our spirits and minds, a sense of significance builds and low self-esteem begins to heal. Unhealthy thoughts melt away because we know He cares; what we do matters, what we say matters, and how we pray matters.

The true mystery of prayer is that we can pray. That the Lord and King of the universe would invite us into His presence to fellowship with Him is more unthinkable than being invited to a private dinner at Windsor Castle with Queen Elizabeth II and her family. Yet this is precisely what the King of kings does! He invites us personally to a feast of joy and affirmation, a place where we can open our hearts to Him and He can open His heart to us, a place where we can tell Him our plans and dreams and He can tell us His dreams and plans for us and the scarred world we live in. While we rush about fixing things and believing that everything depends upon our efforts, He waits to meet us in prayer and to deliberate with us about the way He wants to effect change and transformation.

Some have tried to demean and belittle prayer with the view that God has so preplanned everything that prayer is pointless and insignificant. If you believe this, you also will ask the question, "So, why pray?" But as we look at the prayers prayed in Scripture, we see people who prayed boldly because they knew their prayers could change things, even the mind of God. Moses' prayer for the preservation of the idolatrous partyers in Exodus 32 reveals his belief that prayer could change things, including the mind of God.

Richard Foster explains the transformative power of prayer by saying, "In fact, the Bible stresses so forcefully the openness of our universe, that in an anthropomorphism hard for modern ears, it speaks of God...changing his mind in accordance with his unchanging love.... This comes as a genuine liberation to many of us, but it also sets tremendous responsibility before us. We are working with God to determine the future! Certain things will happen in history if we pray rightly. We are to change the world by prayer."[1] This reveals the significance and power of prayer and places a mandate on the people of God to pray unceasingly, desperately, and responsibly until God moves His hand and changes things.

Jeannette Storm

1. Richard J. Foster, *Celebration of Discipline* (San Francisco: Harper and Row, 1988), 35.

The Vision of Joshua the High Priest

3 Then he showed me Joshua, the high priest, standing before the angel of the LORD, and Satan standing at his right hand to accuse him. 2 And the LORD said to Satan, "The LORD rebuke you, Satan! The LORD who has chosen Jerusalem rebukes you! Is this not a burning brand taken out of the fire?"

> Satan, the Lord rebuke you (Zec 3:2).

3 Now Joshua had on filthy garments and was standing before the angel. 4 And he said to those standing before him, "Take off his filthy garments."

Then he said, "See that I have removed from you your iniquity, and I will clothe you with rich robes."

5 And I said, "Let them place a pure turban on his head." So they put a pure turban on his head and garments on him. And the angel of the LORD was standing by.

6 And the angel of the LORD admonished Joshua, saying, 7 "Thus says the LORD of Hosts: If you walk in My ways and keep My charge, then you will judge My house and guard My courts, and I will give to you access to these who are standing here.

8 "Hear this, O Joshua the high priest, you and your friends sitting before you, for these men are a sign. I am bringing My servant, the Branch. 9 The stone that I have set before Joshua, on that single stone is seven eyes. And I will engrave an inscription, says the LORD of Hosts, and I will remove the iniquity of this land in one day.

10 "On that day, says the LORD of Hosts, each of you will invite your companion to come and sit under the vine and under the fig tree."

The Vision of the Gold Lampstand

4 And the angel who was speaking with me returned and woke me up like a man who is roused from his sleep. 2 And he said to me, "What do you see?"

And I responded, "I see a completely gold lampstand and a bowl at its top, with seven lights on it, and seven pipes on it for each lamp in order to light them. 3 And there are two olive trees next to it, one on the right of the bowl and one on the left."

4 So I answered and I asked the angel speaking with me, "What are these, my lord?"

5 Then the angel speaking with me responded, "Do you really not know what these are?"

And I said, "No, my lord."

3:1 Ps 109:6
3:2 Am 4:11
3:3 Isa 64:6
3:4 Isa 61:10
3:6 Zec 3:1
3:8 Isa 11:1
3:9 Isa 28:16
3:10 1Ki 4:25
4:1 Jer 31:26
4:2 Rev 4:5
4:3 Rev 11:4
4:5 Zec 4:13
4:6 Hos 1:7
4:7 Jer 51:25
4:10 Hag 2:3
4:11 Zec 4:3
4:13 Zec 4:5
4:14 Ex 29:7
5:2 Zec 4:2
5:3 Ex 20:15

6 And he said to me: "This is the word of the LORD to Zerubbabel, saying: Not by might nor by power, but by My Spirit, says the LORD of Hosts.

> Every mountain in my way will become a plain (Zec 4:7).

7 "Who are you, O great mountain? Before Zerubbabel you will be made level ground, and he will bring out the top stone amidst shouting of 'Grace! Grace to *the stone*!' "

8 Then the word of the LORD came to me, saying: 9 "The hands of Zerubbabel have established the foundation of this house, and they will even complete it. Then you will know that the LORD of Hosts has sent Me to all of you.

> I will walk in the ways of the Lord and keep His charge all the days of my life (Zec 3:7).

10 "For who has despised the day of small things? These seven will rejoice and see the plumb line in the hand of Zerubbabel. These are the eyes of the LORD, which survey to and fro throughout the earth."

11 Then I answered and I asked, "What are these two olives trees on the right and left of the lampstand?"

12 And I asked a second time, "What are these two branches of the olive trees that are next to the two golden pipes from which they pour out the gold *oil*?"

13 And he asked me, "Do you not know what these are?"

I responded, "No, my lord."

14 He answered, "These are the two anointed ones who stand by the Lord of all the earth."

The Vision of the Flying Scroll

5 Then I turned and lifted up my eyes and saw a flying scroll.

2 He asked me, "What do you see?"

And I responded, "I see a flying scroll with its length as twenty cubits and its width as ten cubits."[1]

3 He said to me, "This is the curse going out over the surface of all the land. Everyone who steals will be purged according to the writing on one side, and everyone who swears falsely will be purged according to the writing on the other side. 4 I will send it out, says the LORD of Hosts, and it will enter the house of the thief,

[1] *2* About 30 feet long and 15 feet wide, or 9 meters long and 4.5 meters wide.

and the house of him who swears falsely by
My name. It will remain in his house and con-
sume it, with its timber and stones."

The Vision of the Woman in the Basket

5 Then the angel who was speaking with me
came out, saying, "Now lift up your eyes and
see what this is that is going forth."

6 And I asked, "What is it?"

He said, "This is the ephah basket going
forth. This represents their iniquity through-
out all the land."

7 The lead cover was lifted, and there was a
woman sitting in the ephah basket. 8 And he
said, "This is wickedness." And he threw her
back into the basket and then thrust back the
lead stone over its opening.

9 Then I lifted my eyes and saw coming for-
ward two women. There was wind in their
wings, and the wings were like those of a
stork, and they lifted up and carried the ephah
basket between heaven and earth.

10 Then I said to the angel who was speaking
with me, "Where are they carrying the basket?"

11 He responded, "To build a house for it in
the land of Shinar. And when the house is
established, the basket will be set there on a
pedestal."

The Vision of the Four Chariots

6 And I turned around and lifted my eyes,
and I saw four chariots coming out from
between two mountains, which were bronze
mountains. 2 The first chariot had red horses,
the second black horses, 3 the third white hors-
es, and the fourth chariot dappled horses—all
of them strong. 4 Then I answered the angel
speaking with me, "What are these, my lord?"

5 The angel responded, "These are the four
winds of heaven going out after standing be-
fore the Lord of all the earth. 6 The one with
the black horses is going toward the north
country, the white ones are going after them,
while the dappled ones are going toward the
south country."

7 When the strong horses went out, they were
seeking to go to and fro throughout the earth.
And he said, "Go out to and fro throughout the
earth." And they went out to walk to and fro
throughout the earth.

8 Then he cried out to me, "Look, the ones
going out to the northern land have given rest
to my Spirit in the north."

The Coronation of Joshua

9 Then the word of the LORD came to me,
saying: 10 Take from the exiles Heldai, Tobijah,
and Jedaiah who have come from Babylon,
and go on that day to the house of Josiah, the
son of Zephaniah. 11 Take the silver and gold
and make a crown, and set it on the head of

5:5 Zec 1:9
5:6 Am 8:5
5:11 Ge 10:10
6:1 Da 8:22
6:2 Zec 1:8
6:3 Rev 6:2
6:4 Zec 1:9
6:7 Zec 1:10
6:8 Eze 5:13
6:10 Ezr 7:14–16
6:11 Zec 3:1

....

6:12 Zec 3:8
6:13 Ps 110:4
6:15 Isa 60:10
7:1 Ne 1:1
7:2 Zec 8:21
7:3 Zec 8:19
7:5 Zec 1:12
7:6 1Co 11:20–21
7:7 Jer 17:26
7:9 Mic 6:8
7:11 Ne 9:29
7:12 Ne 9:29–30
7:13 Isa 1:15
7:14 Dt 28:33

Joshua, the son of Jehozadak, the high priest.
12 And say to him: Thus says the LORD of Hosts:
Here is a man whose name is Branch; for he
shall branch out from his place, and he shall
build the temple of the LORD. 13 It is he who
shall build the temple of the LORD; he shall
bear the glory, and shall sit and rule on his
throne. He shall be a priest on his throne, and
the counsel of peace shall be between them
both. 14 And the crown shall be for a memorial
to Helem, Tobijah, Jedaiah, and Hen the son
of Zephaniah, in the temple of the LORD. 15 And
those who are far off shall come and help to
build the temple of the LORD; and you all shall
know that the LORD of Hosts has sent me to
you. This shall happen if you diligently obey
the voice of the LORD your God.

A Call for Justice and Mercy

7 And in the fourth year of King Darius,
on the fourth day of the ninth month,
Kislev, the word of the LORD came to Zecha-
riah. 2 Those in Bethel sent Sharezer and Re-
gem-Melek and their men to entreat the graces
of the LORD, 3 saying to the priests and proph-
ets of the house of the LORD of Hosts, "Should
I weep and dedicate myself during the fifth
month as I have done in these many years?"

4 Then the word of the LORD came to me,
saying: 5 Say to all the people in the land and
to the priests: When you fasted and lamented
during the fifth and seventh months for these
seventy years, did you really fast for Me? 6 And
when you eat and when you drink, do you
not eat and drink for yourselves? 7 Were these
not the very words that the former prophets
proclaimed when Jerusalem dwelled with ease
along with her surrounding cities, and when
the Negev and the Lowland were inhabited?

Punishment for Rejecting God's Demands

8 And the word of the LORD came to Zechari-
ah, saying: 9 Thus says the LORD of Hosts: Exe-
cute true justice, show mercy and compassion,
every man to his brother. 10 Do not oppress
the widow, orphan, sojourner, or poor. And let
none of you contemplate evil deeds in your
hearts against his brother.

11 But they refused to pay attention and
turned a stubborn shoulder, and stopped their
ears so that they should not hear. 12 They made
their hearts hard like a diamond so as not to
hear the instruction and words that the LORD
of Hosts sent by His Spirit through the former
prophets, and there was great anger from the
LORD of Hosts.

13 Therefore it happened that as I called, and
they would not hear, so they called, and I would
not hear, says the LORD of Hosts. 14 So I scattered

them about among all the nations whom they did not know, so the land was left desolate behind them with no one coming or going. And they made a desirable land desolate.

The Holy City of Peace and Prosperity

8 And the word of the LORD came, saying: 2 Thus says the LORD of Hosts: I am exceedingly jealous for Zion, and *with* great wrath I am jealous for her.

3 Thus says the LORD: I have returned to Zion and will dwell in the midst of Jerusalem, and Jerusalem will be called a city of faithfulness and the mountain of the LORD of Hosts, the holy mountain.

4 Thus says the LORD of Hosts: Older men and women will again sit in the streets of Jerusalem, each having a staff in his hand because of advanced age. 5 And the plazas of the city will be filled with young boys and girls playing in her open places.

6 Thus says the LORD of Hosts: If it is marvelous in the eyes of the remnant of this people in these days, will it also be marvelous in My eyes? says the LORD of Hosts.

7 Thus says the LORD of Hosts: I will deliver My people from the eastern lands and from the western lands. 8 And I will bring them, and they will reside in Jerusalem, and they will be for Me as a people, and I will be for them as God, with faithfulness and righteousness.

9 Thus says the LORD of Hosts: Let your hands be strengthened, whoever is hearing these words in these days, from the mouth of the prophets who were there in the day that the house of the LORD of Hosts was founded, that the temple might be built. 10 For before those days there were no wages for a man nor any hire for an animal; and there was no peace from an enemy for him who went out or came in; for I set every man against his neighbor. 11 But now I will not be as in the former days against this remnant people, says the LORD of Hosts.

12 For sowing will be done in peace, and the vine will produce its fruit, and the ground will provide its produce, and the heavens will give their rain. And I will cause the remnant of this people to inherit all of these benefits. 13 And as you have been like a curse among the nations, O house of Israel and house of Judah, I will deliver you, and you will be a blessing. Fear not, and strengthen your hands!

14 Thus says the LORD of Hosts: Just as I had determined to punish you when your fathers incited Me to wrath, says the LORD of Hosts, I did not relent. 15 So again have I purposed in these days to do good to Jerusalem and to the house of Judah. Do not fear! 16 These are the things you will do: Speak truth each to his neighbor, and make judgments in your gates that are for truth, and justice, and peace. 17 Let none of you consider evil plans in your heart against your neighbor, and do not love false oaths, for I hate all these things, says the LORD.

18 And the word of the LORD of Hosts came to me, saying:

19 Thus says the LORD of Hosts: The fast during the fourth and fifth months, and the fasts during the seventh and tenth months, will become rejoicing and joy and pleasant feasts for the house of Judah. So love what brings truth and peace.

20 Thus says the LORD of Hosts: Peoples will still come, even those who live in many cities. 21 Those who live in one city will journey to another, saying, "Let us surely go to seek the LORD of Hosts. I myself am going." 22 Many peoples and strong nations will seek out the LORD of Hosts in Jerusalem and to entreat the favor of the LORD.

23 Thus says the LORD of Hosts: In those days ten men from every language of the nations will take hold of the garment of a Jew, saying, "Let us go with you, for we have heard that God is with you."

Judgment on Israel's Enemies

9 An oracle of the word of the LORD that is
against the land of Hadrak,
and Damascus is the place where it will
rest.
For the eyes of men and the tribes of Israel
are on the LORD.
2 Also Hamath borders it,
even Tyre and Sidon, cities that are very
wise.
3 Tyre has built a rampart for herself
and stored up silver like it were dust,
and even gold like it were mud in the
streets.
4 The Lord will dispossess her of her
possessions
and strike down her power in the sea,
and she will be devoured with fire.
5 Ashkelon will observe this and fear;
Gaza as well and will writhe in anguish;
even Ekron, her hope will be
confounded.
The king of Gaza will perish,
and no one will inhabit Ashkelon.
6 A mongrel people will dwell in Ashdod,
and I will cut down the pride of Philistia.
7 I will take away the bloodshed from its
mouth,
and the abominations from between its
teeth.
Even it will be a remnant for our God.

8:3 Zec 1:16
8:5 Jer 30:19–20
8:6 Jer 32:17
8:8 Jer 4:2
8:11 Isa 12:1
8:12 Ge 27:28
8:13 Zec 8:9
8:14 Jer 31:28
8:15 Zec 8:13
8:16 Zec 7:9
8:17 Pr 3:29
8:19 Jer 39:2
8:21 Zec 7:2
8:23 1Co 14:25
9:2 Jer 49:23
9:3 Jos 19:29
9:4 Eze 28:18
9:6 Am 1:8

SPIRITLED WOMAN

COUNSEL FROM THE SPIRIT BASICS

Double for Our Trouble

God promises to give us twofold recompense for our former shame, pain, and disgrace (Isa 61:7). Whatever your pain, your faith in God's goodness will be rewarded and will bless the heart of your Father because faith pleases Him, and He delights to bless you more than you will ever know. He has a way of taking the pain we experience and turning it around so that we end up being blessed because of it. He bears fruit in our lives even through the worst things that happen to us. Adversity doesn't limit our capacity for the supernatural; it enhances it.

Zechariah 9:12 echoes the promise of Isaiah and assures us He will restore double to us: "Return to your stronghold, prisoners who now have hope. Today I declare that I will return to you a double portion." Job went through incredible hardship but ended up having everything he lost restored to him twofold (Job 42:10). God sees the whole story; He notices everything we have been through, and He will not stand back and withhold glorious, divine recompense for long. The blessings He gives will be greater than the losses we experience. We will receive at least double for our trouble, if not more.

Katherine Ruonala

It will be like a tribe of a clan in Judah,
and Ekron like the Jebusites.
8 Then I will make camp at My house with a garrison,
so that no one can pass back and forth.
And no oppressor will pass through them,
for now I see with My eyes.

The Coming King of Zion

9 Rejoice greatly, O daughter of Zion!
And cry aloud, O daughter of Jerusalem!
See, your king is coming to you;
he is righteous and able to deliver,
he is humble and riding on a donkey,
a colt, the offspring of a donkey.
10 I will cut off the chariot from Ephraim
and the horse from Jerusalem;
and the bow for battle will be cut off.
He will speak peace to the nations;
and his dominion will be from one sea to another,
and from the Great River to the ends of the earth.
11 And as for you, because of the blood of your covenant,
I will send your prisoners from the empty, waterless pits.
12 Return to your stronghold, prisoners who now have hope.
Today I declare that I will return to you a double portion.
13 Because I have bent Judah as My bow
and fitted the bow with Ephraim.
I will stir up your sons, O Zion,
against your sons, O Greece,
and will set you like the sword of a warrior.

Let Your arrow go forth as lightning against the enemy (Zec 9:14).

14 Then the LORD will appear over them,
and His arrow will go out like lightning.
The Lord GOD will sound His trumpet,
and will march forth like storm winds of southern Teman.
15 The LORD of Hosts will protect them.
They will devour up
and subdue them with stone slingers.
And they will drink and make noise as with wine;
they will be filled *with blood* as a bowl,
saturated like the corners of the altar.
16 The LORD their God will deliver them that day
like the flock of His people.
For like jewels embedded in a crown,
they will shine in His land.
17 For how great is His goodness, and how great His beauty!
There will be grain for the young men
and new wine to prosper the young women.

The Restoration of Judah and Israel

10 Ask for rain from the LORD
during the season of the latter spring rains.
And the LORD will make the storm winds;
and He will give them showers of rain;
all will have vegetation in the field.
2 For the household Teraphim idols speak wickedness,
and the diviners envision lies.
They utter false dreams,

9:8 Isa 52:1
9:9 Isa 9:6–7
9:10 Hos 1:7
9:11 Ex 24:8
9:12 Isa 61:7
9:14 Isa 21:1
9:15 Ex 27:2
9:16 Isa 62:3
10:2 Eze 34:5

and provide comfort that does not last.
So the people wander about like sheep;
they are afflicted because there is no shepherd.

3 My anger burns against the shepherds,
and I will visit judgment on the male goats.
For the LORD of Hosts will visit His flock,
the house of Judah,
and will make them like His majestic horse in battle.
4 From him comes the cornerstone,
and from him the tent peg.
From him comes the bow for battle,
and from him every ruler goes out, all these together.
5 And they will be as mighty men,
who trample down in the muddy streets in battle.
They will fight because the LORD is with them,
and He will put to shame those riding on horses.
6 I will make strong the house of Judah,
and will deliver the house of Joseph.
I will restore them
because I have compassion on them.
They will be like
I had never rejected them;
for I am the LORD their God,
and I will respond to them.
7 Then Ephraim shall be like a mighty man,
and their hearts shall rejoice as with wine.
Their children shall see this and be glad;
their hearts shall rejoice in the LORD.
8 I will whistle to them
and gather them in,
for I have ransomed them;
they will be numerous as they were numerous before.
9 When I scatter them among the nations,
they will remember Me in the distant lands;
they will live with their children
and then return.
10 I will bring them home from the land of Egypt,
and gather them from Assyria.
I will bring them into the land of Gilead and Lebanon,
until there is no room for them.
11 He will pass through the sea of distress,
and will put down the waves in the sea:
All the depths of the Nile will be dried up;
and the arrogance of Assyria will be brought down,

10:3 Zep 2:7
10:4 Zec 9:10
10:5 Hag 2:22
10:6 Zec 13:9
10:7 Zec 9:15
10:8 Isa 5:26
10:9 Eze 6:9
10:11 Eze 30:13
....
10:12 Mic 4:5
11:1 Jer 22:6–7
11:3 Jer 50:44
11:4 Zec 11:7
11:5 Jer 50:7
11:6 Jer 13:14
11:7 Zec 11:4
11:9 Jer 43:11
11:10 Zec 11:7
11:11 Zep 3:12
11:12 Mt 26:15
11:13 Ac 1:18–19
11:14 Isa 9:21
11:15 Isa 6:10–12

and the scepter of Egypt will turn away.
12 I will make them strong in the LORD,
and they will go to and fro in His name,
says the LORD.

11 Open your doors, O Lebanon,
so the fire can consume your cedar.
2 Wail, O cypress, for the cedar has fallen;
the majestic trees are destroyed.
Wail, O oaks of Bashan,
because the unassailable forest has been brought down.
3 *There is* the sound of wailing shepherds,
because their glory is ruined.
There is the sound of roaring lions,
because the pride of Jordan is ruined.

Two Kinds of Shepherds

4 Thus says the LORD my God: Shepherd the
flock of slaughter. 5 The ones who buy them
then slaughter them and have no guilt, and
those who sell them say, "Blessed is the LORD
because I am rich." Their own shepherds do
not take pity on them. 6 For I will no longer
have pity on those who dwell in the land, says
the LORD. But I will cause each of them to fall
into the hands of his neighbor, even into the
hands of his king. They will crush the land, and
I will not deliver any from their hands.

7 So I shepherded the flock that was for
slaughter, even the afflicted of the flock. And
I took for myself two staffs. One I called Favor and the other I gave the name Union. So I
pastured the flock. 8 I destroyed the three shepherds in the span of one month.

For my soul was impatient with them, and
their souls detested me. 9 Then I said, "I will not
shepherd you. What is to die, let it die. What is
to be destroyed, let it be destroyed. Let those
who are left devour each other's flesh."

10 I took the staff named Favor and cut it into
pieces, to break the covenant that I made with
all the peoples. 11 So it was broken that day, and
the afflicted of the flock were watching me
and knew that this was the word of the LORD.

12 Then I said to them, "If this is good in your
eyes, then give my wages to me, but if not,
then keep it." They weighed my wages at thirty
pieces of silver.

13 Then the LORD said to me, "Throw it to the
potter, the splendid price by which I was valued by them." So I took the thirty silver pieces
and threw them to the house of the LORD to
the potter.

14 Then I cut up the second staff, Union, to
break the brotherhood between Judah and
Israel.

15 Then the LORD said to me: Take for yourself
again the vessels carried by a foolish shepherd.
16 I am raising up a shepherd in the land who

will not care for those who are perishing, nor
seek the young, nor heal the broken, nor feed
those who are standing still. But he will eat the
flesh of the fat and tear their hoofs in pieces.

17 Woe to this worthless shepherd
who abandons his flock.
May the sword take his arm and right eye;
may his arm surely wither up,
and his right eye become blind.

The Deliverance of Judah

12 The oracle of the word of the LORD
against Israel.

Thus says the LORD, the One who stretches
out the heavens and establishes the earth and
forms the spirit of man within him: 2 I am go-
ing to make Jerusalem a cup of reeling be-
fore all the surrounding nations. And when
there is a siege against Judah, it is also against
Jerusalem. 3 And it will be on that day that I
will set Jerusalem as a weighty stone to all
the peoples. All who carry it will surely gash
themselves, and all the nations of the land will
be gathered against it. 4 On that day I will strike
every horse with confusion and its rider with
madness, but for the house of Judah I will keep
My eyes open although I will strike with blind-
ness every horse of the peoples. 5 Then the
clans of Judah will say in their hearts, "There
is strength for us with those residing in Jerusa-
lem by the LORD of Hosts, their God."
6 On that day I will set Judah like a fiery pot
among wood and as a flaming torch among
cut grain. And they will devour to the right
and left all the surrounding peoples, while Je-
rusalem will still reside in her place, the place
of Jerusalem.
7 The LORD will deliver the tents of Judah as
before, so that the glory of the house of David
and the glory of those dwelling in Jerusalem
will not eclipse Judah. 8 On that day the LORD
will defend those residing in Jerusalem; and
even the one who stumbles among them will
be as David on that day. And the house of Da-
vid will be like God, like the angel of the LORD
going out before them. 9 On that day I will seek
to destroy all the nations who come out against
Jerusalem.

Mourning for Him Whom They Have Pierced

10 And I will pour out on the house of David
and over those dwelling in Jerusalem a spirit
of favor and supplication so that they look to
Me, whom they have pierced through. And
they will mourn over him as one mourns for
an only child and weep bitterly over him as a
firstborn. 11 On that day the mourning in Jeru-
salem will be as great as that of Hadad Rim-

11:17 Jer 23:1
12:1 Isa 42:5
12:2 Zec 14:14
12:3 Mt 21:44
12:6 Ob 1:18
12:8 Mic 7:8
12:10 Rev 1:7

13:1 Ps 51:2
13:2 1Ki 22:22
13:3 Dt 13:6–11
13:4 2Ki 1:8
13:5 Am 7:14
13:7 Isa 40:11
13:8 Eze 5:2–4
13:9 Ps 50:15

mon in the plain of Megiddo. 12 The land will
mourn with each family by itself: the family of
the house of David by themselves, and their
wives by themselves; the family of the house
of Nathan by themselves, and their wives by
themselves; 13 the family of the house of Levi
by themselves, and their wives by themselves;
the family of Shimei by themselves, and their
wives also by themselves; 14 and all the families
that remain, each by itself and their wives by
themselves.

The Cleansing of God's People

13 On that day there will be a spring
opened up for the house of David and
for the inhabitants of Jerusalem for sin and
impurity.
2 And on that day, says the LORD of Hosts, I
will cut off the names of the idols from the
land, and they will not be remembered any
more. And I will also remove from the land the
prophets and the unclean spirit. 3 And it will
be if a man again prophesies, then his father
and mother who gave birth to him will say,
"You will not live because you speak decep-
tion in the name of the LORD." Then when he
prophesies, his father and mother will pierce
him through.
4 On that day each prophet will be ashamed
of his vision when he prophesies. He will not
put on a robe of coarse hair in order to deceive.
5 But he will say, "I am not a prophet. I am a
man who works the ground, for a man pur-
chased me when I was young." 6 If someone
asks, "What are these wounds on your arms?"
he will say, "I was struck in the house of my
close friends."

Striking the Shepherd, Scattering the Sheep

7 "Awake, O sword, against My shepherd
and the man of My association,"
says the LORD of Hosts.
Strike the shepherd,
and the sheep will scatter.
I will turn My hand against the small
ones.
8 And it will happen in all the land, says the
LORD,
that two-thirds will be cut off and die,
and one-third will be left in the land.
9 And I will bring this one-third left into the
fire,
and will refine them as the refinement
of silver,
and will test them as the testing of gold.
They will call on My name,
and I will answer them.
I will say, "They are My people";
and they will say, "The LORD is my God."

The Day of the Lord

14 A day of the Lord is coming when your spoil will be divided in your midst.

2 For I will gather all the nations against Jerusalem for battle. The city will be captured and the houses plundered and the women ravished. Half of the city will go to exile, but the remainder of the people will not be cut off from the city. 3 Then the Lord will go out and fight those nations as He fights in the day of war. 4 On that day His feet will stand on the Mount of Olives, which is to the east of Jerusalem. And from east to west the Mount of Olives will be split in two halves by a very great valley so that one half moves to the north and the other to the south. 5 And you will flee to my mountain valley, for the mountain valley will reach to Azal. You will flee just like you fled from the earthquake in the days of Uzziah king of Judah. Then the Lord my God will come and all His holy ones with you.

6 And on that day there will be no light. The lights will diminish. 7 And there will be one day known to the Lord, neither during the day nor the night, but at the evening time there will be light.

8 On that day living water will flow out from Jerusalem, half to the Dead Sea and the other half to the *Mediterranean* Sea. This will happen for the summer as well as the winter.

9 And the Lord will be king over all the earth. In that day it will be—"The Lord is one," and His name is one.

10 All the land will be turned into a plain from Geba to Rimmon to the south of Jerusalem. But Jerusalem will rise and dwell in her place from the Benjamin Gate to the place of the Old Gate, to the Corner Gate, and then from the Tower of Hananel to the winepress of the king. 11 And *people* will live there, and she will never again be devoted for destruction. Jerusalem will reside in security.

14:1 Isa 13:9
14:2 Isa 13:16
14:3 Zec 12:9
14:4 Eze 11:23
14:5 Am 1:1
14:7 Isa 30:26
14:8 Eze 47:1–12
14:0 Eph 1:5–6
14:10 Zec 12:6
14:11 Rev 22:3
....
14:14 Isa 23:18
14:15 Zec 14:12
14:16 Isa 60:6–9
14:17 Jer 14:4
14:21 Ne 8:10

12 And this will be the pestilence with which the Lord will strike all the peoples who go to battle against Jerusalem: Their flesh will rot as they stand on their feet, their eyes will rot in their sockets, and their tongues will rot in their mouths. 13 Then on that day a great tumult from the Lord will come on them as each person will seize the hand of his neighbor, and the hand of one will be raised against the hand of another. 14 And even Judah will fight with Jerusalem, and the wealth of all the surrounding nations will be gathered, a great abundance of gold, silver, and garments. 15 So this plague will come to horses, mules, camels, donkeys, and any other animals that are in the camp. So will this plague be.

16 Then it will be that all the nations who have come against Jerusalem and survived will go up each year to worship the King, the Lord of Hosts, and to celebrate the Feast of Tabernacles. 17 And it will happen that if any of the families of the earth do not go up to Jerusalem to worship the King, the Lord of Hosts, then there will not be rain for them. 18 If the family of Egypt does not go up and enter in, they shall have no rain. This will be the plague with which the Lord strikes the nations that do not go up to celebrate the Feast of Tabernacles. 19 This will be the punishment of Egypt and the punishment of all the nations who do not go up to celebrate the Feast of Tabernacles.

20 On that day "HOLY TO THE LORD" will be engraved on the bells of the horses. And the pots in the house of the Lord will be as the basins before the altar. 21 And every pot in Jerusalem and Judah will be holy to the Lord of Hosts so that all who come to sacrifice will take from those pots and boil the meat in them. And on that day there will no longer be a Canaanite in the house of the Lord of Hosts.

Author: The prophet Malachi

Written: Between 440 and 400 BC

Themes: Restoration, Covenant Blessings

MALACHI

Dear Spirit Led Woman,

In Malachi 4:2 God promises that Jesus will bring healing. God's desire is for us to be healthy in body, mind, and spirit. Sometimes healing occurs in a miraculous instant; other times it is a process. Sometimes this process is physical, but often the issues in our souls keep us from the path to healing.

Your mind is a composite of all your experiences. It can be compared to a deep mountain lake that appears on the surface to be crystal clear but that contains toxic water as a result of the trash thrown into it through the years.

The Holy Spirit once challenged me with this lake illustration and asked me if I was willing to allow Him to make the water of my life refreshing to those who encounter me. I agreed to go through a healing process, and during the next year the Holy Spirit dredged up all the things I had allowed to fill my inner life. Through the power of forgiveness and God's love I was set free from the pain of the past.

Whether the hurts in your past came as a result of another's sin or your own, the keys to healing are the same—and you have to employ them if you want to be free. Will you allow the Holy Spirit to take you through that process? It's never too late to start the path to your healing!

Joy F. Strang

1 The oracle of the word of the LORD to Israel by Malachi.

Israel Preferred to Edom

2 I have loved you, says the LORD.

But you say, "How have You loved us?"

Was not Esau Jacob's brother? says the LORD. Yet I have loved Jacob; 3 but Esau I have hated, and I have made his mountains a desolation and left his inheritance for the jackals of the desert.

4 Whereas Edom says, "We are impoverished, but we will rebuild the ruins," thus says the LORD of Hosts: They may build, but I will tear down. They will be called the Wicked Territory, and the people against whom the LORD has indignation forever. 5 Your eyes will see this, and you will say, "Great is the LORD, beyond the border of Israel!"

Profane Offerings

6 A son honors his father, and a servant his master. If then I am a father, where is My honor? And if I am a master, where is My fear? says the LORD of Hosts to you, O priests, who despise My name.

But you say, "How have we despised Your name?"

7 You offer defiled food on My altar, but say, "How have we defiled You?"

By saying, "The table of the LORD is contemptible." 8 When you offer the blind as a sacrifice, is it not evil? When you offer the lame and sick, is it not evil? Offer it now to your governor! Would he be pleased with you, or accept you? says the LORD of Hosts.

9 But now entreat God's favor, that He may be gracious to us. With such offerings from your hands, will He accept you favorably? says the LORD of Hosts.

10 Who is there among you who would shut the doors, that you might not kindle fire on My altar in vain? I have no pleasure in you, says the LORD of Hosts, nor will I accept an offering from your hand. 11 For from the rising of the sun to its setting, My name will be great among the nations, and in every place incense will be offered to My name, and a pure offering. For My name will be great among the nations, says the LORD of Hosts.

12 But you profane it, in that you say, "The table of the Lord is defiled, and its fruit, that is, its food is contemptible." 13 You also say, "What a weariness it is," and you snort at it, says the LORD of Hosts.

You bring in what is stolen, the lame, or the sick; thus you bring an offering! Should I accept this from your hand? says the LORD. 14 But cursed be the deceiver who has in his flock a male, and vows, and yet sacrifices to the Lord what is blemished. For I am a great king, says the LORD of Hosts, and My name is to be feared among the nations.

Divine Warnings to the Priests

2 And now, O priests, this commandment is for you. 2 If you will not listen, and if you will not take it to heart to give honor to My name, says the LORD of Hosts, I will send a curse on you and I will curse your blessings. Yes, I have cursed them already, because you do not take it to heart.

3 I rebuke your descendants, and spread refuse on your faces, the refuse of your solemn feasts, and you will be taken away with it. 4 And you will know that I have sent this command to you, that My covenant with Levi may remain, says the LORD of Hosts. 5 My covenant with him was for life and peace, and I gave them to him. With awe he feared Me, and he was reverent before My name. 6 True instruction was in his mouth, and injustice was not found on his lips. He walked with Me in peace and with uprightness, and turned many away from iniquity.

7 For a priest's lips should preserve knowledge, and people should seek the law from his mouth; for he is the messenger of the LORD of Hosts. 8 But you have departed from the way. You have caused many to stumble at the law. You have violated the covenant of Levi, says the LORD of Hosts. 9 So I have made you contemptible and base before all the people, because you have not kept My ways, but have shown partiality in the law.

The Covenant Profaned

10 Have we not all one Father? Has not one God created us? Why do we deal treacherously with one another, by profaning the covenant of our fathers?

11 Judah has dealt treacherously, and an abomination has been committed in Israel and Jerusalem. For Judah has profaned the sanctuary of the LORD, which He loves, and has married the daughter of a foreign god. 12 May the LORD cut off from the tents of Jacob any descendant of the man who does this, teacher and student, yet who brings an offering to the LORD of Hosts.

13 This is the second thing you do: You cover the altar of the LORD with tears, with weeping and crying out, because He no longer regards the offering, nor receives it with good will from your hand. 14 Yet you say, "Why?" It is because the LORD has been a witness between you and the wife of your youth, against whom you have dealt treacherously. Yet she is your companion and your wife by covenant.

15 Did He not make them one, having a remnant of the Spirit? And why one? He seeks godly offspring. So take heed to your spirit, that you do not deal treacherously.

1:2 Jer 31:3
1:6 Lk 6:46
1:7 Mal 1:12
1:8 Dt 15:21
1:9 Jer 27:18
1:10 Jer 6:20
1:11 Isa 66:19–20
1:13 Mic 6:3
1:14 Zec 14:9

2:1 Mal 1:6
2:2 Mal 3:9
2:3 Na 3:6
2:5 Nu 25:12–13
2:6 Jer 23:22
2:7 Lev 10:11
2:8 Jer 18:15
2:9 Dt 1:17
2:10 1Co 8:6
2:11 Ezr 9:1–2
2:14 Isa 54:6

SPIRIT-TO-SPIRIT PRAYER

PRAYER FOR WISDOM AS PARENTS

Jesus, children truly are Your best gift. We thank You for this journey You have placed us on. Give us Your complete, unending love for our children and this next generation. Strengthen and anoint us to be the fathers, mothers, and leaders You have called us to be. We ask for Your supernatural guidance in this process and journey.

Let us minister salvation, deliverance, love, and freedom to our young. Let us reflect Your love so freely and without compromise. Cause us to be a strong and shining reflection of Your Father's heart. May there be healing and restoration between us and our young. Where there are breaches of trust, hurt, and emotional pain, bring healing, deliverance, and restoration.

We pray in agreement for the return of the prodigals. We cry in agreement, "Lord, bring them home! Touch their hearts!" We thank You for every good work You are doing that we do not even see with our physical eyes or know about, those things You are doing in their hearts to draw them to You. We thank You for that work.

And for all of our children and in all areas of our lives, make us to be the loving fathers and mothers You have designed for us to be to our physical and spiritual children. Make us tenacious and passionate and ones who do not shrink back but advance forward in Your kingdom. Let the work You have begun in our lives come to complete fruition. May Your abundant love, blessings, and heart touch us, our young, our homes, our youth groups, and our churches in deeper measure. And may Your freedom reign in all of our lives. We love You, Lord. In Jesus' name we pray, amen.

Rebecca Greenwood

[16] For the LORD, the God of Israel, says that He
hates divorce; for it covers one's garment with
violence, says the LORD of Hosts.
Therefore take heed to your spirit, that you
do not deal treacherously.

Injustice Committed

[17] You have wearied the LORD with your
words.
Yet you say, "How have we wearied Him?"
When you say, "Everyone who does evil is
good in the sight of the LORD, and He delights
in them," or, "Where is the God of justice?"

The Coming Messenger

3 I will send My messenger, and he will pre-
pare the way before Me. And the Lord,
whom you seek, will suddenly come to His
temple, even the messenger of the covenant,
in whom you delight. He is coming, says the
LORD of Hosts.
[2] But who can endure the day of his coming,
and who can stand when he appears? For he
is like a refiner's fire and like fullers' soap. [3] He
will sit as a refiner and purifier of silver; he
will purify the sons of Levi, and refine them
like gold and silver, and they will present to
the LORD offerings in righteousness. [4] Then
the offering of Judah and Jerusalem will be
pleasant to the LORD as in the days of old and
as in former years.
[5] Then I will draw near to you for judgment.
I will be a swift witness against the sorcerers,
against the adulterers, against the perjurers,
against those who oppress the hired worker
in his wages, the widow and the fatherless,
against those who turn aside the stranger, and
do not fear Me, says the LORD of Hosts.

Purify my life with Your fire (Mal 3:2).

Withholding Tithes

[6] For I am the LORD, I do not change; there-
fore you, O sons of Jacob, are not consumed.
[7] From the days of your fathers you have gone

2:16 Mt 5:31–32
2:17 Isa 43:24
3:1 Mal 4:5
3:2 Zec 13:9
3:3 Isa 1:25
3:4 2Ch 7:1–3
3:5 Lev 19:13
3:6 Nu 23:19
3:7 Zec 1:3

Let God Take Over

Of course, God's timing is not always our timing. Let's get real. It's almost *never* the same as our timing. We are a society screaming for instant gratification. We have drive-through hamburgers, drive-through med clinics, and drive-through divorces. There is almost nothing for which we are forced to wait in society.

Then, out of the blue, God will allow us to come face-to-face with a seemingly impossible challenge with no resolution in sight. We have a choice: Will we try to handle it on our own, or will we hand the problem over to God?

He is desperately trying to make us into the person He knows we can be, the person created to worship and honor Him. He shows us His love in so many ways, and we sit back and say, "Hey! We don't need You. We can come up with better ideas on our own. Back off!"

And so He does. And in our own foolish wisdom we remain right smack in the middle of our problem.

If we would only realize how limited and painfully shortsighted we are and allow God to work in us, the road to our divine destiny could be paved with unlimited mercy and favor. Does this mean it will be easier? Probably not. God doesn't promise to make our lives easier, but He does promise to walk beside us if we will call upon His name.

David was a great man of God who made poor choices. It makes you wonder what his life could have been like if he would have followed God's plan instead of his own desires. And I don't say this in judgment of David. I have made plenty of mistakes on my own; we all have. But God desires something so much greater for us. His Word says that our minds cannot even grasp the things He has waiting for us. His thoughts are higher than ours, and yet we continue to push Him away.

What if we stop for just a minute and allow God to take over and His will to dominate our lives? What if we admit that we are a hot mess, totally in need of a master planner? What if we start honoring God with our lives and putting His desires first when we are updating our five-year calendar?

He clearly promises to open up the windows of heaven and pour out a blessing, "that there will not be room enough to receive it" (Mal 3:10). I can't speak for you, but as far as I'm concerned, any day God wants to bless me is a very good day. Bring it!

For those of you who think this can't happen in your own life, that it only happens to the people in the Bible or modern-day preachers, continue reading in Malachi. God literally says, "Try Me!" He says if you honor Him in your life, put Him to the test.

He is the Lord, and He does not change. What He has done for others, He can do for you. Put Him to the test, and you will know that He can flood you with goodness and mercy all the days of your life.

Speaking from personal experience, I will say, without hesitation or apology, that when God decides to bless you, there is no mistaking it. And there is no trading it. The peace you find on this path will encapsulate every fiber of your life, no matter the size or intensity of the storm you are facing.

Tish Hagee Tucker

The Importance of God's Tithe

Teach your children early about the importance of giving to God a portion of what He has so graciously allowed you to produce. Know that when you obey the Lord and hearken to His voice, He will cause His blessings to overtake you!

> Bring all the tithes into the storehouse, that there may be food in My house, and test Me now in this, says the LORD of Hosts, if I will not open for you the windows of heaven and pour out for you a blessing, that there will not be room enough to receive it.
>
> —MALACHI 3:10

This portion of Scripture is the only place in the Word of God where God asks His body to test Him.

I minister to many wives who are tormented by the fact their husbands refuse to give back to the Lord one-tenth of what the Provider has allowed them to earn—a man who rejects the principle of tithing.

If you find yourself in the position of being married to a man who will not give the Lord His tithe, you must wait on the Lord to convince your husband of his need to be obedient to God's Word. Wait for your husband to reject the darkness of his choice and embrace the light, yielding fully to the things of God. This is a very difficult position to be in, and hundreds of thousands of believing families are not blessed to their full potential due to their lack of obedience in the tithe.

In some homes one of the reasons the husband feels that he doesn't have enough money to tithe is because of the wife's careless spending habits. As a woman, you will be held accountable for how you help your husband maintain financial order within your marriage.

Read Proverbs 31:11–12. What does this scripture say about the woman's willingness to help her husband maintain financial order?

____

____

____

There are no options for the husband but to provide for his family. And there are no options for the wife but to help her husband maintain financial order by carefully budgeting her own spending habits.

Five hints are given below that can help both the husband and wife follow God's plan for the handling of money. All of these require both the husband and wife to transition from a me-centered life to an others-centered life.

On the lines after each hint, describe how you already do—or how you will in the future—follow that principle for financial order in the family.

1. Identify the problem.

2. Rely on the grace of God.

3. Communicate.

4. Take action.

5. Have compassion.

When you give the Lord His portion, He will bless what you have left and cause it to multiply, bringing you provision beyond what you could ever think possible. Be ready for His blessings, because our God is faithful!

Diana Hagee

SPIRITLED WOMAN

COUNSEL FROM THE SPIRIT BASICS

Money Isn't Everything

There are many different ways we can prosper or do kingdom work. Ecclesiastes 10:19 says, "They make feasts for laughter, and wine gladdens life; but money resolves everything." The necessity of having money is a fact of life. We can all identify with it, because without money we can't eat, keep a roof over our heads, own a car, pay our bills, or do anything! It seems nothing in this world is free. But I have learned that while money "resolves everything," money *isn't* everything!

God does not want us to live in a state of fear, anxiety, or stress. He wants us to live our lives free from poverty, debt, and financial crises. You are anointed to get out of debt. You are anointed to take control of your spending. You are anointed to give generously to the cause of God's kingdom and still be prudent with the resources He has given you. You are anointed to be a good steward of His money. Remember, everything belongs to Him. I always like to remind our church family when it's time to give, "It is God's tithe and your offering." (See Malachi 3:8–12.)

Oh, yes! There is a miracle on the other side of faith and obedience. When we obey the Word of God and walk in His purposes, trusting Him in and through everything we face, He releases His life through us. We experience "greater" in our lives and can do greater works for Him.

Judy Jacobs

away from My ordinances and have not kept
them. Return to Me, and I will return to you,
says the LORD of Hosts.
But you say, "How shall we return?"
8 Will a man rob God? Yet you have robbed
Me.
But you say, "How have we robbed You?"
In tithes and offerings. 9 You are cursed with
a curse, your whole nation, for you are robbing
Me. 10 Bring all the tithes into the storehouse,
that there may be food in My house, and test
Me now in this, says the LORD of Hosts, if I will

3:9 Mal 2:2
3:12 Isa 61:9
3:13 Mal 2:17
3:14 Isa 58:3
3:15 Mal 4:1
3:16 Ps 56:8
3:17 Ex 19:5
3:18 Ge 18:25
4:1 Isa 5:24
4:2 Isa 30:26
4:3 Job 40:12
4:4 Dt 4:10
4:5 Lk 1:17
4:6 Isa 11:4

The floodgates of heaven are opened over my life (Mal 3:10).

not open for you the windows of heaven and
pour out for you a blessing, that *there will* not
be room enough *to receive it*. 11 I will rebuke
the devourer for your sakes, so that it will not
destroy the fruit of your ground, and the vines
in your field will not fail to bear fruit, says the
LORD of Hosts. 12 Then all the nations will call
you blessed, for you will be a delightful land,
says the LORD of Hosts.
13 Your words have been hard against Me,
says the LORD.
Yet you say, "What have we spoken against
You?"
14 You said, "It is vain to serve God. What
profit is it that we have kept His ordinance, and
that we have walked as mourners before the
LORD of Hosts? 15 And now we call the proud
blessed, for those who do wickedness are built
up; they even test God and escape."

The Reward of the Faithful

16 Then those who feared the LORD spoke
to one another. The LORD listened and heard
them, and a book of remembrance was written
before Him for those who fear the LORD and
who esteem His name.
17 They shall be Mine, says the LORD of Hosts,
on the day when I make up My jewels. And I
will spare them as a man spares his son who
serves him. 18 Then you will again discern between the righteous and the wicked, between
one who serves God and one who does not
serve Him.

The Great Day of the LORD

4 Surely the day is coming, burning like an
oven; all the proud, yes, all evildoers will
be stubble. The day that is coming will burn
them up, says the LORD of Hosts, so that it will
leave them neither root nor branch. 2 But for
you who fear My name, the sun of righteousness will rise with healing in its wings. You will
go out and grow up like calves from the stall.
3 And you will tread down the wicked, for they
will be ashes under the soles of your feet, on
the day when I do this, says the LORD of Hosts.
4 Remember the Law of Moses, My servant,
the statutes and judgments which I commanded him at Horeb for all Israel.
5 See, I will send you Elijah the prophet before the coming of the great and dreaded day
of the LORD. 6 He will turn the hearts of the
fathers to their children, and the hearts of the
children to their fathers, lest I come and strike
the earth with a curse.

THE NEW TESTAMENT

Author: Traditionally the apostle Matthew

Written: Between AD 50 and 70, from Judea

Theme: Jesus Christ as the Promised Messiah

MATTHEW

Dear Spirit Led Woman,

As women, we have many responsibilities to our husbands and children, as well as jobs, ministries, and other activities. One time I made a list of major goals for every area of my life, which I then began to pray over, expecting God to give me His seal of approval. Instead I felt His Spirit prompting me to evaluate my list in light of eternity. Only two things on my list had eternal significance: building my relationship with God and pouring eternal things into people. My discovery lined up with what Christ told us to do in the two greatest commandments—to love God fully and to love our neighbor as ourselves (Mt 22:37–39).

Were my other goals related to family, work, and ministry important? Yes. But they could not become the driving force of my life. The point of Matthew 22:37–39 is that we cannot serve God with a divided heart. Obedience begins in the affections, and when your affections are set on God, you won't be pulled in different directions. If you put God first, He will instruct and empower you to do what He requires. As you read Matthew's Gospel, I encourage you to resolve to love God with your heart, soul, mind, and strength, and to love your neighbor as yourself. God will set your priorities, and the fruit you bear will last forever.

Joy F. Strang

The Genealogy of Jesus Christ
Lk 3:23–38

1 The book of the genealogy of Jesus Christ,
the Son of David, the son of Abraham:

2 Abraham was the father of Isaac,
Isaac the father of Jacob,
and Jacob the father of Judah and his brothers.
3 Judah was the father of Perez and Zerah by Tamar,
Perez the father of Hezron,
and Hezron the father of Ram.
4 Ram was the father of Amminadab,
Amminadab the father of Nahshon,
and Nahshon the father of Salmon.
5 Salmon was the father of Boaz by Rahab,
Boaz the father of Obed by Ruth,
and Obed the father of Jesse.
6 Jesse was the father of David the king.

David the king was the father of Solomon,
by her who had been the wife of Uriah.
7 Solomon was the father of Rehoboam,
Rehoboam the father of Abijah,
and Abijah the father of Asa.
8 Asa was the father of Jehoshaphat,
Jehoshaphat the father of Joram,
and Joram the father of Uzziah.
9 Uzziah was the father of Jotham,
Jotham the father of Ahaz,
and Ahaz the father of Hezekiah.
10 Hezekiah was the father of Manasseh,
Manasseh the father of Amon,
and Amon the father of Josiah.
11 Josiah was the father of Jeconiah and his brothers about the time they were exiled to Babylon.

12 And after they were brought to Babylon,
Jeconiah was the father of Shealtiel,
and Shealtiel the father of Zerubbabel.
13 Zerubbabel was the father of Abiud,
Abiud the father of Eliakim,
and Eliakim the father of Azor.
14 Azor was the father of Zadok,
Zadok the father of Akim,
and Akim the father of Eliud.
15 Eliud was the father of Eleazar,
Eleazar the father of Matthan,
and Matthan the father of Jacob.
16 And Jacob the father of Joseph,
the husband of Mary, of whom was born Jesus, who is called Christ.

17 So all the generations from Abraham to
David are fourteen generations, from David
until the exile to Babylon are fourteen generations, and from the exile in Babylon to Christ
are fourteen generations.

1:1 Ge 22:18
1:2 Ge 25:26
1:3 Ge 46:12
1:6 1Sa 16:1
1:8 1Ch 3:11
1:11 Jer 27:20
1:12 1Ch 3:17
1:16 Mt 27:17
....
1:18 Ge 3:15
1:21 Lk 1:31
1:23 Isa 7:14
2:1 Lk 2:4–7
2:2 Nu 24:17
2:5 Ge 35:19
2:6 Mic 5:2
2:11 Ps 72:10

The Birth of Jesus Christ
Lk 2:1–7

18 Now the birth of Jesus Christ happened
this way: After His mother Mary was engaged
to Joseph, before they came together, she was
found with child by the Holy Spirit. 19 Then Jo-
seph her husband, being a just man and not
willing to make her a public example, had in
mind to divorce her privately.
20 But while he thought on these things, the
angel of the Lord appeared to him in a dream
saying, "Joseph, son of David, do not be afraid
to take Mary as your wife, for He who is con-
ceived in her is of the Holy Spirit. 21 She will
bear a Son, and you shall call His name JESUS,
for He will save His people from their sins."
22 Now all this occurred to fulfill what the
Lord had spoken through the prophet, saying,
23 "A virgin shall be with child, and will bear a
Son, and they shall call His name Immanuel,"[1]
which is interpreted, "God with us."
24 Then Joseph, being awakened from sleep,
did as the angel of the Lord had commanded
him, and remained with his wife, 25 and did
not know her until she had given birth to her
firstborn Son. And he called His name JESUS.

The Visit of the Wise Men

2 Now after Jesus was born in Bethlehem of
Judea in the days of Herod the king, wise
men came from the east to Jerusalem, 2 saying,
"Where is He who was born King of the Jews?
For we have seen His star in the east and have
come to worship Him."
3 When Herod the king heard these things,
he was troubled, and all Jerusalem with him.
4 And when he had gathered all the chief
priests and scribes of the people together, he
inquired of them where Christ should be born.
5 They told him, "In Bethlehem of Judea, for
this is what the prophet wrote:

6 'And you, Bethlehem, in the land of Judah,
are no longer least among the princes of Judah;
for out of you shall come a Governor,
who will shepherd My people Israel.'[2]"

7 Then Herod, when he had privately called
the wise men, carefully inquired of them what
time the star appeared. 8 And he sent them to
Bethlehem and said, "Go and search diligently
for the young Child, and when you have found
Him, bring me word again, so that I may come
and worship Him also."
9 When they heard the king, they departed.
And the star which they saw in the east went
before them until it came and stood over where
the young Child was. 10 When they saw the
star, they rejoiced with great excitement. 11 And
when they came into the house, they saw the

[1] 23 Isa 7:14. [2] 6 Mic 5:2.

young Child with Mary, His mother, and fell
down and worshipped Him. And when they
had opened their treasures, they presented
gifts to Him: gold, frankincense, and myrrh.
12 But being warned in a dream that they
should not return to Herod, they returned to
their own country by another route.

The Escape to Egypt

13 Now when they departed, the angel of the
Lord appeared to Joseph in a dream, saying,
"Arise, take the young Child and His mother,
and escape to Egypt, and stay there until I
bring you word. For Herod will seek the young
Child to kill Him."

14 When he rose, he took the young Child and
His mother by night, and departed into Egypt,
15 and remained there until the death of Herod,
to fulfill what the Lord had spoken through the
prophet, "Out of Egypt I have called My Son."[1]

The Killing of the Infants

16 Then Herod, when he saw that he had been
tricked by the wise men, was utterly furious
and sent forth and killed all the male children
who were in Bethlehem and the surrounding
region, from two years old and under, based
on the time which he had diligently inquired
of the wise men. 17 Then was fulfilled what was
spoken by Jeremiah the prophet:

18 "In Ramah a voice was heard,
grieving and weeping and great
mourning,
Rachel weeping for her children,
and she would not be comforted,
because they are no more."[2]

The Return From Egypt

19 But when Herod was dead, an angel of the
Lord appeared in a dream to Joseph in Egypt,
20 saying, "Arise, take the young Child and His
mother, and go into the land of Israel, for those
who sought the young Child's life are dead."

21 And he rose, took the young Child and
His mother, and came into the land of Israel.
22 But when he heard that Archelaus reigned
in Judea instead of his father Herod, he was
afraid to go there. Nevertheless, being warned
by God in a dream, he withdrew to the region
of Galilee. 23 And he went and lived in a city
called Nazareth, that what was spoken by the
prophets might be fulfilled, "He shall be called
a Nazarene."

The Preaching of John the Baptist
Mk 1:1–8; Lk 3:1–9, 15–17; Jn 1:19–28

3 In those days John the Baptist came,
preaching in the wilderness of Judea,
2 and saying, "Repent, for the kingdom of
heaven is at hand." 3 For this is he who was
spoken of by the prophet Isaiah, saying:

"The voice of one crying in the wilderness:
'Prepare the way of the Lord;
make His paths straight.' "[3]

4 This same John had clothing made of cam-
el's hair, a leather belt around his waist, and
his food was locusts and wild honey. 5 Then
Jerusalem, and all Judea, and all the region
around the Jordan went out to him, 6 and were
baptized by him in the Jordan, confessing their
sins.

7 But when he saw many of the Pharisees
and Sadducees come to his baptism, he said
to them, "O generation of vipers, who has
warned you to escape from the wrath to come?
8 Therefore, bear fruit worthy of repentance,
9 and do not think to say within yourselves,
'We have Abraham as our father,' for I say to
you that God is able from these stones to raise
up children for Abraham. 10 Even now the axe
is put to the tree roots. Therefore, every tree
which does not bear good fruit is cut down and
thrown into the fire.

11 "I indeed baptize you with water to repen-
tance, but He who is coming after me is might-
ier than I, whose shoes I am not worthy to
carry. He will baptize you with the Holy Spirit
and with fire. 12 His fan is in His hand, and He
will thoroughly clean His floor and gather His
wheat into the granary, but He will burn up the
chaff with unquenchable fire."

The Baptism of Jesus
Mk 1:9–11; Lk 3:21–22

13 Then Jesus came from Galilee to John at
the Jordan to be baptized by him. 14 But John
prohibited Him, saying, "I need to be baptized
by You, and do You come to me?"

15 But Jesus answered him, "Let it be so now,
for it is fitting for us to fulfill all righteousness."
Then he permitted Him.

16 And when Jesus was baptized, He came up
immediately out of the water. And suddenly
the heavens were opened to Him, and He saw
the Spirit of God descending on Him like a
dove. 17 And a voice came from heaven, saying,
"This is My beloved Son, in whom I am well
pleased."

The Temptation of Jesus
Mk 1:12–13; Lk 4:1–13

4 Then Jesus was led up into the wilder-
ness by the Spirit to be tempted by the
devil. 2 And He had fasted for forty days and
forty nights, and then He was hungry. 3 And
the tempter came to Him and said, "If You are
the Son of God, command that these stones be
turned into bread."

2:12 Mt 2:22
2:13 Ac 5:19
2:15 Hos 11:1
2:16 Isa 59:7
2:18 Jer 31:15
2:19 Mt 1:20
2:20 Ex 4:19
2:22 Lk 2:39
2:23 Jn 1:45–46
3:2 Mt 4:17
3:3 Isa 40:3
3:4 Lev 11:22
3:5 Mk 1:5
3:6 Ac 19:18
3:7 Mt 12:34
3:8 Ac 26:20
3:10 Mt 7:19
3:11 Ac 1:5
3:12 Mal 4:1
3:13 Mt 2:22
3:16 Isa 11:2
3:17 Ps 2:7
4:1 Lk 4:1–13
4:2 1Ki 19:8
4:3 1Th 3:5

[1] *15* Hos 11:1. [2] *18* Jer 31:15. [3] *3* Isa 40:3.

4 But He answered, "It is written, 'Man shall
not live by bread alone, but by every word that
proceeds out of the mouth of God.'[1]"
5 Then the devil took Him up into the holy
city, and set Him on the highest point of the
temple, 6 and said to Him, "If You are the Son
of God, throw Yourself down. For it is written,

'He shall give His angels charge
concerning you,'[2]

and

'In their hands they shall lift you up,
lest at any time you dash your foot
against a stone.'[3]"

7 Jesus said to him, "It is also written, 'You
shall not tempt the Lord your God.'[4]"
8 Again, the devil took Him up on a very high
mountain and showed Him all the kingdoms
of the world and their grandeur, 9 and said to
Him, "All these things I will give You if You will
fall down and worship me."
10 Then Jesus said to him, "Get away from
here, Satan! For it is written, 'You shall wor-
ship the Lord your God, and Him only shall
you serve.'[5]"
11 Then the devil left Him, and immediately
angels came and ministered to Him.

The Beginning of the Galilean Ministry
Mk 1:14–15; Lk 4:14–15

12 Now when Jesus heard that John was put
in prison, He left for Galilee. 13 And leaving
Nazareth, He came and lived in Capernaum,
which is by the sea, in the regions of Zebu-
lun and Naphtali, 14 that what was spoken by
Isaiah the prophet might be fulfilled, saying:

15 "The land of Zebulun and the land of
Naphtali,
the way to the sea, beyond the Jordan,
Galilee of the Gentiles:
16 The people who sat in darkness
saw great light.
And on those who sat in the land of the
shadow of death,
light has dawned."[6]

> God is revealing Himself to the young and old alike so we can see Him with the right lenses (Mt 4:16).

17 From that time Jesus began to preach,
saying, "Repent! For the kingdom of heaven
is at hand."

[1] 4 Dt 8:3. [2] 6 Ps 91:11–12. [3] 6 Ps 91:12. [4] 7 Dt 6:16.
[5] 10 Dt 6:13. [6] 15–16 Isa 9:1–2.

4:4 Dt 8:3
4:5 Mt 27:53
4:6 Ps 91:11–12
4:7 Dt 6:16
4:10 1Ch 21:1
4:11 Mt 26:53
4:12 Mk 1:14
4:13 Mk 1:21
4:14 Mt 1:22
4:16 Lk 2:32
4:17 Mt 3:2

4:18 Jn 1:40–42
4:21 Mt 10:2
4:23 Mt 9:35
4:24 Mt 8:6
4:25 Lk 6:17
5:3 Isa 61:1
5:4 Isa 61:2–3
5:5 Ps 37:11
5:8 Ps 24:4
5:9 Mt 5:45
5:10 Mt 5:3

The Calling of the First Disciples
Mk 1:16–20; Lk 5:1–11

18 As Jesus walked beside the Sea of Galilee,
He saw two brothers, Simon called Peter, and
Andrew his brother, throwing a net into the
sea, for they were fishermen. 19 And He said to
them, "Follow Me, and I will make you fishers
of men." 20 They immediately left their nets and
followed Him.
21 And going on from there, He saw two other
brothers, James the son of Zebedee and John
his brother, in a boat with Zebedee their fa-
ther, mending their nets, and He called them.
22 They immediately left the boat and their fa-
ther and followed Him.

Ministering to Great Crowds
Lk 6:17–19

23 Jesus went throughout all Galilee teaching
in their synagogues, preaching the gospel of
the kingdom, and healing all kinds of sickness
and all sorts of diseases among the people.
24 His fame went throughout all Syria. And they
brought to Him all sick people who were tak-
en with various diseases and tormented with
pain, those who were possessed with demons,
those who had seizures, and those who had
paralysis, and He healed them. 25 Great crowds
followed Him from Galilee, the Decapolis, Je-
rusalem, Judea, and from beyond the Jordan.

The Sermon on the Mount
(Mt 5–7)

5 Now seeing the crowds, He went up on
a mountain. And when He sat down, His
disciples came to Him.

The Beatitudes
Lk 6:20–23

2 And He began speaking and taught them,
saying:

3 "Blessed are the poor in spirit,
for theirs is the kingdom of heaven.
4 Blessed are those who mourn,
for they shall be comforted.
5 Blessed are the meek,
for they shall inherit the earth.
6 Blessed are those who hunger and thirst
for righteousness,
for they shall be filled.
7 Blessed are the merciful,
for they shall obtain mercy.
8 Blessed are the pure in heart,
for they shall see God.
9 Blessed are the peacemakers,
for they shall be called the sons of God.
10 Blessed are those who are persecuted for
righteousness' sake,
for theirs is the kingdom of heaven.

11 “Blessed are you when men revile you, and persecute you, and say all kinds of evil against you falsely for My sake. 12 Rejoice and be very glad, because great is your reward in heaven, for in this manner they persecuted the prophets who were before you.

Salt and Light
Mk 9:50; Lk 14:34–35

I am the salt of the earth (Mt 5:13).

13 “You are the salt of the earth. But if the salt loses its saltiness, how shall it be made salty? It is from then on good for nothing but to be thrown out and to be trampled underfoot by men.

I am the light of the world (Mt 5:14).

14 “You are the light of the world. A city that is set on a hill cannot be hidden. 15 Neither do men light a candle and put it under a basket, but on a candlestick. And it gives light to all who are in the house. 16 Let your light so shine before men that they may see your good works and glorify your Father who is in heaven.

Teaching About the Law

17 “Do not think that I have come to abolish the Law or the Prophets. I have not come to abolish, but to fulfill. 18 For truly I say to you, until heaven and earth pass away, not one dot or one mark will pass from the law until all be fulfilled. 19 Whoever, therefore, breaks one of the least of these commandments and teaches others to do likewise shall be called the least in the kingdom of heaven. But whoever does and teaches them shall be called great in the kingdom of heaven. 20 For I say to you that unless your righteousness exceeds the righteousness of the scribes and Pharisees, you will in no way enter the kingdom of heaven.

Teaching About Anger

21 “You have heard that it was said by the ancients, ‘You shall not murder,’[1] and ‘Whoever murders shall be in danger of the judgment.’ 22 But I say to you that whoever is angry with his brother without a cause shall be in danger of the judgment. And whoever says to his brother, ‘Raca,’ shall be in danger of the Sanhedrin. But whoever says, ‘You fool,’ shall be in danger of hell fire.

23 “Therefore, if you bring your gift to the altar and there remember that your brother has something against you, 24 leave your gift there before the altar and go on your way. First be reconciled to your brother, and then come and offer your gift.

25 “Reconcile with your adversary quickly, while you are on the way with him, lest your adversary deliver you to the judge, and the judge deliver you to the officer, and you be thrown into prison. 26 Truly I say to you, you will by no means come out of there until you have paid the last penny.[2]

Teaching About Adultery

27 “You have heard that it was said by the ancients, ‘You shall not commit adultery.’[3] 28 But I say to you that whoever looks on a woman to lust after her has committed adultery with her already in his heart. 29 And if your right eye causes you to sin, pluck it out and throw it away. For it is profitable that one of your members should perish, and not that your whole body be thrown into hell. 30 And if your right hand causes you to sin, cut it off and throw it away. For it is profitable for you that one of your members should perish, and not that your whole body be thrown into hell.

Teaching About Divorce
Mt 19:9; Mk 10:11–12; Lk 16:18

31 “It was said, ‘Whoever divorces his wife, let him give her a certificate of divorce.’[4] 32 But I say to you that whoever divorces his wife, except for marital unfaithfulness, causes her to commit adultery. And whoever marries her who is divorced commits adultery.

Teaching About Oaths

33 “Again, you have heard that it was said by the ancients, ‘You shall not swear falsely, but shall fulfill your oaths to the Lord.’[5] 34 But I say to you, do not swear at all: neither by heaven, for it is God’s throne; 35 nor by the earth, for it is His footstool; nor by Jerusalem, for it is the city of the great King. 36 Nor shall you swear by your head, because you cannot make one hair white or black. 37 But let your ‘Yes’ mean ‘Yes,’ and ‘No’ mean ‘No.’ For whatever is more than these comes from the evil one.

Teaching About Revenge
Lk 6:29–30

38 “You have heard that it was said, ‘An eye for an eye, and a tooth for a tooth.’[6] 39 But I say to you, do not resist an evil person. But whoever strikes you on your right cheek, turn to him the other as well. 40 And if anyone sues you in a court of law and takes away your tunic, let him have your cloak also. 41 And whoever compels you to go a mile,[7] go with him two. 42 Give to him who asks you, and from him who would borrow from you do not turn away.

5:11 1Pe 4:14
5:12 Lk 6:23
5:14 Jn 8:12
5:15 Mk 4:21
5:16 1Pe 2:12
5:17 Ro 3:31
5:18 Lk 16:17
5:19 Mt 11:11
5:21 Ex 20:13
5:22 Mt 10:28
5:27 Ex 20:14
5:28 Job 31:1
5:29 Mt 18:8–9
5:30 Mt 5:29
5:31 Jer 3:1
5:32 Lk 16:18
5:33 Lev 19:12
5:34 Isa 66:1
5:35 Ps 48:2
5:37 Jas 5:12
5:38 Dt 19:21
5:39 1Co 6:7
5:41 Mt 27:32

[1] *21* Ex 20:13; Dt 5:17. [2] *26* Gk. *kodrantes.* [3] *27* Ex 20:14; Dt 5:18. [4] *31* Dt 24:1, 3. [5] *33* Lev 19:12; Nu 30:2; Dt 23:21. [6] *38* Ex 21:24; Lev 24:20; Dt 19:21. [7] *41* Gk. *milion,* or 1.48 kilometers.

Walking in Peace

Walking in peace with others is often challenging. You cannot always avoid strife. Sometimes you must confront it, get it out in the open, and try to come to some terms of peace.

Jesus taught the importance of choosing to live in peace with others. He said, "Blessed are the peacemakers, for they shall be called the sons of God" (Mt 5:9). He expanded on the importance of being a peacemaker when He said, "Blessed are you when men revile you, and persecute you, and say all kinds of evil against you falsely for My sake. Rejoice and be very glad, because great is your reward in heaven, for in this manner they persecuted the prophets who were before you" (vv. 11–12).

God can heal our relationships and make peace possible. Study each of the points below, which help you to consider how much of a peacemaker you are now and give you important considerations for becoming the peacemaker God wants you to be.

1. List the relationships in your life that have been attacked by conflict and strife.

2. It's possible you are to blame—at least partially—for the problems in some of your relationships. However, it is also possible you are being victimized by someone else's strife. Think carefully and prayerfully about the causes of strife in these relationships. Write down the hard-to-face truth you've discovered.

3. Think about a recent disagreement you had with someone. Then prayerfully consider the principles for how to disagree agreeably, which are listed below. Which of these principles could you have applied in that situation in order to keep peace with the other person? Explain.

Show each other respect.

Drop it for a while.

Be patient.

Search for an answer both parties can be satisfied with.

Give in regularly.

4. Magnifying the positive characteristics in a person is a good way to build relationship bridges. List some of the positive characteristics of a person with whom you've experienced strife.

5. Describe a situation when you felt responsible for changing the opinions of another. What was the outcome? Now suppose you were able to rewrite history. Describe the situation you just mentioned, but change the details to respect and honor the other individual's opinion while still remaining true to your own feelings and opinions.

6. Sometimes we look at a person's faults for so long that we no longer see his or her strengths. Is there a (nonmarital) relationship in your life that is at a similar breaking point? Spend time in prayer asking the Holy Spirit to give you insight on how to handle the division. Write how you sense God is leading you to deal with this situation.

***Dear Lord,** I commit to allowing others the freedom to hold their own opinions and to make their own choices. I trust You to mold and shape others into the people You want them to be. Help me to be a peacemaker in my attitudes, body language, and facial expressions. Please give me the grace to be gracious and positive in all my relationships. If some of my relationships are at the breaking point, show me how I might gain fresh perspective about the people involved. Help me to see the positive in everyone around me, and help me to speak in a positive manner, even when I must bring correction. Thank You, Lord.*

Barbara Dycus

SPIRITLED WOMAN

COUNSEL FROM THE SPIRIT BASICS

Forgiveness Is a Lifestyle Choice

Our heavenly Father is loving, merciful, and gracious toward all of His children. We have done nothing that is meriting of this love. Even so, He faithfully extends forgiveness, liberating each of us from our debt of sin, and He asks us in return to be merciful and gracious to those who have sinned against us

Jesus also said this: "For if you forgive men for their sins, your heavenly Father will also forgive you. But if you do not forgive men for their sins, neither will your Father forgive your sins" (Mt 6:14–15). If we do not forgive the offenses of other people, then our heavenly Father will not forgive our sins.

This does not mean we are to look for an apology from the wrongdoer, nor do we keep a running checklist of wrongs directed at us. The option to forgive is done before any violation has developed and with no anticipation of an apology or repayment. Forgiveness is a lifestyle choice.

Rebecca Greenwood

Love for Enemies
Lk 6:27–28, 32–36

43 "You have heard that it was said, 'You shall love your neighbor[1] and hate your enemy.' 44 But I say to you, love your enemies, bless those who curse you, do good to those who hate you, and pray for those who spitefully use you and persecute you, 45 that you may be sons of your Father who is in heaven. For He makes His sun rise on the evil and on the good and sends rain on the just and on the unjust. 46 For if you love those who love you, what reward do you have? Do not even the tax collectors do the same? 47 And if you greet your brothers only, what are you doing more than others? Do not even the tax collectors do so? 48 Therefore be perfect, even as your Father who is in heaven is perfect.

1 43 Lev 19:18.

5:43 Lev 19:18
5:44 Lk 23:34
5:45 Mt 5:9
5:47 Mt 5:20
5:48 Lev 19:2

....

6:1 Mt 23:5
6:2 Mt 6:5
6:4 Mt 6:6
6:5 Mt 6:2
6:6 2Ki 4:33
6:8 Mt 6:32
6:10 Mt 3:2
6:11 Pr 30:8
6:13 1Co 10:13
6:14 Mk 11:25
6:15 Mt 18:35
6:16 Mt 6:2
6:17 Ru 3:3
6:18 Mt 6:4

Teaching About Charitable Giving

6 "Be sure that you not do your charitable deeds before men to be seen by them. Otherwise you have no reward from your Father who is in heaven.

2 "Therefore, when you do your charitable deeds, do not sound a trumpet before you as the hypocrites do in the synagogues and in the streets, that they may be honored by men. Truly I say to you, they have their reward. 3 But when you do your charitable deeds, do not let your left hand know what your right hand is doing, 4 that your charitable deeds may be in secret. And your Father who sees in secret will Himself reward you openly.

The Lord's Prayer
Lk 11:1–4

5 "When you pray, you shall not be like the hypocrites. For they love to pray standing in the synagogues and on the street corners that they may be seen by men. Truly I say to you, they have their reward. 6 But you, when you pray, enter your closet, and when you have shut your door, pray to your Father who is in secret. And your Father who sees in secret will reward you openly. 7 But when you pray, do not use vain repetitions, as the heathen do. For they think that they will be heard for their much speaking. 8 Do not be like them, for your Father knows what things you have need of before you ask Him.

9 "Therefore pray in this manner:

Our Father who is in heaven,
hallowed be Your name.
10 Your kingdom come;
Your will be done
on earth, as it is in heaven.
11 Give us this day our daily bread.
12 And forgive us our debts,
as we forgive our debtors.
13 And lead us not into temptation,
but deliver us from evil.
For Yours is the kingdom and the power
and the glory forever. Amen.

14 For if you forgive men for their sins, your heavenly Father will also forgive you. 15 But if you do not forgive men for their sins, neither will your Father forgive your sins.

Teaching About Fasting

16 "Moreover, when you fast, do not be like the hypocrites with a sad countenance. For they disfigure their faces so they may appear to men to be fasting. Truly I say to you, they have their reward. 17 But you, when you fast, anoint your head and wash your face, 18 so that you will not appear to men to be fasting, but to your Father who is in secret. And your Father who sees in secret will reward you openly.

Treasures in Heaven
Lk 12:33–34

19 “Do not store up for yourselves treasures on earth where moth and rust destroy and where thieves break in and steal. 20 But store up for yourselves treasures in heaven, where neither moth nor rust destroy and where thieves do not break in nor steal, 21 for where your treasure is, there will your heart be also.

The Light of the Body
Lk 11:34–36

22 “The light of the body is the eye. Therefore, if your eye is clear, your whole body will be full of light. 23 But if your eye is unclear, your whole body will be full of darkness. Therefore, if the light that is in you is darkness, how great is that darkness!

God and Money

24 “No one can serve two masters. For either he will hate the one and love the other, or else he will hold to the one and despise the other. You cannot serve God and money.

Care and Anxiety
Lk 12:22–34

25 “Therefore, I say to you, take no thought about your life, what you will eat, or what you will drink, nor about your body, what you will put on. Is not life more than food and the body than clothing? 26 Look at the birds of the air, for they do not sow, nor do they reap, nor gather into barns. Yet your heavenly Father feeds them. Are you not much better than they? 27 Who among you by taking thought can add a cubit[1] to his stature?

28 “Why take thought about clothing? Consider the lilies of the field, how they grow: They neither work, nor do they spin. 29 Yet I say to you that even Solomon in all his glory was not dressed like one of these. 30 Therefore, if God so clothes the grass of the field, which today is here and tomorrow is thrown into the oven, will He not much more clothe you, O you of little faith? 31 Therefore, take no thought, saying, ‘What shall we eat?’ or ‘What shall we drink?’ or ‘What shall we wear?’ 32 (For the Gentiles seek after all these things.) For your heavenly Father knows that you have need of all these things. 33 But seek first the kingdom of God and His righteousness, and all these things shall be given to you. 34 Therefore, take no thought about tomorrow, for tomorrow will take thought about the things of itself. Sufficient to the day is the trouble thereof.

> I seek first the kingdom of God and His righteousness, and all things are added unto me (Mt 6:33).

6:19 Heb 13:5
6:20 Lk 12:33
6:21 Lk 12:34
6:23 Mt 20:15
6:24 Lk 16:13
6:25 Mt 6:31
6:26 Job 38:41
6:30 Mt 8:26
6:31 1Pe 5:7
6:32 Mt 6:8
6:33 1Ti 4:8
6:34 Mt 6:25

. . . .

7:1 Lk 6:37
7:2 Mk 4:24
7:3 Jn 8:7–9
7:6 Mt 15:26
7:7 Mt 21:22
7:12 Lk 6:31
7:15 1Jn 4:1
7:16 Mt 12:33
7:17 Mt 12:33–35

Judging Others
Lk 6:37–38, 41–42

7 “Judge not, that you be not judged. 2 For with what judgment you judge, you will be judged. And with the measure you use, it will be measured again for you.

3 “And why do you see the speck that is in your brother’s eye, but do not consider the plank that is in your own eye? 4 Or how will you say to your brother, ‘Let me pull the speck out of your eye,’ when a log is in your own eye? 5 You hypocrite! First take the plank out of your own eye, and then you will see clearly to take the speck out of your brother’s eye.

6 “Do not give what is holy to the dogs, nor throw your pearls before swine, lest they trample them under their feet and turn around and attack you.

Ask, Seek, Knock
Lk 11:9–13

7 “Ask and it will be given to you; seek and you will find; knock and it will be opened to you. 8 For everyone who asks receives, and he who seeks finds, and to him who knocks, it will be opened.

9 “What man is there among you who, if his son asks for bread, will give him a stone? 10 Or if he asks for a fish, will he give him a snake? 11 If you then, being evil, know how to give good gifts to your children, how much more will your Father who is in heaven give good things to those who ask Him! 12 Therefore, everything you would like men to do to you, do also to them, for this is the Law and the Prophets.

> Understand that there’s no quick, microwave version of how to “cook up” your moment (Mt 7:7–8, 11).

The Narrow Gate
Lk 13:24

13 “Enter at the narrow gate, for wide is the gate and broad is the way that leads to destruction, and there are many who are going through it, 14 because small is the gate and narrow is the way which leads to life, and there are few who find it.

A Tree and Its Fruit
Lk 6:43–44

15 “Beware of false prophets who come to you in sheep’s clothing, but inwardly they are ravenous wolves. 16 You will know them by their fruit. Do men gather grapes from thorns, or figs from thistles? 17 Even so, every good tree bears good fruit. But a corrupt tree bears

[1] *27* A cubit is about half a meter.

evil fruit. 18 A good tree cannot bear evil fruit,
nor can a corrupt tree bear good fruit. 19 Every
tree that does not bear good fruit is cut down
and thrown into the fire. 20 Therefore, by their
fruit you will know them.

I Never Knew You
Lk 13:25–27

21 "Not everyone who says to Me, 'Lord, Lord,'
shall enter the kingdom of heaven, but he who
does the will of My Father who is in heaven.
22 Many will say to Me on that day, 'Lord, Lord,
have we not prophesied in Your name, cast
out demons in Your name, and done many
wonderful works in Your name?' 23 But then I
will declare to them, 'I never knew you. Depart
from Me, you who practice evil.'[1]

The Two Housebuilders
Lk 6:47–49

24 "Whoever hears these sayings of Mine
and does them, I will liken him to a wise man
who built his house on a rock. 25 And the rain
descended, the floods came, and the winds
blew and beat on that house. And it did not
fall, for it was founded a rock. 26 And every one
who hears these sayings of Mine and does not
do them will be likened to a foolish man who
built his house on the sand. 27 And the rain
descended, the floods came, and the winds
blew and beat on that house. And it fell. And
its fall was great."

28 When Jesus finished these sayings, the
people were astonished at His teaching, 29 for
He taught them as one having authority, and
not as the scribes.

The Cleansing of a Leper
Mk 1:40–45; Lk 5:12–16

8 When He came down from the mountains,
large crowds followed Him. 2 And then a
leper came and worshipped Him, saying,
"Lord, if You are willing, You can make me
clean."

3 Jesus reached out His hand and touched
him, saying, "I will. Be clean." And immedi-
ately his leprosy was cleansed. 4 Then Jesus
said to him, "See that you tell no one. But go
your way, show yourself to the priest, and offer
the gift that Moses commanded as a testimony
to them."

The Healing of a Centurion's Servant
Lk 7:1–10; Jn 4:43–54

5 And when Jesus entered Capernaum, a
centurion[2] came to Him, entreating Him, 6 and
saying, "Lord, my servant is lying at home, sick
with paralysis, terribly tormented."

7 Jesus said to him, "I will come and heal
him."

8 The centurion answered and said, "Lord,
I am not worthy that You should come under
my roof. But speak the word only, and my ser-
vant will be healed. 9 For I am a man under
authority, having soldiers under me. And I say
to this man, 'Go,' and he goes, and to another,
'Come,' and he comes, and to my servant, 'Do
this,' and he does it."

10 When Jesus heard it, He was amazed and
said to those who followed, "Truly I say to
you, I have not found such great faith, no,
not in Israel. 11 And I say to you that many
will come from the east and west and will
dine with Abraham, Isaac, and Jacob in the
kingdom of heaven. 12 But the sons of the
kingdom will be thrown out into outer dark-
ness. There will be weeping and gnashing
of teeth."

13 Then Jesus said to the centurion, "Go your
way. And as you have believed, so let it be
done for you." And his servant was healed that
very moment.

The Healing of Many People
Mk 1:29–34; Lk 4:38–41

14 When Jesus entered Peter's house, He saw
his wife's mother, lying sick with a fever. 15 He
touched her hand, and the fever left her. And
she rose and served them.

16 When the evening came, they brought to
Him many who were possessed with demons.
And He cast out the spirits with His word, and
healed all who were sick, 17 to fulfill what was
spoken by Isaiah the prophet,

"He Himself took our infirmities
and bore our sicknesses."[3]

I have the promise of healing from all illnesses and diseases (Mt 8:17).

The Would-Be Followers of Jesus
Lk 9:57–62

18 Now when Jesus saw large crowds around
Him, He gave a command to depart to the oth-
er side. 19 Then a certain scribe came and said
to Him, "Teacher, I will follow You wherever
You go."

20 Jesus replied, "The foxes have holes and
the birds of the air have nests, but the Son of
Man has no place to lay His head."

21 Another of His other disciples said to
Him, "Lord, let me first go and bury my
father."

22 But Jesus said to him, "Follow Me, and let
the dead bury their dead."

7:19 Mt 3:10
7:20 Mt 7:16
7:21 Mt 25:11–12
7:23 Ps 6:8
7:24 Lk 6:47–49
7:28 Mk 1:22
8:2 Mt 18:26
8:4 Lev 14:2–32
8:5 Lk 7:1–10
8:6 Mt 4:24
8:8 Ps 107:20
8:11 Mal 1:11
8:12 Mt 25:30
8:13 Mt 9:22
8:14 1Co 9:5
8:17 Isa 53:4
8:18 Mk 4:35

1 23 Ps 6:8. *2 5* Commander with the rank of captain over 100 soldiers. *3 17* Isa 53:4.

The Calming of a Storm

Mk 4:35–41; Lk 8:22–25

23 Then He entered the boat, and His disciples followed Him. 24 Suddenly a great storm arose on the sea, so that the boat was covered with the waves. But He was asleep. 25 His disciples went to Him and awoke Him, saying, "Lord, save us! We are perishing!"

26 He replied, "Why are you fearful, O you of little faith?" Then He rose and rebuked the winds and the sea. And there was a great calm.

27 The men were amazed, saying, "What kind of Man is this that even the winds and the sea obey Him!"

The Healing of the Gergesene Demoniacs

Mk 5:1–20; Lk 8:26–39

28 When He came to the other side into the country of the Gergesenes, there met Him two men possessed with demons, coming out of the tombs, extremely fierce, so that no one might pass by that way. 29 Suddenly they cried out, saying, "What have we to do with You, Jesus, Son of God? Have You come here to torment us before the time?"

30 Now a good way off from them was a herd of many swine feeding. 31 So the demons begged Him, saying, "If You cast us out, permit us to go away into the herd of swine."

32 He said to them, "Go!" And when they came out, they went into the herd of swine. And suddenly the whole herd of swine ran violently down a steep place into the sea, and perished in the waters. 33 Those who kept them fled, and went their ways into the city, and told everything, including what had happened to those possessed by the demons. 34 The whole city came out to meet Jesus. And when they saw Him, they begged Him to depart out of their region.

The Healing of a Paralytic

Mk 2:1–12; Lk 5:17–26

9 He entered a boat, crossed over, and came into His own city. 2 They brought to Him a man sick with paralysis, lying on a bed. And Jesus, seeing their faith, said to the paralytic, "Son, be of good cheer. Your sins are forgiven you."

3 Then certain scribes said within themselves, "This Man blasphemes."

4 Jesus, knowing their thoughts, said, "Why do you think evil in your hearts? 5 For which is easier, to say, 'Your sins are forgiven you' or to say, 'Arise and walk'? 6 But that you may know that the Son of Man has authority on earth to forgive sins"—then He said to the paralytic, "Arise, pick up your bed, and go into your house." 7 And he rose and departed to his house. 8 But when the crowds saw it, they were amazed and glorified God who had given such authority to men.

8:26 Mt 6:30
8:27 Mk 1:27
8:29 Mk 1:24
8:34 Ac 16:39
9:1 Mt 4:13
9:2 Mt 9:22
9:3 Mt 26:65
9:4 Mt 12:25
9:8 Mt 15:31

....

9:11 Mt 11:19
9:13 Hos 6:6
9:15 Jn 3:29
9:17 Jos 9:4
9:18 Mt 8:2
9:20 Mt 14:36
9:22 Lk 7:50

The Calling of Matthew

Mk 2:13–17; Lk 5:27–32

9 As Jesus passed on from there, He saw a man named Matthew sitting at the tax collector's station. And He said to him, "Follow Me." And he rose and followed Him.

10 While Jesus sat at supper in the house, many tax collectors and sinners came and sat down with Him and His disciples. 11 When the Pharisees saw it, they said to His disciples, "Why does your Teacher eat with tax collectors and sinners?"

12 But when Jesus heard that, He said to them, "Those who are well do not need a physician, but those who are sick. 13 But go and learn what this means, 'I desire mercy, and not sacrifice.'[1] For I have not come to call the righteous, but sinners, to repentance."

The Question About Fasting

Mk 2:18–22; Lk 5:33–39

14 Then the disciples of John came to Him, asking, "Why do we and the Pharisees fast often, but Your disciples do not fast?"

15 Jesus answered, "Can the guests of the bridegroom mourn as long as the bridegroom is with them? But the days will come when the bridegroom will be taken from them, and then they will fast.

16 "No one sews a piece of new cloth into an old garment, for that which is sewn in to fill it up pulls on the garment, and the tear is made worse. 17 Neither do men put new wine into old wineskins. Or else the wineskins burst, the wine runs out, and the wineskins perish. But they put new wine into new wineskins, and both are preserved."

The Ruler's Daughter and a Woman Healed

Mk 5:21–43; Lk 8:40–56

18 While He was speaking these things to them, a certain ruler came and worshipped Him, saying, "My daughter is even now dead. But come and lay Your hand on her, and she will live." 19 Jesus rose and followed him, and so did His disciples.

20 Then a woman, who was ill with a flow of blood for twelve years, came behind Him and touched the hem of His garment. 21 For she said within herself, "If I may just touch His garment, I shall be healed."

22 But Jesus turned around, and when He saw her, He said, "Daughter, be of good comfort. Your faith has made you well." And the woman was made well instantly.

[1] 13 Hos 6:6.

23 When Jesus came to the ruler's house and saw the musicians and the mourners making a noise, 24 He said to them, "Depart. The girl is not dead, but is sleeping." And they laughed Him to scorn. 25 But when the people were put outside, He went in and took her by the hand, and the girl arose. 26 The news of this went out into all that land.

The Healing of Two Blind Men

27 As Jesus departed from there, two blind men followed Him, crying out and saying, "Son of David, have mercy on us!"

28 When He entered the house, the blind men came to Him. And Jesus said to them, "Do you believe that I am able to do this?"

They said to Him, "Yes, Lord."

29 Then He touched their eyes, saying, "According to your faith, let it be done for you." 30 And their eyes were opened, and Jesus strictly commanded them, saying, "See that no one knows of it." 31 But when they had departed, they spread His fame in all that region.

The Healing of a Mute Man

32 As they went out, they brought to Him a mute man possessed with a demon. 33 And when the demon was cast out, the mute man spoke, and the crowds were amazed, saying, "This has never been seen in Israel."

34 But the Pharisees said, "He casts out demons through the ruler of the demons."

The Compassion of Jesus

35 Jesus went throughout all the cities and villages, teaching in their synagogues, preaching the gospel of the kingdom, and healing every sickness and every disease among the people. 36 But when He saw the crowds, He was moved with compassion for them, because they fainted and were scattered, like sheep without a shepherd. 37 Then He said to His disciples, "The harvest truly is plentiful, but the laborers are few. 38 Therefore, pray to the Lord of the harvest, that He will send out laborers into His harvest."

The Mission of the Twelve Apostles

Mk 3:13–19; Lk 6:12–16

10 He called His twelve disciples to Him and gave them authority over unclean spirits, to cast them out, and to heal all kinds of sickness and all kinds of disease.

2 Now the names of the twelve apostles are these: first, Simon, who is called Peter, and Andrew, his brother; James, the son of Zebedee, and John, his brother; 3 Philip and Bartholomew; Thomas, and Matthew, the tax collector; James, the son of Alphaeus; and Lebbaeus, whose surname was Thaddaeus;

9:23 2Ch 35:25
9:24 Ac 20:10
9:25 Mk 9:27
9:26 Mt 4:24
9:27 Mt 15:22
9:29 Mt 8:13
9:30 Mt 8:4
9:31 Mk 7:36
9:34 Lk 11:15
9:35 Mt 4:23–24
9:36 Mk 6:34
9:37 Lk 10:2
9:38 2Th 3:1
10:1 Mk 3:13–15
10:2 Mt 4:18
10:3 Mk 3:18

....

10:4 Mt 26:14
10:5 Jn 4:9
10:6 Jer 50:6
10:7 Mt 3:2
10:8 Ac 3:6
10:9 Lk 22:35
10:12 1Sa 25:6
10:14 Ac 13:51
10:15 Mt 12:36
10:16 Lk 10:3
10:17 Mk 13:9
10:18 Mt 8:4
10:19 Ex 4:12
10:20 Ac 4:8
10:22 Mt 24:13
10:24 Lk 6:40
10:25 Mk 3:22

4 Simon the Zealot; and Judas Iscariot, who also betrayed Him.

The Commissioning of the Twelve Apostles

Mk 6:7–13; Lk 9:1–6

5 These twelve Jesus sent out, and commanded them, saying, "Do not go into the way of the Gentiles, and do not enter any city of the Samaritans. 6 But go rather to the lost sheep of the house of Israel. 7 As you go, preach, saying, 'The kingdom of heaven is at hand.' 8 Heal the sick, cleanse the lepers, raise the dead, and cast out demons. Freely you have received, freely give.

9 "Provide neither gold nor silver nor copper for your purses, 10 nor bag for your journey, nor two tunics, nor shoes, nor even staffs. For the workman is worthy of his keep.

11 "In whatever city or town you enter, inquire in it who is worthy. And live there until you leave. 12 When you come into a house, greet it. 13 If the house is worthy, let your peace come upon it. But if it is not worthy, let your peace return to you. 14 Whoever will not receive you, nor hear your words, when you depart out of that house or city, shake off the dust of your feet. 15 Truly I say to you, it will be more tolerable for the land of Sodom and Gomorrah on the Day of Judgment than for that town.

Coming Persecutions

Mk 13:9–13; Lk 21:12–17

16 "Look, I am sending you out as sheep in the midst of wolves. Therefore be wise as serpents and harmless as doves. 17 But beware of men, for they will deliver you up to the councils, and they will scourge you in their synagogues. 18 You will be brought before governors and kings for My sake, for a testimony against them and the Gentiles. 19 But when they deliver you up, take no thought of how or what you will speak. For it will be given you at that time what you will speak. 20 For it is not you who speak, but the Spirit of your Father who speaks through you.

21 "The brother will deliver up the brother to death, and the father the child. And the children will rise up against their parents and cause them to be put to death. 22 You will be hated by all men for My name's sake. But he who endures to the end will be saved. 23 But when they persecute you in this city, escape into another. For truly I say to you, you will not have gone through the cities of Israel before the Son of Man comes.

24 "The disciple is not above his teacher, nor the servant above his master. 25 It is enough for the disciple that he be like his teacher, and the servant like his master. If they have called

the master of the house Beelzebub, how much
more will they call those of his household?

Whom to Fear
Lk 12:2–7

26 "Therefore do not fear them. For nothing
is covered that will not be revealed, or hidden
that will not be known. 27 What I tell you in
darkness, speak in the light. And what you
hear in the ear, preach on the housetops. 28 Do
not fear those who kill the body but are not
able to kill the soul. But rather fear Him who
is able to destroy both soul and body in hell.
29 Are not two sparrows sold for a penny? And
not one of them will fall to the ground without
your Father. 30 But the very hairs of your head
are all numbered. 31 Therefore do not fear. You
are more valuable than many sparrows.

Confessing and Denying Christ
Lk 12:8–9

32 "Whoever will confess Me before men, him
will I confess also before My Father who is in
heaven. 33 But whoever will deny Me before
men, him will I also deny before My Father
who is in heaven.

Not Peace, but a Sword
Lk 12:51–53; 14:26–27

34 "Do not think that I have come to bring
peace on earth. I did not come to bring peace,
but a sword. 35 For I have come to turn

'a man against his father,
a daughter against her mother,
and a daughter-in-law against her mother-
in-law;
36 a man's foes will be those of his own
household.'[1]

37 "He who loves father or mother more than
Me is not worthy of Me. And he who loves son
or daughter more than Me is not worthy of
Me. 38 And He who does not take his cross and
follow after Me is not worthy of Me. 39 He who
finds his life will lose it, and he who loses his
life for My sake will find it.

Rewards
Mk 9:41

40 "He who receives you receives Me, and he
who receives Me receives Him who sent Me.
41 He who receives a prophet in the name of a
prophet shall receive a prophet's reward. And
he who receives a righteous man in the name
of a righteous man shall receive a righteous
man's reward. 42 And whoever gives even a cup
of cold water to one of these little ones in the
name of a disciple, truly I tell you, he shall in
no way lose his reward."

11 When Jesus finished instructing His
twelve disciples, He departed from
here to teach and to preach in their cities.

10:26 Mk 4:22
10:27 Ac 5:20
10:28 Isa 8:12–13
10:30 1Sa 14:45
10:31 Mt 6:26
10:32 Rev 3:5
10:33 2Ti 2:12
10:35 Mt 10:21
10:36 Mic 7:6
10:37 Lk 14:26
10:38 Mt 16:24
10:39 Lk 17:33
10:40 Mt 18:5
10:41 3Jn 1:5–8
10:42 Mt 25:40
11:1 Mt 9:35

. . . . . .

11:2 Mt 14:3
11:3 Heb 10:37
11:5 Lk 4:18
11:9 Lk 1:76
11:10 Mal 3:1
11:12 Lk 16:16
11:14 Mal 4:5
11:15 Mt 13:9
11:18 Mt 3:4

The Messengers From John the Baptist
Lk 7:18–35

2 Now when John had heard in prison the
works of Christ, he sent two of his disciples,
3 and said to Him, "Are You He who should
come, or should we look for another?"
4 Jesus answered them, "Go and tell John
what you hear and see: 5 The blind receive
their sight and the lame walk, the lepers are
cleansed and the deaf hear, the dead are raised
up, and the poor have the gospel preached to
them.[2] 6 Blessed is he who does not fall away
because of Me."
7 As they departed, Jesus began to say to the
crowds concerning John, "What did you go out
into the wilderness to see? A reed shaken by
the wind? 8 If not, what did you go out to see?
A man dressed in soft clothing? Indeed, those
who wear soft clothing are in kings' houses.
9 Then what did you go out to see? A prophet?
Yes, I say to you, and more than a prophet.
10 For this is he of whom it is written:

'Look, I am sending My messenger before
Your face,
who will prepare Your way before You.'[3]

> If you pursue everything God wants you to have, God manifests Himself the way He wants to (Mt 11:11).

11 Truly I say to you, among those who are born
of women, there has risen no one greater than
John the Baptist. But he who is least in the
kingdom of heaven is greater than he. 12 From
the days of John the Baptist until now, the
kingdom of heaven has forcefully advanced,
and the strong take it by force. 13 For all the
Prophets and the Law prophesied until John.
14 And if you are willing to receive it, he is Eli-
jah, who is to come. 15 He who has ears to hear,
let him hear.
16 "But to what shall I liken this generation?
It is like children sitting in the markets, calling
to their friends, 17 saying:

'We played the flute for you,
and you did not dance;
we sang a dirge to you,
and you did not mourn.'

18 For John came neither eating nor drinking,
and they say, 'He has a demon.' 19 The Son of
Man came eating and drinking, and they say,
'Here is a gluttonous man, a drunkard, a friend
of tax collectors and sinners.' But wisdom is
justified by her children."

[1] *35–36* Mic 7:6. [2] *5* Taken from Isa 35:5–6; 61:1. [3] *10* Mal 3:1.

Unrepentant Cities
Lk 10:13–15

20 Then He began to reprimand the cities where most of His mighty works were done, because they did not repent: 21 "Woe to you, Chorazin! Woe to you, Bethsaida! For if the mighty works which were done in you had been done in Tyre and Sidon, they would have repented long ago in sackcloth and ashes. 22 But I say to you, it will be more tolerable for Tyre and Sidon on the Day of Judgment than for you. 23 And you, Capernaum, who is exalted toward heaven, will be brought down to Hades. For if the mighty works which have been done in you had been done in Sodom, it would have remained until this day. 24 But I say to you that it shall be more tolerable for the land of Sodom on the Day of Judgment than for you."

Come to Me and Rest
Lk 10:21–22

25 At that time Jesus said, "I thank You, O Father, Lord of heaven and earth, because You have hidden these things from the wise and prudent and revealed them to infants. 26 Even so, Father, for it seemed good in Your sight.

27 "All things are delivered to Me by My Father, and no one knows the Son, except the Father. And no one knows the Father, except the Son and he to whom the Son will reveal Him.

28 "Come to Me, all you who labor and are heavily burdened, and I will give you rest. 29 Take My yoke upon you, and learn from Me. For I am meek and lowly in heart, and you will find rest for your souls.[1] 30 For My yoke is easy, and My burden is light."

The Question About the Sabbath
Mk 2:23–28; Lk 6:1–5

12 At that time Jesus went through the grain fields on the Sabbath. And His disciples were hungry and began to pluck the heads of grain and to eat. 2 But when the Pharisees saw it, they said to Him, "Look, Your disciples are doing that which is not lawful to do on the Sabbath!"

3 But He said to them, "Have you not read what David and those who were with him did when he was hungry, 4 how he entered the house of God and ate the ritual bread, which was not lawful for him to eat, neither for those who were with him, but only for the priests? 5 Or have you not read in the law how on the Sabbath the priests in the temple profane the Sabbath, but are blameless? 6 I say to you, in this place there is One who is greater than the temple. 7 If you had known what this meant, 'I desire mercy, and not sacrifice,' you would not have condemned the innocent. 8 For the Son of Man is Lord even of the Sabbath."

11:21 Mt 15:21
11:22 Mt 10:15
11:23 Isa 14:13–15
11:24 Mt 10:15
11:25 Ps 8:2
11:27 Jn 10:15
11:28 Jn 7:37
11:29 Jer 6:16
11:30 1Jn 5:3
12:1 Dt 23:25
12:2 Mt 12:10
12:5 Nu 28:9–10
12:6 Mt 12:41–42
12:7 Hos 6:6
12:8 Mt 9:6

....

12:9 Lk 6:6–11
12:10 Lk 13:14
12:11 Lk 14:5
12:14 Jn 11:53
12:18 Lk 4:18
12:21 Isa 11:10
12:23 Mt 9:27
12:24 Mt 9:34
12:25 Mt 9:4
12:28 Lk 11:20

The Healing of the Withered Hand
Mk 3:1–6; Lk 6:6–11

9 When He had departed from there, He went into their synagogue. 10 And there was a man whose hand had withered. They asked Him, "Is it lawful to heal on the Sabbath?" that they might accuse Him.

11 He said to them, "What man is there among you who has one sheep, and if it falls into a pit on the Sabbath, will not lay hold of it and lift it out? 12 Then how much better is a man than a sheep? Therefore, it is lawful to do good on the Sabbath."

13 Then He said to the man, "Stretch out your hand." And he stretched it out, and it was restored whole like the other. 14 Then the Pharisees went out and took counsel against Him, how they might kill Him.

The Chosen Servant

15 But when Jesus knew it, He withdrew from there. And great crowds followed Him, and He healed them all, 16 and warned them that they should not make Him known, 17 to fulfill what was spoken by Isaiah the prophet, saying:

18 "Here is My Servant, whom I have chosen,
My Beloved, in whom My soul is well pleased;
I will put My Spirit upon Him,
and He will render judgment to the Gentiles.
19 He shall not struggle nor cry out,
nor will anyone hear His voice in the streets.
20 A bruised reed He will not break,
and a smoldering wick He will not quench,
until He renders judgment unto victory;
21 and in His name will the Gentiles trust."[2]

Jesus and Beelzebub
Mk 3:20–30; Lk 11:14–23; 12:10

22 Then one possessed with a demon was brought to Him, blind and mute, and He healed him, so that the blind and mute man both spoke and saw. 23 All the people were amazed and said, "Is He not the Son of David?"

24 But when the Pharisees heard it, they said, "This Man does not cast out demons, except by Beelzebub the ruler of the demons."

25 Jesus knew their thoughts and said to them, "Every kingdom divided against itself is brought to desolation. And every city or house divided against itself will not stand. 26 If Satan casts out Satan, he is divided against himself. Then how will his kingdom stand? 27 And if I cast out demons by Beelzebub, by whom do your sons cast them out? Therefore, they shall be your judges. 28 But if I cast out demons by

---

[1] *29* Jer 6:16. [2] *18–21* Isa 42:1–4.

the Spirit of God, then the kingdom of God has
come upon you.
[29] "Or else how can one enter a strong
man's house and plunder his goods unless
he first binds the strong man? And then he
will plunder his house.
[30] "He who is not with Me is against Me,
and he who does not gather with Me scatters
abroad. [31] Therefore I say to you, all kinds of
sin and blasphemy will be forgiven men, but
the blasphemy against the Holy Spirit will not
be forgiven men. [32] Whoever speaks a word
against the Son of Man will be forgiven. But
whoever speaks against the Holy Spirit will not
be forgiven, neither in this world, nor in the
world to come.

A Tree and Its Fruit
Lk 6:43–45

[33] "Either make the tree good and its fruit
good, or else make the tree corrupt and its fruit
corrupt. For the tree is known by its fruit. [34] O
generation of vipers, how can you, being evil,
speak good things? For out of the abundance
of the heart the mouth speaks. [35] A good man
out of the good treasure of his heart brings
forth good things. And an evil man out of the
evil treasure brings forth evil things. [36] But I say
to you that for every idle word that men speak,
they will give an account on the Day of Judg-
ment. [37] For by your words you will be justified,
and by your words you will be condemned."

The Demand for a Sign
Mk 8:11–12; Lk 11:29–32

[38] Then some of the scribes and Pharisees
said to Him, "Teacher, we wish to see a sign
from You."
[39] But He answered them, "An evil and adul-
terous generation seeks after a sign, and no
sign will be given to it except the sign of the
prophet Jonah. [40] For as Jonah was three days
and three nights in the belly of the great fish,[1]
so will the Son of Man be three days and three
nights in the heart of the earth. [41] The men of
Nineveh will stand up at the judgment with
this generation and will condemn it, because
they repented at the preaching of Jonah.[2] And
now One greater than Jonah is here. [42] The
Queen of the South will rise up at the judg-
ment with this generation and will condemn
it, for she came from the ends of the earth to
hear the wisdom of Solomon. And now One
greater than Solomon is here.

The Return of the Unclean Spirit
Lk 11:24–26

[43] "When an unclean spirit goes out of a man,
it passes through dry places seeking rest, but
finds none. [44] Then it says, 'I will return to
my house from which I came.' And when it
comes, it finds it empty, swept, and put in or-
der. [45] Then it goes and brings with itself seven
other spirits more evil than itself, and they en-
ter and dwell there. And the last state of that
man is worse than the first. So shall it be also
with this evil generation."

The Mother and Brothers of Jesus
Mk 3:31–35; Lk 8:19–21

[46] While He was still speaking to the people,
right then His mother and His brothers stood
outside asking to speak with Him. [47] Then one
said to Him, "Look, Your mother and Your
brothers are standing outside asking to speak
with You."
[48] But He answered the man who told him,
"Who is My mother, and who are My broth-
ers?" [49] He stretched out His hand toward His
disciples and said, "Here are My mother and
My brothers! [50] For whoever does the will of
My Father who is in heaven is My brother, and
sister, and mother."

The Parable of the Sower
Mk 4:1–9; Lk 8:4–8

13 That same day Jesus went out of the
house and sat beside the sea. [2] Great
crowds assembled around Him, so that He
went into a boat and sat there. And the whole
assembly stood on the shore. [3] Then He told
them many things in parables, saying, "Listen!
A sower went out to sow. [4] While he sowed,
some seeds fell beside the path, and the birds
came and devoured them. [5] But other seeds
fell on rocky ground where they did not have
much soil, and immediately they sprang up
because they did not have deep soil. [6] But
when the sun rose, they were scorched. And
because they did not take root, they withered
away. [7] Some seeds fell among thorns, and the
thorns grew up and choked them. [8] But oth-
er seeds fell into good ground and produced
grain: a hundred, sixty, or thirty times as much.
[9] Whoever has ears to hear, let him hear."

The Purpose of the Parables
Mk 4:10–12; Lk 8:9–10

[10] The disciples came and said to Him, "Why
do You speak to them in parables?"
[11] He answered them, "It is given to you to
know the mysteries of the kingdom of heav-
en, but to them it is not given. [12] For to him
who has, will more be given, and he will have
abundance. But from him who has not, even
what he has will be taken away. [13] Therefore I
speak to them in parables:

'Because they look, but do not see.
And they listen, but they do not hear,
neither do they understand.'[3]

12:30 Mk 9:40
12:31 Lk 12:10
12:33 Lk 6:43–44
12:34 Mt 23:33
12:36 Ecc 12:14
12:38 Mk 8:11–12
12:39 Mt 16:4
12:40 Jnh 1:17
12:41 Mt 12:42
12:43 Ps 63:1
12:46 Ac 1:14
12:50 Jn 15:14
13:2 Lk 5:3
13:8 Ge 26:12
13:9 Mt 11:15
13:11 1Jn 2:27
13:12 Mt 25:29
13:13 Jer 5:21

[1] *40* Jnh 1:17. [2] *41* Jnh 3:5. [3] *13* Dt 29:4; Isa 42:19–20; Jer 5:21; Eze 12:2.

14 In them is fulfilled the prophecy of Isaiah
which says:

'By hearing, you will hear and shall not
understand,
and seeing, you will see and shall not
perceive;[1]
15 for this people's heart has grown dull.
Their ears have become hard of hearing,
and they have closed their eyes,
lest they should see with their eyes
and hear with their ears
and understand with their hearts,
and turn, and I should heal them.'[2]

16 But blessed are your eyes, for they see, and
your ears, for they hear. 17 For truly I say to
you that many prophets and righteous men
have desired to see those things which you
see, and have not seen them, and to hear
those things which you hear, and have not
heard them.

The Parable of the Sower Explained
Mk 4:13–20; Lk 8:11–15

18 "Therefore listen to the parable of the
sower. 19 When anyone hears the word of the
kingdom and does not understand it, the evil
one comes and snatches away what was sown
in his heart. This is the one who received seed
beside the path. 20 But he who received the
seed on rocky ground is he who hears the
word and immediately receives it with joy,
21 yet he has no root in himself, but endures
for a while. For when tribulation or persecu-
tion arises because of the word, eventually he
falls away. 22 He also who received seed among
the thorns is he who hears the word, but the
cares of this world and the deceitfulness of
riches choke the word, and he becomes un-
fruitful. 23 But he who received seed on the
good ground is he who hears the word and
understands it, who indeed bears fruit. Some
produce a hundred, sixty, or thirty times what
was sown."

The Parable of the Weeds

24 He told them another parable, saying, "The
kingdom of heaven is like a man who sowed
good seed in his field. 25 But while men slept,
his enemy came and sowed weeds among the
wheat and went away. 26 But when the shoots
had sprung up and produced fruit, the weeds
also appeared.

27 "So the servants of the landowner came
and said to him, 'Sir, did you not sow good
seed in your field? Then where did the weeds
come from?'

28 "He said to them, 'An enemy did this.'

"The servants said to him, 'Will you then
have us go and gather them up?'

29 "But he said, 'No, lest while you gather up
the weeds, you pull up also the wheat with
them. 30 Let both grow together until the har-
vest, and in the time of harvest I will say to the
reapers: Gather up the weeds first and bind
them in bundles to burn them, but gather the
wheat into my barn.' "

The Parables of the Mustard Seed and the Yeast
Mk 4:30–32; Lk 13:18–21

31 He told them another parable, saying, "The
kingdom of heaven is like a grain of mustard
seed which a man took and sowed in his field.
32 This indeed is the least of all seeds, but when
it has grown, it is the greatest among herbs
and is a tree, so that the birds of the air come
and lodge in its branches."

33 He told them another parable: "The king-
dom of heaven is like yeast which a woman
took and mixed in sixty pounds[3] of meal until
it had leavened the whole batch."

The Use of Parables
Mk 4:33–34

34 Jesus said all these things to the crowds
in parables. And without a parable He did not
speak to them, 35 to fulfill what was spoken by
the prophet, saying:

"I will open My mouth in parables;
I will say things which have been kept
secret since the foundation of the
world."[4]

The Parable of the Weeds Explained

36 Then Jesus sent the crowds away and went
into the house. And His disciples came to Him,
saying, "Explain to us the parable of the weeds
of the field."

37 He answered, "He who sows the good seed
is the Son of Man, 38 the field is the world, and
the good seed are the sons of the kingdom.
But the weeds are the sons of the evil one.
39 The enemy who sowed them is the devil, the
harvest is the end of the world, and the reapers
are the angels.

40 "Therefore as the weeds are gathered and
burned in the fire, so shall it be in the end of
this world. 41 The Son of Man shall send out His
angels, and they shall gather out of His king-
dom all things that offend, and those who do
evil, 42 and will throw them into a fiery furnace.
There will be wailing and gnashing of teeth.
43 Then the righteous will shine forth as the
sun[5] in the kingdom of their Father. Whoever
has ears to hear, let him hear.

13:15 Heb 5:11
13:16 Mt 16:17
13:17 Jn 8:56
13:19 Mt 4:23
13:21 Mt 11:6
13:22 1Ti 6:9–10
13:23 Mt 13:8
13:24 Mt 13:33
13:30 Mt 3:12
13:31 Mt 13:24
13:32 Eze 31:6
13:33 Lk 13:21
13:34 Mk 4:33–34
13:35 Ps 78:2
13:36 Mt 13:1
13:38 Jn 8:44
13:39 Mt 24:3
13:41 Mt 24:31
13:42 Mt 8:12
13:43 Da 12:3

[1] *14* Isa 6:9. [2] *15* Isa 6:10; Ps 119:70; Zec 7:11. [3] *33* Gk. *3 sata,* about 22 liters each. [4] *35* Ps 78:2. [5] *43* Da 12:3.

The Parable of the Hidden Treasure

44 "Again, the kingdom of heaven is like treasure hidden in a field, which a man found and hid. And with joy over it he goes and sells all that he has and buys that field.

The Parable of the Pearl of Great Price

45 "Again, the kingdom of heaven is like a merchant seeking beautiful pearls, 46 who, on finding one pearl of great price, went and sold all that he had and bought it.

The Parable of the Net

47 "Again, the kingdom of heaven is like a net that was cast into the sea and gathered all kinds of fish. 48 When it was full, they drew it to shore, sat down, and gathered the good into baskets, but threw the bad away. 49 So shall it be at the end of the world. The angels will come out and separate the evil from the righteous 50 and throw them into the fiery furnace. There will be wailing and gnashing of teeth."

Treasures New and Old

51 Jesus said to them, "Have you understood all of these things?"

They said to Him, "Yes, Lord."

52 Then He said to them, "Therefore every scribe who is discipled for the kingdom of heaven is like a man who is master of the household who brings out of his treasure new and old things."

The Rejection of Jesus at Nazareth

Mk 6:1–6; Lk 4:16–30

53 When Jesus finished these parables, He departed from there. 54 When He came to His own country, He taught them in their synagogue, so that they were astonished, and said, "Where did this Man get this wisdom and these mighty works? 55 Is He not the carpenter's son? Is His mother not called Mary? And are not His brothers James and Joseph and Simon and Judas? 56 And His sisters, are they not all with us? Where then did this Man get all these things?" 57 And they took offense at Him.

But Jesus said to them, "A prophet is not without honor except in his own country and in his own house."

58 And He did not do many mighty works there because of their unbelief.

The Death of John the Baptist

Mk 6:14–29; Lk 9:7–9

14 At that time Herod the tetrarch heard of the fame of Jesus, 2 and said to his servants, "This is John the Baptist; he has risen from the dead. And therefore mighty works are at work in him."

3 For Herod had laid hold of John, bound him, and put him in prison for the sake of Herodias, his brother Philip's wife. 4 For John said to him, "It is not lawful for you to have her." 5 When Herod would have put him to death, he feared the crowd, because they counted him as a prophet.

6 But when Herod's birthday was celebrated, the daughter of Herodias danced before them and pleased Herod. 7 Therefore he promised with an oath to give her whatever she would ask. 8 Being previously instructed by her mother, she said, "Give me John the Baptist's head on a platter." 9 The king was sorry. Nevertheless, for the oath's sake and those who sat with him at supper, he commanded it to be given to her. 10 He sent and beheaded John in the prison. 11 His head was brought on a platter and given to the girl, and she brought it to her mother. 12 His disciples came and took up the body and buried it. And they went and told Jesus.

The Feeding of the Five Thousand

Mk 6:30–44; Lk 9:10–17; Jn 6:1–14

13 When Jesus heard this, He departed from there by boat for a deserted place. But when the people heard it, they followed Him on foot from the cities. 14 Jesus went ashore and saw a great assembly. And He was moved with compassion toward them, and He healed their sick.

15 When it was evening, His disciples came to Him, saying, "This is a lonely place and the day is now over. Send the crowds away to go into the villages and buy themselves food."

16 But Jesus said to them, "They do not need to depart. You give them something to eat."

17 They said to Him, "We have only five loaves here and two fish."

18 He said, "Bring them here to Me." 19 Then He commanded the crowds to sit down on the grass. He took the five loaves and the two fish, and looking up to heaven, He blessed and broke and gave the loaves to His disciples; and the disciples gave them to the crowds. 20 They all ate and were filled. And they took up twelve baskets full of the fragments that remained. 21 Those who had eaten were about five thousand men, besides women and children.

Walking on the Water

Mk 6:45–52; Jn 6:15–21

22 Then Jesus commanded His disciples to get into the boat and go ahead of Him to the other side, while He sent the crowds away. 23 When He sent the crowds away, He went up into a mountain by Himself to pray. And when evening came, He was there alone. 24 But the boat was now in the middle of the sea, tossed by the waves, for the wind was turbulent.

25 During the fourth watch of the night Jesus went to them, walking on the sea. 26 But when the disciples saw Him walking on the sea, they

13:44 Isa 55:1
13:47 Mt 4:19
13:49 Mt 13:39
13:51 Mt 13:11
13:55 Mk 6:3
13:57 Lk 4:24
14:1 Lk 3:1
14:2 Mt 16:14
14:3 Mt 4:12
14:4 Lev 18:16
....
14:10 Mt 17:12
14:12 Ac 8:2
14:13 Lk 9:10–17
14:14 Mt 9:36
14:15 Mt 15:23
14:16 2Ki 4:42–44
14:19 1Sa 9:13
14:20 Lk 9:17
14:23 Lk 6:12
14:26 Lk 24:37

were troubled, saying, "It is a spirit." And they
cried out in fear.
27 But immediately Jesus spoke to them, say-
ing, "Be of good cheer. It is I. Do not be afraid."
28 Peter answered Him and said, "Lord, if it is
You, bid me come to You on the water."
29 He said, "Come."
And when Peter got out of the boat, he
walked on the water to go to Jesus. 30 But when
he saw the strong wind, he was afraid, and be-
ginning to sink, he cried out, "Lord, save me!"
31 Immediately Jesus reached out His hand
and caught him, and said to him, "O you of
little faith, why did you doubt?"
32 And when they got into the boat, the wind
ceased. 33 Then those who were in the boat
came and worshipped Him, saying, "Truly You
are the Son of God."

The Healing of the Sick in Gennesaret

Mk 6:53–56

34 When they had crossed over, they came to
the land of Gennesaret. 35 And when the men
of that place recognized Him, they sent word to
all the surrounding country and brought to Him
all who were sick, 36 and begged Him that they
might only touch the hem of His garment. And
as many as touched it were made perfectly well.

The Tradition of the Elders

Mk 7:1–23

15 Then scribes and Pharisees who were
from Jerusalem came to Jesus, saying,
2 "Why do Your disciples violate the tradition of
the elders? For they do not wash their hands
when they eat bread."
3 But He answered them, "Why do you also
violate the commandment of God by your
tradition? 4 For God commanded, 'Honor your
father and mother,'[1] and, 'He who speaks evil
of father or mother, let him be put to death.'[2]
5 But you say, 'Whoever shall say to his father
or his mother, "What you would have profited
from me is a gift to God," 6 will be free from
honoring his father or his mother.' So you have
made the commandment of God of no effect
by your tradition. 7 You hypocrites, Isaiah well
prophesied of you, saying:

8 'These people draw near to Me with their
mouth, and honor Me with their lips,
but their heart is far from Me.
9 In vain they do worship Me,
teaching as doctrines the precepts of
men.'[3]"

10 He called the crowds and said to them,
"Hear and understand: 11 That which goes into
the mouth does not defile a man, but that which
comes out of the mouth, this defiles a man."
12 Then His disciples came and said to Him,
"Do You know that the Pharisees were offend-
ed after they heard this saying?"
13 But He answered, "Every plant which My
heavenly Father has not planted will be up-
rooted. 14 Leave them alone. They are blind
leaders of the blind. And if the blind lead the
blind, both will fall into the ditch."
15 Then Peter said to Him, "Explain this par-
able to us."
16 Jesus said, "Are you also still without un-
derstanding? 17 Do you not yet understand that
whatever enters at the mouth goes into the
stomach and is cast out into the sewer? 18 But
those things which proceed out of the mouth
come from the heart, and they defile the man.
19 For out of the heart proceed evil thoughts,
murders, adulteries, sexual immorality, thefts,
false witness, and blasphemies. 20 These are
the things which defile a man. But to eat with
unwashed hands does not defile a man."

> Help me, Holy Spirit, to guard my thoughts, for out of the heart come the things that defile a man (Mt 15:19–20).

The Faith of the Canaanite Woman

Mk 7:24–30

21 Then Jesus went from there and departed
into the regions of Tyre and Sidon. 22 There,
a woman of Canaan came out of the same
regions and cried out to Him, saying, "Have
mercy on me, O Lord, Son of David. My daugh-
ter is severely possessed by a demon."
23 But He did not answer her a word. And His
disciples came and begged Him, saying, "Send
her away, for she cries out after us."
24 But He answered, "I was sent only to the
lost sheep of the house of Israel."
25 Then she came and worshipped Him, say-
ing, "Lord, help me."
26 But He answered, "It is not fair to take the
children's bread and to throw it to dogs."
27 She said, "Yes, Lord, yet even dogs eat the
crumbs that fall from their masters' table."
28 Then Jesus answered her, "O woman, great
is your faith. Let it be done for you as you de-
sire." And her daughter was healed instantly.

The Healing of Many People

29 Jesus departed from there, and passed by
the Sea of Galilee, and went up on a moun-
tain and sat down there. 30 Great crowds came
to Him, having with them those who were
lame, blind, mute, maimed, and many others,
and placed them down at Jesus' feet, and He
healed them, 31 so that the crowds wondered

14:27 Mt 9:2
14:33 Ps 2:7
14:34 Mk 6:53–56
14:36 Mk 3:10
15:4 Ex 20:12
15:8 Isa 29:13
15:11 Ac 10:14–15
15:13 Isa 60:21
15:14 Lk 6:39
15:15 Mt 13:36
15:16 Mt 16:9
15:17 1Co 6:13
15:18 Mt 12:34
15:19 Gal 5:19–21
15:22 Mt 9:27
15:23 Mt 14:15
15:24 Ro 15:8
15:25 Mt 8:2
15:27 Lk 16:21
15:29 Mt 4:18
15:31 Mt 9:8

1 4 Ex 20:12; Dt 5:16. *2 4* Ex 21:17; Lev 20:9. *3 8–9* Isa 29:13.

when they saw the mute speak, the maimed
made whole, the lame walk, and the blind see.
And they glorified the God of Israel.

The Feeding of the Four Thousand
Mk 8:1–10

32 Then Jesus called His disciples to Him
and said, "I have compassion on the crowd,
because they have remained with Me now
for three days and have nothing to eat. I will
not send them away hungry, lest they faint
on the way."

33 His disciples said to Him, "Where will we
get enough bread in the wilderness to feed
such a great crowd?"

34 Jesus said to them, "How many loaves do
you have?"

And they said, "Seven and a few little fish."

35 He commanded the crowd to sit down on
the ground. 36 He took the seven loaves and
the fish, gave thanks, broke them, and gave
them to His disciples, and the disciples gave
them to the crowd. 37 They all ate and were
filled. And they collected seven baskets full
of the broken pieces that were left. 38 Those
who ate were four thousand men, besides
women and children. 39 He sent the crowd
away, and got into the boat, and went to the
region of Magdala.

The Demand for a Sign
Mk 8:11–13; Lk 12:54–56

16 The Pharisees and Sadducees came
and, testing Him, asked Him to show
them a sign from heaven.

2 He answered them, "When it is evening, you
say, 'It will be fair weather, for the sky is red,'
3 and in the morning, 'It will be foul weather
today, for the sky is red and overcast.' O you
hypocrites, you can discern the face of the sky,
but you cannot discern the signs of the times.
4 A wicked and adulterous generation seeks for
a sign, but no sign shall be given to it except
the sign of the prophet Jonah." So He left them
and departed.

The Yeast of Pharisees and Sadducees
Mk 8:14–21

5 But when His disciples reached the other
side, they had forgotten to take bread. 6 Then
Jesus said to them, "Take heed and beware
of the yeast of the Pharisees and Sadducees."

7 They reasoned among themselves, saying,
"It is because we have taken no bread."

8 But when Jesus perceived it, He said to
them, "O you of little faith, why reason among
yourselves, that it is because you have brought
no bread? 9 Do you not yet understand or re-
member the five loaves of the five thousand
and how many baskets you collected? 10 Or the
seven loaves of the four thousand and how

15:32 Mt 9:36
15:36 Lk 22:19
15:39 Mk 8:10
16:1 Lk 11:16
16:3 Lk 12:56
16:6 Lk 12:1
16:8 Mt 6:30
16:9 Mt 14:17–21
16:10 Mt 15:34–38
....
16:11 Mt 16:6
16:13 Lk 9:18–20
16:14 Mt 14:2
16:16 Ps 42:2
16:17 Gal 1:16
16:18 Jn 1:42
16:19 Mt 18:18
16:20 Mk 8:30
16:21 Mt 17:22–23
16:23 Mt 4:10
16:24 Mt 10:38

many baskets you collected? 11 How is it that
you do not understand that I spoke to you not
concerning bread, but that you should beware
of the yeast of the Pharisees and Sadducees?"
12 Then they understood that He did not tell
them to beware of the yeast of bread, but of
the teaching of the Pharisees and Sadducees.

Peter's Declaration About Jesus
Mk 8:27–30; Lk 9:18–21

13 When Jesus came into the region of Caes-
area Philippi, He asked His disciples, "Who do
men say that I, the Son of Man, am?"

14 They said, "Some say that You are John the
Baptist, others say Elijah, and others Jeremiah
or one of the prophets."

15 He said to them, "But who do you say that
I am?"

16 Simon Peter replied, "You are the Christ,
the Son of the living God."

17 Jesus answered him, "Blessed are you,
Simon son of Jonah, for flesh and blood has
not revealed this to you, but My Father who is
in heaven. 18 And I tell you that you are Peter,
and on this rock I will build My church, and
the gates of Hades shall not prevail against it.
19 I will give you the keys of the kingdom of
heaven, and whatever you bind on earth shall
be bound in heaven, and whatever you loose
on earth shall be loosed in heaven." 20 Then He
commanded His disciples to tell no one that
He was Jesus the Christ.

> God wants to release everything that is bound up and to bind everything that is keeping you from Him (Mt 16:19).

Jesus Foretells His Death and Resurrection
Mk 8:31–9:1; Lk 9:22–27

21 From that time on, Jesus began to show
His disciples that He must go to Jerusalem and
suffer many things from the elders and chief
priests and scribes, and be killed, and be raised
on the third day.

22 Then Peter took Him and began rebuking
Him, saying, "Far be it from You, Lord! This
shall not happen to You."

23 But He turned and said to Peter, "Get be-
hind Me, Satan! You are an offense to Me, for
you are not mindful of the things that are of
God, but those that are of men."

24 Then Jesus said to His disciples, "If anyone
will come after Me, let him deny himself, and
take up his cross, and follow Me. 25 For whoev-
er would save his life will lose it, and whoever
loses his life for My sake will find it. 26 For what

will it profit a man if he gains the whole world and loses his own soul? Or what shall a man give in exchange for his soul? 27 For the Son of Man shall come with His angels in the glory of His Father, and then He will repay every man according to his works. 28 Truly I say to you, there are some standing here who shall not taste death before they see the Son of Man coming in His kingdom."

The Transfiguration
Mk 9:2–13; Lk 9:28–36

17 After six days Jesus took Peter, James, and John his brother and brought them up to a high mountain alone, 2 and was transfigured before them. His face shone as the sun, and His garments became white as the light. 3 Suddenly Moses and Elijah appeared to them, talking with Him.

4 Then Peter said to Jesus, "Lord, it is good for us to be here. If You wish, let us make three tabernacles here: one for You, one for Moses, and one for Elijah."

5 While he was still speaking, suddenly a bright cloud overshadowed them, and a voice from the cloud said, "This is My beloved Son, with whom I am well pleased. Listen to Him."

6 When the disciples heard this, they fell on their faces and were filled with awe. 7 But Jesus came and touched them and said, "Rise, and do not be afraid." 8 When they lifted up their eyes, they saw no one but Jesus only.

9 As they came down the mountain, Jesus commanded them, "Tell the vision to no one until the Son of Man is risen from the dead."

10 His disciples asked Him, "Why then do the scribes say that Elijah must come first?"

11 Jesus answered, "Elijah truly does first come and will restore all things. 12 But I tell you that Elijah has already come, and they did not know him, but did to him whatever they pleased. Likewise, the Son of Man will also suffer at their hands." 13 Then the disciples understood that He was speaking to them of John the Baptist.

The Healing of a Boy with a Demon
Mk 9:14–29; Lk 9:37–43

14 When they came to the crowd, a man came to Him and knelt before Him, saying, 15 "Lord, have mercy on my son, for he is an epileptic and suffers terribly. He often falls into the fire and often into the water. 16 I brought him to Your disciples, but they could not heal him."

17 Then Jesus answered, "O faithless and perverse generation, how long shall I be with you? How long shall I bear with you? Bring him here to Me." 18 Jesus rebuked the demon, and he came out of him. And the child was healed instantly.

19 Then the disciples came to Jesus privately and said, "Why could we not cast him out?"

20 Jesus said to them, "Because of your unbelief. For truly I say to you, if you have faith as a grain of mustard seed, you will say to this mountain, 'Move from here to there,' and it will move. And nothing will be impossible for you. 21 But this kind does not go out except by prayer and fasting."

> Sometimes you have to go after God with all that you have, and it will require some intense prayer and fasting (Mt 17:18–20).

Jesus Again Foretells His Death and Resurrection
Mk 9:30–32; Lk 9:43b–45

22 While they were staying in Galilee, Jesus said to them, "The Son of Man is about to be betrayed into the hands of men, 23 and they will kill Him, and He will be raised on the third day." And they were extremely sorrowful.

Payment of the Temple Tax

24 When they came to Capernaum, those who collected tax money came to Peter and said, "Does your Teacher not pay the tax[1]?"

25 He said, "Yes."

And when he came home, Jesus stopped him, saying, "What do you think, Simon? From whom do the kings of the earth take custom or taxes? From their own sons or from strangers?"

26 Peter said to Him, "From strangers."

Jesus said to him, "Then the sons are free. 27 However, lest we offend them, go to the sea and cast a hook, and take the first fish that comes up. And when you open its mouth, you will find a coin. Take it and give it to them for you and Me."

The Greatest in the Kingdom
Mk 9:33–37; Lk 9:46–48

18 At that time the disciples came to Jesus, saying, "Who is the greatest in the kingdom of heaven?"

2 Jesus called a little child to Him and set him in their midst, 3 and said, "Truly I say to you, unless you are converted and become like little children, you will not enter the kingdom of heaven. 4 Therefore whoever humbles himself like this little child is greatest in the kingdom of heaven. 5 And whoever receives one such little child in My name receives Me.

16:27 Ro 2:6
16:28 Mt 10:23
17:1 Mt 26:37
17:4 Lk 9:33
17:5 Mt 3:17
17:6 2Pe 1:18
17:9 Mk 8:30
17:10 Mt 11:14
17:11 Lk 1:16–17
17:12 Mt 16:21
17:15 Mt 4:24
17:17 Jn 20:27
....
17:18 Mt 9:22
17:20 Lk 17:6
17:21 Mk 9:29
17:22 Mt 16:21
17:23 Mt 16:21
17:24 Ex 30:13
17:27 1Co 8:13
18:1 Mk 9:33–37
18:3 1Pe 2:2
18:4 Mt 23:11–12
18:5 Mt 25:40

[1] *24* Gk. *2 drachmas*, or two days' wages.

We must make sure we never allow ourselves to subtly buy the lie that children are just "playing church" or just "in training" (Mt 18:3).

Temptations to Sin
Mk 9:42–48; Lk 17:1–2

6 "But whoever misleads one of these little
ones who believe in Me, it would be better for
him to have a millstone hung about his neck
and to be drowned in the depth of the sea.
7 Woe to the world because of temptations! For
it must be that temptations come, but woe to
that man by whom the temptation comes!
8 Therefore if your hand or your foot causes
you to sin, cut it off and throw it away. It is bet-
ter for you to enter life lame or maimed than
having two hands or two feet to be thrown into
eternal fire. 9 And if your eye causes you to sin,
pluck it out and throw it away. It is better for
you to enter life with one eye than having two
eyes to be thrown into the fire of hell.

The Parable of the Lost Sheep
Lk 15:5–7

10 "See that you do not despise one of these
little ones. For I say to you that in heaven their
angels always see the face of My Father who
is in heaven. 11 For the Son of Man has come
to save that which was lost.

12 "What do you think? If a man has a hun-
dred sheep and one of them goes astray, does
he not leave the ninety-nine on the hills and go
in search for the one which went astray? 13 And
if he finds it, truly I say to you, he rejoices
more over that sheep than over the ninety-nine
which never went astray. 14 So it is not the will
of your Father who is in heaven that one of
these little ones should perish.

The Brother Who Sins
Lk 17:3

15 "Now if your brother sins against you, go
and tell him his fault between you and him
alone. If he listens to you, you have gained
your brother. 16 But if he does not listen, then
take with you one or two others, that by the
testimony of two or three witnesses every word
may be established.[1] 17 If he refuses to listen to
them, tell it to the church. But if he refuses to
listen even to the church, let him be to you as
a Gentile and a tax collector.

God knows that whenever people can get together in unity, *anything is possible* (Mt 18:19).

18:6 Mk 9:42
18:7 Lk 17:1
18:8 Mt 5:29–30
18:10 Lk 1:19
18:11 Lk 19:10
18:12 Lk 15:4–7
18:14 Jn 17:12
18:15 Lev 19:17
18:16 Dt 19:15
18:17 2Th 3:6

....

18:18 Mt 16:19
18:20 Mt 28:20
18:21 Mt 18:15
18:23 Mt 13:24
18:25 Lev 25:39
18:26 Mt 8:2
18:28 Mt 20:2
18:33 Col 3:13
18:34 Mt 5:25–26
19:1 Jn 10:40

18 "Truly I say to you, whatever you bind on
earth will be bound in heaven, and whatever
you loose on earth will be loosed in heaven.

19 "Again I say to you, that if two of you agree
on earth about anything they ask, it will be
done for them by My Father who is in heaven.
20 For where two or three are assembled in My
name, there I am in their midst."

The Parable of the Unforgiving Servant

21 Then Peter came to Him and said, "Lord,
how often shall I forgive my brother who sins
against me? Up to seven times?"

22 Jesus said to him, "I do not say to you up
to seven times, but up to seventy times seven.

23 "Therefore the kingdom of heaven is like
a certain king who wanted to settle accounts
with his servants. 24 When he began to settle
the accounts, one was brought to him who
owed him ten thousand talents.[2] 25 But since
he was not able to pay, his master ordered that
he be sold with his wife, their children, and all
that he had, and payment to be made.

26 "So the servant fell on his knees, pleading
with him, saying, 'Master, have patience with
me, and I will pay you everything.' 27 Then
the master of that servant was moved with
compassion, released him, and forgave him
the debt.

28 "But that same servant went out and found
one of his fellow servants who owed him a
hundred denarii.[3] He laid hands on him and
took him by the throat, saying, 'Pay me what
you owe.'

29 "So his fellow servant fell down at his feet
and entreated him, saying, 'Have patience with
me, and I will pay you everything.'

30 "But he would not and went and threw
him in prison until he should pay the debt.
31 So when his fellow servants saw what took
place, they were very sorry and went and told
their master all that had taken place.

32 "Then his master, after he had summoned
him, said to him, 'O you wicked servant! I
forgave you all that debt because you plead-
ed with me. 33 Should you not also have had
compassion on your fellow servant, even as I
had pity on you?' 34 His master was angry and
delivered him to the jailers until he should pay
all his debt.

35 "So also My heavenly Father will do to each
of you, if from your heart you do not forgive
your brother for his trespasses."

Teaching About Divorce
Mk 10:1–12

19 Now when Jesus finished these say-
ings, He departed from Galilee and
came into the region of Judea beyond the

[1] *16* Dt 19:15. [2] *24* Several million pounds. [3] *28* A few pounds.

Jordan. 2 Large crowds followed Him, and He healed them there.

3 The Pharisees also came to Him, tempting Him and saying, "Is it lawful for a man to divorce his wife for any reason?"

4 He answered, "Have you not read that He who made them at the beginning 'made them male and female,'[1] 5 and said, 'For this reason a man shall leave his father and mother and be joined to his wife, and the two shall become one flesh'?[2] 6 So they are no longer two, but one flesh. Therefore what God has joined together, let no man put asunder."

7 They said to Him, "Then why did Moses command to give a certificate of divorce, and to send her away?"[3]

8 He said to them, "Moses, for the hardness of your hearts, permitted you to divorce your wives, but from the beginning it was not so. 9 But I say to you, whoever divorces his wife, except for sexual immorality, and marries another, commits adultery. And whoever marries her who is divorced commits adultery."

10 His disciples said to Him, "If such is the case of the man with his wife, it is not good to marry."

11 But He said to them, "Not all men can receive this precept, but only those to whom it is given. 12 For there are some eunuchs who have been so from birth, there are some eunuchs who have been made eunuchs by men, and there are some eunuchs who have made themselves eunuchs for the sake of the kingdom of heaven. He who is able to receive this, let him receive it."

Little Children Blessed
Mk 10:13–16; Lk 18:15–17

God longs to bring children into the fullness of who He is (Mt 19:14).

13 Then little children were brought to Him that He might put His hands on them and pray. But the disciples rebuked them.

14 But Jesus said, "Let the little children come to Me, and do not forbid them. For to such belongs the kingdom of heaven." 15 He laid His hands on them and departed from there.

God is passionate about encountering children; for so long children have been held back from the deep things of God (Mt 19:14).

19:2 Mt 12:15
19:3 Jn 8:6
19:4 Ge 1:27
19:5 1Co 6:16
19:7 Dt 24:1–4
19:8 Ge 2:24
19:9 Mt 5:32
19:11 1Co 7:17
19:14 Mt 18:3

19:16 Mt 25:46
19:17 Lev 18:5
19:19 Lev 19:18
19:20 Php 3:6
19:21 Lk 12:33
19:22 Eze 33:31
19:23 Mt 13:22
19:26 Job 42:2
19:28 Rev 3:21
19:29 Lk 14:26
19:30 Mt 20:16
20:1 SS 8:11–12

The Rich Young Man
Mk 10:17–31; Lk 18:18–30

16 Now one came and said to Him, "Good Teacher, what good deed shall I do to have eternal life?"

17 He replied to him, "Why do you call Me good? There is One who is good. But if you would enter life, keep the commandments."

18 He said to Him, "Which ones?"

Jesus said, "You shall not murder, You shall not commit adultery, You shall not steal, You shall not bear false witness,[4] 19 Honor your father and your mother,[5] and, You shall love your neighbor as yourself.[6]"

20 The young man said to Him, "All these I have kept from my youth. What do I still lack?"

21 Jesus said to him, "If you would be perfect, go and sell what you have, and give to the poor, and you will have treasure in heaven. And come, follow Me."

22 But when the young man heard this, he went away sorrowful. For he had great possessions.

23 Then Jesus said to His disciples, "Truly, I say to you that it will be hard for a rich man to enter the kingdom of heaven. 24 And again I say to you, it is easier for a camel to go through the eye of a needle than for a rich man to enter the kingdom of God."

25 When His disciples heard this, they were greatly amazed, saying, "Who then can be saved?"

26 But Jesus looked at them and said, "With men this is impossible, but with God all things are possible."

27 Then Peter answered Him, "See, we have left everything and followed You. What then shall we have?"

28 Jesus said to them, "Truly I say to you, in the regeneration, when the Son of Man sits on His glorious throne, you who have followed Me will also sit on twelve thrones, judging the twelve tribes of Israel. 29 And everyone who has left houses or brothers or sisters or father or mother or wife or children or fields for My name's sake shall receive a hundred times as much and inherit eternal life. 30 But many who are first will be last, and the last first."

The Workers in the Vineyard

20 "For the kingdom of heaven is like a landowner who went out early in the morning to hire laborers for his vineyard. 2 When he had agreed with the laborers for a denarius a day, he sent them into his vineyard.

3 "Then he went out about the third hour and saw others standing idle in the marketplace, 4 and said to them, 'You also go into the vineyard, and whatever is right I will give you.' So

[1] 4 Ge 1:27; 5:2. [2] 5 Ge 2:24. [3] 7 Dt 24:1–4. [4] 18 Ex 20:13–16; Dt 5:17–20. [5] 19 Ex 20:12; Dt 5:16. [6] 19 Lev 19:18.

they went. 5 Again he went out about the sixth hour and the ninth hour and did likewise.

6 "About the eleventh hour he went out and found others standing idle, and said to them, 'Why do you stand here idle all day?'

7 "They said to him, 'Because no one has hired us.'

"He said to them, 'You also go into the vineyard, and whatever is right you will receive.'

8 "So when evening came, the owner of the vineyard said to his steward, 'Call the laborers and give them their wages, beginning with the last to the first.'

9 "When they who were hired about the eleventh hour came, they each received a denarius. 10 But when the first came, they supposed that they would receive more, but each of them likewise received a denarius. 11 When they received it, they grumbled against the landowner, 12 saying, 'These last worked only one hour, and you made them equal to us, who have borne the burden and the heat of the day.'

13 "But he answered one of them, 'Friend, I am doing you no wrong. Did you not agree with me for a denarius? 14 Take what is yours and go your way. I will give to this last one even as I give to you. 15 Is it not lawful for me to do what I wish with my own things? Or is your eye evil because I am good?'

16 "So the last will be first, and the first last. For many are called, but few are chosen."

A Third Time Jesus Foretells His Death and Resurrection

Mk 10:32–34; Lk 18:31–34

17 As Jesus was going up to Jerusalem, He took the twelve disciples aside on the road and said to them, 18 "Now we are going up to Jerusalem, and the Son of Man will be betrayed to the chief priests and scribes. And they will condemn Him to death 19 and deliver Him to the Gentiles to mock, and to scourge, and to crucify Him, but on the third day He will rise."

A Mother's Request

Mk 10:35–45

20 Then the mother of Zebedee's sons came to Him with her sons. And kneeling before Him, she asked for a certain thing.

21 He said to her, "What do you want?"

She said to Him, "Grant that these two sons of mine may sit, one at Your right hand and one at Your left, in Your kingdom."

22 But Jesus answered, "You do not know what you are asking. Are you able to drink from the cup that I am to drink, and to be baptized with the baptism that I am baptized with?"

They said to Him, "We are able."

23 He said to them, "You will indeed drink from My cup and be baptized with the baptism that I am baptized with. But to sit at My right hand and at My left is not Mine to grant, but it is for those for whom it is prepared by My Father."

24 When the ten heard it, they were moved with indignation against the two brothers. 25 But Jesus called them to Him and said, "You know that the rulers of the Gentiles lord it over them, and those who are great exercise authority over them. 26 It shall not be so among you. Whoever would be great among you, let him serve you, 27 and whoever would be first among you, let him be your slave, 28 even as the Son of Man did not come to be served, but to serve and to give His life as a ransom for many."

The Healing of Two Blind Men

Mk 10:46–52; Lk 18:35–43

29 As they departed from Jericho, a large crowd followed Him. 30 There, two blind men sitting by the road, when they heard that Jesus was passing by, cried out, "Have mercy on us, O Lord, Son of David!"

31 The crowd rebuked them, that they should be silent. But they cried out even more, "Have mercy on us, O Lord, Son of David!"

32 Jesus stood still and called them, saying, "What do you want Me to do for you?"

33 They said to Him, "Lord, let our eyes be opened."

34 So Jesus had compassion on them and touched their eyes. Immediately their eyes received sight, and they followed Him.

The Triumphant Entry Into Jerusalem

Mk 11:1–11; Lk 19:28–38; Jn 12:12–19

21 When they drew near to Jerusalem and came to Bethphage, on the Mount of Olives, then Jesus sent two disciples, 2 saying to them, "Go over into the village opposite you, and immediately you will find a donkey tied, and a colt with her. Untie them and bring them to Me. 3 If anyone says anything to you, you shall say, 'The Lord has need of them.' And he will send them immediately."

4 All this was done to fulfill what was spoken by the prophet, saying:

5 "Tell the daughter of Zion,
'Look, your King is coming to you,
humble, and sitting on a donkey,
and on a colt, the foal of a donkey.'[1]"

6 The disciples went and did as Jesus commanded them. 7 They brought the donkey and the colt, laid their garments on them, and He sat on them. 8 A very large crowd spread their garments on the road. Others cut down branches from the trees and spread them on

20:13 Mt 22:12
20:15 Dt 15:9
20:16 Mt 19:30
20:17 Mk 10:32–34
20:18 Mt 16:21
20:19 Mt 16:21
20:20 Mt 4:21
20:21 Mt 19:28
20:22 Mt 26:42
20:23 Ac 12:2
20:25 Lk 22:25–27
20:26 Mk 9:35
20:28 Heb 9:28
20:29 Mk 10:46–52
20:31 Mt 19:13
21:1 Mt 24:3
21:5 Isa 62:11
21:8 2Ki 9:13

[1] 5 Zec 9:9.

the road. 9 The crowds that went before Him
and that followed Him cried out:

"Hosanna to the Son of David!
'Blessed is He who comes in the name of
the Lord!'[1]
Hosanna in the highest!"

10 When He entered Jerusalem, the entire city
was moved, saying, "Who is He?"
11 The crowds said, "This is Jesus, the prophet
from Nazareth of Galilee."

The Cleansing of the Temple
Mk 11:15–19; Lk 19:45–48; Jn 2:13–22

12 Jesus went into the temple of God and
drove out all those who sold and bought in
the temple and overturned the tables of the
moneychangers and the seats of those who
sold doves. 13 He said to them, "It is written, 'My
house shall be called a house of prayer,'[2] but
you have made it 'a den of thieves.'[3] "
14 The blind and the lame came to Him in the
temple, and He healed them. 15 But when the
chief priests and scribes saw the wonderful
things that He did, and the children crying out
in the temple, "Hosanna to the Son of David,"
they were extremely displeased 16 and said to
Him, "Do You hear what these are saying?"
Jesus said to them, "Yes. Have you never
read,

'Out of the mouth of children and infants
You have perfected praise'[4]?"

17 And He left them and went out of the city
into Bethany, and He lodged there.

The Cursing of the Fig Tree
Mk 11:12–14, 20–24

18 Now in the morning as He returned to the
city, He became hungry. 19 When He saw a fig
tree by the road, He went to it but found noth-
ing on it except leaves. He said to it, "Let no
fruit ever grow on you again." Immediately the
fig tree withered away.
20 When the disciples saw it, they were
amazed, saying, "How did the fig tree wither
away instantly?"
21 Jesus answered them, "Truly I say to you,
if you have faith and do not doubt, you will not
only do what was done to the fig tree, but also,
if you say to this mountain, 'Be removed, and
be thrown into the sea,' it will be done. 22 And
whatever you ask in prayer, if you believe, you
will receive."

The Question of Jesus' Authority
Mk 11:27–33; Lk 20:1–8

23 When He entered the temple, the chief
priests and the elders of the people came up
to Him as He was teaching, and said, "By what
authority are You doing these things? And who
gave You this authority?"
24 Jesus answered them, "I also will ask you
one question. If you tell Me, I likewise will
tell you by what authority I do these things.
25 Where did the baptism of John come from?
From heaven or from men?"
They reasoned among themselves, saying,
"If we say, 'From heaven,' He will say to us,
'Then why did you not believe him?' 26 But if
we say, 'From men,' we are afraid of the peo-
ple, for all hold John as a prophet."
27 So they answered Jesus, "We do not know."
Then He said to them, "Neither will I tell you
by what authority I do these things.

The Parable of the Two Sons

28 "What do you think? A man had two sons.
He came to the first and said, 'Son, go work
today in my vineyard.'
29 "He answered, 'I will not,' but afterward he
repented and went.
30 "Then he came to the second, and said
likewise. He answered, 'I will go, sir,' but did
not go.
31 "Which of the two did the will of his father?"
They said, "The first."
Jesus said to them, "Truly I say to you, the tax
collectors and prostitutes enter the kingdom of
God before you. 32 For John came to you in the
way of righteousness, and you did not believe
him. But the tax collectors and prostitutes be-
lieved him. And even when you saw it, you did
not afterward repent and believe him.

The Parable of the Vineyard and the Vinedressers
Mk 12:1–12; Lk 20:9–19

33 "Listen to another parable: There was a
certain landowner who planted a vineyard
and built a wall around it. He dug a winepress
in it and built a tower. Then he rented it to
vinedressers and went into a distant country.
34 When the season of the fruit drew near, he
sent his servants to the vinedressers to receive
his fruit.
35 "The vinedressers took his servants and
beat one, killed another, and stoned another.
36 Again, he sent other servants, more than the
first. And they did likewise to them. 37 Last of
all, he sent his son to them, saying, 'They will
respect my son.'
38 "But when the vinedressers saw the son,
they said to themselves, 'This is the heir.
Come, let us kill him and seize his inheri-
tance.' 39 So they caught him, threw him out
of the vineyard, and killed him.
40 "Therefore, when the owner of the vineyard
comes, what will he do to those vinedressers?"

21:9 Lk 2:14
21:11 Lk 7:16
21:12 Lev 1:14
21:13 Isa 56:7
21:15 Mt 21:9
21:16 Ps 8:2
21:17 Jn 11:18
21:18 Mt 4:2
21:19 Lk 13:6–9
21:21 Mt 17:20
21:22 Mt 7:7
21:23 Ac 4:7
21:26 Mk 6:20
21:31 Lk 7:29
21:33 Mt 25:14–15
21:35 Heb 11:36–37
21:36 Mt 22:4
21:39 Ac 2:23

[1] *9* Ps 118:26. [2] *13* Isa 56:7. [3] *13* Jer 7:11. [4] *16* Ps 8:2.

41 They said, "He will severely destroy those wicked men and rent his vineyard to other vinedressers who will give him the fruits in their seasons."

42 Jesus said to them, "Have you never read in the Scriptures:

'The stone which the builders rejected
has become the cornerstone.
This is the Lord's doing,
and it is marvelous in our eyes'[1]?

43 "Therefore I tell you, the kingdom of God will be taken from you and given to a nation bearing its fruits. 44 Whoever falls on this stone will be broken to pieces. But on whomever it falls, it will crush him."

45 When the chief priests and Pharisees heard His parables, they perceived that He was speaking of them. 46 But as they tried to arrest Him, they feared the crowds, because they held Him as a prophet.

The Parable of the Wedding Banquet
Lk 14:15–24

22 Jesus spoke to them again by parables, saying, 2 "The kingdom of heaven is like a certain king who arranged a marriage for his son, 3 and sent out his servants to call those who were invited to the wedding, but they would not come.

4 "Again, he sent out other servants, saying, 'Tell those who are invited: See, I have prepared my supper. My oxen and fattened calves are killed, and everything is ready. Come to the wedding banquet.'

5 "But they made light of it and went their ways, one to his farm, another to his business; 6 the rest took his servants, treated them spitefully, and killed them. 7 When the king heard about it, he was angry. He sent in his army and destroyed those murderers and burned up their city.

8 "Then he said to his servants, 'The wedding is ready, but those who were invited were not worthy. 9 Go therefore to the streets, and invite to the wedding banquet as many as you find.' 10 So those servants went out into the streets and gathered together as many as they found, both bad and good. So the wedding hall was filled with guests.

11 "But when the king came in to see the guests, he saw a man who was not wearing wedding garments. 12 He said to him, 'Friend, how did you get in here without wedding garments?' And he was speechless.

13 "Then the king told the attendants, 'Bind him hand and foot, take him away, and cast him into outer darkness, where there will be weeping and gnashing of teeth.'

14 "For many are called, but few are chosen."

21:41 Ac 18:6
21:42 Ac 4:11
21:44 Isa 8:14–15
21:46 Mt 21:11
22:2 Mt 13:24
22:4 Mt 21:36
22:5 Heb 2:3
22:7 Lk 19:27
22:10 Mt 13:47–48
22:12 Mt 20:13
22:13 Mt 8:12
22:14 Rev 17:14

. . . .

22:15 Mk 12:13–17
22:16 Mk 3:6
22:17 Lk 2:1
22:18 Jn 8:6
22:21 Ro 13:7
22:22 Mk 12:12
22:23 Mt 3:7
22:29 Jn 20:9
22:31 Mt 21:16
22:32 Ex 3:6
22:35 Lk 7:30
22:37 Dt 6:5

The Question of Paying Taxes
Mk 12:13–17; Lk 20:20–26

15 Then the Pharisees went and took counsel to entangle Him in His words. 16 They sent their disciples to Him with the Herodians, saying, "Teacher, we know that You are truthful and teach the way of God truthfully, and are swayed by no one. For You do not regard the person of men. 17 Tell us then, what do You think? Is it lawful to pay taxes to Caesar, or not?"

18 But Jesus perceived their wickedness and said, "Why test Me, you hypocrites? 19 Show Me the tax money." They brought Him a denarius. 20 He said to them, "Whose is this image and inscription?"

21 They said to Him, "Caesar's."

Then He said to them, "Render therefore to Caesar the things that are Caesar's, and to God the things that are God's."

22 When they heard these words, they were amazed, and left Him and went on their way.

The Question About the Resurrection
Mk 12:18–27; Lk 20:27–40

23 The same day the Sadducees, who say that there is no resurrection, came to Him and asked Him, 24 "Teacher, Moses said, 'If a man dies having no children, his brother must marry his wife and raise up children for his brother.'[2] 25 Now there were seven brothers with us. The first died after he married and, having no children, left his wife to his brother. 26 Likewise the second and third, on to the seventh. 27 Last of all, the woman died also. 28 Therefore, in the resurrection, whose wife shall she be of the seven? For they all had her."

29 Jesus answered, "You err, not knowing the Scriptures nor the power of God. 30 For in the resurrection they neither marry nor are given in marriage, but are like the angels of God in heaven. 31 But concerning the resurrection of the dead, have you not read what was spoken to you by God, 32 'I am the God of Abraham, the God of Isaac, and the God of Jacob'[3]? God is not the God of the dead, but of the living."

33 When the crowds heard this, they were astonished at His teaching.

The Great Commandment
Mk 12:28–34; Lk 10:25–28

34 When the Pharisees heard that He silenced the Sadducees, they came together. 35 One of them, who was a lawyer, tested Him by asking Him, 36 "Teacher, which is the greatest commandment in the law?"

37 Jesus said to him, " 'You shall love the Lord your God with all your heart, and with all your soul, and with all your mind.'[4] 38 This is the first

[1] *42* Ps 118:22–23. [2] *24* Dt 25:5. [3] *32* Ex 3:6. [4] *37* Dt 6:5.

and great commandment. 39 And the second is like it: 'You shall love your neighbor as yourself.'[1] 40 On these two commandments hang all the Law and the Prophets."

The Question About David's Son

Mk 12:35–37; Lk 20:41–44

41 While the Pharisees were assembled, Jesus asked them, 42 "What do you think of the Christ? Whose Son is He?"

They said to Him, "The Son of David."

43 He said to them, "How then does David in the Spirit call Him 'Lord,' saying:

44 'The Lord said to my Lord,
"Sit at My right hand,
until I make Your enemies
Your footstool" '?[2]

45 If David then calls Him 'Lord,' how is He his Son?" 46 No one was able to answer Him a word, nor from that day on did anyone dare to ask Him any more questions.

The Denouncing of the Scribes and Pharisees

Mk 12:38–40; Lk 11:37–52; 20:45–47

23 Then Jesus said to the crowds and to His disciples, 2 "The scribes and the Pharisees sit in Moses' seat. 3 Therefore, whatever they tell you to observe, that observe and do, but do not do their works. For they speak, but do nothing. 4 They fasten heavy loads that are hard to carry and lay them on men's shoulders, but they themselves will not move them with their finger.

5 "They do all their works to be seen by men. They make their Scripture boxes broad and lengthen the tassels on their prayer shawls. 6 They love the places of honor at feasts, and the prominent seats in the synagogues, 7 and greetings in the marketplaces, and being called 'Rabbi' by men.

8 "But do not be called 'Rabbi,' for you have one Teacher, the Christ, and you are all brothers. 9 And call no man on earth your father, for you have one Father, who is in heaven. 10 Nor be called teachers, for you have one Teacher, the Christ. 11 He who is greatest among you shall be your servant. 12 For he who exalts himself will be humbled, and he who humbles himself will be exalted.

13 "Woe to you, scribes and Pharisees, hypocrites! You shut the kingdom of heaven against men. For you neither enter yourselves, nor allow those who are entering to go in. 14 Woe to you, scribes and Pharisees, hypocrites! You devour widows' houses and for pretense make long prayers. Therefore you will receive the greater condemnation.

15 "Woe to you, scribes and Pharisees, hypocrites! You travel sea and land to make one proselyte, and when he becomes one, you make him twice as much a son of hell as yourselves.

16 "Woe to you, blind guides, who say, 'If anyone swears by the temple, it is nothing. But if anyone swears by the gold of the temple, he is obligated.' 17 You blind fools! Which is greater, the gold or the temple that sanctifies the gold? 18 And you say, 'If anyone swears by the altar, it is nothing. But if anyone swears by the gift on it, he is obligated.' 19 You blind fools! Which is greater, the gift or the altar that sanctifies the gift? 20 Therefore he who swears by the altar, swears by it and by all things on it. 21 But he who swears by the temple, swears by it and by Him who dwells in it. 22 And he who swears by heaven, swears by the throne of God and by Him who sits on it.

23 "Woe to you, scribes and Pharisees, hypocrites! You tithe the mint and dill and cumin, but have neglected the weightier matters of the law: justice and mercy and faith. These you ought to have done without leaving the others undone. 24 You blind guides who strain out a gnat and swallow a camel!

25 "Woe to you, scribes and Pharisees, hypocrites! You cleanse the outside of the cup and dish, but inside they are full of extortion and greed. 26 You blind Pharisee, first cleanse the inside of the cup and dish, that the outside of them may also be clean.

27 "Woe to you, scribes and Pharisees, hypocrites! You are like whitewashed tombs, which indeed appear beautiful outwardly, but inside are full of dead men's bones and of all uncleanness. 28 So you also outwardly appear righteous to men, but inside you are full of hypocrisy and iniquity.

29 "Woe to you, scribes and Pharisees, hypocrites! You build the tombs of the prophets, and adorn the memorials of the righteous, 30 and say, 'If we lived in the days of our fathers, we would not have partaken with them in shedding the blood of the prophets.' 31 Therefore you are witnesses against yourselves that you are sons of those who murdered the prophets. 32 Fill up, then, the measure of your fathers' *guilt.*

33 "You serpents! You generation of vipers! How can you escape the judgment of hell? 34 Therefore I send you prophets, and wise men, and scribes. Some of them you will kill and crucify, and some you will scourge in your synagogues and persecute them from city to city, 35 that on you may come all the righteous blood shed on the earth, from the blood of righteous Abel to the blood of Zechariah son

22:39 Lev 19:18
22:40 Mt 7:12
22:41 Mk 12:35–37
22:42 Mt 1:1
22:43 2Sa 23:2
22:44 Ps 110:1
22:45 Ro 1:3–4
22:46 Mk 12:34
23:4 Lk 11:46
23:5 Dt 6:8
23:7 Jn 1:38
23:8 Jas 3:1
23:9 Mal 1:6
23:12 Lk 14:11
23:13 Lk 11:52
23:15 Ac 13:43
23:16 Mt 15:14
23:17 Mt 23:19
23:19 Ex 29:37
23:21 1Ki 8:13
23:22 Mt 5:34
23:23 Lk 11:42
23:24 Mt 19:24
23:27 Lk 11:44
23:28 Mt 23:5
23:29 Lk 11:47–48
23:31 Ac 7:51–52
23:32 Ge 15:16
23:33 Mt 3:7
23:34 Mt 10:16–17
23:35 Ge 4:8

[1] *39* Lev 19:18. [2] *44* Ps 110:1.

Under His Wings

When you picture a magnificent flying bird, it is usually not a chicken that comes to mind. I've never seen a chicken portrayed in flight—many eagles, but no chickens. We quote the scripture from Isaiah 40:31 that talks about being borne up on the wings of eagles or with wings like eagles.

There is a difference, however, between being on His wings and being *under* His wings. The promise of Psalm 91:4 does not elaborate on the *flying* wing but on the *sheltering* wing. One indicates strength and accomplishment, while the other denotes protection and familiarity. When you imagine the warmth of a nest and the security of being under the wings of the nurturing love of a mother hen with chicks, it paints a vivid picture of the sheltering wing of God's protection that the psalmist refers to in this passage.

The Lord gave me a vivid picture of what it means to seek refuge under His wings. My husband, Jack, and I live out in the country, and one spring our old mother hen hatched a brood of baby chickens. One afternoon, when they were scattered all over the yard, I suddenly saw the shadow of a hawk overhead. Then I noticed something that taught me a lesson I will never forget. That mother hen did not run to those little chicks and jump on top of them to try to cover them with her wings. No!

Instead she squatted down, spread out her wings, and began to cluck. And those little chickens, from every direction, came running *to her* to get under those outstretched wings. Then the hen pulled her wings down tight, tucking every little chick safely under her. To get to those babies, the hawk would have to go through the mother.

When I think of those baby chicks running to their mother, I realize it is under His wings that we seek refuge—but we have to run to Him. It is up to us! All that mother hen did was cluck and expand her wings to tell her chicks where to come.

These verses in Matthew show the maternal, hovering side to His protection:

> Jerusalem, Jerusalem...how often I would have gathered your children together as a hen gathers her chicks under her wings, but you would not!
>
> —Matthew 23:37

Notice the contrast between God's willingness and our unwillingness, His wanting against our *not willing to,* His *would* against our *would not.* What an amazing analogy to show us that He offers protection we don't accept!

Peggy Joyce Ruth

of Berekiah, whom you murdered between the temple and the altar. 36 Truly I say to you, all these things will come on this generation.

The Lament Over Jerusalem
Lk 13:34–35

37 "O Jerusalem, Jerusalem, you who kill the prophets and stone those who are sent to you, how often I would have gathered your children together as a hen gathers her chicks under her wings, but you would not! 38 Look, your house is left to you desolate. 39 For I tell you, you shall not see Me again until you say, 'Blessed is He who comes in the name of the Lord.'[1]"

The Destruction of the Temple Foretold
Mk 13:1–2; Lk 21:5–6

24 Jesus departed from the temple and was leaving when His disciples came to show Him the temple buildings. 2 Jesus answered them, "Do you not see all these things? Truly I say to you, not one stone shall be left here upon another that shall not be thrown down."

Troubles and Persecutions
Mk 13:3–13; Lk 21:7–19

3 As He sat on the Mount of Olives, the disciples came to Him privately, saying, "Tell us, when will these things be, and what will be the sign of Your coming and of the end of the age?"

4 Jesus answered them, "Take heed that no one deceives you. 5 For many will come in My name, saying, 'I am the Christ,' and will deceive many. 6 You will hear of wars and rumors of wars. See that you are not troubled. For all these things must happen, but the end is not yet. 7 For nation will rise against nation, and kingdom against kingdom. There will be famines, epidemics, and earthquakes in various places. 8 All these are the beginning of sorrows.

9 "Then they will hand you over to be persecuted and will kill you. And you will be hated by all nations for My name's sake. 10 Then many will fall away, and betray one another, and hate one another. 11 And many false prophets will rise and will deceive many. 12 Because iniquity will abound, the love of many will grow cold. 13 But he who endures to the end shall be saved. 14 And this gospel of the kingdom will be preached throughout the world as a testimony to all nations, and then the end will come.

The Great Tribulation
Mk 13:14–23; Lk 21:20–24

15 "So when you see the 'abomination of desolation,'[2] spoken of by Daniel the prophet, standing in the holy place (let the reader understand), 16 then let those who are in Judea flee to the mountains. 17 Let him who is on the housetop not go down to take anything out of his house. 18 Let him who is in the field not return to take his clothes. 19 Woe to those who are with child and to those who nurse in those days! 20 Pray that your escape will not be in the winter or on the Sabbath. 21 For then will be great tribulation, such as has not happened since the beginning of the world until now, no, nor ever shall be.

22 "Unless those days were shortened, no one would be saved. But for the sake of the elect those days will be shortened. 23 Then if anyone says to you, 'Look, here is the Christ,' or 'There He is,' do not believe it. 24 For false christs and false prophets will arise and show great signs and wonders to deceive, if possible, even the elect. 25 Listen, I have told you beforehand.

26 "So, if they say to you, 'Look, He is in the desert,' do not go there; or, 'Look, He is in the private chambers,' do not believe it. 27 For as the lightning comes from the east and flashes to the west, so will be the coming of the Son of Man. 28 Wherever the carcass is, there the eagles will be gathered together.

The Coming of the Son of Man
Mk 13:24–27; Lk 21:25–28

29 "Immediately after the tribulation of those days,

'the sun will be darkened,
  the moon will not give its light;
the stars will fall from heaven,
  and the powers of the heavens will be
   shaken.'[3]

30 "Then the sign of the Son of Man will appear in heaven, and then all the tribes of the earth will mourn, and they will see the Son of Man coming on the clouds of heaven with power and great glory. 31 And He will send His angels with a great sound of a trumpet, and they shall gather His elect from the four winds, from one end of the heavens to the other.

The Lesson of the Fig Tree
Mk 13:28–31; Lk 21:29–33

32 "Now learn this lesson from the fig tree: When its branch becomes tender and grows leaves, you know that summer is near. 33 So also, when you shall see all these things, you know that it is near, even at the doors. 34 Truly I say to you, this generation will not pass away until all these things take place. 35 Heaven and earth will pass away, but My words will never pass away.

23:36 Mt 24:34
23:37 Ru 2:12
23:38 Jer 22:5
23:39 Ps 118:26
24:2 Lk 19:44
24:3 Mt 21:1
24:4 Jer 29:8
24:5 Mt 24:11
24:6 2Th 2:2
24:7 Isa 19:2
24:9 Jn 16:2
24:11 Mt 7:15
24:13 Mt 10:22
24:14 Ro 10:18
24:15 Da 9:27
24:17 Mt 10:27
24:21 Da 12:1
24:23 Lk 21:8
24:24 Mt 24:11
24:26 Ac 21:38
24:28 Lk 17:37
24:29 Isa 13:10
24:30 Rev 1:7
24:31 Mt 13:41
24:33 Jas 5:9
24:34 Mt 16:28
24:35 Mt 5:18

[1] *39* Ps 118:26. [2] *15* Da 9:27. [3] *29* Joel 2:10.

The Unknown Day and Hour
Mk 13:32–37; Lk 17:26–30, 34–36

36 “Concerning that day and hour no one
knows, not even the angels of heaven, but My
Father only. 37 As were the days of Noah, so will
be the coming of the Son of Man. 38 For as in
the days before the flood, they were eating and
drinking, marrying and giving in marriage,
until the day Noah entered the ark, 39 and did
not know until the flood came and took them
all away, so will be the coming of the Son of
Man. 40 Two will be in the field; one will be
taken, and the other left. 41 Two women will
be grinding at the mill; one will be taken, and
the other left.

42 “Watch therefore, for you do not know
what hour your Lord will come. 43 But know
this, that if the owner of the house had known
what hour the thief would come, he would
have watched and not have let his house be
broken into. 44 Therefore you also must be
ready, for in an hour when you least expect,
the Son of Man is coming.

The Faithful or the Unfaithful Servant
Lk 12:41–48

45 “Who then is a faithful and wise servant,
whom his master has made ruler over his
household to give them food at the appointed
time? 46 Blessed is that servant whom his mas-
ter will find so doing when he comes. 47 Truly,
I say to you that he will make him ruler over
all his goods. 48 But if that evil servant says in
his heart, ‘My master delays his coming,’ 49 and
begins to strike his fellow servants and eat and
drink with the drunkards, 50 the master of that
servant will come on a day when he does not
look for him and in an hour he is not aware of
51 and will cut him in pieces and appoint him
his portion with the hypocrites, where there
shall be weeping and gnashing of teeth.

The Parable of the Ten Virgins

25 “Then the kingdom of heaven shall be
like ten virgins, who took their lamps
and went out to meet the bridegroom. 2 Five of
them were wise and five were foolish. 3 Those
who were foolish took their lamps, but took
no oil with them. 4 But the wise took jars of
oil with their lamps. 5 While the bridegroom
delayed, they all rested and slept.

6 “But at midnight there was a cry, ‘Look, the
bridegroom is coming! Come out to meet him!’

7 “Then all those virgins rose and trimmed
their lamps. 8 But the foolish said to the wise,
‘Give us some of your oil, for our lamps have
gone out.’

9 “The wise answered, ‘No, lest there not be
enough for us and you. Go rather to those who
sell it, and buy some for yourselves.’

24:36 Ac 1:7
24:37 Lk 17:26–27
24:38 Mt 22:30
24:39 Mt 24:37
24:41 Ex 11:5
24:42 Mt 25:13
24:43 Lk 12:39
24:44 Mt 25:10
24:45 Mt 25:21
24:46 Rev 16:15
24:47 Mt 25:21
24:51 Mt 8:12
25:1 Mt 13:24
25:7 Lk 12:35
25:8 Lk 12:35
. . . .
25:10 Lk 13:25
25:11 Mt 7:21–23
25:12 2Ti 2:19
25:13 Mt 24:42–44
25:14 Mt 21:33
25:15 Mt 18:24
25:19 Mt 25:5
25:21 Mt 24:47
25:23 Mt 25:21
25:26 Mt 18:32

10 “But while they went to buy some, the
bridegroom came, and those who were ready
went in with him to the wedding banquet. And
the door was shut.

11 “Afterward, the other virgins came also,
saying, ‘Lord, Lord, open the door for us.’

12 “But he answered, ‘Truly I say to you, I do
not know you.’

13 “Watch therefore, for you know neither the
day nor the hour in which the Son of Man is
coming.

The Parable of the Talents
Lk 19:11–27

14 “Again, the kingdom of heaven is like a
man traveling into a far country, who called
his own servants and entrusted his goods to
them. 15 To one he gave five talents,[1] to another
two, and to another one, to every man accord-
ing to his ability. And immediately he took his
journey. 16 He who had received the five talents
went and traded with them and made another
five talents. 17 So also, he who had received two
gained another two. 18 But he who had received
one went and dug in the ground and hid his
master’s money.

19 “After a long time the master of those ser-
vants came and settled accounts with them.
20 He who had received five talents came and
brought the other five talents, saying, ‘Master,
you entrusted to me five talents. Look, I have
gained five talents more.’

21 “His master said to him, ‘Well done, you
good and faithful servant. You have been faith-
ful over a few things. I will make you ruler over
many things. Enter the joy of your master.’

22 “He who had received two talents also
came and said, ‘Master, you entrusted me
with two talents. See, I have gained two more
talents besides them.’

23 “His master said to him, ‘Well done, you
good and faithful servant. You have been faith-
ful over a few things. I will make you ruler over
many things. Enter the joy of your master.’

24 “Then he who had received the one talent
came and said, ‘Master, I knew that you are a
hard man, reaping where you did not sow, and
gathering where you did not winnow. 25 So I
was afraid, and went and hid your talent in the
ground. Here you have what is yours.’

26 “His master answered, ‘You wicked and
slothful servant! You knew that I reap where
I have not sown, and gather where I have not
winnowed. 27 Then you ought to have given
my money to the bankers, and at my coming I
should have received what was my own with
interest.

[1] *15* A talent was worth several hundred pounds.

28 “ ‘So take the talent from him, and give
it to him who has ten talents. 29 For to every-
one who has will more be given, and he will
have an abundance. But from him who has
nothing, even what he has will be taken away.
30 And throw the unprofitable servant into out-
er darkness, where there will be weeping and
gnashing of teeth.’

The Judgment of the Nations

31 “When the Son of Man comes in His glory,
and all the holy angels with Him, then He will
sit on the throne of His glory. 32 Before Him
will be gathered all nations, and He will sep-
arate them one from another as a shepherd
separates his sheep from the goats. 33 He will
set the sheep at His right hand, but the goats
at the left.

34 “Then the King will say to those at His right
hand, ‘Come, you blessed of My Father, inherit
the kingdom prepared for you since the foun-
dation of the world. 35 For I was hungry and
you gave Me food, I was thirsty and you gave
Me drink, I was a stranger and you took Me
in. 36 I was naked and you clothed Me, I was
sick and you visited Me, I was in prison and
you came to Me.’

37 “Then the righteous will answer Him,
‘Lord, when did we see You hungry and feed
You, or thirsty and give You drink? 38 When
did we see You a stranger and take You in, or
naked and clothe You? 39 And when did we see
You sick or in prison and come to You?’

40 “The King will answer, ‘Truly I say to you,
as you have done it for one of the least of these
brothers of Mine, you have done it for Me.’

41 “Then He will say to those at the left hand,
‘Depart from Me, you cursed, into the eternal
fire, prepared for the devil and his angels.
42 For I was hungry and you gave Me no food,
I was thirsty and you gave Me no drink, 43 I was
a stranger and you did not take Me in, I was
naked and you did not clothe Me, I was sick
and in prison and you did not visit Me.’

44 “Then they also will answer Him, ‘Lord,
when did we see You hungry or thirsty or a
stranger or naked or sick or in prison, and did
not serve You?’

45 “He will answer, ‘Truly I say to you, as you
did it not for one of the least of these, you did
it not for Me.’

46 “And they will go away into eternal pun-
ishment, but the righteous into eternal life.”

The Plot to Kill Jesus
Mk 14:1–2; Lk 22:1–2; Jn 11:45–53

26 When Jesus had finished all these say-
ings, He said to His disciples, 2 “You
know that after two days is the Passover, and
the Son of Man will be betrayed to be cruci-
fied.”

3 Then the chief priests, the scribes, and the
elders of the people gathered in the palace
of the high priest, who was called Caiaphas,
4 and took counsel that they might take Jesus
covertly and kill Him. 5 But they said, “Not on
the feast day, lest there be an uproar among
the people.”

The Anointing at Bethany
Mk 14:3–9; Jn 12:1–8

6 When Jesus was in Bethany in the house of
Simon the leper, 7 a woman came to Him hav-
ing an alabaster jar of very expensive ointment
and poured it on His head as He sat at supper.

8 When His disciples saw it, they were indig-
nant, saying, “For what purpose is this waste?
9 This ointment might have been sold for a
large sum and given to the poor.”

10 When Jesus perceived it, He said to them,
“Why do you trouble the woman? She has
done a good work for Me. 11 For you have the
poor always with you, but you do not always
have Me. 12 In pouring this ointment on My
body, she did it for My burial. 13 Truly I say to
you, wherever this gospel shall be preached in
the whole world, what this woman has done
will be told in memory of her.”

Judas’ Agreement to Betray Jesus
Mk 14:10–11; Lk 22:3–6

14 Then one of the twelve, who was called Ju-
das Iscariot, went to the chief priests 15 and said
to them, “What will you give me if I hand Him
over to you?” And they paid him thirty pieces
of silver. 16 From that moment he searched for
an opportunity to betray Him.

The Passover With the Disciples
Mk 14:12–21; Lk 22:7–14, 21–23; Jn 13:21–30

17 On the first day of the Feast of Unleav-
ened Bread the disciples came to Jesus, saying,
“Where will You have us to prepare for You to
eat the Passover?”

18 He said, “Go into the city to a certain man,
and say to him, ‘The Teacher says, My time
is at hand. I will keep the Passover at your
house with My disciples.’ ” 19 The disciples did
as Jesus had directed them, and they prepared
the Passover.

20 When evening came, He sat down with
the twelve. 21 And as they were eating, He said,
“Truly I say to you, one of you will betray Me.”

22 They were very sorrowful, and each of
them began saying to Him, “Lord, is it I?”

23 He answered and said, “He who has dipped
his hand with Me in the dish will betray Me.
24 The Son of Man goes as it is written of Him,
but woe to that man by whom the Son of Man

25:29 Mt 13:12
25:30 Mt 8:12
25:31 Mt 16:27
25:32 Mt 13:49
25:33 Ps 45:9
25:34 Jas 2:5
25:35 Eze 18:7
25:36 Jas 1:27
25:40 Mt 10:42
25:41 Mt 7:23
25:46 Jn 5:29
26:2 Mk 14:1–2
26:3 Jn 18:24
26:5 Mt 27:24
26:6 Mt 21:17
26:11 Dt 15:11
26:14 Mt 10:4
26:15 Ex 21:32
26:17 Ex 12:18–20
26:18 Jn 7:6
26:20 Mk 14:17–21
26:21 Jn 13:21
26:23 Jn 13:18
26:24 Mk 9:12

is betrayed! It would have been good for that
man if he had not been born."
25 Then Judas, who betrayed Him, answered,
"Master, is it I?"
He said to him, "You have said it."

The Lord's Supper
Mk 14:22–26; Lk 22:15–20; 1Co 11:23–25

26 As they were eating, Jesus took bread,
blessed it and broke it, and gave it to the disci-
ples and said, "Take and eat. This is My body."
27 Then He took the cup, and after He gave
thanks, He gave it to them, saying, "Drink of
it, all of you. 28 For this is My blood of the new
covenant, which is shed for many for the re-
mission of sins. 29 I say to you, I will not drink
of this fruit of the vine from now on until that
day when I drink it new with you in My Fa-
ther's kingdom."
30 And when they had sung a hymn, they
went out to the Mount of Olives.

Peter's Denial Foretold
Mk 14:27–31; Lk 22:31–34; Jn 13:36–38

31 Then Jesus said to them, "All of you will
fall away on account of Me this night, for it
is written:

'I will strike the shepherd,
and the sheep of the flock shall be
scattered.'[1]

32 But after I have risen, I will go before you
to Galilee."
33 Peter answered, "Though all men will fall
away on account of You, yet I will never
fall away."
34 Jesus said to him, "Truly I say to you, this
night, before the rooster crows, you will deny
Me three times."
35 Peter said to Him, "Though I should die
with You, yet I will not deny You." And all the
disciples spoke in this manner.

The Prayer in Gethsemane
Mk 14:32–42; Lk 22:39–46

36 Then Jesus came with them to a place
called Gethsemane and said to the disciples,
"Sit here while I go and pray close by." 37 He
took with Him Peter and the two sons of Zebe-
dee and began to be sorrowful and troubled.
38 Then He said to them, "My soul is very sor-
rowful, even to death. Wait here, and keep
watch with Me."
39 He went a little farther, and falling on His
face, He prayed, "O My Father, if it is possible,
let this cup pass from Me. Nevertheless, not as
I will, but as You will."
40 Then He came to the disciples and found
them sleeping, and said to Peter, "So, could you
not keep watch with Me one hour? 41 Watch and

26:25 Mt 26:64
26:26 Mt 14:19
26:28 Mt 20:28
26:31 Zec 13:7
26:32 Mt 28:10
26:33 Lk 22:33
26:34 Jn 13:38
26:35 Jn 13:37
26:37 Mt 4:21
26:38 Jn 12:27
26:39 Mt 20:22
26:41 Mt 6:13
26:42 Mt 26:39
26:43 Lk 9:32
26:44 2Co 12:8
26:45 Jn 13:1
26:49 Mt 26:25

SPIRITLED WOMAN

COUNSEL FROM THE SPIRIT BASICS

Your Most Fruitful Investment

Prayer will be your most fruitful investment in your marriage. Prayerlessness will cause weakness and spiritual parasites to eat away at your relationship. Communicate in the spirit with your Abba Father. Allow the Holy Spirit to be your friend and your teacher. The practice of prayer must be a requirement for every Christian home. Without it, all the windows and doors are open for the thief to come in. "Watch and pray that you enter not into temptation," Jesus said. "The spirit indeed is willing, but the flesh is weak" (Mt 26:41).

Your personal growth depends on prayer. A healthy body needs food, and a healthy spirit needs prayer. In God's presence the battles are won. Prayer creates in us a thankful spirit, and a thankful spirit brings joy into a marriage.

Iris Delgado

pray that you enter not into temptation. The
spirit indeed is willing, but the flesh is weak."
42 He went away a second time and prayed,
"O My Father, if this cup cannot pass away
from Me unless I drink it, Your will be done."
43 Again, He came and found them sleeping,
for their eyes were heavy. 44 So leaving them
again, He went away and prayed the third
time, saying the same words.
45 Then He came to His disciples and said to
them, "Sleep on now, and take your rest. Look,
the hour is near, and the Son of Man is be-
trayed into the hands of sinners. 46 Rise, let us
be going. Look, he who betrays Me is at hand."

The Betrayal and Arrest of Jesus
Mk 14:43–50; Lk 22:47–53; Jn 18:3–12

47 While He was still speaking, Judas, one of
the twelve, came. And with him was a great
crowd with swords and clubs, from the chief
priests and elders of the people. 48 Now he who
betrayed Him had given them a sign, saying,
"Whomever I shall kiss is the Man. Seize Him."
49 He immediately came to Jesus and said,
"Hail, Rabbi!" and kissed Him.

[1] *31* Zec 13:7.

50 And Jesus said to him, "Friend, why have
you come?"
Then they came and laid hands on Jesus and
took Him. 51 Immediately, one of those who
were with Jesus stretched out his hand, and
drew his sword, and struck the servant of the
high priest, and cut off his ear.
52 Then Jesus said to him, "Put your sword
back in its place. For all those who take up the
sword will perish by the sword. 53 Do you think
that I cannot now pray to My Father, and He
will at once give Me more than twelve legions
of angels? 54 But how then would the Scrip-
tures be fulfilled, that it must be so?"
55 At that same moment Jesus said to the
crowds, "Have you come out as against a thief
to take Me with swords and clubs? Daily I sat
with you in the temple teaching, and you did
not seize Me. 56 But all this was done that the
Scriptures of the prophets might be fulfilled."
Then all the disciples forsook Him and fled.

Jesus Before the Sanhedrin

Mk 14:53–65; Lk 22:54–55, 63–71; Jn 18:13–14, 19–24

57 Those who had seized Jesus led Him away
to Caiaphas the high priest, where the scribes
and the elders had assembled. 58 But Peter fol-
lowed Him from afar to the high priest's court-
yard and went in, and sat with the servants to
see the end.
59 The chief priests and the elders and the
entire Sanhedrin searched for false witness
against Jesus to put Him to death, 60 but they
found none. Yes, though many false witnesses
came forward, they found none.
At last two false witnesses came forward
61 and said, "This fellow said, 'I am able to
destroy the temple of God and to build it in
three days.' "
62 Then the high priest stood up and said
to Him, "Do You answer nothing? What is it
these men testify against You?" 63 But Jesus
remained silent.
The high priest said to Him, "I adjure You
by the living God, tell us whether You are the
Christ, the Son of God."
64 Jesus said to him, "You have said so. But
I say to you, hereafter you will see the Son of
Man seated at the right hand of Power and
coming on the clouds of heaven."
65 Then the high priest tore his clothes, say-
ing, "He has uttered blasphemy. What further
need do we have for witnesses? See, now you
have heard His blasphemy. 66 What do you
think?"
They answered, "He is guilty unto death."
67 Then they spat in His face and struck Him.
And others slapped Him with the palms of
their hands, 68 saying, "Prophesy to us, You
Christ! Who is it that struck You?"

Peter's Denial of Jesus

Mk 14:66–72; Lk 22:56–62; Jn 18:15–18, 25–27

69 Now Peter sat outside in the courtyard. And
a girl came to him, saying, "You also were with
Jesus of Galilee."
70 But he denied it before them all, saying, "I
do not know what you are saying."
71 Then when he went out onto the porch,
another girl saw him and said to those who
were there, "This man was also with Jesus of
Nazareth."
72 Again he denied with an oath, "I do not
know the Man."
73 After a while those who stood by came to
Peter and said, "Surely you also are one of
them, for your accent betrays you."
74 Then he began to invoke a curse on himself
and he swore, "I do not know the Man."
Then immediately a rooster crowed. 75 Then
Peter remembered the word Jesus had spoken,
"Before a rooster crows, you will deny Me three
times." Then he went out and wept bitterly.

Jesus Brought Before Pilate

Mk 15:1; Lk 23:1–2; Jn 18:28–32

27 When the morning came, all the chief
priests and elders of the people took
counsel against Jesus to put Him to death.
2 When they had bound Him, they led Him
away and handed Him over to Pontius Pilate
the governor.

The Death of Judas

Ac 1:18–19

3 When Judas, who had betrayed Him, saw
that He was condemned, he repented and
brought back the thirty pieces of silver to
the chief priests and elders, 4 saying, "I have
sinned in that I have betrayed innocent blood."
They said, "What is that to us? You must see
to that."
5 So he threw down the pieces of silver in
the temple and departed. And he went and
hanged himself.
6 The chief priests took the silver pieces and
said, "It is not lawful to put them into the trea-
sury, because this is the price of blood." 7 So
they took counsel, and bought with them the
potter's field to bury strangers in. 8 Therefore
that field has been called the Field of Blood to
this day. 9 Then what was spoken by Jeremiah
the prophet was fulfilled: "They took the thirty
pieces of silver, the value of that the sons of
Israel set on Him, 10 and gave them for the
potter's field, as the Lord appointed me."[1]

26:50 Mt 20:13
26:51 Mk 14:47
26:52 Ge 9:6
26:53 Mt 4:11
26:54 Mt 26:24
26:55 Mk 12:35
26:57 Mt 26:3
26:58 Jn 7:32
26:60 Dt 19:15
26:61 Mt 27:40
26:63 Lev 5:1
26:64 Ps 110:1
26:66 Jn 19:7

26:67 Isa 50:6
26:69 Mt 26:71
26:73 Jdg 12:6
26:75 Mt 26:34
27:1 Mk 15:1
27:2 Mt 20:19
27:8 Ac 1:19
27:9 Zec 11:12–13

[1] *9–10* Zec 11:12–13; Jer 32:6–9.

Jesus Questioned by Pilate
Mk 15:2–5; Lk 23:3–5; Jn 18:33–38

11 Jesus stood before the governor. And the
governor asked Him, "Are You the King of the
Jews?"
Jesus said to him, "You have said so."
12 When He was accused by the chief priests
and elders, He gave no answer. 13 Then Pilate
said to Him, "Do You not hear how many
things they testify against You?" 14 But He nev-
er answered him a word, so that the governor
was greatly amazed.

Jesus Sentenced to Die
Mk 15:6–15; Lk 23:13–25; Jn 18:39–19:16

15 Now at the feast, the governor was accus-
tomed to releasing to the people a prisoner
whom they chose. 16 They had then a notorious
prisoner called Barabbas. 17 So when they had
gathered together, Pilate said to them, "Whom
do you want me to release to you—Barabbas,
or Jesus who is called Christ?" 18 For he knew
that they had handed Him over out of envy.
19 When he was sitting on the judgment seat,
his wife sent word to him, "Have nothing to do
with that righteous Man, for I have suffered
much today in a dream on account of Him."
20 But the chief priests and elders persuaded
the crowd to ask for Barabbas and kill Jesus.
21 The governor answered, "Which of the two
do you want me to release to you?"
They said, "Barabbas."
22 Pilate said to them, "Then what shall I do
with Jesus who is called Christ?"
They all said to him, "Let Him be crucified!"
23 The governor said, "Why, what evil has He
done?"
But they cried out all the more, "Let Him be
crucified!"
24 When Pilate saw that he could not prevail,
but rather that unrest was beginning, he took
water and washed his hands before the crowd,
saying, "I am innocent of the blood of this righ-
teous Man. See to it yourselves."
25 Then all the people answered, "His blood
be on us and on our children!"
26 Then he released Barabbas to them. But
when he had scourged Jesus, he handed Him
over to be crucified.

The Soldiers Mock Jesus
Mk 15:16–20; Jn 19:2–3

27 Then the soldiers of the governor took
Jesus into the Praetorium, and gathered the
whole detachment of soldiers before Him.
28 They stripped Him and put a scarlet robe on
Him, 29 and when they wove a crown of thorns,
they put it on His head and put a staff in His
right hand. They knelt before Him and mocked
Him, saying, "Hail, King of the Jews!" 30 They
spit on Him, and took the staff and hit Him on
the head. 31 After they had mocked Him, they
took the robe off Him, put His own garments
on Him, and led Him away to crucify Him.

The Crucifixion
Mk 15:21–32; Lk 23:26–43; Jn 19:17–27

32 As they came out, they found a man of
Cyrene, Simon by name. This man they com-
pelled to bear His cross. 33 When they came
to a place called Golgotha, which means
The Place of the Skull, 34 they gave Him sour
wine mingled with gall to drink. But when He
tasted it, He would not drink it. 35 When they
crucified Him, they divided His garments by
casting lots to fulfill what was spoken by the
prophet, "They divided My garments among
themselves and for My clothing they cast lots."[1]
36 And sitting down, they kept watch over Him
there. 37 They put His accusation over His head,
which read:

THIS IS JESUS THE KING OF THE JEWS.

38 Then two thieves were crucified with
Him, one on the right and another on the left.
39 Those who passed by insulted Him, wag-
ging their heads, 40 saying, "You who would
destroy the temple and build it in three days,
save Yourself! If You are the Son of God, come
down from the cross." 41 Likewise the chief
priests, with the scribes and elders, mocked
Him, saying, 42 "He saved others. He cannot
save Himself. If He is the King of Israel, let
Him now come down from the cross, and we
will believe Him. 43 He trusted in God. Let Him
deliver Him now, if He will have Him. For He
said, 'I am the Son of God.'" 44 Even the thieves
who were crucified with Him insulted Him in
the same way.

The Death of Jesus
Mk 15:33–41; Lk 23:44–49; Jn 19:28–30

45 Now from the sixth hour until the ninth
hour there was darkness over all the land.
46 About the ninth hour Jesus cried out with a
loud voice, "*Eli, Eli, lama sabachthani?*" which
means, "My God, My God, why have You for-
saken Me?"[2]
47 Some of those who stood there heard it and
said, "This Man is calling for Elijah."
48 Immediately one of them ran, took a
sponge, filled it with wine, and put it on a
stick, and gave it to Him to drink. 49 The rest
said, "Leave Him alone. Let us see if Elijah will
come to save Him."
50 And Jesus, when He had cried out again
with a loud voice, released His spirit.
51 At that moment the curtain of the temple
was torn in two, from the top to the bottom.
And the ground shook, and the rocks split

27:12 Mt 26:63
27:13 Mt 26:62
27:18 Pr 27:4
27:19 Mt 27:24
27:24 Mt 27:4
27:25 Jos 2:19
27:26 Jn 19:1
27:27 Jn 18:28
27:30 Mt 26:67

27:31 Isa 53:7
27:32 Mk 15:21
27:34 Ps 69:21
27:35 Ps 22:18
27:36 Mt 27:54
27:37 Mk 15:26
27:38 Isa 53:12
27:39 Ps 109:25
27:40 Mt 26:61
27:42 Jn 1:49
27:43 Ps 22:8
27:46 Ps 22:1
27:48 Ps 69:21
27:50 Jn 19:30
27:51 Mk 15:38

[1] *35* Ps 22:18. [2] *46* Ps 22:1.

apart. 52 The graves also were opened, and many bodies of the saints who had died were raised, 53 and coming out of the graves after His resurrection, they went into the Holy City and appeared to many.

54 When the centurion and those with him, keeping watch over Jesus, saw the earthquake and what took place, they feared greatly and said, "Truly He was the Son of God!"

55 Many women who were there watching from afar followed Jesus from Galilee, serving Him, 56 among whom was Mary Magdalene, and Mary the mother of James and Joseph, and the mother of Zebedee's sons.

The Burial of Jesus

Mk 15:42–47; Lk 23:50–56; Jn 19:38–42

57 When the evening came, there came a rich man of Arimathea, named Joseph, who also was a disciple of Jesus. 58 He went to Pilate and asked for the body of Jesus. Then Pilate commanded the body to be given to him. 59 When Joseph had taken the body, he wrapped it in a clean linen cloth, 60 and laid it in his own new tomb, which he had cut out of the rock. And he rolled a large stone to the door of the tomb and departed. 61 Mary Magdalene and the other Mary were there, sitting opposite the tomb.

The Guard at the Tomb

62 The next day, following the Day of Preparation, the chief priests and Pharisees gathered before Pilate, 63 saying, "Sir, we remember that deceiver saying while He was still alive, 'After three days I will rise.' 64 Therefore command that the tomb be made secure until the third day, lest His disciples come by night and steal Him away, and tell the people, 'He has risen from the dead.' The last deception will be worse than the first."

65 Pilate said to them, "You have a guard. Go your way. Make it as secure as you can." 66 So they went and made the tomb secure by sealing the stone and posting the guard.

The Resurrection

Mk 16:1–8; Lk 24:1–12; Jn 20:1–10

28 At the end of the Sabbath, as it began to dawn on the first day of the week, Mary Magdalene and the other Mary went to see the tomb.

2 And then there was a great earthquake. For the angel of the Lord descended from heaven and came and rolled back the stone from the door and sat on it. 3 His countenance was like lightning, and his garments white as snow. 4 The soldiers shook for fear of him and became like dead men.

5 The angel said to the women, "Do not be afraid. For I know that you are looking for Jesus who was crucified. 6 He is not here. For He has risen, as He said. Come, see the place where the Lord lay. 7 Then go quickly and tell His disciples that He has risen from the dead, and indeed, He is going before you to Galilee. There you will see Him. Listen, I have told you."

8 So they departed quickly from the tomb with fear and great joy, and ran to bring His disciples word. 9 As they went to tell His disciples, suddenly Jesus met them, saying, "Greetings!" They came and took hold of His feet and worshipped Him. 10 Then Jesus said to them, "Do not be afraid. Go tell My brothers to go to Galilee, and there they will see Me."

The Report of the Guard

11 While they were going, indeed, some of the soldiers went into the city and described to the chief priests everything that had happened. 12 When the chief priests were assembled with the elders and had taken counsel, they gave much money to the soldiers, 13 saying, "You are to say, 'His disciples came by night and stole Him away while we were sleeping.' 14 If this comes to the governor's ears, we will satisfy him and keep you secure." 15 So they took the money and did as they were instructed. And this saying has been commonly reported among the Jews to this day.

The Commissioning of the Disciples

Mk 16:14–18; Lk 24:36–49; Jn 20:19–23; Ac 1:6–8

16 Then the eleven disciples went away to Galilee, to the mountain to which Jesus had directed them. 17 When they saw Him, they worshipped Him. But some doubted. 18 Then Jesus came and spoke to them, saying, "All authority has been given to Me in heaven and on earth. 19 Go therefore and make disciples of all nations, baptizing them in the name of the Father and of the Son and of the Holy Spirit, 20 teaching them to observe all things I have commanded you. And remember, I am with you always, even to the end of the age." Amen.

I am to do what Christ commanded His disciples (Mt 28:20).

27:53 Mt 4:5
27:54 Mt 27:36
27:55 Lk 8:2–3
27:56 Jn 19:25
27:57 Jn 19:38–42
27:60 Mt 27:66
27:62 Mk 15:42
27:63 Mt 16:21
27:64 Mt 28:13
27:66 Da 6:17
28:1 Mt 27:56
28:3 Mk 9:3
28:4 Rev 1:17
28:5 Heb 1:14
28:6 Mt 16:21
28:7 Mt 26:32
28:8 Ps 2:11
28:10 Jn 20:17
28:11 Mt 27:65–66
28:14 Mt 27:2
28:15 Mt 27:8
28:16 Mt 28:7
28:17 Mt 28:9
28:18 Mt 11:27
28:19 Mk 16:15–16
28:20 Mt 18:20

Author: The apostle Mark (with the apostle Peter)

Written: Mid- to late-AD 50s, possibly from Rome

Themes: Jesus' Servanthood to the Father, Jesus' Power Over the Demonic Realm

MARK

Dear Spirit Led Woman,

One of my favorite verses from the Book of Mark is Mark 10:27: "With men it is impossible, but not with God. For with God all things are possible." I read this when I need to remember that nothing is too big to believe God for.

If there's a need in your life that you've felt was too big for God to meet, the Book of Mark will build your faith and encourage you that God is more than able to do anything we ask of Him. You can bring His presence into every situation by seeking Him with your whole heart. His presence will change any circumstance in your home, church, workplace, community, region—even our country and the world! Nothing is too big for Him. Spend time in His presence today. Allow your faith to grow, ask Him for bigger and bigger things, and watch with great expectancy to see what He brings to pass!

Joy F. Strang

The Preaching of John the Baptist
Mt 3:1–12; Lk 3:1–9, 15–17; Jn 1:19–28

1 The beginning of the gospel of Jesus Christ, the Son of God. 2 As it is written in the Prophets:

> "Look, I am sending My messenger before
> Your face,
> who will prepare Your way before You."[1]
> 3 "The voice of one crying in the wilderness:
> 'Prepare the way of the Lord,
> make His paths straight.' "[2]

4 John came baptizing in the wilderness and preaching a baptism of repentance for the remission of sins. 5 The whole region of Judea and all the people of Jerusalem went out to him and were all baptized by him in the Jordan River, confessing their sins. 6 John was clothed with camel's hair and with a leather belt around his waist. And he ate locusts and wild honey. 7 He preached saying, "After me is coming One mightier than I, the straps of whose shoes I am not worthy to stoop down and untie. 8 I indeed have baptized you with water, but He will baptize you with the Holy Spirit."

The Baptism of Jesus
Mt 3:13–17; Lk 3:21–22

9 In those days Jesus came from Nazareth in Galilee and was baptized by John in the Jordan. 10 Coming up out of the water, He immediately saw the heavens opened and the Spirit descending on Him like a dove. 11 And a voice came from heaven, saying, "You are My beloved Son in whom I am well pleased."

The Temptation of Jesus
Mt 4:1–11; Lk 4:1–13

12 The Spirit immediately drove Him into the wilderness. 13 And He was there in the wilderness for forty days, tempted by Satan, and was with the wild beasts. And the angels ministered to Him.

The Beginning of the Galilean Ministry
Mt 4:12–17; Lk 4:14–15

14 After John was put in prison, Jesus came to Galilee preaching the gospel of the kingdom of God, 15 saying, "The time is fulfilled, and the kingdom of God is at hand. Repent and believe the gospel."

The Calling of the First Disciples
Mt 4:18–22; Lk 5:1–11

16 As He walked by the Sea of Galilee, He saw Simon and Andrew, his brother, throwing a net into the sea, for they were fishermen. 17 Jesus said to them, "Come, follow Me, and I will make you fishers of men." 18 Immediately they left their nets and followed Him.

[1] 2 Mal 3:1. [2] 3 Isa 40:3.

1:1 Mt 14:33
1:2 Mal 3:1
1:3 Mt 3:3
1:4 Lk 1:77
1:5 Ac 19:18
1:6 Lev 11:22
1:7 Ac 13:25
1:8 Ac 1:5
1:9 Mt 2:23
1:11 Ps 2:7
1:12 Mt 4:1–11
1:14 Mt 4:12
1:15 Gal 4:4
1:16 Mt 4:18–22

1:21 Mt 4:23
1:22 Mt 7:28–29
1:24 Ac 3:14
1:25 Mk 1:34
1:29 Mt 8:14–15
1:30 1Co 9:5
1:31 Ac 9:41
1:32 Mt 8:16
1:34 Mk 3:12
1:37 Jn 12:19
1:39 Mt 4:23

19 When He had gone a little farther from there, He saw James the son of Zebedee and John, his brother, who also were in the boat mending their nets. 20 Immediately He called them. And they left their father Zebedee in the boat with the hired servants and followed Him.

The Man With an Unclean Spirit
Lk 4:31–37

21 They went to Capernaum, and immediately on the Sabbath He entered the synagogue and taught. 22 They were astonished at His teaching, for He taught them as one having authority, and not as the scribes. 23 In their synagogue there was a man with an unclean spirit. 24 And he cried out, "Leave us alone! What do You have to do with us, Jesus of Nazareth? Have You come to destroy us? I know who You are, the Holy One of God."

25 Jesus rebuked him, saying, "Be silent and come out of him!" 26 When the unclean spirit had convulsed him and cried out with a loud voice, it came out of him.

27 They were all amazed, so that they questioned among themselves, "What is this? What new teaching is this? With authority He commands even the unclean spirits, and they obey Him." 28 Immediately His fame spread everywhere throughout the region surrounding Galilee.

The Healing of Many People
Mt 8:14–17; Lk 4:38–41

29 When He came out of the synagogue with James and John, they went directly to the house of Simon and Andrew. 30 The mother of Simon's wife lay sick with a fever, and immediately they told Him of her. 31 So He came and took her by the hand and lifted her up, and immediately the fever left her. And she served them.

32 In the evening, when the sun had set, they brought to Him all who were sick and those who were possessed with demons. 33 The whole city was gathered at the door, 34 and He healed many who were sick with various diseases and cast out many demons. And He did not let the demons speak, because they knew Him.

A Preaching Tour
Lk 4:42–44

35 In the morning, rising up a great while before sunrise, He went out and departed to a solitary place. And there He prayed. 36 Simon and those who were with Him followed Him, 37 and when they found Him, they said to Him, "Everyone is searching for You."

38 He said to them, "Let us go into the nearby towns, that I may preach there also. For that is why I have come." 39 So He preached in their

synagogues throughout Galilee and cast out demons.

The Cleansing of a Leper

Mt 8:1–4; Lk 5:12–16

40 A leper came to Him, pleading with Him and kneeling before Him, saying, "If You are willing, You can make me clean."

41 Then Jesus, moved with compassion, extended His hand and touched him, and said to him, "I will. Be clean." 42 As soon as He had spoken, the leprosy immediately departed from him, and he was cleansed.

43 He sternly warned him, and sent him away at once, 44 saying, "See that you say nothing to anyone. But go your way, show yourself to the priest, and offer for your cleansing what Moses commanded, as a testimony to them." 45 Instead he went out and began to proclaim it widely and to spread the news around, so that Jesus could no more openly enter the city, but was out in remote places. And they came to Him from every quarter.

The Healing of a Paralytic

Mt 9:1–8; Lk 5:17–26

2 Again, He entered Capernaum after some days. And it was reported that He was in the house. 2 Immediately many were gathered together, so that there was no room to receive them, not even at the door. And He preached the word to them. 3 They came to Him bringing one sick with paralysis, who was carried by four men. 4 When they could not come near Him due to the crowding, they uncovered the roof where He was. When they had broken it open, they let down the bed on which the paralytic lay. 5 When Jesus saw their faith, He said to the paralytic, "Son, your sins are forgiven you."

6 But some of the scribes were sitting there, reasoning in their hearts, 7 "Why does this Man speak such blasphemies? Who can forgive sins but God alone?"

8 Immediately, when Jesus perceived in His spirit that they so reasoned within themselves, He said to them, "Why do you contemplate these things in your hearts? 9 Which is easier to say to the paralytic: 'Your sins are forgiven you,' or to say, 'Rise, take up your bed and walk'? 10 But that you may know that the Son of Man has authority on earth to forgive sins," He said to the paralytic, 11 "I say to you, rise, and take up your bed, and go your way to your house." 12 Immediately he rose, picked up the bed, and went out in front of them all, so that they were all amazed and glorified God, saying, "We never saw anything like this!"

1:40 Mk 10:17
1:43 Mt 9:30
1:45 Mk 2:13
2:1 Mt 9:1
2:2 Mk 1:45
2:3 Lk 5:18–26
2:4 Lk 5:19
2:7 Isa 43:25
2:12 Mt 9:8

2:13 Mk 1:45
2:14 Mk 3:18
2:16 Ac 23:9
2:20 Lk 17:22
2:22 Jos 9:4
2:23 Mt 12:1–8
2:24 Ex 20:10
2:26 2Sa 8:17
2:27 Col 2:16
2:28 Rev 1:10

The Calling of Levi

Mt 9:9–13; Lk 5:27–32

13 He went out again by the seaside, and the whole crowd came to Him, and He taught them. 14 As He passed by, He saw Levi the son of Alphaeus sitting at the tax collector's station, and He said to him, "Follow Me." And he rose and followed Him.

15 As Jesus was at supper in his house, many tax collectors and sinners also sat together with Jesus and His disciples. For there were many, and they followed Him. 16 When the scribes and Pharisees saw Him eating with tax collectors and sinners, they said to His disciples, "How is it that He eats and drinks with tax collectors and sinners?"

17 When Jesus heard it, He said to them, "Those who are well have no need of a physician, but those who are sick. I came not to call the righteous, but sinners to repentance."

The Question About Fasting

Mt 9:14–17; Lk 5:33–39

18 Now the disciples of John and of the Pharisees were fasting. And people came and said to Him, "Why do the disciples of John and of the Pharisees fast, but Your disciples do not fast?"

19 Jesus said to them, "Can the wedding guests fast while the bridegroom is with them? As long as they have the bridegroom with them, they cannot fast. 20 But the days will come when the bridegroom will be taken away from them, and then they will fast in those days.

21 "No one sews a piece of new cloth on an old garment, or else the new piece that covered it tears away from the old, and the tear is made worse. 22 And no one pours new wine into old wineskins, or else the new wine bursts the wineskins, and the wine is spilled, and the wineskins will be marred. But new wine must be poured into new wineskins."

The Question About the Sabbath

Mt 12:1–8; Lk 6:1–5

23 He went through the grain fields on the Sabbath. As they went, His disciples began to pluck the heads of grain. 24 The Pharisees said to Him, "Look, why are they doing on the Sabbath what is not lawful?"

25 He said to them, "Have you never read what David did, when he and those who were with him were in need and hungry: 26 how he went into the house of God, in the days Abiathar was the high priest, and ate the ritual bread, which is lawful only for the priests to eat, and also gave it to those who were with him?"

27 Then He said to them, "The Sabbath was made for man, and not man for the Sabbath. 28 So the Son of Man is Lord even of the Sabbath."

The Man With a Withered Hand
Mt 12:9–14; Lk 6:6–11

3 Again, He entered the synagogue, and there was a man who had a withered hand. 2 They watched Him to see whether He would heal him on the Sabbath, so that they might accuse Him. 3 He said to the man who had the withered hand, "Stand up."

4 Then He said to them, "Is it lawful to do good or to do evil on the Sabbath, to save life or to kill?" But they kept silent.

5 When He had looked around at them with anger, being grieved for the hardness of their hearts, He said to the man, "Stretch your hand forward." He stretched it out, and his hand was restored as whole as the other. 6 Then the Pharisees went out and immediately took counsel with the Herodians against Him, how to kill Him.

The Crowd at the Seaside

7 Jesus withdrew with His disciples to the sea. And a great crowd followed Him from Galilee and Judea 8 and Jerusalem, and Idumea, and from beyond the Jordan. And those from Tyre and Sidon, a great crowd, when they heard what great things He did, came to Him. 9 He told the disciples to have a small boat ready for Him because of the crowd, lest they should crush Him. 10 For He had healed many, so that all who had diseases pressed on Him to touch Him. 11 When unclean spirits saw Him, they fell down before Him, crying out, "You are the Son of God." 12 But He sternly ordered them not to make Him known.

The Choosing of the Twelve Apostles
Mt 10:1–4; Lk 6:12–16

13 He went up into the mountain and called to Him those whom He desired, and they came to Him. 14 He ordained twelve to be with Him, and to be sent out to preach, 15 and to have authority to heal sicknesses and to cast out demons: 16 Simon, whom He named Peter; 17 James, the son of Zebedee, and John, the brother of James, whom he surnamed Boanerges (meaning Sons of Thunder); 18 Andrew, and Philip, and Bartholomew, and Matthew, and Thomas; and James the son of Alphaeus; and Thaddaeus, and Simon the Zealot; 19 and Judas Iscariot, who betrayed Him.

Jesus and Beelzebub
Mt 12:22–32; Lk 11:14–23; 12:10

20 Then they entered a house, and the crowd came together again, so that they could not even eat bread. 21 When His family heard of it, they went out to seize Him, for they said, "He is beside Himself."

22 And the scribes who came down from Jerusalem said, "He is possessed by Beelzebub, and by the ruler of the demons He casts out demons."

23 So He called them to Him and said to them in parables, "How can Satan cast out Satan? 24 If a kingdom is divided against itself, that kingdom cannot stand. 25 If a house is divided against itself, that house cannot stand. 26 And if Satan rises up against himself and is divided, he cannot stand, but is coming to an end. 27 No one can enter a strong man's house and plunder his goods, unless he first binds the strong man. Then he will plunder his house. 28 Truly I say to you, all sins will be forgiven the sons of men, and whatever blasphemies they speak. 29 But he who blasphemes against the Holy Spirit never has forgiveness, but is in danger of eternal condemnation."

30 For they said, "He has an unclean spirit."

The Mother and Brothers of Jesus
Mt 12:46–50; Lk 8:19–21

31 Then His mother and His brothers came, and standing outside, they sent to Him, calling Him. 32 The crowd sat around Him and said to Him, "Your mother and Your brothers are outside asking for You."

33 He answered, "Who are My mother and My brothers?"

34 Then He looked around at those who sat around Him and said, "Here are My mother and My brothers! 35 For whoever does the will of God is My brother, and My sister, and My mother."

The Parable of the Sower
Mt 13:1–9; Lk 8:4–8

4 Again He began to teach by the seaside. A large crowd was gathered before Him, so that He entered a boat and sat in it on the sea. And the whole crowd was by the sea on the land. 2 He taught them many things in parables and said to them in His teaching: 3 "Listen! And take note: A sower went out to sow. 4 As he sowed, some seed fell beside the path, and the birds of the air came and devoured it. 5 Some seed fell on rocky ground, where it did not have much soil, and soon it sprang up because it did not have deep soil. 6 But when the sun rose, it was scorched. And because it had no root, it withered away. 7 Other seed fell among thorns, and the thorns grew up and choked it, and it yielded no grain. 8 And other seed fell on good ground, and it yielded grain that sprang up and increased by thirty, sixty, or a hundred times as much."

9 Then He said to them, "He who has ears to hear, let him hear."

3:1 Mt 12:9–14
3:2 Lk 14:1
3:5 Lk 6:10
3:6 Mt 22:16
3:7 Mt 4:25
3:8 Eze 35:15
3:10 Mt 14:36
3:11 Mt 4:3
3:16 Jn 1:42
3:18 Ac 1:13
3:20 Mk 6:31
3:21 Jn 10:20
3:22 Mt 9:34
3:23 Mt 13:34
3:28 Mt 12:31–32
3:31 Lk 8:19–21
4:1 Mk 2:13
4:2 Mk 3:23
4:6 Jas 1:11
4:7 Jer 4:3
4:9 Mt 11:15

The Purpose of the Parables
Mt 13:10–17; Lk 8:9–10

10 When He was alone, those who were around Him with the twelve asked Him about the parable. 11 He said to them, "To you is given the secret of the kingdom of God, but to those who are outside, everything is said in parables, 12 so that

'seeing they may see, and not perceive,
and hearing they may hear and not understand;
lest they should turn, and their sins be forgiven them.'[1]"

The Parable of the Sower Explained
Mt 13:18–23; Lk 8:11–15

13 Then He said to them, "Do you not understand this parable? How then will you understand all the parables? 14 The sower sows the word. 15 These are those beside the path, where the word is sown. But when they hear, Satan comes immediately and takes away the word which is sown in their hearts. 16 Others, likewise, are seed sown on rocky ground, who, when they hear the word, immediately receive it with gladness, 17 but have no root in themselves, and so endure for a time. Afterward, when affliction or persecution rises for the word's sake, immediately they fall away. 18 And others are seed sown among thorns, the ones who hear the word. 19 But the cares of this world, and the deceitfulness of riches, and the desires for other things entering in choke the word, and it proves unfruitful. 20 Still others are seed sown on good ground, those who hear the word, and receive it, and bear fruit: thirty, sixty, or a hundred times as much."

A Light Under a Basket
Lk 8:16–18

21 He said to them, "Is a candle brought to be put under a basket or under a bed and not to be set on a candlestick? 22 For there is nothing hidden except to be revealed; neither is anything kept secret except to be proclaimed. 23 If anyone has ears to hear, let him hear."

24 He said to them, "Take heed what you hear. The measure you give will be measured for you, and to you who hear will more be given. 25 For to him who has will more be given. And from him who has not will be taken, even what he has."

The Parable of the Growing Seed

26 He said, "The kingdom of God is like a man who scatters seed on the ground. 27 He sleeps and rises night and day, and the seed sprouts and grows; he does not know how. 28 For the earth bears fruit by itself: first the blade, then the head, then the full seed in the head. 29 But when the grain is ripe, immediately he applies the sickle because the harvest has come."

The Parable of the Mustard Seed
Mt 13:31–32; Lk 13:18–19

30 He said, "To what shall we liken the kingdom of God, or with what parable shall we compare it? 31 It is like a grain of mustard seed which, when it is sown in the ground, is the smallest seed on earth. 32 Yet when it is sown, it grows up and becomes greater than all shrubs, and shoots out great branches, so that the birds of the air may nest in its shade."

The Use of Parables
Mt 13:34–35

33 With many such parables He spoke the word to them as they were able to hear it. 34 Without a parable He did not speak to them. But when they were alone, He expounded on all things to His disciples.

The Calming of a Storm
Mt 8:23–27; Lk 8:22–25

> I'm going to keep moving forward with God's plan for my life, even when storms come along (Mk 4:35–41).

35 That same day, when the evening came, He said to them, "Let us go cross to the other side." 36 When they had sent the crowd away, they took Him in the boat just as He was. There were also other little boats with Him. 37 A great wind storm arose, and the waves splashed into the boat, so that it was now filling the boat. 38 He was in the stern asleep on a pillow. They woke Him and said, "Teacher, do You not care that we are perishing?"

39 He rose and rebuked the wind, and said to the sea, "Peace, be still!" Then the wind ceased and there was a great calm.

> I rebuke all the winds and storms of the enemy sent against my life (Mk 4:39).

40 He said to them, "Why are you so fearful? How is that you have no faith?"

41 They feared greatly and said to one another, "What kind of Man is He, that even the wind and the sea obey Him?"

The Healing of the Gadarene Demoniac
Mt 8:28–34; Lk 8:26–39

5 They went to the other side of the sea to the region of the Gadarenes. 2 When He had come out of the boat, immediately a man

4:10 Mk 4:34
4:11 Col 4:5
4:12 Isa 6:9–10
4:17 Mt 11:6
4:19 1Ti 6:9–10
4:21 Mt 5:15
4:22 Lk 8:17
4:23 Mk 4:9
4:24 Mt 7:2
4:25 Mt 13:12
4:26 Mt 13:24
4:27 Ecc 11:5
4:29 Joel 3:13
....
4:33 Jn 16:12
4:35 Mt 8:18
4:36 Mk 3:9
4:40 Mt 14:31
5:1 Mt 8:28–34
5:2 Mk 1:23

[1] *12* Isa 6:9–10.

SPIRITLED WOMAN

COUNSEL FROM THE SPIRIT BASICS

Acts of God?

Destruction encompasses the evils over which mankind has no control, those things the world ignorantly calls *acts of God*—tornadoes, floods, hail, hurricanes, or fire. God very plainly tells us we are not to fear destruction. These natural disasters are not from God.

In Mark 4:39 Jesus rebuked the storm, and it became perfectly calm. This demonstrates God is not the author of such things; otherwise, Jesus would never have contradicted His Father by rebuking something sent by Him.

There is no place in the world you can go and be safe from every destruction or natural disaster. We can never anticipate what might come when we least expect it. But no matter where you are in the world, God says to run to His shelter, where you will not be afraid of the destruction—*it will not approach you!*

Peggy Joyce Ruth

with an unclean spirit came out of the tombs and met Him. 3 He lived among the tombs. And no one could constrain him, not even with chains, 4 because he had often been bound with shackles and chains. But he had pulled the chains apart and broken the shackles to pieces. And no one could subdue him. 5 Always, night and day, he was in the mountains and in the tombs, crying out and cutting himself with stones.

6 But when he saw Jesus afar off, he ran up and kneeled before Him, 7 and cried out with a loud voice, "What have You to do with me, Jesus, Son of the Most High God? I adjure You by God, do not torment me." 8 For Jesus said to him, "Come out of the man, you unclean spirit!"

9 Then He asked him, "What is your name?"

He answered, "My name is Legion. For we are many." 10 And he begged Him repeatedly not to send them away out of the country.

5:7 Mt 8:29
5:9 Mt 26:53
....
5:15 Mk 5:9
5:17 Ac 16:39
5:18 Lk 8:38–39
5:19 Ps 66:16
5:20 Mt 4:25
5:21 Mt 9:1
5:22 Lk 13:14
5:23 Mk 16:18
5:24 Mk 5:31
5:25 Lev 15:25–27
5:29 Mk 3:10
5:30 Lk 6:19

11 Now there was a great herd of swine feeding near the mountains. 12 All the demons pleaded with Him, asking, "Send us to the swine, so that we may enter them." 13 At once, Jesus gave them leave. Then the unclean spirits came out and entered the swine. And the herd, numbering about two thousand, ran wildly down a steep hill into the sea and were drowned in the sea.

14 Those who fed the swine fled and reported it in the city and in the country. And people went out to see what it was that had happened. 15 They came to Jesus and saw him who had been possessed with the legion of demons sitting and clothed and in his right mind. And they were afraid. 16 Those who saw it told them how it befell him who had been possessed with the demons and also concerning the swine. 17 Then they began to plead with Him to depart out of their region.

18 When He entered the boat, he who had been possessed with the demons prayed Him that he might be with Him. 19 Jesus did not let him, but said to him, "Go home to your friends and tell them what great things the Lord has done for you and how He has had compassion on you." 20 So he departed and began to proclaim in the Decapolis[1] what great things Jesus had done for him. And everyone was amazed.

Jairus' Daughter and the Woman Who Touched Jesus' Garment
Mt 9:18–26; Lk 8:40–56

21 When Jesus had crossed again by boat to the other side, many people gathered to Him. And He was beside the sea. 22 One of the rulers of the synagogue, named Jairus, saw Jesus and came and fell at His feet 23 and earnestly asked Him, "My little daughter is lying at the point of death. I ask You, come and lay Your hands on her, so that she may be healed. And she will live." 24 So Jesus went with him.

And many people followed Him and pressed in on Him. 25 And a certain woman had a hemorrhage for twelve years, 26 and had suffered much under many physicians. She had spent all that she had, and was not better but rather grew worse. 27 When she had heard of Jesus, she came in the crowd behind Him and touched His garment. 28 For she said, "If I may touch His garments, I shall be healed." 29 And immediately her hemorrhage dried up, and she felt in her body that she was healed of the affliction.

30 At once, Jesus knew within Himself that power had gone out of Him. He turned around in the crowd and said, "Who touched My garments?"

[1]*20* The Ten Cities.

31 His disciples said to Him, "You see the
crowd pressing against You, and You say, 'Who
touched Me?' "
32 And He looked around to see her who had
done it. 33 But the woman, fearing and trem-
bling, knowing what had happened to her,
came and fell down before Him and told Him
the entire truth. 34 He said to her, "Daughter,
your faith has made you well. Go in peace, and
be healed of your affliction."
35 While He was still speaking, some came
from the house of the synagogue ruler and
said, "Your daughter is dead. Why trouble the
Teacher any further?"
36 As soon as Jesus heard the word that was
spoken, He said to the ruler of the synagogue,
"Do not be afraid, only believe."
37 He let no one follow Him, except Peter,
and James, and John the brother of James.
38 He came to the house of the ruler of the
synagogue, and saw the tumult, and those
who wept and wailed loudly. 39 When He came
in, He said to them, "Why make this uproar
and weep? The girl is not dead, but sleeping."
40 They laughed at Him in ridicule.
But when He had put them all out, He took
the father and the mother of the girl and those
who were with Him and entered where the
girl was lying. 41 He took the girl by the hand
and said to her, "*Talitha cumi*," which means,
"Little girl, I say to you, arise." 42 Immediately
the girl arose and walked, for she was twelve
years of age. And they were greatly astonished.
43 He strictly ordered them to let no one know
of it and directed them to give her something
to eat.

The Rejection of Jesus at Nazareth
Mt 13:53–58; Lk 4:16–30

6 He went away from there and came into
His own country. And His disciples fol-
lowed Him. 2 When the Sabbath came, He
began to teach in the synagogue. And many
hearing Him were astonished, saying, "Where
did this Man get this? What is this wisdom that
is given Him, that even miracles are done by
His hands? 3 Is this not the carpenter, the Son
of Mary and the brother of James and Joseph
and Judas and Simon? Are not His sisters here
with us?" And they took offense at Him.
4 Jesus said to them, "A prophet is not without
honor, except in his own country, and among
his own relatives, and in his own house." 5 He
could not do any miracles there, except that
He laid His hands on a few sick people and
healed them. 6 And He was amazed because
of their unbelief.

5:34 Lk 8:48
5:36 Lk 8:50
5:39 Ac 20:10
5:41 Mk 1:31
5:43 Mt 8:4
6:1 Lk 4:16–30
6:3 Mt 11:6
6:4 Jn 4:44
6:6 Mt 9:35
6:7 Mk 3:13–14
6:9 Ac 12:8
6:12 Mt 4:17
6:14 Lk 9:7–9
6:15 Mt 21:11
6:17 Mt 11:2
6:18 Lev 18:16
6:20 Mt 21:26
6:21 Est 2:18
6:23 Est 5:3

The Mission of the Twelve
Mt 10:1, 5–15; Lk 9:1–6

Then He went to the surrounding villages,
teaching. 7 He called to Him the twelve, and
began to send them out two by two, and gave
them authority over unclean spirits.
8 He commanded them to take nothing for
their journey except a staff: no bag, no bread,
and no money in their purse, 9 but to wear
sandals, and not put on two tunics. 10 He said
to them, "Wherever you enter a house, remain
there until you depart from that place. 11 And
whoever will not receive you or hear you,
when you depart from there, shake the dust
off your feet as a testimony against them. Truly
I say to you, it will be more tolerable for Sodom
and Gomorrah on the Day of Judgment than
for that city."
12 So they went out and preached that men
should repent. 13 And they cast out many de-
mons and anointed with oil many who were
sick and healed them.

The Death of John the Baptist
Mt 14:1–12; Lk 9:7–9

14 King Herod heard of Him, for His name
was spread publicly. He said, "John the Baptist
has been raised from the dead, and therefore
these miracles are at work in him."
15 But others said, "He is Elijah."
And yet others said, "He is the Prophet, or
like one of the prophets."
16 But when Herod heard of it, he said, "It is
John, whom I beheaded. He has been raised
from the dead!"
17 Herod had sent and seized John and
bound him in prison for the sake of Herodias,
his brother Philip's wife, for he had married
her. 18 For John said to Herod, "It is not law-
ful for you to have your brother's wife." 19 So
Herodias had a grudge against him and would
have killed him, but she could not, 20 for Herod
feared John, knowing that he was a righteous
and holy man, and protected him. When he
heard him, he was greatly perplexed, but
heard him gladly.
21 But a convenient day came when Herod
on his birthday prepared a ceremonial dinner
for his lords and commanding officers and
leading men of Galilee. 22 When the daughter
of Herodias came in and danced and pleased
Herod and those who sat with him, the king
said to the girl, "Ask of me whatever you de-
sire, and I will give it to you." 23 And he swore
to her, "Whatever you ask of me, I will give
you, up to half of my kingdom."
24 She went out and said to her mother, "What
shall I ask?"
She said, "The head of John the Baptist."

25 She came in immediately with haste to the king and asked, "I want you to give me the head of John the Baptist on a platter at once."

26 The king was extremely sorrowful. Yet for the sake of his oath and those who sat with him, he would not reject her. 27 So the king immediately sent an executioner and commanded his head to be brought. He went and beheaded him in the prison, 28 and brought his head on a platter, and gave it to the girl. And the girl gave it to her mother. 29 When his disciples heard of it, they came and took up his corpse and laid it in a tomb.

The Feeding of the Five Thousand
Mt 14:13–21; Lk 9:10–17; Jn 6:1–14

30 The apostles met with Jesus and told him everything, both what they had done and what they had taught. 31 Then He said to them, "Come away by yourselves to a remote place and rest a while," for many were coming and going, and they had no leisure even to eat.

32 So they went into a remote place privately by boat. 33 But the people saw them departing, and many knew Him and ran there on foot out of every city. They arrived first and came together to Him. 34 When Jesus came out and saw many people, He was moved with compassion on them, because they were like sheep without a shepherd. And He began to teach them many things.

35 When the day was now getting late, His disciples came to Him and said, "This is a remote place, and now the time is passing. 36 Send them away into the surrounding country and villages to buy themselves bread, for they have nothing to eat."

37 But He answered, "You give them something to eat."

They said to Him, "Shall we go and buy two hundred denarii[1] worth of bread and give it to them to eat?"

38 He said to them, "How many loaves have you? Go and see."

When they found out, they said, "Five, and two fish."

39 Then He commanded them to make everyone sit down by companies on the green grass. 40 So they sat down in ranks, by hundreds and by fifties. 41 When He had taken the five loaves and the two fish, He looked up to heaven, and blessed and broke the loaves, and gave them to His disciples to set before them. And He divided the two fish among them all. 42 They all ate and were filled. 43 And they took up twelve baskets full of the fragments and of the fish. 44 Those who ate of the loaves were about five thousand men.

[1] *37* Eight months' wages.

6:30 Lk 9:10
6:31 Mk 3:20
6:34 Mt 9:36
6:36 Mt 15:23
6:37 2Ki 4:42–44
6:41 Mt 14:19
6:45 Mk 8:22
6:49 Lk 24:37
6:50 Mt 14:27
6:51 Mk 4:39
6:53 Mt 14:34–36
6:55 Mt 4:24
6:56 Mt 9:20
7:1 Mk 3:22
7:2 Ac 10:28
7:3 Mk 7:13
7:6 Isa 29:13

Walking on the Water
Mt 14:22–33; Jn 6:15–21

45 Immediately He compelled His disciples to get into the boat and to go before Him to the other side, to Bethsaida, while He sent the crowd away. 46 When He had sent them away, He departed to a mountain to pray.

47 When evening came, the boat was in the midst of the sea. And He was alone on the land. 48 He saw them straining at rowing, for the wind was against them. About the fourth watch of the night He came to them, walking on the sea and would have passed by them. 49 But when they saw Him walking on the sea, they supposed it was a ghost, and cried out. 50 For they all saw Him and were troubled.

Immediately He spoke to them and said, "Be of good cheer, it is I. Do not be afraid." 51 Then He went up to them in the boat and the wind ceased. They were greatly astonished in themselves beyond measure, and wondered. 52 For they had not comprehended the miracle of the loaves, for their hearts were hardened.

The Healing of the Sick in Gennesaret
Mt 14:34–36

53 When they had crossed over, they came to the land of Gennesaret and anchored on the shore. 54 When they had come out of the boat, immediately the people recognized Him, 55 and ran throughout the surrounding region, and began to carry the sick on beds to wherever they heard He was. 56 And wherever He entered, into villages, cities, or the country, they laid the sick in the marketplaces and pleaded with Him that they might touch even the fringe of His garment. And as many as touched Him were healed.

The Tradition of the Elders
Mt 15:1–20

7 The Pharisees and certain scribes who came from Jerusalem gathered around Him. 2 When they saw some of His disciples eat bread with defiled, that is, ritually unwashed hands, they found fault. 3 For the Pharisees and all the Jews, unless they wash their hands ritually, do not eat, keeping the tradition of the elders. 4 When they come from the market, unless they wash, they do not eat. And there are many other traditions which they have received and observe, such as the washing of cups and pitchers and bronze vessels and dining couches.

5 So the Pharisees and scribes asked Him, "Why do Your disciples not live according to the tradition of the elders, but eat bread with unwashed hands?"

6 He answered, "Well has Isaiah prophesied of you hypocrites, as it is written:

'These people honor Me with their lips,
but their hearts are far from Me.
7 In vain do they worship Me,
teaching as doctrines the precepts of
men.'[1]

8 For laying aside the commandment of God,
you hold the tradition of men—the washing
of pitchers and cups, and many other such
things you do."

9 And He said to them, "You full well reject
the commandment of God so that you may
keep your own tradition. 10 For Moses said,
'Honor your father and your mother,'[2] and,
'Whoever curses father or mother, let him be
put to death.'[3] 11 But you say, 'If a man says to
his father or mother, "It is Corban," that is to
say, "What you would have profited from me
is a gift to God," he shall be free.' 12 Then you
no longer let him do anything for his father or
his mother, 13 making the word of God of no
effect through your tradition, which you have
delivered. And you do many similar things."

14 When He had called all the people to Him,
He said, "Listen to Me, every one of you, and
understand: 15 There is nothing from outside
a man that by entering him can defile him.
But the things which come out of the man are
what defile him. 16 If anyone has ears to hear,
let him hear."

17 When He had left the people and entered
the house, His disciples asked Him concerning
the parable. 18 He said to them, "Are you so
without understanding also? Do you not know
that anything from the outside that enters a
man cannot defile him, 19 because it does not
enter his heart, but into his stomach, and goes
out into the sewer, thus purifying all foods?"

20 And He said, "What comes out of a man
is what defiles a man. 21 For from within, out
of the heart of men, proceed evil thoughts,
adultery, fornication, murder, 22 theft, covet-
ousness, wickedness, deceit, licentiousness,
an evil eye, blasphemy, pride and foolishness.
23 All these evil things come from within and
defile a man."

The Syrophoenician Woman's Faith
Mt 15:21–28

24 From there He arose and went to the re-
gion of Tyre and Sidon. He entered a house
and would have no one know it. Yet He could
not be hidden. 25 For a certain woman, whose
young daughter had an unclean spirit, heard
of Him, and came and fell at His feet. 26 The
woman was a Greek, a Syrophoenician by race.
And she begged Him to cast the demon out of
her daughter.

27 Jesus said to her, "Let the children first be
filled. For it is not fitting to take the children's
bread and throw it to the dogs."

28 She answered, "Yes, Lord. Yet the dogs un-
der the table eat the children's crumbs."

29 Then He said to her, "For this answer, go
your way. The demon has gone out of your
daughter."

30 When she had come to her house, she
found the demon had gone out, and her
daughter lying on the bed.

> I command all devils to leave my children, in the name of Jesus (Mk 7:29).

The Deaf and Mute Man Healed

31 Again, departing from the region of Tyre
and Sidon, He came to the Sea of Galilee,
through the region of the Decapolis. 32 They
brought to Him one who was deaf and had
difficulty speaking. And they pleaded with Him
to put His hand on him.

33 He took him aside from the crowd, and
put His fingers into his ears, and spat and
touched his tongue. 34 Looking up to heaven,
He sighed, and said to him, "*Ephphatha*," that
is, "Be opened." 35 Immediately his ears were
opened, and the impediment of his tongue
was loosened, and he spoke correctly.

36 He ordered them to tell no one. But the
more He ordered them, the more they greatly
proclaimed it. 37 They were astonished beyond
measure, saying, "He has done all things well.
He makes both the deaf to hear and the mute
to speak."

The Feeding of the Four Thousand
Mt 15:32–39

8 In those days, the crowds being very great
with nothing to eat, Jesus called His dis-
ciples to Him and said to them, 2 "I have com-
passion on the crowd, because they have now
been with Me three days and have nothing to
eat. 3 If I send them away fasting to their own
houses, they will faint on the way, for some of
them have come from afar."

4 His disciples answered, "Where can one
get bread to feed these men here in the wil-
derness?"

5 He asked them, "How many loaves do you
have?"

They said, "Seven."

6 He commanded the people to sit down
on the ground. Taking the seven loaves and
giving thanks, He broke them and gave them
to His disciples to serve. And they served the
crowd. 7 And they had a few small fish. And

7:10 Ex 20:12
7:11 Mt 23:18
7:13 Mk 7:9
7:17 Mt 15:15
7:20 Jas 3:6
7:21 Jer 17:9
7:22 Mt 20:15
7:24 Mt 15:21–28

7:27 Mt 7:6
7:31 Mt 4:25
7:33 Mk 8:23
7:34 Mk 8:12
7:35 Isa 35:5–6
7:36 Mt 8:4
8:1 Mt 15:32–39
8:2 Mt 9:36
8:7 Mt 14:19

[1] *6–7* Isa 29:13. [2] *10* Ex 20:12; Dt 5:16. [3] *10* Ex 21:17; Lev 20:9.

blessing them, He commanded that these also be served them. 8 So they ate and were filled. And they collected seven baskets of the broken pieces that were left. 9 There were about four thousand who had eaten, and He sent them away. 10 He immediately entered a boat with His disciples and came to the region of Dalmanutha.

The Demand for a Sign
Mt 16:1–4

11 The Pharisees came up and began to debate with Him, seeking from Him a sign from heaven to test Him. 12 He sighed deeply in His spirit and said, "Why does this generation look for a sign? Truly I say to you, no sign shall be given to this generation." 13 Then He left them and, entering the boat again, departed to the other side.

The Yeast of the Pharisees and of Herod
Mt 16:5–12

14 Now the disciples had forgotten to take bread and did not have more than one loaf with them in the boat. 15 He warned them, "Take heed. Beware of the yeast of the Pharisees and the yeast of Herod."

16 They reasoned among themselves, saying, "It is because we have no bread."

17 Being aware of it, Jesus said to them, "Why do you reason that you have no bread? Do you still not perceive or understand? Are your hearts still hardened? 18 Having eyes, do you not see? Having ears, do you not hear?[1] And do you not remember? 19 When I broke the five loaves for the five thousand, how many baskets full of broken pieces did you collect?"

They said to Him, "Twelve."

20 "And the seven among the four thousand, how many baskets full of broken pieces did you collect?"

They said, "Seven."

21 He said to them, "Do you still not understand?"

The Healing of a Blind Man at Bethsaida

22 He came to Bethsaida. And they brought a blind man to Him and entreated Him to touch him. 23 He took the blind man by the hand and led him out of the town. When He had spit on his eyes and put His hands on him, He asked him, "Do you see anything?"

24 He looked up and said, "I see men as trees, walking."

25 Then again He put His hands on his eyes and made him look up. And he was restored and saw everyone clearly. 26 He sent him home away to his house, saying, "Neither go into the town, nor tell it to anyone in the town."

Peter's Declaration About Jesus
Mt 16:13–20; Lk 9:18–21

27 Jesus and His disciples went out into the towns of Caesarea Philippi. On the way He asked His disciples, "Who do men say that I am?"

28 They answered, "John the Baptist, but some say, Elijah; and others, one of the prophets."

29 He said to them, "But who do you say that I am?"

Peter answered Him, "You are the Christ."

30 He warned them that they should tell no one about Him.

Jesus Foretells His Death and Resurrection
Mt 16:21–18; Lk 9:22–27

31 He began to teach them that the Son of Man must suffer many things, and be rejected by the elders and the chief priests and the scribes, and be killed, and after three days rise again. 32 He said this openly. And Peter took Him and began to rebuke Him.

33 But when He had turned around and looked at His disciples, He rebuked Peter, saying, "Get behind Me, Satan! For you are not mindful of the things of God, but the things of men."

34 When He had called the people to Him, with His disciples, He said to them, "If any man would come after Me, let him deny himself and take up his cross and follow Me. 35 For whoever would save his life will lose it. But whoever would lose his life for My sake and the gospel's will save it. 36 For what does it profit a man if he gains the whole world and loses his own soul? 37 Or what will a man give in exchange for his soul? 38 Whoever therefore is ashamed of Me and of My words in this adulterous and sinful generation, of him will the Son of Man also be ashamed when He comes in the glory of His Father with the holy angels."

9 And He said to them, "Truly I say to you, there are some standing here who will not taste death before they see the kingdom of God come with power."

The Transfiguration
Mt 17:1–13; Lk 9:28–36

2 After six days Jesus took with Him Peter and James and John and led them up a high mountain, alone by themselves. And He was transfigured before them. 3 His garments became shiny, extremely white as snow, such as no launderer on earth could whiten them. 4 And there appeared to them Elijah with Moses. And they were talking with Jesus.

8:8 2Ki 4:42–44
8:10 Mt 15:39
8:11 Mt 12:38
8:12 Mk 7:34
8:15 Mk 12:13
8:17 Mk 6:52
8:18 Jer 5:21
8:21 Mk 6:52
8:22 Mt 11:21
8:23 Mk 7:33
8:26 Mt 8:4

. . . .

8:27 Lk 9:18–20
8:29 Jn 6:69
8:30 Mt 16:20
8:32 Jn 16:25
8:33 Mt 4:10
8:34 Mt 10:38
8:37 Ps 49:7–8
8:38 Mt 16:27
9:1 Mt 25:31
9:2 Mk 5:37
9:3 Mt 28:3

[1] *18* Jer 5:21; Isa 6:9–10.

5 Peter said to Jesus, "Rabbi, it is good for us
to be here. Let us make three sanctuaries: one
for You, and one for Moses, and one for Elijah."
6 For he did not know what to say, because they
were very afraid.
7 Then a cloud overshadowed them, and a
voice came out of the cloud, saying, "This is
My beloved Son. Listen to Him."
8 Suddenly, when they looked around, they
no longer saw anyone with them except Jesus
only.
9 As they came down the mountain, He
warned them to tell no one what they had
seen, until the Son of Man had risen from the
dead. 10 They kept that statement to them-
selves, questioning each other what the rising
from the dead meant.
11 And they asked Him, "Why do the scribes
say that Elijah must first come?"
12 He answered, "Elijah indeed comes first
to restore all things. Yet how is it written of
the Son of Man that He should suffer many
things and be treated with contempt? 13 But
I say to you that Elijah has indeed come, and
they have done to him whatever they wished,
as it is written of him."

The Healing of a Boy With an Unclean Spirit
Mt 17:14–20; Lk 9:37–43

14 When He came to His other disciples,
He saw a great crowd around them, and the
scribes disputing with them. 15 Immediately
when all the people saw Him, they were great-
ly amazed, and running to Him, greeted Him.
16 He asked the scribes, "What are you debat-
ing with them?"
17 One in the crowd answered, "Teacher, I
brought You my son, who has a mute spirit.
18 Wherever it takes hold on him, it dashes him
to the ground. And he foams at the mouth and
gnashes with his teeth and becomes rigid. And
I told Your disciples so that they would cast it
out, but they could not."
19 He answered, "O faithless generation, how
long shall I be with you? How long shall I bear
with you? Bring him to Me."
20 So they brought the boy to Him. When he
saw Him, immediately the spirit dashed him,
and he fell on the ground and wallowed, foam-
ing at the mouth.
21 He asked his father, "How long has it been
since it came to him?"
He said, "From childhood. 22 Often it has
thrown him into the fire and into the water
to kill him. But if You can do anything, have
compassion on us and help us."
23 Jesus said, "If you can believe, all things
are possible to him who believes."
24 Immediately the father of the child cried out
with tears, "Lord, I believe. Help my unbelief!"
25 When Jesus saw that the people came run-
ning together, He rebuked the foul spirit, say-
ing to it, "You mute and deaf spirit, I command
you, come out of him, and enter him no more."
26 The spirit cried out and convulsed him
greatly. But it came out of him, and he was as
dead, so that many said, "He is dead." 27 But
Jesus took him by the hand and lifted him up,
and he arose.
28 When He had entered the house, His dis-
ciples asked Him privately, "Why could we not
cast it out?"
29 He said to them, "This kind cannot come
out except by prayer and fasting."

Jesus Again Foretells His Death and Resurrection
Mt 17:22–23; Lk 9:43b–45

30 They departed from there and passed
through Galilee, and He did not want anyone
to know it. 31 For He was teaching His disciples,
saying, "The Son of Man will be delivered into
the hands of men, and they will kill Him. After
He is killed, He will rise the third day." 32 But
they did not understand the teaching and were
afraid to ask Him.

Who Is the Greatest?
Mt 18:1–5; Lk 9:46–48

33 He came to Capernaum. And being in the
house, He asked them, "What was it that you
disputed among yourselves on the way?" 34 But
they kept silent, for on the way they had disput-
ed among themselves who was the greatest.
35 He sat down and called the twelve. And He
said to them, "If anyone desires to be first, he
must be last of all and servant of all."
36 He took a child and set him in their midst.
And when He had taken him in His arms, He
said to them, 37 "Whoever receives one of these
children in My name receives Me. And whoev-
er receives Me receives not Me, but Him who
sent Me."

He Who Is Not Against Us Is for Us
Lk 9:49–50

38 John answered Him, "Teacher, we saw one
who does not follow us casting out demons in
Your name, and we forbade him because he
was not following us."
39 But Jesus said, "Do not forbid him, for
no one who does a miracle in My name can
quickly speak evil of Me. 40 For he who is not
against us is for us. 41 Truly I say to you, who-
ever gives you a cup of water to drink in My
name, because you belong to Christ, will not
lose his reward.

9:7 Mt 3:17
9:9 Mk 5:43
9:11 Mt 11:14
9:12 Lk 23:11
9:13 Mt 11:14
9:19 Jn 20:27
9:20 Mk 1:26
9:22 Mt 9:28
9:23 Mt 17:20
9:25 Mk 9:15
9:26 Mk 9:20
9:27 Mk 1:31
9:28 Mk 7:17
9:31 Mt 16:21
9:32 Lk 2:50
9:33 Mt 17:24
9:35 Lk 22:26
9:36 Mk 10:16
9:37 Lk 10:16
9:38 Lk 9:49–50
9:40 Mt 12:30
9:41 Mt 10:42

Temptations to Sin
Mt 18:6–9; Lk 17:1–2

42 “Whoever causes one of these little ones
who believe in Me to sin, it would be better
for him if a millstone were hung around his
neck and he were thrown into the sea. 43 If your
hand causes you to sin, cut it off. It is better for
you to enter life maimed than with two hands
to go into hell, into the fire that shall never be
quenched, 44 where

‘their worm does not die,
and the fire is not quenched.’[1]

45 And if your foot causes you to sin, cut it off.
It is better for you to enter life lame than with
two feet to be thrown into hell, into the fire that
shall never be quenched, 46 where

‘their worm does not die,
and the fire is not quenched.’[2]

47 And if your eye causes you to sin, pluck it
out. It is better for you to enter the kingdom
of God with one eye than with two eyes to be
thrown into the fire of hell, 48 where

‘their worm does not die,
and the fire is not quenched.’[3]

49 Everyone will be salted with fire, and every
sacrifice will be salted with salt.
50 “Salt is good. But if the salt loses its salt-
iness, how will you season it? Have salt in
yourselves, and have peace with one another.”

Teaching About Divorce
Mt 19:1–12

10 He arose and went from there to the
region of Judea to the other side of
the Jordan, and the people came to Him again.
And again, as was His custom, He taught them.
2 The Pharisees came to test Him, asking, “Is
it lawful for a man to divorce his wife?”
3 He answered them, “What did Moses com-
mand you?”
4 They said, “Moses permitted a man to write
a certificate of divorce and to divorce her.”
5 Jesus answered them, “Due to the hardness
of your heart he wrote you this precept. 6 But
from the beginning of the creation, God ‘made
them male and female.’[4] 7 ‘For this cause shall
a man leave his father and mother, and cleave
to his wife, 8 and the two shall be one flesh.’[5]
So then they are no longer two, but one flesh.
9 What therefore God has joined together, let
not man put asunder.”
10 In the house His disciples asked Him con-
cerning this matter again. 11 He said to them,
“Whoever divorces his wife and marries an-
other commits adultery against her. 12 And if
a woman divorces her husband and marries
another, she commits adultery.”

Little Children Blessed
Mt 19:13–18; Lk 18:15–17

13 They brought young children to Him, that
He might touch them. But the disciples re-
buked those who brought them. 14 But when
Jesus saw it, He was very displeased and said
to them, “Allow the little children to come to
Me, and do not forbid them, for of such is the
kingdom of God. 15 Truly I say to you, whoever
does not receive the kingdom of God as a little
child shall not enter it.” 16 And He took them
up in His arms, put His hands on them, and
blessed them.

> Children and youth truly are power tools in the kingdom of God (Mk 10:15).

The Rich Man
Mt 19:16–30; Lk 18:18–30

17 When He set out on His way, a man came
running and knelt before Him, and asked Him,
“Good Teacher, what must I do to inherit eter-
nal life?”
18 He said to him, “Why do you call Me good?
No one is good, except God alone. 19 You know
the commandments, Do not commit adultery,
Do not murder, Do not steal, Do not bear false
witness, Do not defraud, Honor your father
and mother.[6]”
20 He answered Him, “Teacher, all these have
I observed from my youth.”
21 Then Jesus, looking upon him, loved him
and said to him, “You lack one thing: Go your
way, sell whatever you have and give to the
poor, and you will have treasure in heaven.
And come, take up the cross and follow Me.”
22 He was saddened by that word, and he
went away grieving. For he had many pos-
sessions.
23 Jesus looked around and said to His disci-
ples, “How hard it will be for those who have
wealth to enter the kingdom of God!”
24 The disciples were astonished at His words.
But Jesus answered again, “Children, how
hard it is for those who trust in riches to enter
the kingdom of God! 25 It is easier for a camel to
go through the eye of a needle than for a rich
man to enter the kingdom of God.”
26 They were astonished beyond measure,
saying among themselves, “Who then can be
saved?”
27 Jesus, looking at them, said, “With men it
is impossible, but not with God. For with God
all things are possible.”

9:42 Mt 18:6
9:43 Mt 5:29–30
9:45 Mk 9:43
9:47 Mt 18:9
9:48 Isa 66:24
9:49 Lev 2:13
9:50 Ro 12:18
10:1 Jn 10:40
10:2 Jn 8:6
10:4 Dt 24:1–4
10:5 Mt 19:8
10:6 Ge 1:27
10:7 Ge 2:24
10:8 1Co 6:16
10:11 Lk 16:18
10:12 1Co 7:11

10:13 Mt 19:13–15
10:15 Mt 18:3
10:16 Mk 9:36
10:17 Mk 1:40
10:21 Lk 12:33
10:22 Eze 33:31
10:27 Mt 19:26

[1] *44* Isa 66:24. [2] *46* Isa 66:24. [3] *48* Isa 66:24. [4] *6* Ge 1:27. [5] *7–8* Ge 2:24. [6] *19* Ex 20:12–16; Dt 5:16–20.

28 Peter began to say to Him, "Look, we have
left everything and have followed You."
29 Jesus answered, "Truly I say to you, there
is no one who has left a house or brothers or
sisters or father or mother or wife or children
or fields, for My sake and for the gospel's sake,
30 who shall not receive a hundred times as
much now in this age, houses and brothers
and sisters and mothers and children and
fields, with persecution, and in the age to
come, eternal life. 31 But many who are first
will be last, and the last first."

Jesus Foretells His Death and Resurrection a Third Time
Mt 20:17–19; Lk 18:31–34

32 They were on the way, going up to Jeru-
salem, and Jesus went ahead of them. And
they were amazed, and those who followed
were afraid. Again, He took the twelve aside
and began to tell them what would happen
to Him, 33 saying, "Listen! We are going up to
Jerusalem. The Son of Man will be handed
over to the chief priests and the scribes, and
they will condemn Him to death and hand Him
over to the Gentiles. 34 They will mock Him, and
scourge Him, and spit on Him, and kill Him.
Then after three days He will rise."

The Request of James and John
Mt 20:20–28

35 Then James and John, the sons of Zebedee,
came to Him, saying, "Teacher, we want that
whatever we may ask, You would do for us."
36 He said to them, "What do you want Me
to do for you?"
37 They said to Him, "Grant us to sit, one at
Your right hand and the other at Your left hand,
in Your glory."
38 But Jesus said to them, "You do not know
what you are asking. Can you drink the cup
that I drink and be baptized with the baptism
with which I am baptized?"
39 They said to Him, "We can."
Jesus said to them, "You will indeed drink
the cup that I drink and be baptized with the
baptism with which I am baptized. 40 But to
sit at My right hand or at My left hand is not
Mine to grant. It is for those for whom it has
been prepared."
41 When the ten heard it, they began to be
very displeased with James and John. 42 But
Jesus called them together, and said, "You
know that those who are appointed to rule
over the Gentiles lord it over them, and their
great ones exercise authority over them.
43 But it shall not be so among you. Whoev-
er would be great among you must be your
servant, 44 and whoever among you would be
greatest must be servant of all. 45 For even
the Son of Man came not to be served, but
to serve, and to give His life as a ransom
for many."

The Healing of Blind Bartimaeus
Mt 20:29–34; Lk 18:35–43

46 Then they came to Jericho. And as He
went out of Jericho with His disciples and a
great number of people, blind Bartimaeus, the
son of Timaeus, sat along the way begging.
47 When he heard that it was Jesus of Nazareth,
he began to cry out, "Jesus, Son of David, have
mercy on me!"
48 Many ordered him to keep silent. But he
cried out even more, "Son of David, have mercy
on me!"
49 Jesus stood still and commanded him to
be called.
So they called the blind man, saying, "Be of
good comfort. Rise, He is calling you." 50 Throw-
ing aside his garment, he rose and came to
Jesus.
51 Jesus answered him, "What do you want
Me to do for you?"
The blind man said to Him, "Rabbi, that I
might receive my sight."
52 Jesus said to him, "Go your way. Your faith
has made you well." Immediately he received
his sight and followed Jesus on the way.

The Triumphant Entry Into Jerusalem
Mt 21:1–11; Lk 19:28–40; Jn 12:12–19

11 When they drew near Jerusalem and
came to Bethphage and Bethany at the
Mount of Olives, He sent out two of His dis-
ciples 2 and said to them, "Go into the village
opposite you. As soon as you enter it, you will
find a colt tied, on which no one has ever sat.
Untie it and bring it here. 3 If anyone says to
you, 'Why are you doing this?' say 'The Lord
has need of it,' and immediately he will send
it here."
4 They went their way and found the colt tied
by the door outside on the street. And they un-
tied it. 5 Some of those who stood there said to
them, "What are you doing untying the colt?"
6 They answered just as Jesus had command-
ed. And they let them go. 7 They brought the
colt to Jesus and threw their garments on it.
And He sat upon it. 8 Many spread their gar-
ments on the street. And others cut down
branches off the trees and scattered them on
the street. 9 Those who went before and those
who followed cried out, saying:

"Hosanna!
'Blessed is He who comes in the name of
the Lord!'[1]

10:29 Mk 8:35
10:30 Mt 12:32
10:31 Mt 19:30
10:32 Mt 20:17–19
10:33 Mt 27:2
10:34 Mt 16:21
10:35 Mt 20:20–28
10:36 Mk 10:51
10:37 Mt 19:28
10:38 Lk 12:50
10:39 Ac 12:2
10:40 Mt 25:34
10:43 Mk 9:35
10:45 Mt 20:28
10:46 Mt 20:29–34
10:47 Mt 9:27
10:48 Mt 19:13
10:51 Mk 10:36
10:52 Mt 9:22
11:9 Ps 118:25–26

[1] *9* Ps 118:26.

10 Blessed is the kingdom of our father David
that is coming in the name of the Lord!
Hosanna in the highest!"

11 Jesus entered Jerusalem and went into the temple. When He had looked around at everything, as the hour was now late, He went out to Bethany with the twelve.

The Cursing of the Fig Tree
Mt 21:18–19

12 On the next day when they had returned from Bethany, He was hungry. 13 Seeing from afar a fig tree with leaves, He went to see if perhaps He might find anything on it. When He came to it, He found nothing except leaves, for it was not the season for figs. 14 Jesus said to it, "May no one ever eat fruit from you again." And His disciples heard it.

The Cleansing of the Temple
Mt 21:12–17; Lk 19:45–48; Jn 2:13–22

15 And they came to Jerusalem. Jesus went into the temple and began to drive out those who sold and bought in the temple, and He overturned the tables of the moneychangers and the seats of those who sold doves. 16 And He would not allow anyone to carry any vessel through the temple. 17 And He taught them, and said, "Is it not written, 'My house shall be called a house of prayer for all nations'[1]? But you have made it a 'den of thieves.'[2]"

18 The scribes and chief priests heard it and looked for a way to kill Him. For they feared Him, because all the people were astonished at His teaching.

19 When evening came, He went out of the city.

The Lesson From the Fig Tree
Mt 21:20–22

20 In the morning, as they passed by, they saw the fig tree withered from the roots. 21 Peter, calling to remembrance, said to Him, "Rabbi, look! The fig tree which You cursed has withered away."

> If I speak to my mountain of problems and command it to go in the name of Jesus, it must obey me if I believe without doubting in my heart (Mk 11:23)!

22 Jesus answered them, "Have faith in God. 23 For truly I say to you, whoever says to this mountain, 'Be removed and be thrown into the sea,' and does not doubt in his heart, but believes that what he says will come to pass, he will have whatever he says. 24 Therefore I say to you, whatever things you ask when you pray, believe that you will receive them, and you will have them. 25 And when you stand praying, forgive if you have anything against anyone, so that your Father who is in heaven may also forgive you your sins. 26 But if you do not forgive, neither will your Father who is in heaven forgive your sins."

The Question of Jesus' Authority
Mt 21:23–27; Lk 20:1–8

27 They came again to Jerusalem, and as He was walking in the temple, the chief priests and the scribes and the elders came to Him, 28 and said, "By what authority are You doing these things, and who gave You this authority to do them?"

29 Jesus answered them, "I will also ask of you one question. Answer Me, and I will tell you by what authority I do these things. 30 Was the baptism of John from heaven or from men? Answer Me."

31 They debated among themselves, saying, "If we say, 'From heaven,' He will say, 'Why then did you not believe him?' 32 But if we say, 'From men'"—they feared the people, for everyone held John to be a real prophet.

33 So they answered Jesus, "We do not know."

Jesus answered them, "Neither will I tell you by what authority I do these things."

The Parable of the Vineyard and the Vinedressers
Mt 21:33–46; Lk 20:9–10

12 He began to speak to them in parables. "A man planted a vineyard, and set a hedge around it, and dug a pit for the winepress, and built a tower, and rented it to vinedressers, and went to a far country. 2 At harvest time he sent a servant to the vinedressers to receive from them some of the fruit of the vineyard. 3 But they seized him and beat him and sent him away empty-handed. 4 Then he sent another servant to them. They threw stones at him, and wounded him in the head, and sent him away shamefully handled. 5 Still he sent another, and they killed him. And there were many others. Some they beat, and some they killed.

6 "Having yet his one well-beloved son, he sent him last to them, saying, 'They will revere my son.'

7 "But those vinedressers said among themselves, 'This is the heir. Come, let us kill him, and the inheritance will be ours.' 8 So they took him and killed him and threw him out of the vineyard.

9 "What then will the owner of the vineyard do? He will come and kill the vinedressers and

11:10 Lk 2:14
11:13 Lk 13:6–9
11:14 Mt 21:19
11:15 Mt 21:12–16
11:17 Isa 56:7
11:18 Mt 7:28
11:19 Lk 21:37
11:23 Mt 17:20
11:24 1 Jn 3:22
11:25 Col 3:13
11:27 Mt 21:23–27
11:28 Ex 2:14

[1] *17* Isa 56:7. [2] *17* Jer 7:11.

give the vineyard to others. 10 Have you not
read this Scripture:

'The stone which the builders rejected
has become the cornerstone.
11 This was the Lord's doing,
and it is marvelous in our eyes'[1]?"

12 Then they tried to seize Him, but feared
the people, for they knew that He had spoken
the parable against them. So they left Him and
went their way.

The Question of Paying Taxes
Mt 22:15–22; Lk 20:20–26

13 They sent to Him some of the Pharisees
and some of the Herodians to trap Him in
His words. 14 When they came to Him, they
said, "Teacher, we know that You are true and
swayed by no man. For You do not regard the
person of men, but truthfully teach the way
of God. Is it lawful to pay taxes to Caesar, or
not? 15 Should we pay, or should we not pay?"
But He, knowing their hypocrisy, said to
them, "Why test Me? Bring Me a denarius that
I may see it." 16 They brought it, and He said to
them, "Whose image and inscription is this?"
They said to Him, "Caesar's."
17 Then Jesus answered them, "Render to
Caesar the things that are Caesar's, and to God
the things that are God's."
And they were amazed at Him.

The Question About the Resurrection
Mt 22:23–33; Lk 20:27–40

18 Then the Sadducees, who say there is no
resurrection, came to Him, saying, 19 "Teach-
er, Moses wrote for us that if a man's brother
dies and leaves his wife behind, but leaves no
children, that man must take the wife and raise
up children for his brother.[2] 20 Now there were
seven brothers. The first took a wife, and when
he died, he left no children. 21 The second took
her and died, leaving no children, and the third
likewise. 22 The seven had her and left no chil-
dren. Last of all, the woman died too. 23 In the
resurrection, when they rise, whose wife will
she be? For the seven had her as wife."
24 Jesus answered them, "Do you not err,
because you know neither the Scriptures nor
the power of God? 25 When they rise from the
dead, they neither marry nor are given in mar-
riage, but are like angels in heaven. 26 Now
concerning the dead rising, have you not read
in the book of Moses, in the account about the
bush, how God spoke to him, saying, 'I am
the God of Abraham and the God of Isaac and
the God of Jacob'[3]? 27 He is not the God of the
dead, but the God of the living. You therefore
do greatly err."

12:12 Mk 11:18
12:13 Mk 3:6
12:17 Ro 13:7
12:26 Lk 20:37

12:28 Mt 22:34–40
12:29 Dt 6:4
12:31 Lev 19:18
12:33 1Sa 15:22
12:34 Mt 22:46
12:35 Lk 20:41–44
12:36 Ps 110:1
12:37 Ro 1:3–4
12:38 Lk 11:43
12:40 Lk 20:47
12:41 2Ki 12:9

The Great Commandment
Mt 22:34–40; Lk 10:25–28

28 One of the scribes came and heard them
reasoning together. Perceiving that Jesus had
answered them well, he asked Him, "Which is
the first commandment of all?"
29 Jesus answered him, "The first of all the
commandments is, 'Hear, O Israel, the Lord
our God is one Lord. 30 You shall love the Lord
your God with all your heart, and with all
your soul, and with all your mind, and with
all your strength.'[4] This is the first command-
ment. 31 The second is this: 'You shall love your
neighbor as yourself.'[5] There is no other com-
mandment greater than these."
32 The scribe said to Him, "Well said, Teacher.
You have spoken the truth, that there is one
God and there is no other but Him. 33 To love
Him with all the heart, and with all the under-
standing, and with all the soul, and with all the
strength, and to love one's neighbor as oneself,
is more than all burnt offerings and sacrifices."
34 When Jesus saw that he answered wisely,
He said to him, "You are not far from the king-
dom of God." After that, no one dared to ask
Him any question.

The Question About David's Son
Mt 22:41–46; Lk 20:41–44

35 While Jesus taught in the temple, He said,
"How can the scribes say that Christ is the Son
of David? 36 David himself, speaking by the
Holy Spirit, declared:

'The Lord said to my Lord,
"Sit at My right hand,
until I put Your enemies
under Your feet." '[6]

37 David himself calls Him 'Lord.' How then is
He his Son?"
And the large crowd heard him gladly.

The Denouncing of the Scribes
Mt 23:1–36; Lk 20:45–47

38 He said to them in His teaching, "Beware
of the scribes, who love to go about in long
robes and love greetings in the marketplaces,
39 and the prominent seats in the synagogues,
and the places of honor at banquets, 40 who
devour widows' houses and for a pretense
make long prayers. They will receive greater
condemnation."

The Widow's Offering
Lk 21:1–4

41 Jesus sat opposite the treasury and saw
how the people put money into the treasury.
Many who were rich put in much. 42 But a

[1] *10–11* Ps 118:22–23. [2] *19* Dt 25:5. [3] *26* Ex 3:6.
[4] *30* Dt 6:4–5. [5] *31* Lev 19:18. [6] *36* Ps 110:1.

Obstacles to Love

The heart is the spiritual organ that may be flooded with the love of God or become cold and distant toward Him. That is the reason it is named first in the greatest commandment: "You shall love the Lord your God with all your heart" (Mk 12:30).

Ultimately God's love cannot be hindered. But we can slow the flow of it through us if we allow any of the three obstacles described below to prevent our hearts from being filled with love for Christ.

Obstacle #1: Unbelief

The beginning point of our falling in love with Jesus is our trusting the Holy Spirit to put Christ's own faith within our hearts to believe the Scripture. The primary word Jesus spoke concerning our falling in love with Him is John 17:26: "I [Jesus] have declared Your name to them [the disciples], and will declare it, that the love with which You [the Father] loved Me may be in them, and I in them."

Therefore faith must always be the first aspect in any spiritual advance. We cannot love Jesus until we trust Him to be in us what He requires of us (1Co 1:30). Christianity is not a way of life in which we do more and more and therefore appear to be more Christlike. Christianity is a way of life in which *we get out of the way* more and more and allow Christ to manifest Himself through us (2Co 4:10–11).

Obstacle #2: Unforgiveness

A second hindrance to Christ's love flowing through us is unforgiveness. We are always to remember the inestimable love of God in His forgiveness of our past sins through Christ Jesus.

Extending full forgiveness to others who may have wronged us is a key to keeping our hearts open to allow the love of Christ to flow through them. Paul said we must be committed to "forgive one another. If anyone has a quarrel against anyone, even as Christ forgave you, so you must do" (Col 3:13). Of ourselves, we are unable to forgive others as He forgave us—fully and forever. But Christ's divine love through us for others includes His forgiveness of them.

Obstacle #3: Divided heart

The Bible tells us another major impediment to our loving Jesus as His Father does is a divided heart. In order for divine love to be effective, one's heart needs to be fully available for Christ to dwell there. We are to be strengthened with power through Jesus' spirit in our inner person, "that Christ may dwell in [our] hearts through faith" (Eph 3:17).

Therefore set yourself to know Him—really know Him—and learn to love Him above all else. Do not let the enemy deceive you by telling you there are equally glorious pursuits and equally great attainments. There are not. He is the Prize—and when you pursue Him, all things, all things, all things are added unto you (Mt 6:33; Rom 8:32; 1Cor 3:21–23; Col 2:10).

Anna Rountree

certain poor widow came and put in two mites, which make a farthing.[1]

43 He called His disciples to Him and said to them, "Truly I say to you, this poor widow has put in more than all those who are contributing to the treasury. 44 They all contributed out of their abundance. But she, out of her poverty, put in all that she had, her entire livelihood."

The Destruction of the Temple Foretold
Mt 24:1–2; Lk 21:5–6

13 As He went out of the temple, one of His disciples said to Him, "Teacher, see what great stones and what great buildings are here."

2 Jesus answered him, "Do you see these great buildings? Not one stone shall be left upon another that shall not be thrown down."

Troubles and Persecutions
Mt 24:3–14; Lk 21:7–19

3 As He sat on the Mount of Olives opposite the temple, Peter, James, John, and Andrew asked Him privately, 4 "Tell us, when will these things happen, and what will be the sign when all these things will be fulfilled?"

5 Jesus answered them, "Take heed lest anyone deceive you. 6 Many will come in My name, saying, 'I am He,' and will deceive many. 7 When you hear of wars and rumors of wars, do not be troubled. For such things must happen, but the end is still to come. 8 For nation will rise against nation, and kingdom against kingdom. And there will be earthquakes in various places, and there will be famines and troubles. These are the beginning of sorrows.

9 "But take heed. For they will hand you over to councils, and in the synagogues you will be beaten. You will be brought before rulers and kings for My sake, as a testimony to them. 10 And the gospel must first be preached to all nations. 11 But when they arrest you and hand you over, take no thought beforehand, or premeditate what you should speak. But speak whatever is given you in that time, for it is not you who speaks, but the Holy Spirit.

12 "Now a brother will betray his brother to death, and the father the son; children will rise up against their parents, and will cause them to be put to death. 13 You will be hated by all men for My name's sake. But he who endures to the end shall be saved.

The Great Tribulation
Mt 24:15–28; Lk 21:20–24

14 "When you see the 'abomination of desolation'[2] spoken of by Daniel the prophet standing where it should not be (let the reader understand), then let those who are in Judea flee to the mountains. 15 Let him who is on the housetop not go down or enter the house to take anything out of his house. 16 Let him who is in the field not turn back to take his garment. 17 But woe to women who are pregnant and to those who nurse in those days! 18 Pray that your escape may not be in winter. 19 For in those days there will be distress as has not been from the beginning of the creation which God created to this time, nor ever shall be.

20 "Except the Lord shortened the days, no flesh would be saved. But for the sake of the elect, whom He chose, He shortened the days. 21 Then if anyone says to you, 'Look, here is the Christ!' or 'Look, there He is!' do not believe it. 22 For false christs and false prophets will rise and show signs and wonders to deceive, if possible, even the elect. 23 But take heed. I have told you all things beforehand.

The Coming of the Son of Man
Mt 24:29–31; Lk 21:25–28

24 "But in those days, after that distress,
'the sun will be darkened,
and the moon will not give her light;
25 the stars of heaven will fall,
and the powers that are in heaven will
be shaken.'[3]

26 "Then they will see the Son of Man coming in clouds with great power and glory. 27 Then He will send His angels and gather His elect from the four winds, from the farthest part of the earth to the farthest part of heaven.

The Lesson of the Fig Tree
Mt 24:32–35; Lk 21:29–33

28 "Now learn a parable of the fig tree: When her branch is yet tender and puts outs leaves, you know that summer is near. 29 So also, when you see these things come to pass, know that it is near, even at the doors. 30 Truly I say to you, this generation will not pass away until all these things happen. 31 Heaven and earth will pass away, but My words will not pass away.

The Unknown Day and Hour
Mt 24:36–44

32 "But concerning that day or hour no one knows, not even the angels in heaven, nor the Son, but only the Father. 33 Take heed, watch and pray. For you do not know when the time will come. 34 For the Son of Man is like a man leaving on a far journey who left his house and gave authority to his servants and to every man his work, and commanded the porter to watch.

35 "Watch therefore—for you do not know when the master of the house is coming, in the evening, or at midnight, or at the crowing of the rooster, or in the morning— 36 lest he

12:44 Lk 8:43
13:4 Ac 1:6–7
13:5 Jer 29:8
13:6 Mk 13:22
13:9 Mt 10:17–18
13:13 Mt 10:22
13:14 Da 9:27
....
13:17 Lk 23:29
13:19 Da 12:1
13:20 Isa 65:8–9
13:21 Lk 21:8
13:22 Mt 24:24
13:23 2Pe 3:17
13:24 Isa 13:10
13:25 Isa 34:4
13:26 Mt 16:27
13:27 Dt 30:4
13:29 Jas 5:9
13:31 Mt 5:18
13:32 Ac 1:7
13:33 Eph 6:18
13:34 Jn 10:3
13:35 Mt 24:42
13:36 Mk 14:40

[1] *42* Gk. *2 lepta.* A *lepton*, meaning "small" or "thin," was a fraction of a penny and the smallest coin circulated. [2] *14* Da 9:27; 11:31. [3] *24–25* Isa 13:10; 34:4.

come suddenly and find you sleeping. 37 What I say to you I say to all: Watch!"

The Plot to Kill Jesus

Mt 26:1–5; Lk 22:1–2; Jn 11:45–53

14 Now the feasts of the Passover and of Unleavened Bread were two days away. And the chief priests and the scribes looked for a way to seize Him secretly and kill Him. 2 But they said "Not on the feast day, lest there will be an uproar among the people."

The Anointing at Bethany

Mt 26:6–13; Jn 12:1–8

3 While He was in Bethany in the house of Simon the leper, as He sat at supper, a woman came with an alabaster jar of ointment, a very costly spikenard. She broke the jar and poured the ointment on His head.

4 There were some with indignation within themselves, saying, "Why was this ointment wasted? 5 It might have been sold for more than three hundred denarii[1] and given to the poor." And they grumbled against her.

6 Jesus said, "Leave her alone. Why do you trouble her? She has done a good work for Me. 7 You always have the poor with you, and whenever you wish, you may do good to them. But you will not always have Me. 8 She has done what she could. She has come beforehand to anoint My body for burial. 9 Truly I say to you, wherever this gospel will be preached throughout the whole world, what she has done will also be spoken of as a memorial to her."

Judas' Agreement to Betray Jesus

Mt 26:14–18; Lk 22:3–6

10 Then Judas Iscariot, who was one of the twelve, went to the chief priests to betray Him to them. 11 When they heard it, they were glad and promised to give him silver. So he looked for how he might conveniently betray Him.

The Passover With the Disciples

Mt 26:17–28; Lk 22:7–14, 21–23; Jn 13:21–30

12 On the first day of Unleavened Bread, when they sacrificed the Passover lamb, His disciples said to Him, "Where do You want us to prepare for You to eat the Passover?"

13 So He sent two of His disciples and said to them, "Go into the city, and a man carrying a pitcher of water will meet you there. Follow him. 14 Wherever he enters, say to the owner of the house, 'The Teacher says, Where is the guest room where I may eat the Passover with My disciples?' 15 He will show you a large upper room, furnished and ready. Make preparations for us there."

16 His disciples went out, and came into the city, and found it as He had told them. And they prepared the Passover.

17 In the evening He came with the twelve. 18 As they sat and ate, Jesus said, "Truly I say to you, one of you who is eating with Me will betray Me."

19 They began to be sorrowful and to say to Him one by one, "Is it I?" and another, "Is it I?"

20 He answered them, "It is one of the twelve, one who is dipping bread in the dish with Me. 21 The Son of Man indeed goes as it is written concerning Him, but woe to that man by whom the Son of Man is betrayed! It would have been good for that man if he had never been born."

The Lord's Supper

Mt 26:26–30; Lk 22:15–20; 1Co 11:23–25

22 As they were eating, Jesus took bread, blessed and broke it, and gave it to them, saying, "Take and eat it. This is My body."

23 Then He took the cup, and when He had given thanks, He gave it to them. And they all drank from it.

24 He said to them, "This is My blood of the new covenant, which is shed for many. 25 Truly I say to you, I will drink no more of the fruit of the vine until that day when I drink it new in the kingdom of God."

26 When they had sung a hymn, they went out to the Mount of Olives.

Peter's Denial Foretold

Mt 26:31–35; Lk 22:31–34; Jn 13:36–38

27 Jesus said to them, "All of you will fall away on account of Me this night, for it is written:

'I will strike the shepherd,
    and the sheep will be scattered.'[2]

28 But after I have risen, I will go before you to Galilee."

29 Peter said to Him, "Even if all fall away, I will not."

30 Jesus said to him, "Truly, I say to you that this day, during the night, before the rooster crows twice, you will deny Me three times."

31 But he said more vehemently, "If I must die with You, I will not deny You." They all said the same thing.

The Prayer in Gethsemane

Mt 26:36–46; Lk 22:39–46

32 They came to a place which was named Gethsemane. And He said to His disciples, "Sit here while I pray." 33 He took Peter and James and John with Him and began to be greatly distressed and very troubled. 34 And He said to them, "My soul is deeply sorrowful unto death. Remain here and keep watch."

35 He went a little farther and fell on the ground and prayed that, if it were possible, the

13:37 Mk 13:35
14:1 Lk 22:1–2
14:5 Jn 13:29
14:7 Dt 15:11
14:8 2Co 8:12
14:9 Mk 16:15
14:10 Jn 13:2
14:14 Jn 11:28
14:15 Ac 1:13
14:17 Lk 22:14
14:20 Jn 13:26
14:21 Mk 14:49
14:22 Mt 26:26–29
14:23 1Co 10:16
14:24 Ex 24:8
14:25 Mt 26:29
14:26 Mt 26:30
14:27 Zec 13:7
14:28 Mt 28:16
14:32 Mt 26:36–46
14:34 Jn 12:27

[1] *5* A year's wages. [2] *27* Zec 13:7.

hour might pass from Him. 36 He said, "*Abba*, Father, all things are possible for You. Remove this cup from Me; yet not what I will, but what You will."

37 Then He came and found them sleeping and said to Peter, "Simon, are you sleeping? Could you not keep watch one hour? 38 Watch and pray, lest you enter into temptation. The spirit indeed is willing, but the flesh is weak."

39 Again He went away and prayed the same words. 40 When He returned, He again found them sleeping, for their eyes were heavy. And they did not know what to answer Him.

41 When He returned a third time, He said to them, "Are you still sleeping and taking your rest? It is enough! The hour has come. Look, the Son of Man is betrayed into the hands of sinners. 42 Rise up, let us go. Look! He who betrays Me is at hand."

The Betrayal and Arrest of Jesus
Mt 26:47–56; Lk 22:47–53; Jn 18:3–12

43 Immediately, while He was still speaking, Judas, one of the twelve, and with him a great crowd with swords and clubs, came from the chief priests and the scribes and the elders.

44 Now he who betrayed Him had given them a sign, saying, "Whomever I kiss, He is the One. Seize Him and lead Him away safely." 45 So as soon as he came, he went to Him immediately and said, "Rabbi, Rabbi!" and kissed Him. 46 They laid hands on Him and seized Him. 47 Then one of those who stood by drew his sword and struck the servant of the high priest and cut off his ear.

48 Jesus said to them, "Have you come out with swords and clubs to arrest Me as you would a thief? 49 Every day I was with you in the temple teaching, and you did not seize Me. But the Scriptures must be fulfilled." 50 Then they all deserted Him and fled.

The Young Man Who Fled

51 A young man followed Him, wearing a linen cloth around himself. And the young men laid hold of him, 52 so he left the linen cloth, and fled from them unclothed.

Jesus Before the Sanhedrin
Mt 26:57–68; Lk 22:54–55, 63–71; Jn 18:13–14, 19–24

53 They led Jesus away to the high priest. And all the chief priests and the elders and the scribes were assembled with him. 54 Peter followed Him at a distance into the courtyard of the high priest. He sat with the guards and warmed himself by the fire.

55 Now the chief priests and the entire Sanhedrin requested testimony against Jesus to put Him to death, but found none. 56 Many bore false witness against Him, but their testimonies did not agree.

57 Then some rose up and bore false witness against Him, saying, 58 "We heard Him say, 'I will destroy this temple that is made with hands, and within three days I will build another not made with hands.' " 59 But still their testimony did not agree.

60 Then the high priest stood up in the midst and asked Jesus, "Do You answer nothing? What is it which these men testify against You?" 61 But He kept silent and answered nothing.

Again the high priest asked Him, "Are You the Christ, the Son of the Blessed One?"

62 Jesus said, "I am. And you will see the Son of Man sitting at the right hand of Power and coming with the clouds of heaven."

63 The high priest tore his robes, saying, "What need do we have of any further witnesses? 64 You have heard the blasphemy. What do you think?"

They all condemned Him as guilty unto death. 65 Then some began to spit on Him, and to blindfold Him, and to strike Him, saying to Him, "Prophesy!" And the guards struck Him with the palms of their hands.

Peter's Denial of Jesus
Mt 26:69–75; Lk 22:56–62; Jn 18:15–18, 25–27

66 While Peter was below in the courtyard, one of the servant girls of the high priest came. 67 When she saw Peter warming himself, she looked at him and said, "You also were with Jesus of Nazareth."

68 But he denied it, saying, "I neither know nor understand what you are saying." Then he went out to the porch, and a rooster crowed.

69 The servant girl saw him again and began to say to those who stood by, "This man is one of them." 70 But again, he denied it.

A little while later, those who stood by said again to Peter, "Surely, you are one of them. For you are a Galilean, and your speech confirms it."

71 Peter began to invoke a curse on himself, and to swear, "I do not know this Man of whom you speak."

72 And the rooster crowed a second time. And Peter called to mind the word that Jesus said to him, "Before the rooster crows twice, you will deny Me three times." And when he thought on this, he wept.

Jesus Before Pilate
Mt 27:1–2, 11–14; Lk 23:1–5; Jn 18:28–38

15 Early in the morning the chief priests held a consultation with the elders and scribes and the whole Sanhedrin. And they

14:36 Gal 4:6
14:43 Ac 1:16
14:50 Mk 14:27
14:53 Mt 26:57–68
14:54 Jn 18:18
....
14:57 Mt 26:60–61
14:61 Isa 53:7
14:62 Ps 110:1
14:63 Nu 14:6
14:64 Lev 24:16
14:66 Mk 14:54
14:67 Mk 14:54
14:70 Ac 2:7
14:72 Mk 14:30
15:1 Mt 27:1–2

bound Jesus and took Him away and handed
Him over to Pilate.
2 Pilate asked Him, "Are You the King of the
Jews?"
He answered him, "You have said so."
3 The chief priests accused Him of many
things, but He answered nothing. 4 So Pilate
asked Him again, "Do You answer nothing?
See how many things they testify against You."
5 But Jesus still answered nothing, so that
Pilate was astonished.

Jesus Sentenced to Die
Mt 27:15–26; Lk 23:13–25; Jn 18:39–19:16

6 Now at the feast he always released to
them one prisoner, whomever they requested.
7 There was one named Barabbas, who had
committed murder in the insurrection and was
bound with the rebels. 8 The crowd began cry-
ing aloud, asking Pilate to do as he had always
done for them.
9 He answered them, "Do you want me to
release to you the King of the Jews?" 10 For he
knew that the chief priests had handed Him
over out of envy. 11 But the chief priests stirred
the people, so that he should instead release
Barabbas to them.
12 Pilate answered them again, "What then
would you have me do to Him whom you call
the King of the Jews?"
13 They again cried out, "Crucify Him!"
14 Pilate said to them, "Why, what evil has
He done?"
But they cried out even more, "Crucify Him!"
15 So Pilate, resolving to satisfy the people,
released Barabbas to them. And when he had
scourged Jesus, he handed Him over to be
crucified.

The Soldiers Mock Jesus
Mt 27:27–31; Jn 19:2–3

16 The soldiers led Him away to Praetorium
Hall, and they called together the entire bat-
talion. 17 They clothed Him with a purple robe.
And they wove a crown of thorns and put it
on His head, 18 and began to salute Him, "Hail,
King of the Jews!" 19 They struck His head with
a staff and spit on Him. And bowing their
knees, they worshipped Him. 20 When they had
mocked Him, they took the purple robe off of
Him and put His own garments on Him. Then
they led Him out to crucify Him.

The Crucifixion
Mt 27:32–44; Lk 23:26–43; Jn 19:17–27

21 They compelled a man named Simon from
Cyrene, the father of Alexander and Rufus, as
he was passing through from the country, to
bear Jesus' cross. 22 They brought Him to the
place called Golgotha, which means, "Place
of a Skull." 23 They gave Him wine mingled
with myrrh to drink, but He did not take it.
24 When they had crucified Him, they divided
His garments, casting lots for them, to decide
what each man should take.
25 Now it was the third hour, and they cruci-
fied Him. 26 The inscription of His accusation
was written above:

THE KING OF THE JEWS.

27 With Him they crucified two thieves, one
on His right and the other on His left. 28 And
the Scripture was fulfilled, which says, "He was
numbered with the lawless ones."[1] 29 Those
who passed by blasphemed Him, shaking
their heads and saying, "Ah, You who would
destroy the temple and build it in three days,
30 save Yourself, and come down from the
cross!" 31 Likewise the chief priests mocked
Him among themselves with the scribes and
said, "He saved others, but He cannot save
Himself! 32 Let the Christ, the King of Israel,
descend now from the cross, that we may see
and believe." Those who were crucified with
Him also reviled Him.

The Death of Jesus
Mt 27:45–56; Lk 23:44–49; Jn 19:28–30

33 When the sixth hour had come, there was
darkness over the whole land until the ninth
hour. 34 And at the ninth hour Jesus cried out
with a loud voice, saying, "*Eloi, Eloi, lama sa-
bachthani?*" which means, "My God, My God,
why have You forsaken Me?"[2]
35 Some of those who stood by, when they
heard it, said, "Listen, He is calling Elijah!"
36 One man ran and filled a sponge with vin-
egar, put it on a stick, and gave it to Him to
drink, saying, "Leave Him alone. Let us see if
Elijah will come to take Him down."
37 But Jesus cried with a loud voice and gave
up the spirit.
38 And the curtain of the temple was torn in
two from top to bottom. 39 When the centurion[3]
who stood facing Him saw that He cried out
and gave up the spirit, he said, "Truly, this Man
was the Son of God."
40 There were also women looking on from a
distance, among whom were Mary Magdalene,
and Mary the mother of James the Less and of
Joseph, and Salome. 41 They also had followed
Him and had ministered to Him when He was
in Galilee. And many other women who came
up with Him to Jerusalem were there.

The Burial of Jesus
Mt 27:57–61; Lk 23:50–56; Jn 19:38–42

42 When the evening had come, because it
was the Day of Preparation, that is, the day

15:2 Mt 2:2
15:3 Isa 53:7
15:4 Jn 19:10
15:6 Jn 18:39–40
15:11 Ac 3:14
15:14 Lk 23:41
15:15 Mt 27:26
15:16 Jn 18:28
15:17 Lk 23:11
15:19 Mk 14:65
15:21 Mt 27:32
15:22 Mt 27:33–44
15:23 Mt 27:34
15:26 Mt 27:37
15:29 Ps 109:25
15:32 Lk 23:39–43
15:33 Mt 27:45
15:34 Ps 22:1
15:36 Ps 69:21
15:37 Jn 19:30
15:38 Lk 23:45
15:39 Mt 27:54
15:40 Ps 38:11
15:41 Lk 8:2–3

[1] *28* Isa 53:12. [2] *34* Ps 22:1. [3] *39* Commander with the rank of captain over 100 soldiers.

before the Sabbath, 43 Joseph of Arimathea, an honorable member of the Council, who also waited for the kingdom of God, came and went in boldly to Pilate, and requested the body of Jesus. 44 Pilate wondered if He were already dead. And calling for the centurion, he asked him whether He had been dead for a while. 45 When he learned about it from the centurion, he granted the body to Joseph. 46 So he bought fine linen, and taking Him down, wrapped Him in the linen and laid Him in a tomb which had been hewn out of the rock. And he rolled a stone against the door of the tomb. 47 Mary Magdalene and Mary the mother of Joseph saw where He was laid.

The Resurrection of Jesus

Mt 28:1–8; Lk 24:1–12; Jn 20:1–10

16 When the Sabbath was past, Mary Magdalene, and Mary the mother of James, and Salome, bought spices, so that they might go and anoint Him. 2 Very early in the morning, on the first day of the week, they came to the tomb at the rising of the sun. 3 They said among themselves, "Who will roll the stone away from the door of the tomb for us?"

4 But when they looked, they saw that the stone had been rolled away. For it was very large. 5 And entering the tomb, they saw a young man sitting on the right side, clothed in a long white robe. And they were frightened.

6 He said to them, "Do not be frightened. You are looking for Jesus of Nazareth, who was crucified. He is risen. He is not here. See the place where they laid Him. 7 But go your way, tell His disciples and Peter that He is going before you to Galilee. There you will see Him, as He told you."

8 They went out quickly and fled from the tomb, for they trembled and were amazed. And they said nothing to anyone, for they were afraid.

The Appearance to Mary Magdalene

Mt 28:9–10; Jn 20:11–18

9 Now when Jesus rose early on the first day of the week, He appeared first to Mary Magdalene, out of whom He had cast seven demons. 10 She went and told those who had been with Him as they mourned and wept. 11 When they heard that He was alive and had been seen by her, they did not believe it.

The Appearance to Two Disciples

Lk 24:13–35

12 After that He appeared in another form to two of them as they walked and went into the country. 13 And they went and told it to the rest, but they did not believe them either.

15:43 Lk 2:25
15:47 Mk 15:40
16:1 Mk 15:40
16:5 Jn 20:11–12
16:7 Mk 14:28
16:11 Lk 24:11
16:12 Lk 24:13–32

....

16:14 1Co 15:5
16:15 Mt 28:19
16:16 Jn 3:36
16:17 Ac 5:16
16:18 Lk 10:19

SPIRITLED WOMAN

COUNSEL FROM THE SPIRIT BASICS

Worship Is...

When worship is who we are and what we do, when it is our lifestyle, we have the ability to change the atmosphere around us and be an influence for good in any situation. Why? God's dynamic power, His anointing, goes to work in ways we could never imagine.

This reminds me of Mark 16:15–18. Jesus said:

> Go into all the world, and preach the gospel to every creature.... These signs will accompany those who believe: In My name they will cast out demons; they will speak with new tongues; they will take up serpents; if they drink any deadly thing, it will not hurt them; they will lay hands on the sick, and they will recover.

In other words, by the power of the Holy Spirit, we can take charge of the atmosphere around us, injecting a dynamic, positive anointing into negative situations. We can bring light into darkness, declare healing to displace sickness, declare deliverance to set captives free, and, yes, even make dead things come alive again.

Judy Jacobs

The Commissioning of the Disciples

Mt 28:16–20; Lk 24:36–49; Jn 20:19–23; Ac 1:6–8

14 Afterward He appeared to the eleven as they sat at supper, and He reprimanded them for their unbelief and hardness of heart, because they did not believe those who had seen Him after He had risen.

15 He said to them, "Go into all the world, and preach the gospel to every creature. 16 He who believes and is baptized will be saved. But he who does not believe will be condemned. 17 These signs will accompany those who believe: In My name they will cast out demons; they will speak with new tongues; 18 they will

Signs should accompany my work (Mk 16:17–20).

take up serpents; if they drink any deadly thing, it will not hurt them; they will lay hands on the sick, and they will recover."

The Ascension
Lk 24:50–53; Ac 1:9–11

19 After the Lord had spoken to them, He was received up into heaven and sat at the right hand of God. 20 Then they went forth and preached everywhere, the Lord working with them and confirming the word through the accompanying signs. Amen.

16:19 1Pe 3:22

If we are wholehearted followers of Christ, we will in turn make more followers, or disciples, of Christ naturally through authentic and loving relationships (Mk 16:20).

Author: The apostle Luke

Written: Early AD 60s, possibly from Rome or Achaia

Themes: Compassion and Healing Ministry of Jesus

LUKE

Dear SpiritLed Woman,

Do you sometimes feel overwhelmed by the difficulties that confront you in your life? Our enemy, Satan, wants us to feel powerless in the face of the problems we encounter, but we don't have to be defeated by them. God has given us the authority we need to overcome the things that rise up to hinder us. In fact, He has given us authority over all Satan's power. In Luke 10:19 Jesus assures us, "Look, I give you authority to trample on serpents and scorpions, and over all the power of the enemy. And nothing shall by any means hurt you."

Though you can't control the will of another person, you can take authority over the spirits that may be motivating him or her to act in a certain way. Webster's Dictionary defines *authority* as "the right to govern, control, or command." It is delegated power from one at a higher level. As a SpiritLed woman, you have this authority. Stay in close fellowship with the Holy Spirit, and you will be able to operate in this authority to bring God's power and rulership into earthly situations.

Joy F. Strang

The Prologue

1 Whereas many have undertaken to write a narrative of those things which are most surely believed among us, 2 just as they were handed down to us by those who from the beginning were eyewitnesses and ministers of the word, 3 it seemed good to me also, having accurately investigated all things from the very beginning, to write to you an orderly account, most excellent Theophilus, 4 that you might know the certainty of the things which you have been told.

The Birth of John the Baptist Foretold

5 There was in the days of Herod, the king of Judea, a certain priest named Zechariah, of the division of Abijah. And his wife was of the daughters of Aaron, and her name was Elizabeth. 6 They were both righteous before God, walking in all the commandments and ordinances of the Lord blamelessly. 7 But they had no child, because Elizabeth was barren, and they both were now well advanced in years.

8 Now while he served as priest before God, when his division was on duty, 9 according to the custom of the priest's office, his lot was to burn incense when he went into the temple of the Lord. 10 And the whole crowd of people were praying outside at the hour of incense.

11 Then an angel of the Lord appeared to him, standing on the right side of the altar of incense. 12 When Zechariah saw him, he was troubled, and fear fell upon him. 13 But the angel said to him, "Do not fear, Zechariah, for your prayer has been heard, and your wife Elizabeth will bear you a son, and you shall call his name John. 14 You will have joy and gladness, and many will rejoice at his birth. 15 For he will be great in the sight of the Lord, and shall drink neither wine nor strong drink, and he will be filled with the Holy Spirit, even from his mother's womb. 16 He will turn many of the sons of Israel to the Lord their God. 17 And he will go before Him in the spirit and power of Elijah, to turn the hearts of the fathers to the children[1] and the disobedient to the wisdom of the just, to make ready a people prepared for the Lord."

18 Zechariah said to the angel, "How shall I know this? For I am an old man and my wife well advanced in years."

19 The angel answered him, "I am Gabriel, who stands in the presence of God. And I was sent to speak to you and to bring you this good news. 20 And now you will be silent and unable to speak until the day that these things happen, because you did not believe my words, which will be fulfilled in their season."

[1] *17* Mal 4:5–6.

1:2 Jn 15:27
1:3 Ac 1:1
1:4 Jn 20:31
1:5 1Ch 24:10
1:6 Ge 7:1
1:8 1Ch 24:19
1:9 Ex 30:7–8
1:10 Lev 16:17
1:11 Ex 40:26–27
1:13 Ac 10:31
1:14 Lk 1:58
1:15 Lk 7:33
1:17 Mt 11:14
1:18 Ge 17:17
1:19 Mt 18:10
1:20 Eze 3:26
....
1:22 Lk 1:62
1:23 1Ch 9:25
1:25 Isa 4:1
1:26 Mt 2:23
1:27 Mt 1:18
1:28 Jdg 6:12
1:29 Lk 1:12
1:30 Lk 1:13
1:31 Isa 7:14
1:32 Mk 5:7
1:33 Da 2:44
1:35 Mt 1:18
1:37 Mt 19:26
1:39 Lk 1:65
1:41 Lk 1:67
1:42 Jdg 5:24
1:43 Jn 20:28

21 The people waited for Zechariah, and wondered why he waited so long in the temple. 22 When he came out, he could not speak to them. They perceived that he had seen a vision in the temple, for he made signs to them and remained speechless.

23 As soon as the days of his service were fulfilled, he departed to his own home. 24 After those days his wife Elizabeth conceived, and for five months she hid herself, saying, 25 "Thus the Lord has dealt with me in the days when He looked on me, to take away my reproach among men."

The Birth of Jesus Foretold

26 In the sixth month the angel Gabriel was sent from God to a city of Galilee named Nazareth, 27 to a virgin betrothed to a man whose name was Joseph, of the house of David. And the virgin's name was Mary. 28 The angel came to her and said, "Greetings, you who are highly favored. The Lord is with you. Blessed are you among women."

29 When she saw him, she was troubled by his words, and considered in her mind what kind of greeting this might be. 30 But the angel said to her, "Do not be afraid, Mary, for you have found favor with God. 31 Listen, you will conceive in your womb and bear a Son and shall call His name JESUS. 32 He will be great, and will be called the Son of the Highest. And the Lord God will give Him the throne of His father David, 33 and He will reign over the house of Jacob forever. And of His kingdom there will be no end."

34 Then Mary said to the angel, "How can this be, since I do not know a man?"

35 The angel answered her, "The Holy Spirit will come upon you, and the power of the Highest will overshadow you. Therefore the Holy One who will be born will be called the Son of God. 36 Listen, your cousin Elizabeth has also conceived a son in her old age. And this is the sixth month with her who was declared barren. 37 For with God nothing will be impossible."

38 Mary said, "I am the servant of the Lord. May it be unto me according to your word." Then the angel departed from her.

Mary Visits Elizabeth

39 In those days Mary arose and quickly went into the hill country, to a city of Judah, 40 and entered the house of Zechariah and greeted Elizabeth. 41 When Elizabeth heard the greeting of Mary, the baby leaped in her womb. And Elizabeth was filled with the Holy Spirit. 42 She spoke out with a loud voice, "Blessed are you among women, and blessed is the fruit of your womb! 43 But why is this granted to me, that

MARY, THE MOTHER OF JESUS

"LET IT BE UNTO ME"

Declaring "Let it be unto me" to God's Word is saying a resounding yes to the Lord. Many scholars believe Mary was a very beautiful young lady in her early teens when the angel came and said, "Greetings, you who are highly favored. The Lord is with you. Blessed are you among women." Furthermore, "when she saw him, she was troubled by his words, and considered in her mind what kind of greeting this might be" (Lk 1:28–29).

At this point the world was in a terrible predicament and needed a Savior. We all know this story well, and we know Mary's response. But let's walk through the process a little.

As Mary listened to the angel, thinking deeply about the repercussions this would bring, she counted the cost and determined there was only one thing for her to say: "I am the servant of the Lord. May it be unto me according to your word" (v. 38).

Let me put her response another way: "Lord, I don't know what this is going to be like, what everyone will think, especially Joseph, or how this is going to turn out—all I know is I believe what I've been told. I agree with Your word." And the anointing of God went to work.

Many believers know what God has spoken—prophesied, decreed, and declared—over their lives. Yet many still wonder about, doubt, and analyze God's revealed word to them, trying to cross every *t* and dot every *i*...but let that not be said of you and me! God is saying, "Come on in. The water feels good. Just jump. I'm going to catch you. Don't worry about what people think. Just get in the river of My anointing and see how glorious it will be to walk on water."

What would have happened if Mary had not said yes? I'll tell you what would have happened: God would have moved on to someone else, because the work of the Lord must go on, either with or without us. Young Mary was willing to say yes to God in spite of the unknown and to follow His leading. Thousands of years later she is honored because of it.

At some point you will have to start saying, "Let it be to me according to Your Word, Lord. Whatever You have for me, I am ready." I declare to you today, let it be!

Going to the nations...*let it be!*

Starting a homeless ministry...*let it be!*

Starting your own business to finance the kingdom...*let it be!*

Witnessing to your neighbors...*let it be!*

Starting a Bible study at work...*let it be!*

Financing this "last day" outpouring...*let it be!*

You have to be willing to say yes to God and really mean it. Here's the thing: when you say yes, God knows if you are totally sincere because He knows your heart, so you might as well go ahead and be honest with Him the first time. He's waiting for you to believe and respond. Be like Mary and say yes, without doubt or hesitation. *You are anointed for this!*

Judy Jacobs

the mother of my Lord should come to me?
44 Indeed, as soon as the sound of your greet-
ing came to my ears, the baby in my womb
leaped for joy. 45 Blessed is she who believed,
for there will be a completion to those things
which were told her by the Lord."

The Song of Mary

46 And Mary said:

"My soul magnifies the Lord,
47 and my spirit rejoices in God my Savior.
48 For He has regarded
the low estate of His servant;
surely, from now on all generations will call
me blessed.
49 For He who is mighty has done great
things for me,
and holy is His name.
50 His mercy is on those who fear Him
from generation to generation.
51 He has shown strength with His arm;
He has scattered the proud in the
imagination of their hearts.

> Show strength with Your arm, and scatter the proud (Lk 1:51).

52 He has pulled down the mighty from their
thrones
and exalted those of low degree.
53 He has filled the hungry with good things,
and the rich He has sent away empty.
54 He has helped His servant Israel,
in remembrance of His mercy,
55 as He spoke to our fathers,
to Abraham and to his descendants
forever."[1]

56 Mary remained with her about three
months and returned to her own house.

The Birth of John the Baptist

57 Now Elizabeth's time had come to give
birth, and she gave birth to a son. 58 Her
neighbors and cousins heard how the Lord
had shown her great mercy, and they rejoiced
with her.

59 On the eighth day they came to circumcise
the child. And they were calling him Zechariah,
after the name of his father. 60 But his mother
answered, "Not so! He shall be called John."

61 They said to her, "There is no one among
your relatives who is called by this name."

62 They made signs to his father, asking what
he would have him called. 63 He asked for a
writing tablet and wrote, "His name is John."
And they all were amazed. 64 Immediately his
mouth was opened and his tongue was loosed,
and he spoke and praised God. 65 Fear came
on all who lived around them. And all these
facts were talked about throughout all the hill
country of Judea. 66 All those who heard them
laid them up in their hearts, saying, "What kind
of child will he be?" For the hand of the Lord
was with him.

The Prophecy of Zechariah

67 His father Zechariah was filled with the
Holy Spirit and prophesied, saying,

68 "Blessed be the Lord God of Israel,
for He has visited and redeemed His
people,
69 and has raised up a horn of salvation for us
in the house of His servant David,
70 as He spoke by the mouth of His holy
prophets of long ago,
71 that we should be saved from our enemies
and from the hand of all who hate us,
72 to perform the mercy promised to our
fathers
and to remember His holy covenant,
73 the oath which He swore to our father
Abraham,
74 to grant us that we, being delivered out of
the hand of our enemies,
might serve Him without fear,
75 in holiness and righteousness before
Him all the days of our lives.
76 "And you, child, will be called the prophet
of the Highest;
for you will go before the face of the
Lord to prepare His ways,
77 to give knowledge of salvation to His
people
by the remission of their sins,
78 through the tender mercy of our God,
whereby the sunrise from on high has
visited us;
79 to give light to those who sit in darkness
and in the shadow of death,
to guide our feet into the way of peace."

80 And the child grew and became strong in
spirit, and he remained in the wilderness until
the day of his appearance to Israel.

The Birth of Jesus

Mt 1:18–25

2 In those days a decree went out from
Caesar Augustus that the entire inhabit-
ed earth should be taxed. 2 This taxation was
first made when Quirinius was governor of
Syria. 3 And everyone went to his own city to
be taxed.

4 So Joseph also departed from the city of
Nazareth in Galilee to the City of David which
is called Bethlehem, in Judea, because he was
of the house and lineage of David, 5 to be taxed

1:45 Lk 1:20
1:46 Ps 34:2–3
1:47 1Ti 1:1
1:48 Ps 138:6
1:49 Ps 111:9
1:50 Ex 20:6
1:51 Ps 98:1
1:54 Ps 98:3
1:55 Ge 17:19
1:59 Ge 17:12
1:60 Lk 1:13
1:62 Lk 1:22
1:63 Lk 1:60
1:64 Lk 1:20
....
1:65 Lk 1:39
1:66 Ac 11:21
1:67 Joel 2:28
1:68 1Ki 1:48
1:69 1Sa 2:10
1:71 Ps 106:10
1:72 Ps 106:45
1:74 Heb 9:14
1:75 Eph 4:24
1:76 Mal 3:1
1:78 Mal 4:2
1:79 Isa 9:2
1:80 Lk 2:40
2:1 Lk 3:1
2:2 Lk 3:1
2:4 Jn 7:42

[1] *46–55* 1Sa 2:1–10; Mic 7:20; Ge 17:7; 18:18; 22:17.

SPIRIT-TO-SPIRIT PRAYER

PRAYER FOR JOY

Heavenly Father, may Your Spirit fill us with Your glory and joy unspeakable. May we come to know You in a very real and true way, as the guiding light for our lives. For where there is light, darkness must flee. May Your light shine through us, like a beacon of truth for others seeking help. We have been settling for survival mode, struggling through a life of our own making. We ask You to please forgive us for making foolish choices that have led us down a weary and painful path. We know this is not the abundant life You planned for us, and we ask You to please help us begin anew today. We want to serve You above all others. We want to trust You in good times and bad—with money in the bank and when we're flat broke. If we are feeling the fiery flames of life licking our heels, let us not give in to temptation or take the easy way out, but let us follow the commands found in Your Word so that we might obtain the rich fulfillment You have promised. In Jesus's name, amen.

Tish Hagee Tucker

with Mary, his betrothed wife, who was with
child. 6 So while they were there, the day came
for her to give birth. 7 And she gave birth to her
firstborn Son, and wrapped Him in strips of
cloth, and laid Him in a manger, because there
was no room for them in the inn.

The Shepherds and the Angels

8 And in the same area there were shepherds
living in the fields, keeping watch over their
flock by night. 9 And then an angel of the Lord
appeared to them, and the glory of the Lord
shone around them, and they were very afraid.
10 But the angel said to them, "Listen! Do not
fear. For I bring you good news of great joy,
which will be to all people. 11 For unto you is
born this day in the City of David a Savior, who
is Christ the Lord. 12 And this will be a sign to
you: You will find the Baby wrapped in strips
of cloth, lying in a manger."
13 Suddenly there was with the angel a com-
pany of the heavenly host praising God and
saying,

14 "Glory to God in the highest,
and on earth peace, and good will
toward men."

15 When the angels went away from them into
heaven, the shepherds said to each other, "Let
us now go to Bethlehem and see what has hap-
pened, which the Lord has made known to us."
16 So they came hurrying and found Mary
and Joseph, and the Baby lying in a manger.
17 When they had seen Him, they made widely
known the word which was told them concern-
ing this Child. 18 And all those who heard it mar-
veled at what the shepherds told them. 19 But
Mary kept all these things and pondered them
in her heart. 20 The shepherds returned, glori-
fying and praising God for all the things they
had heard and seen, as it had been told them.

The Presentation of Jesus in the Temple

21 When eight days had passed and the Child
was circumcised, He was named JESUS, the
name given by the angel before He was con-
ceived in the womb.
22 When the days of her purification accord-
ing to the Law of Moses were completed, they
brought Him to Jerusalem to present Him to
the Lord 23 (as it is written in the law of the
Lord, "Every firstborn male shall be called holy
to the Lord"[1]) 24 and to offer a sacrifice accord-
ing to what is said in the law of the Lord, "a
pair of turtledoves, or two young pigeons."[2]
25 Now there was a man in Jerusalem whose
name was Simeon, and this man was righteous
and devout, waiting for the consolation of
Israel, and the Holy Spirit was upon him. 26 It
was revealed to him by the Holy Spirit that he
would not die before he had seen the Lord's
Christ. 27 Led by the Spirit, he came into the
temple. And when the parents brought in
the Child Jesus, to do for Him according to

2:9 2Co 3:18
2:11 Mt 1:21
2:14 Lk 1:79

2:19 Lk 2:51
2:21 Lk 1:31
2:23 Ex 13:2
2:25 Lk 1:6
2:26 Jn 8:51

[1] *23* Ex 13:2, 12; Nu 3:13; 8:17. [2] *24* Lev 5:11; 12:8.

the custom of the law, 28 he received Him in
his arms and blessed God and said:

29 "Lord, now let Your servant depart in
peace,
according to Your word;
30 for my eyes have seen Your salvation
31 which You have prepared in the sight of
all people,
32 a light for revelation to the Gentiles,
and the glory of Your people Israel."

33 Joseph and His mother were amazed at
those things which were spoken about Him.
34 Then Simeon blessed them and said to Mary
His mother, "Listen, this Child is destined to
cause the fall and rising of many in Israel and
to be a sign which will be spoken against, 35 so
that the thoughts of many hearts may be re-
vealed. And a sword will pierce through your
own soul also."
36 And there was Anna a prophetess, a daugh-
ter of Phanuel, of the tribe of Asher. She was
of a great age and had lived with her husband
seven years from her virginity. 37 And she was a
widow of about eighty-four years of age who
did not depart from the temple, but served God
with fasting and prayer night and day. 38 Com-
ing at that moment she gave thanks to the Lord
and spoke of Him to all those who looked for
the redemption of Jerusalem.

The Return to Nazareth

39 When they had performed everything ac-
cording to the law of the Lord, they returned
to Galilee, to their own city of Nazareth. 40 And
the Child grew and became strong in spirit,
filled with wisdom. And the grace of God was
upon Him.

The Boy Jesus in the Temple

41 Now His parents went to Jerusalem every
year at the Feast of the Passover. 42 When He
was twelve years old, they went up to Jeru-
salem according to the custom of the feast.
43 When the days of the feast were complete,
as they returned, the Child Jesus remained be-
hind in Jerusalem. And Joseph and His mother
did not know of it. 44 But supposing Him to be
in their company, they went a day's journey.
Then they searched for Him among their rela-
tives and acquaintances. 45 When they did not
find Him, they returned to Jerusalem, search-
ing for Him. 46 After three days they found
Him in the temple, sitting in the midst of the
teachers, listening to them and asking them
questions. 47 All who heard Him were aston-
ished at His understanding and His answers.
48 When they saw Him, they were amazed. And
His mother said to Him, "Son, why have You
dealt with us like this? Look, Your father and I
have anxiously searched for You."
49 He said to them, "How is it that you
searched for Me? Did you not know that I
must be about My Father's business?" 50 But
they did not understand the word which He
spoke to them.
51 Then He went down with them and came
to Nazareth and was obedient to them. But His
mother kept all these words in her heart. 52 And
Jesus increased in wisdom and in stature and
in favor with God and men.

I have favor with God and with man (Lk 2:52).

The Preaching of John the Baptist

Mt 3:1–12; Mk 1:1–8; Jn 1:19–28

3 In the fifteenth year of the reign of Caesar
Tiberius, Pontius Pilate was governor of
Judea, Herod was tetrarch of Galilee, his broth-
er Philip was tetrarch of Iturea and the region
of Traconitis, and Lysanias was the tetrarch of
Abilene. 2 Annas and Caiaphas being the high
priests, the word of God came to John the son
of Zechariah in the wilderness. 3 He came into
the region surrounding the Jordan, preaching
the baptism of repentance for the remission of
sins. 4 As it is written in the book of the words
of Isaiah the prophet, saying:

"The voice of one crying in the wilderness:
'Prepare the way of the Lord;
make His paths straight.
5 Every valley shall be filled
and every mountain and hill shall be
brought low;
and the crooked shall be made straight
and the rough ways shall be made
smooth;
6 and all flesh shall see the salvation of God.' "[1]

Let every valley place in my life be exalted (Lk 3:5).

7 Then he said to the crowds that came out
to be baptized by him, "You children of vipers!
Who warned you to flee from the wrath to
come? 8 Therefore bear fruit worthy of repen-
tance, and do not begin to say to yourselves,
'We have Abraham as our father.' For I say to
you that God is able from these stones to raise
up children for Abraham. 9 Even now the axe is
put to the root of the trees. Every tree therefore
which does not bear good fruit is cut down and
thrown into the fire."

2:28 Lk 1:64
2:30 Lk 3:6
2:32 Isa 49:6
2:34 1Co 1:23
2:36 Ac 21:9
2:37 1Ti 5:5
2:38 Lk 2:25
2:39 Lk 2:4
2:40 Lk 2:52
2:46 Lk 5:17
2:47 Mt 7:28
....
2:49 Jn 4:34
2:50 Lk 18:34
2:51 Lk 2:19
2:52 1Sa 2:26
3:2 Ac 4:6
3:3 Lk 1:77
3:6 Isa 40:5
3:7 Mt 23:33
3:8 Jn 8:33
3:9 Mt 7:19

[1] 4–6 Isa 40:3–5.

[10] The people asked him, "What then must
we do?"
[11] John answered, "He who has two tunics,
let him give to him who has none. And he who
has food, let him do likewise."
[12] Then tax collectors also came to be bap-
tized and said to him, "Teacher, what must we
do?"
[13] He said to them, "Collect no more than
what is appointed you."
[14] Then the soldiers likewise demanded of
him, "And what must we do?"

He said to them, "Do no violence to anyone
nor accuse any falsely, and be content with
your wages."
[15] As the people were in expectation, and
everyone reflected in their hearts upon John,
whether he might be the Christ or not, [16] John
answered them all, "I indeed baptize you with
water. But One mightier than I is coming, the
strings of whose shoes I am not worthy to un-
tie. He will baptize you with the Holy Spirit and
with fire. [17] His fan is in His hand, and He will
thoroughly cleanse His threshing floor, and
will gather the wheat into His granary. But He
will burn the chaff with unquenchable fire."
[18] Then he preached many other things in his
exhortation to the people.
[19] But Herod the tetrarch, being rebuked by
him because of Herodias, his brother Philip's
wife, and for all the evils which Herod had
done, [20] added also this above them all: He
locked John up in prison.

The Baptism of Jesus
Mt 3:13–17; Mk 1:9–11

[21] Now when all the people were baptized,
and when Jesus also had been baptized and
was praying, the heavens were opened, [22] and
the Holy Spirit descended in a bodily form like
a dove on Him, and a voice came from heaven
which said, "You are My beloved Son. In You I
am well pleased."

The Genealogy of Jesus
Mt 1:1–17

[23] Now Jesus Himself began His ministry at
about thirty years of age, being, as was sup-
posed, the son of Joseph,

who was the son of Heli, [24] who was the son of Matthat,
who was the son of Levi, who was the son of Melchi,
who was the son of Jannai, who was the son of Joseph,
[25] who was the son of Mattathias, who was the son of Amos,
who was the son of Nahum, who was the son of Esli,
who was the son of Naggai, [26] who was the son of Maath,
who was the son of Mattathias, who was the son of Semein,
who was the son of Josech, who was the son of Joda,
[27] who was the son of Joanan, who was the son of Rhesa,
who was the son of Zerubbabel, who was the son of Shealtiel,

3:10 Ac 2:37
3:12 Lk 7:29
3:13 Lk 19:8
3:14 Ex 23:1
3:16 Ac 1:5
3:17 Mt 13:30
3:21 Jn 1:32–34
3:22 Ps 2:7
3:23 Mt 13:55
3:27 Mt 1:12

SPIRITLED WOMAN

COUNSEL FROM THE SPIRIT BASICS

Affirmation From Above

If you have a tendency to judge yourself... if you are a works-oriented rather than a grace-oriented person, measuring your worth based on what you do, you need to remember this one thing. I know you have heard it before, but I need to tell you again: God doesn't love you because of what you do for Him. He loves you because, with or without your good works, you're His beloved, delightful child.

Satan, the accuser, wants you to judge yourself based on your works—because either way you lose. If you judge yourself as "good," pride takes you down. If you judge yourself as "bad," depression, low self-esteem, and anxiety takes you down.

As a TV pastor once said in a sermon, "There's a ditch on both sides of the road." So you need to turn away from the accuser and stop listening to him as he tries to get you to judge. Don't even engage in conversation with him.

Instead turn toward God, who loves you and finds you delightful. Read His Word, and listen hard and try to understand what He is telling you. You may have to hear the same message five or even five hundred times before you get it, because it's easier to receive negative words than it is to receive positive words. But hear it as many times as it takes, receive the message, and refuse to give up!

Listen to God say to you: "This is My beloved daughter, with whom I am well pleased."

Rita Hancock

who was the son of Neri, [28] who was the son of Melchi,
who was the son of Addi, who was the son of Cosam,
who was the son of Elmadam, who was the son of Er,
[29] who was the son of Joshua, who was the son of Eliezer,
who was the son of Jorim, who was the son of Matthat,
who was the son of Levi, [30] who was the son of Simeon,
who was the son of Judah, who was the son of Joseph,
who was the son of Jonan, who was the son of Eliakim,
[31] who was the son of Melea, who was the son of Menna,
who was the son of Mattatha, who was the son of Nathan,
who was the son of David, [32] who was the son of Jesse,
who was the son of Obed, who was the son of Boaz,
who was the son of Salmon, who was the son of Nahshon,
[33] who was the son of Amminadab, who was the son of Ram,
who was the son of Hezron, who was the son of Perez,
who was the son of Judah, [34] who was the son of Jacob,
who was the son of Isaac, who was the son of Abraham,
who was the son of Terah, who was the son of Nahor,
[35] who was the son of Serug, who was the son of Reu,
who was the son of Peleg, who was the son of Eber,
who was the son of Shelah, [36] who was the son of Cainan,
who was the son of Arphaxad, who was the son of Shem,
who was the son of Noah, who was the son of Lamech,
[37] who was the son of Methuselah, who was the son of Enoch,
who was the son of Jared, who was the son of Mahalalel,
who was the son of Cainan, [38] who was the son of Enosh,
who was the son of Seth, who was the son of Adam,
who was the son of God.

[1]4 Dt 8:3. [2]8 Dt 6:13. [3]11 Ps 91:11–12. [4]12 Dt 6:16.

3:31 2Sa 5:14
3:33 Ru 4:19–20

4:1 Mt 4:1–11
4:2 1Ki 19:8
4:4 Dt 8:3
4:8 Dt 6:13
4:10 Ps 91:11–12
4:12 Dt 6:16
4:13 Jn 14:30
4:14 Mt 4:12
4:15 Mt 4:23
4:16 Lk 2:51
4:18 Mt 11:5

The Temptation of Jesus
Mt 4:1–11; Mk 1:12–13

4 Jesus, being filled with the Holy Spirit,
returned from the Jordan and was led by
the Spirit into the wilderness, [2] being tempted
by the devil for forty days. During those days
He ate nothing. And when they were ended,
He was hungry.
[3] The devil said to Him, "If You are the Son of
God, command this stone to become bread."
[4] Jesus answered him, "It is written, 'Man
shall not live by bread alone, but by every
word of God.'[1]"
[5] The devil, taking Him up onto a high
mountain, showed Him all the kingdoms of
the world in a moment of time. [6] And the devil
said to Him, "I will give You all this power and
their glory, for it has been delivered to me. And
I give it to whomever I will. [7] If You, then, will
worship me, all will be Yours."
[8] And Jesus answered him, "Get behind Me,
Satan! For it is written, 'You shall worship
the Lord your God, and Him only shall you
serve.'[2]"
[9] He brought Him to Jerusalem, set Him on
the pinnacle of the temple, and said to Him, "If
You are the Son of God, throw Yourself down
from here. [10] For it is written:

'He shall give His angels charge
concerning you,
to preserve you,'

[11] and

'In their hands they shall hold you up,
lest you strike your foot against a
stone.'[3]"

[12] Jesus answered him, "It is said, 'You shall
not tempt the Lord your God.'[4]"
[13] When the devil had ended all the temptations, he departed from Him until another time.

The Beginning of the Galilean Ministry
Mt 4:12–17; Mk 1:14–15

[14] Jesus returned in the power of the Spirit
to Galilee. And His fame went throughout the
surrounding region. [15] He taught in their synagogues, being glorified by everyone.

The Rejection of Jesus at Nazareth
Mt 13:53–58; Mk 6:1–6

[16] He came to Nazareth, where He had been
brought up. And as His custom was, He went
to the synagogue on the Sabbath day. And He
stood up to read. [17] The scroll of the prophet
Isaiah was handed to Him. When He had unrolled the scroll, He found the place where it
was written:

[18] "The Spirit of the Lord is upon Me,
because He has anointed Me

to preach the gospel to the poor;
He has sent Me to heal the broken-hearted,
to preach deliverance to the captives
and recovery of sight to the blind,
to set at liberty those who are oppressed;
19 to preach the acceptable year of the
Lord."[1]

20 Then He rolled up the scroll, and He gave
it back to the attendant, and sat down. The
eyes of all those who were in the synagogue
were fixed on Him. 21 And He began to say
to them, "Today this Scripture is fulfilled in
your hearing."

22 All bore witness to Him, and wondered
at the gracious words which came from His
mouth. Then they said, "Is this not Joseph's
son?"

23 He said to them, "You will surely say to Me
this proverb, 'Physician, heal Yourself. What-
ever we have heard done in Capernaum, do
also here in Your country.' "

24 He also said, "Truly, I say to you, no proph-
et is accepted in his own country. 25 But I tell
you truthfully, many widows were in Israel in
the days of Elijah, when the heavens were
closed for three years and six months, when
great famine was throughout all the land. 26 Yet
to none of them was Elijah sent except to Zare-
phath, a city of Sidon, to a woman who was a
widow. 27 And many lepers were in Israel in the
time of Elisha the prophet. But none of them
was cleansed except Naaman the Syrian."

28 All those in the synagogue, when they
heard these things, were filled with wrath.
29 They rose up and thrust Him out of the city
and led Him to the brow of the hill on which
their city was built, that they might throw Him
down headlong. 30 But passing through the
midst of them, He went His way.

The Man With an Unclean Spirit
Mk 1:21–28

31 Then He went down to Capernaum, a city
of Galilee, and was teaching them on the Sab-
baths. 32 They were astonished at His teaching,
for His word was with authority.

33 In the synagogue there was a man who
had the spirit of an unclean demon. And he
cried out with a loud voice, 34 "Leave us alone!
What have You to do with us, Jesus of Naza-
reth? Have You come to destroy us? I know
who You are—the Holy One of God!"

35 Jesus rebuked him, saying, "Be silent,
and come out of him!" When the demon had
thrown him down in their midst, he came out
of him and did not hurt him.

36 They were all amazed and said among
themselves, "What a word this is! For with au-
thority and power He commands the unclean
spirits, and they come out." 37 And His fame
went out to every place in the surrounding
countryside.

The Healing of Many People
Mt 8:14–17; Mk 1:29–34

38 He went out of the synagogue and entered
Simon's house. Now Simon's mother-in-law
was taken ill with a high fever, and they asked
Him about her. 39 So He stood over her and
rebuked the fever, and it left her. And imme-
diately she rose and served them.

40 Now when the sun was setting, all those
who had anyone sick with various diseases
brought them to Him. And He laid His hands
on every one of them and healed them. 41 And
demons came out of many, crying out, "You
are the Christ, the Son of God!" But He rebuked
them and did not permit them to speak, be-
cause they knew that He was the Christ.

Preaching in the Synagogues
Mk 1:35–39

42 When it was day He departed and went
into a remote place. And searching for Him,
the people came to Him and tried to prevent
Him from leaving them. 43 But He said to them,
"I must preach the kingdom of God to other
cities also, for this is why I was sent." 44 And He
was preaching in the synagogues of Galilee.

The Calling of the First Disciples
Mt 4:18–22; Mk 1:16–20

5 As the people pressed upon Him to hear
the word of God, He stood by the Lake
of Gennesaret 2 and saw two boats beside the
lake. But the fishermen had gone out of them
and were washing their nets. 3 He entered
one of the boats, which was Simon's, and
asked him to thrust it out a little from the
land. Then He sat down and taught the peo-
ple from the boat.

4 When He had finished speaking, He said to
Simon, "Launch out into the deep and let down
your nets for a catch."

5 Simon answered Him, "Master, we have
worked all night and have caught nothing. But
at Your word I will let down the net."

6 When they had done this, they caught a
great number of fish, and their net was tear-
ing. 7 So they signaled to their partners in the
other boat to come and help them. And they
came and filled both boats, so that they began
to sink.

8 When Simon Peter saw it, he fell down at
Jesus' knees, saying, "Depart from me, for I
am a sinful man, O Lord." 9 For he and all who
were with him were astonished at the catch
of fish which they had taken, 10 and so were

4:19 Isa 61:2
4:20 Lk 4:17
4:22 Jn 6:42
4:24 Mt 13:57
4:25 1Ki 17:1
4:29 Nu 15:35
4:30 Jn 10:39
4:31 Mt 4:13
4:32 Lk 4:36
4:34 Mk 1:24
4:35 Lk 4:41
4:36 Lk 4:32
4:37 Lk 4:14
4:38 Mt 8:14–15
4:39 Lk 4:35
4:44 Mt 4:23
5:1 Nu 34:11
5:2 Mk 1:19
5:4 Jn 21:6
5:5 Jn 21:3
5:8 Isa 6:5

[1] *18–19* Isa 61:1–2.

James and John, the sons of Zebedee, who
were partners with Simon.
Then Jesus said to Simon, "Do not fear. From
now on you will catch men." 11 So when they
had brought their boats to land, they left ev-
erything and followed Him.

The Cleansing of a Leper
Mt 8:1–4; Mk 1:40–45

12 When He was in a certain city, a man full
of leprosy, upon seeing Jesus, fell on his face
and begged Him, "Lord, if You will, You can
make me clean."
13 He reached out His hand and touched him,
saying, "I will. Be clean." And immediately the
leprosy left him.
14 Then He commanded him to tell no one,
"But go and show yourself to the priest and
make an offering for your cleansing, as Moses
commanded, as a testimony to them."
15 Yet even more so His fame went every-
where. And great crowds came together to
hear and to be healed by Him of their infir-
mities. 16 But He withdrew to the wilderness
and prayed.

The Healing of a Paralytic
Mt 9:1–8; Mk 2:1–12

17 On a certain day, as He was teaching, Phar-
isees and teachers of the law were sitting near-
by, who had come from every town of Galilee
and Judea and from Jerusalem. And the power
of the Lord was present to heal the sick. 18 Now
some men brought in a bed a man who was
paralyzed. They searched for ways to bring
him in and lay him before Him. 19 When they
could not find a way to bring him in, because
of the crowd, they went up on the roof and let
him down through the tiles with his bed into
their midst before Jesus.

Release Your power in healing and deliverance (Lk 5:17).

20 When He saw their faith, He said to him,
"Man, your sins are forgiven you."
21 The scribes and the Pharisees began to
question, "Who is He who speaks blasphe-
mies? Who can forgive sins but God alone?"
22 When Jesus perceived their thoughts, He
answered them, "Why question in your hearts?
23 Which is easier, to say, 'Your sins are forgiven
you,' or to say, 'Rise up and walk'? 24 But that
you may know that the Son of Man has au-
thority on earth to forgive sins," He said to the
paralyzed man, "I say to you, rise, take up your
bed, and go to your house." 25 Immediately he
rose before them, and took up that on which he
lay, and departed to his own house, glorifying
God. 26 They were all amazed, and they glori-
fied God and were filled with fear, saying, "We
have seen wonderful things today."

The Calling of Levi
Mt 9:9–13; Mk 2:13–17

27 After these things He went out and saw
a tax collector, named Levi, sitting at the tax
collector's station. He said to him, "Follow Me."
28 And he left everything, rose up, and followed
Him.
29 Then Levi made Him a great feast in his
house. And there was a group of many tax
collectors and others who sat down with them.
30 But their scribes and Pharisees murmured
against His disciples, saying, "Why do you eat
and drink with tax collectors and sinners?"
31 Jesus answered them, "Those who are well
do not need a physician, but those who are
sick. 32 I have not come to call the righteous,
but sinners to repentance."

The Question About Fasting
Mt 9:14–17; Mk 2:18–22

33 They said to Him, "Why do the disciples of
John fast often and offer prayers, and likewise
the disciples of the Pharisees, but Yours eat
and drink?"
34 He said to them, "Can you make the atten-
dants of the bridegroom fast while the bride-
groom is with them? 35 But the days will come
when the bridegroom will be taken away from
them. Then in those days they will fast."
36 He told them a parable also: "No one sews
a piece of a new material on an old one. Oth-
erwise the new would tear, for the new piece
does not match the old. 37 And no one puts
new wine into old wineskins. Otherwise the
new wine will burst the wineskins, and it will
be spilled, and the wineskins will be destroyed.
38 But new wine must be put into new wine-
skins, and both are preserved. 39 And no one,
having drunk old wine, immediately desires
new. For he says, 'The old is better.' "

Plucking Grain on the Sabbath
Mt 12:1–8; Mk 2:23–28

6 On the second Sabbath after the first, He
went through the grain fields, and His
disciples plucked and ate the heads of grain,
rubbing them in their hands. 2 Some of the
Pharisees said to them, "Why are you doing
what is not lawful to do on the Sabbath?"
3 Jesus answered them, "Have you not read
what David did when he and those who were
with him were hungry? 4 He went into the
house of God, and took and ate the ritual
bread, and also gave it to those who were with
him. This was not lawful, but for the priests
only to eat." 5 Then He said to them, "The Son
of Man is Lord even of the Sabbath."

5:12 Mt 8:2–4
5:15 Mt 9:26
5:16 Mt 14:23
5:17 Mt 15:1
5:18 Mt 9:2–8
5:19 Mk 2:4
5:20 Lk 7:48
5:21 Isa 43:25
5:26 Mt 9:8
5:28 Lk 5:11
5:29 Lk 15:1
5:30 Ac 23:9
5:34 Jn 3:29
5:35 Lk 17:22
5:37 Jos 9:4
6:1 Dt 23:25
6:2 Mt 12:2
6:4 Lev 24:5–9

The Man With a Withered Hand
Mt 12:9–14; Mk 3:1–6

6 On another Sabbath, when He entered
the synagogue and taught, there was a man
whose right hand had withered. 7 The scribes
and the Pharisees watched Him to see whether
He would heal on the Sabbath, so that they
might find an accusation against Him. 8 But
He knew their thoughts, and He said to the
man who had the withered hand, "Rise and
stand in front." So he rose and stood in front.
9 Then Jesus said to them, "I will ask you one
thing: Is it lawful on the Sabbath to do good or
to do evil, to save life or to destroy it?"
10 Then looking around at them all, He said
to the man, "Stretch out your hand." He did
so, and his hand was restored as whole as the
other. 11 But they were filled with madness and
discussed with each other what they might do
to Jesus.

The Choosing of the Twelve Apostles
Mt 10:1–4; Mk 3:13–19

12 In these days He went out to the moun-
tain to pray and continued all night in prayer
to God. 13 When it was day, He called for His
disciples, and of them He chose twelve, whom
He named apostles: 14 Simon, whom He named
Peter, and Andrew his brother, and James and
John, and Philip and Bartholomew, 15 and
Matthew and Thomas, and James the son of
Alphaeus, and Simon called the Zealot, 16 and
Judas the son of James, and Judas Iscariot,
who became a traitor.

Ministering to a Great Crowd
Mt 4:23–25

17 He came down with them and stood on a
level place with a crowd of His disciples and
a great crowd of people from all Judea and
Jerusalem, and from the seacoast of Tyre
and Sidon, who came to hear Him and be
healed of their diseases, 18 including those
who were vexed by unclean spirits. And they
were healed. 19 The whole crowd tried to touch
Him, for power went out from Him and healed
them all.

Blessings and Woes
Mt 5:1–12

20 He lifted up His eyes on His disciples, and
said:

"Blessed are you poor,
for yours is the kingdom of God.
21 Blessed are you who hunger now,
for you shall be filled.
Blessed are you who weep now,
for you shall laugh.
22 Blessed are you when men hate you,
and when they separate you from their
company and insult you,
and cast out your name as evil,
on account of the Son of Man.

23 "Rejoice in that day, and leap for joy, for
indeed, your reward is great in heaven. For in
like manner their fathers treated the prophets.

24 "But woe to you who are rich,
for you have received your consolation.
25 Woe to you who are filled,
for you shall hunger.
Woe to you who laugh now,
for you shall mourn and weep.
26 Woe to you, when all men speak well of
you,
for so their fathers spoke of the false
prophets.

Love for Enemies
Mt 5:38–48

27 "But I say to you who hear, love your ene-
mies, do good to those who hate you, 28 bless
those who curse you, and pray for those who
spitefully use you. 29 To him who strikes you on
the one cheek, offer also the other. And from
him who takes away your cloak, do not with-
hold your tunic as well. 30 Give to everyone who
asks of you. And of him who takes away your
goods, do not ask for them back. 31 Do unto
others as you would have others do unto you.
32 "For if you love those who love you, what
thanks do you receive? For even sinners love
those who love them. 33 And if you do good to
those who do good to you, what thanks do you
receive? For even sinners do the same. 34 And
if you lend to those from whom you hope to
receive, what thanks do you receive? Even
sinners lend to sinners, to receive as much in
return. 35 But love your enemies, and do good,
and lend, hoping for nothing in return. Then
your reward will be great, and you will be the
sons of the Highest. For He is kind to the un-
thankful and the evil. 36 Be therefore merciful,
even as your Father is merciful.

Judging Others
Mt 7:1–5

37 "Judge not, and you shall not be judged.
Condemn not, and you will not be condemned.
Forgive, and you shall be forgiven. 38 Give, and
it will be given to you: Good measure, pressed
down, shaken together, and running over will
men give unto you. For with the measure you
use, it will be measured unto you."

Your gift will return to you in full—pressed down, shaken together to make room for more, running over, and poured into your lap (Lk 6:38).

6:6 Mt 12:9–14
6:8 Mt 9:4
6:9 Lk 14:3
6:10 Mk 3:5
6:11 Ac 5:33
6:12 Mk 1:35
6:14 Ac 1:13
6:15 Mt 9:9
6:16 Jn 14:22
6:17 Mt 11:21
6:19 Mt 14:36
6:21 Mt 5:4
6:22 Mt 10:22
6:23 Mt 5:12
6:24 Mt 6:2
6:25 Isa 65:13
6:27 Lk 6:35
6:28 1Pe 3:9
6:30 Pr 21:26
6:31 Mt 7:12
6:34 Mt 5:42
6:35 2Co 8:9
6:36 Mt 5:48
6:38 Ps 79:12

39 He spoke a parable to them: "Can the
blind lead the blind? Will they not both fall
into the ditch? 40 The disciple is not above his
teacher, but everyone who is trained will be
like his teacher.

41 "Why do you see the speck that is in your
brother's eye, but do not see the beam that is
in your own eye? 42 How can you say to your
brother, 'Brother, let me remove the speck that
is in your eye,' when you yourself do not see
the beam that is in your own eye? You hypo-
crite! First remove the beam from your own
eye, and then you will see clearly to remove
the speck that is in your brother's eye.

A Tree and Its Fruit
Mt 7:17–20

43 "A good tree does not bear corrupt fruit, nor
does a corrupt tree bear good fruit. 44 Each tree
is known by its own fruit. Men do not gather
figs from thorns, nor do they gather grapes
from a wild bush. 45 A good man out of the
good treasure of his heart bears what is good,
and an evil man out of the evil treasure of his
heart bears what is evil. For of the abundance
of the heart his mouth speaks.

The Two Housebuilders
Mt 7:24–27

46 "Why do you call Me, 'Lord, Lord,' and not
do what I say? 47 Whoever comes to Me and
hears My words and does them, I will show
whom he is like: 48 He is like a man who built a
house, and dug deep, and laid the foundation
on rock. When the flood arose, the stream beat
vehemently against that house, but could not
shake it, for it was founded on rock. 49 But he
who hears and does not obey is like a man
who built a house on the ground without a
foundation, against which the stream beat ve-
hemently. Immediately it fell, and the ruin of
that house was great."

The Healing of a Centurion's Servant
Mt 8:5–13; Jn 4:43–54

7 When He had completed all His words
in the hearing of the people, He entered
Capernaum. 2 Now a centurion's[1] servant, who
was dear to him, was sick and ready to die.
3 When he heard of Jesus, he sent the elders
of the Jews to Him, asking Him to come and
heal his servant. 4 When they came to Jesus,
they asked Him earnestly, saying, "You should
do this for him for he is worthy, 5 for he loves
our nation, and he has built us a synagogue."
6 So Jesus went with them.

When He was not far from the house, the
centurion sent friends to Him, saying, "Lord,
do not trouble Yourself, for I am not worthy to
have You come under my roof. 7 Likewise, I did
not think myself worthy to come to You. But
say the word, and my servant will be healed.
8 For I myself am a man placed under authori-
ty, having soldiers under me. I say to one, 'Go,'
and he goes, and to another, 'Come,' and he
comes, and to my servant, 'Do this,' and he
does it."

9 When Jesus heard these words, He mar-
veled at him, and turned and said to the people
who followed Him, "I tell you, I have not found
such great faith even in Israel." 10 Then those
who were sent, returning to the house, found
the servant well who had been sick.

The Raising of the Widow's Son

11 The following day He went into a city called
Nain, and many of His disciples and a large
crowd went with Him. 12 When He came near
the gate of the city, a man who had died was
being carried out, the only son of his mother,
and she was a widow. And a large crowd from
the city was with her. 13 When the Lord saw
her, He had compassion on her and said to
her, "Do not weep."

14 Then He came and touched the coffin, and
those who carried it stood still. He said, "Young
man, I say to you, arise." 15 He who was dead
sat up and began to speak. And He gave him
to his mother.

16 Fear came on everyone. And they glori-
fied God, saying, "A great prophet has risen up
among us!" and "God has visited His people!"
17 This rumor of Him went throughout all Ju-
dea and the surrounding region.

The Messengers From John the Baptist
Mt 11:2–19

18 The disciples of John told him of all these
things. 19 John, calling for two of his disciples,
sent them to Jesus, saying, "Are You the One
who is coming, or shall we look for another?"

20 When the men had come to Him, they said,
"John the Baptist has sent us to You, saying,
'Are You the One who is coming, or shall we
look for another?' "

21 In that same hour He cured many of their
infirmities and afflictions and evil spirits. And
to many who were blind He gave sight. 22 So
Jesus answered them, "Go and tell John what
you have seen and heard: that the blind see,
the lame walk, the lepers are cleansed, the
deaf hear, the dead are raised, and the gospel
is preached to the poor. 23 Blessed is he who
does not fall away on account of Me."

24 When the messengers of John had depart-
ed, He began to speak to the crowd concerning
John: "What did you go out into the wilderness
to see? A reed shaken by the wind? 25 If not,
what did you go out to see? A man dressed in
fine clothes? Now those who are splendidly

6:39 Mt 15:14
6:40 Jn 13:16
6:41 Jn 8:7
6:44 Mt 12:33
6:45 Eph 4:29
6:46 Mal 1:6
6:47 Jas 1:22–25
7:1 Mt 8:5–13
7:3 Mt 8:5
7:6 Lk 8:49
7:7 Ps 107:20
7:9 Mt 8:10
7:12 Lk 8:42
7:16 Mt 9:8
7:21 Mk 3:10
7:22 Lk 4:18
7:23 Isa 8:14–15

1 2 Commander with the rank of captain over 100 soldiers.

Those Who Are Forgiven Much, Love Much

A heroine of mine who taught me about mercy is named Helena. Though she only had one leg, Helena's life was truly blessed. She taught me about the blessing of extending mercy and living a life embodying the Beatitudes.

I asked Helena why she only had one leg. She told me she had been burned in a fire. Since her leg was burned off, her family thought she would no longer be of any use. So her grandmother took her outside and told her brothers to kill her. The brothers took her to a field, threw rocks at her, and left her there to die.

At first Helena still talked about how she hated her family for trying to kill her. But as she grew in love with Jesus, she also grew in mercy. The love of God flowing through that girl just amazed me. We were able to get her a makeshift prosthetic leg, and after a few months she came to me and told me she wanted to go home. She wanted to go and tell her brothers about Jesus, and she wanted her grandmother to meet Him too.

I was really concerned, though, knowing how difficult her family background was. But when you know you are truly forgiven, you then learn how to forgive. Jesus, when speaking about a woman whose sins had been great, challenged His disciples by saying, "I say to you, her sins, which are many, are forgiven, for she loved much. But he who is forgiven little loves little" (Lk 7:47).

Helena, who had been full of hatred and anger, received God's mercy and forgiveness. Even if her family killed her when she went back home, she was determined to show mercy to them and to let the light of Jesus shine.

When Helena got home, she led one of her brothers into a relationship with Jesus. Her grandmother, however, continued to be a witch doctor. Helena moved into a small reed hut that was next to her family's home and continued to love them. Her life of pain and prostitution was over.

I remember when I performed her wedding sometime later. I recall as she walked down the aisle of our church toward her bridegroom. She wore a dress that had been worn by others many times before, but she looked stunning, purified, and filled with radiant joy. She had truly been forgiven of much.

Helena had poured out great mercy to her family, and she received great mercy from God in return. God blessed her with a wedding, a family, and beautiful children of her own. She also forgave everyone who had abused her.

But—a very important part—she also forgave herself and let the hatred and rage go. In doing so, she was able to receive the mercy of God and then could pour His mercy out on all those around her.

Heidi Baker

clothed and live luxuriously are in royal palaces. 26 What then did you go out to see? A prophet? Yes, I say to you, and much more than a prophet. 27 This is he of whom it is written:

'Look, I am sending My messenger before
Your face,
who shall prepare Your way before You.'[1]

28 I say to you, among those who are born of women there is no greater prophet than John the Baptist. Yet he who is least in the kingdom of God is greater than he."

29 All the people who heard Him, including the tax collectors, justified God, having been baptized with the baptism of John. 30 But the Pharisees and lawyers rejected the counsel of God for themselves, not having been baptized by John.

31 Then the Lord said, "To what then shall I compare the men of this generation, and what are they like? 32 They are like children sitting in the marketplace, calling to each other, saying:

'We played the flute for you,
and you did not dance;
we mourned to you,
and you did not weep.'

33 For John the Baptist came neither eating bread nor drinking wine. But you say, 'He has a demon.' 34 The Son of Man has come eating and drinking. But you say, 'Look, a glutton and a drunkard, a friend of tax collectors and sinners!' 35 But wisdom is justified by all her children."

A Sinful Woman Forgiven

36 One of the Pharisees asked Him to eat with him. So He went to the Pharisee's house and sat down for supper. 37 There, a woman of the city who was a sinner, when she learned that Jesus was sitting for supper in the Pharisee's house, brought an alabaster jar of ointment, 38 and stood behind Him at His feet, weeping, and began to wash His feet with tears, and wiped them with the hair of her head, and kissed His feet, and anointed them with the ointment.

39 Now when the Pharisee who had invited Him saw it, he said to himself, "If this Man were a prophet, He would have known who and what kind of woman she is who is touching Him, for she is a sinner."

40 Jesus answered him, "Simon, I have something to say to you."

He said, "Teacher, say it."

41 "A creditor had two debtors. The one owed five hundred denarii,[2] and the other fifty. 42 When they had no money to pay, he freely forgave them both. Tell Me, therefore, which of them will love him more?"

43 Simon answered, "I suppose he whom he forgave more."

He said to him, "You have judged rightly."

44 Then He turned to the woman and said to Simon, "Do you see this woman? I entered your house. You gave Me no water for My feet, but she has washed My feet with her tears and wiped them with the hair of her head. 45 You gave Me no kiss, but this woman, since the time I came in, has not ceased to kiss My feet. 46 You did not anoint My head with oil, but this woman has anointed My feet with ointment. 47 Therefore I say to you, her sins, which are many, are forgiven, for she loved much. But he who is forgiven little loves little."

48 Then He said to her, "Your sins are forgiven."

49 Those who sat at supper with Him began to say to themselves, "Who is He who even forgives sins?"

50 He said to the woman, "Your faith has saved you. Go in peace."

Women Who Accompany Jesus

8 Afterward, He went throughout every city and village, preaching and bringing the good news of the kingdom of God. With Him were the twelve 2 and some women who had been healed of evil spirits and infirmities: Mary, called Magdalene, from whom seven demons had come out, 3 and Joanna, the wife of Chuza, Herod's steward, and Susanna, and many others, who supported Him with their possessions.

The Parable of the Sower

Mt 13:1–9; Mk 4:1–9

4 When a large crowd had gathered together and people were coming to Him from every city, He told this parable: 5 "A sower went out to sow his seed. As he sowed, some fell along the path and was trampled down, and the birds of the air devoured it. 6 Some fell on a rock. And as soon as it sprang up, it withered away, because it lacked moisture. 7 Yet some fell among thorns. And the thorns sprang up with it and choked it. 8 And other seed fell on good ground and sprang up and yielded a hundred times the amount sown."

When He had said these things, He cried out, "He who has ears to hear, let him hear."

The Purpose of the Parables

Mt 13:10–17; Mk 4:10–12

9 His disciples asked Him, "What might this parable mean?" 10 He said, "To you it has been given to know the secrets of the kingdom of God, but to others they are in parables, so that

'seeing they may not see,
and hearing they may not understand.'[3]

7:27 Mal 3:1
7:29 Lk 3:12
7:30 Mt 22:35
7:33 Lk 1:15
7:34 Lk 15:2
7:39 Lk 7:16
7:41 Mt 18:28

7:44 1Ti 5:10
7:45 2Sa 15:5
7:46 Ps 23:5
7:47 1Jn 4:19
7:48 Mt 9:2
7:50 Mt 9:22
8:1 Mt 4:23
8:2 Mt 27:55–56
8:3 Lk 24:10
8:7 Jer 4:3
8:8 Mt 11:15
8:10 Isa 6:9

[1] *27* Mal 3:1. [2] *41* Gk. *denarius*, a coin worth about a day's wage.
[3] *10* Isa 6:9.

The Parable of the Sower Explained

Mt 13:18–23; Mk 4:13–20

[11] "Now the parable means this: The seed is the word of God. [12] Those along the path are those who hear. Then comes the devil, who takes away the word from their hearts, lest they should believe and be saved. [13] Those on the rock are the ones who, when they hear the word, receive it with joy. But these have no root, for they believe for a while, then in the time of temptation fall away. [14] That which fell among thorns are those who, when they have heard, go out and are choked with the cares and riches and pleasures of this life, and bring no fruit to maturity. [15] But the seed on the good ground are those who, having heard the word, keep it in an honest and good heart and bear fruit with patience.

A Light Under a Vessel

Mk 4:21–25

[16] "No one, when he lights a candle, covers it with a vessel or puts it under a bed, but sets it on a candlestick, that those who enter may see the light. [17] For nothing is secret that will not be revealed, nor anything hidden that will not be known and revealed. [18] Take heed therefore how you hear. For whoever has, to him will be given. And whoever has not, from him will be taken even what he thinks he has."

The Mother and Brothers of Jesus

Mt 12:46–50; Mk 3:31–35

[19] Then His mother and His brothers came to Him, but could not reach Him because of the crowd. [20] Someone told Him, "Your mother and Your brothers are standing outside, desiring to see You."

[21] He answered them, "My mother and My brothers are these who hear the word of God and do it."

The Calming of a Storm

Mt 8:23–27; Mk 4:35–41

[22] One day He went into a boat with His disciples, and He said to them, "Let us go over to the other side of the lake." So they launched out. [23] As they sailed, He fell asleep. Then a wind storm came down on the lake, and they were filling with water, and were in danger.

[24] They came to Him and awoke Him, saying, "Master, Master, we are perishing!"

Then He arose and rebuked the wind and the raging of the water. And they ceased, and there was a calm. [25] He said to them, "Where is your faith?"

Being afraid, they marveled, saying to each other, "Who then is this Man? He commands even the winds and water, and they obey Him."

8:16 Lk 11:33
8:17 Mt 10:26
8:18 Mt 13:12
8:19 Mt 12:46–50
8:21 Jas 1:22
8:22 Mt 8:23–27

. . . .

8:26 Mt 8:28–34
8:28 Mt 8:29
8:30 Mt 26:53
8:31 Rev 9:1–2
8:35 Lk 10:39
8:37 Ac 16:39
8:38 Mk 5:18–20
8:39 Ps 66:16
8:41 Mk 5:22–43

The Healing of the Gadarene Demoniac

Mt 8:28–34; Mk 5:1–20

[26] They sailed to the country of the Gadarenes, which is across from Galilee. [27] When He stepped out on land, a man from the city who had demons for a long time met Him. He wore no clothes, nor did he live in a house but in the tombs. [28] When he saw Jesus, he cried out and fell down before Him, and with a loud voice said, "What have You to do with me, Jesus, Son of the Most High God? I plead with You, do not torment me." [29] For He had commanded the unclean spirit to come out of the man. It often had seized him, and he was kept under guard, bound with chains and shackles. But he broke the shackles and was driven by the demon into the wilderness.

[30] Jesus asked him, "What is your name?"

He said, "Legion," because many demons had entered him. [31] And they begged Him not to command them to go out into the abyss.

[32] There was a large herd of swine feeding on the mountain. They begged Him to permit them to enter them, and He permitted them. [33] Then the demons went out of the man and entered the swine, and the herd ran violently down the steep bank into the lake and was drowned.

[34] When those who fed them saw what had happened, they fled and reported it in the city and in the country. [35] Then they went out to see what had happened, and came to Jesus, and found the man from whom the demons had departed sitting at the feet of Jesus, clothed, and in his right mind. And they were afraid. [36] Those who had seen it told them how he who had been possessed by demons was healed. [37] Then the whole crowd from the surrounding country of the Gadarenes asked Him to depart from them, for they were seized with great fear. So He went into the boat and returned.

[38] Now the man from whom the demons had departed asked Him if he could stay with Him. But Jesus sent him away, saying, [39] "Return to your own house, and tell what great things God has done for you." So he went his way and proclaimed throughout the whole city what great things Jesus had done for him.

Jairus' Daughter and the Woman Who Touched Jesus' Garment

Mt 9:18–26; Mk 5:21–43

[40] When Jesus returned, the crowd gladly received Him, for they were all waiting for Him. [41] Then a man named Jairus, who was a ruler of the synagogue, came and fell down at Jesus' feet, and begged Him to come to his house, [42] for he had an only daughter, about twelve years of age, and she was dying.

As He went, the people crowded Him. 43 And a woman having a hemorrhage for twelve years, who had spent all her living on physicians, but could not be healed by anyone, 44 came behind Him, and touched the fringe of His garment. And immediately her hemorrhage dried up.

45 Jesus said, "Who touched Me?"

When everyone denied it, Peter and those who were with Him said, "Master, the crowds are pressing against You, and You say, 'Who touched Me?' "

46 But Jesus said, "Someone touched Me, for I perceive that power has gone out from Me."

47 When the woman saw that she was not hidden, she came trembling. And falling down before Him, she declared to Him before all the people why she had touched Him and how she was healed immediately. 48 Then He said to her, "Daughter, be of good cheer. Your faith has made you well. Go in peace."

49 While He was still speaking, someone from the synagogue ruler's house came, saying to Jairus, "Your daughter is dead. Do not trouble the Teacher."

50 But when Jesus heard it, He answered him, "Do not fear. Only believe, and she will be made well."

51 When He came into the house, He permitted no one to go in except Peter, John and James, and the father and mother of the girl. 52 All wept and mourned for her. But He said, "Do not weep. She is not dead but sleeping."

53 They laughed at Him, knowing that she was dead. 54 But He put them all outside and took her by the hand and called, saying, "Little girl, arise." 55 Her spirit returned, and she arose immediately. And He told them to give her food. 56 Her parents were astonished, but He commanded them to tell no one what had happened.

The Mission of the Twelve Apostles
Mt 10:1, 5–15; Mk 6:7–13

9 Then He called His twelve disciples together and gave them power and authority over all demons and to cure diseases. 2 And He sent them to preach the kingdom of God and to heal the sick. 3 He said to them, "Take nothing for your journey: no staff, no bag, no bread, no money. And do not take two tunics apiece. 4 Whatever house you enter, stay there, and from there depart. 5 Whoever will not receive you, when you go out of that city, shake off the very dust from your feet as a testimony against them." 6 So they departed and went through the towns, preaching the gospel and healing everywhere.

8:44 Dt 22:12
8:46 Lk 6:19
8:48 Mt 9:22
8:49 Lk 7:6
8:50 Mk 5:36
8:55 Jn 11:44
8:56 Mt 8:4
9:3 Lk 22:35
9:5 Ac 13:51

....

9:9 Lk 23:8
9:10 Mt 11:21
9:12 Mt 15:23
9:13 2Ki 4:42–43
9:19 Lk 9:7–8
9:21 Mt 16:20
9:22 Lk 24:7

Herod's Anxiety
Mt 14:1–12; Mk 6:14–29

7 Now Herod the tetrarch heard of all that was done by Him. And he was perplexed, because it was said by some that John had risen from the dead, 8 and by some that Elijah had appeared, and by others that one of the old prophets had risen. 9 But Herod said, "I have beheaded John. But who is this of whom I hear such things?" And he tried to see Him.

The Feeding of the Five Thousand
Mt 14:13–21; Mk 6:30–44; Jn 6:1–14

10 When the apostles returned, they told Jesus all that they had done. Then He took them and went aside privately into a deserted place belonging to the city called Bethsaida. 11 But when the crowds knew it, they followed Him. And He welcomed them and spoke to them about the kingdom of God, and healed those who had need of healing.

12 When the day began to end, the twelve came and said to Him, "Send the crowds away, so they can go into the towns and surrounding countryside and lodge and get food. For we are in a deserted place here."

13 He said to them, "You give them something to eat."

They said, "We have no more than five loaves and two fish, unless we go and buy food for all these people." 14 There were about five thousand men.

But He said to His disciples, "Make them sit down in groups of fifty." 15 They did so, and made them all sit down. 16 Then He took the five loaves and the two fish, and looking up to heaven, He blessed them, and broke them, and gave them to the disciples to set before the crowd. 17 They all ate and were filled, and twelve baskets of broken pieces that remained were collected.

Peter's Declaration About Jesus
Mt 16:13–19; Mk 8:27–29

18 As He was alone praying, His disciples were with Him. And He asked them, "Who do the people say that I am?"

19 They answered, "John the Baptist. But some say Elijah. And others say that one of the old prophets has risen."

20 He said to them, "But who do you say that I am?"

Peter answered, "The Christ of God."

Jesus Foretells His Death and Resurrection
Mt 16:20–28; Mk 8:30–9:1

21 Jesus strictly commanded them to tell no one of this, 22 saying, "The Son of Man must suffer many things, and be rejected by the

elders and chief priests and scribes, and be killed, and be raised the third day."

23 Then He said to them all, "If anyone will come after Me, let him deny himself, and take up his cross daily, and follow Me. 24 For whoever will save his life will lose it, but whoever loses his life for My sake will save it. 25 For what does it profit a man if he gains the whole world, yet loses or forfeits himself? 26 For whoever is ashamed of Me and My words, of him will the Son of Man be ashamed when He comes in His own glory and in the glory of His Father and of the holy angels.

27 "But I tell you truly, there are some standing here who shall not taste death before they see the kingdom of God."

The Transfiguration
Mt 17:1–8; Mk 9:2–8

28 About eight days after these sayings, He took Peter and John and James and went up onto a mountain to pray. 29 As He prayed, the appearance of His countenance was altered, and His clothing was white and glistening. 30 And suddenly two men were talking with Him, who were Moses and Elijah, 31 who appeared in glory and spoke of His departure which He was to accomplish in Jerusalem. 32 Peter and those who were with him were heavy with sleep. But waking thoroughly, they saw His glory and the two men who stood with Him. 33 As they departed from Him, Peter said to Jesus, "Master, it is good for us to be here. Let us make three sanctuaries: one for You, and one for Moses, and one for Elijah," not knowing what he said.

34 While he was speaking, a cloud came and overshadowed them. And they were afraid as they entered the cloud. 35 A voice came from out of the cloud, saying, "This is My beloved Son. Listen to Him." 36 When the voice had spoken, Jesus was found alone. They kept silent and told no one in those days anything they had seen.

The Healing of a Boy With an Unclean Spirit
Mt 17:14–18; Mk 9:14–27

37 The next day, when they came down from the mountain, a great crowd met Him. 38 Suddenly a man cried out from the crowd, saying, "Teacher, I beg You, look upon my son, for he is my only child. 39 A spirit seizes him, and he suddenly cries out. It convulses him until he foams at the mouth, and bruises him, and scarcely leaves him. 40 I begged Your disciples to cast it out, but they could not."

41 Jesus said, "O faithless and perverse generation, how long shall I be with you and bear with you? Bring your son here."

9:23 Mt 10:38–39
9:24 Lk 17:33
9:26 Mt 16:27
9:33 Mk 9:5–6
9:35 Mt 3:17
9:36 Mt 17:9
9:38 Lk 7:12
9:40 Lk 9:1

....

9:42 Lk 7:15
9:44 Lk 9:22
9:45 Mk 9:32
9:46 Mt 18:1–5
9:49 Mk 9:38–40
9:50 Mt 12:30
9:51 Mk 16:19
9:52 Mt 10:5
9:53 Jn 4:9
9:54 2Ki 1:10–14
9:57 Lk 9:51

42 While he was coming, the demon threw him down and convulsed him. But Jesus rebuked the unclean spirit, and healed the child, and returned him to his father. 43 And they were all amazed at the mighty power of God.

Jesus Foretells His Death a Second Time
Mt 17:22–23; Mk 9:30–32

But while everyone marveled at all the things Jesus did, He said to His disciples, 44 "Let these words sink down into your ears, for the Son of Man is about to be betrayed into the hands of men." 45 But they did not understand this statement, and it was hidden from them, so that they did not perceive it. And they were afraid to ask Him about this statement.

Who Is the Greatest?
Mt 18:1–5; Mk 9:33–37

46 A dispute arose among them as to which of them was the greatest. 47 Jesus, perceiving the thought of their heart, took a child and put him by Him, 48 and said to them, "Whoever receives this child in My name receives Me, and whoever receives Me receives Him who sent Me. For he who is least among you all will be great."

He Who Is Not Against You Is for You
Mk 9:38–40

49 John answered, "Master, we saw a man casting out demons in Your name and we forbade him, because he does not follow with us."

50 Jesus said, "Do not forbid him, for he who is not against you is for you."

A Samaritan Village Refuses to Receive Jesus

51 When the time came for Him to be received up, He was steadfastly set to go to Jerusalem, 52 and sent messengers ahead of Him. They went and entered a village of the Samaritans to make things ready for Him, 53 but they did not receive Him, because He was set to go to Jerusalem. 54 When His disciples James and John saw this, they said, "Lord, do You want us to command fire to come down from heaven and consume them, even as Elijah did?" 55 But He turned and rebuked them and said, "You do not know what kind of spirit you are of. 56 For the Son of Man did not come to destroy men's lives but to save them." And they went to another village.

The Would-Be Followers of Jesus
Mt 8:19–22

57 As they went along the way, a man said to Him, "Lord, I will follow You wherever You go."

58 Jesus said to him, "Foxes have holes and birds of the air have nests. But the Son of Man has no place to lay His head."

59 He said to another man, "Follow Me."

But he said, "Lord, let me first go and bury my father."

60 Jesus said to him, "Leave the dead to bury their own dead. But you go and preach the kingdom of God."

61 Yet another said, "Lord, I will follow You, but let me first go bid farewell to those at my house."

62 Jesus said to him, "No one who puts his hand to the plow and looks back at things is fit for the kingdom of God."

The Mission of the Seventy

10 After this the Lord appointed seventy others, and sent them two by two ahead of Him into every city and place where He Himself was about to come. 2 He said to them, "The harvest truly is plentiful, but the laborers are few. Pray therefore the Lord of the harvest to send out laborers into His harvest. 3 Go your ways. Listen, I am sending you out as lambs among wolves. 4 Carry no purse, no bag, no shoes, and greet no one on the road.

5 "When you enter a house, first say, 'Peace be to this house.' 6 If a son of peace is there, your peace will rest upon him; but if not, it will return upon you. 7 Remain in the same house, eating and drinking what they give, for the laborer is worthy of his hire. Do not go from house to house.

8 "When you enter a city and they receive you, eat what is set before you. 9 Heal the sick who are there and say to them, 'The kingdom of God has come near to you.' 10 But when you enter a city and they do not receive you, go your way out into their streets and say, 11 'Even the dust of your city which clings to us, we wipe off against you. Yet be sure of this, that the kingdom of God has come near to you.' 12 But I say to you, it will be more tolerable on that Day for Sodom than for that city.

Unrepentant Cities

Mt 11:20–24

13 "Woe to you, Chorazin! Woe to you, Bethsaida! For if the mighty works had been done in Tyre and Sidon which have been done for you, they would have repented long ago, sitting in sackcloth and ashes. 14 But it will be more tolerable for Tyre and Sidon at the judgment than for you. 15 And you, Capernaum, will you be exalted to heaven? You will be thrust down to hell.

16 "He who listens to you listens to Me, he who rejects you rejects Me, and he who rejects Me rejects Him who sent Me."

9:61 1Ki 19:20
10:1 Lk 9:52
10:2 2Th 3:1
10:3 Mt 10:16
10:5 1Sa 25:6
10:6 Ps 35:13
10:8 1Co 10:27
10:9 Mt 3:2
10:11 Lk 10:9
10:12 Mt 10:15
10:13 Isa 23:1–18
10:14 Lk 12:47–48
10:15 Isa 14:13–15
10:16 1Th 4:8
....
10:18 Rev 9:1
10:19 Mk 16:18
10:20 Ex 32:32
10:22 Jn 1:18
10:23 Mt 13:16–17
10:25 Lk 18:18
10:27 Lev 19:18
10:28 Lev 18:5
10:29 Lk 16:15

The Return of the Seventy

17 The seventy returned with joy, saying, "Lord, even the demons are subject to us through Your name."

18 He said to them, "I saw Satan as lightning fall from heaven. 19 Look, I give you authority to trample on serpents and scorpions, and over all the power of the enemy. And nothing shall by any means hurt you. 20 Nevertheless do not rejoice that the spirits are subject to you, but rather rejoice that your names are written in heaven."

> I have dominion over all the power of the enemy (Lk 10:19).

The Rejoicing of Jesus

Mt 11:25–27; 13:16–17

21 At that time Jesus rejoiced in the Holy Spirit and said, "I thank You, O Father, Lord of heaven and earth, because You have hidden these things from the wise and intelligent and revealed them to infants. Yes, Father, for it was Your good pleasure.

22 "All things have been handed over to Me by My Father. And no one knows who the Son is but the Father, and who the Father is but the Son and he to whom the Son desires to reveal Him."

23 Then He turned to His disciples and said privately, "Blessed are the eyes which see what you see. 24 For I tell you, many prophets and kings have desired to see what you see, and have not seen it, and to hear what you hear, and have not heard it."

The Good Samaritan

25 Now, a lawyer stood up and tested Him, saying, "Teacher, what must I do to inherit eternal life?"

26 He said to him, "What is written in the law? How do you read?"

27 He answered, " 'You shall love the Lord your God with all your heart, and with all your soul, and with all your strength, and with all your mind'[1] and 'your neighbor as yourself.'[2]"

28 He said to him, "You have answered correctly. Do this, and you will live."

29 But he, desiring to justify himself, said to Jesus, "And who is my neighbor?"

30 Jesus answered, "A man went down from Jerusalem to Jericho and fell among thieves, who stripped him of his clothing and wounded him and departed, leaving him half dead. 31 By chance a priest came down that way. And when he saw him, he passed by on the other side. 32 So likewise a Levite, when he came to that place, looked at him and passed by on the

1 27 Dt 6:5. *2 27* Lev 19:18.

other side. 33 But a Samaritan, as he journeyed,
came where he was. And when he saw him,
he had compassion on him, 34 and went to him
and bound up his wounds, pouring in oil and
wine. Then he set him on his own donkey and
brought him to an inn, and took care of him.
35 The next day when he departed, he took out
two denarii[1] and gave them to the innkeeper
and said to him, 'Take care of him. I will repay
you whatever else you spend when I return.'
36 "Now which of these three do you think
was a neighbor to him who fell among the
thieves?"
37 He said, "The one who showed mercy on
him."
Then Jesus said to him, "Go and do likewise."

Visiting Martha and Mary

38 As they went, He entered a village. And a
woman named Martha welcomed Him into her
house. 39 She had a sister called Mary, who also
sat at Jesus' feet and listened to His teaching.
40 But Martha was distracted with much serv-
ing, and she came to Him and said, "Lord, do
You not care that my sister has left me to serve
alone? Then tell her to help me."
41 Jesus answered her, "Martha, Martha, you
are anxious and troubled about many things.
42 But one thing is needed. And Mary has cho-
sen the good part, which shall not be taken
from her."

Teaching About Prayer
Mt 6:9–15; 7:7–11

11 He was praying in a certain place, and
when He ceased, one of His disciples
said to Him, "Lord, teach us to pray, as John
also taught his disciples."
2 He said to them, "When you pray, say:

Our Father, who is in heaven,
hallowed be Your name.
Your kingdom come;
Your will be done
on earth, as it is in heaven.
3 Give us each day our daily bread.
4 And forgive us our sins,
for we also forgive everyone who is
indebted to us.
And lead us not into temptation,
but deliver us from evil."

5 Then He said to them, "Which of you has
a friend and shall go to him at midnight and
say to him, 'Friend, lend me three loaves, 6 for
a friend of mine on his journey has come to
me, and I have nothing to set before him'; 7 and
he will answer from within, 'Do not trouble
me; the door is now shut, and my children
are with me in bed; I cannot rise and give you
anything'? 8 I say to you, though he will not rise
and give him anything because he is his friend,
yet because of his persistence he will rise and
give him as much as he needs.
9 "And I tell you, ask, and it will be given to
you; seek, and you will find; knock, and it will

10:33 Mt 10:5
10:39 Lk 8:35
10:41 Mt 6:25–34
10:42 Ps 27:4
11:1 Lk 9:18
11:2 Ecc 5:2
11:4 Mt 26:41

SPIRITLED WOMAN

COUNSEL FROM THE SPIRIT BASICS

Self-Denial or Self-Neglect?

Jesus answered her, "Martha, Martha, you are anxious and troubled about many things. But one thing is needed. And Mary has chosen the good part, which shall not be taken from her."

—LUKE 10:41–42

I had become a Martha mom. I deprived myself of sleep, exercise, and recreation. I neglected the joy of my marriage and children. For what reason? To take care of "things."

Worst of all, I neglected myself spiritually, always giving out and never taking in. This neglect was not for spiritual gain but for busyness. I was such a Martha! I'd kneel down to pray and notice a toy under the sofa. After putting it away, I discovered something else amiss. Soon I was cleaning the entire house, totally forgetting I had knelt down to pray.

Sometimes we have to let the toys lie, close our eyes, tune out all that would distract us, and press in to God. At first this may be more difficult than cleaning the house, because we are used to activity. That's how we feel needed. But I challenge you to examine your lifestyle honestly. Are you so busy that you neglect yourself and those you love? Have you mistaken self-neglect for self-denial? Are you drawing your security from the little things, or have you focused on the eternal?

If your answer to any of these questions is yes, don't use them as an excuse for a guilt trip. Instead, let them motivate you to change.

Lisa Bevere

[1] *35* Gk. *denarius*, a coin worth about a day's wage.

be opened to you. 10 For everyone who asks receives, and he who seeks finds, and to him who knocks it will be opened.

11 "If a son asks for bread from any of you who is a father, will you give him a stone? Or if he asks for a fish, will you give him a serpent instead of a fish? 12 Or if he asks for an egg, will you offer him a scorpion? 13 If you then, being evil, know how to give good gifts to your children, how much more will your heavenly Father give the Holy Spirit to those who ask Him?"

Jesus and Beelzebub

Mt 12:22–30; Mk 3:20–27

14 He was casting out a demon, and it was mute. When the demon had gone out, the mute man spoke, and the crowd marveled. 15 But some of them said, "He casts out demons through Beelzebub, the ruler of the demons." 16 Others, testing Him, asked Him for a sign from heaven.

17 But He, knowing their thoughts, said to them, "Every kingdom divided against itself is made desolate. And a house divided against itself falls. 18 If Satan also is divided against himself, how will his kingdom stand? For you say that I cast out demons through Beelzebub. 19 Now if I cast out demons by Beelzebub, by whom do your sons cast them out? Therefore they will be your judges. 20 But if I cast out demons with the finger of God, no doubt the kingdom of God has come upon you.

21 "When a strong man, fully armed, guards his own palace, his goods are peacefully kept. 22 But when a stronger man than he attacks and overpowers him, he seizes all the armor in which the man trusted and divides his spoils.

23 "He who is not with Me is against Me, and he who does not gather with Me scatters.

The Return of the Unclean Spirit

Mt 12:43–45

24 "When an unclean spirit goes out of a man, it goes through dry places seeking rest. Finding none, it says, 'I will return to my house, from which I came.' 25 When it comes, it finds it swept and furnished. 26 Then it goes and brings seven other spirits more wicked than itself, and they enter and dwell there. And the last state of that man is worse than the first."

True Blessedness

27 As He spoke these things, a woman from the crowd raised her voice and said to Him, "Blessed is the woman who gave You birth and nursed You."

28 But He said, "Indeed, blessed are those who hear the word of God and keep it."

11:13 Mt 7:11
11:15 Mt 9:34
11:17 Mt 9:4
11:20 Ex 8:19
11:23 Mt 12:30
11:24 Mt 12:43–45
11:27 Lk 1:48
11:28 Lk 8:21
....
11:30 Jnh 1:17
11:31 2Ch 9:1
11:34 Mt 6:22–23
11:37 Lk 7:36
11:40 Lk 12:20
11:41 Lk 12:33
11:42 Mt 23:23
11:43 Lk 20:46

The Demand for a Sign

Mt 12:38–42; Mk 8:12

29 When the crowds pressed upon Him, He began to say, "This is an evil generation. It looks for a sign, but no sign will be given it except the sign of Jonah the prophet. 30 For as Jonah was a sign to the Ninevites, so will the Son of Man be to this generation. 31 The Queen of the South will rise up in the judgment with the men of this generation and condemn them, for she came from the ends of the earth to hear the wisdom of Solomon. And now one greater than Solomon is here. 32 The men of Nineveh will rise up in the judgment with this generation and will condemn it, for they repented at the preaching of Jonah. And now one greater than Jonah is here.

The Light of the Body

Mt 5:15; 6:22–23

33 "No one, when he has lit a candle, puts it in a secret place or under a basket, but on a candlestick, that those who come in may see the light. 34 The eye is the lamp of the body. Therefore when your eye is good, your whole body also is full of light. But when your eye is bad, your body also is full of darkness. 35 Take heed therefore lest the light which is in you is darkness. 36 If your whole body, then, is full of light, no part being dark, the whole body will be full of light, as when the shining candle gives you light."

The Denouncing of the Pharisees and Lawyers

Mt 23:1–36; Mk 12:38–40; Lk 20:45–47

37 As He spoke, a Pharisee asked Him to dine with him. So He went in and sat down to eat. 38 When the Pharisee saw it, he marveled that He had not first washed before dinner.

39 Then the Lord said to him, "Now you Pharisees clean the outside of the cup and the dish. But inside you are full of extortion and wickedness. 40 You fools! Did not he who made the outside make the inside also? 41 But give alms from what is within. And then all things are clean to you.

42 "Woe to you, Pharisees! For you tithe mint and rue and every herb and pass over justice and the love of God. These you ought to have done, without leaving the others undone.

43 "Woe to you, Pharisees! For you love the prominent seats in the synagogues and greetings in the marketplaces.

44 "Woe to you, scribes and Pharisees, hypocrites! For you are like unseen graves, and the men who walk over them are not aware of them."

45 One of the lawyers answered, "Teacher, by saying these things You insult us also."

46 He said, "Woe to you also, you lawyers! For
you load men with burdens difficult to carry,
and you yourselves do not touch the burdens
with one of your fingers.
47 "Woe to you! For you build the tombs of
the prophets, and your fathers killed them.
48 So you are witnesses and entirely approve
the deeds of your fathers, because they killed
them, and you build their tombs. 49 Therefore
also the wisdom of God said, 'I will send them
prophets and apostles, and some of them they
will kill and persecute,' 50 that the blood of all
the prophets, shed since the beginning of the
world, may be required from this generation,
51 from the blood of Abel to the blood of Zecha-
riah, who was killed between the altar and the
sanctuary. Yes, I tell you, it shall be required
from this generation.
52 "Woe to you, lawyers! For you have taken
away the key of knowledge. You did not enter
yourselves, and you hindered those who were
entering."
53 As He said these things to them, the scribes
and the Pharisees began to incite Him vehe-
mently and angrily draw Him out concerning
many things, 54 lying in wait for Him and seek-
ing to catch something out of His mouth, that
they might accuse Him.

A Warning Against Hypocrisy

12 Meanwhile, when thousands of the
crowd were assembled, so as to tram-
ple on one another, He began to say to His dis-
ciples first, "Beware of the yeast of the Phari-
sees, which is hypocrisy. 2 For there is nothing
covered that will not be revealed, or hidden
that will not be known. 3 Therefore what you
have said in the darkness will be heard in the
light. And what you have whispered in the
ear in private rooms will be proclaimed on
the housetops.

God takes care of the birds, and He will take care of me (Lk 12:6).

Whom to Fear
Mt 10:28–31

4 "I say to you, My friends, do not be afraid
of those who kill the body, and after that can
do no more. 5 But I will warn you whom you
shall fear: Fear Him who, after He has killed,
has power to cast into hell. Yes, I say to you,
fear Him. 6 Are not five sparrows sold for two
pennies[1]? Yet not one of them is forgotten by
God. 7 Indeed, even the hairs of your head are
all numbered. Therefore do not fear. You are
more valuable than many sparrows.

11:47 Mt 23:29–33
11:49 1Co 1:30
11:52 Mt 23:13
11:54 Mk 12:13
12:1 Jas 3:17
12:2 Mk 4:22
12:3 Mt 10:27
12:6 Mt 10:29
....
12:9 Mk 8:38
12:10 Mt 12:31–32
12:11 Mt 23:34
12:12 Lk 21:15
12:14 Ro 2:1
12:15 1Ti 6:6–10
12:19 Ecc 11:9
12:20 Jer 17:11
12:21 Lk 12:33
12:24 Job 38:41

Confessing Christ Before Men
Mt 10:19–20, 32–33; 12:32

8 "I say to you, whoever confesses Me before
men, him will the Son of Man also confess be-
fore the angels of God. 9 But he who denies Me
before men will be denied before the angels
of God. 10 And everyone who speaks a word
against the Son of Man will be forgiven, but
he who blasphemes against the Holy Spirit will
not be forgiven.
11 "When they bring you to the synagogues,
rulers, and authorities, do not be anxious how
you will answer or what you will say. 12 For the
Holy Spirit will teach you at that time what you
should say."

The Parable of the Rich Fool

13 Someone in the crowd said to Him, "Teach-
er, tell my brother to divide the inheritance
with me."
14 Jesus said to him, "Man, who appointed Me
a judge or an arbitrator between you?" 15 Then
He said to them, "Take heed and beware of
covetousness. For a man's life does not consist
in the abundance of his possessions."
16 And He told a parable to them, saying, "The
land of a rich man produced plentifully. 17 He
thought to himself, 'What shall I do, for I have
no room to store my crops?'
18 "Then he said, 'This I will do: I will pull
down my barns and build greater ones, and
there I will store all my grain and my goods.
19 And I will say to my soul, Soul, you have
many goods laid up for many years. Take rest.
Eat, drink, and be merry.'
20 "But God said to him, 'You fool! This night
your soul will be required of you. Then whose
will those things be which you have provided?'
21 "So is he who stores up treasure for himself,
and is not rich toward God."

Care and Anxiety
Mt 6:25–34, 19–21

22 Then He said to His disciples, "Therefore
I say to you, do not be anxious for your life,
what you will eat, nor for your body, what you
will wear. 23 Life is more than food, and the
body is more than clothes. 24 Consider the ra-
vens: They neither sow nor reap, they have
neither storehouses nor barns. Yet God feeds
them. How much more valuable are you than
birds? 25 Who of you by worrying can add one
cubit[2] to his height? 26 If you then cannot do
what is least, why are you anxious about the
other things?
27 "Consider how the lilies grow. They neither
spin nor weave. Yet I say to you that Solomon
in all his glory was not arrayed like one of

[1] *6* Gk. *2 assaria.* An *assarion* was worth 1/16 of a denarius, which was a day's wage. [2] *25* A cubit is about half a meter.

SPIRITLED WOMAN

COUNSEL FROM THE SPIRIT BASICS

God Is Our Glue

Today's married couples, especially the younger ones, are so wrapped up in their jobs and the world of social networking and media entertainment that little time or patience is left to nurture their relationship, and even less to spend quality time with their children.

I was immensely glad to see my daughter's Facebook post advising other couples on her recent fourteenth wedding anniversary: "Today I celebrate a fourteen-year anniversary with my honey. Don't give up on your relationships. Remember the 'crazy in love' feelings you started out with and do whatever it takes to keep them or ask God to help you get them back. God is our glue. It's all worth it!"

Now, that's awesome advice for any couple at any stage of their marriage. Without demonstrative love in a marriage, life is like a cold overcast day. Love is affection, tenderness, desire, intimacy, kindness, enthusiasm, and so much more.

Today's marriages are faced with tremendous opposition of evil forces. But always remember that if you belong to God, you have a supernatural covering and awesome spiritual power at your disposal. If you're not there yet, keep persevering, and make a decision to work at your marriage. Make it a safe haven for all your passions and marital needs. Put God first in your life, and all good things will be added unto you.

Iris Delgado

these. 28 If God so clothes the grass, which today is in the field and tomorrow is thrown into the oven, how much more will He clothe you, O you of little faith? 29 And do not seek what you will eat or what you will drink, nor be of an anxious mind. 30 For the nations of the world seek all these things, and your Father knows that you need them. 31 But seek the kingdom of God, and all these things shall be given to you.

32 "Do not be afraid, little flock, for it is your Father's good pleasure to give you the kingdom. 33 Sell your possessions and give alms. Provide yourselves purses that do not grow old, an unfailing treasure in the heavens, where no thief comes near and no moth destroys. 34 For where your treasure is, there will your heart be also.

12:29 Mt 6:31
12:30 Mt 6:8
12:33 Mt 19:21
12:34 Mt 6:21
12:35 Eph 6:14
12:36 Rev 3:20
12:37 Mt 24:42
12:39 Mt 24:43–44
12:41 Mk 13:37
12:46 Lk 12:40
12:47 Jas 4:17
12:48 Lev 5:17
12:50 Jn 19:30
12:51 Mt 10:34–36

Watchful Servants

Mt 24:45–51

35 "Let your waist be girded and your lights be burning, 36 and you be like men waiting for their master to return from the wedding banquet, so that they may open the door immediately for him when he comes and knocks. 37 Blessed are those servants whom the master will find watching when he comes. Truly I say to you, he will dress himself and have them sit down to dine, and he will come and serve them. 38 If he comes in the second watch, or comes in the third watch, and finds them so, blessed are those servants. 39 But know this: If the owner of the house had known at what hour the thief was coming, he would have watched and not have allowed his house to be broken into. 40 Therefore be ready, for the Son of Man is coming at an hour you do not expect."

41 Peter said to Him, "Lord, are You telling this parable to us, or to everyone?"

42 The Lord said, "Who then is the faithful and wise steward, whom his master will make ruler over his house servants, to give them their portion of food at the proper time? 43 Blessed is that servant whom his master will find so doing when he comes. 44 Truly, I say to you, he will appoint him over all his possessions. 45 But if that servant says in his heart, 'My master delays his coming,' and begins to beat the house servants, both men and women, and to eat and drink and get drunk, 46 the master of that servant will come on a day when he does not look for him, and at an hour when he is not aware, and will cut him to pieces and will appoint him his portion with the unbelievers.

47 "That servant who knew his master's will, but did not prepare himself or do according to his will, shall be beaten with many stripes. 48 But he who unknowingly committed acts worthy of punishment shall be beaten with few stripes. For to whom much is given, of him much shall be required. And from him to whom much was entrusted, much will be asked.

Jesus the Cause of Division

Mt 10:34–36

49 "I have come to send fire upon the earth and wish that it were already kindled! 50 But I have a baptism to be baptized with, and how pressed I am until it is accomplished! 51 Do you

suppose that I have come to give peace on earth? No, I tell you, but rather division. 52 For there will be from now on five divided in one house, three against two and two against three. 53 They will be divided, father against son and son against father, mother against daughter and daughter against mother, and mother-in-law against her daughter-in-law and daughter-in-law against her mother-in-law."

Discerning the Appointed Time
Mt 16:2–3

54 Then He said to the crowd: "When you see a cloud rise out of the west, immediately you say, 'A shower is coming,' and so it is. 55 And when a south wind blows, you say, 'There will be heat,' and it happens. 56 You hypocrites! You can discern the face of the sky and of the earth. But why do you not know how to discern this time?

Settling With Your Accuser
Mt 5:25–26

57 "Why even among yourselves do you not judge what is right? 58 When you go with your adversary to the magistrate, as you are on the way, diligently try to settle matters with him, lest he drag you to the judge, and the judge will hand you over to the officer, and the officer will throw you into prison. 59 I tell you, you shall not come out from there until you have paid the very last penny."[1]

Repent or Perish

13 There were present at that time some who told Him of the Galileans whose blood Pilate had mingled with their sacrifices. 2 Jesus answered, "Do you suppose that these Galileans were worse sinners than all the other Galileans, because they suffered such things? 3 I tell you, no! But unless you repent, you will all likewise perish. 4 Or those eighteen, upon whom the tower in Siloam fell and killed them, do you think that they were worse offenders than all men living in Jerusalem? 5 I tell you, no! But unless you repent, you will all likewise perish."

The Parable of the Barren Fig Tree

6 Then He told this parable: "A man had a fig tree planted in his vineyard. He came and looked for fruit on it and found none. 7 So he said to the vinedresser of his vineyard, 'Now these three years I have come looking for fruit on this fig tree, and I find none. Cut it down. Why should it deplete the soil?'

8 "He answered him, 'Sir, leave it alone this year also, until I dig around it and fertilize it. 9 And if it bears fruit, well. But if not, after that you shall cut it down.'"

12:53 Mic 7:6
12:56 Mt 16:3
12:59 Mk 12:42
13:2 Jn 9:2
13:3 Lk 24:47
13:4 Jn 9:7
13:5 Lk 13:3
13:7 Ex 32:10

....

13:10 Mt 4:23
13:11 Lk 13:16
13:14 Ex 20:9
13:15 Lk 14:5
13:16 Lk 19:9
13:18 Lk 13:20
13:19 Mt 17:20
13:21 Mt 13:33
13:22 Lk 9:51
13:25 Mt 25:10–12

Healing a Woman on the Sabbath

10 He was teaching in one of the synagogues on the Sabbath. 11 And there was a woman who had a spirit of infirmity for eighteen years and was bent over and could not straighten herself up. 12 When Jesus saw her, He called her and said to her, "Woman, you are loosed from your infirmity." 13 Then He laid His hands on her, and immediately she was made straight and glorified God.

14 But the ruler of the synagogue answered with indignation, because Jesus had healed on the Sabbath, and said to the people, "There are six days in which men ought to work. Therefore come and be healed on those days, but not on the Sabbath day."

15 The Lord answered him, "You hypocrite! Does not each one of you on the Sabbath untie his ox or his donkey from the stall and lead it away to water it? 16 Then should not this woman, being a daughter of Abraham whom Satan has bound these eighteen years, be loosed from this bondage on the Sabbath?"

17 When He said this, all His adversaries were ashamed. And all the people rejoiced for all the glorious things that were done by Him.

The Parables of the Mustard Seed and the Yeast
Mt 13:31–33; Mk 4:30–32

18 Then He said, "What is the kingdom of God like? To what shall I compare it? 19 It is like a grain of mustard seed which a man took and planted in his garden. It grew and became a large tree, and the birds of the air nested in its branches."

20 Again He said, "To what shall I compare the kingdom of God? 21 It is like yeast, which a woman took and hid in sixty pounds[2] of meal until all of it was leavened."

The Narrow Gate
Mt 7:13–14, 21–23

22 Then He went through the cities and villages, teaching, and journeying toward Jerusalem. 23 Someone said to Him, "Lord, will those who are saved be few?"

He said to them, 24 "Strive to enter through the narrow gate. For many, I tell you, will try to enter and will not be able. 25 Once the Master of the house has risen up and shut the door, and you begin to stand outside and knock at the door, saying, 'Lord, Lord, open for us,' He will answer you, 'I do not know where you come from.'

26 "Then you will begin to say, 'We ate and drank in your presence, and you taught in our streets.'

[1] 59 Gk. *lepton*, the smallest coin circulated, means "small" or "thin."
[2] 21 Gk. *3 sata*, or 27 kilograms.

27 “But He will say, ‘I tell you, I do not know
you, or where you come from. Depart from Me,
all you workers of iniquity.’
28 “There will be weeping and gnashing of
teeth when you see Abraham, and Isaac, and
Jacob, and all the prophets in the kingdom
of God, and you yourselves thrust out. 29 They
will come from the east and from the west and
from the north and from the south and will sit
down to dine in the kingdom of God. 30 Listen,
there are the last who will be first, and the first
who will be last.”

The Lament Over Jerusalem
Mt 23:37–39

31 On the same day certain Pharisees came,
saying to Him, “Get out and depart from here,
for Herod wants to kill You.”
32 He said to them, “Go and tell that fox, ‘Look,
I cast out demons. And I perform healings
today and tomorrow, and on the third day I
shall be perfected.’ 33 Nevertheless I must travel
today and tomorrow and the day following.
For it cannot be that a prophet should perish
outside Jerusalem.
34 “O Jerusalem, Jerusalem, which kills the
prophets and stones those who are sent to
you! How often would I have gathered your
children together, as a hen gathers her chicks
under her wings, and you were not willing!
35 Look, your house is forsaken. Truly I say to
you, you shall not see Me until the time comes
when you say, ‘Blessed is He who comes in the
name of the Lord.’[1]”

The Healing of the Man With Edema

14 On the Sabbath they watched Him as
He went into the house of one of the
leaders of the Pharisees to eat bread. 2 There
before Him was a man who had edema.[2]
3 Jesus said to the lawyers and Pharisees, “Is
it lawful to heal on the Sabbath?” 4 But they
remained silent. So He took him and healed
him, and let him go.
5 Then He said, “Which of you having a don-
key or an ox that has fallen into a pit will not
immediately pull him out on the Sabbath day?”
6 And they could not answer Him regarding
these things.

A Lesson to Guests and a Host

7 When He marked how they chose the seats
of honor, He told a parable to those who were
invited, saying to them, 8 “When you are in-
vited by any man to a wedding banquet, do
not sit down in a seat of honor, lest a more
honorable man than you be invited by him;
9 and he who invited you both will come and
say to you, ‘Give this man the seat,’ and then
you will begin with shame to take the lowest
seat. 10 But when you are invited, go and sit
down in the lowest seat, so that when he who
invited you comes, he may say to you, ‘Friend,
go up higher.’ Then you will have respect in the
presence of those who sit at dinner with you.
11 For whoever exalts himself will be humbled,
and he who humbles himself will be exalted.”
12 Then He said also to the one who invited
Him, “When you prepare a dinner or a supper,
do not call your friends or your brothers or
your kinsmen or your rich neighbors, lest they
also invite you in return, and you be repaid.
13 But when you prepare a banquet, call the
poor, the maimed, the lame, the blind, 14 and
you will be blessed, for they cannot repay
you. You shall be repaid at the resurrection
of the just.”

The Parable of the Great Banquet
Mt 22:1–10

15 When one of those who sat at dinner with
Him heard this, he said to Him, “Blessed is he
who shall eat bread in the kingdom of God!”
16 Then He said to him, “A man prepared
a banquet and invited many, 17 and sent his
servant at supper time to say to those who
had been invited, ‘Come, for everything is now
prepared.’
18 “But they all with one mind began to make
excuses. The first said to him, ‘I have bought
a piece of land, and I must go and see it. I ask
you to excuse me.’
19 “Another said, ‘I have bought five yoke of
oxen, and I am going to prove them. I ask you
to excuse me.’
20 “Still another said, ‘I have married a wife,
and therefore I cannot come.’
21 “The servant came and reported this to
his master. Then the master of the house in
anger said to his servant, ‘Go out quickly into
the streets and lanes of the city, and bring in
here the poor and the maimed and the lame
and the blind.’
22 “The servant said, ‘Master, what you com-
manded has been done, and yet there is room.’
23 “Then the master said to the servant, ‘Go
out to the highways and hedges, and compel
them to come in, so that my house may be
filled. 24 For I tell you, none of those men who
were invited shall taste my supper.’ ”

The Cost of Discipleship
Mt 10:37–38

25 Large crowds went with Him. And He
turned and said to them, 26 “If anyone comes
to Me and does not hate his father and mother
and wife and children and brothers and sisters,
yes, and even his own life, he cannot be My

13:27 Mt 25:41
13:30 Mt 19:30
13:32 Heb 2:10
13:33 Mt 21:11
13:34 Mt 23:37–39
13:35 Ps 118:26
14:1 Mk 3:2
14:3 Mt 12:10
14:5 Lk 13:15
14:6 Lk 20:40
14:7 Lk 11:43
14:8 Pr 25:6–7
14:10 Pr 25:6–7
14:11 Lk 18:14
14:13 Lk 14:21
14:14 Ac 24:15
14:15 Rev 19:9
14:16 Mt 22:2–14
14:20 1Co 7:33
14:21 Lk 14:13
14:24 Mt 21:43
14:26 Mt 10:37

1 35 Ps 118:26. *2 2* Or *dropsy*.

disciple. 27 And whoever does not bear his cross
and follow Me cannot be My disciple.
28 "For who among you, intending to build
a tower, does not sit down first and count the
cost to see whether he has resources to com-
plete it? 29 Otherwise, perhaps, after he has laid
the foundation and is not able to complete it,
all who see it will begin to mock him, 30 saying,
'This man began to build and was not able to
complete it.'
31 "Or what king, going to wage war against
another king, does not sit down first and take
counsel whether he is able with ten thousand
to meet him who comes against him with
twenty thousand? 32 Otherwise, while the other
is yet at a distance, he sends a delegation and
requests conditions of peace. 33 So likewise,
any of you who does not forsake all that he
has cannot be My disciple.

Tasteless Salt
Mt 5:13; Mk 9:50

34 "Salt is good. But if the salt has lost its
saltiness, how shall it be made salty? 35 It is fit
neither for the land nor for the manure pile.
So men throw it out.
"He who has ears to hear, let him hear."

The Parable of the Lost Sheep
Mt 18:12–14

15 Now all the tax collectors and sinners
drew near to Him to hear Him. 2 But the
Pharisees and scribes murmured, saying, "This
Man receives sinners and eats with them."
3 So He told them this parable, saying,
4 "What man among you having a hundred
sheep and losing one of them does not leave
the ninety-nine in the wilderness and go after
the one which is lost until he finds it? 5 And
when he has found it, he places it on his shoul-
ders, rejoicing. 6 Then when he comes home,
he calls together his friends and neighbors,
saying to them, 'Rejoice with me, for I have
found my sheep which was lost.' 7 Likewise, I
tell you, there will be more joy in heaven over
one sinner who repents than over ninety-nine
righteous men who need no repentance.

The Parable of the Lost Coin

8 "Or what woman, having ten silver coins[1]
and losing one, does not light a candle and
sweep the house and search diligently until
she finds it? 9 And when she has found it, she
calls together her friends and neighbors, say-
ing, 'Rejoice with me, for I have found the coin
which I had lost.' 10 Likewise, I tell you, there is
joy in the presence of the angels of God over
one sinner who repents."

14:27 Mt 10:38
14:28 Pr 24:27
14:31 Pr 20:18
14:34 Mt 5:13
14:35 Mt 11:15
15:2 Mt 9:11
15:4 Eze 34:11–12
15:6 1Pe 2:25
15:7 Lk 5:32
15:10 Heb 1:14
....
15:12 Mk 12:44
15:19 Lk 7:6–7
15:20 Ac 20:37
15:22 Ge 41:42
15:24 Lk 15:32
15:32 Lk 15:24

The Parable of the Prodigal Son

11 Then He said, "A man had two sons. 12 The
younger of them said to his father, 'Father, give
me the share of the property that falls to me.'
So he divided his estate between them.
13 "Not many days later, the younger son
gathered everything together, and journeyed
to a distant country, and there squandered his
possessions in prodigal living. 14 When he had
spent everything, there came a severe famine
in that country, and he began to be in want.
15 So he went and hired himself to a citizen
of that county, who sent him into his fields to
feed swine. 16 He would gladly have filled his
stomach with the husks that the swine were
eating, but no one gave him any.
17 "When he came to himself, he said, 'How
many of my father's hired servants have an
abundance of bread, and here I am perish-
ing with hunger! 18 I will arise and go to my
father, and I will say to him, "Father, I have
sinned against heaven and before you. 19 I am
no longer worthy to be called your son. Make
me like one of your hired servants." ' 20 So he
arose and came to his father.
"But while he was yet far away, his father saw
him and was moved with compassion, and ran
and embraced his neck and kissed him.
21 "The son said to him, 'Father, I have sinned
against heaven and before you. I am no longer
worthy to be called your son.'
22 "But the father said to his servants, 'Bring
out the best robe and put it on him. And put a
ring on his hand and shoes on his feet. 23 Bring
here the fattened calf and kill it, and let us eat
and be merry. 24 For this son of mine was dead,
and is alive again; he was lost, and is found.'
So they began to be merry.
25 "Now his older son was in the field. As he
came and drew near the house, he heard mu-
sic and dancing. 26 So he called one of the ser-
vants and asked what this meant. 27 He said to
him, 'Your brother has come, and your father
has killed the fattened calf, because he has
received him safe and sound.'
28 "He was angry and would not go in. There-
fore his father came out and entreated him.
29 But he answered his father, 'Look! These
many years have I served you. Nor have I ever
transgressed your commands, yet never have
you given me a goat, so that I might be merry
with my friends. 30 But when this son of yours
came, who has devoured your living with har-
lots, you killed the fattened calf for him.'
31 "He said to him, 'Son, you are always with
me, and all that I have is yours. 32 But it was
fitting to be merry and be glad, for this brother

[1] 8 Gk. *drachmas*, each worth about a day's wage.

of yours was dead and is alive again; he was
lost and is found.' "

The Parable of the Dishonest Steward

16 He told His disciples: "There was a rich
man who had a steward who was ac-
cused to the man of wasting his resources. 2 So
he called him and said, 'How is it that I hear
this about you? Give an account of your stew-
ardship, for you may no longer be steward.'
3 "Then the steward said to himself, 'What
shall I do, for my master is taking away the
stewardship from me? I cannot dig. I am
ashamed to beg. 4 I know what to do so that,
when I am removed from the stewardship, oth-
ers may receive me into their houses.'
5 "So he called each of his master's debtors,
and said to the first, 'How much do you owe
my master?'
6 "He said, 'Eight hundred gallons[1] of oil.'
"He said to him, 'Take your bill, and sit down
quickly and write four hundred.'
7 "Then he said to another, 'And how much
do you owe?'
"He said, 'One thousand bushels[2] of wheat.'
"He said to him, 'Take your bill, and write
eight hundred.'
8 "The master commended the dishonest
steward, because he had acted prudently. For
the sons of this world are wiser in their own
generation than the sons of light. 9 I say to you,
make friends for yourself by means of unrigh-
teous wealth, so that when you fall short, they
may receive you into eternal dwellings.
10 "He who is faithful in what is least is faith-
ful also in much. And he who is dishonest in
the least is dishonest also in much. 11 So if
you have not been faithful in the unrighteous
wealth, who will commit to your trust the true
riches? 12 And if you have not been faithful in
that which is another man's, who will give you
that which is your own?
13 "No servant can serve two masters. Either
he will hate the one and love the other, or he
will be loyal to the one and despise the other.
You cannot serve God and wealth."

The Law and the Kingdom of God
Mt 11:12–13

14 The Pharisees, who were lovers of money,
heard all these things and derided Him. 15 He
said to them, "You are those who justify your-
selves before men, but God knows your hearts.
For that which is highly esteemed before men
is an abomination before God.
16 "The Law and the Prophets were preached
until John. Since then the kingdom of God has
been preached, and everyone is pressing into
it. 17 It is easier for heaven and earth to pass
away than for one stroke of the law to fail.
18 "Whoever divorces his wife and marries
another commits adultery, and whoever
marries her who is divorced by her husband
commits adultery.

The Rich Man and Lazarus

19 "There was a rich man who was clothed
in purple and fine linen and fared sumptu-
ously every day. 20 There was also a beggar
named Lazarus, covered with sores, who had
been placed at his gate, 21 desiring to be fed
the crumbs falling from the rich man's table.
Moreover the dogs came and licked his sores.
22 "It came to pass that the beggar died and
was carried by the angels to Abraham's pres-
ence. The rich man also died and was buried.
23 In Hades, being in torment, he lifted up his
eyes and saw Abraham from a distance and
Lazarus in his presence. 24 So he cried out, 'Fa-
ther Abraham, have mercy on me, and send
Lazarus to dip the tip of his finger in water
and cool my tongue. For I am tormented in
this flame.'
25 "But Abraham said, 'Son, remember that
you in your lifetime received your good things,
and Lazarus in like manner evil things. But
now he is comforted and you are tormented.
26 And besides all this, between us and you
there is a great gulf, so that those who would
pass from here to you cannot, nor can those
from there pass to us.'
27 "He said, 'Then I pray you, father, to send
him to my father's house, 28 for I have five
brothers, to testify to them, lest they also come
to this place of torment.'
29 "Abraham said to him, 'They have Moses
and the Prophets. Let them hear them.'
30 "He said, 'No, father Abraham. But if
someone from the dead goes to them, they
will repent.'
31 "He said to him, 'If they do not hear Moses
and the Prophets, neither will they be persuad-
ed if someone should rise from the dead.' "

Some Sayings of Jesus
Mt 18:6–7, 21–22; Mk 9:42

17 Then He said to the disciples, "It is im-
possible except that offenses will come.
But woe to him through whom they come! 2 It
would be better for him if a millstone were
hung around his neck and he was thrown into
the sea, than to offend one of these little ones.
3 Take heed to yourselves.
"If your brother sins against you, rebuke
him. And if he repents, forgive him. 4 If he sins
against you seven times in a day, and seven
times in a day turns to you, saying, 'I repent,'
you must forgive him."

16:1 Lk 15:13
16:8 Jn 12:36
16:9 Mt 19:21
16:10 Mt 25:21
16:13 Mt 6:24
16:14 Lk 23:35
16:15 1Sa 16:7
16:16 Mt 3:2
....
16:17 Mt 5:18
16:18 Mt 19:9
16:19 Est 8:15
16:20 Ac 3:2
16:21 Mt 15:27
16:22 Jn 13:23
16:24 Mt 25:41
16:25 Lk 6:24
16:29 Ac 15:21
16:30 Lk 16:24
16:31 Jn 12:10–11
17:1 Mt 18:7
17:2 Mk 9:42
17:4 Mt 18:21–22

[1]6 Gk. *100 batous*, or 3 kiloliters. [2]7 Gk. *100 korous*, or 35 kiloliters.

I pray as Your anointed disciples
prayed: "Increase my faith!" (Lk 17:5).

5 The apostles said to the Lord, "Increase
our faith."
6 The Lord said, "If you had faith as a grain of
mustard seed, you could say to this mulberry
tree, 'Be uprooted and be planted in the sea,'
and it would obey you.
7 "Which of you, having a servant plowing
or herding sheep, will say to him when he
has come in from the field, 'Come now and
sit down for dinner'? 8 Will he not rather say
to him, 'Prepare my supper, and dress your-
self and serve me until I eat and drink. And
afterward you will eat and drink'? 9 Does he
thank the servant because he did what was
commanded? I think not. 10 So you also, when
you have done everything commanded you,
say, 'We are unprofitable servants. We have
done our duty.' "

The Cleansing of Ten Lepers

11 As Jesus went to Jerusalem, He passed be-
tween Samaria and Galilee. 12 As He entered
a village, there met Him ten men who were
lepers, who stood at a distance. 13 They lifted
up their voices, saying, "Jesus, Master, have
pity on us!"
14 When He saw them, He said to them, "Go,
show yourselves to the priests." And as they
went, they were cleansed.
15 One of them, when he saw that he was
healed, returned with a loud voice glorifying
God, 16 and fell down on his face at His feet,
giving Him thanks. And he was a Samaritan.
17 Jesus said, "Were not the ten cleansed?
Where are the nine? 18 Were there not any
found to return and give glory to God except
this foreigner?" 19 Then He said to him, "Rise,
go your way. Your faith has made you well."

The Coming of the Kingdom

Mt 24:23–28, 37–41

20 When He was asked by the Pharisees when
the kingdom of God would come, He answered
them, "The kingdom of God does not come
with observation. 21 Nor will they say, 'Here it
is!' or 'There it is!' For remember, the kingdom
of God is within you."
22 Then He said to the disciples, "The days
will come when you will desire to see one of
the days of the Son of Man, but you will not
see it. 23 They will say to you, 'Look here,' or
'Look there!' Do not follow after them. 24 For
as the lightning flashes and lights up the
heavens from one side to the other, so will
the Son of Man be in His day. 25 But first He
must suffer many things and be rejected by
this generation.
26 "Just as it was in the days of Noah, so will it
be in the days of the Son of Man. 27 They were
eating, drinking, marrying, and were given in
marriage until the day when Noah entered
the ark. Then the flood came and destroyed
them all.
28 "Likewise as it was in the days of Lot: They
ate, they drank, they bought, they sold, they
planted, they built. 29 But on the day that Lot
departed from Sodom, fire and brimstone
rained from heaven and destroyed them all.
30 "So will it be on the day when the Son of
Man is revealed. 31 On that day let him who is
on the housetop, with his goods in the house,
not come down to take them away. And like-
wise let him who is in the field not return to
the things behind. 32 Remember Lot's wife.
33 Whoever seeks to save his life will lose it,
and whoever loses his life will preserve it. 34 I
tell you, on that night two men will be in one
bed; the one will be taken and the other will
be left. 35 Two women will be grinding grain
together; the one will be taken and the other
will be left. 36 Two men will be in the field; the
one will be taken and the other will be left."
37 They asked, "Where, Lord?"
He replied, "Where the body is, there the ea-
gles will be gathered together."

The Parable of the Widow and the Judge

18 He told them a parable to illustrate
that it is necessary always to pray and
not lose heart. 2 He said: "In a city there was
a judge who did not fear God or regard man.
3 And a widow was in that city. She came to
him, saying, 'Avenge me against my adversary.'
4 "He would not for a while. Yet afterward he
said to himself, 'Though I do not fear God or
respect man, 5 yet because this widow troubles
me, I will avenge her, lest by her continual
coming she will weary me.' "
6 And the Lord said, "Hear what the unjust
judge says. 7 And shall not God avenge His own
elect and be patient with them, who cry day
and night to Him? 8 I tell you, He will avenge
them speedily. Nevertheless, when the Son of
Man comes, will He find faith on the earth?"

The Parable of the Pharisee and the Tax Collector

9 He told this parable to some who trusted
in themselves, as though they were righteous,
and despised others: 10 "Two men went up to
the temple to pray, the one a Pharisee and
the other a tax collector. 11 The Pharisee stood
and prayed these things about himself, 'God,
I thank You that I am not like other men: ex-
tortioners, unjust, adulterers, or even like this

17:6 Mt 17:20
17:8 Lk 12:37
17:11 Lk 9:51–52
17:12 Lev 13:45–46
17:14 Lk 5:14
17:16 Mt 10:5
17:19 Mt 9:22
17:20 Lk 19:11
17:21 Lk 17:23
17:22 Mt 9:15
17:23 Lk 21:8
17:24 Mt 24:27
17:25 Mt 16:21
17:29 2Pe 2:6
17:30 2Th 1:7
17:32 Ge 19:26
17:33 Mt 10:39
17:37 Mt 24:28
18:1 Col 4:2
18:2 Lk 18:4
18:3 Isa 1:17
18:5 Lk 11:8
18:7 Rev 6:10
18:9 Lk 16:15
18:10 Ac 3:1
18:11 Mt 6:5

tax collector. 12 I fast twice a week, and I tithe
of all that I earn.'

13 "But the tax collector, standing at a dis-
tance, would not even lift his eyes to heaven,
but struck his chest, saying, 'God, be merciful
to me a sinner.'

14 "I tell you, this man went down to his house
justified rather than the other. For everyone
who exalts himself will be humbled, and he
who humbles himself will be exalted."

Little Children Blessed
Mt 19:13–15; Mk 10:13–16

15 They also brought infants to Him that He
might touch them. When the disciples saw it,
they rebuked them. 16 But Jesus called them
to Him and said, "Permit the little children to
come to Me, and do not hinder them. For to
such belongs the kingdom of God. 17 Truly, I
say to you, whoever will not receive the king-
dom of God as a little child will in no wise
enter it."

The Rich Ruler
Mt 19:16–30; Mk 10:17–31

18 A certain ruler asked Him, "Good Teacher,
what must I do to inherit eternal life?"

19 Jesus said to him, "Why do you call Me
good? No one is good, except God alone. 20 You
know the commandments: Do not commit
adultery, Do not murder, Do not steal, Do not
bear false witness, Honor your father and your
mother.[1]"

21 He said, "All these I have kept since my
youth."

22 When Jesus heard this, He said to him, "Yet
you lack one thing. Sell all that you have and
distribute to the poor, and you will have trea-
sure in heaven. And come, follow Me."

23 When he heard this he became very sor-
rowful, for he was very rich. 24 When Jesus saw
that he became very sorrowful, He said, "How
hard it is for those who have riches to enter the
kingdom of God! 25 For it is easier for a camel
to go through the eye of a needle than for a
rich man to enter the kingdom of God."

26 Those who heard this said, "Who then can
be saved?"

27 He said, "What is impossible with men is
possible with God."

28 Peter said, "Look, we have left everything
and followed You."

29 He said to them, "Truly, I tell you, there is
no man who has left his home or parents or
brothers or wife or children, for the sake of
the kingdom of God, 30 who shall not receive
many times more in this age and, in the age
to come, eternal life."

[1] *20* Ex 20:12–16; Dt 5:16–20.

18:12 Lk 11:42
18:13 Lk 23:48
18:14 Lk 14:11
18:15 Mt 19:13–15
18:17 Mk 10:15
18:20 Ro 13:9
18:21 Php 3:6
18:22 Lk 12:33
18:23 Eze 33:31
18:24 Pr 11:28
18:27 Mt 19:26
18:28 Lk 5:11

18:31 Ps 22:1–31
18:32 Lk 23:11
18:34 Mk 9:32
18:35 Jn 9:8
18:37 Mt 2:23
18:38 Mt 9:27
18:39 Lk 18:15
19:1 Lk 18:35
19:3 Jn 12:21
19:4 1Ki 10:27
19:8 2Sa 12:6

Jesus Foretells His Death and Resurrection a Third Time
Mt 20:17–19; Mk 10:32–34

31 Taking the twelve, He said, "Listen! We
are going up to Jerusalem, and everything
that is written by the prophets concerning the
Son of Man will be accomplished, 32 for He
will be handed over to the Gentiles and will
be mocked and insulted and spit upon. 33 They
will scourge Him and put Him to death, and
on the third day He will rise again."

34 They understood none of these things. This
saying was hidden from them, and they did not
comprehend what was spoken.

The Healing of a Blind Beggar Near Jericho
Mt 20:29–34; Mk 10:46–52

35 As He was drawing near Jericho, a cer-
tain blind man sat along the way begging.
36 Hearing a crowd passing by, he asked what
it meant. 37 They told him that Jesus of Naza-
reth was passing by.

38 He cried out, "Jesus, Son of David, have
mercy on me!"

39 Those who went in front rebuked him, so
that he would keep quiet. But he cried out
much more, "Son of David, have mercy on
me!"

40 Jesus stood and commanded him to be
brought to Him. When he came near, He asked
him, 41 "What do you want Me to do for you?"

He said, "Lord, grant that I may receive my
sight."

42 Jesus said to him, "Receive your sight.
Your faith has saved you." 43 Immediately he
received his sight and followed Him, glorifying
God. When all the people saw it, they gave
praise to God.

Jesus and Zacchaeus

19 Jesus entered and passed through Jer-
icho. 2 A man was there named Zac-
chaeus who was a chief tax collector, and he
was rich. 3 He tried to see who Jesus was, but
was not able from the crowd, because he was
little in stature. 4 So he ran ahead and climbed
up into a sycamore tree to see Him, for He was
to pass that way.

5 When Jesus came to the vicinity, He looked
up and saw him, and said to him, "Zacchaeus,
hurry and come down, for today I must re-
main at your house." 6 So he hurried and came
down, and received Him joyfully.

7 When they saw it, they all murmured, say-
ing, "He has gone to be the guest of a man
who is a sinner."

8 But Zacchaeus stood and said to the Lord,
"Look, Lord, I give half of my possessions to
the poor. And if I have taken anything from

anyone by false accusation, I will repay him
four times as much."
9 Jesus said to him, "Today salvation has
come to this house, because he also is a son
of Abraham. 10 For the Son of Man has come to
seek and to save that which was lost."

The Parable of the Ten Pounds
Mt 25:14–30

11 As they heard these things, He continued
and told them a parable, because He was
near Jerusalem and because they thought the
kingdom of God would immediately appear.
12 Therefore He said, "A nobleman went to a
distant country to receive a kingdom and to
return. 13 So he called his ten servants and en-
trusted to them ten pounds[1] and said to them,
'Trade until I come.'
14 "But his citizens hated him and sent a del-
egation after him, saying, 'We do not want this
man to reign over us.'
15 "When he returned, having received the
kingdom, he summoned these servants, to
whom he had entrusted the money, that he
might know what everyone gained by trading.
16 "The first came, saying, 'Master, your
pound has made ten pounds more.'
17 "He said to him, 'Well done, good servant!
Because you have been faithful in very little,
take authority over ten cities.'
18 "The second came, saying, 'Master, your
pound has made five pounds more.'
19 "He said in like manner to him, 'You, take
authority over five cities.'
20 "Then another came, saying, 'Master, look,
here is your pound, which I have kept put away
in a napkin. 21 For I feared you, because you
are an exacting man. You collect what you did
not deposit, and reap what you did not sow.'
22 "He said to him, 'Out of your own mouth
will I judge you, you wicked servant. You knew
that I was an exacting man, collecting what I
did not deposit and reaping what I did not sow.
23 Why then did you not deposit my money in
the bank, so that at my coming I might have
collected it with interest?'
24 "Then he said to those who stood by, 'Take
the pound from him and give it to him who
has ten pounds.'
25 "They said to him, 'Master, he has ten
pounds.'
26 " 'I tell you that to everyone who has will be
given. But from him who has not, even what
he has will be taken away from him. 27 But as
for those enemies of mine, who would not let
me reign over them, bring them here and slay
them before me.' "

The Triumphant Entry in Jerusalem
Mt 21:1–11; Mk 11:1–11; Jn 12:12–19

28 When He had said this, He went before
them, ascending up to Jerusalem. 29 When He
came near to Bethphage and Bethany, at the
mountain called the Mount of Olives, He sent
two of His disciples, 30 saying, "Go over into the
village opposite you, where, as you enter, you
will find a colt tied, on which no one has ever
yet sat. Untie it and bring it here. 31 If anyone
asks you, 'Why are you untying it?' you shall
say to him, 'Because the Lord has need of it.' "
32 Those who were sent went and found it just
as He had told them. 33 As they were untying
the colt, its owners said to them, "Why are you
untying the colt?"
34 They said, "The Lord has need of it."
35 They brought it to Jesus. And they threw
their garments on the colt, and they set Jesus
on it. 36 As He went, they spread their clothes
in the street.
37 When He was coming near the descent of
the Mount of Olives, the whole crowd of the
disciples began to rejoice and praise God with
loud voices for all the mighty works that they
had seen, 38 saying:

'Blessed is the King who comes in the
name of the Lord!'[2]
Peace in heaven and glory in the highest!"

39 Some of the Pharisees from the crowd said
to Him, "Teacher, rebuke Your disciples."
40 He answered them, "I tell you, if these should
be silent, the stones would immediately cry out."
41 When He came near, He beheld the city and
wept over it, 42 saying, "If you, even you, had
known even today what things would bring you
peace! But now they are hidden from your eyes.
43 For the days will come upon you when your
enemies will build an embankment around you
and surround you, and press you in on every
side. 44 They will dash you, and your children
within you, to the ground. They will not leave
one stone upon another within you, because
you did not know the time of your visitation."

The Cleansing of the Temple
Mt 21:12–17; Mk 11:15–19; Jn 2:13–22

45 Then He entered the temple and began
to drive out those who sold and bought in it,
46 saying to them, "It is written, 'My house will
be a house of prayer,'[3] but you have made it
'a den of thieves.'[4]"
47 He taught daily in the temple. But the chief
priests, the scribes, and the leaders of the peo-
ple tried to kill Him. 48 Yet they could not find
a way to do it, for all the people were very
attentive to hear Him.

19:9 Ro 4:16
19:10 Eze 34:16
19:11 Lk 17:20
19:12 Mt 25:14–30
19:17 Lk 16:10
19:22 2Sa 1:16
19:26 Mt 13:12
19:27 Mt 22:7

....

19:28 Lk 9:51
19:29 Ac 1:12
19:38 Lk 13:35
19:40 Hab 2:11
19:42 Dt 32:29
19:44 Lk 21:6
19:45 Mt 21:12–13
19:46 Jer 7:11

[1] *13* Gk. *mina*, worth about 3 months' wages. [2] *38* Ps 118:26.
[3] *46* Isa 56:7. [4] *46* Jer 7:11.

The Question of Jesus' Authority

Mt 21:23–27; Mk 11:27–33

20 One day, as He taught the people in the temple and preached the gospel, the chief priests and the scribes with the elders came up to Him, 2 and said to Him, "Tell us, by what authority are You doing these things? Who is he who gave You this authority?"

3 He answered them, "I will also ask you one thing. Answer Me: 4 Was the baptism of John from heaven or from men?"

5 They debated with themselves, saying, "If we say, 'From heaven,' He will say, 'Why then did you not believe him?' 6 But if we say, 'From men,' all the people will stone us, for they are persuaded that John was a prophet."

7 So they answered that they did not know where it was from.

8 Jesus said to them, "Neither will I tell you by what authority I do these things."

The Parable of the Vineyard and the Vinedressers

Mt 21:33–46; Mk 12:1–12

9 He began to tell the people this parable: "A man planted a vineyard, and leased it to vinedressers, and went to a distant country for a long time. 10 At harvest time he sent a servant to the vinedressers so they might give him some fruit of the vineyard. But the vinedressers beat him and sent him away empty-handed. 11 Again, he sent another servant. But they beat him also, and treated him shamefully, and sent him away empty-handed. 12 Once again, he sent a third. And they wounded him also and drove him out.

13 "Then the owner of the vineyard said, 'What shall I do? I will send my beloved son. Perhaps they will respect him when they see him.'

14 "But when the vinedressers saw him, they debated among themselves, saying, 'This is the heir. Come, let us kill him, that the inheritance may be ours.' 15 So they drove him out of the vineyard and killed him.

"What then will the owner of the vineyard do to them? 16 He will come and kill these vinedressers and will give the vineyard to others."

When they heard this, they said, "May it not be so!"

17 He looked at them and said, "What then is this that is written:

'The stone which the builders rejected
has become the cornerstone'[1]?

18 Whoever falls on that stone will be broken. But he on whom it falls will be crushed to powder."[2]

20:4 Lk 15:18
20:6 Mt 21:26
20:9 Mt 21:33–46
20:13 Mt 3:17
20:15 Heb 13:12
20:16 Lk 19:27
20:17 Ps 118:22
20:18 Isa 8:14–15

....

20:19 Lk 19:47–48
20:20 Mt 27:2
20:21 Jn 3:2
20:23 1Co 3:19
20:24 Mt 18:28
20:26 Lk 20:20
20:34 Lk 16:8
20:37 Ex 3:2–6
20:40 Mt 22:46

19 The chief priests and the scribes tried to lay their hands on Him that same hour, but they feared the people. For they perceived that He had told this parable against them.

The Question of Paying Taxes

Mt 22:18–22; Mk 12:13–17

20 They watched Him and sent out spies who pretended to be righteous men, that they might seize Him in His words to hand Him over to the power and authority of the governor. 21 So they asked Him, "Teacher, we know that You speak and teach rightly. And You do not show partiality, but You truly teach the way of God. 22 Is it lawful for us to pay taxes to Caesar, or not?"

23 He perceived their craftiness and said to them, "Why do you test Me? 24 Show Me a denarius.[3] Whose image and inscription does it have?"

They said, "Caesar's."

25 He said to them, "Then render to Caesar what is Caesar's, and to God what is God's."

26 They could not catch Him in His words before the people. And they marveled at His answer and were silent.

The Question About the Resurrection

Mt 22:23–33; Mk 12:18–27

27 Some of the Sadducees, who deny that there is any resurrection, came to Him and asked Him, 28 "Teacher, Moses wrote for us that if a man's brother dies, having a wife but no children, then this man should take the wife and raise up children for his brother.[4] 29 Now there were seven brothers. The first took a wife and died childless. 30 The second took her as wife, and he died childless. 31 And then the third took her, and in like manner, all seven died and left no children. 32 Last of all, the woman died also. 33 Therefore in the resurrection whose wife will she be? For the seven had her as a wife."

34 Jesus answered them, "The sons of this age marry and are given in marriage. 35 But those who are counted worthy to attain that age, and the resurrection from the dead, neither marry nor are given in marriage. 36 For they cannot die any more, for they are equal to the angels and are the sons of God, being sons of the resurrection. 37 Now, at the bush, even Moses pointed out that the dead are raised when he called the Lord 'the God of Abraham, and the God of Isaac, and the God of Jacob.'[5] 38 For He is not the God of the dead, but of the living. For to Him all live."

39 Some of the scribes said, "Teacher, You have spoken well." 40 After that they dared not ask Him any question at all.

[1] *17* Ps 118:22. [2] *18* Isa 8:14–15. [3] *24* Gk. *denarius,* a coin worth about a day's wage. [4] *28* Dt 25:5–6. [5] *37* Ex 3:6.

The Question About David's Son
Mt 22:41–46; Mk 12:35–37

41 Then Jesus said to them, "How do they say that Christ is David's Son? 42 David himself says in the Book of Psalms,

'The Lord said to my Lord,
"Sit at My right hand,
43 until I make Your enemies
Your footstool."'[1]

44 David therefore calls Him 'Lord.' How is He then his Son?"

The Denouncing of the Scribes
Mt 23:1–36; Mk 12:38–40; Lk 11:37–54

45 Then as all the people heard, He said to His disciples, 46 "Beware of the scribes who desire to walk in long robes and who love greetings in the marketplaces and the prominent seats in the synagogues and the seats of honor at banquets, 47 who devour widows' houses and for a pretense make long prayers. They will receive greater condemnation."

The Widow's Offering
Mk 12:41–44

21 He looked up and saw the rich putting their gifts in the treasury. 2 He also saw a poor widow putting in two mites,[2] 3 and He said, "Truly I tell you, this poor widow has put in more than all of them. 4 For all these out of their abundance have put in their gifts for God. But she out of her poverty has put in all the living she had."

The Destruction of the Temple Foretold
Mt 24:1–2; Mk 13:1–2

5 As some spoke of how the temple was adorned with beautiful stones and gifts, He said, 6 "As for these things which you see, the days will come when not one stone shall be left on another that will not be thrown down."

Signs and Persecutions
Mt 24:3–14; Mk 13:3–13

7 They asked Him, "Teacher, when will these things be, and what will be the sign when this is about to happen?"

8 He said, "Beware lest you be deceived. For many will come in My name, saying, 'I am He,' and 'The time has drawn near.' Therefore do not go after them. 9 When you hear of wars and commotions, do not be afraid. For these things must first take place, but the end will not be at hand."

10 Then He said to them, "Nation will rise against nation, and kingdom against kingdom. 11 Great earthquakes will occur in various places, and there will be famines and pestilence. And there will be terrors and great signs from heaven.

12 "But before all these things, they will seize you and persecute you, delivering you up to the synagogues and prisons, and you will be brought before kings and governors for My name's sake. 13 It will turn out as a testimony for you. 14 Therefore resolve in your hearts beforehand not to practice your defense. 15 For I will give you a mouth and wisdom, which all your opponents will be able to neither refute nor resist. 16 You will be betrayed by parents and brothers and relatives and friends. And they will put some of you to death. 17 You will be hated by all men for My name's sake, 18 but not a hair of your head shall perish. 19 In your endurance you will gain your souls.

I will allow the spirit of patience and joy to rule my life and possess my soul (Lk 21:19).

The Destruction of Jerusalem Foretold
Mt 24:15–21; Mk 13:14–19

20 "When you see Jerusalem surrounded by armies, then you know that its desolation has drawn near. 21 Then let those who are in Judea flee to the mountains, and let those who are in the city depart, and let not those who are in the country enter it. 22 For these are the days of vengeance, that all things which are written may be fulfilled. 23 But woe to those who are pregnant and to those who nurse in those days! For there will be great distress in the land and wrath upon this people. 24 They will fall by the edge of the sword and will be led away captive to all nations. And Jerusalem will be trampled on by the Gentiles until the times of the Gentiles are fulfilled.

The Coming of the Son of Man
Mt 24:29–31; Mk 13:24–27

25 "There will be signs in the sun and the moon and the stars; and on the earth distress of nations, with perplexity, the sea and the waves roaring; 26 men fainting from fear and expectation of what is coming on the inhabited earth. For the powers of heaven will be shaken. 27 Then they will see the Son of Man coming in a cloud with power and great glory. 28 When these things begin to happen, look up and lift up your heads, for your redemption is drawing near."

The Lesson of the Fig Tree
Mt 24:32–35; Mk 13:28–31

29 He told them this parable: "Look at the fig tree, and all the trees. 30 When they are sprouting leaves already, you see and know for yourselves that summer is now near. 31 So

20:41 Mt 1:1
20:42 Ps 110:1
20:46 Lk 11:43
20:47 Mk 12:40
21:1 Mk 12:41–44
21:2 Mk 12:42
21:3 2Co 8:12
21:4 Lk 8:43
21:7 Ac 1:6–7
21:12 Ac 8:3
21:17 Jn 15:21
21:18 Mt 10:30
21:19 Ro 5:3
21:20 Lk 19:43
21:24 Rev 11:2
21:26 Mt 24:29
21:27 Da 7:13

[1] 43 Ps 110:1. [2] 2 Gk. *2 lepta*. A *lepton*, meaning "small" or "thin," is a fraction of a penny and about 1/128 of a *denarius*, which was a day's wage. A Jewish bronze or copper coin, it was the smallest coin circulated.

in like manner, when you see these things
happening, you know that the kingdom of
God is near.
32 “Truly, I tell you, this generation will not
pass away until all these things are fulfilled.
33 Heaven and earth will pass away, but My
words will not pass away.

Exhortation to Watch

34 “Take heed to yourselves, lest your hearts
become burdened by excessiveness and
drunkenness and anxieties of life, and that Day
comes on you unexpectedly. 35 For as a snare it
will come on all those who dwell on the face
of the whole earth. 36 Therefore watch always
and pray that you may be counted worthy to
escape all these things that will happen and
to stand before the Son of Man.”
37 Each day He was teaching in the temple,
and each night He went out and stayed on the
mountain called the Mount of Olives. 38 And all
the people came early in the morning to hear
Him in the temple.

The Plot to Kill Jesus

Mt 26:1–5, 14–16; Mk 14:1–2, 10–11; Jn 11:45–53

22 Now the Feast of Unleavened Bread,
which is called the Passover, drew
near. 2 And the chief priests and scribes were
seeking how to kill Jesus, for they feared
the people. 3 Then Satan entered into Judas,
called Iscariot, who was one of the twelve.
4 He went and discussed with the chief priests
and captains how he might betray Him to
them. 5 They were glad and agreed to give him
money. 6 He fully consented and searched for
an opportunity to betray Him to them apart
from the crowds.

The Preparation of the Passover

Mt 26:17–25; Mk 14:12–21; Jn 13:21–30

7 Then the Day of Unleavened Bread came,
when the Passover lamb must be killed. 8 He
sent Peter and John, saying, “Go and prepare
the Passover for us to eat it.”
9 They said to Him, “Where will You have us
prepare it?”
10 He said to them, “Now, as you enter the
city, a man carrying a pitcher of water will
meet you there. Follow him into the house
which he enters, 11 and say to the owner of
the house, ‘The Teacher says to you, “Where is
the guest room where I may eat the Passover
with My disciples?” ’ 12 He will show you a large
furnished upper room. Prepare there.”
13 They went and found it as He had told
them. So they prepared the Passover.

The Lord’s Supper

Mt 26:26–30; Mk 14:22–26; 1Co 11:23–25

14 When the hour had come, He and the
twelve apostles with Him sat down. 15 And He

21:33 Mt 5:18
21:34 Mk 4:19
21:36 Mt 26:41
22:1 Mk 14:1–2
22:3 Jn 13:2
22:7 Ex 12:18
22:11 Jn 11:28
22:12 Ac 1:13
22:14 Mt 26:20
....
22:16 Lk 14:15
22:18 Mt 26:29
22:19 1Co 10:16
22:20 Ex 24:8
22:21 Ps 41:9
22:22 Ac 2:23
22:24 Mk 9:34
22:25 Mt 20:25–28
22:26 Lk 9:48
22:27 Mt 20:28
22:28 Heb 2:18
22:29 2Ti 2:12
22:30 Mt 19:28
22:31 Am 9:9
22:32 Jn 21:15–17
22:35 Lk 9:3

said to them, “I have earnestly desired to eat
this Passover with you before I suffer. 16 For
I tell you, I will never eat it again until it is
fulfilled in the kingdom of God.”
17 And He took the cup and gave thanks and
said, “Take this and divide it among your-
selves. 18 For I tell you, I will not drink of the
fruit of the vine until the kingdom of God
comes.”
19 Then He took the bread, and when He had
given thanks, He broke it and gave it to them,
saying, “This is My body which is given for you.
Do this in remembrance of Me.”
20 In like manner, He took the cup after sup-
per, saying, “This cup is the new covenant in
My blood which is shed for you. 21 But see the
hand of him who betrays Me is with Me at
the table. 22 Indeed, the Son of Man goes as it
has been determined. But woe to that man by
whom He is betrayed!” 23 They began to inquire
among themselves which of them it was who
would do this.

The Dispute About Greatness

24 There was also rivalry among them con-
cerning which of them was to be counted
the greatest. 25 He said to them, “The kings
of the Gentiles exercise lordship over them,
and those who exercise authority over them
are called benefactors. 26 But you are not so.
Instead, let him who is greatest among you be
as the younger, and he who rules as he who
serves. 27 For who is greater: he who sits at the
table, or he who serves? Is it not he who sits
at the table? But I am among you as He who
serves. 28 You are those who have continued
with Me in My trials. 29 And I appoint to you a
kingdom as My Father has appointed one to
Me, 30 so that you may eat and drink at My table
in My kingdom, and sit on thrones judging the
twelve tribes of Israel.”

Peter’s Denial Foretold

31 Then the Lord said, “Simon, Simon, listen!
Satan has demanded to have you to sift you as
wheat. 32 But I have prayed for you that your
faith may not fail. And when you have repent-
ed, strengthen your brothers.”
33 He said to Him, “Lord, I am ready to go
with You to prison and to death.”
34 He said, “I tell you, Peter, before the rooster
crows today, you will deny three times that you
know Me.”

Purse, Bag, and Sword

35 Then He said to them, “When I sent you
without purse or bag or sandals, did you lack
anything?”
They said, “Nothing.”
36 He said to them, “But now, let him who has
a purse take it and also a bag. And let him who

has no sword sell his garment and buy one.
37 For I tell you, what is written must yet be
accomplished in Me, 'And He was numbered
with the transgressors.'[1] Indeed, what is writ-
ten concerning Me has a fulfillment."
38 They said, "Lord, look, here are two swords."
He said to them, "It is enough."

The Prayer on the Mount of Olives
Mt 26:36–46; Mk 14:32–42

39 According to His custom, He came out and
went to the Mount of Olives. And His disci-
ples followed Him. 40 When He came there, He
said to them, "Pray that you may not fall into
temptation." 41 He withdrew from them about a
stone's throw, and He knelt down and prayed,
42 "Father, if You are willing, remove this cup
from Me. Nevertheless not My will, but Yours,
be done." 43 An angel from heaven appeared
to Him, strengthening Him. 44 And being in
anguish, He prayed more earnestly. And His
sweat became like great drops of blood falling
down to the ground.
45 When He rose from prayer and had come
to His disciples, He found them sleeping from
sorrow. 46 He said to them, "Why do you sleep?
Rise and pray, lest you fall into temptation."

The Betrayal and Arrest of Jesus
Mt 26:47–56; Mk 14:43–50; Jn 18:3–11

47 While He was yet speaking, a crowd came.
And he who was called Judas, one of the
twelve, was leading them. He drew near to
Jesus to kiss Him. 48 But Jesus said to him, "Ju-
das, do you betray the Son of Man with a kiss?"
49 When those who were around Him saw
what would follow, they said, "Lord, shall we
strike with the sword?" 50 And one of them
struck the servant of the high priest and cut
off his right ear.
51 But Jesus said, "This is enough!" And He
touched his ear and healed him.
52 Then Jesus said to the chief priests, and
captains of the temple guard, and the elders
who had come for Him, "Have you come out
with swords and clubs as against a rebel?
53 Daily, while I was with you in the temple,
you did not lay hands on Me. But this is your
hour, and the power of darkness!"

Peter's Denial of Jesus
Mt 26:57–58, 69–75; Mk 14:53–54, 66–72; Jn 18:12–18, 25–27

54 Then they arrested Him, and led Him away,
and brought Him into the high priest's house.
Peter followed at a distance. 55 But when they
had kindled a fire in the middle of the court-
yard and sat down together, Peter sat among
them. 56 Then a servant girl saw him as he sat
near the fire, and gazed at him, and said, "This
man was with Him."

22:37 Isa 53:12
22:39 Lk 21:37
22:40 Mt 6:13
22:42 Mt 20:22
22:43 Mt 4:11
22:44 La 1:12
22:46 Lk 22:40
22:49 Lk 22:38
22:52 Lk 22:4
22:53 Jn 12:27
22:54 Mt 26:57–58
22:61 Lk 22:34
22:63 Jn 18:22
22:66 Mt 27:1
22:68 Lk 20:3–7
22:69 Mk 16:19
22:70 Lk 23:3
23:2 Jn 19:12
23:3 1Ti 6:13
23:4 Jn 18:38
23:5 Mk 1:14

57 But he denied Him, saying, "Woman, I do
not know Him."
58 A little later someone else saw him and
said, "You also are one of them."
Peter said, "Man, I am not!"
59 About an hour later another man firmly
declared, "Certainly, this man also was with
Him, for he is a Galilean."
60 Peter said, "Man, I do not know what
you are saying." Immediately, while he was
yet speaking, the rooster crowed. 61 The Lord
turned and looked at Peter. Then Peter remem-
bered the word of the Lord, how He had told
him, "Before the rooster crows, you will deny
Me three times." 62 And Peter went outside and
wept bitterly.

The Mocking and Whipping of Jesus
Mt 26:67–68; Mk 14:65

63 The men who guarded Jesus mocked Him
and whipped Him. 64 When they had blind-
folded Him, they struck Him on the face and
asked Him, "Prophesy! Who struck You?"
65 And many other things they blasphemously
spoke against Him.

Jesus Before the Council
Mt 26:59–66; Mk 14:55–64; Jn 18:19–24

66 When day came, the assembly of the el-
ders of the people, both the chief priests and
scribes, came together and led Him away to
their council, saying, 67 "Are You the Christ?
Tell us!"
He said to them, "If I tell you, you will not
believe. 68 And if I also question you, you will
not answer Me or release Me. 69 From now on
the Son of Man will be seated at the right hand
of the power of God."
70 They all said, "Are You then the Son of God?"
He said to them, "You truly say that I am."
71 Then they said, "What further testimony
do we need? We have heard it from His own
mouth."

Jesus Brought Before Pilate
Mt 27:1–2, 11–14; Mk 15:1–5; Jn 18:28–38

23 Then the whole assembly rose and
led Him to Pilate. 2 And they began
to accuse Him, saying, "We found this Man
perverting our nation, and forbidding us to pay
taxes to Caesar, and saying that He Himself is
Christ a King."
3 So Pilate asked Him, "Are You the King of
the Jews?"
He answered, "You truly say so."
4 Then Pilate said to the chief priests and to
the people, "I find no fault in this Man."
5 But they insisted, saying, "He stirs up the
people, teaching throughout all Judea, begin-
ning from Galilee to here."

[1] *37* Isa 53:12.

Jesus Before Herod

6 When Pilate heard of Galilee, he asked whether the Man was a Galilean. 7 When he learned that He belonged to Herod's jurisdiction, he sent Him to Herod, who was also in Jerusalem at that time.

8 When Herod saw Jesus, he greatly rejoiced, for he had desired to see Him for a long time, because he had heard many things of Him, and he was hoping to see some miracle performed by Him. 9 He questioned Him with many words, but He gave no answer. 10 The chief priests and the scribes stood by, vehemently accusing Him. 11 Then Herod with his soldiers despised Him, and mocked Him, and dressed Him in a fine robe, and sent Him back to Pilate. 12 On the same day Pilate and Herod became friends with each other, having previously been at enmity with each other.

Jesus Sentenced to Die

Mt 27:15–26; Mk 15:6–15; Jn 18:39–19:16

13 Pilate called together the chief priests and the rulers and the people, 14 and said to them, "You have brought this Man to me as one who incites the people. And truly, I, having examined Him before you, have found no fault in this Man concerning those things of which you accuse Him. 15 No, neither has Herod, for he sent him back to us. Look, nothing worthy of death has been done by Him. 16 I will therefore chastise Him and release Him." 17 For he was obligated to release one man to them at the feast.

18 But they all cried out at once saying, "Take this Man away and release Barabbas to us!" 19 This man had been thrown in prison for an insurrection in the city and for murder.

20 Therefore Pilate spoke to them again, desiring to release Jesus. 21 But they cried out, "Crucify Him! Crucify Him!"

22 He said to them a third time, "Why, what evil has He done? I have found in Him no cause worthy of death. I will therefore chastise Him and release Him."

23 But they insisted with loud voices, asking that He be crucified. And the voices of these men and of the chief priests prevailed. 24 So Pilate gave the sentence as they demanded. 25 He released to them the man who was thrown in prison for insurrection and murder, whom they asked for. But he sentenced Jesus according to their will.

The Crucifixion

Mt 27:32–44; Mk 15:21–32; Jn 19:17–27

26 As they led Him away, they seized Simon of Cyrene, who was coming from the country, and they laid the cross on him to carry it behind Jesus. 27 A large number of people followed Him, including women who mourned and lamented Him. 28 Jesus turned to them, saying, "Daughters of Jerusalem, weep not for Me, but weep for yourselves and for your children. 29 Listen, the days are coming when they will say, 'Blessed are the barren, who never bore and never nursed!' 30 Then

> they will begin to say to the mountains,
> 'Fall on us,'
> and to the hills, 'Cover us.'

31 For if men do these things when the tree is green, what will happen when it is dry?"

32 Two different men, who were criminals, also were led with Him to be killed. 33 When they came to the place which is called The Skull, there they crucified Him and the criminals, one on the right and one on the left. 34 Jesus said, "Father, forgive them, for they know not what they do." And they divided His clothes by casting lots.

35 The people stood by watching. But the rulers with them scoffed, saying, "He saved others. Let Him save Himself if He is the Christ, the Chosen One of God."

36 And the soldiers also mocked Him, coming to Him and offering Him sour wine, 37 saying, "If You are the King of the Jews, save Yourself."

38 An inscription was written over Him in letters of Greek and Latin and Hebrew:

THIS IS THE KING OF THE JEWS.

39 One of the criminals who were hanged blasphemed Him, saying, "If You are the Christ, save Yourself and us!"

40 But the other rebuked him, saying, "Do you not fear God, seeing you are under the same sentence? 41 And we indeed, justly. For we are receiving the due reward of our deeds. But this Man has done nothing amiss."

42 Then he said to Jesus, "Lord, remember me when You come into Your kingdom."

43 Jesus said to him, "Truly, I tell you, today you will be with Me in Paradise."

The Death of Jesus

Mt 27:45–56; Mk 15:33–41; Jn 19:28–30

44 It was now about the sixth hour, and darkness came over all the land until the ninth hour, 45 while the sun was darkened. And the veil of the temple was torn in the middle. 46 And Jesus cried out with a loud voice, "Father, into Your hands I commit My spirit." Having said this, He gave up the spirit.

47 When the centurion saw what had happened, he glorified God and said, "Certainly, this was a righteous Man." 48 All the crowds who came together to that sight, witnessing what occurred, struck their chests and

23:7 Lk 3:1
23:9 Mt 27:14
23:11 Mk 9:12
23:12 Ac 4:27
23:16 Mt 27:26
23:19 Ac 3:14
23:24 Ex 23:2
23:27 Lk 8:52
....
23:29 Mt 24:19
23:30 Isa 2:19
23:31 Pr 11:31
23:32 Mk 15:27
23:34 Ps 22:18
23:35 Ps 22:17
23:36 Mt 27:48
23:38 Mt 27:37
23:39 Mt 27:44
23:43 Rev 2:7
23:44 Am 8:9
23:46 Jn 19:30
23:47 Mt 27:54
23:48 Lk 18:13

returned. 49 But all those who knew Him and the women accompanying Him from Galilee stood at a distance, seeing these things.

The Burial of Jesus
Mt 27:57–61; Mk 15:42–47; Jn 19:38–42

50 Now there was a man named Joseph, a member of the Council, who was a good and just man. 51 He had not consented to their counsel and deed. He was from Arimathea, a city of the Jews, and he himself was also waiting for the kingdom of God. 52 This man went to Pilate and asked for the body of Jesus. 53 Then he took Him down, and wrapped Him in linen, and placed Him in a hewn tomb, where no one had ever been buried. 54 It was the Day of Preparation, and the Sabbath was drawing near.

55 The women who came with Him from Galilee followed, and saw the tomb and how His body was placed. 56 Then they returned and prepared spices and ointments. On the Sabbath they rested according to the commandment.

The Resurrection of Jesus
Mt 28:1–10; Mk 16:1–8; Jn 20:1–10

24 Now on the first day of the week, very early in the morning, they, and certain other women with them, came to the tomb bringing the spices they had prepared. 2 They found the stone rolled away from the tomb. 3 But when they entered, they did not find the body of the Lord Jesus. 4 While they were greatly perplexed concerning this, suddenly two men stood by them in shining garments. 5 As they were afraid and bowed their faces to the ground, they said to them, "Why do you seek the living among the dead? 6 He is not here, but has risen! Remember how He spoke to you while He was still in Galilee, 7 saying, 'The Son of Man must be delivered into the hands of sinful men, and be crucified, and on the third day rise again.'" 8 Then they remembered His words.

9 And they returned from the tomb and reported all these things to the eleven and to all the rest. 10 It was Mary Magdalene and Joanna, Mary the mother of James, and other women with them, who told these things to the apostles. 11 But their words seemed like fables to them, and they did not believe them. 12 But Peter rose and ran to the tomb. Stooping down, he saw the linen clothes lying by themselves. He departed, wondering in himself what had happened.

The Walk to Emmaus
Mk 16:12–13

13 Now that same day two of them were going to a village called Emmaus, about seven miles[1] from Jerusalem. 14 They were talking with each other about all these things that had happened. 15 While they communed and reasoned together, Jesus Himself drew near and went with them. 16 But their eyes were kept from recognizing Him.

17 He said to them, "What kind of communication are you sharing with one another while you are walking and are sad?"

18 One of them, named Cleopas, answered Him, "Are You the only foreigner in Jerusalem who does not know what has happened there in these days?"

19 He said to them, "What things?"

They said to Him, "Concerning Jesus of Nazareth, who was a prophet, powerful in deed and word before God and all the people, 20 and how our chief priests and rulers handed Him over to be sentenced to death and crucified Him. 21 But we were hoping that it was He who was to redeem Israel. Moreover, today is the third day since these things happened. 22 Even some women from among us, who arrived early at the tomb, surprised us. 23 When they did not find His body, they returned saying that they had even seen a vision of angels, who said that He was alive. 24 Then some of those who were with us went to the tomb and found it just as the women had said. But they did not see Him."

25 He said to them, "O fools! And slow of heart to believe what the prophets have spoken! 26 Was it not necessary for the Christ to suffer these things and to enter His glory?" 27 And beginning with Moses and all the Prophets, He explained to them the things concerning Himself in all the Scriptures.

28 They drew near the village where they were traveling, and He seemed to be going farther. 29 But they urged Him, saying, "Stay with us. For it is nearly evening and the day is far spent." So He went in to stay with them.

30 As He sat at supper with them, He took the bread, blessed it and broke it, and gave it to them. 31 Then their eyes were opened, and they recognized Him. And He vanished out of their sight. 32 They said to each other, "Did not our hearts burn within us while He talked to us on the way and while He opened the Scriptures to us?"

33 They rose up and returned to Jerusalem at once. And they found the eleven and those who were with them assembled together, 34 saying, "The Lord has risen indeed, and has appeared to Simon!" 35 Then they reported what had happened on the way, and how He was recognized by them in the breaking of the bread.

23:49 Lk 8:2
23:51 Lk 2:25
23:53 Isa 53:9
23:54 Mt 27:62
23:55 Lk 23:49
23:56 Mk 16:1
24:3 Lk 24:23
24:6 Mt 17:22–23
24:11 Mk 16:11

24:15 Lk 24:36
24:16 Jn 20:14
24:18 Jn 19:25
24:19 Mt 21:11
24:20 Lk 23:13
24:21 Lk 1:68
24:24 Lk 24:12
24:26 1Pe 1:11
24:27 Ge 3:15
24:28 Mk 6:48
24:30 Mt 14:19
24:31 Lk 24:16
24:32 Lk 24:45
24:34 1Co 15:5

[1] *13* Gk. *60 stadia*, or 11 kilometers.

The Appearance to the Disciples
Mt 28:16–20; Mk 16:14–18; Jn 20:19–23; Ac 1:6–8

[36] As they were saying this, Jesus Himself stood among them and said to them, "Peace be unto you."

[37] They were terrified and frightened, and supposed that they saw a spirit. [38] He said to them, "Why are you troubled, and why do doubts arise in your hearts? [39] See My hands and My feet, that it is I Myself. Feel Me and see. For a spirit does not have flesh and bones as you see that I have."

[40] When He said this, He showed them His hands and His feet. [41] And while they yet disbelieved for joy and wondered, He said to them, "Do you have any food here?" [42] They gave Him a piece of broiled fish and some honeycomb. [43] And He took it and ate it before them.

[44] He said to them, "These are the words which I spoke to you while I was still with you, that all things must be fulfilled which were written in the Law of Moses and in the

24:36 Mk 16:14
24:39 Jn 20:27
24:41 Jn 21:5
24:43 Ac 10:41
24:44 Ps 72:1–20

....

24:45 Ac 16:14
24:46 Lk 24:44
24:47 Ac 5:31
24:48 Ac 1:8
24:49 Ac 1:4
24:50 Ac 1:12

Prophets and in the Psalms concerning Me."

[45] Then He opened their minds to understand the Scriptures. [46] He said to them, "Thus it is written, and accordingly it was necessary for the Christ to suffer and to rise from the dead the third day, [47] and that repentance and remission of sins should be preached in His name to all nations, beginning at Jerusalem. [48] You are witnesses of these things. [49] And look, I am sending the promise of My Father upon you. But wait in the city of Jerusalem until you are clothed with power from on high."

The Ascension
Mk 16:19–20; Ac 1:9–11

[50] Then He led them out as far as Bethany, and He lifted up His hands and blessed them. [51] While He blessed them, He parted from them and was carried up into heaven. [52] Then they worshipped Him, and returned to Jerusalem with great joy, [53] and were continually in the temple, praising and blessing God. Amen.

Author: The apostle John

Written: Between AD 70 and 90, from Ephesus

Theme: The Divinity, Messiahship, and Eternal Sonship of Jesus Christ

JOHN

Dear Spirit Led Woman,

One of my favorite passages from John's Gospel is when Jesus commands us to abide in Him: "Remain in Me, as I also remain in you. As the branch cannot bear fruit by itself, unless it remains in the vine, neither can you, unless you remain in Me" (Jn 15:4). In this way of life your spirit maintains an inner connection with the Holy Spirit, and your mind and body do the work. It is not an optional way of life; it is the *only* way for those who truly want to fulfill their destinies.

This word picture of the branch and the vine strikes me with one important thought: a branch does not detach itself from the vine to carry out its required function of producing grapes, any more than you are to "disconnect" from Christ to take care of the demands of your life. You must remain in Him in order to do that which you are appointed to do. God created you to live your life from the spirit realm—fulfilling a dual call to intimacy and fruitful labor.

Joy F. Strang

The Word Became Flesh

1 In the beginning was the Word, and the Word was with God, and the Word was God. 2 He was in the beginning with God. 3 All things were created through Him, and without Him nothing was created that was created. 4 In Him was life, and the life was the light of mankind. 5 The light shines in darkness, but the darkness has not overcome it.

6 There was a man sent from God whose name was John. 7 This man came as a witness in order to testify concerning the Light, that all men through Him might believe. 8 He was not this Light, but was sent in order to testify concerning the Light.

9 The true Light, which enlightens everyone, was coming into the world. 10 He was in the world, and the world was created through Him, yet the world did not know Him. 11 He came to His own, and His own people did not receive Him. 12 Yet to all who received Him, He gave the power to become sons of God, to those who believed in His name, 13 who were born not of blood, nor of the will of the flesh, nor of the will of man, but of God.

- **1:1** Jn 17:5
- **1:3** Jn 1:10
- **1:4** Jn 5:26
- **1:7** Jn 1:19
- **1:8** Jn 1:20
- **1:9** Isa 49:6
- **1:10** 1Jn 3:1
- **1:11** Jn 3:32
- **1:12** Gal 3:26
- **1:13** Jas 1:18
- **1:14** Gal 4:4
- **1:15** Mt 3:11
- **1:16** Col 1:19
- **1:18** Mt 11:27
- **1:19** Jn 10:24
- **1:21** Mt 11:14
- **1:23** Mt 3:3
- **1:26** Mt 3:11
- **1:27** Jn 1:30
- **1:28** Jn 10:40
- **1:29** Isa 53:7
- **1:30** Jn 1:15
- **1:31** Lk 1:17
- **1:32** Mt 3:16
- **1:33** Mt 3:11
- **1:34** Mt 4:3
- **1:36** Jn 1:29
- **1:38** Jn 1:49
- **1:41** Jn 4:25
- **1:42** Jn 21:15–17

> I am a child of God and one with Christ (Jn 1:12).

14 The Word became flesh and dwelt among us, and we saw His glory, the glory as the only Son of the Father, full of grace and truth.

15 John bore witness of Him and cried out, "This was He of whom I said, 'He who comes after me is preferred before me, for He was before me.' " 16 We have all received from His fullness grace upon grace. 17 For the law was given through Moses; grace and truth came through Jesus Christ. 18 No one has seen God at any time. The only Son, who is at the Father's side, has made Him known.

The Testimony of John the Baptist

Mt 3:1–12; Mk 1:2–8; Lk 3:15–17

19 Now this is the testimony of John, when the Jews sent priests and Levites from Jerusalem to ask him, "Who are you?" 20 He confessed, and did not deny, but confessed, "I am not the Christ."

21 They asked him, "Who then? Are you Elijah?"

He said, "I am not."

"Are you the Prophet?"

He answered, "No."

22 They said to him then, "Who are you? Tell us so that we may give an answer to those who sent us. What do you say concerning yourself?"

23 John said, "I am the voice of one crying out in the wilderness, 'Make straight the way of the Lord,'[1] just as the prophet Isaiah said."

24 Now those who were sent were from the Pharisees. 25 They asked him, "Why do you baptize then, if you are not the Christ, nor Elijah, nor the Prophet?"

26 John answered them, "I baptize with water, but One stands among you, whom you do not know. 27 This is He who comes after me, who is preferred before me, the strap of whose sandal I am not worthy to untie."

28 These things took place in Bethany beyond the Jordan, where John was baptizing.

The Lamb of God

29 The next day John saw Jesus coming toward him and said, "Look, the Lamb of God, who takes away the sin of the world. 30 This is He of whom I said, 'After me comes a Man who is preferred before me, for He was before me.' 31 I did not know Him, but for this reason I came baptizing with water: so that He might be revealed to Israel."

32 Then John bore witness, saying, "I saw the Spirit descending from heaven like a dove, and it remained on Him. 33 I did not know Him, but He who sent me to baptize with water said to me, 'The One on whom you see the Spirit descending and remaining, this is He who baptizes with the Holy Spirit.' 34 I have seen and have borne witness that He is the Son of God."

The First Disciples

35 Again, the next day John was standing with two of his disciples. 36 Looking upon Jesus as He walked, he said, "Look, the Lamb of God!"

37 The two disciples heard him speak, and they followed Jesus. 38 Then Jesus turned, saw them following, and said to them, "What do you seek?"

And they said to Him, "Rabbi" (which means Teacher), "where are You staying?"

39 Jesus said to them, "Come and see."

So they came and saw where He stayed and remained with Him that day, for it was about the tenth hour.

40 One of the two who heard John speak, and followed Him, was Andrew, Simon Peter's brother. 41 He first found his own brother Simon, and said to him, "We have found the Messiah" (which means the Christ). 42 Then he brought him to Jesus.

When Jesus saw him, He said, "You are Simon the son of John. You shall be called Cephas" (which means Peter).

The Calling of Philip and Nathanael

43 The next day Jesus wanted to go to Galilee, and He found Philip, and said to him, "Follow Me."

---

[1] 23 Isa 40:3.

44 Now Philip was from Bethsaida, the city of
Andrew and Peter. 45 Philip found Nathanael
and said to him, "We have found Him of whom
Moses in the law, as well as the prophets,
wrote, Jesus of Nazareth, the son of Joseph."
46 Nathanael said to him, "Can any good
thing come out of Nazareth?"
Philip said to him, "Come and see."
47 Jesus saw Nathanael coming to Him and
said concerning him, "Here is an Israelite in-
deed, in whom is no guile."
48 Nathanael said to Him, "How do You know
me?"
Jesus answered him, "Before Philip called
you, when you were under the fig tree, I saw
you."
49 Nathanael answered Him, "Rabbi, You are
the Son of God! You are the King of Israel!"
50 Jesus answered him, "Because I said to
you, 'I saw you under the fig tree,' do you be-
lieve? You will see greater things than these."
51 And He said to him, "Truly, truly I say to you,
hereafter you shall see heaven opened and the
angels of God ascending and descending upon
the Son of Man."

The Wedding at Cana

2 On the third day there was a wedding
in Cana of Galilee. The mother of Jesus
was there. 2 Both Jesus and His disciples were
invited to the wedding. 3 When the wine ran
out, the mother of Jesus said to Him, "They
have no wine."
4 Jesus said to her, "Woman, what does this
have to do with Me? My hour has not yet
come."
5 His mother said to the servants, "Whatever
He says to you, do it."
6 Six water pots made of stone were sitting
there, used for ceremonial cleansing by the
Jews, containing twenty to thirty gallons[1] each.
7 Jesus said to them, "Fill the water pots with
water." And they filled them up to the brim.
8 Then He said to them, "Now draw some out,
and take it to the master of the feast."
And they took it. 9 When the master of the
feast tasted the water that had been turned
into wine, and did not know where it came
from (though the servants who drew the wa-
ter knew), the master of the feast called the
bridegroom, 10 and he said to him, "Every man
serves the good wine first, and after men have
drunk freely, then the poor wine is served. But
you have kept the good wine until now."
11 This, the first of His signs, Jesus did in Cana
of Galilee, and He revealed His glory, and His
disciples believed in Him.

1:44 Jn 12:21
1:45 Lk 24:27
1:46 Jn 7:52
1:47 Ps 32:2
1:48 Jn 2:25
1:49 Mt 27:42
1:51 Ge 28:12
2:1 Jn 4:46
2:4 Jn 7:6
2:6 Jn 3:25
2:9 Jn 4:46
2:11 Jn 1:14

. . . .

2:12 Mt 12:46
2:13 Lk 2:41
2:14 Mk 11:15
2:16 Lk 2:49
2:17 Ps 69:9
2:18 Jn 6:30
2:19 Mt 27:40
2:21 1Co 6:19
2:22 Jn 12:16
2:23 Jn 3:2
3:1 Jn 19:39
3:2 Ac 2:22
3:3 Jn 1:13
3:5 Ac 2:38

12 After this He, and His mother, and His
brothers, and His disciples went down to
Capernaum. They remained there a few days.

The Cleansing of the Temple
Mt 21:12–17; Mk 11:15–17; Lk 19:45–48

13 The Passover of the Jews was at hand, and
Jesus went up to Jerusalem. 14 In the temple He
found those who were selling oxen and sheep
and doves, and the moneychangers sitting
there. 15 When He had made a whip of cords,
He drove them all out of the temple, with the
sheep and oxen. He poured out the changers'
money and overturned the tables. 16 He said
to those who sold doves, "Take these things
away! Do not make My Father's house a house
of merchandise!" 17 His disciples remembered
that it was written, "Zeal for Your house will
consume Me."[2]
18 Then the Jews said to Him, "What sign do
You show us, seeing that You do these things?"
19 Jesus answered them, "Destroy this temple,
and in three days I will raise it up."
20 Then the Jews said, "It has taken forty-six
years to build this temple, and will You raise
it up in three days?" 21 But He was speaking
concerning the temple of His body. 22 There-
fore, when He was raised from the dead, His
disciples remembered that He had said this to
them. And they believed the Scripture and the
word which Jesus had spoken.

Jesus Knows All Men

23 Now when He was in Jerusalem at the
Passover Feast, many believed in His name
when they saw the signs which He did. 24 But
Jesus did not entrust Himself to them, because
He knew all men, 25 and did not need anyone
to bear witness of man, for He knew what was
in man.

Jesus and Nicodemus

3 There was a man of the Pharisees named
Nicodemus, a ruler of the Jews. 2 He came
to Jesus by night and said to Him, "Rabbi, we
know that You are a teacher who has come
from God. For no one can do these signs that
You do unless God is with him."
3 Jesus answered him, "Truly, truly I say to
you, unless a man is born again,[3] he cannot
see the kingdom of God."
4 Nicodemus said to Him, "How can a man
be born when he is old? Can he enter a second
time into his mother's womb and be born?"
5 Jesus answered, "Truly, truly I say to you,
unless a man is born of water and the Spirit, he
cannot enter the kingdom of God. 6 That which
is born of the flesh is flesh, and that which is

[1] *6* Gk. *2 to 3 metretes*, or 75 to 115 liters. [2] *17* Ps 69:9. [3] *3* Or *born from above*.

born of the Spirit is spirit. 7 Do not marvel that I said to you, 'You must be born again.' 8 The wind blows where it wishes, and you hear its sound, but you do not know where it comes from or where it goes. So it is with everyone who is born of the Spirit."

9 Nicodemus said to Him, "How can this be?"

10 Jesus answered him, "Are you the teacher of Israel, but you do not know these things? 11 Truly, truly I say to you, We speak of what We know and bear witness of what We have seen, but you do not receive Our testimony. 12 If I have told you earthly things and you do not believe, how will you believe if I tell you heavenly things? 13 No one has ascended to heaven except He who descended from heaven, even the Son of Man who is in heaven. 14 Just as Moses lifted up the serpent in the wilderness, even so must the Son of Man be lifted up, 15 that whoever believes in Him should not perish, but may have eternal life.

16 "For God so loved the world that He gave His only begotten Son, that whoever believes in Him should not perish, but have eternal life. 17 For God did not send His Son into the world to condemn the world, but that the world through Him might be saved. 18 He who believes in Him is not condemned. But he who does not believe is condemned already, because he has not believed in the name of the only begotten Son of God. 19 This is the verdict, that light has come into the world, and men loved darkness rather than light, because their deeds were evil. 20 For everyone who does evil hates the light and does not come to the light, lest his deeds should be exposed. 21 But he who does the truth comes to the light, that it may be revealed that his deeds have been done in God."

Jesus and John the Baptist

22 After these things Jesus and His disciples came into the land of Judea. He remained with them there and baptized. 23 John also was baptizing in Aenon toward Salim, because much water was there. And people came and were baptized. 24 For John had not yet been put in prison. 25 Then a dispute arose between some of John's disciples and the Jews about ceremonial cleansing. 26 They came to John and said to him, "Rabbi, He who was with you beyond the Jordan, to whom you bore witness, look, He is baptizing, and everyone is going to Him."

27 John answered, "A man can receive nothing unless it has been given to him from heaven. 28 You yourselves bear witness of me, that I said, 'I am not the Christ,' but 'I have been sent before Him.' 29 He who has the bride is the bridegroom. But the friend of the bridegroom, who stands and hears him, rejoices greatly at the bridegroom's voice. Therefore this joy of mine is fulfilled. 30 He must increase, but I must decrease."

He Who Comes From Heaven

31 He who comes from above is above all. He who is of the earth is earthly and speaks of the earth. He who comes from heaven is above all. 32 He bears witness of what He has seen and heard, yet no one receives His testimony. 33 He who has received His testimony has certified that God is true. 34 For He whom God has sent speaks the words of God, for God gives the Spirit without measure to Him. 35 The Father loves the Son, and has placed all things into His hand. 36 He who believes in the Son has eternal life. He who does not believe the Son shall not see life, but the wrath of God remains on him.

Jesus and the Samaritan Woman

4 Now when the Lord learned that the Pharisees had heard that Jesus was making and baptizing more disciples than John 2 (though Jesus Himself did not baptize, but His disciples), 3 He left Judea and departed again to Galilee.

4 Now it was necessary that He go through Samaria. 5 So He came to a city of Samaria which is called Sychar, near the plot of ground that Jacob gave to his son Joseph. 6 Jacob's well was there. Jesus, therefore, being exhausted from His journey, sat down by the well. It was about the sixth hour.

7 A woman of Samaria came there to draw water. Jesus said to her, "Give Me a drink." 8 For His disciples had gone away into the city to buy food.

9 Then the woman of Samaria said to Him, "How is it that You, being a Jew, ask a drink from me, a woman of Samaria?" For Jews have no dealings with Samaritans.

10 Jesus answered her, "If you knew the gift of God, and who it is who is saying to you, 'Give Me a drink,' you would have asked Him, and He would have given you living water."

11 The woman said to Him, "Sir, You have nothing to draw with, and the well is deep. Where then do You get that living water? 12 Are You greater than our father Jacob, who gave us the well and drank from it himself, along with his sons and his livestock?"

13 Jesus said to her, "Everyone who drinks of this water will thirst again, 14 but whoever drinks of the water that I shall give him will never thirst. Indeed, the water that I shall give him will become in him a well of water springing up into eternal life."

3:7 Jn 3:3
3:8 Eze 37:9
3:9 Jn 6:52
3:11 Jn 1:18
3:13 Pr 30:4
3:14 Jn 8:28
3:15 Jn 3:16
3:16 Ro 5:8
3:17 1Jn 4:14
3:18 Jn 5:24
3:19 Jn 1:4
3:21 1Jn 1:6
3:22 Jn 3:26
3:24 Mt 4:12
3:25 Jn 2:6
3:26 Jn 1:7
3:27 1Co 4:7
3:28 Jn 1:20
3:29 Mt 9:15
3:31 Jn 8:23
3:32 Jn 3:11
3:34 Jn 3:17
3:35 Mt 28:18
3:36 Jn 5:24
4:1 Jn 3:22
4:5 Ge 33:19
4:9 Jn 8:48
4:10 Jer 2:13
4:12 Jn 8:53
4:14 Jn 6:35

SPIRIT-TO-SPIRIT PRAYER

SACRIFICE OF PRAISE AND WORSHIP

Heavenly Father, I enter Your courts with praise and adoration, for You alone are holy and worthy to be praised. I lift up my hands in surrender to You, and I exalt and glorify Your name. I will praise You, Lord, for Your mercy endures forever. My heart draws near to You, seeking to worship You in spirit and truth. Your Word declares in 1 Peter 2:5 that we are a holy priesthood to offer up spiritual sacrifices acceptable to God through Jesus Christ. I glorify, honor, and magnify Your holy name.

Iris Delgado

15 The woman said to Him, "Sir, give me this
water, so that I will not thirst, nor come here
to draw."
16 Jesus said to her, "Go, call your husband,
and come here."
17 The woman answered, "I have no hus-
band."
Jesus said to her, "You are right in saying,
'I have no husband,' 18 for you have had five
husbands, and he whom you now have is not
your husband. So you have spoken truthfully."
19 The woman said to Him, "Sir, I perceive
that You are a prophet. 20 Our fathers wor-
shipped on this mountain, but you all say that
in Jerusalem is the place where men ought
to worship."
21 Jesus said to her, "Woman, believe Me, the
hour is coming when neither on this mountain
nor in Jerusalem will you worship the Father.
22 You worship what you do not know; we
know what we worship, for salvation is of the
Jews. 23 Yet the hour is coming, and is now
here, when the true worshippers will worship
the Father in spirit and truth. For the Father
seeks such to worship Him. 24 God is Spirit, and
those who worship Him must worship Him in
spirit and truth."
25 The woman said to Him, "I know that Mes-
siah is coming" (who is called Christ). "When
He comes, He will tell us all things."
26 Jesus said to her, "I who speak to you
am He."
27 Then His disciples came. They marveled
that He talked with a woman. Yet no one said,
"What do You seek?" or, "Why are You talking
with her?"

4:15 Jn 6:34
4:19 Lk 7:16
4:21 Mal 1:11
4:22 Isa 2:3
4:23 Php 3:3
4:25 Jn 4:29

4:29 Jn 4:17–18
4:32 Job 23:12
4:34 Jn 6:38
4:36 Ro 1:13
4:37 Mic 6:15
4:38 Ac 8:14–17
4:39 Jn 4:29

28 The woman then left her water pot, went
her way into the city, and said to the men,
29 "Come, see a Man who told me all things that
I ever did. Could this be the Christ?" 30 They
went out of the city and came to Him.
31 Meanwhile His disciples urged Him, say-
ing, "Rabbi, eat."
32 But He said to them, "I have food to eat of
which you do not know."
33 Therefore the disciples said one to another,
"Has anyone brought Him anything to eat?"
34 Jesus said to them, "My food is to do the
will of Him who sent Me, and to finish His
work. 35 Do you not say, 'There are yet four
months, and then comes the harvest'? Listen!
I say to you, lift up your eyes and look at the
fields, for they are already white for harvest.
36 He who reaps receives wages, and gathers
fruit that leads to eternal life, that both he who
sows and he who reaps may rejoice together.
37 For in this is the saying true, 'One sows, and
another reaps.' 38 I sent you to reap a crop for
which you did not labor. And you have bene-
fited from their labor."

The Lord of the harvest has heard the prayers of the saints, and He has responded (Jn 4:35).

39 Many of the Samaritans of that city be-
lieved in Him because of the word of the
woman who testified, "He told me all that I
ever did." 40 So when the Samaritans came to
Him, they asked Him to remain with them. And

He stayed there two days. 41 And many more
believed because of His word.
42 They said to the woman, "Now we believe,
not because of what you said, for we have
heard for ourselves and know that this Man
is indeed the Christ, the Savior of the world."

The Healing of the Nobleman's Son
Mt 8:5–13; Lk 7:1–10

43 After the two days He departed from there
and went to Galilee. 44 For Jesus Himself tes-
tified that a prophet has no honor in his own
country. 45 Then, when He came to Galilee, the
Galileans welcomed Him, having seen all the
things He did at Jerusalem at the feast. For
they had also gone to the feast.
46 So Jesus came again to Cana of Galilee
where He had made the water wine. And there
was a certain nobleman whose son was sick
in Capernaum. 47 When he heard that Jesus
had come out of Judea into Galilee, he went to
Him, pleading that He would come down and
heal his son, for he was at the point of death.
48 Then Jesus said to him, "Unless you see
signs and wonders, you will not believe."
49 The nobleman said to Him, "Sir, come
down before my child dies."
50 Jesus said to him, "Go your way. Your son
lives."
And the man believed the word that Jesus
spoke to him, and he went his way. 51 While
he was going down, his servants met him and
told him, "Your son lives!" 52 When he inquired
of them the hour when he began to heal, they
answered, "Yesterday at the seventh hour the
fever left him."
53 Then the father knew that it was at the
same hour in which Jesus said to him, "Your
son lives." So he and his whole household
believed.
54 This was the second sign that Jesus did
when He had come from Judea to Galilee.

The Healing at the Pool

5 After this there was a feast of the Jews,
and Jesus went up to Jerusalem. 2 Now in
Jerusalem by the Sheep Gate there is a pool,
which in Hebrew is called Bethesda, having
five porches. 3 In these lay a great crowd of
invalids, blind, lame, and paralyzed, waiting
for the moving of the water. 4 For an angel
went down at a certain time into the pool and
stirred up the water. After the stirring of the
water, whoever stepped in first was healed
of whatever disease he had. 5 A certain man
was there who had an illness for thirty-eight
years. 6 When Jesus saw him lying there, and
knew that he had been in that condition now
a long time, He said to him, "Do you want to
be healed?"
7 The sick man answered Him, "Sir, I have no
one to put me into the pool when the water is
stirred. But while I am coming, another steps
down before me."
8 Jesus said to him, "Rise, take up your bed
and walk." 9 Immediately the man was healed,
took up his bed, and walked.
That day was the Sabbath. 10 The Jews there-
fore said to him who was cured, "It is the Sab-
bath day. It is not lawful for you to carry your
bed."
11 He answered them, "He who healed me
said to me, 'Take up your bed and walk.' "
12 So they asked him, "Who is the Man who
said to you, 'Take up your bed and walk'?"
13 Now the man who was healed did not
know who it was, for Jesus had withdrawn,
as there was a crowd in that place.
14 Afterward Jesus found him in the temple,
and said to him, "See, you have become whole.
Sin no more lest something worse happens to
you." 15 The man departed and told the Jews
that it was Jesus who had healed him.
16 So the Jews persecuted Jesus and sought
to kill Him, because He had done these things
on the Sabbath day. 17 Jesus answered them,
"My Father is working still, and I am working."
18 So the Jews sought even more to kill Him,
because He not only had broken the Sabbath,
but also said that God was His Father, making
Himself equal with God.

The Authority of the Son

19 Then Jesus said to them, "Truly, truly I say
to you, the Son can do nothing of Himself, but
what He sees the Father do. For whatever He
does, likewise the Son does. 20 For the Father
loves the Son and shows Him all things that
He Himself does. And He will show Him great-
er works than these so that you may marvel.
21 For as the Father raises the dead and gives
them life, even so the Son gives life to whom
He will. 22 The Father judges no one, but has
committed all judgment to the Son, 23 that all
men should honor the Son, just as they honor
the Father. He who does not honor the Son
does not honor the Father who sent Him.

I have eternal life (Jn 5:24).

24 "Truly, truly I say to you, whoever hears
My word and believes in Him who sent Me
has eternal life and shall not come into con-
demnation, but has passed from death into life.
25 Truly, truly I say to you, the hour is coming,
and is now here, when the dead will hear the
voice of the Son of God, and those who hear

4:42 1Jn 4:14
4:43 Jn 4:40
4:44 Mt 13:57
4:45 Jn 2:23
4:46 Jn 2:1–11
4:48 Ac 2:22
4:50 Mt 8:13
5:1 Jn 2:13
5:2 Ne 3:1

5:8 Mt 9:6
5:9 Jn 9:14
5:10 Jer 17:21
5:14 Jn 8:11
5:18 Jn 10:33
5:19 Jn 8:28
5:20 Jn 3:35
5:21 Jn 11:25
5:22 Jn 5:27
5:23 1Jn 2:23
5:24 Jn 3:18
5:25 Jn 4:23

will live. 26 For as the Father has life in Himself, so He has given to the Son to have life in Himself, 27 and has given Him authority to execute judgment also, because He is the Son of Man.

28 "Do not marvel at this. For the hour is coming in which all who are in the graves will hear His voice 29 and come out—those who have done good to the resurrection of life, and those who have done evil to the resurrection of judgment. 30 I can do nothing of Myself. As I hear, I judge. My judgment is just, because I seek not My own will, but the will of the Father who sent Me.

Witnesses to Jesus

31 "If I bear witness of Myself, My testimony is not true. 32 There is another who bears witness of Me, and I know that the testimony which He bears of Me is true.

33 "You sent to John, and he bore witness of the truth. 34 I do not receive testimony from man, but I say these things that you may be saved. 35 He was a burning and a shining lamp, and you were willing for a season to rejoice in his light.

36 "I have greater testimony than that of John. The works which the Father has given Me to finish, the very works that I do, bear witness of Me, that the Father has sent Me. 37 The Father Himself, who has sent Me, has borne witness of Me. You have neither heard His voice at any time, nor seen His form. 38 You do not have His word abiding in you, for you do not believe the One He has sent. 39 You search the Scriptures, because you think in them you have eternal life. These are they who bear witness of Me. 40 Yet you are not willing to come to Me that you may have life.

41 "I do not receive honor from men. 42 But I know you, that you do not have the love of God in you. 43 I have come in My Father's name, but you do not receive Me. If another comes in his own name, you will receive him. 44 How can you believe, who receive glory from one another and do not seek the glory that comes from the only God?

45 "Do not think that I shall accuse you to the Father. There is one who accuses you—Moses, in whom you trust. 46 For if you believed Moses, you would believe Me, for he wrote of Me. 47 But if you do not believe his writings, how will you believe My words?"

The Feeding of the Five Thousand
Mt 14:13–21; Mk 6:30–44; Lk 9:10–17

6 After these things Jesus went across the Sea of Galilee, which is the Sea of Tiberias. 2 And a great crowd followed Him, because they saw His signs which He did for the sick. 3 Then Jesus went up on a mountain, and He sat there with His disciples. 4 Now the Passover, the feast of the Jews, was near.

5 When Jesus looked up and saw a great crowd coming to Him, He said to Philip, "Where shall we buy bread that these may eat?" 6 He said this to test him, for He Himself knew what He would do.

7 Philip answered Him, "Two hundred denarii[1] worth of bread is not sufficient for each of them to receive but a little."

8 One of His disciples, Andrew, Simon Peter's brother, said to Him, 9 "There is a boy is here who has five barley loaves and two small fish. But what are they among so many?"

10 Jesus said, "Make the people sit down." Now there was much grass in the place. So the men sat down, numbering about five thousand. 11 Jesus then took the loaves, and when He had given thanks, He distributed them to the disciples, and the disciples to those who were sitting down; and likewise, they distributed the fish, as much as they wanted.

12 When they were filled, He told His disciples, "Collect the fragments that remain, that nothing may be lost." 13 So they collected them and filled twelve baskets with the fragments of the five barley loaves which were left over by those who had eaten.

14 When those men saw the sign which He had done, they then said, "This is truly the Prophet who is to come into the world." 15 Therefore, knowing that they would come and take Him by force to make Him king, Jesus departed again to a mountain by Himself alone.

Walking on the Water
Mt 14:22–27; Mk 6:45–52

16 Now when evening came, His disciples went down to the sea. 17 They got into a boat and went across the sea toward Capernaum. It was now dark, and Jesus had not come to them. 18 The sea was stirred up because a strong wind was blowing. 19 So when they had rowed about three or four miles,[2] they saw Jesus walking on the sea and coming near the boat. And they were afraid. 20 But He said to them, "It is I. Do not be afraid." 21 Then they gladly received Him into the boat, and immediately the boat was at the land to which they were going.

Jesus the Bread of Life

22 The following day the people who stood on the other side of the sea saw that there was no other boat there, except the one which His disciples had entered, and that Jesus had not entered the boat with His disciples, but that His disciples had gone away alone. 23 However,

5:26 Jn 1:4
5:27 Jn 5:22
5:29 Ac 24:15
5:30 Jn 4:34
5:34 1Jn 5:9
5:35 2Pe 1:19
5:36 Jn 10:25
5:37 Jn 8:18
5:38 1Jn 2:14
5:39 Lk 24:27
5:41 1Th 2:6
5:42 Jn 2:25
5:43 Mt 24:5
5:44 Ro 2:29
5:47 Lk 16:31
6:1 Mt 4:18
6:3 Jn 6:15

6:4 Jn 2:13
6:7 Mk 6:37
6:11 Jn 6:23
6:14 Mt 11:3
6:15 Jn 18:36
6:17 Mk 6:45
6:19 Job 9:8

[1] *7* Eight months' wages. [2] *19* Gk. *25 to 30 stadia*, or 5 or 6 kilometers.

other boats came from Tiberias near the place where they ate bread when the Lord had given thanks. 24 When the people therefore saw that neither Jesus nor His disciples were there, they also got into boats and came to Capernaum, looking for Jesus.

25 When they found Him on the other side of the sea, they said to Him, "Rabbi, when did You come here?"

26 Jesus answered them, "Truly, truly I say to you, you seek Me not because you saw signs, but because you ate of the loaves and were filled. 27 Do not work for the food which perishes, but for that food which endures to eternal life, which the Son of Man will give you. For God the Father has set His seal on Him."

28 Then they asked Him, "What shall we do that we may work the works of God?"

29 Jesus answered them, "This is the work of God, that you believe in Him whom He has sent."

30 Therefore they said to Him, "What sign do You show then, that we may see and believe You? What work will You perform? 31 Our fathers ate manna in the desert. As it is written, 'He gave them bread from heaven to eat.'[1]"

32 Then Jesus said, "Truly, truly I say to you, Moses did not give you the bread from heaven, but My Father gives you the true bread from heaven. 33 For the bread of God is He who comes down from heaven and gives life to the world."

34 Then they said to Him, "Lord, give us this bread always."

35 Jesus said to them, "I am the bread of life. Whoever comes to Me shall never hunger, and whoever believes in Me shall never thirst. 36 But I told you that you have seen Me, and yet do not believe. 37 All whom the Father gives Me will come to Me, and he who comes to Me I will never cast out. 38 For I came down from heaven, not to do My own will, but the will of Him who sent Me. 39 This is the will of the Father who has sent Me, that of all whom He has given Me, I should lose nothing, but should raise it up at the last day. 40 This is the will of Him who sent Me, that everyone who sees the Son and believes in Him may have eternal life, and I will raise him up on the last day."

41 The Jews then murmured about Him, because He said, "I am the bread which came down from heaven." 42 They said, "Is this not Jesus, the son of Joseph, whose father and mother we know? How is it then that He says, 'I have come down from heaven'?"

43 Jesus therefore answered them, "Do not murmur among yourselves. 44 No one can come to Me unless the Father who has sent Me draws him. And I will raise him up on the last day. 45 It is written in the Prophets, 'They shall all be taught by God.'[2] Therefore everyone who has heard and has learned of the Father comes to Me. 46 Not that anyone has seen the Father, except He who is from God. He has seen the Father. 47 Truly, truly I say to you, whoever believes in Me has eternal life. 48 I am the bread of life. 49 Your fathers ate manna in the wilderness, and they died. 50 This is the bread which comes down from heaven, that one may eat of it and not die. 51 I am the living bread which came down from heaven. If anyone eats of this bread, he will live forever. The bread which I shall give for the life of the world is My flesh."

52 The Jews therefore quarreled among themselves, saying, "How can this Man give us His flesh to eat?"

53 Jesus said to them, "Truly, truly I say to you, unless you eat the flesh of the Son of Man and drink His blood, you have no life in you. 54 Whoever eats My flesh and drinks My blood has eternal life. And I will raise him up on the last day. 55 For My flesh is food indeed, and My blood is drink indeed. 56 Whoever eats My flesh and drinks My blood remains in Me, and I in him. 57 As the living Father sent Me, and I live because of the Father, so whoever feeds on Me also will live because of Me. 58 This is the bread which came down from heaven, not as your fathers ate manna and died. He who eats this bread will live forever." 59 He said these things in the synagogue, as He taught in Capernaum.

The Words of Eternal Life

60 When they heard this, many of His disciples said, "This is a hard saying. Who can listen to it?"

61 Knowing in Himself that His disciples murmured about it, Jesus said to them, "Does this offend you? 62 Then what if you see the Son of Man ascend to where He was before? 63 It is the Spirit who gives life. The flesh profits nothing. The words that I speak to you are spirit and are life. 64 But there are some of you who do not believe." For Jesus knew from the beginning who they were who did not believe, and who it was who would betray Him. 65 Then He said, "For this reason I have said to you that no one can come to Me unless it were given him by My Father."

66 From that time many of His disciples went back and walked no more with Him.

67 So Jesus said to the twelve, "Do you also want to go away?"

68 Simon Peter answered Him, "Lord, to whom shall we go? You have the words of

6:24 Jn 6:17
6:26 Jn 6:24
6:27 Isa 55:2
6:29 1 Jn 3:23
6:31 Ne 9:15
6:34 Jn 4:15
6:36 Jn 6:26
6:37 Jn 6:39
6:38 Jn 4:34
6:39 Jn 6:40
6:40 Jn 6:54
6:41 Jn 6:33
6:42 Lk 4:22
6:44 Jn 6:65
6:45 Isa 54:13
6:46 Jn 1:18
6:47 Jn 3:36
6:48 Jn 6:51
6:50 Jn 6:33
6:52 Jn 9:16
6:53 Jn 3:3
6:54 Jn 6:39–40
6:56 Jn 15:4–5
6:57 Jn 5:26
6:58 Jn 6:41
6:59 Jn 6:24
6:60 Jn 6:66
6:62 Mk 16:19
6:63 Jn 6:68
6:64 Jn 6:61
6:65 Jn 6:37
6:66 Jn 6:60

[1] *31* Ex 16:4, 15; Ne 9:15; Ps 78:24–25. [2] *45* Isa 54:13.

eternal life. 69 We have believed and have come
to know that You are the Christ, the Son of the
living God."

70 Jesus answered them, "Have I not chosen
you, the twelve, and yet one of you is a devil?"
71 He spoke of Judas Iscariot, the son of Simon.
For it was he who would betray Him, being
one of the twelve.

The Unbelief of Jesus' Brothers

7 After these things Jesus walked in Galilee.
He would not walk in Judea, because the
Jews were seeking to kill Him. 2 Now the Jews'
Feast of Tabernacles was at hand. 3 His broth-
ers therefore said to Him, "Depart from here
and go into Judea, that Your disciples also may
see the works that You do. 4 For no one does
anything in secret, while he himself seeks to
be known openly. If You do these things, reveal
Yourself to the world." 5 For even His brothers
did not believe in Him.

6 Therefore Jesus told them, "My time has
not yet come, but your time is always fitting.
7 The world cannot hate you. But it hates Me,
because I testify concerning it, that its works
are evil. 8 You go up to this feast. I am not going
up to this feast yet, because My time has not
yet fully come." 9 Having said these things to
them, He remained in Galilee.

Jesus at the Feast of Tabernacles

10 However, after His brothers had gone up
to the feast, then He also went up, not publicly,
but secretly. 11 Then the Jews looked for Him at
the feast, and said, "Where is He?"

12 There was much complaining among the
people concerning Him. For some said, "He
is a good Man."

Others said, "No, He deceives the people."
13 Yet no one spoke openly of Him for fear of
the Jews.

14 Now about the middle of the feast Jesus
went up into the temple and began teaching.
15 The Jews marveled, saying, "How has this
Man become educated, having never been
taught?"

16 Jesus answered them, "My teaching is
not Mine, but His who sent Me. 17 If any man
desires to do His will, he shall know whether
the teaching is from God or whether I speak
on My own authority. 18 He who speaks on his
own authority seeks his own glory. But He who
seeks the glory of Him who sent Him is true,
and no unrighteousness is in Him. 19 Did Moses
not give you the law, and yet none of you keeps
the law? Why do you seek to kill Me?"

20 The people answered and said, "You have
a demon. Who is seeking to kill You?"

21 Jesus answered them, "I did one work, and
you all marvel. 22 Yet, because Moses gave you
circumcision, you circumcise a man on the
Sabbath day (although it did not come from
Moses, but from the Patriarchs). 23 If a man
receives circumcision on the Sabbath day, so
that the Law of Moses should not be broken,
are you angry at Me because I completely
healed a man on the Sabbath day? 24 Do not
judge according to appearance, but practice
righteous judgment."

Is He the Christ?

25 Then some of them from Jerusalem said,
"Is this not He whom they seek to kill? 26 Look!
He speaks publicly, and they say nothing to
Him. Do the rulers indeed know that this is
really the Christ? 27 But we know where this
Man is from. When the Christ comes, no one
will know where He is from."

28 Then Jesus, still teaching in the temple,
cried out, "You know Me and you likewise
know where I am from. I have not come on
My own authority, but He who sent Me is true,
whom you do not know. 29 But I know Him, for
I am from Him, and He sent Me."

30 So they tried to seize Him, but no one laid
hands on Him, because His hour had not yet
come. 31 Still, many of the people believed in
Him and said, "When the Christ comes, will
He do more signs than these which this Man
has done?"

Officials Sent to Arrest Jesus

32 The Pharisees heard the people mur-
muring these things concerning Him. So the
Pharisees and the chief priests sent officers
to arrest Him.

33 Then Jesus said to them, "I shall be with
you a little while longer, and then I go to Him
who sent Me. 34 You will look for Me and you
will not find Me. And where I am, you cannot
come."

35 The Jews said among themselves, "Where
does He intend to go that we shall not find
Him? Does He intend to go to the Dispersion
among the Greeks and teach the Greeks?
36 What kind of saying is this which He said,
'You will look for Me and you will not find Me.
And where I am, you cannot come'?"

Rivers of Living Water

37 On the last and greatest day of the feast, Je-
sus stood and cried out, "If anyone is thirsty, let
him come to Me and drink. 38 He who believes
in Me, as the Scripture has said, out of his heart
shall flow rivers of living water." 39 By this He
spoke of the Spirit, whom those who believe in
Him would receive. For the Holy Spirit was not
yet given, because Jesus was not yet glorified.

6:69 Mk 8:29
6:70 Jn 13:27
7:2 Zec 14:16–19
7:3 Mt 12:46
7:4 Jn 18:20
7:5 Mk 3:21
7:6 Jn 2:4
7:7 Jn 3:19
7:8 Jn 7:6
7:11 Jn 11:56
7:12 Jn 7:40–43
7:13 Jn 9:22
7:14 Jn 7:28
7:16 Jn 3:11
7:17 Jn 8:43
7:18 Jn 5:41
7:19 Jn 1:17
7:20 Jn 8:48
7:22 Lev 12:3
7:24 Jn 8:15
7:26 Jn 7:48
7:27 Jn 6:42
7:28 Jn 8:42
7:29 Jn 8:55
7:30 Jn 10:39
7:31 Jn 12:42
7:33 Jn 13:33
7:35 Jas 1:1
7:36 Jn 7:34
7:37 Isa 55:1
7:38 Isa 58:11
7:39 Ac 2:17

Division Among the People

40 Therefore when they heard these words,
many of the people said, “Truly, this is the
Prophet.”
41 Others said, “This is the Christ.”
But some said, “Will the Christ come out of
Galilee? 42 Has the Scripture not said that the
Christ comes from the seed of David, out of
the town of Bethlehem where David was?”
43 So there was a division among the people
because of Him. 44 Some of them wanted to
arrest Him, but no one laid hands on Him.

The Unbelief of Those in Authority

45 Then the officers came to the chief priests
and Pharisees, who said to them, “Why did
you not bring Him?”
46 The officers answered, “No man has ever
spoken like this Man.”
47 Then the Pharisees answered them, “Are
you also deceived? 48 Have any of the rulers
or the Pharisees believed in Him? 49 Not at
all. This crowd who does not know the law
is accursed.”
50 Nicodemus, being one of them who came
to Jesus by night, said to them, 51 “Does our law
judge a man before it hears him and knows
what he is doing?”
52 They answered him, “Are you also from
Galilee? Search and see that no prophet arises
out of Galilee.”

The Woman Caught in Adultery

53 Then everyone went to his own house.[1]
8 But Jesus went to the Mount of Olives.
2 Early in the morning He returned to the
temple. All the people came to Him, and He
sat down and taught them. 3 The scribes and
Pharisees brought a woman caught in adul-
tery. When they had put her in the middle,
4 they said to Him, “Teacher, this woman was
caught in the very act of adultery. 5 Now Moses
in the law commanded us to stone such, but
what do You say?” 6 They said this, testing Him,
that they might have something of which to
accuse Him.
But Jesus stooped down and wrote on the
ground with His finger, as though He did not
hear them. 7 So when they continued asking
Him, He stood up and said to them, “Let him
who is without sin among you be the first to
throw a stone at her.” 8 Again He stooped down
and wrote on the ground.
9 Being convicted by their conscience, those
who heard it went out one by one, beginning
with the eldest even to the last. Jesus was left
alone, and the woman standing in the midst.
10 When Jesus had stood up and saw no one
but the woman, He said to her, “Woman, where
are your accusers? Did no one condemn you?”
11 She said, “No one, Lord.”
Jesus said to her, “Neither do I condemn you.
Go and sin no more.”

Jesus the Light of the World

12 Again, Jesus spoke to them, saying, “I am
the light of the world. Whoever follows Me
shall not walk in the darkness, but shall have
the light of life.”
13 The Pharisees therefore said to Him, “You
bear witness of Yourself. Your testimony is
not true.”
14 Jesus answered them, “Though I bear
witness of Myself, My testimony is true. For
I know where I came from and where I am
going. But you do not know where I came from
or where I am going. 15 You judge according
to the flesh. I judge no one. 16 Yet if I do judge,
My judgment is true. For I am not alone, but
I am with the Father who sent Me. 17 Even in
your law it is written that the testimony of two
men is true. 18 I am One who bears witness
of Myself, and the Father that sent Me bears
witness of Me.”
19 Then they said to Him, “Where is Your
Father?”
Jesus answered, “You know neither Me nor
My Father. If you knew Me, you would know
My Father also.” 20 Jesus spoke these words in
the treasury, as He taught in the temple. No one
arrested Him, for His hour had not yet come.

Where I Am Going You Cannot Come

21 Again, Jesus said to them, “I am going away,
and you will seek Me, and you will die in your
sins. Where I am going, you cannot come.”
22 So the Jews said, “Will He kill Himself? For
He said, ‘Where I am going, you cannot come.’ ”
23 He said to them, “You are from below; I am
from above. You are of this world; I am not of
this world. 24 Therefore I said to you that you
will die in your sins. For unless you believe that
I am He, you will die in your sins.”
25 They said to Him, “Who are You?”
Jesus said to them, “Just who I have been
telling you from the beginning. 26 I have many
things to say and to judge concerning you, but
He who sent Me is true. So I tell the world what
I heard from Him.”
27 They did not understand that He spoke to
them of the Father. 28 So Jesus said to them,
“When you lift up the Son of Man, then you
will know that I am He, and I do nothing of
Myself. But I speak these things as My Father
taught Me. 29 He who sent Me is with Me. The
Father has not left Me alone, for I always do
those things that please Him.” 30 As He spoke
these words, many believed in Him.

7:41 Jn 1:46
7:42 Mic 5:2
7:43 Jn 9:16
7:44 Jn 7:30
7:45 Jn 7:32
7:47 Jn 7:12
7:48 Jn 12:42
7:50 Jn 19:39
7:51 Pr 18:13
7:52 Jn 7:41
8:1 Mt 21:1
8:2 Mt 26:55
8:5 Lev 20:10
8:6 Mt 19:3
. . . .
8:11 Jn 3:17
8:12 Jn 12:35
8:14 Jn 13:3
8:15 Jn 7:24
8:17 Dt 17:6
8:19 Jn 16:3
8:20 Jn 7:30
8:21 Jn 7:34
8:23 Jn 3:31
8:24 Jn 8:21
8:25 Jn 1:19
8:26 Jn 7:28
8:28 Jn 3:14
8:29 Jn 4:34
8:30 Jn 7:31

[1] *53* The earliest Gk. manuscripts lack 7:53–8:11.

The Truth Will Set You Free

31 Then Jesus said to those Jews who be-
lieved Him, "If you remain in My word, then
you are truly My disciples. 32 You shall know
the truth, and the truth shall set you free."
33 They answered Him, "We are Abraham's
seed and have never been in bondage to any-
one. Why do You say, 'You shall be set free'? "
34 Jesus answered them, "Truly, truly I say
to you, whoever commits sin is a slave of sin.
35 Now a slave does not remain in the house
forever, but a son remains forever. 36 Therefore
if the Son sets you free, you shall be free in-
deed. 37 I know that you are Abraham's seed.
But you seek to kill Me, because My word has
no place in you. 38 I am telling what I have seen
with My Father, and you are doing what you
have seen with your father."

Your Father the Devil

39 They answered Him, "Abraham is our
father."
Jesus said to them, "If you were Abraham's
children, you would do the works of Abraham.
40 But now you seek to kill Me, a Man who
has told you the truth which I heard from God.
Abraham did not do this. 41 You are doing the
works of your father."
Then they said to Him, "We were not born of
sexual immorality. We have one Father: God."
42 Jesus said to them, "If God were your Fa-
ther, you would love Me, for I came from God
and proceeded into the world. I did not come
of My own authority, but He sent Me. 43 Why
do you not understand My speaking? Because
you cannot bear to hear My word. 44 You are
of your father the devil, and you want to do
the desires of your father. He was a murderer
from the beginning, and does not stand in the
truth, because there is no truth in him. When
he lies, he speaks from his own nature, for he
is a liar and the father of lies. 45 Yet because I
tell the truth, you do not believe Me. 46 Which
of you convicts Me of sin? If I speak the truth,
why do you not believe Me? 47 He who is of God
hears God's words. Therefore, you do not hear
them, because you are not of God."

The Preexistence of Jesus

48 The Jews answered Him, "Do we not right-
ly say that You are a Samaritan and have a
demon?"
49 Jesus answered, "I do not have a demon.
But I honor My Father, and you dishonor Me.
50 I do not seek glory for Myself. There is One
who seeks it and judges. 51 Truly, truly I say to
you, if anyone keeps My word, he shall never
see death."
52 Then the Jews said to Him, "Now we know
that You have a demon. Abraham and the
prophets died, and You say, 'If a man keeps My
word, he shall never taste death.' 53 "Are You
greater than our father Abraham, who died?
The prophets are dead! Who do You make
Yourself out to be?"
54 Jesus answered, "If I glorify Myself, My
glory is nothing. It is My Father who glorifies
Me, of whom you say that He is your God. 55 Yet
you have not known Him, but I know Him.
If I say, 'I do not know Him,' I shall be a liar
like you. But I know Him and keep His word.
56 Your father Abraham rejoiced to see My day.
He saw it and was glad."
57 Then the Jews said to Him, "You are not
yet fifty years old. Have You seen Abraham?"
58 Jesus said to them, "Truly, truly I say to
you, before Abraham was born, I AM." 59 Then
they took up stones to throw at Him. But Jesus
hid Himself and went out of the temple. Going
through their midst, He passed by.

The Healing of a Man Born Blind

9 As Jesus passed by, He saw a man blind
from birth. 2 His disciples asked Him,
"Rabbi, who sinned, this man or his parents,
that he was born blind?"

> God uses plans gone awry as the raw materials for His good purposes (Jn 9:3).

3 Jesus answered, "Neither this man nor his
parents sinned. But it happened so that the
works of God might be displayed in him. 4 I
must do the works of Him who sent Me while
it is day. Night is coming when no one can
work. 5 While I am in the world, I am the light
of the world."
6 When He had said this, He spat on the
ground and made clay with the saliva. He
anointed the eyes of the blind man with the
clay, 7 and said to him, "Go, wash in the pool
of Siloam" (which means "Sent"). So he went
away and washed, and returned seeing.
8 The neighbors and those who had previous-
ly seen that he was blind said, "Is this not he
who sat and begged?" 9 Some said, "This is he."
Others said, "He is like him."
But he said, "I am he."
10 So they said to him, "How were your eyes
opened?"
11 He answered, "A Man called Jesus made
clay, anointed my eyes, and said to me, 'Go to
the pool of Siloam and wash.' So I went away
and washed, and I received my sight."
12 They said to him, "Where is He?"
He said, "I do not know."

8:31 2Jn 1:9
8:32 Ro 8:2
8:33 Mt 3:9
8:34 Ro 6:16
8:35 Ge 21:10
8:37 Jn 7:1
8:38 Jn 5:19
8:39 Gal 3:7
8:40 Jn 8:26
8:41 Isa 63:16
8:42 Jn 17:8
8:44 Jn 8:38
8:46 Heb 4:15
8:48 Jn 7:20
8:50 Jn 5:41
8:51 Lk 2:26
8:52 Heb 2:9
8:53 Jn 4:12
8:54 Jn 8:50
8:55 Jn 8:19
8:56 Heb 11:13
8:58 Ex 3:14
8:59 Jn 11:8
9:2 Jn 9:34
9:3 Jn 11:4
9:4 Jn 12:35
9:5 Jn 8:12
9:6 Mk 7:33
9:7 Jn 11:37
9:11 Jn 9:6–7

The Pharisees Investigate the Healing

13 They brought the man who had been blind to the Pharisees. 14 Now it was a Sabbath day when Jesus made the clay and opened his eyes. 15 Therefore the Pharisees also asked him how he received his sight. He said to them, "He put clay on my eyes, and I washed, and I see."

16 Some of the Pharisees said, "This Man is not from God, because He does not keep the Sabbath day."

Others said, "How can a man who is a sinner do such signs?" So there was division among them.

17 Then they said to the blind man again, "What do you say about Him, since He opened your eyes?"

He said, "He is a prophet."

18 But the Jews did not believe concerning him, that he had been blind and received his sight, until they called the parents of the one who had received his sight. 19 They asked them, "Is this your son, whom you say was born blind? How then does he now see?"

20 His parents answered them, "We know that this is our son and that he was born blind. 21 But how he now sees, we do not know, or who opened his eyes, we do not know. He is of age. Ask him. He will speak for himself." 22 His parents said this, because they feared the Jews. For the Jews had already agreed that if anyone confessed that He was the Christ, he would be put out of the synagogue. 23 Therefore his parents said, "He is of age. Ask him."

24 So again they called the man who was blind and said to him, "Give glory to God. We know that this Man is a sinner."

25 He said, "I do not know if He is a sinner. I know one thing: I was blind, but now I see."

26 Then they said to him again, "What did He do to you? How did He open your eyes?"

27 He answered them, "I told you already, and you did not listen. Why do you want to hear it again? Do you also want to become His disciples?"

28 Then they insulted him and said, "You are His disciple, but we are Moses' disciples. 29 We know that God has spoken to Moses. As for this fellow, we do not know where He is from."

30 The man answered, "Well, here is an amazing thing! You do not know where He is from, and yet He opened my eyes. 31 We know that God does not listen to sinners. But if anyone is a worshipper of God and does His will, He hears him. 32 Since the world began, it has never been heard that anyone opened the eyes of someone born blind. 33 If this Man were not from God, He could do nothing."

9:14 Jn 5:9
9:16 Jn 7:43
9:22 Jn 7:13
9:23 Jn 9:21
9:24 Jos 7:19
9:28 Ro 2:17
9:29 Jn 8:14
9:31 Pr 15:29
9:33 Jn 3:2

....

9:34 Jn 9:2
9:35 1Jn 5:13
9:36 Ro 10:14
9:37 Jn 4:26
9:38 Mt 28:9
9:39 Lk 4:18
9:41 Pr 26:12
10:2 Jn 10:14
10:3 Jn 10:4
10:4 Jn 10:16
10:7 Jn 10:9
10:11 Isa 40:11
10:14 Jn 10:27
10:15 Mt 11:27

34 They answered him, "You were completely born in sin. Are you teaching us?" And they threw him out.

Spiritual Blindness

35 Jesus heard that they had thrown him out, and when He found him, He said, "Do you believe in the Son of God?"

36 He answered, "Who is He, Lord, that I may believe in Him?"

37 Jesus said to him, "You have seen Him, and it is He who speaks with you."

38 Then he said, "Lord, I believe." And he worshipped Him.

39 Jesus said, "I came into this world for judgment, that those who do not see may see, and that those who see may become blind."

40 Some Pharisees who were with Him heard these words, and said to Him, "Are we also blind?"

41 Jesus said, "If you were blind, you would have no sin. But now you say, 'We see.' Therefore your sin remains.

The Parable of the Shepherd

10 "Truly, truly I say to you, he who does not enter by the door into the sheepfold, but climbs up some other way, is a thief and a robber. 2 But he who enters by the door is the shepherd of the sheep. 3 To him the doorkeeper opens, and the sheep hear his voice. He calls his own sheep by name, and he leads them out. 4 When he brings out his own sheep, he goes before them. And the sheep follow him, for they know his voice. 5 Yet they will never follow a stranger, but will run away from him. For they do not know the voice of strangers." 6 Jesus told them this parable, but they did not understand what He was telling them.

Jesus the Good Shepherd

7 Then Jesus said to them again, "Truly, truly I say to you, I am the door of the sheep. 8 All who came before Me are thieves and robbers, but the sheep did not listen to them. 9 I am the door. If anyone enters through Me, he will be saved and will go in and out and find pasture. 10 The thief does not come, except to steal and kill and destroy. I came that they may have life, and that they may have it more abundantly.

11 "I am the good shepherd. The good shepherd lays down His life for the sheep. 12 But he who is a hired hand, and not a shepherd, who does not own the sheep, sees the wolf coming, and leaves the sheep, and runs away. So the wolf catches the sheep and scatters them. 13 The hired hand runs away because he is a hired hand and does not care about the sheep.

14 "I am the good shepherd. I know My sheep and am known by My own. 15 Even as the Father knows Me, so I know the Father. And I

lay down My life for the sheep. 16 I have oth-
er sheep who are not of this fold. I must also
bring them, and they will hear My voice. There
will be one flock and one shepherd. 17 There-
fore My Father loves Me, because I lay down
My life that I may take it up again. 18 No one
takes it from Me, but I lay it down Myself. I
have power to lay it down, and I have power
to take it up again. I received this command
from My Father."

19 Therefore there was a division again
among the Jews because of these sayings.
20 Many of them said, "He has a demon and is
insane. Why do you listen to Him?"

21 Others said, "These are not the words of
one who has a demon. Can a demon open the
eyes of the blind?"

Jesus Rejected by the Jews

22 The Feast of the Dedication[1] was at Jeru-
salem, and it was winter. 23 Jesus walked in the
temple in Solomon's Porch. 24 Then the Jews
surrounded Him, saying, "How long will You
keep us in suspense? If You are the Christ, tell
us plainly."

25 Jesus answered them, "I told you, and you
did not believe. The works that I do in My Fa-
ther's name bear witness of Me. 26 But you do
not believe, because you are not of My sheep,
as I said to you. 27 My sheep hear My voice,
and I know them, and they follow Me. 28 I give
them eternal life. They shall never perish, nor
shall anyone snatch them from My hand. 29 My
Father, who has given them to Me, is greater
than all. No one is able to snatch them from
My Father's hand. 30 My Father and I are one."

I hear my Shepherd's voice
and follow Him (Jn 10:27).

31 Again the Jews took up stones to stone
Him. 32 Jesus answered them, "I have shown
you many good works from My Father. For
which of those works do you stone Me?"

33 The Jews answered Him, "We are not ston-
ing You for a good work, but for blasphemy, and
because You, being a Man, claim to be God."

34 Jesus answered them, "Is it not written
in your law, 'I said, "You are gods"'[2]? 35 If He
called them 'gods,' to whom the word of God
came, and the Scripture cannot be broken,
36 do you say of Him, whom the Father has
sanctified and sent into the world, 'You blas-
pheme,' because I said, 'I am the Son of God'?
37 If I am not doing the works of My Father, do
not believe Me. 38 But if I do them, though you
do not believe Me, believe the works, that you
may know and believe that the Father is in Me,

10:16 Isa 56:8
10:17 Jn 10:11
10:18 Jn 15:10
10:19 Jn 9:16
10:20 Mk 3:21
10:21 Ex 4:11
10:23 Ac 3:11
10:24 Jn 1:19
10:25 Jn 8:58
10:26 Jn 8:47
10:27 Jn 10:14
10:28 Jn 6:37
10:29 Jn 14:28
10:30 Jn 14:9
10:31 Jn 8:59
10:33 Jn 5:18
10:34 Jn 12:34
10:36 Jn 3:17
10:37 Jn 15:24
10:38 Jn 14:20
....
10:39 Jn 7:30
10:40 Jn 1:28
10:42 Jn 7:31
11:1 Mt 21:17
11:2 Jn 12:3
11:3 Jn 11:5
11:4 Jn 9:3
11:8 Jn 10:31
11:9 Jn 9:4
11:10 Jer 13:16
11:11 Da 12:2
11:16 Mt 10:3
11:17 Jn 11:39
11:19 Job 2:11
11:20 Lk 10:38–42

and I in Him." 39 Again they tried to seize Him,
but He escaped from their hands.

40 Then He went away again beyond the Jor-
dan into the place where John was baptizing
at first, and He remained there. 41 Many came
to Him and said, "John did no sign. But every-
thing that John said about this Man was true."
42 And many believed in Him there.

The Death of Lazarus

11 Now a man was sick, Lazarus from
Bethany, the village of Mary and her
sister Martha. 2 This was Mary who anointed
the Lord with ointment and wiped His feet with
her hair, whose brother Lazarus was sick. 3 So
the sisters sent word to Him, saying, "Lord, he
whom You love is sick."

4 When Jesus heard this, He said, "This sick-
ness is not unto death, but for the glory of God,
that the Son of God may be glorified by it."
5 Now Jesus loved Martha, and her sister, and
Lazarus. 6 So when He heard that he was sick,
He remained where He was two more days.
7 Then after this He said to the disciples, "Let
us go into Judea again."

8 His disciples said to Him, "Rabbi, the Jews
were just trying to stone You. Are You going
there again?"

9 Jesus answered, "Are there not twelve hours
in the day? If anyone walks during the day, he
does not stumble, because he sees the light of
this world. 10 But if anyone walks during the
night, he stumbles, because the light is not
in him."

11 After He said this, He said to them, "Our
friend Lazarus has fallen asleep. But I am go-
ing that I may awaken him from sleep."

12 Then His disciples said, "Lord, if he is
sleeping, he will be well." 13 Jesus had spoken
of his death. But they thought that He was
speaking of getting rest through sleep.

14 So then Jesus plainly told them, "Lazarus
is dead. 15 And I am glad for your sakes that I
was not there, so that you may believe. Nev-
ertheless let us go to him."

16 Then Thomas, who is called Didymus, said
to his fellow disciples, "Let us go also, that we
may die with Him."

Jesus the Resurrection and the Life

17 When Jesus arrived, He found that he had
been in the tomb four days already. 18 Now
Bethany was near Jerusalem, less than two
miles away.[3] 19 Many of the Jews had come to
Martha and Mary, to comfort them concerning
their brother. 20 When Martha heard that Jesus
was coming, she went and met Him, but Mary
remained in the house.

[1] 22 Or *Hanukkah*. [2] 34 Ps 82:6. [3] 18 Gk. *15 stadia*, or about 3 kilometers.

PROFILE OF A SPIRITLED WOMAN

MARY

DELAYS ARE NOT DENIALS

When Mary and Martha sent news to Jesus that their brother, Lazarus, was about to die, Jesus didn't respond the way His friends expected. He actually snubbed their request. The Bible says that when Jesus heard Lazarus was sick, "He remained where He was two more days" (Jn 11:6).

For those two anxious women, that was a very, very, very long time. Doubts tormented them. They thought: "What kind of friend is Jesus, anyway? Why didn't He rush to our aid?" Mary was especially troubled by Jesus' seemingly insensitive delay.

When Jesus finally arrived in Bethany, everybody in the village was mourning. And Mary's faith was as cold as Lazarus' corpse.

She didn't even want to talk to Jesus. She stayed in the house while her sister went to ask Jesus why He took so long (v. 20). Most likely Mary was sulking, maybe even struggling with feelings of anger toward Jesus because He was so late.

Many of us get stuck in this place of disappointment. We get upset and confused when God doesn't work according to our timetable.

Perhaps you have been asking Jesus to intervene in your crisis. You may need Him to rescue a wayward child, restore a broken relationship, heal your body (or someone else's), or salvage a dream that is on its deathbed. It may seem that Jesus is so busy meeting the needs of others that He dropped you from His priority list.

Like Mary of Bethany, you may feel that Jesus has waited too long. Your problem seems so serious, and your dream so lifeless, that now Jesus can't help you. It's over.

When we face these frustrating delays, we automatically assume that He is denying us, neglecting us, or rejecting us. So we throw a childish pity party. We go in our rooms, close our doors, shut out the pain, and stay as far away from Jesus as possible.

We find it difficult to pray when we are in a faith crisis. The devil tells us that Jesus doesn't care, that our prayers are meaningless, and that there is no reward for believing in Him. Some of us, if we have melancholy tendencies, also beat ourselves up with the classic "I guess I just don't have enough faith" line.

Thankfully Mary did not stay in her self-made prison of discouragement. The Bible says that when Jesus arrived at Lazarus' tomb, Mary ran to him and knelt at His feet—the place where she began her journey of discipleship (Lk 10:39). After all her moping, she returned to the only place where life's struggles make sense. She stopped asking *why*. She focused on *who*.

She knelt in His presence, not to ask Him why He let Lazarus die but simply to gain strength from being with Him. She left behind the whining immaturity that demands Jesus must act a certain way. She chose to grow up.

When Mary surrendered her life to Him that day, she was saying that she would follow Him not only in the good times but also on the dark days when she couldn't see His love through the clouds of grief, suffering, and pain.

There, at Jesus' feet, Mary caught a glimpse of Jesus as she'd never seen Him before. He wept for Lazarus, and then He commanded his lifeless body to come to life. Mary would have missed the miracle if she'd stayed in seclusion. She needed to see that God's delays are not denials—and that Jesus' timing is perfect.

Have you been sinking into despair because your dream has died—and you think Jesus doesn't care? Run back to Him and take your place at His feet. True disciples know that life operates on God's schedule, not ours. Press through your doubts, surrender your deadlines, renounce your impatience, and renew your trust in Jesus, who is the sovereign Lord over your circumstances.

J. Lee Grady

21 Martha said to Jesus, "Lord, if You had
been here, my brother would not have died.
22 But even now I know that whatever You may
ask of God, God will give You."
23 Jesus said to her, "Your brother will rise
again."
24 Martha said to Him, "I know that he will
rise again in the resurrection on the last day."
25 Jesus said to her, "I am the resurrection
and the life. He who believes in Me, though
he may die, yet shall he live. 26 And whoever
lives and believes in Me shall never die. Do
you believe this?"
27 She said to Him, "Yes, Lord, I believe that
You are the Christ, the Son of God, who is to
come into the world."

Jesus Weeps

28 When she had said this, she went her
way and secretly called her sister Mary, say-
ing, "The Teacher has come and is calling for
you." 29 When she heard this, she rose quickly
and went to Him. 30 Now Jesus had not yet
entered the village, but was in the place where
Martha met Him. 31 When the Jews who were
with Mary in the house, comforting her, saw
that she quickly rose up and went out, they
followed her, saying, "She is going to the tomb
to weep there."
32 When Mary came to where Jesus was, and
saw Him, she fell down at His feet, saying to
Him, "Lord, if You had been here, my brother
would not have died."
33 When Jesus saw her weeping, and the Jews
who came with her weeping, He groaned in
the spirit and was troubled. 34 He said, "Where
have you laid him?"
They said to Him, "Lord, come and see."
35 Jesus wept.
36 Then the Jews said, "See how He loved
him."
37 But some of them said, "Could not this
Man, who opened the eyes of the blind man,
have also kept this man from dying?"

Lazarus Brought to Life

38 Then Jesus, again groaning within Himself,
came to the tomb. It was a cave, and a stone
was lying against it. 39 Jesus said, "Take away
the stone."
Martha, the sister of him who was dead, said
to Him, "Lord, by this time there is a stench,
for he has been dead four days."
40 Jesus said to her, "Did I not tell you that if
you believed, you would see the glory of God?"
41 So they took away the stone from the place
where the dead man was lying. Jesus lifted up
His eyes and said, "Father, I thank You that
You have heard Me. 42 I know that You always
hear Me. But because of the people standing

11:21 Jn 11:32
11:22 Jn 9:31
11:24 Jn 5:28–29
11:25 Jn 1:4
11:27 Mt 16:16
11:28 Jn 13:13
11:31 Jn 11:19
11:32 Jn 11:21
11:33 Jn 11:38
11:35 Lk 19:41
11:36 Jn 11:3
11:37 Jn 9:6–7
11:38 Mt 27:60
11:39 Jn 11:17
11:40 Jn 11:4
11:41 Jn 17:1
11:42 Jn 3:17
....
11:44 Jn 20:7
11:45 Jn 2:23
11:47 Mt 26:3
11:50 Jn 18:14
11:52 Jn 10:16
11:54 Jn 7:1
11:56 Jn 7:11
12:1 Jn 11:55
12:2 Lk 10:38–42
12:3 Jn 11:2

around, I said this, that they may believe that
You sent Me."
43 When He had said this, He cried out with a
loud voice, "Lazarus, come out!" 44 He who was
dead came out, his hands and feet wrapped
with grave clothes, and his face wrapped with
a cloth.
Jesus said to them, "Unbind him, and let
him go."

The Plot to Kill Jesus
Mt 26:1–5; Mk 14:1–2; Lk 22:1–2

45 Therefore many of the Jews who came
to Mary, and saw what Jesus had done, be-
lieved in Him. 46 But some of them went away
to the Pharisees and told them what Jesus
had done. 47 Then the chief priests and the
Pharisees assembled the Sanhedrin and said,
"What shall we do? This Man is performing
many signs. 48 If we leave Him alone like this,
everyone will believe in Him, and the Romans
will come and take away both our temple and
our nation."
49 Then one of them named Caiaphas, who
was the high priest that year, said to them,
"You know nothing at all, 50 nor do you con-
sider that it is expedient for us that one man
should die for the people, that the whole na-
tion should not perish."
51 He did not say this on his own authority.
But being the high priest that year, he prophe-
sied that Jesus would die for the nation, 52 and
not for the nation only, but that He might also
gather together in unity the children of God
who were scattered abroad. 53 So from that day
forward they planned to put Him to death.
54 Therefore Jesus no longer walked openly
among the Jews, but went away from there
to the country near the wilderness, into a city
called Ephraim, and remained there with His
disciples.
55 Now the Passover of the Jews was at
hand. Many went up to Jerusalem from the
country before the Passover to purify them-
selves. 56 Then they searched for Jesus and said
among themselves as they stood in the temple,
"What do you think, that He will not come to
the feast?" 57 Now both the chief priests and
the Pharisees had given orders that if anyone
knew where He was, he should report it, that
they might seize Him.

The Anointing at Bethany
Mt 26:6–13; Mk 14:3–9

12 Six days before the Passover Jesus
came to Bethany, where Lazarus was,
who had been dead, whom He had raised from
the dead. 2 They prepared a supper for Him
there. Martha served, but Lazarus was one of
those who sat at the table with Him. 3 Then

Mary took a pint[1] of very costly ointment made from pure nard, and anointed the feet of Jesus, and wiped His feet with her hair. The house was filled with the fragrance of the ointment.

4 But one of His disciples, Judas Iscariot, Simon's son, who would betray Him, said, 5 "Why was this ointment not sold for three hundred denarii[2] and given to the poor?" 6 He said this, not because he cared for the poor, but because he was a thief. And having the money box, he used to steal what was put in it.

7 But Jesus said, "Leave her alone. She has kept this for the day of My burial. 8 For you always have the poor with you, but you do not always have Me."

The Plot Against Lazarus

9 When many of the Jews learned that He was there, they came, not for Jesus' sake only, but that they might also see Lazarus, whom He had raised from the dead. 10 So the chief priests planned to put Lazarus to death also, 11 because on account of him many of the Jews went away and believed in Jesus.

The Triumphant Entry into Jerusalem

Mt 21:1–11; Mk 11:1–11; Lk 19:28–40

12 On the next day a great crowd that had come to the feast heard that Jesus was coming to Jerusalem. 13 They took branches of palm trees, and went out to meet Him, and cried out:

"Hosanna!
'Blessed is He who comes in the name of
the Lord!'[3]
The King of Israel!"

14 Then Jesus, having found a young donkey, sat on it. As it is written:

15 "Fear not, daughter of Zion;
see, your King is coming,
sitting on a donkey's colt."[4]

16 His disciples did not understand these things at first. But when Jesus was glorified, they remembered that these things were written about Him and that they had done these things to Him.

17 Now the crowd that was with Him when He called Lazarus out of the tomb and raised him from the dead bore witness. 18 The crowd went and met Him for this reason: They heard that He had performed this sign. 19 So the Pharisees said among themselves, "See, you are gaining nothing! Look, the world has followed Him!"

Some Greeks Seek Jesus

20 Now there were some Greeks among those who went up to worship at the feast. 21 They came to Philip, who was from Bethsaida of Galilee, and asked him, "Sir, we want to see Jesus." 22 Philip came and told Andrew, and in turn Andrew and Philip told Jesus.

23 Jesus answered them, "The hour has come for the Son of Man to be glorified. 24 Truly, truly I say to you, unless a grain of wheat falls into the ground and dies, it remains alone. But if it dies, it bears much fruit. 25 He who loves his life will lose it. And he who hates his life in this world will keep it for eternal life. 26 If anyone serves Me, he must follow Me. Where I am, there will My servant be also. If anyone serves Me, the Father will honor him.

The Son of Man Must Be Lifted Up

27 "Now My soul is troubled. What shall I say? 'Father, save Me from this hour'? Instead, for this reason I came to this hour. 28 Father, glorify Your name."

Then a voice came from heaven, saying, "I have glorified it, and will glorify it again." 29 The crowd that stood by and heard it said that it had thundered. Others said, "An angel has spoken to Him."

30 Jesus answered, "This voice came not for My sake, but for your sakes. 31 Now judgment is upon this world. Now the ruler of this world will be cast out. 32 And if I be lifted up from the earth, I will draw all men to Myself." 33 He said this to signify by what kind of death He would die.

34 The crowd answered Him, "We have heard from the law that the Christ remains forever. Why do You say, 'The Son of Man must be lifted up'? Who is this Son of Man?"

35 Then Jesus said to them, "Yet a little while the light is with you. Walk while you have the light, lest darkness overtake you. He who walks in darkness does not know where he is going. 36 While you have light, believe in the light that you may become sons of light." Jesus said these things, and departed and hid Himself from them.

The Unbelief of the Jews

37 Though He had done so many signs before them, yet they did not believe in Him. 38 This fulfilled the word spoken by Isaiah the prophet:

"Lord, who has believed our report,
and to whom has the arm of the Lord
been revealed?"[5]

39 Therefore they could not believe. For Isaiah said again:

40 "He has blinded their eyes
and hardened their hearts,
lest they should see with their eyes
and perceive with their hearts and turn,
and I would heal them."[6]

12:4 Mt 10:4
12:6 Jn 13:29
12:8 Dt 15:11
12:10 Lk 16:31
12:11 Jn 11:45
12:13 Jn 1:49
12:15 Zec 9:9
12:16 Jn 2:22
12:18 Jn 12:11
12:19 Jn 3:26
12:20 Jn 7:35

12:23 Jn 13:31–32
12:25 Mt 10:39
12:26 Jn 14:3
12:27 Lk 22:53
12:28 Mt 3:17
12:30 Jn 11:42
12:31 Jn 14:30
12:32 Jn 6:44
12:33 Jn 18:32
12:34 Ps 110:4
12:35 Jn 12:46
12:36 Lk 16:8
12:38 Isa 53:1
12:39 Jn 5:44

[1] 3 Gk. *a litra*, or half a liter. [2] 5 About a year's wages. [3] 13 Ps 118:25–26. [4] 15 Zec 9:9. [5] 38 Isa 53:1. [6] 40 Isa 6:10.

41 Isaiah said this when he saw His glory and spoke of Him.

42 Yet many of the rulers also believed in Him. But because of the Pharisees they did not confess Him, lest they be put out of the synagogue. 43 For they loved the praise of men more than the praise of God.

Judgment by Jesus' Word

44 Jesus cried out, "He who believes in Me believes not only in Me, but in Him who sent Me. 45 He who sees Me sees Him who sent Me. 46 I have come as a light into the world, that whoever believes in Me should not remain in darkness.

47 "If anyone hears My words and does not believe, I do not judge him. For I did not come to judge the world, but to save the world. 48 He who rejects Me, and does not receive My words, has that which judges him. The word I have spoken will judge him on the last day. 49 For I have not spoken on My own authority, but the Father who sent Me gave Me a command, what I should say and what I should speak. 50 I know that His command is eternal life. Therefore what I say, I say as the Father tells me."

Washing the Disciples' Feet

13 Now before the Passover Feast, Jesus knew that His hour had come to depart from this world to the Father. Having loved His own who were in the world, He loved them to the end.

2 Now supper being concluded, the devil had put into the heart of Judas Iscariot, Simon's son, to betray Him. 3 Jesus, knowing that the Father had given all things into His hands and that He came from God and was going to God, 4 rose from supper, laid aside His garments, and took a towel and wrapped Himself. 5 After that, He poured water into a basin and began to wash the disciples' feet and to wipe them with the towel with which He was wrapped.

6 Then He came to Simon Peter, and Peter said to Him, "Lord, are You washing my feet?"

7 Jesus answered him, "You do not understand what I am doing now. But later you will understand."

8 Peter said to Him, "You shall never wash my feet!"

Jesus answered him, "If I do not wash you, you have no part with Me."

9 Simon Peter said to Him, "Lord, not my feet only, but also my hands and my head!"

10 Jesus said to him, "He who is bathed needs only to wash his feet, but is completely clean. You are clean, but not all of you." 11 For He knew who would betray Him. Therefore He said, "Not all of you are clean."

12:42 Jn 7:13
12:43 Jn 5:44
12:44 Mt 10:40
12:46 Jn 8:12
12:47 Jn 3:17
12:48 Lk 10:16
12:50 Jn 6:68
13:1 Jn 12:23
13:2 Ac 5:3
13:3 Jn 8:42
13:5 Lk 7:44
13:7 Jn 12:16
13:8 1Co 6:11
13:10 Jn 15:3
13:11 Jn 2:25

....

13:12 Jn 13:7
13:13 1Co 12:3
13:14 1Pe 5:5
13:15 Mt 11:29
13:16 Jn 15:20
13:17 Mt 7:24–25
13:18 Ps 41:9
13:19 Jn 14:29
13:20 Lk 10:16
13:21 Mt 26:21
13:22 Lk 22:23
13:23 Jn 19:26
13:25 Jn 21:20
13:26 Mt 26:23
13:27 Lk 22:3
13:29 Jn 12:5–6
13:31 Jn 7:39

12 So when He had washed their feet, and put on His garments, and sat down again, He said to them, "Do you know what I have done to you? 13 You call Me Teacher and Lord. You speak accurately, for so I am. 14 If I then, your Lord and Teacher, have washed your feet, you also ought to wash one another's feet. 15 For I have given you an example, that you should do as I have done to you. 16 Truly, truly I say to you, a servant is not greater than his master, nor is he who is sent greater than he who sent him. 17 If you know these things, blessed are you if you do them.

18 "I do not speak concerning all of you. I know whom I have chosen, but that the Scripture may be fulfilled, 'He who eats bread with Me has lifted up his heel against Me.'[1]

19 "Now I tell you before it happens, that when it does happen, you may believe that I am He. 20 Truly, truly I say to you, he who receives whomever I send receives Me. And he who receives Me receives Him who sent Me."

Jesus Foretells His Betrayal
Mt 26:20–25; Mk 14:17–21; Lk 22:21–23

21 When Jesus had said this, He was troubled in spirit, and testified, "Truly, truly I say to you that one of you will betray Me."

22 The disciples looked at one another, uncertain of whom He spoke. 23 Now there was leaning against Jesus' bosom one of His disciples whom Jesus loved. 24 Therefore Simon Peter motioned to him to ask who it was of whom He spoke.

25 Leaning back against Jesus' bosom, he said to Him, "Lord, who is it?"

26 Jesus answered, "It is he to whom I shall give a piece of bread when I have dipped it." When He had dipped the bread, He gave it to Judas Iscariot, the son of Simon. 27 After receiving the piece of bread, Satan entered him.

Then Jesus said to him, "What you are going to do, do quickly." 28 But no one at the table knew why He said this to him. 29 Since Judas had the moneybox, some thought that Jesus said to him, "Buy what we need for the feast," or that he should give something to the poor. 30 Having received the piece of bread, he then left immediately. And it was night.

The New Commandment

31 When he had gone out, Jesus then said, "Now is the Son of Man glorified, and in Him God is glorified. 32 If God is glorified in Him, God will also glorify Him in Himself and will immediately glorify Him.

33 "Little children, yet a little while I am with you. You will seek Me. And as I said to the

[1] *18* Ps 41:9.

SPIRITLED WOMAN

COUNSEL FROM THE SPIRIT BASICS

He Knows the Way

When you are following God's plan for your life, it makes sense to follow someone who knows where He is going.

Of course, Jesus knows the way. In fact, He told us in His Word that He is the way (Jn 14:6)! As you seek Him, the plan He has for your life will unfold. As you follow Him closely, that plan will come into focus.

Jesus knows the way to victory! He knows the way through the valley of shadows, through the pain and the disappointments. I'm sure you'll agree it's good to follow someone like that.

Karen Jensen Salisbury

Jews, so now I tell you, 'Where I am going,
you cannot come.'
34 "A new commandment I give to you, that
you love one another, even as I have loved
you, that you also love one another. 35 By this
all men will know that you are My disciples, if
you have love for one another."

Peter's Denial Foretold
Mt 26:31–35; Mk 14:27–31; Lk 22:31–34

36 Simon Peter said to Him, "Lord, where are
You going?"
Jesus answered him, "Where I am going, you
cannot follow Me now. But you shall follow
Me afterward."
37 Peter said to Him, "Lord, why can I not
follow You now? I will lay down my life for
Your sake."
38 Jesus answered Him, "Will you lay down
your life for My sake? Truly, truly I say to you,
the rooster shall not crow until you have de-
nied Me three times."

Jesus the Way to the Father

14 "Let not your heart be troubled. You
believe in God. Believe also in Me. 2 In
My Father's house are many dwelling places.
If it were not so, I would have told you. I am
going to prepare a place for you. 3 And if I go
and prepare a place for you, I will come again
and receive you to Myself, that where I am, you
may be also. 4 You know where I am going, and
you know the way."

13:34 Lev 19:18
13:35 Jn 17:21
13:36 2Pe 1:14
13:38 Mk 14:30
14:2 Jn 13:33
14:3 Jn 12:26
14:5 Jn 11:16
14:6 Jn 10:9
14:7 Jn 8:19
14:9 Heb 1:3
14:10 Jn 5:19
14:11 Jn 5:36
14:12 Mt 21:21
14:13 Mt 7:7
14:15 Eph 6:24
14:16 Jn 15:26
14:17 Jn 15:26
14:18 Jn 14:3
14:19 Jn 7:33
14:20 Jn 10:38
14:21 Jn 14:15
14:22 Lk 6:16
14:23 Jn 14:15
14:24 Jn 7:16
14:26 Jn 15:26
14:27 Jn 16:33

5 Thomas said to Him, "Lord, we do not know
where You are going. How can we know the
way?"
6 Jesus said to him, "I am the way, the truth,
and the life. No one comes to the Father except
through Me. 7 If you had known Me, you would
have known My Father also. From now on you
do know Him and have seen Him."
8 Philip said to Him, "Lord, show us the Fa-
ther, and that is sufficient for us."
9 Jesus said to him, "Have I been with you
such a long time, and yet you have not known
Me, Philip? He who has seen Me has seen the
Father. So how can you say, 'Show us the Fa-
ther'? 10 Do you not believe that I am in the Fa-
ther and the Father is in Me? The words that I
say to you I do not speak on My own authority.
But the Father who lives in Me does the works.
11 Believe Me that I am in the Father, and the
Father is in Me. Or else believe Me on account
of the works themselves. 12 Truly, truly I say to
you, he who believes in Me will do the works
that I do also. And he will do greater works
than these, because I am going to My Father.
13 I will do whatever you ask in My name, that
the Father may be glorified in the Son. 14 If you
ask anything in My name, I will do it.

The Promise of the Spirit

15 "If you love Me, keep My commandments.
16 I will pray the Father, and He will give you
another Counselor, that He may be with you
forever: 17 the Spirit of truth, whom the world
cannot receive, for it does not see Him, neither
does it know Him. But you know Him, for He
lives with you, and will be in you. 18 I will not
leave you fatherless. I will come to you. 19 Yet a
little while and the world will see Me no more.
But you will see Me. Because I live, you will
live also. 20 On that day you will know that I
am in My Father, and you are in Me, and I am
in you. 21 He who has My commandments and
keeps them is the one who loves Me. And he
who loves Me will be loved by My Father. And
I will love him and will reveal Myself to him."
22 Then Judas (not Iscariot) said to Him, "Lord,
how is it that You will reveal Yourself to us, but
not to the world?"
23 Jesus answered him, "If a man loves Me,
he will keep My word. My Father will love him,
and We will come to him, and make Our home
with him. 24 He who does not love Me does not
keep My words. The word which you hear is
not Mine, but the Father's who sent Me.
25 "I have spoken these things to you while I
am still with you. 26 But the Counselor, the Holy
Spirit, whom the Father will send in My name,
will teach you everything and remind you of
all that I told you. 27 Peace I leave with you. My

peace I give to you. Not as the world gives do
I give to you. Let not your heart be troubled,
neither let it be afraid.
28 "You have heard Me say to you, 'I am going
away and am returning to you.' If you loved
Me, you would rejoice because I said, 'I am
going to the Father,' for My Father is greater
than I. 29 Now I have told you before it happens
so that, when it happens, you may believe.
30 After this I will not speak much with you, for
the ruler of this world is coming. He has no
power over Me. 31 But I do as the Father has
commanded Me so that the world may know
that I love the Father.
"Rise, let us go from here.

Jesus the True Vine

15 "I am the true vine, and My Father is
the vinedresser. 2 Every branch in Me
that bears no fruit, He takes away. And every
branch that bears fruit, He prunes, that it may
bear more fruit. 3 You are already clean through
the word which I have spoken to you. 4 Remain
in Me, as I also remain in you. As the branch
cannot bear fruit by itself, unless it remains in
the vine, neither can you, unless you remain
in Me.
5 "I am the vine, you are the branches. He
who remains in Me, and I in him, bears much
fruit. For without Me you can do nothing. 6 If
a man does not remain in Me, he is thrown
out as a branch and withers. And they gather
them and throw them into the fire, and they are
burned. 7 If you remain in Me, and My words
remain in you, you will ask whatever you de-
sire, and it shall be done for you. 8 My Father
is glorified by this, that you bear much fruit;
so you will be My disciples.

Father, Your Word declares that if I abide in You and Your words abide in me, I can ask what I desire and it shall be done for me (Jn 15:7).

9 "As the Father loved Me, I also loved you.
Remain in My love. 10 If you keep My com-
mandments, you will remain in My love, even
as I have kept My Father's commandments
and remain in His love. 11 I have spoken these
things to you, that My joy may remain in you,
and that your joy may be full. 12 This is My
commandment: that you love one another, as
I have loved you. 13 Greater love has no man
than this: that a man lay down his life for his
friends. 14 You are My friends if you do what-
ever I command you. 15 I no longer call you
servants, for a servant does not know what
his master does. But I have called you friends,
for everything that I have heard from My Fa-
ther have I made known to you. 16 You did not
choose Me, but I chose you, and appointed
you, that you should go and bear fruit, and
that your fruit should remain, that the Father
may give you whatever you ask Him in My
name. 17 This I command you: that you love
one another.

I am chosen by God to produce fruit (Jn 15:16).

The World's Hatred

18 "If the world hates you, you know that it
hated Me before it hated you. 19 If you were of
the world, the world would love you as its own.
But because you are not of the world, since I
chose you out of the world, the world therefore
hates you. 20 Remember the word that I said to
you: 'A servant is not greater than his master.'
If they persecuted Me, they will also perse-
cute you. If they kept My words, they will keep
yours also. 21 But all these things they will do to
you for My name's sake, because they do not
know Him who sent Me. 22 If I had not come
and spoken to them, they would not have had
sin. But now they have no excuse for their sin.
23 He who hates Me hates My Father also. 24 If
I had not performed among them the works
which no one else did, they would have no
sin. But now have they seen and hated both
My Father and Me. 25 But that the word which
is written in their law might be fulfilled, 'They
hated Me without a cause.'[1]
26 "But when the Counselor comes, whom I
shall send to you from the Father, the Spirit of
truth who proceeds from the Father, He will
bear witness of Me. 27 And you also will bear
witness, because you have been with Me from
the beginning.
16 "I have spoken these things to you so
that you will not fall away. 2 They will
put you out of the synagogues. Yes, the time
is coming that whoever kills you will think that
he is offering a service to God. 3 They will do
these things to you, because they have not
known the Father nor Me. 4 I have told you
these things, so that when the time comes,
you may remember that I told you about them.

The Work of the Spirit

"I did not tell you these things at the begin-
ning, because I was with you. 5 But now I am go-
ing to Him who sent Me, and none of you asks
Me, 'Where are You going?' 6 Rather, sorrow has

14:28 Jn 14:12
14:29 Jn 13:19
14:30 Jn 12:31
14:31 Jn 10:18
15:1 Isa 5:1–7
15:3 Jn 13:10
15:4 1Jn 2:6
15:5 Php 4:13
15:8 Mt 5:16
15:9 Jn 17:26
15:10 Jn 14:15
15:11 Jn 17:13
15:12 Jn 13:34
15:13 Jn 10:11
15:14 Mt 12:50
15:16 Jn 13:18
15:17 Jn 15:12
15:18 1Jn 3:13
15:19 Jn 15:16
15:20 Jn 13:16
15:21 Mt 10:22
15:22 Jn 9:41
15:24 Jn 5:36
15:25 Ps 35:19
15:26 Jn 14:16–17
15:27 Lk 24:48
16:1 Mt 11:6
16:2 Jn 9:22
16:3 Jn 15:21
16:4 Jn 13:19
16:5 Jn 13:36
16:6 Jn 14:1

[1] 25 Ps 35:19; 69:4.

A GOD WHO NEVER CHANGES

The circumstances in your life may change, but God's covenant with you will never change. His love and care for you are constant. Let these truths from God's Word build your confidence in His unchanging love and concern for you.

In the table below, draw lines from each promise from God to the scripture reference where the promise is found.

Promise From God	Scripture Reference
I am grounded on the rock, Christ Jesus, and will not be shaken by the storms of life.	MALACHI 3:6
He is my refuge and fortress; I will trust in Him.	HEBREWS 13:8
The devil kills, steals, and destroys, but Jesus came to give me abundant life.	LUKE 6:47–48
The Lord never changes.	PSALM 91:2
There will be tests and trials in life, but Jesus has overcome those troubles and given me His authority.	PROVERBS 18:10
I will keep my eyes on God's Word and will not be moved by the wind and waves of life's circumstances.	JOHN 10:10
Jesus is the same yesterday, today, and forever.	JOHN 16:33
Jesus is my strong tower. There is no safer place to be.	MATTHEW 14:31

Karen Jensen Salisbury

filled your heart because I have told you these things. 7 Nevertheless I tell you the truth: It is expedient for you that I go away. For if I do not go away, the Counselor will not come to you. But if I go, I will send Him to you. 8 When He comes, He will convict the world of sin and of righteousness and of judgment: 9 of sin, because they do not believe in Me; 10 of righteousness, because I am going to My Father, and you will see Me no more; 11 and of judgment, because the ruler of this world stands condemned.

12 "I have yet many things to tell you, but you cannot bear them now. 13 But when the Spirit of truth comes, He will guide you into all truth. For He will not speak on His own authority. But He will speak whatever He hears, and He will tell you things that are to come. 14 He will glorify Me, for He will receive from Me and will declare it to you. 15 All that the Father has is Mine. Therefore I said that He will take what is Mine and will declare it to you.

Guide me into all truth (Jn 16:13).

Sorrow Will Turn Into Joy

16 "In a little while you will not see Me. And then after a little while you will see Me, because I am going to the Father."

17 Then some of His disciples said among themselves, "What is this He is telling us: 'In a little while you will not see Me; and then after a little while you will see Me,' and, 'because I am going to the Father'? " 18 Then they said, "What is this He is telling us: 'In a little while'? We do not know what He is saying."

19 Then Jesus knew that they wanted to ask Him. So He said to them, "Do you inquire among yourselves concerning what I said: 'In a little while you will not see Me; and then after a little while you will see Me'? 20 Truly, truly I say to you that you will weep and lament, but the world will rejoice. You will be sorrowful, but your sorrow will be turned into joy. 21 When a woman is giving birth, she has pain, because her hour has come. But as soon as she delivers the child, she no longer remembers the anguish for joy that a child is born into the world. 22 Therefore you now have sorrow. But I will see you again, and your heart will rejoice, and no one will take your joy from you. 23 On that day you will ask Me nothing. Truly, truly I say to you, whatever you ask the Father in My name, He will give it to you. 24 Until now you have asked nothing in My name. Ask, and you will receive, that your joy may be full.

16:7 Jn 14:26
16:8 Jn 8:46
16:11 Jn 12:31
16:12 Mk 4:33
16:13 Jn 14:17
16:14 1Jn 4:13–14
16:15 Jn 17:10
16:16 Jn 7:33
16:17 Jn 16:5
16:20 Mk 16:10
16:21 1Th 5:3
16:22 Jn 16:6
16:23 Jn 16:19
16:24 Jn 15:11

....

16:25 Jn 16:2
16:27 Jn 14:21
16:28 Jn 13:3
16:29 Jn 16:25
16:30 Jn 21:17
16:32 Mt 26:31
16:33 Jn 14:27
17:1 Jn 11:41
17:2 Jn 6:37
17:3 1Jn 5:20
17:4 Jn 4:34
17:5 Jn 17:24
17:6 Jn 17:2
17:8 Jn 16:27
17:9 Lk 22:32
17:10 2Th 1:10
17:11 Jn 13:1

I Have Overcome the World

25 "I have told you these things in proverbs. But the time is coming when I will no longer speak to you in proverbs, for I will speak to you plainly about the Father. 26 On that day you will ask in My name. I am not saying to you that I shall ask the Father on your behalf. 27 For the Father Himself loves you, because you have loved Me, and have believed that I came from God. 28 I came from the Father and have come into the world. As I said, I am leaving the world and am going to the Father."

29 His disciples said to Him, "Yes! Now You are speaking plainly and with no figure of speech. 30 Now we know that You know everything and do not need anyone to question You. By this we believe that You came from God."

31 Jesus answered them, "Do you now believe? 32 Listen, the hour is coming. Yes, it has now come that you will be scattered, each to his own home, and will leave Me alone. Yet I am not alone, for the Father is with Me.

33 "I have told you these things so that in Me you may have peace. In the world you will have tribulation. But be of good cheer. I have overcome the world."

The Prayer of Jesus

17 When Jesus spoke these words, He lifted His eyes toward heaven and said:

"Father, the hour has come. Glorify Your Son, that Your Son may also glorify You. 2 As You have given Him authority over all flesh, He will give eternal life to all whom You have given Him. 3 This is eternal life: that they may know You, the only true God, and Jesus Christ, whom You have sent. 4 I have glorified You on the earth. I have finished the work You have given Me to do. 5 And now, O Father, glorify Me in Your own presence with the glory which I had with You before the world existed.

6 "I have revealed Your name to the men whom You have given Me out of the world. They were Yours, and You gave them to Me, and they have kept Your word. 7 Now they know that all things You have given Me are from You. 8 For I have given them the words which You gave Me. They have received them and certainly know that I came from You, and they have believed that You sent Me. 9 I pray for them. I do not pray for the world, but for those whom You have given Me. For they are Yours. 10 All that are Mine are Yours, and all that are Yours are Mine. And I am glorified in them. 11 I am to be no longer in the world, though these are in the world, for I am coming to You. Holy Father, through Your name keep those whom You

Walking Hand in Hand

Let's look at how Jesus interacted with the Father. In Philippians 2:5–8 we see that Jesus, although He had every right to access the benefits of being God, walked in absolute servanthood and humility. He always directed people to the Father; He lived and breathed to point people to the Father. He refused to do things alone but walked closely connected to the Father. Jesus didn't live for His own will. He lived for His Father's will. He taught us to pray, "Your kingdom come; Your will be done on earth, as it is in heaven" (Mt 6:10).

Then again, in Luke 22:42, He prayed to the Father, saying, "Nevertheless not My will, but Yours, be done."

Jesus lived to honor and exalt the Father in everything He did. He wasn't trying to build a name for Himself. He gave every ounce of Himself to demonstrate to people how good and beautiful His Father is. Jesus lived so connected to His Father, He would steal away from the masses to press into His Daddy's heart and draw His strength from that place. He lived to please and honor His Father.

Both the Father and Son were passionate about each other—seeing, loving, and serving the other above Himself. They refused to do anything without the other, but hand in hand they walked.

Their relationship is our model of what true generational unity should look like. And this beautiful, mutually honoring relationship is what Jesus prayed you and I would have as well. Jesus prayed that as fathers and sons and mothers and daughters we would walk in this same manner—refusing to do things alone, always making a way for the other, serving, backing up, putting our approval and affection on display, and seeking the will of the other. In fact, He went as far as to say, "That they may all be one, as You, Father, are in Me, and I in You" (Jn 17:21).

The Father and the Son needed to walk in complete unity so that the world could come into belief. I believe the same holds true for us. God is awakening us to the vital need for fathers and sons and mothers and daughters to learn to walk in such generational unity that the world is provoked to belief. Jesus was able to confidently make the statement in John 10:30, "My Father and I are one." I pray that we too will be able to boldly make that statement and that we would walk as one across generational lines.

Jennifer Toledo

have given Me, that they may be one as We are one. 12 While I was with them in the world, I kept them in Your name. I have kept those whom You have given Me. And none of them is lost except the son of perdition, that the Scripture might be fulfilled.

13 "But now I am coming to You, and I say these things in the world, that they may have My joy fulfilled in themselves. 14 I have given them Your word. And the world has hated them because they are not of the world, just as I am not of the world. 15 I do not pray that You should take them out of the world, but that You should keep them from the evil one. 16 They are not of the world even as I am not of the world. 17 Sanctify them by Your truth. Your word is truth. 18 As You sent Me into the world, so I sent them into the world. 19 For their sakes I sanctify Myself, that they also may be sanctified by the truth.

> When we figure out how to walk in union with God and with one another, something happens (Jn 17:20–23).

20 "I do not pray for these alone, but also for those who will believe in Me through their word, 21 that they may all be one, as You, Father, are in Me, and I in You. May they also be one in Us, that the world may believe that You have sent Me. 22 I have given them the glory which You gave Me, that they may be one even as We are one: 23 I in them and You in Me, that they may be perfect in unity, and that the world may know that You have sent Me, and have loved them as You have loved Me.

> When we walk in true union with God, we start to look like Jesus, and the world takes notice (Jn 17).

24 "Father, I desire that they also, whom You have given Me, be with Me where I am, that they may see My glory which You have given Me. For You loved Me before the creation of the world.

25 "O righteous Father, the world has not known You, but I have known You, and these have known that You sent Me. 26 I have declared Your name to them, and will declare it, that the love with which You loved Me may be in them, and I in them."

17:12 Jn 13:18
17:13 Jn 3:29
17:14 Jn 8:23
17:16 Jn 17:14
17:17 Jn 15:3
17:18 Jn 20:21
17:21 Jn 10:38
17:24 Jn 12:26
17:25 Jn 7:29
17:26 Jn 15:9

18:1 Mt 26:36
18:2 Lk 21:37
18:3 Jn 18:12
18:4 Jn 13:1
18:7 Jn 18:4
18:9 Jn 17:12
18:10 Mk 14:47
18:11 Mt 20:22
18:12 Jn 18:3
18:13 Jn 18:24
18:15 Mk 14:54
18:18 Mk 14:54

The Betrayal and Arrest of Jesus
Mt 26:47–56; Mk 14:43–50; Lk 22:47–53

18 When Jesus had spoken these words, He went out with His disciples across the Kidron Valley. There was a garden which He and His disciples entered.

2 Now Judas, who betrayed Him, also knew the place, for Jesus often met there with His disciples. 3 So Judas, having taken a detachment of soldiers and officers from the chief priests and Pharisees, came there with lanterns and torches and weapons.

4 Jesus therefore, knowing everything that would happen to Him, went forward and said to them, "Whom do you seek?"

5 They answered Him, "Jesus of Nazareth."

Jesus said to them, "I am He." And Judas, who betrayed Him, was standing with them. 6 When He said, "I am He," they drew back and fell to the ground.

7 Again Jesus asked them, "Whom do you seek?"

They said, "Jesus of Nazareth."

8 Jesus answered, "I told you that I am He. So then let these go their way if you are looking for Me." 9 This was to fulfill the word which He had spoken, "I have lost none of those whom You have given Me."

10 Then Simon Peter, having a sword, drew it and struck the high priest's servant, and cut off his right ear. The servant's name was Malchus.

11 Then Jesus said to Peter, "Put your sword into the sheath. Shall I not drink the cup which My Father has given Me?"

Jesus Before the High Priest
Mt 26:57–58; Mk 14:53–54; Lk 22:54

12 Then the detachment of soldiers and the commander and the officers of the Jews arrested Jesus and bound Him. 13 First they led Him to Annas, for he was the father-in-law to Caiaphas, who was the high priest that year. 14 Now it was Caiaphas who advised the Jews that it was expedient that one man should die for the people.

Peter's Denial of Jesus
Mt 26:69–70; Mk 14:66–68; Lk 22:55–57

15 Simon Peter followed Jesus, and so did another disciple. That disciple was known to the high priest and went with Jesus into the courtyard of the high priest. 16 But Peter stood at the door outside. Then the other disciple, who was known to the high priest, went out and spoke to the doorkeeper and brought Peter in.

17 Then the servant girl, being the doorkeeper, said to Peter, "Are you not also one of this Man's disciples?"

He said, "I am not."

18 Now the servants and officers stood there and warmed themselves, having made a fire

of coals, for it was cold. Peter also stood with
them and warmed himself.

The High Priest Questions Jesus
Mt 26:59–66; Mk 14:55–64; Lk 22:66–71

19 The high priest then asked Jesus about His
disciples and His teaching.
20 Jesus answered him, "I spoke openly to the
world. I always taught in the synagogue and
in the temple, where the Jews always meet,
and I said nothing in secret. 21 Why do you ask
Me? Ask those who heard Me and what I have
said to them. Certainly they know what I said."
22 When He had said this, one of the officers
who stood by struck Jesus with the palm of
his hand, saying, "Is that how You answer the
high priest?"
23 Jesus answered him, "If I have spoken evil,
bear witness of the evil, but if well, why do you
strike me?" 24 Then Annas sent Him bound to
Caiaphas the high priest.

Peter Denies Jesus Again
Mt 26:71–75; Mk 14:69–72; Lk 22:58–62

25 Meanwhile Simon Peter was standing and
warming himself. So they said to him, "Are you
not also one of His disciples?"
He denied it and said, "I am not!"
26 One of the servants of the high priest, be-
ing a relative of the man whose ear Peter cut
off, said, "Did I not see you in the garden with
Him?" 27 Peter then denied it again, and imme-
diately a rooster crowed.

Jesus Before Pilate
Mt 27:1–2, 11–14; Mk 15:1–5; Lk 23:1–5

28 Then they led Jesus from Caiaphas to
the Praetorium. It was early. Yet they them-
selves did not enter the Praetorium, so that
they might not be defiled, but might eat the
Passover. 29 Pilate then went out to them and
said, "What accusation do you bring against
this Man?"
30 They answered him, "If He were not an
evildoer, we would not have handed Him over
to you."
31 Then Pilate said, "Take Him and judge Him
according to your law."
The Jews said to him, "It is not lawful for
us to put anyone to death," 32 that the saying
of Jesus might be fulfilled which He spoke,
signifying what death He would die.
33 Again Pilate entered the Praetorium, called
Jesus, and said to Him, "Are You the King of
the Jews?"
34 Jesus answered him, "Are you speaking
of your own accord, or did others tell you
about Me?"
35 Pilate answered, "Am I a Jew? Your own
nation and the chief priests handed You over
to me. What have You done?"

18:20 Jn 7:26
18:24 Jn 18:13
18:27 Jn 13:38
18:28 Jn 18:33
18:32 Mt 20:19
18:33 Jn 19:9

....

18:36 Jn 6:15
18:37 Jn 8:47
18:38 Jn 19:4
18:39 Mt 27:15–18
19:3 Mt 27:29
19:4 Jn 18:38
19:5 Jn 19:2
19:7 Jn 5:18
19:9 Jn 18:33
19:11 Ro 13:1
19:12 Jn 18:33–36

36 Jesus answered, "My kingdom is not of this
world. If My kingdom were of this world, then
My servants would fight, that I would not be
handed over to the Jews. But now My kingdom
is not from here."
37 Therefore Pilate said to Him, "Then are
You a king?"
Jesus answered, "You say correctly that I am
a king. For this reason I was born, and for this
reason I came into the world, to bear witness
to the truth. Everyone who is of the truth hears
My voice."
38 Pilate said to Him, "What is truth?" When
he had said this, he went out again to the Jews
and said to them, "I find no guilt in Him at all.

Jesus Sentenced to Die
Mt 27:15–31; Mk 15:6–20; Lk 23:13–25

39 "But you have a custom, that I should re-
lease someone to you at the Passover. Do you
therefore want me to release to you the King
of the Jews?"
40 They all shouted again, "Not this Man, but
Barabbas!" Now Barabbas was a robber.

19

Then Pilate took Jesus and flogged
Him. 2 The soldiers twisted a crown of
thorns and put it on His head, and they put a
purple robe on Him. 3 They said, "Hail, King of
the Jews!" And they hit Him with their hands.
4 Again Pilate went out and said to them,
"Look, I am bringing Him out to you, that you
may know that I find no guilt in Him." 5 Then
Jesus came out, wearing the crown of thorns
and the purple robe. Pilate said to them, "Here
is the Man!"
6 When the chief priests and officers saw
Him, they cried out, "Crucify Him! Crucify
Him!"
Pilate said to them, "Take Him yourselves
and crucify Him, for I find no guilt in Him."
7 The Jews answered him, "We have a law,
and by our law He ought to die, because He
made Himself the Son of God!"
8 When Pilate heard these words, he was
more afraid, 9 and entered the Praetorium
again, and said to Jesus, "Where are You
from?" But Jesus gave him no answer. 10 Pilate
said to Him, "Are You not speaking to me? Do
You not know that I have power to release You,
and power to crucify You?"
11 Jesus answered, "You would have no pow-
er at all over Me, unless it were given to you
from above. Therefore he who handed Me over
to you has the greater sin."
12 From then on, Pilate tried to release Him.
But the Jews cried out, "If you release this
Man, you are not Caesar's friend. Whoever
makes himself a king speaks against Caesar!"

13 When Pilate heard these words, he brought
Jesus out and sat down on the judgment seat
at a place called The Pavement (which in He-
brew is Gabbatha). 14 It was the Day of Prepara-
tion of the Passover and about the sixth hour.

He said to the Jews, "Here is your King!"

15 But they shouted, "Away with Him! Away
with Him! Crucify Him!"

Pilate said to them, "Shall I crucify your
King?"

The chief priests answered, "We have no
king but Caesar!"

16 Then he handed Him over to them to be
crucified.

The Crucifixion
Mt 27:32–44; Mk 15:21–32; Lk 23:26–43

So they took Jesus and led Him away. 17 He
went out, carrying His own cross, to a place
called The Place of a Skull, which in Hebrew
is called Golgotha. 18 There they crucified Him,
and two others with Him, one on either side,
and Jesus in the middle.

19 Pilate wrote a title and put it on the cross.
The writing was:

JESUS OF NAZARETH, THE
KING OF THE JEWS.

20 Many of the Jews read this title, for the place
where Jesus was crucified was near the city.
And it was written in Hebrew, in Greek, and in
Latin. 21 The chief priests of the Jews said to
Pilate, "Do not write, 'The King of the Jews,'
but 'He said, I am King of the Jews.'"

22 Pilate answered, "What I have written, I
have written."

23 When the soldiers had crucified Jesus, they
took His garments and divided them into four
parts, a part for each soldier; and also His tu-
nic. Now the tunic was seamless, woven from
top to bottom.

24 So they said to one another, "Let us not
tear it, but cast lots for it to decide whose it
shall be."

This happened to fulfill the Scripture which
says:

"They divided My garments among them,
and for My clothing they cast lots."[1]

Therefore the soldiers did these things.

25 But standing by the cross of Jesus were His
mother, and His mother's sister, Mary the wife
of Clopas, and Mary Magdalene. 26 When Je-
sus saw His mother and the disciple whom He
loved standing nearby, He said to His mother,
"Woman, here is your son." 27 Then He said to
the disciple, "Here is your mother." From that
time, this disciple took her to his own home.

19:13 Mt 27:19
19:14 Mt 27:62
19:15 Lk 23:18
19:17 Lk 23:33
19:19 Mt 27:37
19:20 Jn 19:13
19:21 Jn 19:14
19:23 Lk 23:34
19:24 Ps 22:18
19:25 Lk 23:49
19:26 Jn 13:23
19:27 Jn 16:32

....

19:28 Ps 69:21
19:29 Mt 27:48
19:30 Lk 23:46
19:31 Jn 19:14
19:32 Jn 19:18
19:34 1 Jn 5:6
19:35 Jn 21:24
19:36 Ps 34:20
19:37 Zec 12:10
19:39 SS 4:14
19:40 Jn 11:44
19:41 Lk 23:53
19:42 Jn 19:14
20:1 Mt 27:60
20:2 Jn 13:23

The Death of Jesus
Mt 27:45–56; Mk 15:33–41; Lk 23:44–49

28 After this, Jesus, knowing that everything
was now accomplished, that the Scripture
might be fulfilled, said, "I thirst." 29 A bowl full
of sour wine was placed there. So they put a
sponge full of sour wine on hyssop and held
it to His mouth. 30 When Jesus had received
the sour wine, He said, "It is finished." And He
bowed His head and gave up His spirit.

The Piercing of Jesus' Side

31 Since it was the Day of Preparation, to
prevent bodies from remaining on the cross
on the Sabbath day (for that Sabbath day was
a high day), the Jews asked Pilate that their
legs might be broken, and that they might be
taken away. 32 Therefore the soldiers came and
broke the legs of the first and of the other who
was crucified with Him. 33 But when they came
to Jesus and saw that He was dead already,
they did not break His legs. 34 However, one of
the soldiers pierced His side with a spear, and
immediately blood and water came out. 35 He
who saw it has testified, and his testimony is
true. He knows that he is telling the truth, that
you may believe. 36 For these things happened
so that the Scripture should be fulfilled, "Not
one of His bones shall be broken,"[2] 37 and
again another Scripture says, "They shall look
on Him whom they have pierced."[3]

The Burial of Jesus
Mt 27:57–61; Mk 15:42–47; Lk 23:50–56

38 After this, Joseph of Arimathea, being a
disciple of Jesus, but secretly for fear of the
Jews, asked Pilate that he might take away the
body of Jesus. Pilate gave him permission. So
he came and took away His body. 39 Nicode-
mus, who at first came to Jesus by night, also
came, bringing a mixture of myrrh and aloes,
weighing about seventy-five pounds.[4] 40 Then
they took the body of Jesus and wrapped it in
linen cloths with the spices, as is the burial cus-
tom of the Jews. 41 Now in the place where He
was crucified there was a garden, and in the
garden was a new tomb in which no one had
ever been buried. 42 So because of the Jewish
Day of Preparation, and since the tomb was
nearby, they buried Jesus there.

The Resurrection of Jesus
Mt 28:1–10; Mk 16:1–8; Lk 24:1–12

20 Early on the first day of the week, Mary
Magdalene went to the tomb while it
was still dark and saw that the stone had been
taken away from the tomb. 2 So she came run-
ning to Simon Peter and to the other disciple
whom Jesus loved, and said to them, "They

[1] *24* Ps 22:18. [2] *36* Ex 12:46; Nu 9:12; Ps 34:20. [3] *37* Zec 12:10.
[4] *39* Gk. *a hundred litrai* or 34 kilograms.

SPIRITLED WOMAN

COUNSEL FROM THE SPIRIT BASICS

We Are Created Differently

I realized something this morning that I had not seen quite so clearly before. It jumped out and surprised me today. I was considering that the power of God's Word, which created the universe, is as powerful now as it was in the beginning.

I started thinking about how God breathed the breath of life into the human He created on the sixth day—the pinnacle of His creation. That led me to consider (and here is the picture that took me by surprise) that He created the human differently than the way He created everything else.

Everything else was formed by His Word, but the human was formed by His hands.

The man formed of earth is filled with the life of the heavenlies. Heaven and earth meet, and life as God intended appears. What was not, now had become. When God breathed, He breathed into the human—not around him or over him, but into him.

With the Fall, the man who started out earthy—all earth—was once again earthy. When Jesus, the last Adam, appeared in the earth's environment, once again heaven and earth met. When the day came for the Word to indwell mankind again, He breathed (Jn 20:22).

Jennifer Kennedy Dean

have taken the Lord out of the tomb, and we do
not know where they have put Him."
3 So Peter came out with the other disciple
and they went toward the tomb. 4 They both
ran together, and the other disciple outran Pe-
ter and came to the tomb first. 5 Stooping down
and looking in, he saw the linen cloths lying.
Yet he did not enter. 6 Then Simon Peter came,
following him, and went inside the tomb. He
saw the linen cloths lying there, 7 and the cloth
that was around His head, not lying with the
linen cloths, but wrapped in a place by itself.
8 Then the other disciple, who came first to the
tomb, went in also. He saw and believed. 9 For
as yet they did not know the Scripture, that He
must rise from the dead. 10 Then the disciples
went away again to their own homes.

20:3 Lk 24:12
20:5 Jn 19:40
20:7 Jn 11:44
20:8 Jn 20:4
20:9 Lk 24:26

20:13 Jn 20:15
20:14 Mt 28:9
20:16 Jn 1:38
20:18 Lk 24:10
20:19 Jn 20:26
20:20 Jn 16:22
20:23 Mt 16:19
20:24 Jn 11:16
20:25 Mk 16:11

The Appearance of Jesus to Mary Magdalene

Mk 16:9–11

11 But Mary stood outside at the tomb weep-
ing. As she wept, she stooped down and
looked into the tomb, 12 and she saw two an-
gels in white sitting where the body of Jesus
had lain, one at the head and one at the feet.
13 They said to her, "Woman, why are you
weeping?"

She said to them, "Because they have taken
away my Lord, and I do not know where they
have put Him." 14 When she had said this, she
turned around and saw Jesus standing, but she
did not know that it was Jesus.
15 Jesus said to her, "Woman, why are you
weeping? Whom are you seeking?"

Supposing Him to be the gardener, she said
to Him, "Sir, if You have carried Him away, tell
me where You have put Him, and I will take
Him away."
16 Jesus said to her, "Mary."

She turned and said to Him, "Rabboni!"
(which means Teacher).
17 Jesus said to her, "Stop holding on to Me,
for I have not yet ascended to My Father. But
go to My brothers and tell them, 'I am ascend-
ing to My Father and your Father, to My God
and your God.' "
18 Mary Magdalene came and told the disci-
ples that she had seen the Lord and that He
had said these things to her.

The Appearance of Jesus to His Disciples

Mt 28:16–20; Mk 16:14–18; Lk 24:36–49

19 On the evening of that first day of the week,
the doors being locked where the disciples were
assembled, for fear of the Jews, Jesus came and
stood in their midst, and said to them, "Peace
be with you." 20 When He had said this, He
showed them His hands and His side. The dis-
ciples were then glad when they saw the Lord.
21 So Jesus said to them again, "Peace be with
you. As My Father has sent Me, even so I send
you." 22 When He had said this, He breathed
on them and said to them, "Receive the Holy
Spirit. 23 If you forgive the sins of anyone, they
are forgiven them. If you retain the sins of any-
one, they are retained."

Jesus and Thomas

24 But Thomas, one of the twelve, called The
Twin, was not with them when Jesus came.
25 So the other disciples told him, "We have
seen the Lord!"

But he said to them, "Unless I see the nail
prints in His hands, and put my finger in the

nail prints, and put my hand in His side, I will
not believe."
26 After eight days His disciples were again
inside with the doors shut, and Thomas was
with them. Jesus came and stood among them,
and said, "Peace be with you." 27 Then He said
to Thomas, "Put your finger here, and look at
My hands. Put your hand here and place it in
My side. Do not be faithless, but believing."
28 Thomas answered Him, "My Lord and
my God!"
29 Jesus said to him, "Thomas, because you
have seen Me, you have believed. Blessed
are those who have not seen, and have yet
believed."

The Purpose of the Book

30 Jesus performed many other signs in the
presence of His disciples, which are not written
in this book. 31 But these are written that you
might believe that Jesus is the Christ, the Son
of God, and that believing you may have life
in His name.

The Appearance of Jesus to the Seven Disciples

21 After this, Jesus revealed Himself
again to the disciples at the Sea of Ti-
berias. He revealed Himself this way: 2 Simon
Peter; Thomas, called The Twin; Nathanael of
Cana in Galilee; the sons of Zebedee; and two
more of His disciples were together. 3 Simon
Peter said to them, "I am going fishing." Then
they said to him, "We will go with you." They
went out and immediately entered the boat.
But that night they caught nothing.
4 When the morning came, Jesus stood on
the shore. But the disciples did not know that
it was Jesus.
5 Jesus said to them, "Children, do you have
any fish?"
They answered Him, "No."
6 He said to them, "Throw the net on the right
side of the boat, and you will find some." So
they threw it, and now they were not able to
draw it in because of the abundance of fish.
7 Then the disciple whom Jesus loved said to
Peter, "It is the Lord!" When Simon Peter heard
that it was the Lord, he put on his outer garment,
for he had taken it off, and jumped into the sea.
8 The other disciples came in the little boat, drag-
ging the net full of fish. For they were not far
from land, but about three hundred feet away.[1]
9 When they came to land, they saw a charcoal
fire there with fish lying on it, and bread.
10 Jesus said to them, "Bring some of the
fish which you have just caught." 11 Simon Pe-
ter went up and dragged the net, full of one
hundred and fifty-three large fish, to land.
Although there were so many, the net was
not torn. 12 Jesus said to them, "Come and eat
breakfast." None of the disciples dared ask,
"Who are You?" They knew it was the Lord.
13 Jesus came and took the bread and gave it
to them, and likewise the fish. 14 This was now
the third time that Jesus was revealed to His
disciples after He was raised from the dead.

Jesus and Peter

15 So when they had eaten breakfast, Jesus
said to Simon Peter, "Simon, son of John, do
you love Me more than these?"
He said to Him, "Yes, Lord. You know that
I love You."
He said to him, "Feed My lambs."
16 He said to him again a second time, "Si-
mon, son of John, do you love Me?"
He said to Him, "Yes, Lord. You know that
I love You."
He said to him, "Tend My sheep."
17 He said to him the third time, "Simon, son
of John, do you love Me?"
Peter was grieved because He asked him the
third time, "Do you love Me?" He said to Him,
"Lord, You know everything. You know that I
love You."
Jesus said to him, "Feed My sheep. 18 Truly,
truly I say to you, when you were young, you
dressed yourself and walked where you desired.
But when you are old, you will stretch out your
hands, and another will dress you and carry
you where you do not want to go." 19 He said
this, signifying by what kind of death he would
glorify God. When He had said this, He said to
him, "Follow Me."

Jesus and the Beloved Disciple

20 Peter turned and saw following them the
disciple whom Jesus loved, who also leaned
against His bosom at the supper and had said,
"Lord, who is it that is going to betray You?"
21 When Peter saw him, he said to Jesus, "Lord,
what about this man?"
22 Jesus said to him, "If it is My will that he
remain until I come, what is that to you? Fol-
low Me!" 23 The saying went out among the
brothers that this disciple would not die. Yet
Jesus did not say to him that he would not die,
but, "If it is My will that he remain until I come,
what is that to you?"
24 This is the disciple who testifies about these
things, and wrote these things. We know that
his testimony is true.
25 There are also many other things which
Jesus did. Were every one of them to be
written, I suppose that not even the world
itself could contain the books that would be
written. Amen.

20:26 Jn 20:19
20:27 Jn 20:25
20:29 1Pe 1:8
20:30 Jn 21:25
21:1 Jn 6:1
21:3 Lk 5:5
21:4 Jn 20:14
21:6 Lk 5:4–7
21:7 Jn 13:23
....
21:12 Ac 10:41
21:13 Jn 21:9
21:14 Jn 20:19
21:15 Mt 26:33
21:16 Ac 20:28
21:17 Jn 13:38
21:18 Jn 13:36
21:19 2Pe 1:14
21:20 Jn 21:7
21:21 Ac 1:6–7
21:22 1Co 4:5
21:24 Jn 19:35

[1] 8 About 200 cubits, or 90 meters.

Author: The apostle Luke

Written: AD 62, possibly from Rome or Achaia

Theme: Work of the Holy Spirit and the Apostles, Spread of the Early Church

ACTS

Dear Spirit Led Woman,

I love the fact that this book, which we typically call "Acts" or "the Acts of the Apostles," was called "the Acts of the Holy Spirit" early in church history because the Holy Spirit plays such an important role in its pages by spreading the gospel throughout the world.

As you read the Book of Acts, keep in mind that you were designed by God to live supernaturally as the disciples did. You are a spirit being, and the supernatural realm is where He has called you to walk. When your spirit is awakened to new life in Christ, the relationship you have with God makes it possible for you to be in continual fellowship with Him and to hear His voice. Receiving the fullness of the Holy Spirit equips you to utilize His gifts in all areas of your life, just as the disciples did in the Book of Acts. Read through the pages of Acts with enthusiasm, and be inspired to start recording "the acts of the Holy Spirit"—miracles, dreams, visitations with angels, and other supernatural encounters—in your own life!

Joy F. Strang

The Promise of the Holy Spirit

1 The former treatise have I made, O Theophilus, concerning all that Jesus began both to do and teach, 2 until the day when He was taken up, after He had given commandments through the Holy Spirit to the apostles whom He had chosen, 3 to whom He presented Himself alive after His passion by many infallible proofs, appearing to them for forty days, and speaking concerning the kingdom of God. 4 Being assembled with them, He commanded them, "Do not depart from Jerusalem, but wait for the promise of the Father, of which you have heard from Me.[1] 5 For John baptized with water, but you shall be baptized with the Holy Spirit not many days from now."

The Ascension

6 So when they had come together, they asked Him, "Lord, will You at this time restore the kingdom to Israel?"

7 He said to them, "It is not for you to know the times or the dates, which the Father has fixed by His own authority. 8 But you shall receive power when the Holy Spirit comes upon you. And you shall be My witnesses in Jerusalem, and in all Judea and Samaria, and to the ends of the earth."

> Father, Your Word declares that I shall receive power when the Holy Spirit comes upon me (Ac 1:8).

9 When He had spoken these things, while they looked, He was taken up. And a cloud received Him from their sight.

10 While they looked intently toward heaven as He ascended, suddenly two men stood by them in white garments. 11 They said, "Men of Galilee, why stand looking toward heaven? This same Jesus, who was taken up from you to heaven, will come in like manner as you saw Him go into heaven."

Judas' Successor

12 Then they returned to Jerusalem from the Mount of Olives, which is a Sabbath day's walk[2] from Jerusalem. 13 When they had entered, they went up into the upper room, where they were staying: Peter, James, John, and Andrew; Philip and Thomas; Bartholomew and Matthew; James the son of Alphaeus and Simon the Zealot; and Judas the son of James. 14 These all continued with one accord in prayer and supplication, with the women and Mary the mother of Jesus, and with His brothers.

15 In those days Peter stood up among the disciples (the number of people together was about a hundred and twenty), and said, 16 "Brothers, this Scripture had to be fulfilled, which the Holy Spirit previously spoke by the mouth of David concerning Judas, who became the guide to those who seized Jesus. 17 For he was numbered with us and took part in this ministry."

18 (Now this man purchased a field with the reward of iniquity. And falling headlong, he burst asunder in the middle and all his organs spilled out. 19 It became known to all the residents of Jerusalem. So this field is called in their dialect Akeldama, that is, Field of Blood.)

20 "For it is written in the Book of Psalms,

'Let his habitation become desolate,
and let no one live in it,'[3]

and,

'Let another take his office.'[4]

21 Therefore, of these men who have accompanied us while the Lord Jesus went in and out among us, 22 beginning from the baptism of John until the very day that He was taken up from us, one of these men must become with us a witness of His resurrection."

23 So they proposed two, Joseph, called Barsabbas, who was surnamed Justus, and Matthias. 24 Then they prayed, "You, Lord, who knows the hearts of all men, show which of these two You have chosen 25 to take the place in this ministry and apostleship, from which Judas by transgression fell, to go to his own place." 26 Then they cast lots, and the lot fell on Matthias. So he was numbered with the eleven apostles.

The Coming of the Holy Spirit

2 When the day of Pentecost had come, they were all together in one place. 2 Suddenly a sound like a mighty rushing wind came from heaven, and it filled the whole house where they were sitting. 3 There appeared to them tongues as of fire, being distributed and resting on each of them, 4 and they were all filled with the Holy Spirit and began to speak in other tongues, as the Spirit enabled them to speak.

5 Now dwelling in Jerusalem were Jews, devout men, from every nation under heaven. 6 When this sound occurred, the crowd came together and were confounded, because each man heard them speaking in his own language. 7 They were all amazed and marveled, saying to each other, "Are not all these who are speaking Galileans? 8 How is it that we hear, each in our own native language? 9 Parthians, Medes and Elamites, residents of Mesopotamia, Judea and Cappadocia, Pontus and Asia,

1:1 Lk 1:3
1:2 Jn 13:18
1:3 1Co 15:5–7
1:4 Lk 24:49
1:5 Mt 3:11
1:6 Mt 17:11
1:7 Mt 24:36
1:8 Mt 28:19
1:9 Ac 1:2
1:10 Lk 24:4
1:11 Ac 2:7
1:12 Lk 24:52
1:13 Mt 10:2–4
1:14 Mt 12:46
....
1:16 Mt 26:47
1:17 Ac 1:25
1:18 Mt 27:3–10
1:20 Ps 69:25
1:22 Ac 1:2
1:23 Ac 15:22
1:24 1Sa 16:7
1:26 Lev 16:8
2:1 Ac 20:16
2:2 Ac 4:31
2:3 Mt 3:11
2:4 Mk 16:17
2:5 Ac 8:2
2:7 Ac 1:11
2:9 1Pe 1:1

[1]4 Lk 24:49. [2]12 About half a mile. [3]20 Ps 69:25. [4]20 Ps 109:8.

SPIRIT-TO-SPIRIT PRAYER

PRAYER FOR THE POWER OF THE HOLY SPIRIT

Father God, I thank You for the power of the Holy Spirit residing in me to overcome all the evil strategies of the enemy. Thank You because You have given me the ability to walk in the Spirit. Thank You because the same power that raised Christ from the dead dwells in me. I will not fear, but I will continue walking in the spirit. For it's "not by might nor by power, but by My Spirit, says the LORD of Hosts" (Zec 4:6).

Iris Delgado

10 Phrygia and Pamphylia, Egypt and the regions of Libya near Cyrene, and visitors from Rome, both Jews and proselytes, 11 Cretans and Arabs—we hear them speaking in our own languages the mighty works of God." 12 They were all amazed and perplexed, saying to each other, "What does this mean?"

13 Others mocking said, "These men are full of new wine."

Peter's Speech at Pentecost

14 But Peter, standing up with the eleven, lifted up his voice and said to them, "Men of Judea and all you who dwell in Jerusalem, let this be known to you, and listen to my words.
15 For these are not drunk, as you suppose, since it is the third hour of the day. 16 But this is what was spoken by the prophet Joel:

17 'In the last days it shall be,' says God,
'that I will pour out My Spirit on all flesh;
your sons and your daughters shall prophesy,
your young men shall see visions,
and your old men shall dream dreams.
18 Even on My menservants and maidservants
I will pour out My Spirit in those days;
and they shall prophesy.
19 And I will show wonders in heaven above
and signs on the earth below:
blood, and fire, and vapor of smoke.
20 The sun shall be turned into darkness,
and the moon into blood,
before that great and glorious day of the
Lord comes.
21 And whoever calls
on the name of the Lord shall be saved.'[1]

2:10 Ac 13:13
2:11 Ex 15:11
2:13 1Co 14:23
2:14 Ac 1:26
2:17 Isa 44:3
2:20 Mt 24:29
2:21 Ac 22:16

2:22 Jn 3:2
2:23 Lk 22:22
2:24 Ac 2:32
2:25 Ps 16:8–11
2:27 Ac 2:31
2:29 1Ki 2:10
2:30 2Sa 23:2
2:31 Ac 2:27
2:32 Ac 2:24
2:33 Ac 1:4

22 "Men of Israel, hear these words: Jesus of Nazareth was a man attested to you by God with powerful works and wonders and signs, which God did through Him in your midst, as you yourselves know. 23 You have taken Him, who was handed over to you by the ordained counsel and foreknowledge of God, and by lawless hands have crucified and killed Him, 24 whom God raised up by loosening the pull of death, because it was not possible that He should be held by it. 25 For David says concerning Him:

'I foresaw the Lord always before me,
for He is at my right hand,
that I may not be shaken.
26 Therefore my heart was glad, and my
tongue rejoiced;
moreover my flesh will dwell in hope.
27 For You will not abandon my soul to Hades,
nor will You allow Your Holy One to see
corruption.
28 You have made known to me the ways
of life;
You will make me full of joy with Your
presence.'[2]

29 "Brothers, I may speak confidently to you concerning the patriarch David, that he both died and was buried, and his tomb is with us to this day. 30 But being a prophet, and knowing that God had sworn with an oath to him, that of his seed according to the flesh, He would raise up the Christ to sit on his throne, 31 he foresaw this and spoke concerning the resurrection of the Christ, that His soul was not abandoned to Hades, nor did His flesh see corruption. 32 God raised up this Jesus, of which we all are witnesses. 33 Therefore being exalted to the right hand

[1] *16–21* Joel 2:28–32. [2] *25–28* Ps 16:8–11.

of God, and having received from the Father the promise of the Holy Spirit, He has poured out this which you now see and hear. 34 For David has not ascended to the heavens, yet he says:

'The Lord said to my Lord,
"Sit at My right hand,
35 Until I make Your enemies
Your footstool." '[1]

36 "Therefore, let all the house of Israel assuredly know that God has made this Jesus, whom you have crucified, both Lord and Christ."

37 When they heard this, they were stung in the heart and said to Peter and to the rest of the apostles, "Brothers, what shall we do?"

38 Peter said to them, "Repent and be baptized, every one of you, in the name of Jesus Christ for the forgiveness of sins, and you shall receive the gift of the Holy Spirit. 39 For the promise is to you, and to your children, and to all who are far away, as many as the Lord our God will call."

40 With many other words he testified and exhorted them, saying, "Be saved from this perverse generation." 41 Then those who gladly received his word were baptized, and that day about three thousand souls were added to them.

Life Among the Believers

42 They continued steadfastly in the apostles' teaching and fellowship, in the breaking of bread and in the prayers. 43 Fear came to every soul. And many wonders and signs were done through the apostles. 44 All who believed were together and had all things in common. 45 They sold their property and goods and distributed them to all, according to their need. 46 And continuing daily with one mind in the temple, and breaking bread from house to house, they ate their food with gladness and simplicity of heart, 47 praising God and having favor with all the people. And the Lord added to the church daily those who were being saved.

The Lame Man Healed at the Temple Gate

3 Now Peter and John went up together to the temple at the ninth hour, the hour of prayer. 2 A man lame from birth was being carried, whom people placed daily at the gate of the temple called Beautiful to ask alms from those who entered the temple. 3 Seeing Peter and John about to go into the temple, he asked for alms. 4 Peter, gazing at him with John, said, "Look at us." 5 So he paid attention to them, expecting to receive something from them.

6 Then Peter said, "I have no silver and gold, but I give you what I have. In the name of Jesus Christ of Nazareth, rise up and walk." 7 He took him by the right hand and raised him up. Immediately his feet and ankles were strengthened. 8 Jumping up, he stood and walked and entered the temple with them, walking and jumping and praising God. 9 All the people saw him walking and praising God. 10 They knew that it was he who sat for alms at the Beautiful Gate of the temple. And they were filled with wonder and amazement at what happened to him.

Peter's Speech at Solomon's Porch

11 As the lame man who was healed held on to Peter and John, all the people ran together to them in the entrance that is called Solomon's Porch, greatly amazed. 12 When Peter saw it, he answered the people: "Men of Israel, why do you marvel at this man? Or why do you stare at us, as if by our own power or piety we had made him walk? 13 The God of Abraham and Isaac and Jacob, the God of our fathers, has glorified His Son Jesus, whom you handed over and denied in the presence of Pilate, when he had decided to release Him. 14 You denied the Holy and Righteous One and asked for a murderer to be granted to you, 15 and you killed the Creator of Life, whom God has raised from the dead, of which we are witnesses. 16 And His name, by faith in His name, has made this man strong, whom you see and know. And faith which comes through Him has given him perfect health in your presence.

17 "Now brothers, I know that you acted in ignorance, as did also your rulers. 18 But what God foretold through all the prophets, that His Christ should suffer, He thus fulfilled. 19 Therefore repent and be converted, that your sins may be wiped away, that times of refreshing may come from the presence of the Lord, 20 and that He may send the One who previously was preached to you, Jesus Christ, 21 whom the heavens must receive until the time of restoring what God spoke through all His holy prophets since the world began. 22 For Moses indeed said to the fathers, 'The Lord your God will raise up for you a prophet like me from your brothers. You shall hear whatever He may say to you. 23 And it shall be that every soul who will not hear that prophet shall be utterly eliminated from the people.'[2]

24 "Indeed, all the prophets since Samuel and those who follow, as many as have spoken, have likewise foretold these days. 25 You are the sons of the prophets and of the covenant which God made with our fathers, saying to Abraham, 'And in your seed shall all the families of the earth be blessed.'[3] 26 God, having raised up His Son Jesus, sent Him to you first, to bless you in turning every one of you from your iniquities."

2:34 Ps 110:1
2:37 Lk 3:10
2:38 Lk 24:47
2:39 Joel 2:32
2:40 Mt 17:17
2:42 Ac 1:14
2:44 Ac 4:32
2:46 Ac 5:42
2:47 Ac 11:24
3:1 Ps 55:17
3:2 Lk 16:20
3:6 Ac 3:16
....
3:8 Ac 14:10
3:10 Ac 3:2
3:11 Jn 10:23
3:13 Mt 22:32
3:14 Mk 1:24
3:15 Ac 2:24
3:16 Ac 3:6
3:17 Lk 23:34
3:18 Ac 26:22–23
3:19 Ac 2:38
3:21 Lk 1:70
3:22 Ac 7:37
3:23 Dt 18:19
3:25 Ge 22:18
3:26 Ac 3:22

[1] *34–35* Ps 110:1. [2] *23* Dt 18:15, 18–19. [3] *25* Ge 22:18; 26:4.

Peter and John Before the Sanhedrin

4 As they spoke to the people, the priests, the captain of the temple, and the Sadducees came upon them, 2 being greatly troubled because they taught the people and preached through Jesus the resurrection from the dead. 3 And they seized them and put them in custody until the next day, for it was already evening. 4 But many of those who heard the word believed, and the number of the men grew to about five thousand.

5 On the next day their rulers and elders and scribes 6 were assembled at Jerusalem with Annas the high priest, and Caiaphas, and John and Alexander, and all who were of the family of the high priest. 7 When they had stood them in the midst, they asked, "By what power or by what name have you done this?"

8 Then Peter, filled with the Holy Spirit, said to them, "Rulers of the people and elders of Israel: 9 If we today are being examined concerning a good deed done to a crippled man, how this man has been healed, 10 be it known to you all, and to all the people of Israel, that by the name of Jesus Christ of Nazareth, whom you crucified, whom God raised from the dead, by Him this man stands before you whole. 11 He is

'the stone you builders rejected,
 which has become the cornerstone.'[1]

12 There is no salvation in any other, for there is no other name under heaven given among men by which we must be saved."

13 When they saw the boldness of Peter and John and perceived that they were illiterate and uneducated men, they marveled. And they recognized that they had been with Jesus. 14 But seeing the man who was healed standing with them, they had nothing to say against it. 15 So when they had commanded them to go outside of the Sanhedrin, they conferred among themselves, 16 saying, "What shall we do to these men? For, indeed, that an acknowledged miracle has been done through them is revealed to all who dwell in Jerusalem, and we cannot deny it. 17 But lest it spread further among the people, let us threaten them that they no longer speak to anyone in this name."

18 Then they called them and commanded them not to speak or teach at all in the name of Jesus. 19 But Peter and John answered them, "Whether it is right in the sight of God to listen to you more than to God, you judge. 20 For we cannot help but declare what we have seen and heard."

21 When they had further threatened them, they let them go, finding no way to punish them, because of the people. For all glorified God for what was done, 22 for the man on whom this miracle of healing was performed was over forty years old.

The Believers Pray for Boldness

23 On being released, they went to their own people and reported what the chief priests and elders had said to them. 24 When they heard this, they lifted their voices in unity to God and prayed, "Lord, You are God, who has made the heaven and the earth and the sea and everything in them, 25 and who by the mouth of Your servant David said:

'Why did the nations rage,
 and the people devise vain things?
26 The kings of the earth came,
 and the rulers were assembled together
against the Lord
 and against His Christ.'[2]

27 Indeed, both Herod and Pontius Pilate, with the Gentiles and the people of Israel, were assembled together against Your holy Son Jesus whom You have anointed, 28 to do what Your hand and Your counsel had foreordained to be done. 29 Now, Lord, look on their threats and grant that Your servants may speak Your word with great boldness, 30 by stretching out Your hand to heal and that signs and wonders may be performed in the name of Your holy Son Jesus."

31 When they had prayed, the place where they were assembled together was shaken. And they were all filled with the Holy Spirit and spoke the word of God with boldness.

All Things in Common

32 All the believers were of one heart and one soul, and no one said that what he possessed was his own. But to them all things were in common. 33 With great power the apostles testified to the resurrection of the Lord Jesus, and great grace was on them all. 34 There was no one among them who lacked, for all those who were owners of land or houses sold them, and brought the income from what was sold, 35 and placed it at the apostles' feet. And it was distributed to each according to his need.

Let great power be released through Your apostles (Ac 4:33).

36 Joseph, whom the apostles called Barnabas (which means, Son of Encouragement), a Levite from the land of Cyprus, 37 sold a field he owned, and brought the money and placed it at the apostles' feet.

4:1 Lk 22:4
4:2 Ac 17:18
4:3 Ac 5:18
4:4 Ac 2:41
4:5 Ac 4:8
4:6 Lk 3:2
4:8 Ac 2:4
4:9 Ac 3:7
4:10 Ac 3:6
4:11 Isa 28:16
4:12 Mt 1:21
4:13 Jn 7:15
4:17 Ac 5:28
4:18 Ac 5:40
4:19 Ac 5:29
4:20 Ac 22:15
4:21 Ac 5:26

4:24 Ne 9:6
4:25 Ac 1:16
4:27 Mt 27:2
4:28 Ac 2:23
4:29 Ac 4:13
4:30 Ac 4:27
4:31 Ac 2:2
4:33 Ac 1:8
4:34 Ac 2:45
4:35 Ac 5:2
4:36 1Co 9:6

[1] *11* Ps 118:22. [2] *25–26* Ps 2:1–2.

Anananias and Sapphira

5 Now a man named Ananias, with his wife
Sapphira, sold a piece of property. 2 He
kept back part of the proceeds with his wife's
knowledge, and brought a part of it and placed
it at the apostles' feet.
3 Then Peter said, "Ananias, why has Satan
filled your heart to deceive the Holy Spirit and
keep back part of the proceeds of the land?
4 While it remained unsold, was it not your
own? And when it was sold, was it not under
your authority? Why have you conceived this
deed in your heart? You did not lie to men,
but to God."
5 On hearing these words, Ananias fell down
and died. And great fear came on all those
who heard these things. 6 The young men rose
and wrapped him up and carried him out and
buried him.
7 About three hours later his wife came in,
not knowing what had happened. 8 Peter said
to her, "Tell me whether you sold the land for
this amount?"
She said, "Yes, for that much."
9 Peter said to her, "How is it that you have
agreed together to test the Spirit of the Lord?
Look! The feet of those who have buried your
husband are at the door, and they will carry
you out."
10 At once she fell down at his feet and died.
Upon entering, the young men found her dead
and carried her out and buried her beside her
husband. 11 Great fear came on the entire
church and on all those who heard these things.

Signs and Wonders

12 Many signs and wonders were performed
among the people by the hands of the apos-
tles. And they were all together in Solomon's
Porch. 13 No one else dared join them, but the
people respected them. 14 Believers were in-
creasingly added to the Lord, crowds of both
men and women, 15 so that they even brought
the sick out into the streets and placed them
on beds and mats, that at least the shadow of
Peter passing by might touch some of them.
16 Crowds also came out of the cities surround-
ing Jerusalem, bringing the sick and those
who were afflicted by evil spirits, and they
were all healed.

Persecution of the Apostles

17 Then the high priest and all those who
were with him (that is, the sect of the Saddu-
cees) rose up and were filled with jealousy.
18 They seized the apostles and put them in
the common prison. 19 But during the night
an angel of the Lord opened the prison doors
and led them out, and said, 20 "Go, stand and
speak in the temple to the people all the words
of this life."
21 Having heard this, they entered the temple
at dawn and taught.
But the high priest and those who were with
him came and called together the Sanhedrin
and the senate of all the sons of Israel, and sent
to the prison to have them brought out. 22 But
when the officers came and did not find them
in the prison, they returned and reported, 23 "We
found the prison securely shut and the guards
standing outside before the doors. But when
we opened it, we found no one inside." 24 Now
when the high priest, the captain of the temple,
and the chief priests heard these things, they
were in doubt of what might become of this.
25 Then one came and told them, "Look, the
men whom you put in prison are standing in
the temple and teaching the people." 26 Then
the captain with his escorts went and brought
them, without force lest they should be stoned,
for they feared the people.
27 When they had brought them, they stood
them before the Sanhedrin. And the high priest
questioned them, 28 saying, "Did we not strict-
ly command you not to teach in this name?
Yet now you have filled Jerusalem with your
teaching, and you intend to bring on us this
Man's blood."
29 Peter and the other apostles answered, "We
must obey God rather than men. 30 The God of
our fathers raised Jesus, whom you killed by
hanging on a tree. 31 God exalted this Man to
His right hand to be a Ruler and a Savior, to
give repentance to Israel and forgiveness of
sins. 32 We are His witnesses to these words,
as is the Holy Spirit whom God has given to
those who obey Him."

I obey God rather than man (Ac 5:29).

33 When they heard this, they were cut to the
heart and took counsel to kill them. 34 But a
Pharisee in the Sanhedrin named Gamaliel, a
teacher of the law honored by all the people,
stood and ordered the apostles to be put out-
side for a little while. 35 Then he said to them,
"Men of Israel, take heed to yourselves what
you intend to do concerning these men. 36 For
in previous days Theudas rose up, boasting
to be somebody, to whom a number of about
four hundred men joined themselves. He was
killed, and all who obeyed him were dispersed
and came to nothing. 37 After Theudas, Judas
the Galilean rose up in the days of the census
and drew away many people after him. This
man also perished, and all who obeyed him

5:2 Ac 4:37
5:3 Jn 13:2
5:4 Ac 5:3
5:5 Ac 5:10–11
5:6 Jn 19:40
5:9 Ac 5:3–4
5:11 Ac 5:5
5:12 Ac 3:11
5:13 Ac 2:47
5:14 Ac 2:47
5:15 Mt 14:36
5:16 Mk 16:17–18
5:18 Ac 4:3
5:19 Ac 8:26
5:20 Jn 6:63
....
5:21 Jn 8:2
5:24 Ac 4:1
5:26 Ac 5:13
5:28 Mt 27:25
5:29 Ac 4:19
5:30 Ac 10:39
5:31 Lk 24:47
5:33 Ac 2:37
5:34 Ac 22:3
5:36 Ac 8:9
5:37 Lk 2:1–2

were scattered. 38 Now I tell you, keep away
from these men and leave them alone, because
if this intention or this activity is of men, it will
come to nothing. 39 But if it is of God, you will
not be able to overthrow them, lest perhaps
you be found even fighting against God."
40 They agreed with him. When they had
called in the apostles, they beat them, and
commanded them not to speak in the name
of Jesus, and released them.
41 Then they departed from the presence of
the Sanhedrin, rejoicing that they were count-
ed worthy to suffer shame for His name. 42 Dai-
ly, in the temple and from house to house, they
did not cease to teach and preach Jesus Christ.

The Seven Helpers

6 Now in those days, as the disciples were
multiplied, there was murmuring among
the Hellenists against the Hebrews, because
their widows were overlooked in the daily dis-
tribution. 2 So the twelve called the multitude of
disciples together and said, "It is not reasonable
for us to leave the word of God and serve tables.
3 Brothers, look among yourselves for seven
men who are known to be full of the Holy Spirit
and of wisdom, whom we will appoint over this
duty. 4 But we will give ourselves continually to
prayer and to the ministry of the word."
5 And what was said pleased the whole multi-
tude, and they chose Stephen, who was a man
full of faith and of the Holy Spirit, and Philip,
and Procorus, and Nicanor, and Timon, and
Parmenas, and Nicolas, a proselyte from An-
tioch, 6 whom they presented before the apos-
tles. And when they had prayed, they placed
their hands on them.
7 So the word of God spread, and the number
of the disciples grew rapidly in Jerusalem, and
a great number of the priests were obedient
to the faith.

The Arrest of Stephen

8 Now Stephen, full of faith and power, did
great wonders and miracles among the people.
9 Then some men rose up from what is called
the Synagogue of the Freedmen (Cyrenians,
Alexandrians, and those from Cilicia and of
Asia), disputing with Stephen. 10 But they were
not able to withstand the wisdom and the Spirit
by which he spoke.
11 Then they secretly instigated men who
said, "We have heard him speak blasphemous
words against Moses and God."
12 So they stirred up the people and the el-
ders and the scribes, and came upon him and
seized him and led him to the Sanhedrin, 13 and
set up false witnesses who said, "This man
does not cease to speak blasphemous words
against this holy place and the law. 14 For we
have heard him say that this Jesus of Naza-
reth will destroy this place, and will change
the customs which Moses handed down to us."
15 All who sat in the Sanhedrin, gazing at him,
saw his face as the face of an angel.

Stephen's Speech

7 Then the high priest said, "Are these
things so?"
2 He said, "Brothers and fathers, listen! The
God of glory appeared to our father Abraham,
when he was in Mesopotamia, before he lived
in Harran, 3 and said to him, 'Leave your coun-
try and your relatives, and come to the land
which I will show you.'[1]
4 "Then he departed from the land of the
Chaldeans and lived in Harran. When his father
died, He removed him from there to this land
in which you now live. 5 He gave him no inheri-
tance in it, nor a foothold, and promised to give
it to him as a possession and to his descendants
after him while he had no child. 6 God spoke in
this way, 'Your descendants shall be sojourners
in a land belonging to others, who will enslave
them and mistreat them four hundred years.[2]
7 And I will judge the nation to whom they will
be enslaved,'[3] said God. 'After that they shall
come out and worship Me in this place.'[4] 8 Then
He gave him the covenant of circumcision.
And Abraham became the father of Isaac and
circumcised him on the eighth day. And Isaac
became the father of Jacob, and Jacob of the
twelve patriarchs.
9 "The patriarchs, moved with envy, sold Jo-
seph into Egypt. But God was with him, 10 and
delivered him out of all his afflictions, and
gave him favor and wisdom before Pharaoh,
king of Egypt, who appointed him governor
over Egypt and all his house.
11 "Then a famine came over all Egypt and
Canaan with great affliction, and our fathers
found no sustenance. 12 But when Jacob heard
that there was grain in Egypt, he sent out our
fathers the first time. 13 During the second time
Joseph was made known to his brothers, and
Joseph's family became known to Pharaoh.
14 Then Joseph sent and called for his father
Jacob and all his kindred, seventy-five souls.
15 Then Jacob went down into Egypt. And he
and our fathers died, 16 and were carried to
Shechem and put in the tomb that Abraham
had bought for a price of silver from the sons
of Hamor, the father of Shechem.
17 "When the time of the promise drew near,
which God had sworn to Abraham, the people
grew and multiplied in Egypt 18 until another
king rose up who did not know Joseph.[5] 19 He

5:40 Mt 10:17
5:41 Jn 15:21
5:42 Ac 2:46
6:1 Ac 4:35
6:4 Ac 1:14
6:5 Ac 11:24
6:6 Ac 1:24
6:7 Ac 12:24
6:9 Mt 27:32
6:10 Lk 21:15
6:11 Mt 26:59–60
6:15 Ecc 8:1
7:2 Ge 11:31
7:3 Ge 12:1
7:4 Ge 12:4–5
7:5 Ge 12:7
7:6 Ge 15:13
7:7 Ex 3:12
7:8 Ge 17:9–14
7:9 Ge 39:2
7:10 Ge 42:6
7:11 Ps 105:16
7:14 Dt 10:22
7:15 Ge 49:33
7:16 Jos 24:32
7:18 Ex 1:8

[1] *3* Ge 12:1. [2] *6* Ge 15:13. [3] *7* Ge 15:14. [4] *7* Ex 3:12. [5] *18* Ex 1:8.

dealt deceitfully with our people and mistreated our fathers, forcing them to put out their young children, that they might not live.

20 “At that time Moses was born, and was fair in the sight of God. And he was reared for three months in his father’s house. 21 When he was put out, Pharaoh’s daughter took him up and reared him as her own son. 22 Moses was educated in all the wisdom of the Egyptians and was powerful in words and in deeds.

23 “When he was forty years old, it came to his heart to visit his brothers, the sons of Israel. 24 But seeing one being wronged, he defended him, and avenged him who was oppressed, and struck the Egyptian. 25 He supposed that his brothers would understand that God would deliver them by his hand, but they did not understand. 26 On the next day he appeared to them as they fought and tried to reconcile them in peace, saying, ‘Men, you are brothers. Why do you wrong each other?’[1]

27 “But the one wronging his neighbor pushed him away, saying, ‘Who appointed you a ruler and a judge over us? 28 Will you kill me as you killed the Egyptian yesterday?’[2] 29 Moses fled at this word and became a sojourner in the land of Midian,[3] where he became the father of two sons.

30 “When forty years had passed, an angel of the Lord appeared to him in the wilderness of Mount Sinai, in a flame of fire in a bush.[4] 31 When Moses saw it, he marveled at the sight. As he drew near to look at it, the voice of the Lord came to him, saying, 32 ‘I am the God of your fathers, the God of Abraham and the God of Isaac and the God of Jacob.’[5] Moses trembled and dared not look.

33 “Then the Lord said to him, ‘Take off the shoes from your feet, for the place where you are standing is holy ground.[6] 34 I have indeed seen the oppression of My people who are in Egypt. I have heard their groaning, and I have come down to deliver them. Now come, I will send you to Egypt.’[7]

35 “This Moses, whom they rejected, saying, ‘Who appointed you a ruler and a judge?’[8] God sent as both ruler and redeemer by the hand of the angel who appeared to him in the bush. 36 He led them out after he had shown wonders and signs in the land of Egypt, and at the Red Sea, and for forty years in the wilderness.

37 “This is the Moses who said to the sons of Israel, ‘The Lord your God will raise up for you a prophet like me from your brothers. Him you shall hear.’[9] 38 This is he who was in the congregation in the wilderness with the angel who spoke to him on Mount Sinai, and with our fathers, who received living oracles to give to us, 39 whom our fathers would not obey, but thrust away. And in their hearts they turned back to Egypt, 40 saying to Aaron, ‘Make for us gods to go before us. For we do not know what has become of this Moses, who led us out of the land of Egypt.’[10] 41 So they made a calf in those days, and offered a sacrifice to the idol, and rejoiced in the works of their hands. 42 But God turned and gave them up to worship the host of heaven, as it is written in the book of the Prophets:

‘O House of Israel, have you offered to Me
slain animals and sacrifices
for forty years in the wilderness?
43 Yes, you even raised the shrine of Moloch,
and the star of your god Remphan,
idols which you made to worship;
therefore I will exile you beyond Babylon.’[11]

44 “Our fathers had the tabernacle of witness in the wilderness, telling Moses to make it as He had commanded, according to the pattern that he had seen, 45 which our fathers, having received it, brought with Joshua into the land possessed by the Gentiles, whom God drove out in front of our fathers until the days of David, 46 who found favor in the presence of God and asked to find a tabernacle for the God of Jacob. 47 But Solomon built Him a house.

48 “However, the Most High does not dwell in houses made with hands. As the prophet says:

49 ‘Heaven is My throne,
and the earth is My footstool.
What house will you build for Me? says the Lord,
or what is the place of My rest?
50 Has not My hand made all these things?’[12]

51 “You stiff-necked people, uncircumcised in heart and ears! You always resist the Holy Spirit. As your fathers did, so do you. 52 Which of the prophets have your fathers not persecuted? They have even killed those who foretold the coming of the Righteous One, of whom you have now become the betrayers and murderers, 53 who have received the law by the disposition of angels, but have not kept it.”

The Stoning of Stephen

54 When they heard these things, they were cut to the heart, and they gnashed their teeth at him. 55 But being full of the Holy Spirit, he gazed into heaven and saw the glory of God, and Jesus standing at the right hand of God, 56 and said, “Look! I see the heavens opened and the Son of Man standing at the right hand of God.”

57 Then they cried out with a loud voice, closed their ears, and rushed at him in unison. 58 And they threw him out of the city and

7:20 Heb 11:23
7:22 Isa 19:11
7:27 Ac 7:35
7:30 Ac 7:35
7:31 Ex 3:3–4
7:32 Ex 3:6
7:33 Ex 3:5
7:34 Ex 3:7–10
7:36 Ex 12:41
7:38 Ro 3:2
7:39 Nu 14:3–4
7:40 Ex 32:1
7:42 Jer 19:13
7:44 Ex 25:40
7:45 Ps 44:2
7:46 Ps 132:1–5
7:47 1Ki 8:20
7:48 1Ki 8:27
7:49 Mt 5:34–35
7:51 Ex 32:9
7:52 Mt 5:12
7:53 Gal 3:19
7:54 Ac 5:33
7:56 Mt 3:16
7:58 Ac 22:20

[1] *26* Ex 2:13. [2] *28* Ex 2:14. [3] *29* Ex 2:11–15. [4] *30* Ex 3:1–4. [5] *32* Ex 3:6. [6] *33* Ex 3:5. [7] *34* Ex 3:7, 10. [8] *35* Ex 2:14. [9] *37* Dt 18:15. [10] *40* Ex 32:1, 23. [11] *42–43* Am 5:25–27. [12] *49–50* Isa 66:1–2.

stoned him. The witnesses laid down their gar-
ments at the feet of a young man named Saul.
59 They stoned Stephen as he was calling on
God, praying, "Lord Jesus, receive my spirit."
60 Then he knelt down and cried with a loud
voice, "Lord, do not hold this sin against them."
Having said this, he fell asleep.

8 And Saul was consenting to his death.

Saul Persecutes the Church

On that day a great persecution broke out
against the church in Jerusalem. And they
were all scattered throughout the regions of
Judea and Samaria, except the apostles. 2 De-
vout men carried Stephen to his burial and
made great lamentation over him. 3 But Saul
ravaged the church, entering house by house
and dragging out both men and women and
committing them to prison.

The Gospel Preached in Samaria

4 Therefore those who were scattered went
everywhere preaching the word. 5 Philip went
down to the city of Samaria and preached
Christ to them. 6 When the crowds heard Phil-
ip and saw the miracles which he did, they
listened in unity to what he said. 7 For unclean
spirits, crying with a loud voice, came out of
many who were possessed. And many who
were paralyzed or lame were healed. 8 So there
was much joy in that city.

Simon the Sorcerer Believes

9 Now a man named Simon was previously
in the city practicing sorcery and astonishing
the nation of Samaria, saying he was some-
one great, 10 to whom they all listened, from the
least to the greatest, saying, "This man is the
great power of God." 11 They listened to him, be-
cause for a long time he had astonished them
by his sorceries. 12 But when they believed Phil-
ip preaching about the kingdom of God and the
name of Jesus Christ, both men and women
were baptized. 13 Even Simon himself believed.
And when he was baptized, he continued with
Philip and was amazed as he watched the mir-
acles and signs which were done.

Samaritans Receive the Holy Spirit

14 Now when the apostles who were at Je-
rusalem heard that Samaria had received the
word of God, they sent Peter and John to them.
15 When they came down, they prayed for them
that they might receive the Holy Spirit, 16 for
still He had come on none of them. They were
only baptized in the name of the Lord Jesus.
17 Then they laid their hands on them, and they
received the Holy Spirit.

18 When Simon saw that through the laying
on of the apostles' hands the Holy Spirit was
given, he offered them money, 19 saying, "Give
me also this power, that whomever I lay hands
on may receive the Holy Spirit."

20 Peter said to him, "May your money per-
ish with you, because you thought you could
purchase the gift of God with money! 21 You
have neither part nor share in this matter, for
your heart is not right before God. 22 There-
fore repent of your wickedness, and ask God
if perhaps the intention of your heart may be
forgiven you. 23 For I see that you are in the
gall of bitterness and in the bond of iniquity."

24 Then Simon answered, "Pray to the Lord
for me that nothing you have spoken may
come upon me."

25 When they had testified and preached the
word of the Lord, they returned to Jerusalem
and preached the gospel in many villages of
the Samaritans.

Philip and the Ethiopian Eunuch

26 Now an angel of the Lord said to Philip,
"Rise up and go toward the south on the way
that goes down from Jerusalem to Gaza." This
is desert. 27 So he rose up and went. And there
was a man of Ethiopia, a eunuch of great
authority under Candace, queen of the Ethi-
opians, who was in command of her entire
treasury. He had come to Jerusalem to wor-
ship. 28 He was returning, sitting in his chariot
and reading the book of Isaiah the prophet.
29 The Spirit said to Philip, "Go to this chariot
and stay with it."

30 Then Philip ran to him, and heard him read
the book of Isaiah the prophet, and said, "Do
you understand what you are reading?"

31 He said, "How can I, unless someone
guides me?" So he invited Philip to come up
and sit with him.

32 The passage of Scripture which he was
reading was this:

"He was led as a sheep to slaughter;
and as a lamb before its shearer is silent,
so He opened not His mouth.
33 In His humiliation justice was denied Him;
who will speak of His generation?
For His life is taken from the earth."[1]

34 The eunuch said to Philip, "I ask you, of
whom does the prophet speak, of himself or
of someone else?" 35 Then Philip spoke, begin-
ning with the same Scripture, and preached
Jesus to him.

36 As they went on their way, they came to
some water. And the eunuch said, "Look, here is
water. What hinders me from being baptized?"
37 Philip said, "If you believe with all your heart,
you may." He answered, "I believe that Jesus

7:59 Ps 31:5
7:60 Mt 5:44
8:1 Ac 7:58
8:3 1Co 15:9
8:4 Ac 8:1
8:5 Ac 6:5
8:7 Mk 16:17–18
8:9 Ac 5:36
8:11 Gal 3:1
8:12 Ac 1:3
8:14 Ac 8:1
8:15 Ac 2:38
8:16 Mt 28:19
8:17 Ac 6:6

8:20 Da 5:17
8:22 Da 4:27
8:23 Heb 12:15
8:24 Ex 8:8
8:26 Ac 5:19
8:27 Ps 68:31
8:29 Ac 10:19
8:31 Ro 10:14
8:32 Isa 53:7–8
8:33 Isa 53:8
8:35 Lk 24:27
8:36 Ac 10:47

[1] *32–33* Isa 53:7–8.

Christ is the Son of God." 38 And he commanded
the chariot to halt. Then both Philip and the
eunuch went down into the water, and he
baptized him. 39 When they came up out of the
water, the Spirit of the Lord took Philip away.
And the eunuch saw him no more, and he went
his way rejoicing. 40 But Philip was found at
Azotus. And passing through, he preached the
gospel in all the cities until he came to Caesarea.

The Conversion of Saul

> If God was so keen on encountering a murderous sinner like Saul, how much more do you think He wants to encounter His children who have been brought near through the cross and want to know Him (Ac 9)?

Ac 22:6–16; 26:12–18

9 Saul, still breathing out threats and mur-
der against the disciples of the Lord, went
to the high priest, 2 and requested letters from
him to the synagogues of Damascus, so that
if he found any there of the Way, either men
or women, he might bring them bound to Je-
rusalem. 3 As he went he drew near Damas-
cus, and suddenly a light from heaven shone
around him. 4 He fell to the ground and heard
a voice saying to him, "Saul, Saul, why do you
persecute Me?"
5 He said, "Who are You, Lord?"
The Lord said, "I am Jesus, whom you are
persecuting. It is hard for you to kick against
the goads." 6 Trembling and astonished, he
said, "Lord, what will You have me do?" The
Lord said to him, "Rise up and go into the city,
and you will be told what you must do."
7 The men traveling with him stood speech-
less, hearing the voice, but seeing no one.
8 Saul rose up from the ground. And when his
eyes were opened, he saw nothing. So they led
him by the hand and brought him into Damas-
cus. 9 For three days he was without sight, and
neither ate nor drank.
10 A disciple named Ananias was in Damas-
cus. The Lord said to him in a vision, "Ananias."
He said, "Here I am, Lord."
11 The Lord said to him, "Rise and go to
Straight Street, and inquire at Judas' house for
someone named Saul of Tarsus, for he is pray-
ing, 12 and has seen in a vision a man named
Ananias coming in and putting his hand on
him, so that he may see again."
13 Ananias answered, "Lord, I have heard
from many about this man, how many evil
things he has done to Your saints at Jerusa-
lem. 14 And here he has authority from the chief
priests to bind all who call on Your name."

8:39 1Ki 18:12
8:40 Ac 10:1
9:1 Ac 8:3
9:2 Ac 19:9
9:3 1Co 15:8
9:7 Ac 22:9
9:8 Ac 22:11
9:9 Est 4:16
9:10 Ac 10:3
9:11 Ac 21:39
9:12 Mk 5:23
9:13 Ac 8:3
9:14 Ac 9:21
9:15 Ac 13:2
9:16 Ac 21:11
9:17 Ac 2:4
9:18 Ac 22:16
9:19 Ac 26:20
9:21 Ac 8:3
9:22 Ac 18:5
9:24 Ac 25:3
9:25 2Co 11:33
9:26 Ac 26:20
9:27 Ac 4:36
9:28 Ac 1:21
9:29 Ac 6:1
9:30 Ac 8:40

15 But the Lord said to him, "Go your way. For
this man is a chosen vessel of Mine, to bear My
name before the Gentiles and their kings, and
before the sons of Israel. 16 For I will show him
how much he must suffer for My name's sake."
17 Then Ananias went his way and entered
the house. Putting his hands on him, he said,
"Brother Saul, the Lord Jesus, who appeared
to you on the way as you came, has sent me
so that you may see again and be filled with
the Holy Spirit." 18 Immediately something
like scales fell from his eyes, and he could
see again. And he rose up and was baptized.
19 When he had eaten, he was strengthened.

Saul Preaches in Damascus

> Help me, Lord, to increase all the more with Your Holy Spirit's power, just as Paul did (Ac 9:20–22).

For several days Saul was with the disciples
in Damascus. 20 Immediately he preached in
the synagogues that the Christ is the Son of
God. 21 All who heard him were amazed and
said, "Is not this he who killed those who called
on this name in Jerusalem, and came here with
that intent, to bring them bound to the chief
priests?" 22 Yet Saul increased all the more with
power and confounded the Jews living in Da-
mascus, proving that this One is the Christ.

> Let me increase in strength and confound the adversaries (Ac 9:22).

Saul Escapes from the Jews

23 After many days had passed, the Jews
arranged to kill him. 24 But their scheme was
known by Saul. They watched the gates day
and night to kill him. 25 But the disciples took
him by night, and lowered him in a basket
through the wall.

Saul in Jerusalem

26 When Saul had come to Jerusalem, he tried
to join the disciples. But they all feared him,
not believing he was a disciple. 27 But Barna-
bas took him, and led him to the apostles, and
declared to them how on the road he had seen
the Lord, and that He had spoken to him, and
how he had boldly preached in Damascus in
the name of Jesus. 28 So he stayed with them
while coming in and going out of Jerusalem.
29 And he spoke boldly in the name of the Lord
Jesus and disputed against the Hellenists. But
they tried to kill him. 30 When the brothers
learned this, they brought him down to Cae-
sarea, and sent him off to Tarsus.

31 Then the churches throughout all Judea and Galilee and Samaria had peace and were built up. And walking in the fear of the Lord and in the comfort of the Holy Spirit, they were multiplied.

The Healing of Aeneas

32 As Peter passed through every region, he came down also to the saints who lived in Lydda. 33 There he found a man named Aeneas, who had been bedridden for eight years and was paralyzed. 34 Peter said to him, "Aeneas, Jesus the Christ heals you. Rise up and make your bed." And immediately he rose up. 35 All those who lived in Lydda and Sharon saw him and turned to the Lord.

> Jesus Christ makes me whole (Ac 9:34).

Dorcas Restored to Life

36 In Joppa there was a disciple named Tabitha, which is translated Dorcas. This woman was full of good works and almsgiving. 37 In those days she became ill and died. And when they had washed her, they placed her in an upper room. 38 Since Lydda was near Joppa, the disciples, hearing that Peter was there, sent two men to him, pleading, "Do not delay to come to us."

39 Peter rose up and went with them. When he arrived, they led him into the upper room. All the widows stood by him weeping, and showing the tunics and garments which Dorcas had made while she was with them.

40 Peter put them all outside and knelt down and prayed. And turning to the body he said, "Tabitha, arise." She opened her eyes, and when she saw Peter she sat up. 41 He gave her his hand and lifted her up. And when he had called the saints and widows, he presented her alive. 42 It became known throughout all Joppa, and many believed in the Lord. 43 He remained in Joppa for many days with Simon, a tanner.

Peter and Cornelius

10 In Caesarea there was a man named Cornelius, the centurion[1] of a band of soldiers called the Italian Detachment, 2 a devout man and one who feared God with all his household, who gave many alms to the people and continually prayed to God. 3 About the ninth hour of the day he saw clearly in a vision an angel of God coming in and saying to him, "Cornelius."

4 When he looked at him he was afraid, and said, "What is it, Lord?"

He said to him, "Your prayers and your alms have come up as a memorial before God. 5 Now send men to Joppa, and bring back Simon whose surname is Peter. 6 He is lodging with Simon, a tanner, whose house is by the sea. He will tell you what you must do."

7 When the angel who spoke to him had departed, Cornelius called two of his household servants and a devout soldier from among those who continually waited on him. 8 When he had explained everything to them, he sent them to Joppa.

9 The next day as they went on their journey and drew near the city, Peter went up on the housetop to pray about the sixth hour. 10 He became very hungry and desired to eat. But while they prepared a meal, he fell into a trance 11 and saw heaven opened, and a vessel like a great sheet, tied at the four corners, descending to him, and let down to the earth. 12 In it were all kinds of four-footed animals of the earth and wild beasts and reptiles and birds of the air. 13 Then a voice came to him, "Rise, Peter; kill and eat."

14 Peter said, "Not at all, Lord. For I have never eaten anything that is common or unclean."

15 The voice spoke to him a second time: "What God has cleansed, do not call common."

16 This happened three times. And again the vessel was taken up into heaven.

17 Now while Peter wondered what this vision which he had seen might mean, the men who were sent by Cornelius had inquired for Simon's house and stood at the gate, 18 and called and asked whether Simon, who was surnamed Peter, was lodging there.

19 While Peter thought about the vision, the Spirit said to him, "Three men are looking for you. 20 So rise and go down, and go with them, doubting nothing. For I have sent them."

21 Then Peter went down to the men who were sent to him by Cornelius and said, "Here I am, the one you are seeking. Why have you come?"

22 They said, "Cornelius, a centurion, a man who is righteous and fears God and is of good report throughout the nation of the Jews, was directed by a holy angel to summon you to his house to hear your words." 23 Then he invited them in and gave them lodging.

The next day Peter went with them, and some brothers from Joppa accompanied him. 24 And the next day they entered Caesarea. Cornelius was waiting for them and had called together his relatives and close friends. 25 As Peter entered the house, Cornelius met him and fell down at his feet and worshipped him. 26 But Peter lifted him up, saying, "Stand up. I myself am a man."

27 As he talked with him, he went in and found many who had come together. 28 He

9:31 Ac 8:1
9:32 Ac 9:13
9:34 Ac 3:6
9:35 1Ch 5:16
9:36 2Ch 2:16
9:37 Ac 1:13
9:38 Ac 9:36
9:40 Mt 9:25
9:41 Ac 6:1
9:43 Ac 10:6
10:1 Ac 27:1
10:2 Ac 10:22
10:3 Ac 3:1
10:4 Heb 6:10
10:6 Ac 9:43
10:9 Ps 55:17
10:10 Ac 22:17
10:11 Jn 1:51
10:14 Eze 4:14
10:15 Mt 15:11
10:19 Ac 8:29
10:20 Ac 15:7–9
10:22 Ac 11:14
10:23 Ac 10:45
10:25 Mt 8:2
10:26 Rev 19:10
10:27 Ac 10:24
10:28 Jn 4:9

[1] 1 Commander with the rank of captain over 100 soldiers.

said to them, "You know how unlawful it is
for a Jew to visit or approach a foreigner. But
God has shown me not to call any man com-
mon or unclean. 29 So when I was sent for, I
came without question. Therefore I ask why
you have sent for me."
30 Cornelius said, "Four days ago I was fast-
ing until this hour. At the ninth hour I prayed
in my house, and suddenly a man stood before
me in bright clothing, 31 and said, 'Cornelius,
your prayer has been heard, and your alms are
remembered before God. 32 Therefore send to
Joppa for Simon, whose surname is Peter. He
is lodging in the house of Simon, a tanner, by
the sea. When he comes, he will speak to you.'
33 So immediately I sent for you, and you have
done well to come. Now therefore we are all
here, present before God, to hear everything
the Lord has commanded you."

Peter Speaks in Cornelius' House

34 Then Peter began to speak, saying, "Truth-
fully, I perceive that God is no respecter of per-
sons. 35 But in every nation he who fears Him
and works righteousness is accepted by Him.
36 The word which He sent to the children of
Israel, preaching peace through Jesus Christ,
who is Lord of all, 37 the word, which you know,
that was proclaimed throughout all Judea, be-
ginning from Galilee after the baptism which
John preached: 38 how God anointed Jesus of
Nazareth with the Holy Spirit and with power,
who went about doing good and healing all
who were oppressed by the devil, for God was
with Him.

> My "God moments" are when I see in operation in me the same power that dwelled in Jesus Christ of Nazareth when He walked on this earth (Ac 10:38).

39 "We are witnesses of all that He did both in
the land of the Jews and in Jerusalem, whom
they killed by hanging on a tree. 40 But God
raised Him on the third day and presented Him
publicly, 41 not to all the people, but to witness-
es previously chosen by God, to us who ate and
drank with Him after He rose from the dead.
42 He commanded us to preach to the people
and to testify that it is He who was ordained by
God to be the Judge of the living and the dead.
43 To Him all the prophets bear witness that
whoever believes in Him will receive remission
of sins through His name."

Gentiles Receive the Holy Spirit

44 While Peter was still speaking these words,
the Holy Spirit fell on all those who heard the
word. 45 All the believers of the circumcision
who had come with Peter were astonished,
because the gift of the Holy Spirit had been
poured out even on the Gentiles. 46 For they
heard them speaking in other tongues and
magnifying God.
Then Peter continued, 47 "Can anyone forbid
water for baptizing these, who have received
the Holy Spirit as we have?" 48 So he command-
ed them to be baptized in the name of the
Lord. Then they asked him to stay a few days.

Peter's Report to the Church in Jerusalem

11 The apostles and the brothers through-
out Judea heard that the Gentiles also
had received the word of God. 2 So when Peter
went up to Jerusalem, those who were circum-
cised disputed with him, 3 saying, "You went in
and ate with uncircumcised men!"
4 Peter began explaining it to them in order,
saying, 5 "I was in the city of Joppa praying.
And in a trance I saw a vision: A vessel like
a great sheet was descending, let down from
heaven by four corners, and it came to me.
6 I considered what I had observed and saw
four-footed creatures and wild beasts and rep-
tiles and birds of the air. 7 Then I heard a voice
saying to me, 'Rise, Peter; kill and eat.'
8 "I said, 'Not at all, Lord. For nothing common
or unclean has at any time entered my mouth.'
9 "The voice answered from heaven a second
time, 'What God has cleansed, do not call com-
mon.' 10 This happened three times. And again
everything was taken up into heaven.
11 "And immediately three men sent from
Caesarea to me came to the house where I was.
12 The Spirit told me to go with them without
hesitation. Moreover these six brothers came
with me, and we entered the man's house.
13 He told us how he had seen an angel in his
house, who stood and said to him, 'Send men
to Joppa, and call for Simon whose surname
is Peter. 14 He will speak words to you by which
you and all your household will be saved.'
15 "As I began to speak, the Holy Spirit fell on
them, as He fell on us at the beginning. 16 Then
I remembered the word of the Lord, how He
said, 'John indeed baptized with water, but you
shall be baptized with the Holy Spirit.'[1] 17 If
then God gave them the same gift as He gave
us when we believed in the Lord Jesus Christ,
who was I to be able to hinder God?"
18 When they heard these things, they were
silent. And they glorified God, saying, "Then
God has granted to the Gentiles also repen-
tance unto life."

10:30 Ac 10:3
10:31 Ac 10:4
10:34 Dt 10:17
10:36 Mt 28:18
10:38 Lk 4:18
10:39 Lk 24:48
10:40 Ac 2:24
10:41 Jn 14:22
10:42 Ac 17:31
10:43 Ac 15:9
10:44 Ac 11:15
10:45 Ac 10:23
10:46 Ac 2:4
10:47 Ac 8:36
10:48 Ac 2:38
11:2 Ac 10:45
11:3 Ac 10:28
11:4 Lk 1:3
11:5 Ac 10:9–32
11:8 Ro 14:14
11:12 Ac 8:29
11:14 Ac 16:15
11:16 Ac 1:5
11:17 Ac 10:47
11:18 Ro 10:12–13

[1] *16* Ac 1:5.

The Church in Antioch

19 Now those who were scattered by the
persecution that arose over Stephen traveled
as far as Phoenicia and Cyprus and Antioch,
preaching the word to no one except Jews.
20 Some of them were men of Cyprus and
Cyrene, who, when they had come to Antioch,
spoke to the Hellenists, preaching the Lord
Jesus. 21 The hand of the Lord was with them,
and a great number believed and turned to
the Lord.

22 News of these things came to the ears of
the church which was in Jerusalem, and they
sent Barnabas to Antioch. 23 When he arrived
and saw the grace of God, he rejoiced and ex-
horted them all to remain with the Lord with
a loyal heart. 24 For he was a good man, full of
the Holy Spirit and of faith. And many people
were added to the Lord.

25 Then Barnabas went to Tarsus to look for
Saul. 26 When he had found him, he brought
him to Antioch. For a whole year they met with
the church and taught a considerable crowd.
And the disciples were first called Christians
in Antioch.

27 In these days prophets came down from
Jerusalem to Antioch. 28 One of them, named
Agabus, stood up and prophesied by the Spirit
that there would be a great famine throughout
all the world, which came to pass in the days
of Claudius Caesar. 29 Then every disciple, ac-
cording to his ability, determined to send relief
to the brothers who lived in Judea. 30 Indeed
they did, and sent it to the elders by the hands
of Barnabas and Saul.

James Killed and Peter Imprisoned

12 About that time King Herod extended
his hands to harm certain ones from
the church. 2 He killed James the brother of
John with the sword. 3 Seeing that it pleased
the Jews, he proceeded further to arrest Peter
also. This happened during the Days of Un-
leavened Bread. 4 When he had seized him, he
put him in prison and handed him over to four
squads of soldiers to guard him, intending to
bring him before the people after the Passover.
5 So Peter was kept in prison. But the church
prayed to God without ceasing for him.

Peter Delivered From Prison

6 The very night when Herod would have
brought him out, Peter was sleeping between
two soldiers, bound with two chains. And the
guards before the door were securing the pris-
on. 7 And suddenly an angel of the Lord ap-
proached him, and a light shone in the prison.
He struck Peter on the side and woke him up,
saying, "Rise up, quickly." And the chains fell
off his hands.

11:20 Mt 27:32
11:21 Lk 1:66
11:23 Ac 13:43
11:24 Ac 5:14
11:25 Ac 9:11
11:26 Ac 26:28
11:27 Ac 13:1
11:28 Ac 21:10
11:30 Ac 12:25
12:2 Mt 20:23
12:3 Ex 23:15
12:4 Lk 21:12
12:5 2Co 1:11
12:6 Ac 21:33
12:7 Ac 16:26

....

12:9 Ps 126:1
12:10 Ac 5:19
12:11 Da 3:28
12:12 Ac 12:5
12:14 Lk 24:41
12:15 Mt 18:10
12:17 Ac 13:16
12:19 Ac 16:27
12:20 Eze 27:17
12:24 Ac 6:7

8 Then the angel said to him, "Dress yourself
and put your sandals on." And he did so. Then
he said to him, "Wrap your cloak around you
and follow me." 9 He went out and followed
him, and did not know that what was done by
the angel was real, but thought he was seeing
a vision. 10 When they had passed the first and
the second guards, they came to the iron gate
leading to the city, which opened to them by
itself. And they went out and went forward one
street. And immediately the angel left him.

11 When Peter had come to himself, he said,
"Now I certainly know that the Lord has sent
His angel and delivered me from the hand of
Herod and from all that the Jewish people
were expecting."

12 Realizing this, he came to the house of
Mary, the mother of John, whose other name
was Mark, where many were gathered togeth-
er praying. 13 As Peter knocked at the door of
the porch, a servant girl named Rhoda came to
answer. 14 When she recognized Peter's voice,
from joy she did not open the door, but ran
in and announced that Peter was standing at
the door.

15 They said to her, "You are insane." But she
insisted that it was really so. So they said, "It
is his angel."

16 But Peter continued knocking. And when
they opened the door and saw him, they were
astonished. 17 Motioning to them with his hand
to be quiet, he described to them how the Lord
had led him out of the prison. And he said, "Go,
tell these things to James and to the brothers."
Then he departed and went to another place.

18 Now when day came, there was a great dis-
turbance among the soldiers about what had
become of Peter. 19 When Herod had searched
for him and did not find him, he examined the
guards and commanded that they should be
put to death.

Then he went down from Judea to Caesarea,
and stayed there.

The Death of Herod

20 Now Herod was very angry with the peo-
ple of Tyre and Sidon. But they came to him
in unity, and having made Blastus, the king's
personal servant, their friend, they asked for
peace, because their country was fed by the
king's country.

21 On an appointed day, Herod, dressed in
royal apparel, sat on his throne and gave a
public speech to them. 22 The mob shouted,
"It is the voice of a god, and not of a man!"
23 Immediately an angel of the Lord struck him,
because he did not give God the glory. And he
was eaten by worms and died.

24 But the word of God spread and increased.

25 When Barnabas and Saul had fulfilled their
ministry, they returned from Jerusalem and took
with them John, whose surname was Mark.

Barnabas and Saul Commissioned

13 In the church that was in Antioch there
were prophets and teachers: Barna-
bas, Simeon who was called Niger, Lucius of
Cyrene, Manaen who had been brought up
with Herod the tetrarch, and Saul. 2 As they
worshipped the Lord and fasted, the Holy Spir-
it said, "Set apart for Me Barnabas and Saul for
the work to which I have called them." 3 Then
after fasting and praying, they laid their hands
on them and sent them off.

The Apostles Preach in Cyprus

4 So, being sent out by the Holy Spirit, they
went down to Seleucia, and from there they
sailed to Cyprus. 5 When they arrived at Sal-
amis, they preached the word of God in the
synagogues of the Jews. And they had John
as an assistant.

6 When they had gone through the whole
island to Paphos, they found a certain sor-
cerer, a Jewish false prophet, whose name
was Bar-Jesus, 7 who was with the proconsul,
Sergius Paulus, an intelligent man. This man
called for Barnabas and Saul and sought to
hear the word of God. 8 But Elymas the sor-
cerer (which is his name by interpretation)
opposed them, trying to divert the proconsul
from the faith. 9 Then Saul, who also is called
Paul, filled with the Holy Spirit, stared at him
and said, 10 "You son of the devil, enemy of all
righteousness, full of deceit and of all fraud,
will you not cease perverting the right ways of
the Lord? 11 Now, look! The hand of the Lord is
against you, and you shall be blind, not seeing
the sun for a time."

Immediately mist and darkness fell on him,
and he went about seeking someone to lead
him by the hand. 12 When the proconsul saw
what had happened, he believed and was as-
tonished at the doctrine of the Lord.

Paul and Barnabas in Antioch of Pisidia

13 Now when Paul and his companions set
sail from Paphos, they came to Perga in Pam-
phylia. And John departed from them and re-
turned to Jerusalem. 14 But they departed from
Perga and came to Antioch in Pisidia. And they
went into the synagogue on the Sabbath day
and sat down. 15 After the reading from the
Law and the Prophets, the rulers of the syna-
gogue sent word to them, saying, "Brothers,
if you have any word of exhortation for the
people, say it."

16 Then Paul stood up, and motioning with
his hand said: "Men of Israel, and you who
fear God, listen. 17 The God of this people of
Israel chose our fathers, and exalted the peo-
ple when they lived as foreigners in the land
of Egypt, and with great power He led them
out of it. 18 For about forty years He endured
their conduct in the desert. 19 When He had
destroyed seven nations in the land of Canaan,
He gave them their land as an inheritance by
lot.

20 "After about four hundred and fifty years,
God gave them judges until Samuel the proph-
et. 21 Then they requested a king. And God gave
them Saul the son of Kish, a man of the tribe
of Benjamin, for forty years. 22 When He had
removed him, He raised up David to be their
king, of whom He testified, saying, 'I have
found David[1] the son of Jesse, a man after
My own heart, who will fulfill My entire will.'[2]
23 "From this man's descendants God has
raised a Savior for Israel, Jesus, according to
His promise. 24 Before His coming John had
preached a baptism of repentance to all the
people of Israel. 25 As John was fulfilling his
course, he said, 'Who do you think I am? I
am not He. But look! He is coming after me,
the sandals of whose feet I am not worthy
to untie.'[3]

26 "Brothers, sons of the family of Abraham,
and those of you who fear God, the word of this
salvation has been sent to us. 27 Because those
who live in Jerusalem, and their rulers, did not
know Him, in condemning Him they have ful-
filled the voices of the Prophets which are read
every Sabbath. 28 Though they found in Him no
cause worthy of death, yet they asked Pilate to
have Him killed. 29 When they had fulfilled all
that was written of Him, they took Him down
from the tree and placed Him in a tomb. 30 But
God raised Him from the dead, 31 and for many
days He appeared to those who came up with
Him from Galilee to Jerusalem, who are now
His witnesses to the people.

32 "We preach to you good news: The prom-
ise which was made to the fathers, 33 God has
fulfilled to us, their children, raising Jesus. As
it is written in the second Psalm:

'You are My Son;
today I have become Your Father.'[4]

34 That He raised Him from the dead, no more to
return to corruption, He has spoken in this way:

'I will give You the holy and sure blessings
of David.'[5]

35 So He says in another Psalm:

'You will not let Your Holy One see decay.'[6]

12:25 Ac 12:12
13:1 Ac 11:22–27
13:2 Ac 9:15
13:3 Ac 6:6
13:4 Ac 4:36
13:5 Ac 13:14
13:6 Mt 7:15
13:7 Ac 13:12
13:9 Ac 4:8
13:10 Hos 14:9
13:11 Ex 9:3
13:12 Ac 13:7
13:14 Ac 16:13
13:15 Ac 15:21
13:16 Ac 12:17
13:17 Dt 7:6–8
13:18 Ac 7:36
13:19 Ps 78:55
13:20 Jdg 2:16
13:21 1Sa 10:1
13:22 1Sa 16:1
13:23 Mt 1:1
13:24 Ac 1:22
13:25 Mt 3:11
13:27 Ac 3:17
13:28 Mt 27:22–25
13:29 Lk 23:53
13:30 Ac 2:24
13:31 Lk 24:48
13:32 Ac 26:6
13:33 Ps 2:7
13:34 Isa 55:3
13:35 Ps 16:10

[1] *22* Ps 89:20. [2] *22* 1Sa 13:14. [3] *25* Jn 1:20, 27. [4] *33* Ps 2:7. [5] *34* Isa 55:3. [6] *35* Ps 16:10.

SPIRITLED WOMAN

COUNSEL FROM THE SPIRIT BASICS

Christ in Them

In Acts 14 we read about Paul and Barnabas in Iconium preaching at the Jewish synagogue. Paul and Barnabas spoke with power and influence, and the Lord our God was with them. Clearly they loved God more than their personal safety. There was nothing self-serving about their ministry. Christ in them was their hope of glory. And as a result, Christ could trust them with his glory.

Read Acts 14:1–3. At Iconium Paul and Barnabas went, as usual, into the Jewish synagogue. There they spoke so effectively that a great number of Jews and Gentiles believed. But the Jews who refused to believe stirred up the Gentiles and poisoned their minds against their brothers. So Paul and Barnabas spent considerable time there, speaking boldly for the Lord, who confirmed the message of His grace by enabling them to do miraculous signs and wonders.

Even now, within the kingdom of God, we have plenty of people building their own kingdoms. Maybe it's a kingdom of comfort or association or reputation. Maybe it's a kingdom of celebrity or mega-status or political correctness.

But the kingdom of God is always about Christ's saving work in our lives—moving and advancing to reach others with that same saving message.

Susie Larson

36 "For after David had served by the counsel
of God in his own generation, he fell asleep,
was buried with his fathers, and saw decay.
37 But He whom God raised up saw no decay.
38 "Therefore, brothers, let it be known to
you that through this Man forgiveness of sins
is proclaimed to you, 39 and by Him everyone
who believes is justified from everything from
which you could not be justified by the Law of
Moses. 40 Therefore beware, lest what is spoken
of in the prophets come upon you:

41 'Look, you scoffers,
marvel and perish!
For I will perform a work in your days
which you will never believe,
even if someone declares it to you.'[1]"

42 When Paul and Barnabas went out of the
synagogue, the Gentiles asked that these words
might be preached to them the next Sabbath.
43 When the congregation was dismissed, many
of the Jews and devout proselytes followed
Paul and Barnabas, who spoke to them and
urged them to continue in the grace of God.
44 On the next Sabbath almost the whole
city assembled to hear the word of God. 45 But
when the Jews saw the crowds, they were filled
with jealousy, blaspheming and contradicting
what Paul was saying.
46 Then Paul and Barnabas boldly said, "It
was necessary that the word of God should
be spoken to you first. But seeing you reject
it, and judge yourselves unworthy of eternal
life, we are turning to the Gentiles. 47 For thus
has the Lord commanded us:

'I have established you to be a light of the
Gentiles,
that you may bring salvation to the ends
of the earth.'[2]"

48 When the Gentiles heard this, they were
glad and glorified the word of the Lord. And
all who were ordained to eternal life believed.
49 The word of the Lord was spread through-
out the entire region. 50 But the Jews stirred
up the devout and honorable women and the
chief men of the city, and raised up persecu-
tion against Paul and Barnabas, and drove
them from their region. 51 So they shook off
the dust of their feet against them and went to
Iconium. 52 And the disciples were filled with
joy and with the Holy Spirit.

Paul and Barnabas in Iconium

14 At Iconium they entered the synagogue
of the Jews together and so spoke
that a great crowd of both Jews and Greeks
believed. 2 But the unbelieving Jews stirred
up the Gentiles and embittered their minds
against the brothers. 3 So they continued there
a long time, speaking boldly for the Lord, who
bore witness to His gracious word, granting
signs and wonders to be done by their hands.
4 But the people of the city were divided. Some
sided with the Jews, and others with the apos-
tles. 5 When an assault was planned by both
Gentiles and Jews, with their leaders, to attack
them and to stone them, 6 they learned of it
and fled to Lystra and Derbe, cities of Lycao-
nia, and to the surrounding region. 7 And there
they preached the gospel.

13:36 1Ki 2:10
13:37 Ac 13:30
13:38 Lk 24:47
13:39 Ro 8:3
13:41 Hab 1:5
13:43 Ac 11:23
13:45 Ac 18:6
13:46 Ac 3:26
13:47 Isa 49:6
13:50 Ac 14:2
13:51 Mt 10:14
13:52 Ac 2:4
14:1 Ac 18:4
14:2 Ac 13:50
14:3 Heb 2:4
14:4 Ac 28:24
14:5 Ac 14:19
14:6 Mt 10:23
14:7 Ac 14:21

[1] *41* Hab 1:5. [2] *47* Isa 42:6; 49:6.

Paul and Barnabas in Lystra

8 In Lystra there sat a man, crippled in his
feet, who had never walked and was lame
from birth. 9 He heard Paul speaking, who
looked intently at him and perceived that he
had faith to be healed 10 and said with a loud
voice, "Stand upright on your feet." And he
jumped up and walked.

11 When the crowds saw what Paul had done,
they lifted up their voices, saying in Lycaonian,
"The gods have come down to us in the likeness
of men!" 12 Barnabas they called Zeus, and Paul
they called Hermes, because he was the main
speaker. 13 The priest of Zeus, who was in front
of the city, brought bulls and garlands to the
gates to offer sacrifices with the crowds.

14 But when the apostles Barnabas and Paul
heard this, they tore their clothes and rushed out
into the crowd, crying out, 15 "Men, why are you
doing this? We also are men, of like nature with
you, preaching to you to turn from these vain
things to the living God, who made the heaven
and the earth and the sea, and everything that is
in them, 16 who in times past allowed all nations
to walk in their own ways. 17 Yet He did not leave
Himself without witness, for He did good and
gave us rain from heaven and fruitful seasons,
satisfying our hearts with food and gladness."
18 With these words they scarcely restrained the
crowds from sacrificing to them.

19 Then some Jews from Antioch and Iconium
came there and persuaded the crowds. They
stoned Paul and dragged him out of the city,
supposing he was dead. 20 But as the disciples
gathered around him, he rose up and went
into the city. The next day he departed with
Barnabas for Derbe.

The Return to Antioch in Syria

21 When they had preached the gospel to that
city and had made many disciples, they re-
turned to Lystra and to Iconium and to Antioch,
22 strengthening the minds of the disciples and
exhorting them to continue in the faith, to go
through many afflictions and thus enter the
kingdom of God. 23 When they had appointed
elders for them in every church, with prayer
and fasting, they commended them to the Lord
in whom they believed. 24 Then they passed
throughout Pisidia and came to Pamphylia,
25 and when they had preached the word in
Perga, they went down into Attalia.

26 From there they sailed to Antioch, where
they had been commended to the grace of
God for the work which they had completed.
27 When they arrived and had assembled the
church, they reported what God had done
through them and how He had opened the
door of faith to the Gentiles. 28 And there they
stayed a long time with the disciples.

The Council in Jerusalem

15 Some men came down from Judea and
were teaching the brothers, "Unless
you are circumcised in the tradition of Moses,
you cannot be saved." 2 Therefore when Paul
and Barnabas had no small dissension and dis-
pute with them, they determined that Paul and
Barnabas, and certain others among them,
should go up to Jerusalem to the apostles and
elders about this question. 3 So being sent on
their way by the church, they passed through
Phoenicia and Samaria, declaring the conver-
sion of the Gentiles, and they brought great joy
to all the brothers. 4 When they arrived in Jeru-
salem, they were welcomed by the church and
the apostles and the elders, and they declared
what God had done through them.

5 Then some believers of the sect of the Phar
isees rose up, saying, "It is necessary to circum-
cise them, and to command them to keep the
Law of Moses."

6 The apostles and elders assembled to con-
sider this matter. 7 After much disputing, Peter
rose up and said to them, "Brothers, you know
that some time ago God decided among us,
that by my mouth the Gentiles should hear the
word of the gospel and believe. 8 God, who
knows the heart, approved of them, giving
them the Holy Spirit just as He did to us, 9 and
made no distinction between them and us, and
purified their hearts by faith. 10 Now then, why
test God by putting a yoke upon the neck of
the disciples, which neither our fathers nor we
have been able to bear? 11 But we believe that
through the grace of the Lord Jesus Christ we
shall be saved, even as they."

12 The entire assembly remained silent and
listened to Barnabas and Paul declaring what
signs and wonders God had done through
them among the Gentiles. 13 After they had
become silent, James answered, "Brothers,
listen to me. 14 Simon has declared how God
first visited the Gentiles to take from among
them a people for His name. 15 With this the
words of the prophets agree. As it is written:

16 'After this I will return,
and I will rebuild the tabernacle of
David, which has fallen;
I will rebuild its ruins,
and I will set it up;[1]
17 that the rest of men may seek the Lord,
and all the Gentiles who are called by My
name,[2]
says the Lord who does all these things.'[3]

14:8 Ac 3:2
14:10 Isa 35:6
14:11 Ac 8:10
14:12 Ac 19:35
14:13 Da 2:46
14:15 1Sa 12:21
14:16 Ac 17:30
14:17 Dt 11:14
14:19 Ac 13:45
14:20 Ac 14:6
14:21 Ac 13:51
14:22 Jn 16:33
14:23 Titus 1:5
14:24 Ac 13:13–14
14:26 Ac 15:40
14:27 Ac 15:12
14:28 Ac 11:26
15:1 Ac 15:5
15:2 Ac 15:22–23
15:3 Ac 14:27
15:4 Ac 14:27
15:5 Ac 15:1
15:6 Ac 15:25
15:7 Ac 15:2
15:8 Ac 1:24
15:9 Ac 10:28
15:10 Mt 23:4
15:11 Ro 3:24
15:12 Ac 14:27
15:13 Ac 12:17
15:16 Am 9:11–12
15:17 Isa 43:7

[1] *16* Am 9:11; Jer 12:15. [2] *17* Am 9:12; Dt 28:10; Isa 63:19; Jer 14:9; Da 9:19. [3] *17* Am 9:11–12.

> 18 Known to God are all His works since the beginning of the world.

19 "Therefore my judgment is that we should not trouble those of the Gentiles who are turning to God, 20 but that we write to them to abstain from food offered to idols, from sexual immorality, from strangled animals, and from blood. 21 For Moses has had in every city since early generations those who preach him, being read in the synagogues every Sabbath."

Lord, cleanse the pollution of idols from the land (Ac 15:20).

The Reply of the Council

22 Then it pleased the apostles and the elders, with the whole church, to send chosen men from among them to Antioch with Paul and Barnabas, namely, Judas called Barsabas, and Silas, leading men among the brothers. 23 They wrote this letter by their hand:

> The apostles and the elders and the brothers,
>
> To the brothers who are of the Gentiles in Antioch and Syria and Cilicia:
>
> Greetings.
>
> 24 Since we have heard that some of us, whom we did not commission, have gone out and have troubled you with words, unsettling your minds, saying, "You must be circumcised and keep the law," 25 it seemed good to us, being assembled in unity, to send chosen men to you with our beloved Barnabas and Paul, 26 men who have risked their lives for the name of our Lord Jesus Christ. 27 Therefore we have sent Judas and Silas, who will also speak to you, saying the same things. 28 For it seemed good to the Holy Spirit and to us to put on you no greater burden than these necessary things: 29 Abstain from food offered to idols, from sexual immorality, from strangled animals, and from blood. If you keep yourselves from these, you will do well.
>
> Farewell.

30 So when they were dismissed, they went down to Antioch. And when they had assembled the congregation, they delivered the letter. 31 When they had read it, they rejoiced over the exhortation. 32 Judas and Silas, being prophets themselves, exhorted the brothers with many words and strengthened them. 33 After they had remained there for a time, they were sent off in peace by the brothers to the apostles.

15:19 Ac 15:28
15:20 Lev 3:17
15:21 Ac 13:15
15:22 Ac 15:27
15:23 Ac 23:26
15:24 Ac 15:1
15:26 Ac 14:19
15:27 Ac 15:22
15:29 Ac 15:20
15:32 Ac 11:23
15:33 1Co 16:11

....

15:35 Ac 13:1
15:36 Ac 13:4
15:37 Ac 12:12
15:38 Ac 13:13
15:39 Ac 4:36
15:40 Ac 14:26
15:41 Ac 15:23
16:1 Ac 14:6
16:3 Gal 2:3
16:4 Ac 15:28–29
16:5 Ac 9:31
16:6 Ac 18:23
16:8 2Co 2:12
16:12 Php 1:1
16:13 Ac 13:14

34 But it seemed good to Silas to remain there. 35 And Paul and Barnabas remained in Antioch, teaching and preaching the word of the Lord, with many others also.

Paul and Barnabas Separate

36 After some days Paul said to Barnabas, "Let us return and visit our brothers in every city where we preached the word of the Lord and see how they are doing." 37 Barnabas determined to take with them John, who was called Mark. 38 But Paul thought it was not good to take with them one who had withdrawn from them in Pamphylia and had not gone with them to the work. 39 Then there arose a sharp contention, so that they separated from each other. Barnabas took Mark and sailed to Cyprus, 40 but Paul chose Silas and departed, being commended by the brothers to the grace of God. 41 And he went through Syria and Cilicia, strengthening the churches.

Timothy Accompanies Paul and Silas

16 Then he came to Derbe and then to Lystra. A disciple was there, named Timothy, the son of a Jewess who believed, but his father was a Greek. 2 He was well spoken of by the brothers who were at Lystra and Iconium. 3 Paul wanted him to travel with him. So he took him and circumcised him because of the Jews who were in those places, for they all knew that his father was a Greek. 4 As they went through the cities, they delivered to them the decrees to observe, that were set forth by the apostles and elders at Jerusalem. 5 So the churches were strengthened in the faith, and increased in number daily.

Paul's Vision of the Macedonian

6 They went through the region of Phrygia and Galatia and were forbidden by the Holy Spirit to speak the word in Asia. 7 When they came near Mysia, they tried to go into Bithynia, but the Spirit did not allow them. 8 So they passed by Mysia and went down to Troas. 9 During the night a vision appeared to Paul: A man of Macedonia stood and pleaded with him, saying, "Come over to Macedonia and help us." 10 After he had seen the vision, immediately we sought to go into Macedonia, concluding that the Lord had called us to preach the gospel to them.

The Conversion of Lydia

11 From Troas we set sail on a straight course to Samothrace and the next day to Neapolis, 12 and from there to Philippi, which is the main city of that part of Macedonia, and a colony. We stayed in this city several days.

13 On the Sabbath we went out of the city to a riverside, where prayer was customarily

offered. And we sat down and spoke to the women who had assembled. [14] A woman named Lydia, a seller of purple fabric of the city of Thyatira, who worshipped God, heard us. The Lord opened her heart to acknowledge what Paul said. [15] When she and her household were baptized, she entreated us, saying, "If you have judged me to be faithful to the Lord, come to my house and remain there." And she persuaded us.

The Imprisonment in Philippi

[16] On one occasion, as we went to the place of prayer, a servant girl possessed with a spirit of divination met us, who brought her masters much profit by fortune-telling. [17] She followed Paul and us, shouting, "These men are servants of the Most High God, who proclaim to us the way of salvation." [18] She did this for many days. But becoming greatly troubled, Paul turned to the spirit and said, "I command you in the name of Jesus Christ to come out of her." And it came out at that moment.

[19] When her masters saw that the hope of their profits was gone, they seized Paul and Silas, and dragged them into the marketplace to the rulers. [20] And they brought them to the magistrates, saying, "These men, being Jews, greatly trouble our city [21] and teach customs which are not lawful for us, being Romans, to receive or observe."

[22] The crowd rose up together against them. And the magistrates tore the garments off them and gave orders to beat them. [23] After they had laid many stripes on them, they threw them into prison, commanding the jailer to guard them securely. [24] Having received such an order, he threw them into the inner prison and fastened their feet in the stocks.

[25] At midnight Paul and Silas were praying and singing hymns to God, and the prisoners were listening to them. [26] Suddenly there was a great earthquake, so that the foundations of the prison were shaken. And immediately all the doors were opened and everyone's shackles were loosened. [27] When the jailer awoke and saw the prison doors open, he drew his sword and would have killed himself, supposing that the prisoners had escaped. [28] But Paul shouted, "Do not harm yourself, for we are all here."

True worship converts doubt to deliverance (Ac 16:22–26).

[29] He called for lights and rushed in, trembling, and fell down before Paul and Silas. [30] He then led them out and asked, "Sirs, what must I do to be saved?"

16:14 Lk 24:45
16:15 Ac 11:14
16:16 1Sa 28:7
16:17 Mk 5:7
16:18 Mk 16:17
16:19 Ac 21:30
16:20 Ac 28:22
16:22 1Th 2:2
16:24 Job 13:27
16:26 Ac 4:31
16:27 Ac 12:19
16:30 Ac 2:37

....

16:31 Mk 16:16
16:34 Ac 2:46
16:36 Ac 15:33
16:37 Ac 22:25–29
16:38 Ac 22:29
16:39 Mt 8:34
16:40 Ac 16:14
17:1 Php 4:16
17:2 Ac 9:20
17:3 Ac 9:22
17:4 Ac 14:4
17:5 Ac 17:13
17:7 Lk 23:2

[31] They said, "Believe in the Lord Jesus Christ, and you and your household will be saved." [32] And they spoke the word of the Lord to him and to all who were in his household. [33] In that hour of the night he took them and washed their wounds. And immediately he and his entire household were baptized. [34] Then he brought them up to his house and set food before them. And he rejoiced with his entire household believing in God.

My children belong to the kingdom of God (Ac 16:31).

[35] When it was day, the magistrates sent the sergeants, saying, "Release those men." [36] The prison guard reported these words to Paul, saying, "The magistrates have sent to release you. Now therefore depart, and go in peace." [37] But Paul said to them, "They have publicly beaten us, who are uncondemned Romans, and have thrown us into prison. And now do they secretly throw us out? Certainly not! Let them come themselves and bring us out."

[38] The sergeants reported these words to the magistrates, and they were afraid when they heard that they were Romans. [39] So they came and entreated them. And they brought them out, asking them to leave the city. [40] They went out of the prison and entered the house of Lydia. When they had seen the brothers, they exhorted them and departed.

The Uproar in Thessalonica

17 When they had traveled through Amphipolis and Apollonia, they came to Thessalonica, where there was a synagogue of the Jews. [2] According to his custom, Paul went in, and on three Sabbaths he lectured to them from the Scriptures, [3] explaining and proving that the Christ had to suffer and to rise from the dead, and saying, "This Jesus, whom I preach to you, is the Christ." [4] Some of them were persuaded and joined with Paul and Silas, including a great crowd of devout Greeks and many leading women.

[5] But the Jews who did not believe became jealous and, taking some evil men from the marketplace, gathered a crowd, stirred up the city, and attacked the house of Jason, trying to bring them out to the mob. [6] But when they did not find them, they dragged Jason and some brothers to the city officials, crying out, "These men who have turned the world upside down have come here also, [7] and Jason has received them. They are all acting contrary to the decrees of Caesar, saying that there is another king, Jesus." [8] They troubled the crowd and

the city officials when they heard these things.
9 When they had taken a bail payment from
Jason and the rest, they released them.

The Apostles in Berea

10 The brothers immediately sent Paul and
Silas away by night to Berea. When they ar-
rived, they went into the synagogue of the
Jews. 11 These were more noble than those in
Thessalonica, for they received the word with
all eagerness, daily examining the Scriptures,
to find out if these things were so. 12 Therefore
many of them believed, including honorable
Greek women and many Greek men.

13 But when the Jews of Thessalonica learned
that the word of God was preached by Paul
at Berea, they came there also, stirring up
the crowds. 14 The brothers immediately sent
Paul away to the sea. But Silas and Timothy
remained there. 15 Those who escorted Paul
brought him to Athens and departed with in-
structions for Silas and Timothy to come to
him quickly.

Paul in Athens

16 While Paul waited for them in Athens, his
spirit was provoked within him as he saw that
the city was full of idols. 17 Therefore he dis-
puted in the synagogue with the Jews and the
devout persons, and in the marketplace daily
with those who happened to there. 18 Then
some of the Epicurean and Stoic philosophers
encountered him. And some said, "What will
this babbler say?" Others said, "He seems to
be a proclaimer of foreign gods," because he
preached Jesus and the resurrection to them.
19 They took hold of him and led him to the Ar-
eopagus, saying, "May we know what this new
doctrine is of which you speak? 20 For you are
bringing strange things to our ears. Therefore
we want to know what these things mean."
21 For all the Athenians and foreigners who
lived there spent their time in nothing else,
but either telling or hearing something new.

22 Then Paul stood in the middle of the Are-
opagus, and said: "Men of Athens, I perceive
that in all things you are very religious. 23 For
as I passed by and looked up at your objects of
worship, I found an altar with this inscription:

TO THE UNKNOWN GOD.

Whom you therefore unknowingly worship,
Him I proclaim to you.

24 "God who made the world and all things in
it, being Lord of heaven and earth, does not
live in temples made by hands. 25 Nor is He
served by men's hands, as though He need-
ed anything, since He gives all men life and
breath and all things. 26 He has made from one
blood every nation of men to live on the entire

17:10 Ac 17:13–14
17:11 Jn 5:39
17:12 Ac 13:50
17:14 Ac 17:10
17:15 Ac 18:1
17:18 Ac 4:2
17:19 Mk 1:27
17:22 Ac 25:19
17:23 Jn 4:22
17:24 Mt 11:25
17:25 Job 22:2
17:26 Mal 2:10

....

17:27 Ac 14:17
17:28 Job 12:10
17:30 Lk 24:47
17:32 Ac 17:18
17:34 Ac 17:19
18:1 Ac 19:1
18:2 1Co 16:19
18:3 1Co 4:12
18:4 Ac 17:17
18:5 Ac 17:3
18:6 2Sa 1:16
18:7 Ac 16:14

face of the earth, having appointed fixed times
and the boundaries of their habitation, 27 that
they should seek the Lord so perhaps they
might reach for Him and find Him, though
He is not far from each one of us. 28 'For in
Him we live and move and have our being.'
As some of your own poets have said, 'We are
His offspring.'

29 "Therefore since we are the offspring of
God, we ought not to suppose that the Deity
is like gold or silver or stone or an engraved
work of art or an image of the reflection of
man. 30 God overlooked the times of ignorance,
but now He commands all men everywhere to
repent. 31 For He has appointed a day on which
He will judge the world in righteousness by a
Man whom He has appointed, having given
assurance of this to all men by raising Him
from the dead."

32 When they heard of the resurrection of the
dead, some scoffed. But others said, "We will
hear you again concerning this matter." 33 So
Paul departed from them. 34 However, some
men joined him and believed. Among them
were Dionysius the Areopagite, and a woman
named Damaris, and others with them.

Paul in Corinth

18 After this, Paul left Athens and went
to Corinth. 2 He found a Jew named
Aquila, a native of Pontus, who had recently
come from Italy with his wife Priscilla, because
Claudius had commanded all the Jews to leave
Rome. And he went to them. 3 And because he
was of the same trade, he remained with them
and worked, for they were tentmakers by trade.
4 He lectured in the synagogue every Sabbath
and persuaded Jews and Greeks.

5 When Silas and Timothy came from Mace-
donia, Paul was pressed by the Spirit and tes-
tified to the Jews that Jesus was the Christ.
6 But when they opposed him and blasphemed,
he shook out his garments and said to them,
"Your blood be upon your heads. I am inno-
cent. From now on I will go to the Gentiles."

7 Then he departed from there and entered
the house of a man named Justus, one who
worshipped God, whose house was next door
to the synagogue. 8 Crispus, the ruler of the
synagogue, believed in the Lord with his entire
household. And many of the Corinthians, who
heard, believed and were baptized.

9 The Lord spoke to Paul in the night through
a vision, "Do not be afraid, but speak and do
not be silent. 10 For I am with you, and no
one shall attack you and hurt you, for I have
many people in this city." 11 So for a year and
six months he sat among them, teaching the
word of God.

12 When Gallio was proconsul of Achaia, the
Jews in unity attacked Paul and brought him to
court, 13 saying, "This man is persuading men
to worship God contrary to the law."
14 When Paul was about to speak, Gallio said
to the Jews, "O Jews, if it were a matter of a
misdemeanor or serious crime, I would right-
ly bear with you. 15 But if it is a question of
words and names and your law, look into it
yourselves. For I do not intend to be a judge
of these matters." 16 So he drove them out of
court. 17 Then all the Greeks seized Sosthenes,
the ruler of the synagogue, and beat him
before the judgment seat. But none of these
things mattered to Gallio.

Paul's Return to Antioch

18 Yet Paul remained many days. He had
his hair cut in Cenchrea, for he had taken a
vow. Then, bidding farewell to the brothers,
he sailed to Syria, and Priscilla and Aquila
were with him. 19 He arrived at Ephesus and
left them there. But he himself went into the
synagogue and lectured the Jews. 20 When they
asked him to remain for a while longer, he did
not consent, 21 but, bidding farewell, said, "I
must by all means attend this upcoming feast
in Jerusalem, but I will return to you if God
wills." And he set sail from Ephesus. 22 When he
had landed at Caesarea, he went up and greet-
ed the church and then went down to Antioch.
23 After spending some time there, he depart-
ed and passed through the entire region of Ga-
latia and Phrygia in sequence, strengthening
all the disciples.

Apollos Preaches in Ephesus

24 Meanwhile a Jew named Apollos, born in
Alexandria, who was an eloquent man and
powerful in the Scriptures, came to Ephesus.
25 This man was instructed in the way of the
Lord, knowing only the baptism of John, but
being fervent in spirit, he accurately spoke and
taught the things concerning the Lord. 26 He
began to speak boldly in the synagogue. When
Aquila and Priscilla heard him, they took him
and explained the way of God more accurately.
27 When Apollos intended to pass into Achaia,
the brothers wrote to encourage the disciples
to welcome him. On arriving, he greatly helped
those who had believed through grace. 28 For he
vehemently refuted the Jews publicly, proving
from the Scriptures that Jesus was the Christ.

Ephesians Receive the Holy Spirit

19 While Apollos was at Corinth, Paul
passed through the upper regions
and came to Ephesus. He found some disci-
ples 2 and said to them, "Have you received
the Holy Spirit since you believed?"
They said to him, "No, we have not even
heard that there is a Holy Spirit."
3 He said to them, "Into what then were you
baptized?"
They said, "Into John's baptism."
4 Paul said, "John indeed baptized with the
baptism of repentance, telling the people that
they should believe in the One coming after
him, that is, in Christ Jesus." 5 When they heard
this, they were baptized in the name of the
Lord Jesus. 6 When Paul had laid his hands on
them, the Holy Spirit came on them, and they
spoke in other tongues and prophesied. 7 There
were about twelve men in all.
8 He went into the synagogue and spoke
boldly for three months, lecturing and per-
suading concerning the kingdom of God.
9 But when some were hardened and did not
believe, but spoke evil of the Way before the
crowd, he withdrew from them and took the
disciples, lecturing daily in the school of Tyran-
nus. 10 This continued for two years, so that all
who lived in Asia heard the word of the Lord
Jesus, both Jews and Greeks.

The Sons of Sceva

11 God worked powerful miracles by the
hands of Paul. 12 So handkerchiefs or aprons
he had touched were brought to the sick, and
the diseases left them, and the evil spirits went
out of them.
13 Then some of the itinerant Jewish exorcists
invoked the name of the Lord Jesus over those
who had evil spirits, saying, "We command you
to come out in the name of Jesus whom Paul
preaches." 14 There were seven sons of a Jewish
high priest named Sceva doing this. 15 The evil
spirit answered, "I know Jesus, and I know Paul,
but who are you?" 16 Then the man in whom the
evil spirit was jumped on them, overpowered
them, and prevailed against them, so that they
fled from that house naked and wounded.
17 This became known to all Jews and Greeks
living in Ephesus. And fear fell on them all, and
the name of the Lord Jesus was magnified.
18 Many who believed came confessing and
telling their deeds. 19 Many who practiced mag-
ic brought their books together and burned
them before everyone. They calculated their
value, which equaled fifty thousand drach-
mas.[1] 20 So the word of the Lord powerfully
grew and spread.

The Riot in Ephesus

21 After these things happened, Paul deter-
mined in his spirit to pass through Macedonia
and Achaia and go to Jerusalem, saying, "Af-
ter I have been there, I must also see Rome."

18:12 Ac 13:7
18:15 Ac 23:29
18:17 1Co 1:1
18:18 Nu 6:18
18:19 Ac 18:4
18:21 1Co 4:19
18:22 Ac 8:40
18:23 Ac 16:6
18:24 1Co 1:12
18:25 Ac 19:3
18:28 Ac 18:5
19:2 Jn 7:39

19:3 Ac 18:25
19:5 Ac 8:16
19:6 Ac 2:4
19:8 Ac 1:3
19:9 Ac 9:2
19:10 Ac 20:31
19:11 Ac 5:12
19:12 Ac 5:15
19:13 Mt 12:27
19:18 Mt 3:6
19:20 Ac 6:7
19:21 Ac 20:22

1 19 A drachma was worth about a day's wage.

Stand Strong

When you stand strong, you can stand tall (with confidence) and stand long (with perseverance), because you're drawing from a core strength in your spirit. You have a full a reservoir of spiritual strength that comes from God.

Don't get confused about it—your inner strength is *not* the same as being a tough person, someone who has been hardened by life experiences. To stand strong, you do not necessarily need a degree from the School of Hard Knocks. You don't stand strong in the way I'm talking about just because you happened to grow up on a ranch that your granddaddy homesteaded.

You stand strong in *your* spirit because you are filled with *God's* Spirit. Paul said, "For when I am weak, then I am strong" (2Co 12:10). You have such limited power of your own that you need to keep asking for God's Spirit to fill you up. And that keeps you growing stronger all the time.

To stand strong in God's Spirit is the only way to truly stand strong. All the other kinds of strong standing are like mere shadows of the real thing. It is a level of stamina that believes God regardless. It is simply knowing who God is, knowing that you can trust Him to be who He says He is, trusting Him to do what He says He will do. Your flesh, persistence, or composure doesn't amount to much compared to His way of struggling.

When you stand strong in God's Spirit, you:

- Walk by faith, not by sight
- Walk in boldness and authority
- Speak the Word of God and situations change
- Lay hands on the sick and they recover
- Press forward to do His works no matter what opposition comes your way
- Are strong in adversity
- Are calm in the storm
- Call forth those things that are not as though they were

Standing strong doesn't happen automatically. It's a lifelong process of growth, and you have to cooperate with it. When the disciples wanted to see an example of the kingdom of God, Jesus showed them a child. To become strong in spirit, you must become childlike in your faith.

Sometimes the only way to become strong in spirit is through trials. The early church suffered many trials and tribulations. Paul and Barnabas encouraged them "to continue in the faith, to go through many afflictions and thus enter the kingdom of God" (Ac 14:22).

We grow strongest if we grow where we are planted. We put our roots down in Jesus, and we just grow. Storms come through. Droughts come. Hot and cold weather come. We start out like little saplings, but we just keep on drawing the nourishment out of the soil and the air. We grow taller, our bark gets thicker, and we grow more leaves.

And when that happens, we can say with the apostle Paul, "But none of these things deter me. Nor do I count my life of value to myself, so that I may joyfully finish my course and the ministry which I have received from the Lord Jesus, to testify to the gospel of the grace of God" (Ac 20:24).

Judy Jacobs

22 He sent two who ministered to him, Timothy
and Erastus, into Macedonia, but he delayed
in Asia for a time.
23 About that time great trouble arose about
the Way. 24 For a silversmith named Demetrius,
who made silver shrines for Artemis, brought
much business to the craftsmen. 25 He gathered
them together with the workmen of similar
trades and said, "Men, you know that by this
trade we have our wealth. 26 And you see and
hear, not only at Ephesus, but almost through-
out all Asia, that this Paul has persuaded and
turned away many people, saying that these
things made by hands are not gods. 27 Now
not only is our trade in danger of coming into
disrepute, but also the temple of the great
goddess Artemis, whom all Asia and the world
worship, may be discredited and her magnifi-
cence destroyed."
28 When they heard this, they were full of
anger and cried out, "Great is Artemis of the
Ephesians!" 29 The city was filled with con-
fusion. And in unison they seized Gaius and
Aristarchus, Paul's traveling companions
from Macedonia, and rushed into the the-
ater. 30 When Paul intended to go in among
the crowd, the disciples would not let him.
31 Even some of the rulers of Asia, who were
his friends, sent to him begging him not to
venture into the theater.
32 The assembly was confused. Therefore
some cried out one thing and some another,
and most of them did not know why they had
come together. 33 The Jews pushed Alexan-
der to the front as the crowd prompted him.
Alexander motioned with his hand, wishing
to make his defense to the mob. 34 But when
they learned that he was a Jew, for about two
hours they all with one voice cried out, "Great
is Artemis of the Ephesians!"
35 The city clerk quieted the crowd and said,
"Men of Ephesus, what man is there who does
not know that the city of the Ephesians is the
guardian of the temple of the great Artemis
and of the image which fell from heaven?
36 Seeing then that these things are undeniable,
you ought to be quiet and do nothing rash.
37 For you have brought these men here who
are neither temple robbers nor blasphemers
of your goddess. 38 So if Demetrius and the
craftsmen who are with him have a complaint
against anyone, the courts are open and there
are proconsuls. Let them press charges against
one another. 39 If you seek anything further, it
shall be settled in the legal assembly. 40 For we
are in danger of being charged with rioting
today, since there is no reason we may give to
account for this uproar." 41 When he had said
this, he dismissed the assembly.

19:22 Ac 13:5
19:23 Ac 19:9
19:24 Ac 16:16
19:25 Ac 16:19
19:26 Isa 44:10–20
19:29 Ac 20:4
19:32 Ac 21:34
19:33 Ac 12:17
19:34 Ac 19:28
19:37 Ro 2:22
19:38 Ac 13:7

....

20:1 Ac 19:21
20:3 Ac 20:19
20:4 Ac 19:29
20:5 Ac 16:8
20:6 Ac 12:3
20:7 Ac 20:11
20:8 Ac 1:13
20:10 Mk 5:39
20:11 Ac 20:7
20:15 Ac 20:17
20:16 Ac 2:1
20:17 Ac 11:30
20:18 Ac 18:19
20:19 Ac 20:3
20:20 Ac 20:27

Paul's Journey to Macedonia and Greece

20 After the uproar ceased, Paul sum-
moned the disciples and embraced
them and departed for Macedonia. 2 When he
had gone through that region and had great-
ly exhorted them, he arrived in Greece, 3 and
stayed there three months. When the Jews
plotted against him as he was about to sail to
Syria, he decided to return through Macedo-
nia. 4 Accompanying him to Asia were Sopa-
ter of Berea, and Aristarchus and Secundus
of Thessalonica, Gaius of Derbe, and Timothy,
and Tychicus and Trophimus of Asia. 5 These
men went forward and waited for us at Troas.
6 But we sailed away from Philippi after the
Days of Unleavened Bread, and after five days
we came to them at Troas, where we stayed
for seven days.

Paul's Farewell Visit to Troas

7 On the first day of the week, when the disci-
ples came together to break bread, Paul, ready
to leave the next day, preached to them and
continued his message until midnight. 8 There
were many lamps in the upper room where
they were assembled. 9 A young man named
Eutychus sat in the window, falling into a deep
sleep as Paul spoke for a longer time. Being
overcome by sleep, he fell down from the third
floor and was taken up dead. 10 Paul went
down and leaned over him, and embracing
him said, "Do not be troubled, for he is alive."
11 When he had gone up and had broken bread
and eaten, he conversed for a long while until
dawn and departed. 12 They took the lad in
alive and were greatly comforted.

The Voyage From Troas to Miletus

13 We went ahead to the ship and sailed to
Assos, intending to take Paul on board there.
For he had arranged this, intending to go on
foot. 14 When he met us at Assos, we took him
on board and went to Mitylene. 15 The day after
sailing from there we arrived off Chios. And
the next day we crossed over to Samos and
stayed at Trogyllium, and the following day we
came to Miletus. 16 Paul had decided to sail by
Ephesus, to avoid spending time in Asia. For
he was hurrying so he could be in Jerusalem,
if possible, on the day of Pentecost.

Paul Speaks to the Ephesian Elders

17 From Miletus he sent to Ephesus for the
elders of the church. 18 When they came to him,
he said to them, "You know how I always lived
among you from the first day that I came to
Asia, 19 serving the Lord with all humility and
with many tears and trials which befell me
through the plots of the Jews. 20 I did not keep
from declaring what was beneficial to you,
and teaching you publicly and from house to

house, 21 testifying to both Jews and Greeks of repentance toward God and of faith in our Lord Jesus Christ.

22 "Now, compelled by the Spirit, I am going to Jerusalem, not knowing what shall befall me there, 23 except that the Holy Spirit testifies to me in every city that imprisonment and afflictions await me. 24 But none of these things deter me. Nor do I count my life of value to myself, so that I may joyfully finish my course and the ministry which I have received from the Lord Jesus, to testify to the gospel of the grace of God.

25 "Now I know that all you, among whom I went proclaiming the kingdom of God, will see my face no more. 26 Therefore I testify to you this day that I am innocent of the blood of all men. 27 For I did not keep from declaring to you the whole counsel of God. 28 Therefore take heed to yourselves and to the entire flock, over which the Holy Spirit has made you overseers, to shepherd the church of God which He purchased with His own blood. 29 For I know that after my departure, dreadful wolves will enter among you, not sparing the flock. 30 Even from among you men will arise speaking perverse things, to draw the disciples away after them. 31 Therefore watch, remembering that for three years night and day I did not cease to warn everyone with tears.

32 "Now, brothers, I commend you to God and to the word of His grace, which is able to build you up and give you an inheritance among all who are sanctified. 33 I have not coveted anyone's silver or gold or clothing. 34 Yes, you yourselves know that these hands have provided for my necessities and for those who were with me. 35 In all things I have shown you how, working like this, you must help the weak, remembering the words of the Lord Jesus, how He said, 'It is more blessed to give than to receive.'"

36 Having said these things, he knelt down with all of them and prayed. 37 They all wept much and embraced Paul's neck and kissed him, 38 grieving most over the words he spoke, that they were to see his face no more. Then they escorted him to the ship.

Paul's Journey to Jerusalem

21 When we had withdrawn from them and set sail, we went on a straight course to Cos, the next day to Rhodes, and from there to Patara. 2 We found a ship crossing over to Phoenicia, went aboard, and set sail. 3 Having come in sight of Cyprus, we passed to the south of it and sailed to Syria, and landed at Tyre, for there the ship's cargo was to be unloaded. 4 When we found the disciples, we remained there seven days. They told Paul through the Spirit not to go up to Jerusalem. 5 But when our days were over, we parted and traveled on. Everyone, with wives and children, escorted us until we were outside the city. And we knelt on the shore and prayed. 6 After bidding farewell to one another, we boarded the ship, and they returned home.

7 We finished the voyage from Tyre when we landed at Ptolemais, where we greeted the brothers and stayed with them for one day. 8 The next day we who were Paul's companions departed, and arrived at Caesarea, and entered the house of Philip the evangelist, who was one of the seven, and stayed with him. 9 He had four virgin daughters who prophesied.

10 While we stayed there many days, a prophet named Agabus came down from Judea. 11 When he had arrived, he took Paul's belt and bound his own hands and feet, saying, "The Holy Spirit says, 'In this manner the Jews at Jerusalem shall bind the man who owns this belt and deliver him into the hands of the Gentiles.' "

12 When we heard these things, both we and the residents implored him not to go up to Jerusalem. 13 Then Paul answered, "What are you doing, weeping and breaking my heart? For I am ready not only to be imprisoned, but also to die in Jerusalem for the name of the Lord Jesus." 14 When he would not be persuaded, we kept silent and said, "Let the will of the Lord be done."

15 After those days we got ready and went up to Jerusalem. 16 Some of the disciples from Caesarea went with us and brought with them Mnason of Cyprus, an early disciple, with whom we should lodge.

Paul Visits James

17 When we had come to Jerusalem, the brothers received us gladly. 18 On the next day Paul went with us to James, and all the elders were present. 19 He greeted them and recounted one by one what God had done among the Gentiles through his ministry.

20 When they heard this, they glorified the Lord. Then they said to him, "You see, brother, how many thousands of Jews there are who believe, and they are all zealous for the law. 21 They have been informed concerning you that you teach all the Jews who are among the Gentiles to forsake Moses, telling them not to circumcise their children nor to observe the customs. 22 What then shall be done? The assembly will certainly meet, for they will hear that you have come. 23 Therefore do what we tell you. We have four men who have taken a vow. 24 Take these men and be purified with

20:21 Ac 2:38
20:23 Ac 9:16
20:24 Ac 21:13
20:25 Ac 28:31
20:26 Ac 18:6
20:27 Ac 20:20
20:28 1Co 10:32
20:29 Mt 7:15
20:31 Ac 19:10
20:32 Ac 14:23
20:33 1Co 9:12
20:34 Ac 18:3
20:36 Lk 22:41
20:38 Ac 15:3

21:5 Ac 20:36
21:6 Jn 19:27
21:8 Ac 6:5
21:9 Ac 2:17
21:10 Ac 11:28
21:11 Ac 21:33
21:12 Mt 16:21–23
21:13 Ac 20:24
21:17 Ac 15:4
21:19 Ac 1:17
21:20 Ac 22:3
21:21 Ac 21:28
21:23 Ac 18:18
21:24 Ac 21:26

them, and pay their expenses so that they may have their heads shaved. Then all will know that what they were told concerning you is nothing, but that you yourself live in observance of the law. 25 As for the Gentiles who believe, we have written and concluded that they should observe no such thing, except that they abstain from food offered to idols, from sexual immorality, from strangled animals, and from blood."

26 Then on the next day, Paul took the men and purified himself with them. And he went into the temple, announcing when the days of purification would be complete and an offering would be given for each one of them.

Paul Arrested in the Temple

27 When the seven days were nearly concluded, the Jews from Asia saw him in the temple, stirred up all the people, and laid hands on him, 28 crying out, "Men of Israel, help! This is the man teaching all men everywhere against the people and the law and this place. He even brought Greeks into the temple and has defiled this holy place." 29 For they had previously seen Trophimus the Ephesian in the city with him, whom they supposed Paul had brought into the temple.

30 Then the whole city was provoked, and the people ran together. They seized Paul and dragged him out of the temple. And immediately the doors were shut. 31 While they were trying to kill him, news came up to the commander[1] of the battalion of soldiers that all Jerusalem was in an uproar. 32 He at once took soldiers and centurions, and ran down to them. When they saw the commander and the soldiers, they stopped beating Paul.

33 Then the commander came and arrested him, and ordered that he be bound with two chains. Then he asked who he was and what he had done. 34 Some in the crowd shouted one thing, some another. As he could not learn the truth because of the uproar, he commanded that he be brought into the barracks. 35 When he came onto the stairs, he was carried by the soldiers because of the violence of the people. 36 For the mob of people followed, crying out, "Away with him!"

Paul Defends Himself

37 As Paul was about to be brought into the barracks, he said to the commander, "May I speak to you?"

He replied, "Do you know how to speak Greek? 38 Are you not the Egyptian who in past days caused an uproar and led the four thousand men of the Sicarii[2] out into the wilderness?"

21:25 Ac 15:29
21:26 Ac 24:18
21:27 Ac 24:18
21:28 Ac 24:5–6
21:29 Ac 20:4
21:30 Ac 26:21
21:32 Ac 23:27
21:33 Ac 12:6
21:34 Ac 19:32
21:36 Lk 23:18
21:38 Mt 24:26

....

21:39 Ac 9:11
21:40 Ac 12:17
22:1 Ac 7:2
22:2 Ac 21:40
22:3 Ac 9:11
22:4 Ac 22:19–20
22:5 Lk 22:66
22:9 Ac 9:7
22:10 Ac 16:30
22:12 Ac 10:22
22:14 Ac 26:16
22:15 Ac 23:11
22:16 Ac 2:38

39 Paul said, "I am a Jew, from Tarsus of Cilicia, a citizen of no common city. I beg of you, permit me to speak to the people."

40 When he had given him permission, Paul stood on the stairs and motioned with his hand to the people. When there was great silence, he addressed them in the Hebrew language, saying,

22 "Brothers and fathers, hear my defense which I now make to you."

2 When they heard that he addressed them in the Hebrew language, they became even more quiet.

Then he said, 3 "I am a Jew, born in Tarsus of Cilicia, but brought up in this city. At the feet of Gamaliel I was trained in the strict tradition of the law of the fathers, being zealous toward God as you all are today. 4 I persecuted this Way to the death, arresting and imprisoning both men and women, 5 as even the high priest and the council of elders bear witness of me. From them I received letters to the brothers in Damascus, where I went to take even those who were there and lead them in chains to Jerusalem to be punished.

Paul Tells of His Conversion

Ac 9:1–19; 26:12–18

6 "As I journeyed and came near Damascus, about noon suddenly a great light from heaven shone around me. 7 I fell to the ground and heard a voice saying to me, 'Saul, Saul, why do you persecute Me?'

8 "I answered, 'Who are You, Lord?'

"He said to me, 'I am Jesus of Nazareth, whom you are persecuting.' 9 Those who were with me saw the light and were afraid, but they did not hear the voice of Him who was speaking to me.

10 "I said, 'What shall I do, Lord?'

"The Lord said to me, 'Rise and go into Damascus. There you will be told what you have been appointed to do.' 11 Since I was blinded by the glory of that light, those who were with me led me by the hand into Damascus.

12 "Ananias, a devout man according to the law, who was well spoken of by all the Jews living there, 13 came and stood by me, and said, 'Brother Saul, receive your sight.' And at that moment I looked up at him.

14 "Then he said, 'The God of our fathers has appointed you to know His will and to see the Just One and to hear His voice, 15 for you will be His witness to all men of what you have seen and heard. 16 And now why do you wait? Rise, be baptized and wash away your sins, and call on the name of the Lord.'

[1] *31* Gk. *chiliarch*, a battalion commander with the rank of lieutenant colonel over 1,000 soldiers. [2] *38* Or *men of the Assassins.*

Paul Sent to the Gentiles

17 "When I returned to Jerusalem and was
praying in the temple, I fell into a trance 18 and
saw Him saying to me, 'Hurry! Get out of Je-
rusalem immediately, for they will not receive
your testimony concerning Me.'

19 "I said, 'Lord, they know that I imprisoned
and beat those who believed in You in every
synagogue. 20 And when the blood of Your
martyr Stephen was shed, I was standing by
consenting to his death, guarding the clothes
of those who killed him.'

21 "Then He said to me, 'Depart, for I will send
you far away to the Gentiles.' "

Paul and the Roman Commander

22 They listened to him up to this word, and
then they lifted up their voices and said, "Away
with such a man from the earth, for he is not
fit to live!"

23 As they shouted and threw off their gar-
ments and threw dust into the air, 24 the com-
mander ordered him to be brought into the
barracks and examined with scourging, so that
he might learn what crime they were alleging
against him. 25 As they stretched him forward
with straps, Paul said to the centurion standing
by, "Is it legal for you to flog an uncondemned
Roman citizen?"

26 On hearing this, the centurion reported to
the commander, saying, "What are you doing?
This man is a Roman citizen."

27 The commander came and said to him,
"Tell me, are you a Roman citizen?"

He said, "Yes."

28 The commander answered, "I bought my
citizenship for a large sum."

So Paul said, "But I was born a citizen."

29 Therefore those who were about to examine
Paul immediately backed away from him. And
the commander feared, knowing that he was a
Roman citizen and because he had bound him.

Paul Before the Sanhedrin

30 On the next day, desiring to know exactly
why he was accused by the Jews, he released
him and ordered the chief priests and all the
Sanhedrin to assemble, and he brought Paul
down to stand before them.

23 Paul looked at the Sanhedrin and said,
"Brothers, I have lived in all good con-
science before God until this day." 2 The high
priest Ananias ordered those who stood by him
to strike him on the mouth. 3 Then Paul said
to him, "God will strike you, you whitewashed
wall! Do you sit judging me according to the law,
yet order me to be struck contrary to the law?"

4 Those who stood by said, "Do you criticize
God's high priest?"

5 Paul said, "Brothers, I did not know that he
was the high priest. For it is written, 'You shall
not speak evil of the ruler of your people.'[1]"

6 Then Paul, knowing that one sect were
Sadducees and the other Pharisees, cried out
among the Sanhedrin, "Brothers, I am a Phar-
isee, a son of a Pharisee. I am being judged
for my hope in the resurrection of the dead."
7 When he had said this, dissension arose be-
tween the Pharisees and the Sadducees, and
the assembly was divided. 8 For the Sadducees
say that there is no resurrection, nor angel, nor
spirit. But the Pharisees acknowledge them all.

9 There was a great outcry. The scribes that
were from the sect of Pharisees stood up and
argued, "We find no evil in this man. But if a
spirit or an angel has spoken to him, let us not
fight against God." 10 When much dissension
arose, fearing that Paul would be torn to pieces
by them, the commander ordered the soldiers
to go down and take him from them by force
and bring him into the barracks.

11 The following night the Lord stood by him
and said, "Take courage, Paul. For as you have
testified about Me in Jerusalem, so you must
also testify at Rome."

The Plot Against Paul's Life

12 At daybreak some of the Jews conspired
under oath, saying they would neither eat nor
drink until they had killed Paul. 13 There were
more than forty who had conspired. 14 They
went to the chief priests and elders and said,
"We have bound ourselves under oath not to
eat until we have killed Paul. 15 So now, with
the Sanhedrin, tell the commander to bring
him down to you tomorrow, pretending to in-
quire further concerning him. We are ready to
kill him before he arrives."

16 But when the son of Paul's sister heard of
the treachery, he went and entered the bar-
racks and told Paul.

17 Then Paul called one of the centurions
over and said, "Take this young man to the
commander, for he has something to tell him."
18 So he took him to the commander and said,
"Paul the prisoner sent for me and asked me to
bring you this young man who has something
to tell you."

19 Then the commander took him by the
hand, went aside privately, and asked him,
"What is it you have to tell me?"

20 The boy said, "The Jews have agreed to
ask you to bring Paul down tomorrow to the
Sanhedrin, pretending to inquire further con-
cerning him. 21 Do not trust them. More than
forty men, who have bound themselves with

22:17 2Co 12:1–4
22:19 Mt 10:17
22:20 Ac 7:58
22:21 Ac 9:15
22:22 Ac 25:24
22:25 Ac 16:37
22:30 Ac 23:28
23:1 Ac 24:16
23:2 Ac 24:1
23:3 Jn 7:51

23:5 Ex 22:28
23:6 Ac 24:15
23:8 Mt 22:23
23:9 Ac 22:7
23:10 Ac 22:24
23:11 Ac 18:9
23:12 Ac 23:21
23:16 Ac 23:10
23:18 Eph 3:1
23:20 Ac 23:14–15
23:21 Ac 23:12–14

[1] 5 Ex 22:28.

an oath to neither eat nor drink until they have killed him, are waiting for him. And now they are ready, waiting for your promise."

22 The commander dismissed the young man and ordered him, "Tell no one that you have reported these things to me."

Paul Sent to Felix the Governor

23 Then he summoned two centurions and said, "Prepare two hundred infantrymen, seventy mounted soldiers, and two hundred light infantrymen with spears to go to Caesarea at the third hour of the night. 24 And provide mounts so Paul may ride and take him safely to Felix the governor."

25 He wrote a letter that went like this:

26 Claudius Lysias,

To His Excellency Governor Felix:

Greetings.

27 This man was seized by the Jews and was about to be killed by them. When I learned that he was a Roman citizen, I came with soldiers and rescued him. 28 Being minded to learn what crime they alleged, I took him to their Sanhedrin. 29 I found him being accused of controversial matters about their law, but charged with nothing worthy of death or imprisonment. 30 When it was revealed to me that there was a plot against the man, at once I sent him to you and ordered the accusers to state before you their charges against him.

Farewell.

31 So the soldiers, according to their orders, took Paul by night to Antipatris. 32 The next day they let the cavalry depart with him and they returned to the barracks. 33 When they arrived in Caesarea and delivered the letter to the governor, they presented Paul also to him. 34 Upon reading the letter, the governor asked what province he was from. When he learned that he was from Cilicia, 35 he said, "I will hear you when your accusers also arrive." And he ordered that he be guarded in Herod's Praetorium.

The Case Against Paul

24 After five days Ananias the high priest arrived with some of the elders and a lawyer named Tertullus. They brought before the governor their charges against Paul. 2 When he was summoned, Tertullus began to accuse him, saying, "Since through you we enjoy much peace, and your foresight is bringing reforms to this nation, 3 with all thankfulness, most excellent Felix, we always welcome it everywhere. 4 But not to detain you further, I beg you to briefly hear us in your patience.

23:24 Ac 23:26
23:26 Ac 15:23
23:27 Ac 22:25–29
23:28 Ac 22:30
23:29 Ac 18:15
23:34 Ac 21:39
23:35 Ac 23:30
24:1 Ac 23:2
24:3 Ac 23:26
24:5 Ac 28:22
24:11 Ac 24:1
24:12 Ac 25:8
24:13 Ac 25:7
24:14 Ac 3:13
24:15 Da 12:2
24:16 Ac 23:1
24:17 Gal 2:10
24:18 Ac 26:21
24:19 Ac 23:30
24:21 Ac 23:6
24:23 Ac 27:3
24:24 Ac 20:21
24:25 Ac 10:42

5 "We have found this man a troublemaker, instigating riots among all the Jews throughout the world, and a ringleader of the sect of the Nazarenes. 6 He even tried to profane the temple. So we seized him and wanted to judge him according to our law. 7 But the commander, Lysias, came to us and forcefully took him out of our hands, 8 ordering his accusers to come before you. By examining him yourself you will be able to learn about all these things concerning which we accuse him."

9 The Jews assented, alleging these things to be true.

Paul's Defense Before Felix

10 After the governor motioned to him to speak, Paul answered, "Knowing that for many years you have been a judge over this nation, I cheerfully defend myself. 11 You may verify that it is no more than twelve days since I went up to Jerusalem to worship. 12 They did not find me in the temple or in the synagogues or in the city disputing with anyone or stirring up a crowd. 13 They cannot prove the things concerning which they now accuse me. 14 However, I affirm that in accordance with the Way, which they call a sect, I worship the God of my fathers and believe everything written in the Law and in the Prophets. 15 I have hope in God that there will be a resurrection of the dead, both of the just and the unjust, which they also expect. 16 In this do I always strive to have a clear conscience toward God and toward men.

17 "Now after many years I came to bring alms and offerings to my nation, 18 when some Jews from Asia found me purified in the temple, neither with a crowd nor an uproar. 19 They ought to be here before you to accuse me if they have any charges. 20 Or let these men say what crime they found in me when I stood before the Sanhedrin, 21 unless it is concerning this one statement which I cried out while standing among them, 'Concerning the resurrection of the dead, I am being judged by you this day.' "

22 When Felix, who had more exact knowledge concerning the Way, had heard this, he adjourned the proceedings and said, "When Lysias the commander arrives, I will decide your case." 23 Then he ordered the centurion to guard Paul, and to let him have liberty, and to forbid none of his own people from attending to him.

Paul Held in Custody

24 After several days, when Felix arrived with his wife Drusilla, who was a Jewess, he sent for Paul and heard him speak concerning faith in Christ. 25 As he lectured about righteousness, self-control, and the coming judgment, Felix

SPIRITLED WOMAN

COUNSEL FROM THE SPIRIT BASICS

Get Out of the Way

The kingdom of God is ever moving, always flowing, and God is not interested in our fossilized methods, especially if they serve as obstacles to His presence. He wants us. He wants a living, breathing, freely flowing relationship with us. He wants to move in us and through us, and He reserves the right to disrupt our plans, our methods, and even our ideals in order to accomplish His otherworldly plans upon this earth.

Jesus didn't have a single method of doing things, either. He healed people in a plethora of ways. He is not at all bound by the way we've always done it. If Christ wants to move in our church or in our business or in our family in a new and fresh way, may we be the first to get out of the way and let Him have His way!

What happens when we do such a thing? Fruit happens! Life happens! Power happens! And how will people respond? The sincere, earnest Christ followers and seekers will be drawn to the fresh stream flowing from our lives, churches, and businesses. They will be nourished, healed, saved, and encouraged. Yes, Lord!

And the rigid, unbending Pharisees? Well, they'll hate everything about it. They'll stiffen up. They'll find fault. They'll become territorial. And they'll turn into the sin police and watch for the slightest deviation from what they know to be right and true.

Now, granted, we never want to deviate from the truth. But in following Christ—who is the truth—we must know that He will lead us in ways we have not known before. He loves to do that and invites us to willingly trust Him, even if it disrupts our affection for appearing civilized and packaged at all times.

When God moves, may we move with Him. May we resist the urge to control our zone and to manage our methods. Let's put it all on the table and give God room to work.

Move powerfully in and through us, Lord!

Susie Larson

24:27 Ac 25:9
25:1 Ac 23:34
25:2 Ac 25:15
25:6 Ac 25:17
25:7 Ac 24:13
25:8 Ac 24:12
25:9 Ac 24:27
25:11 Ac 26:32
25:14 Ac 24:27
25:16 Ac 25:4–5

was afraid and answered, "For now, leave!
When time permits, I will send for you." 26 At the
same time he hoped that money would be given
him by Paul, that he might release him. So he
sent for him more often and conversed with him.
27 But after two years Porcius Festus succeeded Felix. And Felix, desiring to do the Jews a
favor, left Paul imprisoned.

Paul Appeals to Caesar

25 Now three days after Festus had come
into the province, he went from Caesarea up to Jerusalem. 2 The high priest and
the elders of the Jews spoke to him against
Paul. And they begged him, 3 asking as a favor
against him, that he would summon him to
Jerusalem, plotting to kill him along the way.
4 Festus said that Paul should be kept at Caesarea and that he himself intended to go there
shortly. 5 He also said, "Let the men in authority
go down with me. If there is anything wrong
in the man, let them accuse him."
6 Having stayed among them more than ten
days, he went down to Caesarea. And the next
day he sat on the judgment seat and ordered
that Paul be brought in. 7 When he arrived,
the Jews who had come down from Jerusalem stood around him and brought many serious charges against him which they could
not prove, 8 while he defended himself, saying, "Neither against the law of the Jews, nor
against the temple, nor against Caesar have I
sinned at all."
9 Desiring to do the Jews a favor, Festus
answered, "Are you willing to go up to Jerusalem to be judged concerning these charges
before me?"
10 Paul said, "I am standing before Caesar's
judgment seat, where I ought to be judged. I
have done no wrong to the Jews, as you know
very well. 11 If I am doing wrong or have done
anything worthy of death, I do not refuse to
die. But if these are empty charges of which
these men accuse me, no one may deliver me
to them. I appeal to Caesar."
12 When Festus had conferred with the council, he then answered, "To Caesar you have
appealed. To Caesar you shall go."

Paul Before Agrippa and Bernice

13 After several days King Agrippa and Bernice arrived at Caesarea to welcome Festus.
14 When they had been there many days,
Festus stated Paul's case to the king, saying,
"There is a man left as a prisoner by Felix.
15 When I was at Jerusalem, the chief priests
and the elders of the Jews informed me about
him, asking for a sentence against him.
16 "I answered, 'It is not the custom of the
Romans to deliver any man to die before he

who is accused meets the accusers face to face
and has the opportunity to make his defense
concerning the charge brought against him.'
17 So when they assembled here, without delay
I sat on the judgment seat the next day and or-
dered that the man be brought in. 18 When the
accusers stood up, they brought no accusation
against him of such crimes as I had supposed.
19 But they had disagreements with him about
their own religion and about a Man named
Jesus, who had died, but whom Paul assert-
ed was alive. 20 Being perplexed about such
questions, I asked if he would be willing to
go to Jerusalem and be tried there concerning
these charges. 21 But when Paul had appealed
to be under guard for the decision of Caesar, I
ordered that he be secured until I could send
him to Caesar."
22 Then Agrippa said to Festus, "I would like
to hear the man myself."
He said, "Tomorrow you shall hear him."
23 The next day Agrippa and Bernice came
with great pomp, and they entered the hall
with the commanders and the leading men
of the city. When Festus gave the order, Paul
was brought in. 24 Festus said, "King Agrippa,
and all the men who are present with us, you
see this man, concerning whom the whole
assembly of the Jews petitioned me, both at
Jerusalem and here, shouting that he ought
not to live any longer. 25 I found that he had
committed nothing worthy of death. But when
he himself appealed to Caesar, I decided to
send him. 26 But I have nothing to write to
His Majesty concerning him. Therefore I have
brought him before you, and especially before
you, King Agrippa, so that upon examination, I
might have something to write. 27 For it seems
unreasonable to me to send a prisoner without
signifying the charges against him."

Paul's Defense Before Agrippa

26 Then Agrippa said to Paul, "You are
permitted to speak for yourself."
So Paul stretched out his hand and made
his defense: 2 "King Agrippa, I consider myself
fortunate that today I shall make my defense
before you against all the accusations of the
Jews, 3 especially because you are an expert
in all customs and controversies of the Jews.
Therefore I beg you to patiently listen to me.
4 "My manner of life from my youth, spent
from the beginning in my own nation and at
Jerusalem, is known by all the Jews. 5 They
knew me from the beginning and could testify,
if they wished, how according to the strictest
sect of our religion I lived as a Pharisee. 6 And
now I stand on trial for hope in the promise
made by God to our fathers, 7 to which our

25:19 Ac 18:15
25:20 Ac 25:9
25:22 Ac 9:15
25:23 Ac 25:13
25:24 Ac 22:22
25:25 Ac 23:29
26:1 Ac 9:15
26:3 Ac 6:14
26:4 Gal 1:13
26:5 Ac 23:6
26:6 Ac 24:15
26:7 Jas 1:1

....

26:9 1Ti 1:13
26:10 Ac 8:3
26:11 Mt 10:17
26:14 Ac 21:40
26:16 Ac 22:14–15
26:17 Ac 9:15
26:18 Ac 20:32
26:20 Mt 3:8
26:21 Ac 21:30–31
26:22 Ac 24:14
26:23 Rev 1:5

twelve tribes hope to attain, as they earnest-
ly serve God day and night. Concerning this
hope, King Agrippa, I am accused by the Jews.
8 Why is it judged incredible by you that God
raises the dead?
9 "I, too, thought that I must do many things
contrary to the name of Jesus of Nazareth,
10 which I indeed did in Jerusalem and locked
up many of the saints in prison by authority
from the chief priests. And when they were
killed, I cast my vote against them. 11 I pun-
ished them often in every synagogue and
compelled them to blaspheme. And being ex-
tremely enraged against them, I persecuted
them even to foreign cities.

Paul Tells of His Conversion

Ac 9:1–19; 22:6–16

12 "So I went to Damascus with authority and
a commission from the chief priests. 13 At mid-
day, O King, I saw along the way a light from
heaven, brighter than the sun, shining around
me and those who journeyed with me. 14 When
we had all fallen to the ground, I heard a voice
saying to me in the Hebrew language, 'Saul,
Saul, why do you persecute Me? It is hard for
you to kick against the goads.'
15 "I said, 'Who are You, Lord?'
"He said, 'I am Jesus whom you are perse-
cuting. 16 But rise and stand on your feet. For
I have appeared to you for this purpose, to
appoint you as a servant and a witness both
of what you have seen and of what I will yet
reveal to you. 17 I will deliver you from your
people and from the Gentiles to whom I now
send you, 18 to open their eyes and to turn them
from darkness to light, and from the power of
Satan to God, that they may receive forgive-
ness of sins and an inheritance among those
who are sanctified by faith in Me.'

I am delivered from the power of Satan unto God (Ac 26:18).

Paul's Testimony to Jews and Gentiles

19 "Therefore, King Agrippa, I was not dis-
obedient to the heavenly vision, 20 but declared
first to those at Damascus, then at Jerusalem
and throughout all the region of Judea, and
also to the Gentiles, that they should repent
and turn to God and do works proving their re-
pentance. 21 For these reasons the Jews seized
me in the temple and tried to kill me. 22 There-
fore having obtained help from God, I continue
to this day, testifying both to small and great,
saying nothing but what the prophets and Mo-
ses said would happen: 23 that the Christ must
suffer, that He would be the first who would

rise from the dead, and would announce light to His own people and to the Gentiles."

Paul Appeals to Agrippa to Believe

24 So as he made his defense, Festus said with a loud voice, "Paul, you are mad. Much learning is turning you to madness."

25 Paul said, "I am not mad, most excellent Festus. I speak the words of truth and reason. 26 The king, before whom I also speak freely, knows about these things. For I am persuaded that none of this is hidden from him, for this was not done in a corner. 27 King Agrippa, do you believe the prophets? I know that you believe."

28 Then Agrippa said to Paul, "You almost persuade me to be a Christian."

29 Paul said, "I pray to God that not only you, but all who hear me this day, might become not only almost, but thoroughly and altogether, what I am, except for these chains."

30 When he had said this, the king rose, as well as the governor and Bernice and those who sat with them. 31 When they had gone aside, they said to one another, "This man is doing nothing deserving death or imprisonment."

32 And Agrippa said to Festus, "This man could have been set free if he had not appealed to Caesar."

Paul Sails for Rome

27 When it was decided that we should sail into Italy, they handed Paul and some other prisoners over to a centurion of the Augustan Regiment, named Julius. 2 Boarding a ship from Adramyttium, we put out to sea, meaning to sail along the coasts of Asia. Aristarchus, a Macedonian of Thessalonica, was with us.

3 The next day we landed at Sidon. And Julius treated Paul kindly and gave him leave to go to his friends and be given care. 4 From there we put out to sea and sailed under the lee of Cyprus, because the winds were against us. 5 Sailing across the sea off of Cilicia and Pamphylia, we came to Myra, a city of Lycia. 6 There the centurion found a ship of Alexandria sailing to Italy, and he put us on board. 7 We sailed slowly for many days, and arrived with difficulty off Cnidus, and as the wind did not allow us to proceed, we sailed under the lee of Crete off Salmone. 8 Sailing past it with difficulty, we came to a place called Fair Havens, near the city of Lasea.

9 As much time had been lost and as the voyage was now dangerous, because the Day of Atonement was already over, Paul advised them, 10 saying, "Men, I perceive that this voyage will be with injury and much loss, not only of the cargo and ship, but also of our lives."

26:24 1Co 4:10
26:25 Ac 23:26
26:28 Ac 11:26
26:31 Ac 23:29
26:32 Ac 28:18
27:1 Ac 25:25
27:2 Ac 19:29
27:3 Ac 24:23
27:4 Ac 4:36
27:5 Ac 6:9
27:6 Ac 28:11
27:7 Ac 27:21
27:9 Lev 23:27–29
27:14 Mk 4:37
27:17 Ac 27:29
27:18 Jnh 1:5
27:22 Ac 27:25
27:23 Ac 5:19
27:24 Ac 23:11
27:25 Ro 4:20–21
27:26 Ac 28:1
27:29 Ac 27:17
27:30 Ac 27:16

11 But the centurion was persuaded more by the captain and the owner of the ship than by what Paul said. 12 Since the harbor was not suitable to winter in, the majority decided to sail on from there, if somehow we might reach Phoenix, a harbor in Crete, facing southwest and northwest, and winter there.

The Storm at Sea

13 When a south wind blew gently, supposing that they had obtained the necessary conditions, they weighed anchor and sailed along the shore of Crete. 14 But soon afterward a tempestuous wind swept through, called the Euroclydon.[1] 15 When the ship was overpowered and could not head into the wind, we let her drift. 16 Drifting under the lee of an island called Cauda, we could scarcely secure the rowboat. 17 When they had hoisted it aboard, they used ropes to undergird the ship. And fearing that they might run aground on the sand of Syrtis, they let down the mast, and so were driven. 18 We were violently tossed by the storm. The next day they threw cargo overboard. 19 On the third day we threw the tackle of the ship overboard with our own hands. 20 When neither sun nor stars appeared for many days, and no small storm was upon us, all hope that we should be saved was lost.

21 After they had long abstained from food, Paul stood in their midst and said, "Men, you should have listened to me and not have set sail from Crete, incurring this injury and loss. 22 But now I advise you to take courage, for there will be no loss of life among you, but only of the ship. 23 For there stood by me this night the angel of God to whom I belong and whom I serve, 24 saying, 'Do not be afraid, Paul. You must stand before Caesar. And, look! God has given you all those who sail with you.' 25 Therefore, men, take courage, for I believe God that it will be exactly as it was told to me. 26 Nevertheless, we must be shipwrecked on a certain island."

27 When the fourteenth night came, while we were drifting in the Adriatic Sea, about midnight the sailors supposed that they were approaching land. 28 They took soundings and found the water to be one hundred and twenty feet deep.[2] When they had gone a little farther, they took soundings again and found it to be ninety feet deep.[3] 29 Fearing that we might run aground on the rocks, they dropped four anchors from the stern and prayed for day to come. 30 When the sailors strove to abandon ship and lowered the rowboat into the sea, under the pretext of lowering anchors out of the bow, 31 Paul said to the centurion and to the soldiers, "Unless these sailors remain in the ship, you cannot be saved." 32 Then the soldiers cut away the ropes of the rowboat and let her fall off.

[1] *14* Or *Northeaster.* [2] *28* Gk. *20 orguias*, about 37 meters. [3] *28* Gk. *15 orguias*, about 27 meters.

33 As day was about to dawn, Paul asked
them all to eat, saying, "Today is the fourteenth
day that you have waited and continued with-
out food, having eaten nothing. 34 So I urge you
to eat. This is for your preservation, for not a
hair shall fall from your head." 35 When he had
said this, he took some bread and gave thanks
to God in the presence of them all. And when
he had broken it he began to eat. 36 Then they
were all encouraged, and they also ate food
themselves. 37 In all we were two hundred and
seventy-six persons on the ship. 38 When they
had eaten enough, they lightened the ship and
threw the wheat into the sea.

The Shipwreck

39 When it was day, they did not recognize
the land. But they noticed a bay with a shore,
into which they were determined to run the
ship if possible. 40 Casting off the anchors, they
left them in the sea while loosening the ropes
that secured the rudders. Then they hoisted
the mainsail to the wind and made for shore.
41 But striking a sandbar where two seas met,
they ran the ship aground. The bow stuck and
remained immovable, but the stern was bro-
ken up by the violent surf.

42 The soldiers' plan was to kill the prison-
ers, lest any of them should swim away and
escape. 43 But the centurion, wanting to save
Paul, prevented them from their intent and or-
dered those who could swim to abandon ship
first and get to land, 44 and the rest on planks
or on pieces of the ship. And in this way they
all escaped safely to land.

Paul in Malta

28 When they had escaped, they learned
that the island was called Malta. 2 The
natives showed extraordinary kindness, for
they kindled a fire and welcomed us all, be-
cause of the rain and the cold. 3 When Paul
had gathered a bundle of sticks and put them
on the fire, a viper driven out by the heat fas-
tened on his hand. 4 When the natives saw the
creature hanging from his hand, they said to
one another, "Surely this man is a murderer.
Though he has escaped from the sea, justice
does not allow him to live." 5 But he shook off
the creature into the fire and suffered no harm.
6 They expected him to swell up or suddenly
fall down dead. But while they waited and saw
no harm befall him, they changed their minds
and said that he was a god.

Let demons be exposed and cast out with Your fire (Ac 28:3).

27:34 Mt 10:30
27:35 Mt 15:36
27:36 Ac 27:22
27:37 Ac 2:41
27:38 Jnh 1:5
27:39 Ac 28:1
27:43 Ac 27:3
27:44 Ac 27:22
28:1 Ac 27:26
28:2 Ac 28:4
28:4 Lk 13:2
28:5 Mk 16:18

28:8 Ac 9:40
28:11 Ac 27:6
28:16 Ac 27:3
28:17 Ac 25:8
28:18 Ac 26:31–32
28:19 Ac 26:32
28:21 Ac 22:5
28:22 Ac 24:14
28:23 Ac 19:8

7 In that area was an estate of the chief man
of the island, named Publius, who had wel-
comed us and courteously housed us for three
days. 8 It happened that the father of Publius
lay sick with a fever and dysentery. Paul visited
him and, placing his hands on him, prayed
and healed him. 9 When this happened, the
rest on the island who had diseases also came
and were healed. 10 They honored us in many
ways. And when we sailed, they provided us
with necessary supplies.

Paul Arrives in Rome

11 After three months we sailed in an Alex-
andrian ship whose figurehead was the Twin
Brothers, which had wintered at the island.
12 Landing at Syracuse, we waited there for
three days. 13 From there we circled around
and sailed to Rhegium. After one day the south
wind blew, and the next day we arrived at Pute-
oli. 14 There we found brothers, and were invited
to remain with them for seven days. And so we
went to Rome. 15 From there, when the brothers
heard of us, they traveled as far as the Forum
of Appius[1] and the Three Taverns[2] to meet us.
When Paul saw them, he thanked God and took
courage. 16 When we arrived at Rome, the cen-
turion handed the prisoners over to the captain
of the guard. But Paul was allowed to remain
by himself with the soldier who guarded him.

Paul Preaches in Rome

17 After three days Paul called the leaders of
the Jews together. When they had assembled,
he said to them, "Brothers, having done nothing
contrary to our people or the customs of our fa-
thers, I was delivered as a prisoner from Jerusa-
lem into the hands of the Romans. 18 When they
had examined me, they were determined to re-
lease me, because there was no charge against
me deserving death. 19 But when the Jews ob-
jected, I was compelled to appeal to Caesar,
not that I had any charge to bring against my
nation. 20 For this reason I have asked to see you
and speak with you, because I am bound with
this chain for the hope of Israel."

21 They said to him, "We have not received
any letters from Judea concerning you, and
none of the brothers that have come have re-
ported or spoken any evil of you. 22 But we
think it is proper to hear from you what you
think. For concerning this sect, we know that
it is spoken against everywhere."

23 When they had arranged a day to be with
him, many came to him at his residence. From
morning until evening he explained and sol-
emnly testified of the kingdom of God to them,
persuading them concerning Jesus from both

[1] *15* A town on the Appian Way about 55 miles from Rome. [2] *15* Or Three Inns, also on the Appian Way and about 10 miles closer to Rome.

the Law of Moses and the Prophets. 24 Some
believed what was said, but some did not be-
lieve. 25 Being in disagreement with one anoth-
er, they were dismissed after Paul had said one
word: "The Holy Spirit accurately spoke to our
fathers through Isaiah the prophet,

26 'Go to this people and say:
You shall certainly hear, but never
understand;
and you shall certainly see, but never
perceive;
27 for the heart of this people has grown dull.
Their ears are hard of hearing,
and they have closed their eyes,
lest they should see with their eyes
and hear with their ears
and understand with their heart
and turn, and I would heal them.'[1]

28 "Therefore let it be known to you that the
salvation of God has been sent to the Gentiles.
They will hear it!"
29 When he had said these words, the Jews
departed and disputed greatly among them-
selves. 30 Paul remained two whole years in
his own rented house. He welcomed all who
came to him, 31 boldly and freely preaching
the kingdom of God and teaching those things
which concern the Lord Jesus Christ.

28:24 Ac 14:4
28:25 Mt 15:7
28:26 Eze 12:2
28:31 Ac 28:23

[1] *26–27* Isa 6:9–10.

Author: The apostle Paul
Written: AD 57, from Corinth
Theme: Foundations for Christian Theology, Righteousness

ROMANS

Dear Spirit Led Woman,

The Bible tells us that "faith comes by hearing, and hearing by the word of God" (Ro 10:17).

Some time ago I had lunch with a friend who had walked through several health crises—breast cancer, multiple sclerosis, and a seriously ill family member. She said that her cry was, "God, where are You in all of this?"

When you are in a storm, it is often easier to hear the sound of the wind and the waves of your circumstance than to stay focused on Jesus and the promises recorded in His Word. When you're facing a difficulty, remember Romans 10:17. Write out relevant passages of Scripture and put them in places where you will see them. Encourage yourself by meditating on what God has promised. When circumstances threaten to bring fear into your heart, respond with scriptures that declare God's point of view. Speak the scriptural promises you've written down. There is power in your words, and your faith to believe God will increase!

Joy F. Strang

Salutation

1 Paul, a servant of Jesus Christ, called to be an apostle and set apart for the gospel of God, 2 which He promised beforehand through His prophets in the Holy Scriptures, 3 concerning His Son, Jesus Christ our Lord, who was born of the seed of David according to the flesh 4 and declared to be the Son of God with power, according to the Spirit of holiness, by the resurrection from the dead. 5 Through Him we have received grace and apostleship for the obedience of faith among all nations for His name, 6 among whom you also are called by Jesus Christ:

7 To all who are in Rome, beloved of God, called to be saints:

Grace to you and peace from God our Father and the Lord Jesus Christ.

Paul's Desire to Visit Rome

8 First, I thank my God through Jesus Christ for you all, because your faith is spoken of throughout the whole world. 9 For God is my witness, whom I serve with my spirit in the gospel of His Son, that without ceasing, I mention you always in my prayers, 10 making request if, by any means, now at last I might find a way in the will of God to come to you.

11 For I long to see you, that I may impart to you some spiritual gift, so that you may be strengthened. 12 This is so that I may be encouraged together with you by each other's faith, both yours and mine. 13 Now I would not have you unaware, brothers, that I often intended to come to you (but was prevented until now), that I might have a harvest among you also, even as among the other Gentiles.

14 I am a debtor both to the Greeks and to the barbarians, both to the wise and to the unwise. 15 So, as much as is in me, I am ready to preach the gospel to you also who are in Rome.

The Definition of the Gospel

16 For I am not ashamed of the gospel of Christ. For it is the power of God for salvation to everyone who believes, to the Jew first, and also to the Greek. 17 For in it the righteousness of God is revealed from faith to faith. As it is written, "The just shall live by faith."[1]

The Guilt of Mankind

18 The wrath of God is revealed from heaven against all ungodliness and unrighteousness of men, who suppress the truth through unrighteousness. 19 For what may be known about God is clear to them since God has shown it to them. 20 The invisible things about Him—His eternal power and deity—have been clearly seen since the creation of the world and are understood by the things that are made, so that they are without excuse.

21 Because, although they knew God, they did not glorify Him or give thanks to Him as God, but became futile in their imaginations, and their foolish hearts were darkened. 22 Claiming to be wise, they became fools. 23 They changed the glory of the incorruptible God into an image made like corruptible man, birds, four-footed beasts, and creeping things.

24 Therefore God gave them up to uncleanness through the lusts of their hearts, to dishonor their own bodies among themselves. 25 They turned the truth of God into a lie and worshipped and served the creature rather than the Creator, who is blessed forever. Amen.

26 For this reason God gave them up to dishonorable passions. Their women exchanged the natural function for what is against nature. 27 Likewise the men, leaving the natural function of the woman, burned in their lust toward one another, men with men doing that which is shameful, and receiving in themselves the due penalty of their error.

28 And since they did not see fit to acknowledge God, God gave them over to a debased mind, to do those things which are not proper. 29 They were filled with all unrighteousness, sexual immorality, wickedness, covetousness, maliciousness; full of envy, murder, strife, deceit. They are gossips, 30 slanderers, God-haters, insolent, proud, boastful, inventors of evil things, and disobedient toward parents, 31 without understanding, covenant breakers, without natural affection, calloused, and unmerciful, 32 who know the righteous requirement of God, that those who commit such things are worthy of death. They not only do them, but also give hearty approval to those who practice them.

The Righteous Judgment of God

2 Therefore you are without excuse, O man, whoever you are who judges, for when you judge another, you condemn yourself, for you who judge do the same things. 2 But we know that the judgment of God is according to truth against those who commit such things. 3 Do you think, O man, who judges those who do such things, and who does the same thing, that you will escape the judgment of God? 4 Do you despise the riches of His goodness, tolerance, and patience, not knowing that the goodness of God leads you to repentance?

5 But because of your hardness and impenitent heart, you are storing up treasures of wrath against yourself on the day of wrath when the righteous judgment of God will be revealed, 6 and He "will render to every man

1:1 Ro 15:16
1:2 Ro 3:21
1:3 Gal 4:4
1:4 2Co 13:4
1:5 Ac 6:7
1:6 Rev 17:14
1:7 Col 1:2
1:8 Ro 16:19
1:9 2Ti 1:3
1:10 Ac 18:21
1:11 Ro 15:23
1:12 2Pe 1:1
1:13 Jn 4:36
1:16 Ro 2:9
1:17 Hab 2:4
1:19 Ro 1:20
1:20 1Ti 1:17
....
1:21 Jer 2:5
1:22 Jer 10:14
1:23 Ps 106:20
1:24 1Th 4:4
1:25 Isa 44:20
1:26 Ro 1:24
1:29 2Co 12:20
1:30 2Ti 3:2
1:31 2Ti 3:3
1:32 Ro 6:21
2:1 2Sa 12:5–7
2:3 Lk 12:14
2:4 Ex 34:6
2:5 Dt 32:34
2:6 Ps 62:12

[1] *17* Hab 2:4.

according to his deeds."[1] 7 To those who by patiently doing good seek for glory and honor and immortality will be eternal life. 8 But to those who are contentious and do not obey the truth, but obey unrighteousness, indignation, and wrath, 9 will be tribulation and anguish, upon every soul of man who does evil, to the Jew first, and then to the Gentile. 10 But glory, honor, and peace will be to every man who does good work—to the Jew first, and then to the Gentile, 11 for there is no partiality with God.

12 As many as have sinned without the law will also perish without the law, and as many as have sinned under the law will be judged by the law, 13 for the hearers of the law are not justified before God, but the doers of the law will be justified. 14 For when Gentiles, who do not have the law, do by nature the things contained in the law, these, not having the law, are a law unto themselves, 15 who show the work of the law written in their hearts, their conscience also bearing witness, while their conflicting thoughts accuse or even excuse them, 16 in the day when, according to my gospel, God will judge the secrets of men through Jesus Christ.

The Jews and the Law

17 Indeed you are called a Jew, and rest in the law, and make your boast in God. 18 You know His will and approve the things that are more excellent, because you are instructed in the law. 19 You are confident that you are a guide to the blind, a light to those who are in darkness, 20 an instructor of the foolish, and a teacher of babes, who have the full content of knowledge and truth in the law: 21 You, therefore, who teach another, do you not teach yourself? You who preach not to steal, do you steal? 22 You who say not to commit adultery, do you commit adultery? You who abhor idols, do you rob temples? 23 You who boast in the law, do you dishonor God through breaking the law? 24 As it is written, "The name of God is blasphemed among the Gentiles because of you."[2]

25 Circumcision indeed has merit, if you keep the law, but if you are a breaker of the law, your circumcision becomes uncircumcision. 26 Therefore, if an uncircumcised man keeps the righteousness of the law, will not his uncircumcision be counted as circumcision? 27 Will the uncircumcised one who is righteous by nature, if he fulfills the law, not judge you who, by the letter of the law and circumcision, violate the law?

28 He is not a Jew who is one outwardly, nor is circumcision that which is external in the flesh. 29 But he is a Jew who is one inwardly. And circumcision is of the heart, by the Spirit, and not by the letter. His praise is not from men, but from God.

2:7 Lk 8:15
2:9 1Pe 4:17
2:10 Isa 32:17
2:11 Ac 10:34
2:12 1Co 9:21
2:14 Ro 2:12
2:16 Ro 16:25
2:17 Mic 3:11
2:18 Php 1:10
2:20 2Ti 1:13
2:21 Ps 50:16–21
2:23 Ro 2:17
2:24 Isa 52:5
2:25 Jer 4:4
2:26 Ro 8:4
2:28 Gal 6:15
2:29 1Pe 3:4

....

3:2 Ac 7:38
3:3 Heb 4:2
3:4 Ps 51:4
3:5 Ro 6:19
3:6 Ge 18:25
3:8 Ro 6:1
3:9 Gal 3:22
3:10 Ps 14:1–3
3:12 Ps 14:3
3:13 Ps 5:9
3:14 Ps 10:7
3:17 Lk 1:79
3:18 Ps 36:1
3:19 Ro 3:9
3:20 Ac 13:39

3 What advantage then does the Jew have? Or what profit is there in circumcision? 2 Much in every way! Chiefly because the oracles of God were entrusted to them.

3 What if some did not believe? Would their unbelief nullify the faithfulness of God? 4 God forbid! Let God be true, and every man a liar. As it is written:

"That You may be justified in Your words,
and may prevail in Your judging."[3]

5 But if our unrighteousness demonstrates the righteousness of God, what shall we say? Is God unrighteous in taking vengeance? (I am speaking in human terms.) 6 God forbid! For then how could God judge the world? 7 If through my lie the truth of God has abounded more to His glory, why am I still being judged as a sinner? 8 Why not rather say, "Let us do evil that good may come," as we are slanderously accused and as some claim that we say? Their condemnation is just.

There Is None Righteous

9 What then? Are we better than they? No, not at all. For we have already charged that both Jews and Gentiles are all under sin. 10 As it is written:

"There is none righteous, no, not one;[4]
11 there is no one who understands;
there is no one who seeks after God.[5]
12 They have all turned aside;
together they have become worthless;
there is no one who does good,
no, not one."[6]
13 "Their throats are an open grave;
with their tongues they have used
deceit";
"the poison of vipers is under their lips";[7]
14 "their mouths are full of cursing and
bitterness."[8]
15 "Their feet are swift to shed blood;[9]
16 destruction and misery are in their paths;[10]
17 and they do not know the way of peace."[11]
18 "There is no fear of God before their
eyes."[12]

19 Now we know that whatever the law says, it says to those who are under the law, so that every mouth may be silenced, and all the world may become accountable to God. 20 Therefore by the works of the law no flesh will be justified in His sight, for through the law comes the knowledge of sin.

[1] *6* Ps 62:12; Pr 24:12. [2] *24* Isa 52:5; Eze 36:22. [3] *4* Ps 51:4.
[4] *10* Ps 14:1; 53:1. [5] *11* Ps 14:2; 53:2. [6] *12* Ps 14:3; 53:3.
[7] *13* Ps 5:9; 140:3. [8] *14* Ps 10:7. [9] *15* Pr 1:16; Isa 59:7.
[10] *16* Isa 59:7. [11] *17* Isa 59:8. [12] *18* Ps 36:1.

Righteousness Through Faith

21 But now, apart from the law, the righteousness of God is revealed, being witnessed by the Law and the Prophets. 22 This righteousness of God comes through faith in Jesus Christ[1] to all and upon all who believe, for there is no distinction. 23 For all have sinned and come short of the glory of God, 24 being justified freely by His grace through the redemption that is in Christ Jesus, 25 whom God has set forth to be a propitiation through faith, in His blood, for a demonstration of His righteousness, because in His forbearance God had passed over the sins previously committed, 26 to prove His righteousness at this present time so that He might be just and be the justifier of him who has faith in Jesus.

27 Where is boasting then? It is excluded. By what law? Of works? No, but by the law of faith. 28 Therefore we conclude that a man is justified by faith without the works of the law. 29 Is He the God of the Jews only? Is He not also the God of the Gentiles? Yes, of the Gentiles also, 30 seeing it is one God, who shall justify the circumcised by faith, and the uncircumcised through faith. 31 Do we then make the law void through faith? God forbid! Instead, we establish the law.

The Example of Abraham

4 What then shall we say that Abraham, our father according to the flesh, has found? 2 If Abraham was justified by works, he has something to boast about, but not before God. 3 What does the Scripture say? "Abraham believed God, and it was credited to him as righteousness."[2]

4 Now to him who works, wages are not given as a gift, but as a debt. 5 But to him who does not work, but believes in Him who justifies the ungodly, his faith is credited as righteousness. 6 Even David describes the blessedness of the man to whom God credits righteousness without works:

7 "Blessed are those
whose iniquities are forgiven,
and whose sins are covered;
8 blessed is the man
to whom the Lord shall not impute sin."[3]

9 Does this blessedness then come upon the circumcised only, or upon the uncircumcised also? We are saying that faith was credited to Abraham as righteousness. 10 How then was it credited? When he was in circumcision? Or in uncircumcision? Not in circumcision, but in uncircumcision. 11 And he received the sign of circumcision, a seal of the righteousness of the faith that he had while being uncircumcised, so that he might be the father of all those who believe, though they are uncircumcised, that righteousness might be credited to them also, 12 and the father of circumcision to those who are not of the circumcision only, but who also walk in the steps of the faith of our father Abraham, which he had while still being uncircumcised.

The Promise Received Through Faith

13 It was not through the law that Abraham and his descendants received the promise that he would be the heir of the world, but through the righteousness of faith. 14 For if those who are of the law become heirs, faith would be made void and the promise nullified, 15 because the law produces wrath, for where there is no law, there is no sin.

16 Therefore the promise comes through faith, so that it might be by grace, that the promise would be certain to all the descendants, not only to those who are of the law, but also to those who are of the faith of Abraham, who is the father of us all 17 (as it is written, "I have made you a father of many nations"[4]) before God whom he believed, and who raises the dead, and calls those things that do not exist as though they did.

18 Against all hope, he believed in hope, that he might become the father of many nations according to what was spoken, "So shall your descendants be."[5] 19 And not being weak in faith, he did not consider his own body to be dead (when he was about a hundred years old), nor yet the deadness of Sarah's womb. 20 He did not waver at the promise of God through unbelief, but was strong in faith, giving glory to God, 21 and being fully persuaded that what God had promised, He was able to perform. 22 Therefore "it was credited to him as righteousness."[6] 23 Now the words, "it was credited to him," were not written for his sake only, 24 but also for us, to whom it shall be credited if we believe in Him who raised Jesus our Lord from the dead, 25 who was delivered for our transgressions, and was raised for our justification.

Results of Justification

I am justified by faith, and I have peace with God (Ro 5:1).

5 Therefore, since we have been justified by faith, we have peace with God through our Lord Jesus Christ, 2 through whom we also have access by faith into this grace in which we stand, and so we rejoice in hope of the glory of God. 3 Not only so, but we also boast in

3:21 Ac 10:43
3:22 Ro 10:12
3:23 Ro 3:9
3:24 Ro 4:16
3:25 Ac 17:30
3:27 Ro 2:17
3:30 Gal 3:8
4:1 Ro 4:16
4:2 1Co 1:31
4:3 Ge 15:6
4:4 Ro 11:6
4:5 Ro 3:22
4:7 Ps 32:1–2
4:9 Ro 4:3
4:11 Ro 3:22

4:13 Gal 3:29
4:15 Gal 3:10
4:16 Ro 9:8
4:17 Jn 5:21
4:19 Ge 17:17
4:21 Ge 18:14
4:22 Ro 4:3
4:23 Ro 15:4
4:24 Ac 2:24
4:25 Isa 53:5–6
5:2 1Co 15:1
5:3 Jas 1:2–3

[1] 22 Or *through the faith of Jesus Christ.* [2] 3 Ge 15:6. [3] 7–8 Ps 32:1–2. [4] 17 Ge 17:5. [5] 18 Ge 15:5. [6] 22 Ge 15:6.

tribulation, knowing that tribulation produces patience, 4 patience produces character, and character produces hope. 5 And hope does not disappoint, because the love of God is shed abroad in our hearts by the Holy Spirit who has been given to us.

6 While we were yet weak, in due time Christ died for the ungodly. 7 Rarely for a righteous man will one die. Yet perhaps for a good man some would even dare to die. 8 But God demonstrates His own love toward us, in that while we were yet sinners, Christ died for us.

9 How much more then, being now justified by His blood, shall we be saved from wrath through Him. 10 For if while we were enemies, we were reconciled to God by the death of His Son, how much more, being reconciled, shall we be saved by His life. 11 Furthermore, we also rejoice in God through our Lord Jesus Christ, through whom we have now received reconciliation.

Adam and Christ

12 Therefore as sin came into the world through one man and death through sin, so death has spread to all men, because all have sinned.

13 For until the law, sin was in the world. But sin is not counted when there is no law. 14 Nevertheless death reigned from Adam to Moses, even over those who had not sinned in the likeness of Adam's sin, who was a type of Him who was to come.

15 But the free gift is not like the trespass. For if through the trespass of one man many died, then how much more has the grace of God and the free gift by the grace of the one Man, Jesus Christ, abounded to many. 16 The gift is not like the result that came through the one who sinned. For the judgment from one sin led to condemnation, but the free gift, which came after many trespasses, leads to justification. 17 For if by one man's trespass death reigned through him, then how much more will those who receive abundance of grace and the gift of righteousness reign in life through the One, Jesus Christ.

18 Therefore just as through the trespass of one man came condemnation for all men, so through the righteous act of One came justification of life for all men. 19 For just as through one man's disobedience the many were made sinners, so by the obedience of One the many will be made righteous.

20 But the law entered, so that sin might increase, but where sin increased, grace abounded much more, 21 so that just as sin reigned in death, grace might reign through righteousness unto eternal life through Jesus Christ our Lord.

5:4 Jas 1:12
5:5 Gal 4:6
5:6 Ro 4:25
5:8 Jn 15:13
5:9 Ro 1:18
5:10 2Co 5:18–19
5:12 Ge 2:17
5:13 Ro 4:15
5:14 1Co 15:45
5:15 Ro 5:12
5:17 Ro 5:12
5:18 Ro 5:12
5:19 Php 2:8
5:20 Ro 6:1
5:21 Ro 5:14

6:1 Ro 6:15
6:2 Col 3:3
6:3 Mt 28:19
6:4 Ro 7:6
6:5 Php 3:10–11
6:6 Gal 2:20
6:7 1Pe 4:1
6:8 2Co 13:4
6:9 Rev 1:18
6:12 Ro 6:16
6:13 Ro 7:5
6:14 Ro 6:12
6:15 Ro 6:1–2
6:16 Jn 8:34
6:17 Ro 1:8
6:18 Ro 6:22
6:19 Ro 3:5

Dead to Sin but Alive in Christ

6 What shall we say then? Shall we continue in sin that grace may increase? 2 God forbid! How shall we who died to sin live any longer in it? 3 Do you not know that we who were baptized into Jesus Christ were baptized into His death? 4 Therefore we were buried with Him by baptism into death, that just as Christ was raised up from the dead by the glory of the Father, even so we also should walk in newness of life.

5 For if we have been united with Him in the likeness of His death, so shall we also be united with Him in the likeness of His resurrection, 6 knowing this, that our old man has been crucified with Him, so that the body of sin might be destroyed, and we should no longer be slaves to sin. 7 For the one who has died is freed from sin.

I am crucified with Christ, and sin does not have dominion over me (Ro 6:1–6).

8 Now if we died with Christ, we believe that we shall also live with Him, 9 knowing that Christ, being raised from the dead, will never die again; death has no further dominion over Him. 10 For the death He died, He died to sin once for all, but the life He lives, He lives to God.

11 Likewise, you also consider yourselves to be dead to sin, but alive to God through Jesus Christ our Lord. 12 Therefore do not let sin reign in your mortal body, that you should obey it in its lusts. 13 Do not yield your members to sin as instruments of unrighteousness, but yield yourselves to God, as those who are alive from the dead, and your bodies to God as instruments of righteousness. 14 For sin shall not have dominion over you, for you are not under the law, but under grace.

Slaves of Righteousness

15 What then? Shall we sin because we are not under the law but under grace? God forbid! 16 Do you not know that to whom you yield yourselves as slaves to obey, you are slaves of the one whom you obey, whether of sin leading to death, or of obedience leading to righteousness? 17 But thanks be to God, for you were slaves of sin, but you have obeyed from the heart that form of teaching to which you were entrusted, 18 and having been freed from sin, you became the slaves of righteousness.

19 I speak in human terms because of the weakness of your flesh, for just as you have yielded your members as slaves to impurity and iniquity leading to more iniquity, even so now yield your members as slaves to righteousness unto holiness. 20 For when you were

SPIRITLED WOMAN

COUNSEL FROM THE SPIRIT BASICS

Guilt and Condemnation

> There is therefore now no condemnation for those who are in Christ Jesus.
>
> —ROMANS 8:1

A very delicate area in which I see many parents fall is the overwhelming feelings of guilt and condemnation for the sins of their children.

You must remember that Satan is the deceiver and the father of all lies. Sin originated with Satan. The enemy will lie to you, telling you it is your fault because of your past sins and mistakes. This is a lie of the enemy that you absolutely must not believe.

Reverse the curse of the enemy, and refuse to continue living under guilt and condemnation. Speak life from now on. The enemy wants to steal your faith; that is his ultimate goal. He couldn't care less about everything you do and how religious you are. He's just interested in robbing you of your faith in Jesus Christ.

Do not let guilt rob you of truth.

Faith is believing that God can and will do what He promises. Take hold of God's precious promises, stand firm, and learn to resist Satan. Speak the Word. Chew and digest the Word. Pray the Word. Believe and trust God's Word for you and your family. Nothing else will help. God is ready to restore everything the enemy has taken from you. Make a decision to serve Him with all your heart.

Iris Delgado

the slaves of sin, you were free from righteousness. 21 What fruit did you have then from the things of which you are now ashamed? The result of those things is death. 22 But now, having been freed from sin and having become slaves of God, you have fruit unto holiness, and the end is eternal life. 23 For the wages of sin is death, but the gift of God is eternal life through Jesus Christ our Lord.

[i]7 Ex 20:17; Dt 5:21.

6:21 Ro 1:32
6:22 Ro 6:18
6:23 Ro 5:12

7:2 1Co 7:39
7:3 Mt 5:32
7:4 Ro 8:2
7:5 Ro 6:13
7:6 Ro 6:4
7:7 Ro 3:20
7:8 Ro 7:11
7:10 Ro 10:5
7:11 Ro 7:8
7:12 1Ti 1:8
7:14 1Ki 21:20
7:15 Gal 5:17
7:16 Ro 7:12

An Analogy From Marriage

7 Do you not know, brothers (for I speak to those who know the law), that the law has dominion over a man as long as he lives? 2 For the woman who has a husband is bound by the law to her husband so long as he lives. But if her husband dies, she is released from the law regarding her husband. 3 So then, she will be called an adulteress if she marries another man while her husband lives. But if her husband dies, she is free from that law, so that she would not be an adulteress if she marries another man.

4 So, my brothers, you also have died to the law through the body of Christ, so that you may be married to another, to Him who has been raised from the dead, so that we may bear fruit for God. 5 When we were in the flesh, the passions of sin, through the law, worked in our members to bear fruit leading to death. 6 But now we are delivered from the law, having died to things in which we were bound, so that we may serve in newness of the Spirit, and not in the oldness of the letter of the law.

> We are a body, and we can be the best version of ourselves only when we make space and have value for one another (Ro 7:4).

The Problem of Indwelling Sin

7 What shall we say then? Is the law sin? God forbid! But I did not know sin, except through the law. I would not have known coveting if the law had not said, "You shall not covet."[i] 8 But sin, taking opportunity through the commandment, produced in me all kinds of coveting. For apart from the law sin is dead. 9 I was alive without the law once, but when the commandment came, sin revived, and I died. 10 And the commandment, which was intended for life, proved to be death in me. 11 For sin, taking opportunity through the commandment, deceived me and killed me through it. 12 So then, the law is holy and the commandment is holy and just and good.

13 Therefore has that which is good become death unto me? God forbid! Rather, sin, that it might be shown to be sin, was working death in me through that which is good, so that sin through the commandment might become exceedingly sinful.

14 We know that the law is spiritual, but I am carnal, sold under sin. 15 For what I am doing, I do not understand, for I do not practice what I will to do, but I do the very thing I hate. 16 But if I practice what I do not will to do, I agree with

the law that it is good. 17 So now it is no longer I that do it, but sin that dwells in me. 18 For I know that in me (that is, in my flesh) dwells no good thing, for the will to do what is right is present with me, but how to perform what is good I do not find. 19 For the good I desire to do, I do not do, but the evil I do not want is what I do. 20 Now if I do what I do not want, it is no longer I who does it, but sin that lives in me.

21 I find then a law that when I desire to do good, evil is present with me. 22 For I delight in the law of God according to the inner man, 23 but I see another law in my members, warring against the law of my mind and bringing me into captivity to the law of sin which is in my members. 24 O wretched man that I am! Who will deliver me from the body of this death? 25 I thank God through Jesus Christ our Lord.

So then, with my mind, I serve the law of God, but with my flesh, the law of sin.

Life in the Spirit

8 There is therefore now no condemnation for those who are in Christ Jesus, who walk not according to the flesh, but according to the Spirit. 2 For the law of the Spirit of life in Christ Jesus has set me free from the law of sin and death. 3 For what the law could not do, in that it was weak through the flesh, God did by sending His own Son in the likeness of sinful flesh, and concerning sin, He condemned sin in the flesh, 4 in order that the righteous requirement of the law might be fulfilled in us, who walk not according to the flesh but according to the Spirit.

5 For those who live according to the flesh set their minds on the things of the flesh, but those who live according to the Spirit, the things of the Spirit. 6 To be carnally minded is death, but to be spiritually minded is life and peace, 7 for the carnal mind is hostile toward God, for it is not subject to the law of God, nor indeed can it be, 8 and those who are in the flesh cannot please God.

> Heavenly Father, help me to set my mind on things that are pure and not on things that feed my flesh (Ro 8:5–7).

9 You, however, are not in the flesh but in the Spirit, if indeed the Spirit of God lives in you. Now if any man does not have the Spirit of Christ, he does not belong to Him. 10 And if Christ is in you, though the body is dead because of sin, the Spirit is alive because of righteousness. 11 But if the Spirit of Him who raised Jesus from the dead lives in you, He who raised Christ from the dead will also give

7:17 Ro 7:20
7:18 Ro 7:25
7:19 Ro 7:15
7:20 Ro 7:17
7:21 Ro 7:23
7:22 Eph 3:16
7:23 Gal 5:17
7:24 Ro 6:6
7:25 1Co 15:57
8:2 1Co 15:45
8:3 Ac 13:39
8:4 Gal 5:16
8:5 1Co 2:14
8:6 Ro 6:21
8:7 Jas 4:4
8:8 Ro 7:5
8:9 Gal 4:6
8:10 Eph 3:17
8:11 Ac 2:24

8:13 Gal 6:8
8:14 Gal 5:18
8:15 Mk 14:36
8:16 Eph 1:13
8:17 Gal 4:7
8:18 1Pe 4:13
8:19 1Jn 3:2
8:20 Ge 3:17–19
8:21 2Pe 3:13
8:22 Jer 12:11
8:23 Ro 7:24
8:24 1Th 5:8
8:25 1Th 1:3
8:26 Eph 6:18
8:27 Ro 8:34
8:28 Gal 1:15
8:29 Ro 11:2

life to your mortal bodies through His Spirit that lives in you.

12 Therefore, brothers, we are debtors not to the flesh, to live according to the flesh. 13 For if you live according to the flesh, you will die, but if through the Spirit you put to death the deeds of the body, you will live.

14 For as many as are led by the Spirit of God, these are the sons of God. 15 For you have not received the spirit of slavery again to fear. But you have received the Spirit of adoption, by whom we cry, "Abba, Father." 16 The Spirit Himself bears witness with our spirits that we are the children of God, 17 and if children, then heirs: heirs of God and joint-heirs with Christ, if indeed we suffer with Him, that we may also be glorified with Him.

> I am an heir and joint-heir with Christ Jesus (Ro 8:17).

The Glory That Is to Be

18 For I consider that the sufferings of this present time are not worthy to be compared with the glory which shall be revealed to us. 19 The eager expectation of the creation waits for the appearance of the sons of God. 20 For the creation was subjected to futility, not willingly, but by the will of Him who subjected it, in hope 21 that the creation itself also will be set free from its slavery to corruption into the glorious freedom of the children of God.

22 We know that the whole creation groans and travails in pain together until now. 23 Not only that, but we also, who have the first fruits of the Spirit, groan within ourselves while eagerly waiting for adoption, the redemption of our bodies. 24 For we are saved through hope, but hope that is seen is not hope, for why does a man still hope for what he sees? 25 But if we hope for what we do not see, we wait for it with patience.

26 Likewise, the Spirit helps us in our weaknesses, for we do not know what to pray for as we ought, but the Spirit Himself intercedes for us with groanings too deep for words. 27 He who searches the hearts knows what the mind of the Spirit is, because He intercedes for the saints according to the will of God.

> I may not understand what God's doing right now, but sooner or later I'll see it (Ro 8:28).

28 We know that all things work together for good to those who love God, to those who are called according to His purpose. 29 For those

WOMAN OF THE SPIRIT

The Impossible Dream

Do you have a dream from God that people have told you is impossible to realize? If you are not getting power from God to live every day in that dream, then you are living in your own strength, not God's. If you are not seeking Him daily for the wisdom and character to see it come into fruition, then what are you doing? Worldly wisdom will never right the world system. Only the wisdom and power of heaven can do that!

Prayer is the conduit to whatever we need to turn this world upside right, because it is in prayer that we become the children of God—by getting in step with the leadership of the Holy Spirit: "For as many as are led by the Spirit of God, these are the sons of God" (Ro 8:14). That is why the apostle Paul told us we needed to "pray without ceasing" (1Th 5:17). You can't be led by someone you never hear from or take the time to talk with.

In his book *Just Courage*, Gary Haugen speaks of the calling and work of Mother Teresa: "Mother Teresa said that she couldn't imagine doing her work for more than thirty minutes without prayer. Do you and I have work that we can't imagine doing for thirty minutes without prayer?"[1] If we don't have instruction and strength from heaven for what we are doing periodically throughout the day, then who are we really working for? If we don't rely on God's abilities and wisdom every minute of every day to accomplish the tasks before us, whose strength are we operating under? Do we really think we can work without God's incredible power to overcome the problems our world faces? If it is something we can accomplish without needing to pray, if we can in essence do it in our own strength and wisdom, are we really striving to accomplish anything that significant?

In John 17, which records Jesus's high-priestly prayer, Christ prays that everything God made available to Him while He was on the earth would be made available to us: His glory, His power, His love. Look for a moment at the end of that prayer:

> I do not pray for these alone, but also for those who will believe in Me through their word, that they may all be one, as You, Father, are in Me, and I in You. May they also be one in Us, that the world may believe that You have sent Me. I have given them the glory which You gave Me, that they may be one even as We are one: I in them and You in Me, that they may be perfect in unity, and that the world may know that You have sent Me, and have loved them as You have loved Me.
>
> Father, I desire that they also, whom You have given Me, be with Me where I am, that they may see My glory which You have given Me. For You loved Me before the creation of the world.
>
> O righteous Father, the world has not known You, but I have known You, and these have known that You sent Me. I have declared Your name to them, and will declare it, that the love with which You loved Me may be in them, and I in them.
>
> —John 17:20–26

The bottom line is that there is no way to be an effective Christian if you do not have a regular time of prayer and Bible reading for at least a half-hour every day. As members of His family, we have the right to go to our Father and ask for His plans, strategies, and resources to fulfill our mission, assignments, and purpose on the earth. Prayer is the conduit that not only reveals the will of God for our individual lives, but also helps make us the people we need to be to do the impossible on the earth. It's time to plug into that power like never before.

Cindy Trimm

1. Gary Haugen, *Just Courage* (Downers Grove, IL: InterVarsity Press, 2008), 23.

whom He foreknew, He predestined to be conformed to the image of His Son, so that He might be the firstborn among many brothers. 30 And those whom He predestined, He also called; and those whom He called, He also justified; and those whom He justified, He also glorified.

The Love of God

God and I are a majority (Ro 8:31).

31 What then shall we say to these things? If God is for us, who can be against us? 32 He who did not spare His own Son, but delivered Him up for us all, how shall He not with Him also freely give us all things? 33 Who shall bring a charge against God's elect? It is God who justifies. 34 Who is he who condemns? It is Christ who died, yes, who is risen, who is also at the right hand of God, who also intercedes for us. 35 Who shall separate us from the love of Christ? Shall tribulation, or distress, or persecution, or famine, or nakedness, or peril, or sword? 36 As it is written:

"For Your sake we are killed all day long;
we are counted as sheep for the
slaughter."[1]

37 No, in all these things we are more than conquerors through Him who loved us. 38 For I am persuaded that neither death nor life, neither angels nor principalities nor powers, neither things present nor things to come, 39 neither height nor depth, nor any other created thing, shall be able to separate us from the love of God, which is in Christ Jesus our Lord.

You cause me to triumph and have victory through Christ Jesus (Ro 8:37).

God's Election of Israel

9 I am speaking the truth in Christ, I am not lying; my conscience testifies with me in the Holy Spirit, 2 that I have great sorrow and continual anguish in my heart. 3 For I could wish that I myself were accursed from Christ for my brothers, my kinsmen by race, 4 who are Israelites, to whom belong the adoption, the glory, the covenants, the giving of the law, the service of God, and the promises, 5 to whom belong the patriarchs, and from whom, according to the flesh, is Christ, who is over all, God forever blessed. Amen.

6 It is not as though the word of God has failed. For they are not all Israel who are descended from Israel, 7 nor are they all children because they are descendants of Abraham, but "In Isaac shall your descendants be called."[2] 8 So those who are the children of the flesh are not the children of God, but the children of the promise are counted as descendants. 9 For this is the word of promise, "At this time I will come, and Sarah shall have a son."[3]

10 Not only that, but Rebekah also had conceived by one man, our father Isaac. 11 For before the children had been born, having done neither evil nor good, so that the purpose of God according to election might stand, not of works, but through Him who calls, 12 it was said to her, "The elder shall serve the younger."[4] 13 As it is written, "Jacob I have loved, but Esau I have hated."[5]

14 What shall we say then? Is there unrighteousness with God? God forbid! 15 For He says to Moses,

"I will have mercy on whom I have mercy,
and I will have compassion on whom I
have compassion."[6]

16 So then it is not of him who wills, nor of him who runs, but of God who shows mercy. 17 For the Scripture says to Pharaoh, "For this very purpose I have raised you up, that I may show My power in you, and that My name may be proclaimed in all the earth."[7] 18 Therefore He has mercy on whom He wills, and He hardens whom He wills.

Wrath and Mercy of God

19 You will then say to me, "Why does He yet find fault? For who can resist His will?" 20 Rather, O man, who are you to answer back to God? Shall the thing formed say to him who formed it, "Why have you made me like this?" 21 Does the potter not have power over the clay to make from the same lump one vessel for honor and another for dishonor?

22 What if God, willing to show His wrath and to make His power known, endured with much patience the vessels of wrath prepared for destruction, 23 in order to make known the riches of His glory on the vessels of mercy, which He previously prepared for glory, 24 even us, whom He has called, not from the Jews only, but also from the Gentiles? 25 As indeed He says in Hosea:

"I will call those who were not My people,
'My people,'
and her who was not beloved, 'Beloved,' "[8]

26 and,

"In the place where it was said to them,
'You are not My people,'

8:30 1Co 6:11
8:31 Ps 118:6
8:32 Jn 3:16
8:33 Rov 12:10 11
8:34 Heb 7:25
8:35 1Co 4:11
8:36 Ps 44:22
8:37 1Co 15:57
8:38 Eph 1:21
8:39 Ro 5:8
9:1 Gal 1:20
9:3 Ex 32:32
9:4 Eph 2:12
9:5 Ro 1:25
9:6 Gal 6:16
9:7 Ge 21:12
9:9 Ge 18:10
9:10 Ro 5:3
9:11 Ro 4:17
9:13 Mal 1:2–3
9:14 2Ch 19:7
9:15 Ex 33:19
9:17 Ex 9:16
9:18 Ex 4:21
9:19 2Ch 20:6
9:20 Isa 29:16
9:21 Isa 64:8
9:22 Pr 16:4
9:23 Ro 2:4
9:25 Hos 2:23

1 36 Ps 44:22. *2 7* Ge 21:12. *3 9* Ge 18:10. *4 12* Ge 25:23. *5 13* Mal 1:2. *6 15* Ex 33:19. *7 17* Ex 9:16. *8 25* Hos 2:23.

there they shall be called 'sons of the living
God.' "[1]

27 Isaiah also cries out concerning Israel:

"Though the number of the children of
Israel be like the sand of the sea,
a remnant shall be saved.[2]
28 For He will finish the work, and cut it short
in righteousness,
because the Lord will make a quick work
upon the earth."[3]

29 And as Isaiah previously said:

"Unless the Lord of Hosts
had left us a seed,
we would have become like Sodom,
and been made like Gomorrah."[4]

Israel and the Gospel

30 What shall we say then? The Gentiles, who did not pursue righteousness, have attained righteousness, even the righteousness which is by faith, 31 but Israel, pursuing the law of righteousness, did not attain the law of righteousness. 32 Why not? Because they did not seek it by faith, but by the works of the law. For they stumbled over the stumbling stone. 33 As it is written:

"Look! I lay in Zion a stumbling stone
and rock of offense,
and whoever believes in Him will not be
ashamed."[5]

10 Brothers, my heart's desire and prayer to God for Israel is that they may be saved. 2 For I testify about them that they have a zeal for God, but not according to knowledge. 3 For, being ignorant of God's righteousness and seeking to establish their own righteousness, they did not submit to the righteousness of God. 4 Christ is the end of the law unto righteousness for every one who believes.

Salvation for All

5 For Moses writes about the righteousness which is based on the law: "The man who does those things shall live by them."[6] 6 But the righteousness which is based on faith says, "Do not say in your heart, 'Who will ascend into heaven?' "[7] (that is, to bring Christ down), 7 or, 'Who will descend into the deep?' "[8] (that is, to bring Christ up from the dead). 8 But what does it say? "The word is near you, in your mouth and in your heart."[9] This is the word of faith that we preach: 9 that if you confess with your mouth Jesus is Lord, and believe in your heart that God has raised Him from the dead, you will be saved, 10 for with the heart one believes unto righteousness, and with the mouth confession is made unto salvation. 11 For the Scripture says, "Whoever believes in Him will not be ashamed."[10] 12 For there is no distinction between Jew and Greek, for the same Lord over all is generous toward all who call upon Him. 13 For, "Everyone who calls on the name of the Lord shall be saved."[11]

14 How then shall they call on Him in whom they have not believed? And how shall they believe in Him of whom they have not heard? And how shall they hear without a preacher? 15 And how shall they preach unless they are sent? As it is written: "How beautiful are the feet of those who preach the gospel of peace, who bring good news of good things!"[12]

16 But they have not all obeyed the gospel. For Isaiah says, "Lord, who has believed our report?"[13] 17 So then faith comes by hearing, and hearing by the word of God. 18 But I say, have they not heard? Yes, indeed:

"Their voice went into all the earth,
and their words to the ends of the
world."[14]

19 But I say, did Israel not know? First, Moses says:

"I will make you jealous by those who are
not a nation,
and by a foolish nation I will anger you."[15]

20 And Isaiah is very bold and says:

"I was found by those who did not
seek Me;
I revealed myself to those who did not
ask for Me."[16]

21 But to Israel He says:

"All day long I have stretched out My hands
to a disobedient and contrary people."[17]

The Remnant of Israel

11 I say then, has God rejected His people? God forbid! For I also am an Israelite, a descendant of Abraham, of the tribe of Benjamin. 2 God has not rejected His people whom He foreknew. Do you not know what the Scripture says of Elijah? How he pleads with God against Israel, saying, 3 "Lord, they have killed Your prophets and destroyed Your altars. I alone am left, and they seek my life"?[18] 4 But what is the divine reply to him? "I have kept for Myself seven thousand men, who have not bowed the knee to Baal."[19] 5 So then at this present time there is a remnant according to the election of grace. 6 And if by grace, then it is no longer by works; otherwise grace would

9:29 Isa 1:9
9:30 Php 3:9
9:31 Ro 11:7
9:32 1Pe 2:8
9:33 Isa 28:16
10:2 Ac 21:20
10:3 Ro 1:17
10:4 Gal 3:24
10:5 Lev 18:5
10:7 Heb 13:20
10:8 Dt 30:14
10:9 Lk 12:8
10:11 Ro 9:33
10:12 Ro 3:22
10:13 Ac 2:21
10:14 Titus 1:3
10:15 Isa 52:7
10:16 Isa 53:1
10:18 Ps 19:4
10:19 Dt 32:21
10:20 Ro 9:30
11:1 1Sa 12:22
11:2 1Pe 1:2
11:4 1Ki 19:18
11:5 Ro 9:27

[1] *26* Hos 1:10. [2] *27* Isa 10:22. [3] *28* Isa 10:23. [4] *29* Isa 1:9. [5] *33* Isa 8:14; 28:16. [6] *5* Lev 18:5. [7] *6* Dt 30:12. [8] *7* Dt 30:13. [9] *8* Dt 30:14. [10] *11* Isa 28:16. [11] *13* Joel 2:32. [12] *15* Isa 52:7. [13] *16* Isa 53:1. [14] *18* Ps 19:4. [15] *19* Dt 32:21. [16] *20* Isa 65:1. [17] *21* Isa 65:2. [18] *3* 1Ki 19:10. [19] *4* 1Ki 19:18.

no longer be grace. But if it is by works, then is it no longer by grace; otherwise work would no longer be work.

7 What then? Israel has not obtained what it was seeking. But the elect obtained it, and the rest were hardened. 8 As it is written:

"God has given them a spirit of slumber,
eyes that would not see
and ears that would not hear,
to this very day."[1]

9 And David says:

"Let their table become a snare and a trap,
a stumbling block and a retribution to them.
10 Let their eyes be darkened, so that they may not see,
and always bow down their backs."[2]

The Salvation of the Gentiles

11 I say then, have they stumbled that they should fall? God forbid! But through their transgression salvation has come to the Gentiles, to make them jealous. 12 Now if their transgression means riches for the world, and their failure means riches for the Gentiles, how much more will their fullness mean?

13 For I am speaking to you Gentiles. Inasmuch as I am the apostle to the Gentiles, I magnify my ministry, 14 if somehow I may make my kinsmen jealous and may save some of them. 15 For if their rejection means the reconciliation of the world, what will their acceptance mean but life from the dead? 16 If the first portion of the dough is holy, the batch is also holy. And if the root is holy, so are the branches.

17 But if some of the branches were broken off, and you, being a wild olive shoot, were grafted in among them and became a partaker with them of the root and richness of the olive tree, 18 do not boast against the branches. If you boast, remember you do not sustain the root, but the root sustains you. 19 You will say then, "The branches were broken off, so that I might be grafted in." 20 This is correct. They were broken off because of unbelief, but you stand by faith. Do not be arrogant, but fear. 21 For if God did not spare the natural branches, neither will He spare you.

22 Therefore consider the goodness and severity of God—severity toward those who fell, but goodness toward you, if you continue in His goodness. Otherwise, you also will be cut off. 23 And these also, if they do not remain in unbelief, will be grafted in, for God is able to graft them in again. 24 For if you were cut out of the olive tree which is wild by nature, and were grafted contrary to nature into a cultivated olive tree, how much more will these, who are the natural branches, be grafted into their own olive tree?

The Restoration of Israel

25 For I do not want you to be ignorant of this mystery, brothers, lest you be wise in your own estimation, for a partial hardening has come upon Israel until the fullness of the Gentiles has come in. 26 And so all Israel will be saved, as it is written:

"The Deliverer will come out of Zion,
and He will remove ungodliness from Jacob";[3]
27 "for this is My covenant with them,
when I shall take away their sins."[4]

28 As concerning the gospel, they are enemies for your sake, but as regarding the election, they are beloved for the sake of the patriarchs. 29 For the gifts and calling of God are irrevocable. 30 For just as you once were disobedient to God, but have now received mercy through their disobedience, 31 so these also have now been disobedient, that they also may receive mercy by the mercy shown to you. 32 For God has imprisoned them all in disobedience, so that He might be merciful to all.

33 O the depth of the riches and wisdom and knowledge of God!
How unsearchable are His judgments
and unfathomable are His ways!
34 "For who has known the mind of the Lord?
Or who has become His counselor?"[5]
35 "Or who has first given to Him,
and it shall be repaid to him?"[6]
36 For from Him and through Him and to Him are all things.
To Him be glory forever! Amen.

The New Life in Christ

12 I urge you therefore, brothers, by the mercies of God, that you present your bodies as a living sacrifice, holy, and acceptable to God, which is your reasonable service of worship. 2 Do not be conformed to this world, but be transformed by the renewing of your mind, that you may prove what is the good and acceptable and perfect will of God.

I will be a living sacrifice—dead to sin but with the power of God flowing through me (Ro 12:1).

3 For I say, through the grace given to me, to everyone among you, not to think of himself more highly than he ought to think, but

11:7 Ro 9:18
11:8 Dt 29:4
11:9 Ps 69:22–23
11:10 Ps 69:23
11:12 Ro 11:25
11:13 Ac 9:15
11:14 1Co 7:16
11:16 Eze 44:30
11:17 Jer 11:16
11:20 Ro 12:16
11:22 Jn 15:2
11:23 2Co 3:16
11:25 Lk 21:24
11:26 Isa 59:20
11:27 Isa 27:9
11:28 Dt 10:15
11:29 Ro 8:28
11:30 Col 3:7
11:32 Ro 3:9
11:33 Ro 2:4
11:34 Isa 40:13
11:35 Job 35:7
11:36 Ro 16:27
12:1 1Pe 2:5
12:2 Ro 12:1
12:3 Ro 1:5

[1] *8* Isa 29:10. [2] *10* Ps 69:22–23. [3] *26* Isa 59:20. [4] *27* Isa 59:20–21; Jer 31:31–34. [5] *34* Isa 40:13. [6] *35* Job 35:7; 41:11.

to think with sound judgment, according to
the measure of faith God has distributed to
every man. 4 For just as we have many parts
in one body, and not all parts have the same
function, 5 so we, being many, are one body in
Christ, and all are parts of one another. 6 We
have diverse gifts according to the grace that
is given to us: if prophecy, according to the
proportion of faith; 7 if service, in serving; he
who teaches, in teaching; 8 he who exhorts,
in exhortation; he who gives, with generosity;
he who rules, with diligence; he who shows
mercy, with cheerfulness.

If I don't want to miss my moment, I need to have expectant faith (Ro 12:3).

Rules of the Christian Life

9 Let love be without hypocrisy. Hate what
is evil. Cleave to what is good. 10 Be devoted
to one another with brotherly love; prefer one
another in honor, 11 do not be lazy in diligence,
be fervent in spirit, serve the Lord, 12 rejoice
in hope, be patient in suffering, persevere in
prayer, 13 contribute to the needs of the saints,
practice hospitality.

14 Bless those who persecute you; bless, and
do not curse. 15 Rejoice with those who rejoice,
and weep with those who weep. 16 Be of the
same mind toward one another. Do not be
haughty, but associate with the lowly. Do not
pretend to be wiser than you are.

17 Repay no one evil for evil. Commend
what is honest in the sight of all men. 18 If it is
possible, as much as it depends on you, live
peaceably with all men. 19 Beloved, do not
avenge yourselves, but rather give place to
God's wrath, for it is written: "Vengeance is
Mine. I will repay,"[1] says the Lord. 20 Therefore

"If your enemy is hungry, feed him;
if he is thirsty, give him a drink;
for in doing so you will heap coals of fire
on his head."[2]

21 Do not be overcome by evil, but overcome
evil with good.

Subjection to Authorities

13 Let every person be subject to the
governing authorities, for there is no
authority except from God, and those that exist
are appointed by God. 2 Therefore whoever
resists the authority resists what God has
appointed, and those who resist will incur
judgment. 3 Rulers are not a terror to good

12:4 1Co 12:12–14
12:5 1Co 10:17
12:6 Ac 13:1
12:8 2Co 9:7
12:9 1Ti 1:5
12:10 Php 2:3
12:11 Ac 18:25
12:12 Heb 10:36
12:13 2Co 9:1
12:14 Mt 5:44
12:15 Heb 13:3
12:16 Ro 11:25
12:17 Pr 20:22
12:18 Mk 9:50
12:19 Dt 32:35
12:20 Pr 25:21–22
12:21 1Pe 3:9
13:1 Da 2:21
13:5 Ecc 8:2
13:8 Ro 13:10
13:9 Lev 19:18
13:10 Ro 13:8
13:11 Eph 5:14
13:12 Eph 5:11
13:13 Gal 5:21
13:14 Gal 3:27
14:1 Ro 15:1
14:2 Ro 14:14
14:3 Lk 18:9
14:4 Ro 9:20
14:5 Ro 14:23
14:6 Mt 14:19

works, but to evil works. Do you wish to have
no fear of the authority? Do what is good,
and you will have praise from him, 4 for he
is the servant of God for your good. But if
you do what is evil, be afraid, for he does not
bear the sword in vain, for he is the servant of
God, an avenger to execute wrath upon him
who practices evil. 5 So it is necessary to be
in subjection, not only because of wrath, but
also for the sake of conscience.

6 For this reason you also pay taxes, for they
are God's servants, devoting themselves to this
very thing. 7 Render to all what is due them:
taxes to whom taxes are due, respect to whom
respect is due, fear to whom fear is due, and
honor to whom honor is due.

Brotherly Love

8 Owe no one anything, except to love one
another, for he who loves another has fulfilled
the law. 9 For the commandments, "You shall
not commit adultery, You shall not murder, You
shall not steal, You shall not give false testi-
mony, You shall not covet,"[3] and if there are
any other commandments, are summed up in
this saying, "You shall love your neighbor as
yourself."[4] 10 Love works no evil to a neighbor.
Therefore love is the fulfillment of the law.

The Approach of the Day of Christ

11 Furthermore, knowing the time, now is the
moment to awake from sleep. For now our sal-
vation is nearer than when we believed. 12 The
night is far spent, the day is at hand. Therefore
let us take off the works of darkness and put
on the armor of light. 13 Let us behave properly,
as in the day, not in carousing and drunken-
ness, not in immorality and wickedness, not
in strife and envy. 14 But put on the Lord Jesus
Christ, and make no provision for the flesh to
fulfill its lusts.

Do Not Judge Your Brother

14 Welcome him who is weak in faith, but
not for the purpose of arguing over
opinions. 2 For one has faith to eat all things,
but he who is weak eats only vegetables. 3 Do
not let him who eats despise him who does
not eat, and do not let him who does not eat
judge him who eats, for God has welcomed
him. 4 Who are you to judge another man's
servant? To his own master he stands or falls.
And he will stand, for God is able to make him
stand.

5 One man judges one day above another;
another judges every day alike. Let each one
be fully persuaded in his own mind. 6 He who
observes the day observes it for the Lord, and
he who does not observe the day, to the Lord
he does not observe it. He who eats, eats in
honor of the Lord, for he gives thanks to God;

[1] 19 Dt 32:35. [2] 20 Pr 25:21–22. [3] 9 Ex 20:13–15, 17; Dt 5:17–19, 21. [4] 9 Lev 19:18.

and the one who does not eat, in honor of the
Lord he does not eat, and gives thanks to God.
7 For none of us lives for himself, and no one
dies for himself. 8 For if we live, we live for
the Lord. And if we die, we die for the Lord.
So, whether we live or die, we are the Lord's.
9 For to this end Christ died and rose and lived
again, so that He might be Lord of both the
dead and living.
10 So why do you judge your brother? Or why
do you despise your brother? For we shall all
stand before the judgment seat of Christ. 11 For
it is written:

"As I live, says the Lord,
every knee shall bow to Me,
and every tongue shall confess to God."[1]

12 So then each of us shall give an account of
himself to God.

Do Not Make Your Brother Stumble

13 Therefore let us no longer pass judgment
on one another, but rather determine not to put
a stumbling block or an obstacle in a brother's
way. 14 I know and am persuaded by the Lord
Jesus that nothing is unclean in itself, but to
him who considers anything to be unclean, to
him it is unclean. 15 If your brother is grieved
because of your food, you are no longer walk-
ing in love. Do not destroy with your food one
for whom Christ died. 16 So do not let what is
good to you be spoken of as evil. 17 For the
kingdom of God does not mean eating and
drinking, but righteousness and peace and joy
in the Holy Spirit. 18 For he who serves Christ
in these things is acceptable to God and ap-
proved by men.

I have righteousness, love, joy, and peace in the Holy Spirit (Ro 14:17).

19 Therefore let us pursue the things which
produce peace and the things that build up
one another. 20 Do not destroy the work of
God for the sake of food. All things indeed are
clean, but it is evil for the man who causes
someone to fall by what he eats. 21 It is good
neither to eat meat nor drink wine, nor do
anything whereby your brother stumbles or is
offended or is made weak.
22 The faith that you have, have as your own
conviction before God. Happy is he who does
not condemn himself in what he approves.
23 But he who doubts is condemned if he eats,
because it is not from faith, for whatever is not
from faith is sin.

14:7 2Co 5:15
14:9 Rev 1:18
14:10 2Co 5:10
14:12 Mt 12:36
14:13 Mt 7:1
14:14 1Co 8:7
14:15 Eph 5:2
14:17 Ro 15:13
14:18 2Co 8:21
14:19 Ps 34:14
14:20 Ro 14:14–15
14:21 1Co 8:13
14:22 1Jn 3:21

....

15:1 Ro 14:1
15:2 Ro 14:19
15:3 Ps 69:9
15:4 Ro 4:23–24
15:5 Ro 12:16
15:6 Eph 1:3

SPIRITLED WOMAN

COUNSEL FROM THE SPIRIT BASICS

Get Your Hopes Up High

I think God wants us to lift up our eyes and hearts and then begin to believe the best. I say get your hopes up as high as you can. Start using your God-given imagination to embrace all the possibilities He has for you. Romans 15:13 says, "Now may the God of hope fill you with all joy and peace in believing, so that you may abound in hope, through the power of the Holy Spirit."

A heart full of hope brings you joy and peace in believing and extends the power of the Holy Spirit toward you so that you, in turn, can extend it to others. You should crank your hope in God all the way up! His plans are bigger than anything you can think up. After all, He is the God of increase.

You and I aren't the same as we were before we knew God. At that time we were "apart from Christ, alienated from the citizenship of Israel and strangers to the covenants of promise, without hope and without God in the world" (Eph 2:12). That is not who we are now. Redeemed by Jesus, we have become God's children, and we should act like it. We should *hope* like it.

Karen Jensen Salisbury

Please Others, Not Yourself

15 We who are strong ought to bear the
weaknesses of the weak and not please
ourselves. 2 Let each of us please his neigh-
bor for his good, leading to edification. 3 For
even Christ did not please Himself. But as it
is written, "The insults of those who insulted
You fell on Me."[2] 4 For whatever was previously
written was written for our instruction, so that
through perseverance and encouragement of
the Scriptures we might have hope.
5 Now may the God of perseverance and en-
couragement grant you to live in harmony with
one another in accordance with Christ Jesus,
6 so that together you may with one voice glori-
fy the God and Father of our Lord Jesus Christ.

[1] 11 Isa 45:23. [2] 3 Ps 69:9.

The Gospel for Jews and Gentiles Alike

7 Therefore welcome one another, just as
Christ also welcomed us, for the glory of God.
8 Now I say that Jesus Christ has become a ser-
vant to the circumcised on behalf of the truth
of God, to confirm the promises made to the
patriarchs, 9 and that the Gentiles might glorify
God for His mercy, as it is written:

"For this reason I will acknowledge You
among the Gentiles,
and I will sing praises to Your name."[1]

10 He also says:

"Rejoice, O Gentiles, with His people!"[2]

11 And again:

"Praise the Lord, all you Gentiles;
let all the peoples praise Him."[3]

12 And again Isaiah says:

"There shall be a root of Jesse;
He who shall rise to reign over the
Gentiles,
in Him shall the Gentiles hope."[4]

13 Now may the God of hope fill you with all
joy and peace in believing, so that you may
abound in hope, through the power of the
Holy Spirit.

Paul's Missionary Commission

14 Now I myself am persuaded concerning
you, my brothers, that you also are full of
goodness, filled with all knowledge, and also
able to instruct one another. 15 Nevertheless,
brothers, I have written even more boldly to
you on some points, to remind you, because of
the grace that is given to me from God, 16 that
I might be a minister of Jesus Christ to the
Gentiles, in the priestly service of the gospel
of God, so that the offering of the Gentiles
might be acceptable, being sanctified by the
Holy Spirit.

Let signs, wonders, and miracles be released through the power of the Holy Spirit (Ro 15:19).

17 In Christ Jesus therefore I have reason to
boast in my service to God. 18 For I will not dare
to speak of anything except what Christ has ac-
complished through me, to make the Gentiles
obedient, by word and deed, 19 by the power
of signs and wonders, by the power of the
Spirit of God, so that from Jerusalem and as far
around as Illyricum, I have fully preached the
gospel of Christ. 20 So I have strived to preach
the gospel, not where Christ was named, so
that I should not build on another man's foun-
dation. 21 But as it is written:

"To whom He was not announced, they
shall see;
and those who have not heard shall
understand."[5]

Paul's Plan to Visit Rome

22 For this reason also I was often hindered
from coming to you. 23 But now, no longer
having a place in these regions, and having
a great desire for many years to come to you,
24 whenever I go to Spain, I shall come to you,
for I hope to see you when I pass through and
to be helped on my way there by you, when
I have first enjoyed your company for a little
while. 25 But now I am going to Jerusalem to
minister to the saints. 26 For Macedonia and
Achaia were pleased to make some contribu-
tion for the poor among the saints who are
in Jerusalem. 27 It has pleased them indeed,
and they are their debtors. For if the Gentiles
have been partakers of their spiritual things,
they also ought to minister to them in material
things. 28 Therefore, when I have completed
this and have given this blessing to them, I
shall come by way of you to Spain, 29 and I
know that when I come to you, I shall come
in the fullness of the blessing of the gospel
of Christ.

30 Now I ask you, brothers, through the Lord
Jesus Christ and through the love of the Spirit,
to strive together with me in your prayers to
God on my behalf, 31 that I may be delivered
from the unbelievers in Judea, and that my
ministry for Jerusalem may be acceptable to
the saints, 32 so that I may come to you with
joy by the will of God, and may be refreshed
together with you. 33 Now the God of peace be
with you all. Amen.

Personal Greetings

16 I commend to you our sister Phoe-
be, who is a servant[6] of the church at
Cenchrea, 2 that you welcome her in the Lord
in a manner worthy of the saints, and that you
assist her in whatever matter she may have
need of you, for she has been a helper of many
and of myself as well.

3 Greet Priscilla and Aquila, my fellow work-
ers in Christ Jesus, 4 who risked their own
necks for my life, to whom not only I, but
also all the churches of the Gentiles, give
thanks.
5 Likewise greet the church that is in their
house.
Greet my beloved Epaenetus, who is the
first convert of Achaia for Christ.

15:8 Mt 15:24
15:9 2Sa 22:50
15:10 Dt 32:43
15:11 Ps 117:1
15:12 Isa 11:10
15:13 Ro 14:17
15:14 1Co 8:1
15:15 Ro 12:3
15:16 Php 2:17
15:17 Heb 5:1
15:18 Ac 15:12
15:20 2Co 10:13–16
15:21 Isa 52:15
15:22 Ro 1:13
15:23 Ro 15:32
15:24 Ro 15:28
15:25 Ac 19:21
15:27 1Co 9:11
15:28 Ro 15:24
15:30 2Co 1:11
15:31 2Th 3:2
15:32 Ac 18:21
15:33 2Co 13:11
16:1 Ac 18:18
16:2 Php 2:29
16:5 1Co 16:15

[1]9 Ps 18:49. [2]10 Dt 32:43. [3]11 Ps 117:1. [4]12 Isa 11:10. [5]21 Isa 52:15. [6]1 Or *deacon.*

SPIRIT-TO-SPIRIT PRAYER

PRAYER FOR MOUNTAIN-MOVING POWER

Father God, I release my faith to move all the mountains of disruption, confusion, sickness, lack, strife, adversity, and attacks of the enemy. In the name of Jesus I bind all evil and command you out of my life. Thank You, Father, that no evil shall befall us, neither shall any destruction come near my dwelling. My home is blessed with Your love, joy, and peace. I proclaim with boldness and faith that every mountain of adversity must bow down to the name of Jesus.

Iris Delgado

6 Greet Mary, who labored much for us.
7 Greet Andronicus and Junia, my kinsmen
and fellow prisoners, who are notewor-
thy among the apostles, who also came
to Christ before me.
8 Greet Ampliatus, my beloved in the Lord.
9 Greet Urbanus, our fellow worker in Christ,
and my beloved Stachys.
10 Greet Apelles, who is approved in Christ.
Greet those who are of the household of
Aristobulus.
11 Greet Herodion, my kinsman.
Greet those who are of the household of
Narcissus, who are in the Lord.
12 Greet Tryphena and Tryphosa, who labor
in the Lord.
Greet the beloved Persis, who also labored
much in the Lord.
13 Greet Rufus, chosen in the Lord, and his
mother, who is like a mother to me.
14 Greet Asyncritus, Phlegon, Hermes,
Patrobas, Hermas, and the brothers who
are with them.
15 Greet Philologus, Julia, Nereus and his
sister, and Olympas, and all the saints
who are with them.
16 Greet one another with a holy kiss.
The churches of Christ greet you.

17 Now I urge you, brothers, to closely watch
those who cause divisions and offenses, con-
trary to the teaching which you have learned,
and avoid them. 18 For such people do not
serve our Lord Jesus Christ, but their own ap-
petites, and through smooth talk and flattery
they deceive the hearts of the unsuspecting.
19 Your obedience has become known to all
men. Therefore I am glad on your behalf. Yet I
want you to be wise to that which is good, and
innocent to that which is evil.
20 The God of peace will soon crush Satan
under your feet.
The grace of our Lord Jesus Christ be with
you.
21 Timothy, my fellow worker, and Lucius,
Jason, and Sosipater, my kinsmen, greet you.
22 I, Tertius, who wrote this epistle, greet you
in the Lord.
23 Gaius, who is host to me and to the whole
church, greets you.
Erastus, who is the city treasurer, and our
brother Quartus greet you.
24 The grace of our Lord Jesus Christ be with
you all. Amen.

Doxology

25 Now to Him who has power to establish you
according to my gospel and the preaching of
Jesus Christ, according to the revelation of the
mystery, which was kept secret for long ages
past, 26 but now is revealed by the prophetic
Scriptures according to the commandment of
the everlasting God, made known to all the
Gentiles for the obedience of faith, 27 to the
only wise God, through Jesus Christ, to whom
be glory forever. Amen.

16:6 Ro 16:12
16:7 Ro 16:11
16:13 Mk 15:21
16:15 Ro 16:2
16:16 1Co 16:20
16:17 2Th 3:6
16:18 Php 3:19

16:19 Mt 10:16
16:20 Ge 3:15
16:21 Ac 20:4
16:22 Gal 6:11
16:23 Ac 19:22
16:25 Ro 2:16
16:26 Ro 1:5
16:27 Ro 11:36

Author: The apostle Paul

Written: Between AD 55 and 57, from Ephesus

Theme: Christian Conduct, Doctrinal and Ethical Matters

1 Corinthians

Dear Spirit Led Woman,

The apostle Paul said of the early church that there were thousands of instructors in Christ but not many fathers (1Co 4:15), and we still lack spiritual fathers and mothers today. A spiritual parent is one who helps another grow to maturity—both spiritually and in other areas of life.

I encourage you to become a spiritual mother and to keep in mind these points I've learned along the way. First, you must be led by the Holy Spirit. God will direct you in the process. Second, have a genuine Christlike love. Third, seek God for His vision for the person you are called to mentor. Then the Holy Spirit can speak through you to activate their spiritual gifts and callings. Fourth, provide training and correction in an attitude of acceptance and love. Fifth, transmit a hunger for God. Finally, make sure your own life is an example that can be followed (1Co 11:1).

Not every person who comes into your life will be one you bring to maturity, but be open to what God asks you to do. You can be one who brings life to others!

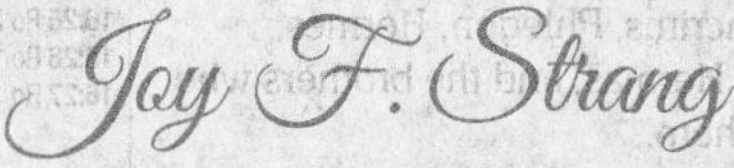

Greeting and Thanksgiving

1 Paul, called to be an apostle of Jesus Christ
through the will of God, and Sosthenes,
our brother,

2 To the church of God which is at Corinth, to
those who are sanctified in Christ Jesus, called
to be saints, with all who in every place call on
the name of Jesus Christ our Lord, both their
Lord and ours:

3 Grace to you and peace from God our Father
and the Lord Jesus Christ.
4 I thank my God always on your behalf for
the grace of God which has been given to you
through Jesus Christ. 5 By Him you are enriched
in everything, in all speech and in all knowl-
edge, 6 even as the testimony of Christ was
confirmed in you, 7 so that you are not lacking
in any gift while waiting for the revelation of
our Lord Jesus Christ. 8 He will strengthen you
to the end, so that you may be blameless on the
day of our Lord Jesus Christ. 9 God is faithful,
and by Him you were called to the fellowship
of His Son, Jesus Christ our Lord.

Divisions in the Church

10 Now I ask you, brothers, by the name of our
Lord Jesus Christ, that you all speak in agree-
ment and that there be no divisions among
you. But be perfectly joined together in the
same mind and in the same judgment. 11 For
it has been declared to me concerning you,
my brothers, by those who are of the house of
Chloe, that there are contentions among you.
12 Now this is what I mean: Every one of you is
saying, "I am of Paul," or "I am of Apollos," or
"I am of Cephas," or "I am of Christ."
13 Is Christ divided? Was Paul crucified for
you? Or were you baptized in the name of Paul?
14 I thank God that I baptized none of you except
Crispus and Gaius, 15 lest any should say that I
had baptized in my own name. 16 I also baptized
the household of Stephanas. Besides them, I do
not know whether I baptized any other. 17 For
Christ did not send me to baptize, but to preach
the gospel, not with eloquent words, lest the
cross of Christ should be made of no effect.

Christ the Power and Wisdom of God

18 For to those who are perishing, the preach-
ing of the cross is foolishness, but to us who
are being saved it is the power of God. 19 For
it is written:

"I will destroy the wisdom of the wise,
and will bring to nothing the
understanding of the prudent."[1]

20 Where is the wise? Where is the scribe?
Where is the debater of this age? Has God not
made the wisdom of this world foolish? 21 For
since, in the wisdom of God, the world through
its wisdom did not know God, it pleased God
through the foolishness of preaching to save
those who believe. 22 For the Jews require a
sign, and the Greeks seek after wisdom. 23 But
we preach Christ crucified, a stumbling block
to the Jews and foolishness to the Greeks.
24 But to those who are called, both Jews and
Greeks, we preach Christ as the power of God
and the wisdom of God. 25 For the foolishness
of God is wiser than men, and the weakness
of God is stronger than men.
26 For observe your calling, brothers. Among
you, not many wise men according to the flesh,
not many mighty men, and not many noble
men were called. 27 But God has chosen the
foolish things of the world to confound the
wise. God has chosen the weak things of the
world to confound the things which are mighty.
28 And God has chosen the base things of the
world and things which are despised. Yes, and
He chose things which did not exist to bring
to nothing things that do, 29 so that no flesh
should boast in His presence. 30 But because of
Him you are in Christ Jesus, whom God made
unto us wisdom, righteousness, sanctification,
and redemption. 31 Therefore, as it is written,
"Let him who boasts, boast in the Lord."[2]

Proclaiming Christ Crucified

2 Brothers, when I came to you, I did not
come with superiority of speech or wis-
dom, declaring to you the testimony of God.
2 For I determined not to know anything among
you except Jesus Christ and Him crucified. 3 I
was with you in weakness and in fear and in
much trembling. 4 My speech and my preach-
ing was not with enticing words of man's wis-
dom, but in demonstration of the Spirit and of
power, 5 so that your faith should not stand in
the wisdom of men, but in the power of God.

The Revelation by God's Spirit

6 Yet we speak wisdom among those who are
mature, although not the wisdom of this age,
nor of the rulers of this age, who are coming
to nothing. 7 But we speak the wisdom of God
in a mystery, the hidden wisdom, which God
ordained before the ages for our glory. 8 None
of the rulers of this age knew it. For had they
known it, they would not have crucified the
Lord of glory. 9 But as it is written,

"Eye has not seen,
nor ear heard,
nor has it entered into the heart of man
the things which God has prepared for
those who love Him."[3]

10 But God has revealed them to us by His Spirit.

1:1 Ro 1:1
1:2 Ro 1:7
1:3 Ro 1:7
1:4 Ro 1:8
1:5 2Co 8:7
1:6 Rev 1:2
1:7 Php 3:20
1:8 1Th 3:13
1:9 1Jn 1:3
1:10 1Co 11:18
1:11 1Co 3:3
1:12 Jn 1:42
1:13 Mt 28:19
1:14 Ac 18:8
1:16 1Co 16:15
1:17 1Co 2:1
1:18 Ro 1:16
1:19 Isa 29:14
1:20 Ro 1:22
....
1:23 Gal 5:11
1:24 1Co 1:30
1:25 1Co 1:18
1:26 1Co 1:20
1:28 Ro 4:17
1:29 Eph 2:9
1:30 Jer 23:5–6
1:31 2Co 10:17
2:1 1Co 1:17
2:2 Gal 6:14
2:3 2Co 13:4
2:4 Ro 15:19
2:5 2Co 4:7
2:6 1Co 1:28
2:8 Ac 7:2
2:9 Isa 64:4
2:10 Jn 14:26

[1] 19 Isa 29:14. [2] 31 Jer 9:24. [3] 9 Isa 64:4.

GROWING AS A SPIRITLED WOMAN

Judging or Misjudging

God is faithful, and by Him you were called to the fellowship of His Son, Jesus Christ our Lord. Now I ask you, brothers, by the name of our Lord Jesus Christ, that you all speak in agreement and that there be no divisions among you. But be perfectly joined together in the same mind and in the same judgment.

—1 Corinthians 1:9–10

Misjudging causes hurt feelings, divisions, and disagreements. Because we have judged by appearances, we often misjudge. Adornment is like a bowl that holds fruit, one that could be displayed on the dining-room table. It is beautifully crafted and forged of cut crystal, yet it holds in its beauty fruit that is artificial and tasteless. The fruit may look initially inviting because it is surrounded by outward beauty, but if handled or sampled, the fruit will soon be revealed or worthless.

1. How often do you judge others by what you see on the outside? What was the result of your judgment? Was it a "misjudgment"?

2. Do you let your misjudgments whittled others down until they no longer intimidate you?

3. Have you been judged by others by your appearance? Do you feel their judgments were fair? Or were you frustrated by their judgments?

4. Do you draw your confidence from the outward appearances or from the inward? Why?

5. What are some things you can do to draw your confidence from inward, not outward appearances?

6. How does misjudgment help to cause divisions and prevent unity in relationships?

7. What steps can you take to not allow misjudgments and intimidation to create divisiveness in your relationships with others?

Father, I am sorry that I have allowed outward appearances to affect my relationship with You and with others. Please forgive me, and help me to grow in my relationship with You to the point where outward appearances no longer have a hold on me.

Lisa Bevere

> Your physical eyes and ears don't always see and hear what God is doing (1Co 2:9–10).

For the Spirit searches all things, yes, the deep things of God. 11 For what man knows the things of a man, except the spirit of man which is in him? Likewise, no one knows the things of God, except the Spirit of God. 12 Now we have received not the spirit of the world, but the Spirit which is of God, so that we might know the things that are freely given to us by God. 13 These things also we proclaim, not in the words which man's wisdom teaches, but which the Holy Spirit teaches, comparing spiritual things with spiritual. 14 But the natural man does not receive the things of the Spirit of God, for they are foolishness to him; nor can he know them, because they are spiritually discerned. 15 But he who is spiritual judges all things. Yet he himself is not judged by anyone. 16 For

"who has known the mind of the Lord
that he may instruct Him?"[1]

But we have the mind of Christ.

> I have the mind of Christ (1Co 2:16).

Fellow Servants of God

3 Brothers, I could not speak to you as to spiritual men, but as to worldly, even as to babes in Christ. 2 I have fed you with milk and not with solid food. For to this day you were not able to endure it. Nor are you able now, 3 for you are still worldly. Since there is envy, strife, and divisions among you, are you not worldly and behaving as mere men? 4 For while one says, "I am of Paul," and another, "I am of Apollos," are you not worldly?

5 Who then is Paul, and who is Apollos, but ministers by whom you believed, even as the Lord gave to each one? 6 I have planted, Apollos watered, but God gave the increase. 7 So then neither is he who plants nor he who waters anything, but God who gives the increase. 8 Now he who plants and he who waters are one, and each one will receive his own reward according to his own labor. 9 For we are laborers together with God: You are God's vineyard; you are God's building.

10 According to the grace of God which has been given to me, as a wise master builder, I have laid the foundation, but another builds on it. Now let each one take heed how he builds on it. 11 For no one can lay another foundation than that which was laid, which is Jesus Christ.

2:11 Pr 20:27
2:13 1Co 1:17
2:14 1Co 1:18
2:15 1Co 3:1
2:16 Jn 15:15
3:1 Ro 7:14
3:2 Jn 16:12
3:3 1Co 1:11
3:4 1Co 1:12
3:5 2Co 6:4
3:6 Ac 18:4–11
3:7 Gal 6:3
3:9 2Co 6:1
3:10 Ro 12:3
3:11 Eph 2:20
3:13 1Co 4:5
3:14 1Co 3:8
3:15 Jude 1:23
3:16 1Co 6:19
3:18 Isa 5:21
3:19 Job 5:13
3:20 Ps 94:11
3:21 1Co 4:6
3:23 2Co 10:7
4:1 Ro 16:25
4:4 Ps 143:2
4:5 Ro 2:16
4:6 1Co 1:12
4:7 Jn 3:27
4:8 Rev 3:17
4:9 Ro 8:36
4:10 1Co 2:3

12 Now if anyone builds on this foundation with gold, silver, precious stones, wood, hay, or stubble, 13 each one's work will be revealed. For the Day will declare it, because it will be revealed by fire, and the fire will test what sort of work each has done. 14 If anyone's work which he has built on the foundation endures, he will receive a reward. 15 If anyone's work is burned, he will suffer loss. But he himself will be saved, still going through the fire.

16 Do you not know that you are the temple of God, and that the Spirit of God dwells in you? 17 If anyone defiles the temple of God, God will destroy him. For the temple of God is holy. And you are His temple.

18 Let no one deceive himself. If anyone among you seems to be wise in this world, let him become a fool that he may be wise. 19 For the wisdom of this world is foolishness with God. For it is written, "He catches the wise in their own craftiness,"[2] 20 and again, "The Lord knows the thoughts of the wise, that they are vain."[3] 21 Therefore let no one boast in men. For all things are yours: 22 whether Paul or Apollos or Cephas or the world or life or death or things present or things to come, all are yours, 23 and you are Christ's, and Christ is God's.

The Ministry of the Apostles

4 Let a man so regard us as the ministers of Christ and stewards of the mysteries of God. 2 Moreover it is required in stewards that a man be found faithful. 3 But with me it is a very small thing that I should be judged by you or by man's judgment. I do not even judge myself. 4 For I know nothing against myself. Yet I am not justified by this. But He who judges me is the Lord. 5 Therefore judge nothing before the appointed time until the Lord comes. He will bring to light the hidden things of darkness and will reveal the purposes of the hearts. Then everyone will have commendation from God.

6 Brothers, I have figuratively applied these things to myself and to Apollos for your sakes, so that you may learn from us not to think of men above that which is written, and that not one of you would be arrogant for one against another. 7 For who makes you differ from another? And what do you have that you did not receive? Now if you received it, why do you boast as if you had not received it?

8 Now you are full, now you are rich; you have begun reigning as kings without us, and I wish to God you reigned, so that we also might reign with you. 9 For I think that God has exhibited us, the apostles, last, as if we were sentenced to death. For we have been made a spectacle to the world, to angels and to men. 10 We are fools for

1 16 Isa 40:13. *2 19* Job 5:13. *3 20* Ps 94:11.

SPIRIT-TO-SPIRIT PRAYER

Prayer for Spiritual Discernment

Father, I thank You for priestly discernment, the gift of discernment, and the discernment of the born-again believer.

I get in place to operate in these anointings where they apply in my life. Connect me with the fivefold ministry gifts that will sharpen my discernment. I draw from the anointing whereby iron sharpens iron. I renounce all false motives and wrong spirits that would affect my discernment in a negative manner. I purpose to pursue things that are after the Spirit and renounce things that are after the flesh. I declare that the righteousness of the law will be fulfilled in me because I have renounced and do not walk in the things of the flesh (Ro 8:4–5). I declare that carnality is my enemy. I am spiritually minded and renounce the death of carnality. The carnal mind is an enemy of God and also an enemy of me. I renounce the things of the flesh, which cannot please God (Ro 6:6–8).

I am giving myself wholly to the Word of God and to the Spirit of God. I am growing daily in the things of God and will never become addicted to spiritual milk. I strive for the maturity of God. My mental faculties are trained by practice to discriminate and distinguish between what is morally good and noble and what is evil or contrary to divine law. God has anointed me to exercise and discern between what is light and what is dark (Heb 5:13–14).

I am striving toward being skilled and experienced in the doctrine of righteousness. I am in conformity with the divine will of God in purpose, thought, and action. I am qualified to speak the oracles of God. I am a sheep, and I will not follow strange voices. I walk in the anointing of eido *("to know God," Jn 10:4–5). I hear what God is saying, and I qualify to repeat it.*

The mantle of discernment is upon me. Lord, stretch Your scepter unto me in every situation so that I will have wisdom and authority to use what You reveal to me. I declare that I am empowered by God to see in the spirit realm. This realm includes what is dark and what is light. I will not fear what God shows me in the dark realm. God has given me power over all the powers of darkness. He has not given me a spirit of fear but of power, love, and a sound mind.

Lord, I thank You for using the spiritual discernment in my life to become an asset to my family. Also allow it to bring a contribution to the kingdom. Let information and revelation come to the saints through teaching. Let gifts be given to the saints through impartation. Let resources come to the church through equipping. Let discernment be turned on in the lives of Your people through activation. I declare that the people of God will not be ignorant of the devices of the enemy, and they will sharply detect the wiles of darkness. In Jesus' name I pray, amen.

Kimberly Daniels

Christ's sake, but you are wise in Christ. We are weak, but you are strong. You are honorable, but we are despised. 11 Even to this present hour we both hunger and thirst, and are poorly clothed and beaten and homeless. 12 We labor, working with our own hands. Being reviled, we bless. Being persecuted, we endure. 13 Being slandered, we encourage. We are made as the filth of the world, and are the refuse of all things to this day.

14 I do not write these things to shame you, but as my beloved sons I warn you. 15 For if you were to have ten thousand instructors in Christ, yet you do not have many fathers. In Christ Jesus I have become a father to you through the gospel. 16 So I implore you, be followers of me. 17 Therefore I have sent Timothy to you. He is my beloved son and is faithful in the Lord. He will remind you of my ways which are in Christ, as I teach everywhere in every church.

18 Now some are arrogant, as though I were not coming to you. 19 But I will come to you shortly if the Lord wills. And I will know not only what those who are arrogant are saying, but also their power. 20 For the kingdom of God is not in word, but in power. 21 What do you desire? Shall I come to you with a rod, or in love and in the spirit of meekness?

Judgment Against Immorality

5 It is actually reported that there is sexual immorality among you, and such immorality as is not even named among the Gentiles, that a man has his father's wife. 2 But you are arrogant. Instead you should have mourned, so that he who has done this deed might be removed from among you. 3 For indeed, though absent in body but present in spirit, I have already, as if I were present, judged him who has done this deed, 4 in the name of our Lord Jesus Christ. When you are assembled, along with my spirit, in the power of our Lord Jesus Christ, 5 deliver him to Satan for the destruction of the flesh, so that the spirit may be saved on the day of the Lord Jesus.

6 Your boasting is not good. Do you not know that a little yeast leavens the whole batch? 7 Therefore purge out the old yeast, that you may be a new batch, since you are unleavened. For even Christ, our Passover, has been sacrificed for us. 8 Therefore let us keep the feast, not with old yeast, nor with the yeast of malice and wickedness, but with the unleavened bread of sincerity and truth.

9 I wrote to you in my letter not to keep company with sexually immoral people. 10 Yet I did not mean the sexually immoral people of this world, or the covetous and extortioners, or the idolaters, since you would then need to go out of the world. 11 But I have written to you not to keep company with any man who is called a brother, who is sexually immoral, or covetous, or an idolater, or a reviler, or a drunkard, or an extortioner. Do not even eat with such a person.

12 For what have I to do with judging those also who are outside? Do you not judge those who are inside? 13 But God judges those who are outside. Therefore "put away from among yourselves that wicked person."[1]

Going to Law Before Unbelievers

6 Dare any of you, having a matter against another, go to the law before the unrighteous, and not before the saints? 2 Do you not know that the saints will judge the world? If the world will be judged by you, are you unworthy to judge the smallest matters? 3 Do you not know that we shall judge angels? How much more the things that pertain to this life? 4 If then you have judgments dealing with matters of this life, do you appoint as judges those who are least esteemed in the church? 5 I speak to your shame. Is it true that there is not even one wise man among you who shall be able to judge between his brothers? 6 But brother goes to the law against brother, and before unbelievers, at that.

7 Now therefore it is already an utter failure for you that you go to law against one another. Why not rather be wronged? Why not rather be defrauded? 8 But you yourselves do wrong and defraud, and do this to your brothers. 9 Do you not know that the unrighteous will not inherit the kingdom of God? Do not be deceived. Neither the sexually immoral, nor idolaters, nor adulterers, nor male prostitutes, nor homosexuals, 10 nor thieves, nor covetous, nor drunkards, nor revilers, nor extortioners will inherit the kingdom of God. 11 Such were some of you. But you were washed, you were sanctified, and you were justified in the name of the Lord Jesus by the Spirit of our God.

> Father God, sanctify and wash me clean as I study and meditate on Your Word (1Co 6:11).

Glorify God in Your Body

12 "All things are lawful to me," but not all things are helpful. "All things are lawful for me," but I will not be brought under the power of anything. 13 "Food is for the belly, and the belly is for food," but God will destroy both of them. Now the body is not for sexual immorality, but for the Lord, and the Lord is for the body. 14 God has raised up the Lord and will also raise us up by His own power. 15 Do you not know

4:11 Ro 8:35
4:12 1Pe 3:9
4:13 La 3:45
4:14 1Th 2:11
4:15 Gal 4:19
4:16 1Co 11:1
4:17 1Co 7:17
4:19 Ac 18:21
4:20 1Co 2:4
4:21 2Co 13:2
5:1 Lev 18:8
5:3 Col 2:5
5:4 Jn 20:23
5:5 1Ti 1:20
5:6 Gal 5:9
5:8 Ex 12:15
5:9 Eph 5:11
5:10 1Co 10:27
5:11 2Th 3:6
5:12 Mk 4:11
5:13 Dt 13:5
6:2 Mt 19:28
6:4 1Co 5:12
6:5 1Co 4:14
6:8 1Th 4:6
6:9 1Co 15:50
6:10 1Co 5:11
6:11 1Co 1:2
6:13 Mt 15:17
6:14 Ac 2:24
6:15 Ro 12:5

[1] 13 Dt 17:7; 19:19; 21:21; 22:21; 24:7.

that your bodies are the parts of Christ? Shall I then take the parts of Christ and make them the parts of a harlot? God forbid! 16 What? Do you not know that he who is joined to a harlot is one body with her? For "the two," He says, "shall become one flesh."[1] 17 But he who is joined to the Lord becomes one spirit with Him.

> I am united in Christ, and I am one spirit with Him (1Co 6:17).

18 Escape from sexual immorality. Every sin that a man commits is outside the body. But he who commits sexual immorality sins against his own body. 19 What? Do you not know that your body is the temple of the Holy Spirit, who is in you, whom you have received from God, and that you are not your own? 20 You were bought with a price. Therefore glorify God in your body and in your spirit, which are God's.

Questions About Marriage

7 Now concerning the things about which you wrote to me: "It is good for a man not to touch a woman." 2 Nevertheless, because of sexual immorality, let every man have his own wife, and let every woman have her own husband. 3 Let the husband render to the wife due affection, and likewise the wife to the husband. 4 The wife does not have authority over her own body, but the husband does. Likewise, the husband does not have authority over his own body, but the wife does. 5 Do not deprive one another except with consent for a time, that you may give yourselves to fasting and prayer. Then come together again, so that Satan does not tempt you for lack of self-control. 6 I speak this as a concession and not as a command. 7 For I would that all men were even as I myself. But every man has his proper gift from God, one after this manner and another after that.

8 I say to the unmarried and widows that it is good for them if they live even as I am. 9 But if they cannot restrain themselves, let them marry. For it is better to marry than to burn with passion.

10 Now to the married I command, not I, but the Lord, do not let the wife depart from her husband. 11 But if she departs, let her remain unmarried or be reconciled to her husband. And do not let the husband divorce his wife.

12 To the rest I speak, not the Lord: If any brother has an unbelieving wife who consents to live with him, he should not divorce her. 13 And if the woman has an unbelieving husband who consents to live with her, she should not divorce him. 14 For the unbelieving husband is sanctified by the wife, and the unbelieving wife is sanctified by the husband. Otherwise, your children would be unclean. But now they are holy.

15 But if the unbeliever departs, let that one depart. A brother or a sister is not bound in such cases. God has called us to peace. 16 For how do you know, O wife, whether you will save your husband? Or how do you know, O husband, whether you will save your wife?

Living as God Called You

17 But as God has given to every man and as the Lord has called every man, so let him walk. This I command in all churches. 18 Is any man called while circumcised? Let him not become uncircumcised. Is any man called while uncircumcised? Let him not be circumcised. 19 Circumcision is nothing, and uncircumcision is nothing, but the keeping of the commandments of God is everything. 20 Let each man remain in the same condition in which he was called.

21 Were you called while a servant? Do not worry about it. But if you may become free, do so. 22 For he who is called in the Lord while a servant is the Lord's freeman. Likewise, he who is called while free is Christ's servant. 23 You were bought at a price. Do not be the servants of men. 24 Brothers, let every man, in whatever condition he is called, remain there with God.

The Unmarried and Widows

25 Now concerning virgins, I have no command from the Lord. Yet I will give my judgment as one who has obtained mercy from the Lord to be faithful. 26 I suppose therefore that this is good because of the present distress, that it is good for a man to remain as he is. 27 Are you committed to a wife? Do not seek to be uncommitted. Are you free from a wife? Do not seek a wife. 28 But if you marry, you have not sinned. And if a virgin marries, she has not sinned. Nevertheless they will have trouble in this life, but I would spare you that.

29 But this I say, brothers, the time is short. It remains that those who have wives should be as though they had none; 30 those who weep, as though they did not weep; those who rejoice, as though they did not rejoice; those who buy, as though they possessed nothing; 31 and those who use this world, as though they did not make full use of it. For the form of this world is passing away.

32 But I prefer that you have no concern. He who is unmarried cares for the things of the Lord, how he may please the Lord. 33 But he who is married cares for the things of the world, how he may please his wife. 34 There

6:16 Ge 2:24
6:17 Jn 17:21–23
6:18 Heb 13:4
6:19 1Co 3:16
6:20 1Co 7:23
7:1 1Co 7:8
7:2 1Co 7:9
7:3 Ex 21:10
7:5 Ex 19:15
7:6 2Co 8:8
7:7 Mt 19:11–12
7:8 1Co 7:1
7:9 1Ti 5:14
7:10 Mt 5:32
7:12 1Co 7:6
7:15 Ro 14:19
7:16 Ro 11:14
7:17 1Co 4:17
7:18 Ac 15:5
7:19 Gal 5:6
7:22 1Pe 2:16
7:23 1Co 6:20
7:24 1Co 7:20
7:25 1Co 7:6
7:26 1Co 7:1
7:29 Ro 13:11–12
7:31 1Jn 2:17
7:32 1Ti 5:5

[1] *16* Ge 2:24.

PROFILE OF A SPIRITLED WOMAN

HANNAH
THE TICKING BIOLOGICAL CLOCK

Getting married and having children is the number-one dream of most women—and for good reason: We were created with a heart for the family, and children are a reward from God, as we read in Psalm 127:3:

> Look, children are a gift of the LORD, and the fruit of the womb is a reward.

But for the single woman who has not yet found her soul mate or for the married woman who, for whatever reason, has not been able to have a child, the ticking of the biological clock can grow so loud at times that it can drown out any voice of reason or sanity. Our arms ache for the husband we long to love and for the children we hope to bear, but if we are not careful, these desires can run rampant and become a fatal distraction in our lives.

What about the heartache of being married, but for whatever reason being unable to bear a child? How can you cope with the deprivation of something so integral to your womanhood? God's Word is true when it likens barrenness to a land that is parched by drought:

> There are three things that are never satisfied, indeed, four things never say, "It is enough": the grave, the barren womb, the earth that is not filled with water, and the fire that never says, "It is enough."
>
> —PROVERBS 30:15–16

God understands the pain and angst of a childless woman—and His response toward Hannah demonstrates how much He cares.

Hannah's story is told in the Book of 1 Samuel, and it takes place at a time in which polygamy was an accepted practice. Because a man would have several wives, it gave the women a certain status in the family when they were able to bear children—especially sons—for their husbands.

Hannah's husband, Elkanah, had another wife named Peninnah who had borne him several children, but Hannah's womb was barren. The Bible tells us Peninnah took joy in making Hannah's life miserable: "Now her rival [Peninnah] provoked her greatly, making her miserable because the LORD had closed her womb" (1Sa 1:6). Sadly there are some wounds women inflict upon each other that cut to the bone, and this is one of them.

Fortunately for Hannah, she had an understanding husband, but nothing but a child would seem to fill the void in her heart.

Hannah reached out to God in her time of need and reorganized her priorities to align with His. As she cried out to God in the temple out of the anguish of her soul, she made a vow that if He would give her a son, she would return the child to the Lord for lifelong service in His temple—and her prayer was answered. She was blessed with a child, Samuel, whom she consecrated to the Lord and who later became one of the Old Testament judges. God performed above and beyond what Hannah had asked in her prayer, and she went on to have five more children besides!

Defeat this distraction and find peace in your spirit by zeroing in on the great love your heavenly Father has for you, His precious daughter. When you center your heart in His love, you will find rest, solace, and comfort, as well as a greater understanding of the destiny God has for your future.

Joyce Rodgers

is a difference between a wife and a virgin. The unmarried woman cares for the things of the Lord, that she may be holy in body and in spirit. But she who is married cares for the things of the world, how she may please her husband. 35 I say this for your own benefit, not to put any restraint upon you, but for what is proper, and that you may serve the Lord without distraction.

36 If any man thinks that he is behaving improperly toward his virgin,[1] and if she is past the flower of her youth, and passions so require, let him do what he will. He does not sin. Let them marry. 37 Nevertheless he who stands steadfast in his heart without necessity, and has power over his own will, and has so decreed in his heart that he will keep his virgin, does well. 38 So then he who gives her in marriage does well, but he who gives her not in marriage does better.

39 The wife is bound by the law as long as her husband lives. But if her husband dies, she is at liberty to be married to whom she will, but only in the Lord. 40 But in my judgment she is happier if she so remains as she is. And I think that I have the Spirit of God.

Food Offered to Idols

8 Now as concerning food offered to idols: We know that "we all have knowledge." Knowledge produces arrogance, but love edifies. 2 So if anyone thinks that he knows anything, he knows nothing yet as he ought to know. 3 But if anyone loves God, this one is known by Him.

4 So concerning the eating of foods that are offered in sacrifice to idols, we know that an idol is nothing in the world, and that there is no other God but one. 5 For there are those who are called gods, whether in heaven or in earth, as there are many gods and many lords. 6 But for us there is but one God, the Father, from whom are all things and for whom we exist. And there is one Lord Jesus Christ, through whom are all things and through whom we exist.

7 However, not everyone has this knowledge. Some, being accustomed to the idol until now, eat the food as a thing offered to an idol. So their weak conscience is defiled. 8 But food does not commend us to God. Neither if we eat are we the better, nor if we do not eat are we the worse.

9 But take heed, lest by any means this liberty of yours becomes a stumbling block to those who are weak. 10 For if anyone sees you, who have knowledge, eating in the idol's temple, shall the conscience of him who is weak not be emboldened to eat those things which are offered to idols, 11 and by your knowledge shall the weak brother perish, for whom Christ died? 12 When you thus sin against the brothers, wounding their weak conscience, you sin against Christ. 13 Therefore, if food causes my brother to stumble, I will never eat meat, lest I cause my brother to stumble.

The Rights of an Apostle

9 Am I not an apostle? Am I not free? Have I not seen Jesus Christ our Lord? Are you not my work in the Lord? 2 If I am not an apostle to others, yet indeed I am to you. For you are the seal of my apostleship in the Lord.

3 This is my answer to those who examine me. 4 Do we have no right to eat and to drink? 5 Do we not have the right to take along a believing wife as do other apostles, the brothers of the Lord, and Cephas? 6 Or is it only Barnabas and I who have no right to refrain from working?

7 Who goes to war at any time at his own expense? Who plants a vineyard, but does not eat of its fruit? Or who feeds a flock, but does not drink of the flock's milk? 8 Do I say these things as a man? Or does the law not say the same thing also? 9 For it is written in the Law of Moses, "You shall not muzzle the mouth of the ox while it treads out the grain."[2] Is God concerned about oxen? 10 Or does He say it completely for our sake? For our sake, no doubt, this is written so that he who plows should plow in hope, and that he who threshes in hope should partake of his hope. 11 If we have sown for you spiritual things, is it a great thing if we shall reap your material things? 12 If others partake of this right over you, should not we instead?

Nevertheless, we have not used this right, but suffer all things, lest we might hinder the gospel of Christ.

13 Do you not know that those who minister unto holy things live from the things of the temple? And do you not know that those who wait at the altar partake of the altar? 14 In the same way, the Lord has ordained that those who preach the gospel should live from the gospel.

15 But I have used none of these rights, nor have I written these things that it should be so done to me. For it would be better for me to die than allow anyone to make my boasting void. 16 Though I preach the gospel, I have nothing to boast of, for the requirement is laid upon me. Yes, woe unto me if I do not preach the gospel! 17 So if I do this willingly, I have a reward, but if against my will, I have

7:35 1Co 7:36
7:38 Heb 13:4
8:1 1Co 8:7
8:3 Gal 4:9
8:4 Dt 6:4
8:5 2Th 2:4
8:6 Jn 1:3
8:7 Ro 14:14
8:8 Ro 14:17
8:9 Gal 5:13
8:11 Ro 14:15

....

8:12 Mt 25:45
8:13 Ro 14:21
9:1 1Co 3:6
9:4 1Th 2:6
9:5 Mt 8:14
9:6 Ac 4:36
9:7 Dt 20:6
9:9 Dt 25:4
9:10 2Ti 2:6
9:11 Ro 15:27
9:12 1Co 9:18
9:13 Lev 6:26
9:14 Mt 10:10
9:16 Ro 1:14
9:17 Gal 2:7

[1] *36* Some versions translate this word as "virgin daughters," others translate it as "fiancée." Since the Greek text itself remains unclear, the editors have chosen to keep the literal translation. [2] *9* Dt 25:4.

been entrusted with a commission. 18 What is my reward then? Truly that when I preach the gospel, I may present the gospel of Christ without charge, so that I may not abuse my authority in the gospel.

19 For though I am free from all men, I have made myself servant to all, that I might win even more. 20 To the Jews, I became as a Jew, that I might win the Jews; to those who are under the law, as under the law, that I might win those who are under the law; 21 to those who are outside the law, as outside the law (being not without God's law, but under Christ's law) that I might win those who are outside the law. 22 To the weak, I became as weak, that I might win the weak. I have become all things to all men, that I might by all means save some. 23 This I do for the gospel's sake, that I might partake of it with you.

24 Do you not know that all those who run in a race run, but one receives the prize? So run, that you may obtain it. 25 Everyone who strives for the prize exercises self-control in all things. Now they do it to obtain a corruptible crown, but we an incorruptible one. 26 So, therefore, I run, not with uncertainty. So I fight, not as one who beats the air. 27 But I bring and keep my body under subjection, lest when preaching to others I myself should be disqualified.

I will exercise self-control in all things (1Co 9:25–26).

Warning Against Idolatry

10 I would not want you to be unaware that all our fathers were under the cloud, and all passed through the sea, 2 and all were baptized into Moses in the cloud and in the sea; 3 all ate the same spiritual food; 4 and all drank the same spiritual drink, for they drank of that spiritual Rock that followed them, and that Rock was Christ. 5 But with many of them God was not well pleased, and they were overthrown in the wilderness.

6 Now these things were our examples to the intent that we should not lust after evil things as they lusted. 7 Neither be idolaters as were some of them. As it is written, "The people sat down to eat and drink and rose up to revel."[1] 8 Neither let us commit sexual immorality as some of them committed, when twenty-three thousand fell in one day. 9 Neither let us tempt Christ, as some of them also tempted and were destroyed by serpents. 10 Neither murmur, as some of them also murmured and were destroyed by the destroyer.

11 Now all these things happened to them for examples. They are written as an admonition to us, upon whom the end of the ages has come. 12 Therefore let him who thinks he stands take heed, lest he fall. 13 No temptation has taken you except what is common to man. God is faithful, and He will not permit you to be tempted above what you can endure, but will with the temptation also make a way to escape, that you may be able to bear it.

14 So, my beloved, flee from idolatry. 15 I speak as to wise men. Judge for yourselves what I say. 16 The cup of blessing which we bless, is it not the communion of the blood of Christ? The bread which we break, is it not the communion of the body of Christ? 17 For we, being many, are one bread and one body, for we are all partakers of that one bread.

18 Consider Israel after the flesh: Are not those who eat of the sacrifices partakers of the altar? 19 What am I saying then, that the idol is anything or that which is offered in sacrifice to idols is anything? 20 But I say that the things which the Gentiles sacrifice, they sacrifice to demons, and not to God. I do not want you to have fellowship with demons. 21 You cannot drink the cup of the Lord and the cup of demons. You cannot be partakers of the Lord's table and of the table of demons. 22 Do we provoke the Lord to jealousy? Are we stronger than He?

Do All to the Glory of God

23 "All things are lawful for me," but not all things are helpful. "All things are lawful for me," but not all things edify. 24 Let no one seek his own, but each one the other's well-being.

25 Eat whatever is sold in the meat market, asking no question for the sake of conscience, 26 for "The earth is the Lord's, and everything in it."[2]

27 If any of those who do not believe invite you to a feast, and you desire to go, eat whatever is set before you, asking no question for the sake of conscience. 28 But if anyone says to you, "This was offered in sacrifice to idols," do not eat it for the sake of him that mentioned it and for the sake of conscience, for "The earth is the Lord's, and everything in it."[3] 29 Conscience, I say, not your own, but that of the other. For why is my liberty judged by another man's conscience? 30 If I partake with thankfulness, why am I slandered concerning that for which I give thanks?

31 Therefore, whether you eat, or drink, or whatever you do, do it all to the glory of God. 32 Give no offense, neither to the Jews, nor to the Gentiles, nor to the church of God, 33 just as I try to please all men in all things, not seeking

9:18 1Co 7:31
9:19 Mt 18:15
9:20 Ac 16:3
9:21 Ro 2:12
9:22 Ro 11:14
9:24 Gal 2:2
9:25 Jas 1:12
9:27 Ro 8:13
10:1 Ex 14:29
10:3 Ex 16:35
10:4 Ex 17:6
10:5 Heb 3:17
10:6 Nu 11:4
10:7 Ex 32:19
10:8 Nu 25:1–9
10:9 Nu 21:5–6
10:10 Ex 12:23
10:11 Ro 13:11
10:12 Ro 11:20
10:13 1Co 1:9
10:14 1Co 10:7
10:16 Mt 26:26–28
10:17 Ro 12:5
10:18 Ro 4:1
10:19 1Co 8:4
10:20 Rev 9:20
10:22 Dt 32:21
10:23 1Co 6:12
10:24 1Co 10:33
10:25 1Co 8:7
10:26 Ps 24:1
10:29 1Co 9:19
10:30 Ro 14:6
10:31 Col 3:17
10:32 Ac 20:28
10:33 1Co 10:24

[1] 7 Ex 32:6. [2] 26 Ps 24:1. [3] 28 Ps 24:1.

my own profit, but the profit of many, that they may be saved.

11 Follow me as I follow Christ.

Covering the Head in Worship

[2] I praise you, brothers, that you remember me in all things and keep the traditions as I delivered them to you. [3] But I would have you know that the head of the woman is the man, the head of every man is Christ, and the head of Christ is God. [4] Every man praying or prophesying having his head covered dishonors his head, [5] but every woman who prays or prophesies with her head uncovered dishonors her head, for that is the same as if she were shaved. [6] For if the woman is not covered, let her also cut off her hair. But if it is a shame for a woman to have her hair cut off or shaved, let her be covered.

[7] For a man indeed ought not to cover his head, because he is the image and glory of God. But the woman is the glory of the man. [8] The man is not from the woman, but the woman from the man. [9] The man was not created for the woman, but the woman for the man. [10] For this reason the woman ought to have a veil of authority over her head, because of the angels. [11] Nevertheless, neither is the man without the woman, nor the woman without the man in the Lord. [12] For just as the woman came from the man, so the man comes through the woman, but all things come from God.

[13] Judge for yourselves. Is it proper for a woman to pray to God uncovered? [14] Does even nature itself not teach you that if a man has long hair it is a shame to him? [15] But if a woman has long hair, it is a glory to her, for her hair is given her for a covering. [16] But if anyone seems to be contentious, we have no such custom, nor have the churches of God.

Abuses at the Lord's Supper

[17] Now in what I have to say to you, I do not praise you. You have come together not for the better, but for the worse. [18] First of all, when you come together as the church, I hear that there are divisions among you, and in part I believe it. [19] For there must also be factions among you so that those who are genuine may become evident among you. [20] Therefore when you come together into one place, it is not to eat the Lord's Supper. [21] For in eating, each one eats his own supper ahead of others. One goes hungry, and another becomes drunk. [22] What? Do you not have houses to eat and to drink in? Or do you despise the church of God and shame those who have nothing? What shall I say to you? Shall I praise you in this? I do not praise you.

11:1 1Co 4:16
11:2 2Th 2:15
11:3 Ge 3:16
11:5 Dt 21:12
11:7 Jas 3:9
11:8 1Ti 2:13
11:9 Ge 2:18
11:11 Gal 3:28
11:12 Ro 11:36
11:13 Lk 12:57
11:16 1Co 7:17
11:17 1Co 11:2
11:18 1Co 3:3
11:19 1Jn 2:19
11:21 Jude 1:12
11:22 1Co 10:32
11:23 1Co 15:3
11:25 Lk 22:20
11:26 Jn 21:22
11:28 2Co 13:5
11:31 1Jn 1:9
11:34 1Co 4:19
12:1 1Co 14:37
12:2 Ps 115:5
12:3 Jn 13:13
12:4 Heb 2:4
12:6 1Co 15:28
12:8 2Co 8:7
12:9 2Co 4:13
12:10 Mk 16:17

The Lord's Supper

Mt 26:26–29; Mk 14:22–25; Lk 22:14–20

[23] I have received of the Lord that which I delivered to you: that the Lord Jesus, on the night in which He was betrayed, took bread. [24] When He had given thanks, He broke it and said, "Take and eat. This is My body which is broken for you. Do this in remembrance of Me."[1] [25] In the same manner He took the cup after He had supper, saying, "This cup is the new covenant in My blood. Do this, as often as you drink it, in remembrance of Me."[2] [26] As often as you eat this bread and drink this cup, you proclaim the Lord's death until He comes.

Partaking of the Supper Unworthily

[27] Therefore whoever eats this bread and drinks this cup of the Lord unworthily will be guilty of the body and blood of the Lord. [28] Let a man examine himself, and so eat of the bread and drink of the cup. [29] For he who eats and drinks unworthily, eats and drinks damnation to himself, not discerning the Lord's body. [30] For this reason many are weak and unhealthy among you, and many die. [31] If we would judge ourselves, we would not be judged. [32] But when we are judged, we are disciplined by the Lord, so that we would not be condemned with the world.

[33] So, my brothers, when you come together to eat, wait for one another. [34] If anyone hungers, let him eat at home, so that you may not come together into condemnation.

I will set the rest in order when I come.

Spiritual Gifts

12 Now concerning spiritual gifts, brothers, I do not want you to be ignorant. [2] You know that you were Gentiles, carried away to these dumb idols, however you were led. [3] Therefore I make known to you that no one speaking by the Spirit of God says, "Jesus be cursed!" And no one can say, "Jesus is the Lord," except by the Holy Spirit.

[4] There are various gifts, but the same Spirit. [5] There are differences of administrations, but the same Lord. [6] There are various operations, but it is the same God who operates all of them in all people.

[7] But the manifestation of the Spirit is given to everyone for the common good. [8] To one is given by the Spirit the word of wisdom, to another the word of knowledge by the same Spirit, [9] to another faith by the same Spirit, to another gifts of healings by the same Spirit, [10] to another the working of miracles, to another prophecy, to another discerning of spirits, to another various kinds of tongues, and to

1 24 Mt 26:26; Mk 14:22; Lk 22:19. *2 25* Mt 26:27–28; Mk 14:24; Lk 22:20.

SPIRITLED WOMAN

COUNSEL FROM THE SPIRIT BASICS

The Reason Love Never Fails

Forgiving your debtors as God has forgiven you is 1 Corinthians 13 in action:

> Love suffers long and is kind; love envies not; love flaunts not itself and is not puffed up, does not behave itself improperly, seeks not its own, is not easily provoked, thinks no evil; rejoices not in iniquity, but rejoices in the truth; bears all things, believes all things, hopes all things, and endures all things. Love never fails.
>
> —1 CORINTHIANS 13:4–8

Take a moment to look at that passage again, but this time, in every place where it says *love*, replace that word with your name. That's you walking in love. That's you walking in proactive forgiveness. That's you cherishing your relationships over your things; over your accomplishments, goals, and tasks; and over yourself. That's you living the richest life possible. It is also a foundational component of living the impossible life Jesus has called us to live in His image. It is faith at work and the key to doing the "greater works" (Jn 14:12) our world needs to manifest God's kingdom.

Cindy Trimm

another the interpretation of tongues. 11 But
that one and very same Spirit works all these,
dividing to each one individually as He will.

One Body With Many Members

12 For as the body is one and has many parts,
and all the many parts of that one body are one
body, so also is Christ. 13 For by one Spirit we
are all baptized into one body, whether we are
Jews or Gentiles, whether we are slaves or free,
and we have all been made to drink of one
Spirit. 14 The body is not one part, but many.
15 If the foot says, "Because I am not the
hand, I am not of the body," is it therefore not
of the body? 16 And if the ear says, "Because
I am not the eye, I am not of the body," is it
therefore not of the body? 17 If the whole body

12:11 1Co 12:4
12:12 1Co 12:27
12:13 Jn 7:37–39
....
12:18 1Co 12:11
12:26 Ro 12:15
12:27 Ro 12:5
12:28 Heb 13:17
12:31 1Co 14:39
13:1 2Co 12:4
13:2 Mt 17:20
13:4 Col 3:12
13:5 1Co 10:24

were an eye, where would the hearing be? If
the whole body were hearing, where would
the sense of smell be? 18 But now God has es-
tablished the parts, every one of them, in the
body as it has pleased Him. 19 If they were all
one part, where would the body be? 20 So there
are many parts, yet one body.
21 The eye cannot say to the hand, "I have no
need of you," nor the head to the feet, "I have
no need of you." 22 No, those parts of the body
which seem to be weaker are necessary. 23 And
those parts of the body which we think are less
honorable, upon these we bestow more abun-
dant honor. And our less respectable parts are
treated with much more respect, 24 whereas our
more respectable parts have no need of this.
But God has composed the body, having given
more abundant honor to that part which lacks
it, 25 so that there should be no division in the
body, but that the parts should have the same
care for one another. 26 If one part suffers, all
the parts suffer with it, and if one part is hon-
ored, all the parts rejoice with it.
27 Now you are the body of Christ and mem-
bers individually. 28 God has put these in the
church: first apostles, second prophets, third
teachers, after that miracles, then gifts of
healings, helps, governments, and various
tongues. 29 Are all apostles? Are all prophets?
Are all teachers? Are all workers of miracles?
30 Do all have the gifts of healings? Do all speak
with tongues? Do all interpret? 31 But earnestly
covet the greater gifts.

I am a member of the body of Christ (1Co 12:27).

Love

Yet I show you a more excellent way.

13 If I speak with the tongues of men and
of angels, and have not love, I have
become as sounding brass or a clanging
cymbal. 2 If I have the gift of prophecy, and
understand all mysteries and all knowledge,
and if I have all faith, so that I could remove
mountains, and have not love, I am nothing.
3 If I give all my goods to feed the poor, and
if I give my body to be burned, and have not
love, it profits me nothing.

Love is the key to a mentor's heart (1Co 13:4–7).

4 Love suffers long and is kind; love envies
not; love flaunts not itself and is not puffed
up, 5 does not behave itself improperly, seeks

Our Problem in America

Coveting will definitely lead to debt. Many people were taken advantage of by the mortgage system in America. Some are in trouble because they coveted what another man had. Coveting comes against the promise of God that we will be lenders and not borrowers.

Before our economic crisis I could not help but notice that many people were living extreme lifestyles in comparison to their income. I wondered how they had such large homes and fancy vehicles. In 2008 all my questions were answered and made clear to me. People were living *above* their means and had become slaves of debt.

Paul warned the church in Rome, "Owe no one anything, except to love one another" (Ro 13:8). Debt is the strongman that rules over the spirit of interest. Interest is a deep hole you can never get out of. People need to get to the place where they are spiritually allergic to interest. It is a bondage that goes deeper than the natural. Many people have been living under the false prosperity of credit cards for years.

As bad as the situation may seem, America has learned a valuable lesson: do not be a brother to the great waster (Pr 18:9). Now we must humble ourselves, repent, and live within the means of our portion. It is the heritage of the just man. Do not attempt to keep up with wicked men in their worldly forms of prosperity.

Paul said that a man should love his neighbor as he loves himself (Ro 13:9). In order to covet, you have to want something from a neighbor (or another person). But Paul teaches that when we love our neighbor, it sums up all the commandments, such as "You shall not kill, steal, or commit adultery." This doesn't take away from the fact that we should not commit these sins. It literally means that we fulfill these commandments by loving our neighbor, because if we love our neighbor, we would not commit these sins against him or her. It is hard to kill someone, steal from someone, or commit adultery with someone when you love that person as Christ called you to love him or her. When we love our neighbors as Christ called us to do, the purpose for God's commandments is manifested in the earth realm.

We can live prosperous lives by displacing ungodly covetousness with godly covetousness. It is scriptural. First Corinthians 12:27–31 teaches that we should covet the best gifts with a sincere heart. First Corinthians 14:39 says that we should covet to prophesy. Whenever deliverance takes place, the spot that was filled with the wrong thing has to be refilled with the right thing. Once a person is delivered from covetousness, they must be filled with contentment.

Kimberly Daniels

not its own, is not easily provoked, thinks no evil; 6 rejoices not in iniquity, but rejoices in the truth; 7 bears all things, believes all things, hopes all things, and endures all things.

8 Love never fails. But if there are prophecies, they shall fail; if there are tongues, they shall cease; and if there is knowledge, it shall vanish. 9 For we know in part, and we prophesy in part. 10 But when that which is perfect comes, then that which is imperfect shall pass away. 11 When I was a child, I spoke as a child, I understood as a child, and I thought as a child. But when I became a man, I put away childish things. 12 For now we see as through a glass, dimly, but then, face to face. Now I know in part, but then I shall know, even as I also am known.

13 So now abide faith, hope, and love, these three. But the greatest of these is love.

Tongues and Prophecy

14 Follow after love and desire spiritual gifts, but especially that you may prophesy. 2 For he who speaks in an unknown tongue does not speak to men, but to God. For no one understands him, although in the spirit, he speaks mysteries. 3 But he who prophesies speaks to men for their edification and exhortation and comfort. 4 He who speaks in an unknown tongue edifies himself, but he who prophesies edifies the church. 5 I desire that you all speak in tongues, but even more that you prophesy. For greater is he who prophesies than he who speaks in tongues, unless he interprets, so that the church may receive edification.

6 Now, brothers, if I come to you speaking in tongues, what shall I profit you, unless I speak to you by revelation or knowledge or prophesying or doctrine? 7 Even when things without life give sound, whether flute or harp, how will it be known what is played unless they give a distinction in the sounds? 8 If the trumpet makes an uncertain sound, who will prepare himself for the battle? 9 So also you, unless with the tongue you speak words easy to understand, how will it be known what is spoken? For you shall speak into the air. 10 There are, it may be, so many kinds of languages in the world, and none of them is without significance. 11 Therefore, if I do not know the meaning of the speech, I shall be a barbarian to him who speaks, and he who speaks will be a barbarian to me. 12 So, seeing that you are zealous of spiritual gifts, seek that you may excel to the edifying of the church.

13 Let him who speaks in an unknown tongue pray that he may interpret. 14 For if I pray in an unknown tongue, my spirit prays, but my understanding is unfruitful. 15 What is it then? I will pray with the spirit, and I will pray with the understanding. I will sing with the spirit, and I will sing with the understanding. 16 Otherwise, when you bless with the spirit, how will he who occupies the place of the unlearned say "Amen" at your giving of thanks, seeing he does not understand what you say? 17 For you indeed give thanks well, but the other is not edified.

18 I thank my God that I speak in tongues more than you all. 19 Yet in the church I had rather speak five words with my understanding, that by my voice I might teach others also, than ten thousand words in an unknown tongue.

20 Brothers, do not be children in your thinking; rather be infants in evil, but in your thinking be mature. 21 In the law it is written:

"With men of other tongues
and other lips
I will speak to this people;
but even then they will not hear Me,"[1]
says the Lord.

22 So tongues are for a sign, not to believers, but to unbelievers. But prophesying does not serve unbelievers, but believers. 23 Therefore if the whole church assembles in one place and all speak with tongues, and those who are unlearned or unbelievers come in, will they not say that you are out of your mind? 24 But if all prophesy and there comes in one who does not believe or one unlearned, he is convinced by all and judged by all. 25 Thus the secrets of his heart are revealed. And so falling down on his face, he will worship God and report that God is truly among you.

All Things to Be Done in Order

26 How is it then, brothers? When you come together, every one of you has a psalm, a teaching, a tongue, a revelation, and an interpretation. Let all things be done for edification. 27 If anyone speaks in an unknown tongue, let it be by two, or at the most by three, and each in turn, and let one interpret. 28 But if there is no interpreter, let him remain silent in the church, and let him speak to himself and to God.

29 Let two or three prophets speak, and let the others judge. 30 If anything is revealed to another that sits by, let the first keep silent. 31 For you may all prophesy one by one, that all may learn and all may be encouraged. 32 The spirits of the prophets are subject to the prophets. 33 For God is not the author of confusion, but of peace, as in all churches of the saints.

13:6 2Jn 1:4
13:7 1Co 13:4
13:9 1Co 8:2
13:12 2Co 5:7
13:13 Gal 5:6
14:1 1Co 12:1
14:2 1Co 13:2
14:3 Ro 14:19
14:5 1Co 12:10
14:6 Eph 1:17
14:8 Nu 10:9
14:9 1Co 9:26
14:11 Ac 28:2
14:12 1Co 14:26
14:14 1Co 14:2
14:15 Col 3:16
14:16 1Ch 16:36
14:17 1Co 14:4
14:20 Ro 16:19
14:21 Jn 10:34
14:22 Mk 16:17
14:23 Ac 2:13
14:25 Isa 45:14
14:26 Ro 14:19
14:29 1Co 12:10
14:30 1Th 5:19–20
14:32 1Jn 4:1
14:33 1Co 7:17

[1]*21* Isa 28:11–12.

34 Let your women remain silent in the churches. For they are not permitted to speak. They are commanded to be under obedience, as the law also says. 35 If they will learn anything, let them ask their husbands at home, for it is a shame for women to speak in the church.

36 What? Did the word of God come from you? Or did it come to you only? 37 If anyone thinks himself to be a prophet or spiritual, let him acknowledge that what I am writing you is a command of the Lord. 38 But if anyone is ignorant, let him be ignorant.

39 Therefore, brothers, eagerly desire to prophesy, and do not forbid speaking in tongues. 40 Let all things be done decently and in order.

The Resurrection of Christ

15 Now, brothers, I declare to you the gospel which I preached to you, which you have received, and in which you stand. 2 Through it you are saved, if you keep in memory what I preached to you, unless you have believed in vain.

3 For I delivered to you first of all that which I also received: how Christ died for our sins according to the Scriptures, 4 was buried, rose again the third day according to the Scriptures, 5 and was seen by Cephas, and then by the twelve. 6 Then He was seen by over five hundred brothers at once, of whom the greater part remain to this present time, though some have passed away. 7 Then He was seen by James and then by all the apostles. 8 Last of all, He was seen by me also, as by one born at the wrong time.

9 For I am the least of the apostles and am not fit to be called an apostle, because I persecuted the church of God. 10 But by the grace of God I am what I am. And His grace toward me was not in vain. I labored more abundantly than all of them, yet not I, but the grace of God which was with me. 11 Therefore, whether it was I or they, so we preach and so you believed.

The Resurrection of the Dead

12 Now if Christ is preached that He rose from the dead, how can some of you say that there is no resurrection of the dead? 13 If there is no resurrection of the dead, then Christ has not risen. 14 If Christ has not risen, then our preaching is vain, and your faith is also vain. 15 Yes, and we would then be found false witnesses of God, because we have testified that God raised up Christ, whom He did not raise up, if in fact the dead do not rise. 16 For if the dead do not rise, then Christ has not been raised. 17 If Christ is not raised, your faith is vain; you are still in your sins. 18 Then they also who have fallen asleep in Christ have perished. 19 If in this life only we have hope in Christ, we are of all men most miserable.

20 But now is Christ risen from the dead and become the first fruits of those who have fallen asleep. 21 For since death came by man, by man came also the resurrection of the dead. 22 For as in Adam all die, even so in Christ shall all be made alive. 23 But every man in his own order: Christ the first fruits; afterward, those who are Christ's at His coming. 24 Then comes the end when He will deliver up the kingdom to God the Father, when He puts an end to all rule and all authority and power. 25 For He will reign until He has put all enemies under His feet. 26 The last enemy that will be destroyed is death. 27 For He "has put all things under His feet."[1] But when He says, "all things are put under Him," it is revealed that He, who has put all things under Him, is the exception. 28 When all things are subjected to Him, then the Son Himself will also be subject to Him who put all things under Him, that God may be all in all.

29 Otherwise, what will they do who are baptized for the dead, if the dead do not rise at all? Why are they then baptized for the dead? 30 And why do we stand in danger every hour? 31 I affirm, by the boasting in you which I have in Christ Jesus our Lord, I die daily. 32 If, in the manner of men, I have fought with beasts at Ephesus, what advantage is it to me if the dead do not rise?

"Let us eat and drink,
for tomorrow we die."[2]

33 Do not be deceived: "Bad company corrupts good morals." 34 Awake to righteousness and do not sin, for some do not have the knowledge of God. I say this to your shame.

The Resurrection Body

35 But someone will say, "How are the dead raised up? With what body do they come?" 36 You fool! What you sow is not made alive unless it dies. 37 When you sow, you do not sow the body that shall be, but a bare kernel, perhaps of wheat or of some other grain. 38 Then God gives it a body as He pleases, and to each seed its own body. 39 All flesh is not the same flesh. There is one kind of flesh of men, another flesh of beasts, another of fish, and another of birds. 40 There are also celestial bodies and terrestrial bodies. The glory of the celestial is one, and the glory of the terrestrial is another. 41 There is one glory of the sun, and another glory of the moon, and another glory of the stars. One star differs from another star in glory.

14:34 1Ti 2:11–12
14:37 2Co 10:7
14:39 1Co 12:31
14:40 Col 2:5
15:1 Ro 5:2
15:2 Gal 3:4
15:3 1Pe 2:24
15:5 Mk 16:14
15:7 Lk 24:50
15:8 1Co 9:1
15:9 Ac 8:3
15:10 Php 2:13
15:13 1Th 4:14
15:15 Ac 2:24
15:17 Ro 4:25
15:18 Rev 14:13
15:19 2Ti 3:12
....
15:20 Ac 26:23
15:23 1Co 15:20
15:24 Da 7:27
15:25 Ps 110:1
15:26 2Ti 1:10
15:27 Ps 8:6
15:28 1Co 3:23
15:31 Ro 8:36
15:32 Isa 22:13
15:34 Ro 13:11
15:35 Eze 37:3
15:36 Jn 12:24

[1] *27* Ps 8:6. [2] *32* Isa 22:13.

42 So also is the resurrection of the dead. *The
body* is sown in corruption; it is raised in in-
corruption. 43 It is sown in dishonor, it is raised
in glory. It is sown in weakness, it is raised in
power. 44 It is sown a natural body, it is raised
a spiritual body.
There is a natural body, and there is a spir-
itual body. 45 So it is written, "The first man
Adam was made a living soul."[1] The last Adam
was made a life-giving spirit. 46 However, that
which is spiritual is not first, but the natural,
and then the spiritual. 47 The first man was of
the earth, made of dust; the second man was
the Lord from heaven. 48 As was the man of
dust, so are those who are of dust; and as is
the man of heaven, so are those who are of
heaven. 49 As we have borne the image of the
man of dust, we shall also bear the image of
the man of heaven.
50 Now this I say, brothers, that flesh and
blood cannot inherit the kingdom of God, nor
does corruption inherit incorruption. 51 Listen,
I tell you a mystery: We shall not all sleep, but
we shall all be changed. 52 In a moment, in the
twinkling of an eye, at the last trumpet, for the
trumpet will sound, the dead will be raised
incorruptible, and we shall be changed. 53 For
this corruptible will put on incorruption, and
this mortal will put on immortality. 54 When this
corruptible will have put on incorruption, and
this mortal will have put on immortality, then
the saying that is written shall come to pass:
"Death is swallowed up in victory."[2]

55 "O death, where is your sting?
O grave, where is your victory?"[3]

56 The sting of death is sin, and the strength of
sin is the law. 57 But thanks be to God, who gives
us the victory through our Lord Jesus Christ!
58 Therefore, my beloved brothers, be stead-
fast, unmovable, always abounding in the
work of the Lord, knowing that your labor in
the Lord is not in vain.

I have victory through Christ
(1Co 15:57).

The Contribution for the Saints

16 Now concerning the collection for the
saints, as I have given instruction to
the churches of Galatia, so even you must do.
2 On the first day of the week let every one of
you lay in store, as God has prospered him,
so that no collections be made when I come.
3 And when I come, I will send whomever you
approve with your letters to take your generous
gifts to Jerusalem. 4 If it is fitting that I go also,
they will go with me.

Paul's Plans for Travel

5 Now I will come to you after I pass through
Macedonia. For I will pass through Macedonia.
6 It may be that I will remain, of course, and
spend the winter with you, that you may send
me on my journey wherever I go. 7 For I do not
wish to see you now in passing. Instead, I trust
to remain a while with you, if the Lord permits.
8 But I will remain at Ephesus until Pentecost.
9 For a great and effective door has opened to
me, and there are many adversaries.
10 Now if Timothy comes, see that he may
remain with you without fear, for he does the
work of the Lord, as I also do. 11 Therefore let
no one despise him. But send him on his way
in peace, that he may come to me. I am expect-
ing him with the brothers.
12 As for our brother Apollos, I greatly wanted
him to come to you with the brothers. But he was
not willing at all to come at this time. However,
he will come when he has a convenient time.
13 Watch, stand fast in the faith, be bold like
men, and be strong. 14 Let all that you do be
done with love.
15 You know the house of Stephanas, that it is
the first fruits of Achaia, and that they have de-
voted themselves to the ministry of the saints.
So I ask you, brothers, 16 that you submit your-
selves to such people, and to everyone who
helps and labors with us. 17 I am happy about
the arrival of Stephanas, Fortunatus, and
Achaicus, for they supplied what was lacking
on your part. 18 They have refreshed my spirit
and yours. Therefore acknowledge these men.

Final Request and Greetings

19 The churches of Asia greet you. Aquila and
Priscilla greet you heartily in the Lord, with the
church that is in their house. 20 All the brothers
greet you. Greet one another with a holy kiss.
21 I, Paul, write this greeting with my own
hand.
22 If anyone does not love the Lord Jesus
Christ, let him be accursed. Come, O Lord!
23 The grace of our Lord Jesus Christ be
with you.
24 My love be with you all in Christ Jesus.
Amen.

15:42 Da 12:3
15:43 Col 3:4
15:45 Ge 2:7
15:47 Jn 3:31
15:48 Php 3:20–21
15:49 Ge 5:3
15:50 Mt 16:17
15:51 1Co 13:2
15:52 Mt 24:31
15:54 Isa 25:8
15:55 Hos 13:14
15:56 Ro 4:15
15:57 Ro 8:37
15:58 1Co 16:10
16:1 Ac 24:17
16:2 Ac 20:7
....
16:5 Ac 19:21
16:6 Ac 15:3
16:7 Ac 18:21
16:8 Ac 2:1
16:9 Ac 14:27
16:10 1Co 15:58
16:11 Ac 15:33
16:12 1Co 1:12
16:13 Gal 5:1
16:15 Ro 16:5
16:16 Heb 13:17
16:17 2Co 11:9
16:18 2Co 7:13
16:19 Ac 18:2
16:20 Ro 16:16
16:21 Gal 6:11
16:22 Ro 9:3
16:23 Ro 16:20

[1] 45 Ge 2:7. [2] 54 Isa 25:8. [3] 55 Hos 13:14.

Author: The apostle Paul

Written: AD 55 or 56, from Macedonia

Themes: Rebuke, General Warnings, Restoration

2 Corinthians

Dear SpiritLed Woman,

According to Paul's second letter to the Corinthians, you are a part of the special operations forces in the army of God! With eyes trained on the spiritual realm, you can see where the enemy is operating. Then you can come into agreement with God regarding His purposes, and His power will be released.

The primary key to spiritual warfare is effective prayer through intimacy with God. Intimacy doesn't come from spending a few minutes a day giving Him a list of desires; it develops as we spend time in worship and true fellowship with Him. From that place we will pray His will. Another key is understanding the power of the Word of God and learning to use it as a sword. The Bible tells us that "the weapons of our warfare are not carnal, but mighty through God to the pulling down of strongholds" (2Co 10:4). As we abide in Christ, we are equipped with the power of His name and can use it against the enemy.

The outcome of this spiritual war will be personal. It will affect you and your household. You must throw off passivity, pick up your weapons, and fight!

Salutation

1 Paul, an apostle of Jesus Christ by the will of God, and Timothy our brother,

To the church of God which is at Corinth, with all the saints who are in all Achaia:

2 Grace to you and peace from God our Father and from the Lord Jesus Christ.

Paul's Thanksgiving After Affliction

3 Blessed be God, the Father of our Lord Jesus Christ, the Father of mercies, and the God of all comfort, 4 who comforts us in all our tribulation, that we may be able to comfort those who are in any trouble by the comfort with which we ourselves are comforted by God. 5 As the sufferings of Christ abound in us, so our consolation also abounds through Christ. 6 If we are afflicted, it is for your consolation and salvation, which is effective in enduring the same sufferings which we also suffer. Or if we are comforted, it is for your consolation and salvation. 7 Our hope for you is steadfast, knowing that as you partake in the sufferings, so also you will partake of the consolation.

8 For we would not, brothers, have you ignorant of our troubles which came to us in Asia. We were pressured beyond measure, above strength, so that we despaired even of life. 9 We had the sentence of death in ourselves, so that we would not trust in ourselves, but in God who raises the dead. 10 He delivered us from so great a death and does deliver us. In Him we trust that He will still deliver us, 11 as you help together by praying for us, so that thanks may be given by many on our behalf for the gift bestowed upon us by means of many persons.

Paul's Travel Plans Change

12 For our rejoicing is this: The testimony of our conscience is that we conducted ourselves in the world, and more abundantly toward you, in simplicity and godly sincerity, not with fleshly wisdom, but by the grace of God. 13 For we write nothing else to you than what you read or understand. And I trust you will understand even to the end, 14 as you have understood us in part, that we are yours, boasting even as you are ours on the day of the Lord Jesus.

15 In this confidence I planned to come to you before, that you might have a second benefit: 16 to visit you while going to Macedonia, and to come again to you from Macedonia, and then be sent by you on my way to Judea. 17 Therefore, when I was planning this, did I do this lightly? Or the things that I plan, do I plan according to the flesh, so that I would tell you "Yes, yes" and "No, no"?

18 But as God is true, we did not tell you "Yes" and "No." 19 For the Son of God, Jesus Christ,

1:1 Eph 1:1
1:2 Ro 1:7
1:3 Eph 1:3
1:4 Isa 51:12
1:5 Col 1:24
1:6 2Ti 2:10
1:8 1Co 15:32
1:9 Lk 18:9
1:10 Ro 15:31
1:11 2Co 4:15
1:12 2Co 2:17
1:14 1Co 1:8
1:15 Ro 1:11
1:16 1Co 16:5–7
1:17 2Co 10:2–3
1:18 1Co 1:9
1:19 Heb 13:8

....

1:20 Rev 3:14
1:21 1Jn 2:20
1:22 2Co 5:5
1:23 Ro 1:9
1:24 Ro 11:20
2:1 2Co 1:23
2:2 2Co 7:8
2:3 Gal 5:10
2:4 2Co 7:12
2:5 Gal 4:12
2:6 1Co 5:4–5
2:7 Eph 4:32
2:9 2Co 10:6
2:10 1Co 5:4
2:11 1Pe 5:8
2:12 Ac 14:27
2:13 2Co 7:5–6
2:14 SS 1:3

who was preached among you by us, even by Silas, Timothy, and me, was not "Yes" and "No." In Him it was "Yes." 20 For all the promises of God in Him are "Yes," and in Him "Amen," to the glory of God through us. 21 Now He who establishes us with you in Christ and has anointed us is God, 22 who also has sealed us and established the guarantee with the Spirit in our hearts.

I am established, anointed, and sealed in Christ (2Co 1:21–22).

23 Moreover I call God as a witness upon my soul, that it is to spare you that I have not yet gone to Corinth. 24 Not that we have dominion over your faith, but we are fellow workers for your joy, for by faith you stand.

2 But I determined this for myself, that I would not come again to you in sorrow. 2 For if I make you sorrowful, who then will there be to make me rejoice, but the one whom I have made sorrowful? 3 I wrote concerning this matter to you, so that when I came, I would not be grieved by those in whom I ought to rejoice, having confidence in you all, that my joy is your joy. 4 For out of much affliction and anguish of heart I wrote to you with many tears, not that you should be grieved, but that you might know the love which I have more abundantly for you.

Forgiveness for the Offender

5 But if anyone has caused grief, he has not grieved me, but to some extent all of you, not to put it too severely. 6 This punishment which was inflicted by many on such a man is sufficient. 7 So on the contrary, you ought to forgive him and comfort him, lest perhaps he might be swallowed up with excessive sorrow. 8 Therefore I ask you to confirm your love toward him. 9 For to this end I also wrote, so that I might know that you are proving yourselves by whether you are being obedient in all things. 10 Whomever you forgive anything, I also forgive. For if I forgave someone anything, for your sakes I forgave it in Christ, 11 lest Satan should take advantage of us. For we are not ignorant of his devices.

Paul's Anxiety in Troas

12 Furthermore, when I came to Troas to preach Christ's gospel, and a door was opened to me by the Lord, 13 I had no rest in my spirit, because I did not find Titus my brother. So taking my leave of them, I went from there into Macedonia.

14 Now thanks be to God who always causes us to triumph in Christ and through us reveals the fragrance of His knowledge in every place.

15 For we are to God a sweet fragrance of Christ among those who are saved and among those who perish. 16 To the one we are the fragrance of death, which brings death, and to the other the fragrance of life, which brings life. Who is sufficient for these things? 17 For we are not as many are who peddle the word of God. Instead, being sent by God, we sincerely speak in Christ in the sight of God.

Ministers of the New Covenant

3 Do we begin again to commend ourselves? Or do we need, as some others, letters of commendation to you, or letters of commendation from you? 2 You are our letter written in our hearts, known and read by all men. 3 For you are prominently declared to be the letter of Christ, prepared by us, written not with ink but with the Spirit of the living God, not on tablets of stone but on human tablets of the heart.

4 We have such trust through Christ toward God, 5 not that we are sufficient in ourselves to take credit for anything of ourselves, but our sufficiency is from God, 6 who has made us able ministers of the new covenant, not of the letter but of the Spirit. For the letter kills, but the Spirit gives life.

7 If the ministry that brought death, written and engraved on stones, was glorious, so that the children of Israel could not look intently at the face of Moses because of the glory of his countenance, the glory which was to fade away, 8 how will the ministry of the Spirit not be more glorious? 9 For if the ministry of condemnation is glorious, the ministry of righteousness much more exceeds it in glory. 10 Even that which was made glorious had no glory in comparison to the glory that excels. 11 For if that which fades was glorious, that which remains is much more glorious.

12 Seeing then that we have such hope, we speak with great boldness, 13 not as Moses, who put a veil over his face, so that the children of Israel could not look intently at the end of what was fading away. 14 Instead, their minds were blinded. For until this day the same veil remains unlifted in the reading of the old covenant, the veil which was done away with in Christ. 15 But even to this day, when Moses is read, the veil is in their hearts. 16 Nevertheless when anyone turns to the Lord, the veil is removed. 17 Now the Lord is the Spirit. And where the Spirit of the Lord is, there is liberty. 18 But we all, seeing the glory of the Lord with unveiled faces, as in a mirror, are being transformed into the same image from glory to glory by the Spirit of the Lord.

2:15 1Co 1:18
2:16 Lk 2:34
2:17 2Co 4:2
3:1 Ac 18:27
3:3 Ex 24:12
3:4 Eph 3:12
3:5 1Co 15:10
3:6 Lk 22:20
3:9 Heb 12:18–21
3:12 2Co 7:4
3:16 Ex 34:34
3:17 Gal 4:6
3:18 Ro 8:29

4:1 1Co 7:25
4:2 2Co 2:17
4:3 1Co 1:18
4:4 2Co 4:6
4:5 1Co 1:23
4:6 Ge 1:3
4:7 2Co 5:1
4:8 2Co 7:5
4:9 Heb 13:5
4:11 Ro 8:36
4:12 2Co 13:9
4:13 Ps 116:10
4:14 1Th 4:14
4:15 2Co 1:11
4:16 Ro 7:22
4:17 Ro 8:18
4:18 Heb 11:1

Treasure in Earthen Vessels

4 Therefore, since we have this ministry through the mercy we have received, we do not lose heart. 2 But we have renounced the secret things of shame, not walking in craftiness nor handling the word of God deceitfully, but by expressing the truth and commending ourselves to every man's conscience in the sight of God. 3 But if our gospel is hidden, it is hidden to those who are lost. 4 The god of this world has blinded the minds of those who do not believe, lest the light of the glorious gospel of Christ, who is the image of God, should shine on them. 5 For we do not preach ourselves, but Christ Jesus the Lord, and ourselves your servants for Jesus' sake. 6 For God, who commanded the light to shine out of darkness, has shone in our hearts to give the light of the knowledge of the glory of God in the face of Jesus Christ.

7 But we have this treasure in earthen vessels, the excellency of the power being from God and not from ourselves. 8 We are troubled on every side, yet not distressed; we are perplexed, but not in despair; 9 persecuted, but not forsaken; cast down, but not destroyed; 10 and always carrying around in the body the death of the Lord Jesus, that also the life of Jesus might be expressed in our bodies. 11 For we who live are always delivered to death for Jesus' sake, that also the life of Jesus might be manifested in our mortal flesh. 12 So then, death works in us, but life in you.

Thank You, Father God, that I am being transformed daily into Your image from glory to glory by the Spirit of the Lord (2Co 3:18).

13 We have the same spirit of faith. As it is written, "I believed, and therefore I have spoken."[1] So we also believe and therefore speak, 14 knowing that He who raised the Lord Jesus will also raise us through Jesus and will present us with you. 15 All these things are for your sakes, so that the abundant grace through the thanksgiving of many might overflow to the glory of God.

Living by Faith

16 For this reason we do not lose heart: Even though our outward man is perishing, yet our inward man is being renewed day by day. 17 Our light affliction, which lasts but for a moment, works for us a far more exceeding and eternal weight of glory, 18 while we do not look at the things which are seen, but at the things

[1] *13* Ps 116:10, LXX (Septuagint).

SPIRITLED WOMAN

COUNSEL FROM THE SPIRIT BASICS

God Is on Your Side

God wants you to know that He is on your side and will never let you go. He wants your spiritual eyes to be open so you can see things from His point of view, not just in the natural. He is there even when you cannot see Him. These things must be seen in the spirit—in other words, by faith.

Second Corinthians 4:18 says, "While we do not look at things which are seen, but at the things which are not seen. For the things which are seen are temporal, but the things which are not seen are eternal."

Your physical eyes and ears don't always see and hear what God is doing—those things have to be discerned by your spirit. But it is possible to hear His voice and follow Him. John 10:27 says, "My sheep hear My voice, and I know them, and they follow Me." God wants to reveal to you that He's with you. He wants you to know He won't let you go!

Karen Jensen Salisbury

which are not seen. For the things which are seen are temporal, but the things which are not seen are eternal.

5 We know that if our earthly house, this tent, were to be destroyed, we have an eternal building of God in the heavens, a house not made with hands. 2 In this one we groan, earnestly desiring to be sheltered with our house which is from heaven. 3 Thus being sheltered, we shall not be found unsheltered. 4 For we who are in this tent groan, being burdened, not because we wish to be unclothed, but to be further clothed, so that what is mortal might be swallowed up by life. 5 Now He who has created us for this very thing is God, who also has given to us the guarantee of the Spirit.

6 Therefore we are always confident, knowing that while we are at home in the body, we are absent from the Lord. 7 For we walk by faith, not by sight. 8 Instead, I say that we are confident and willing to be absent from the body and to be present with the Lord. 9 So whether present or absent, we labor that we may be accepted by Him. 10 For we must all appear before the judgment seat of Christ, that each one may receive his recompense in the body, according to what he has done, whether it was good or bad.

The Ministry of Reconciliation

11 Therefore, knowing the fear of the Lord, we persuade men. But we are revealed to God, and I trust we are also revealed in your consciences. 12 For we are not commending ourselves again to you. Instead, we give you occasion to boast on our behalf, that you may have something to answer those who boast in appearance and not in heart. 13 If we are beside ourselves, it is for God; if we are in our right mind, it is for you. 14 For the love of Christ constrains us, because we thus judge: that if one died for all, then all have died. 15 And He died for all, that those who live should not from now on live for themselves, but for Him who died for them and rose again.

16 So from now on we do not regard anyone according to the flesh. Yes, though we have known Christ according to the flesh, yet we do not regard Him as such from now on. 17 Therefore, if any man is in Christ, he is a new creature. Old things have passed away. Look, all things have become new. 18 All this is from God, who has reconciled us to Himself through Jesus Christ and has given to us the ministry of reconciliation, 19 that is, that God was in Christ reconciling the world to Himself, not counting their sins against them, and has entrusted to us the message of reconciliation. 20 So we are ambassadors for Christ, as though God were pleading through us. We implore you in Christ's stead: Be reconciled to God. 21 God made Him who knew no sin to be sin for us, that we might become the righteousness of God in Him.

I am a new creation (2Co 5:17).

6 As workers together with God, we ask you not to receive the grace of God in vain. 2 For He says:

"In an acceptable time I have listened to you,
and in the day of salvation I have helped you."[1]

Look, now is the accepted time; look, now is the day of salvation.

3 We give no offense in anything, that our service may not be blamed. 4 But in all things we commend ourselves as servants of God: in much patience, in afflictions, in necessities,

5:1 2Co 4:7
5:2 Ro 8:23
5:4 1Co 15:53–54
5:5 Ro 8:23
5:6 Heb 11:13
5:7 1Co 13:12
....
5:10 Mt 16:27
5:11 Heb 10:31
5:12 2Co 1:14
5:13 2Co 11:1
5:14 Ro 5:15
5:15 Ro 14:7–9
5:16 Php 3:7–8
5:17 Jn 3:3
5:20 2Co 6:1
5:21 Ro 1:17
6:1 1Co 3:9
6:2 Isa 49:8
6:3 1Co 9:12

[1]2 Isa 49:8.

Walk by Faith

For we walk by faith, not by sight.

—2 Corinthians 5:7

As I looked in the mirror the other day, I stuck my neck out and pulled up my sagging chin. With the fingers on each hand I raised up the wrinkles on my forehead. I lifted the skin at my temples to smooth out the crinkles around my eyes. Then I declared to myself, "Face it, girlfriend; you could use a facelift. Before you start to go downhill, you need some upkeep!"

You may or may not be to the place where you need a facelift. But no matter how smooth or wrinkled we may be on the outside, our hearts can always use a *faithlift*, a little reconstructive surgery for the soul. There's always room for an encouraging word to elevate our emotions, pull us out of our problems, and help us to soar above our circumstances to a new level of believing. That is what faith will do. It turns things around and heads us in the right direction.

We have a lot in common, you and I. We cook. We clean. We love husbands and raise children. We celebrate our friendships. But we also face health challenges. We worry about our children. We get frustrated with marriage. I know you experience these things because I've met you out there on the road. During a concert in Dallas I saw you wipe away a tear. I hugged your neck and kissed your baby in Brooklyn. I heard your story after my concert in Boise. I received your letter in the mail. That's why I know you hurt as I do sometimes.

Life is filled with circumstances that bog us down, down to the doldrums—so far down that we forget that we do not have to go there. We do not have to live beneath our privilege as believers when Christ has lifted us up to heavenly places.

Walking by faith is hard work. Like building a house with a hammer and nails, it will mean being bumped and bruised. It will require sweat equity. You will shed tears of disappointment. You will even have to tear down some things and start over again. It will demand that you throw off anything that threatens you and your relationship with Christ. But with the help of the Holy Spirit you will be able to run the Christian race with patience. Keeping your eyes on Jesus, the One in whom we place our faith, is the most important thing.

We don't live in a perfect world. Far from it. Sometimes things won't go as you think they should. That is when trusting in God's sovereignty is essential. As you walk by faith, you can speak faith to the issues in your life. You will sing praises to God in the face of your enemies, and you will walk on top of the deep waters of doubt.

A great author and theologian of the church by the name of Charles H. Spurgeon once wrote some words that inspired me to write a song called "Trust His Heart." I think his words say it best: "God is too wise to be mistaken. God is too good to be unkind. And when you can't trace His hand, trust His heart."

Babbie Mason

in distress, 5 in stripes, in imprisonments, in
tumults, in labors, in sleeplessness, and in hun-
ger; 6 by purity, by knowledge, by patience, by
kindness, by the Holy Spirit, by genuine love,
7 by the word of truth, by the power of God, by
the armor of righteousness on the right hand
and on the left, 8 by honor and dishonor, by
evil report and good report; as deceivers, and
yet true; 9 as unknown, and yet well known;
as dying, and look, we live; as punished, but
not killed; 10 as sorrowful, yet always rejoicing;
as poor, yet making many rich; and as having
nothing, and yet possessing all things.
11 O Corinthians, we have spoken frankly to
you; our heart is opened wide. 12 You are not
restrained by us, but you are restrained in your
own affections. 13 In return (I speak as to my
children) you also be open.

The Temple of the Living God

14 Do not be unequally yoked together with
unbelievers. For what fellowship has righteous-
ness with unrighteousness? What communion
has light with darkness? 15 What agreement has
Christ with Belial? Or what part has he who
believes with an unbeliever? 16 What agreement
has the temple of God with idols? For you are
the temple of the living God. As God has said:

"I will live in them
 and walk in them.
I will be their God,
 and they shall be My people."[1]

17 Therefore,

"Come out from among them
 and be separate,
 says the Lord.
Do not touch what is unclean,
 and I will receive you."[2]

18 "I will be a Father to you,
 and you shall be My sons and daughters,
 says the Lord Almighty."[3]

7 Since we have these promises, beloved,
let us cleanse ourselves from all filthiness
of the flesh and spirit, perfecting holiness in
the fear of God.

Paul's Joy at the Church's Repentance

2 Accept us. We have wronged no one, we
have corrupted no one, and we have defraud-
ed no one. 3 I do not say this to condemn you,
for I have said before that you are in our hearts,
so that we would die or live with you. 4 Great is
my boldness of speech toward you; great is my
boasting of you. I am filled with comfort, and
I am exceedingly joyful in all our tribulation.

[1] 16 Lev 26:12; Jer 32:38; Eze 37:27. [2] 17 Isa 52:11; Eze 20:34, 41.
[3] 18 2Sa 7:14.

6:5 2Co 11:23–25
6:6 Ro 12:9
6:7 2Co 4:2
6:8 Mt 27:63
6:9 Ro 8:36
6:10 Jn 16:22
6:14 1Co 5:9
6:16 Lev 26:12
6:17 Isa 52:11
7:2 Ac 20:33
7:3 2Co 6:11–12
7:4 2Co 1:4
....
7:5 Dt 32:25
7:6 2Co 1:3–4
7:9 Ac 20:21
7:10 Ac 11:18
7:11 2Co 7:7
7:12 2Co 2:9
7:13 2Co 7:6
7:14 2Co 7:4
7:15 Php 2:12
7:16 2Co 2:3
8:1 Ac 16:9
8:3 1Co 16:2
8:4 Ac 24:17
8:6 2Co 12:18

5 For when we came to Macedonia, our
bodies had no rest, and we were troubled on
every side. On the outside were conflicts; on
the inside were fears. 6 Nevertheless God, who
comforts the downcast, comforted us through
the coming of Titus, 7 and not only by his com-
ing, but also by the comfort with which he was
comforted in you, when he told us about your
sincere desire, your mourning, and your zeal
toward me, so that I rejoiced even more.
8 Though I caused you sorrow by my letter,
I do not regret it, though I did regret it. For I
perceive that this same letter has caused you
sorrow, though only for a while. 9 Now I re-
joice, not that you were made sorrowful, but
that your sorrow led to repentance. For you
were made sorrowful in a godly way, that you
might not suffer loss in any way through us.
10 Godly sorrow produces repentance that leads
to salvation and brings no regret, but the sor-
row of the world produces death. 11 For observe
this very thing, which you sorrowed in a godly
way: What carefulness it produced in you, what
vindication of yourselves, what indignation,
what fear, what intense desire, what zeal, what
avenging of wrong! In all things you have prov-
en yourselves to be innocent in this matter. 12 So
though I wrote to you, I did it not because of
him who had done the wrong, nor because of
him who suffered wrong, but that our care for
you in the sight of God might be evident to you.
13 Therefore we were comforted in your comfort.
Yes, and we were exceedingly the more joy-
ful for the sake of Titus, because his spirit was
refreshed by you all. 14 So I am not ashamed if
I have boasted of anything to him regarding
you. But as we spoke all things to you in truth,
even our boasting in the presence of Titus is
found to be true. 15 Now his affection abounds
all the more toward you, as he remembers the
obedience of you all, how with fear and trem-
bling you received him. 16 Therefore I rejoice
that I have confidence in you in everything.

Liberal Giving

8 Moreover, brothers, we want you to ex-
perience the grace of God bestowed on
the churches of Macedonia, 2 how in a great
trial of affliction, the abundance of their joy
and their deep poverty overflowed toward the
riches of their generous giving. 3 For I bear
record that according to their means, and be-
yond their means, they freely gave, 4 begging
us with much urgency that we would receive
the gift and the fellowship of ministering to the
saints. 5 This they did, not as we expected. First,
they gave themselves to the Lord, and then
to us by the will of God. 6 So we urged Titus,
that as he had begun, so he would also com-

plete this gracious deed for you. 7 But as you abound in everything—in faith, in utterance, in knowledge, in all diligence, and in your love to us—see that you abound in this grace also.

8 I say this not as a command, but to prove through the authenticity of others, the sincerity also of your love. 9 For you know the grace of our Lord Jesus Christ, that though He was rich, yet for your sakes He became poor, that through His poverty you might be rich.

10 And in this matter I give my advice. It is appropriate for you, who began last year not only to give, but also to willingly give. 11 Now therefore complete the task, so that, as there was a willingness to do so, there may be a performance of it according to your means. 12 For if there is a willing mind first, the gift is accepted according to what a man possesses and not according to what he does not possess.

13 I do not mean that other men have relief, and you be burdened, 14 but for equality, that your abundance now at this time may supply their need, and their abundance may supply your need—that there may be equality. 15 As it is written, "He who gathered much had no excess. And he who gathered little had no lack."[1]

16 But thanks be to God, who placed the same sincere care in the heart of Titus for you. 17 For indeed he accepted the exhortation. But being more zealous, he went to you of his own accord. 18 And we have sent with him the brother whose praise is in the gospel throughout all the churches. 19 And not only that, but he was also chosen by the churches to travel with us with this gift, which we administer to the glory of the same Lord, and to declare your willing mind, 20 to prevent any man from blaming us in administering this abundant gift, 21 providing for honest things, not only in the sight of the Lord but also in the sight of men.

22 Furthermore, we have sent with them our brother whom we have frequently proved diligent in many things, but now is much more diligent, due to the great confidence which he has in you. 23 If anyone inquires about Titus, he is my partner and fellow helper concerning you. Or if our brothers are inquired about, they are the messengers of the churches, and the glory of Christ. 24 Therefore show to them, and before the churches, the proof of your love and of our boasting on your behalf.

The Offering for the Saints

9 It is redundant for me to write to you concerning the ministry to the saints. 2 I know your willingness, for which I boast of you to those in Macedonia, that Achaia was ready a year ago, and your zeal has stirred up most of them. 3 Yet I have sent the brothers, lest our boasting of you might be in vain in this case, that, as I said, you may be ready; 4 and lest if any Macedonians come with me and find you unprepared, we (not to mention you) should be ashamed of this confident boasting. 5 Therefore I thought it necessary to exhort the brothers to go ahead to you and arrange beforehand your bountiful gift you previously promised, that it might be prepared as a gift, not as a matter of greed.

6 But this I say: He who sows sparingly will also reap sparingly, and he who sows bountifully will also reap bountifully. 7 Let every man give according to the purposes in his heart, not grudgingly or out of necessity, for God loves a cheerful giver. 8 God is able to make all grace abound toward you, so that you, always having enough of everything, may abound to every good work. 9 As it is written:

> "He has dispersed abroad, He has given to
> the poor;
> His righteousness remains forever."[2]

10 Now He who supplies seed to the sower and supplies bread for your food will also multiply your seed sown and increase the fruits of your righteousness. 11 So you will be enriched in everything to all bountifulness, which makes us give thanks to God.

12 For the administration of this service not only supplies the need of the saints, but is abundant also through many thanksgivings to God. 13 Meanwhile, through the performance of this ministry, they glorify God for the profession of your faith in the gospel of Christ and for your liberal sharing with them and with all others. 14 And in their prayer for you, they long for you because of the surpassing grace of God in you. 15 Thanks be to God for His indescribable gift.

Heavenly Father, I realize that without You I am open to all of Satan's attacks (2Co 10:5).

Paul Defends His Ministry

10 Now I, Paul, who am lowly in presence among you but bold toward you while absent, appeal to you by the meekness and gentleness of Christ. 2 I beg you that when I am present, I might not have to be bold with that confidence by which I intend to be bold against some, who think of us as if we walked according to the flesh. 3 For though we walk in the flesh, we do not war according to the flesh. 4 For the weapons of our warfare are not carnal, but mighty through God to the pulling down of strongholds, 5 casting down

8:7 2Co 9:8
8:8 1Co 7:6
8:9 Mt 20:28
8:10 1Co 7:25
8:12 2Co 9:7
8:14 2Co 9:12
8:15 Ex 16:18
8:16 Rev 17:17
8:17 2Co 8:6
8:18 2Co 12:18
8:19 1Co 16:3–4
8:21 Ro 12:17
8:23 Php 2:25
8:24 2Co 7:14
9:2 2Co 8:10
9:3 2Co 8:6
9:5 Ge 33:11
9:6 Pr 22:9
9:7 Ex 25:2
9:9 Ps 112:9
9:10 Isa 55:10
9:11 2Co 1:11
9:13 Mt 5:16
9:15 2Co 2:14
10:1 Mt 11:29
10:2 2Co 13:2
10:4 Jer 1:10
10:5 Isa 2:11–12

[1] 15 Ex 16:18. [2] 9 Ps 112:9.

WOMEN OF THE BIBLE

FAITHFULNESS WILL MAKE A SIGNIFICANT IMPACT FOR GOD

There are many examples of women in the New Testament who, although not always in the foreground, gave faithful service to the early church that made a significant impact in the spreading of the gospel. Each of their lives demonstrates how the Holy Spirit stirred up gifts in them to reach the lost and equip the early believers.

Paul recognized the important role that Timothy's grandmother Lois and his mother, Eunice, played in the life of this young godly man. Paul told Timothy, "I thank God, whom I serve with a pure conscience as my forefathers did, as I continually remember you in my prayers night and day, greatly desiring to see you, remembering your tears, that I may be filled with joy, remembering the genuine faith that first lived in your grandmother Lois and your mother Eunice and that I am persuaded lives in you also" (2Ti 1:3–5). Many powerful men and women of God today would be quick to recognize that it was the consistent, loving godliness of their mothers that influenced their lives the most toward faithfulness toward God.

Lydia and Priscilla greatly assisted Paul in his missionary work. Lydia, a "seller of purple fabric" who lived in Thyatira (Ac 16:14), opened her heart to the gospel as she heard it for the first time from the lips of Paul. A person of considerable wealth, she could afford to give a home to Paul and his companions.

Priscilla, the wife of Aquila (Ac 18:2), took part with her husband in instructing and training Apollos to serve alongside Paul.

Dorcas was a woman from Joppa who was "full of good works and almsgiving" (Ac 9:36). However, she became sick and died. Peter was called to her home, where he knelt down and prayed, then said to her, "Tabitha [or Dorcas], arise" (v. 40). He gave her his hand and lifted her up, and life came back into her body. We can only imagine that God must have seen her good works and charitable deeds and counted her worthy of resurrected life so she could continue serving Him.

But the two greatest records of great faith among the women of the New Testament were certainly the lives of Elizabeth, the mother of John the Baptist, and Mary, the mother of Jesus. Elizabeth, the wife of the priest Zechariah, had been barren and childless for all of her life. But Luke tells us that she was "righteous before God, walking in all the commandments and ordinances of the Lord blamelessly" (Lk 1:6). Through a wonderful, supernatural miracle God chose her and Zechariah to be the parents of John the Baptist. The angel Gabriel revealed the miracle of Elizabeth's conception to Mary when he announced to her that she would conceive and bear the baby who would be the Messiah of the world.

When Mary received the news from Gabriel that she was to supernaturally conceive a child who would be the Messiah, she did not for a moment consider all the obstacles and negative factors that such a birth would bring to her life among her people. Instead she immediately burst into exuberant praise and worship to God, exclaiming:

> My soul magnifies the Lord,
> and my spirit rejoices in God my Savior.
> For He has regarded
> the low estate of His servant;
> surely, from now on all generations will call me blessed.
> For He who is mighty has done great things for me,
> and holy is His name.
> His mercy is on those who fear Him
> from generation to generation.
>
> —Luke 1:46–50

Each of these women and so many more were used mightily by God to accomplish His purposes. There is nothing God cannot do through the life of a godly, committed woman. Just as women in the Bible accomplished mighty things through God, so can SpiritLed women today.

Women are "God's secret intelligence weapons." In every way and in every place you look, God will be using mighty women of God committed to His purpose. The devil hates a woman because it is in her to confront issues that need to be dealt with to win the lost for Jesus. She is like the woman with the issue of blood or the woman who would not leave the judge alone until he made a decision in her favor. What she has come out of strengthens her for what she is about to embark upon. God knows the female species will fight for her family just as a lioness guards her territory to ward off danger to her young.

Are you a woman who wants to be used of God? Within you is a spiritual radar to detect darkness. Make a decision today to become one of God's secret intelligence weapons to win the lost in your family, community, and world for God. Be faithful to what He has called you to do, and become a world changer through His power!

Kimberly Daniels

SPIRITLED WOMAN

COUNSEL FROM THE SPIRIT BASICS

Our Powerful Key

Faith is our powerful key for overcoming the powers of Satan. Demonic forces will try to convince you that what you see in the natural with your physical sight is the ultimate truth. This is totally incorrect.

In the spiritual realm faith has the power to change those things that are seen in the natural to things that are congruent with the Word of God: "For we walk by faith, not by sight" (2Co 5:7).

One reason is that genuine faith in the heart of a believer has the power to change outward circumstances to a desired outcome:

> For though we walk in the flesh, we do not war according to the flesh. For the weapons of our warfare are not carnal, but mighty through God to the pulling down of strongholds.
>
> — 2 CORINTHIANS 10:3–4

As Satan wages war against man, one of his tools is the creation of spiritual strongholds. These strongholds cannot be destroyed by the flesh or by the carnal nature of man. They have to be pulled down through fervent intercessory prayers, through praying scriptures, and through other methods of spiritual warfare.

Iris Delgado

imaginations and every high thing that exalts itself against the knowledge of God, bringing every thought into captivity to the obedience of Christ, 6 and being ready to punish all disobedience when your obedience is complete.

7 Do you look at things from the outward appearance? If any man trusts that he is Christ's, let him consider again that, as he is Christ's, even so are we Christ's. 8 For even if I should boast somewhat more of our authority, which the Lord has given us for edification and not for your destruction, I shall not be ashamed, 9 lest I appear to frighten you by my letters. 10 "For his letters," they say, "are weighty and powerful, but his bodily presence is weak, and his speech contemptible." 11 Let such a person consider this: that as we are in word by letters when we are absent, we will also be in deed when we are present.

12 For we dare not count or compare ourselves with those who commend themselves. They who measure themselves by one another and compare themselves with one another are not wise. 13 But we will not boast beyond measure, but within the boundaries which God has appointed us, which reach even you. 14 For we are not overextending ourselves as though we did not reach you, since we have come to you, preaching the gospel of Christ. 15 We are not boasting of things beyond our measure in other men's labors. But we have hope that when your faith is increased, our region shall be greatly enlarged by you, 16 to preach the gospel in the regions beyond you and not to boast in another man's accomplishments. 17 But, "Let him who boasts, boast in the Lord."[1] 18 For it is not he who commends himself who is approved, but he whom the Lord commends.

10:6 2Co 2:9
10:7 2Co 5:12
10:8 2Co 13:10
10:10 1Co 1:17
10:12 2Co 3:1
10:13 Ro 15:20
10:14 1Co 4:15
10:15 Ro 15:20
10:17 1Co 1:31
10:18 Ro 2:29
11:1 2Co 5:13
11:3 Rev 12:9
11:6 1Co 1:17
11:7 2Co 12:13
11:9 1Th 2:6
11:10 Ro 9:1
11:11 2Co 12:15
11:12 1Co 9:12
11:13 Rev 2:2

Paul and the False Apostles

11 I would to God you could bear with me a little in my folly. Indeed, bear with me. 2 For I am jealous over you with godly jealousy. For I have espoused you to one husband, that I may present you as a chaste virgin to Christ. 3 But I fear that somehow, as the serpent deceived Eve through his trickery, so your minds might be led astray from the simplicity that is in Christ. 4 For if he who comes preaches another Jesus, whom we have not preached, or if you receive another spirit, which you have not received, or another gospel, which you have not accepted, you might submit to it readily enough.

5 For I think I am not in any way inferior to the most eminent of the apostles. 6 Even though I am unpolished in speech, yet I am not in knowledge. All things about us have been thoroughly revealed to you. 7 Did I commit a sin in abasing myself that you might be exalted, because I preached to you the gospel of God free of charge? 8 I robbed other churches by accepting wages from them to serve you. 9 Furthermore, when I was present with you and was lacking, I was a burden to no one. For the brothers who came from Macedonia supplied what I lacked. In all things I have kept myself from being burdensome to you, and so will I keep myself. 10 As the truth of Christ is in me, no one shall stop me from this boasting in the regions of Achaia. 11 Why? Because I do not love you? God knows.

12 And I will continue doing what I am doing, that I may cut off the opportunity from those who desire an opportunity to be found equal to us in what they boast about. 13 For such are

[1] *17* Jer 9:24.

false apostles and deceitful workers, disguising themselves as apostles of Christ. 14 And no wonder! For even Satan disguises himself as an angel of light. 15 Therefore it is no great thing if his ministers also disguise themselves as ministers of righteousness, whose end will be according to their works.

Paul's Sufferings as an Apostle

16 I say again, let no one think that I am a fool. Otherwise, at least receive me as a fool, so that I also may boast a little. 17 What I speak, I speak not according to the Lord, but as it were foolishly, in this confidence of boasting. 18 Seeing that many boast according to the flesh, I also will boast. 19 For you tolerate fools gladly, seeing you yourselves are wise. 20 For you permit it if a man brings you into bondage, if a man devours you, if a man takes from you, if a man exalts himself, or if a man strikes you on the face. 21 I say to my reproach that we were too weak for that.

But whenever anyone is bold (I speak foolishly), I am bold also. 22 Are they Hebrews? So am I. Are they Israelites? So am I. Are they the seed of Abraham? So am I. 23 Are they servants of Christ? I speak as a fool. I am more: in labors more abundant, in stripes above measure, in prisons more frequently, in deaths often. 24 Five times I received from the Jews forty lashes minus one. 25 Three times I was beaten with rods; once I was stoned; three times I suffered shipwreck; a night and a day I have been in the deep; 26 in journeys often, in perils of waters, in perils of robbers, in perils by my own countrymen, in perils by the Gentiles, in perils in the city, in perils in the wilderness, in perils in the sea, in perils among false brothers; 27 in weariness and painfulness, in sleeplessness often, in hunger and thirst, in fastings often, and in cold and nakedness. 28 Beside the external things, the care of all the churches pressures me daily. 29 Who is weak, and I am not weak? Who is led into sin, and I am not distressed?

30 If I must boast, I will boast of the things which concern my weakness. 31 The God and Father of our Lord Jesus Christ, who is blessed forevermore, knows that I am not lying. 32 In Damascus the governor under King Aretas secured the city of the Damascenes with a garrison, desiring to arrest me. 33 But I was let down by the wall through a window in a basket and escaped his hands.

Visions and Revelations

12 Doubtless it is not profitable for me to boast. So I will move on to visions and revelations of the Lord. 2 I knew a man in Christ over fourteen years ago—whether in the body or out of the body I cannot tell, God knows—such a one was caught up to the third heaven. 3 And I knew that such a man—whether in the body or out of the body I cannot tell, God knows— 4 was caught up into paradise and heard inexpressible words not permitted for a man to say. 5 Of such a person, I will boast. Yet of myself I will not boast, except in my weaknesses. 6 For if I desire to boast, I will not be a fool, for I will be speaking the truth. But now I resist, lest anyone should think of me above that which he sees me to be or hears from me. 7 And lest I should be exalted above measure by the abundance of revelations, a thorn was given me in the flesh, a messenger of Satan, to torment me, lest I be exalted above measure. 8 I asked the Lord three times that this thing might depart from me. 9 But He said to me, "My grace is sufficient for you, for My strength is made perfect in weakness." Therefore most gladly I will boast in my weaknesses, that the power of Christ may rest upon me. 10 So I take pleasure in weaknesses, in reproaches, in hardships, in persecutions, and in distresses for Christ's sake. For when I am weak, then I am strong.

> The God who is inside me is greater than the whole world put together (2Co 12:10).

Paul's Concern for the Corinthian Church

11 I have become a fool in boasting. You have compelled me, for I ought to have been commended by you, for I am in no way inferior to the leading apostles, though I am nothing. 12 Truly the signs of an apostle were performed among you in all patience, in signs and wonders, and mighty deeds. 13 For in what respect were you inferior to other churches, unless it be that I myself was not burdensome to you? Forgive me this wrong!

14 I am ready to come to you this third time. And I will not be burdensome to you, for I do not seek what is yours, but you. For the children ought not to lay up for the parents, but the parents for the children. 15 And I will very gladly spend and be spent for you. If I love you more, am I to be loved less? 16 But be that as it may. I did not burden you. Nevertheless, being crafty, I caught you with deceit. 17 Did I take advantage of you by any of those whom I sent to you? 18 I urged Titus to go, and with him I sent a brother. Did Titus take advantage of you? Did we not walk in the same spirit? Did we not walk in the same steps?

19 Again, do you think that we are defending ourselves to you? We speak before God in Christ. We do all things, beloved, for your edifying. 20 For I fear that when I come, I shall not find

11:14 Gal 1:8
11:15 Php 3:19
11:16 2Co 11:1
11:17 1Co 7:12
11:19 1Co 4:10
11:20 Gal 2:4
11:21 2Co 10:10
11:22 Php 3:5
11:23 1Co 15:10
11:25 Ac 14:19
11:26 Ac 14:5
11:27 2Co 6:5
11:29 1Co 8:13
11:30 1Co 2:3
11:31 Ro 9:5
11:33 Ac 9:25
12:1 Gal 1:12
12:2 2Co 11:11
....
12:4 Lk 23:43
12:6 2Co 11:16
12:7 Nu 33:55
12:9 Php 4:13
12:10 Ro 5:3
12:11 2Co 11:5
12:13 1Co 9:12
12:14 Pr 19:14
12:15 Php 2:17
12:18 2Co 8:6
12:19 Ro 9:1
12:20 Ro 1:29

you such as I wish, and that I shall be found
by you such as you do not wish. I fear there
are debates, envying, wrath, strife, backbiting,
whispering, arrogance, and disorder. 21 And I
fear that when I come again, my God will hum-
ble me among you, and that I shall mourn for
many who have sinned already, who have not
repented of uncleanness, sexual immorality,
and lasciviousness which they have committed.

Final Warnings and Greetings

13 This is the third time I am coming to
you. "In the mouth of two or three wit-
nesses shall every word be established."[1] 2 I
told you before, and foretell as if I were pres-
ent the second time. And being absent now, I
write to those who have sinned before, and to
all the others, that if I come again, I will not
spare *anyone*, 3 since you seek proof of Christ
speaking through me, who toward you is not
weak, but is mighty in you. 4 For though He
was crucified through weakness, yet He lives
by the power of God. So also we are weak in
Him, but we shall live with Him by the power
of God serving you.

5 Examine yourselves, seeing whether you
are in the faith; test yourselves. Do you not
know that Jesus Christ is in you?—unless in-
deed you are disqualified. 6 I trust that you will
know that we are not disqualified. 7 Now I pray
to God that you do no evil, not that we should
appear approved, but that you should do that
which is honorable, whether or not we may
seem disqualified. 8 For we can do nothing
against the truth, but only for the truth. 9 For
we are glad when we are weak, and you are
strong. We wish even your perfection. 10 There-
fore I write these things being absent, lest be-
ing present I should be sharp, according to
the authority which the Lord has given me for
edification and not for destruction.

11 Finally, brothers, farewell. Be perfect, be
of good comfort, be of one mind, and live in
peace, and the God of love and peace will be
with you.

12 Greet one another with a holy kiss. 13 All the
saints greet you.

14 The grace of the Lord Jesus Christ, and the
love of God, and the communion of the Holy
Spirit be with you all. Amen.

12:21 2Co 13:2
13:1 Dt 19:15
13:2 2Co 1:23
13:3 Mt 10:20
13:4 1Pe 3:18

13:5 1Co 11:28
13:9 2Co 13:11
13:10 2Co 10:8
13:11 Ro 15:33
13:12 Ro 16:16
13:14 Ro 16:20

[1] Dt 19:15.

Author: The apostle Paul

Written: AD 48, possibly from Rome

Theme: Freedom From the Law, the New Covenant

GALATIANS

Dear Spirit Led Woman,

If your motivation is how you measure up to others or what they think, you have fallen into the trap of legalism. Here is a simple challenge for you: do *everything* that the Spirit prompts you to do. Sounds simple, but if you think about it, doing everything the Spirit prompts you to do leaves little time to desire or crave anything from your old nature or judge others for how they are living their lives. You will be focused on hearing from God and only doing what He tells you to do.

I don't mean to imply that the battle between your old nature and your new life in the Spirit will ever cease; it won't. But you have power in the Holy Spirit to make godly choices. When you do, the Holy Spirit produces His fruit in your life. The fruit of the Spirit that Paul articulates in Galatians 5:22–23 is Christ's character being formed in us as we daily live our lives by the Spirit. As you become more like Jesus, you are set free from your past life, from your old sinful nature. This is why you can "stand fast therefore and do not be entangled again with the yoke of bondage" (Gal 5:1).

Joy F. Strang

Salutation

1 Paul, an apostle (not from men nor through
man, but through Jesus Christ and God the
Father, who raised Him from the dead), 2 and
all the brothers who are with me,

To the churches of Galatia:

3 Grace to you and peace from God our Father
and the Lord Jesus Christ, 4 who gave Himself
for our sins, that He might deliver us from this
present evil age, according to the will of our
God and Father, 5 to whom be glory forever
and ever. Amen.

There Is No Other Gospel

6 I marvel that you are turning away so soon
from Him who called you in the grace of Christ
to a different gospel, 7 which is not a gospel.
But there are some who trouble you and would
pervert the gospel of Christ. 8 Although if we or
an angel from heaven preach any other gospel
to you than the one we have preached to you,
let him be accursed. 9 As we said before, so I
say now again: If anyone preaches any other
gospel to you than the one you have received,
let him be accursed.

10 For am I now seeking the approval of men
or of God? Or am I trying to please men? For
if I were still trying to please men, I would not
be the servant of Christ.

How Paul Became an Apostle

11 But I reveal to you, brothers, that the gospel
which was preached by me is not according
to man. 12 For I neither received it from man,
neither was I taught it, except by a revelation
of Jesus Christ.

13 For you have heard of my former life in
Judaism, how I persecuted the church of
God beyond measure and tried to destroy it,
14 and progressed in Judaism above many of
my equals in my own heritage, being more
exceedingly zealous for the traditions of my
fathers. 15 But when it pleased God, who set
me apart since I was in my mother's womb and
called me by His grace, 16 to reveal His Son in
me, that I might preach Him among the na-
tions, I did not immediately confer with flesh
and blood, 17 nor did I go up to Jerusalem to
those who were apostles before me. But I went
into Arabia, and returned again to Damascus.

18 After three years I went up to Jerusalem
to see Peter and stayed with him for fifteen
days. 19 I saw none of the other apostles except
James, the Lord's brother. 20 In what I am writ-
ing to you, before God, I do not lie!

21 Then I went into the regions of Syria and Cili-
cia 22 and was unknown by face to the churches
of Judea which were in Christ. 23 They had heard
only, "He who persecuted us in times past now
preaches the faith which he once destroyed."
24 And they glorified God because of me.

Paul Accepted by the Other Apostles

2 Then after fourteen years I went up again
to Jerusalem with Barnabas and also took
Titus with me. 2 I went up in response to a rev-
elation and communicated to them the gospel
which I preach among the Gentiles. But pri-
vately I communicated to those who were of
reputation, in case I might be running, or had
run, in vain. 3 But even Titus, who was with
me, though he was a Greek, was not compelled
to be circumcised. 4 This happened because
false brothers were secretly brought in, who
sneaked in to spy out our liberty, which we
have in Christ Jesus, that they might bring us
into bondage. 5 We did not yield to subjection
to them, not for an hour, that the truth of the
gospel might continue with you.

I have liberty in Christ (Gal 2:4).

6 But of these who seemed to be something—
whatever they were, it makes no difference to
me; God shows no partiality to anyone—for
those who seemed to be something added
nothing to me. 7 On the contrary, they saw
that I was entrusted with the gospel to the un-
circumcised, as the gospel to the circumcised
was to Peter. 8 For He who worked effectively
in Peter for the apostleship to the circumcised
worked effectively in me toward the Gentiles.
9 When James, Cephas, and John, who seemed
to be pillars, understood the grace that was
given to me, they gave to Barnabas and me
the right hand of fellowship, that we should
go to the Gentiles and they to the circumcised.
10 Only they requested that we should remem-
ber the poor, which I also was eager to do.

Paul Rebukes Peter in Antioch

11 But when Peter came to Antioch, I with-
stood him face to face, because he stood
condemned. 12 Before certain men came from
James, he ate with the Gentiles. But when they
came, he withdrew and separated himself,
fearing those who were of the circumcision.
13 And the other Jews, likewise, joined together
in hypocrisy with him, so that even Barnabas
was carried away by their hypocrisy.

14 But when I saw that they were not straight-
forward about the truth of the gospel, I said to
Peter before them all, "If you, being a Jew, live
like a Gentile and not like a Jew, why do you
compel the Gentiles to live like Jews?"[1]

1:2 1Co 16:1
1:3 1Co 1:3
1:4 Php 4:20
1:5 Ro 11:36
1:6 2Co 11:4
1:7 Ac 15:24
1:8 Ro 9:3
1:10 1Th 2:4
1:13 Ac 8:3
1:15 Isa 49:1
1:16 Mt 16:17
1:19 Mt 13:55
1:20 Ro 9:1
1:21 Ac 6:9
1:22 1Th 2:14

2:2 Gal 2:9
2:3 Ac 16:3
2:4 2Co 11:26
2:5 Gal 2:14
2:6 2Co 12:11
2:7 1Th 2:4
2:9 Ro 12:3
2:10 Ac 24:17
2:14 Gal 2:5

[1] *14* Some interpreters hold that the quotation extends into the following paragraph.

Jews, Like Gentiles, Are Saved by Faith

15 We are Jews by nature, and not Gentile sin-
ners, 16 yet we know that a man is not justified by
the works of the law, but through faith in Jesus
Christ. Even we have believed in Christ Jesus,
so that we might be justified by faith in Christ,
rather than by the works of the law. For by the
works of the law no flesh shall be justified.
17 If, while we seek to be justified by Christ,
we ourselves also are found to be sinners, is
Christ therefore the minister of sin? God for-
bid! 18 For if I build again the things which I
destroyed, I make myself a transgressor.
19 For through the law I am dead to the law,
that I might live for God. 20 I have been cruci-
fied with Christ. It is no longer I who live, but
Christ who lives in me. And the life I now live in
the flesh, I live by faith in the Son of God,[1] who
loved me and gave Himself for me. 21 I do not
nullify the gracc of God. For if righteousness
comes by the law, then Christ died in vain.

I will not "nullify the grace of God" by not appropriating the finished work of the cross (Gal 2:21).

Law or Faith

3 O foolish Galatians! Who has bewitched
you that you should not obey the truth?
Before your eyes Jesus Christ was clearly
portrayed among you as crucified. 2 I want
to learn only this from you: Did you receive
the Spirit through the works of the law, or by
hearing with faith? 3 Are you so foolish? Hav-
ing begun in the Spirit, are you now being
perfected by the flesh? 4 Have you endured so
many things for nothing, if indeed it was for
nothing? 5 Does God give you the Spirit and
work miracles among you by the works of the
law, or by hearing with faith? 6 Even Abraham
"believed God, and it was credited to him as
righteousness."[2] 7 Therefore know that those
who are of faith are the sons of Abraham. 8 And
the Scripture, foreseeing that God would justify
the Gentiles by faith, preached the gospel in
advance to Abraham, saying, "In you shall all
the nations be blessed."[3] 9 So then those who
are of faith are blessed with faithful Abraham.

I am a child of promise (Gal 3:14).

10 For all who rely on the works of the law
are under the curse. For it is written, "Cursed
is everyone who does not continue in all things
which are written in the Book of the Law, to

2:15 Eph 2:3
2:16 Ps 143:2
2:17 Gal 2:15
2:19 Ro 7:4
2:20 Ro 8:37
2:21 Gal 3:21
3:4 2Jn 1:8
3:6 Ge 15:6
3:7 Gal 3:9
3:8 Ge 12:3
3:9 Ro 4:16
3:10 Dt 27:26
3:11 Hab 2:4
3:12 Lev 18:5
3:13 Dt 21:23
3:14 Ac 2:33
3:15 Heb 9:17
3:17 Ge 15:13
3:19 Ac 7:53
3:20 1Ti 2:5
3:21 Gal 2:21
3:22 Ro 11:32
3:24 Gal 2:16

I am redeemed from the curse of the law (Gal 3:13).

do them."[4] 11 Now it is evident that no man is
justified by the law in the sight of God, for "The
just shall live by faith."[5] 12 But the law is not of
faith, for "The man who does them shall live
by them."[6] 13 Christ has redeemed us from the
curse of the law by being made a curse for
us—as it is written, "Cursed is everyone who
hangs on a tree"[7]— 14 so that the blessing of
Abraham might come on the Gentiles through
Jesus Christ, that we might receive the promise
of the Spirit through faith.

I am the seed of Abraham, and his blessing is mine (Gal 3:14).

The Law and the Promise

15 Brothers, I am speaking in human terms:
Though it is only a man's covenant, yet if it is
ratified, no one annuls or adds to it. 16 Now
the promises were made to Abraham and his
Seed. He does not say, "and to seeds," mean-
ing many, but "and to your Seed,"[8] meaning
one, who is Christ. 17 And this I say, that the
law, which came four hundred and thirty years
later, does not annul the covenant that was
ratified by God in Christ, so as to nullify the
promise. 18 For if the inheritance comes from
the law, it no longer comes from the promise.
But God gave it to Abraham through a promise.
19 What purpose then does the law serve? It
was added because of transgressions, until the
Seed should come to whom the promise was
made. And it was ordained through angels by
the hand of a mediator. 20 Now a mediator is not
a mediator for only one party, but God is one.

Slaves and Sons

21 Is the law then contrary to the promises
of God? God forbid! For if there had been a
law given which could have given life, righ-
teousness would indeed come through the law.
22 But the Scripture has confined all things un-
der sin, that the promise through faith in Jesus
Christ[9] might be given to those who believe.
23 But before faith came, we were imprisoned
under the law, kept for the faith which was
later to be revealed. 24 So the law was our tutor
to bring us to Christ, that we might be justified
by faith. 25 But now that faith has come, we are
no longer under a tutor.

[1] *20 Or by the faith of the Son of God.* [2] *6* Ge 15:6. [3] *8* Ge 12:3; 18:18; 22:18. [4] *10* Dt 27:26. [5] *11* Hab 2:4. [6] *12* Lev 18:5. [7] *13* Dt 21:23. [8] *16* Ge 12:7; 13:15; 24:7. [9] *22 Or through the faith of Jesus Christ.*

The Adventure of Prayer in the Spirit

In the third and fourth chapters of the Book of Galatians Paul talks about what it means to grow up in Christ, going from a child tutored by the dos and don'ts of the Scriptures toward an adult who lives in grace by faith as God's own cherished son or daughter. We were in guardianship of the Law as we grew up, but as we became adults, we found we could relate to God for ourselves, not tossing the laws of God aside but instead being able to go straight to their source in the presence of our Father.

When a child is young, right and wrong are very black and white. At that stage of life it is really all our minds can comprehend. A thing either is or it isn't; the light is either on or it's off. But as we grow up, our minds become open to nuance, and an understanding of the Law deepens our perspective.

It is not that the Law changes, but we begin to understand the purpose of the Law and the spirit behind it. We can place it in relationship with other laws and derive from them a sense of living by them that goes beyond what they literally tell us to do or what they each mean on their own. Instead of living by a legal code of fulfilling the letter of the Law, we begin to plug into the *spirit* of what God is saying to us through His Word. As Paul put it:

> So the law was our tutor to bring us to Christ, that we might be justified by faith. But now that faith has come, we are no longer under a tutor. You are all sons of God by faith in Christ Jesus.
>
> —Galatians 3:24–26

Sons and daughters differ from orphans in that they know their parents and can relate to them. Faith in what Jesus did—that He atoned for our sin and gave us right standing with God once again so that we could be in His presence and converse with Him through prayer—puts us in connection with our Father. Grace covers the deficit between whatever bad mistakes we have made in the past and our relationship with God.

When we are immature, we look at Scripture as a book of dos and don'ts, and we live by a code of Christianity. It is a religion, in that it is our own understanding of what to do to pursue God and how to act in order to please Him. Religion is thus humanity, in our own wisdom, reaching out toward God the best that we can.

In and of itself, this is not always a bad thing—it is one way sincere people pursue God as best they can—but if we never allow God to breathe into our religion His way of reaching out toward humanity, it is often more of a stumbling block than a help.

Maturing from a simple seeker of God and follower of His directives, we become children in relationship to Him who have the privilege of intimate conversation with God through prayer. We can go to Him and say, "Dad, I have a question," or, "Dad, can You help me with this for a minute?" Being right with Him allows us to converse with Him about the most private or complex of issues.

Can we really afford to lay that privilege aside and not regularly enter His throne room with whatever concern we might have? Should we neglect our access to heaven and the authority and privileges that go with that for the distractions of this world? This is the responsibility of intercession.

Cindy Trimm

SPIRIT-TO-SPIRIT PRAYER

Prayer for Financial Prosperity

Jehovah Jireh, You are my provider. I thank You because You are the Lord, my God, who teaches me how to profit, and You lead me in the way I should go. Thank You for wisdom, for it causes those who love wisdom to inherit wealth. As I keep Your Word, You make me prosperous. Everything that I endeavor to do according to Your will, will prosper. Thank You for mercy and favor. Thank You for a steady income. Thank You for opening the doors of blessing and closing the doors of lack. Teach me how to become fruitful and how to invest wisely. Father, I will honor You with my tithes and offerings. Thank You, Father, for this great promise. In Jesus' name, amen.

Iris Delgado

26 You are all sons of God by faith in Christ
Jesus. 27 For as many of you as have been bap-
tized into Christ have put on Christ. 28 There is
neither Jew nor Greek, there is neither slave
nor free, and there is neither male nor female,
for you are all one in Christ Jesus. 29 If you
are Christ's, then you are Abraham's seed, and
heirs according to the promise.

4 Now I say that as long as the heir is a
child, he does not differ from a servant
though he is lord of all. 2 But he is under tutors
and governors until the time appointed by the
father. 3 So when we were children, we were
in bondage to the elements of the world. 4 But
when the fullness of time came, God sent forth
His Son, born from a woman, born under the
law, 5 to redeem those who were under the law,
that we might receive the adoption as sons.
6 And because you are sons, God has sent forth
into our hearts the Spirit of His Son, crying,
"Abba, Father!" 7 Therefore you are no longer
a servant, but a son, and if a son, then an heir
of God through Christ.

I am an heir of God through Christ (Gal 4:7).

Paul's Concern for the Galatians

8 Previously, when you did not know God,
you served those who by nature are not gods.
9 But now, after you have known God, or rath-
er are known by God, how do you turn again
to the weak and beggarly elemental forces
to which you desire again to be in bondage?
10 You observe days and months and seasons
and years. 11 I am afraid for you, lest I have
worked for you in vain.

12 Brothers, I ask you, become as I am, for I
also have become as you are. You have done
me no wrong. 13 You know that it was because
of an infirmity of the flesh that I first preached
the gospel to you. 14 Though my infirmity was
a trial to you, you neither despised nor reject-
ed me, but received me as an angel of God,
even as Christ Jesus. 15 So where is your bless-
ing? For I bear witness of you that, if it had
been possible, you would have plucked out
your own eyes and given them to me. 16 Have
I therefore become your enemy because I tell
you the truth?

17 They would zealously influence you, but
not favorably. Yes, they would exclusively con-
trol you, so that you might consult them. 18 But
it is good to be zealous in a good manner al-
ways and not only when I am present with you.
19 My little children, of whom I labor in birth
again until Christ is formed in you, 20 I desire
to be present with you now and to change my
tone, for I am displeased with you.

The Allegory of Hagar and Sarah

21 Tell me, you who desire to be under the
law, do you not hear the law? 22 For it is written
that Abraham had two sons, the one by a slave
woman, the other by a free woman. 23 But he
who was of the slave woman was born ac-
cording to the flesh, but he of the free woman
through the promise.

3:26 Gal 4:5–6
3:27 Ro 13:14
3:28 Col 3:11
4:3 Gal 2:4
4:4 Mk 1:15
4:5 Gal 3:26
4:6 Ro 5:5
4:8 1Co 1:21
4:9 1Co 8:3

4:10 Ro 14:5
4:11 1Th 3:5
4:12 2Co 2:5
4:13 1Co 2:3
4:14 Mt 10:40
4:16 Gal 2:5
4:18 Gal 4:13
4:22 Ge 16:15
4:23 Heb 11:11

JESSIE PENN-LEWIS

HEROINE OF THE FAITH

Jessie was born in South Wales, UK, in 1861. The daughter of a mining engineer and Methodist minister, she married William Penn-Lewis at the age of eighteen. Eighteen months later she realized that if Christ were to return, she wasn't ready, and so she began to seek the Lord. Soon she met Jesus and began a deep walk with Him.

When Jessie turned nineteen, she was found to have tuberculosis and was given six months to live. God miraculously healed her, and she had remarkable resilience and strength to accomplish all God called her to through the rest of her life.

At the age of thirty-one Jessie was filled with the Holy Spirit. She had great insight into the Word of God and taught before huge audiences at conventions around the world, including the Keswick Convention, a famous annual conference on the deeper life. She was also involved in the Welsh revival of 1904–1905, a revival that was cut short by the illness of Evan Roberts, the main leader. Evan Roberts stayed with Jessie and her husband for a couple years following this event.

Jessie's ministry took her to other countries, including Russia, India, Canada, and the United States. She had the privilege of speaking at the Moody Bible Institute's Worker's Conference, where R. A. Torrey introduced her as "one of the most gifted speakers the world has ever known." She had the privilege of being friends with some other spiritual giants of her day, including F. B. Meyer, Andrew Murray, Oswald Chambers, and D. L. Moody. She was a prolific author, and her book *War on the Saints*, written in collaboration with Evan Roberts, is a classic on spiritual warfare.

Jessie Penn-Lewis had an influence on her generation, including such people as Frank Buchman (who founded the Oxford Group) and Norman Grubb (who, as president of WEC International, took a small group of thirty-five missionaries to thousands of workers around the world).

But gender was also an issue. She wrote: "I saw that God had given me a specific commission... but the one objection was the fact that I was a woman. There was no quarrel with the message...no denial of the divine seal...no getting away from the evidence of the results. But none of these...did away with the fact that I was a woman, therefore I could not but see that, whilst God opened doors...in some quarters, others were fast closed to the message I bore, purely, and only, because I was a woman."

The cry of Jessie's heart asked why God not committed this vital message to her when she could not deliver it without restriction. Why didn't God commit it to one who could do so? In her early years of ministry she would often gaze out upon the audience, "watching with eager eyes to see whether there was not some hidden and chosen instrument to whom God could transmit this burden, who would rise up...and let me step aside."

Listen to her deep concerns: "For years I cried to God that He would raise up a man [to fill] the commission He had given to me...many tears did I shed over this...until at last...I saw and could say with the Lord, 'I beheld and there was no man.' ...God had committed this message to me, and at whatever cost, I must go forward."

On one occasion a man who was strongly prejudiced against women in ministry attended a conference where Jessie was speaking. In conversation afterward he confessed, "I would not have believed it possible, had I not seen it, that God would use a woman like that!" Jessie's response? "God never does use a woman like that...or a man either! God only uses the NEW CREATION."

Jessie's heart cry was, "All that I have, all that I am, all that I may be is Thine, wholly, absolutely, and unreservedly."[1]

Felicity Dale

1. Research for this article and its quotes come from "Jessie Penn-Lewis (1861–1927)," Lighthouse Library International, http://tinyurl.com/l5mkg4a (accessed April 29, 2014).

[24] These things are an allegory, for these are
the two covenants. The one is from Mount Si-
nai, which gives birth to bondage; she is Hagar.
[25] Now this Hagar is Mount Sinai in Arabia,
and represents the present Jerusalem, and is
in bondage with her children. [26] But the Jerusa-
lem which is above is free, which is our mother.
[27] For it is written:

"Rejoice, barren woman
who does not bear;
break forth and shout,
you who have no labor pains!
For the desolate has many more children
than she who has a husband."[1]

[28] Now we, brothers, like Isaac, are the chil-
dren of promise. [29] But as it was then, he who
was born after the flesh persecuted him who
was born after the Spirit, so it is now also.
[30] Nevertheless what does the Scripture say?
"Cast out the slave woman and her son, for the
son of the slave woman shall not be heir with
the son of the free woman."[2] [31] So then, broth-
ers, we are not children of the slave woman,
but of the free woman.

Let every yoke of bondage be destroyed in the name of Jesus (Gal 5:1).

5 For freedom Christ freed us. Stand fast
therefore and do not be entangled again
with the yoke of bondage.

Christian Freedom

[2] Indeed I, Paul, say to you that if you become
circumcised, Christ will profit you nothing. [3] I
testify again to every man who is circumcised
that he is obligated to keep the whole law.
[4] You have been cut off from Christ, whoever
of you are justified by law; you have fallen
from grace. [5] For we, through the Spirit, by
faith, eagerly wait for the hope of righteous-
ness. [6] For in Christ Jesus neither circumcision
nor uncircumcision means anything, but faith
which works through love.
[7] You were running well. Who hindered you
from obeying the truth? [8] This persuasion does
not come from Him who calls you. [9] A little yeast
leavens the whole batch. [10] I have confidence
in you through the Lord that you will not think
otherwise. But he who is troubling you shall
bear his judgment, whoever he is. [11] Brothers,
if I am still preaching circumcision, why do
I still suffer persecution? Then the offense of
the cross has ceased. [12] I wish that those who
are troubling you would castrate themselves!
[13] You, brothers, have been called to liberty.
Only do not use liberty to give an opportunity
to the flesh, but by love serve one another. [14] For
the entire law is fulfilled in one word, even in
this: "You shall love your neighbor as yourself."[3]
[15] But if you bite and devour one another, take
heed that you are not consumed by one another.

Spiritual Fruit and Fleshly Works

[16] I say then, walk in the Spirit, and you shall
not fulfill the lust of the flesh. [17] For the flesh
lusts against the Spirit, and the Spirit against
the flesh. These are in opposition to one an-
other, so that you may not do the things that
you please. [18] But if you are led by the Spirit,
you are not under the law.

4:24 1Co 10:11 **4:26** Heb 12:22 **4:28** Gal 3:29 **4:29** Ge 21:9 **4:30** Jn 8:35 **5:1** Gal 2:4 **5:2** Ac 15:1 **5:4** Heb 12:15 **5:5** Ro 8:23–25 **5:6** 1Co 7:19 **5:7** 1Co 9:24 **5:8** Gal 1:6 **5:9** 1Co 15:33 **5:10** 2Co 2:3 **5:11** 1Co 1:23 **5:12** Gal 5:10 **5:13** 1Co 8:9 **5:14** Lev 19:18 **5:16** Eph 2:3 **5:17** Ro 8:5–8 **5:18** Ro 8:14

SPIRITLED WOMAN

COUNSEL FROM THE SPIRIT BASICS

The Very Essence of God

Love is the very essence of God. His love is what motivates Him in every interaction with you. First John 4:8 says that God is love. He doesn't *have* love as you and I do; He *is* love. His very being is love. His response to everything is motivated by love, even when He is correcting you. This love is always looking out for what is best for you.

God's love changes everything. It changes the way you pray. When you realize how much God loves you, you don't have to approach Him with a begging attitude. When you really know that His only motivation toward you is love, you can say, "Father, of course You'll heal me—You love me! Of course You'll protect me—You love me!" This is a supernatural, unconditional, agape love that changes your life.

But you must believe it. Galatians 5:6 says that faith works by love. I like to say it this way: Faith works by *knowing how much you're loved.* If you don't know, you might still be approaching God with begging. When you know how much He loves you, you can approach Him with faith, knowing you have your answer from a loving heavenly Father because He has promised it.

Karen Jensen Salisbury

[1] *27* Isa 54:1. [2] *30* Ge 21:10. [3] *14* Lev 19:18.

Through God's supernatural empowering, I will keep growing and changing (Gal 5:16).

[19] Now the works of the flesh are revealed, which are these: adultery, sexual immorality, impurity, lewdness, [20] idolatry, sorcery, hatred, strife, jealousy, rage, selfishness, dissensions, heresies, [21] envy, murders, drunkenness, carousing, and the like. I warn you, as I previously warned you, that those who do such things shall not inherit the kingdom of God.

[22] But the fruit of the Spirit is love, joy, peace, patience, gentleness, goodness, faith, [23] meekness, and self-control; against such there is no law. [24] Those who are Christ's have crucified the flesh with its passions and lusts. [25] If we live in the Spirit, let us also walk in the Spirit. [26] Let us not be conceited, provoking one another and envying one another.

Bear One Another's Burdens

6 Brothers, if a man is caught in any transgression, you who are spiritual should restore such a one in the spirit of meekness, watching yourselves, lest you also be tempted. [2] Bear one another's burdens, and so fulfill the law of Christ. [3] For if someone thinks himself to be something when he is nothing, he deceives himself. [4] But let each one examine his own work, and then he will have rejoicing in himself alone, and not in another. [5] For each one shall bear his own burden. [6] Let him who is taught in the word share all good things with him who teaches.

[7] Be not deceived. God is not mocked. For whatever a man sows, that will he also reap. [8] For the one who sows to his own flesh will from the flesh reap corruption, but the one who sows to the Spirit will from the Spirit reap eternal life. [9] And let us not grow weary in doing good, for in due season we shall reap, if we do not give up. [10] Therefore, as we have opportunity, let us do good to all people, especially to those who are of the household of faith.

Final Warning and Benediction

[11] You see what large letters I have written to you with my own hand.

[12] It is those who desire to make a good showing in the flesh that try to compel you to be circumcised, only that they may not be persecuted for the cross of Christ. [13] For they themselves who are circumcised do not keep the law. But they desire to have you circumcised, so that they may boast in your flesh. [14] God forbid that I should boast, except in the cross of our Lord Jesus Christ, by whom the world is crucified to me, and I to the world. [15] For in Christ Jesus neither circumcision nor uncircumcision means anything, but a new creation. [16] Peace and mercy be on all who walk according to this rule and upon the Israel of God.

[17] From now on let no one trouble me, for I bear in my body the marks of the Lord Jesus.

[18] Brothers, the grace of our Lord Jesus Christ be with your spirit. Amen.

5:21 Ro 13:13
5:22 Eph 5:9
5:23 Ac 24:25
5:24 Ro 6:6
5:25 Gal 5:16
6:1 Heb 12:13
6:2 Ro 15:1
6:3 1Co 3:18
6:4 1Co 11:28
6:5 1Co 3:8
6:6 Ro 15:27

....

6:7 1Co 6:9
6:8 Jas 3:18
6:9 Heb 12:3
6:10 Eph 2:19
6:12 Gal 5:11
6:14 Ro 6:6
6:15 2Co 5:17
6:16 Gal 3:29
6:18 Ro 16:20

Author: The apostle Paul

Written: AD 62, from Rome

Themes: Christian Unity, Spiritual Warfare

EPHESIANS

Dear Spirit Led Woman,

You are called to look at those around you with eyes that see the invisible. But if you're like many women, you probably do the opposite, focusing on the temporal issues you deal with daily. But this shortsightedness can cause you to overlook the intangible things you should see in people.

We tend to react as though the people around us are the problem. But God's Word makes it clear that "our fight is not against flesh and blood, but against principalities, against powers, against the rulers of the darkness of this world, and against spiritual forces of evil in the heavenly places" (Eph 6:12). You are called to live in the spiritual, eternal realm. It is in this realm that you have the proper view—God's view—of yourself and others and are able to appropriate all God has for you.

For years I prayed that "the eyes of [my] understanding may be enlightened, that [I] may know... the hope of His calling...and the riches of the glory of His inheritance" (Eph 1:18). I challenge you to pray this way also. Your life will take on a completely different dimension as God corrects your vision and helps you to live with the eternal always in sight.

Joy F. Strang

Salutation

1 Paul, an apostle of Jesus Christ by the will of God,

To the saints who are at Ephesus and to the faithful in Christ Jesus:

2 Grace to you and peace from God our Father and the Lord Jesus Christ.

Spiritual Blessings in Christ

> It's time for the daughters of God to come forth and to shine (Eph 1:3–6)!

3 Blessed be the God and Father of our Lord Jesus Christ, who has blessed us with every spiritual blessing in the heavenly places in Christ, 4 just as He chose us in Him before the foundation of the world, to be holy and blameless before Him in love; 5 He predestined us to adoption as sons to Himself through Jesus Christ according to the good pleasure of His will, 6 to the praise of the glory of His grace which He graciously bestowed on us in the Beloved. 7 In Him we have redemption through His blood and the forgiveness of sins according to the riches of His grace, 8 which He lavished on us in all wisdom and insight, 9 making known to us the mystery of His will, according to His good pleasure, which He purposed in Himself, 10 as a plan for the fullness of time, to unite all things in Christ, which are in heaven and on earth.

> I'm redeemed and forgiven (Eph 1:7–8).

11 In Him also we have received an inheritance, being predestined according to the purpose of Him who works all things according to the counsel of His own will, 12 that we, who were the first to hope in Christ, should live for the praise of His glory. 13 In Him you also, after hearing the word of truth, the gospel of your salvation, and after believing in Him, were sealed with the promised Holy Spirit, 14 who is the guarantee of our inheritance until the redemption of the purchased possession, to the praise of His glory.

Paul's Prayer

15 Therefore I also, after hearing of your faith in the Lord Jesus and your love toward all the saints, 16 do not cease giving thanks for you, mentioning you in my prayers, 17 so that the God of our Lord Jesus Christ, the Father of glory, may give you the Spirit of wisdom and revelation in the knowledge of Him, 18 that the eyes of your understanding may be enlightened, that you may know what is the hope of His calling and what are the riches of the glory of His inheritance among the saints,

> I thank You, Father, for granting me the spirit of wisdom and revelation in the knowledge of Christ to understand the deeper things of the Word of God (Eph 1:17).

19 and what is the surpassing greatness of His power toward us who believe, according to the working of His mighty power, 20 which He performed in Christ when He raised Him from the dead and seated Him at His own right hand in the heavenly places, 21 far above all principalities, and power, and might, and dominion, and every name that is named, not only in this age but also in that which is to come. 22 And He put all things in subjection under His feet and made Him the head over all things for the church, 23 which is His body, the fullness of Him who fills all things in all ways.

> I take my position in Christ Jesus, where no plan or strategy of Satan can enter to steal, kill, or destroy (Eph 1:22).

From Death to Life

2 And you were dead in your trespasses and sins, 2 in which you formerly walked according to the age of this world and according to the prince of the power of the air, the spirit who now works in the sons of disobedience,

> Before you go into warfare, recognize it is not you the devil is afraid of—it is Christ in you (Eph 2:2).

3 among them we all also once lived in the lusts of our flesh, doing the desires of the flesh and of the mind, and we were by nature children of wrath, even as the rest. 4 But God, being rich in mercy, because of His great love with which He loved us, 5 even when we were dead in sins, made us alive together with Christ (by grace you have been saved), 6 and He raised us up and seated us together in the heavenly places in Christ Jesus, 7 so that in the coming ages He might show the surpassing riches of His grace in kindness toward us in Christ Jesus. 8 For by grace you have been saved through faith, and this is not of

1:1 2Co 1:1
1:2 Ro 1:7
1:3 2Co 1:3
1:4 Eph 5:27
1:5 Ro 8:29–30
1:6 Mt 3:17
1:7 Ro 3:24
1:9 Ro 8:28
1:10 Col 1:20
1:11 Eph 1:14
1:12 Eph 1:6
1:13 Eph 4:30
1:14 Ro 8:23
1:15 Phm 1:5
1:16 Ro 1:8–9
1:17 Jn 20:17
1:18 Ac 26:18
......
1:19 Col 1:29
1:20 Mk 16:19
1:22 1Co 11:3
1:23 Jn 1:16
2:1 Col 2:13
2:2 Jn 12:31
2:3 Gal 2:15–16
2:5 Eph 2:1
2:6 Eph 1:3
2:7 Titus 3:4
2:8 Eph 2:5

SPIRIT-TO-SPIRIT PRAYER

PRAYER FOR REVELATION

For this reason I bow my knees before You, the Father of my Lord Jesus Christ, from whom every family in heaven and on earth is named. Grant me out of the rich treasury of Your glory to be strengthened with mighty power in my inner man by the [Holy] Spirit indwelling my innermost being [and personality]. May Christ through faith [actually] dwell in my heart! Help me to be rooted deep in love and founded securely on love, that I may have the power and be strong to apprehend and grasp with all the saints [God's devoted people, the experience of that love] what is the breadth and length and height and depth [of it]; [that I may really come] to know [practically, through experience for myself] the love of Christ, which far surpasses mere knowledge [without experience]; that I may be filled [through all my being] unto all the fullness of God [may I have the richest measure of the divine Presence and become a body wholly filled and flooded with God Himself]! Now to You who, by the [action of His] power that is at work within us, is able to [carry out His purpose and] do superabundantly far over and above all that I [dare] ask or think [infinitely beyond my highest prayers, desires, thoughts, hopes, or dreams]—to You be glory in the church and in Christ Jesus throughout all generations forever and ever. Amen (so be it).

Katherine Ruonala

yourselves. It is the gift of God, [9]not of works,
so that no one should boast. [10]For we are His
workmanship, created in Christ Jesus for good
works, which God prepared beforehand, so that
we should walk in them.

I am a citizen of heaven (Eph 2:6).

One in Christ

[11]Therefore remember that formerly you, the
Gentiles in the flesh, who are called the "uncir-
cumcision" by the so-called "circumcision" in
the flesh by human hands, [12]were at that time
apart from Christ, alienated from the citizen-
ship of Israel and strangers to the covenants of
promise, without hope and without God in the
world. [13]But now in Christ Jesus you who were
formerly far away have been brought near by
the blood of Christ.
[14]For He is our peace, who has made both
groups one and has broken down the bar-
rier of the dividing wall, [15]by abolishing in
His flesh the enmity, that is, the law of the
commandments contained in ordinances,
that in Himself He might make the two into
one new man, thus making peace, [16]and that
He might reconcile both to God into one body
through the cross, thereby slaying the enmity.
[17]And He came and preached peace to you
who were far away and peace to those who
were near. [18]For through Him we both have
access by one Spirit to the Father.
[19]Now, therefore, you are no longer strangers
and foreigners, but are fellow citizens with the
saints and members of the household of God,
[20]having been built upon the foundation of the
apostles and prophets, Jesus Christ Himself
being the chief cornerstone, [21]in whom the
entire building, tightly framed together, grows
into a holy temple in the Lord, [22]in whom you
also are being built together into a dwelling
place of God through the Spirit.

Paul's Ministry to the Gentiles

3 For this reason I, Paul, am the prisoner of
Jesus Christ for you Gentiles.
[2]You may have heard of the administration
of the grace of God which was given me for
you, [3]how by revelation He made known to
me the mystery, as I have written briefly al-
ready, [4]by which, when you read it, you may
understand my knowledge of the mystery of
Christ, [5]which in other generations was not

2:9 2Ti 1:9
2:10 Eph 4:24
2:11 Col 2:11
2:12 1Th 4:13
2:13 Ac 2:39
2:14 Gal 3:28
2:15 Col 2:14
....
2:17 Ps 148:14
2:18 1Co 12:13
2:19 Gal 6:10
2:20 Mt 16:18
2:21 1Co 3:16–17
2:22 1Co 3:16
3:1 Eph 4:1
3:2 2Ti 1:11
3:3 Ro 16:25
3:4 2Co 11:6
3:5 Ac 10:28

Looking for Miracles

Many believers long for greater faith because they know that is what moves mountains. If we could "only believe," we would see more miracles. Isn't that what we've always been taught? The Bible tells us anything is possible for those who believe and that God will do great works if we learn to live by faith.

That's true, of course, but there's a deeper issue than faith. So many people struggle with this dynamic of growing in faith in order to see more miracles. It isn't that we doubt the promises of God; actually, we're more inclined to doubt we have enough faith to see those promises manifest in our lives. When we don't see miracles and manifestations of the power of God as often as we want to, we begin to question whether our faith is enough—whether it's big enough or pure enough or consistent enough.

I believe the reason for this is that without knowing the One we put our faith in, our attempts to believe Him are futile. Unless the Holy Spirit gives us a revelation of who God is, believing Him will continue to be a struggle. We have to get a vision of His true nature and know how He sees us. Or, more specifically, we have to have a revelation of His love.

Scripture tells us that faith works by love (Gal 5:6). Experiencing the love of God unleashes the faith God has given us, and it allows us to trust Him with a glorious abandonment. God wants us to become rooted and grounded in His love so we can enter the rest of faith. He wants us to be so confident in His love that we don't even hesitate to boldly approach the throne of grace. When we really get a glimpse of His extravagant, relentless love for us—when we look into His eyes and are overwhelmed by how much He adores us—we stop struggling to have faith. We just have it. We believe because we see who He is.

How can we get this vision of His love? Well, for starters, we can ask for it. Ephesians 3:14–21 is one of my favorite apostolic prayers, and it's all about this very desire we have to know our Father's love:

> For this reason I bow my knees to the Father of our Lord Jesus Christ, from whom the whole family in heaven and earth is named, that He would give you, according to the riches of His glory, power to be strengthened by His Spirit in the inner man, and that Christ may dwell in your hearts through faith; that you, being rooted and grounded in love, may be able to comprehend with all saints what is the breadth and length and depth and height, and to know the love of Christ which surpasses knowledge; that you may be filled with all the fullness of God.
>
> Now to Him who is able to do exceedingly abundantly beyond all that we ask or imagine, according to the power that works in us, to Him be the glory in the church and in Christ Jesus throughout all generations, forever and ever. Amen.

Do you see the heart of this request? Paul prays the Holy Spirit would strengthen us in our inner being for one specific purpose: so we would be able to comprehend this love that completely surpasses natural understanding. He prays that we would know the height and the depth and the width and the breadth of that love, and even that we would be filled with all the fullness of God, who is love.

As God's love overflows in our lives, we are delivered—from fear, from distractions, from obstacles, from all the mess that gets into our lives—and we are released to trust the One who then wants to do exceedingly abundantly above all we can ask, hope, or imagine.

This prayer links His love with our experience of His power, and this is a key to our ability to have faith. We have to be able to live out of the knowledge of God's love in order to know who we are, to know how He sees us, and to know how to enter into the intimacy He calls us to experience. When we can fully rest in His love, faith flourishes and miracles begin to flow.

This relationship between knowing God's love and seeing His power is part of God's plan to reveal Himself through those who know Him. We are gateways, and God wants to step through us. The more we are able to experience His nature, the more we are able to demonstrate His nature to others. Scripture tells us that all of creation longs to see the children of God revealed (Ro 8:19), and as we draw closer to Him and rest in who He is, He shows Himself through us.

I believe God manifesting Himself through us is the result of a great awakening that has already begun. I am seeing this awakening all across the body of Christ and throughout the nations. People from all walks of life and denominations are having the eyes of their understanding enlightened in the knowledge of God, and as a result they are waking up to the hope of their calling, the riches of His glorious inheritance, and the greatness of His power toward those who believe.

Yes, the Spirit of wisdom and revelation is waking people up to the truth of who God really is and to the truly free gift of His amazing grace. As a result of this awakening, the glorious miracles we used to only dream about are happening.

Once people experience a touch from God, they are transformed and immediately want to share their transformation with their family and friends. People all over the world are being provoked to worship God with a fresh awe as they see His power at work. A fresh awakening has begun, and the eyes of our understanding are being enlightened in the knowledge of how good God really is.

It is a glorious time to be alive!

Katherine Ruonala

SPIRITLED WOMAN

COUNSEL FROM THE SPIRIT BASICS

Make an Investment

Speak the truth in love to each other and be transparent. Don't pretend. Be honest. The secret here is to do it in love. Even if your spouse gets angry, God will honor you. When you speak truth, you will have nothing to hide. God always honors and rewards truth.

> But, speaking the truth in love, we may grow up in all things into Him, who is the head, Christ Himself.
> —EPHESIANS 4:15

We make the choice of either speaking creatively or destructively, positively or negatively, in doubt or in faith. Our choice will determine the measure by which God will answer our prayers. A negative confession will hinder a person from receiving the blessing. But if we speak with faith and unwavering confidence in God's Word, then we open the channel of heaven's resources to meet our needs.

Iris Delgado

made known to the sons of men, as it is now revealed to His holy apostles and prophets by the Spirit, [6] how the Gentiles are fellow heirs, and fellow members, and partakers of the promise in Christ by the gospel.

[7] Of this I was made a minister, according to the gift of the grace of God given to me by the effective working of His power. [8] To me, the very least of all saints, this grace was given, to preach to the Gentiles the incomprehensible riches of Christ, [9] and to reveal for all people what is the fellowship of the mystery, which from the beginning of the ages has been hidden in God, who created all things through Jesus Christ, [10] so that now the manifold wisdom of God might be made known by the church to the principalities and powers in the heavenly places, [11] according to the eternal purpose which He completed in Christ Jesus our Lord, [12] in whom we have boldness and confident access through faith in Him. [13] Therefore I ask you not to lose heart at my tribulations for you, which is your glory.

To Know the Love of Christ

[14] For this reason I bow my knees to the Father of our Lord Jesus Christ, [15] from whom the whole family in heaven and earth is named, [16] that He would give you, according to the riches of His glory, power to be strengthened by His Spirit in the inner man, [17] and that Christ may dwell in your hearts through faith; that you, being rooted and grounded in love, [18] may be able to comprehend with all saints what is the breadth and length and depth and height, [19] and to know the love of Christ which surpasses knowledge; that you may be filled with all the fullness of God.

[20] Now to Him who is able to do exceedingly abundantly beyond all that we ask or imagine, according to the power that works in us, [21] to Him be the glory in the church and in Christ Jesus throughout all generations, forever and ever. Amen.

Unity of the Body

4 I, therefore, the prisoner of the Lord, exhort you to walk in a manner worthy of the calling with which you were called. [2] With all humility, meekness, and patience, bearing with one another in love, [3] be eager to keep the unity of the Spirit in the bond of peace. [4] There is one body and one Spirit, even as you were called in one hope of your calling, [5] one Lord, one faith, one baptism, [6] one God and Father of all, who is above all, and through all, and in you all.

[7] But grace was given to each one of us according to the measure of the gift of Christ. [8] Therefore He says:

> "When He ascended on high,
> He led captivity captive,
> and gave gifts to men."[1]

[9] (In saying, "He ascended," what does it mean but that He also descended first into the lower parts of the earth? [10] He who descended is also He who ascended far above all the heavens that He might fill all things.)

[11] He gave some to be apostles, prophets, evangelists, pastors, and teachers, [12] for the equipping of the saints, for the work of service, and for the building up of the body of Christ, [13] until we all come into the unity of the faith and of the knowledge of the Son of God, into a complete man, to the measure of the stature of the fullness of Christ, [14] so we may no longer be children, tossed here and there by waves and carried about with every wind of doctrine by the trickery of men, by craftiness with deceitful scheming. [15] But, speaking the truth in love,

3:7 Eph 1:19
3:8 1Co 15:9
3:9 Col 1:26
3:10 Eph 1:21
3:11 Eph 1:11
3:12 Eph 2:18
3:13 Eph 3:1
3:16 Ro 7:22
3:17 Col 1:23
3:18 Eph 1:15
3:19 Eph 1:23
3:20 Ro 16:25
3:21 Ro 11:36
4:1 Eph 3:1
4:2 Col 3:12–13
4:4 Eph 1:18
4:5 1Co 8:6
4:6 Ro 11:36
4:7 Ro 12:3
4:8 Ps 68:18
4:9 Jn 3:13
4:10 Heb 4:14
4:11 Ac 21:8
4:13 Eph 4:5
4:14 Jas 1:6
4:15 Eph 1:22

1 8 Ps 68:18.

we may grow up in all things into Him, who is the head, Christ Himself, 16 from whom the whole body is joined together and connected by every joint and ligament, as every part effectively does its work and grows, building itself up in love.

The Old Life and New Life

17 Therefore this I say and testify in the Lord, that from now on you walk not as other Gentiles walk, in the vanity of their minds, 18 having their understanding darkened, excluded from the life of God through the ignorance that is within them, due to the hardness of their hearts. 19 Being calloused they have given themselves over to sensuality for the practice of every kind of impurity with greediness.

20 But you did not learn about Christ in this manner, 21 if indeed you have heard Him and have been taught by Him, as the truth is in Jesus: 22 that you put off the former way of life in the old nature, which is corrupt according to the deceitful lusts, 23 and be renewed in the spirit of your mind; 24 and that you put on the new nature, which was created according to God in righteousness and true holiness.

Rules for the New Life

25 Therefore, putting away lying, let every man speak truthfully with his neighbor, for we are members of one another. 26 Be angry but do not sin. Do not let the sun go down on your anger. 27 Do not give place to the devil. 28 Let him who steals steal no more. Instead, let him labor, working with his hands things which are good, that he may have something to share with him who is in need.

29 Let no unwholesome word proceed out of your mouth, but only that which is good for building up, that it may give grace to the listeners. 30 And do not grieve the Holy Spirit of God, in whom you are sealed for the day of redemption. 31 Let all bitterness, wrath, anger, outbursts, and blasphemies, with all malice, be taken away from you. 32 And be kind one to another, tenderhearted, forgiving one another, just as God in Christ also forgave you.

5 Therefore be imitators of God as beloved children. 2 Walk in love, as Christ loved us and gave Himself for us as a fragrant offering and a sacrifice to God.

3 And do not let sexual immorality, or any impurity, or greed be named among you, as these are not proper among saints. 4 Let there be no filthiness, nor foolish talking, nor coarse joking, which are not fitting. Instead, give thanks. 5 For this you know, that no sexually immoral or impure person, or one who is greedy, who is an idolater, has any inheritance in the kingdom of Christ and of God.

4:16 Col 2:19
4:18 Eph 2:12
4:19 1Ti 4:2
4:21 Eph 1:13
4:22 Ro 6:6
4:23 Ro 12:2
4:24 Ro 6:4
4:25 Col 3:9
4:26 Ps 37:8
4:27 Jas 4:7
4:29 Col 4:6
4:30 1Th 5:19
4:31 Col 3:8
4:32 2Co 2:10
5:1 Eph 4:32
5:2 Jn 13:34
5:3 Col 3:5
5:4 Eph 4:29
5:5 Col 3:5

....

5:6 Ro 1:18
5:8 Lk 16:8
5:9 Ro 15:14
5:10 1Th 5:21
5:11 Ro 13:12
5:12 Eph 5:3
5:13 Jn 3:20–21
5:14 Isa 60:1
5:15 Col 4:5
5:16 Eph 6:13
5:17 Ro 12:2
5:18 Pr 20:1
5:19 Col 3:16
5:20 Col 3:17
5:21 Php 2:3
5:22 Ge 3:16
5:25 Eph 5:28
5:26 Ac 22:16
5:27 2Co 11:2
5:28 Eph 5:25
5:30 1Co 6:15
5:31 Ge 2:24

Walk as Children of Light

6 Let no one deceive you with empty words, for because of these things the wrath of God is coming upon the sons of disobedience. 7 Therefore do not be partakers with them.

8 For you were formerly darkness, but now you are light in the Lord. Walk as children of light— 9 for the fruit of the Spirit is in all goodness and righteousness and truth— 10 proving what is pleasing to the Lord. 11 And do not have fellowship with the unfruitful works of darkness; instead, expose them. 12 For it is shameful even to speak of those things which are done by them in secret. 13 But all things are exposed when they are revealed by the light, for everything that becomes visible is light. 14 Therefore He says:

"Awake, you who sleep,
arise from the dead,
and Christ will give you light."

15 See then that you walk carefully, not as fools, but as wise men, 16 making the most of the time because the days are evil. 17 Therefore do not be unwise, but understand what the will of the Lord is. 18 Do not be drunk with wine, for that is reckless living. But be filled with the Spirit. 19 Speak to one another in psalms, hymns, and spiritual songs, singing and making melody in your heart to the Lord. 20 Give thanks always for all things to God the Father in the name of our Lord Jesus Christ, 21 being submissive to one another in the fear of God.

Wives and Husbands

22 Wives, be submissive to your own husbands as unto the Lord. 23 For the husband is the head of the wife, just as Christ is the head and Savior of the church, which is His body. 24 But as the church submits to Christ, so also let the wives be to their own husbands in everything.

We are part of His glorious bride (Eph 5:25–27).

25 Husbands, love your wives, just as Christ also loved the church and gave Himself for it, 26 that He might sanctify and cleanse it with the washing of water by the word, 27 and that He might present to Himself a glorious church, not having spot, or wrinkle, or any such thing, but that it should be holy and without blemish. 28 In this way men ought to love their wives as their own bodies. He who loves his wife loves himself. 29 For no one ever hated his own flesh, but nourishes and cherishes it, just as the Lord cares for the church. 30 For we are members of His body, of His flesh and of His bones. 31 "For this reason a man shall leave his

Putting on the Armor of God

Despite the war Satan has waged against us, we have been given spiritual weaponry to protect, defend, and safeguard what rightfully belongs to us. No matter how organized Satan's regime may be, Jesus has not left us ignorant of his plans. We have been charged to put on the whole armor of God that we may position ourselves in opposition to the enemy. The Bible says:

> Therefore take up the whole armor of God that you may be able to resist in the evil day, and having done all, to stand. Stand therefore, having your waist girded with truth, having put on the breastplate of righteousness, having your feet fitted with the readiness of the gospel of peace, and above all, taking the shield of faith, with which you will be able to extinguish all the fiery arrows of the evil one. Take the helmet of salvation and the sword of the Spirit, which is the word of God.
>
> —Ephesians 6:13–17

The apostle Paul wrote many of his epistles while a prisoner in Rome. During his captivity he was able to observe the protective armor the Roman soldiers who guarded him used. In the passage above Paul used the armor to explain how Christians can defend themselves against the vicious attacks of our adversary. Let's take a look at each component of the Roman soldier's armor and see how it relates to our spiritual armor. On the lines underneath each one, describe how you have used that piece of armor and how it protected you from the enemy's attack in a specific way.

The belt of truth

To a Roman soldier, the belt was essential to keeping the other pieces of armor in place. Paul is telling us that truth keeps the rest of our spiritual armor in place. Operating in truth allows us to be unhindered in warfare.

The breastplate of righteousness

The breastplate covered the chest and protected the vital organs. Righteousness through Jesus Christ allows us to stand before demons with boldness and assurance that we have the victory.

Shoes of peace

The shoes of the Roman soldier were elaborately cut. The soles consisted of layers of metal and leather with hobnail spikes that would plant into the ground and give the soldier stability. Our shoes of peace allow us to take an unmovable stance against our opponent.

The shield of faith

The shield was comprised of layers of animal hide, tanned and woven together, making it as tough and durable as metal yet lightweight. It kept the fiery arrows away from the soldier. Likewise the shield of faith protects us by repelling blows from the enemy.

The helmet of salvation

The helmet of the Roman soldier was designed to deflect blows to the head while allowing the soldier to maintain maximum visibility. The helmet of salvation protects our minds.

The sword of the Spirit

The Roman soldier's sword was a fierce weapon. It was short, lightweight, well balanced, sharp, and deadly. When the sword of the Spirit, which is the Word of God, is spoken in faith, it is a terrifying weapon to the kingdom of darkness.

You may have noticed that all of the armor is defensive except the sword. The sword of the Spirit is our offensive weapon. This is why we must know the Word of God. It does more than protect us from the enemy's attacks; it changes the situation, puts the enemy to fight, and brings the victory.

Kimberly Ray

father and mother and shall be joined to his wife, and the two shall be one flesh."[1] 32 This is a great mystery, but I am speaking about Christ and the church. 33 However, let each one of you love his wife as himself, and let the wife see that she respects her husband.

Children and Parents

6 Children, obey your parents in the Lord, for this is right. 2 "Honor your father and mother," which is the first commandment with a promise, 3 "so that it may be well with you and you may live long on the earth."[2]

4 Fathers, do not provoke your children to anger, but bring them up in the discipline and instruction of the Lord.

Servants and Masters

5 Servants, obey those who are your masters according to the flesh, with fear and trembling, in sincerity of your heart, as to Christ, 6 not serving when eyes are on you, but as pleasing men as the servants of Christ, doing the will of God from the heart, 7 with good will doing service, as to the Lord, and not to men, 8 knowing that whatever good thing any man does, he will receive the same from the Lord, whether he is enslaved or free.

9 And masters, do the same things for them, no longer threatening, knowing that your Master also is in heaven, and there is no partiality with Him.

The Battle Against Evil

10 Finally, my brothers, be strong in the Lord and in the power of His might. 11 Put on the whole armor of God that you may be able to stand against the schemes of the devil. 12 For our fight is not against flesh and blood, but against principalities, against powers, against the rulers of the darkness of this world, and against spiritual forces of evil in the heavenly places. 13 Therefore take up the whole armor of God that you may be able to resist in the evil day, and having done all, to stand. 14 Stand therefore, having your waist girded with truth, having put on the breastplate of righteousness, 15 having your feet fitted with the readiness of the gospel of peace, 16 and above all, taking the shield of faith, with which you will be able to extinguish all the fiery arrows of the evil one. 17 Take the helmet of salvation and the sword of the Spirit, which is the word of God.

I take the shield of faith, and I quench every fiery dart of the enemy (Eph 6:16).

18 Pray in the Spirit always with all kinds of prayer and supplication. To that end be alert with all perseverance and supplication for all the saints. 19 Pray for me, that the power to speak may be given to me, that I may open my mouth boldly to make known the mystery of the gospel, 20 for which I am an ambassador in chains, that I may speak boldly as I ought to speak.

Final Greetings

21 Now that you also may know my activities and how I am doing, Tychicus, a beloved brother and faithful minister in the Lord, will make everything known to you. 22 I have sent him to you for this very purpose, that you might know our activities and that he might comfort your hearts.

23 Peace be to the brothers, and love with faith, from God the Father and the Lord Jesus Christ. 24 Grace be with all those who love our Lord Jesus Christ in sincerity. Amen.

5:33 Eph 5:25
6:1 Pr 6:20
6:2 Ex 20:12
6:4 Ge 18:19
6:8 Col 3:24
6:9 Job 31:13–15
6:10 Eph 1:19
6:11 Eph 6:13
6:12 Eph 1:3
6:13 Eph 5:16
6:14 Isa 11:5
6:15 Isa 52:7
6:17 Heb 4:12
6:18 Col 4:2
6:19 1Th 5:25
6:20 2Co 5:20
6:21 Ac 20:4
6:22 Col 4:7–8
6:23 Gal 6:16
6:24 Mt 22:37

[1] *31* Ge 2:24. [2] *2–3* Dt 5:16

Author: The apostle Paul

Written: Early AD 60s, possibly from Rome or Ephesus

Themes: Having the Mind of Christ, Joy and Rejoicing

PHILIPPIANS

Dear Spirit-Led Woman,

What does God want you to do for Him in this season of your life? Realize that every big accomplishment is made up of a series of little accomplishments. Set a goal for what you need to do next. To make it attainable, the goal needs to be spelled out clearly, along with a course of action and a timeline to accomplish it. Review it periodically to evaluate your progress, and modify your plan if necessary as God gives you new direction or insight.

On the path to fulfilling God's purposes, you may encounter negative feedback. There are always "dream-stealers" who will tell you why you can't accomplish what God has ordained. Instead of listening to them, fill your mind with the Word of God, which tells you that "[you] can do all things because of Christ who strengthens [you]" (Php 4:13). Build up your faith by speaking the truth out loud. Don't allow the enemy or your own flesh to distract you from doing what God wants you to do. Decide that with His help you are going to stay on course and be fruitful for His kingdom.

Joy F. Strang

Salutation

1 Paul and Timothy, servants of Jesus Christ,
To all the saints in Christ Jesus who are
at Philippi, with the overseers and deacons:

2 Grace to you and peace from God our Father
and the Lord Jesus Christ.

Paul's Prayer for the Philippians

3 I thank my God for every reminder of you.
4 In every prayer of mine for you all, I have
always made requests with joy, 5 due to your
fellowship in the gospel from the first day until
now. 6 I am confident of this very thing, that
He who began a good work in you will perfect
it until the day of Jesus Christ.

> I am part of this generation, and I can be sure that He will fulfill His part of the bargain where I am concerned (Php 1:6).

7 It is right for me to think this of you all
because I have you in my heart, since both
in my imprisonments and in the defense and
confirmation of the gospel, you all are fellow
partakers of my grace. 8 For God is my witness,
how I long after you all with the affection of
Jesus Christ.

9 And this I pray, that your love may abound yet
more and more in knowledge and in all discern-
ment, 10 that you may approve things that are
excellent so that you may be pure and blame-
less for the day of Christ, 11 being filled with
the fruit of righteousness, which comes through
Jesus Christ, for the glory and praise of God.

To Live Is Christ

12 But I want you to know, brothers, that
the things which happened to me have re-
sulted in advancing the gospel, 13 so that my
imprisonments in Christ have become known
throughout the entire palace guard and to all
the rest. 14 And a great many of the brothers
in the Lord, having become confident because
of my incarcerations, have dared to speak the
word without fear.

15 Some indeed are preaching Christ out of
envy and strife, and some also from good will.
16 The former preach Christ out of contention,
not sincerely, intending to add trouble to my
circumstance. 17 But the latter preach out of
love, knowing that I am appointed for the
defense of the gospel. 18 What then? Only that
in every way, whether in pretense or in truth,
Christ is preached. And in this I rejoice.

Indeed, I will rejoice. 19 For I know that
through your prayer and the support of the
Spirit of Jesus Christ, this will result in my
deliverance. 20 Accordingly, it is my earnest ex-
pectation and my hope that I shall be ashamed
in nothing, but that with all boldness as always,
so now also, Christ will be magnified in my
body, whether it be by life or by death. 21 For
to me, to continue living is Christ, and to die is
gain. 22 But if I am to live on in the flesh, this
will mean fruitful labor to me. Yet I do not know
what I shall choose. 23 I am in a difficult position
between the two, having a desire to depart and
to be with Christ, which is far better. 24 Never-
theless, to remain in the flesh is more needful
for your sake. 25 Having this confidence, I know
that I shall remain and continue with you all for
your joyful advancement of the faith, 26 so that
your rejoicing for me may be more abundant in
Jesus Christ when I am in your presence again.

27 Only let your conduct be worthy of the gos-
pel of Christ, that whether or not I come and
see you, I may hear of your activities, that you
are standing fast in one spirit, with one mind,
striving together for the faith of the gospel.
28 Do not be frightened by your adversaries.
This is a sign to them of their destruction, but
of your salvation, and this from God. 29 For to
you it was granted on behalf of Christ not only
to believe in Him, but also to suffer for His
sake, 30 having the same conflict which you
saw in me and now hear is in me.

Christian Humility and Christ's Humility

2 If there is any encouragement in Christ, if
any comfort of love, if any fellowship of
the Spirit, if any compassion and mercy, 2 then
fulfill my joy and be like-minded, having the
same love, being in unity with one mind. 3 Let
nothing be done out of strife or conceit, but
in humility let each esteem the other better
than himself. 4 Let each of you look not only
to your own interests, but also to the interests
of others.

5 Let this mind be in you all, which was also
in Christ Jesus,

6 who, being in the form of God,
did not consider equality with God
something to be grasped.
7 But He emptied Himself,
taking upon Himself the form of a servant,
and was made in the likeness of men.
8 And being found in the form of a man,
He humbled Himself
and became obedient to death,
even death on a cross.
9 Therefore God highly exalted Him
and gave Him the name which is above
every name,
10 that at the name of Jesus every knee
should bow,

1:1 2Co 1:1
1:2 Ro 1:7
1:4 Ro 1:9
1:6 1Co 1:8
1:7 2Co 7:3
1:8 Ro 1:9
1:9 1Th 3:12
1:10 1Th 3:13
1:11 Col 1:6
1:13 Php 1:7
1:16 Php 1:7
1:19 2Co 1:11
....
1:20 1Co 6:20
1:21 Gal 2:20
1:23 2Co 5:8
1:25 Php 2:24
1:27 Eph 4:1
1:30 Ac 16:19–40
2:1 2Co 13:14
2:2 Jn 3:29
2:3 Ro 12:10
2:4 Ro 15:1
2:5 Mt 11:29
2:6 Jn 5:18
2:7 Mt 20:28
2:8 Heb 12:2
2:9 Heb 2:9
2:10 Mt 28:18

of those in heaven and on earth and
under the earth,
11 and every tongue should confess that Jesus
Christ is Lord,
to the glory of God the Father.[1]

> The Father fully made a way for
> His Son (Php 2:5–11).

Shining as Lights in the World

12 Therefore, my beloved, as you have al-
ways obeyed, not only in my presence, but
so much more in my absence, work out your
own salvation with fear and trembling. 13 For
God is the One working in you, both to will
and to do His good pleasure.
14 Do all things without murmuring and
disputing, 15 that you may be blameless and
harmless, sons of God, without fault, in the
midst of a crooked and perverse generation, in
which you shine as lights in the world. 16 Hold
forth the word of life that I may rejoice on
the day of Christ that I have not run in vain
or labored in vain. 17 Yes, and even if I am
offered upon the sacrifice and service of your
faith, I take delight and rejoice with you all.
18 For this reason you also take delight and
rejoice with me.

Timothy and Epaphroditus

19 I trust in the Lord Jesus to send Timothy
shortly to you, that I also may be of good
comfort when I get word concerning you.
20 For I have no one like-minded, who will
sincerely care for your welfare. 21 For all seek
their own, not the things of Christ Jesus. 22 But
you know of his proven worth, that as a son
with a father, he has served with me in the
gospel. 23 Therefore I hope to send him soon
after my situation is resolved. 24 But I trust in
the Lord that I, myself, shall also come shortly.
25 Yet I thought it necessary to send to you
Epaphroditus, who is my brother and compan-
ion in labor, fellow soldier, your messenger,
and he who ministered to my necessity. 26 For
he longed after you all and was filled with
heaviness, because you heard that he was
sick. 27 Indeed he was sick, near death. But
God had mercy on him, and not only on him,
but also on me, lest I should have had sorrow
upon sorrow. 28 Therefore I sent him the more
eagerly, that when you see him again, you
may rejoice and I may be less sorrowful. 29 So
receive him in the Lord with all joy. And hold
such ones in high regard, 30 because for the
work of Christ he was near death, not regard-
ing his life, endeavoring to make up for your
lack of service toward me.

2:11 Jn 13:13
2:12 2Co 7:15
2:13 Heb 13:21
2:14 1Pe 4:9
2:15 Mt 5:45
2:16 Gal 2:2
2:17 Ro 15:16
2:20 1Co 16:10
2:21 1Co 10:24
2:22 1Co 4:17
2:24 Phm 1:22
2:25 Php 4:18
2:26 Php 1:8
2:29 1Co 16:18
2:30 1Co 16:17

3:1 Php 4:4
3:2 2Co 11:13
3:5 2Co 11:22
3:6 Ac 8:3
3:7 Lk 14:33
3:8 Jn 17:3
3:9 1Co 1:30
3:10 Ro 8:17
3:11 Ac 26:7
3:12 1Co 13:10
3:13 Lk 9:62

The True Righteousness

3 Finally, my brothers, rejoice in the Lord. To
write the same things to you is no trouble
to me, and it is reassuring for you. 2 Watch out
for dogs, watch out for evil workers, watch out
for those who practice mutilation. 3 For we are
the circumcision who worship God in the Spirit,
and boast in Christ Jesus, and place no trust
in the flesh, 4 though I also have confidence
in the flesh.

> I rejoice in Christ (Php 3:3).

If any other man thinks that he has reason
to trust in the flesh, I have more: 5 I was cir-
cumcised the eighth day, of the stock of Israel,
of the tribe of Benjamin, and a Hebrew of
Hebrews; as concerning the law, a Pharisee;
6 concerning zeal, persecuting the church; and
concerning the righteousness which is in the
law, blameless.
7 But what things were gain to me, I have
counted these things to be loss for the sake
of Christ. 8 Yes, certainly, I count everything
as loss for the excellence of the knowledge of
Christ Jesus my Lord, for whom I have forfeited
the loss of all things and count them as rub-
bish that I may gain Christ, 9 and be found in
Him, not having my own righteousness which
is from the law, but that which is through faith
in Christ,[2] the righteousness which is of God
on the basis of faith, 10 to know Him, and the
power of His resurrection, and the fellowship
of His sufferings, being conformed to His
death, 11 if somehow I might make it to the
resurrection of the dead.

Pressing Toward the Mark

> I have to go after my flesh,
> resist the devil, and apprehend the
> calling God has installed inside me
> (Php 3:12).

12 Not that I have already attained or have
already been perfected, but I follow after it
so that I may lay hold of that for which I
was seized by Christ Jesus. 13 Brothers, I do
not count myself to have attained, but this
one thing I do, forgetting those things which
are behind and reaching forward to those
things which are ahead, 14 I press toward the
goal to the prize of the high calling of God
in Christ Jesus.

1 6–11 A hymn about Jesus' attitude of servanthood. *2 9* Or *through the faith of Christ.*

How to Show Your Kids the Way to God

After bringing children into this world, Christian parents should help them find their way through it. How may we do so? By directing and redirecting them to the One who said, "I am the way" (Jn 14:6). Such godly guidance requires three primary necessities:

1. *Instruction*: We should diligently teach them about the way, His words, and His way of life.
2. *Intercession*: We should faithfully pray for them in the Spirit to come to, receive, walk, and persevere in the way.
3. *Illustration*: We should steadily demonstrate to them a life lived in and for the way and words of God.

Whatever other helpful ways of parenting we discover and practice, these three are essential if we hope to help guide our innocent ones through the wicked wilderness of the world. Naïve and vulnerable to the wily prince of this world, our children need and deserve two parents who walk with God. But with sin and stress ruining many marriages, happy nuclear families are hard to find.

While two Christian parents are preferable, one, if committed, can become an inspirational parental epistle. As Christ was the Word "made flesh" before Israel's attentive eyes, so Christian parents can be Christianity "made flesh" before their children's impressionable gazes.

God's plan is for us to influence our children all their lives, calling and recalling them to the way in which we walk. But our works, ways, and sayings permanently impress our children or grandchildren for Christ only if we are consistent "doers of the word and not hearers only" (Jas 1:22). So, Christian parent, be consistent. Day after day show your children the way.

Demonstrate integrity—a thoroughly honest character that doesn't act deceitfully or unethically or speak falsely. Display humility—a soul that doesn't seek praises, boast of its accomplishments, deny its faults, hold prejudices, or mock anyone. As Micah 6:8 says, "What does the Lord require…but…to walk humbly with your God?"

Exhibit devotion—a deeply dedicated Christian disciple who takes time first daily to fellowship with her King and to strengthen His kingdom and righteousness within (Mt 6:33). Show dutifulness—a parent who steadily pursues her vocational obligations, rain or shine, to provide for her family's needs: "Do not be lazy in diligence, be fervent in spirit, serve the Lord" (Ro 12:11). Demonstrate faith—a parent who relies on God at all times, "anxious for nothing, but in everything, by prayer…with gratitude," asking God's help and resting in His "peace…which surpasses all understanding" (Php 4:6–7).

Display faithfulness—a parent who always honors covenantal and contractual obligations and verbal agreements: "Timothy...is faithful in the Lord" (1Co 4:17). Show submission—a parent who willingly yields to authorities, laws, and rules in the nation, workplace, church, and home: "Be subject to the governing authorities" (Ro 13:1). Exhibit joy—a spirit so free in Jesus that gladness springs and flows out regularly, even during long, dark trials of faith: "strengthened...enduring everything with perseverance and patience joyfully" (Col 1:11).

Demonstrate worship—a parent who freely lavishes adoration on the true God, not the worldly idols of money, materialism, pleasure, or self-promotion: "So David arose... and worshipped" (2Sa 12:20). Display the New Testament overcomer—one who consistently rises above adversaries and adversities by persistently trusting and obeying God, regardless of what others say or do: "Do not be overcome by evil, but overcome evil with good" (Ro 12:21).

Show courage—a parent who consistently obeys God and remains unmoved when the consequences are misunderstanding, criticism, slander, or betrayal: "Be strong and courageous...for the LORD your God is with you" (Jos 1:9).

Exhibit mercy—a parent who doesn't rush to judge or condemn anyone and who forgives all offenders: "Be therefore merciful...judge not...condemn not...forgive" (Lk 6:36–37). And demonstrate love—a parent who is always ready to kindly listen to, counsel, or support her children, whether they excel or fail: "Walk in love, as Christ loved us" (Eph 5:2).

These kinds of living illustrations, combined with intercession, will make your instruction impressive. Your children and grandchildren will remember your parental epistle and find the way—and they will enter into, abide in, and walk in His words and ways and never depart: "Train up a child in the way he should go, and when he is old he will not depart from it" (Pr 22:6). In that day you'll rejoice, knowing you've guided through this world those you brought into it.

Got kids? Grandkids? Go show them the way.

Greg Hinnant

SPIRIT-TO-SPIRIT PRAYER

SACRIFICE OF JOY

My Lord, I offer to You a sacrifice of joy. I will sing praises to the Lord, for You are my exceeding joy, my God, and my King. I rejoice that I belong to You. I rejoice that Christ died for us for the joy of obtaining the prize before Him, enduring the cross so that we could be delivered from the kingdom of darkness and restored to the kingdom of light. I too offer a sacrifice of joy, enduring all hardships for the joy of eternal life. The joy of the Lord is my strength (Heb 12:2; Neh 8:10).

And now I will lift up my head above my enemies all around me, and I will offer sacrifices of joy to You, my Lord. I will sing, yes, I will sing praises to the Lord (Ps 27:6).

Lord, I bring my praises to the altar of God, to God, my exceeding joy. I will always praise You, O God, my God (Ps 43:4).

My King, I praise Your name with songs of joy and with dancing. I rejoice because You alone can fill my heart with gladness (Ps 149:3).

Iris Delgado

15 Therefore let those of us who are mature
be thus minded. And if you think differently
in any way, God will reveal even this to you.
16 Nevertheless, according to what we have
already attained, let us walk by the same rule,
let us be of the same mind.

Paul forgot what was behind; so must I (Php 3:13–14).

17 Brothers, become fellow imitators with me
and observe those who walk according to our
example. 18 For many are walking in such a
way that they are the enemies of the cross
of Christ. I have told you of them often and
tell you again, even weeping. 19 Their destina-
tion is destruction, their god is their appetite,
their glory is in their shame, their minds are
set on earthly things. 20 But our citizenship
is in heaven, from where also we await for
our Savior, the Lord Jesus Christ, 21 who will
transform our body of humiliation, so that
it may be conformed to His glorious body,
according to the working of His power even
to subdue all things to Himself.

3:15 1Co 2:6
3:16 Gal 6:16
3:17 1Co 4:16
3:18 Gal 6:12
3:19 Ro 16:18
3:20 Eph 2:19
3:21 Col 3:4

4:1 Php 1:8
4:2 Php 2:2–3
4:3 Lk 10:20
4:4 Php 3:1
4:5 Jas 5:8–9
4:6 Eph 6:18
4:7 Jn 14:27
4:8 Ac 6:3

4 Therefore, my beloved and longed-for
brothers, my joy and crown, so stand fast
in the Lord, my beloved.

Exhortations

2 I exhort Euodia and Syntyche to be of the
same mind in the Lord. 3 I ask you also, true
companion, help those women who labored
with me in the gospel, with Clement also, and
with my other fellow laborers, whose names
are in the Book of Life.
4 Rejoice in the Lord always. Again I will say,
rejoice! 5 Let everyone come to know your gen-
tleness. The Lord is at hand. 6 Be anxious for
nothing, but in everything, by prayer and sup-
plication with gratitude, make your requests
known to God. 7 And the peace of God, which
surpasses all understanding, will protect your
hearts and minds through Christ Jesus.
8 Finally, brothers, whatever things are true,
whatever things are honest, whatever things

I would do well to rest and allow the peace of God to govern my thoughts toward the care of my children (Php 4:9).

are just, whatever things are pure, whatever
things are lovely, whatever things are of good
report, if there is any virtue, and if there is any
praise, think on these things. 9 Do those things
which you have both learned and received,
and heard and seen in me, and the God of
peace will be with you.

Acknowledgment of the Philippians' Gift

10 I rejoiced in the Lord greatly that now at
last you have revived your concern for me.
Regarding this, you did care, but you lacked
opportunity. 11 I do not speak because I have
need, for I have learned in whatever state I am
to be content. 12 I know both how to face hum-
ble circumstances and how to have abundance.
Everywhere and in all things I have learned the
secret, both to be full and to be hungry, both to
abound and to suffer need. 13 I can do all things
because of Christ who strengthens me.

I can do all things through Christ who gives me the strength (Php 4:13).

14 Nevertheless you did well having shared
in my affliction. 15 Now you Philippians know
also, that in the beginning of the gospel when
I departed from Macedonia, no church shared
with me in the matter of giving and receiv-
ing, except you alone. 16 Even in Thessalonica,
you sent aid once and again for my necessi-
ty, 17 not because I desired a gift, but I desire
fruit that accumulates to your account. 18 But
I have everything and abound. I have been
filled, having received from Epaphroditus the
things which were sent from you, like a sweet
fragrance, an acceptable sacrifice, well pleas-
ing to God. 19 But my God shall supply your
every need according to His riches in glory
by Christ Jesus.

All my needs are met according to His riches in glory (Php 4:19).

20 Now to God and our Father be glory forever
and ever. Amen.

Final Greetings

21 Greet every saint in Christ Jesus. The broth-
ers who are with me greet you. 22 All the saints
greet you, especially those who are of Caesar's
household.

23 The grace of our Lord Jesus Christ be with
you all. Amen.

4:9 Php 3:17
4:10 2Co 11:9
4:12 2Co 11:27
4:13 2Co 12:9–10
4:14 Php 1:7
4:15 Php 1:5
4:16 1Th 2:9
4:17 Titus 3:14
4:19 Ro 2:4
4:20 Ro 11:36
4:21 Gal 1:2
4:22 2Co 13:13
4:23 Ro 16:20

COUNSEL FROM THE SPIRIT BASICS

Manifest God's Love

Be anxious for nothing, but in everything, by prayer and supplication with gratitude, make your requests known to God. And the peace of God, which surpasses all understanding, will protect your hearts and minds through Christ Jesus.

—PHILIPPIANS 4:6–7

When you allow the love of God to be manifested through you to your children, it will be the greatest deterrent against sin and rebellion in your child. This deep love from you will be better than anything that your child can see or have. The greatest deterrent against sin and rebellion in your child is the love of God manifested in your love for your child.

When you feel like screaming, yelling, preaching, or scolding—*stop!* Take a deep breath. This is the time for you to take control of your emotions, mind, and body by refusing to allow your feelings to rule your actions and your words.

Reach out with God's love and kindness toward your loved ones. Be an example. Don't compromise your values or bend your rules, but act in love. Your child may become angry with you, but deep down in his heart he will begin to think maybe you're right and maybe he's wrong. In God's timing, God's love in you will win out.

Examine yourself to see if your prayers are meant to manipulate or to control. If they are, ask God to forgive you. Ask the Holy Spirit to teach you how to pray for your loved ones. It will dramatically change your life and the lives of others.

Iris Delgado

Guard Your Heart

Finally, brothers, whatever things are true, whatever things are honest, whatever things are just, whatever things are pure, whatever things are lovely, whatever things are of good report, if there is any virtue, and if there is any praise, think on these things.

—PHILIPPIANS 4:8

There will come a point in our lives where we must encounter a face-off with past unhealthy behaviors, habits, and faulting thinking. We must be willing to deal with it all! We cannot pick and choose. We need to examine those areas, confront them, and cry out to God, "What have I done to hinder, stagnate, and slow down my assignment?"

God stands before us, never leaving us to deal with our issues alone. He wants us to be free of those things that linger in the corners of our souls. He wants us to be free—free to worship Him, free to move in our assignment, and free to live a full and rich life.

Are you willing to let go of those issues that are holding you back? Rid yourself of all that has hindered your progress? Until you empty yourself, God cannot pour into you. What things do you need to confront and let go? Are you willing to write about some issues or past hurts that you know God is asking you to let go so that healing can take place?

Past hurts

Abuse

Faulty thinking

Fear

Unforgiveness

Bitterness

Betrayal

Disappointment

After praying, think on, meditate on, Philippians 4:8; guard your heart against anything negative that would keep you from your assignment!

Reina Olmeda

Author: The apostle Paul

Written: AD 62, from Rome

Theme: Christ as God in All His Glory, Freedom from the Law, False Religion

COLOSSIANS

Dear SpiritLed Woman,

Colossians 1:9–11 says that when you know what God's will is, you will be able to walk worthy of your calling, being fruitful in every good work and being strengthened by the power of His might. It isn't a matter of being able in yourself. Once you know what His will is, all you have to do is say yes. He will do the rest.

In considering the things God asks of you, you may face some valid concerns. Perhaps you have small children who need constant attention. Perhaps your husband doesn't agree with what you sense God is leading you to do. *How can you fulfill your roles at home and also fulfill God's plan?*

One time when I brought similar concerns to the Lord in prayer, He showed me that although my husband is clearly the head of our home, he won't answer to God for me in eternity. I will have to answer for myself. Obedience has a price—death to our own ways—but it also promises a great reward: the commendation of the Father. So lay aside your excuses. Take hold of His plan for your life, and watch Him do mighty works through you.

Joy F. Strang

Salutation

1 Paul, an apostle of Jesus Christ, by the will of God, and Timothy our brother,

2 To the saints and faithful brothers in Christ who are at Colosse:

Grace to you and peace from God our Father and the Lord Jesus Christ.

Thankfulness for the Colossians

3 We give thanks to God and the Father of our Lord Jesus Christ, praying always for you. 4 For we heard of your faith in Christ Jesus and your love for all the saints, 5 because of the hope which is laid up for you in heaven, of which you have already heard in the word of the truth of the gospel, 6 which has come to you, as it has in all the world, and brings forth fruit, as it has also in you, since the day you heard it and knew the grace of God in truth. 7 And you also learned of Epaphras, our dear fellow servant, who is a faithful minister of Christ for you, 8 who also declared to us your love in the Spirit.

I am delivered from the power of darkness and translated into the kingdom of God's dear Son (Col 1:13).

The Person and Work of Christ

9 For this reason we also, since the day we heard it, do not cease to pray for you and to ask that you may be filled with the knowledge of His will in all wisdom and spiritual understanding; 10 that you may walk in a manner worthy of the Lord, pleasing to all, being fruitful in every good work, and increasing in the knowledge of God, 11 strengthened with all might according to His glorious power, enduring everything with perseverance and patience joyfully, 12 giving thanks to the Father, who has enabled us to be partakers in the inheritance of the saints in light. 13 He has delivered us from the power of darkness and has transferred us into the kingdom of His dear Son, 14 in whom we have redemption through His blood, the forgiveness of sins.

I have forgiveness of sins through the blood of Christ (Col 1:14).

15 He is the image of the invisible God and the firstborn of every creature. 16 For by Him all things were created that are in heaven and that are in earth, visible and invisible, whether they are thrones, or dominions, or principalities, or powers. All things were created by Him and for Him. 17 He is before all things, and in Him all things hold together. 18 He is the head of the body, the church. He is the beginning, the firstborn from the dead, so that in all things He may have the preeminence. 19 For it pleased the Father that in Him all fullness should dwell, 20 and to reconcile all things to Himself by Him, having made peace through the blood of His cross, by Him, I say—whether they are things in earth, or things in heaven.

21 And you, who were formerly alienated and enemies in your mind by wicked works, yet now He has reconciled 22 in the body of His flesh through death, to present you holy and blameless and above reproach in His sight, 23 if you continue in the faith, grounded and settled, and are not removed from the hope of the gospel, which you have heard, and which was preached to every creature which is under heaven, and of which I, Paul, have become a servant.

Paul's Ministry to the Church

24 Now I rejoice in my sufferings for your sake and fill up in my flesh that which is lacking in the afflictions of Christ, for the sake of His body, which is the church. 25 I have been made a servant of it according to the commission of God, which has been given to me for you, to fulfill the word of God, 26 even the mystery which has been hidden from past ages and generations, but now is revealed to His saints. 27 To them God would make known what is the glorious riches of this mystery among the nations. It is Christ in you, the hope of glory, 28 whom we preach, warning everyone and teaching everyone in all wisdom, so that we may present them perfect in Christ Jesus. 29 In this I labor, striving according to His power, which effectively works in me.

Christ Jesus in me is my hope of glory (Col 1:27).

2 I would like you to know what a great struggle I am having for you, and for those at Laodicea, and for everyone who has not seen my face in the flesh, 2 that their hearts may be comforted, being knit together in love, and receive all the riches and assurance of full understanding, and knowledge of the mystery of God, both of the Father and of Christ, 3 in whom are hidden all the treasures of wisdom and knowledge. 4 Now this I say lest anyone beguile you with enticing words. 5 For though I am absent in the flesh, yet I am with you in spirit, rejoicing and seeing your orderliness and the steadfastness of your faith in Christ.

1:1 2Co 1:1
1:2 Ro 1:7
1:3 Eph 1:15
1:4 Gal 5:6
1:5 Ac 23:6
1:6 Jn 15:16
1:7 Col 4:12
1:8 Ro 15:30
1:10 Eph 4:1
1:11 Eph 4:2
1:12 Ac 20:32
1:13 Eph 6:12
1:14 Eph 1:7
1:15 2Co 4:4
1:16 Jn 1:3
....
1:17 Jn 8:58
1:18 Ac 26:23
1:19 Jn 1:16
1:20 Eph 1:10
1:21 Eph 2:12
1:22 Ro 7:4
1:23 Eph 3:17
1:24 2Ti 1:8
1:25 Eph 3:2
1:26 Ro 16:25–26
1:27 1Ti 1:1
1:28 1Co 2:6
1:29 1Co 15:10
2:1 Col 1:29
2:2 Col 4:8
2:3 Ro 11:33
2:4 Eph 5:6
2:5 1Co 14:40

Unleash the Power to Break Through to Victory

There is a new generation arising in the church that can feel something radical stirring inside. These individuals have read the Bible, and the passion of the apostolic leaders of the New Testament church burns in their hearts. This generation confronts sin and the demons that hold souls captive. Their God is the one who can change a nation and lead the church of Jesus Christ out of captivity and into an advancing, invading force. It was their God who led Israel out of Egypt and into the Promised Land. He did not enter into agreement with the Canaanites but utterly cut off the enemy and took their possessions (Ex 23:23).

This is a gate-crashing, wall-breaking, obstacle-removing God. He is the originator of every power and principality, as well as the victor over them through Jesus's death and resurrection (Col 2:10).

This God is our God. He will break open any route through which He has ordained for us to go, even if it seems blocked. God, the breaker, goes up before us. He breaks open the way. This is not an ordinary person on our side. It is the King who will pass through before us. In Old Testament times invading forces used battering rams to break through gates (Eze 21:22). Because God is at the head, up front, He is the battering ram who breaks open the way.

The term *breaker* is foreign to most Christians. According to *Barnes' Notes*, the "Breaker-Through" is one of the titles given to Christ. The breaker crashes a gate in order to move the Israelites into the open place, where they are not confined as they were in prison. The gate of the prison that held them was burst open to set them free.

This is the same image found in Isaiah 43:6, when God said through Isaiah, "I will say to the north, 'Give them up,' and to the south, 'Do not keep them back.'" Breakthrough is something we cannot do by ourselves. It requires divine intervention. God has given apostolic people territories to take and adversity to overcome, and they cannot be victorious alone.

The story of the Exodus is God saying to Moses, "I will do it." God is leading the church today in the same way He led Moses and broke open the way in those days. At the right time God released His intervention and power—but Moses had to believe God and initiate bold action. Moses had to go before Pharaoh and confront him—yet God is the one who broke through for Israel.

Breakthrough occurred when the Israelites were released from captivity in Babylon and returned home to rebuild the temple in Jerusalem and reestablish their land. They had to break through forces exerted by people such as Sanballat and Tobiah, who did not want them to repossess what had been theirs.

God is raising up a people who will reclaim lost land and inheritances, both naturally and spiritually. We will face an enemy who does not want us to have what is rightfully ours, but the Breaker is going before us to give us what is our destined heritage.

Barbara J. Yoder

Fullness of Life in Christ

6 As you have received Christ Jesus the Lord, so walk in Him, 7 rooted and built up in Him and established in the faith, as you have been taught, and abounding with thanksgiving.

8 Beware lest anyone captivate you through philosophy and vain deceit, in the tradition of men and the elementary principles of the world, and not after Christ.

9 For in Him lives all the fullness of the Godhead bodily. 10 And you are complete in Him, who is the head of all authority and power. 11 In Him you were also circumcised with the circumcision made without hands, by putting off the body of the sins of the flesh, by the circumcision of Christ, 12 buried with Him in baptism, in which also you were raised with Him through the faith of the power of God, who has raised Him from the dead.

13 And you, being dead in your sins and the uncircumcision of your flesh, He has resurrected together with Him, having forgiven you all sins. 14 He blotted out the handwriting of ordinances that was against us and contrary to us, and He took it out of the way, nailing it to the cross. 15 And having disarmed authorities and powers, He made a show of them openly, triumphing over them by the cross.

I recognize my real enemy is Satan, and he is already a defeated foe (Col 2:15).

16 Therefore let no one judge you regarding food, or drink, or in respect of a holy day or new moon or sabbath days. 17 These are shadows of things to come, but the substance belongs to Christ. 18 Do not let anyone cheat you of your reward by delighting in false humility and the worship of angels, dwelling on those things which he has not seen, vainly arrogant due to his unspiritual mind, 19 and not supporting the head, from which the entire body, nourished and knit together by joints and sinews, grows as God gives the increase.

The New Life in Christ

20 Therefore, if you died with Christ to the elementary principles of the world, why, as if you were living in the world, do you subject yourself to legalistic rules? 21 "Do not touch! Do not taste! Do not handle!" 22 These all are to perish with use and are aligned with the commandments and doctrines of men. 23 These things have indeed a show of wisdom in self-imposed worship and humility and neglecting of the body, but are worthless against the indulgence of the flesh.

2:7 Eph 3:17
2:8 1Ti 6:20
2:9 Col 1:19
2:11 Ro 2:29
2:12 Ac 2:24
2:13 Eph 2:1
2:15 Eph 4:8
2:16 Heb 9:10
2:17 Heb 8:5
2:18 Col 2:23
2:19 Eph 4:15–16
2:20 Col 2:8
2:21 1Ti 4:3
2:22 Isa 29:13
2:23 Col 2:18

3:2 Mt 16:23
3:3 Ro 6:2
3:4 1Jn 3:2
3:5 Ro 8:13
3:6 Ro 1:18
3:7 Eph 2:2
3:8 Eph 4:22
3:9 Eph 4:22
3:10 Eph 2:10
3:11 Ro 10:12
3:12 Eph 4:2
3:13 Eph 4:32
3:14 Eph 4:3
3:15 Jn 14:27
3:16 Eph 5:19
3:17 1Co 10:31
3:19 Eph 5:25
3:21 Eph 6:4

3 If you then were raised with Christ, desire those things which are above, where Christ sits at the right hand of God. 2 Set your affection on things above, not on things on earth. 3 For you are dead, and your life is hidden with Christ in God. 4 When Christ who is our life shall appear, then you also shall appear with Him in glory.

My life is hidden in Christ (Col 3:3).

5 Therefore put to death the parts of your earthly nature: sexual immorality, uncleanness, inordinate affection, evil desire, and covetousness, which is idolatry. 6 Because of these things, the wrath of God comes on the sons of disobedience. 7 You also once walked in these, when you lived in them. 8 But now you must also put away all these: anger, wrath, malice, blasphemy, and filthy language out of your mouth. 9 Do not lie one to another, since you have put off the old nature with its deeds, 10 and have embraced the new nature, which is renewed in knowledge after the image of Him who created it, 11 where there is neither Greek nor Jew, circumcision nor uncircumcision, barbarian, Scythian, slave nor free, but Christ is all and in all.

12 So embrace, as the elect of God, holy and beloved, a spirit of mercy, kindness, humbleness of mind, meekness, and longsuffering. 13 Bear with one another and forgive one another. If anyone has a quarrel against anyone, even as Christ forgave you, so you must do. 14 And above all these things, embrace love, which is the bond of perfection.

15 Let the peace of God, to which also you are called in one body, rule in your hearts. And be thankful. 16 Let the word of Christ dwell in you richly in all wisdom, teaching and admonishing one another in psalms and hymns and spiritual songs, singing with grace in your hearts to the Lord. 17 And whatever you do in word or deed, do all in the name of the Lord Jesus, giving thanks to God the Father through Him.

Social Duties of the New Life

18 Wives, submit yourselves to your own husbands, as it is fitting in the Lord.

19 Husbands, love your wives, and do not be bitter toward them.

20 Children, obey your parents in all things, for this is well pleasing to the Lord.

21 Fathers, do not provoke your children to anger, lest they be discouraged.

MARITAL PROBLEMS

THE POSITIVE ATTITUDE OF ABIGAIL

First Samuel 25 tells of the marriage of one woman who had every reason to lose her focus on her God-given destiny by the circumstances of a bad marriage. The pain of being married to an alcoholic and abusive husband may have temporarily distracted her, but it did not become a fatal distraction in her life.

Scripture tells us Abigail was "a woman of good understanding" (1Sa 25:3), which meant she was highly intelligent. She was smart, but more importantly, she was wise. In addition to Abigail's wisdom, the Bible also tells us she was beautiful (v. 3). This meant more than that she had a pretty face. The word *countenance* takes into account a person's entire image, including her personality. She may have been pretty, yes, but she was also pleasant. Her attractiveness came from the inside out. This is also a significant point because, as we will see as we look at her situation, Abigail had found a way of not letting her husband's issues affect her in a negative way. She did not wear her unhappy marriage on her person.

Many godly women today can relate to the pain of being married to a substance-abusing spouse. The term substance abuser brings to mind someone who cannot be trusted to keep his word about controlling or quitting his addictive behaviors. It implies someone who wastes the family's resources on his own selfish practices. It describes the demoralizing cycle of sobriety followed by bouts of drunkenness or getting high on drugs—the cycle of hope followed by disappointment each time the substance abuser goes on a binge. It describes the millions of women who are living with husbands who are addicted to things other than alcohol.

The addictive pattern is the same whether the behavior is gambling, legal or illegal drugs, alcohol, pornography, or adultery. Truly, any woman who has lived with a loved one caught in the grip of any one of these obsessive behaviors could testify with Abigail that an entire family can be brought to the brink of ruin by just one person's undisciplined and self-indulgent conduct. And any one of these behaviors is more than just a casual distraction; they can easily become relationship killers—in effect, a fatal distraction.

The Bible tells us Abigail was married to a very wealthy man named Nabal. The name *Nabal* is significant. In biblical times the name of a person was often a reflection of the character of the person bearing that name. A person's name also gave insight into their destiny; it even reflected the gifts a person had or the flaws they possessed.

The same is true of Abigail's husband, Nabal, whose name means "churl." That is an ancient word that means "angry, violent, loud-mouthed, and insulting; a hard-to-please person." The Bible further describes Nabal as being "very drunk" (v. 36). In modern terms, we would describe Nabal as an alcoholic or a substance abuser. He is the prototype of a violent and, at the very least, verbally abusive husband.

Despite his propensity for alcohol, Nabal was a wealthy rancher with extensive holdings of sheep on the open range. As was the case in the early days of our own western frontier, bands of outlaws and thieves roamed the countryside, raiding the camps of the herders and stealing the flocks, which had valuable fleece, and even killing the men who were herding them.

At the time this story takes place, David, the future king of Israel, was living in the mountains and fighting against King Saul. He had a band of six hundred men with him who, although branded as outlaws, cared for Nabal's shepherds who were nearby, seeing to it that no one harmed them or took their sheep.

David's men protected Nabal's far-flung herds, but when they needed provisions of food and other supplies, Nabal's response was surprising. David had sent a messenger to Nabal, asking for a returned favor of food and supplies for the weary men who had protected Nabal's flocks and shepherds. Instead of being gracious and accommodating, as one would expect, Nabal was negative and insulting. He not only replied with an emphatic no, but he also said it in a belittling and demeaning way.

Furious at Nabal's ingratitude and insults, David gathered four hundred of his armed men and declared nothing and no one would be left alive on Nabal's ranch by morning—and that included Abigail.

Fortunately Abigail had an advance warning of the impending crisis. Upon hearing from the messenger how Nabal had responded, Abigail in her wisdom discerned David was on his way to exact vengeance. Immediately she prepared sheep dressed for the men to eat, plus wine, raisins, bread, and cakes of figs—all of the things that David and his men could possibly need—and she prepared them by the wagonload.

She rushed out to intercept David, and when she reached him, she threw herself at his feet, honoring him and speaking of the future he would have as a great warrior. She begged David to accept her gifts and turn from his intent for a bloody revenge.

David's heart was softened by the penitent woman before him, and he relented. He accepted the gifts and commended Abigail for her wisdom in preventing a bloody massacre.

When Abigail returned to her husband's house to tell him what had happened, Nabal was in the midst of a drunken party, and Abigail chose to not tell him the story until the next day, when he finally sobered up. There is a significant lesson in this for women today: Abigail wisely picked an opportune time to discuss a difficult matter with her husband.

Abigail became proactive rather than reactive. She actively sought to find a solution rather than wasting time placing blame. When we are caught in negative situations, it is so much better to determine what we *can* do—whether it is get out of immediate danger or try to minimize the damage—instead of casting blame on someone else. Rather than staying in the same spot and being paralyzed by the circumstances, Abigail was able to present her husband with a situation that was solved, settled, and successfully handled. And when Nabal heard how close he had come to a violent death at the hands of David, the Bible says "his heart died within him, and he became as a stone" (v. 37). Nabal was dead within two weeks' time

When David heard Nabal had died and that Abigail was now a widow, he sent messengers back to gather her and her handmaids and bring them on the road with him and his growing army, and Abigail became David's wife. The story concludes with David being crowned king of Judah in the southern city of Hebron. Abigail, the woman who was once locked in a marriage to a violent, drunken husband, had become a queen!

Joyce Rodgers

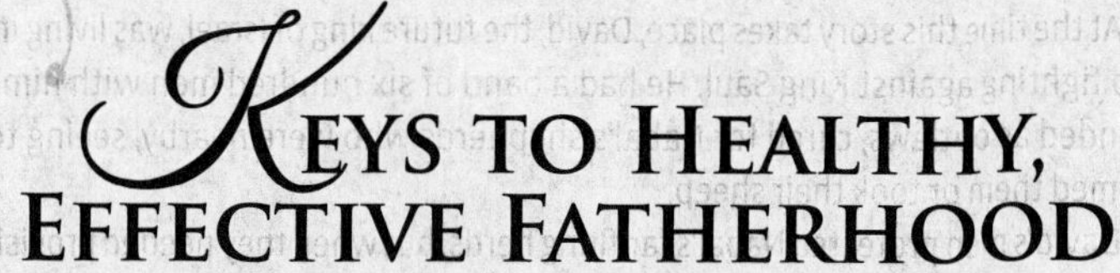

Keys to Healthy, Effective Fatherhood

Fathers, do not provoke your children to anger, lest they be discouraged.

—Colossians 3:21

Obviously, as a SpiritLed woman, you are not a father. But the following keys come from the careful observation of the author's forty years of marriage, parenting, and counseling.

On the lines below each key, if you are a mother, first rate your children's father on his use of each key in his fathering. If you are not a mother, rate your own father's effectiveness in using these keys. Then give a sentence response to each, stating how you can encourage your children's father to make better use of these keys.

1. A good father spends time with his children.

Circle your rating: 1 2 3 4 5 6 7 8 9 10

____

____

2. A good father does things together with his wife to make happy memories with their children.

Circle your rating: 1 2 3 4 5 6 7 8 9 10

____

____

3. A good father loves, affirms, and cares for his wife and his children.

Circle your rating: 1 2 3 4 5 6 7 8 9 10

____

____

4. **The husband and father who loves and cares for his wife and children will be the king of his home.**

Circle your rating: 1 2 3 4 5
6 7 8 9 10

____

____

5. **The father who treats his daughters with respect and tact will have virtuous daughters who will become passionate and good-hearted wives.**

Circle your rating: 1 2 3 4 5
6 7 8 9 10

____

____

6. **The father who abuses his daughter is worse than a criminal.**

Circle your rating: 1 2 3 4 5
6 7 8 9 10

____

____

7. **A good father pays attention to the emotions and the thoughts of his children.**

Circle your rating: 1 2 3 4 5
6 7 8 9 10

____

____

Iris Delgado

SPIRITLED WOMAN

COUNSEL FROM THE SPIRIT BASICS

Take Your Place

There are many benefits to being seated in your place next to Christ in the heavenly places. One benefit is that it is a peaceful, restful place.

From your place at the right hand of the Father, you can gauge your life by peace. Colossians 3:15 says, "Let the peace of God, to which also you are called in one body, rule in your hearts." I like the way the Amplified Bible says it: "And let the peace (soul harmony which comes) from Christ rule (act as umpire continually) in your hearts [deciding and settling with finality all questions that arise in your minds]."

Let peace be in charge of your life. When deciding what to think on, make peace the priority. When making a decision, check your heart and make sure it is at peace. Let peace have the final say-so in every aspect of your life.

Karen Jensen Salisbury

22 Servants, obey your masters in all things according to the flesh, serving not only when they are watching, as the servants of men, but in singleness of heart, fearing God. 23 And whatever you do, do it heartily, as for the Lord and not for men, 24 knowing that from the Lord you will receive the reward of the inheritance. For you serve the Lord Christ. 25 But he who does wrong will receive for the wrong which he has done, and there is no partiality.

3:22 Col 3:20
3:23 Col 3:17
3:24 1Co 7:22
3:25 Ac 10:34

....

4:2 Lk 18:1
4:3 Eph 6:19–20
4:4 Eph 6:20
4:6 Mk 9:50
4:7 Ac 20:4
4:8 Eph 6:22
4:10 Ac 19:29
4:11 Ac 11:2
4:12 Ro 15:30
4:13 Col 2:1
4:14 Phm 1:24
4:15 Ro 16:5
4:16 1Th 5:27
4:17 Phm 1:2
4:18 1Co 16:21

4 Masters, give to your servants that which is just and fair, knowing that you also have a Master in heaven.

Exhortations

2 Continue in prayer, and be watchful with thanksgiving, 3 while praying also for us, that God would open to us a door of utterance to speak the mystery of Christ, for which I am also in chains, 4 that I may reveal it clearly, as I ought to speak. 5 Walk in wisdom toward those who are outside, wisely using the opportunity. 6 Let your speech always be with grace, seasoned with salt, that you may know how you should answer everyone.

Final Greetings

7 Tychicus, who is a beloved brother and a faithful minister and fellow servant in the Lord, will tell you all the news about me. 8 I have sent him to you for this very purpose, that he might know your circumstances and comfort your hearts, 9 with Onesimus, a faithful and beloved brother, who is one of you. They will make known to you everything which is happening here.

10 Aristarchus my fellow prisoner greets you, with Mark, the cousin of Barnabas (concerning whom you received instructions: If he comes to you, receive him), 11 and Jesus, who is called Justus. These are my only fellow workers for the kingdom of God who are of the circumcision. They have been a comfort to me. 12 Epaphras greets you. He is one of you, a servant of Christ, always laboring fervently for you in prayers, that you may stand mature and complete in the entire will of God. 13 I bear witness of him, that he has a great zeal for you, those who are in Laodicea, and those in Hierapolis. 14 Luke, the beloved physician, and Demas greet you. 15 Greet the brothers who are in Laodicea, and Nympha, and the church which is in his house.

16 When this epistle is read among you, ensure that it is read also in the church of the Laodiceans, and that you, likewise, read the epistle from Laodicea.

17 Tell Archippus, "Make sure that you fulfill the ministry which you have received in the Lord."

18 I, Paul, write this greeting with my own hand. Remember my chains. Grace be with you. Amen.

Author: The apostle Paul

Written: AD 50 or 51, from Corinth

Theme: Affirmation of Young Converts, Fundamental Truths of Christian Theology

1 THESSALONIANS

Dear Spirit Led Woman,

Paul says to "pray without ceasing" (1Th 5:17). But you may wonder how to do this when you have so many responsibilities to handle. I've found the answer through the examples of Mary and Martha (Lk 10:38–42). By nature I am a doer—and I like the challenge of taking on big projects. But I have learned that the activity of a Martha is meaningless without the heart of a Mary. You aren't to be one or the other, but both at the same time. In other words, your goal is not to break your daily life into segments, making sure that you are *praying* as much as you are *doing*. The secret to fulfilling 1 Thessalonians 5:17 is to learn how to pray and do simultaneously.

Consumed with the demands of your natural life, you might think you are accomplishing things, but Jesus says you are unproductive when you focus on your outer life to the exclusion of your inner one. He never meant for there to be a conflict between the two; they are not mutually exclusive. You integrate them as you reconcile the Mary and Martha in you, keeping your spirit tuned to God's Spirit and your hands busy with the work He has given you to do.

Joy F. Strang

Salutation

1 Paul, Silas, and Timothy,

To the church of the Thessalonians which is in God the Father and in the Lord Jesus Christ:

Grace to you and peace from God our Father and the Lord Jesus Christ.

The Thessalonians' Faith and Example

2 We give thanks to God always for you all, mentioning you in our prayers, 3 remembering without ceasing your work of faith, labor of love, and patient hope in our Lord Jesus Christ in the sight of God and our Father.

4 For we know, beloved brothers, your election by God. 5 For our gospel did not come to you in word only, but also in power, and in the Holy Spirit, and in much assurance, just as you know what kind of men we were among you for your sake. 6 You became followers of us and the Lord, having received the word in much affliction, with joy of the Holy Spirit. 7 Therefore you were examples to all who believe in Macedonia and Achaia. 8 For the word of the Lord sounded out from you not only in Macedonia and Achaia, but also in every place your faith in God has gone forth, so that we do not need to say anything. 9 For they themselves declare how we were received by you, and how you turned to God from idols, to serve the living and true God, 10 and to wait for His Son from heaven, whom He raised from the dead—Jesus, who delivered us from the wrath to come.

Paul's Ministry in Thessalonica

2 You yourselves know, brothers, that our visit to you was not in vain. 2 But even after we had previously suffered and were shamefully treated at Philippi, as you know, we were bold in our God to declare to you the gospel of God amid much opposition. 3 For our exhortation was not from deceit, nor from uncleanness, nor in guile. 4 But as we were allowed by God to be entrusted with the gospel, even so we speak, not to please men, but God, who examines our hearts. 5 For neither at any time did we come with flattering words, as you know, nor with a pretext for greed. God is our witness. 6 Nor did we seek glory from men, either from you, or from others, even though we might have made demands as the apostles of Christ.

7 But we were gentle among you, like a nurse caring for her own children. 8 So having great love toward you, we were willing to impart to you not only the gospel of God but also our own lives, because you were dear to us. 9 For you remember, brothers, our labor and toil. Laboring night and day so as not to be an expense to any of you, we preached to you the gospel of God. 10 You and God are witnesses of how pure, upright, and blameless we ourselves behaved among you who believe. 11 As you know, we exhorted, comforted, and commanded every one of you, as a father does his own children, 12 that you would walk in a manner worthy of God, who has called you to His kingdom and glory.

13 For this reason we thank God without ceasing because, when you received the word of God, which you heard from us, you received it not as the word of men, but as it truly is, the word of God, which effectively works also in you who believe. 14 For you, brothers, became followers of the churches of God, which in Judea are in Christ Jesus. You also have suffered the same things from your own countrymen, as they have from the Jews, 15 who both killed the Lord Jesus and their own prophets and have persecuted us. They do not please God and are contrary to all men, 16 forbidding us to speak to the Gentiles that they might be saved. In this way they are always piling up their sins, but wrath has come upon them to the extreme.

Paul's Desire to Visit Again

17 But we, brothers, being taken from you for a short time, in presence, not in heart, endeavored all the more abundantly to see your face with great desire. 18 Therefore we wished to come to you—even I, Paul, once and again—but Satan hindered us. 19 For what is our hope, or joy, or crown of rejoicing? Will it not even be you in the presence of our Lord Jesus Christ at His coming? 20 You are our glory and joy.

3 Therefore, when we could no longer endure it, we thought it good to be left at Athens alone. 2 We sent Timothy, who is our brother and minister of God and our fellow laborer in the gospel of Christ, to establish and comfort you with regard to your faith, 3 so that no one would be shaken by these afflictions. For you know that we are appointed to this. 4 Indeed, we told you before when we were with you that we would suffer tribulation, just as it came to pass, as you well know. 5 For this reason, when I could no longer endure it, I sent to inquire about your faith, lest by some means the tempter might have tempted you, and our labor might have been in vain.

6 But just now Timothy has come from you to us and brought us good news of your faith and love, and that you always have good memories of us, desiring greatly to see us, as we also desire to see you. 7 Therefore, brothers, during all our afflictions and distress, we have been encouraged about you through your faith. 8 For now we live, if you stand strong in the

1:1 2Th 1:1
1:2 Ro 1:8–9
1:3 2Th 1:11
1:4 2Th 2:13
1:5 Col 2:2
1:6 Ac 13:52
1:8 Ro 1:8
1:9 1Co 12:2
1:10 Ac 2:24
2:2 Ac 16:22–24
2:3 2Co 2:17
2:4 Gal 1:10
2:5 Ac 20:33
2:6 Jn 5:41
2:7 1Th 2:11
2:8 2Co 12:15
2:9 Ac 18:3

....

2:10 1Th 1:5
2:11 1Th 2:7
2:12 Eph 4:1
2:13 Heb 4:12
2:14 Gal 1:22
2:15 Mt 5:12
2:16 Ac 13:50
2:17 1Co 5:3
2:18 Ro 15:22
2:19 Php 4:1
3:1 Ac 17:15
3:3 Ac 9:16
3:4 1Th 2:14
3:5 Mt 4:3
3:6 Ac 18:5
3:7 2Co 1:4
3:8 1Co 16:13

Lord. [9] For what thanks can we render to God
for you, for all the joy with which we rejoice
for your sakes before our God, [10] night and
day praying earnestly that we might see your
face and might perfect that which is lacking
in your faith?
[11] Now may our God and Father Himself,
and our Lord Jesus Christ, direct our way to
you. [12] And may the Lord make you increase
and abound in love for one another and for
all men, even as we do for you. [13] To this end
may He establish your hearts to be blame-
less in holiness before our God and Father
at the coming of our Lord Jesus Christ with
all His saints.

A Life Pleasing to God

4 Finally, brothers, we urge and exhort
you by the Lord Jesus, that as you have
learned from us how you ought to walk and to
please God, you should excel more and more.
[2] For you know what commands we gave you
through the Lord Jesus.
[3] For this is the will of God, your sanctifica-
tion: that you should abstain from sexual im-
morality, [4] that each one of you should know
how to possess his own vessel in sanctification
and honor, [5] not in the lust of depravity, even
as the Gentiles who do not know God, [6] and
that no man take advantage of and defraud
his brother in any matter, because the Lord
is the avenger in all these things, as we also
have forewarned you and testified. [7] For God
has not called us to uncleanness, but to ho-
liness. [8] Therefore he that despises does not
despise man, but God, who has also given us
His Holy Spirit.
[9] As concerning brotherly love, you do not
need me to write to you. For you yourselves
are taught by God to love one another. [10] And
indeed, you do have love for all the brothers
who are in all Macedonia. But we urge you,
brothers, that you increase more and more.
[11] Learn to be calm, and to conduct your own
business, and to work with your own hands, as
we commanded you, [12] so that you may walk
honestly toward those who are outsiders and
that you may lack nothing.

The Lord's Coming

[13] But I would not have you ignorant, broth-
ers, concerning those who are asleep, that you
may not grieve as others who have no hope.
[14] For if we believe that Jesus died and arose
again, so God will bring with Him those who
sleep in Jesus. [15] For this we say to you by
the word of the Lord, that we who are alive
and remain until the coming of the Lord will
not precede those who are asleep. [16] For the
Lord Himself will descend from heaven with
a shout, with the voice of the archangel, and
with the trumpet call of God. And the dead
in Christ will rise first. [17] Then we who are
alive and remain shall be caught up together
with them in the clouds to meet the Lord in
the air. And so we shall be forever with the
Lord. [18] Therefore comfort one another with
these words.

3:10 2Ti 1:3
3:11 2Th 2:16
3:12 Php 1:9
3:13 1Th 2:19
4:1 Eph 4:1
4:4 1Pe 3:7
4:5 Ro 1:26
4:6 Ro 12:19
4:7 1Th 2:3
4:8 1Jn 3:24
4:9 1Th 5:1
4:10 1Th 1:7
4:11 Eph 4:28
4:12 Mk 4:11
4:13 Eph 2:12
4:15 1Ki 20:35
4:16 1Co 15:23

....

4:17 Jn 12:26

SPIRITLED WOMAN

COUNSEL FROM THE SPIRIT BASICS

Extraordinary Hope

True Christianity offers the world extraordinary hope, but too few believers know this. Tainted by our humanistic culture, modern Christianity seems to have taken on powerless strategies for bringing hope that are no different for the believer than for the unbeliever. Without recognizing Jesus Christ as the ultimate Judge, the comfort we offer those withering under the weight of a wicked and perverse world is reduced to offering them a sympathetic pat on the back and the shallow encouragement, "You will make it through somehow."

Without the revelation of God as Judge, we have no real response to the darkness and torment human beings are bringing upon other human beings. This aspect of God's character and personality makes us wary because we don't want to be seen as bigoted and judgmental or to present God as such. Yet in the process of taming the gospel, we have lost one of the most needed benefits of Jesus as our Judge. Scripture reveals that the entire message of comfort hinges on the statement, "Take comfort, the Judge is coming!" Read the apostle Paul's words to the suffering and persecuted believers in Thessalonica in 1 Thessalonians 4:16–18.

Shelley Hundley

Lord, thank You for filling me with hope, joy, and peace so that I may abound in hope by the power of the Holy Spirit (1Th 4:13–16).

How to Rekindle the Fire for Prayer

A while back I had author Emily Freeman on my radio show, and she said the best thing: Is it more important to please God or to trust Him? She went on to say, "If we focus on pleasing God, we'll quickly get into striving; but if we entrust ourselves to Him and trust Him for all He is, we'll stay in that place of grace, and we'll please Him in the process" (my paraphrase).

Using *TRUST* as an acronym, here are few things I learned about reigniting my prayer life:

T—Thanksgiving: Almost always, when I sense that the fire has gone out and my passion has waned, it's because I stopped being grateful, stopped thanking God for all of the blessings I enjoy.

When we focus too much on what we don't have and on what God is not giving us as the moment, we lose sight of the fact that God is always wonderfully good, is beautifully for us, and will never forsake us. Start today by thanking Him for everything you'd miss tomorrow if you woke up and it wasn't there.

> In everything give thanks, for this is the will of God in Christ Jesus concerning you.
>
> —1 Thessalonians 5:18

R—Repentance: Another fire-quencher is sin and selfish attitudes. Scripture says that His kindness leads us to repentance. When you've spent some time thanking God, conviction returns to your soul. Take the next step and dare to say, "Search me, O God, and know my heart; try me, and know my concerns, and see if there is any rebellious way in me, and lead me in the ancient way" (Ps 139:23–24). Confession is a cleansing, beautiful thing. God draws especially near to the humble, repentant heart.

> Confess your faults to one another and pray for one another, that you may be healed. The effective, fervent prayer of a righteous man accomplishes much.
>
> —James 5:16

U—Understand: Oftentimes when we feel our flame flickering and not burning brightly, it's because we've approached God only for what He can do for us and not for who He is. A sure way to fan our spiritual flame is to seek Him for all He is worth! Still bring your requests before Him, but then lay them down at His feet, and seek to know His heart. He is the star-breathing God, the Lord of lords, the King of kings, and the God of angel armies. He is high and lifted up and yet intimately right here. He loves you. Get to know Him more, and you'll have a better understanding of how He is working in your current circumstances. To better know Him is to love Him more, and to know Him is to be filled to the fullness with Him (Eph 3:14–19).

> The knowledge of the Holy One is understanding.
>
> —Proverbs 9:10

S—Stand: When we don't feel God's presence and His promises don't exactly feel true, it's time to stand on the Word of God because it is true. When I find myself feeling more earthbound than heavenbound, I rise up, walk around my house, and proclaim the promises of God written over my life: "I will not die but live and declare the works of the Lord!" (Because I struggle with health issues.) "God's grace abounds in my life so I can abound in every good work!" (Because I'm constantly in over my head.)

When I stand on God's promises and my ears hear my mouth say what's true, in due time my heart believes again that His Word is true. I challenge you: Walk around, stomp your feet if you have to, and proclaim the promises of God. Take your stand right where you stand!

> For You have exalted Your word above all Your name.
>
> —Psalm 138:2

S—Surrender: Another thing I've noticed is that surrender and spiritual passion are closely linked. When I find myself hanging on to my own understanding or when I rely more heavily on my fears than I do on God's faithfulness, it's like a throwing a wet blanket on my spiritual flame. What's my answer? I get on my knees, open my hands, and surrender everything to the Lord once again.

I give Him my worries, my *what ifs*, and the deep desires of my heart. I'm only dealing with partial information. He knows what's best for me (and for you). Try actually getting on your knees, opening your hands, and releasing the things you've been white-knuckling up to this point. Say to the Lord, "Father, what does obedience look like here? And who do You want to be to me here? My deliverer? Defender? Strong tower? I surrender to You. Show me Your greatness in this place."

> Do not fear, for I am with you; do not be dismayed, for I am your God. I will strengthen you, I will help you, yes, I will uphold you with My righteous right hand.
>
> —Isaiah 41:10

T—Trust: Here we are, back at trust again. When I lose perspective on life, I've somewhere along the line stopped trusting God. Here are a few things that are important to remember:

- He has a plan for your life that is your best-case scenario.
- He is faithful and true and has made Himself available to you.
- He is good and kind and true; you can trust Him to get you safely home.

You can trust Him. If your passion has waned, it's time to reengage your heart, to renew your mind, to humble yourself in His presence, and then to rise up, knowing that you are His and He is yours. You are blessed, indeed.

> Trust in the Lord with all your heart, and lean not on your own understanding; in all your ways acknowledge Him, and He will direct your paths.
>
> —Proverbs 3:5–6

Susie Larson

SPIRIT-TO-SPIRIT PRAYER

PRAYER FOR INNER HEALING

Lord, I confess that as the church, we have sinned against You. Sexual sin, pornography, and abuse are running free and gaining more ground.

I confess that I have embraced a victim spirit as a result of the abuse I have suffered. I admit I have been walking in shame, guilt, and condemnation and have believed the lie of the enemy that I am and will always be a victim. Forgive me for believing these lies.

And now, I choose to walk in obedience to Your Word and forgive those who have inflicted harm, abuse, and neglect. [Name each person aloud.] *I release them to You, Lord. I repent of all thoughts of wanting to get revenge and choose to let go of all bitter-root judgments. I confess and repent of all demonic lies and ungodly thoughts.* [Name them.] *I choose to believe and stand on the promises of the Word of God. I renounce all activity and embracing of a victim spirit and choose to stand on the truth that we are more than conquerors in Christ. We are fearfully and wonderfully made. Your power is in my life. All fear, shame, guilt, and condemnation that have been in operation I renounce, and I command them to go now in Jesus' name.*

Spirits of darkness, I break all unholy soul ties between ________________ [say the name of each person aloud] *and me. I cancel all sexual transference in the powerful name of Jesus. I cancel any control and manipulation between* ________________ [name each person aloud] *and me. I renounce and break all ungodly soul ties between the abusers and me through vows, ceremonies, rituals, secrets, contracts, or demonic alliances. I break the demonic cycle of abuse and say you are no longer welcome. All ties to the demonic realm are broken now. I cut the unfruitful root of darkness off of my life right now. Their hold is over, in Jesus' name!*

Lord, I invite Your healing presence and love. Every place where I have felt abused, victimized, depressed, fearful, and deserving of unjust treatment, I ask that You fill me with acceptance, love, boldness, courage, happiness, joy, and an excitement and expectancy of all the great things You have ahead for me. Help me to focus on Your thoughts toward me, and empower me to walk in a renewed mind. In Jesus' name, amen.

Rebecca Greenwood

5 Concerning the times and the seasons,
brothers, you have no need that I write to
you. 2 For you know perfectly that the day of the
Lord will come like a thief in the night. 3 When
they say, "Peace and safety!" then sudden de-
struction will come upon them as labor upon
a woman with child, and they shall not escape.
4 But you, brothers, are not in darkness so
that this Day should overtake you as a thief.

I am a child of light, not darkness (1Th 5:5).

5:1 Ac 1:7
5:2 2Pe 3:10
5:3 Lk 21:34–35
5:4 1Jn 2:8

5:5 Lk 16:8
5:6 Lk 22:46
5:7 Ac 2:15
5:8 Isa 59:17
5:9 1Th 1:10
5:10 2Co 5:15

5 You are all the sons of light and the sons of
the day. We are not of the night nor of darkness.
6 Therefore let us not sleep as others do. But let
us be alert and sober. 7 For those who sleep,
sleep at night, and those who get drunk, are
drunk at night. 8 But let us, who are of the day,
be sober, putting on the breastplate of faith and
love, and as a helmet, the hope of salvation.
9 For God has not appointed us to wrath, but to
obtain salvation by our Lord Jesus Christ, 10 who
died for us, so that whether we are awake or
asleep, we should live together with Him. 11 So
comfort yourselves together, and edify one
another, just as you are doing.

Prayer Principles for the SpiritLed Woman

The SpiritLed woman of God understands the privilege and the power of an active, godly, intercessory prayer life. The Bible contains many principles regarding the development of your prayer life. In the table below, draw lines from each prayer principle to the Scripture reference where the principle is found. Then start developing these principles in a great measure in your life.

Scripture Reference	Prayer Principle
Matthew 5:44	Do not pray vain, repetitious prayers as the heathens do: to be seen and to get what they can get out of it.
Matthew 6:7	Jesus prayed for God to send the Holy Ghost.
Matthew 26:41	Prayer without ceasing was made for Peter to be released from prison.
John 14:16	Pray for those who spitefully use you and persecute you.
Acts 1:24	The Spirit makes intercession for us with groanings that cannot be uttered.
Acts 12:5	Pray that you will not enter into temptation; the spirit is willing, but the flesh is weak.
Romans 8:26	We are commanded to avoid being anxious in all situations but instead in all situations, with prayer and supplication and with thanksgiving, to make our requests known unto God.
Ephesians 6:18	We should pray for God to set leaders in place because He knows their hearts.
Philippians 4:6	The prayers of the saints come before God out of the hands of angels.
James 5:13–14	The prayers of husbands can be hindered if they do not honor their wives; unto whom much is given, much is required.
James 5:16	We must watch as well as pray.
1 Peter 3:7	We are commanded to be sober and to watch as well as pray.
1 Peter 4:7	The elders of the church are called to pray for the sick.
Revelation 8:4	The effectual, fervent prayer of the righteous produces great results.

God has put a call on my life, and this season is part of its fulfillment (1Th 5:6).

Final Exhortations and Greetings

[12] We ask you, brothers, to acknowledge
those who labor among you, and are ap-
pointed over you in the Lord, and instruct
you. [13] Esteem them very highly in love for
their work's sake. And be at peace among
yourselves. [14] Now we exhort you, broth-
ers, warn those who are unruly, comfort
the faint-hearted, support the weak, and be
patient toward everyone. [15] See that no one
renders evil for evil to anyone. But always
seek to do good to one another and to all.
[16] Rejoice always. [17] Pray without ceasing.
[18] In everything give thanks, for this is the will
of God in Christ Jesus concerning you.
[19] Do not quench the Spirit. [20] Do not despise
prophecies. [21] Examine all things. Firmly hold
onto what is good. [22] Abstain from all appear-
ances of evil.
[23] May the very God of peace sanctify you
completely. And I pray to God that your whole
spirit, soul, and body be preserved blameless
unto the coming of our Lord Jesus Christ.
[24] Faithful is He who calls you, who also will
do it.

[25] Brothers, pray for us. [26] Greet all the
brothers with a holy kiss. [27] I command you
by the Lord that this letter be read to all the
holy brothers.

Let my whole spirit and soul and body be preserved blameless until the coming of my Lord Jesus Christ (1Th 5:23).

[28] The grace of our Lord Jesus Christ be with
you. Amen.

5:12 Heb 13:17
5:13 Mk 9:50
5:14 Ro 14:1
5:15 1Pe 3:9
5:16 Php 4:4
5:17 Eph 6:18
5:18 Eph 5:20
5:19 Eph 4:30
5:21 1Jn 4:1
....
5:23 Ro 15:33
5:24 1Co 1:9
5:26 Ro 16:16
5:27 Col 4:16
5:28 Ro 16:20

Author: The apostle Paul

Written: AD 50 or 51, from Corinth

Theme: Making the Most of Your Time, Awaiting Christ's Return

2 Thessalonians

Dear Spirit Led Woman,

In Paul's second letter to the Thessalonians he writes about the sanctifying work of the Spirit in our lives. The Holy Spirit sanctifies us, or makes us holy, by helping us resist false teaching and ungodly living. He inspires us to work hard and be prepared for the return of the Lord.

You and I live in a fallen world full of temptations and things that can distract us from doing what God has called us to do. If we're not careful, we can drift off course without realizing it.

One way to make sure you stay the course is to listen carefully for the Holy Spirit's guidance in your life. Stay sensitive to Him. He will lead you into a life that will not tolerate compromise or settle for anything less than what God declares in His Word.

Joy F. Strang

SPIRITLED WOMAN

COUNSEL FROM THE SPIRIT BASICS

God Is a Judge

We are ashamed to proclaim that God is a Judge. We hide this truth like a drunken uncle whose unseemly and unpredictable behavior embarrasses us during the annual family reunion. Meanwhile we are oblivious to how bankrupt our faith and witness have become without a living knowledge of God as Judge. Influenced by a relativistic culture, we have backed historic Christian theology on judgment into a corner, where this "inconvenient" message is no longer mentioned in our witness or as part of our experience of the gospel. Consider the apostle Paul's words to the suffering and persecuted believers in Thessalonica:

> And to give you who are troubled rest with us when the Lord Jesus is revealed from heaven with His mighty angels, in flaming fire taking vengeance on those who do not know God and do not obey the gospel of our Lord Jesus Christ. They shall be punished with eternal destruction, isolated from the presence of the Lord and from the glory of His power, when He comes, in that Day, to be glorified in His saints and to be marveled at by all those who believe, because our testimony among you was believed.
>
> —2 THESSALONIANS 1:7–10

This is such a radical departure from our current definition of comfort. The apostle Paul comforted the Thessalonian believers with one truth: The Judge is coming! When God comforts those who are being persecuted, He calls them to look forward to His coming as the day when His people will be fully restored and delivered.

Shelley Hundley

1:1 2Co 1:19
1:2 Ro 1:7
1:3 2Th 2:13
1:4 1Th 2:14
1:5 Php 1:28
1:6 Rev 6:10
1:7 Rev 14:13
1:9 Mt 25:41
1:10 Jn 17:10
1:11 1Th 1:3
2:1 Mk 13:27
2:3 Da 7:25
2:4 Eze 28:2

Salutation

1 Paul, and Silas, and Timothy,

To the church of the Thessalonians in God our Father and the Lord Jesus Christ:

2 Grace to you and peace from God our Father and the Lord Jesus Christ.

The Judgment at Christ's Coming

3 We are bound to thank God always for you, brothers, as it is fitting, because your faith is growing abundantly, and the love of every one of you abounds toward each other. 4 So we boast about you in the churches of God for your patience and faith in all your persecutions and tribulations that you are enduring.

> Let my faith grow exceedingly (2Th 1:3).

5 This is evidence that God's judgment, being righteous, will count you worthy of the kingdom of God for which you are suffering. 6 It is a righteous matter with God to repay with tribulation those who trouble you, 7 and to give you who are troubled rest with us when the Lord Jesus is revealed from heaven with His mighty angels, 8 in flaming fire taking vengeance on those who do not know God and do not obey the gospel of our Lord Jesus Christ. 9 They shall be punished with eternal destruction, isolated from the presence of the Lord and from the glory of His power, 10 when He comes, in that Day, to be glorified in His saints and to be marveled at by all those who believe, because our testimony among you was believed.

11 Therefore we always pray for you that our God would count you worthy of this calling and with power fulfill all your good desires and works done by faith, 12 so that the name of our Lord Jesus Christ may be glorified in you, and you in Him, according to the grace of our God and the Lord Jesus Christ.

The Man of Lawlessness

2 Now, brothers, concerning the coming of our Lord Jesus Christ, and concerning our gathering together unto Him, we ask you 2 not to let your mind be quickly shaken or be troubled, neither in spirit nor by word, nor by letter coming as though from us, as if the day of Christ is already here. 3 Do not let anyone deceive you in any way. For that Day will not come unless a falling away comes first, and the man of sin is revealed, the son of destruction, 4 who opposes and exalts himself above all that is called God or is worshipped, so that he sits as God in the temple of God, showing himself as God.

Freed by the Bridegroom Judge

Through my journey to overcome shame and see Jesus as one who will avenge the wrong done to me, I learned several important truths. I believe they will benefit anyone wanting to know the heart of Jesus as our Judge:

1. ***Vengeance is the Lord's business, not ours.*** We cannot know how God will bring forth His justice or take an account for the wrongs that were done. Hebrews 10:31 tells us that it is a fearful thing to fall into the hands of the living God. The truths of how God works His judgments are too terrifying and mysterious for us to even approach. Vengeance is not our domain (Ro 12:18–20); our job is to give the case to the righteous Judge and know that He will make the wrong things right while giving every chance for mercy and repentance. (See 2 Thessalonians 1:6–10.)

2. ***Someone will pay.*** Either Jesus Christ will accept the just punishment for the wrongs done to us, or the person who sinned against us will pay. The Bible says we all must appear before God, who will judge us (Rev 20:13–15). No one is exempt. Thankfully, those who have accepted Christ are redeemed through His blood, and He has taken upon Himself the penalty for our wrongdoing. (See Ephesians 1:7; Colossians 1:14; 1 John 1:9.) God still judges the wrongs committed against us, but Jesus pays for them through His work on the cross instead of punishing the wrongdoers. Those who have not accepted Christ, however, will receive the weight of God's judgment.

3. ***God will not forget our case when we give it to Him.*** God is a just judge, and He is angry with the wicked (Ps 7:11). Throughout Scripture He promises to remember their iniquity and punish their sins (Jer 14:10; Hos 8:13; 9:9; Ps 90:7–9), and we know the Lord is faithful to keep His promises.

We can have complete assurance that the righteous Judge sees us and will fight for us, but that doesn't absolve us of the responsibility to forgive. Jesus displays an amazing power to forgive our sins, and He invites us to be like Him by forgiving others. For many who have suffered much, this seems almost impossible, but Jesus the Judge, the One whose eyes were lit with jealous fire, gives us a miraculous strength to forgive.

Shelley Hundley

[5] Do you not remember that when I was still with you, I told you these things? [6] Now you know what restrains him that he might be revealed in his time. [7] For the mystery of lawlessness is already working. Only He who is now restraining him will do so until He is taken out of the way. [8] Then the lawless one will be revealed, whom the Lord will consume with the breath of His mouth, and destroy with the brightness of His presence, [9] even him, whose coming is in accordance with the working of Satan with all power and signs and false wonders, [10] and with all deception of unrighteousness among those who perish, because they did not receive the love for the truth that they might be saved. [11] Therefore God will send them a strong delusion, that they should believe the lie: [12] that they all might be condemned who did not believe the truth but had pleasure in unrighteousness.

Chosen for Salvation

[13] But we are bound to always give thanks to God for you, beloved brothers of the Lord, because God has from the beginning called you to salvation through sanctification by the Spirit and belief of the truth. [14] To this He called you by our gospel, to obtain the glory of our Lord Jesus Christ.

[15] Therefore, brothers, stand firm and hold the traditions which you have been taught, whether by word or by our letter.

[16] Now may our Lord Jesus Christ Himself, and God our Father, who has loved us and has given us eternal consolation and good hope through grace, [17] comfort your hearts and establish you in every good word and work.

Pray for Us

3 Finally, brothers, pray for us, that the word of the Lord may quickly spread and be glorified, even as it did with you. [2] And pray that we may be delivered from unreasonable and wicked men, for not all men have faith. [3] But the Lord is faithful, who will establish you and guard you from the evil one. [4] We have confidence in the Lord concerning you, that you are doing and will do the things which we command you. [5] May the Lord direct your hearts to the love of God and to the steadfastness of Christ.

Let Your Word have free course in my life (2Th 3:1).

Deliver me out of the hand of wicked and unreasonable men (2Th 3:2).

Warning Against Idleness

[6] Now we command you, brothers, in the name of our Lord Jesus Christ, that you withdraw yourselves from every brother who walks in idleness and not according to the tradition that he received from us. [7] For you know how you should follow us. For we were not idle among you, [8] neither did we eat anyone's bread without paying for it, but we worked tirelessly and toiled night and day that we might not be a burden to any of you. [9] We did this, not because we did not have that right, but to make ourselves an example for you to follow. [10] For when we were with you, we commanded you that if any will not work, neither shall he eat.

[11] For we hear that there are some among you who live in idleness, mere busybodies, not working at all. [12] Now, concerning those who are such, we command and exhort by our Lord Jesus Christ that they quietly work and eat their own bread. [13] But you, brothers, do not be weary in doing good.

[14] If anyone does not obey our word in this letter, note that man, and do not socialize with him, so that he may be ashamed. [15] Still, do not count him as an enemy, but admonish him as a brother.

Benediction

[16] Now may the Lord of peace Himself give you peace always in every way. The Lord be with you all.

[17] I, Paul, write this greeting with my own hand, and this is the distinguishing mark in every letter: So I write.

[18] The grace of our Lord Jesus Christ be with you all. Amen.

2:7 Rev 17:5
2:8 Isa 11:4
2:9 Mt 24:24
2:10 1Co 1:18
2:11 Ro 1:28
2:12 Ro 1:32
2:13 1Th 1:4
2:14 1Th 2:12
2:15 1Co 11:2
2:16 Jn 3:16
2:17 2Th 3:3
3:1 1Th 5:25
3:2 Ro 15:31
3:3 1Co 1:9
3:4 2Co 2:3
3:5 1Ch 29:18
3:6 1Co 5:4
3:8 Ac 18:3
3:9 1Co 9:4–14
3:10 1Th 4:11
3:11 1Ti 5:13
3:12 1Th 4:11
3:14 2Th 3:6
3:15 1Th 5:14
3:16 Ro 15:33
3:17 1Co 16:21
3:18 Ro 16:20

Author: The apostle Paul

Written: Early AD 60s, possibly from Macedonia

Themes: Church Order, Doctrine and Conduct, Discipline

1 Timothy

Dear Spirit Led Woman,

After hearing a message on being balanced, I did a search on the word *balance*. The only reference I found that contained the word was in Proverbs, and that had to do with a scale—in other words, with weights and measures, not with the way we use our time. So I asked the Holy Spirit to show me the truth, and He replied, "The truth is that being wholehearted for God is the key to balance."

I looked up verses with the concept "whole heart" and found references throughout the Scriptures. The goal is to be able to declare with the psalmist, "There is nothing on earth that I desire besides You" (Ps 73:25). It's why Paul tells Timothy that the purpose of all of his instruction is that Christians be filled with love that comes from a pure heart, a clear conscience, and a sincere faith (1Ti 1:5.)

When you commit to put God first, the other priorities in your life will fall into their proper places. God will direct you by His Spirit as you learn and apply the principles in His Word. He gives you the priorities, and He will help you balance them correctly.

Joy F. Strang

SPIRITLED WOMAN

COUNSEL FROM THE SPIRIT BASICS

Let Your Dream Rise

Let God's dreams be conceived in you and rise up, and you will be able to release faith—the faith of Jesus Himself—that receives the promises He has for you.

You will have to contend for this faith. Your dreams don't just happen accidentally. They do happen as you rest in Him, but it isn't a passive rest. You have to be very resolved and intentional about it. First Timothy 1:18 tells us to wage warfare with the prophetic words spoken over us because it really is a war sometimes. Other people will speak things over you that contradict what God has spoken over you, and they may even ridicule you. Maintaining your faith in what He has said can be a battle.

To walk in the miraculous, we must stay focused on the call. God wants us to be careful to take captive any thought that would try to distract us or exalt itself above the knowledge of who God is. If a thought doesn't line up with the thoughts of God, it needs to be rejected, not reacted to. God is our defense and strong tower; the righteous need only to run into Him to stay safe. We must guard our hearts from these distractions and condemnations with great diligence because it's out of our hearts that the life-giving power of God flows.

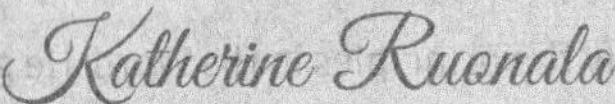

Salutation

1 Paul, an apostle of Jesus Christ by the
command of God our Savior, and of the
Lord Jesus Christ, our hope,

2 To Timothy, my true son in the faith:

Grace, mercy, and peace, from God our Father
and Jesus Christ our Lord.

Warning Against False Doctrine

3 As I urged you when I went into Macedo-
nia, continue to remain at Ephesus so that
you might command some to teach no other
doctrine, 4 nor pay attention to fables and end-
less genealogies, which cause debates rather
than godly edifying, which is in faith. 5 Now
the goal of this command is love from a pure
heart, and from a good conscience, and from
sincere faith. 6 From this, some have lost their
way and turned aside to empty talk, 7 desiring
to be teachers of the law, and understanding
neither what they say nor what they affirm.

8 But we know that the law is good if someone
uses it lawfully. 9 And we know that the law is not
given for a righteous person, but for the lawless
and disobedient, for the ungodly and for sinners,
for the unholy and the profane, for those who kill
their fathers and mothers, for murderers, 10 for
the sexually immoral, for sodomites, for slave
traders, for liars, for perjurers, and for anything
else that is contrary to sound doctrine, 11 accord-
ing to the glorious gospel of the blessed God,
which was committed to my trust.

Thankfulness for Mercy

12 I thank Christ Jesus our Lord, who has
enabled me, because He counted me faith-
ful and appointed me to the ministry. 13 I was
previously a blasphemer, and a persecutor,
and an insolent man. But I was shown mercy,
because I did it ignorantly in unbelief. 14 The
grace of our Lord overflowed with the faith
and love which is in Christ Jesus.

15 This is a faithful saying and worthy of all
acceptance, that Christ Jesus came into the
world to save sinners, of whom I am the worst.
16 But I received mercy for this reason, that in
me, first, Jesus Christ might show all patience,
as an example to those who were to believe
in Him for eternal life. 17 Now to the eternal,
immortal, invisible King, the only wise God, be
honor and glory forever. Amen.

18 This command I commit to you, my son
Timothy, according to the prophecies that
were previously given to you, that by them you
might fight a good fight, 19 keeping faith and
a good conscience, which some have rejected
and suffered shipwreck in regard to their faith.
20 Among these are Hymenaeus and Alexander,
whom I have delivered to Satan that they may
learn not to blaspheme.

Instructions Concerning Prayer

2 Therefore I exhort first of all that you make
supplications, prayers, intercessions, and
thanksgivings for everyone, 2 for kings and for
all who are in authority, that we may lead a
quiet and peaceful life in all godliness and
honesty, 3 for this is good and acceptable in the
sight of God our Savior, 4 who desires all men
to be saved and to come to the knowledge of
the truth. 5 There is one God and one mediator
between God and men, the Man Christ Jesus,
6 who gave Himself as a ransom for all. This
was the testimony given at the proper time.

1:1 Titus 1:3
1:2 2Ti 1:2
1:3 Gal 1:6–7
1:4 1Ti 4:7
. . . .
1:5 2Ti 1:5
1:6 Titus 1:10
1:7 1Ti 6:4
1:8 Ro 7:16
1:9 Gal 5:23
1:10 2Ti 4:3
1:11 Gal 2:7
1:12 Php 4:13
1:13 Ac 8:3
1:14 2Ti 1:13
1:15 1Ti 3:1
1:16 1Ti 1:13
1:17 Col 1:15
1:18 1Ti 4:14
1:20 2Ti 2:17
2:2 Ezr 6:10
2:3 1Ti 1:1
2:4 Eze 18:23
2:5 Gal 3:20
2:6 1Co 1:6

The Intercessor's Authority

There is no question that entering into deep intercession does not happen without a disciplined prayer life. Praying without ceasing does not completely cover this. While there will be times we will enter intercession on a spur-of-the-moment prompting, most intercession will take place in times of regular, premeditated, habitual prayer.

With prayer such an important part of our faith, it is somewhat surprising how little actual instruction we get on prayer in the Scriptures. I think a big part of this is that the school of prayer is prayer itself. As Charles Spurgeon once said, "Pray until you can really pray." It is something you learn to do by doing more than by being instructed in doing. You learn to walk the way or path of prayer.

In the Gospels Jesus gives us the Lord's Prayer—which is what we call it, but, in fact, it is really the "disciple's prayer," as He gives it to us for *our* prayer lives, not for His. While repeating that prayer from memory is good, I think it is even better to use it as an outline for Holy Spirit–led prayer. In that light we enter prayer with praise and worship, "hallowing" the name of the Father.

The second part of that prayer tells us to pray, "Your kingdom come; Your will be done on earth, as it is in heaven" (Mt 6:10).

I believe it is this part of our regular prayer times that Paul discusses and explains in 1 Timothy 2:1–4. I find it quite interesting that Paul and Jesus agree that our first priority in prayer is not to go through our prayer list of personal sins, needs, and concerns, but to first take a global perspective of praying for governments, economies, and societies—or, more specifically, the people who impact them the most. We are instructed to pray for presidents, kings, and other leaders, "that we may lead a quiet and peaceable life in all godliness and honesty" (v. 2). When our leadership is right, the hindrances to the manifestation of the kingdom of God on the earth are greatly reduced. Great things happen when we live in a godly society governed by godly leaders.

In the United States we have fallen into the trap of thinking that our power to vote is greater than our power in prayer. Too many save their season of prayer for election season, praying we will get the right people or party into office, and then we judge the success or failure of our prayers based on whether our candidates won or not. If they did, we celebrate; if they didn't, we think our prayers failed. However, did you know there were Christians in the other party who were praying for their candidates in the same way? Our opinion is often that they were simply wrong or misunderstood the true issues, but I think we are all missing the point if we feel that way. While praying at election times is a good thing, we are making a big mistake if that is the only time we are praying for our government. The truth is, we should actually be praying more between elections than praying *for* them.

God puts prayer for our government leaders at the top of our prayer lists, then prayer for our spiritual leaders, and only then prayer for our families, friends, and loved ones. This overarching approach also helps us love others first as well, making prayer for the common good a priority after seeking God.

Cindy Trimm

JOB CONCERNS
THE "MARTHA SYNDROME"

In millions of homes the only parent is a single female parent who labors outside as well as inside the home. But even in the homes and families in which there are two parents, large numbers of women work outside the home. These women are multitasking themselves to the limit! While most women have a God-given ability to do numerous tasks at the same time, most women in America can relate to having too much to do and too little time, energy, or ability to get it all done. The result is that the next day, the tasks left over from the day before are still there to be done—in addition to the new day's list. And every day the list of undone chores and to-do tasks gets longer and longer.

The story of Lazarus and his two sisters, Mary and Martha, all close friends of Jesus, is a familiar one to most of us. Their home was one where Jesus and His disciples frequently came to visit during their years of ministry. They lived in Bethany, a little town that was near Jerusalem yet far enough away from the hustle and bustle of the big city to be a peaceful respite when Jesus needed to rest.

Hospitality was a trademark of the society in Palestine in that day, and the role of the women of the house was clearly defined: Mary and Martha were the ones who were responsible for serving and attending to the guests in their home. But this was not a task to be taken lightly. In fact, hospitality was so significant in biblical times that one of the qualifications for becoming a minister, according to Paul, was that one must be "hospitable" (1Ti 3:2).

The rules for the treatment of guests were very specific. Throughout the history of many different cultures, guests in the home of a powerful lord could claim protection, sanctuary from pursuers, food, or shelter through the right of hospitality. Moreover, the servants and companions of the traveler and guests also had a claim on the household to share whatever provisions were available.

When all of these cultural and biblical factors are considered, it would not be hard to come to the conclusion that Martha was correct to be the busy sister, hurrying about to see that all of the necessary preparations were on track. I can almost picture Martha, early in the morning, knowing that Jesus was coming, working herself into a frenzy getting the fresh bread baked, the meat dressed for the roasting, the fresh vegetables prepared, the wine, and the fresh fruit, figs, raisins, and dates all arranged on festive platters and in jugs. She would have the foot basins ready to wash the dusty feet of the travelers upon their arrival, as the custom of the day required. She would have made sure there were enough clean straw pallets for each of Jesus' twelve companions who had traveled with Him to rest for the night and that all was ready for the comfort and nourishment of this large crew of hungry men for a visit of several days.

When Jesus and His disciples finally arrived, Martha was still encumbered about many things. But while many are quick to judge Martha for her unwise priorities, it should be noted that her priorities were, in fact, necessary. Those priorities were essential to keep a well-ordered household running smoothly.

Don't women face the same dilemma today? The kids need to get to school. Lunches need to be packed. Projects have to be completed for the science fair. Johnny needs to get to his music lessons, and Janie needs to get to soccer practice. There is a committee meeting for the

PTA, Boy Scouts, and Girl Scouts, but they are all on the same night as choir rehearsal or Bible study. The evaluations for the new employees need to be written. An elderly parent who may be recovering from a stroke needs to be checked on daily. And this does not even include the normal chores that have to be done each day to maintain an active family, even with everyone pitching in, let alone the needed time to be a wife and a person in your own right!

So why did Jesus rebuke Martha? Herein lies the trap: Women are so easily encumbered about many things, most of which are necessary! Taking care of a household is necessary. Caring for a husband and children is necessary. And yes, even jobs outside the home are sometimes necessary. Very few households can operate successfully with only one income in today's economy. Sadly, the reality in America today is that most women need to work outside the home; therefore, women have to multitask. They have to be almost superwomen to meet all of the many necessary demands on their lives.

But as the modern-day Martha falls into bed at the end of the day, she has trouble falling asleep because her mind is already racing over the next day's to-do list, trying to plan how to work "double time" because of what had to be missed from that day. Each day she begins a little further behind, and soon her quiet time with the Lord—the time to meditate on the Word, the time to fellowship with God in prayer, the time to wake up early in the morning to check God's schedule and see what He would have her do that day—is crowded out. Instead of following His pace for her life, she becomes distracted by all that she has to do.

The good news is that this does not have to become a fatal distraction! Martha kept returning to the room where Jesus was seated as He shared His wisdom and teaching with His disciples. Mary, Martha's sister, was sitting quietly at Jesus' feet, drinking in the Master's parables, words, and instructions. She felt the comfort of His presence in an intimate setting where she could ask questions just as the disciples asked and hear Jesus' answers firsthand.

Work and multiple responsibilities can become distractions of the enemy to keep you from focusing on the right priorities. In essence, Jesus told Martha, "Work is good, but keep it in the proper perspective." It should never replace "what is better"—the balance, the love for her Savior—that Mary had chosen.

Woman of God, do the necessary things, but don't become encumbered by them. Don't become a workaholic who leaves her relationship with the Master on the "things to do tomorrow" list.

Instead, "seek first the kingdom of God and His righteousness, and all these things shall be given to you" (Mt 6:33). In other words, you can have it all, as long as your priorities are straight. Feed your soul first. Feed your inner person first. Feed your relationship with God first. Talk to God first about the order of your day. Let Him order your steps and set your schedule. Your days will be more profitable to Him as well as yourself. You don't have to let your distraction of busyness become the fatal distraction of missing God's business for your life.

Joyce Rodgers

7 For this I was appointed a preacher and an
apostle (I speak the truth in Christ and do not
lie), a teacher of the Gentiles in faith and truth.
8 Therefore I desire that the men pray every-
where, lifting up holy hands, without wrath
or contentiousness. 9 In like manner also, that
women clothe themselves in modest clothing,
with decency and self-control, not with braided
hair, gold, pearls, or expensive clothing, 10 but
with good works, which is proper for women
professing godliness.
11 Let a woman learn in silence with all
obedience. 12 I do not permit a woman to
teach or to usurp authority over a man, but
to be silent. 13 For Adam was formed first,
then Eve. 14 And Adam was not deceived,
but the woman, being deceived, fell into sin.
15 Yet she will be saved in childbearing if
they continue in faith, love, and holiness,
with self-control.

Qualifications of Overseers

3 This is a faithful saying: If a man desires
the office of an overseer, he desires a good
work. 2 An overseer then must be blameless,
the husband of one wife, sober, self-controlled,
respectable, hospitable, able to teach; 3 not giv-
en to drunkenness, not violent, not greedy for
money, but patient, not argumentative, not
covetous; 4 and one who manages his own
house well, having his children in submission
with all reverence. 5 For if a man does not
know how to manage his own house, how will
he take care of the church of God? 6 He must
not be newly converted, so that he does not be-
come prideful and fall into the condemnation
of the devil. 7 Moreover he must have a good
reputation among those who are outsiders,
so that he does not fall into reproach and the
snare of the devil.

Qualifications of Deacons

8 Likewise deacons must be serious, not in-
sincere, not given to much wine, not greedy,
9 keeping the mystery of the faith in a pure
conscience. 10 And let them first be tested;
then, being found blameless, let them serve
as deacons.
11 Likewise, their wives must be serious, not
slanderers, sober, and faithful in all things.
12 Let the deacons be the husbands of one
wife, managing their children and their own
houses well. 13 For those who have served well
in the office of deacon purchase for themselves
good standing and great boldness in the faith,
which is in Christ Jesus.

The Mystery of Our Religion

14 I am writing these things to you, hoping to
come to you shortly, 15 but if I am delayed, you
might know how you ought to conduct your-
self in the house of God, which is the church
of the living God, the pillar and foundation
of the truth. 16 Without question, great is the
mystery of godliness:

God was revealed in the flesh,
  justified in the Spirit,
seen by angels,
  preached to the Gentiles,
believed on in the world,
  taken up into glory.

Prediction of Apostasy

4 Now the Spirit clearly says that in the last
times some will depart from the faith and
pay attention to seducing spirits and doctrines
of devils, 2 speaking lies in hypocrisy, having
their consciences seared with a hot iron, 3 for-
bidding to marry, and commanding to abstain
from foods, which God has created to be re-
ceived with thanksgiving by those who believe
and know the truth. 4 For everything created
by God is good, and not to be refused if it is
received with thanksgiving, 5 for it is sanctified
by the word of God and prayer.

Father, help me to discern the spirit of error and the spirit of truth (1Ti 4:1–2).

A Good Minister of Christ Jesus

6 If you remind the brothers of these things,
you will be a good minister of Jesus Christ,
nourished by the words of faith and of good
doctrine, which you have followed closely.
7 But refuse profane and foolish myths. In-
stead, exercise in the ways of godliness. 8 For
bodily exercise profits a little, but godliness
is profitable in all things, holding promise for
the present life and also for the life to come.
9 This is a faithful saying and worthy of all ac-
ceptance. 10 For to this end we both labor and
suffer reproach, because we trust in the living
God, who is the Savior of all men, especially
of those who believe.

I have a promise of life now and life that is to come (1Ti 4:8).

11 Command and teach these things. 12 Let no
one despise your youth, but be an example to
the believers in speech, in conduct, in love, in
spirit, in faith, and in purity. 13 Until I come,
give attention to reading, exhortation, and doc-
trine. 14 Do not neglect the gift that is in you,
which was given to you by prophecy, with the
laying on of hands by the elders.

2:7 Ac 9:15
2:8 Ps 134:2
2:12 1Co 14:34
2:13 Ge 2:22
2:14 Ge 3:6
2:15 1Ti 1:14
3:1 Ac 20:28
3:2 1Ti 5:9
3:3 Titus 1:7
3:4 1Ti 3:12
3:5 1Ti 3:15
3:6 1Ti 6:4
3:7 2Ti 2:26
3:8 Php 1:1
3:9 1Ti 1:19
3:10 1Ti 5:22
3:11 Titus 2:3
3:12 1Ti 3:2
3:13 Mt 25:21
3:16 Jn 1:14
4:1 Jn 16:13
4:2 Eph 4:19
4:3 Ro 14:6
4:6 1Ti 1:10
4:7 1Ti 1:4
4:8 Mt 6:33
4:9 1Ti 1:15
4:10 1Ti 2:4
4:11 1Ti 6:2
4:12 2Ti 2:22
4:14 2Ti 1:6

15 Meditate on these things. Give yourself completely to them, that your progress may be known to everyone. 16 Take heed to yourself and to the doctrine. Continue in them, for in doing this you will save both yourself and those who hear you.

Duties Toward Others

5 Do not rebuke an elder, but exhort him as a father, the younger men as brothers, 2 the elder women as mothers, and the younger women as sisters, with complete purity.

3 Honor widows that are widows indeed. 4 But if any widow has children or grandchildren, let them learn first to show piety at home and to repay their parents. For this is good and acceptable before God. 5 Now she who is a widow indeed, and desolate, trusts in God, and continues in supplications and prayers night and day. 6 But she who lives in pleasure is dead while she lives. 7 And these things command, that they may be blameless. 8 But if any do not care for their own, and especially for those of their own house, they have denied the faith and are worse than unbelievers.

9 Do not let a widow be counted unless she is over sixty years old, has been the wife of one man, 10 is well attested in good works, if she has brought up children, has lodged strangers, has washed the saints' feet, has relieved the afflicted, and has diligently followed every good work.

11 But refuse the younger widows, for when their sensual desires have drawn them away from Christ, they want to marry, 12 and bring judgment on themselves, because they have cast off their first pledge. 13 Besides that, they learn to be idle, and not only idle, wandering around from house to house, but also gossips and busybodies, saying what they ought not. 14 Therefore I desire that the younger women marry, bear children, manage the house, and give no occasion to the adversary to speak reproachfully. 15 For some have already turned aside after Satan.

16 If any believing man or woman has widows, let those assist them. Do not let the church be charged, so that it may relieve those who are widows indeed.

17 Let the elders who rule well be counted worthy of double honor, especially those who labor in the word and doctrine. 18 For the Scripture says, "You shall not muzzle the ox that treads out the grain,"[1] and, "The laborer is worthy of his reward."[2] 19 Do not receive an accusation against an elder, except before two or three witnesses. 20 Rebuke in the presence of everyone those who sin, that the rest also may fear. 21 I command you before God and the Lord Jesus Christ and the elect angels that you observe these things without prejudice, doing nothing by partiality.

22 Do not lay hands suddenly on anyone, and do not partake of other men's sins. Keep yourself pure.

23 No longer drink only water, but use a little wine for your stomach's sake and your frequent illnesses.

24 Some men's sins are evident, pointing to judgment, but other men's sins are revealed later. 25 Likewise, the good works of some are evident, but those that are not cannot be hidden.

6 Let as many servants as are under the yoke of slavery count their own masters worthy of all honor, so that the name of God and His doctrine may not be slandered. 2 Let those who have believing masters not despise them, because they are brothers. Instead, let them serve as slaves, because those who receive their service are faithful and beloved.

False Teaching and True Wealth

Teach and command these things. 3 Anyone who teaches otherwise and does not consent to wholesome words, to the words of our Lord Jesus Christ, and to godly doctrine 4 is conceited and knows nothing. He has a morbid disposition for controversy and verbal disputes, from which come envy, strife, blasphemies, evil speculations, 5 constant disputes by men of corrupt minds, being destitute of the truth, and supposing that financial gain is godliness. Withdraw yourself from such men.

6 But godliness with contentment is great gain. 7 For we brought nothing into this world, and it is certain that we can carry nothing out. 8 If we have food and clothing, we shall be content with these things. 9 But those who desire to be rich fall into temptation and a snare and into many foolish and harmful lusts, which drown men in ruin and destruction. 10 For the love of money is the root of all evil. While coveting after money, some have strayed from the faith and pierced themselves through with many sorrows.

The Good Fight of Faith

11 But you, O man of God, escape these things, and follow after righteousness, godliness, faith, love, patience, and gentleness. 12 Fight the good fight of faith. Lay hold on eternal life, to which you are called and have

4:16 Titus 2:7
5:1 Lev 19:32
5:4 1Ti 2:3
5:5 Lk 2:37
5:6 Lk 15:24
5:7 1Ti 4:11
5:8 Titus 1:16
5:9 1Ti 3:2
5:10 1Ti 6:18
5:11 1Ti 5:14
5:14 Titus 2:5
5:16 1Ti 5:3–5
5:17 Ro 12:8
5:18 Dt 25:4
5:19 Dt 19:15
5:20 Dt 13:11
5:21 1Ti 6:13
5:22 Ac 6:6
5:23 1Ti 3:8
6:1 Titus 2:5
6:2 1Ti 4:11
6:3 1Ti 1:3
6:4 1Ti 1:4
6:5 2Ti 3:8
6:6 1Ti 4:8
6:7 Job 1:21
6:8 Ge 28:20
6:9 Pr 15:27
6:10 Dt 16:19
6:11 2Ti 2:22
6:12 1Ti 1:18

[1] *18* Dt 25:4. [2] *18* Lk 10:7.

I believe God has equipped me with every good thing I will ever need (1Ti 6:11–12).

SPIRIT-TO-SPIRIT PRAYER

Prayer for Inner Healing for Children and Teenagers

Lord, we invite Your presence to come and touch [child's name]. *Bring Your love. Cause* [child's name] *to come to a place of forgiving those who have brought harm and pain.*

Lead the child through a time of forgiving. Use language that is age appropriate. Have the child say this prayer:

Lord, forgive me for being mad. I choose to not be mad at or want to make bad things happen to [name of the abuser].

Once this has been completed, then pray the following prayer over the child:

Lord, we thank You for the prayer that [child's name] *just prayed. We are happy that You have forgiven him/her. We break all negative thoughts and lies the enemy has placed in* [child's name]*'s mind, in Jesus' name. We renounce and break all activity and embracing of a victim spirit. You must go now, in Jesus' name. All shame, guilt, condemnation, and fear, we break your power and command you to go. All perversion and lust that were in operation in the horrible act of abuse, we renounce you and command you to go.*

Spirits of darkness, I break all unholy soul ties between [child's name] *and* [say the name of each abuser aloud]. *We cancel all sexual transference in the powerful name of Jesus. I cancel any control and manipulation between* [child's name] *and* [say the name of each abuser]. *I renounce and break all ungodly soul ties between the abusers and* [child's name] *through vows, ceremonies, rituals, secrets, contracts, or demonic alliances. I break the demonic cycle of abuse and say they are no longer welcome. All ties to the demonic realm are broken now. I cut the unfruitful root of darkness off of* [child's name]. *Your hold is over, in Jesus' name!*

Lord, we invite Your healing presence and love. Every place where [child's name] *has felt abused, victimized, depressed, fearful, and deserving of unjust treatment, I ask that You fill him/her with acceptance, love, boldness, courage, happiness, joy, excitement, and expectancy of all the great things You have for him/her ahead. Help him/her, Lord, to focus on Your thoughts toward him/her, and empower him/her to walk in a renewed mind.* [Child's name] *chooses to stand on the truth that he/she is more than a conqueror in Christ and that he/she is fearfully and wonderfully made. We say* [child's name] *is loved with Your Father's heart and is walking in the peace, comfort, and security of this love from this day forward. In Jesus' name, amen.*

Rebecca Greenwood

professed a good profession before many
witnesses. [13] I command you, in the sight of
God, who gives life to all things, and in the
sight of Christ Jesus, who testified a good con-
fession before Pontius Pilate, [14] to keep this
commandment without blemish, blameless
until the appearing of our Lord Jesus Christ,
[15] which He, who is the blessed and only Ruler,
the King of kings and Lord of lords, will reveal
at the proper time. [16] He alone has immortality,
living in unapproachable light, whom no one
has seen, nor can see. To Him be honor and
everlasting power. Amen.

6:13 1Ti 5:21
6:15 1Ti 1:11
6:16 1Ti 1:17

6:17 Ro 11:20
6:18 Ro 12:8
6:19 Lk 16:9
6:21 2Ti 2:18

[17] Command those who are rich in this world
that they not be conceited, nor trust in uncertain
riches, but in the living God, who richly gives
us all things to enjoy. [18] Command that they do
good, that they be rich in good works, gener-
ous, willing to share, [19] and laying up in store for
themselves a good foundation for the coming
age, so that they may take hold of eternal life.
[20] O Timothy, guard that which is committed to
your trust. Avoid profane babblings and oppos-
ing views from so-called knowledge. [21] By pro-
fessing it, some have erred concerning the faith.
Grace be with you. Amen.

Author: The apostle Paul

Written: AD 64 or 65, from Rome

Theme: Spiritual Mentorship of Paul to Timothy

2 TIMOTHY

Dear SpiritLed Woman,

Fear is one of the devil's favorite weapons to launch at you. It is the atmosphere of his realm, just as faith is the atmosphere of God. Fear causes you to stop thinking about what God has for your future and to focus on mere survival. You live in and for the natural. When you focus on what you fear, you block out God's plans and purposes for your life.

I love Paul's second letter to Timothy because he states a powerful truth: "God has not given us the spirit of fear" (2Ti 1:7). Fear is demonic and is based on a lie. If you agree with the lie, it is easy to fall prey to discouragement, which steals your faith, depresses your spirit, takes your strength, and ultimately causes you to miss the plan God has for your life. That, of course, is the enemy's ultimate goal.

If you have become captive to fear or discouragement, ask God to forgive you for listening to the lie of the enemy. Though He has promised to accomplish His plan through you, you have to do your part. Choose to believe His promises without fear and trust Him to act.

Joy F. Strang

Salutation

1 Paul, an apostle of Jesus Christ by the will of God, according to the promise of life which is in Christ Jesus,

2 To Timothy, my beloved son:

Grace, mercy, and peace, from God the Father and Christ Jesus our Lord.

Loyalty to the Gospel

3 I thank God, whom I serve with a pure conscience as my forefathers did, as I continually remember you in my prayers night and day, 4 greatly desiring to see you, remembering your tears, that I may be filled with joy, 5 remembering the genuine faith that first lived in your grandmother Lois and your mother Eunice and that I am persuaded lives in you also.

6 Therefore I remind you to stir up the gift of God, which is in you by the laying on of my hands. 7 For God has not given us the spirit of fear, but of power, and love, and self-control.

I do not have a spirit of fear but of God's power through the Holy Spirit and His love (2Ti 1:7).

8 So do not be ashamed of the testimony of our Lord, nor of me, His prisoner. But share in the sufferings of the gospel by the power of God, 9 who has saved us and called us with a holy calling, not by our works, but by His own purpose and grace, which was given us in Christ Jesus before the world began, 10 but is

I have been called to live a godly life, be a witness, grow up spiritually, walk in love with my brothers and sisters, and produce the fruit of the Spirit (2Ti 1:9).

now revealed by the appearing of our Savior, Jesus Christ, who has abolished death and has brought life and immortality to light through the gospel, 11 for which I was appointed a preacher, an apostle, and a teacher of the Gentiles. 12 For these things I suffer, but I am not ashamed, for I know whom I have believed, and am persuaded that He is able to keep that which I have committed to Him until that Day.

My Savior has abolished death and brought life (2Ti 1:10–11).

13 Follow the pattern of sound teaching which you have heard from me in the faith and love that is in Christ Jesus. 14 Guard the

1:1 2Co 1:1
1:2 1Ti 1:2
1:3 Ro 1:8–9
1:4 2Ti 4:9
1:5 Ac 16:1
1:6 1Ti 4:14
1:7 Ro 8:15
1:8 Mk 8:38
1:9 Ro 16:25
1:10 Ro 2:7
1:11 1Ti 2:7
1:12 2Ti 1:8
1:13 1Ti 1:14

....

1:15 2Ti 4:16
1:16 2Ti 4:19
1:18 2Ti 1:12
2:1 Eph 6:10
2:2 1Ti 1:18
2:3 1Ti 1:18
2:4 2Pe 2:20
2:8 Mt 1:1
2:9 Php 1:7
2:10 Col 1:24
2:11 Ro 6:8
2:12 Mt 10:33
2:13 Nu 23:19
2:14 1Ti 5:21
2:15 Mt 13:52
2:16 Titus 3:9

treasure that was committed to you through the Holy Spirit who lives in us.

15 You know that all those who are in Asia have turned away from me, including Phygelus and Hermogenes.

16 May the Lord grant mercy to the house of Onesiphorus, for he often refreshed me and was not ashamed of my chains. 17 But when he arrived in Rome, he searched me out very diligently and found me. 18 May the Lord grant that he may find mercy from the Lord on that Day. You know very well how many ways he ministered to me at Ephesus.

A Good Soldier of Christ Jesus

2 So you, my son, be strong in the grace that is in Christ Jesus. 2 Share the things that you have heard from me in the presence of many witnesses with faithful men who will be able to teach others also. 3 Endure hard times as a good soldier of Jesus Christ. 4 No soldier on active duty entangles himself with civilian affairs, that he may please the enlisting officer. 5 Anyone who competes as an athlete is not rewarded without competing legally. 6 The farmer who labors should be first to partake of the crops. 7 Consider what I am saying, and may the Lord grant you understanding in all things.

8 Remember Jesus Christ, raised from the dead, descended from David, according to my gospel, 9 in which I suffer trouble like a criminal, even with chains. But the word of God is not bound. 10 Therefore I endure all things for the sake of the elect, that they also may obtain the salvation which is in Christ Jesus with eternal glory.

11 This is a faithful saying:

If we die with Him,
we shall also live with Him.
12 If we endure,
we shall also reign with Him.
If we deny Him,
He also will deny us.
13 If we are faithless,
He remains faithful;
He cannot deny Himself.

God will not turn His back or walk away (2Ti 2:13).

An Approved Workman

14 Remind them of these things, commanding them before the Lord that they not argue about words, which leads to nothing of value and to the destruction of those who hear them. 15 Study to show yourself approved by God, a workman who need not be ashamed, rightly dividing the word of truth. 16 But avoid profane

Taking Your Stand

When soldiers and warriors are taught to fight, whether it be martial arts, boxing, or how to shoot a gun, one of the first things they are taught is how to stand. The proper stance is crucial to keeping your balance in an attack as well as supporting the power of your strikes against your enemy. If you have ever watched a sumo wrestling match, you will notice that most of the battle is about the preparation of the stance—the fight itself is relatively short. The one with the most solid stance is always the winner; the one thrown off-balance always loses.

The same principle applies in the spiritual realm and in prayer.

Courage is the resolve to do something or become something in spite of fear, hardship, obstacles, and opposition. Courage allows you to accept your fear, embrace it as a legitimate emotion, and use it as fuel to accomplish specific goals. Fear is an irrational emotion that accompanies you as you move from the familiarity of your comfort zone into new and unknown territories. Ambrose Redmoon said, "Courage is not the absence of fear, but rather the judgment that something else is more important than fear."

The courage that overcomes all fear is the courage that is born of God, who placed a divine overcoming, courageous gene within you by His Spirit. He has not given you the spirit of fear (2Ti 1:7). Look deeply within, and you will find the courage to step forward and take a stand.

The Bible tells us in 1 John 4:4, "You are of God...and have overcome them, because He who is in you is greater than he who is in the world." This is manifested when you develop a healthy, realistic perspective of who you are in God and when you realize what He has wired you to do and to become.

Many people have become slaves to unfounded fear. Unfounded fear is a peculiar state of disease within the imagination, arising largely from a lack of knowledge. The Bible states that we perish because we lack knowledge (Hos 4:6). I believe that not only do we dwindle away and die carrying seeds of greatness, unrealized potential, unpublished best sellers, unsung melodies, undiscovered medical breakthroughs, unfinished groundbreaking theories and philosophies, unmanifested multibillion-dollar inventions, and unestablished global businesses with us to the grave, but also our lack of knowledge causes divine opportunities and strategic relationships to die along with them.

When you become a slave to unfounded fear, you also become a slave to faulty beliefs, nonproductive behaviors, self-defeating paradigms, maladaptive practices, and ineffective and inappropriate responses that are inconsistent with your desire for well-being, success, and prosperity. So it is a matter of necessity that you understand the importance of courage and the benefits associated with its application to all facets of your life.

Cindy Trimm

foolish babblings, for they will increase to more ungodliness, 17 and their word will spread like gangrene: Among them are Hymenaeus and Philetus, 18 who have erred concerning the truth, saying that the resurrection has already occurred, and who overthrow the faith of some. 19 But the firm foundation of God stands, having this seal, "The Lord knows those who are His," and, "Let everyone who calls on the name of Christ depart from iniquity."

20 In a large house there are not only gold and silver vessels, but also those of wood and clay; some are for honor, and some for dishonor. 21 One who cleanses himself from these things will be a vessel for honor, sanctified, fit for the Master's use, and prepared for every good work.

22 So flee youthful desires and pursue righteousness, faith, love, and peace, with those who call on the Lord out of a pure heart. 23 But avoid foolish and unlearned debates, knowing that they create strife. 24 The servant of the Lord must not quarrel, but must be gentle toward all people, able to teach, patient, 25 in gentleness instructing those in opposition. Perhaps God will grant them repentance to know the truth, 26 and they may escape from the snare of the devil, after being captured by him to do his will.

The Last Days

3 Know this: In the last days perilous times will come. 2 Men will be lovers of themselves, lovers of money, boastful, proud, blasphemers, disobedient to parents, unthankful, unholy, 3 without natural affection, trucebreakers, slanderers, unrestrained, fierce, despisers of those who are good, 4 traitors, reckless, conceited, lovers of pleasures more than lovers of God, 5 having a form of godliness, but denying its power. Turn away from such people.

6 Those of this nature creep into houses and captivate silly women who are burdened with sins and led away with various desires, 7 always learning, but never able to come to the knowledge of the truth. 8 Now as Jannes and Jambres resisted Moses, so these also resist the truth, men of corrupt minds and worthless concerning the faith. 9 But they shall proceed no further, for their folly will be revealed to everyone, as theirs also was.

Last Charge to Timothy

10 But you have observed my doctrine, manner of life, purpose, faith, tolerance, love, patience, 11 persecutions, and afflictions, which came to me at Antioch, Iconium, and Lystra—what persecutions I endured! But the Lord delivered me out of them all. 12 Yes, and all who desire to live a godly life in Christ Jesus will suffer persecution. 13 But evil men and seducers will grow worse

2:17 1Ti 1:20
2:18 1Co 15:12
2:19 Jn 10:14
2:20 1Ti 3:15
2:21 2Ti 3:17
2:22 1Ti 6:11
2:23 Titus 3:9
2:24 1Ti 3:2–3
2:25 1Ti 2:4
2:26 1Ti 3:7
3:2 Php 2:21
3:3 Ro 1:31
3:4 1Ti 3:6
3:5 1Ti 5:8
3:6 Titus 3:3
3:8 Ex 7:11
3:9 Ex 7:12
3:10 Php 2:22
3:11 Ps 34:19
3:12 Ac 14:22
....
3:14 2Ti 1:13
3:15 2Ti 1:5
3:16 Ro 15:4
3:17 1Ti 6:11
4:1 Ac 10:42
4:2 Titus 1:13
4:3 1Ti 1:10
4:4 1Ti 1:4
4:5 Ac 21:8
4:6 Php 1:23
4:7 Ac 20:24

COUNSEL FROM THE SPIRIT BASICS

SPIRITLED WOMAN

Our Remarkable God

God is remarkable. Even if you're mad at Him, He won't give up on you. He won't turn His back or walk away.

Hebrews 10:23 says, "Let us firmly hold the profession of our faith without wavering, for He who promised is faithful." Rest assured, God is faithful. Even when something bad has happened and you have questions, He is faithful to His promises. He'll never let you go. You can hold fast to that.

Karen Jensen Salisbury

and worse, deceiving and being deceived. 14 But continue in the things that you have learned and have been assured of, knowing those from whom you have learned them, 15 and that since childhood you have known the Holy Scriptures, which are able to make you wise unto salvation through the faith that is in Christ Jesus. 16 All Scripture is inspired by God and is profitable for teaching, for reproof, for correction, and for instruction in righteousness, 17 that the man of God may be complete, thoroughly equipped for every good work.

I am complete and thoroughly equipped for every good work (2Ti 3:17).

4 I charge you therefore before God and the Lord Jesus Christ, who will judge the living and the dead at His appearing and His kingdom: 2 Preach the word, be ready in season and out of season, reprove, rebuke, and exhort, with all patience and teaching. 3 For the time will come when people will not endure sound doctrine, but they will gather to themselves teachers in accordance with their own desires, having itching ears, 4 and they will turn their ears away from the truth and turn to myths. 5 But be self-controlled in all things, endure afflictions, do the work of an evangelist, and prove your ministry.

6 For I am already being poured out as a drink offering, and the time of my departure has come. 7 I have fought a good fight, I have

The Life of God's Soldier

I have fought a good fight, I have finished my course, and I have kept the faith.

—2 Timothy 4:7

As women, we are drawn more often to biblical analogies that compare the woman of God to a daughter of the King, a beautiful rose, a delicately woven tapestry, or an artfully crafted piece of pottery. But the Bible gives us another analogy that women can use to determine to grow in their relationship with Christ, and it is the life of God's soldier. From this analogy we learn the characteristics of a good soldier, the requirements and obligations of a good soldier, and the benefits and rewards for being a good soldier.

These are all foundational principles. It will be important for you to remember that a foundation is just that—the foundation of something bigger. There are important qualities you must add to your foundation of spiritual core values. This study will introduce you to the key qualities you must commit to develop in your spirit as you grow in your commitment to God's army.

The list below will introduce each of these qualities to you, defining how each one applies to the soldier of Christ. Look up each of the scriptures listed, and describe how you can continue to develop each quality in your life to enable you to excel as a soldier in God's army.

1. *Determination*—firmness in purpose because of a resolve in Christ

Read: Ruth 1:18

I will continue developing this quality in my life by:

2. *Backbone*—the ability to stand under the greatest persecution and pressure

Read: Ephesians 6:13

I will continue developing this quality in my life by:

3. *High morale*—being in high praise and having the spirit of a cheerleader to encourage yourself and others in the Lord

Read: Acts 11:23

I will continue developing this quality in my life by:

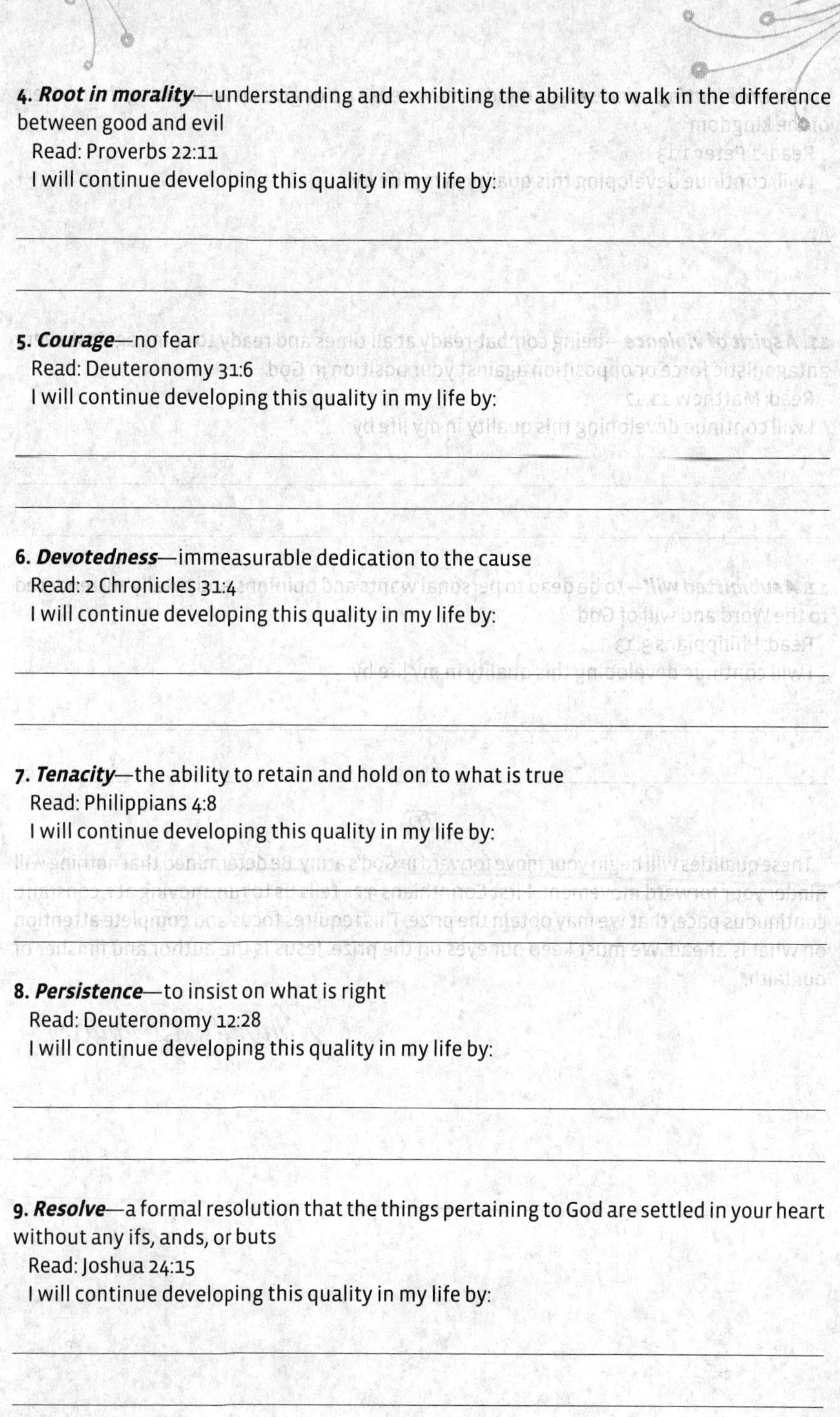

4. ***Root in morality***—understanding and exhibiting the ability to walk in the difference between good and evil

Read: Proverbs 22:11

I will continue developing this quality in my life by:

5. ***Courage***—no fear

Read: Deuteronomy 31:6

I will continue developing this quality in my life by:

6. ***Devotedness***—immeasurable dedication to the cause

Read: 2 Chronicles 31:4

I will continue developing this quality in my life by:

7. ***Tenacity***—the ability to retain and hold on to what is true

Read: Philippians 4:8

I will continue developing this quality in my life by:

8. ***Persistence***—to insist on what is right

Read: Deuteronomy 12:28

I will continue developing this quality in my life by:

9. ***Resolve***—a formal resolution that the things pertaining to God are settled in your heart without any ifs, ands, or buts

Read: Joshua 24:15

I will continue developing this quality in my life by:

10. *An unrelenting mind-set*—a mind to never ease up or give up concerning the matters of the kingdom

Read: 1 Peter 1:13

I will continue developing this quality in my life by:

11. *A spirit of violence*—being combat-ready at all times and ready to come against every antagonistic force or opposition against your position in God

Read: Matthew 11:12

I will continue developing this quality in my life by:

12. *A submitted will*—to be dead to personal wants and opinions and totally surrendered to the Word and will of God

Read: Philippians 3:13

I will continue developing this quality in my life by:

These qualities will begin your move forward in God's army. Be determined that nothing will hinder your forward movement. First Corinthians 9:24 tells us to run, moving at a constant, continuous pace, that we may obtain the prize. This requires focus and complete attention on what is ahead. We must keep our eyes on the prize. Jesus is the author and finisher of our faith.

Kimberly Daniels

finished my course, and I have kept the faith. 8 From now on a crown of righteousness is laid up for me, which the Lord, the righteous Judge, will give me on that Day, and not only to me but also to all who have loved His appearing.

Personal Instructions

9 Diligently try to come to me soon. 10 Demas has forsaken me, having loved this present world, and has departed to Thessalonica, Crescens to Galatia, and Titus to Dalmatia. 11 Only Luke is with me. Get Mark, and bring him with you, for he is profitable to me for the ministry. 12 I sent Tychicus to Ephesus. 13 When you come, bring with you the cloak that I left at Troas with Carpus, and the books, but especially the parchments.

14 Alexander the coppersmith did me much evil. May the Lord reward him according to his works. 15 Beware of him, for he has greatly opposed our words.

4:8 Col 1:5
4:9 2Ti 1:4
4:10 Ac 16:6
4:11 Ac 12:12
4:12 Ac 20:4
4:13 Ac 16:8
4:14 1Ti 1:20

....

4:16 Ac 7:60
4:17 Ac 9:15
4:18 Ro 11:36
4:19 Ac 18:2
4:20 Ac 20:4
4:21 2Ti 4:9
4:22 Gal 6:18

16 At my first defense no one stood with me, but everyone forsook me. May it not be charged against them. 17 But the Lord stood with me and strengthened me, so that through me the preaching might be fully known, and that all the Gentiles might hear. And I was delivered out of the mouth of the lion. 18 The Lord will deliver me from every evil work and will preserve me for His heavenly kingdom, to whom be glory forever and ever. Amen.

Final Greetings

19 Greet Priscilla and Aquila and the household of Onesiphorus. 20 Erastus remained at Corinth, and I have left Trophimus ill in Miletus. 21 Diligently try to come before winter. Eubulus greets you, and so do Pudens, Linus, Claudia, and all the brothers.

22 The Lord Jesus Christ be with your spirit. Grace be with you. Amen.

Author: The apostle Paul

Written: Early AD 60s, from Macedonia

Themes: Church Order, Link Between Belief and Behavior

TITUS

Dear Spirit Led Woman,

In the second chapter of his letter to Titus, Paul reminds us that as we mature in our relationship with God, we are to train up younger women in the faith. I never wanted to be a spiritual mother—except to my two sons—but God placed me in this role. It shouldn't have been a surprise, since I regularly asked Him to use me for His purposes, and He desires to grow the body of Christ to maturity. Simply following His lead brought me to a place of nurturing and training others.

God prepared me for the task of training others through my role as a mother. I found that the things I did to bring my sons to maturity became a pattern for mentoring those God brought into my life to develop spiritually.

But you don't have to be a parent in the natural to be a spiritual parent. Paul had no natural children, yet he was the greatest example in the New Testament of a spiritual father. The victories and defeats you have experienced have prepared you to help someone else mature. Don't keep the lessons you've learned to yourself. Pass them on!

Joy F. Strang

Salutation

1 Paul, a servant of God and an apostle
of Jesus Christ, according to the faith of
God's elect and the knowledge of the truth
which leads to godliness, 2 in hope of eternal
life which God, who cannot lie, promised be-
fore the world began, 3 and has in due time
revealed His word through preaching, with
which I was entrusted according to the com-
mand of God our Savior,

4 To Titus, my own son in the common faith:

Grace, mercy, and peace, from God the Fa-
ther and the Lord Jesus Christ our Savior.

Titus' Work in Crete

5 For this reason I left you in Crete, that you
should set in order the things that are lacking,
and appoint elders in every city, as I command-
ed you: 6 any man who is blameless, the hus-
band of one wife, having faithful children who
are not accused of being wild or unruly. 7 For
an overseer must be blameless, as a steward
of God, not self-willed, not easily angered, not
given to drunkenness, not violent, not greedy
for dishonest gain, 8 but hospitable, a lover of
what is good, self-controlled, just, holy, tem-
perate, 9 holding firmly the trustworthy word
that is in accordance with the teaching, that he
may be able both to exhort with sound doctrine
and to convince those who oppose it.

10 For there are many unruly men, empty
talkers and deceivers, especially those of the
circumcision, 11 who must be silenced, who
subvert whole houses by teaching for dishon-
est gain things they ought not teach. 12 One
of them, a prophet of their own, said, "The
Cretans are always liars, evil beasts, and idle
gluttons!" 13 This witness is true. So rebuke
them sharply that they may be sound in the
faith, 14 not paying attention to Jewish myths
and commandments of men who reject the
truth. 15 To the pure, all things are pure. But to
those who are defiled and unbelieving, noth-
ing is pure. Even their minds and conscienc-
es are defiled. 16 They profess that they know
God, but in their deeds they deny Him, being
abominable, disobedient, and worthless for
every good work.

The Teaching of Sound Doctrine

2 But as for you, teach what is fitting of
sound doctrine: 2 Older men should be
sober, serious, temperate, sound in faith, in
love, in patience.

3 Likewise, older women should be reverent
in behavior, and not be false accusers, not be
enslaved to much wine, but teachers of good
things, 4 that they may teach the young women
to love their husbands, to love their children,

1:1 Ro 1:1
1:2 2Ti 1:1
1:3 1Ti 1:1
1:4 2Ti 1:2
1:5 Ac 14:23
1:7 Lk 12:42
1:8 1Ti 3:2
1:9 1Ti 1:10
1:10 1Ti 1:6
1:11 2Ti 3:6
1:12 Ac 17:28
1:13 2Co 13:10
1:14 Col 2:22
1:15 Ro 14:20
2:1 1Ti 1:10
2:2 1Ti 3:11
2:3 1Ti 3:8
2:4 1Ti 5:14

....

2:5 1Ti 6:1
2:6 1Ti 5:1
2:7 1Ti 4:12
2:8 1Pe 2:12
2:10 Mt 5:16
2:11 1Ti 2:4
2:12 Lk 1:75
2:13 2Ti 4:8

COUNSEL FROM THE SPIRIT BASICS

SPIRITLED WOMAN

Stay on the Path

You cannot live a successful Christian life and stay in the anointing unless you stay on the path of what God has ordained for His church. The truth of the matter is this: I need you, and you need me. You will not get a television to hug you back, I don't care how many times you place your hand on it or on a computer screen. You need to be under the umbrella of a pastor—a man or woman of God who will love you, protect you, encourage you, and visit you if you or your loved ones are in need. Romans 10:17 says, "So then faith comes by hearing, and hearing by the word of God." Receiving an anointed word from a man or woman of God is just how God set things up.

We must stay on God's path to walk consistently in the anointing. Now is the time to "live soberly, righteously, and in godliness in this present world" (Titus 2:12). Hebrews 13:18 encourages us to "live honestly." Peter said, "Live according to God in the spirit" (1Pe 4:6), which means living with eternal life in view.

Judy Jacobs

5 and to be self-controlled, pure, homemakers,
good, obedient to their own husbands, that the
word of God may not be dishonored.

6 Likewise, exhort young men to be self-con-
trolled, 7 in all things presenting yourself as an
example of good works: in doctrine showing
integrity, gravity, incorruptibility, 8 and sound
speech that cannot be condemned, so that the
one who opposes you may be ashamed, hav-
ing nothing evil to say of you.

9 Exhort servants to be obedient to their own
masters, to please them well in everything, not
answering back, 10 or stealing, but showing
complete fidelity, so that they may exemplify
the doctrine of God our Savior in all things.

11 For the grace of God that brings salvation
has appeared to all men, 12 teaching us that,
denying ungodliness and worldly desires, we
should live soberly, righteously, and in godli-
ness in this present world, 13 as we await the
blessed hope and the appearing of the glory of

Five Facts About Faith

What does it mean to live by faith? Why does it please God so greatly? Living by faith is when you know the next "what" on your eternal calendar but not the "how," "when," or "where." It is a great adventure that connects you an invisible realm of provision. Do you remember when the disciples were rowing the boat and Jesus walked on the water to them?

When the invitation came, only Peter climbed out of the boat. Wanting to be in Christ's presence, he left eleven "experts" in the boat, committed to their routine of rowing. I would caution here: Be steadfast in your routines until Jesus invites you to do otherwise. But if you want to please God and walk by faith and not by sight, sooner or later you will have to get out of the boat.

When the invitation came, only faith is agreeing with God and acting on His Word. Although many say they agree with God about an issue, they are just giving mental assent. Assent admires but doesn't act. Others act a certain way, but it is only behavior modification. They confess a certain scripture, but do they *believe?* Faith is *agreeing* with God and *acting* on His Word. Here are five facts that describe real Bible faith.

Fact #1: Faith is a law.

Motorists everywhere understand that if a streetlight turns red, they must stop. You don't even need to feel a peace in your spirit or goose bumps on your arms. If you obey the law, the police will honor you. If you don't, you will suffer the consequences.

The definition of a law is a binding rule of conduct or action, one formally recognized as binding. It is enforced by a controlling authority. The government licenses you to use its roads and will enforce that right—as long as you obey its laws. Faith is a law that entitles you to all of the promises of God. Just as a policeman would enforce the red light law, your Father God enforces His laws of faith.

Fact #2: Faith is a measure.

The typical kitchen contains many different-sized measuring utensils. Yours likely has your favorite scratched-up, three-quart pan that Grandma used, plus a new set of shiny measuring scoops, ranging from one-fourth cup to one cup. I like to stack my little scoopers inside the next larger size.

Likewise, when you accepted Christ, you received a measure or capacity of faith. As you act on God's Word, your one-fourth scoop of faith enlarges to a half scoop.

This is why Jesus said, "According to your faith, let it be done for you" (Mt 9:29). Jesus rebuked the disciples for having no faith in the storm and little faith concerning provision, but He marveled at the Roman centurion's great faith. These are different measures of faith. Believing enlarges yours. And faith pleases God. As Hebrews 11:6 says, "And without faith it is impossible to please God, for he who comes to God must believe that He exists and that He is a rewarder of those who diligently seek Him."

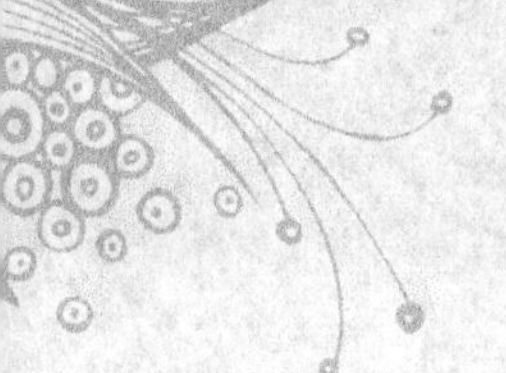

Fact #3: Faith is a muscle.

Imagine a pair of thirty-year-old men smiling at you. One is a tanned bodybuilder; the other looks like a bleached flagpole. One bench-presses five hundred pounds while the other would struggle with the barbell alone. While both have more than six hundred muscles, the difference is that the bodybuilder developed his. Many people don't realize they can develop their faith in the same way a bodybuilder develops his muscles.

Fact #4: Faith is a servant.

Luke contains an interesting story about the role of a servant. Jesus asked His disciples what master—after his servant had plowed a field—would invite him to sit down and eat instead of telling him to prepare the master's supper first. He asked, "Does he thank the servant because he did what was commanded? I think not. So you also, when you have done everything commanded you, say, 'We are unprofitable servants. We have done our duty'" (Lk 17:9–10).

The point is that the master commands the servant. John 1:1 tells us that Jesus, our Master, is the Word. When you speak the Word, your "servant" goes to work to accomplish its assignment. To put it another way, the Word spoke to people, trees, storms, and death, commanding them to obey His voice. When you speak faith-filled words, it is the same as when Jesus spoke them. This is why "with God all things are possible" (Mt 19:26).

Fact #5: Faith is a seed.

The story of the seed and the sower is recorded in all three synoptic Gospels—in Matthew 13, Mark 4, and Luke 8. Repetition alone implies this parable contains a significant message.

The seed is the Word released from our mouths. Isaiah promises that God's Word, described as seed to the sower, will never return empty or be useless (Isa 55:11). The seed has dominion over the soil and makes it bud. When you speak God's Word, you are planting seeds of salvation and abundant life. Just as a gardener waters his plants, speaking and praying God's Word causes His goodness to grow in your life and your loved ones' lives.

Rachel Burchfield

WOMEN ENDURERS

THOSE WHO ENDURED TORTURE, RAPE, AND LOSING FAMILY TO FOLLOW CHRIST

What happens when a woman decides to follow Christ? In the United States it can mean peace, joy, and freedom. In other countries it can mean arrest, torture, rape—even death. Will you allow me to introduce you to some of the women who have endured such things? I warn you that their stories are not pretty. They'll challenge you. They'll make you feel uncomfortable. You may even feel guilty the next time you're in the grocery store.

Anna Kima

Take Anna Kima,[1] for example. I met Anna in Nairobi, Kenya. I flew on a nice comfortable plane to Kenya ("Oh, you're so brave!"), but Anna walked there from war-torn Sudan—with her four children and all their earthly possessions.

"I carried one child on my neck, another on my back, and our luggage on my head," Anna told me. "We walked for three months. All of us were sick with malaria and diarrhea."

Sudan, Anna's homeland, is torn apart by famine and a long-standing civil war that purposely targets Christians, among others. For years the Muslim government of northern Sudan has waged all-out war against Christians and tribal people in the southern part of the country, trying to force them to become Muslims.

Anna was one of the ones who made it out of Sudan rather than being brutally murdered. Today, as a refugee in Kenya, she works with the New Sudan Council of Churches, a ministry that helps people in southern Sudan.

Every Christian woman in southern Sudan has lost a loved one to the war. Like Anna, they are paying the price to follow Jesus.

Lily and Sara

Lily and Sara[2] also live in repressive situations. They pastor a church in Indonesia, the largest Muslim country in the world and one that has been torn apart by war and violence. More than twenty-five hundred people have been killed in Indonesia since early 1999. Most of the dead were Christians.

"[The war has] resulted in murder, rape, persecution, and destruction," Lily says. "There have been many martyrs, including kids. Hundreds of church buildings have been burned to the ground."

Lily and Sara's church went on a forty-day fast and at the same time distributed food to the local poor, regardless of their religious affiliation. When fanatical Islamic mobs went on a rampage against churches, local Muslims remembered how Lily and Sara's church had distributed free food to the poor, so they barricaded the church building, preventing the mob from destroying it. Because of the free food distribution program, "they knew our church,"

1. Not her real name
2. Not their real names

Sara says, "and they protected us in a time of danger."

The women echo a plea that resounds wherever Christians are severely persecuted. "Don't pray that the situation would stop," Sara warns, "but that the churches [in Indonesia] would be strong and able to face this situation. There are many souls coming in right now, and it's very easy to evangelize and win people to the Lord. But many churches are not ready to face this situation [and are not prepared] for the harvest."

Sara and Lily have paid the price to follow Jesus.

Donna Sauñe

Other women I have met stand out in my mind. There's Donna Sauñe, an American who became a missionary to Peru and married a local man well known for his outspoken Christian witness. I met Donna at a memorial service for her husband, who had been brutally murdered by the Shining Path guerrillas. It was the first funeral I ever attended for a martyr, but sadly not the last one.

I'm constantly challenged and inspired by persecuted Christian women such as these—and also by the ones I've never actually met but feel as if I have. There's Zhou Shiu Yon, a Christian woman I interviewed by phone who told me how she had fled China to avoid the abortion the Communist government was trying to force her to have.

Each of these special women represents millions of Christian women all over the world. Anna represents the hundreds of millions of refugees on all continents, women uprooted from their homes and families because of their Christian faith. Lily and Sara represent women in ministry, women who suffer from the devastating effects of repressive governments and false religions. Donna represents the elite circle of women who have paid the ultimate price as wives, mothers, daughters, and sisters of martyrs—and in some cases as martyrs themselves.

Each of these women is real. It's hard for us to imagine the constant terror some of them live with, never knowing if the police, their parents, or their own husbands or children will turn them in or even kill them, simply for practicing their faith.

Someday we'll meet these women in heaven. I don't know about you, but I want to be able to run up to them confident that I did everything on the earth I could to strengthen them. I want to be able to say, "I prayed for you," or, "I wrote you while you were in prison," or, "I gave you a cup of cold water in His name," or, "I read about you and didn't turn the page."

In our comfortable society it's so easy to turn the page or flip the channel. It's much more comfortable to watch reality TV than it is to read the Voice of the Martyrs newsletter or *Jesus Freaks*, the compelling book about persecuted Christians.

But what would Jesus do? Is that a nice little saying on a refrigerator magnet, or does it represent our lives? These women have counted the cost and paid the price to follow Him. We must all ask what we can do to support them—no matter what it costs us.

Elisabeth Farrell

our great God and Savior Jesus Christ, 14 who
gave Himself for us, that He might redeem us
from all lawlessness and purify for Himself a
special people, zealous of good works.
15 Teach these things, exhort, and rebuke with
all authority. Let no one despise you.

Maintain Good Deeds

3 Remind them to be subject to rulers and
authorities, to obey them, to be ready for
every good work, 2 to speak evil of no one,
not to be contentious, but gentle, showing all
humility toward everyone.

Let me be reminded to be ready for every good work, to speak evil of no one, and to be peaceable and gentle, showing all humility to all men (Titus 3:1–2).

3 We also were once foolish, disobedient, de-
ceived, serving various desires and pleasures,
living in evil and envy, filled with hatred and
hating each other. 4 But when the kindness and
the love of God our Savior toward mankind ap-
peared, 5 not by works of righteousness which
we have done, but according to His mercy
He saved us, through the washing of rebirth
and the renewal of the Holy Spirit, 6 whom He
poured out on us abundantly through Jesus
Christ our Savior, 7 so that, being justified by
His grace, we might become heirs according to
the hope of eternal life. 8 This is a faithful say-
ing, and these things I want you constantly to
affirm, so that those who have believed in God
might be careful to maintain good works. These
things are good and profitable to everyone.

Thank You, Holy Spirit, for renewing and regenerating my mind and teaching me how to understand and apply the living Word to my life (Titus 3:4–5).

9 But avoid foolish debates, genealogies, con-
tentions, and arguments about the law, for they
are unprofitable and useless. 10 Reject a divi-
sive man after a first and second admonition,
11 knowing that such a man is perverted and
is sinning, being self-condemned.

Personal Instructions and Greetings

12 When I send Artemas or Tychicus to you,
be diligent to come to me in Nicopolis, for I
have decided to spend the winter there. 13 Dil-
igently send Zenas the lawyer and Apollos
on their journey. See that they lack nothing.
14 And let our people also learn to continue
doing good works to meet urgent needs, that
they may not be unproductive.
15 All who are with me greet you. Greet those
who love us in the faith.
Grace be with you all. Amen.

2:14 Eph 2:10
2:15 2Ti 4:2
3:1 2Ti 2:21
3:2 1Ti 3:3
3:3 Col 3:7
3:4 Titus 2:10–11
3:5 Ro 12:2
3:6 Ro 5:5
3:7 Ro 8:17
3:8 1Ti 1:15
3:9 2Ti 2:14
3:10 Ro 16:17
3:12 Ac 20:4
3:13 Ac 18:24
3:14 Php 1:11
3:15 Col 4:18

Author: The apostle Paul

Written: AD 62, from Rome

Theme: Reconciliation

PHILEMON

Dear Spirit Led Woman,

Forgiving others is an important key to being released from the negative things you've held on to—as well as being forgiven yourself. Jesus said, "And when you stand praying, forgive if you have anything against anyone, so that your Father who is in heaven may also forgive you your sins" (Mk 11:25). Everyone goes through painful experiences in this fallen world, but if we hold on to them, our subconscious minds can become filled with toxic memories and our hearts with unforgiveness, disappointment, and bitterness. God wants us to be filled with His love and light in order to be effective witnesses for Him. We cannot do this if our hearts are filled with contempt.

Just as God loves all of His children, we are called to love everyone. Just as our debts are forgiven, we are to forgive our debtors (Mt 6:12). We should strive to reconcile differences just as Paul did between Onesimus and Philemon.

Joy F. Strang

SPIRITLED WOMAN

COUNSEL FROM THE SPIRIT BASICS

Restore Unity

In his letter to Philemon, Paul pleaded for Philemon to restore his relationship with Onesimus, who apparently displeased Philemon and thus they had severed their relationship. Paul wanted Philemon to receive Onesimus back so that unity between them could once more exist.

The first sin fractured unity. It broke the unity between mankind and heaven. It fractured the unity between man and woman. It destroyed the unity between man and nature.

God is interested in more than just our personal salvation. He wants us to share in the restoration of unity throughout creation, fulfilling His purpose throughout the heavens. Through the church he wants to bring all creation into His eternal purpose.

God wants His children to live in unity: "Behold, how good and how pleasant it is for brothers to dwell together in unity! It is like precious oil upon the head, that runs down on the beard—even Aaron's beard—and going down to the collar of his garments; as the dew of Hermon, that descends upon the mountains of Zion, for there the LORD has commanded the blessing, even life forever" (Ps 133:1–3). In John 17 we can feel the intense yearning of the Lord's heart for us to come into the unity He wants for us.

We were created to live in corporateness; we should never be islands unto ourselves. As we live in unity, we will be refreshed and showered with God's blessings of life!

John Loren and Paula Sandford Lee Bowman

1:1 Eph 3:1
1:2 Ro 16:5
1:3 Ro 1:7
1:4 Ro 1:8
1:5 Eph 1:15
1:7 2Co 7:13
1:8 1Th 2:6
1:9 Eph 4:1
1:10 Col 4:9
1:13 1Co 16:17
1:14 2Co 9:7
1:16 Mt 23:8

Salutation

Paul, a prisoner of Christ Jesus, and Timothy
our brother,

To Philemon, our beloved fellow laborer,
2 and to beloved Apphia, and to Archippus
our fellow soldier, and to the church in your
house:

3 Grace to you and peace from God our Father
and the Lord Jesus Christ.

Philemon's Love and Faith

4 I thank my God, always mentioning you
in my prayers, 5 whenever I hear of your love
and faith, which you have toward the Lord
Jesus and for all the saints, 6 that the sharing
of your faith may be most effective by the
acknowledgment of every good thing which
is in you from Christ Jesus. 7 For we have
great joy and encouragement on account of
your love, because the hearts of the saints
are refreshed through you, brother.

Paul Pleads for Onesimus

8 Therefore, though I might be very bold in
Christ to command you to do that which is
proper, 9 yet for love's sake I rather appeal
to you—I, Paul, an old man, and now also a
prisoner of Jesus Christ— 10 I appeal to you
on behalf of my son Onesimus, whose father
I have become in my imprisonment, 11 who
in the past was unprofitable to you, but now
he is profitable to you and to me.

God has transformed my life from a slave of this world into a prisoner of Jesus Christ (Phm 1:9).

12 I have sent him back. Therefore receive
him as my own heart. 13 I wanted to keep
him with me, so that in your place he might
serve me during my imprisonment for the
gospel. 14 But without your consent I would
do nothing, so that your goodness would
not be forced, but given willingly. 15 Perhaps
this was why he departed for a while, that
you might receive him forever, 16 no longer
as a slave but more than a slave, a beloved
brother, especially to me but how much
more to you, both in the flesh and in the
Lord.

You may have departed from God's plan for a while, but He has received you back as a beloved son (Phm 1:15–16).

The Road of Forgiveness

In his letter to Philemon Paul pleaded with Philemon to offer forgiveness to Onesimus, who had been Philemon's servant and had proved to be "unprofitable" to him. Paul wrote, "That you might receive him forever, no longer as a slave but more than a slave, a beloved brother" (Phm 1:15–16), requiring that Philemon forgive Onesimus.

The Lord gave me an insight into forgiveness years ago when I was in a difficult situation with someone who had taken great offense with me. I do not enjoy confrontation, but I found myself in need of confronting some relational issues that I did not want to keep revisiting. I knew that insecurity was at the root of the discord, but trying to reason with this person had become useless. I was always perceived as defensive whenever we attempted to discuss the disagreement.

Communication between us basically had ceased, and, sadly, for me that brought peace. I had been learning to draw boundary lines, and I felt I was doing the right thing and following God by just praying for the offended person rather than trying to mend trembling fences.

Months had gone by, and one afternoon the Lord asked me to send an e-mail to this person accepting all responsibility for the situation that had created the rift between us. I was in shock. I thought I must have heard God wrong. Take on all the responsibility? I had done little to cause the problems between us, and I felt I had thoroughly repented of what role I did play in the situation. But the Lord again asked me to write this e-mail and accept all the blame, as if I was responsible for the lot of it!

I chose to swallow my pride rather than dishonor God, so I wrote the e-mail, all the while thinking I understood why God would have me do this. By my writing this e-mail, the offended party would be in such shock that person would recognize I was not the guilty party and then ask me for forgiveness. *Yes!*—I mean, great idea, God!

The person responded quickly to my e-mail, and the reply was not at all what I thought it would be. It was a short thank-you for admitting that the fault was mine in the first place!

I was upset with God. He knew my heart was right. Why would He allow the other person to feel righteous in this situation when I was not guilty of what I was being accused of doing? Then God spoke profoundly to me. He simply said, "Rita, I asked you to write that e-mail to show you what I did when I took on all of your offenses. I took all the blame. Without question I laid down My life to set yours free."

That experience was the first of several amazing things I encountered on the road to forgiveness. It was at this point in my life that I first felt the powerful effects of forgiveness. I became a fan of it, because I knew I would need it to greater degrees in the years to come.

Rita Springer

[17] If then you consider me a partner, receive
him as you would me. [18] If he wronged you or
owes you anything, charge this to my account.
[19] I, Paul, have written this with my own hand.
I will repay it—not to mention that you owe
me even your own self. [20] Yes, brother, help
me rejoice in the Lord, refresh my heart in the
Lord. [21] Being convinced of your obedience,
I write to you, knowing that you will also do
more than I say.

1:17 2Co 8:23
1:19 Gal 5:2
1:20 Phm 1:7
1:21 2Co 2:3

1:22 2Co 1:11
1:23 Col 1:7
1:24 Col 4:14
1:25 2Ti 4:22

[22] But, in addition, prepare also lodging for
me, for I hope that through your prayers I shall
be graciously restored to you.

Final Greetings

[23] Epaphras, my fellow prisoner in Christ
Jesus, greets you, [24] as do Mark, Aristarchus,
Demas, and Luke, my fellow laborers.
[25] The grace of our Lord Jesus Christ be with
your spirit. Amen.

Author: Unknown
Written: Before AD 70
Theme: Jesus Christ as the Fulfillment of the Law and Mediator of the New Covenant

HEBREWS

Dear Spirit Led Woman,

One of my favorite chapters in Hebrews is chapter 11. Many people call this the faith chapter. I love it because it reminds me that it takes great faith to live supernaturally. Think about all of the heroes of faith listed in Hebrews 11 and throughout your Bible. Many of them found themselves in places they never would have imagined—from leadership positions and palaces in foreign countries to slavery, chains, and prison cells. These men and women of the Bible had to move in the supernatural realm to fulfill God's assignments for them.

You may not have the same assignments as the women of the Bible did, but whatever God wants you to do, you need His direction and power to do it. Whether you are called to be a witness in the secular marketplace, or disciple your children, or encourage a fellow believer, you will be most effective if you operate in the supernatural realm. Start by developing intimacy with God through worship and prayer. Fellowship with Him in the supernatural realm where He dwells. Then He will do amazing things in your life if you believe Him and follow the leading of His Spirit.

Joy F. Strang

SPIRITLED WOMAN

COUNSEL FROM THE SPIRIT BASICS

The Oil of Joy

You have loved righteousness and hated wickedness; therefore God, Your God, has anointed You with the oil of gladness more than Your companions.

—HEBREWS 1:9

As a believer, the worst thing you can do is not be who you are supposed to be to the world. Jesus is our best model of someone who knew who He was meant to be. Now, I don't mean the bland, boring Jesus you've seen in the movies. They make Him out to be very somber and very blah. The real Jesus loved righteousness and hated wickedness. The real Jesus was anointed with the oil of joy.

This anointing is available for you and for me—and it is who we are supposed to be. Jesus had a spiritual force that sustained Him, and joy is the spiritual force we need to live a life of faith. A life of faith is not always a bed of roses. Tough times might come. Challenges may test you. You must decide now to love righteousness, hate wickedness, and be anointed with joy.

This joy is not a girlfriend giggly kind of thing; that's not the kind of joy my Savior lived. It's deeper than that. It's stronger than that. This is the kind of joy that could carry you into the Garden of Gethsemane sweating drops of blood. This is so much joy dripping all over you that you could proclaim the will of God into the earth today and know God's going to back you up with a demonstration that brings people out of their prisons, takes blinders off their eyes, and heals their broken bodies.

Some of you can't endure anything. You fall apart if you get a flat tire. I'm telling you, if you're going to live a life of faith, you have to decide now to receive the anointing of joy. Grab hold of this special anointing, and let it become who you are this year!

Kathy Gray

1:1 Joel 2:28
1:2 Mt 28:18
1:3 Mk 16:19
1:4 Eph 1:21
1:5 2Sa 7:14
1:6 Ps 97:7
1:7 Ps 104:4
1:9 Isa 61:1
1:10 Ps 102:25–27
1:12 Heb 13:8

God Has Spoken by His Son

1 God, who at various times and in diverse
ways spoke long ago to the fathers through
the prophets, 2 has in these last days spoken to
us by His Son, whom He has appointed heir
of all things, and through whom He made
the world. 3 He is the brightness of His glory,
the express image of Himself, and upholds
all things by the word of His power. When
He had by Himself purged our sins, He sat
down at the right hand of the Majesty on high.
4 He was made so much better than the angels
as He has inherited a more excellent name
than they.

The Son Superior to Angels

5 For to which of the angels did He at any
time say:

"You are My Son;
today I have become Your Father"[1]?

Or again,
"I will be a Father to Him,
and He shall be a Son to Me"[2]?

6 And again, when He brings the firstborn into
the world, He says:

"Let all the angels of God worship Him."[3]

7 Of the angels He says:

"He makes His angels spirits,
and His servants a flame of fire."[4]

8 But to the Son He says:
"Your throne, O God, lasts forever and ever;
a scepter of righteousness is the scepter of Your kingdom.[5]
9 You have loved righteousness and hated wickedness;
therefore God, Your God, has anointed You
with the oil of gladness more than Your companions."[6]

10 And,

"You, Lord, laid the foundation of the earth in the beginning,
and the heavens are the works of Your hands.
11 They will perish, but You remain;
and they all will wear out like a garment;
12 as a cloak You will fold them up,
and they will be changed.
But You are the same,
and Your years will not end."[7]

[1]*5* Ps 2:7. [2]*5* 2Sa 7:8, 14. [3]*6* Ps 97:7. [4]*7* Ps 104:4.
[5]*8* Ps 45:6. [6]*9* Ps 45:7; Isa 61:1, 3. [7]*10–12* Ps 102:25–27.

13 But to which of the angels did He at any
time say:

"Sit at My right hand,
until I make Your enemies
Your footstool"[1]?

14 Are they not all ministering spirits sent out
to minister to those who will inherit salvation?

The Great Salvation

2 Therefore we should be more attentive to
what we have heard, lest we drift away.
2 For if the word spoken by angels was true,
and every sin and disobedience received a
just recompense, 3 how shall we escape if we
neglect such a great salvation, which was first
declared by the Lord, and was confirmed to
us by those who heard Him? 4 God also bore
them witness with signs and wonders and
diverse miracles and with gifts of the Holy
Spirit distributed according to His own will.

The Pioneer of Salvation

5 For it was not to the angels that He has
subjected the world to come, of which we are
speaking. 6 But someone in a certain place
testified, saying:

"What is man that You are mindful of him,
or the son of man that You care for him?
7 You made him a little lower than the angels;
You crowned him with glory and honor,
and set him over the works of Your hands.
8 You have put all things in subjection
under his feet."[2]

For in subjecting all things under him, He left
nothing that is not subjected to him. Yet now
we do not see all things subject to him. 9 But we
see Jesus, who was made a little lower than the
angels to suffer death, crowned with glory and
honor, so that He, by the grace of God, should
experience death for everyone.

10 For it was fitting for Him, for whom and by
whom all things exist, in bringing many sons
to glory, to make the Author of their salvation
perfect through suffering. 11 For both He who
sanctifies and those who are sanctified are all
of One. For this reason He is not ashamed to
call them brothers, 12 saying:

"I will declare Your name to My brothers;
in the midst of the congregation I will
sing praise to You."[3]

13 And again:

"I will put My trust in Him."[4]

And again:

"Here am I and the children whom God has
given Me."[5]

14 So then, as the children share in flesh and
blood, He likewise took part in these, so that
through death He might destroy him who has
the power of death, that is, the devil, 15 and
deliver those who through fear of death were
throughout their lives subject to bondage.
16 For surely He does not help the angels, but
He helps the seed of Abraham. 17 Therefore,
in all things it was necessary for Him to be
made like His brothers, so that He might be a
merciful and faithful High Priest in the things
pertaining to God, to make atonement for the
sins of the people. 18 For since He Himself suf-
fered while being tempted, He is able to help
those who are being tempted.

Jesus Superior to Moses

3 Therefore, holy brothers, partakers in a
heavenly calling, consider the Apostle and
High Priest of our profession, Jesus Christ,

I am a partaker of the heavenly calling (Heb 3:1).

2 who was faithful to Him who appointed Him,
as Moses was faithful in all His house. 3 For the
One was counted worthy of more glory than
Moses, in that He who builds the house has
more honor than the house itself. 4 For every
house is built by someone, but the One who
builds all things is God. 5 Moses was faithful in
all God's house as a servant, testifying about
those things that were to be spoken later.
6 But Christ is faithful over God's house as
a Son, whose house we are if we hold fast
the confidence and the rejoicing of our hope
firm to the end.

A Rest for God's People

7 Therefore, as the Holy Spirit says:

"Today, if you hear His voice,
8 do not harden your hearts
as in the rebellion,
on the day of temptation in the
wilderness,
9 where your fathers tested Me and tried Me
and saw My works for forty years.
10 Therefore I was angry with that generation,
and said, 'They always go astray in their
heart,
and they have not known My ways.'
11 So I swore in My wrath,
'They shall not enter My rest.' "[6]

12 Be attentive, brothers, lest there be in any of
you an evil, unbelieving heart, and you depart
from the living God. 13 But exhort one another

1:13 Ps 110:1
1:14 Ps 34:7
2:1 Pr 3:21
2:2 Ac 7:53
2:3 Lk 1:2
2:4 Eph 1:5
2:5 Heb 6:5
2:6 Heb 4:4
2:8 1Co 15:27
2:9 Jn 3:16
2:10 Lk 24:26
2:11 Heb 10:10
2:12 Ps 22:22

....

2:14 Jn 1:14
2:15 Ro 8:15
3:1 Php 3:14
3:2 Nu 12:7
3:5 Nu 12:7
3:6 1Co 3:16
3:7 Heb 3:15
3:9 Ac 7:36
3:10 Ps 95:10
3:11 Heb 4:3
3:12 Heb 12:25
3:13 Eph 4:22

[1] *13* Ps 110:1. [2] *6–8* Ps 8:4–6. [3] *12* Ps 22:22. [4] *13* Isa 12:2.
[5] *13* Isa 8:18. [6] *7–11* Ps 95:7–11.

The Dynamics of Prayer

Prayer that is initiated by the Father, energized by the Spirit, prayed out by a pure and faith-filled believer, and ushered into the throne room by Jesus is bold and confident. It does not depend upon our ability to pray long, loudly, or perfectly, but upon God Himself, who is the initiator and author of all true prayer. Since such prayer is prayed according to the will of God, we can be confident the answer has already been triggered in heaven, even as we are still praying (1Jn 5:14). The following graphic illustrates such prayer, along with the dynamics of effective prayer.

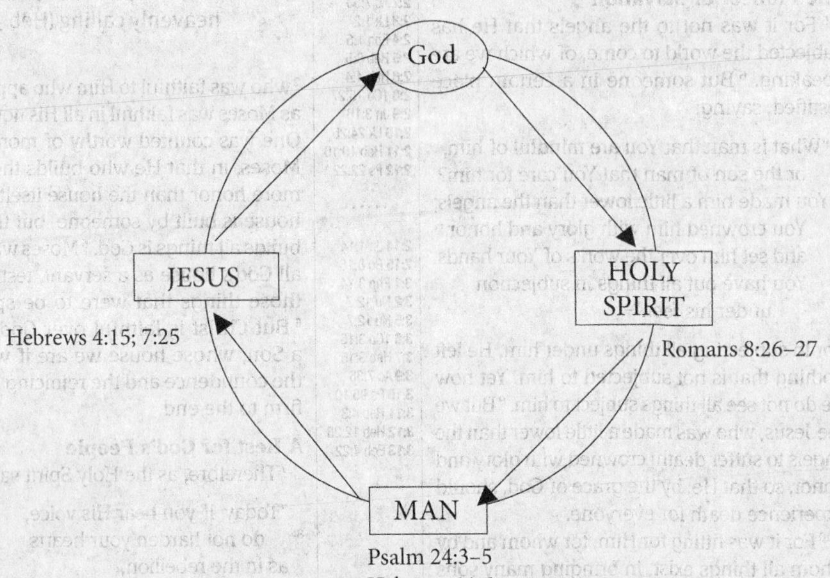

Look up each scripture in the chart below and describe what it tells us about prayer.

Scripture Reference	What Does This Verse Say About Prayer?
HEBREWS 4:15	
HEBREWS 7:25	
ROMANS 8:26–27	
PSALM 24:3–5	
HEBREWS 11:6	

Do you realize what this means? Today, as we carry on the activities of our lives, Jesus Christ is praying for us. Continual prayer is being offered at the throne of God on our behalf by none other than the eternal Son. You are being prayed for right now. I am being prayed for right now. We can rest in this work of the Son on our behalf.[1]

—RICHARD J. FOSTER

Jeannette Storms

1. Richard J. Foster, *Prayer: Finding the Heart's True Home* (San Francisco: Harper San Francisco, 1992), 13

daily, while it is called "Today," lest any of you be hardened through the deceitfulness of sin. 14 For we have become partakers of Christ if we hold the beginning of our confidence firmly to the end, 15 while it is said:

"Today, if you will hear His voice,
do not harden your hearts
as in the rebellion."[1]

16 For who were they who heard and rebelled? Was it not all of those who came out of Egypt, led by Moses? 17 And with whom was He grieved for forty years? Was it not with those who had sinned, whose bodies fell in the wilderness? 18 And to whom did He swear that they would not enter His rest, but to those who disobeyed? 19 So we see that they could not enter because of unbelief.

4 Therefore, since the promise of entering His rest remains, let us fear lest any of you should seem to come short of it. 2 For the gospel was preached to us as well as to them. But the word preached did not benefit them, because it was not mixed with faith in those who heard it. 3 For we who have believed have entered this rest, as He has said,

"As I have sworn in My wrath,
'They shall not enter My rest.' "[2]

However, His works have been finished since the creation of the world. 4 For He spoke somewhere about the seventh day like this: "And God rested on the seventh day from all His works."[3] 5 And again in the present passage He said, "They shall not enter My rest."[4]

6 Since therefore it remains for some to enter it, and they to whom it was first preached did not enter due to unbelief, 7 again He establishes a certain day, "Today," saying through David, after so long a time, as it has been said:

"Today, if you will hear His voice,
do not harden your hearts."[5]

8 For if Joshua had given them rest, He would not have later spoken of another day. 9 Therefore a rest remains for the people of God. 10 For whoever enters His rest will also cease from his own works, as God did from His. 11 Let us labor therefore to enter that rest, lest anyone fall by the same pattern of unbelief.

12 For the word of God is alive, and active, and sharper than any two-edged sword, piercing even to the division of soul and spirit, of joints and marrow, and able to judge the thoughts and intents of the heart. 13 There is no creature that is not revealed in His sight, for all things are bare and exposed to the eyes of Him to whom we must give account.

> God wants to convert my time of hardship into a moment of miraculous provision (Heb 4:12).

Jesus the Great High Priest

14 Since then we have a great High Priest who has passed into the heavens, Jesus the Son of God, let us hold firmly to our confession. 15 For we do not have a High Priest who cannot sympathize with our weaknesses, but One who was in every sense tempted like we are, yet without sin. 16 Let us then come with confidence to the throne of grace, that we may obtain mercy and find grace to help in time of need.

5 For every high priest chosen from among men is appointed to represent men in things pertaining to God, that he may offer both gifts and sacrifices for sins. 2 He is able to have compassion on the ignorant and on those who are wayward, for he himself is also subject to weakness. 3 Because of this he must offer sacrifices for his own sins, just as he does for the people. 4 No man takes this honor for himself, but he who is called by God receives it, just as Aaron did.

5 So also Christ did not glorify Himself to be made a High Priest, but it was He who said to Him:

"You are My Son;
today I have become Your Father."[6]

6 As He also says in another place:

"You are a priest forever
in the order of Melchizedek."[7]

7 In the days of His flesh, Jesus offered up prayers and supplications with loud cries and tears to Him who was able to save Him from death. He was heard because of His godly fear. 8 Though He was a Son, He learned obedience through the things that He suffered, 9 and being made perfect, He became the source of eternal salvation for all those who obey Him, 10 being designated by God a High Priest according to the order of Melchizedek.

Warning Against Apostasy

11 Concerning this we have much to say that is hard to explain, since you have become hard of hearing. 12 For though by now you should be teachers, you need someone to teach you again the first principles of the oracles of God and have come to need milk rather than solid food. 13 Everyone who lives on milk is unskilled in the word of righteousness, for he is a baby.

3:14 Heb 3:6
3:15 Heb 3:7–8
3:16 Nu 14:2
3:17 Nu 14:29
3:18 Dt 1:34–35
3:19 Jn 3:36
4:1 Heb 12:15
4:2 1Th 2:13
4:3 Ps 95:11
4:4 Ex 20:11
4:6 Heb 3:18–19
4:7 Ps 95:7
4:8 Jos 22:4
4:10 Rev 14:13
4:11 Heb 3:12
4:12 Eph 6:17
4:13 Ps 33:13–15
4:14 Heb 6:20
4:15 2Co 5:21
5:1 Heb 8:3
5:2 Heb 2:18
5:3 Heb 7:27
5:4 Ex 28:1
5:5 Jn 8:54
5:6 Heb 7:17
5:7 Mt 27:46
5:8 Php 2:8
5:9 Heb 2:10
5:10 Heb 5:5–6
5:11 2Pe 3:16
5:12 Heb 6:1
5:13 1Co 14:20

1 15 Ps 95:7–8. *2 3* Ps 95:11. *3 4* Ge 2:2. *4 5* Ps 95:11. *5 7* Ps 95:7–8. *6 5* Ps 2:7. *7 6* Ps 110:4.

14 But solid food belongs to those who are mature, for those who through practice have powers of discernment that are trained to distinguish good from evil.

6 Therefore, leaving the elementary principles of the doctrine of Christ, let us go on to maturity, not laying again a foundation of repentance from dead works and of faith toward God, 2 of instruction about washings, the laying on of hands, the resurrection of the dead, and eternal judgment. 3 This we will do if God permits.

4 For it is impossible for those who were once enlightened, who have tasted the heavenly gift, who shared in the Holy Spirit, 5 and have tasted the good word of God and the powers of the age to come, 6 if they fall away, to be renewed once more to repentance, since they again crucify to themselves the Son of God and subject Him to public shame. 7 For land that drinks in the rain that often falls upon it and bears a crop useful to those for whom it is cultivated receives a blessing from God. 8 But land that bears thorns and thistles is rejected and near to being cursed. Its destiny is to be burned.

9 But though we speak in this manner, we are persuaded of better things for you, things that accompany salvation, 10 for God is not unjust so as to forget your work and labor of love that you have shown for His name, in that you have ministered to the saints and continue ministering. 11 We desire that every one of you show the same diligence for the full assurance of hope to the end, 12 so that you may not be lazy, but imitators of those who through faith and patience inherit the promises.

My patience will produce in me God's promises as an inheritance (Heb 6:12).

Sure Promise of God

13 For when God made a promise to Abraham, because He could vow by no one greater, He vowed by Himself, 14 saying, "Surely I will bless you, and surely I will multiply you."[1] 15 So after Abraham had patiently endured, he obtained the promise.

16 For men indeed swear by a greater authority than themselves, and for them an oath of confirmation ends all dispute. 17 So God, wanting to show more abundantly the immutability of His counsel to the heirs of promise, confirmed it by an oath. 18 So that by two immutable things, in which it was impossible for God to lie, we who have fled for refuge might have strong encouragement to hold fast to the hope set before us. 19 We have this hope as a sure and steadfast anchor of the soul, which enters the Inner Place behind the veil. 20 This is where Jesus has entered for us as a forerunner, since He has become the everlasting High Priest in the order of Melchizedek.

The Priestly Order of Melchizedek

7 For this Melchizedek, king of Salem, priest of the Most High God, met Abraham returning from the slaughter of the kings and blessed him. 2 To him Abraham also gave a tenth part of everything. In the first place, his name is translated "king of righteousness," and then also he is king of Salem, which means "king of peace." 3 Without father, without mother, without descent, having neither beginning of days nor end of life, but made like the Son of God, he continually remains a priest.

4 Now consider how great this man was, to whom even the patriarch Abraham gave a tenth of the spoils. 5 Surely the sons of Levi, who receive the office of the priesthood, have a command to take tithes of the people according to the law, that is, from their brothers, though they also come from the seed of Abraham. 6 But this man, whose descent is not numbered among them, received tithes from Abraham and blessed him who had the promises. 7 Without question, the inferior is blessed by the superior. 8 In the one case mortal men receive tithes, but in the other he of whom it is witnessed that he is alive receives them. 9 One might say that Levi also, who receives tithes, paid tithes through Abraham, 10 for he was still in the loins of his father when Melchizedek met Abraham.

11 If perfection were attained through the Levitical priesthood (for through it the people received the law), what further need was there that another priest should rise in the order of Melchizedek, rather than established in the order of Aaron? 12 For a change in the priesthood necessitates a change in the law. 13 For the One concerning whom these things are spoken pertains to another tribe, from which no man served at the altar. 14 For it is evident that our Lord descended from Judah, a tribe concerning which Moses said nothing about priests. 15 This is far more evident when another priest arises in the likeness of Melchizedek, 16 who becomes a priest not by a law pertaining to ancestry, but by the power of an endless life. 17 For He testifies:

"You are a priest forever,
in the order of Melchizedek."[2]

5:14 Isa 7:15
6:1 Heb 9:14
6:2 Ac 6:6
6:3 Ac 18:21
6:4 Gal 3:2
6:6 Heb 10:29
6:8 Ge 3:17–18
6:10 Mt 10:42
6:11 Heb 3:6
6:12 Heb 10:36
6:13 Lk 1:73
6:14 Ge 22:17
6:15 Heb 6:12
6:16 Ex 22:11
6:17 Heb 11:9
6:18 Titus 1:2
6:19 Heb 9:7
6:20 Heb 4:14
7:1 Ge 14:18–20
7:3 Heb 7:6
7:4 Ac 2:29
7:6 Ro 4:13
7:8 Heb 5:6
7:11 Heb 8:7
7:14 Isa 11:1
7:17 Ps 110:4

[1] 14 Ge 22:17. [2] 17 Ps 110:4.

How God Speaks to Us

Jesus told us, "To him the doorkeeper opens, and the sheep hear his voice. He calls his own sheep by name, and he leads them out. When he brings out his own sheep, he goes before them. And the sheep follow him, for they know his voice. Yet they will never follow a stranger, but will run away from him. For they do not know the voice of strangers....I am the good shepherd. The good shepherd lays down His life for the sheep" (Jn 10:3–5, 11).

It is interesting that of all the titles Jesus could have chosen for Himself—king, high priest, revolutionary, prophet, deliverer—He chose to call Himself a shepherd and to refer to His followers as sheep. Not a very world-shattering picture, is it? I am sure none of the disciples were hoping He would choose that title. I doubt they ever imagined themselves triumphantly marching into Jerusalem as a conquering flock of sheep. Once again, He was turning a man-made objective and aspiration firmly on its head.

However, in this passage, Jesus also gives us a key to how we hear His voice. In the same way a flock of sheep comes to distinguish the voice of its shepherd from all the other voices, so we come to know our Father's voice. This is also the same way we come to know the voice of our parents. I remember when I was a young girl, sometimes my family would go into a crowded place—to a busy parade or a marketplace. If I ever got separated from my mother, I knew I had only to call to her, and she would be able to pick my voice out of all the others in the crowd. And when she answered, I would immediately know her voice. Then all I would have to do was follow it until I found her.

God speaks to us in many ways, and we come to recognize His voice from all the others in the world by spending time with Him just as sheep do with their shepherd and children do with their parents. It is a matter of just being together, getting used to each other, and listening. It is not about quality time, though quality time with God is among the things I long for the most in this world, but it's about the practice of daily, consistent prayer. It is about getting up, getting dressed, and eating breakfast together every day. It is about coming home, talking about your day, and sitting down at the dinner table together every day. God controls the quality times when He really wants to bless us, but we control the quantity of time we sit at His feet. I know of no one who has ever had influence with God in prayer who has not spent at least one night with God as Jacob did, wrestling for the blessing. (See Genesis 32:22–32.)

Just as you might read several books by the same author in school to become familiar with his "voice," so the Bible is a great place to start learning the way God speaks to us. And I don't mean that you should get comfortable with King James English; I mean to get so familiar with God's character through His Word that, as we might with a close friend or spouse, we know instantly whether or not something we hear is something He would say. God is not going to ask us to do something that appeals to our selfish ambitions or that contradicts something else He already told us. He is not going to use conniving arguments or ask you to disregard the good of others to profit yourself.

We are taught about the importance of knowing the Scriptures as a means of discerning God's voice in the Book of Hebrews:

> For the word of God is alive, and active, and sharper than any two-edged sword, piercing even to the division of soul and spirit, of joints and marrow, and able to judge the thoughts and intents of the heart.
>
> —Hebrews 4:12

Familiarity with the Word of God is more than memorizing scriptures. The more time we spend reading the Bible, the more it permeates our being and clarifies the voices within us. Many confuse things and divide the world of our existence into the interior and the exterior. These are the people who would say that the spirit and the soul are the same thing, but that is not true. Like the Trinity—God the Father, the Son, and the Holy Spirit—each of us is also three parts—soul, body, and spirit. How can you tell the difference between the thoughts of your own soul, which come from your mind, will, or emotions; your physical desires, hungers, and urges; and the communications of your spirit, which have ears in the spiritual realm? When a thought comes to mind, where is it coming from—God, evil, your physical urges, or your own psyche? The answer to discerning the difference between these "voices in our heads" is learned through practice and repetition, with the Bible as your personal trainer. It is the mirror into which we look and learn who we truly are. (See James 1:23–25.)

Just because something is supernatural does not mean it is instantaneous. The baby who was born in a moment spent nine months in the womb developing from two seeds before he emerged. Though growth is unlikely to be the same in the spirit and in the natural, every endeavor still takes time. People spend years working to become what we think were overnight successes; the fact that we hadn't heard of them before doesn't mean they just appeared out of nowhere.

The same is true with things of the spirit. There are often months, if not years, of things being cultivated in prayer before they happen "overnight" in the natural. A farmer may reap the harvest in a week, but he first had to devote months to planting, weeding, and cultivating or the crop would never have been as large or as healthy. Planting and cultivating, tilling the soil and preparing it for the next season are all hard work. So, oftentimes, is prayer.

Cindy Trimm

18 For there is then an annulling of the previous commandment due to its weakness and uselessness. 19 For the law made nothing perfect, but now a better hope is introduced, by which we draw near to God.

20 And He was not made a priest without an oath. 21 (Other priests were made without an oath, but this One with an oath by the One who said to Him:

"The Lord has sworn
    and will not relent,
'You are a priest forever, in the order of
        Melchizedek.' "[1])

22 Through this oath Jesus became the guarantor of a better covenant.

23 And the former priests were numerous because they were hindered from serving because of death. 24 But He, because He lives forever, has an everlasting priesthood. 25 Therefore He is able to save to the uttermost those who come to God through Him, because He at all times lives to make intercession for them.

26 For such a High Priest was fitting for us, for He is holy, innocent, undefiled, separate from sinners, and is higher than the heavens. 27 Unlike those high priests, He does not need to offer daily sacrifices—first for His own sins and then for the people's, for He did this once for all when He offered up Himself. 28 For the law appoints men who are weak as high priests, but the word of the oath, which came after the law, appoints a Son who is made perfect forever.

Jesus Our High Priest

8 Now this is the main point of the things that we are saying: We have such a High Priest, who is seated at the right hand of the throne of the Majesty in the heavens, 2 a minister in the sanctuary and the true tabernacle, which the Lord, not man, set up.

3 For every high priest is appointed to offer gifts and sacrifices. Therefore it is necessary that this priest also have something to offer. 4 For if He were on earth, He would not be a priest, since there are priests that offer gifts according to the law. 5 They serve in a sanctuary that is an example and shadow of the heavenly one, as Moses was instructed by God when he was about to make the tabernacle, "See that you make all things according to the pattern shown you on the mountain."[2] 6 But now He has obtained a more excellent ministry, because He is the Mediator of a better covenant, which was established on better promises.

7 For if that first covenant had been faultless, then no occasion would have been sought for a second. 8 For finding fault with them, God says:

"Surely the days are coming, says the Lord,
    when I will make a new covenant
with the house of Israel
    and with the house of Judah,
9 not according to the covenant
    that I made with their fathers
in the day when I took them by the hand
    to lead them out of the land of Egypt;
because they did not continue in My
        covenant,
    and I rejected them, says the Lord.
10 This is the covenant that I will make with
        the house of Israel
    after those days, says the Lord:
I will put My laws into their minds
    and write them on their hearts;
and I will be their God,
    and they shall be My people.
11 No longer shall every man teach his
        neighbor,
    and every man his brother, saying,
        'Know the Lord,'
for all shall know Me,
    from the least of them to the greatest.[3]
12 For I will be merciful toward their
        unrighteousness,
    and their sins and their lawless deeds
        I will remember no more."[4]

13 In speaking of a new covenant He has made the first one old. Now that which is decaying and growing old is ready to vanish away.

The Earthly and Heavenly Sanctuaries

9 Then indeed, the first covenant had ordinances for divine services and an earthly sanctuary. 2 A tabernacle was made. In the first part of the tabernacle, called the Holy Place, were the candlestick, the table, and the showbread. 3 Behind the second veil was the second part of the tabernacle called the Most Holy Place, 4 which contained the golden censer and the ark of the covenant overlaid with gold, containing the golden pot holding the manna, Aaron's rod that budded, and the tablets of the covenant. 5 Above the ark were the cherubim of glory overshadowing the mercy seat. Concerning these things we cannot now speak in detail.

6 Now when these things were thus ordained, the priests would regularly go into the first part, conducting the services of God. 7 But only the high priest went into the second part once a year, not without blood, which he offered for himself and for the sins of the people, committed in ignorance. 8 The Holy Spirit was signi-

7:18 Ro 8:3
7:19 Ac 13:39
7:21 Ps 110:4
7:24 Heb 7:28
7:25 Ro 8:34
7:26 Heb 8:1
7:27 Heb 9:28
7:28 Heb 2:10
8:1 Heb 1:3
8:3 Heb 5:1
8:5 Ex 25:40
8:6 Heb 7:22
....
8:7 Heb 7:11
8:8 Jer 31:31–34
8:10 Jer 31:33
8:11 Isa 54:13
8:12 Ro 11:27
8:13 2Co 5:17
9:1 Ex 25:8
9:2 Ex 40:4
9:3 Ex 26:31–33
9:4 Ex 26:33
9:5 Lev 16:2
9:6 Nu 28:3
9:7 Lev 16:34
9:8 Jn 14:6

[1] *21* Nu 23:19; 1Sa 15:29; Ps 110:4. [2] *5* Ex 25:40. [3] *11* Isa 54:13. [4] *8–12* Isa 43:25; Jer 31:31–34; 50:20; Mic 7:18–19.

fying through this that the way into the Most Holy Place was not yet revealed, because the first part of the tabernacle was still standing. 9 This is an illustration for the present time, showing that the gifts and sacrifices offered could not perfect the conscience of those who worshipped, 10 since they are concerned only with foods and drinks, ceremonial cleansings, and fleshly ordinances imposed until the time of reformation.

11 But Christ, when He came as a High Priest of the good things to come, by a greater and more perfect tabernacle, not made with hands, that is to say, not of this creation, 12 neither by the blood of goats and calves, but by His own blood, He entered the Most Holy Place once for all, having obtained eternal redemption. 13 For if the blood of bulls and goats, and the ashes of a heifer, sprinkling the unclean, sanctifies so that the flesh is purified, 14 how much more shall the blood of Christ, who through the eternal Spirit offered Himself without blemish to God, cleanse your conscience from dead works to serve the living God?

15 For this reason He is the Mediator of a new covenant, since a death has occurred for the redemption of the sins that were committed under the first covenant, so that those who are called might receive the promise of eternal inheritance. 16 For where there is a will, there must also of necessity be the death of the testator. 17 For a will has force after men are dead, since it has no force at all while the testator lives. 18 So not even the first covenant was inaugurated without blood. 19 For when Moses had taught every precept to all the people according to the law, he took the blood of calves and goats, with water, scarlet wool, and hyssop, and sprinkled both the book and all the people, 20 saying, "This is the blood of the covenant that God has commanded you to keep."[1] 21 Likewise he sprinkled both the tabernacle and all the vessels of worship with blood. 22 And according to the law almost everything must be cleansed with blood; without the shedding of blood there is no forgiveness.

Christ's Sacrifice Takes Away Sin

23 It was therefore necessary that the replicas of heavenly things be cleansed with these sacrifices, but that the heavenly things themselves be cleansed with better sacrifices than these. 24 For Christ did not enter holy places made with hands, which are patterned after the true one, but into heaven itself, now to appear in the presence of God for us. 25 Nor did He enter to offer Himself often, as the high priest enters the Most Holy Place every year with blood that is not his own. 26 For then He would have had to suffer repeatedly since the world was created, but now He has appeared once at the end of the ages to put away sin by sacrificing Himself. 27 As it is appointed for men to die once, but after this comes the judgment, 28 so Christ was offered once to bear the sins of many, and He will appear a second time, not to bear sin but to save those who eagerly wait for Him.

9:9 Heb 5:1
9:10 Col 2:16
9:11 Heb 10:1
9:12 Heb 10:4
9:14 1Pe 3:18
9:15 Ro 8:28
9:17 Gal 3:15
9:19 Nu 19:6
9:20 Mt 26:28
9:21 Lev 8:15
9:22 Lev 17:11
9:23 Heb 8:5
9:24 Heb 8:2
9:25 Heb 9:7
9:26 Heb 1:2

9:27 Ge 3:19
9:28 Titus 2:13
10:1 Heb 8:5
10:3 Heb 9:7
10:4 Heb 10:11
10:5 Heb 1:6
10:7 Ge 3:15
10:8 Heb 10:5
10:9 Heb 10:7
10:10 Jn 17:19
10:11 Heb 5:1
10:12 Heb 1:3
10:13 Heb 1:13
10:14 Heb 10:1
10:15 Heb 3:7
10:16 Ro 11:27

10 For the law is a shadow of the good things to come, and not the very image of those things. It could never by the same sacrifices, which they offer continually year after year, perfect those who draw near. 2 Otherwise, would they not have ceased to be offered, since the worshippers, once purified, would no longer be conscious of sins? 3 But in those sacrifices there is an annual reminder of sins. 4 For it is not possible for the blood of bulls and goats to take away sins.

5 Therefore, when He came into the world, He said:

"Sacrifices and offerings You did not desire,
but a body You have prepared for Me.
6 In burnt offerings and sacrifices for sin
You have had no pleasure.
7 Then I said, 'See, I have come to do Your
will, O God,' as it is written of Me
in the volume of the book."[2]

8 Previously when He said, "You did not desire sacrifices and offerings. You have had no pleasure in burnt offerings and sacrifices for sin,"[3] which are offered in accordance with the law, 9 then He said, "See, I have come to do Your will, O God."[4] He takes away the first that He may establish the second. 10 By this will we have been sanctified through the offering of the body of Jesus Christ once for all.

11 But every priest stands daily ministering and repetitively offering the same sacrifices, which can never take away sins. 12 But this Man, after He had offered one sacrifice for sins forever, sat down at the right hand of God. 13 Since that time He has been waiting for His enemies to be made His footstool. 14 For by one offering He has forever perfected those who are sanctified.

15 The Holy Spirit also witnesses to us about this. For after saying,

16 "This is the covenant that I will make with
them
after those days, says the Lord:
I will put My laws into their hearts,
and in their minds I will write them,"[5]

[1] *20* Ex 24:8. [2] *5–7* Ps 40:6–8. [3] *8* Ps 40:6. [4] *9* Ps 40:8.
[5] *16* Jer 31:33.

17 then He adds,

"Their sins and lawless deeds
will I remember no more."[1]

> I break the power of sin and iniquity in my life through the blood of Jesus (Heb 10:17).

18 Now where there is forgiveness of these,
there is no longer an offering for sin.

Exhortation and Warning

> I have boldness to enter into the presence of God through the blood (Heb 10:19).

19 Therefore, brothers, we have confidence
to enter the Most Holy Place by the blood of
Jesus, 20 by a new and living way that He has
opened for us through the veil, that is to say,
His flesh, 21 and since we have a High Priest
over the house of God, 22 let us draw near with
a true heart in full assurance of faith, having
our hearts sprinkled to cleanse them from an
evil conscience, and our bodies washed with
pure water. 23 Let us firmly hold the profes-
sion of our faith without wavering, for He who
promised is faithful. 24 And let us consider how
to spur one another to love and to good works.
25 Let us not forsake the assembling of our-
selves together, as is the manner of some, but
let us exhort one another, especially as you see
the Day approaching.

> My heavenly Father has purified my heart with the blood of Jesus and opened my spiritual eyes to discern the wiles of the enemy (Heb 10:22).

26 For if we willfully continue to sin after we
have received the knowledge of the truth,
there no longer remains a sacrifice for sins,
27 but a fearful expectation of judgment and
fiery indignation, which will devour the ad-
versaries. 28 Anyone who despised Moses' law
died without mercy in the presence of two or
three witnesses. 29 How much more severe a
punishment do you suppose he deserves, who
has trampled under foot the Son of God, and
has regarded the blood of the covenant that
sanctified him to be a common thing, and has
insulted the Spirit of grace? 30 For we know
Him who said, "Vengeance is Mine," says the
Lord, "I will repay."[2] And again He says, "The
Lord will judge His people."[3] 31 It is a fearful
thing to fall into the hands of the living God.

> Even when I have questions, I know that God honors His promises and that He will never let me go (Heb 10:23).

32 Remember the former days, after you were
enlightened, in which you endured a great
struggle of afflictions. 33 In part you were made
a spectacle both by reproaches and afflictions.
And in part you became companions of those
who were so abused. 34 For you had compas-
sion on me in my chains and joyfully endured
the confiscation of your property, knowing that
you have in heaven a better and an enduring
possession for yourselves. 35 Therefore do not
throw away your confidence, which will be
greatly rewarded.

36 For you need patience, so that after you
have done the will of God, you will receive the
promise. 37 For,

"In yet a little while,
He who is to come will come, and will
not wait.
38 Now the just shall live by faith;
but if anyone draws back,
My soul shall have no pleasure in him."[4]

39 But we are not of those who draw back to
destruction, but of those who have faith to the
saving of the soul.

Faith

11 Now faith is the substance of things
hoped for, the evidence of things not
seen. 2 For by it the men of old obtained a good
report.

3 By faith we understand that the universe
was framed by the word of God, so that things
that are seen were not made out of things
which are visible.

4 By faith Abel offered to God a more ex-
cellent sacrifice than Cain offered. Through
this he was approved as righteous, with God
testifying concerning his gifts. He still speaks
through his faith, though he is dead.

5 By faith Enoch was taken to heaven so that
he would not see death. He was not found,
because God took him away. For before he
was taken, he had this commendation, that
he pleased God. 6 And without faith it is im-
possible to please God, for he who comes to
God must believe that He exists and that He is
a rewarder of those who diligently seek Him.

> You reward me because I diligently seek You (Heb 11:6).

10:17 Heb 8:12
10:20 Heb 9:3
10:21 Heb 2:17
10:22 Eze 36:25
10:23 1Co 1:9
10:25 Ac 2:42
10:28 Heb 2:2
10:29 Eph 4:30
10:30 Dt 32:35–36
10:32 Heb 6:4
10:33 1Co 4:9
10:34 1Pe 1:4
10:35 Heb 11:26
10:36 Lk 21:19
10:37 Rev 22:20
10:38 Ro 1:17
11:1 2Co 4:18
11:3 Jn 1:3
11:4 Mt 23:35
11:5 2Ki 2:11

1 17 Jer 31:34. *2 30* Dt 32:35. *3 30* Dt 32:36. *4 37–38* Hab 2:3–4.

SPIRIT-TO-SPIRIT PRAYER

PRAYER OF FAITH FOR YOUR CHILDREN

Dear God, please help my children navigate through all the hard places in life—through the pitfalls, the holes, the stumbling blocks, the peer pressures, the pleasures and temptations, the fearful places, and the areas of decision.

Keep their hearts toward You, Lord, I pray. Please remove the bands from their eyes and the veils from their hearts. Cause them to seek You with all their heart.

I bind the unclean spirits and the spirits of fear and rejection from attaching themselves to them. I loose the love and peace of God into their hearts.

Thank You, Father, for placing a hedge of protection around them. Thank You for sending Your angels to protect and deliver them from all evil.

In Jesus' name, amen.

Iris Delgado

7 By faith Noah, being divinely warned about
things not yet seen, moved with godly fear,
prepared an ark to save his family, by which he
condemned the world and became an heir of
the righteousness that comes by faith.
8 By faith Abraham obeyed when he was
called to go out into a place which he would
later receive as an inheritance. He went out
not knowing where he was going. 9 By faith
he dwelt in the promised land, as in a foreign
land, dwelling in tents with Isaac and Jacob,
the heirs of the same promise, 10 for he was
looking for a city which has foundations,
whose builder and maker is God. 11 By faith
Sarah herself also received the ability to con-
ceive seed, and she bore a child when she was
past the age, because she judged Him faithful
who had promised. 12 Therefore from one man,
who was as good as dead, sprang so many, a
multitude as the stars of the sky and innumer-
able as the sand by the seashore.
13 These all died in faith not having received
the promises, but having seen them from
afar were assured of them, embraced them,
and confessed that they were strangers and
pilgrims on the earth. 14 Those who say such
things declare plainly that they are looking
for a homeland. 15 And certainly, if they had
been thinking of the country out of which they
came, they might have had the opportunity
to return. 16 But they desired a better country,
that is, a heavenly one. Therefore God is not
ashamed to be called their God, for He has
prepared a city for them.
17 By faith Abraham, when he was tested, of-
fered up Isaac, and he who had received the
promises offered up his only begotten son.
18 Of him God said, "Through Isaac shall your
seed be named."[1] 19 He reasoned that God was
able to raise him up, even from the dead, from
which he indeed received him in a figurative
sense.
20 By faith Isaac blessed Jacob and Esau con-
cerning things to come.
21 By faith Jacob, when he was dying, blessed
each of the sons of Joseph and worshipped
while leaning on the top of his staff.
22 By faith Joseph, when he was dying, men-
tioned the exodus of the children of Israel and
gave instructions concerning his bones.
23 By faith Moses, when he was born, was
hidden by his parents for three months, be-
cause they saw he was a beautiful child, and
they were not afraid of the king's command.
24 By faith Moses, when he became of age, re-
fused to be called the son of Pharaoh's daugh-
ter, 25 choosing rather to suffer affliction with
the people of God than to enjoy the pleasures
of sin for a time. 26 He esteemed the reproach

11:7 1Pe 3:20
11:8 Ge 12:1–4
11:9 Ge 12:8
11:10 Heb 12:22
11:11 Ge 18:11–14
11:12 Ge 22:17
11:13 Ge 23:4
11:15 Ge 24:6–8
11:16 Ex 3:6
11:18 Ge 21:12
11:19 Ro 4:17–21
11:22 Ex 13:19
11:23 Ex 1:16
11:24 Ex 2:10–11
11:26 Heb 2:2

[1] *18* Ge 21:12.

RAHAB'S STORY

Perhaps no other story of a woman in the Bible is as powerful a testimony of redemption and grace as the story of Rahab, the harlot of Jericho.

According to both our current standards and the standards of her times, Rahab was a fallen woman. She practiced a despised profession in the city of Jericho, a city that had been cursed for the inhospitable way it had treated the children of Israel as they passed on their way from the wilderness to the Promised Land. Rahab had so many strikes against her that anyone looking at her life would believe there was no hope for a positive future.

But this woman became a savior of her family and played an important part in the military conquest of the city by the Jews. In addition, she became an ancestor of Jesus. Her life is a powerful illustration of the redemption Christ provides to us and how He can give power and purpose to the most negative life.

The Bible says that Rahab was a professional harlot. She was so well known and successful that her house was perched high on the city walls—the famous walls of Jericho.

We can determine from the Scriptures that her house was a gathering place for all different kinds and classes of men. No doubt men of all ages and occupations passed through her house—merchants, soldiers, students, scholars, and travelers from distant lands.

As she entertained these men and the after-dinner wine began to flow, she no doubt heard stories about the invisible God of the Jews who fights against those who fight against His people. He was depicted as a warrior God who fights with fire and hail and thunder, who changes the course of rivers, brings down cities, and sweeps all before Him—even pharaohs and kings—for His people's sake.

The guests speak in fearful whispers, saying this band of Jehovah-worshippers is marching two million strong toward her land and moving toward her very city! The information becomes crystal clear when a group of men show up at her house. By their unfamiliar clothing and strange ways, Rahab concludes they must be a scouting party of the very enemy she has heard so much about.

But Rahab, believing the reports of this strange God, Jehovah, is moved to help the spies. She agrees to hide the men from the soldiers of Jericho who are pursuing them. She hides them in a basket on the roof of her house, and as soon as she has sent the soldiers away in a wrong direction, she lets the men down in a basket outside the city walls.

Rahab saves the spies, but in so doing, she makes a powerful agreement with them. She asks them to remember her, her parents, her siblings, and all that pertains to them—to save them when the Jews invade the city.

The Jews tell her she must hang a scarlet cloth from her window high up on the wall as a signal to the invading army. They will pass by her house if they see the red cloth, and everyone in the house will be spared. In this way, Rahab became not only the salvation of her own family but also an Old Testament typology of Christ, the Savior.

There are two compelling life lessons to learn here. One is that God can and will use us as the instruments of salvation for our loved ones. The other is that God does not count our past when He is planning our future!

The end of Rahab's life is a powerful story of faith, trust, salvation, and service. God bestows a tremendous honor on a woman with a bad reputation.

Rahab, the harlot, marries into the aristocracy of the Jews. She becomes Boaz's mother and the great-great-grandmother of David, the greatest king in the history of Israel. But even more important than that, the genealogy of Jesus listed in the Book of Matthew traces Jesus' ancestors back to Rahab! She is an honored ancestor of Jesus, the Christ.

My sisters, be encouraged. We cannot imagine where our lives in God will lead us. You can draw strength, joy, and self-esteem from this wonderful account of Rahab's life.

Remember that God is no respecter of persons. He places His gifts and anointing in a person, not in a pedigree. He honors character, integrity, commitment, a pure heart, and honest motives—not the résumés of our lives, good or bad.

Nothing in our past can disqualify us from a positive, promising, and powerful future in God because God's plans for our future cancel out the failures of the past.

Rahab's life was abundantly blessed with an unexpected future because she uprooted herself based on the spies' description of their God. Her life tells us that in order to cancel our past, it is sometimes necessary to leave familiar situations, surroundings, and people to truly find our place in God.

Rahab's story also shows the power of a positive testimony. The spies talked about their God in such a way as to make Rahab want to leave all to follow Him. We don't know when the words we speak about our relationship with God will touch others so powerfully that they, like Rahab, will want to change their lives, surrender their past, and leave all to follow Him into a bright new future.

Her life shows us too that God will give us opportunities to make choices that will determine our destinies. When we make the right ones, we will walk away from our past into a glorious future of power, purpose, and praise.

God doesn't want us to be bound by society's or the church's ideas of what women can do, nor does He want us to be held back by our own guilt and shame. It's time to let go of all the things that hold you back and step into your true destiny!

Winifred W. Morris

of Christ as greater riches than the treasures in
Egypt, for he looked to the reward. 27 By faith
he forsook Egypt, not fearing the wrath of the
king. He endured by looking to Him who is in-
visible. 28 By faith he kept the Passover and the
sprinkling of blood, lest the one who destroys
the firstborn touch them.
29 By faith they passed through the Red Sea
as on dry land, which the Egyptians attempted
to do, but were drowned.
30 By faith the walls of Jericho fell down after
they were encircled for seven days.
31 By faith the prostitute Rahab, when she
received the spies with peace, did not perish
with those who did not believe.
32 And what more shall I say? For time would
fail me to tell of Gideon, Barak, Samson,
Jephthah, of David and Samuel and the proph-
ets, 33 who through faith subdued kingdoms, ad-
ministered justice, obtained promises, stopped
the mouths of lions, 34 quenched the violence
of fire, escaped the edge of the sword, out of
weakness were made strong, became valiant
in fighting, and turned the armies of foreign
enemies to flight. 35 Women received their dead
raised to life again. Others were tortured and
did not accept deliverance, so that they might
obtain a better resurrection. 36 Still others had
trials of mocking and scourging, and even
chains and imprisonment. 37 They were stoned,
they were sawn in two, were tempted, were
slain with the sword. They wandered around
in sheepskins and goatskins, while destitute,
afflicted, and tormented. 38 The world was not
worthy of them. They wandered in deserts and
mountains, in dens and caves of the earth.
39 These all have obtained a good report
through faith, but they did not receive the
promise. 40 For God provided something
better for us, so that with us they would be
made perfect.

The Discipline of the Lord

12 Therefore, since we are encompassed
with such a great cloud of witnesses,
let us also lay aside every weight and the sin
that so easily entangles us, and let us run with
endurance the race that is set before us. 2 Let
us look to Jesus, the author and finisher of our
faith, who for the joy that was set before Him
endured the cross, despising the shame, and is
seated at the right hand of the throne of God.
3 For consider Him who endured such hostility
from sinners against Himself, lest you become
weary and your hearts give up.
4 You have not yet resisted to bloodshed while
striving against sin. 5 And you have forgotten
the exhortation addressed to you as sons:

"My son, do not despise the discipline from
the Lord,
nor grow weary when you are rebuked
by Him;
6 for whom the Lord loves He disciplines,
and scourges every son whom He
receives."[1]

7 Endure discipline; God is dealing with you
as with sons. For what son is there whom a
father does not discipline? 8 If you are without
discipline, of which everyone has partaken,
then you are illegitimate children and not
sons. 9 Furthermore, we have had human
fathers, and they corrected us, and we gave
them reverence. Shall we not much more be
subject to the Father of spirits and live? 10 For
they indeed disciplined us for a short time ac-
cording to their own judgment, but He does
so for our profit, that we may partake of His
holiness. 11 Now no discipline seems to be joy-
ful at the time, but grievous. Yet afterward it
yields the peaceful fruit of righteousness in
those who have been trained by it.
12 Therefore lift up your tired hands, and
strengthen your weak knees. 13 Make straight
paths for your feet, lest that which is lame go
out of joint, but rather be healed.

Warning Against Rejecting God's Grace

14 Pursue peace with all men, and the holi-
ness without which no one will see the Lord,
15 watching diligently so that no one falls short
of the grace of God, lest any root of bitterness
spring up to cause trouble, and many become
defiled by it, 16 lest there be any sexually im-
moral or profane person, as Esau, who for one
morsel of food sold his birthright. 17 For you
know that afterward, when he wanted to inherit
the blessing, he was rejected. For he found no
place for repentance, though he sought it dili-
gently with tears.

> Let every root of bitterness be cut from my life (Heb 12:15).

18 You have not come to a mountain that
can be touched and that burned with fire,
and to blackness and darkness and storm,
19 and to the sound of a trumpet and to a voice
speaking words, such that those who heard
them begged that the word not be spoken to
them anymore. 20 For they could not endure
that which was commanded: "If so much as a
beast touches the mountain, it must be stoned
or thrust through with a spear."[2] 21 So terrible
was the sight that Moses said, "I am terrified
and trembling."[3]

11:27 Heb 11:13
11:28 Ex 12:21–30
11:31 Jas 2:25
11:32 1Sa 1:20
11:33 Jdg 14:5–6
11:36 Jer 20:2
11:37 1Ki 19:10
11:38 1Ki 18:4
11:39 Heb 11:13
11:40 Rev 6:11
12:2 Heb 1:3
12:3 Gal 6:9
12:4 Heb 10:32–34
12:5 Pr 3:11–12
12:6 Rev 3:19
12:7 Pr 13:24
12:9 Nu 16:22
12:10 2Pe 1:4
12:11 Isa 32:17
12:12 Isa 35:3
12:13 Gal 6:1
12:14 Ro 14:19
12:15 Gal 5:4
12:16 Heb 13:4
12:18 Dt 4:11
12:19 Dt 18:16
12:20 Ex 19:12–13
12:21 Ex 19:16

[1] *5–6* Pr 3:11–12. [2] *20* Ex 19:12–13. [3] *21* Dt 9:19.

[22] But you have come to Mount Zion and to the city of the living God, the heavenly Jerusalem, and to an innumerable company of angels; [23] to the general assembly and church of the firstborn, who are enrolled in heaven; to God, the Judge of all; and to the spirits of the righteous ones made perfect; [24] and to Jesus, the Mediator of a new covenant; and to the sprinkled blood that speaks better than that of Abel.

[25] See that you do not refuse Him who is speaking. For if they did not escape when they refused Him who spoke on earth, much less shall we escape if we turn away from Him who speaks from heaven. [26] At that time His voice shook the earth, but now He has given us a promise, saying, "Yet once more I will shake not only the earth but also heaven."[1] [27] And this statement, "Yet once more," signifies the removal of those things that can be shaken, things that are created, so that only those things that cannot be shaken will remain.

[28] Therefore, since we are receiving a kingdom that cannot be moved, let us be gracious, by which we may serve God acceptably with reverence and godly fear. [29] For our God is a consuming fire.

Service That Pleases God

13 Let brotherly love continue. [2] Do not forget to entertain strangers, for thereby some have entertained angels unknowingly. [3] Remember those who are in chains, as if imprisoned with them, and those who are ill treated, since you are also in the body.

[4] Marriage is to be honored among everyone, and the bed undefiled. But God will judge the sexually immoral and adulterers. [5] Let your lives be without love of money, and be content with the things you have. For He has said:

"I will never leave you,
nor forsake you."[2]

God will not fail me! He won't leave me helpless or without His support (Heb 13:5).

[6] So we may boldly say:

"The Lord is my helper; I will not fear.
What can man do to me?"[3]

[7] Remember those who rule over you, who have proclaimed to you the word of God. Follow their faith, considering the results it has produced in their lives. [8] Jesus Christ is the same yesterday, and today, and forever.

[9] Do not be carried away with diverse and strange doctrines. It is a good thing that the heart be strengthened with grace, not with foods, which have not profited those who have been occupied with them. [10] We have an altar from which those who serve in the tabernacle have no right to eat.

[11] For the bodies of those beasts, whose blood is brought into the sanctuary by the high priest on account of sin, are burned outside the camp. [12] Therefore Jesus also, so that He might sanctify the people with His own blood, suffered outside the gate. [13] Therefore let us go forth to Him outside the camp, bearing the reproach that He bore. [14] For here we have no continuing city, but we seek one to come.

[15] Through Him, then, let us continually offer to God the sacrifice of praise, which is the fruit of our lips, giving thanks to His name. [16] But do not forget to do good and to share. For with such sacrifices God is well pleased.

[17] Obey your leaders and submit to them, for they watch over your souls as those who must give an account. Let them do this with joy and not complaining, for that would not be profitable to you.

[18] Pray for us. For we trust that we have a good conscience and in all things are willing to live honestly. [19] But I implore you to pray, that I may be restored to you very soon.

12:22 Gal 4:26
12:23 Lk 10:20
12:24 Ge 4:10
12:25 Heb 8:5
12:26 Ex 19:18
12:28 Da 2:44
12:29 Dt 4:24
13:1 1Pe 1:22
13:2 Mt 25:35
13:3 Mt 25:36
13:4 1Co 6:9
13:5 Jos 1:5
13:6 Ps 56:4
13:7 Heb 13:17
13:8 Heb 1:12
13:9 Eph 4:14
13:10 1Co 9:13
13:11 Ex 29:14
13:13 Heb 11:26
13:14 Heb 12:22
13:15 Hos 14:2
13:16 Ro 12:13
13:17 Ac 20:28
13:18 1Th 5:25
13:19 Phm 1:22

SPIRITLED WOMAN

COUNSEL FROM THE SPIRIT BASICS

He Never Fails

God will never leave you or forsake you—ever! Let this truth sink deep within your spirit by meditating on and declaring these truths from God's Word:

> Let your lives be without love of money, and be content with the things you have. For He has said: "I will never leave you, nor forsake you."
>
> —Hebrews 13:5

God has hold of me—He won't ever let me down.

God is for me. He loves me! Nothing—nothing that has happened and none of my questions—can stand between Him and me.

Karen Jensen Salisbury

[1]26 Hag 2:6. [2]5 Dt 31:6, 8; Jos 1:5. [3]6 Ps 118:6.

Benediction and Final Greetings

[20] Now may the God of peace, who through
the blood of the eternal covenant brought
again from the dead our Lord Jesus, the Great
Shepherd of the sheep, [21] make you perfect in
every good work to do His will, working in you
that which is pleasing in His sight, through
Jesus Christ, to whom be glory forever and
ever. Amen.

[22] I implore you, brothers, to heed this word
of exhortation, for I have written to you in few
words.
[23] Know that our brother Timothy has been set
free, with whom I shall see you if he comes soon.
[24] Greet all those who rule over you and all
the saints. Those from Italy greet you.
[25] Grace be with you all. Amen.

I am made perfect through the blood of the everlasting covenant (Heb 13:20–21).

13:20 Zec 9:11
13:21 Php 2:13

13:22 1Pe 5:12
13:23 1Th 3:2
13:24 Heb 13:7
13:25 Col 4:18

Author: James, the half-brother of Jesus

Written: AD 46–48, from Jerusalem

Theme: What Christian Faith in Action Looks Like

JAMES

Dear SpiritLed Woman,

I once heard a well-known leader say that God told him, "Where there is no mixture, I will pour out My Spirit without measure." A mixture is a combination of more than one element. The Spirit of God plus our carnal nature is a mixture. God's life plus the ways and ideas of the world is a mixture. God condemns such impurity: "You adulterers and adulteresses, do you not know that the friendship with the world is enmity with God? Whoever therefore will be a friend of the world is the enemy of God" (Jas 4:4).

The world needs to see a church without mixture—operating in God's power with pure hearts. Are you willing to be one He uses for His purpose? Ask Him for a fresh revelation of who He is and begin to look at the world around you from an eternal viewpoint. Just like the believers in the early church, you as a SpiritLed woman are called to change the world!

Joy F. Strang

Salutation

1 James, a servant of God and of the Lord Jesus Christ,

To the twelve tribes which are scattered abroad:

Greetings.

Faith and Wisdom

> When I'm feeling clueless as to how to get my kids to obey, I can fall to my knees and ask God for practical wisdom (Jas 1:5).

2 My brothers, count it all joy when you fall into diverse temptations, 3 knowing that the trying of your faith develops patience. 4 But let patience perfect its work, that you may be perfect and complete, lacking nothing. 5 If any of you lacks wisdom, let him ask of God, who gives to all men liberally and without criticism, and it will be given to him. 6 But let him ask in faith, without wavering. For he who wavers is like a wave of the sea, driven and tossed with the wind. 7 Let not that man think that he will receive anything from the Lord. 8 A double-minded man is unstable in all his ways.

> I must ask without doubting (Jas 1:6).

Poverty and Riches

9 Let the brother of low degree rejoice in that he is exalted, 10 but the rich in that he is made low, because as the flower of the grass he will pass away. 11 For the sun rises with a burning heat and it withers the grass, and its flowers fall, and its beauty perishes. So will the rich man wither away in his ways.

Trial and Temptation

12 Blessed is the man who endures temptation, for when he is tried, he will receive the crown of life, which the Lord has promised to those who love Him.

13 Let no man say when he is tempted, "I am tempted by God," for God cannot be tempted with evil; neither does He tempt anyone. 14 But each man is tempted when he is drawn away by his own lust and enticed. 15 Then, when lust has conceived, it brings forth sin; and when sin is finished, it brings forth death.

16 Do not err, my beloved brothers. 17 Every good gift and every perfect gift is from above and comes down from the Father of lights, with whom is no change or shadow of turning. 18 Of His own will He brought us forth with the word of truth, that we should be a kind of first fruits of His creatures.

> Only good comes from God (Jas 1:17).

Hearing and Doing the Word

19 Therefore, my beloved brothers, let every man be swift to hear, slow to speak, and slow to anger, 20 for the anger of man does not work the righteousness of God. 21 Therefore lay aside all filthiness and remaining wickedness and receive with meekness the engrafted word, which is able to save your souls.

22 Be doers of the word and not hearers only, deceiving yourselves. 23 For if anyone is a hearer of the word and not a doer, he is like a man viewing his natural face in a mirror. 24 He views himself, and goes his way, and immediately forgets what kind of man he was. 25 But whoever looks into the perfect law of liberty, and continues in it, and is not a forgetful hearer but a doer of the work, this man will be blessed in his deeds.

26 If anyone among you seems to be religious and does not bridle his tongue, but deceives his own heart, this man's religion is vain. 27 Religion that is pure and undefiled before God, the Father, is this: to visit the fatherless and widows in their affliction and to keep oneself unstained by the world.

Warning Against Partiality

2 My brothers, have faith in our Lord Jesus Christ, the Lord of glory, without partiality. 2 For if a man with a gold ring, in fine clothing, comes into your assembly, and also a poor man in ragged clothing comes in, 3 and you have respect for him who wears the fine clothing and say to him, "Sit here in a good place," and say to the poor, "Stand there," or "Sit here under my footstool," 4 have you not then become partial among yourselves and become judges with evil thoughts?

5 Listen, my beloved brothers. Has God not chosen the poor of this world to be rich in faith and heirs of the kingdom which He has promised to those who love Him? 6 But you have despised the poor. Do not rich men oppress you and drag you before the judgment seats? 7 Do they not blaspheme that worthy name by which you are called?

8 If you fulfill the royal law according to the Scripture, "You shall love your neighbor as yourself,"[1] you are doing well. 9 But if you show partiality, you are committing sin and are convicted by the law as sinners. 10 For whoever shall keep

1:1 Jn 7:35
1:2 Jas 1:12
1:4 Mt 5:48
1:5 Pr 2:3–6
1:6 Eph 4:14
1:8 Jas 4:8
1:10 1Co 7:31
1:11 Isa 40:7–8
1:12 Jas 2:5
1:15 Job 15:35
1:17 Mal 3:6

1:18 1Pe 1:23
1:19 Pr 10:19
1:21 Eph 1:13
1:22 Ro 2:13
1:25 Jas 2:12
1:26 Ps 34:13
2:1 1Co 2:8
2:4 Jn 7:24
2:5 Mt 5:3
2:6 1Co 11:22
2:7 Ac 11:26
2:8 Lev 19:18
2:10 Gal 3:10

[1] *8* Lev 19:18.

the whole law and yet offend in one point is guilty of breaking the whole law. 11 For He who said, "Do not commit adultery,"[1] also said, "Do not kill."[2] Now if you do not commit adultery, yet you kill, you have become a lawbreaker.

12 So speak and so do as those who will be judged by the law of liberty. 13 For he who has shown no mercy will have judgment without mercy, for mercy triumphs over judgment.

Faith and Works

14 What does it profit, my brothers, if a man says he has faith but has no works? Can faith save him? 15 If a brother or sister is naked and lacking daily food, 16 and one of you says to them, "Depart in peace, be warmed and filled," and yet you give them nothing that the body needs, what does it profit? 17 So faith by itself, if it has no works, is dead.

18 But a man may say, "You have faith and I have works."

Show me your faith without your works, and I will show you my faith by my works. 19 You believe that there is one God; you do well. The demons also believe and tremble.

20 But do you want to be shown, O foolish man, that faith without works is dead? 21 Was not Abraham our father justified by works when he offered his son Isaac on the altar? 22 Do you see how faith worked with his works, and by works faith was made perfect? 23 The Scripture was fulfilled which says, "Abraham believed God, and it was reckoned to him as righteousness,"[3] and he was called the friend of God. 24 You see then how by works a man is justified, and not by faith only.

All the equipping and teaching and excitement and righteousness in the world don't count for much if there's no action (Jas 2:20).

25 Likewise, was not Rahab the prostitute justified by works when she received the messengers and sent them out another way? 26 As the body without the spirit is dead, so faith without works is dead.

The Tongue

3 My brothers, not many of you should become teachers, knowing that we shall receive the greater judgment. 2 We all err in many ways. But if any man does not err in word, he is a perfect man and able also to control the whole body.

3 See how we put bits in the mouths of horses that they may obey us, and we control their whole bodies. 4 And observe ships. Though they are so great and are driven by fierce winds, yet they are directed with a very small rudder wherever the captain pleases. 5 Even so, the tongue is a little part of the body and boasts great things. See how great a forest a little fire kindles. 6 The tongue is a fire, a world of evil. The tongue is among the parts of the body, defiling the whole body, and setting the course of nature on fire, and it is set on fire by hell.

7 All kinds of beasts, and birds, and serpents, and things in the sea are tamed or have been tamed by mankind. 8 But no man can tame the tongue. It is an unruly evil, full of deadly poison.

9 With it we bless the Lord and Father, and with it we curse men, who are made in the image of God. 10 Out of the same mouth proceed blessing and cursing. My brothers, these things ought not to be so. 11 Does a spring yield at the same opening sweet and bitter water? 12 Can the fig tree, my brothers, bear olives, or a vine, figs? So no spring can yield both salt water and fresh water.

The Wisdom From Above

13 Who is wise and understanding among you? Let him show his works by his good life in the meekness of wisdom. 14 But if you have bitter envying and strife in your hearts, do not boast and do not lie against the truth. 15 This wisdom descends not from above, but is earthly, unspiritual, and devilish. 16 For where there is envying and strife, there is confusion and every evil work.

I renounce all earthly, sensual, and demonic wisdom (Jas 3:15).

17 But the wisdom that is from above is first pure, then peaceable, gentle, open to reason, full of mercy and good fruits, without partiality, and without hypocrisy. 18 And the fruit of righteousness is sown in peace by those who make peace.

Friendship With the World

4 Where do wars and fights among you come from? Do they not come from your lusts that war in your body? 2 You lust and do not have, so you kill. You desire to have and cannot obtain. You fight and war. Yet you do not have, because you do not ask. 3 You ask, and do not receive, because you ask amiss, that you may spend it on your passions.

4 You adulterers and adulteresses, do you not know that the friendship with the world is enmity with God? Whoever therefore will

2:11 Ex 20:13–14
2:12 Jas 1:25
2:13 Pr 21:13
2:14 Jas 1:22–25
2:15 Lk 3:11
2:18 Gal 5:6
2:19 Dt 6:4
2:20 Jas 2:26
2:21 Ge 22:16–18
2:22 1Th 1:3
2:23 Ge 15:6
2:25 Heb 11:31
2:26 Jas 2:20
3:1 Mt 23:13
3:2 Mt 12:37
3:3 Ps 32:9
....
3:5 Ps 73:8–9
3:6 Pr 16:27
3:8 Ps 140:3
3:9 1Co 11:7
3:13 Jas 2:18
3:14 Jas 3:16
3:15 Jas 1:17
3:17 Ro 12:9
3:18 Pr 11:18
4:1 Ro 7:23
4:3 1Jn 5:14
4:4 Jn 15:19

[1] *11* Ex 20:14; Dt 5:18. [2] *11* Ex 20:13; Dt 5:17. [3] *23* Ge 15:6.

WOMAN OF THE SPIRIT

Power Is Available

Earnest, heartfelt prayer by a righteous man or woman of God "accomplishes much" (Jas 5:16).

James' use of Elijah as a model of dynamic and effective prayer is well taken. First, James assures us that Elijah did not have an edge over any of us but was "subject to natural passions as we are" (v. 17). Great prayers are prayed by ordinary people who are willing to believe God for the impossible. When we read Elijah's life story, to most of us he seems anything but ordinary. After all, he was a man who was fed by ravens, commanded a starving widow to feed him her last morsel, and called fire down from heaven. How many of us have experienced any of these things?

James 5:17–18 refers specifically to Elijah's prayer challenge and spiritual warfare with the prophets of Baal (1Ki 18). While this incident may seem surreal to some, many would admit that life is a constant war zone spiritually. Elijah's power encounter gives hope to beleaguered believers who wonder where God is when the enemy's bombs start exploding around them.

Are you in hand-to-hand combat and wonder if God is going to show up? Elijah's challenge to the prophets of Baal and the way he structured his worship spelled out in no uncertain terms that Yahweh—not Baal—is God. The outcome of this duel revealed the undeniable, awesome power of God, resulted in the destruction of Baal worship, and eventuated in rain, thus breaking the famine.

But the story does not stop with the power encounter. One may think that after such a dramatic victory, the rest of the journey would be a breeze. But not so. After the victory there was an assassination threat. Elijah experienced isolation and discouragement and even felt abandoned by God. Elijah's emotional and spiritual vulnerability reveals that he was "a man subject to natural passions as we are" (Jas 5:17). His story challenges us to believe that if his prayers were effective in spite of his flaws, spontaneity, and ups and downs, then there is hope that God can use us, ordinary as we are, to pray extraordinary prayers.

Jeannette Storms

be a friend of the world is the enemy of God. 5 Do you think that the Scripture says in vain, "He yearns jealously for the spirit that lives in us"[1]? 6 But He gives more grace. For this reason it says:

> "God resists the proud,
> but gives grace to the humble."[2]

When I draw near to God, He draws near to me (Jas 4:8).

7 Therefore submit yourselves to God. Resist the devil, and he will flee from you. 8 Draw near to God, and He will draw near to you. Cleanse your hands, you sinners, and purify your hearts, you double-minded. 9 Grieve and mourn and weep. Let your laughter be turned to mourning, and your joy to dejection. 10 Humble yourselves in the sight of the Lord, and He will lift you up.

God longs to be seen, known, and encountered (Jas 4:8).

Judging a Brother

11 Do not speak evil of one another, brothers. He who speaks evil of his brother and judges his brother speaks evil of the law and judges the law. If you judge the law, you are not a doer of the law, but a judge. 12 There is one Lawgiver who is able to save and to destroy. Who are you to judge another?

Warning Against Boasting

13 Come now, you who say, "Today or tomorrow we will go into this city, spend a year there, buy and sell, and make a profit," 14 whereas you do not know what will happen tomorrow. What is your life? It is just a vapor that appears for a little while and then vanishes away. 15 Instead you ought to say, "If the Lord wills, we shall live and do this or that." 16 But now you are rejoicing in your boastings. All such rejoicing is evil. 17 Therefore, to him who knows to do good and does not do it, it is sin.

Warning to the Rich

5 Come now, you rich men, weep and howl for your miseries that shall come upon you. 2 Your riches are corrupted and your garments are moth-eaten. 3 Your gold and silver are corroded, and their corrosion will be a witness against you and will eat your flesh like fire. You have stored up treasures for the last days. 4 Indeed the wages that you kept back by fraud from the laborers who harvested your fields are crying, and the cries of those who harvested have entered into the ears of the Lord of Hosts. 5 You have lived in pleasure on the earth and have been wayward. You have nourished your hearts as in a day of slaughter. 6 You have condemned and killed the righteous man who does not resist you.

4:6 Pr 3:34
4:7 Eph 4:27
4:8 2Ch 15:2
4:9 Lk 6:25
4:10 Mt 23:12
4:11 1Pe 2:1
4:12 Mt 10:28
4:13 Pr 27:1
4:14 Ps 102:3
4:15 Ac 18:21
4:16 1Co 5:6
4:17 Jn 9:41
5:2 Job 13:28
5:3 Ro 2:5
5:4 Lev 19:13

5:5 Lk 16:19

SPIRITLED WOMAN

COUNSEL FROM THE SPIRIT BASICS

Mend the Broken Pieces

> Confess your trespasses to one another and pray for one another, that you may be healed. The effective, fervent prayer of a righteous man accomplishes much.
> —JAMES 5:16

I live in a world plagued with evil and suffering. Broken lives walk around me, and I look past their hurting hearts. This is a lost world, a fallen world in need of hope, in need of light. But sometimes I have to recognize not only the darkness but also my own prayerlessness.

This is what has been so heavy in my heart. It is that I sometimes forget how to pray. I say I believe in the power of prayer, yet the time I spend in prayer is insignificant. How is it that I can access the almighty God, yet instead I choose to spend my time browsing through Facebook or researching the best parenting sites?

A tragedy brings us to our knees. It makes us realize how far we have moved away from the Lord and how we have allowed darkness to cover the light we are supposed to give and spread with this world. But darkness cannot destroy light—not when Jesus has already won the battle for us.

So I will fall on my knees, spread out my arms, and ask God to mend the broken pieces of my heart. I will ask Him to make me whole. I will beg Him to move! The same God who parted the sea, the One who made the blind man see and the lame man walk—He can move today too. So move, Lord Jesus. Show us Your power, Your glory, and Your unending love.

Ellen Stumbo

[1] 5 The source of this quotation is uncertain. [2] 6 Pr 3:34.

SPIRIT-TO-SPIRIT PRAYER

PRAYER FOR HEALTH ISSUES

Heavenly Father, as we face overwhelming health issues, may You be our first thought and not our last hope. May we truly come to understand what it means to touch the hem of Your garment, to seek first the kingdom of God. With You we have total and complete healing in our lives, in our health, in our homes, in our finances, in our marriages. There is no area of our being that You cannot touch and bring back to life. Father God, the area that we most need Your healing touch in our lives is ____________________. We ask that You remove all fear and doubt. Satan can use this as a tool against us, and we invite You to step in as Lord and Master, controlling every part of our being. We thank You for healing us, for You alone are the Great Physician. We give You all praise, honor, and glory for the good things that are on the way. In Jesus' name, amen.

Tish Hagee Tucker

Patience and Prayer

7 Therefore be patient, brothers, until the
coming of the Lord. Notice how the farmer
waits for the precious fruit of the earth and is
patient with it until he receives the early and
late rain. 8 You also be patient. Establish your
hearts, for the coming of the Lord is drawing
near. 9 Do not grumble against one another,
brothers, lest you be condemned. Look, the
Judge is standing at the door.

> If I sow good seed and I sow it well and in good soil, the harvest will be plentiful (Jas 5:7).

10 My brothers, take the prophets, who spoke
in the name of the Lord, as an example of
suffering and patience. 11 Indeed we count
them happy who endure. You have heard
of the patience of Job and have seen the
purpose of the Lord, that the Lord is very
gracious and merciful.
12 But above all things, my brothers, do not
swear, either by heaven or by the earth or by
any other oath. But let your "Yes" be "Yes"
and your "No" be "No," that you do not fall
into condemnation.
13 Is anyone among you suffering? Let him
pray. Is anyone merry? Let him sing psalms.
14 Is anyone sick among you? Let him call for
the elders of the church, and let them pray
over him, anointing him with oil in the name
of the Lord. 15 And the prayer of faith will save
the sick, and the Lord will raise him up. And if
he has committed any sins, he will be forgiven.
16 Confess your faults to one another and pray
for one another, that you may be healed. The
effective, fervent prayer of a righteous man
accomplishes much.
17 Elijah was a man subject to natural pas-
sions as we are, and he prayed earnestly that
it might not rain, and it did not rain on the
earth for three years and six months. 18 And he
prayed again, and the sky gave rain, and the
earth brought forth its fruit.
19 Brothers, if any one of you strays from
the truth and someone corrects him, 20 let him
know that he who converts the sinner from the
error of his way will save a soul from death and
will cover a multitude of sins.

5:7 Dt 11:14
5:8 1Pe 4:7
5:9 Mt 24:33
5:11 Ex 34:6

5:13 Ps 50:15
5:14 Mk 6:13
5:16 Ge 20:17
5:17 1Ki 17:1
5:18 1Ki 18:42–45
5:19 Mt 18:15
5:20 Ro 11:14

Author: The apostle Peter

Written: AD 62 or 63, from Babylon (a moniker for Rome or Jerusalem)

Themes: Faithfulness to Jesus Christ, Suffering and Persecution

1 PETER

Dear Spirit Led Woman,

In Peter's first letter he commends us, "But as He who has called you is holy, so be holy in all your conduct, because it is written, 'Be holy, for I am holy'" (1Pe 1:15–16). Holiness is a characteristic that was the primary focus of the Spirit in the late 1800s. It defined the Holiness movement and set the stage for the Pentecostal movement that followed at the turn of the century.

But gradually the emphasis in the Holiness movement changed from seeking to develop a pure heart to simply following a set of rules, and true holiness—taking on the nature of God—was lost. We settled for a doctrine of partial holiness: one that allowed a watered-down purity to coexist with carnal hearts full of compromise, competition, and division.

It's time to embrace true holiness. When you allow the Spirit to work in you, the limitations of the past and the hindrances of your old nature are taken away. Everything the enemy planted in your life is destroyed, and the image of God's Son begins to come forth.

Joy F. Strang

Salutation

1 Peter, an apostle of Jesus Christ,

To the refugees scattered throughout Pon-
tus, Galatia, Cappadocia, Asia, and Bithynia,
2 elect according to the foreknowledge of God
the Father, through sanctification by the Spirit,
for obedience and sprinkling with the blood
of Jesus Christ:

Grace to you and peace be multiplied.

A Living Hope

3 Blessed be the God and Father of our Lord
Jesus Christ, who according to His abundant
mercy has given us a new birth into a living
hope through the resurrection of Jesus Christ
from the dead, 4 to an incorruptible and un-
defiled inheritance that does not fade away,
kept in heaven for you, 5 who are protected by
the power of God through faith for a salvation
ready to be revealed in the last time. 6 In this
you greatly rejoice, even though now, if for
a little while, you have had to suffer various
trials, 7 in order that the genuineness of your
faith, which is more precious than gold that
perishes, though it is tried by fire, may be
found to result in praise, glory, and honor at
the revelation of Jesus Christ, 8 whom, having
not seen, you love; and in whom, though
you do not see Him now, you believe and
you rejoice with joy unspeakable and full of
glory, 9 receiving as the result of your faith
the salvation of your souls.

10 Concerning this salvation, the prophets
who prophesied of the grace that should come
to you have inquired and searched diligently,
11 seeking the events and time the Spirit of
Christ, who was within them, signified when
He foretold the sufferings of Christ and the
glories to follow. 12 It was revealed to them
that they were not serving themselves but you,
concerning the things which are now reported
to you by those who have preached the gospel
to you through the Holy Spirit, who was sent
from heaven—things into which the angels
desire to look.

A Call to Holy Living

13 Therefore guard your minds, be sober,
and hope to the end for the grace that is to
be brought to you at the revelation of Jesus
Christ. 14 As obedient children do not conduct
yourselves according to the former lusts in your
ignorance. 15 But as He who has called you is
holy, so be holy in all your conduct, 16 because
it is written, "Be holy, for I am holy."[1]

17 And if you address as Father the One who
impartially judges according to each one's
work, conduct yourselves in fear during the
time of your sojourning. 18 For you know
that you were not redeemed from your vain
way of life inherited from your fathers with
perishable things, like silver or gold, 19 but
with the precious blood of Christ, as of a
lamb without blemish and without spot. 20 He
was foreordained before the creation of the
world, but was revealed in these last times
for you. 21 Through Him you believe in God
who raised Him up from the dead and gave
Him glory, so that your faith and hope might
be in God.

22 Since your souls have been purified by
obedience to the truth through the Spirit unto
a genuine brotherly love, love one another
deeply with a pure heart, 23 for you have been
born again, not from perishable seed, but im-
perishable, through the word of God which
lives and abides forever. 24 For

"All flesh is as grass,
and all the glory of man as the flower
of grass.
The grass withers, and its flower falls away,
25 but the word of the Lord endures
forever."[2]

This is the word that was preached to you.

The Living Stone and the Holy Nation

2 Therefore put away all wickedness, deceit,
hypocrisy, envy, and all evil speaking. 2 As
newborn babies, desire the pure milk of the
word, that by it you may grow, 3 if it is true that
you have experienced that the Lord is good.

4 Coming to Him as to a living stone who
is rejected by men, but chosen by God and
precious, 5 you also, as living stones, are being
built up into a spiritual house as a holy priest-
hood to offer up spiritual sacrifices that are
acceptable to God through Jesus Christ. 6 For
also it is contained in the Scripture,

"Look! I lay in Zion
a chief cornerstone, elect, precious,
and he who believes in Him
shall never be put to shame."[3]

7 Therefore, to you who believe, He is precious.
But to those who are disobedient,

"The stone that the builders rejected
has become the cornerstone,"[4]

8 and,

"A stone of stumbling,
and a rock of offense."[5]

They stumble because they are disobedient to
the word, to which also they were appointed.

1:1 Ac 16:6–7
1:2 Ro 11:2
1:3 1Co 15:20
1:4 Col 1:5
1:5 Eph 2:8
1:6 Jas 1:2
1:7 Job 23:10
1:8 Jn 20:29
1:9 Ro 6:22
1:10 Mt 13:17
1:11 2Pe 1:21
1:12 Jn 15:26
1:13 1Pe 4:7
1:14 Ro 12:2
1:15 2Co 7:1
1:16 Lev 11:44

1:17 Mt 6:9
1:18 1Co 6:20
1:19 Jn 1:29
1:20 Eph 1:4
1:21 Heb 2:9
1:22 Heb 13:1
1:23 Heb 4:12
1:25 Isa 40:8
2:1 Eph 4:31
2:2 Mt 18:3
2:4 1Pe 2:7
2:5 Php 4:18
2:6 Isa 28:16
2:8 Isa 8:14

[1] *16* Lev 11:44; 19:2; 20:7. [2] *24–25* Isa 40:6–8. [3] *6* Isa 28:16. [4] *7* Ps 118:22. [5] *8* Isa 8:14.

WOMAN OF THE SPIRIT

Challenged by Fear

Did you know everyone is challenged at some point in their life's journey with some kind of fear? Even people whom we may perceive as not having any fear at all have had moments when they had to push past fear. The blessing does not lie in having no fear, because there is healthy fear—like the fear of God. The blessing lies in the efforts you make in working toward becoming mentally, emotionally, and spiritually stronger and more skillful at what you are wired to do until you are empowered to face and conquer your fears. Eleanor Roosevelt said, "The danger lies in refusing to face the fear, in not daring to come to grips with it....You must make yourself succeed every time. You must do the thing you think you cannot do."

God gave Joshua the encouragement he needed, and he went on to become one of the most powerful commanders the nation of Israel ever had. Joshua had to learn the art of conditioning his mind to succeed at life and win.

In the same way, you must learn the art of mental conditioning: "Guard your minds" (1Pe 1:13). Do not quit or give in to your fears. Assume the posture of a conqueror.

Hear the Word of the Lord taken from Isaiah 41:10: "Do not fear, for I am with you; do not be dismayed, for I am your God. I will strengthen you, I will help you, yes, I will uphold you with My righteous right hand."

Courage, boldness, and confidence give us a solid footing in prayer to defeat the enemy. We have to know who we are in the spirit to move heaven; otherwise, we are too timid to make a difference.

It is time to take our positions in the field. But one of the things we need to realize is that authority and power are different things, though we often use them interchangeably. The power is in the government or kingdom that backs the individual; authority is invested in the individual as a representative of the government or kingdom. Our kingdom—the kingdom of heaven—has not only the power but also the authority to rule.

The power of prayer is not merely in the words we speak but in our relationship to the One giving authority. Thus, prayer is first and foremost an essential way of opening communication with the throne room of God.

Cindy Trimm

9 But you are a chosen race, a royal priest-
hood, a holy nation, a people for God's own
possession, so that you may declare the good-
ness of Him who has called you out of dark-
ness into His marvelous light. 10 In times past,
you were not a people, but now you are the
people of God. You had not received mercy,
but now you have received mercy.

Live as Servants of God

11 Dearly beloved, I implore you as aliens
and refugees, abstain from fleshly lusts, which
wage war against the soul. 12 Live your lives
honorably among the Gentiles, so that though
they speak against you as evildoers, they shall
see your good works and thereby glorify God
in the day of visitation.

13 Submit yourselves to every human authority
for the Lord's sake, whether it be to the king,
as supreme, 14 or to governors, as sent by him
for the punishment of evildoers and to praise
those who do right. 15 For it is the will of God
that by doing right you may put to silence the
ignorance of foolish men. 16 As free people, do
not use your liberty as a covering for evil, but
live as servants of God. 17 Honor all people. Love
the brotherhood. Fear God. Honor the king.

The Example of Christ's Suffering

18 Servants, be submissive to your masters
with all fear, not only to the good and gentle, but
also to the harsh. 19 For this is commendable, if
because of conscience toward God a person en-
dures grief, suffering unjustly. 20 For what credit
is it if when you are being beaten for your sins
you patiently endure? But if when doing good
and suffering for it, you patiently endure, this
is favorable before God. 21 For to this you were
called, because Christ suffered for us, leaving us
an example, that you should follow His steps:

22 "He committed no sin,
nor was deceit found in His mouth."[1]

23 When He was reviled, He did not revile
back; when He suffered, He did not threaten,
but He entrusted Himself to Him who judges
righteously. 24 He Himself bore our sins in His
own body on the tree, that we, being dead to
sins, should live unto righteousness. "By His
wounds you were healed."[2] 25 For you were as
sheep going astray, but now have been returned
to the Shepherd and Guardian of your souls.

I am healed by the stripes of Jesus
(1Pe 2:24).

Wives and Husbands

3 Likewise you wives, be submissive to
your own husbands, so that if any do
not obey the word, they may be won without
a word by the conduct of their wives, 2 as they
see the purity and reverence of your lives.
3 Do not let your adorning be the outward
adorning of braiding the hair, wearing gold,
or putting on fine clothing. 4 But let it be the
hidden nature of the heart, that which is not
corruptible, even the ornament of a gentle
and quiet spirit, which is very precious in the
sight of God. 5 For in this manner, in the old
times, the holy women, who trusted in God,
adorned themselves, being submissive to
their own husbands, 6 even as Sarah obeyed
Abraham, calling him lord. You are her children
as long as you do right and are not afraid
with any terror.

7 Likewise, you husbands, live considerately
with your wives, giving honor to the woman
as the weaker vessel, since they too are also
heirs of the grace of life, so that your prayers
will not be hindered.

Suffering for Righteousness' Sake

8 Finally, be all of one mind, be loving toward
one another, be gracious, and be kind. 9 Do not
repay evil for evil, or curse for curse, but on
the contrary, bless, knowing that to this you
are called, so that you may receive a blessing.
10 For

"He who would love life
and see good days,
let him keep his tongue from evil,
and his lips from speaking deceit.
11 Let him turn away from evil and do good;
let him seek peace and pursue it.
12 For the eyes of the Lord are on the
righteous,
and His ears are open to their prayers;
but the face of the Lord is against those
who do evil."[3]

13 Who is he who will harm you if you follow
that which is good? 14 But even if you suffer
for the sake of righteousness, you are bless-
ed. "Do not be afraid of their terror, do not be
troubled."[4] 15 But sanctify the Lord God in your
hearts. Always be ready to give an answer to
every man who asks you for a reason for the
hope that is in you, with gentleness and fear.
16 Have a good conscience so that evildoers
who speak evil of you and falsely accuse your
good conduct in Christ may be ashamed. 17 For
it is better, if it is the will of God, that you suffer
for doing good than for doing evil. 18 For Christ
also has once suffered for sins, the just for the
unjust, so that He might bring us to God, being
put to death in the flesh, but made alive by the

2:9 Dt 7:6
2:10 Hos 1:9–10
2:11 Jas 4:1
2:12 Mt 5:16
2:13 Titus 3:1
2:14 Ro 13:3–4
2:15 1Pe 2:12
2:16 Ro 6:22
2:17 Ro 13:7
2:18 Jas 3:17
2:19 Ro 13:5
2:20 1Pe 2:19
2:21 Ac 14:22
2:22 Isa 53:9
2:23 Isa 53:7
2:24 Ro 6:2
2:25 Isa 53:6

3:1 1Co 7:16
3:3 Isa 3:18–24
3:4 Ro 7:22
3:5 1Ti 5:5
3:6 Ge 18:12
3:7 Col 3:19
3:8 Mt 18:33
3:9 Ro 12:17
3:10 Ps 34:12–16
3:13 Pr 16:7
3:14 1Pe 2:19–20
3:15 Col 4:6
3:16 Heb 13:18
3:18 1Pe 4:1

[1] *22* Isa 53:9. [2] *24* Isa 53:5. [3] *10–12* Ps 34:12–16. [4] *14* Isa 8:12.

SPIRIT-TO-SPIRIT PRAYER

PRAYER OF AGREEMENT FOR A MIRACLE

Ask a prayer partner to pray this prayer with you:

Father God, we stand in agreement with [your name], *believing Your Word, that "if two of you agree on earth about anything they ask, it will be done for them by My Father who is in heaven" (Mt 18:19).*

We believe Your Word will accomplish what we send it to do. We bind the works of the enemy and all manipulation and lying spirits, all sickness, disease, and family curses. We loose the spirit of truth and the power of Your Word to accomplish this miraculous healing.

In the name of the Father, the Son, and the Holy Spirit, we declare it done for Your glory, amen.

Iris Delgado

Spirit, [19] by whom He also went and preached
to the spirits in prison, [20] who in times past
were disobedient, when God waited patiently
in the days of Noah while the ark was being
prepared, in which a few, that is, eight souls,
were saved through water. [21] Figuratively this
is like baptism, which also saves us now. It is
not washing off the dirt from the body, but
a response to God from a good conscience
through the resurrection of Jesus Christ, [22] who
has gone into heaven and is at the right hand
of God, with angels and authorities and powers being made subject to Him.

Good Stewards of God's Grace

4 Therefore, since Christ has suffered for us
in the flesh, arm yourselves likewise with
the same mind, for he who has suffered in the
flesh has ceased from sin, [2] so that he no longer should live the rest of his time in the flesh
serving human desires, but the will of God.
[3] For in earlier times of our lives it may have
sufficed us to do what the Gentiles like to do,
when we walked in immorality: lusts, drunkenness, carousing, debauchery, and abominable
idolatries. [4] They are surprised that you do not
join them in the same excess of wild living,
and so they speak evil of you. [5] They will give
account to Him who is ready to judge the living
and the dead. [6] For this reason the gospel was
preached also to those who are dead, so that
even though they might be judged according
to men in the flesh, they might live according
to God in the spirit.

[7] The end of all things is near. Therefore be
solemn and sober so you can pray. [8] Above all
things, have unfailing love for one another,
because love covers a multitude of sins. [9] Show
hospitality to one another without complaining. [10] As everyone has received a gift, even so
serve one another with it, as good stewards of
the manifold grace of God. [11] If anyone speaks,
let him speak as the oracles of God. If anyone
serves, let him serve with the strength that God
supplies, so that God in all things may be glorified through Jesus Christ, to whom be praise
and dominion forever and ever. Amen.

Suffering as a Christian

[12] Beloved, do not be surprised at the fiery
ordeal that is taking place among you to test
you, as though some strange thing happened
to you. [13] But rejoice insofar as you share in
Christ's sufferings, so that you may rejoice
and be glad also in the revelation of His glory. [14] If you are reproached because of the
name of Christ, you are blessed, because the
Spirit of glory and of God rests upon you. On
their part He is blasphemed, but on your part
He is glorified. [15] Let none of you suffer as a
murderer, or a thief, or an evildoer, or even
as a busybody. [16] Yet if anyone suffers as a
Christian, let him not be ashamed, but let him
glorify God because of it. [17] For the time has
come for judgment to begin at the house of

3:19 1Pe 4:6
3:20 Ge 6:3
3:21 1Pe 1:3
3:22 Ro 8:38
4:1 Ro 6:7
4:4 1Pe 3:16
4:5 Ac 10:42
4:6 1Pe 3:19
4:7 1Pe 1:13
4:8 Pr 10:12
4:9 Php 2:14
4:10 1Co 4:1–2
4:11 Ac 7:38
4:13 Ro 8:17
4:14 Mt 5:11
4:15 1Th 4:11
4:16 Ac 5:41
4:17 Jer 25:29

A Wife's Submission

Submission is one of the most difficult actions you will ever undertake as a Christian woman. It is a difficult task. And if not done under God's empowerment, it is downright impossible! True submission occurs when you follow your spiritual authority's lead, even when every fiber in you feels it's the wrong path to take. And you must do this in a willing and respectful way.

First Peter 3:1–4 lists three main reasons why wives should submit to their husbands:

1. In obedience to the Word of God

2. To bring the lost to the saving knowledge of Jesus Christ

3. To be precious in the eyes of God

God sets up His authority in the home. Throughout His Word we see the pattern of familial authority. To rebel against this divinely appointed authority is to rebel against the kingdom ordained by God Himself. God has set the husband as the delegated authority of Christ, with the wife representative of the church. It is difficult for the wife to be subject to her husband if she does not realize that the real issue is God's authority, not her husband's.

> That they may teach the young women to love their husbands, to love their children, and to be self-controlled, pure, homemakers, good, obedient to their own husbands, that the word of God may not be dishonored.
>
> —Titus 2:4–5

My position on this subject is simple: I want God's blessing on my life! I don't want to be guilty of blaspheming God's Word! What must I do to qualify for His blessing? The answer is *to obey!*

The Bible shares seven rewards for the woman who follows God's instruction to be submissive to her husband. Each of these seven things will help your husband become an effective and godly leader.

Read each verse of scripture shown in the following table, and then draw lines to match the verse with the action you can take as a wife to influence your husband to grow in his godly leadership role in your family.

Scripture Reference	Action of a Wife
1 Timothy 3:11	Be unified with him in purpose and in will.
Ephesians 5:33	Respect him.
Amos 3:3	Be his helpmate.
Genesis 2:19	Praise him.
Ephesians 6:18	Bless him.
Numbers 6:24–27	Be thankful for him.
1 Corinthians 1:4–8	Pray with him and for him.

1. Which of these actions has been the easiest action step for you to take toward your husband?

____

2. Which three actions above are the most difficult for you?

____

____

____

3. How have you been able to see your husband grow into a more effective and godly leader because of your willingness to obey God by following these action steps?

____

____

____

Diana Hagee

SPIRITLED WOMAN

COUNSEL FROM THE SPIRIT BASICS

Sudden Terror

The biblical principle of watching voids out the possibility of an enemy or aggressor gaining entrance to our lives. The devil has a plan with a destination against each of our lives. He has mapped out our destruction and has a specific way he's planned to carry it out. He is very strategic and wants to find the fastest, most efficient way to accomplish his mission.

Although he is anxious to get the job done, he will wait if he has to. This is why so many people who are godly or in ministry and seem to be doing well find that everything is suddenly crashing around them, often without warning. This is called *sudden terror*. Terrorist attacks are always sudden and unexpected. Terrorists get great joy when their plans catch people off guard. Though the attack is sudden, the plan was not made overnight. The plans of the enemy can be long and drawn out. The devil can be very patient in waiting on the right timing to attack his prey.

Just as we have secret agencies that study and are sensitive to the plans of terrorists, God wants us to be prepared for spiritual warfare. We are not to be "ignorant of his devices" (2Co 2:11). The word *devices* in the Greek is *noema*, which means "the mind of the devil." God does not want us to be ignorant of the mind or schemes of the devil.

It is important that prayer warriors have *spiritual secret intelligence*. How do we get information about the enemy? We get it from the Holy Spirit. He knows all things.

Kimberly Daniels

God, and if it begins first with us, what shall the
end be for those who do not obey the gospel
of God? 18 And

"If the righteous one is scarcely saved,
where shall the ungodly and the sinner
appear?"[1]

19 So then, let those who suffer according to
the will of God entrust their souls to a faithful
Creator, while continuing to do good.

Tending the Flock of God

5 I exhort the elders who are among you, as
one who is also an elder and a witness of
the sufferings of Christ as well as a partaker
of the glory that shall be revealed: 2 Shepherd
the flock of God that is among you, take care
of them, not by constraint, but willingly, not for
dishonest gain, but eagerly. 3 Do not lord over
those in your charge, but be examples to the
flock. 4 And when the chief Shepherd appears,
you will receive a crown of glory that will not
fade away.
5 Likewise you younger ones, submit your-
selves to the elders. Yes, all of you be sub-
missive one to another and clothe yourselves
with humility, because

"God resists the proud,
but gives grace to the humble."[2]

I cast my cares upon the Lord (1Pe 5:7).

6 Humble yourselves under the mighty hand
of God, that He may exalt you in due time.
7 Cast all your care upon Him, because He
cares for you.

I am an enemy of the devil (1Pe 5:8).

8 Be sober and watchful, because your ad-
versary the devil walks around as a roaring
lion, seeking whom he may devour. 9 Resist
him firmly in the faith, knowing that the same
afflictions are experienced by your brother-
hood throughout the world.

I am sober and vigilant against my adversary, the devil (1Pe 5:8).

10 But after you have suffered a little while,
the God of all grace, who has called us to
His eternal glory through Christ Jesus, will
restore, support, strengthen, and establish

4:18 Pr 11:31
5:1 Lk 24:48
5:2 1Ti 3:8
5:3 Eze 34:4
5:4 1Co 9:25
5:5 Jas 4:6
5:6 Jas 4:10
5:7 Ps 55:22
5:8 Job 2:2
5:9 Ac 14:22
5:10 2Co 4:17

[1] *18* Pr 11:31. [2] *5* Pr 3:34.

THE WOMAN WITH THE ISSUE OF BLOOD

FAITH FOR HEALING

The sun was already blazing, the gnats biting. It promised to be an uncomfortable day. The wind was blowing gently from the south, a hot, soft whisper. It was still early, but the marketplace was alive with activity when another whisper was heard.

This voice blew through the crowd but spoke not of another relentless day, but of hope, of a promise fulfilled. The busy stalls became energized.

"Have you heard the news? That man Jesus has come across the lake! Jairus is with him! Let's go!"

Jairus, a leader in the synagogue, had gone down to the shore to greet Jesus. Well, not exactly to greet Him, but to fall at His feet and beg for His intervention.

"Would You, Jesus, please come to my house and lay Your hands on my little daughter? For she is dying."

The story is found in Mark 5 and holds a treasure for us today.

Jesus agreed to go, but He wasn't alone. A crowd went with Him. As He walked to Jairus' house, a throng of people surrounded Him, pushed against him, pressed into Him.

Suddenly Jesus stopped and asked the crowd a question, "Who touched me?"

A woman came forward. She fell at His feet and told Him her story. She had been bleeding for twelve years and was getting worse. Doctors couldn't help her, but she knew that if she could just reach out and touch Jesus, she would be healed.

What was Jesus' response? Was He irritated with her? Was He offended by her boldness? Quite the opposite. Jesus was pleased. He told her that her faith had healed her.

Her faith in what? Her faith that Jesus had the power to heal her. Her faith that Jesus had the desire to heal her. Her faith that she could come to Him with all she was and all she was not and He would not withhold what she desired.

With everything in her, she pressed into Him...and she was healed. The "more" that she longed for, she received.

Jesus is the same today as He was when He healed the woman with the issue of blood. He still offers to restore us as women—to heal us, to meet us in our place of deepest need. He still has the power and the desire to restore our femininity, which means the restoration of our hearts.

We have to start there because the heart is the center of it all. Proverbs 4:23 says, "Keep your heart with all diligence, for out of it are the issues of life."

Stasi Eldredge

you. 11 To Him be glory and dominion forever
and ever. Amen.

Final Greetings

12 With the help of Silas, whom I consider
to be a faithful brother to you, I have written
briefly, exhorting you and testifying that this
is the true grace of God in which you stand.
13 The church that is at Babylon, elect to-
gether with you, greets you, and so does
Mark, my son. 14 Greet one another with a
kiss of love.

Peace be with all you who are in Christ Jesus.
Amen.

5:11 1Pe 4:11
5:12 Heb 13:22
5:13 Ac 12:12
5:14 Ro 16:16

Author: The apostle Peter

Written: Between AD 64 and 67, from Babylon (a moniker for Rome or Jerusalem)

Theme: Allusions to the Old Testament

2 PETER

Dear Spirit Led Woman,

There is an abundance of information flowing from every source. The Internet, television, newspapers, and even books strive to tell us what is important. It is difficult to discern the false from the factual. We must all make it a point to identify the counterfeits. If we are called to something that requires boldness, the enemy will try to bring fear. If our call requires discernment, deception and lies can cause detours that last many years.

Once we identify the counterfeits, we will be better equipped to rebuke the enemy and call forth the gifts God has given us. When we seek Him, God will tell us what we need to know. But we have to ask Him continuously—and be aware of what is going on in our surroundings. We will not do everything right, but if we believe we are here for a reason and seek God's wisdom in discovering that reason, then we will be equipped to fulfill our destiny.

Joy F. Strang

SPIRITLED WOMAN

COUNSEL FROM THE SPIRIT BASICS

Our True Identity

God wants to remind us of our identity, and that comes by beholding Him: "But we all, seeing the glory of the Lord with unveiled faces, as in a mirror, are being transformed into the same image from glory to glory by the Spirit of the Lord" (2Co 3:18). As we seek to know God, everything we discover about His character and power is as a mirror to us, reminding us of what we look like. The Bible tells us that when we are born again, it is no longer we who live but Christ who lives in us. In knowing Him, we are reminded of our identity.

Peter put it this way: "His divine power has given to us all things that pertain to life and godliness through the knowledge of Him who has called us by His own glory and excellence" (2Pe 1:3).

Everything pertaining to life and godliness has been given to us, and we activate it all through the supernatural knowledge of what God is like. If we aren't manifesting these qualities and the nature and power of Christ in our lives, it is because we have forgotten our true identity.

Katherine Ruonala

Salutation

1 Simon Peter, a servant and apostle of Jesus Christ,

To those who have received a faith as precious as ours through the righteousness of our God and Savior Jesus Christ.

2 Grace and peace be multiplied to you through the knowledge of God and of Jesus our Lord.

The Christian's Call and Election

> Father, You have given me everything I need to live a godly life (2Pe 1:3).

3 His divine power has given to us all things that pertain to life and godliness through the knowledge of Him who has called us by His own glory and excellence, 4 by which He has given to us exceedingly great and precious promises, so that through these things you might become partakers of the divine nature and escape the corruption that is in the world through lust.

> I've been given great promises (2Pe 1:4).

5 For this reason make every effort to add virtue to your faith; and to your virtue, knowledge; 6 and to your knowledge, self-control; and to your self-control, patient endurance; and to your patient endurance, godliness; 7 and to your godliness, brotherly kindness; and to your brotherly kindness, love. 8 For if these things reside in you and abound, they ensure that you will neither be useless nor unfruitful in the knowledge of our Lord Jesus Christ. 9 But the one who lacks these things is blind and shortsighted because he has forgotten that he was cleansed from his former sins.

10 Therefore, brothers, diligently make your calling and election sure. For if you do these things, you will never stumble. 11 For in this way the entrance into the eternal kingdom of our Lord and Savior Jesus Christ will be abundantly provided for you.

12 Therefore I will not be negligent to always remind you of these things, though you know them and are established in the truth that is present with you. 13 I consider it right, as long as I live in this body, to stir you up by reminding you, 14 knowing that soon I will take off this body, even as our Lord Jesus Christ has shown me. 15 And I will also be diligent to make sure that after my death you will always remember these things.

Christ's Glory and the Prophetic Word

16 For we have not followed cleverly devised myths when we made known to you the power and coming of our Lord Jesus Christ, but we were eyewitnesses of His majesty. 17 For He received honor and glory from God the Father when a voice came to Him from the majestic glory, saying, "This is My beloved Son, in whom I am well pleased."[1] 18 And we ourselves heard this voice, which came from heaven, when we were with Him on the holy mountain.

19 And we have a more reliable word of prophecy, which you would do well to follow, as to a light that shines in a dark place, until the day dawns and the morning star arises in your hearts. 20 But know this first of all, that no prophecy of the Scripture is a matter of one's own interpretation. 21 For no prophecy at any time was produced by the will of man, but holy men moved by the Holy Spirit spoke from God.

1:1 Titus 2:13
1:2 Jn 17:3
1:3 1Th 2:12
1:4 Heb 12:10

1:5 2Pe 3:18
1:6 Ac 24:25
1:8 Jn 15:2
1:9 Eph 5:26
1:10 2Pe 3:17
1:12 Php 3:1
1:13 2Pe 3:1
1:14 2Ti 4:6
1:16 1Ti 1:4
1:17 Mk 9:7
1:18 Mt 17:6
1:19 Rev 22:16
1:20 2Pe 3:3
1:21 1Pe 1:11

All That Pertains to Life and Godliness

In his second letter to the church at large Peter wrote:

> Grace and peace be multiplied to you through the knowledge of God and of Jesus our Lord. His divine power has given to us all things that pertain to life and godliness through the knowledge of Him who has called us by His own glory and excellence, by which He has given to us exceedingly great and precious promises, so that through these things you might become partakers of the divine nature and escape the corruption that is in the world through lust.
>
> —2 Peter 1:2–4

Peter's words here echo the purpose and petitions of Paul's first prayer in the Book of Ephesians. Through the knowledge of God we will receive all things needed for life and godliness—godlikeness, if you will. Or, in other words, being more like Jesus—ushering more of the kingdom of heaven onto this earth and fighting for the same justice Christians throughout history have been fighting for in establishing each generation. We have exceedingly great and precious promises that have been given to us so that we can live by the divine nature God has put into everyone who believes Jesus died for his or her sins and was raised back to life—that we would live by the fullness of the Holy Spirit seeded into us as a down payment on all God plans to do in, through, and for us. (See Ephesians 1:13–21.)

How is this to come about? How would you like to never stumble in the call of God on your life? Peter gives us the key in 2 Peter 1:5–11: add to faith virtue, or moral strength; add to virtue knowledge of God in your fields of study and in your occupations; add to knowledge self-discipline; add to self-discipline perseverance; add to perseverance kindness born out of brotherly love; and add to brotherly kindness the God kind of love that never gives up, never gives in, never wavers, and never fails. (See 1 Corinthians 13:4–8.)

For us to live this kind of life, prayer must be at the center of all we do, for all of these are born out of prayer. When the kingdom of heaven and the kingdom of this world clash, it will be those who have heard from heaven who will supply the strategies to victory. It will be those with the most integrous—pure, honest, sound, strong, untainted, and stable—prayer lives that arise with the answers and the conviction to see the fight to its proper finish.

Cindy Trimm

False Prophets and Teachers

Jude 1:4–13

2 But there were also false prophets among the people, just as there will be false teachers among you, who will secretly bring in destructive heresies, even denying the Lord who bought them, bringing swift destruction upon themselves. 2 And many will follow their destructive ways, because of whom the way of truth will be blasphemed. 3 And in their greed they will exploit you with deceptive words. Their judgment, made long ago, does not linger, and their destruction does not slumber.

4 For if God did not spare the angels that sinned, but cast them down to hell and delivered them into chains of darkness to be kept for judgment; 5 and if He did not spare the ancient world, but saved Noah, a preacher of righteousness, with seven others, when He brought a flood upon the world of the ungodly; 6 and if He condemned the cities of Sodom and Gomorrah to destruction by reducing them to ashes, making them an example to those afterward who would live ungodly lives; 7 and if He delivered righteous Lot, who was distressed by the filthy conduct of the wicked 8 (for that righteous man lived among them, and what he saw and heard of their lawless deeds tormented his righteous soul day after day); 9 then the Lord knows how to rescue the godly from trial, and to keep the unrighteous under punishment for the Day of Judgment, 10 especially those who walk after the flesh in pursuit of unclean desires, and despise authority.

They are presumptuous and arrogant, and are not afraid to slander the angelic beings. 11 Whereas angels, who are greater in power and might, do not bring slanderous accusations against them before the Lord. 12 But these people are like irrational animals, born to be captured and destroyed. They speak evil of the things that they do not understand, and in their corruption they will be destroyed.

13 They shall receive the wages of unrighteousness. They count it a pleasure to carouse in the daytime. They are blots and blemishes who revel in their own deception while they carouse together with you. 14 They have eyes full of adultery that cannot cease from sin. They entice unstable souls. Their hearts are trained in greed. They are cursed children! 15 They have forsaken the right way and have gone astray. They follow the way of Balaam the son of Beor, who loved the wages of wickedness, 16 but who was rebuked for his iniquity. The mute donkey speaking with a man's voice constrained the madness of the prophet.

17 These men are wells without water and clouds that are carried by a storm, for whom the gloom of darkness has been reserved forever. 18 For when they speak arrogant words of vanity, they entice by the lusts of the flesh and by depravity those who barely escaped from those who live in error. 19 Although they promise them freedom, they themselves are slaves of corruption, for by that which a man is overcome, to this he is enslaved. 20 For if after they have escaped the defilements of the world through the knowledge of the Lord and Savior Jesus Christ, and they are again entangled in them and are overcome, the latter end is worse for them than the beginning. 21 For it would have been better for them not to have known the way of righteousness than to have known it and then turn back from the holy commandment that was delivered to them. 22 But it has happened to them according to the true proverb, "The dog returns to his own vomit,"[1] and "the sow that was washed to her wallowing in the mud."

Release Your powerful angels on my behalf to fight my battles in the heavens (2Pe 2:11).

The Promise of the Lord's Coming

3 This is now, beloved, the second epistle I am writing to you, in which I am stirring up your sincere minds by way of reminder, 2 that you should remember the words that were spoken previously by the holy prophets and the commandment of our Lord and Savior spoken through us, the apostles.

3 Know this first, that there shall come scoffers in the last days who walk after their own lusts, 4 and say, "Where is the promise of His coming? For since the fathers fell asleep, all things have continued as they were since the beginning of the creation." 5 For they willingly ignore that, by the word of God the heavens existed long ago, and the earth was formed standing out of the water and in the water, 6 by which the world that then existed was flooded with water and perished. 7 But by the same word, the heavens and the earth that now exist are being reserved for fire, kept for the Day of Judgment and destruction of the ungodly.

8 But, beloved, do not be ignorant of this one thing, that with the Lord one day is as a thousand years, and a thousand years as one day. 9 The Lord is not slow concerning His promise, as some count slowness. But He is patient with us, because He does not want any to perish, but all to come to repentance.

2:1 2Pe 2:3
2:2 Ro 2:24
2:3 Dt 32:35
2:4 Jude 1:6
2:5 2Pe 3:6
2:6 Jude 1:7
2:7 Ge 19:16
2:9 1Co 10:13
2:10 Ex 22:28
2:11 Jude 1:9
2:12 Jude 1:10
2:13 Ro 13:13
2:14 Eph 2:3
2:15 Jude 1:11
2:16 Nu 22:21–33
2:17 Jude 1:12–13
2:18 2Pe 1:4
2:19 Jn 8:34
2:20 2Pe 1:2
2:21 Eze 18:24
2:22 Pr 26:11
3:2 Lk 1:70
3:3 Jude 1:18
3:4 Jer 17:15
3:5 Ge 1:6
3:6 2Pe 2:5
3:7 2Pe 3:10
3:8 Ps 90:4
3:9 1Ti 2:4

[1] *22* Pr 26:11.

SPIRIT-TO-SPIRIT PRAYER

Father, Your Word declares that by Your divine power You have given us everything we need to live a godly life. I thank You for empowering me to overcome all the deception of the enemy. Satan has no place in me, in the name of Jesus (2Pe 1:3).

Father, Your Word declares that if I abide in You and Your words abide in me, I can ask what I desire, and it shall be done for me (Jn 15:7). In the name of Jesus, I command all demonic interruption out of my life and the lives of my family members. Satan, take your hands off my territory, off my children, off my marriage, off my finances.

I speak blessings of health and abundance into my life. No weapon formed against me shall prosper, and every tongue that rises up against me You shall condemn (Isa 54:17). Christ Jesus in me is my hope of glory (Col 1:27). I cast fear, doubt, and unbelief out of my heart. Today I set into motion all of God's blessings and divine protection into my life and home. Thank You, my Father. In Jesus' name, amen.

Iris Delgado

[10] But the day of the Lord will come like a thief
in the night, in which the heavens will pass
away with a loud noise, and the elements will
be destroyed with intense heat. The earth also
and the works that are in it will be burned up.
[11] Seeing then that all these things are to be
destroyed, what sort of people ought you to be
in holy conduct and godliness, [12] while you are
waiting for and desiring the coming of the day
of God, in which the heavens will be destroyed
by fire and the elements will be consumed by
intense heat? [13] But, according to His promise,
we are waiting for new heavens and a new
earth, in which righteousness dwells.
[14] Therefore, beloved, since you are waiting
for these things, be diligent that you may be
found by Him in peace, spotless and blameless.
[15] Keep in mind that the patience of our Lord
means salvation, even as our beloved brother
Paul has also written to you according to the
wisdom given to him. [16] As in all his letters, he
writes about these things, in which some things
are hard to understand, which the unlearned
and unstable distort, as they also do the other
Scriptures, to their own destruction.
[17] You therefore, beloved, since you know
these things beforehand, beware lest you also
fall from your own firm footing, being led away
by the deception of the wicked. [18] But grow
in the grace and knowledge of our Lord and
Savior Jesus Christ. To Him be glory, both now
and forever. Amen.

3:10 Mt 24:35
3:11 1Pe 1:15
3:12 2Pe 3:10
3:13 Isa 65:17
3:14 1Co 15:58

3:15 Ac 15:25
3:16 Heb 5:11
3:17 1Co 10:12
3:18 Col 1:10

Author: The apostle John

Written: AD 90s, from Ephesus

Themes: God's Love, Christian Living

1 JOHN

Dear Spirit Led Woman,

Years ago a dream changed my perspective of loving those who are lost. In my dream my son and I were enjoying a boat ride on the ocean. Suddenly he jumped out of the boat into the water. Although he could swim in a pool, I knew he wasn't prepared for the perilous environment of the ocean.

He splashed around, enjoying his freedom. I warned him of the danger, but he disregarded my plea, laughing as if he were in control. He continued drifting away until he eventually hit an unexpected rip current in the water and went under. I tried to jump into the water to save him but was held in place by a strange force. I began to sob, my heart breaking with the pain of losing him.

As I awoke, I heard, "This is just a glimpse of what I feel over each one who is dying, having rejected My love and offer of eternal life." I could finally identify with the intense pain of helplessly standing by while a beloved child willfully went his own way—a way that led to death.

The harvest fields are ripe. The key to fulfilling your part is to get God's heart. When you really love your neighbors as yourself, you will be motivated to offer them the best gift God can give—eternal life. Do not let the world deceive you into believing its ways are correct. Our Father loved us so much that His Son gave His life for us.

Joy F. Strang

The Word of Life

1 That which was from the beginning, which we have heard, which we have seen with our eyes, which we have looked upon, and our hands have touched, concerning the Word of life— 2 the life was revealed, and we have seen it and testify to it, and announce to you the eternal life, which was with the Father and was revealed to us— 3 we declare to you that which we have seen and heard, that you also may have fellowship with us. And our fellowship is with the Father and with His Son Jesus Christ. 4 We are writing these things to you so that our joy may be complete.

God Is Light

5 This then is the message which we have heard from Him and declare to you: God is light, and in Him is no darkness at all. 6 If we say that we have fellowship with Him, yet walk in darkness, we lie and do not practice the truth. 7 But if we walk in the light as He is in the light, we have fellowship one with another, and the blood of Jesus Christ His Son cleanses us from all sin.

8 If we say that we have no sin, we deceive ourselves, and the truth is not in us. 9 If we confess our sins, He is faithful and just to forgive us our sins and cleanse us from all unrighteousness. 10 If we say that we have not sinned, we make Him a liar and His word is not in us.

Christ Our Advocate

2 My little children, I am writing these things to you, so that you do not sin. But if anyone does sin, we have an Advocate with the Father, Jesus Christ the Righteous One. 2 He is the atoning sacrifice for our sins, and not for ours only, but also for the sins of the whole world.

3 By this we know that we know Him, if we keep His commandments. 4 Whoever says, "I know Him," and does not keep His commandments is a liar, and the truth is not in him. 5 But whoever keeps His word truly has the love of God perfected in him. By this we know we are in Him. 6 Whoever says he remains in Him ought to walk as He walked.

The New Commandment

7 Brothers, I am writing no new commandment to you, but an old commandment which you have had from the beginning. The old commandment is the word which you have heard from the beginning. 8 Yet a new commandment I am writing to you, which holds true in Him and in you, because the darkness is passing away, and the true light is already shining.

9 Whoever says he is in the light but hates his brother is in darkness even until now. 10 Whoever loves his brother lives in the light, and in him there is no cause for stumbling. 11 But whoever hates his brother is in darkness, and walks in darkness, and does not know where he is going, because the darkness has blinded his eyes.

12 I am writing to you, little children,
because your sins are forgiven for His name's sake.
13 I am writing to you, fathers,
because you have known Him who is from the beginning.
I am writing to you, young men,
because you have overcome the evil one.

I am writing to you, little children,
because you have known the Father.
14 I have written to you, fathers,
because you have known Him who is from the beginning.

I have written to you, young men,
because you are strong,
and the word of God lives in you,
and you have overcome the evil one.

15 Do not love the world or the things in the world. If anyone loves the world, the love of the Father is not in him. 16 For all that is in the world—the lust of the flesh, the lust of the eyes, and the pride of life—is not of the Father, but is of the world. 17 The world and its desires are passing away, but the one who does the will of God lives forever.

The Antichrist

18 Little children, it is the last hour. As you have heard that the antichrist will come, even now there are many antichrists. By this we know that it is the last hour. 19 They went out from us, but they were not of us, for if they had been of us, they would no doubt have remained with us. But they went out, revealing that none of them were of us.

20 But you have an anointing from the Holy One, and you know all things. 21 I have written to you, not because you do not know the truth, but because you know it, and because no lie is of the truth. 22 Who is a liar but the one who denies that Jesus is the Christ? Whoever denies the Father and the Son is the antichrist. 23 No one who denies the Son has the Father; the one who confesses the Son has the Father.

24 Let that which you have heard from the beginning remain in you. If that which you have heard from the beginning remains in you, you also will remain in the Son and in the Father. 25 And this is the promise that He has promised us—eternal life.

1:1 Jn 20:27
1:2 Jn 1:4
1:3 1Co 1:9
1:5 1Jn 3:11
1:6 1Jn 4:20
1:7 Isa 2:5
1:8 Jas 3:2
1:9 Ps 32:5
1:10 1Jn 5:10
2:1 Ro 8:34
2:2 1Jn 4:10
2:3 Jn 14:15
2:4 1Jn 1:8
2:5 Jn 14:23
2:6 1Pe 2:21
2:7 1Jn 3:11
2:8 Jn 1:9
....
2:11 Jn 12:35
2:12 Ac 13:38
2:13 1Jn 2:14
2:14 1Jn 2:13
2:15 Jas 4:4
2:16 Ro 13:14
2:17 1Co 7:31
2:18 1Jn 4:3
2:19 Ac 20:30
2:20 1Jn 2:27
2:21 2Pe 1:12
2:22 2Jn 1:7
2:23 1Jn 4:15
2:24 Jn 14:23
2:25 1Jn 1:2

How to Overcome Darkness

Malcolm Gladwell's *Blink* discusses malpractice rates and the momentary decisions doctors make that tend to lower their rates of malpractice. The basic thing Gladwell notes that predicts malpractice rates is the length of time doctors spend explaining situations to their patients, even negative situations of the doctor's own causing. The longer doctors spend with patients and the more open they are about potential and actual problems, the lower the malpractice rates against them.

That was exactly my experience. Our doctor was open and honest about potential problems as well as his own actual mistake, and that up-front transparency on his part reinforced that we were on the same team with the same goals. I would go back to that doctor in a heartbeat (no pun intended) if we were in a similar situation.

The choices we make in a moment involving honesty and transparency about our mistakes have incredible long-term consequences. This isn't just a secular phenomenon but an important Bible principle. God, after all, is the Master Psychologist. Malcolm Gladwell didn't note these statistics about doctors and malpractice suits in a vacuum.

In a world created and ruled by the sovereign God of the universe, transparency concerning our mistakes is a wise choice. God sets this up clearly in His Word, and even secular society notes this truth. We, as believers, are called to operate in the light with other believers, and we are called to operate in the light with unbelievers and our accusers:

> This then is the message which we have heard from Him and declare to you: God is light, and in Him is no darkness at all. If we say that we have fellowship with Him, yet walk in darkness, we lie and do not practice the truth. But if we walk in the light as He is in the light, we have fellowship one with another, and the blood of Jesus Christ His Son cleanses us from all sin.
>
> If we say that we have no sin, we deceive ourselves, and the truth is not in us. If we confess our sins, He is faithful and just to forgive us our sins and cleanse us from all unrighteousness.
>
> —1 John 1:5–9

A few years ago the elders' wives at the church I attended planned a women's retreat entitled "Exposed," taken from Ephesians 5:8–14. I was a women's ministry leader at the time, but to be honest, I dreaded going to this retreat. The title did not in any way naturally draw me. Personally, I did not want to be exposed and did not care to be a part of something that had set that as its agenda.

Then I went to the retreat. Each woman that spoke gave a brutally honest testimony of where she had been in her darkness, how God had brought her from darkness to light, and all the ways God was still meeting her in her failures. Each one was exposing herself, bringing her ugly past and some of her ugly present into the light. It ended up being one of the most powerful retreats with long-lasting outcomes I have ever witnessed.

It took that women's retreat for me to finally understand how radically different God's call to exposure is. In the light of the gospel I do not have to fear exposure. Instead God says, "Bring all of the nooks and crannies of your sin and shame to Me. Let Me shine the light of the gospel into even your deepest and darkest place of fear and guilt." And when these things are exposed to the light, they first become visible. Then they become light. What radical transformation!

Wendy Alsup

26 I have written these things to you concerning those who deceive you. 27 But the anointing which you have received from Him remains in you, and you do not need anyone to teach you. For as the same anointing teaches you concerning all things, and is truth, and is no lie, and just as it has taught you, remain in Him.

God's Spirit fills my thinking and helps me follow the Lord (1Jn 2:27).

Children of God

28 And now, little children, remain in Him, so that when He appears, we may have confidence and not be ashamed before Him when He comes.

29 If you know that He is righteous, you know that everyone who does righteousness is born of Him.

3 Consider how much love the Father has given to us, that we should be called children of God. Therefore the world does not know us, because it did not know Him. 2 Beloved, now are we children of God, and it has not yet been revealed what we shall be. But we know that when He appears, we shall be like Him, for we shall see Him as He is. 3 Everyone who has this hope in Him purifies himself, just as He is pure.

I'm a child of God—He is my Father (1Jn 3:1–2).

4 Whoever practices sin breaks the law, for sin is lawlessness. 5 You know that He was revealed to take away our sins, and in Him there is no sin. 6 Whoever remains in Him does not sin. Whoever sins has not seen Him and does not know Him.

7 Little children, let no one deceive you. The one who does righteousness is righteous, just as Christ is righteous. 8 Whoever practices sin is of the devil, for the devil has been sinning from the beginning. For this purpose the Son of God was revealed, that He might destroy the works of the devil. 9 Whoever has been born of God does not practice sin, for His seed remains in him. And he cannot keep on sinning, because he has been born of God. 10 In this the children of God and the children of the devil are revealed: Whoever does not live in righteousness is not of God, nor is the one who does not love his brother.

Love One Another

11 For this is the message that you heard from the beginning: We should love one another,

2:26 2Jn 1:7
2:27 Jn 14:26
2:28 1Jn 3:2
2:29 1Jn 3:7
3:1 Jn 1:12
3:2 Ro 8:18
3:3 2Co 7:1
3:4 1Jn 5:17
3:5 2Co 5:21
3:6 3Jn 1:11
3:7 1Jn 2:26
3:8 Jn 8:44
3:9 1Jn 5:18
3:10 1Jn 4:8
3:11 1Jn 1:5
....
3:12 Heb 11:4
3:13 Jn 17:14
3:14 Jn 5:24
3:15 Mt 5:21–22

SPIRITLED WOMAN

COUNSEL FROM THE SPIRIT BASICS

We Shall Be Like Him

John wrote, "Consider how much love the Father has given to us, that we should be called children of God. Therefore the world does not know us, because it did not know Him. Beloved, now are we children of God, and it has not yet been revealed what we shall be. But we know that when He appears, we shall be like Him, for we shall see Him as He is" (1Jn 3:1–2).

When He appears, we shall be like Him! We shall see as He sees and feel as He feels. But we do not have to wait until we get to heaven to let Him purify us. We must cry out to be purified and freed from every hidden agenda, rotten motive, and false assumption about God.

My heart's one desire is to be holy in love. I long for the purifying fire of His love to consume every hidden motive within me. As the heart is purified, we can see Him with greater and greater clarity. I want to be fully possessed by His Holy Spirit until I am completely overshadowed by God. I want to be utterly overtaken.

My prayer is for all of us to stay hidden inside God's glorious heart of love until we are manifesting His nature as sons and daughters—living, breathing, moving, healing, and giving life, just as Jesus was. As we are purified, we will see God more clearly. As our hearts become pure, our vision becomes clearer.

Heidi Baker

12 not like Cain, who was of the wicked one and murdered his brother. And why did he murder him? Because his own works were evil, and his brother's works were righteous. 13 Do not marvel, my brothers, if the world hates you. 14 We know that we have passed from death to life, because we love the brothers. Whoever does not love his brother remains in death. 15 Whoever hates his brother is a murderer, and you know that no murderer has eternal life remaining in him.

SPIRIT-TO-SPIRIT PRAYER

PRAYER IN YOUR HOME

Lord, as the homeowners of this house, we want to thank You for the gift You have given us. We are excited about all we are learning about how to protect our home and children. Your Word states in 1 John 4:4, "You are of God, little children, and have overcome them, because He who is in you is greater than he who is in the world." It is from this authority of You living in us that we pray.

We say in agreement that all demonic spirits inhabiting this home must go now, in Jesus's name. All spirits of death, leave now. All perversion and activities of sexual abuse, we command you to leave our property. [You will want to insert here the spirits that are in operation in your home.] *You will no longer harass our family. You have been given your eviction notice. Your assignment here is canceled. We say you will not return to this home or land.*

Lord, we desire holiness as You are holy. We bring our home before You, dedicating it to You and Your purposes. May Your peace, love, and joy fill our dwelling. Where there has been demonic activity, we welcome the activity of Your angels in the walls of this house and the boundaries of this property. And we say, "As for me and our house, we will serve the Lord."

Rebecca Greenwood

16 By this we know the love of God: that He
laid down His life for us, and we ought to lay
down our lives for the brothers. 17 Whoever
has the world's goods and sees his brother in
need, but closes his heart of compassion from
him, how can the love of God remain in him?
18 My little children, let us love not in word and
speech, but in action and truth.

Confidence Before God

19 By this we know that we are of the truth,
and shall reassure our hearts before Him. 20 For
if our heart condemns us, God is greater than
our heart and knows everything. 21 Beloved,
if our heart does not condemn us, then we
have confidence before God. 22 And whatever
we ask, we will receive from Him, because we
keep His commandments and do the things
that are pleasing in His sight. 23 And this is
His commandment: that we should believe
on the name of His Son Jesus Christ and love
one another as He commanded us. 24 Now the
one who keeps His commandments remains
in Him, and He in him. And by this we know
that He remains in us, through the Spirit whom
He has given us.

3:16 Php 2:17
3:17 1Jn 4:20
3:18 1Jn 2:1
3:22 Jn 8:29
3:23 Jn 6:29
3:24 Jn 17:21

4:1 2Pe 2:1
4:2 1Co 12:3
4:3 1Jn 2:18
4:4 Jn 12:31
4:5 Jn 17:14
4:6 Jn 14:17

Test the Spirits

4 Beloved, do not believe every spirit, but
test the spirits to see whether they are
from God, because many false prophets have
gone out into the world. 2 This is how you know
the Spirit of God: Every spirit that confesses
that Jesus Christ has come in the flesh is from
God, 3 and every spirit that does not confess
that Jesus Christ has come in the flesh is not
from God. This is the spirit of the antichrist,
which you have heard is coming and is already
in the world.
4 You are of God, little children, and have
overcome them, because He who is in you is
greater than he who is in the world. 5 They are
of the world, and therefore they speak from
the world, and the world listens to them. 6 We
are of God, and whoever knows God listens to
us. Whoever is not of God does not listen to
us. This is how we know the spirit of truth and
the spirit of error.

I am an overcomer in this world (1Jn 4:4).

God Is Love

[7] Beloved, let us love one another, for love is of God, and everyone who loves is born of God and knows God. [8] Anyone who does not love does not know God, for God is love. [9] In this way the love of God was revealed to us, that God sent His only begotten Son into the world, that we might live through Him. [10] In this is love: not that we loved God, but that He loved us and sent His Son to be the atoning sacrifice for our sins. [11] Beloved, if God so loved us, we must also love one another. [12] No one has seen God at any time. If we love one another, God dwells in us, and His love is perfected in us.

[13] We know that we live in Him, and He in us, because He has given us His Spirit. [14] And we have seen and testify that the Father sent the Son to be the Savior of the world. [15] Whoever confesses that Jesus is the Son of God, God lives in him, and he in God. [16] And we have come to know and to believe the love that God has for us.

God is love. Whoever lives in love lives in God, and God in him. [17] In this way God's love is perfected in us, so that we may have boldness on the Day of Judgment, because as He is, so are we in this world. [18] There is no fear in love, but perfect love casts out fear, because fear has to do with punishment. Whoever fears is not perfect in love.

[19] We love Him because He first loved us. [20] If anyone says, "I love God," and hates his brother, he is a liar. For whoever does not love his brother whom he has seen, how can he love God whom he has not seen? [21] We have this commandment from Him: Whoever loves God must also love his brother.

Overcoming the World

5 Whoever believes that Jesus is the Christ is born of God, and everyone who loves the Father loves the one born of the Father. [2] By this we know that we love the children of God: when we love God and keep His commandments. [3] For this is the love of God, that we keep His commandments. And His commandments are not burdensome, [4] for whoever is born of God overcomes the world, and the victory that overcomes the world is our faith. [5] Who is it that overcomes the world, but the one who believes that Jesus is the Son of God?

The Witness Concerning the Son

[6] This is He who came by water and blood—Jesus Christ. He did not come by water only, but by water and blood. It is the Spirit who bears witness, because the Spirit is the truth. [7] There are three who testify in heaven: the Father, the Word, and the Holy Spirit, and the three are one. [8] There are three that testify on earth: the Spirit, the water, and the blood, and the three are toward the one.[1] [9] If we receive the testimony of men, the testimony of God is greater; for this is the testimony of God which He has given concerning His Son. [10] Whoever believes in the Son of God has this witness in himself. Whoever does not believe God has made Him out to be a liar, because he does not believe the testimony that God gave about His Son. [11] And this is the testimony: that God has given us eternal life, and this life is in His Son. [12] Whoever has the Son has life, and whoever does not have the Son of God does not have life.

Purpose of Writing

[13] I have written these things to you who believe in the name of the Son of God, that you may know that you have eternal life, and that you may continue to believe in the name of the Son of God. [14] This is the confidence that we have in Him, that if we ask anything according to His will, He hears us. [15] So if we know that He hears whatever we ask, we know that we have whatever we asked of Him.

> I can face any circumstance full of confidence because I belong to the God of the universe, and He hears me when I say something to Him (1Jn 5:14–15).

[16] If anyone sees his brother commit a sin which does not lead to death, he shall ask, and He shall give him life. This is for those whose sin does not lead to death. There is a sin that leads to death. I do not say that he should pray for it. [17] All wrongdoing is sin, but there is a sin that does not lead to death.

[18] We know that whoever is born of God does not keep on sinning. But whoever has been born of God guards himself, and the wicked one cannot touch him. [19] We know that we are of God, and the whole world lies in wickedness. [20] And we know that the Son of God has come and has given us understanding, so that we may know Him who is true, and we are in Him who is true—His Son Jesus Christ. He is the true God and eternal life.

[21] Little children, keep yourselves from idols. Amen.

> I am born of God, and the evil one cannot touch me (1Jn 5:18).

4:7 1Jn 2:29
4:8 2Co 13:11
4:9 Jn 3:16
4:10 1Jn 2:2
4:12 Jn 1:18
4:13 1Jn 3:24
4:14 Jn 4:42
4:15 Ro 10:9
4:16 1Jn 3:24
4:17 1Jn 2:5
4:18 Ro 8:15
4:19 1Jn 4:10
4:20 1Jn 2:4
4:21 1Jn 3:11
5:1 1Jn 2:29
5:3 Jn 14:15
5:4 Jn 16:33
5:5 1Jn 4:15
5:6 Jn 15:26
5:7 Mt 28:19
....
5:9 Mt 3:16–17
5:10 Jn 3:33
5:11 Jn 1:4
5:12 Jn 3:36
5:13 Jn 20:31
5:14 1 Jn 3:21–22
5:16 Jer 7:16
5:17 1Jn 3:4
5:18 1Jn 3:9
5:19 Gal 1:4
5:20 Jn 17:3
5:21 1Co 10:14

[1] 7–8 The earliest Greek manuscripts lack *in heaven: the Father, the Word, and the Holy Spirit, and the three are one. There are three that testify on earth.*

Author: The apostle John

Written: AD 90s, from Ephesus

Themes: Christian Conduct, Separation From the World

2 JOHN

Dear Spirit Led Woman,

We forget about prayer when our lives get busy. Our minds become filled with the influence of the media and the world, and we allow these influences to determine how we behave—and often this conflicts with the ways God tells us to.

We were designed to function in the supernatural world. We need to open the door to the kingdom of God that Jesus said is within us. Developing an intimacy with Him through worship and prayer is the only way to be where He is. We must remain alert to the state of our household and strive to guard against the equipment of the deceiver. The best way to do this is through continuous immersion in His Word, remembering: "And this is love: that we walk according to His commandments. This is the commandment, that as you have heard from the beginning, you should walk in it" (2Jn 1:6).

Joy F. Strang

Salutation

The elder,

To the elect lady and her children, whom I love in the truth, and not I only, but also all those who know the truth, 2 for the sake of the truth, which remains in us, and will be with us forever:

3 Grace, mercy, and peace will be with you from God the Father and from the Lord Jesus Christ, the Son of the Father, in truth and love.

Truth and Love

4 I greatly rejoiced that I found some of your children walking in truth as we were commanded by the Father. 5 And now I ask you, lady, not as though I wrote a new commandment to you, but that which we have had from the beginning, that we love one another. 6 And this is love: that we walk according to His commandments. This is the commandment, that as you have heard from the beginning, you should walk in it.

7 For many deceivers, who do not confess that Jesus Christ has come in the flesh, have gone out into the world. Each one is a deceiver and an antichrist. 8 Watch yourselves, so that we do not lose those things for which we have worked, but that we receive a full reward. 9 Whoever transgresses and does not remain in the teaching of Christ does not have God. Whoever remains in the teaching of Christ has both the Father and the Son. 10 If anyone comes to you and does not bring this teaching, do not receive him into your house, nor greet him. 11 For whoever greets him takes part in his evil deeds.

Final Greetings

12 I have many things to write to you, but I prefer not to write with paper and ink. Instead, I hope to come to you and speak face to face that our joy may be complete.

13 The children of your elect sister greet you. Amen.

1:1 Jn 8:32
1:3 Ro 1:7
1:4 3Jn 1:3–4
1:5 1Jn 3:11
1:6 1Jn 2:24
1:7 1Jn 4:1–3
1:8 1Co 3:8
1:10 Titus 3:10
1:11 1Ti 5:22
1:13 2Jn 1:1–13

COUNSEL FROM THE SPIRIT BASICS

SPIRITLED WOMAN

This Is Love

"And this is love: that we walk according to His commandments. This is the commandment, that as you have heard from the beginning, you should walk in it" (2Jn 1:6).

Obedience to God will always lead us to walk in love, which the Lord explicitly taught His disciples to do (Jn 15:12). And the reason Jesus taught us to love one another is that God loved us first—far more than we even realize!

Jenny Swindall

Live in Truth

In his letter to "the elect lady and her children," John spoke of "the truth, which remains in us, and will be with us forever" (2Jn 1:1–2).

The truth is, since the beginning of the world the Creator has been working on a plan. His plan will not fail. Throughout the ages Jesus has been moving toward something and has had a purpose that will be accomplished. As Creator He has a sure plan that will come to fullness, and we have not seen it yet. But even today we are each participating in the beginning stages of that dream. Life as we know it is not the end of the story. This is not "it," but this is part of it. This isn't "as good as it gets," but this is part of the process, and for six thousand years He has been working toward something. The end of the story must be kept in view in order to not lose heart in our individual journeys and to not lose hope when looking at the scope of human history.

The first two chapters of the Scriptures begin with a bride and a bridegroom in the Garden of Eden, and the last two chapters end with the bride and the Bridegroom in the garden of paradise. The story in between the first two chapters of Genesis and the last chapters of Revelation is breathtaking and glorious in the mercy of God. It describes the heroes of faith who rose up and said yes in the grace of God, even in their weakness. It also includes the stories of those who refused the kindness of God and the tragedy that came because of this refusal.

We know that the story of humanity has a happy ending, but we also know that there is a great battle and war for the hearts of men that lead up to that happy ending. This battle will reach its fullness in the generation that the Lord returns. It will be a conflict between two houses of worship, because it will be a war fought for the passion of the human heart.

God wants to restore the world to the Garden of Eden reality. This includes the hearts of women, their physical bodies, creation itself, and the governments of the earth. He is coming as King to set up a kingdom. He is coming as Judge to remove all that hinders love and to cleanse the earth of wickedness. And He is coming as Bridegroom to give those who love Him His name, His throne, and eternal access to His heart in unhindered communication.

Let us live in this truth.

Misty Edwards

Author: The apostle John

Written: AD 90s, from Ephesus

Themes: Instruction, Exhortation

3 JOHN

Dear Spirit Led Woman,

Matthew 14:22–33 tells of Peter walking on the water toward Jesus. When Peter heard the strong wind and saw the boisterous waves, he became afraid and began sinking. Jesus reached out to him and said, "O you of little faith, why did you doubt?" (v. 31).

How many of us doubt our faith and God's promises during our walk with the Lord? How many of us struggle with problems that threaten to separate us from our Father? The apostle John wrote, "Beloved, I pray that all may go well with you and that you may be in good health, even as your soul is well" (3Jn 1:2). God has promised us blessings and health, and we need to maintain our beliefs in Him for those promises, even in times of instability, and acknowledge His authority over our lives.

Joy F. Strang

SPIRITLED WOMAN

COUNSEL FROM THE SPIRIT BASICS

Love Has No Limits

We believe when we die and go to heaven, God will expect the same from us that He did from His Son. He will ask us only one question: Did you learn to love?

I am greatly moved by the words of Mother Teresa, who perfectly expresses this sentiment with us:

> Love has no meaning if it isn't shared. Love has to be put into action. You have to love without expectation, do something for love itself, not for what you may receive.[1]

> Love in action is what gives us grace. We have been created for greater things...to love and to be loved. Love is love—to love a person without any conditions, without any expectations. Small things, done in great love, bring joy and peace. To love, it is necessary to give. To give, it is necessary to be free from selfishness.[2]

We are created to bring the love of Jesus to those who are in need. Love looks like something, yet it has no limits. God did not say the poor will always be good, kind, or thankful, and yet He always calls us to love them.

Heidi Baker

1. Mother Teresa, *One Heart Full of Love* (Ann Arbor, MI: Servant Publications, 1988), 87.
2. Mother Teresa, *No Greater Love*, ed. Becky Benenate and Joseph Durepos, rev. ed. (Novato, CA: New World Library, 1997). Originally published as *The Mother Teresa Reader: A Life for God*, comp. LaVonne Neff, rev. ed. (Ann Arbor, MI: Servant Publications, Inc., 1995).

1:1 1Jn 3:18
1:3 2Jn 1:4
1:4 Gal 4:19
1:6 1Th 2:12
1:11 Ps 37:27
1:12 Jn 21:24
1:13 2Jn 1:12

Salutation

The elder,

To the beloved Gaius, whom I love in the
truth:

2 Beloved, I pray that all may go well with you
and that you may be in good health, even as
your soul is well. 3 For I greatly rejoiced when
brothers came and testified of the truth that is
in you, just as you walk in the truth. 4 I have
no greater joy than to hear that my children
walk in truth.

Working Together

5 Beloved, you are faithful in all you do for the

> I am prosperous as my soul prospers, and I walk in health (3Jn 1:2).

brothers and for strangers, 6 who have testified
of your love before the church. You will do well
to send them along on their journey in a manner worthy of God. 7 For His name's sake they
went out, receiving no help from the Gentiles.
8 Therefore we ought to receive such men, that
we might be fellow workers for the truth.

9 I wrote to the church, but Diotrephes, who
loves to put himself first among them, did not
accept us. 10 Because of this, if I come, I will
bring up what kinds of works he does: ranting
against us with malicious words. Not content
with that, he does not accept the brothers, and
stops those who want to, and throws them out
of the church.

11 Beloved, do not imitate that which is evil,
but that which is good. Whoever does good is
from God, but whoever does evil has not seen
God. 12 Demetrius receives good reports from
everyone and from the truth itself. Yes, and we
also testify, and you know that our testimony
is true.

Final Greetings

13 I had many things to write, but I would
rather not write to you with pen and ink. 14 Instead, I hope to see you soon, and we shall
speak face to face.

Peace be to you. The friends greet you. Greet
the friends by name.

Desire the Word

The application of the truth of the written Word unveils Christ and brings about the soul's prosperity (3Jn 1:2). Every time I open the leather cover of my Bible, I have a sense of wonder. Here in my hands is a treasure chest of wisdom, guidance, counsel, principles for practical, successful living, and spiritual food.

But so often, when I'm reading, I recall the times I've been confused about what I should do in a real-life situation. And I think of the many cries and complaints I've heard through the years I've been in public ministry, heartfelt cries from men and women searching for some solid word from God to direct or to stabilize their lives.

Your need for specific direction in everyday matters is of great concern to God. Questions such as what job to take, whom to marry, where to go to school, what to do about a problem with your friend—these things are important to you. They're important to Him too. And God isn't bothered one bit if we come to Him with the most trivial matter or one that's earthshaking. God wants to give us wisdom; He always wants to speak to us. So I look at it this way: if I lack wisdom on how to handle a certain situation, then the problem is quite likely with my inability to *hear* Him or how His Word applies to me.

Many of us, myself included, are often stumped as to what God is thinking. You pray. Then you get up off your knees, and it's like standing up in a fog. Nothing is clear!

Knowing God's thoughts on a given matter requires that we walk closely with Him every day. It means staying in touch with Him by reading His Word, praying, and having fellowship with our sisters in Christ so we can hear His voice through them too. These are basics for anyone to grow in faith.

If you feel restless, dissatisfied, wanting something more for your spiritual life, then I have great news for you! These are all signs that God wants you to meet His living, active Word in a new way. He wants to break through deadness, dullness, and dryness. He wants to speak a word to you that will settle at the bottom of your soul forever, a foundation stone from which He can call you to come up higher with Him.

God wants your inner man to be energized in a new way—transformed—just as meat and drink become living, healthy tissue to your physical body. God wants not only to change your situation, but He also wants to transform *you*.

When this happens through a desire for His Word, then 3 John 1:2 will manifest in your life: "Beloved, I pray that all may go well with you and that you may be in good health, even as your soul is well."

Marilyn Hickey

SPIRIT-TO-SPIRIT PRAYER

PRAYER OF COMMITMENT

Lord, I give myself to You. Please accept every facet of my life, and use me for Your honor and Your glory. I yield myself to You right now. I desire to know You more intimately and to love You and obey Your Word. I am willing to do Your will and turn my back on all the things that rob my quality time with You. Today I affirm my love for You, my God. Thank You for wisdom, knowledge, and understanding. Today I commit to serve You with all my heart. In the name of Jesus, amen.

Iris Delgado

Author: Jude, the half-brother of Jesus

Written: Mid AD 60s

Themes: Standing Firm in the Faith

JUDE

Dear Spirit Led Woman,

Jude 1:24 says Christ is able to present us blameless before the Father. It does not say we will present ourselves blameless. Many times the goals we set are actually counterproductive; they serve to strengthen the arm of the flesh rather than make us holy. So how do we hold ourselves to a standard without becoming legalistic? By relying on the Holy Spirit for both direction and empowerment. He will tell us what to do to resist temptation and grow in holiness, giving us the grace to overcome and follow through. If our disciplines are not led by the Spirit, they are merely dead works.

We cannot do anything worthwhile of ourselves. Even Jesus admitted this (Jn 5:30). Understanding this truth helps us acquire the humble attitude Brother Lawrence, a seventeenth-century monk, expressed: "When I fail in my duty, I readily acknowledge it, saying, 'I am used to doing so; I shall never do otherwise if I am left to myself.' If I do not fail, then I give God thanks, acknowledging that the strength comes from Him."

Brother Lawrence reminds us that without God we are destined to fail, but that by His grace—and to His glory—we may truly live a life of victory.

Joy F. Strang

SPIRITLED WOMAN

COUNSEL FROM THE SPIRIT BASICS

Keep On the Right Course

The Book of Jude was written to Christians who were dealing with a lot of distractions—false teaching, divisive words, complaining, and more. So Jude says, "But you, beloved, build yourselves up in your most holy faith. Pray in the Holy Spirit. Keep yourselves in the love of God while you are waiting for the mercy of our Lord Jesus Christ, which leads to eternal life" (Jude 1:20–21). These are keys to keep us on the right course.

Jude is talking about positioning yourself to receive God's love—to experience it at a practical level. There's a war going on for your attention. God wants to see your face—to see your eyes gazing at Him, to lift your countenance, to make you shine, to fill you up with love so you can give His love to the "unlovely" of this world. He wants you to be completely absorbed in Him so you can come into union with Him and walk in the power of the Holy Spirit, loving and forgiving and being a catalyst for signs and wonders. When you overflow with God's love, miracles begin to happen all around you.

Katherine Ruonala

Salutation

Jude, a servant of Jesus Christ and a brother of James,

To those who are sanctified and called by God the Father and preserved in Jesus Christ:

I am preserved in Christ (Jude 1:1).

2 May mercy, peace, and love be multiplied to you.

Judgment on False Teachers
2Pe 2:1–17

3 Beloved, while I diligently tried to write to you of the salvation we have in common, I found it necessary to write and appeal to you to contend for the faith which was once delivered to the saints. 4 For there are some men who secretly crept in, who were marked long ago for this condemnation. They are ungodly men, who pervert the grace of our God into immorality and deny the only Lord God and our Lord Jesus Christ.

5 Now I want to remind you, though you already know, that the Lord saved the people out of the land of Egypt and afterward destroyed those who did not believe. 6 Likewise, the angels who did not keep to their first domain, but forsook their own dwelling, He has kept in everlasting chains under darkness for the judgment of the great day. 7 Just as Sodom and Gomorrah, and the surrounding cities in like manner, gave themselves to immorality and went after different flesh, they serve as an example by suffering the punishment of eternal fire.

8 Likewise, these ungodly dreamers defile the flesh, reject authority, and slander celestial beings. 9 Yet Michael the archangel, when contending with the devil in a dispute about the body of Moses, did not dare to pronounce upon him a railing judgment. But he said, "The Lord rebuke you!" 10 But these men slander those things that they do not understand. But they destroy themselves in those things that, like unreasoning animals, they know by instinct.

11 Woe to them! For they have gone in the way of Cain, have run greedily after the error of Balaam for a reward, and perished in the rebellion of Korah.

12 These are the ones who are stains on your love feasts as they feast with you irreverently and care only for themselves. They are clouds without water, carried along by winds; autumn trees without fruit, twice dead, uprooted; 13 raging waves of the sea, which are foaming up their own shame; wandering stars for whom the gloom of darkness has been kept forever.

14 Enoch, the seventh generation from Adam, also prophesied of these men, saying, "Look! The Lord is coming with ten thousand of His holy ones, 15 to execute judgment on everyone, and to convict all who are godless of all their wicked deeds that they have committed, and of all the terrible words that godless sinners have spoken against Him." 16 These men are grumblers, complainers, who walk after their own lusts. Their mouths speak arrogant words, and they flatter others to gain profit.

Warnings and Exhortations

17 But, beloved, remember the words that were previously spoken by the apostles of our Lord Jesus Christ. 18 They said to you, "In the last days there will be scoffers who will walk

1:2 2Pe 1:2
1:3 1Ti 6:12
1:4 Gal 2:4
1:5 Ps 106:26
1:6 2Pe 2:4
1:7 Dt 29:23
1:9 Da 10:13
1:10 2Pe 2:12
1:11 2Pe 2:15
1:12 Pr 25:14
1:13 Isa 57:20
1:14 Ge 5:18
1:16 2Pe 2:18
1:17 2Pe 3:2
1:18 2Pe 3:3

The Perils of Lasciviousness

Jude begins his letter in the Bible by saying he is separated and set apart for Jesus Christ. He addresses the readers of his letter by saying he was impelled and felt it very necessary to make the church aware that certain men had crept into the church of God unnoticed. The King James Version of this scripture says they turned the grace of God into "lasciviousness" (Jude 1:4), denying the only Lord God. The most precious thing a believer can have—the grace of God—has become lasciviousness, or lewdness and immorality.

According to Jude, men like this hang out unnoticed in the church, yet their fates have already been determined. This means they have already been turned over to reprobate and depraved minds with seared consciences that can never experience the true grace and mercy of God. The Bible explains that these people nibble at fake grace because they are eternally doomed to never eat the fruit of the real thing.

Lasciviousness has its greatest power when it operates through fraudulent men in the church. These men are filled with every kind of demonic assignment to lure and trick those who are far away from God and, as a result, have spiritual doors wide open for such infiltration. Let's take a look at some of these people:

- Those who spread a false word (1Ti 4:2)
- Those who give a false witness or testimony (Mt 19:18)
- A false apostle (2Co 11:4)
- A false christ (Mt 24:24)
- A false prophet (Mt 7:15)
- False teachers (2Pe 2:1)

We must beware of pseudo-ministers and false angels of light who operate in the church.

Kimberly Daniels

after their own ungodly desires." 19 These are
the men who cause divisions, sensual, devoid
of the Spirit.
20 But you, beloved, build yourselves up in
your most holy faith. Pray in the Holy Spirit.
21 Keep yourselves in the love of God while you
are waiting for the mercy of our Lord Jesus
Christ, which leads to eternal life.
22 On some have compassion, using discern-
ment. 23 And others save with fear while pulling
them out of the fire, hating even the garment
stained by the flesh.

1:19 1Co 2:14
1:20 Eph 6:18
1:21 2Pe 3:12
1:23 Am 4:11

....

1:24 1Pe 4:13
1:25 1Ti 1:17

Benediction

24 Now to Him who is able to keep you from
falling and to present you blameless before
the presence of His glory with rejoicing, 25 to
the only wise God our Savior, be glory and
majesty, dominion and power, both now and
forever. Amen.

Author: The apostle John

Written: Between AD 54 and 96, from the Isle of Patmos

Themes: Visions, End-Time Prophecy

REVELATION

Dear Spirit Led Woman,

In Revelation 2:1–7 the church at Ephesus is described in a way that makes it seem successful. The people had accomplished a great deal, endured hardships, and persevered without growing weary. They held a high standard of righteousness and operated with great discernment. From a natural perspective, it appeared to be a thriving church.

But God was displeased with them because, for all their great works, they had left their first love. Passion to pursue the Lord was no longer the driving force of their souls.

Where do you stand in your walk with God? Are you as fervent to pursue Him now as you were when you first became a Christian? Renew your commitment to read the Word—not as an assignment but as a love letter. The Holy Spirit is your teacher, and He will guide you in your studies if you ask Him to. Desire to go beyond your present experience with God. Renew your passion for Christ. Commit yourself to growing spiritually, to daily following the Holy Spirit's lead, and to making an impact for eternity in the lives of others.

Joy F. Strang

Introduction and Salutation

1 The Revelation of Jesus Christ, which
God gave to Him to show to His servants
things which must soon take place. He sent
and signified it by His angel to His servant
John, 2 who bears record of the word of God,
and of the testimony of Jesus Christ, and of all
things that he saw. 3 Blessed is he who reads
and those who hear the words of this prophecy
and keep those things which are written in it,
for the time is near.

4 John,

To the seven churches which are in Asia:

Grace to you and peace from Him who is and
who was and who is to come and from the
seven Spirits who are before His throne, 5 and
from Jesus Christ, who is the faithful witness,
the firstborn from the dead, and the ruler of
the kings of the earth.

To Him who loved us and washed us from
our sins in His own blood, 6 and has made
us kings and priests to His God and Father,
to Him be glory and dominion forever and
ever. Amen.

7 Look! He is coming with clouds,
and every eye will see Him,
even those who pierced Him.
And all the tribes of the earth will
mourn because of Him.
Even so, Amen.

8 "I am the Alpha and the Omega, the Begin-
ning and the End," says the Lord, "who is and
who was and who is to come, the Almighty."

A Vision of Christ

9 I, John, both your brother and companion
in the tribulation and kingdom and patience
of Jesus Christ, was on the isle that is called
Patmos on account of the word of God and the
testimony of Jesus Christ. 10 I was in the Spirit
on the Lord's Day, and I heard behind me a
great voice like a trumpet, 11 saying, "I am the
Alpha and the Omega, the First and the Last,"
and "What you see, write in a book, and send
it to the seven churches which are in Asia: to
Ephesus, Smyrna, Pergamum, Thyatira, Sardis,
Philadelphia, and Laodicea."

12 I turned to see the voice that spoke with
me. And when I turned, I saw seven golden
candlesticks, 13 and in the midst of the seven
candlesticks was one like a Son of Man, clothed
with a garment down to the feet and with a
golden sash wrapped around the chest. 14 The
hair on His head was white like wool, as white
as snow. His eyes were like a flame of fire.
15 His feet were like fine brass, as if refined
in a furnace, and His voice as the sound of
many waters. 16 He had in His right hand seven
stars, and out of His mouth went a sharp two-
edged sword. His appearance was like the sun
shining brightly.

17 When I saw Him, I fell at His feet as though
I were dead. Then He laid His right hand on
me, saying to me, "Do not be afraid. I am the
First and the Last. 18 I am He who lives, though I
was dead. Look! I am alive forevermore. Amen.
And I have the keys of Hades and of Death.

19 "Write the things which you have seen, and
the things which are, and the things which
will take place after this. 20 The mystery of the
seven stars which you saw in My right hand,
and the seven golden candlesticks: The seven
stars are the angels of the seven churches, and
the seven candlesticks which you saw are the
seven churches.

The Message to Ephesus

2 "To the angel of the church of Ephesus
write:

"He who holds the seven stars in His
right hand, who walks in the midst of
the seven golden candlesticks, says these
things: 2 I know your works, your labor and
your patience, and that you cannot bear
those who are evil. And you have tested
those who say they are apostles, but are
not, and have found them to be liars. 3 You
have endured, and have been patient, and
for My name's sake have labored and have
not grown weary.

4 "But I have something against you, that
you have abandoned the love you had at first.
5 Remember therefore from where you have
fallen. Repent, and do the works you did at
first, or else I will come to you quickly and re-
move your candlestick from its place, unless
you repent. 6 But this you have: You hate the
works of the Nicolaitans, which I also hate.

7 "He who has an ear, let him hear what
the Spirit says to the churches. To him who
overcomes I will give permission to eat of
the tree of life, which is in the midst of the
Paradise of God.

God has lavished His love on me,
and I renew my vows to put Him first
above all other persons and things
(Rev 2:5–7).

The Message to Smyrna

8 "To the angel of the church in Smyrna write:

"The First and the Last, who was dead
and came to life, says these things: 9 I know
your works and tribulation and poverty (but

1:1 Rev 22:6
1:2 Rev 12:17
1:3 Lk 11:28
1:4 Rev 3:1
1:5 Rev 3:14
1:6 Rev 5:10
1:7 Da 7:13
1:8 Rev 21:6
1:9 Php 4:14
1:10 Ac 20:7
1:11 Rev 1:4
1:12 Ex 25:37
1:13 Da 7:13
1:14 Da 7:9
1:15 Eze 43:2
....
1:16 Isa 49:2
1:17 Isa 44:6
1:18 Ro 6:9
1:20 Rev 2:1
2:1 Rev 1:16
2:2 1Jn 4:1
2:3 Jn 15:21
2:5 Rev 2:16
2:7 Rev 2:11
2:8 Rev 1:17–18
2:9 Rev 3:9

you are rich). And I know the blasphemy of
those who say they are Jews and are not,
but are a synagogue of Satan. 10 Do not fear
any of those things which you are about
to suffer. Look, the devil is about to throw
some of you into prison, that you may be
tried, and you will have tribulation for ten
days. Be faithful unto death, and I will give
you the crown of life.
11 "He who has an ear, let him hear what
the Spirit says to the churches. He who over-
comes shall not be hurt by the second death.

The Message to Pergamum

12 "To the angel of the church in Pergamum
write:

"He who has the sharp two-edged sword
says these things: 13 I know your works and
where you live, where Satan's throne is. Yet
you hold firmly to My name, and did not
deny My faith even in the days of Antipas,
My faithful martyr, who was killed among
you, where Satan dwells.
14 "But I have a few things against you:
You have there those who hold the teach-
ing of Balaam, who taught Balak to cast
a stumbling block before the children of
Israel, to eat things sacrificed to idols and
to commit sexual immorality. 15 So you also
have those who hold the teaching of the
Nicolaitans. 16 Repent, or else I will come
to you quickly and will war against them
with the sword of My mouth.
17 "He who has an ear, let him hear what
the Spirit says to the churches. To him who
overcomes I will give the hidden manna to
eat. And I will give him a white stone, and
on the stone a new name written, which no
one knows except he who receives it.

The Message to Thyatira

18 "To the angel of the church in Thyatira
write:

"The Son of God, who has eyes like a flame
of fire, and whose feet are like fine brass,
says these things: 19 I know your works, love,
service, faith, and your patience, and that
your last works are more than the first.
20 "But I have a few things against you:
You permit that woman Jezebel, who calls
herself a prophetess, to teach and seduce
My servants to commit sexual immorality
and eat food sacrificed to idols. 21 I gave
her time to repent of her sexual immorality,
but she did not repent. 22 Look! I will throw
her onto a sickbed, and those who commit
adultery with her into great tribulation, un-
less they repent of their deeds. 23 I will put
her children to death, and all the churches

2:10 Mt 10:22
2:11 Rev 2:7
2:12 Rev 1:16
2:13 Ac 22:20
2:14 Rev 2:20
2:15 Rev 2:6
2:16 2Th 2:8
2:17 Rev 2:7
2:18 Rev 1:11
2:20 Rev 2:14
2:22 Rev 17:2
2:23 Ro 8:27
2:24 Ac 15:28
2:25 Rev 3:11
2:26 Rev 3:21
2:27 Rev 12:5
2:28 Rev 22:16
2:29 Rev 2:7
3:1 Rev 1:4
3:3 Rev 2:5
3:4 Jude 1:23
3:5 Mt 10:32
3:6 Rev 2:7
3:7 Rev 6:10
3:8 Rev 2:13
3:9 Rev 2:9

shall know that I am He who searches the
hearts and minds. I will give to each one
of you according to your deeds.
24 "Now to you I say, and to the rest in
Thyatira, as many as do not have this teach-
ing, who have not known what some call
the 'depths of Satan,' I will put on you no
other burden. 25 But hold firmly what you
have until I come.
26 "To him who overcomes and keeps My
works to the end, I will give authority over
the nations—

27 He 'shall rule them with a rod of iron;
like the vessels of a potter they shall
be broken in pieces'[1]—

even as I myself have received authority
from My Father. 28 And I will give him the
morning star. 29 He who has an ear, let him
hear what the Spirit says to the churches.

The Message to Sardis

3 "To the angel of the church in Sardis write:
"He who has the seven Spirits of God
and the seven stars says these things: I know
your works, that you have a reputation of
being alive, but you are dead. 2 Be watchful,
and strengthen the things which remain but
are ready to die, for I have not found your
works perfected before God. 3 Remember
therefore how you have received and heard;
hold fast and repent. Therefore if you will
not watch, I will come upon you as a thief,
and you will not know what hour I will come
upon you.
4 "You have a few names even in Sardis
who have not soiled their garments. They
shall walk with Me in white, for they are
worthy. 5 He who overcomes shall be clothed
in white garments. I will not blot his name
out of the Book of Life, but I will confess
his name before My Father and before His
angels. 6 He who has an ear, let him hear
what the Spirit says to the churches.

The Message to Philadelphia

7 "To the angel of the church in Philadelphia
write:

"He who is holy, He who is true, He who
has the key of David, He who opens and no
one shuts, and shuts and no one opens, says
these things: 8 I know your works. Look! I
have set before you an open door, and no
one can shut it. For you have a little strength,
and have kept My word, and have not denied
My name. 9 Listen! I will make them of the
synagogue of Satan, who say they are Jews
and are not, but lie. Listen! I will make them

[1]27 Ps 2:9.

SPIRITLED WOMAN

COUNSEL FROM THE SPIRIT BASICS

God Has Big Plans for You

Being all God has called you to be begins and ends in prayer. It is in hearing from heaven—plugging into the big conversation—that God's will for the earth today will be communicated to His people and put into action. Are you part of the fight to manifest God's kingdom of wholeness, freedom, and sufficiency? Are you a spreader of "righteousness and peace and joy in the Holy Spirit" (Ro 14:17) for every race, creed, culture, and community?

It is my firm conviction that God has big plans for you and is waiting—literally knocking at the door (Rev 3:20)—in order to meet with you and talk about your future and what you need to do today to prepare for it. Spend time in prayer today exercising your spiritual senses and learning to discern God's voice.

The world is waiting for the manifestation of the sons and daughters of God (Ro 8:19–22). It is time for us to step up and be the emissaries of God's goodness. It won't be easy, but it will be worth it. We have God's Word on it. It's time to unleash His kingdom so all of humanity will know the power of love and wisdom as it is manifested in the lives of those who belong to Him.

Cindy Trimm

come and worship before your feet and to
know that I have loved you. 10 Because you
have kept My word of patience, I also will
keep you from the hour of temptation which
shall come upon the entire world, to test
those who dwell on the earth.
11 "Look, I am coming quickly. Hold firmly
what you have, so that no one may take
your crown. 12 He who overcomes will I
make a pillar in the temple of My God, and
he shall go out no more. I will write on him
the name of My God and the name of the
city of My God, the New Jerusalem, which
comes down out of heaven from My God,
and My own new name. 13 He who has an
ear, let him hear what the Spirit says to
the churches.

The Message to Laodicea

14 "To the angel of the church of the Laodiceans write:

"The Amen, the Faithful and True Witness,
the Beginning of the creation of God, says
these things: 15 I know your works, that you
are neither cold nor hot. I wish you were
cold or hot. 16 So then, because you are luke-
warm, and neither cold nor hot, I will spit
you out of My mouth. 17 For you say, 'I am
rich, and have stored up goods, and have
need of nothing,' yet do not realize that you
are wretched, miserable, poor, blind, and
naked. 18 I counsel you to buy from Me gold
refined by fire, that you may be rich, and
white garments, that you may be dressed,
that the shame of your nakedness may not
appear, and anoint your eyes with eye salve,
that you may see.
19 "Those whom I love, I rebuke and dis-
cipline. Therefore be zealous and repent.
20 Listen! I stand at the door and knock. If
anyone hears My voice and opens the door,
I will come in and dine with him, and he
with Me.
21 "To him who overcomes will I grant to
sit with Me on My throne, as I also overcame
and sat down with My Father on His throne.
22 He who has an ear, let him hear what the
Spirit says to the churches."

The Heavenly Worship

4 After this I looked. And there was an open
door in heaven. The first voice I heard was
like a trumpet speaking with me, saying, "Come
up here, and I will show you things which must
take place after this." 2 Immediately I was in the
Spirit. And there was a throne set in heaven
with One sitting on the throne! 3 And He who sat
there appeared like a jasper and a sardius stone.
There was a rainbow around the throne, ap-
pearing like an emerald. 4 Twenty-four thrones
were around the throne. And I saw twenty-four
elders sitting on the thrones, clothed in white
garments. They had crowns of gold on their
heads. 5 Lightnings and thunderings and voices
proceeded from the throne. Seven lamps of fire
were burning before the throne, which are the
seven Spirits of God. 6 Before the throne was a
sea of glass like crystal.

In the midst of the throne, and around the
throne, were four living creatures covered
with eyes in front and in back. 7 The first liv-
ing creature was like a lion, the second living

3:10 2Pe 2:9
3:11 Rev 2:10
3:12 Rev 22:4
3:13 Rev 2:7
3:14 Rev 1:5
3:15 Rev 3:1
3:17 Hos 12:8
3:18 Rev 16:15
3:19 Rev 2:5
3:21 Mt 19:28
3:22 Rev 2:7
4:1 Rev 1:19
4:2 Isa 6:1
4:3 Eze 1:28
4:4 Rev 4:10
4:5 Rev 1:4
4:6 Rev 5:6
4:7 Eze 1:10

SPIRIT-TO-SPIRIT PRAYER

SACRIFICE OF THANKSGIVING

My Lord and Savior, I thank You for giving me life and for breathing Your Spirit into my spirit. Thank You for saving me and transforming my life. Thank You for directing my steps each day. Thank You because I am justified and accepted in Christ Jesus. Thank You for Your provision and protection each day. Thank You for renewing my mind as I study Your Word. Thank You for blessing my family and keeping us from all evil. Thank You for keeping me from all temptations and wrong decisions. Thank You for healing my body and strengthening my bones. Thank You for the Spirit of wisdom and revelation. Amen.

Iris Delgado

creature like a calf, the third living creature
had a face like a man, and the fourth crea-
ture was like a flying eagle. 8 The four living
creatures had six wings each, and they were
covered with eyes all around. All day and night,
without ceasing, they were saying:

"'Holy, holy, holy,
Lord God Almighty,'[1]
who was, and is, and is to come."

9 When the living creatures give glory and hon-
or and thanks to Him who sits on the throne,
who lives forever and ever, 10 the twenty-four
elders fall down before Him who sits on the
throne, and worship Him, who lives forever
and ever. Then they cast their crowns before
the throne, saying,

11 "You are worthy, O Lord,
to receive glory and honor and power;
for You have created all things,
and by Your will they exist
and were created."

The Scroll and the Lamb

5 Then I saw in the right hand of Him
who sat on the throne a scroll written
within and on the back, sealed with seven
seals. 2 And I saw a strong angel proclaiming
with a loud voice, "Who is worthy to open
the scroll and to break its seals?" 3 But no
one in heaven or on earth or under the earth
was able to open the scroll or to look in it. 4 I
began to weep loudly, because no one was
found worthy to open and read the scroll, or
to look in it. 5 Then one of the elders said to
me, "Do not weep. Look! The Lion of the tribe
of Judah, the Root of David, has triumphed.
He is able to open the scroll and to loose its
seven seals."

6 I saw a Lamb in the midst of the throne and
of the four living creatures, and in the midst
of the elders, standing as though it had been
slain, having seven horns and seven eyes,
which are the seven Spirits of God, sent out
into all the earth. 7 He came and took the scroll
out of the right hand of Him who sat on the
throne. 8 When He had taken the scroll, the
four living creatures and the twenty-four elders
fell down before the Lamb, each one having a
harp, and golden bowls full of incense, which
are the prayers of saints. 9 And they sang a
new song, saying:

"You are worthy to take the scroll,
and to open its seals;
for You were slain,
and have redeemed us to God by Your
blood
out of every tribe and tongue and
people and nation,
10 and have made us kings and priests unto
our God;
and we shall reign on the earth."

11 Then I looked, and I heard around the
throne and the living creatures and the elders
the voices of many angels, numbering ten
thousand times ten thousand, and thousands
of thousands, 12 saying with a loud voice:

4:8 Rev 1:8
4:9 Rev 15:7
4:10 Rev 4:4
4:11 Rev 5:12
5:1 Isa 29:11
5:3 Rev 5:13
5:5 Isa 11:1

5:6 Zec 4:10
5:7 Rev 5:1
5:8 Ps 141:2
5:9 Rev 14:6
5:10 Rev 1:6
5:11 Da 7:10
5:12 Rev 4:11

[1]8 Isa 6:3.

"Worthy is the Lamb who was slain,
to receive power and riches and
wisdom and strength
and honor and glory and blessing!"

13 Then I heard every creature which is in
heaven and on the earth and under the earth
and in the sea, and all that are in them, saying:

"To Him who sits on the throne and to the
Lamb
be blessing and honor and glory and
power,
forever and ever!"

14 The four living creatures said, "Amen." And
the twenty-four elders fell down and wor-
shipped Him who lives forever and ever.

The Seals

6 I saw when the Lamb opened one of the
seals. Then I heard one of the four living
creatures saying, with voice like thunder, "Come
and see." 2 And I looked, and there before me
was a white horse. He who sat on it had a bow.
And a crown was given to him, and he went
forth conquering that he might overcome.
3 When He opened the second seal, I heard
the second living creature say, "Come and see."
4 Then another horse that was red went forth.
Power was given to him who sat on it to take
peace from the earth, causing people to kill one
another. Then a great sword was given to him.
5 When He opened the third seal, I heard the
third living creature say, "Come!" I looked, and
there was a black horse, and he who sat on it
had a pair of scales in his hand. 6 Then I heard
a voice in the midst of the four living creatures
saying, "A quart[1] of wheat for a day's wages,
and three quarts of barley for a day's wages,[2]
and do not harm the oil and the wine."
7 When He opened the fourth seal, I heard the
voice of the fourth living creature say, "Come!"
8 So I looked, and there was a pale horse, and
the name of him who sat on it was Death, and
Hades followed him. Power over a fourth of
the earth was given to them, to kill with sword,
with hunger, with death, and by the beasts of
the earth.
9 When He opened the fifth seal, I saw un-
der the altar the souls of those who had been
slain for the word of God and for the testimony
they had held. 10 They cried out with a loud
voice, "How long, O Sovereign Lord, holy and
true, until You judge and avenge our blood on
those who dwell on the earth?" 11 Then a white
robe was given to each of them, and they were
told to rest a little longer, until the number of
their fellow servants and brothers should be
completed, who would be killed as they were.

5:13 Php 2:10
5:14 Rev 19:4
6:2 Rev 14:14
6:3 Rev 4:7
6:4 Zec 6:2
6:5 Zec 6:2
6:6 Rev 9:4
6:7 Rev 4:7
6:8 Hos 13:14
6:9 Rev 14:18
6:10 Zec 1:12
6:11 Heb 11:40

6:12 Mt 24:29
6:13 Rev 9:1
6:14 Rev 16:20
6:15 Isa 2:19
6:16 Hos 10:8
6:17 Ps 76:7
7:1 Da 7:2
7:3 Rev 14:1
7:4 Rev 9:16
7:7 Ge 35:23

12 I watched as He opened the sixth seal. And
suddenly there was a great earthquake. The sun
became black, like sackcloth made from goat
hair, and the moon became like blood. 13 And
the stars of heaven fell to the earth, as a fig
tree drops its unripe figs when it is shaken by a
strong wind. 14 Then the heavens receded like a
scroll when it is rolled up, and every mountain
and island was removed from its place.
15 Then the kings of the earth and the great
men and the rich men and the commanding
officers and the strong and everyone, slave and
free, hid themselves in the caves and in the rocks
of the mountains. 16 They said to the mountains
and rocks, "Fall on us, and hide us from the face
of Him who sits on the throne, and from the
wrath of the Lamb, 17 for the great day of His
wrath has come. Who is able to withstand it?"[3]

The 144,000 of Israel Sealed

7 Then I saw four angels standing at the
four corners of the earth, holding the four
winds of the earth, that the wind would not
blow on the earth or on the sea or on any tree.
2 And I saw another angel ascending from the
east, having the seal of the living God. He cried
out with a loud voice to the four angels who
had been given power to harm the earth and
the sea, 3 saying, "Do not harm the earth or
the sea or the trees, until we have sealed the
servants of our God on their foreheads." 4 Then
I heard the number of those who were sealed,
one hundred and forty-four thousand out of
every tribe of the children of Israel:

5 Twelve thousand from the tribe of Judah
were sealed,
twelve thousand from the tribe of Reuben
were sealed,
twelve thousand from the tribe of Gad were
sealed,
6 twelve thousand from the tribe of Asher
were sealed,
twelve thousand from the tribe of Naphtali
were sealed,
twelve thousand from the tribe of Manasseh
were sealed,
7 twelve thousand from the tribe of Simeon
were sealed,
twelve thousand from the tribe of Levi were
sealed,
twelve thousand from the tribe of Issachar
were sealed,
8 twelve thousand from the tribe of Zebulun
were sealed,
twelve thousand from the tribe of Joseph
were sealed,
and twelve thousand from the tribe of Benja-
min were sealed.

[1]6 Gk. *choenix*, or a kilogram. [2]6 Gk. *denarius*. [3]17 Ho 10:8.

The Multitude From Every Nation

9 Then I looked. And there was a great multi-
tude which no one could count, from all na-
tions and tribes and peoples and tongues,
standing before the throne and before the
Lamb, clothed with white robes, with palm
branches in their hands. 10 They cried out with
a loud voice:

"Salvation belongs to our God
who sits on the throne,
and to the Lamb!"

11 All the angels stood around the throne and
the elders and the four living creatures and
fell on their faces before the throne and wor-
shipped God, 12 saying:

"Amen!
Blessing and glory
and wisdom and thanksgiving and honor
and power and might
be to our God forever and ever!
Amen."

13 Then one of the elders asked me, "Who
are these clothed in white robes, and where
did they come from?"
14 I said to him, "Sir, you know."

Dear Abba Father, help me to obey Your statutes and wise counsel, and to walk in Your freedom so that You may find me washed in the blood of the Lamb (Rev 7:14).

He said to me, "These are those who came
out of great tribulation and washed their
robes and made them white in the blood of
the Lamb. 15 Therefore,

they are before the throne of God,
and serve Him day and night in His
temple.
And He who sits on the throne
will dwell among them.
16 'They shall neither hunger any more,
nor shall they thirst any more;
the sun shall not strike them,'[1]
nor any scorching heat;
17 for the Lamb who is in the midst of the
throne
will shepherd them
and 'He will lead them to springs of living
water.'[2]
'And God will wipe away every tear from
their eyes.'[3]"

The Seventh Seal

8 When He opened the seventh seal, there
was silence in heaven for about half an
hour.
2 And I saw the seven angels who stand
before God, and seven trumpets were given
to them.
3 Another angel, having a golden censer,
came and stood at the altar. He was given
much incense to offer with the prayers of all the
saints on the golden altar which was before
the throne. 4 The smoke of the incense, with
the prayers of the saints, ascended before God
from the angel's hand. 5 Then the angel took
the censer, filled it with fire from the altar, and
threw it onto the earth. And there were noises,
thundering, lightning, and an earthquake.

The Trumpets

6 Then the seven angels who had the seven
trumpets prepared themselves to sound them.
7 The first angel sounded, and there followed
hail and fire mixed with blood, and they were
thrown upon the earth. A third of the trees and
all the green grass were burned up.
8 Then the second angel sounded, and
something like a great mountain, burning
with fire, was thrown into the sea. A third of
the sea became blood, 9 a third of the living
creatures in the sea died, and a third of the
ships were destroyed.
10 The third angel sounded, and a great star
from heaven, burning like a torch, fell on a
third of the rivers and on the springs of waters.
11 The name of this star is Wormwood. A third
of the waters became wormwood, and many
men died from the waters, because they were
made bitter.
12 The fourth angel sounded, and a third of
the sun was struck, and a third of the moon,
and a third of the stars, so that a third of them
were darkened. A third of the day had no light,
and likewise a third of the night.
13 Then I watched, and I heard an angel
flying through the midst of heaven, saying
with a loud voice, "Woe, woe, woe to the
inhabitants of the earth, because of the other
trumpet blasts of the three angels, who are
yet to sound!"

9 The fifth angel sounded, and I saw a star
fallen from heaven to the earth. The star
was given the key to the bottomless pit. 2 He
opened the bottomless pit, and smoke ascended
from the pit, like the smoke of a great furnace.
The sun and the air were darkened by the
smoke from the pit. 3 And out of the smoke
locusts came upon the earth. Power was given
them as the scorpions of the earth have power.

7:9 Rev 5:9
7:10 Ps 3:8
7:11 Rev 4:6
7:12 Rev 5:12–14
7:13 Rev 7:9
7:14 1Jn 1:7
7:15 Rev 22:3
7:16 Isa 49:10
7:17 Isa 25:8

8:1 Rev 6:1
8:2 Rev 11:15
8:3 Rev 9:13
8:4 Ps 141:2
8:5 Rev 4:5
8:6 Rev 8:2
8:7 Rev 9:4
8:8 Jer 51:25
8:9 Isa 2:16
8:10 Isa 14:12
8:11 Jer 9:15
8:12 Isa 13:10
8:13 Rev 11:14
9:1 Rev 8:10
9:2 Ge 19:28

[1] *16* Isa 49:10. [2] *17* Isa 49:10. [3] *17* Isa 25:8.

4 They were commanded not to harm the grass of the earth, or any green thing, or any tree, but only those men who did not have the seal of God on their foreheads. 5 They were given authority, not to kill them, but to torment them for five months. Their torment was like the torment of a scorpion when it stings a man. 6 In those days men will seek death but will not find it. They will desire to die, but death will elude them.

7 The shape of the locusts was like horses prepared for battle. On their heads were something like crowns of gold, and their faces were like faces of men. 8 They had hair like the hair of women, and their teeth were like the teeth of lions. 9 They had breastplates like breastplates of iron, and the sound of their wings was like the sound of chariots with many horses running to battle. 10 They had tails like scorpions and stings in their tails. Their power was to hurt men for five months. 11 They had as king over them the angel of the bottomless pit, whose name in Hebrew is Abaddon, and in Greek his name is Apollyon.[1]

12 The first woe is past. Now, two more woes are yet to come.

13 The sixth angel sounded, and I heard a voice from the four horns of the golden altar which is before God, 14 saying to the sixth angel who had the trumpet, "Release the four angels who are bound at the great Euphrates River." 15 And the four angels, who had been prepared for the hour and day and month and year, were released to kill a third of mankind. 16 The army of horsemen numbered two hundred million. I heard their number.

17 Thus I saw the horses in the vision: Those who sat on them had breastplates of fiery red, hyacinth blue, and sulfur yellow. The heads of the horses were like the heads of lions, and out of their mouths came fire and smoke and brimstone. 18 A third of mankind was killed by these three plagues—by the fire and by the smoke and by the brimstone, which came out of their mouths. 19 The power of the horses is in their mouths and in their tails. For their tails are like serpents, with heads by which they inflict injury.

20 The rest of mankind, who were not killed by these plagues, did not repent of the works of their hands. They did not cease to worship demons, and idols of gold, silver, brass, stone, and wood, which cannot see nor hear nor walk. 21 Nor did they repent of their murders or their magical arts or their sexual immorality or their thefts.

9:4 Rev 6:6
9:5 Rev 9:10
9:6 Jer 8:3
9:7 Da 7:8
9:8 Joel 1:6
9:9 Job 39:25
9:10 Rev 9:5
9:11 Eph 2:2
9:12 Rev 11:14
9:14 Rev 16:12
9:15 Rev 8:7
9:16 Rev 7:4
9:17 Rev 9:18
9:18 Rev 9:15
9:20 Da 5:23
9:21 Rev 17:2

10:1 Mt 17:2
10:2 Rev 10:5
10:4 Da 8:26
10:5 Da 12:7
10:6 Rev 4:11
10:7 Ro 16:25
10:9 Jer 15:16
10:11 Eze 37:4
11:1 Rev 21:15
11:2 Lk 21:24
11:3 Ge 37:34
11:4 Ps 52:8
11:5 Jer 5:14
11:6 1Ki 17:1

The Angel and the Little Scroll

10 Then I saw another mighty angel coming down from heaven, clothed with a cloud and a rainbow on his head. His face was like the sun, and his feet like pillars of fire. 2 He had a little scroll open in his hand. He set his right foot on the sea and his left foot on the land, 3 and cried out with a loud voice, like a lion roaring. When he cried out, seven thunders sounded their voices. 4 And when the seven thunders sounded their voices, I was about to write, but I heard a voice from heaven saying to me, "Seal up those things which the seven thunders said, and do not write them."

5 The angel whom I saw standing on the sea and on the earth lifted up his hand to heaven 6 and swore by Him who lives forever and ever, who created heaven and the things that are in them, and the earth and the things that are in it, and the sea and the things that are in it, that there should be no more delay. 7 But in the days when the seventh angel is about to sound, the mystery of God will be fulfilled, as He has declared to His servants the prophets.

8 Then the voice which I heard from heaven spoke to me again and said, "Go, take the little scroll which is open in the hand of the angel who is standing on the sea and on the earth."

9 So I went to the angel and said to him, "Give me the little scroll." He said to me, "Take it and eat it. 'It will turn your stomach sour, but in your mouth it will be as sweet as honey.'[2]" 10 I took the little scroll from the angel's hand and ate it. It was as sweet as honey in my mouth, but when I had eaten it, my stomach turned sour. 11 Then he said to me, "You must prophesy again about many peoples and nations and tongues and kings."

The Two Witnesses

11 I was given a reed like a measuring rod. The angel stood, saying, "Rise and measure the temple of God and the altar, and those who worship in it. 2 But exclude the court which is outside the temple, and do not measure it, for it has been given to the nations. They will trample on the Holy City for forty-two months. 3 And I will give power to my two witnesses, and they will prophesy for one thousand two hundred and sixty days, clothed in sackcloth." 4 These are the two olive trees and the two candlesticks standing before the God of the earth.[3] 5 If anyone desires to harm them, fire proceeds out of their mouth and devours their enemies. If anyone desires to harm them, he must be killed in this way. 6 They have power to shut heaven, that it may not rain during the days of their prophecy. They have power over waters to turn them into blood and to strike the earth with every plague as often as they desire.

[1] *11* Or *Destroyer.* [2] *9* Eze 3:3. [3] *4* Zec 4:3, 11, 14.

7 When they have finished their testimony,
the beast that ascends from the bottomless
pit will wage war against them and overcome
them and kill them. 8 Their dead bodies will lie
in the street of the great city, which spiritually
is called Sodom and Egypt, where also our
Lord was crucified. 9 Those from every people
and tribe and tongue and nation will see their
dead bodies for three and a half days, and
will not allow their dead bodies to be put in
graves. 10 Those who dwell on the earth will
rejoice over them and make merry and send
gifts to one another, because these two proph-
ets tormented those who dwell on the earth.
11 After the three and a half days, the breath[1]
of life from God entered them, and they stood
on their feet, and great fear fell on those who
saw them. 12 Then they heard a loud voice from
heaven saying to them, "Come up here!" And
they ascended to heaven in a cloud, while their
enemies watched them.
13 At that same hour there was a great earth-
quake, and a tenth of the city fell. Seven thou-
sand men were killed in the earthquake, and
the remnant were frightened and gave glory
to the God of heaven.
14 The second woe is past. Listen, the third
woe is coming quickly.

The Seventh Trumpet

15 The seventh angel sounded, and there
were loud voices in heaven, saying:

"The kingdoms of the world have become
the kingdoms of our Lord, and of His
Christ,
and He shall reign forever and ever."

16 And the twenty-four elders, who sat before
God on their thrones, fell on their faces and
worshipped God, 17 saying:

"We give You thanks, O Lord God Almighty,
who is and was and who is to come,
because You have taken Your great power
and begun to reign.
18 The nations were angry,
and Your wrath has come,
and the time has come for the dead to be
judged,
and to reward Your servants the prophets
and the saints and those who fear Your
name,
small and great,
and to destroy those who destroy the earth."

19 Then the temple of God was opened in
heaven, and the ark of His covenant was seen
in His temple. And there came lightning, noises,
thundering, an earthquake, and great hail.

11:7 Rev 13:7
11:9 Ps 79:2–3
11:10 Rev 3:10
11:11 Ge 2:7
11:12 Ac 1:9
11:13 Rev 6:12
11:14 Rev 8:13
11:15 Rev 12:10
11:16 Rev 4:4
11:17 Rev 1:8
11:18 Rev 19:5
11:19 Rev 16:21
....
12:1 Rev 12:3
12:2 Gal 4:19
12:3 Rev 17:12
12:6 Rev 11:2–3
12:7 Jude 1:9
12:9 Lk 10:18
12:10 Rev 11:15
12:11 Lk 14:26
12:12 Rev 8:13

The Woman and the Dragon

12 A great sign appeared in heaven: a
woman clothed with the sun, with the
moon under her feet, and on her head a crown
of twelve stars. 2 She was with child and cried out
in labor and in pain to give birth. 3 Then another
sign appeared in heaven: There was a great red
dragon with seven heads and ten horns, and
seven diadems on his heads. 4 His tail drew a
third of the stars of heaven, and threw them to
the earth. The dragon stood before the woman
who was ready to give birth, to devour her Child
as soon as He was born. 5 She gave birth to a
male Child, "who was to rule all nations with
an iron scepter."[2] And her Child was caught up
to God and to His throne. 6 The woman fled into
the wilderness where she has a place prepared
by God, that they may nourish her there for one
thousand two hundred and sixty days.
7 Then war broke out in heaven. Michael and
his angels fought against the dragon, and the
dragon and his angels fought, 8 but they did
not prevail, nor was there a place for them in
heaven any longer. 9 The great dragon was cast
out, that ancient serpent called the Devil and
Satan, who deceives the whole world. He was
cast down to the earth, and his angels were
cast down with him.
10 Then I heard a loud voice in heaven, saying:

"Now the salvation and the power and the
kingdom of our God
and the authority of His Christ have come,
for the accuser of our brothers,
who accused them before our God day
and night,
has been cast down.
11 They overcame him
by the blood of the Lamb
and by the word of their testimony,
and they loved not their lives
unto the death.

Thank You, Father, for the blood of
Jesus has redeemed me from every
curse and stronghold of the enemy
(Rev 12:11).

12 Therefore rejoice, O heavens,
and you who dwell in them!
Woe unto the inhabitants of the earth and
the sea!
For the devil has come down to you in
great wrath,
because he knows that his time is short."

[1] 11 Eze 37:5–14. [2] 5 Ps 2:9.

13 When the dragon saw that he was cast
down to the earth, he persecuted the woman
who gave birth to the male Child. 14 The woman
was given two wings of a great eagle, that she
might fly into the wilderness to her place, where
she is to be nourished for a time and times and
half a time, from the presence of the serpent.
15 Then the serpent spewed water out of his
mouth like a flood after the woman, that he
might cause her to be carried away by the flood.
16 But the earth helped the woman. The earth
opened its mouth and swallowed the flood
which the dragon spewed out of his mouth.
17 Then the dragon was angry with the woman,
and he went to wage war with the remnant of
her offspring, who keep the commandments
of God and have the testimony of Jesus Christ.

The Two Beasts

13 I stood on the sand of the sea. And I
saw a beast rising out of the sea, having
seven heads and ten horns, with ten crowns
on his horns, and blasphemous names on
his heads. 2 The beast which I saw was like
a leopard. His feet were like those of a bear,
and his mouth like the mouth of a lion. The
dragon gave him his power and his throne and
great authority. 3 I saw one of his heads as if it
was mortally wounded, but his deadly wound
was healed, and the whole world marveled
and followed the beast. 4 They worshipped the
dragon who gave authority to the beast. And
they worshipped the beast, saying, "Who is like
the beast? Who is able to wage war with him?"

5 He was given a mouth speaking great
things and blasphemies. And he was given
authority to wage war for forty-two months.
6 He opened his mouth to speak blasphemies
against God, to blaspheme His name and His
tabernacle and those who dwell in heaven.
7 It was granted to him to wage war with the
saints and to overcome them. And authority
was given him over every tribe and tongue
and nation. 8 All who dwell on the earth will
worship him, all whose names have not been
written in the Book of Life of the Lamb who
was slain from the foundation of the world.

9 If anyone has an ear, let him hear:

10 "He who is to be taken captive,
into captivity he shall go;
he who kills with the sword,
with the sword he must be killed."[1]

Here is a call for the patience and the faith of
the saints.

11 Then I saw another beast rising out of the
earth. He had two horns like a lamb and he spoke
like a dragon. 12 He exercises all the authority of
the first beast in his presence and causes the
earth and those who dwell on it to worship the
first beast, whose deadly wound was healed.
13 He performs great signs, making fire come
down from heaven on the earth in the sight of
men. 14 He deceives those who dwell on the earth
by the signs which he was granted to do in the
presence of the beast, telling those who dwell
on the earth to make an image to the beast who
was wounded by a sword and lived. 15 He was
allowed to give breath to the image of the beast,
that the image of the beast should both speak
and cause as many as would not worship the
image of the beast to be killed. 16 He causes all,
both small and great, both rich and poor, both
free and slave, to receive a mark on their right
hand or on their forehead, 17 so that no one may
buy or sell, except he who has the mark or the
name of the beast or the number of his name.

18 Here is a call for wisdom: Let him who has
understanding calculate the number of the
beast. It is the number of a man. His number
is six hundred and sixty-six.

The Lamb and the 144,000

14 Then I looked. The Lamb was stand-
ing on Mount Zion and with Him one
hundred and forty-four thousand having His
Father's name written on their foreheads. 2 And
I heard a sound from heaven, like the sound
of many waters and like the sound of a great
thunder. I heard the sound of harpists playing
their harps. 3 They sang a new song before the
throne and before the four living creatures and
the elders. No one could learn that song except
the one hundred and forty-four thousand who
were redeemed from the earth. 4 These are those
who were not defiled with women, for they are
virgins. These are those who follow the Lamb
wherever He goes. These were redeemed from
among men, as first fruits to God and to the
Lamb. 5 No lie was found in their mouths, for
they are without fault before the throne of God.

The Messages of the Three Angels

6 Then I saw another angel flying in the midst
of heaven, having the eternal gospel to preach
to those who dwell on the earth, to every nation
and tribe and tongue and people. 7 He said with
a loud voice, "Fear God and give Him glory, for
the hour of His judgment has come. Worship
Him who made heaven and earth, the sea and
the springs of water."

8 Another angel followed, saying, " 'Fallen!
Fallen is Babylon, that Great City,'[2] because she
made all the nations drink of the wine of the
wrath of her sexual immorality."

9 A third angel followed them, saying with a
loud voice, "If anyone worships the beast and
his image and receives his mark on his fore-

12:14 Rev 12:6
12:15 Isa 59:19
12:17 Rev 14:12
13:1 Rev 12:3
13:2 Rev 16:10
13:3 Rev 17:8
13:4 Rev 13:2
13:5 Da 7:8
13:6 Rev 12:12
13:7 Da 7:21
13:8 Rev 3:5
13:9 Rev 2:7
13:10 Rev 14:12
13:13 1Ki 18:38
13:14 Rev 12:9
13:15 Rev 16:2
13:16 Rev 19:18
13:17 Rev 14:11
13:18 Rev 17:9
14:1 Rev 3:12
14:2 Rev 1:15
14:3 Rev 5:9
14:4 Rev 3:4
14:5 Ps 32:2
14:6 Rev 8:13
14:7 Rev 15:4
14:8 Isa 21:9
14:9 Rev 14:11

[1] *10* Jer 15:2. [2] *8* Isa 21:9.

head or on his hand, 10 he also shall drink of the wine of the wrath of God, which is poured out in full strength into the cup of His anger. He shall be tormented with fire and brimstone in the presence of the holy angels and in the presence of the Lamb. 11 The smoke of their torment will ascend forever and ever. They have no rest day or night, who worship the beast and his image and whoever receives the mark of his name." 12 Here is the patience of the saints; here are those who keep the commandments of God and the faith of Jesus.

13 Then I heard a voice from heaven saying to me, "Write: Blessed are the dead who die in the Lord from now on."

"Yes," says the Spirit, "that they may rest from their labors, for their works follow them."

The Harvest of the Earth

14 I looked. And there was a white cloud, and on the cloud sat One like a Son of Man, having on his head a golden crown, and in His hand a sharp sickle. 15 Then another angel came out of the temple, crying with a loud voice to Him who sat on the cloud, "Thrust in Your sickle and reap. The time has come for You to reap, for the harvest of the earth is ripe." 16 So He who sat on the cloud thrust His sickle on the earth, and the earth was harvested.

17 Another angel came out of the temple which is in heaven. He also had a sharp sickle. 18 Yet another angel who had authority over fire came out from the altar. He cried with a loud voice to him who had the sharp sickle, saying, "Thrust in your sharp sickle and gather the clusters of the vine of the earth, for her grapes are fully ripe." 19 The angel thrust his sickle into the earth and gathered the vintage of the earth, and threw it into the great winepress of the wrath of God. 20 The winepress was trampled outside the city, and blood came out of the winepress, up to the horses' bridles, for one hundred and eighty-six miles.[1]

The Angels With the Last Plagues

15 I saw another great and marvelous sign in heaven: seven angels having the seven last plagues, for in them the wrath of God is complete. 2 And I saw what looked like a sea of glass mixed with fire, and those who have the victory over the beast, over his image and over his mark and over the number of his name, standing on the sea of glass, having harps of God. 3 They sang the song of Moses, the servant of God, and the song of the Lamb, saying:

"Great and marvelous are Your works,
Lord God Almighty!
Just and true are Your ways,
O King of saints!
4 Who shall not fear You, O Lord,
and glorify Your name?
For You alone are holy.
All nations shall come
and worship before You,
for Your judgments have been revealed."[2]

5 After this I looked. And now the temple of the tabernacle of the testimony in heaven was opened. 6 The seven angels came out of the temple with the seven plagues. They were clothed in pure, bright linen, having their chests wrapped with golden sashes. 7 Then one of the four living creatures gave to the seven angels seven golden bowls full of the wrath of God, who lives forever and ever. 8 And the temple was filled with smoke from the glory of God and from His power. No one was able to enter the temple until the seven plagues of the seven angels were completed.

The Seven Bowls of God's Wrath

16 Then I heard a loud voice from the temple saying to the seven angels, "Go, pour out the bowls of the wrath of God on the earth."

2 The first went and poured out his bowl on the earth, and foul and grievous sores came on the men who had the mark of the beast and those who worshipped his image.

3 The second angel poured out his bowl on the sea. It became like the blood of a dead man, and every living creature in the sea died.

4 The third angel poured out his bowl on the rivers and springs of water, and they became blood. 5 Then I heard the angel of the waters saying:

"You are righteous, O Lord,
who is and was and who is to be,
because You have judged these things.
6 For they have shed the blood of saints and prophets,
and You have given them blood to drink.
It is what they deserve!"

7 And I heard another from the altar saying:

"Yes, Lord God Almighty,
true and righteous are Your judgments."

8 The fourth angel poured out his bowl on the sun, and power was given to him to scorch men with fire. 9 Men were scorched with great heat, and they blasphemed the name of God who has power over these plagues, and they did not repent and give Him glory.

10 The fifth angel poured out his bowl on the throne of the beast, and his kingdom was filled with darkness. They gnawed their tongues because of the anguish, 11 and blasphemed the God of heaven because of their pains and their sores, and did not repent of their deeds.

14:10 Isa 51:17
14:11 Isa 34:10
14:12 Rev 12:17
14:13 1Co 15:18
14:14 Rev 1:13
14:15 Jer 51:33
14:18 Joel 3:13
14:20 La 1:15
15:1 Rev 21:9
15:2 Rev 4:6
15:3 Ps 111:2
15:4 Ps 86:9
15:5 Nu 1:50
15:6 Rev 1:13
15:7 Rev 5:8
15:8 Isa 6:4
16:1 Rev 15:1
16:2 Rev 8:7
16:3 Ex 7:17–21
16:4 Ex 7:17–20
16:5 Rev 1:4
16:6 Isa 49:26
16:7 Rev 6:9
16:8 Rev 14:18
16:9 Rev 2:21
16:10 Rev 9:2
16:11 Rev 16:9

[1] 20 Gk. 1,600 stadia or 300 kilometers. [2] 3–4 Phrases from Ps 111:2–3; Dt 32:4; Jer 10:7; Ps 86:9; 98:2.

12 The sixth angel poured out his bowl on the great Euphrates River, and its water was dried up, to prepare the way for the kings from the East. 13 Then I saw three unclean spirits like frogs coming out of the mouth of the dragon, out of the mouth of the beast, and out of the mouth of the false prophet. 14 For they are spirits of demons, performing signs, who go out to the kings of the earth and of the whole world, to gather them to the battle of that great day of God Almighty.

15 "Look, I am coming as a thief. Blessed is
he who watches and keeps his garments
on, lest he walk naked and his shame be
exposed."

16 They gathered them together to the place which in Hebrew is called Armageddon.

17 The seventh angel poured out his bowl into the air, and a loud voice came out of the temple of heaven, from the throne, saying, "It is done!" 18 And there were noises and thundering and lightning and a great earthquake, such a mighty and great earthquake, as had never occurred since men were on the earth. 19 The great city was divided into three parts, and the cities of the nations fell. Babylon the Great was remembered before God, to give to her the cup of the wine of the fierceness of His wrath. 20 Every island fled away, and the mountains were not found. 21 Great hail, about the weight of a hundred pounds,[1] fell from heaven upon man. Men blasphemed God because of the plague of the hail, because that plague was so severe.

The Great Harlot and the Beast

17 One of the seven angels who had the seven bowls came and talked with me, saying to me, "Come, I will show you the judgment of the great prostitute who sits on many waters, 2 with whom the kings of the earth committed adultery, and the inhabitants of the earth were made drunk with the wine of her sexual immorality."

3 Then he carried me away in the Spirit into the wilderness. I saw a woman sitting on a scarlet beast which was full of blasphemous names, having seven heads and ten horns. 4 The woman was arrayed in purple and scarlet, and adorned with gold and precious stones and pearls, having in her hand a golden cup full of abominations and the filth of her sexual immorality. 5 On her forehead a name was written:

MYSTERY,
BABYLON THE GREAT,
THE MOTHER OF PROSTITUTES
AND OF THE ABOMINATIONS
OF THE EARTH.

6 I saw the woman, drunk with the blood of the saints and with the blood of the martyrs of Jesus.

When I saw her, I marveled greatly. 7 Then the angel said to me, "Why do you marvel? I will tell you the mystery of the woman and of the beast that carries her, which has the seven heads and the ten horns. 8 The beast, which you saw, was, and is not, and is to ascend out of the bottomless pit and go to destruction. Those who dwell on the earth whose names are not written in the Book of Life from the foundation of the world will marvel when they see the beast that was, and is not, and is to come.

9 "Here is the mind which has wisdom: The seven heads are seven mountains on which the woman sits. 10 They are also seven kings. Five have fallen, one is, the other has not yet come; and when he comes, he must remain a little while. 11 Concerning the beast who was, and is not, he is the eighth, and is of the seven, and is going to destruction.

12 "The ten horns which you saw are ten kings who have received no kingdom yet, but they will receive authority as kings for one hour with the beast. 13 These are of one mind and will give their power and authority to the beast. 14 These will wage war with the Lamb, but the Lamb will overcome them, for He is Lord of lords and King of kings. Those who are with Him are called and chosen and faithful."

15 Then he said to me, "The waters which you saw, where the prostitute sits, are peoples and multitudes and nations and tongues. 16 These ten horns and the beast which you saw will hate the prostitute; they will make her desolate and naked, and devour her flesh, and burn her with fire. 17 For God has put in their hearts to fulfill His will, and to be of one mind, and to give their kingdom to the beast, until the words of God are fulfilled. 18 The woman whom you saw is that great city, which reigns over the kings of the earth."

The Fall of Babylon

18 After this I saw another angel coming down from heaven, having great authority, and the earth was illuminated with his glory. 2 He cried out mightily with a loud voice, saying:

" 'Fallen! Fallen is Babylon the Great!'[2]
She has become a dwelling place of
demons,
a haunt for every unclean spirit,
and a haunt for every unclean and
hateful bird.
3 For all the nations have drunk
of the wine of the wrath of her sexual
immorality,

16:12 Rev 9:14
16:13 Rev 19:20
16:14 1Ti 4:1
16:15 Rev 3:18
16:16 Jdg 5:19
16:17 Eph 2:2
16:18 Da 12:1
16:19 Rev 18:5
16:20 Rev 6:14
16:21 Rev 11:19
17:1 Jer 51:13
17:2 Rev 14:8
17:3 Rev 12:3
17:4 Jer 51:7
17:5 Rev 14:8
17:6 Rev 16:6
17:8 Rev 11:7
17:9 Rev 13:18
17:11 Rev 17:8
17:12 Da 7:24
17:13 Rev 17:17
17:14 1Ti 6:15
17:15 Rev 17:1
17:16 Rev 18:8
17:17 Rev 10:7
17:18 Rev 16:19
18:1 Eze 43:2
18:2 Rev 14:8
18:3 Rev 14:8

[1] *21* Or 45 kilograms. [2] *2* Isa 21:9.

the kings of the earth have committed
adultery with her,
and the merchants of the earth have
become rich through the
abundance of her luxury."

4 Then I heard another voice from heaven
saying:

" 'Come out of her, my people,'[1]
lest you partake in her sins,
and lest you receive her plagues.
5 For her sins have reached up to heaven,
and God has remembered her iniquities.
6 Render to her as she has rendered to you,
and repay her double for her deeds;
in the cup which she has mixed, mix a
double portion for her.
7 To the extent that she glorified herself and
lived luxuriously,
so give her torment and sorrow;
for in her heart she says,
'I sit as a queen, and am no widow,
and will see no sorrow.'[2]
8 Therefore her plagues will come in one
day—
death and mourning and famine.
And she will be utterly burned with fire,
for strong is the Lord God who judges her.

9 "The kings of the earth, who have commit-
ted adultery and lived luxuriously with her, will
weep and mourn over her when they see the
smoke of her burning. 10 Standing far off for
the fear of her torment, they will say:

'Alas, alas for that great city,
that mighty city, Babylon!
In one hour your judgment has come.'

11 "The merchants of the earth will weep and
mourn over her, for no one buys their mer-
chandise any more: 12 the merchandise of gold,
silver, precious stones and pearls, fine linen,
purple, silk and scarlet, all kinds of scented
wood, all artifacts of ivory, all merchandise of
costly wood, bronze, iron, and marble; 13 and
cinnamon and incense, myrrh and frankin-
cense, wine, oil, fine flour and wheat, cattle
and sheep, horses and chariots, and slaves and
souls of men.

14 'The fruit that your soul lusted after
has departed from you,
and all the things which graceful and
exquisite
have departed from you,
and you shall never find them.'

15 "The merchants of these things, who
gained wealth by her, will stand far off for
fear of her torment, weeping and wailing,
16 and saying:

18:4 2Co 6:17
18:5 Jer 51:9
18:6 Ps 137:8
18:7 Zep 2:15
18:8 Jer 50:31
18:9 Rev 17:2
18:10 Rev 18:19
18:11 Rev 18:3
18:12 Rev 17:4
18:13 Eze 27:13
18:15 Rev 18:3
18:16 Rev 17:4

18:17 Rev 17:16
18:18 Rev 13:4
18:19 Jos 7:6
18:22 Jer 25:10
18:23 Isa 23:8
18:24 Rev 17:6
19:1 Rev 11:15
19:2 Dt 32:43

'Alas, alas, that great city,
that was arrayed in fine linen, in purple
and scarlet,
and decked with gold and precious
stones and pearls!
17 In one hour such great riches came to
nothing!'

"All sea captains and seafaring men, sailors
and all who trade by sea, stood far off, 18 and
cried out when they saw the smoke of her
burning, saying, 'What city is like this great
city?' 19 They threw dust on their heads and
cried out, weeping and wailing, and saying:

'Alas, alas, that great city,
in which all who had ships in the sea
grew rich from her wealth!
In one hour she has been laid waste!'
20 "Rejoice over her, O heaven
and saints and apostles and prophets,
for God has avenged you against her."

21 Then a mighty angel took up a stone like a
great millstone and threw it into the sea, saying:

"With such violence
shall that great city Babylon be thrown
down,
and shall be found no more.
22 The sound of harpists and musicians, flute
players and trumpeters,
shall not be heard in you any more.
No craftsman of any craft
shall be found in you any more,
and the sound of a millstone
shall not be heard in you any more.
23 The light of a lamp
shall shine in you no more,
and the voice of bridegroom and of bride
shall be heard in you no more.
For your merchants were the great men of
the earth,
and all nations were deceived by your
sorcery.
24 In her was found the blood of prophets and
of saints
and of all who were slain on the earth."

19 After these things I heard a great sound
of many people in heaven, shouting:

"Alleluia!
Salvation and glory and honor and power
belong to the Lord our God!
2 For true and righteous are His judgments,
because He has judged the great prostitute
who corrupted the earth with her sexual
immorality;

[2]4 Jer 51:45. [3]7 Isa 47:7–8.

and He has avenged on her the blood of
His servants."

[3] Again they said:

"Alleluia!
Her smoke rises forever and ever."

[4] The twenty-four elders and the four living creatures fell down and worshipped God who sat on the throne, saying:

"Amen! Alleluia!"

The Marriage Supper of the Lamb

[5] Then a voice came from the throne, saying:
"Praise our God,
all you His servants
and those who fear Him,
both small and great!"

[6] Then I heard something like the sound like a great multitude, as the sound of many waters and as the sound of mighty thunderings, saying:

"Alleluia!
For the Lord God Omnipotent reigns!
[7] Let us be glad and rejoice
and give Him glory,
for the marriage of the Lamb has come,
and His wife has made herself ready.
[8] It was granted her to be arrayed in fine linen,
clean and white."
Fine linen is the righteous deeds of the saints.

[9] Then he said to me, "Write: Blessed are
those who are invited to the marriage supper
of the Lamb." And he said to me, "These are
the true sayings of God."
[10] I fell at his feet to worship him. But he said
to me, "See that you not do that. I am your
fellow servant, and of your brothers who hold
the testimony of Jesus. Worship God! For the
testimony of Jesus is the spirit of prophecy."

The Rider on the White Horse

[11] I saw heaven opened. And there was a
white horse. He who sat on it is called Faith-
ful and True, and in righteousness He judges
and wages war. [12] His eyes are like a flame of
fire, and on His head are many crowns. He
has a name written, that no one knows but He
Himself. [13] He is clothed with a robe dipped in
blood. His name is called The Word of God.
[14] The armies in heaven, clothed in fine linen,
white and clean, followed Him on white
horses. [15] Out of His mouth proceeds a sharp
sword, with which He may strike the nations.
"He shall rule them with an iron scepter."[1] He
treads the winepress of the fury and wrath of
God the Almighty. [16] On His robe and on His
thigh He has a name written:

KING OF KINGS
AND LORD OF LORDS.

[17] And I saw an angel standing in the sun,
and he cried with a loud voice to all the birds
flying in the midst of heaven, "Come and gath-
er for the supper of the great God, [18] to eat the
flesh of kings, the flesh of commanders, the
flesh of strong men, the flesh of horses and
their riders, and the flesh of all men, both free
and slave, both small and great!"
[19] Then I saw the beast and the kings of the
earth with their armies gathered to wage war
against Him who sat on the horse and against
His army. [20] But the beast was captured and
with him the false prophet who worked signs
in his presence, by which he deceived those
who received the mark of the beast and those
who worshipped his image. These two were
thrown alive into the lake of fire that burns
with brimstone. [21] The remnant were slain with
the sword which proceeded out of the mouth
of Him who sat on the horse. And all the birds
gorged themselves with their flesh.

Release the sword out of Your mouth against the enemy (Rev 19:15).

19:3 Isa 34:10
19:4 Rev 5:14
19:5 Ps 134:1
19:6 Rev 14:2
19:7 Mt 22:2
19:9 Rev 21:5
19:10 Rev 12:17
19:11 Rev 3:14
19:12 Rev 1:14
19:13 Jn 1:1
19:14 Rev 19:8
19:15 Isa 11:4
19:16 Rev 17:14
19:17 Rev 19:21
19:18 Eze 39:18–20
19:19 Rev 16:16
19:20 Rev 20:10
20:1 Rev 1:18
20:2 2Pe 2:4
20:3 Da 6:17
20:4 Da 7:9
20:6 Rev 1:6
20:7 Rev 20:2
20:8 Rev 16:14

The Thousand Years

20 And I saw an angel coming down out
of heaven, having the key to the bot-
tomless pit and a great chain in his hand. [2] He
seized the dragon, that ancient serpent, who is
the Devil and Satan, and bound him for a thou-
sand years. [3] He cast him into the bottomless
pit, and shut him up, and set a seal on him, that
he should deceive the nations no more, until
the thousand years were ended. After that he
must be set free for a little while.
[4] I saw thrones, and they sat on them, and
the authority to judge was given to them. And
I saw the souls of those who had been behead-
ed for their witness of Jesus and for the word
of God. They had not worshipped the beast or
his image, and had not received his mark on
their foreheads or on their hands. They came
to life and reigned with Christ for a thousand
years. [5] The rest of the dead did not come to
life until the thousand years were ended. This
is the first resurrection. [6] Blessed and holy is
he who takes part in the first resurrection. Over
these the second death has no power, but they
shall be priests of God and of Christ and shall
reign with Him a thousand years.

The Defeat of Satan

[7] When the thousand years are ended, Satan
will be set free from his prison [8] and will go out
to deceive the nations which are in the four

[1] 15 Ps 2:9.

corners of the earth, Gog and Magog, to gather them for battle. Their number is like the sand of the sea. 9 They traveled the breadth of the earth and surrounded the camp of the saints and the beloved city. But fire came down from God out of heaven and devoured them. 10 The devil, who deceived them, was cast into the lake of fire and brimstone where the beast and the false prophet were. They will be tormented day and night forever and ever.

The Great White Throne Judgment

11 Then I saw a great white throne and Him who was seated on it. From His face the earth and the heavens fled away, and no place was found for them. 12 And I saw the dead, small and great, standing before God. Books were opened. Then another book was opened, which is the Book of Life. The dead were judged according to their works as recorded in the books. 13 The sea gave up the dead who were in it, and Death and Hades delivered up the dead who were in them. And they were judged, each one by his works. 14 Then Death and Hades were cast into the lake of fire. This is the second death. 15 Anyone whose name was not found written in the Book of Life was cast into the lake of fire.

The New Heaven and the New Earth

21 Then I saw "a new heaven and a new earth."[1] For the first heaven and the first earth had passed away, and there was no more sea. 2 I, John, saw the Holy City, the New Jerusalem, coming down out of heaven from God, prepared as a bride adorned for her husband. 3 And I heard a loud voice from heaven, saying, "Look! The tabernacle of God is with men, and He will dwell with them. They shall be His people, and God Himself will be with them and be their God. 4 'God shall wipe away all tears from their eyes. There shall be no more death.'[2] Neither shall there be any more sorrow nor crying nor pain, for the former things have passed away."

5 He who was seated on the throne said, "Look! I am making all things new." Then He said to me, "Write, for these words are faithful and true."

6 He said to me, "It is done. I am the Alpha and the Omega, the Beginning and the End. I will give of the spring of the water of life to him who thirsts. 7 He who overcomes shall inherit all things, and I will be his God and he shall be My son.[3] 8 But the cowardly, the unbelieving, the abominable, the murderers, the sexually immoral, the sorcerers, the idolaters, and all liars shall have their portion in the lake which burns with fire and brimstone. This is the second death."

20:9 Eze 38:9
20:10 Rev 19:20
20:11 Da 2:35
20:12 Da 7:10
20:13 Rev 6:8
20:14 1Co 15:26
21:1 Isa 66:22
21:2 Heb 11:10
21:3 2Co 6:16
21:4 Isa 25:8
21:5 Rev 4:9
21:6 Rev 1:8
21:7 Rev 21:3
21:8 Rev 19:20

....

21:9 Rev 19:7
21:10 Rev 17:3
21:11 Rev 4:6
21:12 Eze 48:31–34
21:14 Heb 11:10

SPIRITED WOMAN

COUNSEL FROM THE SPIRIT BASICS

Far Better

What a hope we have! You have much to look forward to because, like the apostle Paul, you know where you're going. Paul said, "For to me, to continue living is Christ, and to die is gain" (Php 1:21). He knew that to be with Christ in heaven is far better than life here on earth.

Revelation 21 describes heaven in great detail. It says, "God shall wipe away all tears from their eyes. There shall be no more death. Neither shall there be any more sorrow nor crying nor pain, for the former things have passed away" (Rev 21:4).

Heaven is such good news! You can rejoice right now because you're headed somewhere great. Yes, hard things may have happened to you on this earth, and you may have questions, but keep everything in perspective. Life is just a blip on the screen of eternity. When Jesus is your Savior, in the end you win.

Karen Jensen Salisbury

The New Jerusalem

9 One of the seven angels who had the seven bowls full of the seven last plagues came to me and said to me, "Come, I will show you the bride, the wife of the Lamb." 10 And he carried me away in the Spirit to a great and high mountain, and showed me the Holy City, Jerusalem, descending out of heaven from God, 11 having the glory of God, her light like a most precious jewel, like a jasper, clear as crystal. 12 It had a great, high wall, with twelve gates, and at the gates twelve angels, and on the gates the names of the twelve tribes of the sons of Israel were written: 13 three gates on the east, three gates on the north, three gates on the south, and three gates on the west. 14 The wall of the city had twelve foundations, and on them were the names of the twelve apostles of the Lamb.

15 He who talked with me had a golden rod to measure the city and its gates and wall.

[1] *1* Isa 65:17. [2] *4* Isa 25:8. [3] *7* 2Sa 7:14; Ps 89:26.

Equally Yoked in Love

And I heard a loud voice from heaven, saying, "Look! The tabernacle of God is with men, and He will dwell with them. They shall be His people, and God Himself will be with them and be their God. 'God shall wipe away all tears from their eyes. There shall be no more death.' Neither shall there be any more sorrow nor crying nor pain, for the former things have passed away."

—Revelation 21:3–4

To inherit the earth, we must be meek. To become a bride equally yoked in love, we must follow the footsteps of Jesus. We must, in love, empty ourselves and become poor in spirit to gain the riches of heaven and be filled with Him. Jesus gave all for His bride when He came to dwell among us. Now we give up our lives to be married to Him and inherit the riches of heaven.

The Christian life is all about union and communion. As Revelation 21 describes, God has chosen to make His dwelling with us, to call us His people. In Jesus, our Servant King, God has united Himself with humanity. In union with Jesus we inherit a new heaven and a new earth. When two people are truly in love, they will each give all that they have for the other. God does not want us to merely love like Jesus. His desire is to possess our very nature with His love.

This bride will be radiant and dazzling, altogether lovely, like her Bridegroom King. She will have the same Spirit, being like-minded, doing nothing out of selfish ambition or vain conceit. She will consider others more than herself. She will be led by Philippians 2, which says, "Let nothing be done out of strife or conceit, but in humility let each esteem the other better than himself. Let each of you look not only to your own interests, but also to the interests of others" (vv. 3–4).

This bride will give up the selfish riches of this world to inherit the earth. She will be so ruined and wrecked by love that she will run full force into the darkness. This will cause His light through her to explode into the world—all for love's sake.

We must give our life in marriage to another—to our Bridegroom, King Jesus. If we embrace the Sermon on the Mount, our life no longer is our own, and yet it is the most fulfilling, exciting, and joyful life imaginable. God knows how to bless us with the true riches of heaven.

Heidi Baker

16 The city lies as a square, its length as long as
its width. He measured the city with the rod:
one thousand four hundred miles.[1] Its length
and breadth and height are equal. 17 He then
measured its wall: two hundred feet[2] by the
measurement of a man, that is, of an angel.
18 The wall was built of jasper and the city was
pure gold, as clear as glass. 19 The foundations
of the wall of the city were garnished with
all kinds of precious jewels. The first foun-
dation was jasper; the second, sapphire; the
third, chalcedony; the fourth, emerald; 20 the
fifth, sardonyx; the sixth, sardius; the seventh,
chrysolite; the eighth, beryl; the ninth, topaz;
the tenth, chrysoprase; the eleventh, jacinth;
and the twelfth, amethyst. 21 The twelve gates
were twelve pearls, each of the gates made of a
single pearl, and the street of the city was pure
gold, transparent as glass.

22 I saw no temple in the city, for the Lord God
Almighty and the Lamb are its temple. 23 The
city has no need of sun or moon to shine in
it, for the glory of God is its light, and its lamp
is the Lamb. 24 And the nations of those who
are saved shall walk in its light, and the kings
of the earth shall bring their glory and honor
into it. 25 Its gates shall never be shut by day,
for there shall be no night there. 26 They shall
bring into it the glory and the honor of the
nations. 27 No unclean thing shall ever enter
it, nor shall anyone who commits abomination
or falsehood, but only those whose names are
written in the Lamb's Book of Life.

22 Then he showed me a pure river of the
water of life, clear as crystal, flowing
from the throne of God and of the Lamb 2 in
the middle of its street. On each side of the
river was the tree of life, which bore twelve
kinds of fruit, yielding its fruit each month. The
leaves of the tree were for the healing of the
nations. 3 There shall be no more curse. The
throne of God and of the Lamb shall be in it,
and His servants shall serve Him. 4 They shall
see His face, and His name shall be on their
foreheads. 5 Night shall be no more. They need
no lamp nor the light of the sun, for the Lord
God will give them light. And they shall reign
forever and ever.

The Coming of Christ

6 The angel said to me, "These words are
faithful and true. The Lord God of the holy
prophets sent His angel to show to His servants
the things which must soon take place."

7 "Look, I am coming soon. Blessed is he who
keeps the words of the prophecy of this book."

8 I, John, am he who saw and heard these
things. When I heard and saw them, I fell
down to worship at the feet of the angel who
showed me these things. 9 But he said to me,
"See that you not do that. For I am your fellow
servant, and of your brothers the prophets,
and of those who keep the words of this book.
Worship God!"

10 Then he said to me, "Do not seal the words
of the prophecy of this book, for the time is at
hand. 11 He who is unjust, let him be unjust
still. He who is filthy, let him be filthy still. He
who is righteous, let him be righteous still.
He who is holy, let him be holy still."

12 "Look, I am coming soon! My reward is
with Me to give to each one according to his
work. 13 I am the Alpha and the Omega, the
Beginning and the End, the First and the Last."

14 Blessed are those who do His command-
ments, that they may have the right to the
tree of life, and may enter through the gates
into the city. 15 Outside are dogs and sorcerers
and the sexually immoral and murderers and
idolaters and everyone who loves and prac-
tices a lie.

16 "I, Jesus, have sent My angel to you with
this testimony for the churches. I am the Root
and the Offspring of David, the Bright and
Morning Star."

17 The Spirit and the bride say, "Come." Let him
who hears say, "Come." Let him who is thirsty
come. Let him who desires take the water of
life freely.

18 I testify to everyone who hears the words
of the prophecy of this book: If anyone adds to
these things, God shall add to him the plagues
that are written in this book. 19 And if anyone
takes away from the words of the book of this
prophecy, God shall take away his part out of
the Book of Life and out of the Holy City and
out of the things which are written in this book.
20 He who testifies to these things says,
"Surely I am coming soon."
Amen. Even so, come Lord Jesus!

21 The grace of our Lord Jesus Christ be with
you all. Amen.

21:18 Rev 21:11
21:19 Isa 54:11–12
21:21 Rev 21:18
21:22 Jn 4:23
21:23 Rev 21:11
21:24 Rev 22:2
21:25 Isa 60:11
21:27 Isa 52:1
22:1 Zec 14:8
22:2 Rev 2:7
22:3 Zec 14:11
22:4 Mt 5:8
22:5 Da 7:27
22:6 Rev 1:1
22:7 Rev 1:3
22:8 Rev 19:10
22:9 Rev 19:10
22:10 Rev 10:4
22:11 Eze 3:27
22:12 Isa 40:10
22:13 Rev 1:8
22:14 Rev 21:27
22:15 Rev 21:8
22:16 Rev 1:1
22:17 Rev 21:6
22:18 Dt 4:2
22:19 Rev 22:2
22:20 Rev 22:7
22:21 Ro 16:20

[1] *16* Gk. 12,000 stadia, or 2,200 kilometers. [2] *17* 144 cubits, or 65 meters.

Epilogue

The doctrine of God's Spirit permeates Scripture. God, who is Spirit, has revealed Himself as the Spirit of God from the very beginning of creation. He continues to manifest His presence in His Holy Spirit to us today as our comforter and guide and energizer. And He will always be the life-giving river to refresh and fructify His new creation throughout the endless ages of eternity.

- The Spirit is God breathing upon the dust of the ground to create the first human being (Ge 2:7), upon the slain of Israel to bring forth a remnant people (Eze 37:11–14), and upon the believing disciples to unite them in new resurrection life with their risen Lord (Jn 20:22).
- The Spirit is the glorious presence of God going before His people as a cloud to lead them and protect them (Ex 13:21; 14:19–20; Isa 63:7–14; Ro 8:14). The Spirit is God empowering and encouraging His servants the prophets to deliver His word to His people (Mic 3:8; Zec 7:12; 2Pet 1:21). He is God enlightening our minds to understand His truth (Jn 16:13; 1Co 2:10–13; Heb 9:8; 10:15).
- The Spirit is God blowing as a searing desert wind to bring judgment upon rebels and idolaters (Hos 13:15–16). He is God as fire, burning up the chaff to purge and sanctify God's people (Isa 4:4; Mt 3:12).
- The Spirit is God coming as a dove to signal life and peace in a new creation (Lk 3:22). He is God anointing His own Son to be the Servant Messiah (Isa 11:2; 42:1; 61:1) and enabling Christ's followers to carry on His ministry (Ac 1:8; 2Co 1:21; 1Jn 2:20).
- The Spirit is God pouring Himself out as water to revive parched souls and to supply the vitalizing power that transforms lives (Isa 32:15; 44:3; Jn 7:38) and floods them with joy (Ac 13:52; Ro 14:17; 15:13; 1Th 1:5–6).

He is the eternal Spirit, the Spirit of Yahweh, the Spirit of Christ, the promised Holy Spirit who was sent forth at Pentecost to empower the church. It is God's will that He, the third Person of the Trinity, be with you and in you and upon you both now and forever. Amen.

John Rea

APPENDIX A

God's Anointing Is for You

> "In the last days it shall be," says God, "that I will pour out My Spirit on all flesh; your sons and your daughters shall prophesy, your young men shall see visions, and your old men shall dream dreams. Even on My menservants and maidservants I will pour out My Spirit in those days; and they shall prophesy."
>
> —Acts 2:17–18

Men and women of God have operated in the anointing throughout eons of time. While being eaten by lions, they sang; while being blindfolded and waiting for bullets to fire through their entire bodies, they prayed in peace; and as Stephen was being stoned, he looked up to heaven and asked God, "Lord, do not hold this sin against them" (Ac 7:60). These saints of God paid the ultimate price for their commitment to the cause of the anointing. We as the church long to be infiltrated with it more and more in our lives.

So, what is the anointing? What does it look like? Why are some people seemingly anointed and others aren't? How can you get the anointing? What will it do for your life? Is it just for people who are in full-time ministry—apostles, prophets, evangelists, pastors, and teachers—those who are seemingly very, very spiritual?

These are questions God's people have frequently asked, passionately motivated to find the right answers for themselves. They have grappled with these questions and longed to experience the anointing, yet many of them still feel left out in the dark on this subject. The questions rumble in their minds over and over again: *How can I be anointed? I know others are, but what about me?*

The anointing is upon your life. My friend, God has anointed you! You just need to believe and receive your impartation through this *now* word that God has given to me for you.

You see, the days we are living in are unprecedented in every respect, yet not surprising. These are the days and times that the prophets, the inspired writers of the Holy Scriptures, and even Jesus Himself warned would come. Things such as:

- Wars and rumors of wars
- The rise of lawlessness
- Apostasy
- Economic and environmental disasters
- Dramatic political, social, cultural, medical, and moral changes

These are, as 2 Timothy 3:1 confirms, "perilous times." Yet even in these times God is still active in His church. He is still moving mightily on people whose hearts are turned toward Him. As we look toward the ultimate escape from all of this mess, we—the people of God and the bride of Christ—are keeping our focus on Jesus, the author and finisher of our faith. We are in a battle for everything that we know is right, and as a community of believers, as a nation, as families, and ultimately as people who know their God, we are confident that our victory is sure. Yet I believe that before the return of the Lord, the things that can be shaken are being removed so that "only those things that cannot be shaken will remain" (Heb 12:27).

I believe this is the time that God is raising up many anointed men and women of God to change societies and cultures as we know them. "How do we change them?" you might ask. We change them through the name of Jesus and through the living Word of God. We appropriate the blood of Christ and use the power of agreement, believing that God hears and answers every prayer that we pray to Him in faith.

Most of all, we use the anointing that God has given to every believer through the power of His Holy Spirit to stand up in the midst of a perverse and wicked generation and declare His Word.

In the book *Personal Faith, Public Policy* he cowrote with Tony Perkins, Bishop Harry R. Jackson says that we as the church must yield "to the ultimate truth test—not what do Republicans or conservatives say or Democrats or liberals think, but rather what does God's Word say."[1]

Everyone has the capacity to be anointed. God is no respecter of persons. The anointing is for every believer: every man, woman, boy, and girl. It is for the young. It is for the old. It is for the rich, and it is for the poor. It is for the one who is near and the one who is far off. The anointing is for you, your children, your children's children, and "as many as the Lord our God will call" (Ac 2:39).

Now, you must first realize one thing. The enemy will come and tell you, "You are not good enough to have the anointing on your life." He'll tell you that because you are divorced or you didn't come from a family in the ministry or you are not a perfect person, you can't experience the anointing. He'll constantly say to you, "Don't you remember when…?" Friend, don't ever forget this one fact: the devil is a liar!

The only thing you have to remember is the anointing that comes upon you is not *your* anointing. It is *God's* anointing, the anointing of the Holy Spirit. God is the one who gives His anointing to us. It is a free gift that comes directly from Him, and once given, it is to be shared with others. The anointing doesn't belong to your mama, your dad, your grandma, or your auntie. The anointing belongs to God.

His anointing destroys the yoke of cancer. It annihilates the HIV/AIDS virus. God's anointing releases healings, deliverances, miracles, signs, and wonders. But this same anointing also helps you live out your everyday life as one of the called-out, chosen, and appointed people of God.

You Are Anointed to Do "Greater Works"

You also need to understand that God wants His people to walk in the supernatural revelation of what He sent Jesus to the earth to do: "For this purpose the Son of God was revealed, that He might destroy the works of the devil" (1Jn 3:8). Jesus' purpose on earth was to ultimately destroy the enemy's works in people's lives and to set every captive free. That's why He, the sinless Lamb of God, was slain from the foundation of the world (Rev 13:8). When He left the earth, He handed it down to us. Sometimes people like to take credit for the anointing, but always remember Romans 11:36, which states, "For from Him and through Him and to Him are all things. To Him be glory forever! Amen."

When Jesus told the disciples to go to the Upper Room and wait for the "promise of the Father" (Ac 1:4), He knew they were going to do the works that He had done, and even greater works. How do I know this? He had already told them: "He who believes in Me will do the works that I do also. And he will do greater works than these, because I am going to My Father" (Jn 14:12). I believe this Bible will give you boldness, power, authority, divine inspiration, and revelation to do "greater works" as you receive and flow in the Lord's anointing.

---

1. Harry R. Jackson Jr. and Tony Perkins, *Personal Faith, Public Policy* (Lake Mary, FL: FrontLine, 2008), vii.

There is another understanding you must have about the anointing, and it comes from Isaiah 61. Jesus declared this to the religious leaders of His day as He stood in the synagogue to read from the scroll of the prophet Isaiah. He boldly said:

> The Spirit of the Lord is upon Me, because He has anointed Me to preach the gospel to the poor; He has sent Me to heal the broken-hearted, to preach deliverance to the captives and recovery of sight to the blind, to set at liberty those who are oppressed; to preach the acceptable year of the Lord.
>
> —Luke 4:18–19

When Jesus declared those words about His own works on the earth, by extension He was also talking about the "greater works" that would be done by the disciples, and ultimately you and me. As you study this *SpiritLed Woman Bible,* it will help you to understand that *the Lord's anointing is for you, right now, and for such a time as this.*

The anointing is not for those you might think deemed worthy of it. Rather, this revelation and word will help you see the anointing comes from God through the power of the Holy Spirit and is for anyone who will seek after it, cradle it with all humility, and guard it. This anointing, as spoken of in Ephesians 4, is for "the equipping of the saints, for the work of service, and for the building up of the body of Christ, until we all come into the unity of the faith and of the knowledge of the Son of God, into a complete man, to the measure of the stature of the fullness of Christ" (vv. 12–13).

That means *you*! With this revelation in your heart and mind you will begin to decree and declare, "The Spirit of the Lord is upon *me*, because the Lord has anointed *me*!"

God has gifted the body of Christ with many supernatural gifts, and He wants you to use every gift He has given you to advance His kingdom with others and see lives changed through the power of the gospel. So whatever gifts you may have, in whatever capacity, and wherever you feel God has called you, I urge you to use those gifts, *because you are anointed for this!*

You Are Anointed for Victory

There is something else that the anointing is for: to help you understand that whatever you may be facing—be it a trial, hardship, or difficulty; a calling; or anything you feel you aren't able to handle or come out of—God wants you to know *you are anointed for this!*

You might be going through a particularly hard season right now in your finances. You need to know that *you are anointed for this!* By God's power and grace, His Word declares, "But my God shall supply your every need according to His riches in glory by Christ Jesus" (Php 4:19). King David said, "I have been young, and now am old; yet I have not seen the righteous forsaken, nor their offspring begging bread" (Ps 37:25). You're coming out of this! There is an anointing upon you to believe God for the unbelievable!

You might have received a bad report from your doctor. You need to understand that *you are anointed for this!* Whose report will you believe? Say it: "I will believe the report of the Lord." Jesus said, "*All things are possible* to him who believes" (Mk 9:23, emphasis added). He said on another occasion, "With men this is impossible, but with God *all things are possible*" (Mt 19:26, emphasis added). You are anointed to get the victory over this illness and come out as the healed of the Lord. God is going to anoint you to increase your level of faith to believe for a miracle.

You might be in the fight of your life for your marriage, your children, or your home—so believe this one thing: *You are anointed for this!* God is going to give you the extra grace and glory you need to believe Him for a miracle.

For everything that you are facing right now, there is an anointing to face it, overcome it, restore it, transform it, and see dynamic change. Why? The Spirit of the Lord God is upon you! He has anointed you, so your "this" becomes "that" which was spoken of by the prophet Joel. Because God is pouring out His Spirit upon your life, *you are anointed for this!* You can come out of every challenge in victory.

With this in mind, as you study this Bible, God wants you to experience His anointing as you never have before. I urge you: take time to make this journey into the anointing personal. God wants to do "greater works," both *in* and *through* you.

Get ready to come face-to-face with an anointing you never knew was possible, simply because you'll recognize and declare, "Hey, you know what? The Spirit of the Lord God is upon *me*, and He has anointed *me* for this! The same power that raised Jesus from the dead is in *me; I* am anointed to do 'greater works' in His name!" I prophesy to you that you are going to find yourself completely overwhelmed with confidence, boldness, and authority that you never dreamed possible. Why? *You are anointed for this!*

Judy Jacobs

APPENDIX B

Ten Tactics of Prayer

I believe prayer is one of the most powerful contributions a Christian can give toward making this world a better place. You don't learn to pray powerfully and effectively by reading a how-to manual. You learn to pray when you pray. When you do, you will discover that there is no continent, no nation, no organization, no city, no office, no situation, no circumstance, no condition, no government, no case, no issue, and no battle that is off limits to the force of its effect. There is no person, no policy, nor any political power on this earth that can keep prayer out.

Prayer is a game changer. Prayer makes a difference. Without prayer, our Christian life is just trying to follow a list of dos and don'ts given to us by someone else. With prayer, Christianity is vital, relevant, transformational, and filled with the knowledge and presence of God.

If prayer was a sport, then it would be a contact sport. Prayer is the contact point between heaven and earth—or perhaps it is better said that the person who prays is that contact point. Your place of prayer is your place of power. Your place of prayer is your place of change management. We can create change through force of will and clever persuasion, but it won't last. Real, irrevocable change only comes through prayer.

With that in mind, I would like to give you sixty different tactics to consider as you pray—but I don't have room to give them all to you in these pages. So I will give you a taste of them here by highlighting the first ten and then urge you to get my MP3 message called "The Unconventional Weapon: Sixty Ways to Pray."[1]

1. Pray faithfully.

When you pray, ensure that you do not waver in your faith. Hold fast to what you have learned and the confidence you have received in your relationship with Christ. God can resurrect a dead life, a dead dream—anything that is dead, if you have faith: "God whom he believed, and who raises the dead, and calls those things that do not exist as though they did" (Ro 4:17). If God can quicken the dead, He can bring your marriage, your business, your job, and your faith back into divine alignment with His promises. But most of the time this takes more than sending up a quick "Help me, God!" It takes dedicated, faithful, faith-filled prayer in which you present yourself to God ready to change and ready to do what He asks of you.

2. Pray decisively.

You cannot be wishy-washy when you pray—one day you trust God, the next day you don't. One day you pray this, the next day you want the opposite. You say one thing to God in faith, and then you go have coffee with your friends and talk about how it can never happen. You are wishy-washy with what you want and where you are going. As the Bible says:

> Let us firmly hold the profession of our faith without wavering, for He who promised is faithful.
>
> —HEBREWS 10:23

1. Available at www.trimminternational.org.

And:

> If any of you lacks wisdom, let him ask of God, who gives to all men liberally and without criticism, and it will be given to him. But let him ask in faith, without wavering. For he who wavers is like a wave of the sea, driven and tossed with the wind. Let not that man think that he will receive anything from the Lord. A double-minded man is unstable in all his ways.
>
> —JAMES 1:5–8

Let there be no misunderstanding: You can speak words in prayer that you do not believe, and they will not produce any result. Parroting something you have heard someone else say or that you read somewhere without conviction does not produce divine alignment. Make a deliberate and conscious decision to agree with the Word of God, and then set your heart to believe it and your mouth to speak it no matter what.

3. Pray forcefully.

Don't be a wimp! Matthew 11:12 tells us, "The kingdom of heaven has forcefully advanced, and the strong take it by force." You are not begging, you are not crying, and you are not persuading; you are coming to take what is legally yours according to the Word of God. You must come boldly as a child would to a father, as a prince or princess would to a king, as a wronged plaintiff would to a court of law.

Hebrews 11:6 tells us, "Without faith it is impossible to please God, for he who comes to God must believe that He exists and that He is a rewarder of those who diligently seek Him." If you feel like you have to beg God for what He has promised, then you don't know the God of heaven. He is a rewarder. He isn't stingy in fulfilling His Word. But if you don't walk into His presence like you belong there, then your faith and understanding need an upgrade. It is not that you aren't humble; it's that you know God for the loving Father He really is.

4. Pray lovingly.

We are not called to take vengeance on anyone or any group of people—if vengeance is to be taken, it will be God taking it, not us. We are not called to be judges over the perpetrators of any crimes, disasters, or diseases. We are called to be deliverers, rescuers, and healers. We are called, like Moses when he lifted up the bronze serpent (Nu 21:4–9), to put ourselves between the people and the harm, lifting up Jesus so that those who will look up from this world to Him might also be saved. (See John 3:14–15.)

Because of this, we must pray to see those who hurt us or the people we are praying for through the eyes of God. We must pray that God stops them in their tracks, as He did Paul, and turns them around. We cannot have faith for something if we are not walking in love, for the only thing that avails is "faith which works through love" (Gal 5:6).

5. Pray truthfully.

There are times when we are honestly in denial about the truth of a situation, or we could just be mistaken about the facts or in how we are interpreting things. But one of the names of the Holy Spirit is the "Spirit of Truth." If we will open ourselves to Him in prayer and listen more than we speak, then there is room for the Holy Spirit to adjust our perspective. He will give us the perspective from the throne room of God that we would never get on our own.

Also, we don't necessarily need to be praying the facts; we need to be praying the truth. The facts might be that the doctor said you will die in six months, but the truth is "by His wounds you were healed" (1Pe 2:24). The facts might be that your husband is not acting lovingly toward you, but the truth is "the unbelieving husband is sanctified by the wife....For how do you know, O wife, whether you will save your husband?" (1Co 7:14, 16). The facts may be that you have a lot of unpaid bills sitting on your desk, but the truth is "my God shall supply your every need according to His riches in glory by Christ Jesus" (Php 4:19).

God doesn't need us to tell Him the facts—He knows them better than we do—but He does need us to agree with His promises so that we can receive the provision He desires to provide. After all, the Bible doesn't say, "You shall recognize the facts and the facts will set you free," but it says, "You shall know the truth, and the truth shall set you free" (Jn 8:32).

6. Pray steadfastly.

Prayer is never wasted. The Bible tells us to "be steadfast, unmovable, always abounding in the work of the Lord, knowing that your labor in the Lord is not in vain" (1Co 15:58). I know from personal experience that one minute in prayer can accomplish more than a lifetime of other activities. Hold fast to God's promises in prayer no matter what things look like in the natural. God will answer you if you seek Him with all of your heart. (See Jeremiah 29:11–14.)

7. Pray earnestly.

Life throws us curveballs, and though we have different backgrounds and personal histories, we all have emotions, dreams, and passions. When we are emotionally involved in a struggle, we tend to pray less rather than pray more. If we are to have overcoming prayer lives, we need to turn those emotions and passions into prayer rather than let them become a hindrance to it. We are told:

> Elijah was a man subject to natural passions as we are, and he prayed earnestly that it might not rain, and it did not rain on the earth for three years and six months. And he prayed again, and the sky gave rain, and the earth brought forth its fruit.
>
> —James 5:17–18

Elijah "was a man subject to natural passions as we are," but when he prayed earnestly, God still heard Him. He knew how to engage the God that answers by fire. Jacob had to wrestle with God to get His blessing. (See Genesis 32:22–32.) We have to come to God earnestly as who we are and be willing to stay in prayer—even if we are angry or frustrated—until we get God's answer. God understands emotions—He created them! We have to be willing to express them earnestly as much as we need to be ready for God to change or correct them.

8. Pray positionally.

We have to know where we stand in order to pray effectively. We know we are seated in heavenly places in Christ Jesus and that Jesus "at all times lives to make intercession" (Heb 7:25). Thus, the best place for us to be praying is from our position in Christ, praying the same intercessions He is praying over every situation. We must pray "in Christ" as the very person the "in Christ" Scriptures tell us we are.

9. Pray authoritatively.

Praying in Jesus' name is not just a closing we are supposed to use before we say amen. Praying in the name of Jesus is coming to the throne of God just as an ambassador would come to the throne of a foreign king in the name of his own king. Using the name of Jesus is another "in Christ" privilege and signet of our authority as a representative of Jesus. As Scripture says:

> I will do whatever you ask in My name, that the Father may be glorified in the Son. If you ask anything in My name, I will do it.
>
> —JOHN 14:13–14

And:

> Therefore God highly exalted Him and gave Him the name which is above every name, that at the name of Jesus every knee should bow, of those in heaven and on earth and under the earth, and every tongue should confess that Jesus Christ is Lord, to the glory of God the Father.
>
> —PHILIPPIANS 2:9–11

When we pray in the name of Jesus, we pray in the authority of Jesus. The name of Jesus will give you the power to overcome when you truly pray in that name.

10. Pray masterfully.

To gain mastery in a thing, you must practice it continually. Malcolm Gladwell talks about the "ten-thousand-hour rule" in his best-selling book *Outliers*. The principle is that those who are most successful at a thing are those who have spent the most time at the right time doing that thing. Charles Spurgeon said it this way: "Pray until you can really pray."

As I have already said, prayer is a journey that is unique for each one of us. Just as each of us has a different calling or job to do for God, each of us will travel a slightly different road in understanding what prayer really is. God will speak to each of us in different ways, and the way God speaks to one person can be markedly different from the way He speaks to another. Why? Because God isn't interested in getting us to learn rules and requirements so we can live life merely by following the dictates of a rulebook.

He wants us to come to Him that we might know Him for ourselves. He wants a unique relationship with each of us, just as He created each of us as unique individuals. He wants to partner with us in our journey and live it out with us day by day. It is why He created human beings in the first place, and it is His great joy when we come to Him without doubt or compromise to wholeheartedly get to know Him and let ourselves be fully known by Him. God is all about relationship, and the key to it is masterful prayer.

Cindy Trimm

APPENDIX C

Family Devotions—Eliminating the Yawn Factor

The chief enterprise of a Christian mom is making God-lovers out of those entrusted to her care. This takes time, skill, prayer, wisdom—and "family devotions."

> Devotions: Religious observance or worship; a form of prayer or worship for special use.

Unfortunately, in many Christian homes, "having devotions" means exactly that—nothing more than a religious observance. But in my home growing up, and in our house today, we apply the word without the *s*:

> Devotion: Profound dedication, consecration; earnest attachment to a cause, person, etc.

In our family we seek to be "profoundly dedicated" and "earnestly attached" to a person—Jesus Christ. A mere religious observance would simply never do for family devotions. It wouldn't suffice in the same way it wouldn't if, in seeking to know my child, I scheduled daily readings on the subject of her life. Or if in an attempt to stay devoted to my husband I recited a greeting to him every time he walked in the front door from work: "Dear Dave, I welcome you into our home once again to receive our bountiful but slightly burnt harvest meal as a reward for your faithful labor. Kindly remove your boots. Amen."

That is not to say we don't have a structured form of family devotions. I *love* my daily routine! But there is a lot of flexibility. In our home family devotions look much as they did when I was a kid. Mom and Dad understood how to apply Deuteronomy 11:19 to leading my siblings and me to a close relationship with God:

> You shall teach them to your children, speaking of them when you sit in your house and when you walk by the way, when you lie down, and when you rise up.

Let's break up that verse into four parts and talk about what an authentic devotional life with our children might look like.

"When You Sit in Your House..."

This presupposes that families will actually sit together at home. Studies show that families who eat meals together on a regular basis turn out kids who are far less likely to use drugs and who are physically and emotionally healthier.[1] But most studies don't point out that sitting around the dinner table as a family can also encourage the *spiritual* health of our children. If a hectic day doesn't allow for morning or evening devotions ("when you lie down" and "when you get up"),

1. Christopher Peterson, "The Family Meal," *The Good Life* (blog), March 20, 2012, http://www.psychologytoday.com/blog/the-good-life/201203/the-family-meal (accessed February 27, 2014).

we can seize dinnertime as a great opportunity for spiritual discussion with our kids.

It helps to come to the table prepared. I have found that if I don't at least have a split-second plan for what we are going to talk about, our thirty precious supper minutes will be spent on militant policing of food pickiness, manners, or—at best—superficial babble (not that one shouldn't be concerned with pickiness or bad manners). So I try to think of something pertinent to recent family happenings or current events, for example, and make a life lesson out of it. If you feel you'd have to pull your brain out of the freezer in order to dream up dinnertime topics of conversation, have no fear! Here are a few suggestions, broken down by main topics, to get your creative juices flowing. Remember, keep it fun.

Church (for Mondays)

- What did you learn about in Sunday school yesterday?
- Can anyone tell me what the pastor preached about yesterday? (It would be a good idea to know the answer yourself.)
- What did you do in youth group last night?
- How can you be a better example of a worshipper for your peers at church?
- What would Jesus think if He watched you at church? Would He think you love Him based on the way you worship? Would your friends think you love Him?
- Why do we go to church?
- Do you like going to church (Sunday school, youth group)? Why or why not?

Politics and current events

- Does God want us to pray for our president?
- According to the Bible, what makes a good leader for a nation?
- Are we living in the last days? What are the signs, according to the Bible?
- What is going on in the world right now? How should we, as a Christian family, respond to this?

Relationships

- How are you kids getting along with one another?
- What can we do to be better parents?

  a. Give you Skittles cereal for breakfast.

  b. Buy you an iPhone.

  c. Let you drive to the store.

  d. Teach you God's ways and show you His kind of love.

- Is anyone bullying you at school? How would God (not Mom) want you to handle that?

  a. Pelt him with your BB gun.

  b. Call him a "snot-nosed warthog."

  c. Pray for him.

  d. Tell your teacher and parents.

  e. Two of the above.

- Tell me about your teachers. Who is your favorite, and why?
- Who is your best friend? Why? Will he/she still be your best friend in twenty years? Why or why not?
- What kind of man (woman) should you marry?
  a. One with a dog.
  b. One who is rich.
  c. One who is rich and has a dog.
  d. One who loves God with all his (her) heart.
- Why is answer D important?

Finances

- Why does God bless some people with a lot of money?
  a. So they can buy an Xbox 360.
  b. So they can give it all away.
  c. So they can keep it under their mattress.
  d. So they can advance God's kingdom by investing and giving to those in need, as God directs them.

I am sure you can expand this list significantly. You may want to keep a small dry-erase board on the fridge to jot down things to talk about as they come to mind. Or you can invest in the Ungame. It's a noncompetitive card game of questions that give rise to a "serious exchange of thoughts, feelings and ideas."[2] It comes in versions for kids, teens, and families. Topics will surely surface that can be turned into spiritual discussion.

Here is an example of one of our most recent "when you sit down" times of family devotion. We'd been counting on receiving a sum of money in the mail for quite some time, and the whole family was aware of it. I'd made the sad mistake of causing my kids to hang all their hopes on getting this money. Every time they asked me for something, I'd say, "Wait until we get our check." I'd started my own personal list of things I was finally going to be able to buy when the magic envelope arrived in the mail. With Dave being unemployed in his field, we'd "made do" for a long time, and the hope of these coming funds was a light at the end of a long financial tunnel, and it kept me holding on to a superficial contentment.

But one evening Dave and I found out the money wouldn't be coming to us as soon as we'd previously been told. In fact, our wait might be significantly longer. Or the money might never arrive. I was disappointed but quickly adjusted my perspective, thanks to what I'd been learning through my own personal devotions and several years of practice in financial disappointment. But now I'd have to help my kids readjust.

During the following dinnertime Dave and I told our girls the news: our proverbial ship wasn't coming in after all. I apologized to the girls for instilling in them a false hope. I explained that I'd been wrong to let them believe the lie that we couldn't be completely happy until we had more money to buy more stuff. We talked about the blessing of learning contentment and how miserable many wealthy people are because they don't have what we have: health, love, and God. We ended that dinner conversation by memorizing Proverbs 15:17 together: "Better is a dinner of herbs where love is than a fatted calf with hatred."

---

2. Ungame.com, "Welcome to the Official Website for the Ungame," http://www.ungame.com (accessed February 27, 2014).

That time of devotions was as natural as, well, sitting down to supper and having a conversation! There was no boring study to read, no yawning faces to call back to attention. The kids were fully engaged and learned something I don't think they'll soon forget.

I do not mean to say that one should strive to converse on a deep level at every single meal. Some days we are tired, stressed, and need nothing more than "Talk Lite"! For those evenings I like to throw out my kids' favorite question—"What was the highlight of your day?"—and leave it at that. If I forget, they remind me!

"When You Walk by the Way..."

We are talking about a lifestyle here. Devotions—learning the ways of God—shouldn't be confined to thirty minutes of Bible reading each morning or to a quaint prayer tower hidden atop a winding staircase above the attic (though that would be nice, and come to think of it, I want one right now). Dave and I are intentional about recognizing teachable moments with our kids throughout each day. These gems of opportunity can be found in the most unlikely places if we keep our eyes and ears open.

When our daughter Sarah was in junior high school, her social studies class was assigned to pick any current event, research it, and give an oral report on it to the class. She was overwhelmed with choices, so I suggested she present a topic rarely covered in mainstream media: the increasing persecution of Christians in some countries. She decided to report on what was happening in northern India: pastors' homes were being burned down and their families tortured, carried off to jail, or executed by Hindu militants. I coached her in being an objective reporter. She used the word *religious* in place of *Christian* and was careful to present only the facts. She wrote an article she could be proud of and read it aloud to her teacher and classmates the next day.

I sat there in her bedroom, observing her live public school cyber class. Sarah was one of the last students to present, so we both had a chance to hear the teacher's reactions to the other kids' reports. Each one received an enthusiastic "Bravo!" or "Nice job!" from the teacher. But after Sarah gave her presentation, the teacher responded with a disappointing, monotone "Thank you." Sarah was crushed. My split-second instinct was to call the school and complain about discrimination. (We had, for weeks, already been getting vibes of intolerance from this teacher.)

But what would that have taught Sarah? That we should be surprised when people mistreat us because of our beliefs? That we should retaliate? Thankfully I was able to shift away from mother-bear emotions and seize the teachable moment. I reminded Sarah of Jesus' words to His disciples: "Blessed are those who are persecuted for righteousness' sake" (Mt 5:10). I told her that we should expect persecution, and we talked about the difference between being persecuted for "righteousness' sake" and for "being right's sake."

I explained that too many Christians are more interested in being right than in being righteous. If I had called the school principal and complained about discrimination on the part of the teacher, I would have had a case. I would have been right. And I would have no doubt brought on more undue persecution from the teacher. But that's not the kind of persecution Jesus blesses. The kingdom of heaven belongs to the righteous. So we prayed blessings for Sarah's teacher instead.

I told Sarah she'd received her "white belt" in handling persecution. This was only the beginning. Instances like these would follow her into adulthood and into the workplace for as long as she followed Jesus. It was better to start training now in how to properly respond to the cruelty of some people who reject our God.

Each of our days is a wealth of wisdom treasures if we approach them with the pickax of intentionality in hand: "Incline your ear to wisdom…cry out for knowledge, and lift up your voice for understanding. If you seek her as silver, and search for her as for hidden treasure" (Pr 2:2–4).

To devote ourselves to seeking divine wisdom from everyday experiences is to fortify the character of our children with precious minerals from the Rock (Christ Jesus). Rather than run from or shelter my children from the world, I see how God can make us more like Him through living in the world. So if my daughter Ruthie gets off the school bus and tells me about the girl who called her a mean name, I talk with her about what pain and losses that child might have to endure at home and how Ruthie can be her nurturer and not her victim.

Or when Ruthie asks whether or not the acquaintance I chat with at the store is a Christian, I say, "No, but isn't she nice?" And we discuss how every person is made in the image of God and is equally valued by Him while not discounting the need for that person's salvation. Or when Rebecca whines because she doesn't like stir-fry for dinner, I talk to her about the murmuring Israelites in the wilderness. Or when I'm helping Anna select a sensible brand of cupcake liners in the baking aisle, I teach her about godly stewardship of our finances and unit pricing. This is how we "walk along the road."

"When You Lie Down…"

My earliest memory of time spent with my mother was when she read to me at night from a two-volume set of Christian storybooks. I still remember the one about "Grumble Glasses," for example, and the kids who had to wear them every time they whined. I now own the nostalgic books with their fifties-style illustrations of mothers cooking in dresses and high heels.

I relish the hours spent reading to Ruthie and Rebecca from these books before bedtime. I want to give them the same memories my mother gave me. I also use *The Bible Story*—the popular blue, ten-volume set for the younger years. Why should I rely entirely on Sunday school to do what is my job as a parent—that is, to lead my kids to a personal relationship with God through the study of His Word?

As I've mentioned before, there is nothing rigorous about our family's lifestyle of devotion to God. I read to Ruthie and Rebecca as often as I can. This may be a quick fifteen-minute "date" with them while their two older sisters are finishing up the dinner dishes. It does not happen every night. Our main family devotion time involves three elements: reading aloud, Scripture memorization, and praying together as a family in the living room after dinner. Again, this is as we are able—usually a few times per week.

Reading

We pick books that will engage the wide age-range of listeners in our family while also teaching biblical truths. In our house, it works out better for me to read and let Dave snuggle with the girls on the couch while they listen. We especially like inspiring, true stories of real heroes of the faith. Here are a few of our recent good reads:

- *Bruchko*: a story about a missionary to the Motilone Indians[3]
- *Hinds' Feet on High Places*: an allegory and timeless classic about spiritual maturity; available in a children's version[4]

3. Bruce R. Olson, *Bruchko* (Lake Mary, FL: Charisma House, 1989).
4. Hannah Hurnard, *Hinds' Feet on High Places* (Carol Stream, IL: Tyndale House Publishers, 1979).

- *Heaven Is for Real*: a young boy's account of his after-death visit to heaven[5]
- *Jesus Freaks*: stories of historical and present-day Christian martyrs[6]
- *I'll Cross the River*: true-to-life story of religious persecution in North Korea[7]
- *Frida*: *Chosen to Die, Destined to Live*: true story of a Rwandan genocide survivor[8]
- *The Chronicles of Narnia: The Lion, the Witch, and the Wardrobe*: a clear portrayal of the gospel[9]

Scripture memorization

Memorizing the Scriptures is important to Dave and me at a time in history in which the possibility of Bibles being outlawed in an increasingly secularized America is easier to imagine than it was when he and I were kids. Dad paid me one dollar per verse to memorize Scripture. Some may criticize his method as a form of bribery and sacrilege. But the truth is, thirty-some years later, I can still recite those chapters I memorized for money. They are my "sleeping pills" on nights when I'm troubled, and they're an emotional anchor for my trying moments as a mom. Those verses course through my mind at times and keep me from sinking into pits of despair, and they have served as "duct tape" to save me from countless relational mishaps. As the Psalms say, "Your word I have hidden in my heart, that I might not sin against You" (Ps 119:11).

At present, our daughters Anna and Sarah have memorized the following chapters of the Bible: Psalm 23, Psalm 91, Matthew 5, John 15, and 1 Corinthians 13 ($142 worth!). Ruthie and Rebecca are learning single verses. After our read-aloud time, we either review some of the scriptures we've memorized, or we work on new chapters or verses. My girls readily assume the task of checking me for mistakes as I quote passages. Perhaps it's due to my habit of replacing words now and then to see if they're still listening ("Blessed are they which do hunger and thirst after vegetables…").

I admit, this requires discipline on Dave's and my part. Some nights I'm tired and Dave has fallen asleep on the couch, and the last thing we want to do is work on Scripture memorization. I try to focus on Sarah's sweet voicing of Psalm 103 (our current endeavor), but my mind drifts to the awaiting pillow upstairs. Other nights I simply don't want to have devotions. I'm tempted to rush through it so Dave and I can get on with our planned evening of Netflix and Nutella. Still, this is one area we believe is too important to let slide. And yet again, we don't want our kids to end up hating it. So there's flexibility and grace, and sometimes a movie with a great spiritual parallel is the order of the day.

Prayer

Our evening devotions always conclude with praying together. We simply remind each other of what needs we or others have and bring them before God. Dave and I encourage the girls to start their prayers with thanksgiving for specific blessings.

---

5. Todd Burpo and Lynn Vincent, *Heaven Is for Real* (Nashville, TN: Thomas Nelson, 2010).
6. DC Talk and the Voice of the Martyrs, *Jesus Freaks* (Tulsa, OK: Albury Publishers, 1999).
7. C. Hope Flinchbaugh, *I'll Cross the River* (Shippensburg, PA: Destiny Image, 2008).
8. Frida Gashumba, *Frida: Chosen to Die, Destined to Live* (Lancaster, England: Sovereign World, 2007).
9. C. S. Lewis, *The Chronicles of Narnia: The Lion, the Witch and the Wardrobe* (New York: HarperCollins, 2005).

I am continually amazed at the willingness of our girls to pray aloud. We rarely have to coax them. One by one they offer up the sweetest, heartfelt prayers. The most memorable one was when Anna, at age thirteen, prayed this: "Dear Lord, thank You that although Dad doesn't have a job right now, You have provided all that we need and more. Thank You for taking such good care of us." Her voice cracked with emotion at the end of the prayer, and my heart flip-flopped with joy at all the things my daughter was learning in life—including how to pray.

"When You Rise Up…"

I'm convinced it was the daily, early-morning talks with my dad over an open Bible that got me through high school with my purity, good grades, and salvation still intact. Those devotional times never felt forced or sounded like a lecture. Dad would simply open the Bible—say, to Proverbs—and expound on a verse or two for as long as it took me to finish my muesli. He applied what he read to my life— to my school friends, teachers, and boyfriends; to my studies and career goals; to my self-esteem. God's Word came alive through my dad's lips. He helped me understand who God is and what He's like—both through the opening of the Scriptures and by just being there for me every day. I cherished those times at the snack bar with Victor Dodzweit, and if I've gained any wisdom at all in life, I owe much of it to those morning devotions with Dad. He was a very busy man, in full-time business and ministry, but I felt like I was a priority every day before I left for school.

I've tried to replicate that model with my own teenagers. These days, before Anna's and Sarah's cyber classes start each morning, I call them to the living room, where we continue our current journey through the four Gospels. I don't have a reading schedule; I place no demands on myself for how much of the New Testament we'll get through within a certain amount of time. In my opinion, this quality time with my teens is too sacred to rush through with man-made guidelines. So we simply pick up where we left off the last time. We read a small section of Scripture and discuss it together. Sometimes there is enough "meat" in a few verses to "chew" on for a while. I try to prevent spiritual indigestion by cramming too much down their throats at a time.

If it's a morning in which we simply don't get to devotions due to a late night before, an appointment, or whatever, I don't sweat it. Our devotional time is about knowing God and feeding our spirits through His Word. This should not involve guilt for the same reason that I don't feel guilt when I skip a meal; I feel *hunger.*

Devotional observances in some families involve enforcing a strict crack-of-dawn schedule in which blurry-eyed kids nod off while potentially life-changing words are being read and wasted. I respect parents who go that route. But family devotions in our home are like a daily Christmas. God's wisdom is waiting for us like packages to unwrap, not like chores to check off a to-do list.

I'm not saying my teens relish every minute of devotions. They meet with me on the sofa before school starts because they have a healthy fear of Mom. But they know that the minute I recognize a hardening of their souls in the way they sometimes stare out the window and refuse to respond, I'll shut the Bible, put my arms around them, and say, "What can I do to be a better mom?" Because I have come to understand that when a child distances herself from a parent, it is often because the parent has first distanced herself from the child through being too busy or too much a nag.

And if there is a hindrance in my kids' relationship with me, how can I expect to ever encourage their relationship with God? So I lay aside devotions in order to devote myself to my daughters for a while, holding them close and letting them hear my prayer: “Lord, please help me to be a better mother. Forgive me for being so impatient. Show me creative ways to spend more time with my precious girls.”

The natural result of this heart devotion is that Anna, Sarah, Rebecca, and Ruthie will be drawn, by God’s grace, back to the Bible, time and time again, to learn more about this God who humbles their mother to listen carefully to the voice of the Holy Spirit. That voice is what helps us distinguish religious duty from an authentic pursuit of relationship.

APPENDIX D

One Hundred Advantages of the Word of the Lord

> Bless the LORD, O my soul, and forget not all his benefits.
>
> —PSALM 103:2

The prophetic word of the Lord releases great benefits to the believer. Understanding these benefits will give us a greater desire to operate in a greater level of prophecy. Benefit is an advantage. This is the prophetic advantage.

1. The prophetic word brings healing and deliverance.

> He sent his word and healed them and delivered them from their destruction.
>
> —PSALM 107:20

I have seen many believers healed and delivered through the prophetic word. Prophecy is a powerful tool that releases miracles. The word of the Lord carries the anointing and virtue of God that brings healing and deliverance to the recipient.

2. The prophetic word resurrects (Eze 37).

When Ezekiel prophesied, the dead bones came to life. Prophecy has resurrection power. God's Word is full of life. I have seen prophecy resurrect visions and dreams that have died. I have seen believers "come alive" when receiving prophecy.

3. The prophetic word is a lamp and a light.

> Your word is a lamp to my feet and a light to my path.
>
> —PSALM 119:105

Every believer needs a lamp and a light helping them see their way. The prophetic word can illuminate the darkness and cause believers to see where they are going. Prophecy shines on our paths and makes it easier to see where we are going.

4. The prophetic word edifies, exhorts, and comforts (1Co 14).

To *edify* means "to build." It is the root of the word *edifice* (a building). The prophetic word builds up the believer and builds up the church. To *exhort* means "to encourage." Every believer needs encouragement. *Comfort* means "to give strength and hope, to cheer."

5. The prophetic word falls like rain (Dt 32:2).

The prophetic word refreshes. Rain is needed to bring forth a harvest. Every believer needs the rain of the Spirit to fall. Rain symbolizes the blessing of heaven. Prophecy is the word coming from heaven that falls upon our lives.

6. The prophetic word roots out, tears down, pulls down, destroys, builds, and plants (Jer 1:10).

Prophecy roots out the things that have been planted by the enemy. Prophecy tears down the strongholds that have been built by the enemy. Prophecy pulls down the high things of the enemy. Prophecy destroys the works of the devil. Prophecy also builds and plants. Things must be rooted out, pulled down, torn down, and destroyed before we can build and plant.

7. The prophetic word is a light that shines in a dark place.

> And we have a more reliable word of prophecy, which you would do well to follow, as to a light that shines in a dark place, until the day dawns and the morning star arises in your hearts.
>
> —2 Peter 1:19

Many believers find themselves in a dark place. They have no light or illumination concerning the will of God or what they are experiencing. Prophecy is a light that shines in our dark places. Prophecy helps us overcome any darkness or blind spots that we are experiencing.

8. The prophetic word causes the winds to blow (Eze 37).

Ezekiel prophesied to the winds. The winds represent the breath of God. Winds are needed to bring change and refreshing. There are many different kinds of winds. The winds of refreshing and life need to blow in our lives. Old things need to be blown away, and new things need to be blown in.

9. The prophetic word can change you into another person (1Sa 10).

Saul was turned into another man when he came into contact with the company of prophets. Saul was changed and began to prophesy. I have seen people change as a result of prophecy. Many have said what they experienced was life-changing.

10. The prophetic word is like a fire and a hammer.

> Is not My word like fire, says the Lord, and like a hammer that breaks the rock in pieces?
>
> —Jeremiah 23:29

Fire burns and hammers break. The word of the Lord can burn things out of your life. The prophetic word is like a hammer that breaks the rock. Hard things are demolished through the prophetic word.

11. The prophetic word reveals the secrets of the heart.

> Thus the secrets of his heart are revealed.
>
> —1 Corinthians 14:25

God knows the heart and uses the prophetic word to reveal the secrets of the heart. People who experience prophecy know it could only be God who revealed what was in their heart. Prophecy is a powerful sign that God knows and understands what we are thinking.

12. The prophetic word provokes worship.

> And so falling down on his face, he will worship God and report that God is truly among you.
>
> —1 CORINTHIANS 14:25

Prophecy can stir men to worship and acknowledge the omniscient God. God knows all and causes wonder and amazement when He speaks only what we know in our hearts. I have seen many fall down and bow as a result of prophecy.

13. Gifts can be imparted through the prophetic word.

> Do not neglect the gift that is in you, which was given to you by prophecy, with the laying on of hands by the elders.
>
> —1 TIMOTHY 4:14

Prophetic presbytery is an important function in imparting gifts into the life of the recipient.

14. The prophetic word blesses.

> Now this is the blessing with which Moses, the man of God, blessed the children of Israel before his death.
>
> —DEUTERONOMY 33:1

Moses blessed the tribes of Israel through prophecy. To *bless* means "to confer well-being or prosperity on." The word of the Lord can release tremendous blessings upon the recipient. Moses blessed the people of Israel and spoke concerning their future. Prophetic blessing helps release us into our destinies with the favor of God.

15. The prophetic word can come in a vision.

> After this the word of the LORD came to Abram in a vision, saying, "Do not fear, Abram. I am your shield, your exceedingly great reward."
>
> —GENESIS 15:1

God revealed His word to Abraham in a vision. The prophetic word is not limited to what we speak but can come through what we see in a vision or a dream.

16. The prophetic word releases signs and judgments.

> The altar also was torn, and the ashes poured out from the altar, just as the man of God had said it would as a sign of the LORD.
>
> —1 KINGS 13:5

The prophetic word can bring judgment. Judgments are a sign of the power and righteousness of God.

17. Through the prophetic word the Lord reveals Himself.

> And the LORD appeared again in Shiloh. For the LORD revealed Himself to Samuel in Shiloh by the word of the LORD.
>
> —1 SAMUEL 3:21

The Lord reveals Himself through prophecy. He reveals His character, love, power, righteousness, wisdom, compassion, mercy, and judgment through prophecy. Those who prophesy will have a greater revelation of the God who speaks.

18. The prophetic word gives revelation of God's purpose for your life.

> Where there is no [prophetic] vision, the people perish; but happy is he who keeps the teaching.
>
> —Proverbs 29:18

19. The Holy Spirit puts the prophetic word on your tongue.

> The Spirit of the Lord spoke by me, and His word was on my tongue.
>
> —2 Samuel 23:2

We prophesy by the Holy Spirit. The Holy Spirit puts the words of God on our tongue (in our mouth and on our lips), and we simply release it.

20. The prophetic word allows us to see God.

> And he said, "Hear, therefore, the word of the Lord: I saw the Lord sitting on His throne, and all the host of heaven standing beside Him on His right hand and on His left."
>
> —1 Kings 22:19

Sometimes the word of the Lord is delivered by what we see. Some prophesy by the *nabi* flow (bubbling up), and some prophesy with a visionary flow (what they see). We can also have a combination of both.

21. The prophetic allows us to inquire of the Lord.

> Jehoshaphat said to the king of Israel, "Please ask for a word from the Lord today."
>
> —1 Kings 22:5

It was a common practice to inquire of the Lord through prophets. We can ask for prophetic direction and insight from those who prophesy.

22. The word of the Lord changes things quickly.

> Then Elisha said, "Hear the word of the Lord: Thus says the Lord: Tomorrow about this time a measure of fine flour will be sold for a shekel, and two measures of barley for a shekel, at the gate of Samaria."
>
> —2 Kings 7:1

I have seen miracle turnarounds in the lives of those who receive prophecy. The prophetic word can change a person's finances, marriage, family, ministry, and so on. There is nothing impossible with God.

23. The word of the Lord destroys Jezebel.

> They returned and told Jehu, and he said, "This is the word of the Lord, which He spoke by His servant Elijah the Tishbite, saying, 'On the property of Jezreel dogs will eat the flesh of Jezebel.'"
>
> —2 Kings 9:36

Judgment came upon Jezebel after Elijah delivered the word of the Lord. The word of the Lord can bring judgment, and there were few people more wicked than Jezebel. The spirit of Jezebel hates the true prophetic anointing and will attack it viciously. The prophetic is a weapon against Jezebel spirits and helps defeat this evil entity.

24. The word of the Lord brings restoration.

> He restored the border of Israel from the entrance of Lebo Hamath to the Sea of the Arabah, according to the word of the LORD God of Israel, which He spoke by His servant Jonah the son of Amittai, the prophet, who was from Gath Hepher.
>
> —2 KINGS 14:25

There are multitudes of people who need restoration in their marriages, finances, and ministries. The word of the Lord is a powerful way to bring restoration.

25. The word of the Lord can bring evil upon a place.

> Thus says the LORD: See, I will bring evil on this place and on its inhabitants—all the words of the book that the king of Judah has read.
>
> —2 KINGS 22:16

God rewards wickedness with evil. God allows evil to come upon a place for disobedience and rebellion. The word of the Lord releases judgment and cleanses wickedness from the land.

26. The word of the Lord comes to those who humble themselves.

> So when the LORD observed that they had humbled themselves, the word of the LORD came to Shemaiah, "They have humbled themselves, so I will not destroy them. I will let some of them escape, and My anger will not pour out against Jerusalem by the hand of Shishak."
>
> —2 CHRONICLES 12:7

God gives grace to the humble. Humility always attracts the blessing of the Lord. Grace is released through prophecy. Humility brings deliverance. The prophetic word also brings deliverance.

27. The word of the Lord releases wrath upon those who despise it.

> But they continued to jest regarding the messengers of God, despising His word and making fun of His prophets until the wrath of the LORD came up against His people, until there was no remedy.
>
> —2 CHRONICLES 36:16

It is dangerous to despise prophecy. Prophecy often brings warning, and those who despise it do so at their own peril.

28. The word of the Lord stirs the spirits of kings.

> In the first year of King Cyrus of Persia, that the word of the LORD spoken by the mouth of Jeremiah might be fulfilled, the LORD stirred up the spirit of King Cyrus of Persia, so that he sent a proclamation throughout all his kingdom and also declared in a written edict.
>
> —2 CHRONICLES 36:22

Jeremiah prophesied a seventy-year captivity in Babylon. After the seventy years the Lord stirred the spirit of Cyrus to issue a decree for the rebuilding of the temple.

29. The word of the Lord is pure.

> The words of the LORD are pure words; they are silver tried in an earthen furnace refined seven times.
>
> —PSALM 12:6

True prophecy is pure. Those who corrupt the word of the Lord are often false prophets or those with hidden agendas. Those who prophesy must have pure motives. Prophecy should be done in love and sincerity.

30. The word of the Lord is right.

> The word of the LORD is upright, and all His work is done in truth.
>
> —PSALM 33:4

Right means "morally good or acceptable." We must speak right things and avoid speaking that which is corrupt or unclean.

31. The word of the Lord causes praise.

> In God whose word I praise, in the LORD whose word I praise.
>
> —PSALM 56:10

Prophecy releases praise. Churches that operate in the prophetic will have a high level of praise.

32. The word of the Lord will test you.

> Until the time that his word came to pass, the word of the LORD tested him.
>
> —PSALM 105:19

The word of the Lord sometimes requires patience before fulfillment. The word will test your obedience and love for the Lord.

33. The word of the Lord will quicken you.

> I am greatly afflicted; revive me, O LORD, according to Your word.
>
> —PSALM 119:107

To *quicken* means "to make alive." It means "to give life." This is much needed, especially for those in affliction.

34. The word of the Lord gives hope.

> I wait for the LORD, with bated breath I wait; I long for His Word!
>
> —PSALM 130:5

Hope is the anchor of the soul. Without hope, our lives are anchorless, and we drift. Hopelessness causes discouragement and despair. Prophecy restores hope and brings encouragement.

35. The word of the Lord gives understanding.

> Let my cry come near before You, O LORD; give me understanding according to Your word.
>
> —PSALM 119:169

Prophecy helps us understand the will of God. Prophecy also gives us a better understanding of what we are dealing with in life. Life can be perplexing, and there are many who end up confused. Prophecy gives us answers and helps us live our lives with confidence and assurance.

36. The word of the Lord empties and spoils.

> The land shall be utterly emptied, and utterly despoiled, for the LORD has spoken this word.
>
> —ISAIAH 24:3

The prophetic word can release judgments upon wickedness and rebellion.

37. The word of the Lord brings trembling.

> For My hand made all those things, thus all those things have come to be, says the LORD. But to this man I will look, even to him who is poor and of a contrite spirit, and trembles at My word.
>
> —ISAIAH 66:2

Prophecy releases the fear of the Lord. We desperately need the reverential fear of the Lord to walk properly and to please God.

38. The word of the Lord comes in famine.

> The word of the LORD which came to Jeremiah concerning the drought.
>
> —JEREMIAH 14:1

Prophecy can give us the reason why we are experiencing famine, and prophecy can help break the famine.

39. The earth hears the word of the Lord.

> O land, land, land, hear the word of the LORD!
>
> —JEREMIAH 22:29

This also includes man who was taken from the earth. The land is very important to God and His purposes.

40. The word of the Lord comes from those who stand in the counsel of the Lord.

> For who has stood in the counsel of the LORD and has perceived and heard His word? Who has given heed to His word and listened to it?
>
> —JEREMIAH 23:18

Prophets stand in the counsel of the Lord. They have insight into the plans and purposes of God for individuals, churches, and nations.

41. The prophetic word gives courage.

> And when Asa heard these words of the prophecy of Azariah son of Oded the prophet, he was encouraged and removed the detestable idols from the entire land of Judah and Benjamin and from the cities that he captured in the hills of Ephraim. And he repaired the altar of the LORD that was before the vestibule of the LORD.
>
> —2 CHRONICLES 15:8

We need courage to deal with life's challenges. Asa received the courage he needed to carry out the reforms needed in Israel. Asa received courage and was able to overcome any hesitancy in carrying out the needed reforms.

42. The prophetic word delivered in love means everything.

> If I have the gift of prophecy, and understand all mysteries and all knowledge, and if I have all faith, so that I could remove mountains, and have not love, I am nothing.
>
> —1 CORINTHIANS 13:2

Prophets and prophetic people must operate in a high degree of love. Prophetic people who become bitter, angry, and harsh will release tainted words.

43. The prophetic word can be elevated by musical instruments.

> Then David and the officers of the army also set apart for the service some of the sons of Asaph, and of Heman, and of Jeduthun, those who prophesied with lyres, harps, and cymbals.
>
> —1 CHRONICLES 25:1

Music is an important aspect of the prophetic ministry. There are many musical prophets who have the anointing to prophesy on the instruments.

44. Prophets can help us prosper in building.

> The rebuilding by the elders of the Jews prospered through the prophesying of Haggai the prophet and Zechariah the son of Iddo. And they built, and finished it, according to the decree of the God of Israel and according to the decrees of Cyrus, Darius, and Artaxerxes king of Persia.
>
> —EZRA 6:14

The Jews prospered in rebuilding the temple through the help of the prophets Haggai and Zechariah. Prophets help us prosper in the work of the Lord.

45. The word of the Lord compels us to prophesy.

> The lion has roared, who will not fear? The Lord GOD has spoken, who can but prophesy?
>
> —AMOS 3:8

Those who receive the word must release it. The prophet is moved by God to declare what he or she hears from the Lord.

46. The prophetic word of the Lord encourages team ministry.

> For we know in part, and we prophesy in part.
>
> —1 CORINTHIANS 13:9

We can only speak the part that God gives us to speak. Team ministry is important because each prophetic minister has a part to release.

47. The word of the Lord makes us desire to prophesy.

> Follow after love and desire spiritual gifts, but especially that you may prophesy.
>
> —1 CORINTHIANS 14:1

Desire is an important part of walking stronger in the prophetic. Teaching and preaching on prophecy will increase the desire in the church to operate in the prophetic.

48. The prophetic word teaches and comforts.

> For you may all prophesy one by one, that all may learn and all may be encouraged.
>
> —1 CORINTHIANS 14:31

Prophecy can bring instruction and great comfort to the recipient.

49. The word of the Lord makes us want to prophesy more.

> Therefore, brothers, eagerly desire to prophesy, and do not forbid speaking in tongues.
>
> —1 Corinthians 14:39

Covet, which is used in the King James Version, is a strong word. It means "to desire strongly." Where there is no desire, there will be a low level of prophecy.

50. The word of the Lord makes us confident in prophecy.

> Do not despise prophecies.
>
> —1 Thessalonians 5:20

There is a danger of despising prophecy. This can be due to misuse or bad experiences with the prophetic ministry. Some are simply afraid of prophecy.

51. The voice of the Lord comes with His presence.

> Then they heard the sound of the Lord God walking in the garden in the cool of the day, and the man and his wife hid themselves from the presence of the Lord God among the trees of the garden.
>
> —Genesis 3:8

Prophecy releases the presence of the Lord. I have seen the atmosphere of church services dramatically change after a strong prophetic utterance.

52. Obeying the voice of the Lord brings health.

> He said, "If you diligently listen to the voice of the Lord your God, and do what is right in His sight, and give ear to His commandments, and keep all His statutes, I will not afflict you with any of the diseases with which I have afflicted the Egyptians. For I am the Lord who heals you."
>
> —Exodus 15:26

Obeying the prophetic word brings great blessings, including health and prosperity.

53. The voice of the Lord is powerful.

> The voice of the Lord sounds with strength; the voice of the Lord—with majesty.
>
> —Psalm 29:4

The power of God is released through prophecy. This can include deliverance, healing, and breakthrough. Majesty is royal power.

54. The voice of the Lord breaks the cedars.

> The voice of the Lord breaks the cedars; the Lord breaks the cedars of Lebanon.
>
> —Psalm 29:5

Cedars are tall and strong trees. This again represents the power of the prophetic word.

55. The voice of the Lord shakes the wilderness.

> The voice of the Lord shakes the wilderness; the Lord shakes the Wilderness of Kadesh.
>
> —Psalm 29:8

Many people have been shaken out of wilderness and dry places through prophecy.

56. The prophetic word confirms.

> Judas and Silas, being prophets themselves, exhorted the brothers with many words and strengthened them.
>
> —Acts 15:32

We all need confirmation concerning our callings, gifts, and destiny. The prophetic word confirms believers and gives them strength.

57. The word of the Lord causes us to excel in prophecy.

> So, seeing that you are zealous of spiritual gifts, seek that you may excel to the edifying of the church.
>
> —1 Corinthians 14:12

We should excel in prophecy. *Excel* means "to abound."

58. The word of the Lord makes our proportion of faith grow.

> We have diverse gifts according to the grace that is given to us: if prophecy, according to the proportion of faith.
>
> —Romans 12:6

Faith is essential to prophecy. The more you operate in the prophetic, the more your faith will develop in this area.

59. The rebellious can be hewed by the prophets.

> Therefore I have hewn them by the prophets. I have killed them by the words of My mouth, and My judgments go forth like light.
>
> —Hosea 6:5

God used the prophets to hew Israel. To *hew* means "to chop or cut." This is another aspect of the power of prophecy to release judgment.

60. All God's people can be prophetic.

> Moses said to him, "Are you jealous for my sake? Oh, that all the people of the Lord were prophets, and that the Lord would put His Spirit upon them!"
>
> —Numbers 11:29

Moses reveals the heart of a leader who desires to see the entire church operate to some degree in the prophetic. I believe this should be the heart and attitude of every leader.

61. We prosper by believing God's prophets.

> So they rose up early in the morning and went out to the Wilderness of Tekoa. And when they went out, Jehoshaphat stood and said, "Listen to me, Judah and those dwelling in Jerusalem. Believe in the Lord your God, and you will be supported. Believe His prophets, and you will succeed."
>
> —2 Chronicles 20:20

Prophets have an anointing to break lack and release prosperity. We benefit when we believe the prophets of God. Prophets are sent to be a blessing to us.

62. The prophetic establishes worship.

> And he set the Levites at the house of the LORD with cymbals, harps, and lyres according to the commandment of David, and Gad the seer of the king, and Nathan the prophet. For the commandment came from the LORD through His prophets.
>
> —2 CHRONICLES 29:25

Worship is important to prophets. Prophets rebuked Israel for vain and false worship. The prophetic ministry will enhance true worship.

63. The prophetic word helps us.

> Then Zerubbabel the son of Shealtiel and Joshua the son of Jozadak rose up and began to build the house of God which is at Jerusalem, and the prophets of God were with them, helping them.
>
> —EZRA 5:2

Prophets bring great help and assistance to leaders. God used Haggai and Zechariah to encourage Joshua and Zerubbabel, the leaders who were restoring the temple.

64. The prophets of God are protected.

> Do not touch my anointed ones, and do no harm to my prophets.
>
> —PSALM 105:15

God is jealous over His prophets. God protects, defends, and avenges His sent ones.

65. The prophetic word brings correction and speaks right things.

> They say to the seers, "You must not see visions," and to the prophets, "You must not prophesy to us right things. Speak to us pleasant things, prophesy illusions."
>
> —ISAIAH 30:10

Sometimes the word of the Lord is corrective. The prophetic word can also bring rebuke and sometimes appear to be hard.

66. The prophetic word reveals secrets.

> Surely the Lord GOD does nothing without revealing His purpose to His servants the prophets.
>
> —AMOS 3:7

Prophets and prophetic people have revelation of the secrets of God. This shows the importance of prophets in the plan of God.

67. The prophetic word of the Lord causes us to know the deep, hidden things of God.

> But as it is written, "Eye has not seen, nor ear heard, nor has it entered into the heart of man the things which God has prepared for those who love Him." But God has revealed them to us by His Spirit. For the Spirit searches all things, yes, the deep things of God.
>
> —1 CORINTHIANS 2:9–10

68. The prophetic word causes a noise and a shaking.

> So I prophesied as I was commanded. And as I prophesied, there was a noise and a shaking. And the bones came together, bone to its bone.
>
> —EZEKIEL 37:7

Prophecy shakes things up and causes things to move in our lives. Nations, churches, and individuals can be shaken by the word. Prophecy can cause things that are disjointed to come together in your life.

69. The prophetic word causes breath to come back.

> So I prophesied as He commanded me, and the breath came into them, and they lived and stood up upon their feet, an exceeding great army.
>
> —EZEKIEL 37:10

Breath is spirit and life. Prophecy restores breath and life to those who are weary and without strength. We need breath and spirit to live.

70. The baptism of the Holy Spirit releases prophecy.

> When Paul had laid his hands on them, the Holy Spirit came on them, and they spoke in other tongues and prophesied.
>
> —ACTS 19:6

The baptism of the Holy Spirit is the doorway to the prophetic realm. Those who receive the Holy Spirit can operate in the prophetic to some degree. Do not limit the baptism of the Holy Spirit to tongues, but include the blessing of prophecy.

71. The word of the Lord causes us to hear.

> Therefore Eli said to Samuel, "Go, lie down. And it will be, if He calls you, that you will say, 'Speak, Lord, for Your servant listens.'" So Samuel went and lay down in his place.
>
> —1 SAMUEL 3:9

We should all be open to hear the Lord's voice and release what He gives us. Samuel was young and did not recognize the voice of the Lord. Young prophets need mature prophets to help them learn the ways of the prophetic.

72. The word of the Lord causes us to speak what the Lord commands.

> But Balaam answered and said to Balak, "Did I not tell you, saying, 'All that the LORD speaks, I must do'?"
>
> —NUMBERS 23:26

We can only speak what the Lord commands. To speak outside of His command is to operate in presumption.

73. The prophetic word reveals that God is always speaking, yet many don't perceive.

> For God speaks once, yes twice, yet man does not perceive it.
>
> —JOB 33:14

God is always speaking, yet hardness of heart causes men not to perceive what He is saying.

74. The prophetic word can be like wine ready to burst.

> See, my belly is like wine that has no vent; it is ready to burst like new wineskins.
>
> —Job 32:19

Prophets who carry the word must release it. Those who have no outlet often become frustrated.

75. The prophetic word delivers the people from slavery.

> And afterward Moses and Aaron went in and said to Pharaoh, "Thus says the Lord, the God of Israel, 'Let My people go, that they may hold a feast to Me in the wilderness.'"
>
> —Exodus 5:1

The prophetic word breaks bondages and liberates. The prophetic word brings deliverance. God used a prophet to bring Israel out of bondage.

76. The prophetic word breaks barrenness.

> He went out to the spring of water and threw the salt into it and said, "Thus says the Lord: I have healed this water. No more death or unfruitfulness will come from it."
>
> —2 Kings 2:21

Fruitfulness is the result of the prophet's ministry. Prophets can identify the cause of barrenness and break lack through the prophetic word.

77. The prophetic word identifies God's anointed.

> So he arose, went into the house, poured the oil on his head, and said to him, "Thus says the Lord, God of Israel: I am anointing you king over the people of the Lord, over Israel."
>
> —2 Kings 9:6

Prophets are used by God to identify leaders. Churches need prophets to help identify emerging leaders and impart into their lives. God used Samuel to identify Saul and David as the first kings of Israel.

78. The prophetic word releases healing.

> Turn back and say to Hezekiah the leader of My people: Thus says the Lord, the God of David your father: I have heard your prayer; I have seen your tears. I will heal you. On the third day you shall go up to the house of the Lord.
>
> —2 Kings 20:5

Prophets can also be used in the healing ministry. The prophetic word can release healing. Prophets can reveal the will of God to heal as an answer to prayer.

79. The prophetic word drives out fear.

> And he said, "Pay attention all Judah, and those dwelling in Jerusalem, and King Jehoshaphat: Thus says the Lord to you, 'Do not fear, nor be dismayed because of this great army, for the battle is not yours, but God's.'"
>
> —2 Chronicles 20:15

Fear is one of the greatest enemies of progress. Prophecy can release boldness and courage to overcome fear and hesitancy. Prophecy encourages us that God is on our side.

80. The prophetic word stops the plans of the enemy.

> Thus says the Lord God: It shall not stand, nor shall it come to pass.
>
> —Isaiah 7:7

Prophecy is a weapon against the plans of hell. The plans of hell are brought to nothing through prophetic intercession and declaration.

81. The prophetic word establishes a foundation.

> Therefore, thus says the Lord God: See, I lay in Zion a stone, a tested stone, a precious cornerstone, firmly placed; he who believes shall not act hastily.
>
> —Isaiah 28:16

A strong foundation is important to build upon. Prophecy speaks to the foundational issues of our life.

82. The prophetic word makes a path.

> Thus says the Lord, who makes a way in the sea and a path in the mighty waters.
>
> —Isaiah 43:16

Prophecy opens the way for us to prosper. God opens doors and establishes our path through the prophetic ministry.

83. The prophetic word teaches us to profit.

> Thus says the Lord, your Redeemer, the Holy One of Israel: I am the Lord your God, who teaches you to profit, who leads you in the way that you should go.
>
> —Isaiah 48:17

This is another aspect of prosperity. Prophecy helps direct our way so that we can prosper. Prophecy encourages us to prosper.

84. The prophetic word releases peace.

> For thus says the Lord: I will extend peace to her like a river and the glory of the nations like a flowing stream. Then you shall nurse, you shall be carried on her sides, and dandled on her knees.
>
> —Isaiah 66:12

Peace is shalom. *Shalom* means "peace, prosperity, health, and favor." Prophecy releases the favor and encouragement we need to move forward.

85. The prophetic word encourages us to seek God.

> Indeed, thus says the Lord to the house of Israel: Seek Me and live!
>
> —Amos 5:4

The prophetic word can stir us up to draw closer to God. God's voice draws us to Him. Prophets encourage us to seek God.

86. The prophetic word challenges us to consider our ways.

> Now, therefore, thus says the Lord of Hosts: Consider your ways.
>
> —Haggai 1:5

Prophets can challenge us to consider our ways when they are contrary to the will of God. Prophecy can bring conviction and repentance.

87. Prophetic words shake the heavens, earth, and sea.

> For thus says the Lord of Hosts: Once more, in a little while, I will shake the heavens and earth, the sea and dry land.
>
> —Haggai 2:6

The prophetic word can shake kingdoms and nations. The heavens, earth, and sea were always prophetic terms representing kingdoms and peoples.

88. The prophetic word challenges men to repent.

> So you will say to them, Thus says the Lord of Hosts: Return to Me, and I will return to you, says the Lord of Hosts.
>
> —Zechariah 1:3

The prophetic word brings conviction and challenges men to turn away from things that are destructive. Repentance can save your life.

89. The prophetic word releases strength.

> Thus says the Lord of Hosts: Let your hands be strengthened, whoever is hearing these words in these days, from the mouth of the prophets who were there in the day that the house of the Lord of Hosts was founded, that the temple might be built.
>
> —Zechariah 8:9

We need the strength of the Lord. We cannot do the will of God in our own strength. Prophecy can strengthen our spirits.

90. The prophetic word is a word in season.

> The Lord God has given me the tongue of the learned, that I may know how to sustain him who is weary with a word; He awakens me morning by morning; He awakens my ear to listen as the learned.
>
> —Isaiah 50:4

The word of the Lord is released at a *kairos* time. This means it is a word delivered in the perfect timing of the Lord at a right time in someone's life for breakthrough and progress.

91. The right word carries power.

> How forceful are right words!
>
> —Job 6:25

The right word at the right time carries tremendous power and force. Power and force are needed for breakthrough.

92. The prophetic word is sweet to the taste.

> How sweet are Your words to the taste of my mouth! Sweeter than honey to my mouth!
>
> —Psalm 119:103

We should enjoy the word of the Lord as something pleasant to the taste.

93. The prophetic word gives light and understanding to the simple.

> The giving of Your words gives light; it grants understanding to the simple.
>
> —PSALM 119:130

Light is needed to move forward. Understanding is needed to make the right decisions. Those who lack light and understanding can receive it through the prophetic word. God does not desire us to be ignorant.

94. The prophetic word releases wisdom.

> Get wisdom! Get understanding! Do not forget it, nor turn away from the words of my mouth.
>
> —PROVERBS 4:5

Wisdom is needed to avoid bad decisions. Your decisions affect your life and destiny.

95. The prophetic word can release health to the bones.

> Pleasant words are as a honeycomb, sweet to the soul and health to the bones.
>
> —PROVERBS 16:24

Healthy bones are essential to good health. Pleasant words release health to the bones.

96. The prophetic word guarantees we have God's words in our mouth.

> I have put My words in your mouth, and I have covered you in the shadow of My hand that I may plant the heavens, and lay the foundations of the earth, and say to Zion, "You are My people."
>
> —ISAIAH 51:16

Prophecy is God putting His words in our mouth. We simply speak the word placed in our mouth by God. The heavens were planted and the foundations of the earth laid through the word of the Lord.

97. The prophetic guarantees our seed will have God's word in their mouths.

> As for Me, this is My covenant with them, says the LORD: My Spirit who is upon you, and My words which I have put in your mouth shall not depart out of your mouth, nor out of the mouth of your descendants, nor out of the mouth of your descendants' descendants, says the LORD, from this time forth and forever.
>
> —ISAIAH 59:21

God desires His word to go from generation to generation. Our children should also prophesy. Each generation can experience the blessing of prophecy.

98. The prophetic word causes joy and rejoicing.

> Your words were found and I ate them. And Your word became to me the joy and rejoicing of my heart, for I am called by Your name, O LORD God of Hosts.
>
> —JEREMIAH 15:16

Prophecy releases great joy to the recipient. The joy of the Lord is our strength. Jeremiah found the word, and it brought great joy to his life. We should rejoice in receiving and speaking the word of the Lord.

CONCORDANCE

A

ABBA
Mk 14:36 He said, "*A*
Ro 8:15 whom we cry, "*A*

ABHOR
Lev 26:11 I shall not *a*
Lev 26:30 I shall *a* you
Job 42:6 Therefore I *a* myself
Jer 14:21 Do not *a* us.
Am 6:8 I *a* the pride of Jacob

ABIDE
Job 24:13 nor *a* in its paths
Ps 91:1 the Most High shall *a*
Jer 49:18 LORD, no man will *a*

ABILITY
Dt 8:18 He who gives you the *a*
Mt 25:15 according to his *a*

ABLE
Dt 16:17 must give as he is *a*
Da 3:17 whom we serve is *a*
Mt 3:9 God is *a* from these
Mt 10:28 fear Him who is *a*
Mt 20:22 Are you *a* to drink
2Ti 1:12 that He is *a*
Heb 11:19 that God was *a* to

ABOLISHED
2Ti 1:10 Christ, who has *a*

ABOMINABLE
Jer 16:18 detestable and *a* things
Eze 4:14 *a* meat come into my mouth
Titus 1:16 deny him, being *a*
1Pe 4:3 and *a* idolatries
Rev 21:8 unbelieving, the *a*

ABOMINATION
Lev 18:22 It is an *a*
Dt 12:31 every *a* to the LORD
Dt 18:12 these things are an *a*
Dt 24:4 is *a* before the LORD
1Ki 11:7 Chemosh, the *a* of Moab
Ps 88:8 You have made me an *a*
Pr 11:1 false balance is *a*
Da 11:31 *a* that makes desolate
Mt 24:15 the '*a* of desolation,'
Rev 21:27 anyone who commits *a*

ABOUND
2Co 9:8 to make all grace *a*
Php 1:9 that your love may *a*

ABOUNDED
Ro 5:20 grace *a* much more

ABOUNDING
Ex 34:6 *a* in goodness and truth
1Co 15:58 unmovable, always *a*

ABOVE
Ex 20:4 that is in heaven *a*
Isa 6:2 *A* it stood the seraphim
Jn 3:31 He who comes from *a*
Jn 8:23 I am from *a*
Jn 19:11 given to you from *a*
Col 3:1 things which are *a*

ABROAD
Ge 28:14 you will spread *a*
Isa 44:24 spreads *a* the earth
Ro 5:5 love of God is shed *a*

ABSENT
2Co 5:6 in the body, we are *a*

ABSTAIN
Ac 15:20 we write to them to *a*
1Th 5:22 *A* from all appearances

ABUNDANCE
Dt 28:47 of heart, for the *a*
Ps 52:7 but trusted in the *a*
Isa 47:9 great *a* of your enchantments
Eze 26:10 By reason of the *a*
Mt 12:34 of the *a* of the heart
Mt 13:12 he will have *a*

ABUNDANT
2Co 11:23 in labors more *a*

ABUNDANTLY
Jn 10:10 may have it more *a*
Eph 3:20 to do exceedingly *a*

ACCEPT
Dt 16:19 must not *a* a bribe
Job 2:10 *a* the good…not *a* the
Jer 14:10 the LORD does not *a* them
Eze 20:40 There I will *a* them,
Hos 14:2 *a* that which is good
2Co 7:2 *A* us.
Heb 11:35 did not *a* deliverance

ACCEPTABLE
Isa 49:8 *a* time I have heard
Isa 61:2 proclaim the *a* year
Lk 4:19 preach the *a* year
Ro 12:2 is the good and *a*

ACCEPTED
Ge 4:7 shall you not be *a*?
Isa 56:7 shall be *a* on My altar
Jer 37:20 my supplication be *a*
Lk 4:24 no prophet is *a*
2Co 6:2 now is the *a* time

ACCESS
Ro 5:2 whom we also have *a*

ACCOMPLISHED
Jn 19:28 everything was now *a*

ACCORD
Ac 1:14 continued with one *a*

ACCOUNT
Mt 12:36 they will give an *a*
Phm 1:18 charge this to my *a*

ACCURSED
Jn 7:49 not know the law is *a*

ACCUSE
Lk 3:14 nor *a* any falsely
Lk 23:2 they began to *a* Him

ACCUSER
Ps 109:6 let an *a* stand
Rev 12:10 *a* of our brothers

ACKNOWLEDGE
Ps 51:3 *a* my transgressions
Pr 3:6 In all your ways *a*

ACQUAINTED
Isa 53:3 A man of sorrows and *a*

ACT
Jn 8:4 in the very *a*

ACTS
Ps 106:2 the mighty *a* of the Lord

ACTIONS
1Sa 2:3 *a* are examined

ADAM
Ge 2:20 *A* there was not found
Ge 4:1 *A* had relations
Lk 3:38 son of *A*
Ro 5:14 from *A* to Moses
1Co 15:45 man *A* was made

ADD
Pr 30:6 Do not *a* to His words

ADDER
Ps 91:13 the lion and *a*

ADMONISH
2Th 3:15 *a* him as a

ADMONITION
1Co 10:11 written as an *a*

ADOPTION
Ro 8:15 received the Spirit of *a*
Eph 1:5 predestined us to *a*

ADORNED
1Pe 3:5 in God, *a* themselves
Rev 21:2 prepared as a bride *a*

ADULTEROUS
Pr 30:20 the way of an *a* woman
Mt 16:4 *a* generation seeks for a
Mk 8:38 this *a* and sinful generation

ADULTERY
Ex 20:14 shall not commit *a*
Pr 6:32 commits *a* with a woman
Jer 7:9 murder, and commit *a*
Mt 5:28 committed *a* with her
Jn 8:3 a woman caught in *a*
Jas 2:11 "Do not commit *a*,"

ADVERSARIES
1Co 16:9 and there are many *a*
Php 1:28 frightened by your *a*

ADVERSARY
Mt 5:25 "Reconcile with your *a*
1Ti 5:14 occasion to the *a*
1Pe 5:8 *a* the devil walks

ADVOCATE
1Jn 2:1 sin, we have an *A*

AFAR
Heb 11:13 seen them from *a*

AFFECTION
1Co 7:3 to the wife due *a*

AFFIRM
Titus 3:8 you constantly to *a*

AFFLICT
Ex 1:11 taskmasters over them to *a*
Jer 31:28 destroy, and to *a*

AFFLICTED
Job 34:28 hears the cry of the *a*
Ps 44:2 how You *a* peoples
Pr 15:15 days of the *a* are evil
Isa 49:13 have mercy on His *a*
Isa 53:4 smitten of God, and *a*
Isa 53:7 oppressed, and he was *a*
Isa 54:11 O *a* one
Isa 60:14 those who *a* you
Isa 63:9 In all their affliction He was *a*
Heb 11:37 while destitute, *a*

AFFLICTION
Dt 16:3 the bread of *a*
Job 30:16 *a* have taken hold of me
2Co 4:17 Our light *a*

AFRAID
Jos 1:9 Do not be *a*
Ps 91:5 *a* of the terror
Pr 3:24 you will not be *a*
Mt 14:27 Do not be *a*
Mk 5:36 Do not be *a*
Lk 1:30 not be *a*, Mary,
Lk 2:9 they were very *a*
Lk 12:4 do not be *a* of those
Jn 19:8 he was more *a*
Ac 27:24 Do not be *a*, Paul.
Heb 11:23 *a* of the king's command
Rev 1:17 Do not be *a*.

AGAINST
Mt 10:35 come to turn 'a man *a*
Mt 12:25 or house divided *a*
Mt 12:30 Me is *a* Me
Mt 12:31 *a* the Holy Spirit
Jn 13:18 lifted up his heel *a*
Ac 4:26 Lord and *a* His Christ
Ac 9:5 to kick *a* the goads
Eph 6:12 our fight is not *a*
Rev 2:20 I have a few things *a*

AGE
Job 5:26 the grave in a full *a*
Mk 10:30 in the *a* to come

AGES
1Co 2:7 ordained before the *a*

AGREE
Mt 18:19 if two of you *a*

AGREED
Am 3:3 if they have not *a*

AIR
Ge 1:26 the birds of the *a*
Lk 9:58 of the *a* have nests
Eph 2:2 of the power of the *a*
1Th 4:17 the Lord in the *a*

ALIENATED
Col 1:21 who were formerly *a*

ALIKE
Ro 14:5 judges every day *a*

ALIVE
Lev 26:36 are left *a* of you I
Nu 21:35 not a survivor left to him *a*

Dt 20:16 must not leave *a*
Dt 31:27 even now, while I am yet *a*
Dt 32:39 kill, and I make *a*
1Sa 2:6 kills and makes *a*

ALMIGHTY
Ge 17:1 "I am *A* God
Ge 28:3 God *A* bless you
Ge 43:14 *A* give you mercy
Ge 48:3 *A* appeared to me
Ru 1:20 *A* has brought
Job 8:3 does the *A* pervert
Ps 91:1 shadow of the *A*
Eze 1:24 voice of the *A*
Joel 1:15 devastation from the *A*
Rev 1:8 who is to come, the *A*
Rev 4:8 holy, Lord God *A*
Rev 15:3 your works, Lord God *A*
Rev 16:14 great day of God *A*
Rev 21:22 the Lord God *A*

ALMOND
Ecc 12:5 *a* tree blossoms

ALMOST
Ac 26:28 *a* persuade me to

ALOES
Jn 19:39 of myrrh and *a*

ALPHA
Rev 1:8 "I am the *A*
Rev 22:13 I am the *A*

ALTAR
Ge 8:20 Noah built an *a*
Ex 20:24 an *a* of earth
Lev 17:11 it to you on the *a*
Mt 5:23 your gift to the *a*
Heb 13:10 We have an *a* from

ALTARS
Ex 34:13 destroy their *a*, break
Dt 7:5 shall destroy their *a*
1Ki 19:10 *a*, and killed Your prophets
2Ki 21:3 erected *a* for Baal
2Ki 21:4 he built *a* in the house
Hos 10:8 will grow on their *a*

ALWAYS
Pr 8:30 *a* before him
Mt 26:11 the poor *a* with you
Mt 28:20 I am with you *a*
Php 4:4 Rejoice in the Lord *a*
1Pe 3:15 *a* be ready to give

AM
Ex 3:14 to Moses, "I *A* WHO I
Isa 44:6 I *a* the last

Mt 18:20 in My name, there I *a*
Jn 6:35 *a* the bread of life
Jn 8:12 *a* the light of the
Jn 8:23 I *a* from above
Jn 8:58 Abraham was born, I *A*
Jn 10:9 I *a* the door
Jn 10:11 *a* the good shepherd
Jn 11:25 *a* the resurrection
Jn 14:6 "I *a* the way
1Co 15:10 of God I *a* what I *a*

AMBASSADOR
Eph 6:20 for which I am an *a*

AMBASSADORS
2Co 5:20 we are *a* for Christ

AMEN
Dt 27:15 answer and say, "*A*
Ne 5:13 congregation said, "*A*,"
Ps 41:13 to everlasting. *A* and *A*
Mt 6:13 the glory forever. *A*
1Co 14:16 unlearned say "*A*"
2Co 1:20 and in Him "*A*
Rev 3:14 The *A*, the Faithful
Rev 5:14 creatures said, "*A*

ANCHOR
Heb 6:19 Sure and steadfast *a*

ANCIENT
Da 7:9 The *A* of Days was seated
Da 7:22 until the *A* of Days

ANGEL
Ex 23:20 I am going to send an *a*
Jdg 13:17 Manoah said to the *a*
Isa 63:9 the *a* of His presence
Mt 1:20 the *a* of the Lord
Mt 28:2 for the *a* of the Lord
Lk 1:11 Then an *a* of the Lord
Lk 2:9 And then an *a*
Lk 22:43 *a* from heaven appeared
Jn 5:4 For an *a* went down at
Jn 12:29 *a* has spoken to Him
Ac 5:19 during the night an *a*
Ac 7:35 *a* who appeared to him
Ac 12:23 immediately an *a*
2Co 11:14 himself as an *a*
Gal 1:8 although if we or an *a*
Rev 5:2 And I saw a strong *a*
Rev 22:16 Jesus, have sent My *a*

ANGELS
Mt 16:27 shall come with His *a*
Mt 24:31 send His *a* with a great
Mt 25:31 and all the holy *a*
Mt 25:41 the devil and his *a*
Mt 26:53 twelve legions of *a*
Mk 8:38 Father with the holy *a*

ANGER
Ex 4:14 *a* of the LORD
Ps 6:1 rebuke me in Your *a*
Ps 30:5 His *a* endures
Hos 11:9 fierceness of My *a*
Jnh 4:2 slow to *a*
Ac 19:28 full of *a*
Eph 4:26 down on your *a*
Eph 4:31 wrath, *a*, outbursts,
Eph 6:4 children to *a*
Jas 1:20 *a* of man

ANGERED
Ps 106:32 They *a* Him also
Titus 1:7 not easily *a*, not given

ANGRY
Ge 4:5 Cain was very *a*
Ge 18:30 Let not the Lord be *a*,
Ps 2:12 lest He become *a*
Ps 80:4 long will You be *a*
Ps 85:5 be *a* with us forever
Pr 21:19 and *a* woman
Pr 29:22 an *a* man stirs up strife
Ecc 7:9 your spirit to be *a*
Zec 1:12 *a* these seventy years
Mt 5:22 is *a* with his brother
Eph 4:26 Be *a* but do not sin

ANGUISH
Jn 16:21 remembers the *a*
Ro 2:9 tribulation and *a*

ANIMAL
Ge 7:2 of every clean *a*

ANIMALS
Dt 14:4 *a* which you may eat

ANOINT
Ps 23:5 *a* my head with oil
Mt 6:17 when you fast, *a*
Mk 14:8 *a* My body for burial
Rev 3:18 *a* your eyes with eye

ANOINTED
1Sa 16:6 "Surely the *a* of the LORD
2Sa 1:14 destroy the *a*
1Ch 16:22 "Do not touch My *a*
Lk 4:18 because He has *a*
Lk 7:46 this woman has *a*
Jn 9:6 *a* the eyes of the
Jn 11:2 Mary who *a*
Ac 4:27 Jesus whom You have *a*
2Co 1:21 and has *a* us is God

ANOINTING
Ex 29:7 shall you take the *a*
Lev 8:12 poured some of the *a* oil
Lev 8:30 *a* oil and some of the blood
1Jn 2:27 *a* which you have received

ANSWER
Job 13:22 Call, and I will *a*
Job 31:14 what will I *a* Him
Ps 102:2 the day when I call *a*
Ps 143:1 In Your faithfulness *a*
Pr 15:1 *a* turns away wrath
Pr 26:4 *a* a fool according
2Co 5:12 have something to *a*

ANT
Pr 6:6 Go to the *a*

ANTICHRIST
1Jn 2:18 the *a* will come

ANXIOUS
Php 4:6 Be *a* for nothing

APOSTLE
Ro 1:1 called to be an *a*
1Co 9:1 Am I not an *a*?
2Co 12:12 signs of an *a*

APOSTLES
Mt 10:2 of the twelve *a*
Lk 6:13 whom He named *a*
Ac 1:26 with the eleven *a*
1Co 15:9 the least of the *a*
Gal 1:19 none of the other *a*
Eph 4:11 gave some to be *a*

APOSTLESHIP
Ac 1:25 in this ministry and *a*
1Co 9:2 are the seal of my *a*

APPEAL
Phm 1:9 love's sake I rather *a*

APPEAR
Ge 1:9 let the dry land *a*
Lk 19:11 would immediately *a*
2Co 5:10 For we must all *a*

APPEARANCE
1Sa 16:7 Do not look on his *a*
Jn 7:24 judge according to *a*
2Co 5:12 those who boast in *a*

APPEARED
Lk 1:11 angel of the Lord *a*
Lk 9:31 who *a* in glory and
Titus 2:11 brings salvation has *a*
Heb 9:26 has *a* once at the end

APPEARING
1Ti 6:14 *a* of our Lord Jesus Christ
2Ti 4:1 the dead at His *a*
2Ti 4:8 who have loved His *a*

APPEARS
Mal 3:2 can stand when He *a*

Col 3:4 who is our life shall *a*
1Pe 5:4 the Chief Shepherd *a*
1Jn 2:28 that when He *a*

APPETITE
Pr 23:2 are a man given to *a*
Ecc 6:7 his *a* is not satisfied

APPLE
Pr 7:2 my teaching as the *a*

APPLES
Pr 25:11 fitly spoken is like *a*

APPOINT
Nu 3:10 You will *a* Aaron
Jer 49:19 and I will *a*
Eze 21:22 to *a* battering rams
Hos 1:11 gathered together, and *a*

APPOINTED
1Th 5:9 God has not *a*
Heb 9:27 as it is *a* for men

APPROACHING
Heb 10:25 as you see the Day *a*

APPROVED
Ro 14:18 to God and *a* by men
2Ti 2:15 to show yourself *a*

ARCHANGEL
1Th 4:16 the voice of the *a*

ARISE
Isa 60:1 *A*, shine
Eph 5:14 you who sleep, *a*

ARK
Ge 6:14 *a* of cypress wood
Ex 25:10 *a* of acacia wood
Jos 3:3 *a* of the covenant
1Sa 6:21 *a* of the LORD
2Sa 15:29 returned the *a* of God
1Ki 8:4 the *a* of the LORD
Heb 9:5 Above the *a*
1Pe 3:20 *a* was being prepared

ARM
Ex 6:6 with a stretched-out *a*
Job 40:9 Have you an *a* like God
Lk 1:51 strength with His *a*
1Pe 4:1 *a* yourselves likewise

ARMIES
Lk 21:20 surrounded by *a*
Rev 19:14 The *a* in heaven
Rev 19:19 the earth with their *a*

ARMOR
1Sa 17:38 clothed David with his *a*
Jer 46:4 and put on the *a*
Ro 13:12 put on the *a* of light
Eph 6:11 whole *a* of God

ARMY
Ps 33:16 No king is saved by a great *a*
Mt 22:7 He sent in his *a*

ARROGANCE
Pr 8:13 Pride and *a* and the

ARROW
2Ki 13:17 *a* of the deliverance
Isa 49:2 made me a select *a*

ARROWS
Job 6:4 For the *a* of the Almighty
Ps 18:14 out His *a* and scattered
Ps 57:4 teeth are spears and *a*
Ps 127:4 As *a* in the hand
Jer 51:11 Sharpen the *a*
Hab 3:9 oaths were the *a*
Eph 6:16 the fiery *a*

ASCEND
Ps 24:3 Who may *a* the hill
Ps 139:8 If I *a* to heaven
Isa 14:13 "I will *a* into heaven
Jn 6:62 see the Son of Man *a*

ASCENDED
Ps 68:18 You have *a* on high
Jn 3:13 No one has *a*
Eph 4:8 "When He *a* on high

ASHAMED
Hos 10:6 And Israel shall be *a*
Mk 8:38 Whoever therefore is *a*
Ro 1:16 am not *a* of the gospel
Heb 11:16 Therefore God is not *a*

ASHES
Job 30:19 become like dust and *a*
Lk 10:13 in sackcloth and *a*

ASK
Jos 4:6 When your children *a*
Isa 7:11 *A* for a sign
Mt 21:22 whatever you *a*
Lk 11:9 *a*, and it will be
Jn 11:22 whatever You may *a*
Jn 14:14 *a* anything in My
Eph 3:20 beyond all that we *a*
Jas 1:5 wisdom, let him *a*
Jas 1:6 But let him *a* in faith

ASKED
Ps 105:40 people *a*, and he brought
Mt 27:11 And the governor *a*
Jn 1:21 they *a* him, who
Jn 4:10 you would have *a*

ASLEEP
Mt 8:24 But He was *a*
1Th 4:15 those who are *a*

ASP
Isa 11:8 play by the hole of the *a*

ASSEMBLED
Jos 18:1 children of Israel *a*
Da 6:6 presidents and officials *a*
Jn 20:19 *a*, for fear of the Jews

ASSEMBLY
Joel 1:14 fast, call a sacred *a*
Heb 12:23 to the general *a*

ASSURANCE
Col 2:2 riches and *a*
1Th 1:5 Spirit, and in much *a*
Heb 6:11 for the full *a* of hope

ASTONISHED
Isa 52:14 Just as many were *a*
Lk 2:47 who heard Him were *a*

ASTRAY
Mt 18:12 one of them goes *a*
1Pe 2:25 as sheep going *a*

ATONEMENT
Lev 16:6 make *a* for himself
Lev 23:27 shall be the Day of *A*
Heb 2:17 make *a* for the sins

ATTAIN
Lk 20:35 worthy to *a* that age

AUTHOR
1Co 14:33 For God is not the *a*
Heb 12:2 look to Jesus, the *a*

AUTHORITIES
Lk 12:11 rulers, and *a*
Ro 13:1 subject to the governing *a*
Col 2:15 disarmed *a* and powers
Titus 3:1 subject to rulers and *a*,

AUTHORITY
Mt 7:29 as one having *a*
Mt 9:6 *a* on earth to forgive
Mt 10:1 *a* over unclean spirits
Mt 28:18 All *a* has been given
Mk 11:28 By what *a* are You
Jn 8:42 come of My own *a*
Ac 5:4 under your *a*

1Co 7:4 *a* over her own body
Heb 6:16 greater *a* than themselves
1Pe 2:13 to every human *a*
Rev 20:4 the *a* to judge

AVENGE
Ro 12:19 Beloved, do not *a*
Rev 6:10 *a* our blood on those

AWAKE
Ps 17:15 be satisfied when I *a*
Ro 13:11 the moment to *a*
1Co 15:34 *A* to righteousness

AWESOME
Ge 28:17 *a* is this place
Dt 7:21 a great and *a* God
Ps 68:35 O God, You are *a*
Ps 99:3 Your great and *a* name

AXE
Mt 3:10 Even now the *a*
Lk 3:9 The *a* is put to the root

B

BABBLER
Ac 17:18 "What will this *b*

BABES
Ps 8:2 Out of the mouth of *b*
1Co 3:1 even as to *b*

BABIES
1Pe 2:2 as newborn *b*

BABY
Lk 1:44 the *b* in my womb
Lk 2:12 You will find the *B*
Heb 5:13 for he is a *b*

BACKSLIDER
Pr 14:14 The *b* in heart

BACKWARD
Isa 1:4 estranged and *b*

BAKER
Ge 40:1 his *b* offended

BALM
Jer 8:22 no *b* in Gilead

BANNERS
Ps 20:5 we will set up our *b*
SS 6:4 as an army with *b*

BAPTISM
Mt 3:7 come to his *b*
Mt 21:25 *b* of John
Mk 10:38 baptized with the *b*
Mk 11:30 Was the *b* of John
Lk 3:3 *b* of repentance
Lk 12:50 But I have *a b*
Lk 20:4 *b* of John from heaven
Ac 1:22 from the *b* of John
Ac 10:37 *b* which John preached
Ac 13:24 a *b* of repentance
Ac 18:25 only the *b* of John,
Ac 19:4 the *b* of repentance
Ro 6:4 buried with Him by *b*
Eph 4:5 one faith, one *b*
Col 2:12 buried with Him in *b*
1Pe 3:21 like *b*, which also saves

BAPTIZE
Mt 3:11 He will *b* you
Jn 4:2 did not *b*, but His
1Co 1:17 not send me to *b*,

BAPTIZED
Mt 3:16 when Jesus was *b*,
Mk 10:38 I drink and be *b*
Mk 16:16 believes and is *b*
Ac 2:38 Repent and be *b*,
Ac 8:36 from being *b*
Ro 6:3 *b* into Jesus Christ
1Co 15:29 *b* for the dead?

BARN
Mt 13:30 the wheat into my *b*

BARNS
Mt 6:26 reap, nor gather into *b*
Lk 12:18 I will pull down my *b*

BARREN
Ge 11:30 But Sarai was *b*
Isa 54:1 Sing, O *b*

BASIN
Jn 13:5 poured water into a *b*

BASKET
Mt 5:15 and put it under a *b*
2Co 11:33 in a *b* and escaped

BASKETS
Mt 14:20 they took up twelve *b*

BATTLE
1Sa 17:47 *b* belongs to the LORD
Ecc 9:11 the *b* to the strong

BEAR
Ge 4:13 more than I can *b*
Ge 17:21 whom Sarah will *b*
Ex 20:16 not *b* false witness
Isa 53:11 *b* their iniquities
Mt 1:23 child, and will *b* a Son
Mt 7:18 A good tree cannot *b*
Mt 17:17 how long shall I *b*
Mk 15:21 to *b* Jesus' cross
Lk 14:27 whoever does not *b*
Ro 15:1 are strong ought to *b*
Gal 6:2 *B* one another's
Heb 9:28 *b* the sins of many

BEARD
Lev 19:27 the edges of your *b*
Ps 133:2 that runs down on the *b*

BEAST
Ge 1:30 every *b* of the earth
Ge 3:1 subtle than any *b*
Ge 37:33 A wild *b* has
Ex 9:9 upon man and *b*
Da 7:5 Another *b* appeared,
Rev 11:7 the *b* that ascends
Rev 13:17 name of the *b*
Rev 19:20 *b* was captured

BEAT
Dt 24:20 when you *b* your olive tree
Isa 2:4 *b* their swords into

BEAUTIFUL
Ge 29:17 Rachel was *b*
Est 2:2 "Let *b* young virgins
Ps 48:2 *B* in elevation,
Ecc 3:11 made everything *b*
Isa 52:7 *b* upon the mountains
Mt 13:45 seeking *b* pearls
Ro 10:15 *b* are the feet

BEAUTY
Job 40:10 with glory and *b*
Ps 27:4 the *b* of the LORD
Ps 50:2 of *b*, God has shined
Pr 6:25 her *b* in your heart
Pr 31:30 and *b* is vain
Isa 13:19 of kingdoms, the *b*
Isa 61:3 *b* for ashes,
La 2:15 the perfection of *b*
Eze 7:20 the *b* of His ornaments
Eze 28:12 and perfect in *b*

BED
Ps 63:6 I remember You on my *b*
Ps 139:8 if I make my *b* in Sheol
Mt 9:6 "Arise, pick up your *b*
Lk 17:34 will be in one *b*
Heb 13:4 and the *b* undefiled

BEGGAR
Lk 16:20 there was also a *b*

BEGINNING
Ge 1:1 *b* God created

Ps 29:11 *b* His people with peace
Ps 34:1 *b* the LORD at all times
Ps 104:1 *B* the LORD, O my soul!
Mt 5:44 *b* those who curse you
Ro 12:14 *B* those who persecute
1Co 10:16 which we *b*, is it not
Jas 3:9 With it we *b* the Lord

BLESSED

Ge 1:22 God *b* them
Ge 22:18 of the earth will be *b*
Ex 20:11 LORD *b* the Sabbath day
2Sa 22:47 *b* be my rock.
Ne 11:2 people *b* all the men
Ps 1:1 *B* is the man who walks
Ps 41:1 *B* are those who consider
Ps 118:26 *B* be he that comes
Ps 119:1 *B* are those whose way
Pr 31:28 and call her *b*
Jer 17:7 *B* is the man who trusts
Mt 5:3 *B* are the poor in spirit,
Mt 21:9 *B* is He who comes
Lk 12:43 *B* is that servant
Ro 4:7 *B* are those whose
Heb 7:7 inferior is *b* by the
Rev 1:3 *B* is he who reads

BLESSING

Ge 27:12 on myself and not a *b*
Dt 11:26 a *b* and a curse
Dt 30:19 life and death, *b*
Mal 3:10 for you a *b*
1Co 10:16 cup of *b* which we
Eph 1:3 every spiritual *b*
Jas 3:10 proceed *b* and cursing
Rev 5:12 and glory and *b*

BLIND

Isa 42:7 To open the *b* eyes
Isa 56:10 His watchmen are *b*
Mt 15:14 *b* lead the *b*
Jn 9:40 to Him, "Are we also *b*
Rev 3:17 miserable, poor, *b*

BLOOD

Ge 4:10 brother's *b* is
Ge 9:4 that is, its *b*
Ex 12:7 of the *b* and put it
Ps 72:14 their *b* be precious
Pr 1:11 lie in wait for *b*
Isa 1:11 the *b* of bulls,
Jer 7:6 shed innocent *b*
Eze 3:20 his *b* I will require
Joel 2:31 the moon to *b*
Mt 9:20 a flow of *b*
Mt 16:17 *b* has not revealed
Mt 26:28 *b* of the new covenant
Mt 27:8 the Field of *B*
Lk 11:51 the *b* of Abel to the *b*
Lk 22:20 new covenant in My *b*
Lk 22:44 drops of *b* falling down
Ac 2:19 *b*, and fire
Ac 20:26 innocent of the *b* of all
Ro 3:15 swift to shed *b*
Ro 5:9 justified by His *b*,
1Co 10:16 of the *b* of Christ
Eph 6:12 not against flesh and *b*,
Heb 9:22 the shedding of *b*
Heb 13:12 with His own *b*
1Jn 1:7 the *b* of Jesus Christ
1Jn 5:6 water and *b*
Rev 5:9 to God by Your *b*
Rev 7:14 the *b* of the Lamb
Rev 19:13 a robe dipped in *b*

BLOT

Ps 51:9 from my sins, and *b*
Rev 3:5 I will not *b*

BLOW

Nu 10:9 you will *b* an alarm
Nu 10:10 months, you shall *b*
Jer 4:5 and say: *b* the trumpet
Jer 6:1 *b* the trumpet in Tekoa
Jer 14:17 a great *b*
Joel 2:1 *B* the ram's horn in Zion

BOAST

Ps 5:5 *b* will not stand
Ps 44:8 In God we *b*
Ps 49:6 *b* in the multitude
Ro 5:3 *b* in tribulation,
1Co 1:31 *b* in the Lord.
2Co 5:12 *b* on our behalf
2Co 10:13 *b* beyond measure
2Co 11:30 If I must *b*, I will *b*
Gal 6:13 *b* in your flesh
2Th 1:4 we *b* about you

BOASTFUL

Da 7:20 spoke *b* words,
Ro 1:30 *b*, inventors of evil
2Ti 3:2 *b*, proud, blasphemers

BOASTING

Ac 5:36 *b* to be somebody,
Ro 3:27 Where is *b* then?
1Co 5:6 Your *b* is not good
2Co 10:15 not *b* of things

BOASTS

Pr 25:14 Whoever *b* himself
2Co 10:17 "Let him who *b*,
Jas 3:5 and *b* great things

BODIES

Ro 8:23 redemption of our *b*
1Co 6:15 *b* are the parts of Christ?

BODY

Mt 10:28 those who kill the *b*
Mt 26:26 This is My *b*
Jn 2:21 the temple of His *b*
Ro 12:4 parts in one *b*
Ro 12:5 are one *b* in Christ
1Co 9:27 my *b* under subjection
1Co 11:24 *b* which is broken
1Co 12:13 baptized into one *b*
1Co 12:27 are the *b* of Christ
1Co 15:44 It is sown a natural *b*
1Pe 2:24 our sins in His own *b*

BOLD

1Sa 2:1 My mouth is *b*
Pr 28:1 *b* as a lion
2Co 10:2 not have to be *b*
1Th 2:2 *b* in our God

BOLDLY

Mk 15:43 went in *b* to Pilate,
Ac 14:3 speaking *b* for the Lord
Eph 6:19 open my mouth *b*

BOLDNESS

Ac 4:31 the word of God with *b*

BONDS

Ps 2:3 "Let us tear off their *b*

BONE

Ge 3:12 *b* of my bones
Pr 25:15 soft tongue breaks the *b*

BONES

Job 19:20 *b* cling to my skin
Ps 22:17 I can count all my *b*
Ps 31:10 and my *b* waste away
Ps 32:3 I kept silent, my *b*
Ecc 11:5 how the *b* grow
Eze 37:4 say to them, O dry *b*
Mt 23:27 of dead men's *b*
Jn 19:36 *b* shall be broken

BOOK

Gal 3:10 are written in the *B*
Rev 21:27 in the Lamb's *B*
Rev 22:18 the prophecy of this *b*

BOOKS

Ecc 12:12 making many *b*
Jn 21:25 contain the *b*
Rev 20:12 *B* were opened

BORN
Ecc 3:2 A time to be *b*
Isa 9:6 unto us a child is *b*
Mt 1:16 *b* Jesus, who is called
Jn 3:3 unless a man is *b* again
Jn 3:6 That which is *b*
1Pe 1:23 You have been *b* again
1Jn 4:7 who loves is *b* of God
1Jn 5:1 loves the one *b*

BOTTOMLESS
Rev 17:8 ascend out of the *b*
Rev 20:1 the key to the *b*

BOUGHT
Ge 17:12 household or *b* with money
Dt 32:6 father, who has *b*
Ac 7:16 tomb that Abraham had *b*
2Pe 2:1 denying the Lord who *b*

BOUND
Mt 16:19 on earth shall be *b*
Ro 7:2 a husband is *b*
Rev 20:2 Satan, and *b*

BOW
Ge 49:8 sons will *b* down
Ex 20:5 *b* down to them
Jos 24:12 sword or your *b*
Job 20:24 bronze *b* will pierce
Ps 37:14 have bent their *b*
Ps 44:6 not trust in my *b*
Mic 6:6 *b* down before God
Ro 14:11 shall *b* to Me
Php 2:10 every knee should *b*
Rev 6:2 He who sat on it had a *b*

BOWED
Ge 42:6 brothers came and *b*
Ex 4:31 *b* down and worshipped
2Ch 7:3 on the temple, and they *b*
Isa 2:11 haughtiness of men shall be *b*
Jn 19:30 *b* His head and gave

BOWLS
Rev 16:1 Go, pour out the *b*

BOWS
2Ch 26:14 armor, *b*, and slings
Isa 2:9 man *b* down,

BRANCH
Jer 23:5 David a righteous *B*
Zec 3:8 My servant, the *B*
Jn 15:2 *b* that bears fruit, He

BRANCHES
Ex 25:32 Six *b* shall go out
Ex 25:33 the six *b* that
Ex 25:35 a bud under two *b*
Ex 25:36 Their buds and their *b*

BRASS
1Co 13:1 become as sounding *b*

BRAVE
2Sa 13:28 Be strong and *b*
2Ch 32:7 Be strong and *b*.

BREAD
Ge 14:18 brought out *b*
Ex 23:15 shall eat unleavened *b*
Dt 8:3 not live by *b* alone
Pr 9:17 *b* eaten in secret is
Pr 20:17 *B* of deceit is sweet
Isa 55:2 that which is not *b*
Mt 4:3 stones be turned into *b*
Mt 4:4 not live by *b* alone
Mt 6:11 this day our daily *b*
Mt 26:26 eating, Jesus took *b*
Jn 6:48 I am the *b* of life
1Co 11:23 betrayed, took *b*

BREAK
Ac 20:7 together to *b* bread

BREASTS
SS 4:5 Your two *b* are like

BREATH
Ge 2:7 nostrils the *b* of life
1Ki 17:17 he had no *b*
Ps 144:4 Man is like a *b*
Ps 150:6 everything that has *b*
Eze 37:5 I will cause *b*
Ac 17:25 gives all men life and *b*
Rev 13:15 allowed to give *b*

BRIBE
Ex 23:8 you shall not take a *b*
Dt 16:19 *b* blinds the eyes

BRICK
Ex 5:7 people straw to make *b*

BRIDE
Rev 21:9 I will show you the *b*
Rev 22:17 the Spirit and the *b*

BRIDEGROOM
Isa 62:5 And as the *b* rejoices
Mt 9:15 mourn as long as the *b*
Mt 25:1 went out to meet the *b*
Jn 3:29 the friend of the *b*

BRIGHTER
Ac 26:13 a light from heaven, *b*

BRIGHTNESS
Isa 60:19 *b* shall the moon give
Eze 1:28 appearance of the *b*
2Th 2:8 destroy with the *b*
Heb 1:3 the *b* of His glory

BRIMSTONE
Ge 19:24 rained *b* and fire
Dt 29:23 the whole land is *b*
Rev 14:10 tormented with fire and *b*
Rev 19:20 fire that burns with *b*
Rev 20:10 lake of fire and *b*
Rev 21:8 burns with fire and *b*

BRING
Job 33:30 *b* back his soul
Isa 46:13 *b* My righteousness
Ro 8:33 Who shall *b* a charge
Ro 10:6 *b* Christ down
1Th 4:14 so God will *b*

BROAD
Mt 7:13 *b* is the way that

BROKEN
Mt 21:44 this stone will be *b*
Jn 10:35 Scripture cannot be *b*
1Co 11:24 body which is *b*

BROOK
Lev 23:40 and willows from a *b*
2Sa 15:23 crossing over the *b* Kidron
1Ki 18:40 the Kishon *b* and executed

BROTHER
Pr 17:17 a *b* is born for
Pr 18:24 sticks closer than a *b*
Isa 19:2 every one against his *b*
Jer 31:34 every man his *b*
Mt 5:22 angry with his *b*
Mt 10:21 *b* will deliver up the *b* to
Mt 18:15 if your *b* sins against you,
Lk 6:42 '*B*, let me remove the speck
Jn 11:23 "Your *b* will rise
Ac 9:17 he said, "*B* Saul
Ro 14:10 why do you despise your *b*
Phm 1:16 a beloved *b*
Jas 4:11 of his *b* and judges his *b*
1Jn 3:15 Whoever hates his *b* is

CARCASS
Jdg 14:9 honey out of a lion's *c*
Mt 24:28 Wherever the *c*

CARE
Lk 10:40 "Lord, do You not *c*
1Ti 3:5 how will he take *c*

CAREFULLY
Eph 5:15 then that you walk *c*

CARES
Ps 142:4 No one *c* for my soul
1Pe 5:7 because He *c* for you

CARNAL
Ro 8:7 *c* mind is hostile

CARNALLY
Ro 8:6 *c* minded is death

CARPENTER
Mk 6:3 Is this not the *c*

CARRY
Dt 28:38 You will *c* a lot of seed
1Ki 21:10 *c* him out and stone
Isa 40:11 with His arm, and *c*
Isa 41:16 and the wind shall *c*
Jer 39:7 him with chains to *c*
Jer 43:12 shall burn them and *c*

CARRYING
Mk 14:13 a man *c* a pitcher

CASE
Ac 25:14 Festus stated Paul's *c*

CAST
Ps 42:5 Why are you *c* down
Mk 16:17 My name they will *c*
Jn 6:37 will never *c* out
1Pe 5:7 *C* all your care
Rev 4:10 *c* their crowns before
Rev 12:9 the great dragon was *c*

CASTING
Mt 27:35 *c* lots to fulfill what was spoken
2Co 10:5 *c* down imaginations

CASTS
1Jn 4:18 perfect love *c* out

CATTLE
Ps 104:14 to grow for the *c*
Isa 46:1 beasts and the *c*
Jer 9:10 the lowing of the *c*

CAULDRON
Eze 11:3 this city is the *c*

CAUSE
Ps 25:3 who transgress without *c*
Jn 15:25 hated Me without a *c*

CAUSED
Ex 14:21 the LORD *c* the sea
2Ki 17:17 They *c* their sons
Ps 78:13 divided the sea and *c*
Isa 19:14 have *c* Egypt to err
Jer 29:14 the place from where I *c*
La 2:17 He has *c* the enemy

CAVES
Heb 11:38 in dens and *c* of the

CEASE
Ge 8:22 and night will not *c*
Ps 46:9 He makes wars *c*
1Co 13:8 tongues, they shall *c*

CEASING
1Th 5:17 pray without *c*

CELESTIAL
1Co 15:40 The glory of the *c*
Jude 1:8 and slander *c* beings

CERTIFICATE
Isa 50:1 Where is the *c* of divorce
Mk 10:4 a man to write a *c*

CHAFF
Isa 17:13 be chased as the *c*
Mt 3:12 He will burn up the *c*

CHAIN
Rev 20:1 pit and a great *c*

CHAINS
Ac 12:7 And the *c* fell off
Ac 26:29 am, except for these *c*

CHAMBERS
Ps 104:3 the upper beams of His *c*
Eze 8:12 every man in the *c*
Eze 40:16 windows in the little *c*
Eze 40:21 Its little *c*, three

CHAMPION
1Sa 17:4 There went out a *c*
Isa 19:20 a Savior and a *C*

CHANGE
Ps 102:26 You shall *c* them
Da 7:25 to *c* times and law
Mal 3:6 I am the LORD, I do not *c*

CHANGED
Nu 32:38 (their names being *c*
Jer 2:11 Has a nation *c* their
Da 7:28 and my countenance *c*
Ro 1:23 *c* the glory of the
1Co 15:51 but we shall all be *c*
Heb 1:12 and they will be *c*

CHARGE
Nu 1:53 Levites will keep the *c*
Nu 9:19 of Israel kept the *c*
Ps 91:11 shall give His angels *c*

CHARIOT
2Ki 2:11 a *c* of fire
Ps 46:9 He burns the *c* in
Ps 104:3 makes the clouds His *c*
Zec 9:10 will cut off the *c*

CHARIOTS
Ps 20:7 trust in *c*
Ps 68:17 The *c* of God are twice

CHARM
Pr 31:30 *C* is deceitful

CHEAT
Col 2:18 *c* you of your reward

CHEATING
Am 8:5 *c* with dishonest scales

CHEEK
Ps 3:7 my enemies on the *c*
Mt 5:39 on your right *c*

CHEERFUL
Pr 15:13 makes a *c* countenance
2Co 9:7 for God loves a *c*

CHERUBIM
Ge 3:24 the *c* and a flaming sword
Ex 25:18 you shall make two *c*
Ex 25:20 The *c* shall stretch
Ex 25:22 from between the two *c*
1Sa 4:4 dwells above the *c*
Ps 80:1 enthroned between the *c*
Ps 99:1 enthroned between the *c*
Heb 9:5 above the ark were the *c*

CHIEF
1Pe 2:6 Zion a *c* cornerstone
1Pe 5:4 when the *c* Shepherd appears

CHILDHOOD
2Ti 3:15 *c* you have known

CHILDLESS

Ge 15:2 give me, seeing I am *c*
Jer 22:30 Write down this man *c*

CHILDREN

Ge 15:3 not given me any *c*
Ge 21:7 Sarah would nurse *c*
Ge 31:43 these *c* are my *c*
Ge 32:11 the mothers with the *c*
Ge 33:1 So he divided the *c*
Ge 45:10 your *c* and your *c*'s *c*
Ex 1:17 kept the male *c* alive
Ex 12:26 your *c* shall say to you
Nu 13:28 we saw the *c* of Anak
Dt 11:19 teach them to your *c*
Jos 1:14 Your wives, your *c*
Ezr 6:19 *c* of the captivity
Ps 127:3 *c* are a gift
Pr 17:6 the glory of *c*
Pr 31:28 *c* rise up and call her
Ecc 6:3 fathers a hundred *c*
Isa 3:4 unweaned *c* shall rule
Mt 10:21 the *c* will rise up
Mt 18:3 and become like little *c*
Mt 19:14 "Let the little *c*
Mk 10:14 "Allow the little *c*
Lk 7:32 like *c* sitting in the
Jn 13:33 Little *c*, yet a little while
1Jn 3:2 now are we *c* of God

CHOOSE

Dt 30:19 therefore *c* life
Jn 15:16 You did not *c*

CHOSE

Ge 13:11 Lot *c* for himself
Eph 1:4 Just as He *c* us in Him

CHOSEN

Isa 43:10 servant whom I have *c*
Jn 13:18 whom I have *c*
1Co 1:27 *c* the foolish things
Jas 2:5 Has God not *c* the

CHRIST

Mt 1:18 the birth of Jesus *C*
Mt 16:16 You are the *C*
Mt 22:42 think of the *C*?
Mk 14:61 Are You the *C*
Lk 2:11 who is *C* the Lord
Lk 23:35 if He is the *C*
Jn 1:17 came through Jesus *C*
Jn 1:20 "I am not the *C*
Jn 4:29 Could this be the *C*?
Jn 7:31 When the *C* comes
Ac 2:38 name of Jesus *C*
Ac 16:18 in the name of Jesus *C*
Ac 17:3 *C* had to suffer
Ro 1:16 of the gospel of *C*
Ro 10:4 *C* is the end of the law
1Co 1:13 Is *C* divided?
1Co 1:23 we preach *c* crucified
1Co 10:16 of the blood of *C*
2Co 1:21 you in *C*
2Co 5:10 the judgment seat of *C*
2Co 10:1 gentleness of *C*
2Co 12:2 I knew a man in *c*
Gal 2:20 crucified with *C*
Gal 3:13 *C* has redeemed us
Gal 3:27 into *C* have put on *C*
Gal 6:14 cross of our Lord Jesus *C*
Eph 1:20 He performed in *C*
Eph 2:5 alive together with *C*
Eph 2:10 created in *C* Jesus
Eph 2:20 Jesus *C* Himself
Eph 3:19 the love of *C*
Eph 5:2 as *C* loved us
Eph 5:25 as *C* also loved
Php 2:11 confess that Jesus *C* is Lord
Php 4:13 all things because of *C*
Col 2:11 circumcision of *C*
1Th 4:16 And the dead in *C*
1Th 5:18 will of God in *C* Jesus
2Th 2:1 coming of our Lord Jesus *C*
1Ti 1:15 *C* Jesus came
2Ti 2:3 soldier of Jesus *C*
Titus 2:13 and Savior Jesus *C*
Heb 3:1 our profession, Jesus *C*
Heb 6:1 doctrine of *C*
Heb 9:28 *C* was offered once
Heb 13:8 Jesus *C* is the same
1Pe 1:2 with the blood of Jesus *C*
1Pe 4:13 you share in *C*'s sufferings
2Pe 1:16 of our Lord Jesus *C*
1Jn 1:7 the blood of Jesus *C*
1Jn 4:2 Jesus *C* has come
2Jn 1:9 in the teaching of *C*
Jude 1:21 mercy of our Lord Jesus *C*
Rev 1:5 from Jesus *C*
Rev 20:4 and reigned with *C*
Rev 20:6 priests of God and of *C*

CHRISTIAN

Ac 26:28 persuade me to be a *C*
1Pe 4:16 suffers as a *C*

CHRISTIANS

Ac 11:26 first called *c* in Antioch

CHRISTS

Mt 24:24 false *c* and false prophets

CHURCH

Mt 16:18 I will build My *c*
Mt 18:17 tell it to the *c*
Ac 2:47 added to the *c* daily
Ac 5:11 fear came on the entire *c*
Ac 8:3 But Saul ravaged the *c*
Ac 14:23 in every *c*, with prayer
Ac 15:3 sent on their way by the *c*
Ac 15:4 welcomed by the *c*
Ac 20:28 to shepherd the *c* of God
Rom 16:5 Likewise greet the *c*
1Co 11:22 do you despise the *c* of God
1Co 12:28 put these in the *c*
1Co 14:4 prophesies edifies the *c*
Gal 1:13 persecuted the *c* of God
Eph 3:10 made known by the *c*
Eph 3:21 glory in the *c*
Eph 5:24 as the *c* submits
Col 1:18 the body, the *c*
1Ti 3:5 take care of the *c* of God
Jas 5:14 call for the elders of the *c*
1Pe 5:13 The *c* that is at Babylon
3Jn 1:6 your love before the *c*
Rev 2:1 angel of the *c* of Ephesus

CHURCHES

Rev 1:4 John, To the seven *c*
Rev 1:11 *c* which are in Asia
Rev 2:7 Spirit says to the *c*
Rev 2:17 Spirit says to the *c*
Rev 2:23 *c* shall know that I
Rev 22:16 testimony for the *c*

CIRCLE

Isa 40:22 who sits upon the *c*

CIRCUMCISE

Ge 17:11 shall *c* the flesh
Dt 10:16 *c* your heart
Lk 1:59 they came to *c* the child

CIRCUMCISED

Ge 17:10 among you shall be *c*
Ge 34:22 will be *c* as they are *c*
Lev 12:3 his foreskin shall be *c*
Lk 2:21 the Child was *c*
Ac 11:2 those who were *c*
Ro 3:30 who shall justify the *c*
Ro 4:9 come upon the *c* only

COMPLETE
Col 2:10 and you are *c* in Him
2Ti 3:17 of God may be *c*

COMPREHEND
Job 37:5 that we cannot *c*
Ecc 8:17 a man cannot *c* the work

conceit
Php 2:3 strife or *c*

CONCEITED
Gal 5:26 Let us not be *c*

CONCEIVE
Isa 7:14 the virgin shall *c*
Lk 1:31 Listen, you will *c*

CONCLUSION
Ecc 12:13 Let us hear the *c*

CONDEMN
Job 9:20 my own mouth would *c* me
Jn 3:17 to *c* the world

CONDEMNATION
Ro 3:8 Their *c* is just
Ro 8:1 therefore now no *c*

CONDEMNED
Jn 3:18 does not believe is *c*
Ro 8:3 *c* sin in the flesh

CONDEMNS
Job 15:6 Your own mouth *c* you
Ro 8:34 Who is he who *c*

CONDUCT
Php 1:27 let your *c* be worthy
1Pe 3:16 accuse your good *c*

CONFESS
Ps 32:5 *c* my transgressions
Ro 10:9 that if you *c* with
Ro 14:11 every tongue shall *c*
1Jn 1:9 If we *c* our sins

CONFESSED
Ne 9:2 *c* their sins and the iniquities
Jn 9:22 *c* that He was the Christ

CONFESSES
Pr 28:13 whoever *c* and forsakes them
1Jn 4:15 *c* that Jesus is the

CONFESSION
Ro 10:10 with the mouth *c*
Heb 4:14 hold firmly to our *c*

CONFIDENCE
Isa 30:15 *c* shall be your
Php 3:4 I also have *c*

CONFORMED
Ro 8:29 predestined to be *c*
Ro 12:2 Do not be *c*

CONFUSE
Ge 11:7 *c* their language

CONFUSION
Ac 19:29 was filled with *c*

CONGREGATION
Ex 12:6 *c* of Israel shall kill
Ex 12:19 cut off from the *c*
Lev 4:13 the whole *c* of Israel
Lev 4:21 offering of the *c*
Lev 24:16 death, and the entire *c*
Nu 1:53 no wrath on the *c*

CONQUERING
Rev 6:2 *c* that he might

CONQUERORS
Ro 8:37 we are more than *c*

CONSCIENCE
Jn 8:9 convicted by their *c*
Ac 24:16 strive to have a clear *c*
1Pe 3:21 a good *c* through the

CONSIDER
Ps 8:3 When I *c* Your heavens
Isa 1:3 My people do not *c*
Mt 6:28 *C* the lilies of the
Lk 12:24 *C* the ravens
Heb 12:3 *c* Him who endured

CONSOLATION
2Th 2:16 us eternal *c*

CONSUME
Jn 2:17 Your house will *c* Me
2Th 2:8 whom the Lord will *c*

CONSUMED
Lev 9:24 before the LORD, and it *c*
Nu 16:35 from the LORD and *c*
1Ki 18:38 the LORD fell and *c*
2Ki 1:12 from heaven and *c*
2Ch 7:1 from the heavens and *c* the burnt

CONSUMING
Dt 4:24 the Lord your God is a *c* fire
Heb 12:29 our God is a *c* fire

CONTENT
Php 4:11 state I am to be *c*
Heb 13:5 money, and be *c*

CONTENTMENT
1Ti 6:6 *c* is great gain

CONTINUALLY
Ex 28:30 before the LORD *c*
Lev 24:8 *c* before the LORD
2Sa 15:12 people with Absalom was *c*
Isa 51:13 and have feared *c* every
Heb 10:1 offer *c* year after year
Heb 13:15 let us *c* offer to God

CONTINUE
Ro 6:1 Shall we *c* in sin
Col 4:2 *C* in prayer
Heb 13:1 Let brotherly love *c*

CONTINUED
Lk 6:12 mountain to pray and *c*
Ac 1:14 all *c* with one accord
Ac 20:7 and *c* his message until

CONTRARY
Lev 26:40 they have walked *c*
Lev 26:41 also have walked *c*
Ac 17:7 all acting *c* to the decrees
1Ti 1:10 is *c* to sound doctrine

CONVERSION
Ac 15:3 declaring the *c*

CONVICTS
Jn 8:46 Which of you *c*

COOL
Lk 16:24 and *c* my tongue

CORD
Jos 2:18 this red *c*
Ecc 4:12 *c* is not quickly broken

CORDS
Pr 5:22 snared in the *c* of his sins
Jn 2:15 made a whip of *c*

CORNERSTONE
Mt 21:42 become the *c*
1Pe 2:6 in Zion a chief *c*

CORRECT
Job 6:26 Do you mean to *c* my words
Pr 29:17 *C* your son

CORRECTED
Pr 29:19 A servant will not be *c* by words
Heb 12:9 fathers, and they *c*

CORRUPT
Ge 6:11 earth was *c*
Ps 14:1 They are *c*
Mt 7:17 a *c* tree bears evil fruit
1Ti 6:5 by men of *c* minds

CORRUPTED
Ge 6:12 for all flesh had *c*
Ex 8:24 land was *c*
2Co 7:2 we have *c* no one
Jas 5:2 Your riches are *c*

CORRUPTION
Ps 16:10 Your godly one to see *c*
Ac 2:31 nor did His flesh see *c*
1Co 15:50 *c* inherit incorruption
2Pe 1:4 and escape the *c*

COST
Nu 16:38 at the *c* of their own lives
Lk 14:28 and count the *c*

COUNSEL
Ps 1:1 who walks not in the *c*
Ps 55:14 We took pleasant *c*
Ps 73:24 guide me with Your *c*
Eph 1:11 according to the *c*
Heb 6:17 immutability of His *c*
Rev 3:18 I *c* you to buy from

COUNTED
Jos 13:3 Ekron, which is *c*
Isa 32:15 fruitful field is *c*
Ro 9:8 of the promise are *c*
1Ti 5:17 rule well be *c* worthy

COUNTRIES
Jer 23:8 *c* where I had driven
Jer 32:37 *c* wherever I have driven
Eze 20:41 gather you out of the *c*
Eze 34:13 gather them from the *c*
Eze 36:24 gather you out of all *c*
Da 9:7 *c* wherever You have

COUNTRY
Ge 12:1 "Go from your *c*
Heb 11:16 *c*, that is, a heavenly

COURAGE
Dt 31:6 strong and of a good *c*
2Sa 4:1 his *c* failed

COURT
Lev 6:16 in the *c* of the tent
Lev 6:26 be eaten in the *c*
Jer 26:2 *c* of the house of the Lord
Jer 32:2 was shut up in the *c*
Jer 37:21 Jeremiah into the *c*
Jer 38:6 Hammelech that was in the *c*
Eze 8:16 *c* of the house of the Lord
Rev 11:2 But exclude the *c*

COVENANT
Ge 6:18 I will establish My *c*
Ge 15:18 made a *c* with Abram
Ge 17:9 you shall keep My *c*
Ex 19:5 keep My *c*
Dt 31:9 bore the ark of the *c*
Jer 31:31 I will make a new *c*
Eze 34:25 a *c* of peace
Mt 26:28 My blood of the new *c*

COVENANTS
Ro 9:4 the glory, the *c*
Gal 4:24 for these are the two c

COVER
Ps 91:4 He shall *c* you with
Jas 5:20 *c* a multitude of sins

COVERING
Ex 25:20 upward, *c* the mercy seat
Nu 4:15 have finished *c* the sanctuary
Eze 28:13 precious stone was your *c*

COVERED
Ps 32:1 whose sin is *c*
Ps 85:2 *c* all their sin
Mt 10:26 For nothing is *c*

COVET
Ex 20:17 shall not *c* your
Dt 5:21 nor shall you *c*
Pr 12:12 The wicked *c*
Mic 2:2 They *c* fields and
Ro 7:7 "You shall not *c*
Ro 13:9 You shall not *c*
1Co 12:31 earnestly *c* the greater gifts

COVETED
Jos 7:21 fifty shekels, I *c* them
Ac 20:33 I have not *c* anyone's

COVETING
Ro 7:8 in me all kinds of *c*
1Ti 6:10 While *c* after money

COVETS
Pr 21:26 He *c* greedily

COWARDLY
Rev 21:8 the *c*, the unbelieving

CRAFTINESS
Job 5:13 catches the wise in their own *c*
Eph 4:14 men, by *c* with

CREATE
Ps 51:10 *C* in me a clean heart
Isa 45:18 who did not *c* it
Isa 65:17 For I *c* new heavens
2Ti 2:23 that they *c* strife

CREATED
Ge 1:1 God *c* the heavens
Ge 1:27 God *c* man in His
Ge 2:3 work which He had *c*
Ge 5:2 He *c* them male and
Ge 6:7 man, whom I have *c*
Dt 4:32 the day that God *c*
Ps 104:30 Your Spirit, they are *c*
Isa 43:1 who *c* you, O Jacob
Isa 45:12 earth and *c* man on it
Jer 31:22 has *c* a new thing in the
Eze 21:30 where you were *c*
Eze 28:15 that you were *c*
Mk 13:19 creation which God *c*
Jn 1:3 nothing was *c* that was *c*
Jn 1:10 the world was *c*
Ro 8:39 nor any other *c* thing
1Co 11:9 was not *c* for the woman
2Co 5:5 He who has *c* us
Eph 2:10 *c* in Christ Jesus
Eph 4:24 was *c* according to God
Col 1:16 all things were *c*
1Ti 4:4 For everything *c* by God
Heb 9:26 since the world was *c*
Heb 12:27 things that are *c*
Rev 4:11 You have *c* all things

CREATES
Am 4:13 and *c* the wind

CREATION
Ro 8:22 know that the whole *c*
Gal 6:15 anything, but a new *c*

CREATOR
Ge 14:19 *C* of heaven and earth
Ecc 12:1 remember your *C*
Isa 27:11 their *c* will show them
Isa 40:28 the Lord, the *c* of the
Isa 43:15 the *c* of Israel, your King
Ac 3:15 killed the *c* of Life
Ro 1:25 creature rather than the *C*

1Pe 4:19 their souls to a faithful *C*

CREATURE

Ge 2:19 every living *c*, that was
Ge 9:10 with every living *c*
Lev 17:14 the life of every *c* is
Job 41:33 a *c* made without fear
Mk 16:15 to every *c*
Ac 28:4 natives saw the *c*
Ro 1:25 served the *c*
2Co 5:17 he is a new *c*
Col 1:15 the firstborn of every *c*
Heb 4:13 is no *c* that is not
Rev 4:7 The first living *c*
Rev 6:3 the second living *c* say
Rev 16:3 living *c* in the sea

CREATURES

Ge 1:20 swarms of living *c*
Ge 1:21 God created great sea *c*
Ge 1:24 earth bring forth living *c*
Ps 50:11 the *c* that move in
Ps 104:24 earth is full of Your *c*
Eze 1:5 the likeness of four living *c*
Eze 1:14 The living *c* ran to and fro
Eze 3:13 of the wings of the living *c*
Eze 10:17 the spirit of the living *c*
Ac 11:6 saw four-footed *c*
Jas 1:18 first fruits of His *c*
Rev 5:6 and of the four living *c*
Rev 6:1 I heard one of the four living *c* saying
Rev 8:9 third of the living *c*
Rev 14:3 four living *c* and the elders
Rev 19:4 four living *c* fell down

CREDIT

1Pe 2:20 For what *c* is it if

CRIED

Ex 14:10 the children of Israel *c* out
Job 29:12 the poor who *c*

CRIMES

Eze 7:23 land is full of bloody *c*

CROOKED

Isa 45:2 make the *c* places straight
Php 2:15 midst of a *c* and perverse

CROSS

Ge 31:52 so that I will not *c* over
Dt 4:21 I should not *c* over
Dt 31:3 God will *c* over before you
Mt 16:24 and take up his *c*
Mt 27:40 come down from the *c*
Lk 23:26 laid the *c* on him
Jn 19:19 and put it on the *c*
1Co 1:17 the *c* of Christ should
Gal 5:11 the offense of the *c*
Eph 2:16 one body through the *c*
Php 2:8 even death on a *c*
Col 2:15 over them by the *c*

CROWD

Ex 23:2 agrees with the *c*

CROWN

Ps 65:11 *c* the year with Your
Mt 27:29 they wove a *c*
1Co 9:25 obtain a corruptible *c*
2Ti 4:8 From now on a *c*
Rev 14:14 on his head a golden *c*

CROWNED

Ps 8:5 angels, and *c*
Pr 14:18 prudent are *c* with knowledge

CRUCIFIED

Mt 26:2 be betrayed to be *c*
Mt 27:22 "Let Him be *c*!"
Mt 28:5 for Jesus who was *c*
Mk 15:25 and they *c* Him
Jn 19:16 over to them to be *c*
Ac 2:36 whom you have *c*
Ro 6:6 man has been *c* with Him
1Co 1:13 Was Paul *c* for
1Co 1:23 we preach Christ *c*
Gal 2:20 I have been *c* with Christ
Gal 6:14 the world is *c* to me

CRUCIFY

Mt 20:19 to *c* Him, but on
Mk 15:13 cried out, "*C* Him!"
Heb 6:6 they again *c* to themselves

CRY

Ex 2:23 and their *c* came up to
Pr 8:1 Does not wisdom *c*
Mt 25:6 at midnight there was a *c*
Lk 18:7 patient with them, who *c*

CUP

Ps 23:5 My *c* runs over
Mt 26:27 Then He took the *c*
Mt 26:39 possible, let this *c*
Lk 22:20 *c* is the new covenant
1Co 10:21 cannot drink the *c*
1Co 11:25 *c* is the new

CURSE

Ge 8:21 *c* the ground
Job 2:9 *C* God and die
Mal 2:2 I will send a *c*
Gal 3:10 law are under the *c*

CURSED

Ge 3:14 *c* above all livestock
Mt 25:41 from Me, you *c*

CURSES

Ge 12:3 and curse him who *c*
Ex 21:17 He who *c* his father

curtain

Ps 104:2 the heavens like a tent *c*
Mt 27:51 the *c* of the temple was torn

D

DAILY

Mt 6:11 Give us this day our *d*
Lk 9:23 take up his cross *d*
Ac 17:11 with all eagerness, *d*

DANCE

Ecc 3:4 and a time to *d*
Jer 31:13 rejoice in the *d*
Mt 11:17 and you did not *d*

DANCED

2Sa 6:14 David *d* before the LORD
Mt 14:6 daughter of Herodias *d*

DANCES

1Sa 29:5 sing for in *d* saying

DANCING

Ex 15:20 timbrels and with *d*
Ex 32:19 the calf and the *d*
2Sa 6:16 leaping and *d*
Ps 30:11 my mourning into *d*
Ps 149:3 His name with *d*
La 5:15 *d* has turned into
Lk 15:25 heard music and *d*

DARE

Ro 5:7 some would even *d*

DARK

2Pe 1:19 shines in a *d* place

DARKENED

Isa 5:30 light is *d* by the clouds

DESCENDED
Eph 4:10 He who *d* is also He
Heb 7:14 our Lord *d* from Judah

DESCENDING
Jn 1:51 God ascending and *d*
Rev 21:10 Holy City Jerusalem, *d*

DESERT
Isa 35:1 *d* shall rejoice
Mt 24:26 'Look, He is in the *d*

DESIRE
Ge 3:16 Your *d* will be for your
Est 6:6 the king *d* to honor
Ps 21:2 given him his heart's *d*
Ps 40:6 offering You did not *d*
Ps 51:6 You *d* truth in the inward
Ps 73:25 earth that I *d* besides
Ps 145:19 He will fulfill the *d* of
Pr 13:12 but when the *d* comes
SS 8:6 fires of *d* are as ardent
Isa 58:3 fast you find your *d*
Mt 9:13 means, 'I *d* mercy
Jn 15:7 ask whatever you *d*
Ro 7:19 For the good I *d* to do
Ro 10:1 my heart's *d* and prayer
1Co 14:1 after love and *d*
Gal 6:12 who *d* to make a good
Col 3:1 *d* those things which
Col 3:5 affection, evil *d*, and
1Ti 2:8 I *d* that the men pray
2Ti 3:12 who *d* to live a godly
Jas 4:2 You *d* to have and
1Pe 2:2 As newborn babies, *d*
Rev 9:6 will *d* to die, but death

DESIRED
Ps 19:10 *d* are they than gold
Lk 22:15 "I have earnestly *d* to eat

desires
Ps 37:4 will give you the *d*
Jn 8:44 do the *d* of your father

DESOLATE
Lev 26:33 your land shall be *d*
Isa 3:26 she, being *d*, shall sit
Isa 6:11 land is utterly *d*
Isa 13:22 cry in their *d* houses
Isa 62:4 your land be termed *D*
Jer 4:7 to make your land *d*

DESOLATION
Jer 25:11 land shall be a *d*
Jer 25:18 to make them a *d*
Jer 49:13 *d*, a reproach, a waste
Jer 49:17 Edom will become a *d*
Zep 2:9 and a perpetual *d*
Zep 2:15 a *d*, a place for beasts
Mt 24:15 'abomination of *d*,' spoken

DESPISE
Mt 6:24 one and *d* the other
Ro 2:4 *d* the riches of His

DESPISED
Isa 53:3 He was *d* and rejected
1Co 1:28 things which are *d*

DESTROY
Ge 6:13 Now I will *d* them
Ge 18:23 also *d* the righteous
Ex 12:13 be upon you to *d* you
Dt 7:5 You shall *d* their
2Sa 1:14 your hand to *d* thc
Est 3:6 sought to *d* all the
Est 9:24 the Jews to *d* them
Ps 5:6 You will *d* those who
Ps 88:16 Your terrors *d* me
Ps 106:34 not *d* the nations
Pr 15:25 The LORD will *d*
Isa 13:9 and He shall *d* its
Isa 65:25 not hurt nor *d* in all
Jer 1:10 *d* and to throw down
Eze 6:3 and I will *d* your
Da 8:24 he shall *d* wonderfully
Zec 12:9 I will seek to *d*
Mt 6:20 moth nor rust *d*
Mt 10:28 who is able to *d*
Mk 1:24 Have You come to *d*
Mk 15:29 would *d* the temple
Lk 9:56 not come to *d*
Jn 2:19 *D* this temple, and
1Co 1:19 I will *d* the wisdom
Heb 2:14 death He might *d* him
Rev 11:18 and to *d* those who *d*

DESTROYED
Ge 19:17 lest you be *d*
Dt 28:61 until you are *d*
Est 4:14 house shall be *d*
Job 4:9 anger they are *d*
Ps 37:38 will be *d* together
Pr 13:13 the word will be *d*
Jer 12:10 have *d* My vineyard
Jer 51:8 suddenly fallen and *d*
Da 7:11 slain, and his body *d*
Am 4:11 *d* some of you, as God *d*
Lk 5:37 wineskins will be *d*
Ro 11:3 and *d* Your altars
1Co 15:26 will be *d* is death
2Co 4:9 cast down, but not *d*
2Pe 3:10 the elements will be *d*
Rev 8:9 of the ships were *d*

DESTROYING
Isa 28:2 hail and a *d* storm
Jer 51:25 you, O *d* mountain

DESTROYS
Pr 6:32 *d* his own soul
Lk 12:33 near and no moth *d*

DESTRUCTION
Jos 6:17 to the LORD for *d*
Jos 7:11 things dedicated for *d*
Job 31:3 Does not *d* belong
Ps 107:20 them from their *d*
Pr 10:14 the foolish is near *d*
Isa 10:23 make a complete *d*
Isa 59:7 Devastation and *d*
Jer 4:20 *D* upon *d* is proclaimed
Da 11:33 captivity and by *d*
Mt 7:13 way that leads to *d*
2Th 1:9 with eternal *d*
Heb 10:39 draw back to *d*
2Pe 3:7 Judgment and *d*

DETERMINED
Da 9:24 "Seventy weeks have been *d*
Da 9:26 desolations are *d*
Da 11:36 for that which is *d*

DEVIL
Mt 4:1 tempted by the *d*
Jn 8:44 your father the *d*
Eph 4:27 place to the *d*
Jas 4:7 Resist the *d*, and
1Pe 5:8 the *d* walks around
Rev 20:2 is the *D* and Satan

DEVOUR
Mt 23:14 you *d* widows'
Gal 5:15 bite and *d* one another
1Pe 5:8 whom he may *d*
Rev 12:4 *d* her Child as

DEVOURED
Ge 37:20 evil beast has *d*
Mt 13:4 birds came and *d* them
Rev 20:9 of heaven and *d* them

DEW
Dt 33:28 will rain down *d*
1Ki 17:1 *d* or rain these years
Ps 133:3 as the *d* of Hermon
Isa 26:19 your *d* is as the *d* of
Da 4:25 wet with the *d*
Hos 14:5 I will be like the *d*

DIADEMS
Rev 12:3 ten horns, and seven *d*

DIAMOND
Jer 17:1 *d* point; it is engraved

DIE
Ge 2:17 it you will surely *d*
Ps 118:17 I shall not *d*
Ecc 3:2 born, and a time to *d*
Jn 6:50 eat of it and not *d*
Jn 8:24 to you that you will *d*
Jn 11:25 though he may *d*
Jn 11:50 one man should *d*
Ro 8:13 the flesh, you will *d*
1Co 15:22 For as in Adam all *d*
Php 1:21 and to *d* is gain
2Ti 2:11 if we *d* with Him
Heb 9:27 for men to *d* once
Rev 14:13 are the dead who *d*

DIED
Ge 7:21 moved on the earth *d*
Ro 5:6 in due time Christ *d*
Ro 5:8 Christ *d* for us
Ro 6:8 Now if we *d* with
2Co 5:15 and He *d* for all

DILIGENT
Pr 10:4 *d* makes rich
Pr 12:24 The hand of the *d* will rule

DIM
Dt 34:7 His eye was not *d*

DIMLY
1Co 13:12 through a glass *d*

DIP
Ru 2:14 *d* your piece

DISARMED
Col 2:15 *d* authorities

DISCIPLE
Am 7:14 I am no prophet's *d*
Mt 10:24 The *d* is not above
Mt 10:42 in the name of a *d*
Lk 6:40 The *d* is not above
Lk 14:26 he cannot be My *d*
Jn 9:28 You are His *d*
Jn 18:15 another *d*. That *d* was
Jn 19:38 being a *d* of Jesus
Jn 20:2 and to the other *d*
Jn 21:23 brothers that this *d*
Ac 9:10 A *d* named Ananias
Ac 9:26 believing he was a *d*
Ac 9:36 a *d* named Tabitha
Ac 11:29 Then every *d*
Ac 16:1 A *d* was there

DISCIPLED
Mt 13:52 scribe who is *d*

DISCIPLES
Isa 8:16 among My *d*
Mt 5:1 His *d* came to Him
Mt 10:1 His twelve *d* to Him
Mt 12:1 His *d* were hungry
Mt 14:19 His *d*; and the *d* gave
Mt 14:26 when the *d* saw Him
Mt 16:21 to show His *d*
Mt 21:1 then Jesus sent two *d*
Mt 26:26 and gave it to the *d*
Mt 28:19 and make *d* of all
Mk 8:33 and looked at His *d*
Mk 14:14 Passover with My *d*
Lk 5:33 Why do the *d*
Jn 3:25 some of John's *d*
Jn 4:1 baptizing more *d*
Jn 13:5 to wash the *d'* feet
Jn 15:8 you will be My *d*
Jn 20:19 being locked where the *d*
Ac 1:15 among the *d*
Ac 6:1 in those days, as the *d*
Ac 11:26 the *d* were first
Ac 14:22 the minds of the *d*
Ac 20:7 when the *d* came

DISCIPLINE
Dt 11:2 have not seen the *d*
Job 5:17 do not despise *d*
Ps 6:1 nor *d* me in the heat
Eph 6:4 bring them up in the *d*
Heb 12:5 do not despise the *d*
Rev 3:19 I rebuke and *d*

DISCIPLINED
Dt 21:18 when they have *d*
Hos 10:10 they are *d* for their
1Co 11:32 we are *d* by the Lord
Heb 12:10 they indeed *d* us

DISCOURAGED
Nu 32:9 *d* the hearts of the children
Col 3:21 lest they be *d*

DISHONEST
Ex 18:21 hating *d* gain
Lk 16:8 commended the *d*
1Pe 5:2 not for *d* gain

DISHONOR
Jn 8:49 Father, and you *d* Me
Ro 1:24 *d* their own bodies among
1Co 15:43 It is sown in *d*

DISMAYED
Dt 31:8 Do not fear, nor be *d*
Jos 1:9 Do not be afraid or *d*
1Ch 22:13 Do not be afraid or *d*
Isa 21:3 I am so *d* at the seeing
Isa 41:10 do not be *d*
Jer 1:17 Do not be *d* at their faces
Jer 30:10 nor be *d*, O Israel

DISPLEASE
Pr 24:18 Lord see it, and it *d*

DISPLEASED
Mk 10:14 it, He was very *d*

DISTINCTION
Ac 15:9 and made no *d* between
Ro 3:22 for there is no *d*
Ro 10:12 no *d* between Jew

DISTRESS
Dt 28:53 during the siege and *d*
Dt 28:55 because of the siege and the *d*
Dt 28:57 during the siege and *d*
Ps 18:6 In my *d* I called on
Ps 120:1 In my *d* I cried unto
Isa 25:4 needy in his *d*, a refuge

DITCH
Mt 15:14 will fall into the *d*

DIVIDE
Pr 16:19 *d* the spoil with the
Lk 22:17 "Take this and *d*

DIVIDED
Ex 14:21 the waters were *d*
Ps 68:12 at home *d* the spoil
Mt 12:25 "Every kingdom *d*
1Co 1:13 Is Christ *d*

DIVIDES
La 4:4 no one *d* it

DIVIDING
Eph 2:14 the barrier of the *d* wall
2Ti 2:15 rightly *d* the word of

DIVISIONS
Ro 16:17 those who cause *d*
Jude 1:19 men who cause *d*

DIVORCE
Dt 24:1 write her a bill of *d*
Mal 2:16 says that He hates *d*
Mk 10:2 man to *d* his wife
1Co 7:11 husband *d* his wife

DO
Mt 7:12 men to *d* to you, *d*
Jn 5:19 He sees the Father *d*
Jn 15:5 without Me you can *d*
Ac 16:30 "Sirs, what must I *d*

Mt 10:14 city, shake off the *d*
1Co 15:49 of the man of *d*

DWELL
Isa 57:15 I *d* in the high and
Eph 3:17 that Christ may *d*
Rev 21:3 men, and He will *d*

DWELLING
Eph 2:22 built together into a *d*
Heb 11:9 a foreign land, *d*

DWELLS
Ps 91:1 He who *d* in the shelter
2Pe 3:13 which righteousness *d*
Rev 2:13 you, where Satan *d*

E

EAGLE
Dt 14:12 cannot eat: the *e*
Pr 30:19 the way of an *e*
Eze 1:10 and the face of an *e*
Mic 1:16 as bald as the *e*
Rev 4:7 like a flying *e*
Rev 12:14 wings of a great *e*

EAGLE'S
Ps 103:5 renewed like the *e*

EAGLES
Isa 40:31 with wings as *e*
Mt 24:28 there the *e* will be

EAR
Ex 15:26 and give *e*
Dt 15:17 through his *e* into
Ps 5:1 Give *e* to my words,
Pr 4:20 incline your *e* to my
Lk 12:3 in the *e* in private
Lk 22:51 touched his *e*
Rev 2:7 He who has an *e*

EARLY
Mk 16:2 Very *e* in the morning
Lk 24:22 arrived *e* at the tomb

EARNESTLY
Lk 22:44 He prayed more *e*
Jas 5:17 *e* that it might not

EARS
Ge 41:7 seven thin *e* devoured
Dt 29:4 and *e* to hear
2Ch 6:40 Your *e* attentive
Ps 135:17 have *e*, but do not hear
Isa 6:10 and their *e* heavy
Mt 11:15 He who has *e*
Ac 7:51 in heart and *e*
2Ti 4:3 having itching *e*

EARTH
Ge 1:2 The *e* was formless
Ge 6:11 The *e* was corrupt
Ge 7:12 rain fell upon the *e*
Ex 20:11 made heaven and *e*
Job 26:7 He hangs the *e*
Ps 8:1 name in all the *e*
Ps 96:1 LORD, all the *e*
Pr 3:19 founded the *e*
Isa 6:3 The whole *e*
Isa 24:1 makes the *e* empty
Isa 40:22 circle of the *e*
Isa 65:17 heavens and a new *e*
Jer 10:10 wrath the *e* trembles
Da 7:17 arise out of the *e*
Joel 2:30 heavens and the *e*
Mt 5:5 inherit the *e*
Mt 18:18 bind on *e* will be
1Co 10:26 "The *e* is the Lord's
Heb 11:13 pilgrims on the *e*
2Pe 3:10 intense heat. The *e*
Rev 6:4 peace from the *e*
Rev 14:16 on the *e*, and the *e*
Rev 21:1 heaven and a new *e*."

EARTHLY
Jn 3:12 If I have told you *e*
2Co 5:1 that if our *e* house
Php 3:19 minds are set on *e* things
Jas 3:15 from above, but is *e*

EARTHQUAKE
1Ki 19:11 after the wind, an *e*
Mt 28:2 there was a great *e*

EARTHQUAKES
Mk 13:8 And there will be *e*

EASIER
Mk 2:9 Which is *e* to say
Mk 10:25 It is *e* for a camel

EAST
Ge 12:8 *e* of Bethel and pitched
Ge 28:14 west and to the *e*
Ex 14:21 back by a strong *e*
Nu 23:7 mountains of the *e*
Jdg 6:3 people from the *e*
Isa 11:14 plunder the sons of the *e*

EAT
Ge 2:16 you may freely *e*
Ge 3:17 'You shall not *e*
Eze 3:1 *E* this scroll
Mt 6:25 life, what you will *e*
Jn 6:52 give us His flesh to *e*
Ro 14:2 one has faith to *e*
Ro 14:21 *e* meat nor drink wine
1Co 8:13 I will never *e*
2Th 3:10 neither shall he *e*

EATS
Lk 15:2 receives sinners and *e*
Jn 6:54 Whoever *e* My flesh
Jn 6:58 *e* this bread will live
Ro 14:6 He who *e*, *e* in honor
1Co 11:29 For he who *e*

EDEN
Ge 2:8 garden in the east, in *E*
Eze 28:13 You were in *E*

EDGE
Nu 21:24 defeated him with the *e*
Jos 19:47 attacked it with the *e*
Jer 21:7 strike them with the *e*
Lk 21:24 will fall by the *e*

EIGHTH
Lev 12:3 On the *e* day the flesh
Lev 14:10 On the *e* day he
Lev 23:36 *e* day it shall be a holy
1Ki 12:32 ordained a feast in the *e*
2Ki 24:12 the *e* year of his reign
2Ch 7:9 *e* day they made a solemn

ELDER
Isa 9:15 The *e* and honorable
1Ti 5:1 Do not rebuke an *e*,

ELDERS
Ex 3:16 Go, and gather the *e*
Pr 31:23 the *e* of the land
La 1:19 *e* perished in the city
Mt 15:2 tradition of the *e*
Ac 14:23 appointed *e* for them
Ac 20:17 the *e* of the church
1Ti 5:17 Let the *e* who rule
Jas 5:14 Let him call for the *e*
Rev 4:4 twenty-four *e* sitting
Rev 5:8 twenty-four *e* fell

ELECT
Mt 24:31 gather His *e* from
Ro 11:7 *e* obtained it
1Pe 1:2 *e* according to the
1Pe 2:6 a chief cornerstone, *e*

ELECTION
Ro 9:11 according to *e* might stand
2Pe 1:10 calling and *e* sure

ELEMENTS
2Pe 3:10 *e* will be destroyed

ELIJAH
1Ki 18:27 By noon, *E* mocked
1Ki 19:19 *E* passed by him

ETERNAL
Isa 9:6 Mighty God, *E* Father,
Mt 25:46 into *e* punishment,
Lk 10:25 to inherit *e* life
Jn 3:16 but have *e* life
1Ti 6:12 Lay hold on *e* life,
1Jn 3:15 no murderer has *e* life

ETERNITY
Isa 57:15 One who inhabits *e*

EUNUCH
Ac 8:27 of Ethiopia, a *e*

EUNUCHS
Isa 56:4 the *e* who keep My Sabbaths
Mt 19:12 there are some *e*

EVANGELIST
Ac 21:8 house of Philip the *e*
2Ti 4:5 do the work of an *e*

EVANGELISTS
Eph 4:11 apostles, prophets, *e*

EVENING
Ex 12:6 shall kill it in the *e*
Ex 27:21 shall arrange it from *e*
2Ki 16:15 the *e* grain offering
2Ch 13:11 every morning and *e*
Ps 141:2 my hands as the *e* sacrifice
Da 8:26 the vision of the *e*

EVERLASTING
Isa 63:16 Your name is from *e*
Da 12:2 awake, some to *e* life

EVIL
Ge 2:9 of good and *e*
Dt 7:15 none of the *e* diseases
1Ki 11:6 did what was *e*
Job 1:8 and avoids *e*
Ps 23:4 I will fear no *e* for
Ps 119:101 feet from every *e*
Pr 3:29 Do not devise *e*
Isa 59:7 feet run to *e*
Jer 26:3 from his *e* way
Mt 5:39 not resist an *e* person
Mt 6:13 but deliver us from *e*
Lk 6:45 an *e* man out of the *e*
Ac 19:12 the *e* spirits went out
Ro 12:9 Hate what is *e*.
Ro 16:19 that which is *e*
Eph 6:12 spiritual forces of *e*
Jas 1:13 tempted with *e*
Jas 4:11 Do not speak *e*
3Jn 1:11 that which is *e*

EXALT
Ps 34:3 *e* His name together
Eze 21:26 *E* what is low

EXALTATION
Isa 13:3 who rejoice in My *e*

EXALTED
2Sa 22:47 my salvation be *e*
Ps 46:10 I will be *e* among the
Ps 97:9 You are *e* far above
Ac 5:31 God *e* this man
2Co 12:7 lest I should be *e*
Php 2:9 God highly *e*

EXALTS
Pr 14:34 Righteousness *e*
2Co 10:5 high thing that *e*
2Th 2:4 *e* himself above all

EXAMINE
1Co 11:28 Let a man *e*
Gal 6:4 But let each one *e*

EXAMPLE
Mt 1:19 to make her a public *e*
Jn 13:15 I have given you an *e*
1Ti 4:12 youth, but be an *e*
1Pe 2:21 us, leaving us an *e*
Jude 1:7 serve as an *e*

EXCEEDINGLY
Ge 15:1 your shield, your *e* great reward
Ex 19:16 sound of an *e* loud trumpet
Eze 9:9 Israel and Judah is *e*

EXCELLENCY
Isa 13:19 of the Chaldean's *e*
Isa 35:2 *e* of Carmel and Sharon

EXCHANGE
Mt 16:26 give in *e* for his soul
Mk 8:37 what will a man give in *e*

EXCUSE
Jn 15:22 now they have no *e*
Ro 1:20 they are without *e*

EXCUSES
Lk 14:18 began to make *e*

EXECUTE
Ex 12:12 gods of Egypt I will *e*
Jer 23:5 *e* justice and righteousness
Eze 5:8 you and will *e* judgments
Eze 5:15 when I *e judgments*
Eze 30:14 Zoan, and will *e* judgments

EXECUTES
Mic 7:9 pleads my case and *e*

EXERCISE
1Ti 4:7 *e* in the ways of

EXHORT
1Ti 5:1 *e* him as a father
Titus 2:15 Teach these things, *e*
Heb 3:13 *e* one another

EXHORTATION
Ro 12:8 he who exhorts, in *e*
1Ti 4:13 to reading, *e*

EXPECTATION
Lk 3:15 the people were in *e*
Heb 10:27 a fearful *e*

EXTORTION
Mt 23:25 they are full of *e*

EXTORTIONERS
1Co 6:10 *e* will inherit

EYE
Ex 21:24 *e* for *e*, tooth for tooth
Pr 7:2 the apple of your *e*
Pr 10:10 who winks with the *e*
Mt 5:38 'An *e* for an *e*
Mt 6:22 of the body is the *e*
Mt 7:3 in your brother's *e*
Mk 9:47 if your *e* causes you
Lk 18:25 the *e* of a needle
1Co 12:17 were an *e*, where
1Co 15:52 twinkling of an *e*
Rev 1:7 every *e* will see Him

EYES
Ge 3:5 eat of it your *e* will be
Ge 6:8 in the *e* of the LORD
Ge 29:17 Leah's *e* were tender
Nu 22:31 the LORD opened the *e*
Dt 6:8 between your *e*
1Ki 8:29 Your *e* may be upon
1Ch 13:4 seemed right in the *e*
Job 10:4 Do You have *e*
Ps 91:8 Only with your *e*
Ps 118:23 marvelous in our *e*
Ps 121:1 I will lift up my *e*
Pr 3:7 wise in your own *e*
Ecc 2:10 everything that my *e*
SS 1:15 Your *e* are doves
Isa 6:5 For my *e* have seen
Isa 6:10 and shut their *e*; lest
Isa 42:7 to open the blind *e*
Jer 14:17 Let my *e* run down
La 3:48 My *e* flow with rivers
Da 10:6 his *e* were like lamps

Mt 13:16 blessed are your *e*
Mt 20:34 *e*. Immediately their *e*
Lk 2:30 For my *e* have seen
Jn 9:6 He anointed the *e*
Jn 12:40 blinded their *e*
Ac 9:18 scales fell from his *e*
Eph 1:18 the *e* of your understanding
1Pe 3:12 For the *e* of the Lord
1Jn 2:16 the lust of the *e*
Rev 4:8 covered with *e* all around
Rev 19:12 His *e* are like a flame

F

FABLES
1Ti 1:4 nor pay attention to *f*

FACE
Ge 32:30 "I have seen God *f*
Ex 34:29 *f* shone while he
Isa 59:2 sins have hidden His *f*
Mt 17:2 *f* shone as the sun
1Co 13:12 dimly, but then, *f*
Gal 2:11 withstood him *f*
Rev 22:4 They shall see His *f*

FACES
Ge 42:6 their *f* to the ground
Nu 16:22 *f* and said, "O God
Nu 16:45 fell on their *f*
2Ch 7:3 their *f* low to the ground
Isa 13:8 *f* shall be as flames
Isa 25:8 tears from all *f*

FADE
Isa 64:6 we all *f* as a leaf
1Pe 1:4 that does not *f*

FAIL
Lk 16:17 stroke of the law to *f*
Lk 22:32 faith may not *f*
1Co 13:8 they shall *f*

FAILS
Ps 143:7 O Lord, my spirit *f*
1Co 13:8 Love never *f*

FAINT
Isa 1:5 And the whole heart *f*
Isa 40:31 shall walk and not *f*

FAITH
Hab 2:4 shall live by his *f*
Mt 6:30 O you of little *f*
Mt 8:10 not found such great *f*
Mt 23:23 justice and mercy and *f*
Mk 10:52 Your *f* has made you
Lk 17:6 *f* as a grain of mustard
Lk 18:8 will He find *f*
Lk 22:32 your *f* may not fail
Ac 6:5 a man full of *f* and
Ac 14:27 opened the door of *f*
Ac 16:5 strengthened in the *f*
Ro 1:5 obedience of *f* among
Ro 1:17 revealed from *f* to *f*
Ro 3:22 God comes through *f*
Ro 4:5 his *f* is credited
Ro 4:16 comes through *f*
Ro 10:17 *f* comes by hearing
1Co 13:2 all *f*, so that I could
1Co 13:13 So now abide *f*, hope
2Co 5:7 For we walk by *f*
Gal 2:16 justified by *f* in Christ,
Gal 3:9 those who are of *f*
Gal 3:11 "The just shall live by *f*
Gal 3:26 all sons of God by *f*
Gal 5:6 but *f* which works
Gal 5:22 gentleness, goodness, *f*
Eph 2:8 been saved through *f*
Eph 3:17 your hearts through *f*
Eph 4:5 one Lord, one *f*
Eph 6:16 taking the shield of *f*
Php 1:27 together for the *f*
Col 1:4 *f* in Christ Jesus
Col 2:5 of your *f* in Christ
Col 2:12 through the *f*
1Th 1:3 work of *f*, labor of
1Ti 4:12 in spirit, in *f*
1Ti 6:12 good fight of *f*
2Ti 2:22 *f*, love, and peace
Titus 2:2 temperate, sound in *f*
Heb 10:38 shall live by *f*
Heb 11:6 without *f* it is impossible
Heb 12:2 finisher of our *f*
Jas 2:17 So *f* by itself
2Pe 1:5 add virtue to your *f*
1Jn 5:4 world is our *f*
Rev 2:19 love, service, *f*

FAITHFUL
Dt 7:9 the *f* God, who keeps
2Sa 22:26 *f* You prove Yourself *f*
Ps 31:23 LORD preserves the *f*
Ps 119:86 commandments are *f*
Pr 20:6 who can find a *f* man
Isa 49:7 LORD who is *f*
Mt 24:45 a *f* and wise servant
Lk 16:10 *f* in what is least is *f*
1Co 1:9 God is *f*, and by Him
1Co 10:13 God is *f*, and He will
1Th 5:24 *F* is He who calls you
1Ti 1:15 a *f* saying and worthy
2Ti 2:13 faithless, He remains *f*
Heb 3:5 Moses was *f* in all
1Jn 1:9 He is *f* and just
Rev 2:10 Be *f* unto death
Rev 3:14 The Amen, the *F*
Rev 22:6 "These words are *f*

FAITHFULNESS
Ge 32:10 the *f* which You
Dt 32:4 He is a God of *f*
Ps 36:5 Your *f* reaches
Ps 40:10 Your *f* and Your
Ps 89:1 make known Your *f*
Ps 91:4 His *f* shall be your
Isa 11:5 *f* the belt about his
La 3:23 great is Your *f*
Ro 3:3 nullify the *f* of God

FALL
Ge 2:21 a deep sleep to *f*
Ps 5:10 May they *f* by their
Pr 24:16 but the wicked will *f*
Mt 15:14 the blind, both will *f*
Mt 24:29 the stars will *f*
Lk 10:18 saw Satan as lightning *f*
1Co 10:12 take heed lest he *f*
Heb 6:6 if they *f* away
Rev 6:16 and rocks, "*F* on us

FALLEN
Isa 21:9 *f* is Babylon
Gal 5:4 you have *f* from grace

FALLING
Lk 22:44 great drops of blood *f*
2Th 2:3 *f* away comes first

FALLS
Pr 24:16 a just man *f*
Pr 24:17 when your enemy *f*
Heb 12:15 no one *f* short of

FALSE
Ex 20:16 You shall not bear *f*
Ps 119:104 I hate every *f* way
Pr 21:28 *f* witness will perish
Mt 7:15 "Beware of *f* prophets
Mt 24:24 *f* christs and *f*
1Co 15:15 would then be found *f*
1Jn 4:1 *f* prophets have gone
Rev 16:13 mouth of the *f* prophet

FALSEHOOD
Ps 119:118 for their deceit is *f*
Isa 57:4 offspring of *f*

FALSELY
Lev 19:12 not swear *f* by My name,
Mt 5:11 of evil against you *f*

FAMILIES
Ge 12:3 in you all *f*

FED
Dt 8:3 and *f* you with manna
1Co 3:2 *f* you with milk and

FEEBLE
Job 4:4 fortified the *f*
Isa 35:3 support the *f* knees

FEED
1Ki 17:4 ravens to *f* you there
Isa 61:5 and *f* your flocks
Ro 12:20 your enemy is hungry, *f*
1Co 13:3 goods to *f* the poor

FEEDS
Mt 6:26 your heavenly Father *f*

FEET
Ps 8:6 all things under his *f*
Ps 18:33 He makes my *f* like the
Ps 31:8 You have set my *f*
Pr 1:16 for their *f* run to
Pr 15:14 the mouth of fools f
Isa 52:7 mountains are the *f*
Isa 60:13 place of My *f* glorious
Zec 14:4 on that day His *f*
Mt 18:8 two hands or two *f*
Lk 7:38 began to wash His *f*
Jn 13:5 wash the disciples' *f*
Jn 13:8 "You shall never wash my *f*
Ro 3:15 *f* are swift to shed
Ro 10:15 beautiful are the *f*
1Co 15:27 things under His *f*
Eph 6:15 having your *f* fitted
Rev 1:17 fell at His *f*

FELL
Ge 17:17 Then Abraham *f* on
Nu 16:22 they *f* on their faces
Nu 16:45 they *f* on their faces
Dt 9:18 I *f* down before
Jos 7:6 elders *f* on their faces
Rev 1:17 When I saw Him, I *f*
Rev 5:8 the twenty-four elders *f*
Rev 5:14 the twenty-four elders *f*
Rev 11:13 a tenth of the city *f*
Rev 16:19 cities of the nations *f*
Rev 16:21 *f* from heaven upon man

FELLOWSHIP
2Ch 31:2 burnt and *f* offerings
Ac 2:42 teaching and *f*
2Co 6:14 *f* has righteousness
Eph 5:11 do not have *f* with
Php 3:10 the *f* of His sufferings
1Jn 1:6 we have *f* with Him

FERVENT
Jas 5:16 *f* prayer of a

FERVENTLY
Col 4:12 *f* for you in prayers

FEW
Ecc 5:2 may your words be *f*
Mt 7:14 and there are *f*
Mt 9:37 but the laborers are *f*
Mt 20:16 called, but *f* are chosen
Lk 13:23 those who are saved be *f*

FIELD
Ps 96:12 Let the *f* be joyful
Mt 13:38 the *f* is the world
Mt 13:44 and buys that *f*

FIELDS
Dt 32:13 produce of the *f*
Jer 8:10 others, and their *f*
Jer 32:44 Men will buy *f* for
Jer 40:7 which were in the *f*
Jas 5:4 who harvested your *f*

FIERCE
Dt 28:50 a nation with a *f* countenance
La 4:11 poured out His *f* anger.
Jnh 3:9 *f* anger, so that we will not perish
Hab 1:8 leopards, more *f*
Zep 3:8 indignation, all My *f*

FIERY
Ps 21:9 will make them as a *f*
Da 3:6 burning *f* furnace
1Pe 4:12 at the *f* ordeal

FIG
Ge 3:7 *f* leaves together
Lk 21:29 "Look at the *f*
Jn 1:50 'I saw you under the *f*

FIGHT
Ex 14:14 The LORD shall *f*
Ne 4:20 Our God shall *f* for us
Jn 18:36 My servants would *f*
Ac 23:9 to him, let us not *f*
1Ti 6:12 *F* the good *f*
2Ti 4:7 have fought a good *f*

FILL
Jer 23:24 Do I not *f* heaven
Hag 2:7 *f* this house with
Jn 2:7 "*F* the water pots
Eph 4:10 that He might *f*

FILLED
Ps 72:19 the whole earth be *f*
Mt 5:6 for they shall be *f*
Mk 7:27 the children first be *f*
Lk 15:16 would gladly have *f*
Ro 1:29 were *f* with all
Eph 5:18 but be *f* with the
Jas 2:16 be warmed and *f*

FILTHY
Zec 3:3 had on *f* garments
2Pe 2:7 distressed by the *f*
Rev 22:11 let him be *f*

FIND
Nu 32:23 sure your sin will *f*
Ecc 11:1 waters, for you will *f*
Mt 7:7 seek and you will *f*
Lk 2:12 *f* the Baby wrapped
Lk 23:4 *f* no fault in this Man
Heb 4:16 *f* grace to help in

FINDS
Pr 8:35 *f* me *f* life
Pr 18:22 *f* a wife *f* a good
Mt 7:8 and he who seeks *f*
Mt 10:39 *f* his life will lose
Lk 11:10 and he who seeks *f*

FINE
Ge 41:42 in clothes of *f* linen
Ps 119:127 above gold, even *f*
Rev 1:15 feet were like *f* brass
Rev 19:8 be arrayed in *f* linen

FINGER
Ex 31:18 written with the *f*
Lk 16:24 dip the tip of his *f*
Jn 20:27 "Put your *f*

FINISH
Jn 4:34 sent Me, and to *f* His work
Jn 5:36 has given Me to *f*

FINISHED
Jn 17:4 *f* the work You
Jn 19:30 He said, "It is *f*
2Ti 4:7 I have *f* my course

FIRE
Ge 22:6 he took the *f* in his hand
Ex 13:21 by night in a pillar of *f*
Nu 11:1 the *f* of the LORD burned
Dt 4:11 mountain burned with *f*
Job 1:16 The *f* of God fell
Ps 66:12 *f* and through water
Isa 66:15 LORD shall come with *f*
Jer 20:9 heart as a burning *f*
Da 3:27 the *f* had no power
Joel 2:30 blood and *f* and columns
Mt 3:11 Holy Spirit and with *f*

1Co 8:13 *f* causes my brother
1Co 10:3 the same spiritual *f*
2Co 9:10 supplies bread for your *f*
1Ti 6:8 If we have *f* and
Heb 5:12 rather than solid *f*
Heb 5:14 But solid *f* belongs to
Heb 12:16 of *f* sold his
Jas 2:15 lacking daily *f*

FOOL
Ps 14:1 *f* has said in his
Pr 10:23 is like sport to a *f*
Pr 12:15 *f* is right in his own
Pr 24:7 is too high for a *f*
Mt 5:22 whoever says, 'You *f*
2Co 12:11 I have become a *f*

FOOLISHNESS
Pr 22:15 *F* is bound in the
Pr 24:9 thought of *f* is sin
1Co 1:18 of the cross is *f*
1Co 1:25 For the *f* of God

FOOLS
Pr 1:7 *f* despise wisdom
Pr 14:8 folly of *f* is deceit
Pr 14:9 *F* make a mock at sin
1Co 4:10 We are *f* for Christ's

FOOT
Ps 121:3 will not let your *f*
Pr 3:23 *f* will not stumble
Isa 1:6 From the sole of the *f*
Mt 18:8 *f* causes you to sin
Lk 4:11 you strike your *f*
1Co 12:15 If the *f* says

FOOTSTOOL
Ps 110:1 Your enemies Your *f*
Mt 22:44 Your enemies Your *f*

FORBID
Mk 9:39 said, "Do not *f*
Ac 10:47 "Can anyone *f*
Gal 6:14 *f* that I should boast

FOREFATHERS
2Ti 1:3 conscience as my *f*

FOREIGNER
Ge 23:4 "I am a stranger and a *f*
Ru 2:10 acknowledge me, a *f*
Lk 17:18 to God except this *f*

FOREIGNERS
Ac 17:21 *f* who lived there
Eph 2:19 longer strangers and *f*

FOREKNEW
Ro 8:29 For those whom He *f*
Ro 11:2 His people whom He *f*

FOREKNOWLEDGE
Ac 2:23 counsel and *f* of God

FOREORDAINED
1Pe 1:20 He was *f*

FORESAW
Ac 2:25 'I *f* the Lord
Ac 2:31 he *f* this and spoke

FORESEEING
Gal 3:8 *f* that God would

FOREST
Isa 32:15 is counted as a *f*
Isa 44:23 you mountains, O *f*
Jer 5:6 a lion out of the *f*
Mic 5:8 the *f*, like a young lion

FOREVER
Ge 3:22 and eat, and live *f*
Dt 29:29 to our children *f*
Ps 29:10 LORD sits as King *f*
Ps 44:23 Do not reject us *f*
Ps 45:6 throne, O God, is *f*
Ps 110:4 "You are a priest *f*
Ps 136:1 His mercy endures *f*
Isa 40:8 of our God shall stand *f*
Isa 51:6 My salvation shall be *f*
La 3:31 will not cast off *f*
Da 12:3 as the stars *f*
Mt 6:13 and the glory *f*
Jn 12:34 the Christ remains *f*
2Co 11:31 who is blessed *f*
Gal 1:5 to whom be glory *f*
Eph 3:21 generations, *f* and ever
Php 4:20 and Father be glory *f*
Heb 1:8 throne, O God, lasts *f*
Jude 1:13 darkness has been kept *f*
Jude 1:25 power, both now and *f*
Rev 22:5 And they shall reign *f*

FOREVERMORE
Ps 37:27 and abide *f*
Rev 1:18 I am alive *f*

FORGET
Dt 4:9 diligently, lest you *f*
1Sa 1:11 and not *f* your maidservant
Ps 9:17 nations that *f* God
Ps 50:22 *f* God, lest I tear
Ps 119:16 I will not *f* Your word
Isa 54:4 you shall *f* the shame

FORGIVE
Ge 50:17 *f* the transgressions
1Sa 25:28 *f* the transgression
Jer 31:34 I will *f* their iniquity
Da 9:19 O Lord, *f*!
Mt 6:12 *f* us our debts, as we *f*
Mk 2:10 authority on earth to *f*
Mk 11:25 *f* if you have anything
Lk 17:3 if he repents, *f* him
2Co 2:10 you *f* anything, I also *f*
1Jn 1:9 just to *f* us our sins

FORGIVEN
Lev 4:20 and they shall be *f*
Ps 32:1 transgression is *f*
Mt 9:2 Your sins are *f* you
Mk 4:12 and their sins be *f*
Lk 7:47 which are many, are *f*
Lk 12:10 Son of Man will be *f*
Ro 4:7 whose iniquities are *f*
Jas 5:15 he will be *f*
1Jn 2:12 your sins are *f*

FORGIVENESS
Ps 130:4 is *f* with You,
Mk 3:29 Holy Spirit never has *f*
Ac 2:38 for the *f* of sins,
Eph 1:7 His blood and the *f*
Heb 9:22 there is no *f*

FORGOTTEN
Ps 10:11 heart, "God has *f*
Jer 30:14 your lovers have *f* you
Jer 50:5 that will not be *f*

FORM
Isa 45:7 *f* the light and create
Lk 3:22 descended in a bodily *f*
Jn 5:37 time, nor seen His *f*
1Co 7:31 For the *f* of this
Php 2:6 who, being in the *f*
2Ti 3:5 having a *f* of

FORMED
Ge 2:7 Then the LORD God *f*
Jer 1:5 "Before I *f* you in
Ro 9:20 Shall the thing *f*
Gal 4:19 until Christ is *f*

FORMER
Zec 1:4 *f* prophets cried
Eph 4:22 the *f* way of life
Rev 21:4 *f* things have passed

FORSAKE
Pr 1:8 father, and do not *f*
Lk 14:33 of you who does not *f*
Heb 13:5 never leave you, nor *f*

FORSAKEN
Ps 22:1 my God, why have You *f*
Ps 37:25 seen the righteous *f*
Isa 54:7 a small moment I have *f*
Mt 27:46 God, why have You *f*

2Co 4:9 persecuted, but not *f*
2Ti 4:10 Demas has *f*

FORTIFIED
Dt 9:1 great cities *f*
Dt 28:52 high and *f* walls
2Ki 18:13 the *f* cities of Judah

FORTRESS
2Sa 22:2 is my rock and my *f*
Ps 31:2 a strong *f*

FOUGHT
Ex 17:10 him and *f* against Amalek
Nu 21:23 came to Jahaz and *f*
Nu 21:26 Amorites, who had *f*
2Ki 12:17 Aram went up, *f*
Isa 63:10 their enemy, and He *f*
1Co 15:32 manner of men, I have *f*

FOUND
Ge 2:20 *f* a helper suitable
Ecc 7:28 a thousand I have *f*
Isa 55:6 LORD while He may be *f*
Lk 13:6 fruit on it and *f* none
Lk 15:24 he was lost, and is *f*
Jn 1:41 *f* the Messiah" (which
Php 3:9 and be *f* in Him

FOUNDATION
Ps 102:25 You have laid the *f*
Lk 6:49 the ground without a *f*
1Co 3:10 I have laid the *f*
1Co 3:11 *f* than that
Eph 1:4 us in Him before the *f*
Heb 6:1 not laying again a *f*
Rev 13:8 who was slain from the *f*

FOUNDATIONS
Job 38:4 when I laid the *f*
Rev 21:19 The *f* of the wall

FOUNTAIN
Pr 14:27 fear of the Lord is a *f* of life
Jer 2:13 the *f* of living waters
Jer 9:1 waters and my eyes a *f*
Jer 17:13 forsaken the LORD, the *f*
Hos 13:15 his *f* shall be dried up

FOUNTAINS
Ge 7:11 the same day, all the *f*

FOWL
Jer 7:33 shall be food for the *f*
Jer 16:4 food for the *f* of heaven

FOWLS
Dt 28:26 be meat for all the *f*

FOX
Ne 4:3 if even a *f* climbed it
Lk 13:32 tell that *f*,

FOXES
SS 2:15 *f* for us, the little *f*
Mt 8:20 "The *f* have holes

FRAGRANCE
Jn 12:3 was filled with the *f*
2Co 2:15 we are to God a sweet *f*

FREE
Jn 8:33 'You shall be set *f*
Ro 8:2 Jesus has set me *f*
Gal 3:28 is neither slave nor *f*
Eph 6:8 he is enslaved or *f*

FRIEND
Pr 18:24 *f* who sticks closer
Mt 11:19 a *f* of tax collectors
Lk 11:5 of you has a *f*
Jn 11:11 *f* Lazarus has fallen
Jas 2:23 he was called the *f*
Jas 4:4 will be a *f*

FRIENDS
Job 16:20 My *f* scorn me
Pr 14:20 the rich has many *f*
Jn 15:13 his life for his *f*
Jn 15:15 I have called you *f*

FROGS
Ex 8:2 your borders with *f*
Rev 16:13 *f* coming out of the

FRUIT
Ge 1:11 and *f* trees on the earth
Ge 1:11 yielding *f*
Lev 19:23 count the *f* as forbidden
Ps 1:3 that brings forth its *f*
Pr 11:30 The *f* of the righteous
SS 2:3 his *f* was sweet
Mt 3:8 bear *f* worthy
Mt 7:16 know them by their *f*
Mk 4:20 bear *f*: thirty, sixty
Jn 15:2 branch that bears *f*
Gal 5:22 the *f* of the Spirit
Jas 3:18 the *f* of righteousness
Rev 22:2 twelve kinds of *f*,
Rev 22:2 yielding its *f* each month

FRUITFUL
Ge 1:22 them, saying, "Be *f*
Ps 128:3 wife shall be as a *f*
Col 1:10 pleasing to all, being *f*

FULFILL
Mt 3:15 for us to *f* all
Gal 6:2 *f* the law of Christ
Php 2:2 *f* my joy and be
2Th 1:11 *f* all your good
Jas 2:8 If you *f*

FULFILLED
Mt 5:18 the law until all be *f*
Lk 21:24 of the Gentiles are *f*
Lk 24:44 all things must be *f*
Ro 8:4 of the law might be *f*
Ro 13:8 loves another has *f*
Gal 5:14 For the entire law is *f*

FULFILLMENT
Ro 13:10 love is the *f* of the

FULL
Eze 37:1 which was *f* of bones
Mt 6:22 whole body will be *f*
Jn 15:11 your joy may be *f*
1Co 4:8 you are *f*
Php 4:12 both to be *f*

FULLNESS
Jn 1:16 all received from His *f*
Gal 4:4 But when the *f* of
Eph 3:19 filled with all the *f*
Col 2:9 Him lives all the *f*

FURNACE
Dt 4:20 you out of the iron *f*
Da 3:6 of a burning fiery *f*
Mt 13:42 throw them into a fiery *f*
Rev 9:2 the smoke of a great *f*

FURY
Eze 6:12 will accomplish My *f*
Rev 19:15 *f* and wrath of God the Almighty.

G

GAIN
Php 1:21 and to die is *g*
Php 3:8 rubbish that I may *g*
1Ti 6:6 contentment is great *g*
1Pe 5:2 for dishonest *g*

GALL
Mt 27:34 wine mingled with *g*

GARDEN
Ge 2:8 God planted a *g*
Ne 3:15 Shelah by the king's *g*
SS 4:16 Blow upon my *g*
Isa 51:3 desert like the *g*
Jer 31:12 be as a watered *g*

Mt 25:29 has more will more be *g*
Lk 12:48 to whom much is *g*
Jn 6:39 *g* Me, I should lose
Jn 7:39 Spirit was not yet *g*

GIVES
Jn 6:33 *g* life to the world
Jn 6:37 All whom the Father *g*
Jn 14:27 Not as the world *g*
1Ti 6:17 richly *g* us all things
Jas 1:5 who *g* to all men liberally
Jas 4:6 *g* more grace

GIVING
Ezr 3:11 praising and *g* thanks
Heb 13:15 fruit of our lips, *g*

GLAD
Ps 46:4 streams make *g*
Ps 122:1 I was *g* when they said
Lk 15:32 be merry and be *g*
Jn 8:56 He saw it and was *g*

GLADNESS
Ps 51:8 me to hear joy and *g*
Ps 100:2 Serve the LORD with *g*

GLORIFIED
Mt 15:31 And they *g* the God of
Jn 7:39 Jesus was not yet *g*
Jn 12:16 when Jesus was *g*
Jn 15:8 My Father is *g*
Jn 17:4 I have *g* You on the
Ac 3:13 *g* His Son Jesus
Ro 8:30 He also *g*
1Pe 4:11 all things may be *g*

GLORIFY
Mt 5:16 *g* your Father
Jn 12:28 Father, *g* Your name
Jn 16:14 He will *g* Me
Jn 17:5 And now, O Father, *g*
Jn 21:19 death he would *g*
1Co 6:20 therefore *g* God in
Heb 5:5 also Christ did not *g*
1Pe 4:16 ashamed, but let him *g*

GLORIOUS
Ex 15:11 like You, *g* in holiness
Dt 28:58 may fear this *g*
Isa 4:2 be beautiful and *g*
Isa 11:10 his rest shall be *g*
Isa 30:30 His *g* voice to be heard
Isa 63:1 *g* in His apparel, traveling

GLORY
Ex 24:16 The *g* of the LORD rested
1Ch 16:24 Declare His *g* among
Ps 8:5 crowned him with *g* and
Pr 17:6 and the *g* of children are
Isa 6:3 earth is full of His *g*
Jer 9:24 who glories *g* in this
Eze 43:2 earth shone with His *g*
Mt 25:31 Son of Man comes in His *g*
Jn 8:50 I do not seek *g* for Myself.
Ro 1:23 changed the *g* of the
Ro 3:23 come short of the *g* of God
2Co 3:10 had no *g* in comparison
Eph 3:16 the riches of His *g*, power
Heb 2:9 crowned with *g* and honor
1Pe 1:24 all the *g* of man as the
Rev 4:9 creatures give *g* and honor
Rev 21:23 the *g* of God is its light

GLUTTON
Pr 23:21 the *g* will come to poverty,
Lk 7:34 you say, 'Look, a *g*

GNASHING
Mt 8:12 will be weeping and *g*

GO
Ge 25:18 east of Egypt, as you *g*
Ge 28:15 protect you wherever you *g*
Ex 4:21 Moses, "When you *g*
Ex 5:1 'Let My people *g*
Dt 28:6 and blessed when you *g*
Dt 28:19 cursed when you *g*
Dt 28:63 land which you *g*
Ru 1:16 For wherever you *g*
Ps 139:7 Where shall I *g* from
Jn 6:68 to whom shall we *g*
Jn 14:3 if I *g* and prepare a place
Rev 3:12 shall *g* out no more

GOADS
Ecc 12:11 Words of the wise are like *g*,
Ac 9:5 to kick against the *g*

GOAL
Php 3:14 I press toward the *g*
1Ti 1:5 Now the *g* of this command

GOATS
Mt 25:32 his sheep from the *g*
Heb 9:12 by the blood of *g*
Heb 10:4 *g* to take away

GOD
Ge 1:1 In the beginning *G*
Ge 9:26 Blessed be the LORD *G*
Ge 14:18 the priest of *G* Most High
Ge 16:13 You are the *G* who sees
Ge 17:1 I am Almighty *G*
Ge 21:33 the Everlasting *G*
Ge 24:3 *G* of heaven and the *G* of
Ge 26:24 "I am the *G* of Abraham
Ge 31:13 I am the *G* of Bethel
Ex 3:16 the *G* of your fathers
Ex 5:1 the LORD, the *G* of Israel
Ex 7:16 the *G* of the Hebrews, has
Ex 8:10 like the LORD our *G*
Dt 10:17 your *G* is the *G* of gods
Dt 32:4 a *G* of faithfulness and
Jdg 5:3 to the LORD *G* of Israel
1Sa 2:3 is the *G* of knowledge
2Sa 5:10 the *G* of Hosts, was with
2Sa 22:3 the *G* of my strength
2Sa 22:47 *G* of the rock of my
1Ki 1:47 'May *G* make the name
2Ch 34:3 the *G* of David his father
Ezr 4:3 build the temple of our *G*
Ne 1:4 prayed before the *G* of
Job 1:1 upright, fearing *G* and
Ps 4:1 O *G* of my righteousness
Ps 14:1 "There is no *G*
Ps 22:1 My *G*, my *G*, why
Ps 52:1 goodness of *G* endures
Ps 57:2 to *G* Most High, to *G* who
Ps 78:35 Most High *G* their redeemer
Ps 78:56 provoked the Most High *G*
Isa 40:28 the everlasting *G*, the LORD
Eze 1:1 I saw visions of *G*
Da 3:26 servants of the Most High *G*
Da 4:2 the Most High *G* has done
Da 5:18 the Most High *G* gave

Mt 16:16 Son of the living *G*
Mt 22:29 nor the power of *G*
Mk 5:7 Son of the Most High *G*
Lk 2:14 "Glory to *G* in the highest
Lk 2:52 in favor with *G* and men
Lk 7:28 in the kingdom of *G* is greater
Jn 1:1 Word was with *G*... was *G*
Jn 3:16 "For *G* so loved the world
Jn 14:1 You believe in *G*
Ac 16:17 servants of the Most High *G*
Ro 3:29 Is He the *G* of the Jews
Ro 6:11 to *G* through Jesus Christ
Ro 10:9 heart that *G* has raised Him
Ro 16:26 of the everlasting *G*
1Co 1:2 the church of *G* which is
1Co 1:18 it is the power of *G*
1Co 11:7 the image and glory of *G*
2Co 1:19 Son of *G*, Jesus Christ
Gal 3:26 all sons of *G* by faith
Heb 7:1 priest of the Most High *G*

GODLY

2Ti 3:12 who desire to live a *g*
Heb 12:28 reverence and *g* fear

GODS

Ge 31:30 have you stolen my *g*
Ex 20:3 no other *g* before Me
Dt 31:16 themselves after the *g*
1Sa 17:43 cursed David by his *g*
1Ki 18:24 call on the name of your *g*
Ps 82:1 judgment among the *g*
Ps 95:3 King above all *g*
Isa 36:18 the *g* of the nations
Jer 7:9 walk after other *g*
Jer 16:13 you will serve other *g*
Da 3:12 do not serve your *g*
Jn 10:35 called them '*g*,' to
1Co 8:5 those who are called *g*

GOLD

Ac 3:6 no silver and *g*
1Ti 2:9 with braided hair, *g*
Jas 2:2 a man with *g* ring
Jas 5:3 Your *g* and silver are
1Pe 1:7 more precious than *g*
1Pe 1:18 like silver or *g*
Rev 21:21 of the city was pure *g*

GOLDEN

Jer 51:7 Babylon has been a *g*
Heb 9:4 *g* pot holding the manna
Rev 5:8 *g* bowls full of incense
Rev 8:3 angel, having a *g* censer

GOLIATH

1Sa 17:4 *G* was his name, from Gath
1Sa 21:9 sword of *G* the Philistine

GONE

Isa 53:6 like sheep have *g*

GOOD

Ge 1:4 that the light was *g*
Ge 2:9 of knowledge of *g* and evil
Ex 18:17 are doing is not *g*
Dt 1:39 knowledge between *g* and
Dt 4:22 and possess that *g* land
1Ki 8:18 you had *g* intentions
Ps 14:3 there is none who does *g*
Ps 37:3 Trust in the LORD, and do *g*
Ps 73:1 God is *g* to Israel
Ps 100:5 the LORD is *g*
Ps 107:1 unto the LORD, for He is *g*
Ps 119:66 Teach me *g* discernment
Ps 147:1 For it is *g* to sing
Pr 3:27 Do not withhold *g*
Pr 16:20 matter wisely will find *g*
Ecc 4:9 there is a *g* reward
Ecc 7:1 A *g* name is better
Isa 1:17 do *g*; seek justice
Isa 40:9 bearer of *g* news
Isa 52:7 him who brings *g* news
Isa 53:10 the *g* pleasure of
Jer 14:11 Do not pray for the *g*
Jer 18:20 be recompensed for *g*
Jer 24:3 "Figs, the *g* figs, very *g*
Jer 32:40 from them, to do them *g*
La 3:25 The LORD is *g* to those
Hos 8:3 Israel has cast off the *g*
Mic 6:8 O man, what is *g*
Na 1:7 The LORD is *g*
Mal 2:17 who does evil is *g*
Mt 5:16 see your *g* works and
Mt 7:17 *g* tree bears *g* fruit
Mt 12:33 the tree *g* and its fruit *g*
Mt 12:35 A *g* man out of the *g*
Mk 3:4 lawful to do *g* or to
Mk 6:50 "Be of *g* cheer, it is I
Mk 9:5 it is *g* for us to be here
Mk 10:18 do you call Me *g*?
Lk 2:10 I bring you *g* news
Lk 6:27 do *g* to those who hate
Lk 8:1 bringing the *g* news
Lk 8:8 other seed fell on *g* ground
Lk 8:48 be of *g* cheer
Lk 11:34 your eye is *g*
Lk 18:18 *G* Teacher, what must
Jn 10:14 "I am the *g* shepherd
Jn 10:33 You for a *g* work
Ac 4:9 concerning a *g* deed done
Ac 10:22 *g* report throughout
Ac 11:24 a *g* man, full of
Ac 15:28 it seemed *g* to
Ro 2:7 doing *g* seek for glory
Ro 3:12 there is no one who does *g*
Ro 7:12 is holy and just and *g*
Ro 7:18 to perform what is *g* I
Ro 8:28 work together for *g*
Ro 12:9 Cleave to what is *g*
Ro 12:21 overcome evil with *g*
Ro 16:19 wise to that which is *g*
1Co 7:8 it is *g* for them if
1Co 15:33 Bad company corrupts *g*
2Co 13:11 be of *g* comfort
Gal 4:18 *g* to be zealous in a *g*
Eph 2:10 in Christ Jesus for *g* works
Eph 4:29 which is *g* for building up
Php 1:6 who began a *g* work
Php 4:8 things are of *g* report
1Th 5:15 always seek to do *g*
1Th 5:21 hold onto what is *g*
2Th 3:13 do not be weary in doing *g*
1Ti 2:10 with *g* works
1Ti 3:7 he must have a *g* reputation
1Ti 4:6 you will be a *g* minister
1Ti 6:12 Fight the *g* fight of faith
2Ti 2:3 hard times as a *g* soldier
2Ti 2:21 prepared for every *g* work
2Ti 4:7 fought a *g* fight

Titus 1:8 a lover of what is *g*
Titus 2:7 an example of *g* works
Heb 5:14 distinguish *g* from evil
Heb 6:5 tasted the *g* word of God
Heb 10:24 to love and to *g* works
Heb 11:39 all have obtained a *g* report
Heb 13:16 do not forget to do *g* and to
Jas 1:17 Every *g* gift and every
Jas 4:17 knows to do *g* and does
1Pe 2:20 doing *g* and suffering for it
1Pe 3:13 follow that which is *g*
3Jn 1:11 does *g* is from God

GOODNESS
Ex 33:19 all My *g* pass before you
Ps 21:3 with the blessings of *g*
Ps 23:6 *g* and mercy shall follow
Ps 27:13 see the *g* of the LORD
Ps 52:1 The *g* of God endures
Ps 107:8 praise the LORD for His *g*
Zec 9:17 great is His *g*, and how
Ro 2:4 the *g* of God leads you
Ro 11:22 *g* toward you…in His *g*
Gal 5:22 gentleness, *g*, faith
Eph 5:9 fruit of the Spirit is in all *g*
1Pe 2:9 may declare the *g* of Him

GOSPEL
Mk 1:1 beginning of the *g*
Mk 1:15 Repent and believe the *g*
Mk 13:10 *g* must first be
Ro 1:1 set apart for the *g*
Ro 1:16 not ashamed of the *g*
Gal 1:6 to a different *g*
Rev 14:6 the eternal *g*

GOVERNMENT
Isa 9:6 And the *g* shall be upon

GOVERNOR
Ge 42:6 Now Joseph was the *g*
Jer 40:7 the son of Ahikam *g*
Hag 1:1 son of Shealtiel, *g*
Mt 27:2 Pontius Pilate the *g*
Mt 27:11 stood before the *g*
Lk 20:20 authority of the *g*

GRACE
Ge 6:8 *g* in the eyes of the LORD
1Sa 1:18 find *g* in your sight
Est 2:17 she had gained *g*
Pr 3:22 and *g* to your neck
Jer 31:2 survived the sword found *g*
Lk 2:40 the *g* of God was upon Him
Jn 1:14 full of *g* and truth
Ro 1:5 we have received *g*
Ro 3:24 justified freely by His *g*
Ro 5:15 the *g* of God…by the *g*
Ro 6:14 but under *g*
Ro 11:6 if by *g*, then it is no
1Co 15:10 by the *g* of God I am what I
2Co 8:7 you abound in this *g* also
Eph 2:8 by *g* you have been saved
Col 4:6 speech always be with *g*
2Ti 2:1 be strong in the *g*
Heb 4:16 to the throne of *g*
Heb 12:15 falls short of the *g* of God
1Pe 4:10 of the manifold *g* of God
Jude 1:4 pervert the *g* of our God

GRACIOUS
Ge 43:29 he said, "God be *g*
Ex 33:19 I will be *g* to whom I
Lk 4:22 at the *g* words
Jas 5:11 the Lord is very *g*

GRAFTED
Ro 11:23 In unbelief, will be *g*

GRAIN
Dt 25:4 he treads out the *g*
Mt 12:1 to pluck the heads of *g*
Jn 12:24 unless a *g* of wheat

GRAPES
Isa 5:2 brought forth wild *g*
Eze 18:2 have eaten sour *g*
Mt 7:16 Do men gather *g*
Rev 14:18 *g* are fully ripe

GRASS
Isa 40:7 The *g* withers
Mt 6:30 so clothes the *g*
1Pe 1:24 flesh is as *g*

GRAVE
Ge 18:20 because their sin is very *g*
Ge 35:20 the pillar of Rachel's *g*
Job 10:19 from the womb to the *g*
Ps 30:3 up my soul from the *g*
Ps 88:4 those who go down to the *g*
Pr 30:16 the *g*, the barren womb
Isa 53:9 His *g* was assigned with
Jn 11:44 wrapped with *g* clothes
Ro 3:13 "Their throats are an open *g*
1Co 15:55 O *g*, where is your victory

GRAVES
Ex 14:11 there were no *g* in Egypt
Ps 49:11 *g* become their perpetual
Eze 32:22 Her *g* are around her
Eze 37:12 open your *g* and cause
Mt 27:52 The *g* also were opened
Rev 11:9 dead bodies to be put in *g*

GREAT
Ge 12:2 and make your name *g*
1Ch 16:25 For *g* is the LORD
Job 5:9 Who does the *g*
Isa 12:6 *g* is the Holy One
La 3:23 *g* is Your faithfulness
Mt 5:19 shall be called *g*
Mt 13:46 one pearl of *g* price
Mt 20:26 would be *g*
Lk 22:44 *g* drops of blood
Titus 2:13 glory of our *g*
Rev 6:15 *g* men and the rich men
Rev 17:5 MYSTERY, BABYLON THE *G*
Rev 20:12 the dead, small and *g*

GREATER
Mt 11:11 *g* than John the Baptist
Mt 12:6 One who is *g*
Mt 12:41 *g* than Jonah is here
Mt 12:42 *g* than Solomon is
Jn 13:16 a servant is not *g*
Jn 15:13 *G* love has no man
Jn 15:20 'A servant is not *g*
1Co 14:5 for *g* is he
1Jn 3:20 God is *g*

GREATEST
Mt 18:4 little child is *g*
Mt 22:36 which is the *g* commandment

GREATLY
Ge 3:16 I will *g* multiply your

Ecc 4:5 The fool folds his *h*
Ecc 9:10 your *h* find to do
SS 5:5 My *h* dripped with myrrh
Isa 49:16 on the palms of My *h*
Isa 55:12 shall clap their *h*
Isa 59:3 your *h* are defiled
La 3:41 and *h* to God in heaven
Zep 3:16 let not your *h* be slack
Mt 15:2 do not wash their *h*
Mt 19:13 put His *h* on them and pray
Mt 27:24 his *h* before the crowd
Mk 8:23 put His *h* on him
Mk 14:46 They laid *h* on Him
Lk 24:40 showed them His *h*
Jn 13:9 only, but also my *h*
Jn 20:25 nail prints in His *h*
Ac 2:23 lawless *h* have crucified
Ac 6:6 they placed their *h* on them
Ac 12:7 the chains fell off his *h*
Ro 10:21 stretched out My *h*
1Ti 2:8 lifting up holy *h*
1Ti 5:22 Do not lay *h* suddenly
Heb 2:7 over the works of Your *h*
Heb 10:31 the *h* of the living God
Rev 9:20 of the works of their *h*
Rev 20:4 foreheads or on their *h*

HANDWRITING
Col 2:14 He blotted out the *h*

HANGED
2Sa 17:23 h himself and died;
Mt 27:5 went and *h* himself

HAPPIER
1Co 7:40 she is *h* if she so remains

HAPPY
Ps 127:5 *H* is the man who has

HARD
Mt 25:24 I knew that you are a *h*
Jn 6:60 "This is a *h* saying
2Pe 3:16 some things are *h*

HARDEN
Ex 4:21 But I will *h* his heart
Heb 3:8 *h* your hearts as

HARDENED
Ex 8:32 Pharaoh *h* his
Mk 6:52 their hearts were *h*
Jn 12:40 and *h* their hearts
Heb 3:13 lest any of you be *h*

HARDENS
Pr 28:14 he who *h* his heart
Ro 9:18 whom He wills, and He *h*

HARLOT
Jer 2:20 wander, playing the *h*
Jer 3:6 has played the *h*
Jer 3:8 went and played the *h*

HARP
Ps 33:2 thanks to the Lord with the *h*
Rev 5:8 Lamb, each one having a *h*

HARPS
Ps 137:2 We hung our *h* upon the

HARVEST
Ge 8:22 Seedtime and *h*
Jer 8:20 "The *h* is past
Mt 9:37 *h* truly is plentiful
Mk 4:29 sickle because the *h*
Jn 4:35 already white for *h*

HATE
Ge 50:15 "Perhaps Joseph will *h* us
Ex 20:5 of them who *h* Me
Lev 19:17 shall not *h* your brother
Ps 5:5 You *h* all workers
Ps 41:7 All who *h* me
Ps 50:17 You *h* instruction
Ps 119:113 I *h* those who
Pr 8:13 is to *h* evil; pride
Pr 9:8 lest he *h* you
Ecc 3:8 and a time to *h*
Da 4:19 for those who *h* you
Am 5:15 *H* evil and love good
Mt 5:43 neighbor and *h* your enemy
Lk 6:22 you when men *h* you
Lk 16:13 Either he will *h* the one
Jn 7:7 The world cannot *h* you
Ro 7:15 but I do the very thing I *h*
Rev 2:6 You *h* the works of

HATED
Ge 27:41 So Esau *h* Jacob
2Sa 22:41 destroyed those who *h* me
Est 9:1 over those who *h* them
Ps 26:5 I have *h* the congregation
Pr 1:29 Because they *h* knowledge
Mt 10:22 will be *h* by all men
Jn 15:18 it *h* Me before it *h* you
Jn 17:14 And the world has *h* them
Ro 9:13 but Esau I have *h*
Heb 1:9 and *h* wickedness

HATES
Job 34:17 he who *h* justice govern
Pr 6:16 six things the LORD *h*
Pr 13:24 spares his rod *h* his son
Jn 3:20 who does evil *h* the light
Jn 7:7 But it *h* Me, because I
Jn 15:23 He who *h* Me *h* My Father
1Jn 2:11 But whoever *h* his brother
1Jn 3:13 if the world *h* you

HATRED
Nu 35:21 in *h* struck him with
Ps 109:3 me with words of *h*
Pr 10:12 *H* stirs up strife
Gal 5:20 sorcery, *h*, strife, jealousy
Titus 3:3 filled with *h* and hating

HEAD
Ge 3:15 He will bruise your *h*
Eph 1:22 and made Him the *h*
Eph 5:23 For the husband is the *h*

HEADS
Jos 7:6 dirt upon their *h*
Ps 74:14 You crushed the *h*
Isa 15:2 their *h* shall be baldness
Isa 35:10 everlasting joy upon their *h*
Eze 1:26 their *h* was the likeness
Eze 24:23 your *h*, and your shoes

HEAL
Ps 6:2 O LORD, *h* me
Jer 3:22 *h* your backslidings
Hos 6:1 torn, and He will *h*
Mt 10:8 *H* the sick
Lk 4:18 sent Me to *h* the
Lk 4:23 'Physician, *h* Yourself

HEALED
Isa 6:10 and turn and be *h*
Isa 53:5 his stripes we are *h*
Mt 4:24 and He *h* them
Jas 5:16 that you may be *h*
Rev 13:3 his deadly wound was *h*

HEATHEN

Mt 6:7 repetitions, as the *h*

HEAVEN

Ge 1:8 God called the expanse *H*
Ge 8:2 the floodgates of *h*
Ge 11:4 whose top will reach to *h*
Ge 15:5 Look up toward *h* and
Ex 16:4 bread from *h* for you
Ex 20:4 anything that is in *h* above
Ex 20:11 the LORD made *h* and earth
Dt 1:10 numerous as the stars of *h*
Dt 30:12 It is not in *h*, that you
Dt 30:19 I call *h* and earth
2Sa 22:14 LORD thundered from *h*
1Ki 8:27 *h* and the *h* of heavens
1Ki 8:32 hear in *h* and act and
2Ki 1:10 fire come down from *h*
2Ki 2:11 by a whirlwind into *h*
2Ch 6:21 from *h*, the place of Your
2Ch 36:23 The LORD God of *h*
Ezr 5:11 servants of the God of *h*
Ne 1:4 prayed before the God of *h*
Ne 9:6 made *h*, the *h* of heavens
Job 16:19 witness is in *h*, and
Ps 11:4 His throne is in *h*
Ps 14:2 LORD looks down from *h*
Ps 78:24 gave them the grain of *h*
Ps 139:8 If I ascend to *h*
Pr 30:4 has ascended up into *h*
Ecc 3:1 for every purpose under *h*
Isa 55:10 and the snow from *h*
Isa 66:1 *H* is My throne
Jer 33:22 As the host of *h*
Jer 51:9 her judgment reaches to *h*
La 3:41 and hands to God in *h*
Da 4:34 lifted up my eyes to *h*
Da 11:4 toward the four winds of *h*
Mt 3:2 the kingdom of *h* is at hand
Mt 5:10 theirs is the kingdom of *h*
Mt 5:19 great in the kingdom of *h*
Mt 6:10 done on earth, as it is in *h*
Mt 10:7 kingdom of *h* is at hand
Mt 13:11 of the kingdom of *h*
Mt 13:24 kingdom of *h* is like
Mt 14:19 looking up to *h*, He
Mt 16:19 keys of the kingdom of *h*
Mt 19:21 will have treasure in *h*
Mt 24:30 Son of Man will appear in *h*
Mt 24:35 *H* and earth will pass away
Mk 8:11 from Him a sign from *h*
Mk 11:30 baptism of John from *h*
Lk 9:54 to come down from *h*
Lk 10:18 as lightning fall from *h*
Lk 15:7 joy in *h* over one sinner
Lk 22:43 An angel from *h* appeared
Jn 1:51 see *h* opened and the
Jn 3:31 comes from *h* is above all
Jn 6:31 bread from *h* to eat
Jn 6:41 which came down from *h*
Ac 1:10 looked intently toward *h*
Ac 4:12 no other name under *h*
Ac 7:49 *H* is My throne
Ac 9:3 a light from *h* shone
Ro 1:18 of God is revealed from *h*
1Co 15:47 man was the Lord from *h*
2Co 12:2 caught up to the third *h*
Php 2:10 of those in *h* and
1Th 4:16 will descend from *h*
Heb 9:24 into *h* itself, now to
Heb 11:5 Enoch was taken to *h*
Jas 5:12 do not swear, either by *h*
Rev 4:1 there was an open door in *h*
Rev 6:13 stars of *h* fell to the earth
Rev 11:19 of God was opened in *h*
Rev 12:7 war broke out in *h*
Rev 16:17 out of the temple of *h*
Rev 21:1 "a new *h* and a new earth."
Rev 21:2 coming down out of *h*

HEAVENLY

2Ch 18:18 the *h* assembly was
Mt 6:14 your *h* Father will also
Eph 1:3 blessing in the *h* places
Eph 3:10 powers in the *h* places
Eph 6:12 forces of evil in the *h* places
Heb 6:4 who have tasted the *h* gift
Heb 9:23 replicas of *h* things
Heb 11:16 that is, a *h* one

HEAVENS

Ge 1:1 God created the *h* and
Ge 1:9 Let the waters under the *h*
Ge 1:14 in the expanse of the *h*
Ge 7:11 of the *h* were opened
Ge 22:17 as the stars of the *h*
Ps 2:4 He who sits in the *h* laughs
Ps 8:3 consider Your *h*
Ps 68:8 the *h* also poured down rain
Ps 103:11 *h* are high above the earth
Ps 103:19 His throne in the *h*
Pr 8:27 When He prepared the *h*
Isa 40:22 who stretches out the *h*
Isa 65:17 I create new *h* and a
Jer 4:23 And to the *h*, and
Jer 32:17 Truly, You have made the *h*
Eze 1:1 the *h* were opened and
Mt 3:16 the *h* were opened to Him
Lk 17:24 and lights up the *h*
Eph 4:10 far above all the *h*
Heb 4:14 who has passed into the *h*
2Pe 3:12 *h* will be destroyed by fire
Rev 6:14 Then the *h* receded

HEAVY

Ex 17:12 Moses' hands became *h*
Isa 6:10 their ears *h*

HEED

Dt 4:9 Only give *h* to yourself
Dt 12:30 take *h* to yourself
Jer 18:18 and let us not give *h*
Mk 8:15 Take *h*. Beware of the yeast
Lk 21:34 "Take *h* to yourselves
Ac 20:28 take *h* to yourselves

HEEL

Ge 3:15 you will bruise his *h*
Ps 41:9 has lifted up the *h*
Jn 13:18 Me has lifted up his *h*

HEIGHT
Ro 8:39 neither *h* nor depth
Eph 3:18 length and depth and *h*

HEIR
Heb 1:2 He has appointed *h*
Heb 11:7 world and became an *h*

HEIRS
Ro 8:17 if children, then *h*
Eph 3:6 the Gentiles are fellow *h*

HELD
1Ki 8:65 time, Solomon *h* a feast
Da 12:7 the river, when he *h*

HELL
Isa 14:11 is brought down to *H*
Mt 5:22 shall be in danger of *h* fire
Lk 12:5 has power to cast into *h*
Jas 3:6 and it is set on fire by *h*

HELMET
Ps 60:7 Ephraim also is My *h*
Isa 59:17 breastplate and a *h* of salvation
Eph 6:17 *h* of salvation and
1Th 5:8 and as a *h*, the hope

HELP
Ge 4:1 with the *h* of the LORD
Dt 33:7 and may You *h* him
2Ki 15:19 that he might *h* him
1Ch 23:28 *h* the sons of Aaron
2Ch 19:2 How do you *h* those
2Ch 32:8 our God who will *h*
Ps 3:2 There is no *h* for him
Ps 20:2 may He send you *h*
Ps 33:20 He is our *h* and our shield
Ps 40:17 You are my *h* and
Ps 115:9 He is their *h* and their
Hos 13:9 but in Me is your *h*
Mt 15:25 saying, "Lord, *h* me."
Lk 10:40 Then tell her to *h* me
Ac 4:20 For we cannot *h* but
Heb 2:16 surely He does not *h* the
Heb 4:16 grace to *h* in time

HELPED
Ex 2:17 Moses stood up and *h* them
2Sa 8:6 The LORD *h* David
1Ch 15:26 Since God *h* the Levites
Lk 1:54 He has *h* His servant Israel
2Co 6:2 salvation I have *h* you
Rev 12:16 But the earth *h* the woman

HELPER
Ge 2:18 a *h* suitable for him
Ps 10:14 the *h* of the orphan
2Co 8:23 fellow *h* concerning you
Heb 13:6 The Lord is my *h*

HELPFUL
1Co 6:12 but not all things are *h*

HELPING
Est 9:3 were *h* the Jews

HELPS
Ro 8:26 *h* us in our weaknesses

HEM
Mt 9:20 and touched the *h*

HERE
Isa 6:8 Then I said, "*H* am I

HERESIES
Gal 5:20 dissensions, *h*

HERITAGE
Isa 54:17 This is the *h* of the
Joel 3:2 regarding My people and My *h*

HEROD
Mt 2:1 in the days of *H* the king
Mt 14:3 *H* had laid hold of John
Mk 6:22 danced and pleased *H*
Lk 13:31 *H* wants to kill You
Lk 23:8 When *H* saw Jesus
Lk 23:12 and *H* became friends
Ac 12:1 *H* extended his hands to

HID
Ex 3:6 And Moses *h* his face
1Ki 18:4 hundred prophets and *h*
Ps 140:5 proud have *h* a snare
Isa 28:15 falsehood we have *h*
Isa 53:3 *h*, as it were, our faces
Isa 54:8 wrath I *h* My face from

HIDDEN
Ps 69:5 and my sins are not *h*
Ps 119:11 Your word I have *h*
Mt 10:26 *h* that will not
1Co 2:7 the *h* wisdom, which
1Co 4:5 bring to light the *h*
1Pe 3:4 let it be the *h*
Rev 2:17 give the *h*

HIDE
Ge 18:17 Should I *h* from Abraham
Ex 2:3 could no longer *h* him
Lev 8:17 the bull, and its *h*, its flesh
Dt 31:17 I will *h* My face from them
Job 13:24 Why do You *h* Your face
Ps 10:1 do You *h* Yourself in times
Ps 17:8 *h* me under the shadow of
Ps 64:2 *H* me from the secret
Pr 2:1 and *h* my commandments
Isa 30:20 will no longer *h* Himself
Eze 39:29 Nor will I *h* My face from
Rev 6:16 and *h* us from the face

HIDES
Job 42:3 who *h* counsel
Pr 10:18 He who *h* hatred
Pr 27:12 the evil and *h* himself
Isa 45:15 a God who *h* Yourself

HIGH
Ge 14:18 priest of God Most *H*
Ps 47:2 For the LORD Most *H*
Isa 57:15 I dwell in the *h*
Da 4:17 know that the Most *H*
Mt 17:1 up to a *h* mountain
2Co 10:5 *h* thing that exalts
Heb 2:17 and faithful *H* Priest

HIGHEST
Mt 21:9 Hosanna in the *h*
Lk 1:32 called the Son of the *H*
Lk 1:35 the power of the *H*

HIGHWAY
Isa 40:3 the desert a h

HIGHWAYS
Isa 49:11 *h* shall be raised up

HILL
Ps 2:6 on Zion My holy *h*
Mt 5:14 *h* cannot be hidden
Lk 3:5 and *h* shall be brought low

HILLS
Ge 49:26 of the everlasting *h*
Ps 121:1 up my eyes to the *h*

HINDER
1Co 9:12 all things, lest we might *h*

HIRED

Lev 19:13 wages of him who is *h*
Jdg 9:4 *h* unprincipled and undisciplined men
2Sa 10:6 *h* the Arameans of Beth Rehob

HISS

Isa 5:26 from afar and will *h*
Jer 50:13 be astonished and *h*
La 2:15 *h* and shake their heads
La 2:16 *h* and gnash their teeth

HOLD

Ex 14:14 while you *h* your peace
Ex 15:14 sorrow has taken *h*
Ex 15:15 trembling takes *h*
Ex 20:7 the LORD will not *h*
Isa 13:8 sorrows shall take *h*
Isa 21:3 pangs have taken *h*

HOLINESS

Ex 15:11 You, glorious in *h*
Ex 28:36 a signet, *H* TO THE LORD
Ps 77:13 Your way, O God, is *h*
Ps 89:35 I have sworn by My *h*
Isa 35:8 the Highway of *H*
Ro 1:4 to the Spirit of *h*
Ro 6:19 to righteousness unto *h*
2Co 7:1 spirit, perfecting *h*
1Ti 2:15 in faith, love, and *h*
1Th 4:7 uncleanness, but to *h*
Heb 12:10 may partake of His *h*

HOLY

Ge 2:3 seventh day and made it *h*
Ex 3:5 standing is *h* ground
Ex 12:16 shall be a *h* convocation
Ex 20:8 Sabbath day and keep it *h*
Ex 22:31 You will be *h* men to Me
Ex 26:34 testimony in the Most *H*
Ex 30:10 most *h* to the LORD
Lev 10:10 what is *h* and common
Lev 11:44 shall be *h*, for I am *h*
Lev 20:26 shall be *h* unto Me
Lev 22:2 not defile My *h* name
Nu 5:10 Every man's *h* things
Nu 6:8 he is *h* to the LORD
Dt 5:12 Sabbath day, to keep it *h*
Dt 33:2 ten thousands of *h* ones
Jos 5:15 you are standing is *h*
Jos 24:19 for He is a *h* God
2Ki 4:9 he is a *h* man of God
1Ch 16:10 Glory in His *h* name
2Ch 3:8 of the Most *H* Place
2Ch 5:7 into the Most *H* Place
Ezr 9:2 *h* seed has been mingled
Ne 8:9 This day is *h* to the
Job 5:1 to whom among the *h* ones
Ps 2:6 on Zion, My *h* hill
Ps 11:4 is in His *h* temple
Ps 24:3 may stand in His *h* place?
Ps 48:1 in His *h* mountain
Ps 51:11 do not take Your *H* Spirit
Ps 68:5 God in His *h* habitation
Ps 79:1 Your *h* temple they have
Ps 103:1 bless His *h* name
Pr 9:10 knowledge of the *H* One
Isa 1:4 have provoked the *H* One
Isa 6:3 *H*, *h*, *h*, is the LORD of Hosts
Isa 6:13 so the *h* seed is its stump
Isa 11:9 all My *h* mountain
Isa 29:19 rejoice in the *H* One of
Isa 48:17 the *H* One of Israel
Isa 52:10 has bared His *h* arm
Isa 57:15 *H*: I dwell…*h* place
Isa 58:13 the *h* day of the LORD
Isa 63:18 Your *h* people possessed
Jer 2:3 Israel is *h* to the LORD
Eze 20:39 do not pollute My *h* name
Eze 44:13 My *h* things in the Most *H*
Eze 45:1 be *h* throughout its
Eze 48:10 shall be this *h* allotment
Da 4:13 a *h* watcher coming down
Zec 2:13 stirred from His *h* habitation
Zec 14:20 "*H* TO THE LORD" will be
Mt 1:18 with child by the *H* Spirit
Mt 3:11 you with the *H* Spirit
Mt 4:5 took Him up into the *h* city
Mt 12:31 against the *H* Spirit will not
Mt 25:31 the *h* angels with Him
Mk 1:24 You are, the *H* One of God
Mk 13:11 who speaks, but the *H* Spirit
Lk 1:35 *H* Spirit will come upon you
Lk 2:23 male shall be called *h* to
Lk 3:22 the *H* Spirit descended
Lk 4:1 being filled with the *H* Spirit
Lk 12:12 the *H* Spirit will teach you
Jn 1:33 baptizes with the *H* Spirit
Jn 14:26 the Counselor, the *H* Spirit
Jn 20:22 Receive the *H* Spirit
Ac 2:4 filled with the *H* Spirit and
Ac 2:38 the gift of the *H* Spirit
Ac 10:47 received the *H* Spirit
Ac 13:34 the *h* and sure blessings
Ro 7:12 law is *h* and
Ro 11:16 the dough is *h*
Ro 12:1 a living sacrifice, *h*, and
Ro 16:16 another with a *h* kiss
1Co 7:34 she may be *h* in body
Eph 1:4 to be *h* and blameless
Eph 2:21 grows into a *h* temple
Eph 4:30 do not grieve the *H* Spirit
Eph 5:27 it should be *h* and
Col 3:12 elect of God, *h* and beloved
1Ti 2:8 lifting up *h* hands
Titus 1:8 just, *h*, temperate
Heb 9:12 entered the Most *H* Place
1Pe 1:16 Be *h*, for I am *h*
1Pe 2:5 house as a *h* priesthood
1Pe 3:5 the *h* women, who trusted
2Pe 3:11 in *h* conduct and godliness
Jude 1:14 ten thousand of His *h* ones
Rev 3:7 "He who is *h*, He who is true
Rev 4:8 "*H*, *h*, *h*, Lord God Almighty

Rev 11:2 *H* City for forty-two months
Rev 20:6 Blessed and *h* is he who takes part
Rev 21:2 *H* City, the New Jerusalem
Rev 22:11 He who is *h*, let him be *h*

HOME

Dt 21:12 you are to bring her *h*
Jos 2:15 her *h* was set into the wall
Jos 22:8 "Return *h* with great wealth
1Sa 25:1 they buried him at his *h*
2Ch 18:16 man return to his *h* in peace
Ezr 10:10 bringing *h* foreign women
Job 39:6 whose *h* I have made the
Ps 52:5 pluck you from your *h*
Ps 126:6 shall come *h* again with
Pr 7:19 my husband is not at *h*
Ecc 12:5 goes to his eternal *h*
Mt 8:6 servant is lying at *h*, sick
Lk 18:29 left his *h* or parents
Jn 14:23 and make Our *h* with him
Jn 19:27 took her to his own *h*
Ac 21:6 ship, and they returned *h*
1Co 14:35 ask their husbands at *h*
2Co 5:6 we are at *h* in the body
1Ti 5:4 learn first to show piety at *h*

HOMOSEXUALS

1Co 6:9 nor male prostitutes, nor *h*

HONEY

Ps 81:16 and with *h* out of
Mt 3:4 was locusts and wild *h*

HONEYCOMB

Ps 19:10 than honey and the *h*
Lk 24:42 fish and some *h*

HONOR

Ex 20:12 *H* your father and
Lev 19:32 *h* the face of an old man
Jos 3:7 I will begin to *h* you in
1Sa 2:30 for those who *h* Me, I will *h*,
1Ch 16:27 *H* and majesty are before
Est 1:20 the wives shall give *h* to
Ps 8:5 him with glory and *h*
Pr 3:9 *H* the LORD with your
Pr 11:16 A gracious woman retains *h*
Pr 20:3 an *h* for a man to cease
Pr 25:2 *h* of kings is to search out a
Ecc 6:2 wealth, possessions, and *h*
Isa 29:13 and *h* Me with their lips
Da 11:38 he shall *h* the god of forces
Mt 13:57 "A prophet is not without *h*
Mt 19:19 *H* your father and your
Mt 23:6 the places of *h* at feasts
Lk 14:7 chose the seats of *h*
Jn 5:23 *h* the Son, just as they *h* the
Ro 2:7 *h* and immortality will
Ro 9:21 vessel for *h* and another
1Co 12:23 bestow more abundant *h*
1Th 4:4 in sanctification and *h*
1Ti 1:17 God, be *h* and glory forever
1Ti 5:3 *H* widows that are widows
1Ti 5:17 worthy of double *h*
Heb 2:7 him with glory and *h*
1Pe 2:17 *H* all people
1Pe 3:7 giving *h* to the woman
Rev 4:9 give glory and *h* and thanks
Rev 21:26 the glory and the *h* of the

HONORABLE

Isa 9:15 The elder and *h*
Na 3:10 cast lots for her *h*
Ac 13:50 the devout and *h* women

HONORED

Ex 14:4 be *h* because of Pharaoh
Ex 20:24 cause My name to be *h*
Pr 13:18 regards reproof will be *h*
Isa 43:23 have you *h* Me with your
Mt 6:2 that they may be *h* by men
1Co 12:26 if one part is *h*, all the
Heb 13:4 Marriage is to be *h*

HONORS

Ps 15:4 who *h* those who fear
Mal 1:6 A son *h* his father

HOPE

Ru 1:12 that there was still *h* for me
Job 17:15 now is my *h*? As for my *h*
Ps 9:18 Nor will the *h* of the poor
Ps 37:34 *H* in the LORD, and
Ps 39:7 My *h* is in You
Ps 119:81 but I *h* in Your word
Ps 131:3 Israel *h* in the LORD from
Pr 13:12 *H* deferred makes the heart
Jer 17:7 and whose *h* is the LORD
La 3:21 and therefore I have *h*
Lk 6:34 from whom you *h* to receive
Ac 2:26 my flesh will dwell in *h*
Ac 23:6 judged for my *h* in the
Ro 5:4 and character produces *h*
Ro 12:12 rejoice in *h*
1Co 9:10 in *h* should partake of his *h*
1Co 13:13 abide faith, *h*, and love
2Co 3:12 such *h*, we speak with
Eph 1:12 were the first to *h* in Christ
Eph 1:18 what is the *h* of His calling
Eph 4:4 in one *h* of your calling
Col 1:5 the *h* which is laid up for
Col 1:27 the *h* of glory
1Th 1:3 and patient *h* in our Lord
1Th 2:19 our *h*, or joy, or crown
Titus 2:13 we await the blessed *h*
Heb 6:19 *h* as a sure and steadfast
1Pe 1:3 into a living *h* through
1Jn 3:3 this *h* in Him purifies

HORN

1Sa 16:1 Fill your *h* with oil
1Sa 16:13 the *h* of oil, and anointed

Ps 18:2 shield, and the *h*
Ps 112:9 his *h* shall be exalted
Jer 48:25 The *h* of Moab has been cut
Da 7:8 them another little *h*

HORNS
Ex 27:2 You shall make its *h*
Ex 30:3 all around, and its *h*
Ex 30:10 atonement on its *h*
Lev 4:7 *h* of the altar of fragrant
Lev 4:18 the blood on the *h*
Da 7:7 and it had ten *h*
Da 7:8 I considered the *h*

HORSE
Ex 15:1 thrown the *h* and his rider
Ne 3:28 Up to the *H* Gate the priests
Est 6:8 a *h* on which the king
Ps 32:9 Do not be as the *h* or
Ps 147:10 in the strength of the *h*
Pr 26:3 A whip for the *h*
Zec 1:8 a man riding on a red *h*
Rev 6:2 before me was a white *h*
Rev 19:11 white *h*. He who sat on

HORSES
Ex 14:9 all the *h* and chariots
Jos 11:6 Hamstring their *h* and
1Ki 10:28 Solomon had *h* brought
2Ki 2:11 and *h* of fire separated
2Ki 5:9 Naaman came with his *h*
2Ki 6:17 mountain was full of *h*
2Ch 9:25 four thousand stalls for *h*
Ps 20:7 chariots, and some in *h*
Jer 4:13 His *h* are swifter than
Joel 2:4 have the appearance of *h*
Hab 3:8 on Your *h*, on Your
Zec 6:2 first chariot had red *h*
Jas 3:3 bits in the mouths of *h*
Rev 9:7 the locusts was like *h*
Rev 19:18 the flesh of *h* and their

HOSANNA
Mt 21:9 *H* in the highest
Mk 11:9 "*H*! 'Blessed is He

HOSTS
Ps 46:7 The LORD of *H* is with
Ps 148:2 praise Him, all His heavenly *h*

HOUR
Mt 24:44 for in an *h*
Jn 4:23 "Yet the *h* is coming
Jn 12:27 save Me from this *h*
Rev 3:10 keep you from the *h*

HOUSE
Ps 127:1 the LORD build the *h*,
Lk 6:48 like a man who built a *h*

HOUSEHOLD
Ge 7:1 your entire *h* go into the ark
Ge 31:19 Rachel stole the *h* idols that
Ge 50:4 spoke to the *h* of Pharaoh
1Sa 24:21 name out of my father's *h*
1Ki 17:15 and her *h* ate many days
Pr 31:15 to her *h* and a portion to
Mt 10:36 will be those of his own *h*
Jn 4:53 he and his whole *h* believed
Ac 10:2 feared God with all his *h*
Ac 16:31 and your *h* will be saved
1Co 1:16 baptized the *h* of Stephanas
Eph 2:19 members of the *h* of God

HUMBLE
Nu 12:3 Moses was very *h*
Dt 8:2 in the wilderness, to *h* you
2Ch 7:14 *h* themselves and pray
Ps 9:12 not forget the cry of the *h*
Ps 10:17 The desire of the *h*
Ps 69:32 The *h* will see this
Pr 3:34 He gives favor to the *h*
Zec 9:9 He is *h* and riding on
Mt 21:5 coming to you, *h*, and
Php 4:12 how to face *h* circumstances
Jas 4:10 *H* yourselves in the sight
1Pe 5:6 *H* yourselves under the

HUMBLED
Lev 23:29 whoever is not *h*
Dt 8:3 He *h* you and let
Jdg 8:28 The Midianites were *h*
2Ki 22:19 *h* yourself before the LORD
2Ch 12:6 the rulers of Israel *h* themselves
Ps 35:13 I *h* my soul with fasting
Isa 10:33 and the haughty shall be *h*
Isa 58:3 we *h* ourselves and You
La 3:20 soul remembers and is *h*
Da 5:22 have not *h* your heart
Mt 23:12 who exalts himself will be *h*
Php 2:8 He *h* Himself and became

HUMBLES
Isa 2:9 the great man *h* himself
Mt 18:4 whoever *h* himself like
Lk 18:14 he who *h* himself will

HUMILITY
Pr 15:33 before honor is *h*
Pr 18:12 and before honor is *h*
Pr 22:4 By *h* and the fear of the
Ac 20:19 serving the Lord with all *h*
Eph 4:2 With all *h*, meekness, and
Php 2:3 but in *h* let each esteem the
Titus 3:2 showing all *h* toward
1Pe 5:5 clothe yourselves with *h*

HUNGER
Isa 49:10 They shall not *h*
Mt 5:6 are those who *h*
Lk 6:25 for you shall *h*
Jn 6:35 to Me shall never *h*
1Co 4:11 hour we both *h*
Rev 7:16 "'They shall neither *h*

HUNGRY
Ps 107:9 and fills the *h*
Ps 146:7 gives food to the *h*
Mt 25:35 'For I was *h* and you
Mt 25:37 did we see You *h*
Php 4:12 to be full and to be *h*

HUNTER
Ge 10:9 Nimrod the mighty *h*
Ge 25:27 Esau was a cunning *h*

HURT
Ex 21:22 *h* a pregnant woman

Ecc 8:9 another to the other's *h*
Isa 11:9 They shall not *h*
Mk 16:18 it will not *h*
Rev 2:11 shall not be *h* by the

HUSBAND
Ge 3:6 she gave to her *h* with her
Ge 29:32 therefore my *h* will love me
Pr 12:4 woman is a crown to her *h*
Pr 31:23 Her *h* is known in the gates
Hos 2:2 wife, and am I not her *h*
Hos 2:16 you will call Me, "My *h*,"
Mk 10:12 divorces her *h* and marries
Jn 4:16 call your *h*, and come here
Ac 5:9 buried your *h* are at the
1Co 7:2 woman have her own *h*
Eph 5:23 the *h* is the head of the wife
1Ti 3:2 blameless, the *h* of one wife
Rev 21:2 as a bride adorned for her *h*

HUSBANDS
Ru 1:11 who could become your *h*
Est 1:20 shall give honor to their *h*
Jn 4:18 for you have had five *h*
Eph 5:22 submissive to your own *h*
Eph 5:25 *H*, love your wives, just as
1Ti 3:12 be the *h* of one wife
Titus 2:4 women to love their *h*
1Pe 3:7 you *h*, live considerately

HYMN
Mt 26:30 they had sung a *h*
Mk 14:26 they had sung a h

HYMNS
Ac 16:25 praying and singing *h*
Eph 5:19 in psalms, *h*

HYPOCRISY
Mt 23:28 you are full of *h*
Lk 12:1 Pharisees, which is *h*
Ro 12:9 Let love be without *h*
Gal 2:13 away by their *h*
Jas 3:17 and without *h*
1Pe 2:1 wickedness, deceit, *h*

HYPOCRITE
Job 20:5 the joy of the *h*
Isa 9:17 every one of them is a *h*

HYPOCRITES
Mt 6:5 not be like the *h*
Mt 22:18 "Why test Me, you *h*
Mt 23:13 and Pharisees, *h*

I

IDLE
Pr 19:15 *i* soul will suffer
Mt 12:36 *i* word that men
Mt 20:3 saw others standing *i*
1Ti 5:13 they learn to be *i*

IDOL
Ex 20:4 for yourself any graven *i*
1Sa 19:13 Michal took an *i* and laid it
Jer 10:14 is put to shame by an *i*
Ac 7:41 offered a sacrifice to the *i*
1Co 8:4 that an *i* is nothing
1Co 10:19 then, that the *i* is anything

IDOLATER
1Co 5:11 or covetous, or an *i*

IDOLATRY
1Sa 15:23 is as iniquity and *i*
1Co 10:14 So, my beloved, flee from *i*
Col 3:5 covetousness, which is *i*

IDOLS
Ge 31:19 stole the household *i*
Lev 26:1 not make for yourselves *i*
Jdg 17:5 an ephod and household *i*
2Ki 23:24 the *i*, and all the
1Ch 16:26 gods of the peoples are *i*
Ps 97:7 who boast in worthless *i*
Ps 106:36 served their *i*
Isa 2:8 land also is full of *i*
Jer 50:2 *i* have been humiliated
Eze 6:4 slain men before your *i*
Eze 20:7 yourselves with the *i*
Hos 4:17 Ephraim is joined to *i*
Mic 1:7 All her *i* will be
Zec 13:2 the names of the *i* from
Ac 15:20 from food offered to *i*
Ac 17:16 the city was full of *i*
Ro 2:22 who abhor *i*, do you rob
1Co 8:1 concerning food offered to *i*
1Jn 5:21 keep yourselves from *i*
Rev 9:20 and *i* of gold, silver

IDOLATER
Eph 5:5 who is an i

IDOLATRY
Col 3:5 covetousness, which is i

IDOLS
Ps 106:38 sacrificed to the *i*
Isa 19:1 and the *i* of Egypt
Isa 46:1 Nebo stoops, their *i*
Eze 20:8 nor did they forsake the *i*

IGNORANCE
Ac 3:17 that you acted in *i*
Ac 17:30 the times of *i*
Heb 9:7 committed in *i*

IMAGE
Ge 1:26 make man in our *i*
1Co 11:7 because he is the *i*
Col 1:15 He is the *i* of the
Heb 10:1 and not the very *i*
Rev 14:9 the beast and his *i*

IMAGES
Ex 23:24 break down their *i*
Dt 7:5 break down their *i*
1Ki 14:9 gods and molded *i*
1Ki 14:23 high places and *i*
2Ki 17:16 made themselves cast *i*
Isa 21:9 graven *i* of her gods

IMMANUEL
Isa 7:14 shall call his name *I*
Mt 1:23 shall call His name *I*

IMMORAL
Pr 5:3 lips of an *i* woman
Pr 7:5 keep you from the *i* woman
1Co 5:9 company with sexually *i*
Eph 5:5 no sexually *i* or impure
1Ti 1:10 for the sexually *i*, for sodomites

Heb 13:4 will judge the sexually *i*
Rev 21:8 murderers, the sexually *i*
Rev 22:15 sexually *i* and murderers

IMMORALITY
Mt 15:19 adulteries, sexual *i*, thefts
Mt 19:9 except for sexual *i*
Ac 15:20 from sexual *i*
Ro 1:29 sexual *i*, wickedness
Ro 13:13 not in *i* and wickedness
1Co 6:13 the body is not for sexual *i*
1Co 6:18 Escape from sexual *i*
2Co 12:21 not repented of uncleanness, sexual *i*
1Th 4:3 abstain from sexual *i*
Jude 1:4 the grace of our God into *i*
Jude 1:7 gave themselves to *i*
Rev 2:21 to repent of her sexual *i*
Rev 19:2 the earth with her sexual *i*

IMMORTAL
1Ti 1:17 to the eternal, *i*

IMMORTALITY
Ro 2:7 *i* will be eternal life.
1Co 15:53 mortal will put on *i*
1Ti 6:16 He alone has *i*

IMMOVABLE
Ac 27:41 and remained *i*

IMMUTABLE
Heb 6:18 that by two *i* things

IMPOSSIBLE
Lk 1:37 God nothing will be *i*
Heb 11:6 without faith it is *i*

INCENSE
Ex 30:7 burn sweet *i* on it
Ex 30:8 a perpetual *i*
Lev 4:7 the altar of fragrant *i*
Lev 10:1 and put *i* on it
Nu 16:35 men that offered *i*
Nu 16:46 altar, and put in *i*

INCORRUPTIBLE
Ro 1:23 the glory of the *i*
1Co 15:52 dead will be raised *i*

INCORRUPTION
1Co 15:50 corruption inherit *i*

INCREASE
Lev 26:4 shall yield its *i*
Dt 28:4 the *i* of your herd
Isa 9:7 Of the *i* of his government
Eze 18:13 and has taken *i*
Eze 34:27 shall yield its *i*

INCREASED
Jer 5:6 backslidings have *i*
Lk 2:52 And Jesus *I* in wisdom

INDIGNATION
Heb 10:27 *i*, which will devour

INEXPRESSIBLE
2Co 12:4 paradise and heard *i*

INFALLIBLE
Ac 1:3 by many *i* proofs

INFANTS
Mt 11:25 revealed them to *i*
Mt 21:16 mouth of children and *i*

INFIRMITIES
Mt 8:17 "He Himself took our *i*
Lk 5:15 healed by Him of their *i*

INHABITANT
Isa 12:6 shout for joy, *O i* of Zion
Jer 4:7 waste without an *i*
Jer 9:11 desolate, without an *i*
Jer 21:13 you, O *i* of the valley

INHABITANTS
Ex 15:15 *i* of Canaan are melted
Ex 23:31 will deliver the *i*
Dt 13:13 have seduced the *i*
Jos 2:9 the *i* of the land melt
1Ki 17:1 Tishbite, who was one of the *i*
Isa 40:22 earth, and the *i*

INHABITED
Isa 13:20 It shall never be *i*
Isa 45:18 formed it to be *i*
Jer 50:13 she will not be *i*
Eze 26:17 destroyed, O *i* one
Eze 34:13 *i* places of the country

INHERIT
Pr 8:21 love me to *i* wealth
Mt 25:34 *i* the kingdom
1Co 6:9 unrighteous will not *i*
Rev 21:7 who overcomes shall *i*

INHERITANCE
Nu 18:20 "You will not have an *i*
Dt 32:9 is the allotment of His *i*
Ps 16:5 the portion of my *i*
Ps 37:18 *i* will be forever
Ps 47:4 He chose our *i*
Ac 7:5 He gave him no *i*
Ac 20:32 and give you an *i*
Gal 3:18 For if the *i* comes from
Eph 1:11 we have received an *i*
Col 1:12 be partakers in the *i*
Heb 11:8 receive as an *i*
1Pe 1:4 and undefiled *i*

INIQUITIES
Lev 16:21 confess over it all the *i*
Ezr 9:6 our *i* have expanded
Ne 9:2 their sins and the *i*
Ps 51:9 and blot out all my *i*
Ps 103:10 repay us according to our *i*
Ps 130:8 Israel from all their *i*
Isa 53:5 He was bruised for our *i*
Mic 7:19 He will tread down our *i*

INIQUITY
Ex 20:5 visiting the *i* of the fathers
Ex 34:9 Pardon our *i*
Lev 26:40 *i*, and the *i* of their fathers
Nu 14:18 *i* and transgression
1Sa 15:23 stubbornness is as *i* and
Job 4:8 those who plow *i* and
Job 31:3 to the workers of *i*
Ps 6:8 all you workers of *i*
Ps 18:23 kept myself from my *i*
Ps 31:10 fails because of my *i*
Ps 51:2 thoroughly from my *i*
Ps 106:6 committed *i*; we have
Ps 119:133 let not any *i* have
Pr 16:6 and truth *i* is purged
Pr 22:8 He who sows *i* will reap
Isa 6:7 your *i* is taken away
Isa 53:6 the *i* of us all
Isa 59:3 and your fingers with *i*
Jer 31:30 will die for his own *i*
Eze 3:18 man shall die in his *i*
Eze 7:13 strengthen his life by his *i*
Eze 33:13 that he commits *i*
Da 9:24 to make atonement for *i*
Zec 3:4 removed from you your *i*
Mt 23:28 are full of hypocrisy and *i*
Lk 13:27 all you workers of *i*
1Co 13:6 rejoices not in *i*

INN
Lk 2:7 room for them in the *i*
Lk 10:34 brought him to an *i*

INNOCENCE
Ps 73:13 washed my hands in *i*
Da 6:22 because *i* was found

INNOCENT
Mt 27:24 saying, "I am *i*
Ac 20:26 this day that I am *i*

INQUIRED
1Sa 23:2 Therefore David *i*
1Pe 1:10 should come to you have *i*

INSTRUCT
Ps 32:8 I will *i* you and teach
1Co 2:16 Lord that he may *i*

INSTRUCTED
Ac 18:25 This man was *i*
Ro 2:18 because you are *i*
Heb 8:5 Moses was *i*

INSTRUCTION
Ps 50:17 you hate *i*
Pr 8:33 Hear *i*, and be wise
Pr 9:9 Give *i* to a wise man
2Ti 3:16 for correction, and for *i*

INSTRUMENTS
Ro 6:13 your bodies to God as *i*

INSULTED
Lk 18:32 will be mocked and *i*
Heb 10:29 *i* the Spirit of grace

INTEGRITY
Ge 20:5 in the *i* of my heart
Titus 2:7 in doctrine showing *i*

INTERCESSION
Isa 53:12 of many and made *i*
Heb 7:25 lives to make *i*

INTERPRETATION
Da 2:4 we will tell the *i*
Da 5:7 writing and show me its *i*
Da 5:16 make known to me its *i*
1Co 12:10 to another the *i*
2Pe 1:20 of one's own *i*

INTERPRETATIONS
Ge 40:8 "Do not *i* belong to

INVISIBLE
Ro 1:20 the *i* things about him
Col 1:15 is the image of the *i*
1Ti 1:17 eternal, immortal, *i*
Heb 11:27 looking to Him who is *i*

IRON
Pr 27:17 *i* sharpens *i*
Da 2:33 its feet partly of *i*

ISRAEL
Ge 32:28 be called Jacob, but *I*
Ge 49:24 Shepherd, the Rock of *I*
Ex 3:14 the children of *I*
Ex 12:35 the children of *I* did
Dt 6:4 Hear, O *I*
Jdg 2:11 children of *I* did evil
1Ki 2:11 David reigned over *I*
Ps 25:22 Redeem *I*, O God
Ps 73:1 Truly God is good to *I*
Isa 10:17 light of *I* shall be a fire
Eze 3:17 watchman to the house of *I*
Mt 2:6 shepherd My people *I*
Ro 11:26 so all *I* will be saved
Rev 21:12 sons of *I* were written

ISRAELITE
Jos 2:2 *I* men came here tonight to
Jn 1:47 an *I* indeed, in whom is no
Ro 11:1 *I*, a descendant of Abraham

ISRAELITES
Ro 9:4 *I*, to whom belong the
2Co 11:22 So am I. Are they *I*?

J

JACKALS
Isa 13:22 desolate houses and *j*
Isa 35:7 the habitation of *j*
Jer 9:11 heap of ruins and a den of *j*
Mal 1:3 left his inheritance for the *j*

JAMES
Mt 4:21 *J* the son of Zebedee
Mt 17:1 Peter, *J*, and John
Mk 6:3 and the brother of *J*
Mk 10:41 very displeased with *J*
Mk 16:1 Mary the mother of *J*
Ac 1:13 *J*, John, and Andrew
Ac 12:2 killed *J* the brother of John
Ac 21:18 Paul went with us to *J*
Gal 1:19 apostles except *J*

JEALOUS
Ge 30:1 she became *j*
Ge 37:11 his brothers were *j*
Ex 20:5 am a *j* God
Ex 34:14 name is Jealous, is a *j* God
Nu 5:14 he is *j* of his wife
Nu 11:29 *j* for my sake?
Dt 4:24 He is a *j* God
Dt 5:9 am a *j* God
Dt 32:16 They made Him *j*
Jos 24:19 He is a *j* God
Ps 37:1 nor be *j* of those
Eze 39:25 *j* for My holy name
Joel 2:18 became *j* for His land
Na 1:2 a *j* and avenging God
Zec 8:2 exceedingly *j* for Zion
Ac 17:5 But the Jews… became *j*
Ro 10:19 make you *j*
Ro 11:14 make my kinsmen *j*
2Co 11:2 For I am *j* over you

JEALOUSY
Dt 29:20 His *j* will smolder
1Ki 14:22 people provoked Him to *j*
Job 5:2 *j* kills the gullible
Ps 78:58 moved Him to *j*
Ps 79:5 *j* burn like fire?
Pr 6:34 For *j* is the rage
Eze 8:3 the image of *j* was
Eze 16:42 My *j* shall depart
Eze 36:5 in the fire of My *j*
Zep 1:18 by the fire of His *j*
Zec 1:14 great *j* for Jerusalem
Ac 5:17 and were filled with *j*
1Co 10:22 provoke the Lord to *j*?
Gal 5:20 hatred, strife, *j*, rage

JERUSALEM
1Ki 11:7 hill that is close to *J*
1Ki 12:28 you to go up to *J*
2Ki 24:15 into exile from *J*
2Ch 36:10 king over Judah and *J*
Ps 137:7 Edom in the day of *J*
Isa 2:3 word of the LORD from *J*

JESUS
Mt 1:1 genealogy of *J* Christ
Mt 1:21 His name *J*, for He will save
Mt 4:17 *J* began to preach
Mt 8:5 *J* entered Capernaum
Mt 11:1 *J* finished instructing
Mt 14:25 *J* went to them
Mt 16:20 tell no one that He was *J*
Mt 18:1 came to *J*, saying
Mt 18:2 *J* called a little child
Mt 20:34 *J* had compassion

Mt 21:11 This is *J*, the prophet
Mt 21:12 *J* went into the temple
Mt 22:1 *J* spoke to them again
Mt 26:4 take *J* covertly
Mt 26:6 *J* was in Bethany
Mt 26:69 with *J* of Galilee
Mt 27:46 *J* cried out
Mt 27:57 Joseph…a disciple of *J*
Mt 28:5 *J* who was crucified
Mk 1:9 *J* came from Nazareth
Mk 1:14 *J* came to Galilee
Mk 1:24 *J* of Nazareth?
Mk 1:45 *J* could no more
Mk 5:7 have You to do with me, *J*
Mk 5:22 saw *J* and…fell at His feet
Mk 9:2 *J* took with Him Peter
Mk 10:47 *J*, Son of David
Mk 11:7 They brought the colt to *J*
Mk 12:35 While *J* taught
Mk 14:53 They led *J* away
Mk 15:1 they bound *J* and took Him
Mk 16:6 for *J* of Nazareth
Mk 16:9 *J* rose early on the first day
Lk 2:52 *J* increased in wisdom
Lk 3:21 *J* also had been baptized
Lk 4:1 *J*, being filled with
Lk 5:10 *J* said to Simon
Lk 8:28 When he saw *J*, he cried
Lk 9:42 *J* rebuked the unclean spirit
Lk 10:21 *J* rejoiced in the Holy Spirit
Lk 13:14 *J* had healed on the
Lk 17:13 *J*, Master, have pity
Lk 22:2 seeking how to kill *J*
Lk 22:47 He drew near to *J*
Lk 22:63 men who guarded *J*
Lk 23:8 Herod saw *J*
Lk 23:25 he sentenced *J*
Lk 23:26 to carry it behind *J*
Lk 23:34 *J* said, "Father, forgive
Lk 23:52 asked for the body of *J*
Lk 24:15 *J* Himself drew near
Jn 1:17 truth came through *J* Christ
Jn 1:45 *J* of Nazareth
Jn 2:1 The mother of *J*
Jn 2:11 *J* did in Cana
Jn 3:2 He came to *J* by night
Jn 4:2 *J* Himself did not baptize
Jn 4:7 *J* said to her, "Give Me a
Jn 6:11 *J* then took the loaves
Jn 6:19 *J* walking on the sea
Jn 6:35 *J* said to them, "I am
Jn 8:6 *J* stooped down and wrote
Jn 11:5 *J* loved Martha
Jn 11:25 *J* said to her, "I am
Jn 11:35 *J* wept
Jn 11:51 prophesied that *J* would die
Jn 14:6 *J* said to him, "I am the way
Jn 17:3 and *J* Christ, whom You
Jn 18:12 the Jews arrested *J*
Jn 19:20 where *J* was crucified
Jn 19:40 took the body of *J*
Jn 20:14 know that it was *J*
Jn 20:30 *J* performed many
Jn 21:13 *J*…took the bread
Ac 1:1 *J* began…to do and teach
Ac 1:11 *J*, who was taken up
Ac 2:36 *J*, whom you have crucified
Ac 5:42 to teach and preach *J*
Ac 9:5 *J*, whom you are
Ac 16:18 in the name of *J* Christ
Ac 19:5 in the name of the Lord *J*
Ro 3:24 that is in Christ *J*
Ro 6:3 baptized into *J* Christ
Ro 6:23 eternal life through *J*
1Co 2:2 among you except *J*
1Co 8:6 there is one Lord *J*
1Co 15:57 through our Lord *J*
2Co 4:14 raised the Lord *J*
Gal 2:16 through faith in *J*
Gal 3:28 all one in Christ *J*
Gal 6:14 cross of our Lord *J*
Eph 2:10 created in Christ *J*
Php 2:10 at the name of *J* every knee
Col 3:17 name of the Lord *J*
1Th 3:13 coming of our Lord *J*
1Th 4:14 believe that *J* died
1Ti 4:6 good minister of *J* Christ
Titus 2:13 great God and Savior *J*
Heb 10:19 by the blood of *J*
Heb 12:2 *J*, the author and finisher
Heb 13:20 *J*, the Great Shepherd
1Pe 3:21 resurrection of *J* Christ
1Jn 1:7 blood of *J* Christ His Son
1Jn 4:2 that *J* Christ has come
1Jn 5:1 believes that *J* is the Christ
Rev 14:12 and the faith of *J*
Rev 22:20 Even so, come Lord *J*

JOHN

Mt 3:1 *J* the Baptist came
Mt 4:12 *J* was put in prison
Mt 11:4 tell *J* what you hear
Mt 11:13 prophesied until *J*
Mt 14:2 *J* the Baptist
Mk 1:6 *J* was clothed with
Mk 6:20 Herod feared *J*
Mk 11:32 everyone held *J* to be
Lk 1:60 shall be called *J*
Lk 9:19 *J* the Baptist
Jn 1:28 where *J* was baptizing
Jn 5:36 greater testimony than…*J*
Jn 21:15 Simon, son of *J*, do you
Ac 3:1 Peter and *J* went up
Ac 12:12 *J*, whose other name was
Rev 1:9 I, *J*, both your brother

JOINED

Ge 2:24 mother and be *j*
Mt 19:6 what God has *j*
Eph 4:16 the whole body is *j*

JOINT

Ps 22:14 bones are out of *j*
Pr 25:19 a foot out of *j*

JOINTS

Col 2:19 knit together by *j*
Heb 4:12 and spirit, of *j*

JOURNEYED

Ex 12:37 children of Israel *j*
Nu 9:17 children of Israel *j*
Nu 9:20 of the LORD they *j*
Nu 9:21 was lifted up, they *j*

JOY

Ge 31:27 sent you away with *j*
Dt 24:5 must bring *j* to his wife
1Ch 16:27 strength and *j* are
Ezr 3:13 noise of the shout of *j*
Ezr 6:16 house of God with *j*
Est 8:16 To the Jews belonged…*j*
Job 38:7 sons of God shouted for *j*
Job 41:22 sorrow is turned into *j*
Ps 16:11 fullness of *j*
Ps 30:5 *j* comes in the morning
Ps 51:8 Make me to hear *j*
Ps 51:12 Restore to me the *j*

Ps 126:5 sow in tears…reap in *j*
Ecc 2:26 wisdom, knowledge, and *j*
Isa 9:3 and increased the *j*
Isa 12:6 Cry out and shout for *j*
Isa 24:11 *j* is turned to gloom.
Isa 29:19 shall increase their *j*
Isa 51:11 and everlasting *j* shall be
Isa 55:12 you shall go out with *j*
Isa 61:3 oil of *j* for mourning
La 2:15 the *j* of the whole earth
Mt 13:20 receives it with *j*
Lk 1:14 You will have *j*
Lk 2:10 good news of great *j*
Lk 15:7 *j* in heaven over one
Jn 15:11 My *j* may remain in you
Jn 16:20 sorrow…turned into *j*
Ro 14:17 *j* in the Holy Spirit
2Co 8:2 abundance of their *j*
Php 2:2 fulfill my *j*
1Th 2:19 our hope, or *j*
Phm 1:7 we have great *j*
Heb 12:2 *j* that was set before Him
Jas 1:2 count it all *j*
1Jn 1:4 our *j* may be complete

JOYFUL
Ps 100:1 Make a *j* noise
Isa 56:7 and make them *j*

JUDAH
Ge 29:35 she called his name *J*
Ge 38:6 *J* took a wife for Er
Ge 44:14 *J* and his brothers
Ge 49:10 shall not depart from *J*
Zec 14:14 And even *J* will fight
Mt 2:6 Bethlehem, in the land of *J*
Heb 7:14 descended from *J*
Rev 5:5 Lion of the tribe of *J*
Rev 7:5 from the tribe of *J*

JUDAS
Mt 10:4 *J* Iscariot, who also
Mt 26:47 *J*, one of the twelve, came
Lk 22:3 Then Satan entered into *J*
Lk 22:48 *J*, do you betray
Jn 14:22 *J* (not Iscariot) said
Ac 1:25 *J* by transgression fell
Ac 15:22 *J* called Barsabas

JUDGE
Ge 16:5 The LORD *j* between
1Ch 16:33 coming to *j* the earth
Mt 5:25 deliver you to the *j*
Mt 7:1 "*J* not
Lk 12:14 who appointed Me a *j*
Lk 18:2 *j* who did not fear God
Jn 5:30 As I hear, I *j*
Jn 7:24 Do not *j* according
Jn 8:15 I *j* no one
Jn 12:47 *j* the world but to
2Ti 4:1 Christ, who will *j*
Jas 4:11 If you *j* the law

JUDGES
Isa 40:23 He makes the *j* of the
Jn 5:22 The Father *j*
Ro 2:3 O man, who *j*
1Co 2:15 he who is spiritual *j*
1Co 4:4 *j* me is the Lord
1Pe 2:23 Him who *j* righteously

JUDGMENT
Ps 37:6 *j* as the noonday
Mt 5:21 be in danger of the *j*
Mt 23:33 can you escape the *j*
Jn 5:30 My *j* is just
Jn 8:16 if I do judge, My *j*
Ro 5:16 *j* from one sin
Ro 14:13 let us no longer pass *j*
2Co 5:10 appear before the *j*
Heb 9:27 after this comes the *j*
1Pe 4:17 time has come for *j*
2Pe 2:3 Their *j*, made long ago
Jude 1:6 darkness for the *j*

JUDGMENTS
Ps 19:9 The *j* of the LORD are
Ro 11:33 unsearchable are His *j*

JUST
Ge 6:9 Noah was a *j* man
Hab 2:4 *j* shall live by his
Mt 1:19 her husband, being a *j*
Lk 14:14 resurrection of the *j*
Ac 24:15 dead, both of the *j*
Ro 1:17 *j* shall live by faith
Ro 3:26 that He might be *j*
1Jn 1:9 He is faithful and *j*

JUSTICE
Ps 72:2 And Your poor with *j*
Isa 28:17 *j* the measuring line
Isa 30:18 the LORD is a God of *j*
Isa 42:1 He shall bring forth *j*
Isa 59:14 *J* is turned backward
Isa 61:8 I, the LORD, love *j*
Da 4:37 truth, and His ways *j*
Zec 7:9 Execute true *j*
Mal 2:17 "Where is the God of *j*
Ac 8:33 His humiliation *j*

JUSTIFICATION
Ro 4:25 was raised for our *j*
Ro 5:16 trespasses, leads to *j*

JUSTIFIED
Job 13:18 that I will be *j*
Ps 51:4 You are *j* when
Isa 45:25 seed of Israel be *j*
Mt 12:37 you will be *j*
Lk 7:29 tax collectors, *j* God
Lk 7:35 wisdom is *j* by all
Ro 2:13 the hearers…are not *j*
Ro 3:24 *j* freely by His grace
Ro 4:2 Abraham was *j* by works
Ro 5:1 we have been *j* by faith
Ro 8:30 those…He also *j*
1Co 6:11 you were *j* in the name
Gal 2:16 a man is not *j* by
Gal 3:24 we might be *j* by faith
Titus 3:7 *j* by His grace
Jas 2:21 Abraham our father *j* by

JUSTIFIES
Pr 17:15 who *j* the wicked
Ro 8:33 It is God who *j*

JUSTIFY
Ex 23:7 will not *j* the wicked
Isa 5:23 *j* the wicked for a reward
Isa 53:11 My righteous servant shall *j*
Lk 10:29 desiring to *j* himself
Gal 3:8 that God would *j*

K

KEEP
Ex 20:8 day and *k* it holy
Hab 2:20 Let all the earth *k*
Mt 19:17 *k* the commandments
Jn 14:15 "If you love Me, *k*
Jn 17:11 through Your name *k*
Eph 4:3 *k* the unity of the
1Jn 2:3 *k* His commandments

KEEPER
Ge 4:9 Am I my brother's *k*

KEPT
2Sa 22:22 For I have *k* the
Mt 19:20 "All these I have *k*
Jn 15:10 love, even as I have *k*
Ac 5:2 *k* back part of the
2Ti 4:7 I have *k* the faith

KEY
Lk 11:52 taken away the *k*
Rev 3:7 He who has the *k*

KEYS
Mt 16:19 I will give you the *k*
Rev 1:18 And I have the *k*

KILL
Ex 12:21 *k* the Passover lamb
Dt 32:39 I *k* and I make alive
2Ki 5:7 "Am I God, to *k*
Ecc 3:3 A time to *k*
Mt 23:37 you who *k* the prophets
Lk 11:49 of them they will *k*
Lk 12:4 afraid of those who *k*
Jn 7:19 Why do you seek to *k*
Ac 10:13 *k* and eat

KILLED
Ge 4:8 his brother Abel and *k*
Ps 44:22 for Your sake we are *k*
Mt 16:21 and scribes, and be *k*
Lk 13:4 Siloam fell and *k* them
Ac 3:15 *k* the Creator of Life
Ro 8:36 Your sake we are *k*
1Th 2:15 both *k* the Lord

KILLS
2Co 3:6 for the letter *k*

KIND
Ge 6:20 every *k* of animal
Mk 9:29 *k* cannot come out
1Co 13:4 suffers long and is *k*
Eph 4:32 And be *k* one to

KINDLY
Ac 27:3 Julius treated Paul *k*

KINDNESS
Ps 117:2 For His merciful *k*
Isa 54:10 *k* shall not depart
Jer 2:2 I remember you, the *k*
2Co 6:6 by patience, by *k*
2Pe 1:7 and to your brotherly *k*

KING
Ge 14:18 Melchizedek *k* of Salem
Ge 41:46 Pharaoh, the *k* of Egypt
Ex 2:23 the *k* of Egypt died
1Sa 11:15 Saul *k* before the LORD
1Sa 16:1 a *k* for Myself from among
Ezr 7:12 Artaxerxes, *k* of kings
Da 2:37 You, O *k*, are the *k*
Mt 1:6 David the *k* was the father
Mt 2:2 born *K* of the Jews?
Mt 5:35 city of the great *K*
Mt 21:5 your *K* is coming
Mt 25:34 the *K* will say to those
Mt 27:37 THE *K* OF THE JEWS
Mk 15:18 Hail, *K* of the Jews
Lk 19:38 Blessed is the *K* who comes
Lk 23:2 He Himself is Christ a *K*
Jn 1:49 You are the *K* of Israel!
Jn 19:15 Shall I crucify your *K*
Ac 26:27 *K* Agrippa, do you believe
1Ti 6:15 the *K* of kings
Heb 7:1 Melchizedek, *k* of Salem
1Pe 2:17 Fear God. Honor the *k*
Rev 15:3 O *K* of saints
Rev 19:16 *K* OF KINGS

KINGDOM
Ex 19:6 be to Me a *k* of priests
Ps 145:13 Your *k* is an everlasting *k*
Isa 9:7 and over his *k*
Da 4:17 over the *k* of men
Mt 3:2 the *k* of heaven is at hand
Mt 13:11 mysteries of the *k*
Mk 4:30 liken the *k* of God
Gal 5:21 shall not inherit the *k*
Rev 17:17 their *k* to the beast

KISS
Ge 27:26 *k* me, my son
Ps 2:12 *K* the son, lest He
SS 1:2 Let him *k* me with
Mt 26:48 "Whomever I shall *k*
Lk 7:45 You gave Me no *k*
Ro 16:16 with a holy *k*

KISSED
Ge 27:27 He came near and *k*
Ge 29:11 Jacob *k* Rachel and wept
Ru 1:9 she *k* them, and they
Ps 85:10 and peace have *k*
Pr 7:13 caught him, and *k* him
Mt 26:49 "Hail, Rabbi!" and *k* Him
Lk 15:20 embraced his neck and *k*

KISSES
Pr 27:6 but the *k* of an enemy
Ss 1:2 with the *k* of his mouth

KNEE
Isa 45:23 That to Me every *k*
Ro 11:4 have not bowed the *k*
Php 2:10 of Jesus every *k*

KNEES
Isa 35:3 support the feeble *k*
Eph 3:14 this reason I bow my *k*
Heb 12:12 your weak *k*

KNEW
Jer 1:5 in the womb I *k*
Mt 7:23 to them, 'I never *k*
2Co 5:21 God made Him who *k*

KNOW
Ge 15:8 I *k* that I will possess it
Ex 3:7 for I *k* their sorrows
Dt 8:2 to *k* what was in your heart
1Sa 17:46 all the earth may *k* that
Ps 46:10 Be still and *k*
Ps 139:2 You *k* when I sit down
Pr 27:1 you do not *k* what a day
Ecc 1:17 to *k* wisdom and to *k*
Jer 31:34 "*K* the LORD," . . . all shall *k*
Eze 6:7 you shall *k* that I am
Mt 1:25 and did not *k* her until
Mt 7:16 You will *k* them by
Mt 24:42 do not *k* what hour
Mk 2:10 may *k* that the Son of Man
Lk 1:4 you might *k* the certainty
Lk 11:13 being evil, *k* how to give
Lk 18:20 *k* the commandments
Jn 1:10 yet the world did not *k* Him
Jn 8:19 You *k* neither Me
Jn 9:21 we do not *k*
Jn 21:17 You *k* everything. You *k* that
Ac 1:7 It is not for you to *k*
Ro 3:17 they do not *k* the way
Ro 7:14 We *k* that the law
Ro 8:28 We *k* that all things
1Co 2:2 I determined not to *k*
1Co 13:9 For we *k* in part, and
Eph 1:18 may *k* what is the hope
Php 3:10 to *k* Him, and the power
1Th 5:2 you *k* perfectly that the
2Ti 1:12 I *k* whom I have believed
1Jn 2:3 By this we *k* that we *k*
1Jn 3:14 We *k* that we have passed
Rev 2:2 I *k* your works, your labor

KNOWLEDGE
Ge 2:9 tree of *k* of good and evil

2Ch 1:10 give wisdom and *k* to me
Job 21:22 “Can anyone teach God *k*
Ps 53:4 workers of iniquity no *k*
Pr 1:7 is the beginning of *k*
Pr 18:15 prudent gets *k*
Ecc 1:18 who increases in *k* also
Isa 11:2 the Spirit of *k* and of the
Isa 53:11 By His *k*
Da 1:17 God gave them *k* and skill
Hos 6:6 the *k* of God more than
Lk 1:77 to give *k* of salvation
Ro 3:20 comes the *k* of sin
1Co 8:1 all have *k*.” *K* produces
1Co 13:2 all mysteries and all *k*
2Co 10:5 against the *k* of God
Eph 3:19 Christ which surpasses *k*
2Pe 3:18 grace and *k* of our Lord

KNOWS
Est 4:14 who *k* if you may
Jer 9:24 he understands and *k* Me

L

LABOR
Ex 20:9 Six days you shall *l*
Ecc 2:22 man with all his *l*
Mt 11:28 to Me, all you who *l*
1Co 15:58 knowing that your *l*
Eph 4:28 I instead, let him *l*
Php 1:22 mean fruitful *l*
1Th 1:3 your work of faith, *l*
Heb 6:10 forget your work and *l*
Rev 2:2 your works, your *l*

LABORED
1Co 15:10 *l* more abundantly

LABORERS
Mt 9:37 but the *l* are few

LABORING
1Th 2:9 *l* night and day

LABORS
Jn 4:38 benefited from their *l*
2Co 11:23 *l* more abundant
Rev 14:13 may rest from their *l*

LADDER
Ge 28:12 and saw a *l*

LAID
Ge 9:23 *l* it upon both
Ge 22:6 and *l* it on Isaac
Ex 5:9 more work *l* upon
Dt 32:34 Is not this *l* up in store
Ru 4:16 took the child, *l* him
1Ki 3:20 *l* him at her bosom and *l*
1Ki 18:33 and *l* him on the wood
Ezr 3:6 the temple…was not yet *l*
Job 31:9 I have *l* wait at my
Job 38:4 I *l* the foundations
Ps 88:6 You have *l* me in the
Ps 119:30 I have *l* before me
Ps 142:3 they have *l* a snare
Isa 6:7 he *l* it on my mouth
Isa 23:1 for Tyre is *l* waste
Isa 47:6 you have *l* your yoke
Jer 17:11 which it has not *l*
Eze 4:5 have *l* upon you the years
Eze 6:6 cities shall be *l* waste
Eze 24:2 king of Babylon has *l* siege
Hag 2:15 stone was *l* upon stone
Mt 14:3 Herod had *l* hold of John
Mt 21:7 *l* their garments
Mt 26:50 and *l* hands on Jesus
Mt 27:60 *l* it in his own new tomb
Mk 6:5 He *l* His hands on a few
Mk 15:47 saw where He was *l*
Lk 2:7 and *l* Him in a manger
Lk 6:48 and *l* the foundation
Lk 12:19 have many goods *l* up
Jn 7:30 no one *l* hands on Him
Ac 7:58 witnesses *l* down their
Ac 19:6 Paul had *l* his hands
1Co 3:10 I have *l* the foundation
2Ti 4:8 crown of righteousness is *l*
1Jn 3:16 He *l* down His life

LAKE
Lk 8:33 steep bank into the *l*
Rev 19:20 thrown alive into the *l*

LAMB
Ge 22:7 where is the *l* for the
2Sa 12:3 a single small ewe *l*
Isa 11:6 shall dwell with the *l*
Isa 53:7 as a *l* to the slaughter
Jn 1:29 the *L* of God, who takes
Ac 8:32 as a *l* before its shearer
Rev 5:6 I saw a *L* in the midst
Rev 21:9 the bride, the wife of the *L*

LAMP
Ps 119:105 Your word is a *l* to
Lk 11:34 The eye is the *l* of

LAMPS
Ex 25:37 shall make its seven *l*
Ex 30:7 *l*, he must burn incense
Ex 30:8 Aaron lights the *l*
2Ch 13:11 *l* to burn every evening
Rev 4:5 Seven *l* of fire were burning

LAMPSTAND
Ex 25:31 make a *l* of pure gold.
Ex 25:32 branches of the *l*

LAND
Ge 1:9 let the dry *l* appear
Ge 2:12 gold of that *l* is good
Ge 11:31 into the *l* of Canaan
Ex 20:2 out of the *l* of Egypt
Ex 20:12 days may be long in the *l*
Lev 25:4 complete rest for the *l*
Lev 25:10 throughout all the *l*
Nu 13:2 explore the *l* of Canaan
Dt 6:3 *l* that flows with milk
Jos 13:1 much of the *l* still remains
Jos 14:1 the *l* of Canaan
Jos 18:1 The *l* was subdued
Job 10:22 a *l* of darkness
Ps 27:13 in the *l* of the living
Ps 37:34 to inherit the *l*
Ps 63:1 in a dry and thirsty *l*
Ps 85:9 glory may dwell in our *l*
Ps 105:23 Jacob sojourned in the *l*
Pr 12:11 tills his *l* will be satisfied
Isa 7:24 all the *l* shall become
Isa 9:1 the *l* of Zebulun and the *l*
Isa 9:2 dwell in the *l* of
Jer 30:3 to return to the *l*
Hos 1:2 for the *l* has committed
Joel 2:18 jealous for His *l*
Jnh 2:10 Jonah out upon dry *l*
Zep 2:3 all you humble of the *l*
Mt 2:6 Bethlehem, in the *l* of
Mt 9:26 went out into all that *l*
Mt 10:15 for the *l* of Sodom
Mk 4:1 by the sea on the *l*

Lk 5:3 a little from the *l*
Lk 12:16 "The *l* of a rich man
Ac 4:34 owners of *l* or houses
Ac 7:6 sojourners in a *l*
Heb 6:7 *l* that drinks in the rain
Heb 11:9 he dwelt in the promised *l*

LANDS
Lev 26:36 their hearts in the *l*
Lev 26:39 in your enemies' *l*
Ezr 9:2 people of the *l*
Jer 27:6 I have given all these *l*
Eze 20:6 the glory of all *l*
Eze 20:15 the glory of all *l*

LANGUAGE
Ge 11:1 whole earth had one *l*
Ac 2:6 speaking in his own *l*
Col 3:8 blasphemy, and filthy *l*

LANGUAGES
Ge 10:20 according to their *l*
Da 3:4 peoples, nations, and *l*

LAUGH
Ge 18:13 "Why did Sarah *l*
Ps 37:13 The Lord will *l* at him
Lk 6:25 Woe to you who *l*

LAW
Ex 24:12 stone tablets with *l*
Nu 5:29 the *l* of jealousies
Dt 4:44 the *l* which Moses set
Dt 17:18 write a copy of this *l*
Dt 28:58 the words of this *l*
Jos 1:8 the *L* must not depart
2Ki 22:8 the *L* in the house
Ezr 7:10 his heart to seek the *l*
Ne 8:1 the Book of the *L*
Ps 1:2 *l* of the Lord, and in His *l*
Ps 119:18 things from Your *l*
Isa 8:16 Seal the *l* among
Jer 31:33 I will put My *l* within
Da 6:12 the *l* of the Medes and
Mt 5:17 to abolish the *L*
Lk 16:16 "The *L* and the Prophets
Ro 2:12 *l* will be judged by the *l*
Ro 3:20 works of the *l* no flesh
Ro 7:1 the *l* has dominion
Gal 2:19 *l* I am dead to the *l*
Heb 7:12 a change in the *l*
Jas 2:10 keep the whole *l* and yet
1Jn 3:4 sin breaks the *l*, for sin

LAWFUL
Mt 22:17 Is it *l* to pay taxes
1Co 6:12 All things are *l*

LAWLESSNESS
Am 6:3 session of *l*
2Th 2:7 *l* is already working

LAY
Ge 9:21 and *l* uncovered
Ge 22:12 "Do not *l* your hands
Ge 37:22 but *l* no hand on him
Ex 16:14 *l* a small flaky thing
Lev 1:4 he shall *l* his hand
Nu 11:11 You *l* the burden
Dt 20:19 When you *l* siege to
Jdg 9:34 *l* in wait by Shechem
Ru 3:7 his feet, and *l* down
1Sa 19:24 he *l* down naked
2Sa 11:4 and he *l* with her
1Ki 5:17 to *l* the foundation
Est 3:6 disdained to *l* hands on
Job 22:22 and *l* up His words
Job 34:23 He will not *l* upon man
Ps 3:5 I *l* down and slept
Isa 28:16 I *l* in Zion a stone
Isa 42:15 I will *l* waste mountains
Jer 6:21 I will *l* stumbling blocks
Eze 4:2 Then *l* siege against it
Eze 19:2 She *l* down among
Mt 8:20 has no place to *l* His head
Mt 28:6 where the Lord *l*
Mk 16:18 *l* hands on the sick
Lk 22:53 did not *l* hands on Me
Jn 10:15 And I *l* down My life
Jn 15:13 a man *l* down his life
Ac 8:19 I *l* hands on may receive
Ro 9:33 "Look! I *l* in Zion
1Co 3:11 no one can *l* another
1Ti 5:22 Do not *l* hands suddenly
1Ti 6:12 *L* hold on eternal life
Heb 12:1 let us also *l* aside every
1Jn 3:16 we ought to *l* down

LEAD
Ps 25:5 *L* me in Your truth
Mt 6:13 And *l* us not into
Mt 15:14 And if the blind *l*
Lk 6:39 "Can the blind *l*

LEADS
Ps 23:3 He *l* me in paths
Pr 2:18 her house *l* down to death

LEAP
Isa 35:6 the lame man shall *l*
Lk 6:23 *l* for joy

LEARN
Isa 1:17 *L* to do good
Mt 11:29 yoke upon you, and *l*

LEARNING
Ac 26:24 *l* is turning you to madness

LEAVE
Ge 2:24 a man will *l* his
Ps 16:10 For You will not *l*
Heb 13:5 "I will never *l*

LEAVEN
Ex 12:15 you shall put away *l*
Ex 12:19 *l* found in your houses
Lev 6:17 not be baked with *l*

LEAVENED
Ex 12:15 whoever eats *l*
Ex 12:19 eats that which is *l*
Ex 12:20 shall eat nothing *l*
Ex 13:3 nothing *l* shall be eaten
Dt 16:3 You must not eat *l*

LED
Ps 107:7 *l* them on a level road
Ro 8:14 For as many as are *l*

LEFT
Dt 17:11 to the right or to the *l*
Mt 6:3 *l* hand know what

LEND
Ps 37:26 are gracious and *l*
Lk 6:34 And if you *l*

LENGTH
Pr 3:2 *l* of days and long
Pr 3:16 *L* of days is in her
Eze 40:21 its *l* was fifty

leopard
Isa 11:6 the *l* shall lie down
Jer 13:23 or the *l* his spots

LEPER
Lev 14:2 the *l* in the day of his cleansing
Nu 5:2 the camp every *l*
Mt 8:2 then a *l* came
Mt 26:6 of Simon the *l*

LEPERS
Mt 10:8 cleanse the *l*
Lk 4:27 many *l* were in Israel
Lk 7:22 the *l* are cleansed
Lk 17:12 ten men who were *l*

LEPROSY
Lev 13:8 unclean. It is *l*
2Ki 5:1 but he had *l*
Mk 1:42 the *l* immediately
Lk 5:12 a man full of *l*

LET
Ge 1:3 "*L* there be light

LEVIATHAN
Job 41:1 "Can you draw out *L*

LEVITE
Lk 10:32 likewise a *L*

LIAR
Jn 8:44 for he is a *l* and the
Ro 3:4 and every man a *l*
1Jn 1:10 we make Him a *l*
1Jn 4:20 his brother, he is a *l*

LIBERALLY
Jas 1:5 who gives to all men *l*

LIBERTY
Lev 25:10 year, and proclaim *l*
Lk 4:18 to set at *l* those who are
2Co 3:17 Lord is, there is *l*

LIE
Ge 19:32 let us *l* with him
Ge 28:13 land on which you *l*
Ge 39:7 "*L* with me."
Ex 23:11 let it rest and *l*
Lev 18:22 *l* with a man
Lev 19:11 nor deal falsely, nor *l*
Nu 23:19 that He should *l*
Dt 6:7 when you *l* down
Dt 31:16 You are about to *l* down
1Sa 15:29 will not *l* nor repent
Ps 4:8 *l* down in peace
Ps 23:2 He makes me *l* down
Ps 89:35 I will not *l* to David
Pr 1:18 They *l* in wait
Pr 3:24 When you *l* down
Isa 11:6 leopard shall *l* down
Isa 21:9 of her gods *l* shattered
Jer 3:25 We *l* down in
Eze 32:21 *l* still, uncircumcised
Am 6:4 who *l* upon beds of ivory
Mic 7:2 All of them *l* in wait
Ac 5:4 You did not *l* to men
Ro 1:25 truth of God into a *l*
Ro 3:7 through my *l* the truth
Heb 6:18 impossible for God to *l*
1Jn 1:6 we *l* and do not
Rev 11:8 will *l* in the street
Rev 14:5 No *l* was found

LIED
Ps 78:36 they *l* to Him with
Isa 57:11 when you *l* and you
Jer 5:12 They have *l* about

LIES
Lev 20:11 If a man *l* with
Jdg 16:10 You have told me *l*
Ps 4:2 seek after *l*
Ps 58:3 those who speak *l*
Ps 101:7 who tells *l* shall not
Ps 119:69 spoken *l* against me
Pr 23:28 She also *l* in wait
Jer 14:14 prophets prophesy *l*
Zep 3:13 nor speak *l*
Jn 8:44 When he *l*, he speaks from
Rev 21:16 The city *l* as a square

LIFE
Ge 2:7 the breath of *l*
Lev 17:11 For the *l* of the
Dt 30:15 before you *l*
Ps 72:14 he redeem their *l*
Pr 3:18 She is a tree of *l*
Pr 8:35 finds me finds *l*
Lk 12:23 *L* is more than
Jn 1:4 *l* was the light
Jn 5:21 so the Son gives *l*
Jn 6:63 who gives *l*…and are *l*
Jn 8:12 have the light of *l*
Jn 10:15 And I lay down My *l*
Jn 11:25 resurrection and the *l*
Jn 13:38 you lay down your *l*
Gal 2:20 *l* I now live
Col 3:3 *l* is hidden with
Jas 4:14 What is your *l*
1Jn 1:2 *l* was revealed
1Jn 2:16 and the pride of *l*
1Jn 5:11 has given us eternal *l*
Rev 20:4 They came to *l* and
Rev 21:27 Lamb's Book of *L*
Rev 22:14 right to the tree of *l*
Rev 22:17 the water of *l* freely
Rev 22:19 out of the Book of *L*

LIFT
Ps 121:1 I will *l* up my eyes to
Jas 4:10 Lord, and He will *l*

LIFTED
Eze 28:2 your heart is *l*
Lk 16:23 he *l* up his eyes
Jn 3:14 the Son of Man be *l*
Jn 12:32 And if I be *l*

LIGHT
Ge 1:3 "Let there be *l*
Ps 27:1 The LORD is my *l*
Ps 119:105 and a *l* to my path
Pr 13:9 The *l* of the righteous
Pr 29:13 The LORD gives *l*
Ecc 11:7 *l* is sweet
Isa 2:5 let us walk in the *l*
Isa 58:8 *l* shall break forth
Mt 5:14 "You are the *l*
Mt 5:16 Let your *l* so shine
Lk 16:8 than the sons of *l*
Jn 1:4 and the life was the *l*
Jn 3:19 darkness rather than *l*
Jn 8:12 saying, "I am the *l*
2Co 4:6 who commanded the *l*
Eph 5:8 Walk as children of *l*
1Th 5:5 You are all the sons of *l*
1Pe 2:9 into His marvelous *l*
1Jn 1:5 to you: God is *l*
1Jn 1:7 *l* as He is in the
1Jn 2:9 says he is in the *l*
Rev 21:23 glory of God is its *l*, and

LIGHTNING
Ex 20:18 witnessed the thunder and the *l*
Mt 24:27 'For as the *l*
Mt 28:3 countenance was like *l*

LIGHTNINGS
Rev 4:5 *L* and thunderings and voices

LIGHTS
Ge 1:14 "Let there be *l*
Php 2:15 which you shine as *l*

LIKENESS
Ge 1:26 after our *l*
Ex 20:4 any graven idol, or any *l*
Ps 17:15 I awake with Your *l*
Php 2:7 was made in the *l*

LILY
2Ch 4:5 the flower of a *l*
SS 2:2 As a *l* among thorns

LINE
2Ki 21:13 over Jerusalem the measuring *l*
Ps 19:4 their *l* has gone out

LINEN
Lev 16:4 put on the holy *l* tunic
Mk 15:46 wrapped Him in the *l*

LION
Ge 49:9 lies down like a *l*
Dt 33:20 He dwells as a *l*
Jdg 14:6 he tore the *l* in two

1Sa 17:36 the *l* and the bear
Ps 7:2 tear my soul like a *l*
Ps 22:13 a preying and roaring *l*
Ps 91:13 tread upon the *l* and
Pr 28:1 are bold as a *l*
Pr 28:15 As a roaring *l* and
Isa 11:6 the young *l* and the
Isa 65:25 and the *l* shall eat
Eze 10:14 the face of a *l*
Da 7:4 first was like a *l* and
Hos 11:10 who roars like a *l*
Joel 1:6 like the teeth of a *l*
1Pe 5:8 as a roaring *l*
Rev 5:5 *L* of the tribe of Judah
Rev 13:2 like the mouth of a *l*

LION'S
Ge 49:9 Judah is a *l* cub

LIONS
2Ch 9:18 two *l* standing beside the
Ps 35:17 my life from the *l*
Da 6:16 into the den of *l*
Rev 9:17 like the heads of *l*

LIPS
Ps 12:3 off all flattering *l*
Pr 10:21 The *l* of the righteous
Pr 20:15 But the *l* of
Isa 6:5 am a man of unclean *l*
1Co 14:21 other *l* I will speak
1Pe 3:10 from evil, and his *l*

LISTEN
Dt 18:15 You must *l* to him.
Ac 13:16 you who fear God, *l*

LITTLE
Mt 10:42 one of these *l* ones
Mt 14:31 "O you of *l* faith
Lk 7:47 he who is forgiven *l*
Lk 19:17 faithful in very *l*

LIVE
Ge 3:22 eat, and *l* forever
Lev 18:5 he shall *l*
Am 5:4 Seek Me and *l*
Hab 2:4 but the just shall *l*
Mt 4:4 *l* by bread alone
Ac 17:28 'For in Him we *l*
Ro 12:18 *l* peaceably with all
Gal 2:20 the life I now *l*
Gal 5:25 If we *l* in the Spirit

LIVED
Ro 14:9 died and rose and *l*

LIVES
Dt 8:3 but man *l* by every
Gal 2:20 Christ who *l* in me
1Jn 3:16 to lay down our *l*
Rev 1:18 "I am He who *l*

LIVING
Ge 2:7 and man became a *l*
Ps 56:13 in the light of the *l*
Mt 22:32 the dead, but of the *l*
Lk 24:5 do you seek the *l*
Php 1:21 *l* is Christ, and to
Rev 4:7 *l* creature was like a

LOAVES
Mt 14:17 have only five *l*
Jn 6:26 you ate of the *l*

LOCUST
Dt 28:38 the *l* will consume it
Joel 1:4 What the adult *l*

LONG
1Ki 18:21 How *l* will you stay
Mk 12:38 go about in *l* robes

LONGED
Ps 119:174 *l* for Your salvation

LOOK
Pr 6:17 a proud *l*
Zec 12:10 *l* to Me, whom they
Lk 17:23 say to you, '*L* here
2Co 4:18 while we do not *l*

LOOKED
Ps 102:19 For He has *l* down
Isa 5:7 He *l* for justice
Lk 22:61 Lord turned and *l*
Heb 11:26 he *l* to the reward

LOOKS
Isa 2:11 The lofty *l* of man
Mt 5:28 to you that whoever *l*
Lk 9:62 the plow and *l* back

LOOSE
Job 6:9 let *l* His hand
Mt 16:19 and whatever you *l*

LORD
Ge 18:12 my *l* is old also
Ge 22:14 The *L* Will Provide
Ge 42:30 the *l* of the land
Ex 17:15 The *L* Is My Banner
Ex 31:13 I am the *L* who
Jdg 5:3 praise to the *L* God
Jdg 6:24 The *L* Is Peace
1Sa 1:3 to sacrifice to the *L*
Ps 23:1 The *L* is my shepherd
Ps 105:21 He made Joseph *l* of
Ps 117:2 *L* endures…forever
Jer 23:6 *L* OUR RIGHTEOUSNESS
Eze 48:35 The *L* is there
Zec 1:9 "What are these, my *l*?"
Mk 10:42 Gentiles *l* it over
Lk 6:46 you call Me, '*L*, *L*,'
Ac 2:36 both *L* and Christ
1Ti 6:15 *L* of lords
1Pe 5:3 Do not *l* over those

LORDS
Ge 19:2 "Here, my *l*, please
Dt 10:17 and Lord of *l*
Da 5:1 for a thousand of his *l*
1Co 8:5 many gods and many *l*
Rev 19:16 LORD OF *L*

LORD'S
Ex 9:29 the earth is the *L*
Ex 12:11 It is the *L* Passover
Dt 32:9 For the *L* portion
La 2:22 day of the *L* anger
La 3:22 of the *L* mercies
Hab 2:16 cup of the *L* right hand
Mt 21:42 the *L* doing
Ro 14:8 we are the *L*
1Co 10:26 The earth is the *L*
1Co 11:26 proclaim the *L* death
Rev 1:10 on the *L* Day

LOSE
Mt 16:25 save his life will *l*

LOSES
Mt 5:13 But if the salt *l*
Mt 16:26 and *l* his own soul

LOSS
Php 3:8 count everything as *l*

LOST
Mt 18:11 save that which was *l*
Jn 17:12 And none of them is *l*
Jn 18:9 I have *l* none of those

LOTS
Mk 15:24 garments, casting *l*
Ac 1:26 they cast *l*

LOUD
Ex 19:16 exceedingly *l* trumpet
Eze 8:18 My ears with a *l*
Eze 11:13 cried out with a *l* voice
Mk 5:7 cried out with a *l* voice
Lk 23:46 cried out with a *l* voice
Ac 7:60 a *l* voice, "Lord, do not
Rev 5:12 with a *l* voice: "Worthy
Rev 6:10 cried out with a *l* voice

LOVE
Ex 20:6 who *l* Me and keep
Dt 30:20 *l* the LORD your God
2Sa 1:26 *l* was more…than the *l*

2Sa 19:6 those who *l* you
Ps 4:2 will you *l* vanity
Ps 40:16 who *l* Your salvation
Ps 45:7 You *l* righteousness
Ps 52:3 You *l* evil more
Ps 97:10 You who *l* the LORD
Ps 119:127 *l* Your commandments
Pr 7:18 take our fill of *l*
Pr 8:36 those who hate me *l*
Pr 15:12 scorner does not *l* one
Pr 17:9 transgression seeks *l*
SS 2:7 awaken *l* until it pleases
SS 8:7 cannot quench *l*
Isa 63:7 *l* of the LORD
Jer 31:3 with an everlasting *l*
Eze 23:11 in her inordinate *l*
Hos 3:1 again, *l* a woman
Joel 2:13 abounding in steadfast *l*
Zec 8:19 So *l* what brings truth
Mt 5:46 *l* those who *l* you
Mt 19:19 *l* your neighbor
Mk 12:33 To *l* Him with all
Lk 6:35 But *l* your enemies
Jn 15:10 remain in My *l*
Jn 21:15 do you *l* Me more
Ro 5:8 His own *l* toward us
Ro 8:35 from the *l* of Christ
Ro 12:9 Let *l* be without
1Co 8:1 but *l* edifies
1Co 13:1 and have not *l*
1Co 13:13 now abide faith, hope, and *l*
1Co 14:1 Follow after *l*
2Co 13:11 the God of *l* and peace
Eph 1:15 your *l* toward all
Eph 3:19 know the *l* of Christ
Php 2:1 if any comfort of *l*
1Th 1:3 labor of *l*, and
1Ti 2:15 faith, *l*, and holiness
Titus 2:4 young women to *l*
Heb 10:24 spur one another to *l*
1Pe 1:22 brotherly *l*, *l* one
1Jn 2:5 has the *l* of God
1Jn 3:1 how much *l* the Father
Rev 2:19 works, *l*, service, faith

LOVED

Ge 24:67 and he *l* her
Ge 37:3 Israel *l* Joseph
Dt 21:15 the *l* one and
1Sa 1:5 because he *l* Hannah
1Ki 3:3 Solomon *l* the LORD
1Ki 11:1 Solomon *l* many
Est 2:17 The king *l* Esther
Ps 26:8 I have *l* the refuge
Ps 119:47 which I have *l*
Jer 14:10 they have *l* to wander
Hos 9:1 *l* a prostitute's wages
Mk 10:21 Jesus…*l* him
Jn 11:5 Jesus *l* Martha
Jn 11:36 how He *l* him
Jn 13:1 Having *l* His own
Jn 14:21 will be *l* by My Father
Jn 19:26 the disciple whom He *l*
Ro 8:37 through Him who *l* us
Eph 5:2 as Christ *l* us
2Ti 4:8 to all who have *l*
Heb 1:9 have *l* righteousness
1Jn 4:10 *l* God, but that He *l*
Rev 12:11 they *l* not their lives

LOVELY

Est 2:7 was *l* to look at
Ps 84:1 How *l* is Your
SS 1:5 dark, but still *l*

LOVES

Ps 11:7 LORD *l* righteousness
Pr 3:12 whom the LORD *l*
Pr 13:24 he who *l* him
Pr 19:8 *l* his own soul
Ecc 5:10 he who *l* money
Jn 5:20 the Father *l* the Son
Eph 5:28 He who *l* his wife *l*
1Jn 2:10 Whoever *l* his brother
3Jn 1:9 *l* to put himself first
Rev 22:15 everyone who *l* and

LOVINGKINDNESS

Ge 32:10 worthy of all the *l*
Ex 20:6 showing *l* to
Ps 26:3 For Your *l* is
Ps 36:7 excellent is Your *l*
Ps 59:16 Your *l* in the morning
Ps 63:3 Your *l* is better than
Jer 32:18 You show *l* to

LOW

Job 40:12 proud and bring him *l*
Pr 29:23 will bring him *l*
Isa 2:12 shall be brought *l*
Isa 2:17 men shall be brought *l*
Eze 17:24 exalted the *l* tree

LOWER

Ps 8:5 *l* than the angels
Heb 2:7 made him a little *l*

LOWLY

Mt 11:29 for I am meek and *l*
2Co 10:1 *l* in presence

LUKE

Col 4:14 *L*, the beloved
2Ti 4:11 Only *L* is with me
Phm 1:24 Demas, and *L*

LUKEWARM

Rev 3:16 because you are *l*

LUST

Ex 15:9 My *l* shall be satisfied
Pr 6:25 Do not *l* after her
Ro 1:27 their *l* toward one
1Co 10:6 not *l* after evil
Jas 1:14 by his own *l*
Jas 1:15 when *l* has conceived

LUSTS

Gal 5:24 its passions and *l*
Eph 2:3 once lived in the *l*
1Ti 6:9 foolish and harmful *l*
1Pe 2:11 abstain from fleshly *l*

LYING

Ge 34:7 disgraced Israel by *l*
Ge 39:10 about *l* with her
Nu 31:17 by *l* with him
Ru 3:8 was *l* at his feet
1Ki 22:22 and be a *l* spirit
Ps 31:18 Let the *l* lips
Ps 52:3 *l* rather than speaking
Pr 6:17 a *l* tongue
Pr 12:22 *L* lips are abomination
Pr 21:6 by a *l* tongue
Isa 30:9 *l* children
Jer 7:8 you trust in *l* words
La 3:10 a bear *l* in wait
Hos 4:2 Swearing, *l*, and killing
Mt 8:14 *l* sick
Lk 2:12 *l* in a manger
Jn 11:41 the dead man was *l*
Ro 9:1 I am not *l*
Eph 4:25 putting away *l*

M

MADE

Ge 1:16 *m* the stars also
Isa 66:2 My hand *m*
Php 1:4 *m* requests with joy

MAGIC

Eze 13:20 against your *m* bands
Ac 19:19 *m* brought their books

MAGICIANS

Ge 41:8 called for all the *m*
Ex 7:11 Then the *m* of Egypt
Da 2:2 command to call the *m*
Da 5:11 made him master of the *m*

MAGNIFIED

2Sa 7:26 may Your name be *m*
Ac 19:17 the Lord Jesus was *m*
Php 1:20 also, Christ will be *m*

MAGNIFIES
Lk 1:46 "My soul *m* the Lord

MAGNIFY
Ps 34:3 *m* the LORD with me

MAJESTY
Heb 1:3 right hand of the *M*
2Pe 1:16 eyewitnesses of His *m*
Jude 1:25 be glory and *m*

MAKE
Ge 1:26 "Let us *m* man in our
Ge 12:2 *m* of you a great nation
Ex 20:4 You shall not *m*
Jn 14:23 *m* Our home with

MAKER
Isa 54:5 *M* is your husband
Hos 8:14 has forgotten his *M*
Heb 11:10 builder and *m* is God

MALE
Ge 1:27 *m* and female He created
Ex 12:5 without blemish, a *m*
Lev 1:3 herd, he shall offer a *m*
Lev 7:6 Every *m* among the priests
Nu 18:10 every *m* shall eat it
Gal 3:28 is neither *m* nor female

MALES
Ex 13:12 *m* shall be the LORD's
Ex 23:17 the year all your *m*
Lev 6:29 the *m* among the priests
Dt 16:16 year all your *m* must

MAN
Ge 2:7 *m* from the dust
Ge 2:23 was taken out of *M*
Ge 6:6 He had made *m*
Ex 13:13 firstborn of *m*
Nu 21:9 serpent had bitten any *m*
Dt 4:32 day that God created *m*
Dt 22:5 *m* to put on
Jdg 21:11 will kill every *m*
1Sa 9:6 a *m* of God
1Sa 16:18 *m* of valor, a *m* of battle
2Sa 12:2 *m* had a very large flock
1Ki 2:2 yourself to be a *m*
Ne 7:2 faithful *m* and feared God
Est 1:22 *m* should rule over
Job 4:17 *m* be more pure
Ps 40:4 *m* who places trust
Ps 119:9 *m* keep his way pure
Pr 3:13 Happy is the *m*...and the *m*
Pr 9:8 rebuke a wise *m*
Pr 18:12 the heart of *m*
Pr 24:5 A wise *m*...yes, a *m*
Ecc 2:19 *m* will be wise or a fool
Isa 3:2 *m* and the *m* of war
Isa 53:3 a *m* of sorrows
Jer 9:23 the wise *m* glory in
Eze 1:10 the face of a *m*
Eze 2:1 Son of *m*, stand
Eze 33:8 O wicked *m*, you
Da 5:11 a *m* in your kingdom
Mt 7:24 to a wise *m* who
Mt 10:35 'a *m* against his father
Mt 12:32 against the Son of *M*
Mt 25:13 Son of *M* is coming
Mk 2:27 made for *m*, and not *m*
Mk 8:36 does it profit a *m*
Lk 6:5 Son of *M* is Lord
Lk 10:30 A *m* went down from
Jn 1:6 a *m* sent from God
Jn 5:34 receive testimony from *m*
Jn 9:1 *m* blind from birth
Jn 15:13 Greater love has no *m*
Ac 3:2 A *m* lame from birth
Ac 13:38 this *M* forgiveness of sins
Ro 1:23 made like corruptible *m*
Ro 3:28 *m* is justified by faith
Ro 10:5 *m* who does those things
1Co 2:9 into the heart of *m*
1Co 5:1 *m* has his father's wife
1Co 11:3 head of the woman is the *m*
Eph 2:15 two into one new *m*
1Ti 3:1 *m* desires the office
Heb 2:6 What is *m* that You
Jas 1:14 each *m* is tempted
Jas 3:8 no *m* can tame

MANGER
Lk 2:7 and laid Him in a *m*
Lk 2:12 lying in a *m*.
manifold
Eph 3:10 the *m* wisdom of God

MANNA
Ex 16:35 of Israel ate *m*
Dt 8:3 and fed you with *m*
Jn 6:31 Our fathers ate *m*
Jn 6:58 your fathers ate *m*
Heb 9:4 golden pot holding the *m*
Rev 2:17 the hidden *m to eat*

MANNER
Ex 12:16 no *m* of work shall
Lev 11:44 any *m* of crawling thing
Isa 51:6 shall die in like *m*
Ac 1:11 come in like *m* as you saw
1Co 15:32 *m* of men, I have fought
Jude 1:7 cities in like *m*, gave

MARK
Ge 4:15 the LORD put a *m*
Lev 13:2 *m* of a leprous sore
Ps 104:19 set the moon to *m*
Eze 9:4 *m* upon the foreheads
Mt 5:18 not one dot or one *m*
2Th 3:17 *m* in every letter
Rev 13:16 to receive a *m*
Rev 14:11 receives the *m*
Rev 16:2 men who had the *m*

MARK
Ac 12:12 other name was *M*
Ac 15:39 Barnabas took *M*
2Ti 4:11 Get *M*, and bring him

MARRED
Isa 52:14 his visage was so *m*

MARRIAGE
Mt 22:30 nor are given in *m*
Mt 24:38 and giving in *m*
Heb 13:4 *M* is to be honored
Rev 19:7 the *m* of the Lamb

MARRIED
Pr 30:23 hateful woman when she is m,
1Co 7:33 But he who is *m*

MARRY
Mt 22:30 they neither *m* nor
1Ti 4:3 forbidding to *m*

MARRYING
Mt 24:3 8 and drinking, *m*

MARTYRS
Rev 17:6 the blood of the *m*

MARVELOUS
Ps 118:23 it is *m* in our eyes
1Pe 2:9 of darkness into His *m*

MASTER
Mt 10:25 servant like his *m*
Jn 15:20 greater than his *m*

MATURE
1Co 14:20 in your thinking be *m*
Php 3:15 us who are *m*

MEANS
Ex 34:7 by no *m* clear the guilty
Nu 14:18 no *m* clear the guilty
Ac 18:21 said, "I must by all *m*

MEASURE
Dt 25:15 a perfect and just *m*
Jn 3:34 gives the Spirit without *m*
Ro 12:3 according to the *m*

MEASURED
Isa 40:12 *m* the waters in the
Mt 7:2 you use, it will be *m*

MEAT
Pr 23:20 riotous eaters of m;
1Co 8:13 will never eat *m*

MEDIATOR
Gal 3:19 by the hand of a *m*
Gal 3:20 *m* is not a *m*
1Ti 2:5 is one God and one *m*
Heb 8:6 *M* of a better covenant
Heb 12:24 to Jesus, the *M* of

MEDICINE
Pr 17:22 does good like a *m*

MEDICINES
Jer 46:11 you shall use many *m*

MEDITATE
Jos 1:8 *M* on it day and night
Ps 119:15 I will *m* on Your

MEDITATION
Ps 19:14 of my mouth and the *m*
Ps 119:97 It is my *m* all the day

MEDIUM
Lev 20:27 speaks to spirits as a *m*

MEDIUMS
Isa 8:19 "Seek after the *m*

MEEK
Ps 22:26 *m* will eat and
Ps 37:11 *m* will inherit the earth
Ps 149:4 He will beautify the *m*
Isa 11:4 with fairness for the *m*
Isa 29:19 *m* also shall increase
Mt 5:5 Blessed are the *m*
Mt 11:29 *m* and lowly in heart

MEET
Ex 25:22 I will *m* with you
Ex 29:42 I will with *m* you, to speak
1Sa 10:5 city, you will *m* a group
2Ch 15:2 he went out to *m* Asa
2Ch 19:2 seer went out to *m*

MELT
Isa 13:7 man's heart shall *m*
Isa 19:1 heart of Egypt shall *m*
Na 1:5 hills *m*; the land

MEMBERS
Mt 5:29 that one of your *m*
Ro 6:13 do not yield your *m*
Eph 4:25 neighbor, for we are *m*

MEN
Ge 4:26 *m* began to call on
Ge 6:2 the daughters of *m*
Ge 18:16 *m* rose up and looked
Ex 21:22 If *m* fight and hurt
Ex 36:4 the skilled *m* who
Nu 31:53 fighting *m* of Israel
Jos 2:4 had taken the two *m*
Jdg 7:7 "With three hundred *m*
1Sa 2:26 and also with *m*
1Sa 10:26 band of valiant *m*
1Sa 17:24 Israel's fighting *m* saw
2Ch 13:3 hundred thousand choice *m*
Ne 2:12 a few *m* who were with me
Job 29:21 *M* listened to me
Ps 45:2 all the sons of *m*
Ps 116:11 "All *m* are liars
Pr 10:14 Wise *m* store up
Pr 24:19 because of evil *m*
Ecc 3:10 given to sons of *m*
Isa 31:3 Now the Egyptians are *m*
Isa 53:3 despised and rejected of *m*
Jer 27:5 earth, the *m*, and the
Jer 51:30 mighty *m* of Babylon
Eze 36:12 cause *m* to walk
Da 3:12 These *m*, O king, have
Mt 2:1 wise *m* came from
Mt 4:19 make you fishers of *m*
Mt 6:14 if you forgive *m*
Mt 22:16 regard the person of *m*
Mk 6:12 that *m* should repent
Mk 13:13 will be hated by all *m*
Lk 2:14 good will toward *m*
Lk 6:26 *m* speak well of you
Lk 12:8 confesses Me before *m*
Lk 15:7 ninety-nine righteous *m*
Lk 20:4 heaven or from *m*
Jn 6:10 *m* sat down
Ac 2:5 *m*, from every nation
Ac 15:17 *m* may seek the Lord
Ac 27:25 Therefore, *m*, take courage
Ro 1:27 *m* leaving the natural
Ro 12:18 live peaceably with all *m*
1Co 3:21 no one boast in *m*
1Co 16:13 be bold like *m*
Eph 6:7 the Lord, and not to *m*
1Ti 2:4 all *m* to be saved
1Ti 2:5 between God and *m*
Heb 9:27 appointed for *m* to die
1Jn 5:9 the testimony of *m*
Rev 9:6 In those days *m* will
Rev 21:3 tabernacle of God is with *m*

MERCIES
Ps 106:45 greatness of His *m*
Isa 55:3 the sure *m* of David
Isa 63:15 heart and Your *m*
Ro 12:1 *m* of God, that you present

MERCIFUL
Ex 34:6 LORD, the LORD God, *m*
Dt 21:8 Be *m*, O LORD
Ps 117:2 His *m* kindness is great
Mt 5:7 Blessed are the *m*
Lk 6:36 Be therefore *m*… Father is *m*
Lk 18:13 saying, 'God be *m*
Heb 2:17 a *m* and faithful High Priest
Heb 8:12 For I will be *m*

MERCY
Ge 19:19 have shown your *m*
Ge 39:21 and showed him *m*
Ex 25:17 a *m* seat of pure gold
Nu 14:18 and abounding in *m*
Dt 5:10 showing *m* to thousands
Jos 11:20 destroyed them without *m*
1Ch 16:34 *m* endures forever
Ne 9:19 You in Your great *m*
Ps 4:1 have *m* on me
Ps 23:6 Surely goodness and *m*
Ps 85:7 Show us Your *m*
Ps 89:14 *m* and truth shall go
Ps 100:5 *m* endures forever
Ps 103:8 and abounding in *m*
Ps 115:1 for the sake of Your *m*
Ps 118:2 "His *m* endures forever
Ps 123:3 Have *m* upon us… have *m*
Ps 136:1 His *m* endures forever
Pr 14:21 has *m* on the poor
Isa 9:17 *m* on their fatherless
Isa 49:10 For He who has *m*
Isa 63:9 in His *m* He redeemed

Ro 6:12 sin reign in your *m*
Ro 8:11 give life to your *m* bodies
1Co 15:53 this *m* will have put
2Co 5:4 that what is *m* might be swallowed

MOSES

Ex 2:10 she called his name *M*
Ex 3:4 and said, "*M*, *M*."
Ex 3:11 *M* said to God
Ex 15:1 *M* and the children of
Ex 16:2 against *M* and Aaron
Ex 20:21 *M* drew near
Dt 31:30 *M* spoke the words
Dt 34:7 *M* was a hundred and
2Ch 34:14 Law of the Lord from *M*
Ne 8:1 Book of the Law of *M*
Ps 77:20 by the hand of *M* and Aaron
Jer 15:1 *M* and Samuel were to
Mt 8:4 gift that *M* commanded
Mt 17:3 *M* and Elijah appeared
Mk 10:4 *M* permitted a man
Lk 16:29 *M* and the Prophets
Lk 20:37 *M* pointed out
Jn 1:17 given through *M*
Jn 3:14 *M* lifted up the
Jn 7:22 *M* gave you circumcision
Ac 6:11 against *M* and God
Ac 7:22 *M* was educated
Ro 5:14 from Adam to *M*
1Co 10:2 all were baptized into *M*
2Co 3:15 when *M* is read
2Ti 3:8 Jambres resisted *M*
Heb 3:2 as *M* was faithful
Heb 11:23 *M*, when he was born
Jude 1:9 about the body of *M*
Rev 15:3 sang the song of *M*

MOTH

Mt 6:19 where *m* and rust

MOTHER

Ge 2:24 father and his *m*
Ge 3:20 she was the *m*
Ge 24:53 her brother and to her *m*
Ex 2:8 called the child's *m*
Ex 20:12 father and your *m*
Ex 21:15 strikes his father or his *m*
Ex 21:17 curses his father or his *m*
Lev 18:7 your *m*. She is your *m*
Lev 20:14 and also her *m*
Jdg 5:7 like a *m* in Israel
Ru 2:11 and *m* and your homeland
Est 2:7 her father and *m* died
Ps 27:10 my *m* forsake me
Ps 35:14 mourns for a *m*
Ps 113:9 joyful *m* of children
Pr 6:20 instruction of your *m*
Pr 10:1 grief of his *m*
Pr 23:22 despise your *m*
Ecc 5:15 his *m*'s womb
SS 8:1 at my *m*'s breasts
Jer 20:14 in which my *m* bore
Eze 16:44 "Like *m*, like daughter
Hos 2:5 their *m* has played
Mic 7:6 rises up against her *m*
Mt 1:18 *m* Mary was engaged
Mt 2:11 with Mary, His *m*
Mt 10:35 daughter against her *m*
Mt 12:50 and sister, and *m*
Mt 19:5 leave his father and *m*
Mt 19:19 your father and your *m*
Mk 1:30 The *m* of Simon's wife
Mk 3:33 "Who are My *m* and
Mk 7:11 father or *m*, "It is Corban
Lk 1:43 that the *m* of my Lord
Lk 2:51 His *m* kept all these words
Lk 14:26 hate his father and *m*
Jn 2:3 *m* of Jesus said to Him
Jn 19:25 cross of Jesus were His *m*
Jn 19:27 "Here is your *m*
Eph 5:31 *m* and shall be joined
Heb 7:3 without *m*, without descent
Rev 17:5 THE *M* OF PROSTITUTES

MOTHER-IN-LAW

Dt 27:23 lies with his *m*
Ru 1:14 Orpah kissed her *m*
Ru 2:23 lived with her *m*
Mic 7:6 against her *m*
Mt 10:35 against her *m*
Lk 4:38 Simon's *m* was taken ill

MOUNT

Ex 19:23 come up to *M* Sinai
Isa 40:31 They shall *m* up with

MOUNTAIN

1Ki 19:8 Horeb, the *m* of God
Isa 2:3 let us go up to the *m*
Da 2:35 became a great *m*
Zec 4:7 are you, O great *m*
Mt 17:20 you will say to this *m*
2Pe 1:18 Him on the holy *m*

MOUNTAINS

Ps 90:2 *m* were brought forth
Isa 54:10 *m* may be removed
Mt 24:16 in Judea flee to the *m*
1Co 13:2 that I could remove *m*

MOURN

Mt 5:4 are those who *m*
Rev 1:7 of the earth will *m*

MOURNING

Zec 12:11 *m* in Jerusalem
Jas 4:9 be turned to *m*, and

MOUTH

Nu 16:32 earth opened its *m*
Nu 22:28 the *m* of the donkey
Dt 8:3 the *m* of the Lord
Dt 30:14 near to you, in your *m*
Jos 1:8 depart from your *m*
Jos 10:18 the *m* of the cave
1Sa 1:12 Eli watched her *m*
1Sa 2:1 My *m* is bold
2Ch 36:21 by the *m* of Jeremiah
Job 3:1 Job opened his *m*
Job 8:21 fills your *m* with laughing
Ps 10:7 *m* is filled with cursing
Ps 19:14 words of my *m*
Ps 37:30 *m* of the righteous
Ps 55:21 *m* were smoother than
Ps 89:1 *m* I will make known
Pr 4:24 a deceitful *m*
Pr 6:2 words of your *m*
Pr 10:11 The *m* of a righteous man
Pr 12:6 *m* of the upright
Pr 31:26 She opens her *m*
Ecc 5:2 speak with your *m*
Isa 49:2 *m* like a sharp sword
Isa 51:16 My words in your *m*
Isa 53:7 he opened not his *m*
Jer 5:14 words in your *m* fire
Jer 9:8 neighbor with his *m*
La 3:38 *m* of the Most High
Eze 3:2 I opened my *m*
Eze 33:7 word from My *m*
Da 3:26 near to the *m* of
Da 10:3 or wine entered my *m*
Mic 7:5 doors of your *m*
Mal 2:6 instruction was in his *m*
Mt 4:4 out of the *m* of God
Mt 13:35 My *m* in parables
Mt 15:17 enters at the *m* goes
Lk 1:64 *m* was opened
Lk 6:45 heart his *m* speaks
Jn 19:29 and held it to His *m*
Ro 10:9 confess with your *m*
1Co 9:9 muzzle the *m* of the ox

P

PASS
Ex 12:13 I will *p* over you
Isa 43:2 When you *p* through waters
Mt 24:35 and earth will *p* away

PASSED
Ro 3:25 forbearance God had *p*
Heb 4:14 High Priest who has *p*
1Jn 3:14 know that we have *p*

PASSIONS
Ro 1:26 gave them up to dishonorable *p*
Ro 7:5 the *p* of sin,

PASSOVER
Ex 12:11 It is the LORD's *P*
Mt 26:18 I will keep the *P*
1Co 5:7 even Christ, our *P*
Heb 11:28 By faith he kept the *P*

PASTORS
Eph 4:11 evangelists, *p*, and teachers

PASTURE
Ps 74:1 the sheep of Your *p*
Jn 10:9 in and out and find *p*

PASTURES
Ps 23:2 lie down in green *p*

PATH
Ps 16:11 make known to me the *p*

PATHS
Ps 23:3 He leads me in *p*
Mt 3:3 make His *p* straight
Heb 12:13 Make straight *p*

PATIENCE
Ro 2:4 goodness, tolerance, and *p*
Ro 5:3 tribulation produces *p*
Gal 5:22 love, joy, peace, *p*
Eph 4:2 humility, meekness, and *p*
Heb 6:12 through faith and *p* inherit
Jas 5:11 the *p* of Job
2Pe 3:15 the *p* of our Lord
Rev 2:19 service, faith, and your *p*

PATIENT
Ecc 7:8 the *p* in spirit
1Ti 3:3 but *p*, not argumentative
Jas 5:7 *p*, brothers
2Pe 1:6 *p* endurance; and to your *p*
Rev 2:3 and have been *p*

PATIENTLY
Ps 37:7 the Lord, and wait *p* for Him;
Ps 40:1 I waited *p* for the Lord
Ac 26:3 I beg you to *p* listen to me
Heb 6:15 So after Abraham had *p* endured,
1Pe 3:20 when God waited *p* in the days

PATRIARCHS
Ac 7:8 of the twelve *p*

PATTERN
Ex 25:40 according to their *p* which was shown to you
2Ti 1:13 the *p* of sound teaching
Heb 8:5 according to the *p* shown you

PAUL
Ac 16:18 *P* turned to the spirit
Ac 17:22 *P* stood in the middle
Ac 19:11 miracles by the hands of *P*
Ac 20:9 as *P* spoke
Ac 20:37 and embraced *P*'s neck
Ac 22:28 *P* said, "But I was born a
Ac 23:12 until they had killed *P*
Ac 26:28 Agrippa said to *P*
1Co 1:12 "I am of *P*," or
2Pe 3:15 beloved brother *P* has also

PAY
Ps 22:25 I will *p* my vows before
Ps 50:14 and *p* your vows

PEACE
Ge 15:15 to your fathers in *p*
Ge 43:23 "Be at *p*, do not be afraid
Ex 4:18 "Go in *p*
Ex 20:24 and your *p* offerings
Lev 3:1 is a *p* sacrifice
Lev 26:6 I will give *p* in the land
Nu 25:12 My covenant of *p*
Dt 20:11 it gives you a reply of *p*
Dt 23:6 not ever to seek their *p*
Jos 9:15 Joshua made *p* with them
Jdg 3:30 land had *p* for eighty years
Jdg 18:6 "Go in *p*
1Ki 22:44 Jehoshaphat made *p*
2Ki 22:20 to your grave in *p*
1Ch 12:18 *P*, *p* to you, and *p* to
1Ch 22:9 I will give *p* and tranquility
Est 10:3 spoke of *p* and prosperity
Job 3:13 and would be at *p*
Job 3:26 I am not at *p*
Ps 34:14 do good; seek *p*
Ps 85:10 righteousness and *p*
Ps 122:6 the *p* of Jerusalem
Ps 147:14 *p* in your borders
Pr 3:2 long life and *p*
Pr 11:12 understanding holds his *p*
Isa 45:7 I make *p* and create
Isa 48:22 "There is no *p*," says
Isa 52:7 who proclaims *p*
Isa 53:5 of our *p* was upon him
Jer 8:15 We looked for *p*
Jer 29:11 plans for *p* and
Zec 8:16 and justice, and *p*
Zec 9:10 speak *p* to the nations
Mk 9:50 have *p* with one
Ac 10:36 preaching *p* through Jesus
Ro 2:10 glory, honor, and *p*
Ro 16:20 The God of *p* will
Col 1:20 *p* through the blood
1Th 5:23 God of *p* sanctify you
2Th 3:16 the Lord of *p*...give you *p*
Heb 12:14 Pursue *p* with all men
Jas 3:18 righteousness is sown in *p*
1Pe 3:11 Let him seek *p*
2Pe 3:14 in *p*, spotless and
Rev 6:4 take *p* from the earth

PEACEABLE
Isa 32:18 in a *p* habitation
Jas 3:17 is first pure, then *p*

PEACEMAKERS
Mt 5:9 Blessed are the *p*, for they shall be

PEARL
Mt 13:46 on finding one *p*
Rev 21:21 gates made of a single *p*

PEARLS
Mt 7:6 nor throw your *p*
Rev 21:21 gates were twelve *p*

Jude 1:25 majesty, dominion and *p*
Rev 4:11 and honor and *p*
Rev 6:4 *P* was given to him
Rev 6:8 *P* over a fourth of the
Rev 7:2 who had been given *p*
Rev 13:2 dragon gave him his *p*
Rev 17:13 give their *p* and authority
Rev 20:6 the second death has no *p*

POWERFUL

Est 9:4 Mordecai grew more *p*.
Ps 106:42 under their *p* hand
Lk 24:19 *p* in deed and word before God

POWERS

Mt 24:29 the *p* of the heavens
Ro 8:38 nor principalities nor *p*
Eph 6:12 against principalities, against *p*,
Col 2:15 disarmed authorities and *p*

PRACTICE

Lev 19:26 *p* divination or fortune-telling
Ps 141:4 to *p* wicked deeds
Eze 13:23 see vanity or *p* divinations
Ro 12:13 needs of the saints, *p* hospitality.

PRAISE

Ge 29:35 "Now I will *p* the LORD!"
Ge 49:8 your brothers shall *p* you
Ex 15:2 and I will *p* Him
Jdg 5:3 I will sing *p* to the LORD God
Ps 7:17 sing *p* to the name
Ps 22:22 I will *p* You
Ps 40:3 even *p* to our God
Ps 51:15 will declare Your *p*
Ps 67:3 Let the peoples *p* You
Ps 71:14 add to all Your *p*
Ps 107:8 Let them *p* the LORD
Ps 119:7 I will *p* You
Ps 135:1 *P* the LORD!
Ps 148:1 *P* the LORD from the
Ps 150:1 *P* God in His sanctuary
Jer 17:14 You are my *p*
Mt 21:16 You have perfected *p*
Lk 18:43 they gave *p* to God
Jn 12:43 loved the *p* of men

Ro 13:3 you will have *p* from
Php 4:8 if there is any *p*
1Pe 1:7 *p*, glory, and honor
Rev 19:5 *P* our God, all

PRAISED

Ps 113:3 LORD's name is to be *p*
Ps 145:3 and greatly to be *p*
Da 4:34 the Most High and I *p*

PRAISES

Ps 9:11 Sing *p* to the LORD
Ps 75:9 I will sing *p* to
Ps 78:4 generation the *p* of the LORD
Pr 31:28 her husband also, and he *p*

PRAISING

Lk 2:13 of the heavenly host *p*
Lk 24:53 in the temple *p*

PRAY

Mt 6:5 when you *p*
Mt 6:9 *p* in this manner
Mt 26:41 Watch and *p*
Lk 11:1 "Lord, teach us to *p*
Jn 14:16 I will *p*
Jn 17:9 I do not *p* for the
Jn 17:20 "I do not *p* for
1Th 5:17 *p* without ceasing
Jas 5:13 Let him *p*
Jas 5:16 to one another and *p*

PRAYED

Lk 22:44 *p* more earnestly
Jas 5:17 *p* earnestly that it

PRAYER

2Ch 7:15 *p* of this place
Job 16:17 and my *p* is pure
Ps 42:8 a *p* to the God of my
Ps 102:17 He will regard the *p*
Mt 17:21 go out except by *p*
Lk 6:12 all night in *p* to God
Ac 6:4 continually to *p*
Ac 16:13 where *p* was
Ro 12:12 persevere in *p*
1Co 7:5 to fasting and *p*
Eph 6:18 all kinds of *p*
Php 4:6 but in everything, by *p*
1Ti 4:5 the word of God and *p*
Jas 5:15 And the *p* of faith

PRAYERS

Isa 1:15 when You make many *p*
Mt 23:14 pretense make long *p*
Col 4:12 fervently for you in *p*
1Pe 3:7 *p* will not be hindered
Rev 5:8 which are the *p*

PRAYING

1Sa 1:12 As she was *p* before the Lord,
Mk 11:25 when you stand *p*, forgive
Lk 3:21 *p*, the heavens were opened
Ac 9:11 Saul of Tarsus, for he is *p*.
Ac 16:25 Silas were *p* and singing hymns

PREACH

Isa 61:1 to *p* good news
Mic 2:11 "I will *p* for you
Mt 4:17 Jesus began to *p*
Mk 16:15 *p* the gospel to every creature.
Lk 4:18 anointed Me to *p*
Ac 5:42 to teach and *p*
Ro 1:15 to *p* the gospel
1Co 1:17 to baptize, but to *p*
1Co 9:14 those who *p* the gospel
2Co 10:16 to *p* the gospel
Eph 3:8 to *p* to the Gentiles

PREACHED

Mk 1:39 He *p* in their
Mk 13:10 be *p* to all nations
Ac 9:27 he had boldly *p* in
Ac 17:18 *p* Jesus and the resurrection
1Co 15:1 the gospel which I *p*
Heb 4:2 the gospel was *p* to
1Pe 3:19 *p* to the spirits

PREACHER

Ecc 1:1 the *P*, the son of David
Ro 10:14 shall they hear without a *p*
2Ti 1:11 was appointed a *p*
2Pe 2:5 Noah, a *p* of righteousness

PREACHES

Gal 1:9 *p* any other gospel

PREACHING

Mt 3:1 John the Baptist came, *p*
Mt 12:41 they repented at the *p*
Lk 3:3 *p* the baptism of
Ac 15:35 *p* the word of the Lord
Ac 28:31 *p* the kingdom of God
1Co 1:18 the *p* of the cross is
1Co 15:14 not risen, then our *p*

PRECEPTS

Ps 119:4 keep Your *p* diligently.
Ps 119:159 how I love Your *p*

PRECIOUS
Ps 116:15 *P* in the sight of the
Pr 3:15 She is more *p* than
Jas 5:7 farmer waits for the *p*
1Pe 1:7 more *p* than gold
1Pe 2:7 who believe, He is *p*
1Pe 3:4 *p* in the sight of

PREDESTINED
Ro 8:29 foreknew, He *p*
Eph 1:5 He *p* us to
Eph 1:11 inheritance, being *p*

PREEMINENCE
Col 1:18 He may have the *p*

PREGNANT
Gen 16:11 You are *p* and will bear a son
Ex 21:22 if men fight and hurt a *p*

prejudice
1Ti 5:21 these things without *p*

PREPARATION
Jn 19:14 it was the Day of *P*

PREPARE
Ps 23:5 *p* a table before me in
Mk 1:3 *P* the way of the Lord
Jn 14:2 *p* a place for you

PREPARED
Mt 20:23 for whom it is *p*
Lk 2:31 which You have *p*
Ro 9:23 He previously *p*
1Co 2:9 things which God has *p*
Eph 2:10 *p* beforehand, so that we
Heb 11:16 God, for He has *p*

PRESENCE
Ge 3:8 themselves from the *p*
Ge 4:16 went out from the *p*
Ex 33:14 *P* will go with you
Dt 1:17 afraid in any man's *p*
Ps 16:11 *p* is fullness of joy
Ps 140:13 shall dwell in Your *p*
Jer 5:22 not tremble at My *p*
Eze 38:20 shall shake at My *p*
Lk 13:26 and drank in Your *p*
Ac 2:28 full of joy with Your *p*
2Co 10:10 but his bodily *p*
Php 2:12 obeyed, not only in my *p*

PRESENT
Ac 10:33 we are all here *p* before
Ro 7:21 evil is *p* with me
Ro 12:1 *p* your bodies as a living
1Co 3:22 or death or things *p*
1Co 5:3 absent in body but *p*
Eph 5:27 that He might *p*
Jude 1:24 *p* you blameless

PRESERVE
Ps 121:7 He shall *p* your soul
Ps 121:8 The LORD shall *p*
Lk 17:33 loses his life will *p*
2Ti 4:18 every evil work and *p*

PRESERVED
1Th 5:23 soul, and body be *p*

PRESERVES
Ps 31:23 For the LORD *p* the
Ps 97:10 *p* the lives of His
Pr 16:17 who keeps his way *p*

PREVAIL
1Sa 2:9 strength shall no man *p*
Jer 1:19 not *p* against you
Jer 5:22 yet they cannot *p*
Jer 20:10 enticed so that we can *p*

PREY
Nu 14:3 children should become *p*
Isa 10:6 the *p*, and to tread
Eze 22:27 wolves ravening the *p*
Eze 29:19 spoil and take her *p*
Eze 36:5 cast it out for a *p*
Na 2:13 will cut off your *p*

PRICE
Mt 13:46 one pearl of great *p*
1Co 6:20 were bought with a *p*

PRIDE
Lev 26:19 break the *p* of your
Pr 16:18 *P* goes before
Isa 25:11 bring down his *p*
Jer 49:16 the *p* of your heart
Eze 7:10 *p* has budded
Da 4:37 in *p* He is able to abase
Ob 1:3 The *p* of your heart
Mk 7:22 *p* and foolishness
1Jn 2:16 and the *p* of life

PRIEST
Ge 14:18 he was the *p* of God
Ps 110:4 You are a *p* forever
Zec 6:13 He shall be a *p*
Heb 2:17 and faithful High *P*
Heb 4:14 we have a great High *P*
Heb 5:6 *p* forever in the order
Heb 9:11 He came as High *P*

PRIESTHOOD
Heb 7:12 change in the *p*
Heb 7:24 has an everlasting *p*
1Pe 2:9 race, a royal *p*

PRIESTS
Ex 19:6 to Me a kingdom of *p*
Mic 3:11 Her *p* teach for a price
Rev 1:6 made us kings and *p*

PRINCE
Ge 23:6 a mighty *p* among us
Ex 2:14 Who made you a *p* and
Pr 25:7 in the presence of the *p*
Isa 9:6 Eternal Father, *P* of Peace
Eze 37:25 David shall be their *p*
Eph 2:2 *p* of the power of the air

PRINCES
Ps 118:9 to put confidence in *p*
Isa 40:23 He brings the *p*

PRINCIPALITIES
Ro 8:38 neither angels nor *p*
Eph 1:21 far above all *p*, and
Eph 6:12 but against *p*
Col 1:16 or dominions, or *p*, or

PRISON
Ge 39:20 and put him into the *p*
Ps 142:7 Bring my soul out of *p*
Isa 42:7 in darkness out of the *p*
Isa 61:1 the opening of the *p*
Mt 11:2 John had heard in *p*
Mt 25:36 I was in *p* and you

PRISONERS
Ps 68:6 brings out *p* into prosperity
Ps 79:11 groans of the *p* come before You;
Ps 107:10 being *p* in affliction and irons
Ps 146:7 The Lord releases the p
Isa 20:4 away the Egyptians as *p*
Isa 42:7 to bring out the *p*
Zec 9:11 I will send your *p*
Zec 9:12 p who now have hope
Ac 16:25 and the *p* were listening to them

PRIZE
1Co 9:24 but one receives the p?
Php 3:14 the goal to the *p*

PROCEEDED
Jn 8:42 from God and *p*

PROCEEDS
Dt 8:3 by every word that *p*
Mt 4:4 by every word that *p*
Jn 15:26 Spirit of truth who *p*

PROCLAIM
Mk 1:45 began to *p* it widely
Ac 17:23 Him I *p*
1Co 11:26 drink this cup, you *p*

PROCLAIMED
Ps 40:9 *p* righteousness in
Lk 8:39 he went his way and *p*

PROCLAIMER
Ac 17:18 "He seems to be a *p*

PROCLAIMS
Isa 52:7 good news, who *p*

PRODIGAL
Lk 15:13 in *p* living

PROFESS
Dt 26:3 "I *p* this day to the Lord
Titus 1:16 They *p* that they know

PROFIT
Mk 8:36 For what does it *p*
Lk 9:25 For what does it *p* a man
Ac 16:16 her masters much *p*
Ro 3:1 what *p* is there
1Co 10:33 seeking my own *p*
Gal 5:2 Christ will *p* you
Heb 12:10 He does so for our *p*
Jas 2:14 What does it *p*
Jas 4:13 sell, and make a *p*

PROFITABLE
Pr 3:14 benefit is more *p*
2Ti 3:16 by God, and is *p*

PROFITS
1Co 13:3 have not love, it *p*

PROLONG
Dt 5:33 you may *p* your days
Ps 61:6 *p* the king's life
Pr 28:16 hates covetousness will *p*
Isa 53:10 he shall *p* his days,

PROMISE
Lk 24:49 I am sending the *p*
Ac 1:4 but wait for the *p*
Ac 2:39 For the *p* is to you
Ac 26:6 for hope in the *p*
Ro 4:16 *p* would be certain
Heb 4:1 Therefore, since the *p*
Heb 6:17 to the heirs of *p*
Heb 11:39 did not receive the *p*

PROMISED
Dt 15:6 as He *p* you,
Heb 11:11 faithful who had *p*

PROMISES
2Co 1:20 For all the *p* of God
Gal 3:16 *p* were made
Heb 11:13 having received the *p*
2Pe 1:4 great and precious *p*

PROPER
1Co 7:35 but for what is *p*
1Ti 2:10 which is *p*

PROPHECY
Da 9:24 the vision and *p*
Mt 13:14 the *p* of Isaiah
1Co 12:10 to another *p*,
1Co 13:2 If I have the gift of *p*
1Ti 4:14 given to you by *p*
2Pe 1:21 no *p* at any time
Rev 1:3 hear the words of this *p*
Rev 22:7 the words of the *p*
Rev 22:19 the book of this *p*

PROPHESIED
Mt 7:22 Lord, have we not *p*
Mt 11:13 and the Law *p*

PROPHESIES
1Ki 22:8 he never *p* good for me
1Co 14:4 *p* edifies the church

PROPHESY
Isa 30:10 You must not *p*
Jer 5:31 The prophets *p* falsely
Joel 2:28 your daughters will *p*
Am 3:8 Who can but *p*
Mt 26:68 saying, "*P* to us
Ac 2:17 your daughters shall *p*
1Co 13:9 in part and we *p*

PROPHET
Ge 20:7 for he is a *p*
Ex 7:1 brother will be your *p*
Dt 18:15 raise up for you a *p*
1Ki 13:11 an old *p* in Bethel
Isa 9:15 the *p* that teaches lies
Jer 1:5 I ordained you a *p*
Jer 28:5 *p* Jeremiah said to the *p*
Mt 2:17 spoken by Jeremiah the *p*
Mt 10:41 a *p* in the name of a *p*
Mt 11:9 A *p*? Yes...more than a *p*
Mk 6:15 He is the *P*
Mk 11:32 held John to be a real *p*
Lk 1:76 will be called the *p*
Lk 4:17 scroll of the *p* Isaiah
Lk 7:39 If this Man were a *p*
Lk 24:19 who was a *p*
Jn 7:52 see that no *p* arises
Ac 2:16 spoken by the *p* Joel
Ac 21:10 a *p* named Agabus
1Co 14:37 thinks himself to be a *p*
2Pe 2:16 the madness of the *p*
Rev 19:20 with him the false *p*
Rev 20:10 beast and the false *p* were

PROPHETS
1Sa 10:10 a group of *p* met him
1Ki 18:4 killed the *p* of the Lord
Ps 105:15 do no harm to my *p*
Isa 30:10 and to the *p*
Jer 2:8 the *p* prophesied by
Jer 27.9 do not listen to your *p*
Eze 13:2 against the *p* of Israel
Zec 13:2 remove from the land the *p*
Mt 5:12 they persecuted the *p* who
Mt 5:17 abolish the Law or the *P*
Mt 11:13 the *P* and the Law
Mk 13:22 and false *p* will rise
Lk 10:24 many *p* and kings
Lk 11:47 the tombs of the *p*
Jn 6:45 It is written in the *P*
Ac 7:52 Which of the *p*
Ac 13:15 from the Law and the *P*
Ro 3:21 by the Law and the *P*
Ro 11:3 they have killed Your *p*
1Co 12:29 Are all *p*?
1Co 14:29 two or three *p* speak
Eph 2:20 of the apostles and *p*
Jas 5:10 take the *p*
Rev 11:10 two *p* tormented
Rev 22:6 God of the holy *p*

PROPITIATION
Ro 3:25 set forth to be a *p*

PROSPER
Ps 122:6 they *p* who love you
Isa 53:10 of the Lord shall *p*
Isa 54:17 against you shall *p*

PROSPERITY
Dt 23:6 *p* all your days
Job 15:21 *p* the destroyer
Ps 30:6 In my *p* I said
Ps 73:3 I saw the *p*

PROSTITUTE
Dt 31:16 begin to *p* themselves
Jos 2:1 a *p* named Rahab

Heb 11:31 By faith the *p* Rahab
Rev 17:1 great *p* who sits on

PROSTITUTES
1Ki 3:16 two women who were *p*
1Ki 14:24 male cult *p* in the land
Mt 21:32 the tax collectors and *p*
Rev 17:5 THE MOTHER OF *P*

PROTECT
Ps 121:7 The Lord shall *p* you
Ps 140:1 *p* me from violent men

PROTECTION
Ps 91:4 you shall find *p*
Ps 143:9 I flee unto You for my *p*

PROUD
Dt 8:14 become *p* and you
Ps 40:4 does not turn toward the *p*
Ps 119:85 the *p* have dug pits
Pr 6:17 a *p* look, a lying tongue,
Pr 28:25 a *p* heart stirs up strife
Lk 1:51 scattered the *p* in
2Ti 3:2 boastful, *p*, blasphemers
1Pe 5:5 "God resists the *p*

PROVE
Dt 8:2 humble you, and to *p*
Dt 8:16 *p* you, to do good for you
Ro 12:2 mind, that you may *p*

PROVED
Ro 7:10 *p* to be death in me

PROVERB
2Pe 2:22 to the true *p*

PROVERBS
1Ki 4:32 three thousand *p*
Ecc 12:9 arranged many *p*

PROVIDE
Ge 22:8 "My son, God will *p*
Mt 10:9 "*P* neither gold nor

PROVIDES
Ps 147:8 *p* rain for the earth
Pr 6:8 *p* her bread in the summer

PROVIDED
Ac 20:34 these hands have *p*
Heb 11:40 *p* something better

PROVINCE
Ne 1:3 *p* enduring great affliction
Est 8:11 of any people or any *p*
Da 2:48 *p* of Babylon and chief
Da 8:2 palace which is in the *p*

PROVING
Ac 9:22 in Damascus, *p* that this One is
Ac 17:3 *p* that the Christ had to suffer
Ac 18:28 *p* from the Scriptures that Jesus

PROVISION
Ro 13:14 no *p* for the flesh

PROVOKE
Jer 7:19 Do they *p* Me to
Eph 6:4 Fathers, do not *p*

PROVOKED
Ps 78:56 *p* the Most High
Ac 17:16 his spirit was *p*
1Co 13:5 is not easily *p*

PRUDENCE
Pr 8:12 I, wisdom, dwell with p

PRUNES
Jn 15:2 that bears fruit, He *p*

PSALMS
Eph 5:19 to one another in *p*
Jas 5:13 Let him sing *p*

PUNISH
Pr 17:26 *p* the just is
Jer 5:9 Shall I not *p*

PUNISHED
Ac 26:11 *p* them often in every
2Th 1:9 They shall be *p*

PUNISHMENT
Ge 4:13 *p* is more than I
Isa 10:3 in the day of *p*
Jer 10:15 *p* they shall perish
Am 1:3 not revoke the *p*
Mt 25:46 into eternal *p*
2Co 2:6 *p* which was inflicted
Heb 10:29 more severe a *p*
1Pe 2:14 sent by him for the *p*
2Pe 2:9 unrighteous under *p*

PURE
Ex 25:11 overlay it with *p* gold
Lev 24:2 to you *p* olive oil
2Sa 22:27 the *p* You…*p*
Job 4:17 a man be more *p*
Ps 19:8 of the LORD is *p*
Ps 24:4 and a *p* heart
Ps 119:9 keep his way *p*
Pr 20:9 I am *p* from my sin
Pr 30:5 word of God is *p*
Da 7:9 head like the *p* wool
Hab 1:13 are too *p* to look
Mt 5:8 Blessed are the *p*
Php 1:10 you may be *p*
Php 4:8 whatever things are *p*
1Ti 3:9 in a *p* conscience
Titus 1:15 To the *p*, all things are *p*
Titus 2:5 *p*, homemakers
Heb 10:22 washed with *p* water
Jas 1:27 Religion that is *p*
Jas 3:17 from above is first *p*
1Pe 2:2 desire the *p* milk of the
Rev 21:18 the city was *p* gold

PURIFICATION
Nu 31:23 with the water of *p*

PURIFIED
Ne 12:30 the Levites *p* themselves
Ac 15:9 *p* their hearts by
1Pe 1:22 your souls have been *p*

PURIFIES
1Jn 3:3 hope in Him *p* himself

PURIFY
Ge 35:2 *P* yourselves and
Titus 2:14 and *p* for Himself
Jas 4:8 and *p* your hearts

PURIFYING
Lev 12:4 blood of her *p*

PURIM
Est 9:26 these days *P*

PURITY
1Ti 4:12 in faith, and in *p*

PURPOSE
Ecc 3:1 A time for every *p*

PURPOSED
Isa 14:24 *p*, so shall it stand
Isa 14:27 For the Lord of Hosts has *p*,
Eph 1:9 pleasure, which He *p* in Himself

PURPOSES
Ps 33:10 He restrains the *p* of the people.
Jer 15:11 free for good *p*
Jer 49:20 *p* that He has purposed
Jer 51:29 *p* of the Lord will be performed

REFRESHED
2Co 7:13 his spirit was *r*
2Ti 1:16 for he often *r*

REFRESHES
Pr 25:13 *r* the soul of his

REFRESHING
Ac 3:19 *r* may come from the

REFUGE
Dt 33:27 eternal God is your *r*
Ps 46:1 God is our *r* and
Heb 6:18 who have fled for *r*

REFUSED
Ge 37:35 but he *r* to be comforted
1Ki 20:35 But the man *r* to strike
Ne 9:17 They *r* to obey
Jer 5:3 have *r* to receive correction
Zec 7:11 *r* to pay attention and turned

REGARD
Ps 66:18 *r* iniquity in my heart
Lk 18:2 did not fear God or *r*

REGARDED
Pr 1:24 my hand and no man *r*
Lk 1:48 *r* the low estate

REGARDS
Pr 13:18 *r* reproof will be

REGENERATION
Mt 19:28 to you, in the *r*

REGULATIONS
Est 2:12 under the *r* for the women
Col 2:20 yourselves to *r*

REIGN
Lk 1:33 and He will *r*
Ro 5:17 righteousness *r*
Ro 5:21 grace might *r*
Ro 6:12 do not let sin *r*
1Co 15:25 For He will *r* until He
Rev 20:6 of Christ, and shall *r*

REIGNED
Ro 5:21 so that just as sin *r*
Rev 20:4 They came to life and *r*

REIGNS
Isa 52:7 to Zion, "Your God *r*
Rev 19:6 Lord God Omnipotent *r*

REJECT
Mk 7:9 "You full well *r*
Titus 3:10 *R* a divisive man

REJECTED
Isa 53:3 He was despised and *r*
Mt 21:42 *r* has become the
Lk 17:25 many things and be *r*
Ac 7:35 Moses whom they *r*
1Pe 2:4 a living stone who is *r*

REJECTS
Lk 10:16 he who *r* Me *r*

REJOICE
Ps 33:1 *R* in the LORD
Ps 63:7 of Your wings I will *r*
Ps 68:3 Let them *r* before God
Ps 96:11 Let the heavens *r*
Ps 97:1 Let the earth *r*
Ps 118:24 We will *r* and be glad
Pr 31:25 she will *r* in time to
Ecc 11:9 *R*, O young man
Isa 66:14 your heart shall *r*
Mic 7:8 Do not *r* over me
Lk 10:20 do not *r*
Jn 14:28 you would *r*
Jn 16:20 but the world will *r*
Jn 16:22 and your heart will *r*
Ro 12:15 *R* with those who
Php 1:18 in this I *r*
Php 2:17 take delight and *r*
Php 4:4 *R* in the Lord
1Th 5:16 *R* always
1Pe 1:8 you *r* with joy

REJOICED
Lk 10:21 At that time Jesus *r*
Jn 8:56 Abraham *r*

REJOICES
Ps 16:9 glad, and my glory *r*
1Co 13:6 but *r* in the truth

REJOICING
Ps 126:6 come home again with *r*
Ac 8:39 he went his way *r*
Heb 3:6 confidence and the *r*

RELATIVES
Mk 6:4 among his own *r* and in his own house
Lk 1:61 "There is no one among your *r*

RELEASED
Ro 7:2 she is *r* from the law

RELENT
Dt 32:36 *r* in regard to His servants
Heb 7:21 sworn and will not *r*

RELENTING
Jer 15:6 I am weary of *r*

RELIEF
Job 14:14 I will wait, until my *r*
Ps 4:1 You have given me *r*

RELIGION
Ac 25:19 about their own *r*
Jas 1:27 *R* that is pure

RELIGIOUS
Ac 17:22 things you are very *r*
Jas 1:26 seems to be *r*

RELY
Isa 27:5 let him *r* on My strength
Isa 50:10 and *r* upon his God
Eze 33:26 You *r* upon your sword
Gal 3:10 For all who *r* on the works

REMAIN
Jn 15:11 that My joy may *r*
Jn 15:16 your fruit should *r*
Jn 21:22 "If it is My will that he *r*
1Co 15:6 the greater part *r*
1Th 4:15 are alive and *r*
Rev 3:2 the things which *r*

REMAINS
Ge 8:22 While the earth *r*
Jn 9:41 Therefore your sin *r*
Heb 4:9 Therefore a rest *r*

REMEMBER
Ex 20:8 *R* the Sabbath day
Ps 20:7 we will *r* the name
Ps 77:6 I *r* my song
Ecc 12:1 *R* your Creator
Isa 43:18 *r* the former things
Jer 31:34 I will *r* their sin
Hab 3:2 In wrath *r* mercy
Lk 1:72 to *r* His holy
Lk 17:32 *R* Lot's wife
2Ti 2:8 *R* Jesus Christ
Heb 13:7 *R* those who rule

REMEMBERED
Ge 8:1 God *r* Noah
Ex 2:24 *r* His covenant with
Ps 137:1 wept when we *r*
Mt 26:75 Then Peter *r* the word
Ac 11:16 *r* the word of the Lord

REMEMBRANCE
Isa 43:26 Put Me in *r*
Lk 22:19 Do this in *r* of Me
1Co 11:24 Do this in *r* of Me

REMISSION
Mk 1:4 for the *r*

REMNANT
Isa 10:21 The *r* shall return
Ro 11:5 time there is a *r*

REMOVE
Rev 2:5 *r* your candlestick

REMOVED
Ps 46:2 Though the earth be *r*
Isa 54:10 the mountains may be *r*
Mt 21:21 this mountain, 'Be *r*

RENDER
Nu 18:9 which they *r*
Isa 66:15 *r* His anger with fury
Jer 51:6 will *r* to her a recompense

RENDERS
1Th 5:15 no one *r* evil for evil

RENEW
Ps 51:10 *r* a right spirit
Isa 40:31 upon the LORD shall *r*

RENEWED
Ps 103:5 that your youth is *r*
2Co 4:16 inward man is being *r*
Eph 4:23 and be *r* in the spirit

RENEWING
Ro 12:2 transformed by the *r*

RENOWN
Ge 6:4 were of old, men of *r*
Ps 135:13 Your *r*, O Lord,

REPAY
Lk 10:35 I will *r*
Lk 14:14 they cannot *r*
Ro 12:17 *R* no one evil for evil
Ro 12:19 I will *r*
1Ti 5:4 *r* their parents

REPENT
Nu 23:19 that He should *r*
Jer 18:11 *R* now
Mt 3:2 "*R*, for the kingdom
Mk 1:15 *R* and believe
Lk 13:3 unless you *r*
Lk 17:4 saying, 'I *r*,'
Rev 16:9 they did not *r*

REPENTANCE
2Ch 6:38 if they turn in *r* to You
Mt 3:8 bear fruit worthy of *r*
Mk 1:4 a baptism of *r*
Mk 2:17 but sinners to *r*
Lk 15:7 men who need no *r*
Ac 20:21 Greeks of *r*
Ac 26:20 do works proving their *r*
Heb 6:1 a foundation of *r*
Heb 6:6 once more to *r*
2Pe 3:9 but all to come to *r*

REPENTED
Jer 31:19 after I turned back, I *r*
Mt 12:41 they *r* at the preaching
Mt 21:29 he *r* and went
Lk 10:13 they would have *r* long

REPENTS
Jer 23:14 no one *r* from his
Lk 17:3 if he *r*, forgive him

REPETITIONS
Mt 6:7 *r*, as the heathen do

REPORT
Ex 23:1 not give a false *r*
Isa 53:1 Who has believed our *r*

REPROACH
Pr 18:3 with dishonor *r*
Isa 54:4 not remember the *r*
Jer 31:19 Because I bore the *r*
1Ti 3:7 he does not fall into *r*
Heb 11:26 esteemed the *r*

REPROACHED
1Pe 4:14 you are *r* because of the

REPROACHES
Ps 55:12 is not an enemy who *r*
2Co 12:10 in weaknesses, in *r*

REQUEST
Ps 106:15 He gave them their *r*

REQUESTS
Php 4:6 make your *r* known

REQUIRE
Mic 6:8 what does the LORD *r*
1Co 1:22 For the Jews *r* a sign

REQUIRED
Ps 40:6 offering You have not *r*
Lk 12:20 your soul will be *r*
Lk 12:48 him much shall be *r*

RESCUE
Ps 22:8 let Him *r* him
2Pe 2:9 the Lord knows how to *r* the godly

RESCUES
Da 6:27 He delivers and *r*

RESIST
Mt 5:39 *r* an evil person
Ac 7:51 *r* the Holy Spirit
Ro 9:19 For who can *r* His will
Jas 4:7 *R* the devil, and he

RESISTED
Heb 12:4 You have not yet *r*

RESISTS
Jas 4:6 "God *r* the proud
1Pe 5:5 because "God *r* the proud

RESPECT
Ge 4:4 the LORD had *r* for Abel
Ps 119:117 I will have *r* for Your
Jas 2:3 have *r* for him who wears

REST
Ex 31:15 Sabbath of complete *r*
1Ch 28:2 to build a house of *r*
Ps 37:7 *R* in the LORD
Ps 55:6 fly away and be at *r*
Isa 28:12 "This is the *r*
Isa 66:1 is the place of My *r*
Mt 11:28 and I will give you *r*
Heb 3:11 shall not enter My *r*
Heb 4:9 therefore a *r* remains
Rev 6:11 they were told to *r*
Rev 14:13 "that they may *r*
Rev 20:5 The *r* of the dead

RESTED
Ge 2:2 had done, and He *r*
Heb 4:4 "And God *r* on the

RESTITUTION
Ex 22:3 He must make full *r*
Lev 5:15 *R* offering to the Lord

RESTORE
Ps 51:12 *R* to me the joy
Mt 17:11 and will *r* all things
Ac 1:6 You at this time *r*
Gal 6:1 who are spiritual should *r*

RESTORED
Eze 18:7 oppressed anyone, but has *r*

RESTORES
Ps 23:3 He *r* my soul

RESTS
Pr 14:33 *r* in the heart

RESULT
Ro 6:21 The *r* of those things is death

1Pe 1:7 found to *r* in praise
1Pe 1:9 *R* of your faith
resurrected
Col 2:13 He has *r* together with Him

RESURRECTION
Mt 22:23 that there is no *r*
Mt 22:30 in the *r* they neither marry
Mt 27:53 of the graves after His *r*
Lk 14:14 at the *r* of the just
Jn 11:25 "I am the *r* and the life
Ac 4:33 testified to the *r*
Ac 17:18 Jesus and the *r*
1Co 15:13 If there is no *r* of
Php 3:10 the power of His *r*
1Pe 3:21 the *r* of Jesus Christ

RETRIBUTION
Ro 11:9 a stumbling block and a *r* to them.

RETURN
Ecc 5:15 naked shall he *r*
Isa 55:7 Let him *r* to the Lord
Zec 1:3 *R* to Me
Mt 12:44 it says, 'I will *r*

RETURNED
1Pe 2:25 now have been *r* to the Shepherd

RETURNS
Pr 26:11 As a dog *r* to its
2Pe 2:22 "The dog *r* to his own

REVEAL
Mt 11:27 the Son will *r* Him.
Gal 1:16 *r* His Son in me

REVEALED
Dt 29:29 things which are *r*
Isa 56:1 righteousness to be *r*
Lk 17:30 the Son of Man is *r*
Ro 1:18 the wrath of God is *r*
Ro 8:18 glory which shall be *r*
2Th 1:7 the Lord Jesus is *r*
2Th 2:8 lawless one will be *r*
1Pe 1:5 ready to be *r* in the
1Jn 3:2 *r* what we shall be

REVEALER
Da 2:47 Lord of kings, and a *r*

REVEALING
Am 3:7 *r* His purpose to His

REVEALS
Pr 20:19 as a talebearer *r*

REVELATION
Ro 16:25 to the *r* of the mystery
Gal 1:12 except by a *r*
Gal 2:2 I went up in response to a *r*
Eph 1:17 Spirit of wisdom and *r*
Eph 3:3 *r* He made known to
1Pe 1:7 and honor at the *r*
1Pe 1:13 at the *r* of Jesus Christ

REVERENCE
Heb 12:28 God acceptably with *r*

REVERENT
Titus 2:3 women should be *r* in behavior

REVILED
Mk 15:32 crucified with Him also *r*
1Pe 2:23 When He was *r*

REVIVE
Ps 85:6 Will You not *r* us
Hos 6:2 two days He will *r*

REVIVED
Ro 7:9 came, sin *r*, and I died

REWARD
Ge 15:1 exceedingly great *r*
Ps 91:8 behold and see the *r*
Isa 40:10 see, His *r* is with
Mt 5:12 because great is your *r*
Mt 6:2 you, they have their *r*
Mt 10:42 no way lose his *r*
Lk 23:41 we are receiving the due *r*
1Co 3:8 will receive his own *r*
Col 2:18 cheat you of your *r*
Heb 11:26 for he looked to the *r*
Rev 22:12 My *r* is with me

REWARDED
Ps 18:20 the Lord *r* me according
Pr 13:13 who fears the commandment will be *r*
Jer 31:16 for your work shall be *r*
Heb 10:35 which will be greatly r.

REWARDS
Pr 17:13 Whoever *r* evil for
Isa 1:23 and follows after *r*

RICH
Ge 14:23 'I have made Abram *r*'
Ex 30:15 *r* must not give more
Job 34:19 nor does He regard the *r*
Ps 49:2 *r* and poor together
Pr 10:4 of the diligent makes *r*
Pr 18:11 The *r* man's wealth is
Pr 21:17 will not be *r*
Pr 22:2 The *r* and poor
Pr 28:20 makes haste to be *r*
Ecc 5:12 the abundance of the *r*
Jer 9:23 let not the *r* man
Mt 19:23 hard for a *r* man
Mt 27:57 a *r* man of Arimathea
Mk 10:25 than for a *r* man to
Lk 12:16 land of a *r* man produced
Lk 16:1 "There was a *r* man
Lk 21:1 the *r* putting their gifts in
1Ti 6:9 who desire to be *r* fall
Jas 2:5 to be *r* in faith
Rev 2:9 poverty (but you are *r*).
Rev 13:16 both *r* and poor

RICHES
Pr 8:18 *R* and honor are
Pr 11:4 *R* do not profit
Pr 11:28 in his *r* will fall
Pr 14:24 of the wise is their *r*
Pr 19:14 and *r* are the
Pr 22:4 of the Lord are *r*
Pr 27:24 *r* are not forever
Ro 2:4 Do you despise the *r*
Ro 9:23 make known the *r*
Eph 1:18 what are the *r*
Eph 2:7 show the surpassing *r*
Eph 3:8 the incomprehensible *r*
Heb 11:26 *r* than the treasures
Rev 5:12 to receive power and *r*

RICHLY
Col 3:16 dwell in you *r*
1Ti 6:17 who *r* gives us all

RIDE
Dt 32:13 made him *r* on the high
1Ki 1:38 had Solomon *r*
Isa 58:14 *r* upon the high places
Jer 50:42 sea; and they shall *r*

RIGHT
Ge 13:9 I will go to the *r*
Ex 15:6 "Your *r* hand, O Lord
Dt 12:8 whatever is *r* in
Jdg 21:25 was *r* in his own eyes
1Sa 26:23 to every man his *r*
1Ki 2:6 Do the *r* thing
1Ki 15:11 Asa did what was *r*
Ps 9:4 have maintained my *r*
Ps 51:10 renew a *r* spirit
Pr 4:27 Do not turn to the *r*
Pr 11:24 withholds more than is *r*

Pr 14:12 that seems *r* to a man
Lk 6:6 whose *r* hand had withered
Jn 4:17 "You are *r* in saying
Ac 8:21 heart is not *r* before
1Co 9:4 we have no *r* to eat
Eph 6:1 for this is *r*
Rev 13:16 a mark on their *r* hand
Rev 22:14 the *r* to the tree of life

RIGHTEOUS
Ge 7:1 to be *r* before Me
Ge 18:23 also destroy the *r*
Ex 23:7 the innocent and the *r*
Ps 7:9 vindicate the *r* one.
Ps 34:15 are on the *r*
Ps 37:12 wicked plot against the *r*
Ps 94:15 return to those who are *r*
Ps 119:106 will keep Your *r* judgments
Pr 29:2 the *r* are in authority
Ecc 7:15 the *r* man who dies
Ecc 9:1 deeds of the *r* and
Jer 23:5 for David a *r* Branch
Eze 18:26 When a *r* man turns away
Mt 9:13 have not come to call the *r*
Mt 13:17 *r* men have desired to see
Ac 3:14 the Holy and *R* One
Ro 1:32 the *r* requirement of God
Ro 3:10 "There is none *r*
Ro 5:7 for a *r* man will one die
1Jn 2:29 know that He is *r*
1Jn 3:7 righteousness is *r*
Rev 22:11 is *r*, let him be *r*

RIGHTEOUSLY
Titus 2:12 should live soberly, *r*
1Pe 2:23 to Him who judges *r*

RIGHTEOUSNESS
Ge 15:6 it to him as *r*
Job 29:14 I put on *r*
Ps 4:1 I call, O God of my *r*
Ps 23:3 He leads me in paths of *r*
Ps 24:5 from the LORD, and *r*
Ps 35:28 will speak of Your *r*
Ps 40:9 have proclaimed *r*
Ps 50:6 heavens will declare His *r*
Ps 71:2 Deliver me in Your *r*
Ps 85:10 *r* and peace have
Ps 85:13 *R* shall go before Him
Ps 111:3 *r* endures forever
Pr 10:2 *r* delivers from death
Pr 11:4 but *r* delivers from death
Pr 11:5 The *r* of the upright
Pr 12:28 the way of *r* is life
Pr 14:34 *R* exalts a nation
Pr 21:21 He who follows after *r*
Isa 1:21 *r* lodged in her
Isa 45:24 in the LORD are *r*
Isa 51:5 My *r* is near
Isa 51:8 *r* shall be forever
Isa 57:12 I will declare your *r*
Isa 59:17 *r* as a breastplate
Isa 61:3 called trees of *r*
Isa 62:1 *r* goes forth as
Isa 64:6 all our *r* is as filthy rags
Jer 23:6 THE LORD OUR *R*
Jer 33:15 *r* in the earth
Jer 33:16 called: THE LORD OUR *R*
Eze 18:20 The *r* of the righteous
Da 12:3 who turn the many to *r*
Hos 10:12 Sow to yourselves *r*
Am 5:24 *r* like an ever-flowing
Zep 2:3 Seek *r*
Mt 3:15 to fulfill all *r*
Mt 5:20 exceeds the *r* of the
Mt 21:32 to you in the way of *r*
Jn 16:8 the world of sin and of *r*
Ro 1:17 For in it the *r*
Ro 3:22 This *r* of God
Ro 4:13 but through the *r* of faith
Ro 4:22 credited to him as *r*
Ro 5:17 *r* reign in life
Ro 5:21 might reign through *r*
Ro 6:16 or of obedience leading to *r*
Ro 10:3 ignorant of God's *r*
Ro 10:10 one believes unto *r*
2Co 5:21 might become the *r*
Gal 3:6 was credited to him as *r*
Eph 6:14 the breastplate of *r*
Php 3:9 not having my own *r*
2Ti 3:16 for instruction in *r*
Titus 3:5 *r* which we have
Jas 1:20 not work the *r*
2Pe 2:5 a preacher of *r*
2Pe 3:13 a new earth, in which *r*
1Jn 2:29 who does *r*
1Jn 3:7 one who does *r*
Rev 19:11 and in *r* He judges

RISE
Mt 5:45 For He makes His sun *r*
Mt 20:19 third day He will *r*
Lk 18:33 third day He will *r*
Ac 26:23 be the first who would *r*
1Th 4:16 in Christ will *r*

RISEN
Mt 11:11 there has *r* no
Mt 28:7 disciples that He has *r*
Lk 24:34 "The Lord has *r*
1Co 15:13 then Christ has not *r*
1Co 15:20 But now is Christ *r*

RISING
Jer 7:13 I spoke to you, *r*
Jer 26:5 *r* up early and sending
Jer 32:33 though I taught them, *r*
Jer 35:15 servants the prophets, *r*
Mal 1:11 from the *r* of the sun
Lk 2:34 to cause the fall and *r*

RIVER
Isa 66:12 peace to her like a *r*
Rev 22:1 he showed me a pure *r*

RIVERS
Ps 137:1 By the *r* of Babylon
Jn 7:38 his heart shall flow *r*

ROAR
1Ch 16:22 Let the sea *r*

ROARING
Lk 21:25 and the waves *r*
1Pe 5:8 walks around as a *r*
Rev 10:3 like a lion *r*

ROARS
Joel 3:16 The LORD *r*
Am 1:2 The LORD *r* from

ROB
Mal 3:8 Will a man *r* God

ROBBED
2Co 11:8 *r* other churches

ROBBER
Jn 10:1 is a thief and a *r*
Jn 18:40 Barabbas was a *r*

ROBBERS
Jer 7:11 a den of *r*
Jn 10:8 Me are thieves and *r*

ROBE
Lk 15:22 'Bring out the best *r*
Jn 19:2 a purple *r* on Him
Rev 6:11 Then a white *r* was

ROBES
Lk 20:46 walk in long *r*
Rev 7:9 clothed with white *r*

ROCK
Ge 49:24 the *R* of Israel
Nu 20:8 speak to the *r*
Dt 32:4 He is the *R*
1Sa 2:2 there is no *r* like our God
2Sa 22:2 The LORD is my *r*
Ps 18:2 my God, my *r*, in
Ps 18:46 blessed be my *R*!
Isa 8:14 and a *r* of offense
Mt 7:24 built his house on a *r*
Mk 15:46 hewn out of the *r*
Ro 9:33 and *r* of offense

ROCKS
1Sa 13:6 among *r*, and in cellars
Isa 2:19 the holes of the *r*
Jer 16:16 the holes of the *r*
Na 1:6 like fire, and the *r*
Rev 6:16 mountains and *r*, "Fall

ROD
Ps 23:4 Your *r* and Your staff
Rev 2:27 rule them with a *r*

ROOM
Mk 14:15 you a large upper *r*
Lk 2:7 no *r* for them in the
Ac 1:13 into the upper *r*

ROOMS
Ge 6:14 Make *r* in the ark

ROOT
Isa 11:10 day there shall be a *R*
Isa 53:2 and as a *r* out of a dry ground
Mt 13:6 they did not take *r*
Mt 13:21 he has no *r* in himself
Ro 11:16 if the *r* is holy, so are the branches.
Ro 15:12 There shall be a *r* of Jesse
1Ti 6:10 of money is the *r*
Heb 12:15 lest any *r* of
Rev 5:5 the tribe of Judah, the *r* of David
Rev 22:16 I am the *R* and the

ROOTED
Eph 3:17 *r* and grounded in love,
Col 2:7 *r* and built up in Him

ROSE
Ro 14:9 end Christ died and *r*
1Co 15:4 buried, *r* again

RUBIES
Job 28:18 the price of wisdom is above *r*.
Pr 3:15 She is more precious than *r*
Pr 8:11 wisdom is better than *r*.
Pr 31:10 For her worth is far above *r*.

RUIN
Pr 24:22 who knows the *r* of them both
Eze 21:27 A *r*, a *r*, a *r* I shall make it
1Ti 6:9 drown men in *r* and destruction

RULE
Ge 3:16 and he will *r*
1Co 15:24 puts an end to all *r*
Col 3:15 *r* in your hearts
1Ti 5:17 Let the elders who *r*
Heb 13:7 Remember those who *r*

RULER
Ex 22:28 God or curse the *r*
Ps 105:21 lord of his house and *r*
Pr 29:12 If a *r* listens to lies
Mt 24:47 make him *r* over all his
Mk 3:22 by the *r* of the
Mk 5:36 the *r* of the synagogue
Lk 8:41 a *r* of the synagogue
Jn 16:11 *r* of this world stands
1Ti 6:15 blessed and only *R*

RULERS
Ex 18:21 to be *r* of thousands
Ps 2:2 the *r* take counsel
Isa 22:3 All your *r* have fled
Da 3:2 all the *r* of the provinces
Mt 20:25 the *r* of the Gentiles
Mk 13:9 brought before *r* and kings
Ac 4:5 On the next day their *r*
Ro 13:3 *R* are not a terror
Eph 6:12 against the *r*
Titus 3:1 be subject to *r*

RULES
Da 4:17 that the Most High *r*
Da 4:32 that the Most High *r*

RUMORS
Mt 24:6 hear of wars and *r*

RUN
Isa 40:31 *r* and not be weary
Heb 12:1 us, and let us *r*

RUNNING
Gal 2:2 in case I might be r
Gal 5:7 You were *r* well

S

SABBATH
Ex 16:23 the *S*, a holy *S*
Ex 20:8 Remember the *S* day
Ex 31:14 "You shall keep the *S*
Lev 23:3 seventh day is the *S*
Nu 28:10 burnt offering of every *S*
Dt 5:12 Keep the *S* day
Jer 17:21 load on the *S* day
Mk 1:21 on the *S* He entered
Lk 6:7 He would heal on the *S*
Jn 7:22 a man on the *S* day
Ac 18:4 the synagogue every *S*

SABBATHS
Isa 56:4 who keep My *S*
Lk 4:31 teaching them on the *S*

SACRIFICE
Pr 21:3 to the LORD than *s*
Isa 34:6 For the LORD has a *s*
Hos 8:13 of My offerings they *s*
Zep 1:7 LORD has prepared the *s*
Mt 9:13 desire mercy, and not *s*
Eph 5:2 offering and a *s*
Heb 10:26 no longer remains a *s*
Heb 13:15 offer to God the *s* of praise

SACRIFICED
Ps 106:37 *s* their sons and their
1Co 5:7 our Passover, has been *s*

SACRIFICES
Ps 51:17 The *s* of God are a
Isa 1:11 multitude of your *s*
Heb 7:27 need to offer daily *s*
Heb 13:16 *s* God is well pleased

SAFELY
Hos 2:18 make them to lie down *s*

SAFETY
1Th 5:3 say, "Peace and *s*

SAINTS
Ps 37:28 does not forsake His *s*
1Sa 2:9 the feet of His *s*
Da 7:21 warring with the *s*
Da 7:25 shall wear out the *s*
Da 7:27 the people of the *s*
Ro 1:7 God, called to be *s*
1Co 1:2 Jesus, called to be *s*
Eph 3:8 least of all *s*
2Th 1:10 be glorified in His *s*
Jude 1:3 delivered to the *s*
Rev 16:6 shed the blood of *s*

SALT
Lev 2:13 your grain offerings with *s*
Mt 5:13 "You are the *s*

SALVATION
Ge 49:18 I wait for Your *s*
Ex 14:13 see the *s* of the LORD
Ex 15:2 has become my *s*
1Sa 2:1 I rejoice in Your *s*
2Sa 22:47 God of the rock of my *s*
1Ch 16:23 good tidings of His *s*
Ps 3:8 *S* belongs to the LORD
Ps 27:1 my light and my *s*
Ps 37:39 the *s* of the righteous
Ps 43:5 the *s* of my countenance
Ps 51:12 the joy of Your *s*
Ps 62:1 from Him comes my *s*
Ps 67:2 Your *s* among all
Ps 74:12 working *s* in the midst
Ps 79:9 O God of our *s*
Ps 85:9 His *s* is near to them
Ps 98:2 has made known His *s*
Isa 12:2 Certainly God is my *s*
Isa 45:17 with an everlasting *s*
Isa 52:7 who proclaims *s*
Isa 59:16 brought *s* to Him
Isa 59:17 helmet of *s* on His head
Isa 62:11 "See, your *s* comes
La 3:26 for the *s* of the LORD
Lk 1:69 a horn of *s* for us
Lk 19:9 *s* has come to this house
Ac 4:12 There is no *s* in any other
2Co 6:2 day of *s* I have helped
Eph 6:17 Take the helmet of *s*
Php 2:12 work out your own *s*
2Th 2:13 called you to *s*
Heb 2:3 neglect such a great *s*
Heb 2:10 Author of their *s* perfect
2Pe 3:15 of our Lord means *s*

SAMARITANS
Jn 4:9 have no dealings with *S*

SANCTIFICATION
1Th 4:3 the will of God, your *s*

SANCTIFIED
Ex 19:14 and *s* the people
Lev 10:3 'I will be *s* by those
Nu 8:17 I *s* them for Myself
2Ch 2:4 my God, *s* for Him
Jn 10:36 the Father has *s*
Ro 15:16 being *s* by the Holy Spirit
1Co 6:11 you were *s*
1Co 7:14 *s* by the wife
1Co 7:14 *s* by the husband
Heb 2:11 who are *s* are all of One

SANCTIFIES
Eze 20:12 I am the LORD who *s* them
Mt 23:17 the temple that *s* the gold
Heb 9:13 *s* so that the flesh is purified

SANCTIFY
Ex 13:2 *S* unto me all the firstborn
Jer 17:24 but *s* the Sabbath
Jn 17:17 *S* them by Your
Eph 5:26 that He might *s*
1Pe 3:15 But *s* the Lord God

SANCTUARY
Ex 25:8 Let them make Me a *s*
Heb 9:1 and an earthly *s*

SAND
Ge 32:12 descendants as the *s*
Heb 11:12 innumerable as the *s*

SANDAL
Dt 25:9 remove his *s* from his foot
Ru 4:7 a man would remove his *s*

SANDALS
Ex 3:5 Remove your *s* from off your feet
Jos 5:15 Remove your *s* from your feet

SANG
Ex 15:1 children of Israel *s* this
Jdg 5:1 Barak son of Abinoam *s*
Job 38:7 morning stars *s* together
Ps 106:12 they *s* His praise
Mt 11:17 we *s* a dirge to you

SAT
Ge 18:1 he *s* in the tent door
Ge 37:25 *s* down to eat
Ex 12:29 firstborn of Pharaoh that *s*
Ex 16:3 we *s* by the pots of meat
Ex 17:12 him, and he *s* on
1Ki 21:13 children of Belial, came in and *s*
Ps 137:1 By the rivers of Babylon, there we *s*
Mk 16:19 *s* at the right hand of God.
Lk 10:39 who also *s* at Jesus' feet
Heb 1:3 He *s* down at the right hand
Heb 10:12 *s* down at the right hand of God.

SATAN
Mt 4:10 away from here, *S*
Mt 16:23 "Get behind Me, *S*
Mk 3:23 "How can *S* cast out
Lk 22:31 *S* has demanded
2Th 2:9 with the working of *S*
Rev 2:24 the, 'depths of *S*,'
Rev 20:7 years are ended, *S*

SATISFIED
Ps 17:15 I will be *s* when I
Pr 30:15 that are never *s*
Isa 53:11 of his soul and be *s*

SATISFIES
Ps 103:5 who *s* your mouth
Ps 107:9 *s* the longing soul

SATISFY
Ps 90:14 *s* us in the early morning
Ps 91:16 long life I will *s*
Isa 55:2 for that which does not *s*

SAUL
1Sa 9:2 whose name was *S*
1Sa 10:21 *S* the son of Kish
1Sa 13:1 *S* was thirty years old
1Sa 13:13 said to *S*, "You have
1Sa 15:11 set up *S* to be king
1Sa 31:4 *S* said to his armor bearer,
2Sa 1:1 After the death of *S*

SAVE
1Sa 19:11 If you do not *s* your life
2Ki 19:19 *s* us from his hand
Ps 6:4 *S* me for the sake of
Ps 55:16 the LORD will *s* me
Ps 69:1 *S* me, O God!
Ps 109:26 *S* me according to
Isa 59:1 it cannot *s*
Jer 2:28 if they can *s* you
Zep 3:17 One, who will *s*
Mt 1:21 He will *s* His people

Mt 16:25	would *s* his life will lose it
Mt 18:11	has come to *s*
Mt 27:42	He cannot *s* Himself
Mk 3:4	to *s* life or to kill
Jn 12:27	*s* Me from this
1Co 1:21	preaching to *s* those
1Co 7:16	you will *s* your husband
Heb 11:7	prepared an ark to *s* his
Jas 5:15	prayer of faith will *s* the
Jude 1:23	others *s* with fear

SAVED

Ex 14:30	*s* Israel that day
Nu 22:33	slain you and *s* her alive
Ps 18:3	*s* from my enemies
Ps 106:8	He *s* them for
Pr 28:18	walks uprightly will be *s*
Isa 45:22	Turn to Me and be *s*
Jer 23:6	Judah will be *s*
Mt 10:22	to the end will be *s*
Mt 24:22	no one would be *s*
Mk 16:16	is baptized will be *s*
Jn 3:17	might be *s*
Ac 2:47	who were being *s*
Ac 16:31	household will be *s*
Ro 5:9	shall we be *s* from
1Co 1:18	who are being *s*
1Ti 2:4	desires all men to be *s*
Titus 3:5	He *s* us
1Pe 3:20	were *s* through water

SAVES

1Sa 17:47	that the Lord *s*
1Pe 3:21	baptism, which also *s*

SAVING

Heb 10:39	to the *s* of the soul

SAVIOR

Isa 60:16	I, the Lord, am your *S*
Lk 1:47	rejoices in God my *S*
Lk 2:11	the City of David a *S*
Ac 13:23	raised a *S* for Israel
1Ti 4:10	God, who is the *S*
Titus 2:13	and *S* Jesus Christ

SAWN

Heb 11:37	stoned, they were *s*

SAY

Mt 5:22	But I *s* to you that
Mt 16:15	"But who do you *s*

SAYING

1Ti 1:15	This is a faithful *s*

SAYINGS

Mt 7:24	"Whoever hears these *s*

SCALES

Lev 11:9	Fins and *s* in the waters
Rev 6:5	on it had a pair of *s*

SCARLET

Isa 1:18	your sins be as *s*
Mt 27:28	*s* robe on Him,

SCATTER

Lev 26:33	I will *s* you among the

SCATTERED

Jer 50:17	Israel is a *s* flock
Mk 14:27	the sheep will be *s*

SCATTERS

Mt 12:30	not gather with Me *s*

SCEPTER

Ge 49:10	*s* shall not depart
Heb 1:8	*s* of Your kingdom.

SCHEMER

Pr 24:8	will be called a *s*

SCHEMES

Ecc 7:29	sought out many *s*
Eph 6:11	stand against the *s* of the devil

SCHOOL

Ac 19:9	daily in the *s* of

SCOFF

Hab 1:10	They *s* at kings

SCOFFERS

2Pe 3:3	*s* in the last days

SCORCHED

Rev 16:9	Men were *s* with

SCORN

Job 16:20	My friends *s* me

SCORNS

Pr 3:34	He *s* the scornful

SCORPIONS

Lk 10:19	on serpents and *s*
Rev 9:10	They had tails like *s*

SCRIBES

Mk 12:38	"Beware of the *s*

SCRIPTURE

Lk 4:21	"Today this *S* is fulfilled in your hearing
Ac 8:35	beginning with the same *S*
2Ti 3:16	All *S* is inspired by God
2Pe 1:20	no prophecy of the *S*

SCRIPTURES

Lk 24:45	to understand the *S*
2Ti 3:15	known the Holy *S*
2Pe 3:16	as they also do the other *S*

SCROLL

Eze 3:1	Eat this *s*
Rev 6:14	heavens receded like a *s*

SEA

Ex 15:4	drowned in the Red *S*
Ps 107:23	went down to the *s*
Mt 8:27	and the *s* obey Him
Rev 4:6	throne was a *s*
Rev 21:1	there was no more *s*

SEAL

Jn 6:27	His *s* on Him.
2Ti 2:19	stands, having this *s*

SEALED

Eph 4:30	in whom you are *s*
Rev 5:1	*s* with seven seals.

SEARCH

Pr 25:2	honor of kings is to *s*
Jn 5:39	*s* the Scriptures

SEARCHED

Ps 139:1	You have *s* me
1Pe 1:10	inquired and *s* diligently

SEARCHES

1Co 2:10	For the Spirit *s*
Rev 2:23	*s* the hearts and minds

SEASON

Lev 26:4	rain in due *s*,
2Ti 4:2	Be ready in *s* and out

SEAT

Ex 25:17	shall make a mercy *s*
2Co 5:10	before the judgment *s*

SECRET

Dt 29:29	*s* things belong
Mt 6:6	Father who sees in *s*

SECRETLY

Ps 10:9	He lies in wait *s*
2Pe 2:1	*s* bring in destructive heresies

SECRETS

Ps 44:21	For He knows the *s*
Ro 2:16	God will judge the *s*

SECT
Ac 26:5 to the strictest *s*

SECURE
2Sa 13:17 *s* the door behind her
Ps 69:29 set me *s* on high
Pr 1:33 *S* from fear of evil

SECURELY
Jer 49:31 at ease, that dwells *s*

SEDUCED
Pr 7:21 flattering of her lips she *s*

SEE
Job 19:26 in my flesh I will *s*
Mt 5:8 For they shall *s* God
Mt 13:13 look, but do not *s*
Jn 8:56 rejoiced to *s* My day
Rev 22:4 They shall *s* His face

SEED
Mt 13:38 the good *s* are the
Gal 3:16 Abraham and his *S*
Gal 3:29 you are Abraham's *s*

SEEDS
Gal 3:16 He does not say "and to *s*,"

SEEK
2Ch 7:14 pray, and *s* My face
Isa 55:6 *S* the LORD while He
Mt 7:7 *s* and you will find
Lk 19:10 of Man has come to *s*
Php 2:21 For all *s* their own

SEEKING
1Co 10:33 *s* my own profit,
1Pe 5:8 as a roaring lion, *s*

SEEKS
Ps 36:7 mankind *s* refuge in the shadow
Ro 3:11 There is no one who *s*

SEEMS
Pr 14:12 is a way that *s*

SEEN
Ge 32:30 *s* God face to face
Jn 1:18 No one has *s* God at
Jn 14:9 *s* Me has *s* the
2Co 4:18 things which are not *s*

SELF
Phm 1:19 even your own *s*

SELF-CONTROL
Ac 24:25 about righteousness, *s*
Gal 5:23 meekness, and *s*
1Ti 2:15 and holiness, with *s*
2Pe 1:6 to your knowledge, *s*
2Pe 1:6 and to your *s*, patient endurance

SELF-CONTROLLED
1Ti 3:2 one wife, sober, *s*
Titus 1:8 *s*, just, holy

SELL
Mk 10:21 *s* whatever you have
Rev 13:17 no one may buy or *s*,

SEND
Jn 20:21 sent Me, even so I *s*

SENDING
Mt 10:16 "Look, I am *s* you
Ro 8:3 *s* His own Son

SENT
Ro 10:15 unless they are *s*
1Jn 4:10 *s* His Son to be the atoning sacrifice

SEPARATE
Ro 8:35 Who shall *s* us from the love
2Co 6:17 "Come out from among them and be *s*

SEPARATES
Ru 1:17 if anything but death *s*
Pr 16:28 a whisperer *s* the best of friends
Pr 17:9 who repeats a matter *s* friends

SERAPHIM
Isa 6:2 Above it stood the *s*
Isa 6:6 one of the *s* flew to me

SERPENT
Ge 3:1 *s* was more subtle
Nu 21:8 "Make a poisonous *s*
Isa 27:1 Leviathan the fleeing *s*,
Jn 3:14 Moses lifted up the *s*
2Co 11:3 *s* deceived Eve
Rev 12:9 that ancient *s* called the Devil
Rev 20:2 that ancient *s*, who is the Devil

SERPENTS
Mt 10:16 be wise as *s*

SERVANT
Pr 17:2 *s* will have rule over a son
Mt 25:21 good and faithful *s*

SERVANTS
Lk 17:10 are unprofitable *s*
Eph 6:5 *S*, obey those who
Col 4:1 give to your *s*
Heb 1:7 His *s* a flame of fire."

SERVE
Mt 20:28 to be served, but to *s*
Ro 12:11 fervent in spirit, *s*
Gal 5:13 but by love *s*

SERVED
Dt 12:2 you will possess *s*
Dt 17:3 *s* other gods and worshipped
Dt 29:26 *s* other gods, and worshipped
Jdg 3:7 LORD their God and *s*
1Ki 4:21 brought presents and *s*
1Ki 9:9 worshipped and *s* them
Mt 20:28 Son of Man did not come to be *s*
Jn 12:2 Martha *s*, but Lazarus was
Ac 17:25 Nor is He *s* by men's hands,
Ro 1:25 *s* the creature rather than the Creator
1Ti 3:13 those who have *s* well in the office

SERVES
Jn 12:26 If anyone *s* Me
Ro 14:18 he who *s* Christ

SERVICE
Ro 12:1 is your reasonable *s*
Eph 6:7 with good will doing *s*

SET
Lev 26:17 I will *s* my face
Num 4:15 the camp is to *s* out
Dt 28:36 you will *s* over you
Jos 18:1 at Shiloh and *s* up
1 Ki 12:29 he *s* one in Bethel

SEVEN
Ge 7:2 Take with you *s* each of every clean
Jos 6:4 *S* priests shall carry *s*
1Ki 19:18 *s* thousand men in Israel
Pr 6:16 hates, yes, *s* are an abomination to Him
Pr 24:16 a just man falls *s* times
Isa 4:1 that day *s* women shall take hold

SEVERELY
2Co 2:5 not to put it too *s*

Heb 4:1	should seem to come *s* of it.

SHOULDER

Isa 9:4	*s*, the rod of his oppressor
Isa 9:6	shall be upon his *s*

SHOULDERS

Dt 33:12	he will dwell between His *s*.
Lk 15:5	he places it on his *s*, rejoicing

SHOUT

Ps 47:1	*S* to God with a joyful voice.
1Th 4:16	heaven with a *s*

SHOW

Ex 18:20	and shall *s* them the way
Ex 33:18	*s* me Your glory
Ps 17:7	*S* marvelously Your lovingkindness
Ps 85:7	*S* us Your mercy, O Lord
Zec 7:9	*s* mercy and compassion
Ac 2:19	I will *s* wonders in heaven above

SHOWED

Lk 24:40	this, He *s* them His hands and His feet.

SHOWERS

Ps 65:10	soften it with *s*
Eze 34:26	cause the *s* to come down

SHRINES

Ac 19:24	who made silver *s*

SHUT

Ge 7:16	then the Lord *s* him in.
Isa 22:22	shall open, and no one shall *s*
Isa 60:11	they shall not be *s* day nor night,
Da 6:22	has *s* the lions' mouths
Rev 21:25	its gates shall never be *s*,

SICK

Mt 25:36	I was *s* and you
Jas 5:15	faith will save the *s*

SICKLE

Joel 3:13	Swing the *s*,
Rev 14:15	"Thrust in Your *s*

SICKNESS

Mt 4:23	healing all kinds of *s*
Jn 11:4	"This *s* is not unto

SICKNESSES

Mt 8:17	and bore our *s*

SIDE

Ps 91:7	A thousand may fall at your *s*
Ps 124:1	the Lord who was on our *s*
Jn 20:20	He showed them His hands and His *s*.

SIGHT

Ex 3:3	and see this great *s*
2Co 5:7	by faith, not by *s*

SIGN

Isa 7:14	shall give you a *s*
Mt 12:39	seeks after a *s*
1Co 1:22	the Jews require a *s*

SIGNS

Ge 1:14	and let them be *s*
Mt 16:3	cannot discern the *s*
Jn 20:30	performed many other *s*

SILENCE

Ps 8:2	to *s* the enemy
Rev 8:1	seal, there was *s*

SILENT

Est 4:14	For if you remain *s* at this time,
Ps 30:12	may sing praise to You and not be *s*.
Ps 32:3	When I kept *s*, my bones wasted
Ps 39:2	I was *s* to no avail
Isa 53:7	as a sheep before its shearers is *s*,
Isa 62:1	For the sake of Zion I will not keep *s*,

silver

Am 8:6	may buy the poor for *s*
Mt 26:15	him thirty pieces of *s*

SIMPLE

Ps 19:7	making wise the *s*
Pr 8:5	O you *s*, understand wisdom

SIMPLICITY

2Co 11:3	led astray from the *s*

SIN

Ge 4:7	*s* is crouching at
Ex 20:20	so that you do not *s*
Ex 32:21	so great a *s* upon them
Lev 6:25	law of the *s* offering
Nu 5:7	confess his *s*
Dt 24:16	put to death for his own *s*
2Ch 7:14	and will forgive their *s*
Ps 32:1	whose *s* is covered
Ps 51:3	and my *s* is ever before me
Ps 119:11	I might not *s* against You
Pr 20:9	I am pure from my *s*
Isa 6:7	and your *s* purged
Jer 17:1	*s* of Judah is written
Eze 43:19	a young bull as a *s* offering
Mt 5:29	right eye causes you to *s*
Mk 9:42	who believe in Me to *s*
Jn 1:29	away the *s* of the world
Jn 8:34	commits *s* is a slave of *s*
Jn 16:8	convict the world of *s*
Ro 3:9	and Gentiles are all under *s*
Ro 5:16	the judgment from one *s*
Ro 6:23	the wages of *s* is death
Ro 8:2	from the law of *s* and death
1Co 6:18	Every *s* that a man commits
Gal 2:17	the minister of *s*?
Eph 4:26	Be angry but do not *s*
1Ti 2:14	being deceived, fell into *s*
Heb 9:28	not to bear *s* but to save
Jas 4:17	and does not do it, it is *s*
1Pe 2:22	He committed no *s*,
1Jn 1:8	If we say that we have no *s*
1Jn 3:4	practices *s* breaks the law
1Jn 5:17	All wrongdoing is *s*

SINCERE

1Ti 1:5	and from *s* faith

SINCERITY

1Co 5:8	with the unleavened bread of *s*
2Co 1:12	in simplicity and godly *s*.
2Co 8:8	the *s* also of your love
Eph 6:5	with fear and trembling, in *s*

SINFUL
Lk 5:8 from me, for I am a *s* man
Ro 8:3 in the likeness of *s* flesh

SING
Ex 15:1 I will *s* to the LORD
1Ch 16:9 *S* to Him, *s* praise to Him
Ps 21:13 may we *s* and make
Ps 89:1 I will *s* of the mercies
Ps 96:1 O *s* unto the LORD
Isa 5:1 I will *s* to my well-beloved
Jas 5:13 Let him *s* psalms

SINGING
Zep 3:17 He will rejoice over you with *s*.
Ac 16:25 were praying and *s* hymns to God
Col 3:16 *s* with grace in your

SINNED
Ps 51:4 You only, have I *s*
Lk 15:18 "Father, I have *s*
Ro 3:23 For all have *s* and
1Jn 1:10 that we have not *s*

SINNER
Lk 15:7 *s* who repents than
1Pe 4:18 the ungodly and the *s*

SINNERS
Ps 1:1 in the path of *s*
Mt 9:13 the righteous, but *s*
Ro 5:8 while we were yet *s*
Ro 5:19 many were made *s*
1Ti 1:15 the world to save *s*
Heb 12:3 such hostility from *s*

SINS
Lev 4:2 a person *s* unintentionally
Dt 19:15 any sin that he *s*
1Sa 2:25 man *s* against another
Ne 9:2 confessed their *s*
Ps 19:13 from presumptuous *s*
Ps 25:7 the *s* of my youth
Isa 1:18 your *s* be as scarlet
Eze 18:4 soul who *s* shall die
Mt 18:15 brother *s* against you
Mk 1:4 remission of *s*
Mk 2:7 can forgive *s* but God
Lk 5:24 on earth to forgive *s*
Jn 8:24 you will die in your *s*
Ac 2:38 for the forgiveness of *s*
Ro 3:25 God had passed over the *s*
1Co 15:3 how Christ died for our *s*
2Co 5:19 their *s* against them
Eph 2:1 your trespasses and *s*
1Ti 5:22 partake of other men's *s*
Jas 5:20 will cover a multitude of *s*
1Pe 2:24 He Himself bore our *s*
1Jn 1:9 If we confess our *s*
Rev 18:5 her *s* have reached

SISTER
Mt 12:50 is My brother, and *s*
1Co 7:15 a brother or a *s* is not bound

SISTERS
Mt 13:56 and His *s*, are they
Mt 19:29 left houses or brothers or *s* or
Jn 11:3 So the *s* sent word to Him
1Ti 5:2 the younger women as *s*,

SIT
Mt 20:23 but to *s* at My right
Heb 1:13 "*S* at My right hand
Rev 3:21 will I grant to *s*

SKIN
Ge 3:21 God made garments of *s*
Job 2:4 LORD, saying, "*S*
Jer 13:23 Ethiopian change his *s*

SKIP
Ps 29:6 He makes them *s*

SKULL
Mt 27:33 the Place of the *S*

SLAIN
1Sa 18:7 Saul has *s* his thousands,
Eze 37:9 breathe upon these *s*,
Rev 5:6 as though it had been *s*,
Rev 5:12 who was *s*, to receive power
Rev 6:9 those who had been *s*
Rev 5:12 is the Lamb who was *s*

SLANDER
Ps 15:3 who does not *s* with the tongue
Pr 10:18 he who spreads *s*

SLANDERED
1Co 4:13 Being *s*, we encourage.
1Co 10:30 why am I *s*

SLANDERERS
Ro 1:30 *s*, God-haters, insolent,

SLAUGHTER
Isa 53:7 as a lamb to the *s*
Ro 8:36 as sheep for the *s*

SLAVE
Dt 15:15 you were a *s* in the land
Jn 8:34 commits sin is a *s*

SLAVES
Ro 6:6 should no longer be *s*
2Pe 2:19 They themselves are *s* of corruption

SLEEP
Ge 2:21 God caused a deep *s*
Ge 15:12 a deep *s* fell on Abram
2Sa 11:11 *s* with my wife
Ps 78:65 awoke as one out of *s*
Ps 121:4 neither slumber nor *s*
Ps 127:2 gives *s* to His beloved
Pr 6:4 no *s* to your eyes
Pr 6:10 a little *s*
Ecc 5:12 Sweet is the *s* of
Da 2:1 his *s* left him
Mt 26:45 "*S* on now, and take
Ac 20:9 overcome by *s*, he fell
1Co 15:51 We shall not all *s*
Eph 5:14 "Awake, you who *s*
1Th 4:14 bring with Him those who *s*
1Th 5:6 let us not *s* as others
1Th 5:7 those who *s*, *s* at night

SLEEPING
Mk 13:36 find you *s*.
Mk 14:41 "Are you still *s*

SLEPT
Ps 3:5 I lay down and *s*

SLING
1Sa 17:40 And his *s*

SLIP
Dt 32:35 their foot will *s*
Ps 121:3 He will not let your foot *s*;

SLOW
Jas 1:19 hear, *s* to speak, and *s*
2Pe 3:9 The Lord is not *s*

SLUMBER
Ps 121:3 he who keeps you will not *s*
Pr 6:10 little sleep, a little *s*

SMELL
Ge 27:27 and he smelled the *s*

SOWER
Mt 13:3 “Listen! A *s* went
2Co 9:10 who supplies seed to the *s*

SOWN
Ex 23:16 labors, which you have *s*

SOWS
Mt 13:37 *s* the good seed is the
Jn 4:37 ‘One *s*, and another
Gal 6:7 For whatever a man *s*

SPARE
Ro 8:32 He who did not *s*
2Pe 2:4 if God did not *s*

SPARROWS
Mt 10:29 Are not two *s* sold
Mt 10:31 than many *s*

SPEAK
Nu 22:35 only *s* the word that I
Job 11:5 oh, that God would *s*
Ecc 3:7 and a time to *s*
Jer 20:9 *s* any more in His name
Mt 10:19 or what you will *s*
Lk 6:26 to you, when all men *s*
Jn 16:13 He will *s* whatever
Ac 2:4 Spirit and began to *s*

SPEAKS
Ex 33:11 to face, just as a man *s*
Jn 3:34 God has sent *s*
Jn 8:44 When he lies, he *s*
Heb 11:4 He still *s*
Heb 12:24 sprinkled blood that *s*

SPEAR
1Sa 19:10 He struck the *s* into the wall.
Jn 19:34 His side with a *s*

SPECK
Mt 7:3 do you see the *s*

SPECTACLE
1Co 4:9 We have been made a *s*
Heb 10:33 you were made a *s*

SPEECH
2Co 10:10 his *s* contemptible
Col 4:6 *s* always be with grace

SPEND
Isa 55:2 you *s* money for
Jas 4:3 amiss, that you may *s*

SPIES
Jos 6:23 men who had been *s*

SPIN
Mt 6:28 work, nor do they *s*

SPIRIT
Ge 1:2 *S* of God was moving
Ge 6:3 My *S* will not always
Dt 34:9 full of the *s* of wisdom
Jdg 3:10 *S* of the LORD came on him
1Sa 16:14 an evil *s* from the LORD
1Ki 22:22 be a lying *s* in the mouth
2Ch 18:22 put a *s* of deception
Ps 51:10 renew a right *s* within me
Pr 14:29 is hasty of *s* exalts folly
Ecc 7:8 *s* than the haughty in *s*
Isa 42:1 I have put My *S* upon him
Isa 42:5 and *s* to those
Isa 61:1 The *S* of the Lord GOD
Eze 18:31 a new heart and a new *s*
Eze 37:1 in the *S* of the LORD
Eze 39:29 poured out My *S*
Da 2:1 his *s* was troubled
Zec 4:6 nor by power, but by My *S*
Mt 1:18 with child by the Holy *S*
Mt 5:3 “Blessed are the poor in *s*
Mt 10:20 the *S* of your Father
Mt 12:28 out demons by the *S* of God
Mt 28:19 and of the Holy *S*
Mk 1:26 *s* had convulsed him
Mk 3:29 against the Holy *S*
Mk 9:17 my son, who has a mute *s*
Mk 15:37 and gave up the *s*
Lk 1:80 and became strong in *s*
Lk 2:40 became strong in *s*
Lk 4:18 *S* of the Lord is upon Me
Lk 9:42 Jesus rebuked the unclean *s*
Lk 11:13 Holy *S* to those who ask
Lk 24:39 a *s* does not have flesh
Jn 1:32 I saw the *S* descending
Jn 14:26 the Counselor, the Holy *S*
Ac 2:4 filled with the Holy *S*
Ac 2:38 the gift of the Holy *S*
Ac 8:17 they received the Holy *S*
Ac 16:16 a *s* of divination
Ro 8:1 according to the *S*
Ro 8:15 the *s* of slavery
Ro 8:26 *S* helps us in our
1Co 2:12 the *s* of the world
1Co 3:16 *S* of God dwells in you
1Co 14:14 my *s* prays
1Co 15:45 made a life-giving *s*
Gal 5:22 the fruit of the *S*
Eph 1:17 may give you the *S*
Eph 4:4 one body and one *S*
Eph 6:17 the sword of the *S*
Heb 4:12 to the division of soul and *s*
Heb 6:4 shared in the Holy *S*
Heb 10:15 The Holy *S* also
1Jn 4:13 He has given us His *S*

SPIRITS
1Co 12:10 to another discerning of *s*,
1Ti 4:1 attention to seducing *s*

SPIRITUAL
1Co 2:15 *s* judges all things
1Co 15:46 that which is *s* is not
Gal 6:1 *s* should restore such a one

SPIRITUALLY
Ro 8:6 *s* minded is life

SPIT
Mt 27:30 They *s* on Him

SPLENDOR
Ps 29:2 the Lord in holy *s*
Ps 45:3 with your *s* and your majesty

SPOKE
1Co 13:11 I was a child, I *s*
Heb 1:1 in diverse ways *s*
2Pe 1:21 by the Holy Spirit *s*

SPOKEN
Isa 45:19 I have not *s* in secret
Jn 7:46 “No man has ever *s*

SPONGE
Mt 27:48 them ran, took a *s*

SPOT
Eph 5:27 church, not having *s*

SPREAD
Ge 28:14 earth, and you will *s*
Ps 140:5 they have *s* a net; they have
Isa 42:5 who *s* forth the earth
Jer 43:10 shall *s* his royal pavilion
Jer 49:22 eagle and *s* his wings
Eze 12:13 My net also I will *s*

SPREADS
Pr 10:18 lying lips and he who *s* slander is a fool.

SPRING
Jas 3:11 *s* yield at the same
Jas 3:12 No *s* can yield both salt water

SPRINGING
Jn 4:14 a well of water *s*

SPRINGS
Ps 85:11 Truth *s* from
Isa 35:7 and the thirsty land *s*

SPRINKLE
Lev 16:14 *s* it with his finger
Eze 36:25 Then I will *s*

SPRINKLED
Ex 24:8 took the blood, and *s* it
Heb 10:22 having our hearts *s*

STAFF
Ge 32:10 with my *s* I crossed over
Ps 23:4 Your rod and Your *s*
Heb 11:21 on the top of his *s*

STAND
Dt 7:24 man will be able to *s*
Job 19:25 lives, and He will *s*
Ps 1:5 ungodly will not *s*
Jer 35:19 not lack a man to *s*
Mal 3:2 and who can *s* when he
Mk 3:24 that kingdom cannot *s*
Ro 14:4 he will *s*
1Co 16:13 Watch, *s* fast in the
2Co 1:24 for by faith you *s*
Eph 6:13 having done all, to *s*
Eph 6:14 *S* therefore
1Pe 5:12 of God in which you *s*
Rev 3:20 Listen! I *s* at the

STANDARD
Isa 59:19 LORD shall lift up a *s*

STANDING
Ex 3:5 you are *s* is holy ground."
Jos 5:15 the place where you are *s* is holy."
1Ti 3:13 for themselves good *s* and great

STANDS
Nu 14:14 Your cloud *s* over them
2Ti 2:19 But the firm foundation of God *s*

STAR
Mt 2:2 For we have seen His *s*
Rev 22:16 Bright and Morning *S*

STARS
Ge 1:16 He made the *s* also
Heb 11:12 a multitude as the *s*

STATUTES
Ps 93:5 Your *s* are very sure

STAY
2Sa 24:16 Now *s* your hand
Da 4:35 no one can *s* His hand

STEADFAST
1Co 15:58 brothers, be *s*
Heb 6:19 sure and *s* anchor

STEADFASTLY
Lk 9:51 He was *s* set to go
Ac 2:42 They continued *s*

STEADFASTNESS
Col 2:5 orderliness and the *s*

STEAL
Ex 20:15 You shall not *s*
Pr 30:9 lest I be poor, and *s*
Mt 6:19 thieves break in and *s*
Mt 19:18 adultery, You shall not *s*
Mt 27:64 come by night and *s* Him
Ro 2:21 preach not to *s*, do you *s*
Ro 13:9 murder, You shall not *s*
Eph 4:28 Let him who steals *s*

STEALS
Pr 6:30 if he *s* to satisfy himself

STEPS
Ps 37:23 The *s* of a man
Ps 40:2 and established my *s*
Pr 16:9 the LORD directs his *s*
1Pe 2:21 should follow His *s*

STEWARD
Titus 1:7 be blameless, as a *s*

STEWARDS
1Co 4:1 of Christ and *s*

STILL
Jos 10:13 So the sun stood *s*, and the moon
Ps 46:10 Be *s* and know that *I* am God;
Ps 89:9 waves arise, You *s* them.
Zec 2:13 Be *s*, all flesh before the Lord

Mk 4:39 be *s*!" Then the wind ceased

STIRS
Pr 10:12 Hatred *s* up strife, but love
Pr 15:18 A wrathful man *s* up strife,
Pr 29:22 An angry man *s* up strife

STOIC
Ac 17:18 and *S* philosophers

STOLE
2Sa 15:6 Absalom *s* the hearts of the

STOLEN
Ex 22:4 If the *s* item is in fact
Jos 7:11 They have *s*
Pr 9:17 "*S* waters are sweet

STOMACH'S
1Ti 5:23 little wine for your *s*

STONE
Ge 35:14 him, a pillar of *s*
Jos 24:27 *s* will be a witness
Ps 118:22 *s* that the builders
Isa 28:16 I lay in Zion a *s*
Mt 7.9 will give him a *s*
Mt 21:44 *s* will be broken
Lk 20:17 *s* which the builders
Jn 10:32 those works do you *s*
1Pe 2:4 Him as to a living *s*

STONED
Ac 7:59 *s* Stephen as he was
Heb 11:37 They were *s*

STONES
Ex 28:21 The *s* shall be according to the
Jos 4:3 twelve *s* from the middle
1Sa 17:40 chose for himself five smooth *s*
Mt 3:9 God is able from these *s*
Mt 4:3 command that these *s*
1Co 3:12 silver, precious *s*, wood, hay, or stubble
1Pe 2:5 living *s*, are being built

STONY
Eze 36:26 take away the *s* heart

STORE
1Co 16:2 in *s*, as God has prospered

STORM
Ps 107:29 He made the *s* calm

STRANGE
Lev 10:1 on it, and offered *s*
Dt 32:16 jealous with *s* gods
Jer 2:21 degenerate plant of a *s*

STRANGER
Mt 25:35 I was a *s* and you
Jn 10:5 They will never follow a *s*,

STRANGERS
Jn 10:5 know the voice of *s*
Eph 2:19 you are no longer *s*

STREAM
Isa 66:12 like a flowing *s*
Am 5:24 like an ever-flowing *s*.

STREAMS
Ps 78:16 He brought *s*
Ecc 1:7 All the *s* flow into the sea,

STRENGTH
Ge 49:3 the beginning of my *s*
1Sa 15:29 the *S* of Israel will not lie
1Ch 16:11 and His *s*
Job 12:16 With Him are *s* and
Job 39:11 because his *s* is great?
Ps 18:1 O LORD, my *s*
Ps 28:7 The LORD is my *s*
Ps 31:10 my *s* fails because
Ps 59:9 My *S*, I will wait
Ps 93:1 put on *s* as His belt
Ps 118:14 LORD is my *s* and song
Isa 51:9 awake, put on *s*,
Jer 16:19 my *s* and my fortress
Da 2:37 power, and *s*, and glory
Mk 12:30 and with all your *s*
1Co 15:56 and the *s* of sin is the law
Rev 3:8 For you have a little *s*
Rev 5:12 wisdom and *s* and honor

STRENGTHEN
Dt 3:28 him and *s* him
Ps 68:28 *s*, O God
Heb 12:12 and *s* your weak knees
1Pe 5:10 support, *s*, and establish
Rev 3:2 *s* the things which remain

STRENGTHENED
Ge 48:2 Israel *s* himself
2Ch 11:11 He *s* the fortresses
Ne 2:18 So they *s* their hands
Ac 9:19 he had eaten, he was *s*

STRENGTHENING
Ac 14:22 *s* the minds of the

STRENGTHENS
Php 4:13 Christ who *s*

STRIFE
Pr 15:18 man stirs up *s*
Php 1:15 out of envy and *s*
1Ti 6:4 which come envy, *s*
Jas 3:16 is envying and *s*

STRIKE
Zec 13:7 *S* the shepherd
Mt 26:31 'I will *s* the shepherd

STRIPES
Isa 53:5 *s* we are healed

STRIVE
Ge 6:3 will not always *s*
Lk 13:24 "*S* to enter through

STRONG
Ex 13:9 with a *s* hand the
Lev 10:9 wine nor *s* drink
Jos 1:9 Be *s* and courageous
1Sa 4:9 Be *s* and be men
Job 8:2 mouth be like a *s* wind
Ps 24:8 The LORD *s* and mighty
Ps 76:5 *s* of heart have been
Pr 18:10 of the LORD is a *s* tower
Jer 32:21 with a *s* hand
Eze 19:11 *s* rods for the scepters
Da 4:22 grown and become *s*
Zec 6:7 the *s* horses went out
Lk 1:80 and became *s* in spirit
Lk 2:40 became *s* in spirit
1Co 16:13 be bold like men, and be *s*
Eph 6:10 be *s* in the Lord
Rev 5:2 I saw a *s* angel

STRUCK
Nu 20:11 *s* the rock twice
Job 19:21 the hand of God has *s*
Ps 78:20 Behold, He *s* the rock
Isa 60:10 in My wrath I *s*

STUBBLE
Mal 4:1 evildoers will be *s*

STUBBORNNESS
Dt 9:27 do not look at the *s*

STUDY
Ecc 12:12 end, and much *s* is a weariness to the flesh

STUMBLE
Ps 119:165 and nothing shall cause them to *s*
Pr 3:23 and your foot will not *s*.
Jer 13:16 before your feet *s* on the dark
Jer 31:9 a straight way in which they shall not *s*
Hos 14:9 but the transgressors *s* in them.
Mal 2:8 have caused many to *s*
Jn 11:9 during the day, he does not *s*
Jn 11:10 walks during the night, he *s*

STUMBLED
Ro 11:11 *s* that they should

STUMP
Isa 6:13 whose *s* remains
Isa 11:1 forth a shoot from the *s*

SUBDUE
Ge 1:28 replenish the earth and *s* it.
Php 3:21 *s* all things to

SUBJECT
Ro 8:7 for it is not *s*
Ro 13:1 Let every person be *s*
Heb 2:15 throughout their lives *s*

SUBJECTION
Heb 2:8 put all things in *s*

SUBMISSION
1Ti 3:4 his children in *s*

SUBMISSIVE
1Pe 5:5 Yes, all of you be *s*

SUBMIT
Jas 4:7 Therefore *s* yourselves to God
1Pe 2:13 *s* yourselves to every

SUCCESS
Ge 24:12 please let me have *s*
1Ki 22:13 declare *s* for the king

SUFFER
Lk 24:46 for the Christ to *s*
Ro 8:17 Christ, if indeed we *s*
Php 1:29 in Him, but also to *s*

SUFFERED
1Pe 5:10 after you have *s*

SUFFERING
Heb 2:10 perfect through *s*
Jas 5:13 anyone among you *s*

SUFFERINGS
Ro 8:18 I consider that the *s*

SUFFERS
1Co 12:26 If one part *s*,
1Co 13:4 Love *s* long and is

SUMMER
Ps 32:4 into the drought of *s*
Isa 16:9 shouting for your *s*
Jer 40:12 gathered very much wine and *s*
Jer 48:32 fallen upon your *s* fruits

SUN
Jos 10:13 So the *s* stood still
Ps 121:6 *s* shall not harm you
Isa 38:8 *s* on the sundial
Joel 2:10 The *s* and moon darken
Mic 3:6 *s* will set upon the
Mt 5:45 For He makes His *s*
Lk 23:45 the *s* was darkened
Eph 4:26 do not let the *s*
Rev 6:12 *s* became black
Rev 21:23 has no need of *s*

SUPPER
1Co 11:20 to eat the Lord's *S*
1Co 11:25 took the cup after He had *s*
Rev 19:17 and gather for the *s*

SUPPLY
2Co 8:14 *s* their need,
Php 4:19 But my God shall *s*

SUPREME
1Pe 2:13 to the king as *s*

SURE
Nu 28:31 *s* they are without blemish.
Nu 32:23 be *s* your sin will find
Ps 132:11 sworn with a *s* oath to David

SURPASSES
Eph 3:19 the love of Christ which *s* knowledge

SURPASSING
2Co 9:14 of the *s* grace of God in you.

SURPRISED
1Pe 4:4 are *s* that you do not join them
1Pe 4:12 do not be *s* at the fiery ordeal

SURROUND
Ps 5:12 You *s* him with favor
Ps 32:7 You will *s* me with shouts of deliverance.
Ps 89:7 awesome to all those who *s* Him.

SURROUNDS
Ps 125:2 so the Lord *s* His people

SUSTAIN
Isa 50:4 that *I* may know how to *s* him

SWEAR
Mt 5:33 'You shall not *s*
Mt 5:34 do not *s* at all;

SWEARING
Hos 4:2 *s*, lying, and killing

SWEARS
Mt 23:18 if anyone *s* by the

SWEET
Ps 119:103 *s* are Your words
Rev 10:9 it will be as *s*

SWIFT
Dt 28:49 as *s* as the eagle flies
Isa 19:1 LORD is riding on a *s*
Mal 3:5 I will be a *s* witness

SWORD
Ge 3:24 a flaming *s* which
Ge 27:40 will live by your *s*
Lev 26:6 and the *s* shall not go
Nu 22:23 His *s* was drawn in
Jos 8:18 *s* in his hand
Jdg 7:14 than the *s* of Gideon
1Sa 17:45 a *s*, a spear, and a shield
Est 9:5 struck all their enemies by *s*
Pr 25:18 is like a club, a *s*, and
Isa 34:6 The *s* of the LORD is
Eze 5:1 take a sharp *s*
Eze 5:12 fall by the *s* all around
Eze 30:4 *s* shall come upon Egypt
Eze 32:10 when I brandish My *s*
Na 3:15 the *s* will cut you off
Mt 10:34 to bring peace, but a *s*
Mt 26:51 drew his *s*, and struck
Lk 2:35 And a *s* will pierce
Eph 6:17 the *s* of the Spirit
Heb 11:37 were slain with the *s*
Rev 2:12 has the sharp two-edged *s*
Rev 13:10 he who kills with the *s*
Rev 19:15 mouth proceeds a sharp *s*

SWORN
Ps 110:4 The Lord has *s* and will not
Heb 7:21 "The Lord has *s* and will not

SWORDS
Ge 34:25 took their *s*
Lk 22:52 *s* and clubs as against a

SWORE
Mt 26:74 *s*, "I do not know
Heb 3:11 So I *s* in My wrath

SYMPATHIZE
Heb 4:15 Priest who cannot *s*

SYNAGOGUE
Lk 4:16 to the *s* on the Sabbath day.
Rev 2:9 but are a *s* of Satan

SYNAGOGUES
Mt 4:23 teaching in their *s*
Mt 10:17 scourge you in their *s*
Jn 16:2 put you out of the *s*
Ac 9:2 to the *s* of Damascus

T

TABERNACLE
Ps 27:5 *t* He will hide me
Ac 15:16 will rebuild the *t*
Heb 9:11 and more perfect *t*

TABERNACLES
Lev 23:34 Feast of *t* for seven days
Jn 7:2 Feast of *T* was at hand

TABLE
Ps 23:5 prepare a *t* before me
Mk 7:28 dogs under the *t*
1Co 10:21 of the Lord's *t*

TABLET
Pr 3:3 write them on the *t*
Jer 17:1 is engraved on the *t*

TABLETS
Ex 31:18 Mount Sinai, He gave Moses the two *t*
Ex 31:18 *t* of stone, written with the finger
Dt 10:5 put the *t* in the ark which I had made,
2Co 3:3 not on *t* of stone but on human *t*

TAKE
Ps 51:11 *t* Your Holy Spirit
Mt 11:29 *T* My yoke upon
Mk 8:34 and *t* up his cross
Jn 10:17 My life that I may *t*

TAKES
1Ki 20:11 boast himself as he who *t* it off."
Ps 34:8 blessed is the man who *t* refuge
Lk 6:30 of him who *t* away your goods
Jn 1:29 who *t* away the sin of the world
Jn 10:18 No one *t* it from Me, but I lay it
Rev 22:19 if anyone *t* away from

TALENT
Mt 25:25 went and hid your *t*

TASTE
Pr 24:13 honeycomb that is sweet to your *t*
Ps 34:8 Oh, *t* and see that the

TASTED
Heb 6:4 *t* the heavenly gift

TAUGHT
Isa 40:13 as His counselor has *t*
Gal 1:12 from man, neither was I *t*

TAX
Mt 5:46 *t* collectors do the
Mt 11:19 a friend of *t* collectors

TAXES
Ro 13:7 *t* to whom *t*

TEACH
Job 21:22 "Can anyone *t*
Ps 25:4 *t* me Your paths
Ps 34:11 *t* you the fear of the
Ps 51:13 *t* transgressors Your
Ps 90:12 So *t* us to number our
Heb 5:12 *t* you again the first

TEACHER
Mt 23:8 you have one *T*
Jn 3:2 know that You are a *t*
Ac 5:34 named Gamaliel, a *t*
1Ti 2:7 a *t* of the Gentiles in

TEACHERS
Ps 119:99 than all my *t*
1Co 12:28 prophets, third *t*
Eph 4:11 pastors and *t*
1Ti 1:7 desiring to be *t*
2Pe 2:1 there will be false *t*

TEACHES
1Co 2:13 the Holy Spirit *t*
1Jn 2:27 the same anointing *t*

TEACHING
Mt 28:20 *t* them to observe all
Col 1:28 *t* everyone in all

TEETH
Ps 3:7 You have broken the *t*
Ps 57:4 sons of men who blaze like fire, whose *t*
La 2:16 hiss and gnash their *t*
Da 7:7 it had great iron *t*
Mt 8:12 and gnashing of *t*

TELL
Mt 18:15 *t* him his fault
Mt 23:3 whatever they *t*
Jn 4:25 He comes, He will *t*

TEMPLE
Jdg 16:30 *t* fell upon the rulers
1Ki 6:3 porch in front of the *t*
2Ch 3:17 in front of the *t*
Ezr 3:6 the *t* of the LORD
Ps 5:7 worship at Your holy *t*
Eze 9:3 to the threshold of the *t*
Eze 40:5 around the outside of the *t*
Joel 2:17 the *t* porch and the altar
Hab 2:20 in His holy *t*
Mt 21:12 into the *t* of God and
Mt 26:61 destroy the *t* of God
Mk 13:1 He went out of the *t*
Lk 2:27 he came into the *t*
Lk 18:10 went up to the *t* to pray
Jn 2:15 drove them all out of the *t*
Jn 2:19 "Destroy this *t*
Ac 2:46 with one mind in the *t*
1Co 3:16 you are the *t* of God
2Co 6:16 agreement has the *t* of God
Rev 15:5 *t* of the tabernacle
Rev 21:22 and the Lamb are its *t*

TEMPT
Mt 4:7 *t* the Lord your God
Jas 1:13 neither does He *t*

TEMPTATION
Mt 6:13 lead us not into *t*
Mk 14:38 lest you enter into *t*
1Co 10:13 with the *t* also make
Jas 1:12 man who endures *t*
Rev 3:10 keep you from the hour of *t*

TEMPTED
Mk 1:13 forty days, *t* by Satan
Gal 6:1 lest you also be *t*
Heb 4:15 in every sense *t*

TEMPTER
Mt 4:3 And the *t* came to Him

TENT
Ex 27:21 In the *t* of meeting,
2Co 5:1 earthly house, this *t*

TENTH
Ex 29:40 lamb will be a *t*
Nu 28:5 one-*t* of an ephah
Eze 20:1 month, on the *t* day of
Rev 11:13 *t* of the city fell

TENTMAKERS
Ac 18:3 they were *t*

TENTS
Nu 24:2 Israel dwelling in their *t*
Ps 84:10 than to dwell in the *t*

TERRIBLE
Dt 8:15 that great and *t* wilderness
Da 7:7 beast, dreadful and *t*

TERRIFIED
Dt 20:3 do not tremble or be *t* because of them.
Ps 90:7 by Your wrath we are *t*

TERROR
Ps 91:5 You shall not be afraid of the *t* by night,
Isa 24:17 *T* and the pit and the snare are upon you
Isa 54:14 *t*, for it shall not come near you
Ro 13:3 Rulers are not a *t* to good works,

TEST
Mt 22:18 "Why *t* Me
1Jn 4:1 but *t* the spirits

TESTED
Ge 22:1 God *t* Abraham
Heb 3:9 where your fathers *t*

TESTIFIED
Jn 19:35 who saw it has *t*

TESTIFIES
Ac 20:23 that the Holy Spirit *t*

TESTIFY
Jn 1:7 *t* concerning the Light,
1Jn 4:14 *t* that the Father

TESTIMONIES
Ps 119:2 those who keep His *t*
Ps 119:99 *t* are my meditation

TESTIMONY
Ex 25:16 put into the ark the *t*
Ex 31:18 two tablets of *t*
Ps 119:88 keep the *t* from Your mouth
Isa 8:16 Bind up the *t*
Mt 8:4 Moses commanded as a *t*
Mk 6:11 off your feet as a *t*
Mk 14:59 their *t* did not agree
Jn 3:32 no one receives His *t*
Jn 19:35 and his *t* is true
2Th 1:10 because our *t*
2Ti 1:8 of the *t* of our Lord
1Jn 5:10 not believe the *t*
Rev 6:9 for the *t* they had held
Rev 19:10 For the *t* of Jesus is

THANK
Mt 11:25 "I *t* You, O Father
Lk 18:11 *t* You that I am not

THANKFUL
Col 3:15 one body, rule in your hearts. And be *t*.

THANKFULNESS
1Co 10:30 if I partake with *t*,

THANKS
Lk 22:17 the cup and gave *t*
2Co 9:15 *T* be to God for His

THANKSGIVING
Ps 95:2 His presence with *t*
Ps 100:4 into His gates with *t*

THICK
Ex 19:16 *t* cloud on the mountain
Dt 32:15 fat, you grew *t*
Isa 44:22 as a *t* cloud, your transgressions
Joel 2:2 clouds and *t* darkness

THIEF
Ex 22:2 If a *t* is caught
Mt 26:55 come out as against a *t*
Lk 12:33 where no *t* comes near
Jn 10:1 some other way, is a *t*
1Th 5:2 like a *t* in the night
1Pe 4:15 as a murderer, or a *t*

THIEVES
Isa 1:23 companions of *t*
Mt 6:19 where *t* break in
Mt 21:13 'a den of *t*
Mt 27:38 Then two *t* were
Lk 10:30 and fell among *t*
Jn 10:8 before Me are *t*
1Co 6:10 nor *t*, nor covetous

THINK
Jn 5:39 *t* in them you have eternal
Ro 12:3 not to *t* of himself

THINKS
Ps 40:17 Yet the LORD *t* about
Pr 23:7 for as he *t* in his
1Co 10:12 *t* he stands take heed

THIRST
Mt 5:6 those who hunger and *t*
Jn 6:35 in Me shall never *t*
Rev 7:16 nor shall they *t*

THIRSTS
Ps 42:2 My soul *t* for God
Rev 21:6 to him who *t*

THIRSTY
Mt 25:35 I was *t* and you gave
Jn 7:37 "If anyone is *t*

THISTLES
Mt 7:16 or figs from *t*

THOMAS
Mt 10:3 *T*, and Matthew
Jn 14:5 *T* said to Him
Jn 20:27 Then He said to *T*

THORN
2Co 12:7 a *t* was given me

THORNS
Ge 3:18 *T* and thistles it
Lk 8:7 some fell among *t*
Jn 19:5 wearing the crown of *t*

THOUGHT
Ps 139:2 You understand my *t*
1Co 13:11 I *t* as a child

THOUGHTS
Ps 94:11 The LORD, He knows the *t*
Isa 55:7 unrighteous man his *t*
Isa 55:8 For My *t* are not your
Mt 9:4 Jesus, knowing their *t*
Mt 15:19 heart proceed evil *t*
1Co 3:20 The LORD knows the *t*

THROAT
Ps 5:9 their *t* is an open tomb
Ps 69:3 my *t* is parched

THROATS
Ro 3:13 Their *t* are an open grave

THRONE
Ps 45:6 Your *t*, O God, is
Isa 6:1 Lord sitting on a *t*
Isa 66:1 Heaven is My *t*
Mt 5:34 for it is God's *t*
Lk 1:32 will give Him the *t*
Heb 1:8 "Your *t*, O God, lasts
Heb 4:16 to the *t* of grace
Rev 3:21 My Father on His *t*
Rev 20:11 I saw a great white *t*

THRONES
Mt 19:28 sit on twelve t,
Col 1:16 *t* or dominions

THROWN
Ex 15:1 He has *t* the horse
Jer 50:15 fallen, her walls have been *t*
La 2:17 has *t* down and has

THUNDER
Ps 77:18 The sound of Your *t*
Rev 14:2 the sound of a great *t*

THUNDERED
2Sa 22:14 The LORD *t* from

THUNDERINGS
Rev 19:6 the sound of mighty *t*

THUNDERS
Ps 29:3 The God of glory *t*
Rev 10:3 seven *t* sounded their voices.

TIMES
Mt 16:3 the signs of the *t*
Ac 1:7 for you to know the *t*
2Ti 3:1 last days perilous *t*

TIMOTHY
Ro 16:21 *T*, my fellow worker

TITHE
Lev 27:30 Any *t* of the land
Dt 12:17 the *t* of your grain
Dt 14:23 the *t* of your grain
Mt 23:23 You *t* mint and dill

TITHES
Nu 18:21 all the *t* in Israel
Ne 10:38 a tenth of the *t*
Mal 3:10 Bring all the *t* into

TITHING
Dt 26:12 have finished *t* all the tithes

TODAY
Lk 23:43 *t* you will be with Me
Heb 3:7 "*T*, if you will hear
Heb 13:8 the same yesterday, and *t*

TOMB
Mt 27:66 made the *t* secure
Jn 19:41 in the garden was a new *t*

TOMBS
Mt 23:27 like whitewashed *t*

TOMORROW
Isa 22:13 drink, for *t* we may die
Mt 6:34 take no thought about *t*
Jas 4:14 what will happen *t*

TONGUE
Ps 137:6 remember you, let my *t*
Pr 12:19 forever, but a lying *t*
Pr 25:15 *t* breaks the bone
Php 2:11 *t* should confess that
Jas 1:26 does not bridle his *t*
Jas 3:8 no man can tame the *t*
Rev 14:6 every nation and tribe and *t*

TONGUES
Ps 31:20 from the strife of *t*
Mk 16:17 speak with new *t*
Ac 2:3 *t* as of fire
1Co 13:1 I speak with the *t*

TOOTH
Ex 21:24 t for *t*,
Mt 5:38 eye for an eye, and a *t*

TORMENT
Mt 8:29 You come here to *t*
Lk 16:23 being in *t*, he
Rev 14:11 *t* will ascend forever

TORMENTED
Rev 20:10 They will be *t*

TORN
Mt 27:51 of the temple was *t*

TOUCH
Nu 4:15 not *t* any holy thing
Isa 52:11 *t* no unclean thing
Mk 3:10 pressed on Him to *t*

TOUCHED
Jer 1:9 hand and *t* my mouth
Da 8:18 *t* me and set me upright
Da 10:16 sons of men *t* my lips

TOWER
Ne 3:1 *T* of Hananel, they sanctified
Ne 12:39 Fish Gate, the *t* of Hananel
Ps 18:2 salvation, my high *t*
Isa 5:2 vine. And He built a *t*

TRADITION
Mt 15:2 violate the *t*
Col 2:8 *t* of men

TRAIN
Pr 22:6 *T* up a child in the
Is 6:1 His *t* filled the temple.

TRAINED
Lk 6:40 everyone who is *t*
Heb 12:11 those who have been *t*

TRAITOR
Lk 6:16 who became a *t*

TRAITORS
2Ti 3:4 *t*, reckless

TRAMPLE
Ps 91:13 serpent you shall *t*
Mt 7:6 swine, lest they *t*

TRAMPLED
Heb 10:29 *t* under foot the Son of God
Rev 14:20 the winepress was *t*

TRANCE
Ac 10:10 fell into a *t*
Ac 11:5 in a *t* I saw

TRANSFIGURED
Mt 17:2 and was *t* before them
Mk 9:2 He was *t* before them.

TRANSFORMED
Ro 12:2 but be *t* by
2Co 3:18 *t* into the same image

TRANSGRESSED
Da 9:11 all Israel has *t*
Lk 15:29 *t* your commands

TRANSGRESSIONS
Ps 51:1 Blot out my *t*
Ps 51:3 For I acknowledge my *t*
Isa 53:5 was wounded for our *t*

TRAP
Ps 69:22 may security become a *t*.
Isa 8:14 a *t* and a snare
Ro 11:9 their table became a snare and a *t*,

TREACHEROUS
Zep 3:4 reckless, *t* men; her priests

TREASURE
Dt 28:12 to you His good *t*
Da 1:2 *t* house of his god
Mt 19:21 and you will have *t*
Lk 12:21 he who stores up *t*
2Co 4:7 But we have this *t*

TREASURES
Job 3:21 more than for hidden *t*
Isa 45:3 I will give you the *t*
Mt 6:19 for yourselves *t*
Col 2:3 are hidden all the *t*
Heb 11:26 the *t* in Egypt

TREAT
Ps 103:10 He does not *t* us according to our sins

TREE
Ge 3:11 from the *t* of which
Ps 1:3 *t* planted by the
Ps 37:35 like a luxuriant *t*
Mt 7:17 *t* bears good fruit
1Pe 2:24 His own body on the *t*
Rev 22:2 was the *t* of life

TREMBLE
Ps 99:1 let the peoples *t*
Jer 5:22 not *t* at My presence
Jer 33:9 they will fear and *t*
Joel 2:1 inhabitants of the earth will *t*

TREMBLED
Ezr 9:4 every one that *t*
Jer 4:24 and they *t*

TREMBLING
1Co 2:3 in fear, and in much *t*
2Co 7:15 *t* you received
Eph 6:5 flesh, with fear and *t*

TRESPASS
Ex 22:9 For any kind of *t*
Eze 18:24 *t* that he has committed
Da 9:7 *t* that they have trespassed

TRESPASSES
Rom 5:16 came after many *t*,
Eph 2:1 you were dead in *t*

TRIAL
2Co 8:2 how in a great *t* of affliction
2Pe 2:9 how to rescue the godly from t

TRIALS
Dt 7:19 the great *t* which your eyes saw
Lk 22:28 who have continued with Me in My *t*
1Pe 1:6 had to suffer various t

TRIBE
Rev 5:5 the Lion of the *t*
Rev 5:9 blood out of every *t*

TRIBES
Mt 19:28 judging the twelve *t* of Israel.
Jas 1:1 *t* which are scattered

TRIBULATION
Mt 24:21 then will be great *t*
Jn 16:33 world you will have *t*
Ro 5:3 but we also boast in *t*
Rev 2:22 with her into great *t*
Rev 7:14 out of great *t*

TRIBULATIONS
2Th 1:4 *t* that you are enduring

TRIED
Ps 95:9 *t* me, though they had seen
Heb 3:9 your fathers tested Me and *t* Me,

TRIMMED
Mt 25:7 and *t* their lamps

TRIUMPH
Ps 25:2 may my enemies not *t* over me.
2Co 2:14 always causes us to *t*

TROUBLE
Job 14:1 few days and full of *t*
Ps 27:5 in the time of *t*
Ps 73:5 not in *t* as other people
Ps 91:15 will be with him in *t*
Jer 14:8 Savior in time of *t*
Gal 1:7 there are some who *t*

TROUBLED
Lk 10:41 anxious and *t*
2Th 2:2 shaken or be *t*

TROUBLES
Ps 25:22 Out of all their *t*
Mk 13:8 will be famines and *t*

TRUE
Ru 3:12 it is *t* that I am
2Sa 7:28 Your words are *t*
2Ch 15:3 without the *t* God
Ps 19:9 are *t* and righteous
Ps 119:140 word is pure and *t*
Da 4:37 all His works are *t*
Zec 7:9 Execute *t* justice
Mk 12:14 that You are *t* and
Jn 15:1 the *t* vine
Php 4:8 whatever things are *t*
Titus 1:13 This witness is *t*
1Jn 2:8 *t* light is already shining
Rev 15:3 Just and *t* are Your ways
Rev 21:5 words are faithful and *t*

TRUMPET
Mt 6:2 do not sound a *t*
1Co 14:8 *t* makes an uncertain
1Co 15:52 For the *t* will sound

TRUMPETS
Lev 23:24 memorial with the blowing of *t*
Nu 10:10 *t* over your burnt offerings
2Ch 5:13 *t* and cymbals and all the instruments

TRUST
2Sa 22:3 in whom I will *t*
Ps 20:7 Some *t* in chariots
Ps 56:11 in God I *t*
Ps 118:8 better to *t* in the LORD
Pr 3:5 *T* in the LORD
Isa 50:10 Let him *t* in the name
Jer 7:8 you *t* in lying words
2Co 1:10 In Him we *t*
Php 3:3 place no *t* in the flesh

TRUSTED
Ps 26:1 *t* in the LORD
Ps 41:9 friend, in whom I *t*
Ps 52:7 but *t* in the abundance
Jer 48:7 you have *t* in your
Da 3:28 His servants who *t*

TRUSTWORTHY
Titus 1:9 holding firmly the *t* word

TRUTH
Ge 24:27 His mercy and His *t*
Ex 34:6 in goodness and *t*
Ps 51:6 You desire *t* in the
Ps 89:14 mercy and *t* shall go
Pr 12:17 He who speaks *t* shows forth righteousness
Isa 29:24 shall know the *t*
Isa 59:14 For *t* is fallen
Mk 12:32 You have spoken the *t*
Jn 1:14 full of grace and *t*
Jn 5:33 bore witness of the *t*
Jn 8:32 know the *t*, and the *t*
Jn 14:6 I am the way, the *t*
Jn 15:26 Spirit of *t* who proceeds
Jn 19:35 he is telling the *t*
Ro 1:18 who suppress the *t*
1Co 13:6 but rejoices in the *t*
2Co 13:8 *t*, but only for the *t*
Eph 4:15 speaking the *t* in love
Eph 6:14 waist girded with *t*
2Th 2:12 did not believe the *t*
2Ti 2:15 the word of *t*
1Pe 1:22 by obedience to the *t*
1Jn 1:6 do not practice the *t*
3Jn 1:3 testified of the *t*

TRUTHFUL
Pr 12:19 The *t* lip will be established forever

TRY
Ps 26:2 *t* my affections and my heart
Lk 12:58 *t* to settle matters
Lk 13:24 will *t* to enter and will not be able
1Co 10:33 even as I *t* to please all men

TRYING
Gal 1:10 Or am I *t* to please men

TURN
Eze 14:6 Repent, and *t* away from
Mt 5:39 on your right cheek, *t*
Ac 26:18 *t* them from darkness

TURNED
Dt 23:5 *t* the curse into a blessing on you
1Ki 11:4 old, his wives *t* his heart away after other
2Ch 15:4 their trouble they *t* to the Lord
Est 9:1 things were *t* around
Est 9:22 things *t* around for them
Ps 30:11 You have *t* my mourning into dancing;

TURNING
2Ki 21:13 bowl, wiping it and *t*
2Ch 36:13 hardened his heart against *t*
Jas 1:17 no change or shadow of *t*

TURNS
Pr 15:1 A soft answer *t* away wrath,
Isa 44:25 *T* wise men backward

TWELVE
Lev 24:5 wheat flour and bake *t*
2Sa 10:6 Tob, *t* thousand men
Mt 19:28 will also sit on *t* thrones
Mt 26:53 than *t* legions of angels
Ac 7:8 Jacob of the *t* patriarchs
Rev 22:2 bore *t* kinds of fruit

U

UNBELIEF
Mt 13:58 because of their *u*
Mk 9:24 help my *u*
1Ti 1:13 did it ignorantly in *u*
Heb 3:19 enter because of *u*

UNBELIEVERS
2Co 6:14 yoked together with *u*

UNBELIEVING
Titus 1:15 *u* nothing is pure
Rev 21:8 But the cowardly, the *u*

UNCIRCUMCISED
Ex 12:48 no *u* person shall eat
Isa 52:1 the *u* and the unclean
Jer 9:25 and yet *u*
Ac 7:51 *u* in heart and ears
Ro 2:26 if an *u* man keeps
Ro 2:27 will the *u* one
Ro 4:11 while being *u*
Gal 2:7 the gospel to the *u*

UNCLEAN
Isa 6:5 I am a man of *u* lips
Ac 10:28 man common or *u*
Ro 14:14 nothing is *u*

UNCLOTHED
2Co 5:4 we wish to be *u*

UNCOVERED
Ru 3:7 softly, *u* his feet, and lay down
1Co 11:5 her head *u* dishonors her head
1Co 11:13 to pray to God u?

UNDEFILED
1Pe 1:4 incorruptible and *u*

UNDERSTAND
Ps 14:2 if there are any who *u*
Isa 6:9 hearing, but do not *u*
Jn 8:43 Why do you not *u*
Ac 28:27 *u* with their heart
2Pe 3:16 some things are hard to *u*

UNDERSTANDING
1Ki 4:29 of *u* as well as compassion
Job 12:12 and *u* comes with long life.
Job 28:12 Where is the place of *u*?
Job 28:28 and to depart from evil is *u*.' "
Job 32:8 of the Almighty gives him *u*.
Ps 147:5 His *u* is without
Pr 3:5 lean not on your own *u*
Pr 14:29 who is slow to wrath is of great *u*
Pr 19:8 *u* will find good
Isa 40:28 His *u* is inscrutable
Mt 15:16 also still without *u*
1Co 14:15 pray with the *u*
2Ti 2:7 the Lord grant you *u*
Jas 3:13 Who is wise and *u*

UNDERSTANDS
Ro 3:11 there is no one who *u*

UNDERSTOOD
Ps 73:17 then I *u* their end
Ro 1:20 are *u* by the things

UNFRUITFUL
Mk 4:19 and it proves *u*

UNGODLINESS
Ro 1:18 heaven against all *u*

UNGODLY
Ps 1:1 the counsel of the *u*
Ps 1:4 The *u* are not so
Ps 1:5 *u* will not stand
Ro 5:6 Christ died for the *u*
2Pe 2:6 who would live *u*
2Pe 3:7 destruction of the *u*
Jude 1:4 They are *u* men

UNINTENTIONALLY
Dt 4:42 killed his neighbor *u*

UNITED
Ro 6:5 be *u* with Him in the likeness

UNITY
Jn 17:23 they may be perfect in *u*

UNJUST
Ac 24:15 of the just and the *u*
Heb 6:10 for God is not *u*

UNJUSTLY
Ps 82:2 long will you all judge *u*

UNKNOWN
Ac 17:23 TO THE *U* GOD

UNLEAVENED
Ex 12:17 the Feast of *U* Bread

UNPROFITABLE
Lk 17:10 'We are *u* servants

UNPUNISHED
Pr 11:21 wicked will not be *u*
Pr 19:5 A false witness will not be *u*,

UNQUENCHABLE
Mt 3:12 up the chaff with *u*

UNRIGHTEOUS
Isa 55:7 *u* man his thoughts
1Co 6:9 *u* will not inherit the

UNRIGHTEOUSNESS
Ro 1:18 all ungodliness and *u*
1Jn 1:9 cleanse us from all *u*

UNWISE
Eph 5:17 Therefore do not be *u*

UNWORTHILY
1Co 11:27 cup of the Lord *u*
1Co 11:29 he who eats and drinks *u*

UPHOLD
Ps 119:116 *U* me according to

UPHOLDS
Ps 145:14 LORD *u* all who fall
Heb 1:3 *u* all things by the

UPPER
Mk 14:15 a large *u* room

UPRIGHT
Dt 32:4 righteous and *u* is He.
Job 1:1 That man was blameless and *u*
Ps 11:7 His countenance beholds the *u*
Ps 33:1 for praise is fitting for the *u*

URIM
Dt 33:8 Thummim and Your *U*

USELESS
Titus 3:9 they are unprofitable and *u*.
2Pe 1:8 you will neither be *u*

UTTERLY
Ex 17:14 for I will *u* wipe out
Ex 23:24 but you shall *u* overthrow

Eze 9:6 *u* slay old and young
Eze 17:10 shall it not *u* wither

UTTERMOST
Ps 65:8 dwell in the *u* parts
Isa 7:18 *u* part of the rivers
Heb 7:25 to save to the *u*

V

VAIN
Lev 26:20 shall be spent in *v*
Job 9:29 do I labor in *v*
Ps 2:1 the peoples plot in *v*
Ps 127:1 labor in *v*
Isa 1:13 no more *v* offerings
Jer 18:15 incense to *v* gods
Jnh 2:8 who follow *v* idols
Mt 6:7 do not use *v* repetitions
Ro 13:4 bear the sword in *v*
1Co 15:2 have believed in *v*
2Co 6:1 the grace of God in *v*
Jas 1:26 this man's religion is *v*

VAINLY
La 4:17 watching *v* for help

VALLEY
Jos 7:26 place is called the *V*
Jos 10:12 moon, in the *V* of Aijalon
Jos 15:8 *V* of Ben Hinnom
Jdg 7:12 covered the *v*
2 Ki 23:10 Topheth, which is in the *V*
2 Ch 33:6 pass through the fire in the *V*
Isa 40:4 *v* be lifted up

VALOR
1Sa 16:18 a mighty man of *v*

VANITIES
Ecc 1:2 "Vanity of *v*...vanity of *v*

VANITY
Ps 4:2 will you love *v*
Ecc 1:14 all is *v*
Eph 4:17 in the *v*

VAPOR
Jas 4:14 It is just a *v*

VEGETABLES
Da 1:12 let them give us *v*
Ro 14:2 eats only *v*

VEIL
Ex 26:33 testimony within the *v*
Ex 27:21 tent of meeting, outside the *v*
Lev 4:6 LORD in front of the *v*
Lev 16:2 Holy Place within the *v*
Heb 6:19 behind the *v*

VENGEANCE
Dt 32:35 "*V* is Mine

VERDICT
Jn 3:19 This is the *v*

VESSEL
Ps 2:9 like a potter's *v*
Ac 9:15 is a chosen *v*

VESSELS
2Co 4:7 treasure in earthen *v*

VICTORY
1Co 15:54 "Death is swallowed up in *v*."
1Co 15:57 who gives us the *v* through our Lord
1Jn 5:4 *v* that overcomes

VINE
Jn 15:1 "I am the true *v*

VINEDRESSER
Jn 15:1 My Father is the *v*

VINEGAR
Pr 10:26 As *v* to the teeth and

VINEYARD
1Ki 21:1 *v* in Jezreel,
Pr 31:16 she plants a *v*.
Ss 1:6 my own *v* I have not kept.
Isa 5:1 a song of my beloved concerning His *v*:
1Co 9:7 Who plants a *v*, but

VINEYARDS
Dt 28:39 You will plant *v*
Ne 5:5 fields and *v* belong to others
Am 5:11 planted pleasant *v*
Am 9:14 plant *v* and drink

VIOLENCE
Ge 6:11 filled with *v*
Isa 53:9 because he had done no *v*
Isa 60:18 *V* shall no more be
Jer 22:3 do no wrong or *v*
Jer 22:17 oppression and *v*
Eze 7:23 city is full of *v*
Eze 18:7 *v*, has given his bread

VIOLENT
1Ti 3:3 to drunkenness, not *v*
Titus 1:7 not *v*, not greedy for dishonest gain

VIPER
Pr 23:32 and stings like a *v*

VIPERS
Mt 3:7 "O generation of *v*

VIRGIN
Ex 22:16 If a man seduces a *v*
Lev 21:14 a *v* of his own people
Isa 7:14 The *v* shall conceive
Jer 31:4 O *v* of Israel
Mt 1:23 "A *v* shall be with child
Lk 1:27 *v* betrothed to a man
1Co 7:28 And if a *v* marries

VIRGINS
Mt 25:1 *v*, who took their lamps

VIRTUE
2Pe 1:5 to your *v*

VIRTUOUSLY
Pr 31:29 have done *v*

VISION
Ac 11:5 in a trance I saw a *v*
Ac 26:19 to the heavenly *v*

VISIONS
Joel 2:28 young men shall see *v*

VISIT
Jas 1:27 *v* the fatherless and

VISITED
Ex 4:31 LORD had *v* the children
Ps 17:3 You have *v* me in the
Lk 1:68 for He has *v* and redeemed
Lk 1:78 from on high has *v*
Lk 7:16 God has *v* His people

VOICE
1Ki 19:12 fire, a still, small *v*
Ps 95:7 if you hear His *v*
Mt 3:3 "The *v* of one crying
Mt 3:17 And a *v*
Jn 10:4 for they know his *v*
Jn 18:37 the truth hears My *v*
Rev 3:20 If anyone hears My *v*

VOICES
Rev 11:15 And there were loud *v*

VOMIT
2Pe 2:22 returns to his own *v*

VOW
Ac 18:18 for he had taken a *v*

WATCHMEN
1Sa 14:16 The *w* of Saul
SS 3:3 The *w* found me
Isa 62:6 I have set *w*
Jer 51:12 set up the *w*

WATCHTOWER
2Ch 20:24 the *w* of the wilderness
Isa 21:5 watch in the *w*
Hab 2:1 on the *w*

WATCHTOWERS
La 4:17 in our *w* we watched

WATER
Ge 1:2 the surface of the *w*
Ge 2:10 to *w* the garden
Ge 7:17 the *w* increased
Ge 26:18 the wells of *w*
Ex 2:10 out of the *w*
Ex 4:9 the *w* which you take
Ex 15:27 twelve wells of *w*
Ex 17:1 *w* for the people
Jos 3:13 *w* of the Jordan
1Ki 13:8 nor drink *w*
2Ki 2:8 and struck the *w*
Ps 22:14 I am poured out like *w*
Ps 63:1 thirsty land with no *w*
Eze 7:17 knees shall be weak as *w*
Da 1:12 and *w* to drink
Mt 3:11 baptize you with *w*
Mt 14:29 he walked on the *w*
Mk 14:13 carrying a pitcher of *w*
Jn 2:7 "Fill the *w* pots with *w*
Jn 13:5 poured *w* into a basin
Jn 19:34 blood and *w* came out
Eph 5:26 the washing of *w*
Heb 10:22 washed with pure *w*
1Pe 3:20 were saved through *w*
Rev 12:15 serpent spewed *w* out
Rev 21:6 spring of the *w* of life

WATERED
1Co 3:6 planted, Apollos *w*

WATERS
Ge 1:6 the midst of the *w*
Ge 6:17 a flood of *w*
Ex 14:22 the *w* were a wall
Jos 2:10 the LORD dried up the *w*
Ps 33:7 He gathers the *w* of the sea
Ps 77:16 The *w* saw You…The *w*
Ps 105:29 turned their *w* into blood
Ps 105:41 and the *w* gushed out
Pr 9:17 "Stolen *w* are sweet
Isa 17:13 the rumbling of many *w*
Jer 2:13 the fountain of living *w*
Jnh 2:5 The *w* encompassed me
Rev 1:15 the sound of many *w*

WAVER
Ro 4:20 He did not *w* at the

WAVERING
Heb 10:23 of our faith without *w*

WAVES
Mt 14:24 tossed by the *w*
Eph 4:14 tossed here and there by *w*

WAX
Ps 22:14 my heart is like *w*

WAY
2Sa 22:31 As for God, His *w*
Ps 1:6 the LORD knows the *w*
Ps 27:11 Teach me Your *w*
Ps 139:24 in the ancient *w*
Pr 14:12 *w* that seems right
Isa 26:7 The *w* of the righteous is
Isa 55:7 wicked forsake his *w*
Mal 3:1 he will prepare the *w*
Mt 7:13 and broad is the *w*
Mt 11:10 will prepare Your *w*
Jn 14:6 to him, "I am the *w*
Ac 18:26 explained the *w* of god
2Pe 2:21 to have known the *w*

WAYS
Dt 32:4 for all His *w* are
Ps 51:13 transgressors Your *w*
Pr 16:7 *w* please the LORD
Jer 6:16 Stand in the *w*
Da 5:23 all your *w*
Hab 3:6 *w* are everlasting
Jas 1:8 unstable in all his *w*
Rev 15:3 and true are Your *w*

WEAK
Ge 27:1 his eyes were so *w*
Jdg 6:6 Israel was made *w*
Ps 6:2 for I am *w*
Ps 109:24 My knees are *w*
Eze 16:30 How *w* is your
Mt 26:41 the flesh is *w*
Ac 20:35 help the *w*
Ro 5:6 While we were yet *w*
Ro 14:1 who is *w* in faith
1Co 1:27 God has chosen the *w*
1Co 8:7 their *w* conscience
1Co 9:22 To the *w*, I became as *w*
2Co 11:29 Who is *w*, and I am not *w*?
2Co 12:10 For when I am *w*, then
Gal 4:9 turn again to the *w*
1Th 5:14 support the *w*
Heb 7:28 appoints men who are *w*
Heb 12:12 strengthen your *w* knees

WEAKENED
Ps 102:23 He has *w* my strength

WEAKENS
Jer 38:4 *w* the hands of the men

WEAKER
1Pe 3:7 the woman as the *w*

WEAKNESS
1Co 1:25 the *w* of God is stronger
1Co 15:43 It is sown in *w*
2Co 13:4 crucified through *w*
Heb 11:34 of *w* were made strong

WEAKNESSES
Ro 15:1 bear the *w* of the weak
2Co 12:10 I take pleasure in *w*

WEALTH
Pr 13:11 *W* gained by

WEAPON
Isa 54:17 *w* that is formed

WEAPONS
2Co 10:4 For the *w* of our

WEAR
Mt 6:31 'What shall we *w*

WEARING
Jn 19:5 Jesus came out, *w* the crown
1Pe 3:3 *w* gold

WEARY
Isa 40:31 shall run and not be *w*
Gal 6:9 And let us not grow *w*
2Th 3:13 do not be *w* in

WEDDING
Jn 2:1 there was a *w*

WEEP
Ecc 3:4 a time to *w*
Isa 30:19 you shall *w* no more
Lk 6:21 are you who *w*
Lk 23:28 *w* not for Me
Ro 12:15 *w* with those who *w*

WEEPING
Ezr 3:13 the noise of the *w*

WIND

Ps 1:4 the chaff which the *w*
Mt 11:7 reed shaken by the *w*
Jn 3:8 The *w* blows where
Ac 2:2 like a mighty rushing *w*

WIND STORM

Mk 4:37 A great *w* arose

WINDOW

Jos 2:21 she tied the red cord in the *w*.
Ac 20:9 Eutychus sat in the *w*
2Co 11:33 Through a *w* in a basket

WINDS

Na 1:3 gale *w* and a storm
Mt 8:27 that even the *w*

WINE

Pr 20:1 *W* is a mocker
SS 1:2 love is better than *w*
Isa 55:1 Come, buy *w*
Mt 27:34 they gave Him sour *w*
Eph 5:18 Do not be drunk with *w*
Titus 2:3 enslaved to much *w*

WINEPRESS

Isa 63:3 "I have trodden the *w*
Rev 14:19 into the great *w*
Rev 19:15 He treads the *w*

WINESKINS

Jos 9:13 These *w* that we filled
Mt 9:17 new wine into old *w*

WING

1Ki 6:24 One *w* of the cherub

WINGS

Ps 36:7 the shadow of Your *w*
Mal 4:2 with healing in its *w*

WINS

Pr 11:30 *w* souls is wise

WINTER

SS 2:11 For now the *w* has past
Mt 24:20 Escape will not be in the *w*

WIPE

Rev 21:4 *w* away all tears

WISDOM

Dt 34:9 was full of the spirit of *w*
1Ki 4:30 Solomon's *w* excelled the *w*
Ps 111:10 the beginning of *w*
Pr 3:21 keep sound *w*
Pr 16:16 better to get *w*
Da 1:17 of learning and *w*
Mt 11:19 But *w* is justified
Lk 2:52 Jesus increased in *w*
Ac 6:3 the Holy Spirit and of *w*
Ro 11:33 and *w* and knowledge
1Co 3:19 the *w* of this world
Jas 1:5 If any of you lacks *w*
Jas 3:17 the *w* that is from above
Rev 5:12 power and riches and *w*
Rev 13:18 Here is a call for *w*

WISE

Ge 3:6 to make one *w*
Ge 41:33 discerning and *w*
Dt 1:13 Choose *w*...men
Job 5:13 He catches the *w*
Ps 19:7 making *w* the simple
Pr 1:5 A *w* man will hear
Pr 3:7 Do not be *w* in your
Pr 11:30 who wins souls is *w*
Pr 13:20 with *w* men will be *w*
Pr 17:10 deeper into a *w* man
Pr 27:11 My son, be *w*
Ecc 7:5 rebuke from a *w* man
Jer 9:23 Let not the *w* man glory
Da 2:12 destroy all the *w* men
Mt 2:1 *w* men came from the east
Mt 10:16 Therefore be *w* as
Mt 25:2 Five of them were *w*
Ro 16:19 be *w* to that which
Ro 16:27 to the only *w* God
1Co 1:19 the wisdom of the *w*
1Co 1:20 Where is the *w*
2Ti 3:15 able to make you *w*

WISER

1Ki 4:31 *w* than all other men
1Co 1:25 God is *w* than men

WISH

Lk 12:49 *w* that it were already

WITCHCRAFT

1Sa 15:23 is as the sin of *w*

WITHER

Ps 1:3 leaf will not *w*

WITHERS

Isa 40:7 The grass *w*
1Pe 1:24 The grass *w*

WITHOUT

1Th 5:17 Pray *w* ceasing
Jas 2:26 *w* works is dead

WITNESS

Ge 31:44 a *w* between you and me
Ex 20:16 You shall not bear false *w*
1Sa 12:3 *W* against me
Mt 19:18 You shall not bear false *w*
Mk 14:56 Many bore false *w* against
Lk 4:22 All bore *w* to Him
Jn 1:15 John bore *w* of Him
Ac 7:44 the tabernacle of *w*
Ac 10:43 bear *w* that whoever believes
Ac 22:15 you will be His *w*
1Jn 5:6 the Spirit who bears *w*
Rev 1:5 the faithful *w*, the firstborn
Rev 3:14 the Faithful and True *W*

WITNESSES

Dt 17:6 testimony of two or three *w*
Dt 30:19 heaven and earth to *w* against you
Ps 27:12 *w* have risen against me
Isa 43:9 Let them bring their *w*
Jer 32:10 and summoned *w*
Lk 11:48 So you are *w*
Heb 10:15 The Holy Spirit also *w* to us
Heb 12:1 a great cloud of *w*
Rev 11:3 give power to my two *w*

WITNESSING

Lk 23:48 *w* what occurred

WIVES

Ge 4:19 Lamech took two *w*
Ge 6:2 took as *w* any they chose
Ge 31:17 sons and his *w* on camels
Dt 21:15 If a man has two *w*
1Sa 30:5 David's two *w* were taken
Da 5:2 his *w*, and his concubines
Mt 19:8 you to divorce your *w*
1Co 7:29 those who have *w*
Eph 5:25 Husbands, love your *w*
Col 3:19 love your *w*
1Ti 3:11 their *w* must be serious

WOLF

Isa 65:25 The *w* and the lamb

WORMS
Ac 12:23 he was eaten by *w*

WORSHIP
Ge 22:5 I will go over there and *w*
Ps 22:27 nations will *w* before You
Mt 4:9 fall down and *w* me
Ac 17:23 unknowingly *w*, Him I
Rev 4:10 *w* Him, who lives forever

WORSHIPPED
Rev 11:16 on their faces and *w*

WORSHIPPER
Jn 9:31 if anyone is a *w*

WORST
1Ti 1:15 of whom I am the *w*

WORTH
Pr 31:10 her *w* is far above rubies.

WORTHY
Ro 8:18 present time are not *w*
Eph 4:1 to walk in a manner *w*
Heb 11:38 The world was not *w*
Rev 5:12 "*W* is the Lamb who

WOUND
Jer 15:18 and my *w* incurable
Rev 13:3 but his deadly *w*

WOUNDED
Isa 53:5 But he was *w* for our

WOUNDS
Pr 27:6 Faithful are the *w*

WRATH
Ps 2:5 speak to them in His *w*
Ps 76:10 Surely the *w* of
Ps 95:11 I swore in My *w*
Pr 27:4 *W* is cruel, and anger
Isa 60:10 in My *w* I struck you
Hab 3:2 *w* remember mercy
Ro 1:18 The *w* of God is
Ro 2:5 storing up treasures of *w*
Eph 2:3 nature children of *w*
Eph 4:31 Let all bitterness, *w*
1Ti 2:8 holy hands, without *w*
Heb 3:11 So I swore in My *w*
Heb 11:27 not fearing the *w*
Rev 14:8 of the wine of the *w*
Rev 15:1 for in them the *w*
Rev 16:19 fierceness of His *w*

WRINGING
Pr 30:33 *w* of the nose

WRINKLE
Eph 5:27 not having spot, or *w*

WRITE
Heb 8:10 *w* them on their hearts

WRITING
Ex 32:16 the *w* was God's *w*

WRITINGS
Jn 5:47 do not believe his *w*

WRITTEN
Ex 31:18 tablets of stone, *w*
Lk 10:20 your names are *w*
Jn 19:22 "What I have *w*

WRONG
Col 3:25 But he who does *w*

WRONGED
2Co 7:2 We have *w* no one

WROTE
Jn 8:6 stooped down and *w*

Y

YEAR
Isa 61:2 the acceptable *y*

YEARS
Ge 1:14 and days, and *y*
Ps 90:10 the *y* of our life are seventy
Lk 2:42 when He was twelve *y*
Rev 20:6 with Him a thousand *y*

YEAST
Mt 16:6 Take heed and beware of the *y*
1Co 5:6 a little *y* leavens the whole batch

YES
Mt 5:37 let your '*Y*' mean '*Y*,'

YESTERDAY
Heb 13:8 Christ is the same *y*, and today

YOKE
Mt 11:29 Take My *y* upon you

YOKED
2Co 6:14 Do not be unequally *y*

YOUNG
2Ch 10:14 with the advice of the *y* men
Ps 37:25 I have been *y*, and now am old
Ps 119:9 shall a *y* man keep his way pure
Pr 20:29 glory of *y* men is their strength,
Isa 40:11 shall gently lead those that are with *y*.
1Jn 2:13 I am writing to you, *y* men,

YOUTH
Ps 25:7 the sins of my *y*
Ecc 11:10 *y* and the dawn are vanity
Mt 19:20 I have kept from my *y*

YOUTHFUL
2Ti 2:22 flee *y* desires

YOUTHS
Isa 40:30 *y* shall faint and be

Z

ZEAL
2Ki 10:16 see my *z* for the LORD
Ps 69:9 the *z* of Your house
Isa 9:7 The *z* of the LORD of Hosts
Jn 2:17 "*Z* for Your house
Col 4:13 he has a great *z*

ZEALOUS
1Co 14:12 are *z* of spiritual gifts
Gal 4:18 it is good to be *z*

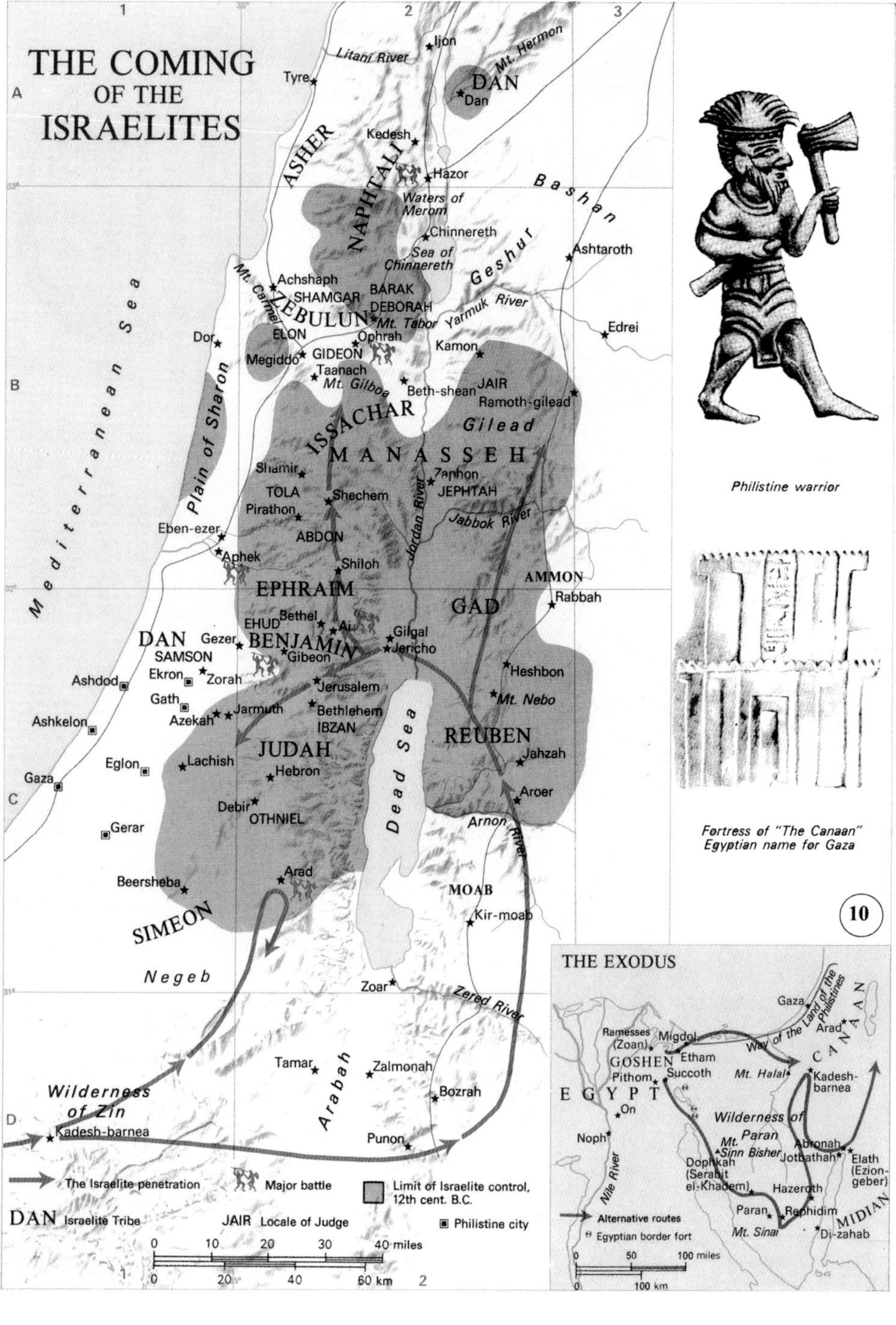
THE COMING OF THE ISRAELITES
Mediterranean Sea
Philistine warrior
Fortress of "The Canaan" Egyptian name for Gaza
10
THE EXODUS
The Israelite penetration
Major battle
Limit of Israelite control, 12th cent. B.C.
DAN Israelite Tribe
JAIR Locale of Judge
Philistine city
Alternative routes
Egyptian border fort

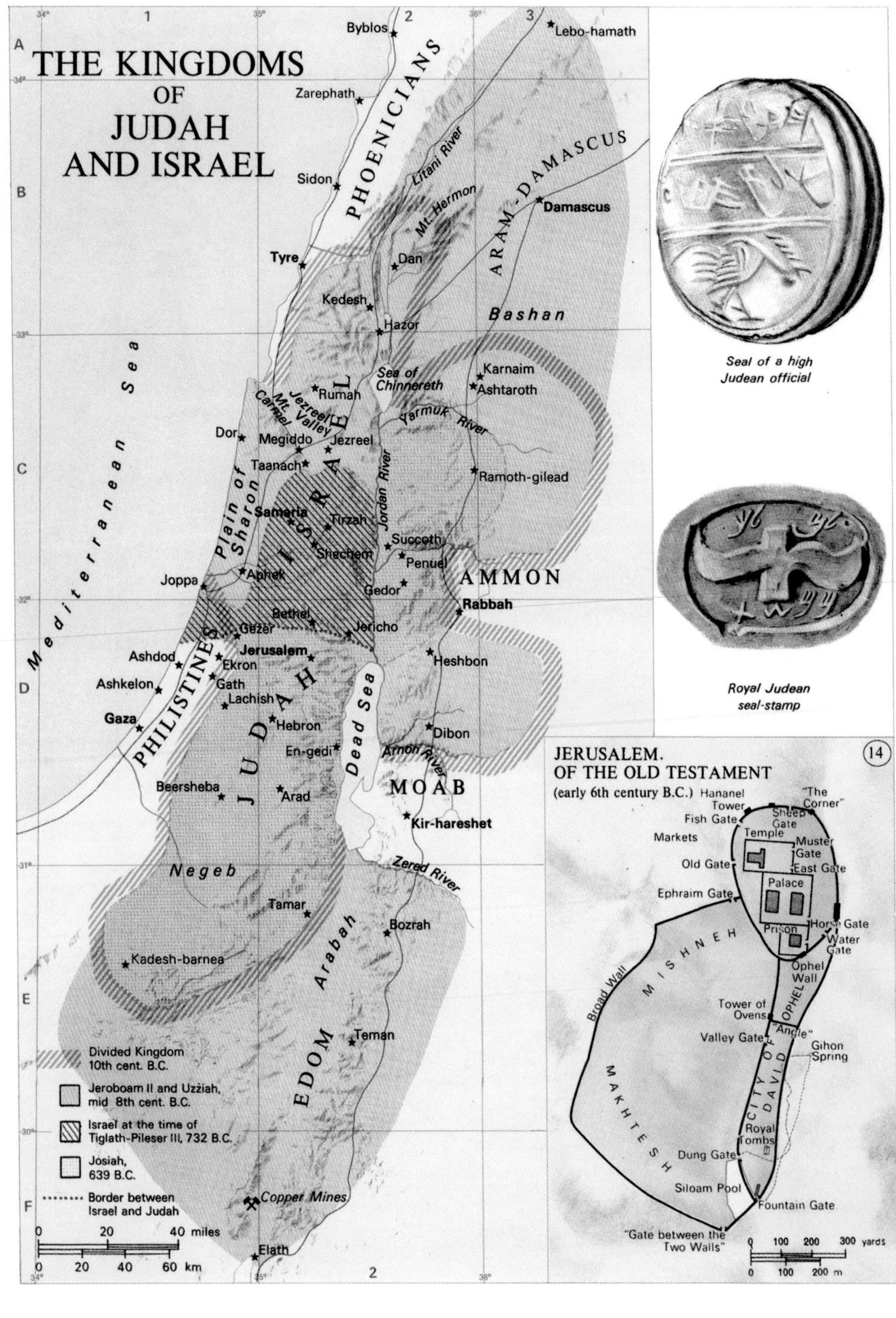

Seal of a high Judean official

Royal Judean seal-stamp

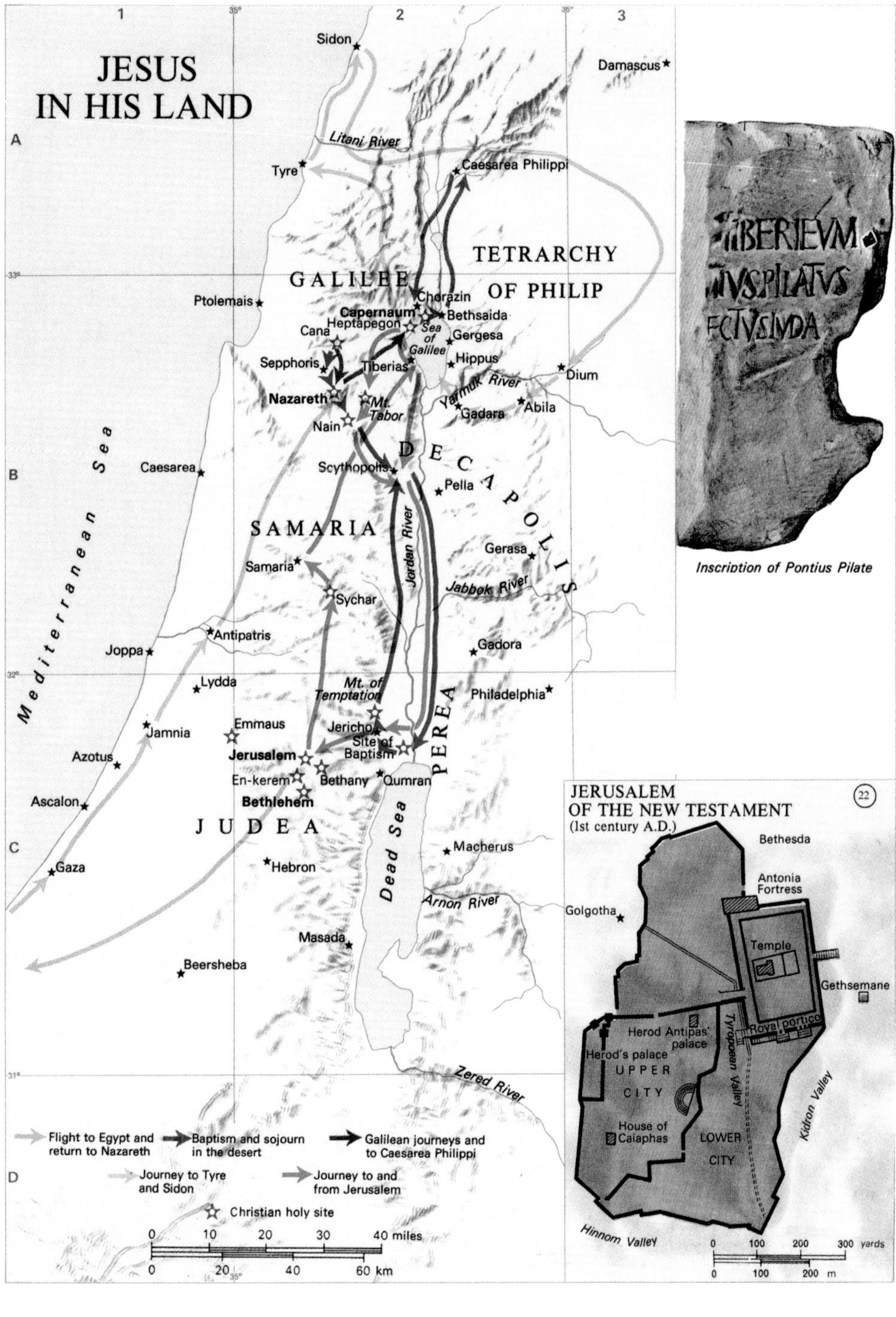

Inscription of Pontius Pilate

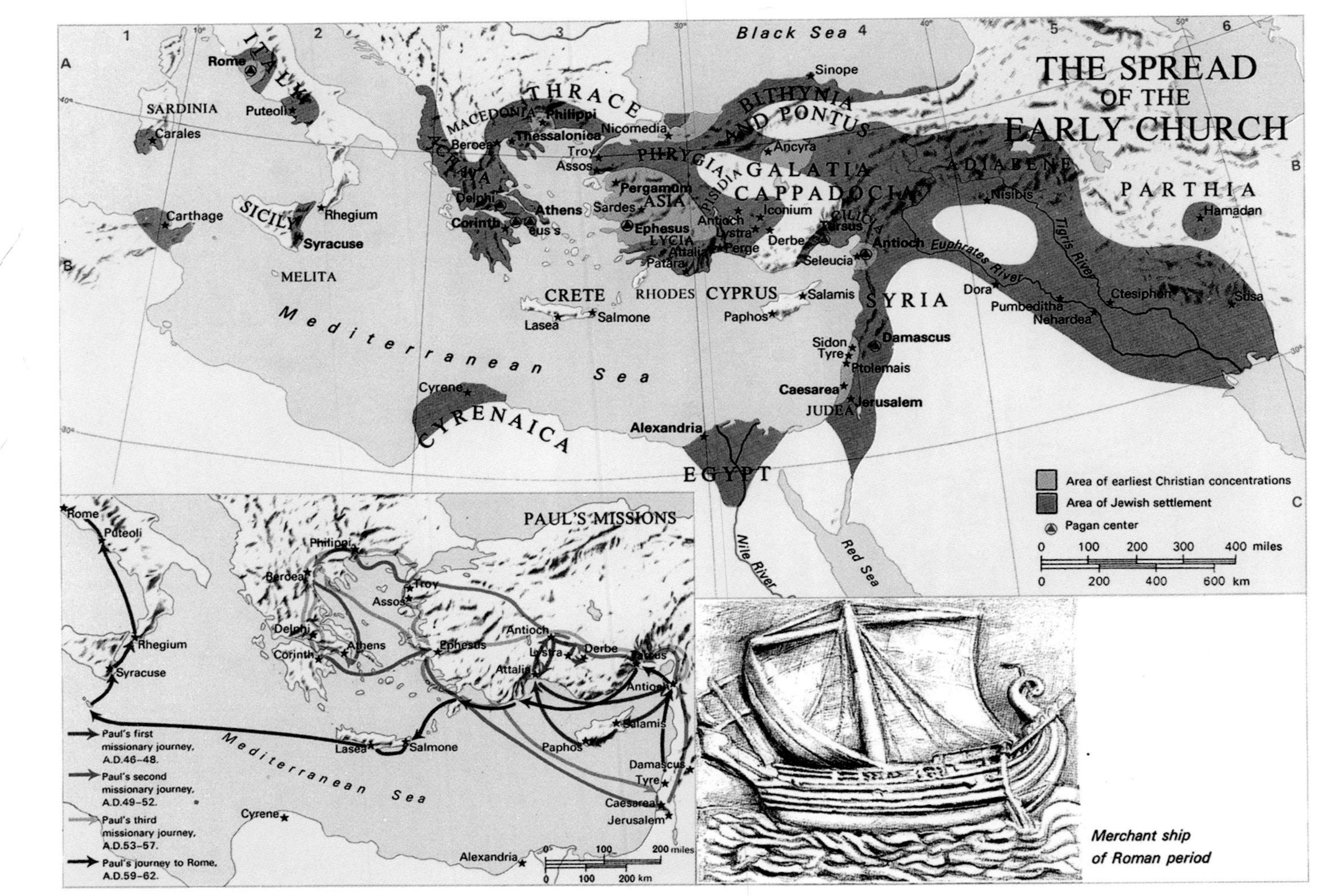

Merchant ship of Roman period

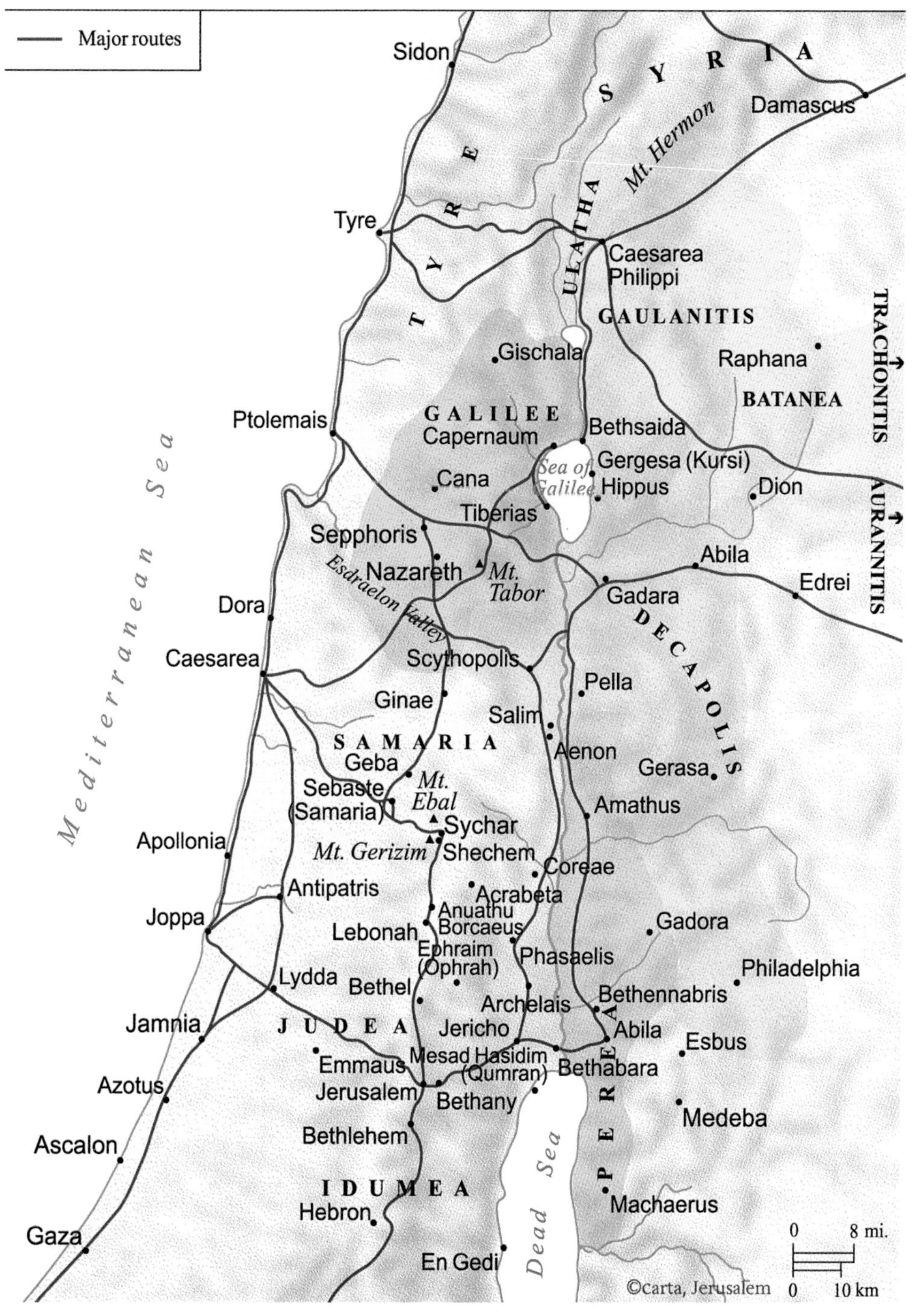
Major routes
Sidon
SYRIA
Damascus
Mt. Hermon
TYRE
ULATHA
Tyre
Caesarea
Philippi
GAULANITIS
TRACHONITIS
Gischala
Raphana
BATANEA
Ptolemais
GALILEE
Bethsaida
Capernaum
Gergesa (Kursi)
Sea of Galilee
Hippus
Cana
Dion
Mediterranean Sea
Tiberias
AURANITIS
Sepphoris
Abila
Nazareth
Mt. Tabor
Esdraelon Valley
Edrei
Gadara
Dora
DECAPOLIS
Caesarea
Scythopolis
Pella
Ginae
Salim
SAMARIA
Aenon
Geba
Mt. Ebal
Gerasa
Sebaste (Samaria)
Sychar
Amathus
Apollonia
Mt. Gerizim
Shechem
Coreae
Antipatris
Acrabeta
Anuathu
Joppa
Borcaeus
Gadora
Lebonah
Ephraim (Ophrah)
Phasaelis
Philadelphia
Lydda
Bethel
Bethennabris
Archelais
Jamnia
JUDEA
Jericho
Abila
Esbus
Emmaus
Mesad Hasidim (Qumran)
Bethabara
Azotus
Jerusalem
Bethany
Medeba
Bethlehem
Ascalon
PEREA
Dead Sea
IDUMEA
Hebron
Machaerus
Gaza
En Gedi
0 8 mi.
0 10 km
©carta, Jerusalem

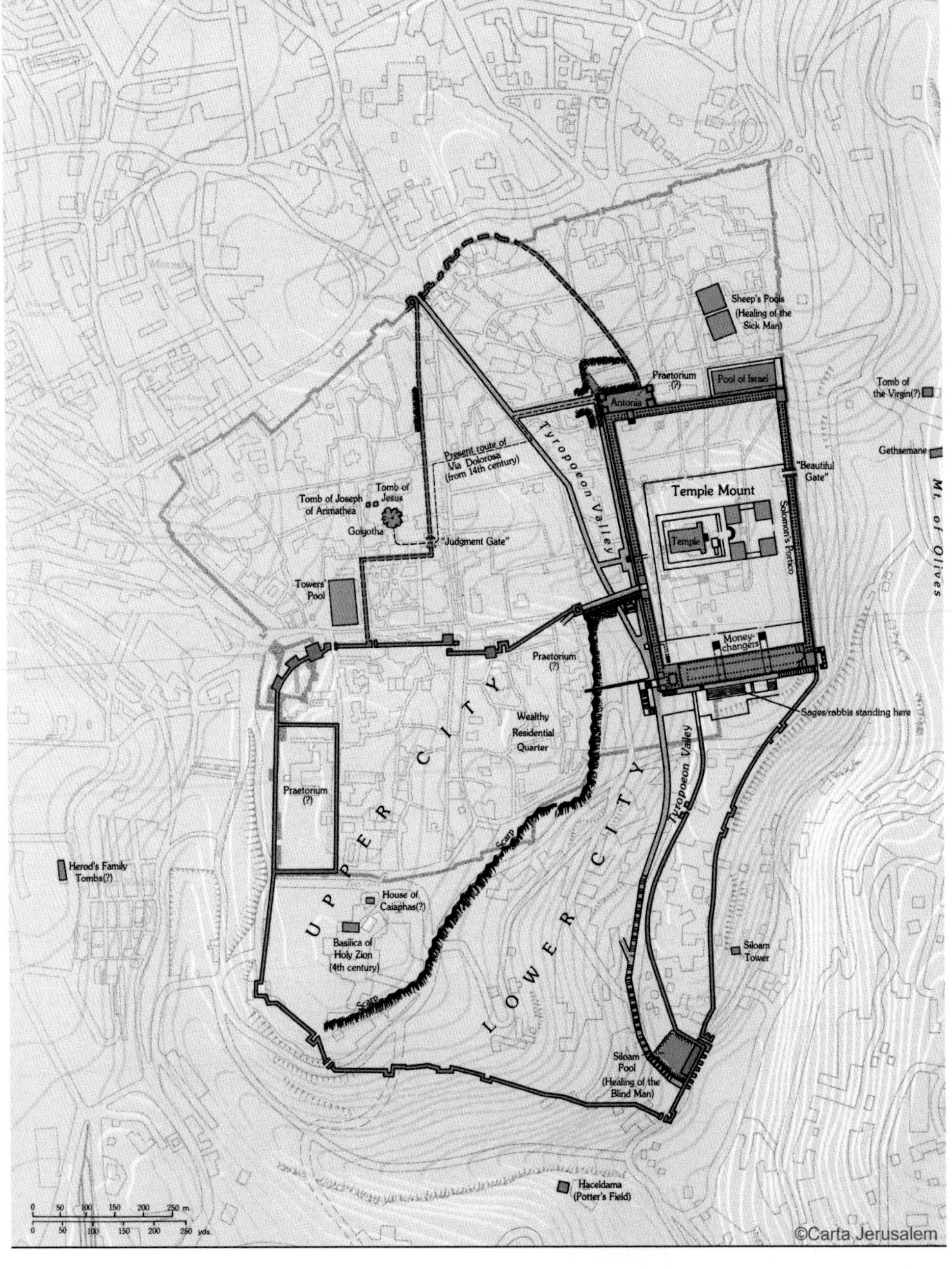

Sheep's Pools (Healing of the Sick Man)
Praetorium (?)
Pool of Israel
Antonia
Tomb of the Virgin(?)
Gethsemane
Mt. of Olives
Present route of Via Dolorosa (from 14th century)
Tyropoeon Valley
"Beautiful Gate"
Temple Mount
Solomon's Portico
Temple
Tomb of Joseph of Arimathea
Tomb of Jesus
Golgotha
"Judgment Gate"
Towers' Pool
Money-changers
Praetorium (?)
Sages/rabbis standing here
Wealthy Residential Quarter
UPPER CITY
LOWER CITY
Tyropoeon Valley
Praetorium (?)
Herod's Family Tombs(?)
Scarp
House of Caiaphas(?)
Basilica of Holy Zion (4th century)
Siloam Tower
Scarp
Siloam Pool (Healing of the Blind Man)
Haceldama (Potter's Field)
0 50 100 150 200 250 m.
0 50 100 150 200 250 yds.
©Carta Jerusalem

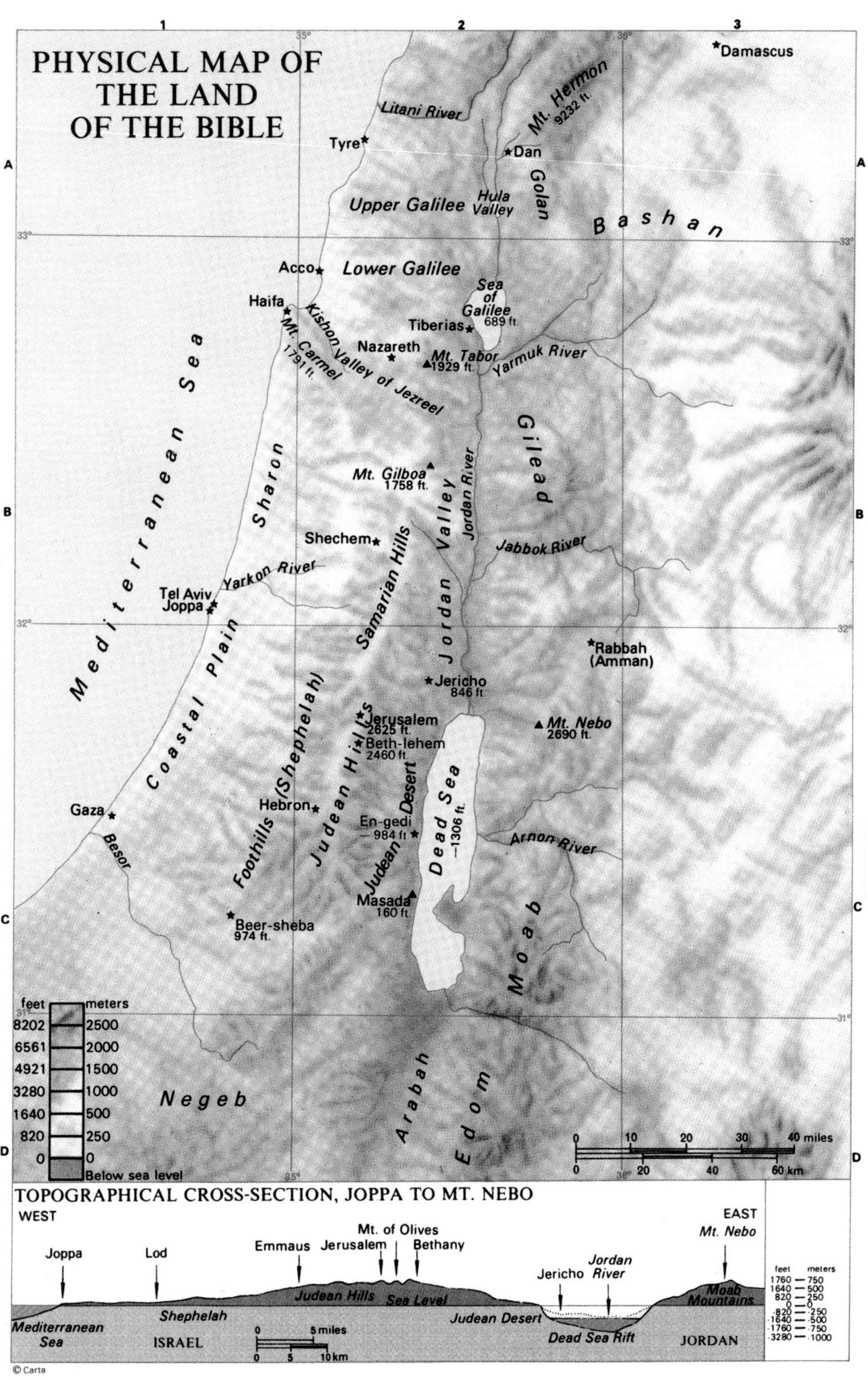
PHYSICAL MAP OF THE LAND OF THE BIBLE
Damascus
Litani River
Mt. Hermon 9232 ft.
Tyre
Dan
Golan
Upper Galilee
Hula Valley
Bashan
Acco
Lower Galilee
Sea of Galilee 689 ft.
Haifa
Mt. Carmel 1791 ft.
Kishon
Tiberias
Nazareth
Mt. Tabor 1929 ft.
Yarmuk River
Valley of Jezreel
Mediterranean Sea
Sharon
Gilead
Mt. Gilboa 1758 ft.
Jordan Valley
Jordan River
Shechem
Samarian Hills
Jabbok River
Yarkon River
Tel Aviv
Joppa
Coastal Plain
Rabbah (Amman)
Jericho 846 ft.
Jerusalem 2625 ft.
Beth-lehem 2460 ft.
Mt. Nebo 2690 ft.
Foothills (Shephelah)
Judean Hills
Judean Desert
Dead Sea −1306 ft.
Gaza
Hebron
En-gedi −984 ft
Besor
Arnon River
Masada 160 ft.
Moab
Beer-sheba 974 ft.
Negeb
Arabah
Edom
feet meters
8202 2500
6561 2000
4921 1500
3280 1000
1640 500
820 250
0 0
Below sea level
0 10 20 30 40 miles
0 20 40 60 km
TOPOGRAPHICAL CROSS-SECTION, JOPPA TO MT. NEBO
WEST
EAST
Joppa
Lod
Emmaus
Jerusalem
Mt. of Olives
Bethany
Jericho
Jordan River
Mt. Nebo
Judean Hills
Sea Level
Moab Mountains
Shephelah
Judean Desert
Mediterranean Sea
ISRAEL
Dead Sea Rift
JORDAN
0 5 miles
0 5 10 km
feet meters
1760 — 750
1640 — 500
820 — 250
0 — 0
-820 — -250
-1640 — -500
-1760 — -750
-3280 — -1000

THE HOLY LAND TODAY
33
THE NEAR EAST, PHYSICAL
32
Black Sea
Caspian Sea
Caucasus Mountains
Pontic Mountains
Mt. Ararat
Azerbaijan
Elburz Mountains
Zagros Mountains
Ankara
Kizil Irmak
Anatolia
Taurus Mountains
Amanus Mountains
Lake Van
Lake Urmia
El Jazira
Nicosia
Cyprus
Mediterranean Sea
Beirut
Mt. Lebanon
Anti-Lebanon
Damascus
Syrian Desert
Baghdad
Tigris
Euphrates
Shatt al Arab
Kuwait
Persian Gulf
Jerusalem
Amman
Jordan
Wadi Sirhan
Nafud Desert
Cairo
Sinai
El Faiyum
Nile
Gulf of Suez
Gulf of Eilat
Wadi Araba
Red Sea
Emblem of the state of Israel
LEBANON
SYRIA
Tyre
Qiryat Shemona
Bint Jubail
Quneitra
Maalot
Quzrin
Nahariya
Safad
Akko
GALILEE
Haifa
Shefaram
Tiberias
Sea of Galilee
En Gev
Atlit
Nazareth
Dor
Afula
Zikron Yaaqov
Irbid
Bet Shean
Jenin
Hadera
Tubas
Hayarden (Jordan)
Jarash
Netanya
Herzliya
Shechem (Nablus)
Tel Aviv Yafo
Bat Yam
SAMARIA
Under Israel Administration
Salt
Shunat Nimrin
Ashdod
Jerusalem
Jericho
Medeba
Bethlehem
Ashqelon
JUDEA
Qiryat Gat
Bet Guvrin
Yam Hamelah (Dead Sea)
Gaza
Sederot
Hebron
Dhiban
En Gedi
Rafah
Beer Sheba
Arad
Karak
Gevulot
El Arish
NEGEV
Sedom
JORDAN
Nizzana
Sede Boqer
Tafila
Hazeva
Quseima
SINAI
Mitzpe Ramon
Shaubak
Maan
Kuntilla
Ras en Naqb
Nakhl
Yotvata
Timna
(Including Palestinian autonomous areas)
Et Tamad
Eilat
Aqaba
Gulf of Eilat
Gulf of Suez
© carta